Global Development Finance

Financing the Poorest Countries

Country Tables

Global Development Finance

Financing the Poorest Countries

COUNTRY TABLES 2002

THE WORLD BANK

Manufactured in the United States of America
First printing March 2002
1 2 3 4 05 04 03 02

ISBN 0-8213-5086-2
ISSN 1020-5454

Table of Contents

Preface

Global Development Finance consists of two volumes: *Analysis and Summary Tables* and *Country Tables. Analysis and Summary Tables* contains analysis and commentary on recent developments in international finance for developing countries, together with summary statistical tables for selected regional and analytical groups comprising 148 developing countries.

Country Tables contains statistical tables on the external debt of the 136 countries that report public and publicly guaranteed debt under the Debtor Reporting System (DRS). Also included are tables of selected debt and resource flow statistics for individual reporting countries as well as summary tables for regional and income groups.

Earlier this year, country tables and summary statistics were also made available on CD-ROM through an advance release edition.

For the convenience of readers, charts on pages xx to xxii summarize graphically the relation between debt stock and its components; the computation of net flows, aggregate net resource flows, and aggregate net transfers; and the relation between net resource flows and the balance of payments. Exact definitions of these and other terms used in *Global Development Finance* are found in the Sources and Definitions section.

The economic aggregates presented in the tables are prepared for the convenience of users. Although debt indicators can give useful information about developments in debt-servicing capacity, conclusions drawn from them will not be valid unless accompanied by careful economic evaluation. The macroeconomic information provided is from standard sources, but many of them are subject to considerable margins of error, and the usual care must be taken in interpreting the indicators. This is particularly the case for the most recent year or two, when figures are preliminary and subject to revision.

This volume was prepared by the Financial Data Team of the Development Data Group, led by Punam Chuhan. The team consisted of Nanasamudd Chhim, Mahyar Eshragh-Tabary, Nevin Fahmy, Kabinah Fofanah, Shelley Fu, Ibrahim Levent, Gloria Moreno, Mohey Ragab, and Alagiri Venkatesan. The team was assisted by Rosario Alipio and Saida Mamedova. Soong Sup Lee provided the macroeconomic data. Many others inside the World Bank provided helpful input, especially the staff of the Development Prospects Group, and the country economists who reviewed the data. The principal editor was Meta de Coquereaumont and the volume was laid out by Wendy Guyette with Communications Development Incorporated. The work was carried out under the direction of Shaida Badiee.

Acronyms and Abbreviations

BIS	Bank for International Settlements
CRS	Creditor Reporting System (of the OECD)
DAC	Development Assistance Committee (of the OECD)
DDSR	Debt and debt service reduction
DRS	Debtor Reporting System (of the World Bank)
GNI	Gross national income
IBRD	International Bank for Reconstruction and Development/World Bank
IDA	International Development Association (of the World Bank)
IMF	International Monetary Fund
LDOD	Long-term debt outstanding and disbursed
LIBOR	London interbank offer rate
MYRA	Multiyear rescheduling agreement
ODA	Official development assistance
OECD	Organisation for Economic Co-operation and Development
OPEC	Organization of Petroleum Exporting Countries
SDR	Special drawing right (of the IMF)
WBXD	World Bank External Debt system

An early release of the data and the cross-country tables presented in this book is available each year in the Global Development Finance online database, GDF Online. For more information, please visit the World Bank's publications Web site at www.worldbank.org/publications or call 202-473-7824 or 800-590-1906.

Methodology

The World Bank is the sole repository for statistics on the external debt of developing countries on a loan-by-loan basis. The Debtor Reporting System (DRS), set up in 1951 to monitor these statistics, is maintained by the staff of the Financial Data Team (FIN), part of the Development Data Group of Development Economics.

Methodology for aggregating data

Using the DRS data, in combination with information obtained from creditors through the debt data collection systems of other agencies such as the Bank for International Settlements (BIS) and the Organisation for Economic Co-operation and Development (OECD), the staff of the Financial Data Team estimate the total external indebtedness of developing countries. The data are also supplemented by estimates made by country economists of the World Bank and desk officers of the International Monetary Fund (IMF).

Converting to a common currency

Since debt data are normally reported to the World Bank in the currency of repayment, they have to be converted into a common currency (usually U.S. dollars) to produce summary tables. Stock figures (such as the amount of debt outstanding) are converted using end-period exchange rates, as published in the IMF's *International Financial Statistics* (line ae). Flow figures are converted at annual average exchange rates (line rf). Projected debt service is converted using end-period exchange rates. Debt repayable in multiple currencies, goods, or services and debt with a provision for maintenance of value of the currency of repayment are shown at book value. Because flow data are converted at annual average exchange rates and stock data at year-end exchange rates, year-to-year changes in debt outstanding and disbursed are sometimes not equal to net flows (disbursements less principal repayments); similarly, changes in debt outstanding including undisbursed debt differ from commitments less repayments. Discrepancies are particularly significant when exchange rates have moved sharply during the year; cancellations and reschedulings of other liabilities into long-term public debt also contribute to the differences.

Public and publicly guaranteed debt

All data related to public and publicly guaranteed debt are from debtors except for lending by some multilateral agencies, in which case data are taken from the creditors' records. These creditors include the African Development Bank, the Asian Development Bank, the IMF, the Inter-American Development Bank, and the International Bank for Reconstruction and Development (IBRD) and the International Development Association (IDA). (The IBRD and IDA are components of the World Bank.)

Starting with the 1988–89 edition of *World Debt Tables* (as this book was previously titled), all data pertaining to World Bank loans from 1985 onward are recorded at their current market value. Starting with the 1991–92 edition, all data pertaining to Asian Development Bank loans from 1989 onward are recorded at their current market value. Starting with the 1998 edition, all data pertaining to African Development Bank and African Development Fund loans from 1997 onward are recorded at their current market value as well.

Private nonguaranteed debt

The DRS was expanded in 1970 to incorporate private nonguaranteed long-term debt. Reports, submitted annually, contain aggregate data for disbursed and outstanding debt, disbursements, principal repayments, interest payments, principal and interest rescheduled for the reporting year, and projected payments of principal and interest. Data are usually presented in dollars and currency conversion is not necessary. A few reporting countries choose to provide data on their private nonguaranteed debt in the loan-by-loan format used for reporting public and publicly guaranteed debt. In those cases the currency conversion and projection methodology just described is used.

Although the reporting countries fully recognize the importance of collecting data on private nonguaranteed debt when it constitutes a significant portion of total external debt, detailed data are available only in countries that have registration requirements covering private debt, most commonly in connection with exchange controls. Where formal registration of foreign borrowing is not mandatory, compilers must rely on balance of payments data and financial surveys.

This edition includes data on private nonguaranteed debt, either as reported or as estimated, for 79 countries for which this type of debt is known to be significant.

For private nonguaranteed debt that is not reported, the standard estimation approach starts from a calculation of the stock of debt outstanding, using data available from creditors. Figures on guaranteed export credits, obtained from the OECD's Creditor Reporting System (CRS), are supplemented by loan-by-loan information on official lending to private borrowers and by information on noninsured commercial bank lending to the private sector.

Disbursements and debt service payments for private nonguaranteed debt are more difficult to estimate. Amortization is estimated by making an assumption regarding the proportion of debt repaid each year and then applying these ratios to generate a first approximation of annual principal repayments. Disbursements are then estimated as a residual between net flows (equal to the change in the stock of debt) and estimated amortization. Interest payments are estimated by applying an assumed average interest rate to the stock of debt outstanding.

Data on the balance of payments flows provide useful guidelines in the process of building a time series because private nonguaranteed debt can be treated as a residual between total net long-term borrowing and net long-term borrowing recorded in the DRS for public and publicly guaranteed debt.

Short-term debt

The World Bank regards the individual reporting country as the authoritative source of information on its own external liabilities. But for short-term debt, defined as debt with an original maturity of one year or less, accurate information is not widely available from debtors. By its nature, short-term debt is difficult to monitor; loan-by-loan registration is normally impractical, and most reporting arrangements involve periodic returns to a country's central bank from its banking sector. Since 1982 the quality of such reporting has improved, but only a few developing countries have figures available for short-term debt.

Where information from debtors is not available, data from creditors can indicate the magnitude of a country's short-term debt. The most important source is the BIS's semiannual series showing the maturity distribution of commercial banks' claims on developing countries. Those data are reported residually. However, an estimate of short-term liabilities by original maturity can be calculated by deducting from claims due in one year those that had a maturity of between one and two years 12 months earlier.

There are several problems with this method. Valuation adjustments caused by exchange rate movements will affect the calculations, as will prepayment and refinancing of long-term maturities falling due. Moreover, not all countries' commercial banks report in a way that allows the full maturity distribution to be determined, and the BIS data include liabilities only to banks within the reporting area. Nevertheless, combining these estimates with data on officially guaranteed short-term suppliers' credits compiled by the OECD gives what may be thought of as a lower-bound estimate of a country's short-term debt. Even on this basis, however, the results need to be interpreted with caution. Where short-term debt has been rescheduled, the effect of lags in reporting and differences in the treatment of the rescheduled debt by debtors and creditors may result in double counting if short-term debt derived from creditor sources is added to long-term debt reported by the country to obtain total external liabilities.

Some of the short-term debt estimates published are drawn from debtor and creditor sources, but most are from creditor sources. Only for a few countries can the data be regarded as authoritative, but they offer a guide to the size of a country's short-term (and, hence, its total) external debt. The quality of these data is likely to improve.

Use of IMF credit

Data related to the operations of the IMF come from the IMF Treasurer's Department and are converted from special drawing rights (SDRs) into dollars using end-of-period exchange rates for stocks and average over the period exchange rates for converting flows, as described earlier. IMF trust fund loans and operations under the structural adjustment and enhanced structural adjustment facilities are presented together with all of the Fund's special facilities (the buffer stock, compensatory financing, extended fund, and oil facilities).

Treatment of arrears

The DRS collects information on arrears in both principal and interest. Principal in arrears is included and identified in the amount of long-term debt outstanding. Interest in arrears of long-term debt and the use of IMF credit is included and identified in the amount of short-term debt outstanding. If and when interest in arrears is capitalized under a debt reorganization agreement, the amount of interest capitalized will be added to the amount of long-term debt outstanding and the corresponding deduction made from the amount of short-term debt outstanding.

Treatment of debt restructurings

The DRS attempts to capture accurately the effects of the different kinds of restructurings on both debt stocks and debt flows, consistent with the circumstances under which the restructuring takes place. Whether a flow has taken place is sometimes difficult to determine.

In compiling and presenting the debt data, a distinction is made between cash flows and imputed flows. Based on this criterion, rescheduled service payments and the shift in liabilities from one financial instrument to another as a result of rescheduling are considered to be imputed flows.

The imputed flows are recorded separately in the World Bank External Debt (WBXD) system, but these debt restructuring transactions are not evident in the main body of the debt data—only the resulting effect of these transactions is reflected.

Changes in creditor and debtor status that can result from debt restructuring are also reflected. For example, when insured commercial credits are rescheduled, the creditor classification shifts from private sources to official sources (bilateral). This reflects the assumption of the assets by the official credit insurance agencies of the creditor countries. The debts to the original creditors are reduced by the amounts rescheduled, and a new obligation to the official creditor agencies is created. This shift also applies to private nonguaranteed debt that is reduced by the amounts rescheduled, which in turn are included in the public and publicly guaranteed debt owed to official creditors. On the debtor side, when a government accepts responsibility for the payment of rescheduled debt previously owed by private enterprises, the DRS registers a change in debtor categories in the DRS. Similarly, when short-term debt is included in a restructuring agreement, the rescheduled amount is shifted from short-term to long-term debt.

Methodology for projecting data

An important feature of the WBXD system of the DRS is its ability to project future disbursements of unutilized commitments and future debt service payments.

Undisbursed debt

Projections of disbursements help underpin future capital requirements in the implementation of externally financed projects. In addition, they help determine the interest portion of projected debt service. Future interest payments are based on projected debt outstanding that is itself determined by projected disbursements and repayments. The underlying assumptions of these projections are that loan commitments will be fully utilized and that the debtor country will repay all sums due. Future disbursements and debt service refer only to existing debt and do not reflect any assumptions on future borrowing.

Disbursement projections use two methods:

- *Specific schedules.* Debtor countries are requested to submit a calendar of future disbursements, if available, at the time individual loans are first reported. Country authorities are in a better position to provide estimated disbursement schedules when there is a solid public sector investment program in place.
- *Standard schedules.* In the absence of specific schedules, the WBXD system projects disbursements by applying a set of profiles to the last actual undisbursed balance of individual loans. The profiles are

derived under the assumption that specific sources of funds have some common characteristics that cause them to disburse, in the aggregate, in some observable pattern. Accordingly, some thirty profiles have been derived that roughly correspond to creditor type. Profiles exist for concessional and nonconcessional loans from official creditors. For bilateral lending, profiles have been developed for the Development Assistance Committee, the Organization of Petroleum Exporting Countries (OPEC), and other creditor groupings. For multilateral lending, specific profiles are available for major international organizations. An estimating equation for each profile is derived by applying regression analysis techniques to a body of data that contains actual disbursement information for more than 100,000 loans. Although these standard profiles are reestimated from time to time, under the best scenario they can only approximate the disbursement pattern of any single loan.

Future debt service payments

Most projections of future debt service payments generated by the WBXD system are based on the repayment terms of the loans. Principal repayments (amortization) are based on the amount of loan commitments, and the amortization profile of most loans follows a set pattern. Using the first and final payment dates and the frequency of the payments, the system calculates the stream of principal payments due. If future payments are irregular, the WBXD system requires a schedule.

Projected future interest payments are calculated similarly. Interest is based on the amount of debt disbursed and outstanding at the beginning of the period. Again, using the first and final interest payment dates and the frequency of payments, the system calculates the stream of interest payments due. If interest payments are irregular, the WBXD system requires a schedule.

The published figures for projected debt service obligations are converted into U.S. dollars using the end-December 2000 exchange rates. Likewise the projection routine for variable interest rate debt, such as commercial bank debt based on the London interbank offer rate (LIBOR), assumes that the rate prevailing at the end of December 2000 will be effective throughout.

Sources and definitions

This edition of *Global Development Finance* presents reported or estimated data on the total external debt of all low- and middle-income countries.

Format

The *Country Tables* volume of *Global Development Finance* has been expanded to include summary tables along with the standard country tables for the 136 individual countries that report to the World Bank's Debtor Reporting System (DRS). Summary tables present selected debt and resource flow statistics for the individual reporting countries and external debt data for regional and income groups. Regional and income group totals in the summary tables include estimates for the 12 low- and middle-income countries that do not report to the DRS. Because these estimates are not shown separately in the tables, most group totals are larger than the sum of the DRS figures shown. The format of the regional and income group tables draws on the individual country table format and includes graphic presentations.

For the 136 individual countries that report to the World Bank's DRS, tables are presented in a four-page layout containing 10 sections.

SECTION 1 summarizes the external debt of the country.

Total external debt stocks (EDT) consist of public and publicly guaranteed long-term debt, private nonguaranteed long-term debt (whether reported or estimated by the staff of the World Bank), the use of IMF credit, and estimated short-term debt. Interest in arrears on long-term debt and the use of IMF credit are added to the short-term debt estimates and are shown as separate lines. Arrears of principal and of interest have been disaggregated to show the arrears owed to official creditors and the arrears owed to private creditors. Export credits and principal in arrears on long-term debt are shown as memorandum items.

Total debt flows are consolidated data on disbursements, principal repayments, and interest payments for total long-term debt and transactions with the IMF.

Net flows on debt are disbursements on long-term debt and IMF purchases minus principal repayments on long-term debt and IMF repurchases up to 1984. Beginning in 1985 this line includes the change in stock of short-term debt (including interest arrears for long-term debt). Thus if the change in stock is positive, a disbursement is assumed to have taken place; if negative, a repayment is assumed to have taken place.

Total debt service (TDS) shows the debt service payments on total long-term debt (public and publicly guaranteed and private nonguaranteed), use of IMF credit, and interest on short-term debt.

SECTION 2 provides data series for aggregate net resource flows and net transfers (long term).

Net resource flows (long term) are the sum of net resource flows on long-term debt (excluding IMF credit) plus net foreign direct investment, portfolio equity flows, and official grants (excluding technical cooperation). Grants for technical cooperation are shown as a memorandum item. Also shown as memorandum items are official net resource flows and private net resource flows. Official net resource flows are the sum of net flows on long-term debt to official creditors (excluding the IMF) plus official grants (excluding technical cooperation). Private net resource flows are the sum of net flows on debt to private creditors plus net foreign direct investment and portfolio equity flows. Official net transfers and private net transfers are shown as memorandum items as well.

Net transfers (long term) are equal to net long-term resource flows minus interest payments on long-term loans and foreign direct investment profits.

SECTION 3 provides data series for major economic aggregates. The gross national income (GNI) series uses yearly average exchange rates in converting GNI from local currency into U.S. dollars. The economic aggregates are prepared for the convenience of users; the usual caution should be exercised in using them for economic analysis.

SECTION 4 provides debt indicators: ratios of debt and debt service to some of the economic aggregates.

SECTION 5 provides detailed information on stocks and flows of long-term debt and its various components. Data on bonds issued by private entities without public guarantee, compiled for major borrowers, are included in private nonguaranteed debt. IBRD loans and IDA credits are shown as memorandum items.

SECTION 6 provides information on the currency composition of long-term debt. The six major currencies in which the external debt of low- and middle-income countries is contracted are separately identified, as is debt denominated in special drawing rights and debt repayable in multiple currencies.

SECTION 7 provides information on restructurings of long-term debt starting in 1985. It shows both the stock and flows rescheduled each year. In addition, the amount of debt forgiven (interest forgiven is shown as a memorandum item) and the amount of debt stock reduction (including debt buyback) are also shown separately. (See the Methodology section for a detailed explanation of restructuring data.)

SECTION 8 reconciles the stock and flow data on total external debt for each year, beginning with 1989. This section is designed to illustrate the changes in stock that have taken place due to five factors: the net flow on debt, the net change in interest arrears, the capitalization of interest, the reduction in debt resulting from debt forgiveness or other debt reduction mechanisms, and the cross-currency valuation effects. The residual difference—the change in stock not explained by any of the factors identified above—is also presented. The residual is calculated as the sum of identified accounts minus the change in stock. Where the residual is large it can, in some cases, serve as an illustration of the inconsistencies in the reported data. More often, however, it can be explained by specific borrowing phenomena in individual countries. These are explained in the Country Notes section.

SECTION 9 provides information on the average terms of new commitments on public and publicly guaranteed debt and information on the level of commitments from official and private sources.

SECTION 10 provides anticipated disbursements and contractual obligations on long-term debt contracted up to December 2000.

Sources

The principal sources of information for the tables in these two volumes are reports to the World Bank through the DRS from member countries that have received either IBRD loans or IDA credits. Additional information has been drawn from the files of the World Bank and the IMF.

Reporting countries submit detailed (loan-by-loan) reports through the DRS on the annual status, transactions, and terms of the long-term external debt of public agencies and that of private ones guaranteed by a public agency in the debtor country. This information forms the basis for the tables in these volumes.

Aggregate data on private debt without public guarantee are compiled and published as reliable reported and estimated information becomes available. This edition includes data on private nonguaranteed debt, either as reported or as estimated, for 79 countries.

The short-term debt data are as reported by the debtor countries or are estimates derived from creditor sources. The principal creditor sources are the semiannual series of commercial banks' claims on developing countries, published by the Bank for International Settlements (BIS), and data on officially guaranteed suppliers' credits compiled by the Organisation for Economic Co-operation and Development (OECD). For some countries, estimates were prepared by pooling creditor and debtor information.

Interest in arrears on long-term debt and the use of IMF credit are added to the short-term debt estimates and shown as separate lines in section 1. Arrears of interest and of principal owed to official and to private creditors are identified separately.

Export credits are shown as a memorandum item in section 1. Data prior to 1998 include official export credits, and suppliers' credits and bank credits officially guaranteed or insured by an export credit agency. Both long-term and short-term exports credits are included. For 1998 to 2000 export credits include all export credits extended, guaranteed, insured, or rescheduled by the official sector of OECD countries. The source for this information is the Creditor Reporting System (CRS) of the OECD.

Data on long-term debt reported by member countries are checked against, and supplemented by, data from several other sources. Among these are the statements and reports of several regional development banks and government lending agencies, as well as the reports received by the World Bank under the CRS from the members of the Development Assistance Committee (DAC) of the OECD.

Every effort has been made to ensure the accuracy and completeness of the debt statistics. Nevertheless, quality and coverage vary among debtors and may also vary for the same debtor from year to year. Coverage has been improved through the efforts of the reporting agencies and the work of World Bank missions, which visit member countries to gather data and to provide technical assistance on debt issues.

Definitions

For all regional, income, and individual country tables, data definitions are presented below or footnoted where appropriate. Data definitions for other summary tables are, likewise, consistent with those below.

Summary debt data

TOTAL DEBT STOCKS are defined as the sum of public and publicly guaranteed long-term debt, private nonguaranteed long-term debt, the use of IMF credit, and short-term debt. The relation between total debt stock and its components is illustrated on page xx.

Long-term external debt is defined as debt that has an original or extended maturity of more than one year and that is owed to nonresidents and repayable in foreign currency, goods, or services. Long-term debt has three components:

- *Public debt*, which is an external obligation of a public debtor, including the national government, a political subdivision (or an agency of either), and autonomous public bodies.
- *Publicly guaranteed debt,* which is an external obligation of a private debtor that is guaranteed for repayment by a public entity.
- *Private nonguaranteed external debt,* which is an external obligation of a private debtor that is not guaranteed for repayment by a public entity.

In the tables, public and publicly guaranteed long-term debt are aggregated.

Short-term external debt is defined as debt that has an original maturity of one year or less. Available data permit no distinction between public and private nonguaranteed short-term debt.

Interest in arrears on long-term debt is defined as interest payment due but not paid, on a cumulative basis.

Principal in arrears on long-term debt is defined as principal repayment due but not paid, on a cumulative basis.

The memorandum item *export credits* includes official export credits, suppliers' credits, the official non-ODA lending, and bank credits officially guaranteed or insured by an export credit agency. Both long-term and short-term credits are included here.

Use of IMF credit denotes repurchase obligations to the IMF with respect to all uses of IMF resources (excluding those resulting from drawings in the reserve tranche) shown for the end of the year specified. Use of IMF credit comprises purchases outstanding under the credit tranches, including enlarged access resources and all special facilities (the buffer stock, compensatory financing, extended fund, and oil facilities), trust fund loans, and operations under the structural adjustment and enhanced structural adjustment facilities. Data are from the Treasurer's Department of the IMF.

- *IMF purchases* are total drawings on the general resources account of the IMF during the year specified, excluding drawings in the reserve tranche.
- *IMF repurchases* are total repayments of outstanding drawings from the general resources account during the year specified, excluding repayments due in the reserve tranche.

To maintain comparability between data on transactions with the IMF and data on long-term debt, use of IMF credit outstanding at year end (stock) is converted to dollars at the SDR exchange rate in effect at the end of the year. Purchases and repurchases (flows) are converted at the average SDR exchange rate for the year in which transactions take place.

Net purchases will usually not reconcile changes in the use of IMF credit from year to year. Valuation effects from the use of different exchange rates frequently explain much of the difference, but not all. Other factors are increases in quotas (which expand a country's reserve tranche and can thereby lower the use of IMF credit as defined here), approved purchases of a country's currency by another member country drawing on the general resources account, and various administrative uses of a country's currency by the IMF.

TOTAL DEBT FLOWS include disbursements, principal repayments, net flows and transfers on debt, and interest payments.

Disbursements are drawings on loan commitments during the year specified.

Principal repayments are the amounts of principal (amortization) paid in foreign currency, goods, or services in the year specified.

Net flows on debts (or net lending or net disbursements) are disbursements minus principal repayments.

Interest payments are the amounts of interest paid in foreign currency, goods, or services in the year specified.

Net transfers on debt are net flows minus interest payments (or disbursements minus total debt service payments).

The concepts of net flows on debt, net transfers on debt, and aggregate net flows and net transfers are illustrated on pages xxi and xxii.

Total debt service paid (TDS) is debt service payments on total long-term debt (public and publicly guaranteed and private nonguaranteed), use of IMF credit, and interest on short-term debt.

Aggregate net resource flows and transfers

NET RESOURCE FLOWS (LONG TERM) are the sum of net resource flows on long-term debt (excluding IMF) plus non–debt-creating flows.

NON–DEBT-CREATING FLOWS are net foreign direct investment, portfolio equity flows, and official grants (excluding technical cooperation). Net foreign direct investment and portfolio equity flows are treated as private source flows. Grants for technical cooperation are shown as a memorandum item.

Foreign direct investment (FDI) is defined as investment that is made to acquire a lasting management interest (usually 10 percent of voting stock) in an enterprise operating in a country other than that of the investor (defined according to residency), the investor's purpose being an effective voice in the management of the enterprise. It is the sum of equity capital, reinvestment of earnings, other long-term capital, and short-term capital as shown in the balance of payments.

Portfolio equity flows are the sum of country funds, depository receipts (American or global), and direct purchases of shares by foreign investors.

Grants are defined as legally binding commitments that obligate a specific value of funds available for disbursement for which there is no repayment requirement.

The memorandum item *technical cooperation grants* includes free-standing technical cooperation grants, which are intended to finance the transfer of technical and managerial skills or of technology for the purpose of building up general national capacity without reference to any specific investment projects; and investment-related technical cooperation grants, which are provided to strengthen the capacity to execute specific investment projects.

Profit remittances on foreign direct investment are the sum of reinvested earnings on direct investment and other direct investment income and are part of net transfers.

Major economic aggregates

Five economic aggregates are provided for the reporting economies.

Gross national income, or GNI (Gross national product, or GNP, in previous editions) is the sum of value added by all resident producers plus any product taxes (less subsidies) not included in the valuation of output plus net receipts of primary income (compensation of employees and property income) from abroad. The national accounts data for most developing countries are collected from national statistical organizations and central banks by visiting and resident World Bank missions. Data on GNI are from the Macroeconomic Data Team of the Development Economics Development Data Group of the World Bank.

Exports of goods and services (XGS) are the total value of goods and services exported as well as income and worker remittances received.

Imports of goods and services (MGS) are the total value of goods and services imported and income paid.

International reserves (RES) are the sum of a country's monetary authority's holdings of special drawing rights (SDRs), its reserve position in the IMF, its holdings of foreign exchange, and its holdings of gold (valued at year-end London prices).

Current account balance is the sum of the credits less the debits arising from international transactions in goods, services, income, and current transfers. It represents the transactions that add to or subtract from an economy's stock of foreign financial items.

Data on exports and imports (on a balance of payments basis), international reserves, and current account balances are drawn mainly from the files of the IMF, supplemented by World Bank staff estimates. Balance of payments data are presented according to the fifth edition of the IMF's *Balance of Payments Manual,* which made several adjustments to its presentation of trade statistics. Coverage of goods was expanded to include in imports the value of goods received for processing and repair (on a gross basis). Their subsequent re-export is recorded in exports (also on a gross basis). This approach will cause a country's imports and exports to increase without affecting the balance of goods. In addition, all capital transfers, which were included with current transfers in the fourth edition of the *Balance of Payments Manual,* are now shown in a separate capital (as opposed to financial) account, and so do not contribute to the current account balance.

Debt indicators

The macroeconomic aggregates and debt data provided in the tables are used to generate ratios that analysts use to assess the external situations of developing countries. Different analysts give different weights to these indicators, but no single indicator or set of indicators can substitute for a thorough analysis of the overall situation of an economy. The advantage of the indicators in *Global Development Finance* is that they are calculated from standardized data series that are compiled on a consistent basis by the World Bank and the IMF. The ratios offer various measures of the cost of, or capacity for, servicing debt in terms of the foreign exchange or output forgone. The following ratios are provided based on total external debt:

EDT/XGS is total external debt to exports of goods and services (including workers' remittances).

EDT/GNI is total external debt to gross national income.

TDS/XGS, also called the debt service ratio, is total debt service to exports of goods and services (including workers' remittances).

INT/XGS, also called the interest service ratio, is total interest payments to exports of goods and services (including workers' remittances).

INT/GNI is total interest payments to gross national income.

RES/EDT is international reserves to total external debt.

RES/MGS is international reserves to imports of goods and services.

Short-term/EDT is short-term debt to total external debt.

Concessional/EDT is concessional debt to total external debt.

Multilateral/EDT is multilateral debt to total external debt.

Long-term debt

Data on long-term debt include eight main elements:

DEBT OUTSTANDING AND DISBURSED is the total outstanding debt at year end.

DISBURSEMENTS are drawings on loan commitments by the borrower during the year.

PRINCIPAL REPAYMENTS are amounts paid by the borrower during the year.

NET FLOWS received by the borrower during the year are disbursements minus principal repayments.

INTEREST PAYMENTS are amounts paid by the borrower during the year.

NET TRANSFERS are net flows minus interest payments during the year; negative transfers show net transfers made by the borrower to the creditor during the year.

DEBT SERVICE (LTDS) is the sum of principal repayments and interest payments actually made.

UNDISBURSED DEBT is total debt undrawn at year end; data for private nonguaranteed debt are not available.

Data from individual reporters are aggregated by type of creditor. *Official creditors* includes multilateral and bilateral debt.

- *Loans from multilateral organizations* are loans and credits from the World Bank, regional development banks, and other multilateral and intergovernmental agencies. Excluded are loans from funds administered by an international organization on behalf of a single donor government; these are classified as loans from governments.
- *Bilateral loans* are loans from governments and their agencies (including central banks), loans from autonomous bodies, and direct loans from official export credit agencies.

Private creditors include bonds, commercial banks, and other private creditors. Commercial banks and other private creditors comprise bank and trade-related lending.

- *Bonds* include publicly issued or privately placed bonds.

- *Commercial banks* are loans from private banks and other private financial institutions.
- *Other private* includes credits from manufacturers, exporters, and other suppliers of goods, and bank credits covered by a guarantee of an export credit agency.

Four characteristics of a country's debt are given as memorandum items for long-term debt outstanding and disbursed (LDOD).

Concessional LDOD conveys information about the borrower's receipt of aid from official lenders at concessional terms as defined by the DAC, that is, loans with an original grant element of 25 percent or more. Loans from major regional development banks—African Development Bank, Asian Development Bank, and the Inter-American Development Bank—and from the World Bank are classified as concessional according to each institution's classification and not according to the DAC definition, as was the practice in earlier reports.

Variable interest rate LDOD is long-term debt with interest rates that float with movements in a key market rate such as the London interbank offer rate (LIBOR) or the U.S. prime rate. This item conveys information about the borrower's exposure to changes in international interest rates.

Public sector LDOD and private sector LDOD convey information about the distribution of long-term debt for DRS countries by type of debtor (central government, state and local government, central bank; private bank, private debt).

Currency composition of long-term debt

The six major currencies in which the external debt of low- and middle-income countries is contracted are separately identified, as is debt denominated in special drawing rights and debt repayable in multiple currencies.

Debt restructurings

Debt restructurings include restructurings in the context of the Paris Club, commercial banks, debt-equity swaps, buybacks, and bond exchanges. Debt restructuring data capture the noncash or inferred flows associated with rescheduling and restructuring. These are presented to complement the cash-basis transactions recorded in the main body of the data.

Debt stock rescheduled is the amount of debt outstanding rescheduled in any given year.

Principal rescheduled is the amount of principal due or in arrears that was rescheduled in any given year.

Interest rescheduled is the amount of interest due or in arrears that was rescheduled in any given year.

Debt forgiven is the amount of principal due or in arrears that was written off or forgiven in any given year.

Interest forgiven is the amount of interest due or in arrears that was written off or forgiven in any given year.

Debt stock reduction is the amount that has been netted out of the stock of debt using debt conversion schemes such as buybacks and equity swaps or the discounted value of long-term bonds that were issued in exchange for outstanding debt.

Debt stock-flow reconciliation

Stock and flow data on total external debt are reconciled for each year, beginning with 1989. The data show the changes in stock that have taken place due to the net flow on debt, the net change in interest arrears, the capitalization of interest, the reduction in debt resulting from debt forgiveness or other debt reduction mechanisms, and the cross-currency valuation effects. The residual difference—the change in stock not explained by any of these factors—is also presented, calculated as the sum of identified accounts minus the change in stock.

Average terms of new commitments

The average terms of borrowing on public and publicly guaranteed debt are given for all new loans contracted during the year and separately for loans from official and private creditors. To obtain averages, the interest rates, maturities, and grace periods in each category have been weighted by the amounts of the loans. The grant equivalent of a loan is its commitment (present) value, less the discounted present value of its contractual debt service; conventionally, future service payments are discounted at 10 percent. The grant element of a loan is the grant equivalent expressed as a percentage of the amount committed. It is used as a measure of the overall cost of borrowing. Loans with an original grant element of 25 percent or more are defined as concessional. The average grant element has been weighted by the amounts of the loans.

Commitments cover the total amount of loans for which contracts were signed in the year specified; data for private nonguaranteed debt are not available.

Projections on existing pipeline

Projected *debt service* payments are estimates of payments due on existing debt outstanding, including undisbursed. They do not include service payments that may become due as a result of new loans contracted in subsequent years. Nor do they allow for effects on service payments of changes in repayment patterns owing to prepayment of loans or to rescheduling or refinancing, including repayment of outstanding arrears, that occurred after the last year of reported data.

Projected *disbursements* are estimates of drawings of unutilized balances. The projections do not take into account future borrowing by the debtor country. (See the Methodology section for a detailed explanation of how undisbursed balances are projected.)

Exchange rates

Data received by the World Bank from its members are expressed in the currencies in which the debts are repayable or in which the transactions took place. For aggregation, the Bank converts these amounts to U.S. dollars using the IMF par values or central rates, or the current market rates where appropriate. Service payments, commitments, and disbursements (flows) are converted to U.S. dollars at the average rate for the year. Debt outstanding and disbursed at the end of a given year (a stock) is converted at the rate in effect at the end of that year. Projected debt service, however, is converted to U.S. dollars at rates in effect at end-December 2000. Debt repayable in multiple currencies, goods, or services and debt with a provision for maintenance of value of the currency of repayment are shown at book value.

Adjustments

Year-to-year changes in debt outstanding and disbursed are sometimes not equal to net flows; similarly, changes in debt outstanding, including undisbursed, differ from commitments less repayments. The reasons for these differences are cancellations, adjustments caused by the use of different exchange rates, and the rescheduling of other liabilities into long-term public debt.

Symbols

The following symbols have been used throughout:

- 0.0 indicates that a datum exists, but is negligible, or is a true zero.
- .. indicates that a datum is not available.
- Dollars are current U.S. dollars unless otherwise specified.

Debt stock and its components

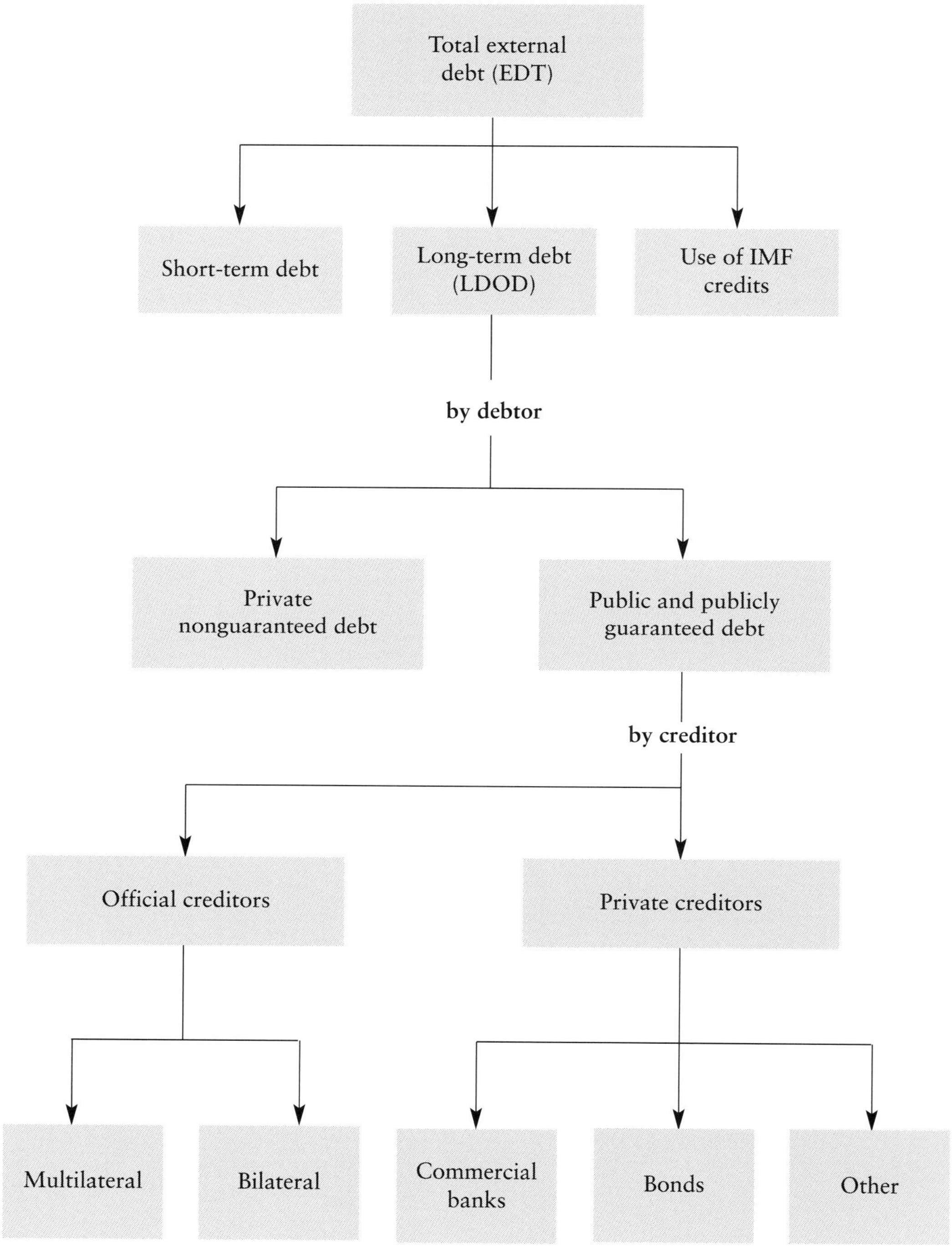

Aggregate net resource flows and net transfers (long-term) to developing countries

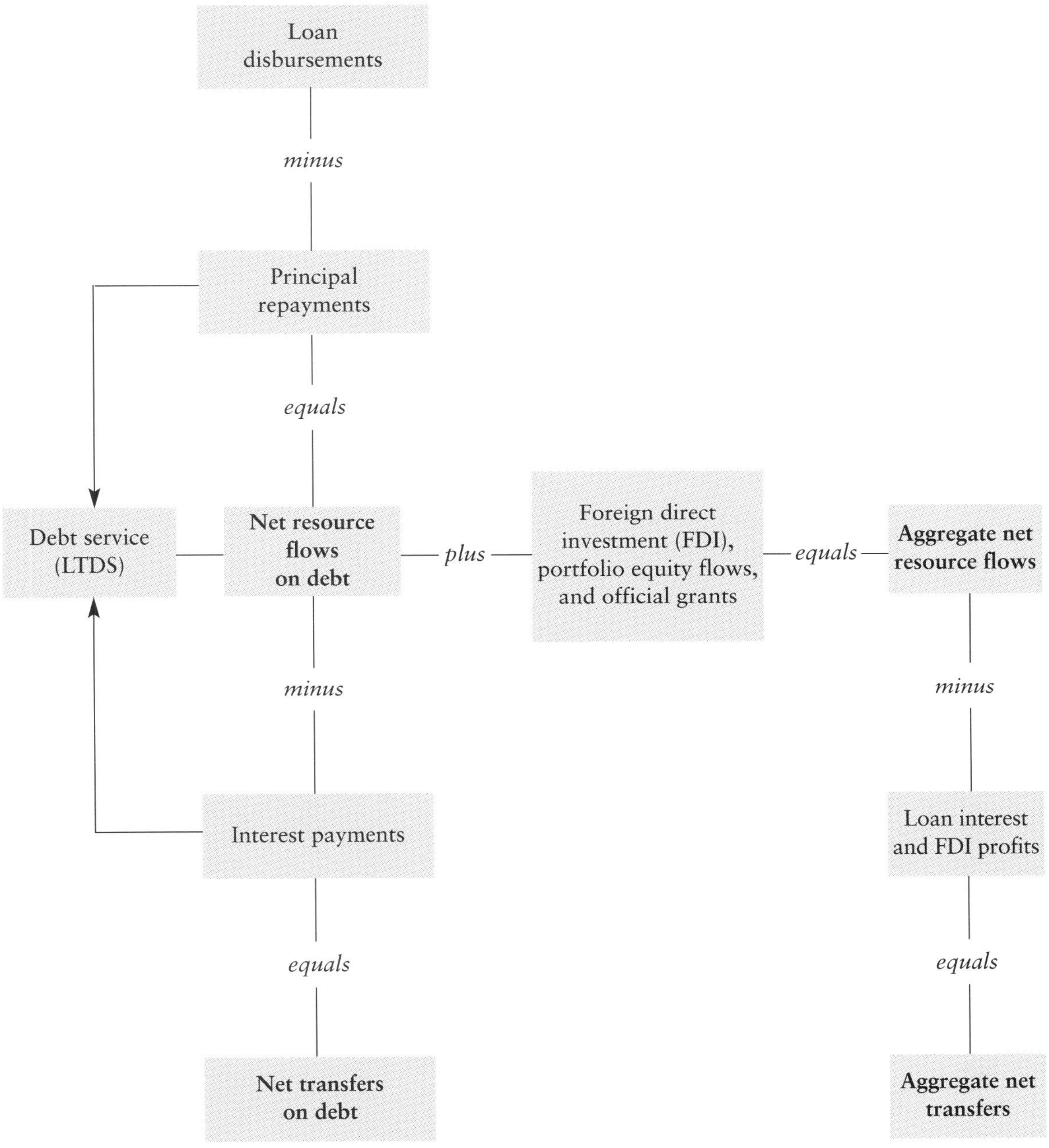

Aggregate net resource flows (long-term) and the balance of payments

	Credits	Debits
Current account	• Exports of goods and services • Income received • Current transfers Including workers' remittances and private grants	• Imports of goods and services • Income paid • Current transfers
	• Official unrequited transfers (by foreign governments)	• Official unrequited transfers (by national government)
Capital and financial account	• Official unrequited transfers (by foreign governments) • Foreign direct investment (by nonresidents) (disinvestment shown as negative)	• Official unrequited transfers (by national government) • Foreign direct investment (by residents) (disinvestment shown as negative)
	• Portfolio investment (by nonresidents) (amortizations shown as negative) • Other long-term capital inflows (by nonresidents) (amortizations shown as negative)	• Portfolio investment (abroad by residents) (amortizations shown as negative) • Other long-term capital outflow (by residents) (amortizations shown as negative)
	• Short-term capital inflow	• Short-term capital outflow
Reserve account	Net changes in reserves	

Aggregate net resource flows

Net resource flows on debt (long-term)

Country groups

Regional groups

East Asia and the Pacific

Cambodia (P)
China (E)
Fiji (A)
Indonesia (P)
Korea, Rep. (A)
Lao PDR (P)
Malaysia (E)
Mongolia (E)
Myanmar (E)
Papua New Guinea (A)
Philippines (A)
Samoa (A)
Solomon Islands (A)
Thailand (P)
Tonga (E)
Vanuatu (E)
Vietnam (P)
Kiribati
Korea, Dem. Rep.

Europe and Central Asia

Albania (A)
Armenia (A)
Azerbaijan (A)
Belarus (A)
Bosnia and Herzegovina[a] (P)
Bulgaria (A)
Croatia (A)
Czech Republic (P)
Estonia (E)
Georgia (A)
Hungary (A)
Kazakhstan (A)
Kyrgyz Republic (A)
Latvia (A)
Lithuania (A)
Macedonia, FYR (A)
Moldova (A)
Poland (A)
Romania (A)
Russian Federation[b] (E)
Slovak Republic (A)
Tajikistan (A)
Turkey (A)
Turkmenistan (E)
Ukraine (A)
Uzbekistan (A)
Yugoslavia, Fed. Rep.[a] (E)
Gibraltar

Latin America and the Caribbean

Argentina (A)
Belize (A)
Bolivia (A)
Brazil (P)
Chile (A)
Colombia (A)
Costa Rica (A)
Dominica (A)
Dominican Republic (A)
Ecuador (E)
El Salvador (A)
Grenada (A)
Guatemala (A)
Guyana (A)
Haiti (P)
Honduras (A)
Jamaica (A)
Mexico (A)
Nicaragua (A)
Panama (A)
Paraguay (A)
Peru (A)
St. Kitts and Nevis (A)
St. Lucia (A)
St.Vincent and the Grenadines (A)
Trinidad and Tobago (E)
Uruguay (A)
Venezuela, R.B. de (P)
Antigua and Barbuda
Cuba
Suriname

Middle East and North Africa

Algeria (A)
Djibouti (P)
Egypt, Arab Rep. (A)
Iran, Islamic Rep. (E)
Jordan (P)
Lebanon (P)
Morocco (A)
Oman (A)
Syrian Arab Republic (E)
Tunisia (A)
Yemen, Rep. (P)
Bahrain
Iraq
Libya
Saudi Arabia

South Asia

Bangladesh (A)
Bhutan (A)
India (P)
Maldives (A)
Nepal (A)
Pakistan (P)
Sri Lanka (A)
Afghanistan

Sub-Saharan Africa

Angola (P)
Benin (A)
Botswana (A)
Burkina Faso (A)
Burundi (E)
Cameroon (P)
Cape Verde (A)
Central African Republic (E)
Chad (P)
Comoros (P)
Congo, Dem. Rep. (A)
Congo, Rep. (E)
Côte d'Ivoire (E)
Equatorial Guinea (E)
Eritrea (A)
Ethiopia (P)
Gabon (A)
Gambia, The (A)
Ghana (E)
Guinea (E)
Guinea-Bissau (E)
Kenya (A)
Lesotho (P)
Liberia (E)
Madagascar (P)
Malawi (E)
Mali (P)
Mauritania (A)
Mauritius (A)
Mozambique (P)
Niger (P)
Nigeria (E)
Rwanda (E)
São Tomé and Principe (P)
Senegal (P)
Seychelles (E)
Sierra Leone (A)
Somalia (E)
South Africa (E)
Sudan (E)
Swaziland (E)
Tanzania (P)
Togo (P)
Uganda (P)
Zambia (P)
Zimbabwe (P)
Namibia

Note: Countries printed in normal type are reporters to the Debtor Reporting System (DRS); those printed in italics do not report to the DRS but are included in aggregate tables. Letters in parenthesis indicate DRS reporters' status: (A) as reported, (P) preliminary, and (E) estimated. The status "as reported" indicates that the country was fully current in its reporting under the DRS and that World Bank staff are satisfied that the reported data give an adequate and fair representation of the country's total public debt. "Preliminary" data are based on reported or collected information but, because of incompleteness or other reasons, include an element of staff estimation. "Estimated" data indicate that countries are not current in their reporting and that a significant element of staff estimation has been necessary in producing the data tables.

a. For Bosnia and Herzegovina total debt before 1999, excluding IBRD and IMF obligations and short-term debt, is included under Yugoslavia, Fed. Rep.

b. Includes the debt of the former Soviet Union on the assumption that 100 percent of all outstanding external debt as of December 1991 has become a liability of the Russian Federation.

Income groups

Low-income countries

Angola
Armenia
Azerbaijan
Bangladesh
Benin
Bhutan
Burkina Faso
Burundi
Cambodia
Cameroon
Central African Republic
Chad
Comoros
Congo, Dem. Rep.
Congo, Rep.
Côte d'Ivoire
Eritrea
Ethiopia
Gambia, The
Georgia
Ghana
Guinea
Guinea-Bissau
Haiti
India
Indonesia
Kenya
Kyrgyz Republic
Lao PDR
Lesotho
Liberia
Madagascar
Malawi
Mali
Mauritania
Moldova
Mongolia
Mozambique
Myanmar
Nepal
Nicaragua
Niger
Nigeria
Pakistan
Rwanda
São Tomé and Principe
Senegal
Sierra Leone
Solomon Islands
Somalia
Sudan
Tajikistan
Tanzania
Togo
Uganda
Ukraine
Uzbekistan
Vietnam
Yemen, Rep.
Zambia
Zimbabwe
Afghanistan
Korea, Dem. Rep.

Middle-income countries

Albania
Algeria
Argentina
Belarus
Belize
Bolivia
Bosnia and Herzegovina
Botswana
Brazil
Bulgaria
Cape Verde
Chile
China
Colombia
Costa Rica
Croatia
Czech Republic
Djibouti
Dominica
Dominican Republic
Ecuador
Egypt, Arab Rep.
El Salvador
Equatorial Guinea
Estonia
Fiji
Gabon
Grenada
Guatemala
Guyana
Honduras
Hungary
Iran, Islamic Rep.
Jamaica
Jordan
Kazakhstan
Korea, Rep.
Latvia
Lebanon
Lithuania
Macedonia, FYR
Malaysia
Maldives
Mauritius
Mexico
Morocco
Oman
Panama
Papua New Guinea
Paraguay
Peru
Philippines
Poland
Romania
Russian Federation
Samoa
Seychelles
Slovak Republic
South Africa
Sri Lanka
St. Kitts and Nevis
St. Lucia
St. Vincent and the Grenadines
Swaziland
Syrian Arab Republic
Thailand
Tonga
Trinidad and Tobago
Tunisia
Turkey
Turkmenistan
Uruguay
Vanuatu
Venezuela, R.B. de
Yugoslavia, Fed. Rep.
Antigua and Barbuda
Bahrain
Cuba
Gibraltar
Iraq
Kiribati
Libya
Namibia
Saudi Arabia
Suriname

Note: Countries printed in normal type are reporters to the Debtor Reporting System (DRS); those printed in italics do not report to the DRS but are included in aggregate tables. Low-income countries are those in which 2000 GNI per capita (calculated using the *World Bank Atlas* method) was no more than $755; middle-income countries are those in which GNI per capita was between $756 and $9,265.

Debt tables

Note to users

Long-term public and publicly guaranteed debt data are as reported for 70 countries; for 33 other countries the data are preliminary (that is, substantially based on reported data) or estimated by World Bank staff. The status of each country is given in the Country Groups section.

This edition includes data on private nonguaranteed debt, either as reported or as estimated, for 79 countries.

Data for exports, imports, and international reserves are standard series drawn from the International Monetary Fund (IMF) and maintained in the data files of the World Bank. Data for gross national income denominated in U.S. dollars are drawn directly from the files of the Macroeconomic Data Team of the Development Data Group of the World Bank. Data for direct foreign investment are drawn from the IMF, and data for grants are drawn from the OECD and supplemented by World Bank staff estimates. The charts on pages xx to xxii are intended to help the reader interpret the debt stocks and flows reported in the tables.

Beginning with 1991 all ruble debt owed to the former Soviet Union is converted at a rate of $1 = 0.6 ruble, except in cases where a bilateral agreement specifying a different conversion rate is in place. This valuation method does not constitute an endorsement by World Bank staff of the appropriateness or validity of this method or the exchange rate used. The appropriate valuation is a matter to be resolved bilaterally between the Russian Federation and its debtor countries.

The following abbreviations are used in the principal ratios and indicator tables:

EDT	Total external debt, including short-term and use of IMF credit
LDOD	Total long-term debt outstanding and disbursed
INT	Total interest payments on long-term and short-term debt, including IMF charges
TDS	Total debt service on long-term debt and short-term (interest only), including IMF credits
FDI	Foreign direct investment
GNI	Gross national income
XGS	Exports of goods and services
MGS	Imports of goods and services
RES	International reserves

Table 1: EXTERNAL DEBT

(US$ millions)

	Total debt stock		Total debt / GNI (%)		Long-term debt / total debt (%)		Distribution of long-term debt (%)					
							Multilateral		Bilateral		Private	
	1995	2000	1995	2000	1995	2000	1995	2000	1995	2000	1995	2000
Albania	456	784	18	20	72	84	35	61	58	33	8	6
Algeria	32,772	25,002	83	49	95	92	13	18	37	57	50	26
Angola	11,380	10,146	469	214	83	86	2	3	20	38	78	59
Argentina	98,802	146,172	39	53	72	77	13	14	16	4	71	82
Armenia	371	898	13	46	80	76	70	72	30	26	0	3
Azerbaijan	321	1,184	11	24	64	58	48	46	52	26	0	27
Bangladesh	15,924	15,609	42	33	95	97	64	73	34	26	2	1
Belarus	1,694	851	8	3	77	81	14	32	45	26	41	42
Belize	255	499	45	65	86	90	41	31	39	19	20	50
Benin	1,614	1,599	82	74	92	90	59	66	41	34	0	0
Bhutan	106	198	35	40	99	99	65	49	29	51	6	0
Bolivia	5,275	5,762	82	72	89	89	55	54	39	25	6	20
Bosnia and Herzegovina	..	2,828	..	61	..	91	..	48	..	20	..	31
Botswana	703	413	14	8	99	96	70	72	23	21	7	7
Brazil	160,505	237,953	23	42	80	86	7	9	14	5	78	86
Bulgaria	10,259	10,026	81	86	88	83	13	17	18	12	69	71
Burkina Faso	1,267	1,332	58	61	90	85	87	85	13	14	0	0
Burundi	1,158	1,100	117	163	95	93	85	86	15	14	0	0
Cambodia	2,035	2,357	70	74	96	93	6	17	93	83	1	0
Cameroon	9,385	9,241	126	112	88	83	20	18	65	74	14	8
Cape Verde	214	327	44	60	86	96	78	73	19	25	3	2
Central African Republic	946	872	86	92	90	93	75	72	23	24	2	4
Chad	902	1,116	64	80	92	90	81	83	19	15	0	1
Chile	22,038	36,978	35	54	84	93	15	4	4	1	81	94
China	118,090	149,800	17	14	81	89	17	20	22	19	61	62
Colombia	25,048	34,081	28	43	78	92	27	20	9	5	64	75
Comoros	214	232	92	115	94	87	78	80	22	20	0	0
Congo, Dem. Rep.	13,239	11,645	271	..	73	67	25	27	66	67	9	6
Congo, Rep.	6,004	4,887	390	219	83	77	14	15	67	65	18	20
Costa Rica	3,802	4,466	33	31	88	79	40	37	34	17	26	45
Cote d'Ivoire	18,899	12,138	210	141	77	87	27	28	37	35	37	37
Croatia	3,829	12,120	20	65	81	93	10	5	42	8	48	87
Czech Republic	16,218	21,299	31	43	69	58	8	6	4	3	88	92
Djibouti	282	262	55	46	95	91	51	58	49	42	0	0
Dominica	103	108	49	45	92	82	66	72	34	28	0	0
Dominican Republic	4,448	4,598	40	25	83	73	28	34	53	43	18	23
Ecuador	13,994	13,281	82	107	89	91	24	29	18	22	58	50
Egypt, Arab Rep.	33,337	28,957	55	29	93	86	13	15	80	80	7	4
El Salvador	2,610	4,023	28	31	80	72	66	65	29	20	5	15
Equatorial Guinea	292	248	191	50	79	80	44	47	49	47	7	6
Eritrea	37	311	5	45	100	96	66	51	34	49	0	0
Estonia	286	3,280	6	71	58	71	65	5	20	1	15	94
Ethiopia	10,308	5,481	180	87	95	97	24	51	70	46	6	2
Fiji	251	136	13	9	94	89	63	74	8	10	29	16
Gabon	4,360	3,995	103	94	91	88	15	13	80	83	5	3
Gambia, The	427	471	113	113	90	90	84	80	16	20	0	0
Georgia	1,240	1,633	68	54	84	80	24	37	67	60	10	3
Ghana	5,936	6,657	94	132	79	87	64	63	25	24	11	13
Grenada	146	207	56	55	90	88	49	39	45	41	6	19
Guatemala	3,655	4,622	25	25	81	71	34	45	39	32	27	22
Guinea	3,242	3,388	90	116	92	87	49	55	48	44	3	1

Table 1: EXTERNAL DEBT

(US$ millions)

	Total debt stock		Total debt / GNI (%)		Long-term debt / total debt (%)		Distribution of long-term debt (%)					
							Multilateral		Bilateral		Private	
	1995	2000	1995	2000	1995	2000	1995	2000	1995	2000	1995	2000
Guinea-Bissau	898	942	381	464	89	87	46	48	50	52	4	0
Guyana	2,129	1,455	389	221	85	83	35	49	60	47	5	4
Haiti	816	1,169	31	29	93	89	80	87	20	13	0	0
Honduras	4,791	5,487	130	95	90	89	50	55	39	31	11	14
Hungary	31,649	29,415	74	67	89	86	13	6	3	2	84	93
India	94,469	100,367	27	21	92	97	35	33	31	25	34	42
Indonesia	124,398	141,803	63	99	79	76	20	18	32	32	48	49
Iran, Islamic Rep.	21,879	7,953	25	8	71	54	2	12	71	14	26	73
Jamaica	4,270	4,287	94	61	83	81	34	32	53	31	13	36
Jordan	8,064	8,226	123	99	87	86	17	25	55	60	27	15
Kazakhstan	3,750	6,664	19	39	78	92	13	24	65	12	22	64
Kenya	7,412	6,295	85	62	86	85	46	53	36	34	18	13
Korea, Rep.	85,810	134,417	18	30	46	66	7	14	6	4	86	82
Kyrgyz Republic	616	1,829	19	150	78	83	39	48	61	31	0	21
Lao PDR	2,165	2,499	123	150	97	98	30	43	70	57	0	0
Latvia	463	3,379	9	47	59	61	51	26	23	2	26	71
Lebanon	2,966	10,311	26	59	54	75	12	9	14	5	73	87
Lesotho	688	716	52	63	93	97	73	68	22	21	5	11
Liberia	2,154	2,032	..	..	54	51	39	38	43	43	18	19
Lithuania	770	4,855	12	44	60	73	35	12	34	6	31	82
Macedonia, FYR	1,277	1,465	29	42	84	89	27	43	29	24	44	33
Madagascar	4,322	4,701	144	124	86	91	46	43	52	57	2	1
Malawi	2,243	2,716	162	164	93	94	82	80	16	19	1	1
Malaysia	34,343	41,797	41	51	79	89	6	4	14	8	80	88
Maldives	155	207	69	39	98	90	60	65	34	19	6	17
Mali	2,958	2,956	122	131	93	89	51	57	49	43	0	0
Mauritania	2,350	2,500	231	275	89	86	44	46	55	53	0	1
Mauritius	1,757	2,374	45	55	81	68	19	14	28	19	53	67
Mexico	166,874	150,288	61	27	68	87	16	13	18	3	66	84
Moldova	695	1,233	23	91	66	85	47	39	47	12	6	49
Mongolia	526	859	57	90	88	93	37	55	47	42	17	2
Morocco	22,665	17,944	72	55	99	99	30	33	43	35	26	32
Mozambique	7,458	7,135	350	198	94	89	18	18	56	54	26	28
Myanmar	5,771	6,046	..	..	93	89	25	24	68	58	7	18
Nepal	2,418	2,823	54	50	97	99	83	88	14	12	3	0
Nicaragua	10,402	7,019	704	333	82	83	17	36	71	53	12	11
Niger	1,587	1,638	87	89	92	90	60	65	31	30	9	5
Nigeria	34,093	34,134	132	93	83	97	17	10	55	79	28	11
Oman	5,777	6,267	55	..	91	79	4	5	9	8	87	86
Pakistan	30,229	32,091	51	54	84	91	48	47	41	40	11	14
Panama	6,098	7,056	81	75	62	92	16	16	17	4	67	80
Papua New Guinea	2,506	2,604	56	71	95	97	39	35	21	23	39	43
Paraguay	2,562	3,091	28	41	69	81	44	45	31	19	26	36
Peru	30,852	28,560	59	55	66	84	18	23	57	37	25	40
Philippines	37,829	50,063	50	63	84	84	27	17	43	29	30	54
Poland	44,263	63,561	35	41	95	89	5	4	72	38	23	58
Romania	6,784	10,224	19	28	65	92	38	32	30	13	32	55
Russian Federation	121,735	160,300	37	67	84	83	2	5	55	48	43	47
Rwanda	1,029	1,271	80	72	94	90	84	87	16	13	0	0
Samoa	170	197	88	83	99	75	93	94	7	6	0	0
Sao Tome and Principe	246	316	614	726	94	93	66	58	34	41	0	1

Table 1: EXTERNAL DEBT

(US$ millions)

	Total debt stock		Total debt / GNI (%)		Long-term debt / total debt (%)		Distribution of long-term debt (%)					
							Multilateral		Bilateral		Private	
	1995	2000	1995	2000	1995	2000	1995	2000	1995	2000	1995	2000
Senegal	3,841	3,372	89	79	84	88	57	62	39	37	4	1
Seychelles	159	163	32	28	92	76	41	43	34	41	25	16
Sierra Leone	1,178	1,273	134	207	77	76	48	59	51	40	1	1
Slovak Republic	5,744	9,462	31	50	62	88	12	8	5	6	83	87
Solomon Islands	159	155	49	54	94	98	53	66	10	11	36	23
Somalia	2,678	2,562	..	..	73	71	40	39	58	59	2	2
South Africa	25,358	24,861	17	20	58	62	0	0	0	0	100	100
Sri Lanka	8,370	9,066	65	55	86	90	39	42	50	46	10	12
St. Kitts and Nevis	57	140	26	51	95	97	55	39	35	36	10	25
St. Lucia	128	237	25	35	87	71	71	59	29	13	0	29
St. Vincent and the Grenadines	119	192	47	62	77	84	67	42	28	22	5	36
Sudan	17,603	15,741	280	161	58	58	21	21	56	59	23	20
Swaziland	235	262	17	17	95	76	55	74	45	26	0	0
Syrian Arab Republic	21,415	21,657	185	136	79	74	6	4	86	90	7	7
Tajikistan	634	1,170	28	125	93	85	0	17	88	41	12	42
Tanzania	7,415	7,445	145	83	84	85	45	52	48	45	7	4
Thailand	100,039	79,675	60	66	56	77	6	9	14	26	80	66
Togo	1,476	1,435	117	120	87	86	55	62	41	38	4	0
Tonga	64	58	39	38	98	100	66	88	27	12	7	0
Trinidad and Tobago	2,746	2,467	56	37	74	65	26	40	21	0	53	60
Tunisia	10,820	10,610	63	57	85	91	41	36	39	27	20	38
Turkey	73,790	116,209	43	58	78	72	16	7	15	9	70	85
Turkmenistan	402	..	7	..	96	..	15	..	42	..	43	..
Uganda	3,573	3,409	63	55	86	88	72	88	25	11	3	1
Ukraine	8,429	12,166	17	39	79	79	10	25	55	27	35	48
Uruguay	5,318	8,196	29	42	74	75	32	31	8	5	60	64
Uzbekistan	1,787	4,340	..	..	79	91	17	12	55	40	28	49
Vanuatu	48	69	22	31	90	98	72	89	27	11	1	0
Venezuela, R.B.	35,538	38,196	47	32	85	95	11	9	5	8	84	83
Vietnam	25,427	12,787	128	41	86	90	1	16	92	44	6	40
Yemen, Rep.	6,654	5,616	164	76	89	81	22	46	49	51	29	4
Yugoslavia, FR	11,137	11,960	..	142	77	56	15	22	39	40	46	38
Zambia	6,953	5,730	215	205	76	79	40	53	56	44	4	2
Zimbabwe	5,007	4,002	74	56	77	79	42	47	30	36	27	17
All developing countries	2,154,585	2,491,975	38	39	77	82	17	17	34	24	48	59
East Asia & Pacific	547,489	632,953	31	31	71	79	14	16	29	23	56	62
Europe & Central Asia	350,925	499,344	36	54	82	79	9	9	39	27	52	64
Latin America & Caribbean	649,398	774,419	40	41	76	85	15	14	24	10	62	76
Middle East & North Africa	214,228	203,785	44	32	78	75	14	15	56	49	30	36
South Asia	157,289	165,680	33	27	91	95	40	40	37	31	24	29
Sub-Saharan Africa	235,256	215,794	78	71	79	81	29	31	44	47	26	22
Low income	550,532	550,548	59	53	84	86	29	31	45	40	26	28
Middle income	1,604,053	1,941,427	34	36	75	81	13	13	30	20	57	68
Heavily indebted poor countries	224,904	190,443	149	102	83	83	30	39	54	45	16	16

Note: Individual country data are shown for Debtor Reporting System (DRS) countries only. Totals include estimates for countries not part of the DRS.

Table 1: EXTERNAL DEBT

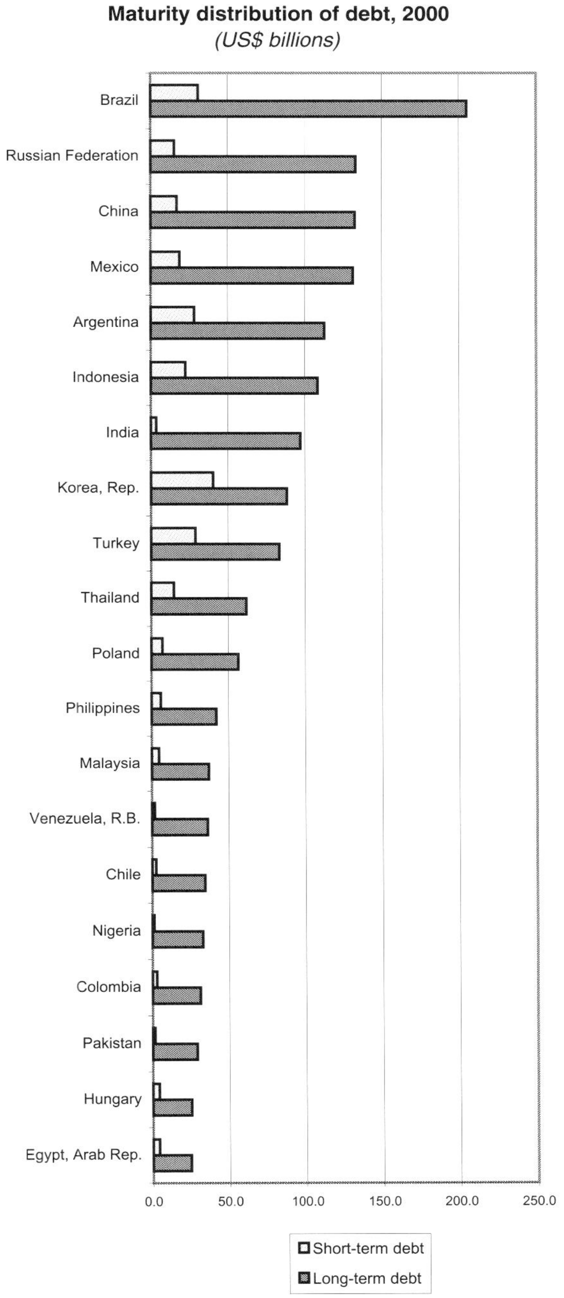

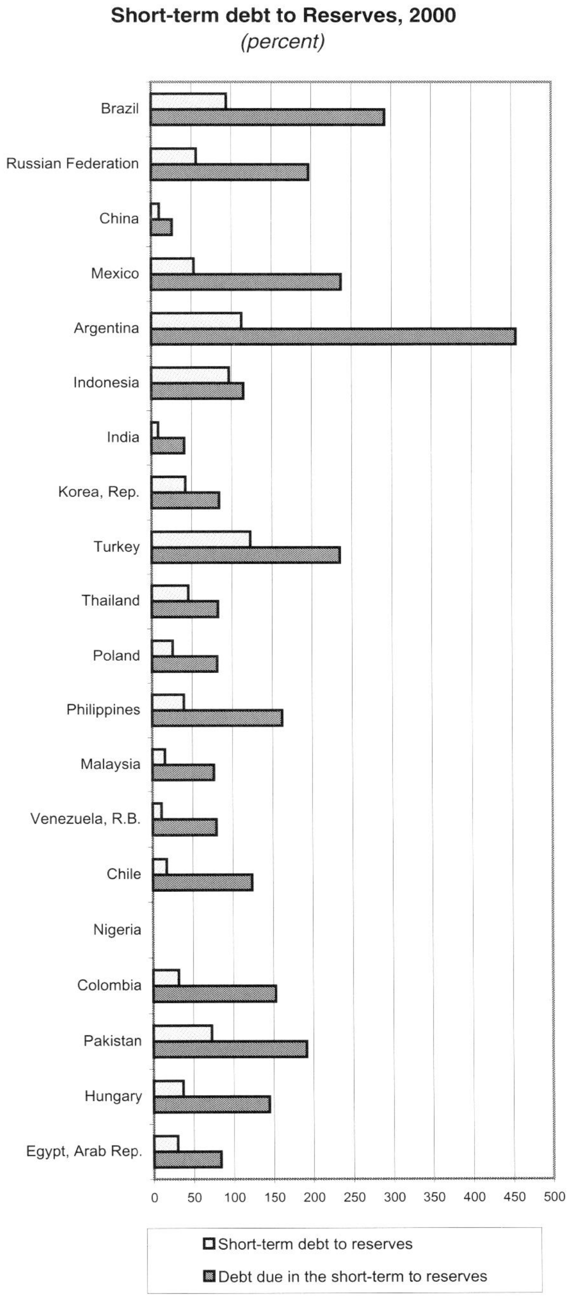

Note: Country selection is based on size of external debt at end-2000. Short-term debt is debt with an original maturity of one year or less (and includes interest arrears). Debt due in the short term is debt due within a year and comprises liabilities to banks, debt securities issued abroad, and nonbank credits. Debt due in the short term is larger than short-term debt, but when these data are derived from different sources this may not hold. Reserves are the sum of a country's monetary authority's holdings of special drawing rights, its reserve position in the IMF, its holding of foreign exchange, and its holdings of gold (valued at year-end London prices)
Source: Debtor Reporting System and Joint BIS-IMF-OECD-World Bank statistics on external debt (also available on the World Bank website: http://www.worldbank.org/data).

Table 2: AGGREGATE NET RESOURCE FLOWS (long-term)

(US$ millions)

	Aggregate net resource flows (excl. IMF)		Private flows: Foreign direct investment		Private flows: Portfolio equity		Private flows: Bonds		Private flows: Bank and trade-related lending		Official flows (including grants)	
	1995-99	2000	1995-99	2000	1995-99	2000	1995-99	2000	1995-99	2000	1995-99	2000
Albania	273	396	59	143	0	0	0	0	-1	-1	215	254
Algeria	-198	-1,678	6	10	4	4	-56	0	-513	-1,227	361	-465
Angola	1,335	1,407	930	1,698	0	0	0	0	102	-492	303	201
Argentina	21,030	16,719	10,599	11,665	753	450	7,731	4,847	1,152	-343	795	100
Armenia	234	270	88	140	0	0	0	0	0	19	146	111
Azerbaijan	877	305	721	130	0	0	0	0	33	45	123	130
Bangladesh	1,101	1,207	105	280	16	3	0	0	-25	-14	1,005	938
Belarus	325	125	224	90	0	0	0	0	14	33	88	3
Belize	53	184	23	18	0	0	0	0	6	145	24	22
Benin	204	192	31	30	0	0	0	0	0	0	173	162
Bhutan	50	46	0	0	0	0	0	0	-2	0	52	46
Bolivia	1,274	1,230	714	733	0	0	-1	0	82	190	479	307
Bosnia and Herzegovina	967	486	0	0	0	0	0	0	0	4	967	483
Botswana	76	11	75	30	0	0	0	0	-3	-3	4	-16
Brazil	33,118	43,934	19,240	32,779	2,946	5,016	2,816	164	7,723	7,713	393	-1,738
Bulgaria	749	1,363	410	1,002	240	5	-62	0	22	107	140	249
Burkina Faso	302	437	13	10	0	0	0	0	0	0	289	427
Burundi	109	98	1	12	0	0	0	0	0	0	108	87
Cambodia	432	398	183	126	0	0	0	0	0	0	249	272
Cameroon	194	185	35	31	0	0	0	0	-42	-52	200	205
Cape Verde	103	71	18	10	0	0	0	0	1	-2	84	63
Central African Republic	112	69	6	5	0	0	0	0	0	0	106	64
Chad	177	94	15	15	0	0	0	0	0	-1	162	79
Chile	8,113	4,733	5,334	3,675	194	18	990	672	2,158	469	-563	-101
China	52,012	60,525	40,554	38,399	3,947	22,198	1,417	-2,451	1,663	148	4,431	2,230
Colombia	5,738	3,312	2,788	2,376	118	26	1,381	1,225	1,328	-497	123	182
Comoros	23	13	2	0	0	0	0	0	0	0	22	13
Congo, Dem. Rep.	121	138	1	1	0	0	0	0	0	0	120	137
Congo, Rep.	119	40	6	14	0	0	0	0	-13	0	126	26
Costa Rica	567	573	491	409	0	0	99	220	5	-20	-29	-36
Cote d'Ivoire	537	56	320	106	13	6	-14	-46	-158	-113	375	103
Croatia	1,678	2,529	712	926	63	0	236	833	587	692	80	78
Czech Republic	4,763	3,441	3,060	4,583	178	617	285	-325	1,153	-1,576	86	142
Djibouti	55	27	5	0	0	0	0	0	0	0	50	27
Dominica	41	18	24	11	0	0	0	0	0	0	18	8
Dominican Republic	656	1,103	594	953	15	74	-2	-4	5	119	44	-40
Ecuador	1,063	1,172	618	710	0	0	65	0	171	194	208	268
Egypt, Arab Rep.	2,450	2,312	853	1,235	818	619	20	0	-194	114	952	345
El Salvador	547	467	285	185	0	0	30	132	6	22	226	129
Equatorial Guinea	149	138	133	120	0	0	0	0	0	0	15	18
Eritrea	152	190	29	35	0	0	0	0	0	0	123	155
Estonia	701	514	301	387	51	-29	37	110	243	16	68	29
Ethiopia	635	587	135	50	0	0	0	0	-49	-8	549	545
Fiji	25	-6	32	0	0	0	0	0	-13	-6	5	-1
Gabon	-217	-24	-225	150	0	0	0	0	-26	-8	34	-166
Gambia, The	43	47	11	14	0	0	0	0	0	0	32	33
Georgia	283	207	128	131	0	0	0	0	2	24	154	52
Ghana	802	483	86	110	94	17	50	0	42	-57	530	412
Grenada	39	84	32	37	0	0	0	0	-1	30	8	17
Guatemala	428	415	213	230	0	0	11	-31	-29	-22	233	238
Guinea	265	177	25	63	0	0	0	0	-6	0	246	113

Table 2: AGGREGATE NET RESOURCE FLOWS (long-term)

(US$ millions)

	Aggregate net resource flows (excl. IMF)		Private flows: Foreign direct investment		Private flows: Portfolio equity		Private flows: Bonds		Private flows: Bank and trade-related lending		Official flows (including grants)	
	1995-99	2000	1995-99	2000	1995-99	2000	1995-99	2000	1995-99	2000	1995-99	2000
Guinea-Bissau	67	61	3	0	0	0	0	0	0	0	64	61
Guyana	163	128	63	67	0	0	0	0	-4	0	104	61
Haiti	296	136	11	13	0	0	0	0	0	0	285	123
Honduras	450	707	120	282	0	0	-18	0	84	19	264	406
Hungary	4,328	1,643	2,595	1,692	830	0	327	-1,218	845	1,247	-268	-78
India	5,957	9,928	2,590	2,315	1,935	2,117	994	4,916	-250	-577	689	1,157
Indonesia	6,989	-9,156	2,423	-4,550	1,959	379	1,503	-2,050	-552	-4,988	1,657	2,053
Iran, Islamic Rep.	-2,648	-2,253	31	39	0	0	0	0	56	-649	-2,735	-1,643
Jamaica	271	972	285	456	0	0	90	485	-10	-43	-94	74
Jordan	630	807	172	558	26	12	13	-95	-120	-20	539	352
Kazakhstan	2,093	1,979	1,232	1,250	10	0	150	350	321	300	380	80
Kenya	141	374	18	111	13	4	0	0	-124	-61	234	321
Korea, Rep.	15,469	13,875	4,338	9,283	5,008	7,784	6,004	1,333	-2,339	-5,185	2,459	660
Kyrgyz Republic	267	112	76	-2	0	0	0	0	-1	-62	192	177
Lao PDR	328	262	94	72	0	0	0	0	0	0	233	190
Latvia	753	669	357	407	6	0	56	-30	182	206	151	86
Lebanon	1,378	2,258	143	298	79	4	801	1,040	124	687	231	230
Lesotho	332	179	252	118	0	0	0	0	18	-7	62	68
Liberia	99	58	16	12	0	0	0	0	0	0	83	47
Lithuania	938	910	398	379	5	151	189	312	194	-43	152	111
Macedonia, FYR	200	417	38	176	0	0	0	0	17	12	145	230
Madagascar	412	298	22	83	0	0	0	0	-2	0	393	215
Malawi	385	360	44	45	5	0	0	0	-6	0	342	315
Malaysia	8,214	3,411	3,622	1,660	1,455	542	1,488	477	1,634	550	15	182
Maldives	41	23	10	13	0	0	0	0	5	1	26	10
Mali	343	420	54	76	0	0	0	0	0	0	289	344
Mauritania	182	183	3	5	0	0	0	0	4	-2	174	180
Mauritius	246	46	34	266	15	0	150	-150	42	-123	5	53
Mexico	21,745	11,035	10,954	13,286	1,671	3,517	4,847	-2,636	5,100	-2,631	-827	-502
Moldova	189	269	49	128	0	0	15	0	51	81	74	60
Mongolia	162	154	20	30	0	0	0	0	-12	-3	154	127
Morocco	134	-460	37	10	176	147	52	-30	-53	-419	-78	-167
Mozambique	1,080	971	155	139	0	0	0	0	1	-1	924	833
Myanmar	514	244	308	255	5	0	0	0	133	-66	68	55
Nepal	274	237	13	4	0	0	0	0	-10	-8	271	240
Nicaragua	770	797	166	254	0	0	-2	0	-5	141	611	401
Niger	199	179	12	15	0	0	0	0	-17	-2	204	166
Nigeria	684	706	1,253	1,083	4	2	0	0	-313	-177	-259	-201
Oman	69	69	59	23	18	11	45	0	-104	23	51	12
Pakistan	2,508	526	680	308	336	0	92	0	305	-361	1,095	578
Panama	1,075	946	777	603	6	0	226	249	35	95	31	-1
Papua New Guinea	553	335	200	130	174	48	-6	0	-19	-50	204	207
Paraguay	420	99	184	82	0	0	0	0	125	-98	112	115
Peru	4,002	2,291	2,271	680	1,101	205	-212	0	409	668	432	738
Philippines	4,608	2,401	1,415	2,029	849	290	2,120	797	147	-657	77	-57
Poland	8,630	13,413	5,340	9,342	856	871	793	2,450	571	532	1,070	218
Romania	1,820	2,606	994	1,025	11	0	154	-75	212	950	449	706
Russian Federation	11,135	2,508	3,441	2,714	1,459	1,075	3,242	-1,018	942	-571	2,051	308
Rwanda	355	253	3	14	0	0	0	0	0	0	351	238
Samoa	16	7	3	0	0	0	0	0	0	0	13	7
Sao Tome and Principe	24	30	0	10	0	0	0	0	0	0	24	20

Table 2: AGGREGATE NET RESOURCE FLOWS (long-term)

(US$ millions)

	Aggregate net resource flows (excl. IMF)		Private flows: Foreign direct investment		Private flows: Portfolio equity		Private flows: Bonds		Private flows: Bank and trade-related lending		Official flows (including grants)	
	1995-99	2000	1995-99	2000	1995-99	2000	1995-99	2000	1995-99	2000	1995-99	2000
Senegal	442	349	89	107	0	0	0	0	-9	-2	361	243
Seychelles	55	64	48	56	0	0	0	0	-3	-4	10	13
Sierra Leone	103	186	3	1	0	0	0	0	-6	0	106	185
Slovak Republic	1,118	2,234	336	2,053	22	0	120	758	425	-625	216	49
Solomon Islands	31	56	12	10	0	0	0	0	-3	-4	22	49
Somalia	88	86	0	0	0	0	0	0	0	0	87	86
South Africa	4,305	2,957	1,586	961	2,439	864	745	1,193	-664	-282	199	221
Sri Lanka	733	530	195	173	48	6	23	-50	36	133	431	268
St. Kitts and Nevis	52	99	33	96	0	0	0	0	6	-1	14	4
St. Lucia	84	89	53	49	0	0	0	0	5	24	26	15
St. Vincent and the Grenadines	97	31	62	28	0	0	0	0	11	0	23	3
Sudan	341	563	168	392	0	0	0	0	0	0	173	171
Swaziland	83	-31	63	-44	0	0	0	0	0	0	20	13
Syrian Arab Republic	135	68	88	111	0	0	0	0	-5	-4	51	-40
Tajikistan	104	134	17	24	0	0	0	0	5	40	81	70
Tanzania	791	1,020	157	193	0	0	0	0	-9	-11	643	838
Thailand	9,885	-525	4,365	3,366	1,653	1,044	1,127	-1,218	613	-4,575	2,127	858
Togo	139	93	27	30	0	0	0	0	-1	0	113	63
Tonga	14	8	2	2	0	0	0	0	-1	-1	12	8
Trinidad and Tobago	537	633	603	650	0	0	63	128	-109	-106	-21	-40
Tunisia	868	1,009	368	752	8	0	311	-371	55	585	126	44
Turkey	4,821	12,217	827	982	737	2,701	1,548	6,484	2,097	1,250	-388	801
Turkmenistan	..	..	85	100	0	0	0	0	..	..	..	..
Uganda	724	936	170	220	0	0	0	0	-4	11	558	705
Ukraine	1,292	169	530	595	0	0	200	-33	171	365	391	-759
Uruguay	556	719	164	298	2	0	161	284	70	-8	160	145
Uzbekistan	749	303	143	100	0	0	0	0	356	-82	250	284
Vanuatu	42	41	27	20	0	0	0	0	0	0	15	21
Venezuela, R.B.	5,157	5,708	3,298	4,464	552	71	167	-751	740	1,670	401	254
Vietnam	2,808	1,790	2,007	1,298	90	0	0	0	-56	-717	767	1,209
Yemen, Rep.	55	-12	-166	-201	0	0	0	0	0	0	221	189
Yugoslavia, FR	461	1,298	0	0	0	0	0	0	0	0	461	1,298
Zambia	495	778	156	200	0	0	0	0	-23	-9	362	587
Zimbabwe	404	108	167	79	11	1	-30	0	-31	-50	287	79
All developing countries	303,339	261,133	154,541	166,691	33,021	50,867	42,588	16,879	28,009	-8,591	45,180	35,287
East Asia & Pacific	102,915	74,557	59,610	52,130	15,139	32,285	13,650	-3,113	1,261	-15,609	13,255	8,864
Europe & Central Asia	52,310	54,000	22,160	28,495	4,467	5,391	7,290	8,598	8,682	2,962	9,711	8,554
Latin America & Caribbean	109,330	99,315	60,039	75,088	7,358	9,378	18,445	4,986	19,087	7,853	4,402	2,010
Middle East & North Africa	6,768	1,470	2,871	1,209	1,128	795	1,193	544	210	-1,474	1,366	396
South Asia	11,355	13,265	3,594	3,093	2,336	2,126	1,109	4,866	56	-831	4,262	4,011
Sub-Saharan Africa	20,660	18,527	6,267	6,676	2,594	893	901	997	-1,286	-1,492	12,185	11,453
Low income	43,299	25,173	14,603	6,562	4,480	2,528	2,808	2,787	-450	-7,296	21,857	20,592
Middle income	260,041	235,959	139,938	160,129	28,541	48,340	39,780	14,091	28,459	-1,295	23,323	14,695
Heavily indebted poor countries	17,748	16,364	6,024	6,572	220	27	17	-46	-87	-1,235	11,574	11,046

Note: Individual country data are shown for Debtor Reporting System (DRS) countries only. Totals include estimates for countries not part of the DRS.

Data for 1995-99 represent average annual flows.

Table 2: AGGREGATE NET RESOURCE FLOWS (long-term)

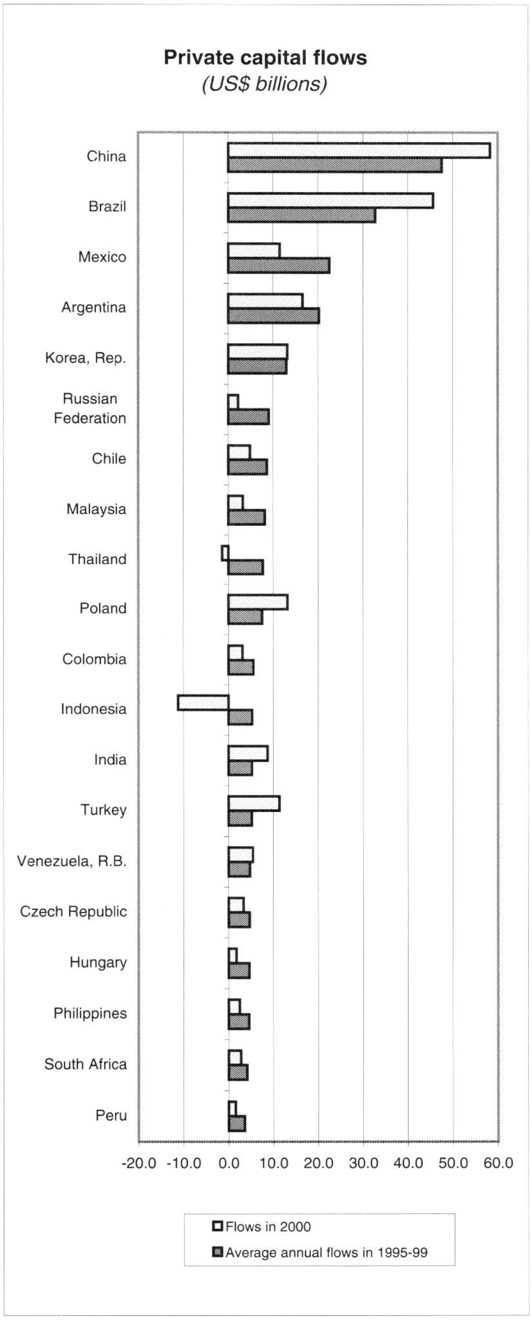

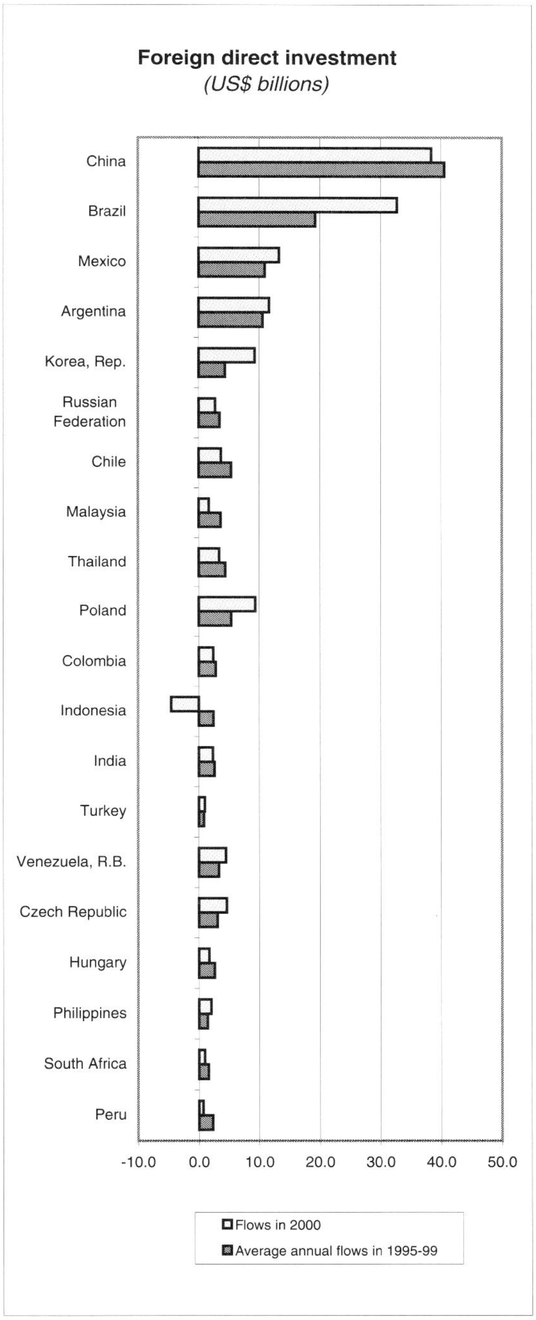

Note: Country selection is based on average annual capital flows during 1995-99, and shows the largest recipients.

Table 3: NET FLOWS AND TRANSFERS ON DEBT

(US$ millions)

	Net flows on debt		Net transfers on debt		Net flows on debt / GNI (%)		Net flows on long-term debt: Total		Official (excl. IMF)		Private	
	1995-99	2000	1995-99	2000	1995-99	2000	1995-99	2000	1995-99	2000	1995-99	2000
Albania	43	112	34	101	1.3	2.9	80	92	80	93	-1	-1
Algeria	-190	-1,820	-2,141	-3,475	-0.3	-3.6	-277	-1,754	291	-527	-569	-1,226
Angola	73	-745	-131	-908	1.1	-15.7	140	-497	38	-5	102	-492
Argentina	14,240	4,288	6,635	-7,325	5.2	1.5	9,645	4,574	762	69	8,883	4,505
Armenia	137	42	122	28	7.2	2.2	90	69	90	50	0	19
Azerbaijan	199	201	181	143	5.3	4.1	110	125	77	80	33	45
Bangladesh	290	287	101	95	0.7	0.6	340	332	365	346	-25	-14
Belarus	78	-103	15	-150	0.4	-0.3	52	8	38	-24	14	32
Belize	25	154	10	129	4.2	20.1	18	155	12	11	6	145
Benin	73	-36	50	-55	3.5	-1.7	50	17	50	17	0	0
Bhutan	17	24	14	22	4.3	4.9	16	25	18	25	-2	0
Bolivia	297	251	122	63	4.0	3.1	268	276	187	86	81	190
Bosnia and Herzegovina	91	-57	-75	-191	1.9	-1.2	116	-84	116	-87	0	4
Botswana	-31	-41	-67	-58	-0.6	-0.8	-34	-37	-32	-34	-3	-3
Brazil	12,351	1,223	287	-13,842	1.5	0.2	10,853	6,084	314	-1,792	10,539	7,877
Bulgaria	65	444	-448	-85	0.5	3.8	-4	227	35	120	-40	107
Burkina Faso	93	31	75	15	4.0	1.4	64	52	64	52	0	0
Burundi	18	14	8	6	2.2	2.0	16	27	16	27	0	0
Cambodia	68	126	60	108	2.3	4.0	55	71	55	71	0	0
Cameroon	108	-74	-133	-363	1.3	-0.9	-52	-19	-10	33	-42	-52
Cape Verde	29	11	25	6	5.4	2.0	27	18	25	20	1	-2
Central African Republic	10	-14	4	-20	0.9	-1.5	9	9	9	9	0	0
Chad	70	29	59	19	4.6	2.1	63	18	63	18	0	-1
Chile	1,950	2,382	608	151	2.8	3.5	2,549	1,022	-599	-119	3,149	1,141
China	7,241	-882	683	-8,476	1.0	-0.1	7,201	-374	4,122	1,928	3,080	-2,302
Colombia	2,647	-264	514	-2,516	2.8	-0.3	2,751	831	41	102	2,710	728
Comoros	6	4	5	2	2.7	1.8	5	2	5	2	0	0
Congo, Dem. Rep.	42	20	25	-4	1.0	..	2	0	2	0	0	0
Congo, Rep.	-20	-52	-100	-90	-2.2	-2.3	-48	-5	-35	-5	-13	0
Costa Rica	113	318	-103	57	0.8	2.2	47	139	-58	-61	104	201
Cote d'Ivoire	299	-617	-258	-1,156	3.4	-7.2	-223	-294	-52	-135	-171	-159
Croatia	982	1,540	588	855	4.9	8.2	871	1,557	48	32	823	1,525
Czech Republic	2,542	-1,241	1,349	-2,638	4.7	-2.5	1,450	-1,853	12	48	1,438	-1,901
Djibouti	9	-2	6	-5	1.7	-0.4	6	-1	6	-1	0	0
Dominica	3	3	0	-1	1.3	1.3	1	3	1	3	0	0
Dominican Republic	89	297	-106	34	0.6	1.6	-11	31	-14	-84	3	115
Ecuador	206	358	-592	-253	1.0	2.9	384	394	148	200	237	194
Egypt, Arab Rep.	133	-695	-958	-1,421	0.2	-0.7	-301	-506	-127	-620	-174	114
El Salvador	333	295	184	74	3.1	2.3	160	210	124	56	36	153
Equatorial Guinea	1	-12	-1	-14	-0.4	-2.5	1	0	1	0	0	0
Eritrea	45	61	43	59	5.7	8.8	45	50	45	50	0	0
Estonia	468	192	371	69	10.5	4.2	305	106	25	-21	280	126
Ethiopia	102	88	48	35	1.7	1.4	98	112	147	120	-49	-8
Fiji	-24	-17	-36	-25	-1.4	-1.2	-24	-16	-11	-10	-13	-6
Gabon	-19	-399	-254	-615	-0.6	-9.4	-54	-213	-29	-205	-26	-8
Gambia, The	11	23	4	17	2.7	5.6	15	11	15	11	0	0
Georgia	52	29	15	-21	0.2	0.9	86	18	84	-6	2	24
Ghana	362	-8	206	-164	5.3	-0.2	399	130	307	187	92	-57
Grenada	5	36	1	32	1.8	9.4	3	40	3	10	-1	30
Guatemala	238	20	59	-225	1.4	0.1	72	40	90	92	-18	-52
Guinea	120	-19	67	-76	3.3	-0.6	72	2	78	2	-6	0

Table 3: NET FLOWS AND TRANSFERS ON DEBT

(US$ millions)

	Net flows on debt		Net transfers on debt		Net flows on debt / GNI (%)		Net flows on long-term debt: Total		Official (excl. IMF)		Private	
	1995-99	2000	1995-99	2000	1995-99	2000	1995-99	2000	1995-99	2000	1995-99	2000
Guinea-Bissau	15	29	11	26	6.3	14.1	14	10	14	10	0	0
Guyana [a]	17	-7	-28	-56	2.6	-1.1	12	22	16	23	-4	0
Haiti	92	24	71	3	2.8	0.6	76	32	76	32	0	0
Honduras	227	192	23	0	4.8	3.3	178	239	112	220	66	19
Hungary	818	413	-892	-1,088	1.8	0.9	820	-196	-352	-225	1,172	29
India	42	4,311	-4,569	569	0.0	0.9	899	5,031	155	691	744	4,340
Indonesia	4,793	-2,753	-1,785	-10,229	1.5	-1.9	2,341	-5,348	1,391	1,691	950	-7,039
Iran, Islamic Rep.	-2,342	-2,267	-3,435	-2,871	-2.3	-2.2	-2,721	-2,328	-2,777	-1,679	56	-649
Jamaica	-54	431	-275	185	-1.2	6.2	-66	471	-146	29	80	442
Jordan	301	-335	-64	-636	4.3	-4.0	194	-148	301	-33	-107	-115
Kazakhstan	908	217	702	-231	4.4	1.3	818	686	347	36	471	650
Kenya	-125	99	-361	-32	-1.2	1.0	-97	57	27	118	-124	-61
Korea, Rep.	12,773	2,526	5,811	-3,276	2.6	0.6	6,121	-3,193	2,456	660	3,664	-3,852
Kyrgyz Republic	177	148	131	72	9.6	12.1	143	71	144	133	-1	-62
Lao PDR	101	52	93	42	6.1	3.1	101	55	101	55	0	0
Latvia	531	377	446	194	9.3	5.2	338	195	100	18	238	176
Lebanon	1,249	2,163	950	1,513	8.2	12.4	1,075	1,824	150	97	925	1,727
Lesotho	37	29	17	5	2.8	2.5	41	34	23	41	18	-7
Liberia	-1	-5	-2	-5	..	..	0	0	0	0	0	0
Lithuania	694	330	571	53	8.1	3.0	475	313	92	44	383	269
Macedonia, FYR	128	47	81	-5	3.3	1.3	101	68	84	56	17	12
Madagascar	119	69	64	31	3.4	1.8	97	100	99	101	-2	0
Malawi	130	86	100	65	7.3	5.2	127	88	133	88	-6	0
Malaysia	3,089	-171	949	-2,461	3.0	-0.2	3,124	1,200	2	174	3,122	1,027
Maldives	20	-3	16	-9	6.9	-0.6	15	0	10	0	5	1
Mali	130	-26	94	-54	5.3	-1.2	85	36	85	36	0	0
Mauritania	47	40	8	7	4.3	4.4	27	53	23	56	4	-2
Mauritius	239	-35	117	-184	5.9	-0.8	181	-229	-11	44	192	-273
Mexico	6,411	-15,221	-5,189	-28,942	2.1	-2.7	9,082	-5,792	-865	-525	9,947	-5,267
Moldova	136	96	90	41	6.9	7.1	130	104	64	23	66	81
Mongolia	86	34	76	24	9.3	3.6	83	42	95	46	-12	-3
Morocco	-382	-836	-1,562	-1,791	-1.2	-2.6	-361	-807	-359	-358	-2	-449
Mozambique [a]	224	71	172	40	7.5	2.0	182	104	181	105	1	-1
Myanmar	139	-16	109	-31	..	..	112	-56	-22	10	133	-66
Nepal	107	68	77	39	2.2	1.2	117	89	128	97	-10	-8
Nicaragua	204	312	90	203	11.5	14.8	219	288	225	147	-6	141
Niger	33	54	20	44	1.7	3.0	27	52	45	54	-17	-2
Nigeria	-640	-187	-1,359	-615	-2.1	-0.5	-606	-428	-292	-251	-313	-177
Oman	245	-536	-88	-921	1.1	..	-27	0	32	-23	-59	23
Pakistan	1,329	-306	222	-1,221	2.2	-0.5	1,306	93	908	454	397	-361
Panama	80	302	-256	-154	0.6	3.2	280	333	19	-11	261	344
Papua New Guinea	-10	30	-108	-60	-0.5	0.8	-12	59	13	110	-25	-50
Paraguay	242	-181	132	-313	2.9	-2.4	210	-9	85	89	125	-98
Peru	828	467	-591	-1,214	1.5	0.9	403	1,246	206	579	197	668
Philippines	2,283	434	18	-2,291	2.5	0.5	2,125	-75	-143	-215	2,267	140
Poland	1,952	3,549	219	976	1.3	2.3	1,183	2,526	-181	-456	1,364	2,982
Romania	409	1,391	-78	803	1.2	3.8	696	1,389	330	513	366	875
Russian Federation	7,475	-2,831	2,845	-8,432	2.2	-1.2	5,686	-1,943	1,502	-354	4,184	-1,589
Rwanda	78	25	69	14	4.6	1.4	61	27	61	27	0	0
Samoa	9	17	6	12	3.9	7.0	1	2	1	2	0	0
Sao Tome and Principe	10	9	8	7	23.7	20.2	9	6	9	6	0	0

Table 3: NET FLOWS AND TRANSFERS ON DEBT

(US$ millions)

	Net flows on debt		Net transfers on debt		Net flows on debt / GNI (%)		Net flows on long-term debt					
							Total		Official (excl. IMF)		Private	
	1995-99	2000	1995-99	2000	1995-99	2000	1995-99	2000	1995-99	2000	1995-99	2000
Senegal	53	-170	-44	-244	1.2	-4.0	38	-5	47	-3	-9	-2
Seychelles	3	-7	-4	-13	0.4	-1.2	0	-3	3	1	-3	-4
Sierra Leone	1	59	-10	50	0.6	9.6	30	69	36	69	-6	0
Slovak Republic	687	-428	202	-986	3.4	-2.3	718	118	173	-15	545	133
Solomon Islands	4	-4	1	-7	1.2	-1.5	4	-3	6	1	-3	-4
Somalia	0	-7	-1	-7	..	..	0	0	0	0	0	0
South Africa	544	1,186	-896	65	0.3	1.0	81	914	0	3	81	911
Sri Lanka	350	-62	174	-279	2.4	-0.4	358	242	299	159	59	83
St. Kitts and Nevis	18	1	14	-6	7.2	0.2	18	1	12	2	6	-1
St. Lucia	18	42	11	23	3.2	6.2	9	29	4	5	5	24
St. Vincent and the Grenadines	17	-2	12	-9	5.7	-0.6	15	-1	4	-1	11	0
Sudan	-96	-97	-108	-100	-1.1	-1.0	10	-4	10	-4	0	0
Swaziland	13	14	2	3	0.7	0.9	4	3	4	3	0	0
Syrian Arab Republic	242	-708	29	-930	1.8	-4.4	-19	-103	-15	-99	-5	-4
Tajikistan	61	47	46	16	5.3	5.0	31	61	26	21	5	40
Tanzania	164	169	80	107	2.3	1.9	127	97	135	108	-9	-11
Thailand	3,314	-13,708	-2,037	-18,559	1.0	-11.4	3,780	-4,972	2,040	820	1,740	-5,793
Togo	54	-45	38	-55	3.9	-3.8	40	14	41	14	-1	0
Tonga	1	-1	0	-1	0.7	-0.3	1	0	2	1	-1	-1
Trinidad and Tobago	7	10	-154	-158	0.0	0.2	-74	-18	-29	-41	-46	23
Tunisia	434	-456	-122	-1,009	2.4	-2.5	390	213	25	-1	366	214
Turkey	5,617	17,259	570	10,401	3.0	8.6	3,065	8,447	-580	714	3,645	7,733
Turkmenistan	..	..	..	..	..	..	..	..	..	..	..	..
Uganda [a]	167	146	125	100	2.7	2.4	156	189	160	178	-4	11
Ukraine	1,132	-1,297	554	-2,006	2.4	-4.2	603	-726	233	-1,058	371	332
Uruguay	518	535	90	-102	2.5	2.8	380	412	150	136	230	276
Uzbekistan	693	-240	546	-520	..	..	582	169	226	251	356	-82
Vanuatu	3	9	2	8	1.1	4.0	3	9	4	9	0	0
Venezuela, R.B.	647	336	-1,712	-2,217	0.6	0.3	1,290	1,139	384	220	906	919
Vietnam	513	393	223	43	2.2	1.3	445	256	501	973	-56	-717
Yemen, Rep.	211	240	165	144	3.5	3.2	97	26	98	26	0	0
Yugoslavia, FR	103	81	54	-23	-3.4	1.0	0	0	0	0	0	0
Zambia	79	159	-111	71	2.5	5.7	41	163	64	172	-23	-9
Zimbabwe	94	-389	-130	-554	1.1	-5.4	39	-85	100	-35	-61	-50
All developing countries	107,329	-834	-4,887	-127,549	1.8	0.0	86,638	13,634	16,041	5,347	70,597	8,288
East Asia & Pacific	34,403	-14,051	3,761	-45,616	1.8	-0.7	25,543	-12,397	10,631	6,325	14,912	-18,721
Europe & Central Asia	26,348	20,285	8,239	-2,941	2.6	2.2	18,876	11,596	2,904	36	15,972	11,560
Latin America & Caribbean	41,637	-3,343	-793	-56,637	2.3	-0.2	38,809	12,316	1,278	-523	37,531	12,839
Middle East & North Africa	3	-7,509	-9,546	-16,238	0.0	-1.2	-973	-4,308	-2,370	-3,377	1,403	-931
South Asia	2,144	4,308	-4,151	-1,325	0.4	0.7	3,044	5,798	1,880	1,763	1,164	4,035
Sub-Saharan Africa	2,793	-523	-2,397	-4,792	0.9	-0.2	1,333	629	1,719	1,123	-385	-494
Low income	12,509	467	-5,255	-17,214	1.3	0.0	9,131	893	6,772	5,402	2,359	-4,509
Middle income	94,819	-1,301	368	-110,335	1.9	0.0	77,508	12,741	9,269	-55	68,239	12,796
Heavily indebted poor countries	4,157	726	880	-2,267	2.4	0.4	3,014	1,726	3,085	3,007	-70	-1,281

Note: Individual country data are shown for Debtor Reporting System (DRS) countries only. Totals include estimates for countries not part of the DRS.

Data for 1995-99 represent average annual flows. a.Debt service payments to IDA do not include payments from the HIPC Trust Fund and IDA Grants under the HIPC initiative.

Table 3: NET FLOWS AND TRANSFERS ON DEBT

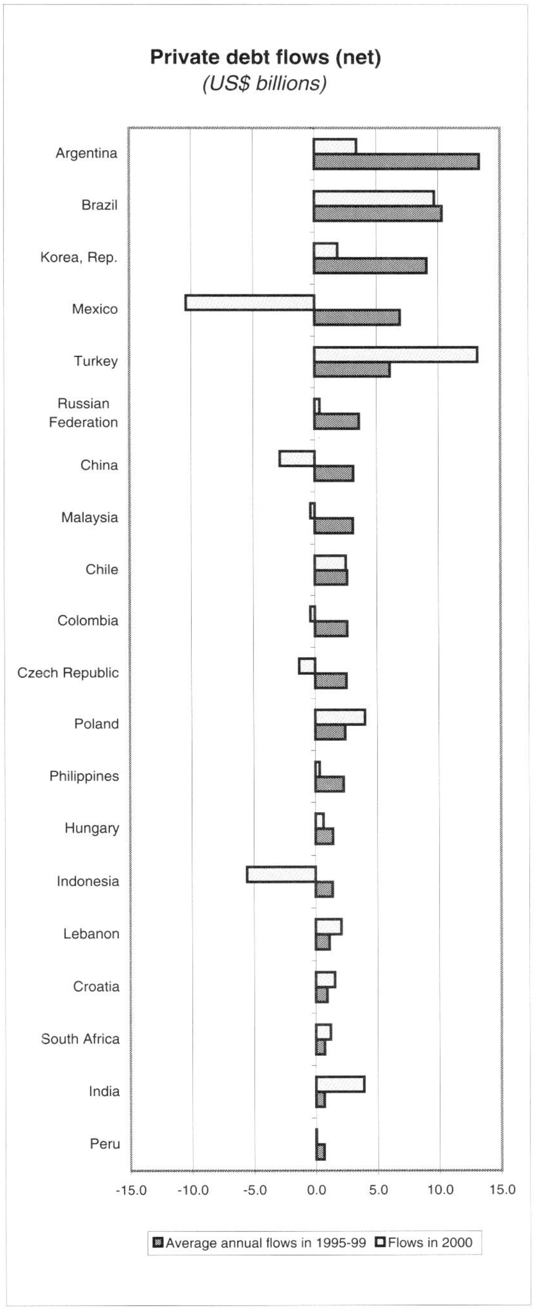

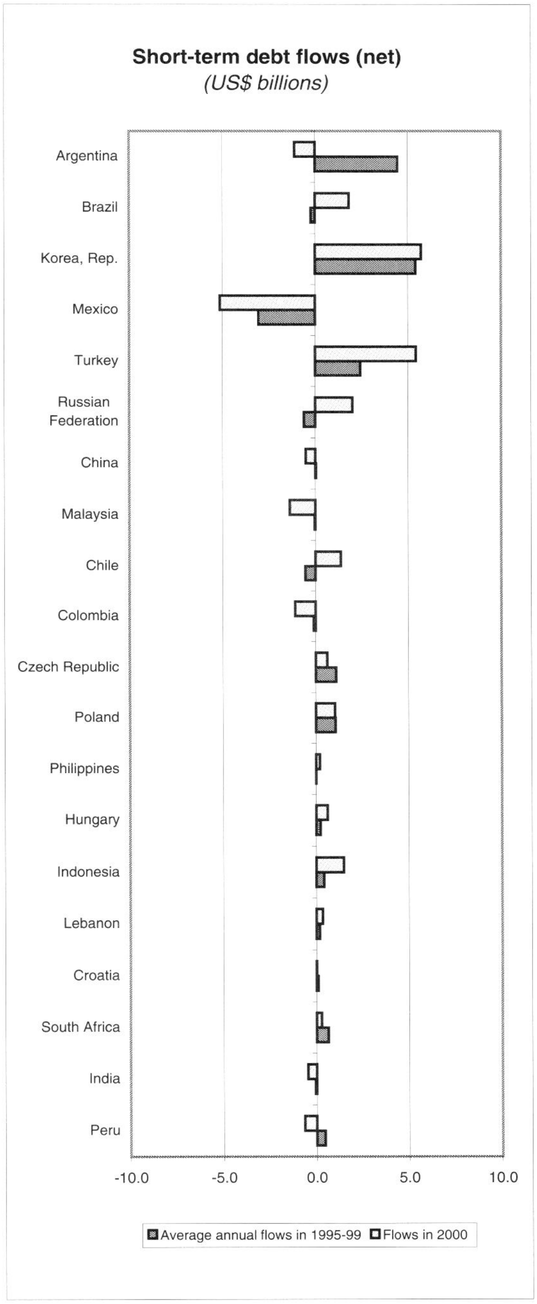

Note: Figures show the largest recipients based on the size of average annual private debt flows during 1995-99.

Table 4: NET FINANCIAL FLOWS FROM MULTILATERAL INSTITUTIONS, 2000

(US $ millions)

		Public and publicly guaranteed								
		World Bank		IMF		Regional development banks		Others	EBRD	IFC
	Total	IBRD	IDA	conc.	non-conc.	conc.	non-conc.			
Albania	94.8	0.0	64.4	11.6	0.0	0.0	0.0	15.4	0.0	3.4
Algeria	-108.0	-113.7	0.0	0.0	-92.6	0.3	38.3	60.8	0.0	-1.2
Angola	-3.5	0.0	23.7	0.0	0.0	-1.5	-23.6	-2.4	0.0	0.3
Argentina	1,918.0	480.7	0.0	0.0	814.7	-0.9	618.4	0.0	0.0	5.1
Armenia	54.2	-0.4	54.4	0.0	-15.8	0.0	-5.2	1.8	19.4	0.0
Azerbaijan	2.3	0.0	27.2	0.0	-51.4	0.0	9.6	10.7	-1.8	8.1
Bangladesh	404.0	-5.3	275.2	0.0	-85.7	184.9	11.3	17.0	0.0	6.6
Belarus	-76.1	-8.8	0.0	0.0	-55.6	0.0	-11.7	0.0	0.0	0.0
Belize	13.6	-1.3	0.0	0.0	0.0	0.0	11.1	4.0	0.0	-0.2
Benin	36.8	0.0	30.3	0.0	-3.6	11.1	0.0	-1.0	0.0	0.0
Bhutan	5.5	0.0	3.3	0.0	0.0	1.2	0.0	1.0	0.0	0.0
Bolivia	100.1	-11.9	50.6	-14.8	0.0	62.5	-25.4	17.0	0.0	22.0
Bosnia and Herzegovina	-79.8	0.0	44.1	0.0	15.8	0.0	15.0	-159.9	3.7	1.4
Botswana	-22.5	-7.4	-0.5	0.0	0.0	0.2	-13.8	-3.0	0.0	2.0
Brazil	-6,512.6	805.4	0.0	0.0	-6,693.0	3.0	2,488.1	-3,136.7	0.0	20.6
Bulgaria	307.9	44.3	0.0	0.0	137.0	0.0	0.7	57.7	47.1	21.1
Burkina Faso [a]	38.5	0.0	35.2	0.0	-2.5	10.0	-1.9	-2.4	0.0	0.0
Burundi	22.8	0.0	27.6	-4.5	0.0	-0.3	0.0	0.0	0.0	0.0
Cambodia	81.4	0.0	36.6	4.1	0.0	38.4	0.0	1.8	0.0	0.5
Cameroon	22.3	-53.3	48.7	0.0	49.9	3.2	-16.7	-2.6	0.0	-6.9
Cape Verde	16.9	0.0	10.2	0.0	0.0	7.9	-0.4	-0.4	0.0	-0.5
Central African Republic	8.3	0.0	7.2	-0.8	0.0	0.0	0.0	1.9	0.0	0.0
Chad	35.1	0.0	13.3	12.9	0.0	9.4	0.0	-0.5	0.0	0.0
Chile	-92.4	-66.7	-0.7	0.0	0.0	-1.3	4.6	0.6	0.0	-28.9
China	1,684.7	949.7	313.6	0.0	0.0	0.0	417.2	8.8	0.0	-4.6
Colombia	46.8	24.5	-0.7	0.0	0.0	-12.3	63.2	-8.2	0.0	-19.7
Comoros	0.8	0.0	1.4	-0.6	0.0	0.0	0.0	0.0	0.0	0.0
Congo, Dem. Rep.	-0.5	0.0	0.0	0.0	0.0	0.0	0.0	0.0	0.0	-0.5
Congo, Rep.	8.6	-2.4	-0.9	0.0	13.9	-0.4	-1.7	0.1	0.0	0.0
Costa Rica	-12.2	-27.2	-0.2	0.0	0.0	-11.1	16.0	21.8	0.0	-11.5
Cote d'Ivoire	-30.7	-57.5	75.4	-39.3	0.0	43.3	-35.4	-20.9	0.0	3.7
Croatia	106.0	33.5	0.0	0.0	-28.8	0.0	-4.0	9.3	60.1	35.8
Czech Republic	8.6	-42.9	0.0	0.0	0.0	0.0	0.0	51.0	3.7	-3.2
Djibouti	5.0	0.0	3.4	0.0	1.3	2.9	0.0	-2.6	0.0	0.0
Dominica	2.8	0.7	-0.2	0.0	0.0	0.0	0.0	2.3	0.0	0.0
Dominican Republic	54.6	17.8	-0.7	0.0	0.0	-4.2	24.1	8.7	0.0	8.9
Ecuador	326.3	-20.6	-1.1	0.0	149.5	-15.5	167.3	46.3	0.0	0.4
Egypt, Arab Rep.	-157.8	-80.5	26.3	0.0	0.0	3.4	-83.1	16.6	0.0	-40.5
El Salvador	78.7	17.0	-0.8	0.0	0.0	-13.0	89.0	-25.9	0.0	12.4
Equatorial Guinea	-2.0	0.0	-0.4	0.0	-2.7	1.5	-0.4	0.0	0.0	0.0
Eritrea	38.7	0.0	31.6	0.0	0.0	0.7	0.0	6.4	0.0	0.0
Estonia	-14.1	-9.4	0.0	0.0	-5.1	0.0	-2.7	-6.1	-8.3	17.5
Ethiopia	112.2	0.0	115.6	-13.0	0.0	22.7	-18.4	5.3	0.0	0.0
Fiji	-9.0	-6.8	0.0	0.0	0.0	0.0	0.6	-2.7	0.0	-0.1
Gabon	-26.3	-3.9	0.0	0.0	7.6	0.0	-30.1	0.1	0.0	0.0
Gambia, The	17.9	0.0	5.4	7.5	0.0	1.6	-0.7	4.2	0.0	0.0
Georgia	42.0	0.0	18.1	0.0	-25.9	0.0	0.7	1.2	24.0	23.9
Ghana	154.1	-8.1	178.9	0.0	-1.8	0.7	-13.5	1.6	0.0	-3.7
Grenada	7.0	1.9	0.7	0.0	0.0	0.0	0.0	4.4	0.0	0.0
Guatemala	80.1	38.2	0.0	0.0	0.0	-5.4	20.6	33.7	0.0	-7.0
Guinea	9.0	0.0	17.5	-8.0	0.0	0.6	-8.8	9.2	0.0	-1.5

Table 4: NET FINANCIAL FLOWS FROM MULTILATERAL INSTITUTIONS, 2000

(US $ millions)

		Public and publicly guaranteed								
		World Bank		IMF		Regional development banks		Others	EBRD	IFC
	Total	IBRD	IDA	conc.	non-conc.	conc.	non-conc.			
Guinea-Bissau	18.9	0.0	10.7	6.5	1.9	0.0	0.0	-0.3	0.0	0.1
Guyana	30.9	-3.2	5.3	0.0	-15.9	51.0	-8.1	1.2	0.0	0.7
Haiti	33.1	0.0	1.5	-3.0	0.0	35.1	0.0	-0.5	0.0	0.0
Honduras	198.0	-32.9	35.9	0.0	16.4	51.5	-15.1	165.1	0.0	-22.9
Hungary	-62.8	-56.7	0.0	0.0	0.0	0.0	3.3	-12.1	6.5	-3.8
India	302.8	-304.8	655.2	-251.0	0.0	0.0	159.8	41.5	0.0	2.0
Indonesia	1,633.6	290.1	33.2	0.0	1,122.7	17.9	203.9	-10.5	0.0	-23.7
Iran, Islamic Rep.	16.5	44.4	0.0	0.0	0.0	0.0	0.0	-27.9	0.0	0.0
Jamaica	111.3	37.1	0.0	0.0	-19.1	-4.7	88.8	10.8	0.0	-1.6
Jordan	-42.4	-14.8	-2.6	0.0	-11.3	0.0	0.0	-15.3	0.0	1.6
Kazakhstan	-329.0	29.7	0.0	0.0	-442.1	3.6	18.0	13.0	49.0	-0.2
Kenya	110.6	-40.4	141.5	1.9	0.0	1.6	-15.2	-5.7	0.0	26.9
Korea, Rep.	-176.5	-187.6	-3.5	0.0	0.0	0.0	-39.7	0.0	0.0	54.3
Kyrgyz Republic	99.7	0.0	51.7	0.0	7.4	37.7	0.0	7.6	0.0	-4.7
Lao PDR	61.4	0.0	16.7	-7.7	0.0	39.2	0.0	13.1	0.0	0.2
Latvia	6.0	53.8	0.0	0.0	-10.1	0.0	14.1	-30.7	-20.3	-0.8
Lebanon	66.6	25.8	0.0	0.0	0.0	0.0	0.0	42.0	0.0	-1.2
Lesotho	3.0	6.0	5.3	0.0	-5.2	1.0	-1.8	-2.4	0.0	0.0
Liberia	2.9	0.0	0.0	0.0	-0.6	0.0	0.0	0.0	0.0	3.5
Lithuania	45.3	56.9	0.0	0.0	-27.3	0.0	1.2	-3.3	-5.5	23.3
Macedonia, FYR	82.4	9.6	38.4	2.3	-17.8	0.0	0.6	10.5	24.9	13.9
Madagascar	150.7	0.0	76.9	45.1	0.0	19.6	-5.6	15.4	0.0	-0.7
Malawi	89.1	-7.6	81.2	-0.6	0.0	15.6	-1.1	0.0	0.0	1.6
Malaysia	-78.9	-85.9	0.0	0.0	0.0	0.0	9.4	-2.4	0.0	0.0
Maldives	2.4	0.0	3.0	0.0	0.0	0.9	0.0	-0.3	0.0	-1.2
Mali [a]	31.7	0.0	40.7	0.0	-8.2	4.7	0.0	3.4	0.0	-9.0
Mauritania	56.0	-1.9	53.1	-3.0	0.0	6.3	-5.8	10.8	0.0	-3.5
Mauritius	-5.8	-14.4	-0.6	0.0	0.0	-0.5	-2.8	12.9	0.0	-0.4
Mexico	-3,483.4	418.0	0.0	-4,298.9	0.0	-1.1	300.6	0.0	0.0	98.1
Moldova	15.6	0.8	30.1	12.2	-24.6	0.0	0.4	-4.2	-2.8	3.7
Mongolia	35.7	0.0	14.1	1.5	0.0	19.8	0.0	0.3	0.0	0.0
Morocco	-71.5	-168.8	-1.4	0.0	0.0	3.5	22.3	-4.4	0.0	77.4
Mozambique	182.5	0.0	93.7	0.0	30.4	12.6	1.8	6.3	0.0	37.7
Myanmar	-1.2	0.0	0.0	0.0	0.0	0.0	0.0	-1.2	0.0	0.0
Nepal	116.6	0.0	34.4	0.0	-4.4	67.5	0.0	4.7	0.0	14.3
Nicaragua	155.3	-4.8	85.5	0.0	21.3	59.9	-9.1	0.9	0.0	1.5
Niger	65.1	0.0	59.8	9.4	0.0	-0.4	0.0	-3.7	0.0	0.0
Nigeria	-236.4	-242.4	51.0	0.0	0.0	12.7	-70.2	-2.0	0.0	14.4
Oman	-1.8	-2.9	0.0	0.0	0.0	0.0	0.0	1.5	0.0	-0.4
Pakistan	115.5	-67.2	76.8	-14.5	-73.1	153.7	119.0	-31.4	0.0	-47.8
Panama	42.4	-2.4	0.0	0.0	-51.8	-9.6	37.7	4.5	0.0	64.1
Papua New Guinea	31.4	14.5	-2.7	0.0	18.7	-0.7	0.0	1.6	0.0	-0.2
Paraguay	105.8	27.9	-1.5	0.0	0.0	-1.1	83.1	-2.6	0.0	0.0
Peru	194.3	172.9	0.0	0.0	-141.3	-6.6	5.3	137.2	0.0	26.8
Philippines	73.9	-197.5	7.2	0.0	305.3	21.8	-77.2	-2.7	0.0	17.0
Poland	175.1	149.8	0.0	0.0	0.0	0.0	0.0	0.0	26.8	-1.5
Romania	487.6	293.2	0.0	0.0	18.3	0.0	19.0	163.5	-12.0	5.6
Russian Federation	-2,874.0	273.6	0.0	0.0	-2,888.0	0.0	-9.4	-2.4	-272.6	24.8
Rwanda	43.4	0.0	30.9	0.0	14.0	-0.9	-0.1	-0.5	0.0	0.0
Samoa	2.5	0.0	5.0	0.0	0.0	-1.7	0.0	-0.9	0.0	0.1
Sao Tome and Principe	8.9	0.0	1.3	0.0	2.5	1.8	0.0	3.3	0.0	0.0

Table 4: NET FINANCIAL FLOWS FROM MULTILATERAL INSTITUTIONS, 2000

(US $ millions)

		Public and publicly guaranteed								
						Regional				
		World Bank		IMF		development banks		Others	EBRD	IFC
	Total	IBRD	IDA	conc.	non-conc.	conc.	non-conc.			
Senegal	42.0	-2.8	76.7	-3.7	0.0	2.5	-12.0	-21.4	0.0	2.6
Seychelles	-0.3	-0.6	0.0	0.0	0.0	1.1	-0.6	1.6	0.0	-1.8
Sierra Leone	54.7	-0.3	68.3	-25.2	13.7	1.4	0.0	-2.5	0.0	-0.6
Slovak Republic	-189.3	-22.2	0.0	0.0	-127.3	0.0	-33.7	27.8	-12.0	-21.9
Solomon Islands	0.3	0.0	0.4	0.0	0.0	-0.2	0.0	0.1	0.0	0.0
Somalia	0.0	0.0	0.0	0.0	0.0	0.0	0.0	0.0	0.0	0.0
South Africa	59.4	2.7	0.0	0.0	0.0	0.0	0.0	0.0	0.0	56.7
Sri Lanka	-0.6	-5.3	28.3	-85.6	0.0	44.6	0.0	2.8	0.0	14.6
St. Kitts and Nevis	4.2	1.0	0.0	0.0	0.0	0.0	0.0	3.2	0.0	0.0
St. Lucia	9.0	0.4	0.6	0.0	0.0	0.0	0.0	8.0	0.0	0.0
St. Vincent and the Grenadines	1.1	0.0	-0.1	0.0	0.0	0.0	0.0	1.2	0.0	0.0
Sudan	-58.6	-2.1	-2.2	0.0	-54.2	0.0	0.0	-0.1	0.0	0.0
Swaziland	7.1	-0.1	-0.3	0.0	0.0	1.2	8.1	-0.7	0.0	-1.1
Syrian Arab Republic	-57.7	-14.2	-1.5	0.0	0.0	0.0	0.0	-42.0	0.0	0.0
Tajikistan	51.3	0.0	22.8	25.5	-9.9	3.2	0.0	9.5	0.9	-0.7
Tanzania	172.8	-4.4	109.4	0.0	27.4	27.2	-2.2	13.5	0.0	2.0
Thailand	-241.0	275.1	-3.4	0.0	-197.9	-2.1	-269.8	-2.3	0.0	-40.6
Togo	8.7	0.0	9.9	-9.4	0.0	2.5	0.0	-0.1	0.0	5.7
Tonga	1.7	0.0	-0.1	0.0	0.0	2.5	0.0	-0.7	0.0	0.0
Trinidad and Tobago	9.5	3.8	0.0	0.0	0.0	-0.1	-11.1	-0.8	0.0	17.6
Tunisia	-46.9	-14.5	-2.1	0.0	-40.1	0.0	-65.0	73.7	0.0	1.2
Turkey	3,817.6	805.8	-5.9	0.0	3,372.0	0.0	0.0	-316.8	0.0	-37.5
Turkmenistan	19.0	19.6	0.0	0.0	0.0	0.0	-2.7	-0.7	2.8	0.0
Uganda	171.0	0.0	175.6	0.0	-37.2	17.8	-0.8	17.3	0.0	-1.7
Ukraine	-491.9	88.2	0.0	0.0	-598.1	0.0	-29.4	0.0	46.2	1.2
Uruguay	175.7	76.3	0.0	0.0	0.0	-1.7	107.3	-4.3	0.0	-1.8
Uzbekistan	27.4	26.8	0.0	0.0	-65.1	1.2	56.9	0.0	6.5	1.1
Vanuatu	8.4	0.0	-0.2	0.0	0.0	9.3	0.0	0.0	0.0	-0.7
Venezuela, R.B.	-373.3	-157.6	0.0	0.0	-507.1	0.0	159.5	77.8	0.0	54.0
Vietnam	325.4	0.0	172.5	-15.9	-5.3	146.4	0.0	21.3	0.0	6.5
Yemen, Rep.	-28.9	0.0	51.3	0.0	-71.4	0.0	0.0	-16.5	0.0	7.7
Yugoslavia, FR	80.8	0.0	0.0	0.0	80.8	0.0	0.0	0.0	0.0	0.0
Zambia	237.2	-7.8	205.8	0.0	26.4	25.0	-14.9	-9.8	0.0	12.5
Zimbabwe	-115.4	-27.4	7.3	-35.7	-34.8	3.7	-7.3	-25.0	0.0	3.6
All developing countries	64.7	3,394.1	4,174.6	-4,694.9	-6,284.1	1,241.2	4,407.4	-2,692.1	-13.9	532.5
East Asia & Pacific	3,433.8	1,051.8	589.6	-18.1	1,243.6	290.7	244.4	23.0	0.0	8.8
Europe & Central Asia	1,406.8	1,745.4	345.2	51.5	-761.3	45.7	40.5	-156.9	-13.9	110.6
Latin America & Caribbean	-6,775.3	1,795.0	174.3	-4,316.6	-6,426.1	174.4	4,215.8	-2,630.7	0.0	238.7
Middle East & North Africa	-472.1	-339.2	73.5	0.0	-214.1	10.1	-87.5	40.5	0.0	44.6
South Asia	946.2	-382.6	1,076.1	-351.1	-163.1	452.8	290.0	35.5	0.0	-11.4
Sub-Saharan Africa	1,525.3	-476.2	1,916.0	-60.6	37.0	267.5	-295.9	-3.9	0.0	141.2
Low income	4,514.7	-428.9	3,545.6	-309.4	153.0	1,062.0	261.8	51.5	92.4	86.8
Middle income	-4,449.9	3,823.0	629.0	-4,385.5	-6,437.0	179.2	4,145.6	-2,743.6	-106.3	445.6
Heavily indebted poor countries	2,660.2	-241.2	2,230.3	-63.3	17.2	648.4	-234.5	219.2	0.0	84.1

a. Debt service payments to IDA do not include payments from the HIPC Trust Fund and IDA Grants under the HIPC initiative.

Note: Loans from major regional developments banks, the IMF, and the World Bank are classified as concessional according to each institutions's classification. Otherwise, concessionality of flows is as defined by DAC. EBRD and IFC data are for loans to the private sector without government guarantees. Data include only debt flows.

Table 4: NET FINANCIAL FLOWS FROM MULTILATERAL INSTITUTIONS, 2000

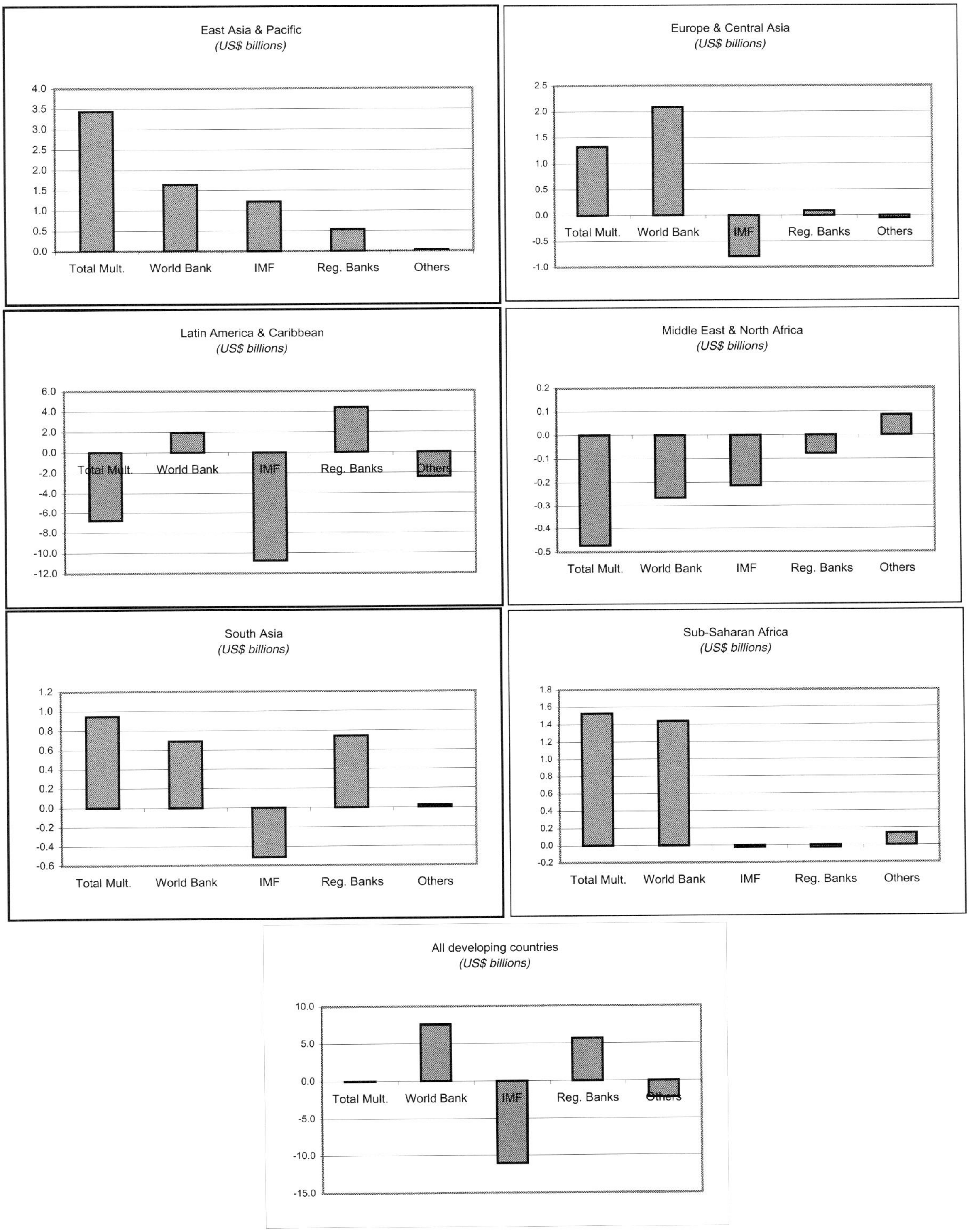

Table 5: INTERNATIONAL BOND ISSUES, NEW AND OUTSTANDING

(US $ millions)

	Outstanding						New Issues						Repayments	
	1999			2000			1999			2000				
	PPG Bonds	Brady Bonds	PNG Bonds	PPG Bonds	Brady Bonds	PNG Bonds	Total	PPG Bonds	PNG Bonds	Total	PPG Bonds	PNG Bonds	1999	2000
Argentina	45,640	16,662	12,130	54,450	11,073	11,138	13,872	12,542	1,330	14,019	12,611	1,408	5,872	9,172
Bosnia and Herzegovina	333	..	..	333	..	..	..	..	..	..	..	..	..	..
Brazil	20,416	31,941	16,823	26,308	25,250	16,846	9,865	8,521	1,345	11,336	8,450	2,886	7,001	11,173
Bulgaria	57	4,977	..	53	4,976	..	53	53	..	..	..	..	35	..
Chile	0	..	5,677	0	..	6,339	873	..	873	672	..	672	11	..
China	14,601	..	1,248	12,294	..	1,068	1,660	1,660	..	390	..	390	1,000	2,841
Colombia	7,367	..	885	8,592	..	762	1,926	1,750	176	1,804	1,804	..	691	579
Congo, Dem. Rep.	4	..	..	3	..	..	..	..	..	..	..	..	..	..
Costa Rica	534	538	..	777	515	..	300	300	..	250	250	..	17	30
Cote d'Ivoire	0	2,389	..	0	2,343	..	..	..	..	..	..	..	46	46
Croatia	1,142	..	..	1,884	..	..	539	539	..	833	833	..	..	..
Czech Republic	1,662	..	486	1,259	..	483	427	427	..	..	..	..	251	325
Dominican Republic	0	510	..	0	506	..	..	..	..	..	..	..	4	4
Ecuador	500	5,806	..	3,950	..	..	..	..	..	..	..	..	19	..
Egypt, Arab Rep.	..	..	100	..	..	100	100	..	100	..	..	..	..	..
El Salvador	150	..	..	282	..	..	150	150	..	132	132	..	..	..
Estonia	34	..	130	31	..	232	78	19	58	139	..	139	33	28
Ghana	..	..	250	..	..	250	..	..	..	..	..	..	..	..
Guatemala	276	..	..	245	..	..	..	..	..	..	..	..	31	31
Hungary	12,720	..	203	10,577	..	188	3,103	2,969	133	630	630	..	1,844	1,847
India	5,722	..	2,874	10,627	..	2,819	..	..	..	5,497	5,497	..	1,126	581
Indonesia	971	..	8,433	971	..	6,337	..	..	..	350	..	350	1,458	2,400
Jamaica	463	..	55	1,004	..	..	..	..	..	553	553	..	65	68
Jordan	154	711	..	153	583	..	..	..	..	..	..	..	9	95
Kazakhstan	650	..	100	1,000	..	100	300	300	..	350	350	..	200	..
Korea, Rep.	24,286	..	19,495	21,754	..	21,995	3,878	2,665	1,213	4,866	1,472	3,394	5,638	3,533
Latvia	226	..	30	209	..	..	240	240	..	..	..	..	..	30
Lebanon	3,681	..	671	4,602	..	736	1,286	1,240	46	1,490	1,375	115	160	450
Lithuania	903	..	..	1,131	..	37	745	745	..	337	300	37	..	25
Malaysia	9,256	..	3,841	9,945	..	3,402	1,010	1,010	..	1,422	1,061	361	263	945
Mauritius	150	..	600	..	..	600	..	..	..	..	..	..	..	150
Mexico	32,826	23,551	13,700	36,039	16,143	13,493	11,512	5,637	5,875	10,172	6,826	3,346	5,880	12,807
Moldova	75	..	..	75	..	..	..	..	..	..	..	..	..	..
Morocco	197	..	..	152	..	..	..	..	..	..	..	..	35	30
Nigeria	0	2,051	..	0	2,051	..	..	..	..	..	..	..	..	..
Oman	225	..	..	225	..	..	..	..	..	..	..	..	..	..
Pakistan	623	..	45	623	..	45	..	..	..	..	..	..	75	..
Panama	2,053	1,872	266	2,422	1,718	266	537	517	20	370	370	..	156	120
Peru	0	3,727	150	0	3,727	150	..	..	..	..	..	..	255	..
Philippines	8,526	1,482	6,137	9,711	1,384	5,690	5,345	4,550	795	1,636	1,631	5	1,135	839
Poland	1,912	5,426	11,009	2,177	4,483	13,981	1,146	..	1,146	5,441	554	4,887	50	2,991
Romania	652	..	75	597	..	..	..	..	..	..	..	..	456	75
Russian Federation	15,644	..	2,171	36,368	..	1,412	..	..	..	75	..	75	..	1,093
Slovak Republic	889	..	251	1,409	..	449	408	248	160	956	748	208	5	199
South Africa	3,969	..	395	4,749	..	1,110	1,627	1,627	..	1,477	765	712	374	284
Sri Lanka	115	..	..	65	..	..	..	..	..	..	..	..	..	50
Thailand	2,840	..	9,501	2,630	..	8,414	..	..	..	..	..	..	1,358	1,218
Trinidad and Tobago	652	..	110	780	..	110	230	230	..	250	250	..	..	122
Tunisia	1,825	..	..	1,327	..	..	240	240	..	..	..	..	..	371
Turkey	17,766	..	1,338	22,783	..	1,784	5,782	5,230	552	8,353	7,899	454	2,019	1,869
Uganda	4	..	..	4	..	..	..	..	..	..	..	..	..	..
Ukraine	2,329	..	..	2,377	..	..	..	..	..	..	..	..	107	33
Uruguay	1,874	593	351	2,226	549	300	137	37	100	616	616	..	322	332
Venezuela, R.B.	6,814	10,448	3,895	6,843	9,554	3,880	1,213	..	1,213	462	462	..	1,079	1,213
Vietnam	..	560	..	..	560	..	..	..	..	..	..	..	..	..
Zimbabwe	..	..	..	..	..	..	..	..	..	..	..	..	30	..

Table 5: INTERNATIONAL BOND ISSUES, NEW AND OUTSTANDING

(US $ millions)

	Outstanding						New Issues						Repayments	
	1999			2000			1999			2000				
	PPG Bonds	Brady Bonds	PNG Bonds	PPG Bonds	Brady Bonds	PNG Bonds	Total	PPG Bonds	PNG Bonds	Total	PPG Bonds	PNG Bonds	1999	2000
All developing countries	253,702	113,243	123,423	306,987	85,414	124,516	68,582	53,446	15,136	74,877	55,440	19,437	39,110	57,999
East Asia & Pacific	60,479	2,041	48,654	57,305	1,944	46,906	11,893	9,885	2,008	8,664	4,164	4,500	10,851	11,777
Europe & Central Asia	56,991	10,403	15,792	82,262	9,459	18,666	12,821	10,771	2,050	17,114	11,315	5,800	5,001	8,516
Latin America & Caribbean	119,563	95,648	54,041	143,918	69,035	53,285	40,615	29,683	10,932	40,635	32,324	8,311	21,403	35,649
Middle East & North Africa	6,082	711	771	7,432	583	836	1,626	1,480	146	1,490	1,375	115	204	946
South Asia	6,460	0	2,919	11,315	0	2,864	..	..	..	..	5,497	..	1,201	631
Sub-Saharan Africa	4,126	4,440	1,245	4,756	4,394	1,960	..	1,627	..	1,477	765	712	450	480
Low income	9,727	4,999	11,602	14,680	4,953	9,451	..	..	..	5,847	5,497	350	2,841	3,060
Middle income	243,976	108,244	111,821	292,307	80,461	115,066	68,582	53,446	15,136	69,030	49,943	19,087	36,269	54,939
Special Program of Assistance	2,392	..	250	2,347	..	250	..	..	..	..	..	..	46	46
Heavily indebted poor countries	7	2,948	250	7	2,902	250	..	..	..	..	..	..	46	46

Note: PPG bonds exclude Brady bonds. PPG is public and publicly guaranteed; PNG is private non-guaranteed.

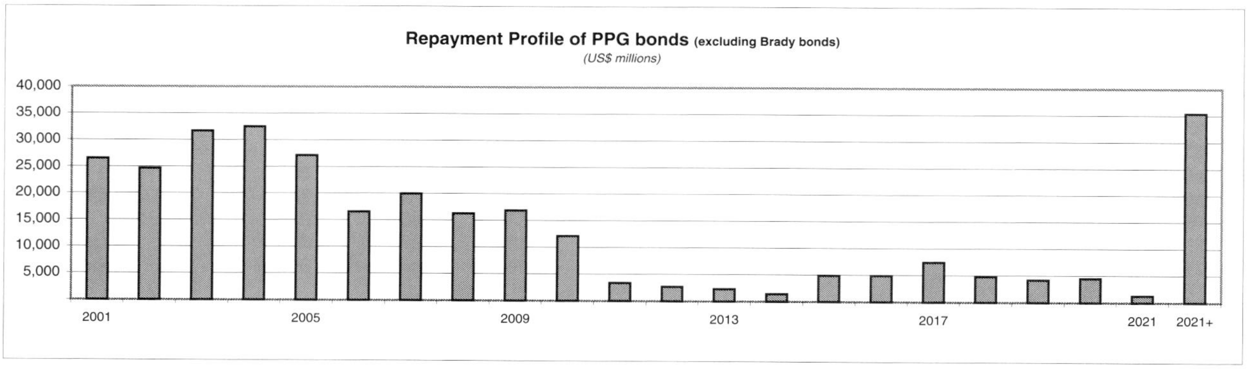

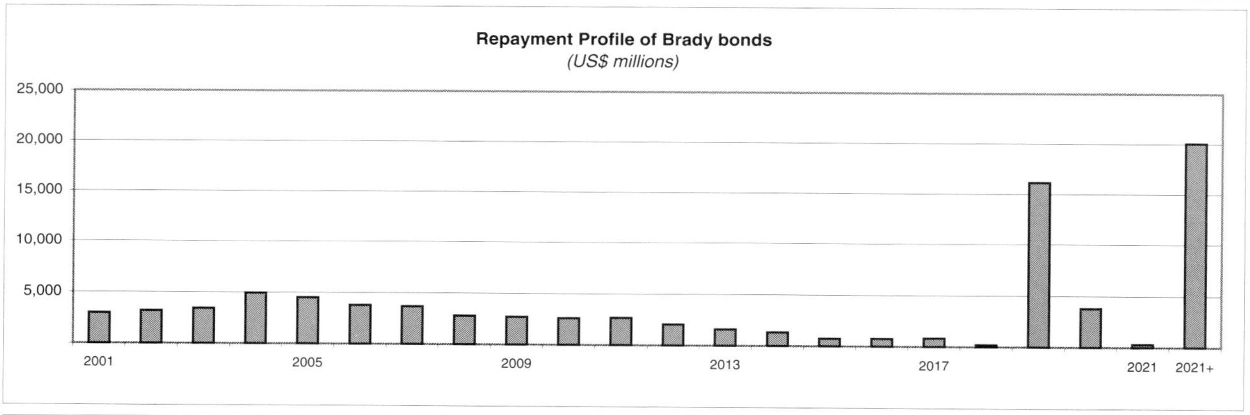

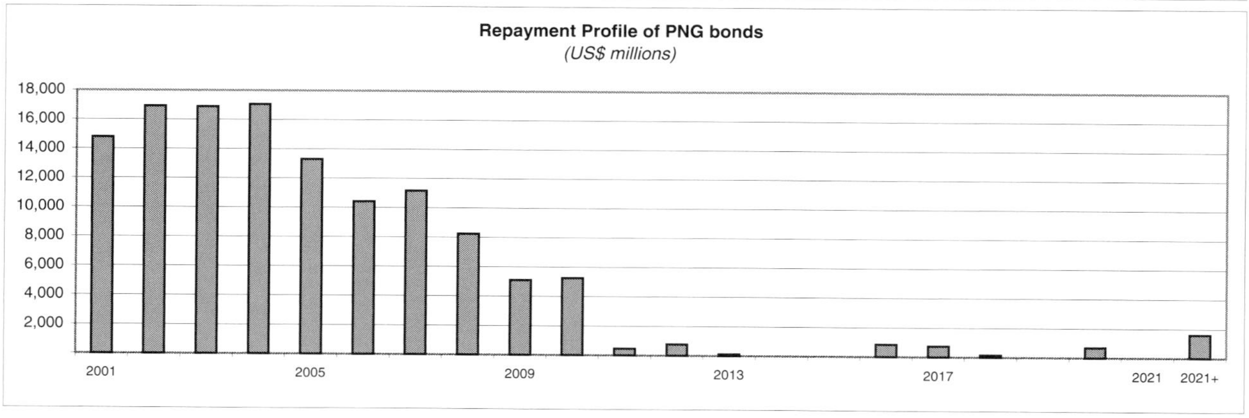

Summary tables

ALL DEVELOPING COUNTRIES

(US$ million, unless otherwise indicated)

1. SUMMARY DEBT DATA

	1970	1980	1990	1995	1996	1997	1998	1999	2000	2001
TOTAL DEBT STOCKS (EDT)	**72,751**	**609,450**	**1,458,389**	**2,154,585**	**2,241,825**	**2,329,296**	**2,546,952**	**2,565,784**	**2,491,975**	**2,442,082**
Long-term debt (LDOD)	**62,627**	**451,635**	**1,179,328**	**1,669,043**	**1,721,723**	**1,798,897**	**2,044,467**	**2,093,021**	**2,047,697**	**1,998,668**
Public and publicly guaranteed	47,250	381,065	1,113,815	1,431,464	1,421,366	1,409,743	1,513,793	1,542,035	1,490,445	1,467,574
Private nonguaranteed	15,377	70,571	65,513	237,579	300,357	389,154	530,674	550,986	557,251	531,094
Use of IMF credit	**756**	**12,244**	**34,651**	**61,064**	**60,096**	**70,798**	**93,839**	**78,888**	**64,262**	**74,810**
Short-term debt	**..**	**145,571**	**244,410**	**424,478**	**460,005**	**459,601**	**408,646**	**393,867**	**380,016**	**368,604**
of which interest arrears on LDOD	..	2,478	52,705	44,524	39,089	30,086	36,139	40,265	33,318	30,761
Official creditors	..	2,030	19,645	26,563	26,022	24,117	28,343	29,072	23,490	..
Private creditors	..	447	33,061	17,961	13,067	5,969	7,796	11,193	9,828	..
Memo: principal arrears on LDOD	..	2,547	59,506	106,981	101,577	75,270	85,086	83,382	64,707	..
Official creditors	..	1,246	27,297	60,457	61,722	59,131	65,042	64,477	47,889	..
Private creditors	..	1,301	32,209	46,525	39,855	16,138	20,044	18,905	16,818	..
Memo: export credits	..	4,570	296,688	369,120	366,941	369,747	219,320	216,257	195,478	..
TOTAL DEBT FLOWS										
Disbursements	**13,445**	**113,824**	**136,647**	**241,509**	**276,135**	**328,918**	**332,398**	**286,089**	**274,801**	**253,040**
Long-term debt	13,114	107,808	128,405	213,595	267,475	305,720	303,273	271,395	264,686	222,586
IMF purchases	331	6,016	8,242	27,914	8,660	23,198	29,125	14,694	10,114	30,455
Principal repayments	**6,821**	**44,506**	**93,484**	**140,131**	**176,292**	**202,037**	**198,313**	**275,864**	**272,146**	**259,737**
Long-term debt	6,079	42,510	85,312	129,058	168,689	193,498	188,419	248,604	251,052	242,074
IMF repurchases	743	1,996	8,171	11,073	7,603	8,539	9,894	27,260	21,093	17,663
Net flows on debt	**6,675**	**102,422**	**59,664**	**170,382**	**142,603**	**138,773**	**96,676**	**-11,789**	**-834**	**-15,693**
of which short-term debt	..	33,104	16,501	69,003	42,760	11,891	-37,410	-22,015	-3,489	-8,996
Interest payments (INT)	**..**	**48,854**	**70,316**	**100,815**	**106,584**	**112,969**	**118,738**	**121,974**	**126,716**	**122,197**
Long-term debt	2,366	32,791	54,545	77,195	81,046	87,687	95,017	99,535	104,104	101,912
IMF charges	0	471	2,500	2,788	2,309	2,207	3,406	3,565	3,181	2,769
Short-term debt	..	15,592	13,271	20,832	23,229	23,075	20,315	18,752	19,232	17,516
Net transfers on debt	**..**	**53,568**	**-10,652**	**69,567**	**36,019**	**25,804**	**-22,063**	**-133,763**	**-127,549**	**-137,889**
Total debt service paid (TDS)	**..**	**93,360**	**163,800**	**240,945**	**282,876**	**315,006**	**317,051**	**397,838**	**398,861**	**381,934**
Long-term debt	8,444	75,301	139,858	206,252	249,734	281,185	283,436	348,138	355,355	343,985
IMF repurchases and charges	743	2,467	10,671	13,861	9,913	10,746	13,300	30,825	24,274	20,432
Short-term debt (interest only)	..	15,592	13,271	20,832	23,229	23,075	20,315	18,752	19,232	17,516

2. AGGREGATE NET RESOURCE FLOWS AND NET TRANSFERS (LONG-TERM)

	1970	1980	1990	1995	1996	1997	1998	1999	2000	2001
NET RESOURCE FLOWS	**11,177**	**82,816**	**99,148**	**260,193**	**306,574**	**341,407**	**336,653**	**271,871**	**261,133**	**196,477**
Net flow of long-term debt (ex. IMF)	7,035	65,298	43,093	84,537	98,787	112,222	114,854	22,791	13,634	-19,488
Foreign direct investment (net)	2,198	4,397	24,119	106,817	130,780	172,494	178,263	184,353	166,691	168,238
Portfolio equity flows	-2	-1	3,743	36,060	48,929	30,094	15,567	34,456	50,867	18,527
Grants (excluding technical coop.)	1,946	13,123	28,193	32,779	28,079	26,597	27,969	30,271	29,940	29,200
Memo: technical coop. grants	1,753	6,353	14,094	20,104	18,685	15,737	16,285	16,628	15,545	15,200
official net resource flows	5,383	34,993	55,591	54,053	30,334	40,734	53,400	47,379	35,287	36,508
private net resource flows	5,794	47,823	43,557	206,139	276,241	300,673	283,252	224,492	225,846	159,970
NET TRANSFERS	**3,522**	**27,345**	**27,044**	**156,498**	**195,548**	**221,958**	**206,412**	**131,876**	**111,464**	**39,265**
Interest on long-term debt	2,366	32,791	54,545	77,195	81,046	87,687	95,017	99,535	104,104	101,912
Profit remittances on FDI	5,290	22,680	17,559	26,500	29,981	31,762	35,224	40,338	45,367	55,300
Memo: official net transfers	4,510	28,869	35,492	23,819	-413	12,380	25,520	18,755	6,419	7,908
private net transfers	-988	-1,524	-8,448	132,679	195,961	209,578	180,891	113,121	105,045	31,358

3. MAJOR ECONOMIC AGGREGATES

	1970	1980	1990	1995	1996	1997	1998	1999	2000	2001
Gross national income (GNI)	669,015	2,901,176	4,273,945	5,626,595	6,206,210	6,452,474	5,992,426	5,873,821	6,376,078	6,388,830
Exports of goods & services (XGS)	..	692,508	906,058	1,523,773	1,684,083	1,819,693	1,724,734	1,816,011	2,198,805	2,175,718
of which workers remittances	..	14,009	25,446	40,858	45,834	51,129	47,961	50,463	52,354	53,360
Imports of goods & services (MGS)	..	680,411	935,706	1,649,596	1,814,911	1,936,848	1,815,536	1,830,202	2,158,779	2,165,903
International reserves (RES)	..	212,086	223,169	539,522	629,182	658,406	708,637	763,963	830,728	1,137,940
Current account balance	..	-7,833	-24,977	-113,425	-116,513	-105,680	-67,728	10,329	48,909	1,509

4. DEBT INDICATORS

	1970	1980	1990	1995	1996	1997	1998	1999	2000	2001
EDT / XGS (%)	..	88.0	161.0	141.4	133.1	128.0	147.7	141.3	113.3	112.2
EDT / GNI (%)	..	21.0	34.1	38.3	36.1	36.1	42.5	43.7	39.1	38.2
TDS / XGS (%)	..	13.5	18.1	15.8	16.8	17.3	18.4	21.9	18.1	17.6
INT / XGS (%)	..	7.1	7.8	6.6	6.3	6.2	6.9	6.7	5.8	5.6
INT / GNI (%)	..	1.7	1.7	1.8	1.7	1.8	2.0	2.1	2.0	1.9
RES / EDT (%)	..	34.8	15.3	25.0	28.1	28.3	27.8	29.8	33.3	46.6
RES / MGS (months)	..	3.7	2.9	3.9	4.2	4.1	4.7	5.0	4.6	6.3
Short-term / EDT (%)	..	23.9	16.8	19.7	20.5	19.7	16.0	15.4	15.3	15.1
Concessional / EDT (%)	..	18.2	21.5	19.4	18.1	16.1	14.9	15.6	15.4	15.4
Multilateral / EDT (%)	..	8.0	14.2	13.5	12.8	12.4	12.9	13.5	13.9	14.2

ALL DEVELOPING COUNTRIES

(US$ million, unless otherwise indicated)

	1970	1980	1990	1995	1996	1997	1998	1999	2000	2001
5. LONG-TERM DEBT										
DEBT OUTSTANDING (LDOD)	**62,627**	**451,635**	**1,179,328**	**1,669,043**	**1,721,723**	**1,798,897**	**2,044,467**	**2,093,021**	**2,047,697**	**1,998,668**
Public and publicly guaranteed	**47,250**	**381,065**	**1,113,815**	**1,431,464**	**1,421,366**	**1,409,743**	**1,513,793**	**1,542,035**	**1,490,445**	**1,467,574**
Official creditors	33,631	178,221	604,192	863,227	829,457	791,908	841,758	865,525	843,843	827,779
Multilateral	7,328	48,815	207,405	289,903	285,850	289,499	328,505	345,681	346,551	346,751
Concessional	2,072	18,250	68,763	106,775	111,181	113,726	124,358	129,957	131,395	131,009
Bilateral	26,304	129,407	396,787	573,325	543,607	502,409	513,252	519,844	497,293	481,029
Concessional	22,632	92,476	245,002	310,182	295,567	260,940	254,020	269,308	251,089	245,974
Private creditors	13,619	202,843	509,623	568,237	591,909	617,834	672,036	676,518	646,602	639,795
Bonds	1,797	13,086	107,305	256,985	292,878	308,453	346,084	366,945	392,401	408,833
Commercial banks	3,650	127,491	257,034	172,939	173,182	206,864	235,983	227,587	178,238	160,978
Other private	8,172	62,266	145,285	138,312	125,849	102,517	89,969	81,986	75,963	69,984
Private nonguaranteed	**15,377**	**70,571**	**65,513**	**237,579**	**300,357**	**389,154**	**530,674**	**550,986**	**557,251**	**531,094**
Bonds	0	0	837	61,557	85,031	107,068	116,603	123,423	124,516	123,496
Commercial banks and other	15,377	70,571	64,677	176,022	215,326	282,087	414,071	427,564	432,735	407,598
Memo:										
IBRD	4,387	22,154	95,537	113,850	107,145	106,022	115,907	119,608	120,150	120,127
IDA	1,832	11,889	45,103	71,631	75,219	77,473	84,160	86,672	88,942	88,847
DISBURSEMENTS	**13,114**	**107,808**	**128,405**	**213,595**	**267,475**	**305,720**	**303,273**	**271,395**	**264,686**	**222,586**
Public and publicly guaranteed	**8,956**	**86,354**	**109,551**	**144,751**	**163,706**	**180,015**	**178,048**	**156,831**	**143,582**	**143,511**
Official creditors	4,992	29,125	52,915	66,291	55,972	65,938	68,963	62,632	54,167	53,343
Multilateral	1,206	9,321	27,537	32,356	33,682	41,004	46,432	38,000	33,627	30,757
Concessional	256	2,837	6,826	8,795	9,974	9,201	8,915	8,781	8,081	9,084
Bilateral	3,786	19,804	25,379	33,935	22,290	24,934	22,531	24,633	20,540	22,587
Concessional	3,022	11,257	15,325	14,079	11,699	10,292	13,516	16,348	13,734	15,338
Private creditors	3,964	57,229	56,635	78,460	107,734	114,077	109,085	94,198	89,416	90,168
Bonds	149	1,681	6,140	29,862	58,465	61,576	57,955	53,446	55,440	54,037
Commercial banks	1,394	34,047	17,926	26,982	29,049	33,124	36,683	26,801	23,196	24,762
Other private	2,421	21,501	32,569	21,616	20,219	19,377	14,447	13,952	10,781	11,369
Private nonguaranteed	**4,158**	**21,454**	**18,855**	**68,844**	**103,770**	**125,705**	**125,225**	**114,565**	**121,104**	**79,075**
Bonds	0	0	701	19,124	32,623	35,544	20,603	15,136	19,437	13,657
Commercial banks and other	4,158	21,454	18,154	49,721	71,147	90,161	104,622	99,428	101,667	65,418
Memo:										
IBRD	679	4,477	13,582	13,234	13,357	17,657	17,514	15,142	13,448	12,203
IDA	174	1,587	4,345	5,476	6,315	5,937	5,556	5,397	5,219	5,920
PRINCIPAL REPAYMENTS	**6,079**	**42,510**	**85,312**	**129,058**	**168,689**	**193,498**	**188,419**	**248,604**	**251,052**	**242,074**
Public and publicly guaranteed	**3,624**	**30,759**	**75,940**	**97,676**	**122,554**	**129,792**	**111,741**	**132,613**	**141,125**	**143,437**
Official creditors	1,555	7,255	25,517	45,016	53,717	51,801	43,532	45,524	48,820	46,036
Multilateral	386	1,668	12,539	21,296	20,989	19,796	18,713	19,267	23,100	19,187
Concessional	30	104	898	1,578	1,750	1,805	1,932	2,057	2,273	2,678
Bilateral	1,169	5,587	12,978	23,720	32,728	32,004	24,818	26,258	25,720	26,849
Concessional	670	2,555	5,826	9,071	9,211	10,479	10,570	9,753	11,395	11,178
Private creditors	2,069	23,504	50,423	52,660	68,837	77,991	68,209	87,089	92,305	97,401
Bonds	143	514	5,637	12,994	21,767	35,165	24,765	25,707	40,809	43,519
Commercial banks	685	13,756	23,496	19,746	28,926	26,335	25,633	46,903	38,197	38,481
Other private	1,241	9,235	21,289	19,920	18,144	16,491	17,811	14,478	13,299	15,402
Private nonguaranteed	**2,454**	**11,751**	**9,373**	**31,382**	**46,135**	**63,706**	**76,678**	**115,991**	**109,927**	**98,637**
Bonds	0	0	0	5,332	7,034	12,349	12,878	13,403	17,190	14,667
Commercial banks and other	2,454	11,751	9,373	26,050	39,101	51,357	63,800	102,588	92,737	83,970
Memo:										
IBRD	248	1,063	8,481	12,129	11,995	10,942	10,712	10,050	10,054	10,004
IDA	0	31	250	546	593	650	742	887	1,044	1,184
NET FLOWS ON DEBT	**7,035**	**65,298**	**43,093**	**84,537**	**98,787**	**112,222**	**114,854**	**22,791**	**13,634**	**-19,488**
Public and publicly guaranteed	**5,332**	**55,595**	**33,611**	**47,075**	**41,152**	**50,223**	**66,308**	**24,218**	**2,457**	**74**
Official creditors	3,437	21,871	27,399	21,275	2,255	14,137	25,431	17,108	5,347	7,308
Multilateral	820	7,653	14,997	11,060	12,693	21,207	27,719	18,733	10,526	11,570
Concessional	226	2,732	5,927	7,218	8,223	7,396	6,983	6,725	5,808	6,406
Bilateral	2,617	14,217	12,401	10,214	-10,438	-7,070	-2,287	-1,625	-5,179	-4,262
Concessional	2,352	8,702	9,499	5,007	2,488	-187	2,945	6,595	2,339	4,160
Private creditors	1,895	33,725	6,213	25,800	38,897	36,086	40,876	7,110	-2,889	-7,234
Bonds	6	1,167	503	16,867	36,698	26,411	33,190	27,738	14,631	10,518
Commercial banks	709	20,291	-5,571	7,236	123	6,789	11,050	-20,102	-15,002	-13,719
Other private	1,180	12,266	11,280	1,697	2,076	2,886	-3,364	-527	-2,519	-4,033
Private nonguaranteed	**1,703**	**9,703**	**9,482**	**37,463**	**57,635**	**61,999**	**48,546**	**-1,426**	**11,177**	**-19,562**
Bonds	0	0	701	13,792	25,589	23,194	7,725	1,734	2,247	-1,010
Commercial banks and other	1,703	9,703	8,781	23,670	32,046	38,805	40,822	-3,160	8,930	-18,552
Memo:										
IBRD	431	3,414	5,101	1,105	1,362	6,715	6,803	5,091	3,394	2,199
IDA	174	1,556	4,095	4,930	5,723	5,287	4,814	4,510	4,175	4,737

ALL DEVELOPING COUNTRIES

(US$ million, unless otherwise indicated)

	1970	1980	1990	1995	1996	1997	1998	1999	2000	2001
INTEREST PAYMENTS (LINT)	**2,366**	**32,791**	**54,545**	**77,195**	**81,046**	**87,687**	**95,017**	**99,535**	**104,104**	**101,912**
Public and publicly guaranteed	**1,608**	**25,763**	**49,458**	**63,766**	**64,883**	**65,669**	**67,258**	**70,927**	**73,337**	**73,856**
Official creditors	873	6,124	20,100	30,234	30,747	28,354	27,880	28,624	28,868	28,600
Multilateral	309	2,550	10,807	13,965	13,760	12,841	13,257	15,570	16,003	15,532
Concessional	20	166	629	1,011	1,065	1,090	1,130	1,206	1,239	1,315
Bilateral	565	3,574	9,293	16,270	16,986	15,514	14,623	13,054	12,865	13,068
Concessional	397	1,838	4,319	6,279	6,146	5,445	5,515	5,673	5,314	5,080
Private creditors	734	19,638	29,358	33,532	34,136	37,315	39,378	42,303	44,469	45,256
Bonds	97	950	4,587	16,914	16,776	19,623	21,398	25,151	28,624	29,914
Commercial banks	253	14,431	17,808	9,340	10,656	11,652	12,510	12,392	11,485	11,109
Other private	384	4,257	6,963	7,278	6,704	6,040	5,470	4,759	4,360	4,233
Private nonguaranteed	**758**	**7,029**	**5,087**	**13,428**	**16,163**	**22,017**	**27,759**	**28,731**	**30,966**	**28,056**
Bonds	0	0	8	4,439	5,464	7,431	8,516	7,534	8,313	8,044
Commercial banks and other	758	7,029	5,080	8,990	10,700	14,586	19,243	21,197	22,653	20,011
Memo:										
IBRD	243	1,814	7,128	8,137	7,806	6,892	7,028	7,724	8,249	8,047
IDA	12	79	302	504	512	532	554	600	622	618
NET TRANSFERS ON DEBT	**4,670**	**32,507**	**-11,452**	**7,343**	**17,741**	**24,535**	**19,837**	**-76,866**	**-90,668**	**-121,400**
Public and publicly guaranteed	**3,724**	**29,833**	**-15,847**	**-16,692**	**-23,731**	**-15,446**	**-951**	**-46,709**	**-70,879**	**-73,782**
Official creditors	2,564	15,746	7,299	-8,960	-28,492	-14,217	-2,449	-11,516	-23,521	-21,292
Multilateral	512	5,103	4,190	-2,905	-1,067	8,366	14,462	3,163	-5,477	-3,962
Concessional	206	2,566	5,299	6,207	7,159	6,306	5,853	5,519	4,569	5,091
Bilateral	2,053	10,643	3,109	-6,055	-27,425	-22,583	-16,910	-14,679	-18,044	-17,330
Concessional	1,955	6,865	5,180	-1,272	-3,658	-5,633	-2,570	922	-2,974	-920
Private creditors	1,160	14,086	-23,146	-7,732	4,761	-1,229	1,498	-35,193	-47,358	-52,490
Bonds	-91	218	-4,084	-47	19,922	6,789	11,792	2,587	-13,993	-19,396
Commercial banks	456	5,860	-23,379	-2,104	-10,532	-4,863	-1,460	-32,495	-26,487	-24,828
Other private	795	8,009	4,317	-5,581	-4,628	-3,154	-8,834	-5,286	-6,879	-8,266
Private nonguaranteed	**945**	**2,674**	**4,395**	**24,034**	**41,472**	**39,981**	**20,788**	**-30,157**	**-19,789**	**-47,617**
Bonds	0	0	693	9,354	20,126	15,763	-791	-5,801	-6,066	-9,055
Commercial banks and other	945	2,674	3,701	14,680	21,346	24,218	21,579	-24,357	-13,723	-38,563
Memo:										
IBRD	187	1,600	-2,027	-7,033	-6,444	-177	-226	-2,633	-4,855	-5,847
IDA	161	1,476	3,793	4,426	5,210	4,756	4,260	3,909	3,553	4,119
DEBT SERVICE (LTDS)	**8,444**	**75,301**	**139,858**	**206,252**	**249,734**	**281,185**	**283,436**	**348,138**	**355,355**	**343,985**
Public and publicly guaranteed	**5,232**	**56,521**	**125,397**	**161,442**	**187,436**	**195,461**	**178,999**	**203,540**	**214,462**	**217,293**
Official creditors	2,428	13,379	45,616	75,251	84,464	80,155	71,412	74,148	77,688	74,635
Multilateral	695	4,218	23,346	35,261	34,749	32,637	31,970	34,836	39,103	34,718
Concessional	49	271	1,527	2,588	2,815	2,894	3,062	3,262	3,512	3,993
Bilateral	1,733	9,161	22,270	39,990	49,715	47,518	39,441	39,312	38,584	39,917
Concessional	1,067	4,393	10,145	15,350	15,357	15,925	16,085	15,427	16,708	16,258
Private creditors	2,804	43,143	79,781	86,192	102,973	115,306	107,587	129,392	136,774	142,658
Bonds	240	1,463	10,224	29,908	38,544	54,788	46,163	50,858	69,433	73,433
Commercial banks	938	28,187	41,304	29,086	39,582	37,988	38,144	59,296	49,682	49,589
Other private	1,626	13,492	28,253	27,198	24,847	22,531	23,281	19,238	17,659	19,635
Private nonguaranteed	**3,212**	**18,780**	**14,460**	**44,810**	**62,298**	**85,724**	**104,437**	**144,722**	**140,893**	**126,692**
Bonds	0	0	8	9,770	12,498	19,781	21,394	20,937	25,503	22,711
Commercial banks and other	3,212	18,780	14,452	35,040	49,801	65,943	83,044	123,785	115,390	103,981
Memo:										
IBRD	492	2,876	15,609	20,267	19,801	17,834	17,740	17,775	18,303	18,051
IDA	12	110	553	1,050	1,105	1,181	1,296	1,487	1,666	1,802
UNDISBURSED DEBT	**17,477**	**142,198**	**215,632**	**258,657**	**245,878**	**237,850**	**259,919**	**301,258**	**212,095**	..
Official creditors	13,500	91,371	162,768	205,895	191,913	185,509	208,444	257,792	173,824	..
Private creditors	3,977	50,828	52,865	52,762	53,965	52,341	51,475	43,466	38,271	..
Memorandum items										
Concessional LDOD	24,704	110,726	313,764	416,957	406,747	374,666	378,378	399,265	382,484	..
Variable rate LDOD	16,160	191,483	441,445	709,549	762,458	865,440	1,045,330	1,049,344	979,961	..
Public sector LDOD	44,969	341,033	1,048,580	1,360,005	1,348,795	1,336,076	1,425,598	1,447,842	1,407,302	..
Private sector LDOD	17,639	84,006	73,655	243,002	306,835	393,350	618,749	644,708	640,025	..

6. CURRENCY COMPOSITION OF LONG-TERM DEBT (PERCENT)

	1970	1980	1990	1995	1996	1997	1998	1999	2000	2001
Deutsche mark	8.5	6.6	8.6	8.2	8.3	7.6	7.8	6.2	5.3	..
French franc	5.2	5.5	5.7	4.9	4.6	3.8	3.7	3.0	2.7	..
Japanese yen	2.3	6.9	10.5	12.7	11.7	10.5	10.9	12.4	11.3	..
Pound sterling	10.9	3.4	2.2	1.4	1.5	1.5	1.4	1.3	0.9	..
Swiss franc	1.1	1.6	1.9	1.0	0.8	0.6	0.5	0.4	0.4	..
U.S.dollars	47.4	49.7	41.2	45.2	47.7	52.8	56.5	57.0	60.0	..
Multiple currency	11.5	10.9	14.7	13.6	12.8	11.4	7.8	7.7	7.1	..
Special drawing rights	0.0	0.0	0.2	0.3	0.3	0.3	0.3	0.3	0.4	..
All other currencies	13.2	8.5	9.8	8.0	7.7	6.4	6.6	6.6	6.8	..

ALL DEVELOPING COUNTRIES

(US$ million, unless otherwise indicated)

	1970	1980	1990	1995	1996	1997	1998	1999	2000	2001
7. DEBT RESTRUCTURINGS										
Total amount rescheduled	117	3,325	79,328	31,321	33,742	49,099	40,372	30,973	60,761	..
Debt stock rescheduled	0	1	61,849	6,900	6,896	1,326	31,995	7,588	23,134	..
Principal rescheduled	0	393	10,277	15,371	15,832	35,350	6,513	13,256	20,991	..
Official	0	137	5,826	6,997	6,374	6,846	4,596	9,776	17,260	..
Private	0	257	4,451	8,374	9,457	28,504	1,917	3,479	3,732	..
Interest rescheduled	..	..	5,799	5,224	7,212	9,039	1,600	7,187	14,009	..
Official	0	38	4,577	2,281	2,064	2,462	1,219	6,533	11,205	..
Private	0	33	1,221	2,943	5,148	6,577	381	654	2,804	..
Debt forgiven	10	280	12,628	2,263	5,997	3,349	590	4,924	728	..
Memo: interest forgiven	0	0	2,890	962	1,870	622	595	515	1,927	..
Debt stock reduction	0	0	26,145	4,220	9,907	18,823	3,902	7,859	41,541	..
of which debt buyback	0	0	4,360	162	3,665	10,050	3,008	5,407	17,016	..
8. DEBT STOCK-FLOW RECONCILIATION										
Total change in debt stocks	..	..	103,434	186,298	87,240	87,471	217,656	18,832	-73,809	..
Net flows on debt	6,675	102,422	59,664	170,382	142,603	138,773	96,676	-11,789	-834	-15,693
Net change in interest arrears	..	..	15,547	521	-5,435	-9,003	6,053	4,126	-6,947	..
Interest capitalized	..	..	5,799	5,224	7,212	9,039	1,600	7,187	14,009	..
Debt forgiveness or reduction	..	..	-34,414	-6,321	-12,240	-12,122	-1,484	-7,376	-25,253	..
Cross-currency valuation	..	..	47,404	1,711	-68,922	-79,018	30,994	-15,887	-50,896	..
Residual	..	..	9,434	14,781	24,022	39,803	83,818	42,570	-3,887	..
9. AVERAGE TERMS OF NEW COMMITMENTS										
ALL CREDITORS										
Interest (%)	5.0	9.2	7.0	6.1	6.4	6.5	7.0	6.2	7.4	..
Maturity (years)	21.0	16.3	17.7	13.9	13.3	14.1	12.0	14.9	13.6	..
Grace period (years)	6.5	4.8	5.7	4.4	5.4	6.4	5.5	5.6	7.7	..
Grant element (%)	32.1	7.7	19.4	20.7	18.6	17.6	16.2	20.7	13.3	..
Official creditors										
Interest (%)	3.6	5.5	5.5	5.8	4.8	5.4	6.1	4.0	5.2	..
Maturity (years)	28.3	25.1	23.6	19.7	22.3	20.5	15.7	18.4	21.7	..
Grace period (years)	9.0	6.3	6.6	4.8	5.3	5.6	4.5	5.1	6.0	..
Grant element (%)	45.2	29.5	31.3	27.4	33.8	28.6	25.4	36.7	33.8	..
Private creditors										
Interest (%)	7.2	12.0	8.5	6.4	7.2	7.3	7.7	8.1	8.3	..
Maturity (years)	9.8	9.8	11.5	7.5	8.4	10.1	9.0	11.9	10.2	..
Grace period (years)	2.6	3.7	4.8	3.9	5.5	7.0	6.4	6.0	8.5	..
Grant element (%)	12.0	-8.5	6.9	13.2	10.2	10.7	8.5	7.0	4.8	..
Memorandum items										
Commitments	12,054	98,573	123,522	153,984	171,719	190,062	194,649	152,369	124,924	..
Official creditors	7,303	41,838	63,194	80,705	60,601	73,054	88,402	69,995	36,609	..
Private creditors	4,751	56,735	60,327	73,279	111,118	117,008	106,293	82,374	88,315	..

10. GRAPH OF AGGREGATE NET RESOURCE FLOWS

(current prices, US$ billion)

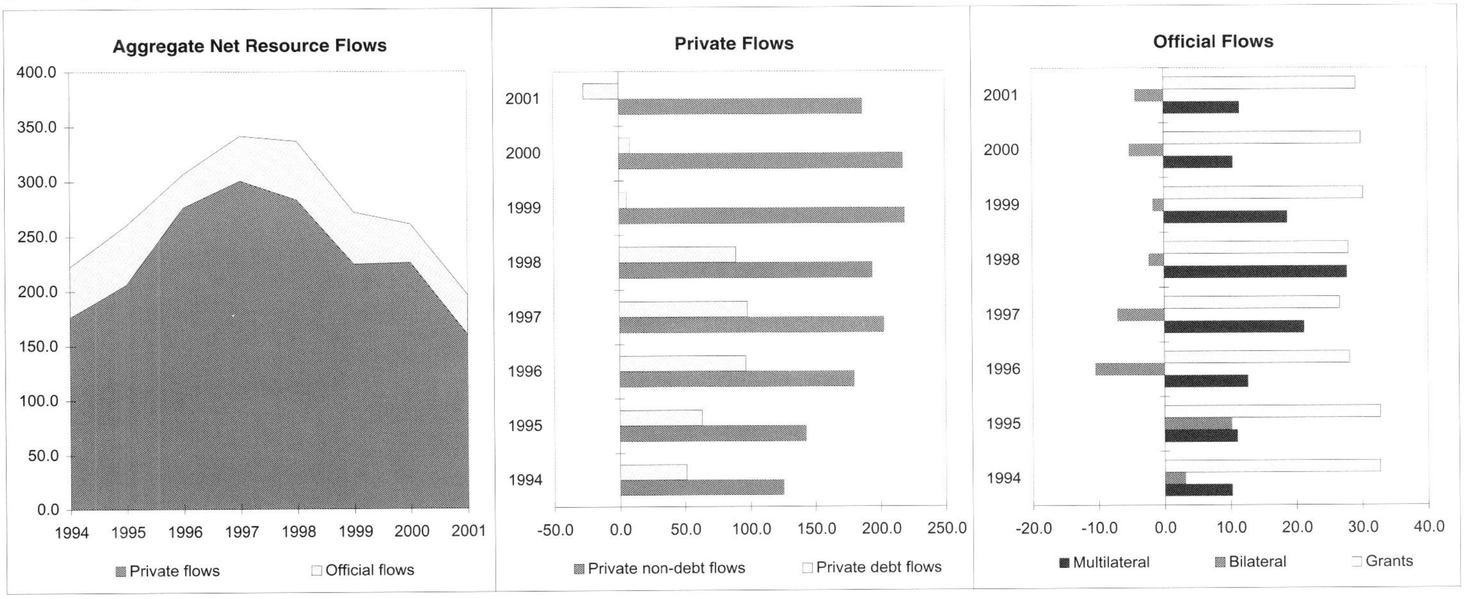

EAST ASIA AND PACIFIC

(US$ million, unless otherwise indicated)

	1970	1980	1990	1995	1996	1997	1998	1999	2000	2001
1. SUMMARY DEBT DATA										
TOTAL DEBT STOCKS (EDT)	**11,162**	**94,080**	**273,983**	**547,489**	**608,302**	**665,477**	**684,819**	**673,379**	**632,953**	**604,322**
Long-term debt (LDOD)	**9,083**	**66,674**	**222,722**	**389,470**	**415,799**	**460,791**	**528,439**	**539,366**	**502,238**	**483,689**
Public and publicly guaranteed	6,903	55,620	195,687	283,662	287,140	305,045	338,620	364,458	333,852	326,798
Private nonguaranteed	2,179	11,054	27,035	105,808	128,659	155,746	189,819	174,908	168,386	156,890
Use of IMF credit	**224**	**2,234**	**2,085**	**1,337**	**1,175**	**17,997**	**31,407**	**22,180**	**22,266**	**13,384**
Short-term debt	**..**	**25,172**	**49,176**	**156,682**	**191,328**	**186,689**	**124,973**	**111,825**	**108,449**	**107,250**
of which interest arrears on LDOD	..	2	1,889	2,869	3,116	1,792	2,016	5,713	5,218	5,218
Official creditors	..	1	1,139	2,292	2,551	1,734	1,958	2,159	540	..
Private creditors	..	1	751	577	565	59	58	3,554	4,678	..
Memo: principal arrears on LDOD	..	5	2,965	10,877	12,579	9,549	13,246	14,478	7,314	..
Official creditors	..	1	1,790	10,149	11,858	9,306	10,284	11,223	4,079	..
Private creditors	..	4	1,175	729	721	243	2,962	3,256	3,235	..
Memo: export credits	..	310	35,516	75,150	74,640	86,131	42,352	39,403	35,727	..
TOTAL DEBT FLOWS										
Disbursements	**2,060**	**17,400**	**35,476**	**72,729**	**92,592**	**115,135**	**70,240**	**56,880**	**49,994**	**44,114**
Long-term debt	1,994	16,251	35,418	72,527	92,398	97,629	55,122	54,362	48,501	43,518
IMF purchases	66	1,149	58	203	195	17,506	15,118	2,518	1,493	596
Principal repayments	**836**	**5,857**	**24,516**	**38,160**	**46,748**	**45,444**	**50,056**	**78,768**	**61,166**	**64,200**
Long-term debt	817	5,619	23,230	37,770	46,434	45,169	47,105	67,847	60,898	55,510
IMF repurchases	18	238	1,286	390	314	276	2,951	10,921	268	8,690
Net flows on debt	**1,224**	**18,319**	**20,005**	**76,881**	**80,244**	**66,376**	**-14,753**	**-36,733**	**-14,051**	**-21,286**
of which short-term debt	..	6,776	9,044	42,313	34,399	-3,315	-34,938	-14,845	-2,880	-1,200
Interest payments (INT)	**..**	**7,677**	**15,247**	**26,816**	**29,029**	**32,110**	**33,042**	**32,212**	**31,564**	**29,623**
Long-term debt	238	4,636	11,934	18,647	19,345	22,219	24,405	25,476	25,161	23,956
IMF charges	0	77	245	69	41	51	1,265	1,287	1,093	817
Short-term debt	..	2,964	3,068	8,100	9,644	9,839	7,372	5,450	5,311	4,850
Net transfers on debt	**..**	**10,642**	**4,758**	**50,066**	**51,214**	**34,266**	**-47,795**	**-68,945**	**-45,616**	**-50,908**
Total debt service paid (TDS)	**..**	**13,534**	**39,762**	**64,976**	**75,777**	**77,554**	**83,098**	**110,979**	**92,730**	**93,822**
Long-term debt	1,055	10,256	35,164	56,417	65,779	67,388	71,509	93,323	86,059	79,466
IMF repurchases and charges	18	314	1,531	459	355	327	4,216	12,208	1,360	9,506
Short-term debt (interest only)	..	2,964	3,068	8,100	9,644	9,839	7,372	5,450	5,311	4,850
2. AGGREGATE NET RESOURCE FLOWS AND NET TRANSFERS (LONG-TERM)										
NET RESOURCE FLOWS	**2,147**	**13,098**	**27,709**	**109,243**	**127,367**	**129,137**	**82,559**	**66,272**	**74,557**	**52,243**
Net flow of long-term debt (ex. IMF)	1,177	10,632	12,189	34,757	45,964	52,460	8,018	-13,485	-12,397	-11,992
Foreign direct investment (net)	267	1,318	11,135	53,130	60,970	65,057	62,997	55,899	52,130	48,528
Portfolio equity flows	0	-4	2,290	18,274	18,089	9,192	9,006	21,133	32,285	13,408
Grants (excluding technical coop.)	703	1,152	2,095	3,082	2,344	2,428	2,539	2,724	2,539	2,300
Memo: technical coop. grants	402	1,045	2,537	3,455	3,243	2,881	2,869	2,851	2,919	2,700
official net resource flows	1,317	4,186	8,306	11,795	5,597	18,328	15,764	14,790	8,864	7,234
private net resource flows	830	8,912	19,402	97,448	121,770	110,809	66,795	51,481	65,693	45,009
NET TRANSFERS	**1,556**	**3,488**	**10,665**	**81,428**	**97,481**	**95,807**	**46,243**	**27,249**	**34,292**	**10,987**
Interest on long-term debt	238	4,636	11,934	18,647	19,345	22,219	24,405	25,476	25,161	23,956
Profit remittances on FDI	354	4,973	5,110	9,168	10,541	11,111	11,911	13,547	15,104	17,300
Memo: official net transfers	1,241	3,107	4,005	4,991	-602	12,134	8,913	7,125	751	-1,120
private net transfers	315	381	6,660	76,437	98,083	83,673	37,331	20,124	33,540	12,107
3. MAJOR ECONOMIC AGGREGATES										
Gross national income (GNI)	133,528	445,379	920,935	1,764,037	1,977,871	1,975,612	1,645,123	1,854,214	2,025,548	2,053,906
Exports of goods & services (XGS)	..	..	252,826	568,606	626,430	694,166	650,010	706,223	854,883	814,789
of which workers remittances	..	310	1,116	1,810	3,335	6,411	1,571	1,732	1,999	2,005
Imports of goods & services (MGS)	..	..	261,293	612,363	679,535	689,945	559,542	630,637	800,327	782,959
International reserves (RES)	..	..	86,264	200,582	247,422	245,307	298,819	348,778	380,358	433,713
Current account balance	..	-10,201	-5,610	-39,863	-49,780	7,582	99,058	84,860	58,185	30,785
4. DEBT INDICATORS										
EDT / XGS (%)	..	..	108.4	96.3	97.1	95.9	105.4	95.4	74.0	74.2
EDT / GNI (%)	..	21.1	29.8	31.0	30.8	33.7	41.6	36.3	31.3	29.4
TDS / XGS (%)	..	..	15.7	11.4	12.1	11.2	12.8	15.7	10.9	11.5
INT / XGS (%)	..	..	6.0	4.7	4.6	4.6	5.1	4.6	3.7	3.6
INT / GNI (%)	..	1.7	1.7	1.5	1.5	1.6	2.0	1.7	1.6	1.4
RES / EDT (%)	..	..	31.5	36.6	40.7	36.9	43.6	51.8	60.1	71.8
RES / MGS (months)	..	..	4.0	3.9	4.4	4.3	6.4	6.6	5.7	6.7
Short-term / EDT (%)	..	26.8	18.0	28.6	31.5	28.1	18.3	16.6	17.1	17.8
Concessional / EDT (%)	..	18.4	28.1	18.8	16.3	11.8	13.3	15.7	15.9	16.9
Multilateral / EDT (%)	..	8.3	14.2	10.3	8.9	8.8	10.4	11.4	12.4	13.1

(US$ million, unless otherwise indicated)

	1970	1980	1990	1995	1996	1997	1998	1999	2000	2001
5. LONG-TERM DEBT										
DEBT OUTSTANDING (LDOD)	**9,083**	**66,674**	**222,722**	**389,470**	**415,799**	**460,791**	**528,439**	**539,366**	**502,238**	**483,689**
Public and publicly guaranteed	**6,903**	**55,620**	**195,687**	**283,662**	**287,140**	**305,045**	**338,620**	**364,458**	**333,852**	**326,798**
Official creditors	4,722	27,349	117,601	170,493	162,777	160,151	183,042	206,080	191,585	194,255
Multilateral	497	7,818	38,784	56,463	53,814	58,368	71,204	76,822	78,311	79,414
Concessional	36	1,308	7,448	13,520	14,321	14,803	16,752	17,771	17,753	17,159
Bilateral	4,225	19,531	78,817	114,030	108,964	101,783	111,838	129,259	113,274	114,841
Concessional	3,632	16,002	69,464	89,173	84,736	63,375	74,495	88,108	83,145	84,675
Private creditors	2,182	28,271	78,086	113,169	124,362	144,894	155,578	158,385	142,267	132,544
Bonds	125	1,946	14,360	34,443	42,562	52,711	57,876	62,520	59,249	61,679
Commercial banks	330	13,888	38,029	44,282	43,624	55,216	70,352	68,464	52,322	40,101
Other private	1,727	12,437	25,698	34,445	38,176	36,967	27,350	27,401	30,697	30,764
Private nonguaranteed	**2,179**	**11,054**	**27,035**	**105,808**	**128,659**	**155,746**	**189,819**	**174,908**	**168,386**	**156,890**
Bonds	0	0	650	26,074	39,709	51,064	50,677	48,654	46,906	45,966
Commercial banks and other	2,179	11,054	26,386	79,734	88,950	104,682	139,141	126,254	121,480	110,924
Memo:										
IBRD	444	4,952	23,416	30,075	28,079	29,699	35,490	38,047	38,508	38,149
IDA	33	961	5,228	9,774	10,545	10,983	12,203	12,581	12,703	12,764
DISBURSEMENTS	**1,994**	**16,251**	**35,418**	**72,527**	**92,398**	**97,629**	**55,122**	**54,362**	**48,501**	**43,518**
Public and publicly guaranteed	**1,199**	**12,789**	**24,048**	**43,185**	**46,293**	**60,691**	**42,455**	**45,233**	**30,813**	**32,443**
Official creditors	700	3,958	11,701	17,870	14,065	25,468	21,612	23,021	16,605	15,526
Multilateral	81	1,575	4,944	6,285	6,427	12,222	12,897	8,124	5,941	5,278
Concessional	8	151	1,027	1,336	1,537	1,449	1,311	1,130	1,108	966
Bilateral	619	2,383	6,757	11,585	7,638	13,246	8,715	14,897	10,663	10,248
Concessional	546	1,380	5,892	6,052	5,446	4,313	7,072	10,463	7,154	7,188
Private creditors	499	8,831	12,348	25,315	32,228	35,223	20,843	22,212	14,209	16,917
Bonds	0	280	1,816	8,903	13,901	14,036	7,781	9,885	4,164	9,418
Commercial banks	116	4,288	4,680	9,230	9,040	11,032	8,560	8,096	3,930	2,197
Other private	384	4,263	5,851	7,182	9,288	10,155	4,502	4,232	6,115	5,302
Private nonguaranteed	**796**	**3,462**	**11,370**	**29,342**	**46,104**	**36,938**	**12,668**	**9,129**	**17,688**	**11,075**
Bonds	0	0	530	10,721	18,428	16,039	1,798	2,008	4,500	4,995
Commercial banks and other	796	3,462	10,840	18,621	27,676	20,899	10,869	7,121	13,188	6,080
Memo:										
IBRD	64	1,047	2,677	3,312	3,095	6,465	6,963	4,866	3,281	2,678
IDA	5	92	604	934	1,135	1,013	920	705	700	732
PRINCIPAL REPAYMENTS	**817**	**5,619**	**23,230**	**37,770**	**46,434**	**45,169**	**47,105**	**67,847**	**60,898**	**55,510**
Public and publicly guaranteed	**427**	**3,674**	**18,571**	**24,635**	**30,086**	**25,743**	**20,416**	**43,036**	**38,134**	**32,940**
Official creditors	86	924	5,489	9,158	10,813	9,569	8,386	10,955	10,280	10,592
Multilateral	22	268	2,683	3,600	5,097	3,782	2,946	3,173	3,742	3,475
Concessional	0	7	80	131	141	136	141	185	214	233
Bilateral	64	656	2,806	5,558	5,715	5,786	5,440	7,781	6,538	7,117
Concessional	39	340	1,491	3,352	3,708	3,214	3,776	3,668	3,937	4,129
Private creditors	341	2,750	13,082	15,477	19,274	16,175	12,030	32,082	27,854	22,348
Bonds	32	41	3,148	2,759	4,030	2,678	2,775	6,640	6,245	6,709
Commercial banks	41	795	6,014	6,249	10,316	8,799	5,628	22,223	18,433	11,938
Other private	268	1,914	3,921	6,469	4,927	4,697	3,628	3,219	3,177	3,701
Private nonguaranteed	**391**	**1,945**	**4,658**	**13,135**	**16,348**	**19,426**	**26,688**	**24,811**	**22,764**	**22,570**
Bonds	0	0	0	1,410	2,176	3,634	4,934	4,211	5,532	5,934
Commercial banks and other	391	1,945	4,658	11,725	14,171	15,792	21,754	20,600	17,232	16,636
Memo:										
IBRD	22	184	2,009	2,612	2,957	2,617	2,114	2,197	2,229	2,509
IDA	0	2	21	54	61	64	72	93	111	135
NET FLOWS ON DEBT	**1,177**	**10,632**	**12,189**	**34,757**	**45,964**	**52,460**	**8,018**	**-13,485**	**-12,397**	**-11,992**
Public and publicly guaranteed	**772**	**9,115**	**5,477**	**18,550**	**16,207**	**34,948**	**22,038**	**2,197**	**-7,321**	**-497**
Official creditors	614	3,034	6,212	8,712	3,252	15,900	13,225	12,066	6,325	4,934
Multilateral	59	1,307	2,260	2,686	1,330	8,440	9,951	4,950	2,200	1,803
Concessional	8	144	948	1,205	1,396	1,313	1,171	945	894	733
Bilateral	555	1,727	3,951	6,027	1,923	7,460	3,274	7,116	4,125	3,132
Concessional	508	1,040	4,401	2,700	1,739	1,099	3,295	6,795	3,216	3,060
Private creditors	158	6,081	-735	9,838	12,955	19,048	8,813	-9,869	-13,646	-5,431
Bonds	-32	238	-1,332	6,143	9,871	11,358	5,006	3,245	-2,081	2,709
Commercial banks	74	3,493	-1,333	2,981	-1,277	2,233	2,933	-14,127	-14,503	-9,742
Other private	116	2,350	1,930	713	4,361	5,458	874	1,013	2,938	1,602
Private nonguaranteed	**405**	**1,517**	**6,712**	**16,206**	**29,757**	**17,512**	**-14,021**	**-15,682**	**-5,075**	**-11,496**
Bonds	0	0	530	9,311	16,252	12,405	-3,136	-2,203	-1,032	-940
Commercial banks and other	405	1,517	6,182	6,896	13,505	5,107	-10,885	-13,479	-4,044	-10,556
Memo:										
IBRD	42	862	668	700	138	3,848	4,849	2,669	1,052	169
IDA	5	89	583	880	1,073	949	848	612	590	597

EAST ASIA AND PACIFIC

(US$ million, unless otherwise indicated)

	1970	1980	1990	1995	1996	1997	1998	1999	2000	2001
INTEREST PAYMENTS (LINT)	**238**	**4,636**	**11,934**	**18,647**	**19,345**	**22,219**	**24,405**	**25,476**	**25,161**	**23,956**
Public and publicly guaranteed	**165**	**3,417**	**10,137**	**13,516**	**13,163**	**14,307**	**15,474**	**18,195**	**17,778**	**17,208**
Official creditors	76	1,079	4,301	6,804	6,199	6,194	6,851	7,665	8,112	8,354
Multilateral	26	548	2,450	3,271	3,024	2,781	3,288	3,830	4,224	4,305
Concessional	0	12	64	126	132	129	127	143	146	156
Bilateral	50	531	1,852	3,533	3,175	3,412	3,563	3,836	3,888	4,049
Concessional	40	295	1,217	2,191	1,899	1,762	1,609	2,244	2,167	2,217
Private creditors	89	2,338	5,836	6,713	6,964	8,114	8,623	10,529	9,666	8,854
Bonds	9	103	1,108	1,724	1,948	3,029	3,550	4,286	4,258	3,829
Commercial banks	13	1,340	3,013	2,757	2,810	2,752	3,059	4,661	3,866	3,385
Other private	67	895	1,715	2,231	2,207	2,333	2,014	1,583	1,542	1,640
Private nonguaranteed	**73**	**1,219**	**1,797**	**5,130**	**6,182**	**7,912**	**8,931**	**7,281**	**7,383**	**6,748**
Bonds	0	0	6	1,770	2,347	3,395	3,584	2,183	2,138	2,047
Commercial banks and other	73	1,219	1,791	3,360	3,834	4,517	5,347	5,098	5,245	4,701
Memo:										
IBRD	25	406	1,783	2,168	2,033	1,866	2,142	2,430	2,716	2,624
IDA	0	7	35	70	73	76	78	85	88	87
NET TRANSFERS ON DEBT	**939**	**5,996**	**255**	**16,110**	**26,619**	**30,242**	**-16,387**	**-38,960**	**-37,558**	**-35,948**
Public and publicly guaranteed	**607**	**5,698**	**-4,660**	**5,034**	**3,044**	**20,641**	**6,564**	**-15,998**	**-25,099**	**-17,705**
Official creditors	538	1,955	1,910	1,909	-2,946	9,706	6,374	4,401	-1,788	-3,420
Multilateral	33	759	-189	-586	-1,694	5,658	6,663	1,120	-2,025	-2,503
Concessional	8	132	884	1,079	1,264	1,184	1,044	802	748	577
Bilateral	505	1,196	2,099	2,494	-1,252	4,048	-289	3,280	237	-917
Concessional	468	746	3,184	509	-161	-663	1,687	4,551	1,050	843
Private creditors	70	3,743	-6,571	3,125	5,990	10,935	190	-20,399	-23,312	-14,285
Bonds	-41	135	-2,440	4,419	7,923	8,329	1,457	-1,042	-6,339	-1,120
Commercial banks	61	2,153	-4,346	224	-4,087	-520	-127	-18,787	-18,370	-13,127
Other private	49	1,454	216	-1,518	2,154	3,126	-1,140	-570	1,397	-38
Private nonguaranteed	**332**	**298**	**4,915**	**11,076**	**23,575**	**9,601**	**-22,951**	**-22,962**	**-12,458**	**-18,244**
Bonds	0	0	524	7,541	13,905	9,010	-6,720	-4,385	-3,170	-2,987
Commercial banks and other	332	298	4,391	3,536	9,670	591	-16,232	-18,577	-9,288	-15,257
Memo:										
IBRD	17	457	-1,115	-1,469	-1,895	1,982	2,707	239	-1,664	-2,455
IDA	5	82	548	811	1,000	873	771	527	502	510
DEBT SERVICE (LTDS)	**1,055**	**10,256**	**35,164**	**56,417**	**65,779**	**67,388**	**71,509**	**93,323**	**86,059**	**79,466**
Public and publicly guaranteed	**591**	**7,091**	**28,708**	**38,151**	**43,250**	**40,050**	**35,891**	**61,231**	**55,913**	**50,148**
Official creditors	162	2,003	9,790	15,961	17,012	15,762	15,238	18,620	18,392	18,946
Multilateral	48	816	5,133	6,871	8,121	6,564	6,234	7,003	7,966	7,781
Concessional	0	20	143	257	273	264	268	328	360	389
Bilateral	114	1,187	4,657	9,090	8,890	9,198	9,003	11,617	10,426	11,165
Concessional	78	634	2,708	5,543	5,607	4,976	5,385	5,912	6,104	6,345
Private creditors	430	5,088	18,918	22,190	26,238	24,288	20,653	42,611	37,520	31,202
Bonds	41	144	4,256	4,484	5,978	5,707	6,325	10,926	10,503	10,538
Commercial banks	54	2,135	9,027	9,006	13,126	11,552	8,687	26,883	22,299	15,324
Other private	335	2,809	5,635	8,700	7,134	7,030	5,642	4,801	4,718	5,341
Private nonguaranteed	**464**	**3,165**	**6,455**	**18,266**	**22,529**	**27,337**	**35,619**	**32,091**	**30,147**	**29,318**
Bonds	0	0	6	3,180	4,524	7,029	8,518	6,393	7,670	7,982
Commercial banks and other	464	3,165	6,449	15,085	18,006	20,309	27,101	25,698	22,477	21,337
Memo:										
IBRD	47	590	3,792	4,780	4,990	4,483	4,256	4,627	4,945	5,133
IDA	0	10	56	124	135	140	149	178	198	222
UNDISBURSED DEBT	**2,112**	**29,808**	**46,988**	**70,973**	**68,781**	**67,691**	**69,641**	**117,654**	**63,899**	**..**
Official creditors	1,495	20,993	34,873	55,057	52,298	53,249	62,976	112,074	56,728	..
Private creditors	617	8,815	12,115	15,916	16,483	14,442	6,665	5,579	7,170	..
Memorandum items										
Concessional LDOD	3,668	17,310	76,913	102,693	99,056	78,178	91,246	105,879	100,898	..
Variable rate LDOD	2,205	25,278	82,111	176,251	199,770	248,625	308,937	298,665	282,184	..
Public sector LDOD	5,881	46,077	188,670	274,545	277,091	296,802	314,258	344,384	321,419	..
Private sector LDOD	3,202	17,240	30,137	108,379	132,229	157,449	214,178	194,990	180,819	..

6. CURRENCY COMPOSITION OF LONG-TERM DEBT (PERCENT)

	1970	1980	1990	1995	1996	1997	1998	1999	2000	2001
Deutsche mark	7.7	5.0	3.7	2.8	2.5	2.3	2.4	1.9	1.8	..
French franc	3.5	3.2	2.3	1.6	1.5	1.2	1.8	1.3	1.2	..
Japanese yen	6.1	18.0	28.8	28.3	24.9	21.6	23.4	26.3	25.9	..
Pound sterling	4.3	1.7	0.9	0.4	0.5	0.7	0.6	0.5	0.4	..
Swiss franc	0.7	1.0	0.9	0.5	0.4	0.3	0.2	0.2	0.2	..
U.S.dollars	53.5	40.8	24.0	36.0	41.9	51.6	56.1	54.6	58.4	..
Multiple currency	6.7	16.6	22.0	18.0	16.3	13.2	7.2	7.6	6.6	..
Special drawing rights	0.0	0.0	0.1	0.1	0.1	0.1	0.2	0.2	0.2	..
All other currencies	17.6	7.6	15.3	9.9	9.8	6.8	6.0	5.5	3.3	..

EAST ASIA AND PACIFIC

(US$ million, unless otherwise indicated)

	1970	1980	1990	1995	1996	1997	1998	1999	2000	2001
7. DEBT RESTRUCTURINGS										
Total amount rescheduled	0	0	1,478	329	179	892	25,641	4,974	2,316	..
Debt stock rescheduled	0	0	0	0	0	0	27,002	3,557	0	..
Principal rescheduled	0	0	848	170	115	410	496	1,477	2,268	..
Official	0	0	172	156	115	15	307	700	1,541	..
Private	0	0	676	14	0	395	189	778	727	..
Interest rescheduled	..	..	186	104	4	305	5	0	1	..
Official	0	0	107	104	4	2	5	0	1	..
Private	0	0	80	0	0	303	0	0	0	..
Debt forgiven	0	45	0	44	9	1	6	1	5	..
Memo: interest forgiven	0	0	0	7	0	0	0	0	1,631	..
Debt stock reduction	0	0	1,803	0	0	249	0	1,065	8,759	..
of which debt buyback	0	0	721	0	0	31	0	921	0	..
8. DEBT STOCK-FLOW RECONCILIATION										
Total change in debt stocks	..	..	32,807	84,482	60,813	57,176	19,341	-11,439	-40,426	..
Net flows on debt	1,224	18,319	20,005	76,881	80,244	66,376	-14,753	-36,733	-14,051	-21,286
Net change in interest arrears	..	..	521	167	247	-1,324	223	3,698	-496	..
Interest capitalized	..	..	186	104	4	305	5	0	1	..
Debt forgiveness or reduction	..	..	-1,082	-44	-9	-219	-6	-145	-8,763	..
Cross-currency valuation	..	..	11,233	-1,877	-16,349	-15,021	11,640	7,172	-15,714	..
Residual	..	..	1,945	9,250	-3,323	7,058	22,233	14,568	-1,404	..
9. AVERAGE TERMS OF NEW COMMITMENTS										
ALL CREDITORS										
Interest (%)	5.0	9.7	6.7	5.7	5.9	6.0	5.7	4.6	5.9	..
Maturity (years)	23.0	16.3	19.2	14.7	14.2	12.6	14.7	14.4	13.7	..
Grace period (years)	6.4	4.8	5.4	5.1	6.3	5.1	5.0	5.2	4.4	..
Grant element (%)	35.4	6.6	22.7	23.6	22.0	20.1	24.7	28.4	22.1	..
Official creditors										
Interest (%)	4.1	6.0	5.0	5.3	4.7	5.8	4.6	3.2	5.0	..
Maturity (years)	28.6	22.9	24.5	21.9	23.6	18.8	19.5	17.2	23.1	..
Grace period (years)	7.4	6.9	7.1	5.6	6.2	5.7	5.8	4.7	5.9	..
Grant element (%)	45.7	29.2	37.5	32.5	38.3	27.0	34.3	38.3	35.9	..
Private creditors										
Interest (%)	6.8	13.0	8.4	6.0	6.5	6.2	7.4	6.6	6.6	..
Maturity (years)	12.2	10.3	13.7	8.7	10.0	7.8	7.7	10.4	7.2	..
Grace period (years)	4.4	2.9	3.6	4.7	6.4	4.7	4.0	5.9	3.4	..
Grant element (%)	15.8	-13.8	7.4	16.3	14.7	14.7	10.7	14.4	12.6	..
Memorandum items										
Commitments	1,716	19,464	26,882	51,577	49,502	59,863	42,230	45,690	26,859	..
Official creditors	1,125	9,231	13,627	23,384	15,441	26,467	25,066	26,857	10,940	..
Private creditors	591	10,232	13,255	28,193	34,061	33,397	17,164	18,833	15,919	..

10. GRAPH OF AGGREGATE NET RESOURCE FLOWS

(current prices, US$ billion)

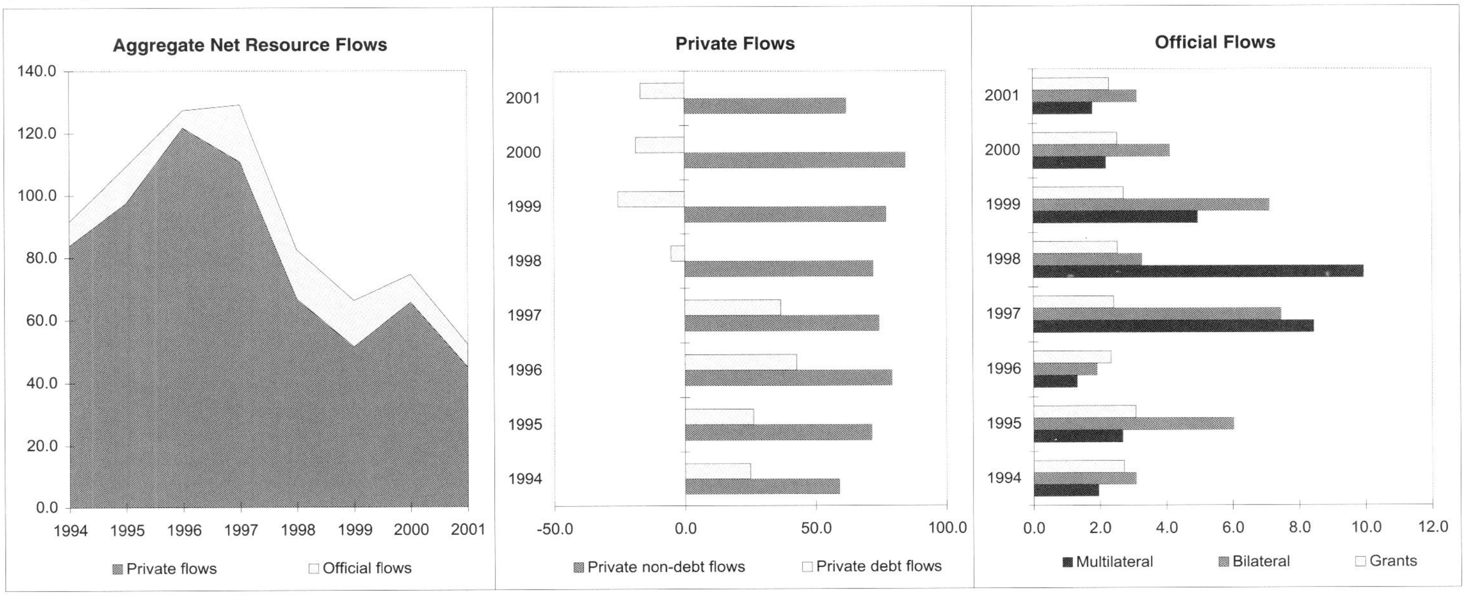

EUROPE AND CENTRAL ASIA

(US$ million, unless otherwise indicated)

	1970	1980	1990	1995	1996	1997	1998	1999	2000	2001
1. SUMMARY DEBT DATA										
TOTAL DEBT STOCKS (EDT)	**5,028**	**75,627**	**219,850**	**350,925**	**368,994**	**388,529**	**482,515**	**496,400**	**499,344**	**485,913**
Long-term debt (LDOD)	**3,965**	**56,430**	**177,688**	**288,199**	**297,059**	**311,911**	**385,791**	**398,931**	**396,428**	**384,287**
Public and publicly guaranteed	3,069	44,890	172,767	270,048	268,775	269,318	294,717	294,890	284,369	284,391
Private nonguaranteed	896	11,540	4,921	18,150	28,284	42,593	91,074	104,041	112,060	99,896
Use of IMF credit	**74**	**2,143**	**1,305**	**16,942**	**20,052**	**21,195**	**27,661**	**23,862**	**21,951**	**27,156**
Short-term debt	**..**	**17,055**	**40,857**	**45,784**	**51,883**	**55,423**	**69,064**	**73,607**	**80,965**	**74,470**
of which interest arrears on LDOD	..	312	13,041	8,519	9,644	4,963	7,953	10,318	9,268	6,843
Official creditors	..	13	6,573	2,641	2,855	2,996	5,487	6,542	7,349	..
Private creditors	..	299	6,468	5,879	6,789	1,967	2,466	3,776	1,919	..
Memo: principal arrears on LDOD	..	56	6,324	29,316	30,624	11,800	12,441	13,721	14,994	..
Official creditors	..	21	4,584	8,203	8,188	8,376	8,342	10,671	11,354	..
Private creditors	..	35	1,740	21,113	22,436	3,425	4,100	3,050	3,640	..
Memo: export credits	..	10	66,608	84,510	88,965	80,735	60,307	58,187	52,589	..
TOTAL DEBT FLOWS										
Disbursements	**1,082**	**21,295**	**30,016**	**37,147**	**43,356**	**49,481**	**74,542**	**63,375**	**62,563**	**54,258**
Long-term debt	1,007	20,057	29,269	28,993	38,139	46,109	67,135	60,568	58,194	42,263
IMF purchases	75	1,238	748	8,155	5,217	3,372	7,407	2,807	4,369	11,994
Principal repayments	**584**	**7,186**	**19,768**	**22,897**	**26,864**	**26,038**	**36,047**	**48,193**	**51,677**	**56,805**
Long-term debt	512	6,857	19,036	19,849	25,345	25,093	33,981	42,297	46,598	50,795
IMF repurchases	72	329	732	3,047	1,520	945	2,066	5,896	5,079	6,010
Net flows on debt	**497**	**13,532**	**3,124**	**21,830**	**21,459**	**31,664**	**41,745**	**15,044**	**20,285**	**-6,618**
of which short-term debt	..	-577	-7,125	7,579	4,967	8,220	3,251	-137	9,399	-4,070
Interest payments (INT)	**..**	**5,400**	**12,293**	**14,724**	**16,103**	**18,468**	**20,539**	**20,713**	**23,226**	**22,624**
Long-term debt	148	3,414	9,610	12,104	13,112	15,206	16,895	16,413	18,195	18,184
IMF charges	0	103	128	711	783	909	1,058	1,013	1,080	1,155
Short-term debt	..	1,884	2,555	1,909	2,208	2,352	2,586	3,287	3,952	3,285
Net transfers on debt	**..**	**8,132**	**-9,169**	**7,106**	**5,356**	**13,196**	**21,207**	**-5,669**	**-2,941**	**-29,241**
Total debt service paid (TDS)	**..**	**12,586**	**32,060**	**37,620**	**42,967**	**44,505**	**56,586**	**68,906**	**74,903**	**79,429**
Long-term debt	660	10,271	28,646	31,953	38,457	40,299	50,876	58,710	64,793	68,978
IMF repurchases and charges	72	432	860	3,758	2,302	1,854	3,124	6,910	6,159	7,166
Short-term debt (interest only)	..	1,884	2,555	1,909	2,208	2,352	2,586	3,287	3,952	3,285
2. AGGREGATE NET RESOURCE FLOWS AND NET TRANSFERS (LONG-TERM)										
NET RESOURCE FLOWS	**608**	**13,510**	**12,537**	**37,955**	**43,270**	**54,912**	**67,406**	**58,009**	**54,000**	**29,851**
Net flow of long-term debt (ex. IMF)	495	13,200	10,233	9,143	12,795	21,016	33,153	18,271	11,596	-8,531
Foreign direct investment (net)	58	28	1,051	16,906	16,120	23,696	25,996	28,084	28,495	28,506
Portfolio equity flows	0	0	235	2,729	8,345	4,809	2,903	3,550	5,391	1,276
Grants (excluding technical coop.)	56	283	1,018	9,177	6,011	5,391	5,354	8,104	8,518	8,600
Memo: technical coop. grants	47	156	419	4,668	4,072	2,861	4,270	4,407	3,049	3,100
official net resource flows	346	3,633	4,845	10,741	10,936	9,523	7,050	10,306	8,554	7,372
private net resource flows	262	9,878	7,692	27,214	32,333	45,389	60,356	47,703	45,446	22,479
NET TRANSFERS	**426**	**10,065**	**2,709**	**24,934**	**28,922**	**38,265**	**48,751**	**39,026**	**32,728**	**7,567**
Interest on long-term debt	148	3,414	9,610	12,104	13,112	15,206	16,895	16,413	18,195	18,184
Profit remittances on FDI	34	31	218	918	1,235	1,441	1,761	2,570	3,077	4,100
Memo: official net transfers	272	2,859	2,616	5,968	5,658	3,767	2,342	6,693	4,616	3,742
private net transfers	154	7,207	93	18,965	23,264	34,498	46,409	32,333	28,112	3,826
3. MAJOR ECONOMIC AGGREGATES										
Gross national income (GNI)	..	..	1,236,346	970,036	1,083,883	1,106,460	995,949	853,870	926,691	986,926
Exports of goods & services (XGS)	..	..	..	310,829	346,305	367,653	362,972	340,669	414,297	431,739
of which workers remittances	..	..	..	4,974	5,489	5,932	7,435	6,234	6,701	6,651
Imports of goods & services (MGS)	..	..	..	325,654	369,285	402,859	397,657	355,291	409,123	421,111
International reserves (RES)	..	..	..	91,183	94,753	100,898	105,928	113,851	129,468	134,674
Current account balance	..	..	..	-7,238	-15,883	-27,400	-25,894	-5,935	14,630	19,530
4. DEBT INDICATORS										
EDT / XGS (%)	..	..	..	112.9	106.6	105.7	132.9	145.7	120.5	112.6
EDT / GNI (%)	..	..	17.8	36.2	34.0	35.1	48.5	58.1	53.9	49.2
TDS / XGS (%)	..	..	..	12.1	12.4	12.1	15.6	20.2	18.1	18.4
INT / XGS (%)	..	..	..	4.7	4.7	5.0	5.7	6.1	5.6	5.2
INT / GNI (%)	..	..	1.0	1.5	1.5	1.7	2.1	2.4	2.5	2.3
RES / EDT (%)	..	..	..	26.0	25.7	26.0	22.0	22.9	25.9	27.7
RES / MGS (months)	..	..	..	3.4	3.1	3.0	3.2	3.9	3.8	3.8
Short-term / EDT (%)	..	22.6	18.6	13.1	14.1	14.3	14.3	14.8	16.2	15.3
Concessional / EDT (%)	..	9.2	5.8	6.8	6.3	5.2	4.6	5.1	4.7	4.9
Multilateral / EDT (%)	..	5.8	7.6	7.4	7.3	7.5	6.7	6.8	6.9	6.9

EUROPE AND CENTRAL ASIA

(US$ million, unless otherwise indicated)

5. LONG-TERM DEBT

	1970	1980	1990	1995	1996	1997	1998	1999	2000	2001
DEBT OUTSTANDING (LDOD)	**3,965**	**56,430**	**177,688**	**288,199**	**297,059**	**311,911**	**385,791**	**398,931**	**396,428**	**384,287**
Public and publicly guaranteed	**3,069**	**44,890**	**172,767**	**270,048**	**268,775**	**269,318**	**294,717**	**294,890**	**284,369**	**284,391**
Official creditors	2,647	18,605	64,347	139,251	140,086	134,928	144,042	146,357	143,081	138,964
Multilateral	635	4,363	16,604	26,103	26,867	29,041	32,536	33,850	34,540	33,425
Concessional	113	242	920	1,756	1,961	2,274	2,842	3,415	3,658	3,952
Bilateral	2,013	14,243	47,743	113,148	113,220	105,888	111,506	112,508	108,541	105,539
Concessional	1,739	6,744	11,731	22,103	21,426	17,955	19,431	21,732	19,734	19,907
Private creditors	422	26,284	108,421	130,797	128,689	134,390	150,675	148,533	141,288	145,428
Bonds	41	200	11,890	46,776	45,595	47,966	63,001	67,395	91,720	97,486
Commercial banks	10	16,733	66,529	47,200	50,761	66,832	69,477	66,497	37,715	38,496
Other private	371	9,352	30,002	36,821	32,333	19,592	18,197	14,640	11,853	9,445
Private nonguaranteed	**896**	**11,540**	**4,921**	**18,150**	**28,284**	**42,593**	**91,074**	**104,041**	**112,060**	**99,896**
Bonds	0	0	16	188	851	3,622	5,815	15,792	18,666	16,896
Commercial banks and other	896	11,540	4,905	17,962	27,432	38,971	85,260	88,250	93,394	83,000
Memo:										
IBRD	297	3,323	10,272	16,057	16,798	19,187	20,953	21,753	22,788	23,962
IDA	83	189	157	669	1,117	1,483	1,991	2,441	2,667	2,891
DISBURSEMENTS	**1,007**	**20,057**	**29,269**	**28,993**	**38,139**	**46,109**	**67,135**	**60,568**	**58,194**	**42,263**
Public and publicly guaranteed	**540**	**16,759**	**27,508**	**22,320**	**27,838**	**30,604**	**38,576**	**26,697**	**25,607**	**26,697**
Official creditors	480	5,051	6,970	6,575	10,735	9,320	9,301	7,320	7,361	8,487
Multilateral	163	1,023	2,298	4,393	5,344	6,554	5,953	4,981	4,848	4,301
Concessional	7	10	14	413	525	594	579	699	459	419
Bilateral	317	4,028	4,672	2,183	5,391	2,766	3,348	2,339	2,513	4,186
Concessional	271	1,925	941	1,113	1,161	933	1,049	1,379	1,424	2,279
Private creditors	61	11,707	20,538	15,745	17,103	21,285	29,275	19,377	18,246	18,210
Bonds	0	80	1,959	5,791	6,215	10,018	19,200	10,771	11,315	8,967
Commercial banks	0	5,069	4,344	5,410	6,970	8,131	7,141	6,539	6,308	8,086
Other private	61	6,559	14,236	4,544	3,918	3,136	2,934	2,068	624	1,156
Private nonguaranteed	**466**	**3,298**	**1,761**	**6,672**	**10,302**	**15,504**	**28,559**	**33,871**	**32,587**	**15,567**
Bonds	0	0	0	36	671	2,894	2,146	2,050	5,800	697
Commercial banks and other	466	3,298	1,761	6,636	9,631	12,611	26,414	31,822	26,787	14,870
Memo:										
IBRD	55	833	1,218	2,696	3,326	4,677	3,357	2,635	3,102	3,182
IDA	7	0	0	370	477	433	450	495	351	332
PRINCIPAL REPAYMENTS	**512**	**6,857**	**19,036**	**19,849**	**25,345**	**25,093**	**33,981**	**42,297**	**46,598**	**50,795**
Public and publicly guaranteed	**305**	**4,816**	**17,539**	**16,953**	**19,895**	**17,614**	**24,352**	**18,514**	**21,072**	**25,822**
Official creditors	189	1,701	3,143	5,011	5,809	5,188	7,604	5,118	7,325	9,715
Multilateral	81	154	1,455	3,033	3,060	2,437	3,724	2,107	2,828	2,527
Concessional	22	2	23	66	197	140	131	71	32	33
Bilateral	108	1,547	1,688	1,978	2,749	2,751	3,881	3,012	4,497	7,188
Concessional	47	532	434	524	525	717	784	1,006	2,231	1,444
Private creditors	116	3,114	14,395	11,941	14,086	12,426	16,748	13,396	13,747	16,107
Bonds	2	15	66	3,764	4,618	3,586	6,285	4,788	5,791	4,763
Commercial banks	2	1,366	8,778	4,306	6,206	5,854	6,450	5,325	5,146	7,716
Other private	112	1,734	5,552	3,871	3,262	2,986	4,012	3,284	2,810	3,628
Private nonguaranteed	**208**	**2,041**	**1,497**	**2,897**	**5,450**	**7,479**	**9,629**	**23,783**	**25,526**	**24,973**
Bonds	0	0	0	0	0	86	0	214	2,725	2,457
Commercial banks and other	208	2,041	1,497	2,897	5,450	7,394	9,629	23,569	22,801	22,516
Memo:										
IBRD	13	133	1,133	1,191	1,605	1,186	2,233	1,258	1,357	1,407
IDA	0	1	4	6	6	6	6	6	6	6
NET FLOWS ON DEBT	**495**	**13,200**	**10,233**	**9,143**	**12,795**	**21,016**	**33,153**	**18,271**	**11,596**	**-8,531**
Public and publicly guaranteed	**236**	**11,943**	**9,969**	**5,368**	**7,943**	**12,991**	**14,224**	**8,183**	**4,535**	**875**
Official creditors	291	3,350	3,827	1,564	4,926	4,132	1,696	2,201	36	-1,228
Multilateral	82	869	843	1,360	2,284	4,117	2,229	2,875	2,020	1,774
Concessional	-15	9	-10	346	327	454	448	628	427	386
Bilateral	209	2,481	2,984	205	2,641	15	-533	-673	-1,984	-3,002
Concessional	224	1,393	507	589	635	216	265	373	-807	834
Private creditors	-55	8,593	6,143	3,804	3,017	8,859	12,527	5,981	4,499	2,103
Bonds	-2	65	1,893	2,026	1,598	6,432	12,915	5,983	5,524	4,204
Commercial banks	-2	3,703	-4,435	1,104	764	2,277	691	1,214	1,162	370
Other private	-51	4,825	8,684	673	656	150	-1,078	-1,216	-2,187	-2,472
Private nonguaranteed	**259**	**1,257**	**264**	**3,775**	**4,852**	**8,025**	**18,930**	**10,089**	**7,061**	**-9,406**
Bonds	0	0	0	36	671	2,808	2,146	1,836	3,074	-1,760
Commercial banks and other	259	1,257	264	3,740	4,181	5,217	16,784	8,252	3,987	-7,646
Memo:										
IBRD	42	700	85	1,505	1,722	3,490	1,124	1,378	1,745	1,775
IDA	7	-1	-4	364	471	427	444	489	345	326

(US$ million, unless otherwise indicated)

	1970	1980	1990	1995	1996	1997	1998	1999	2000	2001
INTEREST PAYMENTS (LINT)	**148**	**3,414**	**9,610**	**12,104**	**13,112**	**15,206**	**16,895**	**16,413**	**18,195**	**18,184**
Public and publicly guaranteed	**115**	**2,565**	**9,169**	**11,390**	**12,160**	**13,285**	**12,489**	**11,536**	**12,605**	**13,171**
Official creditors	74	774	2,228	4,773	5,278	5,756	4,708	3,612	3,938	3,630
Multilateral	24	298	1,199	1,535	1,764	1,601	1,786	1,827	1,873	1,645
Concessional	2	4	39	49	43	35	36	36	42	47
Bilateral	50	476	1,029	3,238	3,513	4,155	2,921	1,785	2,065	1,985
Concessional	35	157	246	751	735	736	686	641	624	454
Private creditors	41	1,792	6,940	6,617	6,882	7,528	7,781	7,924	8,668	9,540
Bonds	1	36	738	3,301	3,102	3,043	3,664	4,699	5,739	6,483
Commercial banks	1	1,176	4,737	1,920	2,598	3,472	3,253	2,353	2,247	2,370
Other private	38	580	1,466	1,396	1,182	1,014	864	872	682	687
Private nonguaranteed	**34**	**849**	**442**	**714**	**952**	**1,922**	**4,406**	**4,876**	**5,590**	**5,013**
Bonds	0	0	1	13	16	54	259	468	981	804
Commercial banks and other	34	849	440	701	936	1,868	4,147	4,408	4,608	4,209
Memo:										
IBRD	16	257	809	939	1,181	1,032	1,136	1,210	1,297	1,301
IDA	1	1	1	3	5	8	11	15	19	20
NET TRANSFERS ON DEBT	**346**	**9,786**	**623**	**-2,960**	**-318**	**5,810**	**16,259**	**1,859**	**-6,599**	**-26,715**
Public and publicly guaranteed	**121**	**9,378**	**801**	**-6,022**	**-4,217**	**-294**	**1,735**	**-3,354**	**-8,071**	**-12,296**
Official creditors	217	2,576	1,598	-3,209	-352	-1,625	-3,012	-1,411	-3,902	-4,859
Multilateral	58	571	-356	-175	520	2,516	443	1,047	147	129
Concessional	-17	5	-48	298	285	419	412	592	385	339
Bilateral	159	2,005	1,955	-3,034	-872	-4,141	-3,454	-2,458	-4,049	-4,987
Concessional	189	1,236	261	-162	-100	-520	-421	-268	-1,432	380
Private creditors	-95	6,801	-798	-2,813	-3,865	1,330	4,747	-1,943	-4,169	-7,437
Bonds	-4	30	1,156	-1,274	-1,505	3,390	9,251	1,284	-215	-2,279
Commercial banks	-3	2,527	-9,171	-817	-1,835	-1,195	-2,563	-1,139	-1,085	-1,999
Other private	-89	4,245	7,218	-722	-526	-864	-1,942	-2,088	-2,869	-3,159
Private nonguaranteed	**225**	**408**	**-178**	**3,062**	**3,899**	**6,104**	**14,524**	**5,212**	**1,472**	**-14,419**
Bonds	0	0	-1	23	655	2,755	1,887	1,368	2,093	-2,564
Commercial banks and other	225	408	-176	3,039	3,244	3,349	12,637	3,844	-622	-11,855
Memo:										
IBRD	26	443	-724	566	541	2,459	-12	167	449	474
IDA	7	-2	-5	361	466	419	432	474	327	306
DEBT SERVICE (LTDS)	**660**	**10,271**	**28,646**	**31,953**	**38,457**	**40,299**	**50,876**	**58,710**	**64,793**	**68,978**
Public and publicly guaranteed	**419**	**7,381**	**26,707**	**28,342**	**32,055**	**30,898**	**36,841**	**30,051**	**33,678**	**38,993**
Official creditors	263	2,475	5,372	9,784	11,087	10,944	12,312	8,731	11,263	13,345
Multilateral	105	452	2,654	4,568	4,824	4,038	5,510	3,934	4,702	4,172
Concessional	25	6	62	115	240	175	167	107	75	80
Bilateral	158	2,023	2,718	5,216	6,263	6,906	6,802	4,797	6,562	9,173
Concessional	82	689	680	1,276	1,260	1,453	1,470	1,648	2,855	1,898
Private creditors	156	4,906	21,336	18,558	20,968	19,954	24,529	21,320	22,415	25,647
Bonds	4	50	803	7,065	7,720	6,629	9,950	9,487	11,530	11,246
Commercial banks	3	2,542	13,515	6,227	8,804	9,326	9,704	7,678	7,393	10,086
Other private	150	2,314	7,018	5,267	4,444	4,000	4,876	4,156	3,492	4,316
Private nonguaranteed	**241**	**2,890**	**1,939**	**3,611**	**6,403**	**9,401**	**14,035**	**28,659**	**31,115**	**29,986**
Bonds	0	0	1	13	16	139	259	682	3,706	3,261
Commercial banks and other	241	2,890	1,937	3,598	6,386	9,262	13,777	27,977	27,409	26,725
Memo:										
IBRD	29	390	1,943	2,130	2,785	2,218	3,369	2,468	2,653	2,708
IDA	1	3	5	9	11	14	17	21	25	26
UNDISBURSED DEBT	**1,935**	**13,750**	**17,065**	**33,214**	**35,109**	**31,742**	**32,295**	**33,856**	**27,683**	**..**
Official creditors	1,613	6,155	9,220	21,526	22,862	21,568	22,191	24,616	18,189	..
Private creditors	322	7,596	7,846	11,688	12,247	10,174	10,104	9,240	9,494	..
Memorandum items										
Concessional LDOD	1,851	6,986	12,652	23,859	23,387	20,229	22,273	25,147	23,392	..
Variable rate LDOD	952	25,866	89,396	142,555	151,364	179,244	232,901	233,304	207,326	..
Public sector LDOD	2,843	44,026	171,111	267,768	265,871	266,117	290,603	290,445	280,324	..
Private sector LDOD	1,122	12,379	5,937	20,008	30,385	44,803	95,071	108,170	115,735	..

6. CURRENCY COMPOSITION OF LONG-TERM DEBT (PERCENT)

	1970	1980	1990	1995	1996	1997	1998	1999	2000	2001
Deutsche mark	16.0	11.0	25.1	22.3	22.9	20.5	21.8	17.5	15.1	..
French franc	2.7	9.3	5.0	3.3	3.4	2.6	2.5	2.1	2.0	..
Japanese yen	0.1	2.4	7.5	9.6	9.1	7.2	6.3	6.3	5.9	..
Pound sterling	5.0	2.6	1.8	1.0	1.0	0.8	0.7	0.7	0.6	..
Swiss franc	1.4	4.5	6.5	2.1	1.7	0.7	0.5	0.4	0.3	..
U.S.dollars	44.7	41.8	32.2	43.7	45.5	55.0	55.5	58.2	58.8	..
Multiple currency	15.2	21.5	10.6	9.2	9.2	7.9	7.2	7.1	7.1	..
Special drawing rights	0.0	0.0	0.0	0.0	0.0	0.0	0.0	0.0	0.0	..
All other currencies	14.9	6.8	11.0	7.7	5.6	3.4	3.3	4.8	7.4	..

EUROPE AND CENTRAL ASIA

(US$ million, unless otherwise indicated)

	1970	1980	1990	1995	1996	1997	1998	1999	2000	2001
7. DEBT RESTRUCTURINGS										
Total amount rescheduled	0	1,757	3,559	11,081	11,836	36,151	5,642	17,529	29,063	..
Debt stock rescheduled	0	0	0	225	1,735	953	224	2,080	19,307	..
Principal rescheduled	0	20	1,366	7,461	6,288	29,068	4,084	7,800	3,663	..
Official	0	17	746	4,029	2,988	3,753	2,993	6,001	2,929	..
Private	0	3	620	3,432	3,300	25,315	1,091	1,800	734	..
Interest rescheduled	..	..	2,163	1,381	1,151	5,356	553	5,818	4,383	..
Official	0	7	1,998	777	525	587	395	5,346	2,207	..
Private	0	1	165	604	626	4,769	158	472	2,176	..
Debt forgiven	0	0	233	3	610	50	41	247	15	..
Memo: interest forgiven	0	0	61	0	15	3	0	0	0	..
Debt stock reduction	0	0	1,779	146	33	1,826	748	154	12,545	..
of which debt buyback	0	0	883	30	0	0	748	30	943	..
8. DEBT STOCK-FLOW RECONCILIATION										
Total change in debt stocks	..	..	21,153	25,533	18,069	19,535	93,987	13,885	2,944	..
Net flows on debt	497	13,532	3,124	21,830	21,459	31,664	41,745	15,044	20,285	-6,618
Net change in interest arrears	..	..	5,213	1,131	1,125	-4,681	2,990	2,365	-1,049	..
Interest capitalized	..	..	2,163	1,381	1,151	5,356	553	5,818	4,383	..
Debt forgiveness or reduction	..	..	-1,129	-119	-643	-1,875	-41	-370	-11,617	..
Cross-currency valuation	..	..	10,086	6,649	-12,413	-17,338	8,630	-10,687	-9,820	..
Residual	..	..	1,697	-5,339	7,391	6,410	40,110	1,715	762	..
9. AVERAGE TERMS OF NEW COMMITMENTS										
ALL CREDITORS										
Interest (%)	4.2	10.2	8.4	6.3	6.4	6.9	7.5	6.4	7.5	..
Maturity (years)	19.2	12.5	11.9	11.7	11.5	10.6	11.9	11.1	11.0	..
Grace period (years)	6.8	4.4	6.1	2.9	2.8	4.9	7.7	4.5	6.8	..
Grant element (%)	37.3	2.1	8.7	18.5	17.7	15.0	10.7	18.5	10.9	..
Official creditors										
Interest (%)	3.8	7.5	7.9	5.7	5.5	5.6	5.2	4.4	6.2	..
Maturity (years)	20.1	16.7	13.6	16.5	15.2	17.6	16.3	17.5	17.1	..
Grace period (years)	7.3	5.3	5.9	0.5	2.1	5.3	5.1	4.8	5.4	..
Grant element (%)	40.3	19.6	12.0	25.6	25.8	27.1	28.0	34.0	23.8	..
Private creditors										
Interest (%)	6.3	11.2	8.6	6.7	7.1	7.5	8.2	7.6	7.8	..
Maturity (years)	13.4	10.9	11.1	8.3	8.4	7.2	10.4	7.5	9.2	..
Grace period (years)	3.6	4.1	6.2	4.6	3.5	4.7	8.6	4.3	7.2	..
Grant element (%)	18.2	-4.4	7.2	13.5	10.9	9.1	4.7	9.7	7.1	..
Memorandum items										
Commitments	759	12,696	30,305	23,659	33,018	31,622	39,030	27,646	24,400	..
Official creditors	654	3,415	9,392	9,691	15,032	10,435	9,999	10,035	5,565	..
Private creditors	105	9,281	20,914	13,968	17,986	21,186	29,031	17,611	18,835	..

10. GRAPH OF AGGREGATE NET RESOURCE FLOWS

(current prices, US$ billion)

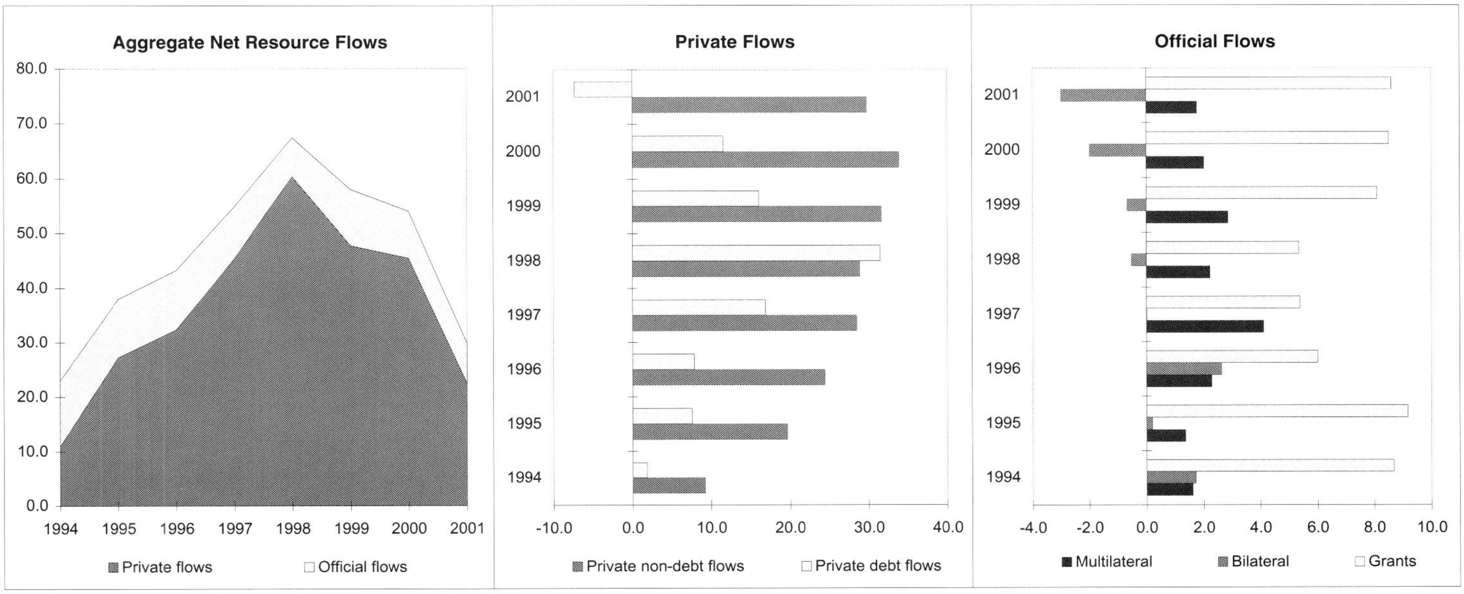

LATIN AMERICA AND CARIBBEAN

(US$ million, unless otherwise indicated)

	1970	1980	1990	1995	1996	1997	1998	1999	2000	2001
1. SUMMARY DEBT DATA										
TOTAL DEBT STOCKS (EDT)	**32,548**	**257,197**	**474,720**	**649,398**	**670,538**	**701,916**	**776,266**	**796,192**	**774,419**	**787,145**
Long-term debt (LDOD)	**27,633**	**187,255**	**379,206**	**495,164**	**525,932**	**556,300**	**635,290**	**665,789**	**661,735**	**659,746**
Public and publicly guaranteed	15,760	144,797	354,155	407,507	408,678	393,813	414,157	421,491	415,077	415,701
Private nonguaranteed	11,873	42,458	25,051	87,657	117,253	162,487	221,133	244,297	246,658	244,045
Use of IMF credit	**128**	**1,410**	**18,297**	**26,682**	**23,882**	**18,564**	**21,969**	**20,498**	**8,846**	**23,900**
Short-term debt	**..**	**68,532**	**77,217**	**127,552**	**120,724**	**127,053**	**119,008**	**109,906**	**103,837**	**103,499**
of which interest arrears on LDOD	..	60	25,560	10,211	3,564	2,785	3,120	1,916	1,654	1,650
Official creditors	..	16	3,858	3,576	2,034	1,834	1,320	1,375	1,248	..
Private creditors	..	44	21,702	6,635	1,530	951	1,800	542	406	..
Memo: principal arrears on LDOD	..	644	24,460	16,307	7,537	6,354	5,653	5,906	4,177	..
Official creditors	..	78	7,388	6,249	3,479	2,768	2,778	3,079	2,216	..
Private creditors	..	566	17,072	10,058	4,058	3,587	2,875	2,828	1,961	..
Memo: export credits	..	554	71,969	79,360	76,889	70,467	34,163	32,271	28,999	..
TOTAL DEBT FLOWS										
Disbursements	**6,576**	**44,754**	**34,043**	**91,095**	**103,020**	**124,633**	**146,791**	**133,291**	**127,501**	**119,392**
Long-term debt	6,452	44,339	29,207	75,323	101,565	123,855	141,755	125,545	123,992	102,403
IMF purchases	124	415	4,836	15,772	1,455	777	5,036	7,746	3,510	16,989
Principal repayments	**3,751**	**21,691**	**22,712**	**43,803**	**66,921**	**91,895**	**79,592**	**113,974**	**125,928**	**105,623**
Long-term debt	3,453	21,204	19,061	40,927	63,520	87,196	77,059	105,296	111,676	104,001
IMF repurchases	298	487	3,651	2,876	3,402	4,699	2,532	8,679	14,252	1,622
Net flows on debt	**2,825**	**46,067**	**20,427**	**62,184**	**35,918**	**39,845**	**58,819**	**11,418**	**-3,343**	**13,432**
of which short-term debt	..	23,003	9,097	14,892	-181	7,107	-8,380	-7,898	-4,917	-338
Interest payments (INT)	**..**	**24,596**	**22,734**	**37,035**	**39,525**	**41,603**	**44,335**	**49,652**	**53,294**	**51,144**
Long-term debt	1,395	17,567	18,745	29,321	30,725	34,009	36,867	42,284	46,068	44,244
IMF charges	0	95	1,459	1,104	1,105	928	828	1,040	778	601
Short-term debt	..	6,934	2,530	6,609	7,695	6,666	6,640	6,328	6,449	6,300
Net transfers on debt	**..**	**21,471**	**-2,307**	**25,149**	**-3,607**	**-1,758**	**14,484**	**-38,234**	**-56,637**	**-37,712**
Total debt service paid (TDS)	**..**	**46,287**	**45,446**	**80,838**	**106,446**	**133,498**	**123,927**	**163,626**	**179,222**	**156,767**
Long-term debt	4,848	38,771	37,806	70,248	94,245	121,204	113,926	147,580	157,743	148,244
IMF repurchases and charges	298	582	5,110	3,980	4,507	5,627	3,360	9,718	15,030	2,222
Short-term debt (interest only)	..	6,934	2,530	6,609	7,695	6,666	6,640	6,328	6,449	6,300
2. AGGREGATE NET RESOURCE FLOWS AND NET TRANSFERS (LONG-TERM)										
NET RESOURCE FLOWS	**4,234**	**29,866**	**21,782**	**75,427**	**98,666**	**114,832**	**142,542**	**115,184**	**99,315**	**73,764**
Net flow of long-term debt (ex. IMF)	2,999	23,135	10,145	34,396	38,045	36,660	64,696	20,250	12,316	-1,598
Foreign direct investment (net)	1,083	6,145	8,177	30,024	43,771	65,540	72,829	88,033	75,088	70,761
Portfolio equity flows	0	0	1,111	7,646	13,652	9,850	1,748	3,893	9,378	2,201
Grants (excluding technical coop.)	153	587	2,349	3,362	3,197	2,782	3,270	3,009	2,533	2,400
Memo: technical coop. grants	258	773	1,966	2,760	2,539	2,440	2,303	2,506	2,952	2,800
official net resource flows	983	5,272	9,152	12,489	-5,577	-1,930	11,662	5,365	2,010	4,367
private net resource flows	3,251	24,594	12,630	62,937	104,243	116,762	130,880	109,819	97,305	69,398
NET TRANSFERS	**815**	**7,427**	**-3,312**	**35,526**	**55,534**	**67,278**	**90,165**	**55,132**	**32,510**	**5,221**
Interest on long-term debt	1,395	17,567	18,745	29,321	30,725	34,009	36,867	42,284	46,068	44,244
Profit remittances on FDI	2,024	4,872	6,349	10,579	12,407	13,545	15,511	17,768	20,737	24,300
Memo: official net transfers	681	3,294	3,024	3,240	-14,450	-9,435	4,082	-3,577	-6,885	-4,167
private net transfers	134	4,132	-6,337	32,286	69,984	76,713	86,082	58,709	39,395	9,387
3. MAJOR ECONOMIC AGGREGATES										
Gross national income (GNI)	160,646	745,562	1,064,676	1,636,190	1,777,823	1,949,033	1,947,896	1,716,530	1,891,329	1,819,458
Exports of goods & services (XGS)	..	127,386	185,903	304,971	334,653	371,615	372,996	389,145	463,072	471,315
of which workers remittances	..	1,187	4,762	11,548	11,310	12,064	13,244	15,250	17,398	17,248
Imports of goods & services (MGS)	..	159,836	193,958	349,386	381,220	444,971	470,975	453,458	518,358	517,322
International reserves (RES)	5,464	57,301	58,639	139,224	164,835	175,122	165,701	158,126	159,568	158,360
Current account balance	..	-30,177	-1,044	-36,989	-39,036	-65,472	-89,136	-55,100	-46,738	-51,438
4. DEBT INDICATORS										
EDT / XGS (%)	..	201.9	255.4	212.9	200.4	188.9	208.1	204.6	167.2	167.0
EDT / GNI (%)	..	34.5	44.6	39.7	37.7	36.0	39.9	46.4	41.0	43.3
TDS / XGS (%)	..	36.3	24.5	26.5	31.8	35.9	33.2	42.1	38.7	33.3
INT / XGS (%)	..	19.3	12.2	12.1	11.8	11.2	11.9	12.8	11.5	10.9
INT / GNI (%)	..	3.3	2.1	2.3	2.2	2.1	2.3	2.9	2.8	2.8
RES / EDT (%)	..	22.3	12.4	21.4	24.6	25.0	21.4	19.9	20.6	20.1
RES / MGS (months)	..	4.3	3.6	4.8	5.2	4.7	4.2	4.2	3.7	3.7
Short-term / EDT (%)	..	26.7	16.3	19.6	18.0	18.1	15.3	13.8	13.4	13.2
Concessional / EDT (%)	..	9.3	10.2	9.8	9.0	8.5	4.3	4.3	4.0	4.0
Multilateral / EDT (%)	..	5.5	12.6	11.2	10.5	10.0	10.8	11.5	12.0	12.4

LATIN AMERICA AND CARIBBEAN

(US$ million, unless otherwise indicated)

	1970	1980	1990	1995	1996	1997	1998	1999	2000	2001
5. LONG-TERM DEBT										
DEBT OUTSTANDING (LDOD)	**27,633**	**187,255**	**379,206**	**495,164**	**525,932**	**556,300**	**635,290**	**665,789**	**661,735**	**659,746**
Public and publicly guaranteed	**15,760**	**144,797**	**354,155**	**407,507**	**408,678**	**393,813**	**414,157**	**421,491**	**415,077**	**415,701**
Official creditors	8,125	44,961	146,012	190,466	170,184	157,256	158,356	162,330	160,745	161,020
Multilateral	2,950	14,108	59,874	72,632	70,483	70,451	83,571	91,383	92,906	97,439
Concessional	305	2,342	5,886	7,905	8,450	9,210	9,693	10,370	10,435	10,813
Bilateral	5,176	30,852	86,139	117,834	99,701	86,806	74,785	70,947	67,839	63,581
Concessional	3,922	21,592	42,591	55,765	52,185	50,179	23,537	24,043	20,677	20,965
Private creditors	7,634	99,837	208,142	217,041	238,495	236,557	255,801	259,161	254,333	254,681
Bonds	1,227	9,582	75,907	165,526	195,512	193,223	205,022	215,211	212,953	217,291
Commercial banks	3,072	77,088	103,087	37,593	31,323	32,368	41,376	34,022	32,183	29,864
Other private	3,336	13,167	29,148	13,923	11,660	10,967	9,403	9,928	9,196	7,526
Private nonguaranteed	**11,873**	**42,458**	**25,051**	**87,657**	**117,253**	**162,487**	**221,133**	**244,297**	**246,658**	**244,045**
Bonds	0	0	171	33,829	40,983	46,404	53,999	54,041	53,285	54,045
Commercial banks and other	11,873	42,458	24,880	53,828	76,270	116,083	167,134	190,256	193,374	190,000
Memo:										
IBRD	2,067	7,706	34,724	36,371	33,974	31,793	34,501	36,080	37,518	38,212
IDA	112	427	1,117	2,186	2,411	2,621	2,989	3,369	3,387	3,517
DISBURSEMENTS	**6,452**	**44,339**	**29,207**	**75,323**	**101,565**	**123,855**	**141,755**	**125,545**	**123,992**	**102,403**
Public and publicly guaranteed	**3,692**	**31,379**	**24,504**	**46,693**	**58,091**	**56,968**	**62,919**	**56,693**	**55,948**	**53,830**
Official creditors	1,340	6,815	13,782	23,721	12,373	13,521	22,314	17,477	16,531	14,700
Multilateral	582	2,955	8,962	9,999	9,546	11,160	17,476	14,783	13,654	11,311
Concessional	76	482	451	812	905	820	813	1,010	690	810
Bilateral	757	3,860	4,821	13,723	2,827	2,361	4,838	2,695	2,876	3,388
Concessional	435	1,118	2,534	1,489	982	935	992	1,280	1,608	1,999
Private creditors	2,352	24,564	10,722	22,972	45,718	43,447	40,605	39,216	39,417	39,131
Bonds	132	1,203	1,938	13,654	36,750	33,615	25,224	29,683	32,324	29,911
Commercial banks	1,229	19,932	5,657	7,528	7,253	8,089	14,367	6,336	6,201	7,590
Other private	991	3,430	3,126	1,790	1,715	1,744	1,014	3,198	892	1,630
Private nonguaranteed	**2,760**	**12,960**	**4,702**	**28,630**	**43,474**	**66,888**	**78,836**	**68,852**	**68,044**	**48,573**
Bonds	0	0	171	7,412	12,129	14,120	15,986	10,932	8,311	6,456
Commercial banks and other	2,760	12,960	4,531	21,218	31,345	52,768	62,850	57,920	59,733	42,116
Memo:										
IBRD	354	1,586	6,134	4,639	4,420	4,389	5,760	5,483	5,609	4,857
IDA	9	60	119	277	304	343	309	499	202	276
PRINCIPAL REPAYMENTS	**3,453**	**21,204**	**19,061**	**40,927**	**63,520**	**87,196**	**77,059**	**105,296**	**111,676**	**104,001**
Public and publicly guaranteed	**1,682**	**14,244**	**16,845**	**27,837**	**42,402**	**55,277**	**40,274**	**44,727**	**53,434**	**56,349**
Official creditors	509	2,129	6,979	14,594	21,147	18,233	13,922	15,121	17,053	12,733
Multilateral	171	711	4,737	8,321	7,023	6,875	6,152	7,777	9,926	6,694
Concessional	7	36	145	279	249	268	270	264	273	283
Bilateral	339	1,419	2,242	6,273	14,124	11,358	7,769	7,344	7,128	6,040
Concessional	119	370	736	1,035	1,243	1,178	1,359	1,478	1,313	1,621
Private creditors	1,173	12,115	9,867	13,243	21,255	37,044	26,352	29,606	36,381	43,616
Bonds	77	401	1,964	5,833	11,577	28,206	15,308	13,708	26,801	30,204
Commercial banks	618	9,366	5,199	4,308	6,453	6,334	7,748	13,659	7,718	10,176
Other private	478	2,348	2,703	3,102	3,226	2,503	3,296	2,239	1,862	3,236
Private nonguaranteed	**1,771**	**6,960**	**2,216**	**13,090**	**21,118**	**31,919**	**36,786**	**60,569**	**58,242**	**47,652**
Bonds	0	0	0	3,922	4,858	8,480	7,694	7,695	8,848	5,696
Commercial banks and other	1,771	6,960	2,216	9,169	16,261	23,439	29,091	52,874	49,393	41,956
Memo:										
IBRD	105	395	3,303	4,980	4,335	3,958	3,637	3,830	3,814	3,859
IDA	0	2	9	21	16	18	21	23	28	28
NET FLOWS ON DEBT	**2,999**	**23,135**	**10,145**	**34,396**	**38,045**	**36,660**	**64,696**	**20,250**	**12,316**	**-1,598**
Public and publicly guaranteed	**2,010**	**17,135**	**7,659**	**18,856**	**15,689**	**1,691**	**22,646**	**11,966**	**2,514**	**-2,518**
Official creditors	830	4,686	6,804	9,128	-8,774	-4,712	8,393	2,356	-523	1,967
Multilateral	412	2,244	4,225	1,678	2,523	4,285	11,324	7,006	3,729	4,618
Concessional	69	446	306	533	656	552	543	746	418	527
Bilateral	419	2,441	2,579	7,450	-11,297	-8,998	-2,932	-4,650	-4,251	-2,651
Concessional	316	748	1,798	454	-261	-243	-367	-198	295	378
Private creditors	1,180	12,450	856	9,728	24,463	6,403	14,253	9,610	3,036	-4,485
Bonds	55	802	-26	7,820	25,174	5,408	9,916	15,975	5,523	-293
Commercial banks	612	10,566	458	3,220	800	1,755	6,618	-7,323	-1,516	-2,587
Other private	513	1,082	423	-1,312	-1,510	-760	-2,282	959	-970	-1,605
Private nonguaranteed	**989**	**6,000**	**2,486**	**15,540**	**22,356**	**34,969**	**42,050**	**8,283**	**9,802**	**921**
Bonds	0	0	171	3,491	7,271	5,639	8,291	3,237	-537	760
Commercial banks and other	989	6,000	2,315	12,049	15,085	29,330	33,759	5,046	10,340	160
Memo:										
IBRD	249	1,191	2,830	-341	85	431	2,123	1,653	1,795	998
IDA	9	59	110	257	288	325	288	475	174	247

(US$ million, unless otherwise indicated)

	1970	1980	1990	1995	1996	1997	1998	1999	2000	2001
INTEREST PAYMENTS (LINT)	**1,395**	**17,567**	**18,745**	**29,321**	**30,725**	**34,009**	**36,867**	**42,284**	**46,068**	**44,244**
Public and publicly guaranteed	**767**	**13,138**	**16,483**	**23,174**	**23,080**	**23,036**	**23,851**	**27,174**	**29,760**	**29,561**
Official creditors	302	1,978	6,128	9,249	8,873	7,505	7,580	8,942	8,895	8,533
Multilateral	157	999	4,115	4,877	4,687	4,489	4,489	6,072	6,369	6,173
Concessional	7	48	103	150	132	140	166	160	170	169
Bilateral	145	979	2,013	4,372	4,186	3,015	3,091	2,870	2,526	2,360
Concessional	75	401	778	893	882	654	851	766	712	728
Private creditors	465	11,161	10,355	13,924	14,208	15,531	16,271	18,232	20,865	21,028
Bonds	72	727	2,390	11,285	10,656	12,913	13,263	14,970	17,296	17,786
Commercial banks	228	9,449	6,685	1,716	2,834	2,031	2,359	2,675	2,697	2,472
Other private	165	985	1,281	923	717	587	649	587	872	770
Private nonguaranteed	**628**	**4,429**	**2,262**	**6,148**	**7,645**	**10,973**	**13,016**	**15,111**	**16,308**	**14,683**
Bonds	0	0	0	2,597	2,983	3,690	4,228	4,437	4,797	4,761
Commercial banks and other	628	4,429	2,262	3,551	4,662	7,283	8,788	10,674	11,510	9,922
Memo:										
IBRD	114	633	2,535	2,656	2,487	2,174	2,115	2,475	2,809	2,826
IDA	1	3	8	23	17	18	20	23	25	23
NET TRANSFERS ON DEBT	**1,604**	**5,568**	**-8,600**	**5,075**	**7,320**	**2,651**	**27,829**	**-22,035**	**-33,752**	**-45,841**
Public and publicly guaranteed	**1,244**	**3,997**	**-8,824**	**-4,318**	**-7,391**	**-21,345**	**-1,206**	**-15,207**	**-27,246**	**-32,079**
Official creditors	528	2,708	676	-122	-17,647	-12,217	813	-6,586	-9,418	-6,567
Multilateral	254	1,245	110	-3,199	-2,164	-204	6,836	934	-2,640	-1,555
Concessional	62	399	202	383	524	412	377	587	247	358
Bilateral	274	1,463	566	3,077	-15,483	-12,013	-6,023	-7,520	-6,777	-5,011
Concessional	241	346	1,020	-439	-1,142	-897	-1,218	-964	-417	-351
Private creditors	715	1,289	-9,500	-4,196	10,256	-9,128	-2,018	-8,622	-17,829	-25,512
Bonds	-16	75	-2,416	-3,465	14,518	-7,505	-3,347	1,004	-11,773	-18,079
Commercial banks	384	1,117	-6,227	1,504	-2,034	-276	4,259	-9,997	-4,213	-5,058
Other private	348	97	-857	-2,234	-2,228	-1,347	-2,931	371	-1,842	-2,375
Private nonguaranteed	**360**	**1,571**	**224**	**9,392**	**14,711**	**23,996**	**29,034**	**-6,828**	**-6,505**	**-13,763**
Bonds	0	0	171	894	4,288	1,949	4,063	-1,200	-5,335	-4,000
Commercial banks and other	360	1,571	53	8,498	10,423	22,047	24,971	-5,628	-1,170	-9,762
Memo:										
IBRD	135	558	295	-2,996	-2,402	-1,743	8	-821	-1,014	-1,828
IDA	8	55	102	234	271	307	268	453	150	225
DEBT SERVICE (LTDS)	**4,848**	**38,771**	**37,806**	**70,248**	**94,245**	**121,204**	**113,926**	**147,580**	**157,743**	**148,244**
Public and publicly guaranteed	**2,449**	**27,382**	**33,328**	**51,011**	**65,482**	**78,312**	**64,125**	**71,901**	**83,194**	**85,909**
Official creditors	812	4,107	13,106	23,843	30,020	25,738	21,501	24,063	25,948	21,266
Multilateral	328	1,710	8,852	13,198	11,709	11,364	10,641	13,848	16,295	12,867
Concessional	14	83	249	429	380	408	436	423	443	451
Bilateral	484	2,397	4,255	10,645	18,310	14,374	10,861	10,214	9,653	8,400
Concessional	193	771	1,514	1,927	2,124	1,832	2,210	2,244	2,026	2,349
Private creditors	1,637	23,275	20,222	27,167	35,462	52,575	42,623	47,838	57,246	64,643
Bonds	148	1,128	4,354	17,119	22,233	41,120	28,571	28,678	44,097	47,990
Commercial banks	846	18,815	11,884	6,024	9,287	8,365	10,107	16,333	10,415	12,648
Other private	643	3,333	3,984	4,024	3,943	3,091	3,945	2,826	2,734	4,006
Private nonguaranteed	**2,400**	**11,389**	**4,478**	**19,238**	**28,763**	**42,892**	**49,802**	**75,680**	**74,549**	**62,335**
Bonds	0	0	0	6,518	7,841	12,170	11,922	12,132	13,646	10,457
Commercial banks and other	2,400	11,389	4,478	12,719	20,922	30,722	37,879	63,547	60,903	51,879
Memo:										
IBRD	219	1,027	5,838	7,635	6,822	6,132	5,752	6,304	6,622	6,685
IDA	1	5	17	44	33	36	40	46	52	51
UNDISBURSED DEBT	**5,070**	**34,949**	**43,359**	**55,747**	**54,408**	**58,504**	**74,496**	**73,817**	**59,716**	**..**
Official creditors	3,255	20,423	30,528	44,250	40,836	43,518	59,307	61,821	50,381	..
Private creditors	1,815	14,526	12,831	11,497	13,572	14,987	15,189	11,996	9,335	..
Memorandum items										
Concessional LDOD	4,227	23,933	48,476	63,670	60,635	59,389	33,231	34,413	31,113	..
Variable rate LDOD	12,501	117,257	195,990	273,202	296,856	325,810	392,246	413,444	392,755	..
Public sector LDOD	15,263	124,642	324,031	373,680	374,891	359,947	387,837	394,689	390,148	..
Private sector LDOD	12,350	48,182	28,395	89,602	119,092	163,952	247,453	270,936	271,588	..
6. CURRENCY COMPOSITION OF LONG-TERM DEBT (PERCENT)										
Deutsche mark	7.8	5.5	5.9	5.1	5.9	5.7	5.4	4.3	3.7	..
French franc	2.3	1.8	3.6	3.2	2.7	2.2	1.7	1.3	1.0	..
Japanese yen	0.1	4.4	5.7	7.6	7.1	6.4	6.1	6.4	6.1	..
Pound sterling	4.5	1.3	1.4	1.0	1.1	1.3	1.2	1.0	0.7	..
Swiss franc	1.9	1.2	0.9	0.5	0.4	0.4	0.3	0.3	0.2	..
U.S.dollars	63.0	63.1	55.0	57.7	58.8	60.5	68.9	69.7	70.5	..
Multiple currency	16.9	9.4	17.4	15.0	13.7	12.4	7.0	6.5	5.9	..
Special drawing rights	0.0	0.0	0.0	0.0	0.0	0.0	0.0	0.0	0.0	..
All other currencies	3.5	3.3	2.5	2.2	2.4	2.8	4.0	5.4	6.6	..

LATIN AMERICA AND CARIBBEAN

(US$ million, unless otherwise indicated)

	1970	*1980*	*1990*	*1995*	*1996*	*1997*	*1998*	*1999*	*2000*	*2001*
7. DEBT RESTRUCTURINGS										
Total amount rescheduled	117	1,124	63,739	7,922	11,046	2,163	5,017	1,212	5,143	..
Debt stock rescheduled	0	1	59,026	3,355	3,158	370	4,459	582	3,784	..
Principal rescheduled	0	104	3,055	1,026	3,203	786	105	365	832	..
Official	0	0	1,533	826	1,307	691	99	349	715	..
Private	0	104	1,522	200	1,896	95	6	17	118	..
Interest rescheduled	..	..	1,507	2,481	4,757	943	457	101	233	..
Official	0	0	960	641	756	509	307	94	215	..
Private	0	0	547	1,840	4,001	434	150	7	19	..
Debt forgiven	6	28	180	534	1,294	328	227	162	81	..
Memo: interest forgiven	0	0	259	734	1,690	15	24	22	13	..
Debt stock reduction	0	0	21,301	3,702	8,487	11,936	2,809	5,821	19,728	..
of which debt buyback	0	0	2,756	102	3,363	9,850	2,158	4,131	15,851	..
8. DEBT STOCK-FLOW RECONCILIATION										
Total change in debt stocks	..	..	22,288	63,664	21,140	31,378	74,350	19,926	-21,773	..
Net flows on debt	2,825	46,067	20,427	62,184	35,918	39,845	58,819	11,418	-3,343	13,432
Net change in interest arrears	..	..	9,067	-3,124	-6,647	-779	335	-1,204	-262	..
Interest capitalized	..	..	1,507	2,481	4,757	943	457	101	233	..
Debt forgiveness or reduction	..	..	-18,724	-4,133	-6,418	-2,414	-878	-1,852	-3,959	..
Cross-currency valuation	..	..	11,524	2,122	-13,211	-16,605	6,168	-4,790	-9,102	..
Residual	..	..	-1,513	4,134	6,742	10,387	9,449	16,253	-5,340	..
9. AVERAGE TERMS OF NEW COMMITMENTS										
ALL CREDITORS										
Interest (%)	7.0	11.5	7.9	7.2	7.6	7.6	8.4	8.1	9.0	..
Maturity (years)	14.4	12.5	15.0	9.8	9.7	14.1	8.5	15.1	13.8	..
Grace period (years)	3.6	4.2	5.1	3.6	5.9	8.4	5.0	6.6	11.0	..
Grant element (%)	16.7	-5.9	12.3	12.4	9.6	11.4	7.2	8.9	3.0	..
Official creditors										
Interest (%)	6.0	7.8	7.0	7.6	5.9	6.4	8.4	5.6	6.6	..
Maturity (years)	23.4	21.2	18.0	14.2	19.9	16.6	8.6	14.6	16.9	..
Grace period (years)	5.5	4.5	4.9	4.0	5.2	4.1	2.4	4.8	5.0	..
Grant element (%)	27.4	14.7	18.8	15.8	26.7	20.0	8.7	25.0	20.6	..
Private creditors										
Interest (%)	7.7	13.0	9.1	6.8	8.0	8.1	8.5	9.5	9.5	..
Maturity (years)	8.9	9.0	11.0	4.1	7.2	13.1	8.5	15.4	13.0	..
Grace period (years)	2.4	4.1	5.2	2.9	6.1	10.2	7.4	7.6	12.4	..
Grant element (%)	10.1	-14.2	3.8	8.0	5.5	7.8	5.8	-0.2	-1.1	..
Memorandum items										
Commitments	4,378	33,219	25,963	49,589	60,162	68,096	80,612	57,301	49,963	..
Official creditors	1,647	9,617	14,841	28,174	11,702	19,928	39,550	20,659	9,518	..
Private creditors	2,731	23,602	11,121	21,415	48,460	48,168	41,063	36,642	40,446	..

10. GRAPH OF AGGREGATE NET RESOURCE FLOWS

(current prices, US$ billion)

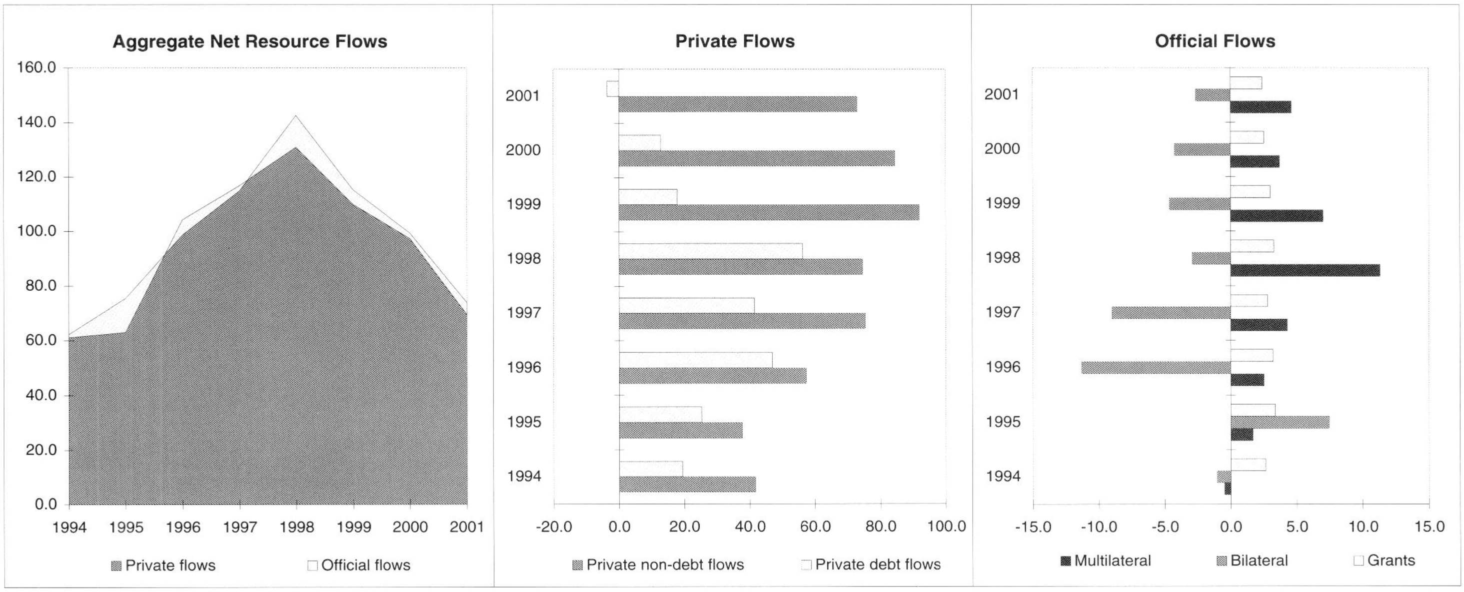

MIDDLE EAST AND NORTH AFRICA

(US$ million, unless otherwise indicated)

1. SUMMARY DEBT DATA

	1970	1980	1990	1995	1996	1997	1998	1999	2000	2001
TOTAL DEBT STOCKS (EDT)	**4,822**	**83,832**	**183,471**	**214,228**	**207,656**	**197,119**	**211,032**	**216,166**	**203,785**	**196,555**
Long-term debt (LDOD)	**4,167**	**61,766**	**137,762**	**167,429**	**161,853**	**153,003**	**162,152**	**162,963**	**153,794**	**150,283**
Public and publicly guaranteed	4,152	61,171	136,260	161,570	155,463	145,728	153,450	156,482	147,031	143,652
Private nonguaranteed	15	595	1,502	5,859	6,390	7,276	8,701	6,481	6,763	6,631
Use of IMF credit	**100**	**916**	**1,815**	**2,177**	**2,752**	**2,874**	**2,954**	**2,901**	**2,542**	**2,340**
Short-term debt	**..**	**21,150**	**43,894**	**44,622**	**43,051**	**41,242**	**45,927**	**50,303**	**47,448**	**43,932**
of which interest arrears on LDOD	..	391	2,882	2,348	2,555	2,257	2,436	2,601	2,735	2,719
Official creditors	..	391	1,650	2,036	2,244	2,095	2,268	2,432	2,570	..
Private creditors	..	0	1,231	312	311	162	169	169	164	..
Memo: principal arrears on LDOD	..	114	8,208	9,101	9,995	8,759	9,633	10,733	11,650	..
Official creditors	..	108	3,599	7,079	7,816	7,548	8,385	9,471	10,426	..
Private creditors	..	6	4,608	2,022	2,179	1,210	1,248	1,262	1,224	..
Memo: export credits	..	3,668	62,532	67,229	64,970	64,964	47,454	44,390	38,743	..
TOTAL DEBT FLOWS										
Disbursements	**891**	**12,328**	**14,603**	**14,397**	**14,888**	**12,944**	**17,008**	**14,317**	**11,670**	**14,973**
Long-term debt	853	11,978	14,538	13,807	13,899	12,205	16,557	13,816	11,646	14,810
IMF purchases	38	350	65	590	989	739	451	501	24	163
Principal repayments	**413**	**5,062**	**15,630**	**14,199**	**15,779**	**16,232**	**14,259**	**16,791**	**16,192**	**15,212**
Long-term debt	382	4,829	15,234	13,810	15,441	15,791	13,765	16,311	15,954	14,938
IMF repurchases	31	233	397	390	338	442	494	480	238	275
Net flows on debt	**478**	**8,664**	**634**	**-441**	**-863**	**-4,799**	**7,255**	**-1,135**	**-7,509**	**-3,739**
of which short-term debt	..	1,397	1,661	-638	28	-1,511	4,505	1,339	-2,988	-3,500
Interest payments (INT)	**..**	**6,455**	**8,569**	**10,258**	**10,035**	**9,340**	**9,100**	**9,017**	**8,729**	**8,344**
Long-term debt	100	3,935	5,185	7,380	7,662	6,731	6,885	6,683	6,496	6,322
IMF charges	0	33	180	112	107	127	127	111	130	103
Short-term debt	..	2,488	3,203	2,767	2,266	2,486	2,092	2,224	2,103	1,919
Net transfers on debt	**..**	**2,208**	**-7,935**	**-10,699**	**-10,898**	**-14,139**	**-1,845**	**-10,151**	**-16,238**	**-12,084**
Total debt service paid (TDS)	**..**	**11,517**	**24,199**	**24,457**	**25,814**	**25,572**	**23,359**	**25,808**	**24,921**	**23,556**
Long-term debt	482	8,764	20,419	21,189	23,103	22,518	20,646	22,994	22,450	21,260
IMF repurchases and charges	31	265	577	501	445	568	621	591	368	377
Short-term debt (interest only)	..	2,488	3,203	2,767	2,266	2,486	2,092	2,224	2,103	1,919

2. AGGREGATE NET RESOURCE FLOWS AND NET TRANSFERS (LONG-TERM)

	1970	1980	1990	1995	1996	1997	1998	1999	2000	2001
NET RESOURCE FLOWS	**1,150**	**8,536**	**10,070**	**2,852**	**6,047**	**7,750**	**14,406**	**2,785**	**1,470**	**6,166**
Net flow of long-term debt (ex. IMF)	471	7,149	-696	-2	-1,559	-3,600	2,792	-2,495	-4,308	-128
Foreign direct investment (net)	294	-3,313	2,458	-597	1,953	5,107	6,562	1,328	1,209	2,645
Portfolio equity flows	-1	0	0	203	1,632	2,259	879	669	795	49
Grants (excluding technical coop.)	385	4,700	8,307	3,249	4,003	3,969	4,173	3,283	3,773	3,600
Memo: technical coop. grants	277	1,024	2,600	2,638	2,444	1,898	1,781	2,281	1,756	1,800
official net resource flows	578	9,572	9,686	1,620	2,577	-313	2,343	601	396	1,864
private net resource flows	572	-1,035	384	1,231	3,470	8,063	12,063	2,184	1,074	4,302
NET TRANSFERS	**-1,078**	**-5,249**	**3,601**	**-5,784**	**-3,003**	**-411**	**6,016**	**-5,449**	**-6,337**	**-2,956**
Interest on long-term debt	100	3,935	5,185	7,380	7,662	6,731	6,885	6,683	6,496	6,322
Profit remittances on FDI	2,128	9,851	1,284	1,256	1,388	1,434	1,509	1,551	1,310	2,800
Memo: official net transfers	513	8,618	7,247	-2,756	-2,376	-4,465	-1,682	-3,121	-3,301	-1,597
private net transfers	-1,592	-13,867	-3,646	-3,028	-627	4,054	7,698	-2,327	-3,035	-1,358

3. MAJOR ECONOMIC AGGREGATES

	1970	1980	1990	1995	1996	1997	1998	1999	2000	2001
Gross national income (GNI)	39,130	380,322	401,262	487,504	552,171	564,102	560,926	586,365	643,723	598,663
Exports of goods & services (XGS)	..	206,124	161,142	169,230	191,204	193,061	154,951	182,878	238,469	230,098
of which workers remittances	..	5,104	10,507	9,394	9,284	9,571	10,110	10,301	9,709	10,109
Imports of goods & services (MGS)	..	147,513	147,546	161,137	172,811	175,733	169,138	166,429	185,312	194,003
International reserves (RES)	4,477	76,217	39,150	56,949	68,043	72,822	72,513	75,551	87,769	94,903
Current account balance	..	46,988	1,884	-6,527	2,777	85	-27,217	4,015	28,092	19,292

4. DEBT INDICATORS

	1970	1980	1990	1995	1996	1997	1998	1999	2000	2001
EDT / XGS (%)	..	40.7	113.9	126.6	108.6	102.1	136.2	118.2	85.5	85.4
EDT / GNI (%)	..	22.0	45.7	43.9	37.6	34.9	37.6	36.9	31.7	32.8
TDS / XGS (%)	..	5.6	15.0	14.5	13.5	13.3	15.1	14.1	10.5	10.2
INT / XGS (%)	..	3.1	5.3	6.1	5.3	4.8	5.9	4.9	3.7	3.6
INT / GNI (%)	..	1.7	2.1	2.1	1.8	1.7	1.6	1.5	1.4	1.4
RES / EDT (%)	..	90.9	21.3	26.6	32.8	36.9	34.4	35.0	43.1	48.3
RES / MGS (months)	..	6.2	3.2	4.2	4.7	5.0	5.1	5.5	5.7	5.9
Short-term / EDT (%)	..	25.2	23.9	20.8	20.7	20.9	21.8	23.3	23.3	22.4
Concessional / EDT (%)	..	21.5	24.2	26.7	29.3	29.2	28.5	27.5	27.9	28.0
Multilateral / EDT (%)	..	6.7	8.6	10.7	11.3	11.3	11.5	11.3	11.4	11.2

MIDDLE EAST AND NORTH AFRICA

(US$ million, unless otherwise indicated)

	1970	1980	1990	1995	1996	1997	1998	1999	2000	2001
5. LONG-TERM DEBT										
DEBT OUTSTANDING (LDOD)	**4,167**	**61,766**	**137,762**	**167,429**	**161,853**	**153,003**	**162,152**	**162,963**	**153,794**	**150,283**
Public and publicly guaranteed	**4,152**	**61,171**	**136,260**	**161,570**	**155,463**	**145,728**	**153,450**	**156,482**	**147,031**	**143,652**
Official creditors	3,043	31,470	80,956	116,506	115,300	107,412	110,195	105,441	98,316	93,674
Multilateral	172	5,606	15,756	23,010	23,500	22,247	24,325	24,449	23,271	21,920
Concessional	32	2,554	3,629	5,337	5,957	6,337	7,279	7,975	8,040	8,268
Bilateral	2,871	25,865	65,200	93,496	91,800	85,165	85,870	80,992	75,045	71,754
Concessional	2,466	15,478	40,752	51,943	54,865	51,264	52,931	51,509	48,734	46,781
Private creditors	1,108	29,701	55,304	45,064	40,163	38,316	43,255	51,041	48,715	49,978
Bonds	38	720	2,234	2,036	2,486	3,513	5,067	6,793	8,015	12,285
Commercial banks	56	10,331	18,126	16,423	15,486	18,722	21,439	29,435	28,744	26,230
Other private	1,014	18,650	34,944	26,605	22,191	16,081	16,750	14,813	11,957	11,462
Private nonguaranteed	**15**	**595**	**1,502**	**5,859**	**6,390**	**7,276**	**8,701**	**6,481**	**6,763**	**6,631**
Bonds	0	0	0	50	410	885	785	771	836	896
Commercial banks and other	15	595	1,502	5,809	5,980	6,391	7,916	5,710	5,927	5,735
Memo:										
IBRD	139	2,384	8,301	10,671	10,053	8,789	8,823	8,371	7,667	7,297
IDA	32	669	1,774	2,105	2,219	2,360	2,559	2,698	2,685	2,680
DISBURSEMENTS	**853**	**11,978**	**14,538**	**13,807**	**13,899**	**12,205**	**16,557**	**13,816**	**11,646**	**14,810**
Public and publicly guaranteed	**845**	**11,724**	**14,399**	**12,289**	**12,476**	**10,869**	**13,505**	**12,583**	**10,233**	**13,832**
Official creditors	420	5,781	6,341	5,876	6,578	5,011	3,705	4,050	2,734	3,363
Multilateral	32	705	2,387	3,475	3,626	2,905	2,586	2,742	1,760	2,072
Concessional	8	182	242	777	940	793	796	916	559	843
Bilateral	388	5,076	3,954	2,401	2,952	2,106	1,119	1,307	974	1,290
Concessional	255	3,451	1,894	1,833	1,663	1,185	820	749	636	861
Private creditors	425	5,943	8,058	6,413	5,898	5,858	9,800	8,534	7,498	10,469
Bonds	5	66	0	888	531	1,556	1,450	1,480	1,375	4,812
Commercial banks	17	1,631	804	1,229	2,548	1,865	3,747	3,654	3,980	3,502
Other private	403	4,245	7,254	4,296	2,819	2,437	4,604	3,400	2,144	2,155
Private nonguaranteed	**8**	**254**	**139**	**1,518**	**1,423**	**1,336**	**3,052**	**1,233**	**1,414**	**979**
Bonds	0	0	0	85	360	475	0	146	115	160
Commercial banks and other	8	254	139	1,433	1,063	861	3,052	1,087	1,299	819
Memo:										
IBRD	23	421	1,164	1,455	1,231	832	610	991	533	731
IDA	8	82	38	128	179	250	180	207	118	118
PRINCIPAL REPAYMENTS	**382**	**4,829**	**15,234**	**13,810**	**15,441**	**15,791**	**13,765**	**16,311**	**15,954**	**14,938**
Public and publicly guaranteed	**380**	**4,716**	**15,057**	**13,293**	**14,522**	**15,298**	**12,194**	**14,080**	**14,621**	**13,828**
Official creditors	228	910	4,962	7,505	8,005	9,293	5,535	6,732	6,111	5,098
Multilateral	16	202	1,306	2,089	1,936	2,701	2,049	2,075	2,063	2,264
Concessional	0	6	143	196	205	234	261	265	346	469
Bilateral	212	708	3,656	5,416	6,069	6,592	3,486	4,656	4,048	2,835
Concessional	137	386	1,617	711	1,033	1,207	1,228	1,198	1,399	1,346
Private creditors	152	3,806	10,094	5,788	6,517	6,005	6,659	7,349	8,510	8,729
Bonds	3	33	148	278	5	410	10	44	896	542
Commercial banks	2	1,465	2,119	1,631	2,457	2,157	2,650	3,114	3,728	5,153
Other private	146	2,309	7,827	3,879	4,056	3,438	3,999	4,191	3,885	3,035
Private nonguaranteed	**3**	**114**	**177**	**517**	**919**	**492**	**1,571**	**2,231**	**1,333**	**1,110**
Bonds	0	0	0	0	0	0	100	160	50	100
Commercial banks and other	3	114	177	517	919	492	1,471	2,071	1,283	1,010
Memo:										
IBRD	16	140	761	1,118	1,071	1,310	936	945	872	832
IDA	0	1	14	28	30	42	36	40	45	55
NET FLOWS ON DEBT	**471**	**7,149**	**-696**	**-2**	**-1,559**	**-3,600**	**2,792**	**-2,495**	**-4,308**	**-128**
Public and publicly guaranteed	**466**	**7,009**	**-658**	**-1,003**	**-2,046**	**-4,429**	**1,311**	**-1,497**	**-4,388**	**4**
Official creditors	193	4,872	1,379	-1,629	-1,426	-4,282	-1,830	-2,682	-3,377	-1,736
Multilateral	16	503	1,081	1,387	1,690	204	537	667	-303	-191
Concessional	8	175	99	581	735	559	536	651	214	374
Bilateral	176	4,368	298	-3,015	-3,117	-4,486	-2,367	-3,349	-3,074	-1,545
Concessional	118	3,065	277	1,122	630	-22	-408	-449	-763	-485
Private creditors	273	2,137	-2,037	625	-620	-147	3,141	1,185	-1,011	1,740
Bonds	2	34	-148	610	526	1,146	1,440	1,436	479	4,270
Commercial banks	15	167	-1,316	-402	91	-292	1,097	540	252	-1,651
Other private	257	1,937	-573	417	-1,237	-1,001	604	-791	-1,742	-880
Private nonguaranteed	**5**	**140**	**-38**	**1,001**	**504**	**844**	**1,482**	**-999**	**81**	**-132**
Bonds	0	0	0	85	360	475	-100	-14	65	60
Commercial banks and other	5	140	-38	916	144	369	1,582	-985	16	-192
Memo:										
IBRD	8	281	403	337	160	-478	-325	46	-339	-101
IDA	8	81	24	100	149	208	144	167	74	63

MIDDLE EAST AND NORTH AFRICA

(US$ million, unless otherwise indicated)

	1970	1980	1990	1995	1996	1997	1998	1999	2000	2001
INTEREST PAYMENTS (LINT)	**100**	**3,935**	**5,185**	**7,380**	**7,662**	**6,731**	**6,885**	**6,683**	**6,496**	**6,322**
Public and publicly guaranteed	**99**	**3,885**	**5,077**	**7,111**	**7,316**	**6,320**	**6,491**	**6,370**	**6,173**	**6,038**
Official creditors	65	954	2,439	4,376	4,953	4,152	4,025	3,723	3,697	3,461
Multilateral	9	239	862	1,395	1,402	1,322	1,307	1,375	1,298	1,216
Concessional	0	19	58	114	139	159	171	176	181	216
Bilateral	56	715	1,577	2,981	3,550	2,830	2,718	2,348	2,399	2,245
Concessional	42	336	456	973	1,124	962	994	818	755	701
Private creditors	34	2,931	2,638	2,734	2,363	2,168	2,466	2,648	2,477	2,577
Bonds	2	71	158	88	145	173	249	360	482	563
Commercial banks	0	1,488	942	1,169	897	722	1,010	1,222	1,242	1,362
Other private	32	1,372	1,537	1,477	1,321	1,273	1,207	1,066	753	652
Private nonguaranteed	**1**	**50**	**108**	**269**	**346**	**407**	**390**	**312**	**323**	**284**
Bonds	0	0	0	0	2	37	77	69	69	77
Commercial banks and other	1	50	108	269	344	370	312	244	254	207
Memo:										
IBRD	9	198	598	750	688	625	582	617	603	577
IDA	0	5	13	15	16	20	18	19	20	20
NET TRANSFERS ON DEBT	**371**	**3,214**	**-5,881**	**-7,382**	**-9,204**	**-10,313**	**-4,088**	**-9,178**	**-10,804**	**-6,450**
Public and publicly guaranteed	**367**	**3,124**	**-5,735**	**-8,114**	**-9,362**	**-10,749**	**-5,180**	**-7,867**	**-10,562**	**-6,034**
Official creditors	128	3,918	-1,060	-6,005	-6,379	-8,434	-5,856	-6,405	-7,074	-5,197
Multilateral	7	264	219	-8	288	-1,118	-770	-708	-1,600	-1,408
Concessional	8	156	41	467	596	401	365	476	33	158
Bilateral	121	3,654	-1,279	-5,996	-6,667	-7,316	-5,085	-5,697	-5,474	-3,790
Concessional	76	2,729	-179	148	-494	-983	-1,402	-1,267	-1,518	-1,185
Private creditors	239	-794	-4,674	-2,109	-2,983	-2,315	675	-1,463	-3,488	-837
Bonds	-1	-38	-307	522	382	973	1,191	1,076	-3	3,707
Commercial banks	14	-1,321	-2,258	-1,571	-806	-1,014	87	-682	-990	-3,012
Other private	225	565	-2,110	-1,060	-2,558	-2,274	-602	-1,857	-2,495	-1,532
Private nonguaranteed	**4**	**90**	**-146**	**732**	**158**	**436**	**1,092**	**-1,311**	**-242**	**-415**
Bonds	0	0	0	85	358	438	-177	-83	-4	-17
Commercial banks and other	4	90	-146	647	-200	-2	1,269	-1,228	-238	-399
Memo:										
IBRD	-1	83	-195	-413	-528	-1,103	-907	-571	-942	-677
IDA	8	76	11	85	134	189	127	148	54	43
DEBT SERVICE (LTDS)	**482**	**8,764**	**20,419**	**21,189**	**23,103**	**22,518**	**20,646**	**22,994**	**22,450**	**21,260**
Public and publicly guaranteed	**479**	**8,601**	**20,133**	**20,403**	**21,838**	**21,618**	**18,685**	**20,451**	**20,794**	**19,866**
Official creditors	292	1,864	7,401	11,881	12,957	13,445	9,560	10,454	9,808	8,560
Multilateral	25	441	2,168	3,484	3,338	4,023	3,356	3,450	3,361	3,480
Concessional	0	25	201	310	344	392	432	441	526	686
Bilateral	268	1,422	5,233	8,397	9,619	9,422	6,204	7,004	6,448	5,080
Concessional	179	722	2,074	1,685	2,157	2,169	2,222	2,016	2,154	2,046
Private creditors	186	6,737	12,732	8,522	8,881	8,173	9,125	9,996	10,986	11,306
Bonds	6	104	307	366	150	583	259	404	1,378	1,105
Commercial banks	3	2,952	3,062	2,800	3,354	2,879	3,660	4,336	4,969	6,514
Other private	178	3,681	9,364	5,356	5,377	4,711	5,206	5,257	4,638	3,687
Private nonguaranteed	**3**	**164**	**285**	**786**	**1,265**	**900**	**1,960**	**2,543**	**1,656**	**1,394**
Bonds	0	0	0	0	2	37	177	229	119	177
Commercial banks and other	3	164	285	786	1,263	863	1,783	2,315	1,537	1,217
Memo:										
IBRD	24	338	1,359	1,868	1,759	1,935	1,518	1,562	1,475	1,408
IDA	0	6	27	42	45	61	54	59	65	74
UNDISBURSED DEBT	**1,915**	**28,071**	**32,050**	**32,183**	**26,661**	**23,481**	**31,116**	**30,733**	**24,172**	**..**
Official creditors	1,541	16,000	19,053	23,897	19,595	17,478	16,542	17,411	13,450	..
Private creditors	374	12,071	12,997	8,286	7,066	6,003	14,574	13,322	10,723	..
Memorandum items										
Concessional LDOD	2,498	18,032	44,381	57,279	60,822	57,600	60,210	59,484	56,774	..
Variable rate LDOD	41	10,209	29,820	52,224	49,269	45,120	45,218	39,383	35,303	..
Public sector LDOD	4,129	53,440	115,472	141,627	136,130	123,540	126,559	120,926	112,921	..
Private sector LDOD	37	741	1,583	4,225	4,518	5,446	35,593	42,037	40,873	..

6. CURRENCY COMPOSITION OF LONG-TERM DEBT (PERCENT)

	1970	1980	1990	1995	1996	1997	1998	1999	2000	2001
Deutsche mark	7.7	6.4	6.6	7.1	6.4	5.9	5.5	4.4	4.1	..
French franc	18.6	9.3	11.1	11.5	11.4	10.2	9.9	8.1	8.3	..
Japanese yen	0.0	5.7	6.3	8.6	8.2	7.8	7.9	8.8	8.1	..
Pound sterling	4.1	1.3	1.4	1.0	1.1	1.1	1.0	0.9	0.8	..
Swiss franc	1.1	1.3	0.9	0.7	0.6	0.6	0.6	0.7	0.7	..
U.S.dollars	33.0	46.4	38.2	37.5	38.3	39.7	41.6	38.6	38.8	..
Multiple currency	3.1	4.7	7.5	8.8	8.6	8.1	4.1	3.6	3.4	..
Special drawing rights	0.0	0.0	0.4	0.2	0.2	0.2	0.2	0.2	0.3	..
All other currencies	32.5	12.4	12.5	12.4	13.1	11.5	12.0	12.1	12.4	..

MIDDLE EAST AND NORTH AFRICA

(US$ million, unless otherwise indicated)

	1970	1980	1990	1995	1996	1997	1998	1999	2000	2001
7. DEBT RESTRUCTURINGS										
Total amount rescheduled	0	0	4,565	8,949	6,140	3,359	1,183	612	289	..
Debt stock rescheduled	0	0	2,732	3,178	1,805	0	0	0	0	..
Principal rescheduled	0	0	1,039	4,934	3,728	2,944	758	292	166	..
Official	0	0	679	697	520	598	214	168	119	..
Private	0	0	360	4,237	3,208	2,346	545	125	48	..
Interest rescheduled	..	..	219	527	397	250	81	138	112	..
Official	0	0	137	131	96	107	54	107	91	..
Private	0	0	82	396	301	143	27	31	21	..
Debt forgiven	0	2	10,614	357	52	2,264	17	4	170	..
Memo: interest forgiven	0	0	2,481	7	5	340	1	0	0	..
Debt stock reduction	0	0	0	13	9	0	0	0	120	..
of which debt buyback	0	0	0	0	0	0	0	0	85	..
8. DEBT STOCK-FLOW RECONCILIATION										
Total change in debt stocks	..	..	-5,746	2,803	-6,573	-10,537	13,914	5,134	-12,382	..
Net flows on debt	478	8,664	634	-441	-863	-4,799	7,255	-1,135	-7,509	-3,739
Net change in interest arrears	..	..	-1,483	277	207	-298	180	165	133	..
Interest capitalized	..	..	219	527	397	250	81	138	112	..
Debt forgiveness or reduction	..	..	-10,614	-370	-61	-2,264	-17	-4	-205	..
Cross-currency valuation	..	..	5,265	2,042	-6,012	-7,471	3,793	-3,363	-3,973	..
Residual	..	..	234	767	-240	4,046	2,622	9,333	-939	..
9. AVERAGE TERMS OF NEW COMMITMENTS										
ALL CREDITORS										
Interest (%)	4.6	6.4	7.4	5.9	5.3	5.4	5.7	5.1	5.8	..
Maturity (years)	18.6	18.1	13.5	14.3	13.8	15.0	12.2	15.1	11.9	..
Grace period (years)	6.2	4.7	4.0	4.5	4.3	6.1	2.6	4.2	4.8	..
Grant element (%)	33.5	24.1	15.8	22.4	25.0	26.3	20.6	26.6	20.1	..
Official creditors										
Interest (%)	3.7	4.7	5.5	5.3	5.1	4.5	3.8	3.4	4.2	..
Maturity (years)	23.6	24.1	21.4	17.8	17.4	17.7	20.4	22.3	19.6	..
Grace period (years)	8.4	5.9	6.3	5.0	5.1	5.2	5.6	4.9	5.8	..
Grant element (%)	43.6	38.8	32.4	28.1	30.3	33.2	41.4	42.8	38.4	..
Private creditors										
Interest (%)	6.3	8.6	8.8	6.8	5.6	6.7	6.2	6.5	6.7	..
Maturity (years)	9.4	10.7	7.6	8.3	9.2	11.0	10.0	9.4	8.0	..
Grace period (years)	2.0	3.1	2.4	3.6	3.2	7.4	1.8	3.7	4.3	..
Grant element (%)	14.7	5.7	3.4	12.9	18.2	16.1	15.0	13.9	10.5	..
Memorandum items										
Commitments	1,207	11,467	15,339	11,708	8,543	7,353	15,101	10,059	6,956	..
Official creditors	785	6,363	6,569	7,377	4,793	4,369	3,222	4,436	2,382	..
Private creditors	423	5,104	8,770	4,331	3,750	2,984	11,879	5,623	4,574	..

10. GRAPH OF AGGREGATE NET RESOURCE FLOWS

(current prices, US$ billion)

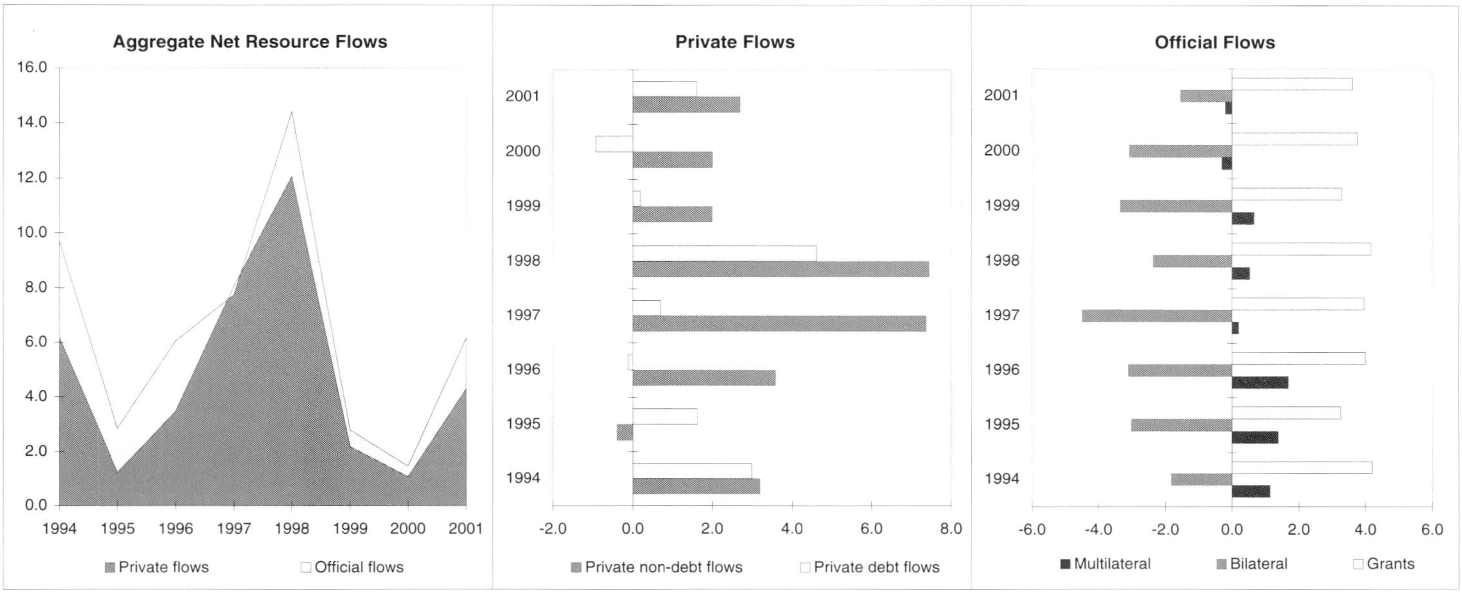

SOUTH ASIA

(US$ million, unless otherwise indicated)

	1970	1980	1990	1995	1996	1997	1998	1999	2000	2001
1. SUMMARY DEBT DATA										
TOTAL DEBT STOCKS (EDT)	**12,270**	**37,816**	**129,481**	**157,289**	**155,208**	**154,952**	**162,897**	**167,320**	**165,680**	**159,289**
Long-term debt (LDOD)	**11,721**	**32,855**	**112,573**	**142,952**	**141,083**	**143,949**	**153,318**	**157,961**	**157,724**	**151,945**
Public and publicly guaranteed	11,616	32,498	110,845	134,651	131,618	132,319	142,221	147,710	146,351	140,574
Private nonguaranteed	105	357	1,727	8,301	9,465	11,630	11,097	10,251	11,373	11,372
Use of IMF credit	**124**	**2,508**	**4,537**	**5,252**	**3,795**	**2,781**	**2,461**	**2,323**	**1,918**	**1,707**
Short-term debt	**..**	**2,454**	**12,371**	**9,084**	**10,330**	**8,222**	**7,118**	**7,036**	**6,038**	**5,637**
of which interest arrears on LDOD	..	0	17	53	123	118	353	155	133	120
Official creditors	..	0	7	18	21	24	171	30	25	..
Private creditors	..	0	11	35	102	94	181	126	107	..
Memo: principal arrears on LDOD	..	0	34	66	182	201	831	290	267	..
Official creditors	..	0	34	21	44	47	548	74	67	..
Private creditors	..	0	1	45	138	154	283	217	201	..
Memo: export credits	..	28	9,370	14,595	13,888	13,898	5,310	5,819	6,062	..
TOTAL DEBT FLOWS										
Disbursements	**1,578**	**6,259**	**12,136**	**12,076**	**12,008**	**14,052**	**15,361**	**9,568**	**14,395**	**9,360**
Long-term debt	1,568	4,612	10,261	11,875	11,853	13,770	15,048	8,957	14,200	9,230
IMF purchases	10	1,647	1,875	202	156	281	313	611	195	130
Principal repayments	**786**	**1,537**	**5,274**	**11,631**	**10,556**	**11,387**	**9,363**	**9,322**	**9,111**	**8,108**
Long-term debt	525	1,211	4,119	9,634	9,123	10,275	8,626	8,626	8,402	7,801
IMF repurchases	260	326	1,155	1,998	1,433	1,112	738	696	709	307
Net flows on debt	**792**	**5,767**	**8,417**	**2,512**	**2,628**	**562**	**4,659**	**361**	**4,308**	**864**
of which short-term debt	..	1,045	1,555	2,067	1,175	-2,102	-1,339	115	-975	-388
Interest payments (INT)	**..**	**1,214**	**6,163**	**6,609**	**6,070**	**6,575**	**6,658**	**5,566**	**5,633**	**5,732**
Long-term debt	291	860	4,709	5,748	5,387	5,804	6,128	5,078	5,257	5,379
IMF charges	0	61	249	233	151	91	63	60	58	60
Short-term debt	..	292	1,204	627	533	680	467	305	318	292
Net transfers on debt	**..**	**4,553**	**2,254**	**-4,097**	**-3,442**	**-6,013**	**-1,999**	**-5,205**	**-1,325**	**-4,867**
Total debt service paid (TDS)	**..**	**2,751**	**11,436**	**18,240**	**16,626**	**17,962**	**16,021**	**14,888**	**14,744**	**13,839**
Long-term debt	816	2,072	8,827	15,382	14,510	16,079	14,753	13,705	13,659	13,180
IMF repurchases and charges	260	387	1,404	2,231	1,583	1,203	801	755	767	367
Short-term debt (interest only)	..	292	1,204	627	533	680	467	305	318	292
2. AGGREGATE NET RESOURCE FLOWS AND NET TRANSFERS (LONG-TERM)										
NET RESOURCE FLOWS	**1,367**	**6,386**	**9,130**	**10,062**	**13,764**	**13,256**	**12,585**	**7,110**	**13,265**	**8,915**
Net flow of long-term debt (ex. IMF)	1,043	3,401	6,142	2,241	2,730	3,495	6,423	331	5,798	1,429
Foreign direct investment (net)	69	185	464	2,940	3,510	4,899	3,548	3,073	3,093	4,196
Portfolio equity flows	0	0	105	2,340	5,198	2,477	351	1,312	2,126	890
Grants (excluding technical coop.)	255	2,800	2,419	2,542	2,326	2,385	2,264	2,394	2,248	2,400
Memo: technical coop. grants	138	690	1,565	1,572	1,456	1,253	1,143	1,181	1,122	1,200
official net resource flows	1,272	5,149	6,968	3,157	4,641	3,509	5,034	4,969	4,011	4,600
private net resource flows	95	1,237	2,162	6,905	9,123	9,747	7,552	2,141	9,254	4,315
NET TRANSFERS	**1,062**	**5,504**	**4,329**	**4,161**	**8,183**	**7,166**	**6,127**	**1,524**	**7,680**	**2,636**
Interest on long-term debt	291	860	4,709	5,748	5,387	5,804	6,128	5,078	5,257	5,379
Profit remittances on FDI	14	23	92	152	194	286	330	384	328	900
Memo: official net transfers	1,029	4,499	4,676	138	1,850	842	2,366	2,260	1,346	2,121
private net transfers	33	1,005	-346	4,024	6,333	6,324	3,762	-736	6,334	515
3. MAJOR ECONOMIC AGGREGATES										
Gross national income (GNI)	82,076	234,017	399,651	471,741	507,198	536,496	546,784	580,397	608,439	651,030
Exports of goods & services (XGS)	4,268	23,010	39,881	73,326	78,920	84,028	86,682	92,835	106,930	112,598
of which workers remittances	..	4,563	5,040	11,640	14,779	14,592	13,436	15,031	15,843	16,243
Imports of goods & services (MGS)	6,125	30,371	54,721	85,886	93,988	98,534	97,029	104,469	116,369	121,745
International reserves (RES)	..	15,404	8,893	30,699	30,940	34,784	37,375	42,700	47,280	55,091
Current account balance	..	-6,251	-14,172	-10,582	-12,395	-11,209	-7,239	-9,081	-6,637	-9,937
4. DEBT INDICATORS										
EDT / XGS (%)	..	164.4	324.7	214.5	196.7	184.4	187.9	180.2	154.9	141.5
EDT / GNI (%)	..	16.2	32.4	33.3	30.6	28.9	29.8	28.8	27.2	24.5
TDS / XGS (%)	..	12.0	28.7	24.9	21.1	21.4	18.5	16.0	13.8	12.3
INT / XGS (%)	..	5.3	15.5	9.0	7.7	7.8	7.7	6.0	5.3	5.1
INT / GNI (%)	..	0.5	1.5	1.4	1.2	1.2	1.2	1.0	0.9	0.9
RES / EDT (%)	..	40.7	6.9	19.5	19.9	22.5	22.9	25.5	28.5	34.6
RES / MGS (months)	..	6.1	2.0	4.3	4.0	4.2	4.6	4.9	4.9	5.4
Short-term / EDT (%)	..	6.5	9.6	5.8	6.7	5.3	4.4	4.2	3.6	3.5
Concessional / EDT (%)	..	74.1	56.3	56.4	51.6	49.2	50.0	53.5	52.4	52.4
Multilateral / EDT (%)	..	24.7	29.5	36.3	36.4	36.0	36.7	37.7	38.1	38.4

SOUTH ASIA

(US$ million, unless otherwise indicated)

	1970	1980	1990	1995	1996	1997	1998	1999	2000	2001
5. LONG-TERM DEBT										
DEBT OUTSTANDING (LDOD)	**11,721**	**32,855**	**112,573**	**142,952**	**141,083**	**143,949**	**153,318**	**157,961**	**157,724**	**151,945**
Public and publicly guaranteed	**11,616**	**32,498**	**110,845**	**134,651**	**131,618**	**132,319**	**142,221**	**147,710**	**146,351**	**140,574**
Official creditors	10,911	30,091	86,536	109,229	105,865	101,568	107,600	116,717	112,162	108,327
Multilateral	2,205	9,321	38,199	57,010	56,502	55,812	59,788	63,143	63,045	61,236
Concessional	1,347	7,818	26,887	39,381	39,993	39,946	42,912	45,320	46,427	44,776
Bilateral	8,706	20,770	48,337	52,219	49,363	45,757	47,812	53,574	49,117	47,090
Concessional	7,913	20,205	45,980	49,305	40,106	36,287	38,607	44,239	40,403	38,721
Private creditors	706	2,407	24,309	25,422	25,753	30,750	34,621	30,993	34,189	32,247
Bonds	14	2	2,613	3,421	1,674	2,683	6,796	6,460	11,315	11,038
Commercial banks	54	1,671	16,810	14,173	16,779	22,059	22,895	20,005	18,655	17,458
Other private	638	734	4,886	7,829	7,301	6,008	4,930	4,529	4,219	3,751
Private nonguaranteed	**105**	**357**	**1,727**	**8,301**	**9,465**	**11,630**	**11,097**	**10,251**	**11,373**	**11,372**
Bonds	0	0	0	1,065	2,478	3,847	3,692	2,919	2,864	2,528
Commercial banks and other	105	357	1,727	7,236	6,987	7,783	7,406	7,332	8,509	8,844
Memo:										
IBRD	852	1,242	9,646	13,035	11,861	11,253	11,188	11,182	10,193	9,606
IDA	1,347	7,065	21,071	29,001	29,433	29,761	31,377	32,131	33,880	32,468
DISBURSEMENTS	**1,568**	**4,612**	**10,261**	**11,875**	**11,853**	**13,770**	**15,048**	**8,957**	**14,200**	**9,230**
Public and publicly guaranteed	**1,541**	**4,316**	**10,008**	**9,940**	**10,367**	**11,207**	**13,937**	**8,456**	**13,667**	**8,280**
Official creditors	1,391	3,274	6,942	6,379	6,936	7,677	7,731	6,935	7,138	6,696
Multilateral	198	1,386	4,402	3,975	4,573	4,091	4,078	4,312	4,325	4,132
Concessional	84	1,152	2,327	2,280	2,695	2,255	2,493	2,324	2,425	2,703
Bilateral	1,193	1,888	2,539	2,404	2,363	3,586	3,653	2,623	2,813	2,564
Concessional	1,075	1,687	1,977	2,091	1,600	2,247	2,948	1,846	2,366	2,325
Private creditors	150	1,042	3,067	3,561	3,431	3,530	6,206	1,521	6,529	1,585
Bonds	0	0	427	86	435	1,075	4,299	0	5,497	0
Commercial banks	16	797	2,067	1,919	1,857	1,906	1,223	738	384	908
Other private	134	245	573	1,557	1,139	548	684	783	648	677
Private nonguaranteed	**28**	**297**	**253**	**1,934**	**1,486**	**2,564**	**1,111**	**501**	**533**	**949**
Bonds	0	0	0	520	785	1,371	300	0	0	99
Commercial banks and other	28	297	253	1,414	701	1,193	811	501	533	850
Memo:										
IBRD	108	190	1,576	860	1,056	1,032	665	1,078	849	700
IDA	84	928	1,558	1,374	1,635	1,502	1,598	1,522	1,654	2,020
PRINCIPAL REPAYMENTS	**525**	**1,211**	**4,119**	**9,634**	**9,123**	**10,275**	**8,626**	**8,626**	**8,402**	**7,801**
Public and publicly guaranteed	**500**	**1,113**	**3,760**	**9,136**	**8,581**	**9,641**	**8,034**	**7,092**	**7,695**	**6,852**
Official creditors	374	925	2,393	5,764	4,622	6,553	4,962	4,361	5,375	4,496
Multilateral	64	135	1,009	2,227	1,873	2,026	1,978	2,243	2,853	2,358
Concessional	0	24	239	470	502	564	626	711	834	886
Bilateral	310	790	1,384	3,537	2,749	4,527	2,984	2,118	2,522	2,138
Concessional	219	716	1,237	3,016	2,283	3,604	2,556	1,592	1,935	1,990
Private creditors	126	188	1,367	3,372	3,960	3,087	3,072	2,732	2,319	2,356
Bonds	3	0	280	319	1,242	2	264	436	596	277
Commercial banks	12	44	371	1,992	1,704	1,377	965	1,159	927	1,366
Other private	111	145	716	1,061	1,013	1,708	1,843	1,137	796	713
Private nonguaranteed	**26**	**98**	**359**	**498**	**542**	**635**	**592**	**1,534**	**708**	**949**
Bonds	0	0	0	0	0	150	149	765	35	435
Commercial banks and other	26	98	359	498	542	485	443	769	673	514
Memo:										
IBRD	64	99	553	1,173	1,077	1,036	1,049	1,134	1,232	941
IDA	0	19	151	318	340	367	421	489	578	617
NET FLOWS ON DEBT	**1,043**	**3,401**	**6,142**	**2,241**	**2,730**	**3,495**	**6,423**	**331**	**5,798**	**1,429**
Public and publicly guaranteed	**1,041**	**3,202**	**6,248**	**804**	**1,786**	**1,566**	**5,903**	**1,364**	**5,972**	**1,429**
Official creditors	1,017	2,349	4,549	615	2,315	1,124	2,769	2,575	1,763	2,200
Multilateral	134	1,250	3,393	1,748	2,701	2,065	2,101	2,069	1,472	1,774
Concessional	84	1,129	2,088	1,810	2,193	1,691	1,867	1,613	1,591	1,817
Bilateral	883	1,098	1,156	-1,132	-386	-941	669	505	291	426
Concessional	856	971	740	-925	-683	-1,357	392	254	430	335
Private creditors	24	854	1,700	189	-528	442	3,134	-1,211	4,210	-771
Bonds	-3	0	147	-234	-807	1,073	4,035	-436	4,901	-277
Commercial banks	4	753	1,696	-73	153	529	258	-421	-544	-459
Other private	23	100	-143	495	126	-1,160	-1,160	-354	-148	-36
Private nonguaranteed	**2**	**199**	**-107**	**1,436**	**944**	**1,929**	**519**	**-1,033**	**-174**	**0**
Bonds	0	0	0	520	785	1,221	151	-765	-35	-336
Commercial banks and other	2	199	-107	916	159	708	368	-268	-139	336
Memo:										
IBRD	44	91	1,023	-314	-21	-5	-384	-56	-383	-241
IDA	84	909	1,407	1,056	1,295	1,135	1,178	1,033	1,076	1,403

SOUTH ASIA

(US$ million, unless otherwise indicated)

	1970	1980	1990	1995	1996	1997	1998	1999	2000	2001
INTEREST PAYMENTS (LINT)	**291**	**860**	**4,709**	**5,748**	**5,387**	**5,804**	**6,128**	**5,078**	**5,257**	**5,379**
Public and publicly guaranteed	**285**	**829**	**4,561**	**5,086**	**4,837**	**5,483**	**5,510**	**4,420**	**4,373**	**4,567**
Official creditors	243	650	2,292	3,019	2,790	2,667	2,668	2,709	2,665	2,479
Multilateral	57	181	1,070	1,645	1,511	1,429	1,360	1,465	1,380	1,341
Concessional	9	55	203	318	321	325	327	368	379	373
Bilateral	185	469	1,222	1,374	1,279	1,238	1,308	1,244	1,285	1,139
Concessional	144	439	1,060	1,113	1,014	897	746	730	744	671
Private creditors	42	179	2,269	2,067	2,047	2,816	2,842	1,711	1,708	2,088
Bonds	1	0	180	194	590	117	130	287	288	666
Commercial banks	3	123	1,806	1,315	937	2,251	2,343	1,134	1,140	1,200
Other private	38	56	283	558	520	448	369	291	280	222
Private nonguaranteed	**6**	**32**	**148**	**663**	**550**	**321**	**618**	**781**	**885**	**813**
Bonds	0	0	0	58	91	156	267	245	227	206
Commercial banks and other	6	32	148	604	459	165	351	536	658	606
Memo:										
IBRD	48	104	753	995	891	789	723	699	612	540
IDA	9	47	150	216	216	218	224	235	253	238
NET TRANSFERS ON DEBT	**752**	**2,541**	**1,433**	**-3,508**	**-2,657**	**-2,309**	**295**	**-4,871**	**541**	**-3,951**
Public and publicly guaranteed	**756**	**2,374**	**1,688**	**-4,281**	**-3,051**	**-3,917**	**394**	**-3,057**	**1,599**	**-3,138**
Official creditors	774	1,699	2,257	-2,404	-476	-1,543	101	-135	-903	-279
Multilateral	77	1,070	2,323	103	1,190	637	741	605	92	433
Concessional	75	1,074	1,885	1,491	1,872	1,365	1,540	1,246	1,212	1,444
Bilateral	697	629	-66	-2,507	-1,666	-2,180	-639	-739	-994	-713
Concessional	712	531	-320	-2,038	-1,697	-2,253	-354	-476	-314	-335
Private creditors	-18	675	-569	-1,878	-2,575	-2,374	292	-2,922	2,502	-2,859
Bonds	-4	0	-33	-427	-1,397	956	3,905	-722	4,613	-943
Commercial banks	1	631	-110	-1,388	-785	-1,722	-2,085	-1,555	-1,683	-1,659
Other private	-15	44	-426	-63	-394	-1,608	-1,529	-645	-428	-257
Private nonguaranteed	**-4**	**167**	**-255**	**774**	**394**	**1,608**	**-99**	**-1,814**	**-1,059**	**-812**
Bonds	0	0	0	462	694	1,065	-117	-1,010	-262	-542
Commercial banks and other	-4	167	-255	312	-300	543	18	-804	-797	-270
Memo:										
IBRD	-4	-13	270	-1,309	-911	-794	-1,107	-755	-994	-781
IDA	75	862	1,257	841	1,079	918	954	798	823	1,165
DEBT SERVICE (LTDS)	**816**	**2,072**	**8,827**	**15,382**	**14,510**	**16,079**	**14,753**	**13,705**	**13,659**	**13,180**
Public and publicly guaranteed	**784**	**1,942**	**8,321**	**14,221**	**13,418**	**15,124**	**13,543**	**11,513**	**12,067**	**11,419**
Official creditors	616	1,575	4,685	8,783	7,412	9,220	7,630	7,070	8,040	6,975
Multilateral	121	316	2,079	3,872	3,384	3,455	3,338	3,708	4,234	3,699
Concessional	10	78	443	788	823	890	953	1,078	1,213	1,259
Bilateral	495	1,259	2,606	4,911	4,029	5,766	4,292	3,362	3,807	3,276
Concessional	364	1,155	2,296	4,129	3,296	4,500	3,302	2,322	2,680	2,661
Private creditors	168	367	3,636	5,439	6,006	5,904	5,914	4,443	4,027	4,444
Bonds	4	0	460	513	1,832	119	394	722	884	943
Commercial banks	15	166	2,177	3,307	2,642	3,629	3,308	2,293	2,067	2,567
Other private	149	201	998	1,619	1,533	2,156	2,212	1,428	1,077	934
Private nonguaranteed	**32**	**130**	**507**	**1,161**	**1,092**	**956**	**1,210**	**2,315**	**1,592**	**1,762**
Bonds	0	0	0	58	91	306	417	1,010	262	641
Commercial banks and other	32	130	507	1,102	1,001	649	793	1,305	1,330	1,120
Memo:										
IBRD	112	203	1,306	2,169	1,968	1,826	1,772	1,833	1,843	1,481
IDA	10	66	300	534	556	584	645	724	832	854
UNDISBURSED DEBT	**3,712**	**14,819**	**42,028**	**37,626**	**36,289**	**34,398**	**31,170**	**27,351**	**21,610**	**..**
Official creditors	3,317	13,476	38,922	35,160	33,845	30,670	28,143	25,391	20,533	..
Private creditors	394	1,343	3,106	2,466	2,444	3,728	3,027	1,960	1,078	..
Memorandum items										
Concessional LDOD	9,260	28,023	72,867	88,686	80,099	76,233	81,518	89,559	86,829	..
Variable rate LDOD	105	1,009	14,678	27,440	30,097	34,062	35,159	34,444	34,876	..
Public sector LDOD	11,164	30,811	105,033	128,398	125,181	126,154	135,916	141,093	139,901	..
Private sector LDOD	557	850	2,494	8,975	10,307	12,332	17,402	16,868	17,823	..

6. CURRENCY COMPOSITION OF LONG-TERM DEBT (PERCENT)

	1970	1980	1990	1995	1996	1997	1998	1999	2000	2001
Deutsche mark	9.3	8.4	5.9	5.8	5.2	4.6	4.6	4.0	3.7	..
French franc	1.4	2.3	1.6	2.0	1.8	1.6	1.5	1.4	1.3	..
Japanese yen	5.3	8.9	11.9	16.1	14.8	13.5	15.0	16.5	14.9	..
Pound sterling	21.7	17.8	4.8	3.4	3.2	3.1	2.9	2.6	2.5	..
Swiss franc	0.4	0.3	0.5	0.6	0.4	0.4	0.3	0.2	0.2	..
U.S.dollars	41.1	41.3	51.6	44.3	47.1	51.0	50.8	50.9	55.4	..
Multiple currency	9.2	7.4	13.7	19.2	18.7	17.6	17.1	17.0	15.0	..
Special drawing rights	0.0	0.0	0.8	1.1	1.3	1.3	1.4	1.4	1.4	..
All other currencies	11.5	10.0	4.5	3.4	3.2	2.7	2.5	2.1	2.0	..

(US$ million, unless otherwise indicated)

	1970	1980	1990	1995	1996	1997	1998	1999	2000	2001
7. DEBT RESTRUCTURINGS										
Total amount rescheduled	0	0	0	0	0	0	0	3,421	918	..
Debt stock rescheduled	0	0	0	0	0	0	0	615	29	..
Principal rescheduled	0	0	0	0	0	0	0	2,158	741	..
Official	0	0	0	0	0	0	0	1,453	663	..
Private	0	0	0	0	0	0	0	705	78	..
Interest rescheduled	..	..	0	0	0	0	0	643	236	..
Official	0	0	0	0	0	0	0	508	200	..
Private	0	0	0	0	0	0	0	135	37	..
Debt forgiven	1	10	0	7	0	0	0	2	0	..
Memo: interest forgiven	0	0	0	0	0	0	0	0	0	..
Debt stock reduction	0	0	0	0	0	0	0	0	0	..
of which debt buyback	0	0	0	0	0	0	0	0	0	..
8. DEBT STOCK-FLOW RECONCILIATION										
Total change in debt stocks	..	..	13,135	-4,300	-2,081	-256	7,945	4,423	-1,641	..
Net flows on debt	792	5,767	8,417	2,512	2,628	562	4,659	361	4,308	864
Net change in interest arrears	..	..	5	9	70	-5	235	-198	-23	..
Interest capitalized	..	..	0	0	0	0	0	643	236	..
Debt forgiveness or reduction	..	..	0	-7	0	0	0	-2	0	..
Cross-currency valuation	..	..	1,586	-8,068	-10,933	-8,845	808	2,460	-5,665	..
Residual	..	..	3,128	1,254	6,154	8,032	2,244	1,159	-498	..
9. AVERAGE TERMS OF NEW COMMITMENTS										
ALL CREDITORS										
Interest (%)	2.5	4.7	4.6	3.8	4.5	4.6	3.7	3.1	6.6	..
Maturity (years)	32.6	32.6	24.7	24.4	21.7	20.0	17.4	26.7	13.6	..
Grace period (years)	9.7	7.4	7.7	7.4	6.9	6.2	6.3	6.8	5.5	..
Grant element (%)	45.1	27.1	34.2	31.9	29.6	26.8	37.4	51.7	20.6	..
Official creditors										
Interest (%)	2.2	2.2	3.6	3.6	4.0	3.6	3.7	2.9	5.2	..
Maturity (years)	34.9	39.2	29.0	26.2	27.1	27.2	27.7	28.2	23.1	..
Grace period (years)	10.5	8.6	8.1	7.8	7.8	7.7	7.5	7.3	6.2	..
Grant element (%)	48.7	34.5	40.8	33.4	34.5	34.7	49.3	54.5	35.0	..
Private creditors										
Interest (%)	5.9	12.8	6.7	5.6	5.6	6.3	3.7	4.7	7.7	..
Maturity (years)	11.7	10.9	15.3	6.7	7.5	7.9	7.3	13.2	5.4	..
Grace period (years)	2.6	3.6	6.8	3.6	4.5	3.8	5.1	1.9	5.0	..
Grant element (%)	12.5	2.6	19.7	17.0	16.5	13.3	25.7	26.4	8.2	..
Memorandum items										
Commitments	2,106	8,442	13,542	8,188	12,572	12,656	11,496	4,985	10,760	..
Official creditors	1,899	6,487	9,308	7,426	9,162	7,945	5,672	4,480	4,975	..
Private creditors	207	1,955	4,234	762	3,410	4,710	5,824	505	5,785	..

10. GRAPH OF AGGREGATE NET RESOURCE FLOWS

(current prices, US$ billion)

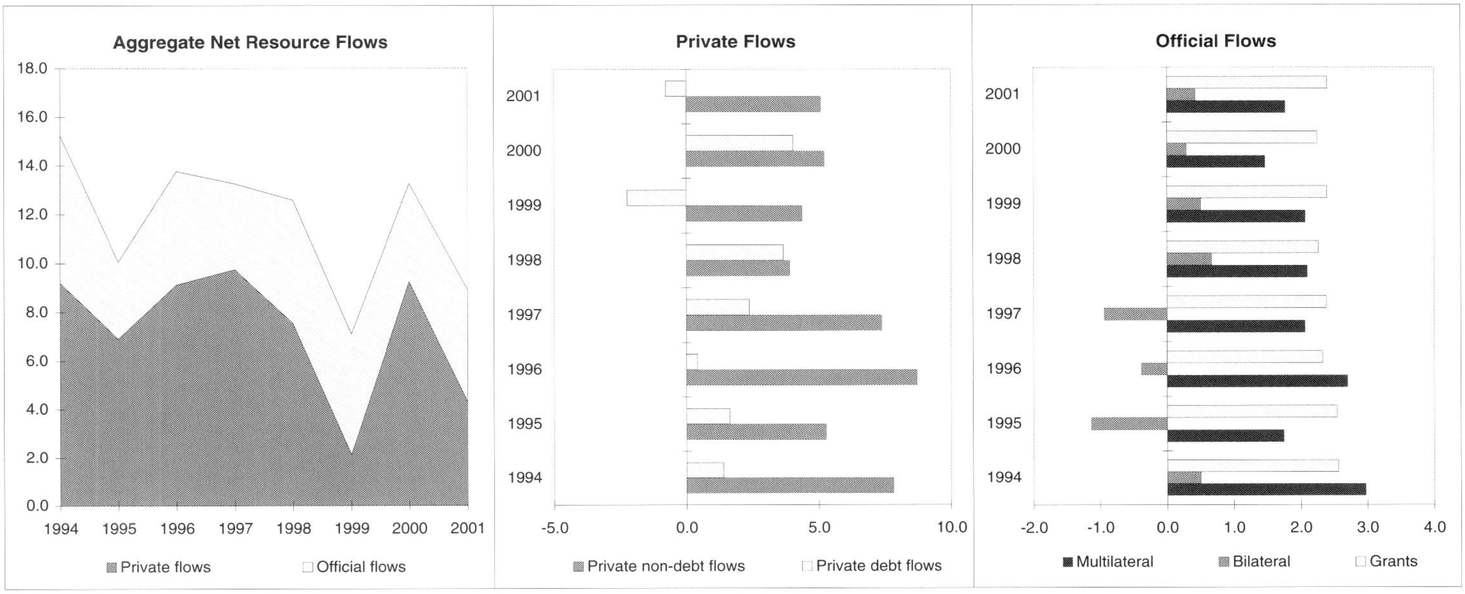

SUB-SAHARAN AFRICA

(US$ million, unless otherwise indicated)

	1970	1980	1990	1995	1996	1997	1998	1999	2000	2001
1. SUMMARY DEBT DATA										
TOTAL DEBT STOCKS (EDT)	**6,921**	**60,898**	**176,883**	**235,256**	**231,128**	**221,303**	**229,423**	**216,326**	**215,794**	**208,857**
Long-term debt (LDOD)	**6,059**	**46,655**	**149,377**	**185,829**	**179,998**	**172,943**	**179,478**	**168,012**	**175,777**	**168,719**
Public and publicly guaranteed	5,751	42,089	144,101	174,025	169,692	163,520	170,629	157,004	163,765	156,458
Private nonguaranteed	309	4,567	5,276	11,804	10,307	9,423	8,849	11,007	12,012	12,260
Use of IMF credit	**106**	**3,033**	**6,612**	**8,673**	**8,441**	**7,388**	**7,388**	**7,124**	**6,739**	**6,323**
Short-term debt	**..**	**11,209**	**20,894**	**40,754**	**42,689**	**40,972**	**42,557**	**41,190**	**33,278**	**33,816**
of which interest arrears on LDOD	..	1,713	9,315	20,524	20,087	18,171	20,261	19,562	14,311	14,198
Official creditors	..	1,609	6,418	16,001	16,318	15,436	17,140	16,534	11,757	..
Private creditors	..	104	2,898	4,523	3,770	2,736	3,122	3,028	2,554	..
Memo: principal arrears on LDOD	..	1,729	17,515	41,315	40,661	38,606	43,282	38,254	26,305	..
Official creditors	..	1,038	9,902	28,756	30,337	31,087	34,705	29,961	19,747	..
Private creditors	..	690	7,613	12,559	10,324	7,519	8,576	8,293	6,558	..
Memo: export credits	..	0	50,693	48,277	47,589	53,552	29,734	36,187	33,359	..
TOTAL DEBT FLOWS										
Disbursements	**1,259**	**11,787**	**10,374**	**14,065**	**10,270**	**12,674**	**8,457**	**8,659**	**8,678**	**10,944**
Long-term debt	1,240	10,570	9,714	11,071	9,622	12,152	7,656	8,147	8,154	10,362
IMF purchases	19	1,217	660	2,994	648	523	801	512	525	582
Principal repayments	**452**	**3,173**	**5,585**	**9,440**	**9,423**	**11,041**	**8,995**	**8,816**	**8,073**	**9,791**
Long-term debt	389	2,789	4,634	7,068	8,827	9,975	7,883	8,227	7,525	9,030
IMF repurchases	63	384	951	2,372	597	1,065	1,112	589	548	760
Net flows on debt	**859**	**10,074**	**7,058**	**7,416**	**3,218**	**5,126**	**-1,049**	**-745**	**-523**	**1,653**
of which short-term debt	..	1,459	2,269	2,791	2,372	3,492	-511	-588	-1,128	500
Interest payments (INT)	**..**	**3,512**	**5,312**	**5,374**	**5,823**	**4,875**	**5,065**	**4,815**	**4,269**	**4,730**
Long-term debt	193	2,379	4,363	3,996	4,815	3,722	3,842	3,601	3,126	3,827
IMF charges	0	103	238	559	124	101	65	55	43	34
Short-term debt	..	1,030	712	819	884	1,052	1,158	1,159	1,101	870
Net transfers on debt	**..**	**6,562**	**1,746**	**2,042**	**-2,605**	**251**	**-6,114**	**-5,561**	**-4,792**	**-3,077**
Total debt service paid (TDS)	**..**	**6,685**	**10,897**	**14,814**	**15,246**	**15,915**	**14,060**	**13,631**	**12,343**	**14,521**
Long-term debt	582	5,167	8,996	11,064	13,642	13,697	11,726	11,828	10,650	12,857
IMF repurchases and charges	63	487	1,189	2,931	720	1,166	1,177	644	591	794
Short-term debt (interest only)	..	1,030	712	819	884	1,052	1,158	1,159	1,101	870
2. AGGREGATE NET RESOURCE FLOWS AND NET TRANSFERS (LONG-TERM)										
NET RESOURCE FLOWS	**1,671**	**11,419**	**17,922**	**24,655**	**17,461**	**21,519**	**17,154**	**22,512**	**18,527**	**25,537**
Net flow of long-term debt (ex. IMF)	851	7,781	5,080	4,003	795	2,176	-228	-80	629	1,332
Foreign direct investment (net)	428	33	834	4,415	4,456	8,195	6,332	7,937	6,676	13,602
Portfolio equity flows	-1	3	2	4,869	2,013	1,507	681	3,899	893	703
Grants (excluding technical coop.)	394	3,601	12,006	11,368	10,197	9,641	10,370	10,756	10,330	9,900
Memo: technical coop. grants	632	2,665	5,008	5,012	4,931	4,404	3,920	3,401	3,747	3,600
official net resource flows	886	7,182	16,635	14,251	12,160	11,617	11,548	11,348	11,453	11,071
private net resource flows	785	4,237	1,287	10,404	5,301	9,903	5,607	11,164	7,074	14,466
NET TRANSFERS	**741**	**6,110**	**11,832**	**16,232**	**8,430**	**13,853**	**9,109**	**14,393**	**10,591**	**15,811**
Interest on long-term debt	193	2,379	4,363	3,996	4,815	3,722	3,842	3,601	3,126	3,827
Profit remittances on FDI	737	2,930	1,728	4,427	4,216	3,945	4,203	4,518	4,811	5,900
Memo: official net transfers	773	6,492	13,924	12,238	9,506	9,536	9,500	9,375	9,893	8,929
private net transfers	-32	-382	-2,092	3,995	-1,075	4,317	-390	5,018	698	6,881
3. MAJOR ECONOMIC AGGREGATES										
Gross national income (GNI)	60,575	258,841	280,890	302,767	316,249	327,464	305,891	302,219	302,595	294,425
Exports of goods & services (XGS)	..	92,733	84,907	96,820	106,627	109,055	97,013	103,735	121,328	116,815
of which workers remittances	..	775	776	1,491	1,637	2,561	2,164	1,914	704	1,104
Imports of goods & services (MGS)	..	93,459	91,670	114,983	118,243	125,447	122,829	119,923	127,758	128,755
International reserves (RES)	3,085	22,940	15,364	20,886	23,189	29,473	28,301	24,957	26,285	26,588
Current account balance	..	83	-1,773	-12,226	-2,196	-9,267	-17,300	-8,429	1,377	-623
4. DEBT INDICATORS										
EDT / XGS (%)	..	65.7	208.3	243.0	216.8	202.9	236.5	208.5	177.9	178.8
EDT / GNI (%)	..	23.5	63.0	77.7	73.1	67.6	75.0	71.6	71.3	70.9
TDS / XGS (%)	..	7.2	12.8	15.3	14.3	14.6	14.5	13.1	10.2	12.4
INT / XGS (%)	..	3.8	6.3	5.6	5.5	4.5	5.2	4.6	3.5	4.1
INT / GNI (%)	..	1.4	1.9	1.8	1.8	1.5	1.7	1.6	1.4	1.6
RES / EDT (%)	..	37.7	8.7	8.9	10.0	13.3	12.3	11.5	12.2	12.7
RES / MGS (months)	..	3.0	2.0	2.2	2.4	2.8	2.8	2.5	2.5	2.5
Short-term / EDT (%)	..	18.4	11.8	17.3	18.5	18.5	18.6	19.0	15.4	16.2
Concessional / EDT (%)	..	27.0	33.1	34.3	35.8	37.5	39.2	39.2	38.7	38.8
Multilateral / EDT (%)	..	12.5	21.6	23.2	23.7	24.2	24.9	25.9	25.3	25.5

SUB-SAHARAN AFRICA

(US$ million, unless otherwise indicated)

	1970	1980	1990	1995	1996	1997	1998	1999	2000	2001
5. LONG-TERM DEBT										
DEBT OUTSTANDING (LDOD)	**6,059**	**46,655**	**149,377**	**185,829**	**179,998**	**172,943**	**179,478**	**168,012**	**175,777**	**168,719**
Public and publicly guaranteed	**5,751**	**42,089**	**144,101**	**174,025**	**169,692**	**163,520**	**170,629**	**157,004**	**163,765**	**156,458**
Official creditors	4,183	25,745	108,741	137,282	135,244	130,592	138,523	128,599	137,955	131,540
Multilateral	869	7,599	38,189	54,684	54,684	53,581	57,082	56,035	54,478	53,316
Concessional	240	3,986	23,992	38,876	40,500	41,157	44,880	45,106	45,082	46,042
Bilateral	3,314	18,147	70,552	82,598	80,560	77,011	81,442	72,564	83,477	78,224
Concessional	2,961	12,455	34,483	41,894	42,248	41,881	45,021	39,678	38,397	34,926
Private creditors	1,567	16,343	35,360	36,743	34,448	32,928	32,105	28,405	25,811	24,919
Bonds	352	637	301	4,784	5,048	8,357	8,322	8,566	9,150	9,055
Commercial banks	128	7,780	14,453	13,269	15,210	11,667	10,444	9,164	8,619	8,829
Other private	1,086	7,927	20,606	18,691	14,190	12,904	13,340	10,675	8,042	7,035
Private nonguaranteed	**309**	**4,567**	**5,276**	**11,804**	**10,307**	**9,423**	**8,849**	**11,007**	**12,012**	**12,260**
Bonds	0	0	0	350	600	1,245	1,636	1,245	1,960	3,165
Commercial banks and other	309	4,567	5,276	11,454	9,707	8,178	7,213	9,762	10,051	9,095
Memo:										
IBRD	587	2,548	9,179	7,641	6,381	5,302	4,953	4,175	3,477	2,902
IDA	226	2,578	15,756	27,895	29,494	30,267	33,041	33,452	33,621	34,527
DISBURSEMENTS	**1,240**	**10,570**	**9,714**	**11,071**	**9,622**	**12,152**	**7,656**	**8,147**	**8,154**	**10,362**
Public and publicly guaranteed	**1,139**	**9,388**	**9,083**	**10,323**	**8,640**	**9,677**	**6,657**	**7,168**	**7,315**	**8,429**
Official creditors	662	4,246	7,180	5,869	5,285	4,941	4,301	3,830	3,798	4,572
Multilateral	150	1,678	4,545	4,230	4,166	4,072	3,441	3,058	3,097	3,662
Concessional	72	860	2,764	3,179	3,373	3,291	2,923	2,702	2,839	3,344
Bilateral	512	2,568	2,635	1,640	1,119	870	860	773	701	910
Concessional	441	1,697	2,087	1,500	847	680	635	631	547	685
Private creditors	477	5,142	1,903	4,454	3,355	4,735	2,356	3,338	3,517	3,857
Bonds	13	52	0	541	632	1,278	0	1,627	765	929
Commercial banks	16	2,331	374	1,666	1,383	2,101	1,646	1,439	2,394	2,479
Other private	448	2,759	1,529	2,247	1,340	1,356	710	272	358	448
Private nonguaranteed	**101**	**1,183**	**630**	**749**	**982**	**2,475**	**999**	**979**	**839**	**1,933**
Bonds	0	0	0	350	250	645	373	0	712	1,250
Commercial banks and other	101	1,183	630	399	732	1,830	626	979	127	683
Memo:										
IBRD	75	400	813	274	229	263	159	89	75	56
IDA	61	424	2,027	2,392	2,585	2,397	2,099	1,969	2,193	2,443
PRINCIPAL REPAYMENTS	**389**	**2,789**	**4,634**	**7,068**	**8,827**	**9,975**	**7,883**	**8,227**	**7,525**	**9,030**
Public and publicly guaranteed	**332**	**2,197**	**4,168**	**5,823**	**7,068**	**6,220**	**6,471**	**5,163**	**6,169**	**7,647**
Official creditors	169	665	2,551	2,986	3,322	2,965	3,123	3,238	2,675	3,401
Multilateral	33	198	1,349	2,027	2,001	1,976	1,865	1,892	1,688	1,869
Concessional	0	30	268	435	457	463	505	561	574	775
Bilateral	136	467	1,202	959	1,322	990	1,258	1,346	987	1,532
Concessional	110	212	312	433	420	560	867	811	579	649
Private creditors	163	1,532	1,617	2,838	3,746	3,254	3,348	1,925	3,494	4,246
Bonds	27	24	31	40	296	283	123	92	480	1,024
Commercial banks	10	721	1,015	1,260	1,790	1,813	2,192	1,424	2,246	2,131
Other private	126	787	571	1,538	1,660	1,158	1,033	409	768	1,090
Private nonguaranteed	**57**	**592**	**466**	**1,245**	**1,758**	**3,756**	**1,413**	**3,064**	**1,356**	**1,383**
Bonds	0	0	0	0	0	0	0	358	0	45
Commercial banks and other	57	592	466	1,245	1,758	3,756	1,413	2,706	1,356	1,338
Memo:										
IBRD	29	111	721	1,056	950	834	743	687	552	456
IDA	0	5	51	120	140	154	187	236	277	343
NET FLOWS ON DEBT	**851**	**7,781**	**5,080**	**4,003**	**795**	**2,176**	**-228**	**-80**	**629**	**1,332**
Public and publicly guaranteed	**807**	**7,191**	**4,915**	**4,500**	**1,572**	**3,457**	**186**	**2,005**	**1,146**	**781**
Official creditors	493	3,581	4,629	2,883	1,963	1,976	1,178	592	1,123	1,171
Multilateral	117	1,480	3,196	2,202	2,165	2,096	1,577	1,166	1,409	1,793
Concessional	72	830	2,497	2,743	2,916	2,828	2,418	2,141	2,266	2,569
Bilateral	376	2,101	1,433	681	-202	-120	-399	-574	-285	-622
Concessional	331	1,486	1,776	1,067	427	120	-232	-180	-32	36
Private creditors	315	3,610	286	1,616	-391	1,481	-992	1,413	23	-390
Bonds	-14	28	-31	501	336	995	-123	1,535	285	-95
Commercial banks	6	1,610	-641	406	-408	288	-547	15	148	348
Other private	322	1,972	958	710	-319	198	-323	-137	-410	-642
Private nonguaranteed	**44**	**590**	**165**	**-496**	**-777**	**-1,281**	**-414**	**-2,085**	**-518**	**550**
Bonds	0	0	0	350	250	645	373	-358	712	1,205
Commercial banks and other	44	590	165	-846	-1,027	-1,926	-787	-1,727	-1,230	-655
Memo:										
IBRD	46	289	92	-782	-721	-572	-584	-598	-476	-400
IDA	61	419	1,976	2,273	2,446	2,243	1,912	1,733	1,916	2,100

SUB-SAHARAN AFRICA

(US$ million, unless otherwise indicated)

	1970	1980	1990	1995	1996	1997	1998	1999	2000	2001
INTEREST PAYMENTS (LINT)	**193**	**2,379**	**4,363**	**3,996**	**4,815**	**3,722**	**3,842**	**3,601**	**3,126**	**3,827**
Public and publicly guaranteed	**178**	**1,928**	**4,032**	**3,491**	**4,326**	**3,239**	**3,444**	**3,231**	**2,647**	**3,312**
Official creditors	113	690	2,711	2,013	2,654	2,081	2,048	1,973	1,561	2,141
Multilateral	35	286	1,111	1,242	1,372	1,218	1,027	1,001	859	851
Concessional	1	29	162	254	299	303	302	324	321	354
Bilateral	79	405	1,600	771	1,282	863	1,021	972	702	1,290
Concessional	61	209	562	358	492	435	630	474	311	310
Private creditors	64	1,238	1,321	1,478	1,672	1,158	1,396	1,258	1,086	1,170
Bonds	12	13	13	322	336	348	542	549	561	588
Commercial banks	8	857	625	462	579	425	486	348	294	320
Other private	45	368	682	694	757	386	368	361	231	262
Private nonguaranteed	**16**	**451**	**331**	**505**	**489**	**483**	**399**	**370**	**479**	**515**
Bonds	0	0	0	0	25	99	101	133	101	149
Commercial banks and other	16	451	331	505	465	384	298	237	378	365
Memo:										
IBRD	32	217	651	630	527	407	332	294	213	180
IDA	1	16	97	178	185	192	204	223	218	230
NET TRANSFERS ON DEBT	**658**	**5,403**	**717**	**8**	**-4,020**	**-1,545**	**-4,070**	**-3,681**	**-2,497**	**-2,495**
Public and publicly guaranteed	**630**	**5,263**	**884**	**1,009**	**-2,754**	**218**	**-3,258**	**-1,226**	**-1,501**	**-2,530**
Official creditors	380	2,891	1,918	870	-691	-105	-870	-1,381	-438	-971
Multilateral	83	1,194	2,085	960	793	878	550	165	550	942
Concessional	71	801	2,335	2,490	2,618	2,526	2,116	1,817	1,945	2,215
Bilateral	297	1,696	-166	-90	-1,485	-982	-1,420	-1,545	-987	-1,912
Concessional	269	1,277	1,214	710	-65	-316	-862	-654	-343	-274
Private creditors	250	2,372	-1,034	139	-2,062	323	-2,388	155	-1,063	-1,560
Bonds	-26	15	-44	179	1	646	-665	986	-276	-684
Commercial banks	-2	753	-1,266	-56	-986	-137	-1,032	-334	-146	28
Other private	277	1,604	276	16	-1,077	-187	-690	-498	-642	-904
Private nonguaranteed	**28**	**140**	**-166**	**-1,001**	**-1,266**	**-1,764**	**-812**	**-2,455**	**-996**	**36**
Bonds	0	0	0	350	226	546	272	-491	611	1,056
Commercial banks and other	28	140	-166	-1,351	-1,492	-2,309	-1,085	-1,964	-1,607	-1,020
Memo:										
IBRD	14	72	-559	-1,412	-1,248	-978	-915	-892	-689	-580
IDA	60	403	1,879	2,094	2,260	2,051	1,709	1,509	1,698	1,869
DEBT SERVICE (LTDS)	**582**	**5,167**	**8,996**	**11,064**	**13,642**	**13,697**	**11,726**	**11,828**	**10,650**	**12,857**
Public and publicly guaranteed	**510**	**4,125**	**8,200**	**9,314**	**11,394**	**9,458**	**9,914**	**8,394**	**8,816**	**10,959**
Official creditors	283	1,355	5,262	4,999	5,977	5,046	5,171	5,211	4,236	5,543
Multilateral	68	483	2,460	3,270	3,373	3,194	2,891	2,893	2,547	2,720
Concessional	1	59	429	689	755	765	807	885	895	1,129
Bilateral	215	872	2,802	1,729	2,604	1,852	2,280	2,318	1,689	2,822
Concessional	171	420	873	790	913	995	1,497	1,286	890	959
Private creditors	227	2,769	2,938	4,315	5,418	4,413	4,744	3,183	4,580	5,416
Bonds	38	37	44	362	632	631	665	641	1,041	1,613
Commercial banks	18	1,577	1,640	1,722	2,369	2,238	2,678	1,772	2,539	2,451
Other private	171	1,155	1,254	2,231	2,417	1,544	1,400	770	1,000	1,353
Private nonguaranteed	**72**	**1,043**	**797**	**1,750**	**2,248**	**4,239**	**1,811**	**3,434**	**1,835**	**1,898**
Bonds	0	0	0	0	25	99	101	491	101	194
Commercial banks and other	72	1,043	797	1,750	2,223	4,139	1,711	2,943	1,734	1,703
Memo:										
IBRD	61	328	1,372	1,686	1,477	1,241	1,074	981	765	635
IDA	1	22	148	298	325	346	390	459	495	574
UNDISBURSED DEBT	**2,734**	**20,801**	**34,142**	**28,913**	**24,630**	**22,034**	**21,202**	**17,847**	**15,016**	**..**
Official creditors	2,279	14,325	30,171	26,005	22,477	19,026	19,285	16,479	14,543	..
Private creditors	455	6,476	3,971	2,909	2,154	3,007	1,917	1,369	473	..
Memorandum items										
Concessional LDOD	3,201	16,441	58,476	80,770	82,748	83,037	89,901	84,783	83,479	..
Variable rate LDOD	356	11,865	29,450	37,878	35,102	32,580	30,868	30,104	27,517	..
Public sector LDOD	5,689	42,037	144,264	173,986	169,631	163,515	170,427	156,305	162,590	..
Private sector LDOD	370	4,614	5,109	11,814	10,306	9,368	9,051	11,707	13,187	..

6. CURRENCY COMPOSITION OF LONG-TERM DEBT (PERCENT)

	1970	1980	1990	1995	1996	1997	1998	1999	2000	2001
Deutsche mark	6.6	7.0	6.4	5.7	5.1	4.6	4.7	4.3	2.6	..
French franc	14.4	13.8	14.1	12.9	12.4	10.7	10.8	9.9	7.6	..
Japanese yen	0.1	5.4	4.0	5.4	5.1	4.9	5.5	6.8	4.2	..
Pound sterling	22.5	5.7	5.4	3.6	4.0	4.0	3.8	3.9	2.0	..
Swiss franc	0.3	1.7	2.1	1.7	1.5	1.5	1.4	1.3	1.2	..
U.S.dollars	21.4	35.4	36.5	40.9	43.0	46.3	46.8	50.0	61.6	..
Multiple currency	11.2	8.8	10.4	10.0	9.4	8.8	7.6	7.7	7.0	..
Special drawing rights	0.0	0.0	0.6	1.0	1.1	1.1	1.1	1.2	1.2	..
All other currencies	23.4	22.2	20.5	18.7	18.5	18.0	18.1	14.6	12.5	..

SUB-SAHARAN AFRICA

(US$ million, unless otherwise indicated)

	1970	1980	1990	1995	1996	1997	1998	1999	2000	2001
7. DEBT RESTRUCTURINGS										
Total amount rescheduled	0	444	5,987	3,040	4,541	6,535	2,890	3,225	23,032	..
Debt stock rescheduled	0	0	91	142	198	2	310	755	14	..
Principal rescheduled	0	269	3,969	1,780	2,498	2,141	1,071	1,162	13,321	..
Official	0	120	2,696	1,290	1,445	1,789	984	1,107	11,293	..
Private	0	149	1,274	490	1,053	353	87	56	2,028	..
Interest rescheduled	..	..	1,724	730	903	2,184	505	488	9,043	..
Official	0	31	1,376	627	683	1,257	459	479	8,491	..
Private	0	31	348	102	220	927	46	9	552	..
Debt forgiven	3	194	1,602	1,319	4,032	706	299	4,509	457	..
Memo: interest forgiven	0	0	87	214	161	264	571	494	283	..
Debt stock reduction	0	0	1,262	360	1,378	4,813	346	819	390	..
of which debt buyback	0	0	0	29	301	169	102	325	137	..
8. DEBT STOCK-FLOW RECONCILIATION										
Total change in debt stocks	..	..	19,796	14,117	-4,128	-9,825	8,119	-13,097	-532	..
Net flows on debt	859	10,074	7,058	7,416	3,218	5,126	-1,049	-745	-523	1,653
Net change in interest arrears	..	..	2,224	2,062	-437	-1,916	2,090	-700	-5,251	..
Interest capitalized	..	..	1,724	730	903	2,184	505	488	9,043	..
Debt forgiveness or reduction	..	..	-2,864	-1,649	-5,108	-5,350	-543	-5,003	-709	..
Cross-currency valuation	..	..	7,711	844	-10,004	-13,738	-44	-6,679	-6,623	..
Residual	..	..	3,944	4,714	7,300	3,869	7,161	-457	3,531	..
9. AVERAGE TERMS OF NEW COMMITMENTS										
ALL CREDITORS										
Interest (%)	3.7	7.0	4.3	3.8	3.8	4.8	2.4	3.6	3.2	..
Maturity (years)	23.9	17.3	32.6	27.3	29.0	24.7	29.7	22.5	24.8	..
Grace period (years)	9.7	5.1	6.9	5.3	6.2	5.9	7.3	6.2	6.2	..
Grant element (%)	47.5	21.8	43.5	41.9	43.7	34.1	59.3	45.2	48.7	..
Official creditors										
Interest (%)	2.0	4.1	3.5	1.9	1.8	1.6	1.3	1.3	0.9	..
Maturity (years)	32.0	25.1	37.1	42.3	43.4	49.2	35.4	34.8	39.1	..
Grace period (years)	14.3	6.8	7.8	8.7	8.7	9.1	8.8	8.8	9.6	..
Grant element (%)	67.4	42.8	51.2	65.9	66.5	70.2	71.8	70.9	77.5	..
Private creditors										
Interest (%)	6.6	10.0	8.1	5.9	6.4	6.6	6.5	6.2	5.9	..
Maturity (years)	10.2	9.4	11.7	12.2	10.3	10.1	8.9	8.8	8.1	..
Grace period (years)	1.8	3.3	2.8	1.9	2.9	4.0	1.6	3.3	2.3	..
Grant element (%)	13.3	0.2	7.7	17.7	14.2	12.6	13.0	16.6	15.0	..
Memorandum items										
Commitments	1,888	13,286	11,491	9,264	7,921	10,473	6,180	6,688	5,986	..
Official creditors	1,194	6,724	9,457	4,653	4,471	3,909	4,893	3,528	3,230	..
Private creditors	694	6,562	2,034	4,611	3,450	6,564	1,332	3,160	2,756	..

10. GRAPH OF AGGREGATE NET RESOURCE FLOWS

(current prices, US$ billion)

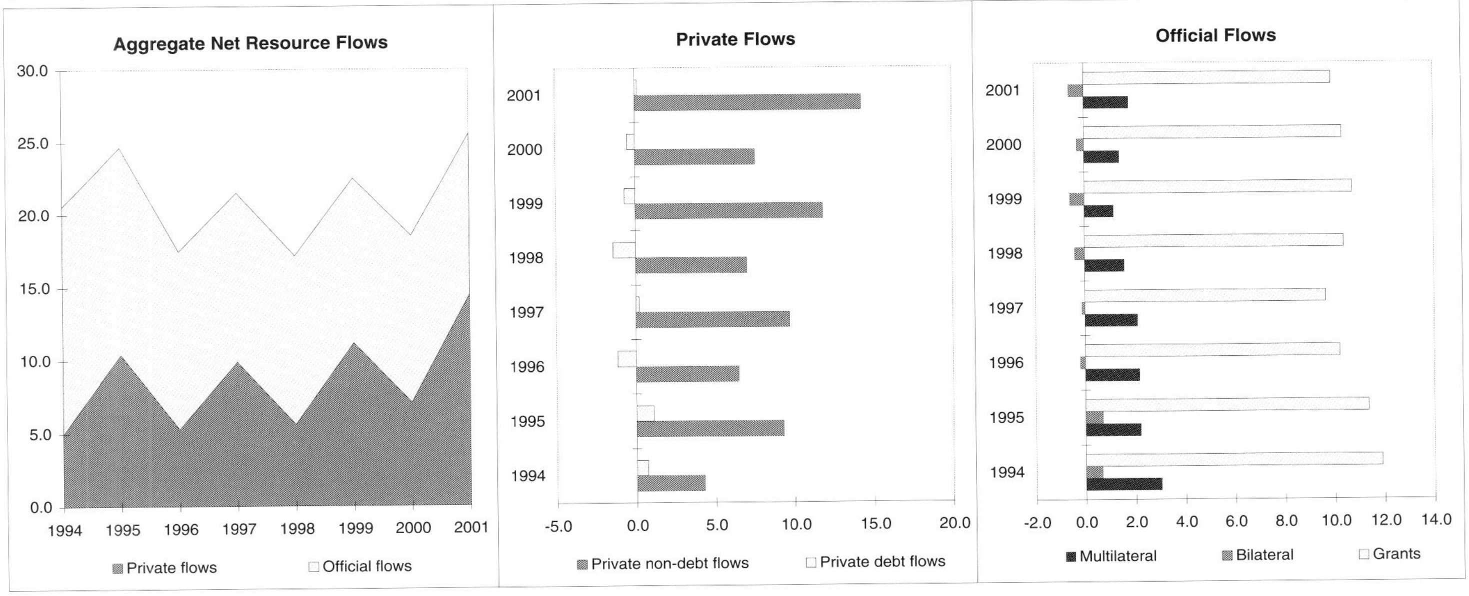

LOW-INCOME COUNTRIES

(US$ million, unless otherwise indicated)

	1970	1980	1990	1994	1995	1996	1997	1998	1999	2000
1. SUMMARY DEBT DATA										
TOTAL DEBT STOCKS (EDT)	**23,503**	**125,207**	**418,588**	**526,238**	**550,532**	**546,820**	**540,596**	**576,782**	**574,010**	**550,548**
Long-term debt (LDOD)	**21,657**	**102,905**	**357,323**	**449,398**	**462,308**	**451,270**	**447,996**	**491,500**	**487,537**	**471,077**
Public and publicly guaranteed	20,783	94,866	340,308	410,910	414,229	398,455	384,566	418,648	422,372	412,834
Private nonguaranteed	875	8,039	17,015	38,488	48,078	52,815	63,430	72,852	65,165	58,243
Use of IMF credit	**318**	**5,277**	**11,250**	**14,678**	**15,270**	**14,948**	**16,775**	**23,636**	**24,786**	**23,580**
Short-term debt	**..**	**17,025**	**50,015**	**62,162**	**72,955**	**80,602**	**75,825**	**61,647**	**61,687**	**55,892**
of which interest arrears on LDOD	..	1,727	12,909	23,778	25,471	24,225	20,625	23,200	26,141	20,599
Official creditors	..	1,615	8,637	18,102	20,173	19,668	17,773	19,857	19,444	13,160
Private creditors	..	112	4,272	5,676	5,298	4,557	2,852	3,342	6,697	7,439
Memo: principal arrears on LDOD	..	1,765	23,545	51,877	58,535	57,055	49,968	59,268	55,419	36,130
Official creditors	..	1,047	13,535	37,486	43,831	44,512	41,746	47,086	43,111	25,516
Private creditors	..	717	10,010	14,390	14,704	12,543	8,222	12,182	12,309	10,614
Memo: export credits	..	337	69,659	73,868	80,697	80,250	86,913	48,258	55,919	52,930
TOTAL DEBT FLOWS										
Disbursements	**3,489**	**21,784**	**33,017**	**36,236**	**40,108**	**45,474**	**49,237**	**45,416**	**31,267**	**30,796**
Long-term debt	3,423	19,001	30,546	34,200	35,101	43,260	44,696	37,908	27,603	28,644
IMF purchases	66	2,783	2,471	2,036	5,007	2,214	4,541	7,508	3,664	2,152
Principal repayments	**1,341**	**6,127**	**16,785**	**23,995**	**30,077**	**33,246**	**31,840**	**29,081**	**30,349**	**30,075**
Long-term debt	1,034	5,423	14,610	22,250	25,738	31,232	30,067	27,481	28,397	27,752
IMF repurchases	308	704	2,175	1,745	4,340	2,014	1,773	1,600	1,953	2,324
Net flows on debt	**2,200**	**19,281**	**23,696**	**12,269**	**19,316**	**21,121**	**19,514**	**2,578**	**18**	**467**
of which short-term debt	..	3,624	7,464	27	9,286	8,894	2,116	-13,757	-901	-254
Interest payments (INT)	**..**	**6,012**	**15,403**	**15,653**	**17,657**	**17,801**	**18,024**	**18,818**	**16,522**	**17,682**
Long-term debt	521	4,331	12,409	13,207	14,437	14,880	14,821	15,898	13,876	14,753
IMF charges	0	152	510	411	818	351	312	452	637	800
Short-term debt	..	1,529	2,483	2,035	2,402	2,570	2,891	2,468	1,886	2,129
Net transfers on debt	**..**	**13,270**	**8,293**	**-3,384**	**1,659**	**3,320**	**1,490**	**-16,240**	**-16,505**	**-17,214**
Total debt service paid (TDS)	**..**	**12,138**	**32,188**	**39,648**	**47,735**	**51,047**	**49,863**	**47,899**	**46,871**	**47,757**
Long-term debt	1,555	9,754	27,019	35,457	40,175	46,113	44,888	43,379	42,272	42,504
IMF repurchases and charges	308	856	2,685	2,156	5,158	2,364	2,085	2,052	2,590	3,124
Short-term debt (interest only)	..	1,529	2,483	2,035	2,402	2,570	2,891	2,468	1,886	2,129
2. AGGREGATE NET RESOURCE FLOWS AND NET TRANSFERS (LONG-TERM)										
NET RESOURCE FLOWS	**3,669**	**20,961**	**33,503**	**48,949**	**47,371**	**53,358**	**50,110**	**38,778**	**26,876**	**25,173**
Net flow of long-term debt (ex. IMF)	2,390	13,579	15,936	11,950	9,363	12,028	14,629	10,427	-793	893
Foreign direct investment (net)	261	244	2,201	9,008	13,824	17,569	18,993	12,910	9,721	6,562
Portfolio equity flows	0	-1	416	10,727	7,617	8,846	2,671	649	2,616	2,528
Grants (excluding technical coop.)	1,018	7,139	14,949	17,263	16,567	14,916	13,818	14,792	15,332	15,191
Memo: technical coop. grants	1,032	3,842	7,323	7,317	8,120	7,932	6,811	6,497	6,501	6,716
official net resource flows	2,860	14,598	26,867	26,826	22,326	19,756	18,883	23,670	24,652	20,592
private net resource flows	809	6,363	6,636	22,122	25,045	33,603	31,227	15,108	2,223	4,581
NET TRANSFERS	**2,260**	**10,830**	**17,739**	**31,755**	**28,714**	**33,700**	**30,376**	**18,294**	**7,132**	**4,900**
Interest on long-term debt	521	4,331	12,409	13,207	14,437	14,880	14,821	15,898	13,876	14,753
Profit remittances on FDI	888	5,800	3,354	3,987	4,220	4,778	4,913	4,587	5,745	5,521
Memo: official net transfers	2,491	12,938	20,311	19,133	14,123	11,634	11,429	16,243	17,064	13,245
private net transfers	-231	-2,108	-2,571	12,622	14,591	22,067	18,947	2,051	-9,932	-8,346
3. MAJOR ECONOMIC AGGREGATES										
Gross national income (GNI)	165,768	595,356	851,697	850,208	930,177	1,015,810	1,047,334	918,454	983,252	1,031,101
Exports of goods & services (XGS)	..	..	140,110	179,247	213,294	238,127	253,625	235,613	251,020	303,276
of which workers remittances	..	5,253	7,009	12,600	14,061	17,549	18,227	16,920	18,487	18,195
Imports of goods & services (MGS)	..	..	172,254	213,313	258,285	283,169	299,388	276,650	278,179	315,707
International reserves (RES)	..	36,734	26,230	55,725	58,800	69,519	74,989	81,165	88,452	97,013
Current account balance	..	-9,458	-22,038	-22,536	-32,497	-29,089	-31,393	-24,786	-10,673	6,327
4. DEBT INDICATORS										
EDT / XGS (%)	..	..	298.8	293.6	258.1	229.6	213.2	244.8	228.7	181.5
EDT / GNI (%)	..	21.0	49.2	61.9	59.2	53.8	51.6	62.8	58.4	53.4
TDS / XGS (%)	..	..	23.0	22.1	22.4	21.4	19.7	20.3	18.7	15.8
INT / XGS (%)	..	..	11.0	8.7	8.3	7.5	7.1	8.0	6.6	5.8
INT / GNI (%)	..	1.0	1.8	1.8	1.9	1.8	1.7	2.1	1.7	1.7
RES / EDT (%)	..	29.3	6.3	10.6	10.7	12.7	13.9	14.1	15.4	17.6
RES / MGS (months)	..	..	1.8	3.1	2.7	3.0	3.0	3.5	3.8	3.7
Short-term / EDT (%)	..	13.6	12.0	11.8	13.3	14.7	14.0	10.7	10.8	10.2
Concessional / EDT (%)	..	45.5	43.6	43.3	41.9	40.4	36.8	37.2	39.6	40.1
Multilateral / EDT (%)	..	15.5	21.9	24.5	24.5	24.3	24.3	24.8	25.9	26.8

LOW-INCOME COUNTRIES

(US$ million, unless otherwise indicated)

	1970	1980	1990	1994	1995	1996	1997	1998	1999	2000
5. LONG-TERM DEBT										
DEBT OUTSTANDING (LDOD)	**21,657**	**102,905**	**357,323**	**449,398**	**462,308**	**451,270**	**447,996**	**491,500**	**487,537**	**471,077**
Public and publicly guaranteed	**20,783**	**94,866**	**340,308**	**410,910**	**414,229**	**398,455**	**384,566**	**418,648**	**422,372**	**412,834**
Official creditors	18,163	70,170	262,113	336,877	341,675	328,777	310,339	334,030	344,775	337,164
Multilateral	3,064	19,369	91,833	129,151	134,832	132,991	131,530	143,055	148,817	147,658
Concessional	1,593	13,072	53,783	76,792	82,054	85,018	86,888	95,012	98,796	100,506
Bilateral	15,099	50,802	170,281	207,726	206,844	195,787	178,809	190,975	195,959	189,505
Concessional	13,610	43,866	128,539	151,140	148,620	136,130	112,050	119,641	128,719	120,455
Private creditors	2,620	24,696	78,194	74,033	72,554	69,677	74,227	84,618	77,596	75,670
Bonds	340	833	3,611	6,722	8,028	6,084	10,155	15,674	14,726	19,633
Commercial banks	201	12,177	41,614	33,219	31,299	35,774	40,788	45,517	41,858	37,702
Other private	2,079	11,686	32,970	34,092	33,227	27,819	23,284	23,427	21,013	18,335
Private nonguaranteed	**875**	**8,039**	**17,015**	**38,488**	**48,078**	**52,815**	**63,430**	**72,852**	**65,165**	**58,243**
Bonds	0	0	120	2,953	4,485	9,394	13,758	13,538	11,602	9,451
Commercial banks and other	875	8,039	16,895	35,535	43,593	43,421	49,672	59,314	53,563	48,792
Memo:										
IBRD	1,414	4,770	28,080	34,070	33,629	30,247	27,701	28,483	28,922	27,603
IDA	1,572	10,465	38,613	55,645	59,315	61,941	63,585	68,676	70,496	72,868
DISBURSEMENTS	**3,423**	**19,001**	**30,546**	**34,200**	**35,101**	**43,260**	**44,696**	**37,908**	**27,603**	**28,644**
Public and publicly guaranteed	**3,100**	**16,834**	**24,706**	**27,523**	**25,782**	**27,377**	**28,421**	**32,463**	**23,478**	**24,161**
Official creditors	2,398	9,375	18,608	19,862	18,145	18,407	18,796	19,986	19,358	16,318
Multilateral	355	3,630	10,596	12,363	11,506	11,931	11,729	11,534	11,700	10,232
Concessional	161	2,222	5,194	6,960	6,225	7,027	6,657	6,482	6,218	6,258
Bilateral	2,043	5,745	8,012	7,499	6,639	6,476	7,066	8,452	7,658	6,086
Concessional	1,864	4,521	6,561	5,698	5,530	4,682	4,659	6,923	6,536	4,937
Private creditors	702	7,459	6,098	7,661	7,637	8,969	9,625	12,477	4,120	7,843
Bonds	6	97	427	150	691	945	1,150	5,657	0	5,497
Commercial banks	44	3,953	2,874	2,332	3,837	4,914	5,700	4,435	2,452	1,566
Other private	652	3,409	2,797	5,179	3,110	3,110	2,775	2,386	1,668	780
Private nonguaranteed	**323**	**2,167**	**5,840**	**6,677**	**9,319**	**15,883**	**16,275**	**5,445**	**4,126**	**4,484**
Bonds	0	0	120	907	2,283	4,566	4,749	800	0	350
Commercial banks and other	323	2,167	5,720	5,770	7,036	11,317	11,526	4,645	4,126	4,134
Memo:										
IBRD	185	915	3,350	2,757	2,779	2,592	2,496	2,438	3,135	2,109
IDA	146	1,461	3,586	4,992	4,154	4,905	4,573	4,340	4,227	4,434
PRINCIPAL REPAYMENTS	**1,034**	**5,423**	**14,610**	**22,250**	**25,738**	**31,232**	**30,067**	**27,481**	**28,397**	**27,752**
Public and publicly guaranteed	**890**	**4,044**	**12,580**	**17,817**	**20,429**	**23,329**	**21,527**	**18,534**	**19,137**	**18,095**
Official creditors	556	1,916	6,690	10,299	12,387	13,568	13,731	11,108	10,037	10,917
Multilateral	96	372	2,976	5,772	5,732	6,830	5,815	4,985	5,202	5,739
Concessional	0	60	558	901	1,046	1,065	1,121	1,215	1,334	1,485
Bilateral	460	1,544	3,715	4,527	6,655	6,738	7,916	6,124	4,836	5,178
Concessional	347	1,124	2,349	3,259	4,779	3,949	5,280	4,468	3,304	3,921
Private creditors	334	2,128	5,890	7,519	8,043	9,762	7,796	7,425	9,100	7,179
Bonds	26	29	405	434	549	1,433	32	352	838	625
Commercial banks	30	792	3,062	3,393	4,201	4,994	4,161	3,823	5,923	4,795
Other private	278	1,307	2,423	3,692	3,292	3,335	3,603	3,251	2,339	1,759
Private nonguaranteed	**143**	**1,379**	**2,030**	**4,433**	**5,308**	**7,903**	**8,541**	**8,947**	**9,260**	**9,656**
Bonds	0	0	0	0	120	225	459	790	2,003	2,435
Commercial banks and other	143	1,379	2,030	4,433	5,188	7,678	8,082	8,157	7,257	7,221
Memo:										
IBRD	91	234	1,762	3,273	3,129	3,384	2,973	2,484	2,549	2,538
IDA	0	26	217	400	478	515	552	633	755	888
NET FLOWS ON DEBT	**2,390**	**13,579**	**15,936**	**11,950**	**9,363**	**12,028**	**14,629**	**10,427**	**-793**	**893**
Public and publicly guaranteed	**2,210**	**12,790**	**12,126**	**9,706**	**5,353**	**4,047**	**6,894**	**13,929**	**4,341**	**6,066**
Official creditors	1,842	7,459	11,918	9,564	5,758	4,840	5,065	8,878	9,321	5,402
Multilateral	258	3,258	7,620	6,591	5,774	5,102	5,914	6,550	6,499	4,493
Concessional	161	2,162	4,637	6,059	5,179	5,963	5,536	5,268	4,884	4,773
Bilateral	1,584	4,201	4,298	2,972	-16	-262	-849	2,328	2,822	909
Concessional	1,518	3,397	4,212	2,438	751	732	-622	2,454	3,232	1,015
Private creditors	368	5,332	209	142	-406	-792	1,829	5,052	-4,980	664
Bonds	-20	69	22	-284	141	-488	1,118	5,305	-838	4,872
Commercial banks	14	3,161	-188	-1,061	-365	-80	1,539	612	-3,471	-3,229
Other private	374	2,102	375	1,487	-182	-225	-828	-865	-671	-979
Private nonguaranteed	**180**	**788**	**3,810**	**2,245**	**4,011**	**7,980**	**7,734**	**-3,502**	**-5,134**	**-5,173**
Bonds	0	0	120	907	2,163	4,341	4,291	10	-2,003	-2,085
Commercial banks and other	180	788	3,690	1,337	1,848	3,639	3,444	-3,512	-3,131	-3,088
Memo:										
IBRD	93	681	1,588	-516	-350	-792	-476	-46	586	-429
IDA	146	1,435	3,369	4,592	3,676	4,391	4,021	3,707	3,471	3,546

LOW-INCOME COUNTRIES

(US$ million, unless otherwise indicated)

	1970	1980	1990	1994	1995	1996	1997	1998	1999	2000
INTEREST PAYMENTS (LINT)	**521**	**4,331**	**12,409**	**13,207**	**14,437**	**14,880**	**14,821**	**15,898**	**13,876**	**14,753**
Public and publicly guaranteed	**479**	**3,493**	**11,334**	**11,556**	**12,366**	**12,562**	**12,256**	**12,352**	**11,854**	**11,458**
Official creditors	369	1,660	6,556	7,693	8,203	8,122	7,454	7,427	7,589	7,347
Multilateral	91	593	3,109	4,367	4,324	4,130	3,779	3,610	3,872	3,843
Concessional	11	103	394	588	640	675	684	702	762	785
Bilateral	278	1,068	3,447	3,326	3,879	3,992	3,675	3,817	3,717	3,504
Concessional	221	783	2,139	2,383	2,399	2,309	2,124	2,091	2,071	1,933
Private creditors	110	1,833	4,778	3,863	4,163	4,440	4,802	4,925	4,265	4,111
Bonds	11	27	256	360	420	894	480	622	982	1,009
Commercial banks	13	1,158	3,107	1,748	2,156	1,978	3,204	3,321	2,368	2,296
Other private	86	649	1,415	1,755	1,586	1,568	1,118	982	915	806
Private nonguaranteed	**43**	**838**	**1,076**	**1,651**	**2,072**	**2,318**	**2,565**	**3,546**	**2,145**	**3,295**
Bonds	0	0	0	112	197	367	721	1,159	1,083	975
Commercial banks and other	43	838	1,076	1,539	1,875	1,951	1,844	2,387	1,062	2,320
Memo:										
IBRD	78	407	2,090	2,567	2,536	2,286	1,959	1,851	1,920	1,902
IDA	10	69	259	357	418	421	431	450	485	503
NET TRANSFERS ON DEBT	**1,868**	**9,247**	**3,527**	**-1,257**	**-5,074**	**-2,853**	**-193**	**-5,471**	**-14,792**	**-13,860**
Public and publicly guaranteed	**1,731**	**9,297**	**793**	**-1,851**	**-7,013**	**-8,515**	**-5,362**	**1,577**	**-7,513**	**-5,392**
Official creditors	1,473	5,798	5,362	1,870	-2,445	-3,283	-2,389	1,450	1,732	-1,945
Multilateral	168	2,665	4,511	2,224	1,450	971	2,136	2,939	2,627	649
Concessional	150	2,059	4,242	5,471	4,539	5,288	4,852	4,566	4,122	3,988
Bilateral	1,306	3,133	850	-354	-3,895	-4,254	-4,525	-1,489	-895	-2,595
Concessional	1,297	2,615	2,073	56	-1,648	-1,577	-2,745	364	1,160	-918
Private creditors	258	3,498	-4,569	-3,721	-4,568	-5,233	-2,973	127	-9,245	-3,447
Bonds	-31	42	-233	-644	-279	-1,382	638	4,683	-1,820	3,863
Commercial banks	1	2,003	-3,295	-2,809	-2,521	-2,058	-1,665	-2,709	-5,839	-5,525
Other private	288	1,453	-1,040	-267	-1,768	-1,793	-1,945	-1,847	-1,586	-1,785
Private nonguaranteed	**137**	**-50**	**2,734**	**594**	**1,939**	**5,663**	**5,169**	**-7,048**	**-7,279**	**-8,468**
Bonds	0	0	120	795	1,966	3,974	3,569	-1,149	-3,086	-3,061
Commercial banks and other	137	-50	2,614	-201	-27	1,688	1,600	-5,899	-4,194	-5,407
Memo:										
IBRD	15	274	-502	-3,082	-2,886	-3,078	-2,435	-1,897	-1,334	-2,331
IDA	135	1,366	3,110	4,235	3,258	3,970	3,590	3,258	2,986	3,043
DEBT SERVICE (LTDS)	**1,555**	**9,754**	**27,019**	**35,457**	**40,175**	**46,113**	**44,888**	**43,379**	**42,272**	**42,504**
Public and publicly guaranteed	**1,369**	**7,537**	**23,914**	**29,373**	**32,795**	**35,892**	**33,783**	**30,886**	**30,991**	**29,553**
Official creditors	925	3,576	13,246	17,992	20,590	21,690	21,184	18,536	17,626	18,263
Multilateral	187	964	6,084	10,139	10,056	10,960	9,594	8,595	9,073	9,582
Concessional	11	163	952	1,489	1,686	1,739	1,804	1,917	2,096	2,271
Bilateral	738	2,612	7,162	7,853	10,534	10,730	11,591	9,941	8,553	8,681
Concessional	568	1,906	4,488	5,642	7,178	6,258	7,404	6,559	5,375	5,854
Private creditors	444	3,961	10,667	11,382	12,205	14,202	12,598	12,351	13,365	11,290
Bonds	37	55	660	794	969	2,327	512	974	1,820	1,634
Commercial banks	43	1,949	6,169	5,141	6,358	6,972	7,365	7,144	8,291	7,091
Other private	364	1,956	3,838	5,447	4,879	4,904	4,720	4,233	3,254	2,565
Private nonguaranteed	**186**	**2,217**	**3,106**	**6,083**	**7,380**	**10,221**	**11,106**	**12,493**	**11,405**	**12,951**
Bonds	0	0	0	112	317	592	1,180	1,949	3,086	3,411
Commercial banks and other	186	2,217	3,106	5,971	7,063	9,629	9,926	10,544	8,319	9,541
Memo:										
IBRD	169	641	3,852	5,839	5,665	5,670	4,931	4,335	4,469	4,441
IDA	11	95	476	757	895	936	983	1,082	1,241	1,391
UNDISBURSED DEBT	**6,967**	**47,089**	**97,634**	**96,786**	**98,223**	**92,026**	**85,707**	**78,114**	**69,125**	**55,543**
Official creditors	6,090	36,582	84,093	84,787	86,067	81,669	76,262	72,163	65,220	52,771
Private creditors	877	10,506	13,541	11,999	12,156	10,358	9,445	5,951	3,906	2,771
Memorandum items										
Concessional LDOD	15,204	56,938	182,321	227,932	230,674	221,148	198,938	214,654	227,515	220,962
Variable rate LDOD	920	18,563	71,836	107,490	118,594	123,457	136,707	154,219	146,542	134,870
Public sector LDOD	20,287	89,800	330,849	398,219	401,437	385,416	371,731	405,147	408,572	399,618
Private sector LDOD	1,370	8,561	17,526	39,114	48,761	53,796	64,271	86,413	78,878	71,369

6. CURRENCY COMPOSITION OF LONG-TERM DEBT (PERCENT)

	1970	1980	1990	1994	1995	1996	1997	1998	1999	2000
Deutsche mark	8.0	7.2	5.4	5.2	5.3	4.9	4.5	4.7	4.0	3.1
French franc	5.5	7.0	6.5	5.9	6.2	6.0	5.3	5.1	4.3	3.6
Japanese yen	4.3	9.1	10.9	14.8	13.6	12.8	12.0	13.1	15.4	13.5
Pound sterling	18.2	8.7	4.0	2.8	2.7	2.9	3.0	2.7	2.6	1.8
Swiss franc	0.4	0.9	1.1	1.0	1.0	0.9	0.9	0.8	0.7	0.6
U.S.dollars	37.4	37.7	37.7	35.9	36.4	38.3	43.3	46.5	48.1	55.5
Multiple currency	8.1	8.1	12.8	14.9	15.0	14.3	13.7	10.4	10.3	9.6
Special drawing rights	0.0	0.0	0.6	0.7	0.8	0.9	1.0	1.0	1.0	1.0
All other currencies	18.1	16.5	18.5	15.6	15.5	15.3	12.6	12.0	9.6	7.3

LOW-INCOME COUNTRIES

(US$ million, unless otherwise indicated)

	1970	1980	1990	1994	1995	1996	1997	1998	1999	2000
7. DEBT RESTRUCTURINGS										
Total amount rescheduled	0	1,202	6,254	5,821	5,802	6,107	9,023	7,309	14,868	28,227
Debt stock rescheduled	0	0	91	201	142	1,366	1,042	3,429	6,565	1,933
Principal rescheduled	0	269	3,879	2,339	2,947	3,042	2,989	1,635	4,864	16,417
Official	0	120	2,762	1,425	2,319	1,944	1,950	1,272	3,314	13,252
Private	0	149	1,117	913	628	1,099	1,039	363	1,549	3,165
Interest rescheduled	..	..	1,676	1,752	1,026	1,124	2,559	532	1,788	9,135
Official	0	31	1,378	1,444	872	895	1,283	485	1,639	8,530
Private	0	31	298	307	154	230	1,275	48	149	605
Debt forgiven	3	201	1,575	3,269	1,769	4,103	3,099	338	4,673	489
Memo: interest forgiven	0	0	87	429	947	1,084	607	581	502	1,922
Debt stock reduction	0	0	1,262	468	1,559	4,460	5,177	346	858	9,148
of which debt buyback	0	0	0	8	119	301	200	102	325	137
8. DEBT STOCK-FLOW RECONCILIATION										
Total change in debt stocks	..	..	47,712	47,327	24,294	-3,712	-6,224	36,186	-2,772	-23,462
Net flows on debt	2,200	19,281	23,696	12,269	19,316	21,121	19,514	2,578	18	467
Net change in interest arrears	..	..	3,035	2,936	1,693	-1,246	-3,600	2,575	2,941	-5,542
Interest capitalized	..	..	1,676	1,752	1,026	1,124	2,559	532	1,788	9,135
Debt forgiveness or reduction	..	..	-2,838	-3,730	-3,209	-8,262	-8,077	-582	-5,206	-9,501
Cross-currency valuation	..	..	14,272	14,593	-8,446	-27,574	-28,612	4,071	-2,423	-17,991
Residual	..	..	7,871	19,507	13,914	11,124	11,993	27,011	111	-32
9. AVERAGE TERMS OF NEW COMMITMENTS										
ALL CREDITORS										
Interest (%)	3.0	6.3	4.8	4.0	4.3	4.3	4.4	4.0	3.1	4.8
Maturity (years)	28.9	22.9	26.5	24.3	24.2	23.8	22.6	20.4	23.8	20.2
Grace period (years)	9.7	6.0	6.9	6.9	6.5	6.7	5.9	6.2	6.4	6.6
Grant element (%)	47.7	24.2	35.8	40.3	37.2	36.3	33.4	40.4	49.3	37.0
Official creditors										
Interest (%)	2.1	3.5	4.0	3.5	3.6	3.7	3.3	3.3	2.7	3.2
Maturity (years)	33.8	30.9	30.5	27.3	28.3	29.3	31.4	26.2	26.0	29.7
Grace period (years)	11.8	7.7	7.5	7.7	7.5	7.7	7.7	7.2	7.0	7.8
Grant element (%)	56.9	39.4	42.4	45.5	43.9	44.0	45.2	50.1	53.9	54.8
Private creditors										
Interest (%)	6.4	10.8	7.2	6.3	6.7	6.1	6.3	5.7	5.6	7.4
Maturity (years)	10.3	10.0	14.1	10.4	9.5	8.6	7.7	6.5	9.4	5.5
Grace period (years)	1.9	3.3	5.2	3.2	3.1	4.0	2.9	3.9	2.5	4.8
Grant element (%)	12.9	-0.3	15.6	15.9	13.4	15.5	13.5	17.3	19.4	9.2
Memorandum items										
Commitments	4,502	26,497	31,499	28,008	30,274	31,038	27,185	32,074	17,363	17,604
Official creditors	3,561	16,364	23,733	23,064	23,644	22,703	17,068	22,589	15,042	10,744
Private creditors	942	10,133	7,767	4,944	6,630	8,336	10,117	9,485	2,321	6,860

10. GRAPH OF AGGREGATE NET RESOURCE FLOWS

(current prices, US$ billion)

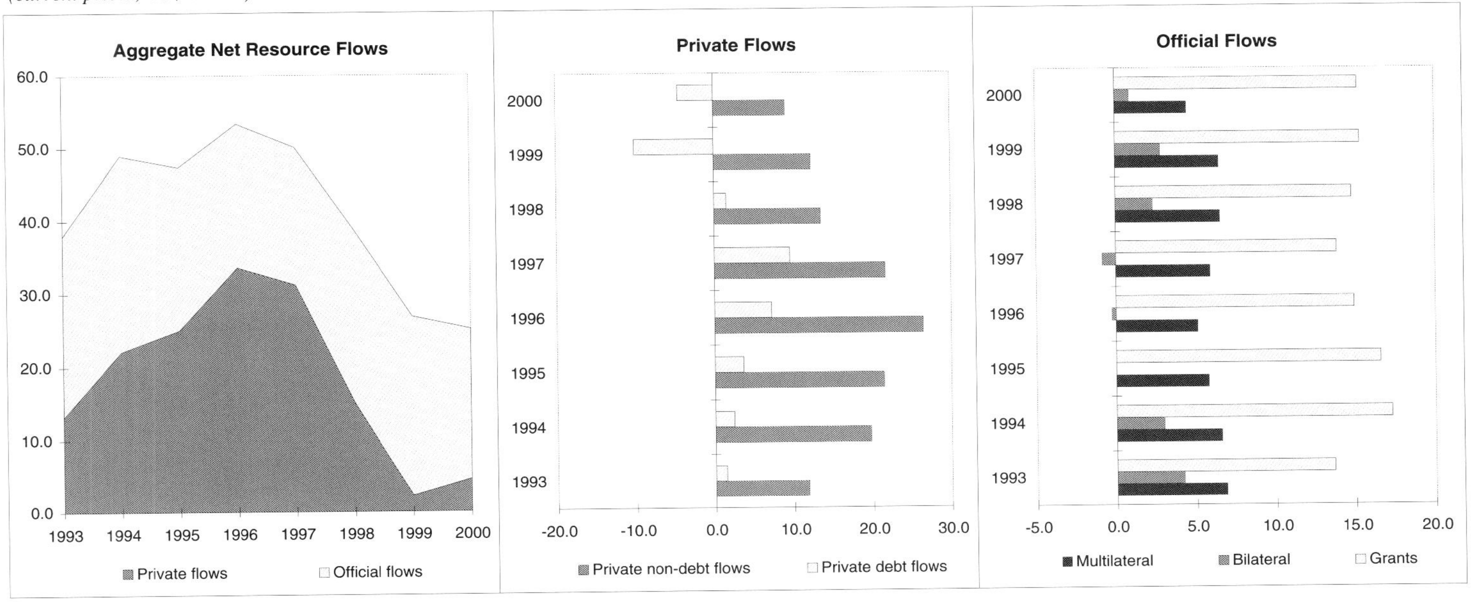

MIDDLE-INCOME COUNTRIES

(US$ million, unless otherwise indicated)

1. SUMMARY DEBT DATA

	1970	1980	1990	1994	1995	1996	1997	1998	1999	2000
TOTAL DEBT STOCKS (EDT)	**49,248**	**484,243**	**1,039,801**	**1,442,048**	**1,604,053**	**1,695,005**	**1,788,699**	**1,970,170**	**1,991,774**	**1,941,427**
Long-term debt (LDOD)	**40,970**	**348,730**	**822,006**	**1,116,140**	**1,206,735**	**1,270,453**	**1,350,901**	**1,552,967**	**1,605,484**	**1,576,620**
Public and publicly guaranteed	26,467	286,198	773,507	963,009	1,017,234	1,022,911	1,025,177	1,095,145	1,119,663	1,077,611
Private nonguaranteed	14,502	62,532	48,498	153,132	189,501	247,542	325,724	457,822	485,821	499,009
Use of IMF credit	**438**	**6,967**	**23,401**	**29,412**	**45,794**	**45,149**	**54,023**	**70,203**	**54,101**	**40,683**
Short-term debt	..	**128,546**	**194,395**	**296,496**	**351,523**	**379,403**	**383,776**	**347,000**	**332,180**	**324,125**
of which interest arrears on LDOD	..	751	39,797	20,225	19,053	14,864	9,462	12,939	14,125	12,719
Official creditors	..	416	11,008	5,933	6,391	6,354	6,345	8,485	9,628	10,330
Private creditors	..	335	28,788	14,292	12,663	8,511	3,117	4,454	4,497	2,389
Memo: principal arrears on LDOD	..	783	35,961	41,186	48,447	44,522	25,301	25,818	27,963	28,577
Official creditors	..	199	13,762	11,509	16,626	17,210	17,385	17,956	21,367	22,373
Private creditors	..	584	22,199	29,678	31,821	27,312	7,916	7,862	6,596	6,205
Memo: export credits	..	4,233	227,029	303,973	288,423	286,691	282,834	171,062	160,338	142,549
TOTAL DEBT FLOWS										
Disbursements	**9,956**	**92,040**	**103,630**	**149,459**	**201,401**	**230,661**	**279,681**	**286,982**	**254,822**	**244,005**
Long-term debt	9,690	88,807	97,859	143,107	178,494	224,215	261,024	265,365	243,792	236,042
IMF purchases	265	3,233	5,771	6,352	22,907	6,446	18,657	21,617	11,030	7,963
Principal repayments	**5,480**	**38,379**	**76,699**	**95,628**	**110,053**	**143,046**	**170,197**	**169,232**	**245,515**	**242,070**
Long-term debt	5,045	37,087	70,703	90,553	103,320	137,456	163,431	160,938	220,207	223,301
IMF repurchases	435	1,292	5,996	5,075	6,733	5,590	6,766	8,294	25,307	18,770
Net flows on debt	**4,476**	**83,141**	**35,968**	**91,717**	**151,066**	**121,481**	**119,259**	**94,097**	**-11,807**	**-1,301**
of which short-term debt	..	29,480	9,037	37,885	59,718	33,866	9,775	-23,653	-21,114	-3,235
Interest payments (INT)	..	**42,843**	**54,913**	**61,912**	**83,157**	**88,783**	**94,946**	**99,920**	**105,452**	**109,034**
Long-term debt	1,844	28,460	42,136	47,056	62,757	66,166	72,866	79,119	85,659	89,549
IMF charges	0	319	1,989	1,392	1,970	1,958	1,895	2,953	2,928	2,381
Short-term debt	..	14,064	10,788	13,463	18,430	20,659	20,185	17,848	16,866	17,104
Net transfers on debt	..	**40,298**	**-18,945**	**29,805**	**67,908**	**32,698**	**24,314**	**-5,823**	**-117,259**	**-110,335**
Total debt service paid (TDS)	..	**81,222**	**131,612**	**157,539**	**193,210**	**231,829**	**265,143**	**269,152**	**350,967**	**351,104**
Long-term debt	6,889	65,547	112,838	137,609	166,077	203,622	236,297	240,057	305,866	312,850
IMF repurchases and charges	435	1,611	7,986	6,467	8,703	7,548	8,661	11,247	28,235	21,150
Short-term debt (interest only)	..	14,064	10,788	13,463	18,430	20,659	20,185	17,848	16,866	17,104

2. AGGREGATE NET RESOURCE FLOWS AND NET TRANSFERS (LONG-TERM)

	1970	1980	1990	1994	1995	1996	1997	1998	1999	2000
NET RESOURCE FLOWS	**7,508**	**61,855**	**64,662**	**173,466**	**212,822**	**253,216**	**291,296**	**297,875**	**244,996**	**235,959**
Net flow of long-term debt (ex. IMF)	4,645	51,719	27,157	52,554	75,174	86,759	97,594	104,427	23,585	12,741
Foreign direct investment (net)	1,937	4,153	21,918	81,019	92,993	113,212	153,501	165,353	174,633	160,129
Portfolio equity flows	-2	0	2,343	24,438	28,443	40,083	27,423	14,918	31,839	48,340
Grants (excluding technical coop.)	928	5,983	13,244	15,455	16,212	13,163	12,778	13,177	14,939	14,750
Memo: technical coop. grants	721	2,511	6,770	9,540	11,984	10,753	8,926	9,788	10,127	8,829
official net resource flows	2,523	20,395	28,725	19,214	31,728	10,578	21,851	29,731	22,727	14,695
private net resource flows	4,985	41,460	35,937	154,252	181,094	242,638	269,446	268,144	222,269	221,265
NET TRANSFERS	**1,262**	**16,515**	**11,100**	**105,504**	**127,784**	**161,847**	**191,582**	**188,118**	**124,744**	**106,564**
Interest on long-term debt	1,844	28,460	42,136	47,056	62,757	66,166	72,866	79,119	85,659	89,549
Profit remittances on FDI	4,403	16,880	11,427	20,906	22,280	25,203	26,849	30,638	34,593	39,846
Memo: official net transfers	2,019	15,931	15,181	1,778	9,696	-12,047	950	9,278	1,692	-6,826
private net transfers	-757	584	-4,081	103,726	118,088	173,894	190,631	178,840	123,053	113,390

3. MAJOR ECONOMIC AGGREGATES

	1970	1980	1990	1994	1995	1996	1997	1998	1999	2000
Gross national income (GNI)	504,270	2,316,315	3,428,265	4,139,450	4,697,574	5,191,456	5,406,048	5,073,642	4,892,645	5,346,183
Exports of goods & services (XGS)	..	566,826	766,904	1,063,812	1,310,802	1,446,394	1,566,440	1,489,349	1,565,285	1,895,876
of which workers remittances	..	8,756	18,437	25,261	26,797	28,285	32,903	31,041	31,976	34,159
Imports of goods & services (MGS)	..	544,927	764,699	1,133,061	1,391,749	1,532,239	1,637,926	1,539,251	1,552,373	1,843,148
International reserves (RES)	..	175,352	196,939	373,151	480,722	559,663	583,417	627,472	675,510	733,715
Current account balance	..	1,625	-2,939	-70,123	-80,927	-87,424	-74,286	-42,942	21,003	42,582

4. DEBT INDICATORS

	1970	1980	1990	1994	1995	1996	1997	1998	1999	2000
EDT / XGS (%)	..	85.4	135.6	135.6	122.4	117.2	114.2	132.3	127.3	102.4
EDT / GNI (%)	..	20.9	30.3	34.8	34.2	32.7	33.1	38.8	40.7	36.3
TDS / XGS (%)	..	14.3	17.2	14.8	14.7	16.0	16.9	18.1	22.4	18.5
INT / XGS (%)	..	7.6	7.2	5.8	6.3	6.1	6.1	6.7	6.7	5.8
INT / GNI (%)	..	1.9	1.6	1.5	1.8	1.7	1.8	2.0	2.2	2.0
RES / EDT (%)	..	36.2	18.9	25.9	30.0	33.0	32.6	31.9	33.9	37.8
RES / MGS (months)	..	3.9	3.1	4.0	4.1	4.4	4.3	4.9	5.2	4.8
Short-term / EDT (%)	..	26.6	18.7	20.6	21.9	22.4	21.5	17.6	16.7	16.7
Concessional / EDT (%)	..	11.1	12.6	12.3	11.6	11.0	9.8	8.3	8.6	8.3
Multilateral / EDT (%)	..	6.1	11.1	10.1	9.7	9.0	8.8	9.4	9.9	10.2

MIDDLE-INCOME COUNTRIES

(US$ million, unless otherwise indicated)

	1970	1980	1990	1994	1995	1996	1997	1998	1999	2000
5. LONG-TERM DEBT										
DEBT OUTSTANDING (LDOD)	**40,970**	**348,730**	**822,006**	**1,116,140**	**1,206,735**	**1,270,453**	**1,350,901**	**1,552,967**	**1,605,484**	**1,576,620**
Public and publicly guaranteed	**26,467**	**286,198**	**773,507**	**963,009**	**1,017,234**	**1,022,911**	**1,025,177**	**1,095,145**	**1,119,663**	**1,077,611**
Official creditors	15,469	108,051	342,079	494,133	521,552	500,679	481,569	507,728	520,750	506,680
Multilateral	4,264	29,446	115,573	145,064	155,071	152,860	157,969	185,450	196,865	198,892
Concessional	479	5,178	14,980	22,379	24,721	26,163	26,838	29,345	31,161	30,888
Bilateral	11,205	78,605	226,506	349,069	366,481	347,820	323,600	322,277	323,885	307,787
Concessional	9,022	48,610	116,463	154,582	161,562	159,437	148,890	134,379	140,589	130,634
Private creditors	10,999	178,147	431,429	468,876	495,682	522,232	543,608	587,417	598,922	570,932
Bonds	1,458	12,253	103,694	227,971	248,957	286,794	298,298	330,410	352,220	372,768
Commercial banks	3,449	115,315	215,420	134,226	141,641	137,408	166,076	190,466	185,730	140,535
Other private	6,093	50,579	112,315	106,679	105,085	98,030	79,233	66,542	60,973	57,628
Private nonguaranteed	**14,502**	**62,532**	**48,498**	**153,132**	**189,501**	**247,542**	**325,724**	**457,822**	**485,821**	**499,009**
Bonds	0	0	717	53,921	57,072	75,637	93,310	103,066	111,821	115,066
Commercial banks and other	14,502	62,532	47,782	99,211	132,429	171,905	232,415	354,757	374,001	383,943
Memo:										
IBRD	2,973	17,384	67,456	76,019	80,220	76,898	78,321	87,424	90,686	92,548
IDA	261	1,424	6,490	10,860	12,315	13,278	13,888	15,484	16,176	16,074
DISBURSEMENTS	**9,690**	**88,807**	**97,859**	**143,107**	**178,494**	**224,215**	**261,024**	**265,365**	**243,792**	**236,042**
Public and publicly guaranteed	**5,856**	**69,520**	**84,845**	**88,957**	**118,968**	**136,329**	**151,595**	**145,585**	**133,353**	**119,422**
Official creditors	2,594	19,751	34,308	30,184	48,146	37,565	47,143	48,977	43,275	37,849
Multilateral	852	5,692	16,941	17,041	20,851	21,751	29,274	34,898	26,299	23,395
Concessional	95	615	1,632	2,147	2,570	2,946	2,544	2,433	2,563	1,823
Bilateral	1,742	14,059	17,366	13,143	27,295	15,814	17,868	14,079	16,975	14,454
Concessional	1,158	6,736	8,764	7,156	8,548	7,017	5,634	6,593	9,813	8,797
Private creditors	3,262	49,770	50,537	58,773	70,822	98,764	104,452	96,608	90,078	81,573
Bonds	143	1,584	5,713	23,976	29,171	57,520	60,426	52,298	53,446	49,943
Commercial banks	1,350	30,095	15,052	15,780	23,145	24,135	27,424	32,249	24,349	21,630
Other private	1,769	18,092	29,772	19,017	18,506	17,109	16,601	12,062	12,284	10,001
Private nonguaranteed	**3,834**	**19,287**	**13,015**	**54,150**	**59,525**	**87,886**	**109,430**	**119,780**	**110,439**	**116,621**
Bonds	0	0	581	23,267	16,841	28,057	30,794	19,803	15,136	19,087
Commercial banks and other	3,834	19,287	12,434	30,883	42,685	59,830	78,636	99,978	95,303	97,533
Memo:										
IBRD	494	3,562	10,232	8,821	10,456	10,765	15,160	15,077	12,006	11,339
IDA	28	126	760	1,060	1,322	1,410	1,364	1,216	1,170	785
PRINCIPAL REPAYMENTS	**5,045**	**37,087**	**70,703**	**90,553**	**103,320**	**137,456**	**163,431**	**160,938**	**220,207**	**223,301**
Public and publicly guaranteed	**2,734**	**26,715**	**63,360**	**65,659**	**77,246**	**99,224**	**108,265**	**93,207**	**113,476**	**123,030**
Official creditors	999	5,338	18,827	26,425	32,630	40,149	38,070	32,423	35,487	37,903
Multilateral	290	1,296	9,564	13,400	15,564	14,159	13,981	13,729	14,065	17,362
Concessional	29	44	341	493	531	686	684	717	723	788
Bilateral	709	4,042	9,263	13,025	17,066	25,990	24,089	18,695	21,422	20,542
Concessional	324	1,431	3,477	3,840	4,292	5,262	5,199	6,102	6,450	7,474
Private creditors	1,735	21,377	44,533	39,234	44,617	59,075	70,195	60,784	77,989	85,126
Bonds	117	485	5,232	6,726	12,445	20,335	35,133	24,413	24,869	40,184
Commercial banks	655	12,964	20,434	15,715	15,544	23,932	22,174	21,810	40,980	33,402
Other private	963	7,928	18,867	16,793	16,627	14,809	12,888	14,561	12,140	11,540
Private nonguaranteed	**2,311**	**10,372**	**7,343**	**24,894**	**26,074**	**38,232**	**55,166**	**67,731**	**106,731**	**100,271**
Bonds	0	0	0	2,997	5,212	6,809	11,891	12,088	11,400	14,755
Commercial banks and other	2,311	10,372	7,343	21,897	20,862	31,423	43,275	55,643	95,332	85,516
Memo:										
IBRD	157	829	6,719	8,608	9,001	8,611	7,969	8,228	7,501	7,516
IDA	0	5	33	58	68	78	98	109	132	156
NET FLOWS ON DEBT	**4,645**	**51,719**	**27,157**	**52,554**	**75,174**	**86,759**	**97,594**	**104,427**	**23,585**	**12,741**
Public and publicly guaranteed	**3,122**	**42,805**	**21,485**	**23,298**	**41,722**	**37,104**	**43,329**	**52,378**	**19,877**	**-3,608**
Official creditors	1,595	14,412	15,481	3,759	15,516	-2,585	9,072	16,554	7,788	-55
Multilateral	562	4,395	7,377	3,641	5,286	7,592	15,293	21,169	12,234	6,033
Concessional	66	570	1,291	1,653	2,039	2,261	1,860	1,715	1,840	1,036
Bilateral	1,033	10,017	8,104	119	10,230	-10,176	-6,221	-4,615	-4,447	-6,088
Concessional	834	5,305	5,287	3,316	4,256	1,755	434	491	3,363	1,324
Private creditors	1,527	28,393	6,004	19,539	26,206	39,689	34,257	35,824	12,089	-3,553
Bonds	26	1,099	481	17,250	16,726	37,186	25,293	27,885	28,576	9,759
Commercial banks	695	17,130	-5,382	65	7,601	203	5,250	10,438	-16,631	-11,773
Other private	806	10,164	10,905	2,224	1,879	2,300	3,713	-2,499	144	-1,540
Private nonguaranteed	**1,523**	**8,914**	**5,672**	**29,256**	**33,452**	**49,654**	**54,264**	**52,049**	**3,708**	**16,350**
Bonds	0	0	581	20,270	11,629	21,248	18,903	7,715	3,737	4,333
Commercial banks and other	1,523	8,914	5,091	8,986	21,823	28,406	35,361	44,334	-29	12,017
Memo:										
IBRD	337	2,733	3,513	213	1,455	2,155	7,191	6,849	4,505	3,823
IDA	28	121	726	1,001	1,254	1,332	1,266	1,107	1,038	629

MIDDLE-INCOME COUNTRIES

(US$ million, unless otherwise indicated)

	1970	1980	1990	1994	1995	1996	1997	1998	1999	2000
INTEREST PAYMENTS (LINT)	**1,844**	**28,460**	**42,136**	**47,056**	**62,757**	**66,166**	**72,866**	**79,119**	**85,659**	**89,549**
Public and publicly guaranteed	**1,129**	**22,269**	**38,124**	**39,227**	**51,401**	**52,320**	**53,414**	**54,906**	**59,073**	**61,879**
Official creditors	504	4,464	13,544	17,436	22,032	22,625	20,901	20,453	21,035	21,521
Multilateral	218	1,958	7,698	9,204	9,641	9,630	9,062	9,647	11,698	12,160
Concessional	9	63	234	337	371	390	406	428	443	454
Bilateral	286	2,507	5,845	8,232	12,390	12,995	11,838	10,806	9,337	9,361
Concessional	176	1,055	2,180	3,384	3,880	3,837	3,322	3,424	3,602	3,381
Private creditors	625	17,805	24,581	21,791	29,370	29,695	32,513	34,453	38,038	40,358
Bonds	86	923	4,332	10,802	16,494	15,882	19,142	20,776	24,170	27,615
Commercial banks	240	13,273	14,701	5,924	7,184	8,678	8,448	9,189	10,024	9,189
Other private	299	3,608	5,548	5,065	5,692	5,135	4,922	4,488	3,844	3,554
Private nonguaranteed	**715**	**6,191**	**4,012**	**7,829**	**11,356**	**13,846**	**19,452**	**24,213**	**26,586**	**27,671**
Bonds	0	0	8	2,811	4,241	5,097	6,710	7,357	6,451	7,338
Commercial banks and other	715	6,191	4,004	5,019	7,115	8,749	12,743	16,856	20,134	20,333
Memo:										
IBRD	165	1,407	5,037	5,434	5,601	5,520	4,934	5,178	5,805	6,347
IDA	2	10	44	74	87	91	101	104	115	119
NET TRANSFERS ON DEBT	**2,801**	**23,259**	**-14,979**	**5,498**	**12,417**	**20,593**	**24,728**	**25,308**	**-62,074**	**-76,808**
Public and publicly guaranteed	**1,993**	**20,536**	**-16,639**	**-15,929**	**-9,679**	**-15,216**	**-10,084**	**-2,528**	**-39,196**	**-65,487**
Official creditors	1,091	9,948	1,937	-13,677	-6,515	-25,209	-11,828	-3,899	-13,248	-21,576
Multilateral	344	2,438	-321	-5,563	-4,355	-2,038	6,231	11,522	536	-6,126
Concessional	57	507	1,056	1,317	1,668	1,871	1,454	1,287	1,397	582
Bilateral	747	7,510	2,258	-8,114	-2,161	-23,171	-18,059	-15,421	-13,784	-15,449
Concessional	658	4,250	3,108	-68	377	-2,081	-2,887	-2,933	-239	-2,057
Private creditors	902	10,588	-18,577	-2,252	-3,164	9,994	1,744	1,371	-25,949	-43,911
Bonds	-60	176	-3,851	6,448	232	21,303	6,151	7,109	4,407	-17,856
Commercial banks	455	3,857	-20,083	-5,858	417	-8,475	-3,198	1,249	-26,656	-20,962
Other private	507	6,556	5,357	-2,841	-3,813	-2,835	-1,209	-6,987	-3,700	-5,094
Private nonguaranteed	**808**	**2,724**	**1,660**	**21,427**	**22,096**	**35,809**	**34,812**	**27,836**	**-22,878**	**-11,321**
Bonds	0	0	573	17,460	7,388	16,151	12,194	358	-2,715	-3,005
Commercial banks and other	808	2,724	1,087	3,967	14,707	19,658	22,618	27,478	-20,163	-8,316
Memo:										
IBRD	172	1,327	-1,525	-5,221	-4,147	-3,366	2,257	1,672	-1,299	-2,524
IDA	26	111	683	927	1,168	1,241	1,165	1,003	923	510
DEBT SERVICE (LTDS)	**6,889**	**65,547**	**112,838**	**137,609**	**166,077**	**203,622**	**236,297**	**240,057**	**305,866**	**312,850**
Public and publicly guaranteed	**3,863**	**48,984**	**101,484**	**104,886**	**128,647**	**151,545**	**161,679**	**148,113**	**172,549**	**184,909**
Official creditors	1,503	9,803	32,370	43,861	54,661	62,774	58,971	52,876	56,522	59,424
Multilateral	508	3,254	17,262	22,604	25,205	23,789	23,044	23,375	25,763	29,521
Concessional	39	108	575	830	902	1,076	1,090	1,146	1,166	1,242
Bilateral	995	6,549	15,108	21,257	29,456	38,985	35,927	29,501	30,759	29,903
Concessional	499	2,486	5,656	7,223	8,172	9,099	8,521	9,527	10,052	10,854
Private creditors	2,360	39,182	69,114	61,025	73,986	88,770	102,708	95,237	116,027	125,484
Bonds	203	1,408	9,564	17,528	28,939	36,217	54,275	45,189	49,039	67,799
Commercial banks	895	26,238	35,135	21,639	22,728	32,610	30,622	30,999	51,005	42,591
Other private	1,262	11,536	24,415	21,858	22,319	19,944	17,810	19,048	15,984	15,095
Private nonguaranteed	**3,026**	**16,563**	**11,354**	**32,723**	**37,430**	**52,078**	**74,618**	**91,944**	**133,317**	**127,941**
Bonds	0	0	8	5,807	9,453	11,906	18,600	19,445	17,851	22,093
Commercial banks and other	3,026	16,563	11,347	26,916	27,977	40,172	56,018	72,500	115,466	105,849
Memo:										
IBRD	322	2,235	11,757	14,042	14,602	14,131	12,903	13,405	13,306	13,863
IDA	2	16	77	133	155	169	199	213	247	275
UNDISBURSED DEBT	**10,510**	**95,110**	**117,999**	**160,000**	**160,434**	**153,851**	**152,142**	**181,806**	**232,132**	**156,553**
Official creditors	7,411	54,788	78,675	116,579	119,828	110,244	109,247	136,281	192,572	121,053
Private creditors	3,100	40,321	39,324	43,421	40,606	43,607	42,896	45,525	39,560	35,500
Memorandum items										
Concessional LDOD	9,501	53,788	131,443	176,961	186,283	185,600	175,728	163,725	171,750	161,522
Variable rate LDOD	15,240	172,920	369,609	527,713	590,955	639,000	728,733	891,111	902,802	845,091
Public sector LDOD	24,682	251,233	717,731	904,953	958,568	963,379	964,345	1,020,451	1,039,270	1,007,684
Private sector LDOD	16,268	75,444	56,129	157,521	194,241	253,039	329,079	532,336	565,831	568,656

6. CURRENCY COMPOSITION OF LONG-TERM DEBT (PERCENT)

	1970	1980	1990	1994	1995	1996	1997	1998	1999	2000
Deutsche mark	9.0	6.4	10.1	8.9	9.4	9.7	8.7	9.0	7.1	6.2
French franc	4.9	4.9	5.3	4.2	4.3	4.0	3.3	3.2	2.5	2.4
Japanese yen	0.7	6.1	10.3	12.3	12.4	11.2	9.9	10.1	11.2	10.5
Pound sterling	5.1	1.7	1.5	1.0	0.9	0.9	1.0	0.9	0.8	0.6
Swiss franc	1.6	1.8	2.2	1.0	1.0	0.8	0.5	0.4	0.3	0.3
U.S.dollars	55.2	53.7	42.8	48.5	48.8	51.3	56.4	60.3	60.3	61.7
Multiple currency	14.2	11.8	15.5	13.4	13.0	12.2	10.5	6.9	6.7	6.1
Special drawing rights	0.0	0.0	0.1	0.1	0.1	0.1	0.1	0.1	0.1	0.1
All other currencies	9.4	5.8	6.0	5.0	5.0	4.7	4.1	4.5	5.5	6.6

MIDDLE-INCOME COUNTRIES

(US$ million, unless otherwise indicated)

	1970	*1980*	*1990*	*1994*	*1995*	*1996*	*1997*	*1998*	*1999*	*2000*
7. DEBT RESTRUCTURINGS										
Total amount rescheduled	117	2,123	73,074	85,420	25,519	27,634	40,076	33,064	16,105	32,535
Debt stock rescheduled	0	1	61,758	53,849	6,758	5,530	284	28,566	1,023	21,201
Principal rescheduled	0	124	6,398	13,296	12,424	12,789	32,361	4,878	8,392	4,574
Official	0	17	3,064	3,046	4,679	4,431	4,896	3,324	6,462	4,008
Private	0	107	3,334	10,250	7,745	8,359	27,465	1,554	1,930	567
Interest rescheduled	..	..	4,122	14,834	4,198	6,087	6,480	1,068	5,399	4,873
Official	0	7	3,199	1,888	1,409	1,169	1,179	735	4,894	2,675
Private	0	1	923	12,947	2,788	4,918	5,301	333	505	2,199
Debt forgiven	7	79	11,053	4,433	494	1,895	250	252	251	238
Memo: interest forgiven	0	0	2,803	267	15	786	15	14	13	6
Debt stock reduction	0	0	24,883	12,798	2,661	5,447	13,646	3,557	7,001	32,393
of which debt buyback	0	0	4,360	1,702	43	3,363	9,850	2,906	5,082	16,879
8. DEBT STOCK-FLOW RECONCILIATION										
Total change in debt stocks	..	..	55,722	143,580	162,004	90,952	93,695	181,471	21,604	-50,347
Net flows on debt	4,476	83,141	35,968	91,717	151,066	121,481	119,259	94,097	-11,807	-1,301
Net change in interest arrears	..	..	12,513	-5,678	-1,171	-4,189	-5,403	3,477	1,185	-1,406
Interest capitalized	..	..	4,122	14,834	4,198	6,087	6,480	1,068	5,399	4,873
Debt forgiveness or reduction	..	..	-31,576	-15,529	-3,112	-3,978	-4,046	-903	-2,169	-15,753
Cross-currency valuation	..	..	33,133	34,408	10,157	-41,348	-50,407	26,923	-13,464	-32,906
Residual	..	..	1,562	23,829	867	12,899	27,810	56,808	42,459	-3,856
9. AVERAGE TERMS OF NEW COMMITMENTS										
ALL CREDITORS										
Interest (%)	6.2	10.3	7.7	6.1	6.5	6.8	6.9	7.5	6.6	7.8
Maturity (years)	16.3	13.8	14.6	13.1	11.4	11.0	12.7	10.4	13.7	12.5
Grace period (years)	4.5	4.3	5.3	4.7	3.8	5.2	6.5	5.4	5.5	7.9
Grant element (%)	22.8	1.6	13.8	20.3	16.6	14.6	14.9	11.4	17.0	9.4
Official creditors										
Interest (%)	5.0	6.7	6.4	5.7	6.7	5.5	6.0	7.0	4.3	6.1
Maturity (years)	23.1	21.3	19.4	18.9	16.2	18.1	17.2	12.1	16.3	18.5
Grace period (years)	6.4	5.4	6.0	5.5	3.7	3.9	4.9	3.6	4.6	5.2
Grant element (%)	34.1	23.2	24.6	27.5	20.6	27.7	23.6	17.0	32.0	25.1
Private creditors										
Interest (%)	7.4	12.2	8.7	6.3	6.4	7.3	7.4	7.9	8.2	8.3
Maturity (years)	9.6	9.7	11.1	9.0	7.3	8.4	10.3	9.2	11.9	10.6
Grace period (years)	2.7	3.7	4.8	4.1	4.0	5.6	7.3	6.6	6.1	8.8
Grant element (%)	11.8	-10.3	5.7	15.1	13.2	9.8	10.4	7.6	6.6	4.5
Memorandum items										
Commitments	7,552	72,076	92,022	92,864	123,710	140,681	162,876	162,575	135,006	107,320
Official creditors	3,742	25,474	39,462	38,870	57,061	37,898	55,986	65,813	54,953	25,865
Private creditors	3,809	46,602	52,560	53,993	66,650	102,783	106,891	96,808	80,053	81,455

10. GRAPH OF AGGREGATE NET RESOURCE FLOWS

(current prices, US$ billion)

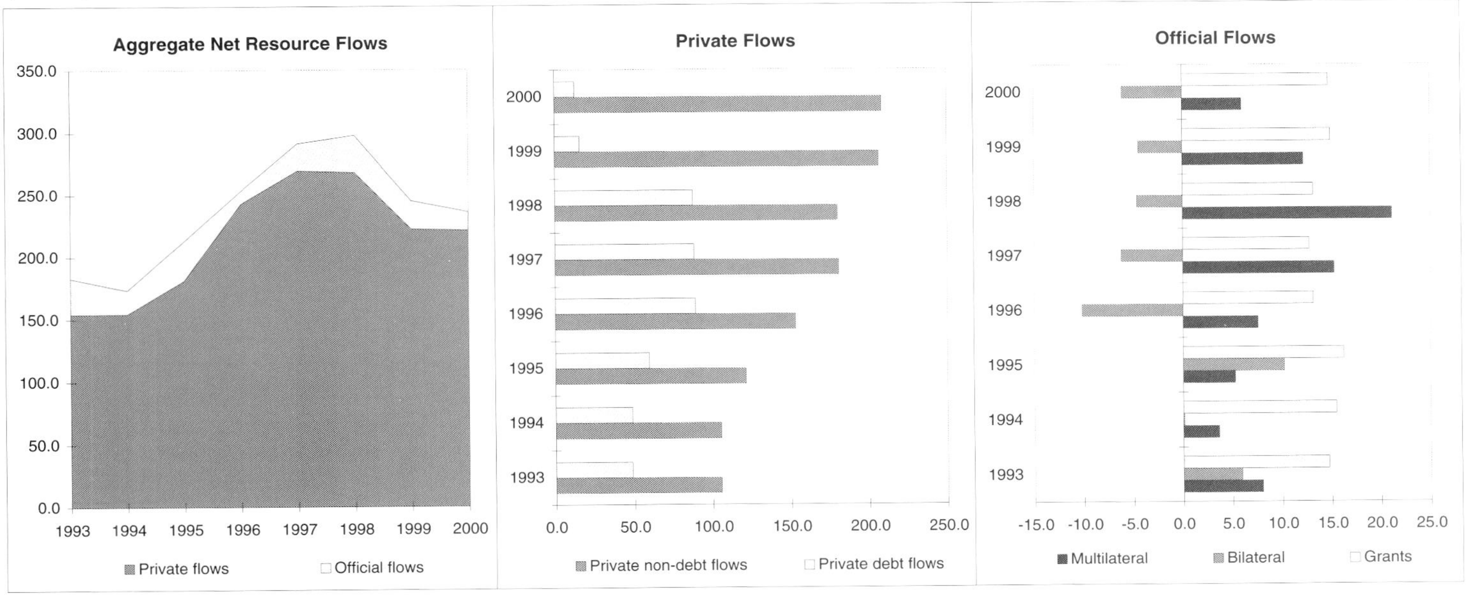

Country tables

ALBANIA

(US$ million, unless otherwise indicated)

	1970	1980	1990	1994	1995	1996	1997	1998	1999	2000
1. SUMMARY DEBT DATA										
TOTAL DEBT STOCKS (EDT)	..	..	**348.6**	**883.1**	**456.4**	**490.9**	**514.9**	**626.5**	**706.4**	**784.1**
Long-term debt (LDOD)	..	..	**35.7**	**247.6**	**329.6**	**405.1**	**412.1**	**527.1**	**596.8**	**659.1**
Public and publicly guaranteed	..	..	35.7	247.6	329.6	405.1	412.1	506.1	580.7	644.2
Private nonguaranteed	..	..	0.0	0.0	0.0	0.0	0.0	21.0	16.1	14.9
Use of IMF credit	**0.0**	**0.0**	**0.0**	**54.2**	**64.5**	**54.2**	**55.0**	**64.4**	**80.6**	**87.9**
Short-term debt	..	..	**312.9**	**581.3**	**62.3**	**31.6**	**47.8**	**34.9**	**29.0**	**37.1**
of which interest arrears on LDOD	..	..	0.0	1.6	1.6	1.5	3.8	3.8	3.9	3.8
Official creditors	..	..	0.0	1.3	1.6	1.5	1.0	1.0	1.1	1.0
Private creditors	..	..	0.0	0.3	0.0	0.0	2.8	2.8	2.8	2.8
Memo: principal arrears on LDOD	..	..	0.0	25.7	27.0	33.4	33.4	33.4	33.4	33.4
Official creditors	..	..	0.0	17.7	17.7	17.7	17.7	17.7	17.7	17.7
Private creditors	..	..	0.0	8.0	9.4	15.8	15.8	15.8	15.8	15.8
Memo: export credits	..	..	16.0	29.5	33.5	37.5	25.5	217.6	180.5	25.9
TOTAL DEBT FLOWS										
Disbursements	..	..	**33.1**	**93.7**	**80.5**	**90.0**	**64.6**	**97.5**	**153.1**	**120.0**
Long-term debt	..	..	33.1	71.5	69.7	90.0	52.4	89.5	132.0	101.2
IMF purchases	0.0	0.0	0.0	22.2	10.7	0.0	12.1	8.0	21.1	18.8
Principal repayments	..	..	**0.0**	**8.1**	**1.6**	**13.6**	**15.9**	**11.6**	**14.4**	**16.1**
Long-term debt	..	..	0.0	8.1	0.4	5.3	8.0	10.4	10.9	8.8
IMF repurchases	0.0	0.0	0.0	0.0	1.2	8.3	8.0	1.2	3.5	7.3
Net flows on debt	..	..	**271.6**	**88.9**	**-99.2**	**45.8**	**62.6**	**73.0**	**132.8**	**112.1**
of which short-term debt	..	..	238.5	3.2	-178.0	-30.6	13.9	-12.9	-6.0	8.2
Interest payments (INT)	..	..	**3.1**	**10.2**	**8.8**	**7.7**	**8.2**	**9.9**	**8.4**	**10.9**
Long-term debt	..	..	3.1	9.1	4.5	5.4	5.7	7.0	6.4	8.3
IMF charges	0.0	0.0	0.0	1.1	1.3	0.9	0.5	0.8	0.8	1.0
Short-term debt	..	..	0.0	0.0	3.0	1.4	2.0	2.1	1.3	1.6
Net transfers on debt	..	..	**268.5**	**78.7**	**-108.0**	**38.1**	**54.4**	**63.1**	**124.4**	**101.2**
Total debt service paid (TDS)	..	..	**3.1**	**18.3**	**10.4**	**21.2**	**24.1**	**21.5**	**22.8**	**27.0**
Long-term debt	..	..	3.1	17.2	5.0	10.7	13.6	17.4	17.3	17.1
IMF repurchases and charges	0.0	0.0	0.0	1.1	2.5	9.2	8.4	2.0	4.3	8.2
Short-term debt (interest only)	..	..	0.0	0.0	3.0	1.4	2.0	2.1	1.3	1.6
2. AGGREGATE NET RESOURCE FLOWS AND NET TRANSFERS (LONG-TERM)										
NET RESOURCE FLOWS	..	..	**35.0**	**184.8**	**216.0**	**288.3**	**167.8**	**251.2**	**442.2**	**395.9**
Net flow of long-term debt (ex. IMF)	..	..	33.1	63.4	69.3	84.7	44.5	79.1	121.1	92.3
Foreign direct investment (net)	..	..	0.0	53.0	70.0	90.1	48.0	45.0	41.0	143.0
Portfolio equity flows	..	..	0.0	0.0	0.0	0.0	0.0	0.0	0.0	0.0
Grants (excluding technical coop.)	..	..	1.9	68.4	76.7	113.5	75.3	127.2	280.1	160.6
Memo: technical coop. grants	..	..	9.2	27.3	33.1	54.4	34.3	33.6	68.9	56.0
official net resource flows	..	..	3.8	139.9	146.4	193.7	120.9	208.0	404.9	253.9
private net resource flows	..	..	31.2	44.9	69.6	94.6	46.9	43.2	37.3	142.0
NET TRANSFERS	..	..	**31.9**	**175.6**	**211.5**	**282.9**	**162.1**	**244.2**	**435.8**	**387.6**
Interest on long-term debt	..	..	3.1	9.1	4.5	5.4	5.7	7.0	6.4	8.3
Profit remittances on FDI	..	..	0.0	0.0	0.0	0.0	0.0	0.0	0.0	0.0
Memo: official net transfers	..	..	3.8	132.2	142.5	188.8	115.7	202.2	399.7	246.8
private net transfers	..	..	28.1	43.4	69.0	94.1	46.4	42.0	36.1	140.8
3. MAJOR ECONOMIC AGGREGATES										
Gross national income (GNI)	..	..	2,098.6	1,953.8	2,537.2	2,754.0	2,344.6	3,126.4	3,744.8	3,859.1
Exports of goods & services (XGS)	..	..	353.6	540.2	760.3	956.2	550.7	832.9	986.5	1,350.2
of which workers remittances	..	..	0.0	264.7	384.6	499.6	266.9	452.3	356.6	530.8
Imports of goods & services (MGS)	..	..	486.9	774.8	864.6	1,123.3	820.6	949.6	1,111.3	1,508.6
International reserves (RES)	..	..	..	223.6	265.3	323.4	342.4	382.2	403.9	382.9
Current account balance	..	..	-118.3	-157.3	-11.5	-107.3	-272.2	-65.1	-155.4	-156.3
4. DEBT INDICATORS										
EDT / XGS (%)	..	..	98.6	163.5	60.0	51.3	93.5	75.2	71.6	58.1
EDT / GNI (%)	..	..	16.6	45.2	18.0	17.8	22.0	20.0	18.9	20.3
TDS / XGS (%)	..	..	0.9	3.4	1.4	2.2	4.4	2.6	2.3	2.0
INT / XGS (%)	..	..	0.9	1.9	1.2	0.8	1.5	1.2	0.9	0.8
INT / GNI (%)	..	..	0.2	0.5	0.4	0.3	0.4	0.3	0.2	0.3
RES / EDT (%)	..	..	..	25.3	58.1	65.9	66.5	61.0	57.2	48.8
RES / MGS (months)	..	..	..	3.5	3.7	3.5	5.0	4.8	4.4	3.1
Short-term / EDT (%)	..	..	89.8	65.8	13.7	6.4	9.3	5.6	4.1	4.7
Concessional / EDT (%)	..	..	0.6	21.5	57.1	67.4	66.9	70.8	72.4	70.9
Multilateral / EDT (%)	..	..	0.0	7.4	25.1	30.8	31.9	38.6	48.2	51.6

ALBANIA

(US$ million, unless otherwise indicated)

	1970	1980	1990	1994	1995	1996	1997	1998	1999	2000
5. LONG-TERM DEBT										
DEBT OUTSTANDING (LDOD)	..	..	**35.7**	**247.6**	**329.6**	**405.1**	**412.1**	**527.1**	**596.8**	**659.1**
Public and publicly guaranteed	..	..	**35.7**	**247.6**	**329.6**	**405.1**	**412.1**	**506.1**	**580.7**	**644.2**
Official creditors	..	..	2.0	228.4	304.6	375.9	384.8	480.3	557.3	622.2
Multilateral	..	..	0.0	65.7	114.6	151.1	164.0	241.9	340.8	404.3
Concessional	..	..	0.0	65.5	109.8	141.6	154.6	232.1	318.0	369.6
Bilateral	..	..	2.0	162.6	190.0	224.8	220.8	238.3	216.5	217.9
Concessional	..	..	2.0	124.5	150.8	189.0	190.0	211.6	193.4	186.1
Private creditors	..	..	33.7	19.2	25.0	29.2	27.3	25.9	23.5	22.0
Bonds	..	..	0.0	0.0	0.0	0.0	0.0	0.0	0.0	0.0
Commercial banks	..	..	0.0	0.0	0.0	0.0	0.0	0.0	0.0	0.0
Other private	..	..	33.7	19.2	25.0	29.2	27.3	25.9	23.5	22.0
Private nonguaranteed	..	..	**0.0**	**0.0**	**0.0**	**0.0**	**0.0**	**21.0**	**16.1**	**14.9**
Bonds	..	..	0.0	0.0	0.0	0.0	0.0	0.0	0.0	0.0
Commercial banks and other	..	..	0.0	0.0	0.0	0.0	0.0	21.0	16.1	14.9
Memo:										
IBRD	0.0	0.0	0.0	0.0	0.0	0.0	0.0	0.0	0.0	0.0
IDA	0.0	0.0	0.0	64.7	109.0	137.2	148.2	220.1	296.3	345.7
DISBURSEMENTS	..	..	**33.1**	**71.5**	**69.7**	**90.0**	**52.4**	**89.5**	**132.0**	**101.2**
Public and publicly guaranteed	..	..	**33.1**	**71.5**	**69.7**	**90.0**	**52.4**	**89.5**	**130.9**	**101.2**
Official creditors	..	..	1.9	71.5	69.7	84.4	51.8	89.5	130.9	101.2
Multilateral	..	..	0.0	36.0	48.0	41.4	22.3	70.3	105.8	82.1
Concessional	..	..	0.0	35.8	43.3	35.9	21.5	69.1	90.4	67.5
Bilateral	..	..	1.9	35.5	21.8	43.0	29.5	19.1	25.1	19.0
Concessional	..	..	1.9	35.5	21.8	43.0	29.5	19.1	25.1	10.5
Private creditors	..	..	31.2	0.0	0.0	5.6	0.7	0.0	0.0	0.0
Bonds	..	..	0.0	0.0	0.0	0.0	0.0	0.0	0.0	0.0
Commercial banks	..	..	0.0	0.0	0.0	0.0	0.0	0.0	0.0	0.0
Other private	..	..	31.2	0.0	0.0	5.6	0.7	0.0	0.0	0.0
Private nonguaranteed	..	..	**0.0**	**0.0**	**0.0**	**0.0**	**0.0**	**0.0**	**1.1**	**0.0**
Bonds	..	..	0.0	0.0	0.0	0.0	0.0	0.0	0.0	0.0
Commercial banks and other	..	..	0.0	0.0	0.0	0.0	0.0	0.0	1.1	0.0
Memo:										
IBRD	0.0	0.0	0.0	0.0	0.0	0.0	0.0	0.0	0.0	0.0
IDA	0.0	0.0	0.0	35.0	43.3	32.3	18.9	63.7	80.6	64.4
PRINCIPAL REPAYMENTS	..	..	**0.0**	**8.1**	**0.4**	**5.3**	**8.0**	**10.4**	**10.9**	**8.8**
Public and publicly guaranteed	..	..	**0.0**	**8.1**	**0.4**	**5.3**	**8.0**	**10.4**	**7.7**	**8.8**
Official creditors	..	..	0.0	0.0	0.0	4.2	6.1	8.6	6.1	7.8
Multilateral	..	..	0.0	0.0	0.0	0.8	1.3	0.8	1.5	2.3
Concessional	..	..	0.0	0.0	0.0	0.0	0.4	0.0	0.0	0.5
Bilateral	..	..	0.0	0.0	0.0	3.4	4.9	7.8	4.6	5.6
Concessional	..	..	0.0	0.0	0.0	0.9	1.4	3.2	1.8	2.4
Private creditors	..	..	0.0	8.1	0.4	1.1	1.8	1.8	1.6	1.0
Bonds	..	..	0.0	0.0	0.0	0.0	0.0	0.0	0.0	0.0
Commercial banks	..	..	0.0	0.0	0.0	0.0	0.0	0.0	0.0	0.0
Other private	..	..	0.0	8.1	0.4	1.1	1.8	1.8	1.6	1.0
Private nonguaranteed	..	..	**0.0**	**0.0**	**0.0**	**0.0**	**0.0**	**0.0**	**3.2**	**0.0**
Bonds	..	..	0.0	0.0	0.0	0.0	0.0	0.0	0.0	0.0
Commercial banks and other	..	..	0.0	0.0	0.0	0.0	0.0	0.0	3.2	0.0
Memo:										
IBRD	0.0	0.0	0.0	0.0	0.0	0.0	0.0	0.0	0.0	0.0
IDA	0.0	0.0	0.0	0.0	0.0	0.0	0.0	0.0	0.0	0.0
NET FLOWS ON DEBT	..	..	**33.1**	**63.4**	**69.3**	**84.7**	**44.5**	**79.1**	**121.1**	**92.3**
Public and publicly guaranteed	..	..	**33.1**	**63.4**	**69.3**	**84.7**	**44.5**	**79.1**	**123.2**	**92.3**
Official creditors	..	..	1.9	71.5	69.7	80.2	45.6	80.8	124.8	93.3
Multilateral	..	..	0.0	36.0	48.0	40.6	21.0	69.5	104.3	79.8
Concessional	..	..	0.0	35.8	43.3	35.9	21.1	69.1	90.4	67.0
Bilateral	..	..	1.9	35.5	21.8	39.6	24.6	11.4	20.5	13.5
Concessional	..	..	1.9	35.5	21.8	42.1	28.1	15.9	23.3	8.1
Private creditors	..	..	31.2	-8.1	-0.4	4.5	-1.1	-1.8	-1.6	-1.0
Bonds	..	..	0.0	0.0	0.0	0.0	0.0	0.0	0.0	0.0
Commercial banks	..	..	0.0	0.0	0.0	0.0	0.0	0.0	0.0	0.0
Other private	..	..	31.2	-8.1	-0.4	4.5	-1.1	-1.8	-1.6	-1.0
Private nonguaranteed	..	..	**0.0**	**0.0**	**0.0**	**0.0**	**0.0**	**0.0**	**-2.1**	**0.0**
Bonds	..	..	0.0	0.0	0.0	0.0	0.0	0.0	0.0	0.0
Commercial banks and other	..	..	0.0	0.0	0.0	0.0	0.0	0.0	-2.1	0.0
Memo:										
IBRD	0.0	0.0	0.0	0.0	0.0	0.0	0.0	0.0	0.0	0.0
IDA	0.0	0.0	0.0	35.0	43.3	32.3	18.9	63.7	80.6	64.4

ALBANIA

(US$ million, unless otherwise indicated)

	1970	1980	1990	1994	1995	1996	1997	1998	1999	2000
INTEREST PAYMENTS (LINT)	..	..	**3.1**	**9.1**	**4.5**	**5.4**	**5.7**	**7.0**	**6.4**	**8.3**
Public and publicly guaranteed	..	..	**3.1**	**9.1**	**4.5**	**5.4**	**5.7**	**6.2**	**5.5**	**7.4**
Official creditors	..	..	0.0	7.7	3.9	4.9	5.2	5.8	5.2	7.1
Multilateral	..	..	0.0	0.2	0.6	1.4	1.9	2.1	2.9	4.1
Concessional	..	..	0.0	0.2	0.6	0.9	1.1	1.4	2.0	2.6
Bilateral	..	..	0.0	7.4	3.3	3.5	3.3	3.7	2.3	3.0
Concessional	..	..	0.0	3.1	1.8	2.0	2.1	2.7	1.9	2.6
Private creditors	..	..	3.1	1.5	0.6	0.5	0.5	0.4	0.3	0.3
Bonds	..	..	0.0	0.0	0.0	0.0	0.0	0.0	0.0	0.0
Commercial banks	..	..	0.0	0.0	0.0	0.0	0.0	0.0	0.0	0.0
Other private	..	..	3.1	1.5	0.6	0.5	0.5	0.4	0.3	0.3
Private nonguaranteed	..	..	**0.0**	**0.0**	**0.0**	**0.0**	**0.0**	**0.8**	**0.9**	**0.9**
Bonds	..	..	0.0	0.0	0.0	0.0	0.0	0.0	0.0	0.0
Commercial banks and other	..	..	0.0	0.0	0.0	0.0	0.0	0.8	0.9	0.9
Memo:										
IBRD	0.0	0.0	0.0	0.0	0.0	0.0	0.0	0.0	0.0	0.0
IDA	0.0	0.0	0.0	0.2	0.6	0.9	1.0	1.2	1.7	2.2
NET TRANSFERS ON DEBT	..	..	**30.0**	**54.3**	**64.8**	**79.3**	**38.8**	**72.1**	**114.7**	**84.0**
Public and publicly guaranteed	..	..	**30.0**	**54.3**	**64.8**	**79.3**	**38.8**	**72.8**	**117.7**	**85.0**
Official creditors	..	..	1.9	63.8	65.8	75.3	40.4	75.0	119.6	86.3
Multilateral	..	..	0.0	35.7	47.4	39.2	19.1	67.3	101.4	75.7
Concessional	..	..	0.0	35.6	42.8	35.0	20.0	67.7	88.5	64.4
Bilateral	..	..	1.9	28.1	18.4	36.1	21.3	7.7	18.2	10.5
Concessional	..	..	1.9	32.5	20.0	40.1	26.0	13.2	21.4	5.5
Private creditors	..	..	28.1	-9.5	-1.0	4.0	-1.6	-2.2	-1.9	-1.3
Bonds	..	..	0.0	0.0	0.0	0.0	0.0	0.0	0.0	0.0
Commercial banks	..	..	0.0	0.0	0.0	0.0	0.0	0.0	0.0	0.0
Other private	..	..	28.1	-9.5	-1.0	4.0	-1.6	-2.2	-1.9	-1.3
Private nonguaranteed	..	..	**0.0**	**0.0**	**0.0**	**0.0**	**0.0**	**-0.8**	**-3.0**	**-0.9**
Bonds	..	..	0.0	0.0	0.0	0.0	0.0	0.0	0.0	0.0
Commercial banks and other	..	..	0.0	0.0	0.0	0.0	0.0	-0.8	-3.0	-0.9
Memo:										
IBRD	0.0	0.0	0.0	0.0	0.0	0.0	0.0	0.0	0.0	0.0
IDA	0.0	0.0	0.0	34.8	42.8	31.5	17.9	62.5	78.9	62.1
DEBT SERVICE (LTDS)	..	..	**3.1**	**17.2**	**5.0**	**10.7**	**13.6**	**17.4**	**17.3**	**17.1**
Public and publicly guaranteed	..	..	**3.1**	**17.2**	**5.0**	**10.7**	**13.6**	**16.7**	**13.2**	**16.2**
Official creditors	..	..	0.0	7.7	3.9	9.1	11.4	14.4	11.3	14.9
Multilateral	..	..	0.0	0.2	0.6	2.3	3.2	3.0	4.4	6.4
Concessional	..	..	0.0	0.2	0.6	0.9	1.5	1.4	2.0	3.1
Bilateral	..	..	0.0	7.4	3.3	6.8	8.2	11.5	6.9	8.5
Concessional	..	..	0.0	3.1	1.8	2.9	3.5	5.9	3.7	5.0
Private creditors	..	..	3.1	9.5	1.0	1.6	2.3	2.2	1.9	1.3
Bonds	..	..	0.0	0.0	0.0	0.0	0.0	0.0	0.0	0.0
Commercial banks	..	..	0.0	0.0	0.0	0.0	0.0	0.0	0.0	0.0
Other private	..	..	3.1	9.5	1.0	1.6	2.3	2.2	1.9	1.3
Private nonguaranteed	..	..	**0.0**	**0.0**	**0.0**	**0.0**	**0.0**	**0.8**	**4.1**	**0.9**
Bonds	..	..	0.0	0.0	0.0	0.0	0.0	0.0	0.0	0.0
Commercial banks and other	..	..	0.0	0.0	0.0	0.0	0.0	0.8	4.1	0.9
Memo:										
IBRD	0.0	0.0	0.0	0.0	0.0	0.0	0.0	0.0	0.0	0.0
IDA	0.0	0.0	0.0	0.2	0.6	0.9	1.0	1.2	1.7	2.2
UNDISBURSED DEBT	..	..	**20.1**	**231.4**	**328.2**	**394.9**	**334.2**	**421.5**	**471.3**	**444.6**
Official creditors	..	..	0.0	212.5	315.1	394.1	334.2	421.5	471.3	444.6
Private creditors	..	..	20.1	19.0	13.1	0.8	0.0	0.0	0.0	0.0
Memorandum items										
Concessional LDOD	..	..	2.0	190.0	260.5	330.6	344.6	443.6	511.5	555.8
Variable rate LDOD	..	..	33.7	49.2	54.2	58.6	54.8	73.3	74.5	91.2
Public sector LDOD	..	..	35.7	247.6	329.6	405.1	412.1	504.9	579.7	643.2
Private sector LDOD	..	..	0.0	0.0	0.0	0.0	0.0	22.3	17.2	15.9

6. CURRENCY COMPOSITION OF LONG-TERM DEBT (PERCENT)

	1970	1980	1990	1994	1995	1996	1997	1998	1999	2000
Deutsche mark	..	..	100.0	17.3	14.4	13.5	14.3	13.1	10.6	8.7
French franc	..	..	0.0	0.2	0.2	0.1	0.1	0.1	0.0	0.0
Japanese yen	..	..	0.0	3.4	2.5	3.9	4.1	4.0	5.3	4.5
Pound sterling	..	..	0.0	0.0	0.0	0.0	0.0	0.0	0.0	0.0
Swiss franc	..	..	0.0	0.0	0.0	0.0	0.0	0.0	0.0	0.0
U.S.dollars	..	..	0.0	55.9	60.9	61.0	59.6	60.8	62.7	65.2
Multiple currency	..	..	0.0	0.0	0.0	0.0	0.0	0.0	0.0	0.0
Special drawing rights	..	..	0.0	0.0	0.0	0.2	0.3	0.7	1.3	1.3
All other currencies	..	..	0.0	23.2	22.0	21.3	21.6	21.3	20.1	20.3

ALBANIA

(US$ million, unless otherwise indicated)

	1970	1980	1990	1994	1995	1996	1997	1998	1999	2000
7. DEBT RESTRUCTURINGS										
Total amount rescheduled	..	..	0.0	0.0	5.9	0.0	0.0	4.5	0.0	8.3
Debt stock rescheduled	..	..	0.0	0.0	225.0	0.0	0.0	0.0	0.0	0.0
Principal rescheduled	..	..	0.0	0.0	0.0	0.0	0.0	0.0	0.0	6.7
Official	..	..	0.0	0.0	0.0	0.0	0.0	0.0	0.0	6.5
Private	..	..	0.0	0.0	0.0	0.0	0.0	0.0	0.0	0.1
Interest rescheduled	..	..	0.0	0.0	0.0	0.0	0.0	0.0	0.0	1.0
Official	..	..	0.0	0.0	0.0	0.0	0.0	0.0	0.0	1.0
Private	..	..	0.0	0.0	0.0	0.0	0.0	0.0	0.0	0.0
Debt forgiven	..	..	0.0	8.4	0.0	0.0	0.0	0.0	0.0	0.0
Memo: interest forgiven	..	..	0.0	0.0	0.0	0.0	0.0	0.0	0.0	0.0
Debt stock reduction	..	..	0.0	0.0	146.0	0.0	0.0	0.0	0.0	0.0
of which debt buyback	..	..	0.0	0.0	30.0	0.0	0.0	0.0	0.0	0.0
8. DEBT STOCK-FLOW RECONCILIATION										
Total change in debt stocks	..	..	274.2	97.1	-426.7	34.5	24.0	111.6	79.9	77.7
Net flows on debt	..	..	271.6	88.9	-99.2	45.8	62.6	73.0	132.8	112.1
Net change in interest arrears	..	..	0.0	0.7	0.0	-0.1	2.3	0.0	0.1	-0.1
Interest capitalized	..	..	0.0	0.0	0.0	0.0	0.0	0.0	0.0	1.0
Debt forgiveness or reduction	..	..	0.0	-8.4	-116.0	0.0	0.0	0.0	0.0	0.0
Cross-currency valuation	..	..	0.0	11.4	7.6	-10.7	-31.0	21.5	-31.4	-34.6
Residual	..	..	2.6	4.5	-219.1	-0.5	-9.9	17.1	-21.6	-0.7
9. AVERAGE TERMS OF NEW COMMITMENTS										
ALL CREDITORS										
Interest (%)	..	..	10.0	1.7	3.2	1.4	0.5	2.6	1.9	2.0
Maturity (years)	..	..	4.7	34.6	25.6	33.5	39.8	32.6	33.6	32.0
Grace period (years)	..	..	2.8	9.2	7.7	10.6	10.3	9.9	8.5	11.5
Grant element (%)	..	..	-0.4	69.5	51.9	72.3	82.6	61.1	66.9	67.6
Official creditors										
Interest (%)	..	..	0.0	1.7	3.2	1.4	0.5	2.6	1.9	2.0
Maturity (years)	..	..	0.0	34.6	25.7	33.5	39.8	32.6	33.6	32.0
Grace period (years)	..	..	0.0	9.2	7.6	10.6	10.3	9.9	8.5	11.5
Grant element (%)	..	..	0.0	69.5	51.8	72.3	82.6	61.1	66.9	67.6
Private creditors										
Interest (%)	..	..	10.0	0.0	3.0	0.0	0.0	0.0	0.0	0.0
Maturity (years)	..	..	4.7	0.0	22.7	0.0	0.0	0.0	0.0	0.0
Grace period (years)	..	..	2.8	0.0	11.7	0.0	0.0	0.0	0.0	0.0
Grant element (%)	..	..	-0.4	0.0	55.9	0.0	0.0	0.0	0.0	0.0
Memorandum items										
Commitments	..	..	49.8	120.3	174.9	182.8	33.8	156.6	214.1	147.7
Official creditors	..	..	0.0	120.3	168.7	182.8	33.8	156.6	214.1	147.7
Private creditors	..	..	49.8	0.0	6.2	0.0	0.0	0.0	0.0	0.0

10. CONTRACTUAL OBLIGATIONS ON OUTSTANDING LONG-TERM DEBT

	2001	2002	2003	2004	2005	2006	2007	2008	2009	2010
TOTAL										
Disbursements	131.6	124.2	83.6	53.9	29.0	10.9	6.3	2.7	1.7	0.6
Principal	12.2	24.0	26.6	29.1	31.2	35.9	29.9	30.8	33.1	35.8
Interest	12.5	14.4	14.9	14.9	14.4	13.3	12.4	11.6	10.7	9.8
Official creditors										
Disbursements	131.6	124.2	83.6	53.9	29.0	10.9	6.3	2.7	1.7	0.6
Principal	10.0	19.9	22.5	25.3	29.7	33.4	29.9	30.6	33.0	35.6
Interest	11.5	13.7	14.5	14.5	14.1	13.3	12.4	11.5	10.7	9.8
Bilateral creditors										
Disbursements	45.0	49.2	31.8	20.9	12.4	7.1	4.3	2.1	1.2	0.6
Principal	5.2	11.4	11.3	12.3	14.4	17.3	13.3	14.3	15.0	15.4
Interest	4.9	5.9	6.2	6.3	6.2	5.9	5.6	5.3	5.0	4.6
Multilateral creditors										
Disbursements	86.5	75.0	51.9	33.0	16.6	3.8	2.0	0.6	0.5	0.0
Principal	4.8	8.5	11.2	13.0	15.3	16.1	16.6	16.3	18.0	20.3
Interest	6.6	7.8	8.3	8.2	7.9	7.4	6.8	6.2	5.7	5.2
Private creditors										
Disbursements	0.0	0.0	0.0	0.0	0.0	0.0	0.0	0.0	0.0	0.0
Principal	2.2	4.1	4.1	3.8	1.5	2.5	0.0	0.2	0.2	0.2
Interest	0.9	0.7	0.5	0.3	0.3	0.0	0.0	0.0	0.0	0.0
Commercial banks										
Disbursements	0.0	0.0	0.0	0.0	0.0	0.0	0.0	0.0	0.0	0.0
Principal	0.0	0.0	0.0	0.0	0.0	0.0	0.0	0.0	0.0	0.0
Interest	0.0	0.0	0.0	0.0	0.0	0.0	0.0	0.0	0.0	0.0
Other private										
Disbursements	0.0	0.0	0.0	0.0	0.0	0.0	0.0	0.0	0.0	0.0
Principal	2.2	4.1	4.1	3.8	1.5	2.5	0.0	0.2	0.2	0.2
Interest	0.9	0.7	0.5	0.3	0.3	0.0	0.0	0.0	0.0	0.0

ALGERIA

(US$ million, unless otherwise indicated)

	1970	1980	1990	1994	1995	1996	1997	1998	1999	2000
1. SUMMARY DEBT DATA										
TOTAL DEBT STOCKS (EDT)	**940**	**19,365**	**27,877**	**29,959**	**32,772**	**33,419**	**30,894**	**30,676**	**28,005**	**25,002**
Long-term debt (LDOD)	**940**	**17,040**	**26,416**	**28,164**	**31,033**	**31,060**	**28,715**	**28,480**	**25,903**	**23,062**
Public and publicly guaranteed	940	17,040	26,416	28,164	31,033	31,060	28,715	28,480	25,903	23,062
Private nonguaranteed	0	0	0	0	0	0	0	0	0	0
Use of IMF credit	**0**	**0**	**670**	**1,159**	**1,478**	**2,031**	**2,018**	**2,011**	**1,906**	**1,718**
Short-term debt	**0**	**2,325**	**791**	**637**	**261**	**328**	**162**	**186**	**195**	**222**
of which interest arrears on LDOD	0	0	0	1	3	0	0	0	0	0
Official creditors	0	0	0	0	0	0	0	0	0	0
Private creditors	0	0	0	1	3	0	0	0	0	0
Memo: principal arrears on LDOD	0	2	1	1	1	0	0	0	0	0
Official creditors	0	0	0	1	0	0	0	0	0	0
Private creditors	0	2	0	1	1	0	0	0	0	0
Memo: export credits	0	0	13,220	16,814	18,158	19,681	19,181	13,518	12,858	12,260
TOTAL DEBT FLOWS										
Disbursements	**313**	**3,398**	**6,935**	**5,617**	**4,157**	**3,629**	**2,110**	**1,510**	**1,449**	**965**
Long-term debt	313	3,398	6,935	4,775	3,683	2,885	1,645	1,166	1,144	965
IMF purchases	0	0	0	841	475	744	465	344	306	0
Principal repayments	**35**	**2,529**	**6,779**	**3,546**	**2,391**	**2,077**	**2,370**	**3,139**	**3,386**	**2,812**
Long-term debt	35	2,529	6,779	3,351	2,220	1,941	2,019	2,704	3,027	2,719
IMF repurchases	0	0	0	195	171	136	350	435	359	93
Net flows on debt	**279**	**1,261**	**-892**	**2,006**	**1,389**	**1,622**	**-426**	**-1,606**	**-1,927**	**-1,820**
of which short-term debt	0	392	-1,049	-64	-378	70	-166	24	9	27
Interest payments (INT)	**10**	**1,556**	**2,025**	**1,561**	**1,813**	**2,094**	**2,048**	**1,992**	**1,810**	**1,655**
Long-term debt	10	1,440	1,784	1,496	1,722	2,005	1,943	1,879	1,722	1,552
IMF charges	0	0	62	31	69	75	93	99	78	92
Short-term debt	0	116	179	33	22	13	13	15	10	10
Net transfers on debt	**269**	**-294**	**-2,917**	**446**	**-424**	**-472**	**-2,474**	**-3,598**	**-3,737**	**-3,475**
Total debt service paid (TDS)	**45**	**4,084**	**8,803**	**5,107**	**4,204**	**4,170**	**4,418**	**5,131**	**5,196**	**4,467**
Long-term debt	45	3,968	8,562	4,847	3,942	3,946	3,962	4,583	4,749	4,271
IMF repurchases and charges	0	0	62	226	240	211	443	534	437	185
Short-term debt (interest only)	0	116	179	33	22	13	13	15	10	10
2. AGGREGATE NET RESOURCE FLOWS AND NET TRANSFERS (LONG-TERM)										
NET RESOURCE FLOWS	**381**	**1,295**	**202**	**1,515**	**1,539**	**1,042**	**-325**	**-1,423**	**-1,824**	**-1,678**
Net flow of long-term debt (ex. IMF)	279	869	156	1,424	1,463	945	-374	-1,538	-1,883	-1,754
Foreign direct investment (net)	47	349	0	18	5	4	7	5	7	10
Portfolio equity flows	0	0	0	5	1	5	8	2	3	4
Grants (excluding technical coop.)	56	77	45	67	70	88	35	108	48	62
Memo: technical coop. grants	44	96	106	96	101	126	110	106	93	76
official net resource flows	88	399	626	922	1,018	1,021	198	-102	-330	-465
private net resource flows	294	896	-424	593	521	20	-523	-1,321	-1,495	-1,212
NET TRANSFERS	**221**	**-831**	**-1,734**	**-111**	**-328**	**-1,103**	**-2,403**	**-3,417**	**-3,667**	**-3,354**
Interest on long-term debt	10	1,440	1,784	1,496	1,722	2,005	1,943	1,879	1,722	1,552
Profit remittances on FDI	150	687	152	130	145	140	135	115	120	124
Memo: official net transfers	84	239	314	524	215	-213	-928	-1,298	-1,519	-1,595
private net transfers	137	-1,071	-2,047	-635	-543	-891	-1,475	-2,119	-2,147	-1,758
3. MAJOR ECONOMIC AGGREGATES										
Gross national income (GNI)	4,742	41,147	59,955	40,808	39,574	44,285	45,649	45,357	45,305	50,606
Exports of goods & services (XGS)	..	14,906	13,887	10,536	12,044	14,711	15,904	12,049	14,062	22,757
of which workers remittances	..	406	352	948	1,101	889	914	918	942	..
Imports of goods & services (MGS)	..	14,552	12,448	11,627	12,973	12,415	11,479	11,893	12,622	13,315
International reserves (RES)	352	7,064	2,703	4,813	4,164	6,296	9,667	8,452	6,146	13,556
Current account balance	..	249	1,420	..	..	..	..	..	..	..
4. DEBT INDICATORS										
EDT / XGS (%)	..	129.9	200.7	284.3	272.1	227.2	194.3	254.6	199.2	109.9
EDT / GNI (%)	19.8	47.1	46.5	73.4	82.8	75.5	67.7	67.6	61.8	49.4
TDS / XGS (%)	..	27.4	63.4	48.5	34.9	28.4	27.8	42.6	37.0	19.6
INT / XGS (%)	..	10.4	14.6	14.8	15.1	14.2	12.9	16.5	12.9	7.3
INT / GNI (%)	0.2	3.8	3.4	3.8	4.6	4.7	4.5	4.4	4.0	3.3
RES / EDT (%)	37.5	36.5	9.7	16.1	12.7	18.8	31.3	27.6	22.0	54.2
RES / MGS (months)	..	5.8	2.6	5.0	3.9	6.1	10.1	8.5	5.8	12.2
Short-term / EDT (%)	0.0	12.0	2.8	2.1	0.8	1.0	0.5	0.6	0.7	0.9
Concessional / EDT (%)	50.0	6.6	3.1	6.9	9.4	9.9	10.2	10.7	11.8	11.7
Multilateral / EDT (%)	1.7	1.5	7.3	11.2	12.0	12.2	12.5	14.3	15.2	16.5

ALGERIA

(US$ million, unless otherwise indicated)

	1970	1980	1990	1994	1995	1996	1997	1998	1999	2000
5. LONG-TERM DEBT										
DEBT OUTSTANDING (LDOD)	**940**	**17,040**	**26,416**	**28,164**	**31,033**	**31,060**	**28,715**	**28,480**	**25,903**	**23,062**
Public and publicly guaranteed	**940**	**17,040**	**26,416**	**28,164**	**31,033**	**31,060**	**28,715**	**28,480**	**25,903**	**23,062**
Official creditors	485	3,495	5,594	10,649	15,385	17,936	18,249	19,425	18,473	17,181
Multilateral	16	284	2,031	3,344	3,915	4,085	3,854	4,390	4,244	4,124
Concessional	0	14	76	155	292	334	362	385	518	545
Bilateral	470	3,211	3,563	7,305	11,470	13,851	14,395	15,036	14,230	13,056
Concessional	470	1,255	784	1,904	2,796	2,961	2,789	2,909	2,773	2,385
Private creditors	454	13,545	20,822	17,514	15,647	13,124	10,465	9,054	7,430	5,881
Bonds	5	410	1,420	261	0	0	0	0	0	0
Commercial banks	20	5,503	6,051	4,904	4,911	4,623	4,261	3,948	3,612	2,948
Other private	430	7,632	13,351	12,349	10,737	8,501	6,204	5,107	3,818	2,934
Private nonguaranteed	**0**	**0**	**0**	**0**	**0**	**0**	**0**	**0**	**0**	**0**
Bonds	0	0	0	0	0	0	0	0	0	0
Commercial banks and other	0	0	0	0	0	0	0	0	0	0
Memo:										
IBRD	16	253	1,208	1,709	2,049	1,939	1,795	1,676	1,540	1,425
IDA	0	0	0	0	0	0	0	0	0	0
DISBURSEMENTS	**313**	**3,398**	**6,935**	**4,775**	**3,683**	**2,885**	**1,645**	**1,166**	**1,144**	**965**
Public and publicly guaranteed	**313**	**3,398**	**6,935**	**4,775**	**3,683**	**2,885**	**1,645**	**1,166**	**1,144**	**965**
Official creditors	45	566	1,753	1,507	1,591	1,577	1,207	767	743	524
Multilateral	0	54	612	701	932	823	792	594	432	337
Concessional	0	1	9	6	149	64	54	64	175	79
Bilateral	45	512	1,141	806	659	755	415	173	311	187
Concessional	45	78	282	386	501	323	158	70	70	48
Private creditors	268	2,832	5,182	3,268	2,092	1,308	438	400	401	441
Bonds	5	30	0	0	0	0	0	0	0	0
Commercial banks	17	891	406	119	255	141	33	22	8	6
Other private	246	1,911	4,776	3,149	1,837	1,167	405	378	393	435
Private nonguaranteed	**0**	**0**	**0**	**0**	**0**	**0**	**0**	**0**	**0**	**0**
Bonds	0	0	0	0	0	0	0	0	0	0
Commercial banks and other	0	0	0	0	0	0	0	0	0	0
Memo:										
IBRD	0	39	300	300	554	286	250	56	62	58
IDA	0	0	0	0	0	0	0	0	0	0
PRINCIPAL REPAYMENTS	**35**	**2,529**	**6,779**	**3,351**	**2,220**	**1,941**	**2,019**	**2,704**	**3,027**	**2,719**
Public and publicly guaranteed	**35**	**2,529**	**6,779**	**3,351**	**2,220**	**1,941**	**2,019**	**2,704**	**3,027**	**2,719**
Official creditors	13	244	1,172	653	643	644	1,044	976	1,122	1,051
Multilateral	3	42	312	450	454	411	698	412	425	351
Concessional	0	1	6	7	11	16	12	31	38	51
Bilateral	10	203	861	203	189	233	346	565	697	700
Concessional	10	72	97	54	43	96	116	146	196	219
Private creditors	22	2,284	5,606	2,698	1,577	1,297	975	1,728	1,905	1,668
Bonds	0	15	16	445	278	0	0	0	0	0
Commercial banks	2	918	1,330	382	220	178	132	501	491	485
Other private	19	1,352	4,261	1,872	1,078	1,119	843	1,227	1,414	1,182
Private nonguaranteed	**0**	**0**	**0**	**0**	**0**	**0**	**0**	**0**	**0**	**0**
Bonds	0	0	0	0	0	0	0	0	0	0
Commercial banks and other	0	0	0	0	0	0	0	0	0	0
Memo:										
IBRD	3	13	130	208	260	252	234	208	199	172
IDA	0	0	0	0	0	0	0	0	0	0
NET FLOWS ON DEBT	**279**	**869**	**156**	**1,424**	**1,463**	**945**	**-374**	**-1,538**	**-1,883**	**-1,754**
Public and publicly guaranteed	**279**	**869**	**156**	**1,424**	**1,463**	**945**	**-374**	**-1,538**	**-1,883**	**-1,754**
Official creditors	32	322	580	855	948	933	163	-210	-378	-527
Multilateral	-3	13	300	252	478	412	94	182	7	-14
Concessional	0	0	3	-1	138	49	43	33	137	28
Bilateral	35	309	281	603	470	522	69	-392	-386	-513
Concessional	35	6	185	332	459	226	42	-76	-126	-171
Private creditors	247	548	-424	570	515	11	-537	-1,328	-1,504	-1,226
Bonds	5	15	-16	-445	-278	0	0	0	0	0
Commercial banks	15	-27	-924	-263	35	-37	-99	-479	-483	-480
Other private	227	559	515	1,278	759	49	-438	-849	-1,022	-747
Private nonguaranteed	**0**	**0**	**0**	**0**	**0**	**0**	**0**	**0**	**0**	**0**
Bonds	0	0	0	0	0	0	0	0	0	0
Commercial banks and other	0	0	0	0	0	0	0	0	0	0
Memo:										
IBRD	-3	26	170	92	294	34	17	-152	-137	-114
IDA	0	0	0	0	0	0	0	0	0	0

ALGERIA

(US$ million, unless otherwise indicated)

	1970	1980	1990	1994	1995	1996	1997	1998	1999	2000
INTEREST PAYMENTS (LINT)	**10**	**1,440**	**1,784**	**1,496**	**1,722**	**2,005**	**1,943**	**1,879**	**1,722**	**1,552**
Public and publicly guaranteed	**10**	**1,440**	**1,784**	**1,496**	**1,722**	**2,005**	**1,943**	**1,879**	**1,722**	**1,552**
Official creditors	4	159	312	398	804	1,234	1,125	1,196	1,189	1,130
Multilateral	1	29	117	203	251	281	252	279	319	297
Concessional	0	1	6	6	8	15	16	18	21	19
Bilateral	3	130	195	196	553	954	873	917	871	833
Concessional	3	35	17	50	83	129	103	107	109	103
Private creditors	6	1,280	1,472	1,098	918	771	818	683	533	422
Bonds	0	45	105	49	13	0	0	0	0	0
Commercial banks	0	672	526	343	253	206	259	229	189	163
Other private	6	563	841	707	653	565	559	454	344	259
Private nonguaranteed	**0**	**0**	**0**	**0**	**0**	**0**	**0**	**0**	**0**	**0**
Bonds	0	0	0	0	0	0	0	0	0	0
Commercial banks and other	0	0	0	0	0	0	0	0	0	0
Memo:										
IBRD	1	25	73	119	137	139	120	124	126	128
IDA	0	0	0	0	0	0	0	0	0	0
NET TRANSFERS ON DEBT	**269**	**-570**	**-1,628**	**-72**	**-259**	**-1,061**	**-2,317**	**-3,417**	**-3,605**	**-3,306**
Public and publicly guaranteed	**269**	**-570**	**-1,628**	**-72**	**-259**	**-1,061**	**-2,317**	**-3,417**	**-3,605**	**-3,306**
Official creditors	28	162	268	457	144	-301	-963	-1,406	-1,568	-1,658
Multilateral	-4	-17	183	49	227	131	-158	-97	-312	-311
Concessional	0	-1	-2	-7	130	34	27	15	117	10
Bilateral	32	179	85	408	-83	-432	-804	-1,309	-1,256	-1,346
Concessional	32	-29	168	282	376	97	-61	-184	-235	-275
Private creditors	240	-733	-1,896	-528	-403	-760	-1,355	-2,011	-2,037	-1,648
Bonds	5	-30	-120	-493	-291	0	0	0	0	0
Commercial banks	14	-699	-1,450	-606	-218	-243	-358	-708	-672	-643
Other private	221	-4	-326	571	105	-517	-996	-1,303	-1,365	-1,006
Private nonguaranteed	**0**	**0**	**0**	**0**	**0**	**0**	**0**	**0**	**0**	**0**
Bonds	0	0	0	0	0	0	0	0	0	0
Commercial banks and other	0	0	0	0	0	0	0	0	0	0
Memo:										
IBRD	-4	0	97	-27	157	-105	-103	-276	-263	-242
IDA	0	0	0	0	0	0	0	0	0	0
DEBT SERVICE (LTDS)	**45**	**3,968**	**8,562**	**4,847**	**3,942**	**3,946**	**3,962**	**4,583**	**4,749**	**4,271**
Public and publicly guaranteed	**45**	**3,968**	**8,562**	**4,847**	**3,942**	**3,946**	**3,962**	**4,583**	**4,749**	**4,271**
Official creditors	17	404	1,485	1,051	1,447	1,878	2,170	2,172	2,311	2,182
Multilateral	4	71	429	652	705	692	951	691	744	648
Concessional	0	2	12	13	19	31	28	48	59	70
Bilateral	13	333	1,056	399	742	1,186	1,219	1,481	1,568	1,533
Concessional	13	107	114	104	125	226	219	253	304	323
Private creditors	28	3,564	7,078	3,796	2,495	2,068	1,793	2,411	2,438	2,090
Bonds	0	60	120	493	291	0	0	0	0	0
Commercial banks	3	1,590	1,856	725	473	384	391	730	680	649
Other private	25	1,915	5,102	2,579	1,732	1,684	1,401	1,680	1,758	1,441
Private nonguaranteed	**0**	**0**	**0**	**0**	**0**	**0**	**0**	**0**	**0**	**0**
Bonds	0	0	0	0	0	0	0	0	0	0
Commercial banks and other	0	0	0	0	0	0	0	0	0	0
Memo:										
IBRD	4	39	203	327	397	391	353	332	325	300
IDA	0	0	0	0	0	0	0	0	0	0
UNDISBURSED DEBT	**738**	**11,717**	**12,857**	**11,596**	**10,077**	**7,107**	**6,033**	**5,625**	**5,209**	**5,152**
Official creditors	579	4,169	5,159	5,971	5,937	4,889	4,362	3,953	3,464	2,516
Private creditors	159	7,548	7,698	5,625	4,140	2,218	1,671	1,672	1,745	2,637
Memorandum items										
Concessional LDOD	470	1,269	860	2,059	3,088	3,296	3,150	3,294	3,291	2,930
Variable rate LDOD	26	4,265	10,711	14,681	16,657	16,723	15,833	15,316	13,640	11,974
Public sector LDOD	940	17,040	26,336	28,068	30,944	30,970	28,598	28,320	25,759	22,935
Private sector LDOD	0	0	80	95	89	90	116	160	144	127

6. CURRENCY COMPOSITION OF LONG-TERM DEBT (PERCENT)

	1970	1980	1990	1994	1995	1996	1997	1998	1999	2000
Deutsche mark	1.9	9.9	10.5	6.3	7.2	6.9	6.6	6.7	5.8	5.5
French franc	36.0	10.9	16.8	13.9	16.2	16.9	15.5	15.1	13.2	12.6
Japanese yen	0.0	13.4	15.2	15.2	13.2	12.2	11.8	12.1	15.1	13.7
Pound sterling	8.3	2.2	1.5	1.0	0.9	1.0	1.1	1.0	1.0	1.0
Swiss franc	0.2	2.7	0.8	0.6	0.7	0.5	0.5	0.4	0.4	0.5
U.S.dollars	37.0	41.5	33.8	40.9	38.3	39.0	41.5	44.8	44.5	45.2
Multiple currency	1.7	3.4	4.9	7.5	8.0	7.7	7.9	1.8	1.9	2.0
Special drawing rights	0.0	0.0	0.0	0.0	0.0	0.0	0.0	0.0	0.0	0.0
All other currencies	14.9	16.0	16.5	14.6	15.5	15.8	15.1	18.1	18.1	19.5

ALGERIA

(US$ million, unless otherwise indicated)

	1970	1980	1990	1994	1995	1996	1997	1998	1999	2000
7. DEBT RESTRUCTURINGS										
Total amount rescheduled	..	..	0	4,229	5,096	3,674	2,295	559	2	0
Debt stock rescheduled	..	..	0	0	0	0	0	0	0	0
Principal rescheduled	..	..	0	3,737	4,405	3,244	2,114	543	0	0
Official	..	..	0	538	529	357	219	81	0	0
Private	..	..	0	3,199	3,875	2,887	1,895	462	0	0
Interest rescheduled	..	..	0	457	380	289	89	0	0	0
Official	..	..	0	79	68	45	20	0	0	0
Private	..	..	0	377	312	243	69	0	0	0
Debt forgiven	..	..	0	0	0	4	10	0	0	0
Memo: interest forgiven	..	..	0	0	0	0	0	0	0	0
Debt stock reduction	..	..	0	0	0	0	0	0	0	0
of which debt buyback	..	..	0	0	0	0	0	0	0	0
8. DEBT STOCK-FLOW RECONCILIATION										
Total change in debt stocks	..	..	805	3,934	2,813	647	-2,524	-218	-2,672	-3,003
Net flows on debt	279	1,261	-892	2,006	1,389	1,622	-426	-1,606	-1,927	-1,820
Net change in interest arrears	..	..	0	-1	3	-3	0	0	0	0
Interest capitalized	..	..	0	457	380	289	89	0	0	0
Debt forgiveness or reduction	..	..	0	0	0	-4	-10	0	0	0
Cross-currency valuation	..	..	1,648	1,325	662	-1,397	-2,199	1,186	-1,028	-1,144
Residual	..	..	50	147	379	141	21	202	283	-39
9. AVERAGE TERMS OF NEW COMMITMENTS										
ALL CREDITORS										
Interest (%)	5.7	8.1	8.4	5.5	6.5	5.5	5.5	5.3	5.1	5.6
Maturity (years)	12.7	12.5	9.1	10.2	9.7	10.7	11.1	11.2	22.8	8.3
Grace period (years)	3.6	3.5	2.5	3.1	2.8	2.9	3.2	3.1	2.0	2.0
Grant element (%)	23.0	8.3	7.0	17.5	13.5	18.8	17.0	19.5	21.4	10.4
Official creditors										
Interest (%)	2.8	7.7	7.0	5.0	6.2	5.8	5.5	6.0	4.5	3.9
Maturity (years)	23.9	17.7	16.8	14.3	10.2	11.3	11.1	14.9	47.2	13.8
Grace period (years)	9.2	5.2	4.0	5.8	3.3	3.7	3.6	3.6	3.1	3.7
Grant element (%)	54.3	13.5	19.5	25.8	15.1	18.5	17.2	19.6	34.1	33.1
Private creditors										
Interest (%)	6.4	8.4	8.9	5.7	7.1	4.8	5.8	4.7	5.4	6.0
Maturity (years)	9.8	9.7	6.5	8.0	8.7	9.2	11.1	7.6	11.7	6.9
Grace period (years)	2.1	2.6	2.0	1.7	1.9	1.3	1.7	2.7	1.5	1.5
Grant element (%)	14.8	5.5	2.9	13.1	10.3	19.6	16.3	19.3	15.5	4.6
Memorandum items										
Commitments	378	3,538	8,052	3,438	2,426	2,303	1,562	951	1,222	2,487
Official creditors	79	1,258	1,983	1,201	1,630	1,580	1,239	463	382	506
Private creditors	299	2,279	6,069	2,237	795	723	323	488	839	1,981

10. CONTRACTUAL OBLIGATIONS ON OUTSTANDING LONG-TERM DEBT

	2001	2002	2003	2004	2005	2006	2007	2008	2009	2010
TOTAL										
Disbursements	1,029	698	444	220	98	42	22	4	3	0
Principal	2,942	2,473	2,168	2,098	2,197	2,133	2,371	2,536	2,481	1,527
Interest	1,553	1,422	1,285	1,151	1,010	860	719	550	379	221
Official creditors										
Disbursements	610	465	315	179	88	40	22	4	3	0
Principal	1,715	1,456	1,323	1,373	1,469	1,565	1,811	2,086	2,148	1,366
Interest	1,156	1,085	1,003	919	826	725	616	487	346	209
Bilateral creditors										
Disbursements	115	42	24	14	8	3	0	0	0	0
Principal	961	730	787	882	1,011	1,162	1,439	1,725	1,843	1,082
Interest	830	783	736	683	623	553	472	370	255	140
Multilateral creditors										
Disbursements	495	423	291	165	80	37	21	4	3	0
Principal	754	727	536	492	458	403	372	361	306	284
Interest	326	301	267	237	203	173	144	117	91	69
Private creditors										
Disbursements	419	232	129	41	11	1	1	0	0	0
Principal	1,227	1,017	845	725	728	567	560	449	332	161
Interest	397	337	282	231	184	135	103	63	34	11
Commercial banks										
Disbursements	44	27	10	5	3	1	1	0	0	0
Principal	434	397	378	364	362	308	217	209	235	104
Interest	194	168	142	117	93	68	50	35	21	5
Other private										
Disbursements	375	206	120	36	8	0	0	0	0	0
Principal	794	621	467	361	366	260	342	240	98	58
Interest	203	169	140	114	92	67	53	28	13	6

ANGOLA

(US$ million, unless otherwise indicated)

1. SUMMARY DEBT DATA

	1970	1980	1990	1994	1995	1996	1997	1998	1999	2000
TOTAL DEBT STOCKS (EDT)	..	..	**8,594**	**11,172**	**11,380**	**10,425**	**9,839**	**11,071**	**11,029**	**10,146**
Long-term debt (LDOD)	..	..	**7,605**	**9,001**	**9,422**	**9,257**	**8,572**	**9,362**	**9,398**	**8,758**
Public and publicly guaranteed	..	..	7,605	9,001	9,422	9,257	8,572	9,362	9,398	8,758
Private nonguaranteed	..	..	0	0	0	0	0	0	0	0
Use of IMF credit	**0**	**0**	**0**	**0**	**0**	**0**	**0**	**0**	**0**	**0**
Short-term debt	..	..	**989**	**2,171**	**1,958**	**1,169**	**1,267**	**1,709**	**1,632**	**1,389**
of which interest arrears on LDOD	..	..	204	1,138	1,233	493	547	809	935	940
Official creditors	..	..	52	234	276	170	188	259	284	254
Private creditors	..	..	152	904	957	323	359	550	651	686
Memo: principal arrears on LDOD	..	..	497	3,767	4,192	1,627	1,722	2,414	2,743	3,013
Official creditors	..	..	86	895	1,098	381	414	569	682	735
Private creditors	..	..	412	2,873	3,094	1,246	1,308	1,845	2,061	2,278
Memo: export credits	..	..	1,639	2,084	2,290	2,100	2,208	1,546	1,866	1,902
TOTAL DEBT FLOWS										
Disbursements	..	..	**862**	**417**	**550**	**778**	**1,190**	**790**	**943**	**545**
Long-term debt	..	..	862	417	550	778	1,190	790	943	545
IMF purchases	0	0	0	0	0	0	0	0	0	0
Principal repayments	..	..	**183**	**153**	**332**	**653**	**806**	**912**	**848**	**1,042**
Long-term debt	..	..	183	153	332	653	806	912	848	1,042
IMF repurchases	0	0	0	0	0	0	0	0	0	0
Net flows on debt	..	..	**977**	**305**	**-90**	**76**	**429**	**58**	**-108**	**-745**
of which short-term debt	..	..	298	42	-308	-50	45	180	-203	-248
Interest payments (INT)	..	..	**143**	**106**	**132**	**333**	**186**	**216**	**153**	**163**
Long-term debt	..	..	100	51	79	284	140	171	108	137
IMF charges	0	0	0	0	0	0	0	0	0	0
Short-term debt	..	..	43	55	53	49	46	45	45	26
Net transfers on debt	..	..	**834**	**200**	**-222**	**-257**	**243**	**-157**	**-261**	**-908**
Total debt service paid (TDS)	..	..	**326**	**259**	**464**	**986**	**992**	**1,128**	**1,000**	**1,205**
Long-term debt	..	..	283	204	411	937	945	1,083	955	1,179
IMF repurchases and charges	0	0	0	0	0	0	0	0	0	0
Short-term debt (interest only)	..	..	43	55	53	49	46	45	45	26

2. AGGREGATE NET RESOURCE FLOWS AND NET TRANSFERS (LONG-TERM)

	1970	1980	1990	1994	1995	1996	1997	1998	1999	2000
NET RESOURCE FLOWS	..	..	**536**	**734**	**1,018**	**582**	**1,039**	**1,208**	**2,827**	**1,407**
Net flow of long-term debt (ex. IMF)	..	..	679	263	218	125	385	-122	95	-497
Foreign direct investment (net)	..	..	-335	170	472	181	412	1,114	2,471	1,698
Portfolio equity flows	..	..	0	0	0	0	0	0	0	0
Grants (excluding technical coop.)	..	..	192	301	328	276	242	216	261	206
Memo: technical coop. grants	..	..	36	69	73	114	57	52	58	52
official net resource flows	..	..	302	340	423	297	240	235	317	201
private net resource flows	..	..	235	394	595	285	798	973	2,510	1,206
NET TRANSFERS	..	..	**122**	**273**	**489**	**-102**	**474**	**588**	**2,225**	**770**
Interest on long-term debt	..	..	100	51	79	284	140	171	108	137
Profit remittances on FDI	..	..	314	410	450	400	425	450	495	500
Memo: official net transfers	..	..	283	330	411	279	228	227	315	169
private net transfers	..	..	-161	-57	78	-381	246	360	1,910	601

3. MAJOR ECONOMIC AGGREGATES

	1970	1980	1990	1994	1995	1996	1997	1998	1999	2000
Gross national income (GNI)	..	..	8,214	1,943	2,428	3,987	4,544	3,230	2,759	4,750
Exports of goods & services (XGS)	..	..	4,003	3,180	3,852	5,406	5,258	3,700	5,335	7,965
of which workers remittances	..	..	0	0	0	0	0	0	0	0
Imports of goods & services (MGS)	..	..	4,161	3,765	4,302	5,980	6,236	5,718	7,100	8,058
International reserves (RES)	..	..	..	..	213	552	396	203	496	1,198
Current account balance	..	..	-236	-340	-295	3,266	-872	-1,858	-1,702	-4

4. DEBT INDICATORS

	1970	1980	1990	1994	1995	1996	1997	1998	1999	2000
EDT / XGS (%)	..	..	214.7	351.4	295.4	192.9	187.1	299.2	206.7	127.4
EDT / GNI (%)	..	..	104.6	575.0	468.6	261.5	216.5	342.8	399.7	213.6
TDS / XGS (%)	..	..	8.1	8.2	12.0	18.2	18.9	30.5	18.7	15.1
INT / XGS (%)	..	..	3.6	3.3	3.4	6.2	3.5	5.8	2.9	2.0
INT / GNI (%)	..	..	1.7	5.5	5.4	8.4	4.1	6.7	5.5	3.4
RES / EDT (%)	..	..	..	..	1.9	5.3	4.0	1.8	4.5	11.8
RES / MGS (months)	..	..	..	..	0.6	1.1	0.8	0.4	0.8	1.8
Short-term / EDT (%)	..	..	11.5	19.4	17.2	11.2	12.9	15.4	14.8	13.7
Concessional / EDT (%)	..	..	13.9	12.6	13.1	20.7	22.5	24.7	25.0	27.1
Multilateral / EDT (%)	..	..	0.7	1.5	1.7	2.1	2.4	2.5	2.8	2.9

ANGOLA

(US$ million, unless otherwise indicated)

	1970	1980	1990	1994	1995	1996	1997	1998	1999	2000
5. LONG-TERM DEBT										
DEBT OUTSTANDING (LDOD)	..	..	**7,605**	**9,001**	**9,422**	**9,257**	**8,572**	**9,362**	**9,398**	**8,758**
Public and publicly guaranteed	..	..	**7,605**	**9,001**	**9,422**	**9,257**	**8,572**	**9,362**	**9,398**	**8,758**
Official creditors	..	..	1,839	1,970	2,104	2,745	2,758	3,663	3,664	3,616
Multilateral	..	..	57	164	192	218	234	279	312	294
Concessional	..	..	20	88	119	151	168	212	246	253
Bilateral	..	..	1,782	1,806	1,912	2,528	2,525	3,383	3,351	3,322
Concessional	..	..	1,177	1,318	1,371	2,002	2,044	2,523	2,508	2,495
Private creditors	..	..	5,767	7,031	7,318	6,511	5,813	5,699	5,734	5,142
Bonds	..	..	0	0	0	0	0	0	0	0
Commercial banks	..	..	196	612	924	4,064	3,574	2,944	3,080	2,641
Other private	..	..	5,571	6,420	6,394	2,447	2,239	2,755	2,654	2,501
Private nonguaranteed	..	..	**0**	**0**	**0**	**0**	**0**	**0**	**0**	**0**
Bonds	..	..	0	0	0	0	0	0	0	0
Commercial banks and other	..	..	0	0	0	0	0	0	0	0
Memo:										
IBRD	0	0	0	0	0	0	0	0	0	0
IDA	0	0	0	50	81	115	136	179	214	226
DISBURSEMENTS	..	..	**862**	**417**	**550**	**778**	**1,190**	**790**	**943**	**545**
Public and publicly guaranteed	..	..	**862**	**417**	**550**	**778**	**1,190**	**790**	**943**	**545**
Official creditors	..	..	169	73	119	55	36	81	68	34
Multilateral	..	..	5	33	30	38	28	36	39	24
Concessional	..	..	5	33	30	38	28	36	39	24
Bilateral	..	..	164	40	89	17	8	45	29	10
Concessional	..	..	54	40	33	5	8	45	29	10
Private creditors	..	..	693	344	431	723	1,154	709	875	511
Bonds	..	..	0	0	0	0	0	0	0	0
Commercial banks	..	..	17	299	396	685	1,126	665	869	511
Other private	..	..	676	45	35	38	28	45	7	0
Private nonguaranteed	..	..	**0**	**0**	**0**	**0**	**0**	**0**	**0**	**0**
Bonds	..	..	0	0	0	0	0	0	0	0
Commercial banks and other	..	..	0	0	0	0	0	0	0	0
Memo:										
IBRD	0	0	0	0	0	0	0	0	0	0
IDA	0	0	0	33	30	38	28	36	39	24
PRINCIPAL REPAYMENTS	..	..	**183**	**153**	**332**	**653**	**806**	**912**	**848**	**1,042**
Public and publicly guaranteed	..	..	**183**	**153**	**332**	**653**	**806**	**912**	**848**	**1,042**
Official creditors	..	..	60	33	24	33	37	62	12	39
Multilateral	..	..	4	0	2	0	1	0	1	28
Concessional	..	..	0	0	0	0	0	0	0	4
Bilateral	..	..	56	33	22	33	37	62	10	12
Concessional	..	..	1	9	3	8	8	13	6	6
Private creditors	..	..	123	120	308	619	768	850	836	1,003
Bonds	..	..	0	0	0	0	0	0	0	0
Commercial banks	..	..	24	48	108	410	621	720	787	947
Other private	..	..	100	73	200	209	147	130	49	56
Private nonguaranteed	..	..	**0**	**0**	**0**	**0**	**0**	**0**	**0**	**0**
Bonds	..	..	0	0	0	0	0	0	0	0
Commercial banks and other	..	..	0	0	0	0	0	0	0	0
Memo:										
IBRD	0	0	0	0	0	0	0	0	0	0
IDA	0	0	0	0	0	0	0	0	0	0
NET FLOWS ON DEBT	..	..	**679**	**263**	**218**	**125**	**385**	**-122**	**95**	**-497**
Public and publicly guaranteed	..	..	**679**	**263**	**218**	**125**	**385**	**-122**	**95**	**-497**
Official creditors	..	..	110	40	95	21	-2	19	56	-5
Multilateral	..	..	1	33	29	38	27	36	38	-4
Concessional	..	..	5	33	30	38	28	36	39	20
Bilateral	..	..	109	7	67	-16	-29	-18	19	-1
Concessional	..	..	53	31	30	-2	-1	31	23	5
Private creditors	..	..	570	224	123	104	386	-141	39	-492
Bonds	..	..	0	0	0	0	0	0	0	0
Commercial banks	..	..	-7	252	288	275	505	-56	82	-436
Other private	..	..	577	-28	-165	-171	-119	-85	-43	-56
Private nonguaranteed	..	..	**0**	**0**	**0**	**0**	**0**	**0**	**0**	**0**
Bonds	..	..	0	0	0	0	0	0	0	0
Commercial banks and other	..	..	0	0	0	0	0	0	0	0
Memo:										
IBRD	0	0	0	0	0	0	0	0	0	0
IDA	0	0	0	33	30	38	28	36	39	24

ANGOLA

(US$ million, unless otherwise indicated)

	1970	1980	1990	1994	1995	1996	1997	1998	1999	2000
INTEREST PAYMENTS (LINT)	..	..	**100**	**51**	**79**	**284**	**140**	**171**	**108**	**137**
Public and publicly guaranteed	..	..	**100**	**51**	**79**	**284**	**140**	**171**	**108**	**137**
Official creditors	..	..	19	10	12	18	12	8	3	32
Multilateral	..	..	2	0	1	1	1	1	2	28
Concessional	..	..	0	0	0	1	1	1	1	4
Bilateral	..	..	16	10	12	17	12	6	1	4
Concessional	..	..	1	7	7	2	5	3	1	2
Private creditors	..	..	81	41	67	266	127	163	105	105
Bonds	..	..	0	0	0	0	0	0	0	0
Commercial banks	..	..	8	11	33	227	92	153	92	87
Other private	..	..	74	30	34	39	36	10	13	19
Private nonguaranteed	..	..	**0**	**0**	**0**	**0**	**0**	**0**	**0**	**0**
Bonds	..	..	0	0	0	0	0	0	0	0
Commercial banks and other	..	..	0	0	0	0	0	0	0	0
Memo:										
IBRD	0	0	0	0	0	0	0	0	0	0
IDA	0	0	0	0	0	1	1	1	1	2
NET TRANSFERS ON DEBT	..	..	**579**	**213**	**139**	**-159**	**245**	**-292**	**-13**	**-634**
Public and publicly guaranteed	..	..	**579**	**213**	**139**	**-159**	**245**	**-292**	**-13**	**-634**
Official creditors	..	..	91	30	83	3	-14	11	54	-37
Multilateral	..	..	-2	33	28	37	27	35	36	-32
Concessional	..	..	4	33	30	37	27	35	37	16
Bilateral	..	..	92	-3	55	-34	-40	-24	18	-5
Concessional	..	..	52	24	23	-5	-6	29	23	2
Private creditors	..	..	488	183	56	-162	259	-304	-66	-597
Bonds	..	..	0	0	0	0	0	0	0	0
Commercial banks	..	..	-15	241	255	48	414	-208	-10	-523
Other private	..	..	503	-58	-199	-210	-155	-95	-56	-75
Private nonguaranteed	..	..	**0**	**0**	**0**	**0**	**0**	**0**	**0**	**0**
Bonds	..	..	0	0	0	0	0	0	0	0
Commercial banks and other	..	..	0	0	0	0	0	0	0	0
Memo:										
IBRD	0	0	0	0	0	0	0	0	0	0
IDA	0	0	0	33	30	37	27	35	37	22
DEBT SERVICE (LTDS)	..	..	**283**	**204**	**411**	**937**	**945**	**1,083**	**955**	**1,179**
Public and publicly guaranteed	..	..	**283**	**204**	**411**	**937**	**945**	**1,083**	**955**	**1,179**
Official creditors	..	..	78	43	36	51	50	70	14	71
Multilateral	..	..	6	1	3	1	1	1	3	56
Concessional	..	..	0	0	0	1	1	1	1	8
Bilateral	..	..	72	43	34	51	48	68	11	15
Concessional	..	..	2	15	10	10	14	16	6	8
Private creditors	..	..	205	161	375	885	895	1,013	941	1,108
Bonds	..	..	0	0	0	0	0	0	0	0
Commercial banks	..	..	31	58	141	638	713	873	879	1,033
Other private	..	..	173	103	234	248	183	140	62	75
Private nonguaranteed	..	..	**0**	**0**	**0**	**0**	**0**	**0**	**0**	**0**
Bonds	..	..	0	0	0	0	0	0	0	0
Commercial banks and other	..	..	0	0	0	0	0	0	0	0
Memo:										
IBRD	0	0	0	0	0	0	0	0	0	0
IDA	0	0	0	0	0	1	1	1	1	2
UNDISBURSED DEBT	..	..	**1,351**	**1,219**	**1,112**	**713**	**779**	**562**	**365**	**316**
Official creditors	..	..	488	705	612	344	320	246	164	155
Private creditors	..	..	863	515	500	369	459	316	200	161
Memorandum items										
Concessional LDOD	..	..	1,197	1,405	1,490	2,153	2,212	2,736	2,754	2,748
Variable rate LDOD	..	..	450	548	850	1,379	1,521	1,218	959	794
Public sector LDOD	..	..	7,600	8,972	9,392	9,231	8,543	9,336	9,371	8,731
Private sector LDOD	..	..	5	29	30	25	28	26	26	26

6. CURRENCY COMPOSITION OF LONG-TERM DEBT (PERCENT)

	1970	1980	1990	1994	1995	1996	1997	1998	1999	2000
Deutsche mark	..	..	0.3	0.2	0.2	0.2	0.2	0.3	0.3	0.3
French franc	..	..	3.6	4.0	4.5	4.3	4.0	3.9	3.4	3.4
Japanese yen	..	..	0.3	0.4	0.3	0.3	0.3	0.4	0.5	0.4
Pound sterling	..	..	1.4	0.9	0.9	1.0	1.1	1.0	0.9	0.9
Swiss franc	..	..	0.7	0.1	0.1	0.1	0.1	0.1	0.1	0.1
U.S.dollars	..	..	80.7	81.7	80.7	86.7	87.2	86.2	87.2	87.3
Multiple currency	..	..	0.5	1.0	1.0	0.9	0.9	0.9	0.9	0.6
Special drawing rights	..	..	0.0	0.3	0.5	0.7	0.9	1.1	1.3	1.5
All other currencies	..	..	12.5	11.4	11.8	5.8	5.3	6.1	5.4	5.5

ANGOLA

(US$ million, unless otherwise indicated)

	1970	1980	1990	1994	1995	1996	1997	1998	1999	2000
7. DEBT RESTRUCTURINGS										
Total amount rescheduled	..	..	252	151	437	1,580	95	528	0	0
Debt stock rescheduled	..	..	53	0	0	0	0	0	0	0
Principal rescheduled	..	..	160	205	360	1,216	28	17	3	3
Official	..	..	16	33	0	267	0	0	0	0
Private	..	..	143	172	360	950	28	17	3	3
Interest rescheduled	..	..	43	44	70	235	0	34	0	0
Official	..	..	8	7	0	38	0	0	0	0
Private	..	..	35	37	70	196	0	34	0	0
Debt forgiven	..	..	0	0	0	3,746	0	0	0	0
Memo: interest forgiven	..	..	0	0	0	3	0	0	0	0
Debt stock reduction	..	..	0	0	0	0	0	0	0	0
of which debt buyback	..	..	0	0	0	0	0	0	0	0
8. DEBT STOCK-FLOW RECONCILIATION										
Total change in debt stocks	..	..	1,303	586	207	-954	-587	1,233	-42	-883
Net flows on debt	..	..	977	305	-90	76	429	58	-108	-745
Net change in interest arrears	..	..	130	247	95	-739	54	262	125	5
Interest capitalized	..	..	43	44	70	235	0	34	0	0
Debt forgiveness or reduction	..	..	0	0	0	-3,746	0	0	0	0
Cross-currency valuation	..	..	150	94	76	-75	-133	59	-115	-78
Residual	..	..	3	-105	56	3,296	-936	820	55	-65
9. AVERAGE TERMS OF NEW COMMITMENTS										
ALL CREDITORS										
Interest (%)	..	..	6.9	6.9	8.1	7.3	7.6	7.2	7.8	4.7
Maturity (years)	..	..	10.1	3.8	8.7	4.5	5.6	7.6	3.6	8.1
Grace period (years)	..	..	2.6	0.8	0.4	1.3	0.9	0.9	0.6	2.5
Grant element (%)	..	..	14.2	5.1	5.4	6.4	6.4	11.2	3.4	19.3
Official creditors										
Interest (%)	..	..	5.7	10.2	8.1	2.8	3.0	1.4	0.0	0.8
Maturity (years)	..	..	14.1	7.8	9.9	29.6	22.3	29.5	0.0	39.8
Grace period (years)	..	..	3.7	1.9	0.4	7.1	4.1	1.9	0.0	10.3
Grant element (%)	..	..	22.0	2.3	6.4	57.5	46.9	59.0	0.0	80.6
Private creditors										
Interest (%)	..	..	7.7	6.2	8.1	7.5	7.7	7.8	7.8	5.0
Maturity (years)	..	..	7.5	3.0	8.6	3.3	5.1	5.1	3.6	6.0
Grace period (years)	..	..	1.8	0.6	0.4	1.0	0.8	0.8	0.6	2.0
Grant element (%)	..	..	9.0	5.6	5.4	4.0	5.3	5.7	3.4	15.2
Memorandum items										
Commitments	..	..	523	329	420	781	1,556	521	787	533
Official creditors	..	..	210	56	3	36	43	54	0	33
Private creditors	..	..	313	273	417	745	1,513	466	787	500

10. CONTRACTUAL OBLIGATIONS ON OUTSTANDING LONG-TERM DEBT

	2001	2002	2003	2004	2005	2006	2007	2008	2009	2010
TOTAL										
Disbursements	161	48	24	9	5	1	1	1	0	0
Principal	1,359	835	601	476	413	307	239	234	224	221
Interest	320	239	193	160	133	111	95	82	69	56
Official creditors										
Disbursements	45	23	14	9	5	1	1	1	0	0
Principal	325	259	192	174	173	169	161	160	154	153
Interest	143	127	115	105	95	86	77	69	60	52
Bilateral creditors										
Disbursements	20	9	6	3	2	1	1	1	0	0
Principal	312	246	179	165	163	159	154	153	147	145
Interest	138	123	111	102	93	84	75	67	58	50
Multilateral creditors										
Disbursements	26	14	9	6	3	0	0	0	0	0
Principal	14	14	13	10	10	9	7	7	7	8
Interest	5	4	4	3	3	2	2	2	2	2
Private creditors										
Disbursements	116	25	9	0	0	0	0	0	0	0
Principal	1,034	576	410	302	240	139	79	74	70	68
Interest	177	112	78	55	37	25	18	13	9	4
Commercial banks										
Disbursements	74	21	9	0	0	0	0	0	0	0
Principal	685	476	348	252	193	91	35	35	35	33
Interest	129	85	57	37	23	13	9	7	5	3
Other private										
Disbursements	42	5	0	0	0	0	0	0	0	0
Principal	349	100	61	50	48	48	44	40	35	35
Interest	48	27	21	18	15	12	9	6	4	2

ARGENTINA

(US$ million, unless otherwise indicated)

	1970	1980	1990	1994	1995	1996	1997	1998	1999	2000
1. SUMMARY DEBT DATA										
TOTAL DEBT STOCKS (EDT)	**5,810**	**27,157**	**62,232**	**75,139**	**98,802**	**111,419**	**128,411**	**141,549**	**145,294**	**146,172**
Long-term debt (LDOD)	**5,171**	**16,774**	**48,676**	**63,757**	**71,316**	**81,629**	**90,555**	**105,151**	**111,401**	**112,801**
Public and publicly guaranteed	1,880	10,181	46,876	50,634	55,250	62,560	67,144	77,285	84,082	86,599
Private nonguaranteed	3,291	6,593	1,800	13,123	16,066	19,068	23,411	27,866	27,320	26,202
Use of IMF credit	**0**	**0**	**3,083**	**4,211**	**6,131**	**6,293**	**5,868**	**5,442**	**4,478**	**5,056**
Short-term debt	**639**	**10,383**	**10,473**	**7,171**	**21,355**	**23,498**	**31,988**	**30,956**	**29,415**	**28,315**
of which interest arrears on LDOD	0	0	7,590	1	0	0	0	0	0	0
Official creditors	0	0	132	0	0	0	0	0	0	0
Private creditors	0	0	7,458	1	0	0	0	0	0	0
Memo: principal arrears on LDOD	0	0	4,371	0	0	0	0	0	0	0
Official creditors	0	0	224	0	0	0	0	0	0	0
Private creditors	0	0	4,147	0	0	0	0	0	0	0
Memo: export credits	0	0	8,964	12,514	12,262	12,191	10,951	5,902	5,042	4,493
TOTAL DEBT FLOWS										
Disbursements	**907**	**4,708**	**1,587**	**9,586**	**11,333**	**18,690**	**19,539**	**25,289**	**23,322**	**21,121**
Long-term debt	907	4,708	1,149	8,709	8,968	17,894	19,097	25,289	23,322	19,027
IMF purchases	0	0	437	876	2,365	796	442	0	0	2,094
Principal repayments	**772**	**1,853**	**3,443**	**1,909**	**3,542**	**6,781**	**10,892**	**12,549**	**15,455**	**15,733**
Long-term debt	772	1,853	2,745	1,494	3,057	6,350	10,414	11,892	14,631	14,453
IMF repurchases	0	0	697	415	484	431	479	657	824	1,280
Net flows on debt	**135**	**6,328**	**-1,856**	**6,195**	**21,976**	**14,052**	**17,137**	**11,708**	**6,326**	**4,288**
of which short-term debt	0	3,472	0	-1,482	14,185	2,143	8,491	-1,032	-1,541	-1,100
Interest payments (INT)	**338**	**2,329**	**2,716**	**3,862**	**5,348**	**6,183**	**7,332**	**8,937**	**10,226**	**11,613**
Long-term debt	338	1,337	2,208	3,157	4,346	4,679	5,724	7,099	8,467	9,686
IMF charges	0	0	277	203	275	270	276	264	197	195
Short-term debt	0	992	231	502	727	1,233	1,332	1,574	1,562	1,732
Net transfers on debt	**-203**	**3,998**	**-4,572**	**2,333**	**16,628**	**7,869**	**9,805**	**2,771**	**-3,900**	**-7,325**
Total debt service paid (TDS)	**1,110**	**4,182**	**6,158**	**5,771**	**8,889**	**12,963**	**18,225**	**21,486**	**25,681**	**27,345**
Long-term debt	1,110	3,190	4,953	4,651	7,403	11,029	16,138	18,992	23,099	24,139
IMF repurchases and charges	0	0	975	618	759	701	755	921	1,021	1,475
Short-term debt (interest only)	0	992	231	502	727	1,233	1,332	1,574	1,562	1,732
2. AGGREGATE NET RESOURCE FLOWS AND NET TRANSFERS (LONG-TERM)										
NET RESOURCE FLOWS	**143**	**3,535**	**274**	**12,071**	**11,768**	**19,383**	**20,117**	**20,777**	**33,103**	**16,719**
Net flow of long-term debt (ex. IMF)	135	2,855	-1,596	7,215	5,911	11,544	8,683	13,397	8,691	4,574
Foreign direct investment (net)	11	678	1,836	3,635	5,610	6,949	9,161	7,292	23,984	11,665
Portfolio equity flows	0	0	13	1,205	211	864	2,236	50	404	450
Grants (excluding technical coop.)	-3	2	21	16	36	27	37	38	24	31
Memo: technical coop. grants	12	35	71	80	84	85	77	72	91	77
official net resource flows	49	60	477	747	1,473	52	-43	1,737	753	100
private net resource flows	94	3,476	-203	11,324	10,294	19,331	20,160	19,041	32,349	16,620
NET TRANSFERS	**-268**	**1,593**	**-2,571**	**7,794**	**6,122**	**13,205**	**12,793**	**11,878**	**22,435**	**4,034**
Interest on long-term debt	338	1,337	2,208	3,157	4,346	4,679	5,724	7,099	8,467	9,686
Profit remittances on FDI	73	605	637	1,120	1,300	1,500	1,600	1,800	2,200	3,000
Memo: official net transfers	16	-86	21	-438	74	-1,279	-1,297	540	-647	-1,494
private net transfers	-284	1,679	-2,592	8,232	6,048	14,483	14,090	11,339	23,083	5,527
3. MAJOR ECONOMIC AGGREGATES										
Gross national income (GNI)	30,396	76,287	135,150	254,012	253,636	266,928	286,937	291,838	276,077	277,735
Exports of goods & services (XGS)	..	11,202	16,654	22,883	29,336	32,792	36,368	37,215	33,869	38,342
of which workers remittances	..	0	0	47	41	41	41	43	29	0
Imports of goods & services (MGS)	..	15,999	13,100	34,456	35,055	40,073	49,124	52,196	46,261	47,601
International reserves (RES)	682	9,297	6,222	16,003	15,979	19,719	22,425	24,856	26,350	25,152
Current account balance	..	-4,774	4,552	-11,158	-5,210	-6,877	-12,344	-14,626	-12,039	-8,970
4. DEBT INDICATORS										
EDT / XGS (%)	..	242.4	373.7	328.4	336.8	339.8	353.1	380.4	429.0	381.2
EDT / GNI (%)	19.1	35.6	46.1	29.6	39.0	41.7	44.8	48.5	52.6	52.6
TDS / XGS (%)	..	37.3	37.0	25.2	30.3	39.5	50.1	57.7	75.8	71.3
INT / XGS (%)	..	20.8	16.3	16.9	18.2	18.9	20.2	24.0	30.2	30.3
INT / GNI (%)	1.1	3.1	2.0	1.5	2.1	2.3	2.6	3.1	3.7	4.2
RES / EDT (%)	11.7	34.2	10.0	21.3	16.2	17.7	17.5	17.6	18.1	17.2
RES / MGS (months)	..	7.0	5.7	5.6	5.5	5.9	5.5	5.7	6.8	6.3
Short-term / EDT (%)	11.0	38.2	16.8	9.5	21.6	21.1	24.9	21.9	20.3	19.4
Concessional / EDT (%)	2.9	1.3	0.9	3.0	2.8	2.2	1.8	1.6	1.4	1.2
Multilateral / EDT (%)	4.8	4.0	8.1	10.3	9.5	8.8	8.0	9.4	10.6	11.1

ARGENTINA

(US$ million, unless otherwise indicated)

	1970	1980	1990	1994	1995	1996	1997	1998	1999	2000
5. LONG-TERM DEBT										
DEBT OUTSTANDING (LDOD)	**5,171**	**16,774**	**48,676**	**63,757**	**71,316**	**81,629**	**90,555**	**105,151**	**111,401**	**112,801**
Public and publicly guaranteed	**1,880**	**10,181**	**46,876**	**50,634**	**55,250**	**62,560**	**67,144**	**77,285**	**84,082**	**86,599**
Official creditors	637	1,903	11,226	18,830	20,963	19,812	18,352	20,492	20,991	20,534
Multilateral	281	1,087	5,007	7,748	9,373	9,784	10,268	13,317	15,324	16,235
Concessional	1	36	30	10	9	7	5	3	1	0
Bilateral	356	816	6,219	11,082	11,590	10,028	8,084	7,175	5,667	4,299
Concessional	166	329	498	2,251	2,737	2,487	2,270	2,197	2,056	1,686
Private creditors	1,243	8,278	35,649	31,804	34,287	42,748	48,792	56,794	63,091	66,065
Bonds	386	832	11,514	30,430	32,670	41,435	47,563	55,696	62,302	65,522
Commercial banks	121	6,065	22,631	916	1,207	1,050	1,059	982	718	503
Other private	735	1,381	1,504	459	410	264	171	116	71	39
Private nonguaranteed	**3,291**	**6,593**	**1,800**	**13,123**	**16,066**	**19,068**	**23,411**	**27,866**	**27,320**	**26,202**
Bonds	0	0	21	7,366	7,582	8,760	10,311	11,873	12,130	11,138
Commercial banks and other	3,291	6,593	1,779	5,757	8,484	10,308	13,100	15,992	15,189	15,064
Memo:										
IBRD	181	404	2,609	4,109	4,913	5,372	5,495	7,188	8,314	8,789
IDA	0	0	0	0	0	0	0	0	0	0
DISBURSEMENTS	**907**	**4,708**	**1,149**	**8,709**	**8,968**	**17,894**	**19,097**	**25,289**	**23,322**	**19,027**
Public and publicly guaranteed	**482**	**2,839**	**1,128**	**4,370**	**6,618**	**13,024**	**11,868**	**15,289**	**15,373**	**14,550**
Official creditors	162	276	910	1,469	2,803	1,678	1,887	3,504	2,814	1,937
Multilateral	64	208	736	787	1,936	1,584	1,673	3,487	2,798	1,923
Concessional	0	6	0	0	0	0	0	0	0	0
Bilateral	98	69	174	683	867	94	215	17	16	14
Concessional	46	13	149	238	630	34	97	11	11	11
Private creditors	321	2,563	219	2,901	3,815	11,346	9,981	11,785	12,560	12,613
Bonds	119	136	0	2,713	3,630	11,204	9,927	11,768	12,542	12,611
Commercial banks	53	2,173	183	110	119	142	54	17	18	2
Other private	149	253	36	77	66	0	0	0	0	0
Private nonguaranteed	**424**	**1,869**	**21**	**4,339**	**2,350**	**4,870**	**7,229**	**10,001**	**7,949**	**4,477**
Bonds	0	0	21	2,430	834	2,490	3,084	3,976	1,330	1,408
Commercial banks and other	424	1,869	0	1,910	1,516	2,380	4,145	6,025	6,619	3,069
Memo:										
IBRD	32	71	405	548	941	1,077	797	2,029	1,573	1,019
IDA	0	0	0	0	0	0	0	0	0	0
PRINCIPAL REPAYMENTS	**772**	**1,853**	**2,745**	**1,494**	**3,057**	**6,350**	**10,414**	**11,892**	**14,631**	**14,453**
Public and publicly guaranteed	**344**	**1,146**	**2,745**	**1,004**	**1,792**	**3,258**	**6,946**	**6,298**	**5,852**	**8,950**
Official creditors	110	218	454	738	1,366	1,653	1,967	1,806	2,084	1,868
Multilateral	16	121	405	665	512	565	571	669	770	825
Concessional	0	4	2	2	2	2	2	2	2	1
Bilateral	94	97	49	74	854	1,088	1,396	1,137	1,314	1,043
Concessional	11	34	0	20	58	103	144	205	254	262
Private creditors	234	928	2,292	266	427	1,606	4,979	4,492	3,767	7,082
Bonds	20	178	878	136	128	1,275	4,738	4,244	3,515	6,863
Commercial banks	69	481	1,342	63	173	208	153	178	209	189
Other private	145	268	72	67	125	122	88	70	44	31
Private nonguaranteed	**428**	**707**	**0**	**490**	**1,265**	**3,092**	**3,468**	**5,595**	**8,780**	**5,503**
Bonds	0	0	0	290	631	1,311	1,468	2,462	2,357	2,309
Commercial banks and other	428	707	0	200	634	1,781	2,000	3,133	6,423	3,194
Memo:										
IBRD	5	34	233	425	259	282	299	350	445	538
IDA	0	0	0	0	0	0	0	0	0	0
NET FLOWS ON DEBT	**135**	**2,855**	**-1,596**	**7,215**	**5,911**	**11,544**	**8,683**	**13,397**	**8,691**	**4,574**
Public and publicly guaranteed	**139**	**1,693**	**-1,617**	**3,366**	**4,826**	**9,766**	**4,923**	**8,991**	**9,522**	**5,600**
Official creditors	52	58	456	731	1,437	25	-80	1,699	729	69
Multilateral	47	86	332	122	1,424	1,019	1,101	2,818	2,028	1,098
Concessional	0	3	-2	-2	-2	-2	-2	-2	-2	-1
Bilateral	5	-29	125	609	13	-994	-1,181	-1,120	-1,298	-1,029
Concessional	35	-20	149	219	572	-69	-48	-194	-243	-252
Private creditors	87	1,635	-2,073	2,635	3,388	9,740	5,002	7,293	8,792	5,531
Bonds	99	-42	-878	2,577	3,502	9,930	5,190	7,523	9,027	5,748
Commercial banks	-16	1,692	-1,159	48	-54	-67	-99	-161	-191	-187
Other private	4	-16	-36	10	-60	-122	-88	-70	-44	-31
Private nonguaranteed	**-4**	**1,162**	**21**	**3,849**	**1,085**	**1,778**	**3,761**	**4,406**	**-831**	**-1,026**
Bonds	0	0	21	2,140	203	1,179	1,616	1,514	-1,027	-901
Commercial banks and other	-4	1,162	0	1,710	882	599	2,145	2,892	196	-125
Memo:										
IBRD	27	37	172	123	682	795	498	1,678	1,128	481
IDA	0	0	0	0	0	0	0	0	0	0

ARGENTINA

(US$ million, unless otherwise indicated)

	1970	1980	1990	1994	1995	1996	1997	1998	1999	2000
INTEREST PAYMENTS (LINT)	**338**	**1,337**	**2,208**	**3,157**	**4,346**	**4,679**	**5,724**	**7,099**	**8,467**	**9,686**
Public and publicly guaranteed	**121**	**841**	**2,064**	**2,597**	**3,461**	**3,737**	**4,494**	**5,428**	**6,276**	**7,645**
Official creditors	33	146	456	1,185	1,399	1,331	1,254	1,197	1,401	1,593
Multilateral	18	98	375	588	617	635	692	728	1,022	1,256
Concessional	0	1	1	1	0	0	0	0	0	0
Bilateral	16	49	81	597	782	697	562	470	379	338
Concessional	4	15	0	73	114	114	103	100	88	92
Private creditors	88	695	1,608	1,412	2,062	2,405	3,241	4,230	4,875	6,052
Bonds	23	80	973	1,346	1,960	2,290	3,155	4,129	4,805	5,910
Commercial banks	9	504	621	42	72	93	71	92	63	138
Other private	56	111	14	25	30	23	15	10	7	4
Private nonguaranteed	**217**	**496**	**144**	**560**	**885**	**942**	**1,230**	**1,672**	**2,191**	**2,041**
Bonds	0	0	0	469	641	691	806	907	1,157	1,109
Commercial banks and other	217	496	144	92	244	251	424	765	1,035	932
Memo:										
IBRD	11	37	182	284	306	326	335	375	537	701
IDA	0	0	0	0	0	0	0	0	0	0
NET TRANSFERS ON DEBT	**-203**	**1,518**	**-3,804**	**4,058**	**1,565**	**6,865**	**2,959**	**6,298**	**224**	**-5,112**
Public and publicly guaranteed	**18**	**852**	**-3,681**	**769**	**1,365**	**6,029**	**428**	**3,563**	**3,246**	**-2,045**
Official creditors	18	-88	0	-454	38	-1,306	-1,334	501	-671	-1,524
Multilateral	30	-11	-44	-466	807	385	409	2,091	1,006	-157
Concessional	0	1	-2	-2	-2	-2	-2	-2	-2	-1
Bilateral	-11	-77	44	12	-769	-1,690	-1,743	-1,589	-1,677	-1,367
Concessional	31	-35	149	145	458	-183	-150	-294	-331	-344
Private creditors	0	940	-3,681	1,223	1,327	7,335	1,762	3,062	3,917	-521
Bonds	77	-122	-1,851	1,231	1,542	7,640	2,035	3,395	4,222	-161
Commercial banks	-25	1,189	-1,780	6	-126	-160	-171	-252	-254	-325
Other private	-52	-127	-50	-14	-89	-145	-102	-80	-50	-35
Private nonguaranteed	**-221**	**666**	**-123**	**3,289**	**200**	**835**	**2,531**	**2,734**	**-3,022**	**-3,067**
Bonds	0	0	21	1,671	-438	487	810	607	-2,184	-2,010
Commercial banks and other	-221	666	-144	1,618	638	348	1,721	2,127	-838	-1,057
Memo:										
IBRD	16	0	-10	-161	376	469	162	1,304	591	-220
IDA	0	0	0	0	0	0	0	0	0	0
DEBT SERVICE (LTDS)	**1,110**	**3,190**	**4,953**	**4,651**	**7,403**	**11,029**	**16,138**	**18,992**	**23,099**	**24,139**
Public and publicly guaranteed	**464**	**1,987**	**4,809**	**3,601**	**5,253**	**6,995**	**11,440**	**11,726**	**12,128**	**16,595**
Official creditors	143	364	910	1,923	2,765	2,984	3,221	3,003	3,485	3,461
Multilateral	34	219	780	1,252	1,129	1,199	1,264	1,397	1,792	2,081
Concessional	0	5	2	2	2	2	2	2	2	1
Bilateral	109	146	130	671	1,636	1,785	1,957	1,606	1,693	1,380
Concessional	15	48	0	93	171	216	247	305	341	354
Private creditors	321	1,623	3,899	1,678	2,488	4,011	8,219	8,723	8,643	13,134
Bonds	42	258	1,851	1,482	2,088	3,564	7,893	8,373	8,320	12,772
Commercial banks	78	985	1,963	105	245	301	224	269	272	327
Other private	201	380	86	92	155	145	102	80	50	35
Private nonguaranteed	**646**	**1,203**	**144**	**1,050**	**2,150**	**4,035**	**4,698**	**7,266**	**10,971**	**7,544**
Bonds	0	0	0	759	1,272	2,003	2,274	3,369	3,514	3,418
Commercial banks and other	646	1,203	144	292	878	2,032	2,424	3,898	7,457	4,126
Memo:										
IBRD	16	71	414	709	565	608	635	725	982	1,239
IDA	0	0	0	0	0	0	0	0	0	0
UNDISBURSED DEBT	**577**	**2,176**	**2,355**	**4,862**	**6,699**	**6,032**	**6,435**	**9,088**	**9,045**	**5,731**
Official creditors	325	1,122	1,936	4,260	6,205	5,669	6,022	8,965	7,928	5,367
Private creditors	252	1,054	419	602	494	364	412	123	1,118	364
Memorandum items										
Concessional LDOD	167	365	529	2,261	2,745	2,493	2,274	2,200	2,057	1,686
Variable rate LDOD	3,291	12,417	28,167	33,288	36,521	39,238	45,532	54,173	55,369	52,008
Public sector LDOD	1,780	7,979	44,707	50,619	55,228	62,518	67,063	77,222	84,020	86,547
Private sector LDOD	3,390	8,795	3,969	13,139	16,088	19,111	23,492	27,929	27,381	26,254

6. CURRENCY COMPOSITION OF LONG-TERM DEBT (PERCENT)

	1970	1980	1990	1994	1995	1996	1997	1998	1999	2000
Deutsche mark	15.7	9.5	10.4	9.4	11.5	14.9	13.3	14.0	10.4	8.6
French franc	1.8	1.2	1.5	1.0	1.3	1.0	0.7	0.7	0.4	0.4
Japanese yen	0.2	5.8	6.7	6.5	9.4	8.5	6.8	6.2	5.7	5.8
Pound sterling	2.9	1.6	1.1	0.2	0.2	0.4	0.8	0.7	0.6	0.5
Swiss franc	1.9	3.4	2.2	1.2	1.6	1.3	1.0	0.7	0.5	0.4
U.S.dollars	47.7	64.5	54.5	64.9	59.3	57.4	61.7	63.8	64.5	62.8
Multiple currency	17.7	10.3	19.5	13.0	13.1	11.9	10.5	4.0	3.4	3.0
Special drawing rights	0.0	0.0	0.0	0.0	0.0	0.0	0.0	0.0	0.0	0.0
All other currencies	12.1	3.7	4.1	3.8	3.6	4.6	5.2	9.9	14.5	18.5

ARGENTINA

(US$ million, unless otherwise indicated)

	1970	1980	1990	1994	1995	1996	1997	1998	1999	2000
7. DEBT RESTRUCTURINGS										
Total amount rescheduled	..	..	932	847	248	0	0	0	0	0
Debt stock rescheduled	..	..	0	0	0	0	0	0	0	0
Principal rescheduled	..	..	512	844	198	0	0	0	0	0
Official	..	..	381	834	158	0	0	0	0	0
Private	..	..	131	10	40	0	0	0	0	0
Interest rescheduled	..	..	420	3	50	0	0	0	0	0
Official	..	..	382	3	22	0	0	0	0	0
Private	..	..	38	0	29	0	0	0	0	0
Debt forgiven	..	..	0	0	0	0	0	0	0	0
Memo: interest forgiven	..	..	0	0	0	0	0	0	0	0
Debt stock reduction	..	..	7,202	399	863	0	2,700	2,729	767	3,434
of which debt buyback	..	..	1,232	0	0	0	2,085	2,100	667	2,745
8. DEBT STOCK-FLOW RECONCILIATION										
Total change in debt stocks	..	..	-3,024	10,421	23,663	12,617	16,992	13,138	3,745	878
Net flows on debt	135	6,328	-1,856	6,195	21,976	14,052	17,137	11,708	6,326	4,288
Net change in interest arrears	..	..	1,949	0	-1	0	0	0	0	0
Interest capitalized	..	..	420	3	50	0	0	0	0	0
Debt forgiveness or reduction	..	..	-5,970	-399	-863	0	-615	-629	-100	-689
Cross-currency valuation	..	..	1,346	768	-147	-3,051	-4,212	734	-2,546	-2,520
Residual	..	..	1,087	3,854	2,646	1,616	4,682	1,325	65	-202
9. AVERAGE TERMS OF NEW COMMITMENTS										
ALL CREDITORS										
Interest (%)	7.3	13.7	6.4	7.2	6.9	8.4	8.2	8.9	9.5	9.9
Maturity (years)	11.9	8.6	17.0	9.8	11.2	8.3	14.5	12.2	8.8	11.7
Grace period (years)	2.9	4.5	3.5	4.0	4.7	7.2	12.1	10.1	7.4	11.5
Grant element (%)	12.6	-17.5	19.3	12.8	14.1	4.0	8.5	5.9	0.2	-2.7
Official creditors										
Interest (%)	7.5	6.1	6.5	5.8	6.5	6.8	6.7	8.5	7.9	7.2
Maturity (years)	16.7	14.5	19.1	16.8	16.3	15.2	16.3	9.5	11.0	17.3
Grace period (years)	3.4	5.2	4.0	4.9	4.7	5.1	4.1	4.0	3.3	5.0
Grant element (%)	11.4	20.2	20.6	25.0	19.7	18.4	18.4	7.6	10.3	16.8
Private creditors										
Interest (%)	7.3	14.3	6.0	8.3	7.4	8.6	8.5	9.1	9.7	10.0
Maturity (years)	10.6	8.2	8.4	4.4	4.7	7.5	14.0	13.8	8.4	11.6
Grace period (years)	2.7	4.4	1.4	3.3	4.6	7.4	13.9	13.8	8.1	11.6
Grant element (%)	13.0	-20.5	14.1	3.4	7.2	2.3	6.2	4.8	-1.4	-3.0
Memorandum items										
Commitments	494	3,062	572	5,395	8,386	12,494	15,724	18,777	15,712	11,977
Official creditors	105	225	460	2,342	4,672	1,310	2,997	6,996	2,142	188
Private creditors	389	2,837	112	3,053	3,714	11,183	12,727	11,781	13,570	11,789

10. CONTRACTUAL OBLIGATIONS ON OUTSTANDING LONG-TERM DEBT

	2001	2002	2003	2004	2005	2006	2007	2008	2009	2010
TOTAL										
Disbursements	1,921	1,477	1,101	650	376	204	104	48	27	9
Principal	13,262	12,767	17,581	14,393	9,279	4,731	5,170	6,324	5,173	3,145
Interest	8,708	8,066	7,252	6,231	5,163	4,552	4,151	3,534	2,945	2,664
Official creditors										
Disbursements	1,402	1,455	1,092	650	376	204	104	48	27	9
Principal	2,044	4,382	4,284	2,035	1,911	1,860	1,834	1,681	1,283	1,114
Interest	1,625	1,516	1,221	958	842	725	602	477	370	284
Bilateral creditors										
Disbursements	123	72	32	12	8	0	0	0	0	0
Principal	821	649	527	527	503	449	425	361	79	48
Interest	245	201	169	139	108	79	53	27	10	6
Multilateral creditors										
Disbursements	1,279	1,383	1,060	638	368	204	104	48	27	9
Principal	1,224	3,733	3,756	1,508	1,408	1,411	1,409	1,321	1,204	1,066
Interest	1,380	1,315	1,052	820	733	645	549	450	360	278
Private creditors										
Disbursements	520	22	9	0	0	0	0	0	0	0
Principal	11,218	8,385	13,297	12,358	7,368	2,871	3,336	4,642	3,890	2,031
Interest	7,084	6,549	6,031	5,273	4,321	3,827	3,549	3,057	2,575	2,381
Commercial banks										
Disbursements	65	22	9	0	0	0	0	0	0	0
Principal	126	118	71	67	60	55	55	14	12	10
Interest	41	34	27	22	16	12	7	4	2	1
Other private										
Disbursements	454	0	0	0	0	0	0	0	0	0
Principal	11,092	8,267	13,226	12,291	7,308	2,815	3,281	4,628	3,877	2,021
Interest	7,043	6,515	6,004	5,251	4,305	3,816	3,541	3,053	2,573	2,379

ARMENIA

(US$ million, unless otherwise indicated)

	1970	1980	1990	1994	1995	1996	1997	1998	1999	2000
1. SUMMARY DEBT DATA										
TOTAL DEBT STOCKS (EDT)	..	..	..	**214.3**	**370.7**	**520.5**	**638.5**	**799.2**	**882.9**	**897.5**
Long-term debt (LDOD)	..	..	..	**188.6**	**298.3**	**402.7**	**484.4**	**563.6**	**632.5**	**677.7**
Public and publicly guaranteed	..	..	..	188.6	298.3	402.7	484.4	563.6	632.5	658.1
Private nonguaranteed	..	..	..	0.0	0.0	0.0	0.0	0.0	0.0	19.5
Use of IMF credit	..	..	..	**24.6**	**70.2**	**116.5**	**132.1**	**190.4**	**201.2**	**175.5**
Short-term debt	..	..	..	**1.1**	**2.1**	**1.4**	**22.0**	**45.2**	**49.2**	**44.4**
of which interest arrears on LDOD	..	..	..	1.1	1.1	0.0	0.0	0.0	0.0	6.1
Official creditors	..	..	..	1.1	1.1	0.0	0.0	0.0	0.0	6.1
Private creditors	..	..	..	0.0	0.0	0.0	0.0	0.0	0.0	0.0
Memo: principal arrears on LDOD	..	..	..	31.2	75.4	64.0	53.2	0.0	0.0	4.4
Official creditors	..	..	..	31.2	75.4	64.0	53.2	0.0	0.0	4.4
Private creditors	..	..	..	0.0	0.0	0.0	0.0	0.0	0.0	0.0
Memo: export credits	..	..	..	0.0	0.0	1.6	0.0	7.0	0.2	0.3
TOTAL DEBT FLOWS										
Disbursements	..	..	..	**84.7**	**148.5**	**195.1**	**131.2**	**158.6**	**123.6**	**81.8**
Long-term debt	..	..	..	60.5	102.4	146.1	108.0	107.3	95.0	81.8
IMF purchases	..	..	..	24.2	46.1	49.0	23.2	51.3	28.6	0.0
Principal repayments	..	..	..	**0.0**	**2.8**	**32.8**	**7.5**	**40.7**	**38.7**	**28.6**
Long-term debt	..	..	..	0.0	2.8	32.8	7.5	40.2	25.7	12.8
IMF repurchases	..	..	..	0.0	0.0	0.0	0.0	0.6	13.1	15.8
Net flows on debt	..	..	..	**84.7**	**146.6**	**162.7**	**144.3**	**141.0**	**88.9**	**42.3**
of which short-term debt	..	..	..	0.0	1.0	0.4	20.6	23.2	4.0	-10.9
Interest payments (INT)	..	..	..	**4.4**	**8.5**	**9.9**	**16.4**	**20.5**	**19.5**	**14.4**
Long-term debt	..	..	..	4.4	6.7	6.6	12.5	15.2	14.1	9.1
IMF charges	..	..	..	0.0	1.7	3.2	3.3	3.4	3.0	2.9
Short-term debt	..	..	..	0.0	0.0	0.1	0.6	1.8	2.5	2.4
Net transfers on debt	..	..	..	**80.2**	**138.2**	**152.8**	**127.9**	**120.5**	**69.4**	**27.9**
Total debt service paid (TDS)	..	..	..	**4.4**	**11.3**	**42.7**	**24.0**	**61.2**	**58.3**	**43.0**
Long-term debt	..	..	..	4.4	9.6	39.5	20.0	55.4	39.8	21.9
IMF repurchases and charges	..	..	..	0.0	1.7	3.2	3.3	4.0	16.1	18.6
Short-term debt (interest only)	..	..	..	0.0	0.0	0.1	0.6	1.8	2.5	2.4
2. AGGREGATE NET RESOURCE FLOWS AND NET TRANSFERS (LONG-TERM)										
NET RESOURCE FLOWS	..	..	..	**239.5**	**215.5**	**187.4**	**186.9**	**341.4**	**238.5**	**270.3**
Net flow of long-term debt (ex. IMF)	..	..	..	60.5	99.5	113.3	100.5	67.1	69.3	69.0
Foreign direct investment (net)	..	..	..	8.0	25.3	17.6	51.9	220.8	122.0	140.0
Portfolio equity flows	..	..	..	0.0	0.0	0.0	0.0	0.0	0.0	0.0
Grants (excluding technical coop.)	..	..	..	171.0	90.7	56.5	34.5	53.5	47.2	61.4
Memo: technical coop. grants	..	..	..	14.8	38.6	85.0	14.9	25.6	55.9	94.2
official net resource flows	..	..	..	231.5	190.2	169.8	135.0	120.6	116.5	110.9
private net resource flows	..	..	..	8.0	25.3	17.6	51.9	220.8	122.0	159.4
NET TRANSFERS	..	..	..	**235.1**	**208.8**	**179.8**	**172.4**	**323.2**	**222.4**	**258.2**
Interest on long-term debt	..	..	..	4.4	6.7	6.6	12.5	15.2	14.1	9.1
Profit remittances on FDI	..	..	..	0.0	0.0	1.0	2.0	3.0	2.0	3.0
Memo: official net transfers	..	..	..	227.1	183.5	163.2	122.5	105.4	102.4	101.8
private net transfers	..	..	..	8.0	25.3	16.6	49.9	217.8	120.0	156.4
3. MAJOR ECONOMIC AGGREGATES										
Gross national income (GNI)	..	..	..	2,358.5	2,883.1	1,599.5	1,641.9	1,919.5	1,857.5	1,931.5
Exports of goods & services (XGS)	..	..	..	229.0	366.5	457.3	477.9	473.2	491.6	564.0
of which workers remittances	..	..	..	..	12.4	11.1	8.7	10.1	14.9	13.4
Imports of goods & services (MGS)	..	..	..	438.4	740.8	921.5	992.9	1,058.5	957.9	1,017.1
International reserves (RES)	..	..	..	36.1	111.2	168.2	239.2	327.7	331.2	330.6
Current account balance	..	..	..	-103.8	-218.4	-290.7	-306.5	-418.0	-307.0	-278.5
4. DEBT INDICATORS										
EDT / XGS (%)	..	..	..	93.6	101.2	113.8	133.6	168.9	179.6	159.1
EDT / GNI (%)	..	..	..	9.1	12.9	32.5	38.9	41.6	47.5	46.5
TDS / XGS (%)	..	..	..	1.9	3.1	9.3	5.0	12.9	11.9	7.6
INT / XGS (%)	..	..	..	1.9	2.3	2.2	3.4	4.3	4.0	2.6
INT / GNI (%)	..	..	..	0.2	0.3	0.6	1.0	1.1	1.1	0.8
RES / EDT (%)	..	..	..	16.9	30.0	32.3	37.5	41.0	37.5	36.8
RES / MGS (months)	..	..	..	1.0	1.8	2.2	2.9	3.7	4.2	3.9
Short-term / EDT (%)	..	..	..	0.5	0.6	0.3	3.5	5.7	5.6	5.0
Concessional / EDT (%)	..	..	..	9.7	28.5	38.8	40.5	43.5	47.6	51.1
Multilateral / EDT (%)	..	..	..	48.6	56.1	59.8	57.7	50.1	51.6	54.0

ARMENIA

(US$ million, unless otherwise indicated)

	1970	1980	1990	1994	1995	1996	1997	1998	1999	2000
5. LONG-TERM DEBT										
DEBT OUTSTANDING (LDOD)	..	..	..	**188.6**	**298.3**	**402.7**	**484.4**	**563.6**	**632.5**	**677.7**
Public and publicly guaranteed	..	..	..	**188.6**	**298.3**	**402.7**	**484.4**	**563.6**	**632.5**	**658.1**
Official creditors	..	..	..	188.6	298.3	402.7	484.4	563.6	632.5	658.1
Multilateral	..	..	..	104.1	208.0	311.2	368.6	400.4	455.7	484.9
Concessional	..	..	..	5.6	90.9	175.3	242.1	300.4	369.6	406.7
Bilateral	..	..	..	84.6	90.3	91.5	115.8	163.2	176.8	173.2
Concessional	..	..	..	15.1	14.9	26.4	16.6	46.9	51.0	52.0
Private creditors	..	..	..	0.0	0.0	0.0	0.0	0.0	0.0	0.0
Bonds	..	..	..	0.0	0.0	0.0	0.0	0.0	0.0	0.0
Commercial banks	..	..	..	0.0	0.0	0.0	0.0	0.0	0.0	0.0
Other private	..	..	..	0.0	0.0	0.0	0.0	0.0	0.0	0.0
Private nonguaranteed	..	..	..	**0.0**	**0.0**	**0.0**	**0.0**	**0.0**	**0.0**	**19.5**
Bonds	..	..	..	0.0	0.0	0.0	0.0	0.0	0.0	0.0
Commercial banks and other	..	..	..	0.0	0.0	0.0	0.0	0.0	0.0	19.5
Memo:										
IBRD	..	..	..	1.6	4.8	9.8	9.9	9.7	9.2	8.3
IDA	..	..	..	5.6	90.9	174.0	240.3	292.8	352.1	388.3
DISBURSEMENTS	..	..	..	**60.5**	**102.4**	**146.1**	**108.0**	**107.3**	**95.0**	**81.8**
Public and publicly guaranteed	..	..	..	**60.5**	**102.4**	**146.1**	**108.0**	**107.3**	**95.0**	**62.4**
Official creditors	..	..	..	60.5	102.4	146.1	108.0	107.3	95.0	62.4
Multilateral	..	..	..	37.3	102.4	122.0	81.3	50.0	78.7	58.1
Concessional	..	..	..	5.5	88.5	88.3	77.1	48.3	75.8	56.2
Bilateral	..	..	..	23.2	0.0	24.1	26.8	57.2	16.3	4.3
Concessional	..	..	..	0.0	0.0	15.3	1.2	30.4	1.6	4.3
Private creditors	..	..	..	0.0	0.0	0.0	0.0	0.0	0.0	0.0
Bonds	..	..	..	0.0	0.0	0.0	0.0	0.0	0.0	0.0
Commercial banks	..	..	..	0.0	0.0	0.0	0.0	0.0	0.0	0.0
Other private	..	..	..	0.0	0.0	0.0	0.0	0.0	0.0	0.0
Private nonguaranteed	..	..	..	**0.0**	**0.0**	**0.0**	**0.0**	**0.0**	**0.0**	**19.4**
Bonds	..	..	..	0.0	0.0	0.0	0.0	0.0	0.0	0.0
Commercial banks and other	..	..	..	0.0	0.0	0.0	0.0	0.0	0.0	19.4
Memo:										
IBRD	..	..	..	1.0	3.4	5.4	0.9	0.0	0.0	0.0
IDA	..	..	..	5.5	88.5	87.0	76.5	42.9	65.7	54.4
PRINCIPAL REPAYMENTS	..	..	..	**0.0**	**2.8**	**32.8**	**7.5**	**40.2**	**25.7**	**12.8**
Public and publicly guaranteed	..	..	..	**0.0**	**2.8**	**32.8**	**7.5**	**40.2**	**25.7**	**12.8**
Official creditors	..	..	..	0.0	2.8	32.8	7.5	40.2	25.7	12.8
Multilateral	..	..	..	0.0	0.0	10.1	5.3	30.3	12.6	7.5
Concessional	..	..	..	0.0	0.0	0.0	0.0	0.0	0.0	0.0
Bilateral	..	..	..	0.0	2.8	22.7	2.2	9.9	13.1	5.3
Concessional	..	..	..	0.0	0.0	3.7	0.1	0.0	4.9	2.8
Private creditors	..	..	..	0.0	0.0	0.0	0.0	0.0	0.0	0.0
Bonds	..	..	..	0.0	0.0	0.0	0.0	0.0	0.0	0.0
Commercial banks	..	..	..	0.0	0.0	0.0	0.0	0.0	0.0	0.0
Other private	..	..	..	0.0	0.0	0.0	0.0	0.0	0.0	0.0
Private nonguaranteed	..	..	..	**0.0**	**0.0**	**0.0**	**0.0**	**0.0**	**0.0**	**0.0**
Bonds	..	..	..	0.0	0.0	0.0	0.0	0.0	0.0	0.0
Commercial banks and other	..	..	..	0.0	0.0	0.0	0.0	0.0	0.0	0.0
Memo:										
IBRD	..	..	..	0.0	0.0	0.0	0.0	0.2	0.4	0.4
IDA	..	..	..	0.0	0.0	0.0	0.0	0.0	0.0	0.0
NET FLOWS ON DEBT	..	..	..	**60.5**	**99.5**	**113.3**	**100.5**	**67.1**	**69.3**	**69.0**
Public and publicly guaranteed	..	..	..	**60.5**	**99.5**	**113.3**	**100.5**	**67.1**	**69.3**	**49.5**
Official creditors	..	..	..	60.5	99.5	113.3	100.5	67.1	69.3	49.5
Multilateral	..	..	..	37.3	102.4	111.9	76.0	19.8	66.1	50.6
Concessional	..	..	..	5.5	88.5	88.3	77.1	48.3	75.8	56.2
Bilateral	..	..	..	23.2	-2.8	1.4	24.5	47.4	3.2	-1.0
Concessional	..	..	..	0.0	0.0	11.7	1.1	30.3	-3.3	1.4
Private creditors	..	..	..	0.0	0.0	0.0	0.0	0.0	0.0	0.0
Bonds	..	..	..	0.0	0.0	0.0	0.0	0.0	0.0	0.0
Commercial banks	..	..	..	0.0	0.0	0.0	0.0	0.0	0.0	0.0
Other private	..	..	..	0.0	0.0	0.0	0.0	0.0	0.0	0.0
Private nonguaranteed	..	..	..	**0.0**	**0.0**	**0.0**	**0.0**	**0.0**	**0.0**	**19.4**
Bonds	..	..	..	0.0	0.0	0.0	0.0	0.0	0.0	0.0
Commercial banks and other	..	..	..	0.0	0.0	0.0	0.0	0.0	0.0	19.4
Memo:										
IBRD	..	..	..	1.0	3.4	5.4	0.9	-0.2	-0.4	-0.4
IDA	..	..	..	5.5	88.5	87.0	76.5	42.9	65.7	54.4

ARMENIA

(US$ million, unless otherwise indicated)

	1970	1980	1990	1994	1995	1996	1997	1998	1999	2000
INTEREST PAYMENTS (LINT)	..	..	..	**4.4**	**6.7**	**6.6**	**12.5**	**15.2**	**14.1**	**9.1**
Public and publicly guaranteed	..	..	..	**4.4**	**6.7**	**6.6**	**12.5**	**15.2**	**14.1**	**9.1**
Official creditors	..	..	..	4.4	6.7	6.6	12.5	15.2	14.1	9.1
Multilateral	..	..	..	4.4	6.7	2.9	9.6	9.6	7.2	8.0
Concessional	..	..	..	0.0	0.2	0.8	1.2	1.7	2.2	2.9
Bilateral	..	..	..	0.0	0.1	3.7	2.9	5.6	6.9	1.1
Concessional	..	..	..	0.0	0.1	0.3	0.4	0.5	0.8	0.9
Private creditors	..	..	..	0.0	0.0	0.0	0.0	0.0	0.0	0.0
Bonds	..	..	..	0.0	0.0	0.0	0.0	0.0	0.0	0.0
Commercial banks	..	..	..	0.0	0.0	0.0	0.0	0.0	0.0	0.0
Other private	..	..	..	0.0	0.0	0.0	0.0	0.0	0.0	0.0
Private nonguaranteed	..	..	..	**0.0**	**0.0**	**0.0**	**0.0**	**0.0**	**0.0**	**0.0**
Bonds	..	..	..	0.0	0.0	0.0	0.0	0.0	0.0	0.0
Commercial banks and other	..	..	..	0.0	0.0	0.0	0.0	0.0	0.0	0.0
Memo:										
IBRD	..	..	..	0.1	0.2	0.4	0.6	0.6	0.6	0.5
IDA	..	..	..	0.0	0.2	0.8	1.2	1.7	2.1	2.7
NET TRANSFERS ON DEBT	..	..	..	**56.1**	**92.8**	**106.7**	**88.0**	**51.9**	**55.3**	**59.9**
Public and publicly guaranteed	..	..	..	**56.1**	**92.8**	**106.7**	**88.0**	**51.9**	**55.3**	**40.5**
Official creditors	..	..	..	56.1	92.8	106.7	88.0	51.9	55.3	40.5
Multilateral	..	..	..	32.9	95.7	109.0	66.3	10.1	59.0	42.6
Concessional	..	..	..	5.5	88.3	87.5	75.9	46.7	73.6	53.3
Bilateral	..	..	..	23.2	-2.9	-2.3	21.6	41.8	-3.7	-2.1
Concessional	..	..	..	0.0	-0.1	11.4	0.7	29.9	-4.0	0.6
Private creditors	..	..	..	0.0	0.0	0.0	0.0	0.0	0.0	0.0
Bonds	..	..	..	0.0	0.0	0.0	0.0	0.0	0.0	0.0
Commercial banks	..	..	..	0.0	0.0	0.0	0.0	0.0	0.0	0.0
Other private	..	..	..	0.0	0.0	0.0	0.0	0.0	0.0	0.0
Private nonguaranteed	..	..	..	**0.0**	**0.0**	**0.0**	**0.0**	**0.0**	**0.0**	**19.4**
Bonds	..	..	..	0.0	0.0	0.0	0.0	0.0	0.0	0.0
Commercial banks and other	..	..	..	0.0	0.0	0.0	0.0	0.0	0.0	19.4
Memo:										
IBRD	..	..	..	0.9	3.2	5.1	0.3	-0.8	-0.9	-0.9
IDA	..	..	..	5.5	88.3	86.2	75.3	41.2	63.5	51.6
DEBT SERVICE (LTDS)	..	..	..	**4.4**	**9.6**	**39.5**	**20.0**	**55.4**	**39.8**	**21.9**
Public and publicly guaranteed	..	..	..	**4.4**	**9.6**	**39.5**	**20.0**	**55.4**	**39.8**	**21.9**
Official creditors	..	..	..	4.4	9.6	39.5	20.0	55.4	39.8	21.9
Multilateral	..	..	..	4.4	6.7	13.0	14.9	39.9	19.7	15.5
Concessional	..	..	..	0.0	0.2	0.8	1.2	1.7	2.2	2.9
Bilateral	..	..	..	0.0	2.9	26.4	5.1	15.5	20.0	6.4
Concessional	..	..	..	0.0	0.1	4.0	0.5	0.5	5.6	3.7
Private creditors	..	..	..	0.0	0.0	0.0	0.0	0.0	0.0	0.0
Bonds	..	..	..	0.0	0.0	0.0	0.0	0.0	0.0	0.0
Commercial banks	..	..	..	0.0	0.0	0.0	0.0	0.0	0.0	0.0
Other private	..	..	..	0.0	0.0	0.0	0.0	0.0	0.0	0.0
Private nonguaranteed	..	..	..	**0.0**	**0.0**	**0.0**	**0.0**	**0.0**	**0.0**	**0.0**
Bonds	..	..	..	0.0	0.0	0.0	0.0	0.0	0.0	0.0
Commercial banks and other	..	..	..	0.0	0.0	0.0	0.0	0.0	0.0	0.0
Memo:										
IBRD	..	..	..	0.1	0.2	0.4	0.6	0.8	0.9	0.9
IDA	..	..	..	0.0	0.2	0.8	1.2	1.7	2.1	2.7
UNDISBURSED DEBT	..	..	..	**171.2**	**188.9**	**117.7**	**191.1**	**267.4**	**210.8**	**197.4**
Official creditors	..	..	..	171.2	188.9	117.7	191.1	267.4	210.8	197.4
Private creditors	..	..	..	0.0	0.0	0.0	0.0	0.0	0.0	0.0
Memorandum items										
Concessional LDOD	..	..	..	20.7	105.9	201.8	258.7	347.4	420.6	458.7
Variable rate LDOD	..	..	..	163.8	189.3	198.8	152.0	128.8	124.7	134.8
Public sector LDOD	..	..	..	188.6	298.3	402.7	484.4	563.6	632.5	658.1
Private sector LDOD	..	..	..	0.0	0.0	0.0	0.0	0.0	0.0	19.5

6. CURRENCY COMPOSITION OF LONG-TERM DEBT (PERCENT)

	1970	1980	1990	1994	1995	1996	1997	1998	1999	2000
Deutsche mark	..	..	..	0.0	0.0	0.0	0.0	0.0	0.0	0.4
French franc	..	..	..	0.0	0.0	0.3	0.5	0.5	0.4	0.4
Japanese yen	..	..	..	0.0	0.0	0.0	0.0	0.0	0.0	0.0
Pound sterling	..	..	..	0.0	0.0	0.0	0.0	0.0	0.0	0.0
Swiss franc	..	..	..	0.0	0.0	0.0	0.0	0.0	0.0	0.0
U.S.dollars	..	..	..	42.0	62.6	75.7	86.0	91.3	92.2	93.2
Multiple currency	..	..	..	0.8	1.6	2.4	2.0	1.7	1.5	1.3
Special drawing rights	..	..	..	0.0	0.0	0.3	0.4	0.7	1.1	1.1
All other currencies	..	..	..	57.2	35.8	21.3	11.1	5.8	4.8	3.6

ARMENIA

(US$ million, unless otherwise indicated)

	1970	1980	1990	1994	1995	1996	1997	1998	1999	2000
7. DEBT RESTRUCTURINGS										
Total amount rescheduled	..	..	..	0.0	0.0	0.0	73.7	31.3	0.0	14.4
Debt stock rescheduled	..	..	..	0.0	0.0	0.0	73.7	31.3	0.0	0.0
Principal rescheduled	..	..	..	0.0	0.0	0.0	0.0	0.0	0.0	14.4
Official	..	..	..	0.0	0.0	0.0	0.0	0.0	0.0	14.4
Private	..	..	..	0.0	0.0	0.0	0.0	0.0	0.0	0.0
Interest rescheduled	..	..	..	0.0	0.0	0.0	0.0	0.0	0.0	0.0
Official	..	..	..	0.0	0.0	0.0	0.0	0.0	0.0	0.0
Private	..	..	..	0.0	0.0	0.0	0.0	0.0	0.0	0.0
Debt forgiven	..	..	..	0.0	0.0	0.0	0.0	0.0	0.0	0.0
Memo: interest forgiven	..	..	..	0.0	0.0	0.0	0.0	0.0	0.0	0.0
Debt stock reduction	..	..	..	0.0	0.0	0.0	0.0	0.0	0.0	0.0
of which debt buyback	..	..	..	0.0	0.0	0.0	0.0	0.0	0.0	0.0
8. DEBT STOCK-FLOW RECONCILIATION										
Total change in debt stocks	..	..	..	80.4	156.3	149.9	117.9	160.7	83.7	14.6
Net flows on debt	..	..	..	84.7	146.6	162.7	144.3	141.0	88.9	42.3
Net change in interest arrears	..	..	..	1.1	0.1	-1.1	0.0	0.0	0.0	6.1
Interest capitalized	..	..	..	0.0	0.0	0.0	0.0	0.0	0.0	0.0
Debt forgiveness or reduction	..	..	..	0.0	0.0	0.0	0.0	0.0	0.0	0.0
Cross-currency valuation	..	..	..	-15.7	-6.1	-82.0	-90.2	-106.6	44.0	-31.5
Residual	..	..	..	10.3	15.7	70.3	63.9	126.3	-49.2	-2.3
9. AVERAGE TERMS OF NEW COMMITMENTS										
ALL CREDITORS										
Interest (%)	..	..	..	3.6	1.3	1.8	2.0	1.7	0.8	0.8
Maturity (years)	..	..	..	20.7	32.6	33.7	29.3	29.8	34.7	34.8
Grace period (years)	..	..	..	6.1	9.2	9.1	8.4	8.8	10.2	10.3
Grant element (%)	..	..	..	44.6	72.4	68.6	63.9	66.3	78.7	78.8
Official creditors										
Interest (%)	..	..	..	3.6	1.3	1.8	2.0	1.7	0.8	0.8
Maturity (years)	..	..	..	20.7	32.6	33.7	29.3	29.8	34.7	34.8
Grace period (years)	..	..	..	6.1	9.2	9.1	8.4	8.8	10.2	10.3
Grant element (%)	..	..	..	44.6	72.4	68.6	63.9	66.3	78.7	78.8
Private creditors										
Interest (%)	..	..	..	0.0	0.0	0.0	0.0	0.0	0.0	0.0
Maturity (years)	..	..	..	0.0	0.0	0.0	0.0	0.0	0.0	0.0
Grace period (years)	..	..	..	0.0	0.0	0.0	0.0	0.0	0.0	0.0
Grant element (%)	..	..	..	0.0	0.0	0.0	0.0	0.0	0.0	0.0
Memorandum items										
Commitments	..	..	..	172.8	131.1	78.8	189.6	192.7	47.6	60.0
Official creditors	..	..	..	172.8	131.1	78.8	189.6	192.7	47.6	60.0
Private creditors	..	..	..	0.0	0.0	0.0	0.0	0.0	0.0	0.0

10. CONTRACTUAL OBLIGATIONS ON OUTSTANDING LONG-TERM DEBT

	2001	2002	2003	2004	2005	2006	2007	2008	2009	2010
TOTAL										
Disbursements	61.0	52.4	37.3	25.1	14.0	5.1	2.6	0.0	0.0	0.0
Principal	26.9	27.4	26.1	33.2	34.2	38.8	32.6	21.4	21.2	24.3
Interest	16.7	15.9	14.8	14.4	12.6	10.7	8.9	7.6	6.9	6.3
Official creditors										
Disbursements	61.0	52.4	37.3	25.1	14.0	5.1	2.6	0.0	0.0	0.0
Principal	26.9	27.4	26.1	28.8	29.8	34.5	28.3	19.4	21.2	24.3
Interest	16.7	15.9	14.8	13.4	11.9	10.2	8.5	7.5	6.9	6.3
Bilateral creditors										
Disbursements	15.3	10.7	5.9	3.2	1.3	0.8	0.3	0.0	0.0	0.0
Principal	18.1	18.7	17.4	19.4	18.3	19.9	14.3	8.8	5.6	5.1
Interest	8.2	7.6	6.8	5.8	4.8	3.7	2.7	2.0	1.5	1.3
Multilateral creditors										
Disbursements	45.7	41.7	31.4	21.9	12.6	4.3	2.3	0.0	0.0	0.0
Principal	8.8	8.8	8.8	9.4	11.4	14.6	14.0	10.6	15.5	19.2
Interest	8.4	8.3	8.0	7.6	7.1	6.5	5.9	5.5	5.3	5.0
Private creditors										
Disbursements	0.0	0.0	0.0	0.0	0.0	0.0	0.0	0.0	0.0	0.0
Principal	0.0	0.0	0.0	4.3	4.5	4.3	4.3	2.1	0.0	0.0
Interest	0.0	0.0	0.0	0.9	0.7	0.5	0.4	0.1	0.0	0.0
Commercial banks										
Disbursements	0.0	0.0	0.0	0.0	0.0	0.0	0.0	0.0	0.0	0.0
Principal	0.0	0.0	0.0	0.0	0.0	0.0	0.0	0.0	0.0	0.0
Interest	0.0	0.0	0.0	0.0	0.0	0.0	0.0	0.0	0.0	0.0
Other private										
Disbursements	0.0	0.0	0.0	0.0	0.0	0.0	0.0	0.0	0.0	0.0
Principal	0.0	0.0	0.0	4.3	4.5	4.3	4.3	2.1	0.0	0.0
Interest	0.0	0.0	0.0	0.9	0.7	0.5	0.4	0.1	0.0	0.0

AZERBAIJAN

(US$ million, unless otherwise indicated)

	1970	1980	1990	1994	1995	1996	1997	1998	1999	2000
1. SUMMARY DEBT DATA										
TOTAL DEBT STOCKS (EDT)	..	..	..	**112.8**	**321.0**	**438.3**	**506.7**	**708.2**	**1,038.1**	**1,184.2**
Long-term debt (LDOD)	..	..	..	**103.2**	**206.1**	**247.9**	**235.9**	**385.5**	**601.8**	**692.1**
Public and publicly guaranteed	..	..	..	103.2	206.1	247.9	235.9	313.1	493.3	593.5
Private nonguaranteed	..	..	..	0.0	0.0	0.0	0.0	72.3	108.5	98.6
Use of IMF credit	..	..	..	**0.0**	**100.9**	**175.0**	**266.8**	**321.2**	**407.3**	**335.8**
Short-term debt	..	..	..	**9.6**	**14.0**	**15.5**	**4.0**	**1.5**	**29.0**	**156.2**
of which interest arrears on LDOD	..	..	..	3.6	6.0	2.5	0.0	0.0	0.0	0.0
Official creditors	..	..	..	3.6	6.0	2.5	0.0	0.0	0.0	0.0
Private creditors	..	..	..	0.0	0.0	0.0	0.0	0.0	0.0	0.0
Memo: principal arrears on LDOD	..	..	..	20.3	35.5	35.5	0.0	24.8	24.8	0.0
Official creditors	..	..	..	20.3	35.5	35.5	0.0	24.8	24.8	0.0
Private creditors	..	..	..	0.0	0.0	0.0	0.0	0.0	0.0	0.0
Memo: export credits	..	..	..	0.0	0.0	0.0	17.7	73.6	159.1	347.5
TOTAL DEBT FLOWS										
Disbursements	..	..	..	**67.4**	**205.0**	**124.7**	**196.0**	**183.9**	**378.0**	**196.2**
Long-term debt	..	..	..	67.4	102.1	46.6	91.3	142.7	268.2	196.2
IMF purchases	..	..	..	0.0	103.0	78.1	104.7	41.3	109.8	0.0
Principal repayments	..	..	..	**0.0**	**0.0**	**0.0**	**57.6**	**2.7**	**57.7**	**122.8**
Long-term debt	..	..	..	0.0	0.0	0.0	57.6	2.7	41.6	71.4
IMF repurchases	..	..	..	0.0	0.0	0.0	0.0	0.0	16.0	51.4
Net flows on debt	..	..	..	**73.4**	**207.0**	**129.7**	**129.4**	**178.7**	**347.9**	**200.6**
of which short-term debt	..	..	..	6.0	2.0	5.0	-9.0	-2.5	27.5	127.2
Interest payments (INT)	..	..	..	**0.4**	**10.1**	**9.8**	**20.3**	**21.2**	**27.8**	**58.1**
Long-term debt	..	..	..	0.0	8.7	4.3	11.6	11.2	14.9	38.9
IMF charges	..	..	..	0.0	1.1	4.9	8.1	9.8	11.5	14.0
Short-term debt	..	..	..	0.4	0.3	0.6	0.5	0.1	1.5	5.2
Net transfers on debt	..	..	..	**73.0**	**196.9**	**119.9**	**109.1**	**157.6**	**320.1**	**142.5**
Total debt service paid (TDS)	..	..	..	**0.4**	**10.1**	**9.8**	**77.9**	**23.8**	**85.4**	**180.9**
Long-term debt	..	..	..	0.0	8.7	4.3	69.3	13.9	56.5	110.3
IMF repurchases and charges	..	..	..	0.0	1.1	4.9	8.1	9.8	27.5	65.4
Short-term debt (interest only)	..	..	..	0.4	0.3	0.6	0.5	0.1	1.5	5.2
2. AGGREGATE NET RESOURCE FLOWS AND NET TRANSFERS (LONG-TERM)										
NET RESOURCE FLOWS	..	..	..	**233.5**	**493.0**	**716.1**	**1,184.2**	**1,199.0**	**790.5**	**305.3**
Net flow of long-term debt (ex. IMF)	..	..	..	67.4	102.1	46.6	33.7	140.0	226.6	124.8
Foreign direct investment (net)	..	..	..	22.0	330.0	627.0	1,115.0	1,023.0	510.3	130.0
Portfolio equity flows	..	..	..	0.0	0.0	0.0	0.0	0.0	0.0	0.0
Grants (excluding technical coop.)	..	..	..	144.1	60.9	42.5	35.4	36.1	53.6	50.5
Memo: technical coop. grants	..	..	..	3.3	27.8	17.9	15.6	31.9	22.2	30.4
official net resource flows	..	..	..	211.5	163.0	89.1	61.1	109.3	192.4	130.0
private net resource flows	..	..	..	22.0	330.0	627.0	1,123.1	1,089.7	598.1	175.3
NET TRANSFERS	..	..	..	**233.5**	**484.3**	**711.8**	**1,172.6**	**1,187.8**	**775.6**	**251.3**
Interest on long-term debt	..	..	..	0.0	8.7	4.3	11.6	11.2	14.9	38.9
Profit remittances on FDI	..	..	..	0.0	0.0	0.0	0.0	0.0	0.0	15.0
Memo: official net transfers	..	..	..	211.5	154.3	84.8	49.5	101.5	184.6	96.9
private net transfers	..	..	..	22.0	330.0	627.0	1,123.1	1,086.3	591.0	154.4
3. MAJOR ECONOMIC AGGREGATES										
Gross national income (GNI)	..	..	..	3,287.8	2,878.1	3,114.1	3,896.7	4,429.7	4,507.7	4,920.7
Exports of goods & services (XGS)	..	..	..	819.0	858.4	943.3	1,165.6	1,049.5	1,315.0	2,251.9
of which workers remittances	..	..	..	0.0	0.0	0.0	0.0	16.0	9.0	57.1
Imports of goods & services (MGS)	..	..	..	1,017.5	1,286.5	1,830.8	2,182.7	2,465.4	1,988.2	2,418.1
International reserves (RES)	..	..	..	2.0	120.9	211.3	466.1	447.3	672.6	679.6
Current account balance	..	..	..	-123.5	-317.4	-820.9	-971.5	-1,363.4	-601.1	-150.0
4. DEBT INDICATORS										
EDT / XGS (%)	..	..	..	13.8	37.4	46.5	43.5	67.5	78.9	52.6
EDT / GNI (%)	..	..	..	3.4	11.2	14.1	13.0	16.0	23.0	24.1
TDS / XGS (%)	..	..	..	0.1	1.2	1.0	6.7	2.3	6.5	8.0
INT / XGS (%)	..	..	..	0.1	1.2	1.0	1.7	2.0	2.1	2.6
INT / GNI (%)	..	..	..	0.0	0.4	0.3	0.5	0.5	0.6	1.2
RES / EDT (%)	..	..	..	1.8	37.7	48.2	92.0	63.2	64.8	57.4
RES / MGS (months)	..	..	..	0.0	1.1	1.4	2.6	2.2	4.1	3.4
Short-term / EDT (%)	..	..	..	8.5	4.4	3.5	0.8	0.2	2.8	13.2
Concessional / EDT (%)	..	..	..	0.0	9.4	14.7	23.0	23.1	29.1	33.3
Multilateral / EDT (%)	..	..	..	7.5	30.8	31.4	30.0	28.2	27.3	27.0

AZERBAIJAN

(US$ million, unless otherwise indicated)

	1970	1980	1990	1994	1995	1996	1997	1998	1999	2000
5. LONG-TERM DEBT										
DEBT OUTSTANDING (LDOD)	..	..	..	**103.2**	**206.1**	**247.9**	**235.9**	**385.5**	**601.8**	**692.1**
Public and publicly guaranteed	..	..	..	**103.2**	**206.1**	**247.9**	**235.9**	**313.1**	**493.3**	**593.5**
Official creditors	..	..	..	103.2	206.1	247.9	227.8	307.7	449.2	503.3
Multilateral	..	..	..	8.4	98.8	137.5	151.9	199.4	283.3	320.0
Concessional	..	..	..	0.0	30.2	64.3	115.5	144.9	205.8	226.8
Bilateral	..	..	..	94.8	107.3	110.3	75.9	108.3	165.9	183.4
Concessional	..	..	..	0.0	0.0	0.0	1.1	19.0	96.2	167.0
Private creditors	..	..	..	0.0	0.0	0.0	8.1	5.4	44.1	90.2
Bonds	..	..	..	0.0	0.0	0.0	0.0	0.0	0.0	0.0
Commercial banks	..	..	..	0.0	0.0	0.0	0.0	0.0	18.6	65.2
Other private	..	..	..	0.0	0.0	0.0	8.1	5.4	25.5	25.0
Private nonguaranteed	..	..	..	**0.0**	**0.0**	**0.0**	**0.0**	**72.3**	**108.5**	**98.6**
Bonds	..	..	..	0.0	0.0	0.0	0.0	0.0	0.0	0.0
Commercial banks and other	..	..	..	0.0	0.0	0.0	0.0	72.3	108.5	98.6
Memo:										
IBRD	..	..	..	0.0	0.0	0.0	0.0	0.0	0.0	0.0
IDA	..	..	..	0.0	30.2	64.3	115.5	141.3	199.3	216.2
DISBURSEMENTS	..	..	..	**67.4**	**102.1**	**46.6**	**91.3**	**142.7**	**268.2**	**196.2**
Public and publicly guaranteed	..	..	..	**67.4**	**102.1**	**46.6**	**91.3**	**73.2**	**218.1**	**190.6**
Official creditors	..	..	..	67.4	102.1	46.6	83.3	73.2	171.1	141.3
Multilateral	..	..	..	8.2	89.5	43.5	82.1	42.3	93.8	55.8
Concessional	..	..	..	0.0	30.2	35.8	55.4	24.1	63.5	31.7
Bilateral	..	..	..	59.3	12.5	3.0	1.2	30.9	77.3	85.5
Concessional	..	..	..	0.0	0.0	0.0	1.2	16.4	71.9	85.4
Private creditors	..	..	..	0.0	0.0	0.0	8.1	0.0	47.0	49.3
Bonds	..	..	..	0.0	0.0	0.0	0.0	0.0	0.0	0.0
Commercial banks	..	..	..	0.0	0.0	0.0	0.0	0.0	19.9	46.0
Other private	..	..	..	0.0	0.0	0.0	8.1	0.0	27.1	3.4
Private nonguaranteed	..	..	..	**0.0**	**0.0**	**0.0**	**0.0**	**69.4**	**50.1**	**5.5**
Bonds	..	..	..	0.0	0.0	0.0	0.0	0.0	0.0	0.0
Commercial banks and other	..	..	..	0.0	0.0	0.0	0.0	69.4	50.1	5.5
Memo:										
IBRD	..	..	..	0.0	0.0	0.0	0.0	0.0	0.0	0.0
IDA	..	..	..	0.0	30.2	35.8	55.4	20.6	60.5	27.2
PRINCIPAL REPAYMENTS	..	..	..	**0.0**	**0.0**	**0.0**	**57.6**	**2.7**	**41.6**	**71.4**
Public and publicly guaranteed	..	..	..	**0.0**	**0.0**	**0.0**	**57.6**	**2.7**	**40.6**	**64.0**
Official creditors	..	..	..	0.0	0.0	0.0	57.6	0.0	32.3	61.7
Multilateral	..	..	..	0.0	0.0	0.0	57.6	0.0	7.3	8.3
Concessional	..	..	..	0.0	0.0	0.0	0.0	0.0	0.0	0.0
Bilateral	..	..	..	0.0	0.0	0.0	0.0	0.0	25.0	53.5
Concessional	..	..	..	0.0	0.0	0.0	0.0	0.0	0.0	0.0
Private creditors	..	..	..	0.0	0.0	0.0	0.0	2.7	8.3	2.2
Bonds	..	..	..	0.0	0.0	0.0	0.0	0.0	0.0	0.0
Commercial banks	..	..	..	0.0	0.0	0.0	0.0	0.0	0.0	0.0
Other private	..	..	..	0.0	0.0	0.0	0.0	2.7	8.3	2.2
Private nonguaranteed	..	..	..	**0.0**	**0.0**	**0.0**	**0.0**	**0.0**	**1.1**	**7.4**
Bonds	..	..	..	0.0	0.0	0.0	0.0	0.0	0.0	0.0
Commercial banks and other	..	..	..	0.0	0.0	0.0	0.0	0.0	1.1	7.4
Memo:										
IBRD	..	..	..	0.0	0.0	0.0	0.0	0.0	0.0	0.0
IDA	..	..	..	0.0	0.0	0.0	0.0	0.0	0.0	0.0
NET FLOWS ON DEBT	..	..	..	**67.4**	**102.1**	**46.6**	**33.7**	**140.0**	**226.6**	**124.8**
Public and publicly guaranteed	..	..	..	**67.4**	**102.1**	**46.6**	**33.7**	**70.5**	**177.5**	**126.7**
Official creditors	..	..	..	67.4	102.1	46.6	25.7	73.2	138.8	79.5
Multilateral	..	..	..	8.2	89.5	43.5	24.5	42.3	86.5	47.5
Concessional	..	..	..	0.0	30.2	35.8	55.4	24.1	63.5	31.7
Bilateral	..	..	..	59.3	12.5	3.0	1.2	30.9	52.3	32.1
Concessional	..	..	..	0.0	0.0	0.0	1.2	16.4	71.9	85.4
Private creditors	..	..	..	0.0	0.0	0.0	8.1	-2.7	38.7	47.1
Bonds	..	..	..	0.0	0.0	0.0	0.0	0.0	0.0	0.0
Commercial banks	..	..	..	0.0	0.0	0.0	0.0	0.0	19.9	46.0
Other private	..	..	..	0.0	0.0	0.0	8.1	-2.7	18.8	1.1
Private nonguaranteed	..	..	..	**0.0**	**0.0**	**0.0**	**0.0**	**69.4**	**49.1**	**-1.8**
Bonds	..	..	..	0.0	0.0	0.0	0.0	0.0	0.0	0.0
Commercial banks and other	..	..	..	0.0	0.0	0.0	0.0	69.4	49.1	-1.8
Memo:										
IBRD	..	..	..	0.0	0.0	0.0	0.0	0.0	0.0	0.0
IDA	..	..	..	0.0	30.2	35.8	55.4	20.6	60.5	27.2

AZERBAIJAN

(US$ million, unless otherwise indicated)

	1970	1980	1990	1994	1995	1996	1997	1998	1999	2000
INTEREST PAYMENTS (LINT)	..	..	..	**0.0**	**8.7**	**4.3**	**11.6**	**11.2**	**14.9**	**38.9**
Public and publicly guaranteed	..	..	..	**0.0**	**8.7**	**4.3**	**11.6**	**8.8**	**9.2**	**34.0**
Official creditors	..	..	..	0.0	8.7	4.3	11.6	7.8	7.8	33.1
Multilateral	..	..	..	0.0	1.9	0.3	2.0	1.5	2.7	7.2
Concessional	..	..	..	0.0	0.0	0.3	0.5	0.9	1.4	1.7
Bilateral	..	..	..	0.0	6.8	4.0	9.7	6.3	5.1	25.9
Concessional	..	..	..	0.0	0.0	0.0	0.0	0.0	0.7	23.6
Private creditors	..	..	..	0.0	0.0	0.0	0.0	1.0	1.4	1.0
Bonds	..	..	..	0.0	0.0	0.0	0.0	0.0	0.0	0.0
Commercial banks	..	..	..	0.0	0.0	0.0	0.0	0.0	0.2	0.0
Other private	..	..	..	0.0	0.0	0.0	0.0	1.0	1.2	0.9
Private nonguaranteed	..	..	..	**0.0**	**0.0**	**0.0**	**0.0**	**2.4**	**5.7**	**4.9**
Bonds	..	..	..	0.0	0.0	0.0	0.0	0.0	0.0	0.0
Commercial banks and other	..	..	..	0.0	0.0	0.0	0.0	2.4	5.7	4.9
Memo:										
IBRD	..	..	..	0.0	0.0	0.0	0.0	0.0	0.0	0.0
IDA	..	..	..	0.0	0.0	0.3	0.5	0.9	1.2	1.5
NET TRANSFERS ON DEBT	..	..	..	**67.4**	**93.4**	**42.2**	**22.1**	**128.8**	**211.7**	**85.9**
Public and publicly guaranteed	..	..	..	**67.4**	**93.4**	**42.2**	**22.1**	**61.8**	**168.3**	**92.6**
Official creditors	..	..	..	67.4	93.4	42.2	14.0	65.4	131.0	46.5
Multilateral	..	..	..	8.2	87.6	43.2	22.5	40.8	83.8	40.3
Concessional	..	..	..	0.0	30.2	35.5	54.9	23.2	62.1	30.1
Bilateral	..	..	..	59.3	5.7	-1.0	-8.5	24.6	47.2	6.2
Concessional	..	..	..	0.0	0.0	0.0	1.2	16.4	71.2	61.8
Private creditors	..	..	..	0.0	0.0	0.0	8.1	-3.7	37.3	46.2
Bonds	..	..	..	0.0	0.0	0.0	0.0	0.0	0.0	0.0
Commercial banks	..	..	..	0.0	0.0	0.0	0.0	0.0	19.7	46.0
Other private	..	..	..	0.0	0.0	0.0	8.1	-3.7	17.7	0.2
Private nonguaranteed	..	..	..	**0.0**	**0.0**	**0.0**	**0.0**	**67.0**	**43.4**	**-6.7**
Bonds	..	..	..	0.0	0.0	0.0	0.0	0.0	0.0	0.0
Commercial banks and other	..	..	..	0.0	0.0	0.0	0.0	67.0	43.4	-6.7
Memo:										
IBRD	..	..	..	0.0	0.0	0.0	0.0	0.0	0.0	0.0
IDA	..	..	..	0.0	30.2	35.5	54.9	19.7	59.3	25.7
DEBT SERVICE (LTDS)	..	..	..	**0.0**	**8.7**	**4.3**	**69.3**	**13.9**	**56.5**	**110.3**
Public and publicly guaranteed	..	..	..	**0.0**	**8.7**	**4.3**	**69.3**	**11.5**	**49.8**	**98.0**
Official creditors	..	..	..	0.0	8.7	4.3	69.3	7.8	40.1	94.8
Multilateral	..	..	..	0.0	1.9	0.3	59.6	1.5	10.0	15.5
Concessional	..	..	..	0.0	0.0	0.3	0.5	0.9	1.4	1.7
Bilateral	..	..	..	0.0	6.8	4.0	9.7	6.3	30.1	79.3
Concessional	..	..	..	0.0	0.0	0.0	0.0	0.0	0.7	23.6
Private creditors	..	..	..	0.0	0.0	0.0	0.0	3.7	9.7	3.2
Bonds	..	..	..	0.0	0.0	0.0	0.0	0.0	0.0	0.0
Commercial banks	..	..	..	0.0	0.0	0.0	0.0	0.0	0.2	0.0
Other private	..	..	..	0.0	0.0	0.0	0.0	3.7	9.5	3.2
Private nonguaranteed	..	..	..	**0.0**	**0.0**	**0.0**	**0.0**	**2.4**	**6.7**	**12.2**
Bonds	..	..	..	0.0	0.0	0.0	0.0	0.0	0.0	0.0
Commercial banks and other	..	..	..	0.0	0.0	0.0	0.0	2.4	6.7	12.2
Memo:										
IBRD	..	..	..	0.0	0.0	0.0	0.0	0.0	0.0	0.0
IDA	..	..	..	0.0	0.0	0.3	0.5	0.9	1.2	1.5
UNDISBURSED DEBT	..	..	..	**329.4**	**413.3**	**226.8**	**303.3**	**645.8**	**731.0**	**539.0**
Official creditors	..	..	..	329.4	413.3	226.8	279.1	550.7	689.0	538.5
Private creditors	..	..	..	0.0	0.0	0.0	24.2	95.1	42.0	0.6
Memorandum items										
Concessional LDOD	..	..	..	0.0	30.2	64.3	116.7	163.8	302.0	393.8
Variable rate LDOD	..	..	..	103.2	175.9	183.6	119.2	221.6	286.7	281.3
Public sector LDOD	..	..	..	103.2	206.1	247.9	235.9	313.1	493.3	593.5
Private sector LDOD	..	..	..	0.0	0.0	0.0	0.0	72.3	108.5	98.6

6. CURRENCY COMPOSITION OF LONG-TERM DEBT (PERCENT)

	1970	1980	1990	1994	1995	1996	1997	1998	1999	2000
Deutsche mark	..	..	..	0.0	0.0	0.0	0.5	3.6	4.5	4.3
French franc	..	..	..	0.0	0.0	0.0	0.0	0.0	0.0	0.0
Japanese yen	..	..	..	0.0	0.0	0.0	0.0	2.5	17.4	25.8
Pound sterling	..	..	..	0.0	0.0	0.0	0.0	0.0	0.0	0.0
Swiss franc	..	..	..	0.0	0.0	0.0	0.0	0.0	3.8	8.1
U.S.dollars	..	..	..	57.4	51.4	60.0	99.5	92.8	72.9	57.8
Multiple currency	..	..	..	0.0	0.0	0.0	0.0	0.0	0.0	0.0
Special drawing rights	..	..	..	0.0	0.0	0.0	0.0	0.0	0.0	0.0
All other currencies	..	..	..	42.6	48.6	40.0	0.0	1.1	1.4	4.0

AZERBAIJAN

(US$ million, unless otherwise indicated)

	1970	1980	1990	1994	1995	1996	1997	1998	1999	2000
7. DEBT RESTRUCTURINGS										
Total amount rescheduled	..	..	..	0.0	0.0	0.0	0.0	0.0	0.0	0.0
Debt stock rescheduled	..	..	..	0.0	0.0	0.0	0.0	0.0	0.0	0.0
Principal rescheduled	..	..	..	0.0	0.0	0.0	0.0	0.0	0.0	0.0
Official	..	..	..	0.0	0.0	0.0	0.0	0.0	0.0	0.0
Private	..	..	..	0.0	0.0	0.0	0.0	0.0	0.0	0.0
Interest rescheduled	..	..	..	0.0	0.0	0.0	0.0	0.0	0.0	0.0
Official	..	..	..	0.0	0.0	0.0	0.0	0.0	0.0	0.0
Private	..	..	..	0.0	0.0	0.0	0.0	0.0	0.0	0.0
Debt forgiven	..	..	..	0.0	0.0	0.0	35.5	0.0	0.0	0.0
Memo: interest forgiven	..	..	..	0.0	0.0	0.0	2.5	0.0	0.0	0.0
Debt stock reduction	..	..	..	0.0	0.0	0.0	0.0	0.0	0.0	0.0
of which debt buyback	..	..	..	0.0	0.0	0.0	0.0	0.0	0.0	0.0
8. DEBT STOCK-FLOW RECONCILIATION										
Total change in debt stocks	..	..	..	77.3	208.2	117.3	68.3	201.5	329.9	146.1
Net flows on debt	..	..	..	73.4	207.0	129.7	129.4	178.7	347.9	200.6
Net change in interest arrears	..	..	..	3.6	2.4	-3.6	-2.5	0.0	0.0	0.0
Interest capitalized	..	..	..	0.0	0.0	0.0	0.0	0.0	0.0	0.0
Debt forgiveness or reduction	..	..	..	0.0	0.0	0.0	-35.5	0.0	0.0	0.0
Cross-currency valuation	..	..	..	-23.0	-7.2	-16.5	-53.7	-49.4	-11.3	-42.8
Residual	..	..	..	23.3	5.9	7.7	30.6	72.2	-6.6	-11.7
9. AVERAGE TERMS OF NEW COMMITMENTS										
ALL CREDITORS										
Interest (%)	..	..	..	6.3	1.4	2.4	3.8	2.7	1.7	1.5
Maturity (years)	..	..	..	9.4	32.2	27.9	21.7	26.7	34.8	29.4
Grace period (years)	..	..	..	3.7	9.4	7.8	6.4	7.1	8.9	8.6
Grant element (%)	..	..	..	15.3	71.8	59.5	45.9	56.3	70.0	66.9
Official creditors										
Interest (%)	..	..	..	6.3	1.4	2.4	3.0	1.4	1.7	0.8
Maturity (years)	..	..	..	9.4	32.2	27.9	24.9	31.5	34.8	34.8
Grace period (years)	..	..	..	3.7	9.4	7.8	7.4	8.1	8.9	10.3
Grant element (%)	..	..	..	15.3	71.8	59.5	54.0	67.9	70.0	78.9
Private creditors										
Interest (%)	..	..	..	0.0	0.0	0.0	8.0	8.8	0.0	4.6
Maturity (years)	..	..	..	0.0	0.0	0.0	5.1	4.8	0.0	5.8
Grace period (years)	..	..	..	0.0	0.0	0.0	1.3	2.3	0.0	1.3
Grant element (%)	..	..	..	0.0	0.0	0.0	4.3	2.7	0.0	14.8
Memorandum items										
Commitments	..	..	..	144.1	187.8	40.5	197.4	374.7	271.8	51.7
Official creditors	..	..	..	144.1	187.8	40.5	165.1	308.1	271.8	42.0
Private creditors	..	..	..	0.0	0.0	0.0	32.2	66.6	0.0	9.7

10. CONTRACTUAL OBLIGATIONS ON OUTSTANDING LONG-TERM DEBT

	2001	2002	2003	2004	2005	2006	2007	2008	2009	2010
TOTAL										
Disbursements	170.1	154.8	96.4	60.3	32.6	17.4	7.1	0.4	0.0	0.0
Principal	73.1	74.6	68.3	45.4	55.5	35.4	29.0	42.7	39.5	41.6
Interest	24.0	23.7	20.4	16.8	15.0	13.3	10.9	10.1	8.6	7.4
Official creditors										
Disbursements	169.5	154.8	96.4	60.3	32.6	17.4	7.1	0.4	0.0	0.0
Principal	29.0	34.5	26.7	26.7	24.8	27.1	29.0	36.9	39.5	41.6
Interest	12.3	14.6	14.4	13.8	12.8	11.9	10.9	9.8	8.6	7.4
Bilateral creditors										
Disbursements	92.3	87.7	56.1	33.1	17.4	10.5	3.6	0.0	0.0	0.0
Principal	9.2	13.2	13.2	13.2	9.1	9.1	9.2	15.6	18.5	21.2
Interest	3.5	4.7	4.6	4.3	4.0	3.9	3.8	3.6	3.4	3.1
Multilateral creditors										
Disbursements	77.2	67.1	40.3	27.2	15.2	6.8	3.5	0.4	0.0	0.0
Principal	19.8	21.3	13.5	13.5	15.7	18.0	19.8	21.3	21.1	20.4
Interest	8.9	9.9	9.8	9.4	8.8	8.0	7.1	6.2	5.2	4.4
Private creditors										
Disbursements	0.6	0.0	0.0	0.0	0.0	0.0	0.0	0.0	0.0	0.0
Principal	44.1	40.1	41.6	18.8	30.7	8.3	0.0	5.8	0.0	0.0
Interest	11.7	9.1	5.9	3.0	2.2	1.4	0.0	0.3	0.0	0.0
Commercial banks										
Disbursements	0.6	0.0	0.0	0.0	0.0	0.0	0.0	0.0	0.0	0.0
Principal	20.6	20.6	20.6	2.0	2.0	0.0	0.0	0.0	0.0	0.0
Interest	5.3	3.5	1.6	0.2	0.1	0.0	0.0	0.0	0.0	0.0
Other private										
Disbursements	0.0	0.0	0.0	0.0	0.0	0.0	0.0	0.0	0.0	0.0
Principal	23.5	19.5	21.0	16.8	28.8	8.3	0.0	0.0	0.0	0.0
Interest	6.4	5.6	4.3	2.8	2.1	1.4	0.0	0.0	0.0	0.0

BANGLADESH

(US$ million, unless otherwise indicated)

	1970	1980	1990	1994	1995	1996	1997	1998	1999	2000
1. SUMMARY DEBT DATA										
TOTAL DEBT STOCKS (EDT)	..	**3,918**	**12,439**	**15,622**	**15,924**	**15,337**	**14,421**	**15,671**	**16,533**	**15,609**
Long-term debt (LDOD)	..	**3,282**	**11,657**	**14,758**	**15,103**	**14,658**	**13,874**	**15,100**	**15,961**	**15,098**
Public and publicly guaranteed	..	3,282	11,657	14,758	15,103	14,658	13,874	15,100	15,961	15,098
Private nonguaranteed	..	0	0	0	0	0	0	0	0	0
Use of IMF credit	..	**424**	**626**	**669**	**622**	**517**	**372**	**422**	**318**	**216**
Short-term debt	..	**212**	**156**	**195**	**199**	**163**	**175**	**150**	**254**	**295**
of which interest arrears on LDOD	..	0	1	10	15	0	0	0	0	0
Official creditors	..	0	1	10	15	0	0	0	0	0
Private creditors	..	0	0	0	0	0	0	0	0	0
Memo: principal arrears on LDOD	..	0	11	20	15	3	3	4	4	4
Official creditors	..	0	11	16	15	3	3	4	4	4
Private creditors	..	0	0	4	0	0	0	0	0	0
Memo: export credits	..	0	329	913	466	437	430	388	305	311
TOTAL DEBT FLOWS										
Disbursements	..	**858**	**1,273**	**1,003**	**762**	**898**	**628**	**846**	**808**	**844**
Long-term debt	..	631	1,213	1,003	762	898	628	712	808	844
IMF purchases	..	227	61	0	0	0	0	135	0	0
Principal repayments	..	**168**	**548**	**374**	**591**	**465**	**508**	**472**	**524**	**598**
Long-term debt	..	34	344	319	530	380	394	371	431	513
IMF repurchases	..	134	204	55	61	86	115	101	93	86
Net flows on debt	..	**792**	**813**	**666**	**169**	**411**	**132**	**349**	**388**	**287**
of which short-term debt	..	102	88	37	-1	-21	12	-25	105	41
Interest payments (INT)	..	**73**	**201**	**182**	**189**	**207**	**182**	**172**	**194**	**192**
Long-term debt	..	44	151	171	176	194	171	162	173	167
IMF charges	..	13	41	3	3	3	2	2	7	7
Short-term debt	..	16	9	7	10	10	9	8	14	17
Net transfers on debt	..	**719**	**612**	**484**	**-19**	**204**	**-50**	**177**	**194**	**95**
Total debt service paid (TDS)	..	**241**	**749**	**556**	**780**	**672**	**690**	**644**	**718**	**790**
Long-term debt	..	78	495	490	706	574	564	532	605	680
IMF repurchases and charges	..	147	245	59	64	88	117	103	99	93
Short-term debt (interest only)	..	16	9	7	10	10	9	8	14	17
2. AGGREGATE NET RESOURCE FLOWS AND NET TRANSFERS (LONG-TERM)										
NET RESOURCE FLOWS	..	**1,598**	**1,644**	**1,503**	**959**	**1,157**	**966**	**1,191**	**1,235**	**1,207**
Net flow of long-term debt (ex. IMF)	..	597	869	684	231	518	234	341	376	332
Foreign direct investment (net)	..	0	3	11	2	14	141	190	180	280
Portfolio equity flows	..	0	0	48	33	30	11	3	4	3
Grants (excluding technical coop.)	..	1,001	772	760	693	596	579	657	675	592
Memo: technical coop. grants	..	159	234	294	293	277	233	203	170	212
official net resource flows	..	1,588	1,585	1,465	946	1,144	844	1,027	1,063	938
private net resource flows	..	11	58	38	14	14	122	164	171	269
NET TRANSFERS	..	**1,554**	**1,492**	**1,332**	**784**	**951**	**770**	**999**	**1,026**	**998**
Interest on long-term debt	..	44	151	171	176	194	171	162	173	167
Profit remittances on FDI	..	0	0	0	0	12	25	30	35	42
Memo: official net transfers	..	1,546	1,445	1,302	779	961	683	873	897	778
private net transfers	..	9	47	30	5	-10	87	126	130	220
3. MAJOR ECONOMIC AGGREGATES										
Gross national income (GNI)	..	17,609	29,998	33,738	37,899	39,698	42,212	43,992	45,827	46,885
Exports of goods & services (XGS)	..	1,174	2,731	4,293	5,490	5,907	6,647	7,495	7,828	8,657
of which workers remittances	..	197	761	1,089	1,198	1,217	1,475	1,525	1,706	1,949
Imports of goods & services (MGS)	..	2,622	4,345	4,871	6,783	7,802	7,851	8,240	8,753	9,378
International reserves (RES)	..	331	660	3,175	2,376	1,869	1,611	1,936	1,634	1,516
Current account balance	..	-844	-1,573	-89	-664	-1,291	-534	-253	-394	2
4. DEBT INDICATORS										
EDT / XGS (%)	..	333.8	455.4	363.9	290.1	259.7	217.0	209.1	211.2	180.3
EDT / GNI (%)	..	22.3	41.5	46.3	42.0	38.6	34.2	35.6	36.1	33.3
TDS / XGS (%)	..	20.5	27.4	12.9	14.2	11.4	10.4	8.6	9.2	9.1
INT / XGS (%)	..	6.2	7.4	4.2	3.4	3.5	2.7	2.3	2.5	2.2
INT / GNI (%)	..	0.4	0.7	0.5	0.5	0.5	0.4	0.4	0.4	0.4
RES / EDT (%)	..	8.5	5.3	20.3	14.9	12.2	11.2	12.4	9.9	9.7
RES / MGS (months)	..	1.5	1.8	7.8	4.2	2.9	2.5	2.8	2.2	1.9
Short-term / EDT (%)	..	5.4	1.3	1.3	1.3	1.1	1.2	1.0	1.5	1.9
Concessional / EDT (%)	..	80.4	90.7	92.7	92.9	93.8	94.5	94.9	95.1	95.3
Multilateral / EDT (%)	..	31.9	51.8	58.9	60.8	63.6	66.0	67.0	67.6	70.5

BANGLADESH

(US$ million, unless otherwise indicated)

5. LONG-TERM DEBT

	1970	1980	1990	1994	1995	1996	1997	1998	1999	2000
DEBT OUTSTANDING (LDOD)	..	**3,282**	**11,657**	**14,758**	**15,103**	**14,658**	**13,874**	**15,100**	**15,961**	**15,098**
Public and publicly guaranteed	..	**3,282**	**11,657**	**14,758**	**15,103**	**14,658**	**13,874**	**15,100**	**15,961**	**15,098**
Official creditors	..	3,226	11,435	14,555	14,848	14,433	13,679	14,922	15,796	14,934
Multilateral	..	1,252	6,441	9,205	9,678	9,751	9,520	10,498	11,178	10,999
Concessional	..	1,191	6,344	9,147	9,623	9,701	9,472	10,449	11,112	10,933
Bilateral	..	1,975	4,994	5,350	5,170	4,683	4,160	4,424	4,619	3,936
Concessional	..	1,960	4,941	5,337	5,164	4,681	4,158	4,424	4,618	3,935
Private creditors	..	56	223	203	255	225	195	178	165	164
Bonds	..	0	0	0	0	0	0	0	0	0
Commercial banks	..	0	21	15	12	7	1	0	0	15
Other private	..	56	202	188	242	218	193	178	165	149
Private nonguaranteed	..	**0**	**0**	**0**	**0**	**0**	**0**	**0**	**0**	**0**
Bonds	..	0	0	0	0	0	0	0	0	0
Commercial banks and other	..	0	0	0	0	0	0	0	0	0
Memo:										
IBRD	..	55	64	58	55	47	38	36	31	24
IDA	..	926	4,095	5,378	5,638	5,713	5,701	6,168	6,428	6,431
DISBURSEMENTS	..	**631**	**1,213**	**1,003**	**762**	**898**	**628**	**712**	**808**	**844**
Public and publicly guaranteed	..	**631**	**1,213**	**1,003**	**762**	**898**	**628**	**712**	**808**	**844**
Official creditors	..	614	1,123	982	676	890	628	712	793	830
Multilateral	..	276	822	806	494	642	520	619	724	652
Concessional	..	275	792	806	494	639	513	617	704	641
Bilateral	..	338	301	176	182	248	109	93	69	178
Concessional	..	338	301	176	181	248	109	93	69	177
Private creditors	..	17	90	21	86	8	0	0	15	15
Bonds	..	0	0	0	0	0	0	0	0	0
Commercial banks	..	0	22	6	0	0	0	0	0	15
Other private	..	17	67	14	86	8	0	0	15	0
Private nonguaranteed	..	**0**	**0**	**0**	**0**	**0**	**0**	**0**	**0**	**0**
Bonds	..	0	0	0	0	0	0	0	0	0
Commercial banks and other	..	0	0	0	0	0	0	0	0	0
Memo:										
IBRD	..	0	0	0	0	0	0	0	0	0
IDA	..	156	464	405	198	279	301	350	413	357
PRINCIPAL REPAYMENTS	..	**34**	**344**	**319**	**530**	**380**	**394**	**371**	**431**	**513**
Public and publicly guaranteed	..	**34**	**344**	**319**	**530**	**380**	**394**	**371**	**431**	**513**
Official creditors	..	28	310	277	423	343	364	342	405	484
Multilateral	..	1	62	79	104	111	124	132	154	169
Concessional	..	1	44	75	100	106	119	127	150	163
Bilateral	..	27	248	199	319	232	240	210	250	316
Concessional	..	23	239	190	309	228	239	209	250	316
Private creditors	..	6	34	42	107	37	30	29	27	28
Bonds	..	0	0	0	0	0	0	0	0	0
Commercial banks	..	0	2	4	2	6	6	1	0	0
Other private	..	6	32	38	105	32	25	28	27	28
Private nonguaranteed	..	**0**	**0**	**0**	**0**	**0**	**0**	**0**	**0**	**0**
Bonds	..	0	0	0	0	0	0	0	0	0
Commercial banks and other	..	0	0	0	0	0	0	0	0	0
Memo:										
IBRD	..	0	2	4	5	5	5	4	5	5
IDA	..	0	13	32	41	50	55	61	73	82
NET FLOWS ON DEBT	..	**597**	**869**	**684**	**231**	**518**	**234**	**341**	**376**	**332**
Public and publicly guaranteed	..	**597**	**869**	**684**	**231**	**518**	**234**	**341**	**376**	**332**
Official creditors	..	587	814	705	253	548	264	370	388	346
Multilateral	..	275	761	727	390	531	396	487	570	483
Concessional	..	275	749	732	395	533	394	490	554	477
Bilateral	..	311	53	-22	-137	16	-132	-117	-182	-138
Concessional	..	315	62	-14	-128	20	-131	-116	-181	-138
Private creditors	..	11	55	-21	-21	-30	-30	-29	-12	-14
Bonds	..	0	0	0	0	0	0	0	0	0
Commercial banks	..	0	20	2	-2	-6	-6	-1	0	15
Other private	..	11	35	-23	-19	-24	-25	-28	-12	-28
Private nonguaranteed	..	**0**	**0**	**0**	**0**	**0**	**0**	**0**	**0**	**0**
Bonds	..	0	0	0	0	0	0	0	0	0
Commercial banks and other	..	0	0	0	0	0	0	0	0	0
Memo:										
IBRD	..	0	-2	-4	-5	-5	-5	-4	-5	-5
IDA	..	156	451	373	156	230	246	289	340	275

BANGLADESH

(US$ million, unless otherwise indicated)

	1970	1980	1990	1994	1995	1996	1997	1998	1999	2000
INTEREST PAYMENTS (LINT)	..	**44**	**151**	**171**	**176**	**194**	**171**	**162**	**173**	**167**
Public and publicly guaranteed	..	**44**	**151**	**171**	**176**	**194**	**171**	**162**	**173**	**167**
Official creditors	..	42	140	163	167	183	161	154	167	160
Multilateral	..	11	52	77	87	85	84	85	94	93
Concessional	..	7	46	73	83	82	81	82	92	91
Bilateral	..	31	89	86	80	98	77	69	73	67
Concessional	..	30	84	84	79	97	77	69	73	67
Private creditors	..	2	11	9	9	11	10	8	7	7
Bonds	..	0	0	0	0	0	0	0	0	0
Commercial banks	..	0	1	1	0	1	0	0	0	0
Other private	..	2	11	8	9	11	10	8	7	7
Private nonguaranteed	..	**0**	**0**	**0**	**0**	**0**	**0**	**0**	**0**	**0**
Bonds	..	0	0	0	0	0	0	0	0	0
Commercial banks and other	..	0	0	0	0	0	0	0	0	0
Memo:										
IBRD	..	3	4	4	4	3	3	2	2	2
IDA	..	6	28	38	42	42	42	43	46	47
NET TRANSFERS ON DEBT	..	**553**	**718**	**513**	**56**	**324**	**64**	**179**	**203**	**165**
Public and publicly guaranteed	..	**553**	**718**	**513**	**56**	**324**	**64**	**179**	**203**	**165**
Official creditors	..	545	673	542	86	365	104	216	222	186
Multilateral	..	264	709	651	303	446	313	402	476	390
Concessional	..	267	702	659	312	451	313	408	462	386
Bilateral	..	281	-36	-108	-217	-81	-209	-186	-254	-205
Concessional	..	285	-23	-98	-207	-77	-208	-185	-254	-205
Private creditors	..	8	44	-30	-30	-41	-40	-37	-19	-21
Bonds	..	0	0	0	0	0	0	0	0	0
Commercial banks	..	0	20	2	-3	-6	-6	-1	0	14
Other private	..	8	24	-31	-28	-35	-34	-36	-19	-35
Private nonguaranteed	..	**0**	**0**	**0**	**0**	**0**	**0**	**0**	**0**	**0**
Bonds	..	0	0	0	0	0	0	0	0	0
Commercial banks and other	..	0	0	0	0	0	0	0	0	0
Memo:										
IBRD	..	-3	-5	-7	-8	-8	-7	-7	-7	-7
IDA	..	150	424	334	114	187	204	246	293	228
DEBT SERVICE (LTDS)	..	**78**	**495**	**490**	**706**	**574**	**564**	**532**	**605**	**680**
Public and publicly guaranteed	..	**78**	**495**	**490**	**706**	**574**	**564**	**532**	**605**	**680**
Official creditors	..	70	450	440	590	525	524	495	571	644
Multilateral	..	12	113	155	191	196	207	217	249	262
Concessional	..	8	90	148	183	188	200	210	242	254
Bilateral	..	58	337	285	399	329	317	279	323	383
Concessional	..	53	323	274	388	325	316	277	322	383
Private creditors	..	8	45	50	116	49	40	37	33	36
Bonds	..	0	0	0	0	0	0	0	0	0
Commercial banks	..	0	2	5	3	6	6	1	0	0
Other private	..	8	43	46	113	42	34	36	33	35
Private nonguaranteed	..	**0**	**0**	**0**	**0**	**0**	**0**	**0**	**0**	**0**
Bonds	..	0	0	0	0	0	0	0	0	0
Commercial banks and other	..	0	0	0	0	0	0	0	0	0
Memo:										
IBRD	..	3	5	7	8	8	7	7	7	7
IDA	..	6	41	71	84	92	96	105	119	129
UNDISBURSED DEBT	..	**2,189**	**4,318**	**4,514**	**4,447**	**3,504**	**3,390**	**3,686**	**4,240**	**3,761**
Official creditors	..	2,139	4,128	4,191	4,130	3,195	3,081	3,595	3,848	3,303
Private creditors	..	50	190	323	317	309	309	91	392	459
Memorandum items										
Concessional LDOD	..	3,150	11,284	14,484	14,787	14,381	13,630	14,873	15,731	14,868
Variable rate LDOD	..	5	21	15	12	7	1	0	0	0
Public sector LDOD	..	3,282	11,657	14,758	15,103	14,658	13,874	15,100	15,961	15,098
Private sector LDOD	..	0	0	0	0	0	0	0	0	0

6. CURRENCY COMPOSITION OF LONG-TERM DEBT (PERCENT)

	1970	1980	1990	1994	1995	1996	1997	1998	1999	2000
Deutsche mark	..	0.1	0.0	0.0	0.0	0.0	0.0	0.0	0.0	0.0
French franc	..	1.2	1.2	0.8	0.6	0.5	0.4	0.4	0.3	0.3
Japanese yen	..	23.6	24.8	27.4	25.9	23.9	22.0	22.2	22.5	20.5
Pound sterling	..	18.6	5.0	3.6	3.5	3.5	3.5	3.1	2.8	3.0
Swiss franc	..	0.2	0.1	0.0	0.0	0.0	0.0	0.0	0.0	0.0
U.S.dollars	..	38.1	48.1	41.2	41.9	42.4	43.3	42.9	42.8	44.4
Multiple currency	..	8.1	15.4	21.8	22.9	23.7	23.7	24.4	24.9	24.7
Special drawing rights	..	0.2	1.0	2.8	3.2	3.9	4.7	4.9	4.6	4.8
All other currencies	..	9.9	4.4	2.4	2.0	2.1	2.4	2.1	2.1	2.3

BANGLADESH

(US$ million, unless otherwise indicated)

	1970	1980	1990	1994	1995	1996	1997	1998	1999	2000
7. DEBT RESTRUCTURINGS										
Total amount rescheduled	..	..	0	0	0	0	0	0	0	0
Debt stock rescheduled	..	..	0	0	0	0	0	0	0	0
Principal rescheduled	..	..	0	0	0	0	0	0	0	0
Official	..	..	0	0	0	0	0	0	0	0
Private	..	..	0	0	0	0	0	0	0	0
Interest rescheduled	..	..	0	0	0	0	0	0	0	0
Official	..	..	0	0	0	0	0	0	0	0
Private	..	..	0	0	0	0	0	0	0	0
Debt forgiven	..	..	0	0	0	0	0	0	0	0
Memo: interest forgiven	..	..	0	0	0	0	0	0	0	0
Debt stock reduction	..	..	0	0	0	0	0	0	0	0
of which debt buyback	..	..	0	0	0	0	0	0	0	0
8. DEBT STOCK-FLOW RECONCILIATION										
Total change in debt stocks	..	..	1,594	1,366	302	-586	-916	1,250	862	-925
Net flows on debt	..	792	813	666	169	411	132	349	388	287
Net change in interest arrears	..	..	1	5	6	-15	0	0	0	0
Interest capitalized	..	..	0	0	0	0	0	0	0	0
Debt forgiveness or reduction	..	..	0	0	0	0	0	0	0	0
Cross-currency valuation	..	..	925	859	-244	-1,132	-1,241	725	809	-1,087
Residual	..	..	-145	-164	372	150	193	176	-335	-125
9. AVERAGE TERMS OF NEW COMMITMENTS										
ALL CREDITORS										
Interest (%)	..	1.7	1.8	1.5	1.9	1.0	1.6	1.6	1.7	2.6
Maturity (years)	..	36.0	34.1	32.3	38.2	33.8	37.2	39.1	30.3	26.1
Grace period (years)	..	9.0	9.2	8.6	10.0	9.1	9.8	10.1	7.2	7.2
Grant element (%)	..	68.5	68.5	68.5	69.5	74.1	70.9	72.8	64.3	55.8
Official creditors										
Interest (%)	..	1.5	1.1	1.0	1.9	1.0	1.6	1.6	1.2	2.4
Maturity (years)	..	36.9	37.6	35.1	38.2	33.8	37.2	39.1	34.5	28.0
Grace period (years)	..	9.2	10.2	9.3	10.0	9.1	9.8	10.1	8.4	7.4
Grant element (%)	..	70.4	76.1	74.5	69.5	74.1	70.9	72.8	72.4	58.4
Private creditors										
Interest (%)	..	7.5	5.4	4.8	0.0	0.0	0.0	0.0	3.5	3.5
Maturity (years)	..	10.7	14.1	13.2	0.0	0.0	0.0	0.0	15.1	13.2
Grace period (years)	..	2.4	3.5	3.9	0.0	0.0	0.0	0.0	2.9	5.9
Grant element (%)	..	11.4	25.0	27.6	0.0	0.0	0.0	0.0	35.1	37.7
Memorandum items										
Commitments	..	1,029	1,317	1,476	716	334	1,109	1,102	1,445	590
Official creditors	..	997	1,122	1,288	716	334	1,109	1,102	1,130	516
Private creditors	..	32	196	189	0	0	0	0	315	75

10. CONTRACTUAL OBLIGATIONS ON OUTSTANDING LONG-TERM DEBT

	2001	2002	2003	2004	2005	2006	2007	2008	2009	2010
TOTAL										
Disbursements	1,238	1,040	680	409	227	87	53	20	8	1
Principal	498	533	568	601	632	645	669	709	704	706
Interest	172	177	176	171	167	171	167	160	151	142
Official creditors										
Disbursements	1,057	875	603	384	216	87	53	20	8	1
Principal	459	482	505	538	569	586	622	664	666	669
Interest	159	160	158	154	153	160	158	153	145	137
Bilateral creditors										
Disbursements	271	202	128	77	43	27	16	6	3	1
Principal	270	279	285	292	294	290	289	287	262	248
Interest	62	60	57	54	50	46	41	37	32	28
Multilateral creditors										
Disbursements	786	672	475	307	173	60	38	14	5	0
Principal	189	203	220	246	274	296	333	377	404	421
Interest	97	100	101	101	103	115	116	116	113	109
Private creditors										
Disbursements	181	165	77	25	11	0	0	0	0	0
Principal	38	51	63	63	63	58	46	44	38	38
Interest	14	18	18	16	14	11	9	8	6	5
Commercial banks										
Disbursements	8	4	0	0	0	0	0	0	0	0
Principal	0	0	3	3	3	3	3	3	3	3
Interest	1	2	2	1	1	1	1	1	1	0
Other private										
Disbursements	173	161	77	25	11	0	0	0	0	0
Principal	38	51	60	60	60	56	44	42	35	35
Interest	12	16	17	15	13	10	8	7	5	4

BELARUS

(US$ million, unless otherwise indicated)

	1970	1980	1990	1994	1995	1996	1997	1998	1999	2000
1. SUMMARY DEBT DATA										
TOTAL DEBT STOCKS (EDT)	..	..	..	**1,297**	**1,694**	**1,105**	**1,171**	**1,154**	**982**	**851**
Long-term debt (LDOD)	..	..	..	**1,124**	**1,302**	**730**	**683**	**798**	**710**	**693**
Public and publicly guaranteed	..	..	..	1,124	1,301	729	681	796	708	692
Private nonguaranteed	..	..	..	1	0	1	1	2	1	1
Use of IMF credit	..	..	..	**102**	**283**	**274**	**257**	**243**	**178**	**114**
Short-term debt	..	..	..	**70**	**110**	**102**	**232**	**113**	**95**	**43**
of which interest arrears on LDOD	..	..	..	15	19	10	3	6	9	14
Official creditors	..	..	..	0	0	2	1	4	7	12
Private creditors	..	..	..	15	19	8	2	3	2	2
Memo: principal arrears on LDOD	..	..	..	135	140	12	1	9	24	29
Official creditors	..	..	..	0	0	1	1	6	11	28
Private creditors	..	..	..	135	140	11	0	4	13	1
Memo: export credits	..	..	..	379	399	352	279	49	56	69
TOTAL DEBT FLOWS										
Disbursements	..	..	..	**352**	**441**	**93**	**85**	**146**	**64**	**138**
Long-term debt	..	..	..	352	258	93	85	146	64	138
IMF purchases	..	..	..	0	182	0	0	0	0	0
Principal repayments	..	..	..	**88**	**108**	**59**	**70**	**85**	**149**	**185**
Long-term debt	..	..	..	88	108	59	70	61	91	130
IMF repurchases	..	..	..	0	0	0	0	24	58	56
Net flows on debt	..	..	..	**319**	**369**	**35**	**152**	**-62**	**-106**	**-103**
of which short-term debt	..	..	..	55	36	1	137	-123	-21	-56
Interest payments (INT)	..	..	..	**31**	**74**	**54**	**73**	**61**	**53**	**47**
Long-term debt	..	..	..	22	59	38	52	41	41	37
IMF charges	..	..	..	5	10	12	12	12	9	7
Short-term debt	..	..	..	4	4	4	9	9	4	3
Net transfers on debt	..	..	..	**288**	**295**	**-19**	**79**	**-123**	**-159**	**-150**
Total debt service paid (TDS)	..	..	..	**119**	**182**	**113**	**143**	**147**	**202**	**232**
Long-term debt	..	..	..	110	167	97	122	101	131	167
IMF repurchases and charges	..	..	..	5	10	12	12	36	67	63
Short-term debt (interest only)	..	..	..	4	4	4	9	9	4	3
2. AGGREGATE NET RESOURCE FLOWS AND NET TRANSFERS (LONG-TERM)										
NET RESOURCE FLOWS	..	..	..	**354**	**301**	**177**	**407**	**303**	**437**	**125**
Net flow of long-term debt (ex. IMF)	..	..	..	264	150	34	16	85	-27	8
Foreign direct investment (net)	..	..	..	11	15	105	352	203	444	90
Portfolio equity flows	..	..	..	0	0	0	0	0	0	0
Grants (excluding technical coop.)	..	..	..	79	136	38	40	15	20	27
Memo: technical coop. grants	..	..	..	13	27	27	15	24	20	14
official net resource flows	..	..	..	230	183	72	83	106	-5	3
private net resource flows	..	..	..	123	118	106	324	197	442	122
NET TRANSFERS	..	..	..	**331**	**243**	**140**	**355**	**263**	**397**	**88**
Interest on long-term debt	..	..	..	22	59	38	52	41	41	37
Profit remittances on FDI	..	..	..	0	0	0	0	0	0	0
Memo: official net transfers	..	..	..	223	151	54	60	80	-30	-15
private net transfers	..	..	..	108	92	86	294	183	427	103
3. MAJOR ECONOMIC AGGREGATES										
Gross national income (GNI)	..	..	..	20,447	20,328	21,602	24,121	25,782	26,837	29,960
Exports of goods & services (XGS)	..	..	..	2,762	5,299	6,795	7,898	7,156	6,474	8,107
of which workers remittances	..	..	..	0	29	23	29	32	54	101
Imports of goods & services (MGS)	..	..	..	3,228	5,805	7,379	8,806	8,236	6,718	8,325
International reserves (RES)	..	..	..	101	377	469	394	703	294	350
Current account balance	..	..	..	-444	-458	-516	-859	-1,017	-194	-162
4. DEBT INDICATORS										
EDT / XGS (%)	..	..	..	46.9	32.0	16.3	14.8	16.1	15.2	10.5
EDT / GNI (%)	..	..	..	6.3	8.3	5.1	4.9	4.5	3.7	2.8
TDS / XGS (%)	..	..	..	4.3	3.4	1.7	1.8	2.1	3.1	2.9
INT / XGS (%)	..	..	..	1.1	1.4	0.8	0.9	0.9	0.8	0.6
INT / GNI (%)	..	..	..	0.2	0.4	0.3	0.3	0.2	0.2	0.2
RES / EDT (%)	..	..	..	7.8	22.3	42.5	33.6	60.9	30.0	41.2
RES / MGS (months)	..	..	..	0.4	0.8	0.8	0.5	1.0	0.5	0.5
Short-term / EDT (%)	..	..	..	5.4	6.5	9.2	19.8	9.8	9.6	5.1
Concessional / EDT (%)	..	..	..	35.6	28.1	7.8	7.3	7.4	8.6	9.8
Multilateral / EDT (%)	..	..	..	13.3	11.1	19.8	22.1	24.6	25.7	25.8

BELARUS

(US$ million, unless otherwise indicated)

	1970	1980	1990	1994	1995	1996	1997	1998	1999	2000
5. LONG-TERM DEBT										
DEBT OUTSTANDING (LDOD)	..	..	..	**1,124**	**1,302**	**730**	**683**	**798**	**710**	**693**
Public and publicly guaranteed	..	..	..	**1,124**	**1,301**	**729**	**681**	**796**	**708**	**692**
Official creditors	..	..	..	718	769	361	384	488	442	403
Multilateral	..	..	..	173	188	219	259	283	253	220
Concessional	..	..	..	0	0	0	0	0	0	0
Bilateral	..	..	..	545	582	142	125	205	189	183
Concessional	..	..	..	461	477	86	86	86	85	84
Private creditors	..	..	..	406	532	368	298	309	267	289
Bonds	..	..	..	0	0	0	0	0	0	0
Commercial banks	..	..	..	24	46	49	50	64	45	71
Other private	..	..	..	382	486	318	248	244	222	218
Private nonguaranteed	..	..	..	**1**	**0**	**1**	**1**	**2**	**1**	**1**
Bonds	..	..	..	0	0	0	0	0	0	0
Commercial banks and other	..	..	..	1	0	1	1	2	1	1
Memo:										
IBRD	..	..	..	101	116	121	124	135	122	105
IDA	..	..	..	0	0	0	0	0	0	0
DISBURSEMENTS	..	..	..	**352**	**258**	**93**	**85**	**146**	**64**	**138**
Public and publicly guaranteed	..	..	..	**352**	**258**	**93**	**85**	**145**	**64**	**138**
Official creditors	..	..	..	211	131	57	64	111	19	25
Multilateral	..	..	..	111	77	47	64	30	19	25
Concessional	..	..	..	0	0	0	0	0	0	0
Bilateral	..	..	..	100	54	10	0	81	0	0
Concessional	..	..	..	30	20	10	0	0	0	0
Private creditors	..	..	..	141	127	36	21	34	44	112
Bonds	..	..	..	0	0	0	0	0	0	0
Commercial banks	..	..	..	23	20	8	10	13	0	56
Other private	..	..	..	117	107	28	11	21	44	56
Private nonguaranteed	..	..	..	**0**	**0**	**1**	**0**	**1**	**1**	**1**
Bonds	..	..	..	0	0	0	0	0	0	0
Commercial banks and other	..	..	..	0	0	1	0	1	1	1
Memo:										
IBRD	..	..	..	100	11	14	13	4	13	6
IDA	..	..	..	0	0	0	0	0	0	0
PRINCIPAL REPAYMENTS	..	..	..	**88**	**108**	**59**	**70**	**61**	**91**	**130**
Public and publicly guaranteed	..	..	..	**87**	**108**	**59**	**69**	**61**	**90**	**129**
Official creditors	..	..	..	60	84	23	20	20	44	50
Multilateral	..	..	..	60	70	4	7	16	27	46
Concessional	..	..	..	0	0	0	0	0	0	0
Bilateral	..	..	..	0	15	19	13	4	17	4
Concessional	..	..	..	0	0	0	0	0	1	1
Private creditors	..	..	..	27	24	36	49	40	46	80
Bonds	..	..	..	0	0	0	0	0	0	0
Commercial banks	..	..	..	0	0	1	2	3	7	30
Other private	..	..	..	27	24	35	47	38	39	49
Private nonguaranteed	..	..	..	**1**	**0**	**0**	**0**	**0**	**1**	**1**
Bonds	..	..	..	0	0	0	0	0	0	0
Commercial banks and other	..	..	..	1	0	0	0	0	1	1
Memo:										
IBRD	..	..	..	0	0	0	0	0	11	14
IDA	..	..	..	0	0	0	0	0	0	0
NET FLOWS ON DEBT	..	..	..	**264**	**150**	**34**	**16**	**85**	**-27**	**8**
Public and publicly guaranteed	..	..	..	**265**	**150**	**34**	**15**	**84**	**-27**	**8**
Official creditors	..	..	..	152	47	33	43	91	-25	-24
Multilateral	..	..	..	51	8	43	56	13	-8	-21
Concessional	..	..	..	0	0	0	0	0	0	0
Bilateral	..	..	..	100	39	-9	-13	77	-17	-4
Concessional	..	..	..	30	20	10	0	0	-1	-1
Private creditors	..	..	..	113	103	0	-28	-6	-2	33
Bonds	..	..	..	0	0	0	0	0	0	0
Commercial banks	..	..	..	23	20	7	8	10	-7	26
Other private	..	..	..	90	83	-7	-36	-17	6	7
Private nonguaranteed	..	..	..	**-1**	**0**	**0**	**0**	**1**	**0**	**0**
Bonds	..	..	..	0	0	0	0	0	0	0
Commercial banks and other	..	..	..	-1	0	0	0	1	0	0
Memo:										
IBRD	..	..	..	100	11	14	13	4	1	-9
IDA	..	..	..	0	0	0	0	0	0	0

BELARUS

(US$ million, unless otherwise indicated)

	1970	1980	1990	1994	1995	1996	1997	1998	1999	2000
INTEREST PAYMENTS (LINT)	..	..	..	**22**	**59**	**38**	**52**	**41**	**41**	**37**
Public and publicly guaranteed	..	..	..	**22**	**59**	**37**	**52**	**40**	**41**	**37**
Official creditors	..	..	..	7	32	17	23	26	25	18
Multilateral	..	..	..	6	23	13	17	19	19	16
Concessional	..	..	..	0	0	0	0	0	0	0
Bilateral	..	..	..	2	10	4	5	7	6	2
Concessional	..	..	..	1	1	2	2	2	2	2
Private creditors	..	..	..	15	26	20	30	15	16	19
Bonds	..	..	..	0	0	0	0	0	0	0
Commercial banks	..	..	..	0	1	2	2	2	2	5
Other private	..	..	..	15	25	18	28	13	14	14
Private nonguaranteed	..	..	..	**0**	**0**	**0**	**0**	**0**	**0**	**0**
Bonds	..	..	..	0	0	0	0	0	0	0
Commercial banks and other	..	..	..	0	0	0	0	0	0	0
Memo:										
IBRD	..	..	..	2	8	8	8	8	8	6
IDA	..	..	..	0	0	0	0	0	0	0
NET TRANSFERS ON DEBT	..	..	..	**242**	**92**	**-4**	**-37**	**45**	**-67**	**-29**
Public and publicly guaranteed	..	..	..	**242**	**92**	**-4**	**-37**	**44**	**-67**	**-29**
Official creditors	..	..	..	144	15	16	21	65	-50	-42
Multilateral	..	..	..	46	-15	30	39	-6	-27	-37
Concessional	..	..	..	0	0	0	0	0	0	0
Bilateral	..	..	..	98	30	-14	-18	70	-23	-5
Concessional	..	..	..	29	19	8	-2	-2	-3	-3
Private creditors	..	..	..	98	77	-20	-58	-21	-18	13
Bonds	..	..	..	0	0	0	0	0	0	0
Commercial banks	..	..	..	23	19	5	5	8	-10	21
Other private	..	..	..	75	58	-25	-63	-29	-8	-7
Private nonguaranteed	..	..	..	**-1**	**0**	**0**	**0**	**1**	**0**	**0**
Bonds	..	..	..	0	0	0	0	0	0	0
Commercial banks and other	..	..	..	-1	0	0	0	1	0	0
Memo:										
IBRD	..	..	..	98	4	6	6	-4	-7	-15
IDA	..	..	..	0	0	0	0	0	0	0
DEBT SERVICE (LTDS)	..	..	..	**110**	**167**	**97**	**122**	**101**	**131**	**167**
Public and publicly guaranteed	..	..	..	**110**	**167**	**96**	**122**	**101**	**131**	**166**
Official creditors	..	..	..	67	117	41	43	46	69	67
Multilateral	..	..	..	65	92	17	25	35	46	62
Concessional	..	..	..	0	0	0	0	0	0	0
Bilateral	..	..	..	2	24	24	18	11	23	5
Concessional	..	..	..	1	1	2	2	2	3	3
Private creditors	..	..	..	42	50	56	79	55	62	99
Bonds	..	..	..	0	0	0	0	0	0	0
Commercial banks	..	..	..	0	1	3	4	5	10	36
Other private	..	..	..	42	49	53	75	50	52	63
Private nonguaranteed	..	..	..	**1**	**0**	**0**	**0**	**0**	**1**	**1**
Bonds	..	..	..	0	0	0	0	0	0	0
Commercial banks and other	..	..	..	1	0	0	0	0	1	1
Memo:										
IBRD	..	..	..	2	8	8	8	8	19	20
IDA	..	..	..	0	0	0	0	0	0	0
UNDISBURSED DEBT	..	..	..	**409**	**274**	**218**	**248**	**173**	**158**	**52**
Official creditors	..	..	..	280	255	190	203	95	64	41
Private creditors	..	..	..	129	19	28	45	78	94	11
Memorandum items										
Concessional LDOD	..	..	..	461	477	86	86	86	85	84
Variable rate LDOD	..	..	..	592	697	503	451	530	451	413
Public sector LDOD	..	..	..	1,124	1,301	729	681	796	708	692
Private sector LDOD	..	..	..	1	0	1	1	2	1	1

6. CURRENCY COMPOSITION OF LONG-TERM DEBT (PERCENT)

	1970	1980	1990	1994	1995	1996	1997	1998	1999	2000
Deutsche mark	..	..	..	23.9	27.5	42.2	35.5	30.7	25.0	20.3
French franc	..	..	..	0.0	0.0	0.0	0.0	0.0	0.0	0.0
Japanese yen	..	..	..	2.9	2.3	2.8	2.1	2.1	2.6	2.2
Pound sterling	..	..	..	0.0	0.0	0.0	0.0	0.0	0.0	0.0
Swiss franc	..	..	..	0.0	0.7	0.9	0.7	0.5	0.3	0.1
U.S.dollars	..	..	..	54.3	50.8	26.2	33.8	39.2	43.9	49.7
Multiple currency	..	..	..	9.2	10.8	16.6	18.2	16.9	17.3	15.2
Special drawing rights	..	..	..	0.0	0.0	0.0	0.0	0.0	0.0	0.0
All other currencies	..	..	..	9.7	7.9	11.3	9.7	10.6	10.9	12.5

BELARUS

(US$ million, unless otherwise indicated)

	1970	1980	1990	1994	1995	1996	1997	1998	1999	2000
7. DEBT RESTRUCTURINGS										
Total amount rescheduled	..	..	..	0	0	0	0	0	0	50
Debt stock rescheduled	..	..	..	0	0	0	0	0	0	49
Principal rescheduled	..	..	..	0	0	0	0	0	0	0
Official	..	..	..	0	0	0	0	0	0	0
Private	..	..	..	0	0	0	0	0	0	0
Interest rescheduled	..	..	..	0	0	0	0	0	0	0
Official	..	..	..	0	0	0	0	0	0	0
Private	..	..	..	0	0	0	0	0	0	0
Debt forgiven	..	..	..	0	0	553	0	0	0	0
Memo: interest forgiven	..	..	..	0	0	15	0	0	0	0
Debt stock reduction	..	..	..	0	0	0	0	0	0	0
of which debt buyback	..	..	..	0	0	0	0	0	0	0
8. DEBT STOCK-FLOW RECONCILIATION										
Total change in debt stocks	..	..	..	327	398	-589	66	-18	-171	-132
Net flows on debt	..	..	..	319	369	35	152	-62	-106	-103
Net change in interest arrears	..	..	..	8	4	-9	-7	3	3	5
Interest capitalized	..	..	..	0	0	0	0	0	0	0
Debt forgiveness or reduction	..	..	..	0	0	-553	0	0	0	0
Cross-currency valuation	..	..	..	1	29	-60	-81	42	-61	-25
Residual	..	..	..	-1	-3	-2	1	-2	-7	-8
9. AVERAGE TERMS OF NEW COMMITMENTS										
ALL CREDITORS										
Interest (%)	..	..	..	6.4	5.7	6.2	6.1	4.9	6.0	6.7
Maturity (years)	..	..	..	12.0	14.0	17.7	6.7	8.0	5.2	1.5
Grace period (years)	..	..	..	3.9	4.8	4.3	1.7	2.9	1.9	0.9
Grant element (%)	..	..	..	17.8	25.3	22.9	12.3	19.7	9.9	3.2
Official creditors										
Interest (%)	..	..	..	6.9	5.2	4.5	5.8	5.7	0.0	0.0
Maturity (years)	..	..	..	13.0	16.0	16.8	8.3	9.8	0.0	0.0
Grace period (years)	..	..	..	4.0	5.6	6.8	1.6	1.8	0.0	0.0
Grant element (%)	..	..	..	16.9	29.9	35.6	14.6	16.9	0.0	0.0
Private creditors										
Interest (%)	..	..	..	4.9	8.1	6.4	6.6	4.9	6.0	6.7
Maturity (years)	..	..	..	8.2	5.8	17.9	3.3	8.0	5.2	1.5
Grace period (years)	..	..	..	3.6	1.6	3.9	1.9	2.9	1.9	0.9
Grant element (%)	..	..	..	21.1	5.9	20.9	7.5	19.7	9.9	3.2
Memorandum items										
Commitments	..	..	..	288	145	54	125	66	70	57
Official creditors	..	..	..	226	117	8	85	1	0	0
Private creditors	..	..	..	62	28	47	40	65	70	57

10. CONTRACTUAL OBLIGATIONS ON OUTSTANDING LONG-TERM DEBT

	2001	2002	2003	2004	2005	2006	2007	2008	2009	2010
TOTAL										
Disbursements	30	15	4	2	0	0	0	0	0	0
Principal	140	110	102	93	85	45	31	25	13	11
Interest	34	29	24	18	13	9	6	5	4	3
Official creditors										
Disbursements	22	13	3	2	0	0	0	0	0	0
Principal	58	62	59	54	51	25	22	20	7	6
Interest	23	20	16	12	9	6	5	3	3	2
Bilateral creditors										
Disbursements	0	0	0	0	0	0	0	0	0	0
Principal	19	20	20	15	15	4	4	4	4	4
Interest	7	6	5	4	3	2	2	2	2	2
Multilateral creditors										
Disbursements	22	13	3	2	0	0	0	0	0	0
Principal	39	42	39	39	36	21	19	16	4	2
Interest	16	14	11	8	6	4	2	1	1	0
Private creditors										
Disbursements	8	2	1	0	0	0	0	0	0	0
Principal	81	47	43	40	34	20	8	5	5	5
Interest	12	10	8	6	4	2	2	1	1	1
Commercial banks										
Disbursements	0	0	0	0	0	0	0	0	0	0
Principal	37	10	9	8	4	1	0	0	0	0
Interest	2	2	1	1	0	0	0	0	0	0
Other private										
Disbursements	8	2	1	0	0	0	0	0	0	0
Principal	44	37	34	31	30	19	8	5	5	5
Interest	10	8	7	5	4	2	2	1	1	1

BELIZE

(US$ million, unless otherwise indicated)

	1970	1980	1990	1994	1995	1996	1997	1998	1999	2000
1. SUMMARY DEBT DATA										
TOTAL DEBT STOCKS (EDT)	**4.1**	**63.0**	**153.8**	**200.2**	**255.2**	**281.5**	**450.1**	**333.5**	**346.6**	**499.0**
Long-term debt (LDOD)	**4.1**	**47.0**	**147.3**	**184.0**	**219.4**	**250.4**	**268.1**	**282.9**	**295.6**	**449.0**
Public and publicly guaranteed	4.1	47.0	136.2	182.4	219.4	250.4	268.1	282.9	295.6	449.0
Private nonguaranteed	0.0	0.0	11.1	1.5	0.0	0.0	0.0	0.0	0.0	0.0
Use of IMF credit	**0.0**	**0.0**	**0.4**	**0.0**	**0.0**	**0.0**	**0.0**	**0.0**	**0.0**	**0.0**
Short-term debt	**0.0**	**16.0**	**6.1**	**16.2**	**35.7**	**31.1**	**182.0**	**50.5**	**51.0**	**50.0**
of which interest arrears on LDOD	0.0	0.0	0.9	2.2	0.6	0.6	0.0	0.0	0.0	0.0
Official creditors	0.0	0.0	0.4	1.2	0.3	0.6	0.0	0.0	0.0	0.0
Private creditors	0.0	0.0	0.5	1.0	0.3	0.0	0.0	0.0	0.0	0.0
Memo: principal arrears on LDOD	0.0	0.0	2.0	6.1	1.0	0.6	0.0	0.0	0.0	0.0
Official creditors	0.0	0.0	0.8	3.9	1.0	0.6	0.0	0.0	0.0	0.0
Private creditors	0.0	0.0	1.2	2.1	0.0	0.0	0.0	0.0	0.0	0.0
Memo: export credits	0.0	0.0	30.0	47.1	41.8	38.2	34.0	2.1	3.4	3.5
TOTAL DEBT FLOWS										
Disbursements	**4.3**	**13.7**	**22.2**	**19.3**	**31.2**	**60.5**	**48.8**	**38.7**	**40.0**	**195.6**
Long-term debt	4.3	13.7	22.2	19.3	31.2	60.5	48.8	38.7	40.0	195.6
IMF purchases	0.0	0.0	0.0	0.0	0.0	0.0	0.0	0.0	0.0	0.0
Principal repayments	**0.0**	**0.6**	**12.9**	**18.8**	**26.9**	**27.3**	**25.5**	**25.0**	**24.5**	**40.2**
Long-term debt	0.0	0.6	9.9	18.8	26.9	27.3	25.5	25.0	24.5	40.2
IMF repurchases	0.0	0.0	3.0	0.0	0.0	0.0	0.0	0.0	0.0	0.0
Net flows on debt	**4.3**	**-8.9**	**10.0**	**-2.5**	**25.5**	**28.5**	**174.9**	**-117.8**	**15.9**	**154.4**
of which short-term debt	0.0	-22.0	0.8	-3.0	21.2	-4.7	151.5	-131.5	0.5	-1.0
Interest payments (INT)	**0.0**	**3.1**	**7.2**	**8.3**	**11.3**	**13.0**	**14.2**	**20.9**	**19.3**	**25.9**
Long-term debt	0.0	0.9	6.6	7.3	9.9	11.1	9.4	15.1	16.4	22.5
IMF charges	0.0	0.0	0.2	0.0	0.0	0.0	0.0	0.0	0.0	0.0
Short-term debt	0.0	2.2	0.4	0.9	1.4	1.9	4.9	5.8	2.8	3.4
Net transfers on debt	**4.3**	**-11.9**	**2.9**	**-10.8**	**14.2**	**15.5**	**160.6**	**-138.7**	**-3.3**	**128.5**
Total debt service paid (TDS)	**0.0**	**3.6**	**20.1**	**27.1**	**38.2**	**40.3**	**39.7**	**46.0**	**43.8**	**66.1**
Long-term debt	0.0	1.5	16.5	26.1	36.8	38.4	34.8	40.1	41.0	62.7
IMF repurchases and charges	0.0	0.0	3.2	0.0	0.0	0.0	0.0	0.0	0.0	0.0
Short-term debt (interest only)	0.0	2.2	0.4	0.9	1.4	1.9	4.9	5.8	2.8	3.4
2. AGGREGATE NET RESOURCE FLOWS AND NET TRANSFERS (LONG-TERM)										
NET RESOURCE FLOWS	**6.1**	**22.0**	**33.6**	**28.5**	**32.9**	**52.6**	**39.8**	**62.4**	**77.3**	**184.0**
Net flow of long-term debt (ex. IMF)	4.3	13.1	12.3	0.5	4.3	33.2	23.3	13.7	15.5	155.4
Foreign direct investment (net)	0.0	0.0	17.0	15.0	21.0	16.6	12.0	17.7	47.4	17.7
Portfolio equity flows	0.0	0.0	0.0	0.0	0.0	0.0	0.0	0.0	0.0	0.0
Grants (excluding technical coop.)	1.8	8.8	4.4	13.0	7.6	2.9	4.5	31.1	14.4	11.0
Memo: technical coop. grants	1.1	2.4	12.9	9.2	11.9	11.4	6.9	3.5	4.4	4.6
official net resource flows	6.1	16.2	11.0	16.0	15.6	29.7	19.4	38.5	17.4	21.6
private net resource flows	0.0	5.8	22.6	12.5	17.3	22.9	20.4	23.9	59.9	162.4
NET TRANSFERS	**6.1**	**21.1**	**19.6**	**8.4**	**9.9**	**29.5**	**17.4**	**32.3**	**46.8**	**146.5**
Interest on long-term debt	0.0	0.9	6.6	7.3	9.9	11.1	9.4	15.1	16.4	22.5
Profit remittances on FDI	0.0	0.0	7.5	12.8	13.0	12.0	13.0	15.0	14.0	15.0
Memo: official net transfers	6.1	15.3	6.8	10.6	7.9	21.3	12.2	28.7	6.8	9.5
private net transfers	0.0	5.8	12.8	-2.2	2.0	8.2	5.2	3.6	40.0	137.0
3. MAJOR ECONOMIC AGGREGATES										
Gross national income (GNI)	51.5	192.8	396.0	529.5	570.5	606.7	625.3	639.6	687.8	767.3
Exports of goods & services (XGS)	..	..	268.9	293.5	314.1	328.6	356.5	352.8	398.8	411.2
of which workers remittances	..	..	13.7	13.0	13.9	13.2	17.8	19.0	21.3	21.8
Imports of goods & services (MGS)	..	..	269.2	348.0	350.6	353.2	405.4	429.2	492.2	582.2
International reserves (RES)	..	12.7	69.8	34.5	37.6	58.4	59.4	44.1	71.3	122.9
Current account balance	..	..	15.4	-40.1	-17.2	-6.6	-31.9	-59.8	-65.7	-131.0
4. DEBT INDICATORS										
EDT / XGS (%)	..	..	57.2	68.2	81.3	85.7	126.3	94.5	86.9	121.4
EDT / GNI (%)	8.0	32.7	38.8	37.8	44.7	46.4	72.0	52.1	50.4	65.0
TDS / XGS (%)	..	..	7.5	9.2	12.2	12.3	11.1	13.0	11.0	16.1
INT / XGS (%)	..	..	2.7	2.8	3.6	4.0	4.0	5.9	4.8	6.3
INT / GNI (%)	0.0	1.6	1.8	1.6	2.0	2.1	2.3	3.3	2.8	3.4
RES / EDT (%)	..	20.1	45.4	17.2	14.7	20.8	13.2	13.2	20.6	24.6
RES / MGS (months)	..	..	3.1	1.2	1.3	2.0	1.8	1.2	1.7	2.5
Short-term / EDT (%)	0.0	25.4	4.0	8.1	14.0	11.1	40.4	15.1	14.7	10.0
Concessional / EDT (%)	0.0	48.7	52.6	41.5	36.4	41.7	25.0	32.6	29.5	19.9
Multilateral / EDT (%)	0.0	35.7	37.3	35.3	35.1	31.9	23.3	35.6	36.7	28.0

BELIZE

(US$ million, unless otherwise indicated)

	1970	1980	1990	1994	1995	1996	1997	1998	1999	2000
5. LONG-TERM DEBT										
DEBT OUTSTANDING (LDOD)	**4.1**	**47.0**	**147.3**	**184.0**	**219.4**	**250.4**	**268.1**	**282.9**	**295.6**	**449.0**
Public and publicly guaranteed	**4.1**	**47.0**	**136.2**	**182.4**	**219.4**	**250.4**	**268.1**	**282.9**	**295.6**	**449.0**
Official creditors	4.1	39.9	118.0	151.2	175.0	199.6	208.8	217.5	217.7	226.2
Multilateral	0.0	22.5	57.4	70.7	89.5	89.7	104.8	118.6	127.1	139.7
Concessional	0.0	19.6	30.0	34.2	43.0	40.5	38.5	38.2	36.7	36.8
Bilateral	4.1	17.4	60.6	80.4	85.5	109.9	104.0	98.9	90.6	86.4
Concessional	0.0	11.1	50.9	48.9	49.9	76.9	74.2	70.5	65.6	62.5
Private creditors	0.0	7.1	18.2	31.3	44.5	50.8	59.2	65.5	77.9	222.8
Bonds	0.0	0.0	0.0	0.0	0.0	0.0	0.0	0.0	0.0	0.0
Commercial banks	0.0	0.0	16.4	24.3	38.7	47.9	47.7	55.3	67.9	204.2
Other private	0.0	7.1	1.8	7.0	5.8	2.9	11.5	10.2	10.1	18.6
Private nonguaranteed	**0.0**	**0.0**	**11.1**	**1.5**	**0.0**	**0.0**	**0.0**	**0.0**	**0.0**	**0.0**
Bonds	0.0	0.0	0.0	0.0	0.0	0.0	0.0	0.0	0.0	0.0
Commercial banks and other	0.0	0.0	11.1	1.5	0.0	0.0	0.0	0.0	0.0	0.0
Memo:										
IBRD	0.0	0.0	17.5	25.6	29.5	32.5	39.9	41.4	41.3	40.0
IDA	0.0	0.0	0.0	0.0	0.0	0.0	0.0	0.0	0.0	0.0
DISBURSEMENTS	**4.3**	**13.7**	**22.2**	**19.3**	**31.2**	**60.5**	**48.8**	**38.7**	**40.0**	**195.6**
Public and publicly guaranteed	**4.3**	**13.7**	**17.9**	**19.3**	**31.2**	**60.5**	**48.8**	**38.7**	**40.0**	**195.6**
Official creditors	4.3	7.9	13.2	14.7	25.8	45.0	31.8	24.7	20.5	29.4
Multilateral	0.0	4.6	5.8	10.6	12.4	10.0	26.5	19.0	18.2	22.8
Concessional	0.0	3.2	2.2	1.5	3.4	1.0	2.4	1.7	2.6	3.9
Bilateral	4.3	3.3	7.5	4.1	13.4	35.0	5.3	5.7	2.3	6.6
Concessional	0.0	0.7	4.6	0.0	3.5	30.4	1.8	0.8	1.4	3.9
Private creditors	0.0	5.8	4.6	4.6	5.3	15.5	17.0	14.0	19.5	166.2
Bonds	0.0	0.0	0.0	0.0	0.0	0.0	0.0	0.0	0.0	0.0
Commercial banks	0.0	0.0	4.6	4.6	4.8	15.5	7.0	14.0	19.5	156.4
Other private	0.0	5.8	0.0	0.0	0.5	0.0	10.0	0.0	0.0	9.8
Private nonguaranteed	**0.0**	**0.0**	**4.3**	**0.0**	**0.0**	**0.0**	**0.0**	**0.0**	**0.0**	**0.0**
Bonds	0.0	0.0	0.0	0.0	0.0	0.0	0.0	0.0	0.0	0.0
Commercial banks and other	0.0	0.0	4.3	0.0	0.0	0.0	0.0	0.0	0.0	0.0
Memo:										
IBRD	0.0	0.0	3.4	6.4	5.6	7.5	12.6	4.0	3.2	2.3
IDA	0.0	0.0	0.0	0.0	0.0	0.0	0.0	0.0	0.0	0.0
PRINCIPAL REPAYMENTS	**0.0**	**0.6**	**9.9**	**18.8**	**26.9**	**27.3**	**25.5**	**25.0**	**24.5**	**40.2**
Public and publicly guaranteed	**0.0**	**0.6**	**9.0**	**16.7**	**25.4**	**27.3**	**25.5**	**25.0**	**24.5**	**40.2**
Official creditors	0.0	0.5	6.6	11.8	17.8	18.2	16.9	17.3	17.5	18.8
Multilateral	0.0	0.4	2.7	5.3	7.2	6.8	6.5	6.2	7.6	9.0
Concessional	0.0	0.3	1.5	2.1	3.2	3.0	2.8	2.5	2.7	3.1
Bilateral	0.0	0.1	3.9	6.5	10.6	11.3	10.4	11.1	9.9	9.8
Concessional	0.0	0.1	1.1	1.6	2.6	4.1	3.7	4.8	5.7	6.0
Private creditors	0.0	0.1	2.4	4.9	7.6	9.1	8.6	7.8	7.0	21.4
Bonds	0.0	0.0	0.0	0.0	0.0	0.0	0.0	0.0	0.0	0.0
Commercial banks	0.0	0.0	2.3	2.3	4.7	6.3	7.2	6.4	6.9	20.1
Other private	0.0	0.1	0.1	2.7	2.9	2.9	1.4	1.4	0.1	1.3
Private nonguaranteed	**0.0**	**0.0**	**0.9**	**2.1**	**1.5**	**0.0**	**0.0**	**0.0**	**0.0**	**0.0**
Bonds	0.0	0.0	0.0	0.0	0.0	0.0	0.0	0.0	0.0	0.0
Commercial banks and other	0.0	0.0	0.9	2.1	1.5	0.0	0.0	0.0	0.0	0.0
Memo:										
IBRD	0.0	0.0	0.6	2.3	2.5	2.3	2.3	2.7	3.2	3.6
IDA	0.0	0.0	0.0	0.0	0.0	0.0	0.0	0.0	0.0	0.0
NET FLOWS ON DEBT	**4.3**	**13.1**	**12.3**	**0.5**	**4.3**	**33.2**	**23.3**	**13.7**	**15.5**	**155.4**
Public and publicly guaranteed	**4.3**	**13.1**	**8.8**	**2.6**	**5.8**	**33.2**	**23.3**	**13.7**	**15.5**	**155.4**
Official creditors	4.3	7.4	6.6	3.0	8.0	26.8	14.9	7.4	3.0	10.6
Multilateral	0.0	4.2	3.0	5.3	5.2	3.2	20.0	12.8	10.6	13.8
Concessional	0.0	2.8	0.7	-0.6	0.3	-2.0	-0.5	-0.8	-0.1	0.8
Bilateral	4.3	3.1	3.6	-2.4	2.8	23.6	-5.1	-5.4	-7.6	-3.2
Concessional	0.0	0.7	3.5	-1.6	0.9	26.2	-1.9	-4.0	-4.2	-2.1
Private creditors	0.0	5.8	2.2	-0.4	-2.2	6.3	8.4	6.2	12.5	144.7
Bonds	0.0	0.0	0.0	0.0	0.0	0.0	0.0	0.0	0.0	0.0
Commercial banks	0.0	0.0	2.3	2.3	0.2	9.2	-0.1	7.6	12.6	136.3
Other private	0.0	5.8	-0.1	-2.7	-2.4	-2.9	8.6	-1.4	-0.1	8.4
Private nonguaranteed	**0.0**	**0.0**	**3.4**	**-2.1**	**-1.5**	**0.0**	**0.0**	**0.0**	**0.0**	**0.0**
Bonds	0.0	0.0	0.0	0.0	0.0	0.0	0.0	0.0	0.0	0.0
Commercial banks and other	0.0	0.0	3.4	-2.1	-1.5	0.0	0.0	0.0	0.0	0.0
Memo:										
IBRD	0.0	0.0	2.8	4.1	3.1	5.2	10.3	1.3	-0.1	-1.3
IDA	0.0	0.0	0.0	0.0	0.0	0.0	0.0	0.0	0.0	0.0

BELIZE

(US$ million, unless otherwise indicated)

	1970	1980	1990	1994	1995	1996	1997	1998	1999	2000
INTEREST PAYMENTS (LINT)	**0.0**	**0.9**	**6.6**	**7.3**	**9.9**	**11.1**	**9.4**	**15.1**	**16.4**	**22.5**
Public and publicly guaranteed	**0.0**	**0.9**	**5.6**	**7.2**	**9.9**	**11.1**	**9.4**	**15.1**	**16.4**	**22.5**
Official creditors	0.0	0.9	4.2	5.4	7.7	8.4	7.2	9.8	10.6	12.1
Multilateral	0.0	0.6	2.7	2.8	4.0	4.2	3.8	5.2	6.0	7.8
Concessional	0.0	0.5	1.0	0.8	1.1	1.1	0.8	0.8	0.8	0.9
Bilateral	0.0	0.3	1.5	2.6	3.7	4.2	3.3	4.6	4.6	4.3
Concessional	0.0	0.0	0.6	0.6	0.8	1.5	1.2	2.5	2.5	2.4
Private creditors	0.0	0.0	1.4	1.8	2.2	2.7	2.2	5.3	5.9	10.4
Bonds	0.0	0.0	0.0	0.0	0.0	0.0	0.0	0.0	0.0	0.0
Commercial banks	0.0	0.0	1.4	1.2	1.6	2.4	2.0	4.2	4.9	9.0
Other private	0.0	0.0	0.0	0.6	0.6	0.4	0.2	1.1	1.0	1.5
Private nonguaranteed	**0.0**	**0.0**	**0.9**	**0.1**	**0.1**	**0.0**	**0.0**	**0.0**	**0.0**	**0.0**
Bonds	0.0	0.0	0.0	0.0	0.0	0.0	0.0	0.0	0.0	0.0
Commercial banks and other	0.0	0.0	0.9	0.1	0.1	0.0	0.0	0.0	0.0	0.0
Memo:										
IBRD	0.0	0.0	1.1	1.5	1.9	2.0	2.1	2.4	3.1	3.4
IDA	0.0	0.0	0.0	0.0	0.0	0.0	0.0	0.0	0.0	0.0
NET TRANSFERS ON DEBT	**4.3**	**12.2**	**5.7**	**-6.9**	**-5.7**	**22.1**	**14.0**	**-1.4**	**-1.0**	**132.9**
Public and publicly guaranteed	**4.3**	**12.2**	**3.2**	**-4.6**	**-4.1**	**22.1**	**14.0**	**-1.4**	**-1.0**	**132.9**
Official creditors	4.3	6.5	2.4	-2.4	0.4	18.5	7.7	-2.4	-7.6	-1.4
Multilateral	0.0	3.6	0.3	2.5	1.2	-1.0	16.2	7.6	4.6	6.0
Concessional	0.0	2.3	-0.4	-1.4	-0.9	-3.1	-1.3	-1.6	-0.9	-0.1
Bilateral	4.3	2.9	2.1	-5.0	-0.9	19.5	-8.4	-10.0	-12.2	-7.4
Concessional	0.0	0.7	3.0	-2.2	0.0	24.7	-3.0	-6.5	-6.8	-4.5
Private creditors	0.0	5.8	0.8	-2.2	-4.4	3.6	6.2	0.9	6.6	134.3
Bonds	0.0	0.0	0.0	0.0	0.0	0.0	0.0	0.0	0.0	0.0
Commercial banks	0.0	0.0	1.0	1.1	-1.5	6.8	-2.2	3.3	7.7	127.3
Other private	0.0	5.8	-0.2	-3.3	-3.0	-3.2	8.4	-2.4	-1.1	7.0
Private nonguaranteed	**0.0**	**0.0**	**2.5**	**-2.2**	**-1.6**	**0.0**	**0.0**	**0.0**	**0.0**	**0.0**
Bonds	0.0	0.0	0.0	0.0	0.0	0.0	0.0	0.0	0.0	0.0
Commercial banks and other	0.0	0.0	2.5	-2.2	-1.6	0.0	0.0	0.0	0.0	0.0
Memo:										
IBRD	0.0	0.0	1.7	2.6	1.2	3.2	8.2	-1.1	-3.1	-4.6
IDA	0.0	0.0	0.0	0.0	0.0	0.0	0.0	0.0	0.0	0.0
DEBT SERVICE (LTDS)	**0.0**	**1.5**	**16.5**	**26.1**	**36.8**	**38.4**	**34.8**	**40.1**	**41.0**	**62.7**
Public and publicly guaranteed	**0.0**	**1.5**	**14.6**	**23.9**	**35.3**	**38.4**	**34.8**	**40.1**	**41.0**	**62.7**
Official creditors	0.0	1.4	10.8	17.2	25.5	26.6	24.0	27.1	28.1	30.8
Multilateral	0.0	1.0	5.4	8.1	11.2	11.1	10.3	11.4	13.6	16.8
Concessional	0.0	0.9	2.5	2.9	4.3	4.1	3.6	3.3	3.5	4.0
Bilateral	0.0	0.4	5.4	9.1	14.3	15.5	13.7	15.7	14.5	14.1
Concessional	0.0	0.1	1.6	2.2	3.5	5.7	4.9	7.3	8.2	8.4
Private creditors	0.0	0.1	3.8	6.7	9.8	11.9	10.8	13.1	12.9	31.9
Bonds	0.0	0.0	0.0	0.0	0.0	0.0	0.0	0.0	0.0	0.0
Commercial banks	0.0	0.0	3.7	3.4	6.3	8.6	9.2	10.7	11.8	29.1
Other private	0.0	0.1	0.2	3.3	3.5	3.2	1.6	2.4	1.1	2.8
Private nonguaranteed	**0.0**	**0.0**	**1.8**	**2.2**	**1.6**	**0.0**	**0.0**	**0.0**	**0.0**	**0.0**
Bonds	0.0	0.0	0.0	0.0	0.0	0.0	0.0	0.0	0.0	0.0
Commercial banks and other	0.0	0.0	1.8	2.2	1.6	0.0	0.0	0.0	0.0	0.0
Memo:										
IBRD	0.0	0.0	1.8	3.8	4.4	4.3	4.4	5.1	6.3	6.9
IDA	0.0	0.0	0.0	0.0	0.0	0.0	0.0	0.0	0.0	0.0
UNDISBURSED DEBT	**0.0**	**22.7**	**60.9**	**93.1**	**97.3**	**78.7**	**73.5**	**97.5**	**219.8**	**231.5**
Official creditors	0.0	17.9	49.8	78.1	85.5	70.3	66.5	82.5	156.9	179.7
Private creditors	0.0	4.8	11.1	15.0	11.8	8.3	7.0	15.0	62.9	51.7
Memorandum items										
Concessional LDOD	0.0	30.7	80.9	83.1	92.9	117.4	112.7	108.7	102.3	99.3
Variable rate LDOD	0.0	0.0	38.6	42.8	56.6	57.2	61.4	61.9	62.2	99.6
Public sector LDOD	4.1	47.0	136.2	182.4	219.4	250.4	268.1	282.9	295.6	449.0
Private sector LDOD	0.0	0.0	11.1	1.5	0.0	0.0	0.0	0.0	0.0	0.0

6. CURRENCY COMPOSITION OF LONG-TERM DEBT (PERCENT)

	1970	1980	1990	1994	1995	1996	1997	1998	1999	2000
Deutsche mark	0.0	0.8	0.7	0.3	0.2	0.1	0.1	0.1	0.0	0.0
French franc	0.0	0.0	0.0	0.0	0.0	0.0	0.0	0.0	0.0	0.0
Japanese yen	0.0	0.0	0.0	0.0	0.0	0.0	0.0	0.0	0.0	0.0
Pound sterling	100.0	15.3	23.6	13.0	10.0	7.7	6.2	5.2	4.3	2.3
Swiss franc	0.0	0.0	0.0	0.0	0.1	0.0	0.0	0.0	0.0	0.0
U.S.dollars	0.0	29.3	45.3	55.8	62.7	67.8	68.8	84.1	87.0	90.9
Multiple currency	0.0	23.5	23.4	20.0	17.6	16.1	17.2	2.8	2.1	1.0
Special drawing rights	0.0	0.0	0.5	0.8	0.6	0.5	0.4	0.3	0.3	0.1
All other currencies	0.0	31.1	6.5	10.1	8.8	7.8	7.3	7.5	6.3	5.7

BELIZE

(US$ million, unless otherwise indicated)

	1970	1980	1990	1994	1995	1996	1997	1998	1999	2000
7. DEBT RESTRUCTURINGS										
Total amount rescheduled	..	..	0.0	0.0	0.0	0.0	0.0	0.0	0.0	0.0
Debt stock rescheduled	..	..	0.0	0.0	0.0	0.0	0.0	0.0	0.0	0.0
Principal rescheduled	..	..	0.0	0.0	0.0	0.0	0.0	0.0	0.0	0.0
Official	..	..	0.0	0.0	0.0	0.0	0.0	0.0	0.0	0.0
Private	..	..	0.0	0.0	0.0	0.0	0.0	0.0	0.0	0.0
Interest rescheduled	..	..	0.0	0.0	0.0	0.0	0.0	0.0	0.0	0.0
Official	..	..	0.0	0.0	0.0	0.0	0.0	0.0	0.0	0.0
Private	..	..	0.0	0.0	0.0	0.0	0.0	0.0	0.0	0.0
Debt forgiven	..	..	9.1	0.0	0.0	0.0	0.0	0.0	0.0	0.0
Memo: interest forgiven	..	..	0.0	0.0	0.0	0.0	0.0	0.0	0.0	0.0
Debt stock reduction	..	..	0.0	0.0	0.0	0.0	0.0	0.0	0.0	0.0
of which debt buyback	..	..	0.0	0.0	0.0	0.0	0.0	0.0	0.0	0.0
8. DEBT STOCK-FLOW RECONCILIATION										
Total change in debt stocks	..	..	9.0	2.0	55.0	26.4	168.6	-116.6	13.2	152.4
Net flows on debt	4.3	-8.9	10.0	-2.5	25.5	28.5	174.9	-117.8	15.9	154.4
Net change in interest arrears	..	..	0.3	0.3	-1.7	0.1	-0.6	0.0	0.0	0.0
Interest capitalized	..	..	0.0	0.0	0.0	0.0	0.0	0.0	0.0	0.0
Debt forgiveness or reduction	..	..	-9.1	0.0	0.0	0.0	0.0	0.0	0.0	0.0
Cross-currency valuation	..	..	6.9	3.9	1.1	-1.5	-5.7	1.1	-2.7	-2.1
Residual	..	..	0.9	0.3	30.1	-0.7	0.0	0.1	-0.1	0.1
9. AVERAGE TERMS OF NEW COMMITMENTS										
ALL CREDITORS										
Interest (%)	7.0	5.5	5.0	5.8	6.0	4.3	6.8	6.6	5.9	8.9
Maturity (years)	26.0	18.6	10.0	14.7	17.6	17.4	15.1	17.7	19.1	11.7
Grace period (years)	3.0	4.7	2.5	4.2	3.9	12.6	4.3	4.2	4.5	3.6
Grant element (%)	20.7	29.7	21.2	22.5	23.0	37.1	20.1	20.1	25.4	5.4
Official creditors										
Interest (%)	7.0	4.4	5.0	5.8	5.9	5.2	5.0	6.4	6.3	7.1
Maturity (years)	26.0	26.0	10.0	17.6	17.9	20.7	17.7	22.1	21.7	22.1
Grace period (years)	3.0	6.8	2.5	5.2	3.9	15.4	5.3	4.9	4.9	5.2
Grant element (%)	20.7	43.8	21.2	26.4	23.3	38.7	31.8	23.9	24.4	19.3
Private creditors										
Interest (%)	0.0	7.3	0.0	5.9	8.6	1.8	10.4	6.9	5.3	9.5
Maturity (years)	0.0	7.7	0.0	5.5	4.8	7.0	10.0	9.6	15.7	8.1
Grace period (years)	0.0	1.7	0.0	1.0	0.3	3.5	2.3	2.9	4.0	3.0
Grant element (%)	0.0	8.6	0.0	10.0	2.7	32.0	-2.6	13.2	26.7	0.7
Memorandum items										
Commitments	4.3	11.7	5.0	23.5	29.2	49.9	46.7	62.5	170.0	209.7
Official creditors	4.3	7.0	5.0	17.8	28.7	37.9	30.7	40.5	96.2	53.5
Private creditors	0.0	4.7	0.0	5.6	0.5	12.0	16.0	22.0	73.8	156.2

10. CONTRACTUAL OBLIGATIONS ON OUTSTANDING LONG-TERM DEBT

	2001	2002	2003	2004	2005	2006	2007	2008	2009	2010
TOTAL										
Disbursements	83.6	68.2	40.6	20.4	10.5	5.5	1.4	1.0	0.3	0.0
Principal	49.9	45.6	45.0	49.0	70.8	41.2	69.4	34.8	30.5	29.1
Interest	34.6	35.8	35.8	34.1	30.0	26.1	22.2	18.1	15.9	13.9
Official creditors										
Disbursements	54.0	53.4	34.4	19.6	10.1	5.5	1.4	1.0	0.3	0.0
Principal	21.2	22.5	20.7	24.5	23.3	24.6	24.6	22.8	21.7	20.4
Interest	15.5	17.7	18.6	18.6	17.8	16.7	15.2	13.8	12.4	11.1
Bilateral creditors										
Disbursements	4.0	2.4	1.6	0.9	0.5	0.5	0.4	0.3	0.0	0.0
Principal	9.0	9.3	8.8	7.9	5.6	5.3	5.3	4.9	4.4	3.3
Interest	3.9	3.6	3.2	2.9	2.6	2.4	2.2	2.0	1.8	1.6
Multilateral creditors										
Disbursements	50.0	51.0	32.8	18.7	9.6	4.9	0.9	0.7	0.3	0.0
Principal	12.2	13.2	12.0	16.7	17.7	19.3	19.3	17.8	17.3	17.1
Interest	11.6	14.1	15.4	15.7	15.2	14.3	13.0	11.8	10.6	9.5
Private creditors										
Disbursements	29.6	14.9	6.2	0.7	0.4	0.0	0.0	0.0	0.0	0.0
Principal	28.7	23.1	24.2	24.5	47.4	16.6	44.9	12.1	8.8	8.7
Interest	19.1	18.1	17.2	15.5	12.2	9.4	7.0	4.3	3.5	2.8
Commercial banks										
Disbursements	25.9	11.7	4.6	0.3	0.2	0.0	0.0	0.0	0.0	0.0
Principal	25.5	20.3	20.3	20.6	43.9	15.1	39.0	11.6	8.3	8.3
Interest	17.3	16.5	15.5	14.1	11.1	8.5	6.2	4.1	3.3	2.7
Other private										
Disbursements	3.7	3.1	1.6	0.4	0.2	0.0	0.0	0.0	0.0	0.0
Principal	3.1	2.8	4.0	3.8	3.5	1.5	5.9	0.5	0.4	0.4
Interest	1.8	1.6	1.7	1.4	1.1	0.9	0.7	0.2	0.2	0.1

BENIN

(US$ million, unless otherwise indicated)

	1970	1980	1990	1994	1995	1996	1997	1998	1999	2000
1. SUMMARY DEBT DATA										
TOTAL DEBT STOCKS (EDT)	**41**	**424**	**1,292**	**1,589**	**1,614**	**1,592**	**1,627**	**1,651**	**1,686**	**1,599**
Long-term debt (LDOD)	**41**	**334**	**1,219**	**1,487**	**1,483**	**1,446**	**1,396**	**1,471**	**1,472**	**1,443**
Public and publicly guaranteed	41	334	1,219	1,487	1,483	1,446	1,396	1,471	1,472	1,443
Private nonguaranteed	0	0	0	0	0	0	0	0	0	0
Use of IMF credit	**0**	**16**	**18**	**71**	**84**	**99**	**95**	**94**	**92**	**84**
Short-term debt	**1**	**73**	**55**	**31**	**47**	**47**	**136**	**86**	**122**	**72**
of which interest arrears on LDOD	1	5	21	8	8	8	8	8	8	7
Official creditors	0	0	19	7	7	7	7	7	7	6
Private creditors	1	5	2	1	1	1	1	1	1	1
Memo: principal arrears on LDOD	4	14	69	72	71	72	71	73	73	17
Official creditors	1	1	60	68	67	68	68	69	70	14
Private creditors	2	13	9	4	4	4	3	4	3	3
Memo: export credits	0	0	303	144	174	152	125	163	154	141
TOTAL DEBT FLOWS										
Disbursements	**2**	**71**	**120**	**130**	**115**	**128**	**57**	**62**	**81**	**70**
Long-term debt	2	62	120	104	101	109	51	62	71	61
IMF purchases	0	10	0	26	14	20	6	0	10	9
Principal repayments	**1**	**6**	**21**	**21**	**26**	**28**	**32**	**35**	**45**	**57**
Long-term debt	1	6	19	20	24	26	28	29	36	45
IMF repurchases	0	0	2	1	2	2	4	5	9	13
Net flows on debt	**1**	**42**	**92**	**112**	**105**	**101**	**114**	**-24**	**72**	**-36**
of which short-term debt	0	-24	-8	3	16	0	89	-50	36	-49
Interest payments (INT)	**0**	**14**	**18**	**20**	**24**	**18**	**23**	**26**	**25**	**19**
Long-term debt	0	3	14	19	21	16	18	21	20	14
IMF charges	0	0	0	0	0	1	1	1	1	0
Short-term debt	0	11	4	1	2	2	4	5	5	5
Net transfers on debt	**1**	**27**	**74**	**92**	**81**	**82**	**91**	**-50**	**47**	**-55**
Total debt service paid (TDS)	**2**	**20**	**38**	**41**	**50**	**46**	**55**	**61**	**70**	**77**
Long-term debt	2	9	33	39	46	42	46	50	56	59
IMF repurchases and charges	0	0	2	1	2	3	5	6	9	13
Short-term debt (interest only)	0	11	4	1	2	2	4	5	5	5
2. AGGREGATE NET RESOURCE FLOWS AND NET TRANSFERS (LONG-TERM)										
NET RESOURCE FLOWS	**17**	**101**	**213**	**205**	**239**	**242**	**176**	**190**	**173**	**192**
Net flow of long-term debt (ex. IMF)	1	56	102	84	77	83	23	32	35	17
Foreign direct investment (net)	7	4	1	14	13	36	27	38	41	30
Portfolio equity flows	0	0	0	0	0	0	0	0	0	0
Grants (excluding technical coop.)	9	41	110	108	149	123	126	120	98	145
Memo: technical coop. grants	6	26	49	52	61	67	78	67	65	68
official net resource flows	9	97	212	192	226	206	149	152	133	162
private net resource flows	8	4	1	14	13	36	27	38	41	30
NET TRANSFERS	**13**	**96**	**199**	**187**	**218**	**226**	**158**	**169**	**153**	**177**
Interest on long-term debt	0	3	14	19	21	16	18	21	20	14
Profit remittances on FDI	4	3	0	0	0	0	0	0	0	0
Memo: official net transfers	9	95	198	173	205	190	131	131	113	147
private net transfers	4	1	1	14	13	36	27	38	41	30
3. MAJOR ECONOMIC AGGREGATES										
Gross national income (GNI)	330	1,402	1,806	1,462	1,965	2,162	2,023	2,256	2,314	2,150
Exports of goods & services (XGS)	..	318	465	641	730	772	632	674	697	607
of which workers remittances	..	77	89	82	92	81	67	87	70	79
Imports of goods & services (MGS)	..	428	492	655	926	806	795	808	891	807
International reserves (RES)	16	15	69	262	202	266	256	265	403	458
Current account balance	..	-36	-18	11	-167	-41	-154	-133	-156	-168
4. DEBT INDICATORS										
EDT / XGS (%)	..	133.1	277.9	247.9	221.0	206.4	257.3	244.8	242.0	263.4
EDT / GNI (%)	12.6	30.2	71.5	108.7	82.1	73.7	80.4	73.2	72.9	74.4
TDS / XGS (%)	..	6.4	8.2	6.4	6.8	5.9	8.7	9.0	10.0	12.6
INT / XGS (%)	..	4.5	3.8	3.2	3.2	2.4	3.6	3.9	3.6	3.2
INT / GNI (%)	0.1	1.0	1.0	1.4	1.2	0.8	1.1	1.2	1.1	0.9
RES / EDT (%)	37.5	3.5	5.4	16.5	12.5	16.7	15.8	16.0	23.9	28.7
RES / MGS (months)	..	0.4	1.7	4.8	2.6	4.0	3.9	3.9	5.4	6.8
Short-term / EDT (%)	2.2	17.3	4.3	1.9	2.9	2.9	8.4	5.2	7.2	4.5
Concessional / EDT (%)	70.3	39.2	78.1	79.9	77.7	81.2	77.8	80.8	80.6	84.0
Multilateral / EDT (%)	1.0	24.5	41.6	49.0	54.0	56.6	53.6	56.5	56.8	59.3

BENIN

(US$ million, unless otherwise indicated)

	1970	1980	1990	1994	1995	1996	1997	1998	1999	2000
5. LONG-TERM DEBT										
DEBT OUTSTANDING (LDOD)	**41**	**334**	**1,219**	**1,487**	**1,483**	**1,446**	**1,396**	**1,471**	**1,472**	**1,443**
Public and publicly guaranteed	**41**	**334**	**1,219**	**1,487**	**1,483**	**1,446**	**1,396**	**1,471**	**1,472**	**1,443**
Official creditors	29	217	1,202	1,483	1,479	1,443	1,393	1,468	1,469	1,440
Multilateral	0	104	537	779	871	902	871	933	957	947
Concessional	0	84	497	755	847	878	852	904	933	928
Bilateral	29	113	665	704	608	541	521	535	512	493
Concessional	29	82	512	515	407	415	413	429	426	414
Private creditors	11	118	17	4	4	4	3	4	3	3
Bonds	0	0	0	0	0	0	0	0	0	0
Commercial banks	0	0	0	0	0	0	0	0	0	0
Other private	11	118	17	4	4	4	3	4	3	3
Private nonguaranteed	**0**	**0**	**0**	**0**	**0**	**0**	**0**	**0**	**0**	**0**
Bonds	0	0	0	0	0	0	0	0	0	0
Commercial banks and other	0	0	0	0	0	0	0	0	0	0
Memo:										
IBRD	0	0	0	0	0	0	0	0	0	0
IDA	0	52	326	464	498	520	510	543	574	578
DISBURSEMENTS	**2**	**62**	**120**	**104**	**101**	**109**	**51**	**62**	**71**	**61**
Public and publicly guaranteed	**2**	**62**	**120**	**104**	**101**	**109**	**51**	**62**	**71**	**61**
Official creditors	2	58	120	104	101	109	51	62	71	61
Multilateral	0	24	91	95	84	81	42	45	70	60
Concessional	0	19	82	91	79	77	41	34	70	60
Bilateral	1	35	29	9	18	27	9	17	1	2
Concessional	1	16	29	9	18	27	9	17	1	2
Private creditors	1	4	0	0	0	0	0	0	0	0
Bonds	0	0	0	0	0	0	0	0	0	0
Commercial banks	0	0	0	0	0	0	0	0	0	0
Other private	1	4	0	0	0	0	0	0	0	0
Private nonguaranteed	**0**	**0**	**0**	**0**	**0**	**0**	**0**	**0**	**0**	**0**
Bonds	0	0	0	0	0	0	0	0	0	0
Commercial banks and other	0	0	0	0	0	0	0	0	0	0
Memo:										
IBRD	0	0	0	0	0	0	0	0	0	0
IDA	0	12	56	29	31	41	20	20	49	37
PRINCIPAL REPAYMENTS	**1**	**6**	**19**	**20**	**24**	**26**	**28**	**29**	**36**	**45**
Public and publicly guaranteed	**1**	**6**	**19**	**20**	**24**	**26**	**28**	**29**	**36**	**45**
Official creditors	1	2	18	20	24	26	28	29	36	45
Multilateral	0	1	18	13	17	16	18	18	20	19
Concessional	0	0	7	9	12	12	14	15	17	17
Bilateral	1	2	0	7	8	10	10	11	16	26
Concessional	1	1	0	3	3	3	4	5	5	22
Private creditors	0	3	0	0	0	0	0	0	0	0
Bonds	0	0	0	0	0	0	0	0	0	0
Commercial banks	0	0	0	0	0	0	0	0	0	0
Other private	0	3	0	0	0	0	0	0	0	0
Private nonguaranteed	**0**	**0**	**0**	**0**	**0**	**0**	**0**	**0**	**0**	**0**
Bonds	0	0	0	0	0	0	0	0	0	0
Commercial banks and other	0	0	0	0	0	0	0	0	0	0
Memo:										
IBRD	0	0	0	0	0	0	0	0	0	0
IDA	0	0	1	3	3	3	4	4	6	6
NET FLOWS ON DEBT	**1**	**56**	**102**	**84**	**77**	**83**	**23**	**32**	**35**	**17**
Public and publicly guaranteed	**1**	**56**	**102**	**84**	**77**	**83**	**23**	**32**	**35**	**17**
Official creditors	0	56	102	84	77	83	23	32	35	17
Multilateral	0	23	73	82	67	65	24	27	50	40
Concessional	0	19	75	82	67	65	27	19	53	43
Bilateral	0	33	29	3	10	18	-2	5	-15	-24
Concessional	0	15	29	7	15	25	4	12	-5	-20
Private creditors	1	0	0	0	0	0	0	0	0	0
Bonds	0	0	0	0	0	0	0	0	0	0
Commercial banks	0	0	0	0	0	0	0	0	0	0
Other private	1	0	0	0	0	0	0	0	0	0
Private nonguaranteed	**0**	**0**	**0**	**0**	**0**	**0**	**0**	**0**	**0**	**0**
Bonds	0	0	0	0	0	0	0	0	0	0
Commercial banks and other	0	0	0	0	0	0	0	0	0	0
Memo:										
IBRD	0	0	0	0	0	0	0	0	0	0
IDA	0	12	55	26	28	37	16	16	43	30

BENIN

(US$ million, unless otherwise indicated)

	1970	1980	1990	1994	1995	1996	1997	1998	1999	2000
INTEREST PAYMENTS (LINT)	**0**	**3**	**14**	**19**	**21**	**16**	**18**	**21**	**20**	**14**
Public and publicly guaranteed	**0**	**3**	**14**	**19**	**21**	**16**	**18**	**21**	**20**	**14**
Official creditors	0	2	14	19	21	16	18	21	20	14
Multilateral	0	1	13	8	9	9	10	10	10	10
Concessional	0	1	6	6	7	8	9	8	8	9
Bilateral	0	1	1	11	13	7	8	11	10	4
Concessional	0	0	1	3	4	2	3	4	4	3
Private creditors	0	1	0	0	0	0	0	0	0	0
Bonds	0	0	0	0	0	0	0	0	0	0
Commercial banks	0	0	0	0	0	0	0	0	0	0
Other private	0	1	0	0	0	0	0	0	0	0
Private nonguaranteed	**0**	**0**	**0**	**0**	**0**	**0**	**0**	**0**	**0**	**0**
Bonds	0	0	0	0	0	0	0	0	0	0
Commercial banks and other	0	0	0	0	0	0	0	0	0	0
Memo:										
IBRD	0	0	0	0	0	0	0	0	0	0
IDA	0	0	2	3	4	4	4	4	4	4
NET TRANSFERS ON DEBT	**1**	**53**	**88**	**66**	**56**	**67**	**5**	**11**	**15**	**2**
Public and publicly guaranteed	**1**	**53**	**88**	**66**	**56**	**67**	**5**	**11**	**15**	**2**
Official creditors	0	54	88	66	56	67	5	11	15	2
Multilateral	0	21	60	74	58	56	14	17	40	30
Concessional	0	18	69	76	60	57	18	11	45	35
Bilateral	0	33	28	-8	-3	11	-9	-6	-25	-28
Concessional	0	15	28	4	11	23	2	8	-9	-23
Private creditors	1	-1	0	0	0	0	0	0	0	0
Bonds	0	0	0	0	0	0	0	0	0	0
Commercial banks	0	0	0	0	0	0	0	0	0	0
Other private	1	-1	0	0	0	0	0	0	0	0
Private nonguaranteed	**0**	**0**	**0**	**0**	**0**	**0**	**0**	**0**	**0**	**0**
Bonds	0	0	0	0	0	0	0	0	0	0
Commercial banks and other	0	0	0	0	0	0	0	0	0	0
Memo:										
IBRD	0	0	0	0	0	0	0	0	0	0
IDA	0	12	53	23	24	34	12	12	39	26
DEBT SERVICE (LTDS)	**2**	**9**	**33**	**39**	**46**	**42**	**46**	**50**	**56**	**59**
Public and publicly guaranteed	**2**	**9**	**33**	**39**	**46**	**42**	**46**	**50**	**56**	**59**
Official creditors	2	4	32	39	46	42	46	50	56	59
Multilateral	0	2	31	21	25	25	28	28	30	29
Concessional	0	1	13	15	18	19	23	23	25	25
Bilateral	2	2	1	18	21	16	18	22	26	30
Concessional	2	1	1	5	6	4	7	9	10	24
Private creditors	0	4	0	0	0	0	0	0	0	0
Bonds	0	0	0	0	0	0	0	0	0	0
Commercial banks	0	0	0	0	0	0	0	0	0	0
Other private	0	4	0	0	0	0	0	0	0	0
Private nonguaranteed	**0**	**0**	**0**	**0**	**0**	**0**	**0**	**0**	**0**	**0**
Bonds	0	0	0	0	0	0	0	0	0	0
Commercial banks and other	0	0	0	0	0	0	0	0	0	0
Memo:										
IBRD	0	0	0	0	0	0	0	0	0	0
IDA	0	0	3	6	7	7	8	8	10	10
UNDISBURSED DEBT	**15**	**532**	**414**	**358**	**368**	**356**	**322**	**381**	**392**	**375**
Official creditors	15	154	414	358	368	356	322	381	392	375
Private creditors	0	379	0	0	0	0	0	0	0	0
Memorandum items										
Concessional LDOD	29	166	1,009	1,270	1,253	1,293	1,265	1,333	1,359	1,343
Variable rate LDOD	0	2	26	109	120	15	13	14	12	11
Public sector LDOD	41	334	1,219	1,487	1,483	1,446	1,396	1,471	1,472	1,443
Private sector LDOD	0	0	0	0	0	0	0	0	0	0

6. CURRENCY COMPOSITION OF LONG-TERM DEBT (PERCENT)

	1970	1980	1990	1994	1995	1996	1997	1998	1999	2000
Deutsche mark	5.3	0.3	0.3	0.2	0.3	0.2	0.2	0.2	0.2	0.2
French franc	16.7	27.2	18.7	20.0	13.1	10.1	9.2	8.5	7.2	6.6
Japanese yen	0.0	0.0	0.0	0.0	0.0	1.1	1.0	2.2	2.5	2.3
Pound sterling	0.0	0.0	0.9	0.4	0.4	0.3	0.3	0.3	0.3	0.3
Swiss franc	0.0	0.1	0.0	0.0	0.0	0.0	0.0	0.0	0.0	0.0
U.S.dollars	6.6	18.9	50.8	49.3	51.8	54.2	55.2	54.5	56.3	61.1
Multiple currency	0.0	6.7	7.3	11.0	13.6	14.6	14.4	14.7	14.6	14.2
Special drawing rights	0.0	0.0	1.9	1.9	1.9	2.0	1.9	1.9	1.9	1.9
All other currencies	71.4	46.8	20.1	17.2	18.9	17.5	17.8	17.7	17.0	13.4

BENIN

(US$ million, unless otherwise indicated)

	1970	1980	1990	1994	1995	1996	1997	1998	1999	2000
7. DEBT RESTRUCTURINGS										
Total amount rescheduled	..	..	12	6	6	129	0	0	0	53
Debt stock rescheduled	..	..	0	0	0	120	0	0	0	0
Principal rescheduled	..	..	9	2	0	0	0	0	0	37
Official	..	..	4	2	0	0	0	0	0	37
Private	..	..	5	0	0	0	0	0	0	0
Interest rescheduled	..	..	1	4	3	6	0	0	0	6
Official	..	..	0	4	3	6	0	0	0	6
Private	..	..	1	0	0	0	0	0	0	0
Debt forgiven	..	..	122	5	137	0	1	0	0	0
Memo: interest forgiven	..	..	3	2	2	4	0	0	0	0
Debt stock reduction	..	..	0	0	0	80	0	0	0	0
of which debt buyback	..	..	0	0	0	0	0	0	0	0
8. DEBT STOCK-FLOW RECONCILIATION										
Total change in debt stocks	..	..	50	142	25	-22	35	24	36	-88
Net flows on debt	1	42	92	112	105	101	114	-24	72	-36
Net change in interest arrears	..	..	-8	-5	0	0	0	0	0	-2
Interest capitalized	..	..	1	4	3	6	0	0	0	6
Debt forgiveness or reduction	..	..	-122	-5	-137	-80	-1	0	0	0
Cross-currency valuation	..	..	62	-16	-4	-99	-143	-38	-34	-53
Residual	..	..	24	52	58	50	65	85	-3	-4
9. AVERAGE TERMS OF NEW COMMITMENTS										
ALL CREDITORS										
Interest (%)	1.8	8.3	1.3	0.8	1.3	1.1	1.7	1.9	2.1	1.1
Maturity (years)	32.0	11.7	39.2	40.5	33.1	35.1	22.5	33.0	30.2	40.9
Grace period (years)	7.0	3.7	8.4	9.9	8.7	9.2	6.4	8.7	8.1	9.2
Grant element (%)	59.9	8.9	72.0	79.7	70.4	74.1	56.0	65.5	62.8	75.4
Official creditors										
Interest (%)	1.1	4.4	1.3	0.8	1.3	1.1	1.7	1.9	2.1	1.1
Maturity (years)	36.0	26.1	39.2	40.5	33.1	35.1	22.5	33.0	30.2	40.9
Grace period (years)	8.0	5.3	8.4	9.9	8.7	9.2	6.4	8.7	8.1	9.2
Grant element (%)	67.7	40.8	72.0	79.7	70.4	74.1	56.0	65.5	62.8	75.4
Private creditors										
Interest (%)	6.0	8.8	0.0	0.0	0.0	0.0	0.0	0.0	0.0	0.0
Maturity (years)	7.5	9.9	0.0	0.0	0.0	0.0	0.0	0.0	0.0	0.0
Grace period (years)	0.5	3.5	0.0	0.0	0.0	0.0	0.0	0.0	0.0	0.0
Grant element (%)	11.7	4.8	0.0	0.0	0.0	0.0	0.0	0.0	0.0	0.0
Memorandum items										
Commitments	7	448	85	57	111	120	43	115	101	81
Official creditors	6	51	85	57	111	120	43	115	101	81
Private creditors	1	397	0	0	0	0	0	0	0	0

10. CONTRACTUAL OBLIGATIONS ON OUTSTANDING LONG-TERM DEBT

	2001	2002	2003	2004	2005	2006	2007	2008	2009	2010
TOTAL										
Disbursements	98	107	76	49	31	18	12	4	2	0
Principal	35	40	65	66	69	74	74	76	75	77
Interest	19	20	21	20	20	19	18	17	16	15
Official creditors										
Disbursements	98	107	76	49	31	18	12	4	2	0
Principal	35	40	65	66	69	74	74	76	75	77
Interest	19	20	21	20	20	19	18	17	16	15
Bilateral creditors										
Disbursements	15	15	11	8	6	4	3	1	1	0
Principal	9	12	37	35	35	36	36	37	36	36
Interest	9	9	9	9	8	8	7	7	6	6
Multilateral creditors										
Disbursements	83	92	65	41	26	15	9	3	2	0
Principal	26	28	29	31	34	38	38	38	39	42
Interest	10	11	12	12	12	11	11	10	10	9
Private creditors										
Disbursements	0	0	0	0	0	0	0	0	0	0
Principal	0	0	0	0	0	0	0	0	0	0
Interest	0	0	0	0	0	0	0	0	0	0
Commercial banks										
Disbursements	0	0	0	0	0	0	0	0	0	0
Principal	0	0	0	0	0	0	0	0	0	0
Interest	0	0	0	0	0	0	0	0	0	0
Other private										
Disbursements	0	0	0	0	0	0	0	0	0	0
Principal	0	0	0	0	0	0	0	0	0	0
Interest	0	0	0	0	0	0	0	0	0	0

BHUTAN

(US$ million, unless otherwise indicated)

	1970	1980	1990	1994	1995	1996	1997	1998	1999	2000
1. SUMMARY DEBT DATA										
TOTAL DEBT STOCKS (EDT)	..	..	**83.5**	**104.5**	**105.8**	**113.0**	**119.6**	**171.0**	**183.8**	**198.4**
Long-term debt (LDOD)	..	..	**80.3**	**103.8**	**105.2**	**112.9**	**117.6**	**171.0**	**181.8**	**197.3**
Public and publicly guaranteed	..	..	80.3	103.8	105.2	112.9	117.6	171.0	181.8	197.3
Private nonguaranteed	..	..	0.0	0.0	0.0	0.0	0.0	0.0	0.0	0.0
Use of IMF credit	**0.0**	**0.0**	**0.0**	**0.0**	**0.0**	**0.0**	**0.0**	**0.0**	**0.0**	**0.0**
Short-term debt	..	..	**3.3**	**0.7**	**0.6**	**0.1**	**2.0**	**0.0**	**2.0**	**1.1**
of which interest arrears on LDOD	..	..	0.3	0.7	0.6	0.0	0.0	0.0	0.0	0.0
Official creditors	..	..	0.3	0.7	0.6	0.0	0.0	0.0	0.0	0.0
Private creditors	..	..	0.0	0.0	0.0	0.0	0.0	0.0	0.0	0.0
Memo: principal arrears on LDOD	..	..	1.5	1.3	0.2	0.0	0.0	0.0	0.0	0.0
Official creditors	..	..	1.5	1.3	0.2	0.0	0.0	0.0	0.0	0.0
Private creditors	..	..	0.0	0.0	0.0	0.0	0.0	0.0	0.0	0.0
Memo: export credits	..	..	17.0	16.8	25.9	38.2	14.8	7.3	2.8	2.6
TOTAL DEBT FLOWS										
Disbursements	..	..	**8.4**	**10.8**	**9.9**	**15.2**	**16.8**	**60.3**	**8.3**	**29.9**
Long-term debt	..	..	8.4	10.8	9.9	15.2	16.8	60.3	8.3	29.9
IMF purchases	0.0	0.0	0.0	0.0	0.0	0.0	0.0	0.0	0.0	0.0
Principal repayments	..	..	**2.9**	**5.1**	**7.2**	**4.3**	**4.9**	**7.0**	**4.9**	**4.7**
Long-term debt	..	..	2.9	5.1	7.2	4.3	4.9	7.0	4.9	4.7
IMF repurchases	0.0	0.0	0.0	0.0	0.0	0.0	0.0	0.0	0.0	0.0
Net flows on debt	..	..	**6.5**	**4.7**	**2.7**	**11.0**	**13.8**	**51.3**	**5.4**	**24.2**
of which short-term debt	..	..	1.0	-1.0	0.0	0.1	1.9	-2.0	2.0	-1.0
Interest payments (INT)	..	..	**2.3**	**2.4**	**2.6**	**2.6**	**2.3**	**2.1**	**2.1**	**1.9**
Long-term debt	..	..	2.0	2.4	2.6	2.6	2.2	2.1	2.0	1.8
IMF charges	0.0	0.0	0.0	0.0	0.0	0.0	0.0	0.0	0.0	0.0
Short-term debt	..	..	0.2	0.0	0.0	0.0	0.1	0.0	0.1	0.1
Net transfers on debt	..	..	**4.2**	**2.2**	**0.1**	**8.4**	**11.5**	**49.1**	**3.3**	**22.3**
Total debt service paid (TDS)	..	..	**5.2**	**7.5**	**9.8**	**6.9**	**7.2**	**9.2**	**7.0**	**6.6**
Long-term debt	..	..	5.0	7.5	9.8	6.9	7.1	9.2	6.9	6.5
IMF repurchases and charges	0.0	0.0	0.0	0.0	0.0	0.0	0.0	0.0	0.0	0.0
Short-term debt (interest only)	..	..	0.2	0.0	0.0	0.0	0.1	0.0	0.1	0.1
2. AGGREGATE NET RESOURCE FLOWS AND NET TRANSFERS (LONG-TERM)										
NET RESOURCE FLOWS	..	..	**22.4**	**48.1**	**42.2**	**37.2**	**47.6**	**81.5**	**41.2**	**45.7**
Net flow of long-term debt (ex. IMF)	..	..	5.5	5.7	2.7	10.9	11.9	53.3	3.4	25.1
Foreign direct investment (net)	..	..	0.0	0.0	0.0	0.0	0.0	0.0	0.0	0.0
Portfolio equity flows	..	..	0.0	0.0	0.0	0.0	0.0	0.0	0.0	0.0
Grants (excluding technical coop.)	..	..	16.9	42.5	39.5	26.4	35.7	28.3	37.8	20.6
Memo: technical coop. grants	..	..	23.7	26.5	27.1	27.7	23.6	19.9	22.4	21.9
official net resource flows	..	..	25.0	50.4	44.5	39.5	49.9	83.8	41.2	45.7
private net resource flows	..	..	-2.6	-2.3	-2.3	-2.3	-2.3	-2.3	0.0	0.0
NET TRANSFERS	..	..	**20.4**	**45.7**	**39.6**	**34.6**	**45.3**	**79.4**	**39.2**	**43.9**
Interest on long-term debt	..	..	2.0	2.4	2.6	2.6	2.2	2.1	2.0	1.8
Profit remittances on FDI	..	..	0.0	0.0	0.0	0.0	0.0	0.0	0.0	0.0
Memo: official net transfers	..	..	24.6	48.8	42.5	37.4	47.9	81.8	39.2	43.9
private net transfers	..	..	-4.2	-3.1	-2.9	-2.8	-2.6	-2.4	0.0	0.0
3. MAJOR ECONOMIC AGGREGATES										
Gross national income (GNI)	..	..	284.7	271.0	305.1	330.2	398.3	409.6	446.5	497.6
Exports of goods & services (XGS)	..	..	94.9	83.7	90.2	120.8	121.2	145.8	138.6	156.8
of which workers remittances	..	..	0.0	0.0	0.0	0.0	0.0	0.0	0.0	0.0
Imports of goods & services (MGS)	..	..	122.9	130.4	132.3	163.8	183.3	203.0	246.9	293.5
International reserves (RES)	..	..	86.0	115.2	124.3	184.0	181.2	249.6	274.4	295.4
Current account balance	..	..	-28.0	-40.0	-34.1	-37.2	-56.2	-46.6	-97.9	-126.8
4. DEBT INDICATORS										
EDT / XGS (%)	..	..	88.0	124.9	117.3	93.5	98.7	117.3	132.6	126.5
EDT / GNI (%)	..	..	29.3	38.6	34.7	34.2	30.0	41.8	41.2	39.9
TDS / XGS (%)	..	..	5.5	9.0	10.9	5.7	5.9	6.3	5.1	4.2
INT / XGS (%)	..	..	2.4	2.9	2.9	2.2	1.9	1.4	1.5	1.2
INT / GNI (%)	..	..	0.8	0.9	0.9	0.8	0.6	0.5	0.5	0.4
RES / EDT (%)	..	..	103.0	110.2	117.5	162.8	151.5	146.0	149.3	148.9
RES / MGS (months)	..	..	8.4	10.6	11.3	13.5	11.9	14.8	13.3	12.1
Short-term / EDT (%)	..	..	4.0	0.7	0.6	0.1	1.7	0.0	1.1	0.6
Concessional / EDT (%)	..	..	74.0	90.7	93.0	96.0	96.4	69.5	71.2	64.8
Multilateral / EDT (%)	..	..	50.2	59.5	64.5	61.7	61.5	47.5	50.8	48.2

BHUTAN

(US$ million, unless otherwise indicated)

	1970	1980	1990	1994	1995	1996	1997	1998	1999	2000
5. LONG-TERM DEBT										
DEBT OUTSTANDING (LDOD)	..	..	**80.3**	**103.8**	**105.2**	**112.9**	**117.6**	**171.0**	**181.8**	**197.3**
Public and publicly guaranteed	..	..	**80.3**	**103.8**	**105.2**	**112.9**	**117.6**	**171.0**	**181.8**	**197.3**
Official creditors	..	..	61.8	94.8	98.4	108.4	115.4	171.0	181.8	197.3
Multilateral	..	..	41.9	62.2	68.2	69.7	73.5	81.2	93.4	95.7
Concessional	..	..	41.9	62.2	68.2	69.7	73.5	81.2	93.4	95.7
Bilateral	..	..	19.9	32.6	30.2	38.8	41.8	89.8	88.4	101.6
Concessional	..	..	19.9	32.6	30.2	38.8	41.8	37.7	37.5	32.9
Private creditors	..	..	18.5	9.0	6.8	4.5	2.3	0.0	0.0	0.0
Bonds	..	..	0.0	0.0	0.0	0.0	0.0	0.0	0.0	0.0
Commercial banks	..	..	0.0	0.0	0.0	0.0	0.0	0.0	0.0	0.0
Other private	..	..	18.5	9.0	6.8	4.5	2.3	0.0	0.0	0.0
Private nonguaranteed	..	..	**0.0**	**0.0**	**0.0**	**0.0**	**0.0**	**0.0**	**0.0**	**0.0**
Bonds	..	..	0.0	0.0	0.0	0.0	0.0	0.0	0.0	0.0
Commercial banks and other	..	..	0.0	0.0	0.0	0.0	0.0	0.0	0.0	0.0
Memo:										
IBRD	0.0	0.0	0.0	0.0	0.0	0.0	0.0	0.0	0.0	0.0
IDA	0.0	0.0	16.1	20.9	22.5	22.8	22.5	23.9	24.1	26.1
DISBURSEMENTS	..	..	**8.4**	**10.8**	**9.9**	**15.2**	**16.8**	**60.3**	**8.3**	**29.9**
Public and publicly guaranteed	..	..	**8.4**	**10.8**	**9.9**	**15.2**	**16.8**	**60.3**	**8.3**	**29.9**
Official creditors	..	..	8.4	10.8	9.9	15.2	16.8	60.3	8.3	29.9
Multilateral	..	..	7.2	4.8	5.8	4.8	9.2	5.6	3.1	6.8
Concessional	..	..	7.2	4.8	5.8	4.8	9.2	5.6	3.1	6.8
Bilateral	..	..	1.2	6.0	4.1	10.3	7.5	54.7	5.2	23.0
Concessional	..	..	1.2	6.0	4.1	10.3	7.5	0.9	5.2	0.9
Private creditors	..	..	0.0	0.0	0.0	0.0	0.0	0.0	0.0	0.0
Bonds	..	..	0.0	0.0	0.0	0.0	0.0	0.0	0.0	0.0
Commercial banks	..	..	0.0	0.0	0.0	0.0	0.0	0.0	0.0	0.0
Other private	..	..	0.0	0.0	0.0	0.0	0.0	0.0	0.0	0.0
Private nonguaranteed	..	..	**0.0**	**0.0**	**0.0**	**0.0**	**0.0**	**0.0**	**0.0**	**0.0**
Bonds	..	..	0.0	0.0	0.0	0.0	0.0	0.0	0.0	0.0
Commercial banks and other	..	..	0.0	0.0	0.0	0.0	0.0	0.0	0.0	0.0
Memo:										
IBRD	0.0	0.0	0.0	0.0	0.0	0.0	0.0	0.0	0.0	0.0
IDA	0.0	0.0	2.0	1.3	1.2	1.4	1.1	0.7	1.0	3.6
PRINCIPAL REPAYMENTS	..	..	**2.9**	**5.1**	**7.2**	**4.3**	**4.9**	**7.0**	**4.9**	**4.7**
Public and publicly guaranteed	..	..	**2.9**	**5.1**	**7.2**	**4.3**	**4.9**	**7.0**	**4.9**	**4.7**
Official creditors	..	..	0.3	2.8	4.9	2.0	2.6	4.8	4.9	4.7
Multilateral	..	..	0.0	0.6	0.6	0.8	0.9	1.0	1.3	1.3
Concessional	..	..	0.0	0.6	0.6	0.8	0.9	1.0	1.3	1.3
Bilateral	..	..	0.3	2.2	4.3	1.2	1.7	3.8	3.6	3.4
Concessional	..	..	0.3	2.2	4.3	1.2	1.7	3.8	3.6	3.4
Private creditors	..	..	2.6	2.3	2.3	2.3	2.3	2.3	0.0	0.0
Bonds	..	..	0.0	0.0	0.0	0.0	0.0	0.0	0.0	0.0
Commercial banks	..	..	0.0	0.0	0.0	0.0	0.0	0.0	0.0	0.0
Other private	..	..	2.6	2.3	2.3	2.3	2.3	2.3	0.0	0.0
Private nonguaranteed	..	..	**0.0**	**0.0**	**0.0**	**0.0**	**0.0**	**0.0**	**0.0**	**0.0**
Bonds	..	..	0.0	0.0	0.0	0.0	0.0	0.0	0.0	0.0
Commercial banks and other	..	..	0.0	0.0	0.0	0.0	0.0	0.0	0.0	0.0
Memo:										
IBRD	0.0	0.0	0.0	0.0	0.0	0.0	0.0	0.0	0.0	0.0
IDA	0.0	0.0	0.0	0.1	0.1	0.2	0.2	0.2	0.3	0.3
NET FLOWS ON DEBT	..	..	**5.5**	**5.7**	**2.7**	**10.9**	**11.9**	**53.3**	**3.4**	**25.1**
Public and publicly guaranteed	..	..	**5.5**	**5.7**	**2.7**	**10.9**	**11.9**	**53.3**	**3.4**	**25.1**
Official creditors	..	..	8.1	7.9	5.0	13.1	14.2	55.5	3.4	25.1
Multilateral	..	..	7.2	4.2	5.3	4.0	8.4	4.6	1.8	5.5
Concessional	..	..	7.2	4.2	5.3	4.0	8.4	4.6	1.8	5.5
Bilateral	..	..	0.9	3.7	-0.3	9.1	5.8	50.9	1.6	19.6
Concessional	..	..	0.9	3.7	-0.3	9.1	5.8	-2.9	1.6	-2.5
Private creditors	..	..	-2.6	-2.3	-2.3	-2.3	-2.3	-2.3	0.0	0.0
Bonds	..	..	0.0	0.0	0.0	0.0	0.0	0.0	0.0	0.0
Commercial banks	..	..	0.0	0.0	0.0	0.0	0.0	0.0	0.0	0.0
Other private	..	..	-2.6	-2.3	-2.3	-2.3	-2.3	-2.3	0.0	0.0
Private nonguaranteed	..	..	**0.0**	**0.0**	**0.0**	**0.0**	**0.0**	**0.0**	**0.0**	**0.0**
Bonds	..	..	0.0	0.0	0.0	0.0	0.0	0.0	0.0	0.0
Commercial banks and other	..	..	0.0	0.0	0.0	0.0	0.0	0.0	0.0	0.0
Memo:										
IBRD	0.0	0.0	0.0	0.0	0.0	0.0	0.0	0.0	0.0	0.0
IDA	0.0	0.0	2.0	1.3	1.1	1.2	0.9	0.5	0.7	3.3

BHUTAN

(US$ million, unless otherwise indicated)

	1970	1980	1990	1994	1995	1996	1997	1998	1999	2000
INTEREST PAYMENTS (LINT)	..	..	**2.0**	**2.4**	**2.6**	**2.6**	**2.2**	**2.1**	**2.0**	**1.8**
Public and publicly guaranteed	..	..	**2.0**	**2.4**	**2.6**	**2.6**	**2.2**	**2.1**	**2.0**	**1.8**
Official creditors	..	..	0.4	1.6	2.0	2.1	2.0	2.0	2.0	1.8
Multilateral	..	..	0.3	0.5	0.6	0.7	0.6	0.7	0.9	0.9
Concessional	..	..	0.3	0.5	0.6	0.7	0.6	0.7	0.9	0.9
Bilateral	..	..	0.1	1.1	1.4	1.5	1.3	1.3	1.1	0.9
Concessional	..	..	0.1	1.1	1.4	1.5	1.3	1.3	1.1	0.9
Private creditors	..	..	1.6	0.8	0.6	0.5	0.3	0.1	0.0	0.0
Bonds	..	..	0.0	0.0	0.0	0.0	0.0	0.0	0.0	0.0
Commercial banks	..	..	0.0	0.0	0.0	0.0	0.0	0.0	0.0	0.0
Other private	..	..	1.6	0.8	0.6	0.5	0.3	0.1	0.0	0.0
Private nonguaranteed	..	..	**0.0**	**0.0**	**0.0**	**0.0**	**0.0**	**0.0**	**0.0**	**0.0**
Bonds	..	..	0.0	0.0	0.0	0.0	0.0	0.0	0.0	0.0
Commercial banks and other	..	..	0.0	0.0	0.0	0.0	0.0	0.0	0.0	0.0
Memo:										
IBRD	0.0	0.0	0.0	0.0	0.0	0.0	0.0	0.0	0.0	0.0
IDA	0.0	0.0	0.1	0.1	0.2	0.2	0.2	0.2	0.2	0.2
NET TRANSFERS ON DEBT	..	..	**3.4**	**3.2**	**0.1**	**8.3**	**9.7**	**51.1**	**1.4**	**23.3**
Public and publicly guaranteed	..	..	**3.4**	**3.2**	**0.1**	**8.3**	**9.7**	**51.1**	**1.4**	**23.3**
Official creditors	..	..	7.7	6.3	3.0	11.0	12.2	53.5	1.4	23.3
Multilateral	..	..	6.9	3.7	4.7	3.4	7.7	4.0	0.9	4.6
Concessional	..	..	6.9	3.7	4.7	3.4	7.7	4.0	0.9	4.6
Bilateral	..	..	0.8	2.6	-1.7	7.6	4.5	49.5	0.5	18.7
Concessional	..	..	0.8	2.6	-1.7	7.6	4.5	-4.3	0.5	-3.5
Private creditors	..	..	-4.2	-3.1	-2.9	-2.7	-2.6	-2.4	0.0	0.0
Bonds	..	..	0.0	0.0	0.0	0.0	0.0	0.0	0.0	0.0
Commercial banks	..	..	0.0	0.0	0.0	0.0	0.0	0.0	0.0	0.0
Other private	..	..	-4.2	-3.1	-2.9	-2.7	-2.6	-2.4	0.0	0.0
Private nonguaranteed	..	..	**0.0**	**0.0**	**0.0**	**0.0**	**0.0**	**0.0**	**0.0**	**0.0**
Bonds	..	..	0.0	0.0	0.0	0.0	0.0	0.0	0.0	0.0
Commercial banks and other	..	..	0.0	0.0	0.0	0.0	0.0	0.0	0.0	0.0
Memo:										
IBRD	0.0	0.0	0.0	0.0	0.0	0.0	0.0	0.0	0.0	0.0
IDA	0.0	0.0	1.9	1.1	0.9	1.0	0.8	0.4	0.6	3.1
DEBT SERVICE (LTDS)	..	..	**5.0**	**7.5**	**9.8**	**6.9**	**7.1**	**9.2**	**6.9**	**6.5**
Public and publicly guaranteed	..	..	**5.0**	**7.5**	**9.8**	**6.9**	**7.1**	**9.2**	**6.9**	**6.5**
Official creditors	..	..	0.7	4.5	6.9	4.2	4.6	6.8	6.9	6.5
Multilateral	..	..	0.3	1.1	1.2	1.5	1.5	1.7	2.2	2.2
Concessional	..	..	0.3	1.1	1.2	1.5	1.5	1.7	2.2	2.2
Bilateral	..	..	0.4	3.3	5.7	2.7	3.1	5.1	4.8	4.3
Concessional	..	..	0.4	3.3	5.7	2.7	3.1	5.1	4.8	4.3
Private creditors	..	..	4.2	3.1	2.9	2.7	2.6	2.4	0.0	0.0
Bonds	..	..	0.0	0.0	0.0	0.0	0.0	0.0	0.0	0.0
Commercial banks	..	..	0.0	0.0	0.0	0.0	0.0	0.0	0.0	0.0
Other private	..	..	4.2	3.1	2.9	2.7	2.6	2.4	0.0	0.0
Private nonguaranteed	..	..	**0.0**	**0.0**	**0.0**	**0.0**	**0.0**	**0.0**	**0.0**	**0.0**
Bonds	..	..	0.0	0.0	0.0	0.0	0.0	0.0	0.0	0.0
Commercial banks and other	..	..	0.0	0.0	0.0	0.0	0.0	0.0	0.0	0.0
Memo:										
IBRD	0.0	0.0	0.0	0.0	0.0	0.0	0.0	0.0	0.0	0.0
IDA	0.0	0.0	0.1	0.2	0.3	0.3	0.3	0.4	0.4	0.4
UNDISBURSED DEBT	..	..	**48.4**	**77.4**	**86.6**	**225.3**	**189.7**	**146.0**	**133.5**	**172.2**
Official creditors	..	..	48.4	77.4	86.6	225.3	189.7	146.0	133.5	172.2
Private creditors	..	..	0.0	0.0	0.0	0.0	0.0	0.0	0.0	0.0
Memorandum items										
Concessional LDOD	..	..	61.8	94.8	98.4	108.4	115.4	118.9	130.8	128.6
Variable rate LDOD	..	..	0.0	0.0	0.0	0.0	0.0	0.0	0.0	0.0
Public sector LDOD	..	..	80.3	103.8	105.2	112.9	117.6	171.0	181.8	197.3
Private sector LDOD	..	..	0.0	0.0	0.0	0.0	0.0	0.0	0.0	0.0

6. CURRENCY COMPOSITION OF LONG-TERM DEBT (PERCENT)

	1970	1980	1990	1994	1995	1996	1997	1998	1999	2000
Deutsche mark	..	..	0.0	0.0	0.0	0.0	0.0	0.0	0.0	0.0
French franc	..	..	0.0	0.0	0.0	0.0	0.0	0.0	0.0	0.0
Japanese yen	..	..	0.0	0.0	0.0	0.0	0.0	0.0	0.0	0.0
Pound sterling	..	..	0.0	0.0	0.0	0.0	0.0	0.0	0.0	0.0
Swiss franc	..	..	0.0	0.0	0.0	0.0	0.0	0.0	0.0	0.0
U.S.dollars	..	..	43.1	29.6	28.6	24.9	21.6	15.7	15.5	15.6
Multiple currency	..	..	22.8	28.7	31.4	30.2	32.6	24.2	29.0	26.3
Special drawing rights	..	..	9.3	11.1	12.1	11.3	10.8	7.9	7.1	6.7
All other currencies	..	..	24.8	30.6	27.9	33.6	35.0	52.2	48.4	51.4

BHUTAN

(US$ million, unless otherwise indicated)

	1970	1980	1990	1994	1995	1996	1997	1998	1999	2000
7. DEBT RESTRUCTURINGS										
Total amount rescheduled	..	..	0.0	0.0	0.0	0.0	0.0	0.0	0.0	0.0
Debt stock rescheduled	..	..	0.0	0.0	0.0	0.0	0.0	0.0	0.0	0.0
Principal rescheduled	..	..	0.0	0.0	0.0	0.0	0.0	0.0	0.0	0.0
Official	..	..	0.0	0.0	0.0	0.0	0.0	0.0	0.0	0.0
Private	..	..	0.0	0.0	0.0	0.0	0.0	0.0	0.0	0.0
Interest rescheduled	..	..	0.0	0.0	0.0	0.3	0.0	0.0	0.0	0.0
Official	..	..	0.0	0.0	0.0	0.3	0.0	0.0	0.0	0.0
Private	..	..	0.0	0.0	0.0	0.0	0.0	0.0	0.0	0.0
Debt forgiven	..	..	0.0	0.0	0.0	0.0	0.0	0.0	0.0	0.0
Memo: interest forgiven	..	..	0.0	0.0	0.0	0.0	0.0	0.0	0.0	0.0
Debt stock reduction	..	..	0.0	0.0	0.0	0.0	0.0	0.0	0.0	0.0
of which debt buyback	..	..	0.0	0.0	0.0	0.0	0.0	0.0	0.0	0.0
8. DEBT STOCK-FLOW RECONCILIATION										
Total change in debt stocks	..	..	9.7	7.9	1.3	7.3	6.6	51.4	12.8	14.5
Net flows on debt	..	..	6.5	4.7	2.7	11.0	13.8	51.3	5.4	24.2
Net change in interest arrears	..	..	0.3	0.0	-0.1	-0.6	0.0	0.0	0.0	0.0
Interest capitalized	..	..	0.0	0.0	0.0	0.3	0.0	0.0	0.0	0.0
Debt forgiveness or reduction	..	..	0.0	0.0	0.0	0.0	0.0	0.0	0.0	0.0
Cross-currency valuation	..	..	1.1	2.2	-2.0	-4.0	-7.9	0.0	-2.2	-10.6
Residual	..	..	1.8	1.0	0.7	0.6	0.7	0.2	9.6	1.0
9. AVERAGE TERMS OF NEW COMMITMENTS										
ALL CREDITORS										
Interest (%)	..	..	0.0	9.4	1.3	9.0	0.0	2.1	0.0	3.8
Maturity (years)	..	..	0.0	26.6	33.4	22.0	0.0	39.5	0.0	32.0
Grace period (years)	..	..	0.0	11.7	11.2	10.0	0.0	10.0	0.0	10.1
Grant element (%)	..	..	0.0	4.0	73.8	7.7	0.0	68.8	0.0	51.7
Official creditors										
Interest (%)	..	..	0.0	9.4	1.3	9.0	0.0	2.1	0.0	3.8
Maturity (years)	..	..	0.0	26.6	33.4	22.0	0.0	39.5	0.0	32.0
Grace period (years)	..	..	0.0	11.7	11.2	10.0	0.0	10.0	0.0	10.1
Grant element (%)	..	..	0.0	4.0	73.8	7.7	0.0	68.8	0.0	51.7
Private creditors										
Interest (%)	..	..	0.0	0.0	0.0	0.0	0.0	0.0	0.0	0.0
Maturity (years)	..	..	0.0	0.0	0.0	0.0	0.0	0.0	0.0	0.0
Grace period (years)	..	..	0.0	0.0	0.0	0.0	0.0	0.0	0.0	0.0
Grant element (%)	..	..	0.0	0.0	0.0	0.0	0.0	0.0	0.0	0.0
Memorandum items										
Commitments	..	..	0.0	37.9	24.0	159.0	0.0	27.9	0.0	78.4
Official creditors	..	..	0.0	37.9	24.0	159.0	0.0	27.9	0.0	78.4
Private creditors	..	..	0.0	0.0	0.0	0.0	0.0	0.0	0.0	0.0

10. CONTRACTUAL OBLIGATIONS ON OUTSTANDING LONG-TERM DEBT

	2001	2002	2003	2004	2005	2006	2007	2008	2009	2010
TOTAL										
Disbursements	77.0	44.6	25.3	14.9	5.9	2.2	1.3	0.6	0.4	0.0
Principal	4.9	5.0	5.0	4.7	4.5	18.0	18.5	17.1	17.8	18.6
Interest	10.2	14.5	16.3	17.0	17.3	17.4	16.1	14.9	13.7	12.5
Official creditors										
Disbursements	77.0	44.6	25.3	14.9	5.9	2.2	1.3	0.6	0.4	0.0
Principal	4.9	5.0	5.0	4.7	4.5	18.0	18.5	17.1	17.8	18.6
Interest	10.2	14.5	16.3	17.0	17.3	17.4	16.1	14.9	13.7	12.5
Bilateral creditors										
Disbursements	57.8	25.0	10.7	5.0	0.0	0.0	0.0	0.0	0.0	0.0
Principal	3.7	3.7	3.7	3.1	2.7	15.6	15.9	13.7	13.3	13.3
Interest	9.2	13.3	15.0	15.6	15.8	15.6	14.3	13.0	11.8	10.6
Multilateral creditors										
Disbursements	19.2	19.6	14.5	9.9	5.9	2.2	1.3	0.6	0.4	0.0
Principal	1.2	1.3	1.3	1.6	1.9	2.4	2.6	3.4	4.5	5.3
Interest	1.1	1.2	1.3	1.4	1.4	1.7	1.8	1.9	1.9	1.9
Private creditors										
Disbursements	0.0	0.0	0.0	0.0	0.0	0.0	0.0	0.0	0.0	0.0
Principal	0.0	0.0	0.0	0.0	0.0	0.0	0.0	0.0	0.0	0.0
Interest	0.0	0.0	0.0	0.0	0.0	0.0	0.0	0.0	0.0	0.0
Commercial banks										
Disbursements	0.0	0.0	0.0	0.0	0.0	0.0	0.0	0.0	0.0	0.0
Principal	0.0	0.0	0.0	0.0	0.0	0.0	0.0	0.0	0.0	0.0
Interest	0.0	0.0	0.0	0.0	0.0	0.0	0.0	0.0	0.0	0.0
Other private										
Disbursements	0.0	0.0	0.0	0.0	0.0	0.0	0.0	0.0	0.0	0.0
Principal	0.0	0.0	0.0	0.0	0.0	0.0	0.0	0.0	0.0	0.0
Interest	0.0	0.0	0.0	0.0	0.0	0.0	0.0	0.0	0.0	0.0

BOLIVIA

(US$ million, unless otherwise indicated)

	1970	1980	1990	1994	1995	1996	1997	1998	1999	2000
1. SUMMARY DEBT DATA										
TOTAL DEBT STOCKS (EDT)	**588**	**2,702**	**4,275**	**4,877**	**5,275**	**5,195**	**5,237**	**5,616**	**5,549**	**5,762**
Long-term debt (LDOD)	**491**	**2,274**	**3,864**	**4,313**	**4,701**	**4,544**	**4,559**	**4,938**	**4,889**	**5,140**
Public and publicly guaranteed	480	2,182	3,687	4,122	4,462	4,259	4,133	4,296	4,246	4,120
Private nonguaranteed	11	92	177	191	239	285	426	643	643	1,020
Use of IMF credit	**6**	**126**	**257**	**264**	**268**	**276**	**248**	**264**	**247**	**220**
Short-term debt	**91**	**303**	**154**	**300**	**307**	**374**	**430**	**413**	**413**	**403**
of which interest arrears on LDOD	0	3	6	34	20	26	4	3	3	3
Official creditors	0	2	2	21	7	14	4	3	3	3
Private creditors	0	1	4	13	13	12	0	0	0	0
Memo: principal arrears on LDOD	3	22	31	103	30	56	28	28	18	19
Official creditors	3	15	9	82	21	50	18	19	18	19
Private creditors	0	7	22	20	9	5	9	9	0	0
Memo: export credits	0	0	794	602	638	581	495	270	239	224
TOTAL DEBT FLOWS										
Disbursements	**58**	**553**	**331**	**437**	**520**	**497**	**666**	**492**	**442**	**735**
Long-term debt	58	457	300	393	494	448	643	446	419	720
IMF purchases	0	96	31	44	26	49	23	46	23	15
Principal repayments	**19**	**145**	**241**	**188**	**199**	**230**	**263**	**277**	**307**	**474**
Long-term debt	19	145	196	173	173	199	229	236	274	444
IMF repurchases	0	0	46	15	26	32	34	41	34	30
Net flows on debt	**39**	**180**	**32**	**322**	**341**	**329**	**480**	**199**	**135**	**251**
of which short-term debt	0	-228	-57	73	20	62	78	-16	0	-10
Interest payments (INT)	**7**	**220**	**144**	**160**	**173**	**183**	**212**	**167**	**137**	**188**
Long-term debt	7	173	117	148	155	164	190	144	115	166
IMF charges	0	3	13	1	1	2	1	1	1	1
Short-term debt	0	45	14	11	17	17	21	21	21	20
Net transfers on debt	**32**	**-40**	**-112**	**162**	**168**	**146**	**268**	**33**	**-3**	**63**
Total debt service paid (TDS)	**26**	**366**	**385**	**348**	**372**	**413**	**475**	**443**	**444**	**662**
Long-term debt	26	319	313	321	328	362	418	380	389	611
IMF repurchases and charges	0	3	59	16	28	34	36	42	35	31
Short-term debt (interest only)	0	45	14	11	17	17	21	21	21	20
2. AGGREGATE NET RESOURCE FLOWS AND NET TRANSFERS (LONG-TERM)										
NET RESOURCE FLOWS	**-34**	**407**	**333**	**632**	**1,042**	**1,116**	**1,444**	**1,400**	**1,368**	**1,230**
Net flow of long-term debt (ex. IMF)	39	312	104	221	321	250	414	210	145	276
Foreign direct investment (net)	-76	47	27	130	393	474	731	957	1,016	733
Portfolio equity flows	0	0	0	0	0	0	0	0	0	0
Grants (excluding technical coop.)	3	48	202	281	328	392	299	233	206	221
Memo: technical coop. grants	9	41	108	190	217	195	199	185	193	150
official net resource flows	39	204	330	496	608	596	503	334	351	307
private net resource flows	-73	203	3	136	434	519	941	1,065	1,017	923
NET TRANSFERS	**-58**	**214**	**199**	**454**	**853**	**912**	**1,212**	**1,196**	**1,169**	**964**
Interest on long-term debt	7	173	117	148	155	164	190	144	115	166
Profit remittances on FDI	17	19	17	30	33	40	43	60	83	100
Memo: official net transfers	35	161	230	366	475	448	355	198	242	189
private net transfers	-94	53	-30	88	379	464	857	998	927	775
3. MAJOR ECONOMIC AGGREGATES										
Gross national income (GNI)	1,134	2,784	4,627	5,793	6,468	7,191	7,706	8,257	8,065	8,056
Exports of goods & services (XGS)	..	1,046	998	1,201	1,264	1,344	1,580	1,546	1,540	1,694
of which workers remittances	..	0	2	1	2	2	68	64	73	101
Imports of goods & services (MGS)	..	1,112	1,354	1,554	1,809	1,968	2,357	2,490	2,342	2,442
International reserves (RES)	46	553	511	793	1,005	1,302	1,359	1,118	1,153	1,038
Current account balance	..	-6	-199	-90	-303	-380	-554	-678	-488	-464
4. DEBT INDICATORS										
EDT / XGS (%)	..	258.4	428.6	406.0	417.4	386.6	331.4	363.3	360.2	340.1
EDT / GNI (%)	51.9	97.1	92.4	84.2	81.6	72.2	68.0	68.0	68.8	71.5
TDS / XGS (%)	..	35.0	38.6	28.9	29.4	30.7	30.1	28.7	28.8	39.1
INT / XGS (%)	..	21.1	14.4	13.3	13.7	13.6	13.4	10.8	8.9	11.1
INT / GNI (%)	0.6	7.9	3.1	2.8	2.7	2.5	2.8	2.0	1.7	2.3
RES / EDT (%)	7.9	20.5	12.0	16.3	19.1	25.1	26.0	19.9	20.8	18.0
RES / MGS (months)	..	6.0	4.5	6.1	6.7	7.9	6.9	5.4	5.9	5.1
Short-term / EDT (%)	15.5	11.2	3.6	6.2	5.8	7.2	8.2	7.4	7.4	7.0
Concessional / EDT (%)	45.0	24.6	44.2	49.8	51.7	56.5	56.7	57.3	57.5	54.1
Multilateral / EDT (%)	4.4	16.6	37.2	46.7	49.0	50.8	51.2	47.9	50.1	48.4

BOLIVIA

(US$ million, unless otherwise indicated)

	1970	1980	1990	1994	1995	1996	1997	1998	1999	2000
5. LONG-TERM DEBT										
DEBT OUTSTANDING (LDOD)	**491**	**2,274**	**3,864**	**4,313**	**4,701**	**4,544**	**4,559**	**4,938**	**4,889**	**5,140**
Public and publicly guaranteed	**480**	**2,182**	**3,687**	**4,122**	**4,462**	**4,259**	**4,133**	**4,296**	**4,246**	**4,120**
Official creditors	275	1,110	3,362	4,040	4,399	4,223	4,100	4,258	4,221	4,086
Multilateral	26	447	1,589	2,276	2,582	2,640	2,680	2,691	2,777	2,787
Concessional	26	178	882	1,231	1,400	1,537	1,689	1,794	1,909	1,970
Bilateral	249	663	1,773	1,764	1,817	1,583	1,420	1,568	1,444	1,300
Concessional	239	487	1,006	1,197	1,327	1,397	1,279	1,422	1,281	1,150
Private creditors	205	1,072	325	83	63	37	33	38	25	33
Bonds	67	73	35	17	17	17	9	9	0	0
Commercial banks	2	603	4	13	9	4	4	9	10	9
Other private	136	395	286	53	37	16	20	19	14	24
Private nonguaranteed	**11**	**92**	**177**	**191**	**239**	**285**	**426**	**643**	**643**	**1,020**
Bonds	0	0	0	0	0	0	0	0	0	0
Commercial banks and other	11	92	177	191	239	285	426	643	643	1,020
Memo:										
IBRD	0	175	194	116	95	61	37	26	13	0
IDA	18	64	393	648	770	843	930	1,045	1,097	1,096
DISBURSEMENTS	**58**	**457**	**300**	**393**	**494**	**448**	**643**	**446**	**419**	**720**
Public and publicly guaranteed	**55**	**441**	**300**	**369**	**427**	**357**	**374**	**316**	**291**	**258**
Official creditors	45	198	291	360	427	350	365	309	288	245
Multilateral	2	108	204	301	383	285	352	251	255	221
Concessional	2	28	90	130	174	188	227	194	168	152
Bilateral	43	91	86	59	45	65	14	58	34	25
Concessional	33	31	85	57	45	63	14	54	22	21
Private creditors	10	242	9	8	0	8	8	7	3	13
Bonds	0	0	0	0	0	0	0	0	0	0
Commercial banks	0	55	0	8	0	1	2	6	3	1
Other private	10	187	9	0	0	6	6	1	0	12
Private nonguaranteed	**3**	**16**	**0**	**25**	**67**	**91**	**269**	**131**	**127**	**462**
Bonds	0	0	0	0	0	0	0	0	0	0
Commercial banks and other	3	16	0	25	67	91	269	131	127	462
Memo:										
IBRD	0	73	0	0	0	0	0	0	0	0
IDA	2	2	49	80	113	100	136	88	82	61
PRINCIPAL REPAYMENTS	**19**	**145**	**196**	**173**	**173**	**199**	**229**	**236**	**274**	**444**
Public and publicly guaranteed	**17**	**126**	**172**	**154**	**155**	**155**	**168**	**209**	**147**	**163**
Official creditors	9	43	163	145	147	145	162	207	143	159
Multilateral	2	7	117	110	120	135	152	193	119	128
Concessional	2	1	14	20	22	24	26	26	26	31
Bilateral	7	36	46	35	27	10	10	14	24	32
Concessional	5	15	9	9	3	2	4	9	17	22
Private creditors	8	84	9	9	8	9	6	3	4	4
Bonds	0	1	0	0	0	0	3	0	0	0
Commercial banks	1	49	2	5	4	6	2	1	1	1
Other private	7	33	8	4	4	3	2	2	2	3
Private nonguaranteed	**2**	**19**	**24**	**19**	**18**	**44**	**61**	**27**	**127**	**281**
Bonds	0	0	0	0	0	0	0	0	0	0
Commercial banks and other	2	19	24	19	18	44	61	27	127	281
Memo:										
IBRD	0	3	21	24	27	25	19	13	14	12
IDA	0	0	2	2	2	3	4	6	8	10
NET FLOWS ON DEBT	**39**	**312**	**104**	**221**	**321**	**250**	**414**	**210**	**145**	**276**
Public and publicly guaranteed	**38**	**315**	**128**	**215**	**273**	**203**	**206**	**106**	**145**	**95**
Official creditors	36	156	128	215	281	204	204	102	145	86
Multilateral	0	101	87	191	263	149	200	58	135	93
Concessional	0	28	77	110	152	165	202	167	142	121
Bilateral	36	55	41	24	18	55	4	44	10	-7
Concessional	28	17	76	48	42	61	10	45	5	-1
Private creditors	2	159	0	0	-8	-2	2	4	-1	9
Bonds	0	-1	0	0	0	0	-3	0	0	0
Commercial banks	-1	6	-2	3	-4	-5	1	5	2	-1
Other private	3	154	1	-4	-4	3	4	-1	-2	10
Private nonguaranteed	**1**	**-3**	**-24**	**6**	**49**	**47**	**208**	**104**	**1**	**181**
Bonds	0	0	0	0	0	0	0	0	0	0
Commercial banks and other	1	-3	-24	6	49	47	208	104	1	181
Memo:										
IBRD	0	70	-21	-24	-27	-25	-19	-13	-14	-12
IDA	2	2	47	77	111	97	132	82	74	51

BOLIVIA

(US$ million, unless otherwise indicated)

	1970	1980	1990	1994	1995	1996	1997	1998	1999	2000
INTEREST PAYMENTS (LINT)	**7**	**173**	**117**	**148**	**155**	**164**	**190**	**144**	**115**	**166**
Public and publicly guaranteed	**7**	**164**	**103**	**132**	**137**	**150**	**150**	**138**	**111**	**120**
Official creditors	4	43	101	130	133	148	149	137	109	118
Multilateral	1	21	69	90	100	104	100	92	85	89
Concessional	1	2	10	16	17	18	20	22	21	23
Bilateral	3	21	32	40	33	44	49	44	24	29
Concessional	3	11	6	22	24	33	41	37	20	23
Private creditors	3	121	2	3	4	1	1	1	1	1
Bonds	1	3	0	0	0	0	0	0	0	0
Commercial banks	0	96	1	1	1	1	0	0	0	1
Other private	2	22	2	2	3	1	1	1	1	1
Private nonguaranteed	**1**	**9**	**14**	**16**	**19**	**14**	**40**	**6**	**5**	**47**
Bonds	0	0	0	0	0	0	0	0	0	0
Commercial banks and other	1	9	14	16	19	14	40	6	5	47
Memo:										
IBRD	0	10	15	11	9	7	4	3	2	1
IDA	0	1	3	4	6	5	6	7	8	8
NET TRANSFERS ON DEBT	**32**	**138**	**-13**	**73**	**166**	**86**	**225**	**66**	**30**	**110**
Public and publicly guaranteed	**31**	**151**	**25**	**82**	**136**	**53**	**56**	**-32**	**34**	**-25**
Official creditors	33	113	28	85	147	56	55	-35	36	-32
Multilateral	0	79	18	101	163	45	100	-34	50	3
Concessional	0	25	66	94	135	147	182	146	121	98
Bilateral	33	34	9	-16	-16	11	-45	0	-14	-36
Concessional	26	6	71	26	18	28	-31	8	-15	-24
Private creditors	-1	38	-3	-3	-11	-3	1	3	-2	8
Bonds	-1	-4	0	0	0	0	-3	0	0	0
Commercial banks	-1	-90	-2	2	-5	-6	1	5	2	-1
Other private	1	132	-1	-6	-7	3	3	-2	-3	9
Private nonguaranteed	**0**	**-12**	**-38**	**-10**	**30**	**33**	**168**	**98**	**-4**	**134**
Bonds	0	0	0	0	0	0	0	0	0	0
Commercial banks and other	0	-12	-38	-10	30	33	168	98	-4	134
Memo:										
IBRD	0	60	-36	-35	-36	-32	-24	-16	-15	-13
IDA	2	1	45	73	105	92	126	75	66	43
DEBT SERVICE (LTDS)	**26**	**319**	**313**	**321**	**328**	**362**	**418**	**380**	**389**	**611**
Public and publicly guaranteed	**23**	**290**	**275**	**286**	**291**	**304**	**317**	**347**	**257**	**283**
Official creditors	13	85	263	275	280	294	310	343	252	277
Multilateral	3	28	186	200	220	239	251	285	205	217
Concessional	3	3	24	36	39	41	46	48	48	54
Bilateral	10	57	77	75	60	54	59	58	48	60
Concessional	7	25	14	31	27	35	45	46	37	46
Private creditors	11	205	12	12	11	11	7	4	5	5
Bonds	1	4	0	0	0	0	3	0	0	0
Commercial banks	1	145	2	6	5	7	2	1	1	2
Other private	8	56	10	6	7	4	3	3	3	3
Private nonguaranteed	**3**	**28**	**38**	**34**	**37**	**58**	**101**	**33**	**132**	**328**
Bonds	0	0	0	0	0	0	0	0	0	0
Commercial banks and other	3	28	38	34	37	58	101	33	132	328
Memo:										
IBRD	0	13	36	35	36	32	24	16	15	13
IDA	0	1	4	7	8	8	10	13	16	18
UNDISBURSED DEBT	**72**	**954**	**1,123**	**1,195**	**1,447**	**1,346**	**1,099**	**1,265**	**1,243**	**1,123**
Official creditors	66	804	1,107	1,189	1,434	1,332	1,088	1,246	1,229	1,122
Private creditors	6	150	16	7	14	14	12	19	14	1
Memorandum items										
Concessional LDOD	265	665	1,888	2,428	2,727	2,934	2,968	3,215	3,190	3,120
Variable rate LDOD	11	719	918	734	840	752	888	1,079	1,048	1,414
Public sector LDOD	467	2,166	3,687	4,122	4,462	4,259	4,133	4,296	3,839	3,758
Private sector LDOD	24	107	177	191	239	285	426	643	1,050	1,382

6. CURRENCY COMPOSITION OF LONG-TERM DEBT (PERCENT)

	1970	1980	1990	1994	1995	1996	1997	1998	1999	2000
Deutsche mark	2.3	6.8	7.0	9.6	10.0	9.6	8.6	9.1	7.9	7.3
French franc	0.1	0.8	2.2	2.2	2.1	1.4	1.3	1.4	0.8	0.7
Japanese yen	0.0	1.7	10.0	14.0	13.1	12.2	11.3	12.2	13.5	12.3
Pound sterling	0.0	2.0	0.9	0.6	0.7	0.5	0.5	0.4	0.2	0.2
Swiss franc	0.0	0.3	0.7	0.1	0.0	0.0	0.0	0.0	0.0	0.0
U.S.dollars	85.9	65.1	41.3	31.0	32.7	35.1	37.1	39.0	42.2	44.8
Multiple currency	11.7	18.1	29.4	34.4	33.6	34.2	34.8	31.3	30.7	30.0
Special drawing rights	0.0	0.0	0.0	0.0	0.1	0.1	0.1	0.2	0.3	0.4
All other currencies	0.0	5.2	8.5	8.1	7.7	6.9	6.3	6.4	4.4	4.3

BOLIVIA

(US$ million, unless otherwise indicated)

	1970	1980	1990	1994	1995	1996	1997	1998	1999	2000
7. DEBT RESTRUCTURINGS										
Total amount rescheduled	..	..	153	0	196	433	301	0	551	0
Debt stock rescheduled	..	..	0	0	10	0	0	0	532	0
Principal rescheduled	..	..	81	0	138	427	300	0	3	0
Official	..	..	69	0	137	420	300	0	3	0
Private	..	..	12	0	1	7	0	0	0	0
Interest rescheduled	..	..	63	0	46	4	0	0	0	0
Official	..	..	59	0	46	4	0	0	0	0
Private	..	..	4	0	1	1	0	0	0	0
Debt forgiven	..	..	92	17	74	181	83	15	26	18
Memo: interest forgiven	..	..	60	0	8	0	12	0	0	1
Debt stock reduction	..	..	20	0	0	0	0	0	102	18
of which debt buyback	..	..	4	0	0	0	0	0	0	0
8. DEBT STOCK-FLOW RECONCILIATION										
Total change in debt stocks	..	..	143	570	399	-80	42	379	-67	214
Net flows on debt	39	180	32	322	341	329	480	199	135	251
Net change in interest arrears	..	..	-44	20	-14	5	-22	0	-1	0
Interest capitalized	..	..	63	0	46	4	0	0	0	0
Debt forgiveness or reduction	..	..	-109	-17	-74	-181	-83	-15	-128	-36
Cross-currency valuation	..	..	114	124	-27	-384	-415	3	-27	-196
Residual	..	..	86	120	125	146	81	192	-47	195
9. AVERAGE TERMS OF NEW COMMITMENTS										
ALL CREDITORS										
Interest (%)	1.9	8.4	4.2	3.4	3.8	1.8	4.8	1.7	1.9	4.2
Maturity (years)	47.7	15.5	29.2	28.2	28.7	31.7	20.2	35.1	35.3	28.4
Grace period (years)	4.0	4.5	7.9	7.3	7.7	8.7	5.7	9.6	9.3	7.8
Grant element (%)	66.6	13.0	47.8	51.2	49.7	63.1	36.2	69.1	68.3	47.9
Official creditors										
Interest (%)	1.8	8.1	4.1	3.4	3.8	1.8	4.8	1.7	1.9	4.2
Maturity (years)	48.2	21.5	29.5	28.2	28.9	32.5	20.7	35.9	36.3	28.4
Grace period (years)	4.0	5.3	7.9	7.3	7.8	9.0	5.8	9.7	9.4	7.8
Grant element (%)	67.4	20.4	48.4	51.2	50.1	64.3	37.1	70.0	69.1	47.9
Private creditors										
Interest (%)	12.0	8.7	9.4	0.0	6.7	0.3	5.5	1.5	0.8	4.2
Maturity (years)	5.5	10.1	5.8	0.0	5.6	6.9	6.0	9.4	10.0	5.3
Grace period (years)	3.5	3.9	1.5	0.0	1.0	0.6	1.3	5.3	5.9	0.8
Grant element (%)	-6.9	6.4	1.0	0.0	8.2	27.7	12.6	43.9	48.8	14.2
Memorandum items										
Commitments	24	370	549	501	677	291	174	468	355	180
Official creditors	24	176	542	501	671	281	168	453	342	180
Private creditors	0	194	7	0	6	9	6	15	13	0

10. CONTRACTUAL OBLIGATIONS ON OUTSTANDING LONG-TERM DEBT

	2001	2002	2003	2004	2005	2006	2007	2008	2009	2010
TOTAL										
Disbursements	312	314	222	138	79	38	18	2	1	0
Principal	314	320	331	312	298	288	284	271	275	274
Interest	138	134	125	112	102	94	88	83	72	60
Official creditors										
Disbursements	311	314	222	138	79	38	18	2	1	0
Principal	206	215	226	206	193	183	179	166	172	172
Interest	110	108	102	93	85	80	76	71	65	59
Bilateral creditors										
Disbursements	31	20	12	5	3	1	1	0	0	0
Principal	39	40	45	42	39	39	38	38	37	37
Interest	21	22	22	21	21	21	23	24	24	23
Multilateral creditors										
Disbursements	280	294	210	132	76	37	18	2	1	0
Principal	167	175	181	164	154	144	141	128	135	134
Interest	88	86	80	72	65	59	53	47	41	36
Private creditors										
Disbursements	1	0	0	0	0	0	0	0	0	0
Principal	107	105	105	106	105	105	105	105	103	103
Interest	29	26	23	20	17	14	13	12	7	1
Commercial banks										
Disbursements	1	0	0	0	0	0	0	0	0	0
Principal	2	2	2	1	1	1	1	1	1	1
Interest	0	0	0	0	0	0	0	0	0	0
Other private										
Disbursements	0	0	0	0	0	0	0	0	0	0
Principal	105	103	103	105	105	105	105	105	102	102
Interest	28	25	22	20	17	14	13	12	7	1

BOSNIA AND HERZEGOVINA

(US$ million, unless otherwise indicated)

	1970	1980	1990	1994	1995	1996	1997	1998	1999	2000
1. SUMMARY DEBT DATA										
TOTAL DEBT STOCKS (EDT)	..	..	..	..	..	..	..	..	**2,968**	**2,828**
Long-term debt (LDOD)	..	..	..	..	..	..	..	..	**2,769**	**2,575**
Public and publicly guaranteed	..	..	..	..	..	..	..	..	2,766	2,569
Private nonguaranteed	..	..	..	..	..	..	..	..	3	7
Use of IMF credit	..	..	..	**30**	**48**	**45**	**41**	**77**	**94**	**105**
Short-term debt	..	..	..	**39**	**31**	**73**	**57**	**104**	**105**	**148**
of which interest arrears on LDOD	..	..	..	..	..	..	..	..	68	100
Official creditors	..	..	..	..	..	..	..	..	2	1
Private creditors	..	..	..	..	..	..	..	..	66	98
Memo: principal arrears on LDOD	..	..	..	..	..	..	..	..	89	144
Official creditors	..	..	..	..	..	..	..	..	4	2
Private creditors	..	..	..	..	..	..	..	..	85	142
Memo: export credits	..	..	..	166	187	245	234	143	256	219
TOTAL DEBT FLOWS										
Disbursements	..	..	..	..	..	..	..	..	**160**	**132**
Long-term debt	..	..	..	..	..	..	..	..	120	96
IMF purchases	..	..	..	0	46	0	0	33	40	36
Principal repayments	..	..	..	..	..	..	..	..	**25**	**200**
Long-term debt	..	..	..	..	..	..	..	..	4	180
IMF repurchases	..	..	..	0	28	2	1	0	21	20
Net flows on debt	..	..	..	..	..	..	..	..	**91**	**-57**
of which short-term debt	..	..	..	..	..	..	..	..	-44	11
Interest payments (INT)	..	..	..	..	..	..	..	..	**166**	**134**
Long-term debt	..	..	..	..	..	..	..	..	160	126
IMF charges	..	..	..	0	5	2	2	3	3	5
Short-term debt	..	..	..	..	..	..	..	..	3	3
Net transfers on debt	..	..	..	..	..	..	..	..	**-75**	**-191**
Total debt service paid (TDS)	..	..	..	..	..	..	..	..	**191**	**334**
Long-term debt	..	..	..	..	..	..	..	..	164	306
IMF repurchases and charges	..	..	..	0	33	4	3	3	24	25
Short-term debt (interest only)	..	..	..	..	..	..	..	..	3	3
2. AGGREGATE NET RESOURCE FLOWS AND NET TRANSFERS (LONG-TERM)										
NET RESOURCE FLOWS	..	..	..	..	..	..	..	..	**967**	**486**
Net flow of long-term debt (ex. IMF)	..	..	..	..	..	..	..	..	116	-84
Foreign direct investment (net)	..	..	..	..	..	..	..	..	0	0
Portfolio equity flows	..	..	..	..	..	..	..	..	0	0
Grants (excluding technical coop.)	..	..	..	384	870	636	700	498	851	570
Memo: technical coop. grants	..	..	..	7	62	93	86	243	111	103
official net resource flows	..	..	..	..	..	..	..	..	967	483
private net resource flows	..	..	..	..	..	..	..	..	0	4
NET TRANSFERS	..	..	..	..	..	..	..	..	**808**	**360**
Interest on long-term debt	..	..	..	..	..	..	..	..	160	126
Profit remittances on FDI	..	..	..	..	..	..	..	..	0	0
Memo: official net transfers	..	..	..	..	..	..	..	..	831	396
private net transfers	..	..	..	..	..	..	..	..	-24	-36
3. MAJOR ECONOMIC AGGREGATES										
Gross national income (GNI)	..	..	..	..	1,625	2,519	3,299	4,499	4,812	4,619
Exports of goods & services (XGS)	..	..	..	194	381	658	1,002	1,669	1,554	1,510
of which workers remittances	..	..	..	..	..	..	..	..	..	..
Imports of goods & services (MGS)	..	..	..	1,250	1,576	2,500	2,834	2,919	2,809	2,636
International reserves (RES)	..	..	..	53	71	235	80	175	455	508
Current account balance	..	..	..	-177	-193	-748	-1,060	-789	-971	-909
4. DEBT INDICATORS										
EDT / XGS (%)	..	..	..	..	..	..	..	..	191.0	187.3
EDT / GNI (%)	..	..	..	..	..	..	..	..	61.7	61.2
TDS / XGS (%)	..	..	..	..	..	..	..	..	12.3	22.1
INT / XGS (%)	..	..	..	..	..	..	..	..	10.7	8.9
INT / GNI (%)	..	..	..	..	..	..	..	..	3.5	2.9
RES / EDT (%)	..	..	..	..	..	..	..	..	15.3	18.0
RES / MGS (months)	..	..	..	0.5	0.5	1.1	0.3	0.7	1.9	2.3
Short-term / EDT (%)	..	..	..	..	..	..	..	..	3.6	5.2
Concessional / EDT (%)	..	..	..	..	..	..	..	..	28.8	30.7
Multilateral / EDT (%)	..	..	..	..	..	..	..	..	47.5	43.9

BOSNIA AND HERZEGOVINA

(US$ million, unless otherwise indicated)

	1970	1980	1990	1994	1995	1996	1997	1998	1999	2000
5. LONG-TERM DEBT										
DEBT OUTSTANDING (LDOD)	..	..	..	..	..	..	..	..	**2,769**	**2,575**
Public and publicly guaranteed	..	..	..	..	..	..	..	..	**2,766**	**2,569**
Official creditors	..	..	..	..	..	..	..	..	1,955	1,767
Multilateral	..	..	..	..	..	..	..	..	1,410	1,241
Concessional	..	..	..	..	..	..	..	..	419	446
Bilateral	..	..	..	..	..	..	..	..	544	526
Concessional	..	..	..	..	..	..	..	..	436	422
Private creditors	..	..	..	..	..	..	..	..	812	802
Bonds	..	..	..	..	..	..	..	..	333	333
Commercial banks	..	..	..	..	..	..	..	..	135	125
Other private	..	..	..	..	..	..	..	..	344	344
Private nonguaranteed	..	..	..	..	..	..	..	..	**3**	**7**
Bonds	..	..	..	..	..	..	..	..	0	0
Commercial banks and other	..	..	..	..	..	..	..	..	3	7
Memo:										
IBRD	..	..	..	452	472	589	566	581	578	562
IDA	..	..	..	0	0	109	167	312	373	398
DISBURSEMENTS	..	..	..	..	..	..	..	..	**120**	**96**
Public and publicly guaranteed	..	..	..	..	..	..	..	..	**120**	**91**
Official creditors	..	..	..	..	..	..	..	..	120	91
Multilateral	..	..	..	..	..	..	..	..	118	66
Concessional	..	..	..	..	..	..	..	..	105	48
Bilateral	..	..	..	..	..	..	..	..	2	26
Concessional	..	..	..	..	..	..	..	..	2	14
Private creditors	..	..	..	..	..	..	..	..	0	0
Bonds	..	..	..	..	..	..	..	..	0	0
Commercial banks	..	..	..	..	..	..	..	..	0	0
Other private	..	..	..	..	..	..	..	..	0	0
Private nonguaranteed	..	..	..	..	..	..	..	..	**0**	**5**
Bonds	..	..	..	..	..	..	..	..	0	0
Commercial banks and other	..	..	..	..	..	..	..	..	0	5
Memo:										
IBRD	..	..	..	0	0	0	0	0	0	0
IDA	..	..	..	0	0	110	65	135	68	44
PRINCIPAL REPAYMENTS	..	..	..	..	..	..	..	..	**4**	**180**
Public and publicly guaranteed	..	..	..	..	..	..	..	..	**4**	**179**
Official creditors	..	..	..	..	..	..	..	..	4	179
Multilateral	..	..	..	..	..	..	..	..	4	166
Concessional	..	..	..	..	..	..	..	..	0	0
Bilateral	..	..	..	..	..	..	..	..	0	12
Concessional	..	..	..	..	..	..	..	..	0	4
Private creditors	..	..	..	..	..	..	..	..	0	0
Bonds	..	..	..	..	..	..	..	..	0	0
Commercial banks	..	..	..	..	..	..	..	..	0	0
Other private	..	..	..	..	..	..	..	..	0	0
Private nonguaranteed	..	..	..	..	..	..	..	..	**0**	**1**
Bonds	..	..	..	..	..	..	..	..	0	0
Commercial banks and other	..	..	..	..	..	..	..	..	0	1
Memo:										
IBRD	..	..	..	0	0	25	0	0	0	0
IDA	..	..	..	0	0	0	0	0	0	0
NET FLOWS ON DEBT	..	..	..	..	..	..	..	..	**116**	**-84**
Public and publicly guaranteed	..	..	..	..	..	..	..	..	**116**	**-87**
Official creditors	..	..	..	..	..	..	..	..	116	-87
Multilateral	..	..	..	..	..	..	..	..	114	-101
Concessional	..	..	..	..	..	..	..	..	105	48
Bilateral	..	..	..	..	..	..	..	..	2	13
Concessional	..	..	..	..	..	..	..	..	2	10
Private creditors	..	..	..	..	..	..	..	..	0	0
Bonds	..	..	..	..	..	..	..	..	0	0
Commercial banks	..	..	..	..	..	..	..	..	0	0
Other private	..	..	..	..	..	..	..	..	0	0
Private nonguaranteed	..	..	..	..	..	..	..	..	**0**	**4**
Bonds	..	..	..	..	..	..	..	..	0	0
Commercial banks and other	..	..	..	..	..	..	..	..	0	4
Memo:										
IBRD	..	..	..	0	0	-25	0	0	0	0
IDA	..	..	..	0	0	110	65	135	68	44

BOSNIA AND HERZEGOVINA

(US$ million, unless otherwise indicated)

	1970	1980	1990	1994	1995	1996	1997	1998	1999	2000
INTEREST PAYMENTS (LINT)	..	..	..	..	..	..	..	..	**160**	**126**
Public and publicly guaranteed	..	..	..	..	..	..	..	..	**159**	**126**
Official creditors	..	..	..	..	..	..	..	..	136	87
Multilateral	..	..	..	..	..	..	..	..	131	73
Concessional	..	..	..	..	..	..	..	..	3	4
Bilateral	..	..	..	..	..	..	..	..	5	14
Concessional	..	..	..	..	..	..	..	..	2	8
Private creditors	..	..	..	..	..	..	..	..	23	39
Bonds	..	..	..	..	..	..	..	..	21	37
Commercial banks	..	..	..	..	..	..	..	..	3	3
Other private	..	..	..	..	..	..	..	..	0	0
Private nonguaranteed	..	..	..	..	..	..	..	..	**0**	**0**
Bonds	..	..	..	..	..	..	..	..	0	0
Commercial banks and other	..	..	..	..	..	..	..	..	0	0
Memo:										
IBRD	..	..	..	0	0	180	36	35	34	33
IDA	..	..	..	0	0	0	1	1	2	3
NET TRANSFERS ON DEBT	..	..	..	..	..	..	..	..	**-44**	**-210**
Public and publicly guaranteed	..	..	..	..	..	..	..	..	**-43**	**-214**
Official creditors	..	..	..	..	..	..	..	..	-20	-174
Multilateral	..	..	..	..	..	..	..	..	-17	-174
Concessional	..	..	..	..	..	..	..	..	101	44
Bilateral	..	..	..	..	..	..	..	..	-3	0
Concessional	..	..	..	..	..	..	..	..	0	2
Private creditors	..	..	..	..	..	..	..	..	-23	-39
Bonds	..	..	..	..	..	..	..	..	-21	-37
Commercial banks	..	..	..	..	..	..	..	..	-3	-3
Other private	..	..	..	..	..	..	..	..	0	0
Private nonguaranteed	..	..	..	..	..	..	..	..	**0**	**4**
Bonds	..	..	..	..	..	..	..	..	0	0
Commercial banks and other	..	..	..	..	..	..	..	..	0	4
Memo:										
IBRD	..	..	..	0	0	-205	-36	-35	-34	-33
IDA	..	..	..	0	0	110	64	134	66	41
DEBT SERVICE (LTDS)	..	..	..	..	..	..	..	..	**164**	**306**
Public and publicly guaranteed	..	..	..	..	..	..	..	..	**163**	**305**
Official creditors	..	..	..	..	..	..	..	..	140	266
Multilateral	..	..	..	..	..	..	..	..	135	240
Concessional	..	..	..	..	..	..	..	..	4	4
Bilateral	..	..	..	..	..	..	..	..	5	26
Concessional	..	..	..	..	..	..	..	..	2	12
Private creditors	..	..	..	..	..	..	..	..	23	39
Bonds	..	..	..	..	..	..	..	..	21	37
Commercial banks	..	..	..	..	..	..	..	..	3	3
Other private	..	..	..	..	..	..	..	..	0	0
Private nonguaranteed	..	..	..	..	..	..	..	..	**0**	**1**
Bonds	..	..	..	..	..	..	..	..	0	0
Commercial banks and other	..	..	..	..	..	..	..	..	0	1
Memo:										
IBRD	..	..	..	0	0	205	36	35	34	33
IDA	..	..	..	0	0	0	1	1	2	3
UNDISBURSED DEBT	..	..	..	..	..	..	..	..	**369**	**299**
Official creditors	..	..	..	..	..	..	..	..	369	299
Private creditors	..	..	..	..	..	..	..	..	0	0
Memorandum items										
Concessional LDOD	..	..	..	..	..	..	..	..	855	868
Variable rate LDOD	..	..	..	..	..	..	..	..	2,243	2,080
Public sector LDOD	..	..	..	..	..	..	..	..	2,766	2,569
Private sector LDOD	..	..	..	..	..	..	..	..	3	7

6. CURRENCY COMPOSITION OF LONG-TERM DEBT (PERCENT)

	1970	1980	1990	1994	1995	1996	1997	1998	1999	2000
Deutsche mark	..	..	..	..	..	..	..	..	8.4	8.8
French franc	..	..	..	..	..	..	..	..	0.0	0.0
Japanese yen	..	..	..	..	..	..	..	..	0.0	0.0
Pound sterling	..	..	..	..	..	..	..	..	0.0	0.0
Swiss franc	..	..	..	..	..	..	..	..	1.3	1.3
U.S.dollars	..	..	..	..	..	..	..	..	42.0	46.6
Multiple currency	..	..	..	..	..	..	..	..	21.1	22.1
Special drawing rights	..	..	..	..	..	..	..	..	0.0	0.0
All other currencies	..	..	..	..	..	..	..	..	27.2	21.2

BOSNIA AND HERZEGOVINA

(US$ million, unless otherwise indicated)

	1970	1980	1990	1994	1995	1996	1997	1998	1999	2000
7. DEBT RESTRUCTURINGS										
Total amount rescheduled	..	..	..	..	..	..	..	..	566	4
Debt stock rescheduled	..	..	..	..	..	..	..	..	0	0
Principal rescheduled	..	..	..	..	..	..	..	..	0	0
Official	..	..	..	..	..	..	..	..	0	0
Private	..	..	..	..	..	..	..	..	0	0
Interest rescheduled	..	..	..	..	..	..	..	..	0	0
Official	..	..	..	..	..	..	..	..	0	0
Private	..	..	..	..	..	..	..	..	0	0
Debt forgiven	..	..	..	..	..	..	..	..	0	0
Memo: interest forgiven	..	..	..	..	..	..	..	..	0	0
Debt stock reduction	..	..	..	..	..	..	..	..	0	0
of which debt buyback	..	..	..	..	..	..	..	..	0	0
8. DEBT STOCK-FLOW RECONCILIATION										
Total change in debt stocks	..	..	..	..	..	..	..	..	576	-141
Net flows on debt	..	..	..	..	..	..	..	..	91	-57
Net change in interest arrears	..	..	..	..	..	..	..	..	46	31
Interest capitalized	..	..	..	..	..	..	..	..	0	0
Debt forgiveness or reduction	..	..	..	..	..	..	..	..	0	0
Cross-currency valuation	..	..	..	..	..	..	..	..	-96	-113
Residual	..	..	..	..	..	..	..	..	535	-2
9. AVERAGE TERMS OF NEW COMMITMENTS										
ALL CREDITORS										
Interest (%)	..	..	..	..	..	..	..	..	1.3	0.8
Maturity (years)	..	..	..	..	..	..	..	..	31.7	34.6
Grace period (years)	..	..	..	..	..	..	..	..	9.4	10.1
Grant element (%)	..	..	..	..	..	..	..	..	71.5	78.6
Official creditors										
Interest (%)	..	..	..	..	..	..	..	..	1.2	0.8
Maturity (years)	..	..	..	..	..	..	..	..	31.7	34.6
Grace period (years)	..	..	..	..	..	..	..	..	9.4	10.1
Grant element (%)	..	..	..	..	..	..	..	..	71.5	78.6
Private creditors										
Interest (%)	..	..	..	..	..	..	..	..	0.0	0.0
Maturity (years)	..	..	..	..	..	..	..	..	0.0	0.0
Grace period (years)	..	..	..	..	..	..	..	..	0.0	0.0
Grant element (%)	..	..	..	..	..	..	..	..	0.0	0.0
Memorandum items										
Commitments	..	..	..	..	..	..	..	..	242	38
Official creditors	..	..	..	..	..	..	..	..	242	38
Private creditors	..	..	..	..	..	..	..	..	0	0

10. CONTRACTUAL OBLIGATIONS ON OUTSTANDING LONG-TERM DEBT

	2001	2002	2003	2004	2005	2006	2007	2008	2009	2010
TOTAL										
Disbursements	108	84	56	29	14	5	3	0	0	0
Principal	241	88	90	102	125	125	122	96	102	103
Interest	105	102	98	93	87	79	72	66	61	56
Official creditors										
Disbursements	108	84	56	29	14	5	3	0	0	0
Principal	212	59	60	60	62	62	58	61	64	69
Interest	59	58	56	54	51	48	45	42	40	37
Bilateral creditors										
Disbursements	45	35	20	11	6	3	1	0	0	0
Principal	19	29	29	29	31	31	22	22	22	22
Interest	14	14	14	14	13	11	10	10	9	8
Multilateral creditors										
Disbursements	63	49	36	18	8	3	2	0	0	0
Principal	192	30	31	31	31	32	36	39	42	46
Interest	45	43	42	40	38	36	34	33	31	29
Private creditors										
Disbursements	0	0	0	0	0	0	0	0	0	0
Principal	29	29	29	42	64	63	64	35	38	34
Interest	46	44	42	40	36	32	27	23	21	19
Commercial banks										
Disbursements	0	0	0	0	0	0	0	0	0	0
Principal	0	0	0	0	10	10	10	10	10	10
Interest	9	9	9	9	9	8	7	7	6	5
Other private										
Disbursements	0	0	0	0	0	0	0	0	0	0
Principal	29	29	29	42	54	54	54	25	28	25
Interest	37	35	33	31	28	24	20	17	15	13

BOTSWANA

(US$ million, unless otherwise indicated)

1. SUMMARY DEBT DATA

	1970	1980	1990	1994	1995	1996	1997	1998	1999	2000
TOTAL DEBT STOCKS (EDT)	**17.4**	**146.7**	**561.3**	**688.7**	**703.4**	**613.5**	**562.0**	**515.6**	**474.4**	**413.0**
Long-term debt (LDOD)	**17.4**	**142.7**	**555.5**	**677.5**	**693.2**	**607.5**	**522.0**	**508.2**	**454.7**	**397.6**
Public and publicly guaranteed	17.4	142.7	555.5	677.5	693.2	607.5	522.0	508.2	454.7	397.6
Private nonguaranteed	0.0	0.0	0.0	0.0	0.0	0.0	0.0	0.0	0.0	0.0
Use of IMF credit	**0.0**	**0.0**	**0.0**	**0.0**	**0.0**	**0.0**	**0.0**	**0.0**	**0.0**	**0.0**
Short-term debt	**0.0**	**4.0**	**5.8**	**11.2**	**10.2**	**6.0**	**40.0**	**7.4**	**19.7**	**15.4**
of which interest arrears on LDOD	0.0	0.0	2.6	7.8	6.2	0.0	0.0	0.0	0.0	0.0
Official creditors	0.0	0.0	1.3	2.3	0.2	0.0	0.0	0.0	0.0	0.0
Private creditors	0.0	0.0	1.3	5.5	6.0	0.0	0.0	0.0	0.0	0.0
Memo: principal arrears on LDOD	0.0	0.0	2.7	12.6	8.9	0.0	0.0	0.0	0.0	0.0
Official creditors	0.0	0.0	0.9	6.7	2.9	0.0	0.0	0.0	0.0	0.0
Private creditors	0.0	0.0	1.8	5.9	6.0	0.0	0.0	0.0	0.0	0.0
Memo: export credits	0.0	0.0	128.0	102.0	85.1	75.1	82.1	12.3	8.0	6.9
TOTAL DEBT FLOWS										
Disbursements	**5.7**	**27.5**	**29.7**	**52.0**	**65.9**	**28.1**	**22.0**	**20.0**	**18.0**	**14.7**
Long-term debt	5.7	27.5	29.7	52.0	65.9	28.1	22.0	20.0	18.0	14.7
IMF purchases	0.0	0.0	0.0	0.0	0.0	0.0	0.0	0.0	0.0	0.0
Principal repayments	**0.2**	**6.4**	**66.8**	**61.9**	**64.6**	**73.2**	**74.5**	**53.3**	**60.7**	**51.5**
Long-term debt	0.2	6.4	66.8	61.9	64.6	73.2	74.5	53.3	60.7	51.5
IMF repurchases	0.0	0.0	0.0	0.0	0.0	0.0	0.0	0.0	0.0	0.0
Net flows on debt	**5.6**	**8.1**	**-37.0**	**-9.7**	**1.9**	**-43.1**	**-18.4**	**-65.9**	**-30.4**	**-41.1**
of which short-term debt	0.0	-13.0	0.1	0.2	0.6	2.0	34.0	-32.6	12.3	-4.3
Interest payments (INT)	**0.4**	**9.1**	**39.3**	**30.9**	**27.7**	**78.5**	**29.2**	**23.4**	**21.6**	**16.5**
Long-term debt	0.4	7.6	39.1	30.7	27.5	78.2	27.8	23.0	20.9	15.3
IMF charges	0.0	0.0	0.0	0.0	0.0	0.0	0.0	0.0	0.0	0.0
Short-term debt	0.0	1.5	0.2	0.2	0.2	0.3	1.4	0.4	0.8	1.2
Net transfers on debt	**5.1**	**-1.0**	**-76.3**	**-40.6**	**-25.8**	**-121.6**	**-47.7**	**-89.2**	**-52.0**	**-57.6**
Total debt service paid (TDS)	**0.6**	**15.5**	**106.0**	**92.8**	**92.3**	**151.7**	**103.7**	**76.7**	**82.3**	**68.0**
Long-term debt	0.6	14.0	105.8	92.6	92.1	151.4	102.3	76.3	81.6	66.8
IMF repurchases and charges	0.0	0.0	0.0	0.0	0.0	0.0	0.0	0.0	0.0	0.0
Short-term debt (interest only)	0.0	1.5	0.2	0.2	0.2	0.3	1.4	0.4	0.8	1.2

2. AGGREGATE NET RESOURCE FLOWS AND NET TRANSFERS (LONG-TERM)

	1970	1980	1990	1994	1995	1996	1997	1998	1999	2000
NET RESOURCE FLOWS	**14.9**	**183.3**	**136.2**	**9.3**	**100.0**	**56.0**	**88.7**	**106.9**	**26.8**	**11.3**
Net flow of long-term debt (ex. IMF)	5.6	21.1	-37.1	-9.9	1.3	-45.1	-52.4	-33.3	-42.7	-36.7
Foreign direct investment (net)	0.0	111.6	95.0	-14.0	70.0	71.0	100.0	95.0	36.7	30.0
Portfolio equity flows	0.0	0.0	0.0	0.1	0.0	0.1	0.0	0.0	0.0	0.0
Grants (excluding technical coop.)	9.3	50.6	78.4	33.1	28.6	30.0	41.2	45.2	32.8	18.1
Memo: technical coop. grants	2.7	47.5	59.1	45.0	51.4	37.0	41.0	31.8	27.3	18.2
official net resource flows	12.0	68.9	59.7	25.2	36.2	-6.5	-6.3	16.4	-19.7	-15.6
private net resource flows	2.9	114.4	76.5	-15.9	63.8	62.5	95.0	90.5	46.5	26.9
NET TRANSFERS	**14.5**	**68.2**	**-200.5**	**-301.5**	**-227.6**	**-332.2**	**-279.2**	**-216.0**	**-314.1**	**-354.0**
Interest on long-term debt	0.4	7.6	39.1	30.7	27.5	78.2	27.8	23.0	20.9	15.3
Profit remittances on FDI	0.0	107.5	297.7	280.0	300.0	310.0	340.0	300.0	320.0	350.0
Memo: official net transfers	11.6	62.3	23.7	-4.4	11.7	-76.2	-31.8	-5.0	-38.8	-29.6
private net transfers	2.9	5.9	-224.2	-297.1	-239.2	-256.0	-247.4	-211.0	-275.3	-324.4

3. MAJOR ECONOMIC AGGREGATES

	1970	1980	1990	1994	1995	1996	1997	1998	1999	2000
Gross national income (GNI)	101.0	1,097.4	3,659.9	4,179.6	4,866.5	4,869.1	4,797.2	4,880.4	4,670.7	5,278.1
Exports of goods & services (XGS)	..	747.5	2,421.1	2,291.2	2,903.8	2,890.5	3,652.1	2,939.0	3,473.6	3,778.7
of which workers remittances	..	0.0	..	..	..	8.3	0.1	0.4	0.2	0.2
Imports of goods & services (MGS)	..	953.5	2,508.9	2,141.4	2,565.3	2,566.1	3,132.0	3,008.7	3,208.4	3,495.7
International reserves (RES)	..	334.0	3,331.5	4,401.5	4,695.5	5,027.7	5,675.0	5,940.7	6,298.7	6,318.2
Current account balance	..	-151.1	-19.3	211.6	299.7	495.0	721.5	170.1	516.8	..

4. DEBT INDICATORS

	1970	1980	1990	1994	1995	1996	1997	1998	1999	2000
EDT / XGS (%)	..	19.6	23.2	30.1	24.2	21.2	15.4	17.5	13.7	10.9
EDT / GNI (%)	17.2	13.4	15.3	16.5	14.5	12.6	11.7	10.6	10.2	7.8
TDS / XGS (%)	..	2.1	4.4	4.1	3.2	5.3	2.8	2.6	2.4	1.8
INT / XGS (%)	..	1.2	1.6	1.4	1.0	2.7	0.8	0.8	0.6	0.4
INT / GNI (%)	0.4	0.8	1.1	0.7	0.6	1.6	0.6	0.5	0.5	0.3
RES / EDT (%)	..	227.7	593.5	639.1	667.5	819.5	1,009.8	1,152.2	1,327.7	1,529.8
RES / MGS (months)	..	4.2	15.9	24.7	22.0	23.5	21.7	23.7	23.6	21.7
Short-term / EDT (%)	0.0	2.7	1.0	1.6	1.5	1.0	7.1	1.4	4.2	3.7
Concessional / EDT (%)	64.4	40.5	32.9	42.6	48.3	52.5	51.6	57.4	56.9	60.6
Multilateral / EDT (%)	29.9	57.5	69.5	72.2	69.1	70.5	68.1	72.1	68.0	69.0

BOTSWANA

(US$ million, unless otherwise indicated)

	1970	1980	1990	1994	1995	1996	1997	1998	1999	2000
5. LONG-TERM DEBT										
DEBT OUTSTANDING (LDOD)	**17.4**	**142.7**	**555.5**	**677.5**	**693.2**	**607.5**	**522.0**	**508.2**	**454.7**	**397.6**
Public and publicly guaranteed	**17.4**	**142.7**	**555.5**	**677.5**	**693.2**	**607.5**	**522.0**	**508.2**	**454.7**	**397.6**
Official creditors	14.2	134.9	528.1	627.5	646.3	571.6	494.4	484.0	422.7	369.7
Multilateral	5.2	84.3	389.9	497.2	486.1	432.5	382.5	371.5	322.7	285.0
Concessional	5.2	31.5	112.6	194.3	206.1	202.0	192.2	194.0	177.0	169.9
Bilateral	9.0	50.6	138.2	130.2	160.2	139.2	111.8	112.5	100.0	84.7
Concessional	6.0	27.9	71.9	98.8	133.7	120.3	97.6	101.8	92.8	80.2
Private creditors	3.2	7.8	27.4	50.0	47.0	35.9	27.6	24.2	32.0	27.9
Bonds	2.6	2.5	0.0	0.0	0.0	0.0	0.0	0.0	0.0	0.0
Commercial banks	0.0	0.0	10.5	42.0	40.3	33.6	25.8	22.4	30.4	26.4
Other private	0.6	5.3	16.9	8.0	6.7	2.3	1.8	1.8	1.6	1.5
Private nonguaranteed	**0.0**	**0.0**	**0.0**	**0.0**	**0.0**	**0.0**	**0.0**	**0.0**	**0.0**	**0.0**
Bonds	0.0	0.0	0.0	0.0	0.0	0.0	0.0	0.0	0.0	0.0
Commercial banks and other	0.0	0.0	0.0	0.0	0.0	0.0	0.0	0.0	0.0	0.0
Memo:										
IBRD	0.0	50.0	155.2	113.6	96.3	68.8	47.1	36.2	24.3	15.6
IDA	5.2	15.6	13.6	12.0	11.5	11.0	10.6	10.1	9.6	9.1
DISBURSEMENTS	**5.7**	**27.5**	**29.7**	**52.0**	**65.9**	**28.1**	**22.0**	**20.0**	**18.0**	**14.7**
Public and publicly guaranteed	**5.7**	**27.5**	**29.7**	**52.0**	**65.9**	**28.1**	**22.0**	**20.0**	**18.0**	**14.7**
Official creditors	2.8	24.7	29.7	52.0	65.9	28.1	22.0	20.0	7.3	11.0
Multilateral	1.6	15.5	23.2	45.7	21.9	26.3	20.3	17.9	6.4	8.3
Concessional	1.6	5.8	14.1	26.8	13.0	13.0	11.5	6.7	3.1	6.5
Bilateral	1.2	9.2	6.5	6.3	44.0	1.9	1.7	2.1	1.0	2.7
Concessional	1.2	2.7	3.9	6.1	44.0	1.9	1.7	2.1	1.0	2.7
Private creditors	2.9	2.8	0.0	0.0	0.0	0.0	0.0	0.0	10.7	3.8
Bonds	2.6	0.0	0.0	0.0	0.0	0.0	0.0	0.0	0.0	0.0
Commercial banks	0.0	0.0	0.0	0.0	0.0	0.0	0.0	0.0	10.7	3.8
Other private	0.3	2.8	0.0	0.0	0.0	0.0	0.0	0.0	0.0	0.0
Private nonguaranteed	**0.0**	**0.0**	**0.0**	**0.0**	**0.0**	**0.0**	**0.0**	**0.0**	**0.0**	**0.0**
Bonds	0.0	0.0	0.0	0.0	0.0	0.0	0.0	0.0	0.0	0.0
Commercial banks and other	0.0	0.0	0.0	0.0	0.0	0.0	0.0	0.0	0.0	0.0
Memo:										
IBRD	0.0	9.7	7.0	1.1	0.6	0.0	0.0	0.0	0.0	0.0
IDA	1.6	0.0	0.0	0.0	0.0	0.0	0.0	0.0	0.0	0.0
PRINCIPAL REPAYMENTS	**0.2**	**6.4**	**66.8**	**61.9**	**64.6**	**73.2**	**74.5**	**53.3**	**60.7**	**51.5**
Public and publicly guaranteed	**0.2**	**6.4**	**66.8**	**61.9**	**64.6**	**73.2**	**74.5**	**53.3**	**60.7**	**51.5**
Official creditors	0.1	6.4	48.3	59.9	58.4	64.6	69.5	48.8	59.9	44.6
Multilateral	0.0	5.7	36.6	50.1	48.7	49.4	46.7	40.7	41.3	32.8
Concessional	0.0	0.1	2.7	9.1	6.3	9.1	10.9	9.4	10.2	7.6
Bilateral	0.1	0.7	11.7	9.9	9.7	15.3	22.8	8.2	18.6	11.8
Concessional	0.0	0.0	3.4	4.5	4.6	6.1	18.8	4.4	15.5	9.7
Private creditors	0.0	0.0	18.5	2.0	6.2	8.6	5.0	4.5	0.8	6.9
Bonds	0.0	0.0	0.0	0.0	0.0	0.0	0.0	0.0	0.0	0.0
Commercial banks	0.0	0.0	0.2	0.2	4.5	4.3	4.5	4.4	0.7	6.7
Other private	0.0	0.0	18.3	1.8	1.7	4.3	0.5	0.0	0.2	0.1
Private nonguaranteed	**0.0**	**0.0**	**0.0**	**0.0**	**0.0**	**0.0**	**0.0**	**0.0**	**0.0**	**0.0**
Bonds	0.0	0.0	0.0	0.0	0.0	0.0	0.0	0.0	0.0	0.0
Commercial banks and other	0.0	0.0	0.0	0.0	0.0	0.0	0.0	0.0	0.0	0.0
Memo:										
IBRD	0.0	5.4	19.0	21.0	23.7	20.9	16.5	12.9	11.2	7.4
IDA	0.0	0.1	0.3	0.4	0.5	0.5	0.5	0.5	0.5	0.5
NET FLOWS ON DEBT	**5.6**	**21.1**	**-37.1**	**-9.9**	**1.3**	**-45.1**	**-52.4**	**-33.3**	**-42.7**	**-36.7**
Public and publicly guaranteed	**5.6**	**21.1**	**-37.1**	**-9.9**	**1.3**	**-45.1**	**-52.4**	**-33.3**	**-42.7**	**-36.7**
Official creditors	2.7	18.3	-18.7	-7.9	7.6	-36.5	-47.5	-28.8	-52.5	-33.7
Multilateral	1.6	9.8	-13.4	-4.3	-26.8	-23.1	-26.4	-22.7	-34.9	-24.5
Concessional	1.6	5.7	11.4	17.7	6.7	3.9	0.6	-2.7	-7.1	-1.1
Bilateral	1.1	8.5	-5.2	-3.6	34.4	-13.4	-21.1	-6.1	-17.7	-9.2
Concessional	1.2	2.7	0.5	1.7	39.4	-4.3	-17.1	-2.3	-14.6	-7.0
Private creditors	2.9	2.8	-18.5	-2.0	-6.2	-8.6	-5.0	-4.5	9.8	-3.1
Bonds	2.6	0.0	0.0	0.0	0.0	0.0	0.0	0.0	0.0	0.0
Commercial banks	0.0	0.0	-0.2	-0.2	-4.5	-4.3	-4.5	-4.4	10.0	-3.0
Other private	0.3	2.8	-18.3	-1.8	-1.7	-4.3	-0.5	0.0	-0.2	-0.1
Private nonguaranteed	**0.0**	**0.0**	**0.0**	**0.0**	**0.0**	**0.0**	**0.0**	**0.0**	**0.0**	**0.0**
Bonds	0.0	0.0	0.0	0.0	0.0	0.0	0.0	0.0	0.0	0.0
Commercial banks and other	0.0	0.0	0.0	0.0	0.0	0.0	0.0	0.0	0.0	0.0
Memo:										
IBRD	0.0	4.3	-11.9	-19.9	-23.1	-20.9	-16.5	-12.9	-11.2	-7.4
IDA	1.6	0.0	-0.3	-0.4	-0.5	-0.5	-0.5	-0.5	-0.5	-0.5

BOTSWANA

(US$ million, unless otherwise indicated)

	1970	1980	1990	1994	1995	1996	1997	1998	1999	2000
INTEREST PAYMENTS (LINT)	**0.4**	**7.6**	**39.1**	**30.7**	**27.5**	**78.2**	**27.8**	**23.0**	**20.9**	**15.3**
Public and publicly guaranteed	**0.4**	**7.6**	**39.1**	**30.7**	**27.5**	**78.2**	**27.8**	**23.0**	**20.9**	**15.3**
Official creditors	0.4	6.6	36.0	29.5	24.5	69.7	25.5	21.4	19.1	14.0
Multilateral	0.0	4.7	27.8	24.9	21.0	63.0	20.8	17.6	15.7	11.0
Concessional	0.0	0.2	2.5	1.8	1.6	4.1	4.0	3.5	2.9	2.5
Bilateral	0.4	1.9	8.3	4.7	3.5	6.7	4.7	3.8	3.4	3.0
Concessional	0.2	0.5	1.8	1.5	1.0	4.3	3.0	2.5	2.4	2.4
Private creditors	0.0	1.0	3.0	1.2	3.0	8.5	2.4	1.5	1.8	1.3
Bonds	0.0	0.2	0.0	0.0	0.0	0.0	0.0	0.0	0.0	0.0
Commercial banks	0.0	0.5	0.1	0.3	2.7	6.5	2.2	1.4	1.6	1.2
Other private	0.0	0.3	3.0	0.8	0.3	2.0	0.2	0.2	0.2	0.2
Private nonguaranteed	**0.0**	**0.0**	**0.0**	**0.0**	**0.0**	**0.0**	**0.0**	**0.0**	**0.0**	**0.0**
Bonds	0.0	0.0	0.0	0.0	0.0	0.0	0.0	0.0	0.0	0.0
Commercial banks and other	0.0	0.0	0.0	0.0	0.0	0.0	0.0	0.0	0.0	0.0
Memo:										
IBRD	0.0	4.4	14.2	9.3	8.6	6.2	4.3	2.9	2.0	1.2
IDA	0.0	0.1	0.1	0.1	0.1	0.1	0.1	0.1	0.1	0.1
NET TRANSFERS ON DEBT	**5.1**	**13.5**	**-76.2**	**-40.6**	**-26.2**	**-123.3**	**-80.3**	**-56.2**	**-63.6**	**-52.1**
Public and publicly guaranteed	**5.1**	**13.5**	**-76.2**	**-40.6**	**-26.2**	**-123.3**	**-80.3**	**-56.2**	**-63.6**	**-52.1**
Official creditors	2.2	11.7	-54.7	-37.5	-16.9	-106.2	-72.9	-50.2	-71.6	-47.7
Multilateral	1.6	5.1	-41.2	-29.2	-47.8	-86.1	-47.2	-40.4	-50.6	-35.5
Concessional	1.6	5.5	8.9	15.9	5.1	-0.2	-3.5	-6.2	-10.0	-3.6
Bilateral	0.7	6.6	-13.5	-8.3	30.9	-20.1	-25.7	-9.9	-21.0	-12.2
Concessional	1.0	2.1	-1.4	0.2	38.4	-8.6	-20.1	-4.8	-17.0	-9.4
Private creditors	2.9	1.9	-21.5	-3.1	-9.3	-17.1	-7.4	-6.0	8.0	-4.4
Bonds	2.6	-0.2	0.0	0.0	0.0	0.0	0.0	0.0	0.0	0.0
Commercial banks	0.0	-0.5	-0.2	-0.5	-7.2	-10.8	-6.7	-5.8	8.4	-4.1
Other private	0.2	2.5	-21.3	-2.6	-2.0	-6.3	-0.7	-0.2	-0.3	-0.3
Private nonguaranteed	**0.0**	**0.0**	**0.0**	**0.0**	**0.0**	**0.0**	**0.0**	**0.0**	**0.0**	**0.0**
Bonds	0.0	0.0	0.0	0.0	0.0	0.0	0.0	0.0	0.0	0.0
Commercial banks and other	0.0	0.0	0.0	0.0	0.0	0.0	0.0	0.0	0.0	0.0
Memo:										
IBRD	0.0	-0.1	-26.1	-29.2	-31.7	-27.1	-20.8	-15.8	-13.2	-8.6
IDA	1.6	-0.2	-0.4	-0.5	-0.6	-0.6	-0.6	-0.6	-0.6	-0.5
DEBT SERVICE (LTDS)	**0.6**	**14.0**	**105.8**	**92.6**	**92.1**	**151.4**	**102.3**	**76.3**	**81.6**	**66.8**
Public and publicly guaranteed	**0.6**	**14.0**	**105.8**	**92.6**	**92.1**	**151.4**	**102.3**	**76.3**	**81.6**	**66.8**
Official creditors	0.6	13.0	84.4	89.5	82.8	134.3	95.0	70.3	79.0	58.6
Multilateral	0.0	10.4	64.4	74.9	69.7	112.4	67.5	58.3	57.0	43.8
Concessional	0.0	0.3	5.2	10.9	8.0	13.1	15.0	12.9	13.1	10.2
Bilateral	0.5	2.6	20.0	14.5	13.1	21.9	27.5	11.9	22.0	14.9
Concessional	0.2	0.5	5.2	5.9	5.6	10.4	21.8	6.8	18.0	12.1
Private creditors	0.1	1.0	21.5	3.1	9.3	17.1	7.4	6.0	2.6	8.2
Bonds	0.0	0.2	0.0	0.0	0.0	0.0	0.0	0.0	0.0	0.0
Commercial banks	0.0	0.5	0.2	0.5	7.2	10.8	6.7	5.8	2.3	7.9
Other private	0.1	0.3	21.3	2.6	2.0	6.3	0.7	0.2	0.3	0.3
Private nonguaranteed	**0.0**	**0.0**	**0.0**	**0.0**	**0.0**	**0.0**	**0.0**	**0.0**	**0.0**	**0.0**
Bonds	0.0	0.0	0.0	0.0	0.0	0.0	0.0	0.0	0.0	0.0
Commercial banks and other	0.0	0.0	0.0	0.0	0.0	0.0	0.0	0.0	0.0	0.0
Memo:										
IBRD	0.0	9.7	33.1	30.3	32.2	27.1	20.8	15.8	13.2	8.6
IDA	0.0	0.2	0.4	0.5	0.6	0.6	0.6	0.6	0.6	0.5
UNDISBURSED DEBT	**31.1**	**159.6**	**410.4**	**189.2**	**101.6**	**101.7**	**83.7**	**69.2**	**52.3**	**34.1**
Official creditors	31.1	118.1	373.2	185.8	101.6	87.2	69.3	54.7	48.5	34.1
Private creditors	0.0	41.6	37.2	3.4	0.0	14.4	14.4	14.4	3.8	0.0
Memorandum items										
Concessional LDOD	11.2	59.4	184.6	293.1	339.9	322.3	289.7	295.8	269.8	250.1
Variable rate LDOD	0.0	0.0	73.1	110.3	105.8	87.4	67.2	58.0	54.8	43.7
Public sector LDOD	17.4	142.7	555.5	645.2	662.7	583.4	505.2	494.8	443.1	392.2
Private sector LDOD	0.0	0.0	0.0	32.3	30.5	24.1	16.7	13.4	11.6	5.4

6. CURRENCY COMPOSITION OF LONG-TERM DEBT (PERCENT)

	1970	1980	1990	1994	1995	1996	1997	1998	1999	2000
Deutsche mark	0.0	0.0	0.3	4.9	4.5	4.1	3.3	2.7	2.6	1.4
French franc	0.0	0.0	1.6	1.1	1.0	0.6	0.6	0.6	0.5	0.5
Japanese yen	0.0	0.0	4.3	6.5	11.3	11.4	9.6	11.1	11.2	10.5
Pound sterling	81.6	27.3	11.0	5.0	4.2	4.3	4.2	3.5	3.1	2.9
Swiss franc	0.0	0.0	0.0	0.0	0.0	0.0	0.0	0.0	0.0	0.0
U.S.dollars	0.0	23.7	11.7	10.7	11.3	11.7	12.5	12.0	14.2	16.5
Multiple currency	0.0	44.2	54.5	51.5	47.4	45.3	44.5	42.7	40.1	38.1
Special drawing rights	0.0	0.0	0.0	1.4	1.4	1.7	1.9	2.0	2.0	2.1
All other currencies	18.4	4.8	16.6	18.9	18.9	20.9	23.4	25.4	26.3	28.0

BOTSWANA

(US$ million, unless otherwise indicated)

	1970	1980	1990	1994	1995	1996	1997	1998	1999	2000
7. DEBT RESTRUCTURINGS										
Total amount rescheduled	..	..	0.0	0.0	0.0	0.0	0.0	0.0	0.0	0.0
Debt stock rescheduled	..	..	0.0	0.0	0.0	0.0	0.0	0.0	0.0	0.0
Principal rescheduled	..	..	0.0	0.0	0.0	0.0	0.0	0.0	0.0	0.0
Official	..	..	0.0	0.0	0.0	0.0	0.0	0.0	0.0	0.0
Private	..	..	0.0	0.0	0.0	0.0	0.0	0.0	0.0	0.0
Interest rescheduled	..	..	0.0	0.0	0.0	0.0	0.0	0.0	0.0	0.0
Official	..	..	0.0	0.0	0.0	0.0	0.0	0.0	0.0	0.0
Private	..	..	0.0	0.0	0.0	0.0	0.0	0.0	0.0	0.0
Debt forgiven	..	..	0.0	0.0	0.0	0.0	0.0	0.0	0.0	0.0
Memo: interest forgiven	..	..	0.0	0.0	0.0	0.0	0.0	0.0	0.0	0.0
Debt stock reduction	..	..	0.0	0.0	0.0	0.0	0.0	0.0	0.0	0.0
of which debt buyback	..	..	0.0	0.0	0.0	0.0	0.0	0.0	0.0	0.0
8. DEBT STOCK-FLOW RECONCILIATION										
Total change in debt stocks	..	..	6.5	29.1	14.7	-89.9	-51.5	-46.3	-41.2	-61.4
Net flows on debt	5.6	8.1	-37.0	-9.7	1.9	-43.1	-18.4	-65.9	-30.4	-41.1
Net change in interest arrears	..	..	2.1	3.3	-1.6	-6.2	0.0	0.0	0.0	0.0
Interest capitalized	..	..	0.0	0.0	0.0	0.0	0.0	0.0	0.0	0.0
Debt forgiveness or reduction	..	..	0.0	0.0	0.0	0.0	0.0	0.0	0.0	0.0
Cross-currency valuation	..	..	22.1	12.2	0.1	-44.9	-24.1	4.7	-1.5	-9.5
Residual	..	..	19.3	23.3	14.4	4.2	-9.0	14.8	-9.3	-10.8
9. AVERAGE TERMS OF NEW COMMITMENTS										
ALL CREDITORS										
Interest (%)	0.6	6.0	6.9	3.6	0.0	3.8	2.5	4.3	4.0	0.0
Maturity (years)	38.9	18.4	14.9	11.8	0.0	13.9	19.1	17.6	11.6	0.0
Grace period (years)	10.0	4.0	4.3	4.0	0.0	4.0	3.6	3.4	4.1	0.0
Grant element (%)	79.7	24.2	17.1	32.7	0.0	33.8	46.6	33.8	30.4	0.0
Official creditors										
Interest (%)	0.1	6.0	5.7	3.6	0.0	3.5	2.5	4.3	4.0	0.0
Maturity (years)	40.7	18.4	17.0	11.8	0.0	16.1	19.1	17.6	11.6	0.0
Grace period (years)	9.4	4.0	4.4	4.0	0.0	4.4	3.6	3.4	4.1	0.0
Grant element (%)	84.9	24.2	25.0	32.7	0.0	38.6	46.6	33.8	30.4	0.0
Private creditors										
Interest (%)	7.3	0.0	8.9	0.0	0.0	4.2	0.0	0.0	0.0	0.0
Maturity (years)	16.9	0.0	11.6	0.0	0.0	11.6	0.0	0.0	0.0	0.0
Grace period (years)	16.3	0.0	4.1	0.0	0.0	3.6	0.0	0.0	0.0	0.0
Grant element (%)	19.6	0.0	4.6	0.0	0.0	28.6	0.0	0.0	0.0	0.0
Memorandum items										
Commitments	37.6	69.3	79.5	6.2	0.0	30.0	9.9	11.1	2.7	0.0
Official creditors	34.7	69.3	48.4	6.2	0.0	15.6	9.9	11.1	2.7	0.0
Private creditors	2.9	0.0	31.0	0.0	0.0	14.4	0.0	0.0	0.0	0.0

10. CONTRACTUAL OBLIGATIONS ON OUTSTANDING LONG-TERM DEBT

	2001	2002	2003	2004	2005	2006	2007	2008	2009	2010
TOTAL										
Disbursements	14.3	9.9	5.0	2.3	1.3	0.8	0.5	0.1	0.0	0.0
Principal	49.9	40.2	35.6	31.3	29.0	28.0	27.4	22.0	17.6	15.2
Interest	15.1	12.9	11.0	9.4	7.9	6.7	5.4	4.1	3.2	2.5
Official creditors										
Disbursements	14.3	9.9	5.0	2.3	1.3	0.8	0.5	0.1	0.0	0.0
Principal	42.0	37.7	33.1	28.8	26.4	25.5	24.9	19.5	16.9	14.6
Interest	13.2	11.4	9.8	8.3	7.0	5.9	4.8	3.7	3.0	2.4
Bilateral creditors										
Disbursements	3.6	2.5	1.6	0.9	0.5	0.5	0.1	0.1	0.0	0.0
Principal	10.3	8.5	7.3	6.7	6.7	6.3	6.1	5.8	5.6	5.6
Interest	2.5	2.2	2.0	1.9	1.7	1.5	1.3	1.1	1.0	0.8
Multilateral creditors										
Disbursements	10.7	7.4	3.3	1.4	0.8	0.3	0.3	0.0	0.0	0.0
Principal	31.7	29.2	25.7	22.1	19.8	19.1	18.8	13.6	11.3	9.0
Interest	10.6	9.2	7.7	6.5	5.4	4.4	3.5	2.6	2.0	1.6
Private creditors										
Disbursements	0.0	0.0	0.0	0.0	0.0	0.0	0.0	0.0	0.0	0.0
Principal	7.9	2.5	2.5	2.5	2.5	2.5	2.5	2.5	0.7	0.5
Interest	1.9	1.5	1.3	1.1	0.9	0.7	0.5	0.4	0.2	0.1
Commercial banks										
Disbursements	0.0	0.0	0.0	0.0	0.0	0.0	0.0	0.0	0.0	0.0
Principal	7.7	2.4	2.4	2.4	2.4	2.4	2.4	2.3	0.5	0.5
Interest	1.8	1.3	1.2	1.0	0.8	0.7	0.5	0.3	0.2	0.1
Other private										
Disbursements	0.0	0.0	0.0	0.0	0.0	0.0	0.0	0.0	0.0	0.0
Principal	0.2	0.2	0.2	0.2	0.2	0.2	0.2	0.2	0.2	0.0
Interest	0.1	0.1	0.1	0.1	0.1	0.1	0.0	0.0	0.0	0.0

BRAZIL

(US$ million, unless otherwise indicated)

	1970	1980	1990	1994	1995	1996	1997	1998	1999	2000
1. SUMMARY DEBT DATA										
TOTAL DEBT STOCKS (EDT)	**5,735**	**71,527**	**119,964**	**152,430**	**160,505**	**181,321**	**198,023**	**241,010**	**243,651**	**237,953**
Long-term debt (LDOD)	**5,020**	**57,987**	**94,428**	**120,068**	**129,125**	**145,327**	**163,138**	**206,291**	**205,593**	**205,210**
Public and publicly guaranteed	3,314	41,382	87,757	95,367	98,295	96,352	87,305	98,175	92,057	92,590
Private nonguaranteed	1,706	16,605	6,671	24,701	30,830	48,975	75,833	108,116	113,536	112,620
Use of IMF credit	**0**	**0**	**1,821**	**186**	**142**	**68**	**31**	**4,825**	**8,827**	**1,768**
Short-term debt	**714**	**13,540**	**23,716**	**32,176**	**31,238**	**35,927**	**34,854**	**29,894**	**29,231**	**30,976**
of which interest arrears on LDOD	0	14	8,791	2,125	1,546	1,927	1,354	1,674	265	179
Official creditors	0	0	332	1,614	1,185	903	813	246	148	107
Private creditors	0	13	8,459	510	361	1,024	541	1,428	117	72
Memo: principal arrears on LDOD	3	446	3,694	3,319	3,972	3,035	2,959	1,937	2,099	1,783
Official creditors	0	3	789	905	884	821	813	384	259	599
Private creditors	3	443	2,905	2,415	3,088	2,214	2,146	1,552	1,840	1,183
Memo: export credits	0	0	23,906	26,389	21,591	21,526	20,873	10,606	10,290	8,909
TOTAL DEBT FLOWS										
Disbursements	**1,783**	**11,419**	**4,087**	**11,985**	**20,207**	**29,695**	**43,823**	**66,639**	**46,634**	**47,114**
Long-term debt	1,783	11,419	4,087	11,985	20,207	29,695	43,823	62,000	40,549	47,114
IMF purchases	0	0	0	0	0	0	0	4,639	6,085	0
Principal repayments	**531**	**6,848**	**5,913**	**9,742**	**11,054**	**14,766**	**29,104**	**35,906**	**53,332**	**47,723**
Long-term debt	456	6,848	5,147	9,608	11,005	14,696	29,071	35,885	51,355	41,030
IMF repurchases	75	0	765	134	49	70	33	21	1,977	6,693
Net flows on debt	**1,252**	**9,463**	**-1,727**	**8,891**	**8,794**	**19,238**	**14,220**	**25,454**	**-5,952**	**1,223**
of which short-term debt	0	4,892	99	6,648	-359	4,308	-500	-5,280	746	1,831
Interest payments (INT)	**221**	**7,910**	**2,260**	**6,198**	**10,522**	**10,452**	**12,157**	**12,453**	**14,736**	**15,065**
Long-term debt	221	6,385	2,029	4,681	8,720	8,587	10,771	10,952	12,968	13,235
IMF charges	0	0	231	14	10	5	2	1	464	336
Short-term debt	0	1,525	0	1,503	1,792	1,860	1,384	1,500	1,305	1,494
Net transfers on debt	**1,031**	**1,553**	**-3,986**	**2,694**	**-1,727**	**8,786**	**2,063**	**13,000**	**-20,688**	**-13,842**
Total debt service paid (TDS)	**752**	**14,757**	**8,173**	**15,940**	**21,576**	**25,217**	**41,261**	**48,359**	**68,067**	**62,788**
Long-term debt	677	13,232	7,176	14,289	19,724	23,282	39,842	46,837	64,322	54,264
IMF repurchases and charges	75	0	996	148	59	75	35	22	2,441	7,029
Short-term debt (interest only)	0	1,525	0	1,503	1,792	1,860	1,384	1,500	1,305	1,494
2. AGGREGATE NET RESOURCE FLOWS AND NET TRANSFERS (LONG-TERM)										
NET RESOURCE FLOWS	**1,777**	**6,495**	**-31**	**10,600**	**18,537**	**30,261**	**38,321**	**58,673**	**19,797**	**43,934**
Net flow of long-term debt (ex. IMF)	1,327	4,571	-1,060	2,377	9,202	15,000	14,752	26,116	-10,806	6,084
Foreign direct investment (net)	421	1,911	989	3,072	4,859	11,200	19,650	31,913	28,576	32,779
Portfolio equity flows	0	0	0	5,082	4,411	3,981	3,835	542	1,961	5,016
Grants (excluding technical coop.)	28	14	41	69	65	80	83	103	65	54
Memo: technical coop. grants	32	83	145	195	239	246	230	236	272	277
official net resource flows	212	840	-593	-2,225	-1,649	-671	-1,103	4,944	445	-1,738
private net resource flows	1,565	5,656	563	12,825	20,186	30,932	39,423	53,730	19,352	45,672
NET TRANSFERS	**1,168**	**-844**	**-3,952**	**3,469**	**7,217**	**18,474**	**24,250**	**43,721**	**2,169**	**25,200**
Interest on long-term debt	221	6,385	2,029	4,681	8,720	8,587	10,771	10,952	12,968	13,235
Profit remittances on FDI	387	955	1,892	2,450	2,600	3,200	3,300	4,000	4,660	5,500
Memo: official net transfers	161	396	-1,867	-3,538	-3,217	-2,168	-2,342	3,451	-1,714	-3,658
private net transfers	1,008	-1,240	-2,085	7,007	10,434	20,642	26,592	40,270	3,883	28,857
3. MAJOR ECONOMIC AGGREGATES										
Gross national income (GNI)	41,729	227,300	452,628	537,368	693,103	762,769	791,353	767,697	510,212	569,770
Exports of goods & services (XGS)	..	23,331	36,854	53,046	58,989	59,722	65,846	64,644	60,326	69,202
of which workers remittances	..	56	527	1,834	2,891	1,866	1,324	963	1,190	1,113
Imports of goods & services (MGS)	..	36,250	40,949	54,788	77,855	83,545	96,827	98,946	86,224	94,243
International reserves (RES)	1,190	6,875	9,200	38,492	51,477	59,685	51,706	43,902	35,717	33,008
Current account balance	..	-12,831	-3,823	-1,153	-18,136	-23,248	-30,491	-33,829	-25,400	-24,632
4. DEBT INDICATORS										
EDT / XGS (%)	..	306.6	325.5	287.4	272.1	303.6	300.7	372.8	403.9	343.9
EDT / GNI (%)	13.7	31.5	26.5	28.4	23.2	23.8	25.0	31.4	47.8	41.8
TDS / XGS (%)	..	63.3	22.2	30.1	36.6	42.2	62.7	74.8	112.8	90.7
INT / XGS (%)	..	33.9	6.1	11.7	17.8	17.5	18.5	19.3	24.4	21.8
INT / GNI (%)	0.5	3.5	0.5	1.2	1.5	1.4	1.5	1.6	2.9	2.6
RES / EDT (%)	20.8	9.6	7.7	25.3	32.1	32.9	26.1	18.2	14.7	13.9
RES / MGS (months)	..	2.3	2.7	8.4	7.9	8.6	6.4	5.3	5.0	4.2
Short-term / EDT (%)	12.5	18.9	19.8	21.1	19.5	19.8	17.6	12.4	12.0	13.0
Concessional / EDT (%)	22.9	2.5	2.5	4.0	3.8	2.9	2.3	1.8	1.9	0.9
Multilateral / EDT (%)	6.6	4.3	9.5	6.2	5.8	5.2	5.1	6.8	7.6	7.7

BRAZIL

(US$ million, unless otherwise indicated)

	1970	1980	1990	1994	1995	1996	1997	1998	1999	2000
5. LONG-TERM DEBT										
DEBT OUTSTANDING (LDOD)	**5,020**	**57,987**	**94,428**	**120,068**	**129,125**	**145,327**	**163,138**	**206,291**	**205,593**	**205,210**
Public and publicly guaranteed	**3,314**	**41,382**	**87,757**	**95,367**	**98,295**	**96,352**	**87,305**	**98,175**	**92,057**	**92,590**
Official creditors	1,779	7,313	29,348	28,694	27,837	25,351	22,194	27,832	28,870	29,356
Multilateral	376	3,092	11,391	9,375	9,366	9,404	10,065	16,320	18,557	18,240
Concessional	7	72	16	1	1	0	0	0	0	3
Bilateral	1,403	4,221	17,957	19,318	18,471	15,947	12,129	11,513	10,313	11,116
Concessional	1,308	1,685	3,002	6,048	6,073	5,300	4,573	4,397	4,599	2,185
Private creditors	1,535	34,069	58,409	66,674	70,458	71,000	65,111	70,343	63,188	63,233
Bonds	0	3,233	2,339	53,566	54,615	57,403	51,736	51,512	52,357	51,558
Commercial banks	748	24,329	47,461	8,712	12,159	10,727	11,165	17,252	9,545	10,707
Other private	787	6,507	8,609	4,395	3,683	2,870	2,210	1,578	1,285	968
Private nonguaranteed	**1,706**	**16,605**	**6,671**	**24,701**	**30,830**	**48,975**	**75,833**	**108,116**	**113,536**	**112,620**
Bonds	0	0	0	9,391	11,290	14,135	14,820	16,779	16,823	16,846
Commercial banks and other	1,706	16,605	6,671	15,310	19,541	34,840	61,013	91,338	96,713	95,774
Memo:										
IBRD	206	2,035	8,427	6,311	6,038	5,876	5,743	6,298	6,822	7,377
IDA	0	0	0	0	0	0	0	0	0	0
DISBURSEMENTS	**1,783**	**11,419**	**4,087**	**11,985**	**20,207**	**29,695**	**43,823**	**62,000**	**40,549**	**47,114**
Public and publicly guaranteed	**883**	**8,227**	**3,212**	**3,617**	**8,111**	**10,169**	**10,484**	**19,622**	**14,640**	**16,704**
Official creditors	260	1,344	1,322	1,048	2,005	3,149	3,011	9,512	5,706	5,256
Multilateral	108	535	1,001	950	1,257	2,263	2,718	6,978	4,542	4,468
Concessional	0	3	0	0	0	0	0	0	0	3
Bilateral	152	810	321	98	747	886	293	2,533	1,164	788
Concessional	96	47	86	3	146	3	4	353	568	525
Private creditors	623	6,883	1,890	2,569	6,107	7,021	7,472	10,110	8,934	11,448
Bonds	0	378	200	402	1,661	4,345	4,262	2,935	8,521	8,450
Commercial banks	333	4,874	864	1,820	4,342	2,527	3,051	7,159	394	2,986
Other private	290	1,631	826	347	103	149	158	17	20	12
Private nonguaranteed	**900**	**3,192**	**875**	**8,368**	**12,096**	**19,526**	**33,340**	**42,379**	**25,909**	**30,410**
Bonds	0	0	0	3,516	4,563	5,058	5,750	3,489	1,345	2,886
Commercial banks and other	900	3,192	875	4,853	7,533	14,468	27,590	38,890	24,564	27,524
Memo:										
IBRD	61	343	782	640	838	1,500	1,416	1,240	1,533	1,692
IDA	0	0	0	0	0	0	0	0	0	0
PRINCIPAL REPAYMENTS	**456**	**6,848**	**5,147**	**9,608**	**11,005**	**14,696**	**29,071**	**35,885**	**51,355**	**41,030**
Public and publicly guaranteed	**256**	**3,878**	**4,139**	**5,085**	**6,525**	**7,406**	**10,763**	**12,176**	**18,282**	**17,223**
Official creditors	76	518	1,956	3,342	3,719	3,900	4,197	4,671	5,326	7,048
Multilateral	32	164	1,518	1,674	1,683	1,517	1,335	1,265	2,596	4,308
Concessional	1	2	6	1	1	1	0	0	0	0
Bilateral	45	354	439	1,667	2,035	2,383	2,862	3,406	2,731	2,740
Concessional	40	97	29	275	408	543	302	461	441	243
Private creditors	180	3,360	2,183	1,744	2,806	3,506	6,566	7,506	12,956	10,175
Bonds	0	32	71	604	919	1,272	3,825	3,475	5,859	8,397
Commercial banks	137	2,430	1,616	370	1,051	1,548	2,127	3,278	6,812	1,544
Other private	43	898	496	770	837	686	615	752	285	234
Private nonguaranteed	**200**	**2,970**	**1,008**	**4,523**	**4,480**	**7,290**	**18,308**	**23,708**	**33,072**	**23,807**
Bonds	0	0	0	1,507	2,670	2,132	4,967	1,591	1,142	2,775
Commercial banks and other	200	2,970	1,008	3,016	1,810	5,158	13,341	22,117	31,931	21,031
Memo:										
IBRD	14	98	1,251	1,346	1,377	1,222	1,049	994	952	887
IDA	0	0	0	0	0	0	0	0	0	0
NET FLOWS ON DEBT	**1,327**	**4,571**	**-1,060**	**2,377**	**9,202**	**15,000**	**14,752**	**26,116**	**-10,806**	**6,084**
Public and publicly guaranteed	**627**	**4,349**	**-927**	**-1,468**	**1,586**	**2,764**	**-280**	**7,446**	**-3,642**	**-519**
Official creditors	184	826	-634	-2,294	-1,714	-751	-1,186	4,841	380	-1,792
Multilateral	76	371	-517	-725	-426	746	1,383	5,714	1,946	160
Concessional	-1	2	-6	-1	-1	-1	0	0	0	3
Bilateral	108	455	-117	-1,569	-1,288	-1,498	-2,569	-873	-1,566	-1,952
Concessional	57	-49	57	-271	-262	-540	-298	-108	127	283
Private creditors	444	3,523	-293	826	3,300	3,515	906	2,605	-4,022	1,273
Bonds	0	346	129	-202	743	3,074	438	-541	2,661	53
Commercial banks	196	2,444	-753	1,450	3,291	978	924	3,880	-6,418	1,442
Other private	247	733	330	-423	-733	-538	-456	-735	-265	-223
Private nonguaranteed	**700**	**222**	**-133**	**3,845**	**7,616**	**12,236**	**15,032**	**18,670**	**-7,163**	**6,604**
Bonds	0	0	0	2,009	1,894	2,925	783	1,898	203	111
Commercial banks and other	700	222	-133	1,836	5,722	9,311	14,249	16,773	-7,367	6,493
Memo:										
IBRD	47	245	-469	-706	-539	278	368	246	580	805
IDA	0	0	0	0	0	0	0	0	0	0

BRAZIL

(US$ million, unless otherwise indicated)

	1970	1980	1990	1994	1995	1996	1997	1998	1999	2000
INTEREST PAYMENTS (LINT)	**221**	**6,385**	**2,029**	**4,681**	**8,720**	**8,587**	**10,771**	**10,952**	**12,968**	**13,235**
Public and publicly guaranteed	**132**	**4,253**	**1,569**	**3,532**	**6,624**	**5,531**	**5,211**	**5,135**	**6,632**	**6,883**
Official creditors	51	444	1,273	1,313	1,568	1,497	1,240	1,492	2,159	1,920
Multilateral	21	255	966	781	750	679	689	738	1,550	1,400
Concessional	0	3	1	0	0	0	0	0	0	0
Bilateral	30	189	307	533	817	818	551	755	609	520
Concessional	28	48	13	66	247	244	50	194	195	90
Private creditors	81	3,809	296	2,219	5,057	4,034	3,971	3,642	4,474	4,963
Bonds	0	234	14	1,735	4,416	3,123	3,168	2,467	3,395	4,173
Commercial banks	45	3,128	46	301	376	706	687	977	1,014	751
Other private	36	447	236	183	265	205	116	198	65	39
Private nonguaranteed	**89**	**2,132**	**460**	**1,149**	**2,095**	**3,056**	**5,560**	**5,818**	**6,335**	**6,352**
Bonds	0	0	0	656	837	1,028	1,323	1,399	1,503	1,562
Commercial banks and other	89	2,132	460	493	1,258	2,028	4,237	4,419	4,832	4,790
Memo:										
IBRD	11	177	725	537	491	416	380	378	428	464
IDA	0	0	0	0	0	0	0	0	0	0
NET TRANSFERS ON DEBT	**1,106**	**-1,814**	**-3,089**	**-2,304**	**483**	**6,413**	**3,982**	**15,164**	**-23,773**	**-7,150**
Public and publicly guaranteed	**495**	**96**	**-2,496**	**-5,001**	**-5,038**	**-2,768**	**-5,490**	**2,311**	**-10,275**	**-7,402**
Official creditors	132	382	-1,907	-3,607	-3,281	-2,248	-2,425	3,349	-1,779	-3,712
Multilateral	55	116	-1,483	-1,505	-1,176	67	695	4,976	397	-1,240
Concessional	-1	-1	-6	-1	-1	-1	0	0	0	3
Bilateral	78	266	-425	-2,102	-2,105	-2,316	-3,120	-1,627	-2,175	-2,472
Concessional	29	-97	44	-338	-509	-784	-347	-302	-68	193
Private creditors	363	-286	-589	-1,394	-1,757	-519	-3,065	-1,038	-8,496	-3,690
Bonds	0	112	115	-1,937	-3,673	-49	-2,730	-3,008	-734	-4,120
Commercial banks	151	-684	-799	1,150	2,915	273	237	2,903	-7,432	691
Other private	212	287	94	-606	-998	-743	-572	-933	-330	-261
Private nonguaranteed	**611**	**-1,910**	**-593**	**2,696**	**5,521**	**9,181**	**9,472**	**12,853**	**-13,499**	**252**
Bonds	0	0	0	1,353	1,057	1,897	-540	499	-1,300	-1,451
Commercial banks and other	611	-1,910	-593	1,343	4,464	7,283	10,012	12,354	-12,199	1,703
Memo:										
IBRD	36	68	-1,193	-1,242	-1,031	-138	-12	-133	152	341
IDA	0	0	0	0	0	0	0	0	0	0
DEBT SERVICE (LTDS)	**677**	**13,232**	**7,176**	**14,289**	**19,724**	**23,282**	**39,842**	**46,837**	**64,322**	**54,264**
Public and publicly guaranteed	**388**	**8,131**	**5,709**	**8,617**	**13,149**	**12,937**	**15,974**	**17,311**	**24,915**	**24,106**
Official creditors	127	962	3,230	4,655	5,286	5,397	5,437	6,163	7,485	8,968
Multilateral	53	419	2,484	2,455	2,434	2,196	2,024	2,002	4,145	5,708
Concessional	1	4	6	1	1	1	0	0	0	0
Bilateral	75	544	746	2,200	2,852	3,201	3,413	4,161	3,340	3,260
Concessional	68	144	42	341	655	787	352	655	636	333
Private creditors	261	7,169	2,479	3,963	7,863	7,540	10,537	11,148	17,430	15,139
Bonds	0	266	85	2,339	5,335	4,395	6,993	5,943	9,255	12,570
Commercial banks	182	5,558	1,663	671	1,427	2,254	2,814	4,255	7,826	2,295
Other private	79	1,345	732	953	1,101	892	730	950	349	273
Private nonguaranteed	**289**	**5,102**	**1,468**	**5,672**	**6,575**	**10,346**	**23,868**	**29,526**	**39,408**	**30,158**
Bonds	0	0	0	2,163	3,507	3,160	6,290	2,990	2,645	4,337
Commercial banks and other	289	5,102	1,468	3,509	3,069	7,185	17,578	26,536	36,763	25,821
Memo:										
IBRD	25	275	1,975	1,883	1,868	1,638	1,428	1,373	1,381	1,351
IDA	0	0	0	0	0	0	0	0	0	0
UNDISBURSED DEBT	**1,509**	**14,060**	**12,962**	**17,035**	**14,858**	**15,034**	**17,341**	**30,468**	**31,162**	**27,428**
Official creditors	821	6,373	6,882	10,625	9,494	9,048	11,637	25,082	26,459	22,446
Private creditors	688	7,687	6,080	6,410	5,365	5,987	5,704	5,386	4,703	4,982
Memorandum items										
Concessional LDOD	1,315	1,757	3,018	6,049	6,074	5,300	4,573	4,397	4,599	2,188
Variable rate LDOD	2,111	41,557	66,630	88,800	96,241	110,472	132,997	166,688	166,652	156,927
Public sector LDOD	3,206	39,303	87,186	94,901	97,428	95,570	86,676	96,064	90,050	92,132
Private sector LDOD	1,814	18,685	7,241	25,167	31,698	49,757	76,462	110,227	115,543	113,078

6. CURRENCY COMPOSITION OF LONG-TERM DEBT (PERCENT)

	1970	1980	1990	1994	1995	1996	1997	1998	1999	2000
Deutsche mark	7.3	8.1	8.9	4.2	5.1	5.7	5.1	3.3	2.6	3.9
French franc	0.2	2.5	6.6	5.9	6.0	4.9	4.2	3.1	2.3	2.0
Japanese yen	0.0	8.5	7.4	7.5	8.6	8.2	7.3	5.9	7.3	7.1
Pound sterling	7.6	2.5	1.8	2.1	1.8	2.2	2.3	1.7	1.2	1.1
Swiss franc	2.2	1.3	1.0	0.3	0.3	0.2	0.3	0.2	0.2	0.3
U.S.dollars	72.1	67.8	60.3	69.5	68.2	68.0	68.8	74.7	73.2	71.9
Multiple currency	9.6	7.2	12.7	10.0	9.5	9.3	9.7	7.7	7.6	6.6
Special drawing rights	0.0	0.0	0.0	0.0	0.0	0.0	0.0	0.0	0.0	0.0
All other currencies	1.0	2.1	1.3	0.5	0.5	1.5	2.3	3.4	5.6	7.1

BRAZIL

(US$ million, unless otherwise indicated)

	1970	1980	1990	1994	1995	1996	1997	1998	1999	2000
7. DEBT RESTRUCTURINGS										
Total amount rescheduled	..	..	1,316	43,451	234	298	288	148	0	0
Debt stock rescheduled	..	..	0	35,758	0	0	0	0	0	0
Principal rescheduled	..	..	1,064	76	0	0	0	0	0	0
Official	..	..	212	0	0	0	0	0	0	0
Private	..	..	852	76	0	0	0	0	0	0
Interest rescheduled	..	..	274	7,273	0	298	288	148	0	0
Official	..	..	69	0	0	0	0	0	0	0
Private	..	..	205	7,273	0	298	288	148	0	0
Debt forgiven	..	..	0	0	0	0	0	0	0	0
Memo: interest forgiven	..	..	0	0	0	0	0	0	0	0
Debt stock reduction	..	..	1,259	4,104	0	0	3,294	0	4,151	6,479
of which debt buyback	..	..	776	204	0	0	2,694	0	2,971	6,342
8. DEBT STOCK-FLOW RECONCILIATION										
Total change in debt stocks	..	..	5,327	8,326	8,075	20,817	16,702	42,986	2,641	-5,698
Net flows on debt	1,252	9,463	-1,727	8,891	8,794	19,238	14,220	25,454	-5,952	1,223
Net change in interest arrears	..	..	5,603	-5,796	-579	381	-573	320	-1,409	-86
Interest capitalized	..	..	274	7,273	0	298	288	148	0	0
Debt forgiveness or reduction	..	..	-483	-3,900	0	0	-600	0	-1,181	-137
Cross-currency valuation	..	..	3,031	2,402	664	-2,582	-3,390	1,871	-817	-2,415
Residual	..	..	-1,371	-544	-804	3,483	6,757	15,194	11,999	-4,282
9. AVERAGE TERMS OF NEW COMMITMENTS										
ALL CREDITORS										
Interest (%)	7.0	12.2	8.2	8.0	7.1	8.3	7.7	9.6	8.8	9.7
Maturity (years)	14.0	10.9	11.7	11.9	7.7	8.1	15.8	4.6	7.8	16.6
Grace period (years)	3.4	4.0	3.7	3.7	2.9	3.8	3.6	2.1	4.8	14.7
Grant element (%)	17.2	-9.8	9.0	10.4	10.3	7.6	10.8	1.8	3.2	-1.3
Official creditors										
Interest (%)	5.7	9.5	7.4	6.7	5.6	7.0	6.0	9.3	6.2	6.7
Maturity (years)	24.8	13.9	15.2	18.9	19.7	16.4	17.9	4.5	10.1	13.0
Grace period (years)	5.9	3.7	4.1	5.2	4.8	3.7	4.1	1.1	3.6	4.0
Grant element (%)	29.3	4.2	14.9	20.3	26.4	15.7	22.2	2.6	16.4	15.6
Private creditors										
Interest (%)	7.5	13.0	9.0	9.0	7.7	8.7	9.1	10.5	10.9	10.3
Maturity (years)	9.4	10.0	7.9	6.8	3.1	5.0	14.2	4.9	5.9	17.3
Grace period (years)	2.2	4.1	3.2	2.5	2.2	3.9	3.1	4.5	5.7	16.8
Grant element (%)	12.0	-14.0	2.6	3.0	4.1	4.5	2.1	0.0	-7.8	-4.6
Memorandum items										
Commitments	1,441	10,066	2,979	5,717	7,303	10,921	13,919	32,719	16,111	17,613
Official creditors	433	2,303	1,552	2,431	2,020	3,006	6,071	22,856	7,298	2,860
Private creditors	1,008	7,762	1,427	3,286	5,283	7,916	7,848	9,863	8,814	14,753

10. CONTRACTUAL OBLIGATIONS ON OUTSTANDING LONG-TERM DEBT

	2001	2002	2003	2004	2005	2006	2007	2008	2009	2010
TOTAL										
Disbursements	6,228	3,110	1,929	1,104	588	346	196	78	42	21
Principal	36,945	27,028	21,574	25,777	16,133	12,575	12,700	10,390	9,868	7,182
Interest	10,211	8,616	7,657	6,680	5,251	4,584	4,102	3,373	2,990	2,446
Official creditors										
Disbursements	2,613	2,388	1,659	1,017	588	346	196	78	42	21
Principal	3,279	4,285	5,637	4,770	3,428	3,062	1,749	1,615	1,550	1,445
Interest	1,773	1,734	1,556	1,251	1,027	879	743	648	560	465
Bilateral creditors										
Disbursements	730	707	429	237	114	62	21	2	2	0
Principal	1,853	1,706	1,664	1,623	1,632	1,598	383	358	440	397
Interest	469	422	370	308	244	176	121	104	89	61
Multilateral creditors										
Disbursements	1,883	1,680	1,230	780	474	284	175	76	40	21
Principal	1,426	2,578	3,973	3,147	1,796	1,464	1,366	1,257	1,110	1,049
Interest	1,304	1,312	1,187	943	783	703	622	545	471	404
Private creditors										
Disbursements	3,615	722	269	87	0	0	0	0	0	0
Principal	33,667	22,743	15,937	21,007	12,706	9,513	10,952	8,775	8,318	5,736
Interest	8,437	6,882	6,101	5,429	4,225	3,705	3,359	2,725	2,430	1,981
Commercial banks										
Disbursements	3,576	708	268	87	0	0	0	0	0	0
Principal	8,056	3,443	920	603	471	359	318	177	150	125
Interest	907	376	189	137	100	70	46	26	16	6
Other private										
Disbursements	40	15	2	0	0	0	0	0	0	0
Principal	25,611	19,301	15,017	20,404	12,234	9,154	10,633	8,599	8,168	5,611
Interest	7,530	6,506	5,912	5,291	4,124	3,634	3,313	2,699	2,415	1,975

BULGARIA

(US$ million, unless otherwise indicated)

1. SUMMARY DEBT DATA

	1970	1980	1990	1994	1995	1996	1997	1998	1999	2000
TOTAL DEBT STOCKS (EDT)	..	..	**10,890**	**9,748**	**10,259**	**9,975**	**9,719**	**9,742**	**9,810**	**10,026**
Long-term debt (LDOD)	..	..	**9,834**	**8,371**	**9,031**	**8,509**	**8,041**	**8,208**	**8,188**	**8,282**
Public and publicly guaranteed	..	..	9,834	8,371	8,689	8,096	7,617	7,654	7,497	7,513
Private nonguaranteed	..	..	0	0	342	413	424	554	691	769
Use of IMF credit	**0**	**0**	**0**	**941**	**717**	**586**	**942**	**1,116**	**1,250**	**1,322**
Short-term debt	..	..	**1,056**	**436**	**512**	**881**	**736**	**419**	**372**	**422**
of which interest arrears on LDOD	..	..	226	110	74	115	178	179	34	5
Official creditors	..	..	5	16	5	10	9	8	0	4
Private creditors	..	..	221	94	68	105	169	170	34	0
Memo: principal arrears on LDOD	..	..	356	277	227	95	329	89	164	17
Official creditors	..	..	1	21	25	25	24	23	0	16
Private creditors	..	..	354	256	201	71	305	66	164	1
Memo: export credits	..	..	4,798	1,360	1,492	1,427	1,207	1,034	841	671
TOTAL DEBT FLOWS										
Disbursements	..	..	**876**	**730**	**247**	**316**	**696**	**991**	**1,312**	**1,024**
Long-term debt	..	..	876	397	247	200	207	681	1,026	748
IMF purchases	0	0	0	333	0	116	489	311	286	276
Principal repayments	..	..	**865**	**518**	**566**	**703**	**462**	**769**	**750**	**660**
Long-term debt	..	..	865	450	319	478	374	586	626	522
IMF repurchases	0	0	0	69	246	225	89	183	124	139
Net flows on debt	..	..	**-14**	**499**	**-206**	**-60**	**26**	**-96**	**660**	**444**
of which short-term debt	..	..	-24	288	113	327	-208	-318	98	80
Interest payments (INT)	..	..	**510**	**170**	**575**	**549**	**511**	**527**	**402**	**529**
Long-term debt	..	..	452	113	501	485	450	460	340	447
IMF charges	0	0	0	40	50	29	31	45	44	63
Short-term debt	..	..	58	16	24	35	30	22	18	19
Net transfers on debt	..	..	**-523**	**330**	**-780**	**-609**	**-486**	**-623**	**259**	**-85**
Total debt service paid (TDS)	..	..	**1,375**	**688**	**1,140**	**1,252**	**973**	**1,296**	**1,152**	**1,189**
Long-term debt	..	..	1,317	563	820	963	824	1,046	965	969
IMF repurchases and charges	0	0	0	109	296	254	120	228	168	202
Short-term debt (interest only)	..	..	58	16	24	35	30	22	18	19

2. AGGREGATE NET RESOURCE FLOWS AND NET TRANSFERS (LONG-TERM)

	1970	1980	1990	1994	1995	1996	1997	1998	1999	2000
NET RESOURCE FLOWS	..	..	**17**	**556**	**440**	**429**	**609**	**805**	**1,461**	**1,363**
Net flow of long-term debt (ex. IMF)	..	..	11	-53	-72	-278	-167	94	401	227
Foreign direct investment (net)	..	..	4	105	90	109	505	537	806	1,002
Portfolio equity flows	..	..	0	400	400	500	130	66	102	5
Grants (excluding technical coop.)	..	..	3	103	22	98	141	108	153	130
Memo: technical coop. grants	..	..	1	43	91	57	44	114	93	150
official net resource flows	..	..	60	452	48	120	59	171	300	249
private net resource flows	..	..	-42	104	392	309	551	634	1,161	1,114
NET TRANSFERS	..	..	**-434**	**441**	**-64**	**-68**	**147**	**331**	**1,105**	**894**
Interest on long-term debt	..	..	452	113	501	485	450	460	340	447
Profit remittances on FDI	..	..	0	2	3	11	12	14	16	22
Memo: official net transfers	..	..	46	379	-130	-54	-88	29	171	119
private net transfers	..	..	-481	62	67	-14	236	302	935	775

3. MAJOR ECONOMIC AGGREGATES

	1970	1980	1990	1994	1995	1996	1997	1998	1999	2000
Gross national income (GNI)	..	..	19,083	9,586	12,679	9,442	9,796	11,974	12,189	11,674
Exports of goods & services (XGS)	..	..	7,070	5,277	6,926	6,437	6,488	6,288	6,058	7,323
of which workers remittances	..	..	0	..	..	..	..	..	..	..
Imports of goods & services (MGS)	..	..	8,905	5,475	7,084	6,526	6,298	6,580	7,043	8,314
International reserves (RES)	..	..	..	1,397	1,635	864	2,548	3,127	3,383	3,625
Current account balance	..	..	-1,710	-32	-26	16	427	-62	-685	-701

4. DEBT INDICATORS

	1970	1980	1990	1994	1995	1996	1997	1998	1999	2000
EDT / XGS (%)	..	..	154.0	184.7	148.1	155.0	149.8	154.9	161.9	136.9
EDT / GNI (%)	..	..	57.1	101.7	80.9	105.7	99.2	81.4	80.5	85.9
TDS / XGS (%)	..	..	19.4	13.0	16.5	19.5	15.0	20.6	19.0	16.2
INT / XGS (%)	..	..	7.2	3.2	8.3	8.5	7.9	8.4	6.6	7.2
INT / GNI (%)	..	..	2.7	1.8	4.5	5.8	5.2	4.4	3.3	4.5
RES / EDT (%)	..	..	..	14.3	15.9	8.7	26.2	32.1	34.5	36.2
RES / MGS (months)	..	..	..	3.1	2.8	1.6	4.9	5.7	5.8	5.2
Short-term / EDT (%)	..	..	9.7	4.5	5.0	8.8	7.6	4.3	3.8	4.2
Concessional / EDT (%)	..	..	0.7	1.6	1.8	1.8	1.6	1.7	2.2	4.0
Multilateral / EDT (%)	..	..	2.0	8.1	11.8	12.1	10.6	12.5	13.3	13.7

BULGARIA

(US$ million, unless otherwise indicated)

	1970	1980	1990	1994	1995	1996	1997	1998	1999	2000
5. LONG-TERM DEBT										
DEBT OUTSTANDING (LDOD)	..	..	**9,834**	**8,371**	**9,031**	**8,509**	**8,041**	**8,208**	**8,188**	**8,282**
Public and publicly guaranteed	..	..	**9,834**	**8,371**	**8,689**	**8,096**	**7,617**	**7,654**	**7,497**	**7,513**
Official creditors	..	..	1,669	2,320	2,831	2,659	2,295	2,424	2,392	2,398
Multilateral	..	..	222	793	1,208	1,209	1,034	1,214	1,304	1,371
Concessional	..	..	0	0	0	0	0	0	0	0
Bilateral	..	..	1,447	1,527	1,623	1,450	1,261	1,210	1,088	1,027
Concessional	..	..	77	153	186	179	159	165	212	397
Private creditors	..	..	8,165	6,051	5,857	5,437	5,322	5,230	5,106	5,115
Bonds	..	..	327	5,411	5,412	5,155	5,072	5,020	5,035	5,029
Commercial banks	..	..	7,084	577	394	244	212	205	3	27
Other private	..	..	753	62	51	38	39	5	68	59
Private nonguaranteed	..	..	**0**	**0**	**342**	**413**	**424**	**554**	**691**	**769**
Bonds	..	..	0	0	0	0	0	0	0	0
Commercial banks and other	..	..	0	0	342	413	424	554	691	769
Memo:										
IBRD	0	0	0	415	444	453	501	697	829	824
IDA	0	0	0	0	0	0	0	0	0	0
DISBURSEMENTS	..	..	**876**	**397**	**247**	**200**	**207**	**681**	**1,026**	**748**
Public and publicly guaranteed	..	..	**876**	**397**	**247**	**139**	**182**	**375**	**513**	**435**
Official creditors	..	..	80	375	118	139	176	375	388	411
Multilateral	..	..	44	365	26	122	173	372	299	154
Concessional	..	..	0	0	0	0	0	0	0	0
Bilateral	..	..	36	10	92	17	2	3	89	256
Concessional	..	..	0	0	32	15	2	3	59	256
Private creditors	..	..	796	22	129	0	6	0	125	24
Bonds	..	..	65	16	33	0	0	0	53	0
Commercial banks	..	..	652	6	96	0	0	0	4	24
Other private	..	..	79	0	0	0	6	0	68	0
Private nonguaranteed	..	..	**0**	**0**	**0**	**61**	**25**	**306**	**514**	**313**
Bonds	..	..	0	0	0	0	0	0	0	0
Commercial banks and other	..	..	0	0	0	61	25	306	514	313
Memo:										
IBRD	0	0	0	246	15	53	101	197	221	71
IDA	0	0	0	0	0	0	0	0	0	0
PRINCIPAL REPAYMENTS	..	..	**865**	**450**	**319**	**478**	**374**	**586**	**626**	**522**
Public and publicly guaranteed	..	..	**865**	**450**	**319**	**455**	**352**	**377**	**310**	**293**
Official creditors	..	..	23	27	92	117	258	312	241	291
Multilateral	..	..	22	20	25	23	193	205	52	52
Concessional	..	..	0	0	0	0	0	0	0	0
Bilateral	..	..	1	7	67	94	64	107	189	240
Concessional	..	..	0	0	0	9	8	7	20	50
Private creditors	..	..	842	423	228	338	95	65	69	2
Bonds	..	..	0	223	39	205	62	56	35	0
Commercial banks	..	..	241	200	183	122	28	7	33	1
Other private	..	..	601	0	7	12	5	2	1	1
Private nonguaranteed	..	..	**0**	**0**	**0**	**23**	**21**	**209**	**316**	**229**
Bonds	..	..	0	0	0	0	0	0	0	0
Commercial banks and other	..	..	0	0	0	23	21	209	316	229
Memo:										
IBRD	0	0	0	0	0	13	16	20	22	27
IDA	0	0	0	0	0	0	0	0	0	0
NET FLOWS ON DEBT	..	..	**11**	**-53**	**-72**	**-278**	**-167**	**94**	**401**	**227**
Public and publicly guaranteed	..	..	**11**	**-53**	**-72**	**-316**	**-171**	**-2**	**203**	**142**
Official creditors	..	..	57	348	26	22	-82	63	147	120
Multilateral	..	..	21	345	1	100	-20	168	247	103
Concessional	..	..	0	0	0	0	0	0	0	0
Bilateral	..	..	36	3	25	-77	-62	-104	-99	17
Concessional	..	..	0	0	32	6	-6	-5	40	207
Private creditors	..	..	-46	-401	-98	-338	-88	-65	56	22
Bonds	..	..	65	-207	-6	-205	-62	-56	18	0
Commercial banks	..	..	411	-194	-86	-122	-28	-7	-29	24
Other private	..	..	-522	0	-7	-12	2	-2	67	-1
Private nonguaranteed	..	..	**0**	**0**	**0**	**38**	**4**	**96**	**198**	**85**
Bonds	..	..	0	0	0	0	0	0	0	0
Commercial banks and other	..	..	0	0	0	38	4	96	198	85
Memo:										
IBRD	0	0	0	246	15	40	85	176	199	44
IDA	0	0	0	0	0	0	0	0	0	0

BULGARIA

(US$ million, unless otherwise indicated)

	1970	1980	1990	1994	1995	1996	1997	1998	1999	2000
INTEREST PAYMENTS (LINT)	..	..	**452**	**113**	**501**	**485**	**450**	**460**	**340**	**447**
Public and publicly guaranteed	..	..	**452**	**113**	**501**	**466**	**437**	**447**	**318**	**415**
Official creditors	..	..	14	72	178	174	147	142	129	130
Multilateral	..	..	13	27	61	73	64	62	61	72
Concessional	..	..	0	0	0	0	0	0	0	0
Bilateral	..	..	0	45	118	101	83	80	68	58
Concessional	..	..	0	2	4	9	8	7	6	10
Private creditors	..	..	438	41	323	292	290	305	189	285
Bonds	..	..	16	36	315	279	275	304	188	284
Commercial banks	..	..	337	5	7	12	14	1	1	0
Other private	..	..	85	0	1	1	0	0	0	0
Private nonguaranteed	..	..	**0**	**0**	**0**	**20**	**13**	**13**	**22**	**32**
Bonds	..	..	0	0	0	0	0	0	0	0
Commercial banks and other	..	..	0	0	0	20	13	13	22	32
Memo:										
IBRD	0	0	0	15	31	30	31	37	42	49
IDA	0	0	0	0	0	0	0	0	0	0
NET TRANSFERS ON DEBT	..	..	**-441**	**-166**	**-573**	**-764**	**-617**	**-365**	**61**	**-220**
Public and publicly guaranteed	..	..	**-441**	**-166**	**-573**	**-782**	**-607**	**-449**	**-116**	**-273**
Official creditors	..	..	43	276	-153	-152	-229	-79	18	-11
Multilateral	..	..	8	317	-60	27	-84	106	186	31
Concessional	..	..	0	0	0	0	0	0	0	0
Bilateral	..	..	35	-42	-93	-178	-145	-184	-168	-41
Concessional	..	..	0	-2	28	-2	-13	-12	34	197
Private creditors	..	..	-484	-442	-421	-630	-378	-370	-134	-262
Bonds	..	..	49	-243	-321	-484	-337	-360	-170	-284
Commercial banks	..	..	74	-199	-93	-133	-42	-8	-30	23
Other private	..	..	-608	0	-7	-12	1	-2	66	-1
Private nonguaranteed	..	..	**0**	**0**	**0**	**18**	**-9**	**84**	**176**	**53**
Bonds	..	..	0	0	0	0	0	0	0	0
Commercial banks and other	..	..	0	0	0	18	-9	84	176	53
Memo:										
IBRD	0	0	0	230	-16	10	54	140	157	-5
IDA	0	0	0	0	0	0	0	0	0	0
DEBT SERVICE (LTDS)	..	..	**1,317**	**563**	**820**	**963**	**824**	**1,046**	**965**	**969**
Public and publicly guaranteed	..	..	**1,317**	**563**	**820**	**921**	**789**	**824**	**628**	**708**
Official creditors	..	..	37	99	270	291	405	454	370	421
Multilateral	..	..	36	47	86	96	257	267	113	124
Concessional	..	..	0	0	0	0	0	0	0	0
Bilateral	..	..	1	52	184	195	148	187	257	298
Concessional	..	..	0	2	4	17	16	14	26	60
Private creditors	..	..	1,280	464	550	630	385	370	258	287
Bonds	..	..	16	259	354	484	337	360	223	284
Commercial banks	..	..	578	205	189	133	42	8	33	1
Other private	..	..	686	0	7	12	5	2	1	1
Private nonguaranteed	..	..	**0**	**0**	**0**	**43**	**34**	**222**	**337**	**261**
Bonds	..	..	0	0	0	0	0	0	0	0
Commercial banks and other	..	..	0	0	0	43	34	222	337	261
Memo:										
IBRD	0	0	0	15	31	43	47	57	64	76
IDA	0	0	0	0	0	0	0	0	0	0
UNDISBURSED DEBT	..	..	**271**	**393**	**783**	**725**	**740**	**590**	**557**	**779**
Official creditors	..	..	25	362	775	718	740	580	545	666
Private creditors	..	..	246	31	8	7	0	10	12	112
Memorandum items										
Concessional LDOD	..	..	77	153	186	179	159	165	212	397
Variable rate LDOD	..	..	7,714	6,661	7,145	7,024	6,786	7,066	7,210	7,220
Public sector LDOD	..	..	9,834	8,371	8,689	8,096	7,617	7,654	7,497	7,513
Private sector LDOD	..	..	0	0	342	413	424	554	691	769

6. CURRENCY COMPOSITION OF LONG-TERM DEBT (PERCENT)

	1970	1980	1990	1994	1995	1996	1997	1998	1999	2000
Deutsche mark	..	..	33.9	6.2	7.1	4.9	4.1	4.4	4.6	3.6
French franc	..	..	0.5	0.5	0.5	0.5	0.4	0.4	0.3	0.2
Japanese yen	..	..	6.6	8.8	8.2	6.5	5.5	4.8	5.0	4.9
Pound sterling	..	..	0.3	0.2	0.2	0.3	0.3	0.3	0.2	0.1
Swiss franc	..	..	7.7	1.1	1.1	1.0	1.0	0.8	0.5	0.3
U.S.dollars	..	..	42.1	72.0	67.0	70.1	75.4	82.8	82.7	83.4
Multiple currency	..	..	2.5	5.0	5.1	5.6	6.1	1.0	1.2	1.3
Special drawing rights	..	..	0.0	0.0	0.0	0.0	0.0	0.0	0.0	0.0
All other currencies	..	..	6.4	6.2	10.8	11.1	7.2	5.5	5.5	6.2

BULGARIA

(US$ million, unless otherwise indicated)

	1970	1980	1990	1994	1995	1996	1997	1998	1999	2000
7. DEBT RESTRUCTURINGS										
Total amount rescheduled	..	..	0	5,306	54	17	0	0	0	0
Debt stock rescheduled	..	..	0	3,420	0	0	0	0	0	0
Principal rescheduled	..	..	0	222	41	0	0	0	0	0
Official	..	..	0	153	36	0	0	0	0	0
Private	..	..	0	69	5	0	0	0	0	0
Interest rescheduled	..	..	0	1,678	10	0	0	0	0	0
Official	..	..	0	57	9	0	0	0	0	0
Private	..	..	0	1,621	1	0	0	0	0	0
Debt forgiven	..	..	0	0	0	5	0	0	2	10
Memo: interest forgiven	..	..	0	0	0	0	0	0	0	0
Debt stock reduction	..	..	0	2,871	0	16	7	0	150	1
of which debt buyback	..	..	0	423	0	0	0	0	30	0
8. DEBT STOCK-FLOW RECONCILIATION										
Total change in debt stocks	..	..	753	-2,430	512	-284	-256	23	68	216
Net flows on debt	..	..	-14	499	-206	-60	26	-96	660	444
Net change in interest arrears	..	..	226	-1,704	-36	41	64	0	-145	-29
Interest capitalized	..	..	0	1,678	10	0	0	0	0	0
Debt forgiveness or reduction	..	..	0	-2,448	0	-21	-7	-8	-122	-12
Cross-currency valuation	..	..	617	639	110	-250	-302	177	-146	-183
Residual	..	..	-77	-1,094	634	6	-37	-52	-180	-4
9. AVERAGE TERMS OF NEW COMMITMENTS										
ALL CREDITORS										
Interest (%)	..	..	9.1	6.6	5.5	6.5	6.2	4.6	5.0	6.1
Maturity (years)	..	..	3.5	13.3	15.4	14.8	15.1	17.4	16.5	16.8
Grace period (years)	..	..	2.4	4.9	5.1	6.0	6.3	4.9	6.5	4.7
Grant element (%)	..	..	2.3	16.6	24.5	20.0	22.5	33.2	29.2	23.2
Official creditors										
Interest (%)	..	..	9.3	6.7	6.0	6.5	6.2	4.5	4.6	5.8
Maturity (years)	..	..	7.2	14.7	17.5	14.8	15.1	17.7	16.5	17.0
Grace period (years)	..	..	3.0	5.7	5.4	6.0	6.3	5.0	4.6	4.7
Grant element (%)	..	..	2.8	18.0	25.0	20.0	22.5	33.9	31.5	24.9
Private creditors										
Interest (%)	..	..	9.1	6.1	3.4	0.0	0.0	5.7	6.2	7.6
Maturity (years)	..	..	3.2	5.3	4.7	0.0	0.0	9.7	16.2	16.0
Grace period (years)	..	..	2.3	0.7	3.2	0.0	0.0	0.9	11.8	4.9
Grant element (%)	..	..	2.3	8.7	21.7	0.0	0.0	15.7	22.8	13.2
Memorandum items										
Commitments	..	..	563	339	635	140	281	246	482	826
Official creditors	..	..	52	288	530	140	281	237	355	701
Private creditors	..	..	511	51	105	0	0	10	128	125

10. CONTRACTUAL OBLIGATIONS ON OUTSTANDING LONG-TERM DEBT

	2001	2002	2003	2004	2005	2006	2007	2008	2009	2010
TOTAL										
Disbursements	182	213	146	100	60	35	20	12	4	3
Principal	581	648	566	561	598	510	625	587	590	572
Interest	476	490	466	444	413	375	342	304	268	229
Official creditors										
Disbursements	127	176	131	93	60	35	20	12	4	3
Principal	428	290	251	210	220	237	234	229	171	104
Interest	142	126	118	109	100	88	74	60	48	38
Bilateral creditors										
Disbursements	20	16	11	6	3	1	1	0	0	0
Principal	288	206	121	106	32	39	27	27	27	26
Interest	49	30	20	14	10	9	7	7	6	5
Multilateral creditors										
Disbursements	107	160	120	86	57	34	19	12	4	3
Principal	140	84	130	104	187	198	207	202	144	79
Interest	94	96	98	95	90	80	67	54	42	33
Private creditors										
Disbursements	54	37	15	7	0	0	0	0	0	0
Principal	153	358	315	351	379	273	391	358	420	467
Interest	334	363	348	335	314	286	268	243	220	191
Commercial banks										
Disbursements	54	37	15	7	0	0	0	0	0	0
Principal	1	1	1	3	14	14	27	12	12	5
Interest	5	8	9	10	10	9	7	6	5	4
Other private										
Disbursements	0	0	0	0	0	0	0	0	0	0
Principal	152	357	314	349	365	259	364	347	408	462
Interest	328	355	338	325	304	278	260	238	215	187

BURKINA FASO

(US$ million, unless otherwise indicated)

	1970	1980	1990	1994	1995	1996	1997	1998	1999	2000
1. SUMMARY DEBT DATA										
TOTAL DEBT STOCKS (EDT)	**21**	**330**	**834**	**1,129**	**1,267**	**1,294**	**1,297**	**1,406**	**1,522**	**1,332**
Long-term debt (LDOD)	**21**	**281**	**750**	**1,040**	**1,136**	**1,160**	**1,139**	**1,234**	**1,298**	**1,135**
Public and publicly guaranteed	21	281	750	1,040	1,136	1,160	1,139	1,234	1,298	1,135
Private nonguaranteed	0	0	0	0	0	0	0	0	0	0
Use of IMF credit	**0**	**15**	**0**	**48**	**75**	**81**	**92**	**112**	**121**	**112**
Short-term debt	**0**	**35**	**84**	**41**	**56**	**53**	**66**	**59**	**103**	**84**
of which interest arrears on LDOD	0	0	21	11	12	10	7	7	6	5
Official creditors	0	0	14	10	11	8	5	5	4	4
Private creditors	0	0	7	1	1	2	2	2	2	2
Memo: principal arrears on LDOD	0	0	64	36	37	38	33	39	39	40
Official creditors	0	0	34	34	35	35	30	35	35	37
Private creditors	0	0	30	2	3	3	3	4	3	3
Memo: export credits	0	0	200	65	98	83	86	70	65	44
TOTAL DEBT FLOWS										
Disbursements	**2**	**70**	**79**	**132**	**139**	**113**	**89**	**106**	**122**	**89**
Long-term debt	2	65	79	107	112	103	71	88	105	81
IMF purchases	1	4	0	25	27	10	18	18	17	7
Principal repayments	**2**	**11**	**19**	**27**	**29**	**31**	**33**	**35**	**42**	**39**
Long-term debt	2	11	18	27	29	30	32	32	37	29
IMF repurchases	0	0	1	0	0	1	2	3	5	10
Net flows on debt	**1**	**56**	**70**	**117**	**124**	**81**	**71**	**64**	**126**	**31**
of which short-term debt	0	-3	10	12	14	0	15	-7	46	-19
Interest payments (INT)	**0**	**12**	**16**	**17**	**20**	**17**	**18**	**18**	**19**	**16**
Long-term debt	0	6	10	15	17	15	15	15	16	14
IMF charges	0	0	0	0	0	1	0	1	1	1
Short-term debt	0	5	6	2	2	2	3	3	3	1
Net transfers on debt	**0**	**45**	**54**	**100**	**104**	**64**	**53**	**46**	**106**	**15**
Total debt service paid (TDS)	**2**	**22**	**34**	**44**	**49**	**49**	**52**	**53**	**61**	**55**
Long-term debt	2	17	28	42	46	45	47	47	52	43
IMF repurchases and charges	0	0	1	0	0	2	2	3	6	10
Short-term debt (interest only)	0	5	6	2	2	2	3	3	3	1
2. AGGREGATE NET RESOURCE FLOWS AND NET TRANSFERS (LONG-TERM)										
NET RESOURCE FLOWS	**13**	**142**	**218**	**310**	**335**	**325**	**262**	**280**	**307**	**437**
Net flow of long-term debt (ex. IMF)	0	55	61	80	83	73	39	56	68	52
Foreign direct investment (net)	0	0	0	18	10	17	13	10	13	10
Portfolio equity flows	0	0	0	0	0	0	0	0	0	0
Grants (excluding technical coop.)	13	88	158	212	242	235	210	214	226	375
Memo: technical coop. grants	8	73	112	111	123	117	95	91	80	77
official net resource flows	13	138	219	292	325	308	249	270	294	427
private net resource flows	0	4	-1	18	10	17	13	10	13	10
NET TRANSFERS	**11**	**128**	**209**	**295**	**317**	**310**	**247**	**265**	**292**	**423**
Interest on long-term debt	0	6	10	15	17	15	15	15	16	14
Profit remittances on FDI	2	9	0	0	0	0	0	0	0	0
Memo: official net transfers	13	135	209	277	307	293	234	255	279	413
private net transfers	-1	-7	-1	18	10	17	13	10	13	10
3. MAJOR ECONOMIC AGGREGATES										
Gross national income (GNI)	421	1,698	2,757	1,739	2,172	2,469	2,274	2,473	2,447	2,172
Exports of goods & services (XGS)	..	376	506	361	434	420	380	487	393	316
of which workers remittances	..	150	140	80	89	89	71	75	66	46
Imports of goods & services (MGS)	..	596	776	521	691	762	694	832	763	684
International reserves (RES)	36	75	305	241	352	343	348	377	298	244
Current account balance	..	-49	-77	15	-81	-232	-27	-34	-40	-65
4. DEBT INDICATORS										
EDT / XGS (%)	..	88.0	164.6	312.6	292.1	308.4	341.0	288.5	387.8	421.8
EDT / GNI (%)	4.9	19.5	30.2	64.9	58.3	52.4	57.1	56.8	62.2	61.3
TDS / XGS (%)	..	5.9	6.8	12.1	11.2	11.6	13.5	10.9	15.5	17.3
INT / XGS (%)	..	3.1	3.1	4.6	4.5	4.2	4.8	3.8	4.8	4.9
INT / GNI (%)	0.1	0.7	0.6	1.0	0.9	0.7	0.8	0.7	0.8	0.7
RES / EDT (%)	174.8	22.6	36.6	21.4	27.8	26.5	26.8	26.8	19.6	18.3
RES / MGS (months)	..	1.5	4.7	5.6	6.1	5.4	6.0	5.4	4.7	4.3
Short-term / EDT (%)	0.0	10.6	10.1	3.6	4.4	4.1	5.1	4.2	6.8	6.3
Concessional / EDT (%)	84.1	67.0	71.6	80.2	79.0	83.9	83.1	83.6	82.3	82.4
Multilateral / EDT (%)	0.0	42.9	67.7	78.1	77.7	78.9	77.3	78.2	75.2	72.8

BURKINA FASO

(US$ million, unless otherwise indicated)

	1970	1980	1990	1994	1995	1996	1997	1998	1999	2000
5. LONG-TERM DEBT										
DEBT OUTSTANDING (LDOD)	**21**	**281**	**750**	**1,040**	**1,136**	**1,160**	**1,139**	**1,234**	**1,298**	**1,135**
Public and publicly guaranteed	**21**	**281**	**750**	**1,040**	**1,136**	**1,160**	**1,139**	**1,234**	**1,298**	**1,135**
Official creditors	21	261	712	1,036	1,131	1,155	1,135	1,230	1,295	1,132
Multilateral	0	142	565	881	984	1,021	1,003	1,100	1,144	969
Concessional	0	133	460	810	916	960	953	1,053	1,106	939
Bilateral	21	119	147	154	147	134	132	130	151	163
Concessional	18	89	138	96	86	125	124	122	146	159
Private creditors	0	20	38	4	5	4	4	4	4	3
Bonds	0	0	0	0	0	0	0	0	0	0
Commercial banks	0	1	1	0	0	0	0	0	0	0
Other private	0	19	37	4	5	4	4	4	3	3
Private nonguaranteed	**0**	**0**	**0**	**0**	**0**	**0**	**0**	**0**	**0**	**0**
Bonds	0	0	0	0	0	0	0	0	0	0
Commercial banks and other	0	0	0	0	0	0	0	0	0	0
Memo:										
IBRD	0	0	0	0	0	0	0	0	0	0
IDA	0	77	282	518	608	636	636	710	753	593
DISBURSEMENTS	**2**	**65**	**79**	**107**	**112**	**103**	**71**	**88**	**105**	**81**
Public and publicly guaranteed	**2**	**65**	**79**	**107**	**112**	**103**	**71**	**88**	**105**	**81**
Official creditors	2	59	79	107	112	103	71	88	105	81
Multilateral	0	26	45	100	106	90	66	86	89	66
Concessional	0	22	34	98	104	89	65	85	89	65
Bilateral	2	33	34	7	6	13	5	2	16	16
Concessional	1	19	34	7	6	13	5	2	16	16
Private creditors	0	6	0	0	0	0	0	0	0	0
Bonds	0	0	0	0	0	0	0	0	0	0
Commercial banks	0	0	0	0	0	0	0	0	0	0
Other private	0	6	0	0	0	0	0	0	0	0
Private nonguaranteed	**0**	**0**	**0**	**0**	**0**	**0**	**0**	**0**	**0**	**0**
Bonds	0	0	0	0	0	0	0	0	0	0
Commercial banks and other	0	0	0	0	0	0	0	0	0	0
Memo:										
IBRD	0	0	0	0	0	0	0	0	0	0
IDA	0	12	15	79	85	50	35	58	63	38
PRINCIPAL REPAYMENTS	**2**	**11**	**18**	**27**	**29**	**30**	**32**	**32**	**37**	**29**
Public and publicly guaranteed	**2**	**11**	**18**	**27**	**29**	**30**	**32**	**32**	**37**	**29**
Official creditors	2	8	18	27	29	30	32	32	37	29
Multilateral	0	3	13	25	24	25	26	27	29	25
Concessional	0	2	10	17	16	20	21	22	24	20
Bilateral	2	5	4	2	5	5	5	5	8	5
Concessional	1	3	3	1	4	4	4	5	5	5
Private creditors	0	2	1	0	0	0	0	0	0	0
Bonds	0	0	0	0	0	0	0	0	0	0
Commercial banks	0	0	0	0	0	0	0	0	0	0
Other private	0	2	1	0	0	0	0	0	0	0
Private nonguaranteed	**0**	**0**	**0**	**0**	**0**	**0**	**0**	**0**	**0**	**0**
Bonds	0	0	0	0	0	0	0	0	0	0
Commercial banks and other	0	0	0	0	0	0	0	0	0	0
Memo:										
IBRD	0	0	0	0	0	0	0	0	0	0
IDA	0	0	1	3	4	4	4	6	6	2
NET FLOWS ON DEBT	**0**	**55**	**61**	**80**	**83**	**73**	**39**	**56**	**68**	**52**
Public and publicly guaranteed	**0**	**55**	**61**	**80**	**83**	**73**	**39**	**56**	**68**	**52**
Official creditors	0	51	61	80	83	73	39	56	68	52
Multilateral	0	23	32	75	82	65	40	59	60	41
Concessional	0	21	24	81	88	70	45	64	65	46
Bilateral	0	28	29	5	1	7	-1	-3	8	11
Concessional	1	16	31	6	2	9	0	-3	12	11
Private creditors	0	4	-1	0	0	0	0	0	0	0
Bonds	0	0	0	0	0	0	0	0	0	0
Commercial banks	0	0	0	0	0	0	0	0	0	0
Other private	0	4	-1	0	0	0	0	0	0	0
Private nonguaranteed	**0**	**0**	**0**	**0**	**0**	**0**	**0**	**0**	**0**	**0**
Bonds	0	0	0	0	0	0	0	0	0	0
Commercial banks and other	0	0	0	0	0	0	0	0	0	0
Memo:										
IBRD	0	0	0	0	0	0	0	0	0	0
IDA	0	12	14	76	81	46	30	53	57	35

BURKINA FASO

(US$ million, unless otherwise indicated)

	1970	1980	1990	1994	1995	1996	1997	1998	1999	2000
INTEREST PAYMENTS (LINT)	**0**	**6**	**10**	**15**	**17**	**15**	**15**	**15**	**16**	**14**
Public and publicly guaranteed	**0**	**6**	**10**	**15**	**17**	**15**	**15**	**15**	**16**	**14**
Official creditors	0	4	10	15	17	15	15	15	16	14
Multilateral	0	2	7	11	11	13	12	12	12	12
Concessional	0	1	4	6	7	10	9	9	10	10
Bilateral	0	2	3	4	6	2	4	3	4	2
Concessional	0	1	3	1	1	1	3	3	4	2
Private creditors	0	3	0	0	0	0	0	0	0	0
Bonds	0	0	0	0	0	0	0	0	0	0
Commercial banks	0	0	0	0	0	0	0	0	0	0
Other private	0	2	0	0	0	0	0	0	0	0
Private nonguaranteed	**0**	**0**	**0**	**0**	**0**	**0**	**0**	**0**	**0**	**0**
Bonds	0	0	0	0	0	0	0	0	0	0
Commercial banks and other	0	0	0	0	0	0	0	0	0	0
Memo:										
IBRD	0	0	0	0	0	0	0	0	0	0
IDA	0	1	2	3	4	5	5	5	5	6
NET TRANSFERS ON DEBT	**-1**	**49**	**51**	**65**	**65**	**58**	**24**	**41**	**53**	**38**
Public and publicly guaranteed	**-1**	**49**	**51**	**65**	**65**	**58**	**24**	**41**	**53**	**38**
Official creditors	0	47	51	65	65	58	24	41	53	38
Multilateral	0	22	25	64	70	52	29	47	48	29
Concessional	0	20	20	75	81	60	36	55	55	36
Bilateral	0	26	27	1	-5	6	-4	-6	5	9
Concessional	0	16	28	5	1	8	-3	-6	8	9
Private creditors	0	1	-1	0	0	0	0	0	0	0
Bonds	0	0	0	0	0	0	0	0	0	0
Commercial banks	0	0	0	0	0	0	0	0	0	0
Other private	0	2	-1	0	0	0	0	0	0	0
Private nonguaranteed	**0**	**0**	**0**	**0**	**0**	**0**	**0**	**0**	**0**	**0**
Bonds	0	0	0	0	0	0	0	0	0	0
Commercial banks and other	0	0	0	0	0	0	0	0	0	0
Memo:										
IBRD	0	0	0	0	0	0	0	0	0	0
IDA	0	11	12	73	77	42	26	48	52	30
DEBT SERVICE (LTDS)	**2**	**17**	**28**	**42**	**46**	**45**	**47**	**47**	**52**	**43**
Public and publicly guaranteed	**2**	**17**	**28**	**42**	**46**	**45**	**47**	**47**	**52**	**43**
Official creditors	2	12	28	42	46	45	47	47	52	43
Multilateral	0	5	21	36	36	38	38	39	41	36
Concessional	0	3	14	23	23	29	30	31	34	29
Bilateral	2	7	7	5	11	7	9	8	11	7
Concessional	1	3	6	1	5	5	8	8	8	7
Private creditors	0	5	1	0	0	0	0	0	0	0
Bonds	0	0	0	0	0	0	0	0	0	0
Commercial banks	0	0	0	0	0	0	0	0	0	0
Other private	0	5	1	0	0	0	0	0	0	0
Private nonguaranteed	**0**	**0**	**0**	**0**	**0**	**0**	**0**	**0**	**0**	**0**
Bonds	0	0	0	0	0	0	0	0	0	0
Commercial banks and other	0	0	0	0	0	0	0	0	0	0
Memo:										
IBRD	0	0	0	0	0	0	0	0	0	0
IDA	0	1	3	6	8	9	9	11	11	8
UNDISBURSED DEBT	**10**	**218**	**540**	**540**	**463**	**366**	**411**	**451**	**435**	**390**
Official creditors	9	214	525	525	448	351	398	437	435	390
Private creditors	1	4	15	14	16	15	13	14	0	0
Memorandum items										
Concessional LDOD	18	221	597	906	1,001	1,085	1,077	1,175	1,252	1,098
Variable rate LDOD	0	12	2	6	7	0	0	0	0	0
Public sector LDOD	21	276	749	1,040	1,136	1,160	1,139	1,234	1,298	1,135
Private sector LDOD	0	5	1	0	0	0	0	0	0	0

6. CURRENCY COMPOSITION OF LONG-TERM DEBT (PERCENT)

	1970	1980	1990	1994	1995	1996	1997	1998	1999	2000
Deutsche mark	10.0	12.1	0.0	0.1	0.1	0.1	0.1	0.1	0.1	0.1
French franc	32.6	31.3	16.6	7.0	6.5	3.6	3.5	3.2	3.9	2.7
Japanese yen	0.0	0.0	0.0	0.0	0.0	0.0	0.0	0.0	0.0	0.0
Pound sterling	20.2	0.7	0.5	0.4	0.3	0.0	0.0	0.0	0.0	0.0
Swiss franc	0.0	0.0	0.0	0.0	0.0	0.0	0.0	0.0	0.0	0.0
U.S.dollars	0.0	28.8	39.2	52.8	56.0	61.0	62.4	63.7	64.8	62.3
Multiple currency	0.0	8.9	15.3	19.2	18.8	19.2	19.1	19.4	18.7	20.3
Special drawing rights	0.0	0.0	2.1	2.3	2.2	2.1	2.0	1.7	1.6	1.5
All other currencies	37.2	18.2	26.3	18.2	16.1	14.0	12.9	11.9	10.9	13.1

BURKINA FASO

(US$ million, unless otherwise indicated)

	1970	1980	1990	1994	1995	1996	1997	1998	1999	2000
7. DEBT RESTRUCTURINGS										
Total amount rescheduled	..	..	0	0	0	44	1	0	14	13
Debt stock rescheduled	..	..	0	0	0	44	0	0	0	12
Principal rescheduled	..	..	0	0	0	0	0	0	0	0
Official	..	..	0	0	0	0	0	0	0	0
Private	..	..	0	0	0	0	0	0	0	0
Interest rescheduled	..	..	0	0	0	0	0	0	0	1
Official	..	..	0	0	0	0	0	0	0	1
Private	..	..	0	0	0	0	0	0	0	0
Debt forgiven	..	..	5	123	15	3	1	1	0	0
Memo: interest forgiven	..	..	0	0	0	0	0	0	0	1
Debt stock reduction	..	..	0	0	0	16	0	0	0	161
of which debt buyback	..	..	0	0	0	0	0	0	0	92
8. DEBT STOCK-FLOW RECONCILIATION										
Total change in debt stocks	..	..	116	12	138	27	3	108	117	-190
Net flows on debt	1	56	70	117	124	81	71	64	126	31
Net change in interest arrears	..	..	6	-1	1	-2	-3	1	-2	0
Interest capitalized	..	..	0	0	0	0	0	0	0	1
Debt forgiveness or reduction	..	..	-5	-123	-15	-18	-1	-1	0	-69
Cross-currency valuation	..	..	27	1	-21	-114	-146	-63	-33	-222
Residual	..	..	19	18	49	81	81	107	26	69
9. AVERAGE TERMS OF NEW COMMITMENTS										
ALL CREDITORS										
Interest (%)	2.3	4.3	2.5	0.9	0.8	1.2	0.7	2.8	1.0	1.4
Maturity (years)	36.3	21.5	27.6	38.0	39.9	31.6	41.6	21.8	32.7	37.1
Grace period (years)	8.1	6.5	8.7	9.8	10.4	8.5	10.1	5.9	8.8	7.8
Grant element (%)	61.9	37.8	59.1	78.4	80.8	70.3	81.1	48.9	72.3	70.2
Official creditors										
Interest (%)	1.7	4.0	2.5	0.9	0.8	1.2	0.7	2.8	1.0	1.4
Maturity (years)	40.6	23.0	27.6	38.0	39.9	31.6	41.6	21.8	32.7	37.1
Grace period (years)	8.9	7.0	8.7	9.8	10.4	8.5	10.1	5.9	8.8	7.8
Grant element (%)	69.4	40.9	59.1	78.4	80.8	70.3	81.1	48.9	72.3	70.2
Private creditors										
Interest (%)	6.8	7.3	0.0	0.0	0.0	0.0	0.0	0.0	0.0	0.0
Maturity (years)	7.2	5.6	0.0	0.0	0.0	0.0	0.0	0.0	0.0	0.0
Grace period (years)	2.8	1.1	0.0	0.0	0.0	0.0	0.0	0.0	0.0	0.0
Grant element (%)	11.3	6.6	0.0	0.0	0.0	0.0	0.0	0.0	0.0	0.0
Memorandum items										
Commitments	9	115	90	100	37	24	141	118	119	54
Official creditors	8	104	90	100	37	24	141	118	119	54
Private creditors	1	10	0	0	0	0	0	0	0	0

10. CONTRACTUAL OBLIGATIONS ON OUTSTANDING LONG-TERM DEBT

	2001	2002	2003	2004	2005	2006	2007	2008	2009	2010
TOTAL										
Disbursements	103	106	73	47	28	16	10	4	2	0
Principal	31	34	37	41	43	44	46	47	49	49
Interest	13	14	15	15	15	14	14	13	12	12
Official creditors										
Disbursements	103	106	73	47	28	16	10	4	2	0
Principal	31	34	37	41	43	44	46	47	49	49
Interest	13	14	15	15	15	14	14	13	12	12
Bilateral creditors										
Disbursements	16	23	16	11	7	4	2	1	0	0
Principal	7	7	9	9	11	11	11	11	13	12
Interest	4	4	4	4	4	4	4	4	3	3
Multilateral creditors										
Disbursements	87	84	57	37	21	13	8	3	1	0
Principal	24	27	29	32	33	33	35	37	37	37
Interest	10	10	11	11	11	10	10	10	9	9
Private creditors										
Disbursements	0	0	0	0	0	0	0	0	0	0
Principal	0	0	0	0	0	0	0	0	0	0
Interest	0	0	0	0	0	0	0	0	0	0
Commercial banks										
Disbursements	0	0	0	0	0	0	0	0	0	0
Principal	0	0	0	0	0	0	0	0	0	0
Interest	0	0	0	0	0	0	0	0	0	0
Other private										
Disbursements	0	0	0	0	0	0	0	0	0	0
Principal	0	0	0	0	0	0	0	0	0	0
Interest	0	0	0	0	0	0	0	0	0	0

BURUNDI

(US$ million, unless otherwise indicated)

	1970	1980	1990	1994	1995	1996	1997	1998	1999	2000
1. SUMMARY DEBT DATA										
TOTAL DEBT STOCKS (EDT)	**15**	**166**	**907**	**1,123**	**1,158**	**1,127**	**1,066**	**1,119**	**1,131**	**1,100**
Long-term debt (LDOD)	**7**	**118**	**851**	**1,062**	**1,095**	**1,081**	**1,022**	**1,079**	**1,050**	**1,028**
Public and publicly guaranteed	7	118	851	1,062	1,095	1,081	1,022	1,079	1,050	1,028
Private nonguaranteed	0	0	0	0	0	0	0	0	0	0
Use of IMF credit	**8**	**36**	**43**	**56**	**48**	**38**	**28**	**20**	**12**	**7**
Short-term debt	**0**	**12**	**13**	**6**	**15**	**8**	**16**	**20**	**70**	**65**
of which interest arrears on LDOD	0	0	0	1	2	5	9	12	15	20
Official creditors	0	0	0	1	2	5	9	12	15	20
Private creditors	0	0	0	0	0	0	0	0	0	0
Memo: principal arrears on LDOD	0	0	0	12	3	15	27	44	63	82
Official creditors	0	0	0	12	3	15	27	44	62	82
Private creditors	0	0	0	0	0	0	0	0	1	1
Memo: export credits	0	0	15	5	2	0	0	0	0	0
TOTAL DEBT FLOWS										
Disbursements	**4**	**45**	**96**	**53**	**45**	**35**	**19**	**31**	**20**	**36**
Long-term debt	1	39	96	53	45	35	19	31	20	36
IMF purchases	3	6	0	0	0	0	0	0	0	0
Principal repayments	**1**	**4**	**28**	**28**	**27**	**21**	**20**	**21**	**21**	**14**
Long-term debt	0	4	28	22	18	12	12	13	14	9
IMF repurchases	0	0	1	6	9	9	8	9	7	5
Net flows on debt	**3**	**40**	**65**	**25**	**26**	**4**	**3**	**10**	**46**	**14**
of which short-term debt	0	-1	-3	1	8	-10	4	1	47	-9
Interest payments (INT)	**0**	**4**	**14**	**13**	**12**	**10**	**9**	**9**	**8**	**8**
Long-term debt	0	2	12	12	11	9	9	8	6	4
IMF charges	0	1	0	0	0	0	0	0	0	0
Short-term debt	0	2	2	1	1	0	0	1	2	3
Net transfers on debt	**3**	**36**	**51**	**12**	**15**	**-5**	**-6**	**1**	**38**	**6**
Total debt service paid (TDS)	**1**	**9**	**42**	**41**	**39**	**31**	**29**	**30**	**29**	**21**
Long-term debt	1	6	40	34	29	21	21	21	20	14
IMF repurchases and charges	0	1	1	6	9	9	8	9	7	5
Short-term debt (interest only)	0	2	2	1	1	0	0	1	2	3
2. AGGREGATE NET RESOURCE FLOWS AND NET TRANSFERS (LONG-TERM)										
NET RESOURCE FLOWS	**8**	**74**	**204**	**274**	**258**	**95**	**53**	**71**	**66**	**98**
Net flow of long-term debt (ex. IMF)	1	35	68	31	27	23	7	18	6	27
Foreign direct investment (net)	0	0	1	0	2	0	0	2	0	12
Portfolio equity flows	0	0	0	0	0	0	0	0	0	0
Grants (excluding technical coop.)	7	39	135	243	229	72	46	51	60	59
Memo: technical coop. grants	11	45	60	49	44	30	19	13	21	15
official net resource flows	8	76	209	275	257	96	53	68	66	87
private net resource flows	0	-3	-5	-1	1	-1	0	3	0	12
NET TRANSFERS	**7**	**72**	**189**	**258**	**244**	**84**	**43**	**62**	**60**	**94**
Interest on long-term debt	0	2	12	12	11	9	9	8	6	4
Profit remittances on FDI	0	0	3	3	3	2	1	1	0	0
Memo: official net transfers	7	76	198	262	246	87	44	60	60	82
private net transfers	0	-4	-9	-4	-2	-3	-1	2	0	12
3. MAJOR ECONOMIC AGGREGATES										
Gross national income (GNI)	235	922	1,117	914	988	886	945	870	703	674
Exports of goods & services (XGS)	..	..	98	104	140	57	100	75	63	58
of which workers remittances	..	..	0	0	0	0	0	0	0	..
Imports of goods & services (MGS)	..	..	341	286	282	159	158	185	141	166
International reserves (RES)	15	105	112	211	216	146	118	70	53	38
Current account balance	..	..	-69	-17	10	-40	-1	-54	-27	-49
4. DEBT INDICATORS										
EDT / XGS (%)	..	..	928.6	1,083.4	828.5	1,964.7	1,060.6	1,486.8	1,791.9	1,910.9
EDT / GNI (%)	6.4	18.0	81.2	122.9	117.2	127.1	112.8	128.7	161.0	163.3
TDS / XGS (%)	..	..	43.4	39.5	27.6	53.4	29.0	40.1	45.6	37.2
INT / XGS (%)	..	..	14.4	12.6	8.5	16.7	9.0	11.7	12.5	13.6
INT / GNI (%)	0.1	0.5	1.3	1.4	1.2	1.1	1.0	1.0	1.1	1.2
RES / EDT (%)	102.6	63.2	12.3	18.8	18.7	13.0	11.1	6.3	4.7	3.4
RES / MGS (months)	..	..	3.9	8.9	9.2	11.0	9.0	4.6	4.5	2.7
Short-term / EDT (%)	0.0	7.2	1.5	0.5	1.3	0.8	1.5	1.8	6.2	5.9
Concessional / EDT (%)	16.0	62.6	85.9	90.1	90.4	92.3	92.8	93.7	90.4	91.2
Multilateral / EDT (%)	30.0	35.7	72.8	78.4	80.0	81.8	81.9	82.3	79.4	80.5

BURUNDI

(US$ million, unless otherwise indicated)

	1970	1980	1990	1994	1995	1996	1997	1998	1999	2000
5. LONG-TERM DEBT										
DEBT OUTSTANDING (LDOD)	**7**	**118**	**851**	**1,062**	**1,095**	**1,081**	**1,022**	**1,079**	**1,050**	**1,028**
Public and publicly guaranteed	**7**	**118**	**851**	**1,062**	**1,095**	**1,081**	**1,022**	**1,079**	**1,050**	**1,028**
Official creditors	6	110	842	1,060	1,093	1,080	1,021	1,078	1,049	1,027
Multilateral	5	59	660	881	926	921	872	921	899	885
Concessional	1	55	597	833	880	882	840	891	873	861
Bilateral	1	51	182	179	167	159	149	157	150	142
Concessional	1	49	182	179	167	159	149	157	150	142
Private creditors	2	8	9	2	2	1	1	1	1	1
Bonds	0	0	0	0	0	0	0	0	0	0
Commercial banks	0	5	1	0	0	0	0	0	0	0
Other private	1	4	8	2	2	1	1	1	1	1
Private nonguaranteed	**0**	**0**	**0**	**0**	**0**	**0**	**0**	**0**	**0**	**0**
Bonds	0	0	0	0	0	0	0	0	0	0
Commercial banks and other	0	0	0	0	0	0	0	0	0	0
Memo:										
IBRD	3	0	0	0	0	0	0	0	0	0
IDA	1	37	398	556	591	588	567	603	599	601
DISBURSEMENTS	**1**	**39**	**96**	**53**	**45**	**35**	**19**	**31**	**20**	**36**
Public and publicly guaranteed	**1**	**39**	**96**	**53**	**45**	**35**	**19**	**31**	**20**	**36**
Official creditors	1	39	93	53	45	35	19	30	20	36
Multilateral	1	21	64	48	41	34	16	30	20	36
Concessional	0	20	60	47	40	33	16	30	20	36
Bilateral	0	18	30	5	4	1	3	0	0	0
Concessional	0	18	30	5	4	1	3	0	0	0
Private creditors	0	0	2	0	0	0	0	1	0	0
Bonds	0	0	0	0	0	0	0	0	0	0
Commercial banks	0	0	0	0	0	0	0	0	0	0
Other private	0	0	2	0	0	0	0	1	0	0
Private nonguaranteed	**0**	**0**	**0**	**0**	**0**	**0**	**0**	**0**	**0**	**0**
Bonds	0	0	0	0	0	0	0	0	0	0
Commercial banks and other	0	0	0	0	0	0	0	0	0	0
Memo:										
IBRD	0	0	0	0	0	0	0	0	0	0
IDA	0	12	49	28	27	17	12	24	15	36
PRINCIPAL REPAYMENTS	**0**	**4**	**28**	**22**	**18**	**12**	**12**	**13**	**14**	**9**
Public and publicly guaranteed	**0**	**4**	**28**	**22**	**18**	**12**	**12**	**13**	**14**	**9**
Official creditors	0	1	19	21	17	12	12	13	14	9
Multilateral	0	0	11	15	12	11	12	12	13	9
Concessional	0	0	6	10	8	5	8	8	11	9
Bilateral	0	1	8	6	5	1	0	0	0	0
Concessional	0	1	8	6	5	1	0	0	0	0
Private creditors	0	3	8	1	1	1	0	0	0	0
Bonds	0	0	0	0	0	0	0	0	0	0
Commercial banks	0	2	5	0	0	0	0	0	0	0
Other private	0	1	3	1	1	1	0	0	0	0
Private nonguaranteed	**0**	**0**	**0**	**0**	**0**	**0**	**0**	**0**	**0**	**0**
Bonds	0	0	0	0	0	0	0	0	0	0
Commercial banks and other	0	0	0	0	0	0	0	0	0	0
Memo:										
IBRD	0	0	0	0	0	0	0	0	0	0
IDA	0	0	1	2	3	3	4	6	8	9
NET FLOWS ON DEBT	**1**	**35**	**68**	**31**	**27**	**23**	**7**	**18**	**6**	**27**
Public and publicly guaranteed	**1**	**35**	**68**	**31**	**27**	**23**	**7**	**18**	**6**	**27**
Official creditors	1	38	74	32	28	23	7	17	6	27
Multilateral	1	20	52	33	29	23	4	18	7	27
Concessional	0	20	55	37	32	28	8	22	9	27
Bilateral	0	17	22	-1	-1	1	3	0	0	0
Concessional	0	17	22	-1	-1	1	3	0	0	0
Private creditors	0	-3	-6	-1	-1	-1	0	1	0	0
Bonds	0	0	0	0	0	0	0	0	0	0
Commercial banks	0	-1	-5	0	0	0	0	0	0	0
Other private	0	-1	-1	-1	-1	-1	0	1	0	0
Private nonguaranteed	**0**	**0**	**0**	**0**	**0**	**0**	**0**	**0**	**0**	**0**
Bonds	0	0	0	0	0	0	0	0	0	0
Commercial banks and other	0	0	0	0	0	0	0	0	0	0
Memo:										
IBRD	0	0	0	0	0	0	0	0	0	0
IDA	0	12	48	26	24	14	7	19	8	28

BURUNDI

(US$ million, unless otherwise indicated)

	1970	1980	1990	1994	1995	1996	1997	1998	1999	2000
INTEREST PAYMENTS (LINT)	**0**	**2**	**12**	**12**	**11**	**9**	**9**	**8**	**6**	**4**
Public and publicly guaranteed	**0**	**2**	**12**	**12**	**11**	**9**	**9**	**8**	**6**	**4**
Official creditors	0	1	11	12	11	9	9	8	6	4
Multilateral	0	1	9	9	9	9	9	7	6	4
Concessional	0	0	5	6	6	6	7	6	6	4
Bilateral	0	0	2	3	2	0	0	1	0	0
Concessional	0	0	2	3	2	0	0	1	0	0
Private creditors	0	1	1	0	0	0	0	0	0	0
Bonds	0	0	0	0	0	0	0	0	0	0
Commercial banks	0	1	1	0	0	0	0	0	0	0
Other private	0	0	1	0	0	0	0	0	0	0
Private nonguaranteed	**0**	**0**	**0**	**0**	**0**	**0**	**0**	**0**	**0**	**0**
Bonds	0	0	0	0	0	0	0	0	0	0
Commercial banks and other	0	0	0	0	0	0	0	0	0	0
Memo:										
IBRD	0	0	0	0	0	0	0	0	0	0
IDA	0	0	3	4	5	4	5	4	5	4
NET TRANSFERS ON DEBT	**1**	**33**	**56**	**19**	**16**	**14**	**-2**	**10**	**0**	**23**
Public and publicly guaranteed	**1**	**33**	**56**	**19**	**16**	**14**	**-2**	**10**	**0**	**23**
Official creditors	1	37	63	19	17	15	-2	10	0	23
Multilateral	1	20	43	24	20	14	-5	11	0	23
Concessional	0	20	50	31	26	22	1	16	3	23
Bilateral	0	17	20	-5	-3	1	3	-1	0	0
Concessional	0	17	20	-5	-3	1	3	-1	0	0
Private creditors	0	-4	-7	-1	-1	-1	0	1	0	0
Bonds	0	0	0	0	0	0	0	0	0	0
Commercial banks	0	-2	-6	0	0	0	0	0	0	0
Other private	0	-2	-1	-1	-1	-1	0	1	0	0
Private nonguaranteed	**0**	**0**	**0**	**0**	**0**	**0**	**0**	**0**	**0**	**0**
Bonds	0	0	0	0	0	0	0	0	0	0
Commercial banks and other	0	0	0	0	0	0	0	0	0	0
Memo:										
IBRD	0	0	0	0	0	0	0	0	0	0
IDA	0	11	45	21	20	10	3	15	3	23
DEBT SERVICE (LTDS)	**1**	**6**	**40**	**34**	**29**	**21**	**21**	**21**	**20**	**14**
Public and publicly guaranteed	**1**	**6**	**40**	**34**	**29**	**21**	**21**	**21**	**20**	**14**
Official creditors	1	2	30	33	28	21	21	21	20	14
Multilateral	1	1	20	24	20	20	21	19	20	14
Concessional	0	0	10	16	15	11	15	14	17	14
Bilateral	0	1	10	9	8	1	0	1	0	0
Concessional	0	1	10	9	8	1	0	1	0	0
Private creditors	0	4	9	1	1	1	0	0	0	0
Bonds	0	0	0	0	0	0	0	0	0	0
Commercial banks	0	2	6	0	0	0	0	0	0	0
Other private	0	2	4	1	1	1	0	0	0	0
Private nonguaranteed	**0**	**0**	**0**	**0**	**0**	**0**	**0**	**0**	**0**	**0**
Bonds	0	0	0	0	0	0	0	0	0	0
Commercial banks and other	0	0	0	0	0	0	0	0	0	0
Memo:										
IBRD	0	0	0	0	0	0	0	0	0	0
IDA	0	0	4	6	8	7	9	10	12	13
UNDISBURSED DEBT	**2**	**184**	**457**	**369**	**311**	**232**	**145**	**119**	**121**	**77**
Official creditors	2	184	457	368	311	232	145	119	86	77
Private creditors	0	0	0	0	0	0	0	0	35	0
Memorandum items										
Concessional LDOD	2	104	779	1,012	1,047	1,041	989	1,048	1,023	1,003
Variable rate LDOD	0	0	0	0	0	0	0	0	0	0
Public sector LDOD	6	117	849	1,062	1,095	1,081	1,022	1,079	1,050	1,028
Private sector LDOD	2	1	2	0	0	0	0	0	0	0

6. CURRENCY COMPOSITION OF LONG-TERM DEBT (PERCENT)

	1970	1980	1990	1994	1995	1996	1997	1998	1999	2000
Deutsche mark	17.8	1.8	0.5	0.1	0.1	0.1	0.1	0.1	0.0	0.0
French franc	0.0	1.1	4.4	5.8	6.1	5.8	5.3	5.4	4.7	4.5
Japanese yen	0.0	0.0	2.0	3.1	2.9	2.6	2.5	2.6	3.1	2.8
Pound sterling	0.0	0.0	0.0	0.0	0.0	0.0	0.0	0.0	0.0	0.0
Swiss franc	0.0	0.0	0.0	0.0	0.0	0.0	0.0	0.0	0.0	0.0
U.S.dollars	15.7	34.4	50.3	53.5	54.9	55.3	56.4	56.9	57.9	59.3
Multiple currency	34.6	16.1	21.6	22.0	22.4	22.9	22.3	21.7	21.4	20.8
Special drawing rights	0.0	0.0	2.8	2.3	2.0	1.9	1.8	1.8	1.7	1.6
All other currencies	31.9	46.6	18.4	13.2	11.6	11.4	11.6	11.5	11.2	11.0

BURUNDI

(US$ million, unless otherwise indicated)

	1970	1980	1990	1994	1995	1996	1997	1998	1999	2000
7. DEBT RESTRUCTURINGS										
Total amount rescheduled	..	..	0	0	0	0	0	0	0	0
Debt stock rescheduled	..	..	0	0	0	0	0	0	0	0
Principal rescheduled	..	..	0	0	0	0	0	0	0	0
Official	..	..	0	0	0	0	0	0	0	0
Private	..	..	0	0	0	0	0	0	0	0
Interest rescheduled	..	..	0	0	0	0	0	0	0	0
Official	..	..	0	0	0	0	0	0	0	0
Private	..	..	0	0	0	0	0	0	0	0
Debt forgiven	..	..	105	0	16	0	0	0	0	0
Memo: interest forgiven	..	..	1	0	1	0	0	0	0	0
Debt stock reduction	..	..	0	0	0	0	0	0	0	0
of which debt buyback	..	..	0	0	0	0	0	0	0	0
8. DEBT STOCK-FLOW RECONCILIATION										
Total change in debt stocks	..	..	18	62	35	-31	-62	53	13	-31
Net flows on debt	3	40	65	25	26	4	3	10	46	14
Net change in interest arrears	..	..	-1	0	1	3	3	4	3	4
Interest capitalized	..	..	0	0	0	0	0	0	0	0
Debt forgiveness or reduction	..	..	-105	0	-16	0	0	0	0	0
Cross-currency valuation	..	..	26	-29	-30	-88	-105	-30	-37	-37
Residual	..	..	33	66	53	49	37	70	1	-12
9. AVERAGE TERMS OF NEW COMMITMENTS										
ALL CREDITORS										
Interest (%)	2.9	1.3	0.9	0.8	0.8	0.0	0.0	2.0	1.5	1.8
Maturity (years)	4.7	41.8	40.1	49.8	38.0	0.0	0.0	3.1	25.7	33.7
Grace period (years)	2.2	8.9	10.3	10.3	9.9	0.0	0.0	0.2	7.0	8.8
Grant element (%)	20.3	73.5	78.7	83.3	78.4	0.0	0.0	12.2	60.8	68.0
Official creditors										
Interest (%)	2.3	1.3	0.9	0.8	0.8	0.0	0.0	0.0	0.8	1.8
Maturity (years)	4.8	41.8	40.1	49.8	38.0	0.0	0.0	0.0	38.3	33.7
Grace period (years)	2.5	8.9	10.3	10.3	9.9	0.0	0.0	0.0	9.2	8.8
Grant element (%)	22.5	73.5	78.7	83.3	78.4	0.0	0.0	0.0	75.9	68.0
Private creditors										
Interest (%)	7.6	0.0	0.0	0.0	0.0	0.0	0.0	2.0	2.0	0.0
Maturity (years)	3.6	0.0	0.0	0.0	0.0	0.0	0.0	3.1	15.3	0.0
Grace period (years)	0.1	0.0	0.0	0.0	0.0	0.0	0.0	0.2	5.3	0.0
Grant element (%)	3.8	0.0	0.0	0.0	0.0	0.0	0.0	12.2	48.3	0.0
Memorandum items										
Commitments	1	102	126	7	39	0	0	1	64	42
Official creditors	1	102	126	7	39	0	0	0	29	42
Private creditors	0	0	0	0	0	0	0	1	35	0

10. CONTRACTUAL OBLIGATIONS ON OUTSTANDING LONG-TERM DEBT

	2001	2002	2003	2004	2005	2006	2007	2008	2009	2010
TOTAL										
Disbursements	26	22	14	8	4	1	1	0	0	0
Principal	33	33	30	29	26	28	29	29	31	31
Interest	9	8	8	8	7	7	7	6	6	6
Official creditors										
Disbursements	26	22	14	8	4	1	1	0	0	0
Principal	33	33	30	29	26	28	29	29	31	31
Interest	9	8	8	8	7	7	7	6	6	6
Bilateral creditors										
Disbursements	2	3	2	1	0	0	0	0	0	0
Principal	9	11	10	8	5	5	5	5	4	3
Interest	2	2	1	1	1	1	1	1	1	1
Multilateral creditors										
Disbursements	25	19	13	7	4	1	1	0	0	0
Principal	23	21	20	21	21	23	24	24	27	28
Interest	7	7	7	6	6	6	6	6	6	5
Private creditors										
Disbursements	0	0	0	0	0	0	0	0	0	0
Principal	0	0	0	0	0	0	0	0	0	0
Interest	0	0	0	0	0	0	0	0	0	0
Commercial banks										
Disbursements	0	0	0	0	0	0	0	0	0	0
Principal	0	0	0	0	0	0	0	0	0	0
Interest	0	0	0	0	0	0	0	0	0	0
Other private										
Disbursements	0	0	0	0	0	0	0	0	0	0
Principal	0	0	0	0	0	0	0	0	0	0
Interest	0	0	0	0	0	0	0	0	0	0

CAMBODIA

(US$ million, unless otherwise indicated)

	1970	1980	1990	1994	1995	1996	1997	1998	1999	2000
1. SUMMARY DEBT DATA										
TOTAL DEBT STOCKS (EDT)	..	..	**1,854**	**1,915**	**2,035**	**2,100**	**2,129**	**2,210**	**2,262**	**2,357**
Long-term debt (LDOD)	..	..	**1,688**	**1,745**	**1,946**	**2,013**	**2,031**	**2,102**	**2,136**	**2,180**
Public and publicly guaranteed	..	..	1,688	1,745	1,946	2,013	2,031	2,102	2,136	2,180
Private nonguaranteed	..	..	0	0	0	0	0	0	0	0
Use of IMF credit	**0**	**0**	**27**	**30**	**72**	**69**	**65**	**67**	**73**	**73**
Short-term debt	..	..	**140**	**140**	**17**	**19**	**33**	**42**	**53**	**104**
of which interest arrears on LDOD	..	..	107	110	5	5	7	11	10	10
Official creditors	..	..	106	110	5	5	7	11	10	10
Private creditors	..	..	0	0	0	0	0	0	0	0
Memo: principal arrears on LDOD	..	..	393	577	588	708	828	949	1,065	1,181
Official creditors	..	..	393	577	588	708	828	949	1,065	1,181
Private creditors	..	..	0	0	0	0	0	0	0	0
Memo: export credits	..	..	8	22	17	10	13	5	5	5
TOTAL DEBT FLOWS										
Disbursements	..	..	**0**	**75**	**128**	**77**	**40**	**56**	**60**	**89**
Long-term debt	..	..	0	55	85	77	40	56	49	78
IMF purchases	0	0	0	20	43	0	0	0	11	11
Principal repayments	..	..	**0**	**0**	**4**	**4**	**4**	**6**	**18**	**14**
Long-term debt	..	..	0	0	4	4	4	4	14	7
IMF repurchases	0	0	0	0	0	0	0	1	3	7
Net flows on debt	..	..	**15**	**73**	**106**	**74**	**49**	**56**	**55**	**126**
of which short-term debt	..	..	15	-2	-18	1	13	5	12	51
Interest payments (INT)	..	..	**30**	**2**	**2**	**6**	**6**	**7**	**15**	**18**
Long-term debt	..	..	29	0	1	4	5	5	13	13
IMF charges	0	0	0	1	1	1	1	1	1	1
Short-term debt	..	..	1	1	1	1	1	2	2	5
Net transfers on debt	..	..	**-15**	**71**	**103**	**68**	**43**	**48**	**39**	**108**
Total debt service paid (TDS)	..	..	**30**	**2**	**6**	**10**	**10**	**13**	**33**	**31**
Long-term debt	..	..	29	0	5	8	9	9	27	19
IMF repurchases and charges	0	0	0	1	1	1	1	2	4	8
Short-term debt (interest only)	..	..	1	1	1	1	1	2	2	5

	1970	1980	1990	1994	1995	1996	1997	1998	1999	2000
2. AGGREGATE NET RESOURCE FLOWS AND NET TRANSFERS (LONG-TERM)										
NET RESOURCE FLOWS	..	..	**23**	**287**	**544**	**560**	**411**	**343**	**300**	**398**
Net flow of long-term debt (ex. IMF)	..	..	0	55	81	73	36	52	35	71
Foreign direct investment (net)	..	..	0	69	151	294	204	121	144	126
Portfolio equity flows	..	..	0	0	0	0	0	0	0	0
Grants (excluding technical coop.)	..	..	23	163	312	194	171	170	122	201
Memo: technical coop. grants	..	..	19	116	143	150	123	121	94	102
official net resource flows	..	..	23	218	381	270	210	225	160	272
private net resource flows	..	..	0	69	164	290	201	118	140	126
NET TRANSFERS	..	..	**-6**	**284**	**541**	**556**	**407**	**338**	**287**	**385**
Interest on long-term debt	..	..	29	0	1	4	5	5	13	13
Profit remittances on FDI	..	..	0	2	2	0	0	0	0	0
Memo: official net transfers	..	..	-6	217	380	265	206	221	147	259
private net transfers	..	..	0	67	162	290	201	118	140	126

	1970	1980	1990	1994	1995	1996	1997	1998	1999	2000
3. MAJOR ECONOMIC AGGREGATES										
Gross national income (GNI)	..	..	1,115	2,399	2,907	3,111	3,040	2,845	2,979	3,173
Exports of goods & services (XGS)	..	..	..	556	989	829	922	1,037	1,143	1,546
of which workers remittances	..	..	..	10	10	10	10	10	12	17
Imports of goods & services (MGS)	..	..	..	933	1,442	1,385	1,311	1,300	1,478	1,853
International reserves (RES)	..	..	..	118	192	266	299	324	393	502
Current account balance	..	..	..	-157	-186	-185	-210	-49	-113	-19

	1970	1980	1990	1994	1995	1996	1997	1998	1999	2000
4. DEBT INDICATORS										
EDT / XGS (%)	..	..	..	344.1	205.8	253.4	230.8	213.1	197.9	152.5
EDT / GNI (%)	..	..	166.4	79.8	70.0	67.5	70.0	77.7	75.9	74.3
TDS / XGS (%)	..	..	..	0.3	0.7	1.2	1.1	1.2	2.9	2.0
INT / XGS (%)	..	..	..	0.3	0.2	0.7	0.6	0.7	1.3	1.1
INT / GNI (%)	..	..	2.7	0.1	0.1	0.2	0.2	0.3	0.5	0.6
RES / EDT (%)	..	..	..	6.2	9.4	12.7	14.0	14.7	17.4	21.3
RES / MGS (months)	..	..	..	1.5	1.6	2.3	2.7	3.0	3.2	3.3
Short-term / EDT (%)	..	..	7.5	7.3	0.9	0.9	1.5	1.9	2.3	4.4
Concessional / EDT (%)	..	..	91.0	90.9	93.0	93.6	93.3	93.2	93.0	91.2
Multilateral / EDT (%)	..	..	0.1	3.0	5.8	8.9	10.1	12.5	14.4	16.1

CAMBODIA

(US$ million, unless otherwise indicated)

	1970	1980	1990	1994	1995	1996	1997	1998	1999	2000
5. LONG-TERM DEBT										
DEBT OUTSTANDING (LDOD)	..	..	**1,688**	**1,745**	**1,946**	**2,013**	**2,031**	**2,102**	**2,136**	**2,180**
Public and publicly guaranteed	..	..	**1,688**	**1,745**	**1,946**	**2,013**	**2,031**	**2,102**	**2,136**	**2,180**
Official creditors	..	..	1,688	1,745	1,934	2,003	2,025	2,099	2,136	2,180
Multilateral	..	..	1	58	118	188	215	276	325	380
Concessional	..	..	1	58	118	188	215	276	325	380
Bilateral	..	..	1,686	1,687	1,816	1,815	1,810	1,822	1,811	1,800
Concessional	..	..	1,686	1,683	1,776	1,778	1,771	1,783	1,779	1,769
Private creditors	..	..	0	0	13	10	6	3	0	0
Bonds	..	..	0	0	0	0	0	0	0	0
Commercial banks	..	..	0	0	0	0	0	0	0	0
Other private	..	..	0	0	13	10	6	3	0	0
Private nonguaranteed	..	..	**0**	**0**	**0**	**0**	**0**	**0**	**0**	**0**
Bonds	..	..	0	0	0	0	0	0	0	0
Commercial banks and other	..	..	0	0	0	0	0	0	0	0
Memo:										
IBRD	0	0	0	0	0	0	0	0	0	0
IDA	0	0	0	39	65	108	132	157	180	207
DISBURSEMENTS	..	..	**0**	**55**	**85**	**77**	**40**	**56**	**49**	**78**
Public and publicly guaranteed	..	..	**0**	**55**	**85**	**77**	**40**	**56**	**49**	**78**
Official creditors	..	..	0	55	69	77	40	56	49	78
Multilateral	..	..	0	50	61	77	40	47	48	77
Concessional	..	..	0	50	61	77	40	47	48	77
Bilateral	..	..	0	4	9	0	0	9	1	1
Concessional	..	..	0	0	9	0	0	9	1	1
Private creditors	..	..	0	0	16	0	0	0	0	0
Bonds	..	..	0	0	0	0	0	0	0	0
Commercial banks	..	..	0	0	0	0	0	0	0	0
Other private	..	..	0	0	16	0	0	0	0	0
Private nonguaranteed	..	..	**0**	**0**	**0**	**0**	**0**	**0**	**0**	**0**
Bonds	..	..	0	0	0	0	0	0	0	0
Commercial banks and other	..	..	0	0	0	0	0	0	0	0
Memo:										
IBRD	0	0	0	0	0	0	0	0	0	0
IDA	0	0	0	38	25	46	30	19	27	37
PRINCIPAL REPAYMENTS	..	..	**0**	**0**	**4**	**4**	**4**	**4**	**14**	**7**
Public and publicly guaranteed	..	..	**0**	**0**	**4**	**4**	**4**	**4**	**14**	**7**
Official creditors	..	..	0	0	1	1	1	1	11	7
Multilateral	..	..	0	0	0	0	0	0	0	0
Concessional	..	..	0	0	0	0	0	0	0	0
Bilateral	..	..	0	0	1	1	1	1	11	7
Concessional	..	..	0	0	0	0	0	0	7	7
Private creditors	..	..	0	0	3	3	3	3	3	0
Bonds	..	..	0	0	0	0	0	0	0	0
Commercial banks	..	..	0	0	0	0	0	0	0	0
Other private	..	..	0	0	3	3	3	3	3	0
Private nonguaranteed	..	..	**0**	**0**	**0**	**0**	**0**	**0**	**0**	**0**
Bonds	..	..	0	0	0	0	0	0	0	0
Commercial banks and other	..	..	0	0	0	0	0	0	0	0
Memo:										
IBRD	0	0	0	0	0	0	0	0	0	0
IDA	0	0	0	0	0	0	0	0	0	0
NET FLOWS ON DEBT	..	..	**0**	**55**	**81**	**73**	**36**	**52**	**35**	**71**
Public and publicly guaranteed	..	..	**0**	**55**	**81**	**73**	**36**	**52**	**35**	**71**
Official creditors	..	..	0	55	68	76	39	55	38	71
Multilateral	..	..	0	50	61	77	40	47	48	77
Concessional	..	..	0	50	61	77	40	47	48	77
Bilateral	..	..	0	4	8	-1	-1	8	-10	-6
Concessional	..	..	0	0	9	0	0	9	-6	-6
Private creditors	..	..	0	0	13	-3	-3	-3	-3	0
Bonds	..	..	0	0	0	0	0	0	0	0
Commercial banks	..	..	0	0	0	0	0	0	0	0
Other private	..	..	0	0	13	-3	-3	-3	-3	0
Private nonguaranteed	..	..	**0**	**0**	**0**	**0**	**0**	**0**	**0**	**0**
Bonds	..	..	0	0	0	0	0	0	0	0
Commercial banks and other	..	..	0	0	0	0	0	0	0	0
Memo:										
IBRD	0	0	0	0	0	0	0	0	0	0
IDA	0	0	0	38	25	46	30	19	27	37

CAMBODIA

(US$ million, unless otherwise indicated)

	1970	1980	1990	1994	1995	1996	1997	1998	1999	2000
INTEREST PAYMENTS (LINT)	..	..	**29**	**0**	**1**	**4**	**5**	**5**	**13**	**13**
Public and publicly guaranteed	..	..	**29**	**0**	**1**	**4**	**5**	**5**	**13**	**13**
Official creditors	..	..	29	0	1	4	5	5	13	13
Multilateral	..	..	0	0	1	1	2	2	2	3
Concessional	..	..	0	0	1	1	2	2	2	3
Bilateral	..	..	29	0	0	3	3	3	11	10
Concessional	..	..	29	0	0	1	1	1	9	9
Private creditors	..	..	0	0	0	0	0	0	0	0
Bonds	..	..	0	0	0	0	0	0	0	0
Commercial banks	..	..	0	0	0	0	0	0	0	0
Other private	..	..	0	0	0	0	0	0	0	0
Private nonguaranteed	..	..	**0**	**0**	**0**	**0**	**0**	**0**	**0**	**0**
Bonds	..	..	0	0	0	0	0	0	0	0
Commercial banks and other	..	..	0	0	0	0	0	0	0	0
Memo:										
IBRD	0	0	0	0	0	0	0	0	0	0
IDA	0	0	0	0	0	1	1	1	1	1
NET TRANSFERS ON DEBT	..	..	**-29**	**54**	**80**	**68**	**32**	**47**	**22**	**59**
Public and publicly guaranteed	..	..	**-29**	**54**	**80**	**68**	**32**	**47**	**22**	**59**
Official creditors	..	..	-29	54	67	72	35	50	25	59
Multilateral	..	..	0	50	60	76	39	45	45	74
Concessional	..	..	0	50	60	76	39	45	45	74
Bilateral	..	..	-29	4	8	-4	-4	5	-21	-15
Concessional	..	..	-29	0	9	-1	-1	8	-15	-14
Private creditors	..	..	0	0	13	-3	-3	-3	-3	0
Bonds	..	..	0	0	0	0	0	0	0	0
Commercial banks	..	..	0	0	0	0	0	0	0	0
Other private	..	..	0	0	13	-3	-3	-3	-3	0
Private nonguaranteed	..	..	**0**	**0**	**0**	**0**	**0**	**0**	**0**	**0**
Bonds	..	..	0	0	0	0	0	0	0	0
Commercial banks and other	..	..	0	0	0	0	0	0	0	0
Memo:										
IBRD	0	0	0	0	0	0	0	0	0	0
IDA	0	0	0	38	24	45	30	18	26	35
DEBT SERVICE (LTDS)	..	..	**29**	**0**	**5**	**8**	**9**	**9**	**27**	**19**
Public and publicly guaranteed	..	..	**29**	**0**	**5**	**8**	**9**	**9**	**27**	**19**
Official creditors	..	..	29	0	2	5	6	6	24	19
Multilateral	..	..	0	0	1	1	2	2	2	3
Concessional	..	..	0	0	1	1	2	2	2	3
Bilateral	..	..	29	0	1	4	4	4	22	17
Concessional	..	..	29	0	0	1	1	1	16	15
Private creditors	..	..	0	0	3	3	3	3	3	0
Bonds	..	..	0	0	0	0	0	0	0	0
Commercial banks	..	..	0	0	0	0	0	0	0	0
Other private	..	..	0	0	3	3	3	3	3	0
Private nonguaranteed	..	..	**0**	**0**	**0**	**0**	**0**	**0**	**0**	**0**
Bonds	..	..	0	0	0	0	0	0	0	0
Commercial banks and other	..	..	0	0	0	0	0	0	0	0
Memo:										
IBRD	0	0	0	0	0	0	0	0	0	0
IDA	0	0	0	0	0	1	1	1	1	1
UNDISBURSED DEBT	..	..	**651**	**131**	**201**	**212**	**226**	**209**	**332**	**404**
Official creditors	..	..	651	115	201	212	226	209	332	404
Private creditors	..	..	0	16	0	0	0	0	0	0
Memorandum items										
Concessional LDOD	..	..	1,688	1,741	1,894	1,965	1,985	2,059	2,104	2,150
Variable rate LDOD	..	..	0	0	0	0	0	0	0	0
Public sector LDOD	..	..	1,688	1,745	1,946	2,013	2,031	2,102	2,136	2,180
Private sector LDOD	..	..	0	0	0	0	0	0	0	0

6. CURRENCY COMPOSITION OF LONG-TERM DEBT (PERCENT)

	1970	1980	1990	1994	1995	1996	1997	1998	1999	2000
Deutsche mark	..	..	0.4	0.0	0.3	0.2	0.2	0.2	0.2	0.2
French franc	..	..	0.5	0.4	1.0	0.9	1.1	1.1	0.9	0.8
Japanese yen	..	..	0.6	0.7	1.2	1.1	0.9	1.0	1.1	1.0
Pound sterling	..	..	0.0	0.0	0.0	0.0	0.0	0.0	0.0	0.0
Swiss franc	..	..	0.0	0.0	0.0	0.0	0.0	0.0	0.0	0.0
U.S.dollars	..	..	12.6	14.6	20.2	21.7	22.3	22.6	23.1	23.9
Multiple currency	..	..	0.0	1.1	2.7	4.0	4.1	5.6	6.5	7.2
Special drawing rights	..	..	0.0	0.0	0.0	0.0	0.0	0.0	0.0	0.1
All other currencies	..	..	85.9	83.2	74.6	72.1	71.4	69.5	68.2	66.8

CAMBODIA

(US$ million, unless otherwise indicated)

	1970	1980	1990	1994	1995	1996	1997	1998	1999	2000
7. DEBT RESTRUCTURINGS										
Total amount rescheduled	..	..	0	0	240	12	5	0	0	0
Debt stock rescheduled	..	..	0	0	0	0	0	0	0	0
Principal rescheduled	..	..	0	0	109	7	3	0	0	0
Official	..	..	0	0	108	7	3	0	0	0
Private	..	..	0	0	0	0	0	0	0	0
Interest rescheduled	..	..	..	0	103	4	2	0	0	0
Official	..	..	0	0	103	4	2	0	0	0
Private	..	..	0	0	0	0	0	0	0	0
Debt forgiven	..	..	0	0	6	0	0	0	0	0
Memo: interest forgiven	..	..	0	0	7	0	0	0	0	0
Debt stock reduction	..	..	0	0	0	0	0	0	0	0
of which debt buyback	..	..	0	0	0	0	0	0	0	0
8. DEBT STOCK-FLOW RECONCILIATION										
Total change in debt stocks	..	..	..	86	120	65	28	81	52	95
Net flows on debt	..	..	15	73	106	74	49	56	55	126
Net change in interest arrears	..	..	..	7	-105	0	1	4	-1	0
Interest capitalized	..	..	..	0	103	4	2	0	0	0
Debt forgiveness or reduction	..	..	..	0	-6	0	0	0	0	0
Cross-currency valuation	..	..	..	6	1	-14	-24	18	-2	-30
Residual	..	..	..	0	22	1	0	3	0	0
9. AVERAGE TERMS OF NEW COMMITMENTS										
ALL CREDITORS										
Interest (%)	..	..	0.0	0.7	1.8	3.3	1.1	0.5	1.1	1.4
Maturity (years)	..	..	0.0	25.0	37.5	39.7	38.3	39.5	37.6	30.4
Grace period (years)	..	..	0.0	6.7	9.7	10.2	9.7	10.0	9.7	8.0
Grant element (%)	..	..	0.0	58.5	69.8	57.9	76.0	82.5	76.2	68.0
Official creditors										
Interest (%)	..	..	0.0	1.1	1.8	3.3	1.1	0.5	1.1	1.4
Maturity (years)	..	..	0.0	33.6	37.5	39.7	38.3	39.5	37.6	30.4
Grace period (years)	..	..	0.0	9.2	9.7	10.2	9.7	10.0	9.7	8.0
Grant element (%)	..	..	0.0	73.2	69.8	57.9	76.0	82.5	76.2	68.0
Private creditors										
Interest (%)	..	..	0.0	0.0	0.0	0.0	0.0	0.0	0.0	0.0
Maturity (years)	..	..	0.0	5.0	0.0	0.0	0.0	0.0	0.0	0.0
Grace period (years)	..	..	0.0	1.0	0.0	0.0	0.0	0.0	0.0	0.0
Grant element (%)	..	..	0.0	24.3	0.0	0.0	0.0	0.0	0.0	0.0
Memorandum items										
Commitments	..	..	0	53	161	94	75	31	175	153
Official creditors	..	..	0	37	161	94	75	31	175	153
Private creditors	..	..	0	16	0	0	0	0	0	0

10. CONTRACTUAL OBLIGATIONS ON OUTSTANDING LONG-TERM DEBT

	2001	2002	2003	2004	2005	2006	2007	2008	2009	2010
TOTAL										
Disbursements	98	95	66	41	22	10	6	3	3	0
Principal	38	40	42	44	48	49	50	54	52	46
Interest	15	16	16	16	17	17	18	17	17	16
Official creditors										
Disbursements	98	95	66	41	22	10	6	3	3	0
Principal	38	40	42	44	48	49	50	54	52	46
Interest	15	16	16	16	17	17	18	17	17	16
Bilateral creditors										
Disbursements	18	14	10	6	4	2	1	1	1	0
Principal	38	40	40	41	43	41	38	38	34	28
Interest	10	10	10	10	10	9	9	8	8	7
Multilateral creditors										
Disbursements	80	80	56	35	18	8	5	2	2	0
Principal	0	0	2	3	5	9	12	16	18	18
Interest	5	5	6	6	7	8	9	9	9	9
Private creditors										
Disbursements	0	0	0	0	0	0	0	0	0	0
Principal	0	0	0	0	0	0	0	0	0	0
Interest	0	0	0	0	0	0	0	0	0	0
Commercial banks										
Disbursements	0	0	0	0	0	0	0	0	0	0
Principal	0	0	0	0	0	0	0	0	0	0
Interest	0	0	0	0	0	0	0	0	0	0
Other private										
Disbursements	0	0	0	0	0	0	0	0	0	0
Principal	0	0	0	0	0	0	0	0	0	0
Interest	0	0	0	0	0	0	0	0	0	0

CAMEROON

(US$ million, unless otherwise indicated)

	1970	1980	1990	1994	1995	1996	1997	1998	1999	2000
1. SUMMARY DEBT DATA										
TOTAL DEBT STOCKS (EDT)	**145**	**2,588**	**6,676**	**8,270**	**9,385**	**9,582**	**9,334**	**9,922**	**9,444**	**9,241**
Long-term debt (LDOD)	**145**	**2,251**	**5,595**	**7,481**	**8,298**	**8,251**	**7,927**	**8,368**	**7,970**	**7,674**
Public and publicly guaranteed	136	2,073	5,365	7,248	8,010	7,951	7,730	8,189	7,616	7,357
Private nonguaranteed	9	178	230	233	288	300	198	179	355	317
Use of IMF credit	**0**	**59**	**121**	**44**	**51**	**72**	**93**	**156**	**196**	**235**
Short-term debt	**0**	**278**	**960**	**745**	**1,036**	**1,260**	**1,314**	**1,398**	**1,278**	**1,332**
of which interest arrears on LDOD	0	9	191	264	395	788	185	172	154	313
Official creditors	0	3	87	134	247	650	78	64	56	144
Private creditors	0	6	105	130	147	138	108	109	98	169
Memo: principal arrears on LDOD	0	7	350	538	619	774	490	528	471	564
Official creditors	0	2	103	198	243	377	170	199	175	265
Private creditors	0	5	246	340	376	398	320	328	296	299
Memo: export credits	0	0	2,193	2,575	2,929	2,858	2,620	2,586	2,488	2,361
TOTAL DEBT FLOWS										
Disbursements	**40**	**626**	**718**	**478**	**121**	**230**	**296**	**266**	**306**	**304**
Long-term debt	40	614	718	447	108	201	259	192	244	236
IMF purchases	0	12	0	31	13	29	37	73	62	69
Principal repayments	**6**	**131**	**270**	**204**	**217**	**248**	**277**	**292**	**286**	**273**
Long-term debt	6	114	269	198	211	242	266	276	268	254
IMF repurchases	0	17	1	6	6	6	11	16	18	19
Net flows on debt	**33**	**538**	**685**	**305**	**64**	**-188**	**676**	**70**	**-82**	**-74**
of which short-term debt	0	43	237	30	160	-170	657	97	-102	-105
Interest payments (INT)	**5**	**149**	**252**	**181**	**214**	**262**	**232**	**236**	**263**	**289**
Long-term debt	5	119	198	155	173	235	189	178	202	216
IMF charges	0	2	11	2	2	3	3	3	2	2
Short-term debt	0	28	43	24	39	24	40	55	59	72
Net transfers on debt	**28**	**389**	**433**	**123**	**-150**	**-449**	**444**	**-166**	**-345**	**-363**
Total debt service paid (TDS)	**11**	**280**	**522**	**385**	**431**	**510**	**509**	**528**	**549**	**562**
Long-term debt	11	233	467	354	384	477	455	454	470	470
IMF repurchases and charges	0	19	13	7	9	9	15	19	20	20
Short-term debt (interest only)	0	28	43	24	39	24	40	55	59	72
2. AGGREGATE NET RESOURCE FLOWS AND NET TRANSFERS (LONG-TERM)										
NET RESOURCE FLOWS	**70**	**659**	**649**	**573**	**109**	**233**	**178**	**244**	**206**	**185**
Net flow of long-term debt (ex. IMF)	33	500	449	249	-103	-41	-7	-84	-24	-19
Foreign direct investment (net)	16	130	-113	-9	7	35	45	50	40	31
Portfolio equity flows	0	0	0	0	0	0	0	0	0	0
Grants (excluding technical coop.)	21	29	313	333	205	239	139	278	190	172
Memo: technical coop. grants	17	85	126	101	124	117	95	107	97	94
official net resource flows	44	250	774	641	167	221	158	238	218	205
private net resource flows	26	409	-125	-68	-58	12	20	6	-13	-21
NET TRANSFERS	**61**	**424**	**451**	**418**	**-64**	**-2**	**-11**	**66**	**4**	**-31**
Interest on long-term debt	5	119	198	155	173	235	189	178	202	216
Profit remittances on FDI	4	115	0	0	0	0	0	0	0	0
Memo: official net transfers	40	208	649	507	14	0	-16	79	39	7
private net transfers	21	216	-198	-90	-79	-2	4	-13	-35	-38
3. MAJOR ECONOMIC AGGREGATES										
Gross national income (GNI)	1,025	5,618	10,674	7,307	7,437	8,518	8,506	8,234	8,719	8,284
Exports of goods & services (XGS)	306	1,912	2,320	1,744	2,060	2,061	2,323	2,321	2,256	2,738
of which workers remittances	..	11	61	0	0	0	0	0	0	0
Imports of goods & services (MGS)	329	2,478	2,418	2,087	2,188	2,471	2,667	2,660	2,750	2,988
International reserves (RES)	81	206	37	14	15	14	10	1	4	212
Current account balance	1	-495	-196	-324	-71	-375	-258	-235	-377	-153
4. DEBT INDICATORS										
EDT / XGS (%)	47.4	135.4	287.7	474.3	455.6	464.9	401.8	427.5	418.6	337.5
EDT / GNI (%)	14.1	46.1	62.5	113.2	126.2	112.5	109.7	120.5	108.3	111.6
TDS / XGS (%)	3.7	14.6	22.5	22.1	20.9	24.7	21.9	22.7	24.3	20.5
INT / XGS (%)	1.6	7.8	10.8	10.4	10.4	12.7	10.0	10.2	11.6	10.6
INT / GNI (%)	0.5	2.7	2.4	2.5	2.9	3.1	2.7	2.9	3.0	3.5
RES / EDT (%)	55.8	8.0	0.6	0.2	0.2	0.1	0.1	0.0	0.1	2.3
RES / MGS (months)	3.0	1.0	0.2	0.1	0.1	0.1	0.0	0.0	0.0	0.9
Short-term / EDT (%)	0.0	10.8	14.4	9.0	11.0	13.1	14.1	14.1	13.5	14.4
Concessional / EDT (%)	74.1	33.7	27.4	42.4	43.7	43.3	45.3	46.0	45.2	45.2
Multilateral / EDT (%)	14.0	16.7	19.7	20.1	17.9	16.4	15.7	15.0	15.4	14.9

CAMEROON

(US$ million, unless otherwise indicated)

	1970	1980	1990	1994	1995	1996	1997	1998	1999	2000
5. LONG-TERM DEBT										
DEBT OUTSTANDING (LDOD)	**145**	**2,251**	**5,595**	**7,481**	**8,298**	**8,251**	**7,927**	**8,368**	**7,970**	**7,674**
Public and publicly guaranteed	**136**	**2,073**	**5,365**	**7,248**	**8,010**	**7,951**	**7,730**	**8,189**	**7,616**	**7,357**
Official creditors	124	1,237	3,882	6,292	7,112	7,182	7,177	7,710	7,243	7,027
Multilateral	20	432	1,317	1,665	1,678	1,568	1,465	1,487	1,456	1,379
Concessional	12	210	341	558	611	670	735	835	901	917
Bilateral	104	805	2,566	4,627	5,434	5,614	5,712	6,223	5,787	5,648
Concessional	95	663	1,486	2,945	3,490	3,482	3,498	3,725	3,368	3,260
Private creditors	12	836	1,483	956	898	769	553	479	372	330
Bonds	0	0	0	0	0	0	0	0	0	0
Commercial banks	0	193	503	415	418	365	314	327	279	256
Other private	12	643	980	541	480	404	239	152	93	75
Private nonguaranteed	**9**	**178**	**230**	**233**	**288**	**300**	**198**	**179**	**355**	**317**
Bonds	0	0	0	0	0	0	0	0	0	0
Commercial banks and other	9	178	230	233	288	300	198	179	355	317
Memo:										
IBRD	3	152	651	695	639	520	410	350	276	218
IDA	9	146	238	406	443	513	609	701	749	769
DISBURSEMENTS	**40**	**614**	**718**	**447**	**108**	**201**	**259**	**192**	**244**	**236**
Public and publicly guaranteed	**29**	**564**	**665**	**440**	**108**	**176**	**245**	**182**	**189**	**197**
Official creditors	27	250	558	440	108	176	245	182	189	197
Multilateral	10	72	200	280	82	106	147	106	119	78
Concessional	6	22	2	217	38	85	122	92	101	68
Bilateral	18	178	359	159	26	70	98	76	70	119
Concessional	15	120	106	154	26	70	98	75	70	112
Private creditors	1	314	107	0	0	0	0	0	0	0
Bonds	0	0	0	0	0	0	0	0	0	0
Commercial banks	0	115	11	0	0	0	0	0	0	0
Other private	1	199	97	0	0	0	0	0	0	0
Private nonguaranteed	**11**	**50**	**53**	**7**	**0**	**25**	**14**	**10**	**56**	**39**
Bonds	0	0	0	0	0	0	0	0	0	0
Commercial banks and other	11	50	53	7	0	25	14	10	56	39
Memo:										
IBRD	3	28	75	22	6	6	6	3	1	0
IDA	4	19	0	180	35	84	120	79	65	55
PRINCIPAL REPAYMENTS	**6**	**114**	**269**	**198**	**211**	**242**	**266**	**276**	**268**	**254**
Public and publicly guaranteed	**5**	**82**	**139**	**155**	**183**	**229**	**241**	**256**	**166**	**168**
Official creditors	4	29	97	131	146	194	227	222	160	164
Multilateral	0	10	68	119	130	146	163	124	116	99
Concessional	0	2	7	9	10	10	30	14	15	15
Bilateral	4	19	29	12	16	48	64	98	44	65
Concessional	3	12	17	4	3	4	20	61	33	45
Private creditors	0	53	41	24	36	35	14	34	6	4
Bonds	0	0	0	0	0	0	0	0	0	0
Commercial banks	0	18	28	23	26	29	8	7	4	4
Other private	0	35	14	1	11	7	6	27	2	0
Private nonguaranteed	**2**	**32**	**130**	**43**	**28**	**13**	**25**	**20**	**102**	**86**
Bonds	0	0	0	0	0	0	0	0	0	0
Commercial banks and other	2	32	130	43	28	13	25	20	102	86
Memo:										
IBRD	0	4	42	82	92	82	76	69	65	53
IDA	0	1	3	4	4	5	5	5	6	7
NET FLOWS ON DEBT	**33**	**500**	**449**	**249**	**-103**	**-41**	**-7**	**-84**	**-24**	**-19**
Public and publicly guaranteed	**24**	**482**	**527**	**284**	**-75**	**-53**	**4**	**-74**	**23**	**29**
Official creditors	23	221	461	308	-39	-18	18	-40	28	33
Multilateral	9	63	131	161	-49	-40	-17	-18	3	-21
Concessional	6	21	-4	209	28	75	92	78	87	53
Bilateral	14	159	330	147	10	22	35	-22	26	54
Concessional	12	109	89	150	24	67	79	13	37	67
Private creditors	1	261	66	-24	-36	-35	-14	-34	-6	-4
Bonds	0	0	0	0	0	0	0	0	0	0
Commercial banks	0	97	-17	-23	-26	-29	-8	-7	-4	-4
Other private	1	164	83	-1	-11	-7	-6	-27	-2	0
Private nonguaranteed	**9**	**18**	**-77**	**-35**	**-28**	**12**	**-11**	**-10**	**-47**	**-48**
Bonds	0	0	0	0	0	0	0	0	0	0
Commercial banks and other	9	18	-77	-35	-28	12	-11	-10	-47	-48
Memo:										
IBRD	3	24	33	-60	-85	-76	-70	-65	-63	-53
IDA	4	19	-3	176	31	80	115	74	59	49

CAMEROON

(US$ million, unless otherwise indicated)

	1970	1980	1990	1994	1995	1996	1997	1998	1999	2000
INTEREST PAYMENTS (LINT)	**5**	**119**	**198**	**155**	**173**	**235**	**189**	**178**	**202**	**216**
Public and publicly guaranteed	**4**	**104**	**181**	**141**	**163**	**230**	**179**	**174**	**181**	**199**
Official creditors	4	42	125	134	152	221	174	159	180	198
Multilateral	1	18	73	112	80	100	91	59	56	49
Concessional	0	2	4	4	6	4	10	6	7	8
Bilateral	3	24	52	23	72	121	82	100	123	150
Concessional	2	13	28	15	48	32	51	56	48	59
Private creditors	1	62	56	6	10	9	6	15	1	1
Bonds	0	0	0	0	0	0	0	0	0	0
Commercial banks	0	23	40	6	5	7	2	5	1	1
Other private	1	39	16	1	5	2	4	10	0	0
Private nonguaranteed	**1**	**15**	**17**	**15**	**11**	**5**	**10**	**4**	**21**	**17**
Bonds	0	0	0	0	0	0	0	0	0	0
Commercial banks and other	1	15	17	15	11	5	10	4	21	17
Memo:										
IBRD	0	13	49	58	56	47	37	28	26	22
IDA	0	1	2	2	3	3	4	5	5	5
NET TRANSFERS ON DEBT	**28**	**381**	**251**	**93**	**-277**	**-276**	**-196**	**-262**	**-226**	**-234**
Public and publicly guaranteed	**19**	**378**	**346**	**144**	**-238**	**-283**	**-175**	**-248**	**-158**	**-170**
Official creditors	19	180	336	174	-191	-239	-155	-199	-151	-165
Multilateral	9	45	59	49	-129	-140	-108	-77	-54	-69
Concessional	6	19	-8	205	23	71	82	72	80	45
Bilateral	11	135	277	125	-62	-99	-47	-122	-98	-96
Concessional	10	96	60	136	-24	34	28	-42	-11	9
Private creditors	0	199	10	-31	-47	-44	-19	-49	-7	-5
Bonds	0	0	0	0	0	0	0	0	0	0
Commercial banks	0	73	-57	-29	-31	-36	-10	-12	-5	-5
Other private	0	125	66	-2	-16	-8	-10	-37	-2	0
Private nonguaranteed	**9**	**3**	**-94**	**-50**	**-39**	**7**	**-21**	**-14**	**-68**	**-65**
Bonds	0	0	0	0	0	0	0	0	0	0
Commercial banks and other	9	3	-94	-50	-39	7	-21	-14	-68	-65
Memo:										
IBRD	3	12	-16	-119	-141	-123	-107	-94	-90	-75
IDA	4	18	-4	174	28	76	110	69	54	43
DEBT SERVICE (LTDS)	**11**	**233**	**467**	**354**	**384**	**477**	**455**	**454**	**470**	**470**
Public and publicly guaranteed	**9**	**186**	**320**	**296**	**345**	**459**	**420**	**430**	**346**	**367**
Official creditors	8	71	222	265	299	415	400	381	340	362
Multilateral	1	28	141	231	211	246	255	183	173	148
Concessional	0	4	11	13	15	14	40	19	22	23
Bilateral	7	43	81	34	88	169	146	198	167	215
Concessional	6	25	46	18	50	36	70	117	81	103
Private creditors	1	115	97	31	47	44	19	49	7	5
Bonds	0	0	0	0	0	0	0	0	0	0
Commercial banks	0	42	67	29	31	36	10	12	5	5
Other private	1	74	30	2	16	8	10	37	2	0
Private nonguaranteed	**2**	**47**	**147**	**58**	**39**	**18**	**35**	**24**	**124**	**103**
Bonds	0	0	0	0	0	0	0	0	0	0
Commercial banks and other	2	47	147	58	39	18	35	24	124	103
Memo:										
IBRD	0	17	91	140	147	129	113	97	91	75
IDA	0	2	4	6	8	8	10	10	11	12
UNDISBURSED DEBT	**104**	**619**	**1,843**	**1,341**	**1,111**	**991**	**812**	**1,060**	**952**	**689**
Official creditors	103	545	1,526	1,125	1,021	987	809	1,056	952	689
Private creditors	1	74	318	216	90	4	4	4	0	0
Memorandum items										
Concessional LDOD	107	873	1,826	3,503	4,101	4,152	4,233	4,560	4,269	4,177
Variable rate LDOD	9	499	854	1,276	1,381	1,462	1,326	1,287	1,370	1,258
Public sector LDOD	128	2,006	5,243	7,177	7,933	7,879	7,670	8,130	7,565	7,310
Private sector LDOD	17	245	353	304	365	372	257	238	406	364

6. CURRENCY COMPOSITION OF LONG-TERM DEBT (PERCENT)

	1970	1980	1990	1994	1995	1996	1997	1998	1999	2000
Deutsche mark	10.7	8.6	16.9	16.9	17.6	17.8	17.5	17.5	16.6	16.3
French franc	15.8	36.8	31.4	34.3	34.9	35.2	33.6	33.4	31.1	30.0
Japanese yen	0.0	0.0	0.3	0.4	0.3	0.3	0.3	0.3	0.3	0.3
Pound sterling	2.8	2.0	2.3	1.2	1.0	1.0	2.0	1.8	2.0	1.8
Swiss franc	0.0	0.0	1.1	1.1	1.1	1.0	1.0	0.9	0.7	0.7
U.S.dollars	22.7	19.2	11.0	11.2	10.8	11.9	16.5	22.8	26.3	27.6
Multiple currency	4.9	10.5	16.5	14.7	12.6	10.8	9.1	4.1	4.0	3.6
Special drawing rights	0.0	0.0	0.0	0.1	0.2	0.2	0.2	0.2	0.2	0.2
All other currencies	43.1	22.9	20.5	20.1	21.5	21.8	19.8	19.0	18.8	19.5

CAMEROON

(US$ million, unless otherwise indicated)

	1970	1980	1990	1994	1995	1996	1997	1998	1999	2000
7. DEBT RESTRUCTURINGS										
Total amount rescheduled	..	..	75	1,298	642	656	1,075	370	482	158
Debt stock rescheduled	..	..	0	0	0	0	0	0	0	0
Principal rescheduled	..	..	26	479	294	185	406	208	218	20
Official	..	..	7	244	204	147	306	147	181	9
Private	..	..	19	235	90	39	99	61	38	12
Interest rescheduled	..	..	22	470	154	66	564	151	141	16
Official	..	..	6	376	131	59	538	141	137	15
Private	..	..	16	94	24	8	26	9	4	0
Debt forgiven	..	..	10	533	0	1	73	23	20	2
Memo: interest forgiven	..	..	0	13	0	0	89	17	16	2
Debt stock reduction	..	..	0	0	0	0	0	0	0	0
of which debt buyback	..	..	0	0	0	0	0	0	0	0
8. DEBT STOCK-FLOW RECONCILIATION										
Total change in debt stocks	..	..	1,236	883	1,115	197	-248	588	-478	-203
Net flows on debt	33	538	685	305	64	-188	676	70	-82	-74
Net change in interest arrears	..	..	115	-220	130	393	-602	-13	-19	160
Interest capitalized	..	..	22	470	154	66	564	151	141	16
Debt forgiveness or reduction	..	..	-10	-533	0	-1	-73	-23	-20	-2
Cross-currency valuation	..	..	337	394	277	-680	-1,052	118	-807	-418
Residual	..	..	87	467	490	606	240	285	308	116
9. AVERAGE TERMS OF NEW COMMITMENTS										
ALL CREDITORS										
Interest (%)	4.7	6.9	6.6	2.3	2.2	1.3	0.6	1.1	2.1	0.8
Maturity (years)	28.4	23.3	15.1	31.9	26.7	35.2	32.8	36.8	26.3	44.1
Grace period (years)	8.0	5.9	5.3	9.3	8.0	8.8	7.9	9.8	8.5	10.0
Grant element (%)	39.9	25.9	21.2	63.7	58.8	71.7	75.6	75.1	61.0	81.4
Official creditors										
Interest (%)	4.6	6.1	6.6	2.3	2.2	1.3	0.6	1.1	2.1	0.8
Maturity (years)	28.8	24.8	15.2	31.9	26.7	35.2	32.8	36.8	26.3	44.1
Grace period (years)	8.1	6.3	5.3	9.3	8.0	8.8	7.9	9.8	8.5	10.0
Grant element (%)	40.4	30.6	21.3	63.7	58.8	71.7	75.6	75.1	61.0	81.4
Private creditors										
Interest (%)	6.0	14.7	7.0	0.0	0.0	0.0	0.0	0.0	0.0	0.0
Maturity (years)	7.2	8.2	13.2	0.0	0.0	0.0	0.0	0.0	0.0	0.0
Grace period (years)	1.7	2.4	2.7	0.0	0.0	0.0	0.0	0.0	0.0	0.0
Grant element (%)	13.0	-21.2	14.4	0.0	0.0	0.0	0.0	0.0	0.0	0.0
Memorandum items										
Commitments	42	170	479	403	143	351	43	385	378	70
Official creditors	41	155	473	403	143	351	43	385	378	70
Private creditors	1	15	6	0	0	0	0	0	0	0

10. CONTRACTUAL OBLIGATIONS ON OUTSTANDING LONG-TERM DEBT

	2001	2002	2003	2004	2005	2006	2007	2008	2009	2010
TOTAL										
Disbursements	203	195	123	69	41	21	11	2	1	0
Principal	433	411	413	419	439	416	356	349	314	256
Interest	318	296	274	250	229	206	187	172	162	149
Official creditors										
Disbursements	203	195	123	69	41	21	11	2	1	0
Principal	347	367	395	413	435	413	355	348	314	255
Interest	304	288	269	249	227	204	186	171	161	148
Bilateral creditors										
Disbursements	89	93	58	36	19	9	4	0	0	0
Principal	234	267	307	331	359	346	301	296	259	213
Interest	260	249	236	221	205	186	171	158	150	139
Multilateral creditors										
Disbursements	114	103	65	34	22	12	7	2	1	0
Principal	112	100	88	82	76	68	54	52	54	42
Interest	45	39	33	28	22	18	15	12	10	9
Private creditors										
Disbursements	0	0	0	0	0	0	0	0	0	0
Principal	87	44	18	6	4	3	1	1	1	0
Interest	13	9	6	2	2	1	1	1	1	1
Commercial banks										
Disbursements	0	0	0	0	0	0	0	0	0	0
Principal	3	3	0	0	0	0	0	0	0	0
Interest	0	0	0	0	0	0	0	0	0	0
Other private										
Disbursements	0	0	0	0	0	0	0	0	0	0
Principal	84	41	18	6	4	3	1	1	1	0
Interest	13	8	6	2	2	1	1	1	1	1

CAPE VERDE

(US$ million, unless otherwise indicated)

	1970	1980	1990	1994	1995	1996	1997	1998	1999	2000
1. SUMMARY DEBT DATA										
TOTAL DEBT STOCKS (EDT)	..	..	**133.8**	**176.3**	**214.3**	**202.1**	**206.5**	**246.5**	**327.4**	**327.2**
Long-term debt (LDOD)	..	..	**129.1**	**166.4**	**185.0**	**196.0**	**199.5**	**240.9**	**308.0**	**314.6**
Public and publicly guaranteed	..	..	129.1	166.4	185.0	196.0	199.5	240.9	308.0	314.6
Private nonguaranteed	..	..	0.0	0.0	0.0	0.0	0.0	0.0	0.0	0.0
Use of IMF credit	**0.0**	**0.0**	**0.0**	**0.0**	**0.0**	**0.0**	**0.0**	**0.0**	**0.0**	**0.0**
Short-term debt	..	..	**4.7**	**9.9**	**29.3**	**6.1**	**7.0**	**5.7**	**19.4**	**12.6**
of which interest arrears on LDOD	..	..	2.3	3.9	4.7	5.0	4.0	2.7	3.7	4.0
Official creditors	..	..	1.9	3.4	4.0	4.2	3.4	2.7	3.6	4.0
Private creditors	..	..	0.4	0.5	0.7	0.8	0.5	0.0	0.1	0.0
Memo: principal arrears on LDOD	..	..	11.1	16.2	20.0	21.5	19.6	15.4	24.8	34.1
Official creditors	..	..	10.4	14.9	18.5	19.7	17.4	15.4	23.0	32.9
Private creditors	..	..	0.7	1.3	1.6	1.8	2.2	0.0	1.8	1.2
Memo: export credits	..	..	11.0	12.5	19.3	27.9	27.0	13.8	15.2	12.8
TOTAL DEBT FLOWS										
Disbursements	..	..	**12.1**	**28.5**	**21.4**	**23.6**	**21.6**	**54.5**	**66.0**	**28.8**
Long-term debt	..	..	12.1	28.5	21.4	23.6	21.6	54.5	66.0	28.8
IMF purchases	0.0	0.0	0.0	0.0	0.0	0.0	0.0	0.0	0.0	0.0
Principal repayments	..	..	**3.7**	**6.0**	**5.5**	**5.0**	**10.3**	**15.6**	**16.2**	**11.1**
Long-term debt	..	..	3.7	6.0	5.5	5.0	10.3	15.6	16.2	11.1
IMF repurchases	0.0	0.0	0.0	0.0	0.0	0.0	0.0	0.0	0.0	0.0
Net flows on debt	..	..	**10.7**	**24.5**	**34.5**	**-5.0**	**13.3**	**38.7**	**62.6**	**10.7**
of which short-term debt	..	..	2.4	2.0	18.7	-23.6	2.0	-0.1	12.8	-7.1
Interest payments (INT)	..	..	**2.0**	**3.2**	**4.1**	**2.8**	**4.2**	**3.8**	**3.8**	**5.0**
Long-term debt	..	..	1.9	3.0	3.4	2.6	4.1	3.7	3.3	4.8
IMF charges	0.0	0.0	0.0	0.0	0.0	0.0	0.0	0.0	0.0	0.0
Short-term debt	..	..	0.1	0.2	0.8	0.3	0.1	0.2	0.5	0.3
Net transfers on debt	..	..	**8.7**	**21.3**	**30.4**	**-7.9**	**9.1**	**34.9**	**58.8**	**5.6**
Total debt service paid (TDS)	..	..	**5.7**	**9.2**	**9.6**	**7.8**	**14.5**	**19.5**	**20.0**	**16.1**
Long-term debt	..	..	5.6	9.0	8.9	7.6	14.4	19.3	19.5	15.9
IMF repurchases and charges	0.0	0.0	0.0	0.0	0.0	0.0	0.0	0.0	0.0	0.0
Short-term debt (interest only)	..	..	0.1	0.2	0.8	0.3	0.1	0.2	0.5	0.3
2. AGGREGATE NET RESOURCE FLOWS AND NET TRANSFERS (LONG-TERM)										
NET RESOURCE FLOWS	..	..	**85.9**	**87.4**	**103.4**	**106.8**	**86.0**	**109.3**	**110.6**	**71.3**
Net flow of long-term debt (ex. IMF)	..	..	8.3	22.5	15.9	18.6	11.3	38.8	49.8	17.7
Foreign direct investment (net)	..	..	0.0	2.1	26.2	28.5	11.6	9.0	15.0	10.0
Portfolio equity flows	..	..	0.0	0.0	0.0	0.0	0.0	0.0	0.0	0.0
Grants (excluding technical coop.)	..	..	77.5	62.8	61.4	59.8	63.0	61.5	45.8	43.6
Memo: technical coop. grants	..	..	18.0	37.6	40.4	37.3	33.9	36.0	30.9	29.6
official net resource flows	..	..	86.0	85.3	73.0	73.0	74.1	102.5	96.2	63.1
private net resource flows	..	..	-0.1	2.1	30.4	33.8	11.9	6.8	14.4	8.2
NET TRANSFERS	..	..	**84.0**	**84.4**	**100.0**	**104.3**	**81.8**	**105.7**	**107.3**	**66.5**
Interest on long-term debt	..	..	1.9	3.0	3.4	2.6	4.1	3.7	3.3	4.8
Profit remittances on FDI	..	..	0.0	0.0	0.0	0.0	0.0	0.0	0.0	0.0
Memo: official net transfers	..	..	84.1	82.3	69.6	70.8	71.1	99.5	93.2	59.2
private net transfers	..	..	-0.1	2.1	30.4	33.5	10.7	6.2	14.1	7.3
3. MAJOR ECONOMIC AGGREGATES										
Gross national income (GNI)	..	..	340.5	407.3	485.3	495.4	498.3	534.0	579.6	546.6
Exports of goods & services (XGS)	..	..	119.3	148.5	191.4	203.1	213.7	193.6	200.2	215.0
of which workers remittances	..	..	56.0	83.1	103.9	98.7	74.2	71.9	74.0	67.3
Imports of goods & services (MGS)	..	..	153.1	234.4	300.7	284.9	295.5	317.0	362.2	346.8
International reserves (RES)	..	..	77.0	42.1	36.9	27.6	19.3	8.3	43.5	28.2
Current account balance	..	..	-3.8	-45.7	-61.6	-35.0	-29.7	-58.0	-78.7	-64.8
4. DEBT INDICATORS										
EDT / XGS (%)	..	..	112.2	118.7	112.0	99.5	96.7	127.3	163.5	152.2
EDT / GNI (%)	..	..	39.3	43.3	44.2	40.8	41.4	46.2	56.5	59.9
TDS / XGS (%)	..	..	4.8	6.2	5.0	3.8	6.8	10.1	10.0	7.5
INT / XGS (%)	..	..	1.7	2.2	2.1	1.4	2.0	2.0	1.9	2.3
INT / GNI (%)	..	..	0.6	0.8	0.8	0.6	0.8	0.7	0.7	0.9
RES / EDT (%)	..	..	57.5	23.9	17.2	13.6	9.4	3.4	13.3	8.6
RES / MGS (months)	..	..	6.0	2.2	1.5	1.2	0.8	0.3	1.4	1.0
Short-term / EDT (%)	..	..	3.5	5.6	13.7	3.0	3.4	2.3	5.9	3.9
Concessional / EDT (%)	..	..	70.2	75.6	68.6	76.3	78.3	78.3	78.3	82.0
Multilateral / EDT (%)	..	..	65.0	74.5	67.2	72.7	73.3	73.3	67.8	70.1

CAPE VERDE

(US$ million, unless otherwise indicated)

	1970	1980	1990	1994	1995	1996	1997	1998	1999	2000
5. LONG-TERM DEBT										
DEBT OUTSTANDING (LDOD)	..	..	**129.1**	**166.4**	**185.0**	**196.0**	**199.5**	**240.9**	**308.0**	**314.6**
Public and publicly guaranteed	..	..	**129.1**	**166.4**	**185.0**	**196.0**	**199.5**	**240.9**	**308.0**	**314.6**
Official creditors	..	..	126.6	164.3	178.6	184.3	187.5	231.0	298.7	307.1
Multilateral	..	..	87.0	131.4	143.9	147.0	151.3	180.7	222.0	229.2
Concessional	..	..	68.4	111.0	122.6	127.0	135.0	165.1	210.1	220.0
Bilateral	..	..	39.6	32.9	34.6	37.3	36.2	50.3	76.8	77.9
Concessional	..	..	25.5	22.3	24.5	27.1	26.7	28.0	46.3	48.4
Private creditors	..	..	2.5	2.2	6.4	11.8	12.0	9.9	9.3	7.5
Bonds	..	..	0.0	0.0	0.0	0.0	0.0	0.0	0.0	0.0
Commercial banks	..	..	0.0	0.0	0.0	0.0	0.0	0.0	0.0	0.0
Other private	..	..	2.5	2.2	6.4	11.8	12.0	9.9	9.3	7.5
Private nonguaranteed	..	..	**0.0**	**0.0**	**0.0**	**0.0**	**0.0**	**0.0**	**0.0**	**0.0**
Bonds	..	..	0.0	0.0	0.0	0.0	0.0	0.0	0.0	0.0
Commercial banks and other	..	..	0.0	0.0	0.0	0.0	0.0	0.0	0.0	0.0
Memo:										
IBRD	0.0	0.0	0.0	0.0	0.0	0.0	0.0	0.0	0.0	0.0
IDA	0.0	0.0	13.6	26.6	33.0	39.3	45.1	70.2	92.5	97.9
DISBURSEMENTS	..	..	**12.1**	**28.5**	**21.4**	**23.6**	**21.6**	**54.5**	**66.0**	**28.8**
Public and publicly guaranteed	..	..	**12.1**	**28.5**	**21.4**	**23.6**	**21.6**	**54.5**	**66.0**	**28.8**
Official creditors	..	..	12.1	28.5	17.1	18.3	20.2	54.5	66.0	28.8
Multilateral	..	..	6.0	28.0	14.9	15.4	19.5	29.3	40.9	23.5
Concessional	..	..	6.0	27.1	13.7	14.5	19.2	29.3	40.9	23.5
Bilateral	..	..	6.1	0.6	2.2	2.9	0.7	25.1	25.2	5.3
Concessional	..	..	0.7	0.6	2.2	2.9	0.7	2.6	15.8	5.3
Private creditors	..	..	0.0	0.0	4.2	5.3	1.5	0.0	0.0	0.0
Bonds	..	..	0.0	0.0	0.0	0.0	0.0	0.0	0.0	0.0
Commercial banks	..	..	0.0	0.0	0.0	0.0	0.0	0.0	0.0	0.0
Other private	..	..	0.0	0.0	4.2	5.3	1.5	0.0	0.0	0.0
Private nonguaranteed	..	..	**0.0**	**0.0**	**0.0**	**0.0**	**0.0**	**0.0**	**0.0**	**0.0**
Bonds	..	..	0.0	0.0	0.0	0.0	0.0	0.0	0.0	0.0
Commercial banks and other	..	..	0.0	0.0	0.0	0.0	0.0	0.0	0.0	0.0
Memo:										
IBRD	0.0	0.0	0.0	0.0	0.0	0.0	0.0	0.0	0.0	0.0
IDA	0.0	0.0	2.0	5.0	6.0	7.6	8.3	22.7	24.1	10.4
PRINCIPAL REPAYMENTS	..	..	**3.7**	**6.0**	**5.5**	**5.0**	**10.3**	**15.6**	**16.2**	**11.1**
Public and publicly guaranteed	..	..	**3.7**	**6.0**	**5.5**	**5.0**	**10.3**	**15.6**	**16.2**	**11.1**
Official creditors	..	..	3.6	6.0	5.5	5.0	9.1	13.5	15.6	9.3
Multilateral	..	..	2.5	5.3	4.8	4.8	7.0	6.2	5.4	6.1
Concessional	..	..	1.0	3.0	3.5	3.1	5.1	4.7	3.9	4.8
Bilateral	..	..	1.1	0.7	0.7	0.2	2.0	7.2	10.2	3.2
Concessional	..	..	0.2	0.3	0.2	0.2	1.4	1.0	0.5	2.2
Private creditors	..	..	0.1	0.0	0.0	0.0	1.2	2.2	0.6	1.8
Bonds	..	..	0.0	0.0	0.0	0.0	0.0	0.0	0.0	0.0
Commercial banks	..	..	0.0	0.0	0.0	0.0	0.0	0.0	0.0	0.0
Other private	..	..	0.1	0.0	0.0	0.0	1.2	2.2	0.6	1.8
Private nonguaranteed	..	..	**0.0**	**0.0**	**0.0**	**0.0**	**0.0**	**0.0**	**0.0**	**0.0**
Bonds	..	..	0.0	0.0	0.0	0.0	0.0	0.0	0.0	0.0
Commercial banks and other	..	..	0.0	0.0	0.0	0.0	0.0	0.0	0.0	0.0
Memo:										
IBRD	0.0	0.0	0.0	0.0	0.0	0.0	0.0	0.0	0.0	0.0
IDA	0.0	0.0	0.0	0.1	0.1	0.1	0.1	0.2	0.3	0.3
NET FLOWS ON DEBT	..	..	**8.3**	**22.5**	**15.9**	**18.6**	**11.3**	**38.8**	**49.8**	**17.7**
Public and publicly guaranteed	..	..	**8.3**	**22.5**	**15.9**	**18.6**	**11.3**	**38.8**	**49.8**	**17.7**
Official creditors	..	..	8.5	22.5	11.6	13.2	11.1	41.0	50.4	19.5
Multilateral	..	..	3.5	22.7	10.1	10.6	12.4	23.1	35.4	17.4
Concessional	..	..	5.0	24.1	10.2	11.5	14.1	24.7	36.9	18.7
Bilateral	..	..	4.9	-0.2	1.6	2.7	-1.3	17.9	15.0	2.1
Concessional	..	..	0.6	0.2	2.0	2.7	-0.7	1.6	15.2	3.1
Private creditors	..	..	-0.1	0.0	4.2	5.3	0.3	-2.2	-0.6	-1.8
Bonds	..	..	0.0	0.0	0.0	0.0	0.0	0.0	0.0	0.0
Commercial banks	..	..	0.0	0.0	0.0	0.0	0.0	0.0	0.0	0.0
Other private	..	..	-0.1	0.0	4.2	5.3	0.3	-2.2	-0.6	-1.8
Private nonguaranteed	..	..	**0.0**	**0.0**	**0.0**	**0.0**	**0.0**	**0.0**	**0.0**	**0.0**
Bonds	..	..	0.0	0.0	0.0	0.0	0.0	0.0	0.0	0.0
Commercial banks and other	..	..	0.0	0.0	0.0	0.0	0.0	0.0	0.0	0.0
Memo:										
IBRD	0.0	0.0	0.0	0.0	0.0	0.0	0.0	0.0	0.0	0.0
IDA	0.0	0.0	2.0	4.9	5.9	7.4	8.2	22.5	23.8	10.2

CAPE VERDE

(US$ million, unless otherwise indicated)

	1970	1980	1990	1994	1995	1996	1997	1998	1999	2000
INTEREST PAYMENTS (LINT)	..	..	**1.9**	**3.0**	**3.4**	**2.6**	**4.1**	**3.7**	**3.3**	**4.8**
Public and publicly guaranteed	..	..	**1.9**	**3.0**	**3.4**	**2.6**	**4.1**	**3.7**	**3.3**	**4.8**
Official creditors	..	..	1.9	3.0	3.4	2.2	3.0	3.0	3.0	3.9
Multilateral	..	..	1.2	2.8	3.3	2.0	2.2	2.4	2.1	2.7
Concessional	..	..	0.5	2.0	2.3	1.1	1.4	1.8	1.9	2.3
Bilateral	..	..	0.7	0.2	0.1	0.2	0.8	0.6	0.9	1.1
Concessional	..	..	0.0	0.1	0.1	0.2	0.4	0.4	0.3	0.8
Private creditors	..	..	0.0	0.0	0.0	0.3	1.2	0.6	0.3	0.9
Bonds	..	..	0.0	0.0	0.0	0.0	0.0	0.0	0.0	0.0
Commercial banks	..	..	0.0	0.0	0.0	0.0	0.0	0.0	0.0	0.0
Other private	..	..	0.0	0.0	0.0	0.3	1.2	0.6	0.3	0.9
Private nonguaranteed	..	..	**0.0**	**0.0**	**0.0**	**0.0**	**0.0**	**0.0**	**0.0**	**0.0**
Bonds	..	..	0.0	0.0	0.0	0.0	0.0	0.0	0.0	0.0
Commercial banks and other	..	..	0.0	0.0	0.0	0.0	0.0	0.0	0.0	0.0
Memo:										
IBRD	0.0	0.0	0.0	0.0	0.0	0.0	0.0	0.0	0.0	0.0
IDA	0.0	0.0	0.1	0.2	0.2	0.2	0.3	0.4	0.5	0.7
NET TRANSFERS ON DEBT	..	..	**6.5**	**19.5**	**12.5**	**16.0**	**7.2**	**35.2**	**46.5**	**12.9**
Public and publicly guaranteed	..	..	**6.5**	**19.5**	**12.5**	**16.0**	**7.2**	**35.2**	**46.5**	**12.9**
Official creditors	..	..	6.6	19.5	8.3	11.0	8.1	37.9	47.4	15.7
Multilateral	..	..	2.3	19.8	6.8	8.5	10.3	20.7	33.3	14.7
Concessional	..	..	4.6	22.2	7.9	10.4	12.7	22.8	35.1	16.4
Bilateral	..	..	4.3	-0.3	1.5	2.5	-2.2	17.3	14.1	1.0
Concessional	..	..	0.6	0.1	2.0	2.5	-1.1	1.2	15.0	2.3
Private creditors	..	..	-0.2	0.0	4.2	5.0	-0.9	-2.8	-0.9	-2.7
Bonds	..	..	0.0	0.0	0.0	0.0	0.0	0.0	0.0	0.0
Commercial banks	..	..	0.0	0.0	0.0	0.0	0.0	0.0	0.0	0.0
Other private	..	..	-0.2	0.0	4.2	5.0	-0.9	-2.8	-0.9	-2.7
Private nonguaranteed	..	..	**0.0**	**0.0**	**0.0**	**0.0**	**0.0**	**0.0**	**0.0**	**0.0**
Bonds	..	..	0.0	0.0	0.0	0.0	0.0	0.0	0.0	0.0
Commercial banks and other	..	..	0.0	0.0	0.0	0.0	0.0	0.0	0.0	0.0
Memo:										
IBRD	0.0	0.0	0.0	0.0	0.0	0.0	0.0	0.0	0.0	0.0
IDA	0.0	0.0	1.9	4.7	5.7	7.2	7.9	22.1	23.3	9.5
DEBT SERVICE (LTDS)	..	..	**5.6**	**9.0**	**8.9**	**7.6**	**14.4**	**19.3**	**19.5**	**15.9**
Public and publicly guaranteed	..	..	**5.6**	**9.0**	**8.9**	**7.6**	**14.4**	**19.3**	**19.5**	**15.9**
Official creditors	..	..	5.5	9.0	8.9	7.3	12.0	16.5	18.6	13.1
Multilateral	..	..	3.7	8.1	8.1	6.9	9.2	8.7	7.6	8.8
Concessional	..	..	1.4	5.0	5.8	4.2	6.5	6.5	5.8	7.1
Bilateral	..	..	1.8	0.9	0.7	0.4	2.9	7.8	11.1	4.3
Concessional	..	..	0.2	0.4	0.3	0.4	1.8	1.4	0.8	3.0
Private creditors	..	..	0.2	0.0	0.0	0.3	2.4	2.8	0.9	2.7
Bonds	..	..	0.0	0.0	0.0	0.0	0.0	0.0	0.0	0.0
Commercial banks	..	..	0.0	0.0	0.0	0.0	0.0	0.0	0.0	0.0
Other private	..	..	0.2	0.0	0.0	0.3	2.4	2.8	0.9	2.7
Private nonguaranteed	..	..	**0.0**	**0.0**	**0.0**	**0.0**	**0.0**	**0.0**	**0.0**	**0.0**
Bonds	..	..	0.0	0.0	0.0	0.0	0.0	0.0	0.0	0.0
Commercial banks and other	..	..	0.0	0.0	0.0	0.0	0.0	0.0	0.0	0.0
Memo:										
IBRD	0.0	0.0	0.0	0.0	0.0	0.0	0.0	0.0	0.0	0.0
IDA	0.0	0.0	0.1	0.2	0.4	0.4	0.4	0.6	0.8	0.9
UNDISBURSED DEBT	..	..	**99.9**	**175.8**	**168.7**	**132.9**	**116.4**	**146.8**	**153.3**	**126.9**
Official creditors	..	..	99.9	163.8	160.9	130.5	115.5	145.8	152.4	118.6
Private creditors	..	..	0.0	12.0	7.8	2.4	0.9	0.9	0.9	8.3
Memorandum items										
Concessional LDOD	..	..	93.9	133.3	147.1	154.2	161.7	193.1	256.5	268.5
Variable rate LDOD	..	..	109.8	147.5	161.7	167.5	170.8	214.8	264.3	274.6
Public sector LDOD	..	..	129.1	166.4	185.0	196.0	199.5	240.9	308.0	314.6
Private sector LDOD	..	..	0.0	0.0	0.0	0.0	0.0	0.0	0.0	0.0

6. CURRENCY COMPOSITION OF LONG-TERM DEBT (PERCENT)

	1970	1980	1990	1994	1995	1996	1997	1998	1999	2000
Deutsche mark	..	..	0.0	0.0	0.0	0.0	0.0	0.0	3.9	3.3
French franc	..	..	0.0	0.0	0.0	0.0	0.0	0.0	0.0	0.0
Japanese yen	..	..	0.0	0.0	0.0	0.0	0.0	0.0	0.0	0.0
Pound sterling	..	..	0.0	0.0	0.0	0.0	0.0	0.0	0.0	0.0
Swiss franc	..	..	0.0	0.0	0.0	0.0	0.0	0.0	0.0	0.0
U.S.dollars	..	..	38.5	33.1	35.4	39.9	43.4	51.3	54.1	55.7
Multiple currency	..	..	16.1	8.9	7.6	6.2	5.9	4.9	4.0	4.5
Special drawing rights	..	..	0.1	3.4	3.7	3.8	4.1	3.9	3.3	3.1
All other currencies	..	..	45.3	54.6	53.3	50.1	46.6	39.9	34.7	33.4

CAPE VERDE

(US$ million, unless otherwise indicated)

	1970	1980	1990	1994	1995	1996	1997	1998	1999	2000
7. DEBT RESTRUCTURINGS										
Total amount rescheduled	..	..	0.0	0.0	0.0	0.0	2.6	0.0	0.0	0.0
Debt stock rescheduled	..	..	0.0	0.0	0.0	0.0	0.0	0.0	0.0	0.0
Principal rescheduled	..	..	0.0	0.0	0.0	0.0	1.9	0.0	0.0	0.0
Official	..	..	0.0	0.0	0.0	0.0	1.9	0.0	0.0	0.0
Private	..	..	0.0	0.0	0.0	0.0	0.0	0.0	0.0	0.0
Interest rescheduled	..	..	0.0	0.0	0.0	0.0	0.7	0.0	0.0	0.0
Official	..	..	0.0	0.0	0.0	0.0	0.7	0.0	0.0	0.0
Private	..	..	0.0	0.0	0.0	0.0	0.0	0.0	0.0	0.0
Debt forgiven	..	..	8.2	0.0	0.0	0.0	0.0	0.4	0.0	0.0
Memo: interest forgiven	..	..	0.8	0.0	0.0	0.0	0.0	0.0	0.0	0.0
Debt stock reduction	..	..	0.0	0.0	0.0	0.0	0.0	0.0	0.0	0.0
of which debt buyback	..	..	0.0	0.0	0.0	0.0	0.0	0.0	0.0	0.0
8. DEBT STOCK-FLOW RECONCILIATION										
Total change in debt stocks	..	..	7.7	28.5	38.0	-12.2	4.4	40.0	80.9	-0.2
Net flows on debt	..	..	10.7	24.5	34.5	-5.0	13.3	38.7	62.6	10.7
Net change in interest arrears	..	..	-0.2	0.9	0.8	0.4	-1.1	-1.3	1.0	0.3
Interest capitalized	..	..	0.0	0.0	0.0	0.0	0.7	0.0	0.0	0.0
Debt forgiveness or reduction	..	..	-8.2	0.0	0.0	0.0	0.0	-0.4	0.0	0.0
Cross-currency valuation	..	..	2.9	-0.4	1.3	-6.2	-5.0	2.3	-1.5	-7.0
Residual	..	..	2.4	3.5	1.4	-1.3	-3.5	0.7	18.9	-4.2
9. AVERAGE TERMS OF NEW COMMITMENTS										
ALL CREDITORS										
Interest (%)	..	..	1.5	3.2	0.8	0.8	0.8	1.1	0.5	0.3
Maturity (years)	..	..	42.6	22.6	39.8	39.8	50.1	21.6	33.3	28.7
Grace period (years)	..	..	9.1	5.1	10.3	10.3	10.6	5.4	8.8	5.8
Grant element (%)	..	..	73.0	45.9	80.6	80.6	83.5	47.5	69.5	50.2
Official creditors										
Interest (%)	..	..	1.5	2.5	0.8	0.8	0.8	1.2	1.1	0.8
Maturity (years)	..	..	42.6	27.0	39.8	39.8	50.1	21.6	33.3	45.9
Grace period (years)	..	..	9.1	6.1	10.3	10.3	10.6	5.4	8.8	9.3
Grant element (%)	..	..	73.0	55.1	80.6	80.6	83.5	47.5	69.5	80.1
Private creditors										
Interest (%)	..	..	0.0	5.0	0.0	0.0	0.0	0.0	0.0	5.5
Maturity (years)	..	..	0.0	12.0	0.0	0.0	0.0	0.0	0.0	10.6
Grace period (years)	..	..	0.0	2.5	0.0	0.0	0.0	0.0	0.0	2.2
Grant element (%)	..	..	0.0	23.4	0.0	0.0	0.0	0.0	0.0	18.6
Memorandum items										
Commitments	..	..	35.9	41.3	11.5	11.4	10.3	93.3	64.5	15.0
Official creditors	..	..	35.9	29.3	11.5	11.4	10.3	93.3	64.5	7.7
Private creditors	..	..	0.0	12.0	0.0	0.0	0.0	0.0	0.0	7.3

10. CONTRACTUAL OBLIGATIONS ON OUTSTANDING LONG-TERM DEBT

	2001	2002	2003	2004	2005	2006	2007	2008	2009	2010
TOTAL										
Disbursements	37.7	34.6	23.1	15.1	9.0	3.4	2.0	0.8	0.5	0.1
Principal	19.3	14.0	15.6	15.4	14.8	14.3	12.9	13.4	13.8	14.5
Interest	4.6	4.8	4.8	4.6	4.3	4.0	3.7	3.4	3.1	2.8
Official creditors										
Disbursements	33.5	31.9	22.1	14.7	9.0	3.4	2.0	0.8	0.5	0.1
Principal	17.8	12.0	13.5	13.6	12.9	12.5	12.2	12.8	13.2	13.9
Interest	4.2	4.2	4.3	4.2	4.0	3.8	3.5	3.2	3.0	2.8
Bilateral creditors										
Disbursements	2.6	3.4	2.6	2.0	1.3	0.6	0.4	0.3	0.1	0.1
Principal	10.3	4.2	4.7	4.3	4.1	4.3	3.9	3.6	3.6	3.6
Interest	1.4	1.3	1.2	1.0	0.9	0.8	0.6	0.5	0.5	0.4
Multilateral creditors										
Disbursements	30.9	28.5	19.5	12.7	7.7	2.8	1.6	0.5	0.4	0.0
Principal	7.5	7.9	8.8	9.3	8.8	8.1	8.3	9.2	9.6	10.3
Interest	2.8	3.0	3.1	3.1	3.1	3.0	2.9	2.7	2.5	2.4
Private creditors										
Disbursements	4.2	2.7	1.0	0.4	0.0	0.0	0.0	0.0	0.0	0.0
Principal	1.5	2.0	2.1	1.8	1.8	1.8	0.6	0.6	0.6	0.6
Interest	0.4	0.6	0.5	0.4	0.4	0.3	0.2	0.1	0.1	0.1
Commercial banks										
Disbursements	3.5	2.4	1.0	0.4	0.0	0.0	0.0	0.0	0.0	0.0
Principal	0.3	0.8	0.9	0.6	0.6	0.6	0.6	0.6	0.6	0.6
Interest	0.1	0.3	0.3	0.3	0.3	0.2	0.2	0.1	0.1	0.1
Other private										
Disbursements	0.7	0.3	0.0	0.0	0.0	0.0	0.0	0.0	0.0	0.0
Principal	1.2	1.2	1.2	1.2	1.2	1.2	0.0	0.0	0.0	0.0
Interest	0.3	0.3	0.2	0.2	0.1	0.0	0.0	0.0	0.0	0.0

CENTRAL AFRICAN REPUBLIC

(US$ million, unless otherwise indicated)

	1970	1980	1990	1994	1995	1996	1997	1998	1999	2000
1. SUMMARY DEBT DATA										
TOTAL DEBT STOCKS (EDT)	**24.1**	**194.7**	**698.5**	**888.1**	**946.0**	**932.8**	**883.0**	**918.7**	**909.2**	**872.1**
Long-term debt (LDOD)	**24.1**	**146.5**	**624.1**	**802.4**	**853.9**	**850.4**	**801.5**	**841.0**	**826.1**	**810.1**
Public and publicly guaranteed	24.1	146.5	624.1	802.4	853.9	850.4	801.5	841.0	826.1	810.1
Private nonguaranteed	0.0	0.0	0.0	0.0	0.0	0.0	0.0	0.0	0.0	0.0
Use of IMF credit	**0.0**	**23.5**	**36.7**	**41.4**	**34.9**	**27.6**	**18.6**	**17.6**	**23.5**	**21.5**
Short-term debt	**0.1**	**24.6**	**37.7**	**44.3**	**57.1**	**54.7**	**62.8**	**60.1**	**59.6**	**40.6**
of which interest arrears on LDOD	0.1	10.6	15.0	25.3	35.7	38.5	44.8	44.2	22.9	25.5
Official creditors	0.1	1.7	13.1	23.7	31.7	37.2	43.6	43.3	21.6	24.1
Private creditors	0.0	8.8	1.9	1.5	4.0	1.3	1.2	0.8	1.4	1.3
Memo: principal arrears on LDOD	0.3	43.5	23.2	58.1	74.2	85.0	94.9	95.9	84.1	96.1
Official creditors	0.2	16.9	19.6	51.2	60.6	70.8	81.3	85.3	71.5	83.5
Private creditors	0.1	26.7	3.6	7.0	13.6	14.2	13.6	10.6	12.6	12.5
Memo: export credits	0.0	0.0	63.0	42.6	48.6	44.6	34.7	69.4	57.0	38.4
TOTAL DEBT FLOWS										
Disbursements	**1.7**	**39.8**	**121.1**	**59.3**	**32.6**	**26.9**	**6.4**	**14.6**	**16.7**	**16.1**
Long-term debt	1.7	25.2	112.8	44.0	32.6	26.9	6.4	3.4	5.5	16.1
IMF purchases	0.0	14.7	8.3	15.3	0.0	0.0	0.0	11.2	11.3	0.0
Principal repayments	**2.4**	**6.7**	**17.4**	**12.4**	**10.0**	**8.0**	**11.6**	**25.3**	**12.2**	**8.3**
Long-term debt	2.4	1.0	7.6	7.7	2.6	1.8	4.1	12.4	7.2	7.5
IMF repurchases	0.0	5.7	9.8	4.8	7.4	6.2	7.5	13.0	5.0	0.8
Net flows on debt	**-0.7**	**31.1**	**106.6**	**31.8**	**25.1**	**13.8**	**-3.5**	**-12.8**	**25.3**	**-13.8**
of which short-term debt	0.0	-2.0	2.9	-15.1	2.4	-5.1	1.7	-2.0	20.8	-21.6
Interest payments (INT)	**0.7**	**3.3**	**11.8**	**10.7**	**5.7**	**4.9**	**4.0**	**8.0**	**6.6**	**5.9**
Long-term debt	0.7	0.4	9.0	8.1	3.5	3.4	2.4	6.7	4.6	4.3
IMF charges	0.0	0.8	1.2	0.7	1.0	0.8	0.7	0.4	0.1	0.1
Short-term debt	0.0	2.1	1.6	2.0	1.2	0.7	0.9	0.9	1.8	1.4
Net transfers on debt	**-1.4**	**27.8**	**94.9**	**21.1**	**19.3**	**8.9**	**-7.5**	**-20.8**	**18.7**	**-19.7**
Total debt service paid (TDS)	**3.1**	**10.0**	**29.1**	**23.1**	**15.7**	**12.9**	**15.6**	**33.3**	**18.7**	**14.1**
Long-term debt	3.1	1.4	16.6	15.8	6.1	5.3	6.5	19.0	11.9	11.8
IMF repurchases and charges	0.0	6.5	11.0	5.4	8.4	7.0	8.2	13.4	5.1	0.9
Short-term debt (interest only)	0.0	2.1	1.6	2.0	1.2	0.7	0.9	0.9	1.8	1.4
2. AGGREGATE NET RESOURCE FLOWS AND NET TRANSFERS (LONG-TERM)										
NET RESOURCE FLOWS	**6.8**	**85.1**	**192.4**	**137.8**	**142.6**	**149.5**	**81.0**	**98.3**	**90.7**	**69.4**
Net flow of long-term debt (ex. IMF)	-0.7	24.2	105.2	36.3	30.0	25.1	2.3	-9.0	-1.8	8.6
Foreign direct investment (net)	1.2	5.3	1.0	4.0	3.0	5.0	5.5	5.0	13.0	5.0
Portfolio equity flows	0.0	0.0	0.0	0.0	0.0	0.0	0.0	0.0	0.0	0.0
Grants (excluding technical coop.)	6.4	55.7	86.2	97.5	109.6	119.4	73.2	102.3	79.4	55.8
Memo: technical coop. grants	8.1	34.2	56.2	42.7	46.8	44.8	26.1	26.2	38.4	21.7
official net resource flows	6.8	80.7	192.0	134.0	139.6	144.5	75.5	93.3	78.1	64.4
private net resource flows	0.0	4.4	0.4	3.8	3.0	5.0	5.5	5.0	12.6	5.0
NET TRANSFERS	**5.1**	**84.7**	**181.5**	**128.8**	**138.1**	**145.1**	**77.6**	**90.6**	**86.1**	**65.1**
Interest on long-term debt	0.7	0.4	9.0	8.1	3.5	3.4	2.4	6.7	4.6	4.3
Profit remittances on FDI	1.0	0.0	2.0	1.0	1.0	1.0	1.0	1.0	0.0	0.0
Memo: official net transfers	6.5	80.4	183.9	126.1	136.1	141.1	73.1	86.6	73.5	60.1
private net transfers	-1.4	4.3	-2.4	2.7	2.0	4.0	4.5	4.0	12.6	5.0
3. MAJOR ECONOMIC AGGREGATES										
Gross national income (GNI)	186.4	799.6	1,465.1	832.2	1,100.9	1,049.0	987.5	1,028.5	1,038.3	951.6
Exports of goods & services (XGS)	..	205.4	220.4	179.0	200.6	162.9	171.2	147.3	154.3	156.7
of which workers remittances	..	0.0	0.0	..	..	..	..	..	..	..
Imports of goods & services (MGS)	..	329.2	432.5	267.1	323.5	240.8	258.8	273.4	262.1	256.5
International reserves (RES)	1.4	61.7	122.9	214.3	237.9	236.3	181.8	145.7	136.3	133.3
Current account balance	..	-43.1	-89.1	-24.7	-61.9	-79.4	-49.3	-57.3	-41.6	..
4. DEBT INDICATORS										
EDT / XGS (%)	..	94.8	317.0	496.1	471.5	572.8	515.8	623.6	589.4	556.4
EDT / GNI (%)	12.9	24.4	47.7	106.7	85.9	88.9	89.4	89.3	87.6	91.6
TDS / XGS (%)	..	4.9	13.2	12.9	7.8	7.9	9.1	22.6	12.1	9.0
INT / XGS (%)	..	1.6	5.4	6.0	2.8	3.0	2.3	5.4	4.3	3.8
INT / GNI (%)	0.4	0.4	0.8	1.3	0.5	0.5	0.4	0.8	0.6	0.6
RES / EDT (%)	5.8	31.7	17.6	24.1	25.2	25.3	20.6	15.9	15.0	15.3
RES / MGS (months)	..	2.3	3.4	9.6	8.8	11.8	8.4	6.4	6.2	6.2
Short-term / EDT (%)	0.4	12.6	5.4	5.0	6.0	5.9	7.1	6.5	6.6	4.7
Concessional / EDT (%)	62.2	30.1	73.1	81.4	80.9	82.3	82.0	81.1	81.5	83.2
Multilateral / EDT (%)	0.8	27.4	65.2	66.8	67.3	69.2	68.5	67.8	66.9	66.9

CENTRAL AFRICAN REPUBLIC

(US$ million, unless otherwise indicated)

	1970	1980	1990	1994	1995	1996	1997	1998	1999	2000
5. LONG-TERM DEBT										
DEBT OUTSTANDING (LDOD)	**24.1**	**146.5**	**624.1**	**802.4**	**853.9**	**850.4**	**801.5**	**841.0**	**826.1**	**810.1**
Public and publicly guaranteed	**24.1**	**146.5**	**624.1**	**802.4**	**853.9**	**850.4**	**801.5**	**841.0**	**826.1**	**810.1**
Official creditors	17.9	98.3	602.6	784.8	835.6	836.2	787.9	807.9	793.5	777.5
Multilateral	0.2	53.3	455.5	593.2	636.2	645.2	604.5	622.4	608.4	583.1
Concessional	0.2	41.6	429.4	580.0	622.3	631.1	590.6	607.8	595.9	571.6
Bilateral	17.7	44.9	147.0	191.6	199.4	191.0	183.4	185.5	185.1	194.4
Concessional	14.8	17.0	81.5	142.6	142.6	136.9	133.5	137.5	145.3	154.2
Private creditors	6.1	48.3	21.6	17.6	18.4	14.2	13.6	33.2	32.6	32.6
Bonds	0.0	0.0	0.0	0.0	0.0	0.0	0.0	0.0	0.0	0.0
Commercial banks	0.0	0.0	0.0	0.0	0.0	0.0	0.0	0.0	0.0	0.0
Other private	6.1	48.3	21.6	17.6	18.4	14.2	13.6	33.2	32.6	32.6
Private nonguaranteed	**0.0**	**0.0**	**0.0**	**0.0**	**0.0**	**0.0**	**0.0**	**0.0**	**0.0**	**0.0**
Bonds	0.0	0.0	0.0	0.0	0.0	0.0	0.0	0.0	0.0	0.0
Commercial banks and other	0.0	0.0	0.0	0.0	0.0	0.0	0.0	0.0	0.0	0.0
Memo:										
IBRD	0.0	0.0	0.0	0.0	0.0	0.0	0.0	0.0	0.0	0.0
IDA	0.2	28.8	265.1	377.2	414.0	422.0	403.0	413.3	403.3	391.3
DISBURSEMENTS	**1.7**	**25.2**	**112.8**	**44.0**	**32.6**	**26.9**	**6.4**	**3.4**	**5.5**	**16.1**
Public and publicly guaranteed	**1.7**	**25.2**	**112.8**	**44.0**	**32.6**	**26.9**	**6.4**	**3.4**	**5.5**	**16.1**
Official creditors	1.5	25.2	112.8	44.0	32.6	26.9	6.4	3.4	5.5	16.1
Multilateral	0.2	13.7	95.2	44.0	32.6	26.9	6.4	3.4	5.5	16.1
Concessional	0.2	13.5	93.6	44.0	32.0	26.9	5.3	3.4	5.5	16.1
Bilateral	1.3	11.5	17.6	0.0	0.0	0.0	0.0	0.0	0.0	0.0
Concessional	1.0	5.5	16.1	0.0	0.0	0.0	0.0	0.0	0.0	0.0
Private creditors	0.2	0.0	0.0	0.0	0.0	0.0	0.0	0.0	0.0	0.0
Bonds	0.0	0.0	0.0	0.0	0.0	0.0	0.0	0.0	0.0	0.0
Commercial banks	0.0	0.0	0.0	0.0	0.0	0.0	0.0	0.0	0.0	0.0
Other private	0.2	0.0	0.0	0.0	0.0	0.0	0.0	0.0	0.0	0.0
Private nonguaranteed	**0.0**	**0.0**	**0.0**	**0.0**	**0.0**	**0.0**	**0.0**	**0.0**	**0.0**	**0.0**
Bonds	0.0	0.0	0.0	0.0	0.0	0.0	0.0	0.0	0.0	0.0
Commercial banks and other	0.0	0.0	0.0	0.0	0.0	0.0	0.0	0.0	0.0	0.0
Memo:										
IBRD	0.0	0.0	0.0	0.0	0.0	0.0	0.0	0.0	0.0	0.0
IDA	0.2	10.3	70.4	40.1	29.8	22.9	4.6	0.2	2.6	12.9
PRINCIPAL REPAYMENTS	**2.4**	**1.0**	**7.6**	**7.7**	**2.6**	**1.8**	**4.1**	**12.4**	**7.2**	**7.5**
Public and publicly guaranteed	**2.4**	**1.0**	**7.6**	**7.7**	**2.6**	**1.8**	**4.1**	**12.4**	**7.2**	**7.5**
Official creditors	1.1	0.1	7.0	7.5	2.6	1.8	4.1	12.4	6.8	7.4
Multilateral	0.0	0.1	3.2	6.4	2.6	1.8	4.1	12.3	6.2	6.9
Concessional	0.0	0.1	1.8	4.3	2.2	1.7	4.0	10.2	5.1	6.9
Bilateral	1.1	0.0	3.8	1.0	0.0	0.0	0.0	0.1	0.6	0.5
Concessional	0.5	0.0	0.9	1.0	0.0	0.0	0.0	0.1	0.6	0.3
Private creditors	1.4	0.9	0.6	0.2	0.0	0.0	0.0	0.0	0.4	0.0
Bonds	0.0	0.0	0.0	0.0	0.0	0.0	0.0	0.0	0.0	0.0
Commercial banks	0.0	0.0	0.0	0.0	0.0	0.0	0.0	0.0	0.0	0.0
Other private	1.4	0.9	0.6	0.2	0.0	0.0	0.0	0.0	0.4	0.0
Private nonguaranteed	**0.0**	**0.0**	**0.0**	**0.0**	**0.0**	**0.0**	**0.0**	**0.0**	**0.0**	**0.0**
Bonds	0.0	0.0	0.0	0.0	0.0	0.0	0.0	0.0	0.0	0.0
Commercial banks and other	0.0	0.0	0.0	0.0	0.0	0.0	0.0	0.0	0.0	0.0
Memo:										
IBRD	0.0	0.0	0.0	0.0	0.0	0.0	0.0	0.0	0.0	0.0
IDA	0.0	0.1	0.5	1.2	1.3	1.4	1.3	3.6	3.9	5.7
NET FLOWS ON DEBT	**-0.7**	**24.2**	**105.2**	**36.3**	**30.0**	**25.1**	**2.3**	**-9.0**	**-1.8**	**8.6**
Public and publicly guaranteed	**-0.7**	**24.2**	**105.2**	**36.3**	**30.0**	**25.1**	**2.3**	**-9.0**	**-1.8**	**8.6**
Official creditors	0.4	25.0	105.8	36.5	30.0	25.1	2.3	-9.0	-1.3	8.6
Multilateral	0.2	13.6	92.0	37.5	30.0	25.1	2.3	-8.9	-0.7	9.1
Concessional	0.2	13.4	91.8	39.6	29.8	25.2	1.3	-6.8	0.4	9.2
Bilateral	0.2	11.4	13.8	-1.0	0.0	0.0	0.0	-0.1	-0.6	-0.5
Concessional	0.5	5.5	15.2	-1.0	0.0	0.0	0.0	-0.1	-0.6	-0.3
Private creditors	-1.2	-0.9	-0.6	-0.2	0.0	0.0	0.0	0.0	-0.4	0.0
Bonds	0.0	0.0	0.0	0.0	0.0	0.0	0.0	0.0	0.0	0.0
Commercial banks	0.0	0.0	0.0	0.0	0.0	0.0	0.0	0.0	0.0	0.0
Other private	-1.2	-0.9	-0.6	-0.2	0.0	0.0	0.0	0.0	-0.4	0.0
Private nonguaranteed	**0.0**	**0.0**	**0.0**	**0.0**	**0.0**	**0.0**	**0.0**	**0.0**	**0.0**	**0.0**
Bonds	0.0	0.0	0.0	0.0	0.0	0.0	0.0	0.0	0.0	0.0
Commercial banks and other	0.0	0.0	0.0	0.0	0.0	0.0	0.0	0.0	0.0	0.0
Memo:										
IBRD	0.0	0.0	0.0	0.0	0.0	0.0	0.0	0.0	0.0	0.0
IDA	0.2	10.2	69.9	38.9	28.5	21.5	3.3	-3.4	-1.3	7.2

CENTRAL AFRICAN REPUBLIC

(US$ million, unless otherwise indicated)

	1970	1980	1990	1994	1995	1996	1997	1998	1999	2000
INTEREST PAYMENTS (LINT)	**0.7**	**0.4**	**9.0**	**8.1**	**3.5**	**3.4**	**2.4**	**6.7**	**4.6**	**4.3**
Public and publicly guaranteed	**0.7**	**0.4**	**9.0**	**8.1**	**3.5**	**3.4**	**2.4**	**6.7**	**4.6**	**4.3**
Official creditors	0.3	0.3	8.1	7.9	3.5	3.4	2.4	6.7	4.6	4.3
Multilateral	0.0	0.3	5.1	7.8	3.5	3.3	2.4	6.3	3.7	3.4
Concessional	0.0	0.2	2.9	6.3	3.4	3.2	2.4	5.2	3.2	3.4
Bilateral	0.3	0.0	3.1	0.1	0.0	0.1	0.0	0.4	0.9	0.9
Concessional	0.2	0.0	1.9	0.1	0.0	0.0	0.0	0.2	0.9	0.8
Private creditors	0.4	0.1	0.8	0.1	0.0	0.0	0.0	0.0	0.0	0.0
Bonds	0.0	0.0	0.0	0.0	0.0	0.0	0.0	0.0	0.0	0.0
Commercial banks	0.0	0.0	0.0	0.0	0.0	0.0	0.0	0.0	0.0	0.0
Other private	0.4	0.1	0.8	0.1	0.0	0.0	0.0	0.0	0.0	0.0
Private nonguaranteed	**0.0**	**0.0**	**0.0**	**0.0**	**0.0**	**0.0**	**0.0**	**0.0**	**0.0**	**0.0**
Bonds	0.0	0.0	0.0	0.0	0.0	0.0	0.0	0.0	0.0	0.0
Commercial banks and other	0.0	0.0	0.0	0.0	0.0	0.0	0.0	0.0	0.0	0.0
Memo:										
IBRD	0.0	0.0	0.0	0.0	0.0	0.0	0.0	0.0	0.0	0.0
IDA	0.0	0.2	1.5	2.8	2.9	2.9	1.9	4.1	2.9	3.2
NET TRANSFERS ON DEBT	**-1.4**	**23.8**	**96.3**	**28.2**	**26.5**	**21.7**	**-0.2**	**-15.7**	**-6.4**	**4.3**
Public and publicly guaranteed	**-1.4**	**23.8**	**96.3**	**28.2**	**26.5**	**21.7**	**-0.2**	**-15.7**	**-6.4**	**4.3**
Official creditors	0.1	24.7	97.6	28.6	26.5	21.7	-0.2	-15.7	-6.0	4.3
Multilateral	0.2	13.3	86.9	29.7	26.5	21.8	-0.2	-15.3	-4.4	5.7
Concessional	0.2	13.2	88.9	33.3	26.4	22.0	-1.1	-12.0	-2.8	5.7
Bilateral	-0.1	11.4	10.7	-1.1	0.0	-0.1	0.0	-0.4	-1.5	-1.4
Concessional	0.3	5.5	13.4	-1.1	0.0	0.0	0.0	-0.2	-1.5	-1.1
Private creditors	-1.6	-0.9	-1.4	-0.4	0.0	0.0	0.0	0.0	-0.4	0.0
Bonds	0.0	0.0	0.0	0.0	0.0	0.0	0.0	0.0	0.0	0.0
Commercial banks	0.0	0.0	0.0	0.0	0.0	0.0	0.0	0.0	0.0	0.0
Other private	-1.6	-0.9	-1.4	-0.4	0.0	0.0	0.0	0.0	-0.4	0.0
Private nonguaranteed	**0.0**	**0.0**	**0.0**	**0.0**	**0.0**	**0.0**	**0.0**	**0.0**	**0.0**	**0.0**
Bonds	0.0	0.0	0.0	0.0	0.0	0.0	0.0	0.0	0.0	0.0
Commercial banks and other	0.0	0.0	0.0	0.0	0.0	0.0	0.0	0.0	0.0	0.0
Memo:										
IBRD	0.0	0.0	0.0	0.0	0.0	0.0	0.0	0.0	0.0	0.0
IDA	0.2	10.0	68.4	36.1	25.6	18.5	1.4	-7.5	-4.2	4.0
DEBT SERVICE (LTDS)	**3.1**	**1.4**	**16.6**	**15.8**	**6.1**	**5.3**	**6.5**	**19.0**	**11.9**	**11.8**
Public and publicly guaranteed	**3.1**	**1.4**	**16.6**	**15.8**	**6.1**	**5.3**	**6.5**	**19.0**	**11.9**	**11.8**
Official creditors	1.4	0.5	15.2	15.4	6.1	5.3	6.5	19.0	11.4	11.7
Multilateral	0.0	0.4	8.3	14.3	6.1	5.1	6.5	18.6	9.9	10.3
Concessional	0.0	0.3	4.6	10.6	5.6	4.9	6.4	15.4	8.3	10.3
Bilateral	1.4	0.1	6.9	1.1	0.0	0.1	0.0	0.4	1.5	1.4
Concessional	0.6	0.0	2.7	1.1	0.0	0.0	0.0	0.2	1.5	1.1
Private creditors	1.8	0.9	1.4	0.4	0.0	0.0	0.0	0.0	0.4	0.0
Bonds	0.0	0.0	0.0	0.0	0.0	0.0	0.0	0.0	0.0	0.0
Commercial banks	0.0	0.0	0.0	0.0	0.0	0.0	0.0	0.0	0.0	0.0
Other private	1.8	0.9	1.4	0.4	0.0	0.0	0.0	0.0	0.4	0.0
Private nonguaranteed	**0.0**	**0.0**	**0.0**	**0.0**	**0.0**	**0.0**	**0.0**	**0.0**	**0.0**	**0.0**
Bonds	0.0	0.0	0.0	0.0	0.0	0.0	0.0	0.0	0.0	0.0
Commercial banks and other	0.0	0.0	0.0	0.0	0.0	0.0	0.0	0.0	0.0	0.0
Memo:										
IBRD	0.0	0.0	0.0	0.0	0.0	0.0	0.0	0.0	0.0	0.0
IDA	0.0	0.3	2.0	4.0	4.2	4.4	3.2	7.7	6.8	8.9
UNDISBURSED DEBT	**12.6**	**60.7**	**235.8**	**133.3**	**119.1**	**83.0**	**65.5**	**45.7**	**17.2**	**19.9**
Official creditors	10.8	60.7	235.8	133.3	119.1	83.0	65.5	45.7	17.2	19.9
Private creditors	1.7	0.0	0.0	0.0	0.0	0.0	0.0	0.0	0.0	0.0
Memorandum items										
Concessional LDOD	15.1	58.6	510.9	722.6	765.0	768.0	724.1	745.3	741.1	725.9
Variable rate LDOD	0.0	2.8	0.0	5.2	6.3	5.8	5.1	5.3	5.2	7.5
Public sector LDOD	24.1	146.5	624.1	802.2	853.7	850.1	800.3	839.7	824.9	809.1
Private sector LDOD	0.0	0.0	0.0	0.2	0.3	0.2	1.2	1.3	1.2	1.0

6. CURRENCY COMPOSITION OF LONG-TERM DEBT (PERCENT)

	1970	1980	1990	1994	1995	1996	1997	1998	1999	2000
Deutsche mark	19.7	1.2	0.7	0.4	0.4	0.3	0.3	0.3	0.2	0.2
French franc	40.0	16.9	11.0	5.5	5.4	5.1	4.8	4.4	4.1	4.3
Japanese yen	0.0	0.0	0.7	0.7	0.7	0.6	0.6	0.6	0.7	0.6
Pound sterling	0.5	0.7	0.1	0.0	0.0	0.0	0.0	0.0	0.1	0.1
Swiss franc	0.0	7.5	2.6	2.6	2.8	2.4	2.4	2.5	2.3	2.3
U.S.dollars	1.8	35.8	43.6	55.3	56.2	57.5	58.7	59.6	60.2	61.3
Multiple currency	0.0	7.5	21.5	19.3	18.5	18.5	17.5	17.5	17.4	16.3
Special drawing rights	0.0	0.0	7.6	7.2	6.9	7.2	7.1	7.3	7.5	7.6
All other currencies	38.0	30.4	12.2	9.0	9.1	8.4	8.6	7.8	7.5	7.3

CENTRAL AFRICAN REPUBLIC

(US$ million, unless otherwise indicated)

	1970	1980	1990	1994	1995	1996	1997	1998	1999	2000
7. DEBT RESTRUCTURINGS										
Total amount rescheduled	..	..	4.4	38.5	7.6	0.0	0.0	9.2	30.7	17.2
Debt stock rescheduled	..	..	0.0	0.0	0.0	0.0	0.0	0.0	0.0	0.0
Principal rescheduled	..	..	2.6	21.5	4.4	0.0	0.0	6.2	22.7	2.1
Official	..	..	2.6	13.1	4.4	0.0	0.0	6.2	22.7	2.1
Private	..	..	0.0	8.4	0.0	0.0	0.0	0.0	0.0	0.0
Interest rescheduled	..	..	0.3	13.0	0.9	0.0	0.0	3.0	7.4	0.6
Official	..	..	0.3	11.5	0.9	0.0	0.0	3.0	7.4	0.6
Private	..	..	0.0	1.5	0.0	0.0	0.0	0.0	0.0	0.0
Debt forgiven	..	..	153.1	49.2	1.1	3.7	0.0	1.9	0.1	0.4
Memo: interest forgiven	..	..	4.4	4.5	0.2	3.5	0.0	2.2	0.2	0.3
Debt stock reduction	..	..	0.0	0.0	0.0	0.0	0.0	0.0	0.0	0.0
of which debt buyback	..	..	0.0	0.0	0.0	0.0	0.0	0.0	0.0	0.0
8. DEBT STOCK-FLOW RECONCILIATION										
Total change in debt stocks	..	..	5.0	12.9	57.9	-13.2	-49.8	35.8	-9.6	-37.0
Net flows on debt	-0.7	31.1	106.6	31.8	25.1	13.8	-3.5	-12.8	25.3	-13.8
Net change in interest arrears	..	..	-1.9	-13.8	10.5	2.8	6.4	-0.7	-21.2	2.5
Interest capitalized	..	..	0.3	13.0	0.9	0.0	0.0	3.0	7.4	0.6
Debt forgiveness or reduction	..	..	-153.1	-49.2	-1.1	-3.7	0.0	-1.9	-0.1	-0.4
Cross-currency valuation	..	..	38.2	-18.1	-35.4	-72.8	-95.2	-31.2	-18.4	-33.6
Residual	..	..	14.9	49.3	58.0	46.8	42.5	79.4	-2.5	7.6
9. AVERAGE TERMS OF NEW COMMITMENTS										
ALL CREDITORS										
Interest (%)	2.0	0.6	1.0	0.0	0.8	1.0	0.0	0.0	0.0	0.8
Maturity (years)	35.8	12.5	37.6	0.0	39.7	49.8	0.0	0.0	0.0	39.8
Grace period (years)	7.9	4.3	10.2	0.0	10.2	9.3	0.0	0.0	0.0	10.3
Grant element (%)	62.8	39.0	77.0	0.0	80.5	80.2	0.0	0.0	0.0	80.6
Official creditors										
Interest (%)	1.0	0.6	1.0	0.0	0.8	1.0	0.0	0.0	0.0	0.8
Maturity (years)	47.5	12.5	37.6	0.0	39.7	49.8	0.0	0.0	0.0	39.8
Grace period (years)	9.9	4.3	10.2	0.0	10.2	9.3	0.0	0.0	0.0	10.3
Grant element (%)	79.6	39.0	77.0	0.0	80.5	80.2	0.0	0.0	0.0	80.6
Private creditors										
Interest (%)	4.6	0.0	0.0	0.0	0.0	0.0	0.0	0.0	0.0	0.0
Maturity (years)	8.0	0.0	0.0	0.0	0.0	0.0	0.0	0.0	0.0	0.0
Grace period (years)	3.3	0.0	0.0	0.0	0.0	0.0	0.0	0.0	0.0	0.0
Grant element (%)	23.0	0.0	0.0	0.0	0.0	0.0	0.0	0.0	0.0	0.0
Memorandum items										
Commitments	6.5	38.4	174.9	0.0	16.6	4.9	0.0	0.0	0.0	28.0
Official creditors	4.6	38.4	174.9	0.0	16.6	4.9	0.0	0.0	0.0	28.0
Private creditors	1.9	0.0	0.0	0.0	0.0	0.0	0.0	0.0	0.0	0.0

10. CONTRACTUAL OBLIGATIONS ON OUTSTANDING LONG-TERM DEBT

	2001	2002	2003	2004	2005	2006	2007	2008	2009	2010
TOTAL										
Disbursements	6.8	5.5	2.5	2.1	1.6	0.9	0.5	0.0	0.0	0.0
Principal	32.5	31.2	29.4	29.9	22.9	22.3	17.0	17.9	19.2	20.8
Interest	9.9	9.1	8.3	7.5	6.8	6.3	5.9	5.7	5.6	5.4
Official creditors										
Disbursements	6.8	5.5	2.5	2.1	1.6	0.9	0.5	0.0	0.0	0.0
Principal	27.4	26.2	24.3	24.8	22.9	22.3	17.0	17.9	19.2	20.8
Interest	9.3	8.7	8.1	7.4	6.8	6.3	5.9	5.7	5.6	5.4
Bilateral creditors										
Disbursements	0.0	0.0	0.0	0.0	0.0	0.0	0.0	0.0	0.0	0.0
Principal	12.9	12.9	12.9	12.7	10.2	9.3	3.3	3.4	3.6	3.7
Interest	4.8	4.4	3.9	3.3	2.8	2.3	2.0	2.0	2.0	1.9
Multilateral creditors										
Disbursements	6.8	5.5	2.5	2.1	1.6	0.9	0.5	0.0	0.0	0.0
Principal	14.5	13.3	11.5	12.2	12.6	12.9	13.7	14.5	15.6	17.2
Interest	4.5	4.3	4.2	4.1	4.0	3.9	3.8	3.7	3.6	3.5
Private creditors										
Disbursements	0.0	0.0	0.0	0.0	0.0	0.0	0.0	0.0	0.0	0.0
Principal	5.0	5.0	5.0	5.0	0.0	0.0	0.0	0.0	0.0	0.0
Interest	0.6	0.4	0.3	0.1	0.0	0.0	0.0	0.0	0.0	0.0
Commercial banks										
Disbursements	0.0	0.0	0.0	0.0	0.0	0.0	0.0	0.0	0.0	0.0
Principal	0.0	0.0	0.0	0.0	0.0	0.0	0.0	0.0	0.0	0.0
Interest	0.0	0.0	0.0	0.0	0.0	0.0	0.0	0.0	0.0	0.0
Other private										
Disbursements	0.0	0.0	0.0	0.0	0.0	0.0	0.0	0.0	0.0	0.0
Principal	5.0	5.0	5.0	5.0	0.0	0.0	0.0	0.0	0.0	0.0
Interest	0.6	0.4	0.3	0.1	0.0	0.0	0.0	0.0	0.0	0.0

CHAD

(US$ million, unless otherwise indicated)

	1970	1980	1990	1994	1995	1996	1997	1998	1999	2000
1. SUMMARY DEBT DATA										
TOTAL DEBT STOCKS (EDT)	**35**	**284**	**524**	**828**	**902**	**997**	**1,026**	**1,092**	**1,142**	**1,116**
Long-term debt (LDOD)	**33**	**259**	**464**	**759**	**833**	**914**	**939**	**1,005**	**1,045**	**1,009**
Public and publicly guaranteed	33	259	464	759	833	914	939	1,005	1,045	1,009
Private nonguaranteed	0	0	0	0	0	0	0	0	0	0
Use of IMF credit	**3**	**14**	**31**	**43**	**49**	**65**	**61**	**64**	**69**	**78**
Short-term debt	**0**	**12**	**30**	**27**	**20**	**18**	**26**	**23**	**28**	**29**
of which interest arrears on LDOD	0	7	6	19	11	8	7	9	12	14
Official creditors	0	5	4	17	11	8	7	8	11	13
Private creditors	0	2	2	2	0	0	0	0	0	1
Memo: principal arrears on LDOD	2	31	16	32	34	35	30	38	46	54
Official creditors	0	12	13	28	34	35	30	37	44	51
Private creditors	2	20	3	3	0	0	0	2	2	3
Memo: export credits	0	0	52	34	63	85	77	42	31	28
TOTAL DEBT FLOWS										
Disbursements	**10**	**5**	**112**	**83**	**72**	**125**	**92**	**52**	**98**	**47**
Long-term debt	6	5	104	69	60	101	80	40	86	33
IMF purchases	4	0	8	15	13	24	11	11	11	14
Principal repayments	**3**	**5**	**7**	**9**	**10**	**16**	**24**	**23**	**21**	**16**
Long-term debt	3	3	3	8	3	10	12	12	16	15
IMF repurchases	0	3	4	2	7	6	11	11	5	1
Net flows on debt	**7**	**-8**	**107**	**72**	**63**	**110**	**77**	**24**	**78**	**29**
of which short-term debt	0	-8	2	-3	1	2	9	-5	2	-2
Interest payments (INT)	**0**	**1**	**5**	**9**	**6**	**14**	**12**	**12**	**11**	**10**
Long-term debt	0	0	3	8	4	13	10	11	10	9
IMF charges	0	1	0	1	1	1	1	1	0	0
Short-term debt	0	0	2	0	1	0	1	1	1	1
Net transfers on debt	**7**	**-9**	**102**	**63**	**57**	**96**	**65**	**12**	**67**	**19**
Total debt service paid (TDS)	**3**	**6**	**12**	**18**	**16**	**30**	**35**	**35**	**32**	**26**
Long-term debt	3	3	7	15	7	23	22	22	27	24
IMF repurchases and charges	0	3	4	2	8	7	12	12	5	1
Short-term debt (interest only)	0	0	2	0	1	0	1	1	1	1
2. AGGREGATE NET RESOURCE FLOWS AND NET TRANSFERS (LONG-TERM)										
NET RESOURCE FLOWS	**15**	**24**	**247**	**203**	**190**	**233**	**190**	**128**	**146**	**94**
Net flow of long-term debt (ex. IMF)	3	3	100	61	56	91	68	29	70	18
Foreign direct investment (net)	1	0	0	27	13	18	15	16	15	15
Portfolio equity flows	0	0	0	0	0	0	0	0	0	0
Grants (excluding technical coop.)	11	22	147	115	121	124	107	83	61	61
Memo: technical coop. grants	10	12	58	49	63	54	46	44	40	32
official net resource flows	13	24	248	176	177	215	175	112	132	79
private net resource flows	3	0	-1	27	13	18	15	16	14	14
NET TRANSFERS	**13**	**24**	**244**	**195**	**186**	**220**	**180**	**116**	**136**	**85**
Interest on long-term debt	0	0	3	8	4	13	10	11	10	9
Profit remittances on FDI	2	0	0	0	0	0	0	1	0	0
Memo: official net transfers	12	24	244	168	173	202	165	101	123	71
private net transfers	1	0	-1	27	13	18	15	15	14	14
3. MAJOR ECONOMIC AGGREGATES										
Gross national income (GNI)	470	1,038	1,730	1,152	1,410	1,595	1,491	1,680	1,549	1,398
Exports of goods & services (XGS)	..	71	274	196	384	350	346	379	294	283
of which workers remittances	..	0	0	1	..	..	..	..	..	..
Imports of goods & services (MGS)	..	83	511	424	543	518	526	561	522	492
International reserves (RES)	2	12	132	80	147	169	139	120	95	111
Current account balance	..	12	-46	-38	-36	-75	-84	-101	-189	-158
4. DEBT INDICATORS										
EDT / XGS (%)	..	398.2	191.1	422.8	235.0	285.2	296.3	287.9	388.8	394.3
EDT / GNI (%)	7.5	27.4	30.3	71.9	64.0	62.5	68.8	65.0	73.7	79.9
TDS / XGS (%)	..	8.4	4.4	9.2	4.1	8.6	10.2	9.2	11.0	9.3
INT / XGS (%)	..	0.8	1.9	4.4	1.5	4.0	3.4	3.2	3.8	3.6
INT / GNI (%)	0.1	0.1	0.3	0.8	0.4	0.9	0.8	0.7	0.7	0.7
RES / EDT (%)	6.6	4.1	25.2	9.7	16.3	16.9	13.6	11.0	8.3	9.9
RES / MGS (months)	..	1.7	3.1	2.3	3.3	3.9	3.2	2.6	2.2	2.7
Short-term / EDT (%)	0.6	4.1	5.7	3.2	2.2	1.8	2.6	2.1	2.5	2.6
Concessional / EDT (%)	68.5	60.2	76.8	81.4	76.9	76.5	78.6	79.9	81.3	81.0
Multilateral / EDT (%)	4.3	26.2	63.4	72.8	74.8	73.5	73.2	74.6	75.8	75.3

CHAD

(US$ million, unless otherwise indicated)

	1970	1980	1990	1994	1995	1996	1997	1998	1999	2000
5. LONG-TERM DEBT										
DEBT OUTSTANDING (LDOD)	**33**	**259**	**464**	**759**	**833**	**914**	**939**	**1,005**	**1,045**	**1,009**
Public and publicly guaranteed	**33**	**259**	**464**	**759**	**833**	**914**	**939**	**1,005**	**1,045**	**1,009**
Official creditors	25	205	455	753	831	897	922	988	1,029	994
Multilateral	2	75	332	603	675	733	751	814	866	840
Concessional	2	75	322	560	625	687	712	778	835	815
Bilateral	23	131	123	150	156	164	171	174	163	154
Concessional	23	97	80	114	69	77	94	95	93	89
Private creditors	8	54	9	6	2	17	17	17	16	15
Bonds	0	0	0	0	0	0	0	0	0	0
Commercial banks	1	1	0	0	0	0	0	0	0	0
Other private	7	53	9	6	2	17	17	17	16	15
Private nonguaranteed	**0**	**0**	**0**	**0**	**0**	**0**	**0**	**0**	**0**	**0**
Bonds	0	0	0	0	0	0	0	0	0	0
Commercial banks and other	0	0	0	0	0	0	0	0	0	0
Memo:										
IBRD	0	0	0	0	0	0	0	0	0	0
IDA	0	36	186	332	379	433	457	488	527	515
DISBURSEMENTS	**6**	**5**	**104**	**69**	**60**	**101**	**80**	**40**	**86**	**33**
Public and publicly guaranteed	**6**	**5**	**104**	**69**	**60**	**101**	**80**	**40**	**86**	**33**
Official creditors	3	5	104	69	60	101	80	40	86	33
Multilateral	0	5	72	62	60	101	74	40	83	33
Concessional	0	5	71	62	60	99	74	40	83	33
Bilateral	3	0	32	6	0	0	6	0	3	0
Concessional	2	0	25	6	0	0	6	0	3	0
Private creditors	3	0	0	0	0	0	0	0	0	0
Bonds	0	0	0	0	0	0	0	0	0	0
Commercial banks	0	0	0	0	0	0	0	0	0	0
Other private	3	0	0	0	0	0	0	0	0	0
Private nonguaranteed	**0**	**0**	**0**	**0**	**0**	**0**	**0**	**0**	**0**	**0**
Bonds	0	0	0	0	0	0	0	0	0	0
Commercial banks and other	0	0	0	0	0	0	0	0	0	0
Memo:										
IBRD	0	0	0	0	0	0	0	0	0	0
IDA	0	0	48	38	42	68	49	18	53	18
PRINCIPAL REPAYMENTS	**3**	**3**	**3**	**8**	**3**	**10**	**12**	**12**	**16**	**15**
Public and publicly guaranteed	**3**	**3**	**3**	**8**	**3**	**10**	**12**	**12**	**16**	**15**
Official creditors	1	3	3	7	3	10	12	12	15	15
Multilateral	0	2	3	6	3	8	10	11	12	11
Concessional	0	2	2	6	2	7	6	7	10	9
Bilateral	1	1	0	2	1	2	3	1	3	4
Concessional	1	1	0	0	0	0	0	0	2	3
Private creditors	1	0	1	0	0	0	0	0	1	1
Bonds	0	0	0	0	0	0	0	0	0	0
Commercial banks	0	0	0	0	0	0	0	0	0	0
Other private	1	0	1	0	0	0	0	0	1	1
Private nonguaranteed	**0**	**0**	**0**	**0**	**0**	**0**	**0**	**0**	**0**	**0**
Bonds	0	0	0	0	0	0	0	0	0	0
Commercial banks and other	0	0	0	0	0	0	0	0	0	0
Memo:										
IBRD	0	0	0	0	0	0	0	0	0	0
IDA	0	0	1	2	1	2	2	3	5	4
NET FLOWS ON DEBT	**3**	**3**	**100**	**61**	**56**	**91**	**68**	**29**	**70**	**18**
Public and publicly guaranteed	**3**	**3**	**100**	**61**	**56**	**91**	**68**	**29**	**70**	**18**
Official creditors	1	3	101	61	57	91	68	29	71	18
Multilateral	0	3	69	56	57	93	64	30	71	22
Concessional	0	3	68	57	57	92	68	34	73	24
Bilateral	1	-1	32	5	-1	-2	4	-1	0	-4
Concessional	1	-1	25	6	0	0	6	0	1	-3
Private creditors	2	0	-1	0	0	0	0	0	-1	-1
Bonds	0	0	0	0	0	0	0	0	0	0
Commercial banks	0	0	0	0	0	0	0	0	0	0
Other private	2	0	-1	0	0	0	0	0	-1	-1
Private nonguaranteed	**0**	**0**	**0**	**0**	**0**	**0**	**0**	**0**	**0**	**0**
Bonds	0	0	0	0	0	0	0	0	0	0
Commercial banks and other	0	0	0	0	0	0	0	0	0	0
Memo:										
IBRD	0	0	0	0	0	0	0	0	0	0
IDA	0	0	48	36	41	67	47	15	48	13

CHAD

(US$ million, unless otherwise indicated)

	1970	1980	1990	1994	1995	1996	1997	1998	1999	2000
INTEREST PAYMENTS (LINT)	**0**	**0**	**3**	**8**	**4**	**13**	**10**	**11**	**10**	**9**
Public and publicly guaranteed	**0**	**0**	**3**	**8**	**4**	**13**	**10**	**11**	**10**	**9**
Official creditors	0	0	3	8	4	13	10	11	10	9
Multilateral	0	0	2	6	4	9	7	8	7	6
Concessional	0	0	2	4	3	7	5	6	6	5
Bilateral	0	0	1	2	0	3	3	3	3	3
Concessional	0	0	1	1	0	0	0	0	0	0
Private creditors	0	0	0	0	0	0	0	0	0	0
Bonds	0	0	0	0	0	0	0	0	0	0
Commercial banks	0	0	0	0	0	0	0	0	0	0
Other private	0	0	0	0	0	0	0	0	0	0
Private nonguaranteed	**0**	**0**	**0**	**0**	**0**	**0**	**0**	**0**	**0**	**0**
Bonds	0	0	0	0	0	0	0	0	0	0
Commercial banks and other	0	0	0	0	0	0	0	0	0	0
Memo:										
IBRD	0	0	0	0	0	0	0	0	0	0
IDA	0	0	1	3	3	3	3	4	4	3
NET TRANSFERS ON DEBT	**3**	**3**	**97**	**53**	**52**	**78**	**58**	**18**	**60**	**9**
Public and publicly guaranteed	**3**	**3**	**97**	**53**	**52**	**78**	**58**	**18**	**60**	**9**
Official creditors	1	3	98	54	52	78	58	18	61	10
Multilateral	0	3	67	51	53	84	58	22	64	16
Concessional	0	3	66	53	54	85	63	28	68	19
Bilateral	1	-1	31	3	-1	-5	0	-4	-3	-7
Concessional	0	-1	24	5	0	0	6	0	1	-4
Private creditors	2	0	-1	0	0	0	0	0	-2	-1
Bonds	0	0	0	0	0	0	0	0	0	0
Commercial banks	0	0	0	0	0	0	0	0	0	0
Other private	2	0	-1	0	0	0	0	0	-2	-1
Private nonguaranteed	**0**	**0**	**0**	**0**	**0**	**0**	**0**	**0**	**0**	**0**
Bonds	0	0	0	0	0	0	0	0	0	0
Commercial banks and other	0	0	0	0	0	0	0	0	0	0
Memo:										
IBRD	0	0	0	0	0	0	0	0	0	0
IDA	0	0	47	34	38	64	43	11	45	10
DEBT SERVICE (LTDS)	**3**	**3**	**7**	**15**	**7**	**23**	**22**	**22**	**27**	**24**
Public and publicly guaranteed	**3**	**3**	**7**	**15**	**7**	**23**	**22**	**22**	**27**	**24**
Official creditors	2	3	6	15	7	22	22	22	25	23
Multilateral	0	2	5	12	6	17	16	19	19	17
Concessional	0	2	4	10	6	14	11	12	16	14
Bilateral	2	1	1	3	1	5	6	4	6	7
Concessional	2	1	1	1	0	0	0	0	2	4
Private creditors	1	0	1	0	0	0	0	0	2	1
Bonds	0	0	0	0	0	0	0	0	0	0
Commercial banks	0	0	0	0	0	0	0	0	0	0
Other private	1	0	1	0	0	0	0	0	2	1
Private nonguaranteed	**0**	**0**	**0**	**0**	**0**	**0**	**0**	**0**	**0**	**0**
Bonds	0	0	0	0	0	0	0	0	0	0
Commercial banks and other	0	0	0	0	0	0	0	0	0	0
Memo:										
IBRD	0	0	0	0	0	0	0	0	0	0
IDA	0	0	2	4	4	5	5	7	9	8
UNDISBURSED DEBT	**18**	**94**	**372**	**329**	**387**	**318**	**287**	**292**	**183**	**297**
Official creditors	11	76	372	329	387	318	287	292	183	297
Private creditors	7	18	0	0	0	0	0	0	0	0
Memorandum items										
Concessional LDOD	24	171	402	674	694	763	807	873	928	904
Variable rate LDOD	0	1	0	0	0	0	0	0	0	0
Public sector LDOD	33	259	464	758	833	914	939	1,005	1,045	1,009
Private sector LDOD	0	0	0	0	0	0	0	0	0	0

6. CURRENCY COMPOSITION OF LONG-TERM DEBT (PERCENT)

	1970	1980	1990	1994	1995	1996	1997	1998	1999	2000
Deutsche mark	10.7	2.7	1.5	0.7	0.1	0.1	0.0	0.0	0.0	0.0
French franc	35.2	14.5	9.1	8.5	7.6	6.4	5.6	5.8	4.8	4.5
Japanese yen	0.0	0.0	0.0	0.0	0.0	0.0	0.0	0.0	0.0	0.0
Pound sterling	1.2	0.2	0.1	0.0	0.0	0.0	0.0	0.0	0.0	0.0
Swiss franc	0.0	0.0	0.0	0.0	0.0	0.0	0.0	0.0	0.0	0.0
U.S.dollars	4.1	18.9	49.0	50.2	51.6	53.4	56.9	55.9	57.4	58.3
Multiple currency	3.7	9.6	25.7	26.6	26.3	25.4	23.2	23.5	22.5	21.9
Special drawing rights	0.0	0.0	0.0	0.1	0.2	0.2	0.2	0.2	0.2	0.2
All other currencies	45.1	54.1	14.6	13.9	14.2	14.5	14.1	14.6	15.1	15.1

CHAD

(US$ million, unless otherwise indicated)

	1970	1980	1990	1994	1995	1996	1997	1998	1999	2000
7. DEBT RESTRUCTURINGS										
Total amount rescheduled	..	..	8	0	56	33	10	3	0	0
Debt stock rescheduled	..	..	0	0	0	0	0	0	0	0
Principal rescheduled	..	..	3	0	2	3	7	2	0	0
Official	..	..	3	0	1	3	7	2	0	0
Private	..	..	1	0	1	0	0	0	0	0
Interest rescheduled	..	..	1	0	7	1	1	1	0	0
Official	..	..	1	0	7	1	1	1	0	0
Private	..	..	0	0	1	0	0	0	0	0
Debt forgiven	..	..	12	0	55	11	2	2	0	0
Memo: interest forgiven	..	..	0	0	8	1	1	1	0	0
Debt stock reduction	..	..	0	0	0	0	0	0	0	0
of which debt buyback	..	..	0	0	0	0	0	0	0	0
8. DEBT STOCK-FLOW RECONCILIATION										
Total change in debt stocks	..	..	125	61	74	95	29	66	50	-26
Net flows on debt	7	-8	107	72	63	110	77	24	78	29
Net change in interest arrears	..	..	-1	3	-7	-3	-1	1	3	2
Interest capitalized	..	..	1	0	7	1	1	1	0	0
Debt forgiveness or reduction	..	..	-12	0	-55	-11	-2	-2	0	0
Cross-currency valuation	..	..	8	-57	-34	-76	-130	-76	-24	-43
Residual	..	..	22	43	101	74	83	118	-7	-15
9. AVERAGE TERMS OF NEW COMMITMENTS										
ALL CREDITORS										
Interest (%)	5.7	0.0	1.7	1.0	0.9	0.9	0.7	0.4	0.8	0.8
Maturity (years)	8.3	0.0	30.3	37.5	39.8	37.4	47.3	39.8	44.2	40.6
Grace period (years)	1.0	0.0	9.2	9.8	9.1	9.7	10.4	7.3	10.3	10.2
Grant element (%)	14.3	0.0	66.4	76.9	77.5	76.3	83.2	80.8	81.8	80.7
Official creditors										
Interest (%)	3.7	0.0	1.7	1.0	0.9	0.9	0.7	0.4	0.8	0.8
Maturity (years)	10.1	0.0	30.3	37.5	39.8	37.4	47.3	39.8	44.2	40.6
Grace period (years)	1.8	0.0	9.2	9.8	9.1	9.7	10.4	7.3	10.3	10.2
Grant element (%)	25.5	0.0	66.4	76.9	77.5	76.3	83.2	80.8	81.8	80.7
Private creditors										
Interest (%)	6.3	0.0	0.0	0.0	0.0	0.0	0.0	0.0	0.0	0.0
Maturity (years)	7.8	0.0	0.0	0.0	0.0	0.0	0.0	0.0	0.0	0.0
Grace period (years)	0.7	0.0	0.0	0.0	0.0	0.0	0.0	0.0	0.0	0.0
Grant element (%)	11.1	0.0	0.0	0.0	0.0	0.0	0.0	0.0	0.0	0.0
Memorandum items										
Commitments	10	0	85	62	106	45	75	32	54	166
Official creditors	2	0	85	62	106	45	75	32	54	166
Private creditors	8	0	0	0	0	0	0	0	0	0

10. CONTRACTUAL OBLIGATIONS ON OUTSTANDING LONG-TERM DEBT

	2001	2002	2003	2004	2005	2006	2007	2008	2009	2010
TOTAL										
Disbursements	60	74	57	44	31	18	12	1	0	0
Principal	29	29	31	29	30	29	31	30	31	35
Interest	13	12	12	12	12	11	11	10	10	9
Official creditors										
Disbursements	60	74	57	44	31	18	12	1	0	0
Principal	28	28	30	28	28	28	30	29	30	34
Interest	12	12	12	12	12	11	11	10	10	9
Bilateral creditors										
Disbursements	0	0	0	0	0	0	0	0	0	0
Principal	12	12	12	9	9	7	7	7	6	6
Interest	4	4	4	4	3	3	3	3	3	2
Multilateral creditors										
Disbursements	60	74	57	44	31	18	12	1	0	0
Principal	16	16	17	19	20	21	23	22	24	28
Interest	8	8	9	8	8	8	8	7	7	7
Private creditors										
Disbursements	0	0	0	0	0	0	0	0	0	0
Principal	1	1	1	1	1	1	1	1	1	1
Interest	0	0	0	0	0	0	0	0	0	0
Commercial banks										
Disbursements	0	0	0	0	0	0	0	0	0	0
Principal	0	0	0	0	0	0	0	0	0	0
Interest	0	0	0	0	0	0	0	0	0	0
Other private										
Disbursements	0	0	0	0	0	0	0	0	0	0
Principal	1	1	1	1	1	1	1	1	1	1
Interest	0	0	0	0	0	0	0	0	0	0

CHILE

(US$ million, unless otherwise indicated)

	1970	1980	1990	1994	1995	1996	1997	1998	1999	2000
1. SUMMARY DEBT DATA										
TOTAL DEBT STOCKS (EDT)	**2,977**	**12,081**	**19,226**	**22,155**	**22,038**	**23,049**	**22,809**	**30,175**	**34,269**	**36,978**
Long-term debt (LDOD)	**2,567**	**9,399**	**14,687**	**17,999**	**18,607**	**20,414**	**21,522**	**28,565**	**33,098**	**34,447**
Public and publicly guaranteed	2,066	4,705	10,425	8,995	7,178	4,883	4,367	5,005	5,655	5,210
Private nonguaranteed	501	4,693	4,263	9,004	11,429	15,531	17,155	23,560	27,443	29,236
Use of IMF credit	**2**	**123**	**1,157**	**291**	**0**	**0**	**0**	**0**	**0**	**0**
Short-term debt	**409**	**2,560**	**3,382**	**3,865**	**3,431**	**2,635**	**1,287**	**1,610**	**1,171**	**2,531**
of which interest arrears on LDOD	0	0	0	0	0	0	0	0	0	0
Official creditors	0	0	0	0	0	0	0	0	0	0
Private creditors	0	0	0	0	0	0	0	0	0	0
Memo: principal arrears on LDOD	0	0	0	0	0	0	0	0	0	0
Official creditors	0	0	0	0	0	0	0	0	0	0
Private creditors	0	0	0	0	0	0	0	0	0	0
Memo: export credits	0	0	2,062	2,583	2,335	2,037	1,876	1,182	1,016	850
TOTAL DEBT FLOWS										
Disbursements	**655**	**3,551**	**2,253**	**2,922**	**3,821**	**6,644**	**6,217**	**6,784**	**5,879**	**4,954**
Long-term debt	655	3,551	2,253	2,922	3,821	6,644	6,217	6,784	5,879	4,954
IMF purchases	0	0	0	0	0	0	0	0	0	0
Principal repayments	**254**	**1,513**	**980**	**1,692**	**3,671**	**4,677**	**2,857**	**2,345**	**3,351**	**3,933**
Long-term debt	207	1,462	771	1,482	3,369	4,677	2,857	2,345	3,351	3,933
IMF repurchases	47	52	209	211	303	0	0	0	0	0
Net flows on debt	**400**	**2,963**	**1,682**	**1,608**	**-284**	**1,171**	**2,012**	**4,762**	**2,090**	**2,382**
of which short-term debt	0	925	409	378	-434	-796	-1,348	323	-439	1,360
Interest payments (INT)	**104**	**1,193**	**1,792**	**1,141**	**1,293**	**1,291**	**1,134**	**1,418**	**1,578**	**2,230**
Long-term debt	104	918	1,364	929	1,114	1,185	1,070	1,326	1,502	2,076
IMF charges	0	12	118	22	13	0	0	0	0	0
Short-term debt	0	262	310	190	165	105	64	92	76	154
Net transfers on debt	**296**	**1,771**	**-110**	**467**	**-1,577**	**-120**	**878**	**3,345**	**512**	**151**
Total debt service paid (TDS)	**359**	**2,706**	**2,772**	**2,833**	**4,964**	**5,968**	**3,991**	**3,762**	**4,928**	**6,163**
Long-term debt	311	2,380	2,135	2,411	4,483	5,863	3,927	3,671	4,852	6,008
IMF repurchases and charges	47	64	327	232	316	0	0	0	0	0
Short-term debt (interest only)	0	262	310	190	165	105	64	92	76	154
2. AGGREGATE NET RESOURCE FLOWS AND NET TRANSFERS (LONG-TERM)										
NET RESOURCE FLOWS	**381**	**2,312**	**2,465**	**4,958**	**3,738**	**6,751**	**9,101**	**9,191**	**11,783**	**4,733**
Net flow of long-term debt (ex. IMF)	448	2,090	1,481	1,441	452	1,967	3,360	4,439	2,529	1,022
Foreign direct investment (net)	-79	213	590	2,583	2,957	4,634	5,219	4,638	9,221	3,675
Portfolio equity flows	0	0	320	867	274	103	486	87	18	18
Grants (excluding technical coop.)	12	9	73	67	54	47	36	26	15	18
Memo: technical coop. grants	19	37	66	87	97	89	78	73	63	56
official net resource flows	67	-136	367	-122	-1,755	-595	-338	-61	-68	-101
private net resource flows	314	2,447	2,098	5,080	5,493	7,346	9,439	9,252	11,851	4,834
NET TRANSFERS	**173**	**1,307**	**766**	**3,078**	**1,624**	**4,465**	**6,631**	**6,215**	**8,231**	**357**
Interest on long-term debt	104	918	1,364	929	1,114	1,185	1,070	1,326	1,502	2,076
Profit remittances on FDI	104	86	335	950	1,000	1,100	1,400	1,650	2,050	2,300
Memo: official net transfers	28	-216	-16	-501	-2,143	-869	-498	-180	-200	-239
private net transfers	145	1,523	782	3,580	3,767	5,334	7,129	6,395	8,431	596
3. MAJOR ECONOMIC AGGREGATES										
Gross national income (GNI)	8,513	26,544	28,564	48,367	62,504	65,901	72,548	71,002	65,835	68,141
Exports of goods & services (XGS)	..	6,276	10,705	15,000	20,226	19,861	21,858	20,088	20,509	23,699
of which workers remittances	..	0	..	0	..	..	..	..	..	..
Imports of goods & services (MGS)	..	8,360	11,387	16,917	21,883	23,878	26,107	24,690	21,041	25,227
International reserves (RES)	392	4,128	6,784	13,802	14,860	15,520	17,845	16,014	14,761	14,749
Current account balance	..	-1,971	-485	-1,585	-1,350	-3,510	-3,728	-4,139	-80	-991
4. DEBT INDICATORS										
EDT / XGS (%)	..	192.5	179.6	147.7	109.0	116.1	104.4	150.2	167.1	156.0
EDT / GNI (%)	35.0	45.5	67.3	45.8	35.3	35.0	31.4	42.5	52.1	54.3
TDS / XGS (%)	..	43.1	25.9	18.9	24.5	30.1	18.3	18.7	24.0	26.0
INT / XGS (%)	..	19.0	16.7	7.6	6.4	6.5	5.2	7.1	7.7	9.4
INT / GNI (%)	1.2	4.5	6.3	2.4	2.1	2.0	1.6	2.0	2.4	3.3
RES / EDT (%)	13.2	34.2	35.3	62.3	67.4	67.3	78.2	53.1	43.1	39.9
RES / MGS (months)	..	5.9	7.2	9.8	8.2	7.8	8.2	7.8	8.4	7.0
Short-term / EDT (%)	13.7	21.2	17.6	17.4	15.6	11.4	5.6	5.3	3.4	6.8
Concessional / EDT (%)	22.8	5.6	1.9	1.4	1.5	1.4	1.5	1.3	1.2	1.0
Multilateral / EDT (%)	5.9	2.9	21.6	19.7	13.0	9.1	7.0	5.1	4.4	3.8

CHILE

(US$ million, unless otherwise indicated)

	1970	1980	1990	1994	1995	1996	1997	1998	1999	2000
5. LONG-TERM DEBT										
DEBT OUTSTANDING (LDOD)	**2,567**	**9,399**	**14,687**	**17,999**	**18,607**	**20,414**	**21,522**	**28,565**	**33,098**	**34,447**
Public and publicly guaranteed	**2,066**	**4,705**	**10,425**	**8,995**	**7,178**	**4,883**	**4,367**	**5,005**	**5,655**	**5,210**
Official creditors	1,179	1,360	5,182	5,156	3,582	2,711	2,163	2,151	2,095	1,915
Multilateral	176	351	4,143	4,374	2,871	2,092	1,587	1,533	1,497	1,406
Concessional	20	50	33	25	23	21	19	17	21	13
Bilateral	1,003	1,009	1,040	782	711	619	576	619	598	509
Concessional	658	628	334	285	308	307	331	383	377	348
Private creditors	887	3,345	5,243	3,839	3,596	2,172	2,205	2,854	3,559	3,296
Bonds	60	106	39	0	0	0	0	0	0	0
Commercial banks	291	2,420	4,747	3,728	3,509	2,152	2,132	2,784	3,490	3,228
Other private	536	818	457	111	87	20	73	70	69	68
Private nonguaranteed	**501**	**4,693**	**4,263**	**9,004**	**11,429**	**15,531**	**17,155**	**23,560**	**27,443**	**29,236**
Bonds	0	0	0	377	866	2,725	3,764	4,466	5,677	6,339
Commercial banks and other	501	4,693	4,263	8,627	10,563	12,806	13,391	19,094	21,767	22,897
Memo:										
IBRD	111	163	1,860	1,919	1,372	1,093	980	945	877	808
IDA	19	21	14	11	11	10	9	9	8	7
DISBURSEMENTS	**655**	**3,551**	**2,253**	**2,922**	**3,821**	**6,644**	**6,217**	**6,784**	**5,879**	**4,954**
Public and publicly guaranteed	**407**	**857**	**708**	**463**	**342**	**975**	**685**	**1,029**	**1,092**	**382**
Official creditors	130	62	650	351	194	157	167	149	164	161
Multilateral	34	46	583	292	146	126	108	94	138	113
Concessional	0	3	0	0	0	0	0	0	0	0
Bilateral	97	15	67	59	48	31	59	55	27	47
Concessional	44	3	0	59	48	31	59	55	27	17
Private creditors	277	796	58	113	148	818	519	880	928	222
Bonds	0	55	0	0	0	0	0	0	0	0
Commercial banks	119	568	37	113	141	808	458	880	928	222
Other private	158	172	21	0	7	10	60	0	0	0
Private nonguaranteed	**247**	**2,694**	**1,545**	**2,459**	**3,479**	**5,669**	**5,532**	**5,755**	**4,788**	**4,572**
Bonds	0	0	0	91	500	1,870	1,050	863	873	672
Commercial banks and other	247	2,694	1,545	2,368	2,979	3,799	4,482	4,892	3,914	3,900
Memo:										
IBRD	27	14	251	81	83	75	85	71	43	48
IDA	0	0	0	0	0	0	0	0	0	0
PRINCIPAL REPAYMENTS	**207**	**1,462**	**771**	**1,482**	**3,369**	**4,677**	**2,857**	**2,345**	**3,351**	**3,933**
Public and publicly guaranteed	**166**	**891**	**500**	**646**	**2,277**	**2,960**	**995**	**441**	**469**	**752**
Official creditors	75	206	356	539	2,004	799	541	236	247	280
Multilateral	15	15	263	430	1,884	719	476	173	177	177
Concessional	0	0	2	2	2	2	2	2	2	2
Bilateral	61	191	93	109	119	80	64	63	71	103
Concessional	21	69	32	25	29	28	26	30	33	34
Private creditors	90	685	144	107	273	2,162	454	205	221	472
Bonds	5	4	7	0	0	0	0	0	0	0
Commercial banks	32	464	32	4	240	2,086	447	201	221	471
Other private	54	217	105	104	33	76	7	3	1	1
Private nonguaranteed	**41**	**571**	**271**	**835**	**1,092**	**1,717**	**1,863**	**1,904**	**2,882**	**3,181**
Bonds	0	0	0	0	11	11	11	161	11	0
Commercial banks and other	41	571	271	835	1,081	1,706	1,852	1,743	2,871	3,181
Memo:										
IBRD	10	9	119	192	704	263	109	105	111	115
IDA	0	0	1	1	1	1	1	1	1	1
NET FLOWS ON DEBT	**448**	**2,090**	**1,481**	**1,441**	**452**	**1,967**	**3,360**	**4,439**	**2,529**	**1,022**
Public and publicly guaranteed	**242**	**-34**	**208**	**-183**	**-1,935**	**-1,986**	**-309**	**588**	**623**	**-370**
Official creditors	55	-145	294	-189	-1,810	-642	-374	-87	-83	-119
Multilateral	19	31	319	-138	-1,739	-593	-369	-79	-39	-64
Concessional	0	3	-2	-2	-2	-2	-2	-2	-2	-2
Bilateral	36	-176	-25	-51	-71	-49	-5	-9	-44	-56
Concessional	23	-66	-32	34	19	4	33	24	-6	-16
Private creditors	187	111	-86	6	-125	-1,344	65	676	706	-251
Bonds	-5	52	-7	0	0	0	0	0	0	0
Commercial banks	87	104	5	109	-99	-1,278	11	679	707	-249
Other private	105	-45	-85	-104	-26	-66	54	-3	-1	-1
Private nonguaranteed	**206**	**2,123**	**1,274**	**1,624**	**2,387**	**3,952**	**3,669**	**3,851**	**1,906**	**1,391**
Bonds	0	0	0	91	489	1,859	1,039	702	862	672
Commercial banks and other	206	2,123	1,274	1,533	1,898	2,093	2,630	3,149	1,044	719
Memo:										
IBRD	18	5	132	-111	-621	-188	-25	-35	-67	-67
IDA	0	0	-1	-1	-1	-1	-1	-1	-1	-1

CHILE

(US$ million, unless otherwise indicated)

	1970	1980	1990	1994	1995	1996	1997	1998	1999	2000
INTEREST PAYMENTS (LINT)	**104**	**918**	**1,364**	**929**	**1,114**	**1,185**	**1,070**	**1,326**	**1,502**	**2,076**
Public and publicly guaranteed	**78**	**483**	**1,112**	**565**	**653**	**535**	**292**	**254**	**312**	**374**
Official creditors	40	80	384	379	387	274	161	119	132	139
Multilateral	9	26	313	353	348	190	136	99	109	112
Concessional	0	1	1	0	0	0	0	0	0	0
Bilateral	31	54	71	27	39	84	24	21	23	27
Concessional	12	22	9	6	6	60	6	6	8	9
Private creditors	39	403	729	186	266	261	131	135	180	235
Bonds	2	5	2	0	0	0	0	0	0	0
Commercial banks	19	325	688	175	258	256	130	130	176	230
Other private	17	73	39	11	8	5	1	4	4	5
Private nonguaranteed	**26**	**435**	**252**	**365**	**461**	**651**	**778**	**1,072**	**1,190**	**1,702**
Bonds	0	0	0	13	26	59	192	267	321	440
Commercial banks and other	26	435	252	352	435	591	587	806	869	1,262
Memo:										
IBRD	6	16	130	140	137	89	68	58	70	70
IDA	0	0	0	0	0	0	0	0	0	0
NET TRANSFERS ON DEBT	**343**	**1,171**	**118**	**512**	**-662**	**781**	**2,290**	**3,113**	**1,027**	**-1,054**
Public and publicly guaranteed	**163**	**-517**	**-904**	**-748**	**-2,588**	**-2,521**	**-601**	**335**	**312**	**-743**
Official creditors	15	-225	-90	-568	-2,197	-916	-535	-206	-215	-258
Multilateral	10	5	7	-490	-2,087	-783	-505	-177	-149	-176
Concessional	0	2	-3	-2	-2	-2	-2	-2	-2	-2
Bilateral	5	-230	-96	-77	-110	-133	-30	-29	-67	-82
Concessional	11	-88	-42	28	13	-57	27	19	-14	-25
Private creditors	148	-292	-815	-180	-391	-1,605	-67	541	527	-486
Bonds	-7	47	-9	0	0	0	0	0	0	0
Commercial banks	68	-221	-683	-66	-357	-1,534	-119	548	531	-480
Other private	87	-118	-123	-114	-34	-71	52	-8	-5	-6
Private nonguaranteed	**180**	**1,688**	**1,022**	**1,259**	**1,926**	**3,302**	**2,891**	**2,779**	**716**	**-311**
Bonds	0	0	0	78	463	1,800	847	435	542	232
Commercial banks and other	180	1,688	1,022	1,181	1,463	1,502	2,044	2,343	174	-543
Memo:										
IBRD	12	-11	2	-251	-758	-277	-93	-93	-138	-137
IDA	0	0	-1	-1	-1	-1	-1	-1	-1	-1
DEBT SERVICE (LTDS)	**311**	**2,380**	**2,135**	**2,411**	**4,483**	**5,863**	**3,927**	**3,671**	**4,852**	**6,008**
Public and publicly guaranteed	**244**	**1,374**	**1,612**	**1,211**	**2,930**	**3,495**	**1,286**	**694**	**780**	**1,125**
Official creditors	115	287	740	918	2,391	1,073	701	355	379	418
Multilateral	24	41	576	782	2,233	908	613	271	286	289
Concessional	0	1	3	2	2	2	2	2	2	2
Bilateral	91	245	164	136	158	164	89	84	93	129
Concessional	33	90	42	30	36	88	32	36	41	43
Private creditors	129	1,088	872	293	539	2,423	585	339	401	707
Bonds	7	8	9	0	0	0	0	0	0	0
Commercial banks	51	789	720	179	498	2,342	578	332	396	701
Other private	71	290	144	114	41	80	8	8	5	6
Private nonguaranteed	**67**	**1,006**	**523**	**1,200**	**1,553**	**2,368**	**2,641**	**2,976**	**4,072**	**4,883**
Bonds	0	0	0	13	37	70	203	428	332	440
Commercial banks and other	67	1,006	523	1,187	1,516	2,297	2,438	2,549	3,740	4,443
Memo:										
IBRD	16	25	249	332	841	352	178	163	181	185
IDA	0	0	1	1	1	1	1	1	1	1
UNDISBURSED DEBT	**469**	**432**	**1,550**	**1,270**	**1,196**	**952**	**834**	**511**	**621**	**487**
Official creditors	180	186	1,364	1,078	1,101	861	568	214	482	298
Private creditors	289	246	186	192	95	91	266	297	140	190
Memorandum items										
Concessional LDOD	678	678	367	310	331	328	350	400	399	361
Variable rate LDOD	501	7,104	11,124	14,903	16,461	18,854	20,425	27,471	31,286	32,780
Public sector LDOD	1,978	4,587	10,421	8,995	7,178	4,883	4,367	4,865	5,515	5,130
Private sector LDOD	589	4,811	4,267	9,004	11,429	15,531	17,155	23,700	27,583	29,317

6. CURRENCY COMPOSITION OF LONG-TERM DEBT (PERCENT)

	1970	1980	1990	1994	1995	1996	1997	1998	1999	2000
Deutsche mark	5.6	5.9	4.7	3.7	4.5	3.6	2.0	1.9	1.3	1.3
French franc	2.1	6.3	1.1	0.6	0.7	0.8	0.8	0.5	0.4	0.3
Japanese yen	0.0	1.8	8.2	8.8	9.5	8.6	7.2	6.9	6.5	5.6
Pound sterling	7.4	1.0	3.4	2.8	2.9	0.5	0.4	0.3	0.3	0.2
Swiss franc	0.9	0.4	0.6	0.7	0.9	0.3	0.2	0.2	0.1	0.1
U.S.dollars	75.1	74.6	40.2	34.9	42.3	45.8	54.9	79.4	83.2	85.3
Multiple currency	6.7	7.0	39.4	47.5	38.0	39.8	34.2	10.6	8.1	7.1
Special drawing rights	0.0	0.0	0.0	0.0	0.0	0.0	0.0	0.0	0.0	0.0
All other currencies	2.2	3.0	2.4	1.0	1.2	0.6	0.3	0.2	0.1	0.1

CHILE

(US$ million, unless otherwise indicated)

7. DEBT RESTRUCTURINGS

	1970	1980	1990	1994	1995	1996	1997	1998	1999	2000
Total amount rescheduled	..	..	4,172	0	0	1	0	0	0	0
Debt stock rescheduled	..	..	4,169	0	0	0	0	0	0	0
Principal rescheduled	..	..	0	0	0	0	0	0	0	0
Official	..	..	0	0	0	0	0	0	0	0
Private	..	..	0	0	0	0	0	0	0	0
Interest rescheduled	..	..	0	0	0	0	0	0	0	0
Official	..	..	0	0	0	0	0	0	0	0
Private	..	..	0	0	0	0	0	0	0	0
Debt forgiven	..	..	0	0	0	0	0	0	0	0
Memo: interest forgiven	..	..	0	0	0	0	0	0	0	0
Debt stock reduction	..	..	1,100	32	145	34	0	0	0	0
of which debt buyback	..	..	0	0	0	0	0	0	0	0

8. DEBT STOCK-FLOW RECONCILIATION

	1970	1980	1990	1994	1995	1996	1997	1998	1999	2000
Total change in debt stocks	..	..	1,193	2,162	-117	1,011	-240	7,366	4,094	2,709
Net flows on debt	400	2,963	1,682	1,608	-284	1,171	2,012	4,762	2,090	2,382
Net change in interest arrears	..	..	0	0	0	0	0	0	0	0
Interest capitalized	..	..	0	0	0	0	0	0	0	0
Debt forgiveness or reduction	..	..	-1,100	-32	-145	-34	0	0	0	0
Cross-currency valuation	..	..	508	172	14	601	142	382	29	-61
Residual	..	..	104	414	298	-726	-2,395	2,222	1,975	388

9. AVERAGE TERMS OF NEW COMMITMENTS

	1970	1980	1990	1994	1995	1996	1997	1998	1999	2000
ALL CREDITORS										
Interest (%)	6.8	13.9	7.8	7.5	6.2	5.6	6.2	6.0	6.9	7.0
Maturity (years)	12.4	8.4	17.6	13.3	18.0	7.0	6.2	5.0	12.3	6.3
Grace period (years)	3.5	3.7	4.2	6.0	5.4	5.3	3.9	2.6	8.1	3.0
Grant element (%)	15.6	-18.0	12.0	13.9	24.2	19.1	13.5	11.2	18.5	9.8
Official creditors										
Interest (%)	6.5	8.7	7.7	6.3	6.1	4.7	1.0	0.0	6.6	1.0
Maturity (years)	21.0	15.1	18.4	22.1	19.5	20.9	10.0	0.0	16.9	10.0
Grace period (years)	6.7	3.6	4.3	5.0	5.8	8.7	1.5	0.0	4.7	1.5
Grant element (%)	24.4	6.0	12.8	22.6	26.2	38.8	36.4	0.0	19.8	36.4
Private creditors										
Interest (%)	6.9	14.4	9.3	8.3	6.8	5.6	6.3	6.0	7.0	7.0
Maturity (years)	11.1	7.7	7.6	7.7	9.6	5.9	6.1	5.0	9.9	6.3
Grace period (years)	3.0	3.7	2.3	6.7	3.0	5.0	3.9	2.6	9.9	3.0
Grant element (%)	14.3	-20.4	1.7	8.3	13.7	17.5	13.2	11.2	17.9	9.7
Memorandum items										
Commitments	361	835	1,049	181	314	885	711	907	1,249	324
Official creditors	46	74	967	70	265	63	9	0	431	1
Private creditors	314	761	82	111	49	821	702	907	818	323

10. CONTRACTUAL OBLIGATIONS ON OUTSTANDING LONG-TERM DEBT

	2001	2002	2003	2004	2005	2006	2007	2008	2009	2010
TOTAL										
Disbursements	213	128	69	32	20	13	8	4	1	0
Principal	4,762	4,946	5,156	3,272	3,232	3,722	1,796	1,647	2,260	1,417
Interest	1,919	1,630	1,325	1,139	871	720	500	376	294	201
Official creditors										
Disbursements	103	75	48	26	20	13	8	4	1	0
Principal	306	300	271	223	194	166	114	108	92	73
Interest	128	115	100	85	69	55	45	37	30	24
Bilateral creditors										
Disbursements	12	10	6	4	3	1	1	1	1	0
Principal	129	125	88	25	11	12	15	14	13	13
Interest	13	10	7	5	5	5	4	4	4	3
Multilateral creditors										
Disbursements	91	65	42	22	18	11	7	3	0	0
Principal	177	176	184	199	183	153	99	94	79	60
Interest	115	105	93	79	65	51	40	33	26	21
Private creditors										
Disbursements	110	53	22	6	0	0	0	0	0	0
Principal	4,455	4,646	4,885	3,049	3,038	3,556	1,682	1,539	2,167	1,345
Interest	1,790	1,515	1,225	1,054	802	665	455	339	264	177
Commercial banks										
Disbursements	110	53	22	6	0	0	0	0	0	0
Principal	1,066	622	391	226	139	37	35	35	835	25
Interest	214	152	114	86	75	68	65	63	32	2
Other private										
Disbursements	0	0	0	0	0	0	0	0	0	0
Principal	3,389	4,024	4,494	2,823	2,899	3,519	1,647	1,504	1,333	1,319
Interest	1,577	1,364	1,111	969	727	598	390	277	232	175

CHINA

(US$ million, unless otherwise indicated)

	1970	1980	1990	1994	1995	1996	1997	1998	1999	2000
1. SUMMARY DEBT DATA										
TOTAL DEBT STOCKS (EDT)	..	..	**55,301**	**100,457**	**118,090**	**128,817**	**146,697**	**154,599**	**154,223**	**149,800**
Long-term debt (LDOD)	..	..	**45,515**	**82,974**	**95,764**	**103,410**	**115,233**	**126,667**	**136,541**	**132,625**
Public and publicly guaranteed	..	..	45,515	82,391	94,675	102,260	112,821	99,424	108,163	104,709
Private nonguaranteed	..	..	0	583	1,090	1,150	2,412	27,243	28,378	27,916
Use of IMF credit	**0**	**0**	**469**	**0**	**0**	**0**	**0**	**0**	**0**	**0**
Short-term debt	..	..	**9,317**	**17,483**	**22,326**	**25,407**	**31,464**	**27,933**	**17,682**	**17,174**
of which interest arrears on LDOD	..	..	0	0	0	0	0	0	0	0
Official creditors	..	..	0	0	0	0	0	0	0	0
Private creditors	..	..	0	0	0	0	0	0	0	0
Memo: principal arrears on LDOD	..	..	0	0	0	0	0	0	0	0
Official creditors	..	..	0	0	0	0	0	0	0	0
Private creditors	..	..	0	0	0	0	0	0	0	0
Memo: export credits	..	..	8,076	23,371	26,520	28,724	31,951	13,149	12,813	11,747
TOTAL DEBT FLOWS										
Disbursements	..	..	**9,665**	**16,151**	**21,985**	**21,114**	**23,976**	**11,148**	**13,351**	**13,760**
Long-term debt	..	..	9,665	16,151	21,985	21,114	23,976	11,148	13,351	13,760
IMF purchases	0	0	0	0	0	0	0	0	0	0
Principal repayments	..	..	**3,809**	**6,343**	**9,070**	**10,260**	**11,527**	**11,209**	**13,502**	**14,134**
Long-term debt	..	..	3,319	6,343	9,070	10,260	11,527	11,209	13,502	14,134
IMF repurchases	0	0	490	0	0	0	0	0	0	0
Net flows on debt	..	..	**8,267**	**11,995**	**17,758**	**13,936**	**18,506**	**-3,593**	**-10,401**	**-882**
of which short-term debt	..	..	2,410	2,187	4,843	3,082	6,057	-3,532	-10,251	-508
Interest payments (INT)	..	..	**3,248**	**4,792**	**5,996**	**5,496**	**6,918**	**7,226**	**7,153**	**7,594**
Long-term debt	..	..	2,534	3,844	4,657	4,685	5,553	5,575	6,013	6,426
IMF charges	0	0	66	0	0	0	0	0	0	0
Short-term debt	..	..	649	948	1,340	812	1,365	1,651	1,140	1,168
Net transfers on debt	..	..	**5,018**	**7,203**	**11,761**	**8,440**	**11,588**	**-10,818**	**-17,554**	**-8,476**
Total debt service paid (TDS)	..	..	**7,057**	**11,135**	**15,066**	**15,756**	**18,445**	**18,435**	**20,655**	**21,728**
Long-term debt	..	..	5,853	10,187	13,726	14,944	17,080	16,784	19,515	20,561
IMF repurchases and charges	0	0	555	0	0	0	0	0	0	0
Short-term debt (interest only)	..	..	649	948	1,340	812	1,365	1,651	1,140	1,168
2. AGGREGATE NET RESOURCE FLOWS AND NET TRANSFERS (LONG-TERM)										
NET RESOURCE FLOWS	..	..	**10,082**	**47,847**	**51,902**	**54,745**	**65,407**	**45,299**	**42,709**	**60,525**
Net flow of long-term debt (ex. IMF)	..	..	6,346	9,808	12,915	10,854	12,449	-61	-150	-374
Foreign direct investment (net)	..	..	3,487	33,787	35,849	40,180	44,237	43,751	38,753	38,399
Portfolio equity flows	..	..	0	3,915	2,807	3,466	8,457	1,273	3,732	22,198
Grants (excluding technical coop.)	..	..	249	337	330	245	263	336	373	303
Memo: technical coop. grants	..	..	384	484	563	536	466	512	560	541
official net resource flows	..	..	1,975	3,454	8,233	4,646	4,578	2,624	2,076	2,230
private net resource flows	..	..	8,107	44,393	43,669	50,100	60,828	42,675	40,632	58,295
NET TRANSFERS	..	..	**7,502**	**43,503**	**46,495**	**48,561**	**58,053**	**37,124**	**33,596**	**49,899**
Interest on long-term debt	..	..	2,534	3,844	4,657	4,685	5,553	5,575	6,013	6,426
Profit remittances on FDI	..	..	46	500	750	1,500	1,800	2,600	3,100	4,200
Memo: official net transfers	..	..	1,444	2,323	6,945	3,335	2,793	811	253	180
private net transfers	..	..	6,058	41,179	39,550	45,225	55,260	36,313	33,343	49,719
3. MAJOR ECONOMIC AGGREGATES										
Gross national income (GNI)	..	..	355,609	541,498	688,446	804,053	887,240	929,668	973,383	1,065,283
Exports of goods & services (XGS)	..	..	60,515	125,313	152,781	180,668	217,372	213,255	229,678	292,668
of which workers remittances	..	..	124	395	350	1,672	4,423	247	384	556
Imports of goods & services (MGS)	..	..	48,668	118,345	152,248	173,882	181,130	185,815	213,123	277,904
International reserves (RES)	..	..	34,476	57,781	80,288	111,729	146,448	152,843	161,414	171,763
Current account balance	..	..	11,997	6,908	1,618	7,243	36,963	31,472	21,115	20,518
4. DEBT INDICATORS										
EDT / XGS (%)	..	..	91.4	80.2	77.3	71.3	67.5	72.5	67.2	51.2
EDT / GNI (%)	..	..	15.6	18.6	17.2	16.0	16.5	16.6	15.8	14.1
TDS / XGS (%)	..	..	11.7	8.9	9.9	8.7	8.5	8.6	9.0	7.4
INT / XGS (%)	..	..	5.4	3.8	3.9	3.0	3.2	3.4	3.1	2.6
INT / GNI (%)	..	..	0.9	0.9	0.9	0.7	0.8	0.8	0.7	0.7
RES / EDT (%)	..	..	62.3	57.5	68.0	86.7	99.8	98.9	104.7	114.7
RES / MGS (months)	..	..	8.5	5.9	6.3	7.7	9.7	9.9	9.1	7.4
Short-term / EDT (%)	..	..	16.9	17.4	18.9	19.7	21.5	18.1	11.5	11.5
Concessional / EDT (%)	..	..	17.6	15.9	15.2	14.5	12.3	17.4	19.2	18.7
Multilateral / EDT (%)	..	..	11.1	13.5	13.8	13.7	12.9	14.4	15.5	17.6

CHINA

(US$ million, unless otherwise indicated)

5. LONG-TERM DEBT

	1970	1980	1990	1994	1995	1996	1997	1998	1999	2000
DEBT OUTSTANDING (LDOD)	..	..	**45,515**	**82,974**	**95,764**	**103,410**	**115,233**	**126,667**	**136,541**	**132,625**
Public and publicly guaranteed	..	..	**45,515**	**82,391**	**94,675**	**102,260**	**112,821**	**99,424**	**108,163**	**104,709**
Official creditors	..	..	14,514	28,973	36,982	39,433	39,755	45,146	50,416	50,955
Multilateral	..	..	6,111	13,588	16,302	17,695	18,973	22,283	23,856	26,349
Concessional	..	..	3,119	6,231	7,180	7,715	7,954	8,945	9,173	9,033
Bilateral	..	..	8,403	15,385	20,680	21,737	20,782	22,863	26,560	24,606
Concessional	..	..	6,599	9,729	10,792	11,006	10,148	17,892	20,459	18,918
Private creditors	..	..	31,001	53,418	57,693	62,828	73,066	54,278	57,747	53,755
Bonds	..	..	5,426	11,087	10,684	11,106	12,616	13,941	14,601	12,294
Commercial banks	..	..	14,520	21,475	23,869	24,437	34,873	24,400	25,878	20,673
Other private	..	..	11,055	20,856	23,140	27,285	25,577	15,937	17,269	20,788
Private nonguaranteed	..	..	**0**	**583**	**1,090**	**1,150**	**2,412**	**27,243**	**28,378**	**27,916**
Bonds	..	..	0	583	1,090	1,150	2,412	1,198	1,248	1,068
Commercial banks and other	..	..	0	0	0	0	0	26,045	27,131	26,848
Memo:										
IBRD	0	0	2,865	5,933	7,209	7,616	8,239	9,644	10,400	11,118
IDA	0	0	3,016	6,097	7,038	7,579	7,830	8,693	8,907	8,771
DISBURSEMENTS	..	..	**9,665**	**16,151**	**21,985**	**21,114**	**23,976**	**11,148**	**13,351**	**13,760**
Public and publicly guaranteed	..	..	**9,665**	**16,151**	**21,441**	**20,985**	**22,458**	**10,679**	**13,351**	**13,370**
Official creditors	..	..	2,578	4,200	9,073	5,669	6,214	5,012	5,874	5,874
Multilateral	..	..	1,158	2,559	2,838	2,797	2,939	2,830	2,396	2,501
Concessional	..	..	511	686	822	816	715	602	493	401
Bilateral	..	..	1,420	1,642	6,235	2,872	3,275	2,182	3,478	3,374
Concessional	..	..	1,022	1,171	1,533	1,388	248	2,046	2,421	2,004
Private creditors	..	..	7,088	11,951	12,368	15,316	16,244	5,667	7,478	7,496
Bonds	..	..	277	3,337	1,224	2,777	3,105	1,325	1,660	0
Commercial banks	..	..	3,247	2,380	4,977	4,915	5,889	1,537	2,086	1,631
Other private	..	..	3,564	6,234	6,167	7,624	7,249	2,805	3,732	5,865
Private nonguaranteed	..	..	**0**	**0**	**544**	**129**	**1,518**	**469**	**0**	**390**
Bonds	..	..	0	0	544	129	1,518	469	0	390
Commercial banks and other	..	..	0	0	0	0	0	0	0	0
Memo:										
IBRD	0	0	591	1,380	1,457	1,286	1,562	1,474	1,294	1,528
IDA	0	0	507	680	812	811	713	592	460	379
PRINCIPAL REPAYMENTS	..	..	**3,319**	**6,343**	**9,070**	**10,260**	**11,527**	**11,209**	**13,502**	**14,134**
Public and publicly guaranteed	..	..	**3,319**	**6,343**	**9,070**	**10,260**	**11,320**	**8,182**	**10,682**	**11,601**
Official creditors	..	..	851	1,083	1,171	1,269	1,899	2,724	4,171	3,946
Multilateral	..	..	220	359	420	414	554	575	696	811
Concessional	..	..	0	12	19	27	34	40	66	79
Bilateral	..	..	631	725	751	854	1,345	2,150	3,475	3,135
Concessional	..	..	145	276	315	387	385	1,514	1,383	1,638
Private creditors	..	..	2,468	5,260	7,899	8,991	9,421	5,458	6,511	7,654
Bonds	..	..	325	461	1,451	1,716	1,087	0	1,000	2,307
Commercial banks	..	..	808	1,803	2,645	4,132	5,159	3,018	3,134	3,057
Other private	..	..	1,335	2,997	3,803	3,143	3,175	2,440	2,377	2,290
Private nonguaranteed	..	..	**0**	**0**	**0**	**0**	**207**	**3,027**	**2,820**	**2,534**
Bonds	..	..	0	0	0	0	207	207	0	534
Commercial banks and other	..	..	0	0	0	0	0	2,820	2,820	2,000
Memo:										
IBRD	0	0	216	315	350	343	351	396	505	578
IDA	0	0	0	9	14	20	26	38	53	66
NET FLOWS ON DEBT	..	..	**6,346**	**9,808**	**12,915**	**10,854**	**12,449**	**-61**	**-150**	**-374**
Public and publicly guaranteed	..	..	**6,346**	**9,808**	**12,371**	**10,725**	**11,138**	**2,497**	**2,670**	**1,769**
Official creditors	..	..	1,727	3,117	7,902	4,401	4,315	2,288	1,703	1,928
Multilateral	..	..	938	2,200	2,418	2,383	2,385	2,255	1,700	1,689
Concessional	..	..	511	674	804	789	681	563	427	323
Bilateral	..	..	789	917	5,484	2,018	1,930	32	3	239
Concessional	..	..	877	895	1,218	1,001	-137	531	1,039	367
Private creditors	..	..	4,620	6,691	4,469	6,325	6,823	209	967	-159
Bonds	..	..	-48	2,876	-227	1,061	2,019	1,325	660	-2,307
Commercial banks	..	..	2,439	577	2,332	783	730	-1,481	-1,048	-1,426
Other private	..	..	2,229	3,237	2,364	4,481	4,075	366	1,355	3,574
Private nonguaranteed	..	..	**0**	**0**	**544**	**129**	**1,311**	**-2,558**	**-2,820**	**-2,144**
Bonds	..	..	0	0	544	129	1,311	262	0	-144
Commercial banks and other	..	..	0	0	0	0	0	-2,820	-2,820	-2,000
Memo:										
IBRD	0	0	376	1,066	1,107	943	1,211	1,078	788	950
IDA	0	0	507	671	798	791	687	554	407	314

CHINA

(US$ million, unless otherwise indicated)

	1970	1980	1990	1994	1995	1996	1997	1998	1999	2000
INTEREST PAYMENTS (LINT)	..	..	**2,534**	**3,844**	**4,657**	**4,685**	**5,553**	**5,575**	**6,013**	**6,426**
Public and publicly guaranteed	..	..	**2,534**	**3,818**	**4,624**	**4,631**	**5,498**	**4,612**	**4,986**	**5,382**
Official creditors	..	..	531	1,131	1,288	1,310	1,785	1,813	1,824	2,051
Multilateral	..	..	226	480	619	684	731	817	965	1,064
Concessional	..	..	20	44	53	56	58	60	68	69
Bilateral	..	..	305	651	669	626	1,055	996	859	986
Concessional	..	..	193	330	324	293	342	293	530	570
Private creditors	..	..	2,003	2,687	3,336	3,321	3,713	2,799	3,162	3,331
Bonds	..	..	367	363	594	506	568	397	794	797
Commercial banks	..	..	959	1,034	1,333	1,351	1,441	983	1,353	1,463
Other private	..	..	677	1,290	1,409	1,464	1,704	1,419	1,015	1,071
Private nonguaranteed	..	..	**0**	**26**	**33**	**53**	**55**	**963**	**1,027**	**1,045**
Bonds	..	..	0	26	33	53	55	42	96	93
Commercial banks and other	..	..	0	0	0	0	0	922	932	952
Memo:										
IBRD	0	0	200	364	460	497	507	545	637	713
IDA	0	0	19	41	49	52	56	59	64	65
NET TRANSFERS ON DEBT	..	..	**3,813**	**5,964**	**8,258**	**6,170**	**6,896**	**-5,636**	**-6,163**	**-6,801**
Public and publicly guaranteed	..	..	**3,813**	**5,990**	**7,748**	**6,094**	**5,640**	**-2,115**	**-2,316**	**-3,612**
Official creditors	..	..	1,196	1,986	6,614	3,090	2,530	475	-121	-123
Multilateral	..	..	712	1,720	1,799	1,699	1,655	1,438	735	625
Concessional	..	..	491	630	751	734	622	503	359	254
Bilateral	..	..	484	266	4,816	1,392	875	-963	-856	-748
Concessional	..	..	684	565	894	708	-480	239	509	-203
Private creditors	..	..	2,617	4,004	1,133	3,004	3,111	-2,590	-2,195	-3,490
Bonds	..	..	-415	2,513	-821	555	1,451	928	-134	-3,104
Commercial banks	..	..	1,480	-457	999	-568	-711	-2,465	-2,402	-2,889
Other private	..	..	1,551	1,948	955	3,017	2,371	-1,053	340	2,503
Private nonguaranteed	..	..	**0**	**-26**	**511**	**76**	**1,256**	**-3,521**	**-3,847**	**-3,189**
Bonds	..	..	0	-26	511	76	1,256	220	-96	-237
Commercial banks and other	..	..	0	0	0	0	0	-3,742	-3,752	-2,952
Memo:										
IBRD	0	0	176	701	648	447	704	533	151	237
IDA	0	0	488	630	749	738	632	495	342	248
DEBT SERVICE (LTDS)	..	..	**5,853**	**10,187**	**13,726**	**14,944**	**17,080**	**16,784**	**19,515**	**20,561**
Public and publicly guaranteed	..	..	**5,853**	**10,161**	**13,693**	**14,891**	**16,818**	**12,794**	**15,667**	**16,982**
Official creditors	..	..	1,383	2,214	2,459	2,579	3,684	4,537	5,994	5,997
Multilateral	..	..	446	838	1,039	1,099	1,285	1,392	1,660	1,876
Concessional	..	..	20	56	71	82	92	100	134	148
Bilateral	..	..	937	1,376	1,419	1,480	2,400	3,145	4,334	4,121
Concessional	..	..	338	607	639	680	728	1,807	1,912	2,208
Private creditors	..	..	4,470	7,947	11,234	12,312	13,133	8,257	9,673	10,985
Bonds	..	..	692	824	2,045	2,223	1,655	397	1,794	3,104
Commercial banks	..	..	1,767	2,837	3,978	5,483	6,600	4,002	4,487	4,520
Other private	..	..	2,012	4,286	5,212	4,607	4,879	3,858	3,392	3,362
Private nonguaranteed	..	..	**0**	**26**	**33**	**53**	**262**	**3,990**	**3,847**	**3,579**
Bonds	..	..	0	26	33	53	262	249	96	627
Commercial banks and other	..	..	0	0	0	0	0	3,742	3,752	2,952
Memo:										
IBRD	0	0	415	679	810	840	858	941	1,142	1,291
IDA	0	0	19	50	63	73	81	97	118	131
UNDISBURSED DEBT	..	..	**9,298**	**16,252**	**17,041**	**17,906**	**16,883**	**22,267**	**21,095**	**14,617**
Official creditors	..	..	5,280	13,164	13,486	12,141	11,512	21,758	20,607	14,218
Private creditors	..	..	4,019	3,088	3,556	5,765	5,371	510	488	399
Memorandum items										
Concessional LDOD	..	..	9,718	15,960	17,972	18,722	18,101	26,838	29,632	27,951
Variable rate LDOD	..	..	16,491	23,272	28,370	30,652	45,217	62,139	63,621	61,883
Public sector LDOD	..	..	45,449	81,709	93,573	101,163	111,740	99,424	108,163	104,709
Private sector LDOD	..	..	66	1,265	2,192	2,247	3,493	27,243	28,378	27,916

6. CURRENCY COMPOSITION OF LONG-TERM DEBT (PERCENT)

	1970	1980	1990	1994	1995	1996	1997	1998	1999	2000
Deutsche mark	..	..	3.1	1.7	1.7	1.4	1.2	2.3	2.0	2.0
French franc	..	..	0.4	0.3	0.3	0.3	0.2	2.9	1.8	1.7
Japanese yen	..	..	30.4	23.2	20.7	15.9	11.8	14.8	16.4	15.3
Pound sterling	..	..	0.7	0.3	0.2	0.2	0.2	0.1	0.1	0.1
Swiss franc	..	..	0.2	0.1	0.0	0.0	0.0	0.1	0.1	0.1
U.S.dollars	..	..	29.1	53.6	58.1	65.0	74.6	72.4	70.2	74.0
Multiple currency	..	..	31.2	18.7	17.1	15.6	10.8	6.2	8.4	5.8
Special drawing rights	..	..	0.3	0.2	0.1	0.1	0.1	0.3	0.3	0.3
All other currencies	..	..	4.6	1.9	1.8	1.5	1.1	0.9	0.7	0.7

CHINA

(US$ million, unless otherwise indicated)

	1970	1980	1990	1994	1995	1996	1997	1998	1999	2000
7. DEBT RESTRUCTURINGS										
Total amount rescheduled	..	..	0	0	0	0	0	0	0	0
Debt stock rescheduled	..	..	0	0	0	0	0	0	0	0
Principal rescheduled	..	..	0	0	0	0	0	0	0	0
Official	..	..	0	0	0	0	0	0	0	0
Private	..	..	0	0	0	0	0	0	0	0
Interest rescheduled	..	..	0	0	0	0	0	0	0	0
Official	..	..	0	0	0	0	0	0	0	0
Private	..	..	0	0	0	0	0	0	0	0
Debt forgiven	..	..	0	0	0	0	0	0	0	0
Memo: interest forgiven	..	..	0	0	0	0	0	0	0	0
Debt stock reduction	..	..	0	0	0	0	0	0	0	0
of which debt buyback	..	..	0	0	0	0	0	0	0	0
8. DEBT STOCK-FLOW RECONCILIATION										
Total change in debt stocks	..	..	10,369	14,529	17,633	10,727	17,880	7,902	-376	-4,423
Net flows on debt	..	..	8,267	11,995	17,758	13,936	18,506	-3,593	-10,401	-882
Net change in interest arrears	..	..	0	0	0	0	0	0	0	0
Interest capitalized	..	..	0	0	0	0	0	0	0	0
Debt forgiveness or reduction	..	..	0	0	0	0	0	0	0	0
Cross-currency valuation	..	..	1,415	2,424	-375	-3,793	-3,502	2,253	964	-3,118
Residual	..	..	687	111	250	584	2,875	9,242	9,061	-423
9. AVERAGE TERMS OF NEW COMMITMENTS										
ALL CREDITORS										
Interest (%)	..	..	7.5	5.5	6.5	6.6	6.5	6.2	6.1	6.7
Maturity (years)	..	..	16.6	15.6	11.8	10.1	10.1	14.4	13.0	10.9
Grace period (years)	..	..	3.9	5.0	2.9	2.9	3.2	3.4	3.1	2.6
Grant element (%)	..	..	15.6	25.4	15.4	14.2	14.8	19.8	19.0	12.9
Official creditors										
Interest (%)	..	..	3.7	5.6	6.8	5.9	6.6	5.9	5.5	7.3
Maturity (years)	..	..	27.9	21.1	18.3	21.2	19.1	21.6	23.3	21.1
Grace period (years)	..	..	7.9	6.0	3.7	4.5	3.9	5.6	6.1	4.9
Grant element (%)	..	..	49.2	30.4	19.0	27.7	21.2	27.8	31.9	17.3
Private creditors										
Interest (%)	..	..	8.6	5.4	6.3	6.8	6.4	6.4	6.3	6.6
Maturity (years)	..	..	13.3	11.6	7.3	7.0	6.4	9.2	8.8	7.5
Grace period (years)	..	..	2.7	4.2	2.4	2.4	2.9	1.8	1.9	1.8
Grant element (%)	..	..	5.7	21.7	12.9	10.5	12.2	14.0	13.8	11.5
Memorandum items										
Commitments	..	..	9,988	15,960	22,813	22,438	22,108	8,029	10,480	9,854
Official creditors	..	..	2,288	6,824	9,296	4,886	6,323	3,357	3,020	2,438
Private creditors	..	..	7,701	9,135	13,517	17,552	15,785	4,671	7,460	7,417

10. CONTRACTUAL OBLIGATIONS ON OUTSTANDING LONG-TERM DEBT

	2001	2002	2003	2004	2005	2006	2007	2008	2009	2010
TOTAL										
Disbursements	4,715	3,263	2,291	1,675	1,144	748	441	202	104	35
Principal	17,915	18,415	17,288	13,350	12,167	6,380	5,226	5,034	4,613	4,536
Interest	6,246	5,726	5,054	3,699	2,980	2,414	2,132	1,860	1,595	1,323
Official creditors										
Disbursements	4,335	3,252	2,286	1,672	1,143	747	441	202	104	35
Principal	3,956	4,362	4,365	4,199	3,954	4,030	3,917	3,385	3,318	3,242
Interest	2,274	2,338	2,267	2,180	2,061	1,926	1,754	1,573	1,400	1,228
Bilateral creditors										
Disbursements	1,810	892	365	147	29	9	0	0	0	0
Principal	2,681	2,886	2,753	2,386	1,995	1,965	1,878	1,374	1,367	1,308
Interest	911	851	762	672	596	523	449	381	326	271
Multilateral creditors										
Disbursements	2,525	2,360	1,922	1,525	1,114	738	441	202	104	35
Principal	1,275	1,476	1,613	1,813	1,959	2,065	2,039	2,010	1,952	1,934
Interest	1,363	1,487	1,505	1,508	1,465	1,404	1,306	1,192	1,074	957
Private creditors										
Disbursements	380	11	4	3	1	0	0	0	0	0
Principal	13,959	14,053	12,923	9,151	8,213	2,350	1,310	1,649	1,295	1,294
Interest	3,971	3,388	2,787	1,519	919	488	378	287	196	95
Commercial banks										
Disbursements	340	0	0	0	0	0	0	0	0	0
Principal	3,953	3,951	3,946	3,938	3,938	119	103	99	97	95
Interest	1,248	999	740	481	223	28	25	23	20	18
Other private										
Disbursements	40	11	4	3	1	0	0	0	0	0
Principal	10,006	10,101	8,978	5,214	4,275	2,231	1,207	1,550	1,198	1,199
Interest	2,723	2,389	2,048	1,037	696	460	353	264	175	77

COLOMBIA

(US$ million, unless otherwise indicated)

	1970	1980	1990	1994	1995	1996	1997	1998	1999	2000
1. SUMMARY DEBT DATA										
TOTAL DEBT STOCKS (EDT)	**2,237**	**6,941**	**17,222**	**21,940**	**25,048**	**28,900**	**31,800**	**33,338**	**34,678**	**34,081**
Long-term debt (LDOD)	**1,580**	**4,604**	**15,784**	**17,448**	**19,503**	**23,016**	**26,041**	**27,105**	**30,713**	**31,210**
Public and publicly guaranteed	1,297	4,089	14,671	14,358	13,950	14,854	15,295	17,004	20,474	20,951
Private nonguaranteed	283	515	1,113	3,091	5,553	8,162	10,746	10,101	10,239	10,259
Use of IMF credit	**55**	**0**	**0**	**0**	**0**	**0**	**0**	**0**	**0**	**0**
Short-term debt	**602**	**2,337**	**1,438**	**4,492**	**5,545**	**5,884**	**5,759**	**6,232**	**3,965**	**2,871**
of which interest arrears on LDOD	0	0	28	11	2	0	0	0	0	0
Official creditors	0	0	17	8	0	0	0	0	0	0
Private creditors	0	0	11	3	2	0	0	0	0	0
Memo: principal arrears on LDOD	0	0	409	230	224	42	38	42	46	42
Official creditors	0	0	42	138	126	31	28	31	37	33
Private creditors	0	0	367	92	99	11	10	11	9	9
Memo: export credits	0	0	3,908	3,235	2,841	3,370	3,107	1,357	1,130	879
TOTAL DEBT FLOWS										
Disbursements	**362**	**1,074**	**1,994**	**5,709**	**4,181**	**7,422**	**6,108**	**3,351**	**7,462**	**3,749**
Long-term debt	332	1,074	1,994	5,709	4,181	7,422	6,108	3,351	7,462	3,749
IMF purchases	29	0	0	0	0	0	0	0	0	0
Principal repayments	**226**	**263**	**2,189**	**3,892**	**2,347**	**3,365**	**2,508**	**2,604**	**3,948**	**2,919**
Long-term debt	153	263	2,189	3,892	2,347	3,365	2,508	2,604	3,948	2,919
IMF repurchases	73	0	0	0	0	0	0	0	0	0
Net flows on debt	**136**	**1,136**	**-399**	**2,660**	**2,897**	**4,397**	**3,476**	**1,220**	**1,247**	**-264**
of which short-term debt	0	325	-204	844	1,062	341	-125	473	-2,267	-1,094
Interest payments (INT)	**62**	**688**	**1,701**	**1,678**	**1,998**	**2,036**	**2,011**	**1,949**	**2,672**	**2,252**
Long-term debt	62	310	1,558	1,478	1,687	1,722	1,662	1,600	2,387	2,080
IMF charges	0	0	0	0	0	0	0	0	0	0
Short-term debt	0	378	143	200	311	314	349	348	285	172
Net transfers on debt	**74**	**447**	**-2,100**	**982**	**899**	**2,361**	**1,465**	**-728**	**-1,425**	**-2,516**
Total debt service paid (TDS)	**287**	**951**	**3,889**	**5,570**	**4,345**	**5,401**	**4,519**	**4,553**	**6,620**	**5,171**
Long-term debt	215	573	3,746	5,370	4,034	5,087	4,170	4,205	6,336	4,998
IMF repurchases and charges	73	0	0	0	0	0	0	0	0	0
Short-term debt (interest only)	0	378	143	200	311	314	349	348	285	172
2. AGGREGATE NET RESOURCE FLOWS AND NET TRANSFERS (LONG-TERM)										
NET RESOURCE FLOWS	**245**	**976**	**340**	**3,626**	**3,008**	**7,539**	**9,367**	**3,666**	**5,111**	**3,312**
Net flow of long-term debt (ex. IMF)	179	811	-195	1,817	1,834	4,057	3,601	747	3,514	831
Foreign direct investment (net)	43	157	500	1,445	969	3,112	5,562	2,829	1,468	2,376
Portfolio equity flows	0	0	0	320	131	290	116	26	25	26
Grants (excluding technical coop.)	23	8	35	45	74	81	89	64	104	79
Memo: technical coop. grants	14	46	79	85	98	91	75	117	224	183
official net resource flows	175	288	-5	-423	-349	-30	-363	241	1,117	182
private net resource flows	70	688	345	4,049	3,357	7,569	9,731	3,425	3,994	3,130
NET TRANSFERS	**89**	**556**	**-2,182**	**749**	**-179**	**4,068**	**5,806**	**65**	**824**	**-1,068**
Interest on long-term debt	62	310	1,558	1,478	1,687	1,722	1,662	1,600	2,387	2,080
Profit remittances on FDI	94	110	964	1,400	1,500	1,750	1,900	2,000	1,900	2,300
Memo: official net transfers	138	160	-632	-938	-854	-497	-769	-129	410	-359
private net transfers	-49	396	-1,550	1,686	676	4,565	6,575	194	413	-709
3. MAJOR ECONOMIC AGGREGATES										
Gross national income (GNI)	6,995	33,185	38,193	79,164	89,491	93,171	104,317	97,131	82,386	78,855
Exports of goods & services (XGS)	1,025	5,928	9,514	12,302	13,710	14,500	15,759	14,788	15,963	18,081
of which workers remittances	6	68	488	966	739	635	658	483	1,278	1,554
Imports of goods & services (MGS)	1,348	6,231	9,510	16,078	18,296	19,222	21,584	19,986	15,835	17,811
International reserves (RES)	207	6,474	4,869	8,103	8,452	9,938	9,907	8,754	8,103	9,006
Current account balance	-293	-206	542	-3,673	-4,596	-4,761	-5,868	-5,235	190	306
4. DEBT INDICATORS										
EDT / XGS (%)	218.2	117.1	181.0	178.3	182.7	199.3	201.8	225.4	217.2	188.5
EDT / GNI (%)	32.0	20.9	45.1	27.7	28.0	31.0	30.5	34.3	42.1	43.2
TDS / XGS (%)	28.0	16.1	40.9	45.3	31.7	37.3	28.7	30.8	41.5	28.6
INT / XGS (%)	6.0	11.6	17.9	13.6	14.6	14.0	12.8	13.2	16.7	12.5
INT / GNI (%)	0.9	2.1	4.5	2.1	2.2	2.2	1.9	2.0	3.2	2.9
RES / EDT (%)	9.3	93.3	28.3	36.9	33.7	34.4	31.2	26.3	23.4	26.4
RES / MGS (months)	1.8	12.5	6.1	6.1	5.5	6.2	5.5	5.3	6.1	6.1
Short-term / EDT (%)	26.9	33.7	8.4	20.5	22.1	20.4	18.1	18.7	11.4	8.4
Concessional / EDT (%)	28.1	14.2	5.7	4.3	3.9	3.3	2.8	2.7	2.8	2.8
Multilateral / EDT (%)	19.9	19.5	35.4	24.6	21.2	16.5	12.8	13.9	18.3	18.4

COLOMBIA

(US$ million, unless otherwise indicated)

	1970	1980	1990	1994	1995	1996	1997	1998	1999	2000
5. LONG-TERM DEBT										
DEBT OUTSTANDING (LDOD)	**1,580**	**4,604**	**15,784**	**17,448**	**19,503**	**23,016**	**26,041**	**27,105**	**30,713**	**31,210**
Public and publicly guaranteed	**1,297**	**4,089**	**14,671**	**14,358**	**13,950**	**14,854**	**15,295**	**17,004**	**20,474**	**20,951**
Official creditors	1,112	2,393	8,540	7,277	7,066	6,503	5,623	6,017	7,829	7,724
Multilateral	445	1,350	6,103	5,392	5,320	4,765	4,084	4,623	6,360	6,276
Concessional	25	89	219	175	164	152	145	131	117	104
Bilateral	667	1,043	2,437	1,886	1,747	1,738	1,538	1,394	1,470	1,448
Concessional	604	899	769	773	814	790	745	755	850	860
Private creditors	185	1,696	6,131	7,080	6,883	8,351	9,672	10,987	12,645	13,227
Bonds	21	31	275	1,333	1,734	3,410	4,366	6,200	7,367	8,592
Commercial banks	24	1,371	4,208	4,623	4,163	4,095	4,482	4,112	4,370	3,944
Other private	140	294	1,648	1,124	987	847	825	675	908	690
Private nonguaranteed	**283**	**515**	**1,113**	**3,091**	**5,553**	**8,162**	**10,746**	**10,101**	**10,239**	**10,259**
Bonds	0	0	0	125	717	820	809	821	885	762
Commercial banks and other	283	515	1,113	2,966	4,836	7,341	9,937	9,280	9,354	9,497
Memo:										
IBRD	354	991	3,859	2,629	2,548	2,177	1,723	1,740	1,960	1,920
IDA	20	21	15	12	11	10	10	9	8	7
DISBURSEMENTS	**332**	**1,074**	**1,994**	**5,709**	**4,181**	**7,422**	**6,108**	**3,351**	**7,462**	**3,749**
Public and publicly guaranteed	**332**	**1,019**	**1,847**	**3,109**	**1,571**	**3,461**	**2,846**	**3,351**	**6,519**	**2,884**
Official creditors	194	416	698	1,158	687	880	603	851	1,758	660
Multilateral	74	303	559	602	397	428	488	811	1,550	508
Concessional	0	37	4	9	2	0	5	0	0	0
Bilateral	120	113	139	555	290	453	115	41	208	152
Concessional	101	9	26	205	70	50	35	8	105	97
Private creditors	138	603	1,150	1,951	885	2,581	2,242	2,500	4,761	2,224
Bonds	0	0	0	566	535	1,928	1,144	2,132	1,750	1,804
Commercial banks	88	501	874	1,223	257	509	893	329	1,433	415
Other private	50	103	275	162	93	145	205	39	1,578	5
Private nonguaranteed	**0**	**55**	**147**	**2,600**	**2,610**	**3,960**	**3,263**	**0**	**944**	**865**
Bonds	0	0	0	125	592	108	0	0	176	0
Commercial banks and other	0	55	147	2,475	2,018	3,852	3,263	0	768	865
Memo:										
IBRD	58	218	213	310	238	152	189	184	488	266
IDA	0	0	0	0	0	0	0	0	0	0
PRINCIPAL REPAYMENTS	**153**	**263**	**2,189**	**3,892**	**2,347**	**3,365**	**2,508**	**2,604**	**3,948**	**2,919**
Public and publicly guaranteed	**94**	**250**	**1,875**	**2,336**	**2,200**	**2,018**	**1,840**	**1,948**	**3,129**	**2,086**
Official creditors	42	136	737	1,625	1,110	991	1,055	674	745	558
Multilateral	22	80	527	1,299	647	613	833	437	511	441
Concessional	0	1	12	13	13	13	12	14	14	14
Bilateral	20	57	210	326	463	377	222	237	234	116
Concessional	7	30	36	24	39	38	35	29	42	44
Private creditors	52	114	1,138	711	1,090	1,027	785	1,274	2,384	1,528
Bonds	3	3	4	113	120	192	76	380	566	469
Commercial banks	21	52	849	334	723	570	502	700	1,175	840
Other private	28	59	284	265	248	265	208	195	643	220
Private nonguaranteed	**59**	**13**	**314**	**1,556**	**147**	**1,347**	**667**	**656**	**820**	**832**
Bonds	0	0	0	0	0	0	0	0	125	110
Commercial banks and other	59	13	314	1,556	147	1,347	667	656	695	722
Memo:										
IBRD	17	65	434	836	414	350	437	232	270	242
IDA	0	0	1	1	1	1	1	1	1	1
NET FLOWS ON DEBT	**179**	**811**	**-195**	**1,817**	**1,834**	**4,057**	**3,601**	**747**	**3,514**	**831**
Public and publicly guaranteed	**238**	**769**	**-28**	**772**	**-628**	**1,443**	**1,005**	**1,403**	**3,390**	**798**
Official creditors	152	280	-40	-467	-423	-111	-452	177	1,013	102
Multilateral	52	223	32	-697	-250	-186	-345	373	1,039	67
Concessional	0	37	-8	-4	-11	-13	-7	-14	-14	-14
Bilateral	100	57	-72	230	-173	75	-107	-196	-26	36
Concessional	94	-21	-10	181	31	12	0	-21	63	53
Private creditors	86	489	12	1,240	-205	1,554	1,457	1,226	2,378	696
Bonds	-3	-3	-4	453	416	1,736	1,068	1,752	1,184	1,335
Commercial banks	67	449	25	889	-466	-61	391	-371	258	-425
Other private	22	43	-9	-103	-155	-121	-2	-156	935	-215
Private nonguaranteed	**-59**	**42**	**-167**	**1,044**	**2,463**	**2,613**	**2,595**	**-656**	**124**	**32**
Bonds	0	0	0	125	592	108	0	0	51	-110
Commercial banks and other	-59	42	-167	919	1,871	2,505	2,595	-656	73	142
Memo:										
IBRD	41	152	-221	-526	-176	-198	-248	-48	218	25
IDA	0	0	-1	-1	-1	-1	-1	-1	-1	-1

COLOMBIA

(US$ million, unless otherwise indicated)

	1970	1980	1990	1994	1995	1996	1997	1998	1999	2000
INTEREST PAYMENTS (LINT)	**62**	**310**	**1,558**	**1,478**	**1,687**	**1,722**	**1,662**	**1,600**	**2,387**	**2,080**
Public and publicly guaranteed	**47**	**279**	**1,240**	**977**	**962**	**843**	**885**	**977**	**1,656**	**1,462**
Official creditors	37	128	627	515	506	468	406	370	706	541
Multilateral	25	102	476	424	388	366	314	286	497	470
Concessional	0	2	6	5	4	4	3	3	3	3
Bilateral	12	26	150	91	118	102	91	84	210	71
Concessional	8	21	19	18	25	26	24	24	16	26
Private creditors	10	151	613	462	457	375	480	607	949	921
Bonds	1	2	27	57	58	43	145	242	281	558
Commercial banks	3	128	461	305	310	254	269	303	492	298
Other private	6	21	124	100	89	78	66	63	176	65
Private nonguaranteed	**15**	**31**	**318**	**500**	**725**	**879**	**776**	**623**	**732**	**618**
Bonds	0	0	0	0	15	78	82	82	82	84
Commercial banks and other	15	31	318	500	710	801	695	542	650	534
Memo:										
IBRD	20	79	318	218	191	170	137	115	121	127
IDA	0	0	0	0	0	0	0	0	0	0
NET TRANSFERS ON DEBT	**118**	**501**	**-1,753**	**339**	**147**	**2,335**	**1,939**	**-853**	**1,127**	**-1,249**
Public and publicly guaranteed	**192**	**490**	**-1,268**	**-205**	**-1,591**	**601**	**120**	**426**	**1,735**	**-664**
Official creditors	115	152	-666	-982	-928	-578	-858	-193	306	-439
Multilateral	27	121	-445	-1,121	-638	-551	-659	88	542	-403
Concessional	-1	35	-14	-8	-15	-16	-10	-17	-17	-17
Bilateral	88	30	-222	139	-290	-27	-199	-280	-236	-35
Concessional	86	-42	-29	163	6	-14	-23	-45	47	27
Private creditors	77	338	-601	777	-662	1,179	978	619	1,428	-225
Bonds	-3	-5	-32	396	357	1,693	924	1,511	903	777
Commercial banks	64	321	-436	584	-776	-315	122	-674	-234	-723
Other private	16	22	-133	-203	-244	-199	-68	-218	759	-279
Private nonguaranteed	**-74**	**11**	**-485**	**544**	**1,738**	**1,734**	**1,819**	**-1,280**	**-608**	**-586**
Bonds	0	0	0	125	577	30	-82	-82	-32	-194
Commercial banks and other	-74	11	-485	419	1,161	1,704	1,901	-1,198	-576	-391
Memo:										
IBRD	21	74	-538	-744	-367	-368	-385	-163	98	-102
IDA	0	0	-1	-1	-1	-1	-1	-1	-1	-1
DEBT SERVICE (LTDS)	**215**	**573**	**3,746**	**5,370**	**4,034**	**5,087**	**4,170**	**4,205**	**6,336**	**4,998**
Public and publicly guaranteed	**141**	**529**	**3,115**	**3,313**	**3,162**	**2,861**	**2,726**	**2,925**	**4,784**	**3,548**
Official creditors	79	264	1,364	2,140	1,615	1,458	1,461	1,044	1,451	1,099
Multilateral	47	181	1,003	1,723	1,035	979	1,148	723	1,008	911
Concessional	1	2	18	18	17	17	15	17	17	17
Bilateral	32	83	361	417	581	479	313	321	444	187
Concessional	15	51	55	42	64	64	58	53	58	70
Private creditors	62	265	1,751	1,174	1,547	1,402	1,265	1,881	3,333	2,449
Bonds	3	5	32	170	178	235	220	621	847	1,027
Commercial banks	24	179	1,311	639	1,032	824	771	1,002	1,667	1,138
Other private	34	81	409	365	337	343	274	258	819	284
Private nonguaranteed	**74**	**44**	**632**	**2,056**	**872**	**2,226**	**1,444**	**1,280**	**1,551**	**1,450**
Bonds	0	0	0	0	15	78	82	82	207	194
Commercial banks and other	74	44	632	2,056	857	2,148	1,362	1,198	1,344	1,256
Memo:										
IBRD	37	144	751	1,054	604	520	573	347	390	368
IDA	0	0	1	1	1	1	1	1	1	1
UNDISBURSED DEBT	**576**	**2,455**	**4,034**	**2,791**	**2,756**	**2,390**	**2,033**	**2,077**	**2,429**	**2,535**
Official creditors	424	1,781	3,468	2,675	2,434	2,193	1,976	2,073	2,415	2,267
Private creditors	153	674	567	116	322	197	57	3	14	268
Memorandum items										
Concessional LDOD	629	988	988	948	979	943	890	886	968	964
Variable rate LDOD	283	1,877	7,778	9,656	11,660	14,541	17,228	16,901	19,104	19,076
Public sector LDOD	1,224	4,045	14,630	14,354	13,945	14,848	15,289	16,999	20,470	20,948
Private sector LDOD	356	559	1,154	3,094	5,558	8,167	10,752	10,106	10,243	10,262

6. CURRENCY COMPOSITION OF LONG-TERM DEBT (PERCENT)

	1970	1980	1990	1994	1995	1996	1997	1998	1999	2000
Deutsche mark	1.3	3.8	6.0	4.3	5.0	5.7	4.2	3.6	2.4	1.8
French franc	0.4	1.9	0.3	0.4	0.4	0.3	0.2	0.2	0.1	0.1
Japanese yen	0.0	0.1	4.9	4.1	5.6	5.9	4.9	4.7	4.6	3.6
Pound sterling	0.2	0.4	0.3	0.1	0.1	0.1	0.1	5.0	4.0	3.6
Swiss franc	0.3	0.0	0.3	0.2	0.2	0.1	0.1	0.1	0.0	0.0
U.S.dollars	66.1	60.4	44.0	54.9	53.3	59.7	74.8	73.2	78.7	78.5
Multiple currency	29.8	31.3	41.2	34.7	34.3	27.2	15.0	12.9	9.9	8.5
Special drawing rights	0.0	0.0	0.0	0.0	0.0	0.0	0.0	0.0	0.0	0.0
All other currencies	1.9	2.1	3.0	1.3	1.1	1.0	0.7	0.3	0.3	3.9

COLOMBIA

(US$ million, unless otherwise indicated)

	1970	1980	1990	1994	1995	1996	1997	1998	1999	2000
7. DEBT RESTRUCTURINGS										
Total amount rescheduled	..	..	0	0	0	0	0	0	0	0
Debt stock rescheduled	..	..	0	0	0	0	0	0	0	0
Principal rescheduled	..	..	0	0	0	0	0	0	0	0
Official	..	..	0	0	0	0	0	0	0	0
Private	..	..	0	0	0	0	0	0	0	0
Interest rescheduled	..	..	0	0	0	0	0	0	0	0
Official	..	..	0	0	0	0	0	0	0	0
Private	..	..	0	0	0	0	0	0	0	0
Debt forgiven	..	..	2	0	0	0	0	0	0	0
Memo: interest forgiven	..	..	0	0	0	0	0	0	0	0
Debt stock reduction	..	..	0	0	0	0	0	0	0	0
of which debt buyback	..	..	0	0	0	0	0	0	0	0
8. DEBT STOCK-FLOW RECONCILIATION										
Total change in debt stocks	..	..	336	2,998	3,108	3,852	2,900	1,538	1,341	-597
Net flows on debt	136	1,136	-399	2,660	2,897	4,397	3,476	1,220	1,247	-264
Net change in interest arrears	..	..	26	-5	-9	-2	0	0	0	0
Interest capitalized	..	..	0	0	0	0	0	0	0	0
Debt forgiveness or reduction	..	..	-2	0	0	0	0	0	0	0
Cross-currency valuation	..	..	494	213	315	-651	-657	396	-56	-306
Residual	..	..	218	129	-95	107	81	-78	150	-27
9. AVERAGE TERMS OF NEW COMMITMENTS										
ALL CREDITORS										
Interest (%)	6.0	12.9	8.0	5.1	4.8	7.2	7.4	7.8	7.2	7.3
Maturity (years)	21.1	15.5	16.5	12.3	11.6	9.1	12.3	7.8	9.9	11.2
Grace period (years)	4.8	4.4	4.6	5.4	4.3	5.8	7.6	5.4	6.0	6.9
Grant element (%)	25.8	-20.2	12.2	22.9	23.6	12.6	13.0	8.8	12.7	6.1
Official creditors										
Interest (%)	5.2	8.8	7.5	6.5	6.4	6.8	7.2	7.8	4.9	8.6
Maturity (years)	29.8	18.0	18.7	19.3	20.4	17.3	18.6	11.6	10.8	12.6
Grace period (years)	7.2	4.3	5.4	5.2	4.8	4.6	4.4	3.8	4.3	3.7
Grant element (%)	36.9	7.2	15.5	21.8	23.2	18.9	16.4	10.6	24.2	7.4
Private creditors										
Interest (%)	7.2	15.4	9.3	4.0	3.8	7.3	7.4	7.8	9.2	6.9
Maturity (years)	7.2	13.9	9.9	6.9	6.0	7.1	10.9	6.3	9.1	10.7
Grace period (years)	1.1	4.5	2.2	5.6	4.0	6.1	8.4	6.1	7.4	8.0
Grant element (%)	7.9	-37.2	2.3	23.7	23.8	11.0	12.2	8.0	3.0	5.6
Memorandum items										
Commitments	363	1,561	1,269	2,143	1,792	3,064	2,596	3,526	4,365	3,352
Official creditors	224	597	951	933	704	607	493	1,032	1,995	874
Private creditors	139	964	318	1,209	1,088	2,458	2,102	2,494	2,370	2,478

10. CONTRACTUAL OBLIGATIONS ON OUTSTANDING LONG-TERM DEBT

	2001	2002	2003	2004	2005	2006	2007	2008	2009	2010
TOTAL										
Disbursements	997	700	419	191	102	58	25	18	14	8
Principal	3,736	3,615	4,602	3,040	2,686	2,018	2,652	2,296	2,513	1,448
Interest	2,065	1,850	1,690	1,388	1,200	1,036	887	706	553	390
Official creditors										
Disbursements	869	610	383	177	101	58	25	18	14	8
Principal	666	1,133	1,326	929	828	775	725	685	554	494
Interest	543	532	479	410	356	304	255	207	164	130
Bilateral creditors										
Disbursements	87	45	31	9	2	2	0	0	0	0
Principal	116	113	149	142	127	121	121	121	120	83
Interest	69	64	58	51	45	39	33	27	21	16
Multilateral creditors										
Disbursements	782	566	353	168	99	56	25	18	14	8
Principal	551	1,019	1,177	787	701	653	605	564	433	412
Interest	474	468	421	359	312	266	222	180	143	114
Private creditors										
Disbursements	128	90	36	14	1	0	0	0	0	0
Principal	3,069	2,483	3,276	2,111	1,858	1,244	1,926	1,611	1,960	954
Interest	1,522	1,318	1,211	978	844	731	633	499	389	260
Commercial banks										
Disbursements	116	79	31	12	0	0	0	0	0	0
Principal	1,065	694	594	562	205	173	164	154	154	148
Interest	265	208	161	115	84	70	58	47	36	25
Other private										
Disbursements	12	10	5	1	1	0	0	0	0	0
Principal	2,005	1,789	2,682	1,549	1,654	1,071	1,762	1,458	1,806	805
Interest	1,257	1,110	1,050	863	760	661	574	452	353	235

COMOROS

(US$ million, unless otherwise indicated)

	1970	1980	1990	1994	1995	1996	1997	1998	1999	2000
1. SUMMARY DEBT DATA										
TOTAL DEBT STOCKS (EDT)	**1.2**	**44.0**	**187.1**	**201.6**	**213.5**	**217.7**	**219.4**	**227.1**	**228.3**	**231.7**
Long-term debt (LDOD)	**1.2**	**43.0**	**174.7**	**188.4**	**200.1**	**205.0**	**202.7**	**211.6**	**206.2**	**201.9**
Public and publicly guaranteed	1.2	43.0	174.7	188.4	200.1	205.0	202.7	211.6	206.2	201.9
Private nonguaranteed	0.0	0.0	0.0	0.0	0.0	0.0	0.0	0.0	0.0	0.0
Use of IMF credit	**0.0**	**0.0**	**0.0**	**3.3**	**3.3**	**3.2**	**2.8**	**2.7**	**2.2**	**1.5**
Short-term debt	**0.0**	**1.0**	**12.4**	**9.9**	**10.1**	**9.5**	**13.9**	**12.9**	**19.9**	**28.4**
of which interest arrears on LDOD	0.0	0.0	12.2	9.9	8.1	9.5	8.9	11.8	12.9	19.4
Official creditors	0.0	0.0	12.2	9.9	8.1	9.5	8.9	11.8	12.9	19.4
Private creditors	0.0	0.0	0.0	0.0	0.0	0.0	0.0	0.0	0.0	0.0
Memo: principal arrears on LDOD	0.0	0.0	25.5	18.6	26.8	33.0	36.7	40.6	44.4	60.6
Official creditors	0.0	0.0	25.5	18.6	26.8	33.0	36.7	40.6	44.4	60.6
Private creditors	0.0	0.0	0.0	0.0	0.0	0.0	0.0	0.0	0.0	0.0
Memo: export credits	0.0	0.0	2.0	1.7	3.9	3.3	3.3	2.7	4.4	4.1
TOTAL DEBT FLOWS										
Disbursements	**0.0**	**13.0**	**5.4**	**13.7**	**9.7**	**9.6**	**5.8**	**4.2**	**0.7**	**3.1**
Long-term debt	0.0	13.0	5.4	11.8	9.7	9.6	5.8	4.2	0.7	3.1
IMF purchases	0.0	0.0	0.0	1.9	0.0	0.0	0.0	0.0	0.0	0.0
Principal repayments	**0.0**	**0.0**	**0.2**	**2.0**	**0.4**	**0.8**	**1.5**	**1.6**	**2.2**	**1.4**
Long-term debt	0.0	0.0	0.2	2.0	0.4	0.8	1.2	1.4	1.8	0.8
IMF repurchases	0.0	0.0	0.0	0.0	0.0	0.0	0.2	0.2	0.4	0.6
Net flows on debt	**0.0**	**13.0**	**2.2**	**10.8**	**11.3**	**6.9**	**9.3**	**-1.4**	**4.4**	**3.7**
of which short-term debt	0.0	0.0	-3.0	-1.0	2.0	-2.0	5.0	-3.9	5.9	2.0
Interest payments (INT)	**0.0**	**0.4**	**0.8**	**0.8**	**0.6**	**0.6**	**0.8**	**0.4**	**0.9**	**1.3**
Long-term debt	0.0	0.3	0.7	0.7	0.5	0.6	0.5	0.4	0.7	0.8
IMF charges	0.0	0.0	0.0	0.0	0.0	0.0	0.0	0.0	0.0	0.0
Short-term debt	0.0	0.1	0.2	0.0	0.1	0.1	0.3	0.1	0.2	0.5
Net transfers on debt	**-0.1**	**12.6**	**1.3**	**10.0**	**10.7**	**6.2**	**8.5**	**-1.8**	**3.5**	**2.4**
Total debt service paid (TDS)	**0.1**	**0.4**	**1.1**	**2.8**	**1.0**	**1.4**	**2.3**	**2.0**	**3.1**	**2.7**
Long-term debt	0.1	0.3	0.9	2.7	0.9	1.4	1.8	1.7	2.5	1.6
IMF repurchases and charges	0.0	0.0	0.0	0.0	0.0	0.0	0.3	0.3	0.4	0.6
Short-term debt (interest only)	0.0	0.1	0.2	0.0	0.1	0.1	0.3	0.1	0.2	0.5
2. AGGREGATE NET RESOURCE FLOWS AND NET TRANSFERS (LONG-TERM)										
NET RESOURCE FLOWS	**3.1**	**30.8**	**31.9**	**26.4**	**28.0**	**26.4**	**18.9**	**29.0**	**15.2**	**13.0**
Net flow of long-term debt (ex. IMF)	0.0	13.0	5.2	9.8	9.3	8.9	4.6	2.8	-1.1	2.3
Foreign direct investment (net)	0.0	0.0	-1.0	0.2	0.9	2.0	2.0	2.0	1.0	0.0
Portfolio equity flows	0.0	0.0	0.0	0.0	0.0	0.0	0.0	0.0	0.0	0.0
Grants (excluding technical coop.)	3.1	17.8	27.7	16.4	17.8	15.5	12.3	24.2	15.3	10.7
Memo: technical coop. grants	4.8	7.0	15.8	14.3	14.6	17.3	12.1	10.8	10.0	8.4
official net resource flows	3.1	30.4	32.9	26.2	27.1	24.4	16.9	27.0	14.2	13.0
private net resource flows	0.0	0.4	-1.0	0.2	0.9	2.0	2.0	2.0	1.0	0.0
NET TRANSFERS	**3.1**	**30.5**	**30.6**	**25.7**	**27.5**	**25.8**	**18.4**	**28.6**	**14.5**	**12.2**
Interest on long-term debt	0.0	0.3	0.7	0.7	0.5	0.6	0.5	0.4	0.7	0.8
Profit remittances on FDI	0.0	0.0	0.6	0.0	0.0	0.0	0.0	0.0	0.0	0.0
Memo: official net transfers	3.1	30.1	32.2	25.5	26.6	23.8	16.4	26.6	13.5	12.2
private net transfers	0.0	0.4	-1.6	0.2	0.9	2.0	2.0	2.0	1.0	0.0
3. MAJOR ECONOMIC AGGREGATES										
Gross national income (GNI)	24.7	124.1	249.3	186.2	232.9	230.9	212.3	215.0	222.8	202.2
Exports of goods & services (XGS)	..	15.7	48.1	57.5	61.4	56.9	40.9	51.0	54.1	54.0
of which workers remittances	..	1.6	9.9	15.2	12.2	12.1	0.0	..	..	..
Imports of goods & services (MGS)	..	34.3	93.4	93.2	105.7	97.6	93.4	81.0	80.7	66.1
International reserves (RES)	..	6.4	29.9	44.4	44.9	50.9	40.8	39.1	37.1	43.2
Current account balance	..	-8.9	-10.5	-7.2	-19.0	-40.7	..	..	..	..
4. DEBT INDICATORS										
EDT / XGS (%)	..	280.6	389.1	350.7	347.5	382.5	536.9	445.2	421.8	428.9
EDT / GNI (%)	4.9	35.4	75.0	108.3	91.7	94.3	103.3	105.6	102.5	114.6
TDS / XGS (%)	..	2.6	2.3	4.9	1.6	2.5	5.6	3.9	5.7	5.0
INT / XGS (%)	..	2.6	1.7	1.4	1.0	1.1	2.0	0.8	1.7	2.4
INT / GNI (%)	0.0	0.3	0.3	0.4	0.3	0.3	0.4	0.2	0.4	0.6
RES / EDT (%)	..	14.5	16.0	22.0	21.0	23.4	18.6	17.2	16.3	18.7
RES / MGS (months)	..	2.2	3.9	5.7	5.1	6.3	5.2	5.8	5.5	7.8
Short-term / EDT (%)	0.0	2.3	6.6	4.9	4.7	4.4	6.3	5.7	8.7	12.3
Concessional / EDT (%)	100.0	96.8	86.1	89.7	90.1	90.1	88.7	89.3	86.3	83.5
Multilateral / EDT (%)	0.0	48.2	60.9	71.4	72.8	73.8	72.6	74.2	72.2	69.4

COMOROS

(US$ million, unless otherwise indicated)

	1970	1980	1990	1994	1995	1996	1997	1998	1999	2000
5. LONG-TERM DEBT										
DEBT OUTSTANDING (LDOD)	**1.2**	**43.0**	**174.7**	**188.4**	**200.1**	**205.0**	**202.7**	**211.6**	**206.2**	**201.9**
Public and publicly guaranteed	**1.2**	**43.0**	**174.7**	**188.4**	**200.1**	**205.0**	**202.7**	**211.6**	**206.2**	**201.9**
Official creditors	1.2	42.6	174.7	188.4	200.1	205.0	202.7	211.6	206.2	201.9
Multilateral	0.0	21.2	113.9	143.9	155.4	160.7	159.3	168.6	164.9	160.8
Concessional	0.0	21.2	100.2	136.3	147.7	151.7	151.0	159.7	155.7	152.3
Bilateral	1.2	21.4	60.8	44.5	44.7	44.4	43.5	43.0	41.4	41.1
Concessional	1.2	21.4	60.8	44.5	44.7	44.4	43.5	43.0	41.4	41.1
Private creditors	0.0	0.4	0.0	0.0	0.0	0.0	0.0	0.0	0.0	0.0
Bonds	0.0	0.0	0.0	0.0	0.0	0.0	0.0	0.0	0.0	0.0
Commercial banks	0.0	0.0	0.0	0.0	0.0	0.0	0.0	0.0	0.0	0.0
Other private	0.0	0.4	0.0	0.0	0.0	0.0	0.0	0.0	0.0	0.0
Private nonguaranteed	**0.0**	**0.0**	**0.0**	**0.0**	**0.0**	**0.0**	**0.0**	**0.0**	**0.0**	**0.0**
Bonds	0.0	0.0	0.0	0.0	0.0	0.0	0.0	0.0	0.0	0.0
Commercial banks and other	0.0	0.0	0.0	0.0	0.0	0.0	0.0	0.0	0.0	0.0
Memo:										
IBRD	0.0	0.0	0.0	0.0	0.0	0.0	0.0	0.0	0.0	0.0
IDA	0.0	4.2	37.5	53.9	64.1	68.2	69.6	74.8	72.7	70.8
DISBURSEMENTS	**0.0**	**13.0**	**5.4**	**11.8**	**9.7**	**9.6**	**5.8**	**4.2**	**0.7**	**3.1**
Public and publicly guaranteed	**0.0**	**13.0**	**5.4**	**11.8**	**9.7**	**9.6**	**5.8**	**4.2**	**0.7**	**3.1**
Official creditors	0.0	12.6	5.4	11.8	9.7	9.6	5.8	4.2	0.7	3.1
Multilateral	0.0	6.1	1.3	7.7	9.7	9.6	5.8	4.2	0.7	3.1
Concessional	0.0	6.1	1.3	7.7	9.7	9.6	5.8	4.2	0.7	3.1
Bilateral	0.0	6.5	4.2	4.1	0.0	0.0	0.0	0.0	0.0	0.0
Concessional	0.0	6.5	4.2	4.1	0.0	0.0	0.0	0.0	0.0	0.0
Private creditors	0.0	0.4	0.0	0.0	0.0	0.0	0.0	0.0	0.0	0.0
Bonds	0.0	0.0	0.0	0.0	0.0	0.0	0.0	0.0	0.0	0.0
Commercial banks	0.0	0.0	0.0	0.0	0.0	0.0	0.0	0.0	0.0	0.0
Other private	0.0	0.4	0.0	0.0	0.0	0.0	0.0	0.0	0.0	0.0
Private nonguaranteed	**0.0**	**0.0**	**0.0**	**0.0**	**0.0**	**0.0**	**0.0**	**0.0**	**0.0**	**0.0**
Bonds	0.0	0.0	0.0	0.0	0.0	0.0	0.0	0.0	0.0	0.0
Commercial banks and other	0.0	0.0	0.0	0.0	0.0	0.0	0.0	0.0	0.0	0.0
Memo:										
IBRD	0.0	0.0	0.0	0.0	0.0	0.0	0.0	0.0	0.0	0.0
IDA	0.0	1.8	0.7	7.6	9.6	6.4	5.2	3.1	0.0	2.1
PRINCIPAL REPAYMENTS	**0.0**	**0.0**	**0.2**	**2.0**	**0.4**	**0.8**	**1.2**	**1.4**	**1.8**	**0.8**
Public and publicly guaranteed	**0.0**	**0.0**	**0.2**	**2.0**	**0.4**	**0.8**	**1.2**	**1.4**	**1.8**	**0.8**
Official creditors	0.0	0.0	0.2	2.0	0.4	0.8	1.2	1.4	1.8	0.8
Multilateral	0.0	0.0	0.2	0.7	0.4	0.8	1.0	0.5	0.8	0.8
Concessional	0.0	0.0	0.2	0.7	0.4	0.8	1.0	0.5	0.8	0.8
Bilateral	0.0	0.0	0.0	1.3	0.0	0.0	0.2	0.9	1.0	0.0
Concessional	0.0	0.0	0.0	1.3	0.0	0.0	0.2	0.9	1.0	0.0
Private creditors	0.0	0.0	0.0	0.0	0.0	0.0	0.0	0.0	0.0	0.0
Bonds	0.0	0.0	0.0	0.0	0.0	0.0	0.0	0.0	0.0	0.0
Commercial banks	0.0	0.0	0.0	0.0	0.0	0.0	0.0	0.0	0.0	0.0
Other private	0.0	0.0	0.0	0.0	0.0	0.0	0.0	0.0	0.0	0.0
Private nonguaranteed	**0.0**	**0.0**	**0.0**	**0.0**	**0.0**	**0.0**	**0.0**	**0.0**	**0.0**	**0.0**
Bonds	0.0	0.0	0.0	0.0	0.0	0.0	0.0	0.0	0.0	0.0
Commercial banks and other	0.0	0.0	0.0	0.0	0.0	0.0	0.0	0.0	0.0	0.0
Memo:										
IBRD	0.0	0.0	0.0	0.0	0.0	0.0	0.0	0.0	0.0	0.0
IDA	0.0	0.0	0.1	0.3	0.4	0.4	0.4	0.2	0.6	0.8
NET FLOWS ON DEBT	**0.0**	**13.0**	**5.2**	**9.8**	**9.3**	**8.9**	**4.6**	**2.8**	**-1.1**	**2.3**
Public and publicly guaranteed	**0.0**	**13.0**	**5.2**	**9.8**	**9.3**	**8.9**	**4.6**	**2.8**	**-1.1**	**2.3**
Official creditors	0.0	12.6	5.2	9.8	9.3	8.9	4.6	2.8	-1.1	2.3
Multilateral	0.0	6.1	1.0	7.1	9.3	8.9	4.8	3.7	-0.1	2.3
Concessional	0.0	6.1	1.0	7.1	9.3	8.9	4.8	3.7	-0.1	2.3
Bilateral	0.0	6.5	4.1	2.8	0.0	0.0	-0.2	-0.9	-1.0	0.0
Concessional	0.0	6.5	4.1	2.8	0.0	0.0	-0.2	-0.9	-1.0	0.0
Private creditors	0.0	0.4	0.0	0.0	0.0	0.0	0.0	0.0	0.0	0.0
Bonds	0.0	0.0	0.0	0.0	0.0	0.0	0.0	0.0	0.0	0.0
Commercial banks	0.0	0.0	0.0	0.0	0.0	0.0	0.0	0.0	0.0	0.0
Other private	0.0	0.4	0.0	0.0	0.0	0.0	0.0	0.0	0.0	0.0
Private nonguaranteed	**0.0**	**0.0**	**0.0**	**0.0**	**0.0**	**0.0**	**0.0**	**0.0**	**0.0**	**0.0**
Bonds	0.0	0.0	0.0	0.0	0.0	0.0	0.0	0.0	0.0	0.0
Commercial banks and other	0.0	0.0	0.0	0.0	0.0	0.0	0.0	0.0	0.0	0.0
Memo:										
IBRD	0.0	0.0	0.0	0.0	0.0	0.0	0.0	0.0	0.0	0.0
IDA	0.0	1.8	0.6	7.3	9.2	6.1	4.8	2.8	-0.6	1.4

COMOROS

(US$ million, unless otherwise indicated)

	1970	1980	1990	1994	1995	1996	1997	1998	1999	2000
INTEREST PAYMENTS (LINT)	**0.0**	**0.3**	**0.7**	**0.7**	**0.5**	**0.6**	**0.5**	**0.4**	**0.7**	**0.8**
Public and publicly guaranteed	**0.0**	**0.3**	**0.7**	**0.7**	**0.5**	**0.6**	**0.5**	**0.4**	**0.7**	**0.8**
Official creditors	0.0	0.3	0.7	0.7	0.5	0.6	0.5	0.4	0.7	0.8
Multilateral	0.0	0.0	0.4	0.7	0.5	0.6	0.5	0.3	0.7	0.8
Concessional	0.0	0.0	0.4	0.7	0.5	0.6	0.5	0.3	0.7	0.8
Bilateral	0.0	0.3	0.3	0.0	0.0	0.0	0.0	0.0	0.0	0.0
Concessional	0.0	0.3	0.3	0.0	0.0	0.0	0.0	0.0	0.0	0.0
Private creditors	0.0	0.0	0.0	0.0	0.0	0.0	0.0	0.0	0.0	0.0
Bonds	0.0	0.0	0.0	0.0	0.0	0.0	0.0	0.0	0.0	0.0
Commercial banks	0.0	0.0	0.0	0.0	0.0	0.0	0.0	0.0	0.0	0.0
Other private	0.0	0.0	0.0	0.0	0.0	0.0	0.0	0.0	0.0	0.0
Private nonguaranteed	**0.0**	**0.0**	**0.0**	**0.0**	**0.0**	**0.0**	**0.0**	**0.0**	**0.0**	**0.0**
Bonds	0.0	0.0	0.0	0.0	0.0	0.0	0.0	0.0	0.0	0.0
Commercial banks and other	0.0	0.0	0.0	0.0	0.0	0.0	0.0	0.0	0.0	0.0
Memo:										
IBRD	0.0	0.0	0.0	0.0	0.0	0.0	0.0	0.0	0.0	0.0
IDA	0.0	0.0	0.3	0.3	0.4	0.5	0.5	0.3	0.6	0.8
NET TRANSFERS ON DEBT	**-0.1**	**12.7**	**4.5**	**9.1**	**8.8**	**8.3**	**4.0**	**2.5**	**-1.7**	**1.5**
Public and publicly guaranteed	**-0.1**	**12.7**	**4.5**	**9.1**	**8.8**	**8.3**	**4.0**	**2.5**	**-1.7**	**1.5**
Official creditors	-0.1	12.3	4.5	9.1	8.8	8.3	4.0	2.5	-1.7	1.5
Multilateral	0.0	6.1	0.6	6.3	8.8	8.3	4.3	3.4	-0.8	1.5
Concessional	0.0	6.1	0.6	6.3	8.8	8.3	4.3	3.4	-0.8	1.5
Bilateral	-0.1	6.2	3.9	2.8	0.0	0.0	-0.2	-0.9	-1.0	0.0
Concessional	-0.1	6.2	3.9	2.8	0.0	0.0	-0.2	-0.9	-1.0	0.0
Private creditors	0.0	0.4	0.0	0.0	0.0	0.0	0.0	0.0	0.0	0.0
Bonds	0.0	0.0	0.0	0.0	0.0	0.0	0.0	0.0	0.0	0.0
Commercial banks	0.0	0.0	0.0	0.0	0.0	0.0	0.0	0.0	0.0	0.0
Other private	0.0	0.4	0.0	0.0	0.0	0.0	0.0	0.0	0.0	0.0
Private nonguaranteed	**0.0**	**0.0**	**0.0**	**0.0**	**0.0**	**0.0**	**0.0**	**0.0**	**0.0**	**0.0**
Bonds	0.0	0.0	0.0	0.0	0.0	0.0	0.0	0.0	0.0	0.0
Commercial banks and other	0.0	0.0	0.0	0.0	0.0	0.0	0.0	0.0	0.0	0.0
Memo:										
IBRD	0.0	0.0	0.0	0.0	0.0	0.0	0.0	0.0	0.0	0.0
IDA	0.0	1.7	0.3	7.0	8.7	5.6	4.3	2.6	-1.1	0.6
DEBT SERVICE (LTDS)	**0.1**	**0.3**	**0.9**	**2.7**	**0.9**	**1.4**	**1.8**	**1.7**	**2.5**	**1.6**
Public and publicly guaranteed	**0.1**	**0.3**	**0.9**	**2.7**	**0.9**	**1.4**	**1.8**	**1.7**	**2.5**	**1.6**
Official creditors	0.1	0.3	0.9	2.7	0.9	1.4	1.8	1.7	2.5	1.6
Multilateral	0.0	0.0	0.6	1.4	0.9	1.4	1.5	0.8	1.5	1.6
Concessional	0.0	0.0	0.6	1.4	0.9	1.4	1.5	0.8	1.5	1.6
Bilateral	0.1	0.3	0.3	1.3	0.0	0.0	0.2	0.9	1.0	0.0
Concessional	0.1	0.3	0.3	1.3	0.0	0.0	0.2	0.9	1.0	0.0
Private creditors	0.0	0.0	0.0	0.0	0.0	0.0	0.0	0.0	0.0	0.0
Bonds	0.0	0.0	0.0	0.0	0.0	0.0	0.0	0.0	0.0	0.0
Commercial banks	0.0	0.0	0.0	0.0	0.0	0.0	0.0	0.0	0.0	0.0
Other private	0.0	0.0	0.0	0.0	0.0	0.0	0.0	0.0	0.0	0.0
Private nonguaranteed	**0.0**	**0.0**	**0.0**	**0.0**	**0.0**	**0.0**	**0.0**	**0.0**	**0.0**	**0.0**
Bonds	0.0	0.0	0.0	0.0	0.0	0.0	0.0	0.0	0.0	0.0
Commercial banks and other	0.0	0.0	0.0	0.0	0.0	0.0	0.0	0.0	0.0	0.0
Memo:										
IBRD	0.0	0.0	0.0	0.0	0.0	0.0	0.0	0.0	0.0	0.0
IDA	0.0	0.0	0.3	0.6	0.8	0.8	0.9	0.5	1.1	1.5
UNDISBURSED DEBT	**0.0**	**49.8**	**56.8**	**39.8**	**33.9**	**19.9**	**32.9**	**36.2**	**33.0**	**29.2**
Official creditors	0.0	48.8	56.8	39.8	33.9	19.9	32.9	36.2	33.0	29.2
Private creditors	0.0	1.0	0.0	0.0	0.0	0.0	0.0	0.0	0.0	0.0
Memorandum items										
Concessional LDOD	1.2	42.6	161.0	180.9	192.4	196.1	194.5	202.7	197.1	193.4
Variable rate LDOD	0.0	0.0	0.0	0.0	0.0	0.0	0.0	0.0	0.0	0.0
Public sector LDOD	1.2	43.0	174.7	188.4	200.1	205.0	202.7	211.6	206.2	201.9
Private sector LDOD	0.0	0.0	0.0	0.0	0.0	0.0	0.0	0.0	0.0	0.0

6. CURRENCY COMPOSITION OF LONG-TERM DEBT (PERCENT)

	1970	1980	1990	1994	1995	1996	1997	1998	1999	2000
Deutsche mark	0.0	0.0	0.0	0.0	0.0	0.0	0.0	0.0	0.0	0.0
French franc	100.0	2.9	23.5	18.5	17.6	16.5	15.7	15.4	15.3	14.7
Japanese yen	0.0	0.0	0.0	0.0	0.0	0.0	0.0	0.0	0.0	0.0
Pound sterling	0.0	0.0	0.0	0.0	0.0	0.0	0.0	0.0	0.0	0.0
Swiss franc	0.0	0.0	0.0	0.0	0.0	0.0	0.0	0.0	0.0	0.0
U.S.dollars	0.0	38.4	17.1	24.3	27.8	29.7	31.6	32.3	32.6	33.2
Multiple currency	0.0	10.2	8.0	5.3	4.8	4.4	4.1	4.5	4.9	4.9
Special drawing rights	0.0	0.0	0.0	1.3	1.3	2.5	2.7	2.7	2.7	3.0
All other currencies	0.0	48.5	51.4	50.6	48.5	46.9	45.9	45.1	44.5	44.2

COMOROS

(US$ million, unless otherwise indicated)

	1970	1980	1990	1994	1995	1996	1997	1998	1999	2000
7. DEBT RESTRUCTURINGS										
Total amount rescheduled	..	..	0.0	8.6	2.0	2.1	3.5	0.0	0.0	0.0
Debt stock rescheduled	..	..	0.0	0.0	0.0	0.0	0.0	0.0	0.0	0.0
Principal rescheduled	..	..	0.0	4.7	1.8	2.0	0.5	0.0	0.0	0.0
Official	..	..	0.0	4.7	1.8	2.0	0.5	0.0	0.0	0.0
Private	..	..	0.0	0.0	0.0	0.0	0.0	0.0	0.0	0.0
Interest rescheduled	..	..	0.0	3.9	0.2	0.1	0.0	0.0	0.0	0.0
Official	..	..	0.0	3.9	0.2	0.1	0.0	0.0	0.0	0.0
Private	..	..	0.0	0.0	0.0	0.0	0.0	0.0	0.0	0.0
Debt forgiven	..	..	0.1	4.6	0.4	0.2	0.0	0.0	0.0	0.0
Memo: interest forgiven	..	..	0.0	0.7	0.0	0.0	0.0	0.0	0.0	0.0
Debt stock reduction	..	..	0.0	0.0	0.0	0.0	0.0	0.0	0.0	0.0
of which debt buyback	..	..	0.0	0.0	0.0	0.0	0.0	0.0	0.0	0.0
8. DEBT STOCK-FLOW RECONCILIATION										
Total change in debt stocks	..	..	11.0	12.3	11.9	4.2	1.7	7.6	1.2	3.4
Net flows on debt	0.0	13.0	2.2	10.8	11.3	6.9	9.3	-1.4	4.4	3.7
Net change in interest arrears	..	..	2.6	-3.1	-1.9	1.4	-0.5	2.9	1.1	6.5
Interest capitalized	..	..	0.0	3.9	0.2	0.1	0.0	0.0	0.0	0.0
Debt forgiveness or reduction	..	..	-0.1	-4.6	-0.4	-0.2	0.0	0.0	0.0	0.0
Cross-currency valuation	..	..	1.7	-0.8	-3.5	-6.9	-11.9	-1.8	-7.2	-9.0
Residual	..	..	4.6	6.2	6.2	2.9	4.9	7.9	2.9	2.3
9. AVERAGE TERMS OF NEW COMMITMENTS										
ALL CREDITORS										
Interest (%)	0.0	1.3	2.0	1.0	1.0	2.5	0.6	0.8	0.0	1.0
Maturity (years)	0.0	43.1	29.8	36.5	37.3	25.1	39.8	39.9	0.0	10.7
Grace period (years)	0.0	9.0	10.3	9.7	11.5	7.6	10.3	10.4	0.0	1.2
Grant element (%)	0.0	74.5	65.9	76.1	78.4	56.7	81.5	80.8	0.0	36.7
Official creditors										
Interest (%)	0.0	0.8	2.0	1.0	1.0	2.5	0.6	0.8	0.0	1.0
Maturity (years)	0.0	45.6	29.8	36.5	37.3	25.1	39.8	39.9	0.0	10.7
Grace period (years)	0.0	9.5	10.3	9.7	11.5	7.6	10.3	10.4	0.0	1.2
Grant element (%)	0.0	79.1	65.9	76.1	78.4	56.7	81.5	80.8	0.0	36.7
Private creditors										
Interest (%)	0.0	7.6	0.0	0.0	0.0	0.0	0.0	0.0	0.0	0.0
Maturity (years)	0.0	5.2	0.0	0.0	0.0	0.0	0.0	0.0	0.0	0.0
Grace period (years)	0.0	1.5	0.0	0.0	0.0	0.0	0.0	0.0	0.0	0.0
Grant element (%)	0.0	5.6	0.0	0.0	0.0	0.0	0.0	0.0	0.0	0.0
Memorandum items										
Commitments	0.0	23.4	0.9	22.2	2.8	0.6	20.1	8.4	0.0	0.9
Official creditors	0.0	21.9	0.9	22.2	2.8	0.6	20.1	8.4	0.0	0.9
Private creditors	0.0	1.5	0.0	0.0	0.0	0.0	0.0	0.0	0.0	0.0

10. CONTRACTUAL OBLIGATIONS ON OUTSTANDING LONG-TERM DEBT

	2001	2002	2003	2004	2005	2006	2007	2008	2009	2010
TOTAL										
Disbursements	9.0	7.8	5.8	4.2	2.1	0.2	0.1	0.0	0.0	0.0
Principal	10.2	10.2	7.5	5.0	5.3	5.4	4.8	5.2	5.3	5.1
Interest	1.8	1.5	1.3	1.3	1.2	1.2	1.2	1.1	1.1	1.0
Official creditors										
Disbursements	9.0	7.8	5.8	4.2	2.1	0.2	0.1	0.0	0.0	0.0
Principal	10.2	10.2	7.5	5.0	5.3	5.4	4.8	5.2	5.3	5.1
Interest	1.8	1.5	1.3	1.3	1.2	1.2	1.2	1.1	1.1	1.0
Bilateral creditors										
Disbursements	0.0	0.0	0.0	0.0	0.0	0.0	0.0	0.0	0.0	0.0
Principal	1.9	1.6	1.6	1.3	1.6	1.6	1.3	1.3	1.3	1.1
Interest	0.2	0.2	0.2	0.2	0.2	0.2	0.2	0.1	0.1	0.1
Multilateral creditors										
Disbursements	9.0	7.8	5.8	4.2	2.1	0.2	0.1	0.0	0.0	0.0
Principal	8.3	8.6	5.9	3.7	3.8	3.8	3.5	3.9	4.0	4.0
Interest	1.5	1.3	1.1	1.1	1.1	1.0	1.0	1.0	0.9	0.9
Private creditors										
Disbursements	0.0	0.0	0.0	0.0	0.0	0.0	0.0	0.0	0.0	0.0
Principal	0.0	0.0	0.0	0.0	0.0	0.0	0.0	0.0	0.0	0.0
Interest	0.0	0.0	0.0	0.0	0.0	0.0	0.0	0.0	0.0	0.0
Commercial banks										
Disbursements	0.0	0.0	0.0	0.0	0.0	0.0	0.0	0.0	0.0	0.0
Principal	0.0	0.0	0.0	0.0	0.0	0.0	0.0	0.0	0.0	0.0
Interest	0.0	0.0	0.0	0.0	0.0	0.0	0.0	0.0	0.0	0.0
Other private										
Disbursements	0.0	0.0	0.0	0.0	0.0	0.0	0.0	0.0	0.0	0.0
Principal	0.0	0.0	0.0	0.0	0.0	0.0	0.0	0.0	0.0	0.0
Interest	0.0	0.0	0.0	0.0	0.0	0.0	0.0	0.0	0.0	0.0

CONGO, DEMOCRATIC REPUBLIC OF

(US$ million, unless otherwise indicated)

	1970	1980	1990	1994	1995	1996	1997	1998	1999	2000
1. SUMMARY DEBT DATA										
TOTAL DEBT STOCKS (EDT)	**342**	**4,773**	**10,274**	**12,322**	**13,239**	**12,830**	**12,337**	**13,203**	**11,999**	**11,645**
Long-term debt (LDOD)	**308**	**4,071**	**9,010**	**9,294**	**9,636**	**9,275**	**8,628**	**9,214**	**8,221**	**7,842**
Public and publicly guaranteed	308	4,071	9,010	9,294	9,636	9,275	8,628	9,214	8,221	7,842
Private nonguaranteed	0	0	0	0	0	0	0	0	0	0
Use of IMF credit	**0**	**373**	**521**	**478**	**485**	**433**	**407**	**423**	**412**	**391**
Short-term debt	**34**	**329**	**743**	**2,550**	**3,119**	**3,122**	**3,303**	**3,565**	**3,366**	**3,413**
of which interest arrears on LDOD	0	33	265	2,431	2,937	2,998	2,938	3,213	3,007	3,033
Official creditors	0	24	166	2,113	2,611	2,675	2,620	2,890	2,826	2,854
Private creditors	0	8	99	318	326	324	318	323	181	179
Memo: principal arrears on LDOD	0	37	1,049	3,082	4,569	4,685	4,661	5,144	4,881	4,933
Official creditors	0	13	375	2,301	3,752	3,864	3,850	4,279	4,389	4,445
Private creditors	0	23	674	781	817	821	811	866	492	488
Memo: export credits	0	0	4,604	4,911	4,965	5,247	5,659	4,207	3,974	4,101
TOTAL DEBT FLOWS										
Disbursements	**32**	**603**	**315**	**1**	**0**	**3**	**0**	**0**	**8**	**0**
Long-term debt	32	463	315	1	0	3	0	0	8	0
IMF purchases	0	140	0	0	0	0	0	0	0	0
Principal repayments	**25**	**277**	**200**	**5**	**1**	**37**	**0**	**1**	**1**	**0**
Long-term debt	25	192	49	0	0	0	0	0	0	0
IMF repurchases	0	85	152	4	1	37	0	1	1	0
Net flows on debt	**6**	**278**	**88**	**-140**	**61**	**-91**	**242**	**-13**	**13**	**20**
of which short-term debt	0	-48	-27	-137	63	-58	242	-13	7	20
Interest payments (INT)	**9**	**265**	**148**	**11**	**24**	**12**	**13**	**19**	**20**	**25**
Long-term debt	9	205	89	0	0	0	0	0	0	0
IMF charges	0	15	38	1	16	5	0	0	2	0
Short-term debt	0	45	21	9	8	7	12	18	18	25
Net transfers on debt	**-3**	**13**	**-60**	**-151**	**38**	**-103**	**229**	**-32**	**-6**	**-4**
Total debt service paid (TDS)	**34**	**543**	**348**	**16**	**25**	**48**	**13**	**19**	**21**	**25**
Long-term debt	34	397	137	1	0	0	0	0	0	0
IMF repurchases and charges	0	101	190	6	18	42	0	1	3	0
Short-term debt (interest only)	0	45	21	9	8	7	12	18	18	25
2. AGGREGATE NET RESOURCE FLOWS AND NET TRANSFERS (LONG-TERM)										
NET RESOURCE FLOWS	**45**	**368**	**628**	**223**	**162**	**129**	**114**	**98**	**102**	**138**
Net flow of long-term debt (ex. IMF)	6	271	267	1	0	3	0	0	8	0
Foreign direct investment (net)	0	0	-12	1	1	2	1	1	1	1
Portfolio equity flows	0	0	0	0	0	0	0	0	0	0
Grants (excluding technical coop.)	38	96	374	221	161	124	113	97	94	137
Memo: technical coop. grants	42	168	146	38	55	58	49	40	58	54
official net resource flows	45	195	652	222	161	127	113	97	101	137
private net resource flows	-1	173	-24	1	1	2	1	1	1	1
NET TRANSFERS	**6**	**36**	**532**	**182**	**112**	**89**	**76**	**63**	**66**	**103**
Interest on long-term debt	9	205	89	0	0	0	0	0	0	0
Profit remittances on FDI	30	128	8	40	50	40	38	35	36	35
Memo: official net transfers	40	89	576	221	161	127	113	97	101	137
private net transfers	-34	-54	-45	-39	-49	-38	-37	-34	-35	-34
3. MAJOR ECONOMIC AGGREGATES										
Gross national income (GNI)	4,721	13,895	8,579	5,129	4,877	5,141	5,041	4,979	..	..
Exports of goods & services (XGS)	803	2,404	2,584	1,322	1,770	1,793	1,458	1,664	..	..
of which workers remittances	2	0	0	0	0	0	0	..	..	..
Imports of goods & services (MGS)	710	2,679	3,294	1,853	2,263	2,115	2,149	2,295	..	..
International reserves (RES)	189	380	261	131	157	83	..	..	..	..
Current account balance	-7	-87	-738	-530	-465	-348	-658	-583	..	..
4. DEBT INDICATORS										
EDT / XGS (%)	42.6	198.6	397.6	932.1	747.9	715.5	846.0	793.7	..	..
EDT / GNI (%)	7.2	34.4	119.8	240.2	271.5	249.6	244.8	265.2	..	..
TDS / XGS (%)	4.3	22.6	13.5	1.2	1.4	2.7	0.9	1.2	..	..
INT / XGS (%)	1.1	11.0	5.7	0.8	1.3	0.7	0.9	1.1	..	..
INT / GNI (%)	0.2	1.9	1.7	0.2	0.5	0.2	0.3	0.4	..	..
RES / EDT (%)	55.4	8.0	2.5	1.1	1.2	0.6	..	..	..	..
RES / MGS (months)	3.2	1.7	1.0	0.9	0.8	0.5	..	..	..	..
Short-term / EDT (%)	9.9	6.9	7.2	20.7	23.6	24.3	26.8	27.0	28.1	29.3
Concessional / EDT (%)	63.2	18.1	30.6	27.7	26.6	26.3	25.4	26.0	27.0	26.3
Multilateral / EDT (%)	1.7	6.7	18.8	18.9	18.0	18.1	17.7	17.3	18.6	18.3

CONGO, DEMOCRATIC REPUBLIC OF

(US$ million, unless otherwise indicated)

	1970	1980	1990	1994	1995	1996	1997	1998	1999	2000
5. LONG-TERM DEBT										
DEBT OUTSTANDING (LDOD)	**308**	**4,071**	**9,010**	**9,294**	**9,636**	**9,275**	**8,628**	**9,214**	**8,221**	**7,842**
Public and publicly guaranteed	**308**	**4,071**	**9,010**	**9,294**	**9,636**	**9,275**	**8,628**	**9,214**	**8,221**	**7,842**
Official creditors	222	2,609	8,122	8,434	8,758	8,414	7,795	8,316	7,717	7,346
Multilateral	6	322	1,929	2,326	2,382	2,319	2,179	2,281	2,230	2,126
Concessional	1	194	1,426	1,641	1,679	1,626	1,537	1,601	1,552	1,486
Bilateral	216	2,287	6,193	6,108	6,376	6,095	5,616	6,034	5,487	5,220
Concessional	216	667	1,720	1,772	1,842	1,745	1,601	1,832	1,682	1,581
Private creditors	86	1,462	889	860	878	861	834	899	504	496
Bonds	4	7	5	5	5	4	4	4	4	3
Commercial banks	0	553	524	518	523	518	510	555	192	191
Other private	82	902	360	337	350	339	320	340	308	302
Private nonguaranteed	**0**	**0**	**0**	**0**	**0**	**0**	**0**	**0**	**0**	**0**
Bonds	0	0	0	0	0	0	0	0	0	0
Commercial banks and other	0	0	0	0	0	0	0	0	0	0
Memo:										
IBRD	5	87	49	88	92	87	82	84	82	81
IDA	1	159	1,113	1,294	1,321	1,284	1,225	1,261	1,235	1,188
DISBURSEMENTS	**32**	**463**	**315**	**1**	**0**	**3**	**0**	**0**	**8**	**0**
Public and publicly guaranteed	**32**	**463**	**315**	**1**	**0**	**3**	**0**	**0**	**8**	**0**
Official creditors	13	201	312	1	0	3	0	0	8	0
Multilateral	1	69	222	1	0	0	0	0	0	0
Concessional	1	27	125	1	0	0	0	0	0	0
Bilateral	12	132	90	0	0	3	0	0	8	0
Concessional	12	105	88	0	0	3	0	0	8	0
Private creditors	19	263	3	0	0	0	0	0	0	0
Bonds	0	0	0	0	0	0	0	0	0	0
Commercial banks	0	92	0	0	0	0	0	0	0	0
Other private	19	171	3	0	0	0	0	0	0	0
Private nonguaranteed	**0**	**0**	**0**	**0**	**0**	**0**	**0**	**0**	**0**	**0**
Bonds	0	0	0	0	0	0	0	0	0	0
Commercial banks and other	0	0	0	0	0	0	0	0	0	0
Memo:										
IBRD	0	23	21	0	0	0	0	0	0	0
IDA	1	20	89	1	0	0	0	0	0	0
PRINCIPAL REPAYMENTS	**25**	**192**	**49**	**0**	**0**	**0**	**0**	**0**	**0**	**0**
Public and publicly guaranteed	**25**	**192**	**49**	**0**	**0**	**0**	**0**	**0**	**0**	**0**
Official creditors	6	102	34	0	0	0	0	0	0	0
Multilateral	1	12	28	0	0	0	0	0	0	0
Concessional	0	0	3	0	0	0	0	0	0	0
Bilateral	5	90	6	0	0	0	0	0	0	0
Concessional	4	2	5	0	0	0	0	0	0	0
Private creditors	19	90	15	0	0	0	0	0	0	0
Bonds	0	0	0	0	0	0	0	0	0	0
Commercial banks	0	36	5	0	0	0	0	0	0	0
Other private	19	53	10	0	0	0	0	0	0	0
Private nonguaranteed	**0**	**0**	**0**	**0**	**0**	**0**	**0**	**0**	**0**	**0**
Bonds	0	0	0	0	0	0	0	0	0	0
Commercial banks and other	0	0	0	0	0	0	0	0	0	0
Memo:										
IBRD	1	6	5	0	0	0	0	0	0	0
IDA	0	0	2	0	0	0	0	0	0	0
NET FLOWS ON DEBT	**6**	**271**	**267**	**1**	**0**	**3**	**0**	**0**	**8**	**0**
Public and publicly guaranteed	**6**	**271**	**267**	**1**	**0**	**3**	**0**	**0**	**8**	**0**
Official creditors	7	98	279	1	0	3	0	0	8	0
Multilateral	-1	56	194	1	0	0	0	0	0	0
Concessional	1	27	122	1	0	0	0	0	0	0
Bilateral	7	42	85	0	0	3	0	0	8	0
Concessional	8	102	84	0	0	3	0	0	8	0
Private creditors	-1	173	-12	0	0	0	0	0	0	0
Bonds	0	0	0	0	0	0	0	0	0	0
Commercial banks	0	56	-5	0	0	0	0	0	0	0
Other private	-1	117	-7	0	0	0	0	0	0	0
Private nonguaranteed	**0**	**0**	**0**	**0**	**0**	**0**	**0**	**0**	**0**	**0**
Bonds	0	0	0	0	0	0	0	0	0	0
Commercial banks and other	0	0	0	0	0	0	0	0	0	0
Memo:										
IBRD	-1	17	16	0	0	0	0	0	0	0
IDA	1	20	87	1	0	0	0	0	0	0

CONGO, DEMOCRATIC REPUBLIC OF

(US$ million, unless otherwise indicated)

	1970	1980	1990	1994	1995	1996	1997	1998	1999	2000
INTEREST PAYMENTS (LINT)	**9**	**205**	**89**	**0**	**0**	**0**	**0**	**0**	**0**	**0**
Public and publicly guaranteed	**9**	**205**	**89**	**0**	**0**	**0**	**0**	**0**	**0**	**0**
Official creditors	5	105	76	0	0	0	0	0	0	0
Multilateral	0	11	40	0	0	0	0	0	0	0
Concessional	0	2	8	0	0	0	0	0	0	0
Bilateral	5	94	36	0	0	0	0	0	0	0
Concessional	5	45	8	0	0	0	0	0	0	0
Private creditors	4	99	12	0	0	0	0	0	0	0
Bonds	0	1	0	0	0	0	0	0	0	0
Commercial banks	0	69	6	0	0	0	0	0	0	0
Other private	3	30	6	0	0	0	0	0	0	0
Private nonguaranteed	**0**	**0**	**0**	**0**	**0**	**0**	**0**	**0**	**0**	**0**
Bonds	0	0	0	0	0	0	0	0	0	0
Commercial banks and other	0	0	0	0	0	0	0	0	0	0
Memo:										
IBRD	0	8	1	0	0	0	0	0	0	0
IDA	0	1	7	0	0	0	0	0	0	0
NET TRANSFERS ON DEBT	**-3**	**67**	**178**	**1**	**0**	**3**	**0**	**0**	**8**	**0**
Public and publicly guaranteed	**-3**	**67**	**178**	**1**	**0**	**3**	**0**	**0**	**8**	**0**
Official creditors	2	-7	202	1	0	3	0	0	8	0
Multilateral	-1	45	154	1	0	0	0	0	0	0
Concessional	1	25	114	1	0	0	0	0	0	0
Bilateral	3	-52	49	0	0	3	0	0	8	0
Concessional	3	57	76	0	0	3	0	0	8	0
Private creditors	-4	74	-24	0	0	0	0	0	0	0
Bonds	0	-1	-1	0	0	0	0	0	0	0
Commercial banks	0	-14	-11	0	0	0	0	0	0	0
Other private	-4	88	-13	0	0	0	0	0	0	0
Private nonguaranteed	**0**	**0**	**0**	**0**	**0**	**0**	**0**	**0**	**0**	**0**
Bonds	0	0	0	0	0	0	0	0	0	0
Commercial banks and other	0	0	0	0	0	0	0	0	0	0
Memo:										
IBRD	-2	9	14	0	0	0	0	0	0	0
IDA	1	19	80	1	0	0	0	0	0	0
DEBT SERVICE (LTDS)	**34**	**397**	**137**	**1**	**0**	**0**	**0**	**0**	**0**	**0**
Public and publicly guaranteed	**34**	**397**	**137**	**1**	**0**	**0**	**0**	**0**	**0**	**0**
Official creditors	11	208	110	1	0	0	0	0	0	0
Multilateral	2	24	68	1	0	0	0	0	0	0
Concessional	0	2	11	1	0	0	0	0	0	0
Bilateral	10	184	42	0	0	0	0	0	0	0
Concessional	9	48	13	0	0	0	0	0	0	0
Private creditors	23	189	27	0	0	0	0	0	0	0
Bonds	0	1	1	0	0	0	0	0	0	0
Commercial banks	0	105	11	0	0	0	0	0	0	0
Other private	23	83	16	0	0	0	0	0	0	0
Private nonguaranteed	**0**	**0**	**0**	**0**	**0**	**0**	**0**	**0**	**0**	**0**
Bonds	0	0	0	0	0	0	0	0	0	0
Commercial banks and other	0	0	0	0	0	0	0	0	0	0
Memo:										
IBRD	2	14	6	0	0	0	0	0	0	0
IDA	0	1	9	0	0	0	0	0	0	0
UNDISBURSED DEBT	**288**	**818**	**1,654**	**945**	**964**	**452**	**410**	**495**	**235**	**178**
Official creditors	52	743	1,590	893	907	399	364	446	202	151
Private creditors	236	75	65	52	57	53	46	49	33	27
Memorandum items										
Concessional LDOD	216	862	3,146	3,413	3,521	3,371	3,137	3,432	3,234	3,067
Variable rate LDOD	0	508	1,367	1,372	1,406	1,376	1,318	1,344	950	927
Public sector LDOD	308	4,071	9,010	9,279	9,621	9,261	8,615	9,200	8,207	7,829
Private sector LDOD	0	0	0	15	15	15	14	14	14	13

6. CURRENCY COMPOSITION OF LONG-TERM DEBT (PERCENT)

	1970	1980	1990	1994	1995	1996	1997	1998	1999	2000
Deutsche mark	2.2	5.9	6.9	6.5	6.8	6.5	6.0	6.3	6.2	6.0
French franc	3.8	13.6	16.4	15.5	16.3	15.9	14.9	14.9	12.6	12.1
Japanese yen	0.0	1.5	3.0	3.9	3.7	3.4	3.2	4.0	5.1	4.8
Pound sterling	1.8	4.1	1.2	0.9	0.9	1.0	1.0	1.0	1.1	1.0
Swiss franc	0.0	0.4	0.2	0.2	0.3	0.2	0.2	0.2	0.2	0.2
U.S.dollars	41.5	42.2	41.4	42.0	40.8	42.0	44.4	42.9	43.3	44.8
Multiple currency	1.6	2.1	3.2	4.3	4.2	4.1	4.0	4.0	4.5	4.4
Special drawing rights	0.0	0.0	0.2	0.4	0.4	0.4	0.4	0.4	0.4	0.4
All other currencies	49.1	30.2	27.5	26.3	26.6	26.5	25.9	26.3	26.6	26.3

CONGO, DEMOCRATIC REPUBLIC OF

(US$ million, unless otherwise indicated)

	1970	1980	1990	1994	1995	1996	1997	1998	1999	2000
7. DEBT RESTRUCTURINGS										
Total amount rescheduled	..	..	446	0	0	0	0	0	0	0
Debt stock rescheduled	..	..	0	0	0	0	0	0	0	0
Principal rescheduled	..	..	259	0	0	0	0	0	6	0
Official	..	..	252	0	0	0	0	0	6	0
Private	..	..	7	0	0	0	0	0	0	0
Interest rescheduled	..	..	131	0	0	0	0	0	1	0
Official	..	..	129	0	0	0	0	0	1	0
Private	..	..	2	0	0	0	0	0	0	0
Debt forgiven	..	..	9	0	0	0	0	0	1	0
Memo: interest forgiven	..	..	15	0	0	0	0	0	0	0
Debt stock reduction	..	..	0	0	0	0	0	0	0	0
of which debt buyback	..	..	0	0	0	0	0	0	0	0
8. DEBT STOCK-FLOW RECONCILIATION										
Total change in debt stocks	..	..	1,023	1,048	918	-409	-493	866	-1,204	-354
Net flows on debt	6	278	88	-140	61	-91	242	-13	13	20
Net change in interest arrears	..	..	125	648	506	61	-61	275	-206	26
Interest capitalized	..	..	131	0	0	0	0	0	1	0
Debt forgiveness or reduction	..	..	-9	0	0	0	0	0	-1	0
Cross-currency valuation	..	..	416	260	95	-584	-850	93	-612	-351
Residual	..	..	273	281	256	205	176	511	-399	-50
9. AVERAGE TERMS OF NEW COMMITMENTS										
ALL CREDITORS										
Interest (%)	6.5	5.1	5.9	0.0	2.5	0.0	0.0	0.0	0.0	0.0
Maturity (years)	12.5	22.7	23.8	0.0	19.9	0.0	0.0	0.0	0.0	0.0
Grace period (years)	3.6	6.3	6.4	0.0	4.4	0.0	0.0	0.0	0.0	0.0
Grant element (%)	18.3	39.4	30.6	0.0	48.7	0.0	0.0	0.0	0.0	0.0
Official creditors										
Interest (%)	2.6	2.8	5.9	0.0	2.5	0.0	0.0	0.0	0.0	0.0
Maturity (years)	32.6	28.9	23.8	0.0	19.9	0.0	0.0	0.0	0.0	0.0
Grace period (years)	8.6	8.5	6.4	0.0	4.4	0.0	0.0	0.0	0.0	0.0
Grant element (%)	59.8	57.2	30.6	0.0	48.7	0.0	0.0	0.0	0.0	0.0
Private creditors										
Interest (%)	6.9	9.8	0.0	0.0	0.0	0.0	0.0	0.0	0.0	0.0
Maturity (years)	10.1	9.5	0.0	0.0	0.0	0.0	0.0	0.0	0.0	0.0
Grace period (years)	3.0	1.6	0.0	0.0	0.0	0.0	0.0	0.0	0.0	0.0
Grant element (%)	13.3	1.6	0.0	0.0	0.0	0.0	0.0	0.0	0.0	0.0
Memorandum items										
Commitments	258	438	109	0	14	0	0	0	0	0
Official creditors	27	298	109	0	14	0	0	0	0	0
Private creditors	231	140	0	0	0	0	0	0	0	0

10. CONTRACTUAL OBLIGATIONS ON OUTSTANDING LONG-TERM DEBT

	2001	2002	2003	2004	2005	2006	2007	2008	2009	2010
TOTAL										
Disbursements	12	17	12	8	4	2	1	0	0	0
Principal	498	319	219	203	185	174	168	156	145	131
Interest	132	107	92	80	70	61	53	45	39	33
Official creditors										
Disbursements	12	17	12	8	4	2	1	0	0	0
Principal	497	318	218	202	184	174	167	156	145	130
Interest	132	107	92	80	70	61	53	45	39	33
Bilateral creditors										
Disbursements	12	17	12	8	4	2	1	0	0	0
Principal	233	228	128	117	117	112	101	94	90	83
Interest	87	74	64	57	51	45	39	33	28	23
Multilateral creditors										
Disbursements	0	0	0	0	0	0	0	0	0	0
Principal	264	91	90	85	67	63	67	62	55	47
Interest	44	33	28	23	19	17	14	12	11	10
Private creditors										
Disbursements	0	0	0	0	0	0	0	0	0	0
Principal	1	1	1	1	1	0	0	0	0	0
Interest	0	0	0	0	0	0	0	0	0	0
Commercial banks										
Disbursements	0	0	0	0	0	0	0	0	0	0
Principal	0	0	0	0	0	0	0	0	0	0
Interest	0	0	0	0	0	0	0	0	0	0
Other private										
Disbursements	0	0	0	0	0	0	0	0	0	0
Principal	0	0	0	0	0	0	0	0	0	0
Interest	0	0	0	0	0	0	0	0	0	0

CONGO, REPUBLIC OF

(US$ million, unless otherwise indicated)

	1970	1980	1990	1994	1995	1996	1997	1998	1999	2000
1. SUMMARY DEBT DATA										
TOTAL DEBT STOCKS (EDT)	**119**	**1,526**	**4,947**	**5,414**	**6,004**	**5,241**	**5,071**	**5,119**	**5,033**	**4,887**
Long-term debt (LDOD)	**119**	**1,257**	**4,201**	**4,774**	**4,955**	**4,666**	**4,284**	**4,251**	**3,934**	**3,758**
Public and publicly guaranteed	119	1,257	4,201	4,774	4,955	4,666	4,284	4,251	3,934	3,758
Private nonguaranteed	0	0	0	0	0	0	0	0	0	0
Use of IMF credit	**0**	**22**	**11**	**20**	**19**	**38**	**34**	**34**	**29**	**41**
Short-term debt	**0**	**247**	**736**	**619**	**1,030**	**537**	**754**	**834**	**1,070**	**1,088**
of which interest arrears on LDOD	0	4	181	265	441	283	372	511	588	667
Official creditors	0	2	77	170	332	155	227	343	419	496
Private creditors	0	2	104	95	109	128	144	168	169	171
Memo: principal arrears on LDOD	1	10	571	796	1,028	1,011	1,228	1,474	1,623	1,806
Official creditors	0	5	127	400	595	521	671	831	942	1,093
Private creditors	1	5	444	396	433	491	558	642	681	714
Memo: export credits	0	0	1,877	1,865	2,510	2,356	2,420	1,138	1,035	972
TOTAL DEBT FLOWS										
Disbursements	**18**	**526**	**318**	**350**	**15**	**24**	**24**	**10**	**0**	**14**
Long-term debt	18	522	312	332	15	4	24	0	0	0
IMF purchases	0	4	5	18	0	20	0	10	0	14
Principal repayments	**6**	**41**	**362**	**287**	**84**	**140**	**55**	**18**	**4**	**5**
Long-term debt	6	34	355	284	82	140	53	7	0	5
IMF repurchases	0	7	7	3	2	0	2	11	4	0
Net flows on debt	**13**	**541**	**93**	**97**	**166**	**-451**	**96**	**-66**	**154**	**-52**
of which short-term debt	0	56	138	34	236	-335	128	-58	158	-61
Interest payments (INT)	**3**	**68**	**169**	**248**	**97**	**199**	**57**	**23**	**21**	**38**
Long-term debt	3	37	120	228	61	180	40	6	0	7
IMF charges	0	1	1	1	1	1	1	1	1	1
Short-term debt	0	31	48	20	35	18	16	16	20	30
Net transfers on debt	**10**	**473**	**-76**	**-152**	**69**	**-649**	**39**	**-90**	**133**	**-90**
Total debt service paid (TDS)	**9**	**109**	**531**	**535**	**181**	**339**	**112**	**41**	**25**	**43**
Long-term debt	9	71	475	512	142	320	93	13	0	12
IMF repurchases and charges	0	8	8	4	3	1	3	11	5	1
Short-term debt (interest only)	0	31	48	20	35	18	16	16	20	30
2. AGGREGATE NET RESOURCE FLOWS AND NET TRANSFERS (LONG-TERM)										
NET RESOURCE FLOWS	**18**	**548**	**7**	**233**	**22**	**171**	**214**	**51**	**135**	**40**
Net flow of long-term debt (ex. IMF)	13	488	-43	48	-67	-136	-30	-7	0	-5
Foreign direct investment (net)	0	40	0	5	3	8	9	4	5	14
Portfolio equity flows	0	0	0	0	0	0	0	0	0	0
Grants (excluding technical coop.)	5	20	50	181	86	299	235	54	130	32
Memo: technical coop. grants	10	37	51	37	41	39	31	30	21	19
official net resource flows	19	108	106	384	69	177	205	47	130	26
private net resource flows	-1	440	-100	-151	-47	-7	9	4	5	14
NET TRANSFERS	**15**	**505**	**-113**	**2**	**-41**	**-11**	**172**	**43**	**132**	**30**
Interest on long-term debt	3	37	120	228	61	180	40	6	0	7
Profit remittances on FDI	0	6	0	4	3	2	2	2	3	4
Memo: official net transfers	17	83	38	207	49	1	165	41	130	20
private net transfers	-2	421	-151	-205	-90	-12	7	2	2	10
3. MAJOR ECONOMIC AGGREGATES										
Gross national income (GNI)	267	1,544	2,324	1,515	1,541	1,363	1,295	1,405	1,799	2,232
Exports of goods & services (XGS)	..	1,030	1,503	1,028	1,246	1,657	1,805	1,356	1,790	2,720
of which workers remittances	..	1	0	0	0	0	0	..	..	..
Imports of goods & services (MGS)	..	1,195	1,757	1,900	1,889	2,752	2,037	2,253	1,956	2,176
International reserves (RES)	9	93	10	55	64	95	63	1	39	222
Current account balance	..	-167	-251	-793	-650	-1,109	-252	..	..	..
4. DEBT INDICATORS										
EDT / XGS (%)	..	148.2	329.2	526.7	481.8	316.2	280.9	377.7	281.2	179.7
EDT / GNI (%)	44.5	98.8	212.9	357.4	389.6	384.6	391.5	364.4	279.8	219.0
TDS / XGS (%)	..	10.6	35.4	52.1	14.5	20.4	6.2	3.0	1.4	1.6
INT / XGS (%)	..	6.6	11.2	24.1	7.8	12.0	3.2	1.7	1.2	1.4
INT / GNI (%)	1.1	4.4	7.3	16.4	6.3	14.6	4.4	1.7	1.2	1.7
RES / EDT (%)	7.5	6.1	0.2	1.0	1.1	1.8	1.3	0.0	0.8	4.5
RES / MGS (months)	..	0.9	0.1	0.4	0.4	0.4	0.4	0.0	0.2	1.2
Short-term / EDT (%)	0.3	16.2	14.9	11.4	17.2	10.3	14.9	16.3	21.3	22.3
Concessional / EDT (%)	62.8	26.5	35.2	34.8	33.0	38.2	36.6	36.8	34.4	33.7
Multilateral / EDT (%)	24.7	7.7	11.5	13.0	11.7	12.9	12.2	12.2	12.0	11.7

CONGO, REPUBLIC OF

(US$ million, unless otherwise indicated)

	1970	1980	1990	1994	1995	1996	1997	1998	1999	2000
5. LONG-TERM DEBT										
DEBT OUTSTANDING (LDOD)	**119**	**1,257**	**4,201**	**4,774**	**4,955**	**4,666**	**4,284**	**4,251**	**3,934**	**3,758**
Public and publicly guaranteed	**119**	**1,257**	**4,201**	**4,774**	**4,955**	**4,666**	**4,284**	**4,251**	**3,934**	**3,758**
Official creditors	104	605	3,055	3,833	4,043	3,799	3,452	3,437	3,152	2,994
Multilateral	29	118	568	702	703	675	619	625	601	570
Concessional	0	49	151	255	262	252	239	243	234	223
Bilateral	75	487	2,487	3,131	3,340	3,125	2,832	2,812	2,551	2,424
Concessional	75	355	1,588	1,629	1,722	1,750	1,615	1,643	1,496	1,424
Private creditors	14	653	1,145	941	913	866	832	814	782	764
Bonds	0	0	0	0	0	0	0	0	0	0
Commercial banks	0	282	725	814	784	771	748	725	703	692
Other private	14	371	421	127	129	96	84	89	79	73
Private nonguaranteed	**0**	**0**	**0**	**0**	**0**	**0**	**0**	**0**	**0**	**0**
Bonds	0	0	0	0	0	0	0	0	0	0
Commercial banks and other	0	0	0	0	0	0	0	0	0	0
Memo:										
IBRD	29	39	164	116	105	82	73	71	68	65
IDA	0	22	75	172	174	171	165	168	166	159
DISBURSEMENTS	**18**	**522**	**312**	**332**	**15**	**4**	**24**	**0**	**0**	**0**
Public and publicly guaranteed	**18**	**522**	**312**	**332**	**15**	**4**	**24**	**0**	**0**	**0**
Official creditors	16	109	127	331	15	4	24	0	0	0
Multilateral	0	23	11	247	1	4	22	0	0	0
Concessional	0	10	1	110	0	2	1	0	0	0
Bilateral	16	87	116	84	14	0	2	0	0	0
Concessional	16	39	113	84	14	0	2	0	0	0
Private creditors	2	412	185	1	0	0	0	0	0	0
Bonds	0	0	0	0	0	0	0	0	0	0
Commercial banks	0	277	174	0	0	0	0	0	0	0
Other private	2	135	11	1	0	0	0	0	0	0
Private nonguaranteed	**0**	**0**	**0**	**0**	**0**	**0**	**0**	**0**	**0**	**0**
Bonds	0	0	0	0	0	0	0	0	0	0
Commercial banks and other	0	0	0	0	0	0	0	0	0	0
Memo:										
IBRD	0	2	2	0	1	2	0	0	0	0
IDA	0	1	0	101	0	2	1	0	0	0
PRINCIPAL REPAYMENTS	**6**	**34**	**355**	**284**	**82**	**140**	**53**	**7**	**0**	**5**
Public and publicly guaranteed	**6**	**34**	**355**	**284**	**82**	**140**	**53**	**7**	**0**	**5**
Official creditors	2	21	70	127	32	126	53	7	0	5
Multilateral	1	6	30	106	19	32	38	7	0	5
Concessional	0	0	2	6	1	5	0	0	0	1
Bilateral	2	16	40	22	13	94	15	0	0	0
Concessional	1	11	1	3	5	17	0	0	0	0
Private creditors	4	12	285	157	50	15	0	0	0	0
Bonds	0	0	0	0	0	0	0	0	0	0
Commercial banks	0	0	257	117	46	0	0	0	0	0
Other private	4	12	28	40	4	15	0	0	0	0
Private nonguaranteed	**0**	**0**	**0**	**0**	**0**	**0**	**0**	**0**	**0**	**0**
Bonds	0	0	0	0	0	0	0	0	0	0
Commercial banks and other	0	0	0	0	0	0	0	0	0	0
Memo:										
IBRD	1	4	6	57	18	16	3	3	0	2
IDA	0	0	0	4	1	1	0	0	0	1
NET FLOWS ON DEBT	**13**	**488**	**-43**	**48**	**-67**	**-136**	**-30**	**-7**	**0**	**-5**
Public and publicly guaranteed	**13**	**488**	**-43**	**48**	**-67**	**-136**	**-30**	**-7**	**0**	**-5**
Official creditors	14	88	57	204	-17	-122	-30	-7	0	-5
Multilateral	-1	17	-19	142	-19	-28	-16	-7	0	-5
Concessional	0	10	0	105	-1	-3	1	0	0	-1
Bilateral	15	71	76	62	1	-94	-14	0	0	0
Concessional	14	28	113	81	9	-17	2	0	0	0
Private creditors	-1	400	-100	-156	-50	-15	0	0	0	0
Bonds	0	0	0	0	0	0	0	0	0	0
Commercial banks	0	277	-83	-117	-46	0	0	0	0	0
Other private	-1	123	-17	-39	-4	-15	0	0	0	0
Private nonguaranteed	**0**	**0**	**0**	**0**	**0**	**0**	**0**	**0**	**0**	**0**
Bonds	0	0	0	0	0	0	0	0	0	0
Commercial banks and other	0	0	0	0	0	0	0	0	0	0
Memo:										
IBRD	-1	-2	-4	-57	-17	-14	-3	-3	0	-2
IDA	0	1	0	97	-1	1	1	0	0	-1

CONGO, REPUBLIC OF

(US$ million, unless otherwise indicated)

	1970	1980	1990	1994	1995	1996	1997	1998	1999	2000
INTEREST PAYMENTS (LINT)	**3**	**37**	**120**	**228**	**61**	**180**	**40**	**6**	**0**	**7**
Public and publicly guaranteed	**3**	**37**	**120**	**228**	**61**	**180**	**40**	**6**	**0**	**7**
Official creditors	3	25	68	178	20	177	40	6	0	7
Multilateral	2	6	30	65	11	20	37	6	0	7
Concessional	0	1	1	3	1	2	1	1	0	1
Bilateral	1	19	38	113	10	156	4	0	0	0
Concessional	1	11	28	90	8	33	0	0	0	0
Private creditors	1	13	52	50	40	3	0	0	0	0
Bonds	0	0	0	0	0	0	0	0	0	0
Commercial banks	0	2	44	37	39	0	0	0	0	0
Other private	1	11	8	13	2	3	0	0	0	0
Private nonguaranteed	**0**	**0**	**0**	**0**	**0**	**0**	**0**	**0**	**0**	**0**
Bonds	0	0	0	0	0	0	0	0	0	0
Commercial banks and other	0	0	0	0	0	0	0	0	0	0
Memo:										
IBRD	2	4	12	53	10	7	1	1	0	1
IDA	0	0	1	2	1	1	1	1	0	1
NET TRANSFERS ON DEBT	**10**	**451**	**-163**	**-180**	**-127**	**-316**	**-70**	**-13**	**0**	**-12**
Public and publicly guaranteed	**10**	**451**	**-163**	**-180**	**-127**	**-316**	**-70**	**-13**	**0**	**-12**
Official creditors	11	64	-12	26	-37	-298	-70	-13	0	-12
Multilateral	-3	12	-50	77	-29	-48	-53	-13	0	-12
Concessional	0	10	-2	102	-3	-5	0	-1	0	-2
Bilateral	14	52	38	-51	-8	-250	-17	0	0	0
Concessional	14	17	84	-9	1	-50	2	0	0	0
Private creditors	-2	388	-151	-206	-90	-18	0	0	0	0
Bonds	0	0	0	0	0	0	0	0	0	0
Commercial banks	0	275	-127	-153	-84	0	0	0	0	0
Other private	-2	112	-24	-53	-6	-18	0	0	0	0
Private nonguaranteed	**0**	**0**	**0**	**0**	**0**	**0**	**0**	**0**	**0**	**0**
Bonds	0	0	0	0	0	0	0	0	0	0
Commercial banks and other	0	0	0	0	0	0	0	0	0	0
Memo:										
IBRD	-3	-6	-16	-110	-27	-22	-4	-4	0	-4
IDA	0	1	-1	95	-3	-1	0	-1	0	-1
DEBT SERVICE (LTDS)	**9**	**71**	**475**	**512**	**142**	**320**	**93**	**13**	**0**	**12**
Public and publicly guaranteed	**9**	**71**	**475**	**512**	**142**	**320**	**93**	**13**	**0**	**12**
Official creditors	5	46	139	305	52	302	93	13	0	12
Multilateral	3	11	60	170	30	52	75	13	0	12
Concessional	0	1	3	9	3	7	1	1	0	2
Bilateral	2	35	78	135	22	250	19	0	0	0
Concessional	2	22	29	92	13	50	0	0	0	0
Private creditors	4	25	337	207	90	18	0	0	0	0
Bonds	0	0	0	0	0	0	0	0	0	0
Commercial banks	0	2	301	153	84	0	0	0	0	0
Other private	4	23	36	54	6	18	0	0	0	0
Private nonguaranteed	**0**	**0**	**0**	**0**	**0**	**0**	**0**	**0**	**0**	**0**
Bonds	0	0	0	0	0	0	0	0	0	0
Commercial banks and other	0	0	0	0	0	0	0	0	0	0
Memo:										
IBRD	3	8	18	110	27	24	4	4	0	4
IDA	0	0	1	6	3	3	1	1	0	1
UNDISBURSED DEBT	**42**	**735**	**400**	**309**	**340**	**281**	**226**	**6**	**5**	**5**
Official creditors	36	221	338	158	177	128	93	6	5	5
Private creditors	7	514	62	151	163	153	134	0	0	0
Memorandum items										
Concessional LDOD	75	404	1,739	1,884	1,984	2,003	1,854	1,886	1,730	1,648
Variable rate LDOD	0	82	883	1,187	1,155	1,097	1,047	1,001	967	945
Public sector LDOD	119	1,257	4,201	4,774	4,955	4,666	4,284	4,251	3,934	3,758
Private sector LDOD	0	0	0	0	0	0	0	0	0	0

6. CURRENCY COMPOSITION OF LONG-TERM DEBT (PERCENT)

	1970	1980	1990	1994	1995	1996	1997	1998	1999	2000
Deutsche mark	5.2	1.1	2.4	2.7	2.8	2.8	2.7	2.9	2.7	2.6
French franc	14.1	31.0	51.2	45.2	47.1	44.6	41.4	41.7	38.8	37.6
Japanese yen	0.0	0.0	0.2	0.2	0.2	0.2	0.2	0.2	0.2	0.2
Pound sterling	0.6	0.0	5.7	5.0	4.9	5.7	6.3	6.3	6.8	6.5
Swiss franc	0.0	2.1	0.4	0.4	0.5	0.3	0.3	0.3	0.3	0.3
U.S.dollars	2.3	25.1	16.6	25.1	23.7	24.2	26.0	25.9	27.9	29.0
Multiple currency	24.7	3.1	3.9	2.4	2.1	1.8	1.7	0.6	0.6	0.6
Special drawing rights	0.0	0.0	0.6	0.5	0.5	0.5	0.5	0.5	0.5	0.5
All other currencies	53.1	37.6	19.0	18.5	18.2	19.9	20.9	21.6	22.2	22.7

CONGO, REPUBLIC OF

(US$ million, unless otherwise indicated)

	1970	1980	1990	1994	1995	1996	1997	1998	1999	2000
7. DEBT RESTRUCTURINGS										
Total amount rescheduled	..	..	780	1,044	108	269	91	69	36	0
Debt stock rescheduled	..	..	0	0	0	0	0	0	0	0
Principal rescheduled	..	..	386	505	65	193	70	53	25	0
Official	..	..	101	355	60	182	70	53	25	0
Private	..	..	285	150	5	11	0	0	0	0
Interest rescheduled	..	..	370	433	42	69	19	16	7	0
Official	..	..	249	396	41	65	19	16	7	0
Private	..	..	121	38	1	5	0	0	0	0
Debt forgiven	..	..	0	126	24	77	37	36	17	0
Memo: interest forgiven	..	..	0	8	0	24	4	4	2	0
Debt stock reduction	..	..	0	0	0	0	0	0	0	0
of which debt buyback	..	..	0	0	0	0	0	0	0	0
8. DEBT STOCK-FLOW RECONCILIATION										
Total change in debt stocks	..	..	668	332	591	-764	-170	48	-87	-146
Net flows on debt	13	541	93	97	166	-451	96	-66	154	-52
Net change in interest arrears	..	..	-167	-378	176	-158	89	139	77	79
Interest capitalized	..	..	370	433	42	69	19	16	7	0
Debt forgiveness or reduction	..	..	0	-126	-24	-77	-37	-36	-17	0
Cross-currency valuation	..	..	321	180	115	-257	-432	37	-305	-163
Residual	..	..	52	125	115	110	96	-42	-2	-10
9. AVERAGE TERMS OF NEW COMMITMENTS										
ALL CREDITORS										
Interest (%)	2.8	7.6	5.1	0.8	2.2	0.0	0.0	0.0	0.0	0.0
Maturity (years)	18.3	11.1	15.7	31.7	31.8	0.0	0.0	0.0	0.0	0.0
Grace period (years)	6.5	3.2	6.8	7.5	9.0	0.0	0.0	0.0	0.0	0.0
Grant element (%)	49.5	13.1	32.0	70.8	63.7	0.0	0.0	0.0	0.0	0.0
Official creditors										
Interest (%)	2.3	3.5	4.3	0.8	2.2	0.0	0.0	0.0	0.0	0.0
Maturity (years)	19.6	25.3	16.9	31.7	31.8	0.0	0.0	0.0	0.0	0.0
Grace period (years)	6.6	6.7	7.2	7.5	9.0	0.0	0.0	0.0	0.0	0.0
Grant element (%)	53.6	46.5	37.3	70.8	63.7	0.0	0.0	0.0	0.0	0.0
Private creditors										
Interest (%)	4.2	8.5	9.9	0.0	0.0	0.0	0.0	0.0	0.0	0.0
Maturity (years)	14.9	8.1	8.3	0.0	0.0	0.0	0.0	0.0	0.0	0.0
Grace period (years)	6.2	2.4	4.1	0.0	0.0	0.0	0.0	0.0	0.0	0.0
Grant element (%)	38.9	6.2	-0.5	0.0	0.0	0.0	0.0	0.0	0.0	0.0
Memorandum items										
Commitments	31	966	192	249	31	0	0	0	0	0
Official creditors	23	165	165	249	31	0	0	0	0	0
Private creditors	9	801	27	0	0	0	0	0	0	0

10. CONTRACTUAL OBLIGATIONS ON OUTSTANDING LONG-TERM DEBT

	2001	2002	2003	2004	2005	2006	2007	2008	2009	2010
TOTAL										
Disbursements	2	2	1	1	0	0	0	0	0	0
Principal	250	184	183	172	169	164	107	102	103	42
Interest	88	74	65	55	46	38	30	24	18	13
Official creditors										
Disbursements	2	2	1	1	0	0	0	0	0	0
Principal	200	184	183	172	169	164	107	102	103	42
Interest	85	74	64	55	46	38	30	24	18	13
Bilateral creditors										
Disbursements	0	0	0	0	0	0	0	0	0	0
Principal	146	143	144	144	147	143	87	87	89	27
Interest	72	65	58	50	43	35	28	22	16	11
Multilateral creditors										
Disbursements	2	2	1	1	0	0	0	0	0	0
Principal	53	41	38	28	23	22	20	15	14	14
Interest	12	9	7	5	4	3	2	2	2	2
Private creditors										
Disbursements	0	0	0	0	0	0	0	0	0	0
Principal	50	0	0	0	0	0	0	0	0	0
Interest	3	0	0	0	0	0	0	0	0	0
Commercial banks										
Disbursements	0	0	0	0	0	0	0	0	0	0
Principal	50	0	0	0	0	0	0	0	0	0
Interest	3	0	0	0	0	0	0	0	0	0
Other private										
Disbursements	0	0	0	0	0	0	0	0	0	0
Principal	0	0	0	0	0	0	0	0	0	0
Interest	0	0	0	0	0	0	0	0	0	0

COSTA RICA

(US$ million, unless otherwise indicated)

	1970	1980	1990	1994	1995	1996	1997	1998	1999	2000
1. SUMMARY DEBT DATA										
TOTAL DEBT STOCKS (EDT)	**287**	**2,744**	**3,756**	**3,909**	**3,802**	**3,491**	**3,476**	**3,954**	**4,208**	**4,466**
Long-term debt (LDOD)	**246**	**2,112**	**3,367**	**3,446**	**3,348**	**3,116**	**2,938**	**3,263**	**3,430**	**3,510**
Public and publicly guaranteed	134	1,700	3,063	3,218	3,133	2,923	2,767	3,026	3,186	3,274
Private nonguaranteed	112	412	304	228	214	193	172	237	244	236
Use of IMF credit	**0**	**57**	**11**	**66**	**24**	**1**	**0**	**0**	**0**	**0**
Short-term debt	**41**	**575**	**377**	**396**	**430**	**374**	**538**	**690**	**777**	**956**
of which interest arrears on LDOD	0	0	77	40	32	29	29	28	21	21
Official creditors	0	0	76	36	28	25	25	24	18	17
Private creditors	0	0	2	4	4	4	4	4	3	3
Memo: principal arrears on LDOD	0	2	173	132	118	88	77	78	79	78
Official creditors	0	0	167	128	115	85	75	76	77	76
Private creditors	0	2	6	4	3	3	2	2	2	2
Memo: export credits	0	0	297	302	214	204	146	58	83	59
TOTAL DEBT FLOWS										
Disbursements	**62**	**556**	**207**	**202**	**211**	**389**	**276**	**591**	**510**	**529**
Long-term debt	60	536	207	202	211	389	276	591	510	529
IMF purchases	2	20	0	0	0	0	0	0	0	0
Principal repayments	**45**	**176**	**295**	**291**	**399**	**373**	**358**	**326**	**356**	**389**
Long-term debt	41	164	269	271	355	350	358	326	356	389
IMF repurchases	4	12	26	20	44	23	1	0	0	0
Net flows on debt	**17**	**603**	**-109**	**-72**	**-146**	**-36**	**82**	**418**	**249**	**318**
of which short-term debt	0	222	-20	17	42	-53	164	154	94	179
Interest payments (INT)	**14**	**179**	**206**	**215**	**251**	**216**	**208**	**214**	**193**	**261**
Long-term debt	14	171	171	193	224	195	183	180	154	205
IMF charges	0	4	3	4	3	0	0	0	0	0
Short-term debt	0	4	32	18	23	20	26	34	40	56
Net transfers on debt	**3**	**424**	**-315**	**-287**	**-397**	**-252**	**-127**	**204**	**55**	**57**
Total debt service paid (TDS)	**59**	**354**	**501**	**507**	**650**	**588**	**567**	**541**	**549**	**650**
Long-term debt	55	335	440	465	580	544	540	507	509	594
IMF repurchases and charges	4	16	29	24	47	23	1	0	0	0
Short-term debt (interest only)	0	4	32	18	23	20	26	34	40	56
2. AGGREGATE NET RESOURCE FLOWS AND NET TRANSFERS (LONG-TERM)										
NET RESOURCE FLOWS	**48**	**425**	**210**	**268**	**224**	**502**	**357**	**904**	**847**	**573**
Net flow of long-term debt (ex. IMF)	19	373	-63	-69	-144	40	-82	265	155	139
Foreign direct investment (net)	26	53	163	298	337	427	408	613	669	409
Portfolio equity flows	0	0	0	4	1	1	0	0	0	0
Grants (excluding technical coop.)	3	0	110	35	30	34	30	26	24	25
Memo: technical coop. grants	4	14	73	60	77	60	44	50	24	24
official net resource flows	15	178	188	27	-101	97	-90	50	-101	-36
private net resource flows	33	248	23	241	325	404	446	854	948	610
NET TRANSFERS	**30**	**234**	**-21**	**0**	**-80**	**207**	**59**	**604**	**549**	**214**
Interest on long-term debt	14	171	171	193	224	195	183	180	154	205
Profit remittances on FDI	4	20	60	75	80	100	115	120	145	155
Memo: official net transfers	11	135	84	-104	-263	-36	-212	-63	-198	-138
private net transfers	19	99	-104	104	182	243	271	667	747	351
3. MAJOR ECONOMIC AGGREGATES										
Gross national income (GNI)	969	4,615	5,460	10,415	11,491	11,660	12,581	13,660	13,850	14,624
Exports of goods & services (XGS)	..	1,219	2,094	3,472	4,713	5,092	5,650	7,177	8,493	7,964
of which workers remittances	..	0	0	0	116	122	116	112	101	106
Imports of goods & services (MGS)	..	1,897	2,709	3,871	5,089	5,383	6,141	7,698	9,143	8,671
International reserves (RES)	16	197	525	906	1,060	1,001	1,262	1,064	1,461	1,318
Current account balance	..	-664	-424	-234	-358	-264	-481	-521	-649	..
4. DEBT INDICATORS										
EDT / XGS (%)	..	225.2	179.4	112.6	80.7	68.6	61.5	55.1	49.5	56.1
EDT / GNI (%)	29.6	59.5	68.8	37.5	33.1	29.9	27.6	28.9	30.4	30.5
TDS / XGS (%)	..	29.1	23.9	14.6	13.8	11.6	10.0	7.5	6.5	8.2
INT / XGS (%)	..	14.7	9.9	6.2	5.3	4.2	3.7	3.0	2.3	3.3
INT / GNI (%)	1.5	3.9	3.8	2.1	2.2	1.9	1.7	1.6	1.4	1.8
RES / EDT (%)	5.7	7.2	14.0	23.2	27.9	28.7	36.3	26.9	34.7	29.5
RES / MGS (months)	..	1.3	2.3	2.8	2.5	2.2	2.5	1.7	1.9	1.8
Short-term / EDT (%)	14.3	21.0	10.1	10.1	11.3	10.7	15.5	17.5	18.5	21.4
Concessional / EDT (%)	16.2	9.1	23.6	24.6	24.2	23.6	21.0	17.4	15.7	13.0
Multilateral / EDT (%)	19.9	16.4	30.4	33.6	35.6	37.7	36.8	34.7	31.9	29.2

COSTA RICA

(US$ million, unless otherwise indicated)

	1970	1980	1990	1994	1995	1996	1997	1998	1999	2000
5. LONG-TERM DEBT										
DEBT OUTSTANDING (LDOD)	**246**	**2,112**	**3,367**	**3,446**	**3,348**	**3,116**	**2,938**	**3,263**	**3,430**	**3,510**
Public and publicly guaranteed	**134**	**1,700**	**3,063**	**3,218**	**3,133**	**2,923**	**2,767**	**3,026**	**3,186**	**3,274**
Official creditors	96	791	2,359	2,578	2,492	2,284	2,069	2,152	2,040	1,920
Multilateral	57	450	1,141	1,313	1,352	1,318	1,278	1,370	1,344	1,305
Concessional	11	121	246	206	199	188	192	186	191	182
Bilateral	39	341	1,218	1,265	1,139	966	791	782	696	614
Concessional	36	128	642	754	721	637	537	504	471	399
Private creditors	38	909	704	641	642	639	698	874	1,146	1,355
Bonds	1	141	609	576	572	564	605	789	1,072	1,292
Commercial banks	20	712	41	24	33	40	61	55	45	36
Other private	17	55	54	41	37	35	32	31	29	26
Private nonguaranteed	**112**	**412**	**304**	**228**	**214**	**193**	**172**	**237**	**244**	**236**
Bonds	0	0	0	0	0	0	0	0	0	0
Commercial banks and other	112	412	304	228	214	193	172	237	244	236
Memo:										
IBRD	36	178	409	323	300	245	191	172	149	121
IDA	5	5	4	3	3	2	2	2	2	2
DISBURSEMENTS	**60**	**536**	**207**	**202**	**211**	**389**	**276**	**591**	**510**	**529**
Public and publicly guaranteed	**30**	**435**	**202**	**202**	**201**	**389**	**276**	**504**	**482**	**520**
Official creditors	19	200	170	200	190	375	189	302	181	269
Multilateral	13	97	89	150	172	313	181	210	167	148
Concessional	4	42	13	3	6	45	19	9	16	10
Bilateral	7	103	81	51	18	62	8	92	14	122
Concessional	7	20	76	18	12	18	6	10	13	10
Private creditors	10	235	32	2	11	15	87	203	301	250
Bonds	0	97	0	0	0	0	50	200	300	250
Commercial banks	6	120	30	1	11	13	36	0	0	0
Other private	4	17	1	1	0	2	1	3	1	0
Private nonguaranteed	**30**	**102**	**5**	**0**	**10**	**0**	**0**	**87**	**28**	**9**
Bonds	0	0	0	0	0	0	0	0	0	0
Commercial banks and other	30	102	5	0	10	0	0	87	28	9
Memo:										
IBRD	5	29	5	11	16	10	20	20	12	6
IDA	0	0	0	0	0	0	0	0	0	0
PRINCIPAL REPAYMENTS	**41**	**164**	**269**	**271**	**355**	**350**	**358**	**326**	**356**	**389**
Public and publicly guaranteed	**21**	**76**	**263**	**219**	**331**	**328**	**336**	**305**	**334**	**372**
Official creditors	7	23	92	208	321	311	309	278	305	331
Multilateral	3	15	79	120	176	121	159	156	190	148
Concessional	0	2	10	12	14	13	14	15	15	15
Bilateral	4	7	14	88	145	190	150	122	114	182
Concessional	3	3	3	35	44	72	79	63	63	61
Private creditors	14	53	171	11	11	17	27	27	29	42
Bonds	1	0	42	1	4	7	10	16	17	30
Commercial banks	12	41	124	4	2	6	14	7	10	9
Other private	1	12	5	6	5	3	3	4	3	3
Private nonguaranteed	**20**	**88**	**6**	**52**	**24**	**21**	**21**	**21**	**21**	**17**
Bonds	0	0	0	0	0	0	0	0	0	0
Commercial banks and other	20	88	6	52	24	21	21	21	21	17
Memo:										
IBRD	2	7	45	56	55	41	54	40	34	33
IDA	0	0	0	0	0	0	0	0	0	0
NET FLOWS ON DEBT	**19**	**373**	**-63**	**-69**	**-144**	**40**	**-82**	**265**	**155**	**139**
Public and publicly guaranteed	**9**	**359**	**-62**	**-17**	**-130**	**61**	**-60**	**199**	**148**	**147**
Official creditors	12	178	78	-8	-131	64	-120	24	-124	-61
Multilateral	10	82	11	30	-4	192	22	54	-24	-1
Concessional	4	40	4	-9	-7	32	6	-7	1	-5
Bilateral	3	96	67	-38	-127	-128	-142	-30	-101	-61
Concessional	4	17	73	-17	-32	-54	-73	-54	-49	-51
Private creditors	-3	182	-139	-9	1	-2	60	176	272	209
Bonds	-1	97	-42	-1	-4	-7	40	184	283	220
Commercial banks	-5	79	-94	-2	9	7	21	-7	-10	-9
Other private	3	5	-4	-5	-5	-2	-2	-2	-1	-3
Private nonguaranteed	**10**	**14**	**-1**	**-52**	**-14**	**-21**	**-21**	**65**	**7**	**-8**
Bonds	0	0	0	0	0	0	0	0	0	0
Commercial banks and other	10	14	-1	-52	-14	-21	-21	65	7	-8
Memo:										
IBRD	3	23	-40	-45	-39	-32	-34	-21	-23	-27
IDA	0	0	0	0	0	0	0	0	0	0

COSTA RICA

(US$ million, unless otherwise indicated)

	1970	1980	1990	1994	1995	1996	1997	1998	1999	2000
INTEREST PAYMENTS (LINT)	**14**	**171**	**171**	**193**	**224**	**195**	**183**	**180**	**154**	**205**
Public and publicly guaranteed	**7**	**130**	**169**	**171**	**204**	**177**	**167**	**161**	**141**	**189**
Official creditors	4	42	104	131	162	133	122	113	98	101
Multilateral	3	27	77	90	95	87	86	84	82	81
Concessional	0	3	5	4	5	4	3	4	3	3
Bilateral	1	15	27	41	67	46	36	29	15	20
Concessional	1	3	9	23	30	23	20	17	6	14
Private creditors	3	88	65	40	42	44	44	48	43	88
Bonds	0	6	24	35	37	36	37	39	37	80
Commercial banks	2	78	36	1	0	4	4	6	3	4
Other private	1	4	5	4	5	4	4	4	3	3
Private nonguaranteed	**7**	**41**	**2**	**22**	**21**	**18**	**16**	**19**	**13**	**16**
Bonds	0	0	0	0	0	0	0	0	0	0
Commercial banks and other	7	41	2	22	21	18	16	19	13	16
Memo:										
IBRD	2	15	33	27	27	20	16	12	13	12
IDA	0	0	0	0	0	0	0	0	0	0
NET TRANSFERS ON DEBT	**5**	**202**	**-234**	**-262**	**-368**	**-155**	**-264**	**84**	**1**	**-65**
Public and publicly guaranteed	**2**	**229**	**-231**	**-188**	**-334**	**-115**	**-227**	**38**	**7**	**-42**
Official creditors	8	135	-27	-140	-293	-70	-242	-90	-222	-163
Multilateral	6	54	-67	-60	-100	104	-65	-30	-106	-82
Concessional	3	37	-1	-13	-12	28	3	-10	-2	-8
Bilateral	2	81	40	-79	-193	-174	-177	-59	-116	-81
Concessional	3	14	64	-40	-62	-77	-94	-71	-56	-65
Private creditors	-6	94	-204	-49	-41	-46	15	128	229	121
Bonds	-1	91	-66	-36	-41	-43	4	146	246	140
Commercial banks	-7	2	-130	-3	9	3	17	-12	-13	-13
Other private	2	1	-9	-10	-9	-6	-6	-5	-4	-6
Private nonguaranteed	**3**	**-28**	**-3**	**-74**	**-35**	**-40**	**-38**	**46**	**-6**	**-24**
Bonds	0	0	0	0	0	0	0	0	0	0
Commercial banks and other	3	-28	-3	-74	-35	-40	-38	46	-6	-24
Memo:										
IBRD	1	8	-73	-72	-66	-52	-50	-33	-35	-39
IDA	0	0	0	0	0	0	0	0	0	0
DEBT SERVICE (LTDS)	**55**	**335**	**440**	**465**	**580**	**544**	**540**	**507**	**509**	**594**
Public and publicly guaranteed	**28**	**206**	**432**	**391**	**535**	**505**	**503**	**466**	**475**	**561**
Official creditors	11	65	197	340	483	444	431	391	402	432
Multilateral	6	43	156	210	271	209	246	240	273	229
Concessional	0	5	15	16	19	17	17	19	19	18
Bilateral	5	22	40	130	212	236	186	151	130	203
Concessional	4	6	12	58	74	95	99	80	69	75
Private creditors	17	141	236	51	52	61	72	75	73	129
Bonds	1	6	66	36	41	43	46	55	54	110
Commercial banks	14	119	160	5	2	10	18	12	13	13
Other private	2	16	10	10	9	7	7	8	5	6
Private nonguaranteed	**28**	**129**	**8**	**74**	**45**	**40**	**38**	**41**	**34**	**33**
Bonds	0	0	0	0	0	0	0	0	0	0
Commercial banks and other	28	129	8	74	45	40	38	41	34	33
Memo:										
IBRD	4	21	79	83	81	62	70	52	47	45
IDA	0	0	0	0	0	0	0	0	0	0
UNDISBURSED DEBT	**95**	**797**	**1,053**	**1,474**	**1,174**	**1,107**	**995**	**738**	**553**	**465**
Official creditors	93	623	1,038	1,446	1,155	1,099	991	737	553	465
Private creditors	2	174	15	29	19	7	4	2	0	0
Memorandum items										
Concessional LDOD	47	249	888	961	920	825	729	690	662	581
Variable rate LDOD	122	1,203	1,061	961	989	907	881	992	970	895
Public sector LDOD	130	1,655	3,059	3,216	3,131	2,921	2,765	3,025	3,185	3,273
Private sector LDOD	116	457	308	230	216	195	173	239	245	237

6. CURRENCY COMPOSITION OF LONG-TERM DEBT (PERCENT)

	1970	1980	1990	1994	1995	1996	1997	1998	1999	2000
Deutsche mark	2.0	3.1	2.6	2.1	1.9	1.9	1.3	1.0	0.6	0.4
French franc	0.0	0.2	1.0	0.5	0.4	0.3	0.2	0.2	0.1	0.1
Japanese yen	0.0	0.5	3.0	8.9	8.1	7.1	6.0	5.8	5.6	4.5
Pound sterling	2.8	0.5	0.2	0.3	0.1	0.1	0.1	0.0	0.0	0.0
Swiss franc	0.0	0.7	0.0	0.0	0.0	0.0	0.0	0.0	0.0	0.0
U.S.dollars	67.1	69.2	58.2	52.2	52.3	54.6	58.7	67.8	72.3	77.5
Multiple currency	28.2	18.2	31.4	34.1	35.6	34.1	32.1	23.3	19.6	16.0
Special drawing rights	0.0	0.0	0.2	0.1	0.1	0.1	0.1	0.1	0.0	0.0
All other currencies	-0.1	7.6	3.4	1.8	1.5	1.8	1.5	1.8	1.8	1.5

COSTA RICA

(US$ million, unless otherwise indicated)

	1970	1980	1990	1994	1995	1996	1997	1998	1999	2000
7. DEBT RESTRUCTURINGS										
Total amount rescheduled	..	..	641	0	0	0	0	0	0	0
Debt stock rescheduled	..	..	469	0	0	0	0	0	0	0
Principal rescheduled	..	..	20	0	0	0	0	0	0	0
Official	..	..	20	0	0	0	0	0	0	0
Private	..	..	0	0	0	0	0	0	0	0
Interest rescheduled	..	..	151	0	0	0	0	0	0	0
Official	..	..	10	0	0	0	0	0	0	0
Private	..	..	141	0	0	0	0	0	0	0
Debt forgiven	..	..	0	3	3	2	2	0	0	0
Memo: interest forgiven	..	..	187	0	0	0	0	0	0	0
Debt stock reduction	..	..	668	0	0	0	0	0	0	0
of which debt buyback	..	..	0	0	0	0	0	0	0	0
8. DEBT STOCK-FLOW RECONCILIATION										
Total change in debt stocks	..	..	-834	46	-107	-311	-15	478	254	258
Net flows on debt	17	603	-109	-72	-146	-36	82	418	249	318
Net change in interest arrears	..	..	-308	8	-8	-3	-1	-1	-7	0
Interest capitalized	..	..	151	0	0	0	0	0	0	0
Debt forgiveness or reduction	..	..	-668	-3	-3	-2	-2	0	0	0
Cross-currency valuation	..	..	52	62	24	-132	-112	-6	5	-29
Residual	..	..	47	51	26	-138	17	66	8	-31
9. AVERAGE TERMS OF NEW COMMITMENTS										
ALL CREDITORS										
Interest (%)	5.6	11.2	6.9	6.9	2.6	5.3	7.5	7.3	9.3	8.8
Maturity (years)	27.7	13.3	15.4	17.0	7.2	11.4	13.0	4.0	10.1	14.7
Grace period (years)	6.3	5.0	4.4	5.4	1.2	3.7	3.0	4.0	10.1	13.3
Grant element (%)	33.6	-1.2	18.2	18.8	16.8	24.7	12.4	6.8	4.1	2.7
Official creditors										
Interest (%)	5.3	7.2	6.4	6.8	2.2	5.3	7.0	5.3	0.0	7.1
Maturity (years)	29.8	18.3	17.6	17.3	7.3	11.4	15.8	1.1	0.0	6.1
Grace period (years)	7.2	6.3	5.0	5.5	1.2	3.7	4.2	1.1	0.0	2.4
Grant element (%)	37.3	19.4	21.1	19.3	17.4	24.7	16.7	4.6	0.0	6.7
Private creditors										
Interest (%)	7.1	15.8	9.5	12.5	6.9	3.3	8.4	8.0	9.3	10.0
Maturity (years)	14.8	7.6	3.2	7.0	6.0	10.8	7.7	5.1	10.1	20.4
Grace period (years)	0.9	3.6	1.1	1.5	1.5	1.1	0.7	5.1	10.1	20.4
Grant element (%)	12.2	-24.4	2.2	-9.1	8.6	27.4	4.3	7.7	4.1	0.0
Memorandum items										
Commitments	58	625	230	426	25	244	241	275	300	415
Official creditors	49	330	195	417	23	242	157	75	0	165
Private creditors	8	295	36	9	2	3	84	200	300	250

10. CONTRACTUAL OBLIGATIONS ON OUTSTANDING LONG-TERM DEBT

	2001	2002	2003	2004	2005	2006	2007	2008	2009	2010
TOTAL										
Disbursements	161	124	81	55	27	5	4	3	2	1
Principal	450	337	493	265	256	233	230	208	516	168
Interest	229	213	191	168	153	138	124	110	84	59
Official creditors										
Disbursements	161	124	81	55	27	5	4	3	2	1
Principal	374	261	218	192	187	161	161	139	147	111
Interest	106	95	86	76	66	56	46	38	30	23
Bilateral creditors										
Disbursements	20	15	7	4	3	2	2	1	1	0
Principal	197	94	61	44	35	26	25	24	23	22
Interest	17	13	10	8	7	5	5	4	3	2
Multilateral creditors										
Disbursements	141	109	74	52	24	4	3	2	1	1
Principal	177	167	158	148	152	135	136	115	124	89
Interest	88	83	76	68	60	50	42	34	27	21
Private creditors										
Disbursements	0	0	0	0	0	0	0	0	0	0
Principal	76	76	275	72	70	72	69	69	369	57
Interest	124	118	105	91	87	82	77	73	54	36
Commercial banks										
Disbursements	0	0	0	0	0	0	0	0	0	0
Principal	9	9	7	4	3	3	0	0	0	0
Interest	3	2	2	1	1	0	0	0	0	0
Other private										
Disbursements	0	0	0	0	0	0	0	0	0	0
Principal	67	67	268	68	67	69	69	69	369	57
Interest	120	116	103	90	86	82	77	73	54	36

COTE D'IVOIRE

(US$ million, unless otherwise indicated)

	1970	1980	1990	1994	1995	1996	1997	1998	1999	2000
1. SUMMARY DEBT DATA										
TOTAL DEBT STOCKS (EDT)	**374**	**7,462**	**17,251**	**17,395**	**18,899**	**19,524**	**15,609**	**14,852**	**13,170**	**12,138**
Long-term debt (LDOD)	**267**	**6,339**	**13,223**	**13,852**	**14,562**	**13,216**	**12,498**	**12,632**	**11,295**	**10,546**
Public and publicly guaranteed	256	4,327	10,666	11,241	11,902	11,367	10,427	10,800	9,699	9,063
Private nonguaranteed	11	2,012	2,558	2,611	2,660	1,849	2,071	1,833	1,596	1,482
Use of IMF credit	**0**	**65**	**431**	**328**	**427**	**503**	**450**	**644**	**620**	**549**
Short-term debt	**107**	**1,059**	**3,597**	**3,215**	**3,910**	**5,805**	**2,661**	**1,576**	**1,256**	**1,043**
of which interest arrears on LDOD	0	0	819	961	1,020	953	87	9	8	79
Official creditors	0	0	66	45	34	6	78	0	0	70
Private creditors	0	0	753	915	986	947	9	9	8	8
Memo: principal arrears on LDOD	0	0	1,727	2,505	2,686	2,551	147	49	45	169
Official creditors	0	0	16	13	32	11	98	1	1	125
Private creditors	0	0	1,710	2,492	2,655	2,540	48	48	43	44
Memo: export credits	0	0	3,560	3,179	2,970	2,932	2,749	1,755	1,383	1,401
TOTAL DEBT FLOWS										
Disbursements	**82**	**1,777**	**1,172**	**1,405**	**924**	**1,014**	**236**	**613**	**247**	**148**
Long-term debt	82	1,739	1,019	1,235	743	876	236	445	247	148
IMF purchases	0	38	153	171	181	138	0	168	0	0
Principal repayments	**31**	**722**	**621**	**787**	**625**	**860**	**838**	**670**	**832**	**481**
Long-term debt	31	722	498	711	539	812	816	670	823	442
IMF repurchases	0	0	123	77	86	48	22	0	8	39
Net flows on debt	**51**	**1,257**	**1,189**	**-1,002**	**935**	**2,117**	**413**	**-1,064**	**-904**	**-617**
of which short-term debt	0	202	639	-1,620	636	1,963	1,015	-1,007	-319	-284
Interest payments (INT)	**12**	**685**	**641**	**457**	**421**	**515**	**521**	**713**	**618**	**539**
Long-term debt	12	590	443	426	390	473	413	615	544	462
IMF charges	0	0	31	11	8	5	3	3	3	3
Short-term debt	0	95	167	20	23	37	105	96	70	74
Net transfers on debt	**39**	**572**	**548**	**-1,459**	**514**	**1,602**	**-109**	**-1,778**	**-1,522**	**-1,156**
Total debt service paid (TDS)	**43**	**1,407**	**1,262**	**1,244**	**1,046**	**1,375**	**1,360**	**1,384**	**1,449**	**1,020**
Long-term debt	43	1,312	941	1,137	929	1,285	1,229	1,285	1,368	904
IMF repurchases and charges	0	0	155	87	94	53	25	3	11	42
Short-term debt (interest only)	0	95	167	20	23	37	105	96	70	74
2. AGGREGATE NET RESOURCE FLOWS AND NET TRANSFERS (LONG-TERM)										
NET RESOURCE FLOWS	**94**	**1,139**	**855**	**1,292**	**873**	**859**	**157**	**674**	**122**	**56**
Net flow of long-term debt (ex. IMF)	51	1,017	521	524	204	64	-580	-225	-577	-294
Foreign direct investment (net)	31	95	48	78	212	269	415	380	324	106
Portfolio equity flows	0	0	0	7	3	30	18	6	8	6
Grants (excluding technical coop.)	12	27	287	683	454	497	304	513	367	238
Memo: technical coop. grants	21	100	129	114	123	109	100	95	85	73
official net resource flows	46	203	798	1,247	644	452	159	548	74	103
private net resource flows	48	936	57	46	229	408	-3	126	48	-47
NET TRANSFERS	**33**	**361**	**349**	**801**	**420**	**320**	**-324**	**-16**	**-503**	**-476**
Interest on long-term debt	12	590	443	426	390	473	413	615	544	462
Profit remittances on FDI	49	188	64	65	63	66	68	75	80	70
Memo: official net transfers	41	125	611	979	392	123	-109	179	-239	-86
private net transfers	-9	235	-262	-178	28	197	-215	-195	-264	-390
3. MAJOR ECONOMIC AGGREGATES										
Gross national income (GNI)	1,413	9,680	9,209	6,892	9,005	9,930	9,870	10,690	10,288	8,615
Exports of goods & services (XGS)	..	3,640	3,561	3,537	4,526	5,182	5,192	5,390	5,410	4,549
of which workers remittances	..	0	0	0	0	0	0	0	..	..
Imports of goods & services (MGS)	..	4,761	4,594	3,435	4,782	5,002	4,966	5,287	5,145	4,193
International reserves (RES)	119	46	21	221	546	622	631	868	643	668
Current account balance	..	-1,826	-1,214	-14	-492	-162	-155	-290	-121	-13
4. DEBT INDICATORS										
EDT / XGS (%)	..	205.0	484.5	491.8	417.5	376.7	300.6	275.6	243.4	266.8
EDT / GNI (%)	26.4	77.1	187.3	252.4	209.9	196.6	158.1	138.9	128.0	140.9
TDS / XGS (%)	..	38.7	35.4	35.2	23.1	26.5	26.2	25.7	26.8	22.4
INT / XGS (%)	..	18.8	18.0	12.9	9.3	9.9	10.0	13.2	11.4	11.9
INT / GNI (%)	0.9	7.1	7.0	6.6	4.7	5.2	5.3	6.7	6.0	6.3
RES / EDT (%)	31.8	0.6	0.1	1.3	2.9	3.2	4.0	5.9	4.9	5.5
RES / MGS (months)	..	0.1	0.1	0.8	1.4	1.5	1.5	2.0	1.5	1.9
Short-term / EDT (%)	28.7	14.2	20.9	18.5	20.7	29.7	17.1	10.6	9.5	8.6
Concessional / EDT (%)	32.5	5.9	18.0	22.3	24.2	24.6	28.9	33.3	33.6	34.0
Multilateral / EDT (%)	3.8	7.0	20.8	21.4	20.6	18.8	21.2	23.5	23.9	24.4

COTE D'IVOIRE

(US$ million, unless otherwise indicated)

	1970	1980	1990	1994	1995	1996	1997	1998	1999	2000
5. LONG-TERM DEBT										
DEBT OUTSTANDING (LDOD)	**267**	**6,339**	**13,223**	**13,852**	**14,562**	**13,216**	**12,498**	**12,632**	**11,295**	**10,546**
Public and publicly guaranteed	**256**	**4,327**	**10,666**	**11,241**	**11,902**	**11,367**	**10,427**	**10,800**	**9,699**	**9,063**
Official creditors	143	1,247	7,686	8,642	9,217	8,787	7,906	8,302	7,256	6,669
Multilateral	14	523	3,585	3,715	3,900	3,665	3,301	3,491	3,148	2,958
Concessional	8	69	1,150	1,045	1,286	1,435	1,434	1,711	1,679	1,676
Bilateral	129	724	4,101	4,927	5,317	5,122	4,605	4,812	4,108	3,711
Concessional	114	369	1,946	2,837	3,277	3,371	3,070	3,233	2,739	2,450
Private creditors	112	3,080	2,980	2,599	2,685	2,580	2,521	2,497	2,443	2,394
Bonds	21	15	0	0	0	0	2,457	2,434	2,389	2,343
Commercial banks	32	1,611	2,640	2,514	2,630	2,526	16	17	15	14
Other private	59	1,454	340	85	55	54	48	46	40	37
Private nonguaranteed	**11**	**2,012**	**2,558**	**2,611**	**2,660**	**1,849**	**2,071**	**1,833**	**1,596**	**1,482**
Bonds	0	0	0	0	0	0	0	0	0	0
Commercial banks and other	11	2,012	2,558	2,611	2,660	1,849	2,071	1,833	1,596	1,482
Memo:										
IBRD	5	306	1,913	1,691	1,573	1,304	1,044	942	708	600
IDA	0	8	7	576	813	1,019	1,100	1,337	1,360	1,366
DISBURSEMENTS	**82**	**1,739**	**1,019**	**1,235**	**743**	**876**	**236**	**445**	**247**	**148**
Public and publicly guaranteed	**78**	**1,414**	**769**	**927**	**670**	**475**	**185**	**393**	**194**	**148**
Official creditors	43	231	758	918	669	465	185	389	191	148
Multilateral	12	136	460	582	340	321	181	299	111	148
Concessional	8	8	21	453	239	253	147	253	75	131
Bilateral	31	95	298	336	329	144	3	90	80	0
Concessional	25	34	283	314	309	142	3	59	66	0
Private creditors	35	1,183	11	9	1	10	0	4	3	0
Bonds	6	0	0	0	0	0	0	0	0	0
Commercial banks	7	634	2	0	1	2	0	0	0	0
Other private	22	550	9	9	0	8	0	4	3	0
Private nonguaranteed	**4**	**325**	**250**	**308**	**73**	**401**	**52**	**52**	**53**	**0**
Bonds	0	0	0	0	0	0	0	0	0	0
Commercial banks and other	4	325	250	308	73	401	52	52	53	0
Memo:										
IBRD	3	86	261	21	19	18	0	0	0	0
IDA	0	0	0	448	226	235	140	190	53	76
PRINCIPAL REPAYMENTS	**31**	**722**	**498**	**711**	**539**	**812**	**816**	**670**	**823**	**442**
Public and publicly guaranteed	**29**	**517**	**319**	**397**	**514**	**521**	**525**	**380**	**533**	**329**
Official creditors	9	55	247	355	479	510	329	354	485	283
Multilateral	0	17	230	291	286	304	264	255	238	143
Concessional	0	2	70	43	46	47	44	42	42	34
Bilateral	9	38	16	64	193	206	65	99	247	140
Concessional	6	16	5	13	19	34	24	64	174	97
Private creditors	20	462	72	42	36	11	196	26	49	46
Bonds	2	1	1	0	0	0	0	23	46	46
Commercial banks	2	301	25	5	5	5	193	0	0	0
Other private	15	161	46	37	30	6	3	3	3	0
Private nonguaranteed	**2**	**205**	**179**	**314**	**25**	**292**	**292**	**290**	**290**	**113**
Bonds	0	0	0	0	0	0	0	0	0	0
Commercial banks and other	2	205	179	314	25	292	292	290	290	113
Memo:										
IBRD	0	7	125	196	199	178	158	140	121	58
IDA	0	0	0	0	0	0	0	0	0	0
NET FLOWS ON DEBT	**51**	**1,017**	**521**	**524**	**204**	**64**	**-580**	**-225**	**-577**	**-294**
Public and publicly guaranteed	**49**	**897**	**450**	**529**	**156**	**-46**	**-340**	**13**	**-340**	**-181**
Official creditors	34	176	511	563	190	-45	-144	35	-294	-135
Multilateral	12	120	229	291	54	17	-83	44	-127	5
Concessional	8	7	-49	410	194	206	103	212	33	97
Bilateral	22	57	282	272	136	-62	-62	-9	-167	-140
Concessional	19	18	278	300	290	107	-20	-5	-108	-97
Private creditors	15	721	-62	-34	-34	-1	-196	-22	-46	-46
Bonds	4	-1	-1	0	0	0	0	-23	-46	-46
Commercial banks	5	333	-23	-5	-4	-3	-193	0	0	0
Other private	7	389	-38	-29	-30	3	-3	1	-1	0
Private nonguaranteed	**2**	**120**	**71**	**-5**	**49**	**110**	**-240**	**-238**	**-237**	**-113**
Bonds	0	0	0	0	0	0	0	0	0	0
Commercial banks and other	2	120	71	-5	49	110	-240	-238	-237	-113
Memo:										
IBRD	3	78	136	-175	-180	-160	-158	-140	-121	-58
IDA	0	0	0	448	226	235	140	190	53	75

COTE D'IVOIRE

(US$ million, unless otherwise indicated)

	1970	*1980*	*1990*	*1994*	*1995*	*1996*	*1997*	*1998*	*1999*	*2000*
INTEREST PAYMENTS (LINT)	**12**	**590**	**443**	**426**	**390**	**473**	**413**	**615**	**544**	**462**
Public and publicly guaranteed	**12**	**353**	**205**	**296**	**257**	**330**	**270**	**506**	**458**	**342**
Official creditors	4	77	187	267	252	328	269	369	313	189
Multilateral	0	32	176	228	172	213	165	140	129	78
Concessional	0	1	3	4	7	7	10	11	12	11
Bilateral	4	45	12	39	81	116	104	229	184	111
Concessional	3	13	2	28	40	69	65	134	106	47
Private creditors	7	275	18	28	5	2	1	137	146	153
Bonds	1	1	0	0	0	0	0	136	145	153
Commercial banks	3	176	7	2	1	1	0	0	0	0
Other private	4	98	12	27	3	1	1	1	1	0
Private nonguaranteed	**0**	**237**	**237**	**131**	**133**	**143**	**143**	**109**	**86**	**120**
Bonds	0	0	0	0	0	0	0	0	0	0
Commercial banks and other	0	237	237	131	133	143	143	109	86	120
Memo:										
IBRD	0	22	141	144	135	112	87	69	57	32
IDA	0	0	0	2	5	5	8	8	10	8
NET TRANSFERS ON DEBT	**39**	**427**	**78**	**98**	**-186**	**-409**	**-993**	**-840**	**-1,121**	**-756**
Public and publicly guaranteed	**38**	**544**	**245**	**234**	**-101**	**-376**	**-610**	**-493**	**-798**	**-523**
Official creditors	30	99	324	296	-62	-373	-413	-334	-606	-324
Multilateral	11	87	54	63	-117	-196	-248	-96	-256	-73
Concessional	8	6	-52	406	187	199	93	201	20	86
Bilateral	18	11	271	233	55	-178	-165	-238	-350	-251
Concessional	15	5	276	272	250	38	-85	-139	-214	-144
Private creditors	8	446	-80	-62	-39	-2	-197	-159	-192	-198
Bonds	3	-2	-1	0	0	0	0	-159	-190	-198
Commercial banks	2	156	-30	-7	-5	-4	-193	0	0	0
Other private	3	291	-49	-55	-34	2	-4	0	-2	0
Private nonguaranteed	**2**	**-117**	**-167**	**-136**	**-84**	**-34**	**-383**	**-347**	**-323**	**-233**
Bonds	0	0	0	0	0	0	0	0	0	0
Commercial banks and other	2	-117	-167	-136	-84	-34	-383	-347	-323	-233
Memo:										
IBRD	3	56	-5	-319	-315	-271	-245	-209	-178	-90
IDA	0	0	0	446	222	230	132	181	43	68
DEBT SERVICE (LTDS)	**43**	**1,312**	**941**	**1,137**	**929**	**1,285**	**1,229**	**1,285**	**1,368**	**904**
Public and publicly guaranteed	**40**	**870**	**524**	**693**	**771**	**850**	**794**	**886**	**992**	**671**
Official creditors	13	133	434	622	731	838	598	723	797	472
Multilateral	1	49	406	519	457	516	429	394	367	221
Concessional	0	3	73	47	53	54	54	52	55	45
Bilateral	13	84	28	103	274	322	168	328	430	251
Concessional	9	29	7	41	59	104	88	198	280	144
Private creditors	27	738	90	71	40	12	197	163	195	198
Bonds	3	2	1	0	0	0	0	159	190	198
Commercial banks	5	477	32	7	7	6	193	0	0	0
Other private	19	259	58	64	34	7	4	5	4	0
Private nonguaranteed	**2**	**442**	**417**	**444**	**158**	**435**	**435**	**399**	**376**	**233**
Bonds	0	0	0	0	0	0	0	0	0	0
Commercial banks and other	2	442	417	444	158	435	435	399	376	233
Memo:										
IBRD	0	29	266	340	334	289	245	209	178	90
IDA	0	0	0	2	5	5	8	9	10	8
UNDISBURSED DEBT	**169**	**1,723**	**1,221**	**909**	**901**	**909**	**892**	**888**	**687**	**456**
Official creditors	108	747	1,122	898	892	907	885	884	686	456
Private creditors	61	976	99	11	9	3	8	4	1	0
Memorandum items										
Concessional LDOD	121	438	3,096	3,883	4,563	4,806	4,503	4,943	4,418	4,126
Variable rate LDOD	34	3,601	7,400	7,808	7,940	6,742	6,598	6,043	5,418	5,054
Public sector LDOD	255	4,277	10,663	11,240	11,901	11,365	10,427	10,800	9,699	9,063
Private sector LDOD	11	2,061	2,560	2,613	2,661	1,850	2,071	1,833	1,596	1,482

6. CURRENCY COMPOSITION OF LONG-TERM DEBT (PERCENT)

	1970	*1980*	*1990*	*1994*	*1995*	*1996*	*1997*	*1998*	*1999*	*2000*
Deutsche mark	10.5	4.5	3.9	4.1	4.4	4.2	3.5	3.5	3.1	2.9
French franc	47.7	34.6	38.1	38.8	39.1	38.9	27.1	27.9	25.9	25.0
Japanese yen	0.0	0.6	0.9	1.5	1.4	1.3	1.1	1.2	1.5	1.4
Pound sterling	0.0	1.4	1.3	1.0	0.9	0.9	0.8	0.7	0.6	0.6
Swiss franc	0.0	6.3	2.3	0.4	0.5	0.4	0.2	0.2	0.2	0.2
U.S.dollars	25.4	31.5	15.5	21.0	22.0	25.1	40.9	49.4	52.0	53.7
Multiple currency	2.1	9.9	22.7	22.3	20.1	18.1	16.3	6.4	6.4	6.1
Special drawing rights	0.0	0.0	0.4	0.6	0.6	0.6	0.2	0.3	0.3	0.4
All other currencies	14.3	11.2	14.9	10.3	11.0	10.5	9.9	10.4	10.0	9.7

COTE D'IVOIRE

(US$ million, unless otherwise indicated)

	1970	1980	1990	1994	1995	1996	1997	1998	1999	2000
7. DEBT RESTRUCTURINGS										
Total amount rescheduled	..	..	930	645	381	315	2,612	319	67	72
Debt stock rescheduled	..	..	0	0	0	0	0	0	0	0
Principal rescheduled	..	..	590	266	192	139	138	265	34	45
Official	..	..	407	257	189	137	58	264	33	44
Private	..	..	183	9	4	3	80	1	0	0
Interest rescheduled	..	..	287	306	131	106	875	54	30	25
Official	..	..	257	302	129	105	8	53	30	24
Private	..	..	29	4	1	1	867	0	0	0
Debt forgiven	..	..	50	1,352	292	8	0	103	16	22
Memo: interest forgiven	..	..	0	228	30	2	0	20	8	7
Debt stock reduction	..	..	0	0	0	0	4,053	0	0	0
of which debt buyback	..	..	0	0	0	0	163	0	0	0
8. DEBT STOCK-FLOW RECONCILIATION										
Total change in debt stocks	..	..	2,431	-1,676	1,503	625	-3,915	-757	-1,682	-1,032
Net flows on debt	51	1,257	1,189	-1,002	935	2,117	413	-1,064	-904	-617
Net change in interest arrears	..	..	62	-290	59	-67	-866	-78	-1	71
Interest capitalized	..	..	287	306	131	106	875	54	30	25
Debt forgiveness or reduction	..	..	-50	-1,352	-292	-8	-3,890	-103	-16	-22
Cross-currency valuation	..	..	829	298	17	-1,232	-1,715	-327	-761	-446
Residual	..	..	115	365	654	-291	1,269	762	-30	-43
9. AVERAGE TERMS OF NEW COMMITMENTS										
ALL CREDITORS										
Interest (%)	5.8	11.4	5.9	2.1	1.9	1.9	1.7	0.5	0.8	0.8
Maturity (years)	18.6	10.3	20.0	29.8	29.8	31.4	30.2	40.5	48.4	46.2
Grace period (years)	5.4	4.5	6.3	8.6	8.5	8.8	8.4	10.0	10.4	9.6
Grant element (%)	26.1	-5.6	27.5	64.0	63.7	65.2	65.8	82.7	82.9	81.7
Official creditors										
Interest (%)	4.9	6.2	5.9	2.0	1.9	1.8	1.6	0.5	0.8	0.8
Maturity (years)	22.5	18.8	20.0	29.9	29.8	32.0	30.9	40.5	48.4	46.2
Grace period (years)	7.4	5.7	6.3	8.6	8.5	8.9	8.6	10.0	10.4	9.6
Grant element (%)	35.3	25.4	27.5	64.6	63.9	66.4	67.3	82.7	82.9	81.7
Private creditors										
Interest (%)	7.4	11.9	0.0	11.4	14.5	6.0	5.8	0.0	0.0	0.0
Maturity (years)	12.1	9.5	0.0	12.0	19.6	5.4	6.2	0.0	0.0	0.0
Grace period (years)	2.1	4.4	0.0	2.5	0.1	0.9	0.6	0.0	0.0	0.0
Grant element (%)	10.9	-8.5	0.0	-7.8	-27.0	8.7	10.7	0.0	0.0	0.0
Memorandum items										
Commitments	71	1,688	764	907	716	538	241	359	32	72
Official creditors	44	144	764	900	715	526	235	359	32	72
Private creditors	27	1,544	0	7	1	12	6	0	0	0

10. CONTRACTUAL OBLIGATIONS ON OUTSTANDING LONG-TERM DEBT

	2001	2002	2003	2004	2005	2006	2007	2008	2009	2010
TOTAL										
Disbursements	171	128	84	47	17	5	4	1	0	0
Principal	676	714	702	696	554	531	632	600	572	528
Interest	562	578	543	508	475	448	421	390	360	333
Official creditors										
Disbursements	171	128	84	47	17	5	4	1	0	0
Principal	514	553	542	537	395	372	329	297	269	225
Interest	290	309	277	246	216	192	170	151	134	119
Bilateral creditors										
Disbursements	0	0	0	0	0	0	0	0	0	0
Principal	317	351	345	345	219	206	182	158	147	136
Interest	184	214	193	173	154	142	129	119	109	100
Multilateral creditors										
Disbursements	171	128	84	47	17	5	4	1	0	0
Principal	197	202	197	192	176	167	147	138	122	89
Interest	106	96	85	73	61	50	40	32	25	19
Private creditors										
Disbursements	0	0	0	0	0	0	0	0	0	0
Principal	162	161	160	159	159	159	303	303	303	303
Interest	272	269	266	263	259	256	251	239	227	214
Commercial banks										
Disbursements	0	0	0	0	0	0	0	0	0	0
Principal	0	0	0	0	0	0	0	0	0	0
Interest	0	0	0	0	0	0	0	0	0	0
Other private										
Disbursements	0	0	0	0	0	0	0	0	0	0
Principal	162	161	160	159	159	159	303	303	303	303
Interest	272	269	266	263	259	256	251	239	227	214

CROATIA

(US$ million, unless otherwise indicated)

1. SUMMARY DEBT DATA

	1970	1980	1990	1994	1995	1996	1997	1998	1999	2000
TOTAL DEBT STOCKS (EDT)	..	..	..	**2,054**	**3,829**	**6,410**	**8,353**	**10,630**	**11,027**	**12,120**
Long-term debt (LDOD)	..	..	..	**1,685**	**3,117**	**5,769**	**7,553**	**9,747**	**10,139**	**11,264**
Public and publicly guaranteed	..	..	..	643	1,860	4,811	5,729	6,389	6,882	7,686
Private nonguaranteed	..	..	..	1,042	1,257	958	1,824	3,359	3,257	3,578
Use of IMF credit	..	..	..	**127**	**221**	**209**	**233**	**234**	**197**	**158**
Short-term debt	..	..	..	**242**	**492**	**432**	**568**	**649**	**692**	**698**
of which interest arrears on LDOD	..	..	..	70	71	21	29	45	53	47
Official creditors	..	..	..	2	1	1	0	3	7	3
Private creditors	..	..	..	68	70	20	29	41	46	45
Memo: principal arrears on LDOD	..	..	..	619	547	133	180	212	231	209
Official creditors	..	..	..	128	1	1	0	16	0	1
Private creditors	..	..	..	491	546	132	180	196	231	208
Memo: export credits	..	..	..	396	609	666	1,138	779	988	558
TOTAL DEBT FLOWS										
Disbursements	..	..	..	**331**	**618**	**960**	**2,945**	**1,794**	**2,238**	**3,282**
Long-term debt	..	..	..	219	518	960	2,905	1,794	2,238	3,282
IMF purchases	..	..	..	112	99	0	40	0	0	0
Principal repayments	..	..	..	**155**	**240**	**421**	**794**	**1,398**	**1,259**	**1,753**
Long-term debt	..	..	..	146	234	417	792	1,389	1,227	1,724
IMF repurchases	..	..	..	9	6	5	2	9	31	29
Net flows on debt	..	..	..	**293**	**627**	**529**	**2,278**	**462**	**1,014**	**1,540**
of which short-term debt	..	..	..	117	249	-10	127	66	35	11
Interest payments (INT)	..	..	..	**86**	**126**	**109**	**530**	**571**	**635**	**684**
Long-term debt	..	..	..	78	98	83	501	527	593	641
IMF charges	..	..	..	1	10	10	10	11	9	9
Short-term debt	..	..	..	7	18	16	19	34	34	34
Net transfers on debt	..	..	..	**208**	**501**	**420**	**1,748**	**-109**	**380**	**855**
Total debt service paid (TDS)	..	..	..	**241**	**365**	**530**	**1,324**	**1,969**	**1,893**	**2,437**
Long-term debt	..	..	..	224	332	500	1,293	1,915	1,820	2,365
IMF repurchases and charges	..	..	..	10	16	14	12	20	40	38
Short-term debt (interest only)	..	..	..	7	18	16	19	34	34	34

2. AGGREGATE NET RESOURCE FLOWS AND NET TRANSFERS (LONG-TERM)

	1970	1980	1990	1994	1995	1996	1997	1998	1999	2000
NET RESOURCE FLOWS	..	..	..	**284**	**430**	**1,185**	**2,681**	**1,578**	**2,518**	**2,529**
Net flow of long-term debt (ex. IMF)	..	..	..	72	285	543	2,113	405	1,011	1,557
Foreign direct investment (net)	..	..	..	117	115	506	530	932	1,479	926
Portfolio equity flows	..	..	..	0	0	111	0	205	0	0
Grants (excluding technical coop.)	..	..	..	95	31	25	39	36	28	46
Memo: technical coop. grants	..	..	..	8	21	29	18	23	32	31
official net resource flows	..	..	..	69	50	24	177	83	66	78
private net resource flows	..	..	..	215	380	1,162	2,504	1,495	2,452	2,451
NET TRANSFERS	..	..	..	**206**	**332**	**1,102**	**2,180**	**1,051**	**1,889**	**1,846**
Interest on long-term debt	..	..	..	78	98	83	501	527	593	641
Profit remittances on FDI	..	..	..	0	0	0	0	0	36	42
Memo: official net transfers	..	..	..	35	24	-10	75	-8	-23	-2
private net transfers	..	..	..	172	309	1,112	2,106	1,060	1,913	1,848

3. MAJOR ECONOMIC AGGREGATES

	1970	1980	1990	1994	1995	1996	1997	1998	1999	2000
Gross national income (GNI)	..	..	..	14,418	18,782	19,802	20,271	21,464	19,714	18,721
Exports of goods & services (XGS)	..	..	..	7,607	7,812	8,716	9,102	9,484	8,824	9,551
of which workers remittances	..	..	..	340	506	603	524	520	454	531
Imports of goods & services (MGS)	..	..	..	6,939	9,550	10,226	11,773	11,200	10,393	10,277
International reserves (RES)	..	..	..	1,405	1,896	2,314	2,539	2,816	3,025	3,524
Current account balance	..	..	..	854	-1,442	-1,091	-2,325	-1,531	-1,390	-399

4. DEBT INDICATORS

	1970	1980	1990	1994	1995	1996	1997	1998	1999	2000
EDT / XGS (%)	..	..	..	27.0	49.0	73.6	91.8	112.1	125.0	126.9
EDT / GNI (%)	..	..	..	14.3	20.4	32.4	41.2	49.5	55.9	64.7
TDS / XGS (%)	..	..	..	3.2	4.7	6.1	14.6	20.8	21.5	25.5
INT / XGS (%)	..	..	..	1.1	1.6	1.3	5.8	6.0	7.2	7.2
INT / GNI (%)	..	..	..	0.6	0.7	0.6	2.6	2.7	3.2	3.7
RES / EDT (%)	..	..	..	68.4	49.5	36.1	30.4	26.5	27.4	29.1
RES / MGS (months)	..	..	..	2.4	2.4	2.7	2.6	3.0	3.5	4.1
Short-term / EDT (%)	..	..	..	11.8	12.8	6.7	6.8	6.1	6.3	5.8
Concessional / EDT (%)	..	..	..	1.5	8.9	4.9	3.5	3.1	2.8	2.5
Multilateral / EDT (%)	..	..	..	13.5	7.9	5.9	5.8	5.8	5.4	4.9

CROATIA

(US$ million, unless otherwise indicated)

	1970	1980	1990	1994	1995	1996	1997	1998	1999	2000
5. LONG-TERM DEBT										
DEBT OUTSTANDING (LDOD)	..	..	..	**1,685**	**3,117**	**5,769**	**7,553**	**9,747**	**10,139**	**11,264**
Public and publicly guaranteed	..	..	..	**643**	**1,860**	**4,811**	**5,729**	**6,389**	**6,882**	**7,686**
Official creditors	..	..	..	532	1,621	1,542	1,552	1,633	1,501	1,458
Multilateral	..	..	..	278	304	375	481	612	597	599
Concessional	..	..	..	21	11	9	22	47	63	70
Bilateral	..	..	..	255	1,317	1,167	1,071	1,021	904	860
Concessional	..	..	..	9	330	306	269	278	247	227
Private creditors	..	..	..	111	240	3,270	4,177	4,756	5,381	6,227
Bonds	..	..	..	0	0	64	534	644	1,142	1,884
Commercial banks	..	..	..	47	135	3,078	3,297	3,852	4,064	4,181
Other private	..	..	..	64	104	127	346	259	175	162
Private nonguaranteed	..	..	..	**1,042**	**1,257**	**958**	**1,824**	**3,359**	**3,257**	**3,578**
Bonds	..	..	..	0	0	0	0	0	0	0
Commercial banks and other	..	..	..	1,042	1,257	958	1,824	3,359	3,257	3,578
Memo:										
IBRD	..	..	..	84	117	195	276	336	387	395
IDA	..	..	..	0	0	0	0	0	0	0
DISBURSEMENTS	..	..	..	**219**	**518**	**960**	**2,905**	**1,794**	**2,238**	**3,282**
Public and publicly guaranteed	..	..	..	**51**	**203**	**403**	**1,517**	**1,114**	**1,213**	**1,853**
Official creditors	..	..	..	27	72	141	284	222	164	186
Multilateral	..	..	..	2	60	134	182	200	130	85
Concessional	..	..	..	0	0	0	14	29	23	9
Bilateral	..	..	..	25	12	8	101	22	34	101
Concessional	..	..	..	9	6	0	2	12	10	5
Private creditors	..	..	..	24	131	262	1,234	892	1,049	1,667
Bonds	..	..	..	0	0	67	531	101	539	833
Commercial banks	..	..	..	0	100	135	326	751	410	802
Other private	..	..	..	24	31	60	378	40	100	32
Private nonguaranteed	..	..	..	**168**	**316**	**557**	**1,388**	**680**	**1,025**	**1,429**
Bonds	..	..	..	0	0	0	0	0	0	0
Commercial banks and other	..	..	..	168	316	557	1,388	680	1,025	1,429
Memo:										
IBRD	..	..	..	1	50	105	115	108	87	55
IDA	..	..	..	0	0	0	0	0	0	0
PRINCIPAL REPAYMENTS	..	..	..	**146**	**234**	**417**	**792**	**1,389**	**1,227**	**1,724**
Public and publicly guaranteed	..	..	..	**67**	**73**	**283**	**411**	**557**	**401**	**821**
Official creditors	..	..	..	53	52	143	145	175	126	154
Multilateral	..	..	..	53	52	40	36	51	51	47
Concessional	..	..	..	2	12	1	0	6	0	0
Bilateral	..	..	..	0	0	103	109	124	75	107
Concessional	..	..	..	0	0	8	16	13	15	15
Private creditors	..	..	..	14	21	140	266	383	276	668
Bonds	..	..	..	0	0	0	46	11	0	0
Commercial banks	..	..	..	0	0	112	81	229	234	631
Other private	..	..	..	14	21	28	139	142	41	37
Private nonguaranteed	..	..	..	**79**	**161**	**134**	**381**	**831**	**826**	**903**
Bonds	..	..	..	0	0	0	0	0	0	0
Commercial banks and other	..	..	..	79	161	134	381	831	826	903
Memo:										
IBRD	..	..	..	29	20	16	14	17	21	22
IDA	..	..	..	0	0	0	0	0	0	0
NET FLOWS ON DEBT	..	..	..	**72**	**285**	**543**	**2,113**	**405**	**1,011**	**1,557**
Public and publicly guaranteed	..	..	..	**-17**	**130**	**120**	**1,106**	**557**	**812**	**1,032**
Official creditors	..	..	..	-26	20	-2	138	48	38	32
Multilateral	..	..	..	-51	8	93	146	149	79	39
Concessional	..	..	..	-2	-12	-1	13	23	23	9
Bilateral	..	..	..	25	12	-95	-8	-102	-41	-6
Concessional	..	..	..	9	6	-8	-14	-1	-5	-10
Private creditors	..	..	..	10	111	122	968	509	774	999
Bonds	..	..	..	0	0	67	485	89	539	833
Commercial banks	..	..	..	0	100	23	245	522	176	171
Other private	..	..	..	10	11	32	239	-102	58	-5
Private nonguaranteed	..	..	..	**89**	**154**	**423**	**1,007**	**-152**	**199**	**526**
Bonds	..	..	..	0	0	0	0	0	0	0
Commercial banks and other	..	..	..	89	154	423	1,007	-152	199	526
Memo:										
IBRD	..	..	..	-28	29	89	100	92	67	34
IDA	..	..	..	0	0	0	0	0	0	0

CROATIA

(US$ million, unless otherwise indicated)

	1970	1980	1990	1994	1995	1996	1997	1998	1999	2000
INTEREST PAYMENTS (LINT)	..	..	..	**78**	**98**	**83**	**501**	**527**	**593**	**641**
Public and publicly guaranteed	..	..	..	**43**	**32**	**47**	**425**	**372**	**446**	**485**
Official creditors	..	..	..	34	27	34	102	92	90	80
Multilateral	..	..	..	25	25	26	31	32	35	32
Concessional	..	..	..	1	1	1	1	1	2	2
Bilateral	..	..	..	9	2	8	71	60	55	48
Concessional	..	..	..	0	0	1	11	9	10	9
Private creditors	..	..	..	9	5	13	322	280	356	405
Bonds	..	..	..	0	0	1	14	35	40	68
Commercial banks	..	..	..	4	0	8	288	221	310	323
Other private	..	..	..	4	5	4	20	24	6	15
Private nonguaranteed	..	..	..	**35**	**66**	**37**	**76**	**155**	**147**	**156**
Bonds	..	..	..	0	0	0	0	0	0	0
Commercial banks and other	..	..	..	35	66	37	76	155	147	156
Memo:										
IBRD	..	..	..	8	7	11	15	17	20	19
IDA	..	..	..	0	0	0	0	0	0	0
NET TRANSFERS ON DEBT	..	..	..	**-5**	**186**	**460**	**1,612**	**-122**	**418**	**916**
Public and publicly guaranteed	..	..	..	**-59**	**98**	**73**	**682**	**186**	**366**	**546**
Official creditors	..	..	..	-60	-7	-35	36	-44	-52	-48
Multilateral	..	..	..	-76	-17	67	115	117	44	7
Concessional	..	..	..	-3	-14	-1	12	22	21	7
Bilateral	..	..	..	16	10	-103	-79	-161	-96	-55
Concessional	..	..	..	9	6	-9	-25	-11	-15	-19
Private creditors	..	..	..	1	105	109	646	230	417	594
Bonds	..	..	..	0	0	65	470	55	499	766
Commercial banks	..	..	..	-4	100	16	-43	301	-134	-152
Other private	..	..	..	5	5	28	218	-126	52	-19
Private nonguaranteed	..	..	..	**54**	**88**	**386**	**931**	**-307**	**53**	**370**
Bonds	..	..	..	0	0	0	0	0	0	0
Commercial banks and other	..	..	..	54	88	386	931	-307	53	370
Memo:										
IBRD	..	..	..	-36	22	78	86	75	47	14
IDA	..	..	..	0	0	0	0	0	0	0
DEBT SERVICE (LTDS)	..	..	..	**224**	**332**	**500**	**1,293**	**1,915**	**1,820**	**2,365**
Public and publicly guaranteed	..	..	..	**110**	**105**	**330**	**836**	**929**	**847**	**1,307**
Official creditors	..	..	..	87	79	177	248	266	215	234
Multilateral	..	..	..	78	77	66	67	83	85	79
Concessional	..	..	..	3	14	1	2	7	2	2
Bilateral	..	..	..	9	2	111	181	184	130	155
Concessional	..	..	..	0	0	9	27	23	25	24
Private creditors	..	..	..	23	26	153	588	662	632	1,073
Bonds	..	..	..	0	0	1	60	46	40	68
Commercial banks	..	..	..	4	0	120	368	450	544	954
Other private	..	..	..	19	26	32	159	166	48	51
Private nonguaranteed	..	..	..	**114**	**227**	**171**	**457**	**987**	**973**	**1,059**
Bonds	..	..	..	0	0	0	0	0	0	0
Commercial banks and other	..	..	..	114	227	171	457	987	973	1,059
Memo:										
IBRD	..	..	..	37	28	26	29	34	41	41
IDA	..	..	..	0	0	0	0	0	0	0
UNDISBURSED DEBT	..	..	..	**223**	**432**	**883**	**646**	**886**	**1,228**	**707**
Official creditors	..	..	..	161	307	433	429	453	764	429
Private creditors	..	..	..	62	126	451	217	433	463	278
Memorandum items										
Concessional LDOD	..	..	..	30	340	315	290	326	309	297
Variable rate LDOD	..	..	..	1,303	2,030	4,871	5,942	7,828	7,955	7,981
Public sector LDOD	..	..	..	613	1,275	4,294	5,251	5,751	6,147	6,981
Private sector LDOD	..	..	..	1,073	1,842	1,475	2,302	3,997	3,991	4,283

6. CURRENCY COMPOSITION OF LONG-TERM DEBT (PERCENT)

	1970	1980	1990	1994	1995	1996	1997	1998	1999	2000
Deutsche mark	..	..	..	7.3	22.0	11.9	14.7	17.0	16.8	13.4
French franc	..	..	..	2.5	7.2	2.3	1.6	1.3	1.0	0.8
Japanese yen	..	..	..	1.0	3.7	1.2	0.6	0.4	3.9	7.6
Pound sterling	..	..	..	0.5	3.3	1.3	1.0	0.8	0.7	0.5
Swiss franc	..	..	..	2.8	2.7	1.0	1.0	1.2	1.3	1.5
U.S.dollars	..	..	..	25.3	30.2	70.0	66.7	63.7	59.4	47.3
Multiple currency	..	..	..	13.0	6.3	4.0	3.9	3.8	3.9	3.3
Special drawing rights	..	..	..	0.0	0.0	0.0	0.0	0.0	0.0	0.0
All other currencies	..	..	..	47.6	24.6	8.3	10.5	11.8	13.0	25.6

CROATIA

(US$ million, unless otherwise indicated)

	1970	1980	1990	1994	1995	1996	1997	1998	1999	2000
7. DEBT RESTRUCTURINGS										
Total amount rescheduled	..	..	..	16	1,065	2,924	0	16	0	0
Debt stock rescheduled	..	..	..	0	0	975	0	0	0	0
Principal rescheduled	..	..	..	13	781	0	0	0	0	0
Official	..	..	..	0	719	0	0	0	0	0
Private	..	..	..	13	62	0	0	0	0	0
Interest rescheduled	..	..	..	3	70	51	0	0	0	0
Official	..	..	..	0	43	0	0	0	0	0
Private	..	..	..	3	27	51	0	0	0	0
Debt forgiven	..	..	..	0	0	0	0	0	0	0
Memo: interest forgiven	..	..	..	0	0	0	0	0	0	0
Debt stock reduction	..	..	..	0	0	0	0	0	0	0
of which debt buyback	..	..	..	0	0	0	0	0	0	0
8. DEBT STOCK-FLOW RECONCILIATION										
Total change in debt stocks	..	..	..	440	1,775	2,581	1,944	2,277	397	1,093
Net flows on debt	..	..	..	293	627	529	2,278	462	1,014	1,540
Net change in interest arrears	..	..	..	18	1	-50	8	16	8	-5
Interest capitalized	..	..	..	3	70	51	0	0	0	0
Debt forgiveness or reduction	..	..	..	0	0	0	0	0	0	0
Cross-currency valuation	..	..	..	34	29	-97	-184	130	-272	-208
Residual	..	..	..	93	1,048	2,148	-159	1,669	-354	-234
9. AVERAGE TERMS OF NEW COMMITMENTS										
ALL CREDITORS										
Interest (%)	..	..	..	7.0	4.7	7.0	6.3	6.0	6.3	6.0
Maturity (years)	..	..	..	13.5	8.5	6.5	6.8	13.8	8.0	6.3
Grace period (years)	..	..	..	4.5	3.0	2.4	4.2	2.7	3.7	5.2
Grant element (%)	..	..	..	16.0	14.1	10.9	14.6	13.7	13.9	17.3
Official creditors										
Interest (%)	..	..	..	7.0	6.0	5.5	5.6	3.6	5.9	6.0
Maturity (years)	..	..	..	16.4	12.8	13.8	11.6	13.6	11.2	11.8
Grace period (years)	..	..	..	4.2	3.6	5.0	4.0	5.4	4.0	5.7
Grant element (%)	..	..	..	17.0	17.5	26.1	22.1	36.5	16.2	21.1
Private creditors										
Interest (%)	..	..	..	6.9	3.1	7.7	6.6	6.4	6.4	6.0
Maturity (years)	..	..	..	6.3	3.5	3.0	5.3	13.8	7.1	6.2
Grace period (years)	..	..	..	5.2	2.4	1.2	4.2	2.2	3.6	5.2
Grant element (%)	..	..	..	13.4	10.1	3.6	12.3	9.8	13.3	17.2
Memorandum items										
Commitments	..	..	..	213	405	873	1,363	1,277	1,670	1,557
Official creditors	..	..	..	151	217	282	321	189	354	54
Private creditors	..	..	..	62	189	591	1,042	1,088	1,317	1,504

10. CONTRACTUAL OBLIGATIONS ON OUTSTANDING LONG-TERM DEBT

	2001	2002	2003	2004	2005	2006	2007	2008	2009	2010
TOTAL										
Disbursements	318	186	92	46	28	15	11	8	2	1
Principal	1,853	1,741	1,309	1,336	1,795	1,108	997	507	472	400
Interest	723	619	532	443	357	236	158	99	62	38
Official creditors										
Disbursements	161	103	64	38	27	15	11	8	2	1
Principal	152	153	166	185	167	191	206	194	198	81
Interest	86	85	79	71	63	54	43	32	21	12
Bilateral creditors										
Disbursements	43	29	15	6	2	0	0	0	0	0
Principal	84	89	98	99	91	100	108	107	117	11
Interest	51	48	43	38	32	26	20	13	7	1
Multilateral creditors										
Disbursements	118	73	49	32	26	14	10	8	2	1
Principal	67	64	68	85	76	91	97	87	81	70
Interest	36	37	36	34	31	28	23	19	15	10
Private creditors										
Disbursements	157	84	28	8	1	0	0	0	0	0
Principal	1,701	1,587	1,143	1,152	1,628	916	791	313	275	319
Interest	636	533	453	372	294	183	115	67	41	26
Commercial banks										
Disbursements	128	62	19	6	0	0	0	0	0	0
Principal	706	630	461	450	861	384	234	231	225	164
Interest	335	288	245	212	173	107	77	55	33	12
Other private										
Disbursements	30	21	8	2	1	0	0	0	0	0
Principal	995	958	682	701	767	532	558	82	49	154
Interest	301	245	207	160	121	75	38	12	8	14

CZECH REPUBLIC

(US$ million, unless otherwise indicated)

	1970	1980	1990	1994	1995	1996	1997	1998	1999	2000
1. SUMMARY DEBT DATA										
TOTAL DEBT STOCKS (EDT)	..	..	**6,383**	**10,681**	**16,218**	**20,066**	**23,577**	**24,184**	**22,653**	**21,299**
Long-term debt (LDOD)	..	..	**3,983**	**7,792**	**11,148**	**14,346**	**15,009**	**16,568**	**14,266**	**12,282**
Public and publicly guaranteed	..	..	3,983	7,024	9,688	12,218	12,837	12,557	9,912	8,132
Private nonguaranteed	..	..	0	768	1,460	2,128	2,172	4,011	4,354	4,151
Use of IMF credit	**0**	**0**	**0**	**0**	**0**	**0**	**0**	**0**	**0**	**0**
Short-term debt	..	..	**2,400**	**2,889**	**5,070**	**5,720**	**8,568**	**7,615**	**8,387**	**9,017**
of which interest arrears on LDOD	..	..	0	1	28	14	8	11	40	58
Official creditors	..	..	0	1	0	0	0	0	0	0
Private creditors	..	..	0	0	28	14	8	11	40	58
Memo: principal arrears on LDOD	..	..	0	0	105	149	122	48	98	128
Official creditors	..	..	0	0	0	0	0	0	0	0
Private creditors	..	..	0	0	105	149	122	48	98	128
Memo: export credits	..	..	0	1,460	1,909	1,409	1,010	1,174	975	476
TOTAL DEBT FLOWS										
Disbursements	..	..	**1,182**	**1,582**	**4,311**	**5,109**	**4,143**	**5,278**	**2,873**	**1,523**
Long-term debt	..	..	1,182	1,582	4,311	5,109	4,143	5,278	2,873	1,523
IMF purchases	0	0	0	0	0	0	0	0	0	0
Principal repayments	..	..	**537**	**2,009**	**1,667**	**1,664**	**3,331**	**3,558**	**4,246**	**3,376**
Long-term debt	..	..	537	891	1,667	1,664	3,331	3,558	4,246	3,376
IMF repurchases	0	0	0	1,118	0	0	0	0	0	0
Net flows on debt	..	..	**52**	**459**	**4,798**	**4,109**	**3,666**	**764**	**-629**	**-1,241**
of which short-term debt	..	..	-593	886	2,154	664	2,854	-956	743	612
Interest payments (INT)	..	..	**497**	**513**	**744**	**955**	**1,129**	**1,555**	**1,578**	**1,397**
Long-term debt	..	..	196	332	506	768	920	1,134	1,158	1,019
IMF charges	0	0	0	34	0	0	0	0	0	0
Short-term debt	..	..	301	147	238	187	209	421	420	378
Net transfers on debt	..	..	**-446**	**-53**	**4,054**	**3,154**	**2,537**	**-791**	**-2,207**	**-2,638**
Total debt service paid (TDS)	..	..	**1,035**	**2,522**	**2,411**	**2,619**	**4,460**	**5,112**	**5,823**	**4,774**
Long-term debt	..	..	734	1,223	2,173	2,432	4,251	4,692	5,404	4,396
IMF repurchases and charges	0	0	0	1,152	0	0	0	0	0	0
Short-term debt (interest only)	..	..	301	147	238	187	209	421	420	378
2. AGGREGATE NET RESOURCE FLOWS AND NET TRANSFERS (LONG-TERM)										
NET RESOURCE FLOWS	..	..	**862**	**1,786**	**5,340**	**5,115**	**2,192**	**5,605**	**5,562**	**3,441**
Net flow of long-term debt (ex. IMF)	..	..	645	691	2,644	3,445	812	1,720	-1,372	-1,853
Foreign direct investment (net)	..	..	207	878	2,568	1,435	1,286	3,700	6,313	4,583
Portfolio equity flows	..	..	0	114	82	164	16	129	500	617
Grants (excluding technical coop.)	..	..	11	103	46	70	78	56	122	94
Memo: technical coop. grants	..	..	0	39	97	58	38	40	27	20
official net resource flows	..	..	-14	145	92	198	-4	38	106	142
private net resource flows	..	..	876	1,641	5,248	4,917	2,196	5,567	5,457	3,299
NET TRANSFERS	..	..	**666**	**1,324**	**4,694**	**4,182**	**1,072**	**4,071**	**3,910**	**1,822**
Interest on long-term debt	..	..	196	332	506	768	920	1,134	1,158	1,019
Profit remittances on FDI	..	..	0	130	140	165	200	400	495	600
Memo: official net transfers	..	..	-38	64	6	119	-76	-28	41	81
private net transfers	..	..	704	1,261	4,688	4,063	1,148	4,099	3,868	1,741
3. MAJOR ECONOMIC AGGREGATES										
Gross national income (GNI)	..	..	..	41,071	51,931	57,003	52,206	55,926	53,857	50,013
Exports of goods & services (XGS)	..	..	..	21,922	29,399	31,044	31,274	35,336	34,832	37,561
of which workers remittances	..	..	..	..	..	..	..	..	..	..
Imports of goods & services (MGS)	..	..	..	22,869	31,345	35,727	34,910	37,131	36,911	40,095
International reserves (RES)	..	..	..	6,949	14,613	13,085	10,036	12,625	12,936	13,142
Current account balance	..	..	..	-820	-1,374	-4,299	-3,271	-1,387	-1,570	-2,236
4. DEBT INDICATORS										
EDT / XGS (%)	..	..	..	48.7	55.2	64.6	75.4	68.4	65.0	56.7
EDT / GNI (%)	..	..	..	26.0	31.2	35.2	45.2	43.2	42.1	42.6
TDS / XGS (%)	..	..	..	11.5	8.2	8.4	14.3	14.5	16.7	12.7
INT / XGS (%)	..	..	..	2.3	2.5	3.1	3.6	4.4	4.5	3.7
INT / GNI (%)	..	..	..	1.3	1.4	1.7	2.2	2.8	2.9	2.8
RES / EDT (%)	..	..	..	65.1	90.1	65.2	42.6	52.2	57.1	61.7
RES / MGS (months)	..	..	..	3.7	5.6	4.4	3.5	4.1	4.2	3.9
Short-term / EDT (%)	..	..	37.6	27.1	31.3	28.5	36.3	31.5	37.0	42.3
Concessional / EDT (%)	..	..	0.0	0.5	0.5	0.6	0.5	0.7	0.8	1.0
Multilateral / EDT (%)	..	..	2.8	7.2	5.2	4.6	3.3	3.3	3.2	3.3

CZECH REPUBLIC

(US$ million, unless otherwise indicated)

	1970	1980	1990	1994	1995	1996	1997	1998	1999	2000
5. LONG-TERM DEBT										
DEBT OUTSTANDING (LDOD)	..	..	**3,983**	**7,792**	**11,148**	**14,346**	**15,009**	**16,568**	**14,266**	**12,282**
Public and publicly guaranteed	..	..	**3,983**	**7,024**	**9,688**	**12,218**	**12,837**	**12,557**	**9,912**	**8,132**
Official creditors	..	..	252	1,199	1,283	1,323	1,117	1,138	1,058	1,030
Multilateral	..	..	179	773	839	928	766	794	732	695
Concessional	..	..	0	26	28	26	23	24	21	19
Bilateral	..	..	73	426	444	396	351	344	326	335
Concessional	..	..	0	30	51	84	93	152	159	203
Private creditors	..	..	3,732	5,825	8,405	10,895	11,721	11,419	8,854	7,102
Bonds	..	..	50	870	860	480	672	1,376	1,662	1,259
Commercial banks	..	..	1,970	3,776	6,621	9,723	10,537	9,420	6,421	5,293
Other private	..	..	1,712	1,178	924	692	511	623	771	550
Private nonguaranteed	..	..	**0**	**768**	**1,460**	**2,128**	**2,172**	**4,011**	**4,354**	**4,151**
Bonds	..	..	0	0	39	527	457	671	486	483
Commercial banks and other	..	..	0	768	1,421	1,601	1,716	3,340	3,868	3,667
Memo:										
IBRD	0	0	0	367	434	435	382	380	324	260
IDA	0	0	0	0	0	0	0	0	0	0
DISBURSEMENTS	..	..	**1,182**	**1,582**	**4,311**	**5,109**	**4,143**	**5,278**	**2,873**	**1,523**
Public and publicly guaranteed	..	..	**1,182**	**1,394**	**3,376**	**4,140**	**3,422**	**3,012**	**1,145**	**365**
Official creditors	..	..	19	105	151	308	168	121	107	143
Multilateral	..	..	5	79	108	249	137	74	77	71
Concessional	..	..	0	1	0	0	0	0	0	0
Bilateral	..	..	14	26	43	59	32	47	30	73
Concessional	..	..	0	0	18	39	21	46	30	67
Private creditors	..	..	1,163	1,289	3,225	3,832	3,254	2,891	1,038	221
Bonds	..	..	0	0	20	50	264	637	427	0
Commercial banks	..	..	435	910	3,007	3,689	2,902	2,091	407	221
Other private	..	..	729	379	198	92	88	162	204	0
Private nonguaranteed	..	..	**0**	**189**	**935**	**970**	**721**	**2,266**	**1,729**	**1,159**
Bonds	..	..	0	0	36	496	0	200	0	0
Commercial banks and other	..	..	0	189	900	474	721	2,066	1,729	1,159
Memo:										
IBRD	0	0	0	30	57	42	23	26	21	0
IDA	0	0	0	0	0	0	0	0	0	0
PRINCIPAL REPAYMENTS	..	..	**537**	**891**	**1,667**	**1,664**	**3,331**	**3,558**	**4,246**	**3,376**
Public and publicly guaranteed	..	..	**537**	**868**	**1,420**	**1,370**	**2,530**	**2,985**	**2,963**	**1,945**
Official creditors	..	..	43	62	105	180	250	139	123	95
Multilateral	..	..	5	32	71	108	213	54	68	63
Concessional	..	..	0	0	0	0	0	0	0	0
Bilateral	..	..	38	30	34	72	37	86	55	33
Concessional	..	..	0	0	0	0	0	0	26	7
Private creditors	..	..	494	805	1,315	1,190	2,280	2,846	2,840	1,850
Bonds	..	..	0	126	18	375	23	0	88	325
Commercial banks	..	..	20	364	823	503	1,998	2,793	2,701	1,308
Other private	..	..	474	315	475	312	258	53	51	216
Private nonguaranteed	..	..	**0**	**24**	**247**	**294**	**801**	**573**	**1,283**	**1,432**
Bonds	..	..	0	0	0	0	36	0	164	0
Commercial banks and other	..	..	0	24	247	294	765	573	1,119	1,432
Memo:										
IBRD	0	0	0	0	0	10	39	47	56	43
IDA	0	0	0	0	0	0	0	0	0	0
NET FLOWS ON DEBT	..	..	**645**	**691**	**2,644**	**3,445**	**812**	**1,720**	**-1,372**	**-1,853**
Public and publicly guaranteed	..	..	**645**	**526**	**1,955**	**2,770**	**892**	**27**	**-1,819**	**-1,580**
Official creditors	..	..	-24	43	46	128	-82	-18	-16	48
Multilateral	..	..	0	47	37	141	-76	20	9	8
Concessional	..	..	0	1	0	0	0	0	0	0
Bilateral	..	..	-24	-5	9	-13	-6	-38	-25	40
Concessional	..	..	0	0	18	39	21	46	4	60
Private creditors	..	..	669	483	1,909	2,642	974	45	-1,803	-1,628
Bonds	..	..	0	-126	3	-325	241	637	339	-325
Commercial banks	..	..	414	546	2,184	3,187	903	-702	-2,294	-1,087
Other private	..	..	255	63	-278	-219	-170	109	153	-216
Private nonguaranteed	..	..	**0**	**165**	**689**	**676**	**-80**	**1,693**	**446**	**-273**
Bonds	..	..	0	0	36	496	-36	200	-164	0
Commercial banks and other	..	..	0	165	653	180	-44	1,493	610	-273
Memo:										
IBRD	0	0	0	30	57	32	-17	-21	-36	-43
IDA	0	0	0	0	0	0	0	0	0	0

CZECH REPUBLIC

(US$ million, unless otherwise indicated)

	1970	1980	1990	1994	1995	1996	1997	1998	1999	2000
INTEREST PAYMENTS (LINT)	..	..	**196**	**332**	**506**	**768**	**920**	**1,134**	**1,158**	**1,019**
Public and publicly guaranteed	..	..	**196**	**317**	**456**	**637**	**803**	**1,003**	**942**	**685**
Official creditors	..	..	24	82	86	79	72	66	65	61
Multilateral	..	..	18	55	58	52	52	46	48	43
Concessional	..	..	0	1	2	2	2	0	1	1
Bilateral	..	..	7	26	28	27	20	20	16	18
Concessional	..	..	0	2	1	2	4	5	7	9
Private creditors	..	..	172	236	370	559	731	937	877	623
Bonds	..	..	2	69	117	56	35	45	79	106
Commercial banks	..	..	91	127	149	412	639	848	720	435
Other private	..	..	79	39	104	90	57	43	78	82
Private nonguaranteed	..	..	**0**	**14**	**50**	**130**	**117**	**131**	**216**	**335**
Bonds	..	..	0	0	0	4	31	31	47	38
Commercial banks and other	..	..	0	14	50	126	86	101	169	297
Memo:										
IBRD	0	0	0	25	28	29	27	24	22	17
IDA	0	0	0	0	0	0	0	0	0	0
NET TRANSFERS ON DEBT	..	..	**448**	**360**	**2,138**	**2,678**	**-108**	**586**	**-2,530**	**-2,872**
Public and publicly guaranteed	..	..	**448**	**209**	**1,499**	**2,132**	**89**	**-976**	**-2,761**	**-2,265**
Official creditors	..	..	-48	-39	-40	49	-154	-84	-81	-13
Multilateral	..	..	-18	-8	-21	89	-128	-26	-39	-35
Concessional	..	..	0	0	-2	-2	-2	0	-1	-1
Bilateral	..	..	-31	-31	-19	-40	-26	-58	-41	22
Concessional	..	..	0	-2	16	37	17	40	-3	51
Private creditors	..	..	497	248	1,540	2,084	243	-892	-2,680	-2,252
Bonds	..	..	-2	-195	-114	-381	206	592	260	-431
Commercial banks	..	..	323	419	2,036	2,774	265	-1,550	-3,015	-1,523
Other private	..	..	176	25	-382	-309	-227	66	75	-298
Private nonguaranteed	..	..	**0**	**151**	**639**	**545**	**-197**	**1,562**	**230**	**-607**
Bonds	..	..	0	0	36	492	-67	169	-211	-38
Commercial banks and other	..	..	0	151	603	53	-130	1,393	441	-570
Memo:										
IBRD	0	0	0	5	29	3	-44	-44	-58	-60
IDA	0	0	0	0	0	0	0	0	0	0
DEBT SERVICE (LTDS)	..	..	**734**	**1,223**	**2,173**	**2,432**	**4,251**	**4,692**	**5,404**	**4,396**
Public and publicly guaranteed	..	..	**734**	**1,185**	**1,876**	**2,007**	**3,333**	**3,988**	**3,905**	**2,630**
Official creditors	..	..	67	144	191	259	322	206	187	157
Multilateral	..	..	23	87	129	160	265	100	116	106
Concessional	..	..	0	1	2	2	2	0	1	1
Bilateral	..	..	45	57	62	99	57	106	71	50
Concessional	..	..	0	2	1	2	4	5	32	16
Private creditors	..	..	666	1,041	1,685	1,748	3,011	3,783	3,718	2,473
Bonds	..	..	2	195	134	431	59	45	167	431
Commercial banks	..	..	111	491	972	915	2,637	3,641	3,421	1,744
Other private	..	..	553	354	579	402	315	96	129	298
Private nonguaranteed	..	..	**0**	**38**	**297**	**425**	**918**	**704**	**1,499**	**1,766**
Bonds	..	..	0	0	0	4	67	31	211	38
Commercial banks and other	..	..	0	38	297	421	851	673	1,287	1,728
Memo:										
IBRD	0	0	0	25	28	39	66	71	78	60
IDA	0	0	0	0	0	0	0	0	0	0
UNDISBURSED DEBT	..	..	**447**	**885**	**1,206**	**2,399**	**1,973**	**1,439**	**1,021**	**848**
Official creditors	..	..	14	586	966	954	774	729	438	332
Private creditors	..	..	433	299	241	1,445	1,199	709	583	516
Memorandum items										
Concessional LDOD	..	..	0	56	79	110	116	177	180	222
Variable rate LDOD	..	..	1,192	3,844	4,959	5,241	6,397	9,800	8,232	7,333
Public sector LDOD	..	..	3,726	6,732	9,251	11,792	12,416	12,041	9,437	7,760
Private sector LDOD	..	..	258	1,060	1,897	2,553	2,593	4,527	4,829	4,522

6. CURRENCY COMPOSITION OF LONG-TERM DEBT (PERCENT)

	1970	1980	1990	1994	1995	1996	1997	1998	1999	2000
Deutsche mark	..	..	33.5	14.6	5.5	4.1	5.3	11.3	12.0	13.9
French franc	..	..	1.4	0.5	0.2	0.1	0.1	0.0	0.0	0.0
Japanese yen	..	..	9.0	12.1	8.1	5.7	4.5	4.7	5.7	2.3
Pound sterling	..	..	0.6	0.1	0.0	0.0	0.0	0.0	0.0	0.0
Swiss franc	..	..	13.8	3.9	3.1	2.0	1.6	0.6	0.2	0.0
U.S.dollars	..	..	26.6	47.6	66.1	74.3	78.4	73.9	64.9	65.7
Multiple currency	..	..	0.0	15.4	12.2	9.5	7.9	7.3	10.6	9.2
Special drawing rights	..	..	0.0	0.0	0.0	0.0	0.0	0.0	0.0	0.0
All other currencies	..	..	15.1	5.8	4.8	4.3	2.2	2.2	6.6	8.9

CZECH REPUBLIC

(US$ million, unless otherwise indicated)

	1970	1980	1990	1994	1995	1996	1997	1998	1999	2000
7. DEBT RESTRUCTURINGS										
Total amount rescheduled	..	..	0	0	0	0	0	0	0	0
Debt stock rescheduled	..	..	0	0	0	0	0	0	0	0
Principal rescheduled	..	..	0	0	0	0	0	0	0	0
Official	..	..	0	0	0	0	0	0	0	0
Private	..	..	0	0	0	0	0	0	0	0
Interest rescheduled	..	..	0	0	0	0	0	0	0	0
Official	..	..	0	0	0	0	0	0	0	0
Private	..	..	0	0	0	0	0	0	0	0
Debt forgiven	..	..	0	1	2	0	2	0	0	3
Memo: interest forgiven	..	..	0	0	0	0	0	0	0	0
Debt stock reduction	..	..	0	0	0	0	0	0	0	0
of which debt buyback	..	..	0	0	0	0	0	0	0	0
8. DEBT STOCK-FLOW RECONCILIATION										
Total change in debt stocks	..	..	19	1,525	5,537	3,848	3,511	607	-1,530	-1,354
Net flows on debt	..	..	52	459	4,798	4,109	3,666	764	-629	-1,241
Net change in interest arrears	..	..	0	1	27	-13	-7	4	29	18
Interest capitalized	..	..	0	0	0	0	0	0	0	0
Debt forgiveness or reduction	..	..	0	-1	-2	0	-2	0	0	-3
Cross-currency valuation	..	..	240	390	144	-237	-261	176	-187	-212
Residual	..	..	-273	676	570	-11	113	-337	-743	84
9. AVERAGE TERMS OF NEW COMMITMENTS										
ALL CREDITORS										
Interest (%)	..	..	8.2	7.5	7.2	7.5	6.6	6.5	7.5	5.2
Maturity (years)	..	..	5.1	15.0	14.6	14.4	9.2	8.3	12.7	13.4
Grace period (years)	..	..	3.1	2.7	-10.0	-4.7	2.2	4.2	4.9	3.9
Grant element (%)	..	..	4.3	12.4	13.8	12.3	12.5	14.4	15.0	23.8
Official creditors										
Interest (%)	..	..	9.6	7.1	4.5	6.3	5.9	9.5	3.8	4.9
Maturity (years)	..	..	10.8	20.0	17.6	19.1	18.7	9.4	16.4	17.9
Grace period (years)	..	..	5.2	5.5	-79.5	-76.0	5.2	1.4	6.9	5.6
Grant element (%)	..	..	0.6	18.8	33.7	23.8	25.9	1.0	40.5	31.8
Private creditors										
Interest (%)	..	..	8.1	7.5	7.7	7.6	6.6	6.5	7.6	5.5
Maturity (years)	..	..	5.0	14.4	14.0	14.0	8.9	8.3	12.6	7.8
Grace period (years)	..	..	3.1	2.4	2.7	2.7	2.1	4.2	4.9	1.9
Grant element (%)	..	..	4.4	11.6	10.2	11.1	12.2	14.4	14.2	13.9
Memorandum items										
Commitments	..	..	784	1,426	3,383	5,655	3,136	2,788	1,051	360
Official creditors	..	..	18	150	520	534	86	1	34	200
Private creditors	..	..	766	1,276	2,862	5,121	3,051	2,787	1,017	160

10. CONTRACTUAL OBLIGATIONS ON OUTSTANDING LONG-TERM DEBT

	2001	2002	2003	2004	2005	2006	2007	2008	2009	2010
TOTAL										
Disbursements	571	138	65	37	19	10	5	3	0	0
Principal	2,309	1,508	1,655	990	1,332	1,054	910	897	803	421
Interest	922	780	653	537	464	347	285	201	132	83
Official creditors										
Disbursements	107	95	59	34	19	10	5	3	0	0
Principal	105	115	120	118	117	121	91	80	75	70
Interest	63	63	60	55	49	43	37	32	27	23
Bilateral creditors										
Disbursements	63	36	18	9	3	1	0	0	0	0
Principal	36	36	39	37	35	40	34	33	31	29
Interest	18	19	18	17	16	15	13	11	9	8
Multilateral creditors										
Disbursements	44	60	40	25	16	9	5	3	0	0
Principal	69	79	82	82	82	82	57	47	44	42
Interest	46	45	42	38	33	29	24	21	18	15
Private creditors										
Disbursements	463	43	7	3	0	0	0	0	0	0
Principal	2,204	1,393	1,535	872	1,214	932	819	817	728	351
Interest	859	717	593	482	415	304	247	169	105	60
Commercial banks										
Disbursements	449	36	5	2	0	0	0	0	0	0
Principal	1,153	694	628	513	698	475	469	422	389	195
Interest	404	351	300	255	213	159	120	84	50	17
Other private										
Disbursements	14	7	2	1	0	0	0	0	0	0
Principal	1,051	699	907	359	516	458	350	395	339	156
Interest	455	366	294	227	201	145	127	85	55	42

DJIBOUTI

(US$ million, unless otherwise indicated)

	1970	1980	1990	1994	1995	1996	1997	1998	1999	2000
1. SUMMARY DEBT DATA										
TOTAL DEBT STOCKS (EDT)	**2.6**	**31.8**	**205.3**	**263.1**	**281.8**	**295.8**	**273.7**	**287.8**	**274.6**	**262.2**
Long-term debt (LDOD)	**2.6**	**25.8**	**155.2**	**254.9**	**268.9**	**279.3**	**253.0**	**263.8**	**248.4**	**237.9**
Public and publicly guaranteed	2.6	25.8	155.2	254.9	268.9	279.3	253.0	263.8	248.4	237.9
Private nonguaranteed	0.0	0.0	0.0	0.0	0.0	0.0	0.0	0.0	0.0	0.0
Use of IMF credit	**0.0**	**0.0**	**0.0**	**0.0**	**0.0**	**4.1**	**5.4**	**8.9**	**12.7**	**13.4**
Short-term debt	**0.0**	**6.0**	**50.1**	**8.2**	**12.9**	**12.4**	**15.3**	**15.1**	**13.5**	**10.9**
of which interest arrears on LDOD	0.0	0.0	0.1	2.8	3.5	4.2	4.3	6.3	6.6	6.9
Official creditors	0.0	0.0	0.1	2.8	3.5	4.2	4.3	6.3	6.6	6.9
Private creditors	0.0	0.0	0.0	0.0	0.0	0.0	0.0	0.0	0.0	0.0
Memo: principal arrears on LDOD	0.0	0.0	1.2	10.7	13.1	14.6	12.6	20.5	23.5	24.4
Official creditors	0.0	0.0	1.2	10.7	13.1	14.6	12.6	20.5	23.5	24.4
Private creditors	0.0	0.0	0.0	0.0	0.0	0.0	0.0	0.0	0.0	0.0
Memo: export credits	0.0	0.0	27.0	9.7	8.5	5.0	17.4	6.5	3.1	2.3
TOTAL DEBT FLOWS										
Disbursements	**1.4**	**10.2**	**27.0**	**25.8**	**18.4**	**27.8**	**13.5**	**8.2**	**8.3**	**11.3**
Long-term debt	1.4	10.2	27.0	25.8	18.4	23.6	12.0	5.1	3.2	7.7
IMF purchases	0.0	0.0	0.0	0.0	0.0	4.2	1.5	3.2	5.1	3.6
Principal repayments	**0.1**	**2.2**	**8.9**	**8.9**	**9.2**	**8.8**	**5.0**	**3.3**	**7.3**	**10.7**
Long-term debt	0.1	2.2	8.9	8.9	9.2	8.8	5.0	3.3	6.3	8.4
IMF repurchases	0.0	0.0	0.0	0.0	0.0	0.0	0.0	0.0	1.0	2.3
Net flows on debt	**1.3**	**9.0**	**20.8**	**-9.5**	**13.2**	**17.9**	**11.3**	**2.7**	**-0.9**	**-2.2**
of which short-term debt	0.0	1.0	2.8	-26.5	3.9	-1.2	2.8	-2.2	-1.9	-2.9
Interest payments (INT)	**0.0**	**1.7**	**6.0**	**2.9**	**2.5**	**3.2**	**2.2**	**2.1**	**2.7**	**2.8**
Long-term debt	0.0	0.9	2.1	1.8	2.0	2.7	1.5	1.5	1.9	2.2
IMF charges	0.0	0.0	0.0	0.0	0.0	0.1	0.2	0.3	0.4	0.4
Short-term debt	0.0	0.8	3.9	1.1	0.5	0.4	0.5	0.4	0.4	0.2
Net transfers on debt	**1.3**	**7.3**	**14.8**	**-12.4**	**10.7**	**14.6**	**9.0**	**0.6**	**-3.6**	**-5.1**
Total debt service paid (TDS)	**0.1**	**3.9**	**14.9**	**11.8**	**11.6**	**12.0**	**7.3**	**5.4**	**10.0**	**13.5**
Long-term debt	0.1	3.1	11.0	10.7	11.1	11.5	6.6	4.8	8.2	10.6
IMF repurchases and charges	0.0	0.0	0.0	0.0	0.0	0.1	0.2	0.3	1.4	2.7
Short-term debt (interest only)	0.0	0.8	3.9	1.1	0.5	0.4	0.5	0.4	0.4	0.2
2. AGGREGATE NET RESOURCE FLOWS AND NET TRANSFERS (LONG-TERM)										
NET RESOURCE FLOWS	**5.6**	**37.8**	**148.7**	**72.6**	**61.2**	**62.3**	**50.3**	**55.6**	**44.4**	**27.2**
Net flow of long-term debt (ex. IMF)	1.3	8.0	18.0	16.9	9.2	14.9	6.9	1.8	-3.1	-0.7
Foreign direct investment (net)	0.0	0.0	0.0	1.4	3.2	5.0	5.0	6.0	5.0	0.0
Portfolio equity flows	0.0	0.0	0.0	0.0	0.0	0.0	0.0	0.0	0.0	0.0
Grants (excluding technical coop.)	4.3	29.8	130.7	54.3	48.8	42.4	38.4	47.8	42.5	27.9
Memo: technical coop. grants	6.2	27.8	43.8	50.7	45.7	41.0	31.1	28.9	29.2	23.6
official net resource flows	5.6	32.8	149.3	71.2	58.0	57.3	45.3	49.6	39.4	27.2
private net resource flows	0.0	5.0	-0.6	1.4	3.2	5.0	5.0	6.0	5.0	0.0
NET TRANSFERS	**5.6**	**36.9**	**146.6**	**67.8**	**56.2**	**56.6**	**45.8**	**50.1**	**36.5**	**17.0**
Interest on long-term debt	0.0	0.9	2.1	1.8	2.0	2.7	1.5	1.5	1.9	2.2
Profit remittances on FDI	0.0	0.0	0.0	3.0	3.0	3.0	3.0	4.0	6.0	8.0
Memo: official net transfers	5.6	31.9	147.2	69.4	56.0	54.6	43.8	48.1	37.5	25.0
private net transfers	0.0	5.0	-0.6	-1.6	0.2	2.0	2.0	2.0	-1.0	-8.0
3. MAJOR ECONOMIC AGGREGATES										
Gross national income (GNI)	..	..	..	..	515.0	509.7	514.9	524.9	547.0	568.1
Exports of goods & services (XGS)	..	..	..	233.8	211.8	209.6	212.5	244.3	244.2	245.4
of which workers remittances	..	..	..	1.5	1.0	..	..	..	..	..
Imports of goods & services (MGS)	..	..	..	333.8	300.8	296.6	300.4	344.2	338.1	359.0
International reserves (RES)	..	..	93.6	73.8	72.2	77.0	66.6	66.5	70.6	67.8
Current account balance	..	..	..	-46.1	-23.0	..	..	..	..	..
4. DEBT INDICATORS										
EDT / XGS (%)	..	..	..	112.5	133.0	141.1	128.8	117.8	112.4	106.9
EDT / GNI (%)	..	..	..	..	54.7	58.0	53.2	54.8	50.2	46.2
TDS / XGS (%)	..	..	..	5.1	5.5	5.7	3.4	2.2	4.1	5.5
INT / XGS (%)	..	..	..	1.2	1.2	1.5	1.0	0.9	1.1	1.1
INT / GNI (%)	..	..	..	..	0.5	0.6	0.4	0.4	0.5	0.5
RES / EDT (%)	..	..	45.6	28.0	25.6	26.0	24.3	23.1	25.7	25.9
RES / MGS (months)	..	..	..	2.7	2.9	3.1	2.7	2.3	2.5	2.3
Short-term / EDT (%)	0.0	18.9	24.4	3.1	4.6	4.2	5.6	5.3	4.9	4.2
Concessional / EDT (%)	100.0	45.6	74.0	96.1	94.8	94.0	92.1	91.4	90.2	90.5
Multilateral / EDT (%)	0.0	7.2	41.9	48.8	48.4	46.3	49.8	50.2	51.3	52.8

DJIBOUTI

(US$ million, unless otherwise indicated)

	1970	1980	1990	1994	1995	1996	1997	1998	1999	2000
5. LONG-TERM DEBT										
DEBT OUTSTANDING (LDOD)	**2.6**	**25.8**	**155.2**	**254.9**	**268.9**	**279.3**	**253.0**	**263.8**	**248.4**	**237.9**
Public and publicly guaranteed	**2.6**	**25.8**	**155.2**	**254.9**	**268.9**	**279.3**	**253.0**	**263.8**	**248.4**	**237.9**
Official creditors	2.6	21.2	155.2	254.9	268.9	279.3	253.0	263.8	248.4	237.9
Multilateral	0.0	2.3	86.1	128.5	136.4	137.0	136.3	144.6	140.8	138.3
Concessional	0.0	1.0	83.0	126.6	134.7	135.7	135.4	143.8	140.1	137.7
Bilateral	2.6	18.9	69.2	126.4	132.5	142.2	116.7	119.3	107.6	99.6
Concessional	2.6	13.5	68.9	126.3	132.4	142.2	116.7	119.3	107.6	99.6
Private creditors	0.0	4.7	0.0	0.0	0.0	0.0	0.0	0.0	0.0	0.0
Bonds	0.0	0.0	0.0	0.0	0.0	0.0	0.0	0.0	0.0	0.0
Commercial banks	0.0	4.7	0.0	0.0	0.0	0.0	0.0	0.0	0.0	0.0
Other private	0.0	0.0	0.0	0.0	0.0	0.0	0.0	0.0	0.0	0.0
Private nonguaranteed	**0.0**	**0.0**	**0.0**	**0.0**	**0.0**	**0.0**	**0.0**	**0.0**	**0.0**	**0.0**
Bonds	0.0	0.0	0.0	0.0	0.0	0.0	0.0	0.0	0.0	0.0
Commercial banks and other	0.0	0.0	0.0	0.0	0.0	0.0	0.0	0.0	0.0	0.0
Memo:										
IBRD	0.0	0.0	0.0	0.0	0.0	0.0	0.0	0.0	0.0	0.0
IDA	0.0	0.0	31.1	42.8	46.2	45.7	46.1	49.5	49.0	49.9
DISBURSEMENTS	**1.4**	**10.2**	**27.0**	**25.8**	**18.4**	**23.6**	**12.0**	**5.1**	**3.2**	**7.7**
Public and publicly guaranteed	**1.4**	**10.2**	**27.0**	**25.8**	**18.4**	**23.6**	**12.0**	**5.1**	**3.2**	**7.7**
Official creditors	1.4	5.3	27.0	25.8	18.4	23.6	12.0	5.1	3.2	7.7
Multilateral	0.0	2.4	8.9	12.1	10.0	10.6	9.6	4.9	3.2	7.7
Concessional	0.0	1.0	8.9	12.1	10.0	10.6	9.6	4.9	3.2	7.7
Bilateral	1.4	2.9	18.0	13.8	8.4	13.1	2.4	0.2	0.0	0.0
Concessional	1.4	0.0	18.0	13.8	8.4	13.1	2.4	0.2	0.0	0.0
Private creditors	0.0	5.0	0.0	0.0	0.0	0.0	0.0	0.0	0.0	0.0
Bonds	0.0	0.0	0.0	0.0	0.0	0.0	0.0	0.0	0.0	0.0
Commercial banks	0.0	5.0	0.0	0.0	0.0	0.0	0.0	0.0	0.0	0.0
Other private	0.0	0.0	0.0	0.0	0.0	0.0	0.0	0.0	0.0	0.0
Private nonguaranteed	**0.0**	**0.0**	**0.0**	**0.0**	**0.0**	**0.0**	**0.0**	**0.0**	**0.0**	**0.0**
Bonds	0.0	0.0	0.0	0.0	0.0	0.0	0.0	0.0	0.0	0.0
Commercial banks and other	0.0	0.0	0.0	0.0	0.0	0.0	0.0	0.0	0.0	0.0
Memo:										
IBRD	0.0	0.0	0.0	0.0	0.0	0.0	0.0	0.0	0.0	0.0
IDA	0.0	0.0	2.5	1.3	2.8	1.4	3.3	2.0	0.9	3.9
PRINCIPAL REPAYMENTS	**0.1**	**2.2**	**8.9**	**8.9**	**9.2**	**8.8**	**5.0**	**3.3**	**6.3**	**8.4**
Public and publicly guaranteed	**0.1**	**2.2**	**8.9**	**8.9**	**9.2**	**8.8**	**5.0**	**3.3**	**6.3**	**8.4**
Official creditors	0.1	2.2	8.3	8.9	9.2	8.8	5.0	3.3	6.3	8.4
Multilateral	0.0	0.0	3.5	4.0	4.4	4.3	2.1	1.9	3.0	4.0
Concessional	0.0	0.0	3.3	3.8	4.1	4.1	1.9	1.7	3.0	4.0
Bilateral	0.1	2.2	4.8	4.9	4.8	4.4	2.9	1.4	3.3	4.4
Concessional	0.1	1.7	4.7	4.8	4.7	4.4	2.9	1.4	3.3	4.4
Private creditors	0.0	0.0	0.6	0.0	0.0	0.0	0.0	0.0	0.0	0.0
Bonds	0.0	0.0	0.0	0.0	0.0	0.0	0.0	0.0	0.0	0.0
Commercial banks	0.0	0.0	0.4	0.0	0.0	0.0	0.0	0.0	0.0	0.0
Other private	0.0	0.0	0.2	0.0	0.0	0.0	0.0	0.0	0.0	0.0
Private nonguaranteed	**0.0**	**0.0**	**0.0**	**0.0**	**0.0**	**0.0**	**0.0**	**0.0**	**0.0**	**0.0**
Bonds	0.0	0.0	0.0	0.0	0.0	0.0	0.0	0.0	0.0	0.0
Commercial banks and other	0.0	0.0	0.0	0.0	0.0	0.0	0.0	0.0	0.0	0.0
Memo:										
IBRD	0.0	0.0	0.0	0.0	0.0	0.0	0.0	0.0	0.0	0.0
IDA	0.0	0.0	0.0	0.1	0.3	0.3	0.3	0.4	0.3	0.5
NET FLOWS ON DEBT	**1.3**	**8.0**	**18.0**	**16.9**	**9.2**	**14.9**	**6.9**	**1.8**	**-3.1**	**-0.7**
Public and publicly guaranteed	**1.3**	**8.0**	**18.0**	**16.9**	**9.2**	**14.9**	**6.9**	**1.8**	**-3.1**	**-0.7**
Official creditors	1.3	3.0	18.6	16.9	9.2	14.9	6.9	1.8	-3.1	-0.7
Multilateral	0.0	2.4	5.4	8.0	5.6	6.2	7.5	3.0	0.2	3.7
Concessional	0.0	1.0	5.6	8.3	5.9	6.5	7.8	3.2	0.2	3.7
Bilateral	1.3	0.6	13.2	8.9	3.7	8.6	-0.6	-1.2	-3.3	-4.4
Concessional	1.3	-1.7	13.3	8.9	3.7	8.7	-0.6	-1.2	-3.3	-4.4
Private creditors	0.0	5.0	-0.6	0.0	0.0	0.0	0.0	0.0	0.0	0.0
Bonds	0.0	0.0	0.0	0.0	0.0	0.0	0.0	0.0	0.0	0.0
Commercial banks	0.0	5.0	-0.4	0.0	0.0	0.0	0.0	0.0	0.0	0.0
Other private	0.0	0.0	-0.2	0.0	0.0	0.0	0.0	0.0	0.0	0.0
Private nonguaranteed	**0.0**	**0.0**	**0.0**	**0.0**	**0.0**	**0.0**	**0.0**	**0.0**	**0.0**	**0.0**
Bonds	0.0	0.0	0.0	0.0	0.0	0.0	0.0	0.0	0.0	0.0
Commercial banks and other	0.0	0.0	0.0	0.0	0.0	0.0	0.0	0.0	0.0	0.0
Memo:										
IBRD	0.0	0.0	0.0	0.0	0.0	0.0	0.0	0.0	0.0	0.0
IDA	0.0	0.0	2.5	1.2	2.4	1.0	3.0	1.7	0.7	3.4

DJIBOUTI

(US$ million, unless otherwise indicated)

	1970	1980	1990	1994	1995	1996	1997	1998	1999	2000
INTEREST PAYMENTS (LINT)	**0.0**	**0.9**	**2.1**	**1.8**	**2.0**	**2.7**	**1.5**	**1.5**	**1.9**	**2.2**
Public and publicly guaranteed	**0.0**	**0.9**	**2.1**	**1.8**	**2.0**	**2.7**	**1.5**	**1.5**	**1.9**	**2.2**
Official creditors	0.0	0.9	2.1	1.8	2.0	2.7	1.5	1.5	1.9	2.2
Multilateral	0.0	0.0	1.3	1.0	0.9	1.6	1.0	1.1	1.2	1.4
Concessional	0.0	0.0	1.3	0.9	0.9	1.6	1.0	1.1	1.2	1.4
Bilateral	0.0	0.9	0.8	0.9	1.1	1.1	0.5	0.4	0.7	0.8
Concessional	0.0	0.7	0.7	0.9	1.1	1.1	0.5	0.4	0.7	0.8
Private creditors	0.0	0.0	0.0	0.0	0.0	0.0	0.0	0.0	0.0	0.0
Bonds	0.0	0.0	0.0	0.0	0.0	0.0	0.0	0.0	0.0	0.0
Commercial banks	0.0	0.0	0.0	0.0	0.0	0.0	0.0	0.0	0.0	0.0
Other private	0.0	0.0	0.0	0.0	0.0	0.0	0.0	0.0	0.0	0.0
Private nonguaranteed	**0.0**	**0.0**	**0.0**	**0.0**	**0.0**	**0.0**	**0.0**	**0.0**	**0.0**	**0.0**
Bonds	0.0	0.0	0.0	0.0	0.0	0.0	0.0	0.0	0.0	0.0
Commercial banks and other	0.0	0.0	0.0	0.0	0.0	0.0	0.0	0.0	0.0	0.0
Memo:										
IBRD	0.0	0.0	0.0	0.0	0.0	0.0	0.0	0.0	0.0	0.0
IDA	0.0	0.0	0.2	0.2	0.3	0.3	0.3	0.4	0.3	0.4
NET TRANSFERS ON DEBT	**1.3**	**7.1**	**15.9**	**15.1**	**7.3**	**12.1**	**5.4**	**0.3**	**-5.0**	**-2.9**
Public and publicly guaranteed	**1.3**	**7.1**	**15.9**	**15.1**	**7.3**	**12.1**	**5.4**	**0.3**	**-5.0**	**-2.9**
Official creditors	1.3	2.1	16.6	15.1	7.3	12.1	5.4	0.3	-5.0	-2.9
Multilateral	0.0	2.4	4.1	7.1	4.7	4.6	6.5	1.9	-1.0	2.3
Concessional	0.0	1.0	4.3	7.4	5.0	4.9	6.8	2.1	-1.0	2.3
Bilateral	1.3	-0.3	12.5	8.0	2.6	7.5	-1.1	-1.6	-4.0	-5.1
Concessional	1.3	-2.4	12.6	8.1	2.6	7.6	-1.1	-1.6	-4.0	-5.1
Private creditors	0.0	5.0	-0.6	0.0	0.0	0.0	0.0	0.0	0.0	0.0
Bonds	0.0	0.0	0.0	0.0	0.0	0.0	0.0	0.0	0.0	0.0
Commercial banks	0.0	5.0	-0.4	0.0	0.0	0.0	0.0	0.0	0.0	0.0
Other private	0.0	0.0	-0.2	0.0	0.0	0.0	0.0	0.0	0.0	0.0
Private nonguaranteed	**0.0**	**0.0**	**0.0**	**0.0**	**0.0**	**0.0**	**0.0**	**0.0**	**0.0**	**0.0**
Bonds	0.0	0.0	0.0	0.0	0.0	0.0	0.0	0.0	0.0	0.0
Commercial banks and other	0.0	0.0	0.0	0.0	0.0	0.0	0.0	0.0	0.0	0.0
Memo:										
IBRD	0.0	0.0	0.0	0.0	0.0	0.0	0.0	0.0	0.0	0.0
IDA	0.0	0.0	2.3	0.9	2.1	0.7	2.6	1.3	0.3	3.0
DEBT SERVICE (LTDS)	**0.1**	**3.1**	**11.0**	**10.7**	**11.1**	**11.5**	**6.6**	**4.8**	**8.2**	**10.6**
Public and publicly guaranteed	**0.1**	**3.1**	**11.0**	**10.7**	**11.1**	**11.5**	**6.6**	**4.8**	**8.2**	**10.6**
Official creditors	0.1	3.1	10.4	10.7	11.1	11.5	6.6	4.8	8.2	10.6
Multilateral	0.0	0.0	4.9	5.0	5.3	5.9	3.1	3.0	4.3	5.4
Concessional	0.0	0.0	4.6	4.7	5.0	5.6	2.8	2.8	4.3	5.4
Bilateral	0.1	3.1	5.5	5.7	5.9	5.6	3.5	1.7	4.0	5.1
Concessional	0.1	2.4	5.5	5.7	5.8	5.5	3.5	1.7	4.0	5.1
Private creditors	0.0	0.0	0.6	0.0	0.0	0.0	0.0	0.0	0.0	0.0
Bonds	0.0	0.0	0.0	0.0	0.0	0.0	0.0	0.0	0.0	0.0
Commercial banks	0.0	0.0	0.4	0.0	0.0	0.0	0.0	0.0	0.0	0.0
Other private	0.0	0.0	0.2	0.0	0.0	0.0	0.0	0.0	0.0	0.0
Private nonguaranteed	**0.0**	**0.0**	**0.0**	**0.0**	**0.0**	**0.0**	**0.0**	**0.0**	**0.0**	**0.0**
Bonds	0.0	0.0	0.0	0.0	0.0	0.0	0.0	0.0	0.0	0.0
Commercial banks and other	0.0	0.0	0.0	0.0	0.0	0.0	0.0	0.0	0.0	0.0
Memo:										
IBRD	0.0	0.0	0.0	0.0	0.0	0.0	0.0	0.0	0.0	0.0
IDA	0.0	0.0	0.2	0.4	0.7	0.7	0.7	0.8	0.6	0.9
UNDISBURSED DEBT	**0.0**	**23.4**	**161.4**	**107.9**	**88.8**	**59.3**	**49.3**	**50.8**	**99.6**	**120.8**
Official creditors	0.0	23.4	161.4	107.9	88.8	55.7	45.7	47.2	96.0	117.2
Private creditors	0.0	0.0	0.0	0.0	0.0	3.6	3.6	3.6	3.6	3.6
Memorandum items										
Concessional LDOD	2.6	14.5	151.9	252.9	267.1	277.9	252.1	263.1	247.8	237.3
Variable rate LDOD	0.0	0.0	0.0	0.0	0.0	0.0	0.0	0.0	0.0	0.0
Public sector LDOD	2.6	25.8	155.2	254.9	268.9	279.3	253.0	263.8	248.4	237.9
Private sector LDOD	0.0	0.0	0.0	0.0	0.0	0.0	0.0	0.0	0.0	0.0

6. CURRENCY COMPOSITION OF LONG-TERM DEBT (PERCENT)

	1970	1980	1990	1994	1995	1996	1997	1998	1999	2000
Deutsche mark	0.0	0.0	0.0	0.0	0.0	0.0	0.0	0.0	0.0	0.0
French franc	100.0	91.0	3.1	3.6	3.5	3.1	2.8	2.9	2.7	2.6
Japanese yen	0.0	0.0	0.0	0.0	0.0	0.0	0.0	0.0	0.0	0.0
Pound sterling	0.0	0.0	0.0	0.0	0.0	0.0	0.0	0.0	0.0	0.0
Swiss franc	0.0	0.0	0.0	0.0	0.0	0.0	0.0	0.0	0.0	0.0
U.S.dollars	0.0	2.9	13.9	11.9	12.4	11.9	13.6	14.1	14.9	16.2
Multiple currency	0.0	0.6	16.8	23.6	23.5	21.9	22.9	23.1	23.9	24.3
Special drawing rights	0.0	0.4	8.9	6.5	6.3	5.8	5.9	5.8	6.0	5.8
All other currencies	0.0	5.1	57.3	54.4	54.3	57.3	54.8	54.1	52.5	51.1

DJIBOUTI

(US$ million, unless otherwise indicated)

	1970	1980	1990	1994	1995	1996	1997	1998	1999	2000
7. DEBT RESTRUCTURINGS										
Total amount rescheduled	..	..	0.0	0.0	0.0	0.0	0.0	0.0	0.0	0.0
Debt stock rescheduled	..	..	0.0	0.0	0.0	0.0	0.0	0.0	0.0	0.0
Principal rescheduled	..	..	0.0	0.0	0.0	0.0	0.0	0.0	0.0	0.0
Official	..	..	0.0	0.0	0.0	0.0	0.0	0.0	0.0	0.0
Private	..	..	0.0	0.0	0.0	0.0	0.0	0.0	0.0	0.0
Interest rescheduled	..	..	0.0	0.0	0.0	0.0	0.0	0.0	0.0	0.0
Official	..	..	0.0	0.0	0.0	0.0	0.0	0.0	0.0	0.0
Private	..	..	0.0	0.0	0.0	0.0	0.0	0.0	0.0	0.0
Debt forgiven	..	..	0.0	0.0	0.0	0.0	16.1	0.0	0.0	0.0
Memo: interest forgiven	..	..	0.0	0.0	0.0	0.0	0.0	0.0	0.0	0.0
Debt stock reduction	..	..	0.0	0.0	0.0	0.0	0.0	0.0	0.0	0.0
of which debt buyback	..	..	0.0	0.0	0.0	0.0	0.0	0.0	0.0	0.0
8. DEBT STOCK-FLOW RECONCILIATION										
Total change in debt stocks	..	..	26.8	-1.3	18.7	14.0	-22.1	14.1	-13.2	-12.5
Net flows on debt	1.3	9.0	20.8	-9.5	13.2	17.9	11.3	2.7	-0.9	-2.2
Net change in interest arrears	..	..	0.1	1.2	0.8	0.7	0.0	2.1	0.2	0.3
Interest capitalized	..	..	0.0	0.0	0.0	0.0	0.0	0.0	0.0	0.0
Debt forgiveness or reduction	..	..	0.0	0.0	0.0	0.0	-16.1	0.0	0.0	0.0
Cross-currency valuation	..	..	3.0	1.9	1.8	-6.3	-16.4	2.0	-10.5	-6.5
Residual	..	..	2.9	5.1	3.0	1.8	-0.9	7.4	-2.0	-4.0
9. AVERAGE TERMS OF NEW COMMITMENTS										
ALL CREDITORS										
Interest (%)	3.3	2.1	0.8	0.0	0.0	6.9	0.8	0.8	1.6	1.9
Maturity (years)	19.5	18.0	39.7	20.7	0.0	8.2	30.4	47.6	30.0	32.8
Grace period (years)	1.0	7.4	10.2	4.5	0.0	3.4	4.1	10.4	7.0	7.7
Grant element (%)	38.0	55.0	80.5	66.6	0.0	12.8	66.9	82.7	65.6	65.1
Official creditors										
Interest (%)	3.3	1.0	0.8	0.0	0.0	6.9	0.8	0.8	1.6	1.9
Maturity (years)	19.5	20.1	39.7	20.7	0.0	8.4	30.4	47.6	30.0	32.8
Grace period (years)	1.0	8.5	10.2	4.5	0.0	3.7	4.1	10.4	7.0	7.7
Grant element (%)	38.0	64.5	80.5	66.6	0.0	14.1	66.9	82.7	65.6	65.1
Private creditors										
Interest (%)	0.0	7.5	0.0	0.0	0.0	7.0	0.0	0.0	0.0	0.0
Maturity (years)	0.0	7.5	0.0	0.0	0.0	7.9	0.0	0.0	0.0	0.0
Grace period (years)	0.0	2.0	0.0	0.0	0.0	3.0	0.0	0.0	0.0	0.0
Grant element (%)	0.0	8.2	0.0	0.0	0.0	11.3	0.0	0.0	0.0	0.0
Memorandum items										
Commitments	0.2	29.5	6.2	2.6	0.0	7.7	11.9	11.5	59.3	31.3
Official creditors	0.2	24.6	6.2	2.6	0.0	4.1	11.9	11.5	59.3	31.3
Private creditors	0.0	5.0	0.0	0.0	0.0	3.6	0.0	0.0	0.0	0.0

10. CONTRACTUAL OBLIGATIONS ON OUTSTANDING LONG-TERM DEBT

	2001	2002	2003	2004	2005	2006	2007	2008	2009	2010
TOTAL										
Disbursements	22.5	34.0	25.3	17.6	10.4	5.8	3.2	1.3	0.7	0.0
Principal	12.4	13.6	13.2	12.4	13.7	13.7	12.9	12.6	11.9	11.4
Interest	2.8	2.8	2.6	2.8	3.3	3.3	3.1	2.9	2.7	2.6
Official creditors										
Disbursements	20.8	32.9	24.9	17.4	10.4	5.8	3.2	1.3	0.7	0.0
Principal	11.2	12.4	12.2	12.4	13.7	13.7	12.9	12.6	11.9	11.4
Interest	2.7	2.7	2.6	2.8	3.3	3.3	3.1	2.9	2.7	2.6
Bilateral creditors										
Disbursements	4.5	8.3	5.8	4.0	2.2	1.2	0.7	0.5	0.0	0.0
Principal	7.0	8.1	8.1	7.3	7.5	7.4	6.6	6.3	5.4	4.3
Interest	1.4	1.3	1.1	1.0	1.0	0.9	0.8	0.7	0.6	0.5
Multilateral creditors										
Disbursements	16.3	24.6	19.0	13.4	8.1	4.6	2.4	0.8	0.7	0.0
Principal	4.2	4.2	4.1	5.1	6.2	6.2	6.3	6.3	6.5	7.1
Interest	1.4	1.4	1.4	1.8	2.3	2.3	2.3	2.2	2.1	2.0
Private creditors										
Disbursements	1.7	1.2	0.5	0.2	0.0	0.0	0.0	0.0	0.0	0.0
Principal	1.2	1.2	1.0	0.0	0.0	0.0	0.0	0.0	0.0	0.0
Interest	0.1	0.1	0.0	0.0	0.0	0.0	0.0	0.0	0.0	0.0
Commercial banks										
Disbursements	0.0	0.0	0.0	0.0	0.0	0.0	0.0	0.0	0.0	0.0
Principal	0.0	0.0	0.0	0.0	0.0	0.0	0.0	0.0	0.0	0.0
Interest	0.0	0.0	0.0	0.0	0.0	0.0	0.0	0.0	0.0	0.0
Other private										
Disbursements	1.7	1.2	0.5	0.2	0.0	0.0	0.0	0.0	0.0	0.0
Principal	1.2	1.2	1.0	0.0	0.0	0.0	0.0	0.0	0.0	0.0
Interest	0.1	0.1	0.0	0.0	0.0	0.0	0.0	0.0	0.0	0.0

DOMINICA

(US$ million, unless otherwise indicated)

	1970	1980	1990	1994	1995	1996	1997	1998	1999	2000
1. SUMMARY DEBT DATA										
TOTAL DEBT STOCKS (EDT)	..	..	**88.0**	**98.2**	**102.6**	**114.2**	**102.8**	**108.9**	**107.6**	**108.2**
Long-term debt (LDOD)	..	..	**80.2**	**88.7**	**94.1**	**97.8**	**90.6**	**90.9**	**88.7**	**89.2**
Public and publicly guaranteed	..	..	80.2	88.7	94.1	97.8	90.6	90.9	88.7	89.2
Private nonguaranteed	..	..	0.0	0.0	0.0	0.0	0.0	0.0	0.0	0.0
Use of IMF credit	**0.0**	**0.0**	**5.7**	**2.5**	**1.7**	**0.8**	**0.3**	**0.0**	**0.0**	**0.0**
Short-term debt	..	..	**2.0**	**7.0**	**6.7**	**15.6**	**12.0**	**17.9**	**18.8**	**19.0**
of which interest arrears on LDOD	..	..	0.0	0.0	0.2	0.4	0.0	0.0	0.0	0.0
Official creditors	..	..	0.0	0.0	0.2	0.4	0.0	0.0	0.0	0.0
Private creditors	..	..	0.0	0.0	0.0	0.0	0.0	0.0	0.0	0.0
Memo: principal arrears on LDOD	..	..	0.2	0.2	1.8	3.1	0.5	0.4	0.3	0.2
Official creditors	..	..	0.2	0.2	1.8	3.1	0.5	0.4	0.3	0.2
Private creditors	..	..	0.1	0.0	0.0	0.0	0.0	0.0	0.0	0.0
Memo: export credits	..	..	8.0	6.4	6.2	5.6	6.4	2.2	1.1	0.4
TOTAL DEBT FLOWS										
Disbursements	..	..	**11.5**	**4.5**	**8.1**	**7.4**	**2.8**	**5.4**	**7.8**	**9.5**
Long-term debt	..	..	11.5	4.5	8.1	7.4	2.8	5.4	7.8	9.5
IMF purchases	0.0	0.0	0.0	0.0	0.0	0.0	0.0	0.0	0.0	0.0
Principal repayments	..	..	**3.8**	**5.0**	**4.6**	**3.8**	**6.8**	**7.0**	**7.1**	**6.7**
Long-term debt	..	..	2.5	4.2	3.8	3.0	6.2	6.8	7.1	6.7
IMF repurchases	0.0	0.0	1.4	0.8	0.9	0.8	0.6	0.2	0.0	0.0
Net flows on debt	..	..	**7.8**	**5.6**	**3.0**	**12.3**	**-7.1**	**4.2**	**1.6**	**3.0**
of which short-term debt	..	..	0.1	6.1	-0.5	8.7	-3.2	5.8	1.0	0.2
Interest payments (INT)	..	..	**2.0**	**2.4**	**2.5**	**3.0**	**3.9**	**3.3**	**3.3**	**3.5**
Long-term debt	..	..	1.6	2.1	2.1	2.1	2.9	2.6	2.2	2.5
IMF charges	0.0	0.0	0.2	0.0	0.0	0.0	0.0	0.0	0.0	0.0
Short-term debt	..	..	0.2	0.2	0.4	0.9	1.0	0.7	1.0	1.1
Net transfers on debt	..	..	**5.9**	**3.2**	**0.5**	**9.3**	**-11.0**	**0.9**	**-1.7**	**-0.5**
Total debt service paid (TDS)	..	..	**5.8**	**7.4**	**7.1**	**6.8**	**10.7**	**10.3**	**10.4**	**10.2**
Long-term debt	..	..	4.1	6.4	5.8	5.1	9.1	9.4	9.4	9.2
IMF repurchases and charges	0.0	0.0	1.6	0.8	0.9	0.8	0.6	0.2	0.0	0.0
Short-term debt (interest only)	..	..	0.2	0.2	0.4	0.9	1.0	0.7	1.0	1.1
2. AGGREGATE NET RESOURCE FLOWS AND NET TRANSFERS (LONG-TERM)										
NET RESOURCE FLOWS	..	..	**25.1**	**34.9**	**83.0**	**44.8**	**25.5**	**29.2**	**23.6**	**18.4**
Net flow of long-term debt (ex. IMF)	..	..	9.0	0.3	4.3	4.4	-3.4	-1.4	0.7	2.8
Foreign direct investment (net)	..	..	13.0	22.6	54.1	17.8	21.7	6.5	18.0	10.6
Portfolio equity flows	..	..	0.0	0.0	0.0	0.0	0.0	0.0	0.0	0.0
Grants (excluding technical coop.)	..	..	3.1	12.0	24.6	22.6	7.2	24.1	4.9	5.0
Memo: technical coop. grants	..	..	2.9	4.0	3.6	5.5	4.3	5.0	3.7	3.3
official net resource flows	..	..	12.2	12.3	28.9	27.0	3.8	22.7	5.6	7.8
private net resource flows	..	..	12.9	22.6	54.1	17.8	21.7	6.5	18.0	10.6
NET TRANSFERS	..	..	**18.0**	**26.8**	**73.9**	**36.7**	**14.6**	**18.1**	**12.4**	**7.9**
Interest on long-term debt	..	..	1.6	2.1	2.1	2.1	2.9	2.6	2.2	2.5
Profit remittances on FDI	..	..	5.5	6.0	7.0	6.0	8.0	8.5	9.0	8.0
Memo: official net transfers	..	..	10.6	10.2	26.8	24.9	0.9	20.1	3.4	5.3
private net transfers	..	..	7.4	16.6	47.1	11.8	13.7	-2.0	9.0	2.6
3. MAJOR ECONOMIC AGGREGATES										
Gross national income (GNI)	..	..	161.4	204.4	210.7	217.7	227.2	240.9	238.8	239.9
Exports of goods & services (XGS)	..	..	102.8	114.2	114.1	128.0	143.3	154.5	..	..
of which workers remittances	..	..	9.4	10.3	10.8	11.1	11.4	11.8	..	..
Imports of goods & services (MGS)	..	..	142.9	149.4	160.9	167.0	175.9	171.0	..	..
International reserves (RES)	..	..	14.5	15.4	22.1	22.9	23.9	27.7	31.6	29.4
Current account balance	..	..	-43.5	-38.4	-49.8	-39.9	-33.6	-17.5	..	..
4. DEBT INDICATORS										
EDT / XGS (%)	..	..	85.6	86.0	89.9	89.3	71.7	70.5	..	..
EDT / GNI (%)	..	..	54.5	48.0	48.7	52.5	45.3	45.2	45.1	45.1
TDS / XGS (%)	..	..	5.6	6.5	6.2	5.3	7.5	6.7	..	..
INT / XGS (%)	..	..	1.9	2.1	2.2	2.3	2.7	2.1	..	..
INT / GNI (%)	..	..	1.2	1.2	1.2	1.4	1.7	1.4	1.4	1.5
RES / EDT (%)	..	..	16.4	15.7	21.6	20.1	23.2	25.4	29.3	27.2
RES / MGS (months)	..	..	1.2	1.2	1.7	1.7	1.6	1.9	..	..
Short-term / EDT (%)	..	..	2.3	7.1	6.5	13.7	11.7	16.4	17.5	17.6
Concessional / EDT (%)	..	..	87.3	82.8	82.5	77.0	80.0	75.8	74.2	73.1
Multilateral / EDT (%)	..	..	65.7	58.5	60.7	55.0	58.4	55.9	58.3	59.2

DOMINICA

(US$ million, unless otherwise indicated)

	1970	1980	1990	1994	1995	1996	1997	1998	1999	2000
5. LONG-TERM DEBT										
DEBT OUTSTANDING (LDOD)	..	..	**80.2**	**88.7**	**94.1**	**97.8**	**90.6**	**90.9**	**88.7**	**89.2**
Public and publicly guaranteed	..	..	**80.2**	**88.7**	**94.1**	**97.8**	**90.6**	**90.9**	**88.7**	**89.2**
Official creditors	..	..	80.2	88.7	94.1	97.8	90.6	90.9	88.7	89.2
Multilateral	..	..	57.8	57.4	62.3	62.8	60.0	60.9	62.7	64.0
Concessional	..	..	54.4	50.0	52.8	52.9	51.6	52.5	53.7	53.9
Bilateral	..	..	22.4	31.3	31.8	35.0	30.6	30.0	26.1	25.2
Concessional	..	..	22.4	31.3	31.8	35.0	30.6	30.0	26.1	25.2
Private creditors	..	..	0.1	0.0	0.0	0.0	0.0	0.0	0.0	0.0
Bonds	..	..	0.0	0.0	0.0	0.0	0.0	0.0	0.0	0.0
Commercial banks	..	..	0.1	0.0	0.0	0.0	0.0	0.0	0.0	0.0
Other private	..	..	0.0	0.0	0.0	0.0	0.0	0.0	0.0	0.0
Private nonguaranteed	..	..	**0.0**	**0.0**	**0.0**	**0.0**	**0.0**	**0.0**	**0.0**	**0.0**
Bonds	..	..	0.0	0.0	0.0	0.0	0.0	0.0	0.0	0.0
Commercial banks and other	..	..	0.0	0.0	0.0	0.0	0.0	0.0	0.0	0.0
Memo:										
IBRD	0.0	0.0	0.0	0.0	0.0	0.0	0.0	0.4	1.7	2.4
IDA	0.0	0.0	10.4	11.8	12.2	11.7	12.3	14.3	14.5	13.6
DISBURSEMENTS	..	..	**11.5**	**4.5**	**8.1**	**7.4**	**2.8**	**5.4**	**7.8**	**9.5**
Public and publicly guaranteed	..	..	**11.5**	**4.5**	**8.1**	**7.4**	**2.8**	**5.4**	**7.8**	**9.5**
Official creditors	..	..	11.5	4.5	8.1	7.4	2.8	5.4	7.8	9.5
Multilateral	..	..	8.3	2.0	3.5	4.1	2.8	3.5	7.5	6.6
Concessional	..	..	6.7	1.5	2.7	3.2	2.8	3.1	5.4	4.5
Bilateral	..	..	3.2	2.5	4.6	3.3	0.0	2.0	0.3	2.9
Concessional	..	..	3.2	2.5	4.6	3.3	0.0	2.0	0.3	2.9
Private creditors	..	..	0.0	0.0	0.0	0.0	0.0	0.0	0.0	0.0
Bonds	..	..	0.0	0.0	0.0	0.0	0.0	0.0	0.0	0.0
Commercial banks	..	..	0.0	0.0	0.0	0.0	0.0	0.0	0.0	0.0
Other private	..	..	0.0	0.0	0.0	0.0	0.0	0.0	0.0	0.0
Private nonguaranteed	..	..	**0.0**	**0.0**	**0.0**	**0.0**	**0.0**	**0.0**	**0.0**	**0.0**
Bonds	..	..	0.0	0.0	0.0	0.0	0.0	0.0	0.0	0.0
Commercial banks and other	..	..	0.0	0.0	0.0	0.0	0.0	0.0	0.0	0.0
Memo:										
IBRD	0.0	0.0	0.0	0.0	0.0	0.0	0.0	0.4	1.3	0.7
IDA	0.0	0.0	0.9	0.3	0.1	0.0	1.4	1.6	0.6	-0.1
PRINCIPAL REPAYMENTS	..	..	**2.5**	**4.2**	**3.8**	**3.0**	**6.2**	**6.8**	**7.1**	**6.7**
Public and publicly guaranteed	..	..	**2.5**	**4.2**	**3.8**	**3.0**	**6.2**	**6.8**	**7.1**	**6.7**
Official creditors	..	..	2.4	4.2	3.8	3.0	6.2	6.8	7.1	6.7
Multilateral	..	..	2.1	2.8	2.2	2.4	3.4	3.8	4.1	3.8
Concessional	..	..	2.1	2.5	1.9	2.1	2.8	3.1	3.4	3.2
Bilateral	..	..	0.3	1.5	1.6	0.7	2.8	3.0	3.1	2.9
Concessional	..	..	0.3	1.5	1.6	0.7	2.8	3.0	3.1	2.9
Private creditors	..	..	0.1	0.0	0.0	0.0	0.0	0.0	0.0	0.0
Bonds	..	..	0.0	0.0	0.0	0.0	0.0	0.0	0.0	0.0
Commercial banks	..	..	0.1	0.0	0.0	0.0	0.0	0.0	0.0	0.0
Other private	..	..	0.0	0.0	0.0	0.0	0.0	0.0	0.0	0.0
Private nonguaranteed	..	..	**0.0**	**0.0**	**0.0**	**0.0**	**0.0**	**0.0**	**0.0**	**0.0**
Bonds	..	..	0.0	0.0	0.0	0.0	0.0	0.0	0.0	0.0
Commercial banks and other	..	..	0.0	0.0	0.0	0.0	0.0	0.0	0.0	0.0
Memo:										
IBRD	0.0	0.0	0.0	0.0	0.0	0.0	0.0	0.0	0.0	0.0
IDA	0.0	0.0	0.0	0.1	0.1	0.1	0.1	0.1	0.1	0.1
NET FLOWS ON DEBT	..	..	**9.0**	**0.3**	**4.3**	**4.4**	**-3.4**	**-1.4**	**0.7**	**2.8**
Public and publicly guaranteed	..	..	**9.0**	**0.3**	**4.3**	**4.4**	**-3.4**	**-1.4**	**0.7**	**2.8**
Official creditors	..	..	9.1	0.3	4.3	4.4	-3.4	-1.4	0.7	2.8
Multilateral	..	..	6.3	-0.8	1.3	1.8	-0.6	-0.3	3.4	2.8
Concessional	..	..	4.6	-1.0	0.8	1.0	0.1	0.0	2.0	1.3
Bilateral	..	..	2.9	1.1	3.0	2.6	-2.8	-1.1	-2.7	0.0
Concessional	..	..	2.9	1.1	3.0	2.6	-2.8	-1.1	-2.7	0.0
Private creditors	..	..	-0.1	0.0	0.0	0.0	0.0	0.0	0.0	0.0
Bonds	..	..	0.0	0.0	0.0	0.0	0.0	0.0	0.0	0.0
Commercial banks	..	..	-0.1	0.0	0.0	0.0	0.0	0.0	0.0	0.0
Other private	..	..	0.0	0.0	0.0	0.0	0.0	0.0	0.0	0.0
Private nonguaranteed	..	..	**0.0**	**0.0**	**0.0**	**0.0**	**0.0**	**0.0**	**0.0**	**0.0**
Bonds	..	..	0.0	0.0	0.0	0.0	0.0	0.0	0.0	0.0
Commercial banks and other	..	..	0.0	0.0	0.0	0.0	0.0	0.0	0.0	0.0
Memo:										
IBRD	0.0	0.0	0.0	0.0	0.0	0.0	0.0	0.4	1.3	0.7
IDA	0.0	0.0	0.9	0.2	0.0	-0.1	1.3	1.5	0.5	-0.2

DOMINICA

(US$ million, unless otherwise indicated)

	1970	1980	1990	1994	1995	1996	1997	1998	1999	2000
INTEREST PAYMENTS (LINT)	..	..	**1.6**	**2.1**	**2.1**	**2.1**	**2.9**	**2.6**	**2.2**	**2.5**
Public and publicly guaranteed	..	..	**1.6**	**2.1**	**2.1**	**2.1**	**2.9**	**2.6**	**2.2**	**2.5**
Official creditors	..	..	1.6	2.1	2.1	2.1	2.9	2.6	2.2	2.5
Multilateral	..	..	1.4	1.6	1.6	1.4	1.7	1.5	1.6	1.7
Concessional	..	..	1.3	1.3	1.3	1.2	1.2	1.2	1.3	1.2
Bilateral	..	..	0.2	0.5	0.4	0.6	1.2	1.0	0.6	0.8
Concessional	..	..	0.2	0.5	0.4	0.6	1.2	1.0	0.6	0.8
Private creditors	..	..	0.0	0.0	0.0	0.0	0.0	0.0	0.0	0.0
Bonds	..	..	0.0	0.0	0.0	0.0	0.0	0.0	0.0	0.0
Commercial banks	..	..	0.0	0.0	0.0	0.0	0.0	0.0	0.0	0.0
Other private	..	..	0.0	0.0	0.0	0.0	0.0	0.0	0.0	0.0
Private nonguaranteed	..	..	**0.0**	**0.0**	**0.0**	**0.0**	**0.0**	**0.0**	**0.0**	**0.0**
Bonds	..	..	0.0	0.0	0.0	0.0	0.0	0.0	0.0	0.0
Commercial banks and other	..	..	0.0	0.0	0.0	0.0	0.0	0.0	0.0	0.0
Memo:										
IBRD	0.0	0.0	0.0	0.0	0.0	0.0	0.0	0.0	0.0	0.1
IDA	0.0	0.0	0.1	0.1	0.1	0.1	0.1	0.1	0.1	0.1
NET TRANSFERS ON DEBT	..	..	**7.4**	**-1.8**	**2.3**	**2.3**	**-6.3**	**-3.9**	**-1.6**	**0.3**
Public and publicly guaranteed	..	..	**7.4**	**-1.8**	**2.3**	**2.3**	**-6.3**	**-3.9**	**-1.6**	**0.3**
Official creditors	..	..	7.5	-1.8	2.3	2.3	-6.3	-3.9	-1.6	0.3
Multilateral	..	..	4.9	-2.4	-0.3	0.3	-2.2	-1.9	1.8	1.1
Concessional	..	..	3.3	-2.3	-0.5	-0.1	-1.1	-1.2	0.7	0.1
Bilateral	..	..	2.6	0.6	2.6	2.0	-4.1	-2.1	-3.3	-0.8
Concessional	..	..	2.6	0.6	2.6	2.0	-4.1	-2.1	-3.3	-0.8
Private creditors	..	..	-0.1	0.0	0.0	0.0	0.0	0.0	0.0	0.0
Bonds	..	..	0.0	0.0	0.0	0.0	0.0	0.0	0.0	0.0
Commercial banks	..	..	-0.1	0.0	0.0	0.0	0.0	0.0	0.0	0.0
Other private	..	..	0.0	0.0	0.0	0.0	0.0	0.0	0.0	0.0
Private nonguaranteed	..	..	**0.0**	**0.0**	**0.0**	**0.0**	**0.0**	**0.0**	**0.0**	**0.0**
Bonds	..	..	0.0	0.0	0.0	0.0	0.0	0.0	0.0	0.0
Commercial banks and other	..	..	0.0	0.0	0.0	0.0	0.0	0.0	0.0	0.0
Memo:										
IBRD	0.0	0.0	0.0	0.0	0.0	0.0	0.0	0.4	1.3	0.6
IDA	0.0	0.0	0.8	0.2	-0.1	-0.2	1.2	1.4	0.4	-0.3
DEBT SERVICE (LTDS)	..	..	**4.1**	**6.4**	**5.8**	**5.1**	**9.1**	**9.4**	**9.4**	**9.2**
Public and publicly guaranteed	..	..	**4.1**	**6.4**	**5.8**	**5.1**	**9.1**	**9.4**	**9.4**	**9.2**
Official creditors	..	..	4.0	6.4	5.8	5.1	9.1	9.4	9.4	9.2
Multilateral	..	..	3.4	4.4	3.8	3.8	5.1	5.4	5.7	5.5
Concessional	..	..	3.4	3.8	3.2	3.3	4.0	4.3	4.7	4.5
Bilateral	..	..	0.6	2.0	2.0	1.3	4.1	4.0	3.6	3.7
Concessional	..	..	0.6	2.0	2.0	1.3	4.1	4.0	3.6	3.7
Private creditors	..	..	0.1	0.0	0.0	0.0	0.0	0.0	0.0	0.0
Bonds	..	..	0.0	0.0	0.0	0.0	0.0	0.0	0.0	0.0
Commercial banks	..	..	0.1	0.0	0.0	0.0	0.0	0.0	0.0	0.0
Other private	..	..	0.0	0.0	0.0	0.0	0.0	0.0	0.0	0.0
Private nonguaranteed	..	..	**0.0**	**0.0**	**0.0**	**0.0**	**0.0**	**0.0**	**0.0**	**0.0**
Bonds	..	..	0.0	0.0	0.0	0.0	0.0	0.0	0.0	0.0
Commercial banks and other	..	..	0.0	0.0	0.0	0.0	0.0	0.0	0.0	0.0
Memo:										
IBRD	0.0	0.0	0.0	0.0	0.0	0.0	0.0	0.0	0.0	0.1
IDA	0.0	0.0	0.1	0.1	0.2	0.2	0.2	0.2	0.2	0.2
UNDISBURSED DEBT	..	..	**23.0**	**16.2**	**24.0**	**35.2**	**35.8**	**37.0**	**35.9**	**54.0**
Official creditors	..	..	23.0	16.2	24.0	35.2	35.8	37.0	35.9	54.0
Private creditors	..	..	0.0	0.0	0.0	0.0	0.0	0.0	0.0	0.0
Memorandum items										
Concessional LDOD	..	..	76.8	81.3	84.6	87.9	82.2	82.5	79.7	79.0
Variable rate LDOD	..	..	0.0	0.0	0.0	0.0	0.0	0.4	1.7	2.5
Public sector LDOD	..	..	80.2	88.7	94.1	97.8	90.6	90.9	88.7	89.2
Private sector LDOD	..	..	0.0	0.0	0.0	0.0	0.0	0.0	0.0	0.0

6. CURRENCY COMPOSITION OF LONG-TERM DEBT (PERCENT)

	1970	1980	1990	1994	1995	1996	1997	1998	1999	2000
Deutsche mark	..	..	8.7	5.4	3.5	2.8	2.3	2.1	1.6	1.2
French franc	..	..	9.7	16.9	11.4	9.9	8.6	8.3	6.6	5.3
Japanese yen	..	..	0.3	0.1	1.1	0.9	0.8	0.8	0.8	0.6
Pound sterling	..	..	16.5	14.8	13.4	13.9	12.3	9.8	7.4	4.5
Swiss franc	..	..	0.0	0.0	0.0	0.0	0.0	0.0	0.0	0.0
U.S.dollars	..	..	51.7	49.2	58.0	60.2	64.8	67.7	71.8	73.7
Multiple currency	..	..	0.0	0.0	0.0	0.0	0.0	0.4	1.9	2.7
Special drawing rights	..	..	6.0	5.7	4.3	3.9	3.7	3.7	4.3	3.9
All other currencies	..	..	7.1	7.9	8.3	8.4	7.5	7.2	5.6	8.1

DOMINICA

(US$ million, unless otherwise indicated)

	1970	1980	1990	1994	1995	1996	1997	1998	1999	2000
7. DEBT RESTRUCTURINGS										
Total amount rescheduled	..	..	0.0	0.0	0.0	0.0	0.0	0.0	0.0	0.0
Debt stock rescheduled	..	..	0.0	0.0	0.0	0.0	0.0	0.0	0.0	0.0
Principal rescheduled	..	..	0.0	0.0	0.0	0.0	0.0	0.0	0.0	0.0
Official	..	..	0.0	0.0	0.0	0.0	0.0	0.0	0.0	0.0
Private	..	..	0.0	0.0	0.0	0.0	0.0	0.0	0.0	0.0
Interest rescheduled	..	..	0.0	0.0	0.0	0.0	0.0	0.0	0.0	0.0
Official	..	..	0.0	0.0	0.0	0.0	0.0	0.0	0.0	0.0
Private	..	..	0.0	0.0	0.0	0.0	0.0	0.0	0.0	0.0
Debt forgiven	..	..	3.3	0.0	0.0	0.0	0.0	0.0	0.0	0.0
Memo: interest forgiven	..	..	0.0	0.0	0.0	0.0	0.0	0.0	0.0	0.0
Debt stock reduction	..	..	0.0	0.0	0.0	0.0	0.0	0.0	0.0	0.0
of which debt buyback	..	..	0.0	0.0	0.0	0.0	0.0	0.0	0.0	0.0
8. DEBT STOCK-FLOW RECONCILIATION										
Total change in debt stocks	..	..	10.4	1.8	4.4	11.7	-11.4	6.0	-1.3	0.7
Net flows on debt	..	..	7.8	5.6	3.0	12.3	-7.1	4.2	1.6	3.0
Net change in interest arrears	..	..	0.0	0.0	0.2	0.2	-0.4	0.0	0.0	0.0
Interest capitalized	..	..	0.0	0.0	0.0	0.0	0.0	0.0	0.0	0.0
Debt forgiveness or reduction	..	..	-3.3	0.0	0.0	0.0	0.0	0.0	0.0	0.0
Cross-currency valuation	..	..	4.7	3.0	1.2	-2.1	-5.2	0.6	-2.8	-2.6
Residual	..	..	1.2	-6.8	0.0	1.3	1.3	1.2	-0.1	0.3
9. AVERAGE TERMS OF NEW COMMITMENTS										
ALL CREDITORS										
Interest (%)	..	..	3.0	0.0	2.6	2.7	0.5	3.6	3.5	5.6
Maturity (years)	..	..	25.1	0.0	26.4	26.2	19.5	25.0	28.5	19.6
Grace period (years)	..	..	8.5	0.0	8.8	8.1	4.0	7.0	2.6	6.5
Grant element (%)	..	..	53.8	0.0	56.5	56.3	60.8	49.1	45.3	30.0
Official creditors										
Interest (%)	..	..	3.0	0.0	2.6	2.7	0.5	3.6	3.5	5.6
Maturity (years)	..	..	25.1	0.0	26.4	26.2	19.5	25.0	28.5	19.6
Grace period (years)	..	..	8.5	0.0	8.8	8.1	4.0	7.0	2.6	6.5
Grant element (%)	..	..	53.8	0.0	56.5	56.3	60.8	49.1	45.3	30.0
Private creditors										
Interest (%)	..	..	0.0	0.0	0.0	0.0	0.0	0.0	0.0	0.0
Maturity (years)	..	..	0.0	0.0	0.0	0.0	0.0	0.0	0.0	0.0
Grace period (years)	..	..	0.0	0.0	0.0	0.0	0.0	0.0	0.0	0.0
Grant element (%)	..	..	0.0	0.0	0.0	0.0	0.0	0.0	0.0	0.0
Memorandum items										
Commitments	..	..	3.4	0.0	5.1	18.8	4.1	6.2	7.5	28.2
Official creditors	..	..	3.4	0.0	5.1	18.8	4.1	6.2	7.5	28.2
Private creditors	..	..	0.0	0.0	0.0	0.0	0.0	0.0	0.0	0.0

10. CONTRACTUAL OBLIGATIONS ON OUTSTANDING LONG-TERM DEBT

	2001	2002	2003	2004	2005	2006	2007	2008	2009	2010
TOTAL										
Disbursements	15.4	16.3	10.6	6.3	2.9	1.5	0.7	0.2	0.1	0.0
Principal	6.4	6.1	6.0	6.2	6.5	8.2	8.9	8.7	8.4	8.2
Interest	2.8	3.2	3.5	3.5	3.5	3.3	3.0	2.7	2.4	2.1
Official creditors										
Disbursements	15.4	16.3	10.6	6.3	2.9	1.5	0.7	0.2	0.1	0.0
Principal	6.4	6.1	6.0	6.2	6.5	8.2	8.9	8.7	8.4	8.2
Interest	2.8	3.2	3.5	3.5	3.5	3.3	3.0	2.7	2.4	2.1
Bilateral creditors										
Disbursements	1.0	0.6	0.2	0.1	0.0	0.0	0.0	0.0	0.0	0.0
Principal	1.5	1.6	1.5	1.7	1.9	1.9	2.6	2.3	2.1	1.9
Interest	0.6	0.6	0.6	0.6	0.5	0.5	0.4	0.4	0.3	0.3
Multilateral creditors										
Disbursements	14.4	15.8	10.4	6.2	2.9	1.5	0.7	0.2	0.1	0.0
Principal	4.9	4.5	4.4	4.5	4.7	6.3	6.3	6.3	6.3	6.4
Interest	2.1	2.6	2.9	3.0	2.9	2.8	2.6	2.3	2.1	1.8
Private creditors										
Disbursements	0.0	0.0	0.0	0.0	0.0	0.0	0.0	0.0	0.0	0.0
Principal	0.0	0.0	0.0	0.0	0.0	0.0	0.0	0.0	0.0	0.0
Interest	0.0	0.0	0.0	0.0	0.0	0.0	0.0	0.0	0.0	0.0
Commercial banks										
Disbursements	0.0	0.0	0.0	0.0	0.0	0.0	0.0	0.0	0.0	0.0
Principal	0.0	0.0	0.0	0.0	0.0	0.0	0.0	0.0	0.0	0.0
Interest	0.0	0.0	0.0	0.0	0.0	0.0	0.0	0.0	0.0	0.0
Other private										
Disbursements	0.0	0.0	0.0	0.0	0.0	0.0	0.0	0.0	0.0	0.0
Principal	0.0	0.0	0.0	0.0	0.0	0.0	0.0	0.0	0.0	0.0
Interest	0.0	0.0	0.0	0.0	0.0	0.0	0.0	0.0	0.0	0.0

DOMINICAN REPUBLIC

(US$ million, unless otherwise indicated)

	1970	1980	1990	1994	1995	1996	1997	1998	1999	2000
1. SUMMARY DEBT DATA										
TOTAL DEBT STOCKS (EDT)	**360**	**2,002**	**4,372**	**4,275**	**4,448**	**4,332**	**4,246**	**4,455**	**4,759**	**4,598**
Long-term debt (LDOD)	**353**	**1,473**	**3,518**	**3,655**	**3,672**	**3,529**	**3,467**	**3,533**	**3,657**	**3,368**
Public and publicly guaranteed	212	1,219	3,419	3,619	3,653	3,523	3,467	3,533	3,657	3,368
Private nonguaranteed	141	254	99	35	19	5	0	0	0	0
Use of IMF credit	**7**	**49**	**72**	**190**	**160**	**96**	**29**	**56**	**55**	**52**
Short-term debt	**0**	**480**	**782**	**431**	**616**	**708**	**750**	**866**	**1,047**	**1,178**
of which interest arrears on LDOD	0	7	506	173	215	241	135	122	162	28
Official creditors	0	3	304	119	157	177	76	56	90	22
Private creditors	0	4	202	54	58	64	59	66	72	6
Memo: principal arrears on LDOD	1	12	614	302	320	293	273	286	316	62
Official creditors	0	4	444	256	261	242	228	230	255	58
Private creditors	1	8	169	46	59	51	45	56	62	4
Memo: export credits	0	0	967	950	779	1,134	1,103	693	647	626
TOTAL DEBT FLOWS										
Disbursements	**60**	**482**	**139**	**123**	**195**	**133**	**106**	**187**	**293**	**289**
Long-term debt	60	482	139	123	195	133	106	133	293	289
IMF purchases	0	0	0	0	0	0	0	54	0	0
Principal repayments	**32**	**200**	**146**	**294**	**234**	**250**	**259**	**181**	**174**	**258**
Long-term debt	27	135	88	286	200	190	196	153	174	258
IMF repurchases	5	65	58	8	34	60	62	29	0	0
Net flows on debt	**28**	**438**	**15**	**-212**	**105**	**-52**	**-4**	**134**	**260**	**297**
of which short-term debt	0	156	23	-41	143	65	148	128	142	265
Interest payments (INT)	**13**	**179**	**86**	**210**	**175**	**198**	**202**	**193**	**204**	**263**
Long-term debt	13	121	59	183	145	163	174	159	158	211
IMF charges	0	5	9	10	10	7	3	1	2	3
Short-term debt	0	54	19	17	20	28	25	34	44	50
Net transfers on debt	**15**	**259**	**-71**	**-422**	**-70**	**-250**	**-207**	**-60**	**56**	**34**
Total debt service paid (TDS)	**45**	**379**	**232**	**504**	**409**	**448**	**461**	**375**	**378**	**521**
Long-term debt	39	256	147	469	345	354	370	311	332	468
IMF repurchases and charges	5	69	67	18	44	66	66	30	2	3
Short-term debt (interest only)	0	54	19	17	20	28	25	34	44	50
2. AGGREGATE NET RESOURCE FLOWS AND NET TRANSFERS (LONG-TERM)										
NET RESOURCE FLOWS	**114**	**453**	**213**	**83**	**451**	**93**	**381**	**815**	**1,541**	**1,103**
Net flow of long-term debt (ex. IMF)	33	346	51	-163	-5	-57	-90	-20	119	31
Foreign direct investment (net)	72	93	133	207	414	97	421	700	1,338	953
Portfolio equity flows	0	0	0	0	0	0	0	74	0	74
Grants (excluding technical coop.)	9	14	29	39	41	54	51	61	84	44
Memo: technical coop. grants	5	16	44	46	51	50	48	45	47	63
official net resource flows	39	304	83	-9	67	25	-43	35	138	-40
private net resource flows	75	150	130	92	384	68	424	780	1,403	1,142
NET TRANSFERS	**101**	**267**	**64**	**-129**	**271**	**-108**	**163**	**608**	**1,321**	**822**
Interest on long-term debt	13	121	59	183	145	163	174	159	158	211
Profit remittances on FDI	0	66	90	29	35	38	44	48	62	70
Memo: official net transfers	35	278	28	-113	-53	-96	-171	-84	18	-196
private net transfers	66	-11	36	-16	323	-12	334	692	1,302	1,018
3. MAJOR ECONOMIC AGGREGATES										
Gross national income (GNI)	1,476	6,420	6,759	9,780	11,170	12,596	14,277	14,968	16,375	18,628
Exports of goods & services (XGS)	284	1,496	2,233	6,098	6,653	7,237	8,290	8,976	9,724	10,953
of which workers remittances	25	183	315	757	794	914	1,089	1,326	1,519	1,689
Imports of goods & services (MGS)	392	2,237	2,568	6,608	7,034	7,703	8,716	9,975	10,482	12,193
International reserves (RES)	32	279	69	259	373	357	396	507	695	630
Current account balance	-102	-720	-280	-283	-183	-213	-163	-338	-429	-1,027
4. DEBT INDICATORS										
EDT / XGS (%)	126.9	133.8	195.8	70.1	66.9	59.9	51.2	49.6	48.9	42.0
EDT / GNI (%)	24.4	31.2	64.7	43.7	39.8	34.4	29.7	29.8	29.1	24.7
TDS / XGS (%)	15.8	25.3	10.4	8.3	6.2	6.2	5.6	4.2	3.9	4.8
INT / XGS (%)	4.4	12.0	3.9	3.4	2.6	2.7	2.4	2.2	2.1	2.4
INT / GNI (%)	0.9	2.8	1.3	2.1	1.6	1.6	1.4	1.3	1.3	1.4
RES / EDT (%)	9.0	13.9	1.6	6.1	8.4	8.2	9.3	11.4	14.6	13.7
RES / MGS (months)	1.0	1.5	0.3	0.5	0.6	0.6	0.6	0.6	0.8	0.6
Short-term / EDT (%)	0.1	24.0	17.9	10.1	13.9	16.3	17.7	19.4	22.0	25.6
Concessional / EDT (%)	46.5	20.1	27.5	39.1	37.6	37.5	36.6	34.5	32.0	30.9
Multilateral / EDT (%)	3.9	10.2	19.6	21.9	23.2	23.4	22.7	22.6	23.6	24.8

DOMINICAN REPUBLIC

(US$ million, unless otherwise indicated)

	1970	1980	1990	1994	1995	1996	1997	1998	1999	2000
5. LONG-TERM DEBT										
DEBT OUTSTANDING (LDOD)	**353**	**1,473**	**3,518**	**3,655**	**3,672**	**3,529**	**3,467**	**3,533**	**3,657**	**3,368**
Public and publicly guaranteed	**212**	**1,219**	**3,419**	**3,619**	**3,653**	**3,523**	**3,467**	**3,533**	**3,657**	**3,368**
Official creditors	202	786	2,383	2,948	2,996	2,890	2,833	2,890	2,950	2,598
Multilateral	14	205	858	936	1,034	1,014	965	1,008	1,124	1,141
Concessional	0	138	432	413	438	454	454	465	472	460
Bilateral	188	581	1,525	2,012	1,962	1,876	1,867	1,882	1,826	1,458
Concessional	167	264	772	1,259	1,234	1,169	1,100	1,074	1,052	961
Private creditors	10	434	1,036	672	657	634	634	644	707	770
Bonds	0	0	0	520	520	520	518	514	510	507
Commercial banks	0	386	775	27	34	37	59	71	126	248
Other private	9	48	261	125	104	77	58	59	71	15
Private nonguaranteed	**141**	**254**	**99**	**35**	**19**	**5**	**0**	**0**	**0**	**0**
Bonds	0	0	0	0	0	0	0	0	0	0
Commercial banks and other	141	254	99	35	19	5	0	0	0	0
Memo:										
IBRD	11	66	238	276	283	244	209	204	275	292
IDA	0	18	20	18	17	17	16	15	15	14
DISBURSEMENTS	**60**	**482**	**139**	**123**	**195**	**133**	**106**	**133**	**293**	**289**
Public and publicly guaranteed	**38**	**415**	**139**	**123**	**195**	**133**	**106**	**133**	**293**	**289**
Official creditors	36	319	136	114	187	118	77	113	211	132
Multilateral	11	90	84	81	157	95	61	84	177	109
Concessional	0	51	21	22	44	36	26	26	21	22
Bilateral	25	229	53	33	31	24	16	30	35	23
Concessional	24	42	20	7	18	10	6	13	24	23
Private creditors	2	96	2	9	8	15	29	20	81	157
Bonds	0	0	0	0	0	0	0	0	0	0
Commercial banks	0	72	0	8	8	15	29	18	66	157
Other private	2	24	2	2	0	0	0	2	15	0
Private nonguaranteed	**22**	**67**	**0**	**0**	**0**	**0**	**0**	**0**	**0**	**0**
Bonds	0	0	0	0	0	0	0	0	0	0
Commercial banks and other	22	67	0	0	0	0	0	0	0	0
Memo:										
IBRD	11	39	39	33	36	18	13	17	92	39
IDA	0	0	0	0	0	0	0	0	0	0
PRINCIPAL REPAYMENTS	**27**	**135**	**88**	**286**	**200**	**190**	**196**	**153**	**174**	**258**
Public and publicly guaranteed	**7**	**62**	**83**	**271**	**184**	**176**	**191**	**153**	**174**	**258**
Official creditors	6	30	83	162	161	148	171	139	158	216
Multilateral	0	3	38	70	79	70	67	59	61	64
Concessional	0	0	6	18	20	19	21	17	17	18
Bilateral	6	27	44	92	82	78	104	80	97	153
Concessional	3	9	8	51	47	50	57	41	51	93
Private creditors	1	32	0	109	23	29	20	14	16	41
Bonds	0	0	0	0	0	0	2	4	4	4
Commercial banks	0	30	0	79	3	9	5	4	10	33
Other private	1	2	0	30	20	19	14	6	3	4
Private nonguaranteed	**20**	**74**	**5**	**15**	**16**	**14**	**5**	**0**	**0**	**0**
Bonds	0	0	0	0	0	0	0	0	0	0
Commercial banks and other	20	74	5	15	16	14	5	0	0	0
Memo:										
IBRD	0	2	19	36	40	37	29	24	20	21
IDA	0	0	0	1	1	1	1	1	1	1
NET FLOWS ON DEBT	**33**	**346**	**51**	**-163**	**-5**	**-57**	**-90**	**-20**	**119**	**31**
Public and publicly guaranteed	**31**	**353**	**56**	**-148**	**11**	**-43**	**-85**	**-20**	**119**	**31**
Official creditors	30	289	54	-48	26	-29	-94	-26	54	-84
Multilateral	11	87	46	11	78	25	-6	24	116	46
Concessional	0	51	15	5	24	17	5	9	4	4
Bilateral	19	202	8	-59	-52	-54	-87	-50	-62	-130
Concessional	22	33	11	-44	-29	-40	-51	-28	-27	-70
Private creditors	1	64	2	-100	-15	-14	9	6	65	115
Bonds	0	0	0	0	0	0	-2	-4	-4	-4
Commercial banks	0	42	0	-72	5	5	24	14	56	124
Other private	1	22	2	-28	-20	-19	-14	-4	13	-4
Private nonguaranteed	**2**	**-7**	**-5**	**-15**	**-16**	**-14**	**-5**	**0**	**0**	**0**
Bonds	0	0	0	0	0	0	0	0	0	0
Commercial banks and other	2	-7	-5	-15	-16	-14	-5	0	0	0
Memo:										
IBRD	11	37	20	-3	-4	-19	-15	-6	72	18
IDA	0	0	0	-1	-1	-1	-1	-1	-1	-1

DOMINICAN REPUBLIC

(US$ million, unless otherwise indicated)

	1970	1980	1990	1994	1995	1996	1997	1998	1999	2000
INTEREST PAYMENTS (LINT)	**13**	**121**	**59**	**183**	**145**	**163**	**174**	**159**	**158**	**211**
Public and publicly guaranteed	**4**	**92**	**56**	**179**	**143**	**162**	**174**	**159**	**158**	**211**
Official creditors	4	26	55	104	120	121	128	119	120	157
Multilateral	1	5	32	47	51	51	47	45	51	58
Concessional	0	1	4	9	10	9	9	8	8	8
Bilateral	4	21	24	57	69	70	81	74	69	99
Concessional	2	6	7	35	53	48	53	42	40	54
Private creditors	0	66	1	75	23	41	46	40	38	54
Bonds	0	0	0	5	13	34	35	35	32	38
Commercial banks	0	64	0	63	3	4	10	4	6	15
Other private	0	3	1	7	7	3	1	1	1	2
Private nonguaranteed	**8**	**29**	**3**	**4**	**2**	**1**	**0**	**0**	**0**	**0**
Bonds	0	0	0	0	0	0	0	0	0	0
Commercial banks and other	8	29	3	4	2	1	0	0	0	0
Memo:										
IBRD	0	3	14	20	21	19	16	14	16	22
IDA	0	0	0	0	0	0	0	0	0	0
NET TRANSFERS ON DEBT	**21**	**226**	**-9**	**-346**	**-150**	**-221**	**-264**	**-178**	**-40**	**-179**
Public and publicly guaranteed	**27**	**261**	**0**	**-327**	**-132**	**-206**	**-259**	**-178**	**-40**	**-179**
Official creditors	26	264	-1	-153	-94	-150	-221	-145	-66	-241
Multilateral	10	83	14	-36	27	-26	-53	-21	65	-12
Concessional	0	50	11	-4	14	8	-4	0	-4	-4
Bilateral	16	181	-15	-116	-121	-124	-169	-124	-131	-228
Concessional	20	27	4	-80	-82	-87	-104	-70	-67	-125
Private creditors	1	-3	1	-175	-38	-56	-38	-34	27	61
Bonds	0	0	0	-5	-13	-34	-37	-39	-36	-41
Commercial banks	0	-22	0	-135	2	1	14	10	50	109
Other private	1	20	1	-35	-27	-22	-15	-4	12	-6
Private nonguaranteed	**-6**	**-35**	**-8**	**-19**	**-18**	**-15**	**-6**	**0**	**0**	**0**
Bonds	0	0	0	0	0	0	0	0	0	0
Commercial banks and other	-6	-35	-8	-19	-18	-15	-6	0	0	0
Memo:										
IBRD	10	34	6	-23	-25	-38	-31	-20	55	-4
IDA	0	0	0	-1	-1	-1	-1	-1	-1	-1
DEBT SERVICE (LTDS)	**39**	**256**	**147**	**469**	**345**	**354**	**370**	**311**	**332**	**468**
Public and publicly guaranteed	**12**	**154**	**139**	**450**	**327**	**338**	**365**	**311**	**332**	**468**
Official creditors	10	56	138	266	281	268	299	258	277	373
Multilateral	1	7	70	118	130	121	114	105	112	122
Concessional	0	1	10	26	30	28	30	26	24	26
Bilateral	10	48	68	149	151	148	185	154	166	252
Concessional	4	15	15	86	100	98	109	83	91	148
Private creditors	1	98	1	184	46	70	66	53	55	95
Bonds	0	0	0	5	13	34	37	39	36	41
Commercial banks	0	94	0	143	6	14	15	8	16	48
Other private	1	4	1	36	27	22	15	6	3	6
Private nonguaranteed	**28**	**102**	**8**	**19**	**18**	**15**	**6**	**0**	**0**	**0**
Bonds	0	0	0	0	0	0	0	0	0	0
Commercial banks and other	28	102	8	19	18	15	6	0	0	0
Memo:										
IBRD	0	5	33	56	60	56	44	38	37	43
IDA	0	0	0	1	1	1	1	1	1	1
UNDISBURSED DEBT	**64**	**632**	**510**	**523**	**492**	**461**	**595**	**1,235**	**1,455**	**910**
Official creditors	42	537	483	509	480	439	530	875	991	732
Private creditors	22	94	27	14	12	22	65	360	464	178
Memorandum items										
Concessional LDOD	167	402	1,204	1,672	1,671	1,622	1,554	1,539	1,524	1,421
Variable rate LDOD	141	695	1,104	1,204	1,273	1,272	1,228	1,291	1,436	1,423
Public sector LDOD	197	1,185	3,391	3,591	3,626	3,499	3,444	3,511	3,643	3,355
Private sector LDOD	156	289	127	63	46	30	23	22	15	13

6. CURRENCY COMPOSITION OF LONG-TERM DEBT (PERCENT)

	1970	1980	1990	1994	1995	1996	1997	1998	1999	2000
Deutsche mark	0.0	0.6	2.0	2.2	2.2	2.0	1.7	1.8	1.5	1.5
French franc	0.0	0.0	0.5	1.2	1.5	1.4	1.2	1.2	0.9	0.8
Japanese yen	0.0	0.0	6.4	8.4	7.7	6.7	5.7	6.1	6.6	4.9
Pound sterling	0.0	0.0	0.0	0.0	0.0	0.0	0.0	0.0	0.0	0.0
Swiss franc	0.0	0.0	0.0	0.0	0.0	0.0	0.0	0.0	0.0	0.0
U.S.dollars	93.4	81.8	68.4	64.3	63.7	65.0	67.5	71.5	72.6	74.0
Multiple currency	6.6	11.5	21.8	23.2	24.2	24.0	23.1	18.5	17.6	17.7
Special drawing rights	0.0	0.0	0.2	0.1	0.1	0.3	0.3	0.3	0.3	0.6
All other currencies	0.0	6.1	0.7	0.6	0.6	0.6	0.5	0.6	0.5	0.5

DOMINICAN REPUBLIC

(US$ million, unless otherwise indicated)

	1970	1980	1990	1994	1995	1996	1997	1998	1999	2000
7. DEBT RESTRUCTURINGS										
Total amount rescheduled	..	..	8	520	2	22	130	60	0	0
Debt stock rescheduled	..	..	0	506	0	0	0	0	0	0
Principal rescheduled	..	..	1	6	1	14	20	30	0	0
Official	..	..	1	0	1	14	20	30	0	0
Private	..	..	0	6	0	0	0	0	0	0
Interest rescheduled	..	..	2	3	0	7	110	29	0	0
Official	..	..	2	0	0	7	110	29	0	0
Private	..	..	0	3	0	0	0	0	0	0
Debt forgiven	..	..	7	0	0	3	0	0	0	1
Memo: interest forgiven	..	..	0	180	0	4	0	0	0	0
Debt stock reduction	..	..	0	291	0	0	0	0	0	0
of which debt buyback	..	..	0	68	0	0	0	0	0	0
8. DEBT STOCK-FLOW RECONCILIATION										
Total change in debt stocks	..	..	334	-585	173	-116	-86	209	304	-161
Net flows on debt	28	438	15	-212	105	-52	-4	134	260	297
Net change in interest arrears	..	..	267	-360	42	26	-106	-13	40	-135
Interest capitalized	..	..	2	3	0	7	110	29	0	0
Debt forgiveness or reduction	..	..	-7	-223	0	-3	0	0	0	-1
Cross-currency valuation	..	..	52	53	18	-104	-96	43	9	-51
Residual	..	..	5	154	8	9	10	16	-5	-272
9. AVERAGE TERMS OF NEW COMMITMENTS										
ALL CREDITORS										
Interest (%)	2.4	8.9	5.9	3.7	6.6	5.5	7.3	6.7	5.8	7.6
Maturity (years)	28.4	12.3	24.5	28.0	19.8	16.4	19.1	16.9	14.2	14.4
Grace period (years)	4.8	4.0	6.4	7.9	5.1	4.4	4.2	3.3	3.8	2.1
Grant element (%)	53.4	10.2	31.3	49.6	21.2	26.8	16.1	17.7	22.2	11.3
Official creditors										
Interest (%)	2.4	7.5	5.8	3.6	6.6	5.1	7.5	6.6	5.4	7.2
Maturity (years)	28.4	12.8	24.9	28.2	20.2	18.4	21.5	22.1	16.8	22.8
Grace period (years)	4.8	4.3	6.4	8.0	5.2	5.0	5.0	4.0	4.5	1.5
Grant element (%)	53.4	17.5	32.0	50.3	21.7	30.9	16.2	21.6	27.0	16.8
Private creditors										
Interest (%)	0.0	11.8	9.8	9.1	8.4	7.1	6.5	6.8	6.5	7.9
Maturity (years)	0.0	11.3	9.1	8.9	9.5	8.5	12.7	9.6	9.8	9.3
Grace period (years)	0.0	3.4	4.6	1.7	2.0	1.8	2.3	2.2	2.6	2.5
Grant element (%)	0.0	-3.9	-0.2	1.4	5.8	9.9	15.7	12.1	14.2	8.0
Memorandum items										
Commitments	20	519	204	229	167	126	264	764	552	81
Official creditors	20	342	199	226	161	101	192	449	346	31
Private creditors	0	176	5	3	6	25	72	315	205	50

10. CONTRACTUAL OBLIGATIONS ON OUTSTANDING LONG-TERM DEBT

	2001	2002	2003	2004	2005	2006	2007	2008	2009	2010
TOTAL										
Disbursements	315	265	143	87	52	27	14	4	3	1
Principal	408	418	392	353	344	306	253	194	188	158
Interest	195	188	173	156	139	121	104	90	79	69
Official creditors										
Disbursements	216	211	123	82	51	27	14	4	3	1
Principal	337	344	314	278	271	252	201	144	137	126
Interest	139	131	120	108	96	82	69	58	51	44
Bilateral creditors										
Disbursements	41	38	24	14	8	5	3	2	2	1
Principal	241	244	208	165	153	144	94	46	40	36
Interest	70	58	46	36	27	19	12	7	6	5
Multilateral creditors										
Disbursements	175	173	99	67	43	22	11	2	1	0
Principal	96	100	106	113	118	108	108	97	96	90
Interest	69	74	74	72	68	63	57	51	45	39
Private creditors										
Disbursements	99	53	21	5	1	0	0	0	0	0
Principal	71	74	78	75	73	54	52	50	51	32
Interest	57	57	53	49	44	39	35	32	28	25
Commercial banks										
Disbursements	90	44	16	4	0	0	0	0	0	0
Principal	44	47	54	53	51	32	30	28	29	30
Interest	21	22	20	17	13	10	8	6	4	2
Other private										
Disbursements	9	9	5	1	1	0	0	0	0	0
Principal	7	7	4	2	2	2	2	2	2	2
Interest	1	1	1	1	1	1	1	0	0	0

ECUADOR

(US$ million, unless otherwise indicated)

	1970	1980	1990	1994	1995	1996	1997	1998	1999	2000
1. SUMMARY DEBT DATA										
TOTAL DEBT STOCKS (EDT)	**364**	**5,998**	**12,107**	**15,061**	**13,994**	**14,495**	**15,419**	**15,640**	**15,305**	**13,281**
Long-term debt (LDOD)	**245**	**4,422**	**10,029**	**10,769**	**12,508**	**12,764**	**13,216**	**13,299**	**14,059**	**12,151**
Public and publicly guaranteed	195	3,301	9,865	10,545	12,068	12,444	12,876	13,089	13,556	11,366
Private nonguaranteed	49	1,122	164	224	440	320	340	210	503	785
Use of IMF credit	**14**	**0**	**265**	**198**	**174**	**145**	**133**	**70**	**0**	**148**
Short-term debt	**106**	**1,575**	**1,814**	**4,094**	**1,312**	**1,586**	**2,069**	**2,272**	**1,247**	**982**
of which interest arrears on LDOD	0	0	1,522	2,343	13	77	84	85	198	119
Official creditors	0	0	10	3	8	61	75	76	74	1
Private creditors	0	0	1,512	2,340	5	16	9	9	124	118
Memo: principal arrears on LDOD	0	1	1,096	3,420	10	178	251	280	576	6
Official creditors	0	0	6	6	8	121	192	201	497	0
Private creditors	0	1	1,090	3,415	2	58	59	79	79	6
Memo: export credits	0	0	2,090	1,726	1,149	1,410	1,240	458	544	503
TOTAL DEBT FLOWS										
Disbursements	**58**	**1,283**	**638**	**666**	**1,049**	**1,090**	**1,828**	**714**	**1,155**	**1,208**
Long-term debt	48	1,283	606	524	1,049	1,090	1,828	714	1,155	1,059
IMF purchases	10	0	32	142	0	0	0	0	0	150
Principal repayments	**33**	**535**	**610**	**509**	**750**	**646**	**1,069**	**840**	**798**	**665**
Long-term debt	26	535	495	487	721	623	1,066	773	731	665
IMF repurchases	7	0	115	21	29	23	3	67	68	0
Net flows on debt	**25**	**1,174**	**0**	**375**	**-152**	**653**	**1,235**	**76**	**-782**	**358**
of which short-term debt	0	426	-28	218	-451	210	475	202	-1,139	-185
Interest payments (INT)	**10**	**473**	**474**	**491**	**666**	**675**	**823**	**922**	**903**	**611**
Long-term debt	10	365	416	400	574	576	715	812	814	545
IMF charges	0	0	30	3	10	7	6	5	2	4
Short-term debt	0	108	28	88	81	92	101	104	87	62
Net transfers on debt	**15**	**701**	**-474**	**-116**	**-818**	**-22**	**412**	**-846**	**-1,685**	**-253**
Total debt service paid (TDS)	**43**	**1,008**	**1,084**	**1,000**	**1,416**	**1,321**	**1,891**	**1,762**	**1,701**	**1,276**
Long-term debt	36	900	911	888	1,296	1,199	1,781	1,586	1,544	1,210
IMF repurchases and charges	7	0	145	25	39	30	9	72	70	4
Short-term debt (interest only)	0	108	28	88	81	92	101	104	87	62
2. AGGREGATE NET RESOURCE FLOWS AND NET TRANSFERS (LONG-TERM)										
NET RESOURCE FLOWS	**113**	**825**	**290**	**618**	**870**	**1,014**	**1,440**	**824**	**1,168**	**1,172**
Net flow of long-term debt (ex. IMF)	21	748	110	37	328	466	762	-59	425	394
Foreign direct investment (net)	89	70	126	531	470	491	625	814	690	710
Portfolio equity flows	0	0	0	4	1	1	0	0	0	0
Grants (excluding technical coop.)	3	7	53	46	71	55	53	69	53	68
Memo: technical coop. grants	9	28	65	91	110	99	85	84	74	86
official net resource flows	12	231	106	113	329	167	63	257	224	268
private net resource flows	101	594	184	505	541	847	1,377	567	944	904
NET TRANSFERS	**84**	**349**	**-251**	**67**	**144**	**278**	**555**	**-169**	**156**	**422**
Interest on long-term debt	10	365	416	400	574	576	715	812	814	545
Profit remittances on FDI	19	111	125	150	152	160	170	180	198	204
Memo: official net transfers	8	142	-106	-139	1	-104	-256	-20	-67	-9
private net transfers	76	207	-145	206	143	382	811	-149	223	431
3. MAJOR ECONOMIC AGGREGATES										
Gross national income (GNI)	1,642	11,152	9,752	15,427	17,014	17,805	18,858	18,496	17,161	12,380
Exports of goods & services (XGS)	..	2,975	3,337	4,735	5,487	6,086	6,598	5,887	6,396	7,237
of which workers remittances	0	0	50	95	170	282	406	794	1,084	1,281
Imports of goods & services (MGS)	..	3,647	3,754	5,466	6,313	6,010	7,297	8,038	5,458	6,092
International reserves (RES)	76	1,257	1,009	2,003	1,788	2,011	2,213	1,739	1,763	1,180
Current account balance	..	-642	-360	-681	-765	84	-714	-2,169	955	..
4. DEBT INDICATORS										
EDT / XGS (%)	..	201.6	362.8	318.1	255.0	238.2	233.7	265.7	239.3	183.5
EDT / GNI (%)	22.2	53.8	124.2	97.6	82.3	81.4	81.8	84.6	89.2	107.3
TDS / XGS (%)	..	33.9	32.5	21.1	25.8	21.7	28.7	29.9	26.6	17.6
INT / XGS (%)	..	15.9	14.2	10.4	12.1	11.1	12.5	15.7	14.1	8.4
INT / GNI (%)	0.6	4.2	4.9	3.2	3.9	3.8	4.4	5.0	5.3	4.9
RES / EDT (%)	20.8	21.0	8.3	13.3	12.8	13.9	14.4	11.1	11.5	8.9
RES / MGS (months)	..	4.1	3.2	4.4	3.4	4.0	3.6	2.6	3.9	2.3
Short-term / EDT (%)	29.1	26.3	15.0	27.2	9.4	10.9	13.4	14.5	8.1	7.4
Concessional / EDT (%)	23.2	4.8	7.6	11.1	12.9	12.9	11.6	12.4	13.4	15.3
Multilateral / EDT (%)	13.9	5.4	17.6	17.1	21.6	20.3	18.6	20.2	21.9	26.1

ECUADOR

(US$ million, unless otherwise indicated)

	1970	1980	1990	1994	1995	1996	1997	1998	1999	2000
5. LONG-TERM DEBT										
DEBT OUTSTANDING (LDOD)	**245**	**4,422**	**10,029**	**10,769**	**12,508**	**12,764**	**13,216**	**13,299**	**14,059**	**12,151**
Public and publicly guaranteed	**195**	**3,301**	**9,865**	**10,545**	**12,068**	**12,444**	**12,876**	**13,089**	**13,556**	**11,366**
Official creditors	133	1,325	4,065	4,934	5,281	5,149	4,905	5,234	5,741	6,094
Multilateral	51	323	2,127	2,580	3,019	2,944	2,872	3,165	3,351	3,466
Concessional	10	102	451	601	647	654	639	634	631	613
Bilateral	83	1,002	1,938	2,354	2,261	2,206	2,033	2,070	2,390	2,628
Concessional	75	188	469	1,068	1,159	1,215	1,145	1,300	1,415	1,417
Private creditors	62	1,976	5,800	5,611	6,787	7,294	7,971	7,855	7,815	5,273
Bonds	3	55	0	191	5,999	6,013	6,334	6,325	6,306	3,950
Commercial banks	4	1,697	4,884	4,951	453	942	1,317	1,262	1,271	1,187
Other private	55	224	917	469	335	339	320	268	237	136
Private nonguaranteed	**49**	**1,122**	**164**	**224**	**440**	**320**	**340**	**210**	**503**	**785**
Bonds	0	0	0	0	10	10	0	0	0	0
Commercial banks and other	49	1,122	164	224	430	310	340	210	503	785
Memo:										
IBRD	34	109	816	830	1,082	980	851	854	861	840
IDA	6	36	32	28	27	25	24	23	22	21
DISBURSEMENTS	**48**	**1,283**	**606**	**524**	**1,049**	**1,090**	**1,828**	**714**	**1,155**	**1,059**
Public and publicly guaranteed	**41**	**968**	**575**	**524**	**839**	**1,090**	**1,748**	**714**	**756**	**644**
Official creditors	17	348	329	377	744	478	414	614	558	545
Multilateral	5	91	227	310	602	317	355	463	411	445
Concessional	2	11	24	39	62	34	15	16	17	9
Bilateral	12	257	101	67	142	161	59	151	147	100
Concessional	9	4	31	66	128	135	46	146	145	99
Private creditors	25	620	247	147	95	612	1,334	100	198	99
Bonds	0	0	0	0	0	0	500	0	0	0
Commercial banks	2	497	39	131	75	546	793	100	188	99
Other private	22	122	207	16	21	66	41	0	11	0
Private nonguaranteed	**7**	**315**	**30**	**0**	**210**	**0**	**80**	**0**	**399**	**415**
Bonds	0	0	0	0	10	0	0	0	0	0
Commercial banks and other	7	315	30	0	200	0	80	0	399	415
Memo:										
IBRD	2	34	47	112	319	89	45	85	90	69
IDA	2	0	0	0	0	0	0	0	0	0
PRINCIPAL REPAYMENTS	**26**	**535**	**495**	**487**	**721**	**623**	**1,066**	**773**	**731**	**665**
Public and publicly guaranteed	**16**	**272**	**470**	**471**	**711**	**493**	**1,006**	**643**	**625**	**555**
Official creditors	7	125	276	310	486	366	404	426	387	344
Multilateral	3	16	164	225	235	234	288	220	226	268
Concessional	1	0	8	20	23	25	26	22	22	22
Bilateral	4	108	112	85	252	132	116	206	162	76
Concessional	3	8	2	18	46	36	45	53	57	55
Private creditors	8	147	194	160	225	127	602	217	238	211
Bonds	0	14	0	0	10	10	126	10	19	0
Commercial banks	3	110	27	62	60	56	417	155	178	184
Other private	6	23	167	99	155	62	59	53	40	27
Private nonguaranteed	**11**	**263**	**25**	**17**	**10**	**130**	**60**	**130**	**106**	**110**
Bonds	0	0	0	0	0	0	10	0	0	0
Commercial banks and other	11	263	25	17	10	130	50	130	106	110
Memo:										
IBRD	2	10	42	94	98	119	101	79	82	90
IDA	0	0	1	1	1	1	1	1	1	1
NET FLOWS ON DEBT	**21**	**748**	**110**	**37**	**328**	**466**	**762**	**-59**	**425**	**394**
Public and publicly guaranteed	**26**	**696**	**105**	**54**	**128**	**596**	**742**	**71**	**132**	**89**
Official creditors	9	224	53	67	258	112	10	188	171	200
Multilateral	1	75	64	85	368	83	67	243	186	176
Concessional	1	11	16	19	39	9	-11	-7	-5	-13
Bilateral	8	149	-11	-18	-110	29	-57	-55	-15	24
Concessional	6	-4	28	49	82	99	1	93	87	44
Private creditors	16	473	52	-14	-130	485	732	-117	-39	-112
Bonds	0	-14	0	0	-10	-10	374	-10	-19	0
Commercial banks	0	387	12	69	14	490	375	-55	9	-85
Other private	17	99	40	-83	-135	4	-18	-53	-30	-27
Private nonguaranteed	**-4**	**52**	**5**	**-17**	**200**	**-130**	**20**	**-130**	**293**	**305**
Bonds	0	0	0	0	10	0	-10	0	0	0
Commercial banks and other	-4	52	5	-17	190	-130	30	-130	293	305
Memo:										
IBRD	0	24	5	18	221	-30	-56	6	8	-21
IDA	2	0	-1	-1	-1	-1	-1	-1	-1	-1

ECUADOR

(US$ million, unless otherwise indicated)

	1970	1980	1990	1994	1995	1996	1997	1998	1999	2000
INTEREST PAYMENTS (LINT)	**10**	**365**	**416**	**400**	**574**	**576**	**715**	**812**	**814**	**545**
Public and publicly guaranteed	**7**	**288**	**404**	**399**	**573**	**572**	**711**	**811**	**813**	**544**
Official creditors	4	89	212	252	328	271	319	277	291	277
Multilateral	3	19	140	157	171	191	221	179	200	241
Concessional	0	1	8	12	13	12	14	12	11	11
Bilateral	2	71	72	94	157	80	99	98	91	36
Concessional	1	5	8	28	47	33	39	45	47	28
Private creditors	2	199	191	147	245	301	392	535	523	268
Bonds	0	6	0	0	147	241	250	405	391	140
Commercial banks	1	184	132	120	54	43	114	111	118	116
Other private	2	8	59	27	44	17	28	18	14	12
Private nonguaranteed	**3**	**78**	**12**	**2**	**1**	**4**	**4**	**1**	**0**	**1**
Bonds	0	0	0	0	0	1	1	0	0	0
Commercial banks and other	3	78	12	2	1	3	3	1	0	1
Memo:										
IBRD	2	9	62	59	69	75	69	51	58	74
IDA	0	0	0	0	0	0	0	0	0	0
NET TRANSFERS ON DEBT	**11**	**383**	**-305**	**-363**	**-246**	**-109**	**47**	**-871**	**-389**	**-152**
Public and publicly guaranteed	**19**	**408**	**-299**	**-345**	**-445**	**25**	**31**	**-740**	**-682**	**-456**
Official creditors	5	134	-160	-184	-71	-159	-309	-89	-120	-77
Multilateral	-1	56	-77	-72	197	-108	-154	65	-14	-64
Concessional	1	9	8	7	26	-3	-25	-18	-16	-24
Bilateral	6	78	-83	-112	-268	-51	-155	-153	-106	-12
Concessional	5	-9	21	21	35	66	-38	48	40	15
Private creditors	14	274	-139	-161	-375	184	340	-652	-562	-379
Bonds	0	-20	0	0	-157	-250	125	-415	-410	-140
Commercial banks	-1	203	-120	-51	-40	446	261	-166	-108	-201
Other private	15	91	-19	-110	-178	-12	-46	-71	-44	-39
Private nonguaranteed	**-8**	**-26**	**-7**	**-18**	**199**	**-134**	**16**	**-131**	**293**	**304**
Bonds	0	0	0	0	10	-1	-11	0	0	0
Commercial banks and other	-8	-26	-7	-18	189	-133	27	-131	293	304
Memo:										
IBRD	-2	16	-56	-41	152	-105	-125	-45	-50	-95
IDA	2	0	-1	-1	-1	-1	-1	-1	-1	-1
DEBT SERVICE (LTDS)	**36**	**900**	**911**	**888**	**1,296**	**1,199**	**1,781**	**1,586**	**1,544**	**1,210**
Public and publicly guaranteed	**22**	**559**	**874**	**869**	**1,284**	**1,065**	**1,717**	**1,454**	**1,438**	**1,099**
Official creditors	12	214	488	562	815	638	723	703	678	621
Multilateral	6	35	304	383	406	425	509	399	426	509
Concessional	1	2	16	32	36	37	40	34	33	33
Bilateral	6	179	184	179	409	213	214	304	252	112
Concessional	4	13	10	46	93	69	84	97	105	84
Private creditors	11	346	386	308	470	428	994	752	760	478
Bonds	0	20	0	0	157	250	375	415	410	140
Commercial banks	3	294	159	182	114	99	532	266	296	300
Other private	8	31	226	126	199	78	87	71	54	39
Private nonguaranteed	**14**	**341**	**37**	**18**	**11**	**134**	**64**	**131**	**106**	**111**
Bonds	0	0	0	0	0	1	11	0	0	0
Commercial banks and other	14	341	37	18	11	133	53	131	106	111
Memo:										
IBRD	4	19	103	153	167	194	170	130	140	164
IDA	0	0	1	1	1	1	1	1	1	1
UNDISBURSED DEBT	**142**	**1,039**	**1,647**	**2,017**	**2,253**	**2,118**	**1,903**	**1,886**	**1,208**	**945**
Official creditors	60	695	1,533	1,809	1,772	1,535	1,596	1,558	1,078	889
Private creditors	82	345	114	208	482	583	307	328	130	56
Memorandum items										
Concessional LDOD	85	290	920	1,669	1,806	1,868	1,785	1,934	2,046	2,030
Variable rate LDOD	49	2,766	6,245	6,649	6,542	6,755	6,875	7,033	7,598	3,832
Public sector LDOD	195	3,301	9,865	10,545	12,068	12,444	12,876	13,089	13,556	11,366
Private sector LDOD	49	1,122	164	224	440	320	340	210	503	785

6. CURRENCY COMPOSITION OF LONG-TERM DEBT (PERCENT)

	1970	1980	1990	1994	1995	1996	1997	1998	1999	2000
Deutsche mark	4.6	1.7	2.8	2.5	1.1	1.0	0.8	0.7	0.6	0.6
French franc	1.9	0.0	1.5	2.6	2.3	2.1	1.7	1.7	1.3	1.2
Japanese yen	0.0	2.7	6.9	9.6	5.0	4.4	3.6	4.7	5.8	6.3
Pound sterling	0.8	1.1	1.6	1.3	0.7	0.7	0.7	0.6	0.5	0.4
Swiss franc	0.2	0.7	0.5	0.2	0.0	0.0	0.0	0.0	0.0	0.0
U.S.dollars	71.7	64.2	54.5	53.6	70.5	73.9	77.9	83.5	84.0	83.3
Multiple currency	19.6	28.1	29.7	28.1	19.6	17.1	14.5	8.0	7.0	7.4
Special drawing rights	0.0	0.0	0.0	0.0	0.0	0.0	0.0	0.0	0.0	0.1
All other currencies	1.2	1.5	2.5	2.1	0.8	0.8	0.8	0.8	0.8	0.7

ECUADOR

(US$ million, unless otherwise indicated)

	1970	1980	1990	1994	1995	1996	1997	1998	1999	2000
7. DEBT RESTRUCTURINGS										
Total amount rescheduled	..	..	249	533	5,818	29	62	0	0	4,837
Debt stock rescheduled	..	..	16	0	3,345	0	0	0	0	3,783
Principal rescheduled	..	..	152	300	0	0	0	0	0	624
Official	..	..	110	276	0	0	0	0	0	549
Private	..	..	42	24	0	0	0	0	0	74
Interest rescheduled	..	..	81	117	1,750	25	62	0	0	127
Official	..	..	61	115	0	0	0	0	0	121
Private	..	..	19	3	1,750	25	62	0	0	6
Debt forgiven	..	..	1	0	0	1	0	0	0	0
Memo: interest forgiven	..	..	0	0	0	0	0	0	0	0
Debt stock reduction	..	..	45	10	1,180	1	200	0	0	2,522
of which debt buyback	..	..	0	0	0	0	85	0	0	0
8. DEBT STOCK-FLOW RECONCILIATION										
Total change in debt stocks	..	..	791	925	-1,067	502	923	222	-335	-2,024
Net flows on debt	25	1,174	0	375	-152	653	1,235	76	-782	358
Net change in interest arrears	..	..	451	19	-2,330	64	7	1	114	-79
Interest capitalized	..	..	81	117	1,750	25	62	0	0	127
Debt forgiveness or reduction	..	..	-46	-10	-1,180	-2	-115	0	0	-2,522
Cross-currency valuation	..	..	193	170	57	-286	-282	110	21	-173
Residual	..	..	113	254	788	48	17	35	312	265
9. AVERAGE TERMS OF NEW COMMITMENTS										
ALL CREDITORS										
Interest (%)	6.2	10.7	6.4	6.0	6.4	5.8	9.3	7.0	6.9	7.0
Maturity (years)	20.0	14.9	17.4	20.7	15.8	11.0	10.5	14.4	22.1	16.6
Grace period (years)	3.9	3.8	4.2	5.4	5.5	3.3	5.1	3.9	4.8	4.9
Grant element (%)	24.0	-0.9	24.1	27.2	21.9	19.1	5.7	16.5	20.3	17.8
Official creditors										
Interest (%)	4.3	8.6	5.2	5.9	5.6	4.6	6.8	7.0	6.9	6.9
Maturity (years)	35.8	22.1	22.2	21.9	18.0	26.0	17.6	15.9	22.1	17.1
Grace period (years)	8.0	4.4	6.0	5.8	6.7	7.7	4.9	4.1	4.8	5.1
Grant element (%)	48.8	11.4	35.1	29.0	28.4	41.5	20.4	17.5	20.3	18.3
Private creditors										
Interest (%)	7.3	12.7	8.6	6.8	8.1	6.3	10.9	7.0	..	7.5
Maturity (years)	10.2	7.9	8.7	10.6	11.0	4.8	6.0	10.1	..	9.9
Grace period (years)	1.3	3.2	1.0	2.5	2.9	1.4	5.3	3.3	..	2.5
Grant element (%)	8.4	-12.7	4.0	13.5	7.9	9.8	-3.8	13.3	..	10.0
Memorandum items										
Commitments	78	1,148	641	924	1,165	1,024	1,778	780	82	404
Official creditors	30	564	413	820	797	301	700	581	82	379
Private creditors	48	584	228	104	369	723	1,078	199	0	25

10. CONTRACTUAL OBLIGATIONS ON OUTSTANDING LONG-TERM DEBT

	2001	2002	2003	2004	2005	2006	2007	2008	2009	2010
TOTAL										
Disbursements	468	253	104	59	31	15	7	5	3	1
Principal	905	982	902	1,042	597	544	518	419	367	322
Interest	764	730	709	686	628	589	554	522	498	477
Official creditors										
Disbursements	427	244	100	58	30	15	7	5	3	1
Principal	478	483	511	509	501	478	462	382	343	303
Interest	373	358	331	300	268	236	205	177	155	136
Bilateral creditors										
Disbursements	72	48	29	16	6	4	2	2	1	1
Principal	122	122	156	164	171	169	159	144	149	117
Interest	130	126	120	111	101	92	82	74	67	61
Multilateral creditors										
Disbursements	355	196	71	41	24	11	5	3	2	0
Principal	356	361	356	345	330	309	303	238	194	186
Interest	243	233	212	189	166	144	123	103	88	76
Private creditors										
Disbursements	40	9	5	2	1	0	0	0	0	0
Principal	427	499	391	532	96	66	57	37	23	20
Interest	391	372	378	386	360	353	349	345	343	341
Commercial banks										
Disbursements	34	2	1	0	0	0	0	0	0	0
Principal	145	482	112	248	78	47	39	33	20	16
Interest	107	77	48	31	16	10	7	5	3	1
Other private										
Disbursements	7	7	4	1	1	0	0	0	0	0
Principal	282	17	279	284	18	18	18	4	4	4
Interest	284	294	330	355	345	343	342	340	340	340

EGYPT, ARAB REPUBLIC OF

(US$ million, unless otherwise indicated)

	1970	1980	1990	1994	1995	1996	1997	1998	1999	2000
1. SUMMARY DEBT DATA										
TOTAL DEBT STOCKS (EDT)	**1,802**	**19,131**	**33,017**	**32,379**	**33,337**	**31,366**	**29,928**	**32,268**	**30,802**	**28,957**
Long-term debt (LDOD)	**1,351**	**14,693**	**28,438**	**30,253**	**30,861**	**29,002**	**26,935**	**28,006**	**26,508**	**24,852**
Public and publicly guaranteed	1,351	14,428	27,438	29,878	30,548	28,875	26,804	27,622	26,026	24,279
Private nonguaranteed	0	265	1,000	375	313	127	131	384	481	573
Use of IMF credit	**49**	**411**	**125**	**193**	**103**	**16**	**0**	**0**	**0**	**0**
Short-term debt	**401**	**4,027**	**4,453**	**1,933**	**2,372**	**2,348**	**2,993**	**4,262**	**4,294**	**4,105**
of which interest arrears on LDOD	4	383	1,441	3	4	4	5	3	1	1
Official creditors	4	383	873	1	2	1	2	0	0	0
Private creditors	1	0	569	2	2	2	2	2	1	1
Memo: principal arrears on LDOD	82	74	3,542	19	148	154	162	156	145	145
Official creditors	70	74	1,775	0	128	133	142	134	137	141
Private creditors	12	0	1,767	19	20	20	20	21	8	4
Memo: export credits	0	0	14,578	10,237	8,933	9,119	7,656	10,456	8,604	7,969
TOTAL DEBT FLOWS										
Disbursements	**188**	**2,743**	**1,951**	**1,157**	**624**	**671**	**890**	**747**	**584**	**582**
Long-term debt	170	2,680	1,951	1,157	624	671	890	747	584	582
IMF purchases	18	63	0	0	0	0	0	0	0	0
Principal repayments	**234**	**446**	**1,751**	**939**	**989**	**1,111**	**955**	**959**	**1,202**	**1,088**
Long-term debt	225	343	1,704	918	894	1,025	940	959	1,202	1,088
IMF repurchases	9	103	47	22	95	86	16	0	0	0
Net flows on debt	**-46**	**2,465**	**-1,301**	**146**	**74**	**-464**	**579**	**1,059**	**-584**	**-695**
of which short-term debt	0	168	-1,502	-72	438	-24	644	1,271	34	-189
Interest payments (INT)	**37**	**790**	**1,323**	**1,283**	**1,388**	**1,209**	**1,022**	**929**	**905**	**726**
Long-term debt	37	350	1,007	1,143	1,247	1,073	759	702	674	612
IMF charges	0	18	15	10	9	3	0	0	0	0
Short-term debt	0	422	301	130	132	133	262	227	231	113
Net transfers on debt	**-83**	**1,676**	**-2,624**	**-1,137**	**-1,315**	**-1,673**	**-443**	**130**	**-1,489**	**-1,421**
Total debt service paid (TDS)	**270**	**1,235**	**3,074**	**2,223**	**2,377**	**2,321**	**1,977**	**1,888**	**2,106**	**1,813**
Long-term debt	261	693	2,711	2,061	2,142	2,098	1,699	1,661	1,875	1,700
IMF repurchases and charges	9	121	61	32	104	89	16	0	0	0
Short-term debt (interest only)	0	422	301	130	132	133	262	227	231	113
2. AGGREGATE NET RESOURCE FLOWS AND NET TRANSFERS (LONG-TERM)										
NET RESOURCE FLOWS	**99**	**3,051**	**5,183**	**2,697**	**1,336**	**2,739**	**3,682**	**2,732**	**1,760**	**2,312**
Net flow of long-term debt (ex. IMF)	-54	2,337	247	240	-270	-354	-49	-212	-618	-506
Foreign direct investment (net)	0	548	734	1,256	598	636	891	1,076	1,065	1,235
Portfolio equity flows	0	0	0	10	2	1,233	1,813	494	550	619
Grants (excluding technical coop.)	153	165	4,201	1,192	1,006	1,224	1,028	1,374	763	964
Memo: technical coop. grants	14	156	812	594	744	635	573	474	771	472
official net resource flows	129	1,918	4,514	1,715	1,048	1,290	1,016	1,128	280	345
private net resource flows	-30	1,133	668	982	288	1,448	2,667	1,604	1,481	1,967
NET TRANSFERS	**62**	**2,687**	**4,162**	**1,533**	**66**	**1,616**	**2,843**	**1,910**	**915**	**1,515**
Interest on long-term debt	37	350	1,007	1,143	1,247	1,073	759	702	674	612
Profit remittances on FDI	0	15	14	20	23	50	80	120	172	185
Memo: official net transfers	99	1,697	3,795	709	-69	315	327	494	-340	-221
private net transfers	-37	990	367	825	135	1,301	2,516	1,416	1,255	1,736
3. MAJOR ECONOMIC AGGREGATES										
Gross national income (GNI)	7,618	21,453	42,025	51,776	60,300	68,190	76,573	83,919	90,203	99,657
Exports of goods & services (XGS)	991	9,212	13,670	15,247	17,792	18,042	19,842	19,302	19,232	21,555
of which workers remittances	29	2,696	3,743	3,232	3,279	2,798	3,256	3,718	3,772	3,747
Imports of goods & services (MGS)	1,447	9,745	15,398	15,651	18,324	18,951	20,613	22,663	22,038	23,657
International reserves (RES)	165	2,480	3,620	14,413	17,122	18,296	19,371	18,824	15,190	13,785
Current account balance	-452	-438	-634	410	386	-185	119	-2,479	-1,709	-1,171
4. DEBT INDICATORS										
EDT / XGS (%)	181.8	207.7	241.5	212.4	187.4	173.9	150.8	167.2	160.2	134.3
EDT / GNI (%)	23.7	89.2	78.6	62.5	55.3	46.0	39.1	38.5	34.2	29.1
TDS / XGS (%)	27.3	13.4	22.5	14.6	13.4	12.9	10.0	9.8	11.0	8.4
INT / XGS (%)	3.7	8.6	9.7	8.4	7.8	6.7	5.2	4.8	4.7	3.4
INT / GNI (%)	0.5	3.7	3.2	2.5	2.3	1.8	1.3	1.1	1.0	0.7
RES / EDT (%)	9.2	13.0	11.0	44.5	51.4	58.3	64.7	58.3	49.3	47.6
RES / MGS (months)	1.4	3.1	2.8	11.1	11.2	11.6	11.3	10.0	8.3	7.0
Short-term / EDT (%)	22.3	21.1	13.5	6.0	7.1	7.5	10.0	13.2	13.9	14.2
Concessional / EDT (%)	47.9	42.4	37.9	60.3	60.9	76.4	75.3	72.5	73.0	72.7
Multilateral / EDT (%)	1.2	13.7	10.4	12.1	11.9	12.5	13.0	13.0	12.9	13.2

EGYPT, ARAB REPUBLIC OF

(US$ million, unless otherwise indicated)

	1970	1980	1990	1994	1995	1996	1997	1998	1999	2000
5. LONG-TERM DEBT										
DEBT OUTSTANDING (LDOD)	**1,351**	**14,693**	**28,438**	**30,253**	**30,861**	**29,002**	**26,935**	**28,006**	**26,508**	**24,852**
Public and publicly guaranteed	**1,351**	**14,428**	**27,438**	**29,878**	**30,548**	**28,875**	**26,804**	**27,622**	**26,026**	**24,279**
Official creditors	1,189	12,623	21,190	27,734	28,795	27,518	25,729	26,749	25,469	23,741
Multilateral	22	2,625	3,427	3,912	3,974	3,933	3,892	4,195	3,968	3,813
Concessional	0	1,885	1,297	1,486	1,612	1,798	1,970	2,167	2,183	2,223
Bilateral	1,167	9,998	17,763	23,821	24,822	23,585	21,837	22,553	21,501	19,928
Concessional	864	6,231	11,224	18,046	18,673	22,171	20,554	21,239	20,297	18,840
Private creditors	162	1,805	6,249	2,145	1,753	1,357	1,076	874	558	538
Bonds	0	132	0	0	0	0	0	0	0	0
Commercial banks	36	257	624	553	516	437	520	404	242	312
Other private	126	1,416	5,625	1,592	1,237	920	556	470	316	226
Private nonguaranteed	**0**	**265**	**1,000**	**375**	**313**	**127**	**131**	**384**	**481**	**573**
Bonds	0	0	0	0	0	0	0	0	100	100
Commercial banks and other	0	265	1,000	375	313	127	131	384	381	473
Memo:										
IBRD	22	421	1,480	1,411	1,320	1,075	869	847	761	639
IDA	0	307	921	961	1,035	1,090	1,206	1,268	1,273	1,266
DISBURSEMENTS	**170**	**2,680**	**1,951**	**1,157**	**624**	**671**	**890**	**747**	**584**	**582**
Public and publicly guaranteed	**170**	**2,554**	**1,900**	**1,097**	**624**	**671**	**813**	**468**	**241**	**374**
Official creditors	137	1,904	1,198	898	584	638	625	457	230	235
Multilateral	0	242	269	576	384	426	493	300	155	173
Concessional	0	53	56	129	157	206	252	212	110	104
Bilateral	137	1,663	929	322	200	212	133	157	76	61
Concessional	53	1,011	647	308	186	212	132	157	70	50
Private creditors	33	650	703	200	40	33	188	10	10	140
Bonds	0	30	0	0	0	0	0	0	0	0
Commercial banks	0	8	170	76	31	18	187	9	9	132
Other private	33	612	533	123	10	16	1	1	1	8
Private nonguaranteed	**0**	**126**	**51**	**60**	**0**	**0**	**77**	**279**	**343**	**207**
Bonds	0	0	0	0	0	0	0	0	100	0
Commercial banks and other	0	126	51	60	0	0	77	279	243	207
Memo:										
IBRD	0	169	92	149	42	26	103	48	31	6
IDA	0	41	8	50	83	83	158	57	33	49
PRINCIPAL REPAYMENTS	**225**	**343**	**1,704**	**918**	**894**	**1,025**	**940**	**959**	**1,202**	**1,088**
Public and publicly guaranteed	**225**	**297**	**1,572**	**733**	**832**	**839**	**867**	**927**	**956**	**972**
Official creditors	162	151	885	374	543	571	638	704	714	854
Multilateral	6	18	282	287	310	298	351	290	286	291
Concessional	0	0	55	25	30	35	38	52	59	80
Bilateral	156	134	603	87	232	273	286	414	428	564
Concessional	92	119	215	43	121	190	250	380	400	497
Private creditors	63	145	687	359	290	268	229	223	242	118
Bonds	0	4	1	0	0	0	0	0	0	0
Commercial banks	0	65	34	119	74	86	87	133	160	57
Other private	63	76	653	239	216	182	143	91	82	61
Private nonguaranteed	**0**	**46**	**132**	**185**	**62**	**186**	**73**	**32**	**246**	**116**
Bonds	0	0	0	0	0	0	0	0	0	0
Commercial banks and other	0	46	132	185	62	186	73	32	246	116
Memo:										
IBRD	6	7	176	191	198	178	225	115	106	87
IDA	0	0	7	12	14	15	16	18	20	23
NET FLOWS ON DEBT	**-54**	**2,337**	**247**	**240**	**-270**	**-354**	**-49**	**-212**	**-618**	**-506**
Public and publicly guaranteed	**-54**	**2,257**	**328**	**365**	**-208**	**-168**	**-53**	**-459**	**-715**	**-598**
Official creditors	-24	1,753	313	523	41	67	-12	-247	-484	-620
Multilateral	-6	224	-13	289	74	128	142	11	-131	-117
Concessional	0	53	1	103	127	171	214	161	51	24
Bilateral	-19	1,529	326	234	-33	-61	-154	-257	-353	-502
Concessional	-39	893	432	265	65	22	-118	-223	-329	-448
Private creditors	-30	505	15	-159	-249	-235	-41	-213	-232	22
Bonds	0	26	-1	0	0	0	0	0	0	0
Commercial banks	0	-58	137	-43	-43	-68	101	-124	-151	75
Other private	-30	536	-121	-116	-207	-167	-142	-90	-81	-53
Private nonguaranteed	**0**	**80**	**-81**	**-125**	**-62**	**-186**	**4**	**247**	**97**	**91**
Bonds	0	0	0	0	0	0	0	0	100	0
Commercial banks and other	0	80	-81	-125	-62	-186	4	247	-3	91
Memo:										
IBRD	-6	162	-84	-42	-156	-152	-123	-67	-74	-81
IDA	0	41	1	37	69	68	142	39	14	26

EGYPT, ARAB REPUBLIC OF

(US$ million, unless otherwise indicated)

	1970	1980	1990	1994	1995	1996	1997	1998	1999	2000
INTEREST PAYMENTS (LINT)	**37**	**350**	**1,007**	**1,143**	**1,247**	**1,073**	**759**	**702**	**674**	**612**
Public and publicly guaranteed	**37**	**327**	**918**	**1,108**	**1,223**	**1,061**	**752**	**696**	**666**	**596**
Official creditors	30	221	719	1,006	1,117	976	689	633	620	566
Multilateral	2	40	184	204	229	213	197	192	182	142
Concessional	0	7	14	19	22	25	28	32	34	33
Bilateral	28	181	535	803	888	763	492	441	438	424
Concessional	18	146	196	448	545	525	385	346	344	336
Private creditors	7	106	199	102	106	85	63	62	46	30
Bonds	0	11	0	0	0	0	0	0	0	0
Commercial banks	0	36	45	30	40	32	25	35	24	16
Other private	7	59	153	71	67	53	38	28	22	14
Private nonguaranteed	**0**	**23**	**89**	**35**	**24**	**12**	**8**	**7**	**8**	**16**
Bonds	0	0	0	0	0	0	0	0	0	12
Commercial banks and other	0	23	89	35	24	12	8	7	8	4
Memo:										
IBRD	2	29	138	114	114	94	72	56	52	41
IDA	0	2	7	7	7	8	8	9	9	10
NET TRANSFERS ON DEBT	**-91**	**1,988**	**-760**	**-904**	**-1,517**	**-1,427**	**-809**	**-915**	**-1,292**	**-1,119**
Public and publicly guaranteed	**-91**	**1,931**	**-589**	**-744**	**-1,431**	**-1,229**	**-805**	**-1,155**	**-1,381**	**-1,194**
Official creditors	-54	1,532	-406	-483	-1,076	-909	-701	-880	-1,104	-1,186
Multilateral	-7	184	-197	85	-156	-85	-56	-182	-314	-260
Concessional	0	46	-13	84	105	146	186	129	18	-9
Bilateral	-47	1,348	-209	-568	-920	-824	-645	-698	-790	-926
Concessional	-57	746	236	-183	-481	-503	-503	-569	-673	-784
Private creditors	-37	399	-183	-261	-356	-320	-104	-275	-277	-8
Bonds	0	15	-1	0	0	0	0	0	0	0
Commercial banks	0	-94	91	-73	-82	-101	76	-158	-175	59
Other private	-37	478	-274	-187	-274	-220	-180	-117	-103	-67
Private nonguaranteed	**0**	**57**	**-170**	**-160**	**-86**	**-198**	**-4**	**241**	**89**	**75**
Bonds	0	0	0	0	0	0	0	0	100	-12
Commercial banks and other	0	57	-170	-160	-86	-198	-4	241	-11	87
Memo:										
IBRD	-7	133	-222	-157	-270	-246	-195	-123	-126	-122
IDA	0	39	-6	30	62	60	134	30	4	17
DEBT SERVICE (LTDS)	**261**	**693**	**2,711**	**2,061**	**2,142**	**2,098**	**1,699**	**1,661**	**1,875**	**1,700**
Public and publicly guaranteed	**261**	**624**	**2,490**	**1,841**	**2,056**	**1,900**	**1,618**	**1,623**	**1,622**	**1,568**
Official creditors	192	372	1,604	1,381	1,659	1,547	1,326	1,337	1,334	1,420
Multilateral	7	58	466	491	540	511	548	482	469	433
Concessional	0	7	69	44	52	60	66	83	92	113
Bilateral	184	315	1,138	890	1,120	1,036	778	856	865	987
Concessional	110	265	411	491	666	715	635	726	743	834
Private creditors	70	251	886	460	396	353	292	286	288	148
Bonds	0	15	1	0	0	0	0	0	0	0
Commercial banks	0	101	79	150	113	118	112	167	184	73
Other private	70	135	806	311	283	235	180	118	104	75
Private nonguaranteed	**0**	**69**	**221**	**220**	**86**	**198**	**81**	**38**	**254**	**132**
Bonds	0	0	0	0	0	0	0	0	0	12
Commercial banks and other	0	69	221	220	86	198	81	38	254	120
Memo:										
IBRD	7	36	314	306	312	272	297	170	157	128
IDA	0	3	14	19	21	23	24	26	29	32
UNDISBURSED DEBT	**315**	**4,999**	**4,573**	**3,981**	**3,335**	**2,550**	**1,986**	**1,674**	**1,429**	**1,280**
Official creditors	282	4,163	3,335	3,778	3,180	2,445	1,864	1,587	1,400	1,257
Private creditors	33	837	1,237	203	154	106	122	87	30	23
Memorandum items										
Concessional LDOD	864	8,115	12,521	19,532	20,285	23,969	22,524	23,405	22,480	21,063
Variable rate LDOD	0	663	4,399	1,673	1,564	1,278	1,375	1,545	1,461	1,542
Public sector LDOD	1,351	14,427	27,418	29,870	30,546	28,873	26,803	27,620	26,025	24,278
Private sector LDOD	0	266	1,021	383	316	129	133	386	483	574

6. CURRENCY COMPOSITION OF LONG-TERM DEBT (PERCENT)

	1970	1980	1990	1994	1995	1996	1997	1998	1999	2000
Deutsche mark	10.0	4.8	12.3	10.5	11.2	11.1	10.5	10.9	9.9	9.9
French franc	0.9	5.6	14.0	19.5	20.5	19.9	18.2	18.3	16.3	15.7
Japanese yen	0.0	4.0	8.2	14.0	13.2	12.3	11.6	12.5	14.7	13.8
Pound sterling	2.9	1.2	2.5	1.7	1.5	1.5	1.5	1.4	1.3	1.2
Swiss franc	2.4	1.3	3.0	2.4	2.7	2.4	2.3	2.3	2.1	2.1
U.S.dollars	23.0	73.0	41.8	35.1	34.1	35.8	39.1	37.1	38.1	39.8
Multiple currency	1.6	3.3	8.4	8.0	7.4	6.8	6.4	6.6	6.5	6.4
Special drawing rights	0.0	0.0	0.6	0.0	0.0	0.0	0.1	0.1	0.1	0.3
All other currencies	59.2	6.8	9.2	8.8	9.4	10.2	10.3	10.8	11.0	10.8

EGYPT, ARAB REPUBLIC OF

(US$ million, unless otherwise indicated)

7. DEBT RESTRUCTURINGS

	1970	1980	1990	1994	1995	1996	1997	1998	1999	2000
Total amount rescheduled	..	..	0	428	309	192	156	53	96	22
Debt stock rescheduled	..	..	0	0	0	0	0	0	0	0
Principal rescheduled	..	..	0	323	260	131	95	45	85	13
Official	..	..	0	81	50	34	23	24	10	2
Private	..	..	0	242	210	96	73	21	76	11
Interest rescheduled	..	..	0	78	49	31	18	11	10	1
Official	..	..	0	23	10	6	3	2	1	0
Private	..	..	0	55	39	25	15	9	9	1
Debt forgiven	..	..	10,576	39	35	35	27	17	1	25
Memo: interest forgiven	..	..	2,481	81	7	4	2	1	0	0
Debt stock reduction	..	..	0	0	13	9	0	0	0	0
of which debt buyback	..	..	0	0	0	0	0	0	0	0

8. DEBT STOCK-FLOW RECONCILIATION

	1970	1980	1990	1994	1995	1996	1997	1998	1999	2000
Total change in debt stocks	..	..	-12,667	1,811	958	-1,971	-1,438	2,340	-1,466	-1,845
Net flows on debt	-46	2,465	-1,301	146	74	-464	579	1,059	-584	-695
Net change in interest arrears	..	..	-1,938	0	2	-1	1	-2	-1	0
Interest capitalized	..	..	0	78	49	31	18	11	10	1
Debt forgiveness or reduction	..	..	-10,576	-39	-47	-44	-27	-17	-1	-25
Cross-currency valuation	..	..	1,461	1,508	796	-1,548	-2,027	1,065	-991	-894
Residual	..	..	-312	117	85	54	18	224	101	-232

9. AVERAGE TERMS OF NEW COMMITMENTS

	1970	1980	1990	1994	1995	1996	1997	1998	1999	2000
ALL CREDITORS										
Interest (%)	5.2	5.0	5.3	2.3	3.1	1.4	6.0	3.4	0.8	4.2
Maturity (years)	14.3	26.6	25.5	32.5	21.8	32.8	20.3	27.3	34.7	14.9
Grace period (years)	7.8	6.6	6.9	8.2	6.6	9.5	6.1	7.7	10.2	4.5
Grant element (%)	26.5	39.1	36.0	62.5	47.9	72.0	25.1	52.5	78.7	33.3
Official creditors										
Interest (%)	5.2	3.3	4.7	2.1	3.1	1.4	4.5	3.4	0.8	2.8
Maturity (years)	14.9	36.4	28.2	33.5	22.0	32.8	28.9	27.3	34.7	21.3
Grace period (years)	8.2	8.9	7.6	8.5	6.6	9.5	8.5	7.7	10.2	5.4
Grant element (%)	27.5	56.9	41.8	64.7	48.2	72.0	43.7	52.5	78.7	47.0
Private creditors										
Interest (%)	5.9	7.9	8.4	6.2	6.5	0.0	7.4	0.0	0.0	6.7
Maturity (years)	4.7	9.6	11.5	11.7	4.3	0.0	11.8	0.0	0.0	3.0
Grace period (years)	1.5	2.5	3.4	1.1	2.4	0.0	3.7	0.0	0.0	2.9
Grant element (%)	10.6	8.3	6.9	16.7	7.7	0.0	7.1	0.0	0.0	8.0
Memorandum items										
Commitments	306	2,176	1,223	332	207	172	428	286	155	384
Official creditors	288	1,378	1,022	317	206	172	211	286	155	250
Private creditors	18	798	201	16	1	0	217	0	0	135

10. CONTRACTUAL OBLIGATIONS ON OUTSTANDING LONG-TERM DEBT

	2001	2002	2003	2004	2005	2006	2007	2008	2009	2010
TOTAL										
Disbursements	528	319	172	102	60	34	22	15	10	7
Principal	1,079	1,102	1,255	1,348	1,243	1,280	1,296	1,325	1,309	1,333
Interest	634	604	565	525	477	442	407	373	339	307
Official creditors										
Disbursements	515	315	172	102	60	34	22	15	10	7
Principal	982	1,031	1,071	1,198	1,210	1,268	1,288	1,316	1,301	1,325
Interest	589	565	535	502	470	436	402	368	335	304
Bilateral creditors										
Disbursements	124	51	28	16	7	2	0	0	0	0
Principal	668	716	746	879	908	984	1,016	1,066	1,070	1,110
Interest	448	432	414	394	374	353	331	308	286	263
Multilateral creditors										
Disbursements	391	264	144	86	53	31	22	15	10	7
Principal	314	316	326	319	302	284	271	251	231	216
Interest	141	133	121	108	96	83	71	60	50	41
Private creditors										
Disbursements	13	4	1	0	0	0	0	0	0	0
Principal	97	71	184	151	32	12	9	8	8	8
Interest	45	39	30	22	7	5	5	4	4	3
Commercial banks										
Disbursements	10	2	0	0	0	0	0	0	0	0
Principal	46	46	169	39	21	3	1	0	0	0
Interest	22	19	11	4	1	0	0	0	0	0
Other private										
Disbursements	3	2	1	0	0	0	0	0	0	0
Principal	51	25	15	112	11	9	8	8	8	8
Interest	24	20	19	18	6	5	5	4	4	3

EL SALVADOR

(US$ million, unless otherwise indicated)

1. SUMMARY DEBT DATA

	1970	1980	1990	1994	1995	1996	1997	1998	1999	2000
TOTAL DEBT STOCKS (EDT)	**183**	**911**	**2,149**	**2,210**	**2,610**	**2,914**	**3,252**	**3,374**	**3,795**	**4,023**
Long-term debt (LDOD)	**176**	**659**	**1,938**	**2,022**	**2,084**	**2,318**	**2,442**	**2,525**	**2,743**	**2,886**
Public and publicly guaranteed	88	499	1,913	2,014	2,080	2,317	2,397	2,443	2,649	2,775
Private nonguaranteed	88	161	26	8	5	2	45	82	93	111
Use of IMF credit	**7**	**32**	**0**	**0**	**0**	**0**	**0**	**0**	**0**	**0**
Short-term debt	**0**	**220**	**210**	**188**	**525**	**596**	**811**	**849**	**1,053**	**1,138**
of which interest arrears on LDOD	0	0	7	3	3	3	2	1	0	0
Official creditors	0	0	7	2	2	2	1	1	0	0
Private creditors	0	0	0	1	1	1	0	0	0	0
Memo: principal arrears on LDOD	0	0	6	4	6	8	14	5	0	0
Official creditors	0	0	6	0	1	1	13	5	0	0
Private creditors	0	0	0	4	5	6	1	0	0	0
Memo: export credits	0	0	236	337	267	313	427	173	139	116
TOTAL DEBT FLOWS										
Disbursements	**31**	**149**	**108**	**293**	**195**	**474**	**334**	**326**	**389**	**363**
Long-term debt	31	110	108	293	195	474	334	326	389	363
IMF purchases	0	40	0	0	0	0	0	0	0	0
Principal repayments	**27**	**35**	**124**	**241**	**160**	**178**	**127**	**288**	**167**	**153**
Long-term debt	22	35	119	241	160	178	127	288	167	153
IMF repurchases	5	0	5	0	0	0	0	0	0	0
Net flows on debt	**4**	**56**	**2**	**136**	**373**	**368**	**423**	**78**	**427**	**295**
of which short-term debt	0	-58	18	83	337	71	216	39	204	85
Interest payments (INT)	**9**	**61**	**84**	**98**	**124**	**138**	**152**	**159**	**175**	**221**
Long-term debt	9	36	75	91	102	105	110	111	122	148
IMF charges	0	0	0	0	0	0	0	0	0	0
Short-term debt	0	25	9	8	22	33	42	48	53	73
Net transfers on debt	**-5**	**-5**	**-83**	**37**	**249**	**229**	**271**	**-81**	**252**	**74**
Total debt service paid (TDS)	**36**	**96**	**208**	**339**	**284**	**316**	**279**	**447**	**341**	**374**
Long-term debt	31	71	194	332	262	283	237	398	288	300
IMF repurchases and charges	5	0	5	0	0	0	0	0	0	0
Short-term debt (interest only)	0	25	9	8	22	33	42	48	53	73

2. AGGREGATE NET RESOURCE FLOWS AND NET TRANSFERS (LONG-TERM)

	1970	1980	1990	1994	1995	1996	1997	1998	1999	2000
NET RESOURCE FLOWS	**14**	**111**	**151**	**139**	**175**	**394**	**358**	**1,262**	**548**	**467**
Net flow of long-term debt (ex. IMF)	9	74	-11	52	35	297	207	39	222	210
Foreign direct investment (net)	4	6	2	0	38	-5	59	1,104	231	185
Portfolio equity flows	0	0	0	0	0	0	0	0	0	0
Grants (excluding technical coop.)	1	31	160	87	102	102	92	119	95	72
Memo: technical coop. grants	7	9	127	180	130	108	119	64	70	85
official net resource flows	5	104	143	199	168	377	252	186	149	129
private net resource flows	10	7	8	-60	7	17	106	1,075	400	338
NET TRANSFERS	**-2**	**34**	**47**	**24**	**47**	**263**	**221**	**1,123**	**387**	**268**
Interest on long-term debt	9	36	75	91	102	105	110	111	122	148
Profit remittances on FDI	7	41	28	24	26	25	27	28	40	52
Memo: official net transfers	2	82	81	117	76	279	151	83	35	6
private net transfers	-4	-48	-33	-93	-29	-16	69	1,040	352	262

3. MAJOR ECONOMIC AGGREGATES

	1970	1980	1990	1994	1995	1996	1997	1998	1999	2000
Gross national income (GNI)	1,123	3,490	4,727	7,994	9,405	10,273	11,139	11,851	12,158	12,965
Exports of goods & services (XGS)	..	1,282	1,360	2,642	3,154	3,330	4,188	4,498	4,650	5,538
of which workers remittances	..	11	357	967	1,061	1,084	1,199	1,338	1,374	1,751
Imports of goods & services (MGS)	..	1,289	1,785	2,981	3,744	3,669	4,447	4,777	5,107	6,034
International reserves (RES)	64	382	595	829	940	1,110	1,444	1,748	2,140	2,051
Current account balance	..	34	-152	-18	-262	-169	-98	-91	-274	-418

4. DEBT INDICATORS

	1970	1980	1990	1994	1995	1996	1997	1998	1999	2000
EDT / XGS (%)	..	71.1	158.0	83.7	82.7	87.5	77.7	75.0	81.6	72.7
EDT / GNI (%)	16.3	26.1	45.5	27.6	27.8	28.4	29.2	28.5	31.2	31.0
TDS / XGS (%)	..	7.5	15.3	12.8	9.0	9.5	6.7	9.9	7.3	6.8
INT / XGS (%)	..	4.7	6.2	3.7	3.9	4.2	3.6	3.5	3.8	4.0
INT / GNI (%)	0.8	1.7	1.8	1.2	1.3	1.4	1.4	1.3	1.4	1.7
RES / EDT (%)	35.0	41.9	27.7	37.5	36.0	38.1	44.4	51.8	56.4	51.0
RES / MGS (months)	..	3.6	4.0	3.3	3.0	3.6	3.9	4.4	5.0	4.1
Short-term / EDT (%)	0.0	24.2	9.8	8.5	20.1	20.5	24.9	25.2	27.7	28.3
Concessional / EDT (%)	21.3	23.9	56.3	49.0	42.7	40.2	36.1	35.1	30.8	27.9
Multilateral / EDT (%)	22.4	28.3	36.6	57.5	52.8	54.0	51.2	52.2	48.1	46.4

EL SALVADOR

(US$ million, unless otherwise indicated)

5. LONG-TERM DEBT

	1970	1980	1990	1994	1995	1996	1997	1998	1999	2000
DEBT OUTSTANDING (LDOD)	**176**	**659**	**1,938**	**2,022**	**2,084**	**2,318**	**2,442**	**2,525**	**2,743**	**2,886**
Public and publicly guaranteed	**88**	**499**	**1,913**	**2,014**	**2,080**	**2,317**	**2,397**	**2,443**	**2,649**	**2,775**
Official creditors	70	460	1,729	1,880	1,971	2,185	2,267	2,376	2,432	2,440
Multilateral	41	258	786	1,271	1,377	1,573	1,666	1,760	1,825	1,867
Concessional	10	134	414	605	623	648	656	646	632	608
Bilateral	30	202	943	608	594	612	601	616	606	574
Concessional	29	84	795	478	490	522	516	538	537	515
Private creditors	17	39	184	135	109	132	130	68	218	335
Bonds	3	0	0	0	0	0	0	0	150	282
Commercial banks	14	8	127	94	74	82	83	19	26	23
Other private	0	31	57	41	35	50	47	49	42	30
Private nonguaranteed	**88**	**161**	**26**	**8**	**5**	**2**	**45**	**82**	**93**	**111**
Bonds	0	0	0	0	0	0	0	0	0	0
Commercial banks and other	88	161	26	8	5	2	45	82	93	111
Memo:										
IBRD	25	87	140	290	307	282	275	287	293	309
IDA	8	27	23	21	20	20	19	18	17	16
DISBURSEMENTS	**31**	**110**	**108**	**293**	**195**	**474**	**334**	**326**	**389**	**363**
Public and publicly guaranteed	**8**	**110**	**108**	**289**	**195**	**474**	**290**	**261**	**349**	**313**
Official creditors	6	81	78	271	190	381	268	255	182	172
Multilateral	5	36	44	268	166	317	232	236	164	152
Concessional	2	15	34	81	32	40	25	8	8	4
Bilateral	2	45	33	3	25	64	37	19	19	21
Concessional	2	20	18	2	24	64	36	18	19	21
Private creditors	1	29	30	19	5	94	22	6	167	140
Bonds	0	0	0	0	0	0	0	0	150	132
Commercial banks	1	3	25	19	5	71	15	4	15	8
Other private	0	26	5	0	0	23	7	3	2	1
Private nonguaranteed	**24**	**0**	**0**	**4**	**0**	**0**	**44**	**65**	**40**	**50**
Bonds	0	0	0	0	0	0	0	0	0	0
Commercial banks and other	24	0	0	4	0	0	44	65	40	50
Memo:										
IBRD	1	10	3	70	26	21	35	34	23	34
IDA	0	3	0	0	0	0	0	0	0	0
PRINCIPAL REPAYMENTS	**22**	**35**	**119**	**241**	**160**	**178**	**127**	**288**	**167**	**153**
Public and publicly guaranteed	**6**	**17**	**105**	**237**	**157**	**175**	**126**	**260**	**138**	**120**
Official creditors	3	8	94	159	124	106	108	188	129	116
Multilateral	3	5	57	107	78	76	85	164	102	85
Concessional	0	1	11	13	13	15	15	20	25	22
Bilateral	0	3	37	52	45	30	24	24	27	31
Concessional	0	1	8	19	19	17	17	16	19	19
Private creditors	3	10	11	79	33	69	18	72	9	4
Bonds	0	0	0	0	0	0	0	0	0	0
Commercial banks	3	2	9	71	26	63	14	68	7	4
Other private	0	8	2	8	8	6	4	4	3	1
Private nonguaranteed	**16**	**18**	**14**	**4**	**3**	**3**	**1**	**28**	**28**	**33**
Bonds	0	0	0	0	0	0	0	0	0	0
Commercial banks and other	16	18	14	4	3	3	1	28	28	33
Memo:										
IBRD	2	3	15	19	21	22	24	28	17	17
IDA	0	0	1	1	1	1	1	1	1	1
NET FLOWS ON DEBT	**9**	**74**	**-11**	**52**	**35**	**297**	**207**	**39**	**222**	**210**
Public and publicly guaranteed	**2**	**92**	**3**	**52**	**38**	**300**	**164**	**2**	**211**	**192**
Official creditors	3	73	-17	112	66	275	160	67	54	56
Multilateral	2	31	-13	161	87	241	147	72	62	66
Concessional	2	14	23	68	18	26	10	-11	-17	-18
Bilateral	2	42	-4	-49	-21	34	13	-5	-8	-10
Concessional	2	18	11	-18	5	47	19	2	-1	1
Private creditors	-2	19	19	-60	-28	25	4	-66	157	136
Bonds	0	0	0	0	0	0	0	0	150	132
Commercial banks	-2	1	16	-52	-20	9	1	-65	8	4
Other private	0	18	3	-8	-8	17	3	-1	-1	0
Private nonguaranteed	**8**	**-18**	**-14**	**0**	**-3**	**-3**	**43**	**37**	**12**	**18**
Bonds	0	0	0	0	0	0	0	0	0	0
Commercial banks and other	8	-18	-14	0	-3	-3	43	37	12	18
Memo:										
IBRD	-1	8	-13	52	5	-1	12	7	6	17
IDA	0	3	-1	-1	-1	-1	-1	-1	-1	-1

EL SALVADOR

(US$ million, unless otherwise indicated)

	1970	*1980*	*1990*	*1994*	*1995*	*1996*	*1997*	*1998*	*1999*	*2000*
INTEREST PAYMENTS (LINT)	**9**	**36**	**75**	**91**	**102**	**105**	**110**	**111**	**122**	**148**
Public and publicly guaranteed	**4**	**25**	**72**	**90**	**102**	**105**	**107**	**106**	**116**	**141**
Official creditors	2	21	63	82	92	97	101	103	114	123
Multilateral	2	11	50	56	62	74	79	83	93	102
Concessional	0	2	9	9	11	11	11	11	12	11
Bilateral	0	10	13	25	30	23	21	21	21	21
Concessional	0	2	9	14	16	15	14	14	14	15
Private creditors	1	3	10	9	9	8	7	3	2	18
Bonds	0	0	0	0	0	0	0	0	0	17
Commercial banks	1	1	8	6	7	6	5	2	1	1
Other private	0	2	2	3	2	2	2	1	1	1
Private nonguaranteed	**6**	**11**	**3**	**0**	**0**	**0**	**3**	**5**	**6**	**7**
Bonds	0	0	0	0	0	0	0	0	0	0
Commercial banks and other	6	11	3	0	0	0	3	5	6	7
Memo:										
IBRD	1	7	14	17	22	21	19	20	20	24
IDA	0	0	0	0	0	0	0	0	0	0
NET TRANSFERS ON DEBT	**0**	**39**	**-86**	**-39**	**-67**	**191**	**97**	**-72**	**101**	**62**
Public and publicly guaranteed	**-2**	**68**	**-69**	**-38**	**-63**	**195**	**57**	**-104**	**95**	**51**
Official creditors	1	52	-79	30	-26	177	60	-36	-60	-66
Multilateral	0	20	-63	104	25	167	68	-10	-31	-36
Concessional	2	12	14	58	7	15	-1	-22	-29	-29
Bilateral	1	32	-17	-74	-51	10	-8	-26	-29	-31
Concessional	2	16	2	-32	-11	32	5	-12	-15	-13
Private creditors	-3	16	10	-69	-37	17	-3	-68	155	118
Bonds	0	0	0	0	0	0	0	0	150	115
Commercial banks	-3	0	8	-59	-27	2	-4	-66	7	3
Other private	0	16	2	-10	-10	15	2	-2	-1	0
Private nonguaranteed	**2**	**-29**	**-17**	**0**	**-4**	**-3**	**40**	**32**	**6**	**11**
Bonds	0	0	0	0	0	0	0	0	0	0
Commercial banks and other	2	-29	-17	0	-4	-3	40	32	6	11
Memo:										
IBRD	-2	0	-27	35	-17	-22	-7	-13	-14	-7
IDA	0	3	-1	-1	-1	-1	-1	-1	-1	-1
DEBT SERVICE (LTDS)	**31**	**71**	**194**	**332**	**262**	**283**	**237**	**398**	**288**	**300**
Public and publicly guaranteed	**9**	**42**	**177**	**327**	**258**	**280**	**233**	**365**	**254**	**261**
Official creditors	5	29	157	240	216	203	209	291	243	239
Multilateral	5	16	107	163	141	150	164	247	195	187
Concessional	0	3	19	22	24	25	26	30	36	33
Bilateral	1	13	50	77	76	54	45	44	48	51
Concessional	0	3	17	33	35	32	31	30	34	34
Private creditors	4	13	21	87	42	77	25	75	12	23
Bonds	0	0	0	0	0	0	0	0	0	17
Commercial banks	4	3	17	77	32	69	19	70	8	5
Other private	0	10	4	10	10	8	6	5	4	1
Private nonguaranteed	**22**	**29**	**17**	**4**	**4**	**3**	**4**	**33**	**34**	**39**
Bonds	0	0	0	0	0	0	0	0	0	0
Commercial banks and other	22	29	17	4	4	3	4	33	34	39
Memo:										
IBRD	4	10	29	36	43	42	42	47	37	41
IDA	0	0	1	1	1	1	1	1	1	1
UNDISBURSED DEBT	**38**	**424**	**324**	**698**	**1,329**	**1,223**	**910**	**788**	**814**	**791**
Official creditors	38	390	322	693	1,257	1,192	890	768	790	777
Private creditors	0	35	2	5	72	31	20	20	25	14
Memorandum items										
Concessional LDOD	39	218	1,209	1,083	1,113	1,170	1,173	1,184	1,169	1,123
Variable rate LDOD	88	181	192	359	405	498	610	736	876	994
Public sector LDOD	88	496	1,905	2,007	2,073	2,310	2,391	2,438	2,644	2,770
Private sector LDOD	88	163	34	15	11	8	51	87	99	116

6. CURRENCY COMPOSITION OF LONG-TERM DEBT (PERCENT)

	1970	*1980*	*1990*	*1994*	*1995*	*1996*	*1997*	*1998*	*1999*	*2000*
Deutsche mark	0.0	0.2	3.7	3.8	4.0	4.6	4.1	4.4	3.5	3.1
French franc	0.0	5.5	3.3	2.5	2.5	2.0	1.6	1.5	1.2	0.4
Japanese yen	0.0	3.6	1.3	0.8	1.7	2.7	3.7	4.9	5.6	5.3
Pound sterling	0.0	0.3	0.0	0.0	0.0	0.0	0.0	0.0	0.0	0.0
Swiss franc	0.0	0.0	0.0	0.0	0.0	0.0	0.0	0.0	0.0	0.0
U.S.dollars	65.2	37.8	56.5	51.2	50.7	55.1	65.7	66.1	68.3	71.1
Multiple currency	31.1	32.6	33.7	40.7	40.2	34.6	23.7	21.8	20.1	18.8
Special drawing rights	0.0	0.0	0.0	0.2	0.3	0.4	0.4	0.5	0.5	0.5
All other currencies	3.7	20.0	1.5	0.8	0.6	0.6	0.8	0.8	0.8	0.8

EL SALVADOR

(US$ million, unless otherwise indicated)

	1970	1980	1990	1994	1995	1996	1997	1998	1999	2000
7. DEBT RESTRUCTURINGS										
Total amount rescheduled	..	..	86	0	0	0	0	0	0	0
Debt stock rescheduled	..	..	0	0	0	0	0	0	0	0
Principal rescheduled	..	..	42	0	0	0	0	0	0	0
Official	..	..	39	0	0	0	0	0	0	0
Private	..	..	3	0	0	0	0	0	0	0
Interest rescheduled	..	..	43	0	0	0	0	0	0	0
Official	..	..	38	0	0	0	0	0	0	0
Private	..	..	5	0	0	0	0	0	0	0
Debt forgiven	..	..	0	0	0	0	0	0	1	17
Memo: interest forgiven	..	..	0	0	0	0	0	0	0	0
Debt stock reduction	..	..	0	0	0	0	0	0	0	0
of which debt buyback	..	..	0	0	0	0	0	0	0	0
8. DEBT STOCK-FLOW RECONCILIATION										
Total change in debt stocks	..	..	67	177	400	305	338	122	421	228
Net flows on debt	4	56	2	136	373	368	423	78	427	295
Net change in interest arrears	..	..	-17	-5	0	0	-2	-1	-1	0
Interest capitalized	..	..	43	0	0	0	0	0	0	0
Debt forgiveness or reduction	..	..	0	0	0	0	0	0	-1	-17
Cross-currency valuation	..	..	7	13	49	-68	-149	-49	28	-41
Residual	..	..	31	33	-22	5	65	93	-32	-8
9. AVERAGE TERMS OF NEW COMMITMENTS										
ALL CREDITORS										
Interest (%)	4.7	4.2	4.6	3.8	6.5	7.1	7.1	7.0	7.3	8.2
Maturity (years)	23.4	27.6	29.8	24.2	22.6	20.7	16.8	21.9	16.1	12.7
Grace period (years)	6.0	8.4	7.2	7.6	5.2	5.0	3.7	3.8	5.7	3.8
Grant element (%)	37.6	45.8	45.5	45.9	22.6	18.2	16.6	18.0	17.4	10.2
Official creditors										
Interest (%)	4.4	3.3	3.2	3.8	6.5	7.1	7.1	7.1	5.9	7.1
Maturity (years)	25.0	28.4	35.6	24.2	21.9	22.1	17.6	22.5	22.8	19.9
Grace period (years)	6.5	8.9	8.8	7.6	5.1	5.1	3.9	3.9	5.2	4.5
Grant element (%)	40.7	53.5	56.6	45.9	22.6	18.9	17.3	18.4	27.2	18.0
Private creditors										
Interest (%)	7.5	11.7	10.4	0.0	6.4	7.2	7.0	6.6	9.0	9.7
Maturity (years)	7.2	20.7	5.0	0.0	29.0	4.7	6.2	4.9	7.6	3.0
Grace period (years)	0.7	4.3	0.5	0.0	6.7	3.8	1.1	0.9	6.3	3.0
Grant element (%)	6.9	-17.3	-1.4	0.0	22.1	11.0	8.0	7.7	4.9	-0.4
Memorandum items										
Commitments	12	225	131	161	832	705	195	156	394	307
Official creditors	11	200	106	161	760	649	181	151	222	177
Private creditors	1	25	25	0	72	56	14	6	172	130

10. CONTRACTUAL OBLIGATIONS ON OUTSTANDING LONG-TERM DEBT

	2001	2002	2003	2004	2005	2006	2007	2008	2009	2010
TOTAL										
Disbursements	210	211	142	94	62	36	21	7	6	2
Principal	280	197	218	221	221	348	240	182	173	169
Interest	163	160	158	152	143	133	106	93	83	73
Official creditors										
Disbursements	200	208	142	94	62	36	21	7	6	2
Principal	175	177	200	205	205	183	177	172	163	159
Interest	129	132	131	126	118	108	99	90	80	71
Bilateral creditors										
Disbursements	17	13	9	5	5	1	1	1	1	0
Principal	32	32	39	35	34	31	25	25	25	25
Interest	20	19	18	16	14	13	12	11	10	10
Multilateral creditors										
Disbursements	183	195	133	89	58	35	20	6	5	2
Principal	143	145	161	170	171	152	152	147	138	134
Interest	109	113	113	110	103	96	88	79	70	62
Private creditors										
Disbursements	10	3	0	0	0	0	0	0	0	0
Principal	105	20	18	16	16	164	64	11	10	9
Interest	34	29	27	26	25	24	6	3	2	2
Commercial banks										
Disbursements	7	3	0	0	0	0	0	0	0	0
Principal	10	6	5	4	3	3	3	0	0	0
Interest	2	1	1	1	0	0	0	0	0	0
Other private										
Disbursements	3	0	0	0	0	0	0	0	0	0
Principal	96	14	13	13	13	162	61	11	10	9
Interest	32	27	26	26	25	24	6	3	2	2

EQUATORIAL GUINEA

(US$ million, unless otherwise indicated)

	1970	1980	1990	1994	1995	1996	1997	1998	1999	2000
1. SUMMARY DEBT DATA										
TOTAL DEBT STOCKS (EDT)	**5.0**	**75.6**	**241.1**	**287.6**	**291.8**	**282.4**	**283.2**	**306.1**	**271.1**	**247.8**
Long-term debt (LDOD)	**5.0**	**52.5**	**209.2**	**219.3**	**229.6**	**222.2**	**208.6**	**216.5**	**207.9**	**198.9**
Public and publicly guaranteed	5.0	52.5	209.2	219.3	229.6	222.2	208.6	216.5	207.9	198.9
Private nonguaranteed	0.0	0.0	0.0	0.0	0.0	0.0	0.0	0.0	0.0	0.0
Use of IMF credit	**0.0**	**16.1**	**5.8**	**19.6**	**18.9**	**17.2**	**13.2**	**10.8**	**8.0**	**4.9**
Short-term debt	**0.0**	**7.0**	**26.0**	**48.6**	**43.4**	**43.1**	**61.4**	**78.8**	**55.2**	**44.0**
of which interest arrears on LDOD	0.0	0.0	19.7	37.6	41.4	39.6	37.4	39.8	37.2	36.0
Official creditors	0.0	0.0	17.3	32.7	35.9	34.5	32.8	34.9	32.9	32.0
Private creditors	0.0	0.0	2.3	4.9	5.4	5.2	4.6	4.9	4.3	4.0
Memo: principal arrears on LDOD	0.3	5.6	28.4	71.9	94.5	93.7	91.0	97.0	95.0	94.7
Official creditors	0.3	5.6	24.4	59.8	77.8	77.7	76.8	82.0	81.8	82.4
Private creditors	0.0	0.0	4.0	12.1	16.7	16.0	14.3	15.0	13.2	12.3
Memo: export credits	0.0	0.0	37.0	103.1	59.3	60.4	55.4	44.1	50.6	60.2
TOTAL DEBT FLOWS										
Disbursements	**0.0**	**37.6**	**9.9**	**6.6**	**2.2**	**2.0**	**2.6**	**1.1**	**3.8**	**1.7**
Long-term debt	0.0	19.6	9.9	4.0	2.2	2.0	2.6	1.1	3.8	1.7
IMF purchases	0.0	18.0	0.0	2.6	0.0	0.0	0.0	0.0	0.0	0.0
Principal repayments	**0.0**	**1.7**	**4.2**	**0.7**	**1.3**	**3.3**	**4.1**	**3.7**	**3.5**	**4.1**
Long-term debt	0.0	1.7	0.6	0.1	0.2	2.2	1.1	0.8	1.0	1.4
IMF repurchases	0.0	0.0	3.6	0.5	1.1	1.1	3.0	2.9	2.5	2.7
Net flows on debt	**0.0**	**40.9**	**9.7**	**16.7**	**-8.1**	**0.1**	**19.0**	**12.4**	**-20.7**	**-12.3**
of which short-term debt	0.0	5.0	4.0	10.8	-9.0	1.5	20.6	15.0	-21.0	-10.0
Interest payments (INT)	**0.0**	**0.8**	**0.9**	**1.4**	**0.8**	**1.3**	**1.8**	**2.3**	**1.5**	**1.2**
Long-term debt	0.0	0.1	0.5	0.8	0.4	1.0	1.0	0.7	0.7	0.8
IMF charges	0.0	0.2	0.2	0.0	0.1	0.1	0.1	0.1	0.0	0.0
Short-term debt	0.0	0.6	0.2	0.6	0.3	0.2	0.7	1.6	0.8	0.4
Net transfers on debt	**0.0**	**40.0**	**8.8**	**15.3**	**-8.9**	**-1.3**	**17.2**	**10.1**	**-22.2**	**-13.5**
Total debt service paid (TDS)	**0.0**	**2.6**	**5.1**	**2.0**	**2.1**	**4.7**	**5.9**	**6.0**	**5.0**	**5.3**
Long-term debt	0.0	1.8	1.1	0.9	0.6	3.3	2.1	1.5	1.7	2.2
IMF repurchases and charges	0.0	0.2	3.8	0.6	1.2	1.2	3.1	2.9	2.5	2.7
Short-term debt (interest only)	0.0	0.6	0.2	0.6	0.3	0.2	0.7	1.6	0.8	0.4
2. AGGREGATE NET RESOURCE FLOWS AND NET TRANSFERS (LONG-TERM)										
NET RESOURCE FLOWS	**0.0**	**19.3**	**63.9**	**31.8**	**144.0**	**394.1**	**34.5**	**37.2**	**134.1**	**138.2**
Net flow of long-term debt (ex. IMF)	0.0	17.8	9.4	3.8	2.0	-0.3	1.4	0.3	2.8	0.3
Foreign direct investment (net)	0.0	0.0	11.0	17.0	127.0	376.0	20.0	24.0	120.0	120.0
Portfolio equity flows	0.0	0.0	0.0	0.0	0.0	0.0	0.0	0.0	0.0	0.0
Grants (excluding technical coop.)	0.0	1.4	43.5	11.0	15.0	18.4	13.1	12.9	11.3	17.9
Memo: technical coop. grants	0.0	2.0	12.9	13.1	17.2	11.0	12.4	13.2	10.1	7.9
official net resource flows	0.0	14.8	52.9	14.8	17.0	18.1	14.5	13.2	14.1	18.2
private net resource flows	0.0	4.5	11.0	17.0	127.0	376.0	20.0	24.0	120.0	120.0
NET TRANSFERS	**-0.6**	**19.2**	**63.4**	**31.0**	**143.6**	**393.1**	**33.5**	**36.5**	**133.4**	**125.4**
Interest on long-term debt	0.0	0.1	0.5	0.8	0.4	1.0	1.0	0.7	0.7	0.8
Profit remittances on FDI	0.6	0.0	0.0	0.0	0.0	0.0	0.0	0.0	0.0	12.0
Memo: official net transfers	0.0	14.7	52.4	14.0	16.6	17.1	13.5	12.5	13.4	17.4
private net transfers	-0.6	4.5	11.0	17.0	127.0	376.0	20.0	24.0	120.0	108.0
3. MAJOR ECONOMIC AGGREGATES										
Gross national income (GNI)	66.9	..	123.5	115.7	153.1	203.8	415.8	404.9	466.0	498.3
Exports of goods & services (XGS)	..	..	42.3	65.4	94.2	180.4	509.1	804.3	1,415.9	2,362.6
of which workers remittances	..	..	..	..	..	..	..	..	..	..
Imports of goods & services (MGS)	..	..	99.2	69.5	221.1	521.8	818.9	1,257.7	1,653.1	2,481.5
International reserves (RES)	..	..	0.7	0.4	0.0	0.5	4.9	0.8	3.4	23.0
Current account balance	..	..	-19.0	-0.4	-123.4	-344.0	..	..	..	..
4. DEBT INDICATORS										
EDT / XGS (%)	..	..	569.7	440.0	309.7	156.6	55.6	38.1	19.2	10.5
EDT / GNI (%)	7.5	..	195.2	248.5	190.6	138.6	68.1	75.6	58.2	49.7
TDS / XGS (%)	..	..	12.1	3.1	2.2	2.6	1.2	0.8	0.4	0.2
INT / XGS (%)	..	..	2.1	2.1	0.9	0.7	0.4	0.3	0.1	0.1
INT / GNI (%)	0.0	..	0.7	1.2	0.5	0.6	0.4	0.3	0.1	0.1
RES / EDT (%)	..	..	0.3	0.1	0.0	0.2	1.7	0.3	1.2	9.3
RES / MGS (months)	..	..	0.1	0.1	0.0	0.0	0.1	0.0	0.0	0.1
Short-term / EDT (%)	0.0	9.3	10.8	16.9	14.9	15.3	21.7	25.7	20.4	17.8
Concessional / EDT (%)	0.0	41.7	48.9	49.3	50.7	51.4	49.0	47.0	52.5	55.3
Multilateral / EDT (%)	0.0	3.6	28.0	33.7	34.8	35.0	33.1	32.0	36.2	37.8

EQUATORIAL GUINEA

(US$ million, unless otherwise indicated)

	1970	1980	1990	1994	1995	1996	1997	1998	1999	2000
5. LONG-TERM DEBT										
DEBT OUTSTANDING (LDOD)	**5.0**	**52.5**	**209.2**	**219.3**	**229.6**	**222.2**	**208.6**	**216.5**	**207.9**	**198.9**
Public and publicly guaranteed	**5.0**	**52.5**	**209.2**	**219.3**	**229.6**	**222.2**	**208.6**	**216.5**	**207.9**	**198.9**
Official creditors	5.0	45.3	191.5	203.6	212.8	206.2	194.3	201.5	194.7	186.5
Multilateral	0.0	2.7	67.4	96.8	101.4	98.8	93.7	98.0	98.2	93.6
Concessional	0.0	2.0	51.6	84.3	88.2	87.0	83.7	87.6	89.4	85.8
Bilateral	5.0	42.6	124.1	106.8	111.5	107.4	100.5	103.6	96.5	92.9
Concessional	0.0	29.5	66.4	57.6	59.8	58.1	55.1	56.4	53.0	51.2
Private creditors	0.0	7.2	17.8	15.7	16.8	16.0	14.3	15.0	13.2	12.3
Bonds	0.0	0.0	0.0	0.0	0.0	0.0	0.0	0.0	0.0	0.0
Commercial banks	0.0	0.0	0.0	0.0	0.0	0.0	0.0	0.0	0.0	0.0
Other private	0.0	7.2	17.8	15.7	16.8	16.0	14.3	15.0	13.2	12.3
Private nonguaranteed	**0.0**	**0.0**	**0.0**	**0.0**	**0.0**	**0.0**	**0.0**	**0.0**	**0.0**	**0.0**
Bonds	0.0	0.0	0.0	0.0	0.0	0.0	0.0	0.0	0.0	0.0
Commercial banks and other	0.0	0.0	0.0	0.0	0.0	0.0	0.0	0.0	0.0	0.0
Memo:										
IBRD	0.0	0.0	0.0	0.0	0.0	0.0	0.0	0.0	0.0	0.0
IDA	0.0	0.0	37.6	49.9	53.1	52.1	49.9	51.7	50.3	47.3
DISBURSEMENTS	**0.0**	**19.6**	**9.9**	**4.0**	**2.2**	**2.0**	**2.6**	**1.1**	**3.8**	**1.7**
Public and publicly guaranteed	**0.0**	**19.6**	**9.9**	**4.0**	**2.2**	**2.0**	**2.6**	**1.1**	**3.8**	**1.7**
Official creditors	0.0	14.8	9.9	4.0	2.2	2.0	2.6	1.1	3.8	1.7
Multilateral	0.0	1.7	3.7	4.0	2.2	2.0	2.6	1.1	3.8	1.7
Concessional	0.0	1.0	3.1	4.0	2.2	2.0	2.6	1.1	3.8	1.7
Bilateral	0.0	13.1	6.3	0.0	0.0	0.0	0.0	0.0	0.0	0.0
Concessional	0.0	3.3	6.3	0.0	0.0	0.0	0.0	0.0	0.0	0.0
Private creditors	0.0	4.8	0.0	0.0	0.0	0.0	0.0	0.0	0.0	0.0
Bonds	0.0	0.0	0.0	0.0	0.0	0.0	0.0	0.0	0.0	0.0
Commercial banks	0.0	0.0	0.0	0.0	0.0	0.0	0.0	0.0	0.0	0.0
Other private	0.0	4.8	0.0	0.0	0.0	0.0	0.0	0.0	0.0	0.0
Private nonguaranteed	**0.0**	**0.0**	**0.0**	**0.0**	**0.0**	**0.0**	**0.0**	**0.0**	**0.0**	**0.0**
Bonds	0.0	0.0	0.0	0.0	0.0	0.0	0.0	0.0	0.0	0.0
Commercial banks and other	0.0	0.0	0.0	0.0	0.0	0.0	0.0	0.0	0.0	0.0
Memo:										
IBRD	0.0	0.0	0.0	0.0	0.0	0.0	0.0	0.0	0.0	0.0
IDA	0.0	0.0	2.0	2.4	2.2	1.0	1.3	0.3	0.1	0.0
PRINCIPAL REPAYMENTS	**0.0**	**1.7**	**0.6**	**0.1**	**0.2**	**2.2**	**1.1**	**0.8**	**1.0**	**1.4**
Public and publicly guaranteed	**0.0**	**1.7**	**0.6**	**0.1**	**0.2**	**2.2**	**1.1**	**0.8**	**1.0**	**1.4**
Official creditors	0.0	1.4	0.6	0.1	0.2	2.2	1.1	0.8	1.0	1.4
Multilateral	0.0	0.0	0.5	0.1	0.2	2.2	1.1	0.8	1.0	1.0
Concessional	0.0	0.0	0.5	0.1	0.2	0.7	0.7	0.5	0.6	0.6
Bilateral	0.0	1.4	0.1	0.0	0.0	0.0	0.0	0.0	0.0	0.4
Concessional	0.0	0.0	0.0	0.0	0.0	0.0	0.0	0.0	0.0	0.4
Private creditors	0.0	0.3	0.0	0.0	0.0	0.0	0.0	0.0	0.0	0.0
Bonds	0.0	0.0	0.0	0.0	0.0	0.0	0.0	0.0	0.0	0.0
Commercial banks	0.0	0.0	0.0	0.0	0.0	0.0	0.0	0.0	0.0	0.0
Other private	0.0	0.3	0.0	0.0	0.0	0.0	0.0	0.0	0.0	0.0
Private nonguaranteed	**0.0**	**0.0**	**0.0**	**0.0**	**0.0**	**0.0**	**0.0**	**0.0**	**0.0**	**0.0**
Bonds	0.0	0.0	0.0	0.0	0.0	0.0	0.0	0.0	0.0	0.0
Commercial banks and other	0.0	0.0	0.0	0.0	0.0	0.0	0.0	0.0	0.0	0.0
Memo:										
IBRD	0.0	0.0	0.0	0.0	0.0	0.0	0.0	0.0	0.0	0.0
IDA	0.0	0.0	0.0	0.1	0.2	0.2	0.4	0.4	0.4	0.4
NET FLOWS ON DEBT	**0.0**	**17.8**	**9.4**	**3.8**	**2.0**	**-0.3**	**1.4**	**0.3**	**2.8**	**0.3**
Public and publicly guaranteed	**0.0**	**17.8**	**9.4**	**3.8**	**2.0**	**-0.3**	**1.4**	**0.3**	**2.8**	**0.3**
Official creditors	0.0	13.4	9.4	3.8	2.0	-0.3	1.4	0.3	2.8	0.3
Multilateral	0.0	1.7	3.2	3.8	2.0	-0.3	1.4	0.3	2.8	0.7
Concessional	0.0	1.0	2.6	3.8	2.0	1.3	1.9	0.6	3.2	1.1
Bilateral	0.0	11.7	6.2	0.0	0.0	0.0	0.0	0.0	0.0	-0.4
Concessional	0.0	3.3	6.3	0.0	0.0	0.0	0.0	0.0	0.0	-0.4
Private creditors	0.0	4.5	0.0	0.0	0.0	0.0	0.0	0.0	0.0	0.0
Bonds	0.0	0.0	0.0	0.0	0.0	0.0	0.0	0.0	0.0	0.0
Commercial banks	0.0	0.0	0.0	0.0	0.0	0.0	0.0	0.0	0.0	0.0
Other private	0.0	4.5	0.0	0.0	0.0	0.0	0.0	0.0	0.0	0.0
Private nonguaranteed	**0.0**	**0.0**	**0.0**	**0.0**	**0.0**	**0.0**	**0.0**	**0.0**	**0.0**	**0.0**
Bonds	0.0	0.0	0.0	0.0	0.0	0.0	0.0	0.0	0.0	0.0
Commercial banks and other	0.0	0.0	0.0	0.0	0.0	0.0	0.0	0.0	0.0	0.0
Memo:										
IBRD	0.0	0.0	0.0	0.0	0.0	0.0	0.0	0.0	0.0	0.0
IDA	0.0	0.0	2.0	2.4	2.0	0.8	0.8	-0.1	-0.3	-0.4

EQUATORIAL GUINEA

(US$ million, unless otherwise indicated)

	1970	1980	1990	1994	1995	1996	1997	1998	1999	2000
INTEREST PAYMENTS (LINT)	**0.0**	**0.1**	**0.5**	**0.8**	**0.4**	**1.0**	**1.0**	**0.7**	**0.7**	**0.8**
Public and publicly guaranteed	**0.0**	**0.1**	**0.5**	**0.8**	**0.4**	**1.0**	**1.0**	**0.7**	**0.7**	**0.8**
Official creditors	0.0	0.1	0.5	0.8	0.4	1.0	1.0	0.7	0.7	0.8
Multilateral	0.0	0.0	0.3	0.8	0.4	1.0	1.0	0.7	0.7	0.8
Concessional	0.0	0.0	0.3	0.5	0.4	0.8	0.7	0.5	0.6	0.6
Bilateral	0.0	0.1	0.1	0.0	0.0	0.0	0.0	0.0	0.0	0.0
Concessional	0.0	0.1	0.1	0.0	0.0	0.0	0.0	0.0	0.0	0.0
Private creditors	0.0	0.0	0.0	0.0	0.0	0.0	0.0	0.0	0.0	0.0
Bonds	0.0	0.0	0.0	0.0	0.0	0.0	0.0	0.0	0.0	0.0
Commercial banks	0.0	0.0	0.0	0.0	0.0	0.0	0.0	0.0	0.0	0.0
Other private	0.0	0.0	0.0	0.0	0.0	0.0	0.0	0.0	0.0	0.0
Private nonguaranteed	**0.0**	**0.0**	**0.0**	**0.0**	**0.0**	**0.0**	**0.0**	**0.0**	**0.0**	**0.0**
Bonds	0.0	0.0	0.0	0.0	0.0	0.0	0.0	0.0	0.0	0.0
Commercial banks and other	0.0	0.0	0.0	0.0	0.0	0.0	0.0	0.0	0.0	0.0
Memo:										
IBRD	0.0	0.0	0.0	0.0	0.0	0.0	0.0	0.0	0.0	0.0
IDA	0.0	0.0	0.2	0.4	0.4	0.3	0.5	0.3	0.3	0.4
NET TRANSFERS ON DEBT	**0.0**	**17.8**	**8.9**	**3.1**	**1.7**	**-1.3**	**0.4**	**-0.4**	**2.1**	**-0.5**
Public and publicly guaranteed	**0.0**	**17.8**	**8.9**	**3.1**	**1.7**	**-1.3**	**0.4**	**-0.4**	**2.1**	**-0.5**
Official creditors	0.0	13.3	8.9	3.1	1.7	-1.3	0.4	-0.4	2.1	-0.5
Multilateral	0.0	1.7	2.9	3.1	1.7	-1.3	0.4	-0.4	2.1	-0.1
Concessional	0.0	1.0	2.3	3.4	1.7	0.5	1.2	0.1	2.6	0.5
Bilateral	0.0	11.6	6.0	0.0	0.0	0.0	0.0	0.0	0.0	-0.4
Concessional	0.0	3.2	6.1	0.0	0.0	0.0	0.0	0.0	0.0	-0.4
Private creditors	0.0	4.4	0.0	0.0	0.0	0.0	0.0	0.0	0.0	0.0
Bonds	0.0	0.0	0.0	0.0	0.0	0.0	0.0	0.0	0.0	0.0
Commercial banks	0.0	0.0	0.0	0.0	0.0	0.0	0.0	0.0	0.0	0.0
Other private	0.0	4.4	0.0	0.0	0.0	0.0	0.0	0.0	0.0	0.0
Private nonguaranteed	**0.0**	**0.0**	**0.0**	**0.0**	**0.0**	**0.0**	**0.0**	**0.0**	**0.0**	**0.0**
Bonds	0.0	0.0	0.0	0.0	0.0	0.0	0.0	0.0	0.0	0.0
Commercial banks and other	0.0	0.0	0.0	0.0	0.0	0.0	0.0	0.0	0.0	0.0
Memo:										
IBRD	0.0	0.0	0.0	0.0	0.0	0.0	0.0	0.0	0.0	0.0
IDA	0.0	0.0	1.8	2.0	1.7	0.4	0.4	-0.4	-0.7	-0.8
DEBT SERVICE (LTDS)	**0.0**	**1.8**	**1.1**	**0.9**	**0.6**	**3.3**	**2.1**	**1.5**	**1.7**	**2.2**
Public and publicly guaranteed	**0.0**	**1.8**	**1.1**	**0.9**	**0.6**	**3.3**	**2.1**	**1.5**	**1.7**	**2.2**
Official creditors	0.0	1.5	1.1	0.9	0.6	3.3	2.1	1.5	1.7	2.2
Multilateral	0.0	0.0	0.8	0.9	0.6	3.3	2.1	1.5	1.7	1.8
Concessional	0.0	0.0	0.8	0.6	0.6	1.4	1.4	1.0	1.2	1.3
Bilateral	0.0	1.5	0.3	0.0	0.0	0.0	0.0	0.0	0.0	0.4
Concessional	0.0	0.1	0.1	0.0	0.0	0.0	0.0	0.0	0.0	0.4
Private creditors	0.0	0.4	0.0	0.0	0.0	0.0	0.0	0.0	0.0	0.0
Bonds	0.0	0.0	0.0	0.0	0.0	0.0	0.0	0.0	0.0	0.0
Commercial banks	0.0	0.0	0.0	0.0	0.0	0.0	0.0	0.0	0.0	0.0
Other private	0.0	0.4	0.0	0.0	0.0	0.0	0.0	0.0	0.0	0.0
Private nonguaranteed	**0.0**	**0.0**	**0.0**	**0.0**	**0.0**	**0.0**	**0.0**	**0.0**	**0.0**	**0.0**
Bonds	0.0	0.0	0.0	0.0	0.0	0.0	0.0	0.0	0.0	0.0
Commercial banks and other	0.0	0.0	0.0	0.0	0.0	0.0	0.0	0.0	0.0	0.0
Memo:										
IBRD	0.0	0.0	0.0	0.0	0.0	0.0	0.0	0.0	0.0	0.0
IDA	0.0	0.0	0.2	0.5	0.6	0.6	0.9	0.7	0.7	0.8
UNDISBURSED DEBT	**0.0**	**70.6**	**64.9**	**44.4**	**43.0**	**36.6**	**28.3**	**30.8**	**14.4**	**10.9**
Official creditors	0.0	67.6	64.9	44.4	43.0	36.6	28.3	30.8	14.4	10.9
Private creditors	0.0	3.0	0.0	0.0	0.0	0.0	0.0	0.0	0.0	0.0
Memorandum items										
Concessional LDOD	0.0	31.5	118.1	141.9	148.0	145.1	138.7	144.1	142.4	137.0
Variable rate LDOD	0.0	0.0	5.1	4.2	4.2	4.2	4.1	4.1	4.1	4.0
Public sector LDOD	5.0	46.9	209.2	219.3	229.6	222.2	208.6	216.5	207.9	198.9
Private sector LDOD	0.0	5.6	0.0	0.0	0.0	0.0	0.0	0.0	0.0	0.0

6. CURRENCY COMPOSITION OF LONG-TERM DEBT (PERCENT)

	1970	1980	1990	1994	1995	1996	1997	1998	1999	2000
Deutsche mark	0.0	0.0	5.9	5.5	5.6	5.4	5.0	5.1	4.6	4.4
French franc	0.0	0.0	7.0	7.6	7.9	7.6	7.1	7.3	6.5	6.3
Japanese yen	0.0	0.0	0.0	0.0	0.0	0.0	0.0	0.0	0.0	0.0
Pound sterling	0.0	0.0	0.0	0.0	0.0	0.0	0.0	0.0	0.0	0.0
Swiss franc	0.0	0.0	0.0	0.0	0.0	0.0	0.0	0.0	0.0	0.0
U.S.dollars	0.0	16.5	37.8	41.1	40.7	41.6	43.3	42.5	43.6	43.9
Multiple currency	0.0	0.0	5.6	15.0	14.6	15.0	15.3	15.5	17.5	17.9
Special drawing rights	0.0	0.0	0.0	0.0	0.0	0.0	0.0	0.0	0.0	0.0
All other currencies	0.0	83.5	43.7	30.8	31.2	30.4	29.3	29.6	27.8	27.5

EQUATORIAL GUINEA

(US$ million, unless otherwise indicated)

	1970	1980	1990	1994	1995	1996	1997	1998	1999	2000
7. DEBT RESTRUCTURINGS										
Total amount rescheduled	..	..	0.0	0.0	0.0	0.0	0.0	0.0	0.0	0.0
Debt stock rescheduled	..	..	0.0	0.0	0.0	0.0	0.0	0.0	0.0	0.0
Principal rescheduled	..	..	0.0	0.0	0.0	0.0	0.0	0.0	0.0	0.0
Official	..	..	0.0	0.0	0.0	0.0	0.0	0.0	0.0	0.0
Private	..	..	0.0	0.0	0.0	0.0	0.0	0.0	0.0	0.0
Interest rescheduled	..	..	0.0	0.0	0.0	0.0	0.0	0.0	0.0	0.0
Official	..	..	0.0	0.0	0.0	0.0	0.0	0.0	0.0	0.0
Private	..	..	0.0	0.0	0.0	0.0	0.0	0.0	0.0	0.0
Debt forgiven	..	..	18.5	0.0	0.0	0.0	0.0	0.0	0.0	0.0
Memo: interest forgiven	..	..	0.0	0.0	0.0	0.0	0.0	0.0	0.0	0.0
Debt stock reduction	..	..	0.0	0.0	0.0	0.0	0.0	0.0	0.0	0.0
of which debt buyback	..	..	0.0	0.0	0.0	0.0	0.0	0.0	0.0	0.0
8. DEBT STOCK-FLOW RECONCILIATION										
Total change in debt stocks	..	..	12.0	23.5	4.3	-9.4	0.7	22.9	-35.0	-23.3
Net flows on debt	0.0	40.9	9.7	16.7	-8.1	0.1	19.0	12.4	-20.7	-12.3
Net change in interest arrears	..	..	7.2	5.0	3.7	-1.7	-2.2	2.4	-2.6	-1.2
Interest capitalized	..	..	0.0	0.0	0.0	0.0	0.0	0.0	0.0	0.0
Debt forgiveness or reduction	..	..	-18.5	0.0	0.0	0.0	0.0	0.0	0.0	0.0
Cross-currency valuation	..	..	15.4	5.0	6.7	-7.7	-14.9	5.0	-10.8	-7.9
Residual	..	..	-1.9	-3.2	1.9	0.0	-1.1	3.2	-0.9	-1.9
9. AVERAGE TERMS OF NEW COMMITMENTS										
ALL CREDITORS										
Interest (%)	0.0	6.5	0.9	0.8	0.0	0.0	0.0	0.0	0.0	0.0
Maturity (years)	0.0	14.2	38.2	49.7	0.0	0.0	0.0	49.7	0.0	0.0
Grace period (years)	0.0	3.4	10.1	10.2	0.0	0.0	0.0	10.2	0.0	0.0
Grant element (%)	0.0	21.0	77.5	83.1	0.0	0.0	0.0	90.0	0.0	0.0
Official creditors										
Interest (%)	0.0	6.5	0.9	0.8	0.0	0.0	0.0	0.0	0.0	0.0
Maturity (years)	0.0	14.2	38.2	49.7	0.0	0.0	0.0	49.7	0.0	0.0
Grace period (years)	0.0	3.4	10.1	10.2	0.0	0.0	0.0	10.2	0.0	0.0
Grant element (%)	0.0	21.0	77.5	83.1	0.0	0.0	0.0	90.0	0.0	0.0
Private creditors										
Interest (%)	0.0	0.0	0.0	0.0	0.0	0.0	0.0	0.0	0.0	0.0
Maturity (years)	0.0	0.0	0.0	0.0	0.0	0.0	0.0	0.0	0.0	0.0
Grace period (years)	0.0	0.0	0.0	0.0	0.0	0.0	0.0	0.0	0.0	0.0
Grant element (%)	0.0	0.0	0.0	0.0	0.0	0.0	0.0	0.0	0.0	0.0
Memorandum items										
Commitments	0.0	27.2	18.1	6.6	0.0	0.0	0.0	2.7	0.0	0.0
Official creditors	0.0	27.2	18.1	6.6	0.0	0.0	0.0	2.7	0.0	0.0
Private creditors	0.0	0.0	0.0	0.0	0.0	0.0	0.0	0.0	0.0	0.0

10. CONTRACTUAL OBLIGATIONS ON OUTSTANDING LONG-TERM DEBT

	2001	2002	2003	2004	2005	2006	2007	2008	2009	2010
TOTAL										
Disbursements	4.2	2.9	1.8	1.1	0.8	0.2	0.0	0.0	0.0	0.0
Principal	4.4	4.4	3.8	3.6	3.0	3.1	3.3	3.5	3.6	3.5
Interest	1.1	1.0	0.9	0.8	0.8	0.7	0.7	0.7	0.6	0.6
Official creditors										
Disbursements	4.2	2.9	1.8	1.1	0.8	0.2	0.0	0.0	0.0	0.0
Principal	4.4	4.4	3.8	3.6	3.0	3.1	3.3	3.5	3.6	3.5
Interest	1.1	1.0	0.9	0.8	0.8	0.7	0.7	0.7	0.6	0.6
Bilateral creditors										
Disbursements	0.0	0.0	0.0	0.0	0.0	0.0	0.0	0.0	0.0	0.0
Principal	2.9	2.7	1.7	1.4	0.7	0.6	0.6	0.6	0.6	0.5
Interest	0.4	0.3	0.2	0.1	0.1	0.1	0.1	0.1	0.1	0.1
Multilateral creditors										
Disbursements	4.2	2.9	1.8	1.1	0.8	0.2	0.0	0.0	0.0	0.0
Principal	1.5	1.7	2.1	2.2	2.3	2.4	2.7	3.0	3.0	3.0
Interest	0.8	0.8	0.7	0.7	0.6	0.6	0.6	0.6	0.6	0.5
Private creditors										
Disbursements	0.0	0.0	0.0	0.0	0.0	0.0	0.0	0.0	0.0	0.0
Principal	0.0	0.0	0.0	0.0	0.0	0.0	0.0	0.0	0.0	0.0
Interest	0.0	0.0	0.0	0.0	0.0	0.0	0.0	0.0	0.0	0.0
Commercial banks										
Disbursements	0.0	0.0	0.0	0.0	0.0	0.0	0.0	0.0	0.0	0.0
Principal	0.0	0.0	0.0	0.0	0.0	0.0	0.0	0.0	0.0	0.0
Interest	0.0	0.0	0.0	0.0	0.0	0.0	0.0	0.0	0.0	0.0
Other private										
Disbursements	0.0	0.0	0.0	0.0	0.0	0.0	0.0	0.0	0.0	0.0
Principal	0.0	0.0	0.0	0.0	0.0	0.0	0.0	0.0	0.0	0.0
Interest	0.0	0.0	0.0	0.0	0.0	0.0	0.0	0.0	0.0	0.0

ERITREA

(US$ million, unless otherwise indicated)

1. SUMMARY DEBT DATA

	1970	1980	1990	1994	1995	1996	1997	1998	1999	2000
TOTAL DEBT STOCKS (EDT)	..	..	..	29.1	36.7	44.3	75.5	151.3	252.7	311.1
Long-term debt (LDOD)	..	..	..	29.1	36.7	44.3	75.5	146.1	252.6	298.0
Public and publicly guaranteed	..	..	..	29.1	36.7	44.3	75.5	146.1	252.6	298.0
Private nonguaranteed	..	..	..	0.0	0.0	0.0	0.0	0.0	0.0	0.0
Use of IMF credit	..	..	..	0.0	0.0	0.0	0.0	0.0	0.0	0.0
Short-term debt	..	..	..	0.0	0.0	0.0	0.0	5.2	0.2	13.1
of which interest arrears on LDOD	..	..	..	0.0	0.0	0.0	0.0	0.0	0.0	2.0
Official creditors	..	..	..	0.0	0.0	0.0	0.0	0.0	0.0	2.0
Private creditors	..	..	..	0.0	0.0	0.0	0.0	0.0	0.0	0.0
Memo: principal arrears on LDOD	..	..	..	0.0	0.0	0.0	0.0	0.0	0.0	4.9
Official creditors	..	..	..	0.0	0.0	0.0	0.0	0.0	0.0	4.9
Private creditors	..	..	..	0.0	0.0	0.0	0.0	0.0	0.0	0.0
Memo: export credits	..	..	..	1.3	1.7	0.8	0.2	0.2	0.2	1.1
TOTAL DEBT FLOWS										
Disbursements	..	..	..	26.6	7.2	6.9	33.3	67.3	108.2	50.7
Long-term debt	..	..	..	26.6	7.2	6.9	33.3	67.3	108.2	50.7
IMF purchases	..	..	..	0.0	0.0	0.0	0.0	0.0	0.0	0.0
Principal repayments	..	..	..	0.0	0.0	0.0	0.0	0.0	0.0	0.5
Long-term debt	..	..	..	0.0	0.0	0.0	0.0	0.0	0.0	0.5
IMF repurchases	..	..	..	0.0	0.0	0.0	0.0	0.0	0.0	0.0
Net flows on debt	..	..	..	26.6	7.2	6.9	33.3	72.5	103.2	61.2
of which short-term debt	..	..	..	0.0	0.0	0.0	0.0	5.2	-5.0	11.0
Interest payments (INT)	..	..	..	0.0	0.2	0.0	0.5	3.7	3.3	2.5
Long-term debt	..	..	..	0.0	0.2	0.0	0.5	3.6	3.3	2.5
IMF charges	..	..	..	0.0	0.0	0.0	0.0	0.0	0.0	0.0
Short-term debt	..	..	..	0.0	0.0	0.0	0.0	0.1	0.0	0.0
Net transfers on debt	..	..	..	26.6	7.1	6.9	32.8	68.8	99.9	58.7
Total debt service paid (TDS)	..	..	..	0.0	0.2	0.0	0.5	3.7	3.3	3.3
Long-term debt	..	..	..	0.0	0.2	0.0	0.5	3.6	3.3	3.0
IMF repurchases and charges	..	..	..	0.0	0.0	0.0	0.0	0.0	0.0	0.0
Short-term debt (interest only)	..	..	..	0.0	0.0	0.0	0.0	0.1	0.0	0.0

2. AGGREGATE NET RESOURCE FLOWS AND NET TRANSFERS (LONG-TERM)

	1970	1980	1990	1994	1995	1996	1997	1998	1999	2000
NET RESOURCE FLOWS	..	..	..	140.3	110.4	135.9	132.1	172.9	208.5	189.5
Net flow of long-term debt (ex. IMF)	..	..	..	26.6	7.2	6.9	33.3	67.3	108.2	50.2
Foreign direct investment (net)	..	..	..	0.0	0.0	36.7	38.7	31.7	36.0	35.0
Portfolio equity flows	..	..	..	0.0	0.0	0.0	0.0	0.0	0.0	0.0
Grants (excluding technical coop.)	..	..	..	113.7	103.2	92.3	60.1	73.9	64.3	104.3
Memo: technical coop. grants	..	..	..	31.7	42.7	62.3	36.9	31.0	21.2	22.3
official net resource flows	..	..	..	140.3	110.4	99.2	93.4	141.2	172.5	154.5
private net resource flows	..	..	..	0.0	0.0	36.7	38.7	31.7	36.0	35.0
NET TRANSFERS	..	..	..	140.3	110.2	135.9	131.6	169.3	205.2	187.0
Interest on long-term debt	..	..	..	0.0	0.2	0.0	0.5	3.6	3.3	2.5
Profit remittances on FDI	..	..	..	0.0	0.0	0.0	0.0	0.0	0.0	0.0
Memo: official net transfers	..	..	..	140.3	110.2	99.2	92.9	137.6	169.2	152.0
private net transfers	..	..	..	0.0	0.0	36.7	38.7	31.7	36.0	35.0

3. MAJOR ECONOMIC AGGREGATES

	1970	1980	1990	1994	1995	1996	1997	1998	1999	2000
Gross national income (GNI)	..	..	..	664.7	688.8	760.7	829.9	805.1	776.0	694.9
Exports of goods & services (XGS)	..	..	..	..	298.1	344.5	390.5	245.0	207.5	299.1
of which workers remittances	..	..	..	166.4	119.0	136.1	177.2	123.9	127.4	200.2
Imports of goods & services (MGS)	..	..	..	..	447.7	583.4	602.4	604.8	608.6	502.5
International reserves (RES)	..	..	..	..	..	..	..	..	..	..
Current account balance	..	..	..	61.6	-31.2	-104.2	-37.0	-238.2	-284.9	-207.9

4. DEBT INDICATORS

	1970	1980	1990	1994	1995	1996	1997	1998	1999	2000
EDT / XGS (%)	..	..	..	..	12.3	12.9	19.3	61.8	121.8	104.0
EDT / GNI (%)	..	..	..	4.4	5.3	5.8	9.1	18.8	32.6	44.8
TDS / XGS (%)	..	..	..	..	0.1	0.0	0.1	1.5	1.6	1.1
INT / XGS (%)	..	..	..	..	0.1	0.0	0.1	1.5	1.6	0.8
INT / GNI (%)	..	..	..	0.0	0.0	0.0	0.1	0.5	0.4	0.4
RES / EDT (%)	..	..	..	..	..	..	..	..	..	..
RES / MGS (months)	..	..	..	..	..	..	..	..	..	..
Short-term / EDT (%)	..	..	..	0.0	0.0	0.0	0.0	3.4	0.1	4.2
Concessional / EDT (%)	..	..	..	100.0	100.0	95.7	96.0	92.2	93.4	90.5
Multilateral / EDT (%)	..	..	..	63.9	66.2	66.6	55.4	50.3	46.6	48.8

ERITREA

(US$ million, unless otherwise indicated)

	1970	1980	1990	1994	1995	1996	1997	1998	1999	2000
5. LONG-TERM DEBT										
DEBT OUTSTANDING (LDOD)	..	..	..	**29.1**	**36.7**	**44.3**	**75.5**	**146.1**	**252.6**	**298.0**
Public and publicly guaranteed	..	..	..	**29.1**	**36.7**	**44.3**	**75.5**	**146.1**	**252.6**	**298.0**
Official creditors	..	..	..	29.1	36.7	44.3	75.5	146.1	252.6	298.0
Multilateral	..	..	..	18.6	24.3	29.5	41.8	76.1	117.8	151.9
Concessional	..	..	..	18.6	24.3	27.6	38.9	71.5	110.9	144.9
Bilateral	..	..	..	10.5	12.4	14.8	33.6	70.0	134.8	146.1
Concessional	..	..	..	10.5	12.4	14.8	33.6	68.0	125.1	136.5
Private creditors	..	..	..	0.0	0.0	0.0	0.0	0.0	0.0	0.0
Bonds	..	..	..	0.0	0.0	0.0	0.0	0.0	0.0	0.0
Commercial banks	..	..	..	0.0	0.0	0.0	0.0	0.0	0.0	0.0
Other private	..	..	..	0.0	0.0	0.0	0.0	0.0	0.0	0.0
Private nonguaranteed	..	..	..	**0.0**	**0.0**	**0.0**	**0.0**	**0.0**	**0.0**	**0.0**
Bonds	..	..	..	0.0	0.0	0.0	0.0	0.0	0.0	0.0
Commercial banks and other	..	..	..	0.0	0.0	0.0	0.0	0.0	0.0	0.0
Memo:										
IBRD	..	..	..	0.0	0.0	0.0	0.0	0.0	0.0	0.0
IDA	..	..	..	18.6	24.3	26.5	28.8	36.9	55.8	84.5
DISBURSEMENTS	..	..	..	**26.6**	**7.2**	**6.9**	**33.3**	**67.3**	**108.2**	**50.7**
Public and publicly guaranteed	..	..	..	**26.6**	**7.2**	**6.9**	**33.3**	**67.3**	**108.2**	**50.7**
Official creditors	..	..	..	26.6	7.2	6.9	33.3	67.3	108.2	50.7
Multilateral	..	..	..	16.0	5.4	4.5	14.2	31.3	43.1	39.2
Concessional	..	..	..	16.0	5.4	2.5	12.9	29.9	40.0	38.1
Bilateral	..	..	..	10.6	1.8	2.4	19.1	36.0	65.1	11.5
Concessional	..	..	..	10.6	1.8	2.4	19.1	34.0	57.5	11.5
Private creditors	..	..	..	0.0	0.0	0.0	0.0	0.0	0.0	0.0
Bonds	..	..	..	0.0	0.0	0.0	0.0	0.0	0.0	0.0
Commercial banks	..	..	..	0.0	0.0	0.0	0.0	0.0	0.0	0.0
Other private	..	..	..	0.0	0.0	0.0	0.0	0.0	0.0	0.0
Private nonguaranteed	..	..	..	**0.0**	**0.0**	**0.0**	**0.0**	**0.0**	**0.0**	**0.0**
Bonds	..	..	..	0.0	0.0	0.0	0.0	0.0	0.0	0.0
Commercial banks and other	..	..	..	0.0	0.0	0.0	0.0	0.0	0.0	0.0
Memo:										
IBRD	..	..	..	0.0	0.0	0.0	0.0	0.0	0.0	0.0
IDA	..	..	..	16.0	5.4	1.5	3.8	6.3	19.5	31.6
PRINCIPAL REPAYMENTS	..	..	..	**0.0**	**0.0**	**0.0**	**0.0**	**0.0**	**0.0**	**0.5**
Public and publicly guaranteed	..	..	..	**0.0**	**0.0**	**0.0**	**0.0**	**0.0**	**0.0**	**0.5**
Official creditors	..	..	..	0.0	0.0	0.0	0.0	0.0	0.0	0.5
Multilateral	..	..	..	0.0	0.0	0.0	0.0	0.0	0.0	0.5
Concessional	..	..	..	0.0	0.0	0.0	0.0	0.0	0.0	0.0
Bilateral	..	..	..	0.0	0.0	0.0	0.0	0.0	0.0	0.0
Concessional	..	..	..	0.0	0.0	0.0	0.0	0.0	0.0	0.0
Private creditors	..	..	..	0.0	0.0	0.0	0.0	0.0	0.0	0.0
Bonds	..	..	..	0.0	0.0	0.0	0.0	0.0	0.0	0.0
Commercial banks	..	..	..	0.0	0.0	0.0	0.0	0.0	0.0	0.0
Other private	..	..	..	0.0	0.0	0.0	0.0	0.0	0.0	0.0
Private nonguaranteed	..	..	..	**0.0**	**0.0**	**0.0**	**0.0**	**0.0**	**0.0**	**0.0**
Bonds	..	..	..	0.0	0.0	0.0	0.0	0.0	0.0	0.0
Commercial banks and other	..	..	..	0.0	0.0	0.0	0.0	0.0	0.0	0.0
Memo:										
IBRD	..	..	..	0.0	0.0	0.0	0.0	0.0	0.0	0.0
IDA	..	..	..	0.0	0.0	0.0	0.0	0.0	0.0	0.0
NET FLOWS ON DEBT	..	..	..	**26.6**	**7.2**	**6.9**	**33.3**	**67.3**	**108.2**	**50.2**
Public and publicly guaranteed	..	..	..	**26.6**	**7.2**	**6.9**	**33.3**	**67.3**	**108.2**	**50.2**
Official creditors	..	..	..	26.6	7.2	6.9	33.3	67.3	108.2	50.2
Multilateral	..	..	..	16.0	5.4	4.5	14.2	31.3	43.1	38.7
Concessional	..	..	..	16.0	5.4	2.5	12.9	29.9	40.0	38.1
Bilateral	..	..	..	10.6	1.8	2.4	19.1	36.0	65.1	11.5
Concessional	..	..	..	10.6	1.8	2.4	19.1	34.0	57.5	11.5
Private creditors	..	..	..	0.0	0.0	0.0	0.0	0.0	0.0	0.0
Bonds	..	..	..	0.0	0.0	0.0	0.0	0.0	0.0	0.0
Commercial banks	..	..	..	0.0	0.0	0.0	0.0	0.0	0.0	0.0
Other private	..	..	..	0.0	0.0	0.0	0.0	0.0	0.0	0.0
Private nonguaranteed	..	..	..	**0.0**	**0.0**	**0.0**	**0.0**	**0.0**	**0.0**	**0.0**
Bonds	..	..	..	0.0	0.0	0.0	0.0	0.0	0.0	0.0
Commercial banks and other	..	..	..	0.0	0.0	0.0	0.0	0.0	0.0	0.0
Memo:										
IBRD	..	..	..	0.0	0.0	0.0	0.0	0.0	0.0	0.0
IDA	..	..	..	16.0	5.4	1.5	3.8	6.3	19.5	31.6

ERITREA

(US$ million, unless otherwise indicated)

	1970	1980	1990	1994	1995	1996	1997	1998	1999	2000
INTEREST PAYMENTS (LINT)	..	..	..	**0.0**	**0.2**	**0.0**	**0.5**	**3.6**	**3.3**	**2.5**
Public and publicly guaranteed	..	..	..	**0.0**	**0.2**	**0.0**	**0.5**	**3.6**	**3.3**	**2.5**
Official creditors	..	..	..	0.0	0.2	0.0	0.5	3.6	3.3	2.5
Multilateral	..	..	..	0.0	0.2	0.0	0.3	0.6	1.6	1.3
Concessional	..	..	..	0.0	0.2	0.0	0.2	0.5	1.5	1.2
Bilateral	..	..	..	0.0	0.0	0.0	0.2	3.0	1.7	1.2
Concessional	..	..	..	0.0	0.0	0.0	0.2	3.0	1.5	1.2
Private creditors	..	..	..	0.0	0.0	0.0	0.0	0.0	0.0	0.0
Bonds	..	..	..	0.0	0.0	0.0	0.0	0.0	0.0	0.0
Commercial banks	..	..	..	0.0	0.0	0.0	0.0	0.0	0.0	0.0
Other private	..	..	..	0.0	0.0	0.0	0.0	0.0	0.0	0.0
Private nonguaranteed	..	..	..	**0.0**	**0.0**	**0.0**	**0.0**	**0.0**	**0.0**	**0.0**
Bonds	..	..	..	0.0	0.0	0.0	0.0	0.0	0.0	0.0
Commercial banks and other	..	..	..	0.0	0.0	0.0	0.0	0.0	0.0	0.0
Memo:										
IBRD	..	..	..	0.0	0.0	0.0	0.0	0.0	0.0	0.0
IDA	..	..	..	0.0	0.2	0.0	0.2	0.2	0.3	0.4
NET TRANSFERS ON DEBT	..	..	..	**26.6**	**7.1**	**6.9**	**32.8**	**63.7**	**105.0**	**47.8**
Public and publicly guaranteed	..	..	..	**26.6**	**7.1**	**6.9**	**32.8**	**63.7**	**105.0**	**47.8**
Official creditors	..	..	..	26.6	7.1	6.9	32.8	63.7	105.0	47.8
Multilateral	..	..	..	16.0	5.2	4.5	13.9	30.7	41.5	37.4
Concessional	..	..	..	16.0	5.2	2.5	12.7	29.4	38.5	37.0
Bilateral	..	..	..	10.6	1.8	2.4	18.9	33.0	63.4	10.4
Concessional	..	..	..	10.6	1.8	2.4	18.9	31.0	56.0	10.4
Private creditors	..	..	..	0.0	0.0	0.0	0.0	0.0	0.0	0.0
Bonds	..	..	..	0.0	0.0	0.0	0.0	0.0	0.0	0.0
Commercial banks	..	..	..	0.0	0.0	0.0	0.0	0.0	0.0	0.0
Other private	..	..	..	0.0	0.0	0.0	0.0	0.0	0.0	0.0
Private nonguaranteed	..	..	..	**0.0**	**0.0**	**0.0**	**0.0**	**0.0**	**0.0**	**0.0**
Bonds	..	..	..	0.0	0.0	0.0	0.0	0.0	0.0	0.0
Commercial banks and other	..	..	..	0.0	0.0	0.0	0.0	0.0	0.0	0.0
Memo:										
IBRD	..	..	..	0.0	0.0	0.0	0.0	0.0	0.0	0.0
IDA	..	..	..	16.0	5.2	1.5	3.6	6.1	19.2	31.2
DEBT SERVICE (LTDS)	..	..	..	**0.0**	**0.2**	**0.0**	**0.5**	**3.6**	**3.3**	**3.0**
Public and publicly guaranteed	..	..	..	**0.0**	**0.2**	**0.0**	**0.5**	**3.6**	**3.3**	**3.0**
Official creditors	..	..	..	0.0	0.2	0.0	0.5	3.6	3.3	3.0
Multilateral	..	..	..	0.0	0.2	0.0	0.3	0.6	1.6	1.8
Concessional	..	..	..	0.0	0.2	0.0	0.2	0.5	1.5	1.2
Bilateral	..	..	..	0.0	0.0	0.0	0.2	3.0	1.7	1.2
Concessional	..	..	..	0.0	0.0	0.0	0.2	3.0	1.5	1.2
Private creditors	..	..	..	0.0	0.0	0.0	0.0	0.0	0.0	0.0
Bonds	..	..	..	0.0	0.0	0.0	0.0	0.0	0.0	0.0
Commercial banks	..	..	..	0.0	0.0	0.0	0.0	0.0	0.0	0.0
Other private	..	..	..	0.0	0.0	0.0	0.0	0.0	0.0	0.0
Private nonguaranteed	..	..	..	**0.0**	**0.0**	**0.0**	**0.0**	**0.0**	**0.0**	**0.0**
Bonds	..	..	..	0.0	0.0	0.0	0.0	0.0	0.0	0.0
Commercial banks and other	..	..	..	0.0	0.0	0.0	0.0	0.0	0.0	0.0
Memo:										
IBRD	..	..	..	0.0	0.0	0.0	0.0	0.0	0.0	0.0
IDA	..	..	..	0.0	0.2	0.0	0.2	0.2	0.3	0.4
UNDISBURSED DEBT	..	..	..	**29.6**	**133.7**	**154.0**	**277.6**	**313.5**	**201.2**	**184.6**
Official creditors	..	..	..	29.6	133.7	154.0	277.6	313.5	201.2	184.6
Private creditors	..	..	..	0.0	0.0	0.0	0.0	0.0	0.0	0.0
Memorandum items										
Concessional LDOD	..	..	..	29.1	36.7	42.3	72.5	139.5	236.0	281.4
Variable rate LDOD	..	..	..	0.0	0.0	0.0	0.0	0.0	0.0	0.0
Public sector LDOD	..	..	..	29.1	36.7	44.3	75.5	146.1	252.6	298.0
Private sector LDOD	..	..	..	0.0	0.0	0.0	0.0	0.0	0.0	0.0

6. CURRENCY COMPOSITION OF LONG-TERM DEBT (PERCENT)

	1970	1980	1990	1994	1995	1996	1997	1998	1999	2000
Deutsche mark	..	..	..	0.0	0.0	0.0	0.0	0.0	0.0	0.0
French franc	..	..	..	0.0	0.0	0.0	0.0	0.0	0.0	0.0
Japanese yen	..	..	..	0.0	0.0	0.0	0.0	0.0	0.0	0.0
Pound sterling	..	..	..	0.0	0.0	0.0	0.0	0.0	0.0	0.0
Swiss franc	..	..	..	0.0	0.0	0.0	0.0	0.0	0.0	0.0
U.S.dollars	..	..	..	63.9	66.3	59.9	48.9	45.7	52.2	57.0
Multiple currency	..	..	..	0.0	0.0	0.0	0.0	0.0	0.0	0.0
Special drawing rights	..	..	..	0.0	0.0	1.6	1.6	1.4	0.8	0.9
All other currencies	..	..	..	36.1	33.7	38.5	49.5	52.9	47.0	42.1

ERITREA

(US$ million, unless otherwise indicated)

	1970	1980	1990	1994	1995	1996	1997	1998	1999	2000
7. DEBT RESTRUCTURINGS										
Total amount rescheduled	..	..	..	0.0	0.0	0.0	0.0	0.0	0.0	0.0
Debt stock rescheduled	..	..	..	0.0	0.0	0.0	0.0	0.0	0.0	0.0
Principal rescheduled	..	..	..	0.0	0.0	0.0	0.0	0.0	0.0	0.0
Official	..	..	..	0.0	0.0	0.0	0.0	0.0	0.0	0.0
Private	..	..	..	0.0	0.0	0.0	0.0	0.0	0.0	0.0
Interest rescheduled	..	..	..	..	0.0	0.0	0.0	0.0	0.0	0.0
Official	..	..	..	0.0	0.0	0.0	0.0	0.0	0.0	0.0
Private	..	..	..	0.0	0.0	0.0	0.0	0.0	0.0	0.0
Debt forgiven	..	..	..	0.0	0.0	0.0	0.0	0.0	0.0	0.0
Memo: interest forgiven	..	..	..	0.0	0.0	0.0	0.0	0.0	0.0	0.0
Debt stock reduction	..	..	..	0.0	0.0	0.0	0.0	0.0	0.0	0.0
of which debt buyback	..	..	..	0.0	0.0	0.0	0.0	0.0	0.0	0.0
8. DEBT STOCK-FLOW RECONCILIATION										
Total change in debt stocks	..	..	..	..	7.6	7.6	31.2	75.9	101.4	58.4
Net flows on debt	..	..	..	26.6	7.2	6.9	33.3	72.5	103.2	61.2
Net change in interest arrears	..	..	..	..	0.0	0.0	0.0	0.0	0.0	2.0
Interest capitalized	..	..	..	..	0.0	0.0	0.0	0.0	0.0	0.0
Debt forgiveness or reduction	..	..	..	..	0.0	0.0	0.0	0.0	0.0	0.0
Cross-currency valuation	..	..	..	..	0.4	-4.7	-2.1	2.4	-1.5	-4.2
Residual	..	..	..	..	0.0	5.3	-0.1	1.0	-0.3	-0.6
9. AVERAGE TERMS OF NEW COMMITMENTS										
ALL CREDITORS										
Interest (%)	..	..	..	1.2	2.0	1.0	1.2	1.3	0.0	0.7
Maturity (years)	..	..	..	26.6	23.9	38.7	37.3	32.0	0.0	38.9
Grace period (years)	..	..	..	6.1	5.6	9.5	10.9	7.4	0.0	10.3
Grant element (%)	..	..	..	65.9	56.6	76.3	75.0	68.1	0.0	80.8
Official creditors										
Interest (%)	..	..	..	1.2	2.0	1.0	1.2	1.3	0.0	0.7
Maturity (years)	..	..	..	26.6	23.9	38.7	37.3	32.0	0.0	38.9
Grace period (years)	..	..	..	6.1	5.6	9.5	10.9	7.4	0.0	10.3
Grant element (%)	..	..	..	65.9	56.6	76.3	75.0	68.1	0.0	80.8
Private creditors										
Interest (%)	..	..	..	0.0	0.0	0.0	0.0	0.0	0.0	0.0
Maturity (years)	..	..	..	0.0	0.0	0.0	0.0	0.0	0.0	0.0
Grace period (years)	..	..	..	0.0	0.0	0.0	0.0	0.0	0.0	0.0
Grant element (%)	..	..	..	0.0	0.0	0.0	0.0	0.0	0.0	0.0
Memorandum items										
Commitments	..	..	..	29.8	110.5	30.5	159.6	97.0	0.0	43.6
Official creditors	..	..	..	29.8	110.5	30.5	159.6	97.0	0.0	43.6
Private creditors	..	..	..	0.0	0.0	0.0	0.0	0.0	0.0	0.0

10. CONTRACTUAL OBLIGATIONS ON OUTSTANDING LONG-TERM DEBT

	2001	2002	2003	2004	2005	2006	2007	2008	2009	2010
TOTAL										
Disbursements	64.9	47.5	31.3	16.8	7.0	1.2	0.7	0.4	0.3	0.1
Principal	10.2	12.8	13.8	14.6	13.0	13.3	14.0	14.9	15.2	17.0
Interest	5.0	5.1	5.1	4.8	4.6	4.4	4.1	3.8	3.6	3.4
Official creditors										
Disbursements	64.9	47.5	31.3	16.8	7.0	1.2	0.7	0.4	0.3	0.1
Principal	10.2	12.8	13.8	14.6	13.0	13.3	14.0	14.9	15.2	17.0
Interest	5.0	5.1	5.1	4.8	4.6	4.4	4.1	3.8	3.6	3.4
Bilateral creditors										
Disbursements	14.6	9.3	4.8	2.0	0.7	0.5	0.4	0.3	0.3	0.1
Principal	6.9	8.7	8.8	9.4	7.3	7.4	7.6	6.9	6.9	8.3
Interest	2.6	2.6	2.4	2.2	2.0	1.8	1.7	1.6	1.5	1.4
Multilateral creditors										
Disbursements	50.3	38.1	26.5	14.8	6.3	0.7	0.3	0.0	0.0	0.0
Principal	3.3	4.1	5.0	5.3	5.7	5.9	6.4	7.9	8.3	8.7
Interest	2.3	2.6	2.6	2.6	2.7	2.5	2.4	2.3	2.1	2.0
Private creditors										
Disbursements	0.0	0.0	0.0	0.0	0.0	0.0	0.0	0.0	0.0	0.0
Principal	0.0	0.0	0.0	0.0	0.0	0.0	0.0	0.0	0.0	0.0
Interest	0.0	0.0	0.0	0.0	0.0	0.0	0.0	0.0	0.0	0.0
Commercial banks										
Disbursements	0.0	0.0	0.0	0.0	0.0	0.0	0.0	0.0	0.0	0.0
Principal	0.0	0.0	0.0	0.0	0.0	0.0	0.0	0.0	0.0	0.0
Interest	0.0	0.0	0.0	0.0	0.0	0.0	0.0	0.0	0.0	0.0
Other private										
Disbursements	0.0	0.0	0.0	0.0	0.0	0.0	0.0	0.0	0.0	0.0
Principal	0.0	0.0	0.0	0.0	0.0	0.0	0.0	0.0	0.0	0.0
Interest	0.0	0.0	0.0	0.0	0.0	0.0	0.0	0.0	0.0	0.0

ESTONIA

(US$ million, unless otherwise indicated)

	1970	1980	1990	1994	1995	1996	1997	1998	1999	2000
1. SUMMARY DEBT DATA										
TOTAL DEBT STOCKS (EDT)	..	..	..	**186.0**	**286.4**	**1,533.6**	**2,264.3**	**2,583.1**	**2,490.6**	**3,280.4**
Long-term debt (LDOD)	..	..	..	**117.0**	**164.9**	**336.6**	**1,237.8**	**1,586.9**	**1,612.5**	**2,317.3**
Public and publicly guaranteed	..	..	..	108.6	159.3	216.5	197.5	234.4	205.5	206.3
Private nonguaranteed	..	..	..	8.4	5.6	120.0	1,040.2	1,352.5	1,407.0	2,111.0
Use of IMF credit	..	..	..	**61.1**	**91.9**	**77.9**	**54.0**	**30.0**	**25.3**	**18.9**
Short-term debt	..	..	..	**8.0**	**29.7**	**1,119.2**	**972.6**	**966.2**	**852.8**	**944.2**
of which interest arrears on LDOD	..	..	..	0.0	0.0	0.0	0.0	0.0	0.0	0.0
Official creditors	..	..	..	0.0	0.0	0.0	0.0	0.0	0.0	0.0
Private creditors	..	..	..	0.0	0.0	0.0	0.0	0.0	0.0	0.0
Memo: principal arrears on LDOD	..	..	..	0.0	0.0	0.0	0.0	0.0	0.0	0.0
Official creditors	..	..	..	0.0	0.0	0.0	0.0	0.0	0.0	0.0
Private creditors	..	..	..	0.0	0.0	0.0	0.0	0.0	0.0	0.0
Memo: export credits	..	..	..	46.8	73.0	82.7	85.5	53.4	52.7	35.6
TOTAL DEBT FLOWS										
Disbursements	..	..	..	**31.1**	**81.1**	**216.6**	**954.6**	**438.9**	**473.9**	**405.1**
Long-term debt	..	..	..	31.1	49.4	216.6	954.6	438.9	473.9	405.1
IMF purchases	..	..	..	0.0	31.7	0.0	0.0	0.0	0.0	0.0
Principal repayments	..	..	..	**15.6**	**6.8**	**24.2**	**57.6**	**188.2**	**391.7**	**304.7**
Long-term debt	..	..	..	15.6	5.3	13.1	38.1	162.9	387.8	299.5
IMF repurchases	..	..	..	0.0	1.5	11.1	19.5	25.4	4.0	5.1
Net flows on debt	..	..	..	**23.2**	**96.0**	**1,281.9**	**750.4**	**244.3**	**-31.2**	**191.9**
of which short-term debt	..	..	..	7.7	21.7	1,089.5	-146.6	-6.4	-113.4	91.4
Interest payments (INT)	..	..	..	**10.8**	**14.5**	**71.5**	**125.1**	**139.6**	**134.5**	**122.9**
Long-term debt	..	..	..	7.2	8.6	17.3	71.9	88.9	87.9	76.9
IMF charges	..	..	..	3.1	4.7	3.9	3.1	2.3	1.2	1.1
Short-term debt	..	..	..	0.5	1.1	50.4	50.1	48.5	45.5	44.9
Net transfers on debt	..	..	..	**12.4**	**81.5**	**1,210.4**	**625.3**	**104.7**	**-165.7**	**69.0**
Total debt service paid (TDS)	..	..	..	**26.4**	**21.3**	**95.7**	**182.7**	**327.9**	**526.3**	**427.6**
Long-term debt	..	..	..	22.8	13.9	30.4	110.0	251.8	475.6	376.4
IMF repurchases and charges	..	..	..	3.1	6.2	15.0	22.6	27.6	5.1	6.2
Short-term debt (interest only)	..	..	..	0.5	1.1	50.4	50.1	48.5	45.5	44.9
2. AGGREGATE NET RESOURCE FLOWS AND NET TRANSFERS (LONG-TERM)										
NET RESOURCE FLOWS	..	..	..	**257.8**	**272.3**	**394.4**	**1,230.9**	**974.2**	**631.4**	**514.3**
Net flow of long-term debt (ex. IMF)	..	..	..	15.5	44.0	203.5	916.4	276.1	86.2	105.6
Foreign direct investment (net)	..	..	..	214.4	201.5	150.2	266.2	581.0	305.2	387.0
Portfolio equity flows	..	..	..	10.0	7.0	5.0	1.0	53.0	191.4	-28.5
Grants (excluding technical coop.)	..	..	..	17.9	19.8	35.7	47.3	64.1	48.7	50.2
Memo: technical coop. grants	..	..	..	22.6	37.0	23.5	19.9	18.6	12.3	11.9
official net resource flows	..	..	..	46.1	65.0	87.5	54.1	73.1	62.5	29.5
private net resource flows	..	..	..	211.7	207.3	306.9	1,176.8	901.1	568.9	484.8
NET TRANSFERS	..	..	..	**250.5**	**263.7**	**372.2**	**1,151.0**	**873.3**	**529.6**	**417.4**
Interest on long-term debt	..	..	..	7.2	8.6	17.3	71.9	88.9	87.9	76.9
Profit remittances on FDI	..	..	..	0.0	0.0	5.0	8.0	12.0	14.0	20.0
Memo: official net transfers	..	..	..	42.1	58.2	78.9	45.1	63.7	52.9	21.5
private net transfers	..	..	..	208.4	205.5	293.3	1,105.9	809.6	476.7	395.9
3. MAJOR ECONOMIC AGGREGATES										
Gross national income (GNI)	..	..	..	3,887.6	4,792.5	4,360.4	4,488.0	5,132.3	5,026.7	4,610.4
Exports of goods & services (XGS)	..	..	..	1,777.7	2,636.8	3,032.9	3,722.7	4,303.4	4,076.7	4,908.5
of which workers remittances	..	..	..	0.1	0.0	0.0	0.1	0.1	0.1	0.3
Imports of goods & services (MGS)	..	..	..	2,058.5	2,920.9	3,531.7	4,401.0	4,930.0	4,483.7	5,361.3
International reserves (RES)	..	..	..	446.4	583.0	639.8	760.0	812.9	855.8	922.8
Current account balance	..	..	..	-166.3	-157.8	-398.3	-561.7	-478.4	-294.6	-314.9
4. DEBT INDICATORS										
EDT / XGS (%)	..	..	..	10.5	10.9	50.6	60.8	60.0	61.1	66.8
EDT / GNI (%)	..	..	..	4.8	6.0	35.2	50.5	50.3	49.6	71.2
TDS / XGS (%)	..	..	..	1.5	0.8	3.2	4.9	7.6	12.9	8.7
INT / XGS (%)	..	..	..	0.6	0.6	2.4	3.4	3.2	3.3	2.5
INT / GNI (%)	..	..	..	0.3	0.3	1.6	2.8	2.7	2.7	2.7
RES / EDT (%)	..	..	..	240.0	203.6	41.7	33.6	31.5	34.4	28.1
RES / MGS (months)	..	..	..	2.6	2.4	2.2	2.1	2.0	2.3	2.1
Short-term / EDT (%)	..	..	..	4.3	10.4	73.0	43.0	37.4	34.2	28.8
Concessional / EDT (%)	..	..	..	12.8	9.9	2.1	1.4	1.2	1.1	0.8
Multilateral / EDT (%)	..	..	..	35.2	37.7	8.3	5.4	5.3	5.4	3.2

ESTONIA

(US$ million, unless otherwise indicated)

	1970	1980	1990	1994	1995	1996	1997	1998	1999	2000
5. LONG-TERM DEBT										
DEBT OUTSTANDING (LDOD)	..	..	..	**117.0**	**164.9**	**336.6**	**1,237.8**	**1,586.9**	**1,612.5**	**2,317.3**
Public and publicly guaranteed	..	..	..	**108.6**	**159.3**	**216.5**	**197.5**	**234.4**	**205.5**	**206.3**
Official creditors	..	..	..	92.0	140.6	162.2	159.6	173.6	168.1	136.9
Multilateral	..	..	..	65.5	108.0	126.8	122.5	137.3	133.8	105.2
Concessional	..	..	..	0.0	0.0	0.0	0.0	0.0	0.0	0.0
Bilateral	..	..	..	26.4	32.5	35.5	37.1	36.3	34.3	31.7
Concessional	..	..	..	23.8	28.4	31.6	31.6	29.7	28.0	26.1
Private creditors	..	..	..	16.6	18.7	54.3	37.9	60.8	37.5	69.5
Bonds	..	..	..	0.0	0.0	38.6	33.5	53.8	33.5	31.0
Commercial banks	..	..	..	0.0	2.1	0.0	0.0	0.0	0.0	36.2
Other private	..	..	..	16.6	16.6	15.7	4.5	7.0	4.0	2.3
Private nonguaranteed	..	..	..	**8.4**	**5.6**	**120.0**	**1,040.2**	**1,352.5**	**1,407.0**	**2,111.0**
Bonds	..	..	..	0.0	0.0	0.0	80.9	86.7	129.7	231.5
Commercial banks and other	..	..	..	8.4	5.6	120.0	959.3	1,265.8	1,277.3	1,879.4
Memo:										
IBRD	..	..	..	31.0	49.8	62.2	71.5	83.7	87.5	71.1
IDA	..	..	..	0.0	0.0	0.0	0.0	0.0	0.0	0.0
DISBURSEMENTS	..	..	..	**31.1**	**49.4**	**216.6**	**954.6**	**438.9**	**473.9**	**405.1**
Public and publicly guaranteed	..	..	..	**31.1**	**49.4**	**100.4**	**18.0**	**44.5**	**47.3**	**40.1**
Official creditors	..	..	..	28.2	45.2	58.7	15.9	23.7	28.1	4.2
Multilateral	..	..	..	15.8	39.2	54.2	14.3	22.6	28.1	4.2
Concessional	..	..	..	0.0	0.0	0.0	0.0	0.0	0.0	0.0
Bilateral	..	..	..	12.4	6.0	4.5	1.6	1.1	0.0	0.0
Concessional	..	..	..	9.8	4.6	3.2	0.0	0.0	0.0	0.0
Private creditors	..	..	..	2.9	4.2	41.7	2.2	20.8	19.2	35.9
Bonds	..	..	..	0.0	0.0	39.9	0.0	17.1	19.2	0.0
Commercial banks	..	..	..	0.0	2.1	0.0	0.0	0.0	0.0	35.9
Other private	..	..	..	2.9	2.1	1.8	2.2	3.7	0.0	0.0
Private nonguaranteed	..	..	..	**0.0**	**0.0**	**116.2**	**936.5**	**394.4**	**426.7**	**365.1**
Bonds	..	..	..	0.0	0.0	0.0	80.9	0.0	58.3	138.6
Commercial banks and other	..	..	..	0.0	0.0	116.2	855.6	394.4	368.3	226.5
Memo:										
IBRD	..	..	..	9.7	18.0	16.5	10.9	13.0	19.0	4.2
IDA	..	..	..	0.0	0.0	0.0	0.0	0.0	0.0	0.0
PRINCIPAL REPAYMENTS	..	..	..	**15.6**	**5.3**	**13.1**	**38.1**	**162.9**	**387.8**	**299.5**
Public and publicly guaranteed	..	..	..	**12.8**	**2.5**	**11.3**	**21.8**	**16.3**	**49.2**	**26.3**
Official creditors	..	..	..	0.0	0.0	6.9	9.1	14.7	14.3	24.9
Multilateral	..	..	..	0.0	0.0	5.4	9.1	12.9	12.2	22.3
Concessional	..	..	..	0.0	0.0	0.0	0.0	0.0	0.0	0.0
Bilateral	..	..	..	0.0	0.0	1.5	0.0	1.8	2.0	2.6
Concessional	..	..	..	0.0	0.0	0.0	0.0	1.8	1.7	1.9
Private creditors	..	..	..	12.8	2.5	4.4	12.7	1.6	35.0	1.4
Bonds	..	..	..	0.0	0.0	0.0	0.0	0.0	32.7	0.0
Commercial banks	..	..	..	0.0	0.0	2.1	0.0	0.0	0.0	0.0
Other private	..	..	..	12.8	2.5	2.3	12.7	1.6	2.2	1.4
Private nonguaranteed	..	..	..	**2.8**	**2.8**	**1.8**	**16.3**	**146.6**	**338.5**	**273.3**
Bonds	..	..	..	0.0	0.0	0.0	0.0	0.0	0.0	28.3
Commercial banks and other	..	..	..	2.8	2.8	1.8	16.3	146.6	338.5	244.9
Memo:										
IBRD	..	..	..	0.0	0.0	0.0	0.0	2.8	3.3	13.6
IDA	..	..	..	0.0	0.0	0.0	0.0	0.0	0.0	0.0
NET FLOWS ON DEBT	..	..	..	**15.5**	**44.0**	**203.5**	**916.4**	**276.1**	**86.2**	**105.6**
Public and publicly guaranteed	..	..	..	**18.3**	**46.8**	**89.1**	**-3.8**	**28.3**	**-2.0**	**13.8**
Official creditors	..	..	..	28.2	45.2	51.8	6.8	9.0	13.8	-20.7
Multilateral	..	..	..	15.8	39.2	48.8	5.2	9.7	15.8	-18.2
Concessional	..	..	..	0.0	0.0	0.0	0.0	0.0	0.0	0.0
Bilateral	..	..	..	12.4	6.0	3.0	1.6	-0.7	-2.0	-2.6
Concessional	..	..	..	9.8	4.6	3.2	0.0	-1.8	-1.7	-1.9
Private creditors	..	..	..	-9.9	1.6	37.3	-10.6	19.3	-15.8	34.5
Bonds	..	..	..	0.0	0.0	39.9	0.0	17.1	-13.5	0.0
Commercial banks	..	..	..	0.0	2.1	-2.1	0.0	0.0	0.0	35.9
Other private	..	..	..	-9.9	-0.5	-0.5	-10.6	2.2	-2.2	-1.4
Private nonguaranteed	..	..	..	**-2.8**	**-2.8**	**114.4**	**920.2**	**247.8**	**88.1**	**91.8**
Bonds	..	..	..	0.0	0.0	0.0	80.9	0.0	58.3	110.3
Commercial banks and other	..	..	..	-2.8	-2.8	114.4	839.3	247.8	29.8	-18.5
Memo:										
IBRD	..	..	..	9.7	18.0	16.5	10.9	10.3	15.7	-9.4
IDA	..	..	..	0.0	0.0	0.0	0.0	0.0	0.0	0.0

ESTONIA

(US$ million, unless otherwise indicated)

	1970	1980	1990	1994	1995	1996	1997	1998	1999	2000
INTEREST PAYMENTS (LINT)	..	..	..	**7.2**	**8.6**	**17.3**	**71.9**	**88.9**	**87.9**	**76.9**
Public and publicly guaranteed	..	..	..	**6.5**	**8.0**	**9.7**	**12.2**	**11.9**	**11.9**	**10.9**
Official creditors	..	..	..	4.0	6.8	8.6	9.0	9.4	9.6	8.0
Multilateral	..	..	..	3.3	5.6	7.6	7.7	8.0	7.9	6.9
Concessional	..	..	..	0.0	0.0	0.0	0.0	0.0	0.0	0.0
Bilateral	..	..	..	0.6	1.1	1.0	1.2	1.4	1.7	1.1
Concessional	..	..	..	0.5	0.9	0.6	0.7	0.9	1.2	0.6
Private creditors	..	..	..	2.5	1.2	1.1	3.2	2.5	2.3	2.9
Bonds	..	..	..	0.0	0.0	0.0	2.1	2.0	2.0	2.4
Commercial banks	..	..	..	0.0	0.1	0.1	0.0	0.0	0.0	0.2
Other private	..	..	..	2.5	1.1	1.0	1.1	0.4	0.4	0.3
Private nonguaranteed	..	..	..	**0.8**	**0.6**	**7.5**	**59.7**	**77.0**	**75.9**	**66.0**
Bonds	..	..	..	0.0	0.0	0.0	0.1	5.7	5.0	9.0
Commercial banks and other	..	..	..	0.8	0.6	7.5	59.6	71.3	71.0	56.9
Memo:										
IBRD	..	..	..	1.7	2.5	3.6	4.2	4.6	5.0	5.1
IDA	..	..	..	0.0	0.0	0.0	0.0	0.0	0.0	0.0
NET TRANSFERS ON DEBT	..	..	..	**8.3**	**35.4**	**186.2**	**844.6**	**187.2**	**-1.7**	**28.7**
Public and publicly guaranteed	..	..	..	**11.9**	**38.8**	**79.3**	**-15.9**	**16.4**	**-13.9**	**2.9**
Official creditors	..	..	..	24.3	38.4	43.2	-2.2	-0.4	4.1	-28.8
Multilateral	..	..	..	12.5	33.6	41.2	-2.5	1.7	7.9	-25.1
Concessional	..	..	..	0.0	0.0	0.0	0.0	0.0	0.0	0.0
Bilateral	..	..	..	11.8	4.8	2.0	0.3	-2.2	-3.7	-3.7
Concessional	..	..	..	9.3	3.7	2.5	-0.7	-2.7	-2.9	-2.5
Private creditors	..	..	..	-12.4	0.4	36.1	-13.8	16.8	-18.1	31.6
Bonds	..	..	..	0.0	0.0	39.9	-2.1	15.0	-15.5	-2.4
Commercial banks	..	..	..	0.0	2.0	-2.2	0.0	0.0	0.0	35.7
Other private	..	..	..	-12.4	-1.6	-1.5	-11.7	1.7	-2.6	-1.6
Private nonguaranteed	..	..	..	**-3.6**	**-3.4**	**106.9**	**860.5**	**170.8**	**12.2**	**25.8**
Bonds	..	..	..	0.0	0.0	0.0	80.8	-5.7	53.4	101.2
Commercial banks and other	..	..	..	-3.6	-3.4	106.9	779.7	176.5	-41.2	-75.4
Memo:										
IBRD	..	..	..	8.0	15.5	12.9	6.7	5.6	10.8	-14.5
IDA	..	..	..	0.0	0.0	0.0	0.0	0.0	0.0	0.0
DEBT SERVICE (LTDS)	..	..	..	**22.8**	**13.9**	**30.4**	**110.0**	**251.8**	**475.6**	**376.4**
Public and publicly guaranteed	..	..	..	**19.2**	**10.5**	**21.1**	**33.9**	**28.2**	**61.2**	**37.2**
Official creditors	..	..	..	4.0	6.8	15.5	18.0	24.1	23.9	32.9
Multilateral	..	..	..	3.3	5.6	13.0	16.8	20.8	20.2	29.3
Concessional	..	..	..	0.0	0.0	0.0	0.0	0.0	0.0	0.0
Bilateral	..	..	..	0.6	1.1	2.5	1.2	3.3	3.7	3.7
Concessional	..	..	..	0.5	0.9	0.6	0.7	2.7	2.9	2.5
Private creditors	..	..	..	15.3	3.8	5.6	15.9	4.1	37.3	4.3
Bonds	..	..	..	0.0	0.0	0.0	2.1	2.0	34.7	2.4
Commercial banks	..	..	..	0.0	0.1	2.2	0.0	0.0	0.0	0.2
Other private	..	..	..	15.3	3.6	3.3	13.8	2.0	2.6	1.6
Private nonguaranteed	..	..	..	**3.6**	**3.4**	**9.3**	**76.0**	**223.6**	**414.5**	**339.2**
Bonds	..	..	..	0.0	0.0	0.0	0.1	5.7	5.0	37.4
Commercial banks and other	..	..	..	3.6	3.4	9.3	75.9	217.9	409.5	301.9
Memo:										
IBRD	..	..	..	1.7	2.5	3.6	4.2	7.4	8.2	18.6
IDA	..	..	..	0.0	0.0	0.0	0.0	0.0	0.0	0.0
UNDISBURSED DEBT	..	..	..	**154.8**	**128.0**	**112.9**	**75.4**	**53.2**	**13.4**	**24.0**
Official creditors	..	..	..	149.6	126.8	105.2	70.7	52.3	13.4	24.0
Private creditors	..	..	..	5.2	1.3	7.8	4.7	0.9	0.0	0.0
Memorandum items										
Concessional LDOD	..	..	..	23.8	28.4	31.6	31.6	29.7	28.0	26.1
Variable rate LDOD	..	..	..	95.3	132.4	241.6	1,160.9	1,499.5	1,563.5	2,274.8
Public sector LDOD	..	..	..	108.6	159.3	216.5	197.5	234.4	205.5	170.2
Private sector LDOD	..	..	..	8.4	5.6	120.0	1,040.2	1,352.5	1,407.0	2,147.1

6. CURRENCY COMPOSITION OF LONG-TERM DEBT (PERCENT)

	1970	1980	1990	1994	1995	1996	1997	1998	1999	2000
Deutsche mark	..	..	..	9.1	14.7	30.4	64.2	67.5	55.9	61.3
French franc	..	..	..	0.0	0.0	0.0	0.0	0.0	0.0	0.0
Japanese yen	..	..	..	0.0	0.0	0.0	0.0	0.0	0.0	0.0
Pound sterling	..	..	..	0.0	0.0	0.0	0.0	0.0	0.0	0.0
Swiss franc	..	..	..	0.0	0.0	0.0	0.0	0.0	0.0	0.0
U.S.dollars	..	..	..	32.7	27.3	21.2	18.9	16.1	17.7	17.4
Multiple currency	..	..	..	28.6	31.3	28.7	0.0	0.0	0.0	0.0
Special drawing rights	..	..	..	0.0	0.0	0.0	0.0	0.0	0.0	0.0
All other currencies	..	..	..	29.6	26.7	19.7	16.9	16.4	26.4	21.3

ESTONIA

(US$ million, unless otherwise indicated)

	1970	1980	1990	1994	1995	1996	1997	1998	1999	2000
7. DEBT RESTRUCTURINGS										
Total amount rescheduled	..	..	..	0.0	0.0	0.0	0.0	0.0	0.0	0.0
Debt stock rescheduled	..	..	..	0.0	0.0	0.0	0.0	0.0	0.0	0.0
Principal rescheduled	..	..	..	0.0	0.0	0.0	0.0	0.0	0.0	0.0
Official	..	..	..	0.0	0.0	0.0	0.0	0.0	0.0	0.0
Private	..	..	..	0.0	0.0	0.0	0.0	0.0	0.0	0.0
Interest rescheduled	..	..	..	0.0	0.0	0.0	0.0	0.0	0.0	0.0
Official	..	..	..	0.0	0.0	0.0	0.0	0.0	0.0	0.0
Private	..	..	..	0.0	0.0	0.0	0.0	0.0	0.0	0.0
Debt forgiven	..	..	..	0.0	0.0	0.0	0.0	0.0	0.0	0.0
Memo: interest forgiven	..	..	..	0.0	0.0	0.0	0.0	0.0	0.0	0.0
Debt stock reduction	..	..	..	0.0	0.0	0.0	0.0	0.0	0.0	0.0
of which debt buyback	..	..	..	0.0	0.0	0.0	0.0	0.0	0.0	0.0
8. DEBT STOCK-FLOW RECONCILIATION										
Total change in debt stocks	..	..	..	32.2	100.4	1,247.2	730.7	318.8	-92.6	789.9
Net flows on debt	..	..	..	23.2	96.0	1,281.9	750.4	244.3	-31.2	191.9
Net change in interest arrears	..	..	..	0.0	0.0	0.0	0.0	0.0	0.0	0.0
Interest capitalized	..	..	..	0.0	0.0	0.0	0.0	0.0	0.0	0.0
Debt forgiveness or reduction	..	..	..	0.0	0.0	0.0	0.0	0.0	0.0	0.0
Cross-currency valuation	..	..	..	8.5	5.0	-11.0	-20.2	12.2	-25.6	-8.5
Residual	..	..	..	0.5	-0.6	-23.7	0.5	62.3	-35.7	606.5
9. AVERAGE TERMS OF NEW COMMITMENTS										
ALL CREDITORS										
Interest (%)	..	..	..	7.3	7.1	6.3	3.1	6.4	7.4	5.2
Maturity (years)	..	..	..	14.9	15.0	8.7	5.1	5.2	5.0	9.1
Grace period (years)	..	..	..	5.6	5.5	2.7	0.6	5.0	5.0	2.5
Grant element (%)	..	..	..	15.3	16.4	15.3	15.6	13.5	10.0	14.5
Official creditors										
Interest (%)	..	..	..	7.3	7.1	6.5	0.0	8.5	0.0	7.2
Maturity (years)	..	..	..	14.9	15.0	12.4	0.0	14.9	0.0	14.9
Grace period (years)	..	..	..	5.6	5.5	2.7	0.0	5.4	0.0	5.4
Grant element (%)	..	..	..	15.3	16.4	19.2	0.0	8.1	0.0	15.7
Private creditors										
Interest (%)	..	..	..	0.0	0.0	5.9	3.1	6.4	7.4	3.8
Maturity (years)	..	..	..	0.0	0.0	3.6	5.1	5.1	5.0	5.0
Grace period (years)	..	..	..	0.0	0.0	2.8	0.6	5.0	5.0	0.5
Grant element (%)	..	..	..	0.0	0.0	10.1	15.6	13.6	10.0	13.6
Memorandum items										
Commitments	..	..	..	105.6	20.0	116.8	0.0	17.5	19.2	60.9
Official creditors	..	..	..	105.6	20.0	67.6	0.0	0.1	0.0	25.0
Private creditors	..	..	..	0.0	0.0	49.2	0.0	17.3	19.2	35.9

10. CONTRACTUAL OBLIGATIONS ON OUTSTANDING LONG-TERM DEBT

	2001	2002	2003	2004	2005	2006	2007	2008	2009	2010
TOTAL										
Disbursements	3.6	4.7	4.5	3.3	2.4	2.1	1.3	1.1	0.9	0.1
Principal	481.2	549.6	654.3	517.3	26.6	18.5	37.4	16.7	13.7	5.9
Interest	71.0	54.4	30.4	19.3	6.6	5.4	4.0	2.7	1.9	1.4
Official creditors										
Disbursements	3.6	4.7	4.5	3.3	2.4	2.1	1.3	1.1	0.9	0.1
Principal	15.5	19.8	15.3	13.9	15.1	16.2	16.2	12.0	10.8	5.9
Interest	7.1	6.9	6.2	5.6	5.0	4.2	3.4	2.6	1.9	1.4
Bilateral creditors										
Disbursements	0.0	0.0	0.0	0.0	0.0	0.0	0.0	0.0	0.0	0.0
Principal	2.6	6.3	3.2	3.2	3.2	3.2	3.2	1.3	1.0	0.6
Interest	1.0	0.9	0.8	0.7	0.6	0.5	0.3	0.2	0.2	0.1
Multilateral creditors										
Disbursements	3.6	4.7	4.5	3.3	2.4	2.1	1.3	1.1	0.9	0.1
Principal	12.9	13.5	12.1	10.7	11.9	13.1	13.0	10.7	9.9	5.2
Interest	6.1	6.0	5.4	4.9	4.4	3.8	3.0	2.3	1.7	1.2
Private creditors										
Disbursements	0.0	0.0	0.0	0.0	0.0	0.0	0.0	0.0	0.0	0.0
Principal	466.0	530.0	639.0	503.0	11.0	2.0	21.0	5.0	3.0	0.0
Interest	64.0	47.0	24.0	14.0	2.0	1.0	1.0	0.0	0.0	0.0
Commercial banks										
Disbursements	0.0	0.0	0.0	0.0	0.0	0.0	0.0	0.0	0.0	0.0
Principal	8.0	8.0	8.0	8.0	4.0	0.0	0.0	0.0	0.0	0.0
Interest	1.7	1.3	0.9	0.5	0.1	0.0	0.0	0.0	0.0	0.0
Other private										
Disbursements	0.0	0.0	0.0	0.0	0.0	0.0	0.0	0.0	0.0	0.0
Principal	458.0	522.0	631.0	495.0	7.0	2.0	21.0	5.0	3.0	0.0
Interest	62.0	46.0	23.0	13.0	2.0	1.0	1.0	0.0	0.0	0.0

ETHIOPIA

(US$ million, unless otherwise indicated)

	1970	1980	1990	1994	1995	1996	1997	1998	1999	2000
1. SUMMARY DEBT DATA										
TOTAL DEBT STOCKS (EDT)	**169**	**824**	**8,630**	**10,063**	**10,308**	**10,078**	**10,075**	**10,347**	**5,544**	**5,481**
Long-term debt (LDOD)	**169**	**688**	**8,479**	**9,567**	**9,774**	**9,484**	**9,423**	**9,614**	**5,362**	**5,325**
Public and publicly guaranteed	169	688	8,479	9,567	9,774	9,484	9,423	9,614	5,362	5,325
Private nonguaranteed	0	0	0	0	0	0	0	0	0	0
Use of IMF credit	**0**	**79**	**6**	**72**	**74**	**92**	**87**	**107**	**95**	**77**
Short-term debt	**0**	**57**	**145**	**424**	**461**	**502**	**565**	**626**	**87**	**79**
of which interest arrears on LDOD	0	1	43	393	437	481	541	603	62	65
Official creditors	0	0	39	374	417	460	523	584	57	59
Private creditors	0	0	3	19	20	21	18	19	5	6
Memo: principal arrears on LDOD	0	1	236	2,810	3,628	4,303	4,756	5,195	638	652
Official creditors	0	0	196	2,646	3,453	4,103	4,530	4,964	581	609
Private creditors	0	1	40	164	176	200	227	231	57	43
Memo: export credits	0	0	311	234	239	300	248	193	223	202
TOTAL DEBT FLOWS										
Disbursements	**28**	**119**	**374**	**256**	**232**	**315**	**179**	**162**	**231**	**185**
Long-term debt	28	110	374	236	232	294	179	142	231	185
IMF purchases	0	9	0	20	0	21	0	20	0	0
Principal repayments	**15**	**17**	**177**	**68**	**91**	**292**	**52**	**68**	**98**	**86**
Long-term debt	15	17	152	68	91	292	52	65	88	73
IMF repurchases	0	0	25	0	0	0	0	4	10	13
Net flows on debt	**13**	**94**	**204**	**188**	**133**	**21**	**130**	**93**	**134**	**88**
of which short-term debt	0	-8	7	0	-8	-2	3	-1	2	-11
Interest payments (INT)	**6**	**28**	**59**	**44**	**63**	**55**	**47**	**50**	**57**	**53**
Long-term debt	6	17	49	40	61	54	46	48	55	52
IMF charges	0	2	2	0	0	0	0	1	1	0
Short-term debt	0	9	8	4	1	1	1	1	2	1
Net transfers on debt	**7**	**67**	**145**	**144**	**70**	**-34**	**82**	**43**	**77**	**35**
Total debt service paid (TDS)	**21**	**45**	**236**	**112**	**154**	**347**	**100**	**119**	**155**	**139**
Long-term debt	21	34	201	107	152	346	98	113	144	125
IMF repurchases and charges	0	2	27	0	0	0	0	5	10	14
Short-term debt (interest only)	0	9	8	4	1	1	1	1	2	1
2. AGGREGATE NET RESOURCE FLOWS AND NET TRANSFERS (LONG-TERM)										
NET RESOURCE FLOWS	**23**	**217**	**838**	**827**	**630**	**416**	**772**	**769**	**589**	**587**
Net flow of long-term debt (ex. IMF)	13	93	222	168	141	1	127	78	142	112
Foreign direct investment (net)	4	0	12	21	14	22	288	261	90	50
Portfolio equity flows	0	0	0	0	0	0	0	0	0	0
Grants (excluding technical coop.)	6	124	604	638	476	393	357	430	357	425
Memo: technical coop. grants	20	44	250	123	164	200	151	119	109	127
official net resource flows	26	191	883	838	664	604	462	506	511	545
private net resource flows	-3	26	-45	-12	-34	-188	311	263	78	42
NET TRANSFERS	**10**	**201**	**789**	**787**	**569**	**363**	**727**	**721**	**533**	**536**
Interest on long-term debt	6	17	49	40	61	54	46	48	55	52
Profit remittances on FDI	6	0	0	0	0	0	0	0	0	0
Memo: official net transfers	21	177	858	808	632	565	420	461	460	498
private net transfers	-11	24	-69	-21	-63	-202	306	260	73	38
3. MAJOR ECONOMIC AGGREGATES										
Gross national income (GNI)	..	..	6,788	4,825	5,719	5,967	6,286	6,449	6,429	6,331
Exports of goods & services (XGS)	185	591	677	563	808	825	1,040	1,060	945	1,000
of which workers remittances	..	0	0	0	0	0	0	0	0	0
Imports of goods & services (MGS)	226	797	1,141	1,187	1,356	1,462	1,716	1,742	1,960	2,038
International reserves (RES)	72	262	55	588	815	733	502	520	467	312
Current account balance	-40	-126	-244	-291	-90	-191	-191	-104	-521	-346
4. DEBT INDICATORS										
EDT / XGS (%)	91.4	139.5	1,275.7	1,787.4	1,276.3	1,222.0	968.4	975.9	586.7	548.1
EDT / GNI (%)	..	..	127.1	208.6	180.2	168.9	160.3	160.4	86.2	86.6
TDS / XGS (%)	11.4	7.6	34.9	19.8	19.1	42.1	9.6	11.2	16.4	13.9
INT / XGS (%)	3.4	4.7	8.7	7.8	7.8	6.7	4.6	4.7	6.1	5.3
INT / GNI (%)	..	..	0.9	0.9	1.1	0.9	0.8	0.8	0.9	0.8
RES / EDT (%)	42.4	31.8	0.6	5.8	7.9	7.3	5.0	5.0	8.4	5.7
RES / MGS (months)	3.8	4.0	0.6	5.9	7.2	6.0	3.5	3.6	2.9	1.8
Short-term / EDT (%)	0.2	6.9	1.7	4.2	4.5	5.0	5.6	6.1	1.6	1.4
Concessional / EDT (%)	54.6	68.3	87.3	84.3	84.6	86.3	85.7	85.1	86.5	87.7
Multilateral / EDT (%)	41.4	41.2	14.7	21.2	22.7	24.7	24.4	25.4	49.4	50.0

ETHIOPIA

(US$ million, unless otherwise indicated)

	1970	1980	1990	1994	1995	1996	1997	1998	1999	2000
5. LONG-TERM DEBT										
DEBT OUTSTANDING (LDOD)	**169**	**688**	**8,479**	**9,567**	**9,774**	**9,484**	**9,423**	**9,614**	**5,362**	**5,325**
Public and publicly guaranteed	**169**	**688**	**8,479**	**9,567**	**9,774**	**9,484**	**9,423**	**9,614**	**5,362**	**5,325**
Official creditors	140	638	7,902	8,915	9,179	9,130	9,073	9,266	5,235	5,208
Multilateral	70	340	1,268	2,130	2,339	2,484	2,458	2,627	2,738	2,741
Concessional	23	282	1,151	1,968	2,157	2,276	2,231	2,389	2,509	2,547
Bilateral	70	299	6,634	6,785	6,841	6,645	6,615	6,639	2,497	2,467
Concessional	70	281	6,382	6,515	6,559	6,418	6,400	6,421	2,289	2,263
Private creditors	29	49	577	652	594	354	350	348	127	117
Bonds	0	0	0	0	0	0	0	0	0	0
Commercial banks	0	10	116	292	253	27	25	20	16	12
Other private	29	39	461	360	342	327	326	328	111	105
Private nonguaranteed	**0**	**0**	**0**	**0**	**0**	**0**	**0**	**0**	**0**	**0**
Bonds	0	0	0	0	0	0	0	0	0	0
Commercial banks and other	0	0	0	0	0	0	0	0	0	0
Memo:										
IBRD	47	56	27	4	0	0	0	0	0	0
IDA	23	249	824	1,373	1,470	1,555	1,532	1,632	1,739	1,779
DISBURSEMENTS	**28**	**110**	**374**	**236**	**232**	**294**	**179**	**142**	**231**	**185**
Public and publicly guaranteed	**28**	**110**	**374**	**236**	**232**	**294**	**179**	**142**	**231**	**185**
Official creditors	25	77	324	232	232	272	149	132	229	184
Multilateral	8	36	139	232	209	272	145	127	224	181
Concessional	3	34	128	211	177	223	92	110	200	176
Bilateral	17	41	185	0	23	0	4	5	6	3
Concessional	17	37	128	0	23	0	4	5	6	3
Private creditors	2	33	51	4	0	22	30	10	1	2
Bonds	0	0	0	0	0	0	0	0	0	0
Commercial banks	0	2	0	0	0	0	0	0	0	0
Other private	2	31	51	4	0	22	30	10	1	2
Private nonguaranteed	**0**	**0**	**0**	**0**	**0**	**0**	**0**	**0**	**0**	**0**
Bonds	0	0	0	0	0	0	0	0	0	0
Commercial banks and other	0	0	0	0	0	0	0	0	0	0
Memo:										
IBRD	6	0	0	0	0	0	0	0	0	0
IDA	3	28	74	150	84	142	65	69	157	137
PRINCIPAL REPAYMENTS	**15**	**17**	**152**	**68**	**91**	**292**	**52**	**65**	**88**	**73**
Public and publicly guaranteed	**15**	**17**	**152**	**68**	**91**	**292**	**52**	**65**	**88**	**73**
Official creditors	6	11	45	32	43	61	45	57	75	64
Multilateral	3	4	16	28	40	42	42	45	56	56
Concessional	0	0	7	17	22	23	24	27	29	31
Bilateral	3	6	29	3	3	19	3	11	19	8
Concessional	3	6	13	2	3	13	3	11	18	8
Private creditors	9	7	107	36	48	231	8	8	13	10
Bonds	0	0	0	0	0	0	0	0	0	0
Commercial banks	0	3	45	35	39	226	2	5	4	4
Other private	9	4	62	1	9	5	6	3	9	6
Private nonguaranteed	**0**	**0**	**0**	**0**	**0**	**0**	**0**	**0**	**0**	**0**
Bonds	0	0	0	0	0	0	0	0	0	0
Commercial banks and other	0	0	0	0	0	0	0	0	0	0
Memo:										
IBRD	3	4	7	4	4	0	0	0	0	0
IDA	0	0	4	10	12	14	15	18	20	21
NET FLOWS ON DEBT	**13**	**93**	**222**	**168**	**141**	**1**	**127**	**78**	**142**	**112**
Public and publicly guaranteed	**13**	**93**	**222**	**168**	**141**	**1**	**127**	**78**	**142**	**112**
Official creditors	20	67	279	201	189	211	105	75	154	120
Multilateral	5	32	123	204	169	230	104	82	167	125
Concessional	3	33	121	194	154	201	68	83	171	145
Bilateral	14	35	156	-3	19	-19	1	-7	-13	-5
Concessional	14	30	115	-1	20	-12	1	-6	-13	-5
Private creditors	-7	26	-57	-33	-48	-210	23	2	-12	-8
Bonds	0	0	0	0	0	0	0	0	0	0
Commercial banks	0	-1	-45	-35	-39	-226	-2	-5	-4	-4
Other private	-7	27	-12	2	-9	16	25	7	-8	-4
Private nonguaranteed	**0**	**0**	**0**	**0**	**0**	**0**	**0**	**0**	**0**	**0**
Bonds	0	0	0	0	0	0	0	0	0	0
Commercial banks and other	0	0	0	0	0	0	0	0	0	0
Memo:										
IBRD	3	-4	-7	-4	-4	0	0	0	0	0
IDA	3	28	69	140	71	128	50	51	137	116

ETHIOPIA

(US$ million, unless otherwise indicated)

	1970	1980	1990	1994	1995	1996	1997	1998	1999	2000
INTEREST PAYMENTS (LINT)	**6**	**17**	**49**	**40**	**61**	**54**	**46**	**48**	**55**	**52**
Public and publicly guaranteed	**6**	**17**	**49**	**40**	**61**	**54**	**46**	**48**	**55**	**52**
Official creditors	5	15	24	31	32	39	42	45	50	48
Multilateral	3	8	13	25	24	30	33	33	35	33
Concessional	0	2	7	13	14	16	17	17	19	20
Bilateral	2	6	11	6	9	9	8	12	15	14
Concessional	2	5	9	3	6	4	4	8	11	11
Private creditors	2	2	24	9	29	15	4	3	5	4
Bonds	0	0	0	0	0	0	0	0	0	0
Commercial banks	0	2	11	9	27	15	2	1	1	1
Other private	2	1	13	0	2	1	3	2	4	3
Private nonguaranteed	**0**	**0**	**0**	**0**	**0**	**0**	**0**	**0**	**0**	**0**
Bonds	0	0	0	0	0	0	0	0	0	0
Commercial banks and other	0	0	0	0	0	0	0	0	0	0
Memo:										
IBRD	3	7	2	0	0	0	0	0	0	0
IDA	0	2	6	10	11	11	11	11	12	13
NET TRANSFERS ON DEBT	**7**	**76**	**173**	**128**	**80**	**-52**	**81**	**29**	**87**	**61**
Public and publicly guaranteed	**7**	**76**	**173**	**128**	**80**	**-52**	**81**	**29**	**87**	**61**
Official creditors	15	52	254	170	156	172	63	31	104	73
Multilateral	3	23	110	179	146	200	70	49	132	92
Concessional	3	31	114	181	141	185	51	66	152	125
Bilateral	12	29	145	-9	11	-28	-7	-18	-28	-19
Concessional	12	25	106	-4	14	-16	-3	-14	-24	-16
Private creditors	-8	24	-81	-42	-77	-224	18	-1	-17	-12
Bonds	0	0	0	0	0	0	0	0	0	0
Commercial banks	0	-2	-56	-44	-66	-240	-4	-7	-5	-5
Other private	-8	26	-25	2	-11	16	22	5	-12	-7
Private nonguaranteed	**0**	**0**	**0**	**0**	**0**	**0**	**0**	**0**	**0**	**0**
Bonds	0	0	0	0	0	0	0	0	0	0
Commercial banks and other	0	0	0	0	0	0	0	0	0	0
Memo:										
IBRD	0	-10	-9	-4	-4	0	0	0	0	0
IDA	3	26	64	131	60	116	38	40	125	103
DEBT SERVICE (LTDS)	**21**	**34**	**201**	**107**	**152**	**346**	**98**	**113**	**144**	**125**
Public and publicly guaranteed	**21**	**34**	**201**	**107**	**152**	**346**	**98**	**113**	**144**	**125**
Official creditors	11	25	69	62	76	100	86	101	126	111
Multilateral	6	13	29	53	64	72	75	78	91	89
Concessional	0	2	14	30	36	38	41	44	48	51
Bilateral	5	13	40	10	12	28	11	23	34	23
Concessional	5	11	22	4	9	16	7	19	30	19
Private creditors	11	9	131	45	77	246	12	11	18	14
Bonds	0	0	0	0	0	0	0	0	0	0
Commercial banks	0	4	56	44	66	240	4	7	5	5
Other private	11	5	76	1	11	6	8	5	13	8
Private nonguaranteed	**0**	**0**	**0**	**0**	**0**	**0**	**0**	**0**	**0**	**0**
Bonds	0	0	0	0	0	0	0	0	0	0
Commercial banks and other	0	0	0	0	0	0	0	0	0	0
Memo:										
IBRD	6	10	9	4	4	0	0	0	0	0
IDA	0	2	10	19	23	25	26	29	32	34
UNDISBURSED DEBT	**108**	**436**	**2,002**	**1,330**	**1,225**	**1,052**	**859**	**1,760**	**1,439**	**1,255**
Official creditors	105	383	1,565	1,315	1,217	1,021	844	1,756	1,436	1,254
Private creditors	4	54	436	15	8	32	15	4	3	1
Memorandum items										
Concessional LDOD	93	562	7,533	8,483	8,715	8,693	8,631	8,810	4,798	4,809
Variable rate LDOD	0	10	114	84	67	29	26	20	16	12
Public sector LDOD	161	685	8,478	9,567	9,774	9,484	9,423	9,614	5,362	5,325
Private sector LDOD	8	3	1	0	0	0	0	0	0	0

6. CURRENCY COMPOSITION OF LONG-TERM DEBT (PERCENT)

	1970	1980	1990	1994	1995	1996	1997	1998	1999	2000
Deutsche mark	2.7	8.1	1.9	2.2	2.3	2.2	1.8	1.9	2.8	2.6
French franc	0.0	0.0	0.2	0.0	0.1	0.1	0.1	0.1	0.1	0.1
Japanese yen	0.0	2.5	0.5	0.4	0.4	0.2	0.1	0.2	0.3	0.3
Pound sterling	2.1	2.3	0.3	0.1	0.2	0.2	0.2	0.2	0.4	0.3
Swiss franc	0.3	0.1	0.1	0.1	0.1	0.1	0.1	0.1	0.1	0.1
U.S.dollars	41.9	64.5	24.2	29.2	29.0	26.8	27.6	28.1	74.9	76.0
Multiple currency	28.0	14.7	4.4	6.9	7.9	8.6	8.8	9.2	16.1	15.1
Special drawing rights	0.0	0.0	0.2	0.2	0.2	0.2	0.2	0.2	0.4	0.4
All other currencies	25.0	7.8	68.2	60.9	59.8	61.6	61.1	60.0	4.9	5.1

ETHIOPIA

(US$ million, unless otherwise indicated)

	1970	1980	1990	1994	1995	1996	1997	1998	1999	2000
7. DEBT RESTRUCTURINGS										
Total amount rescheduled	..	..	0	47	30	0	105	35	1,246	0
Debt stock rescheduled	..	..	0	0	0	0	0	3	747	0
Principal rescheduled	..	..	0	38	23	0	89	22	220	0
Official	..	..	0	19	12	0	73	14	216	0
Private	..	..	0	19	11	0	16	8	5	0
Interest rescheduled	..	..	0	9	6	0	16	6	100	0
Official	..	..	0	3	2	0	11	4	99	0
Private	..	..	0	6	3	0	5	2	1	0
Debt forgiven	..	..	67	15	7	0	19	6	4,321	0
Memo: interest forgiven	..	..	0	3	1	18	3	1	426	0
Debt stock reduction	..	..	0	0	0	195	0	0	0	0
of which debt buyback	..	..	0	0	0	16	0	0	0	0
8. DEBT STOCK-FLOW RECONCILIATION										
Total change in debt stocks	..	..	789	360	245	-230	-3	272	-4,803	-63
Net flows on debt	13	94	204	188	133	21	130	93	134	88
Net change in interest arrears	..	..	27	55	44	44	61	61	-540	3
Interest capitalized	..	..	0	9	6	0	16	6	100	0
Debt forgiveness or reduction	..	..	-67	-15	-7	-180	-19	-6	-4,321	0
Cross-currency valuation	..	..	585	63	22	-148	-259	-55	-77	-105
Residual	..	..	40	59	48	34	69	172	-99	-49
9. AVERAGE TERMS OF NEW COMMITMENTS										
ALL CREDITORS										
Interest (%)	4.4	3.6	6.6	1.1	1.0	2.2	2.4	0.6	0.0	1.0
Maturity (years)	33.0	19.2	21.7	40.3	36.3	30.4	33.5	40.6	17.7	34.2
Grace period (years)	6.9	3.8	3.5	9.3	9.3	7.6	7.4	10.1	8.7	9.2
Grant element (%)	44.5	39.5	23.7	71.6	76.1	62.1	60.7	81.3	70.4	74.0
Official creditors										
Interest (%)	4.2	2.4	1.9	1.1	1.0	0.9	1.2	0.6	0.0	1.0
Maturity (years)	37.8	24.1	32.7	40.3	36.3	35.4	39.6	40.6	17.7	34.2
Grace period (years)	8.0	4.6	8.0	9.3	9.3	9.4	8.9	10.1	8.7	9.2
Grant element (%)	49.6	50.8	59.0	71.6	76.1	75.4	73.6	81.3	70.4	74.0
Private creditors										
Interest (%)	5.0	6.3	9.8	0.0	0.0	7.5	6.8	0.0	0.0	0.0
Maturity (years)	8.5	8.3	14.1	0.0	0.0	10.4	11.1	0.0	0.0	0.0
Grace period (years)	1.7	2.1	0.4	0.0	0.0	0.7	1.6	0.0	0.0	0.0
Grant element (%)	18.1	14.3	-0.4	0.0	0.0	9.0	13.0	0.0	0.0	0.0
Memorandum items										
Commitments	20	194	580	198	170	244	69	1,032	1	89
Official creditors	17	134	236	198	170	195	55	1,032	1	89
Private creditors	3	60	345	0	0	49	15	0	0	0

10. CONTRACTUAL OBLIGATIONS ON OUTSTANDING LONG-TERM DEBT

	2001	2002	2003	2004	2005	2006	2007	2008	2009	2010
TOTAL										
Disbursements	403	342	241	149	75	24	13	3	1	0
Principal	186	180	179	182	177	176	175	182	190	179
Interest	75	73	71	68	64	60	56	53	50	47
Official creditors										
Disbursements	402	341	241	149	75	24	13	3	1	0
Principal	177	172	171	174	169	168	172	181	189	179
Interest	71	70	68	65	62	59	56	52	49	46
Bilateral creditors										
Disbursements	11	10	7	4	2	1	0	0	0	0
Principal	111	100	93	88	81	79	79	76	77	67
Interest	34	33	31	30	28	27	26	25	23	22
Multilateral creditors										
Disbursements	391	332	234	145	73	23	12	3	1	0
Principal	66	72	78	86	87	89	93	105	112	112
Interest	36	37	37	35	34	32	30	28	26	24
Private creditors										
Disbursements	1	0	0	0	0	0	0	0	0	0
Principal	9	8	8	8	8	8	2	1	0	0
Interest	4	4	3	2	2	1	1	1	1	1
Commercial banks										
Disbursements	0	0	0	0	0	0	0	0	0	0
Principal	0	0	0	0	0	0	0	0	0	0
Interest	0	0	0	0	0	0	0	0	0	0
Other private										
Disbursements	1	0	0	0	0	0	0	0	0	0
Principal	9	8	8	8	8	8	2	1	0	0
Interest	4	4	3	2	2	1	1	1	1	1

FIJI

(US$ million, unless otherwise indicated)

	1970	1980	1990	1994	1995	1996	1997	1998	1999	2000
1. SUMMARY DEBT DATA										
TOTAL DEBT STOCKS (EDT)	**11.7**	**281.2**	**412.7**	**284.2**	**251.2**	**218.1**	**219.1**	**192.9**	**162.7**	**135.9**
Long-term debt (LDOD)	**11.7**	**244.9**	**400.7**	**268.2**	**236.3**	**199.7**	**171.1**	**172.3**	**145.3**	**120.3**
Public and publicly guaranteed	11.7	180.0	306.0	180.7	168.3	147.2	129.9	140.1	120.6	101.2
Private nonguaranteed	0.0	64.9	94.7	87.5	68.0	52.5	41.2	32.2	24.7	19.1
Use of IMF credit	**0.0**	**0.0**	**0.0**	**0.0**	**0.0**	**0.0**	**0.0**	**0.0**	**0.0**	**0.0**
Short-term debt	**0.0**	**36.3**	**12.0**	**16.0**	**14.9**	**18.4**	**48.0**	**20.7**	**17.4**	**15.6**
of which interest arrears on LDOD	0.0	0.3	0.0	0.0	0.0	0.0	0.0	0.0	0.0	0.0
Official creditors	0.0	0.3	0.0	0.0	0.0	0.0	0.0	0.0	0.0	0.0
Private creditors	0.0	0.0	0.0	0.0	0.0	0.0	0.0	0.0	0.0	0.0
Memo: principal arrears on LDOD	0.0	0.0	0.0	0.0	0.0	0.0	0.0	0.0	0.0	0.0
Official creditors	0.0	0.0	0.0	0.0	0.0	0.0	0.0	0.0	0.0	0.0
Private creditors	0.0	0.0	0.0	0.0	0.0	0.0	0.0	0.0	0.0	0.0
Memo: export credits	0.0	0.0	61.0	28.1	31.3	33.5	44.9	7.8	5.9	4.6
TOTAL DEBT FLOWS										
Disbursements	**2.3**	**78.3**	**33.5**	**41.4**	**15.2**	**8.6**	**9.1**	**6.5**	**3.1**	**7.1**
Long-term debt	2.3	78.3	33.5	41.4	15.2	8.6	9.1	6.5	3.1	7.1
IMF purchases	0.0	0.0	0.0	0.0	0.0	0.0	0.0	0.0	0.0	0.0
Principal repayments	**1.6**	**19.7**	**73.0**	**71.7**	**51.3**	**35.2**	**23.2**	**23.9**	**29.6**	**22.8**
Long-term debt	1.6	11.2	72.1	71.7	51.3	35.2	23.2	23.9	29.6	22.8
IMF repurchases	0.0	8.5	0.8	0.0	0.0	0.0	0.0	0.0	0.0	0.0
Net flows on debt	**0.7**	**71.6**	**-41.5**	**-61.0**	**-37.2**	**-23.1**	**15.6**	**-44.8**	**-29.7**	**-17.4**
of which short-term debt	0.0	13.0	-2.0	-30.7	-1.1	3.5	29.6	-27.4	-3.3	-1.7
Interest payments (INT)	**1.1**	**16.2**	**32.9**	**21.0**	**16.0**	**13.5**	**12.5**	**10.6**	**9.7**	**7.3**
Long-term debt	1.1	9.5	31.4	19.1	15.1	12.5	10.5	8.9	8.7	6.5
IMF charges	0.0	0.3	0.0	0.0	0.0	0.0	0.0	0.0	0.0	0.0
Short-term debt	0.0	6.3	1.5	1.9	0.9	1.0	2.0	1.7	1.0	0.8
Net transfers on debt	**-0.4**	**55.4**	**-74.4**	**-82.0**	**-53.2**	**-36.6**	**3.1**	**-55.4**	**-39.4**	**-24.7**
Total debt service paid (TDS)	**2.7**	**35.8**	**105.9**	**92.7**	**67.3**	**48.7**	**35.7**	**34.5**	**39.3**	**30.1**
Long-term debt	2.7	20.7	103.5	90.9	66.4	47.7	33.7	32.8	38.2	29.3
IMF repurchases and charges	0.0	8.8	0.8	0.0	0.0	0.0	0.0	0.0	0.0	0.0
Short-term debt (interest only)	0.0	6.3	1.5	1.9	0.9	1.0	2.0	1.7	1.0	0.8
2. AGGREGATE NET RESOURCE FLOWS AND NET TRANSFERS (LONG-TERM)										
NET RESOURCE FLOWS	**11.3**	**118.8**	**67.6**	**48.1**	**54.7**	**-5.4**	**16.4**	**103.3**	**-45.1**	**-6.3**
Net flow of long-term debt (ex. IMF)	0.7	67.1	-38.7	-30.3	-36.1	-26.6	-14.0	-17.4	-26.4	-15.7
Foreign direct investment (net)	6.4	36.4	92.0	67.5	69.5	2.4	16.0	107.0	-33.2	0.0
Portfolio equity flows	0.0	0.0	0.0	0.0	0.0	0.0	0.0	0.0	0.0	0.0
Grants (excluding technical coop.)	4.2	15.3	14.3	10.9	21.4	18.8	14.4	13.7	14.6	9.3
Memo: technical coop. grants	3.0	16.9	36.2	33.5	30.9	34.1	33.1	25.7	28.1	21.9
official net resource flows	5.8	54.5	-8.7	-23.2	5.7	7.9	11.9	5.3	-4.4	-0.7
private net resource flows	5.5	64.3	76.2	71.3	49.0	-13.3	4.5	98.0	-40.7	-5.6
NET TRANSFERS	**-1.3**	**78.8**	**-3.8**	**-39.1**	**-26.4**	**-80.9**	**-62.1**	**23.4**	**-130.8**	**-97.8**
Interest on long-term debt	1.1	9.5	31.4	19.1	15.1	12.5	10.5	8.9	8.7	6.5
Profit remittances on FDI	11.5	30.4	39.9	68.0	66.0	63.0	68.0	71.0	77.0	85.0
Memo: official net transfers	5.2	48.4	-30.1	-36.7	-4.9	-1.1	4.3	-1.6	-11.6	-6.4
private net transfers	-6.5	30.4	26.3	-2.4	-21.5	-79.8	-66.4	25.0	-119.2	-91.4
3. MAJOR ECONOMIC AGGREGATES										
Gross national income (GNI)	210.8	1,186.2	1,345.8	1,772.4	1,877.6	2,059.4	2,033.2	1,513.5	1,651.3	1,434.7
Exports of goods & services (XGS)	..	597.1	881.6	1,074.0	1,139.1	1,348.4	1,265.3	986.7	1,110.1	1,186.5
of which workers remittances	..	0.0	..	..	..	..	..	..	..	..
Imports of goods & services (MGS)	..	656.6	974.3	1,191.4	1,254.7	1,344.4	1,323.7	1,077.2	1,125.9	1,198.5
International reserves (RES)	27.4	174.1	261.1	273.4	349.3	427.5	360.5	385.7	428.9	409.9
Current account balance	..	-17.5	-94.0	-112.8	-112.7	13.5	-34.1	-59.9	12.7	16.7
4. DEBT INDICATORS										
EDT / XGS (%)	..	47.1	46.8	26.5	22.1	16.2	17.3	19.6	14.7	11.5
EDT / GNI (%)	5.6	23.7	30.7	16.0	13.4	10.6	10.8	12.8	9.9	9.5
TDS / XGS (%)	..	6.0	12.0	8.6	5.9	3.6	2.8	3.5	3.5	2.5
INT / XGS (%)	..	2.7	3.7	2.0	1.4	1.0	1.0	1.1	0.9	0.6
INT / GNI (%)	0.5	1.4	2.4	1.2	0.9	0.7	0.6	0.7	0.6	0.5
RES / EDT (%)	233.8	61.9	63.3	96.2	139.1	196.0	164.6	199.9	263.6	301.6
RES / MGS (months)	..	3.2	3.2	2.8	3.3	3.8	3.3	4.3	4.6	4.1
Short-term / EDT (%)	0.0	12.9	2.9	5.6	5.9	8.4	21.9	10.7	10.7	11.5
Concessional / EDT (%)	14.5	9.2	7.2	7.6	8.3	8.4	8.0	12.6	12.0	13.6
Multilateral / EDT (%)	0.0	23.2	49.0	55.9	59.6	60.0	53.4	63.3	65.3	65.1

FIJI

(US$ million, unless otherwise indicated)

	1970	1980	1990	1994	1995	1996	1997	1998	1999	2000
5. LONG-TERM DEBT										
DEBT OUTSTANDING (LDOD)	**11.7**	**244.9**	**400.7**	**268.2**	**236.3**	**199.7**	**171.1**	**172.3**	**145.3**	**120.3**
Public and publicly guaranteed	**11.7**	**180.0**	**306.0**	**180.7**	**168.3**	**147.2**	**129.9**	**140.1**	**120.6**	**101.2**
Official creditors	8.2	123.7	279.1	179.2	167.8	146.9	129.8	140.0	120.6	101.2
Multilateral	0.0	65.1	202.0	158.8	149.7	130.9	117.0	122.1	106.2	88.5
Concessional	0.0	4.4	14.7	11.3	11.6	10.6	11.2	11.4	8.6	7.7
Bilateral	8.2	58.6	77.1	20.4	18.1	16.0	12.9	18.0	14.3	12.6
Concessional	1.7	21.5	15.2	10.3	9.3	7.8	6.3	12.9	10.9	10.8
Private creditors	3.5	56.3	26.9	1.5	0.6	0.3	0.1	0.1	0.0	0.0
Bonds	3.5	2.5	0.0	0.0	0.0	0.0	0.0	0.0	0.0	0.0
Commercial banks	0.0	41.0	12.1	0.6	0.4	0.2	0.0	0.0	0.0	0.0
Other private	0.0	12.8	14.7	0.9	0.1	0.1	0.1	0.1	0.0	0.0
Private nonguaranteed	**0.0**	**64.9**	**94.7**	**87.5**	**68.0**	**52.5**	**41.2**	**32.2**	**24.7**	**19.1**
Bonds	0.0	0.0	0.0	0.0	0.0	0.0	0.0	0.0	0.0	0.0
Commercial banks and other	0.0	64.9	94.7	87.5	68.0	52.5	41.2	32.2	24.7	19.1
Memo:										
IBRD	0.0	33.5	67.8	39.6	35.3	32.8	30.3	31.8	28.1	19.7
IDA	0.0	0.0	0.0	0.0	0.0	0.0	0.0	0.0	0.0	0.0
DISBURSEMENTS	**2.3**	**78.3**	**33.5**	**41.4**	**15.2**	**8.6**	**9.1**	**6.5**	**3.1**	**7.1**
Public and publicly guaranteed	**2.3**	**78.3**	**19.3**	**16.9**	**15.2**	**8.6**	**9.1**	**6.5**	**3.1**	**7.1**
Official creditors	2.3	43.4	18.6	16.9	15.2	8.6	9.1	6.5	3.1	7.1
Multilateral	0.0	23.2	13.2	16.9	15.2	8.6	9.1	6.5	3.1	5.6
Concessional	0.0	2.3	0.0	0.0	0.0	0.0	2.1	0.0	0.0	0.0
Bilateral	2.3	20.2	5.3	0.0	0.0	0.0	0.0	0.0	0.0	1.5
Concessional	2.3	0.0	1.0	0.0	0.0	0.0	0.0	0.0	0.0	1.5
Private creditors	0.0	34.9	0.7	0.0	0.0	0.0	0.0	0.0	0.0	0.0
Bonds	0.0	0.0	0.0	0.0	0.0	0.0	0.0	0.0	0.0	0.0
Commercial banks	0.0	31.0	0.6	0.0	0.0	0.0	0.0	0.0	0.0	0.0
Other private	0.0	3.9	0.1	0.0	0.0	0.0	0.0	0.0	0.0	0.0
Private nonguaranteed	**0.0**	**0.0**	**14.2**	**24.5**	**0.0**	**0.0**	**0.0**	**0.0**	**0.0**	**0.0**
Bonds	0.0	0.0	0.0	0.0	0.0	0.0	0.0	0.0	0.0	0.0
Commercial banks and other	0.0	0.0	14.2	24.5	0.0	0.0	0.0	0.0	0.0	0.0
Memo:										
IBRD	0.0	5.7	5.1	5.8	5.6	6.6	4.3	4.3	1.5	1.0
IDA	0.0	0.0	0.0	0.0	0.0	0.0	0.0	0.0	0.0	0.0
PRINCIPAL REPAYMENTS	**1.6**	**11.2**	**72.1**	**71.7**	**51.3**	**35.2**	**23.2**	**23.9**	**29.6**	**22.8**
Public and publicly guaranteed	**1.6**	**11.2**	**54.6**	**52.6**	**31.8**	**19.7**	**11.9**	**14.9**	**22.1**	**17.2**
Official creditors	0.7	4.2	41.5	51.0	30.9	19.5	11.7	14.9	22.0	17.2
Multilateral	0.0	1.0	33.8	39.8	28.2	16.9	9.3	11.6	19.1	14.5
Concessional	0.0	0.0	0.3	1.4	0.5	0.5	0.3	0.4	1.3	0.3
Bilateral	0.7	3.2	7.7	11.2	2.7	2.6	2.3	3.3	3.0	2.6
Concessional	0.6	1.4	0.8	1.1	1.4	1.3	1.0	1.8	1.5	1.3
Private creditors	0.9	7.0	13.2	1.6	1.0	0.2	0.2	0.0	0.0	0.0
Bonds	0.9	1.6	0.0	0.0	0.0	0.0	0.0	0.0	0.0	0.0
Commercial banks	0.0	0.0	5.7	0.2	0.2	0.2	0.2	0.0	0.0	0.0
Other private	0.0	5.3	7.5	1.4	0.8	0.0	0.0	0.0	0.0	0.0
Private nonguaranteed	**0.0**	**0.0**	**17.5**	**19.1**	**19.5**	**15.5**	**11.3**	**9.0**	**7.5**	**5.6**
Bonds	0.0	0.0	0.0	0.0	0.0	0.0	0.0	0.0	0.0	0.0
Commercial banks and other	0.0	0.0	17.5	19.1	19.5	15.5	11.3	9.0	7.5	5.6
Memo:										
IBRD	0.0	0.7	9.1	12.9	11.5	6.7	3.9	4.8	4.8	7.7
IDA	0.0	0.0	0.0	0.0	0.0	0.0	0.0	0.0	0.0	0.0
NET FLOWS ON DEBT	**0.7**	**67.1**	**-38.7**	**-30.3**	**-36.1**	**-26.6**	**-14.0**	**-17.4**	**-26.4**	**-15.7**
Public and publicly guaranteed	**0.7**	**67.1**	**-35.4**	**-35.7**	**-16.6**	**-11.1**	**-2.7**	**-8.4**	**-18.9**	**-10.1**
Official creditors	1.6	39.2	-22.9	-34.1	-15.7	-10.9	-2.5	-8.4	-18.9	-10.0
Multilateral	0.0	22.2	-20.5	-22.9	-13.0	-8.2	-0.2	-5.1	-15.9	-8.9
Concessional	0.0	2.3	-0.3	-1.4	-0.5	-0.5	1.9	-0.4	-1.3	-0.3
Bilateral	1.6	17.0	-2.4	-11.2	-2.7	-2.6	-2.3	-3.3	-3.0	-1.1
Concessional	1.7	-1.4	0.1	-1.1	-1.4	-1.3	-1.0	-1.8	-1.5	0.2
Private creditors	-0.9	27.9	-12.5	-1.6	-1.0	-0.2	-0.2	0.0	0.0	0.0
Bonds	-0.9	-1.6	0.0	0.0	0.0	0.0	0.0	0.0	0.0	0.0
Commercial banks	0.0	31.0	-5.1	-0.2	-0.2	-0.2	-0.2	0.0	0.0	0.0
Other private	0.0	-1.5	-7.3	-1.4	-0.8	0.0	0.0	0.0	0.0	0.0
Private nonguaranteed	**0.0**	**0.0**	**-3.3**	**5.4**	**-19.5**	**-15.5**	**-11.3**	**-9.0**	**-7.5**	**-5.6**
Bonds	0.0	0.0	0.0	0.0	0.0	0.0	0.0	0.0	0.0	0.0
Commercial banks and other	0.0	0.0	-3.3	5.4	-19.5	-15.5	-11.3	-9.0	-7.5	-5.6
Memo:										
IBRD	0.0	5.0	-4.0	-7.0	-5.9	-0.1	0.4	-0.5	-3.3	-6.8
IDA	0.0	0.0	0.0	0.0	0.0	0.0	0.0	0.0	0.0	0.0

FIJI

(US$ million, unless otherwise indicated)

	1970	1980	1990	1994	1995	1996	1997	1998	1999	2000
INTEREST PAYMENTS (LINT)	**1.1**	**9.5**	**31.4**	**19.1**	**15.1**	**12.5**	**10.5**	**8.9**	**8.7**	**6.5**
Public and publicly guaranteed	**1.1**	**9.5**	**24.0**	**13.7**	**10.7**	**9.0**	**7.6**	**6.9**	**7.2**	**5.7**
Official creditors	0.6	6.1	21.4	13.5	10.6	9.0	7.6	6.9	7.2	5.7
Multilateral	0.0	3.4	15.0	11.4	9.5	8.0	6.7	6.0	6.5	5.2
Concessional	0.0	0.0	0.1	0.1	0.1	0.1	0.1	0.1	0.1	0.1
Bilateral	0.6	2.7	6.3	2.1	1.1	1.0	0.8	0.9	0.7	0.5
Concessional	0.1	0.8	0.3	0.4	0.3	0.3	0.2	0.4	0.3	0.3
Private creditors	0.5	3.5	2.6	0.2	0.1	0.0	0.0	0.0	0.0	0.0
Bonds	0.5	0.3	0.0	0.0	0.0	0.0	0.0	0.0	0.0	0.0
Commercial banks	0.0	2.1	1.1	0.1	0.1	0.0	0.0	0.0	0.0	0.0
Other private	0.0	1.1	1.5	0.1	0.0	0.0	0.0	0.0	0.0	0.0
Private nonguaranteed	**0.0**	**0.0**	**7.4**	**5.5**	**4.4**	**3.5**	**2.9**	**2.0**	**1.5**	**0.8**
Bonds	0.0	0.0	0.0	0.0	0.0	0.0	0.0	0.0	0.0	0.0
Commercial banks and other	0.0	0.0	7.4	5.5	4.4	3.5	2.9	2.0	1.5	0.8
Memo:										
IBRD	0.0	2.7	5.6	3.4	3.0	2.3	2.1	1.9	1.8	1.4
IDA	0.0	0.0	0.0	0.0	0.0	0.0	0.0	0.0	0.0	0.0
NET TRANSFERS ON DEBT	**-0.4**	**57.6**	**-70.0**	**-49.5**	**-51.2**	**-39.1**	**-24.6**	**-26.3**	**-35.1**	**-22.2**
Public and publicly guaranteed	**-0.4**	**57.6**	**-59.3**	**-49.4**	**-27.3**	**-20.1**	**-10.3**	**-15.3**	**-26.2**	**-15.8**
Official creditors	0.9	33.1	-44.3	-47.6	-26.3	-19.8	-10.1	-15.3	-26.1	-15.7
Multilateral	0.0	18.9	-35.5	-34.3	-22.5	-16.2	-7.0	-11.1	-22.5	-14.1
Concessional	0.0	2.3	-0.4	-1.5	-0.6	-0.6	1.8	-0.5	-1.4	-0.3
Bilateral	0.9	14.3	-8.7	-13.3	-3.8	-3.6	-3.1	-4.1	-3.6	-1.6
Concessional	1.6	-2.2	-0.2	-1.5	-1.7	-1.6	-1.2	-2.1	-1.8	0.0
Private creditors	-1.4	24.4	-15.1	-1.8	-1.0	-0.3	-0.2	0.0	0.0	0.0
Bonds	-1.4	-1.9	0.0	0.0	0.0	0.0	0.0	0.0	0.0	0.0
Commercial banks	0.0	28.9	-6.2	-0.2	-0.3	-0.2	-0.2	0.0	0.0	0.0
Other private	0.0	-2.6	-8.9	-1.5	-0.8	0.0	0.0	0.0	0.0	0.0
Private nonguaranteed	**0.0**	**0.0**	**-10.7**	**-0.1**	**-23.9**	**-19.0**	**-14.3**	**-11.0**	**-9.0**	**-6.4**
Bonds	0.0	0.0	0.0	0.0	0.0	0.0	0.0	0.0	0.0	0.0
Commercial banks and other	0.0	0.0	-10.7	-0.1	-23.9	-19.0	-14.3	-11.0	-9.0	-6.4
Memo:										
IBRD	0.0	2.3	-9.6	-10.5	-8.9	-2.4	-1.7	-2.4	-5.1	-8.1
IDA	0.0	0.0	0.0	0.0	0.0	0.0	0.0	0.0	0.0	0.0
DEBT SERVICE (LTDS)	**2.7**	**20.7**	**103.5**	**90.9**	**66.4**	**47.7**	**33.7**	**32.8**	**38.2**	**29.3**
Public and publicly guaranteed	**2.7**	**20.7**	**78.6**	**66.3**	**42.5**	**28.7**	**19.4**	**21.8**	**29.3**	**22.9**
Official creditors	1.4	10.3	62.8	64.5	41.5	28.5	19.2	21.7	29.3	22.9
Multilateral	0.0	4.4	48.8	51.2	37.7	24.9	16.1	17.6	25.6	19.7
Concessional	0.0	0.0	0.4	1.5	0.6	0.6	0.4	0.5	1.4	0.3
Bilateral	1.4	5.9	14.0	13.3	3.8	3.6	3.1	4.1	3.6	3.1
Concessional	0.7	2.2	1.2	1.5	1.7	1.6	1.2	2.1	1.8	1.5
Private creditors	1.4	10.4	15.8	1.8	1.0	0.3	0.2	0.0	0.0	0.0
Bonds	1.4	1.9	0.0	0.0	0.0	0.0	0.0	0.0	0.0	0.0
Commercial banks	0.0	2.1	6.8	0.2	0.3	0.2	0.2	0.0	0.0	0.0
Other private	0.0	6.4	9.0	1.5	0.8	0.0	0.0	0.0	0.0	0.0
Private nonguaranteed	**0.0**	**0.0**	**24.9**	**24.6**	**23.9**	**19.0**	**14.3**	**11.0**	**9.0**	**6.4**
Bonds	0.0	0.0	0.0	0.0	0.0	0.0	0.0	0.0	0.0	0.0
Commercial banks and other	0.0	0.0	24.9	24.6	23.9	19.0	14.3	11.0	9.0	6.4
Memo:										
IBRD	0.0	3.3	14.7	16.3	14.5	9.0	6.0	6.7	6.7	9.1
IDA	0.0	0.0	0.0	0.0	0.0	0.0	0.0	0.0	0.0	0.0
UNDISBURSED DEBT	**1.4**	**120.8**	**81.2**	**48.8**	**37.5**	**28.8**	**60.1**	**74.3**	**62.9**	**53.2**
Official creditors	1.2	120.8	80.6	48.8	37.5	28.8	60.1	74.3	62.9	53.2
Private creditors	0.2	0.0	0.6	0.0	0.0	0.0	0.0	0.0	0.0	0.0
Memorandum items										
Concessional LDOD	1.7	25.9	29.9	21.6	20.9	18.4	17.5	24.3	19.5	18.5
Variable rate LDOD	0.0	105.9	124.0	125.1	113.9	98.1	84.6	79.6	71.2	59.7
Public sector LDOD	11.7	180.0	306.0	180.7	168.3	147.2	129.9	140.1	120.6	101.2
Private sector LDOD	0.0	64.9	94.7	87.5	68.0	52.5	41.2	32.2	24.7	19.1

6. CURRENCY COMPOSITION OF LONG-TERM DEBT (PERCENT)

	1970	1980	1990	1994	1995	1996	1997	1998	1999	2000
Deutsche mark	0.0	0.0	0.0	0.0	0.0	0.0	0.0	0.0	0.0	0.0
French franc	0.0	0.0	1.4	2.0	2.1	2.1	1.9	2.0	1.8	1.8
Japanese yen	0.0	0.0	0.0	0.0	0.0	0.0	0.0	0.0	0.0	1.4
Pound sterling	34.2	24.7	16.4	7.1	6.3	6.4	5.7	4.0	3.1	1.8
Swiss franc	0.0	0.0	0.0	0.0	0.0	0.0	0.0	0.0	0.0	0.0
U.S.dollars	14.6	26.1	5.2	0.9	0.8	0.7	0.5	5.3	6.4	11.6
Multiple currency	0.0	36.2	58.9	82.0	83.5	84.6	84.9	83.0	84.2	79.9
Special drawing rights	0.0	0.0	0.0	0.0	0.0	0.0	0.0	0.0	0.0	0.0
All other currencies	51.2	13.0	18.1	8.0	7.3	6.2	7.0	5.7	4.5	3.5

FIJI

(US$ million, unless otherwise indicated)

	1970	1980	1990	1994	1995	1996	1997	1998	1999	2000
7. DEBT RESTRUCTURINGS										
Total amount rescheduled	..	..	0.0	0.0	0.0	0.0	0.0	0.0	0.0	0.0
Debt stock rescheduled	..	..	0.0	0.0	0.0	0.0	0.0	0.0	0.0	0.0
Principal rescheduled	..	..	0.0	0.0	0.0	0.0	0.0	0.0	0.0	0.0
Official	..	..	0.0	0.0	0.0	0.0	0.0	0.0	0.0	0.0
Private	..	..	0.0	0.0	0.0	0.0	0.0	0.0	0.0	0.0
Interest rescheduled	..	..	0.0	0.0	0.0	0.0	0.0	0.0	0.0	0.0
Official	..	..	0.0	0.0	0.0	0.0	0.0	0.0	0.0	0.0
Private	..	..	0.0	0.0	0.0	0.0	0.0	0.0	0.0	0.0
Debt forgiven	..	..	0.0	0.0	0.0	0.0	0.0	0.0	0.0	0.0
Memo: interest forgiven	..	..	0.0	0.0	0.0	0.0	0.0	0.0	0.0	0.0
Debt stock reduction	..	..	0.0	0.0	0.0	0.0	0.0	0.0	0.0	0.0
of which debt buyback	..	..	0.0	0.0	0.0	0.0	0.0	0.0	0.0	0.0
8. DEBT STOCK-FLOW RECONCILIATION										
Total change in debt stocks	..	..	-1.5	-45.9	-33.0	-33.2	1.1	-26.2	-30.3	-26.8
Net flows on debt	0.7	71.6	-41.5	-61.0	-37.2	-23.1	15.6	-44.8	-29.7	-17.4
Net change in interest arrears	..	..	0.0	0.0	0.0	0.0	0.0	0.0	0.0	0.0
Interest capitalized	..	..	0.0	0.0	0.0	0.0	0.0	0.0	0.0	0.0
Debt forgiveness or reduction	..	..	0.0	0.0	0.0	0.0	0.0	0.0	0.0	0.0
Cross-currency valuation	..	..	25.4	4.4	-6.1	-11.3	-10.3	9.1	2.8	-8.1
Residual	..	..	14.6	10.7	10.3	1.2	-4.2	9.5	-3.4	-1.3
9. AVERAGE TERMS OF NEW COMMITMENTS										
ALL CREDITORS										
Interest (%)	3.1	8.1	6.6	0.0	4.5	0.0	6.5	2.5	0.0	0.0
Maturity (years)	17.7	14.4	24.7	0.0	12.0	0.0	25.4	24.3	0.0	0.0
Grace period (years)	5.2	3.7	5.1	0.0	4.5	0.0	5.4	7.0	0.0	0.0
Grant element (%)	43.6	9.5	22.9	0.0	28.8	0.0	24.6	55.6	0.0	0.0
Official creditors										
Interest (%)	3.0	7.9	6.6	0.0	4.5	0.0	6.5	2.5	0.0	0.0
Maturity (years)	18.5	14.7	24.8	0.0	12.0	0.0	25.4	24.3	0.0	0.0
Grace period (years)	5.5	3.7	5.1	0.0	4.5	0.0	5.4	7.0	0.0	0.0
Grant element (%)	45.6	10.6	23.0	0.0	28.8	0.0	24.6	55.6	0.0	0.0
Private creditors										
Interest (%)	5.5	10.2	8.8	0.0	0.0	0.0	0.0	0.0	0.0	0.0
Maturity (years)	5.2	10.0	10.4	0.0	0.0	0.0	0.0	0.0	0.0	0.0
Grace period (years)	0.7	3.3	6.3	0.0	0.0	0.0	0.0	0.0	0.0	0.0
Grant element (%)	10.5	-4.3	3.5	0.0	0.0	0.0	0.0	0.0	0.0	0.0
Memorandum items										
Commitments	3.7	89.1	30.0	0.0	10.5	0.0	42.3	17.8	0.0	0.0
Official creditors	3.5	82.6	29.8	0.0	10.5	0.0	42.3	17.8	0.0	0.0
Private creditors	0.2	6.5	0.1	0.0	0.0	0.0	0.0	0.0	0.0	0.0

10. CONTRACTUAL OBLIGATIONS ON OUTSTANDING LONG-TERM DEBT

	2001	2002	2003	2004	2005	2006	2007	2008	2009	2010
TOTAL										
Disbursements	18.6	13.4	9.4	7.2	4.4	0.0	0.0	0.0	0.0	0.0
Principal	19.1	16.6	15.7	9.9	8.5	8.9	8.6	8.3	8.5	7.6
Interest	6.4	6.4	6.2	5.6	5.5	5.1	4.7	4.2	3.8	3.4
Official creditors										
Disbursements	18.6	13.4	9.4	7.2	4.4	0.0	0.0	0.0	0.0	0.0
Principal	13.0	11.1	10.7	7.4	8.5	8.9	8.6	8.3	8.5	7.6
Interest	5.7	5.9	5.8	5.6	5.5	5.1	4.7	4.2	3.8	3.4
Bilateral creditors										
Disbursements	10.7	5.3	1.7	0.8	0.0	0.0	0.0	0.0	0.0	0.0
Principal	1.5	1.5	1.5	0.9	1.8	1.8	1.8	1.8	1.8	1.8
Interest	0.5	0.8	0.8	0.8	0.7	0.7	0.6	0.6	0.5	0.4
Multilateral creditors										
Disbursements	7.9	8.2	7.7	6.5	4.4	0.0	0.0	0.0	0.0	0.0
Principal	11.5	9.6	9.2	6.6	6.7	7.1	6.8	6.5	6.7	5.8
Interest	5.2	5.1	5.0	4.9	4.8	4.5	4.1	3.7	3.3	2.9
Private creditors										
Disbursements	0.0	0.0	0.0	0.0	0.0	0.0	0.0	0.0	0.0	0.0
Principal	6.1	5.5	5.0	2.5	0.0	0.0	0.0	0.0	0.0	0.0
Interest	0.7	0.5	0.4	0.0	0.0	0.0	0.0	0.0	0.0	0.0
Commercial banks										
Disbursements	0.0	0.0	0.0	0.0	0.0	0.0	0.0	0.0	0.0	0.0
Principal	0.0	0.0	0.0	0.0	0.0	0.0	0.0	0.0	0.0	0.0
Interest	0.0	0.0	0.0	0.0	0.0	0.0	0.0	0.0	0.0	0.0
Other private										
Disbursements	0.0	0.0	0.0	0.0	0.0	0.0	0.0	0.0	0.0	0.0
Principal	6.1	5.5	5.0	2.5	0.0	0.0	0.0	0.0	0.0	0.0
Interest	0.7	0.5	0.4	0.0	0.0	0.0	0.0	0.0	0.0	0.0

GABON

(US$ million, unless otherwise indicated)

	1970	1980	1990	1994	1995	1996	1997	1998	1999	2000
1. SUMMARY DEBT DATA										
TOTAL DEBT STOCKS (EDT)	**104**	**1,514**	**3,983**	**4,171**	**4,360**	**4,310**	**4,278**	**4,425**	**3,978**	**3,995**
Long-term debt (LDOD)	**91**	**1,272**	**3,150**	**3,694**	**3,976**	**3,972**	**3,665**	**3,833**	**3,290**	**3,512**
Public and publicly guaranteed	91	1,272	3,150	3,694	3,976	3,972	3,665	3,833	3,290	3,512
Private nonguaranteed	0	0	0	0	0	0	0	0	0	0
Use of IMF credit	**0**	**15**	**140**	**90**	**97**	**120**	**131**	**113**	**86**	**89**
Short-term debt	**13**	**228**	**693**	**387**	**287**	**219**	**482**	**478**	**602**	**395**
of which interest arrears on LDOD	0	0	130	51	0	0	0	79	94	81
Official creditors	0	0	111	36	0	0	0	77	92	77
Private creditors	0	0	20	15	0	0	0	2	2	4
Memo: principal arrears on LDOD	0	0	82	110	26	0	0	85	116	136
Official creditors	0	0	17	47	0	0	0	84	113	128
Private creditors	0	0	65	63	26	0	0	1	3	7
Memo: export credits	0	0	1,917	2,066	2,103	2,210	2,539	1,492	1,531	1,379
TOTAL DEBT FLOWS										
Disbursements	**26**	**171**	**204**	**198**	**279**	**121**	**168**	**46**	**59**	**47**
Long-term debt	26	171	195	134	222	89	145	46	59	30
IMF purchases	0	0	9	64	57	32	23	0	0	17
Principal repayments	**9**	**279**	**40**	**119**	**216**	**137**	**172**	**135**	**281**	**252**
Long-term debt	9	279	26	96	165	131	168	112	256	242
IMF repurchases	0	0	15	23	52	5	4	23	25	10
Net flows on debt	**17**	**-122**	**164**	**-18**	**14**	**-84**	**260**	**-172**	**-112**	**-399**
of which short-term debt	0	-13	0	-97	-49	-69	263	-83	109	-195
Interest payments (INT)	**3**	**153**	**136**	**149**	**240**	**247**	**261**	**172**	**257**	**216**
Long-term debt	3	119	78	103	217	232	238	142	231	184
IMF charges	0	1	13	3	5	4	6	6	4	4
Short-term debt	0	33	45	43	17	11	18	25	23	28
Net transfers on debt	**14**	**-275**	**28**	**-167**	**-226**	**-331**	**-2**	**-344**	**-370**	**-615**
Total debt service paid (TDS)	**12**	**432**	**176**	**268**	**456**	**384**	**433**	**307**	**538**	**468**
Long-term debt	12	398	104	199	382	363	406	254	487	426
IMF repurchases and charges	0	1	27	26	57	10	9	29	29	14
Short-term debt (interest only)	0	33	45	43	17	11	18	25	23	28
2. AGGREGATE NET RESOURCE FLOWS AND NET TRANSFERS (LONG-TERM)										
NET RESOURCE FLOWS	**26**	**-73**	**273**	**85**	**-171**	**-454**	**-276**	**132**	**-315**	**-24**
Net flow of long-term debt (ex. IMF)	17	-109	170	38	57	-43	-23	-66	-197	-213
Foreign direct investment (net)	-1	32	74	-100	-315	-489	-311	147	-157	150
Portfolio equity flows	0	0	0	0	0	0	0	0	0	0
Grants (excluding technical coop.)	10	4	30	147	87	78	58	52	38	39
Memo: technical coop. grants	7	38	36	43	46	43	36	35	35	26
official net resource flows	17	20	170	216	219	86	40	-8	-167	-166
private net resource flows	9	-93	103	-131	-389	-540	-316	140	-148	142
NET TRANSFERS	**15**	**-465**	**79**	**-238**	**-588**	**-896**	**-714**	**-235**	**-776**	**-458**
Interest on long-term debt	3	119	78	103	217	232	238	142	231	184
Profit remittances on FDI	8	273	116	220	200	210	200	225	230	250
Memo: official net transfers	15	1	103	141	45	-133	-188	-141	-388	-343
private net transfers	0	-466	-24	-379	-633	-762	-526	-93	-387	-115
3. MAJOR ECONOMIC AGGREGATES										
Gross national income (GNI)	306	3,856	5,336	3,693	4,241	4,887	4,754	4,067	3,812	4,240
Exports of goods & services (XGS)	..	2,434	2,750	2,597	2,984	3,613	3,308	2,188	2,866	3,113
of which workers remittances	..	0	0	..	4	2	4	3	2	..
Imports of goods & services (MGS)	..	1,926	2,448	2,113	2,473	2,685	2,739	2,727	2,431	2,658
International reserves (RES)	15	115	279	180	153	253	286	15	18	190
Current account balance	..	384	168	317	465	889	531	-596	390	385
4. DEBT INDICATORS										
EDT / XGS (%)	..	62.2	144.8	160.6	146.1	119.3	129.3	202.2	138.8	128.3
EDT / GNI (%)	34.0	39.3	74.6	113.0	102.8	88.2	90.0	108.8	104.4	94.2
TDS / XGS (%)	..	17.8	6.4	10.3	15.3	10.6	13.1	14.0	18.8	15.0
INT / XGS (%)	..	6.3	4.9	5.7	8.0	6.8	7.9	7.9	9.0	6.9
INT / GNI (%)	0.9	4.0	2.5	4.0	5.7	5.1	5.5	4.2	6.8	5.1
RES / EDT (%)	14.2	7.6	7.0	4.3	3.5	5.9	6.7	0.4	0.5	4.8
RES / MGS (months)	..	0.7	1.4	1.0	0.7	1.1	1.3	0.1	0.1	0.9
Short-term / EDT (%)	12.5	15.1	17.4	9.3	6.6	5.1	11.3	10.8	15.1	9.9
Concessional / EDT (%)	34.9	7.5	10.6	13.8	16.1	17.2	20.9	21.4	20.6	35.5
Multilateral / EDT (%)	30.1	2.7	8.0	11.2	13.5	13.5	12.3	12.5	13.2	11.6

GABON

(US$ million, unless otherwise indicated)

	1970	1980	1990	1994	1995	1996	1997	1998	1999	2000
5. LONG-TERM DEBT										
DEBT OUTSTANDING (LDOD)	**91**	**1,272**	**3,150**	**3,694**	**3,976**	**3,972**	**3,665**	**3,833**	**3,290**	**3,512**
Public and publicly guaranteed	**91**	**1,272**	**3,150**	**3,694**	**3,976**	**3,972**	**3,665**	**3,833**	**3,290**	**3,512**
Official creditors	67	316	2,435	3,427	3,778	3,829	3,534	3,708	3,162	3,394
Multilateral	31	40	317	467	588	583	528	554	525	463
Concessional	1	10	29	25	28	30	30	32	28	26
Bilateral	36	276	2,118	2,960	3,189	3,246	3,007	3,154	2,637	2,931
Concessional	35	103	393	549	674	712	863	916	793	1,391
Private creditors	24	955	715	268	199	143	131	125	129	117
Bonds	8	2	0	0	0	0	0	0	0	0
Commercial banks	0	721	181	175	148	117	97	85	91	82
Other private	16	232	535	92	51	26	33	40	37	36
Private nonguaranteed	**0**	**0**	**0**	**0**	**0**	**0**	**0**	**0**	**0**	**0**
Bonds	0	0	0	0	0	0	0	0	0	0
Commercial banks and other	0	0	0	0	0	0	0	0	0	0
Memo:										
IBRD	29	19	69	114	110	92	77	75	68	64
IDA	0	0	0	0	0	0	0	0	0	0
DISBURSEMENTS	**26**	**171**	**195**	**134**	**222**	**89**	**145**	**46**	**59**	**30**
Public and publicly guaranteed	**26**	**171**	**195**	**134**	**222**	**89**	**145**	**46**	**59**	**30**
Official creditors	13	36	158	132	222	89	125	36	27	9
Multilateral	4	2	84	78	150	64	34	22	4	9
Concessional	1	0	4	1	2	5	6	2	0	0
Bilateral	9	33	74	54	72	25	91	14	22	0
Concessional	9	16	63	52	62	22	90	12	21	0
Private creditors	13	135	37	2	0	0	20	10	33	21
Bonds	4	0	0	0	0	0	0	0	0	0
Commercial banks	0	95	0	0	0	0	0	3	31	21
Other private	9	40	37	2	0	0	20	8	2	0
Private nonguaranteed	**0**	**0**	**0**	**0**	**0**	**0**	**0**	**0**	**0**	**0**
Bonds	0	0	0	0	0	0	0	0	0	0
Commercial banks and other	0	0	0	0	0	0	0	0	0	0
Memo:										
IBRD	3	0	10	33	4	3	3	7	4	9
IDA	0	0	0	0	0	0	0	0	0	0
PRINCIPAL REPAYMENTS	**9**	**279**	**26**	**96**	**165**	**131**	**168**	**112**	**256**	**242**
Public and publicly guaranteed	**9**	**279**	**26**	**96**	**165**	**131**	**168**	**112**	**256**	**242**
Official creditors	6	19	18	63	90	80	143	95	232	213
Multilateral	4	3	13	36	43	46	42	23	30	43
Concessional	0	0	1	3	2	2	3	1	2	0
Bilateral	2	17	5	27	48	34	101	72	202	171
Concessional	2	4	0	5	10	7	36	27	43	30
Private creditors	4	260	8	33	75	51	25	17	24	29
Bonds	0	1	0	0	0	0	0	0	0	0
Commercial banks	0	185	3	3	26	31	20	15	23	29
Other private	3	74	5	30	49	20	5	2	1	0
Private nonguaranteed	**0**	**0**	**0**	**0**	**0**	**0**	**0**	**0**	**0**	**0**
Bonds	0	0	0	0	0	0	0	0	0	0
Commercial banks and other	0	0	0	0	0	0	0	0	0	0
Memo:										
IBRD	3	2	1	10	12	13	10	9	10	13
IDA	0	0	0	0	0	0	0	0	0	0
NET FLOWS ON DEBT	**17**	**-109**	**170**	**38**	**57**	**-43**	**-23**	**-66**	**-197**	**-213**
Public and publicly guaranteed	**17**	**-109**	**170**	**38**	**57**	**-43**	**-23**	**-66**	**-197**	**-213**
Official creditors	7	16	141	69	132	9	-18	-60	-205	-205
Multilateral	0	0	71	42	107	17	-8	-1	-25	-34
Concessional	1	0	3	-1	1	4	3	1	-2	0
Bilateral	7	17	70	27	24	-9	-10	-59	-180	-171
Concessional	7	13	63	47	52	14	54	-15	-22	-30
Private creditors	9	-125	29	-31	-75	-51	-5	-7	9	-8
Bonds	4	-1	0	0	0	0	0	0	0	0
Commercial banks	0	-91	-3	-3	-26	-31	-20	-13	8	-8
Other private	6	-34	32	-28	-49	-20	15	6	1	0
Private nonguaranteed	**0**	**0**	**0**	**0**	**0**	**0**	**0**	**0**	**0**	**0**
Bonds	0	0	0	0	0	0	0	0	0	0
Commercial banks and other	0	0	0	0	0	0	0	0	0	0
Memo:										
IBRD	-1	-2	9	23	-8	-11	-7	-3	-6	-4
IDA	0	0	0	0	0	0	0	0	0	0

GABON

(US$ million, unless otherwise indicated)

	1970	1980	1990	1994	1995	1996	1997	1998	1999	2000
INTEREST PAYMENTS (LINT)	**3**	**119**	**78**	**103**	**217**	**232**	**238**	**142**	**231**	**184**
Public and publicly guaranteed	**3**	**119**	**78**	**103**	**217**	**232**	**238**	**142**	**231**	**184**
Official creditors	2	19	68	74	174	219	228	134	221	177
Multilateral	1	2	21	37	26	43	44	21	29	42
Concessional	0	0	0	1	1	1	1	0	1	0
Bilateral	1	17	47	37	148	176	184	113	193	135
Concessional	1	3	2	14	39	38	35	23	26	17
Private creditors	1	100	11	29	44	12	10	8	9	7
Bonds	0	0	0	0	0	0	0	0	0	0
Commercial banks	0	81	5	16	27	9	7	7	7	7
Other private	0	19	6	13	17	3	3	1	3	0
Private nonguaranteed	**0**	**0**	**0**	**0**	**0**	**0**	**0**	**0**	**0**	**0**
Bonds	0	0	0	0	0	0	0	0	0	0
Commercial banks and other	0	0	0	0	0	0	0	0	0	0
Memo:										
IBRD	1	2	5	8	8	9	6	3	5	5
IDA	0	0	0	0	0	0	0	0	0	0
NET TRANSFERS ON DEBT	**14**	**-227**	**92**	**-65**	**-161**	**-274**	**-261**	**-208**	**-427**	**-397**
Public and publicly guaranteed	**14**	**-227**	**92**	**-65**	**-161**	**-274**	**-261**	**-208**	**-427**	**-397**
Official creditors	5	-3	73	-5	-42	-211	-246	-193	-427	-382
Multilateral	-1	-2	51	5	82	-26	-52	-22	-54	-76
Concessional	1	0	2	-2	0	3	2	0	-2	0
Bilateral	6	-1	23	-10	-124	-185	-194	-172	-373	-306
Concessional	7	10	62	33	13	-24	19	-39	-48	-47
Private creditors	9	-224	18	-60	-119	-63	-15	-15	-1	-15
Bonds	3	-1	0	0	0	0	0	0	0	0
Commercial banks	0	-171	-8	-18	-53	-40	-27	-19	1	-14
Other private	6	-53	26	-41	-66	-23	12	4	-2	-1
Private nonguaranteed	**0**	**0**	**0**	**0**	**0**	**0**	**0**	**0**	**0**	**0**
Bonds	0	0	0	0	0	0	0	0	0	0
Commercial banks and other	0	0	0	0	0	0	0	0	0	0
Memo:										
IBRD	-2	-3	4	15	-16	-20	-13	-6	-11	-9
IDA	0	0	0	0	0	0	0	0	0	0
DEBT SERVICE (LTDS)	**12**	**398**	**104**	**199**	**382**	**363**	**406**	**254**	**487**	**426**
Public and publicly guaranteed	**12**	**398**	**104**	**199**	**382**	**363**	**406**	**254**	**487**	**426**
Official creditors	8	39	85	137	264	300	371	229	453	391
Multilateral	5	4	34	74	68	90	86	43	58	85
Concessional	0	0	2	4	2	3	4	1	2	0
Bilateral	3	34	51	64	195	210	285	186	395	306
Concessional	3	6	2	19	49	45	71	50	69	47
Private creditors	4	359	19	61	119	63	35	25	34	36
Bonds	1	1	0	0	0	0	0	0	0	0
Commercial banks	0	266	8	18	53	40	27	22	30	35
Other private	4	93	11	43	66	23	8	4	4	1
Private nonguaranteed	**0**	**0**	**0**	**0**	**0**	**0**	**0**	**0**	**0**	**0**
Bonds	0	0	0	0	0	0	0	0	0	0
Commercial banks and other	0	0	0	0	0	0	0	0	0	0
Memo:										
IBRD	5	4	6	18	20	22	16	12	15	18
IDA	0	0	0	0	0	0	0	0	0	0
UNDISBURSED DEBT	**34**	**164**	**285**	**548**	**409**	**445**	**419**	**444**	**347**	**148**
Official creditors	15	133	268	548	409	445	382	357	299	133
Private creditors	19	31	17	0	0	0	37	87	48	14
Memorandum items										
Concessional LDOD	36	113	422	574	702	742	893	948	821	1,417
Variable rate LDOD	0	500	415	676	723	651	562	543	470	403
Public sector LDOD	65	1,246	3,148	3,694	3,976	3,972	3,665	3,833	3,290	3,512
Private sector LDOD	26	26	2	0	0	0	0	0	0	0

6. CURRENCY COMPOSITION OF LONG-TERM DEBT (PERCENT)

	1970	1980	1990	1994	1995	1996	1997	1998	1999	2000
Deutsche mark	4.9	4.8	8.4	11.9	8.4	7.8	7.1	6.7	6.0	4.4
French franc	43.2	39.0	54.8	47.6	47.4	46.4	45.3	45.6	43.6	35.2
Japanese yen	0.0	1.5	0.7	1.0	0.9	0.8	0.8	0.8	1.0	0.8
Pound sterling	0.0	0.8	5.3	4.4	5.0	5.6	6.0	5.8	6.0	4.6
Swiss franc	0.0	0.5	0.3	0.7	0.8	0.7	0.7	0.7	0.6	0.5
U.S.dollars	7.6	42.7	10.3	12.6	11.5	11.3	11.2	12.0	12.6	30.1
Multiple currency	32.2	1.5	3.7	8.0	8.8	8.9	8.7	6.7	7.7	6.2
Special drawing rights	0.0	0.0	0.0	0.3	0.2	0.2	0.0	0.0	0.0	0.0
All other currencies	12.1	9.2	16.5	13.5	17.0	18.3	20.2	21.7	22.5	18.2

GABON

(US$ million, unless otherwise indicated)

	1970	1980	1990	1994	1995	1996	1997	1998	1999	2000
7. DEBT RESTRUCTURINGS										
Total amount rescheduled	..	..	271	1,571	472	501	315	127	0	687
Debt stock rescheduled	..	..	0	74	0	0	0	0	0	0
Principal rescheduled	..	..	188	766	253	270	191	82	0	457
Official	..	..	32	397	249	266	190	82	0	457
Private	..	..	156	369	4	4	1	0	0	0
Interest rescheduled	..	..	77	449	68	64	45	21	0	230
Official	..	..	27	376	67	64	45	21	0	230
Private	..	..	50	73	1	0	0	0	0	0
Debt forgiven	..	..	0	240	40	0	2	0	0	0
Memo: interest forgiven	..	..	0	0	0	0	0	0	0	0
Debt stock reduction	..	..	0	0	1	0	0	0	0	0
of which debt buyback	..	..	0	0	0	0	0	0	0	0
8. DEBT STOCK-FLOW RECONCILIATION										
Total change in debt stocks	..	..	632	310	189	-50	-32	147	-446	17
Net flows on debt	17	-122	164	-18	14	-84	260	-172	-112	-399
Net change in interest arrears	..	..	88	-399	-51	0	0	79	15	-13
Interest capitalized	..	..	77	449	68	64	45	21	0	230
Debt forgiveness or reduction	..	..	0	-240	-41	0	-2	0	0	0
Cross-currency valuation	..	..	293	214	228	-180	-371	177	-344	-196
Residual	..	..	11	304	-27	151	37	41	-5	396
9. AVERAGE TERMS OF NEW COMMITMENTS										
ALL CREDITORS										
Interest (%)	5.1	11.2	7.9	5.5	4.7	6.2	6.0	4.7	0.0	0.0
Maturity (years)	10.8	11.2	17.9	16.2	13.0	15.5	11.4	9.2	0.0	0.0
Grace period (years)	1.5	3.4	4.8	5.1	5.9	5.4	3.9	2.5	0.0	0.0
Grant element (%)	19.2	-5.3	12.3	25.0	30.4	21.6	19.3	23.6	0.0	0.0
Official creditors										
Interest (%)	4.0	7.4	7.7	5.5	4.7	6.2	5.6	1.6	0.0	0.0
Maturity (years)	17.3	14.8	19.0	16.2	13.0	15.5	13.1	17.5	0.0	0.0
Grace period (years)	3.6	5.0	5.4	5.1	5.9	5.4	4.8	5.3	0.0	0.0
Grant element (%)	34.4	15.0	13.9	25.0	30.4	21.6	23.1	54.2	0.0	0.0
Private creditors										
Interest (%)	5.2	13.0	9.0	0.0	0.0	0.0	6.9	6.0	0.0	0.0
Maturity (years)	10.0	9.5	11.8	0.0	0.0	0.0	7.3	5.9	0.0	0.0
Grace period (years)	1.3	2.6	1.3	0.0	0.0	0.0	1.9	1.4	0.0	0.0
Grant element (%)	17.4	-15.4	3.3	0.0	0.0	0.0	10.2	11.2	0.0	0.0
Memorandum items										
Commitments	33	196	66	184	89	154	175	82	0	0
Official creditors	4	65	56	184	89	154	124	24	0	0
Private creditors	29	131	10	0	0	0	52	58	0	0

10. CONTRACTUAL OBLIGATIONS ON OUTSTANDING LONG-TERM DEBT

	2001	2002	2003	2004	2005	2006	2007	2008	2009	2010
TOTAL										
Disbursements	64	36	24	15	7	1	0	0	0	0
Principal	266	272	282	306	311	318	333	348	353	229
Interest	191	175	158	174	153	132	110	87	62	42
Official creditors										
Disbursements	52	33	24	15	7	1	0	0	0	0
Principal	231	239	254	292	305	315	332	347	352	228
Interest	184	170	154	172	153	132	110	87	62	41
Bilateral creditors										
Disbursements	0	0	0	0	0	0	0	0	0	0
Principal	173	185	198	239	253	266	286	304	315	196
Interest	150	138	125	146	129	112	94	74	51	33
Multilateral creditors										
Disbursements	52	33	24	15	7	1	0	0	0	0
Principal	58	55	56	53	51	49	46	43	37	33
Interest	34	32	29	26	23	20	16	13	10	8
Private creditors										
Disbursements	12	3	0	0	0	0	0	0	0	0
Principal	35	33	28	14	7	3	1	1	1	0
Interest	8	5	3	2	1	1	0	0	0	0
Commercial banks										
Disbursements	12	3	0	0	0	0	0	0	0	0
Principal	30	28	24	10	3	1	0	0	0	0
Interest	5	4	2	1	0	0	0	0	0	0
Other private										
Disbursements	0	0	0	0	0	0	0	0	0	0
Principal	5	5	4	4	4	1	1	1	1	0
Interest	2	2	1	1	1	1	0	0	0	0

GAMBIA, THE

(US$ million, unless otherwise indicated)

	1970	1980	1990	1994	1995	1996	1997	1998	1999	2000
1. SUMMARY DEBT DATA										
TOTAL DEBT STOCKS (EDT)	**5.1**	**136.8**	**369.1**	**423.0**	**427.1**	**452.8**	**425.3**	**459.2**	**464.3**	**470.8**
Long-term debt (LDOD)	**5.1**	**97.3**	**308.4**	**368.1**	**386.5**	**412.8**	**402.0**	**433.5**	**430.7**	**425.2**
Public and publicly guaranteed	5.1	97.3	308.4	368.1	386.5	412.8	402.0	433.5	430.7	425.2
Private nonguaranteed	0.0	0.0	0.0	0.0	0.0	0.0	0.0	0.0	0.0	0.0
Use of IMF credit	**0.0**	**16.2**	**44.9**	**31.3**	**25.8**	**17.6**	**10.2**	**10.4**	**11.3**	**18.1**
Short-term debt	**0.0**	**23.3**	**15.7**	**23.6**	**14.8**	**22.4**	**13.1**	**15.3**	**22.2**	**27.4**
of which interest arrears on LDOD	0.0	0.3	0.6	0.6	0.7	0.0	0.1	0.0	0.1	0.2
Official creditors	0.0	0.2	0.6	0.6	0.7	0.0	0.1	0.0	0.1	0.2
Private creditors	0.0	0.1	0.0	0.0	0.0	0.0	0.0	0.0	0.0	0.0
Memo: principal arrears on LDOD	0.0	0.0	0.9	5.7	3.2	0.2	0.2	0.1	1.3	2.0
Official creditors	0.0	0.0	0.9	5.7	3.1	0.2	0.2	0.1	1.3	2.0
Private creditors	0.0	0.0	0.0	0.1	0.1	0.0	0.0	0.0	0.0	0.0
Memo: export credits	0.0	0.0	32.0	34.4	28.1	23.2	22.3	17.9	12.8	11.3
TOTAL DEBT FLOWS										
Disbursements	**0.8**	**55.7**	**32.8**	**22.7**	**23.0**	**58.1**	**24.0**	**20.9**	**26.2**	**30.3**
Long-term debt	0.8	51.2	23.5	22.7	23.0	58.1	24.0	16.2	21.5	21.3
IMF purchases	0.0	4.4	9.3	0.0	0.0	0.0	0.0	4.7	4.7	9.1
Principal repayments	**0.1**	**0.4**	**25.5**	**23.5**	**20.7**	**22.2**	**19.8**	**20.1**	**14.8**	**12.0**
Long-term debt	0.1	0.4	20.2	19.6	14.5	14.8	13.5	15.2	11.3	10.4
IMF repurchases	0.0	0.0	5.3	3.9	6.2	7.4	6.4	4.9	3.5	1.6
Net flows on debt	**0.7**	**58.3**	**15.5**	**-19.8**	**-6.6**	**44.1**	**-5.3**	**3.0**	**18.2**	**23.4**
of which short-term debt	0.0	3.0	8.1	-19.0	-8.8	8.2	-9.4	2.3	6.8	5.2
Interest payments (INT)	**0.0**	**3.8**	**12.3**	**7.6**	**5.9**	**5.7**	**6.8**	**6.3**	**6.5**	**6.6**
Long-term debt	0.0	0.4	10.2	5.8	4.8	4.5	5.7	5.4	5.5	5.3
IMF charges	0.0	0.5	1.3	0.2	0.2	0.1	0.1	0.1	0.0	0.1
Short-term debt	0.0	2.9	0.8	1.6	0.9	1.1	1.1	0.8	1.0	1.2
Net transfers on debt	**0.7**	**54.5**	**3.2**	**-27.4**	**-12.5**	**38.3**	**-12.1**	**-3.3**	**11.7**	**16.9**
Total debt service paid (TDS)	**0.1**	**4.1**	**37.7**	**31.1**	**26.6**	**28.0**	**26.7**	**26.4**	**21.4**	**18.6**
Long-term debt	0.1	0.8	30.3	25.4	19.3	19.3	19.1	20.7	16.8	15.7
IMF repurchases and charges	0.0	0.5	6.7	4.1	6.4	7.6	6.4	4.9	3.6	1.7
Short-term debt (interest only)	0.0	2.9	0.8	1.6	0.9	1.1	1.1	0.8	1.0	1.2
2. AGGREGATE NET RESOURCE FLOWS AND NET TRANSFERS (LONG-TERM)										
NET RESOURCE FLOWS	**0.9**	**78.0**	**48.1**	**50.4**	**33.7**	**67.2**	**40.1**	**38.0**	**38.1**	**46.6**
Net flow of long-term debt (ex. IMF)	0.7	50.9	3.4	3.1	8.5	43.3	10.5	1.0	10.2	10.8
Foreign direct investment (net)	0.1	0.0	0.0	9.7	7.7	10.7	12.0	13.0	14.0	14.0
Portfolio equity flows	0.0	0.0	0.0	0.0	0.0	0.0	0.0	0.0	0.0	0.0
Grants (excluding technical coop.)	0.1	27.2	44.7	37.6	17.6	13.2	17.6	24.0	13.9	21.7
Memo: technical coop. grants	0.7	12.7	24.2	23.9	22.8	18.0	14.1	11.4	12.2	9.7
official net resource flows	0.8	56.7	55.6	45.0	26.4	56.7	28.1	25.0	23.3	32.7
private net resource flows	0.1	21.3	-7.5	5.4	7.3	10.5	12.0	13.0	14.8	13.9
NET TRANSFERS	**0.9**	**75.6**	**37.9**	**44.6**	**28.9**	**62.7**	**34.4**	**32.6**	**32.6**	**41.3**
Interest on long-term debt	0.0	0.4	10.2	5.8	4.8	4.5	5.7	5.4	5.5	5.3
Profit remittances on FDI	0.0	2.0	0.0	0.0	0.0	0.0	0.0	0.0	0.0	0.0
Memo: official net transfers	0.8	56.3	50.1	39.4	21.6	52.2	22.4	19.6	17.8	27.5
private net transfers	0.1	19.3	-12.2	5.2	7.3	10.5	12.0	13.0	14.8	13.8
3. MAJOR ECONOMIC AGGREGATES										
Gross national income (GNI)	52.3	237.0	291.4	357.8	377.1	385.5	401.3	409.0	424.4	415.3
Exports of goods & services (XGS)	..	66.2	169.7	220.3	181.0	226.0	232.7	267.5	249.7	267.3
of which workers remittances	..	0.0	0.0	0.0	0.0	0.0	0.0	0.0	0.0	0.0
Imports of goods & services (MGS)	..	181.5	205.4	253.8	241.4	303.4	293.1	339.7	320.6	330.7
International reserves (RES)	8.1	5.7	55.4	98.0	106.1	102.1	96.0	106.4	111.2	109.4
Current account balance	..	-86.9	23.4	8.2	-8.2	-47.7	-23.6	-43.1	-45.7	-48.5
4. DEBT INDICATORS										
EDT / XGS (%)	..	206.5	217.5	192.0	235.9	200.4	182.8	171.7	185.9	176.2
EDT / GNI (%)	9.8	57.7	126.7	118.2	113.3	117.5	106.0	112.3	109.4	113.4
TDS / XGS (%)	..	6.2	22.2	14.1	14.7	12.4	11.5	9.9	8.6	7.0
INT / XGS (%)	..	5.7	7.3	3.5	3.3	2.5	2.9	2.4	2.6	2.5
INT / GNI (%)	0.0	1.6	4.2	2.1	1.6	1.5	1.7	1.5	1.5	1.6
RES / EDT (%)	159.0	4.1	15.0	23.2	24.9	22.6	22.6	23.2	24.0	23.2
RES / MGS (months)	..	0.4	3.2	4.6	5.3	4.0	3.9	3.8	4.2	4.0
Short-term / EDT (%)	0.0	17.0	4.3	5.6	3.5	5.0	3.1	3.3	4.8	5.8
Concessional / EDT (%)	96.1	49.9	67.8	79.4	84.9	87.2	91.4	90.9	89.9	88.1
Multilateral / EDT (%)	0.0	29.9	55.0	71.8	76.4	72.3	76.7	75.7	74.4	72.4

GAMBIA, THE

(US$ million, unless otherwise indicated)

	1970	1980	1990	1994	1995	1996	1997	1998	1999	2000
5. LONG-TERM DEBT										
DEBT OUTSTANDING (LDOD)	**5.1**	**97.3**	**308.4**	**368.1**	**386.5**	**412.8**	**402.0**	**433.5**	**430.7**	**425.2**
Public and publicly guaranteed	**5.1**	**97.3**	**308.4**	**368.1**	**386.5**	**412.8**	**402.0**	**433.5**	**430.7**	**425.2**
Official creditors	5.1	73.4	290.1	367.5	386.3	412.8	402.0	433.5	429.9	424.5
Multilateral	0.0	40.9	203.1	303.5	326.2	327.5	326.0	347.4	345.6	340.7
Concessional	0.0	35.8	183.3	278.8	305.4	310.0	312.7	331.2	333.3	330.9
Bilateral	5.1	32.5	87.0	64.0	60.0	85.3	76.0	86.0	84.3	83.7
Concessional	4.9	32.5	66.8	57.1	57.0	84.9	76.0	86.0	84.3	83.7
Private creditors	0.0	23.9	18.3	0.5	0.2	0.0	0.0	0.0	0.8	0.7
Bonds	0.0	0.0	0.0	0.0	0.0	0.0	0.0	0.0	0.0	0.0
Commercial banks	0.0	7.4	16.0	0.0	0.0	0.0	0.0	0.0	0.0	0.0
Other private	0.0	16.5	2.3	0.5	0.2	0.0	0.0	0.0	0.8	0.7
Private nonguaranteed	**0.0**	**0.0**	**0.0**	**0.0**	**0.0**	**0.0**	**0.0**	**0.0**	**0.0**	**0.0**
Bonds	0.0	0.0	0.0	0.0	0.0	0.0	0.0	0.0	0.0	0.0
Commercial banks and other	0.0	0.0	0.0	0.0	0.0	0.0	0.0	0.0	0.0	0.0
Memo:										
IBRD	0.0	0.0	0.0	0.0	0.0	0.0	0.0	0.0	0.0	0.0
IDA	0.0	15.9	101.6	147.8	161.6	165.9	165.6	172.6	172.8	170.7
DISBURSEMENTS	**0.8**	**51.2**	**23.5**	**22.7**	**23.0**	**58.1**	**24.0**	**16.2**	**21.5**	**21.3**
Public and publicly guaranteed	**0.8**	**51.2**	**23.5**	**22.7**	**23.0**	**58.1**	**24.0**	**16.2**	**21.5**	**21.3**
Official creditors	0.8	29.6	23.5	22.7	23.0	58.1	24.0	16.2	20.7	21.3
Multilateral	0.0	18.3	17.7	21.7	19.0	22.4	23.1	14.3	15.6	17.7
Concessional	0.0	16.1	16.6	21.1	18.9	22.4	23.1	14.3	15.6	17.7
Bilateral	0.8	11.3	5.8	1.0	4.0	35.7	0.8	1.9	5.1	3.6
Concessional	0.8	11.3	5.8	1.0	4.0	35.7	0.8	1.9	5.1	3.6
Private creditors	0.0	21.7	0.0	0.0	0.0	0.0	0.0	0.0	0.8	0.0
Bonds	0.0	0.0	0.0	0.0	0.0	0.0	0.0	0.0	0.0	0.0
Commercial banks	0.0	7.0	0.0	0.0	0.0	0.0	0.0	0.0	0.0	0.0
Other private	0.0	14.7	0.0	0.0	0.0	0.0	0.0	0.0	0.8	0.0
Private nonguaranteed	**0.0**	**0.0**	**0.0**	**0.0**	**0.0**	**0.0**	**0.0**	**0.0**	**0.0**	**0.0**
Bonds	0.0	0.0	0.0	0.0	0.0	0.0	0.0	0.0	0.0	0.0
Commercial banks and other	0.0	0.0	0.0	0.0	0.0	0.0	0.0	0.0	0.0	0.0
Memo:										
IBRD	0.0	0.0	0.0	0.0	0.0	0.0	0.0	0.0	0.0	0.0
IDA	0.0	5.2	9.8	9.2	11.6	10.1	9.1	3.1	5.5	7.7
PRINCIPAL REPAYMENTS	**0.1**	**0.4**	**20.2**	**19.6**	**14.5**	**14.8**	**13.5**	**15.2**	**11.3**	**10.4**
Public and publicly guaranteed	**0.1**	**0.4**	**20.2**	**19.6**	**14.5**	**14.8**	**13.5**	**15.2**	**11.3**	**10.4**
Official creditors	0.1	0.0	12.7	15.3	14.1	14.6	13.5	15.2	11.3	10.3
Multilateral	0.0	0.0	4.7	5.5	6.7	6.4	6.6	8.3	6.9	7.2
Concessional	0.0	0.0	2.7	3.2	3.4	3.6	4.0	6.0	4.7	5.6
Bilateral	0.1	0.0	7.9	9.7	7.5	8.2	6.8	6.9	4.4	3.1
Concessional	0.1	0.0	7.9	5.8	3.4	5.7	6.4	6.9	4.4	3.1
Private creditors	0.0	0.3	7.5	4.3	0.4	0.2	0.0	0.0	0.0	0.1
Bonds	0.0	0.0	0.0	0.0	0.0	0.0	0.0	0.0	0.0	0.0
Commercial banks	0.0	0.1	3.0	4.0	0.0	0.0	0.0	0.0	0.0	0.0
Other private	0.0	0.3	4.5	0.3	0.4	0.2	0.0	0.0	0.0	0.1
Private nonguaranteed	**0.0**	**0.0**	**0.0**	**0.0**	**0.0**	**0.0**	**0.0**	**0.0**	**0.0**	**0.0**
Bonds	0.0	0.0	0.0	0.0	0.0	0.0	0.0	0.0	0.0	0.0
Commercial banks and other	0.0	0.0	0.0	0.0	0.0	0.0	0.0	0.0	0.0	0.0
Memo:										
IBRD	0.0	0.0	0.0	0.0	0.0	0.0	0.0	0.0	0.0	0.0
IDA	0.0	0.0	0.3	0.6	0.8	1.0	1.3	1.4	1.9	2.3
NET FLOWS ON DEBT	**0.7**	**50.9**	**3.4**	**3.1**	**8.5**	**43.3**	**10.5**	**1.0**	**10.2**	**10.8**
Public and publicly guaranteed	**0.7**	**50.9**	**3.4**	**3.1**	**8.5**	**43.3**	**10.5**	**1.0**	**10.2**	**10.8**
Official creditors	0.7	29.5	10.9	7.4	8.8	43.5	10.5	1.0	9.4	11.0
Multilateral	0.0	18.3	13.0	16.1	12.3	16.0	16.5	6.0	8.7	10.5
Concessional	0.0	16.1	13.9	17.9	15.5	18.8	19.1	8.3	10.9	12.1
Bilateral	0.7	11.3	-2.1	-8.7	-3.5	27.5	-6.0	-5.0	0.7	0.4
Concessional	0.7	11.3	-2.1	-4.8	0.6	30.0	-5.6	-5.0	0.7	0.4
Private creditors	0.0	21.3	-7.5	-4.3	-0.4	-0.2	0.0	0.0	0.8	-0.1
Bonds	0.0	0.0	0.0	0.0	0.0	0.0	0.0	0.0	0.0	0.0
Commercial banks	0.0	6.9	-3.0	-4.0	0.0	0.0	0.0	0.0	0.0	0.0
Other private	0.0	14.4	-4.5	-0.3	-0.4	-0.2	0.0	0.0	0.8	-0.1
Private nonguaranteed	**0.0**	**0.0**	**0.0**	**0.0**	**0.0**	**0.0**	**0.0**	**0.0**	**0.0**	**0.0**
Bonds	0.0	0.0	0.0	0.0	0.0	0.0	0.0	0.0	0.0	0.0
Commercial banks and other	0.0	0.0	0.0	0.0	0.0	0.0	0.0	0.0	0.0	0.0
Memo:										
IBRD	0.0	0.0	0.0	0.0	0.0	0.0	0.0	0.0	0.0	0.0
IDA	0.0	5.2	9.5	8.6	10.9	9.1	7.8	1.7	3.6	5.4

GAMBIA, THE

(US$ million, unless otherwise indicated)

	1970	1980	1990	1994	1995	1996	1997	1998	1999	2000
INTEREST PAYMENTS (LINT)	**0.0**	**0.4**	**10.2**	**5.8**	**4.8**	**4.5**	**5.7**	**5.4**	**5.5**	**5.3**
Public and publicly guaranteed	**0.0**	**0.4**	**10.2**	**5.8**	**4.8**	**4.5**	**5.7**	**5.4**	**5.5**	**5.3**
Official creditors	0.0	0.4	5.5	5.6	4.8	4.5	5.7	5.4	5.5	5.2
Multilateral	0.0	0.4	2.9	3.5	3.5	3.4	3.4	3.3	3.5	3.5
Concessional	0.0	0.2	1.5	2.4	2.2	2.4	2.7	2.7	3.0	3.1
Bilateral	0.0	0.0	2.6	2.0	1.3	1.2	2.3	2.1	2.0	1.7
Concessional	0.0	0.0	2.6	1.3	0.8	1.0	2.3	2.1	2.0	1.7
Private creditors	0.0	0.0	4.7	0.2	0.0	0.0	0.0	0.0	0.0	0.1
Bonds	0.0	0.0	0.0	0.0	0.0	0.0	0.0	0.0	0.0	0.0
Commercial banks	0.0	0.0	3.8	0.2	0.0	0.0	0.0	0.0	0.0	0.0
Other private	0.0	0.0	0.9	0.0	0.0	0.0	0.0	0.0	0.0	0.1
Private nonguaranteed	**0.0**	**0.0**	**0.0**	**0.0**	**0.0**	**0.0**	**0.0**	**0.0**	**0.0**	**0.0**
Bonds	0.0	0.0	0.0	0.0	0.0	0.0	0.0	0.0	0.0	0.0
Commercial banks and other	0.0	0.0	0.0	0.0	0.0	0.0	0.0	0.0	0.0	0.0
Memo:										
IBRD	0.0	0.0	0.0	0.0	0.0	0.0	0.0	0.0	0.0	0.0
IDA	0.0	0.1	0.7	1.1	1.2	1.2	1.2	1.2	1.3	1.2
NET TRANSFERS ON DEBT	**0.7**	**50.5**	**-6.8**	**-2.7**	**3.7**	**38.8**	**4.8**	**-4.5**	**4.8**	**5.5**
Public and publicly guaranteed	**0.7**	**50.5**	**-6.8**	**-2.7**	**3.7**	**38.8**	**4.8**	**-4.5**	**4.8**	**5.5**
Official creditors	0.7	29.2	5.4	1.9	4.1	39.0	4.8	-4.5	3.9	5.8
Multilateral	0.0	17.9	10.1	12.6	8.8	12.7	13.1	2.7	5.2	7.1
Concessional	0.0	15.9	12.4	15.5	13.4	16.4	16.4	5.6	7.9	9.0
Bilateral	0.7	11.3	-4.7	-10.8	-4.7	26.3	-8.3	-7.1	-1.3	-1.3
Concessional	0.7	11.3	-4.7	-6.1	-0.1	29.0	-7.8	-7.1	-1.3	-1.3
Private creditors	0.0	21.3	-12.1	-4.6	-0.4	-0.2	0.0	0.0	0.8	-0.2
Bonds	0.0	0.0	0.0	0.0	0.0	0.0	0.0	0.0	0.0	0.0
Commercial banks	0.0	6.9	-6.8	-4.2	0.0	0.0	0.0	0.0	0.0	0.0
Other private	0.0	14.4	-5.4	-0.4	-0.4	-0.2	0.0	0.0	0.8	-0.2
Private nonguaranteed	**0.0**	**0.0**	**0.0**	**0.0**	**0.0**	**0.0**	**0.0**	**0.0**	**0.0**	**0.0**
Bonds	0.0	0.0	0.0	0.0	0.0	0.0	0.0	0.0	0.0	0.0
Commercial banks and other	0.0	0.0	0.0	0.0	0.0	0.0	0.0	0.0	0.0	0.0
Memo:										
IBRD	0.0	0.0	0.0	0.0	0.0	0.0	0.0	0.0	0.0	0.0
IDA	0.0	5.1	8.8	7.5	9.7	7.9	6.6	0.4	2.4	4.2
DEBT SERVICE (LTDS)	**0.1**	**0.8**	**30.3**	**25.4**	**19.3**	**19.3**	**19.1**	**20.7**	**16.8**	**15.7**
Public and publicly guaranteed	**0.1**	**0.8**	**30.3**	**25.4**	**19.3**	**19.3**	**19.1**	**20.7**	**16.8**	**15.7**
Official creditors	0.1	0.4	18.2	20.8	18.9	19.1	19.1	20.7	16.8	15.5
Multilateral	0.0	0.4	7.7	9.1	10.2	9.7	10.0	11.6	10.4	10.6
Concessional	0.0	0.2	4.2	5.6	5.6	6.0	6.7	8.7	7.6	8.7
Bilateral	0.1	0.0	10.5	11.8	8.7	9.4	9.1	9.0	6.4	4.9
Concessional	0.1	0.0	10.5	7.2	4.1	6.7	8.7	9.0	6.4	4.9
Private creditors	0.0	0.4	12.1	4.6	0.4	0.2	0.0	0.0	0.0	0.2
Bonds	0.0	0.0	0.0	0.0	0.0	0.0	0.0	0.0	0.0	0.0
Commercial banks	0.0	0.1	6.8	4.2	0.0	0.0	0.0	0.0	0.0	0.0
Other private	0.0	0.3	5.4	0.4	0.4	0.2	0.0	0.0	0.0	0.2
Private nonguaranteed	**0.0**	**0.0**	**0.0**	**0.0**	**0.0**	**0.0**	**0.0**	**0.0**	**0.0**	**0.0**
Bonds	0.0	0.0	0.0	0.0	0.0	0.0	0.0	0.0	0.0	0.0
Commercial banks and other	0.0	0.0	0.0	0.0	0.0	0.0	0.0	0.0	0.0	0.0
Memo:										
IBRD	0.0	0.0	0.0	0.0	0.0	0.0	0.0	0.0	0.0	0.0
IDA	0.0	0.1	1.0	1.7	1.9	2.2	2.5	2.6	3.2	3.5
UNDISBURSED DEBT	**5.5**	**106.3**	**167.7**	**102.8**	**124.5**	**71.2**	**64.7**	**112.1**	**143.7**	**129.7**
Official creditors	5.5	87.7	167.7	102.8	124.5	71.2	64.7	112.1	143.7	129.7
Private creditors	0.0	18.6	0.0	0.0	0.0	0.0	0.0	0.0	0.0	0.0
Memorandum items										
Concessional LDOD	4.9	68.3	250.1	335.9	362.4	394.8	388.7	417.3	417.6	414.6
Variable rate LDOD	0.0	7.7	17.6	0.9	0.6	0.2	0.0	0.0	0.0	0.0
Public sector LDOD	5.1	94.0	306.6	367.6	386.3	412.8	402.0	433.5	430.7	425.2
Private sector LDOD	0.0	3.4	1.8	0.5	0.2	0.0	0.0	0.0	0.0	0.0

6. CURRENCY COMPOSITION OF LONG-TERM DEBT (PERCENT)

	1970	1980	1990	1994	1995	1996	1997	1998	1999	2000
Deutsche mark	0.0	1.8	1.8	0.5	0.3	0.2	0.1	0.1	0.1	0.1
French franc	0.0	1.4	7.7	3.8	3.2	2.2	1.5	0.7	0.3	0.3
Japanese yen	0.0	0.0	0.0	0.0	0.0	0.0	0.0	0.0	0.0	0.0
Pound sterling	100.0	16.3	8.5	6.7	6.3	5.8	5.9	5.3	5.1	5.0
Swiss franc	0.0	0.5	1.3	0.4	0.2	0.0	0.0	0.0	0.0	0.0
U.S.dollars	0.0	32.3	39.1	39.8	43.4	49.3	50.2	50.4	52.1	52.8
Multiple currency	0.0	6.9	19.8	24.6	24.7	22.0	21.6	21.5	21.3	20.5
Special drawing rights	0.0	0.0	0.0	0.0	0.0	0.0	0.1	0.1	0.4	0.7
All other currencies	0.0	40.8	21.8	24.2	21.9	20.5	20.6	21.9	20.7	20.6

GAMBIA, THE

(US$ million, unless otherwise indicated)

	1970	1980	1990	1994	1995	1996	1997	1998	1999	2000
7. DEBT RESTRUCTURINGS										
Total amount rescheduled	..	..	0.0	0.0	0.0	0.0	0.0	0.0	0.0	0.0
Debt stock rescheduled	..	..	0.0	0.0	0.0	0.0	0.0	0.0	0.0	0.0
Principal rescheduled	..	..	0.0	0.0	0.0	0.0	0.0	0.0	0.0	0.0
Official	..	..	0.0	0.0	0.0	0.0	0.0	0.0	0.0	0.0
Private	..	..	0.0	0.0	0.0	0.0	0.0	0.0	0.0	0.0
Interest rescheduled	..	..	0.0	0.0	0.0	0.0	0.0	0.0	0.0	0.0
Official	..	..	0.0	0.0	0.0	0.0	0.0	0.0	0.0	0.0
Private	..	..	0.0	0.0	0.0	0.0	0.0	0.0	0.0	0.0
Debt forgiven	..	..	0.0	0.0	0.0	0.0	0.0	0.0	0.0	0.0
Memo: interest forgiven	..	..	0.0	0.0	0.0	0.0	0.0	0.0	0.0	0.0
Debt stock reduction	..	..	0.0	0.0	0.0	0.0	0.0	0.0	0.0	0.0
of which debt buyback	..	..	0.0	0.0	0.0	0.0	0.0	0.0	0.0	0.0
8. DEBT STOCK-FLOW RECONCILIATION										
Total change in debt stocks	..	..	31.4	-3.0	4.1	25.7	-27.4	33.9	5.0	6.5
Net flows on debt	0.7	58.3	15.5	-19.8	-6.6	44.1	-5.3	3.0	18.2	23.4
Net change in interest arrears	..	..	-3.5	0.0	0.1	-0.7	0.1	0.0	0.0	0.1
Interest capitalized	..	..	0.0	0.0	0.0	0.0	0.0	0.0	0.0	0.0
Debt forgiveness or reduction	..	..	0.0	0.0	0.0	0.0	0.0	0.0	0.0	0.0
Cross-currency valuation	..	..	3.3	-14.8	-17.5	-39.2	-38.9	-19.0	-12.1	-9.5
Residual	..	..	16.1	31.7	28.2	21.4	16.7	49.9	-1.1	-7.6
9. AVERAGE TERMS OF NEW COMMITMENTS										
ALL CREDITORS										
Interest (%)	0.7	3.9	0.8	0.8	3.5	0.4	1.0	1.1	1.4	1.7
Maturity (years)	49.7	20.3	42.1	41.6	21.3	27.2	49.6	33.0	30.9	33.2
Grace period (years)	10.4	4.9	10.0	9.6	6.2	7.1	10.5	8.6	6.2	7.4
Grant element (%)	83.3	39.1	79.7	78.0	45.7	71.3	80.5	71.6	65.7	64.6
Official creditors										
Interest (%)	0.7	1.7	0.8	0.8	3.5	0.4	1.0	1.1	1.3	1.7
Maturity (years)	49.7	25.1	42.1	41.6	21.3	27.2	49.6	33.0	31.3	33.2
Grace period (years)	10.4	5.8	10.0	9.6	6.2	7.1	10.5	8.6	6.3	7.4
Grant element (%)	83.3	55.8	79.7	78.0	45.7	71.3	80.5	71.6	66.6	64.6
Private creditors										
Interest (%)	0.0	7.5	0.0	0.0	0.0	0.0	0.0	0.0	9.0	0.0
Maturity (years)	0.0	12.2	0.0	0.0	0.0	0.0	0.0	0.0	6.4	0.0
Grace period (years)	0.0	3.4	0.0	0.0	0.0	0.0	0.0	0.0	1.4	0.0
Grant element (%)	0.0	11.3	0.0	0.0	0.0	0.0	0.0	0.0	2.4	0.0
Memorandum items										
Commitments	2.1	72.9	37.9	43.8	40.3	9.9	21.6	59.8	60.0	12.5
Official creditors	2.1	45.7	37.9	43.8	40.3	9.9	21.6	59.8	59.2	12.5
Private creditors	0.0	27.3	0.0	0.0	0.0	0.0	0.0	0.0	0.8	0.0

10. CONTRACTUAL OBLIGATIONS ON OUTSTANDING LONG-TERM DEBT

	2001	2002	2003	2004	2005	2006	2007	2008	2009	2010
TOTAL										
Disbursements	39.1	34.1	24.4	16.0	8.8	3.7	2.5	0.6	0.3	0.0
Principal	16.8	16.8	16.3	17.9	18.0	17.6	17.9	17.9	19.0	19.3
Interest	5.4	5.4	5.4	5.2	5.0	4.8	4.5	4.2	4.0	3.7
Official creditors										
Disbursements	39.1	34.1	24.4	16.0	8.8	3.7	2.5	0.6	0.3	0.0
Principal	16.6	16.7	16.2	17.7	17.9	17.6	17.9	17.9	19.0	19.3
Interest	5.4	5.4	5.3	5.2	5.0	4.8	4.5	4.2	4.0	3.7
Bilateral creditors										
Disbursements	5.3	3.6	2.4	1.4	0.7	0.3	0.2	0.0	0.0	0.0
Principal	7.8	7.7	6.4	7.0	6.8	6.3	5.9	5.9	5.9	4.9
Interest	2.0	1.9	1.9	1.8	1.6	1.5	1.4	1.3	1.1	1.0
Multilateral creditors										
Disbursements	33.8	30.5	22.1	14.6	8.1	3.4	2.3	0.6	0.3	0.0
Principal	8.9	9.0	9.7	10.7	11.1	11.4	12.0	12.0	13.1	14.3
Interest	3.4	3.5	3.5	3.4	3.4	3.2	3.1	3.0	2.9	2.7
Private creditors										
Disbursements	0.0	0.0	0.0	0.0	0.0	0.0	0.0	0.0	0.0	0.0
Principal	0.2	0.2	0.2	0.2	0.1	0.0	0.0	0.0	0.0	0.0
Interest	0.1	0.0	0.0	0.0	0.0	0.0	0.0	0.0	0.0	0.0
Commercial banks										
Disbursements	0.0	0.0	0.0	0.0	0.0	0.0	0.0	0.0	0.0	0.0
Principal	0.0	0.0	0.0	0.0	0.0	0.0	0.0	0.0	0.0	0.0
Interest	0.0	0.0	0.0	0.0	0.0	0.0	0.0	0.0	0.0	0.0
Other private										
Disbursements	0.0	0.0	0.0	0.0	0.0	0.0	0.0	0.0	0.0	0.0
Principal	0.2	0.2	0.2	0.2	0.1	0.0	0.0	0.0	0.0	0.0
Interest	0.1	0.0	0.0	0.0	0.0	0.0	0.0	0.0	0.0	0.0

GEORGIA

(US$ million, unless otherwise indicated)

	1970	1980	1990	1994	1995	1996	1997	1998	1999	2000
1. SUMMARY DEBT DATA										
TOTAL DEBT STOCKS (EDT)	..	..	..	**1,450**	**1,240**	**1,361**	**1,466**	**1,648**	**1,652**	**1,633**
Long-term debt (LDOD)	..	..	..	**924**	**1,039**	**1,106**	**1,190**	**1,316**	**1,324**	**1,311**
Public and publicly guaranteed	..	..	..	924	1,039	1,106	1,190	1,301	1,307	1,271
Private nonguaranteed	..	..	..	0	0	0	0	15	17	40
Use of IMF credit	..	..	..	**41**	**116**	**192**	**255**	**304**	**320**	**278**
Short-term debt	..	..	..	**485**	**86**	**64**	**22**	**28**	**7**	**44**
of which interest arrears on LDOD	..	..	..	15	62	43	18	0	1	1
Official creditors	..	..	..	15	54	30	18	0	1	1
Private creditors	..	..	..	0	8	13	0	0	0	0
Memo: principal arrears on LDOD	..	..	..	43	211	135	77	59	113	180
Official creditors	..	..	..	42	203	118	77	59	113	180
Private creditors	..	..	..	1	8	17	0	0	0	0
Memo: export credits	..	..	..	89	106	100	84	90	82	76
TOTAL DEBT FLOWS										
Disbursements	..	..	..	**134**	**174**	**173**	**173**	**279**	**141**	**60**
Long-term debt	..	..	..	94	98	92	96	241	95	60
IMF purchases	..	..	..	40	76	81	76	38	46	0
Principal repayments	..	..	..	**1**	**0**	**1**	**3**	**150**	**62**	**68**
Long-term debt	..	..	..	1	0	1	3	149	40	42
IMF repurchases	..	..	..	0	0	0	0	1	22	26
Net flows on debt	..	..	..	**603**	**-272**	**169**	**153**	**153**	**57**	**29**
of which short-term debt	..	..	..	470	-446	-3	-17	24	-22	36
Interest payments (INT)	..	..	..	**5**	**20**	**12**	**44**	**63**	**47**	**49**
Long-term debt	..	..	..	5	17	6	37	57	42	43
IMF charges	..	..	..	0	3	5	6	6	5	5
Short-term debt	..	..	..	0	0	1	1	1	0	1
Net transfers on debt	..	..	..	**598**	**-292**	**157**	**109**	**90**	**10**	**-21**
Total debt service paid (TDS)	..	..	..	**6**	**20**	**13**	**46**	**213**	**109**	**117**
Long-term debt	..	..	..	6	17	7	40	205	82	85
IMF repurchases and charges	..	..	..	0	3	5	6	7	26	31
Short-term debt (interest only)	..	..	..	0	0	1	1	1	0	1
2. AGGREGATE NET RESOURCE FLOWS AND NET TRANSFERS (LONG-TERM)										
NET RESOURCE FLOWS	..	..	..	**271**	**191**	**214**	**390**	**420**	**203**	**207**
Net flow of long-term debt (ex. IMF)	..	..	..	93	98	91	94	93	55	18
Foreign direct investment (net)	..	..	..	6	8	40	243	265	82	131
Portfolio equity flows	..	..	..	0	0	0	0	0	0	0
Grants (excluding technical coop.)	..	..	..	172	85	83	53	62	66	57
Memo: technical coop. grants	..	..	..	3	37	46	19	26	41	83
official net resource flows	..	..	..	266	183	174	147	148	116	52
private net resource flows	..	..	..	5	8	40	243	272	86	155
NET TRANSFERS	..	..	..	**266**	**173**	**208**	**353**	**364**	**156**	**155**
Interest on long-term debt	..	..	..	5	17	6	37	57	42	43
Profit remittances on FDI	..	..	..	0	0	0	0	0	5	8
Memo: official net transfers	..	..	..	261	165	168	110	92	76	10
private net transfers	..	..	..	5	8	40	243	271	80	146
3. MAJOR ECONOMIC AGGREGATES										
Gross national income (GNI)	..	..	..	1,628	1,816	3,018	3,712	3,737	2,923	3,042
Exports of goods & services (XGS)	..	..	..	473	486	516	848	914	945	1,224
of which workers remittances	..	..	..	..	0	0	0	0	0	0
Imports of goods & services (MGS)	..	..	..	923	890	931	1,419	1,513	1,359	1,486
International reserves (RES)	..	..	..	..	194	189	200	123	132	109
Current account balance	..	..	..	-278	-215	-275	-375	-389	-238	-162
4. DEBT INDICATORS										
EDT / XGS (%)	..	..	..	306.6	255.4	263.9	172.9	180.4	174.8	133.4
EDT / GNI (%)	..	..	..	89.1	68.3	45.1	39.5	44.1	56.5	53.7
TDS / XGS (%)	..	..	..	1.3	4.1	2.5	5.5	23.3	11.5	9.6
INT / XGS (%)	..	..	..	1.0	4.1	2.3	5.1	6.9	5.0	4.0
INT / GNI (%)	..	..	..	0.3	1.1	0.4	1.2	1.7	1.6	1.6
RES / EDT (%)	..	..	..	..	15.6	13.9	13.6	7.5	8.0	6.7
RES / MGS (months)	..	..	..	..	2.6	2.4	1.7	1.0	1.2	0.9
Short-term / EDT (%)	..	..	..	33.5	6.9	4.7	1.5	1.7	0.4	2.7
Concessional / EDT (%)	..	..	..	0.1	6.9	30.3	43.5	46.0	49.6	48.9
Multilateral / EDT (%)	..	..	..	9.7	19.7	23.0	24.7	26.4	29.1	29.4

GEORGIA

(US$ million, unless otherwise indicated)

	1970	1980	1990	1994	1995	1996	1997	1998	1999	2000
5. LONG-TERM DEBT										
DEBT OUTSTANDING (LDOD)	..	..	..	**924**	**1,039**	**1,106**	**1,190**	**1,316**	**1,324**	**1,311**
Public and publicly guaranteed	..	..	..	**924**	**1,039**	**1,106**	**1,190**	**1,301**	**1,307**	**1,271**
Official creditors	..	..	..	833	939	1,014	1,187	1,298	1,305	1,269
Multilateral	..	..	..	141	245	313	363	436	481	480
Concessional	..	..	..	1	84	157	212	275	348	350
Bilateral	..	..	..	692	694	701	824	863	824	788
Concessional	..	..	..	0	2	256	426	484	471	448
Private creditors	..	..	..	91	100	93	3	3	2	2
Bonds	..	..	..	0	0	0	0	0	0	0
Commercial banks	..	..	..	0	0	0	0	0	0	0
Other private	..	..	..	91	100	93	3	3	2	2
Private nonguaranteed	..	..	..	**0**	**0**	**0**	**0**	**15**	**17**	**40**
Bonds	..	..	..	0	0	0	0	0	0	0
Commercial banks and other	..	..	..	0	0	0	0	15	17	40
Memo:										
IBRD	..	..	..	0	0	0	0	0	0	0
IDA	..	..	..	1	84	157	212	274	346	347
DISBURSEMENTS	..	..	..	**94**	**98**	**92**	**96**	**241**	**95**	**60**
Public and publicly guaranteed	..	..	..	**94**	**98**	**92**	**96**	**234**	**90**	**34**
Official creditors	..	..	..	94	98	92	96	234	90	34
Multilateral	..	..	..	34	96	78	77	186	83	25
Concessional	..	..	..	1	85	76	64	54	80	19
Bilateral	..	..	..	60	2	14	20	48	7	10
Concessional	..	..	..	0	2	14	20	48	7	10
Private creditors	..	..	..	0	0	0	0	0	0	0
Bonds	..	..	..	0	0	0	0	0	0	0
Commercial banks	..	..	..	0	0	0	0	0	0	0
Other private	..	..	..	0	0	0	0	0	0	0
Private nonguaranteed	..	..	..	**0**	**0**	**0**	**0**	**7**	**5**	**26**
Bonds	..	..	..	0	0	0	0	0	0	0
Commercial banks and other	..	..	..	0	0	0	0	7	5	26
Memo:										
IBRD	..	..	..	0	0	0	0	0	0	0
IDA	..	..	..	1	85	76	64	53	79	18
PRINCIPAL REPAYMENTS	..	..	..	**1**	**0**	**1**	**3**	**149**	**40**	**42**
Public and publicly guaranteed	..	..	..	**1**	**0**	**1**	**3**	**149**	**39**	**40**
Official creditors	..	..	..	0	0	1	3	149	39	40
Multilateral	..	..	..	0	0	0	0	129	14	5
Concessional	..	..	..	0	0	0	0	0	0	0
Bilateral	..	..	..	0	0	1	3	20	25	35
Concessional	..	..	..	0	0	0	3	0	0	22
Private creditors	..	..	..	1	0	0	0	0	0	0
Bonds	..	..	..	0	0	0	0	0	0	0
Commercial banks	..	..	..	1	0	0	0	0	0	0
Other private	..	..	..	0	0	0	0	0	0	0
Private nonguaranteed	..	..	..	**0**	**0**	**0**	**0**	**0**	**1**	**2**
Bonds	..	..	..	0	0	0	0	0	0	0
Commercial banks and other	..	..	..	0	0	0	0	0	1	2
Memo:										
IBRD	..	..	..	0	0	0	0	0	0	0
IDA	..	..	..	0	0	0	0	0	0	0
NET FLOWS ON DEBT	..	..	..	**93**	**98**	**91**	**94**	**93**	**55**	**18**
Public and publicly guaranteed	..	..	..	**93**	**98**	**91**	**94**	**86**	**51**	**-6**
Official creditors	..	..	..	94	98	91	94	86	51	-6
Multilateral	..	..	..	34	96	78	76	57	69	20
Concessional	..	..	..	1	85	76	64	54	80	19
Bilateral	..	..	..	60	2	13	17	29	-18	-26
Concessional	..	..	..	0	2	14	17	48	7	-13
Private creditors	..	..	..	-1	0	0	0	0	0	0
Bonds	..	..	..	0	0	0	0	0	0	0
Commercial banks	..	..	..	-1	0	0	0	0	0	0
Other private	..	..	..	0	0	0	0	0	0	0
Private nonguaranteed	..	..	..	**0**	**0**	**0**	**0**	**7**	**4**	**24**
Bonds	..	..	..	0	0	0	0	0	0	0
Commercial banks and other	..	..	..	0	0	0	0	7	4	24
Memo:										
IBRD	..	..	..	0	0	0	0	0	0	0
IDA	..	..	..	1	85	76	64	53	79	18

GEORGIA

(US$ million, unless otherwise indicated)

	1970	1980	1990	1994	1995	1996	1997	1998	1999	2000
INTEREST PAYMENTS (LINT)	..	..	..	**5**	**17**	**6**	**37**	**57**	**42**	**43**
Public and publicly guaranteed	..	..	..	**5**	**17**	**6**	**37**	**56**	**41**	**42**
Official creditors	..	..	..	5	17	6	37	56	41	42
Multilateral	..	..	..	5	0	5	8	24	8	8
Concessional	..	..	..	0	0	1	1	2	2	3
Bilateral	..	..	..	0	17	1	29	32	33	34
Concessional	..	..	..	0	0	0	14	15	16	17
Private creditors	..	..	..	0	0	0	0	0	0	0
Bonds	..	..	..	0	0	0	0	0	0	0
Commercial banks	..	..	..	0	0	0	0	0	0	0
Other private	..	..	..	0	0	0	0	0	0	0
Private nonguaranteed	..	..	..	**0**	**0**	**0**	**0**	**1**	**1**	**1**
Bonds	..	..	..	0	0	0	0	0	0	0
Commercial banks and other	..	..	..	0	0	0	0	1	1	1
Memo:										
IBRD	..	..	..	0	0	0	0	0	0	0
IDA	..	..	..	0	0	1	1	2	2	3
NET TRANSFERS ON DEBT	..	..	..	**88**	**81**	**85**	**56**	**36**	**13**	**-25**
Public and publicly guaranteed	..	..	..	**88**	**81**	**85**	**56**	**30**	**10**	**-48**
Official creditors	..	..	..	89	81	85	56	30	10	-48
Multilateral	..	..	..	30	96	73	69	33	61	12
Concessional	..	..	..	1	85	76	63	53	78	17
Bilateral	..	..	..	60	-15	12	-12	-3	-51	-59
Concessional	..	..	..	0	2	14	4	33	-9	-30
Private creditors	..	..	..	-1	0	0	0	0	0	0
Bonds	..	..	..	0	0	0	0	0	0	0
Commercial banks	..	..	..	-1	0	0	0	0	0	0
Other private	..	..	..	0	0	0	0	0	0	0
Private nonguaranteed	..	..	..	**0**	**0**	**0**	**0**	**6**	**3**	**23**
Bonds	..	..	..	0	0	0	0	0	0	0
Commercial banks and other	..	..	..	0	0	0	0	6	3	23
Memo:										
IBRD	..	..	..	0	0	0	0	0	0	0
IDA	..	..	..	1	85	76	63	51	77	15
DEBT SERVICE (LTDS)	..	..	..	**6**	**17**	**7**	**40**	**205**	**82**	**85**
Public and publicly guaranteed	..	..	..	**6**	**17**	**7**	**40**	**205**	**80**	**82**
Official creditors	..	..	..	5	17	7	40	205	80	82
Multilateral	..	..	..	5	0	5	8	153	22	13
Concessional	..	..	..	0	0	1	1	2	2	3
Bilateral	..	..	..	0	17	2	32	52	58	69
Concessional	..	..	..	0	0	0	16	15	16	39
Private creditors	..	..	..	1	0	0	0	0	0	0
Bonds	..	..	..	0	0	0	0	0	0	0
Commercial banks	..	..	..	1	0	0	0	0	0	0
Other private	..	..	..	0	0	0	0	0	0	0
Private nonguaranteed	..	..	..	**0**	**0**	**0**	**0**	**1**	**2**	**3**
Bonds	..	..	..	0	0	0	0	0	0	0
Commercial banks and other	..	..	..	0	0	0	0	1	2	3
Memo:										
IBRD	..	..	..	0	0	0	0	0	0	0
IDA	..	..	..	0	0	1	1	2	2	3
UNDISBURSED DEBT	..	..	..	**46**	**42**	**105**	**181**	**271**	**329**	**337**
Official creditors	..	..	..	46	42	105	181	271	329	337
Private creditors	..	..	..	0	0	0	0	0	0	0
Memorandum items										
Concessional LDOD	..	..	..	1	86	413	638	758	819	798
Variable rate LDOD	..	..	..	388	409	202	141	162	136	157
Public sector LDOD	..	..	..	924	1,039	1,106	1,186	1,293	1,298	1,259
Private sector LDOD	..	..	..	0	0	0	4	24	27	52

6. CURRENCY COMPOSITION OF LONG-TERM DEBT (PERCENT)

	1970	1980	1990	1994	1995	1996	1997	1998	1999	2000
Deutsche mark	..	..	..	0.0	0.2	1.4	2.7	3.8	3.7	4.0
French franc	..	..	..	0.0	0.0	0.0	0.0	0.0	0.0	0.0
Japanese yen	..	..	..	0.0	0.0	0.0	0.0	0.0	0.0	0.2
Pound sterling	..	..	..	0.0	0.0	0.0	0.0	0.0	0.0	0.0
Swiss franc	..	..	..	0.4	0.4	0.3	0.3	0.3	0.2	0.2
U.S.dollars	..	..	..	74.5	75.3	77.0	79.2	78.9	82.2	82.2
Multiple currency	..	..	..	0.0	0.0	0.0	0.0	0.0	0.0	0.0
Special drawing rights	..	..	..	0.0	0.0	0.0	0.0	0.1	0.1	0.2
All other currencies	..	..	..	25.1	24.1	21.3	17.8	16.9	13.8	13.2

GEORGIA

(US$ million, unless otherwise indicated)

	1970	1980	1990	1994	1995	1996	1997	1998	1999	2000
7. DEBT RESTRUCTURINGS										
Total amount rescheduled	..	..	..	459	0	634	167	0	0	0
Debt stock rescheduled	..	..	..	201	0	394	96	0	0	0
Principal rescheduled	..	..	..	3	0	199	35	0	0	0
Official	..	..	..	0	0	199	35	0	0	0
Private	..	..	..	3	0	0	0	0	0	0
Interest rescheduled	..	..	..	5	0	26	17	0	0	0
Official	..	..	..	0	0	26	5	0	0	0
Private	..	..	..	5	0	0	11	0	0	0
Debt forgiven	..	..	..	0	0	46	4	0	0	0
Memo: interest forgiven	..	..	..	0	0	0	0	0	0	0
Debt stock reduction	..	..	..	0	0	0	0	0	0	0
of which debt buyback	..	..	..	0	0	0	0	0	0	0
8. DEBT STOCK-FLOW RECONCILIATION										
Total change in debt stocks	..	..	..	891	-210	121	104	182	3	-19
Net flows on debt	..	..	..	603	-272	169	153	153	57	29
Net change in interest arrears	..	..	..	15	46	-19	-25	-18	1	1
Interest capitalized	..	..	..	5	0	26	17	0	0	0
Debt forgiveness or reduction	..	..	..	0	0	-46	-4	0	0	0
Cross-currency valuation	..	..	..	16	18	-23	-115	-26	-52	-51
Residual	..	..	..	252	-2	14	79	72	-2	3
9. AVERAGE TERMS OF NEW COMMITMENTS										
ALL CREDITORS										
Interest (%)	..	..	..	4.0	1.5	1.2	0.7	4.1	0.5	1.2
Maturity (years)	..	..	..	13.7	32.3	35.0	34.3	23.0	35.4	31.0
Grace period (years)	..	..	..	4.0	9.6	10.5	9.6	8.9	10.4	8.7
Grant element (%)	..	..	..	33.5	71.3	75.3	78.4	45.3	81.0	71.1
Official creditors										
Interest (%)	..	..	..	4.0	1.5	1.2	0.7	4.1	0.5	1.2
Maturity (years)	..	..	..	13.7	32.3	35.0	34.3	23.0	35.4	31.0
Grace period (years)	..	..	..	4.0	9.6	10.5	9.6	8.9	10.4	8.7
Grant element (%)	..	..	..	33.5	71.3	75.3	78.4	45.3	81.0	71.1
Private creditors										
Interest (%)	..	..	..	0.0	0.0	0.0	0.0	0.0	0.0	0.0
Maturity (years)	..	..	..	0.0	0.0	0.0	0.0	0.0	0.0	0.0
Grace period (years)	..	..	..	0.0	0.0	0.0	0.0	0.0	0.0	0.0
Grant element (%)	..	..	..	0.0	0.0	0.0	0.0	0.0	0.0	0.0
Memorandum items										
Commitments	..	..	..	106	91	158	181	312	151	64
Official creditors	..	..	..	106	91	158	181	312	151	64
Private creditors	..	..	..	0	0	0	0	0	0	0

10. CONTRACTUAL OBLIGATIONS ON OUTSTANDING LONG-TERM DEBT

	2001	2002	2003	2004	2005	2006	2007	2008	2009	2010
TOTAL										
Disbursements	111	94	63	37	20	8	4	0	0	0
Principal	139	140	64	66	66	56	53	41	59	61
Interest	34	31	27	25	22	20	18	16	14	12
Official creditors										
Disbursements	111	94	63	37	20	8	4	0	0	0
Principal	118	135	59	61	63	55	52	41	59	60
Interest	33	30	26	24	22	20	17	16	14	12
Bilateral creditors										
Disbursements	32	30	20	12	7	3	2	0	0	0
Principal	113	127	49	50	51	41	37	25	22	23
Interest	21	17	13	11	10	8	6	5	4	3
Multilateral creditors										
Disbursements	79	65	43	25	14	4	2	0	0	0
Principal	5	9	10	11	12	13	15	16	37	37
Interest	12	13	13	13	12	12	11	11	10	8
Private creditors										
Disbursements	0	0	0	0	0	0	0	0	0	0
Principal	21	5	5	5	3	1	1	0	0	0
Interest	2	1	1	1	0	0	0	0	0	0
Commercial banks										
Disbursements	0	0	0	0	0	0	0	0	0	0
Principal	0	0	0	0	0	0	0	0	0	0
Interest	0	0	0	0	0	0	0	0	0	0
Other private										
Disbursements	0	0	0	0	0	0	0	0	0	0
Principal	21	5	5	5	3	1	1	0	0	0
Interest	2	1	1	1	0	0	0	0	0	0

GHANA

(US$ million, unless otherwise indicated)

	1970	1980	1990	1994	1995	1996	1997	1998	1999	2000
1. SUMMARY DEBT DATA										
TOTAL DEBT STOCKS (EDT)	**571**	**1,402**	**3,881**	**5,469**	**5,936**	**6,443**	**6,347**	**6,964**	**7,010**	**6,657**
Long-term debt (LDOD)	**520**	**1,166**	**2,816**	**4,189**	**4,666**	**5,247**	**5,323**	**5,914**	**5,989**	**5,786**
Public and publicly guaranteed	510	1,156	2,783	4,157	4,639	4,976	5,056	5,651	5,729	5,529
Private nonguaranteed	10	10	33	32	27	271	267	263	260	257
Use of IMF credit	**46**	**105**	**745**	**700**	**649**	**543**	**347**	**334**	**310**	**293**
Short-term debt	**5**	**131**	**320**	**580**	**621**	**654**	**677**	**717**	**711**	**579**
of which interest arrears on LDOD	5	5	56	57	28	11	13	11	13	17
Official creditors	1	4	45	19	22	2	5	7	6	10
Private creditors	4	1	11	38	6	9	9	4	8	7
Memo: principal arrears on LDOD	25	6	77	93	89	33	14	43	54	46
Official creditors	7	4	50	50	46	10	7	34	30	22
Private creditors	18	2	27	43	43	23	7	10	24	24
Memo: export credits	0	0	411	427	612	735	883	202	183	165
TOTAL DEBT FLOWS										
Disbursements	**44**	**249**	**503**	**468**	**648**	**940**	**649**	**713**	**457**	**443**
Long-term debt	42	220	438	468	606	900	649	602	396	408
IMF purchases	2	29	65	0	42	40	0	112	61	35
Principal repayments	**39**	**106**	**260**	**248**	**308**	**331**	**398**	**389**	**346**	**315**
Long-term debt	14	77	144	166	201	206	232	250	270	278
IMF repurchases	25	29	117	83	108	125	166	139	76	37
Net flows on debt	**5**	**75**	**341**	**323**	**410**	**658**	**272**	**366**	**103**	**-8**
of which short-term debt	0	-68	98	103	71	50	21	42	-8	-136
Interest payments (INT)	**12**	**53**	**108**	**121**	**98**	**152**	**161**	**194**	**177**	**157**
Long-term debt	12	31	59	84	60	109	127	153	137	117
IMF charges	0	4	37	11	10	7	5	2	2	2
Short-term debt	0	18	12	26	28	36	29	38	38	38
Net transfers on debt	**-7**	**22**	**234**	**202**	**312**	**506**	**111**	**173**	**-74**	**-164**
Total debt service paid (TDS)	**51**	**159**	**368**	**369**	**406**	**483**	**559**	**582**	**523**	**472**
Long-term debt	26	108	203	250	260	314	359	403	408	396
IMF repurchases and charges	25	33	154	93	117	133	171	141	77	39
Short-term debt (interest only)	0	18	12	26	28	36	29	38	38	38
2. AGGREGATE NET RESOURCE FLOWS AND NET TRANSFERS (LONG-TERM)										
NET RESOURCE FLOWS	**101**	**181**	**758**	**1,311**	**1,017**	**1,155**	**709**	**663**	**465**	**483**
Net flow of long-term debt (ex. IMF)	28	143	294	302	405	694	417	352	126	130
Foreign direct investment (net)	68	16	15	233	107	120	83	56	63	110
Portfolio equity flows	0	0	0	557	267	124	46	15	19	17
Grants (excluding technical coop.)	5	22	449	218	238	216	163	240	257	226
Memo: technical coop. grants	15	42	61	88	108	96	108	104	112	126
official net resource flows	35	207	763	463	550	632	496	538	434	412
private net resource flows	66	-26	-5	848	467	523	213	125	31	71
NET TRANSFERS	**76**	**135**	**692**	**1,217**	**937**	**1,016**	**542**	**466**	**286**	**315**
Interest on long-term debt	12	31	59	84	60	109	127	153	137	117
Profit remittances on FDI	12	15	7	10	20	30	40	44	42	51
Memo: official net transfers	28	183	719	400	498	554	417	448	354	337
private net transfers	49	-48	-26	817	439	462	125	18	-68	-23
3. MAJOR ECONOMIC AGGREGATES										
Gross national income (GNI)	2,170	4,426	5,774	5,330	6,324	6,782	6,750	7,322	7,611	5,037
Exports of goods & services (XGS)	..	1,214	996	1,413	1,613	1,778	1,708	2,586	2,519	2,451
of which workers remittances	..	1	6	16	17	28	26	30	31	32
Imports of goods & services (MGS)	..	1,264	1,624	2,123	2,263	2,557	2,791	3,733	4,041	3,462
International reserves (RES)	43	330	309	689	804	930	..	457	535	309
Current account balance	..	30	-223	-255	-145	-325	-550	-443	-932	-413
4. DEBT INDICATORS										
EDT / XGS (%)	..	115.5	389.7	387.2	368.1	362.4	371.7	269.3	278.3	271.7
EDT / GNI (%)	26.3	31.7	67.2	102.6	93.9	95.0	94.0	95.1	92.1	132.2
TDS / XGS (%)	..	13.1	37.0	26.1	25.2	27.2	32.7	22.5	20.8	19.3
INT / XGS (%)	..	4.4	10.8	8.5	6.1	8.5	9.5	7.5	7.0	6.4
INT / GNI (%)	0.6	1.2	1.9	2.3	1.5	2.2	2.4	2.7	2.3	3.1
RES / EDT (%)	7.5	23.5	8.0	12.6	13.5	14.4	..	6.6	7.6	4.6
RES / MGS (months)	..	3.1	2.3	3.9	4.3	4.4	..	1.5	1.6	1.1
Short-term / EDT (%)	0.9	9.3	8.3	10.6	10.5	10.2	10.7	10.3	10.1	8.7
Concessional / EDT (%)	43.1	55.3	54.6	61.1	63.0	62.2	64.2	66.3	68.8	71.4
Multilateral / EDT (%)	9.3	19.9	47.6	49.5	50.2	48.7	50.4	51.2	52.5	55.1

GHANA

(US$ million, unless otherwise indicated)

5. LONG-TERM DEBT

	1970	1980	1990	1994	1995	1996	1997	1998	1999	2000
DEBT OUTSTANDING (LDOD)	**520**	**1,166**	**2,816**	**4,189**	**4,666**	**5,247**	**5,323**	**5,914**	**5,989**	**5,786**
Public and publicly guaranteed	**510**	**1,156**	**2,783**	**4,157**	**4,639**	**4,976**	**5,056**	**5,651**	**5,729**	**5,529**
Official creditors	332	1,034	2,560	3,770	4,141	4,448	4,472	4,995	5,149	5,029
Multilateral	53	279	1,846	2,710	2,982	3,138	3,198	3,563	3,682	3,667
Concessional	11	139	1,510	2,369	2,670	2,855	2,966	3,345	3,490	3,516
Bilateral	279	756	713	1,060	1,159	1,311	1,275	1,432	1,467	1,362
Concessional	236	637	611	974	1,072	1,151	1,111	1,275	1,332	1,235
Private creditors	178	121	224	387	498	528	584	656	580	500
Bonds	0	0	0	0	0	0	0	0	0	0
Commercial banks	12	0	10	36	140	204	183	171	132	113
Other private	166	121	214	352	358	323	401	485	448	387
Private nonguaranteed	**10**	**10**	**33**	**32**	**27**	**271**	**267**	**263**	**260**	**257**
Bonds	0	0	0	0	0	250	250	250	250	250
Commercial banks and other	10	10	33	32	27	21	17	13	10	7
Memo:										
IBRD	43	114	113	70	59	44	30	27	18	9
IDA	11	99	1,310	2,094	2,375	2,530	2,617	2,962	3,099	3,130
DISBURSEMENTS	**42**	**220**	**438**	**468**	**606**	**900**	**649**	**602**	**396**	**408**
Public and publicly guaranteed	**42**	**220**	**430**	**468**	**606**	**650**	**649**	**602**	**396**	**408**
Official creditors	39	220	379	345	428	516	441	438	330	358
Multilateral	4	50	274	224	284	298	291	293	254	228
Concessional	4	21	214	203	269	285	288	291	250	223
Bilateral	35	170	105	121	144	217	150	145	75	131
Concessional	35	93	95	121	138	108	116	125	66	102
Private creditors	3	0	51	123	178	134	208	164	67	50
Bonds	0	0	0	0	0	0	0	0	0	0
Commercial banks	0	0	9	30	108	72	25	25	13	24
Other private	3	0	42	93	70	62	183	139	54	25
Private nonguaranteed	**0**	**0**	**8**	**0**	**0**	**250**	**0**	**0**	**0**	**0**
Bonds	0	0	0	0	0	250	0	0	0	0
Commercial banks and other	0	0	8	0	0	0	0	0	0	0
Memo:										
IBRD	0	25	0	0	0	0	0	0	0	0
IDA	4	5	201	178	242	244	237	261	219	204
PRINCIPAL REPAYMENTS	**14**	**77**	**144**	**166**	**201**	**206**	**232**	**250**	**270**	**278**
Public and publicly guaranteed	**14**	**77**	**136**	**161**	**196**	**200**	**228**	**246**	**267**	**275**
Official creditors	9	35	65	100	116	100	109	140	153	172
Multilateral	2	4	29	51	73	55	52	53	61	68
Concessional	0	0	7	14	17	18	20	26	33	35
Bilateral	8	31	35	50	43	45	57	86	92	104
Concessional	7	14	33	42	38	37	34	57	66	74
Private creditors	5	42	71	61	80	99	120	106	115	103
Bonds	0	0	0	0	0	0	0	0	0	0
Commercial banks	0	22	17	1	2	19	38	40	43	34
Other private	5	20	55	59	78	80	81	66	72	69
Private nonguaranteed	**0**	**0**	**8**	**5**	**5**	**6**	**4**	**4**	**3**	**3**
Bonds	0	0	0	0	0	0	0	0	0	0
Commercial banks and other	0	0	8	5	5	6	4	4	3	3
Memo:										
IBRD	2	3	10	13	15	10	11	4	8	8
IDA	0	0	2	6	8	10	12	16	20	25
NET FLOWS ON DEBT	**28**	**143**	**294**	**302**	**405**	**694**	**417**	**352**	**126**	**130**
Public and publicly guaranteed	**28**	**143**	**294**	**307**	**410**	**450**	**421**	**356**	**129**	**133**
Official creditors	29	185	314	245	312	415	333	298	177	187
Multilateral	3	47	245	173	211	243	239	240	194	160
Concessional	4	21	207	189	252	266	268	265	218	188
Bilateral	27	138	69	71	101	172	93	58	-17	27
Concessional	28	79	62	79	101	70	83	67	0	28
Private creditors	-2	-42	-20	63	98	35	88	58	-48	-54
Bonds	0	0	0	0	0	0	0	0	0	0
Commercial banks	0	-22	-8	29	106	53	-13	-16	-30	-10
Other private	-2	-20	-13	34	-8	-18	101	74	-18	-44
Private nonguaranteed	**0**	**0**	**0**	**-5**	**-5**	**244**	**-4**	**-4**	**-3**	**-3**
Bonds	0	0	0	0	0	250	0	0	0	0
Commercial banks and other	0	0	0	-5	-5	-6	-4	-4	-3	-3
Memo:										
IBRD	-1	21	-10	-13	-15	-10	-11	-4	-8	-8
IDA	4	5	199	172	234	234	225	245	199	179

GHANA

(US$ million, unless otherwise indicated)

	1970	1980	1990	1994	1995	1996	1997	1998	1999	2000
INTEREST PAYMENTS (LINT)	**12**	**31**	**59**	**84**	**60**	**109**	**127**	**153**	**137**	**117**
Public and publicly guaranteed	**12**	**31**	**57**	**82**	**58**	**107**	**112**	**138**	**123**	**103**
Official creditors	7	24	45	63	52	77	79	90	80	75
Multilateral	3	10	30	36	40	43	41	38	39	39
Concessional	0	1	10	16	18	21	21	23	25	26
Bilateral	4	14	15	27	12	35	39	52	42	37
Concessional	4	10	13	23	10	30	22	41	33	25
Private creditors	5	7	12	19	6	30	33	48	42	28
Bonds	0	0	0	0	0	0	0	0	0	0
Commercial banks	0	2	2	0	0	7	11	15	13	6
Other private	5	4	11	19	6	22	22	34	29	22
Private nonguaranteed	**0**	**0**	**2**	**2**	**2**	**1**	**15**	**15**	**15**	**14**
Bonds	0	0	0	0	0	0	14	14	14	14
Commercial banks and other	0	0	2	2	2	1	1	1	1	1
Memo:										
IBRD	3	8	9	6	6	3	4	1	2	1
IDA	0	1	8	14	17	18	19	20	21	22
NET TRANSFERS ON DEBT	**16**	**112**	**235**	**218**	**346**	**586**	**290**	**199**	**-12**	**12**
Public and publicly guaranteed	**16**	**112**	**238**	**225**	**352**	**343**	**309**	**217**	**6**	**30**
Official creditors	22	161	270	182	260	338	254	208	97	111
Multilateral	0	37	216	137	170	200	199	202	155	121
Concessional	4	20	197	173	234	246	246	242	193	162
Bilateral	22	124	54	44	90	138	55	6	-58	-10
Concessional	24	69	49	57	90	40	61	27	-33	3
Private creditors	-7	-48	-32	44	92	5	55	10	-91	-82
Bonds	0	0	0	0	0	0	0	0	0	0
Commercial banks	0	-24	-9	29	106	46	-24	-30	-44	-15
Other private	-7	-25	-23	15	-14	-41	80	40	-47	-66
Private nonguaranteed	**0**	**0**	**-2**	**-7**	**-7**	**243**	**-19**	**-19**	**-18**	**-17**
Bonds	0	0	0	0	0	250	-14	-14	-14	-14
Commercial banks and other	0	0	-2	-7	-7	-7	-5	-5	-4	-4
Memo:										
IBRD	-4	13	-20	-20	-21	-13	-15	-6	-10	-10
IDA	4	4	191	157	218	216	207	225	178	157
DEBT SERVICE (LTDS)	**26**	**108**	**203**	**250**	**260**	**314**	**359**	**403**	**408**	**396**
Public and publicly guaranteed	**26**	**108**	**192**	**243**	**254**	**307**	**340**	**384**	**390**	**378**
Official creditors	16	59	109	163	168	178	188	230	233	247
Multilateral	4	14	59	87	113	98	93	91	100	107
Concessional	0	1	17	31	35	39	42	49	57	61
Bilateral	12	46	50	77	55	80	95	138	133	140
Concessional	11	24	46	64	48	67	56	98	99	99
Private creditors	10	48	83	80	86	129	153	155	157	131
Bonds	0	0	0	0	0	0	0	0	0	0
Commercial banks	0	24	18	1	2	27	50	55	56	40
Other private	10	25	65	79	84	103	103	99	101	92
Private nonguaranteed	**0**	**0**	**10**	**7**	**7**	**7**	**19**	**19**	**18**	**17**
Bonds	0	0	0	0	0	0	14	14	14	14
Commercial banks and other	0	0	10	7	7	7	5	5	4	4
Memo:										
IBRD	4	11	20	20	21	13	15	6	10	10
IDA	0	1	10	21	25	28	30	36	41	47
UNDISBURSED DEBT	**76**	**431**	**1,705**	**1,871**	**2,103**	**1,980**	**1,552**	**1,256**	**1,325**	**953**
Official creditors	76	431	1,591	1,619	1,800	1,696	1,366	1,159	1,139	837
Private creditors	0	0	113	252	303	284	186	97	186	115
Memorandum items										
Concessional LDOD	246	775	2,120	3,343	3,741	4,006	4,077	4,620	4,822	4,751
Variable rate LDOD	10	10	51	58	56	305	293	284	274	266
Public sector LDOD	510	1,128	2,783	4,157	4,639	4,976	5,056	5,651	5,729	5,529
Private sector LDOD	10	38	33	32	27	271	267	263	260	257

6. CURRENCY COMPOSITION OF LONG-TERM DEBT (PERCENT)

	1970	1980	1990	1994	1995	1996	1997	1998	1999	2000
Deutsche mark	12.3	12.9	3.9	4.3	3.9	4.2	4.1	3.8	3.1	2.8
French franc	2.7	1.9	2.2	2.5	3.1	3.0	2.5	2.4	1.7	1.3
Japanese yen	0.0	0.1	6.7	13.2	13.7	12.4	11.8	13.9	16.0	15.5
Pound sterling	28.3	11.8	2.8	4.7	5.7	7.3	7.0	5.8	4.9	3.6
Swiss franc	0.0	0.0	0.6	0.2	0.2	0.3	0.2	0.2	0.1	0.1
U.S.dollars	22.5	38.6	58.7	54.9	55.3	56.0	58.3	59.0	60.5	63.7
Multiple currency	8.4	10.7	7.8	6.1	5.7	5.7	5.8	5.7	5.5	5.3
Special drawing rights	0.0	0.0	0.6	0.7	0.7	0.8	0.7	0.7	0.7	0.8
All other currencies	25.8	24.0	16.7	13.4	11.7	10.3	9.6	8.5	7.5	6.9

GHANA

(US$ million, unless otherwise indicated)

	1970	1980	1990	1994	1995	1996	1997	1998	1999	2000
7. DEBT RESTRUCTURINGS										
Total amount rescheduled	..	..	0	0	0	99	0	0	0	0
Debt stock rescheduled	..	..	0	0	0	0	0	0	0	0
Principal rescheduled	..	..	0	0	0	47	0	0	0	0
Official	..	..	0	0	0	38	0	0	0	0
Private	..	..	0	0	0	9	0	0	0	0
Interest rescheduled	..	..	0	0	0	21	0	0	0	0
Official	..	..	0	0	0	20	0	0	0	0
Private	..	..	0	0	0	2	0	0	0	0
Debt forgiven	..	..	102	12	1	7	7	0	0	0
Memo: interest forgiven	..	..	0	1	0	0	0	0	0	0
Debt stock reduction	..	..	0	0	0	0	0	12	0	0
of which debt buyback	..	..	0	0	0	0	0	0	0	0
8. DEBT STOCK-FLOW RECONCILIATION										
Total change in debt stocks	..	..	479	583	467	507	-96	617	46	-353
Net flows on debt	5	75	341	323	410	658	272	366	103	-8
Net change in interest arrears	..	..	17	3	-29	-17	3	-3	3	4
Interest capitalized	..	..	0	0	0	21	0	0	0	0
Debt forgiveness or reduction	..	..	-102	-12	-1	-7	-7	-12	0	0
Cross-currency valuation	..	..	174	57	-104	-397	-573	-18	-99	-327
Residual	..	..	49	211	191	248	209	283	40	-21
9. AVERAGE TERMS OF NEW COMMITMENTS										
ALL CREDITORS										
Interest (%)	2.0	1.4	3.0	4.2	3.3	2.9	2.5	4.0	2.5	1.1
Maturity (years)	36.7	44.1	32.1	25.4	26.8	25.3	28.6	28.0	29.1	41.9
Grace period (years)	9.7	9.7	8.4	7.0	7.1	6.6	7.3	6.9	7.6	9.8
Grant element (%)	66.8	74.4	58.2	44.0	52.1	50.8	54.7	45.6	57.3	76.7
Official creditors										
Interest (%)	1.8	1.4	2.0	1.9	1.8	2.1	1.4	2.5	2.6	1.1
Maturity (years)	38.6	44.1	35.9	35.1	34.1	29.4	38.8	35.7	30.5	41.9
Grace period (years)	10.2	9.7	9.4	9.7	9.2	7.9	10.1	8.8	8.1	9.8
Grant element (%)	70.2	74.4	67.8	68.3	69.1	60.1	73.2	60.8	59.9	76.7
Private creditors										
Interest (%)	5.3	0.0	8.1	7.2	6.9	5.9	4.6	7.0	2.1	1.0
Maturity (years)	8.4	0.0	11.4	12.4	9.0	10.5	8.3	12.5	25.7	31.3
Grace period (years)	1.4	0.0	2.9	3.3	1.9	2.1	1.9	3.1	6.5	11.3
Grant element (%)	16.3	0.0	6.2	11.4	10.6	16.9	17.9	14.6	50.9	75.9
Memorandum items										
Commitments	51	170	679	477	796	710	380	342	527	139
Official creditors	48	170	573	273	565	556	253	229	376	139
Private creditors	3	0	106	203	231	154	127	113	151	0

10. CONTRACTUAL OBLIGATIONS ON OUTSTANDING LONG-TERM DEBT

	2001	2002	2003	2004	2005	2006	2007	2008	2009	2010
TOTAL										
Disbursements	390	276	138	77	39	17	11	3	0	0
Principal	294	269	508	253	254	223	214	198	196	195
Interest	125	118	103	88	78	69	62	56	51	47
Official creditors										
Disbursements	327	242	125	72	39	17	11	3	0	0
Principal	188	180	179	187	198	177	181	184	186	189
Interest	80	79	76	72	66	61	57	53	49	45
Bilateral creditors										
Disbursements	102	64	36	19	9	3	1	0	0	0
Principal	115	104	98	102	105	78	78	75	73	73
Interest	40	39	36	33	30	26	24	21	19	17
Multilateral creditors										
Disbursements	225	178	89	53	30	14	10	3	0	0
Principal	73	76	81	85	93	98	103	109	113	116
Interest	40	40	40	39	37	35	33	31	30	28
Private creditors										
Disbursements	63	34	13	5	0	0	0	0	0	0
Principal	105	89	329	66	56	46	34	14	10	6
Interest	44	39	27	16	11	8	5	3	2	2
Commercial banks										
Disbursements	3	1	0	0	0	0	0	0	0	0
Principal	33	25	20	14	8	4	2	2	2	1
Interest	6	4	3	2	1	1	0	0	0	0
Other private										
Disbursements	60	34	13	5	0	0	0	0	0	0
Principal	72	64	309	53	48	42	31	12	8	5
Interest	38	35	24	14	10	7	5	3	2	2

GRENADA

(US$ million, unless otherwise indicated)

	1970	1980	1990	1994	1995	1996	1997	1998	1999	2000
1. SUMMARY DEBT DATA										
TOTAL DEBT STOCKS (EDT)	**14.9**	**19.6**	**134.3**	**149.0**	**146.3**	**158.7**	**157.9**	**212.1**	**174.5**	**206.7**
Long-term debt (LDOD)	**14.9**	**15.8**	**121.2**	**133.1**	**131.4**	**137.7**	**143.6**	**141.7**	**144.8**	**180.9**
Public and publicly guaranteed	14.9	15.8	121.2	133.1	131.4	137.7	143.6	141.7	144.8	180.9
Private nonguaranteed	0.0	0.0	0.0	0.0	0.0	0.0	0.0	0.0	0.0	0.0
Use of IMF credit	**0.0**	**2.8**	**0.0**	**0.0**	**0.0**	**0.0**	**0.0**	**0.0**	**0.0**	**0.0**
Short-term debt	**0.0**	**1.0**	**13.1**	**15.9**	**14.9**	**21.1**	**14.2**	**70.4**	**29.7**	**25.8**
of which interest arrears on LDOD	0.0	0.0	7.1	6.9	6.9	7.4	7.2	7.8	8.6	8.8
Official creditors	0.0	0.0	6.8	6.7	6.6	7.1	7.0	7.6	8.3	7.3
Private creditors	0.0	0.0	0.3	0.2	0.3	0.3	0.2	0.2	0.2	1.5
Memo: principal arrears on LDOD	0.0	0.0	22.5	26.0	26.2	27.4	25.0	25.4	27.2	27.2
Official creditors	0.0	0.0	21.0	24.6	25.1	26.4	24.2	24.5	25.5	23.9
Private creditors	0.0	0.0	1.5	1.4	1.1	1.0	0.8	0.9	1.6	3.3
Memo: export credits	0.0	0.0	23.0	17.6	5.1	4.2	22.4	11.6	10.5	8.3
TOTAL DEBT FLOWS										
Disbursements	**5.8**	**1.7**	**14.8**	**12.4**	**5.0**	**9.6**	**14.6**	**6.2**	**13.9**	**47.9**
Long-term debt	5.8	1.0	14.8	12.4	5.0	9.6	14.6	6.2	13.9	47.9
IMF purchases	0.0	0.7	0.0	0.0	0.0	0.0	0.0	0.0	0.0	0.0
Principal repayments	**0.0**	**1.6**	**2.1**	**7.6**	**6.5**	**6.1**	**6.1**	**9.2**	**8.8**	**8.3**
Long-term debt	0.0	0.9	1.6	7.6	6.5	6.1	6.1	9.2	8.8	8.3
IMF repurchases	0.0	0.7	0.5	0.0	0.0	0.0	0.0	0.0	0.0	0.0
Net flows on debt	**5.8**	**-0.9**	**12.7**	**-23.0**	**-2.5**	**9.1**	**1.9**	**52.6**	**-36.3**	**35.5**
of which short-term debt	0.0	-1.0	0.0	-27.8	-1.0	5.7	-6.7	55.5	-41.4	-4.1
Interest payments (INT)	**0.3**	**0.8**	**2.1**	**3.7**	**2.7**	**3.4**	**2.7**	**4.2**	**4.8**	**3.7**
Long-term debt	0.3	0.5	1.7	2.3	2.2	2.6	2.2	2.5	2.5	2.7
IMF charges	0.0	0.1	0.0	0.0	0.0	0.0	0.0	0.0	0.0	0.0
Short-term debt	0.0	0.2	0.4	1.4	0.5	0.8	0.5	1.7	2.3	1.0
Net transfers on debt	**5.6**	**-1.7**	**10.6**	**-26.6**	**-5.2**	**5.7**	**-0.8**	**48.4**	**-41.1**	**31.8**
Total debt service paid (TDS)	**0.3**	**2.3**	**4.2**	**11.3**	**9.2**	**9.5**	**8.7**	**13.4**	**13.6**	**12.0**
Long-term debt	0.3	1.3	3.3	9.9	8.7	8.7	8.2	11.6	11.3	11.0
IMF repurchases and charges	0.0	0.8	0.5	0.0	0.0	0.0	0.0	0.0	0.0	0.0
Short-term debt (interest only)	0.0	0.2	0.4	1.4	0.5	0.8	0.5	1.7	2.3	1.0
2. AGGREGATE NET RESOURCE FLOWS AND NET TRANSFERS (LONG-TERM)										
NET RESOURCE FLOWS	**5.9**	**1.1**	**30.3**	**35.4**	**26.6**	**24.9**	**46.7**	**50.1**	**49.0**	**83.7**
Net flow of long-term debt (ex. IMF)	5.8	0.1	13.2	4.8	-1.5	3.5	8.6	-2.9	5.1	39.6
Foreign direct investment (net)	0.0	0.0	13.0	19.3	20.0	17.0	34.0	49.0	42.0	37.0
Portfolio equity flows	0.0	0.0	0.0	0.0	0.0	0.0	0.0	0.0	0.0	0.0
Grants (excluding technical coop.)	0.0	1.0	4.2	11.3	8.1	4.4	4.1	4.0	1.9	7.1
Memo: technical coop. grants	0.0	0.8	2.8	3.3	3.8	3.4	3.3	3.4	1.6	4.7
official net resource flows	0.3	1.7	17.0	17.4	8.3	8.7	13.2	0.7	8.7	16.7
private net resource flows	5.6	-0.6	13.3	18.0	18.3	16.2	33.5	49.4	40.3	67.0
NET TRANSFERS	**5.6**	**0.4**	**20.2**	**26.1**	**15.4**	**14.3**	**35.5**	**39.7**	**36.5**	**70.0**
Interest on long-term debt	0.3	0.5	1.7	2.3	2.2	2.6	2.2	2.5	2.5	2.7
Profit remittances on FDI	0.0	0.2	8.4	7.0	9.0	8.0	9.0	8.0	10.0	11.0
Memo: official net transfers	0.3	1.4	15.5	15.1	6.3	6.1	11.0	-1.7	6.3	14.0
private net transfers	5.3	-1.0	4.7	11.0	9.1	8.2	24.5	41.4	30.2	56.0
3. MAJOR ECONOMIC AGGREGATES										
Gross national income (GNI)	..	83.6	208.9	253.1	262.9	279.6	298.2	317.1	348.5	377.0
Exports of goods & services (XGS)	..	39.1	105.5	145.1	149.7	156.9	172.6	198.8	264.3	259.4
of which workers remittances	..	0.0	9.9	13.5	19.8	21.0	23.4	18.2	19.6	..
Imports of goods & services (MGS)	..	63.1	153.2	169.3	182.3	213.2	248.2	289.2	302.9	352.7
International reserves (RES)	5.3	12.9	17.6	31.2	36.7	35.7	42.7	46.8	50.8	57.7
Current account balance	..	0.3	-46.2	-21.8	-35.2	-57.9	-78.7	-89.3	-40.3	..
4. DEBT INDICATORS										
EDT / XGS (%)	..	50.1	127.3	102.7	97.7	101.2	91.5	106.7	66.0	79.7
EDT / GNI (%)	..	23.4	64.3	58.9	55.7	56.8	53.0	66.9	50.1	54.8
TDS / XGS (%)	..	5.9	4.0	7.8	6.1	6.1	5.0	6.7	5.2	4.6
INT / XGS (%)	..	2.1	2.0	2.6	1.8	2.2	1.6	2.1	1.8	1.4
INT / GNI (%)	..	1.0	1.0	1.5	1.0	1.2	0.9	1.3	1.4	1.0
RES / EDT (%)	35.7	65.9	13.1	21.0	25.1	22.5	27.0	22.1	29.1	27.9
RES / MGS (months)	..	2.5	1.4	2.2	2.4	2.0	2.1	1.9	2.0	2.0
Short-term / EDT (%)	0.0	5.1	9.8	10.7	10.2	13.3	9.0	33.2	17.0	12.5
Concessional / EDT (%)	32.2	60.7	65.5	64.8	64.7	61.8	62.4	45.6	57.1	50.4
Multilateral / EDT (%)	0.0	29.1	43.0	42.8	43.8	40.7	40.9	29.9	37.1	34.3

GRENADA

(US$ million, unless otherwise indicated)

	1970	1980	1990	1994	1995	1996	1997	1998	1999	2000
5. LONG-TERM DEBT										
DEBT OUTSTANDING (LDOD)	**14.9**	**15.8**	**121.2**	**133.1**	**131.4**	**137.7**	**143.6**	**141.7**	**144.8**	**180.9**
Public and publicly guaranteed	**14.9**	**15.8**	**121.2**	**133.1**	**131.4**	**137.7**	**143.6**	**141.7**	**144.8**	**180.9**
Official creditors	5.0	13.3	118.3	123.6	123.6	130.1	137.0	134.6	139.6	145.9
Multilateral	0.0	5.7	57.8	63.8	64.0	64.6	64.5	63.4	64.7	70.9
Concessional	0.0	4.7	51.9	59.8	58.1	57.0	57.1	56.1	57.3	60.5
Bilateral	5.0	7.5	60.5	59.8	59.6	65.6	72.5	71.2	74.9	75.0
Concessional	4.8	7.2	36.0	36.7	36.6	41.1	41.4	40.6	42.3	43.7
Private creditors	10.0	2.6	2.9	9.5	7.8	7.5	6.7	7.1	5.2	35.0
Bonds	10.0	2.1	0.0	0.0	0.0	0.0	0.0	0.0	0.0	0.0
Commercial banks	0.0	0.0	0.7	0.6	0.4	0.3	0.3	0.3	0.2	30.2
Other private	0.0	0.5	2.2	8.9	7.4	7.2	6.4	6.8	4.9	4.8
Private nonguaranteed	**0.0**	**0.0**	**0.0**	**0.0**	**0.0**	**0.0**	**0.0**	**0.0**	**0.0**	**0.0**
Bonds	0.0	0.0	0.0	0.0	0.0	0.0	0.0	0.0	0.0	0.0
Commercial banks and other	0.0	0.0	0.0	0.0	0.0	0.0	0.0	0.0	0.0	0.0
Memo:										
IBRD	0.0	0.0	0.0	0.0	0.0	0.0	0.0	0.0	0.4	2.2
IDA	0.0	0.0	5.5	7.2	7.3	7.2	7.1	8.2	9.3	9.6
DISBURSEMENTS	**5.8**	**1.0**	**14.8**	**12.4**	**5.0**	**9.6**	**14.6**	**6.2**	**13.9**	**47.9**
Public and publicly guaranteed	**5.8**	**1.0**	**14.8**	**12.4**	**5.0**	**9.6**	**14.6**	**6.2**	**13.9**	**47.9**
Official creditors	0.3	1.0	14.3	12.4	5.0	9.6	14.6	3.8	13.9	16.7
Multilateral	0.0	1.0	2.9	5.8	3.4	4.4	4.2	2.7	6.0	10.9
Concessional	0.0	0.0	2.9	5.4	1.3	2.0	3.4	2.1	4.7	6.9
Bilateral	0.3	0.0	11.4	6.6	1.5	5.2	10.5	1.1	8.0	5.8
Concessional	0.1	0.0	1.2	5.2	1.5	3.9	2.5	0.9	4.4	4.9
Private creditors	5.6	0.0	0.5	0.0	0.0	0.0	0.0	2.5	0.0	31.2
Bonds	5.6	0.0	0.0	0.0	0.0	0.0	0.0	0.0	0.0	0.0
Commercial banks	0.0	0.0	0.0	0.0	0.0	0.0	0.0	0.0	0.0	30.0
Other private	0.0	0.0	0.5	0.0	0.0	0.0	0.0	2.5	0.0	1.2
Private nonguaranteed	**0.0**	**0.0**	**0.0**	**0.0**	**0.0**	**0.0**	**0.0**	**0.0**	**0.0**	**0.0**
Bonds	0.0	0.0	0.0	0.0	0.0	0.0	0.0	0.0	0.0	0.0
Commercial banks and other	0.0	0.0	0.0	0.0	0.0	0.0	0.0	0.0	0.0	0.0
Memo:										
IBRD	0.0	0.0	0.0	0.0	0.0	0.0	0.0	0.0	0.4	1.9
IDA	0.0	0.0	1.0	0.0	0.0	0.3	0.3	0.9	1.4	0.8
PRINCIPAL REPAYMENTS	**0.0**	**0.9**	**1.6**	**7.6**	**6.5**	**6.1**	**6.1**	**9.2**	**8.8**	**8.3**
Public and publicly guaranteed	**0.0**	**0.9**	**1.6**	**7.6**	**6.5**	**6.1**	**6.1**	**9.2**	**8.8**	**8.3**
Official creditors	0.0	0.3	1.5	6.3	4.8	5.3	5.5	7.1	7.1	7.1
Multilateral	0.0	0.0	1.4	4.3	3.7	3.3	3.3	4.2	4.2	3.9
Concessional	0.0	0.0	1.1	3.6	3.3	2.7	2.7	3.5	3.3	2.9
Bilateral	0.0	0.3	0.1	2.1	1.1	2.0	2.2	2.8	2.9	3.2
Concessional	0.0	0.2	0.0	2.0	1.1	1.2	1.3	2.0	1.7	1.9
Private creditors	0.0	0.6	0.2	1.3	1.7	0.8	0.5	2.1	1.7	1.2
Bonds	0.0	0.6	0.0	0.0	0.0	0.0	0.0	0.0	0.0	0.0
Commercial banks	0.0	0.0	0.1	0.0	0.2	0.1	0.0	0.0	0.0	0.0
Other private	0.0	0.0	0.1	1.3	1.5	0.7	0.5	2.1	1.7	1.1
Private nonguaranteed	**0.0**	**0.0**	**0.0**	**0.0**	**0.0**	**0.0**	**0.0**	**0.0**	**0.0**	**0.0**
Bonds	0.0	0.0	0.0	0.0	0.0	0.0	0.0	0.0	0.0	0.0
Commercial banks and other	0.0	0.0	0.0	0.0	0.0	0.0	0.0	0.0	0.0	0.0
Memo:										
IBRD	0.0	0.0	0.0	0.0	0.0	0.0	0.0	0.0	0.0	0.0
IDA	0.0	0.0	0.0	0.0	0.1	0.1	0.1	0.1	0.1	0.1
NET FLOWS ON DEBT	**5.8**	**0.1**	**13.2**	**4.8**	**-1.5**	**3.5**	**8.6**	**-2.9**	**5.1**	**39.6**
Public and publicly guaranteed	**5.8**	**0.1**	**13.2**	**4.8**	**-1.5**	**3.5**	**8.6**	**-2.9**	**5.1**	**39.6**
Official creditors	0.3	0.7	12.8	6.1	0.2	4.3	9.1	-3.3	6.8	9.6
Multilateral	0.0	1.0	1.5	1.5	-0.3	1.1	0.8	-1.5	1.7	7.0
Concessional	0.0	0.0	1.8	1.8	-2.0	-0.7	0.7	-1.4	1.4	3.9
Bilateral	0.3	-0.3	11.4	4.6	0.4	3.2	8.3	-1.7	5.1	2.6
Concessional	0.1	-0.2	1.2	3.2	0.4	2.7	1.2	-1.1	2.7	3.0
Private creditors	5.6	-0.6	0.3	-1.3	-1.7	-0.8	-0.5	0.4	-1.7	30.0
Bonds	5.6	-0.6	0.0	0.0	0.0	0.0	0.0	0.0	0.0	0.0
Commercial banks	0.0	0.0	-0.1	0.0	-0.2	-0.1	0.0	0.0	0.0	30.0
Other private	0.0	0.0	0.4	-1.3	-1.5	-0.7	-0.5	0.4	-1.7	0.0
Private nonguaranteed	**0.0**	**0.0**	**0.0**	**0.0**	**0.0**	**0.0**	**0.0**	**0.0**	**0.0**	**0.0**
Bonds	0.0	0.0	0.0	0.0	0.0	0.0	0.0	0.0	0.0	0.0
Commercial banks and other	0.0	0.0	0.0	0.0	0.0	0.0	0.0	0.0	0.0	0.0
Memo:										
IBRD	0.0	0.0	0.0	0.0	0.0	0.0	0.0	0.0	0.4	1.9
IDA	0.0	0.0	1.0	0.0	-0.1	0.2	0.3	0.9	1.3	0.7

GRENADA

(US$ million, unless otherwise indicated)

	1970	1980	1990	1994	1995	1996	1997	1998	1999	2000
INTEREST PAYMENTS (LINT)	**0.3**	**0.5**	**1.7**	**2.3**	**2.2**	**2.6**	**2.2**	**2.5**	**2.5**	**2.7**
Public and publicly guaranteed	**0.3**	**0.5**	**1.7**	**2.3**	**2.2**	**2.6**	**2.2**	**2.5**	**2.5**	**2.7**
Official creditors	0.0	0.3	1.5	2.3	2.0	2.6	2.2	2.4	2.4	2.7
Multilateral	0.0	0.2	1.5	2.0	1.8	1.8	1.6	1.8	1.9	1.4
Concessional	0.0	0.2	1.4	1.9	1.6	1.5	1.5	1.5	1.6	1.0
Bilateral	0.0	0.1	0.0	0.2	0.2	0.8	0.5	0.6	0.5	1.3
Concessional	0.0	0.0	0.0	0.0	0.2	0.2	0.2	0.4	0.1	0.6
Private creditors	0.3	0.2	0.2	0.0	0.2	0.0	0.0	0.0	0.1	0.0
Bonds	0.3	0.2	0.0	0.0	0.0	0.0	0.0	0.0	0.0	0.0
Commercial banks	0.0	0.0	0.2	0.0	0.0	0.0	0.0	0.0	0.0	0.0
Other private	0.0	0.0	0.0	0.0	0.1	0.0	0.0	0.0	0.1	0.0
Private nonguaranteed	**0.0**	**0.0**	**0.0**	**0.0**	**0.0**	**0.0**	**0.0**	**0.0**	**0.0**	**0.0**
Bonds	0.0	0.0	0.0	0.0	0.0	0.0	0.0	0.0	0.0	0.0
Commercial banks and other	0.0	0.0	0.0	0.0	0.0	0.0	0.0	0.0	0.0	0.0
Memo:										
IBRD	0.0	0.0	0.0	0.0	0.0	0.0	0.0	0.0	0.0	0.0
IDA	0.0	0.0	0.0	0.1	0.1	0.1	0.1	0.1	0.0	0.1
NET TRANSFERS ON DEBT	**5.6**	**-0.3**	**11.5**	**2.5**	**-3.7**	**0.9**	**6.4**	**-5.4**	**2.6**	**36.8**
Public and publicly guaranteed	**5.6**	**-0.3**	**11.5**	**2.5**	**-3.7**	**0.9**	**6.4**	**-5.4**	**2.6**	**36.8**
Official creditors	0.3	0.4	11.3	3.8	-1.8	1.7	7.0	-5.7	4.4	6.9
Multilateral	0.0	0.8	0.0	-0.5	-2.0	-0.7	-0.8	-3.4	-0.2	5.6
Concessional	0.0	-0.2	0.4	-0.2	-3.6	-2.2	-0.8	-2.9	-0.1	2.9
Bilateral	0.3	-0.4	11.3	4.3	0.2	2.4	7.8	-2.3	4.6	1.3
Concessional	0.1	-0.2	1.2	3.2	0.2	2.5	1.1	-1.4	2.6	2.4
Private creditors	5.3	-0.7	0.2	-1.3	-1.9	-0.8	-0.6	0.3	-1.8	30.0
Bonds	5.3	-0.7	0.0	0.0	0.0	0.0	0.0	0.0	0.0	0.0
Commercial banks	0.0	0.0	-0.3	-0.1	-0.2	-0.1	-0.1	-0.1	0.0	30.0
Other private	0.0	0.0	0.4	-1.3	-1.7	-0.7	-0.5	0.4	-1.8	0.0
Private nonguaranteed	**0.0**	**0.0**	**0.0**	**0.0**	**0.0**	**0.0**	**0.0**	**0.0**	**0.0**	**0.0**
Bonds	0.0	0.0	0.0	0.0	0.0	0.0	0.0	0.0	0.0	0.0
Commercial banks and other	0.0	0.0	0.0	0.0	0.0	0.0	0.0	0.0	0.0	0.0
Memo:										
IBRD	0.0	0.0	0.0	0.0	0.0	0.0	0.0	0.0	0.4	1.8
IDA	0.0	0.0	0.9	-0.1	-0.1	0.1	0.2	0.8	1.3	0.6
DEBT SERVICE (LTDS)	**0.3**	**1.3**	**3.3**	**9.9**	**8.7**	**8.7**	**8.2**	**11.6**	**11.3**	**11.0**
Public and publicly guaranteed	**0.3**	**1.3**	**3.3**	**9.9**	**8.7**	**8.7**	**8.2**	**11.6**	**11.3**	**11.0**
Official creditors	0.0	0.6	3.0	8.6	6.8	7.9	7.7	9.5	9.5	9.8
Multilateral	0.0	0.2	2.9	6.3	5.5	5.1	5.0	6.1	6.2	5.3
Concessional	0.0	0.2	2.5	5.5	4.9	4.2	4.3	4.9	4.8	4.0
Bilateral	0.0	0.4	0.1	2.3	1.3	2.8	2.7	3.4	3.3	4.5
Concessional	0.0	0.2	0.0	2.0	1.2	1.5	1.4	2.3	1.8	2.6
Private creditors	0.3	0.7	0.3	1.3	1.9	0.8	0.6	2.1	1.8	1.2
Bonds	0.3	0.7	0.0	0.0	0.0	0.0	0.0	0.0	0.0	0.0
Commercial banks	0.0	0.0	0.3	0.1	0.2	0.1	0.1	0.1	0.0	0.0
Other private	0.0	0.0	0.1	1.3	1.7	0.7	0.5	2.1	1.8	1.1
Private nonguaranteed	**0.0**	**0.0**	**0.0**	**0.0**	**0.0**	**0.0**	**0.0**	**0.0**	**0.0**	**0.0**
Bonds	0.0	0.0	0.0	0.0	0.0	0.0	0.0	0.0	0.0	0.0
Commercial banks and other	0.0	0.0	0.0	0.0	0.0	0.0	0.0	0.0	0.0	0.0
Memo:										
IBRD	0.0	0.0	0.0	0.0	0.0	0.0	0.0	0.0	0.0	0.0
IDA	0.0	0.0	0.0	0.1	0.1	0.1	0.1	0.1	0.1	0.2
UNDISBURSED DEBT	**2.0**	**11.4**	**25.0**	**19.4**	**31.2**	**29.7**	**26.7**	**43.6**	**30.5**	**38.1**
Official creditors	2.0	11.4	25.0	19.4	31.2	29.7	23.0	40.3	29.4	38.1
Private creditors	0.0	0.0	0.0	0.0	0.0	0.0	3.7	3.3	1.2	0.0
Memorandum items										
Concessional LDOD	4.8	11.9	87.9	96.5	94.6	98.1	98.5	96.7	99.6	104.2
Variable rate LDOD	0.0	0.0	13.4	10.9	10.6	11.5	11.2	11.2	13.8	14.8
Public sector LDOD	14.9	15.8	121.2	133.1	131.4	137.7	143.6	141.7	144.8	180.9
Private sector LDOD	0.0	0.0	0.0	0.0	0.0	0.0	0.0	0.0	0.0	0.0

6. CURRENCY COMPOSITION OF LONG-TERM DEBT (PERCENT)

	1970	1980	1990	1994	1995	1996	1997	1998	1999	2000
Deutsche mark	0.0	0.0	0.0	0.0	0.0	0.0	0.0	0.0	0.0	0.0
French franc	0.0	0.0	0.0	1.4	1.7	1.7	1.4	1.5	1.3	0.8
Japanese yen	0.0	0.0	0.0	0.0	0.0	0.0	0.0	0.0	0.0	0.0
Pound sterling	100.0	56.1	27.8	29.8	28.8	29.7	26.8	25.0	21.9	14.9
Swiss franc	0.0	0.0	0.0	0.0	0.0	0.0	0.0	0.0	0.0	0.0
U.S.dollars	0.0	39.4	61.7	62.0	63.3	60.5	63.3	64.8	65.8	71.2
Multiple currency	0.0	0.0	0.0	0.0	0.0	0.0	0.0	0.1	0.4	2.0
Special drawing rights	0.0	0.0	3.5	2.7	2.4	1.9	2.1	2.0	2.1	2.0
All other currencies	0.0	4.5	7.0	4.1	3.8	6.2	6.4	6.6	8.5	9.1

GRENADA

(US$ million, unless otherwise indicated)

	1970	1980	1990	1994	1995	1996	1997	1998	1999	2000
7. DEBT RESTRUCTURINGS										
Total amount rescheduled	..	..	0.0	0.0	0.0	0.0	0.0	0.0	0.0	0.0
Debt stock rescheduled	..	..	0.0	0.0	0.0	0.0	0.0	0.0	0.0	0.0
Principal rescheduled	..	..	0.0	0.0	0.0	0.0	0.0	0.0	0.0	0.0
Official	..	..	0.0	0.0	0.0	0.0	0.0	0.0	0.0	0.0
Private	..	..	0.0	0.0	0.0	0.0	0.0	0.0	0.0	0.0
Interest rescheduled	..	..	0.0	0.0	0.0	0.0	0.0	0.0	0.0	0.0
Official	..	..	0.0	0.0	0.0	0.0	0.0	0.0	0.0	0.0
Private	..	..	0.0	0.0	0.0	0.0	0.0	0.0	0.0	0.0
Debt forgiven	..	..	0.0	0.0	0.6	0.0	0.0	0.0	0.0	0.0
Memo: interest forgiven	..	..	0.0	0.0	0.0	0.0	0.0	0.0	0.0	0.0
Debt stock reduction	..	..	0.0	0.0	0.0	0.0	0.0	0.0	0.0	0.0
of which debt buyback	..	..	0.0	0.0	0.0	0.0	0.0	0.0	0.0	0.0
8. DEBT STOCK-FLOW RECONCILIATION										
Total change in debt stocks	..	..	22.0	-20.0	-2.7	12.5	-0.9	54.2	-37.6	32.3
Net flows on debt	5.8	-0.9	12.7	-23.0	-2.5	9.1	1.9	52.6	-36.3	35.5
Net change in interest arrears	..	..	2.4	0.1	0.0	0.5	-0.2	0.6	0.7	0.2
Interest capitalized	..	..	0.0	0.0	0.0	0.0	0.0	0.0	0.0	0.0
Debt forgiveness or reduction	..	..	0.0	0.0	-0.6	0.0	0.0	0.0	0.0	0.0
Cross-currency valuation	..	..	6.8	2.9	0.4	2.9	-2.6	1.0	-2.1	-3.4
Residual	..	..	0.1	0.0	0.1	-0.1	0.0	0.0	0.0	0.0
9. AVERAGE TERMS OF NEW COMMITMENTS										
ALL CREDITORS										
Interest (%)	7.4	1.1	4.6	4.6	2.6	4.3	4.9	4.7	6.9	4.4
Maturity (years)	12.7	12.5	14.0	17.3	28.2	22.3	13.2	21.1	5.7	18.2
Grace period (years)	12.7	4.4	2.4	4.2	5.6	6.1	0.5	5.6	1.2	3.7
Grant element (%)	17.0	44.2	27.1	32.8	52.2	42.1	22.4	34.8	8.1	33.1
Official creditors										
Interest (%)	0.0	1.1	4.6	4.6	2.6	4.3	4.7	4.7	6.9	3.7
Maturity (years)	29.5	12.5	14.0	17.3	28.2	22.3	14.4	21.1	5.7	25.2
Grace period (years)	29.5	4.4	2.4	4.2	5.6	6.1	0.3	5.6	1.2	7.6
Grant element (%)	94.0	44.2	27.1	32.8	52.2	42.1	24.3	34.8	8.1	48.1
Private creditors										
Interest (%)	7.5	0.0	0.0	0.0	0.0	0.0	5.3	0.0	0.0	5.0
Maturity (years)	12.5	0.0	0.0	0.0	0.0	0.0	10.5	0.0	0.0	12.0
Grace period (years)	12.5	0.0	0.0	0.0	0.0	0.0	1.0	0.0	0.0	0.3
Grant element (%)	16.1	0.0	0.0	0.0	0.0	0.0	18.2	0.0	0.0	19.8
Memorandum items										
Commitments	5.6	11.4	15.9	14.5	17.0	8.8	12.2	20.7	2.5	56.8
Official creditors	0.1	11.4	15.9	14.5	17.0	8.8	8.5	20.7	2.5	26.8
Private creditors	5.6	0.0	0.0	0.0	0.0	0.0	3.7	0.0	0.0	30.0

10. CONTRACTUAL OBLIGATIONS ON OUTSTANDING LONG-TERM DEBT

	2001	2002	2003	2004	2005	2006	2007	2008	2009	2010
TOTAL										
Disbursements	12.2	8.9	6.0	4.2	2.8	1.7	1.1	0.4	0.3	0.2
Principal	19.6	12.9	12.6	12.3	11.7	11.3	11.2	10.5	9.6	9.2
Interest	5.4	5.1	4.8	4.5	4.1	3.8	3.4	3.0	2.6	2.2
Official creditors										
Disbursements	12.2	8.9	6.0	4.2	2.8	1.7	1.1	0.4	0.3	0.2
Principal	16.5	9.9	9.6	9.2	8.8	8.4	8.3	7.8	7.1	6.7
Interest	3.8	3.7	3.6	3.4	3.2	3.0	2.7	2.5	2.2	2.0
Bilateral creditors										
Disbursements	3.8	3.0	1.8	1.1	0.5	0.3	0.2	0.0	0.0	0.0
Principal	10.8	4.2	4.2	4.0	3.8	3.4	3.4	3.4	3.2	3.0
Interest	1.6	1.3	1.2	1.1	1.0	0.9	0.8	0.7	0.6	0.5
Multilateral creditors										
Disbursements	8.4	6.0	4.2	3.1	2.3	1.5	0.9	0.4	0.3	0.2
Principal	5.8	5.7	5.4	5.2	5.0	5.0	4.9	4.4	3.9	3.8
Interest	2.3	2.4	2.4	2.3	2.2	2.1	1.9	1.8	1.6	1.5
Private creditors										
Disbursements	0.0	0.0	0.0	0.0	0.0	0.0	0.0	0.0	0.0	0.0
Principal	3.0	3.0	3.0	3.0	2.9	2.9	2.9	2.7	2.5	2.5
Interest	1.5	1.4	1.2	1.1	0.9	0.8	0.6	0.5	0.4	0.2
Commercial banks										
Disbursements	0.0	0.0	0.0	0.0	0.0	0.0	0.0	0.0	0.0	0.0
Principal	2.5	2.5	2.5	2.5	2.5	2.5	2.5	2.5	2.5	2.5
Interest	1.4	1.3	1.1	1.0	0.9	0.7	0.6	0.5	0.4	0.2
Other private										
Disbursements	0.0	0.0	0.0	0.0	0.0	0.0	0.0	0.0	0.0	0.0
Principal	0.5	0.5	0.5	0.5	0.4	0.4	0.4	0.2	0.0	0.0
Interest	0.1	0.1	0.1	0.1	0.1	0.0	0.0	0.0	0.0	0.0

GUATEMALA

(US$ million, unless otherwise indicated)

	1970	1980	1990	1994	1995	1996	1997	1998	1999	2000
1. SUMMARY DEBT DATA										
TOTAL DEBT STOCKS (EDT)	**159**	**1,180**	**3,080**	**3,430**	**3,655**	**3,772**	**4,122**	**4,555**	**4,644**	**4,622**
Long-term debt (LDOD)	**120**	**845**	**2,605**	**2,900**	**2,966**	**2,876**	**2,975**	**3,174**	**3,287**	**3,287**
Public and publicly guaranteed	106	563	2,478	2,739	2,824	2,755	2,872	2,992	3,126	3,146
Private nonguaranteed	14	282	127	161	142	121	103	182	162	142
Use of IMF credit	**0**	**0**	**67**	**0**	**0**	**0**	**0**	**0**	**0**	**0**
Short-term debt	**39**	**335**	**409**	**531**	**690**	**896**	**1,147**	**1,381**	**1,356**	**1,335**
of which interest arrears on LDOD	0	0	202	92	98	101	96	88	89	87
Official creditors	0	0	47	33	35	38	35	26	27	26
Private creditors	0	0	155	58	63	63	61	61	61	61
Memo: principal arrears on LDOD	0	0	308	429	478	521	523	512	506	505
Official creditors	0	0	102	150	164	187	173	163	157	151
Private creditors	0	0	206	279	314	335	349	349	349	354
Memo: export credits	0	0	545	418	383	353	526	364	286	270
TOTAL DEBT FLOWS										
Disbursements	**43**	**173**	**165**	**336**	**236**	**158**	**361**	**268**	**327**	**233**
Long-term debt	43	173	165	336	236	158	361	268	327	233
IMF purchases	0	0	0	0	0	0	0	0	0	0
Principal repayments	**30**	**78**	**102**	**180**	**198**	**194**	**201**	**195**	**203**	**193**
Long-term debt	22	78	90	180	198	194	201	195	203	193
IMF repurchases	8	0	12	0	0	0	0	0	0	0
Net flows on debt	**13**	**130**	**67**	**153**	**191**	**167**	**416**	**315**	**100**	**20**
of which short-term debt	0	34	4	-2	153	203	256	242	-25	-20
Interest payments (INT)	**7**	**67**	**112**	**127**	**152**	**161**	**162**	**205**	**213**	**245**
Long-term debt	7	60	88	104	120	120	107	137	141	161
IMF charges	0	0	7	0	0	0	0	0	0	0
Short-term debt	0	8	16	23	32	41	55	68	72	84
Net transfers on debt	**6**	**63**	**-45**	**27**	**39**	**6**	**254**	**111**	**-114**	**-225**
Total debt service paid (TDS)	**38**	**145**	**214**	**307**	**350**	**355**	**363**	**400**	**416**	**438**
Long-term debt	29	137	179	284	318	314	307	331	344	354
IMF repurchases and charges	8	0	19	0	0	0	0	0	0	0
Short-term debt (interest only)	0	8	16	23	32	41	55	68	72	84
2. AGGREGATE NET RESOURCE FLOWS AND NET TRANSFERS (LONG-TERM)										
NET RESOURCE FLOWS	**53**	**221**	**192**	**310**	**219**	**158**	**400**	**899**	**466**	**415**
Net flow of long-term debt (ex. IMF)	21	96	75	155	38	-36	160	74	125	40
Foreign direct investment (net)	29	111	48	65	75	77	84	673	155	230
Portfolio equity flows	0	0	0	0	0	0	0	0	0	0
Grants (excluding technical coop.)	2	14	69	89	106	117	156	152	187	146
Memo: technical coop. grants	9	18	87	66	91	79	101	90	84	88
official net resource flows	9	130	148	203	132	152	240	277	365	238
private net resource flows	44	91	44	107	88	6	160	621	101	178
NET TRANSFERS	**16**	**117**	**67**	**161**	**44**	**-21**	**223**	**688**	**251**	**177**
Interest on long-term debt	7	60	88	104	120	120	107	137	141	161
Profit remittances on FDI	30	44	37	45	55	60	71	74	73	78
Memo: official net transfers	6	101	95	124	45	61	153	179	257	118
private net transfers	9	17	-29	37	-1	-83	70	508	-6	58
3. MAJOR ECONOMIC AGGREGATES										
Gross national income (GNI)	1,866	7,834	7,494	12,841	14,484	15,467	17,484	19,137	18,044	18,743
Exports of goods & services (XGS)	..	1,834	1,695	2,574	3,228	3,212	3,672	4,035	4,022	4,637
of which workers remittances	..	0	107	263	358	375	408	457	466	563
Imports of goods & services (MGS)	..	2,107	2,028	3,385	3,933	3,810	4,504	5,323	5,297	5,992
International reserves (RES)	79	753	362	943	783	948	1,173	1,397	1,252	1,806
Current account balance	..	-163	-213	-625	-572	-452	-634	-1,039	-1,026	-1,049
4. DEBT INDICATORS										
EDT / XGS (%)	..	64.3	181.7	133.3	113.3	117.5	112.2	112.9	115.5	99.7
EDT / GNI (%)	8.5	15.1	41.1	26.7	25.2	24.4	23.6	23.8	25.7	24.7
TDS / XGS (%)	..	7.9	12.6	11.9	10.8	11.0	9.9	9.9	10.3	9.4
INT / XGS (%)	..	3.7	6.6	4.9	4.7	5.0	4.4	5.1	5.3	5.3
INT / GNI (%)	0.4	0.9	1.5	1.0	1.1	1.0	0.9	1.1	1.2	1.3
RES / EDT (%)	49.9	63.8	11.8	27.5	21.4	25.1	28.5	30.7	27.0	39.1
RES / MGS (months)	..	4.3	2.1	3.3	2.4	3.0	3.1	3.2	2.8	3.6
Short-term / EDT (%)	24.5	28.4	13.3	15.5	18.9	23.8	27.8	30.3	29.2	28.9
Concessional / EDT (%)	21.2	21.1	22.5	36.6	35.6	33.7	31.2	29.1	28.6	28.7
Multilateral / EDT (%)	20.7	30.9	33.7	29.1	27.7	27.7	26.1	26.7	30.8	32.3

GUATEMALA

(US$ million, unless otherwise indicated)

5. LONG-TERM DEBT

	1970	1980	1990	1994	1995	1996	1997	1998	1999	2000
DEBT OUTSTANDING (LDOD)	**120**	**845**	**2,605**	**2,900**	**2,966**	**2,876**	**2,975**	**3,174**	**3,287**	**3,287**
Public and publicly guaranteed	**106**	**563**	**2,478**	**2,739**	**2,824**	**2,755**	**2,872**	**2,992**	**3,126**	**3,146**
Official creditors	54	548	1,702	2,113	2,165	2,149	2,173	2,330	2,498	2,550
Multilateral	33	364	1,039	997	1,012	1,044	1,074	1,217	1,429	1,495
Concessional	13	153	335	366	371	379	383	387	417	415
Bilateral	21	183	663	1,116	1,153	1,105	1,099	1,113	1,069	1,056
Concessional	21	96	359	891	930	893	903	936	909	910
Private creditors	52	15	776	626	659	607	699	662	628	596
Bonds	14	0	190	220	264	231	337	307	276	245
Commercial banks	36	14	166	150	140	126	116	114	111	111
Other private	3	1	420	257	255	250	245	242	241	239
Private nonguaranteed	**14**	**282**	**127**	**161**	**142**	**121**	**103**	**182**	**162**	**142**
Bonds	0	0	0	0	0	0	0	0	0	0
Commercial banks and other	14	282	127	161	142	121	103	182	162	142
Memo:										
IBRD	14	144	293	177	158	200	188	203	258	296
IDA	0	0	0	0	0	0	0	0	0	0
DISBURSEMENTS	**43**	**173**	**165**	**336**	**236**	**158**	**361**	**268**	**327**	**233**
Public and publicly guaranteed	**37**	**141**	**158**	**336**	**236**	**158**	**361**	**268**	**327**	**233**
Official creditors	12	128	128	235	163	158	211	267	327	233
Multilateral	9	80	68	151	87	143	136	202	292	165
Concessional	5	35	20	42	19	24	19	19	38	24
Bilateral	2	48	59	84	76	15	74	65	35	68
Concessional	2	23	54	60	56	6	56	63	34	67
Private creditors	26	13	30	101	73	1	150	1	1	0
Bonds	0	0	0	89	59	0	150	0	0	0
Commercial banks	25	13	14	9	2	0	0	0	0	0
Other private	0	0	16	3	12	1	0	1	1	0
Private nonguaranteed	**6**	**32**	**7**	**0**	**0**	**0**	**0**	**0**	**0**	**0**
Bonds	0	0	0	0	0	0	0	0	0	0
Commercial banks and other	6	32	7	0	0	0	0	0	0	0
Memo:										
IBRD	4	39	17	29	13	69	17	28	70	51
IDA	0	0	0	0	0	0	0	0	0	0
PRINCIPAL REPAYMENTS	**22**	**78**	**90**	**180**	**198**	**194**	**201**	**195**	**203**	**193**
Public and publicly guaranteed	**20**	**15**	**87**	**158**	**179**	**173**	**183**	**180**	**182**	**173**
Official creditors	5	12	49	122	137	122	127	142	148	141
Multilateral	3	12	28	86	90	75	71	74	88	78
Concessional	0	1	6	14	14	16	14	15	16	15
Bilateral	2	1	21	35	48	47	56	68	61	63
Concessional	2	1	2	15	22	30	25	45	47	50
Private creditors	16	3	39	37	41	51	56	38	34	32
Bonds	8	0	11	14	15	33	44	31	31	31
Commercial banks	6	1	24	16	11	14	8	3	3	0
Other private	1	2	4	7	15	4	4	5	1	2
Private nonguaranteed	**2**	**62**	**3**	**22**	**19**	**21**	**18**	**15**	**20**	**20**
Bonds	0	0	0	0	0	0	0	0	0	0
Commercial banks and other	2	62	3	22	19	21	18	15	20	20
Memo:										
IBRD	2	4	5	44	40	13	12	14	15	13
IDA	0	0	0	0	0	0	0	0	0	0
NET FLOWS ON DEBT	**21**	**96**	**75**	**155**	**38**	**-36**	**160**	**74**	**125**	**40**
Public and publicly guaranteed	**17**	**126**	**71**	**177**	**57**	**-15**	**178**	**88**	**145**	**60**
Official creditors	7	116	79	113	26	35	84	125	178	92
Multilateral	6	69	40	65	-3	68	66	128	205	87
Concessional	5	33	14	27	4	9	5	4	23	9
Bilateral	1	47	38	48	29	-32	19	-3	-26	5
Concessional	1	23	52	45	34	-24	31	18	-13	18
Private creditors	10	10	-8	64	31	-50	94	-37	-33	-32
Bonds	-8	0	-11	75	44	-33	106	-31	-31	-31
Commercial banks	19	11	-10	-8	-10	-14	-8	-3	-3	0
Other private	-1	-2	12	-4	-3	-3	-4	-4	0	-2
Private nonguaranteed	**4**	**-30**	**4**	**-22**	**-19**	**-21**	**-18**	**-15**	**-20**	**-20**
Bonds	0	0	0	0	0	0	0	0	0	0
Commercial banks and other	4	-30	4	-22	-19	-21	-18	-15	-20	-20
Memo:										
IBRD	2	35	11	-15	-26	56	4	14	55	38
IDA	0	0	0	0	0	0	0	0	0	0

GUATEMALA

(US$ million, unless otherwise indicated)

	1970	1980	1990	1994	1995	1996	1997	1998	1999	2000
INTEREST PAYMENTS (LINT)	**7**	**60**	**88**	**104**	**120**	**120**	**107**	**137**	**141**	**161**
Public and publicly guaranteed	**6**	**30**	**78**	**98**	**115**	**116**	**103**	**126**	**132**	**142**
Official creditors	3	29	52	79	87	91	88	98	108	119
Multilateral	2	21	33	53	52	58	56	60	73	86
Concessional	0	3	4	7	8	8	7	8	8	8
Bilateral	1	9	19	26	35	33	32	38	34	33
Concessional	1	3	4	20	26	27	25	28	29	29
Private creditors	4	0	26	19	28	25	15	28	25	23
Bonds	1	0	18	13	23	21	13	27	24	22
Commercial banks	2	0	6	3	3	2	1	0	0	0
Other private	0	0	3	2	3	2	1	1	0	0
Private nonguaranteed	**1**	**30**	**10**	**6**	**5**	**4**	**4**	**11**	**9**	**19**
Bonds	0	0	0	0	0	0	0	0	0	0
Commercial banks and other	1	30	10	6	5	4	4	11	9	19
Memo:										
IBRD	1	11	4	16	14	14	14	12	16	21
IDA	0	0	0	0	0	0	0	0	0	0
NET TRANSFERS ON DEBT	**14**	**36**	**-13**	**52**	**-82**	**-155**	**53**	**-63**	**-17**	**-121**
Public and publicly guaranteed	**11**	**96**	**-8**	**80**	**-58**	**-130**	**75**	**-38**	**13**	**-82**
Official creditors	4	86	26	34	-61	-56	-3	27	71	-27
Multilateral	5	48	7	12	-55	9	10	68	131	1
Concessional	4	31	10	20	-3	0	-3	-4	14	1
Bilateral	0	38	19	23	-6	-65	-13	-41	-61	-28
Concessional	0	19	49	25	7	-51	6	-10	-42	-11
Private creditors	6	10	-34	45	3	-75	79	-65	-58	-55
Bonds	-10	0	-28	62	22	-54	93	-58	-55	-53
Commercial banks	17	11	-15	-11	-13	-16	-9	-3	-3	0
Other private	-1	-2	9	-6	-6	-5	-5	-5	-1	-2
Private nonguaranteed	**3**	**-60**	**-6**	**-28**	**-24**	**-25**	**-22**	**-25**	**-29**	**-39**
Bonds	0	0	0	0	0	0	0	0	0	0
Commercial banks and other	3	-60	-6	-28	-24	-25	-22	-25	-29	-39
Memo:										
IBRD	1	24	8	-31	-40	42	-10	2	40	17
IDA	0	0	0	0	0	0	0	0	0	0
DEBT SERVICE (LTDS)	**29**	**137**	**179**	**284**	**318**	**314**	**307**	**331**	**344**	**354**
Public and publicly guaranteed	**26**	**45**	**166**	**256**	**294**	**289**	**285**	**306**	**315**	**315**
Official creditors	7	42	101	201	224	213	214	240	256	260
Multilateral	4	32	61	139	142	133	127	133	161	165
Concessional	0	4	10	22	22	24	21	23	24	23
Bilateral	3	10	40	61	82	80	88	106	95	95
Concessional	3	4	6	35	49	57	50	73	76	79
Private creditors	19	3	64	55	69	75	71	66	59	55
Bonds	10	0	28	27	38	54	57	58	55	53
Commercial banks	8	2	29	19	14	16	9	3	3	0
Other private	1	2	7	9	17	6	5	6	1	2
Private nonguaranteed	**3**	**92**	**13**	**28**	**24**	**25**	**22**	**25**	**29**	**39**
Bonds	0	0	0	0	0	0	0	0	0	0
Commercial banks and other	3	92	13	28	24	25	22	25	29	39
Memo:										
IBRD	3	15	9	60	53	27	26	26	30	34
IDA	0	0	0	0	0	0	0	0	0	0
UNDISBURSED DEBT	**70**	**507**	**802**	**649**	**496**	**713**	**672**	**834**	**1,016**	**862**
Official creditors	59	397	741	570	488	707	671	833	1,016	862
Private creditors	10	110	61	79	7	6	2	1	0	0
Memorandum items										
Concessional LDOD	34	249	694	1,256	1,301	1,272	1,286	1,323	1,327	1,325
Variable rate LDOD	25	296	409	662	715	722	702	875	1,011	1,039
Public sector LDOD	106	563	2,475	2,739	2,824	2,755	2,872	2,992	3,126	3,146
Private sector LDOD	15	282	130	161	142	121	103	182	162	142

6. CURRENCY COMPOSITION OF LONG-TERM DEBT (PERCENT)

	1970	1980	1990	1994	1995	1996	1997	1998	1999	2000
Deutsche mark	0.0	0.0	1.6	2.4	3.0	3.1	3.0	3.4	2.9	2.7
French franc	0.0	0.0	0.7	1.9	2.0	1.9	1.7	1.7	1.5	1.4
Japanese yen	0.0	0.0	0.0	2.2	2.0	1.8	2.4	2.5	2.6	2.3
Pound sterling	0.0	0.0	0.0	0.0	0.0	0.0	0.0	0.0	0.0	0.0
Swiss franc	0.0	0.0	0.0	0.1	0.4	0.4	0.3	0.3	0.2	0.1
U.S.dollars	76.2	19.3	56.1	61.1	62.0	62.0	65.6	73.0	75.5	78.4
Multiple currency	23.8	80.6	41.1	32.0	30.2	30.6	26.9	19.1	17.2	14.9
Special drawing rights	0.0	0.0	0.0	0.2	0.1	0.1	0.1	0.1	0.1	0.1
All other currencies	0.0	0.1	0.5	0.1	0.3	0.1	0.0	-0.1	0.0	0.1

GUATEMALA

(US$ million, unless otherwise indicated)

	1970	1980	1990	1994	1995	1996	1997	1998	1999	2000
7. DEBT RESTRUCTURINGS										
Total amount rescheduled	..	..	30	0	0	0	0	0	0	0
Debt stock rescheduled	..	..	8	0	0	0	0	0	0	0
Principal rescheduled	..	..	13	0	0	0	0	0	0	0
Official	..	..	13	0	0	0	0	0	0	0
Private	..	..	0	0	0	0	0	0	0	0
Interest rescheduled	..	..	7	0	0	0	0	0	0	0
Official	..	..	7	0	0	0	0	0	0	0
Private	..	..	0	0	0	0	0	0	0	0
Debt forgiven	..	..	0	0	0	0	0	0	0	0
Memo: interest forgiven	..	..	0	0	0	0	0	0	0	0
Debt stock reduction	..	..	0	0	0	0	0	0	0	0
of which debt buyback	..	..	0	0	0	0	0	0	0	0
8. DEBT STOCK-FLOW RECONCILIATION										
Total change in debt stocks	..	..	430	240	225	117	349	433	89	-22
Net flows on debt	13	130	67	153	191	167	416	315	100	20
Net change in interest arrears	..	..	81	19	6	3	-5	-8	1	-2
Interest capitalized	..	..	7	0	0	0	0	0	0	0
Debt forgiveness or reduction	..	..	0	0	0	0	0	0	0	0
Cross-currency valuation	..	..	36	34	10	-62	-72	23	-15	-29
Residual	..	..	239	34	18	8	10	103	3	-11
9. AVERAGE TERMS OF NEW COMMITMENTS										
ALL CREDITORS										
Interest (%)	5.5	7.9	5.9	5.6	4.2	6.3	7.2	6.2	6.2	7.2
Maturity (years)	25.8	15.5	17.8	21.0	30.9	23.3	15.6	19.3	22.2	19.2
Grace period (years)	6.3	3.9	4.7	6.1	8.1	3.5	6.7	4.5	4.5	4.7
Grant element (%)	36.0	10.9	27.2	29.7	47.5	23.6	17.2	23.7	25.3	17.3
Official creditors										
Interest (%)	3.0	7.3	4.9	5.6	4.2	6.3	6.5	6.2	6.2	7.2
Maturity (years)	39.4	17.7	22.6	21.0	30.9	23.3	18.6	19.3	22.2	19.2
Grace period (years)	10.6	3.5	6.2	6.1	8.1	3.5	5.0	4.5	4.5	4.7
Grant element (%)	61.0	14.3	36.1	29.7	47.5	23.6	21.3	23.7	25.3	17.3
Private creditors										
Interest (%)	8.5	8.5	8.8	0.0	0.0	0.0	8.5	0.0	0.0	0.0
Maturity (years)	9.7	13.2	4.0	0.0	0.0	0.0	10.0	0.0	0.0	0.0
Grace period (years)	1.2	4.2	0.5	0.0	0.0	0.0	10.0	0.0	0.0	0.0
Grant element (%)	6.6	7.5	1.7	0.0	0.0	0.0	9.2	0.0	0.0	0.0
Memorandum items										
Commitments	50	247	146	244	97	384	441	435	514	87
Official creditors	27	124	108	244	97	384	291	435	514	87
Private creditors	23	123	38	0	0	0	150	0	0	0

10. CONTRACTUAL OBLIGATIONS ON OUTSTANDING LONG-TERM DEBT

	2001	2002	2003	2004	2005	2006	2007	2008	2009	2010
TOTAL										
Disbursements	296	230	142	85	53	26	15	8	6	3
Principal	211	227	271	253	250	241	387	228	221	205
Interest	158	159	154	145	135	124	112	87	75	64
Official creditors										
Disbursements	296	230	142	85	53	26	15	8	6	3
Principal	166	182	226	239	236	227	223	213	207	191
Interest	131	136	134	128	118	108	96	85	74	64
Bilateral creditors										
Disbursements	42	33	21	13	9	5	3	2	1	0
Principal	58	54	84	87	89	85	82	74	70	65
Interest	31	30	28	26	23	20	17	15	12	10
Multilateral creditors										
Disbursements	253	197	121	71	45	21	12	6	5	2
Principal	108	128	142	152	148	142	141	139	137	126
Interest	100	106	106	102	96	88	79	71	62	53
Private creditors										
Disbursements	0	0	0	0	0	0	0	0	0	0
Principal	45	45	45	14	14	14	164	14	14	14
Interest	27	24	20	18	17	16	15	2	1	0
Commercial banks										
Disbursements	0	0	0	0	0	0	0	0	0	0
Principal	0	0	0	0	0	0	0	0	0	0
Interest	0	0	0	0	0	0	0	0	0	0
Other private										
Disbursements	0	0	0	0	0	0	0	0	0	0
Principal	45	45	45	14	14	14	164	14	14	14
Interest	27	24	20	18	17	16	15	2	1	0

GUINEA

(US$ million, unless otherwise indicated)

	1970	1980	1990	1994	1995	1996	1997	1998	1999	2000
1. SUMMARY DEBT DATA										
TOTAL DEBT STOCKS (EDT)	**328**	**1,134**	**2,476**	**3,110**	**3,242**	**3,240**	**3,519**	**3,546**	**3,522**	**3,388**
Long-term debt (LDOD)	**320**	**1,019**	**2,253**	**2,886**	**2,987**	**2,981**	**3,009**	**3,126**	**3,061**	**2,940**
Public and publicly guaranteed	320	1,019	2,253	2,886	2,987	2,981	3,009	3,126	3,061	2,940
Private nonguaranteed	0	0	0	0	0	0	0	0	0	0
Use of IMF credit	**4**	**35**	**52**	**71**	**94**	**82**	**99**	**127**	**127**	**113**
Short-term debt	**5**	**80**	**172**	**152**	**161**	**177**	**411**	**293**	**334**	**335**
of which interest arrears on LDOD	5	29	55	100	82	103	98	99	106	118
Official creditors	2	23	49	90	71	91	89	96	102	114
Private creditors	3	5	6	10	11	11	10	4	4	4
Memo: principal arrears on LDOD	17	105	190	460	371	434	471	467	515	566
Official creditors	9	89	164	401	314	368	407	452	491	537
Private creditors	7	15	26	59	58	66	64	15	24	29
Memo: export credits	0	0	352	176	192	191	152	190	145	136
TOTAL DEBT FLOWS										
Disbursements	**98**	**129**	**196**	**182**	**200**	**143**	**265**	**180**	**106**	**70**
Long-term debt	94	121	196	169	169	143	232	148	95	70
IMF purchases	4	8	0	12	31	0	33	32	11	0
Principal repayments	**11**	**76**	**110**	**54**	**129**	**67**	**100**	**104**	**73**	**76**
Long-term debt	11	75	96	48	121	58	90	94	66	68
IMF repurchases	0	1	14	6	9	8	10	9	7	8
Net flows on debt	**87**	**23**	**86**	**120**	**98**	**72**	**403**	**-43**	**68**	**-19**
of which short-term debt	0	-31	0	-9	27	-4	238	-120	35	-12
Interest payments (INT)	**4**	**33**	**59**	**43**	**49**	**47**	**55**	**55**	**55**	**57**
Long-term debt	4	23	53	40	44	43	45	43	44	41
IMF charges	0	1	2	0	0	0	1	1	1	1
Short-term debt	0	9	4	3	5	3	10	12	11	15
Net transfers on debt	**83**	**-11**	**27**	**76**	**49**	**25**	**348**	**-99**	**13**	**-76**
Total debt service paid (TDS)	**15**	**109**	**169**	**97**	**178**	**114**	**155**	**159**	**128**	**133**
Long-term debt	15	98	149	88	164	101	134	138	110	110
IMF repurchases and charges	0	2	16	6	9	9	11	10	8	9
Short-term debt (interest only)	0	9	4	3	5	3	10	12	11	15
2. AGGREGATE NET RESOURCE FLOWS AND NET TRANSFERS (LONG-TERM)										
NET RESOURCE FLOWS	**85**	**106**	**212**	**284**	**285**	**258**	**285**	**244**	**251**	**177**
Net flow of long-term debt (ex. IMF)	83	47	100	122	49	85	143	54	30	2
Foreign direct investment (net)	0	34	18	0	1	24	17	18	63	63
Portfolio equity flows	0	0	0	0	0	0	0	0	0	0
Grants (excluding technical coop.)	2	25	93	162	235	149	125	172	158	112
Memo: technical coop. grants	4	19	61	65	72	68	49	49	54	51
official net resource flows	79	26	212	293	299	217	288	237	188	113
private net resource flows	6	80	-1	-9	-14	41	-3	7	63	63
NET TRANSFERS	**80**	**43**	**98**	**204**	**231**	**200**	**224**	**188**	**189**	**115**
Interest on long-term debt	4	23	53	40	44	43	45	43	44	41
Profit remittances on FDI	0	40	61	40	10	15	16	13	18	20
Memo: official net transfers	76	5	165	254	256	174	246	194	144	72
private net transfers	5	38	-68	-51	-25	25	-22	-6	45	43
3. MAJOR ECONOMIC AGGREGATES										
Gross national income (GNI)	..	..	2,665	3,361	3,608	3,773	3,660	3,460	3,350	2,931
Exports of goods & services (XGS)	..	..	841	676	714	775	749	817	822	870
of which workers remittances	..	..	..	0	1	1	1	4	6	1
Imports of goods & services (MGS)	..	..	1,115	1,131	1,109	1,053	955	1,088	1,032	1,024
International reserves (RES)	..	..	..	88	87	87	122	237	200	148
Current account balance	..	..	-203	-248	-216	-177	-91	-154	-138	-165
4. DEBT INDICATORS										
EDT / XGS (%)	..	..	294.3	460.3	454.3	418.4	469.6	434.0	428.6	389.4
EDT / GNI (%)	..	..	92.9	92.5	89.9	85.9	96.2	102.5	105.2	115.6
TDS / XGS (%)	..	..	20.0	14.3	25.0	14.7	20.7	19.5	15.6	15.3
INT / XGS (%)	..	..	7.0	6.4	6.8	6.1	7.3	6.8	6.7	6.5
INT / GNI (%)	..	..	2.2	1.3	1.4	1.3	1.5	1.6	1.7	1.9
RES / EDT (%)	..	..	..	2.8	2.7	2.7	3.5	6.7	5.7	4.4
RES / MGS (months)	..	..	..	0.9	0.9	1.0	1.5	2.6	2.3	1.7
Short-term / EDT (%)	1.5	7.0	7.0	4.9	5.0	5.5	11.7	8.3	9.5	9.9
Concessional / EDT (%)	75.1	59.8	67.7	74.9	75.8	74.9	70.5	74.7	74.3	74.9
Multilateral / EDT (%)	6.2	11.5	27.4	41.9	45.1	45.9	44.2	47.6	47.7	47.7

GUINEA

(US$ million, unless otherwise indicated)

	1970	1980	1990	1994	1995	1996	1997	1998	1999	2000
5. LONG-TERM DEBT										
DEBT OUTSTANDING (LDOD)	**320**	**1,019**	**2,253**	**2,886**	**2,987**	**2,981**	**3,009**	**3,126**	**3,061**	**2,940**
Public and publicly guaranteed	**320**	**1,019**	**2,253**	**2,886**	**2,987**	**2,981**	**3,009**	**3,126**	**3,061**	**2,940**
Official creditors	279	860	2,145	2,789	2,905	2,883	2,933	3,097	3,032	2,911
Multilateral	20	130	678	1,304	1,460	1,486	1,555	1,689	1,679	1,615
Concessional	0	63	602	1,103	1,216	1,221	1,299	1,449	1,459	1,420
Bilateral	259	731	1,467	1,485	1,444	1,397	1,378	1,408	1,352	1,296
Concessional	246	615	1,073	1,225	1,241	1,205	1,181	1,200	1,159	1,117
Private creditors	40	159	108	98	82	98	76	30	29	29
Bonds	0	0	0	0	0	0	0	0	0	0
Commercial banks	0	9	24	24	25	24	12	0	0	0
Other private	40	150	84	74	57	74	63	30	29	29
Private nonguaranteed	**0**	**0**	**0**	**0**	**0**	**0**	**0**	**0**	**0**	**0**
Bonds	0	0	0	0	0	0	0	0	0	0
Commercial banks and other	0	0	0	0	0	0	0	0	0	0
Memo:										
IBRD	20	55	28	0	0	0	0	0	0	0
IDA	0	32	392	773	847	863	922	1,016	1,014	982
DISBURSEMENTS	**94**	**121**	**196**	**169**	**169**	**143**	**232**	**148**	**95**	**70**
Public and publicly guaranteed	**94**	**121**	**196**	**169**	**169**	**143**	**232**	**148**	**95**	**70**
Official creditors	83	64	196	169	169	126	212	142	95	70
Multilateral	15	34	90	139	161	111	194	135	84	70
Concessional	0	31	85	95	115	69	160	115	67	60
Bilateral	68	30	106	30	8	15	18	7	11	0
Concessional	57	24	105	30	8	14	13	3	10	0
Private creditors	10	57	0	0	0	17	20	7	0	0
Bonds	0	0	0	0	0	0	0	0	0	0
Commercial banks	0	4	0	0	0	0	0	0	0	0
Other private	10	53	0	0	0	17	20	7	0	0
Private nonguaranteed	**0**	**0**	**0**	**0**	**0**	**0**	**0**	**0**	**0**	**0**
Bonds	0	0	0	0	0	0	0	0	0	0
Commercial banks and other	0	0	0	0	0	0	0	0	0	0
Memo:										
IBRD	15	0	0	0	0	0	0	0	0	0
IDA	0	10	52	63	59	47	109	66	29	29
PRINCIPAL REPAYMENTS	**11**	**75**	**96**	**48**	**121**	**58**	**90**	**94**	**66**	**68**
Public and publicly guaranteed	**11**	**75**	**96**	**48**	**121**	**58**	**90**	**94**	**66**	**68**
Official creditors	6	63	77	38	106	58	49	77	65	68
Multilateral	0	14	21	15	35	35	33	61	47	51
Concessional	0	0	6	8	26	26	15	15	25	29
Bilateral	6	50	56	23	71	23	16	16	18	17
Concessional	6	44	48	18	60	18	14	16	18	9
Private creditors	5	11	19	9	15	0	40	17	0	0
Bonds	0	0	0	0	0	0	0	0	0	0
Commercial banks	0	0	7	0	0	0	11	17	0	0
Other private	5	11	11	9	15	0	30	0	0	0
Private nonguaranteed	**0**	**0**	**0**	**0**	**0**	**0**	**0**	**0**	**0**	**0**
Bonds	0	0	0	0	0	0	0	0	0	0
Commercial banks and other	0	0	0	0	0	0	0	0	0	0
Memo:										
IBRD	0	3	12	0	0	0	0	0	0	0
IDA	0	0	1	2	2	4	4	5	10	12
NET FLOWS ON DEBT	**83**	**47**	**100**	**122**	**49**	**85**	**143**	**54**	**30**	**2**
Public and publicly guaranteed	**83**	**47**	**100**	**122**	**49**	**85**	**143**	**54**	**30**	**2**
Official creditors	77	1	119	131	64	68	163	64	30	2
Multilateral	15	20	68	124	126	76	160	74	37	19
Concessional	0	31	80	87	89	44	145	100	42	31
Bilateral	62	-19	51	7	-63	-8	3	-10	-7	-17
Concessional	51	-19	57	12	-52	-4	-1	-12	-8	-9
Private creditors	6	46	-19	-9	-15	17	-20	-10	0	0
Bonds	0	0	0	0	0	0	0	0	0	0
Commercial banks	0	4	-7	0	0	0	-11	-17	0	0
Other private	6	43	-11	-9	-15	17	-10	7	0	0
Private nonguaranteed	**0**	**0**	**0**	**0**	**0**	**0**	**0**	**0**	**0**	**0**
Bonds	0	0	0	0	0	0	0	0	0	0
Commercial banks and other	0	0	0	0	0	0	0	0	0	0
Memo:										
IBRD	15	-3	-12	0	0	0	0	0	0	0
IDA	0	10	51	61	57	43	105	61	19	18

GUINEA

(US$ million, unless otherwise indicated)

	1970	1980	1990	1994	1995	1996	1997	1998	1999	2000
INTEREST PAYMENTS (LINT)	**4**	**23**	**53**	**40**	**44**	**43**	**45**	**43**	**44**	**41**
Public and publicly guaranteed	**4**	**23**	**53**	**40**	**44**	**43**	**45**	**43**	**44**	**41**
Official creditors	3	21	47	39	43	43	42	43	44	41
Multilateral	1	8	12	16	15	24	24	25	26	24
Concessional	0	0	5	10	9	11	11	11	15	13
Bilateral	2	13	35	23	28	19	17	18	18	17
Concessional	2	12	23	17	20	11	12	13	10	9
Private creditors	1	2	6	2	1	0	3	0	0	0
Bonds	0	0	0	0	0	0	0	0	0	0
Commercial banks	0	0	6	0	0	0	2	0	0	0
Other private	1	2	1	2	1	0	1	0	0	0
Private nonguaranteed	**0**	**0**	**0**	**0**	**0**	**0**	**0**	**0**	**0**	**0**
Bonds	0	0	0	0	0	0	0	0	0	0
Commercial banks and other	0	0	0	0	0	0	0	0	0	0
Memo:										
IBRD	1	6	2	0	0	0	0	0	0	0
IDA	0	0	2	6	6	7	6	6	9	7
NET TRANSFERS ON DEBT	**79**	**24**	**47**	**81**	**5**	**41**	**98**	**11**	**-15**	**-40**
Public and publicly guaranteed	**79**	**24**	**47**	**81**	**5**	**41**	**98**	**11**	**-15**	**-40**
Official creditors	74	-20	72	92	21	25	121	21	-15	-39
Multilateral	14	12	57	108	111	52	136	49	11	-6
Concessional	0	31	74	78	80	33	134	89	27	18
Bilateral	60	-32	15	-16	-91	-27	-15	-28	-26	-34
Concessional	49	-31	34	-6	-72	-15	-13	-25	-18	-18
Private creditors	5	44	-25	-11	-16	16	-23	-10	0	0
Bonds	0	0	0	0	0	0	0	0	0	0
Commercial banks	0	3	-13	0	0	0	-13	-17	0	0
Other private	5	40	-12	-11	-16	16	-11	7	0	0
Private nonguaranteed	**0**	**0**	**0**	**0**	**0**	**0**	**0**	**0**	**0**	**0**
Bonds	0	0	0	0	0	0	0	0	0	0
Commercial banks and other	0	0	0	0	0	0	0	0	0	0
Memo:										
IBRD	14	-9	-14	0	0	0	0	0	0	0
IDA	0	10	49	55	51	36	99	55	11	11
DEBT SERVICE (LTDS)	**15**	**98**	**149**	**88**	**164**	**101**	**134**	**138**	**110**	**110**
Public and publicly guaranteed	**15**	**98**	**149**	**88**	**164**	**101**	**134**	**138**	**110**	**110**
Official creditors	9	84	124	77	149	101	91	120	110	109
Multilateral	1	22	33	31	50	59	58	86	73	76
Concessional	0	0	11	18	35	36	26	26	40	42
Bilateral	8	63	91	46	99	42	33	35	37	34
Concessional	8	55	71	35	80	29	26	29	28	18
Private creditors	6	14	25	11	16	0	44	17	0	0
Bonds	0	0	0	0	0	0	0	0	0	0
Commercial banks	0	1	13	0	0	0	13	17	0	0
Other private	6	13	12	11	16	0	31	0	0	0
Private nonguaranteed	**0**	**0**	**0**	**0**	**0**	**0**	**0**	**0**	**0**	**0**
Bonds	0	0	0	0	0	0	0	0	0	0
Commercial banks and other	0	0	0	0	0	0	0	0	0	0
Memo:										
IBRD	1	9	14	0	0	0	0	0	0	0
IDA	0	0	3	8	8	11	10	11	19	19
UNDISBURSED DEBT	**196**	**527**	**1,183**	**621**	**680**	**632**	**476**	**356**	**257**	**208**
Official creditors	173	412	1,182	621	637	605	469	356	257	208
Private creditors	24	115	0	0	44	27	7	0	0	0
Memorandum items										
Concessional LDOD	246	678	1,675	2,329	2,457	2,425	2,479	2,649	2,618	2,536
Variable rate LDOD	0	3	173	100	34	30	18	5	5	5
Public sector LDOD	320	1,019	2,253	2,886	2,987	2,981	3,009	3,126	3,061	2,940
Private sector LDOD	0	0	0	0	0	0	0	0	0	0

6. CURRENCY COMPOSITION OF LONG-TERM DEBT (PERCENT)

	1970	1980	1990	1994	1995	1996	1997	1998	1999	2000
Deutsche mark	7.1	5.1	1.3	0.8	0.8	0.7	0.6	0.6	0.5	0.5
French franc	5.1	11.3	14.9	11.8	9.6	8.9	8.3	7.9	6.7	6.3
Japanese yen	0.0	0.1	2.2	3.8	3.5	3.2	2.6	2.7	3.0	2.8
Pound sterling	4.0	4.1	1.8	1.0	0.9	1.0	0.9	0.8	0.7	0.6
Swiss franc	0.0	0.8	0.6	0.5	0.3	0.3	0.3	0.3	0.2	0.2
U.S.dollars	16.0	28.2	33.1	43.5	48.5	49.3	51.5	51.8	53.3	54.1
Multiple currency	6.4	5.5	7.6	7.9	8.0	7.9	7.4	7.6	7.7	7.5
Special drawing rights	0.0	0.0	0.6	1.0	1.1	1.1	1.2	1.5	1.6	1.6
All other currencies	61.4	44.9	37.9	29.7	27.3	27.6	27.2	26.8	26.3	26.4

GUINEA

(US$ million, unless otherwise indicated)

	1970	1980	1990	1994	1995	1996	1997	1998	1999	2000
7. DEBT RESTRUCTURINGS										
Total amount rescheduled	..	..	110	0	131	0	84	22	39	0
Debt stock rescheduled	..	..	0	0	0	0	0	0	0	0
Principal rescheduled	..	..	71	0	94	0	24	15	14	0
Official	..	..	71	0	93	0	24	15	14	0
Private	..	..	0	0	2	0	0	0	0	0
Interest rescheduled	..	..	0	0	16	0	11	7	6	0
Official	..	..	0	0	15	0	11	7	6	0
Private	..	..	0	0	0	0	0	0	0	0
Debt forgiven	..	..	2	1	53	0	7	5	4	0
Memo: interest forgiven	..	..	0	0	8	0	3	2	2	0
Debt stock reduction	..	..	0	0	0	0	0	130	0	0
of which debt buyback	..	..	0	0	0	0	0	17	0	0
8. DEBT STOCK-FLOW RECONCILIATION										
Total change in debt stocks	..	..	300	262	132	-2	279	27	-23	-135
Net flows on debt	87	23	86	120	98	72	403	-43	68	-19
Net change in interest arrears	..	..	25	33	-18	21	-4	1	6	13
Interest capitalized	..	..	0	0	16	0	11	7	6	0
Debt forgiveness or reduction	..	..	-2	-1	-53	0	-7	-118	-4	0
Cross-currency valuation	..	..	106	17	-16	-148	-206	-10	-69	-97
Residual	..	..	85	94	106	54	82	190	-31	-31
9. AVERAGE TERMS OF NEW COMMITMENTS										
ALL CREDITORS										
Interest (%)	2.9	4.6	2.6	1.3	2.1	2.5	0.6	1.4	0.8	0.8
Maturity (years)	12.9	19.3	30.5	32.7	21.3	28.5	43.0	37.2	39.5	45.0
Grace period (years)	5.2	5.6	8.2	8.7	6.8	8.3	10.4	9.0	10.0	10.2
Grant element (%)	40.1	36.2	59.5	70.2	50.6	60.4	83.1	69.7	80.3	81.9
Official creditors										
Interest (%)	0.9	3.4	2.6	1.3	2.0	2.5	0.6	1.4	0.8	0.8
Maturity (years)	15.0	22.8	30.5	32.7	25.9	28.5	43.0	37.2	39.5	45.0
Grace period (years)	7.0	6.6	8.2	8.7	8.5	8.3	10.4	9.0	10.0	10.2
Grant element (%)	55.5	46.5	59.5	70.2	60.8	60.4	83.1	69.7	80.3	81.9
Private creditors										
Interest (%)	6.2	7.9	0.0	0.0	2.7	0.0	0.0	0.0	0.0	0.0
Maturity (years)	9.5	9.8	0.0	0.0	3.5	0.0	0.0	0.0	0.0	0.0
Grace period (years)	2.5	3.0	0.0	0.0	0.1	0.0	0.0	0.0	0.0	0.0
Grant element (%)	15.6	8.0	0.0	0.0	10.8	0.0	0.0	0.0	0.0	0.0
Memorandum items										
Commitments	68	269	487	75	215	131	135	24	51	41
Official creditors	42	197	487	75	171	131	135	24	51	41
Private creditors	26	72	0	0	44	0	0	0	0	0

10. CONTRACTUAL OBLIGATIONS ON OUTSTANDING LONG-TERM DEBT

	2001	2002	2003	2004	2005	2006	2007	2008	2009	2010
TOTAL										
Disbursements	76	59	36	20	11	4	3	1	0	0
Principal	114	112	110	109	94	94	90	91	92	94
Interest	50	47	44	41	38	35	32	30	28	26
Official creditors										
Disbursements	76	59	36	20	11	4	3	1	0	0
Principal	113	112	110	109	94	94	90	91	92	94
Interest	50	47	44	41	38	35	32	30	28	26
Bilateral creditors										
Disbursements	0	0	0	0	0	0	0	0	0	0
Principal	60	57	53	52	36	35	33	32	32	32
Interest	26	24	22	20	19	18	17	16	15	14
Multilateral creditors										
Disbursements	76	59	36	20	11	4	3	1	0	0
Principal	54	56	57	57	58	59	57	59	60	63
Interest	24	23	22	20	19	17	16	14	13	12
Private creditors										
Disbursements	0	0	0	0	0	0	0	0	0	0
Principal	0	0	0	0	0	0	0	0	0	0
Interest	0	0	0	0	0	0	0	0	0	0
Commercial banks										
Disbursements	0	0	0	0	0	0	0	0	0	0
Principal	0	0	0	0	0	0	0	0	0	0
Interest	0	0	0	0	0	0	0	0	0	0
Other private										
Disbursements	0	0	0	0	0	0	0	0	0	0
Principal	0	0	0	0	0	0	0	0	0	0
Interest	0	0	0	0	0	0	0	0	0	0

GUINEA-BISSAU

(US$ million, unless otherwise indicated)

	1970	1980	1990	1994	1995	1996	1997	1998	1999	2000
1. SUMMARY DEBT DATA										
TOTAL DEBT STOCKS (EDT)	**0.0**	**139.6**	**692.1**	**852.5**	**898.3**	**936.8**	**921.3**	**965.6**	**933.7**	**941.5**
Long-term debt (LDOD)	**0.0**	**133.1**	**630.4**	**761.6**	**797.7**	**856.2**	**838.4**	**874.3**	**834.2**	**818.3**
Public and publicly guaranteed	0.0	133.1	630.4	761.6	797.7	856.2	838.4	874.3	834.2	818.3
Private nonguaranteed	0.0	0.0	0.0	0.0	0.0	0.0	0.0	0.0	0.0	0.0
Use of IMF credit	**0.0**	**1.4**	**5.3**	**4.6**	**5.9**	**7.7**	**12.2**	**15.4**	**17.3**	**24.7**
Short-term debt	**0.0**	**5.1**	**56.5**	**86.2**	**94.6**	**73.0**	**70.7**	**76.0**	**82.2**	**98.5**
of which interest arrears on LDOD	0.0	1.1	29.9	79.2	88.6	61.5	62.7	71.9	79.1	85.5
Official creditors	0.0	1.1	27.5	74.0	82.6	61.4	62.7	71.8	79.0	85.4
Private creditors	0.0	0.0	2.4	5.3	6.1	0.0	0.0	0.1	0.1	0.1
Memo: principal arrears on LDOD	0.0	4.5	112.8	230.3	252.0	157.7	161.6	176.9	199.7	217.6
Official creditors	0.0	2.7	107.0	202.9	221.1	157.4	161.3	176.5	199.2	217.0
Private creditors	0.0	1.8	5.9	27.4	30.9	0.3	0.3	0.4	0.5	0.6
Memo: export credits	0.0	0.0	98.0	79.6	106.1	94.7	152.7	167.7	159.6	154.8
TOTAL DEBT FLOWS										
Disbursements	**0.0**	**74.7**	**36.5**	**28.4**	**23.5**	**31.3**	**36.5**	**17.7**	**5.0**	**22.2**
Long-term debt	0.0	74.7	36.5	28.4	21.1	28.3	30.3	14.5	2.1	13.6
IMF purchases	0.0	0.0	0.0	0.0	2.4	3.0	6.1	3.2	2.9	8.6
Principal repayments	**0.0**	**3.0**	**2.3**	**3.5**	**9.3**	**6.7**	**6.1**	**7.0**	**4.0**	**3.5**
Long-term debt	0.0	3.0	2.3	3.1	8.1	5.6	5.0	6.4	3.4	3.3
IMF repurchases	0.0	0.0	0.0	0.4	1.1	1.1	1.0	0.6	0.6	0.2
Net flows on debt	**0.0**	**72.7**	**45.7**	**27.1**	**13.2**	**30.1**	**26.9**	**6.7**	**0.0**	**28.7**
of which short-term debt	0.0	1.0	11.6	2.3	-1.0	5.5	-3.5	-3.9	-1.0	10.0
Interest payments (INT)	**0.0**	**1.6**	**6.1**	**3.9**	**6.1**	**4.5**	**3.6**	**5.1**	**5.1**	**2.7**
Long-term debt	0.0	1.1	3.4	3.6	5.7	4.0	3.0	4.7	4.8	1.9
IMF charges	0.0	0.1	0.0	0.0	0.0	0.0	0.1	0.1	0.1	0.3
Short-term debt	0.0	0.5	2.7	0.3	0.4	0.5	0.5	0.3	0.2	0.5
Net transfers on debt	**0.0**	**71.0**	**39.6**	**23.2**	**7.2**	**25.6**	**23.3**	**1.5**	**-5.1**	**26.0**
Total debt service paid (TDS)	**0.0**	**4.6**	**8.4**	**7.4**	**15.3**	**11.2**	**9.7**	**12.2**	**9.1**	**6.2**
Long-term debt	0.0	4.1	5.7	6.7	13.8	9.6	8.1	11.2	8.1	5.2
IMF repurchases and charges	0.0	0.1	0.0	0.4	1.2	1.1	1.1	0.7	0.7	0.5
Short-term debt (interest only)	0.0	0.5	2.7	0.3	0.4	0.5	0.5	0.3	0.2	0.5
2. AGGREGATE NET RESOURCE FLOWS AND NET TRANSFERS (LONG-TERM)										
NET RESOURCE FLOWS	**0.0**	**108.4**	**96.3**	**75.7**	**68.1**	**77.8**	**87.5**	**56.3**	**42.9**	**60.8**
Net flow of long-term debt (ex. IMF)	0.0	71.7	34.2	25.3	13.0	22.7	25.3	8.0	-1.3	10.4
Foreign direct investment (net)	0.0	0.0	2.0	1.0	1.0	1.0	10.0	0.0	3.0	0.0
Portfolio equity flows	0.0	0.0	0.0	0.0	0.0	0.0	0.0	0.0	0.0	0.0
Grants (excluding technical coop.)	0.0	36.7	60.2	49.4	54.1	54.1	52.2	48.3	41.2	50.4
Memo: technical coop. grants	0.1	12.1	21.4	39.6	46.5	40.5	40.3	31.6	12.6	13.0
official net resource flows	0.0	90.6	94.4	74.8	67.3	76.9	77.5	56.3	39.9	60.8
private net resource flows	0.0	17.8	1.9	0.9	0.8	0.9	10.0	0.0	3.0	0.0
NET TRANSFERS	**0.0**	**107.3**	**92.9**	**72.1**	**62.5**	**73.8**	**84.5**	**51.6**	**38.1**	**58.9**
Interest on long-term debt	0.0	1.1	3.4	3.6	5.7	4.0	3.0	4.7	4.8	1.9
Profit remittances on FDI	0.0	0.0	0.0	0.0	0.0	0.0	0.0	0.0	0.0	0.0
Memo: official net transfers	0.0	90.3	91.3	71.2	61.7	73.0	74.5	51.6	35.1	58.9
private net transfers	0.0	17.0	1.6	0.9	0.8	0.8	10.0	0.0	3.0	0.0
3. MAJOR ECONOMIC AGGREGATES										
Gross national income (GNI)	78.7	104.8	233.3	221.5	236.0	251.9	254.3	191.5	210.1	203.1
Exports of goods & services (XGS)	..	..	27.1	38.8	29.6	30.6	58.9	31.8	58.0	72.1
of which workers remittances	..	..	1.0	..	..	2.0	2.0	1.8	1.8	1.8
Imports of goods & services (MGS)	..	..	110.5	107.2	110.3	104.7	102.9	74.8	93.7	119.7
International reserves (RES)	..	..	18.2	18.4	20.3	11.5	33.7	35.8	35.3	66.7
Current account balance	..	..	-45.3	-45.9	-35.2	-44.5	-6.4	..	..	..
4. DEBT INDICATORS										
EDT / XGS (%)	..	..	2,553.9	2,196.0	3,035.8	3,064.4	1,565.2	3,032.7	1,608.9	1,305.1
EDT / GNI (%)	0.0	133.3	296.6	384.8	380.7	371.9	362.3	504.3	444.5	463.5
TDS / XGS (%)	..	..	31.0	19.1	51.7	36.6	16.5	38.3	15.7	8.6
INT / XGS (%)	..	..	22.5	10.1	20.6	14.7	6.1	16.0	8.8	3.7
INT / GNI (%)	0.0	1.5	2.6	1.8	2.6	1.8	1.4	2.7	2.4	1.3
RES / EDT (%)	..	..	2.6	2.2	2.3	1.2	3.7	3.7	3.8	7.1
RES / MGS (months)	..	..	2.0	2.1	2.2	1.3	3.9	5.7	4.5	6.7
Short-term / EDT (%)	..	3.7	8.2	10.1	10.5	7.8	7.7	7.9	8.8	10.5
Concessional / EDT (%)	..	62.0	56.7	62.6	62.9	72.1	72.2	72.3	71.6	69.6
Multilateral / EDT (%)	..	24.5	39.5	41.2	41.1	40.9	42.0	42.5	42.7	41.5

GUINEA-BISSAU

(US$ million, unless otherwise indicated)

	1970	1980	1990	1994	1995	1996	1997	1998	1999	2000
5. LONG-TERM DEBT										
DEBT OUTSTANDING (LDOD)	**0.0**	**133.1**	**630.4**	**761.6**	**797.7**	**856.2**	**838.4**	**874.3**	**834.2**	**818.3**
Public and publicly guaranteed	**0.0**	**133.1**	**630.4**	**761.6**	**797.7**	**856.2**	**838.4**	**874.3**	**834.2**	**818.3**
Official creditors	0.0	96.9	597.4	733.5	766.2	855.4	837.6	873.5	833.4	817.5
Multilateral	0.0	34.2	273.3	351.2	369.6	382.7	386.9	410.1	398.3	390.5
Concessional	0.0	29.0	244.3	318.8	340.0	365.7	371.9	395.1	384.4	377.4
Bilateral	0.0	62.7	324.1	382.3	396.7	472.7	450.6	463.4	435.1	427.0
Concessional	0.0	57.6	148.2	215.0	224.6	309.6	293.6	302.6	283.7	277.5
Private creditors	0.0	36.2	32.9	28.2	31.5	0.8	0.8	0.8	0.8	0.8
Bonds	0.0	0.0	0.0	0.0	0.0	0.0	0.0	0.0	0.0	0.0
Commercial banks	0.0	2.1	0.0	0.0	0.0	0.0	0.0	0.0	0.0	0.0
Other private	0.0	34.0	32.9	28.2	31.5	0.8	0.8	0.8	0.8	0.8
Private nonguaranteed	**0.0**	**0.0**	**0.0**	**0.0**	**0.0**	**0.0**	**0.0**	**0.0**	**0.0**	**0.0**
Bonds	0.0	0.0	0.0	0.0	0.0	0.0	0.0	0.0	0.0	0.0
Commercial banks and other	0.0	0.0	0.0	0.0	0.0	0.0	0.0	0.0	0.0	0.0
Memo:										
IBRD	0.0	0.0	0.0	0.0	0.0	0.0	0.0	0.0	0.0	0.0
IDA	0.0	4.7	145.5	197.3	209.9	216.2	220.7	233.5	227.9	227.6
DISBURSEMENTS	**0.0**	**74.7**	**36.5**	**28.4**	**21.1**	**28.3**	**30.3**	**14.5**	**2.1**	**13.6**
Public and publicly guaranteed	**0.0**	**74.7**	**36.5**	**28.4**	**21.1**	**28.3**	**30.3**	**14.5**	**2.1**	**13.6**
Official creditors	0.0	54.1	36.5	28.4	21.1	28.3	30.3	14.5	2.1	13.6
Multilateral	0.0	29.5	30.3	12.2	18.8	28.3	30.3	14.5	2.1	13.6
Concessional	0.0	24.3	30.3	11.9	18.5	27.7	30.3	14.5	2.1	13.6
Bilateral	0.0	24.7	6.2	16.2	2.3	0.0	0.0	0.0	0.0	0.0
Concessional	0.0	24.2	6.2	13.9	2.3	0.0	0.0	0.0	0.0	0.0
Private creditors	0.0	20.5	0.0	0.0	0.0	0.0	0.0	0.0	0.0	0.0
Bonds	0.0	0.0	0.0	0.0	0.0	0.0	0.0	0.0	0.0	0.0
Commercial banks	0.0	0.0	0.0	0.0	0.0	0.0	0.0	0.0	0.0	0.0
Other private	0.0	20.5	0.0	0.0	0.0	0.0	0.0	0.0	0.0	0.0
Private nonguaranteed	**0.0**	**0.0**	**0.0**	**0.0**	**0.0**	**0.0**	**0.0**	**0.0**	**0.0**	**0.0**
Bonds	0.0	0.0	0.0	0.0	0.0	0.0	0.0	0.0	0.0	0.0
Commercial banks and other	0.0	0.0	0.0	0.0	0.0	0.0	0.0	0.0	0.0	0.0
Memo:										
IBRD	0.0	0.0	0.0	0.0	0.0	0.0	0.0	0.0	0.0	0.0
IDA	0.0	4.2	15.5	11.1	8.8	14.1	17.7	5.3	2.1	13.6
PRINCIPAL REPAYMENTS	**0.0**	**3.0**	**2.3**	**3.1**	**8.1**	**5.6**	**5.0**	**6.4**	**3.4**	**3.3**
Public and publicly guaranteed	**0.0**	**3.0**	**2.3**	**3.1**	**8.1**	**5.6**	**5.0**	**6.4**	**3.4**	**3.3**
Official creditors	0.0	0.2	2.3	3.0	8.0	5.5	5.0	6.4	3.4	3.3
Multilateral	0.0	0.0	1.5	1.8	7.8	4.1	3.5	6.4	3.4	3.3
Concessional	0.0	0.0	0.6	1.0	4.0	2.5	2.9	5.7	3.3	3.2
Bilateral	0.0	0.2	0.8	1.2	0.2	1.4	1.6	0.0	0.0	0.0
Concessional	0.0	0.0	0.3	1.2	0.2	0.2	1.6	0.0	0.0	0.0
Private creditors	0.0	2.8	0.1	0.1	0.2	0.1	0.0	0.0	0.0	0.0
Bonds	0.0	0.0	0.0	0.0	0.0	0.0	0.0	0.0	0.0	0.0
Commercial banks	0.0	0.4	0.0	0.0	0.0	0.0	0.0	0.0	0.0	0.0
Other private	0.0	2.4	0.1	0.1	0.2	0.1	0.0	0.0	0.0	0.0
Private nonguaranteed	**0.0**	**0.0**	**0.0**	**0.0**	**0.0**	**0.0**	**0.0**	**0.0**	**0.0**	**0.0**
Bonds	0.0	0.0	0.0	0.0	0.0	0.0	0.0	0.0	0.0	0.0
Commercial banks and other	0.0	0.0	0.0	0.0	0.0	0.0	0.0	0.0	0.0	0.0
Memo:										
IBRD	0.0	0.0	0.0	0.0	0.0	0.0	0.0	0.0	0.0	0.0
IDA	0.0	0.0	0.1	0.6	0.9	0.8	1.3	0.5	2.7	2.9
NET FLOWS ON DEBT	**0.0**	**71.7**	**34.2**	**25.3**	**13.0**	**22.7**	**25.3**	**8.0**	**-1.3**	**10.4**
Public and publicly guaranteed	**0.0**	**71.7**	**34.2**	**25.3**	**13.0**	**22.7**	**25.3**	**8.0**	**-1.3**	**10.4**
Official creditors	0.0	53.9	34.2	25.4	13.2	22.8	25.3	8.0	-1.3	10.4
Multilateral	0.0	29.5	28.8	10.4	11.0	24.1	26.9	8.0	-1.3	10.4
Concessional	0.0	24.3	29.7	10.9	14.6	25.1	27.4	8.8	-1.2	10.4
Bilateral	0.0	24.5	5.4	14.9	2.2	-1.4	-1.6	0.0	0.0	0.0
Concessional	0.0	24.2	5.9	12.7	2.2	-0.2	-1.6	0.0	0.0	0.0
Private creditors	0.0	17.8	-0.1	-0.1	-0.2	-0.1	0.0	0.0	0.0	0.0
Bonds	0.0	0.0	0.0	0.0	0.0	0.0	0.0	0.0	0.0	0.0
Commercial banks	0.0	-0.4	0.0	0.0	0.0	0.0	0.0	0.0	0.0	0.0
Other private	0.0	18.1	-0.1	-0.1	-0.2	-0.1	0.0	0.0	0.0	0.0
Private nonguaranteed	**0.0**	**0.0**	**0.0**	**0.0**	**0.0**	**0.0**	**0.0**	**0.0**	**0.0**	**0.0**
Bonds	0.0	0.0	0.0	0.0	0.0	0.0	0.0	0.0	0.0	0.0
Commercial banks and other	0.0	0.0	0.0	0.0	0.0	0.0	0.0	0.0	0.0	0.0
Memo:										
IBRD	0.0	0.0	0.0	0.0	0.0	0.0	0.0	0.0	0.0	0.0
IDA	0.0	4.2	15.4	10.4	7.9	13.3	16.4	4.8	-0.6	10.7

GUINEA-BISSAU

(US$ million, unless otherwise indicated)

	1970	1980	1990	1994	1995	1996	1997	1998	1999	2000
INTEREST PAYMENTS (LINT)	**0.0**	**1.1**	**3.4**	**3.6**	**5.7**	**4.0**	**3.0**	**4.7**	**4.8**	**1.9**
Public and publicly guaranteed	**0.0**	**1.1**	**3.4**	**3.6**	**5.7**	**4.0**	**3.0**	**4.7**	**4.8**	**1.9**
Official creditors	0.0	0.3	3.1	3.6	5.6	3.9	3.0	4.7	4.8	1.9
Multilateral	0.0	0.0	2.6	2.9	4.4	2.8	2.9	2.2	2.6	1.9
Concessional	0.0	0.0	1.8	1.6	3.0	2.2	2.7	1.8	2.6	1.9
Bilateral	0.0	0.2	0.6	0.7	1.2	1.1	0.1	2.5	2.1	0.0
Concessional	0.0	0.2	0.3	0.7	0.3	1.1	0.1	2.5	2.1	0.0
Private creditors	0.0	0.8	0.3	0.0	0.0	0.1	0.0	0.0	0.0	0.0
Bonds	0.0	0.0	0.0	0.0	0.0	0.0	0.0	0.0	0.0	0.0
Commercial banks	0.0	0.1	0.0	0.0	0.0	0.0	0.0	0.0	0.0	0.0
Other private	0.0	0.7	0.3	0.0	0.0	0.1	0.0	0.0	0.0	0.0
Private nonguaranteed	**0.0**	**0.0**	**0.0**	**0.0**	**0.0**	**0.0**	**0.0**	**0.0**	**0.0**	**0.0**
Bonds	0.0	0.0	0.0	0.0	0.0	0.0	0.0	0.0	0.0	0.0
Commercial banks and other	0.0	0.0	0.0	0.0	0.0	0.0	0.0	0.0	0.0	0.0
Memo:										
IBRD	0.0	0.0	0.0	0.0	0.0	0.0	0.0	0.0	0.0	0.0
IDA	0.0	0.0	1.1	1.4	1.6	1.4	1.8	0.8	2.5	1.8
NET TRANSFERS ON DEBT	**0.0**	**70.6**	**30.8**	**21.7**	**7.3**	**18.7**	**22.2**	**3.3**	**-6.0**	**8.4**
Public and publicly guaranteed	**0.0**	**70.6**	**30.8**	**21.7**	**7.3**	**18.7**	**22.2**	**3.3**	**-6.0**	**8.4**
Official creditors	0.0	53.7	31.1	21.7	7.5	18.9	22.2	3.3	-6.0	8.4
Multilateral	0.0	29.4	26.2	7.5	6.6	21.3	23.9	5.8	-3.9	8.4
Concessional	0.0	24.3	27.9	9.3	11.6	22.9	24.7	7.0	-3.8	8.5
Bilateral	0.0	24.2	4.9	14.2	0.9	-2.5	-1.7	-2.5	-2.1	0.0
Concessional	0.0	24.0	5.7	12.0	1.9	-1.3	-1.7	-2.5	-2.1	0.0
Private creditors	0.0	16.9	-0.3	-0.1	-0.2	-0.2	0.0	0.0	0.0	0.0
Bonds	0.0	0.0	0.0	0.0	0.0	0.0	0.0	0.0	0.0	0.0
Commercial banks	0.0	-0.5	0.0	0.0	0.0	0.0	0.0	0.0	0.0	0.0
Other private	0.0	17.4	-0.3	-0.1	-0.2	-0.2	0.0	0.0	0.0	0.0
Private nonguaranteed	**0.0**	**0.0**	**0.0**	**0.0**	**0.0**	**0.0**	**0.0**	**0.0**	**0.0**	**0.0**
Bonds	0.0	0.0	0.0	0.0	0.0	0.0	0.0	0.0	0.0	0.0
Commercial banks and other	0.0	0.0	0.0	0.0	0.0	0.0	0.0	0.0	0.0	0.0
Memo:										
IBRD	0.0	0.0	0.0	0.0	0.0	0.0	0.0	0.0	0.0	0.0
IDA	0.0	4.2	14.2	9.1	6.3	11.9	14.6	4.0	-3.1	8.9
DEBT SERVICE (LTDS)	**0.0**	**4.1**	**5.7**	**6.7**	**13.8**	**9.6**	**8.1**	**11.2**	**8.1**	**5.2**
Public and publicly guaranteed	**0.0**	**4.1**	**5.7**	**6.7**	**13.8**	**9.6**	**8.1**	**11.2**	**8.1**	**5.2**
Official creditors	0.0	0.5	5.4	6.6	13.6	9.4	8.1	11.2	8.1	5.2
Multilateral	0.0	0.0	4.0	4.7	12.2	6.9	6.4	8.7	6.0	5.2
Concessional	0.0	0.0	2.3	2.6	6.9	4.7	5.6	7.4	5.9	5.1
Bilateral	0.0	0.4	1.4	2.0	1.4	2.5	1.7	2.5	2.1	0.0
Concessional	0.0	0.2	0.5	1.9	0.4	1.3	1.7	2.5	2.1	0.0
Private creditors	0.0	3.6	0.3	0.1	0.2	0.2	0.0	0.0	0.0	0.0
Bonds	0.0	0.0	0.0	0.0	0.0	0.0	0.0	0.0	0.0	0.0
Commercial banks	0.0	0.5	0.0	0.0	0.0	0.0	0.0	0.0	0.0	0.0
Other private	0.0	3.1	0.3	0.1	0.2	0.2	0.0	0.0	0.0	0.0
Private nonguaranteed	**0.0**	**0.0**	**0.0**	**0.0**	**0.0**	**0.0**	**0.0**	**0.0**	**0.0**	**0.0**
Bonds	0.0	0.0	0.0	0.0	0.0	0.0	0.0	0.0	0.0	0.0
Commercial banks and other	0.0	0.0	0.0	0.0	0.0	0.0	0.0	0.0	0.0	0.0
Memo:										
IBRD	0.0	0.0	0.0	0.0	0.0	0.0	0.0	0.0	0.0	0.0
IDA	0.0	0.0	1.2	2.0	2.5	2.2	3.1	1.4	5.2	4.7
UNDISBURSED DEBT	**0.0**	**72.6**	**271.9**	**157.1**	**134.6**	**91.4**	**85.2**	**77.8**	**66.4**	**72.8**
Official creditors	0.0	66.6	263.6	157.1	134.6	91.4	85.2	77.8	66.4	72.8
Private creditors	0.0	6.0	8.3	0.0	0.0	0.0	0.0	0.0	0.0	0.0
Memorandum items										
Concessional LDOD	0.0	86.6	392.6	533.8	564.5	675.3	665.5	697.7	668.1	655.0
Variable rate LDOD	0.0	2.1	36.9	45.4	47.1	15.7	15.7	15.7	15.7	15.7
Public sector LDOD	0.0	133.1	630.4	761.6	797.7	856.2	838.4	874.3	834.2	818.3
Private sector LDOD	0.0	0.0	0.0	0.0	0.0	0.0	0.0	0.0	0.0	0.0

6. CURRENCY COMPOSITION OF LONG-TERM DEBT (PERCENT)

	1970	1980	1990	1994	1995	1996	1997	1998	1999	2000
Deutsche mark	0.0	0.0	0.5	0.4	0.4	0.4	0.3	0.3	0.3	0.3
French franc	0.0	14.8	1.8	1.2	1.4	1.1	1.0	1.0	0.9	0.9
Japanese yen	0.0	0.0	0.0	0.0	0.0	0.0	0.0	0.0	0.0	0.0
Pound sterling	0.0	0.0	0.0	0.0	0.0	0.0	0.0	0.0	0.0	0.0
Swiss franc	0.0	2.8	8.6	7.3	6.6	12.7	12.2	12.3	11.1	11.1
U.S.dollars	0.0	25.1	27.3	36.5	38.1	30.1	31.9	31.3	32.4	33.5
Multiple currency	0.0	2.8	26.4	26.0	25.5	24.0	24.1	25.0	25.3	24.5
Special drawing rights	0.0	0.0	0.0	0.0	0.0	0.0	0.0	0.0	0.0	0.0
All other currencies	0.0	54.5	35.4	28.6	28.0	31.7	30.5	30.1	30.0	29.7

GUINEA-BISSAU

(US$ million, unless otherwise indicated)

	1970	1980	1990	1994	1995	1996	1997	1998	1999	2000
7. DEBT RESTRUCTURINGS										
Total amount rescheduled	..	..	16.1	23.4	13.7	228.0	3.0	1.1	0.0	0.0
Debt stock rescheduled	..	..	0.0	0.0	0.0	16.3	0.0	0.0	0.0	0.0
Principal rescheduled	..	..	8.2	21.5	0.0	112.9	0.4	0.3	0.0	0.0
Official	..	..	3.8	21.5	0.0	84.4	0.4	0.3	0.0	0.0
Private	..	..	4.4	0.0	0.0	28.5	0.0	0.0	0.0	0.0
Interest rescheduled	..	..	6.8	0.1	0.0	43.3	0.1	0.1	0.0	0.0
Official	..	..	3.7	0.1	0.0	37.6	0.1	0.1	0.0	0.0
Private	..	..	3.1	0.0	0.0	5.6	0.0	0.0	0.0	0.0
Debt forgiven	..	..	4.5	1.7	11.0	3.4	0.0	0.0	0.0	0.0
Memo: interest forgiven	..	..	0.6	8.6	3.7	2.5	0.0	0.0	0.0	0.0
Debt stock reduction	..	..	0.0	0.0	0.0	0.0	0.0	0.0	0.0	0.0
of which debt buyback	..	..	0.0	0.0	0.0	0.0	0.0	0.0	0.0	0.0
8. DEBT STOCK-FLOW RECONCILIATION										
Total change in debt stocks	..	..	98.9	65.5	45.8	38.5	-15.5	44.3	-31.9	7.8
Net flows on debt	0.0	72.7	45.7	27.1	13.2	30.1	26.9	6.7	0.0	28.7
Net change in interest arrears	..	..	6.6	14.2	9.4	-27.2	1.2	9.2	7.2	6.3
Interest capitalized	..	..	6.8	0.1	0.0	43.3	0.1	0.1	0.0	0.0
Debt forgiveness or reduction	..	..	-4.5	-1.7	-11.0	-3.4	0.0	0.0	0.0	0.0
Cross-currency valuation	..	..	35.1	13.5	11.3	-31.4	-45.6	12.4	-35.0	-19.7
Residual	..	..	9.3	12.3	22.8	27.1	1.8	16.0	-4.2	-7.5
9. AVERAGE TERMS OF NEW COMMITMENTS										
ALL CREDITORS										
Interest (%)	0.0	2.8	2.2	5.1	0.8	2.5	0.7	0.8	0.0	0.8
Maturity (years)	0.0	17.5	28.1	2.9	39.8	25.4	47.9	39.4	0.0	39.7
Grace period (years)	0.0	3.9	10.4	0.4	10.3	5.9	10.8	9.9	0.0	10.2
Grant element (%)	0.0	39.5	61.8	7.0	80.7	55.0	83.7	80.2	0.0	80.5
Official creditors										
Interest (%)	0.0	2.7	2.2	5.1	0.8	2.5	0.7	0.8	0.0	0.8
Maturity (years)	0.0	17.9	28.1	2.9	39.8	25.4	47.9	39.4	0.0	39.7
Grace period (years)	0.0	4.0	10.4	0.4	10.3	5.9	10.8	9.9	0.0	10.2
Grant element (%)	0.0	40.5	61.8	7.0	80.7	55.0	83.7	80.2	0.0	80.5
Private creditors										
Interest (%)	0.0	7.4	0.0	0.0	0.0	0.0	0.0	0.0	0.0	0.0
Maturity (years)	0.0	3.9	0.0	0.0	0.0	0.0	0.0	0.0	0.0	0.0
Grace period (years)	0.0	1.2	0.0	0.0	0.0	0.0	0.0	0.0	0.0	0.0
Grant element (%)	0.0	5.1	0.0	0.0	0.0	0.0	0.0	0.0	0.0	0.0
Memorandum items										
Commitments	0.0	43.6	97.9	2.3	22.0	1.1	39.8	11.7	0.0	25.0
Official creditors	0.0	42.3	97.9	2.3	22.0	1.1	39.8	11.7	0.0	25.0
Private creditors	0.0	1.3	0.0	0.0	0.0	0.0	0.0	0.0	0.0	0.0

10. CONTRACTUAL OBLIGATIONS ON OUTSTANDING LONG-TERM DEBT

	2001	2002	2003	2004	2005	2006	2007	2008	2009	2010
TOTAL										
Disbursements	17.5	18.1	13.5	9.3	5.4	2.7	2.2	0.5	0.0	0.0
Principal	30.3	32.0	32.2	33.5	26.8	20.1	19.0	19.3	17.6	17.7
Interest	10.9	10.0	9.0	8.0	6.9	6.3	5.9	5.5	5.1	4.9
Official creditors										
Disbursements	17.5	18.1	13.5	9.3	5.4	2.7	2.2	0.5	0.0	0.0
Principal	30.2	31.9	32.2	33.5	26.8	20.1	19.0	19.3	17.6	17.7
Interest	10.9	10.0	9.0	8.0	6.9	6.3	5.9	5.5	5.1	4.9
Bilateral creditors										
Disbursements	0.0	0.0	0.0	0.0	0.0	0.0	0.0	0.0	0.0	0.0
Principal	17.3	21.0	22.1	23.0	16.8	9.7	8.0	7.6	5.9	5.1
Interest	7.6	6.9	6.0	5.0	4.0	3.4	3.1	2.8	2.5	2.3
Multilateral creditors										
Disbursements	17.5	18.1	13.5	9.3	5.4	2.7	2.2	0.5	0.0	0.0
Principal	12.8	10.9	10.1	10.5	10.0	10.4	11.0	11.7	11.7	12.6
Interest	3.3	3.1	3.1	3.0	2.9	2.9	2.8	2.7	2.6	2.5
Private creditors										
Disbursements	0.0	0.0	0.0	0.0	0.0	0.0	0.0	0.0	0.0	0.0
Principal	0.1	0.1	0.0	0.0	0.0	0.0	0.0	0.0	0.0	0.0
Interest	0.0	0.0	0.0	0.0	0.0	0.0	0.0	0.0	0.0	0.0
Commercial banks										
Disbursements	0.0	0.0	0.0	0.0	0.0	0.0	0.0	0.0	0.0	0.0
Principal	0.0	0.0	0.0	0.0	0.0	0.0	0.0	0.0	0.0	0.0
Interest	0.0	0.0	0.0	0.0	0.0	0.0	0.0	0.0	0.0	0.0
Other private										
Disbursements	0.0	0.0	0.0	0.0	0.0	0.0	0.0	0.0	0.0	0.0
Principal	0.1	0.1	0.0	0.0	0.0	0.0	0.0	0.0	0.0	0.0
Interest	0.0	0.0	0.0	0.0	0.0	0.0	0.0	0.0	0.0	0.0

GUYANA

(US$ million, unless otherwise indicated)

	1970	1980	1990	1994	1995	1996	1997	1998	1999	2000
1. SUMMARY DEBT DATA										
TOTAL DEBT STOCKS (EDT)	**83**	**835**	**1,969**	**2,062**	**2,129**	**1,654**	**1,635**	**1,516**	**1,514**	**1,455**
Long-term debt (LDOD)	**83**	**631**	**1,781**	**1,811**	**1,806**	**1,394**	**1,370**	**1,229**	**1,230**	**1,213**
Public and publicly guaranteed	83	631	1,781	1,811	1,806	1,394	1,370	1,229	1,226	1,209
Private nonguaranteed	0	0	0	0	0	0	0	0	5	4
Use of IMF credit	**0**	**86**	**113**	**179**	**172**	**168**	**157**	**154**	**140**	**117**
Short-term debt	**0**	**118**	**75**	**72**	**151**	**92**	**108**	**133**	**144**	**125**
of which interest arrears on LDOD	0	8	63	63	135	74	92	86	79	73
Official creditors	0	5	40	49	115	55	71	65	65	65
Private creditors	0	3	23	14	19	20	21	22	14	8
Memo: principal arrears on LDOD	0	61	193	109	123	121	116	95	64	57
Official creditors	0	34	89	70	85	82	76	55	52	45
Private creditors	0	27	104	39	38	39	40	40	12	12
Memo: export credits	0	0	257	204	189	167	207	22	43	37
TOTAL DEBT FLOWS										
Disbursements	**14**	**169**	**264**	**47**	**59**	**109**	**90**	**70**	**63**	**73**
Long-term debt	14	115	160	34	45	83	65	57	51	64
IMF purchases	0	55	104	13	14	26	25	12	12	9
Principal repayments	**2**	**58**	**175**	**61**	**74**	**73**	**76**	**73**	**64**	**67**
Long-term debt	2	43	69	39	51	49	51	52	41	42
IMF repurchases	0	16	107	22	24	24	26	22	22	25
Net flows on debt	**12**	**155**	**256**	**-14**	**-8**	**38**	**12**	**27**	**18**	**-7**
of which short-term debt	0	44	167	0	7	1	-2	30	19	-14
Interest payments (INT)	**3**	**35**	**120**	**37**	**35**	**32**	**56**	**63**	**39**	**48**
Long-term debt	3	31	73	32	31	29	54	60	35	45
IMF charges	0	4	40	4	3	2	1	1	1	1
Short-term debt	0	1	7	1	1	1	1	2	3	3
Net transfers on debt	**8**	**120**	**135**	**-51**	**-43**	**6**	**-44**	**-36**	**-21**	**-56**
Total debt service paid (TDS)	**6**	**94**	**295**	**97**	**109**	**104**	**132**	**136**	**103**	**116**
Long-term debt	6	74	142	71	82	78	104	112	77	87
IMF repurchases and charges	0	19	146	26	27	25	27	22	23	26
Short-term debt (interest only)	0	1	7	1	1	1	1	2	3	3
2. AGGREGATE NET RESOURCE FLOWS AND NET TRANSFERS (LONG-TERM)										
NET RESOURCE FLOWS	**22**	**77**	**165**	**134**	**90**	**164**	**263**	**158**	**139**	**128**
Net flow of long-term debt (ex. IMF)	12	72	91	-5	-5	35	14	6	9	22
Foreign direct investment (net)	9	1	0	107	74	93	53	47	48	67
Portfolio equity flows	0	0	0	0	0	0	0	0	0	0
Grants (excluding technical coop.)	2	4	74	32	21	37	196	105	82	39
Memo: technical coop. grants	3	8	9	12	16	17	14	7	15	18
official net resource flows	14	70	181	31	26	70	214	114	96	61
private net resource flows	8	6	-16	103	64	95	49	43	43	67
NET TRANSFERS	**5**	**45**	**92**	**102**	**59**	**135**	**209**	**97**	**104**	**83**
Interest on long-term debt	3	31	73	32	31	29	54	60	35	45
Profit remittances on FDI	14	0	0	0	0	0	0	0	0	0
Memo: official net transfers	12	59	117	2	-4	43	161	56	63	25
private net transfers	-7	-14	-26	100	63	93	48	42	41	59
3. MAJOR ECONOMIC AGGREGATES										
Gross national income (GNI)	247	561	275	460	547	651	675	662	621	660
Exports of goods & services (XGS)	..	411	..	593	641	723	751	700	..	..
of which workers remittances	..	0	..	..	..	..	..	..	..	..
Imports of goods & services (MGS)	..	538	..	780	838	885	959	900	..	..
International reserves (RES)	20	13	29	247	269	330	316	277	268	305
Current account balance	..	-129	..	-125	-135	..	..	..	..	..
4. DEBT INDICATORS										
EDT / XGS (%)	..	203.3	..	347.8	331.9	228.9	217.6	216.7	..	..
EDT / GNI (%)	33.5	148.7	715.8	448.4	389.4	253.9	242.2	229.2	243.7	220.5
TDS / XGS (%)	..	22.8	..	16.4	17.0	14.4	17.6	19.5	..	..
INT / XGS (%)	..	8.6	..	6.2	5.4	4.4	7.4	9.0	..	..
INT / GNI (%)	1.4	6.3	43.7	7.9	6.4	4.9	8.3	9.5	6.3	7.3
RES / EDT (%)	24.7	1.5	1.5	12.0	12.6	19.9	19.3	18.2	17.7	21.0
RES / MGS (months)	..	0.3	..	3.8	3.9	4.5	4.0	3.7	..	..
Short-term / EDT (%)	0.0	14.1	3.8	3.5	7.1	5.5	6.6	8.8	9.5	8.6
Concessional / EDT (%)	48.5	27.5	56.9	61.4	60.7	54.2	55.6	54.6	70.8	74.1
Multilateral / EDT (%)	0.9	13.5	23.7	29.5	30.0	40.4	40.7	46.2	38.4	41.0

GUYANA

(US$ million, unless otherwise indicated)

	1970	1980	1990	1994	1995	1996	1997	1998	1999	2000
5. LONG-TERM DEBT										
DEBT OUTSTANDING (LDOD)	**83**	**631**	**1,781**	**1,811**	**1,806**	**1,394**	**1,370**	**1,229**	**1,230**	**1,213**
Public and publicly guaranteed	**83**	**631**	**1,781**	**1,811**	**1,806**	**1,394**	**1,370**	**1,229**	**1,226**	**1,209**
Official creditors	66	379	1,610	1,716	1,720	1,308	1,289	1,152	1,183	1,168
Multilateral	1	112	468	609	639	669	666	700	581	597
Concessional	0	69	291	457	498	554	574	620	517	551
Bilateral	66	267	1,142	1,107	1,081	639	623	452	602	570
Concessional	40	160	831	809	794	342	335	209	555	528
Private creditors	17	252	172	95	86	87	81	78	43	42
Bonds	17	15	0	0	0	0	0	0	0	0
Commercial banks	0	124	104	39	37	43	40	37	3	3
Other private	0	113	68	57	49	44	42	41	40	39
Private nonguaranteed	**0**	**0**	**0**	**0**	**0**	**0**	**0**	**0**	**5**	**4**
Bonds	0	0	0	0	0	0	0	0	0	0
Commercial banks and other	0	0	0	0	0	0	0	0	5	4
Memo:										
IBRD	0	36	59	39	35	27	19	16	12	8
IDA	0	18	93	182	203	212	218	235	184	180
DISBURSEMENTS	**14**	**115**	**160**	**34**	**45**	**83**	**65**	**57**	**51**	**64**
Public and publicly guaranteed	**14**	**115**	**160**	**34**	**45**	**83**	**65**	**57**	**48**	**64**
Official creditors	14	84	153	34	45	74	65	57	48	64
Multilateral	1	35	123	33	41	73	53	50	45	64
Concessional	0	29	109	33	41	73	53	50	45	64
Bilateral	13	50	31	1	4	1	12	8	3	0
Concessional	6	21	19	0	3	1	12	8	3	0
Private creditors	0	31	6	0	0	10	0	0	0	0
Bonds	0	0	0	0	0	0	0	0	0	0
Commercial banks	0	21	0	0	0	9	0	0	0	0
Other private	0	9	6	0	0	1	0	0	0	0
Private nonguaranteed	**0**	**0**	**0**	**0**	**0**	**0**	**0**	**0**	**3**	**0**
Bonds	0	0	0	0	0	0	0	0	0	0
Commercial banks and other	0	0	0	0	0	0	0	0	3	0
Memo:										
IBRD	0	2	0	0	0	0	0	0	0	0
IDA	0	2	54	12	18	16	18	9	7	6
PRINCIPAL REPAYMENTS	**2**	**43**	**69**	**39**	**51**	**49**	**51**	**52**	**41**	**42**
Public and publicly guaranteed	**2**	**43**	**69**	**39**	**51**	**49**	**51**	**52**	**37**	**42**
Official creditors	1	18	46	35	40	41	47	48	34	42
Multilateral	0	1	42	22	24	23	28	32	18	18
Concessional	0	0	6	6	6	7	13	17	5	6
Bilateral	1	17	4	13	16	18	19	16	16	24
Concessional	1	9	0	3	5	10	14	11	12	20
Private creditors	1	25	22	4	10	8	4	4	3	0
Bonds	0	0	1	0	0	0	0	0	0	0
Commercial banks	1	11	8	0	2	3	2	3	3	0
Other private	0	14	14	4	8	5	2	1	0	0
Private nonguaranteed	**0**	**0**	**0**	**0**	**0**	**0**	**0**	**0**	**5**	**0**
Bonds	0	0	0	0	0	0	0	0	0	0
Commercial banks and other	0	0	0	0	0	0	0	0	5	0
Memo:										
IBRD	0	1	31	5	6	5	5	5	3	3
IDA	0	0	0	1	1	1	1	1	0	1
NET FLOWS ON DEBT	**12**	**72**	**91**	**-5**	**-5**	**35**	**14**	**6**	**9**	**22**
Public and publicly guaranteed	**12**	**72**	**91**	**-5**	**-5**	**35**	**14**	**6**	**11**	**22**
Official creditors	13	66	107	-1	5	33	18	10	14	23
Multilateral	1	34	80	11	17	50	25	18	27	46
Concessional	0	29	103	27	34	67	40	33	40	58
Bilateral	12	33	27	-12	-12	-17	-7	-8	-13	-24
Concessional	5	12	19	-3	-2	-9	-2	-3	-9	-20
Private creditors	-1	6	-16	-4	-10	2	-4	-4	-3	0
Bonds	0	0	-1	0	0	0	0	0	0	0
Commercial banks	-1	10	-8	0	-2	6	-2	-3	-3	0
Other private	0	-4	-8	-4	-8	-5	-2	-1	0	0
Private nonguaranteed	**0**	**0**	**0**	**0**	**0**	**0**	**0**	**0**	**-2**	**0**
Bonds	0	0	0	0	0	0	0	0	0	0
Commercial banks and other	0	0	0	0	0	0	0	0	-2	0
Memo:										
IBRD	0	1	-31	-5	-6	-5	-5	-5	-3	-3
IDA	0	2	54	12	17	16	17	9	7	5

GUYANA

(US$ million, unless otherwise indicated)

	1970	1980	1990	1994	1995	1996	1997	1998	1999	2000
INTEREST PAYMENTS (LINT)	**3**	**31**	**73**	**32**	**31**	**29**	**54**	**60**	**35**	**45**
Public and publicly guaranteed	**3**	**31**	**73**	**32**	**31**	**29**	**54**	**60**	**35**	**45**
Official creditors	3	11	64	29	30	27	53	59	33	37
Multilateral	0	4	58	18	18	16	17	23	13	11
Concessional	0	1	8	6	6	6	9	17	7	7
Bilateral	3	7	6	11	12	11	36	36	20	25
Concessional	1	4	3	8	8	9	13	19	13	24
Private creditors	1	20	9	3	2	2	1	2	2	8
Bonds	1	1	0	0	0	0	0	0	0	0
Commercial banks	0	14	5	0	1	1	1	1	1	0
Other private	0	5	4	3	1	2	0	1	1	8
Private nonguaranteed	**0**	**0**	**0**	**0**	**0**	**0**	**0**	**0**	**0**	**0**
Bonds	0	0	0	0	0	0	0	0	0	0
Commercial banks and other	0	0	0	0	0	0	0	0	0	0
Memo:										
IBRD	0	3	31	3	3	3	2	1	1	1
IDA	0	0	0	1	1	2	2	2	2	1
NET TRANSFERS ON DEBT	**8**	**41**	**18**	**-37**	**-37**	**6**	**-39**	**-54**	**-26**	**-23**
Public and publicly guaranteed	**8**	**41**	**18**	**-37**	**-37**	**6**	**-39**	**-54**	**-24**	**-22**
Official creditors	10	55	43	-30	-25	6	-35	-49	-19	-14
Multilateral	1	30	23	-7	-1	34	9	-5	14	35
Concessional	0	28	95	21	28	60	31	17	33	51
Bilateral	9	25	20	-23	-24	-28	-43	-44	-33	-49
Concessional	4	8	17	-11	-11	-18	-14	-22	-22	-44
Private creditors	-2	-14	-26	-7	-12	-1	-5	-6	-5	-8
Bonds	-1	-1	-1	0	0	0	0	0	0	0
Commercial banks	-1	-4	-12	0	-3	6	-3	-3	-4	0
Other private	0	-10	-12	-7	-9	-6	-2	-2	-2	-8
Private nonguaranteed	**0**	**0**	**0**	**0**	**0**	**0**	**0**	**0**	**-2**	**-1**
Bonds	0	0	0	0	0	0	0	0	0	0
Commercial banks and other	0	0	0	0	0	0	0	0	-2	-1
Memo:										
IBRD	0	-2	-62	-9	-9	-8	-7	-6	-4	-4
IDA	0	2	54	11	16	14	16	7	5	4
DEBT SERVICE (LTDS)	**6**	**74**	**142**	**71**	**82**	**78**	**104**	**112**	**77**	**87**
Public and publicly guaranteed	**6**	**74**	**142**	**71**	**82**	**78**	**104**	**112**	**72**	**86**
Official creditors	4	29	110	64	70	68	100	106	67	78
Multilateral	0	5	100	40	42	39	44	55	31	29
Concessional	0	1	15	12	13	13	21	33	12	13
Bilateral	4	24	11	24	28	29	56	52	36	49
Concessional	2	13	3	11	14	18	26	30	25	44
Private creditors	2	45	32	7	12	10	5	6	5	8
Bonds	1	1	1	0	0	0	0	0	0	0
Commercial banks	1	25	12	0	3	3	3	3	4	0
Other private	0	19	18	7	9	7	2	2	2	8
Private nonguaranteed	**0**	**0**	**0**	**0**	**0**	**0**	**0**	**0**	**5**	**1**
Bonds	0	0	0	0	0	0	0	0	0	0
Commercial banks and other	0	0	0	0	0	0	0	0	5	1
Memo:										
IBRD	0	4	62	9	9	8	7	6	4	4
IDA	0	0	1	2	2	2	2	2	2	2
UNDISBURSED DEBT	**56**	**226**	**275**	**277**	**258**	**275**	**272**	**280**	**246**	**263**
Official creditors	56	210	271	277	249	275	272	280	246	263
Private creditors	0	16	4	0	9	0	0	0	0	0
Memorandum items										
Concessional LDOD	40	230	1,121	1,266	1,292	896	909	828	1,072	1,078
Variable rate LDOD	0	148	259	239	219	99	95	88	80	80
Public sector LDOD	83	631	1,781	1,811	1,806	1,394	1,370	1,229	1,226	1,209
Private sector LDOD	0	0	0	0	0	0	0	0	5	4

6. CURRENCY COMPOSITION OF LONG-TERM DEBT (PERCENT)

	1970	1980	1990	1994	1995	1996	1997	1998	1999	2000
Deutsche mark	0.0	0.8	2.2	2.5	2.5	1.9	1.5	1.6	1.2	1.1
French franc	0.0	0.1	0.0	0.1	0.1	0.1	0.0	0.1	0.0	0.0
Japanese yen	0.0	0.0	0.3	0.2	0.2	0.2	0.1	0.0	0.0	0.0
Pound sterling	68.9	20.9	10.3	9.5	9.2	9.0	8.9	9.9	9.4	8.5
Swiss franc	0.0	0.0	0.1	0.1	0.1	0.0	0.0	0.0	0.0	0.0
U.S.dollars	24.7	59.9	68.1	64.9	65.0	60.2	62.2	58.4	65.8	68.4
Multiple currency	0.4	9.7	14.7	15.9	16.0	21.7	20.7	22.8	16.9	16.6
Special drawing rights	0.0	0.0	0.1	0.2	0.2	0.3	0.3	0.3	0.3	0.3
All other currencies	6.0	8.6	4.2	6.6	6.7	6.6	6.3	6.9	6.4	5.1

GUYANA

(US$ million, unless otherwise indicated)

	1970	1980	1990	1994	1995	1996	1997	1998	1999	2000
7. DEBT RESTRUCTURINGS										
Total amount rescheduled	..	..	474	49	1	277	0	0	369	0
Debt stock rescheduled	..	..	320	0	0	0	0	0	37	0
Principal rescheduled	..	..	89	14	1	239	0	0	218	0
Official	..	..	89	14	0	239	0	0	218	0
Private	..	..	0	0	0	0	0	0	0	0
Interest rescheduled	..	..	38	16	0	38	0	0	4	0
Official	..	..	38	16	0	38	0	0	4	0
Private	..	..	0	0	0	0	0	0	0	0
Debt forgiven	..	..	31	11	0	459	2	0	24	6
Memo: interest forgiven	..	..	1	3	0	4	0	0	2	0
Debt stock reduction	..	..	0	0	0	0	0	0	111	0
of which debt buyback	..	..	0	0	0	0	0	0	30	0
8. DEBT STOCK-FLOW RECONCILIATION										
Total change in debt stocks	..	..	313	84	67	-474	-19	-119	-2	-59
Net flows on debt	12	155	256	-14	-8	38	12	27	18	-7
Net change in interest arrears	..	..	-37	26	71	-60	18	-6	-8	-6
Interest capitalized	..	..	38	16	0	38	0	0	4	0
Debt forgiveness or reduction	..	..	-31	-11	0	-459	-2	0	-105	-6
Cross-currency valuation	..	..	44	-18	-44	-78	-109	-51	-109	-64
Residual	..	..	44	84	48	47	62	-89	197	24
9. AVERAGE TERMS OF NEW COMMITMENTS										
ALL CREDITORS										
Interest (%)	6.0	10.5	1.3	1.6	3.0	1.6	1.6	1.4	1.7	2.0
Maturity (years)	25.3	8.1	39.7	39.7	37.1	37.3	39.0	38.8	38.9	40.0
Grace period (years)	9.7	2.4	9.9	10.5	9.9	10.0	9.9	10.4	9.9	10.5
Grant element (%)	32.4	2.9	74.9	73.0	60.5	70.8	72.7	74.1	71.3	69.6
Official creditors										
Interest (%)	6.0	9.2	1.3	1.6	1.5	1.6	1.6	1.4	1.7	2.0
Maturity (years)	25.3	9.5	39.7	39.7	38.7	37.5	39.0	38.8	38.9	40.0
Grace period (years)	9.7	3.2	9.9	10.5	10.4	10.1	9.9	10.4	9.9	10.5
Grant element (%)	32.4	11.2	74.9	73.0	73.3	71.2	72.7	74.1	71.3	69.6
Private creditors										
Interest (%)	0.0	12.3	0.0	0.0	8.8	7.4	0.0	0.0	0.0	0.0
Maturity (years)	0.0	6.2	0.0	0.0	31.0	3.8	0.0	0.0	0.0	0.0
Grace period (years)	0.0	1.3	0.0	0.0	8.0	0.3	0.0	0.0	0.0	0.0
Grant element (%)	0.0	-8.9	0.0	0.0	9.6	3.9	0.0	0.0	0.0	0.0
Memorandum items										
Commitments	20	96	282	64	45	106	83	55	28	85
Official creditors	20	56	282	64	36	105	83	55	28	85
Private creditors	0	39	0	0	9	1	0	0	0	0

10. CONTRACTUAL OBLIGATIONS ON OUTSTANDING LONG-TERM DEBT

	2001	2002	2003	2004	2005	2006	2007	2008	2009	2010
TOTAL										
Disbursements	62	64	47	33	23	12	7	1	0	0
Principal	51	51	55	56	55	73	51	49	42	37
Interest	34	33	32	30	28	26	25	23	22	21
Official creditors										
Disbursements	62	64	47	33	23	12	7	1	0	0
Principal	50	50	54	55	54	48	50	49	41	37
Interest	32	31	30	28	27	26	25	23	21	20
Bilateral creditors										
Disbursements	2	1	0	0	0	0	0	0	0	0
Principal	29	31	33	34	33	26	26	26	18	14
Interest	21	20	18	17	16	15	13	12	11	10
Multilateral creditors										
Disbursements	61	63	46	33	23	12	7	1	0	0
Principal	21	20	22	22	22	22	24	22	24	23
Interest	11	11	11	11	11	11	11	11	10	10
Private creditors										
Disbursements	0	0	0	0	0	0	0	0	0	0
Principal	1	1	1	1	1	26	1	1	1	0
Interest	2	2	2	2	2	0	0	0	0	0
Commercial banks										
Disbursements	0	0	0	0	0	0	0	0	0	0
Principal	0	0	0	0	0	0	0	0	0	0
Interest	0	0	0	0	0	0	0	0	0	0
Other private										
Disbursements	0	0	0	0	0	0	0	0	0	0
Principal	1	1	1	1	1	26	1	1	1	0
Interest	2	2	2	1	1	0	0	0	0	0

HAITI

(US$ million, unless otherwise indicated)

	1970	1980	1990	1994	1995	1996	1997	1998	1999	2000
1. SUMMARY DEBT DATA										
TOTAL DEBT STOCKS (EDT)	**43**	**350**	**911**	**729**	**816**	**904**	**1,052**	**1,050**	**1,190**	**1,169**
Long-term debt (LDOD)	**40**	**290**	**772**	**647**	**761**	**843**	**902**	**982**	**1,049**	**1,040**
Public and publicly guaranteed	40	290	772	647	761	843	902	982	1,049	1,040
Private nonguaranteed	0	0	0	0	0	0	0	0	0	0
Use of IMF credit	**3**	**46**	**38**	**35**	**29**	**25**	**43**	**38**	**45**	**39**
Short-term debt	**0**	**14**	**101**	**47**	**26**	**36**	**107**	**30**	**96**	**90**
of which interest arrears on LDOD	0	0	24	34	1	1	1	1	1	1
Official creditors	0	0	14	18	1	1	1	1	1	1
Private creditors	0	0	10	16	0	0	0	0	0	0
Memo: principal arrears on LDOD	4	0	43	121	1	2	2	2	2	2
Official creditors	0	0	14	55	1	2	2	2	2	2
Private creditors	4	0	29	67	0	0	0	0	0	0
Memo: export credits	0	0	117	79	104	100	99	84	81	79
TOTAL DEBT FLOWS										
Disbursements	**4**	**77**	**44**	**0**	**128**	**107**	**119**	**94**	**79**	**51**
Long-term debt	4	47	38	0	104	107	98	94	79	51
IMF purchases	0	30	5	0	25	0	21	0	0	0
Principal repayments	**3**	**21**	**20**	**3**	**65**	**16**	**19**	**22**	**30**	**21**
Long-term debt	3	18	8	3	33	13	17	17	19	18
IMF repurchases	0	3	12	0	32	3	1	5	11	3
Net flows on debt	**1**	**51**	**39**	**-81**	**76**	**100**	**172**	**-5**	**115**	**24**
of which short-term debt	0	-5	16	-78	13	10	71	-77	66	-6
Interest payments (INT)	**0**	**9**	**15**	**1**	**32**	**13**	**19**	**20**	**20**	**20**
Long-term debt	0	6	6	0	25	10	14	15	15	15
IMF charges	0	1	3	0	6	1	1	1	1	1
Short-term debt	0	2	7	1	2	2	4	3	3	5
Net transfers on debt	**1**	**42**	**24**	**-82**	**44**	**87**	**153**	**-24**	**95**	**3**
Total debt service paid (TDS)	**4**	**29**	**36**	**4**	**97**	**29**	**37**	**41**	**50**	**42**
Long-term debt	4	24	14	3	58	23	31	32	34	33
IMF repurchases and charges	0	4	15	0	38	4	2	7	13	4
Short-term debt (interest only)	0	2	7	1	2	2	4	3	3	5
2. AGGREGATE NET RESOURCE FLOWS AND NET TRANSFERS (LONG-TERM)										
NET RESOURCE FLOWS	**6**	**73**	**103**	**595**	**590**	**251**	**218**	**223**	**198**	**136**
Net flow of long-term debt (ex. IMF)	1	29	30	-3	71	93	81	78	60	32
Foreign direct investment (net)	3	13	8	0	7	4	4	11	30	13
Portfolio equity flows	0	0	0	0	0	0	0	0	0	0
Grants (excluding technical coop.)	2	30	65	597	512	154	133	134	109	91
Memo: technical coop. grants	4	32	66	58	112	93	109	96	102	91
official net resource flows	2	52	95	595	583	247	214	212	168	123
private net resource flows	5	20	8	0	7	4	4	11	30	13
NET TRANSFERS	**3**	**56**	**88**	**589**	**560**	**236**	**200**	**203**	**177**	**115**
Interest on long-term debt	0	6	6	0	25	10	14	15	15	15
Profit remittances on FDI	3	11	8	5	6	5	4	5	6	7
Memo: official net transfers	1	48	89	594	558	237	200	197	153	109
private net transfers	1	7	0	-5	1	-1	0	6	24	6
3. MAJOR ECONOMIC AGGREGATES										
Gross national income (GNI)	391	1,446	2,954	1,882	2,623	2,945	3,446	3,854	4,117	4,064
Exports of goods & services (XGS)	..	415	325	67	192	192	379	479	569	521
of which workers remittances	..	106	0	0	..	..	..	..	..	..
Imports of goods & services (MGS)	..	498	540	247	832	792	905	1,033	1,270	..
International reserves (RES)	4	27	10	58	199	223	219	270	265	184
Current account balance	..	-101	-22	-23	-87	-138	-48	-38	..	..
4. DEBT INDICATORS										
EDT / XGS (%)	..	84.3	280.2	1,087.9	424.1	471.8	277.5	219.1	209.2	224.4
EDT / GNI (%)	11.0	24.2	30.8	38.7	31.1	30.7	30.5	27.3	28.9	28.8
TDS / XGS (%)	..	7.0	11.0	5.8	50.2	15.2	9.8	8.6	8.8	8.0
INT / XGS (%)	..	2.1	4.7	1.6	16.6	6.9	4.9	4.1	3.5	3.9
INT / GNI (%)	0.1	0.6	0.5	0.1	1.2	0.5	0.5	0.5	0.5	0.5
RES / EDT (%)	10.1	7.6	1.1	8.0	24.4	24.7	20.8	25.7	22.3	15.7
RES / MGS (months)	..	0.6	0.2	2.8	2.9	3.4	2.9	3.1	2.5	..
Short-term / EDT (%)	0.0	4.0	11.1	6.5	3.2	4.0	10.2	2.8	8.1	7.7
Concessional / EDT (%)	68.5	74.7	79.1	79.2	93.1	93.1	85.6	93.5	88.1	88.8
Multilateral / EDT (%)	0.9	37.8	53.7	71.8	74.8	76.4	71.2	79.1	76.1	77.2

HAITI

(US$ million, unless otherwise indicated)

	1970	1980	1990	1994	1995	1996	1997	1998	1999	2000
5. LONG-TERM DEBT										
DEBT OUTSTANDING (LDOD)	**40**	**290**	**772**	**647**	**761**	**843**	**902**	**982**	**1,049**	**1,040**
Public and publicly guaranteed	**40**	**290**	**772**	**647**	**761**	**843**	**902**	**982**	**1,049**	**1,040**
Official creditors	29	266	725	580	761	843	902	982	1,049	1,040
Multilateral	0	132	489	524	610	691	749	830	905	903
Concessional	0	132	489	524	610	691	749	830	905	903
Bilateral	29	134	236	56	150	152	153	152	144	136
Concessional	29	129	231	54	149	151	152	151	143	136
Private creditors	11	24	47	67	0	0	0	0	0	0
Bonds	4	0	0	0	0	0	0	0	0	0
Commercial banks	0	8	47	67	0	0	0	0	0	0
Other private	7	16	0	0	0	0	0	0	0	0
Private nonguaranteed	**0**	**0**	**0**	**0**	**0**	**0**	**0**	**0**	**0**	**0**
Bonds	0	0	0	0	0	0	0	0	0	0
Commercial banks and other	0	0	0	0	0	0	0	0	0	0
Memo:										
IBRD	0	0	0	0	0	0	0	0	0	0
IDA	0	66	324	346	389	442	458	493	504	480
DISBURSEMENTS	**4**	**47**	**38**	**0**	**104**	**107**	**98**	**94**	**79**	**51**
Public and publicly guaranteed	**4**	**47**	**38**	**0**	**104**	**107**	**98**	**94**	**79**	**51**
Official creditors	0	32	38	0	104	107	98	94	79	51
Multilateral	0	21	27	0	103	101	90	93	79	51
Concessional	0	21	27	0	103	101	90	93	79	51
Bilateral	0	11	11	0	1	6	8	1	0	0
Concessional	0	7	11	0	1	6	8	1	0	0
Private creditors	4	15	0	0	0	0	0	0	0	0
Bonds	0	0	0	0	0	0	0	0	0	0
Commercial banks	0	5	0	0	0	0	0	0	0	0
Other private	4	10	0	0	0	0	0	0	0	0
Private nonguaranteed	**0**	**0**	**0**	**0**	**0**	**0**	**0**	**0**	**0**	**0**
Bonds	0	0	0	0	0	0	0	0	0	0
Commercial banks and other	0	0	0	0	0	0	0	0	0	0
Memo:										
IBRD	0	0	0	0	0	0	0	0	0	0
IDA	0	13	14	0	49	67	40	39	14	8
PRINCIPAL REPAYMENTS	**3**	**18**	**8**	**3**	**33**	**13**	**17**	**17**	**19**	**18**
Public and publicly guaranteed	**3**	**18**	**8**	**3**	**33**	**13**	**17**	**17**	**19**	**18**
Official creditors	1	11	8	3	33	13	17	17	19	18
Multilateral	0	0	5	1	29	10	14	13	14	15
Concessional	0	0	5	1	29	10	14	13	14	15
Bilateral	1	10	3	2	3	3	4	4	5	4
Concessional	1	10	3	2	3	3	4	3	5	4
Private creditors	3	7	0	0	0	0	0	0	0	0
Bonds	0	0	0	0	0	0	0	0	0	0
Commercial banks	0	1	0	0	0	0	0	0	0	0
Other private	3	7	0	0	0	0	0	0	0	0
Private nonguaranteed	**0**	**0**	**0**	**0**	**0**	**0**	**0**	**0**	**0**	**0**
Bonds	0	0	0	0	0	0	0	0	0	0
Commercial banks and other	0	0	0	0	0	0	0	0	0	0
Memo:										
IBRD	0	0	0	0	0	0	0	0	0	0
IDA	0	0	1	0	10	4	5	5	6	7
NET FLOWS ON DEBT	**1**	**29**	**30**	**-3**	**71**	**93**	**81**	**78**	**60**	**32**
Public and publicly guaranteed	**1**	**29**	**30**	**-3**	**71**	**93**	**81**	**78**	**60**	**32**
Official creditors	-1	22	30	-3	71	93	81	78	60	32
Multilateral	0	21	22	-1	74	91	77	81	64	36
Concessional	0	21	22	-1	74	91	77	81	64	36
Bilateral	-1	1	8	-2	-3	3	4	-3	-5	-4
Concessional	-1	-3	8	-2	-2	3	4	-3	-5	-4
Private creditors	2	7	0	0	0	0	0	0	0	0
Bonds	0	0	0	0	0	0	0	0	0	0
Commercial banks	0	5	0	0	0	0	0	0	0	0
Other private	2	3	0	0	0	0	0	0	0	0
Private nonguaranteed	**0**	**0**	**0**	**0**	**0**	**0**	**0**	**0**	**0**	**0**
Bonds	0	0	0	0	0	0	0	0	0	0
Commercial banks and other	0	0	0	0	0	0	0	0	0	0
Memo:										
IBRD	0	0	0	0	0	0	0	0	0	0
IDA	0	13	13	0	39	63	35	34	8	2

HAITI

(US$ million, unless otherwise indicated)

	1970	1980	1990	1994	1995	1996	1997	1998	1999	2000
INTEREST PAYMENTS (LINT)	**0**	**6**	**6**	**0**	**25**	**10**	**14**	**15**	**15**	**15**
Public and publicly guaranteed	**0**	**6**	**6**	**0**	**25**	**10**	**14**	**15**	**15**	**15**
Official creditors	0	4	6	0	25	10	14	15	15	15
Multilateral	0	1	5	0	24	7	9	10	10	9
Concessional	0	1	5	0	24	7	9	10	10	9
Bilateral	0	3	1	0	1	3	6	6	6	5
Concessional	0	3	1	0	1	3	5	5	5	5
Private creditors	0	2	0	0	0	0	0	0	0	0
Bonds	0	0	0	0	0	0	0	0	0	0
Commercial banks	0	1	0	0	0	0	0	0	0	0
Other private	0	1	0	0	0	0	0	0	0	0
Private nonguaranteed	**0**	**0**	**0**	**0**	**0**	**0**	**0**	**0**	**0**	**0**
Bonds	0	0	0	0	0	0	0	0	0	0
Commercial banks and other	0	0	0	0	0	0	0	0	0	0
Memo:										
IBRD	0	0	0	0	0	0	0	0	0	0
IDA	0	0	2	0	10	3	3	4	4	4
NET TRANSFERS ON DEBT	**1**	**23**	**24**	**-3**	**46**	**83**	**67**	**63**	**45**	**18**
Public and publicly guaranteed	**1**	**23**	**24**	**-3**	**46**	**83**	**67**	**63**	**45**	**18**
Official creditors	-1	18	24	-3	46	83	67	63	45	18
Multilateral	0	20	17	-1	50	84	68	71	55	27
Concessional	0	20	17	-1	50	84	68	71	55	27
Bilateral	-1	-2	7	-3	-4	0	-1	-8	-10	-9
Concessional	-1	-6	7	-3	-3	0	-1	-8	-10	-9
Private creditors	1	5	0	0	0	0	0	0	0	0
Bonds	0	0	0	0	0	0	0	0	0	0
Commercial banks	0	4	0	0	0	0	0	0	0	0
Other private	1	2	0	0	0	0	0	0	0	0
Private nonguaranteed	**0**	**0**	**0**	**0**	**0**	**0**	**0**	**0**	**0**	**0**
Bonds	0	0	0	0	0	0	0	0	0	0
Commercial banks and other	0	0	0	0	0	0	0	0	0	0
Memo:										
IBRD	0	0	0	0	0	0	0	0	0	0
IDA	0	13	11	0	29	60	32	31	5	-2
DEBT SERVICE (LTDS)	**4**	**24**	**14**	**3**	**58**	**23**	**31**	**32**	**34**	**33**
Public and publicly guaranteed	**4**	**24**	**14**	**3**	**58**	**23**	**31**	**32**	**34**	**33**
Official creditors	1	15	14	3	58	23	31	32	34	33
Multilateral	0	1	10	1	53	17	22	23	24	24
Concessional	0	1	10	1	53	17	22	23	24	24
Bilateral	1	13	4	3	5	6	9	9	10	9
Concessional	1	13	4	3	3	6	9	9	10	9
Private creditors	3	9	0	0	0	0	0	0	0	0
Bonds	0	0	0	0	0	0	0	0	0	0
Commercial banks	0	2	0	0	0	0	0	0	0	0
Other private	3	8	0	0	0	0	0	0	0	0
Private nonguaranteed	**0**	**0**	**0**	**0**	**0**	**0**	**0**	**0**	**0**	**0**
Bonds	0	0	0	0	0	0	0	0	0	0
Commercial banks and other	0	0	0	0	0	0	0	0	0	0
Memo:										
IBRD	0	0	0	0	0	0	0	0	0	0
IDA	0	0	3	0	20	7	8	9	10	10
UNDISBURSED DEBT	**5**	**145**	**267**	**267**	**393**	**351**	**407**	**300**	**310**	**228**
Official creditors	0	128	267	267	393	351	407	300	310	228
Private creditors	5	17	0	0	0	0	0	0	0	0
Memorandum items										
Concessional LDOD	29	261	721	577	759	842	901	981	1,048	1,039
Variable rate LDOD	0	8	7	5	0	0	0	0	0	0
Public sector LDOD	40	282	772	647	761	843	902	982	1,049	1,040
Private sector LDOD	0	7	0	0	0	0	0	0	0	0

6. CURRENCY COMPOSITION OF LONG-TERM DEBT (PERCENT)

	1970	1980	1990	1994	1995	1996	1997	1998	1999	2000
Deutsche mark	0.0	4.2	0.0	0.0	0.0	0.0	0.0	0.0	0.0	0.0
French franc	0.0	5.8	10.8	3.3	2.8	2.9	3.1	2.9	2.3	1.9
Japanese yen	0.0	0.0	0.0	0.0	0.0	0.0	0.0	0.0	0.0	0.0
Pound sterling	0.0	0.0	0.0	0.0	0.0	0.0	0.0	0.0	0.0	0.0
Swiss franc	0.0	0.0	0.0	0.0	0.0	0.0	0.0	0.0	0.0	0.0
U.S.dollars	100.0	79.3	70.7	72.4	77.3	78.1	78.2	79.7	80.6	82.0
Multiple currency	0.0	10.8	18.5	24.3	19.9	19.0	18.8	17.3	17.0	16.0
Special drawing rights	0.0	0.0	0.0	0.0	0.0	0.0	0.0	0.0	0.0	0.0
All other currencies	0.0	-0.1	0.0	0.0	0.0	0.0	-0.1	0.1	0.1	0.1

HAITI

(US$ million, unless otherwise indicated)

	1970	1980	1990	1994	1995	1996	1997	1998	1999	2000
7. DEBT RESTRUCTURINGS										
Total amount rescheduled	..	..	0	0	108	2	0	0	0	0
Debt stock rescheduled	..	..	0	0	0	0	0	0	0	0
Principal rescheduled	..	..	0	0	71	1	0	0	0	0
Official	..	..	0	0	4	1	0	0	0	0
Private	..	..	0	0	67	0	0	0	0	0
Interest rescheduled	..	..	0	0	17	0	0	0	0	0
Official	..	..	0	0	2	0	0	0	0	0
Private	..	..	0	0	16	0	0	0	0	0
Debt forgiven	..	..	0	23	8	1	0	0	0	0
Memo: interest forgiven	..	..	0	0	3	0	0	0	0	0
Debt stock reduction	..	..	0	0	0	0	0	0	0	0
of which debt buyback	..	..	0	0	0	0	0	0	0	0
8. DEBT STOCK-FLOW RECONCILIATION										
Total change in debt stocks	..	..	81	-88	87	88	148	-2	140	-21
Net flows on debt	1	51	39	-81	76	100	172	-5	115	24
Net change in interest arrears	..	..	8	4	-33	0	0	0	0	0
Interest capitalized	..	..	0	0	17	0	0	0	0	0
Debt forgiveness or reduction	..	..	0	-23	-8	-1	0	0	0	0
Cross-currency valuation	..	..	23	-7	-11	-69	-79	-64	-1	-32
Residual	..	..	11	19	46	58	55	67	26	-13
9. AVERAGE TERMS OF NEW COMMITMENTS										
ALL CREDITORS										
Interest (%)	4.8	5.2	1.4	0.0	1.2	1.8	1.5	0.0	1.5	0.0
Maturity (years)	9.5	19.6	38.9	0.0	39.9	40.0	39.9	0.0	40.0	0.0
Grace period (years)	1.0	6.3	10.4	0.0	10.4	10.5	10.4	0.0	10.5	0.0
Grant element (%)	16.0	32.6	75.0	0.0	76.6	71.8	73.6	0.0	74.1	0.0
Official creditors										
Interest (%)	3.4	2.8	1.4	0.0	1.2	1.8	1.5	0.0	1.5	0.0
Maturity (years)	43.0	29.8	38.9	0.0	39.9	40.0	39.9	0.0	40.0	0.0
Grace period (years)	7.3	10.3	10.4	0.0	10.4	10.5	10.4	0.0	10.5	0.0
Grant element (%)	55.8	54.5	75.0	0.0	76.6	71.8	73.6	0.0	74.1	0.0
Private creditors										
Interest (%)	4.8	8.2	0.0	0.0	0.0	0.0	0.0	0.0	0.0	0.0
Maturity (years)	8.6	7.0	0.0	0.0	0.0	0.0	0.0	0.0	0.0	0.0
Grace period (years)	0.9	1.4	0.0	0.0	0.0	0.0	0.0	0.0	0.0	0.0
Grant element (%)	14.9	5.2	0.0	0.0	0.0	0.0	0.0	0.0	0.0	0.0
Memorandum items										
Commitments	5	51	102	0	254	71	163	0	96	0
Official creditors	0	29	102	0	254	71	163	0	96	0
Private creditors	5	23	0	0	0	0	0	0	0	0

10. CONTRACTUAL OBLIGATIONS ON OUTSTANDING LONG-TERM DEBT

	2001	2002	2003	2004	2005	2006	2007	2008	2009	2010
TOTAL										
Disbursements	28	44	40	38	32	26	16	2	0	0
Principal	23	24	24	25	27	32	36	39	41	43
Interest	16	16	16	15	16	17	17	17	16	16
Official creditors										
Disbursements	28	44	40	38	32	26	16	2	0	0
Principal	23	24	24	25	27	32	36	39	41	43
Interest	16	16	16	15	16	17	17	17	16	16
Bilateral creditors										
Disbursements	0	0	0	0	0	0	0	0	0	0
Principal	5	5	5	5	4	4	4	4	5	5
Interest	5	5	5	5	4	4	4	4	4	4
Multilateral creditors										
Disbursements	28	44	40	38	32	26	16	2	0	0
Principal	19	20	20	20	23	28	32	35	36	39
Interest	11	11	11	11	11	12	13	13	13	12
Private creditors										
Disbursements	0	0	0	0	0	0	0	0	0	0
Principal	0	0	0	0	0	0	0	0	0	0
Interest	0	0	0	0	0	0	0	0	0	0
Commercial banks										
Disbursements	0	0	0	0	0	0	0	0	0	0
Principal	0	0	0	0	0	0	0	0	0	0
Interest	0	0	0	0	0	0	0	0	0	0
Other private										
Disbursements	0	0	0	0	0	0	0	0	0	0
Principal	0	0	0	0	0	0	0	0	0	0
Interest	0	0	0	0	0	0	0	0	0	0

HONDURAS

(US$ million, unless otherwise indicated)

	1970	1980	1990	1994	1995	1996	1997	1998	1999	2000
1. SUMMARY DEBT DATA										
TOTAL DEBT STOCKS (EDT)	**111**	**1,473**	**3,718**	**4,695**	**4,791**	**4,714**	**4,851**	**5,104**	**5,423**	**5,487**
Long-term debt (LDOD)	**111**	**1,168**	**3,487**	**4,256**	**4,310**	**4,237**	**4,318**	**4,455**	**4,759**	**4,897**
Public and publicly guaranteed	91	976	3,420	4,156	4,187	4,021	4,059	4,043	4,216	4,337
Private nonguaranteed	19	191	66	100	123	216	259	412	543	560
Use of IMF credit	**0**	**33**	**32**	**109**	**99**	**58**	**46**	**113**	**210**	**216**
Short-term debt	**0**	**272**	**199**	**330**	**382**	**419**	**487**	**537**	**454**	**374**
of which interest arrears on LDOD	0	0	89	73	63	60	62	69	53	36
Official creditors	0	0	34	45	31	36	38	40	20	10
Private creditors	0	0	55	28	31	24	25	29	33	26
Memo: principal arrears on LDOD	0	3	190	205	197	185	186	196	149	73
Official creditors	0	1	63	124	108	116	120	115	74	16
Private creditors	0	2	128	81	90	68	66	81	75	56
Memo: export credits	0	0	338	487	469	552	468	315	311	338
TOTAL DEBT FLOWS										
Disbursements	**45**	**375**	**457**	**352**	**379**	**456**	**662**	**488**	**810**	**641**
Long-term debt	39	346	429	352	349	456	662	423	706	620
IMF purchases	6	29	29	0	31	0	0	64	104	21
Principal repayments	**6**	**87**	**211**	**278**	**376**	**430**	**352**	**337**	**310**	**387**
Long-term debt	6	87	177	262	332	392	343	335	306	382
IMF repurchases	0	0	35	16	44	38	9	2	4	5
Net flows on debt	**38**	**296**	**129**	**204**	**66**	**65**	**377**	**193**	**435**	**192**
of which short-term debt	0	8	-117	130	62	39	67	43	-66	-63
Interest payments (INT)	**4**	**120**	**178**	**195**	**231**	**186**	**204**	**216**	**186**	**192**
Long-term debt	4	83	157	180	209	164	180	190	159	167
IMF charges	0	1	6	5	5	2	0	0	3	4
Short-term debt	0	36	15	10	18	20	24	26	24	20
Net transfers on debt	**35**	**176**	**-49**	**10**	**-165**	**-121**	**174**	**-23**	**249**	**0**
Total debt service paid (TDS)	**10**	**207**	**389**	**473**	**607**	**616**	**555**	**553**	**496**	**578**
Long-term debt	10	170	333	442	541	556	523	525	465	549
IMF repurchases and charges	0	1	41	21	48	40	9	2	7	9
Short-term debt (interest only)	0	36	15	10	18	20	24	26	24	20
2. AGGREGATE NET RESOURCE FLOWS AND NET TRANSFERS (LONG-TERM)										
NET RESOURCE FLOWS	**41**	**284**	**507**	**207**	**190**	**252**	**519**	**353**	**937**	**707**
Net flow of long-term debt (ex. IMF)	32	259	252	90	17	64	320	88	401	239
Foreign direct investment (net)	8	6	44	35	50	91	122	99	237	282
Portfolio equity flows	0	0	0	0	0	0	0	0	0	0
Grants (excluding technical coop.)	0	19	211	83	123	97	78	166	299	186
Memo: technical coop. grants	6	18	93	55	85	80	76	69	73	123
official net resource flows	27	147	431	159	115	91	395	145	576	406
private net resource flows	14	137	76	48	75	161	124	208	361	301
NET TRANSFERS	**17**	**123**	**278**	**-67**	**-109**	**8**	**253**	**78**	**692**	**449**
Interest on long-term debt	4	83	157	180	209	164	180	190	159	167
Profit remittances on FDI	20	78	72	95	90	80	86	85	86	90
Memo: official net transfers	25	116	282	-4	-70	-54	254	-7	451	276
private net transfers	-8	7	-3	-63	-40	62	-1	85	241	173
3. MAJOR ECONOMIC AGGREGATES										
Gross national income (GNI)	700	2,429	2,848	3,238	3,698	3,821	4,507	5,053	5,264	5,794
Exports of goods & services (XGS)	..	967	1,103	1,453	1,787	2,111	2,421	2,705	2,672	2,991
of which workers remittances	..	0	50	85	120	128	160	220	320	410
Imports of goods & services (MGS)	..	1,306	1,384	1,900	2,111	2,546	2,793	3,081	3,248	3,493
International reserves (RES)	20	159	47	179	270	257	587	824	1,264	1,319
Current account balance	..	-317	-51	-343	-201	-335	-272	-148	-200	-204
4. DEBT INDICATORS										
EDT / XGS (%)	..	152.2	337.0	323.2	268.1	223.3	200.3	188.7	202.9	183.5
EDT / GNI (%)	15.8	60.6	130.6	145.0	129.6	123.4	107.6	101.0	103.0	94.7
TDS / XGS (%)	..	21.4	35.3	32.5	34.0	29.2	22.9	20.5	18.5	19.3
INT / XGS (%)	..	12.4	16.1	13.4	13.0	8.8	8.4	8.0	7.0	6.4
INT / GNI (%)	0.5	5.0	6.2	6.0	6.3	4.9	4.5	4.3	3.5	3.3
RES / EDT (%)	18.3	10.8	1.3	3.8	5.6	5.5	12.1	16.2	23.3	24.0
RES / MGS (months)	..	1.5	0.4	1.1	1.5	1.2	2.5	3.2	4.7	4.5
Short-term / EDT (%)	0.0	18.5	5.4	7.0	8.0	8.9	10.1	10.5	8.4	6.8
Concessional / EDT (%)	49.1	21.8	37.4	45.2	46.5	50.2	49.7	50.0	53.3	53.3
Multilateral / EDT (%)	57.2	31.1	42.5	43.9	44.9	44.7	47.7	46.7	47.8	49.5

HONDURAS

(US$ million, unless otherwise indicated)

	1970	1980	1990	1994	1995	1996	1997	1998	1999	2000
5. LONG-TERM DEBT										
DEBT OUTSTANDING (LDOD)	**111**	**1,168**	**3,487**	**4,256**	**4,310**	**4,237**	**4,318**	**4,455**	**4,759**	**4,897**
Public and publicly guaranteed	**91**	**976**	**3,420**	**4,156**	**4,187**	**4,021**	**4,059**	**4,043**	**4,216**	**4,337**
Official creditors	88	697	2,978	3,787	3,823	3,697	3,817	3,879	4,078	4,231
Multilateral	63	459	1,581	2,062	2,153	2,109	2,315	2,381	2,590	2,717
Concessional	30	202	536	921	1,036	1,186	1,295	1,409	1,737	1,767
Bilateral	24	238	1,396	1,725	1,670	1,588	1,502	1,498	1,489	1,514
Concessional	24	120	855	1,201	1,192	1,180	1,114	1,142	1,156	1,160
Private creditors	4	280	443	369	365	324	242	164	138	106
Bonds	0	0	0	152	139	126	62	0	0	0
Commercial banks	0	205	204	98	115	110	94	92	84	70
Other private	4	75	238	120	111	88	86	72	54	36
Private nonguaranteed	**19**	**191**	**66**	**100**	**123**	**216**	**259**	**412**	**543**	**560**
Bonds	0	0	0	0	0	0	0	0	0	0
Commercial banks and other	19	191	66	100	123	216	259	412	543	560
Memo:										
IBRD	30	152	558	469	443	350	275	235	185	152
IDA	15	64	77	307	386	424	496	579	841	838
DISBURSEMENTS	**39**	**346**	**429**	**352**	**349**	**456**	**662**	**423**	**706**	**620**
Public and publicly guaranteed	**29**	**265**	**421**	**320**	**287**	**309**	**556**	**197**	**452**	**436**
Official creditors	29	151	364	297	258	306	551	195	448	432
Multilateral	21	113	190	195	209	259	478	141	367	396
Concessional	10	37	54	119	132	182	133	117	352	114
Bilateral	7	38	174	102	49	47	72	54	81	36
Concessional	7	12	88	84	45	46	68	43	22	24
Private creditors	0	114	57	23	29	2	5	3	4	4
Bonds	0	0	0	0	0	0	0	0	0	0
Commercial banks	0	59	22	3	26	2	5	3	0	1
Other private	0	55	36	20	4	0	0	0	4	3
Private nonguaranteed	**10**	**81**	**8**	**32**	**62**	**147**	**106**	**226**	**254**	**184**
Bonds	0	0	0	0	0	0	0	0	0	0
Commercial banks and other	10	81	8	32	62	147	106	226	254	184
Memo:										
IBRD	10	24	82	5	7	0	0	0	0	0
IDA	2	18	0	64	78	52	95	64	273	38
PRINCIPAL REPAYMENTS	**6**	**87**	**177**	**262**	**332**	**392**	**343**	**335**	**306**	**382**
Public and publicly guaranteed	**3**	**39**	**151**	**242**	**293**	**338**	**280**	**261**	**182**	**215**
Official creditors	2	23	143	220	266	313	234	216	171	212
Multilateral	2	20	137	158	158	239	137	120	133	192
Concessional	1	2	16	24	22	22	20	25	27	26
Bilateral	0	2	6	63	108	74	97	96	38	21
Concessional	0	1	2	35	50	50	53	54	14	8
Private creditors	1	16	8	22	27	25	46	46	11	3
Bonds	0	0	0	0	13	13	30	32	0	0
Commercial banks	0	14	4	12	6	4	3	3	6	3
Other private	1	3	4	10	8	8	13	11	5	0
Private nonguaranteed	**3**	**48**	**25**	**20**	**39**	**54**	**63**	**74**	**124**	**166**
Bonds	0	0	0	0	0	0	0	0	0	0
Commercial banks and other	3	48	25	20	39	54	63	74	124	166
Memo:										
IBRD	1	4	94	51	58	59	50	48	47	33
IDA	0	0	2	2	2	2	2	2	2	2
NET FLOWS ON DEBT	**32**	**259**	**252**	**90**	**17**	**64**	**320**	**88**	**401**	**239**
Public and publicly guaranteed	**26**	**226**	**270**	**78**	**-6**	**-29**	**276**	**-64**	**270**	**221**
Official creditors	27	128	220	77	-9	-6	317	-21	277	220
Multilateral	20	92	53	37	51	20	341	21	234	205
Concessional	9	35	38	95	110	160	113	91	325	87
Bilateral	7	36	168	39	-59	-26	-24	-42	43	16
Concessional	7	11	86	49	-5	-4	15	-11	8	16
Private creditors	-1	98	49	2	2	-23	-41	-43	-7	1
Bonds	0	0	0	0	-13	-13	-30	-32	0	0
Commercial banks	0	46	18	-9	20	-2	2	0	-6	-2
Other private	-1	52	32	11	-4	-8	-13	-11	-1	3
Private nonguaranteed	**7**	**33**	**-18**	**12**	**23**	**93**	**43**	**153**	**131**	**18**
Bonds	0	0	0	0	0	0	0	0	0	0
Commercial banks and other	7	33	-18	12	23	93	43	153	131	18
Memo:										
IBRD	9	20	-12	-46	-51	-59	-50	-48	-47	-33
IDA	2	18	-2	62	76	50	93	62	271	36

HONDURAS

(US$ million, unless otherwise indicated)

	1970	1980	1990	1994	1995	1996	1997	1998	1999	2000
INTEREST PAYMENTS (LINT)	**4**	**83**	**157**	**180**	**209**	**164**	**180**	**190**	**159**	**167**
Public and publicly guaranteed	**3**	**58**	**156**	**178**	**204**	**158**	**160**	**168**	**127**	**136**
Official creditors	2	31	150	163	184	145	141	152	125	130
Multilateral	2	24	141	104	103	98	82	91	88	96
Concessional	0	4	11	14	14	15	16	19	19	23
Bilateral	0	7	8	59	81	47	60	60	36	35
Concessional	0	2	1	29	35	30	32	30	21	27
Private creditors	0	27	6	14	20	14	19	16	2	6
Bonds	0	0	0	5	7	7	8	9	0	0
Commercial banks	0	26	5	3	7	4	4	2	1	6
Other private	0	1	1	6	6	3	7	4	1	0
Private nonguaranteed	**1**	**25**	**1**	**2**	**5**	**6**	**20**	**23**	**32**	**31**
Bonds	0	0	0	0	0	0	0	0	0	0
Commercial banks and other	1	25	1	2	5	6	20	23	32	31
Memo:										
IBRD	1	12	96	38	38	30	23	20	18	15
IDA	0	0	1	2	3	3	3	4	4	6
NET TRANSFERS ON DEBT	**29**	**176**	**95**	**-90**	**-192**	**-100**	**140**	**-102**	**242**	**71**
Public and publicly guaranteed	**23**	**168**	**114**	**-99**	**-211**	**-187**	**116**	**-232**	**143**	**85**
Official creditors	25	97	71	-87	-193	-151	176	-173	152	90
Multilateral	18	68	-89	-67	-52	-77	259	-71	146	109
Concessional	9	31	27	82	96	145	97	73	306	65
Bilateral	7	29	159	-20	-141	-73	-84	-102	7	-19
Concessional	7	9	85	20	-39	-34	-17	-40	-12	-10
Private creditors	-2	71	43	-13	-18	-37	-59	-59	-9	-5
Bonds	0	0	0	-5	-21	-20	-38	-41	0	0
Commercial banks	0	20	13	-12	13	-6	-2	-2	-7	-8
Other private	-2	51	31	4	-10	-11	-20	-16	-2	3
Private nonguaranteed	**6**	**8**	**-19**	**10**	**18**	**87**	**23**	**130**	**98**	**-14**
Bonds	0	0	0	0	0	0	0	0	0	0
Commercial banks and other	6	8	-19	10	18	87	23	130	98	-14
Memo:										
IBRD	8	8	-108	-85	-89	-89	-73	-68	-65	-48
IDA	2	17	-4	60	73	47	90	58	266	30
DEBT SERVICE (LTDS)	**10**	**170**	**333**	**442**	**541**	**556**	**523**	**525**	**465**	**549**
Public and publicly guaranteed	**6**	**97**	**307**	**420**	**497**	**496**	**439**	**429**	**309**	**352**
Official creditors	4	54	293	384	451	457	375	367	296	343
Multilateral	4	45	278	262	262	336	219	211	221	287
Concessional	1	6	27	38	36	37	36	44	46	49
Bilateral	0	9	15	122	189	121	156	156	74	55
Concessional	0	3	3	65	84	80	85	84	35	35
Private creditors	2	44	14	36	47	39	64	62	13	9
Bonds	0	0	0	5	21	20	38	41	0	0
Commercial banks	0	39	9	15	13	8	7	5	7	9
Other private	2	4	5	16	13	11	20	16	6	0
Private nonguaranteed	**4**	**73**	**27**	**22**	**44**	**60**	**83**	**97**	**156**	**197**
Bonds	0	0	0	0	0	0	0	0	0	0
Commercial banks and other	4	73	27	22	44	60	83	97	156	197
Memo:										
IBRD	2	17	191	90	96	89	73	68	65	48
IDA	0	1	4	3	4	5	5	6	7	8
UNDISBURSED DEBT	**54**	**729**	**664**	**741**	**799**	**802**	**556**	**645**	**655**	**614**
Official creditors	54	716	654	712	787	793	546	637	646	609
Private creditors	0	13	10	29	12	9	10	8	9	5
Memorandum items										
Concessional LDOD	54	321	1,390	2,122	2,228	2,365	2,410	2,551	2,893	2,926
Variable rate LDOD	19	400	753	784	768	790	775	882	960	951
Public sector LDOD	91	841	3,314	4,131	4,164	3,998	4,037	4,022	4,196	4,316
Private sector LDOD	0	324	173	125	147	239	281	433	563	581

6. CURRENCY COMPOSITION OF LONG-TERM DEBT (PERCENT)

	1970	1980	1990	1994	1995	1996	1997	1998	1999	2000
Deutsche mark	0.0	0.0	2.6	3.0	3.2	3.0	2.9	3.1	2.3	2.2
French franc	0.6	0.4	3.1	2.5	2.4	2.5	2.7	2.8	1.8	1.5
Japanese yen	0.0	0.0	8.4	9.9	9.3	8.5	8.9	10.1	9.3	8.3
Pound sterling	0.0	0.0	0.9	0.6	0.6	0.6	0.8	0.7	0.6	0.4
Swiss franc	0.0	0.0	2.1	1.3	1.5	1.3	1.3	1.3	1.0	0.9
U.S.dollars	66.6	62.9	45.2	48.1	48.2	50.9	59.6	57.9	62.9	66.1
Multiple currency	32.8	25.4	34.5	30.5	30.3	28.5	20.0	19.8	18.2	16.2
Special drawing rights	0.0	0.0	0.1	0.2	0.2	0.2	0.1	0.1	0.1	0.3
All other currencies	0.0	11.3	3.1	3.9	4.3	4.5	3.7	4.2	3.8	4.1

HONDURAS

(US$ million, unless otherwise indicated)

	1970	1980	1990	1994	1995	1996	1997	1998	1999	2000
7. DEBT RESTRUCTURINGS										
Total amount rescheduled	..	..	308	45	25	67	109	0	155	158
Debt stock rescheduled	..	..	0	0	0	0	3	0	7	0
Principal rescheduled	..	..	151	29	17	45	100	0	103	113
Official	..	..	68	11	7	39	99	0	95	82
Private	..	..	83	18	9	5	1	0	8	31
Interest rescheduled	..	..	140	14	8	21	3	0	45	45
Official	..	..	78	8	4	17	3	0	43	36
Private	..	..	62	6	4	5	0	0	2	9
Debt forgiven	..	..	10	20	10	2	1	28	32	8
Memo: interest forgiven	..	..	11	0	0	2	0	13	9	5
Debt stock reduction	..	..	41	0	0	0	0	0	0	0
of which debt buyback	..	..	0	0	0	0	0	0	0	0
8. DEBT STOCK-FLOW RECONCILIATION										
Total change in debt stocks	..	..	332	336	96	-78	137	253	319	64
Net flows on debt	38	296	129	204	66	65	377	193	435	192
Net change in interest arrears	..	..	-83	-24	-10	-2	2	7	-16	-17
Interest capitalized	..	..	140	14	8	21	3	0	45	45
Debt forgiveness or reduction	..	..	-51	-20	-10	-2	-1	-28	-32	-8
Cross-currency valuation	..	..	48	49	-74	-325	-234	-101	-29	-133
Residual	..	..	149	113	116	165	-10	182	-83	-14
9. AVERAGE TERMS OF NEW COMMITMENTS										
ALL CREDITORS										
Interest (%)	4.1	6.8	6.5	5.6	2.3	2.7	6.3	2.0	1.3	5.3
Maturity (years)	29.6	104.4	21.2	19.3	29.8	32.2	14.4	33.7	34.7	30.5
Grace period (years)	6.8	6.7	5.9	5.2	7.3	8.3	2.9	8.4	9.6	19.4
Grant element (%)	45.5	26.9	26.5	29.6	58.4	57.7	22.4	63.5	72.9	40.3
Official creditors										
Interest (%)	4.1	5.9	6.1	5.6	2.1	2.7	6.3	2.0	1.2	5.3
Maturity (years)	29.6	113.7	22.7	19.3	29.8	32.2	14.2	33.7	35.0	30.5
Grace period (years)	6.8	7.1	6.5	5.2	7.5	8.3	2.8	8.4	9.7	19.4
Grant element (%)	45.5	31.5	29.3	29.6	59.9	57.7	22.0	63.5	73.6	40.3
Private creditors										
Interest (%)	0.0	16.0	9.9	0.0	7.5	0.0	3.6	0.0	6.6	0.0
Maturity (years)	0.0	6.7	7.1	0.0	29.8	0.0	25.5	0.0	8.1	0.0
Grace period (years)	0.0	2.5	0.6	0.0	2.3	0.0	5.0	0.0	1.1	0.0
Grant element (%)	0.0	-22.3	-0.8	0.0	16.6	0.0	45.8	0.0	10.9	0.0
Memorandum items										
Commitments	23	495	452	144	344	420	449	339	475	404
Official creditors	23	452	410	144	332	420	442	339	469	404
Private creditors	0	43	42	0	12	0	8	0	6	0

10. CONTRACTUAL OBLIGATIONS ON OUTSTANDING LONG-TERM DEBT

	2001	2002	2003	2004	2005	2006	2007	2008	2009	2010
TOTAL										
Disbursements	195	174	108	68	35	21	10	2	0	0
Principal	332	320	290	279	273	263	233	204	205	204
Interest	197	184	174	155	139	125	111	100	91	82
Official creditors										
Disbursements	193	173	107	67	35	21	10	2	0	0
Principal	277	267	236	225	219	211	184	157	157	157
Interest	157	148	139	126	114	104	94	87	81	75
Bilateral creditors										
Disbursements	34	43	23	12	4	3	0	0	0	0
Principal	130	122	109	110	109	97	80	67	69	67
Interest	58	57	56	50	45	40	36	33	30	28
Multilateral creditors										
Disbursements	160	130	84	56	31	18	10	1	0	0
Principal	147	145	127	115	110	114	104	90	88	90
Interest	99	91	83	76	70	65	59	54	50	47
Private creditors										
Disbursements	2	1	1	0	0	0	0	0	0	0
Principal	55	53	54	54	54	52	49	47	47	47
Interest	40	36	35	28	25	21	17	14	10	7
Commercial banks										
Disbursements	2	1	1	0	0	0	0	0	0	0
Principal	6	5	5	5	5	5	3	1	1	1
Interest	3	3	3	2	2	1	1	1	1	1
Other private										
Disbursements	0	0	0	0	0	0	0	0	0	0
Principal	48	48	49	49	49	47	46	46	46	46
Interest	36	33	33	26	23	19	16	13	10	7

HUNGARY

(US$ million, unless otherwise indicated)

	1970	1980	1990	1994	1995	1996	1997	1998	1999	2000
1. SUMMARY DEBT DATA										
TOTAL DEBT STOCKS (EDT)	..	**9,764**	**21,202**	**28,304**	**31,649**	**27,246**	**24,549**	**28,459**	**29,833**	**29,415**
Long-term debt (LDOD)	..	**6,416**	**17,931**	**24,766**	**28,062**	**23,716**	**21,032**	**23,678**	**26,290**	**25,263**
Public and publicly guaranteed	..	6,416	17,931	22,379	23,973	18,711	15,117	15,890	16,828	14,251
Private nonguaranteed	..	0	0	2,388	4,089	5,005	5,915	7,789	9,462	11,012
Use of IMF credit	**0**	**0**	**330**	**1,141**	**385**	**171**	**160**	**0**	**0**	**0**
Short-term debt	..	**3,347**	**2,941**	**2,397**	**3,203**	**3,359**	**3,357**	**4,780**	**3,543**	**4,152**
of which interest arrears on LDOD	..	0	0	0	0	0	0	0	0	0
Official creditors	..	0	0	0	0	0	0	0	0	0
Private creditors	..	0	0	0	0	0	0	0	0	0
Memo: principal arrears on LDOD	..	0	0	0	5	0	0	0	0	0
Official creditors	..	0	0	0	0	0	0	0	0	0
Private creditors	..	0	0	0	5	0	0	0	0	0
Memo: export credits	..	0	1,424	2,252	2,435	1,947	1,840	1,043	788	469
TOTAL DEBT FLOWS										
Disbursements	..	**1,552**	**2,455**	**5,143**	**6,886**	**4,380**	**4,629**	**7,052**	**9,234**	**6,248**
Long-term debt	..	1,552	2,282	5,143	6,886	4,380	4,629	7,052	9,234	6,248
IMF purchases	0	0	173	0	0	0	0	0	0	0
Principal repayments	..	**824**	**2,546**	**3,932**	**4,911**	**6,544**	**5,992**	**5,759**	**6,033**	**6,444**
Long-term debt	..	824	2,216	3,768	4,117	6,340	5,992	5,598	6,033	6,444
IMF repurchases	0	0	330	164	793	203	0	161	0	0
Net flows on debt	..	**903**	**-457**	**1,603**	**2,782**	**-2,008**	**-1,365**	**2,716**	**1,963**	**413**
of which short-term debt	..	176	-366	392	806	156	-2	1,423	-1,238	609
Interest payments (INT)	..	**1,099**	**1,678**	**1,730**	**2,109**	**1,815**	**1,685**	**1,494**	**1,446**	**1,502**
Long-term debt	..	636	1,528	1,501	1,875	1,618	1,516	1,297	1,301	1,332
IMF charges	0	0	35	63	60	17	8	2	0	0
Short-term debt	..	463	115	166	174	180	161	195	145	170
Net transfers on debt	..	**-196**	**-2,135**	**-127**	**673**	**-3,823**	**-3,049**	**1,222**	**517**	**-1,088**
Total debt service paid (TDS)	..	**1,923**	**4,224**	**5,662**	**7,019**	**8,359**	**7,676**	**7,254**	**7,480**	**7,946**
Long-term debt	..	1,460	3,745	5,269	5,992	7,958	7,507	6,895	7,335	7,776
IMF repurchases and charges	0	0	364	228	853	221	8	163	0	0
Short-term debt (interest only)	..	463	115	166	174	180	161	195	145	170
2. AGGREGATE NET RESOURCE FLOWS AND NET TRANSFERS (LONG-TERM)										
NET RESOURCE FLOWS	..	**728**	**219**	**2,998**	**7,804**	**1,428**	**2,698**	**3,837**	**5,876**	**1,643**
Net flow of long-term debt (ex. IMF)	..	728	66	1,375	2,769	-1,961	-1,363	1,454	3,201	-196
Foreign direct investment (net)	..	0	0	1,144	4,519	2,274	2,167	2,037	1,977	1,692
Portfolio equity flows	..	0	150	340	483	1,004	1,810	259	592	0
Grants (excluding technical coop.)	..	0	3	139	33	110	84	88	106	147
Memo: technical coop. grants	..	0	0	61	158	85	54	79	53	39
official net resource flows	..	132	527	234	-99	-589	-8	-851	208	-78
private net resource flows	..	596	-308	2,765	7,903	2,017	2,706	4,688	5,668	1,721
NET TRANSFERS	..	**92**	**-1,346**	**1,408**	**5,819**	**-390**	**932**	**2,261**	**4,244**	**-89**
Interest on long-term debt	..	636	1,528	1,501	1,875	1,618	1,516	1,297	1,301	1,332
Profit remittances on FDI	..	0	37	90	110	200	250	280	330	400
Memo: official net transfers	..	120	343	-47	-402	-844	-204	-1,002	76	-209
private net transfers	..	-28	-1,689	1,455	6,221	454	1,136	3,263	4,168	120
3. MAJOR ECONOMIC AGGREGATES										
Gross national income (GNI)	..	21,775	31,601	40,103	42,876	43,709	44,304	45,177	46,414	44,061
Exports of goods & services (XGS)	..	..	12,315	11,441	18,850	21,376	26,773	27,804	28,298	32,613
of which workers remittances	..	..	0	0	6	11	18	26	26	53
Imports of goods & services (MGS)	..	..	12,724	16,404	21,515	23,000	27,875	30,231	30,718	34,463
International reserves (RES)	..	..	1,185	6,778	12,017	9,757	8,437	9,348	10,983	11,217
Current account balance	..	..	379	-4,054	-2,530	-1,689	-982	-2,304	-2,106	-1,494
4. DEBT INDICATORS										
EDT / XGS (%)	..	..	172.2	247.4	167.9	127.5	91.7	102.4	105.4	90.2
EDT / GNI (%)	..	44.8	67.1	70.6	73.8	62.3	55.4	63.0	64.3	66.8
TDS / XGS (%)	..	..	34.3	49.5	37.2	39.1	28.7	26.1	26.4	24.4
INT / XGS (%)	..	..	13.6	15.1	11.2	8.5	6.3	5.4	5.1	4.6
INT / GNI (%)	..	5.1	5.3	4.3	4.9	4.2	3.8	3.3	3.1	3.4
RES / EDT (%)	..	..	5.6	24.0	38.0	35.8	34.4	32.9	36.8	38.1
RES / MGS (months)	..	..	1.1	5.0	6.7	5.1	3.6	3.7	4.3	3.9
Short-term / EDT (%)	..	34.3	13.9	8.5	10.1	12.3	13.7	16.8	11.9	14.1
Concessional / EDT (%)	..	5.6	0.2	0.8	1.3	1.7	1.8	1.9	1.6	1.0
Multilateral / EDT (%)	..	0.0	11.8	12.7	11.1	10.2	10.0	5.3	5.2	4.8

HUNGARY

(US$ million, unless otherwise indicated)

	1970	1980	1990	1994	1995	1996	1997	1998	1999	2000
5. LONG-TERM DEBT										
DEBT OUTSTANDING (LDOD)	..	**6,416**	**17,931**	**24,766**	**28,062**	**23,716**	**21,032**	**23,678**	**26,290**	**25,263**
Public and publicly guaranteed	..	**6,416**	**17,931**	**22,379**	**23,973**	**18,711**	**15,117**	**15,890**	**16,828**	**14,251**
Official creditors	..	542	2,656	4,445	4,457	3,503	3,123	2,273	2,225	1,862
Multilateral	..	0	2,497	3,594	3,510	2,767	2,462	1,504	1,555	1,412
Concessional	..	0	13	0	0	0	0	0	10	22
Bilateral	..	542	160	851	947	736	661	769	669	449
Concessional	..	542	19	229	415	461	439	525	476	284
Private creditors	..	5,874	15,275	17,934	19,516	15,208	11,994	13,616	14,604	12,389
Bonds	..	25	4,645	13,486	15,814	13,135	10,618	11,977	12,720	10,577
Commercial banks	..	5,523	9,642	3,969	3,372	1,899	1,258	1,535	1,857	1,798
Other private	..	326	988	479	330	174	118	105	28	14
Private nonguaranteed	..	**0**	**0**	**2,388**	**4,089**	**5,005**	**5,915**	**7,789**	**9,462**	**11,012**
Bonds	..	0	0	0	0	0	0	90	203	188
Commercial banks and other	..	0	0	2,388	4,089	5,005	5,915	7,699	9,259	10,824
Memo:										
IBRD	0	0	1,513	2,208	2,218	1,650	1,520	699	654	582
IDA	0	0	0	0	0	0	0	0	0	0
DISBURSEMENTS	..	**1,552**	**2,282**	**5,143**	**6,886**	**4,380**	**4,629**	**7,052**	**9,234**	**6,248**
Public and publicly guaranteed	..	**1,552**	**2,282**	**3,729**	**4,149**	**1,946**	**1,151**	**3,077**	**3,718**	**1,082**
Official creditors	..	187	669	378	687	507	344	664	322	119
Multilateral	..	0	654	265	483	354	274	565	288	67
Concessional	..	0	0	0	0	0	0	0	11	13
Bilateral	..	187	15	114	204	153	71	98	34	53
Concessional	..	187	3	112	204	96	40	73	15	34
Private creditors	..	1,365	1,614	3,351	3,462	1,438	807	2,414	3,397	963
Bonds	..	0	940	2,817	3,102	468	424	2,101	2,969	630
Commercial banks	..	1,240	574	527	343	867	326	294	424	333
Other private	..	125	99	6	17	104	57	20	4	0
Private nonguaranteed	..	**0**	**0**	**1,414**	**2,737**	**2,434**	**3,478**	**3,975**	**5,516**	**5,166**
Bonds	..	0	0	0	0	0	0	85	133	0
Commercial banks and other	..	0	0	1,414	2,737	2,434	3,478	3,889	5,383	5,166
Memo:										
IBRD	0	0	268	168	188	95	185	369	31	38
IDA	0	0	0	0	0	0	0	0	0	0
PRINCIPAL REPAYMENTS	..	**824**	**2,216**	**3,768**	**4,117**	**6,340**	**5,992**	**5,598**	**6,033**	**6,444**
Public and publicly guaranteed	..	**824**	**2,216**	**3,160**	**3,081**	**4,823**	**2,985**	**3,310**	**2,234**	**2,513**
Official creditors	..	55	145	283	819	1,207	436	1,602	220	344
Multilateral	..	0	125	232	723	931	375	1,546	98	132
Concessional	..	0	0	0	0	0	0	0	0	0
Bilateral	..	55	19	52	96	275	61	56	122	212
Concessional	..	55	0	12	14	7	6	30	45	183
Private creditors	..	769	2,072	2,877	2,262	3,617	2,549	1,708	2,014	2,169
Bonds	..	0	19	577	982	1,610	1,616	1,594	1,844	1,847
Commercial banks	..	652	1,894	2,067	1,094	1,860	834	75	90	308
Other private	..	117	159	233	186	147	99	39	80	14
Private nonguaranteed	..	**0**	**0**	**608**	**1,036**	**1,517**	**3,007**	**2,288**	**3,800**	**3,931**
Bonds	..	0	0	0	0	0	0	0	0	0
Commercial banks and other	..	0	0	608	1,036	1,517	3,007	2,288	3,800	3,931
Memo:										
IBRD	0	0	108	196	251	514	218	1,172	55	95
IDA	0	0	0	0	0	0	0	0	0	0
NET FLOWS ON DEBT	..	**728**	**66**	**1,375**	**2,769**	**-1,961**	**-1,363**	**1,454**	**3,201**	**-196**
Public and publicly guaranteed	..	**728**	**66**	**569**	**1,068**	**-2,877**	**-1,834**	**-233**	**1,485**	**-1,431**
Official creditors	..	132	524	95	-132	-699	-92	-939	102	-225
Multilateral	..	0	529	33	-240	-577	-102	-981	190	-66
Concessional	..	0	0	0	0	0	0	0	11	13
Bilateral	..	132	-5	62	108	-122	10	42	-88	-159
Concessional	..	132	2	100	190	89	34	44	-30	-149
Private creditors	..	596	-458	474	1,200	-2,178	-1,742	705	1,383	-1,206
Bonds	..	0	921	2,241	2,120	-1,142	-1,192	506	1,125	-1,218
Commercial banks	..	588	-1,320	-1,540	-750	-993	-508	219	334	26
Other private	..	8	-59	-227	-170	-43	-42	-20	-76	-14
Private nonguaranteed	..	**0**	**0**	**807**	**1,701**	**917**	**472**	**1,687**	**1,716**	**1,235**
Bonds	..	0	0	0	0	0	0	85	133	0
Commercial banks and other	..	0	0	807	1,701	917	472	1,601	1,583	1,235
Memo:										
IBRD	0	0	161	-28	-63	-419	-33	-802	-24	-57
IDA	0	0	0	0	0	0	0	0	0	0

HUNGARY

(US$ million, unless otherwise indicated)

	1970	1980	1990	1994	1995	1996	1997	1998	1999	2000
INTEREST PAYMENTS (LINT)	..	**636**	**1,528**	**1,501**	**1,875**	**1,618**	**1,516**	**1,297**	**1,301**	**1,332**
Public and publicly guaranteed	..	**636**	**1,528**	**1,449**	**1,708**	**1,550**	**1,179**	**978**	**1,001**	**950**
Official creditors	..	12	184	281	303	255	195	152	132	131
Multilateral	..	0	175	234	241	213	163	123	98	95
Concessional	..	0	1	0	0	0	0	0	0	1
Bilateral	..	12	9	47	62	42	32	29	34	36
Concessional	..	12	1	5	14	17	17	17	22	24
Private creditors	..	624	1,344	1,167	1,405	1,295	983	827	869	819
Bonds	..	3	241	878	1,130	1,139	898	761	794	733
Commercial banks	..	583	1,034	261	241	144	76	60	70	84
Other private	..	38	70	28	35	12	9	5	6	2
Private nonguaranteed	..	**0**	**0**	**52**	**166**	**68**	**337**	**319**	**300**	**382**
Bonds	..	0	0	0	0	0	0	1	10	18
Commercial banks and other	..	0	0	52	166	68	337	318	290	364
Memo:										
IBRD	0	0	106	157	160	141	102	70	43	42
IDA	0	0	0	0	0	0	0	0	0	0
NET TRANSFERS ON DEBT	..	**92**	**-1,462**	**-126**	**894**	**-3,579**	**-2,878**	**157**	**1,900**	**-1,528**
Public and publicly guaranteed	..	**92**	**-1,462**	**-880**	**-640**	**-4,427**	**-3,013**	**-1,211**	**484**	**-2,381**
Official creditors	..	120	340	-186	-435	-954	-287	-1,090	-30	-356
Multilateral	..	0	354	-201	-482	-790	-265	-1,103	93	-160
Concessional	..	0	-1	0	0	0	0	0	11	12
Bilateral	..	120	-14	15	46	-164	-22	13	-122	-196
Concessional	..	120	1	96	176	72	18	27	-52	-173
Private creditors	..	-28	-1,802	-694	-205	-3,473	-2,726	-121	514	-2,025
Bonds	..	-3	681	1,362	991	-2,281	-2,090	-255	331	-1,951
Commercial banks	..	5	-2,354	-1,801	-991	-1,136	-584	159	264	-59
Other private	..	-30	-129	-255	-204	-56	-51	-25	-81	-15
Private nonguaranteed	..	**0**	**0**	**754**	**1,534**	**848**	**135**	**1,368**	**1,416**	**854**
Bonds	..	0	0	0	0	0	0	85	123	-18
Commercial banks and other	..	0	0	754	1,534	848	135	1,284	1,292	871
Memo:										
IBRD	0	0	54	-185	-223	-560	-135	-872	-67	-99
IDA	0	0	0	0	0	0	0	0	0	0
DEBT SERVICE (LTDS)	..	**1,460**	**3,745**	**5,269**	**5,992**	**7,958**	**7,507**	**6,895**	**7,335**	**7,776**
Public and publicly guaranteed	..	**1,460**	**3,745**	**4,609**	**4,789**	**6,373**	**4,164**	**4,288**	**3,235**	**3,463**
Official creditors	..	67	329	564	1,122	1,462	632	1,754	351	475
Multilateral	..	0	300	465	964	1,144	539	1,669	195	227
Concessional	..	0	1	0	0	0	0	0	0	1
Bilateral	..	67	29	99	158	317	93	85	156	248
Concessional	..	67	1	16	28	24	22	46	67	207
Private creditors	..	1,393	3,416	4,044	3,667	4,911	3,532	2,535	2,883	2,988
Bonds	..	3	260	1,455	2,111	2,749	2,514	2,356	2,638	2,581
Commercial banks	..	1,236	2,928	2,329	1,335	2,003	910	135	160	392
Other private	..	155	228	261	221	159	108	44	85	15
Private nonguaranteed	..	**0**	**0**	**660**	**1,203**	**1,585**	**3,344**	**2,607**	**4,100**	**4,313**
Bonds	..	0	0	0	0	0	0	1	10	18
Commercial banks and other	..	0	0	660	1,203	1,585	3,344	2,606	4,090	4,295
Memo:										
IBRD	0	0	214	353	411	656	319	1,241	98	137
IDA	0	0	0	0	0	0	0	0	0	0
UNDISBURSED DEBT	..	**930**	**2,945**	**2,611**	**2,862**	**1,465**	**1,296**	**1,254**	**969**	**555**
Official creditors	..	141	2,050	2,293	2,072	1,107	987	642	656	344
Private creditors	..	789	895	318	789	358	309	612	313	212
Memorandum items										
Concessional LDOD	..	542	33	229	415	461	439	525	486	307
Variable rate LDOD	..	2,553	10,833	10,172	11,029	9,596	9,455	11,467	13,795	15,424
Public sector LDOD	..	6,416	17,931	22,254	23,755	18,238	14,719	15,261	16,312	13,778
Private sector LDOD	..	0	0	2,513	4,307	5,478	6,313	8,418	9,979	11,485

6. CURRENCY COMPOSITION OF LONG-TERM DEBT (PERCENT)

	1970	1980	1990	1994	1995	1996	1997	1998	1999	2000
Deutsche mark	..	0.0	26.3	29.7	29.6	29.5	30.6	34.0	26.5	22.2
French franc	..	0.0	0.1	0.9	0.8	1.5	1.6	2.2	1.2	1.2
Japanese yen	..	2.9	25.4	31.5	34.5	37.7	37.4	33.4	29.6	26.5
Pound sterling	..	0.0	0.3	0.7	0.6	0.6	0.7	0.7	0.6	0.7
Swiss franc	..	0.0	3.9	1.9	2.7	2.6	3.0	3.0	1.4	0.6
U.S.dollars	..	1.8	18.5	11.3	10.7	10.7	18.7	19.4	21.0	23.0
Multiple currency	..	95.3	17.9	13.4	12.0	10.2	2.2	2.2	1.7	1.6
Special drawing rights	..	0.0	0.0	0.0	0.0	0.0	0.0	0.0	0.0	0.0
All other currencies	..	0.0	7.6	10.6	9.1	7.2	5.8	5.1	18.0	24.2

HUNGARY

(US$ million, unless otherwise indicated)

	1970	1980	1990	1994	1995	1996	1997	1998	1999	2000
7. DEBT RESTRUCTURINGS										
Total amount rescheduled	..	..	0	0	0	0	0	0	0	0
Debt stock rescheduled	..	..	0	0	0	0	0	0	0	0
Principal rescheduled	..	..	0	0	0	0	0	0	0	0
Official	..	..	0	0	0	0	0	0	0	0
Private	..	..	0	0	0	0	0	0	0	0
Interest rescheduled	..	..	0	0	0	0	0	0	0	0
Official	..	..	0	0	0	0	0	0	0	0
Private	..	..	0	0	0	0	0	0	0	0
Debt forgiven	..	..	0	0	0	0	0	0	0	0
Memo: interest forgiven	..	..	0	0	0	0	0	0	0	0
Debt stock reduction	..	..	0	0	0	0	0	0	0	0
of which debt buyback	..	..	0	0	0	0	0	0	0	0
8. DEBT STOCK-FLOW RECONCILIATION										
Total change in debt stocks	..	..	805	3,901	3,345	-4,404	-2,697	3,910	1,375	-418
Net flows on debt	..	903	-457	1,603	2,782	-2,008	-1,365	2,716	1,963	413
Net change in interest arrears	..	..	0	0	0	0	0	0	0	0
Interest capitalized	..	..	0	0	0	0	0	0	0	0
Debt forgiveness or reduction	..	..	0	0	0	0	0	0	0	0
Cross-currency valuation	..	..	1,113	1,839	638	-1,917	-1,840	1,098	-288	-1,111
Residual	..	..	149	459	-75	-478	507	96	-301	279
9. AVERAGE TERMS OF NEW COMMITMENTS										
ALL CREDITORS										
Interest (%)	..	9.8	8.9	7.6	6.4	5.3	4.1	5.3	4.8	5.1
Maturity (years)	..	13.2	9.9	7.8	10.4	8.7	9.2	7.6	7.6	5.9
Grace period (years)	..	3.0	5.1	6.3	9.1	5.1	5.0	5.8	4.2	4.7
Grant element (%)	..	-0.5	5.0	10.8	21.2	19.5	26.9	19.3	24.6	18.6
Official creditors										
Interest (%)	..	2.5	8.4	7.5	7.3	6.8	6.0	5.8	4.2	4.7
Maturity (years)	..	15.2	12.3	12.7	13.3	16.4	14.0	13.8	16.5	11.6
Grace period (years)	..	1.2	5.1	3.9	4.0	3.5	3.3	3.6	3.6	7.9
Grant element (%)	..	37.5	7.6	11.9	13.3	17.4	20.4	21.7	33.5	30.6
Private creditors										
Interest (%)	..	10.3	9.4	7.6	6.3	5.0	3.2	5.3	4.8	5.2
Maturity (years)	..	13.0	7.2	7.0	9.9	6.9	6.7	6.8	6.7	5.4
Grace period (years)	..	3.2	5.0	6.6	9.9	5.4	5.8	6.1	4.3	4.5
Grant element (%)	..	-3.1	2.0	10.7	22.4	19.9	30.2	19.0	23.7	17.5
Memorandum items										
Commitments	..	1,225	3,547	3,201	4,459	1,371	1,209	3,025	3,503	962
Official creditors	..	80	1,889	405	591	260	406	341	330	78
Private creditors	..	1,145	1,658	2,796	3,868	1,111	804	2,684	3,173	884

10. CONTRACTUAL OBLIGATIONS ON OUTSTANDING LONG-TERM DEBT

	2001	2002	2003	2004	2005	2006	2007	2008	2009	2010
TOTAL										
Disbursements	367	109	50	15	8	5	2	0	0	0
Principal	4,624	2,666	3,989	3,905	3,626	1,719	1,288	880	1,804	224
Interest	1,111	884	770	591	462	253	194	145	154	70
Official creditors										
Disbursements	233	55	26	15	8	5	2	0	0	0
Principal	176	199	190	171	190	187	162	229	113	92
Interest	126	119	109	99	89	74	63	54	37	31
Bilateral creditors										
Disbursements	45	30	18	10	5	3	1	0	0	0
Principal	79	79	66	57	64	63	46	21	21	11
Interest	21	19	16	13	11	8	6	5	4	4
Multilateral creditors										
Disbursements	188	26	8	5	3	2	1	0	0	0
Principal	96	120	124	115	126	124	117	208	92	81
Interest	105	101	94	86	78	66	57	49	33	27
Private creditors										
Disbursements	134	54	24	0	0	0	0	0	0	0
Principal	4,449	2,467	3,800	3,734	3,436	1,532	1,126	650	1,691	132
Interest	985	764	661	492	373	179	132	90	117	39
Commercial banks										
Disbursements	134	54	24	0	0	0	0	0	0	0
Principal	817	108	104	336	66	46	47	47	12	11
Interest	99	50	48	45	30	28	26	24	23	22
Other private										
Disbursements	0	0	0	0	0	0	0	0	0	0
Principal	3,632	2,359	3,696	3,398	3,370	1,486	1,079	604	1,680	121
Interest	886	714	613	447	343	151	106	66	94	17

INDIA

(US$ million, unless otherwise indicated)

	1970	1980	1990	1994	1995	1996	1997	1998	1999	2000
1. SUMMARY DEBT DATA										
TOTAL DEBT STOCKS (EDT)	**8,428**	**20,695**	**83,628**	**102,483**	**94,469**	**93,470**	**94,320**	**97,639**	**98,158**	**100,367**
Long-term debt (LDOD)	**8,145**	**18,447**	**72,462**	**93,907**	**87,046**	**85,431**	**88,610**	**93,022**	**94,199**	**96,903**
Public and publicly guaranteed	8,045	18,111	70,974	87,480	80,428	78,049	79,402	84,613	86,256	87,598
Private nonguaranteed	100	336	1,488	6,427	6,618	7,382	9,208	8,409	7,944	9,305
Use of IMF credit	**0**	**977**	**2,623**	**4,312**	**2,374**	**1,313**	**664**	**288**	**26**	**0**
Short-term debt	**283**	**1,271**	**8,544**	**4,264**	**5,049**	**6,726**	**5,046**	**4,329**	**3,933**	**3,464**
of which interest arrears on LDOD	0	0	0	0	0	0	0	0	0	0
Official creditors	0	0	0	0	0	0	0	0	0	0
Private creditors	0	0	0	0	0	0	0	0	0	0
Memo: principal arrears on LDOD	0	0	0	0	0	0	0	0	0	0
Official creditors	0	0	0	0	0	0	0	0	0	0
Private creditors	0	0	0	0	0	0	0	0	0	0
Memo: export credits	0	0	5,998	8,030	7,928	7,820	7,861	3,194	3,115	3,305
TOTAL DEBT FLOWS										
Disbursements	**930**	**3,492**	**8,344**	**7,552**	**7,140**	**6,682**	**7,620**	**10,737**	**5,474**	**10,798**
Long-term debt	930	2,469	6,590	7,552	7,140	6,682	7,620	10,737	5,474	10,798
IMF purchases	0	1,023	1,754	0	0	0	0	0	0	0
Principal repayments	**549**	**781**	**3,376**	**6,318**	**8,648**	**7,618**	**7,551**	**6,973**	**6,326**	**6,018**
Long-term debt	344	772	2,650	5,144	6,929	6,645	6,938	6,583	6,065	5,768
IMF repurchases	205	9	726	1,174	1,719	973	613	390	262	251
Net flows on debt	**381**	**3,284**	**6,011**	**1,872**	**-723**	**742**	**-1,611**	**3,047**	**-1,248**	**4,311**
of which short-term debt	0	573	1,043	638	785	1,677	-1,680	-717	-396	-469
Interest payments (INT)	**198**	**645**	**4,811**	**4,633**	**4,918**	**4,365**	**4,864**	**5,121**	**3,782**	**3,902**
Long-term debt	198	506	3,779	4,093	4,352	4,010	4,465	4,769	3,566	3,716
IMF charges	0	4	134	228	182	87	50	25	7	1
Short-term debt	0	134	899	312	385	268	349	327	209	185
Net transfers on debt	**183**	**2,639**	**1,200**	**-2,761**	**-5,641**	**-3,623**	**-6,475**	**-2,074**	**-5,030**	**409**
Total debt service paid (TDS)	**747**	**1,426**	**8,187**	**10,951**	**13,566**	**11,982**	**12,415**	**12,094**	**10,108**	**9,921**
Long-term debt	542	1,278	6,429	9,237	11,281	10,655	11,403	11,352	9,630	9,484
IMF repurchases and charges	205	14	859	1,402	1,901	1,059	663	415	269	252
Short-term debt (interest only)	0	134	899	312	385	268	349	327	209	185
2. AGGREGATE NET RESOURCE FLOWS AND NET TRANSFERS (LONG-TERM)										
NET RESOURCE FLOWS	**780**	**2,425**	**4,719**	**8,722**	**4,437**	**7,450**	**6,925**	**7,621**	**3,355**	**9,928**
Net flow of long-term debt (ex. IMF)	586	1,697	3,940	2,408	212	37	683	4,154	-590	5,031
Foreign direct investment (net)	46	79	162	973	2,144	2,426	3,577	2,635	2,169	2,315
Portfolio equity flows	0	0	105	4,729	1,517	4,398	2,116	342	1,302	2,117
Grants (excluding technical coop.)	147	649	512	612	565	589	549	490	475	466
Memo: technical coop. grants	46	151	341	388	437	409	333	313	297	309
official net resource flows	746	1,557	2,846	1,581	-483	773	143	1,469	1,542	1,157
private net resource flows	34	868	1,873	7,141	4,920	6,677	6,781	6,152	1,813	8,771
NET TRANSFERS	**582**	**1,918**	**940**	**4,629**	**85**	**3,440**	**2,459**	**2,852**	**-210**	**6,212**
Interest on long-term debt	198	506	3,779	4,093	4,352	4,010	4,465	4,769	3,566	3,716
Profit remittances on FDI	0	0	0	0	0	0	0	0	0	0
Memo: official net transfers	576	1,206	1,350	-265	-2,350	-907	-1,456	-86	1	-367
private net transfers	6	713	-409	4,894	2,435	4,347	3,916	2,938	-211	6,579
3. MAJOR ECONOMIC AGGREGATES										
Gross national income (GNI)	60,837	183,263	313,138	318,205	350,017	380,333	406,197	414,496	447,986	470,480
Exports of goods & services (XGS)	2,368	14,602	25,271	41,177	48,771	53,872	57,358	58,726	66,243	77,716
of which workers remittances	121	2,436	1,875	7,301	7,685	11,192	10,688	9,307	11,061	11,586
Imports of goods & services (MGS)	3,119	18,413	35,606	45,754	55,847	60,076	64,379	64,044	72,518	81,843
International reserves (RES)	1,023	12,010	5,637	24,221	22,865	24,889	28,385	30,647	36,005	41,059
Current account balance	-755	-3,554	-10,142	-3,785	-6,255	-5,029	-5,879	-4,345	-5,080	-2,915
4. DEBT INDICATORS										
EDT / XGS (%)	356.0	141.7	330.9	248.9	193.7	173.5	164.4	166.3	148.2	129.2
EDT / GNI (%)	13.9	11.3	26.7	32.2	27.0	24.6	23.2	23.6	21.9	21.3
TDS / XGS (%)	31.6	9.8	32.4	26.6	27.8	22.2	21.6	20.6	15.3	12.8
INT / XGS (%)	8.4	4.4	19.0	11.3	10.1	8.1	8.5	8.7	5.7	5.0
INT / GNI (%)	0.3	0.4	1.5	1.5	1.4	1.2	1.2	1.2	0.8	0.8
RES / EDT (%)	12.1	58.0	6.7	23.6	24.2	26.6	30.1	31.4	36.7	40.9
RES / MGS (months)	3.9	7.8	1.9	6.4	4.9	5.0	5.3	5.7	6.0	6.0
Short-term / EDT (%)	3.4	6.1	10.2	4.2	5.3	7.2	5.4	4.4	4.0	3.5
Concessional / EDT (%)	79.8	74.2	46.2	45.5	45.7	43.7	41.2	41.1	45.5	43.7
Multilateral / EDT (%)	18.5	29.3	26.0	30.7	31.8	31.4	31.2	31.3	32.0	32.3

(US$ million, unless otherwise indicated)

	1970	1980	1990	1994	1995	1996	1997	1998	1999	2000
5. LONG-TERM DEBT										
DEBT OUTSTANDING (LDOD)	**8,145**	**18,447**	**72,462**	**93,907**	**87,046**	**85,431**	**88,610**	**93,022**	**94,199**	**96,903**
Public and publicly guaranteed	**8,045**	**18,111**	**70,974**	**87,480**	**80,428**	**78,049**	**79,402**	**84,613**	**86,256**	**87,598**
Official creditors	7,714	16,450	48,337	61,997	57,112	54,541	52,165	53,653	58,544	56,527
Multilateral	1,562	6,070	21,768	31,486	30,048	29,332	29,391	30,517	31,361	32,408
Concessional	1,065	5,244	13,657	18,009	17,814	17,939	18,230	18,875	19,332	21,242
Bilateral	6,153	10,380	26,569	30,511	27,065	25,209	22,775	23,137	27,183	24,119
Concessional	5,658	10,115	25,006	28,599	25,378	22,903	20,607	21,272	25,350	22,609
Private creditors	330	1,661	22,637	25,483	23,315	23,509	27,236	30,960	27,712	31,071
Bonds	2	2	2,613	3,740	3,271	1,364	1,948	5,996	5,722	10,627
Commercial banks	45	1,498	16,130	14,588	13,412	16,061	20,216	20,924	18,360	17,143
Other private	283	161	3,894	7,156	6,632	6,084	5,072	4,040	3,630	3,301
Private nonguaranteed	**100**	**336**	**1,488**	**6,427**	**6,618**	**7,382**	**9,208**	**8,409**	**7,944**	**9,305**
Bonds	0	0	0	1,158	1,020	2,433	3,802	3,647	2,874	2,819
Commercial banks and other	100	336	1,488	5,268	5,598	4,949	5,406	4,763	5,070	6,487
Memo:										
IBRD	496	827	7,685	11,120	9,849	8,769	8,138	7,990	7,816	7,063
IDA	1,065	5,142	13,312	17,666	17,499	17,616	17,912	18,562	18,930	20,804
DISBURSEMENTS	**930**	**2,469**	**6,590**	**7,552**	**7,140**	**6,682**	**7,620**	**10,737**	**5,474**	**10,798**
Public and publicly guaranteed	**905**	**2,184**	**6,376**	**6,685**	**5,961**	**5,897**	**5,734**	**10,237**	**5,174**	**10,498**
Official creditors	864	1,511	3,572	3,334	2,828	3,040	3,708	4,471	3,883	4,185
Multilateral	101	863	2,211	2,230	1,942	2,234	2,021	2,041	2,089	2,316
Concessional	60	689	785	979	736	924	856	885	929	1,128
Bilateral	764	648	1,361	1,104	886	806	1,687	2,430	1,794	1,870
Concessional	710	540	1,129	909	815	681	1,445	1,887	1,485	1,718
Private creditors	41	673	2,804	3,351	3,133	2,857	2,026	5,766	1,292	6,313
Bonds	0	0	427	0	86	275	650	4,234	0	5,497
Commercial banks	16	639	1,983	870	1,719	1,698	903	931	698	346
Other private	25	34	395	2,481	1,329	884	473	602	593	470
Private nonguaranteed	**25**	**285**	**214**	**867**	**1,179**	**785**	**1,886**	**500**	**300**	**300**
Bonds	0	0	0	367	520	785	1,371	300	0	0
Commercial banks and other	25	285	214	500	659	0	515	200	300	300
Memo:										
IBRD	41	174	1,219	741	589	686	542	535	644	689
IDA	60	652	762	966	729	906	830	866	816	1,053
PRINCIPAL REPAYMENTS	**344**	**772**	**2,650**	**5,144**	**6,929**	**6,645**	**6,938**	**6,583**	**6,065**	**5,768**
Public and publicly guaranteed	**319**	**681**	**2,332**	**5,021**	**6,773**	**6,405**	**6,645**	**6,291**	**5,157**	**5,519**
Official creditors	266	603	1,237	2,365	3,876	2,856	4,114	3,491	2,815	3,494
Multilateral	40	86	609	1,102	1,513	1,218	1,217	1,295	1,403	1,764
Concessional	0	15	128	212	245	252	274	313	351	419
Bilateral	226	517	629	1,263	2,364	1,638	2,897	2,196	1,413	1,730
Concessional	167	488	558	1,107	2,106	1,459	2,654	1,924	1,165	1,430
Private creditors	53	78	1,094	2,656	2,897	3,549	2,531	2,800	2,342	2,025
Bonds	0	0	280	404	319	1,242	2	264	361	546
Commercial banks	10	34	250	1,054	1,797	1,484	1,160	837	973	788
Other private	43	44	564	1,198	780	823	1,370	1,699	1,009	691
Private nonguaranteed	**25**	**91**	**318**	**123**	**156**	**240**	**293**	**292**	**908**	**249**
Bonds	0	0	0	0	0	0	150	149	765	35
Commercial banks and other	25	91	318	123	156	240	143	143	143	214
Memo:										
IBRD	40	71	472	827	943	840	820	842	899	994
IDA	0	15	114	194	226	234	250	288	330	397
NET FLOWS ON DEBT	**586**	**1,697**	**3,940**	**2,408**	**212**	**37**	**683**	**4,154**	**-590**	**5,031**
Public and publicly guaranteed	**586**	**1,503**	**4,044**	**1,664**	**-811**	**-508**	**-911**	**3,946**	**17**	**4,979**
Official creditors	598	908	2,334	970	-1,048	184	-406	979	1,068	691
Multilateral	61	777	1,602	1,129	429	1,016	804	745	687	552
Concessional	60	674	657	767	492	672	583	572	578	710
Bilateral	538	132	733	-159	-1,477	-832	-1,210	234	381	139
Concessional	543	51	572	-198	-1,291	-779	-1,209	-37	319	288
Private creditors	-12	595	1,710	695	237	-692	-505	2,966	-1,050	4,288
Bonds	0	0	147	-404	-234	-967	648	3,970	-361	4,951
Commercial banks	6	605	1,733	-184	-78	214	-256	94	-274	-442
Other private	-18	-10	-170	1,283	548	61	-897	-1,098	-415	-221
Private nonguaranteed	**0**	**194**	**-104**	**744**	**1,023**	**545**	**1,594**	**208**	**-608**	**51**
Bonds	0	0	0	367	520	785	1,221	151	-765	-35
Commercial banks and other	0	194	-104	376	503	-240	373	58	158	86
Memo:										
IBRD	1	103	747	-86	-354	-154	-278	-307	-254	-305
IDA	60	637	648	773	503	672	580	579	486	655

INDIA

(US$ million, unless otherwise indicated)

	1970	1980	1990	1994	1995	1996	1997	1998	1999	2000
INTEREST PAYMENTS (LINT)	**198**	**506**	**3,779**	**4,093**	**4,352**	**4,010**	**4,465**	**4,769**	**3,566**	**3,716**
Public and publicly guaranteed	**192**	**476**	**3,644**	**3,702**	**3,820**	**3,584**	**4,292**	**4,302**	**3,064**	**3,058**
Official creditors	170	351	1,497	1,846	1,867	1,680	1,600	1,555	1,541	1,524
Multilateral	34	101	738	1,014	1,061	966	907	887	875	848
Concessional	7	35	101	124	135	135	136	139	144	161
Bilateral	136	250	759	832	806	714	693	668	667	676
Concessional	110	236	635	688	686	614	539	522	524	528
Private creditors	22	125	2,147	1,856	1,954	1,904	2,692	2,747	1,522	1,534
Bonds	0	0	180	221	185	573	99	118	229	221
Commercial banks	3	113	1,751	1,159	1,263	886	2,212	2,297	1,030	1,072
Other private	19	12	216	476	506	446	382	332	264	242
Private nonguaranteed	**6**	**30**	**135**	**391**	**531**	**426**	**173**	**467**	**502**	**658**
Bonds	0	0	0	20	56	88	154	265	243	224
Commercial banks and other	6	30	135	371	475	338	19	202	259	434
Memo:										
IBRD	27	66	615	768	770	674	590	536	491	427
IDA	7	35	97	121	131	130	131	135	139	156
NET TRANSFERS ON DEBT	**388**	**1,191**	**161**	**-1,685**	**-4,140**	**-3,973**	**-3,783**	**-615**	**-4,156**	**1,315**
Public and publicly guaranteed	**394**	**1,027**	**401**	**-2,037**	**-4,632**	**-4,091**	**-5,203**	**-356**	**-3,046**	**1,921**
Official creditors	429	557	837	-876	-2,915	-1,496	-2,005	-576	-474	-833
Multilateral	26	676	864	115	-632	50	-103	-142	-188	-296
Concessional	52	639	557	643	357	537	447	433	435	549
Bilateral	402	-119	-27	-991	-2,283	-1,546	-1,903	-434	-286	-537
Concessional	433	-185	-63	-886	-1,977	-1,393	-1,748	-559	-205	-240
Private creditors	-34	470	-437	-1,161	-1,717	-2,596	-3,198	220	-2,573	2,754
Bonds	0	0	-33	-625	-419	-1,540	549	3,853	-589	4,730
Commercial banks	3	492	-18	-1,343	-1,341	-672	-2,468	-2,204	-1,304	-1,513
Other private	-37	-22	-385	807	43	-385	-1,279	-1,429	-679	-463
Private nonguaranteed	**-6**	**164**	**-239**	**353**	**492**	**119**	**1,420**	**-259**	**-1,110**	**-607**
Bonds	0	0	0	347	464	697	1,067	-114	-1,008	-259
Commercial banks and other	-6	164	-239	6	28	-578	353	-144	-102	-347
Memo:										
IBRD	-26	37	132	-854	-1,124	-828	-868	-843	-745	-732
IDA	52	602	551	651	372	542	449	444	347	499
DEBT SERVICE (LTDS)	**542**	**1,278**	**6,429**	**9,237**	**11,281**	**10,655**	**11,403**	**11,352**	**9,630**	**9,484**
Public and publicly guaranteed	**511**	**1,157**	**5,975**	**8,722**	**10,593**	**9,989**	**10,937**	**10,593**	**8,221**	**8,577**
Official creditors	436	954	2,734	4,211	5,743	4,536	5,713	5,046	4,356	5,018
Multilateral	74	187	1,347	2,116	2,573	2,184	2,123	2,182	2,277	2,612
Concessional	7	50	229	336	379	387	410	452	494	579
Bilateral	362	767	1,388	2,095	3,169	2,352	3,590	2,864	2,079	2,406
Concessional	277	725	1,192	1,795	2,792	2,073	3,193	2,446	1,689	1,958
Private creditors	75	203	3,241	4,512	4,850	5,453	5,224	5,547	3,864	3,559
Bonds	0	0	460	625	504	1,815	101	382	589	767
Commercial banks	12	147	2,001	2,213	3,060	2,370	3,371	3,134	2,002	1,859
Other private	63	56	780	1,673	1,286	1,269	1,751	2,031	1,273	933
Private nonguaranteed	**31**	**121**	**453**	**514**	**688**	**666**	**466**	**759**	**1,410**	**907**
Bonds	0	0	0	20	56	88	304	414	1,008	259
Commercial banks and other	31	121	453	494	631	578	162	344	402	647
Memo:										
IBRD	67	137	1,087	1,595	1,714	1,514	1,410	1,378	1,389	1,421
IDA	7	50	211	315	357	365	381	423	469	554
UNDISBURSED DEBT	**1,862**	**8,267**	**24,971**	**21,863**	**20,055**	**19,738**	**20,129**	**17,351**	**14,073**	**11,266**
Official creditors	1,700	7,370	22,397	19,159	18,539	18,112	17,290	14,872	12,878	10,892
Private creditors	162	898	2,574	2,704	1,517	1,626	2,839	2,479	1,195	374
Memorandum items										
Concessional LDOD	6,723	15,359	38,662	46,608	43,192	40,841	38,837	40,147	44,682	43,851
Variable rate LDOD	100	790	12,169	21,758	21,054	22,841	24,565	24,761	24,934	25,941
Public sector LDOD	7,720	17,697	70,436	86,952	79,969	77,398	78,857	83,938	85,479	86,748
Private sector LDOD	425	750	2,026	6,955	7,077	8,033	9,753	9,084	8,720	10,156

6. CURRENCY COMPOSITION OF LONG-TERM DEBT (PERCENT)

	1970	1980	1990	1994	1995	1996	1997	1998	1999	2000
Deutsche mark	9.4	9.9	6.0	6.8	6.6	6.0	5.3	5.4	4.9	4.4
French franc	1.3	2.3	1.7	2.0	2.1	1.9	1.8	1.6	1.3	1.1
Japanese yen	5.1	6.7	9.7	16.5	14.8	13.3	12.2	13.5	15.1	13.1
Pound sterling	24.1	26.6	6.1	4.5	4.7	4.3	4.1	3.9	3.7	3.3
Swiss franc	0.3	0.1	0.6	0.8	0.9	0.6	0.5	0.4	0.3	0.2
U.S.dollars	40.2	39.0	60.7	50.6	52.4	56.4	60.0	60.6	61.4	67.2
Multiple currency	6.2	6.4	11.0	15.1	14.8	14.0	13.0	11.8	10.9	8.7
Special drawing rights	0.0	0.0	0.3	0.2	0.2	0.2	0.2	0.2	0.2	0.2
All other currencies	13.4	9.0	3.9	3.5	3.5	3.3	2.9	2.6	2.2	1.8

INDIA

(US$ million, unless otherwise indicated)

	1970	1980	1990	1994	1995	1996	1997	1998	1999	2000
7. DEBT RESTRUCTURINGS										
Total amount rescheduled	..	..	0	0	0	0	0	0	0	0
Debt stock rescheduled	..	..	0	0	0	0	0	0	0	0
Principal rescheduled	..	..	0	0	0	0	0	0	0	0
Official	..	..	0	0	0	0	0	0	0	0
Private	..	..	0	0	0	0	0	0	0	0
Interest rescheduled	..	..	0	0	0	0	0	0	0	0
Official	..	..	0	0	0	0	0	0	0	0
Private	..	..	0	0	0	0	0	0	0	0
Debt forgiven	..	..	0	0	0	0	0	0	0	0
Memo: interest forgiven	..	..	0	0	0	0	0	0	0	0
Debt stock reduction	..	..	0	0	0	0	0	0	0	0
of which debt buyback	..	..	0	0	0	0	0	0	0	0
8. DEBT STOCK-FLOW RECONCILIATION										
Total change in debt stocks	..	..	8,222	8,140	-8,013	-999	850	3,319	520	2,209
Net flows on debt	381	3,284	6,011	1,872	-723	742	-1,611	3,047	-1,248	4,311
Net change in interest arrears	..	..	0	0	0	0	0	0	0	0
Interest capitalized	..	..	0	0	0	0	0	0	0	0
Debt forgiveness or reduction	..	..	0	0	0	0	0	0	0	0
Cross-currency valuation	..	..	-849	4,127	-7,898	-7,451	-4,891	-1,495	913	-2,125
Residual	..	..	3,059	2,142	607	5,710	7,351	1,767	854	23
9. AVERAGE TERMS OF NEW COMMITMENTS										
ALL CREDITORS										
Interest (%)	2.5	5.5	5.2	3.9	3.5	4.5	4.9	3.5	3.1	7.1
Maturity (years)	34.1	32.6	22.5	25.0	25.3	20.3	20.0	12.6	29.3	12.0
Grace period (years)	8.2	7.2	7.8	8.0	8.1	6.9	6.7	5.8	7.7	5.6
Grant element (%)	27.6	10.7	23.7	21.9	24.7	22.9	18.9	33.4	55.9	16.6
Official creditors										
Interest (%)	2.2	2.5	3.8	3.5	3.3	3.8	3.8	3.6	3.1	5.7
Maturity (years)	35.5	40.3	28.8	27.2	27.2	28.0	27.1	25.9	29.3	23.8
Grace period (years)	8.5	8.4	8.4	8.6	8.4	8.2	7.9	7.4	7.7	6.5
Grant element (%)	29.6	13.4	27.1	23.3	25.2	26.4	21.0	49.6	55.9	32.0
Private creditors										
Interest (%)	6.3	14.0	6.7	7.0	5.1	5.7	6.5	3.4	0.0	7.8
Maturity (years)	12.9	10.7	15.6	8.2	6.9	7.6	10.0	7.3	0.0	5.1
Grace period (years)	4.5	4.0	7.1	3.6	5.2	4.8	5.1	5.2	0.0	5.1
Grant element (%)	0.0	2.9	19.9	10.9	20.1	17.1	16.0	27.1	0.0	7.6
Memorandum items										
Commitments	954	5,426	8,228	4,600	4,681	7,766	7,423	7,483	1,749	8,741
Official creditors	892	4,014	4,318	4,074	4,229	4,826	4,322	2,111	1,749	3,240
Private creditors	62	1,413	3,910	526	452	2,940	3,101	5,372	0	5,502

10. CONTRACTUAL OBLIGATIONS ON OUTSTANDING LONG-TERM DEBT

	2001	2002	2003	2004	2005	2006	2007	2008	2009	2010
TOTAL										
Disbursements	3,751	2,635	1,704	1,146	783	512	360	146	109	65
Principal	5,467	6,490	9,742	5,399	10,194	4,598	5,336	4,244	4,316	3,242
Interest	3,776	3,611	3,574	3,070	2,943	2,373	2,181	1,982	1,818	1,671
Official creditors										
Disbursements	3,476	2,550	1,691	1,146	783	512	360	146	109	65
Principal	2,761	2,981	3,145	3,227	3,373	3,442	3,414	3,345	3,246	2,795
Interest	1,444	1,398	1,321	1,287	1,258	1,183	1,087	974	863	762
Bilateral creditors										
Disbursements	1,022	559	317	130	42	23	3	0	0	0
Principal	1,239	1,314	1,399	1,454	1,577	1,590	1,598	1,612	1,552	1,134
Interest	579	555	519	529	529	476	434	383	332	288
Multilateral creditors										
Disbursements	2,455	1,991	1,373	1,016	741	489	357	146	109	65
Principal	1,523	1,667	1,746	1,773	1,796	1,852	1,815	1,733	1,695	1,661
Interest	865	843	802	758	728	707	653	591	531	474
Private creditors										
Disbursements	275	86	13	0	0	0	0	0	0	0
Principal	2,705	3,509	6,597	2,172	6,821	1,156	1,923	900	1,070	447
Interest	2,333	2,212	2,253	1,783	1,685	1,190	1,094	1,009	955	909
Commercial banks										
Disbursements	108	29	13	0	0	0	0	0	0	0
Principal	1,055	2,081	1,125	1,079	676	560	564	451	449	28
Interest	1,138	1,080	985	922	873	836	803	772	745	724
Other private										
Disbursements	167	56	1	0	0	0	0	0	0	0
Principal	1,650	1,428	5,472	1,093	6,146	596	1,359	449	621	419
Interest	1,195	1,133	1,269	861	813	354	292	237	210	185

INDONESIA

(US$ million, unless otherwise indicated)

	1970	1980	1990	1994	1995	1996	1997	1998	1999	2000
1. SUMMARY DEBT DATA										
TOTAL DEBT STOCKS (EDT)	**4,528**	**20,938**	**69,872**	**107,824**	**124,398**	**128,937**	**136,161**	**151,236**	**150,844**	**141,803**
Long-term debt (LDOD)	**4,043**	**18,163**	**58,242**	**88,367**	**98,432**	**96,706**	**100,326**	**122,033**	**120,567**	**108,330**
Public and publicly guaranteed	3,582	15,021	47,982	63,926	65,309	60,012	55,857	67,305	73,302	69,161
Private nonguaranteed	461	3,142	10,261	24,441	33,123	36,694	44,469	54,728	47,265	39,169
Use of IMF credit	**139**	**0**	**494**	**0**	**0**	**0**	**2,970**	**9,090**	**10,248**	**10,838**
Short-term debt	**346**	**2,775**	**11,135**	**19,457**	**25,966**	**32,230**	**32,865**	**20,113**	**20,029**	**22,635**
of which interest arrears on LDOD	7	0	0	0	0	0	0	0	3,500	4,635
Official creditors	7	0	0	0	0	0	0	0	0	8
Private creditors	0	0	0	0	0	0	0	0	3,500	4,627
Memo: principal arrears on LDOD	66	0	1	0	0	0	0	2,710	3,000	3,000
Official creditors	55	0	1	0	0	0	0	0	0	0
Private creditors	11	0	0	0	0	0	0	2,710	3,000	3,000
Memo: export credits	0	0	10,032	17,711	19,417	19,191	20,926	10,408	10,912	10,981
TOTAL DEBT FLOWS										
Disbursements	**674**	**3,246**	**10,024**	**12,547**	**13,629**	**20,973**	**22,454**	**16,392**	**9,460**	**7,071**
Long-term debt	636	3,246	10,024	12,547	13,629	20,973	19,425	10,619	8,078	5,948
IMF purchases	38	0	0	0	0	0	3,029	5,772	1,382	1,123
Principal repayments	**123**	**1,633**	**5,969**	**8,951**	**10,197**	**14,896**	**13,011**	**11,203**	**11,711**	**11,296**
Long-term debt	120	1,633	5,812	8,951	10,197	14,896	13,011	11,203	11,711	11,296
IMF repurchases	3	0	157	0	0	0	0	0	0	0
Net flows on debt	**551**	**2,280**	**7,216**	**5,066**	**9,941**	**12,341**	**10,078**	**-4,561**	**-3,834**	**-2,753**
of which short-term debt	0	667	3,160	1,470	6,509	6,264	635	-9,750	-1,584	1,472
Interest payments (INT)	**46**	**1,452**	**3,978**	**5,316**	**6,219**	**6,647**	**6,726**	**7,107**	**6,192**	**7,476**
Long-term debt	46	1,182	3,413	4,174	4,935	5,114	5,116	5,601	4,837	5,793
IMF charges	0	0	59	0	0	0	0	182	366	526
Short-term debt	0	270	506	1,142	1,284	1,533	1,610	1,324	989	1,157
Net transfers on debt	**506**	**828**	**3,238**	**-251**	**3,722**	**5,694**	**3,352**	**-11,668**	**-10,026**	**-10,229**
Total debt service paid (TDS)	**169**	**3,084**	**9,946**	**14,267**	**16,416**	**21,543**	**19,737**	**18,310**	**17,903**	**18,772**
Long-term debt	165	2,814	9,224	13,125	15,132	20,010	18,126	16,804	16,548	17,089
IMF repurchases and charges	3	0	216	0	0	0	0	182	366	526
Short-term debt (interest only)	0	270	506	1,142	1,284	1,533	1,610	1,324	989	1,157
2. AGGREGATE NET RESOURCE FLOWS AND NET TRANSFERS (LONG-TERM)										
NET RESOURCE FLOWS	**686**	**1,902**	**5,901**	**9,594**	**12,901**	**15,560**	**11,588**	**-420**	**-4,685**	**-9,156**
Net flow of long-term debt (ex. IMF)	517	1,613	4,213	3,596	3,432	6,077	6,414	-583	-3,633	-5,348
Foreign direct investment (net)	83	180	1,093	2,109	4,346	6,194	4,677	-356	-2,745	-4,550
Portfolio equity flows	0	0	312	3,672	4,873	3,099	298	250	1,273	379
Grants (excluding technical coop.)	87	109	283	218	250	190	199	269	421	362
Memo: technical coop. grants	26	187	401	444	494	412	373	316	339	422
official net resource flows	441	915	2,666	1,849	1,379	-602	733	2,965	3,809	2,053
private net resource flows	245	987	3,235	7,745	11,522	16,163	10,855	-3,385	-8,494	-11,210
NET TRANSFERS	**513**	**-2,514**	**296**	**2,620**	**4,966**	**7,046**	**3,172**	**-8,821**	**-13,122**	**-18,150**
Interest on long-term debt	46	1,182	3,413	4,174	4,935	5,114	5,116	5,601	4,837	5,793
Profit remittances on FDI	128	3,234	2,192	2,800	3,000	3,400	3,300	2,800	3,600	3,200
Memo: official net transfers	421	603	1,081	-633	-1,286	-3,008	-1,362	915	1,348	-543
private net transfers	92	-3,117	-785	3,253	6,253	10,054	4,534	-9,736	-14,470	-17,607
3. MAJOR ECONOMIC AGGREGATES										
Gross national income (GNI)	9,698	74,806	109,209	172,149	196,188	221,276	209,440	90,063	131,262	142,657
Exports of goods & services (XGS)	..	..	29,870	46,517	54,880	58,793	65,819	57,719	58,821	74,265
of which workers remittances	..	..	166	449	651	796	725	959	1,109	1,190
Imports of goods & services (MGS)	..	..	33,110	49,479	61,641	66,597	71,017	54,002	53,841	66,905
International reserves (RES)	160	6,803	8,657	13,321	14,908	19,396	17,487	23,606	27,345	29,353
Current account balance	..	..	-2,988	-2,792	-6,431	-7,663	-4,889	4,096	5,785	7,986
4. DEBT INDICATORS										
EDT / XGS (%)	..	..	233.9	231.8	226.7	219.3	206.9	262.0	256.5	190.9
EDT / GNI (%)	46.7	28.0	64.0	62.6	63.4	58.3	65.0	167.9	114.9	99.4
TDS / XGS (%)	..	..	33.3	30.7	29.9	36.6	30.0	31.7	30.4	25.3
INT / XGS (%)	..	..	13.3	11.4	11.3	11.3	10.2	12.3	10.5	10.1
INT / GNI (%)	0.5	1.9	3.6	3.1	3.2	3.0	3.2	7.9	4.7	5.2
RES / EDT (%)	3.5	32.5	12.4	12.4	12.0	15.0	12.8	15.6	18.1	20.7
RES / MGS (months)	..	..	3.1	3.2	2.9	3.5	3.0	5.3	6.1	5.3
Short-term / EDT (%)	7.7	13.3	15.9	18.1	20.9	25.0	24.1	13.3	13.3	16.0
Concessional / EDT (%)	62.2	36.4	26.4	25.8	22.5	20.3	17.7	18.4	21.3	21.3
Multilateral / EDT (%)	0.1	8.8	20.4	17.8	16.1	13.4	11.6	11.8	13.1	14.0

INDONESIA

(US$ million, unless otherwise indicated)

	1970	1980	1990	1994	1995	1996	1997	1998	1999	2000
5. LONG-TERM DEBT										
DEBT OUTSTANDING (LDOD)	**4,043**	**18,163**	**58,242**	**88,367**	**98,432**	**96,706**	**100,326**	**122,033**	**120,567**	**108,330**
Public and publicly guaranteed	**3,582**	**15,021**	**47,982**	**63,926**	**65,309**	**60,012**	**55,857**	**67,305**	**73,302**	**69,161**
Official creditors	3,210	9,563	33,007	49,968	51,250	46,148	42,523	49,074	55,900	54,792
Multilateral	6	1,834	14,285	19,165	20,013	17,248	15,799	17,892	19,733	19,794
Concessional	6	661	1,369	1,637	1,668	1,663	1,581	1,652	1,672	1,631
Bilateral	3,204	7,729	18,722	30,804	31,237	28,899	26,723	31,181	36,167	34,999
Concessional	2,810	6,961	17,088	26,226	26,304	24,485	22,508	26,164	30,404	28,496
Private creditors	373	5,458	14,975	13,958	14,059	13,864	13,334	18,231	17,402	14,368
Bonds	0	199	696	99	704	1,141	1,191	1,191	971	971
Commercial banks	2	2,431	8,606	7,426	6,714	5,996	5,877	10,999	11,607	9,545
Other private	371	2,828	5,673	6,434	6,642	6,728	6,266	6,041	4,824	3,852
Private nonguaranteed	**461**	**3,142**	**10,261**	**24,441**	**33,123**	**36,694**	**44,469**	**54,728**	**47,265**	**39,169**
Bonds	0	0	120	1,750	3,420	6,666	9,661	9,596	8,433	6,337
Commercial banks and other	461	3,142	10,141	22,692	29,703	30,029	34,808	45,132	38,832	32,832
Memo:										
IBRD	0	1,040	9,542	12,008	12,503	11,139	9,991	10,692	11,424	11,715
IDA	5	566	842	776	756	736	715	694	682	714
DISBURSEMENTS	**636**	**3,246**	**10,024**	**12,547**	**13,629**	**20,973**	**19,425**	**10,619**	**8,078**	**5,948**
Public and publicly guaranteed	**441**	**2,551**	**5,009**	**7,627**	**6,665**	**7,532**	**6,295**	**7,405**	**6,078**	**3,598**
Official creditors	376	1,130	3,969	4,915	4,254	3,961	3,958	5,239	5,769	3,307
Multilateral	4	431	1,794	1,854	1,777	1,696	1,586	2,369	2,557	1,650
Concessional	4	48	145	61	80	103	35	47	48	108
Bilateral	372	698	2,175	3,061	2,477	2,266	2,372	2,870	3,212	1,657
Concessional	372	592	1,979	2,261	1,923	1,841	1,656	2,476	3,096	1,106
Private creditors	66	1,421	1,041	2,711	2,411	3,571	2,337	2,166	309	291
Bonds	0	45	0	0	605	510	50	0	0	0
Commercial banks	0	1,013	487	831	938	1,784	1,344	1,851	285	285
Other private	66	363	554	1,880	869	1,277	943	315	24	6
Private nonguaranteed	**195**	**695**	**5,015**	**4,920**	**6,963**	**13,441**	**13,129**	**3,215**	**2,000**	**2,350**
Bonds	0	0	120	495	1,763	3,531	3,378	500	0	350
Commercial banks and other	195	695	4,895	4,425	5,200	9,910	9,751	2,715	2,000	2,000
Memo:										
IBRD	0	331	987	1,184	1,045	905	899	1,212	1,495	1,051
IDA	3	42	0	0	0	0	0	0	11	59
PRINCIPAL REPAYMENTS	**120**	**1,633**	**5,812**	**8,951**	**10,197**	**14,896**	**13,011**	**11,203**	**11,711**	**11,296**
Public and publicly guaranteed	**59**	**940**	**4,588**	**5,546**	**5,715**	**8,128**	**5,702**	**4,162**	**5,473**	**3,896**
Official creditors	22	324	1,586	3,284	3,125	4,753	3,425	2,542	2,380	1,616
Multilateral	0	38	677	1,888	1,289	2,980	1,671	989	1,077	1,116
Concessional	0	4	24	43	46	47	44	51	59	69
Bilateral	22	286	909	1,396	1,837	1,774	1,754	1,554	1,303	500
Concessional	19	184	611	1,037	1,271	1,211	1,207	1,109	997	334
Private creditors	37	616	3,001	2,262	2,589	3,374	2,277	1,619	3,093	2,280
Bonds	0	5	94	0	0	73	0	0	220	0
Commercial banks	1	190	1,718	1,188	1,678	2,342	1,380	970	2,580	2,106
Other private	37	421	1,190	1,074	911	960	897	649	292	174
Private nonguaranteed	**61**	**693**	**1,224**	**3,405**	**4,483**	**6,768**	**7,309**	**7,041**	**6,238**	**7,400**
Bonds	0	0	0	0	120	225	309	641	1,238	2,400
Commercial banks and other	61	693	1,224	3,405	4,363	6,543	7,000	6,400	5,000	5,000
Memo:										
IBRD	0	31	551	1,240	955	1,408	1,145	733	762	761
IDA	0	1	11	20	20	20	20	21	24	26
NET FLOWS ON DEBT	**517**	**1,613**	**4,213**	**3,596**	**3,432**	**6,077**	**6,414**	**-583**	**-3,633**	**-5,348**
Public and publicly guaranteed	**383**	**1,611**	**422**	**2,081**	**951**	**-595**	**594**	**3,243**	**605**	**-297**
Official creditors	354	806	2,382	1,631	1,129	-792	534	2,696	3,389	1,691
Multilateral	4	393	1,117	-34	488	-1,284	-85	1,380	1,479	535
Concessional	4	44	122	18	34	57	-9	-4	-11	39
Bilateral	350	413	1,265	1,666	641	492	619	1,316	1,909	1,157
Concessional	353	409	1,368	1,224	652	630	449	1,367	2,099	771
Private creditors	28	805	-1,961	449	-178	197	60	547	-2,784	-1,988
Bonds	0	40	-94	0	605	438	50	0	-220	0
Commercial banks	0	823	-1,231	-357	-740	-558	-36	881	-2,296	-1,821
Other private	29	-58	-636	806	-43	318	46	-334	-268	-168
Private nonguaranteed	**134**	**2**	**3,791**	**1,515**	**2,481**	**6,673**	**5,821**	**-3,826**	**-4,238**	**-5,050**
Bonds	0	0	120	495	1,643	3,306	3,070	-141	-1,238	-2,050
Commercial banks and other	134	2	3,671	1,020	838	3,366	2,751	-3,685	-3,000	-3,000
Memo:										
IBRD	0	301	436	-56	90	-503	-245	479	733	290
IDA	3	40	-11	-20	-20	-20	-20	-21	-12	33

INDONESIA

(US$ million, unless otherwise indicated)

	1970	1980	1990	1994	1995	1996	1997	1998	1999	2000
INTEREST PAYMENTS (LINT)	**46**	**1,182**	**3,413**	**4,174**	**4,935**	**5,114**	**5,116**	**5,601**	**4,837**	**5,793**
Public and publicly guaranteed	**25**	**824**	**2,808**	**3,248**	**3,773**	**3,620**	**3,215**	**2,970**	**3,775**	**3,760**
Official creditors	20	312	1,585	2,482	2,666	2,406	2,095	2,051	2,461	2,596
Multilateral	0	107	990	1,395	1,403	1,238	1,020	1,039	1,229	1,376
Concessional	0	7	16	25	26	29	26	24	24	24
Bilateral	20	205	595	1,087	1,263	1,167	1,075	1,012	1,233	1,220
Concessional	18	130	451	777	875	807	745	706	828	808
Private creditors	5	512	1,223	767	1,108	1,214	1,120	920	1,313	1,164
Bonds	0	14	62	5	6	76	130	107	133	72
Commercial banks	0	268	699	372	656	687	593	443	857	847
Other private	5	230	462	389	446	451	397	370	323	246
Private nonguaranteed	**21**	**358**	**605**	**926**	**1,161**	**1,495**	**1,901**	**2,631**	**1,062**	**2,033**
Bonds	0	0	0	91	139	276	551	878	824	735
Commercial banks and other	21	358	605	835	1,022	1,218	1,350	1,753	238	1,298
Memo:										
IBRD	0	89	731	917	921	841	704	723	822	950
IDA	0	4	6	6	6	6	6	5	5	5
NET TRANSFERS ON DEBT	**471**	**431**	**800**	**-579**	**-1,503**	**963**	**1,298**	**-6,184**	**-8,470**	**-11,141**
Public and publicly guaranteed	**358**	**787**	**-2,386**	**-1,168**	**-2,823**	**-4,215**	**-2,621**	**273**	**-3,170**	**-4,058**
Official creditors	334	494	798	-850	-1,537	-3,198	-1,561	646	927	-905
Multilateral	4	286	128	-1,429	-915	-2,522	-1,105	341	251	-842
Concessional	4	37	105	-8	8	28	-35	-28	-35	15
Bilateral	330	207	670	579	-622	-675	-456	304	677	-64
Concessional	335	278	917	447	-223	-177	-296	661	1,271	-37
Private creditors	24	294	-3,184	-317	-1,286	-1,017	-1,060	-373	-4,097	-3,152
Bonds	0	26	-156	-5	599	362	-80	-107	-353	-72
Commercial banks	0	555	-1,930	-730	-1,396	-1,245	-629	438	-3,153	-2,667
Other private	24	-288	-1,098	417	-488	-134	-351	-703	-592	-414
Private nonguaranteed	**113**	**-356**	**3,186**	**589**	**1,319**	**5,178**	**3,919**	**-6,457**	**-5,300**	**-7,083**
Bonds	0	0	120	404	1,504	3,030	2,518	-1,019	-2,062	-2,785
Commercial banks and other	113	-356	3,066	185	-185	2,148	1,401	-5,439	-3,238	-4,298
Memo:										
IBRD	0	212	-294	-972	-831	-1,344	-949	-244	-89	-659
IDA	3	36	-18	-26	-26	-26	-26	-26	-18	28
DEBT SERVICE (LTDS)	**165**	**2,814**	**9,224**	**13,125**	**15,132**	**20,010**	**18,126**	**16,804**	**16,548**	**17,089**
Public and publicly guaranteed	**83**	**1,763**	**7,395**	**8,794**	**9,488**	**11,747**	**8,916**	**7,132**	**9,248**	**7,656**
Official creditors	42	636	3,171	5,765	5,791	7,159	5,519	4,593	4,841	4,212
Multilateral	0	145	1,667	3,283	2,692	4,218	2,691	2,028	2,306	2,492
Concessional	0	11	40	68	72	75	70	75	83	93
Bilateral	42	491	1,504	2,483	3,099	2,941	2,828	2,565	2,535	1,720
Concessional	37	314	1,062	1,814	2,146	2,018	1,953	1,815	1,825	1,143
Private creditors	42	1,127	4,225	3,029	3,697	4,588	3,397	2,539	4,406	3,444
Bonds	0	19	156	5	6	148	130	107	353	72
Commercial banks	1	458	2,417	1,561	2,334	3,029	1,973	1,413	3,438	2,952
Other private	41	651	1,652	1,463	1,357	1,411	1,294	1,019	616	420
Private nonguaranteed	**82**	**1,051**	**1,829**	**4,331**	**5,644**	**8,263**	**9,210**	**9,672**	**7,300**	**9,433**
Bonds	0	0	0	91	259	501	860	1,519	2,062	3,135
Commercial banks and other	82	1,051	1,829	4,240	5,385	7,762	8,350	8,153	5,238	6,298
Memo:										
IBRD	0	120	1,282	2,156	1,875	2,249	1,848	1,456	1,584	1,710
IDA	0	5	18	26	26	26	26	26	29	31
UNDISBURSED DEBT	**514**	**9,483**	**20,410**	**21,383**	**25,023**	**23,702**	**19,355**	**16,395**	**15,672**	**11,939**
Official creditors	496	7,060	14,369	16,697	19,045	18,663	15,535	15,439	15,148	11,068
Private creditors	18	2,422	6,041	4,687	5,978	5,039	3,821	956	524	871
Memorandum items										
Concessional LDOD	2,816	7,622	18,457	27,864	27,971	26,148	24,089	27,816	32,077	30,127
Variable rate LDOD	461	5,574	25,978	44,171	54,087	56,590	63,622	80,893	77,374	69,066
Public sector LDOD	3,578	15,021	47,982	63,926	65,309	60,012	55,857	67,305	73,301	69,160
Private sector LDOD	465	3,142	10,261	24,441	33,123	36,694	44,469	54,728	47,266	39,170

6. CURRENCY COMPOSITION OF LONG-TERM DEBT (PERCENT)

	1970	1980	1990	1994	1995	1996	1997	1998	1999	2000
Deutsche mark	6.0	7.8	5.0	4.8	4.9	4.8	4.7	4.3	3.2	2.8
French franc	5.5	4.0	3.4	3.3	3.7	3.7	3.3	2.8	2.0	1.8
Japanese yen	8.0	20.0	34.6	38.0	35.3	34.5	32.9	32.4	35.7	33.2
Pound sterling	2.1	0.8	1.4	0.9	0.8	1.2	1.8	1.6	1.4	1.2
Swiss franc	0.6	0.7	0.4	0.7	0.7	0.8	0.8	0.6	0.5	0.6
U.S.dollars	46.3	43.5	20.9	20.0	21.5	24.3	27.2	47.5	46.8	50.1
Multiple currency	0.0	8.6	27.3	26.7	27.2	24.7	23.3	5.4	5.4	5.3
Special drawing rights	0.0	0.0	0.0	0.0	0.0	0.0	0.1	0.1	0.1	0.2
All other currencies	31.5	14.6	7.0	5.6	5.9	6.0	5.9	5.3	4.9	4.8

INDONESIA

(US$ million, unless otherwise indicated)

	1970	1980	1990	1994	1995	1996	1997	1998	1999	2000
7. DEBT RESTRUCTURINGS										
Total amount rescheduled	..	..	0	0	0	0	0	3,891	4,860	2,309
Debt stock rescheduled	..	..	0	0	0	0	0	3,002	3,300	0
Principal rescheduled	..	..	0	0	0	0	0	491	1,477	2,262
Official	..	..	0	0	0	0	0	302	700	1,534
Private	..	..	0	0	0	0	0	189	778	727
Interest rescheduled	..	..	0	0	0	0	0	0	0	0
Official	..	..	0	0	0	0	0	0	0	0
Private	..	..	0	0	0	0	0	0	0	0
Debt forgiven	..	..	0	0	0	0	0	0	0	0
Memo: interest forgiven	..	..	0	0	0	0	0	0	0	0
Debt stock reduction	..	..	0	0	0	0	0	0	0	0
of which debt buyback	..	..	0	0	0	0	0	0	0	0
8. DEBT STOCK-FLOW RECONCILIATION										
Total change in debt stocks	..	..	10,470	18,652	16,574	4,538	7,224	15,075	-392	-9,041
Net flows on debt	551	2,280	7,216	5,066	9,941	12,341	10,078	-4,561	-3,834	-2,753
Net change in interest arrears	..	..	0	0	0	0	0	0	3,500	1,135
Interest capitalized	..	..	0	0	0	0	0	0	0	0
Debt forgiveness or reduction	..	..	0	0	0	0	0	0	0	0
Cross-currency valuation	..	..	3,078	4,237	-44	-5,526	-5,117	3,537	1,780	-4,547
Residual	..	..	176	9,350	6,678	-2,277	2,263	16,099	-1,838	-2,876
9. AVERAGE TERMS OF NEW COMMITMENTS										
ALL CREDITORS										
Interest (%)	2.6	8.1	6.0	5.2	5.7	5.4	5.6	4.5	3.7	4.2
Maturity (years)	34.1	19.8	21.1	20.0	17.7	19.2	16.2	19.0	17.2	19.1
Grace period (years)	9.0	5.6	6.0	5.6	5.1	6.1	4.8	5.6	5.3	6.8
Grant element (%)	59.8	17.7	28.6	31.3	26.8	30.3	25.2	34.6	39.3	41.0
Official creditors										
Interest (%)	2.4	5.4	5.6	4.9	5.1	4.8	6.3	4.5	3.7	2.8
Maturity (years)	35.9	25.6	23.1	23.1	21.3	23.4	19.5	19.0	17.1	25.9
Grace period (years)	9.5	7.3	6.6	6.4	5.8	6.7	4.9	5.6	5.2	7.9
Grant element (%)	62.9	36.4	32.8	35.9	33.3	37.0	22.7	34.6	39.3	56.4
Private creditors										
Interest (%)	6.0	12.0	7.6	6.0	6.8	6.6	4.9	0.0	4.0	6.7
Maturity (years)	8.1	11.4	14.0	12.2	11.0	11.5	12.4	0.0	22.4	6.9
Grace period (years)	2.0	3.3	4.1	3.4	3.9	5.0	4.6	0.0	8.2	4.6
Grant element (%)	14.1	-9.2	14.1	19.8	14.9	17.9	28.0	0.0	42.4	13.2
Memorandum items										
Commitments	520	4,277	6,687	7,712	10,954	7,796	3,425	7,375	5,374	1,903
Official creditors	487	2,524	5,190	5,495	7,108	5,057	1,816	7,375	5,275	1,224
Private creditors	33	1,753	1,498	2,217	3,846	2,738	1,608	0	99	679

10. CONTRACTUAL OBLIGATIONS ON OUTSTANDING LONG-TERM DEBT

	2001	2002	2003	2004	2005	2006	2007	2008	2009	2010
TOTAL										
Disbursements	5,117	3,494	1,706	983	537	301	166	5	2	1
Principal	16,926	13,794	11,567	9,481	9,418	7,860	8,484	7,794	4,430	4,495
Interest	5,787	5,031	4,255	3,661	3,175	2,607	2,186	1,709	1,383	1,148
Official creditors										
Disbursements	4,504	3,285	1,688	978	536	301	166	5	2	1
Principal	4,118	4,870	4,712	4,398	4,591	4,523	4,342	4,323	4,316	3,891
Interest	2,856	2,803	2,609	2,386	2,150	1,912	1,681	1,453	1,232	1,025
Bilateral creditors										
Disbursements	2,530	1,758	984	529	257	115	44	2	1	1
Principal	2,528	2,907	2,636	2,372	2,656	2,656	2,553	2,641	2,705	2,446
Interest	1,351	1,342	1,255	1,168	1,072	970	868	770	670	575
Multilateral creditors										
Disbursements	1,974	1,527	704	449	280	186	122	2	1	0
Principal	1,590	1,962	2,077	2,026	1,935	1,868	1,789	1,682	1,611	1,445
Interest	1,505	1,461	1,354	1,218	1,078	942	812	683	563	451
Private creditors										
Disbursements	612	210	18	5	0	0	0	0	0	0
Principal	12,807	8,924	6,855	5,082	4,827	3,336	4,142	3,471	114	603
Interest	2,930	2,228	1,647	1,274	1,024	694	505	257	151	122
Commercial banks										
Disbursements	570	186	11	3	0	0	0	0	0	0
Principal	3,255	1,551	1,845	2,045	1,193	74	57	24	19	16
Interest	648	467	322	146	51	16	12	9	8	7
Other private										
Disbursements	42	23	7	2	0	0	0	0	0	0
Principal	9,553	7,373	5,010	3,037	3,634	3,263	4,085	3,447	95	588
Interest	2,282	1,761	1,325	1,129	974	678	493	248	143	115

IRAN, ISLAMIC REPUBLIC OF

(US$ million, unless otherwise indicated)

	1970	1980	1990	1994	1995	1996	1997	1998	1999	2000
1. SUMMARY DEBT DATA										
TOTAL DEBT STOCKS (EDT)	..	**4,500**	**9,021**	**22,634**	**21,879**	**16,703**	**11,823**	**13,999**	**10,357**	**7,953**
Long-term debt (LDOD)	..	**4,500**	**1,797**	**15,922**	**15,430**	**11,948**	**8,469**	**9,496**	**6,739**	**4,275**
Public and publicly guaranteed	..	4,500	1,797	15,530	15,116	11,712	8,263	7,584	6,184	3,812
Private nonguaranteed	..	0	0	392	314	236	207	1,912	556	463
Use of IMF credit	**0**	**0**	**0**	**0**	**0**	**0**	**0**	**0**	**0**	**0**
Short-term debt	..	**0**	**7,224**	**6,712**	**6,449**	**4,755**	**3,354**	**4,503**	**3,618**	**3,678**
of which interest arrears on LDOD	..	0	456	5	6	1	1	1	1	0
Official creditors	..	0	6	0	2	0	0	0	0	0
Private creditors	..	0	449	5	5	1	1	1	1	0
Memo: principal arrears on LDOD	..	1	1,517	50	48	33	38	34	33	0
Official creditors	..	1	29	0	0	0	0	0	0	0
Private creditors	..	0	1,488	50	48	33	38	34	33	0
Memo: export credits	..	0	7,826	13,474	12,694	11,550	9,778	3,006	2,480	1,736
TOTAL DEBT FLOWS										
Disbursements	..	**264**	**139**	**1,874**	**979**	**945**	**907**	**3,173**	**2,184**	**506**
Long-term debt	..	264	139	1,874	979	945	907	3,173	2,184	506
IMF purchases	0	0	0	0	0	0	0	0	0	0
Principal repayments	..	**527**	**225**	**2,388**	**4,198**	**5,153**	**5,295**	**2,272**	**4,875**	**2,834**
Long-term debt	..	527	225	2,388	4,198	5,153	5,295	2,272	4,875	2,834
IMF repurchases	0	0	0	0	0	0	0	0	0	0
Net flows on debt	..	**-263**	**2,480**	**-621**	**-305**	**-4,093**	**-5,789**	**2,050**	**-3,576**	**-2,267**
of which short-term debt	..	0	2,566	-108	2,914	116	-1,401	1,149	-885	61
Interest payments (INT)	..	**431**	**430**	**905**	**1,627**	**1,380**	**980**	**806**	**673**	**604**
Long-term debt	..	431	28	273	1,132	1,113	792	603	429	383
IMF charges	0	0	0	0	0	0	0	0	0	0
Short-term debt	..	0	402	632	494	267	188	203	244	221
Net transfers on debt	..	**-694**	**2,050**	**-1,526**	**-1,931**	**-5,472**	**-6,769**	**1,244**	**-4,249**	**-2,871**
Total debt service paid (TDS)	..	**959**	**655**	**3,293**	**5,824**	**6,533**	**6,275**	**3,078**	**5,548**	**3,438**
Long-term debt	..	959	253	2,661	5,330	6,266	6,087	2,875	5,304	3,217
IMF repurchases and charges	0	0	0	0	0	0	0	0	0	0
Short-term debt (interest only)	..	0	402	632	494	267	188	203	244	221
2. AGGREGATE NET RESOURCE FLOWS AND NET TRANSFERS (LONG-TERM)										
NET RESOURCE FLOWS	..	**-262**	**-371**	**-455**	**-3,161**	**-4,140**	**-4,277**	**955**	**-2,619**	**-2,253**
Net flow of long-term debt (ex. IMF)	..	-263	-86	-513	-3,219	-4,209	-4,388	901	-2,691	-2,328
Foreign direct investment (net)	..	0	-362	2	17	26	53	24	35	39
Portfolio equity flows	..	0	0	0	0	0	0	0	0	0
Grants (excluding technical coop.)	..	1	76	56	41	42	58	30	37	36
Memo: technical coop. grants	..	19	99	92	106	103	81	94	85	64
official net resource flows	..	-84	21	-1,509	-3,063	-3,545	-4,014	-947	-2,105	-1,643
private net resource flows	..	-178	-392	1,054	-98	-596	-262	1,902	-514	-610
NET TRANSFERS	..	**-1,091**	**-477**	**-729**	**-4,293**	**-5,253**	**-5,069**	**352**	**-3,048**	**-2,636**
Interest on long-term debt	..	431	28	273	1,132	1,113	792	603	429	383
Profit remittances on FDI	..	398	78	0	0	0	0	0	0	0
Memo: official net transfers	..	-149	7	-1,534	-3,850	-4,424	-4,550	-1,270	-2,359	-1,819
private net transfers	..	-942	-485	805	-443	-829	-519	1,622	-689	-817
3. MAJOR ECONOMIC AGGREGATES										
Gross national income (GNI)	..	93,270	120,782	65,736	86,906	104,325	99,043	101,728	99,345	105,286
Exports of goods & services (XGS)	..	14,073	20,197	20,014	19,269	23,739	20,039	15,141	22,427	30,131
of which workers remittances	..	0	0	0	0	0	0	0	0	0
Imports of goods & services (MGS)	..	16,509	22,370	16,256	15,907	18,970	18,219	17,777	16,363	18,107
International reserves (RES)	..	12,783	..	..	..	..	..	..	..	..
Current account balance	..	-2,438	327	4,956	3,358	5,232	2,213	-2,139	6,589	12,645
4. DEBT INDICATORS										
EDT / XGS (%)	..	32.0	44.7	113.1	113.6	70.4	59.0	92.5	46.2	26.4
EDT / GNI (%)	..	4.8	7.5	34.4	25.2	16.0	11.9	13.8	10.4	7.6
TDS / XGS (%)	..	6.8	3.2	16.5	30.2	27.5	31.3	20.3	24.7	11.4
INT / XGS (%)	..	3.1	2.1	4.5	8.4	5.8	4.9	5.3	3.0	2.0
INT / GNI (%)	..	0.5	0.4	1.4	1.9	1.3	1.0	0.8	0.7	0.6
RES / EDT (%)	..	284.0	..	..	..	..	..	..	..	..
RES / MGS (months)	..	9.3	..	..	..	..	..	..	..	..
Short-term / EDT (%)	..	0.0	80.1	29.7	29.5	28.5	28.4	32.2	34.9	46.3
Concessional / EDT (%)	..	5.9	1.2	0.8	0.9	1.4	2.4	2.2	3.2	3.0
Multilateral / EDT (%)	..	13.8	1.3	1.4	1.7	3.2	4.5	3.7	4.9	6.5

IRAN, ISLAMIC REPUBLIC OF

(US$ million, unless otherwise indicated)

	1970	1980	1990	1994	1995	1996	1997	1998	1999	2000
5. LONG-TERM DEBT										
DEBT OUTSTANDING (LDOD)	..	**4,500**	**1,797**	**15,922**	**15,430**	**11,948**	**8,469**	**9,496**	**6,739**	**4,275**
Public and publicly guaranteed	..	**4,500**	**1,797**	**15,530**	**15,116**	**11,712**	**8,263**	**7,584**	**6,184**	**3,812**
Official creditors	..	903	225	11,423	11,354	8,879	5,910	4,982	2,867	1,140
Multilateral	..	622	116	323	381	535	533	516	503	520
Concessional	..	0	0	0	0	0	0	0	0	0
Bilateral	..	282	110	11,101	10,974	8,343	5,377	4,465	2,363	620
Concessional	..	264	110	176	192	229	279	309	332	241
Private creditors	..	3,597	1,572	4,107	3,761	2,833	2,353	2,602	3,317	2,673
Bonds	..	0	0	0	0	0	0	0	0	0
Commercial banks	..	1,055	1,055	6	5	143	243	856	1,961	1,718
Other private	..	2,542	517	4,101	3,756	2,691	2,109	1,746	1,356	955
Private nonguaranteed	..	**0**	**0**	**392**	**314**	**236**	**207**	**1,912**	**556**	**463**
Bonds	..	0	0	0	0	0	0	0	0	0
Commercial banks and other	..	0	0	392	314	236	207	1,912	556	463
Memo:										
IBRD	0	622	86	260	316	387	421	433	437	481
IDA	0	0	0	0	0	0	0	0	0	0
DISBURSEMENTS	..	**264**	**139**	**1,874**	**979**	**945**	**907**	**3,173**	**2,184**	**506**
Public and publicly guaranteed	..	**264**	**139**	**1,482**	**979**	**945**	**907**	**1,264**	**2,184**	**506**
Official creditors	..	4	30	332	393	580	326	163	315	224
Multilateral	..	4	30	101	123	235	99	39	91	130
Concessional	..	0	0	0	0	0	0	0	0	0
Bilateral	..	0	0	231	270	346	227	124	223	95
Concessional	..	0	0	141	47	64	91	54	35	0
Private creditors	..	261	109	1,151	586	364	581	1,102	1,869	282
Bonds	..	0	0	0	0	0	0	0	0	0
Commercial banks	..	0	0	0	1	150	201	660	1,278	0
Other private	..	261	109	1,151	585	214	380	441	592	282
Private nonguaranteed	..	**0**	**0**	**392**	**0**	**0**	**0**	**1,909**	**0**	**0**
Bonds	..	0	0	0	0	0	0	0	0	0
Commercial banks and other	..	0	0	392	0	0	0	1,909	0	0
Memo:										
IBRD	0	4	0	48	85	137	78	28	74	114
IDA	0	0	0	0	0	0	0	0	0	0
PRINCIPAL REPAYMENTS	..	**527**	**225**	**2,388**	**4,198**	**5,153**	**5,295**	**2,272**	**4,875**	**2,834**
Public and publicly guaranteed	..	**527**	**225**	**2,388**	**4,120**	**5,075**	**5,266**	**2,069**	**3,518**	**2,741**
Official creditors	..	89	86	1,896	3,497	4,167	4,399	1,140	2,457	1,903
Multilateral	..	70	67	19	41	41	86	89	104	113
Concessional	..	0	0	0	0	0	0	0	0	0
Bilateral	..	19	18	1,877	3,456	4,126	4,313	1,051	2,353	1,790
Concessional	..	9	18	19	20	9	26	37	47	47
Private creditors	..	439	139	491	622	908	867	929	1,061	838
Bonds	..	0	0	0	0	0	0	0	0	0
Commercial banks	..	45	0	2	1	10	93	43	96	194
Other private	..	394	139	490	621	899	774	887	965	644
Private nonguaranteed	..	**0**	**0**	**0**	**78**	**78**	**30**	**203**	**1,357**	**93**
Bonds	..	0	0	0	0	0	0	0	0	0
Commercial banks and other	..	0	0	0	78	78	30	203	1,357	93
Memo:										
IBRD	0	70	67	8	6	27	29	50	70	70
IDA	0	0	0	0	0	0	0	0	0	0
NET FLOWS ON DEBT	..	**-263**	**-86**	**-513**	**-3,219**	**-4,209**	**-4,388**	**901**	**-2,691**	**-2,328**
Public and publicly guaranteed	..	**-263**	**-86**	**-905**	**-3,141**	**-4,131**	**-4,359**	**-805**	**-1,334**	**-2,235**
Official creditors	..	-85	-56	-1,565	-3,104	-3,587	-4,073	-977	-2,142	-1,679
Multilateral	..	-66	-37	82	82	193	13	-51	-13	17
Concessional	..	0	0	0	0	0	0	0	0	0
Bilateral	..	-19	-18	-1,647	-3,186	-3,780	-4,086	-927	-2,129	-1,696
Concessional	..	-9	-18	122	27	56	65	17	-13	-47
Private creditors	..	-178	-30	660	-37	-544	-286	172	808	-556
Bonds	..	0	0	0	0	0	0	0	0	0
Commercial banks	..	-45	0	-2	-1	141	108	618	1,181	-194
Other private	..	-133	-30	661	-36	-685	-394	-446	-373	-362
Private nonguaranteed	..	**0**	**0**	**392**	**-78**	**-78**	**-30**	**1,706**	**-1,357**	**-93**
Bonds	..	0	0	0	0	0	0	0	0	0
Commercial banks and other	..	0	0	392	-78	-78	-30	1,706	-1,357	-93
Memo:										
IBRD	0	-66	-67	40	79	110	49	-22	4	44
IDA	0	0	0	0	0	0	0	0	0	0

IRAN, ISLAMIC REPUBLIC OF

(US$ million, unless otherwise indicated)

	1970	1980	1990	1994	1995	1996	1997	1998	1999	2000
INTEREST PAYMENTS (LINT)	..	**431**	**28**	**273**	**1,132**	**1,113**	**792**	**603**	**429**	**383**
Public and publicly guaranteed	..	**431**	**28**	**273**	**1,107**	**1,093**	**777**	**492**	**398**	**357**
Official creditors	..	65	14	25	787	880	535	323	254	176
Multilateral	..	49	10	19	27	33	38	31	41	45
Concessional	..	0	0	0	0	0	0	0	0	0
Bilateral	..	16	4	6	759	846	497	292	214	131
Concessional	..	14	4	3	9	15	13	11	12	11
Private creditors	..	366	14	249	321	213	242	169	144	181
Bonds	..	0	0	0	0	0	0	0	0	0
Commercial banks	..	153	0	0	0	8	14	32	39	93
Other private	..	213	14	248	320	205	228	137	105	88
Private nonguaranteed	..	**0**	**0**	**0**	**25**	**20**	**15**	**111**	**31**	**26**
Bonds	..	0	0	0	0	0	0	0	0	0
Commercial banks and other	..	0	0	0	25	20	15	111	31	26
Memo:										
IBRD	0	49	10	16	19	23	26	19	33	40
IDA	0	0	0	0	0	0	0	0	0	0
NET TRANSFERS ON DEBT	..	**-694**	**-114**	**-787**	**-4,351**	**-5,321**	**-5,180**	**298**	**-3,120**	**-2,711**
Public and publicly guaranteed	..	**-694**	**-114**	**-1,179**	**-4,248**	**-5,223**	**-5,135**	**-1,297**	**-1,732**	**-2,593**
Official creditors	..	-150	-69	-1,590	-3,891	-4,467	-4,608	-1,300	-2,396	-1,855
Multilateral	..	-116	-47	63	55	160	-25	-81	-54	-29
Concessional	..	0	0	0	0	0	0	0	0	0
Bilateral	..	-35	-22	-1,653	-3,945	-4,626	-4,583	-1,219	-2,343	-1,827
Concessional	..	-24	-22	118	18	40	52	6	-25	-57
Private creditors	..	-544	-45	411	-357	-757	-528	3	664	-737
Bonds	..	0	0	0	0	0	0	0	0	0
Commercial banks	..	-198	0	-2	-1	133	94	586	1,142	-287
Other private	..	-346	-45	413	-357	-890	-622	-582	-478	-451
Private nonguaranteed	..	**0**	**0**	**392**	**-103**	**-98**	**-45**	**1,595**	**-1,388**	**-118**
Bonds	..	0	0	0	0	0	0	0	0	0
Commercial banks and other	..	0	0	392	-103	-98	-45	1,595	-1,388	-118
Memo:										
IBRD	0	-116	-77	24	61	87	23	-41	-29	5
IDA	0	0	0	0	0	0	0	0	0	0
DEBT SERVICE (LTDS)	..	**959**	**253**	**2,661**	**5,330**	**6,266**	**6,087**	**2,875**	**5,304**	**3,217**
Public and publicly guaranteed	..	**959**	**253**	**2,661**	**5,227**	**6,168**	**6,043**	**2,561**	**3,916**	**3,099**
Official creditors	..	154	99	1,921	4,284	5,047	4,934	1,463	2,711	2,080
Multilateral	..	119	77	38	68	75	124	120	145	159
Concessional	..	0	0	0	0	0	0	0	0	0
Bilateral	..	35	22	1,884	4,216	4,972	4,810	1,343	2,566	1,921
Concessional	..	24	22	23	29	24	39	48	59	58
Private creditors	..	805	154	740	943	1,121	1,109	1,098	1,205	1,019
Bonds	..	0	0	0	0	0	0	0	0	0
Commercial banks	..	198	0	2	1	17	107	75	135	287
Other private	..	607	154	738	942	1,104	1,002	1,023	1,070	732
Private nonguaranteed	..	**0**	**0**	**0**	**103**	**98**	**45**	**314**	**1,388**	**118**
Bonds	..	0	0	0	0	0	0	0	0	0
Commercial banks and other	..	0	0	0	103	98	45	314	1,388	118
Memo:										
IBRD	0	119	77	24	24	50	55	69	103	109
IDA	0	0	0	0	0	0	0	0	0	0
UNDISBURSED DEBT	..	**1,173**	**1,512**	**3,198**	**3,992**	**4,434**	**3,630**	**2,293**	**2,058**	**945**
Official creditors	..	63	250	1,592	1,583	1,082	761	536	284	476
Private creditors	..	1,109	1,262	1,606	2,409	3,353	2,869	1,757	1,775	468
Memorandum items										
Concessional LDOD	..	264	110	176	192	229	279	309	332	241
Variable rate LDOD	..	1,706	1,273	15,240	14,806	11,350	7,929	8,868	5,951	3,544
Public sector LDOD	..	4,500	1,797	15,505	15,031	11,604	8,150	7,583	6,174	3,796
Private sector LDOD	..	0	0	417	398	345	319	1,913	565	479

6. CURRENCY COMPOSITION OF LONG-TERM DEBT (PERCENT)

	1970	1980	1990	1994	1995	1996	1997	1998	1999	2000
Deutsche mark	..	15.5	0.0	17.9	16.0	13.7	13.4	9.3	5.6	3.7
French franc	..	8.8	0.7	2.2	2.5	2.4	2.4	2.0	1.2	0.4
Japanese yen	..	9.0	4.2	4.4	4.9	5.7	7.2	7.9	8.3	7.7
Pound sterling	..	0.9	0.0	0.0	0.0	0.0	0.0	0.0	0.3	0.6
Swiss franc	..	0.0	0.0	0.8	0.6	0.5	0.7	0.9	4.9	7.3
U.S.dollars	..	43.4	88.6	70.5	71.5	71.6	67.5	75.9	70.9	68.7
Multiple currency	..	13.8	6.4	1.7	2.1	3.3	5.1	0.0	0.0	0.0
Special drawing rights	..	0.0	0.0	0.0	0.0	0.0	0.0	0.0	0.0	0.0
All other currencies	..	8.6	0.1	2.5	2.4	2.8	3.7	4.0	8.8	11.6

IRAN, ISLAMIC REPUBLIC OF

(US$ million, unless otherwise indicated)

	1970	1980	1990	1994	1995	1996	1997	1998	1999	2000
7. DEBT RESTRUCTURINGS										
Total amount rescheduled	..	..	0	10,785	3,178	1,805	0	0	0	0
Debt stock rescheduled	..	..	0	10,785	3,178	1,805	0	0	0	0
Principal rescheduled	..	..	0	0	0	0	0	0	0	0
Official	..	..	0	0	0	0	0	0	0	0
Private	..	..	0	0	0	0	0	0	0	0
Interest rescheduled	..	..	0	0	0	0	0	0	0	0
Official	..	..	0	0	0	0	0	0	0	0
Private	..	..	0	0	0	0	0	0	0	0
Debt forgiven	..	..	0	0	0	0	0	0	0	0
Memo: interest forgiven	..	..	0	0	0	0	0	0	0	0
Debt stock reduction	..	..	0	0	0	0	0	0	0	0
of which debt buyback	..	..	0	0	0	0	0	0	0	0
8. DEBT STOCK-FLOW RECONCILIATION										
Total change in debt stocks	..	..	2,502	-869	-755	-5,176	-4,880	2,176	-3,642	-2,404
Net flows on debt	..	-263	2,480	-621	-305	-4,093	-5,789	2,050	-3,576	-2,267
Net change in interest arrears	..	..	1	1	1	-6	0	0	0	-1
Interest capitalized	..	..	0	0	0	0	0	0	0	0
Debt forgiveness or reduction	..	..	0	0	0	0	0	0	0	0
Cross-currency valuation	..	..	-6	586	-340	-526	-250	82	-37	-159
Residual	..	..	27	-835	-112	-552	1,159	44	-29	23
9. AVERAGE TERMS OF NEW COMMITMENTS										
ALL CREDITORS										
Interest (%)	..	0.0	8.3	6.3	6.6	5.9	6.6	4.9	6.3	7.7
Maturity (years)	..	0.0	9.3	6.1	8.4	9.6	9.1	9.5	10.4	16.8
Grace period (years)	..	0.0	4.0	1.9	3.1	2.8	2.1	2.5	2.6	5.6
Grant element (%)	..	0.0	6.9	11.0	13.6	17.1	13.0	21.4	16.0	13.2
Official creditors										
Interest (%)	..	0.0	7.3	6.4	7.5	8.0	0.0	5.6	7.6	7.9
Maturity (years)	..	0.0	13.5	3.9	7.2	8.2	0.0	6.0	10.2	17.0
Grace period (years)	..	0.0	5.0	3.6	2.2	3.3	0.0	1.5	2.8	5.5
Grant element (%)	..	0.0	14.4	10.7	8.1	6.4	0.0	12.7	9.7	12.1
Private creditors										
Interest (%)	..	0.0	8.6	6.3	6.3	5.7	6.6	4.8	6.2	5.9
Maturity (years)	..	0.0	8.1	6.3	8.8	9.8	9.1	10.5	10.4	14.8
Grace period (years)	..	0.0	3.7	1.8	3.3	2.7	2.1	2.7	2.5	6.8
Grant element (%)	..	0.0	4.7	11.1	15.2	18.1	13.0	23.9	16.6	25.3
Memorandum items										
Commitments	..	0	1,241	335	1,941	1,464	276	9	2,182	254
Official creditors	..	0	280	26	442	122	0	2	188	232
Private creditors	..	0	961	309	1,499	1,343	276	7	1,994	22

10. CONTRACTUAL OBLIGATIONS ON OUTSTANDING LONG-TERM DEBT

	2001	2002	2003	2004	2005	2006	2007	2008	2009	2010
TOTAL										
Disbursements	508	187	80	47	39	28	21	14	10	8
Principal	924	868	748	660	513	357	314	245	195	139
Interest	236	222	189	147	110	84	62	44	29	17
Official creditors										
Disbursements	159	83	66	46	39	28	21	14	10	8
Principal	279	229	138	123	126	111	106	104	97	68
Interest	73	67	61	54	47	40	33	26	20	13
Bilateral creditors										
Disbursements	88	41	19	5	2	0	0	0	0	0
Principal	189	146	61	48	42	40	39	37	35	30
Interest	23	21	20	17	15	13	10	8	6	5
Multilateral creditors										
Disbursements	71	42	46	41	38	28	21	14	10	8
Principal	90	83	77	76	85	71	67	67	62	38
Interest	50	46	42	37	33	27	23	18	13	9
Private creditors										
Disbursements	349	104	14	1	0	0	0	0	0	0
Principal	645	639	610	537	387	246	208	140	98	71
Interest	163	155	128	93	62	44	29	17	9	4
Commercial banks										
Disbursements	211	53	6	1	0	0	0	0	0	0
Principal	267	297	329	323	188	162	144	110	83	64
Interest	87	95	86	65	47	35	24	15	8	3
Other private										
Disbursements	138	51	8	0	0	0	0	0	0	0
Principal	378	342	281	215	199	85	64	31	15	7
Interest	76	61	42	28	16	10	5	2	1	0

JAMAICA

(US$ million, unless otherwise indicated)

	1970	1980	1990	1994	1995	1996	1997	1998	1999	2000
1. SUMMARY DEBT DATA										
TOTAL DEBT STOCKS (EDT)	**982**	**1,913**	**4,674**	**4,317**	**4,270**	**3,994**	**3,920**	**4,024**	**3,921**	**4,287**
Long-term debt (LDOD)	**982**	**1,505**	**3,970**	**3,516**	**3,537**	**3,257**	**3,117**	**3,288**	**3,076**	**3,475**
Public and publicly guaranteed	160	1,430	3,937	3,438	3,409	3,134	2,929	3,109	2,910	3,373
Private nonguaranteed	822	75	34	78	128	123	188	179	166	103
Use of IMF credit	**0**	**309**	**357**	**318**	**240**	**161**	**118**	**105**	**83**	**60**
Short-term debt	**0**	**98**	**347**	**483**	**492**	**575**	**685**	**631**	**762**	**751**
of which interest arrears on LDOD	0	0	125	107	102	98	73	74	97	108
Official creditors	0	0	87	92	87	84	67	67	90	106
Private creditors	0	0	37	15	15	14	7	7	7	2
Memo: principal arrears on LDOD	0	27	157	199	203	200	158	163	160	105
Official creditors	0	8	84	163	166	165	133	137	135	103
Private creditors	0	19	73	36	37	36	25	26	24	2
Memo: export credits	0	0	651	521	523	612	506	214	215	224
TOTAL DEBT FLOWS										
Disbursements	**184**	**363**	**340**	**210**	**301**	**210**	**391**	**393**	**150**	**850**
Long-term debt	180	363	284	161	291	210	391	393	150	850
IMF purchases	4	0	56	49	11	0	0	0	0	0
Principal repayments	**170**	**121**	**401**	**374**	**436**	**444**	**436**	**315**	**371**	**398**
Long-term debt	170	102	290	287	340	373	401	298	352	379
IMF repurchases	0	19	112	87	96	72	35	17	19	19
Net flows on debt	**13**	**234**	**-106**	**58**	**-121**	**-148**	**90**	**23**	**-114**	**431**
of which short-term debt	0	-8	-45	222	14	87	136	-55	108	-21
Interest payments (INT)	**64**	**159**	**261**	**215**	**236**	**227**	**208**	**209**	**225**	**246**
Long-term debt	64	121	203	184	196	193	169	170	186	198
IMF charges	0	23	34	17	17	9	7	5	4	4
Short-term debt	0	15	24	14	24	26	33	34	35	44
Net transfers on debt	**-50**	**75**	**-367**	**-158**	**-357**	**-375**	**-118**	**-187**	**-339**	**185**
Total debt service paid (TDS)	**234**	**280**	**662**	**590**	**672**	**672**	**644**	**524**	**596**	**643**
Long-term debt	234	223	492	471	537	565	570	468	538	577
IMF repurchases and charges	0	42	145	105	112	81	41	22	23	23
Short-term debt (interest only)	0	15	24	14	24	26	33	34	35	44
2. AGGREGATE NET RESOURCE FLOWS AND NET TRANSFERS (LONG-TERM)										
NET RESOURCE FLOWS	**174**	**301**	**249**	**94**	**161**	**60**	**233**	**556**	**346**	**972**
Net flow of long-term debt (ex. IMF)	10	261	-6	-126	-50	-163	-11	95	-202	471
Foreign direct investment (net)	162	28	138	130	147	184	203	369	524	456
Portfolio equity flows	0	0	0	0	0	0	0	0	0	0
Grants (excluding technical coop.)	3	13	117	91	64	39	41	93	25	45
Memo: technical coop. grants	5	17	33	37	51	38	37	32	34	32
official net resource flows	14	293	157	-42	-14	-135	-208	-34	-79	74
private net resource flows	160	9	92	136	175	195	442	591	425	898
NET TRANSFERS	**6**	**66**	**-142**	**-114**	**-66**	**-163**	**30**	**346**	**112**	**721**
Interest on long-term debt	64	121	203	184	196	193	169	170	186	198
Profit remittances on FDI	105	114	189	24	31	30	35	40	48	53
Memo: official net transfers	12	247	-7	-189	-177	-298	-346	-156	-193	-44
private net transfers	-6	-181	-135	75	111	135	375	503	305	765
3. MAJOR ECONOMIC AGGREGATES										
Gross national income (GNI)	1,400	2,425	3,732	4,403	4,539	4,465	6,891	6,970	6,840	6,993
Exports of goods & services (XGS)	..	1,472	2,461	3,591	4,123	4,100	4,189	4,201	4,330	4,563
of which workers remittances	..	51	136	458	582	636	642	661	686	789
Imports of goods & services (MGS)	..	1,678	2,928	3,511	4,246	4,231	4,503	4,502	4,507	4,869
International reserves (RES)	139	105	168	736	681	880	682	709	555	1,054
Current account balance	..	-136	-312	82	-99	-143	-332	-328	-211	-275
4. DEBT INDICATORS										
EDT / XGS (%)	..	129.9	189.9	120.2	103.6	97.4	93.6	95.8	90.6	93.9
EDT / GNI (%)	70.2	78.9	125.2	98.0	94.1	89.4	56.9	57.7	57.3	61.3
TDS / XGS (%)	..	19.0	26.9	16.4	16.3	16.4	15.4	12.5	13.8	14.1
INT / XGS (%)	..	10.8	10.6	6.0	5.7	5.6	5.0	5.0	5.2	5.4
INT / GNI (%)	4.5	6.6	7.0	4.9	5.2	5.1	3.0	3.0	3.3	3.5
RES / EDT (%)	14.2	5.5	3.6	17.1	16.0	22.0	17.4	17.6	14.1	24.6
RES / MGS (months)	..	0.8	0.7	2.5	1.9	2.5	1.8	1.9	1.5	2.6
Short-term / EDT (%)	0.0	5.1	7.4	11.2	11.5	14.4	17.5	15.7	19.4	17.5
Concessional / EDT (%)	2.0	20.3	29.9	29.8	31.5	31.2	27.7	26.5	25.5	20.9
Multilateral / EDT (%)	3.0	14.9	25.0	27.4	28.3	27.6	25.1	24.8	25.9	26.2

JAMAICA

(US$ million, unless otherwise indicated)

	1970	1980	1990	1994	1995	1996	1997	1998	1999	2000
5. LONG-TERM DEBT										
DEBT OUTSTANDING (LDOD)	**982**	**1,505**	**3,970**	**3,516**	**3,537**	**3,257**	**3,117**	**3,288**	**3,076**	**3,475**
Public and publicly guaranteed	**160**	**1,430**	**3,937**	**3,438**	**3,409**	**3,134**	**2,929**	**3,109**	**2,910**	**3,373**
Official creditors	59	920	3,409	3,092	3,086	2,795	2,418	2,368	2,255	2,212
Multilateral	30	284	1,168	1,181	1,209	1,100	984	996	1,014	1,122
Concessional	0	79	175	142	143	142	125	122	120	117
Bilateral	29	636	2,241	1,911	1,876	1,695	1,434	1,371	1,241	1,090
Concessional	19	310	1,223	1,144	1,200	1,104	960	945	879	780
Private creditors	101	510	528	346	324	339	511	742	655	1,161
Bonds	83	19	0	13	25	78	278	528	463	1,004
Commercial banks	17	384	298	265	234	206	194	180	161	149
Other private	0	108	230	68	65	56	40	34	31	7
Private nonguaranteed	**822**	**75**	**34**	**78**	**128**	**123**	**188**	**179**	**166**	**103**
Bonds	0	0	0	55	55	55	55	55	55	0
Commercial banks and other	822	75	34	23	73	68	133	124	111	103
Memo:										
IBRD	30	176	672	595	595	515	431	410	393	415
IDA	0	0	0	0	0	0	0	0	0	0
DISBURSEMENTS	**180**	**363**	**284**	**161**	**291**	**210**	**391**	**393**	**150**	**850**
Public and publicly guaranteed	**15**	**338**	**284**	**106**	**236**	**210**	**321**	**393**	**150**	**850**
Official creditors	14	317	246	83	178	121	108	129	137	276
Multilateral	7	93	102	67	115	89	87	84	133	247
Concessional	0	33	9	1	10	9	9	5	2	15
Bilateral	7	224	144	16	64	32	21	45	4	29
Concessional	2	84	103	10	31	16	9	13	3	8
Private creditors	1	21	39	23	57	89	212	264	13	573
Bonds	0	0	0	13	13	53	200	250	0	553
Commercial banks	1	4	0	10	42	36	12	14	13	21
Other private	0	17	39	0	3	0	0	0	0	0
Private nonguaranteed	**165**	**25**	**0**	**55**	**55**	**0**	**70**	**0**	**0**	**0**
Bonds	0	0	0	55	0	0	0	0	0	0
Commercial banks and other	165	25	0	0	55	0	70	0	0	0
Memo:										
IBRD	7	55	35	22	61	41	26	31	64	98
IDA	0	0	0	0	0	0	0	0	0	0
PRINCIPAL REPAYMENTS	**170**	**102**	**290**	**287**	**340**	**373**	**401**	**298**	**352**	**379**
Public and publicly guaranteed	**6**	**92**	**282**	**282**	**335**	**368**	**396**	**289**	**339**	**315**
Official creditors	2	37	205	216	256	295	357	256	241	248
Multilateral	1	11	100	121	127	124	137	112	113	115
Concessional	0	0	8	11	10	9	23	10	10	10
Bilateral	1	26	105	95	129	171	220	144	128	133
Concessional	1	2	19	24	29	67	97	65	68	65
Private creditors	4	55	76	66	80	73	39	34	98	67
Bonds	2	9	0	0	0	0	0	0	65	13
Commercial banks	2	16	1	10	73	65	24	27	31	32
Other private	0	31	75	56	6	8	15	6	2	23
Private nonguaranteed	**164**	**10**	**8**	**5**	**5**	**5**	**5**	**9**	**13**	**64**
Bonds	0	0	0	0	0	0	0	0	0	55
Commercial banks and other	164	10	8	5	5	5	5	9	13	9
Memo:										
IBRD	1	6	62	76	85	80	72	72	75	61
IDA	0	0	0	0	0	0	0	0	0	0
NET FLOWS ON DEBT	**10**	**261**	**-6**	**-126**	**-50**	**-163**	**-11**	**95**	**-202**	**471**
Public and publicly guaranteed	**9**	**246**	**3**	**-176**	**-100**	**-158**	**-76**	**104**	**-189**	**535**
Official creditors	12	280	41	-133	-78	-174	-249	-127	-104	29
Multilateral	6	82	2	-54	-12	-35	-50	-28	21	132
Concessional	0	33	1	-10	0	0	-14	-4	-8	5
Bilateral	6	198	39	-79	-65	-139	-199	-99	-124	-103
Concessional	1	82	84	-14	2	-51	-88	-52	-65	-57
Private creditors	-3	-34	-38	-43	-22	16	173	230	-86	506
Bonds	-2	-9	0	13	13	53	200	250	-65	540
Commercial banks	-1	-12	-1	0	-31	-28	-12	-13	-19	-11
Other private	0	-13	-37	-56	-4	-8	-15	-6	-2	-23
Private nonguaranteed	**1**	**15**	**-8**	**50**	**50**	**-5**	**65**	**-9**	**-13**	**-64**
Bonds	0	0	0	55	0	0	0	0	0	-55
Commercial banks and other	1	15	-8	-5	50	-5	65	-9	-13	-9
Memo:										
IBRD	6	50	-26	-54	-24	-39	-46	-41	-11	37
IDA	0	0	0	0	0	0	0	0	0	0

JAMAICA

(US$ million, unless otherwise indicated)

	1970	1980	1990	1994	1995	1996	1997	1998	1999	2000
INTEREST PAYMENTS (LINT)	**64**	**121**	**203**	**184**	**196**	**193**	**169**	**170**	**186**	**198**
Public and publicly guaranteed	**9**	**115**	**200**	**182**	**185**	**182**	**156**	**157**	**174**	**185**
Official creditors	2	45	165	147	162	163	138	122	113	117
Multilateral	1	17	86	84	83	75	69	61	58	61
Concessional	0	2	5	4	3	3	5	3	3	3
Bilateral	1	29	79	63	79	88	68	62	56	57
Concessional	1	10	16	24	37	42	35	35	33	27
Private creditors	7	69	35	35	23	19	18	35	60	67
Bonds	6	2	0	0	2	2	3	22	49	50
Commercial banks	1	55	20	13	19	15	14	12	11	12
Other private	0	13	15	22	2	2	2	1	1	6
Private nonguaranteed	**54**	**7**	**3**	**3**	**11**	**11**	**13**	**12**	**12**	**13**
Bonds	0	0	0	1	5	5	5	5	5	2
Commercial banks and other	54	7	3	2	6	6	8	8	8	11
Memo:										
IBRD	1	13	58	49	47	41	34	28	24	22
IDA	0	0	0	0	0	0	0	0	0	0
NET TRANSFERS ON DEBT	**-54**	**140**	**-208**	**-311**	**-246**	**-355**	**-179**	**-75**	**-388**	**273**
Public and publicly guaranteed	**-1**	**132**	**-197**	**-358**	**-285**	**-340**	**-231**	**-54**	**-363**	**350**
Official creditors	9	235	-124	-280	-240	-337	-386	-249	-217	-89
Multilateral	5	66	-84	-138	-95	-110	-119	-89	-37	71
Concessional	0	31	-4	-14	-4	-3	-20	-7	-11	2
Bilateral	4	169	-40	-141	-145	-227	-267	-161	-180	-160
Concessional	0	72	68	-38	-34	-94	-122	-87	-98	-84
Private creditors	-10	-103	-73	-78	-45	-3	155	195	-146	439
Bonds	-7	-10	0	13	11	51	197	228	-114	490
Commercial banks	-3	-66	-22	-14	-50	-44	-26	-25	-30	-23
Other private	0	-26	-51	-77	-6	-10	-16	-8	-2	-29
Private nonguaranteed	**-53**	**8**	**-11**	**47**	**39**	**-16**	**52**	**-21**	**-25**	**-77**
Bonds	0	0	0	54	-5	-5	-5	-5	-5	-57
Commercial banks and other	-53	8	-11	-7	44	-11	57	-17	-21	-20
Memo:										
IBRD	5	37	-85	-102	-71	-80	-80	-68	-35	15
IDA	0	0	0	0	0	0	0	0	0	0
DEBT SERVICE (LTDS)	**234**	**223**	**492**	**471**	**537**	**565**	**570**	**468**	**538**	**577**
Public and publicly guaranteed	**15**	**206**	**482**	**464**	**521**	**550**	**552**	**447**	**513**	**500**
Official creditors	4	82	370	363	418	458	495	378	355	365
Multilateral	2	27	186	205	210	199	206	172	171	176
Concessional	0	2	14	15	13	12	29	13	13	13
Bilateral	2	55	184	158	208	259	289	206	184	189
Concessional	2	12	35	47	66	110	131	100	101	92
Private creditors	11	124	112	101	103	92	57	69	158	135
Bonds	7	10	0	0	2	2	3	22	114	63
Commercial banks	4	70	22	24	92	80	38	39	43	43
Other private	0	44	90	77	9	10	16	8	2	29
Private nonguaranteed	**218**	**17**	**11**	**8**	**16**	**16**	**18**	**21**	**25**	**77**
Bonds	0	0	0	1	5	5	5	5	5	57
Commercial banks and other	218	17	11	7	11	11	13	17	21	20
Memo:										
IBRD	2	18	120	124	132	121	106	99	99	83
IDA	0	0	0	0	0	0	0	0	0	0
UNDISBURSED DEBT	**38**	**325**	**555**	**582**	**504**	**526**	**526**	**426**	**353**	**531**
Official creditors	38	314	547	569	480	514	515	426	353	457
Private creditors	0	11	9	13	24	12	10	0	0	74
Memorandum items										
Concessional LDOD	19	389	1,398	1,286	1,343	1,245	1,085	1,067	999	897
Variable rate LDOD	822	344	1,024	1,016	1,003	962	946	906	855	855
Public sector LDOD	158	1,384	3,937	3,438	3,409	3,134	2,929	3,109	2,910	3,373
Private sector LDOD	824	122	34	78	128	123	188	179	166	103

6. CURRENCY COMPOSITION OF LONG-TERM DEBT (PERCENT)

	1970	1980	1990	1994	1995	1996	1997	1998	1999	2000
Deutsche mark	0.0	0.7	2.0	3.0	3.4	3.1	2.7	2.6	2.2	1.7
French franc	0.0	1.1	0.7	1.0	1.0	0.8	0.5	0.4	0.3	0.2
Japanese yen	0.0	0.6	4.9	8.6	8.8	8.5	7.5	7.5	8.4	5.9
Pound sterling	47.6	8.5	5.6	4.4	4.3	4.5	3.5	2.9	2.5	2.2
Swiss franc	0.0	0.3	0.0	0.0	0.0	0.0	0.0	0.0	0.0	0.0
U.S.dollars	27.7	58.5	49.3	47.1	46.5	48.6	54.7	57.8	57.8	62.6
Multiple currency	18.7	17.1	27.8	28.7	28.6	27.3	25.0	22.6	23.4	17.8
Special drawing rights	0.0	0.0	0.0	0.0	0.0	0.1	0.0	0.1	0.1	0.1
All other currencies	6.0	13.2	9.7	7.2	7.4	7.1	6.1	6.1	5.3	9.5

JAMAICA

(US$ million, unless otherwise indicated)

	1970	1980	1990	1994	1995	1996	1997	1998	1999	2000
7. DEBT RESTRUCTURINGS										
Total amount rescheduled	..	..	469	106	105	0	0	0	0	0
Debt stock rescheduled	..	..	314	0	0	0	0	0	0	0
Principal rescheduled	..	..	99	76	88	0	0	0	0	0
Official	..	..	96	74	87	0	0	0	0	0
Private	..	..	3	1	1	0	0	0	0	0
Interest rescheduled	..	..	55	30	17	0	0	0	0	0
Official	..	..	54	30	16	0	0	0	0	0
Private	..	..	1	0	0	0	0	0	0	0
Debt forgiven	..	..	0	6	0	0	0	0	8	4
Memo: interest forgiven	..	..	1	3	0	0	0	0	0	0
Debt stock reduction	..	..	24	16	0	0	0	0	0	0
of which debt buyback	..	..	0	0	0	0	0	0	0	0
8. DEBT STOCK-FLOW RECONCILIATION										
Total change in debt stocks	..	..	110	211	-47	-276	-74	105	-103	365
Net flows on debt	13	234	-106	58	-121	-148	90	23	-114	431
Net change in interest arrears	..	..	0	-29	-5	-4	-25	1	23	10
Interest capitalized	..	..	55	30	17	0	0	0	0	0
Debt forgiveness or reduction	..	..	-25	-21	0	0	0	0	-8	-4
Cross-currency valuation	..	..	156	120	32	-148	-160	76	-20	-71
Residual	..	..	30	54	30	24	21	5	15	-1
9. AVERAGE TERMS OF NEW COMMITMENTS										
ALL CREDITORS										
Interest (%)	6.0	7.2	8.0	5.2	6.5	4.6	8.6	8.4	6.0	9.3
Maturity (years)	16.0	13.8	16.7	14.4	13.4	15.7	11.1	8.0	17.1	11.0
Grace period (years)	3.2	4.6	3.8	5.3	3.0	4.6	4.9	6.4	3.9	4.7
Grant element (%)	21.7	21.6	10.9	28.0	16.4	28.6	8.3	7.2	19.0	5.9
Official creditors										
Interest (%)	6.0	6.5	7.9	4.9	6.2	5.2	7.0	6.1	5.6	6.1
Maturity (years)	16.0	14.7	18.8	17.9	19.8	20.2	21.0	15.4	20.0	19.7
Grace period (years)	3.2	5.0	4.2	5.4	4.1	5.5	5.0	2.7	4.4	5.4
Grant element (%)	21.7	24.1	12.3	32.0	22.9	32.9	19.2	16.1	22.0	24.9
Private creditors										
Interest (%)	0.0	13.0	8.7	5.8	6.8	3.2	9.5	8.7	8.3	11.2
Maturity (years)	0.0	5.7	1.9	6.0	3.3	4.9	5.3	6.9	2.7	5.8
Grace period (years)	0.0	1.3	0.4	5.0	1.3	2.3	4.8	6.9	1.1	4.3
Grant element (%)	0.0	0.2	0.5	18.2	6.4	18.5	1.9	6.0	4.3	-5.6
Memorandum items										
Commitments	24	245	318	85	175	261	336	288	75	1,036
Official creditors	24	219	279	60	107	184	125	34	62	389
Private creditors	0	26	39	25	69	78	211	254	13	647

10. CONTRACTUAL OBLIGATIONS ON OUTSTANDING LONG-TERM DEBT

	2001	2002	2003	2004	2005	2006	2007	2008	2009	2010
TOTAL										
Disbursements	189	139	92	58	31	14	6	1	0	0
Principal	293	458	410	240	482	235	448	211	194	170
Interest	252	242	212	183	158	132	118	75	62	50
Official creditors										
Disbursements	149	118	83	55	31	14	6	1	0	0
Principal	216	181	174	182	187	203	190	182	165	152
Interest	126	121	115	108	99	88	77	66	55	46
Bilateral creditors										
Disbursements	32	26	15	9	6	3	2	0	0	0
Principal	84	82	72	83	96	94	84	81	70	66
Interest	48	45	42	38	34	29	25	21	17	14
Multilateral creditors										
Disbursements	118	93	68	45	25	11	5	1	0	0
Principal	132	99	102	100	90	109	106	101	95	85
Interest	78	76	73	70	65	59	52	45	39	32
Private creditors										
Disbursements	40	21	9	4	1	0	0	0	0	0
Principal	78	277	236	58	295	33	258	29	29	19
Interest	126	121	97	75	59	44	41	9	6	4
Commercial banks										
Disbursements	23	15	6	3	0	0	0	0	0	0
Principal	68	37	37	31	14	1	1	0	0	0
Interest	10	7	5	3	1	0	0	0	0	0
Other private										
Disbursements	17	6	3	1	1	0	0	0	0	0
Principal	10	240	199	27	282	32	257	29	29	19
Interest	117	114	92	72	58	44	41	9	6	4

JORDAN

(US$ million, unless otherwise indicated)

	1970	1980	1990	1994	1995	1996	1997	1998	1999	2000
1. SUMMARY DEBT DATA										
TOTAL DEBT STOCKS (EDT)	**119**	**1,971**	**8,177**	**7,709**	**8,064**	**8,034**	**8,112**	**8,417**	**8,910**	**8,226**
Long-term debt (LDOD)	**119**	**1,486**	**7,043**	**6,883**	**7,023**	**7,091**	**6,936**	**7,354**	**7,537**	**7,055**
Public and publicly guaranteed	119	1,486	7,043	6,883	7,023	7,091	6,936	7,354	7,537	7,055
Private nonguaranteed	0	0	0	0	0	0	0	0	0	0
Use of IMF credit	**0**	**0**	**94**	**144**	**252**	**340**	**427**	**469**	**498**	**462**
Short-term debt	**0**	**485**	**1,040**	**681**	**790**	**603**	**748**	**594**	**875**	**710**
of which interest arrears on LDOD	0	5	110	60	72	87	87	81	96	106
Official creditors	0	5	34	56	68	86	87	81	92	103
Private creditors	0	0	77	4	4	1	1	0	4	4
Memo: principal arrears on LDOD	0	22	549	187	223	298	304	287	315	327
Official creditors	0	22	54	186	222	252	277	281	306	320
Private creditors	0	0	495	1	2	46	27	7	9	7
Memo: export credits	0	0	2,366	2,040	1,334	1,388	2,811	210	1,033	1,057
TOTAL DEBT FLOWS										
Disbursements	**15**	**369**	**691**	**307**	**748**	**923**	**841**	**469**	**466**	**209**
Long-term debt	15	369	691	213	633	804	708	437	390	189
IMF purchases	0	0	0	94	115	119	133	32	76	20
Principal repayments	**3**	**104**	**251**	**320**	**333**	**587**	**497**	**410**	**272**	**368**
Long-term debt	3	104	241	283	325	565	475	400	237	337
IMF repurchases	0	0	10	37	8	22	22	9	36	31
Net flows on debt	**12**	**462**	**606**	**-97**	**512**	**135**	**489**	**-90**	**461**	**-335**
of which short-term debt	0	196	165	-84	97	-202	145	-149	267	-176
Interest payments (INT)	**2**	**107**	**374**	**245**	**273**	**423**	**402**	**479**	**254**	**301**
Long-term debt	2	79	307	200	220	376	350	424	206	230
IMF charges	0	0	9	5	10	12	17	21	19	24
Short-term debt	0	28	58	40	43	35	35	34	28	46
Net transfers on debt	**10**	**355**	**232**	**-341**	**240**	**-288**	**88**	**-568**	**207**	**-636**
Total debt service paid (TDS)	**5**	**210**	**625**	**564**	**606**	**1,010**	**899**	**888**	**526**	**669**
Long-term debt	5	182	548	483	544	941	825	825	443	567
IMF repurchases and charges	0	0	19	42	18	34	39	30	55	56
Short-term debt (interest only)	0	28	58	40	43	35	35	34	28	46
2. AGGREGATE NET RESOURCE FLOWS AND NET TRANSFERS (LONG-TERM)										
NET RESOURCE FLOWS	**53**	**1,427**	**1,161**	**239**	**552**	**446**	**960**	**632**	**559**	**807**
Net flow of long-term debt (ex. IMF)	12	266	450	-70	309	239	233	36	154	-148
Foreign direct investment (net)	0	34	38	3	13	16	361	310	158	558
Portfolio equity flows	0	0	0	0	11	25	70	11	11	12
Grants (excluding technical coop.)	41	1,127	672	306	219	167	296	275	236	386
Memo: technical coop. grants	31	25	68	130	160	145	69	63	158	120
official net resource flows	49	1,399	907	415	725	559	555	419	439	352
private net resource flows	4	28	254	-177	-172	-113	405	213	120	455
NET TRANSFERS	**50**	**1,348**	**853**	**39**	**333**	**70**	**610**	**208**	**353**	**577**
Interest on long-term debt	2	79	307	200	220	376	350	424	206	230
Profit remittances on FDI	1	0	0	0	0	0	0	0	0	0
Memo: official net transfers	48	1,357	784	305	594	274	277	70	291	182
private net transfers	3	-9	69	-266	-262	-203	333	138	62	395
3. MAJOR ECONOMIC AGGREGATES										
Gross national income (GNI)	658	4,009	3,805	5,982	6,533	6,726	7,115	7,821	7,919	8,313
Exports of goods & services (XGS)	..	1,870	3,079	4,150	4,841	5,337	5,476	5,398	5,499	5,867
of which workers remittances	15	595	500	1,093	1,244	1,562	1,655	1,543	1,664	1,845
Imports of goods & services (MGS)	..	2,476	4,036	4,783	5,298	5,829	5,643	5,535	5,446	6,308
International reserves (RES)	258	1,745	1,139	1,997	2,279	2,055	2,436	1,988	2,770	3,441
Current account balance	-17	280	-411	-400	-257	-222	29	21	404	59
4. DEBT INDICATORS										
EDT / XGS (%)	..	105.4	265.6	185.7	166.6	150.5	148.1	155.9	162.0	140.2
EDT / GNI (%)	18.1	49.2	214.9	128.9	123.4	119.4	114.0	107.6	112.5	99.0
TDS / XGS (%)	..	11.2	20.3	13.6	12.5	18.9	16.4	16.5	9.6	11.4
INT / XGS (%)	..	5.7	12.2	5.9	5.6	7.9	7.3	8.9	4.6	5.1
INT / GNI (%)	0.3	2.7	9.8	4.1	4.2	6.3	5.6	6.1	3.2	3.6
RES / EDT (%)	216.2	88.5	13.9	25.9	28.3	25.6	30.0	23.6	31.1	41.8
RES / MGS (months)	..	8.5	3.4	5.0	5.2	4.2	5.2	4.3	6.1	6.6
Short-term / EDT (%)	0.0	24.6	12.7	8.8	9.8	7.5	9.2	7.1	9.8	8.6
Concessional / EDT (%)	91.4	41.6	31.0	39.8	42.4	43.8	42.5	45.1	45.6	46.0
Multilateral / EDT (%)	7.6	8.1	10.8	13.2	15.0	17.2	18.1	19.7	20.4	21.1

JORDAN

(US$ million, unless otherwise indicated)

	1970	1980	1990	1994	1995	1996	1997	1998	1999	2000
5. LONG-TERM DEBT										
DEBT OUTSTANDING (LDOD)	**119**	**1,486**	**7,043**	**6,883**	**7,023**	**7,091**	**6,936**	**7,354**	**7,537**	**7,055**
Public and publicly guaranteed	**119**	**1,486**	**7,043**	**6,883**	**7,023**	**7,091**	**6,936**	**7,354**	**7,537**	**7,055**
Official creditors	109	1,210	3,603	4,619	5,102	5,417	5,413	5,990	6,275	5,987
Multilateral	9	159	887	1,016	1,209	1,385	1,464	1,659	1,816	1,739
Concessional	9	113	209	244	278	370	434	505	612	618
Bilateral	100	1,052	2,716	3,603	3,893	4,032	3,949	4,331	4,460	4,248
Concessional	100	707	2,328	2,822	3,139	3,151	3,013	3,292	3,449	3,164
Private creditors	10	276	3,440	2,265	1,921	1,674	1,523	1,365	1,262	1,068
Bonds	0	0	263	824	801	796	886	875	866	736
Commercial banks	0	206	1,604	465	337	217	116	58	19	0
Other private	10	70	1,573	976	782	662	521	432	377	332
Private nonguaranteed	**0**	**0**	**0**	**0**	**0**	**0**	**0**	**0**	**0**	**0**
Bonds	0	0	0	0	0	0	0	0	0	0
Commercial banks and other	0	0	0	0	0	0	0	0	0	0
Memo:										
IBRD	0	26	516	635	736	777	749	745	835	798
IDA	9	76	77	71	69	67	65	62	60	57
DISBURSEMENTS	**15**	**369**	**691**	**213**	**633**	**804**	**708**	**437**	**390**	**189**
Public and publicly guaranteed	**15**	**369**	**691**	**213**	**633**	**804**	**708**	**437**	**390**	**189**
Official creditors	10	326	377	213	633	804	608	437	390	189
Multilateral	0	54	142	102	282	358	269	265	324	88
Concessional	0	18	10	24	53	116	90	87	133	38
Bilateral	10	272	235	111	351	447	339	172	66	101
Concessional	10	106	224	111	336	402	319	172	66	58
Private creditors	5	44	315	0	0	0	100	0	0	0
Bonds	0	0	0	0	0	0	100	0	0	0
Commercial banks	0	15	73	0	0	0	0	0	0	0
Other private	5	29	241	0	0	0	0	0	0	0
Private nonguaranteed	**0**	**0**	**0**	**0**	**0**	**0**	**0**	**0**	**0**	**0**
Bonds	0	0	0	0	0	0	0	0	0	0
Commercial banks and other	0	0	0	0	0	0	0	0	0	0
Memo:										
IBRD	0	22	123	58	158	169	94	36	161	38
IDA	0	9	0	0	0	0	0	0	0	0
PRINCIPAL REPAYMENTS	**3**	**104**	**241**	**283**	**325**	**565**	**475**	**400**	**237**	**337**
Public and publicly guaranteed	**3**	**104**	**241**	**283**	**325**	**565**	**475**	**400**	**237**	**337**
Official creditors	2	54	142	103	128	411	349	292	187	222
Multilateral	0	1	94	98	117	122	116	113	123	120
Concessional	0	1	12	19	21	22	23	22	20	28
Bilateral	2	53	48	6	11	289	234	179	64	102
Concessional	2	23	33	2	6	279	208	141	36	85
Private creditors	0	50	99	180	197	153	126	108	50	115
Bonds	0	0	0	0	0	5	10	10	9	95
Commercial banks	0	46	69	131	135	117	98	58	39	19
Other private	0	4	30	48	62	32	18	40	2	1
Private nonguaranteed	**0**	**0**	**0**	**0**	**0**	**0**	**0**	**0**	**0**	**0**
Bonds	0	0	0	0	0	0	0	0	0	0
Commercial banks and other	0	0	0	0	0	0	0	0	0	0
Memo:										
IBRD	0	0	52	57	77	78	69	64	65	53
IDA	0	0	1	2	2	2	2	2	3	3
NET FLOWS ON DEBT	**12**	**266**	**450**	**-70**	**309**	**239**	**233**	**36**	**154**	**-148**
Public and publicly guaranteed	**12**	**266**	**450**	**-70**	**309**	**239**	**233**	**36**	**154**	**-148**
Official creditors	8	272	235	110	505	393	259	145	203	-33
Multilateral	0	52	48	4	165	235	154	152	201	-33
Concessional	0	17	-3	4	32	94	67	65	113	10
Bilateral	7	220	187	106	340	157	105	-7	2	-1
Concessional	7	83	191	109	330	123	111	31	30	-27
Private creditors	4	-6	216	-180	-197	-153	-26	-108	-50	-115
Bonds	0	0	0	0	0	-5	90	-10	-9	-95
Commercial banks	0	-31	4	-131	-135	-117	-98	-58	-39	-19
Other private	4	25	211	-48	-62	-32	-18	-40	-2	-1
Private nonguaranteed	**0**	**0**	**0**	**0**	**0**	**0**	**0**	**0**	**0**	**0**
Bonds	0	0	0	0	0	0	0	0	0	0
Commercial banks and other	0	0	0	0	0	0	0	0	0	0
Memo:										
IBRD	0	22	71	2	81	91	25	-27	95	-15
IDA	0	9	-1	-2	-2	-2	-2	-2	-3	-3

JORDAN

(US$ million, unless otherwise indicated)

	1970	1980	1990	1994	1995	1996	1997	1998	1999	2000
INTEREST PAYMENTS (LINT)	**2**	**79**	**307**	**200**	**220**	**376**	**350**	**424**	**206**	**230**
Public and publicly guaranteed	**2**	**79**	**307**	**200**	**220**	**376**	**350**	**424**	**206**	**230**
Official creditors	1	43	123	110	130	286	277	349	148	171
Multilateral	0	5	54	60	64	67	70	77	84	93
Concessional	0	3	6	6	6	9	14	18	21	24
Bilateral	1	38	69	50	66	219	208	273	64	78
Concessional	1	13	57	28	45	171	160	239	43	47
Private creditors	1	36	184	90	89	91	72	75	58	60
Bonds	0	0	15	31	41	40	39	51	52	54
Commercial banks	0	32	67	34	32	23	15	8	4	1
Other private	1	4	103	25	17	28	18	17	2	5
Private nonguaranteed	**0**	**0**	**0**	**0**	**0**	**0**	**0**	**0**	**0**	**0**
Bonds	0	0	0	0	0	0	0	0	0	0
Commercial banks and other	0	0	0	0	0	0	0	0	0	0
Memo:										
IBRD	0	1	37	46	48	48	47	46	48	53
IDA	0	1	1	1	1	1	1	1	1	0
NET TRANSFERS ON DEBT	**10**	**187**	**143**	**-270**	**89**	**-137**	**-116**	**-388**	**-52**	**-379**
Public and publicly guaranteed	**10**	**187**	**143**	**-270**	**89**	**-137**	**-116**	**-388**	**-52**	**-379**
Official creditors	6	229	112	-1	375	107	-18	-205	55	-204
Multilateral	0	47	-6	-56	102	169	84	76	117	-126
Concessional	0	14	-9	-2	26	85	54	48	92	-13
Bilateral	6	182	118	55	274	-62	-103	-280	-62	-78
Concessional	6	71	134	82	285	-48	-49	-208	-13	-74
Private creditors	4	-42	31	-269	-286	-244	-98	-183	-108	-175
Bonds	0	0	-15	-31	-41	-45	51	-61	-62	-149
Commercial banks	0	-63	-63	-166	-166	-139	-113	-65	-43	-20
Other private	4	20	109	-73	-79	-60	-36	-57	-3	-6
Private nonguaranteed	**0**	**0**	**0**	**0**	**0**	**0**	**0**	**0**	**0**	**0**
Bonds	0	0	0	0	0	0	0	0	0	0
Commercial banks and other	0	0	0	0	0	0	0	0	0	0
Memo:										
IBRD	0	22	33	-44	33	43	-22	-74	47	-68
IDA	0	8	-2	-2	-3	-3	-3	-3	-3	-3
DEBT SERVICE (LTDS)	**5**	**182**	**548**	**483**	**544**	**941**	**825**	**825**	**443**	**567**
Public and publicly guaranteed	**5**	**182**	**548**	**483**	**544**	**941**	**825**	**825**	**443**	**567**
Official creditors	4	97	265	213	258	697	627	641	335	393
Multilateral	0	6	148	158	181	189	185	189	207	213
Concessional	0	4	18	26	27	31	37	40	41	52
Bilateral	4	90	117	56	77	508	441	452	128	179
Concessional	4	36	90	30	52	450	368	380	79	132
Private creditors	1	86	283	269	286	244	198	183	108	175
Bonds	0	0	15	31	41	45	49	61	62	149
Commercial banks	0	78	136	166	166	139	113	65	43	20
Other private	1	8	133	73	79	60	36	57	3	6
Private nonguaranteed	**0**	**0**	**0**	**0**	**0**	**0**	**0**	**0**	**0**	**0**
Bonds	0	0	0	0	0	0	0	0	0	0
Commercial banks and other	0	0	0	0	0	0	0	0	0	0
Memo:										
IBRD	0	1	89	102	125	127	116	110	114	106
IDA	0	1	2	2	3	3	3	3	3	3
UNDISBURSED DEBT	**73**	**1,354**	**1,471**	**1,234**	**1,838**	**1,469**	**1,025**	**1,085**	**1,088**	**1,115**
Official creditors	61	1,136	1,120	1,234	1,838	1,469	1,025	1,085	1,088	1,115
Private creditors	12	217	351	0	0	0	0	0	0	0
Memorandum items										
Concessional LDOD	109	819	2,537	3,066	3,417	3,521	3,447	3,797	4,062	3,782
Variable rate LDOD	0	200	2,501	1,972	2,043	2,079	2,063	2,077	2,253	2,317
Public sector LDOD	118	1,485	7,043	6,883	7,023	7,072	6,915	7,320	7,507	7,030
Private sector LDOD	1	1	0	0	0	19	22	34	30	25

6. CURRENCY COMPOSITION OF LONG-TERM DEBT (PERCENT)

	1970	1980	1990	1994	1995	1996	1997	1998	1999	2000
Deutsche mark	8.7	10.6	7.9	7.7	7.6	6.9	6.0	6.3	5.5	5.2
French franc	2.6	2.0	3.5	8.7	9.9	9.2	8.5	9.3	7.9	7.8
Japanese yen	0.0	1.1	6.0	21.6	24.1	22.3	21.7	23.2	25.6	24.3
Pound sterling	32.6	6.4	8.0	6.7	6.7	7.5	7.3	6.5	6.2	6.7
Swiss franc	0.0	0.0	0.8	0.4	0.5	0.4	0.4	0.4	0.3	0.3
U.S.dollars	30.8	59.6	44.4	35.0	28.9	29.5	30.5	30.5	31.1	32.0
Multiple currency	0.0	4.4	8.4	10.6	11.8	12.3	12.1	8.9	8.0	7.8
Special drawing rights	0.0	0.0	2.8	0.3	0.5	0.5	0.7	0.8	0.7	0.6
All other currencies	25.3	15.9	18.2	9.0	10.0	11.4	12.8	14.1	14.7	15.3

JORDAN

(US$ million, unless otherwise indicated)

	1970	1980	1990	1994	1995	1996	1997	1998	1999	2000
7. DEBT RESTRUCTURINGS										
Total amount rescheduled	..	..	350	337	367	388	224	211	304	243
Debt stock rescheduled	..	..	0	0	0	0	0	0	0	0
Principal rescheduled	..	..	350	218	269	329	176	147	183	136
Official	..	..	193	95	118	105	89	87	135	101
Private	..	..	157	122	152	224	87	60	47	35
Interest rescheduled	..	..	0	119	97	60	48	64	122	107
Official	..	..	0	67	53	27	23	47	100	87
Private	..	..	0	52	45	33	25	17	22	20
Debt forgiven	..	..	0	297	323	11	34	0	2	28
Memo: interest forgiven	..	..	0	0	0	0	0	0	0	0
Debt stock reduction	..	..	0	0	0	0	0	0	0	120
of which debt buyback	..	..	0	0	0	0	0	0	0	85
8. DEBT STOCK-FLOW RECONCILIATION										
Total change in debt stocks	..	..	1,021	86	355	-30	78	306	493	-684
Net flows on debt	12	462	606	-97	512	135	489	-90	461	-335
Net change in interest arrears	..	..	71	-7	12	15	0	-6	15	11
Interest capitalized	..	..	0	119	97	60	48	64	122	107
Debt forgiveness or reduction	..	..	0	-297	-323	-11	-34	0	-2	-63
Cross-currency valuation	..	..	310	326	63	-334	-464	316	-24	-398
Residual	..	..	35	42	-7	106	38	22	-78	-5
9. AVERAGE TERMS OF NEW COMMITMENTS										
ALL CREDITORS										
Interest (%)	3.7	7.3	4.5	4.8	4.7	5.1	5.3	4.0	5.0	4.9
Maturity (years)	23.4	15.4	19.9	22.2	22.1	19.5	15.9	20.4	18.5	20.4
Grace period (years)	5.0	4.0	6.5	6.7	8.5	5.7	5.7	5.8	5.1	7.2
Grant element (%)	42.6	16.5	39.0	36.9	38.4	32.2	28.7	40.1	31.6	35.9
Official creditors										
Interest (%)	2.6	7.3	3.9	4.8	4.7	5.1	4.5	4.0	5.0	4.9
Maturity (years)	31.4	16.0	21.8	22.2	22.1	19.5	20.2	20.4	18.5	20.4
Grace period (years)	6.4	4.3	7.4	6.7	8.5	5.7	6.0	5.8	5.1	7.2
Grant element (%)	56.7	17.2	44.4	36.9	38.4	32.2	36.1	40.1	31.6	35.9
Private creditors										
Interest (%)	6.2	7.2	8.9	0.0	0.0	0.0	7.3	0.0	0.0	0.0
Maturity (years)	5.5	11.5	7.0	0.0	0.0	0.0	5.0	0.0	0.0	0.0
Grace period (years)	1.9	2.4	1.0	0.0	0.0	0.0	5.0	0.0	0.0	0.0
Grant element (%)	10.4	12.0	2.8	0.0	0.0	0.0	10.2	0.0	0.0	0.0
Memorandum items										
Commitments	36	759	749	638	1,225	486	349	473	421	257
Official creditors	25	653	652	638	1,225	486	249	473	421	257
Private creditors	11	106	97	0	0	0	100	0	0	0

10. CONTRACTUAL OBLIGATIONS ON OUTSTANDING LONG-TERM DEBT

	2001	2002	2003	2004	2005	2006	2007	2008	2009	2010
TOTAL										
Disbursements	286	298	209	135	86	50	28	11	6	1
Principal	413	549	470	488	492	477	462	381	386	389
Interest	316	337	323	305	283	260	237	216	198	179
Official creditors										
Disbursements	286	298	209	135	86	50	28	11	6	1
Principal	364	400	420	437	442	434	426	369	375	377
Interest	250	272	268	253	235	216	196	176	159	141
Bilateral creditors										
Disbursements	122	94	59	33	19	10	5	2	1	0
Principal	215	235	255	260	263	260	264	213	219	226
Interest	148	168	166	155	144	133	121	110	101	91
Multilateral creditors										
Disbursements	163	205	150	102	68	40	23	9	6	0
Principal	149	165	165	177	179	173	163	156	155	152
Interest	103	104	103	98	91	83	75	67	58	50
Private creditors										
Disbursements	0	0	0	0	0	0	0	0	0	0
Principal	49	149	50	51	50	43	36	12	12	12
Interest	66	65	55	51	48	45	42	40	39	38
Commercial banks										
Disbursements	0	0	0	0	0	0	0	0	0	0
Principal	0	0	0	0	0	0	0	0	0	0
Interest	0	0	0	0	0	0	0	0	0	0
Other private										
Disbursements	0	0	0	0	0	0	0	0	0	0
Principal	38	38	39	39	38	36	33	9	9	9
Interest	17	16	15	13	10	8	5	3	3	2

KAZAKHSTAN

(US$ million, unless otherwise indicated)

	1970	1980	1990	1994	1995	1996	1997	1998	1999	2000
1. SUMMARY DEBT DATA										
TOTAL DEBT STOCKS (EDT)	..	..	..	**2,790**	**3,750**	**2,922**	**4,078**	**6,085**	**6,105**	**6,664**
Long-term debt (LDOD)	..	..	..	**2,268**	**2,937**	**2,149**	**3,218**	**5,008**	**5,171**	**6,131**
Public and publicly guaranteed	..	..	..	2,227	2,834	1,947	2,622	3,038	3,336	3,602
Private nonguaranteed	..	..	..	41	103	203	596	1,970	1,835	2,529
Use of IMF credit	..	..	..	**289**	**432**	**552**	**511**	**653**	**460**	**0**
Short-term debt	..	..	..	**232**	**381**	**221**	**349**	**424**	**474**	**533**
of which interest arrears on LDOD	..	..	..	105	162	0	0	49	108	194
Official creditors	..	..	..	80	162	0	0	0	0	0
Private creditors	..	..	..	25	0	0	0	49	108	194
Memo: principal arrears on LDOD	..	..	..	0	0	0	0	55	95	120
Official creditors	..	..	..	0	0	0	0	0	0	0
Private creditors	..	..	..	0	0	0	0	55	95	120
Memo: export credits	..	..	..	773	1,119	1,203	1,173	581	440	348
TOTAL DEBT FLOWS										
Disbursements	..	..	..	**806**	**881**	**922**	**1,487**	**2,030**	**1,345**	**1,635**
Long-term debt	..	..	..	611	740	787	1,487	1,820	1,345	1,635
IMF purchases	..	..	..	195	141	135	0	210	0	0
Principal repayments	..	..	..	**23**	**105**	**192**	**273**	**718**	**1,076**	**1,391**
Long-term debt	..	..	..	23	105	192	267	623	900	949
IMF repurchases	..	..	..	0	0	0	6	95	176	442
Net flows on debt	..	..	..	**910**	**868**	**732**	**1,342**	**1,337**	**260**	**217**
of which short-term debt	..	..	..	127	93	2	128	26	-9	-27
Interest payments (INT)	..	..	..	**46**	**130**	**131**	**210**	**273**	**284**	**448**
Long-term debt	..	..	..	32	102	98	170	231	243	417
IMF charges	..	..	..	9	18	22	24	23	22	11
Short-term debt	..	..	..	5	10	10	16	20	19	20
Net transfers on debt	..	..	..	**864**	**739**	**601**	**1,132**	**1,064**	**-25**	**-231**
Total debt service paid (TDS)	..	..	..	**68**	**235**	**322**	**483**	**992**	**1,360**	**1,840**
Long-term debt	..	..	..	55	207	290	437	854	1,143	1,366
IMF repurchases and charges	..	..	..	9	18	22	31	118	198	453
Short-term debt (interest only)	..	..	..	5	10	10	16	20	19	20
2. AGGREGATE NET RESOURCE FLOWS AND NET TRANSFERS (LONG-TERM)										
NET RESOURCE FLOWS	..	..	..	**799**	**1,610**	**1,776**	**2,646**	**2,373**	**2,060**	**1,979**
Net flow of long-term debt (ex. IMF)	..	..	..	588	635	596	1,220	1,196	445	686
Foreign direct investment (net)	..	..	..	185	964	1,137	1,321	1,151	1,587	1,250
Portfolio equity flows	..	..	..	0	0	0	50	0	0	0
Grants (excluding technical coop.)	..	..	..	26	11	44	54	26	28	44
Memo: technical coop. grants	..	..	..	17	55	67	41	97	86	74
official net resource flows	..	..	..	468	405	377	488	366	263	80
private net resource flows	..	..	..	331	1,205	1,399	2,158	2,008	1,797	1,900
NET TRANSFERS	..	..	..	**767**	**1,508**	**1,678**	**2,476**	**2,143**	**1,692**	**1,417**
Interest on long-term debt	..	..	..	32	102	98	170	231	243	417
Profit remittances on FDI	..	..	..	0	0	0	0	0	125	145
Memo: official net transfers	..	..	..	453	346	315	400	265	157	-43
private net transfers	..	..	..	315	1,162	1,363	2,076	1,878	1,535	1,461
3. MAJOR ECONOMIC AGGREGATES										
Gross national income (GNI)	..	..	..	19,687	19,746	20,854	21,855	21,838	16,345	17,052
Exports of goods & services (XGS)	..	..	..	4,246	6,026	7,033	7,833	6,879	7,037	10,953
of which workers remittances	..	..	..	0	7	10	18	10	13	64
Imports of goods & services (MGS)	..	..	..	5,519	6,292	7,832	8,689	8,227	7,418	10,023
International reserves (RES)	..	..	..	1,216	1,660	1,961	2,223	1,965	2,001	2,099
Current account balance	..	..	..	-1,172	-213	-750	-799	-1,236	-236	1,074
4. DEBT INDICATORS										
EDT / XGS (%)	..	..	..	65.7	62.2	41.6	52.1	88.5	86.8	60.8
EDT / GNI (%)	..	..	..	14.2	19.0	14.0	18.7	27.9	37.4	39.1
TDS / XGS (%)	..	..	..	1.6	3.9	4.6	6.2	14.4	19.3	16.8
INT / XGS (%)	..	..	..	1.1	2.2	1.9	2.7	4.0	4.0	4.1
INT / GNI (%)	..	..	..	0.2	0.7	0.6	1.0	1.3	1.7	2.6
RES / EDT (%)	..	..	..	43.6	44.3	67.1	54.5	32.3	32.8	31.5
RES / MGS (months)	..	..	..	2.6	3.2	3.0	3.1	2.9	3.2	2.5
Short-term / EDT (%)	..	..	..	8.3	10.2	7.6	8.6	7.0	7.8	8.0
Concessional / EDT (%)	..	..	..	0.1	2.7	4.4	3.9	4.2	6.4	6.2
Multilateral / EDT (%)	..	..	..	7.8	10.4	20.0	20.2	20.3	24.1	22.2

KAZAKHSTAN

(US$ million, unless otherwise indicated)

	1970	1980	1990	1994	1995	1996	1997	1998	1999	2000
5. LONG-TERM DEBT										
DEBT OUTSTANDING (LDOD)	..	..	..	**2,268**	**2,937**	**2,149**	**3,218**	**5,008**	**5,171**	**6,131**
Public and publicly guaranteed	..	..	..	**2,227**	**2,834**	**1,947**	**2,622**	**3,038**	**3,336**	**3,602**
Official creditors	..	..	..	1,893	2,293	1,291	1,612	2,050	2,317	2,228
Multilateral	..	..	..	217	392	586	824	1,233	1,473	1,477
Concessional	..	..	..	0	0	6	22	37	60	60
Bilateral	..	..	..	1,675	1,901	705	788	817	843	751
Concessional	..	..	..	2	100	122	135	218	328	351
Private creditors	..	..	..	334	541	656	1,009	988	1,019	1,374
Bonds	..	..	..	0	0	200	550	550	650	1,000
Commercial banks	..	..	..	0	17	17	114	148	195	255
Other private	..	..	..	334	523	438	346	290	175	119
Private nonguaranteed	..	..	..	**41**	**103**	**203**	**596**	**1,970**	**1,835**	**2,529**
Bonds	..	..	..	0	0	0	0	100	100	100
Commercial banks and other	..	..	..	41	103	203	596	1,870	1,735	2,429
Memo:										
IBRD	..	..	..	187	295	490	648	899	1,082	1,057
IDA	..	..	..	0	0	0	0	0	0	0
DISBURSEMENTS	..	..	..	**611**	**740**	**787**	**1,487**	**1,820**	**1,345**	**1,635**
Public and publicly guaranteed	..	..	..	**591**	**671**	**639**	**991**	**485**	**727**	**625**
Official creditors	..	..	..	454	421	408	491	442	350	168
Multilateral	..	..	..	184	171	257	284	365	263	95
Concessional	..	..	..	0	0	6	17	12	16	5
Bilateral	..	..	..	269	250	151	208	77	87	73
Concessional	..	..	..	2	108	36	29	60	83	70
Private creditors	..	..	..	137	249	232	500	43	377	457
Bonds	..	..	..	0	0	200	350	0	300	350
Commercial banks	..	..	..	0	17	0	105	42	40	100
Other private	..	..	..	137	232	32	46	1	37	7
Private nonguaranteed	..	..	..	**20**	**69**	**148**	**496**	**1,334**	**618**	**1,010**
Bonds	..	..	..	0	0	0	0	100	0	0
Commercial banks and other	..	..	..	20	69	148	496	1,234	618	1,010
Memo:										
IBRD	..	..	..	182	107	225	202	211	209	50
IDA	..	..	..	0	0	0	0	0	0	0
PRINCIPAL REPAYMENTS	..	..	..	**23**	**105**	**192**	**267**	**623**	**900**	**949**
Public and publicly guaranteed	..	..	..	**18**	**95**	**151**	**152**	**192**	**447**	**215**
Official creditors	..	..	..	12	27	74	57	103	115	131
Multilateral	..	..	..	0	0	32	0	0	24	31
Concessional	..	..	..	0	0	0	0	0	0	0
Bilateral	..	..	..	12	27	43	57	103	92	101
Concessional	..	..	..	0	0	1	1	1	5	8
Private creditors	..	..	..	6	68	77	94	89	331	84
Bonds	..	..	..	0	0	0	0	0	200	0
Commercial banks	..	..	..	0	0	0	8	13	53	31
Other private	..	..	..	6	68	77	87	77	78	53
Private nonguaranteed	..	..	..	**5**	**11**	**41**	**115**	**432**	**453**	**734**
Bonds	..	..	..	0	0	0	0	0	0	0
Commercial banks and other	..	..	..	5	11	41	115	432	453	734
Memo:										
IBRD	..	..	..	0	0	0	0	0	19	20
IDA	..	..	..	0	0	0	0	0	0	0
NET FLOWS ON DEBT	..	..	..	**588**	**635**	**596**	**1,220**	**1,196**	**445**	**686**
Public and publicly guaranteed	..	..	..	**573**	**576**	**488**	**840**	**294**	**280**	**410**
Official creditors	..	..	..	442	395	334	434	340	235	36
Multilateral	..	..	..	184	171	226	284	365	239	64
Concessional	..	..	..	0	0	6	17	12	16	5
Bilateral	..	..	..	258	223	108	151	-26	-5	-28
Concessional	..	..	..	2	108	35	29	60	78	62
Private creditors	..	..	..	131	182	155	406	-46	46	374
Bonds	..	..	..	0	0	200	350	0	100	350
Commercial banks	..	..	..	0	17	0	97	30	-13	69
Other private	..	..	..	131	164	-45	-41	-76	-42	-46
Private nonguaranteed	..	..	..	**15**	**59**	**107**	**380**	**903**	**164**	**276**
Bonds	..	..	..	0	0	0	0	100	0	0
Commercial banks and other	..	..	..	15	59	107	380	803	164	276
Memo:										
IBRD	..	..	..	182	107	225	202	211	190	30
IDA	..	..	..	0	0	0	0	0	0	0

KAZAKHSTAN

(US$ million, unless otherwise indicated)

	1970	1980	1990	1994	1995	1996	1997	1998	1999	2000
INTEREST PAYMENTS (LINT)	..	..	..	**32**	**102**	**98**	**170**	**231**	**243**	**417**
Public and publicly guaranteed	..	..	..	**30**	**100**	**95**	**164**	**206**	**178**	**235**
Official creditors	..	..	..	16	59	63	88	101	106	123
Multilateral	..	..	..	7	15	31	43	58	72	82
Concessional	..	..	..	0	0	0	0	0	1	1
Bilateral	..	..	..	9	44	32	46	43	34	41
Concessional	..	..	..	0	2	7	5	6	8	9
Private creditors	..	..	..	14	41	32	76	104	73	112
Bonds	..	..	..	0	0	0	22	48	47	90
Commercial banks	..	..	..	0	0	1	15	8	8	14
Other private	..	..	..	14	41	31	39	49	17	8
Private nonguaranteed	..	..	..	**3**	**1**	**4**	**6**	**25**	**65**	**182**
Bonds	..	..	..	0	0	0	0	0	11	11
Commercial banks and other	..	..	..	3	1	4	6	25	53	171
Memo:										
IBRD	..	..	..	7	14	24	34	44	52	63
IDA	..	..	..	0	0	0	0	0	0	0
NET TRANSFERS ON DEBT	..	..	..	**556**	**533**	**497**	**1,050**	**966**	**202**	**269**
Public and publicly guaranteed	..	..	..	**543**	**476**	**394**	**676**	**88**	**102**	**175**
Official creditors	..	..	..	426	335	271	346	239	129	-87
Multilateral	..	..	..	177	156	195	241	307	167	-18
Concessional	..	..	..	0	0	6	17	12	15	5
Bilateral	..	..	..	249	180	76	105	-69	-38	-69
Concessional	..	..	..	2	105	28	24	54	70	52
Private creditors	..	..	..	117	141	123	330	-151	-27	262
Bonds	..	..	..	0	0	200	328	-48	53	260
Commercial banks	..	..	..	0	17	-1	83	22	-21	55
Other private	..	..	..	117	123	-76	-81	-125	-58	-54
Private nonguaranteed	..	..	..	**13**	**57**	**104**	**374**	**878**	**100**	**94**
Bonds	..	..	..	0	0	0	0	100	-11	-11
Commercial banks and other	..	..	..	13	57	104	374	778	111	105
Memo:										
IBRD	..	..	..	175	93	201	167	167	138	-33
IDA	..	..	..	0	0	0	0	0	0	0
DEBT SERVICE (LTDS)	..	..	..	**55**	**207**	**290**	**437**	**854**	**1,143**	**1,366**
Public and publicly guaranteed	..	..	..	**47**	**195**	**246**	**316**	**397**	**625**	**450**
Official creditors	..	..	..	27	86	137	145	204	221	255
Multilateral	..	..	..	7	15	62	43	58	96	113
Concessional	..	..	..	0	0	0	0	0	1	1
Bilateral	..	..	..	21	71	75	103	146	125	142
Concessional	..	..	..	0	2	8	5	6	13	17
Private creditors	..	..	..	20	109	109	170	194	404	196
Bonds	..	..	..	0	0	0	22	48	247	90
Commercial banks	..	..	..	0	0	1	22	21	61	46
Other private	..	..	..	20	109	108	126	125	95	61
Private nonguaranteed	..	..	..	**8**	**12**	**44**	**121**	**457**	**518**	**916**
Bonds	..	..	..	0	0	0	0	0	11	11
Commercial banks and other	..	..	..	8	12	44	121	457	507	905
Memo:										
IBRD	..	..	..	7	14	24	34	44	71	83
IDA	..	..	..	0	0	0	0	0	0	0
UNDISBURSED DEBT	..	..	..	**704**	**948**	**1,170**	**1,184**	**1,479**	**1,608**	**1,269**
Official creditors	..	..	..	346	784	977	1,005	1,307	1,457	1,217
Private creditors	..	..	..	357	164	193	179	172	151	52
Memorandum items										
Concessional LDOD	..	..	..	2	100	128	157	256	389	411
Variable rate LDOD	..	..	..	2,077	2,520	1,481	2,196	3,852	3,810	4,370
Public sector LDOD	..	..	..	2,227	2,834	1,947	2,622	3,033	3,331	3,599
Private sector LDOD	..	..	..	41	103	203	596	1,975	1,840	2,532

6. CURRENCY COMPOSITION OF LONG-TERM DEBT (PERCENT)

	1970	1980	1990	1994	1995	1996	1997	1998	1999	2000
Deutsche mark	..	..	..	22.6	21.6	28.0	17.3	13.3	7.9	4.8
French franc	..	..	..	0.4	0.4	0.3	0.6	0.5	0.3	0.2
Japanese yen	..	..	..	3.9	8.9	15.1	11.1	13.2	15.8	13.8
Pound sterling	..	..	..	0.0	0.0	0.0	0.0	0.2	0.7	0.6
Swiss franc	..	..	..	0.2	0.0	0.0	0.0	0.1	0.0	0.0
U.S.dollars	..	..	..	5.7	6.9	23.4	44.2	47.1	53.3	61.2
Multiple currency	..	..	..	8.4	11.8	27.5	24.0	23.4	21.6	19.0
Special drawing rights	..	..	..	0.0	0.0	0.0	0.0	0.0	0.2	0.2
All other currencies	..	..	..	58.8	50.4	5.7	2.8	2.2	0.2	0.2

KAZAKHSTAN

(US$ million, unless otherwise indicated)

	1970	1980	1990	1994	1995	1996	1997	1998	1999	2000
7. DEBT RESTRUCTURINGS										
Total amount rescheduled	..	..	..	0	0	0	0	0	202	0
Debt stock rescheduled	..	..	..	0	0	0	0	0	185	0
Principal rescheduled	..	..	..	0	0	0	0	0	0	0
Official	..	..	..	0	0	0	0	0	0	0
Private	..	..	..	0	0	0	0	0	0	0
Interest rescheduled	..	..	..	0	0	0	0	0	0	0
Official	..	..	..	0	0	0	0	0	0	0
Private	..	..	..	0	0	0	0	0	0	0
Debt forgiven	..	..	..	0	0	0	0	0	0	0
Memo: interest forgiven	..	..	..	0	0	0	0	0	0	0
Debt stock reduction	..	..	..	0	0	0	0	0	0	0
of which debt buyback	..	..	..	0	0	0	0	0	0	0
8. DEBT STOCK-FLOW RECONCILIATION										
Total change in debt stocks	..	..	..	1,062	961	-828	1,156	2,007	20	559
Net flows on debt	..	..	..	910	868	732	1,342	1,337	260	217
Net change in interest arrears	..	..	..	84	56	-162	0	49	60	86
Interest capitalized	..	..	..	0	0	0	0	0	0	0
Debt forgiveness or reduction	..	..	..	0	0	0	0	0	0	0
Cross-currency valuation	..	..	..	-763	-222	-292	-198	141	-38	-161
Residual	..	..	..	831	258	-1,106	12	480	-261	417
9. AVERAGE TERMS OF NEW COMMITMENTS										
ALL CREDITORS										
Interest (%)	..	..	..	5.6	5.5	7.1	6.5	5.3	9.0	11.0
Maturity (years)	..	..	..	13.4	13.3	13.4	13.6	24.2	12.5	6.0
Grace period (years)	..	..	..	5.0	4.3	4.1	5.6	6.2	4.8	5.6
Grant element (%)	..	..	..	22.6	22.3	15.1	21.2	34.3	8.0	-5.5
Official creditors										
Interest (%)	..	..	..	5.6	5.5	6.5	5.5	5.1	6.2	2.0
Maturity (years)	..	..	..	14.1	14.2	17.4	20.5	25.0	18.3	28.1
Grace period (years)	..	..	..	5.3	4.5	4.7	6.5	6.4	5.1	9.1
Grant element (%)	..	..	..	23.7	23.7	19.9	31.1	35.8	23.7	63.4
Private creditors										
Interest (%)	..	..	..	6.1	6.4	8.8	7.6	7.8	12.6	11.0
Maturity (years)	..	..	..	6.6	5.7	3.8	5.8	9.2	5.3	6.0
Grace period (years)	..	..	..	2.1	2.3	2.7	4.6	2.1	4.5	5.6
Grant element (%)	..	..	..	12.2	10.0	3.4	10.1	7.1	-11.6	-5.5
Memorandum items										
Commitments	..	..	..	414	982	903	1,058	729	790	460
Official creditors	..	..	..	374	880	639	559	691	439	0
Private creditors	..	..	..	40	101	264	499	38	352	460

10. CONTRACTUAL OBLIGATIONS ON OUTSTANDING LONG-TERM DEBT

	2001	2002	2003	2004	2005	2006	2007	2008	2009	2010
TOTAL										
Disbursements	479	295	183	103	72	54	38	24	17	3
Principal	1,061	1,273	689	824	538	340	657	259	228	195
Interest	392	344	279	250	184	162	126	92	80	68
Official creditors										
Disbursements	442	281	182	103	72	54	38	24	17	3
Principal	277	273	227	238	236	192	202	194	195	195
Interest	141	139	134	127	118	108	99	89	79	68
Bilateral creditors										
Disbursements	197	121	52	2	1	0	0	0	0	0
Principal	190	171	90	84	63	17	24	30	31	31
Interest	40	34	27	22	17	14	13	12	11	10
Multilateral creditors										
Disbursements	245	160	131	100	71	54	38	24	17	3
Principal	88	102	137	154	174	175	178	164	164	165
Interest	101	105	107	106	101	94	86	77	68	58
Private creditors										
Disbursements	37	15	1	0	0	0	0	0	0	0
Principal	784	1,000	462	586	301	147	456	65	33	0
Interest	251	206	145	123	66	54	28	4	1	0
Commercial banks										
Disbursements	33	14	1	0	0	0	0	0	0	0
Principal	78	71	60	20	20	19	17	14	6	0
Interest	21	16	10	5	4	3	2	1	0	0
Other private										
Disbursements	3	1	0	0	0	0	0	0	0	0
Principal	706	929	402	567	282	128	439	51	27	0
Interest	230	190	135	117	62	51	26	3	1	0

KENYA

(US$ million, unless otherwise indicated)

1. SUMMARY DEBT DATA

	1970	1980	1990	1994	1995	1996	1997	1998	1999	2000
TOTAL DEBT STOCKS (EDT)	**478**	**3,387**	**7,058**	**7,202**	**7,412**	**6,931**	**6,603**	**6,881**	**6,487**	**6,295**
Long-term debt (LDOD)	**409**	**2,493**	**5,642**	**6,119**	**6,405**	**6,060**	**5,550**	**5,841**	**5,543**	**5,355**
Public and publicly guaranteed	321	2,056	4,762	5,589	5,960	5,685	5,225	5,561	5,323	5,180
Private nonguaranteed	88	437	880	530	445	375	325	280	220	175
Use of IMF credit	**0**	**254**	**482**	**405**	**374**	**337**	**250**	**197**	**132**	**127**
Short-term debt	**69**	**640**	**934**	**679**	**634**	**534**	**803**	**844**	**812**	**813**
of which interest arrears on LDOD	0	2	95	83	32	16	34	68	102	62
Official creditors	0	2	49	20	23	9	21	30	48	18
Private creditors	0	0	46	63	9	7	13	38	54	44
Memo: principal arrears on LDOD	0	3	72	9	6	29	76	136	239	216
Official creditors	0	0	22	9	2	17	46	70	137	44
Private creditors	0	3	50	0	4	12	30	66	102	172
Memo: export credits	0	0	1,540	1,617	1,324	1,102	1,093	504	405	418
TOTAL DEBT FLOWS										
Disbursements	**78**	**714**	**778**	**294**	**698**	**467**	**219**	**231**	**259**	**409**
Long-term debt	78	620	642	262	698	431	219	231	259	364
IMF purchases	0	94	136	32	0	36	0	0	0	44
Principal repayments	**33**	**205**	**458**	**552**	**600**	**567**	**449**	**467**	**529**	**350**
Long-term debt	29	195	352	538	561	506	381	404	470	307
IMF repurchases	4	9	106	14	39	61	67	63	60	42
Net flows on debt	**45**	**718**	**615**	**-322**	**104**	**-185**	**21**	**-229**	**-336**	**99**
of which short-term debt	0	209	294	-65	6	-84	251	7	-66	41
Interest payments (INT)	**17**	**229**	**333**	**329**	**301**	**277**	**221**	**205**	**174**	**131**
Long-term debt	17	163	230	290	263	245	190	165	133	89
IMF charges	0	8	26	2	2	2	2	1	1	1
Short-term debt	0	58	78	38	36	30	30	39	40	41
Net transfers on debt	**28**	**489**	**281**	**-652**	**-198**	**-462**	**-199**	**-434**	**-510**	**-32**
Total debt service paid (TDS)	**50**	**434**	**791**	**881**	**901**	**844**	**669**	**672**	**704**	**481**
Long-term debt	46	359	582	827	824	752	571	569	603	397
IMF repurchases and charges	4	17	131	16	41	63	69	64	61	43
Short-term debt (interest only)	0	58	78	38	36	30	30	39	40	41

2. AGGREGATE NET RESOURCE FLOWS AND NET TRANSFERS (LONG-TERM)

	1970	1980	1990	1994	1995	1996	1997	1998	1999	2000
NET RESOURCE FLOWS	**67**	**624**	**1,324**	**39**	**412**	**176**	**72**	**40**	**5**	**374**
Net flow of long-term debt (ex. IMF)	49	424	290	-276	137	-76	-163	-174	-211	57
Foreign direct investment (net)	14	79	57	4	33	13	20	11	14	111
Portfolio equity flows	0	0	0	0	0	43	12	4	5	4
Grants (excluding technical coop.)	3	121	977	311	242	196	202	199	196	202
Memo: technical coop. grants	27	128	207	191	221	192	180	151	140	138
official net resource flows	33	323	1,202	317	538	291	145	142	54	321
private net resource flows	33	301	122	-278	-126	-115	-73	-102	-50	53
NET TRANSFERS	**0**	**311**	**961**	**-351**	**53**	**-170**	**-238**	**-225**	**-234**	**172**
Interest on long-term debt	17	163	230	290	263	245	190	165	133	89
Profit remittances on FDI	49	150	132	100	95	100	120	100	105	112
Memo: official net transfers	25	269	1,068	156	371	128	28	32	-33	269
private net transfers	-25	41	-107	-507	-318	-297	-266	-257	-201	-96

3. MAJOR ECONOMIC AGGREGATES

	1970	1980	1990	1994	1995	1996	1997	1998	1999	2000
Gross national income (GNI)	1,545	7,039	8,089	6,758	8,687	9,037	10,380	11,271	10,368	10,223
Exports of goods & services (XGS)	..	2,061	2,233	2,675	2,974	3,041	3,000	2,889	2,715	2,786
of which workers remittances	..	0	0	0	..	..	..	..	..	..
Imports of goods & services (MGS)	..	3,095	3,128	2,848	3,892	3,694	4,029	3,938	3,493	3,947
International reserves (RES)	220	539	236	588	384	776	811	783	792	898
Current account balance	..	-876	-527	98	-400	-73	-457	-475	-98	-238

4. DEBT INDICATORS

	1970	1980	1990	1994	1995	1996	1997	1998	1999	2000
EDT / XGS (%)	..	164.3	316.0	269.2	249.3	227.9	220.1	238.2	238.9	226.0
EDT / GNI (%)	30.9	48.1	87.3	106.6	85.3	76.7	63.6	61.1	62.6	61.6
TDS / XGS (%)	..	21.0	35.4	32.9	30.3	27.8	22.3	23.3	25.9	17.3
INT / XGS (%)	..	11.1	14.9	12.3	10.1	9.1	7.4	7.1	6.4	4.7
INT / GNI (%)	1.1	3.3	4.1	4.9	3.5	3.1	2.1	1.8	1.7	1.3
RES / EDT (%)	46.0	15.9	3.4	8.2	5.2	11.2	12.3	11.4	12.2	14.3
RES / MGS (months)	..	2.1	0.9	2.5	1.2	2.5	2.4	2.4	2.7	2.7
Short-term / EDT (%)	14.5	18.9	13.2	9.4	8.6	7.7	12.2	12.3	12.5	12.9
Concessional / EDT (%)	35.6	20.2	33.7	47.1	52.3	56.8	57.0	59.9	63.7	65.0
Multilateral / EDT (%)	8.0	18.7	35.3	38.4	39.4	42.5	43.2	43.6	44.5	45.0

KENYA

(US$ million, unless otherwise indicated)

5. LONG-TERM DEBT

	1970	1980	1990	1994	1995	1996	1997	1998	1999	2000
DEBT OUTSTANDING (LDOD)	**409**	**2,493**	**5,642**	**6,119**	**6,405**	**6,060**	**5,550**	**5,841**	**5,543**	**5,355**
Public and publicly guaranteed	**321**	**2,056**	**4,762**	**5,589**	**5,960**	**5,685**	**5,225**	**5,561**	**5,323**	**5,180**
Official creditors	237	1,206	3,715	4,853	5,252	5,106	4,745	5,007	4,801	4,659
Multilateral	38	634	2,492	2,762	2,919	2,943	2,855	2,999	2,884	2,831
Concessional	32	270	1,395	2,040	2,249	2,402	2,390	2,584	2,575	2,607
Bilateral	199	572	1,222	2,091	2,333	2,164	1,890	2,008	1,917	1,828
Concessional	138	414	985	1,355	1,630	1,536	1,372	1,539	1,555	1,482
Private creditors	84	849	1,047	736	708	578	480	554	522	521
Bonds	71	10	0	0	0	0	0	0	0	0
Commercial banks	1	394	924	653	607	500	445	472	424	432
Other private	12	445	124	83	101	79	35	82	98	89
Private nonguaranteed	**88**	**437**	**880**	**530**	**445**	**375**	**325**	**280**	**220**	**175**
Bonds	0	0	0	0	0	0	0	0	0	0
Commercial banks and other	88	437	880	530	445	375	325	280	220	175
Memo:										
IBRD	6	308	872	501	435	312	213	154	91	47
IDA	32	220	1,185	1,789	1,977	2,062	2,032	2,210	2,220	2,262
DISBURSEMENTS	**78**	**620**	**642**	**262**	**698**	**431**	**219**	**231**	**259**	**364**
Public and publicly guaranteed	**37**	**533**	**587**	**262**	**698**	**431**	**219**	**231**	**259**	**364**
Official creditors	36	233	405	256	566	359	171	194	120	308
Multilateral	10	154	297	160	220	197	142	142	87	188
Concessional	7	94	264	124	181	181	128	132	84	184
Bilateral	26	79	108	96	346	161	29	53	33	120
Concessional	20	66	106	74	346	108	29	35	17	102
Private creditors	1	300	182	6	132	72	48	36	139	56
Bonds	0	0	0	0	0	0	0	0	0	0
Commercial banks	0	215	119	5	72	72	48	14	77	52
Other private	1	85	63	0	60	0	0	22	62	4
Private nonguaranteed	**41**	**87**	**55**	**0**	**0**	**0**	**0**	**0**	**0**	**0**
Bonds	0	0	0	0	0	0	0	0	0	0
Commercial banks and other	41	87	55	0	0	0	0	0	0	0
Memo:										
IBRD	3	45	4	0	0	0	0	0	0	0
IDA	7	72	235	97	159	156	84	123	78	170
PRINCIPAL REPAYMENTS	**29**	**195**	**352**	**538**	**561**	**506**	**381**	**404**	**470**	**307**
Public and publicly guaranteed	**17**	**108**	**315**	**468**	**476**	**436**	**331**	**359**	**409**	**262**
Official creditors	6	31	180	251	271	263	229	251	262	190
Multilateral	1	13	127	151	150	135	127	124	124	106
Concessional	0	1	9	18	18	16	19	23	29	36
Bilateral	5	17	54	100	120	128	102	127	138	84
Concessional	3	5	25	50	51	52	40	41	51	49
Private creditors	12	77	135	217	205	173	103	109	146	73
Bonds	10	0	0	0	0	0	0	0	0	0
Commercial banks	0	25	115	169	161	150	88	82	103	67
Other private	1	53	20	48	45	23	15	27	43	6
Private nonguaranteed	**12**	**88**	**37**	**70**	**85**	**70**	**50**	**45**	**61**	**45**
Bonds	0	0	0	0	0	0	0	0	0	0
Commercial banks and other	12	88	37	70	85	70	50	45	61	45
Memo:										
IBRD	1	11	95	106	100	89	74	66	59	40
IDA	0	1	4	8	9	10	11	15	23	29
NET FLOWS ON DEBT	**49**	**424**	**290**	**-276**	**137**	**-76**	**-163**	**-174**	**-211**	**57**
Public and publicly guaranteed	**20**	**425**	**272**	**-206**	**222**	**-6**	**-113**	**-129**	**-150**	**102**
Official creditors	30	202	225	5	295	95	-58	-57	-142	118
Multilateral	9	141	171	10	70	62	15	18	-37	82
Concessional	7	94	255	106	163	165	108	109	55	148
Bilateral	21	62	54	-4	225	33	-73	-75	-106	37
Concessional	17	61	81	24	294	57	-11	-6	-34	52
Private creditors	-10	223	47	-211	-73	-101	-55	-72	-7	-16
Bonds	-10	0	0	0	0	0	0	0	0	0
Commercial banks	0	190	4	-164	-89	-78	-40	-68	-26	-15
Other private	0	33	43	-48	15	-23	-15	-5	19	-1
Private nonguaranteed	**30**	**-1**	**18**	**-70**	**-85**	**-70**	**-50**	**-45**	**-61**	**-45**
Bonds	0	0	0	0	0	0	0	0	0	0
Commercial banks and other	30	-1	18	-70	-85	-70	-50	-45	-61	-45
Memo:										
IBRD	2	35	-92	-106	-100	-89	-74	-66	-59	-40
IDA	7	71	230	89	150	146	72	108	55	142

KENYA

(US$ million, unless otherwise indicated)

	1970	1980	1990	1994	1995	1996	1997	1998	1999	2000
INTEREST PAYMENTS (LINT)	**17**	**163**	**230**	**290**	**263**	**245**	**190**	**165**	**133**	**89**
Public and publicly guaranteed	**13**	**124**	**193**	**244**	**222**	**214**	**158**	**139**	**112**	**71**
Official creditors	8	54	134	161	167	163	117	110	87	52
Multilateral	1	36	100	81	77	73	58	50	43	35
Concessional	0	1	9	16	17	17	18	18	19	19
Bilateral	8	18	34	80	89	90	59	60	44	17
Concessional	4	7	14	31	43	40	29	32	29	12
Private creditors	5	70	59	83	55	50	41	29	25	19
Bonds	4	1	0	0	0	0	0	0	0	0
Commercial banks	0	30	53	69	49	45	40	27	24	17
Other private	1	39	6	14	7	5	2	2	1	2
Private nonguaranteed	**4**	**39**	**38**	**46**	**42**	**32**	**31**	**26**	**21**	**19**
Bonds	0	0	0	0	0	0	0	0	0	0
Commercial banks and other	4	39	38	46	42	32	31	26	21	19
Memo:										
IBRD	0	31	78	49	43	34	23	17	12	7
IDA	0	1	7	13	14	15	15	15	16	16
NET TRANSFERS ON DEBT	**32**	**261**	**60**	**-566**	**-127**	**-321**	**-352**	**-339**	**-344**	**-32**
Public and publicly guaranteed	**7**	**301**	**79**	**-450**	**0**	**-220**	**-271**	**-268**	**-262**	**31**
Official creditors	21	149	91	-155	129	-68	-175	-167	-229	66
Multilateral	8	105	71	-71	-7	-11	-43	-32	-80	47
Concessional	7	92	247	90	147	147	90	92	36	129
Bilateral	13	44	21	-84	136	-57	-132	-135	-149	19
Concessional	13	53	66	-7	252	17	-40	-38	-63	40
Private creditors	-15	152	-12	-294	-129	-151	-96	-101	-33	-35
Bonds	-14	-1	0	0	0	0	0	0	0	0
Commercial banks	0	160	-49	-233	-137	-123	-80	-95	-50	-32
Other private	-1	-6	37	-62	9	-28	-17	-6	17	-3
Private nonguaranteed	**25**	**-40**	**-20**	**-116**	**-127**	**-102**	**-81**	**-71**	**-82**	**-64**
Bonds	0	0	0	0	0	0	0	0	0	0
Commercial banks and other	25	-40	-20	-116	-127	-102	-81	-71	-82	-64
Memo:										
IBRD	2	3	-169	-155	-144	-122	-97	-83	-70	-47
IDA	7	70	223	76	135	131	57	93	39	125
DEBT SERVICE (LTDS)	**46**	**359**	**582**	**827**	**824**	**752**	**571**	**569**	**603**	**397**
Public and publicly guaranteed	**30**	**232**	**507**	**711**	**698**	**650**	**490**	**498**	**521**	**333**
Official creditors	14	84	314	411	437	427	346	361	349	242
Multilateral	2	49	227	231	228	208	185	174	167	141
Concessional	0	2	18	34	35	34	37	40	48	55
Bilateral	13	35	87	180	210	219	161	187	182	101
Concessional	7	13	40	81	94	91	69	73	79	61
Private creditors	16	148	194	300	260	223	144	137	172	92
Bonds	14	1	0	0	0	0	0	0	0	0
Commercial banks	0	55	167	238	209	195	127	109	128	84
Other private	2	91	26	62	52	28	17	29	44	7
Private nonguaranteed	**16**	**127**	**75**	**116**	**127**	**102**	**81**	**71**	**82**	**64**
Bonds	0	0	0	0	0	0	0	0	0	0
Commercial banks and other	16	127	75	116	127	102	81	71	82	64
Memo:										
IBRD	1	42	173	155	144	122	97	83	70	47
IDA	0	2	11	21	24	25	26	30	40	45
UNDISBURSED DEBT	**119**	**1,333**	**1,991**	**1,574**	**1,288**	**1,280**	**1,239**	**1,306**	**1,076**	**940**
Official creditors	119	1,241	1,634	1,409	1,084	1,115	1,117	1,098	973	911
Private creditors	0	92	356	165	203	165	122	208	103	29
Memorandum items										
Concessional LDOD	170	684	2,381	3,394	3,879	3,938	3,762	4,123	4,131	4,089
Variable rate LDOD	88	690	1,090	875	777	703	618	538	415	318
Public sector LDOD	321	2,056	4,762	5,589	5,960	5,685	5,225	5,561	5,323	5,180
Private sector LDOD	88	437	880	530	445	375	325	280	220	175

6. CURRENCY COMPOSITION OF LONG-TERM DEBT (PERCENT)

	1970	1980	1990	1994	1995	1996	1997	1998	1999	2000
Deutsche mark	5.9	9.8	1.7	1.8	2.6	2.8	3.0	3.0	2.8	2.6
French franc	0.0	9.0	6.7	7.0	6.2	5.0	4.8	4.8	3.9	3.7
Japanese yen	0.2	4.6	8.4	16.0	18.3	17.6	16.9	17.8	20.3	19.0
Pound sterling	76.5	14.3	8.7	4.5	3.8	3.8	3.6	4.4	3.5	3.2
Swiss franc	0.0	2.3	3.4	4.7	4.1	3.1	2.9	2.4	1.7	1.4
U.S.dollars	15.7	35.9	30.9	35.1	36.2	39.7	42.1	43.4	46.0	50.8
Multiple currency	1.2	14.9	24.4	15.2	13.4	11.5	10.1	7.4	6.4	5.6
Special drawing rights	0.0	0.0	0.3	0.4	0.4	0.4	0.4	0.4	0.4	0.5
All other currencies	0.5	9.2	15.5	15.3	15.0	16.1	16.2	16.4	15.0	13.2

KENYA

(US$ million, unless otherwise indicated)

	1970	1980	1990	1994	1995	1996	1997	1998	1999	2000
7. DEBT RESTRUCTURINGS										
Total amount rescheduled	..	..	0	550	0	0	0	0	0	199
Debt stock rescheduled	..	..	0	0	0	0	0	0	0	0
Principal rescheduled	..	..	0	367	0	0	0	0	0	160
Official	..	..	0	74	0	0	0	0	0	157
Private	..	..	0	293	0	0	0	0	0	3
Interest rescheduled	..	..	0	162	0	0	0	0	0	39
Official	..	..	0	45	0	0	0	0	0	38
Private	..	..	0	118	0	0	0	0	0	1
Debt forgiven	..	..	84	0	0	0	26	0	0	0
Memo: interest forgiven	..	..	13	0	0	0	0	0	0	0
Debt stock reduction	..	..	0	0	0	0	0	0	0	0
of which debt buyback	..	..	0	0	0	0	0	0	0	0
8. DEBT STOCK-FLOW RECONCILIATION										
Total change in debt stocks	..	..	1,168	91	210	-481	-328	278	-394	-192
Net flows on debt	45	718	615	-322	104	-185	21	-229	-336	99
Net change in interest arrears	..	..	30	-159	-51	-15	18	34	34	-40
Interest capitalized	..	..	0	162	0	0	0	0	0	39
Debt forgiveness or reduction	..	..	-84	0	0	0	-26	0	0	0
Cross-currency valuation	..	..	89	-34	-252	-840	-976	-294	-146	-304
Residual	..	..	518	443	409	558	634	768	54	13
9. AVERAGE TERMS OF NEW COMMITMENTS										
ALL CREDITORS										
Interest (%)	2.5	3.5	4.1	1.9	4.8	1.2	1.7	2.6	5.2	1.2
Maturity (years)	37.3	31.3	25.5	29.5	23.0	34.8	31.7	22.9	17.0	38.1
Grace period (years)	7.9	8.0	7.5	7.0	5.8	8.8	9.2	5.6	3.4	9.7
Grant element (%)	62.6	53.3	46.0	62.7	39.0	70.7	66.9	47.3	27.8	74.8
Official creditors										
Interest (%)	2.4	3.5	3.0	1.9	2.1	0.7	1.6	1.6	0.8	1.2
Maturity (years)	37.9	31.5	29.9	29.5	35.5	37.6	33.3	33.6	49.7	38.1
Grace period (years)	8.0	8.0	8.4	7.0	9.8	9.5	9.7	8.2	10.2	9.7
Grant element (%)	63.7	53.6	57.7	62.7	66.8	76.3	70.1	68.1	83.1	74.8
Private creditors										
Interest (%)	7.0	8.0	7.4	0.0	8.3	6.5	4.3	4.5	7.0	0.0
Maturity (years)	11.2	5.9	13.2	0.0	6.4	5.1	4.1	3.8	3.6	0.0
Grace period (years)	1.7	-0.6	4.9	0.0	0.4	0.9	0.4	1.1	0.6	0.0
Grant element (%)	12.4	5.2	13.5	0.0	2.2	8.6	10.5	10.5	5.0	0.0
Memorandum items										
Commitments	50	518	825	103	389	419	268	357	54	361
Official creditors	49	514	606	103	222	384	254	228	16	361
Private creditors	1	4	219	0	168	35	14	129	38	0

10. CONTRACTUAL OBLIGATIONS ON OUTSTANDING LONG-TERM DEBT

	2001	2002	2003	2004	2005	2006	2007	2008	2009	2010
TOTAL										
Disbursements	277	260	175	99	50	24	13	2	1	0
Principal	520	363	303	206	196	195	201	200	192	198
Interest	122	104	87	77	72	68	67	63	58	54
Official creditors										
Disbursements	261	251	172	98	50	24	13	2	1	0
Principal	330	209	201	175	180	184	189	192	187	193
Interest	88	83	77	72	69	65	65	61	57	53
Bilateral creditors										
Disbursements	77	85	55	34	19	10	4	0	0	0
Principal	230	118	111	94	99	99	107	108	99	97
Interest	55	52	48	45	43	41	41	38	36	33
Multilateral creditors										
Disbursements	184	167	117	64	31	14	9	2	1	0
Principal	100	91	90	81	81	85	82	84	87	96
Interest	33	31	29	28	26	25	23	22	21	20
Private creditors										
Disbursements	16	8	3	2	0	0	0	0	0	0
Principal	190	154	102	31	17	12	12	8	5	5
Interest	34	21	9	5	3	3	2	2	2	1
Commercial banks										
Disbursements	16	8	3	2	0	0	0	0	0	0
Principal	109	78	49	28	15	12	12	8	5	4
Interest	19	12	7	5	3	3	2	2	2	1
Other private										
Disbursements	0	0	0	0	0	0	0	0	0	0
Principal	81	75	53	4	2	0	0	0	0	0
Interest	16	9	3	0	0	0	0	0	0	0

KOREA, REPUBLIC OF

(US$ million, unless otherwise indicated)

	1970	1980	1990	1994	1995	1996	1997	1998	1999	2000
1. SUMMARY DEBT DATA										
Total External Liabilities *	..	..	31,700	97,400	127,500	163,500	159,200	148,700	136,446	136,306
TOTAL DEBT STOCKS (EDT)	**2,580**	**29,480**	**34,968**	**72,414**	**85,810**	**115,803**	**136,984**	**139,097**	**130,316**	**134,417**
Long-term debt (LDOD)	**1,991**	**18,236**	**24,168**	**40,802**	**39,197**	**49,221**	**72,128**	**94,062**	**89,448**	**88,141**
Public and publicly guaranteed	1,816	15,933	18,768	19,253	22,123	25,423	33,852	57,956	57,763	46,941
Private nonguaranteed	175	2,303	5,400	21,550	17,074	23,798	38,276	36,106	31,685	41,200
Use of IMF credit	**0**	**683**	**0**	**0**	**0**	**0**	**11,064**	**16,896**	**6,125**	**5,814**
Short-term debt	**589**	**10,561**	**10,800**	**31,612**	**46,613**	**66,582**	**53,792**	**28,139**	**34,743**	**40,462**
of which interest arrears on LDOD	0	0	0	0	0	0	0	0	0	0
Official creditors	0	0	0	0	0	0	0	0	0	0
Private creditors	0	0	0	0	0	0	0	0	0	0
Memo: principal arrears on LDOD	0	0	0	0	0	0	0	0	0	0
Official creditors	0	0	0	0	0	0	0	0	0	0
Private creditors	0	0	0	0	0	0	0	0	0	0
Memo: export credits	0	0	6,821	4,687	3,247	2,951	4,685	4,073	1,566	1,568
TOTAL DEBT FLOWS										
Disbursements	**476**	**4,605**	**5,719**	**14,131**	**13,610**	**20,133**	**36,345**	**21,255**	**13,433**	**14,210**
Long-term debt	476	3,980	5,719	14,131	13,610	20,133	25,061	13,318	12,937	14,210
IMF purchases	0	625	0	0	0	0	11,284	7,937	496	0
Principal repayments	**218**	**1,586**	**5,678**	**5,222**	**5,905**	**6,802**	**6,781**	**12,412**	**36,141**	**17,403**
Long-term debt	205	1,554	5,678	5,222	5,905	6,802	6,781	9,631	25,338	17,403
IMF repurchases	13	33	0	0	0	0	0	2,781	10,802	0
Net flows on debt	**258**	**6,415**	**1,041**	**28,321**	**22,706**	**33,300**	**16,774**	**7,190**	**-16,104**	**2,526**
of which short-term debt	0	3,396	1,000	19,412	15,001	19,969	-12,790	-1,653	6,604	5,719
Interest payments (INT)	**76**	**2,863**	**2,596**	**3,109**	**5,966**	**6,760**	**6,997**	**8,212**	**6,879**	**5,802**
Long-term debt	76	1,637	1,683	2,262	2,931	2,837	4,110	5,014	4,586	3,998
IMF charges	0	17	0	0	0	0	0	904	722	300
Short-term debt	0	1,210	913	848	3,035	3,923	2,887	2,294	1,572	1,504
Net transfers on debt	**182**	**3,551**	**-1,556**	**25,212**	**16,741**	**26,541**	**9,777**	**-1,022**	**-22,983**	**-3,276**
Total debt service paid (TDS)	**294**	**4,449**	**8,274**	**8,331**	**11,870**	**13,562**	**13,778**	**20,624**	**43,020**	**23,205**
Long-term debt	281	3,190	7,361	7,483	8,835	9,639	10,891	14,645	29,924	21,401
IMF repurchases and charges	13	49	0	0	0	0	0	3,685	11,524	300
Short-term debt (interest only)	0	1,210	913	848	3,035	3,923	2,887	2,294	1,572	1,504
2. AGGREGATE NET RESOURCE FLOWS AND NET TRANSFERS (LONG-TERM)										
NET RESOURCE FLOWS	**411**	**2,440**	**1,351**	**12,244**	**13,045**	**19,359**	**22,383**	**13,199**	**9,361**	**13,875**
Net flow of long-term debt (ex. IMF)	271	2,426	41	8,909	7,705	13,331	18,280	3,687	-12,401	-3,193
Foreign direct investment (net)	66	6	788	810	1,776	2,326	2,844	5,412	9,333	9,283
Portfolio equity flows	0	0	518	2,525	3,559	3,700	1,257	4,096	12,426	7,784
Grants (excluding technical coop.)	75	8	4	0	5	2	2	4	2	0
Memo: technical coop. grants	13	34	101	115	144	145	105	147	156	0
official net resource flows	221	658	313	-629	-625	-517	4,531	5,557	3,349	660
private net resource flows	190	1,782	1,038	12,873	13,670	19,876	17,852	7,641	6,012	13,215
NET TRANSFERS	**330**	**739**	**-598**	**9,713**	**9,819**	**16,202**	**17,922**	**7,810**	**4,207**	**9,177**
Interest on long-term debt	76	1,637	1,683	2,262	2,931	2,837	4,110	5,014	4,586	3,998
Profit remittances on FDI	5	64	266	270	295	320	350	375	568	700
Memo: official net transfers	207	289	-220	-1,056	-990	-826	4,216	4,947	2,622	-280
private net transfers	124	450	-378	10,769	10,810	17,028	13,707	2,862	1,585	9,456
3. MAJOR ECONOMIC AGGREGATES										
Gross national income (GNI)	8,770	61,699	252,534	402,036	487,955	518,392	474,032	311,442	400,910	455,019
Exports of goods & services (XGS)	..	22,050	76,679	114,850	151,237	157,229	168,928	160,451	174,991	212,083
of which workers remittances	..	86	488	245	291	183	129	90	54	63
Imports of goods & services (MGS)	..	27,812	79,343	119,753	159,670	180,006	177,633	123,349	152,376	201,296
International reserves (RES)	610	3,101	14,916	25,764	32,804	34,158	20,465	52,100	74,114	96,251
Current account balance	..	-5,312	-2,003	-3,867	-8,507	-23,006	-8,167	40,365	24,477	11,405
4. DEBT INDICATORS										
EDT / XGS (%)	..	133.7	45.6	63.1	56.7	73.7	81.1	86.7	74.5	63.4
EDT / GNI (%)	29.4	47.8	13.9	18.0	17.6	22.3	28.9	44.7	32.5	29.5
TDS / XGS (%)	..	20.2	10.8	7.3	7.9	8.6	8.2	12.9	24.6	10.9
INT / XGS (%)	..	13.0	3.4	2.7	3.9	4.3	4.1	5.1	3.9	2.7
INT / GNI (%)	0.9	4.6	1.0	0.8	1.2	1.3	1.5	2.6	1.7	1.3
RES / EDT (%)	23.7	10.5	42.7	35.6	38.2	29.5	14.9	37.5	56.9	71.6
RES / MGS (months)	..	1.3	2.3	2.6	2.5	2.3	1.4	5.1	5.8	5.7
Short-term / EDT (%)	22.8	35.8	30.9	43.7	54.3	57.5	39.3	20.2	26.7	30.1
Concessional / EDT (%)	20.4	9.5	12.6	2.4	1.8	1.1	0.8	0.1	1.3	1.1
Multilateral / EDT (%)	1.8	8.0	10.9	4.3	3.3	2.0	5.1	8.3	9.5	9.0

* Total external liabilities include external debt (as per DRS) definition and debt contracted by overseas branches of domestic financial institutions.

KOREA, REPUBLIC OF

(US$ million, unless otherwise indicated)

	1970	1980	1990	1994	1995	1996	1997	1998	1999	2000
5. LONG-TERM DEBT										
DEBT OUTSTANDING (LDOD)	**1,991**	**18,236**	**24,168**	**40,802**	**39,197**	**49,221**	**72,128**	**94,062**	**89,448**	**88,141**
Public and publicly guaranteed	**1,816**	**15,933**	**18,768**	**19,253**	**22,123**	**25,423**	**33,852**	**57,956**	**57,763**	**46,941**
Official creditors	588	6,332	9,262	5,863	5,350	4,563	8,867	12,750	16,500	15,902
Multilateral	46	2,361	3,794	3,100	2,844	2,363	6,923	11,595	12,434	12,078
Concessional	27	113	98	85	82	79	75	72	68	65
Bilateral	542	3,970	5,468	2,763	2,505	2,200	1,944	1,155	4,066	3,824
Concessional	500	2,675	4,309	1,644	1,422	1,200	1,039	0	1,642	1,421
Private creditors	1,228	9,601	9,507	13,390	16,774	20,860	24,985	45,206	41,263	31,039
Bonds	0	291	2,546	7,200	10,753	15,110	21,086	24,454	24,286	21,754
Commercial banks	27	4,213	2,634	4,451	4,520	4,622	3,084	20,752	16,849	9,207
Other private	1,201	5,098	4,327	1,740	1,501	1,129	816	0	129	78
Private nonguaranteed	**175**	**2,303**	**5,400**	**21,550**	**17,074**	**23,798**	**38,276**	**36,106**	**31,685**	**41,200**
Bonds	0	0	490	15,325	10,500	15,848	18,555	20,106	19,495	21,995
Commercial banks and other	175	2,303	4,910	6,225	6,574	7,950	19,721	16,000	12,190	19,205
Memo:										
IBRD	10	1,723	3,240	2,380	2,163	1,841	4,505	7,463	8,290	8,032
IDA	27	113	98	85	82	79	75	72	68	65
DISBURSEMENTS	**476**	**3,980**	**5,719**	**14,131**	**13,610**	**20,133**	**25,061**	**13,318**	**12,937**	**14,210**
Public and publicly guaranteed	**444**	**3,429**	**4,190**	**4,084**	**5,165**	**7,120**	**14,769**	**12,578**	**10,744**	**3,276**
Official creditors	154	916	1,357	396	199	222	5,161	5,872	4,522	1,508
Multilateral	13	344	233	295	150	211	5,161	4,844	1,067	37
Concessional	1	0	0	0	0	0	0	0	0	0
Bilateral	141	572	1,124	101	48	11	0	1,028	3,455	1,472
Concessional	122	178	1,066	1	1	0	0	0	1,544	259
Private creditors	290	2,513	2,833	3,687	4,966	6,899	9,608	6,706	6,223	1,768
Bonds	0	44	964	2,854	4,453	6,229	8,214	5,656	2,665	1,472
Commercial banks	27	1,222	590	834	513	670	1,394	1,050	3,427	241
Other private	264	1,247	1,279	0	0	0	0	0	131	55
Private nonguaranteed	**32**	**551**	**1,529**	**10,047**	**8,445**	**13,013**	**10,292**	**739**	**2,193**	**10,934**
Bonds	0	0	410	8,000	4,990	9,448	6,242	739	1,213	3,394
Commercial banks and other	32	551	1,119	2,047	3,455	3,565	4,050	0	980	7,540
Memo:										
IBRD	7	254	145	282	144	210	3,161	3,144	1,062	35
IDA	1	0	0	0	0	0	0	0	0	0
PRINCIPAL REPAYMENTS	**205**	**1,554**	**5,678**	**5,222**	**5,905**	**6,802**	**6,781**	**9,631**	**25,338**	**17,403**
Public and publicly guaranteed	**198**	**1,490**	**3,589**	**2,522**	**2,974**	**3,820**	**2,780**	**2,819**	**18,720**	**14,259**
Official creditors	7	266	1,049	1,025	828	740	632	318	1,175	849
Multilateral	0	111	652	631	505	483	428	295	242	267
Concessional	0	1	2	4	4	4	4	4	4	4
Bilateral	7	155	397	394	323	257	204	24	933	581
Concessional	2	80	246	249	232	166	117	19	29	329
Private creditors	192	1,224	2,540	1,496	2,146	3,080	2,148	2,500	17,545	13,411
Bonds	0	0	1,223	601	905	996	1,258	1,964	3,809	3,169
Commercial banks	0	301	619	556	912	1,802	692	533	13,735	10,136
Other private	192	923	698	339	329	283	198	4	1	105
Private nonguaranteed	**7**	**64**	**2,090**	**2,700**	**2,931**	**2,982**	**4,001**	**6,812**	**6,618**	**3,144**
Bonds	0	0	0	1,000	1,290	1,826	2,745	3,212	1,828	364
Commercial banks and other	7	64	2,090	1,700	1,641	1,155	1,256	3,600	4,790	2,780
Memo:										
IBRD	0	66	547	588	460	386	363	269	219	223
IDA	0	1	2	4	4	4	4	4	4	4
NET FLOWS ON DEBT	**271**	**2,426**	**41**	**8,909**	**7,705**	**13,331**	**18,280**	**3,687**	**-12,401**	**-3,193**
Public and publicly guaranteed	**246**	**1,940**	**601**	**1,562**	**2,191**	**3,300**	**11,989**	**9,760**	**-7,976**	**-10,983**
Official creditors	147	650	308	-629	-629	-519	4,529	5,554	3,346	660
Multilateral	13	233	-418	-336	-355	-272	4,733	4,550	825	-231
Concessional	1	-1	-2	-4	-4	-4	-4	-4	-4	-4
Bilateral	134	417	727	-293	-274	-247	-204	1,004	2,522	890
Concessional	121	98	821	-248	-231	-166	-117	-19	1,515	-70
Private creditors	99	1,289	293	2,191	2,821	3,819	7,460	4,206	-11,322	-11,643
Bonds	0	44	-260	2,252	3,548	5,234	6,957	3,692	-1,144	-1,698
Commercial banks	27	921	-28	278	-399	-1,132	702	517	-10,308	-9,895
Other private	72	325	580	-339	-329	-283	-198	-4	130	-50
Private nonguaranteed	**25**	**487**	**-561**	**7,347**	**5,514**	**10,032**	**6,291**	**-6,073**	**-4,425**	**7,790**
Bonds	0	0	410	7,000	3,700	7,622	3,497	-2,473	-615	3,030
Commercial banks and other	25	487	-971	347	1,814	2,410	2,794	-3,600	-3,810	4,760
Memo:										
IBRD	7	188	-402	-306	-317	-176	2,798	2,875	844	-188
IDA	1	-1	-2	-4	-4	-4	-4	-4	-4	-4

KOREA, REPUBLIC OF

(US$ million, unless otherwise indicated)

	1970	1980	1990	1994	1995	1996	1997	1998	1999	2000
INTEREST PAYMENTS (LINT)	**76**	**1,637**	**1,683**	**2,262**	**2,931**	**2,837**	**4,110**	**5,014**	**4,586**	**3,998**
Public and publicly guaranteed	**71**	**1,293**	**1,177**	**1,149**	**1,298**	**1,275**	**1,814**	**3,317**	**4,280**	**3,374**
Official creditors	15	369	533	427	366	309	316	610	727	939
Multilateral	1	193	303	233	219	179	200	597	696	851
Concessional	0	1	1	1	1	1	1	1	1	1
Bilateral	14	175	230	194	147	130	116	13	31	88
Concessional	12	86	128	95	52	41	35	1	9	32
Private creditors	56	925	644	722	932	966	1,499	2,707	3,553	2,435
Bonds	0	14	185	338	487	636	1,265	1,815	1,890	1,735
Commercial banks	0	516	218	223	298	215	150	892	1,659	693
Other private	56	394	241	161	147	115	84	0	4	7
Private nonguaranteed	**5**	**343**	**507**	**1,113**	**1,633**	**1,562**	**2,296**	**1,697**	**306**	**624**
Bonds	0	0	5	706	1,267	1,237	1,911	1,531	197	196
Commercial banks and other	5	343	502	407	366	325	385	167	109	428
Memo:										
IBRD	0	145	262	185	170	141	172	417	458	570
IDA	0	1	1	1	1	1	1	1	1	1
NET TRANSFERS ON DEBT	**195**	**790**	**-1,643**	**6,648**	**4,775**	**10,494**	**14,169**	**-1,327**	**-16,986**	**-7,191**
Public and publicly guaranteed	**175**	**646**	**-576**	**413**	**894**	**2,025**	**10,175**	**6,443**	**-12,256**	**-14,357**
Official creditors	132	281	-224	-1,056	-995	-828	4,214	4,944	2,620	-280
Multilateral	12	40	-721	-569	-574	-452	4,533	3,953	128	-1,082
Concessional	1	-2	-3	-4	-4	-4	-4	-4	-4	-4
Bilateral	120	242	497	-487	-421	-376	-319	991	2,491	803
Concessional	109	12	693	-343	-283	-208	-152	-20	1,506	-101
Private creditors	43	365	-351	1,469	1,889	2,853	5,961	1,499	-14,875	-14,077
Bonds	0	30	-445	1,914	3,062	4,598	5,692	1,878	-3,034	-3,432
Commercial banks	27	404	-246	55	-697	-1,347	551	-375	-11,967	-10,588
Other private	16	-69	339	-500	-476	-398	-282	-4	126	-57
Private nonguaranteed	**20**	**144**	**-1,067**	**6,235**	**3,881**	**8,469**	**3,995**	**-7,770**	**-4,731**	**7,166**
Bonds	0	0	405	6,294	2,433	6,385	1,586	-4,003	-812	2,835
Commercial banks and other	20	144	-1,472	-59	1,448	2,084	2,409	-3,767	-3,919	4,332
Memo:										
IBRD	7	43	-664	-491	-486	-317	2,626	2,458	385	-757
IDA	1	-2	-3	-4	-4	-4	-4	-4	-4	-4
DEBT SERVICE (LTDS)	**281**	**3,190**	**7,361**	**7,483**	**8,835**	**9,639**	**10,891**	**14,645**	**29,924**	**21,401**
Public and publicly guaranteed	**269**	**2,783**	**4,765**	**3,670**	**4,271**	**5,095**	**4,594**	**6,135**	**23,000**	**17,633**
Official creditors	22	635	1,581	1,452	1,194	1,050	947	928	1,902	1,788
Multilateral	1	305	954	864	725	663	628	892	939	1,119
Concessional	0	2	3	4	4	4	4	4	4	4
Bilateral	21	330	627	588	469	387	319	37	963	669
Concessional	13	167	373	344	284	208	152	20	38	360
Private creditors	248	2,148	3,184	2,218	3,077	4,046	3,647	5,207	21,098	15,845
Bonds	0	14	1,409	939	1,392	1,631	2,522	3,778	5,699	4,904
Commercial banks	0	817	836	779	1,210	2,017	842	1,425	15,394	10,829
Other private	248	1,317	939	500	476	398	282	4	5	112
Private nonguaranteed	**12**	**407**	**2,596**	**3,813**	**4,564**	**4,544**	**6,297**	**8,509**	**6,924**	**3,768**
Bonds	0	0	5	1,706	2,557	3,063	4,656	4,743	2,025	560
Commercial banks and other	12	407	2,591	2,107	2,007	1,481	1,641	3,767	4,899	3,208
Memo:										
IBRD	0	211	809	773	630	527	535	686	677	792
IDA	0	2	3	4	4	4	4	4	4	4
UNDISBURSED DEBT	**887**	**6,731**	**2,287**	**3,125**	**2,803**	**2,554**	**4,597**	**3,710**	**7,476**	**5,689**
Official creditors	370	3,908	1,824	808	759	530	2,374	1,612	5,959	4,442
Private creditors	517	2,823	463	2,317	2,044	2,024	2,223	2,099	1,518	1,247
Memorandum items										
Concessional LDOD	527	2,789	4,407	1,730	1,504	1,278	1,114	72	1,710	1,485
Variable rate LDOD	196	6,641	9,492	26,626	22,236	29,196	48,562	67,509	61,707	63,600
Public sector LDOD	810	9,770	16,134	18,160	20,833	23,106	33,378	40,725	44,879	41,483
Private sector LDOD	1,180	8,466	8,035	22,642	18,364	26,115	38,750	53,337	44,569	46,658

6. CURRENCY COMPOSITION OF LONG-TERM DEBT (PERCENT)

	1970	1980	1990	1994	1995	1996	1997	1998	1999	2000
Deutsche mark	7.2	3.7	4.7	5.7	5.9	3.3	4.5	2.5	1.6	1.3
French franc	2.1	2.4	8.0	5.0	4.0	3.9	2.3	0.5	0.4	0.5
Japanese yen	5.1	16.6	31.5	34.1	38.2	32.4	22.9	17.6	21.8	21.1
Pound sterling	1.4	3.3	0.7	0.2	0.2	0.1	1.8	1.0	0.5	0.1
Swiss franc	0.4	1.9	1.1	0.5	0.4	0.9	0.6	0.3	0.2	0.3
U.S.dollars	82.1	53.5	33.0	38.5	38.5	47.8	59.9	73.7	71.8	73.0
Multiple currency	1.2	12.9	18.8	15.0	12.0	8.8	5.4	3.1	2.8	2.7
Special drawing rights	0.0	0.0	0.0	0.0	0.0	0.0	0.0	0.0	0.0	0.0
All other currencies	0.5	5.7	2.2	1.0	0.8	2.8	2.6	1.3	0.9	1.0

KOREA, REPUBLIC OF

(US$ million, unless otherwise indicated)

	1970	1980	1990	1994	1995	1996	1997	1998	1999	2000
7. DEBT RESTRUCTURINGS										
Total amount rescheduled	..	..	0	0	0	0	0	21,736	114	0
Debt stock rescheduled	..	..	0	0	0	0	0	24,000	257	0
Principal rescheduled	..	..	0	0	0	0	0	0	0	0
Official	..	..	0	0	0	0	0	0	0	0
Private	..	..	0	0	0	0	0	0	0	0
Interest rescheduled	..	..	0	0	0	0	0	0	0	0
Official	..	..	0	0	0	0	0	0	0	0
Private	..	..	0	0	0	0	0	0	0	0
Debt forgiven	..	..	0	0	0	0	0	0	0	0
Memo: interest forgiven	..	..	0	0	0	0	0	0	0	0
Debt stock reduction	..	..	0	0	0	0	0	0	63	0
of which debt buyback	..	..	0	0	0	0	0	0	63	0
8. DEBT STOCK-FLOW RECONCILIATION										
Total change in debt stocks	..	..	2,170	25,213	13,396	29,993	21,181	2,113	-8,781	4,101
Net flows on debt	258	6,415	1,041	28,321	22,706	33,300	16,774	7,190	-16,104	2,526
Net change in interest arrears	..	..	0	0	0	0	0	0	0	0
Interest capitalized	..	..	0	0	0	0	0	0	0	0
Debt forgiveness or reduction	..	..	0	0	0	0	0	0	0	0
Cross-currency valuation	..	..	883	1,274	-89	-1,490	-1,480	1,694	636	-1,963
Residual	..	..	247	-4,382	-9,221	-1,818	5,888	-6,771	6,687	3,538
9. AVERAGE TERMS OF NEW COMMITMENTS										
ALL CREDITORS										
Interest (%)	5.8	11.3	7.9	5.7	4.4	5.7	6.2	7.5	2.8	5.6
Maturity (years)	19.1	15.3	17.7	10.9	6.1	12.4	11.6	9.0	6.7	4.6
Grace period (years)	5.8	3.9	5.3	6.6	5.8	12.3	6.1	5.6	2.3	4.5
Grant element (%)	27.7	-3.6	13.2	20.5	23.0	20.7	17.7	11.5	24.8	15.3
Official creditors										
Interest (%)	4.5	7.4	6.2	6.5	7.1	0.0	6.4	5.4	1.8	0.0
Maturity (years)	28.0	20.4	23.6	15.0	14.8	0.0	18.7	12.3	7.9	0.0
Grace period (years)	7.7	6.0	7.0	5.5	5.3	0.0	5.9	4.8	2.0	0.0
Grant element (%)	43.1	16.9	26.9	20.2	16.2	0.0	21.8	20.4	30.0	0.0
Private creditors										
Interest (%)	6.7	14.1	8.9	5.6	4.3	5.7	6.1	9.1	5.7	5.6
Maturity (years)	12.9	11.7	14.1	10.6	5.8	12.4	6.6	6.4	3.4	4.6
Grace period (years)	4.6	2.4	4.3	6.7	5.8	12.3	6.3	6.2	3.2	4.5
Grant element (%)	17.2	-17.9	5.1	20.6	23.2	20.7	14.7	4.5	10.7	15.3
Memorandum items										
Commitments	691	4,928	3,701	6,305	5,192	6,920	16,911	11,717	11,608	1,500
Official creditors	282	2,027	1,371	480	175	0	7,015	5,135	8,485	0
Private creditors	409	2,901	2,330	5,825	5,017	6,920	9,896	6,582	3,123	1,500

10. CONTRACTUAL OBLIGATIONS ON OUTSTANDING LONG-TERM DEBT

	2001	2002	2003	2004	2005	2006	2007	2008	2009	2010
TOTAL										
Disbursements	2,812	1,487	662	338	139	54	27	0	0	0
Principal	19,137	21,976	14,034	7,323	5,783	6,147	3,554	6,449	1,612	2,457
Interest	3,575	3,026	2,254	1,758	1,441	1,193	985	706	474	386
Official creditors										
Disbursements	1,942	1,282	661	338	139	54	27	0	0	0
Principal	1,056	1,266	2,090	2,705	2,699	2,116	1,861	1,330	610	582
Interest	897	877	874	793	685	577	482	390	333	292
Bilateral creditors										
Disbursements	1,884	1,257	646	332	138	54	27	0	0	0
Principal	840	1,064	1,465	1,445	1,444	872	627	402	1	0
Interest	99	90	98	75	51	26	14	4	0	0
Multilateral creditors										
Disbursements	59	25	15	6	1	0	0	0	0	0
Principal	216	202	625	1,260	1,255	1,244	1,234	928	609	582
Interest	798	787	776	718	634	551	468	385	333	292
Private creditors										
Disbursements	870	205	1	0	0	0	0	0	0	0
Principal	18,081	20,710	11,944	4,618	3,084	4,031	1,693	5,119	1,003	1,875
Interest	2,678	2,149	1,380	965	756	616	503	317	141	94
Commercial banks										
Disbursements	864	203	0	0	0	0	0	0	0	0
Principal	3,197	2,325	2,059	337	421	351	314	238	238	238
Interest	618	431	274	138	117	96	77	60	45	30
Other private										
Disbursements	5	2	1	0	0	0	0	0	0	0
Principal	14,884	18,385	9,885	4,281	2,663	3,679	1,379	4,881	765	1,637
Interest	2,060	1,718	1,106	827	638	519	426	257	96	64

KYRGYZ REPUBLIC

(US$ million, unless otherwise indicated)

	1970	1980	1990	1994	1995	1996	1997	1998	1999	2000
1. SUMMARY DEBT DATA										
TOTAL DEBT STOCKS (EDT)	..	..	..	**446.8**	**615.5**	**1,143.0**	**1,347.0**	**1,511.1**	**1,741.9**	**1,829.1**
Long-term debt (LDOD)	..	..	..	**356.1**	**478.2**	**994.7**	**1,149.1**	**1,307.7**	**1,490.9**	**1,511.8**
Public and publicly guaranteed	..	..	..	356.1	478.2	632.3	756.6	939.9	1,140.5	1,223.6
Private nonguaranteed	..	..	..	0.0	0.0	362.4	392.4	367.8	350.5	288.2
Use of IMF credit	..	..	..	**77.8**	**124.3**	**139.6**	**164.9**	**175.2**	**190.3**	**188.0**
Short-term debt	..	..	..	**12.8**	**13.0**	**8.7**	**33.0**	**28.2**	**60.7**	**129.3**
of which interest arrears on LDOD	..	..	..	12.8	10.8	0.5	0.0	0.0	10.6	10.1
Official creditors	..	..	..	12.8	10.8	0.5	0.0	0.0	10.4	9.0
Private creditors	..	..	..	0.0	0.0	0.0	0.0	0.0	0.2	1.1
Memo: principal arrears on LDOD	..	..	..	11.6	11.0	3.1	1.1	0.0	21.4	28.0
Official creditors	..	..	..	11.6	11.0	3.1	1.1	0.0	18.7	25.1
Private creditors	..	..	..	0.0	0.0	0.0	0.0	0.0	2.7	2.9
Memo: export credits	..	..	..	0.0	17.1	52.3	53.9	87.0	79.6	74.1
TOTAL DEBT FLOWS										
Disbursements	..	..	..	**131.6**	**207.2**	**199.8**	**209.1**	**178.9**	**244.7**	**175.8**
Long-term debt	..	..	..	118.1	161.2	176.3	164.7	164.3	217.8	156.9
IMF purchases	..	..	..	13.5	46.0	23.4	44.4	14.6	26.8	18.9
Principal repayments	..	..	..	**0.0**	**36.3**	**36.2**	**19.5**	**52.8**	**58.3**	**97.3**
Long-term debt	..	..	..	0.0	36.3	32.4	9.7	41.2	50.9	85.8
IMF repurchases	..	..	..	0.0	0.0	3.9	9.8	11.6	7.4	11.5
Net flows on debt	..	..	..	**131.6**	**173.0**	**169.5**	**214.4**	**121.3**	**208.3**	**147.6**
of which short-term debt	..	..	..	0.0	2.2	6.0	24.8	-4.8	21.9	69.1
Interest payments (INT)	..	..	..	**16.4**	**23.5**	**38.0**	**58.3**	**62.0**	**51.9**	**75.9**
Long-term debt	..	..	..	13.1	19.7	34.5	54.2	57.7	46.8	69.1
IMF charges	..	..	..	3.3	3.7	3.1	3.0	2.6	2.1	2.1
Short-term debt	..	..	..	0.0	0.1	0.4	1.1	1.7	3.0	4.7
Net transfers on debt	..	..	..	**115.2**	**149.5**	**131.5**	**156.1**	**59.3**	**156.4**	**71.7**
Total debt service paid (TDS)	..	..	..	**16.4**	**59.9**	**74.2**	**77.8**	**114.8**	**110.2**	**173.2**
Long-term debt	..	..	..	13.1	56.0	66.9	63.9	98.9	97.7	155.0
IMF repurchases and charges	..	..	..	3.3	3.7	7.0	12.8	14.2	9.4	13.5
Short-term debt (interest only)	..	..	..	0.0	0.1	0.4	1.1	1.7	3.0	4.7
2. AGGREGATE NET RESOURCE FLOWS AND NET TRANSFERS (LONG-TERM)										
NET RESOURCE FLOWS	..	..	..	**228.5**	**274.8**	**236.1**	**284.2**	**280.1**	**260.9**	**112.2**
Net flow of long-term debt (ex. IMF)	..	..	..	118.1	124.8	144.0	155.0	123.1	166.9	71.1
Foreign direct investment (net)	..	..	..	38.2	96.1	47.2	84.0	109.0	44.4	-2.4
Portfolio equity flows	..	..	..	0.0	0.0	0.0	0.0	0.0	0.0	0.0
Grants (excluding technical coop.)	..	..	..	72.2	53.9	44.9	45.2	48.0	49.6	43.5
Memo: technical coop. grants	..	..	..	10.3	28.6	42.7	26.1	42.7	42.3	37.6
official net resource flows	..	..	..	190.3	178.7	181.9	177.2	191.9	229.6	176.7
private net resource flows	..	..	..	38.2	96.1	54.2	107.0	88.2	31.3	-64.5
NET TRANSFERS	..	..	..	**215.4**	**255.1**	**201.7**	**230.0**	**222.3**	**214.1**	**33.1**
Interest on long-term debt	..	..	..	13.1	19.7	34.5	54.2	57.7	46.8	69.1
Profit remittances on FDI	..	..	..	0.0	0.0	0.0	0.0	0.0	0.0	10.0
Memo: official net transfers	..	..	..	177.2	159.0	171.1	158.6	170.3	215.8	156.4
private net transfers	..	..	..	38.2	96.1	30.6	71.4	52.0	-1.7	-123.3
3. MAJOR ECONOMIC AGGREGATES										
Gross national income (GNI)	..	..	..	3,133.8	3,245.8	3,816.4	1,703.2	1,566.8	1,175.1	1,223.4
Exports of goods & services (XGS)	..	..	..	373.6	453.1	569.2	684.9	611.8	538.7	591.8
of which workers remittances	..	..	..	1.0	1.2	2.4	2.7	2.2	1.1	2.2
Imports of goods & services (MGS)	..	..	..	519.6	765.2	1,075.4	888.1	1,022.2	785.3	747.9
International reserves (RES)	..	..	..	26.2	81.0	94.6	169.8	187.7	253.8	261.8
Current account balance	..	..	..	-84.4	-234.7	-424.7	-138.4	-363.9	-179.8	-76.5
4. DEBT INDICATORS										
EDT / XGS (%)	..	..	..	119.6	135.9	200.8	196.7	247.0	323.4	309.1
EDT / GNI (%)	..	..	..	14.3	19.0	30.0	79.1	96.4	148.2	149.5
TDS / XGS (%)	..	..	..	4.4	13.2	13.0	11.4	18.8	20.5	29.3
INT / XGS (%)	..	..	..	4.4	5.2	6.7	8.5	10.1	9.6	12.8
INT / GNI (%)	..	..	..	0.5	0.7	1.0	3.4	4.0	4.4	6.2
RES / EDT (%)	..	..	..	5.9	13.2	8.3	12.6	12.4	14.6	14.3
RES / MGS (months)	..	..	..	0.6	1.3	1.1	2.3	2.2	3.9	4.2
Short-term / EDT (%)	..	..	..	2.9	2.1	0.8	2.5	1.9	3.5	7.1
Concessional / EDT (%)	..	..	..	51.6	60.6	32.7	34.9	42.2	46.3	48.3
Multilateral / EDT (%)	..	..	..	20.3	30.0	25.3	29.3	35.5	37.7	39.3

KYRGYZ REPUBLIC

(US$ million, unless otherwise indicated)

	1970	1980	1990	1994	1995	1996	1997	1998	1999	2000
5. LONG-TERM DEBT										
DEBT OUTSTANDING (LDOD)	..	..	..	**356.1**	**478.2**	**994.7**	**1,149.1**	**1,307.7**	**1,490.9**	**1,511.8**
Public and publicly guaranteed	..	..	..	**356.1**	**478.2**	**632.3**	**756.6**	**939.9**	**1,140.5**	**1,223.6**
Official creditors	..	..	..	356.1	478.2	625.3	726.6	907.2	1,103.7	1,186.9
Multilateral	..	..	..	90.8	184.5	288.7	394.0	536.8	657.0	719.4
Concessional	..	..	..	60.4	173.6	256.1	358.0	493.5	584.8	644.5
Bilateral	..	..	..	265.3	293.7	336.6	332.6	370.5	446.6	467.5
Concessional	..	..	..	170.2	199.2	117.7	112.3	143.8	222.0	238.6
Private creditors	..	..	..	0.0	0.0	7.0	30.0	32.7	36.8	36.7
Bonds	..	..	..	0.0	0.0	0.0	0.0	0.0	0.0	0.0
Commercial banks	..	..	..	0.0	0.0	7.0	30.0	32.7	35.1	36.5
Other private	..	..	..	0.0	0.0	0.0	0.0	0.0	1.7	0.2
Private nonguaranteed	..	..	..	**0.0**	**0.0**	**362.4**	**392.4**	**367.8**	**350.5**	**288.2**
Bonds	..	..	..	0.0	0.0	0.0	0.0	0.0	0.0	0.0
Commercial banks and other	..	..	..	0.0	0.0	362.4	392.4	367.8	350.5	288.2
Memo:										
IBRD	..	..	..	0.0	0.0	0.0	0.0	0.0	0.0	0.0
IDA	..	..	..	60.4	141.2	196.8	251.1	328.0	342.4	376.8
DISBURSEMENTS	..	..	..	**118.1**	**161.2**	**176.3**	**164.7**	**164.3**	**217.8**	**156.9**
Public and publicly guaranteed	..	..	..	**118.1**	**161.2**	**176.3**	**164.7**	**163.2**	**185.8**	**150.4**
Official creditors	..	..	..	118.1	161.2	169.3	141.7	160.5	181.4	146.4
Multilateral	..	..	..	35.7	124.3	110.8	125.3	123.3	119.5	104.9
Concessional	..	..	..	35.7	115.3	89.1	119.2	112.3	90.2	94.4
Bilateral	..	..	..	82.4	36.9	58.5	16.4	37.2	61.8	41.6
Concessional	..	..	..	51.6	32.2	46.1	5.9	21.6	61.0	41.6
Private creditors	..	..	..	0.0	0.0	7.0	23.0	2.7	4.5	3.9
Bonds	..	..	..	0.0	0.0	0.0	0.0	0.0	0.0	0.0
Commercial banks	..	..	..	0.0	0.0	7.0	23.0	2.7	2.5	3.9
Other private	..	..	..	0.0	0.0	0.0	0.0	0.0	2.0	0.0
Private nonguaranteed	..	..	..	**0.0**	**0.0**	**0.0**	**0.0**	**1.1**	**32.0**	**6.5**
Bonds	..	..	..	0.0	0.0	0.0	0.0	0.0	0.0	0.0
Commercial banks and other	..	..	..	0.0	0.0	0.0	0.0	1.1	32.0	6.5
Memo:										
IBRD	..	..	..	0.0	0.0	0.0	0.0	0.0	0.0	0.0
IDA	..	..	..	35.7	81.3	61.2	66.5	65.5	21.6	51.7
PRINCIPAL REPAYMENTS	..	..	..	**0.0**	**36.3**	**32.4**	**9.7**	**41.2**	**50.9**	**85.8**
Public and publicly guaranteed	..	..	..	**0.0**	**36.3**	**32.4**	**9.7**	**16.5**	**1.6**	**17.1**
Official creditors	..	..	..	0.0	36.3	32.4	9.7	16.5	1.4	13.2
Multilateral	..	..	..	0.0	30.4	0.0	0.9	3.9	0.6	7.9
Concessional	..	..	..	0.0	0.0	0.0	0.1	0.2	0.1	0.1
Bilateral	..	..	..	0.0	5.9	32.4	8.8	12.6	0.7	5.3
Concessional	..	..	..	0.0	0.2	0.7	0.6	2.9	0.0	1.4
Private creditors	..	..	..	0.0	0.0	0.0	0.0	0.0	0.2	3.9
Bonds	..	..	..	0.0	0.0	0.0	0.0	0.0	0.0	0.0
Commercial banks	..	..	..	0.0	0.0	0.0	0.0	0.0	0.0	2.3
Other private	..	..	..	0.0	0.0	0.0	0.0	0.0	0.2	1.5
Private nonguaranteed	..	..	..	**0.0**	**0.0**	**0.0**	**0.0**	**24.7**	**49.3**	**68.8**
Bonds	..	..	..	0.0	0.0	0.0	0.0	0.0	0.0	0.0
Commercial banks and other	..	..	..	0.0	0.0	0.0	0.0	24.7	49.3	68.8
Memo:										
IBRD	..	..	..	0.0	0.0	0.0	0.0	0.0	0.0	0.0
IDA	..	..	..	0.0	0.0	0.0	0.0	0.0	0.0	0.0
NET FLOWS ON DEBT	..	..	..	**118.1**	**124.8**	**144.0**	**155.0**	**123.1**	**166.9**	**71.1**
Public and publicly guaranteed	..	..	..	**118.1**	**124.8**	**144.0**	**155.0**	**146.6**	**184.2**	**133.3**
Official creditors	..	..	..	118.1	124.8	137.0	132.0	143.9	180.0	133.2
Multilateral	..	..	..	35.7	93.9	110.8	124.4	119.4	118.9	97.0
Concessional	..	..	..	35.7	115.3	89.1	119.1	112.1	90.0	94.3
Bilateral	..	..	..	82.4	31.0	26.1	7.7	24.6	61.1	36.2
Concessional	..	..	..	51.6	32.0	45.4	5.3	18.7	61.0	40.2
Private creditors	..	..	..	0.0	0.0	7.0	23.0	2.7	4.2	0.1
Bonds	..	..	..	0.0	0.0	0.0	0.0	0.0	0.0	0.0
Commercial banks	..	..	..	0.0	0.0	7.0	23.0	2.7	2.5	1.6
Other private	..	..	..	0.0	0.0	0.0	0.0	0.0	1.7	-1.5
Private nonguaranteed	..	..	..	**0.0**	**0.0**	**0.0**	**0.0**	**-23.5**	**-17.3**	**-62.2**
Bonds	..	..	..	0.0	0.0	0.0	0.0	0.0	0.0	0.0
Commercial banks and other	..	..	..	0.0	0.0	0.0	0.0	-23.5	-17.3	-62.2
Memo:										
IBRD	..	..	..	0.0	0.0	0.0	0.0	0.0	0.0	0.0
IDA	..	..	..	35.7	81.3	61.2	66.5	65.5	21.6	51.7

KYRGYZ REPUBLIC

(US$ million, unless otherwise indicated)

	1970	1980	1990	1994	1995	1996	1997	1998	1999	2000
INTEREST PAYMENTS (LINT)	..	..	..	**13.1**	**19.7**	**34.5**	**54.2**	**57.7**	**46.8**	**69.1**
Public and publicly guaranteed	..	..	..	**13.1**	**19.7**	**11.0**	**19.9**	**23.7**	**15.6**	**22.5**
Official creditors	..	..	..	13.1	19.7	10.8	18.6	21.6	13.8	20.3
Multilateral	..	..	..	5.1	2.6	2.6	4.9	7.0	7.3	10.6
Concessional	..	..	..	0.2	0.7	1.5	2.2	3.2	4.5	5.1
Bilateral	..	..	..	8.0	17.1	8.2	13.7	14.6	6.5	9.7
Concessional	..	..	..	1.7	11.0	2.3	3.2	3.3	4.5	5.9
Private creditors	..	..	..	0.0	0.0	0.2	1.3	2.1	1.8	2.2
Bonds	..	..	..	0.0	0.0	0.0	0.0	0.0	0.0	0.0
Commercial banks	..	..	..	0.0	0.0	0.2	1.3	2.1	1.8	2.2
Other private	..	..	..	0.0	0.0	0.0	0.0	0.0	0.0	0.0
Private nonguaranteed	..	..	..	**0.0**	**0.0**	**23.4**	**34.3**	**34.1**	**31.2**	**46.6**
Bonds	..	..	..	0.0	0.0	0.0	0.0	0.0	0.0	0.0
Commercial banks and other	..	..	..	0.0	0.0	23.4	34.3	34.1	31.2	46.6
Memo:										
IBRD	..	..	..	0.0	0.0	0.0	0.0	0.0	0.0	0.0
IDA	..	..	..	0.2	0.6	1.0	1.5	1.9	2.4	2.6
NET TRANSFERS ON DEBT	..	..	..	**105.0**	**105.1**	**109.5**	**100.9**	**65.4**	**120.1**	**1.9**
Public and publicly guaranteed	..	..	..	**105.0**	**105.1**	**132.9**	**135.2**	**123.0**	**168.7**	**110.8**
Official creditors	..	..	..	105.0	105.1	126.1	113.4	122.4	166.2	112.9
Multilateral	..	..	..	30.6	91.2	108.2	119.5	112.3	111.7	86.4
Concessional	..	..	..	35.5	114.6	87.6	116.9	108.9	85.5	89.1
Bilateral	..	..	..	74.4	13.9	17.9	-6.1	10.0	54.6	26.5
Concessional	..	..	..	49.9	21.0	43.1	2.1	15.4	56.5	34.2
Private creditors	..	..	..	0.0	0.0	6.8	21.7	0.6	2.4	-2.1
Bonds	..	..	..	0.0	0.0	0.0	0.0	0.0	0.0	0.0
Commercial banks	..	..	..	0.0	0.0	6.8	21.7	0.6	0.7	-0.6
Other private	..	..	..	0.0	0.0	0.0	0.0	0.0	1.7	-1.5
Private nonguaranteed	..	..	..	**0.0**	**0.0**	**-23.4**	**-34.3**	**-57.6**	**-48.5**	**-108.9**
Bonds	..	..	..	0.0	0.0	0.0	0.0	0.0	0.0	0.0
Commercial banks and other	..	..	..	0.0	0.0	-23.4	-34.3	-57.6	-48.5	-108.9
Memo:										
IBRD	..	..	..	0.0	0.0	0.0	0.0	0.0	0.0	0.0
IDA	..	..	..	35.5	80.7	60.1	65.0	63.6	19.2	49.2
DEBT SERVICE (LTDS)	..	..	..	**13.1**	**56.0**	**66.9**	**63.9**	**98.9**	**97.7**	**155.0**
Public and publicly guaranteed	..	..	..	**13.1**	**56.0**	**43.4**	**29.6**	**40.2**	**17.2**	**39.6**
Official creditors	..	..	..	13.1	56.0	43.2	28.3	38.1	15.1	33.5
Multilateral	..	..	..	5.1	33.0	2.6	5.8	11.0	7.9	18.5
Concessional	..	..	..	0.2	0.7	1.5	2.3	3.4	4.6	5.3
Bilateral	..	..	..	8.0	23.0	40.6	22.5	27.2	7.3	15.0
Concessional	..	..	..	1.7	11.2	3.0	3.8	6.2	4.5	7.3
Private creditors	..	..	..	0.0	0.0	0.2	1.3	2.1	2.0	6.1
Bonds	..	..	..	0.0	0.0	0.0	0.0	0.0	0.0	0.0
Commercial banks	..	..	..	0.0	0.0	0.2	1.3	2.1	1.8	4.6
Other private	..	..	..	0.0	0.0	0.0	0.0	0.0	0.2	1.5
Private nonguaranteed	..	..	..	**0.0**	**0.0**	**23.4**	**34.3**	**58.7**	**80.6**	**115.4**
Bonds	..	..	..	0.0	0.0	0.0	0.0	0.0	0.0	0.0
Commercial banks and other	..	..	..	0.0	0.0	23.4	34.3	58.7	80.6	115.4
Memo:										
IBRD	..	..	..	0.0	0.0	0.0	0.0	0.0	0.0	0.0
IDA	..	..	..	0.2	0.6	1.0	1.5	1.9	2.4	2.6
UNDISBURSED DEBT	..	..	..	**274.9**	**281.8**	**326.9**	**416.4**	**560.9**	**520.1**	**451.7**
Official creditors	..	..	..	274.9	281.8	326.9	416.4	552.1	514.9	450.8
Private creditors	..	..	..	0.0	0.0	0.0	0.0	8.9	5.3	0.9
Memorandum items										
Concessional LDOD	..	..	..	230.5	372.8	373.7	470.4	637.3	806.9	883.1
Variable rate LDOD	..	..	..	224.2	198.9	587.3	644.2	592.5	585.9	523.4
Public sector LDOD	..	..	..	356.1	478.2	632.3	756.6	939.9	1,140.5	1,223.6
Private sector LDOD	..	..	..	0.0	0.0	362.4	392.4	367.8	350.5	288.2

6. CURRENCY COMPOSITION OF LONG-TERM DEBT (PERCENT)

	1970	1980	1990	1994	1995	1996	1997	1998	1999	2000
Deutsche mark	..	..	..	0.4	2.5	2.5	2.5	2.9	2.3	2.0
French franc	..	..	..	0.0	0.0	0.0	0.1	0.5	0.3	0.3
Japanese yen	..	..	..	14.1	14.1	13.4	10.2	11.3	15.0	15.0
Pound sterling	..	..	..	0.0	0.0	0.0	0.0	0.0	0.0	0.0
Swiss franc	..	..	..	1.5	1.2	0.7	0.1	0.0	0.0	0.0
U.S.dollars	..	..	..	44.6	50.8	73.2	74.9	71.3	66.9	67.7
Multiple currency	..	..	..	0.0	6.8	9.1	11.2	13.2	13.0	11.8
Special drawing rights	..	..	..	0.0	0.0	0.0	0.0	0.0	0.1	0.2
All other currencies	..	..	..	39.4	24.6	1.1	1.0	0.8	2.4	3.0

KYRGYZ REPUBLIC

(US$ million, unless otherwise indicated)

	1970	1980	1990	1994	1995	1996	1997	1998	1999	2000
7. DEBT RESTRUCTURINGS										
Total amount rescheduled	..	..	..	0.0	0.0	194.9	3.0	41.0	0.0	32.2
Debt stock rescheduled	..	..	..	0.0	0.0	106.8	2.9	41.4	0.0	0.0
Principal rescheduled	..	..	..	0.0	0.0	59.9	0.0	0.0	0.0	22.1
Official	..	..	..	0.0	0.0	59.9	0.0	0.0	0.0	22.1
Private	..	..	..	0.0	0.0	0.0	0.0	0.0	0.0	0.0
Interest rescheduled	..	..	..	0.0	0.0	27.9	0.0	0.0	0.0	1.0
Official	..	..	..	0.0	0.0	27.9	0.0	0.0	0.0	1.0
Private	..	..	..	0.0	0.0	0.0	0.0	0.0	0.0	0.0
Debt forgiven	..	..	..	0.0	0.0	0.2	0.0	0.0	0.0	0.0
Memo: interest forgiven	..	..	..	0.0	0.0	0.0	0.0	0.0	0.0	0.0
Debt stock reduction	..	..	..	0.0	0.0	0.0	0.0	0.0	0.0	0.0
of which debt buyback	..	..	..	0.0	0.0	0.0	0.0	0.0	0.0	0.0
8. DEBT STOCK-FLOW RECONCILIATION										
Total change in debt stocks	..	..	..	154.7	168.7	527.5	204.0	164.1	230.8	87.1
Net flows on debt	..	..	..	131.6	173.0	169.5	214.4	121.3	208.3	147.6
Net change in interest arrears	..	..	..	12.7	-2.1	-10.3	-0.5	0.0	10.6	-0.6
Interest capitalized	..	..	..	0.0	0.0	27.9	0.0	0.0	0.0	1.0
Debt forgiveness or reduction	..	..	..	0.0	0.0	-0.2	0.0	0.0	0.0	0.0
Cross-currency valuation	..	..	..	-63.7	-23.6	-34.1	-64.3	-9.4	6.4	-66.7
Residual	..	..	..	74.0	21.4	374.8	54.3	52.2	5.5	5.8
9. AVERAGE TERMS OF NEW COMMITMENTS										
ALL CREDITORS										
Interest (%)	..	..	..	2.1	3.7	2.5	3.7	2.1	1.3	0.9
Maturity (years)	..	..	..	34.0	28.9	32.1	24.2	33.6	23.9	36.1
Grace period (years)	..	..	..	10.2	8.1	9.4	6.8	11.6	7.2	9.6
Grant element (%)	..	..	..	67.0	50.4	61.4	45.7	65.9	58.8	77.0
Official creditors										
Interest (%)	..	..	..	2.1	3.7	2.4	3.4	2.0	1.3	0.9
Maturity (years)	..	..	..	34.0	28.9	32.8	25.9	34.7	24.2	36.1
Grace period (years)	..	..	..	10.2	8.1	9.5	7.3	12.0	7.3	9.6
Grant element (%)	..	..	..	67.0	50.4	62.5	49.2	67.7	59.4	77.0
Private creditors										
Interest (%)	..	..	..	0.0	0.0	5.3	7.0	3.7	1.4	0.0
Maturity (years)	..	..	..	0.0	0.0	5.3	5.1	6.4	1.3	0.0
Grace period (years)	..	..	..	0.0	0.0	5.3	0.5	2.3	0.8	0.0
Grant element (%)	..	..	..	0.0	0.0	18.3	6.3	21.7	8.7	0.0
Memorandum items										
Commitments	..	..	..	194.7	163.9	269.1	281.5	284.4	147.3	185.0
Official creditors	..	..	..	194.7	163.9	262.1	258.5	273.2	145.3	185.0
Private creditors	..	..	..	0.0	0.0	7.0	23.0	11.2	2.0	0.0

10. CONTRACTUAL OBLIGATIONS ON OUTSTANDING LONG-TERM DEBT

	2001	2002	2003	2004	2005	2006	2007	2008	2009	2010
TOTAL										
Disbursements	127.2	123.4	86.0	56.2	32.1	16.3	7.4	1.7	1.3	0.0
Principal	139.0	162.6	107.9	88.3	73.0	59.6	56.8	61.2	66.4	42.0
Interest	32.1	29.1	26.5	24.7	23.6	23.8	23.9	23.0	21.4	19.5
Official creditors										
Disbursements	126.3	123.4	86.0	56.2	32.1	16.3	7.4	1.7	1.3	0.0
Principal	55.7	60.9	45.7	51.3	51.7	48.0	52.6	60.3	65.5	42.0
Interest	29.2	27.8	25.8	24.2	23.2	23.5	23.7	22.9	21.4	19.5
Bilateral creditors										
Disbursements	29.6	24.8	15.7	9.7	6.2	1.5	0.3	0.0	0.0	0.0
Principal	43.5	48.7	36.5	36.6	33.5	25.0	24.7	24.7	25.8	11.7
Interest	17.1	15.2	13.2	11.7	10.1	10.1	9.4	8.2	6.9	6.1
Multilateral creditors										
Disbursements	96.7	98.6	70.3	46.5	25.9	14.9	7.1	1.7	1.3	0.0
Principal	12.2	12.2	9.2	14.7	18.2	23.1	27.9	35.6	39.7	30.3
Interest	12.1	12.5	12.6	12.5	13.1	13.4	14.3	14.7	14.5	13.4
Private creditors										
Disbursements	0.9	0.0	0.0	0.0	0.0	0.0	0.0	0.0	0.0	0.0
Principal	83.0	102.0	62.0	37.0	21.0	12.0	4.0	1.0	1.0	0.0
Interest	3.0	1.0	1.0	0.0	0.0	0.0	0.0	0.0	0.0	0.0
Commercial banks										
Disbursements	0.9	0.0	0.0	0.0	0.0	0.0	0.0	0.0	0.0	0.0
Principal	21.3	9.0	1.3	1.3	1.3	0.6	0.0	0.0	0.0	0.0
Interest	1.7	0.4	0.1	0.1	0.0	0.0	0.0	0.0	0.0	0.0
Other private										
Disbursements	0.0	0.0	0.0	0.0	0.0	0.0	0.0	0.0	0.0	0.0
Principal	62.0	93.0	61.0	36.0	20.0	11.0	4.0	1.0	1.0	0.0
Interest	1.0	1.0	1.0	0.0	0.0	0.0	0.0	0.0	0.0	0.0

LAO PEOPLE'S DEMOCRATIC REPUBLIC

(US$ million, unless otherwise indicated)

	1970	1980	1990	1994	1995	1996	1997	1998	1999	2000
1. SUMMARY DEBT DATA										
TOTAL DEBT STOCKS (EDT)	**8**	**350**	**1,768**	**2,080**	**2,165**	**2,263**	**2,320**	**2,437**	**2,527**	**2,499**
Long-term debt (LDOD)	**8**	**333**	**1,758**	**2,022**	**2,091**	**2,186**	**2,247**	**2,373**	**2,471**	**2,449**
Public and publicly guaranteed	8	333	1,758	2,022	2,091	2,186	2,247	2,373	2,471	2,449
Private nonguaranteed	0	0	0	0	0	0	0	0	0	0
Use of IMF credit	**0**	**16**	**8**	**47**	**64**	**67**	**66**	**62**	**53**	**42**
Short-term debt	**0**	**1**	**2**	**11**	**10**	**11**	**7**	**1**	**3**	**7**
of which interest arrears on LDOD	0	1	0	0	0	0	0	0	0	0
Official creditors	0	1	0	0	0	0	0	0	0	0
Private creditors	0	1	0	0	0	0	0	0	0	0
Memo: principal arrears on LDOD	0	4	1	0	0	2	2	1	1	1
Official creditors	0	1	1	0	0	2	2	1	1	1
Private creditors	0	4	0	0	0	0	0	0	0	0
Memo: export credits	0	0	3	5	3	30	58	23	10	12
TOTAL DEBT FLOWS										
Disbursements	**6**	**60**	**152**	**66**	**110**	**198**	**143**	**95**	**81**	**80**
Long-term debt	6	55	152	58	92	189	135	95	81	80
IMF purchases	0	4	0	8	18	9	8	0	0	0
Principal repayments	**1**	**1**	**6**	**15**	**19**	**22**	**20**	**23**	**28**	**32**
Long-term debt	1	1	6	15	18	19	15	16	20	24
IMF repurchases	0	0	1	0	2	3	5	6	8	8
Net flows on debt	**4**	**59**	**147**	**61**	**90**	**176**	**119**	**66**	**54**	**52**
of which short-term debt	0	0	1	10	-1	0	-4	-6	1	4
Interest payments (INT)	**0**	**1**	**3**	**5**	**7**	**7**	**8**	**8**	**9**	**10**
Long-term debt	0	1	3	5	6	6	7	8	9	9
IMF charges	0	0	0	0	0	0	0	0	0	0
Short-term debt	0	0	0	0	1	1	0	0	0	0
Net transfers on debt	**4**	**57**	**144**	**56**	**83**	**169**	**111**	**58**	**45**	**42**
Total debt service paid (TDS)	**2**	**3**	**9**	**20**	**26**	**29**	**28**	**31**	**37**	**42**
Long-term debt	2	2	8	20	23	25	22	24	29	34
IMF repurchases and charges	0	0	1	0	2	3	5	7	8	8
Short-term debt (interest only)	0	0	0	0	1	1	0	0	0	0
2. AGGREGATE NET RESOURCE FLOWS AND NET TRANSFERS (LONG-TERM)										
NET RESOURCE FLOWS	**33**	**70**	**199**	**200**	**300**	**469**	**343**	**243**	**284**	**262**
Net flow of long-term debt (ex. IMF)	4	54	146	43	75	170	120	78	61	55
Foreign direct investment (net)	0	0	6	59	95	160	91	46	79	72
Portfolio equity flows	0	0	0	0	0	0	0	0	0	0
Grants (excluding technical coop.)	28	16	47	98	130	139	132	119	144	135
Memo: technical coop. grants	40	14	30	56	75	75	64	68	75	74
official net resource flows	33	70	193	141	204	309	252	197	205	190
private net resource flows	0	0	6	59	95	160	91	46	79	72
NET TRANSFERS	**32**	**69**	**196**	**195**	**294**	**463**	**335**	**236**	**275**	**253**
Interest on long-term debt	0	1	3	5	6	6	7	8	9	9
Profit remittances on FDI	0	0	0	0	0	0	0	0	0	0
Memo: official net transfers	33	69	190	136	198	303	244	190	196	181
private net transfers	0	0	6	59	95	160	91	46	79	72
3. MAJOR ECONOMIC AGGREGATES										
Gross national income (GNI)	..	..	865	1,542	1,758	1,867	1,704	1,248	1,420	1,670
Exports of goods & services (XGS)	..	..	105	400	415	436	435	494	479	516
of which workers remittances	..	..	0	0	..	..	..	..	..	..
Imports of goods & services (MGS)	..	..	215	680	761	783	741	644	629	677
International reserves (RES)	..	..	8	67	99	176	117	117	135	144
Current account balance	..	..	-55	-160	-237	-265	-206	-77	90	..
4. DEBT INDICATORS										
EDT / XGS (%)	..	..	1,690.3	520.4	521.5	518.7	533.1	493.3	527.8	484.1
EDT / GNI (%)	..	..	204.5	134.9	123.2	121.3	136.1	195.2	177.9	149.6
TDS / XGS (%)	..	..	8.7	5.0	6.3	6.7	6.4	6.3	7.7	8.1
INT / XGS (%)	..	..	3.0	1.3	1.6	1.7	1.8	1.7	2.0	1.9
INT / GNI (%)	..	..	0.4	0.3	0.4	0.4	0.5	0.7	0.7	0.6
RES / EDT (%)	..	..	0.5	3.2	4.6	7.8	5.1	4.8	5.4	5.8
RES / MGS (months)	..	..	0.5	1.2	1.6	2.7	1.9	2.2	2.6	2.5
Short-term / EDT (%)	0.0	0.4	0.1	0.5	0.5	0.5	0.3	0.1	0.1	0.3
Concessional / EDT (%)	90.4	93.3	99.1	97.0	96.4	96.4	96.7	97.3	97.7	98.0
Multilateral / EDT (%)	0.0	5.9	15.1	25.5	28.7	32.7	35.2	39.1	42.1	42.3

LAO PEOPLE'S DEMOCRATIC REPUBLIC

(US$ million, unless otherwise indicated)

	1970	1980	1990	1994	1995	1996	1997	1998	1999	2000
5. LONG-TERM DEBT										
DEBT OUTSTANDING (LDOD)	**8**	**333**	**1,758**	**2,022**	**2,091**	**2,186**	**2,247**	**2,373**	**2,471**	**2,449**
Public and publicly guaranteed	**8**	**333**	**1,758**	**2,022**	**2,091**	**2,186**	**2,247**	**2,373**	**2,471**	**2,449**
Official creditors	8	327	1,758	2,022	2,091	2,186	2,247	2,373	2,471	2,449
Multilateral	0	21	267	529	621	741	816	953	1,064	1,058
Concessional	0	21	267	529	621	741	816	953	1,064	1,058
Bilateral	8	306	1,491	1,493	1,471	1,445	1,431	1,420	1,407	1,392
Concessional	8	306	1,485	1,489	1,466	1,441	1,427	1,417	1,405	1,390
Private creditors	1	6	0	0	0	0	0	0	0	0
Bonds	0	0	0	0	0	0	0	0	0	0
Commercial banks	0	0	0	0	0	0	0	0	0	0
Other private	1	6	0	0	0	0	0	0	0	0
Private nonguaranteed	**0**	**0**	**0**	**0**	**0**	**0**	**0**	**0**	**0**	**0**
Bonds	0	0	0	0	0	0	0	0	0	0
Commercial banks and other	0	0	0	0	0	0	0	0	0	0
Memo:										
IBRD	0	0	0	0	0	0	0	0	0	0
IDA	0	6	131	253	285	335	358	395	405	403
DISBURSEMENTS	**6**	**55**	**152**	**58**	**92**	**189**	**135**	**95**	**81**	**80**
Public and publicly guaranteed	**6**	**55**	**152**	**58**	**92**	**189**	**135**	**95**	**81**	**80**
Official creditors	6	55	152	58	92	189	135	95	81	80
Multilateral	0	7	78	58	92	189	135	95	81	80
Concessional	0	7	78	58	92	189	135	95	81	80
Bilateral	6	48	74	0	0	0	0	0	0	0
Concessional	6	48	74	0	0	0	0	0	0	0
Private creditors	0	0	0	0	0	0	0	0	0	0
Bonds	0	0	0	0	0	0	0	0	0	0
Commercial banks	0	0	0	0	0	0	0	0	0	0
Other private	0	0	0	0	0	0	0	0	0	0
Private nonguaranteed	**0**	**0**	**0**	**0**	**0**	**0**	**0**	**0**	**0**	**0**
Bonds	0	0	0	0	0	0	0	0	0	0
Commercial banks and other	0	0	0	0	0	0	0	0	0	0
Memo:										
IBRD	0	0	0	0	0	0	0	0	0	0
IDA	0	5	32	27	28	60	42	25	21	20
PRINCIPAL REPAYMENTS	**1**	**1**	**6**	**15**	**18**	**19**	**15**	**16**	**20**	**24**
Public and publicly guaranteed	**1**	**1**	**6**	**15**	**18**	**19**	**15**	**16**	**20**	**24**
Official creditors	1	1	6	15	18	19	15	16	20	24
Multilateral	0	0	3	3	4	3	3	5	6	11
Concessional	0	0	3	3	4	3	3	5	6	11
Bilateral	1	1	3	12	14	16	12	12	14	14
Concessional	1	1	2	11	13	16	11	11	13	13
Private creditors	0	0	0	0	0	0	0	0	0	0
Bonds	0	0	0	0	0	0	0	0	0	0
Commercial banks	0	0	0	0	0	0	0	0	0	0
Other private	0	0	0	0	0	0	0	0	0	0
Private nonguaranteed	**0**	**0**	**0**	**0**	**0**	**0**	**0**	**0**	**0**	**0**
Bonds	0	0	0	0	0	0	0	0	0	0
Commercial banks and other	0	0	0	0	0	0	0	0	0	0
Memo:										
IBRD	0	0	0	0	0	0	0	0	0	0
IDA	0	0	0	1	1	1	1	1	2	4
NET FLOWS ON DEBT	**4**	**54**	**146**	**43**	**75**	**170**	**120**	**78**	**61**	**55**
Public and publicly guaranteed	**4**	**54**	**146**	**43**	**75**	**170**	**120**	**78**	**61**	**55**
Official creditors	5	54	146	43	75	170	120	78	61	55
Multilateral	0	7	75	55	88	186	131	90	75	69
Concessional	0	7	75	55	88	186	131	90	75	69
Bilateral	5	47	71	-12	-14	-16	-12	-12	-14	-14
Concessional	5	47	72	-11	-13	-16	-11	-11	-13	-13
Private creditors	0	0	0	0	0	0	0	0	0	0
Bonds	0	0	0	0	0	0	0	0	0	0
Commercial banks	0	0	0	0	0	0	0	0	0	0
Other private	0	0	0	0	0	0	0	0	0	0
Private nonguaranteed	**0**	**0**	**0**	**0**	**0**	**0**	**0**	**0**	**0**	**0**
Bonds	0	0	0	0	0	0	0	0	0	0
Commercial banks and other	0	0	0	0	0	0	0	0	0	0
Memo:										
IBRD	0	0	0	0	0	0	0	0	0	0
IDA	0	5	32	26	27	59	41	24	19	17

LAO PEOPLE'S DEMOCRATIC REPUBLIC

(US$ million, unless otherwise indicated)

	1970	1980	1990	1994	1995	1996	1997	1998	1999	2000
INTEREST PAYMENTS (LINT)	**0**	**1**	**3**	**5**	**6**	**6**	**7**	**8**	**9**	**9**
Public and publicly guaranteed	**0**	**1**	**3**	**5**	**6**	**6**	**7**	**8**	**9**	**9**
Official creditors	0	1	3	5	6	6	7	8	9	9
Multilateral	0	0	2	4	5	6	7	7	9	9
Concessional	0	0	2	4	5	6	7	7	9	9
Bilateral	0	1	1	1	1	1	1	1	0	0
Concessional	0	1	1	1	1	0	0	0	0	0
Private creditors	0	0	0	0	0	0	0	0	0	0
Bonds	0	0	0	0	0	0	0	0	0	0
Commercial banks	0	0	0	0	0	0	0	0	0	0
Other private	0	0	0	0	0	0	0	0	0	0
Private nonguaranteed	**0**	**0**	**0**	**0**	**0**	**0**	**0**	**0**	**0**	**0**
Bonds	0	0	0	0	0	0	0	0	0	0
Commercial banks and other	0	0	0	0	0	0	0	0	0	0
Memo:										
IBRD	0	0	0	0	0	0	0	0	0	0
IDA	0	0	1	2	2	2	2	3	3	3
NET TRANSFERS ON DEBT	**4**	**53**	**144**	**38**	**69**	**164**	**112**	**71**	**52**	**46**
Public and publicly guaranteed	**4**	**53**	**144**	**38**	**69**	**164**	**112**	**71**	**52**	**46**
Official creditors	4	53	144	38	69	164	112	71	52	46
Multilateral	0	7	73	51	83	181	125	83	66	60
Concessional	0	7	73	51	83	181	125	83	66	60
Bilateral	4	46	70	-12	-15	-17	-12	-12	-14	-14
Concessional	4	46	71	-12	-14	-16	-12	-12	-13	-13
Private creditors	0	0	0	0	0	0	0	0	0	0
Bonds	0	0	0	0	0	0	0	0	0	0
Commercial banks	0	0	0	0	0	0	0	0	0	0
Other private	0	0	0	0	0	0	0	0	0	0
Private nonguaranteed	**0**	**0**	**0**	**0**	**0**	**0**	**0**	**0**	**0**	**0**
Bonds	0	0	0	0	0	0	0	0	0	0
Commercial banks and other	0	0	0	0	0	0	0	0	0	0
Memo:										
IBRD	0	0	0	0	0	0	0	0	0	0
IDA	0	5	32	25	25	57	38	21	16	14
DEBT SERVICE (LTDS)	**2**	**2**	**8**	**20**	**23**	**25**	**22**	**24**	**29**	**34**
Public and publicly guaranteed	**2**	**2**	**8**	**20**	**23**	**25**	**22**	**24**	**29**	**34**
Official creditors	1	2	8	20	23	25	22	24	29	34
Multilateral	0	0	5	7	9	8	10	12	15	20
Concessional	0	0	5	7	9	8	10	12	15	20
Bilateral	1	2	4	12	15	17	12	12	14	14
Concessional	1	2	3	12	14	16	12	12	13	13
Private creditors	0	0	0	0	0	0	0	0	0	0
Bonds	0	0	0	0	0	0	0	0	0	0
Commercial banks	0	0	0	0	0	0	0	0	0	0
Other private	0	0	0	0	0	0	0	0	0	0
Private nonguaranteed	**0**	**0**	**0**	**0**	**0**	**0**	**0**	**0**	**0**	**0**
Bonds	0	0	0	0	0	0	0	0	0	0
Commercial banks and other	0	0	0	0	0	0	0	0	0	0
Memo:										
IBRD	0	0	0	0	0	0	0	0	0	0
IDA	0	0	1	2	3	3	3	4	5	7
UNDISBURSED DEBT	**10**	**254**	**221**	**458**	**484**	**481**	**456**	**478**	**378**	**330**
Official creditors	9	254	221	458	484	481	456	478	378	330
Private creditors	1	0	0	0	0	0	0	0	0	0
Memorandum items										
Concessional LDOD	8	327	1,752	2,018	2,086	2,182	2,244	2,370	2,469	2,448
Variable rate LDOD	0	0	0	0	0	0	0	0	0	0
Public sector LDOD	8	333	1,758	2,022	2,091	2,186	2,247	2,373	2,471	2,449
Private sector LDOD	0	0	0	0	0	0	0	0	0	0

6. CURRENCY COMPOSITION OF LONG-TERM DEBT (PERCENT)

	1970	1980	1990	1994	1995	1996	1997	1998	1999	2000
Deutsche mark	77.3	10.3	1.8	0.0	0.1	0.1	0.0	0.0	0.0	0.0
French franc	12.9	4.3	0.3	0.2	0.2	0.1	0.1	0.1	0.1	0.0
Japanese yen	0.0	7.7	1.5	1.3	1.1	0.8	0.7	0.7	1.1	1.2
Pound sterling	0.0	0.0	0.0	0.0	0.0	0.0	0.0	0.0	0.0	0.0
Swiss franc	0.0	0.0	0.0	0.0	0.0	0.0	0.0	0.0	0.0	0.0
U.S.dollars	9.8	3.6	7.1	12.0	13.1	14.8	15.6	16.6	16.7	17.3
Multiple currency	0.0	3.0	7.1	13.1	15.4	17.8	19.5	22.1	24.3	23.6
Special drawing rights	0.0	0.0	1.1	1.1	1.2	1.4	1.3	1.4	1.5	1.6
All other currencies	0.0	71.1	81.1	72.3	68.9	65.0	62.8	59.1	56.3	56.3

LAO PEOPLE'S DEMOCRATIC REPUBLIC

(US$ million, unless otherwise indicated)

	1970	1980	1990	1994	1995	1996	1997	1998	1999	2000
7. DEBT RESTRUCTURINGS										
Total amount rescheduled	..	..	0	0	0	0	0	0	0	0
Debt stock rescheduled	..	..	0	0	0	0	0	0	0	0
Principal rescheduled	..	..	0	0	0	0	0	0	0	0
Official	..	..	0	0	0	0	0	0	0	0
Private	..	..	0	0	0	0	0	0	0	0
Interest rescheduled	..	..	0	0	0	0	0	0	0	0
Official	..	..	0	0	0	0	0	0	0	0
Private	..	..	0	0	0	0	0	0	0	0
Debt forgiven	..	..	0	0	0	0	0	0	0	0
Memo: interest forgiven	..	..	0	0	0	0	0	0	0	0
Debt stock reduction	..	..	0	0	0	0	0	0	0	0
of which debt buyback	..	..	0	0	0	0	0	0	0	0
8. DEBT STOCK-FLOW RECONCILIATION										
Total change in debt stocks	..	..	296	95	85	99	57	117	90	-28
Net flows on debt	4	59	147	61	90	176	119	66	54	52
Net change in interest arrears	..	..	0	0	0	0	0	0	0	0
Interest capitalized	..	..	0	0	0	0	0	0	0	0
Debt forgiveness or reduction	..	..	0	0	0	0	0	0	0	0
Cross-currency valuation	..	..	141	0	-31	-68	-114	-6	9	-73
Residual	..	..	8	33	26	-9	51	56	26	-7
9. AVERAGE TERMS OF NEW COMMITMENTS										
ALL CREDITORS										
Interest (%)	3.0	0.2	0.9	0.9	2.5	2.0	2.6	1.7	1.2	1.4
Maturity (years)	28.2	33.0	39.9	39.7	37.1	37.6	39.1	39.4	33.8	31.6
Grace period (years)	4.4	25.5	10.0	10.2	9.7	8.8	10.1	9.9	8.7	8.1
Grant element (%)	51.1	91.1	79.0	79.2	62.0	66.7	63.6	71.7	72.8	69.9
Official creditors										
Interest (%)	2.5	0.2	0.9	0.9	2.5	2.0	2.6	1.7	1.2	1.4
Maturity (years)	30.8	33.0	39.9	39.7	37.1	37.6	39.1	39.4	33.8	31.6
Grace period (years)	4.2	25.5	10.0	10.2	9.7	8.8	10.1	9.9	8.7	8.1
Grant element (%)	55.8	91.1	79.0	79.2	62.0	66.7	63.6	71.7	72.8	69.9
Private creditors										
Interest (%)	6.3	0.0	0.0	0.0	0.0	0.0	0.0	0.0	0.0	0.0
Maturity (years)	10.1	0.0	0.0	0.0	0.0	0.0	0.0	0.0	0.0	0.0
Grace period (years)	5.6	0.0	0.0	0.0	0.0	0.0	0.0	0.0	0.0	0.0
Grant element (%)	18.2	0.0	0.0	0.0	0.0	0.0	0.0	0.0	0.0	0.0
Memorandum items										
Commitments	12	96	125	171	110	173	143	128	8	53
Official creditors	11	96	125	171	110	173	143	128	8	53
Private creditors	2	0	0	0	0	0	0	0	0	0

10. CONTRACTUAL OBLIGATIONS ON OUTSTANDING LONG-TERM DEBT

	2001	2002	2003	2004	2005	2006	2007	2008	2009	2010
TOTAL										
Disbursements	109	89	60	36	20	8	4	3	1	0
Principal	25	27	30	32	99	89	93	100	102	104
Interest	11	11	12	12	12	14	16	16	16	16
Official creditors										
Disbursements	109	89	60	36	20	8	4	3	1	0
Principal	25	27	30	32	99	89	93	100	102	104
Interest	11	11	12	12	12	14	16	16	16	16
Bilateral creditors										
Disbursements	0	0	0	0	0	0	0	0	0	0
Principal	13	13	13	12	77	64	63	63	63	63
Interest	0	0	0	0	0	0	0	0	0	0
Multilateral creditors										
Disbursements	109	89	60	36	20	8	4	3	1	0
Principal	12	14	17	20	22	25	29	37	39	41
Interest	11	11	12	12	12	14	16	16	16	16
Private creditors										
Disbursements	0	0	0	0	0	0	0	0	0	0
Principal	0	0	0	0	0	0	0	0	0	0
Interest	0	0	0	0	0	0	0	0	0	0
Commercial banks										
Disbursements	0	0	0	0	0	0	0	0	0	0
Principal	0	0	0	0	0	0	0	0	0	0
Interest	0	0	0	0	0	0	0	0	0	0
Other private										
Disbursements	0	0	0	0	0	0	0	0	0	0
Principal	0	0	0	0	0	0	0	0	0	0
Interest	0	0	0	0	0	0	0	0	0	0

LATVIA

(US$ million, unless otherwise indicated)

	1970	1980	1990	1994	1995	1996	1997	1998	1999	2000
1. SUMMARY DEBT DATA										
TOTAL DEBT STOCKS (EDT)	..	..	..	**373.8**	**462.6**	**1,581.0**	**1,836.6**	**2,324.0**	**3,095.8**	**3,378.7**
Long-term debt (LDOD)	..	..	..	**207.5**	**271.1**	**649.6**	**884.7**	**1,325.1**	**1,970.9**	**2,074.1**
Public and publicly guaranteed	..	..	..	207.5	271.1	300.4	313.7	404.2	864.8	827.1
Private nonguaranteed	..	..	..	0.0	0.0	349.2	571.0	920.9	1,106.1	1,247.0
Use of IMF credit	..	..	..	**160.3**	**160.4**	**129.9**	**85.9**	**63.9**	**47.1**	**34.8**
Short-term debt	..	..	..	**6.0**	**31.2**	**801.4**	**866.0**	**935.0**	**1,077.8**	**1,269.8**
of which interest arrears on LDOD	..	..	..	0.0	0.0	0.0	0.0	0.0	0.0	0.0
Official creditors	..	..	..	0.0	0.0	0.0	0.0	0.0	0.0	0.0
Private creditors	..	..	..	0.0	0.0	0.0	0.0	0.0	0.0	0.0
Memo: principal arrears on LDOD	..	..	..	0.0	0.0	0.0	0.0	0.0	0.0	0.0
Official creditors	..	..	..	0.0	0.0	0.0	0.0	0.0	0.0	0.0
Private creditors	..	..	..	0.0	0.0	0.0	0.0	0.0	0.0	0.0
Memo: export credits	..	..	..	102.2	124.0	118.1	166.4	104.4	78.7	56.3
TOTAL DEBT FLOWS										
Disbursements	..	..	..	**130.0**	**75.2**	**408.5**	**291.7**	**547.6**	**930.9**	**563.6**
Long-term debt	..	..	..	84.2	75.2	408.5	291.7	547.6	930.9	563.6
IMF purchases	..	..	..	45.9	0.0	0.0	0.0	0.0	0.0	0.0
Principal repayments	..	..	..	**9.5**	**10.0**	**39.1**	**200.4**	**183.1**	**237.3**	**378.9**
Long-term debt	..	..	..	9.5	7.1	13.6	163.7	158.3	222.1	368.9
IMF repurchases	..	..	..	0.0	2.9	25.5	36.7	24.8	15.1	10.1
Net flows on debt	..	..	..	**121.2**	**90.4**	**1,139.7**	**155.9**	**433.5**	**836.4**	**376.7**
of which short-term debt	..	..	..	0.7	25.2	770.2	64.6	69.0	142.8	192.0
Interest payments (INT)	..	..	..	**16.0**	**24.3**	**74.6**	**94.6**	**98.0**	**134.3**	**182.7**
Long-term debt	..	..	..	9.5	14.2	31.5	46.1	62.4	80.7	121.9
IMF charges	..	..	..	6.2	9.0	6.7	5.2	3.6	2.2	2.1
Short-term debt	..	..	..	0.3	1.1	36.4	43.3	32.1	51.3	58.7
Net transfers on debt	..	..	..	**105.1**	**66.1**	**1,065.0**	**61.3**	**335.5**	**702.1**	**194.0**
Total debt service paid (TDS)	..	..	..	**25.6**	**34.3**	**113.7**	**295.0**	**281.1**	**371.6**	**561.6**
Long-term debt	..	..	..	19.0	21.3	45.2	209.8	220.6	302.9	490.7
IMF repurchases and charges	..	..	..	6.2	11.8	32.2	41.9	28.4	17.3	12.2
Short-term debt (interest only)	..	..	..	0.3	1.1	36.4	43.3	32.1	51.3	58.7
2. AGGREGATE NET RESOURCE FLOWS AND NET TRANSFERS (LONG-TERM)										
NET RESOURCE FLOWS	..	..	..	**310.2**	**271.5**	**818.0**	**724.7**	**821.5**	**1,126.9**	**669.3**
Net flow of long-term debt (ex. IMF)	..	..	..	74.6	68.1	394.9	128.0	389.4	708.7	194.7
Foreign direct investment (net)	..	..	..	214.5	179.6	382.0	521.0	357.0	347.6	407.0
Portfolio equity flows	..	..	..	0.0	0.0	0.0	26.0	4.0	0.0	0.0
Grants (excluding technical coop.)	..	..	..	21.1	23.8	41.1	49.8	71.1	70.6	67.7
Memo: technical coop. grants	..	..	..	28.0	37.5	29.0	24.4	24.0	20.1	14.6
official net resource flows	..	..	..	81.0	46.4	81.2	112.4	166.2	349.8	86.1
private net resource flows	..	..	..	229.2	225.1	736.8	612.3	655.3	777.1	583.2
NET TRANSFERS	..	..	..	**300.6**	**257.3**	**776.5**	**666.6**	**739.1**	**1,027.1**	**525.4**
Interest on long-term debt	..	..	..	9.5	14.2	31.5	46.1	62.4	80.7	121.9
Profit remittances on FDI	..	..	..	0.0	0.0	10.0	12.0	20.0	19.0	22.0
Memo: official net transfers	..	..	..	72.4	33.6	68.1	97.1	150.3	330.5	52.3
private net transfers	..	..	..	228.2	223.7	708.4	569.5	588.8	696.6	473.1
3. MAJOR ECONOMIC AGGREGATES										
Gross national income (GNI)	..	..	..	5,474.3	4,924.8	5,176.2	5,692.8	6,137.8	6,614.6	7,176.4
Exports of goods & services (XGS)	..	..	..	1,729.6	2,158.7	2,753.6	3,049.8	3,330.0	3,073.7	3,546.7
of which workers remittances	..	..	..	..	..	..	1.7	3.0	2.6	61.2
Imports of goods & services (MGS)	..	..	..	1,661.2	2,245.7	3,126.9	3,470.5	4,101.0	3,818.2	4,077.3
International reserves (RES)	..	..	..	640.7	602.1	746.1	776.3	800.0	912.5	919.2
Current account balance	..	..	..	201.2	-16.2	-279.8	-345.0	-649.5	-654.3	-494.4
4. DEBT INDICATORS										
EDT / XGS (%)	..	..	..	21.6	21.4	57.4	60.2	69.8	100.7	95.3
EDT / GNI (%)	..	..	..	6.8	9.4	30.5	32.3	37.9	46.8	47.1
TDS / XGS (%)	..	..	..	1.5	1.6	4.1	9.7	8.4	12.1	15.8
INT / XGS (%)	..	..	..	0.9	1.1	2.7	3.1	2.9	4.4	5.2
INT / GNI (%)	..	..	..	0.3	0.5	1.4	1.7	1.6	2.0	2.6
RES / EDT (%)	..	..	..	171.4	130.2	47.2	42.3	34.4	29.5	27.2
RES / MGS (months)	..	..	..	4.6	3.2	2.9	2.7	2.3	2.9	2.7
Short-term / EDT (%)	..	..	..	1.6	6.7	50.7	47.2	40.2	34.8	37.6
Concessional / EDT (%)	..	..	..	15.8	12.7	4.0	3.8	3.2	2.3	1.4
Multilateral / EDT (%)	..	..	..	30.7	30.1	10.4	10.8	12.3	17.3	16.1

LATVIA

(US$ million, unless otherwise indicated)

	1970	1980	1990	1994	1995	1996	1997	1998	1999	2000
5. LONG-TERM DEBT										
DEBT OUTSTANDING (LDOD)	..	..	..	**207.5**	**271.1**	**649.6**	**884.7**	**1,325.1**	**1,970.9**	**2,074.1**
Public and publicly guaranteed	..	..	..	**207.5**	**271.1**	**300.4**	**313.7**	**404.2**	**864.8**	**827.1**
Official creditors	..	..	..	173.7	200.4	229.4	272.9	365.0	607.2	591.3
Multilateral	..	..	..	114.8	139.2	163.7	199.1	286.1	534.7	542.8
Concessional	..	..	..	0.0	0.0	0.0	0.0	0.0	0.0	0.0
Bilateral	..	..	..	58.9	61.2	65.8	73.8	78.9	72.5	48.6
Concessional	..	..	..	58.9	58.9	63.7	69.7	75.4	70.3	47.5
Private creditors	..	..	..	33.8	70.6	71.0	40.8	39.2	257.7	235.8
Bonds	..	..	..	0.0	38.9	34.5	0.0	0.0	226.0	209.4
Commercial banks	..	..	..	0.0	0.0	2.2	1.9	2.0	0.0	0.0
Other private	..	..	..	33.8	31.7	34.3	38.9	37.2	31.6	26.4
Private nonguaranteed	..	..	..	**0.0**	**0.0**	**349.2**	**571.0**	**920.9**	**1,106.1**	**1,247.0**
Bonds	..	..	..	0.0	0.0	0.0	30.0	30.0	30.0	0.0
Commercial banks and other	..	..	..	0.0	0.0	349.2	541.0	890.9	1,076.1	1,247.0
Memo:										
IBRD	..	..	..	44.8	54.9	74.8	120.1	186.5	200.0	242.4
IDA	..	..	..	0.0	0.0	0.0	0.0	0.0	0.0	0.0
DISBURSEMENTS	..	..	..	**84.2**	**75.2**	**408.5**	**291.7**	**547.6**	**930.9**	**563.6**
Public and publicly guaranteed	..	..	..	**84.2**	**75.2**	**59.3**	**104.1**	**106.8**	**535.5**	**94.5**
Official creditors	..	..	..	65.4	26.4	46.2	93.1	103.9	290.9	91.2
Multilateral	..	..	..	41.6	23.2	37.8	75.4	100.4	290.9	90.5
Concessional	..	..	..	0.0	0.0	0.0	0.0	0.0	0.0	0.0
Bilateral	..	..	..	23.8	3.2	8.4	17.6	3.5	0.0	0.7
Concessional	..	..	..	23.8	0.8	8.1	14.3	3.1	0.0	0.7
Private creditors	..	..	..	18.8	48.9	13.1	11.0	2.8	244.5	3.3
Bonds	..	..	..	0.0	42.8	0.0	0.0	0.0	240.0	0.0
Commercial banks	..	..	..	0.0	0.0	2.3	0.0	0.0	0.0	0.0
Other private	..	..	..	18.8	6.1	10.9	11.0	2.8	4.5	3.3
Private nonguaranteed	..	..	..	**0.0**	**0.0**	**349.2**	**187.7**	**440.9**	**395.4**	**469.1**
Bonds	..	..	..	0.0	0.0	0.0	30.0	0.0	0.0	0.0
Commercial banks and other	..	..	..	0.0	0.0	349.2	157.7	440.9	395.4	469.1
Memo:										
IBRD	..	..	..	22.0	8.7	24.4	52.8	81.8	27.8	62.9
IDA	..	..	..	0.0	0.0	0.0	0.0	0.0	0.0	0.0
PRINCIPAL REPAYMENTS	..	..	..	**9.5**	**7.1**	**13.6**	**163.7**	**158.3**	**222.1**	**368.9**
Public and publicly guaranteed	..	..	..	**9.5**	**7.1**	**13.6**	**67.9**	**14.5**	**20.9**	**80.5**
Official creditors	..	..	..	5.5	3.8	6.1	30.4	8.8	11.7	72.8
Multilateral	..	..	..	0.0	3.8	5.7	25.2	5.4	7.5	53.3
Concessional	..	..	..	0.0	0.0	0.0	0.0	0.0	0.0	0.0
Bilateral	..	..	..	5.5	0.0	0.5	5.2	3.5	4.2	19.5
Concessional	..	..	..	0.0	0.0	0.0	4.2	2.4	3.1	18.4
Private creditors	..	..	..	4.0	3.3	7.5	37.5	5.6	9.2	7.8
Bonds	..	..	..	0.0	0.0	0.0	33.1	0.0	0.0	0.0
Commercial banks	..	..	..	0.0	0.0	0.0	0.0	0.0	1.4	0.0
Other private	..	..	..	4.0	3.3	7.5	4.4	5.6	7.8	7.8
Private nonguaranteed	..	..	..	**0.0**	**0.0**	**0.0**	**95.8**	**143.8**	**201.2**	**288.3**
Bonds	..	..	..	0.0	0.0	0.0	0.0	0.0	0.0	30.0
Commercial banks and other	..	..	..	0.0	0.0	0.0	95.8	143.8	201.2	258.3
Memo:										
IBRD	..	..	..	0.0	0.0	0.0	0.0	3.6	4.4	9.1
IDA	..	..	..	0.0	0.0	0.0	0.0	0.0	0.0	0.0
NET FLOWS ON DEBT	..	..	..	**74.6**	**68.1**	**394.9**	**128.0**	**389.4**	**708.7**	**194.7**
Public and publicly guaranteed	..	..	..	**74.6**	**68.1**	**45.7**	**36.2**	**92.3**	**514.5**	**14.0**
Official creditors	..	..	..	59.9	22.6	40.1	62.6	95.1	279.2	18.4
Multilateral	..	..	..	41.6	19.4	32.1	50.3	95.0	283.4	37.2
Concessional	..	..	..	0.0	0.0	0.0	0.0	0.0	0.0	0.0
Bilateral	..	..	..	18.3	3.2	8.0	12.4	0.1	-4.2	-18.8
Concessional	..	..	..	23.8	0.8	8.1	10.1	0.7	-3.1	-17.7
Private creditors	..	..	..	14.7	45.5	5.6	-26.5	-2.8	235.3	-4.5
Bonds	..	..	..	0.0	42.8	0.0	-33.1	0.0	240.0	0.0
Commercial banks	..	..	..	0.0	0.0	2.3	0.0	0.0	-1.4	0.0
Other private	..	..	..	14.7	2.8	3.3	6.6	-2.8	-3.3	-4.5
Private nonguaranteed	..	..	..	**0.0**	**0.0**	**349.2**	**91.8**	**297.1**	**194.2**	**180.7**
Bonds	..	..	..	0.0	0.0	0.0	30.0	0.0	0.0	-30.0
Commercial banks and other	..	..	..	0.0	0.0	349.2	61.8	297.1	194.2	210.7
Memo:										
IBRD	..	..	..	22.0	8.7	24.4	52.8	78.2	23.4	53.8
IDA	..	..	..	0.0	0.0	0.0	0.0	0.0	0.0	0.0

LATVIA

(US$ million, unless otherwise indicated)

	1970	1980	1990	1994	1995	1996	1997	1998	1999	2000
INTEREST PAYMENTS (LINT)	..	..	..	**9.5**	**14.2**	**31.5**	**46.1**	**62.4**	**80.7**	**121.9**
Public and publicly guaranteed	..	..	..	**9.5**	**14.2**	**17.2**	**19.4**	**17.2**	**20.4**	**49.6**
Official creditors	..	..	..	8.6	12.8	13.1	15.3	15.9	19.3	33.8
Multilateral	..	..	..	6.3	9.1	10.0	11.2	12.4	16.4	30.7
Concessional	..	..	..	0.0	0.0	0.0	0.0	0.0	0.0	0.0
Bilateral	..	..	..	2.2	3.7	3.2	4.1	3.4	2.9	3.0
Concessional	..	..	..	1.7	3.6	3.0	3.1	3.1	2.7	2.9
Private creditors	..	..	..	1.0	1.4	4.0	4.1	1.4	1.1	15.9
Bonds	..	..	..	0.0	0.0	2.0	1.8	0.0	0.0	14.6
Commercial banks	..	..	..	0.0	0.0	0.0	0.0	0.0	0.1	0.0
Other private	..	..	..	1.0	1.4	2.0	2.3	1.4	1.0	1.2
Private nonguaranteed	..	..	..	**0.0**	**0.0**	**14.4**	**26.7**	**45.1**	**60.4**	**72.2**
Bonds	..	..	..	0.0	0.0	0.0	0.0	2.0	1.8	2.1
Commercial banks and other	..	..	..	0.0	0.0	14.4	26.7	43.2	58.6	70.1
Memo:										
IBRD	..	..	..	2.0	3.5	4.1	5.6	8.3	12.9	12.0
IDA	..	..	..	0.0	0.0	0.0	0.0	0.0	0.0	0.0
NET TRANSFERS ON DEBT	..	..	..	**65.1**	**53.9**	**363.3**	**81.9**	**327.0**	**628.0**	**72.9**
Public and publicly guaranteed	..	..	..	**65.1**	**53.9**	**28.5**	**16.8**	**75.1**	**494.1**	**-35.6**
Official creditors	..	..	..	51.4	9.8	26.9	47.3	79.2	259.9	-15.3
Multilateral	..	..	..	35.3	10.3	22.2	39.0	82.6	267.0	6.5
Concessional	..	..	..	0.0	0.0	0.0	0.0	0.0	0.0	0.0
Bilateral	..	..	..	16.1	-0.5	4.8	8.3	-3.4	-7.1	-21.8
Concessional	..	..	..	22.1	-2.8	5.1	7.0	-2.4	-5.8	-20.6
Private creditors	..	..	..	13.8	44.1	1.6	-30.6	-4.2	234.2	-20.3
Bonds	..	..	..	0.0	42.8	-2.0	-34.9	0.0	240.0	-14.6
Commercial banks	..	..	..	0.0	0.0	2.3	0.0	0.0	-1.4	0.0
Other private	..	..	..	13.8	1.3	1.3	4.3	-4.2	-4.3	-5.7
Private nonguaranteed	..	..	..	**0.0**	**0.0**	**334.8**	**65.1**	**251.9**	**133.8**	**108.5**
Bonds	..	..	..	0.0	0.0	0.0	30.0	-2.0	-1.8	-32.1
Commercial banks and other	..	..	..	0.0	0.0	334.8	35.1	253.9	135.6	140.6
Memo:										
IBRD	..	..	..	20.0	5.2	20.3	47.2	69.9	10.4	41.8
IDA	..	..	..	0.0	0.0	0.0	0.0	0.0	0.0	0.0
DEBT SERVICE (LTDS)	..	..	..	**19.0**	**21.3**	**45.2**	**209.8**	**220.6**	**302.9**	**490.7**
Public and publicly guaranteed	..	..	..	**19.0**	**21.3**	**30.8**	**87.3**	**31.7**	**41.3**	**130.1**
Official creditors	..	..	..	14.0	16.6	19.2	45.7	24.7	31.0	106.5
Multilateral	..	..	..	6.3	12.9	15.6	36.4	17.8	23.9	84.1
Concessional	..	..	..	0.0	0.0	0.0	0.0	0.0	0.0	0.0
Bilateral	..	..	..	7.7	3.7	3.6	9.3	6.9	7.1	22.5
Concessional	..	..	..	1.7	3.6	3.0	7.3	5.5	5.8	21.3
Private creditors	..	..	..	5.0	4.8	11.6	41.6	7.0	10.3	23.6
Bonds	..	..	..	0.0	0.0	2.0	34.9	0.0	0.0	14.6
Commercial banks	..	..	..	0.0	0.0	0.0	0.0	0.0	1.4	0.0
Other private	..	..	..	5.0	4.8	9.6	6.7	7.0	8.8	9.0
Private nonguaranteed	..	..	..	**0.0**	**0.0**	**14.4**	**122.5**	**188.9**	**261.6**	**360.6**
Bonds	..	..	..	0.0	0.0	0.0	0.0	2.0	1.8	32.1
Commercial banks and other	..	..	..	0.0	0.0	14.4	122.5	186.9	259.8	328.5
Memo:										
IBRD	..	..	..	2.0	3.5	4.1	5.6	11.9	17.4	21.1
IDA	..	..	..	0.0	0.0	0.0	0.0	0.0	0.0	0.0
UNDISBURSED DEBT	..	..	..	**183.8**	**224.0**	**312.0**	**245.0**	**257.1**	**261.7**	**189.6**
Official creditors	..	..	..	176.3	207.2	297.3	231.6	245.7	256.2	187.8
Private creditors	..	..	..	7.5	16.8	14.7	13.5	11.3	5.5	1.8
Memorandum items										
Concessional LDOD	..	..	..	58.9	58.9	63.7	69.7	75.4	70.3	47.5
Variable rate LDOD	..	..	..	153.2	172.6	555.5	808.7	1,238.5	1,662.4	1,793.0
Public sector LDOD	..	..	..	196.0	252.1	287.8	302.6	394.2	857.8	818.2
Private sector LDOD	..	..	..	11.5	19.0	361.8	582.0	930.9	1,113.2	1,255.9

6. CURRENCY COMPOSITION OF LONG-TERM DEBT (PERCENT)

	1970	1980	1990	1994	1995	1996	1997	1998	1999	2000
Deutsche mark	..	..	..	3.6	8.5	8.1	10.2	17.6	7.5	7.6
French franc	..	..	..	0.0	0.0	0.0	0.0	0.0	0.3	0.6
Japanese yen	..	..	..	15.6	26.2	23.0	13.7	11.8	5.7	4.7
Pound sterling	..	..	..	0.0	0.0	0.0	0.0	0.0	0.0	0.0
Swiss franc	..	..	..	0.0	0.0	0.0	0.0	0.6	0.4	0.6
U.S.dollars	..	..	..	54.8	45.0	43.9	43.8	40.6	18.5	20.0
Multiple currency	..	..	..	21.6	20.3	24.9	30.9	28.2	14.2	13.7
Special drawing rights	..	..	..	0.0	0.0	0.0	0.0	0.0	0.0	0.0
All other currencies	..	..	..	4.4	0.0	0.1	1.4	1.2	53.4	52.8

LATVIA

(US$ million, unless otherwise indicated)

	1970	1980	1990	1994	1995	1996	1997	1998	1999	2000
7. DEBT RESTRUCTURINGS										
Total amount rescheduled	..	..	..	0.0	0.0	0.0	0.0	0.0	0.0	0.0
Debt stock rescheduled	..	..	..	0.0	0.0	0.0	0.0	0.0	0.0	0.0
Principal rescheduled	..	..	..	0.0	0.0	0.0	0.0	0.0	0.0	0.0
Official	..	..	..	0.0	0.0	0.0	0.0	0.0	0.0	0.0
Private	..	..	..	0.0	0.0	0.0	0.0	0.0	0.0	0.0
Interest rescheduled	..	..	..	0.0	0.0	0.0	0.0	0.0	0.0	0.0
Official	..	..	..	0.0	0.0	0.0	0.0	0.0	0.0	0.0
Private	..	..	..	0.0	0.0	0.0	0.0	0.0	0.0	0.0
Debt forgiven	..	..	..	0.0	0.0	0.0	0.0	0.0	0.0	0.0
Memo: interest forgiven	..	..	..	0.0	0.0	0.0	0.0	0.0	0.0	0.0
Debt stock reduction	..	..	..	0.0	0.0	0.0	0.0	0.0	0.0	0.0
of which debt buyback	..	..	..	0.0	0.0	0.0	0.0	0.0	0.0	0.0
8. DEBT STOCK-FLOW RECONCILIATION										
Total change in debt stocks	..	..	..	138.0	88.9	1,118.3	255.7	487.4	771.8	282.9
Net flows on debt	..	..	..	121.2	90.4	1,139.7	155.9	433.5	836.4	376.7
Net change in interest arrears	..	..	..	0.0	0.0	0.0	0.0	0.0	0.0	0.0
Interest capitalized	..	..	..	0.0	0.0	0.0	0.0	0.0	0.0	0.0
Debt forgiveness or reduction	..	..	..	0.0	0.0	0.0	0.0	0.0	0.0	0.0
Cross-currency valuation	..	..	..	10.7	4.8	-19.6	-25.4	16.6	1.7	-48.9
Residual	..	..	..	6.2	-6.3	-1.8	125.2	37.3	-66.2	-44.9
9. AVERAGE TERMS OF NEW COMMITMENTS										
ALL CREDITORS										
Interest (%)	..	..	..	6.9	5.2	6.0	5.7	5.1	6.2	5.8
Maturity (years)	..	..	..	14.7	9.0	15.3	13.8	17.4	6.6	14.6
Grace period (years)	..	..	..	4.2	3.3	4.0	4.1	4.5	7.6	6.0
Grant element (%)	..	..	..	16.8	19.2	21.5	22.9	30.0	19.5	23.7
Official creditors										
Interest (%)	..	..	..	6.8	5.3	6.3	5.7	5.1	5.9	5.8
Maturity (years)	..	..	..	16.3	14.1	15.7	14.0	17.4	7.1	14.6
Grace period (years)	..	..	..	4.7	4.1	4.2	4.3	4.5	4.8	6.0
Grant element (%)	..	..	..	18.6	25.3	20.8	23.1	30.0	17.5	23.7
Private creditors										
Interest (%)	..	..	..	7.6	5.1	2.5	5.4	0.0	6.6	0.0
Maturity (years)	..	..	..	3.3	3.9	11.1	12.0	0.0	6.0	0.0
Grace period (years)	..	..	..	0.6	2.5	1.2	2.5	0.0	11.0	0.0
Grant element (%)	..	..	..	3.6	13.1	30.6	21.4	0.0	22.0	0.0
Memorandum items										
Commitments	..	..	..	82.7	116.3	188.4	102.0	89.3	534.7	93.5
Official creditors	..	..	..	72.5	58.4	174.0	89.5	89.3	294.7	93.5
Private creditors	..	..	..	10.2	57.9	14.3	12.5	0.0	240.0	0.0

10. CONTRACTUAL OBLIGATIONS ON OUTSTANDING LONG-TERM DEBT

	2001	2002	2003	2004	2005	2006	2007	2008	2009	2010
TOTAL										
Disbursements	53.2	65.5	33.0	16.0	10.3	5.9	2.7	1.8	0.5	0.3
Principal	284.6	288.7	298.9	504.6	296.6	57.4	56.7	52.5	51.8	39.8
Interest	193.7	164.3	132.6	99.8	53.7	21.0	17.9	14.8	11.7	9.1
Official creditors										
Disbursements	52.0	65.0	33.0	16.0	10.3	5.9	2.7	1.8	0.5	0.3
Principal	32.4	36.1	49.5	255.0	48.0	50.3	50.0	49.1	47.2	39.0
Interest	37.9	39.7	39.5	37.8	22.7	20.2	17.4	14.5	11.6	9.1
Bilateral creditors										
Disbursements	2.9	1.7	1.1	0.7	0.4	0.2	0.1	0.0	0.0	0.0
Principal	5.7	5.0	5.0	4.9	4.9	4.9	4.9	4.9	5.0	5.7
Interest	2.1	2.0	1.9	1.7	1.5	1.3	1.1	0.8	0.6	0.5
Multilateral creditors										
Disbursements	49.0	63.3	31.8	15.2	9.9	5.7	2.6	1.8	0.5	0.3
Principal	26.7	31.2	44.5	250.1	43.1	45.4	45.1	44.3	42.3	33.3
Interest	35.7	37.7	37.6	36.1	21.2	18.9	16.3	13.6	11.0	8.6
Private creditors										
Disbursements	1.2	0.6	0.0	0.0	0.0	0.0	0.0	0.0	0.0	0.0
Principal	252.0	253.0	249.0	250.0	249.0	7.0	7.0	3.0	5.0	1.0
Interest	156.0	125.0	93.0	62.0	31.0	1.0	1.0	0.0	0.0	0.0
Commercial banks										
Disbursements	0.0	0.0	0.0	0.0	0.0	0.0	0.0	0.0	0.0	0.0
Principal	0.0	0.0	0.0	0.0	0.0	0.0	0.0	0.0	0.0	0.0
Interest	0.0	0.0	0.0	0.0	0.0	0.0	0.0	0.0	0.0	0.0
Other private										
Disbursements	1.2	0.6	0.0	0.0	0.0	0.0	0.0	0.0	0.0	0.0
Principal	252.0	253.0	249.0	250.0	249.0	7.0	7.0	3.0	5.0	1.0
Interest	156.0	125.0	93.0	62.0	31.0	1.0	1.0	0.0	0.0	0.0

LEBANON

(US$ million, unless otherwise indicated)

	1970	1980	1990	1994	1995	1996	1997	1998	1999	2000
1. SUMMARY DEBT DATA										
TOTAL DEBT STOCKS (EDT)	**64**	**510**	**1,779**	**2,127**	**2,966**	**3,996**	**5,037**	**6,802**	**8,235**	**10,311**
Long-term debt (LDOD)	**64**	**216**	**358**	**778**	**1,601**	**2,343**	**3,242**	**4,841**	**6,033**	**7,770**
Public and publicly guaranteed	64	216	358	778	1,551	1,933	2,357	4,056	5,362	7,034
Private nonguaranteed	0	0	0	0	50	410	885	785	671	736
Use of IMF credit	**0**	**0**	**0**	**0**	**0**	**0**	**0**	**0**	**0**	**0**
Short-term debt	**0**	**294**	**1,421**	**1,349**	**1,366**	**1,653**	**1,795**	**1,961**	**2,202**	**2,541**
of which interest arrears on LDOD	0	0	39	20	11	0	0	0	0	0
Official creditors	0	0	16	2	0	0	0	0	0	0
Private creditors	0	0	23	18	10	0	0	0	0	0
Memo: principal arrears on LDOD	0	0	132	63	43	0	0	0	0	0
Official creditors	0	0	28	12	2	0	0	0	0	0
Private creditors	0	0	104	51	41	0	0	0	0	0
Memo: export credits	0	0	345	303	404	520	730	381	313	318
TOTAL DEBT FLOWS										
Disbursements	**12**	**120**	**12**	**481**	**907**	**830**	**1,390**	**1,730**	**1,575**	**2,995**
Long-term debt	12	120	12	481	907	830	1,390	1,730	1,575	2,995
IMF purchases	0	0	0	0	0	0	0	0	0	0
Principal repayments	**2**	**7**	**27**	**96**	**104**	**69**	**438**	**169**	**280**	**1,171**
Long-term debt	2	7	27	96	104	69	438	169	280	1,171
IMF repurchases	0	0	0	0	0	0	0	0	0	0
Net flows on debt	**10**	**236**	**726**	**755**	**830**	**1,059**	**1,094**	**1,727**	**1,537**	**2,163**
of which short-term debt	0	124	742	370	26	298	142	166	241	339
Interest payments (INT)	**1**	**45**	**72**	**89**	**121**	**231**	**296**	**358**	**490**	**650**
Long-term debt	1	6	11	26	54	149	201	263	362	518
IMF charges	0	0	0	0	0	0	0	0	0	0
Short-term debt	0	39	61	63	67	83	95	95	128	132
Net transfers on debt	**9**	**191**	**654**	**666**	**709**	**828**	**798**	**1,368**	**1,047**	**1,513**
Total debt service paid (TDS)	**4**	**53**	**99**	**185**	**224**	**301**	**734**	**528**	**770**	**1,821**
Long-term debt	4	13	39	122	158	218	639	432	642	1,689
IMF repurchases and charges	0	0	0	0	0	0	0	0	0	0
Short-term debt (interest only)	0	39	61	63	67	83	95	95	128	132
2. AGGREGATE NET RESOURCE FLOWS AND NET TRANSFERS (LONG-TERM)										
NET RESOURCE FLOWS	**12**	**311**	**203**	**489**	**917**	**1,015**	**1,310**	**2,016**	**1,630**	**2,258**
Net flow of long-term debt (ex. IMF)	10	112	-16	385	804	761	952	1,561	1,295	1,824
Foreign direct investment (net)	0	0	6	7	35	80	150	200	250	298
Portfolio equity flows	0	0	0	1	34	122	89	147	3	4
Grants (excluding technical coop.)	3	199	213	96	44	52	119	108	82	133
Memo: technical coop. grants	9	19	39	99	94	98	43	46	59	55
official net resource flows	12	242	190	83	165	276	243	276	195	230
private net resource flows	0	70	12	407	753	740	1,067	1,740	1,435	2,028
NET TRANSFERS	**11**	**305**	**192**	**463**	**863**	**867**	**1,109**	**1,752**	**1,268**	**1,740**
Interest on long-term debt	1	6	11	26	54	149	201	263	362	518
Profit remittances on FDI	0	0	0	0	0	0	0	0	0	0
Memo: official net transfers	11	236	181	62	146	250	213	241	155	185
private net transfers	0	69	11	401	718	617	897	1,511	1,113	1,555
3. MAJOR ECONOMIC AGGREGATES										
Gross national income (GNI)	..	..	3,461	9,235	11,611	13,392	15,297	16,991	17,431	17,420
Exports of goods & services (XGS)	..	..	3,022	3,480	2,102	2,221	2,391	..	..	..
of which workers remittances	..	..	1,818	2,165	..	..	..	..	..	..
Imports of goods & services (MGS)	..	..	2,908	6,222	7,570	8,005	8,004	..	..	..
International reserves (RES)	405	7,025	4,210	7,419	8,100	9,337	8,653	9,210	10,452	8,475
Current account balance	..	..	115	-2,742	-4,587	-4,507	-4,153	-4,399	-3,317	-3,065
4. DEBT INDICATORS										
EDT / XGS (%)	..	..	58.9	61.1	141.1	179.9	210.7	..	..	..
EDT / GNI (%)	..	..	51.4	23.0	25.6	29.8	32.9	40.0	47.2	59.2
TDS / XGS (%)	..	..	3.3	5.3	10.7	13.5	30.7	..	..	..
INT / XGS (%)	..	..	2.4	2.6	5.7	10.4	12.4	..	..	..
INT / GNI (%)	..	..	2.1	1.0	1.0	1.7	1.9	2.1	2.8	3.7
RES / EDT (%)	630.7	1,376.6	236.7	348.8	273.1	233.6	171.8	135.4	126.9	82.2
RES / MGS (months)	..	..	17.4	14.3	12.8	14.0	13.0	..	..	..
Short-term / EDT (%)	0.0	57.6	79.9	63.4	46.0	41.4	35.6	28.8	26.7	24.6
Concessional / EDT (%)	47.5	14.5	6.2	6.3	9.2	10.4	9.4	8.2	7.5	6.5
Multilateral / EDT (%)	28.5	15.2	4.8	5.9	6.7	8.2	7.5	8.1	7.6	6.6

LEBANON

(US$ million, unless otherwise indicated)

	1970	1980	1990	1994	1995	1996	1997	1998	1999	2000
5. LONG-TERM DEBT										
DEBT OUTSTANDING (LDOD)	**64**	**216**	**358**	**778**	**1,601**	**2,343**	**3,242**	**4,841**	**6,033**	**7,770**
Public and publicly guaranteed	**64**	**216**	**358**	**778**	**1,551**	**1,933**	**2,357**	**4,056**	**5,362**	**7,034**
Official creditors	64	146	188	295	428	629	714	905	984	1,047
Multilateral	18	78	85	125	198	326	375	553	629	677
Concessional	0	21	30	45	63	169	190	264	311	347
Bilateral	46	68	104	170	230	304	339	353	355	370
Concessional	31	53	81	89	209	246	281	295	307	327
Private creditors	0	71	169	483	1,123	1,304	1,643	3,151	4,378	5,987
Bonds	0	0	0	400	700	800	1,040	2,499	3,681	4,602
Commercial banks	0	70	0	26	359	482	583	632	680	1,370
Other private	0	1	169	58	64	22	21	19	17	15
Private nonguaranteed	**0**	**0**	**0**	**0**	**50**	**410**	**885**	**785**	**671**	**736**
Bonds	0	0	0	0	50	410	885	785	671	736
Commercial banks and other	0	0	0	0	0	0	0	0	0	0
Memo:										
IBRD	18	27	34	64	113	132	151	199	234	248
IDA	0	0	0	0	0	0	0	0	0	0
DISBURSEMENTS	**12**	**120**	**12**	**481**	**907**	**830**	**1,390**	**1,730**	**1,575**	**2,995**
Public and publicly guaranteed	**12**	**120**	**12**	**481**	**857**	**470**	**915**	**1,730**	**1,529**	**2,880**
Official creditors	12	50	5	69	213	244	150	195	172	163
Multilateral	0	17	0	52	80	147	79	176	125	107
Concessional	0	5	0	24	21	109	29	77	64	56
Bilateral	12	33	5	17	133	97	71	19	46	56
Concessional	6	18	5	17	125	59	63	18	45	51
Private creditors	0	70	6	411	644	227	765	1,536	1,358	2,717
Bonds	0	0	0	400	300	100	644	1,450	1,240	1,375
Commercial banks	0	70	0	8	340	126	121	86	117	1,342
Other private	0	0	6	4	4	1	0	0	0	0
Private nonguaranteed	**0**	**0**	**0**	**0**	**50**	**360**	**475**	**0**	**46**	**115**
Bonds	0	0	0	0	50	360	475	0	46	115
Commercial banks and other	0	0	0	0	0	0	0	0	0	0
Memo:										
IBRD	0	8	0	27	51	32	39	48	49	42
IDA	0	0	0	0	0	0	0	0	0	0
PRINCIPAL REPAYMENTS	**2**	**7**	**27**	**96**	**104**	**69**	**438**	**169**	**280**	**1,171**
Public and publicly guaranteed	**2**	**7**	**27**	**96**	**104**	**69**	**438**	**69**	**120**	**1,121**
Official creditors	2	7	27	83	93	20	26	27	59	66
Multilateral	1	3	7	10	10	8	12	12	32	39
Concessional	0	0	0	3	3	3	4	2	14	18
Bilateral	1	4	21	73	83	12	14	15	27	27
Concessional	1	4	1	6	10	12	13	12	21	21
Private creditors	0	0	0	13	11	49	412	42	61	1,055
Bonds	0	0	0	0	0	0	400	0	0	400
Commercial banks	0	0	0	12	9	9	11	41	59	653
Other private	0	0	0	2	2	40	1	2	2	2
Private nonguaranteed	**0**	**0**	**0**	**0**	**0**	**0**	**0**	**100**	**160**	**50**
Bonds	0	0	0	0	0	0	0	100	160	50
Commercial banks and other	0	0	0	0	0	0	0	0	0	0
Memo:										
IBRD	1	3	7	4	4	4	8	9	12	17
IDA	0	0	0	0	0	0	0	0	0	0
NET FLOWS ON DEBT	**10**	**112**	**-16**	**385**	**804**	**761**	**952**	**1,561**	**1,295**	**1,824**
Public and publicly guaranteed	**10**	**112**	**-16**	**385**	**754**	**401**	**477**	**1,661**	**1,409**	**1,759**
Official creditors	10	43	-22	-13	120	223	124	168	113	97
Multilateral	-1	14	-6	42	70	139	67	164	94	68
Concessional	0	5	0	21	18	106	25	74	50	38
Bilateral	11	29	-16	-55	50	85	57	4	19	30
Concessional	5	14	4	12	115	47	50	7	24	30
Private creditors	0	70	6	398	633	178	353	1,493	1,296	1,662
Bonds	0	0	0	400	300	100	244	1,450	1,240	975
Commercial banks	0	70	0	-4	331	117	110	45	58	688
Other private	0	0	6	2	2	-39	-1	-2	-2	-2
Private nonguaranteed	**0**	**0**	**0**	**0**	**50**	**360**	**475**	**-100**	**-114**	**65**
Bonds	0	0	0	0	50	360	475	-100	-114	65
Commercial banks and other	0	0	0	0	0	0	0	0	0	0
Memo:										
IBRD	-1	5	-7	23	47	27	32	38	36	26
IDA	0	0	0	0	0	0	0	0	0	0

LEBANON

(US$ million, unless otherwise indicated)

	1970	1980	1990	1994	1995	1996	1997	1998	1999	2000
INTEREST PAYMENTS (LINT)	**1**	**6**	**11**	**26**	**54**	**149**	**201**	**263**	**362**	**518**
Public and publicly guaranteed	**1**	**6**	**11**	**26**	**54**	**146**	**164**	**186**	**293**	**461**
Official creditors	1	6	9	21	19	26	31	35	40	45
Multilateral	1	4	4	7	11	15	19	22	27	33
Concessional	0	1	0	2	3	4	8	8	11	13
Bilateral	0	2	5	14	8	11	11	13	13	12
Concessional	0	2	0	2	3	8	8	8	8	9
Private creditors	0	0	2	5	35	120	133	151	254	416
Bonds	0	0	0	0	20	72	81	99	191	300
Commercial banks	0	0	0	3	12	36	50	50	61	115
Other private	0	0	2	2	3	12	2	2	2	2
Private nonguaranteed	**0**	**0**	**0**	**0**	**0**	**2**	**37**	**77**	**69**	**57**
Bonds	0	0	0	0	0	2	37	77	69	57
Commercial banks and other	0	0	0	0	0	0	0	0	0	0
Memo:										
IBRD	1	2	4	4	7	9	10	11	13	14
IDA	0	0	0	0	0	0	0	0	0	0
NET TRANSFERS ON DEBT	**9**	**106**	**-27**	**359**	**750**	**612**	**751**	**1,298**	**933**	**1,306**
Public and publicly guaranteed	**9**	**106**	**-27**	**359**	**700**	**255**	**314**	**1,475**	**1,116**	**1,298**
Official creditors	9	37	-31	-34	101	197	93	133	73	53
Multilateral	-2	10	-11	35	59	124	48	142	66	35
Concessional	0	5	0	18	15	102	17	66	39	25
Bilateral	11	27	-21	-69	42	73	46	-9	7	18
Concessional	5	12	4	10	112	40	42	-1	16	22
Private creditors	0	69	5	393	599	57	220	1,342	1,043	1,245
Bonds	0	0	0	400	280	28	164	1,351	1,049	675
Commercial banks	0	70	0	-7	319	81	59	-5	-2	574
Other private	0	0	5	0	0	-51	-3	-4	-4	-4
Private nonguaranteed	**0**	**0**	**0**	**0**	**50**	**358**	**438**	**-177**	**-183**	**8**
Bonds	0	0	0	0	50	358	438	-177	-183	8
Commercial banks and other	0	0	0	0	0	0	0	0	0	0
Memo:										
IBRD	-2	3	-11	19	40	19	22	28	24	12
IDA	0	0	0	0	0	0	0	0	0	0
DEBT SERVICE (LTDS)	**4**	**13**	**39**	**122**	**158**	**218**	**639**	**432**	**642**	**1,689**
Public and publicly guaranteed	**4**	**13**	**39**	**122**	**158**	**216**	**602**	**255**	**413**	**1,582**
Official creditors	4	13	37	103	112	46	57	61	99	111
Multilateral	2	7	11	17	21	23	32	34	59	72
Concessional	0	1	0	5	6	7	12	10	25	31
Bilateral	1	6	26	86	91	23	25	28	39	39
Concessional	1	6	1	8	13	19	21	20	29	29
Private creditors	0	1	2	18	46	170	545	194	315	1,471
Bonds	0	0	0	0	20	72	481	99	191	700
Commercial banks	0	0	0	15	21	45	61	91	120	768
Other private	0	0	2	4	4	53	3	4	4	4
Private nonguaranteed	**0**	**0**	**0**	**0**	**0**	**2**	**37**	**177**	**229**	**107**
Bonds	0	0	0	0	0	2	37	177	229	107
Commercial banks and other	0	0	0	0	0	0	0	0	0	0
Memo:										
IBRD	2	5	11	8	11	13	18	20	25	31
IDA	0	0	0	0	0	0	0	0	0	0
UNDISBURSED DEBT	**1**	**401**	**116**	**622**	**1,091**	**1,218**	**1,123**	**10,653**	**9,108**	**7,058**
Official creditors	1	164	79	606	773	875	898	813	693	610
Private creditors	0	237	37	16	319	343	224	9,840	8,415	6,448
Memorandum items										
Concessional LDOD	31	74	111	134	272	415	471	559	619	674
Variable rate LDOD	0	70	0	51	164	547	1,048	997	914	1,214
Public sector LDOD	64	216	358	778	1,551	1,933	2,357	4,030	5,336	7,008
Private sector LDOD	0	0	0	0	50	410	885	811	697	762

6. CURRENCY COMPOSITION OF LONG-TERM DEBT (PERCENT)

	1970	1980	1990	1994	1995	1996	1997	1998	1999	2000
Deutsche mark	0.0	0.7	5.3	1.2	1.1	2.7	8.3	5.1	3.2	2.2
French franc	21.9	6.0	31.7	23.5	8.2	6.2	4.6	2.8	1.9	15.8
Japanese yen	0.0	0.0	0.5	0.1	0.0	0.0	0.0	0.0	0.5	0.8
Pound sterling	0.0	0.0	0.7	0.2	0.1	0.1	0.1	0.0	0.0	0.0
Swiss franc	0.0	0.0	0.5	0.0	0.0	0.0	0.0	0.0	0.0	0.0
U.S.dollars	44.7	53.7	41.0	57.5	69.2	65.0	62.0	72.8	67.2	60.6
Multiple currency	0.0	18.4	9.4	8.3	7.4	6.8	6.5	5.0	4.5	3.6
Special drawing rights	0.0	0.0	0.0	0.0	0.0	0.0	0.0	0.0	0.1	0.1
All other currencies	33.4	21.2	10.9	9.2	14.0	19.2	18.5	14.3	22.6	16.9

LEBANON

(US$ million, unless otherwise indicated)

	1970	1980	1990	1994	1995	1996	1997	1998	1999	2000
7. DEBT RESTRUCTURINGS										
Total amount rescheduled	..	..	0	0	0	0	0	0	0	0
Debt stock rescheduled	..	..	0	0	0	0	0	0	0	0
Principal rescheduled	..	..	0	0	0	0	0	0	0	0
Official	..	..	0	0	0	0	0	0	0	0
Private	..	..	0	0	0	0	0	0	0	0
Interest rescheduled	..	..	0	0	0	0	0	0	0	0
Official	..	..	0	0	0	0	0	0	0	0
Private	..	..	0	0	0	0	0	0	0	0
Debt forgiven	..	..	0	0	0	0	0	0	0	0
Memo: interest forgiven	..	..	0	0	0	0	0	0	0	0
Debt stock reduction	..	..	0	0	0	0	0	0	0	0
of which debt buyback	..	..	0	0	0	0	0	0	0	0
8. DEBT STOCK-FLOW RECONCILIATION										
Total change in debt stocks	..	..	755	780	839	1,030	1,040	1,765	1,433	2,076
Net flows on debt	10	236	726	755	830	1,059	1,094	1,727	1,537	2,163
Net change in interest arrears	..	..	10	0	-9	-11	0	0	0	0
Interest capitalized	..	..	0	0	0	0	0	0	0	0
Debt forgiveness or reduction	..	..	0	0	0	0	0	0	0	0
Cross-currency valuation	..	..	17	27	19	-27	-48	40	-68	-89
Residual	..	..	3	-2	0	9	-6	-2	-36	3
9. AVERAGE TERMS OF NEW COMMITMENTS										
ALL CREDITORS										
Interest (%)	2.9	3.0	0.0	8.4	8.0	6.6	6.6	6.3	8.7	9.3
Maturity (years)	20.4	12.4	0.0	8.6	10.4	14.5	12.0	9.9	7.4	6.0
Grace period (years)	1.4	2.6	0.0	3.7	4.2	5.0	8.1	1.6	7.0	5.2
Grant element (%)	42.0	34.3	0.0	11.1	10.2	20.7	21.0	14.5	5.4	2.7
Official creditors										
Interest (%)	2.9	2.7	0.0	4.9	5.6	5.4	2.3	5.9	5.5	7.5
Maturity (years)	20.4	15.1	0.0	20.1	18.6	18.3	21.9	18.7	12.8	14.7
Grace period (years)	1.4	3.9	0.0	5.2	3.8	6.3	6.0	5.7	4.0	5.2
Grant element (%)	42.0	42.2	0.0	34.6	26.7	30.2	53.5	27.0	23.5	14.0
Private creditors										
Interest (%)	0.0	3.0	0.0	10.1	9.0	8.1	8.0	6.3	8.8	9.5
Maturity (years)	0.0	11.9	0.0	3.0	7.2	9.5	8.9	9.8	7.2	5.2
Grace period (years)	0.0	2.4	0.0	3.0	4.3	3.2	8.8	1.5	7.1	5.2
Grant element (%)	0.0	32.9	0.0	-0.3	3.7	8.0	10.6	14.3	4.6	1.6
Memorandum items										
Commitments	7	92	0	594	1,324	622	863	10,844	1,297	1,513
Official creditors	7	14	0	194	373	354	210	136	49	137
Private creditors	0	78	0	400	951	268	654	10,708	1,249	1,376

10. CONTRACTUAL OBLIGATIONS ON OUTSTANDING LONG-TERM DEBT

	2001	2002	2003	2004	2005	2006	2007	2008	2009	2010
TOTAL										
Disbursements	3,560	2,211	751	379	52	40	24	17	11	7
Principal	1,637	1,438	1,937	1,938	2,089	1,454	1,609	1,018	1,108	118
Interest	742	778	750	638	494	364	269	162	109	24
Official creditors										
Disbursements	150	130	96	77	52	40	24	17	11	7
Principal	85	94	98	109	117	190	125	124	124	113
Interest	51	54	55	54	52	49	40	35	29	24
Bilateral creditors										
Disbursements	38	24	12	6	2	1	0	0	0	0
Principal	26	26	27	32	32	32	32	31	31	27
Interest	13	12	12	11	10	9	8	7	6	4
Multilateral creditors										
Disbursements	112	107	85	72	51	39	24	17	11	7
Principal	59	67	71	78	86	159	94	94	93	86
Interest	39	41	43	43	43	40	32	28	24	19
Private creditors										
Disbursements	3,410	2,081	655	302	0	0	0	0	0	0
Principal	1,552	1,345	1,840	1,829	1,972	1,264	1,484	893	984	5
Interest	691	724	695	584	442	315	229	127	80	1
Commercial banks										
Disbursements	3,410	2,081	655	302	0	0	0	0	0	0
Principal	951	949	949	949	946	938	908	892	333	4
Interest	220	308	312	279	227	170	114	60	13	0
Other private										
Disbursements	0	0	0	0	0	0	0	0	0	0
Principal	602	396	891	880	1,026	326	576	1	651	1
Interest	471	417	383	305	215	145	116	67	67	0

LESOTHO

(US$ million, unless otherwise indicated)

	1970	1980	1990	1994	1995	1996	1997	1998	1999	2000
1. SUMMARY DEBT DATA										
TOTAL DEBT STOCKS (EDT)	**8.1**	**71.9**	**395.6**	**625.1**	**687.6**	**704.8**	**702.7**	**748.6**	**731.7**	**715.9**
Long-term debt (LDOD)	**8.1**	**57.7**	**377.7**	**577.4**	**641.4**	**663.0**	**667.2**	**717.1**	**707.2**	**697.8**
Public and publicly guaranteed	8.1	57.7	377.7	577.4	641.4	663.0	667.2	717.1	707.2	697.8
Private nonguaranteed	0.0	0.0	0.0	0.0	0.0	0.0	0.0	0.0	0.0	0.0
Use of IMF credit	**0.0**	**6.2**	**15.1**	**40.3**	**38.4**	**33.8**	**27.5**	**23.6**	**17.1**	**11.1**
Short-term debt	**0.0**	**8.0**	**2.8**	**7.4**	**7.9**	**8.0**	**7.9**	**7.9**	**7.4**	**7.0**
of which interest arrears on LDOD	0.0	0.0	0.8	3.4	3.9	4.0	3.9	3.9	3.4	3.0
Official creditors	0.0	0.0	0.5	1.5	1.8	1.9	1.8	1.6	1.5	1.2
Private creditors	0.0	0.0	0.3	1.8	2.1	2.1	2.1	2.3	1.9	1.8
Memo: principal arrears on LDOD	0.0	0.0	3.6	12.4	9.8	10.2	8.6	8.7	8.4	7.7
Official creditors	0.0	0.0	2.0	7.5	4.6	5.2	4.1	4.0	4.3	3.9
Private creditors	0.0	0.0	1.6	4.9	5.2	5.0	4.5	4.8	4.1	3.8
Memo: export credits	0.0	0.0	115.0	246.3	379.2	298.8	384.7	55.8	44.4	47.0
TOTAL DEBT FLOWS										
Disbursements	**0.4**	**15.0**	**62.0**	**68.9**	**70.4**	**76.0**	**68.2**	**67.0**	**45.7**	**70.6**
Long-term debt	0.4	13.3	57.9	63.5	70.4	76.0	68.2	67.0	45.7	70.6
IMF purchases	0.0	1.7	4.1	5.4	0.0	0.0	0.0	0.0	0.0	0.0
Principal repayments	**0.3**	**3.4**	**15.0**	**18.4**	**24.6**	**21.9**	**28.2**	**33.2**	**35.9**	**41.8**
Long-term debt	0.3	3.4	14.8	16.9	21.9	18.5	24.0	28.3	30.0	36.6
IMF repurchases	0.0	0.0	0.2	1.5	2.7	3.4	4.3	4.9	5.9	5.2
Net flows on debt	**0.1**	**19.6**	**47.0**	**50.5**	**45.8**	**54.2**	**40.0**	**33.7**	**9.8**	**28.8**
of which short-term debt	0.0	8.0	0.0	0.0	0.0	0.0	0.0	0.0	0.0	0.0
Interest payments (INT)	**0.2**	**2.1**	**8.3**	**11.3**	**16.1**	**16.2**	**20.3**	**23.7**	**23.3**	**24.0**
Long-term debt	0.2	1.5	8.0	11.0	15.6	15.7	19.9	23.5	22.9	23.8
IMF charges	0.0	0.0	0.1	0.1	0.2	0.3	0.2	0.1	0.2	0.0
Short-term debt	0.0	0.6	0.2	0.2	0.2	0.2	0.2	0.2	0.2	0.2
Net transfers on debt	**-0.1**	**17.5**	**38.7**	**39.2**	**29.7**	**38.0**	**19.7**	**10.0**	**-13.5**	**4.8**
Total debt service paid (TDS)	**0.5**	**5.5**	**23.3**	**29.7**	**40.7**	**38.0**	**48.5**	**57.0**	**59.2**	**65.8**
Long-term debt	0.5	4.8	22.8	27.9	37.5	34.1	43.9	51.8	52.9	60.4
IMF repurchases and charges	0.0	0.0	0.3	1.6	3.0	3.7	4.4	5.0	6.0	5.2
Short-term debt (interest only)	0.0	0.6	0.2	0.2	0.2	0.2	0.2	0.2	0.2	0.2
2. AGGREGATE NET RESOURCE FLOWS AND NET TRANSFERS (LONG-TERM)										
NET RESOURCE FLOWS	**7.3**	**66.4**	**120.0**	**111.3**	**382.2**	**390.5**	**351.0**	**336.8**	**201.7**	**179.5**
Net flow of long-term debt (ex. IMF)	0.1	10.0	43.1	46.6	48.5	57.6	44.3	38.6	15.7	34.0
Foreign direct investment (net)	0.0	4.5	17.0	18.7	275.0	288.0	268.0	265.0	163.3	118.0
Portfolio equity flows	0.0	0.0	0.0	0.0	0.0	0.0	0.0	0.0	0.0	0.0
Grants (excluding technical coop.)	7.3	52.0	59.9	46.0	58.7	44.9	38.7	33.1	22.7	27.6
Memo: technical coop. grants	2.6	32.0	44.5	35.6	36.8	31.1	29.0	17.9	12.4	11.3
official net resource flows	7.2	59.6	103.0	96.3	95.4	72.6	61.2	47.0	34.5	68.3
private net resource flows	0.1	6.8	17.0	15.0	286.8	317.9	289.8	289.8	167.2	111.2
NET TRANSFERS	**7.1**	**58.9**	**99.3**	**83.3**	**351.6**	**360.8**	**316.1**	**297.3**	**162.8**	**136.7**
Interest on long-term debt	0.2	1.5	8.0	11.0	15.6	15.7	19.9	23.5	22.9	23.8
Profit remittances on FDI	0.0	6.0	12.7	17.0	15.0	14.0	15.0	16.0	16.0	19.0
Memo: official net transfers	7.0	59.0	96.9	86.1	83.1	60.4	47.7	33.0	21.7	51.6
private net transfers	0.1	-0.1	2.4	-2.8	268.5	300.4	268.4	264.3	141.1	85.1
3. MAJOR ECONOMIC AGGREGATES										
Gross national income (GNI)	115.2	694.8	1,028.3	1,216.6	1,321.9	1,331.4	1,378.3	1,208.2	1,205.0	1,132.4
Exports of goods & services (XGS)	..	363.5	555.0	550.8	671.4	683.0	731.2	605.8	541.9	542.7
of which workers remittances	..	0.0	0.0	0.0	0.8	0.6	0.8	1.1	0.7	0.1
Imports of goods & services (MGS)	..	482.4	775.9	913.8	1,203.8	1,174.1	1,202.0	1,041.8	909.8	832.8
International reserves (RES)	..	50.3	72.4	372.6	456.7	460.5	571.7	575.1	499.6	417.9
Current account balance	..	56.3	65.0	108.1	-323.0	-302.5	-269.2	-280.2	-220.8	-151.4
4. DEBT INDICATORS										
EDT / XGS (%)	..	19.8	71.3	113.5	102.4	103.2	96.1	123.6	135.0	131.9
EDT / GNI (%)	7.0	10.4	38.5	51.4	52.0	52.9	51.0	62.0	60.7	63.2
TDS / XGS (%)	..	1.5	4.2	5.4	6.1	5.6	6.6	9.4	10.9	12.1
INT / XGS (%)	..	0.6	1.5	2.1	2.4	2.4	2.8	3.9	4.3	4.4
INT / GNI (%)	0.2	0.3	0.8	0.9	1.2	1.2	1.5	2.0	1.9	2.1
RES / EDT (%)	..	69.9	18.3	59.6	66.4	65.3	81.4	76.8	68.3	58.4
RES / MGS (months)	..	1.3	1.1	4.9	4.6	4.7	5.7	6.6	6.6	6.0
Short-term / EDT (%)	0.0	11.1	0.7	1.2	1.2	1.1	1.1	1.1	1.0	1.0
Concessional / EDT (%)	87.7	61.8	73.7	70.4	68.3	66.4	65.5	65.6	67.1	67.8
Multilateral / EDT (%)	50.6	56.1	73.6	68.7	67.9	67.1	66.8	66.9	66.5	66.1

LESOTHO

(US$ million, unless otherwise indicated)

	1970	1980	1990	1994	1995	1996	1997	1998	1999	2000
5. LONG-TERM DEBT										
DEBT OUTSTANDING (LDOD)	**8.1**	**57.7**	**377.7**	**577.4**	**641.4**	**663.0**	**667.2**	**717.1**	**707.2**	**697.8**
Public and publicly guaranteed	**8.1**	**57.7**	**377.7**	**577.4**	**641.4**	**663.0**	**667.2**	**717.1**	**707.2**	**697.8**
Official creditors	7.6	46.4	344.0	555.8	606.4	602.2	590.7	619.1	613.5	621.6
Multilateral	4.1	40.3	291.0	429.1	466.9	472.9	469.6	500.6	486.7	473.5
Concessional	4.1	40.3	251.6	351.6	374.8	377.1	374.3	401.7	398.2	387.5
Bilateral	3.5	6.1	53.1	126.8	139.5	129.3	121.2	118.5	126.8	148.1
Concessional	3.0	4.1	40.1	88.2	94.6	90.8	85.6	89.3	92.4	97.5
Private creditors	0.5	11.4	33.7	21.6	34.9	60.8	76.5	97.9	93.7	76.2
Bonds	0.0	0.0	0.0	0.0	0.0	0.0	0.0	0.0	0.0	0.0
Commercial banks	0.0	2.0	6.0	7.1	21.8	49.4	66.3	87.4	85.1	68.5
Other private	0.5	9.4	27.7	14.5	13.2	11.3	10.2	10.5	8.6	7.7
Private nonguaranteed	**0.0**	**0.0**	**0.0**	**0.0**	**0.0**	**0.0**	**0.0**	**0.0**	**0.0**	**0.0**
Bonds	0.0	0.0	0.0	0.0	0.0	0.0	0.0	0.0	0.0	0.0
Commercial banks and other	0.0	0.0	0.0	0.0	0.0	0.0	0.0	0.0	0.0	0.0
Memo:										
IBRD	0.0	0.0	0.0	41.7	54.0	57.1	58.3	60.8	56.0	58.6
IDA	4.1	24.1	111.7	143.0	152.8	159.3	162.9	180.1	185.0	183.2
DISBURSEMENTS	**0.4**	**13.3**	**57.9**	**63.5**	**70.4**	**76.0**	**68.2**	**67.0**	**45.7**	**70.6**
Public and publicly guaranteed	**0.4**	**13.3**	**57.9**	**63.5**	**70.4**	**76.0**	**68.2**	**67.0**	**45.7**	**70.6**
Official creditors	0.2	8.0	51.4	61.8	54.5	43.6	43.8	37.7	34.8	70.5
Multilateral	0.0	6.5	32.0	53.4	41.1	35.0	37.3	29.1	13.0	22.3
Concessional	0.0	6.5	28.3	36.0	23.7	19.7	23.4	23.1	12.8	12.0
Bilateral	0.2	1.5	19.4	8.3	13.4	8.6	6.5	8.6	21.9	48.1
Concessional	0.2	0.9	15.2	6.6	4.2	3.9	5.9	6.9	13.1	19.0
Private creditors	0.2	5.3	6.5	1.8	16.0	32.5	24.4	29.3	10.9	0.2
Bonds	0.0	0.0	0.0	0.0	0.0	0.0	0.0	0.0	0.0	0.0
Commercial banks	0.0	2.0	3.0	1.8	16.0	32.5	23.5	29.1	10.9	0.0
Other private	0.2	3.3	3.5	0.0	0.0	0.0	0.9	0.1	0.0	0.1
Private nonguaranteed	**0.0**	**0.0**	**0.0**	**0.0**	**0.0**	**0.0**	**0.0**	**0.0**	**0.0**	**0.0**
Bonds	0.0	0.0	0.0	0.0	0.0	0.0	0.0	0.0	0.0	0.0
Commercial banks and other	0.0	0.0	0.0	0.0	0.0	0.0	0.0	0.0	0.0	0.0
Memo:										
IBRD	0.0	0.0	0.0	13.7	11.2	7.2	8.2	3.4	0.1	9.9
IDA	0.0	3.8	9.2	6.3	8.8	11.7	11.6	14.3	10.2	7.8
PRINCIPAL REPAYMENTS	**0.3**	**3.4**	**14.8**	**16.9**	**21.9**	**18.5**	**24.0**	**28.3**	**30.0**	**36.6**
Public and publicly guaranteed	**0.3**	**3.4**	**14.8**	**16.9**	**21.9**	**18.5**	**24.0**	**28.3**	**30.0**	**36.6**
Official creditors	0.3	0.4	8.3	11.4	17.7	15.9	21.3	23.8	23.1	29.7
Multilateral	0.0	0.2	5.4	7.6	14.1	9.2	13.2	15.4	16.1	14.1
Concessional	0.0	0.2	3.0	4.4	9.1	6.2	7.5	7.5	8.1	7.2
Bilateral	0.3	0.2	2.9	3.8	3.7	6.7	8.1	8.4	6.9	15.6
Concessional	0.2	0.2	0.9	1.1	1.7	4.4	5.8	5.3	4.7	7.9
Private creditors	0.0	3.0	6.5	5.4	4.1	2.6	2.7	4.5	7.0	6.9
Bonds	0.0	0.0	0.0	0.0	0.0	0.0	0.0	0.0	0.0	0.0
Commercial banks	0.0	0.0	0.6	1.2	1.5	1.6	2.1	4.0	6.5	6.5
Other private	0.0	3.0	5.9	4.2	2.6	0.9	0.5	0.5	0.5	0.4
Private nonguaranteed	**0.0**	**0.0**	**0.0**	**0.0**	**0.0**	**0.0**	**0.0**	**0.0**	**0.0**	**0.0**
Bonds	0.0	0.0	0.0	0.0	0.0	0.0	0.0	0.0	0.0	0.0
Commercial banks and other	0.0	0.0	0.0	0.0	0.0	0.0	0.0	0.0	0.0	0.0
Memo:										
IBRD	0.0	0.0	0.0	0.0	0.0	0.0	2.2	4.5	4.2	3.9
IDA	0.0	0.0	0.6	1.1	1.3	1.5	1.6	1.9	2.1	2.5
NET FLOWS ON DEBT	**0.1**	**10.0**	**43.1**	**46.6**	**48.5**	**57.6**	**44.3**	**38.6**	**15.7**	**34.0**
Public and publicly guaranteed	**0.1**	**10.0**	**43.1**	**46.6**	**48.5**	**57.6**	**44.3**	**38.6**	**15.7**	**34.0**
Official creditors	-0.1	7.6	43.1	50.3	36.7	27.7	22.5	13.9	11.8	40.7
Multilateral	0.0	6.4	26.6	45.8	27.0	25.8	24.1	13.7	-3.2	8.2
Concessional	0.0	6.4	25.3	31.7	14.6	13.5	15.9	15.6	4.6	4.8
Bilateral	-0.1	1.3	16.5	4.5	9.8	1.8	-1.6	0.2	15.0	32.5
Concessional	0.0	0.7	14.3	5.4	2.5	-0.5	0.1	1.6	8.4	11.1
Private creditors	0.1	2.3	0.0	-3.7	11.8	29.9	21.8	24.8	3.9	-6.8
Bonds	0.0	0.0	0.0	0.0	0.0	0.0	0.0	0.0	0.0	0.0
Commercial banks	0.0	2.0	2.4	0.5	14.5	30.8	21.4	25.1	4.4	-6.5
Other private	0.1	0.3	-2.5	-4.2	-2.6	-0.9	0.4	-0.4	-0.5	-0.2
Private nonguaranteed	**0.0**	**0.0**	**0.0**	**0.0**	**0.0**	**0.0**	**0.0**	**0.0**	**0.0**	**0.0**
Bonds	0.0	0.0	0.0	0.0	0.0	0.0	0.0	0.0	0.0	0.0
Commercial banks and other	0.0	0.0	0.0	0.0	0.0	0.0	0.0	0.0	0.0	0.0
Memo:										
IBRD	0.0	0.0	0.0	13.7	11.2	7.2	6.0	-1.1	-4.1	6.0
IDA	0.0	3.8	8.6	5.2	7.4	10.3	10.0	12.5	8.1	5.3

LESOTHO

(US$ million, unless otherwise indicated)

	1970	1980	1990	1994	1995	1996	1997	1998	1999	2000
INTEREST PAYMENTS (LINT)	**0.2**	**1.5**	**8.0**	**11.0**	**15.6**	**15.7**	**19.9**	**23.5**	**22.9**	**23.8**
Public and publicly guaranteed	**0.2**	**1.5**	**8.0**	**11.0**	**15.6**	**15.7**	**19.9**	**23.5**	**22.9**	**23.8**
Official creditors	0.2	0.6	6.1	10.2	12.3	12.2	13.5	14.0	12.8	16.7
Multilateral	0.0	0.4	4.7	6.6	8.6	8.1	9.2	9.0	8.9	7.6
Concessional	0.0	0.3	2.1	2.3	3.1	3.1	3.5	3.7	3.7	3.2
Bilateral	0.2	0.2	1.4	3.6	3.7	4.1	4.3	5.0	3.9	9.1
Concessional	0.1	0.0	0.6	1.4	1.6	1.7	1.6	1.8	1.4	5.5
Private creditors	0.0	0.9	1.9	0.8	3.3	3.5	6.4	9.5	10.1	7.1
Bonds	0.0	0.0	0.0	0.0	0.0	0.0	0.0	0.0	0.0	0.0
Commercial banks	0.0	0.3	0.3	0.4	3.0	3.2	6.2	9.1	9.7	6.9
Other private	0.0	0.6	1.6	0.4	0.3	0.3	0.1	0.4	0.3	0.2
Private nonguaranteed	**0.0**	**0.0**	**0.0**	**0.0**	**0.0**	**0.0**	**0.0**	**0.0**	**0.0**	**0.0**
Bonds	0.0	0.0	0.0	0.0	0.0	0.0	0.0	0.0	0.0	0.0
Commercial banks and other	0.0	0.0	0.0	0.0	0.0	0.0	0.0	0.0	0.0	0.0
Memo:										
IBRD	0.0	0.0	0.0	2.5	3.5	3.8	3.7	3.7	3.7	3.2
IDA	0.0	0.2	0.8	1.0	1.1	1.2	1.2	1.2	1.3	1.4
NET TRANSFERS ON DEBT	**-0.1**	**8.5**	**35.1**	**35.6**	**32.9**	**41.9**	**24.3**	**15.2**	**-7.2**	**10.2**
Public and publicly guaranteed	**-0.1**	**8.5**	**35.1**	**35.6**	**32.9**	**41.9**	**24.3**	**15.2**	**-7.2**	**10.2**
Official creditors	-0.2	7.1	37.0	40.1	24.4	15.5	9.0	-0.1	-1.0	24.1
Multilateral	0.0	6.0	21.9	39.2	18.3	17.7	14.9	4.7	-12.1	0.6
Concessional	0.0	6.1	23.1	29.3	11.5	10.4	12.4	11.9	0.9	1.6
Bilateral	-0.2	1.1	15.2	0.9	6.0	-2.2	-5.9	-4.8	11.1	23.4
Concessional	-0.1	0.7	13.7	4.1	0.9	-2.2	-1.5	-0.1	7.0	5.6
Private creditors	0.1	1.4	-2.0	-4.5	8.5	26.4	15.4	15.3	-6.2	-13.9
Bonds	0.0	0.0	0.0	0.0	0.0	0.0	0.0	0.0	0.0	0.0
Commercial banks	0.0	1.8	2.2	0.1	11.4	27.6	15.2	16.0	-5.4	-13.4
Other private	0.1	-0.3	-4.1	-4.6	-2.9	-1.2	0.2	-0.8	-0.8	-0.5
Private nonguaranteed	**0.0**	**0.0**	**0.0**	**0.0**	**0.0**	**0.0**	**0.0**	**0.0**	**0.0**	**0.0**
Bonds	0.0	0.0	0.0	0.0	0.0	0.0	0.0	0.0	0.0	0.0
Commercial banks and other	0.0	0.0	0.0	0.0	0.0	0.0	0.0	0.0	0.0	0.0
Memo:										
IBRD	0.0	0.0	0.0	11.3	7.7	3.4	2.3	-4.7	-7.8	2.8
IDA	0.0	3.6	7.9	4.2	6.3	9.1	8.8	11.2	6.7	3.9
DEBT SERVICE (LTDS)	**0.5**	**4.8**	**22.8**	**27.9**	**37.5**	**34.1**	**43.9**	**51.8**	**52.9**	**60.4**
Public and publicly guaranteed	**0.5**	**4.8**	**22.8**	**27.9**	**37.5**	**34.1**	**43.9**	**51.8**	**52.9**	**60.4**
Official creditors	0.4	1.0	14.4	21.7	30.1	28.1	34.8	37.8	35.9	46.4
Multilateral	0.0	0.5	10.2	14.2	22.7	17.3	22.4	24.4	25.1	21.7
Concessional	0.0	0.4	5.2	6.7	12.2	9.3	11.0	11.2	11.8	10.4
Bilateral	0.4	0.4	4.2	7.5	7.4	10.8	12.4	13.4	10.8	24.7
Concessional	0.3	0.3	1.5	2.5	3.2	6.1	7.3	7.0	6.1	13.4
Private creditors	0.1	3.9	8.5	6.3	7.4	6.1	9.1	14.0	17.1	14.0
Bonds	0.0	0.0	0.0	0.0	0.0	0.0	0.0	0.0	0.0	0.0
Commercial banks	0.0	0.3	0.9	1.6	4.5	4.9	8.4	13.1	16.3	13.4
Other private	0.1	3.6	7.6	4.6	2.9	1.2	0.7	0.9	0.8	0.6
Private nonguaranteed	**0.0**	**0.0**	**0.0**	**0.0**	**0.0**	**0.0**	**0.0**	**0.0**	**0.0**	**0.0**
Bonds	0.0	0.0	0.0	0.0	0.0	0.0	0.0	0.0	0.0	0.0
Commercial banks and other	0.0	0.0	0.0	0.0	0.0	0.0	0.0	0.0	0.0	0.0
Memo:										
IBRD	0.0	0.0	0.0	2.5	3.5	3.8	5.8	8.1	7.9	7.1
IDA	0.0	0.2	1.4	2.2	2.5	2.6	2.8	3.1	3.5	3.9
UNDISBURSED DEBT	**0.8**	**118.0**	**315.0**	**493.7**	**482.0**	**292.8**	**220.9**	**194.6**	**304.0**	**203.4**
Official creditors	0.1	110.0	312.3	341.3	309.7	222.4	173.8	179.4	301.0	201.0
Private creditors	0.7	8.0	2.7	152.4	172.3	70.3	47.1	15.3	3.1	2.3
Memorandum items										
Concessional LDOD	7.1	44.3	291.7	439.8	469.4	467.9	460.0	491.0	490.6	484.9
Variable rate LDOD	0.0	2.0	0.0	41.7	54.0	57.1	58.3	60.8	61.9	87.1
Public sector LDOD	8.1	55.7	376.5	576.7	640.7	662.3	666.6	716.6	706.8	697.5
Private sector LDOD	0.0	2.0	1.2	0.8	0.7	0.7	0.6	0.5	0.4	0.3

6. CURRENCY COMPOSITION OF LONG-TERM DEBT (PERCENT)

	1970	1980	1990	1994	1995	1996	1997	1998	1999	2000
Deutsche mark	0.0	0.0	0.4	0.0	0.0	0.0	0.0	0.0	0.0	0.0
French franc	0.0	0.0	7.5	8.4	8.1	6.9	6.2	6.1	5.0	4.8
Japanese yen	0.0	0.0	0.0	0.0	0.0	0.0	0.0	0.0	0.0	0.0
Pound sterling	43.0	16.4	1.7	1.0	0.8	1.0	1.3	1.8	2.0	1.7
Swiss franc	0.0	0.0	0.0	0.0	0.0	0.0	0.0	0.0	0.0	1.1
U.S.dollars	50.5	46.4	24.8	23.0	22.1	22.6	23.5	24.3	25.2	26.5
Multiple currency	0.0	7.0	5.6	17.1	20.2	20.3	19.9	18.2	17.0	15.5
Special drawing rights	0.0	0.0	9.9	7.6	6.9	6.4	6.0	5.8	5.6	5.3
All other currencies	6.5	30.2	50.1	42.9	41.9	42.8	43.1	43.8	45.2	45.1

LESOTHO

(US$ million, unless otherwise indicated)

	1970	1980	1990	1994	1995	1996	1997	1998	1999	2000
7. DEBT RESTRUCTURINGS										
Total amount rescheduled	..	..	0.0	0.0	0.0	0.0	0.0	0.0	0.0	0.0
Debt stock rescheduled	..	..	0.0	0.0	0.0	0.0	0.0	0.0	0.0	0.0
Principal rescheduled	..	..	0.0	0.0	0.0	0.0	0.0	0.0	0.0	0.0
Official	..	..	0.0	0.0	0.0	0.0	0.0	0.0	0.0	0.0
Private	..	..	0.0	0.0	0.0	0.0	0.0	0.0	0.0	0.0
Interest rescheduled	..	..	0.0	0.0	0.0	0.0	0.0	0.0	0.0	0.0
Official	..	..	0.0	0.0	0.0	0.0	0.0	0.0	0.0	0.0
Private	..	..	0.0	0.0	0.0	0.0	0.0	0.0	0.0	0.0
Debt forgiven	..	..	3.7	0.0	0.0	0.0	0.0	0.0	0.0	0.0
Memo: interest forgiven	..	..	0.0	0.0	0.0	0.0	0.0	0.0	0.0	0.0
Debt stock reduction	..	..	0.0	0.0	0.0	0.0	0.0	0.0	0.0	0.0
of which debt buyback	..	..	0.0	0.0	0.0	0.0	0.0	0.0	0.0	0.0
8. DEBT STOCK-FLOW RECONCILIATION										
Total change in debt stocks	..	..	67.4	82.0	62.5	17.2	-2.1	45.9	-16.8	-15.8
Net flows on debt	0.1	19.6	47.0	50.5	45.8	54.2	40.0	33.7	9.8	28.8
Net change in interest arrears	..	..	0.8	1.6	0.5	0.2	-0.1	-0.1	-0.5	-0.4
Interest capitalized	..	..	0.0	0.0	0.0	0.0	0.0	0.0	0.0	0.0
Debt forgiveness or reduction	..	..	-3.7	0.0	0.0	0.0	0.0	0.0	0.0	0.0
Cross-currency valuation	..	..	7.2	5.8	1.5	-45.2	-35.9	0.0	-19.5	-29.1
Residual	..	..	16.2	24.0	14.7	8.0	-6.1	12.2	-6.7	-15.1
9. AVERAGE TERMS OF NEW COMMITMENTS										
ALL CREDITORS										
Interest (%)	5.0	5.9	1.3	4.9	6.3	8.2	5.1	4.6	2.7	0.8
Maturity (years)	18.1	24.3	24.3	16.6	22.0	31.9	13.1	23.5	17.4	39.6
Grace period (years)	1.9	5.7	6.0	6.1	4.8	16.4	2.7	6.6	3.5	10.1
Grant element (%)	31.9	37.3	63.2	38.0	26.8	13.4	25.5	39.9	40.6	80.4
Official creditors										
Interest (%)	0.0	3.0	1.0	1.0	5.9	0.8	4.0	4.6	2.7	0.8
Maturity (years)	25.0	29.8	25.1	21.5	27.5	39.5	16.1	23.5	17.4	39.6
Grace period (years)	5.5	6.7	6.2	8.9	5.7	10.0	3.3	6.6	3.5	10.1
Grant element (%)	72.7	52.7	65.9	65.4	33.7	80.3	34.7	39.9	40.6	80.4
Private creditors										
Interest (%)	7.5	15.8	8.4	8.9	6.5	16.3	6.7	0.0	0.0	0.0
Maturity (years)	14.6	5.5	5.9	11.4	17.6	23.5	8.6	0.0	0.0	0.0
Grace period (years)	0.1	2.2	1.8	3.1	4.1	23.5	1.8	0.0	0.0	0.0
Grant element (%)	10.9	-15.0	4.3	9.0	21.2	-59.8	12.0	0.0	0.0	0.0
Memorandum items										
Commitments	0.4	58.5	46.4	63.8	67.4	76.6	20.9	66.5	191.9	11.2
Official creditors	0.2	45.2	44.4	32.7	30.1	40.0	12.4	66.5	191.9	11.2
Private creditors	0.3	13.3	2.0	31.1	37.3	36.6	8.5	0.0	0.0	0.0

10. CONTRACTUAL OBLIGATIONS ON OUTSTANDING LONG-TERM DEBT

	2001	2002	2003	2004	2005	2006	2007	2008	2009	2010
TOTAL										
Disbursements	65.2	52.3	36.1	23.2	12.9	6.7	4.3	2.2	0.5	0.0
Principal	47.1	47.7	49.2	51.1	52.7	52.3	49.1	47.1	42.0	26.7
Interest	21.6	21.4	20.5	19.1	17.3	15.4	13.5	11.7	10.0	8.8
Official creditors										
Disbursements	63.6	51.6	36.1	23.2	12.9	6.7	4.3	2.2	0.5	0.0
Principal	40.3	40.9	42.9	45.2	47.1	46.8	45.3	44.4	41.4	26.4
Interest	14.3	14.5	14.2	13.2	11.8	10.3	8.8	7.3	5.7	4.6
Bilateral creditors										
Disbursements	35.3	22.5	14.0	7.3	3.5	1.1	0.6	0.0	0.0	0.0
Principal	20.4	20.7	20.7	21.0	21.9	22.0	20.8	20.0	19.9	7.8
Interest	6.0	6.2	6.0	5.4	4.7	3.9	3.0	2.2	1.4	0.8
Multilateral creditors										
Disbursements	28.3	29.0	22.1	15.9	9.5	5.6	3.7	2.2	0.5	0.0
Principal	19.9	20.2	22.2	24.2	25.2	24.9	24.5	24.4	21.5	18.6
Interest	8.2	8.3	8.2	7.8	7.2	6.5	5.8	5.1	4.3	3.8
Private creditors										
Disbursements	1.7	0.7	0.0	0.0	0.0	0.0	0.0	0.0	0.0	0.0
Principal	6.8	6.8	6.3	5.9	5.6	5.4	3.8	2.7	0.7	0.4
Interest	7.3	6.9	6.4	5.9	5.5	5.1	4.7	4.4	4.3	4.3
Commercial banks										
Disbursements	1.7	0.7	0.0	0.0	0.0	0.0	0.0	0.0	0.0	0.0
Principal	6.2	6.2	5.8	5.4	5.4	5.2	3.6	2.5	0.4	0.1
Interest	7.0	6.6	6.2	5.8	5.4	5.0	4.6	4.4	4.3	4.2
Other private										
Disbursements	0.0	0.0	0.0	0.0	0.0	0.0	0.0	0.0	0.0	0.0
Principal	0.6	0.6	0.5	0.5	0.2	0.2	0.2	0.2	0.2	0.2
Interest	0.3	0.2	0.2	0.1	0.1	0.1	0.1	0.1	0.1	0.0

LIBERIA

(US$ million, unless otherwise indicated)

	1970	1980	1990	1994	1995	1996	1997	1998	1999	2000
1. SUMMARY DEBT DATA										
TOTAL DEBT STOCKS (EDT)	**162**	**686**	**1,849**	**2,056**	**2,154**	**2,107**	**2,012**	**2,103**	**2,077**	**2,032**
Long-term debt (LDOD)	**158**	**516**	**1,116**	**1,137**	**1,161**	**1,110**	**1,061**	**1,092**	**1,062**	**1,040**
Public and publicly guaranteed	158	516	1,116	1,137	1,161	1,110	1,061	1,092	1,062	1,040
Private nonguaranteed	0	0	0	0	0	0	0	0	0	0
Use of IMF credit	**4**	**89**	**322**	**330**	**336**	**325**	**305**	**317**	**309**	**292**
Short-term debt	**0**	**81**	**411**	**589**	**657**	**672**	**646**	**694**	**707**	**699**
of which interest arrears on LDOD	0	2	355	545	613	617	612	656	668	665
Official creditors	0	1	251	390	458	467	466	506	515	516
Private creditors	0	1	104	155	155	151	146	150	153	149
Memo: principal arrears on LDOD	0	3	722	924	961	956	940	991	999	1,053
Official creditors	0	2	530	715	754	756	749	792	795	856
Private creditors	0	1	192	208	208	199	192	199	205	197
Memo: export credits	0	0	203	52	295	382	320	234	282	235
TOTAL DEBT FLOWS										
Disbursements	**9**	**109**	**0**	**0**	**0**	**0**	**0**	**0**	**0**	**0**
Long-term debt	7	76	0	0	0	0	0	0	0	0
IMF purchases	2	34	0	0	0	0	0	0	0	0
Principal repayments	**17**	**18**	**2**	**15**	**0**	**0**	**0**	**1**	**1**	**1**
Long-term debt	11	15	1	14	0	0	0	0	0	0
IMF repurchases	5	3	1	1	0	0	0	1	1	1
Net flows on debt	**-7**	**95**	**-1**	**-14**	**0**	**11**	**-21**	**3**	**1**	**-5**
of which short-term debt	0	4	1	1	0	11	-21	4	1	-5
Interest payments (INT)	**6**	**35**	**1**	**0**	**2**	**1**	**0**	**0**	**2**	**0**
Long-term debt	6	23	1	0	0	0	0	0	0	0
IMF charges	0	2	0	0	2	1	0	0	2	0
Short-term debt	0	11	0	0	0	0	0	0	0	0
Net transfers on debt	**-13**	**60**	**-2**	**-14**	**-2**	**10**	**-21**	**3**	**-2**	**-5**
Total debt service paid (TDS)	**23**	**54**	**3**	**15**	**2**	**1**	**0**	**1**	**3**	**1**
Long-term debt	18	38	2	14	0	0	0	0	0	0
IMF repurchases and charges	5	5	1	1	2	1	0	1	3	1
Short-term debt (interest only)	0	11	0	0	0	0	0	0	0	0
2. AGGREGATE NET RESOURCE FLOWS AND NET TRANSFERS (LONG-TERM)										
NET RESOURCE FLOWS	**-3**	**83**	**59**	**54**	**129**	**112**	**84**	**76**	**92**	**58**
Net flow of long-term debt (ex. IMF)	-4	61	-1	-14	0	0	0	0	0	0
Foreign direct investment (net)	0	0	0	14	21	17	15	16	10	12
Portfolio equity flows	0	0	0	0	0	0	0	0	0	0
Grants (excluding technical coop.)	1	23	60	53	108	95	69	60	82	47
Memo: technical coop. grants	8	24	21	11	16	10	15	18	20	24
official net resource flows	4	84	59	40	108	95	69	60	82	47
private net resource flows	-7	0	0	14	21	17	15	16	10	12
NET TRANSFERS	**-9**	**61**	**59**	**54**	**129**	**111**	**84**	**76**	**92**	**58**
Interest on long-term debt	6	23	1	0	0	0	0	0	0	0
Profit remittances on FDI	0	0	0	0	0	0	0	0	0	0
Memo: official net transfers	1	77	59	40	108	94	69	60	82	47
private net transfers	-10	-16	0	14	21	17	15	16	10	12
3. MAJOR ECONOMIC AGGREGATES										
Gross national income (GNI)	402	1,093	..	..	..	..	..	..	..	..
Exports of goods & services (XGS)	..	613	..	..	..	..	..	..	..	..
of which workers remittances	..	0	..	..	..	..	..	..	..	..
Imports of goods & services (MGS)	..	575	..	..	..	..	..	..	..	..
International reserves (RES)	..	5	..	5	28	0	0	1	0	0
Current account balance	..	46	..	..	..	..	..	..	..	..
4. DEBT INDICATORS										
EDT / XGS (%)	..	111.8	..	..	..	..	..	..	..	..
EDT / GNI (%)	40.3	62.7	..	..	..	..	..	..	..	..
TDS / XGS (%)	..	8.8	..	..	..	..	..	..	..	..
INT / XGS (%)	..	5.8	..	..	..	..	..	..	..	..
INT / GNI (%)	1.5	3.2	..	..	..	..	..	..	..	..
RES / EDT (%)	..	0.8	..	0.3	1.3	0.0	0.0	0.0	0.0	0.0
RES / MGS (months)	..	0.1	..	..	..	..	..	..	..	..
Short-term / EDT (%)	0.0	11.8	22.2	28.7	30.5	31.9	32.1	33.0	34.0	34.4
Concessional / EDT (%)	67.7	30.8	32.1	30.3	29.5	28.9	29.1	28.5	28.0	27.9
Multilateral / EDT (%)	4.7	19.1	23.4	21.4	21.0	20.1	20.1	19.9	19.2	19.5

LIBERIA

(US$ million, unless otherwise indicated)

	1970	1980	1990	1994	1995	1996	1997	1998	1999	2000
5. LONG-TERM DEBT										
DEBT OUTSTANDING (LDOD)	**158**	**516**	**1,116**	**1,137**	**1,161**	**1,110**	**1,061**	**1,092**	**1,062**	**1,040**
Public and publicly guaranteed	**158**	**516**	**1,116**	**1,137**	**1,161**	**1,110**	**1,061**	**1,092**	**1,062**	**1,040**
Official creditors	124	359	924	929	954	911	869	894	858	843
Multilateral	8	131	433	439	453	424	405	418	398	395
Concessional	0	33	184	211	214	202	197	200	198	194
Bilateral	116	229	491	490	501	486	465	476	460	448
Concessional	110	179	410	411	421	408	388	399	384	374
Private creditors	34	156	192	208	208	199	192	199	205	197
Bonds	0	0	0	0	0	0	0	0	0	0
Commercial banks	0	129	172	189	187	180	173	180	187	180
Other private	34	28	20	20	21	20	19	19	18	17
Private nonguaranteed	**0**	**0**	**0**	**0**	**0**	**0**	**0**	**0**	**0**	**0**
Bonds	0	0	0	0	0	0	0	0	0	0
Commercial banks and other	0	0	0	0	0	0	0	0	0	0
Memo:										
IBRD	7	69	143	151	161	146	136	143	125	130
IDA	0	23	105	107	108	106	102	105	103	100
DISBURSEMENTS	**7**	**76**	**0**	**0**	**0**	**0**	**0**	**0**	**0**	**0**
Public and publicly guaranteed	**7**	**76**	**0**	**0**	**0**	**0**	**0**	**0**	**0**	**0**
Official creditors	7	65	0	0	0	0	0	0	0	0
Multilateral	2	33	0	0	0	0	0	0	0	0
Concessional	0	8	0	0	0	0	0	0	0	0
Bilateral	5	32	0	0	0	0	0	0	0	0
Concessional	4	30	0	0	0	0	0	0	0	0
Private creditors	0	11	0	0	0	0	0	0	0	0
Bonds	0	0	0	0	0	0	0	0	0	0
Commercial banks	0	6	0	0	0	0	0	0	0	0
Other private	0	5	0	0	0	0	0	0	0	0
Private nonguaranteed	**0**	**0**	**0**	**0**	**0**	**0**	**0**	**0**	**0**	**0**
Bonds	0	0	0	0	0	0	0	0	0	0
Commercial banks and other	0	0	0	0	0	0	0	0	0	0
Memo:										
IBRD	2	17	0	0	0	0	0	0	0	0
IDA	0	5	0	0	0	0	0	0	0	0
PRINCIPAL REPAYMENTS	**11**	**15**	**1**	**14**	**0**	**0**	**0**	**0**	**0**	**0**
Public and publicly guaranteed	**11**	**15**	**1**	**14**	**0**	**0**	**0**	**0**	**0**	**0**
Official creditors	5	4	1	14	0	0	0	0	0	0
Multilateral	0	2	1	14	0	0	0	0	0	0
Concessional	0	0	0	1	0	0	0	0	0	0
Bilateral	5	1	0	0	0	0	0	0	0	0
Concessional	5	1	0	0	0	0	0	0	0	0
Private creditors	7	12	0	0	0	0	0	0	0	0
Bonds	0	0	0	0	0	0	0	0	0	0
Commercial banks	0	3	0	0	0	0	0	0	0	0
Other private	7	9	0	0	0	0	0	0	0	0
Private nonguaranteed	**0**	**0**	**0**	**0**	**0**	**0**	**0**	**0**	**0**	**0**
Bonds	0	0	0	0	0	0	0	0	0	0
Commercial banks and other	0	0	0	0	0	0	0	0	0	0
Memo:										
IBRD	0	2	0	0	0	0	0	0	0	0
IDA	0	0	0	0	0	0	0	0	0	0
NET FLOWS ON DEBT	**-4**	**61**	**-1**	**-14**	**0**	**0**	**0**	**0**	**0**	**0**
Public and publicly guaranteed	**-4**	**61**	**-1**	**-14**	**0**	**0**	**0**	**0**	**0**	**0**
Official creditors	3	61	-1	-14	0	0	0	0	0	0
Multilateral	2	31	-1	-14	0	0	0	0	0	0
Concessional	0	8	0	-1	0	0	0	0	0	0
Bilateral	0	30	0	0	0	0	0	0	0	0
Concessional	-1	29	0	0	0	0	0	0	0	0
Private creditors	-7	0	0	0	0	0	0	0	0	0
Bonds	0	0	0	0	0	0	0	0	0	0
Commercial banks	0	3	0	0	0	0	0	0	0	0
Other private	-7	-3	0	0	0	0	0	0	0	0
Private nonguaranteed	**0**	**0**	**0**	**0**	**0**	**0**	**0**	**0**	**0**	**0**
Bonds	0	0	0	0	0	0	0	0	0	0
Commercial banks and other	0	0	0	0	0	0	0	0	0	0
Memo:										
IBRD	2	16	0	0	0	0	0	0	0	0
IDA	0	5	0	0	0	0	0	0	0	0

LIBERIA

(US$ million, unless otherwise indicated)

	1970	1980	1990	1994	1995	1996	1997	1998	1999	2000
INTEREST PAYMENTS (LINT)	**6**	**23**	**1**	**0**	**0**	**0**	**0**	**0**	**0**	**0**
Public and publicly guaranteed	**6**	**23**	**1**	**0**	**0**	**0**	**0**	**0**	**0**	**0**
Official creditors	3	7	1	0	0	0	0	0	0	0
Multilateral	0	5	1	0	0	0	0	0	0	0
Concessional	0	0	0	0	0	0	0	0	0	0
Bilateral	3	2	0	0	0	0	0	0	0	0
Concessional	2	2	0	0	0	0	0	0	0	0
Private creditors	3	16	0	0	0	0	0	0	0	0
Bonds	0	0	0	0	0	0	0	0	0	0
Commercial banks	0	14	0	0	0	0	0	0	0	0
Other private	3	2	0	0	0	0	0	0	0	0
Private nonguaranteed	**0**	**0**	**0**	**0**	**0**	**0**	**0**	**0**	**0**	**0**
Bonds	0	0	0	0	0	0	0	0	0	0
Commercial banks and other	0	0	0	0	0	0	0	0	0	0
Memo:										
IBRD	0	4	0	0	0	0	0	0	0	0
IDA	0	0	0	0	0	0	0	0	0	0
NET TRANSFERS ON DEBT	**-10**	**38**	**-2**	**-14**	**0**	**0**	**0**	**0**	**0**	**0**
Public and publicly guaranteed	**-10**	**38**	**-2**	**-14**	**0**	**0**	**0**	**0**	**0**	**0**
Official creditors	-1	54	-2	-14	0	0	0	0	0	0
Multilateral	2	25	-2	-14	0	0	0	0	0	0
Concessional	0	8	0	-1	0	0	0	0	0	0
Bilateral	-2	29	0	0	0	0	0	0	0	0
Concessional	-3	28	0	0	0	0	0	0	0	0
Private creditors	-10	-16	0	0	0	0	0	0	0	0
Bonds	0	0	0	0	0	0	0	0	0	0
Commercial banks	0	-11	0	0	0	0	0	0	0	0
Other private	-10	-5	0	0	0	0	0	0	0	0
Private nonguaranteed	**0**	**0**	**0**	**0**	**0**	**0**	**0**	**0**	**0**	**0**
Bonds	0	0	0	0	0	0	0	0	0	0
Commercial banks and other	0	0	0	0	0	0	0	0	0	0
Memo:										
IBRD	1	12	0	0	0	0	0	0	0	0
IDA	0	5	0	0	0	0	0	0	0	0
DEBT SERVICE (LTDS)	**18**	**38**	**2**	**14**	**0**	**0**	**0**	**0**	**0**	**0**
Public and publicly guaranteed	**18**	**38**	**2**	**14**	**0**	**0**	**0**	**0**	**0**	**0**
Official creditors	8	11	2	14	0	0	0	0	0	0
Multilateral	0	8	2	14	0	0	0	0	0	0
Concessional	0	0	0	1	0	0	0	0	0	0
Bilateral	8	3	0	0	0	0	0	0	0	0
Concessional	7	3	0	0	0	0	0	0	0	0
Private creditors	10	27	0	0	0	0	0	0	0	0
Bonds	0	0	0	0	0	0	0	0	0	0
Commercial banks	0	17	0	0	0	0	0	0	0	0
Other private	10	11	0	0	0	0	0	0	0	0
Private nonguaranteed	**0**	**0**	**0**	**0**	**0**	**0**	**0**	**0**	**0**	**0**
Bonds	0	0	0	0	0	0	0	0	0	0
Commercial banks and other	0	0	0	0	0	0	0	0	0	0
Memo:										
IBRD	0	6	0	0	0	0	0	0	0	0
IDA	0	0	0	0	0	0	0	0	0	0
UNDISBURSED DEBT	**20**	**228**	**84**	**36**	**18**	**17**	**15**	**16**	**3**	**0**
Official creditors	18	220	84	36	18	17	15	16	3	0
Private creditors	2	8	0	0	0	0	0	0	0	0
Memorandum items										
Concessional LDOD	110	211	594	622	635	610	585	599	582	568
Variable rate LDOD	0	100	123	123	123	123	123	123	123	123
Public sector LDOD	158	514	1,116	1,137	1,161	1,110	1,061	1,092	1,062	1,040
Private sector LDOD	0	1	0	0	0	0	0	0	0	0

6. CURRENCY COMPOSITION OF LONG-TERM DEBT (PERCENT)

	1970	1980	1990	1994	1995	1996	1997	1998	1999	2000
Deutsche mark	12.7	9.2	11.1	10.5	11.1	10.7	9.7	10.1	8.9	8.5
French franc	0.0	0.0	1.1	1.0	1.1	1.0	1.0	1.0	0.9	0.8
Japanese yen	0.0	7.6	6.1	8.1	7.7	7.1	6.6	7.3	8.4	7.7
Pound sterling	0.3	1.5	1.2	1.2	1.2	1.2	1.3	1.2	1.3	1.3
Swiss franc	0.0	0.0	0.0	0.0	0.0	0.0	0.0	0.0	0.0	0.0
U.S.dollars	82.1	62.6	51.2	50.3	49.4	51.5	53.5	52.2	53.5	54.4
Multiple currency	4.9	17.4	22.7	20.8	21.4	20.4	20.1	20.4	19.3	19.9
Special drawing rights	0.0	0.0	1.5	1.5	1.5	1.5	1.5	1.5	1.5	1.4
All other currencies	0.0	1.7	5.1	6.6	6.6	6.6	6.3	6.3	6.2	6.0

LIBERIA

(US$ million, unless otherwise indicated)

	1970	1980	1990	1994	1995	1996	1997	1998	1999	2000
7. DEBT RESTRUCTURINGS										
Total amount rescheduled	..	..	0	0	0	0	0	0	0	0
Debt stock rescheduled	..	..	0	0	0	0	0	0	0	0
Principal rescheduled	..	..	0	0	0	0	0	0	0	0
Official	..	..	0	0	0	0	0	0	0	0
Private	..	..	0	0	0	0	0	0	0	0
Interest rescheduled	..	..	0	0	0	0	0	0	0	0
Official	..	..	0	0	0	0	0	0	0	0
Private	..	..	0	0	0	0	0	0	0	0
Debt forgiven	..	..	0	0	0	0	0	0	0	0
Memo: interest forgiven	..	..	0	0	0	0	0	0	0	0
Debt stock reduction	..	..	0	0	0	0	0	0	0	0
of which debt buyback	..	..	0	0	0	0	0	0	0	0
8. DEBT STOCK-FLOW RECONCILIATION										
Total change in debt stocks	..	..	164	99	98	-48	-95	91	-26	-46
Net flows on debt	-7	95	-1	-14	0	11	-21	3	1	-5
Net change in interest arrears	..	..	87	45	68	4	-5	44	12	-3
Interest capitalized	..	..	0	0	0	0	0	0	0	0
Debt forgiveness or reduction	..	..	0	0	0	0	0	0	0	0
Cross-currency valuation	..	..	63	55	23	-63	-66	34	-35	-32
Residual	..	..	15	13	8	1	-3	10	-4	-6
9. AVERAGE TERMS OF NEW COMMITMENTS										
ALL CREDITORS										
Interest (%)	6.6	7.3	4.0	0.0	0.0	0.0	0.0	0.0	0.0	0.0
Maturity (years)	18.7	18.8	24.8	0.0	0.0	0.0	0.0	0.0	0.0	0.0
Grace period (years)	4.4	4.5	5.3	0.0	0.0	0.0	0.0	0.0	0.0	0.0
Grant element (%)	20.7	25.1	42.8	0.0	0.0	0.0	0.0	0.0	0.0	0.0
Official creditors										
Interest (%)	6.4	5.3	4.0	0.0	0.0	0.0	0.0	0.0	0.0	0.0
Maturity (years)	20.8	23.1	24.8	0.0	0.0	0.0	0.0	0.0	0.0	0.0
Grace period (years)	5.0	5.5	5.3	0.0	0.0	0.0	0.0	0.0	0.0	0.0
Grant element (%)	23.5	35.5	42.8	0.0	0.0	0.0	0.0	0.0	0.0	0.0
Private creditors										
Interest (%)	7.9	12.6	0.0	0.0	0.0	0.0	0.0	0.0	0.0	0.0
Maturity (years)	8.1	7.3	0.0	0.0	0.0	0.0	0.0	0.0	0.0	0.0
Grace period (years)	1.5	1.6	0.0	0.0	0.0	0.0	0.0	0.0	0.0	0.0
Grant element (%)	6.6	-3.1	0.0	0.0	0.0	0.0	0.0	0.0	0.0	0.0
Memorandum items										
Commitments	12	40	30	0	0	0	0	0	0	0
Official creditors	10	30	30	0	0	0	0	0	0	0
Private creditors	2	11	0	0	0	0	0	0	0	0

10. CONTRACTUAL OBLIGATIONS ON OUTSTANDING LONG-TERM DEBT

	2001	2002	2003	2004	2005	2006	2007	2008	2009	2010
TOTAL										
Disbursements	0	0	0	0	0	0	0	0	0	0
Principal	28	22	21	18	17	17	14	14	12	11
Interest	6	5	5	4	4	3	3	3	2	2
Official creditors										
Disbursements	0	0	0	0	0	0	0	0	0	0
Principal	28	22	21	18	17	17	14	14	12	11
Interest	6	5	5	4	4	3	3	3	2	2
Bilateral creditors										
Disbursements	0	0	0	0	0	0	0	0	0	0
Principal	13	13	13	12	11	10	8	7	6	5
Interest	3	3	2	2	2	2	1	1	1	1
Multilateral creditors										
Disbursements	0	0	0	0	0	0	0	0	0	0
Principal	14	10	9	6	6	6	6	6	6	6
Interest	3	3	2	2	2	2	2	1	1	1
Private creditors										
Disbursements	0	0	0	0	0	0	0	0	0	0
Principal	0	0	0	0	0	0	0	0	0	0
Interest	0	0	0	0	0	0	0	0	0	0
Commercial banks										
Disbursements	0	0	0	0	0	0	0	0	0	0
Principal	0	0	0	0	0	0	0	0	0	0
Interest	0	0	0	0	0	0	0	0	0	0
Other private										
Disbursements	0	0	0	0	0	0	0	0	0	0
Principal	0	0	0	0	0	0	0	0	0	0
Interest	0	0	0	0	0	0	0	0	0	0

LITHUANIA

(US$ million, unless otherwise indicated)

	1970	1980	1990	1994	1995	1996	1997	1998	1999	2000
1. SUMMARY DEBT DATA										
TOTAL DEBT STOCKS (EDT)	..	..	..	**502.7**	**769.5**	**1,258.2**	**3,262.3**	**3,741.4**	**4,528.5**	**4,854.9**
Long-term debt (LDOD)	..	..	..	**277.3**	**458.6**	**828.2**	**1,961.9**	**2,446.2**	**3,228.2**	**3,549.3**
Public and publicly guaranteed	..	..	..	277.3	429.9	736.2	1,053.4	1,220.6	2,122.6	2,188.2
Private nonguaranteed	..	..	..	0.0	28.7	92.0	908.5	1,225.5	1,105.7	1,361.2
Use of IMF credit	..	..	..	**196.4**	**261.5**	**273.4**	**270.5**	**253.2**	**230.2**	**191.6**
Short-term debt	..	..	..	**29.0**	**49.4**	**156.7**	**1,030.0**	**1,042.0**	**1,070.0**	**1,114.0**
of which interest arrears on LDOD	..	..	..	0.0	0.0	0.0	0.0	0.0	0.0	0.0
Official creditors	..	..	..	0.0	0.0	0.0	0.0	0.0	0.0	0.0
Private creditors	..	..	..	0.0	0.0	0.0	0.0	0.0	0.0	0.0
Memo: principal arrears on LDOD	..	..	..	0.0	0.0	0.0	0.0	0.0	0.0	0.0
Official creditors	..	..	..	0.0	0.0	0.0	0.0	0.0	0.0	0.0
Private creditors	..	..	..	0.0	0.0	0.0	0.0	0.0	0.0	0.0
Memo: export credits	..	..	..	96.6	134.5	178.5	189.3	92.3	86.5	79.5
TOTAL DEBT FLOWS										
Disbursements	..	..	..	**160.8**	**219.4**	**464.3**	**813.5**	**503.8**	**1,500.7**	**914.6**
Long-term debt	..	..	..	94.1	156.6	419.2	756.5	503.8	1,500.7	914.6
IMF purchases	..	..	..	66.7	62.8	45.1	57.0	0.0	0.0	0.0
Principal repayments	..	..	..	**35.2**	**12.2**	**81.8**	**250.0**	**288.2**	**440.2**	**629.0**
Long-term debt	..	..	..	35.2	12.2	57.3	207.2	260.3	423.7	601.7
IMF repurchases	..	..	..	0.0	0.0	24.5	42.7	28.0	16.5	27.3
Net flows on debt	..	..	..	**147.8**	**227.6**	**489.8**	**1,436.9**	**227.6**	**1,088.5**	**329.6**
of which short-term debt	..	..	..	22.2	20.4	107.3	873.3	12.0	28.0	44.0
Interest payments (INT)	..	..	..	**32.5**	**31.3**	**42.2**	**124.9**	**194.2**	**221.3**	**277.0**
Long-term debt	..	..	..	23.1	17.4	23.6	77.0	120.9	150.5	211.6
IMF charges	..	..	..	7.6	11.5	11.5	12.4	12.3	9.5	10.8
Short-term debt	..	..	..	1.8	2.4	7.1	35.5	61.0	61.2	54.6
Net transfers on debt	..	..	..	**115.3**	**196.3**	**447.6**	**1,311.9**	**33.4**	**867.2**	**52.6**
Total debt service paid (TDS)	..	..	..	**67.7**	**43.5**	**124.0**	**374.9**	**482.4**	**661.5**	**906.0**
Long-term debt	..	..	..	58.3	29.6	80.9	284.2	381.2	574.2	813.3
IMF repurchases and charges	..	..	..	7.6	11.5	36.1	55.2	40.2	26.1	38.1
Short-term debt (interest only)	..	..	..	1.8	2.4	7.1	35.5	61.0	61.2	54.6
2. AGGREGATE NET RESOURCE FLOWS AND NET TRANSFERS (LONG-TERM)										
NET RESOURCE FLOWS	..	..	..	**117.3**	**239.0**	**578.4**	**968.0**	**1,259.4**	**1,647.7**	**909.7**
Net flow of long-term debt (ex. IMF)	..	..	..	58.9	144.4	361.9	549.3	243.6	1,077.0	312.9
Foreign direct investment (net)	..	..	..	31.3	72.6	152.4	354.5	926.0	486.5	379.0
Portfolio equity flows	..	..	..	0.0	4.0	21.0	0.0	0.0	0.0	150.5
Grants (excluding technical coop.)	..	..	..	27.0	18.0	43.1	64.3	89.9	84.2	67.3
Memo: technical coop. grants	..	..	..	28.6	116.5	36.1	31.7	25.9	30.2	23.3
official net resource flows	..	..	..	98.0	107.0	154.9	133.3	205.6	158.0	110.9
private net resource flows	..	..	..	19.3	132.0	423.5	834.7	1,053.8	1,489.7	798.8
NET TRANSFERS	..	..	..	**94.1**	**221.6**	**554.9**	**891.0**	**1,138.4**	**1,483.2**	**681.0**
Interest on long-term debt	..	..	..	23.1	17.4	23.6	77.0	120.9	150.5	211.6
Profit remittances on FDI	..	..	..	0.0	0.0	0.0	0.0	0.0	14.0	17.0
Memo: official net transfers	..	..	..	89.1	93.7	140.2	111.6	180.3	126.2	76.0
private net transfers	..	..	..	5.0	127.9	414.7	779.4	958.1	1,357.0	605.0
3. MAJOR ECONOMIC AGGREGATES										
Gross national income (GNI)	..	..	..	5,840.8	6,430.9	7,257.0	8,456.5	9,409.9	9,957.9	11,119.7
Exports of goods & services (XGS)	..	..	..	2,373.3	3,243.3	4,264.5	5,306.5	5,197.2	4,354.6	5,296.9
of which workers remittances	..	..	..	0.7	1.1	1.9	1.8	2.1	1.5	2.3
Imports of goods & services (MGS)	..	..	..	2,623.3	3,965.9	5,129.0	6,516.0	6,728.3	5,709.9	6,212.1
International reserves (RES)	..	..	..	596.7	829.0	841.0	1,064.0	1,462.7	1,249.1	1,362.7
Current account balance	..	..	..	-94.0	-614.4	-722.6	-981.3	-1,298.2	-1,194.0	-674.9
4. DEBT INDICATORS										
EDT / XGS (%)	..	..	..	21.2	23.7	29.5	61.5	72.0	104.0	91.7
EDT / GNI (%)	..	..	..	8.6	12.0	17.3	38.6	39.8	45.5	43.7
TDS / XGS (%)	..	..	..	2.9	1.3	2.9	7.1	9.3	15.2	17.1
INT / XGS (%)	..	..	..	1.4	1.0	1.0	2.4	3.7	5.1	5.2
INT / GNI (%)	..	..	..	0.6	0.5	0.6	1.5	2.1	2.2	2.5
RES / EDT (%)	..	..	..	118.7	107.7	66.8	32.6	39.1	27.6	28.1
RES / MGS (months)	..	..	..	2.7	2.5	2.0	2.0	2.6	2.6	2.6
Short-term / EDT (%)	..	..	..	5.8	6.4	12.5	31.6	27.9	23.6	23.0
Concessional / EDT (%)	..	..	..	17.3	14.3	9.2	3.6	3.4	2.7	2.3
Multilateral / EDT (%)	..	..	..	23.7	21.1	18.1	7.6	9.2	8.5	8.8

LITHUANIA

(US$ million, unless otherwise indicated)

	1970	1980	1990	1994	1995	1996	1997	1998	1999	2000
5. LONG-TERM DEBT										
DEBT OUTSTANDING (LDOD)	..	..	..	**277.3**	**458.6**	**828.2**	**1,961.9**	**2,446.2**	**3,228.2**	**3,549.3**
Public and publicly guaranteed	..	..	..	**277.3**	**429.9**	**736.2**	**1,053.4**	**1,220.6**	**2,122.6**	**2,188.2**
Official creditors	..	..	..	222.8	316.9	410.4	450.2	584.0	628.0	647.4
Multilateral	..	..	..	119.2	162.6	227.9	248.5	344.1	384.3	424.7
Concessional	..	..	..	0.0	0.0	0.0	0.0	0.0	0.0	0.0
Bilateral	..	..	..	103.6	154.3	182.5	201.7	239.9	243.7	222.6
Concessional	..	..	..	86.7	109.7	116.3	118.4	126.3	121.6	113.3
Private creditors	..	..	..	54.5	112.9	325.8	603.1	636.6	1,494.6	1,540.8
Bonds	..	..	..	0.0	0.0	110.0	200.0	200.0	903.1	1,130.5
Commercial banks	..	..	..	0.0	0.0	59.8	168.9	203.7	309.3	189.7
Other private	..	..	..	54.5	112.9	156.0	234.2	232.9	282.2	220.6
Private nonguaranteed	..	..	..	**0.0**	**28.7**	**92.0**	**908.5**	**1,225.5**	**1,105.7**	**1,361.2**
Bonds	..	..	..	0.0	0.0	0.0	0.0	0.0	0.0	37.2
Commercial banks and other	..	..	..	0.0	28.7	92.0	908.5	1,225.5	1,105.7	1,323.9
Memo:										
IBRD	..	..	..	48.9	61.8	101.2	114.3	173.7	200.1	253.4
IDA	..	..	..	0.0	0.0	0.0	0.0	0.0	0.0	0.0
DISBURSEMENTS	..	..	..	**94.1**	**156.6**	**419.2**	**756.5**	**503.8**	**1,500.7**	**914.6**
Public and publicly guaranteed	..	..	..	**94.1**	**156.6**	**383.5**	**556.5**	**208.3**	**1,075.9**	**456.8**
Official creditors	..	..	..	72.1	92.3	130.3	87.3	140.4	106.4	123.8
Multilateral	..	..	..	10.6	38.0	81.3	48.5	95.5	84.7	117.1
Concessional	..	..	..	0.0	0.0	0.0	0.0	0.0	0.0	0.0
Bilateral	..	..	..	61.5	54.3	49.0	38.8	44.9	21.7	6.7
Concessional	..	..	..	47.3	25.1	16.2	8.2	7.3	0.9	2.3
Private creditors	..	..	..	22.0	64.4	253.2	469.2	67.9	969.5	333.0
Bonds	..	..	..	0.0	0.0	110.0	200.0	0.0	745.1	300.3
Commercial banks	..	..	..	0.0	0.0	60.0	150.3	45.8	124.4	31.2
Other private	..	..	..	22.0	64.4	83.2	118.9	22.1	99.9	1.5
Private nonguaranteed	..	..	..	**0.0**	**0.0**	**35.7**	**200.0**	**295.5**	**424.9**	**457.8**
Bonds	..	..	..	0.0	0.0	0.0	0.0	0.0	0.0	37.0
Commercial banks and other	..	..	..	0.0	0.0	35.7	200.0	295.5	424.9	420.8
Memo:										
IBRD	..	..	..	4.2	12.1	43.8	20.7	60.3	30.4	66.2
IDA	..	..	..	0.0	0.0	0.0	0.0	0.0	0.0	0.0
PRINCIPAL REPAYMENTS	..	..	..	**35.2**	**12.2**	**57.3**	**207.2**	**260.3**	**423.7**	**601.7**
Public and publicly guaranteed	..	..	..	**35.2**	**12.2**	**52.3**	**200.5**	**65.2**	**88.5**	**309.8**
Official creditors	..	..	..	1.2	3.2	18.5	18.3	24.7	32.6	80.2
Multilateral	..	..	..	0.0	0.0	6.2	8.5	9.7	10.3	62.3
Concessional	..	..	..	0.0	0.0	0.0	0.0	0.0	0.0	0.0
Bilateral	..	..	..	1.2	3.2	12.3	9.8	15.0	22.3	17.9
Concessional	..	..	..	0.0	0.3	3.5	2.1	3.4	9.7	6.9
Private creditors	..	..	..	34.1	8.9	33.8	182.3	40.5	55.9	229.6
Bonds	..	..	..	0.0	0.0	0.0	110.0	0.0	0.0	25.0
Commercial banks	..	..	..	0.0	0.0	0.0	40.4	11.6	15.1	147.1
Other private	..	..	..	34.1	8.9	33.8	31.9	29.0	40.8	57.4
Private nonguaranteed	..	..	..	**0.0**	**0.0**	**5.0**	**6.7**	**195.0**	**335.2**	**291.9**
Bonds	..	..	..	0.0	0.0	0.0	0.0	0.0	0.0	0.0
Commercial banks and other	..	..	..	0.0	0.0	5.0	6.7	195.0	335.2	291.9
Memo:										
IBRD	..	..	..	0.0	0.0	0.0	2.6	3.2	4.3	9.3
IDA	..	..	..	0.0	0.0	0.0	0.0	0.0	0.0	0.0
NET FLOWS ON DEBT	..	..	..	**58.9**	**144.4**	**361.9**	**549.3**	**243.6**	**1,077.0**	**312.9**
Public and publicly guaranteed	..	..	..	**58.9**	**144.4**	**331.2**	**356.0**	**143.1**	**987.3**	**147.1**
Official creditors	..	..	..	71.0	89.0	111.8	69.0	115.7	73.8	43.6
Multilateral	..	..	..	10.6	38.0	75.2	40.0	85.8	74.3	54.8
Concessional	..	..	..	0.0	0.0	0.0	0.0	0.0	0.0	0.0
Bilateral	..	..	..	60.3	51.1	36.7	29.0	29.9	-0.5	-11.2
Concessional	..	..	..	47.3	24.8	12.7	6.1	3.9	-8.8	-4.6
Private creditors	..	..	..	-12.0	55.4	219.4	286.9	27.4	913.5	103.4
Bonds	..	..	..	0.0	0.0	110.0	90.0	0.0	745.1	275.3
Commercial banks	..	..	..	0.0	0.0	60.0	110.0	34.3	109.3	-116.0
Other private	..	..	..	-12.0	55.4	49.4	87.0	-6.9	59.2	-55.9
Private nonguaranteed	..	..	..	**0.0**	**0.0**	**30.7**	**193.3**	**100.4**	**89.7**	**165.9**
Bonds	..	..	..	0.0	0.0	0.0	0.0	0.0	0.0	37.0
Commercial banks and other	..	..	..	0.0	0.0	30.7	193.3	100.4	89.7	128.9
Memo:										
IBRD	..	..	..	4.2	12.1	43.8	18.1	57.1	26.1	56.9
IDA	..	..	..	0.0	0.0	0.0	0.0	0.0	0.0	0.0

LITHUANIA

(US$ million, unless otherwise indicated)

	1970	1980	1990	1994	1995	1996	1997	1998	1999	2000
INTEREST PAYMENTS (LINT)	..	..	..	**23.1**	**17.4**	**23.6**	**77.0**	**120.9**	**150.5**	**211.6**
Public and publicly guaranteed	..	..	..	**23.1**	**17.4**	**21.3**	**44.0**	**48.8**	**75.6**	**135.6**
Official creditors	..	..	..	8.9	13.3	14.7	21.7	25.3	31.8	34.9
Multilateral	..	..	..	7.8	9.4	10.4	14.2	17.0	21.5	26.1
Concessional	..	..	..	0.0	0.0	0.0	0.0	0.0	0.0	0.0
Bilateral	..	..	..	1.1	3.9	4.3	7.4	8.3	10.3	8.8
Concessional	..	..	..	0.7	2.7	1.8	2.3	2.4	3.6	3.6
Private creditors	..	..	..	14.3	4.1	6.5	22.3	23.6	43.8	100.8
Bonds	..	..	..	0.0	0.0	0.0	8.3	7.1	14.3	62.9
Commercial banks	..	..	..	0.0	0.0	0.2	4.2	5.0	16.6	20.1
Other private	..	..	..	14.3	4.1	6.3	9.8	11.5	13.0	17.7
Private nonguaranteed	..	..	..	**0.0**	**0.0**	**2.3**	**33.0**	**72.1**	**74.9**	**76.0**
Bonds	..	..	..	0.0	0.0	0.0	0.0	0.0	0.0	0.0
Commercial banks and other	..	..	..	0.0	0.0	2.3	33.0	72.1	74.9	76.0
Memo:										
IBRD	..	..	..	3.2	3.6	4.3	7.1	8.4	10.6	14.8
IDA	..	..	..	0.0	0.0	0.0	0.0	0.0	0.0	0.0
NET TRANSFERS ON DEBT	..	..	..	**35.8**	**127.0**	**338.3**	**472.3**	**122.6**	**926.5**	**101.3**
Public and publicly guaranteed	..	..	..	**35.8**	**127.0**	**309.9**	**312.0**	**94.3**	**911.7**	**11.4**
Official creditors	..	..	..	62.1	75.7	97.1	47.4	90.5	42.0	8.8
Multilateral	..	..	..	2.8	28.6	64.8	25.8	68.9	52.8	28.8
Concessional	..	..	..	0.0	0.0	0.0	0.0	0.0	0.0	0.0
Bilateral	..	..	..	59.3	47.1	32.3	21.6	21.6	-10.8	-20.0
Concessional	..	..	..	46.7	22.1	10.9	3.8	1.5	-12.4	-8.1
Private creditors	..	..	..	-26.3	51.3	212.8	264.6	3.8	869.7	2.7
Bonds	..	..	..	0.0	0.0	110.0	81.8	-7.1	730.9	212.4
Commercial banks	..	..	..	0.0	0.0	59.8	105.8	29.3	92.7	-136.1
Other private	..	..	..	-26.3	51.3	43.1	77.1	-18.3	46.2	-73.6
Private nonguaranteed	..	..	..	**0.0**	**0.0**	**28.4**	**160.3**	**28.3**	**14.8**	**89.9**
Bonds	..	..	..	0.0	0.0	0.0	0.0	0.0	0.0	37.0
Commercial banks and other	..	..	..	0.0	0.0	28.4	160.3	28.3	14.8	52.9
Memo:										
IBRD	..	..	..	1.0	8.5	39.5	11.0	48.7	15.4	42.1
IDA	..	..	..	0.0	0.0	0.0	0.0	0.0	0.0	0.0
DEBT SERVICE (LTDS)	..	..	..	**58.3**	**29.6**	**80.9**	**284.2**	**381.2**	**574.2**	**813.3**
Public and publicly guaranteed	..	..	..	**58.3**	**29.6**	**73.6**	**244.5**	**114.0**	**164.1**	**445.4**
Official creditors	..	..	..	10.0	16.6	33.2	39.9	49.9	64.4	115.1
Multilateral	..	..	..	7.8	9.4	16.6	22.7	26.6	31.8	88.4
Concessional	..	..	..	0.0	0.0	0.0	0.0	0.0	0.0	0.0
Bilateral	..	..	..	2.2	7.1	16.6	17.2	23.3	32.6	26.7
Concessional	..	..	..	0.7	3.0	5.3	4.4	5.7	13.3	10.4
Private creditors	..	..	..	48.3	13.0	40.3	204.6	64.1	99.7	330.3
Bonds	..	..	..	0.0	0.0	0.0	118.3	7.1	14.3	87.9
Commercial banks	..	..	..	0.0	0.0	0.2	44.6	16.5	31.7	167.3
Other private	..	..	..	48.3	13.0	40.1	41.7	40.4	53.8	75.1
Private nonguaranteed	..	..	..	**0.0**	**0.0**	**7.3**	**39.7**	**267.2**	**410.1**	**367.9**
Bonds	..	..	..	0.0	0.0	0.0	0.0	0.0	0.0	0.0
Commercial banks and other	..	..	..	0.0	0.0	7.3	39.7	267.2	410.1	367.9
Memo:										
IBRD	..	..	..	3.2	3.6	4.3	9.7	11.6	14.9	24.0
IDA	..	..	..	0.0	0.0	0.0	0.0	0.0	0.0	0.0
UNDISBURSED DEBT	..	..	..	**209.1**	**478.4**	**585.6**	**379.9**	**352.2**	**234.9**	**575.4**
Official creditors	..	..	..	139.0	235.1	380.3	296.0	246.7	208.6	240.5
Private creditors	..	..	..	70.2	243.4	205.3	83.9	105.5	26.3	334.8
Memorandum items										
Concessional LDOD	..	..	..	86.7	109.7	116.3	118.4	126.3	121.6	113.3
Variable rate LDOD	..	..	..	128.4	236.4	427.8	1,412.4	1,868.2	1,976.3	2,098.5
Public sector LDOD	..	..	..	274.4	424.2	726.0	989.9	1,129.8	2,035.5	2,110.8
Private sector LDOD	..	..	..	2.9	34.4	102.2	972.0	1,316.3	1,192.7	1,438.5

6. CURRENCY COMPOSITION OF LONG-TERM DEBT (PERCENT)

	1970	1980	1990	1994	1995	1996	1997	1998	1999	2000
Deutsche mark	..	..	..	11.3	17.3	8.8	6.0	4.6	2.9	1.6
French franc	..	..	..	0.0	0.0	0.0	0.0	0.0	0.2	0.6
Japanese yen	..	..	..	12.4	9.8	8.4	5.9	5.9	3.6	2.9
Pound sterling	..	..	..	0.0	0.0	0.0	0.0	0.2	0.1	0.1
Swiss franc	..	..	..	4.9	3.2	1.3	0.6	0.2	0.1	0.0
U.S.dollars	..	..	..	30.0	34.4	49.8	61.6	58.7	40.7	33.4
Multiple currency	..	..	..	17.6	14.4	13.6	10.6	14.1	9.3	9.1
Special drawing rights	..	..	..	0.0	0.0	0.0	0.0	0.0	0.0	0.0
All other currencies	..	..	..	23.8	20.9	18.1	15.3	16.3	43.1	52.3

LITHUANIA

(US$ million, unless otherwise indicated)

	1970	1980	1990	1994	1995	1996	1997	1998	1999	2000
7. DEBT RESTRUCTURINGS										
Total amount rescheduled	..	..	..	0.0	0.0	0.0	0.0	0.0	0.0	0.0
Debt stock rescheduled	..	..	..	0.0	0.0	0.0	0.0	0.0	0.0	0.0
Principal rescheduled	..	..	..	0.0	0.0	0.0	0.0	0.0	0.0	0.0
Official	..	..	..	0.0	0.0	0.0	0.0	0.0	0.0	0.0
Private	..	..	..	0.0	0.0	0.0	0.0	0.0	0.0	0.0
Interest rescheduled	..	..	..	0.0	0.0	0.0	0.0	0.0	0.0	0.0
Official	..	..	..	0.0	0.0	0.0	0.0	0.0	0.0	0.0
Private	..	..	..	0.0	0.0	0.0	0.0	0.0	0.0	0.0
Debt forgiven	..	..	..	0.0	0.0	0.0	0.0	0.0	0.0	0.0
Memo: interest forgiven	..	..	..	0.0	0.0	0.0	0.0	0.0	0.0	0.0
Debt stock reduction	..	..	..	0.0	0.0	0.0	0.0	0.0	0.0	0.0
of which debt buyback	..	..	..	0.0	0.0	0.0	0.0	0.0	0.0	0.0
8. DEBT STOCK-FLOW RECONCILIATION										
Total change in debt stocks	..	..	..	169.9	266.8	488.7	2,004.1	479.0	787.1	326.5
Net flows on debt	..	..	..	147.8	227.6	489.8	1,436.9	227.6	1,088.5	329.6
Net change in interest arrears	..	..	..	0.0	0.0	0.0	0.0	0.0	0.0	0.0
Interest capitalized	..	..	..	0.0	0.0	0.0	0.0	0.0	0.0	0.0
Debt forgiveness or reduction	..	..	..	0.0	0.0	0.0	0.0	0.0	0.0	0.0
Cross-currency valuation	..	..	..	19.1	12.5	-29.9	-53.3	36.4	-30.4	-95.0
Residual	..	..	..	3.0	26.6	28.8	620.6	215.0	-270.9	91.8
9. AVERAGE TERMS OF NEW COMMITMENTS										
ALL CREDITORS										
Interest (%)	..	..	..	5.0	7.3	6.9	6.3	5.2	7.4	7.6
Maturity (years)	..	..	..	12.7	9.4	11.2	6.0	8.7	5.1	6.8
Grace period (years)	..	..	..	3.6	2.6	2.8	3.7	3.0	3.9	5.5
Grant element (%)	..	..	..	25.1	13.8	13.7	13.2	18.1	8.8	10.1
Official creditors										
Interest (%)	..	..	..	5.3	6.3	6.6	6.5	4.7	4.5	7.2
Maturity (years)	..	..	..	14.9	14.6	15.0	17.1	13.7	15.3	13.2
Grace period (years)	..	..	..	4.9	4.4	4.3	4.2	4.1	6.3	8.0
Grant element (%)	..	..	..	27.5	22.5	18.1	18.6	26.4	34.8	16.9
Private creditors										
Interest (%)	..	..	..	4.7	8.1	7.3	6.2	5.7	7.8	7.7
Maturity (years)	..	..	..	9.9	5.2	6.4	5.6	4.2	4.0	5.0
Grace period (years)	..	..	..	2.1	1.2	0.9	3.6	2.0	3.6	4.7
Grant element (%)	..	..	..	22.1	6.9	7.9	13.0	10.6	6.1	8.1
Memorandum items										
Commitments	..	..	..	150.0	422.2	503.6	458.4	143.0	1,005.5	828.2
Official creditors	..	..	..	82.9	186.4	285.2	18.0	68.2	94.7	184.3
Private creditors	..	..	..	67.1	235.9	218.4	440.5	74.8	910.8	643.9

10. CONTRACTUAL OBLIGATIONS ON OUTSTANDING LONG-TERM DEBT

	2001	2002	2003	2004	2005	2006	2007	2008	2009	2010
TOTAL										
Disbursements	273.3	149.8	70.1	40.5	14.8	9.6	7.0	4.5	3.1	2.1
Principal	463.4	653.7	961.0	440.5	989.9	113.6	70.0	65.5	53.3	36.3
Interest	221.5	217.9	186.1	124.8	76.5	34.1	27.1	23.5	20.2	17.7
Official creditors										
Disbursements	109.9	40.4	27.6	21.1	14.8	9.6	7.0	4.5	3.1	2.1
Principal	59.6	114.5	61.4	56.4	77.7	53.4	53.2	51.2	47.5	36.2
Interest	42.2	41.9	35.9	33.9	31.2	27.9	25.3	22.6	20.0	17.6
Bilateral creditors										
Disbursements	3.5	1.3	0.2	0.0	0.0	0.0	0.0	0.0	0.0	0.0
Principal	30.1	36.3	27.7	21.2	17.6	10.9	10.6	8.7	5.8	4.1
Interest	11.3	9.2	6.8	5.2	4.1	3.1	2.7	2.3	2.1	1.9
Multilateral creditors										
Disbursements	106.4	39.0	27.4	21.1	14.8	9.6	7.0	4.5	3.1	2.1
Principal	29.4	78.1	33.8	35.2	60.0	42.6	42.6	42.6	41.8	32.2
Interest	30.9	32.7	29.2	28.7	27.0	24.8	22.6	20.3	17.9	15.7
Private creditors										
Disbursements	163.4	109.5	42.5	19.4	0.0	0.0	0.0	0.0	0.0	0.0
Principal	404.0	539.0	900.0	384.0	912.0	60.0	17.0	14.0	6.0	0.0
Interest	179.0	176.0	150.0	91.0	45.0	6.0	2.0	1.0	0.0	0.0
Commercial banks										
Disbursements	162.5	109.2	42.4	19.4	0.0	0.0	0.0	0.0	0.0	0.0
Principal	84.2	37.6	31.3	16.6	317.4	11.6	10.5	9.3	4.6	0.0
Interest	21.0	23.9	26.4	26.7	14.5	1.9	1.3	0.6	0.1	0.0
Other private										
Disbursements	0.9	0.2	0.1	0.0	0.0	0.0	0.0	0.0	0.0	0.0
Principal	320.0	502.0	868.0	368.0	595.0	49.0	6.0	5.0	1.0	0.0
Interest	158.0	152.0	124.0	64.0	31.0	4.0	1.0	0.0	0.0	0.1

MACEDONIA, FYR

(US$ million, unless otherwise indicated)

	1970	1980	1990	1994	1995	1996	1997	1998	1999	2000
1. SUMMARY DEBT DATA										
TOTAL DEBT STOCKS (EDT)	..	..	..	**1,104**	**1,277**	**1,818**	**1,234**	**1,481**	**1,438**	**1,465**
Long-term debt (LDOD)	..	..	..	**927**	**1,078**	**1,481**	**1,008**	**1,242**	**1,268**	**1,304**
Public and publicly guaranteed	..	..	..	709	788	856	942	1,054	1,138	1,165
Private nonguaranteed	..	..	..	218	289	625	67	189	130	140
Use of IMF credit	..	..	..	**21**	**57**	**68**	**88**	**102**	**102**	**81**
Short-term debt	..	..	..	**156**	**143**	**269**	**137**	**136**	**68**	**79**
of which interest arrears on LDOD	..	..	..	138	143	183	3	3	2	18
Official creditors	..	..	..	30	26	19	0	2	0	14
Private creditors	..	..	..	108	117	164	3	2	2	4
Memo: principal arrears on LDOD	..	..	..	360	216	85	9	6	8	40
Official creditors	..	..	..	234	24	7	3	4	0	21
Private creditors	..	..	..	126	191	79	6	2	8	19
Memo: export credits	..	..	..	90	139	124	224	206	205	188
TOTAL DEBT FLOWS										
Disbursements	..	..	..	**104**	**112**	**127**	**147**	**264**	**236**	**161**
Long-term debt	..	..	..	86	75	113	122	252	217	157
IMF purchases	..	..	..	18	38	14	25	12	19	4
Principal repayments	..	..	..	**121**	**20**	**27**	**50**	**93**	**106**	**109**
Long-term debt	..	..	..	119	19	26	49	91	89	89
IMF repurchases	..	..	..	2	1	1	0	2	17	19
Net flows on debt	..	..	..	**-15**	**74**	**186**	**146**	**170**	**63**	**47**
of which short-term debt	..	..	..	2	-18	85	48	-1	-67	-5
Interest payments (INT)	..	..	..	**35**	**12**	**32**	**70**	**65**	**53**	**53**
Long-term debt	..	..	..	33	9	25	62	55	45	45
IMF charges	..	..	..	1	2	3	3	3	3	3
Short-term debt	..	..	..	1	1	5	5	7	5	5
Net transfers on debt	..	..	..	**-50**	**63**	**153**	**76**	**105**	**10**	**-5**
Total debt service paid (TDS)	..	..	..	**156**	**32**	**59**	**120**	**158**	**159**	**161**
Long-term debt	..	..	..	152	28	50	111	146	134	134
IMF repurchases and charges	..	..	..	3	3	4	3	5	20	22
Short-term debt (interest only)	..	..	..	1	1	5	5	7	5	5
2. AGGREGATE NET RESOURCE FLOWS AND NET TRANSFERS (LONG-TERM)										
NET RESOURCE FLOWS	..	..	..	**49**	**87**	**141**	**123**	**308**	**339**	**417**
Net flow of long-term debt (ex. IMF)	..	..	..	-33	56	87	73	161	128	68
Foreign direct investment (net)	..	..	..	24	14	11	16	118	30	176
Portfolio equity flows	..	..	..	0	0	0	0	0	0	0
Grants (excluding technical coop.)	..	..	..	58	18	43	34	29	180	174
Memo: technical coop. grants	..	..	..	0	16	19	9	20	26	31
official net resource flows	..	..	..	40	73	130	114	118	289	230
private net resource flows	..	..	..	9	14	11	9	190	50	187
NET TRANSFERS	..	..	..	**16**	**78**	**116**	**61**	**253**	**293**	**372**
Interest on long-term debt	..	..	..	33	9	25	62	55	45	45
Profit remittances on FDI	..	..	..	0	0	0	0	0	0	0
Memo: official net transfers	..	..	..	7	64	106	54	81	263	203
private net transfers	..	..	..	9	14	11	7	172	30	169
3. MAJOR ECONOMIC AGGREGATES										
Gross national income (GNI)	..	..	..	3,335	4,426	4,389	3,680	3,527	3,629	3,524
Exports of goods & services (XGS)	..	..	..	..	..	1,392	1,425	1,511	1,534	1,743
of which workers remittances	..	..	..	..	..	45	56	63	71	80
Imports of goods & services (MGS)	..	..	..	..	..	1,848	1,934	2,086	1,992	2,320
International reserves (RES)	..	..	..	166	275	268	280	335	460	460
Current account balance	..	..	..	..	..	-288	-275	-312	-109	-107
4. DEBT INDICATORS										
EDT / XGS (%)	..	..	..	..	..	130.6	86.6	98.0	93.7	84.0
EDT / GNI (%)	..	..	..	33.1	28.9	41.4	33.5	42.0	39.6	41.6
TDS / XGS (%)	..	..	..	..	..	4.3	8.4	10.5	10.4	9.3
INT / XGS (%)	..	..	..	..	..	2.3	4.9	4.3	3.5	3.0
INT / GNI (%)	..	..	..	1.1	0.3	0.7	1.9	1.8	1.5	1.5
RES / EDT (%)	..	..	..	15.1	21.5	14.7	22.7	22.6	32.0	31.4
RES / MGS (months)	..	..	..	..	..	1.7	1.7	1.9	2.8	2.4
Short-term / EDT (%)	..	..	..	14.2	11.2	14.8	11.1	9.2	4.7	5.4
Concessional / EDT (%)	..	..	..	4.6	8.2	8.3	16.1	17.2	21.2	23.1
Multilateral / EDT (%)	..	..	..	20.3	22.6	19.2	32.5	31.2	36.9	38.4

MACEDONIA, FYR

(US$ million, unless otherwise indicated)

	1970	1980	1990	1994	1995	1996	1997	1998	1999	2000
5. LONG-TERM DEBT										
DEBT OUTSTANDING (LDOD)	..	..	..	**927**	**1,078**	**1,481**	**1,008**	**1,242**	**1,268**	**1,304**
Public and publicly guaranteed	..	..	..	**709**	**788**	**856**	**942**	**1,054**	**1,138**	**1,165**
Official creditors	..	..	..	519	605	675	707	804	860	880
Multilateral	..	..	..	224	288	348	401	462	530	562
Concessional	..	..	..	42	84	125	175	212	266	294
Bilateral	..	..	..	295	317	326	305	341	330	318
Concessional	..	..	..	9	21	26	24	42	39	45
Private creditors	..	..	..	190	184	182	235	250	278	285
Bonds	..	..	..	0	0	0	0	0	0	0
Commercial banks	..	..	..	108	103	100	230	240	269	274
Other private	..	..	..	82	81	82	5	10	10	11
Private nonguaranteed	..	..	..	**218**	**289**	**625**	**67**	**189**	**130**	**140**
Bonds	..	..	..	0	0	0	0	0	0	0
Commercial banks and other	..	..	..	218	289	625	67	189	130	140
Memo:										
IBRD	..	..	..	93	97	78	85	108	110	116
IDA	..	..	..	42	84	125	146	181	223	249
DISBURSEMENTS	..	..	..	**86**	**75**	**113**	**122**	**252**	**217**	**157**
Public and publicly guaranteed	..	..	..	**86**	**75**	**113**	**113**	**144**	**173**	**94**
Official creditors	..	..	..	86	74	112	113	139	148	92
Multilateral	..	..	..	86	74	97	106	88	125	79
Concessional	..	..	..	40	42	44	59	30	62	44
Bilateral	..	..	..	0	0	15	7	51	23	14
Concessional	..	..	..	0	0	7	0	20	3	9
Private creditors	..	..	..	0	0	1	0	6	25	2
Bonds	..	..	..	0	0	0	0	0	0	0
Commercial banks	..	..	..	0	0	0	0	0	25	0
Other private	..	..	..	0	0	1	0	5	0	2
Private nonguaranteed	..	..	..	**0**	**0**	**0**	**10**	**108**	**44**	**63**
Bonds	..	..	..	0	0	0	0	0	0	0
Commercial banks and other	..	..	..	0	0	0	10	108	44	63
Memo:										
IBRD	..	..	..	40	20	2	19	43	12	13
IDA	..	..	..	40	42	44	29	29	45	38
PRINCIPAL REPAYMENTS	..	..	..	**119**	**19**	**26**	**49**	**91**	**89**	**89**
Public and publicly guaranteed	..	..	..	**104**	**19**	**26**	**33**	**50**	**43**	**38**
Official creditors	..	..	..	104	19	25	32	50	40	37
Multilateral	..	..	..	104	19	25	25	25	25	20
Concessional	..	..	..	0	0	0	0	0	0	0
Bilateral	..	..	..	0	0	0	8	25	15	17
Concessional	..	..	..	0	0	0	0	4	1	2
Private creditors	..	..	..	0	0	1	1	1	3	2
Bonds	..	..	..	0	0	0	0	0	0	0
Commercial banks	..	..	..	0	0	1	0	0	3	2
Other private	..	..	..	0	0	0	1	1	0	0
Private nonguaranteed	..	..	..	**15**	**0**	**0**	**16**	**41**	**46**	**51**
Bonds	..	..	..	0	0	0	0	0	0	0
Commercial banks and other	..	..	..	15	0	0	16	41	46	51
Memo:										
IBRD	..	..	..	104	19	15	6	4	3	4
IDA	..	..	..	0	0	0	0	0	0	0
NET FLOWS ON DEBT	..	..	..	**-33**	**56**	**87**	**73**	**161**	**128**	**68**
Public and publicly guaranteed	..	..	..	**-18**	**56**	**87**	**80**	**94**	**131**	**56**
Official creditors	..	..	..	-18	55	87	80	89	109	56
Multilateral	..	..	..	-18	55	72	81	63	100	59
Concessional	..	..	..	40	42	44	59	30	62	44
Bilateral	..	..	..	0	0	15	-1	26	9	-3
Concessional	..	..	..	0	0	7	0	16	2	8
Private creditors	..	..	..	0	0	0	-1	5	22	0
Bonds	..	..	..	0	0	0	0	0	0	0
Commercial banks	..	..	..	0	0	-1	0	0	22	-2
Other private	..	..	..	0	0	1	-1	5	0	1
Private nonguaranteed	..	..	..	**-15**	**0**	**0**	**-7**	**67**	**-2**	**12**
Bonds	..	..	..	0	0	0	0	0	0	0
Commercial banks and other	..	..	..	-15	0	0	-7	67	-2	12
Memo:										
IBRD	..	..	..	-64	1	-13	13	39	9	10
IDA	..	..	..	40	42	44	29	29	45	38

MACEDONIA, FYR

(US$ million, unless otherwise indicated)

	1970	1980	1990	1994	1995	1996	1997	1998	1999	2000
INTEREST PAYMENTS (LINT)	..	..	..	**33**	**9**	**25**	**62**	**55**	**45**	**45**
Public and publicly guaranteed	..	..	..	**33**	**9**	**25**	**61**	**48**	**35**	**37**
Official creditors	..	..	..	33	9	24	61	37	26	27
Multilateral	..	..	..	33	9	16	36	17	18	19
Concessional	..	..	..	0	0	1	1	2	1	3
Bilateral	..	..	..	0	0	8	25	21	8	7
Concessional	..	..	..	0	0	0	1	1	0	1
Private creditors	..	..	..	0	0	1	0	11	10	10
Bonds	..	..	..	0	0	0	0	0	0	0
Commercial banks	..	..	..	0	0	0	0	10	9	10
Other private	..	..	..	0	0	0	0	0	1	0
Private nonguaranteed	..	..	..	**0**	**0**	**0**	**1**	**7**	**10**	**8**
Bonds	..	..	..	0	0	0	0	0	0	0
Commercial banks and other	..	..	..	0	0	0	1	7	10	8
Memo:										
IBRD	..	..	..	32	8	6	6	5	7	7
IDA	..	..	..	0	0	1	1	1	1	2
NET TRANSFERS ON DEBT	..	..	..	**-67**	**46**	**63**	**11**	**106**	**83**	**23**
Public and publicly guaranteed	..	..	..	**-52**	**46**	**63**	**19**	**46**	**95**	**19**
Official creditors	..	..	..	-52	46	63	20	52	83	29
Multilateral	..	..	..	-52	46	57	46	46	82	40
Concessional	..	..	..	40	41	43	58	27	61	41
Bilateral	..	..	..	0	0	7	-26	6	1	-11
Concessional	..	..	..	0	0	7	-1	15	2	7
Private creditors	..	..	..	0	0	0	-1	-6	12	-11
Bonds	..	..	..	0	0	0	0	0	0	0
Commercial banks	..	..	..	0	0	-1	0	-10	13	-12
Other private	..	..	..	0	0	1	-1	5	-1	1
Private nonguaranteed	..	..	..	**-15**	**0**	**0**	**-8**	**59**	**-12**	**4**
Bonds	..	..	..	0	0	0	0	0	0	0
Commercial banks and other	..	..	..	-15	0	0	-8	59	-12	4
Memo:										
IBRD	..	..	..	-96	-7	-19	7	34	2	2
IDA	..	..	..	40	41	44	28	28	44	37
DEBT SERVICE (LTDS)	..	..	..	**152**	**28**	**50**	**111**	**146**	**134**	**134**
Public and publicly guaranteed	..	..	..	**137**	**28**	**50**	**94**	**98**	**78**	**75**
Official creditors	..	..	..	137	28	49	93	87	65	63
Multilateral	..	..	..	137	28	40	60	42	43	39
Concessional	..	..	..	0	0	1	1	2	1	3
Bilateral	..	..	..	0	0	9	33	45	23	24
Concessional	..	..	..	0	0	0	1	5	1	2
Private creditors	..	..	..	0	0	2	1	11	13	12
Bonds	..	..	..	0	0	0	0	0	0	0
Commercial banks	..	..	..	0	0	1	0	10	12	12
Other private	..	..	..	0	0	0	1	1	1	0
Private nonguaranteed	..	..	..	**15**	**0**	**0**	**18**	**48**	**56**	**59**
Bonds	..	..	..	0	0	0	0	0	0	0
Commercial banks and other	..	..	..	15	0	0	18	48	56	59
Memo:										
IBRD	..	..	..	136	27	21	12	9	10	11
IDA	..	..	..	0	0	1	1	1	1	2
UNDISBURSED DEBT	..	..	..	**45**	**176**	**118**	**131**	**275**	**281**	**229**
Official creditors	..	..	..	45	169	112	125	264	276	224
Private creditors	..	..	..	0	7	6	5	11	5	5
Memorandum items										
Concessional LDOD	..	..	..	51	105	151	199	254	305	339
Variable rate LDOD	..	..	..	509	571	961	490	669	618	642
Public sector LDOD	..	..	..	705	785	849	931	1,043	1,131	1,160
Private sector LDOD	..	..	..	222	293	632	77	200	137	145

6. CURRENCY COMPOSITION OF LONG-TERM DEBT (PERCENT)

	1970	1980	1990	1994	1995	1996	1997	1998	1999	2000
Deutsche mark	..	..	..	5.7	13.9	13.6	14.1	15.7	11.5	9.2
French franc	..	..	..	0.6	5.9	5.1	3.7	3.4	2.6	2.2
Japanese yen	..	..	..	6.7	6.5	4.4	0.4	0.4	0.4	0.3
Pound sterling	..	..	..	1.3	1.1	1.4	0.3	0.2	0.2	0.2
Swiss franc	..	..	..	0.9	0.9	5.6	4.6	3.8	2.8	2.4
U.S.dollars	..	..	..	63.2	49.7	51.0	60.6	67.9	70.6	72.6
Multiple currency	..	..	..	21.3	20.2	15.8	11.0	3.6	2.6	2.2
Special drawing rights	..	..	..	0.1	0.1	0.1	0.0	0.1	0.1	0.3
All other currencies	..	..	..	0.2	1.7	3.0	5.3	4.9	9.2	10.6

MACEDONIA, FYR

(US$ million, unless otherwise indicated)

	1970	1980	1990	1994	1995	1996	1997	1998	1999	2000
7. DEBT RESTRUCTURINGS										
Total amount rescheduled	..	..	..	0	256	73	229	0	0	0
Debt stock rescheduled	..	..	..	0	0	0	141	0	0	0
Principal rescheduled	..	..	..	0	242	64	39	0	0	0
Official	..	..	..	0	235	64	0	0	0	0
Private	..	..	..	0	7	0	39	0	0	0
Interest rescheduled	..	..	..	0	14	9	76	0	0	0
Official	..	..	..	0	13	9	0	0	0	0
Private	..	..	..	0	1	0	76	0	0	0
Debt forgiven	..	..	..	0	0	0	0	0	0	0
Memo: interest forgiven	..	..	..	0	0	0	0	0	0	0
Debt stock reduction	..	..	..	0	0	0	129	0	0	0
of which debt buyback	..	..	..	0	0	0	0	0	0	0
8. DEBT STOCK-FLOW RECONCILIATION										
Total change in debt stocks	..	..	..	62	174	541	-585	247	-43	27
Net flows on debt	..	..	..	-15	74	186	146	170	63	47
Net change in interest arrears	..	..	..	30	4	41	-180	0	-1	16
Interest capitalized	..	..	..	0	14	9	76	0	0	0
Debt forgiveness or reduction	..	..	..	0	0	0	-129	0	0	0
Cross-currency valuation	..	..	..	-20	-41	-74	-132	-55	-41	-36
Residual	..	..	..	67	122	380	-365	132	-64	-1
9. AVERAGE TERMS OF NEW COMMITMENTS										
ALL CREDITORS										
Interest (%)	..	..	..	4.2	3.7	3.7	2.8	4.5	3.3	5.0
Maturity (years)	..	..	..	25.1	23.2	20.2	24.1	19.8	22.3	19.9
Grace period (years)	..	..	..	6.9	6.8	5.9	8.2	8.3	6.6	6.7
Grant element (%)	..	..	..	44.2	46.8	43.4	54.0	38.8	49.1	35.2
Official creditors										
Interest (%)	..	..	..	4.2	3.8	3.6	2.8	4.4	3.4	4.9
Maturity (years)	..	..	..	25.1	23.0	20.5	24.1	20.3	22.7	20.1
Grace period (years)	..	..	..	6.9	6.7	6.0	8.2	8.5	6.6	6.8
Grant element (%)	..	..	..	44.2	46.2	44.2	54.0	40.2	49.4	35.6
Private creditors										
Interest (%)	..	..	..	0.0	2.3	6.7	0.0	8.1	3.2	9.2
Maturity (years)	..	..	..	0.0	29.7	3.0	0.0	7.7	19.6	3.4
Grace period (years)	..	..	..	0.0	10.9	0.3	0.0	2.9	6.8	0.5
Grant element (%)	..	..	..	0.0	64.1	4.8	0.0	6.6	47.5	1.0
Memorandum items										
Commitments	..	..	..	101	206	62	140	243	170	113
Official creditors	..	..	..	101	199	61	140	233	149	112
Private creditors	..	..	..	0	7	1	0	10	21	1

10. CONTRACTUAL OBLIGATIONS ON OUTSTANDING LONG-TERM DEBT

	2001	2002	2003	2004	2005	2006	2007	2008	2009	2010
TOTAL										
Disbursements	67	67	44	24	13	9	3	1	1	0
Principal	104	91	91	86	88	89	90	90	107	107
Interest	64	61	57	52	48	43	38	33	28	21
Official creditors										
Disbursements	64	66	43	24	13	9	3	1	1	0
Principal	62	56	65	64	60	61	59	64	72	72
Interest	39	38	37	34	30	27	24	20	17	13
Bilateral creditors										
Disbursements	25	16	8	3	1	0	0	0	0	0
Principal	30	27	33	33	33	33	33	33	33	33
Interest	18	17	17	15	13	11	9	7	5	2
Multilateral creditors										
Disbursements	39	50	36	20	12	8	3	1	1	0
Principal	32	29	32	31	27	28	26	31	39	39
Interest	21	21	20	19	18	16	15	14	12	11
Private creditors										
Disbursements	3	1	1	0	0	0	0	0	0	0
Principal	41	35	26	22	28	28	31	26	36	36
Interest	25	23	21	19	17	16	14	13	11	8
Commercial banks										
Disbursements	3	1	1	0	0	0	0	0	0	0
Principal	1	7	10	10	10	23	24	23	35	35
Interest	18	18	18	17	16	16	14	12	11	8
Other private										
Disbursements	0	0	0	0	0	0	0	0	0	0
Principal	40	28	17	12	19	4	6	3	1	1
Interest	7	4	3	2	1	1	0	0	0	0

MADAGASCAR

(US$ million, unless otherwise indicated)

	1970	1980	1990	1994	1995	1996	1997	1998	1999	2000
1. SUMMARY DEBT DATA										
TOTAL DEBT STOCKS (EDT)	**485**	**1,248**	**3,704**	**4,096**	**4,322**	**4,146**	**4,109**	**4,394**	**4,755**	**4,701**
Long-term debt (LDOD)	**485**	**918**	**3,335**	**3,537**	**3,706**	**3,552**	**3,875**	**4,106**	**4,369**	**4,295**
Public and publicly guaranteed	485	918	3,335	3,537	3,706	3,552	3,875	4,106	4,369	4,295
Private nonguaranteed	0	0	0	0	0	0	0	0	0	0
Use of IMF credit	**0**	**87**	**144**	**86**	**73**	**73**	**69**	**58**	**63**	**104**
Short-term debt	**0**	**244**	**226**	**474**	**544**	**521**	**165**	**230**	**324**	**301**
of which interest arrears on LDOD	0	6	126	426	488	502	154	150	150	204
Official creditors	0	2	116	410	470	482	138	136	136	190
Private creditors	0	4	10	17	18	20	15	14	14	14
Memo: principal arrears on LDOD	0	11	266	976	1,197	1,263	600	604	614	666
Official creditors	0	6	245	931	1,145	1,210	573	584	589	636
Private creditors	0	5	21	45	53	53	27	20	25	30
Memo: export credits	0	0	795	734	774	810	811	511	486	481
TOTAL DEBT FLOWS										
Disbursements	**54**	**444**	**231**	**82**	**90**	**156**	**336**	**102**	**147**	**200**
Long-term debt	54	375	214	82	90	137	318	102	129	150
IMF purchases	0	70	17	0	0	20	19	0	19	50
Principal repayments	**45**	**44**	**121**	**43**	**38**	**60**	**118**	**72**	**76**	**55**
Long-term debt	45	42	70	31	24	43	100	58	64	50
IMF repurchases	0	2	51	12	15	17	18	14	12	5
Net flows on debt	**9**	**476**	**194**	**22**	**59**	**60**	**210**	**100**	**165**	**69**
of which short-term debt	0	75	83	-17	7	-36	-8	69	94	-76
Interest payments (INT)	**16**	**56**	**102**	**22**	**20**	**23**	**94**	**53**	**83**	**38**
Long-term debt	16	27	85	19	16	18	93	51	76	28
IMF charges	0	1	10	1	1	1	0	0	0	0
Short-term debt	0	29	7	2	3	4	1	2	6	9
Net transfers on debt	**-7**	**419**	**91**	**0**	**39**	**37**	**116**	**46**	**82**	**31**
Total debt service paid (TDS)	**61**	**100**	**223**	**65**	**58**	**83**	**212**	**125**	**159**	**93**
Long-term debt	61	68	155	50	40	62	193	109	140	78
IMF repurchases and charges	0	3	61	13	15	17	18	14	13	6
Short-term debt (interest only)	0	29	7	2	3	4	1	2	6	9
2. AGGREGATE NET RESOURCE FLOWS AND NET TRANSFERS (LONG-TERM)										
NET RESOURCE FLOWS	**39**	**361**	**514**	**225**	**240**	**305**	**797**	**416**	**303**	**298**
Net flow of long-term debt (ex. IMF)	9	333	144	51	66	93	217	44	65	100
Foreign direct investment (net)	10	-1	22	6	10	10	14	17	58	83
Portfolio equity flows	0	0	0	0	0	0	0	0	0	0
Grants (excluding technical coop.)	20	30	348	168	164	202	566	355	181	115
Memo: technical coop. grants	21	51	84	105	124	117	111	95	93	86
official net resource flows	30	223	507	224	235	300	784	400	246	215
private net resource flows	9	139	7	1	6	5	13	16	57	83
NET TRANSFERS	**18**	**334**	**428**	**204**	**222**	**284**	**700**	**360**	**220**	**262**
Interest on long-term debt	16	27	85	19	16	18	93	51	76	28
Profit remittances on FDI	5	1	1	2	2	3	4	5	7	8
Memo: official net transfers	14	215	435	206	219	283	692	349	170	187
private net transfers	4	119	-7	-2	3	1	8	11	50	75
3. MAJOR ECONOMIC AGGREGATES										
Gross national income (GNI)	1,109	4,024	2,936	2,827	3,002	3,837	3,454	3,665	3,678	3,804
Exports of goods & services (XGS)	..	519	490	669	765	815	808	854	931	1,210
of which workers remittances	..	0	4	11	9	6	..	..	..	..
Imports of goods & services (MGS)	..	1,121	985	1,032	1,161	1,171	1,195	1,231	1,262	1,584
International reserves (RES)	37	9	92	72	109	241	282	171	227	285
Current account balance	..	-556	-265	-277	-276	-153	-202	-289	-225	-260
4. DEBT INDICATORS										
EDT / XGS (%)	..	240.6	756.0	612.3	564.9	508.8	508.5	514.6	510.9	388.4
EDT / GNI (%)	43.8	31.0	126.2	144.9	144.0	108.1	119.0	119.9	129.3	123.6
TDS / XGS (%)	..	19.3	45.5	9.8	7.6	10.2	26.2	14.7	17.1	7.7
INT / XGS (%)	..	10.9	20.8	3.3	2.6	2.8	11.6	6.3	8.9	3.1
INT / GNI (%)	1.5	1.4	3.5	0.8	0.7	0.6	2.7	1.5	2.3	1.0
RES / EDT (%)	7.7	0.7	2.5	1.8	2.5	5.8	6.9	3.9	4.8	6.1
RES / MGS (months)	..	0.1	1.1	0.8	1.1	2.5	2.8	1.7	2.2	2.2
Short-term / EDT (%)	0.0	19.5	6.1	11.6	12.6	12.6	4.0	5.2	6.8	6.4
Concessional / EDT (%)	93.1	37.4	46.5	51.7	51.9	51.4	65.2	66.3	61.4	61.2
Multilateral / EDT (%)	8.6	14.6	33.2	39.0	39.1	38.7	40.4	40.5	37.9	38.9

MADAGASCAR

(US$ million, unless otherwise indicated)

	1970	1980	1990	1994	1995	1996	1997	1998	1999	2000
5. LONG-TERM DEBT										
DEBT OUTSTANDING (LDOD)	**485**	**918**	**3,335**	**3,537**	**3,706**	**3,552**	**3,875**	**4,106**	**4,369**	**4,295**
Public and publicly guaranteed	**485**	**918**	**3,335**	**3,537**	**3,706**	**3,552**	**3,875**	**4,106**	**4,369**	**4,295**
Official creditors	484	572	3,195	3,451	3,622	3,475	3,830	4,065	4,329	4,256
Multilateral	42	182	1,231	1,596	1,690	1,604	1,661	1,782	1,801	1,828
Concessional	10	148	1,075	1,440	1,536	1,452	1,560	1,692	1,732	1,766
Bilateral	443	390	1,964	1,855	1,931	1,871	2,169	2,284	2,527	2,429
Concessional	442	319	648	678	706	680	1,121	1,221	1,185	1,109
Private creditors	1	346	140	86	84	77	45	41	40	39
Bonds	0	0	0	0	0	0	0	0	0	0
Commercial banks	0	134	38	28	28	25	24	24	23	23
Other private	1	212	102	58	56	51	21	17	17	17
Private nonguaranteed	**0**	**0**	**0**	**0**	**0**	**0**	**0**	**0**	**0**	**0**
Bonds	0	0	0	0	0	0	0	0	0	0
Commercial banks and other	0	0	0	0	0	0	0	0	0	0
Memo:										
IBRD	2	30	26	14	12	7	3	1	0	0
IDA	10	122	770	1,021	1,110	1,147	1,212	1,317	1,361	1,378
DISBURSEMENTS	**54**	**375**	**214**	**82**	**90**	**137**	**318**	**102**	**129**	**150**
Public and publicly guaranteed	**54**	**375**	**214**	**82**	**90**	**137**	**318**	**102**	**129**	**150**
Official creditors	54	212	212	82	89	136	317	102	129	150
Multilateral	6	42	136	75	78	108	210	98	120	143
Concessional	5	38	120	66	78	91	208	98	118	134
Bilateral	48	170	77	8	11	28	107	5	8	7
Concessional	48	115	77	6	10	25	6	5	7	5
Private creditors	0	163	1	0	1	0	0	0	0	0
Bonds	0	0	0	0	0	0	0	0	0	0
Commercial banks	0	62	0	0	0	0	0	0	0	0
Other private	0	101	1	0	1	0	0	0	0	0
Private nonguaranteed	**0**	**0**	**0**	**0**	**0**	**0**	**0**	**0**	**0**	**0**
Bonds	0	0	0	0	0	0	0	0	0	0
Commercial banks and other	0	0	0	0	0	0	0	0	0	0
Memo:										
IBRD	1	2	0	0	0	0	0	0	0	0
IDA	5	25	64	60	76	78	130	77	84	94
PRINCIPAL REPAYMENTS	**45**	**42**	**70**	**31**	**24**	**43**	**100**	**58**	**64**	**50**
Public and publicly guaranteed	**45**	**42**	**70**	**31**	**24**	**43**	**100**	**58**	**64**	**50**
Official creditors	45	19	53	26	19	38	99	57	63	49
Multilateral	3	1	19	22	18	36	65	36	36	37
Concessional	0	0	9	9	9	20	25	20	23	26
Bilateral	41	18	35	4	1	2	34	21	27	12
Concessional	41	17	9	4	1	1	30	20	17	10
Private creditors	1	23	16	5	5	5	2	1	1	0
Bonds	0	0	0	0	0	0	0	0	0	0
Commercial banks	0	12	11	1	1	2	1	1	0	0
Other private	1	12	6	4	4	3	1	0	0	0
Private nonguaranteed	**0**	**0**	**0**	**0**	**0**	**0**	**0**	**0**	**0**	**0**
Bonds	0	0	0	0	0	0	0	0	0	0
Commercial banks and other	0	0	0	0	0	0	0	0	0	0
Memo:										
IBRD	0	0	3	3	4	4	4	2	1	0
IDA	0	0	3	6	7	9	10	12	15	17
NET FLOWS ON DEBT	**9**	**333**	**144**	**51**	**66**	**93**	**217**	**44**	**65**	**100**
Public and publicly guaranteed	**9**	**333**	**144**	**51**	**66**	**93**	**217**	**44**	**65**	**100**
Official creditors	10	193	159	56	70	98	219	45	65	101
Multilateral	3	41	117	52	60	72	145	61	84	106
Concessional	5	38	111	58	69	71	183	78	95	109
Bilateral	7	152	42	4	10	26	73	-16	-19	-6
Concessional	7	97	68	2	10	24	-24	-15	-11	-5
Private creditors	-1	140	-15	-5	-4	-5	-1	-1	-1	0
Bonds	0	0	0	0	0	0	0	0	0	0
Commercial banks	0	50	-10	-1	-1	-2	-1	-1	0	0
Other private	-1	89	-5	-4	-3	-3	-1	0	0	0
Private nonguaranteed	**0**	**0**	**0**	**0**	**0**	**0**	**0**	**0**	**0**	**0**
Bonds	0	0	0	0	0	0	0	0	0	0
Commercial banks and other	0	0	0	0	0	0	0	0	0	0
Memo:										
IBRD	1	1	-3	-3	-4	-4	-4	-2	-1	0
IDA	5	25	61	54	69	69	120	65	69	77

MADAGASCAR

(US$ million, unless otherwise indicated)

	1970	1980	1990	1994	1995	1996	1997	1998	1999	2000
INTEREST PAYMENTS (LINT)	**16**	**27**	**85**	**19**	**16**	**18**	**93**	**51**	**76**	**28**
Public and publicly guaranteed	**16**	**27**	**85**	**19**	**16**	**18**	**93**	**51**	**76**	**28**
Official creditors	16	8	72	18	15	17	93	51	76	28
Multilateral	1	4	18	15	12	15	42	19	17	17
Concessional	0	1	7	8	9	11	16	14	13	14
Bilateral	15	4	54	4	4	2	51	32	60	11
Concessional	15	3	11	3	3	1	26	22	21	4
Private creditors	0	19	13	1	1	2	0	0	0	0
Bonds	0	0	0	0	0	0	0	0	0	0
Commercial banks	0	9	10	0	0	1	0	0	0	0
Other private	0	10	3	1	0	0	0	0	0	0
Private nonguaranteed	**0**	**0**	**0**	**0**	**0**	**0**	**0**	**0**	**0**	**0**
Bonds	0	0	0	0	0	0	0	0	0	0
Commercial banks and other	0	0	0	0	0	0	0	0	0	0
Memo:										
IBRD	0	2	2	1	1	1	0	0	0	0
IDA	0	1	5	7	8	9	9	9	10	10
NET TRANSFERS ON DEBT	**-7**	**306**	**59**	**32**	**50**	**75**	**125**	**-7**	**-12**	**72**
Public and publicly guaranteed	**-7**	**306**	**59**	**32**	**50**	**75**	**125**	**-7**	**-12**	**72**
Official creditors	-7	185	87	38	55	81	126	-6	-11	72
Multilateral	2	37	99	38	48	57	103	43	67	89
Concessional	5	37	104	50	60	61	167	64	83	95
Bilateral	-9	148	-12	0	7	24	23	-48	-78	-17
Concessional	-9	94	57	-1	7	23	-50	-37	-32	-9
Private creditors	-1	121	-28	-6	-5	-6	-2	-1	-1	-1
Bonds	0	0	0	0	0	0	0	0	0	0
Commercial banks	0	42	-21	-2	-1	-3	-1	-1	-1	0
Other private	-1	79	-8	-4	-4	-3	-1	0	0	0
Private nonguaranteed	**0**	**0**	**0**	**0**	**0**	**0**	**0**	**0**	**0**	**0**
Bonds	0	0	0	0	0	0	0	0	0	0
Commercial banks and other	0	0	0	0	0	0	0	0	0	0
Memo:										
IBRD	1	-1	-5	-5	-5	-5	-4	-2	-1	0
IDA	5	24	56	46	62	60	111	56	59	67
DEBT SERVICE (LTDS)	**61**	**68**	**155**	**50**	**40**	**62**	**193**	**109**	**140**	**78**
Public and publicly guaranteed	**61**	**68**	**155**	**50**	**40**	**62**	**193**	**109**	**140**	**78**
Official creditors	61	27	125	44	34	55	191	108	139	78
Multilateral	4	4	37	37	30	51	107	55	53	54
Concessional	0	1	16	17	18	31	41	33	36	39
Bilateral	56	22	89	8	5	4	84	53	87	24
Concessional	56	21	20	7	3	2	56	42	39	14
Private creditors	1	42	29	6	6	7	2	1	1	1
Bonds	0	0	0	0	0	0	0	0	0	0
Commercial banks	0	20	21	2	1	3	1	1	1	0
Other private	1	22	9	4	5	3	1	0	0	0
Private nonguaranteed	**0**	**0**	**0**	**0**	**0**	**0**	**0**	**0**	**0**	**0**
Bonds	0	0	0	0	0	0	0	0	0	0
Commercial banks and other	0	0	0	0	0	0	0	0	0	0
Memo:										
IBRD	0	3	5	5	5	5	4	2	1	0
IDA	0	1	8	13	15	18	19	21	25	27
UNDISBURSED DEBT	**186**	**713**	**889**	**655**	**636**	**540**	**497**	**577**	**555**	**536**
Official creditors	177	472	888	653	636	540	497	577	555	536
Private creditors	10	241	0	2	1	0	0	0	0	0
Memorandum items										
Concessional LDOD	452	467	1,723	2,118	2,242	2,132	2,681	2,913	2,918	2,875
Variable rate LDOD	0	74	337	274	292	280	240	235	217	214
Public sector LDOD	483	904	3,259	3,418	3,573	3,404	3,745	3,951	4,232	4,173
Private sector LDOD	2	14	76	118	133	148	130	156	137	122

6. CURRENCY COMPOSITION OF LONG-TERM DEBT (PERCENT)

	1970	1980	1990	1994	1995	1996	1997	1998	1999	2000
Deutsche mark	2.3	5.0	3.3	3.3	3.3	3.0	1.8	1.8	1.5	1.4
French franc	88.3	12.5	15.7	11.9	12.6	12.9	13.4	13.8	10.9	10.0
Japanese yen	0.0	7.3	7.3	8.8	8.1	7.5	7.5	8.2	8.4	7.6
Pound sterling	0.0	0.1	0.1	0.1	0.1	0.1	0.1	0.1	0.1	0.1
Swiss franc	0.0	0.6	1.4	1.2	1.3	1.1	1.1	1.1	0.9	0.9
U.S.dollars	9.1	53.6	42.3	44.3	44.8	47.9	49.1	49.0	55.0	56.7
Multiple currency	0.3	4.0	8.6	10.5	10.1	10.0	9.1	8.8	8.1	7.7
Special drawing rights	0.0	0.0	3.2	3.3	3.2	3.2	2.7	2.8	2.1	2.1
All other currencies	0.0	16.9	18.1	16.6	16.5	14.3	15.2	14.4	13.0	13.5

MADAGASCAR

(US$ million, unless otherwise indicated)

	1970	1980	1990	1994	1995	1996	1997	1998	1999	2000
7. DEBT RESTRUCTURINGS										
Total amount rescheduled	..	..	88	0	0	0	972	46	41	0
Debt stock rescheduled	..	..	0	0	0	0	0	0	0	0
Principal rescheduled	..	..	65	0	0	0	579	29	27	0
Official	..	..	49	0	0	0	551	29	27	0
Private	..	..	16	0	0	0	28	0	0	0
Interest rescheduled	..	..	16	0	0	0	251	13	12	0
Official	..	..	14	0	0	0	245	13	12	0
Private	..	..	2	0	0	0	6	0	0	0
Debt forgiven	..	..	185	0	0	0	48	6	3	0
Memo: interest forgiven	..	..	0	0	0	0	17	1	1	0
Debt stock reduction	..	..	0	0	0	0	0	0	0	0
of which debt buyback	..	..	0	0	0	0	0	0	0	0
8. DEBT STOCK-FLOW RECONCILIATION										
Total change in debt stocks	..	..	273	292	226	-176	-37	285	361	-54
Net flows on debt	9	476	194	22	59	60	210	100	165	69
Net change in interest arrears	..	..	19	95	62	13	-348	-4	0	54
Interest capitalized	..	..	16	0	0	0	251	13	12	0
Debt forgiveness or reduction	..	..	-185	0	0	0	-48	-6	-3	0
Cross-currency valuation	..	..	182	29	-45	-259	-332	-67	-159	-162
Residual	..	..	48	146	150	10	231	250	347	-16
9. AVERAGE TERMS OF NEW COMMITMENTS										
ALL CREDITORS										
Interest (%)	2.3	5.7	1.1	0.9	1.0	0.6	2.7	0.9	0.8	0.8
Maturity (years)	39.0	18.2	36.2	37.8	36.8	37.9	36.2	35.9	40.4	39.7
Grace period (years)	9.2	4.6	9.7	9.7	9.6	10.0	9.3	9.0	9.9	10.2
Grant element (%)	65.4	27.5	74.9	77.0	75.3	80.7	62.6	74.8	79.6	80.5
Official creditors										
Interest (%)	1.4	3.7	1.1	0.9	1.0	0.6	2.7	0.9	0.8	0.8
Maturity (years)	44.6	28.1	36.4	37.8	36.8	37.9	36.2	35.9	40.4	39.7
Grace period (years)	10.4	6.1	9.7	9.7	9.6	10.0	9.3	9.0	9.9	10.2
Grant element (%)	75.3	46.5	75.2	77.0	75.3	80.7	62.6	74.8	79.6	80.5
Private creditors										
Interest (%)	6.5	7.4	5.0	0.0	0.0	0.0	0.0	0.0	0.0	0.0
Maturity (years)	10.5	9.7	5.1	0.0	0.0	0.0	0.0	0.0	0.0	0.0
Grace period (years)	2.8	3.3	1.1	0.0	0.0	0.0	0.0	0.0	0.0	0.0
Grant element (%)	14.8	11.3	12.4	0.0	0.0	0.0	0.0	0.0	0.0	0.0
Memorandum items										
Commitments	23	468	211	78	80	78	338	180	176	148
Official creditors	19	215	210	78	80	78	338	180	176	148
Private creditors	4	252	1	0	0	0	0	0	0	0

10. CONTRACTUAL OBLIGATIONS ON OUTSTANDING LONG-TERM DEBT

	2001	2002	2003	2004	2005	2006	2007	2008	2009	2010
TOTAL										
Disbursements	160	143	103	70	39	11	8	2	0	0
Principal	111	106	97	99	101	105	110	118	123	125
Interest	105	102	99	97	94	90	87	83	79	75
Official creditors										
Disbursements	160	143	103	70	39	11	8	2	0	0
Principal	105	103	96	99	101	105	110	118	123	125
Interest	105	102	99	97	94	90	87	83	79	75
Bilateral creditors										
Disbursements	4	2	1	1	1	1	1	0	0	0
Principal	60	58	50	52	57	58	59	59	60	58
Interest	88	85	82	80	77	74	71	67	64	61
Multilateral creditors										
Disbursements	156	141	102	69	39	10	7	2	0	0
Principal	45	45	46	47	45	47	52	58	63	67
Interest	17	17	17	17	17	16	16	16	15	14
Private creditors										
Disbursements	0	0	0	0	0	0	0	0	0	0
Principal	6	3	0	0	0	0	0	0	0	0
Interest	0	0	0	0	0	0	0	0	0	0
Commercial banks										
Disbursements	0	0	0	0	0	0	0	0	0	0
Principal	6	3	0	0	0	0	0	0	0	0
Interest	0	0	0	0	0	0	0	0	0	0
Other private										
Disbursements	0	0	0	0	0	0	0	0	0	0
Principal	0	0	0	0	0	0	0	0	0	0
Interest	0	0	0	0	0	0	0	0	0	0

MALAWI

(US$ million, unless otherwise indicated)

	1970	1980	1990	1994	1995	1996	1997	1998	1999	2000
1. SUMMARY DEBT DATA										
TOTAL DEBT STOCKS (EDT)	**135**	**830**	**1,558**	**2,025**	**2,243**	**2,315**	**2,229**	**2,444**	**2,751**	**2,716**
Long-term debt (LDOD)	**135**	**634**	**1,385**	**1,900**	**2,083**	**2,096**	**2,099**	**2,310**	**2,596**	**2,555**
Public and publicly guaranteed	135	634	1,382	1,900	2,083	2,096	2,099	2,310	2,596	2,555
Private nonguaranteed	0	0	3	0	0	0	0	0	0	0
Use of IMF credit	**0**	**80**	**115**	**112**	**116**	**119**	**106**	**102**	**88**	**83**
Short-term debt	**0**	**116**	**58**	**12**	**44**	**100**	**24**	**32**	**67**	**78**
of which interest arrears on LDOD	0	3	6	2	1	5	4	14	24	37
Official creditors	0	2	4	2	1	4	2	12	22	34
Private creditors	0	1	2	1	1	1	1	2	2	2
Memo: principal arrears on LDOD	0	1	19	14	7	15	17	38	48	73
Official creditors	0	1	12	9	3	8	9	27	36	60
Private creditors	0	0	7	4	4	7	8	11	12	12
Memo: export credits	0	0	94	96	101	86	53	45	34	30
TOTAL DEBT FLOWS										
Disbursements	**54**	**190**	**161**	**147**	**227**	**184**	**178**	**173**	**152**	**126**
Long-term debt	53	153	136	121	215	161	168	156	141	117
IMF purchases	1	37	25	26	12	22	11	17	10	9
Principal repayments	**3**	**35**	**86**	**53**	**76**	**56**	**55**	**60**	**50**	**38**
Long-term debt	3	33	67	47	66	41	38	34	28	29
IMF repurchases	0	1	19	6	10	15	17	25	22	9
Net flows on debt	**51**	**154**	**88**	**95**	**183**	**181**	**48**	**112**	**127**	**86**
of which short-term debt	0	-1	13	1	32	53	-75	-2	25	-2
Interest payments (INT)	**4**	**53**	**47**	**27**	**43**	**33**	**30**	**24**	**19**	**20**
Long-term debt	4	35	36	26	39	28	26	22	17	17
IMF charges	0	2	6	1	1	1	1	1	1	0
Short-term debt	0	16	4	1	3	4	3	1	2	3
Net transfers on debt	**48**	**101**	**41**	**69**	**141**	**148**	**18**	**87**	**108**	**65**
Total debt service paid (TDS)	**6**	**87**	**133**	**80**	**118**	**89**	**85**	**84**	**69**	**59**
Long-term debt	6	68	103	73	104	69	64	56	44	46
IMF repurchases and charges	0	3	25	6	11	16	18	26	23	10
Short-term debt (interest only)	0	16	4	1	3	4	3	1	2	3
2. AGGREGATE NET RESOURCE FLOWS AND NET TRANSFERS (LONG-TERM)										
NET RESOURCE FLOWS	**65**	**178**	**296**	**313**	**437**	**364**	**269**	**429**	**428**	**360**
Net flow of long-term debt (ex. IMF)	50	120	69	74	149	121	129	121	114	88
Foreign direct investment (net)	9	10	0	9	25	44	22	70	60	45
Portfolio equity flows	0	0	0	0	0	0	0	24	0	0
Grants (excluding technical coop.)	7	48	227	231	262	200	118	213	254	226
Memo: technical coop. grants	9	36	110	64	87	87	92	80	81	111
official net resource flows	55	148	294	308	435	324	248	336	368	315
private net resource flows	10	30	2	6	2	40	21	93	60	45
NET TRANSFERS	**54**	**134**	**260**	**288**	**398**	**337**	**243**	**407**	**411**	**342**
Interest on long-term debt	4	35	36	26	39	28	26	22	17	17
Profit remittances on FDI	8	9	0	0	0	0	0	0	0	0
Memo: official net transfers	53	139	264	284	400	299	224	314	351	297
private net transfers	1	-4	-4	3	-1	38	19	93	60	45
3. MAJOR ECONOMIC AGGREGATES										
Gross national income (GNI)	283	1,138	1,837	1,139	1,381	2,393	2,492	1,695	1,775	1,660
Exports of goods & services (XGS)	..	315	452	387	463	571	651	638	543	500
of which workers remittances	..	0	0	0	..	..	..	..	..	..
Imports of goods & services (MGS)	..	638	638	961	889	1,150	1,377	1,125	1,208	1,029
International reserves (RES)	29	76	142	48	115	230	166	273	254	250
Current account balance	..	-260	-86	-450	-433	-609	-750	-524	-654	-523
4. DEBT INDICATORS										
EDT / XGS (%)	..	263.7	344.4	523.7	484.8	405.4	342.3	383.0	506.7	543.3
EDT / GNI (%)	47.7	72.9	84.8	177.8	162.4	96.7	89.4	144.2	155.0	163.6
TDS / XGS (%)	..	27.8	29.3	20.6	25.6	15.5	13.1	13.1	12.7	11.7
INT / XGS (%)	..	16.8	10.3	6.9	9.2	5.8	4.7	3.8	3.5	4.1
INT / GNI (%)	1.2	4.7	2.5	2.3	3.1	1.4	1.2	1.4	1.1	1.2
RES / EDT (%)	21.6	9.2	9.1	2.4	5.1	10.0	7.5	11.2	9.3	9.2
RES / MGS (months)	..	1.4	2.7	0.6	1.6	2.4	1.5	2.9	2.5	2.9
Short-term / EDT (%)	0.0	14.0	3.8	0.6	1.9	4.3	1.1	1.3	2.5	2.9
Concessional / EDT (%)	58.0	31.1	67.5	83.0	84.6	84.0	88.5	89.4	90.0	90.3
Multilateral / EDT (%)	12.5	26.4	69.8	79.1	76.4	76.6	80.8	81.4	74.8	75.4

MALAWI

(US$ million, unless otherwise indicated)

	1970	1980	1990	1994	1995	1996	1997	1998	1999	2000
5. LONG-TERM DEBT										
DEBT OUTSTANDING (LDOD)	**135**	**634**	**1,385**	**1,900**	**2,083**	**2,096**	**2,099**	**2,310**	**2,596**	**2,555**
Public and publicly guaranteed	**135**	**634**	**1,382**	**1,900**	**2,083**	**2,096**	**2,099**	**2,310**	**2,596**	**2,555**
Official creditors	116	442	1,305	1,851	2,055	2,072	2,079	2,290	2,577	2,537
Multilateral	17	219	1,088	1,601	1,712	1,773	1,800	1,990	2,057	2,048
Concessional	17	147	902	1,460	1,577	1,665	1,709	1,900	1,972	1,977
Bilateral	99	223	217	250	343	299	279	300	520	490
Concessional	62	111	149	221	321	281	264	284	503	475
Private creditors	20	192	78	49	28	24	21	20	19	18
Bonds	16	2	0	0	0	0	0	0	0	0
Commercial banks	1	153	35	11	0	0	0	0	0	0
Other private	3	38	42	39	28	24	21	20	19	18
Private nonguaranteed	**0**	**0**	**3**	**0**	**0**	**0**	**0**	**0**	**0**	**0**
Bonds	0	0	0	0	0	0	0	0	0	0
Commercial banks and other	0	0	3	0	0	0	0	0	0	0
Memo:										
IBRD	0	26	91	65	55	42	34	25	17	9
IDA	17	131	764	1,160	1,251	1,346	1,375	1,542	1,586	1,592
DISBURSEMENTS	**53**	**153**	**136**	**121**	**215**	**161**	**168**	**156**	**141**	**117**
Public and publicly guaranteed	**53**	**153**	**136**	**121**	**215**	**161**	**168**	**156**	**141**	**117**
Official creditors	50	105	129	111	215	161	166	156	141	117
Multilateral	10	49	118	104	97	161	146	156	141	117
Concessional	10	28	109	101	93	161	142	147	128	115
Bilateral	40	56	10	6	118	0	20	0	0	0
Concessional	19	18	10	6	118	0	20	0	0	0
Private creditors	3	48	7	10	0	0	1	0	1	0
Bonds	0	0	0	0	0	0	0	0	0	0
Commercial banks	0	39	0	0	0	0	0	0	0	0
Other private	3	9	7	10	0	0	1	0	1	0
Private nonguaranteed	**0**	**0**	**0**	**0**	**0**	**0**	**0**	**0**	**0**	**0**
Bonds	0	0	0	0	0	0	0	0	0	0
Commercial banks and other	0	0	0	0	0	0	0	0	0	0
Memo:										
IBRD	0	8	2	0	0	0	0	0	0	0
IDA	10	15	99	59	73	141	107	130	88	97
PRINCIPAL REPAYMENTS	**3**	**33**	**67**	**47**	**66**	**41**	**38**	**34**	**28**	**29**
Public and publicly guaranteed	**3**	**33**	**65**	**47**	**66**	**41**	**38**	**34**	**28**	**29**
Official creditors	2	5	61	33	43	37	35	33	27	29
Multilateral	0	2	20	29	29	26	25	30	27	29
Concessional	0	1	3	7	9	11	11	16	15	18
Bilateral	2	4	41	5	14	11	11	4	0	0
Concessional	1	1	4	3	7	8	9	4	0	0
Private creditors	1	28	4	14	23	4	3	1	0	0
Bonds	1	1	0	0	0	0	0	0	0	0
Commercial banks	0	21	0	8	11	0	0	0	0	0
Other private	0	6	4	6	12	4	3	1	0	0
Private nonguaranteed	**0**	**0**	**1**	**0**	**0**	**0**	**0**	**0**	**0**	**0**
Bonds	0	0	0	0	0	0	0	0	0	0
Commercial banks and other	0	0	1	0	0	0	0	0	0	0
Memo:										
IBRD	0	0	8	7	12	9	6	10	8	8
IDA	0	1	3	6	7	9	9	11	14	16
NET FLOWS ON DEBT	**50**	**120**	**69**	**74**	**149**	**121**	**129**	**121**	**114**	**88**
Public and publicly guaranteed	**50**	**120**	**70**	**74**	**149**	**121**	**129**	**121**	**114**	**88**
Official creditors	48	100	68	77	172	125	131	122	114	88
Multilateral	10	48	98	76	69	135	122	126	114	88
Concessional	10	27	106	93	84	150	130	132	113	97
Bilateral	39	52	-31	1	104	-11	9	-4	0	0
Concessional	19	17	6	3	111	-8	11	-4	0	0
Private creditors	2	20	3	-3	-23	-4	-2	-1	0	0
Bonds	-1	-1	0	0	0	0	0	0	0	0
Commercial banks	0	18	0	-8	-11	0	0	0	0	0
Other private	3	4	3	5	-12	-4	-2	-1	0	0
Private nonguaranteed	**0**	**0**	**-1**	**0**	**0**	**0**	**0**	**0**	**0**	**0**
Bonds	0	0	0	0	0	0	0	0	0	0
Commercial banks and other	0	0	-1	0	0	0	0	0	0	0
Memo:										
IBRD	0	8	-6	-7	-12	-9	-6	-10	-8	-8
IDA	10	14	96	53	66	133	98	120	75	81

MALAWI

(US$ million, unless otherwise indicated)

	1970	1980	1990	1994	1995	1996	1997	1998	1999	2000
INTEREST PAYMENTS (LINT)	**4**	**35**	**36**	**26**	**39**	**28**	**26**	**22**	**17**	**17**
Public and publicly guaranteed	**4**	**35**	**36**	**26**	**39**	**28**	**26**	**22**	**17**	**17**
Official creditors	2	10	31	23	35	25	25	22	17	17
Multilateral	0	3	19	19	25	19	17	19	17	17
Concessional	0	1	6	10	12	12	12	14	13	15
Bilateral	2	7	12	4	10	6	8	3	0	0
Concessional	1	3	3	3	7	5	6	3	0	0
Private creditors	1	25	6	2	4	2	1	0	0	0
Bonds	1	0	0	0	0	0	0	0	0	0
Commercial banks	0	22	3	0	1	0	0	0	0	0
Other private	0	2	2	2	3	2	1	0	0	0
Private nonguaranteed	**0**	**0**	**0**	**0**	**0**	**0**	**0**	**0**	**0**	**0**
Bonds	0	0	0	0	0	0	0	0	0	0
Commercial banks and other	0	0	0	0	0	0	0	0	0	0
Memo:										
IBRD	0	1	8	4	7	4	2	3	2	1
IDA	0	1	5	8	9	10	10	10	11	12
NET TRANSFERS ON DEBT	**47**	**85**	**33**	**48**	**111**	**93**	**103**	**99**	**97**	**71**
Public and publicly guaranteed	**47**	**85**	**34**	**48**	**111**	**93**	**103**	**99**	**97**	**71**
Official creditors	46	90	37	54	137	99	106	100	97	71
Multilateral	10	45	79	57	44	116	104	107	97	71
Concessional	10	26	100	83	72	138	118	118	99	82
Bilateral	37	45	-42	-3	94	-17	2	-7	0	0
Concessional	18	14	3	1	104	-12	5	-6	0	0
Private creditors	0	-5	-3	-6	-26	-6	-3	-1	0	0
Bonds	-2	-1	0	0	0	0	0	0	0	0
Commercial banks	0	-5	-3	-9	-11	0	0	0	0	0
Other private	2	1	1	3	-15	-6	-3	-1	0	0
Private nonguaranteed	**0**	**0**	**-2**	**0**	**0**	**0**	**0**	**0**	**0**	**0**
Bonds	0	0	0	0	0	0	0	0	0	0
Commercial banks and other	0	0	-2	0	0	0	0	0	0	0
Memo:										
IBRD	0	6	-13	-11	-18	-13	-8	-13	-10	-9
IDA	10	13	91	45	57	123	89	109	63	70
DEBT SERVICE (LTDS)	**6**	**68**	**103**	**73**	**104**	**69**	**64**	**56**	**44**	**46**
Public and publicly guaranteed	**6**	**68**	**102**	**73**	**104**	**69**	**64**	**56**	**44**	**46**
Official creditors	4	15	92	57	78	62	60	55	44	46
Multilateral	0	5	39	48	54	46	42	49	44	46
Concessional	0	2	9	18	21	23	23	29	28	33
Bilateral	4	11	53	9	24	17	18	7	0	0
Concessional	1	4	7	6	14	12	16	6	0	0
Private creditors	3	53	10	16	26	6	4	1	1	0
Bonds	2	1	0	0	0	0	0	0	0	0
Commercial banks	0	44	3	9	11	0	0	0	0	0
Other private	1	8	7	7	15	6	4	1	1	0
Private nonguaranteed	**0**	**0**	**2**	**0**	**0**	**0**	**0**	**0**	**0**	**0**
Bonds	0	0	0	0	0	0	0	0	0	0
Commercial banks and other	0	0	2	0	0	0	0	0	0	0
Memo:										
IBRD	0	1	16	11	18	13	8	13	10	9
IDA	0	2	8	14	16	18	18	21	25	28
UNDISBURSED DEBT	**39**	**162**	**574**	**701**	**579**	**601**	**478**	**557**	**478**	**358**
Official creditors	39	152	563	701	579	598	472	551	472	358
Private creditors	0	10	12	0	0	3	6	6	5	0
Memorandum items										
Concessional LDOD	78	258	1,051	1,681	1,897	1,946	1,973	2,184	2,475	2,452
Variable rate LDOD	0	145	51	20	9	8	7	6	6	5
Public sector LDOD	135	585	1,372	1,896	2,080	2,092	2,096	2,307	2,593	2,552
Private sector LDOD	0	49	13	4	4	3	3	3	3	3

6. CURRENCY COMPOSITION OF LONG-TERM DEBT (PERCENT)

	1970	1980	1990	1994	1995	1996	1997	1998	1999	2000
Deutsche mark	4.1	2.5	0.7	0.1	0.3	0.3	0.2	0.2	0.2	0.2
French franc	0.0	1.2	2.0	1.5	1.2	1.0	0.8	0.8	0.6	0.6
Japanese yen	0.0	4.1	9.3	9.8	12.3	10.6	9.1	9.2	9.3	8.4
Pound sterling	56.2	17.4	16.7	10.0	9.0	8.5	8.0	7.4	6.4	6.1
Swiss franc	0.0	0.0	0.1	0.1	0.1	0.1	0.1	0.1	0.1	0.1
U.S.dollars	12.9	46.5	46.9	48.0	47.4	51.8	54.5	56.4	59.9	61.5
Multiple currency	0.0	12.4	21.9	22.1	20.4	18.6	18.5	17.6	15.5	15.0
Special drawing rights	0.0	0.0	0.0	6.8	6.6	6.7	6.4	6.1	5.5	5.4
All other currencies	26.8	15.9	2.4	1.6	2.7	2.4	2.4	2.2	2.5	2.7

MALAWI

(US$ million, unless otherwise indicated)

	1970	1980	1990	1994	1995	1996	1997	1998	1999	2000
7. DEBT RESTRUCTURINGS										
Total amount rescheduled	..	..	0	0	0	0	0	0	0	0
Debt stock rescheduled	..	..	0	0	0	0	0	0	0	0
Principal rescheduled	..	..	0	0	0	0	0	0	0	0
Official	..	..	0	0	0	0	0	0	0	0
Private	..	..	0	0	0	0	0	0	0	0
Interest rescheduled	..	..	0	0	0	0	0	0	0	0
Official	..	..	0	0	0	0	0	0	0	0
Private	..	..	0	0	0	0	0	0	0	0
Debt forgiven	..	..	51	0	0	0	0	0	0	0
Memo: interest forgiven	..	..	0	0	0	0	0	0	0	0
Debt stock reduction	..	..	0	0	0	0	0	0	0	0
of which debt buyback	..	..	0	0	0	0	0	0	0	0
8. DEBT STOCK-FLOW RECONCILIATION										
Total change in debt stocks	..	..	148	199	218	73	-87	216	307	-35
Net flows on debt	51	154	88	95	183	181	48	112	127	86
Net change in interest arrears	..	..	-2	1	-1	4	-1	10	10	13
Interest capitalized	..	..	0	0	0	0	0	0	0	0
Debt forgiveness or reduction	..	..	-51	0	0	0	0	0	0	0
Cross-currency valuation	..	..	22	-21	-91	-212	-231	-50	-21	-111
Residual	..	..	91	124	127	101	98	144	190	-22
9. AVERAGE TERMS OF NEW COMMITMENTS										
ALL CREDITORS										
Interest (%)	3.8	6.0	1.3	1.8	1.0	1.2	1.0	0.8	0.8	0.8
Maturity (years)	29.5	23.6	37.7	27.7	38.6	37.5	46.8	39.7	47.8	43.4
Grace period (years)	6.0	5.9	9.2	6.7	9.6	9.8	10.3	10.2	10.6	10.1
Grant element (%)	47.1	32.4	74.2	60.2	78.2	75.9	79.8	80.5	82.9	81.4
Official creditors										
Interest (%)	3.1	4.0	1.1	1.8	1.0	1.1	0.7	0.8	0.8	0.8
Maturity (years)	35.4	28.6	38.3	27.7	38.6	37.9	49.3	39.7	47.8	43.4
Grace period (years)	7.6	6.9	9.4	6.7	9.6	9.9	11.0	10.2	10.6	10.1
Grant element (%)	56.9	44.9	75.6	60.2	78.2	76.8	83.9	80.5	82.9	81.4
Private creditors										
Interest (%)	6.5	13.2	8.6	0.0	0.0	9.2	5.5	0.0	0.0	0.0
Maturity (years)	8.4	5.7	11.8	0.0	0.0	4.7	10.5	0.0	0.0	0.0
Grace period (years)	0.3	2.6	3.5	0.0	0.0	1.2	1.0	0.0	0.0	0.0
Grant element (%)	12.0	-12.3	6.2	0.0	0.0	1.5	17.5	0.0	0.0	0.0
Memorandum items										
Commitments	14	130	259	153	102	207	80	214	102	47
Official creditors	11	102	253	153	102	205	75	214	102	47
Private creditors	3	28	5	0	0	3	5	0	0	0

10. CONTRACTUAL OBLIGATIONS ON OUTSTANDING LONG-TERM DEBT

	2001	2002	2003	2004	2005	2006	2007	2008	2009	2010
TOTAL										
Disbursements	107	95	67	44	25	10	6	1	0	0
Principal	60	62	66	68	83	87	88	81	86	89
Interest	31	30	29	28	27	25	24	22	21	20
Official creditors										
Disbursements	107	95	67	44	25	10	6	1	0	0
Principal	59	61	66	68	83	87	88	80	86	89
Interest	31	30	29	28	27	25	24	22	21	20
Bilateral creditors										
Disbursements	0	0	0	0	0	0	0	0	0	0
Principal	23	23	23	23	37	36	35	25	23	23
Interest	12	11	11	10	9	8	7	7	6	5
Multilateral creditors										
Disbursements	107	95	67	44	25	10	6	1	0	0
Principal	36	38	42	45	46	51	53	56	63	66
Interest	19	18	18	18	17	17	16	16	15	15
Private creditors										
Disbursements	0	0	0	0	0	0	0	0	0	0
Principal	1	0	0	0	0	0	0	0	0	0
Interest	0	0	0	0	0	0	0	0	0	0
Commercial banks										
Disbursements	0	0	0	0	0	0	0	0	0	0
Principal	0	0	0	0	0	0	0	0	0	0
Interest	0	0	0	0	0	0	0	0	0	0
Other private										
Disbursements	0	0	0	0	0	0	0	0	0	0
Principal	1	0	0	0	0	0	0	0	0	0
Interest	0	0	0	0	0	0	0	0	0	0

MALAYSIA

(US$ million, unless otherwise indicated)

1. SUMMARY DEBT DATA

	1970	1980	1990	1994	1995	1996	1997	1998	1999	2000
TOTAL DEBT STOCKS (EDT)	**502**	**6,611**	**15,328**	**30,336**	**34,343**	**39,673**	**47,228**	**42,409**	**41,902**	**41,797**
Long-term debt (LDOD)	**440**	**5,256**	**13,422**	**24,147**	**27,069**	**28,605**	**32,289**	**33,940**	**35,891**	**37,157**
Public and publicly guaranteed	390	4,008	11,592	14,693	16,023	15,702	16,808	18,155	18,929	19,090
Private nonguaranteed	50	1,248	1,830	9,454	11,046	12,903	15,482	15,786	16,961	18,067
Use of IMF credit	**0**	**0**	**0**	**0**	**0**	**0**	**0**	**0**	**0**	**0**
Short-term debt	**62**	**1,355**	**1,906**	**6,189**	**7,274**	**11,068**	**14,939**	**8,469**	**6,012**	**4,640**
of which interest arrears on LDOD	0	0	0	0	0	0	0	0	0	0
Official creditors	0	0	0	0	0	0	0	0	0	0
Private creditors	0	0	0	0	0	0	0	0	0	0
Memo: principal arrears on LDOD	0	0	0	0	0	0	0	0	0	0
Official creditors	0	0	0	0	0	0	0	0	0	0
Private creditors	0	0	0	0	0	0	0	0	0	0
Memo: export credits	0	0	1,395	3,445	4,373	3,350	3,289	1,409	1,246	998
TOTAL DEBT FLOWS										
Disbursements	**58**	**1,456**	**1,683**	**7,672**	**8,503**	**8,936**	**8,803**	**6,724**	**4,017**	**4,878**
Long-term debt	58	1,456	1,683	7,672	8,503	8,936	8,803	6,724	4,017	4,878
IMF purchases	0	0	0	0	0	0	0	0	0	0
Principal repayments	**57**	**345**	**3,167**	**4,690**	**4,450**	**6,343**	**4,276**	**3,806**	**2,486**	**3,678**
Long-term debt	57	345	3,167	4,690	4,450	6,343	4,276	3,806	2,486	3,678
IMF repurchases	0	0	0	0	0	0	0	0	0	0
Net flows on debt	**1**	**1,592**	**-1,851**	**2,220**	**5,138**	**6,387**	**8,397**	**-3,552**	**-927**	**-171**
of which short-term debt	0	481	-367	-762	1,085	3,794	3,871	-6,470	-2,457	-1,372
Interest payments (INT)	**25**	**589**	**1,166**	**1,432**	**1,591**	**2,084**	**2,833**	**2,268**	**1,922**	**2,289**
Long-term debt	25	338	997	1,007	1,151	1,432	1,588	1,612	1,603	2,023
IMF charges	0	0	0	0	0	0	0	0	0	0
Short-term debt	0	251	169	424	441	652	1,245	656	319	266
Net transfers on debt	**-25**	**1,003**	**-3,017**	**788**	**3,547**	**4,303**	**5,565**	**-5,820**	**-2,848**	**-2,461**
Total debt service paid (TDS)	**82**	**934**	**4,333**	**6,121**	**6,041**	**8,427**	**7,109**	**6,074**	**4,408**	**5,967**
Long-term debt	82	683	4,164	5,697	5,600	7,776	5,864	5,418	4,089	5,701
IMF repurchases and charges	0	0	0	0	0	0	0	0	0	0
Short-term debt (interest only)	0	251	169	424	441	652	1,245	656	319	266

2. AGGREGATE NET RESOURCE FLOWS AND NET TRANSFERS (LONG-TERM)

	1970	1980	1990	1994	1995	1996	1997	1998	1999	2000
NET RESOURCE FLOWS	**99**	**2,052**	**1,184**	**8,680**	**10,542**	**12,031**	**9,187**	**5,695**	**3,618**	**3,411**
Net flow of long-term debt (ex. IMF)	1	1,111	-1,484	2,982	4,053	2,593	4,527	2,918	1,531	1,200
Foreign direct investment (net)	94	934	2,333	4,342	4,178	5,078	5,137	2,163	1,553	1,660
Portfolio equity flows	0	0	293	1,320	2,299	4,353	-489	592	522	542
Grants (excluding technical coop.)	4	6	42	36	11	7	13	21	13	9
Memo: technical coop. grants	13	54	125	113	121	100	86	80	89	82
official net resource flows	27	139	414	222	393	-774	-156	243	371	182
private net resource flows	71	1,913	770	8,458	10,149	12,805	9,343	5,451	3,247	3,229
NET TRANSFERS	**-93**	**524**	**-1,739**	**4,423**	**5,391**	**6,599**	**3,399**	**-418**	**-2,385**	**-3,512**
Interest on long-term debt	25	338	997	1,007	1,151	1,432	1,588	1,612	1,603	2,023
Profit remittances on FDI	166	1,190	1,926	3,250	4,000	4,000	4,200	4,500	4,400	4,900
Memo: official net transfers	14	53	182	-30	109	-1,017	-358	36	126	-67
private net transfers	-107	471	-1,921	4,453	5,282	7,616	3,756	-454	-2,511	-3,446

3. MAJOR ECONOMIC AGGREGATES

	1970	1980	1990	1994	1995	1996	1997	1998	1999	2000
Gross national income (GNI)	4,167	24,057	42,152	70,895	84,689	96,161	94,803	68,470	75,130	82,392
Exports of goods & services (XGS)	..	14,836	34,514	68,526	85,992	94,813	95,750	84,942	97,974	113,221
of which workers remittances	..	0	0	0	0	0	0	0	0	..
Imports of goods & services (MGS)	..	15,100	35,486	73,275	93,618	98,093	100,176	72,950	83,640	105,265
International reserves (RES)	667	5,755	10,659	26,339	24,699	27,892	21,470	26,236	30,931	29,844
Current account balance	..	-266	-870	-4,520	-8,644	-4,462	-5,935	9,529	12,606	..

4. DEBT INDICATORS

	1970	1980	1990	1994	1995	1996	1997	1998	1999	2000
EDT / XGS (%)	..	44.6	44.4	44.3	39.9	41.8	49.3	49.9	42.8	36.9
EDT / GNI (%)	12.0	27.5	36.4	42.8	40.6	41.3	49.8	61.9	55.8	50.7
TDS / XGS (%)	..	6.3	12.6	8.9	7.0	8.9	7.4	7.2	4.5	5.3
INT / XGS (%)	..	4.0	3.4	2.1	1.9	2.2	3.0	2.7	2.0	2.0
INT / GNI (%)	0.6	2.5	2.8	2.0	1.9	2.2	3.0	3.3	2.6	2.8
RES / EDT (%)	133.0	87.1	69.5	86.8	71.9	70.3	45.5	61.9	73.8	71.4
RES / MGS (months)	..	4.6	3.6	4.3	3.2	3.4	2.6	4.3	4.4	3.4
Short-term / EDT (%)	12.4	20.5	12.4	20.4	21.2	27.9	31.6	20.0	14.4	11.1
Concessional / EDT (%)	18.8	8.6	14.6	11.0	10.6	6.4	4.3	5.5	6.0	5.4
Multilateral / EDT (%)	28.2	11.3	11.8	5.7	4.8	3.5	2.6	3.5	3.4	3.1

MALAYSIA

(US$ million, unless otherwise indicated)

	1970	1980	1990	1994	1995	1996	1997	1998	1999	2000
5. LONG-TERM DEBT										
DEBT OUTSTANDING (LDOD)	**440**	**5,256**	**13,422**	**24,147**	**27,069**	**28,605**	**32,289**	**33,940**	**35,891**	**37,157**
Public and publicly guaranteed	**390**	**4,008**	**11,592**	**14,693**	**16,023**	**15,702**	**16,808**	**18,155**	**18,929**	**19,090**
Official creditors	265	1,444	4,191	5,687	5,490	4,205	3,983	4,508	4,588	4,428
Multilateral	141	745	1,812	1,721	1,644	1,404	1,228	1,487	1,438	1,314
Concessional	0	3	9	3	1	0	0	0	0	0
Bilateral	124	699	2,378	3,966	3,846	2,802	2,755	3,021	3,150	3,115
Concessional	94	565	2,225	3,322	3,651	2,548	2,033	2,333	2,498	2,267
Private creditors	125	2,564	7,401	9,006	10,533	11,497	12,824	13,647	14,341	14,662
Bonds	111	278	4,090	4,080	6,062	7,789	8,265	8,338	9,256	9,945
Commercial banks	0	1,397	2,285	3,384	4,171	3,121	3,119	3,346	3,161	2,987
Other private	14	889	1,026	1,542	300	587	1,440	1,963	1,925	1,729
Private nonguaranteed	**50**	**1,248**	**1,830**	**9,454**	**11,046**	**12,903**	**15,482**	**15,786**	**16,961**	**18,067**
Bonds	0	0	0	1,285	1,765	1,937	3,752	3,785	3,841	3,402
Commercial banks and other	50	1,248	1,830	8,169	9,281	10,966	11,730	12,001	13,120	14,665
Memo:										
IBRD	141	504	1,103	1,118	1,059	907	758	970	900	812
IDA	0	0	0	0	0	0	0	0	0	0
DISBURSEMENTS	**58**	**1,456**	**1,683**	**7,672**	**8,503**	**8,936**	**8,803**	**6,724**	**4,017**	**4,878**
Public and publicly guaranteed	**45**	**1,015**	**798**	**3,646**	**4,150**	**3,528**	**3,566**	**1,624**	**1,878**	**2,417**
Official creditors	39	211	737	881	837	297	662	600	768	546
Multilateral	22	119	273	198	135	128	138	386	71	61
Concessional	0	0	2	0	0	0	0	0	0	0
Bilateral	18	93	464	684	702	168	524	214	697	485
Concessional	16	78	460	615	604	94	271	214	97	241
Private creditors	6	804	61	2,765	3,313	3,231	2,904	1,024	1,111	1,872
Bonds	0	0	0	1,060	2,100	2,252	746	0	1,010	1,061
Commercial banks	0	510	57	1,578	1,205	703	900	456	101	811
Other private	6	294	4	127	8	276	1,259	568	0	0
Private nonguaranteed	**12**	**441**	**885**	**4,026**	**4,353**	**5,408**	**5,237**	**5,100**	**2,139**	**2,461**
Bonds	0	0	0	1,285	480	172	1,844	0	0	361
Commercial banks and other	12	441	885	2,741	3,873	5,236	3,393	5,100	2,139	2,100
Memo:										
IBRD	21	80	205	144	88	85	51	325	42	15
IDA	0	0	0	0	0	0	0	0	0	0
PRINCIPAL REPAYMENTS	**57**	**345**	**3,167**	**4,690**	**4,450**	**6,343**	**4,276**	**3,806**	**2,486**	**3,678**
Public and publicly guaranteed	**47**	**127**	**2,697**	**3,360**	**1,701**	**3,264**	**1,867**	**1,135**	**1,192**	**1,549**
Official creditors	16	79	365	695	455	1,078	830	378	410	372
Multilateral	5	34	216	241	261	230	191	179	156	140
Concessional	0	0	2	2	2	1	0	0	0	0
Bilateral	11	45	149	454	195	848	640	199	253	233
Concessional	4	17	123	435	188	840	535	164	218	198
Private creditors	32	48	2,332	2,665	1,246	2,186	1,037	757	783	1,177
Bonds	30	11	1,239	1,100	140	362	86	299	263	200
Commercial banks	0	17	664	1,235	420	1,616	779	339	401	864
Other private	2	20	428	330	686	208	172	119	118	112
Private nonguaranteed	**9**	**218**	**470**	**1,330**	**2,749**	**3,079**	**2,409**	**2,671**	**1,294**	**2,129**
Bonds	0	0	0	0	0	0	0	15	0	745
Commercial banks and other	9	218	470	1,330	2,749	3,079	2,409	2,656	1,294	1,384
Memo:										
IBRD	5	26	164	185	194	161	126	117	111	100
IDA	0	0	0	0	0	0	0	0	0	0
NET FLOWS ON DEBT	**1**	**1,111**	**-1,484**	**2,982**	**4,053**	**2,593**	**4,527**	**2,918**	**1,531**	**1,200**
Public and publicly guaranteed	**-2**	**889**	**-1,899**	**286**	**2,450**	**264**	**1,699**	**489**	**686**	**869**
Official creditors	23	133	372	186	382	-781	-168	222	358	174
Multilateral	17	85	57	-44	-126	-102	-53	207	-85	-79
Concessional	0	0	0	-2	-2	-1	0	0	0	0
Bilateral	7	48	315	230	507	-679	-115	15	443	252
Concessional	12	61	337	180	416	-745	-263	50	-122	43
Private creditors	-25	756	-2,271	99	2,068	1,045	1,868	267	328	695
Bonds	-30	-11	-1,239	-40	1,960	1,890	659	-299	747	861
Commercial banks	0	493	-608	342	785	-913	121	118	-301	-54
Other private	5	274	-424	-204	-678	68	1,087	449	-118	-112
Private nonguaranteed	**3**	**223**	**415**	**2,697**	**1,604**	**2,329**	**2,828**	**2,429**	**845**	**331**
Bonds	0	0	0	1,285	480	172	1,844	-15	0	-384
Commercial banks and other	3	223	415	1,412	1,124	2,157	984	2,444	845	716
Memo:										
IBRD	16	54	41	-41	-106	-76	-75	208	-69	-86
IDA	0	0	0	0	0	0	0	0	0	0

MALAYSIA

(US$ million, unless otherwise indicated)

	1970	1980	1990	1994	1995	1996	1997	1998	1999	2000
INTEREST PAYMENTS (LINT)	**25**	**338**	**997**	**1,007**	**1,151**	**1,432**	**1,588**	**1,612**	**1,603**	**2,023**
Public and publicly guaranteed	**22**	**250**	**956**	**763**	**805**	**856**	**903**	**1,000**	**1,086**	**1,161**
Official creditors	13	86	232	253	284	243	202	207	245	249
Multilateral	8	60	145	127	129	108	90	82	100	98
Concessional	0	0	1	0	0	0	0	0	0	0
Bilateral	5	26	87	126	155	135	112	125	145	151
Concessional	3	19	75	123	146	133	81	70	92	85
Private creditors	9	163	724	511	522	612	702	792	841	912
Bonds	8	18	414	234	251	318	509	536	592	611
Commercial banks	0	108	199	174	190	229	142	161	156	208
Other private	1	37	111	102	80	65	50	96	94	93
Private nonguaranteed	**3**	**88**	**41**	**244**	**345**	**577**	**685**	**613**	**517**	**862**
Bonds	0	0	0	1	28	48	60	161	157	159
Commercial banks and other	3	88	41	243	318	529	625	451	360	703
Memo:										
IBRD	8	39	86	83	83	70	57	50	67	66
IDA	0	0	0	0	0	0	0	0	0	0
NET TRANSFERS ON DEBT	**-25**	**774**	**-2,481**	**1,975**	**2,903**	**1,161**	**2,939**	**1,306**	**-72**	**-823**
Public and publicly guaranteed	**-24**	**639**	**-2,855**	**-477**	**1,644**	**-592**	**796**	**-511**	**-400**	**-292**
Official creditors	10	46	140	-66	98	-1,025	-370	15	114	-75
Multilateral	9	25	-88	-170	-254	-210	-144	125	-185	-177
Concessional	0	0	0	-2	-2	-1	0	0	0	0
Bilateral	1	22	228	104	352	-814	-227	-110	298	102
Concessional	9	42	262	57	270	-879	-345	-19	-214	-42
Private creditors	-34	593	-2,995	-411	1,546	433	1,166	-526	-514	-217
Bonds	-38	-29	-1,654	-274	1,709	1,572	150	-835	155	250
Commercial banks	0	384	-806	168	595	-1,142	-21	-43	-456	-262
Other private	4	237	-535	-305	-758	3	1,037	353	-212	-205
Private nonguaranteed	**0**	**135**	**374**	**2,452**	**1,258**	**1,752**	**2,143**	**1,817**	**328**	**-531**
Bonds	0	0	0	1,284	452	124	1,784	-176	-157	-544
Commercial banks and other	0	135	374	1,169	806	1,628	359	1,993	485	13
Memo:										
IBRD	9	15	-46	-124	-189	-146	-132	159	-135	-152
IDA	0	0	0	0	0	0	0	0	0	0
DEBT SERVICE (LTDS)	**82**	**683**	**4,164**	**5,697**	**5,600**	**7,776**	**5,864**	**5,418**	**4,089**	**5,701**
Public and publicly guaranteed	**70**	**376**	**3,653**	**4,123**	**2,506**	**4,120**	**2,770**	**2,135**	**2,278**	**2,710**
Official creditors	29	165	597	948	739	1,321	1,032	585	654	621
Multilateral	13	94	361	368	389	339	281	261	256	238
Concessional	0	0	2	2	2	1	0	0	0	0
Bilateral	16	71	237	580	350	983	751	324	398	384
Concessional	7	37	198	559	334	973	616	234	311	283
Private creditors	40	211	3,056	3,176	1,767	2,798	1,738	1,550	1,624	2,088
Bonds	38	29	1,654	1,334	391	680	595	835	855	811
Commercial banks	0	126	863	1,410	610	1,845	921	500	557	1,073
Other private	2	57	539	432	766	273	222	215	212	205
Private nonguaranteed	**13**	**307**	**511**	**1,574**	**3,094**	**3,656**	**3,094**	**3,284**	**1,811**	**2,991**
Bonds	0	0	0	1	28	48	60	176	157	904
Commercial banks and other	13	307	511	1,572	3,066	3,608	3,034	3,107	1,654	2,087
Memo:										
IBRD	13	65	251	268	277	231	183	167	177	166
IDA	0	0	0	0	0	0	0	0	0	0
UNDISBURSED DEBT	**201**	**1,761**	**2,068**	**3,647**	**3,147**	**2,243**	**1,193**	**913**	**4,096**	**5,842**
Official creditors	181	1,404	1,795	2,235	2,069	1,621	831	559	2,314	2,421
Private creditors	20	357	274	1,413	1,078	622	362	353	1,782	3,421
Memorandum items										
Concessional LDOD	94	567	2,234	3,326	3,652	2,548	2,033	2,333	2,498	2,267
Variable rate LDOD	50	2,665	6,559	13,722	15,779	16,593	19,457	20,286	21,274	22,585
Public sector LDOD	390	4,008	11,592	14,693	16,023	15,702	16,808	18,155	18,929	18,991
Private sector LDOD	50	1,248	1,830	9,454	11,046	12,903	15,482	15,786	16,961	18,166

6. CURRENCY COMPOSITION OF LONG-TERM DEBT (PERCENT)

	1970	1980	1990	1994	1995	1996	1997	1998	1999	2000
Deutsche mark	6.9	3.3	5.9	2.2	1.1	0.8	0.5	0.4	0.3	0.2
French franc	0.0	13.0	2.8	0.7	0.6	0.5	0.4	0.4	0.3	0.2
Japanese yen	2.2	19.0	36.5	37.5	34.6	28.2	26.5	29.6	29.9	27.8
Pound sterling	37.8	3.6	1.6	2.4	1.0	1.2	1.1	0.9	0.8	0.7
Swiss franc	0.0	2.3	3.6	3.0	3.1	1.7	0.5	0.1	0.0	0.0
U.S.dollars	14.0	36.7	31.8	35.1	48.5	55.6	55.8	58.7	60.0	63.2
Multiple currency	36.3	21.0	15.0	18.7	10.7	11.5	15.0	9.7	8.6	7.7
Special drawing rights	0.0	0.0	0.0	0.0	0.0	0.0	0.0	0.0	0.0	0.0
All other currencies	2.8	1.1	2.8	0.4	0.4	0.5	0.2	0.2	0.1	0.2

MALAYSIA

(US$ million, unless otherwise indicated)

	1970	1980	1990	1994	1995	1996	1997	1998	1999	2000
7. DEBT RESTRUCTURINGS										
Total amount rescheduled	..	..	0	0	0	0	0	0	0	0
Debt stock rescheduled	..	..	0	0	0	0	0	0	0	0
Principal rescheduled	..	..	0	0	0	0	0	0	0	0
Official	..	..	0	0	0	0	0	0	0	0
Private	..	..	0	0	0	0	0	0	0	0
Interest rescheduled	..	..	0	0	0	0	0	0	0	0
Official	..	..	0	0	0	0	0	0	0	0
Private	..	..	0	0	0	0	0	0	0	0
Debt forgiven	..	..	0	0	0	0	0	0	0	0
Memo: interest forgiven	..	..	0	0	0	0	0	0	0	0
Debt stock reduction	..	..	0	0	0	0	0	0	0	0
of which debt buyback	..	..	0	0	0	0	0	0	0	0
8. DEBT STOCK-FLOW RECONCILIATION										
Total change in debt stocks	..	..	-950	4,187	4,007	5,331	7,555	-4,819	-507	-106
Net flows on debt	1	1,592	-1,851	2,220	5,138	6,387	8,397	-3,552	-927	-171
Net change in interest arrears	..	..	0	0	0	0	0	0	0	0
Interest capitalized	..	..	0	0	0	0	0	0	0	0
Debt forgiveness or reduction	..	..	0	0	0	0	0	0	0	0
Cross-currency valuation	..	..	926	809	-104	-898	-676	607	711	-689
Residual	..	..	-25	1,159	-1,027	-158	-166	-1,874	-291	755
9. AVERAGE TERMS OF NEW COMMITMENTS										
ALL CREDITORS										
Interest (%)	6.1	11.2	4.8	6.6	5.8	6.5	5.9	4.1	5.2	6.4
Maturity (years)	18.7	13.8	20.9	13.8	18.3	18.1	12.8	14.2	18.1	10.0
Grace period (years)	4.8	5.4	6.0	4.5	12.5	13.1	4.7	3.6	6.6	4.7
Grant element (%)	22.8	-6.6	37.3	17.1	27.6	19.0	21.2	32.8	31.6	17.3
Official creditors										
Interest (%)	6.4	6.7	4.0	7.5	3.4	0.0	7.4	6.3	4.3	4.3
Maturity (years)	21.0	18.3	22.9	24.8	24.4	0.0	22.3	15.8	18.9	18.9
Grace period (years)	5.7	5.0	6.7	3.6	6.3	0.0	4.2	3.8	5.1	6.9
Grant element (%)	24.0	20.9	44.2	16.0	48.1	0.0	15.8	20.9	36.0	38.6
Private creditors										
Interest (%)	5.1	14.1	8.9	6.5	6.3	6.5	5.9	3.4	5.8	7.0
Maturity (years)	8.8	10.9	11.4	11.6	16.9	18.1	12.5	13.7	17.5	7.6
Grace period (years)	1.3	5.7	2.6	4.7	14.0	13.1	4.7	3.5	7.6	4.0
Grant element (%)	17.3	-23.9	4.3	17.4	22.7	19.0	21.3	36.4	28.5	11.4
Memorandum items										
Commitments	84	1,423	701	3,704	3,772	3,435	2,405	1,278	4,364	4,625
Official creditors	68	550	579	625	730	0	74	300	1,775	1,000
Private creditors	16	873	122	3,079	3,042	3,435	2,330	978	2,590	3,625

10. CONTRACTUAL OBLIGATIONS ON OUTSTANDING LONG-TERM DEBT

	2001	2002	2003	2004	2005	2006	2007	2008	2009	2010
TOTAL										
Disbursements	2,419	1,698	848	455	164	84	64	50	40	20
Principal	2,986	3,619	3,643	4,106	5,574	3,273	4,903	2,591	5,917	795
Interest	2,331	2,308	2,182	2,049	1,895	1,667	1,491	1,385	1,277	279
Official creditors										
Disbursements	752	611	424	250	139	77	57	50	40	20
Principal	360	461	508	496	464	448	422	404	368	291
Interest	260	258	243	220	193	166	141	117	95	75
Bilateral creditors										
Disbursements	659	517	339	215	135	77	57	50	40	20
Principal	226	302	343	343	311	302	294	288	256	208
Interest	156	158	150	137	122	107	93	78	64	53
Multilateral creditors										
Disbursements	93	94	85	35	3	0	0	0	0	0
Principal	134	160	165	153	153	146	128	116	112	82
Interest	104	100	93	83	71	59	48	39	30	23
Private creditors										
Disbursements	1,666	1,087	424	205	26	6	6	0	0	0
Principal	2,625	3,157	3,135	3,610	5,110	2,825	4,481	2,187	5,549	504
Interest	2,071	2,050	1,939	1,830	1,702	1,501	1,350	1,267	1,182	203
Commercial banks										
Disbursements	1,666	1,087	424	205	26	6	6	0	0	0
Principal	441	1,078	883	787	787	759	704	204	110	40
Interest	267	309	258	213	161	109	59	22	10	6
Other private										
Disbursements	0	0	0	0	0	0	0	0	0	0
Principal	2,185	2,080	2,252	2,823	4,323	2,066	3,777	1,983	5,439	464
Interest	1,805	1,741	1,682	1,617	1,541	1,392	1,291	1,246	1,172	198

MALDIVES

(US$ million, unless otherwise indicated)

	1970	1980	1990	1994	1995	1996	1997	1998	1999	2000
1. SUMMARY DEBT DATA										
TOTAL DEBT STOCKS (EDT)	..	**25.8**	**78.0**	**123.5**	**154.9**	**168.2**	**171.3**	**193.6**	**218.9**	**206.7**
Long-term debt (LDOD)	..	**24.8**	**64.0**	**122.5**	**151.9**	**163.5**	**164.3**	**183.4**	**194.1**	**185.3**
Public and publicly guaranteed	..	24.8	64.0	122.5	151.9	163.5	164.3	183.4	194.1	185.3
Private nonguaranteed	..	0.0	0.0	0.0	0.0	0.0	0.0	0.0	0.0	0.0
Use of IMF credit	**0.0**	**0.0**	**0.0**	**0.0**	**0.0**	**0.0**	**0.0**	**0.0**	**0.0**	**0.0**
Short-term debt	..	**1.0**	**14.0**	**1.0**	**3.0**	**4.7**	**7.0**	**10.2**	**24.8**	**21.4**
of which interest arrears on LDOD	..	0.0	0.0	0.0	0.0	0.0	0.0	0.0	0.0	0.0
Official creditors	..	0.0	0.0	0.0	0.0	0.0	0.0	0.0	0.0	0.0
Private creditors	..	0.0	0.0	0.0	0.0	0.0	0.0	0.0	0.0	0.0
Memo: principal arrears on LDOD	..	0.0	0.0	0.0	0.0	0.0	0.0	0.0	0.0	0.0
Official creditors	..	0.0	0.0	0.0	0.0	0.0	0.0	0.0	0.0	0.0
Private creditors	..	0.0	0.0	0.0	0.0	0.0	0.0	0.0	0.0	0.0
Memo: export credits	..	0.0	8.0	28.6	26.2	28.8	39.2	20.7	21.3	17.1
TOTAL DEBT FLOWS										
Disbursements	..	**17.9**	**13.0**	**15.4**	**34.7**	**23.5**	**32.7**	**30.7**	**17.4**	**14.3**
Long-term debt	..	17.9	13.0	15.4	34.7	23.5	32.7	30.7	17.4	14.3
IMF purchases	0.0	0.0	0.0	0.0	0.0	0.0	0.0	0.0	0.0	0.0
Principal repayments	..	**0.0**	**6.0**	**6.4**	**7.1**	**7.8**	**24.2**	**11.6**	**12.3**	**13.9**
Long-term debt	..	0.0	6.0	6.4	7.1	7.8	24.2	11.6	12.3	13.9
IMF repurchases	0.0	0.0	0.0	0.0	0.0	0.0	0.0	0.0	0.0	0.0
Net flows on debt	..	**12.9**	**8.6**	**7.0**	**29.6**	**17.4**	**10.8**	**22.3**	**19.7**	**-3.1**
of which short-term debt	..	-5.0	1.6	-2.0	2.0	1.7	2.3	3.2	14.6	-3.5
Interest payments (INT)	..	**0.5**	**2.8**	**3.1**	**3.7**	**3.9**	**4.4**	**4.3**	**5.4**	**5.9**
Long-term debt	..	0.3	1.3	3.0	3.6	3.7	4.1	3.9	4.4	4.8
IMF charges	0.0	0.0	0.0	0.0	0.0	0.0	0.0	0.0	0.0	0.0
Short-term debt	..	0.3	1.5	0.1	0.2	0.2	0.4	0.4	0.9	1.2
Net transfers on debt	..	**12.4**	**5.8**	**3.9**	**25.8**	**13.5**	**6.4**	**18.0**	**14.3**	**-9.0**
Total debt service paid (TDS)	..	**0.5**	**8.8**	**9.5**	**10.8**	**11.7**	**28.6**	**15.9**	**17.7**	**19.9**
Long-term debt	..	0.3	7.3	9.3	10.7	11.5	28.2	15.5	16.7	18.7
IMF repurchases and charges	0.0	0.0	0.0	0.0	0.0	0.0	0.0	0.0	0.0	0.0
Short-term debt (interest only)	..	0.3	1.5	0.1	0.2	0.2	0.4	0.4	0.9	1.2
2. AGGREGATE NET RESOURCE FLOWS AND NET TRANSFERS (LONG-TERM)										
NET RESOURCE FLOWS	..	**19.0**	**24.3**	**33.4**	**58.4**	**34.7**	**32.9**	**43.8**	**34.0**	**23.3**
Net flow of long-term debt (ex. IMF)	..	17.9	7.0	9.0	27.6	15.7	8.5	19.1	5.1	0.3
Foreign direct investment (net)	..	0.0	6.0	9.0	7.0	9.3	11.4	11.5	11.5	13.0
Portfolio equity flows	..	0.0	0.0	0.0	0.0	0.0	0.0	0.0	0.0	0.0
Grants (excluding technical coop.)	..	1.1	11.3	15.4	23.7	9.8	13.0	13.2	17.5	10.0
Memo: technical coop. grants	..	2.8	5.8	8.1	10.1	8.7	8.0	7.0	8.3	7.6
official net resource flows	..	19.0	17.2	24.8	49.8	23.1	15.5	21.7	18.2	9.6
private net resource flows	..	0.0	7.1	8.6	8.6	11.6	17.4	22.1	15.8	13.7
NET TRANSFERS	..	**17.2**	**9.1**	**11.4**	**36.9**	**15.0**	**11.9**	**19.9**	**11.6**	**-2.5**
Interest on long-term debt	..	0.3	1.3	3.0	3.6	3.7	4.1	3.9	4.4	4.8
Profit remittances on FDI	..	1.5	13.9	19.0	18.0	16.0	17.0	20.0	18.0	21.0
Memo: official net transfers	..	18.7	16.4	22.5	47.1	20.2	12.5	19.0	15.5	7.0
private net transfers	..	-1.5	-7.3	-11.1	-10.2	-5.2	-0.6	0.9	-3.9	-9.5
3. MAJOR ECONOMIC AGGREGATES										
Gross national income (GNI)	..	..	124.7	198.4	224.6	254.4	287.0	309.8	528.4	526.2
Exports of goods & services (XGS)	..	65.2	183.8	276.6	322.3	374.9	412.6	435.5	443.2	467.5
of which workers remittances	..	0.0	0.0	0.0	0.0	0.0	0.0	0.0	0.0	0.0
Imports of goods & services (MGS)	..	89.8	177.7	281.9	337.0	381.1	436.1	447.1	502.1	492.1
International reserves (RES)	..	0.9	24.5	31.8	48.5	76.8	98.8	119.1	127.6	123.3
Current account balance	..	-22.2	9.9	-11.2	-18.3	-7.3	-34.2	-23.3	-81.7	-53.1
4. DEBT INDICATORS										
EDT / XGS (%)	..	39.6	42.4	44.7	48.1	44.9	41.5	44.5	49.4	44.2
EDT / GNI (%)	..	..	62.6	62.3	69.0	66.1	59.7	62.5	41.4	39.3
TDS / XGS (%)	..	0.8	4.8	3.4	3.4	3.1	6.9	3.7	4.0	4.3
INT / XGS (%)	..	0.8	1.5	1.1	1.2	1.0	1.1	1.0	1.2	1.3
INT / GNI (%)	..	..	2.3	1.6	1.7	1.5	1.5	1.4	1.0	1.1
RES / EDT (%)	..	3.7	31.4	25.7	31.3	45.7	57.7	61.5	58.3	59.7
RES / MGS (months)	..	0.1	1.7	1.4	1.7	2.4	2.7	3.2	3.1	3.0
Short-term / EDT (%)	..	3.9	18.0	0.8	1.9	2.8	4.1	5.3	11.3	10.4
Concessional / EDT (%)	..	96.1	70.9	79.6	81.6	81.0	79.2	73.8	68.7	68.8
Multilateral / EDT (%)	..	13.6	41.7	58.8	58.8	58.0	58.7	58.3	57.1	58.3

MALDIVES

(US$ million, unless otherwise indicated)

	1970	1980	1990	1994	1995	1996	1997	1998	1999	2000
5. LONG-TERM DEBT										
DEBT OUTSTANDING (LDOD)	..	**24.8**	**64.0**	**122.5**	**151.9**	**163.5**	**164.3**	**183.4**	**194.1**	**185.3**
Public and publicly guaranteed	..	**24.8**	**64.0**	**122.5**	**151.9**	**163.5**	**164.3**	**183.4**	**194.1**	**185.3**
Official creditors	..	24.8	60.2	115.1	142.6	152.0	147.5	155.4	163.4	154.8
Multilateral	..	3.5	32.5	72.6	91.1	97.6	100.6	112.9	124.9	120.5
Concessional	..	3.5	32.5	72.6	91.1	97.3	99.1	109.9	120.4	115.4
Bilateral	..	21.3	27.6	42.5	51.5	54.3	47.0	42.5	38.5	34.3
Concessional	..	21.3	22.8	25.7	35.3	39.0	36.5	32.9	30.0	26.9
Private creditors	..	0.0	3.8	7.4	9.4	11.5	16.8	28.1	30.7	30.6
Bonds	..	0.0	0.0	0.0	0.0	0.0	0.0	0.0	0.0	0.0
Commercial banks	..	0.0	0.0	1.6	3.4	6.5	10.7	18.7	24.0	25.5
Other private	..	0.0	3.8	5.8	5.9	5.0	6.1	9.3	6.7	5.0
Private nonguaranteed	..	**0.0**	**0.0**	**0.0**	**0.0**	**0.0**	**0.0**	**0.0**	**0.0**	**0.0**
Bonds	..	0.0	0.0	0.0	0.0	0.0	0.0	0.0	0.0	0.0
Commercial banks and other	..	0.0	0.0	0.0	0.0	0.0	0.0	0.0	0.0	0.0
Memo:										
IBRD	0.0	0.0	0.0	0.0	0.0	0.0	0.0	0.0	0.0	0.0
IDA	0.0	1.6	10.0	31.6	36.1	37.3	39.0	44.1	45.6	46.4
DISBURSEMENTS	..	**17.9**	**13.0**	**15.4**	**34.7**	**23.5**	**32.7**	**30.7**	**17.4**	**14.3**
Public and publicly guaranteed	..	**17.9**	**13.0**	**15.4**	**34.7**	**23.5**	**32.7**	**30.7**	**17.4**	**14.3**
Official creditors	..	17.9	9.6	14.0	30.9	18.5	23.5	15.0	7.2	6.3
Multilateral	..	2.6	3.6	9.9	18.7	11.8	11.0	14.8	6.8	6.1
Concessional	..	2.6	3.6	9.9	18.7	11.5	9.9	13.4	5.1	5.4
Bilateral	..	15.3	5.9	4.1	12.2	6.7	12.5	0.2	0.4	0.2
Concessional	..	15.3	1.1	4.1	12.2	6.7	1.8	0.2	0.4	0.2
Private creditors	..	0.0	3.5	1.4	3.8	5.0	9.2	15.8	10.2	8.0
Bonds	..	0.0	0.0	0.0	0.0	0.0	0.0	0.0	0.0	0.0
Commercial banks	..	0.0	0.0	1.0	2.4	3.9	5.7	10.7	10.0	8.0
Other private	..	0.0	3.5	0.4	1.4	1.1	3.4	5.0	0.2	0.0
Private nonguaranteed	..	**0.0**	**0.0**	**0.0**	**0.0**	**0.0**	**0.0**	**0.0**	**0.0**	**0.0**
Bonds	..	0.0	0.0	0.0	0.0	0.0	0.0	0.0	0.0	0.0
Commercial banks and other	..	0.0	0.0	0.0	0.0	0.0	0.0	0.0	0.0	0.0
Memo:										
IBRD	0.0	0.0	0.0	0.0	0.0	0.0	0.0	0.0	0.0	0.0
IDA	0.0	1.6	1.2	5.6	3.9	2.5	3.8	3.7	2.7	3.3
PRINCIPAL REPAYMENTS	..	**0.0**	**6.0**	**6.4**	**7.1**	**7.8**	**24.2**	**11.6**	**12.3**	**13.9**
Public and publicly guaranteed	..	**0.0**	**6.0**	**6.4**	**7.1**	**7.8**	**24.2**	**11.6**	**12.3**	**13.9**
Official creditors	..	0.0	3.7	4.6	4.8	5.2	21.0	6.5	6.5	6.7
Multilateral	..	0.0	1.5	1.3	1.4	1.5	1.5	1.7	2.2	2.5
Concessional	..	0.0	1.5	1.3	1.4	1.5	1.5	1.7	2.2	2.5
Bilateral	..	0.0	2.2	3.3	3.4	3.6	19.5	4.8	4.3	4.2
Concessional	..	0.0	1.9	2.6	2.7	2.9	4.0	3.8	3.3	3.2
Private creditors	..	0.0	2.3	1.8	2.3	2.7	3.2	5.1	5.8	7.3
Bonds	..	0.0	0.0	0.0	0.0	0.0	0.0	0.0	0.0	0.0
Commercial banks	..	0.0	1.5	0.4	0.6	0.9	1.3	2.9	4.0	6.1
Other private	..	0.0	0.9	1.4	1.7	1.7	1.8	2.2	1.9	1.2
Private nonguaranteed	..	**0.0**	**0.0**	**0.0**	**0.0**	**0.0**	**0.0**	**0.0**	**0.0**	**0.0**
Bonds	..	0.0	0.0	0.0	0.0	0.0	0.0	0.0	0.0	0.0
Commercial banks and other	..	0.0	0.0	0.0	0.0	0.0	0.0	0.0	0.0	0.0
Memo:										
IBRD	0.0	0.0	0.0	0.0	0.0	0.0	0.0	0.0	0.0	0.0
IDA	0.0	0.0	0.0	0.1	0.1	0.1	0.1	0.1	0.3	0.4
NET FLOWS ON DEBT	..	**17.9**	**7.0**	**9.0**	**27.6**	**15.7**	**8.5**	**19.1**	**5.1**	**0.3**
Public and publicly guaranteed	..	**17.9**	**7.0**	**9.0**	**27.6**	**15.7**	**8.5**	**19.1**	**5.1**	**0.3**
Official creditors	..	17.9	5.9	9.4	26.1	13.3	2.5	8.5	0.7	-0.4
Multilateral	..	2.6	2.2	8.6	17.3	10.3	9.5	13.1	4.6	3.6
Concessional	..	2.6	2.2	8.6	17.3	10.0	8.4	11.7	2.9	2.9
Bilateral	..	15.3	3.7	0.8	8.7	3.0	-7.0	-4.6	-3.8	-4.0
Concessional	..	15.3	-0.8	1.5	9.5	3.7	-2.3	-3.7	-2.9	-3.0
Private creditors	..	0.0	1.1	-0.4	1.6	2.3	6.0	10.6	4.3	0.7
Bonds	..	0.0	0.0	0.0	0.0	0.0	0.0	0.0	0.0	0.0
Commercial banks	..	0.0	-1.5	0.6	1.8	3.0	4.4	7.9	6.0	1.9
Other private	..	0.0	2.6	-1.1	-0.3	-0.6	1.6	2.8	-1.6	-1.2
Private nonguaranteed	..	**0.0**	**0.0**	**0.0**	**0.0**	**0.0**	**0.0**	**0.0**	**0.0**	**0.0**
Bonds	..	0.0	0.0	0.0	0.0	0.0	0.0	0.0	0.0	0.0
Commercial banks and other	..	0.0	0.0	0.0	0.0	0.0	0.0	0.0	0.0	0.0
Memo:										
IBRD	0.0	0.0	0.0	0.0	0.0	0.0	0.0	0.0	0.0	0.0
IDA	0.0	1.6	1.2	5.5	3.8	2.4	3.7	3.6	2.4	3.0

MALDIVES

(US$ million, unless otherwise indicated)

	1970	1980	1990	1994	1995	1996	1997	1998	1999	2000
INTEREST PAYMENTS (LINT)	..	**0.3**	**1.3**	**3.0**	**3.6**	**3.7**	**4.1**	**3.9**	**4.4**	**4.8**
Public and publicly guaranteed	..	**0.3**	**1.3**	**3.0**	**3.6**	**3.7**	**4.1**	**3.9**	**4.4**	**4.8**
Official creditors	..	0.3	0.8	2.3	2.7	2.9	3.0	2.7	2.7	2.6
Multilateral	..	0.0	0.3	0.9	1.0	1.2	1.3	1.3	1.5	1.5
Concessional	..	0.0	0.3	0.9	1.0	1.2	1.2	1.3	1.4	1.4
Bilateral	..	0.3	0.5	1.3	1.7	1.7	1.8	1.4	1.2	1.1
Concessional	..	0.3	0.3	0.4	0.4	0.6	0.6	0.6	0.6	0.5
Private creditors	..	0.0	0.5	0.7	0.8	0.8	1.0	1.2	1.7	2.2
Bonds	..	0.0	0.0	0.0	0.0	0.0	0.0	0.0	0.0	0.0
Commercial banks	..	0.0	0.1	0.1	0.2	0.3	0.7	0.9	1.2	1.8
Other private	..	0.0	0.4	0.6	0.6	0.4	0.4	0.3	0.5	0.4
Private nonguaranteed	..	**0.0**	**0.0**	**0.0**	**0.0**	**0.0**	**0.0**	**0.0**	**0.0**	**0.0**
Bonds	..	0.0	0.0	0.0	0.0	0.0	0.0	0.0	0.0	0.0
Commercial banks and other	..	0.0	0.0	0.0	0.0	0.0	0.0	0.0	0.0	0.0
Memo:										
IBRD	0.0	0.0	0.0	0.0	0.0	0.0	0.0	0.0	0.0	0.0
IDA	0.0	0.0	0.1	0.2	0.3	0.3	0.3	0.3	0.3	0.3
NET TRANSFERS ON DEBT	..	**17.6**	**5.7**	**6.0**	**24.0**	**12.0**	**4.4**	**15.2**	**0.6**	**-4.4**
Public and publicly guaranteed	..	**17.6**	**5.7**	**6.0**	**24.0**	**12.0**	**4.4**	**15.2**	**0.6**	**-4.4**
Official creditors	..	17.6	5.0	7.2	23.3	10.4	-0.5	5.8	-2.0	-3.0
Multilateral	..	2.6	1.8	7.7	16.3	9.1	8.2	11.7	3.1	2.1
Concessional	..	2.6	1.8	7.7	16.3	8.8	7.2	10.4	1.5	1.4
Bilateral	..	15.0	3.2	-0.5	7.0	1.3	-8.8	-6.0	-5.0	-5.1
Concessional	..	15.0	-1.1	1.1	9.1	3.2	-2.9	-4.3	-3.4	-3.5
Private creditors	..	0.0	0.6	-1.1	0.7	1.6	5.0	9.5	2.6	-1.4
Bonds	..	0.0	0.0	0.0	0.0	0.0	0.0	0.0	0.0	0.0
Commercial banks	..	0.0	-1.6	0.6	1.6	2.7	3.7	7.0	4.7	0.1
Other private	..	0.0	2.2	-1.7	-0.9	-1.1	1.2	2.5	-2.1	-1.6
Private nonguaranteed	..	**0.0**	**0.0**	**0.0**	**0.0**	**0.0**	**0.0**	**0.0**	**0.0**	**0.0**
Bonds	..	0.0	0.0	0.0	0.0	0.0	0.0	0.0	0.0	0.0
Commercial banks and other	..	0.0	0.0	0.0	0.0	0.0	0.0	0.0	0.0	0.0
Memo:										
IBRD	0.0	0.0	0.0	0.0	0.0	0.0	0.0	0.0	0.0	0.0
IDA	0.0	1.6	1.1	5.3	3.5	2.1	3.4	3.3	2.1	2.6
DEBT SERVICE (LTDS)	..	**0.3**	**7.3**	**9.3**	**10.7**	**11.5**	**28.2**	**15.5**	**16.7**	**18.7**
Public and publicly guaranteed	..	**0.3**	**7.3**	**9.3**	**10.7**	**11.5**	**28.2**	**15.5**	**16.7**	**18.7**
Official creditors	..	0.3	4.5	6.8	7.6	8.1	24.0	9.2	9.2	9.3
Multilateral	..	0.0	1.8	2.2	2.4	2.7	2.8	3.0	3.7	4.0
Concessional	..	0.0	1.8	2.2	2.4	2.7	2.7	3.0	3.7	3.9
Bilateral	..	0.3	2.7	4.6	5.1	5.4	21.2	6.2	5.5	5.3
Concessional	..	0.3	2.2	3.0	3.1	3.5	4.7	4.5	3.8	3.7
Private creditors	..	0.0	2.8	2.5	3.1	3.4	4.2	6.3	7.6	9.4
Bonds	..	0.0	0.0	0.0	0.0	0.0	0.0	0.0	0.0	0.0
Commercial banks	..	0.0	1.6	0.5	0.8	1.3	2.0	3.8	5.2	7.9
Other private	..	0.0	1.2	2.1	2.3	2.2	2.2	2.5	2.3	1.6
Private nonguaranteed	..	**0.0**	**0.0**	**0.0**	**0.0**	**0.0**	**0.0**	**0.0**	**0.0**	**0.0**
Bonds	..	0.0	0.0	0.0	0.0	0.0	0.0	0.0	0.0	0.0
Commercial banks and other	..	0.0	0.0	0.0	0.0	0.0	0.0	0.0	0.0	0.0
Memo:										
IBRD	0.0	0.0	0.0	0.0	0.0	0.0	0.0	0.0	0.0	0.0
IDA	0.0	0.0	0.1	0.3	0.4	0.4	0.4	0.4	0.6	0.7
UNDISBURSED DEBT	..	**21.0**	**51.3**	**63.9**	**58.7**	**46.7**	**38.9**	**48.0**	**66.1**	**87.3**
Official creditors	..	19.1	49.6	59.5	54.5	38.5	28.9	38.1	57.8	75.7
Private creditors	..	1.9	1.7	4.4	4.2	8.2	10.0	9.9	8.4	11.6
Memorandum items										
Concessional LDOD	..	24.8	55.4	98.3	126.4	136.3	135.6	142.9	150.4	142.3
Variable rate LDOD	..	0.0	0.0	16.1	16.4	16.8	6.6	13.2	16.7	17.0
Public sector LDOD	..	24.8	64.0	122.5	151.9	163.5	164.3	183.4	192.5	184.1
Private sector LDOD	..	0.0	0.0	0.0	0.0	0.0	0.0	0.0	1.5	1.2

6. CURRENCY COMPOSITION OF LONG-TERM DEBT (PERCENT)

	1970	1980	1990	1994	1995	1996	1997	1998	1999	2000
Deutsche mark	..	0.0	13.0	4.1	2.3	0.9	0.1	2.6	1.9	1.5
French franc	..	0.0	0.0	0.0	0.0	0.0	0.0	0.0	0.0	0.0
Japanese yen	..	0.0	0.0	0.0	0.0	0.3	0.8	0.2	0.0	0.0
Pound sterling	..	0.0	0.4	0.0	0.0	0.9	0.7	0.5	0.3	0.2
Swiss franc	..	0.0	0.0	0.0	0.0	0.0	0.0	0.0	0.0	0.0
U.S.dollars	..	14.2	25.4	49.8	51.3	49.5	49.2	49.6	50.4	53.6
Multiple currency	..	0.0	12.4	19.3	20.3	21.2	21.7	20.7	24.0	22.2
Special drawing rights	..	0.0	0.0	0.0	0.7	1.7	1.7	1.6	1.7	1.8
All other currencies	..	85.8	48.8	26.8	25.4	25.5	25.8	24.8	21.7	20.7

MALDIVES

(US$ million, unless otherwise indicated)

	1970	1980	1990	1994	1995	1996	1997	1998	1999	2000
7. DEBT RESTRUCTURINGS										
Total amount rescheduled	..	..	0.0	0.0	0.0	0.0	0.0	0.0	0.0	0.0
Debt stock rescheduled	..	..	0.0	0.0	0.0	0.0	0.0	0.0	0.0	0.0
Principal rescheduled	..	..	0.0	0.0	0.0	0.0	0.0	0.0	0.0	0.0
Official	..	..	0.0	0.0	0.0	0.0	0.0	0.0	0.0	0.0
Private	..	..	0.0	0.0	0.0	0.0	0.0	0.0	0.0	0.0
Interest rescheduled	..	..	0.0	0.0	0.0	0.0	0.0	0.0	0.0	0.0
Official	..	..	0.0	0.0	0.0	0.0	0.0	0.0	0.0	0.0
Private	..	..	0.0	0.0	0.0	0.0	0.0	0.0	0.0	0.0
Debt forgiven	..	..	0.0	0.0	0.0	0.0	0.0	0.0	0.0	0.0
Memo: interest forgiven	..	..	0.0	0.0	0.0	0.0	0.0	0.0	0.0	0.0
Debt stock reduction	..	..	0.0	0.0	0.0	0.0	0.0	0.0	0.0	0.0
of which debt buyback	..	..	0.0	0.0	0.0	0.0	0.0	0.0	0.0	0.0
8. DEBT STOCK-FLOW RECONCILIATION										
Total change in debt stocks	..	..	11.2	11.2	31.3	13.3	3.1	22.3	25.3	-12.2
Net flows on debt	..	12.9	8.6	7.0	29.6	17.4	10.8	22.3	19.7	-3.1
Net change in interest arrears	..	..	0.0	0.0	0.0	0.0	0.0	0.0	0.0	0.0
Interest capitalized	..	..	0.0	0.0	0.0	0.0	0.0	0.0	0.0	0.0
Debt forgiveness or reduction	..	..	0.0	0.0	0.0	0.0	0.0	0.0	0.0	0.0
Cross-currency valuation	..	..	1.2	3.5	1.1	-5.5	-8.4	2.4	-3.3	-6.5
Residual	..	..	1.3	0.7	0.6	1.5	0.7	-2.5	8.9	-2.5
9. AVERAGE TERMS OF NEW COMMITMENTS										
ALL CREDITORS										
Interest (%)	..	2.9	0.8	4.8	3.2	6.4	5.6	4.1	2.8	3.7
Maturity (years)	..	14.7	37.3	14.0	31.3	9.6	8.6	17.2	19.9	26.6
Grace period (years)	..	4.4	9.2	3.7	9.1	2.8	1.9	3.9	4.6	6.9
Grant element (%)	..	41.2	77.2	30.9	56.1	17.8	17.1	33.4	47.8	47.7
Official creditors										
Interest (%)	..	2.5	0.8	2.1	2.5	2.4	5.1	2.3	1.6	2.5
Maturity (years)	..	15.5	37.3	19.8	34.8	16.5	9.3	27.9	24.4	34.7
Grace period (years)	..	4.7	9.2	5.6	10.1	5.0	1.7	6.6	5.7	9.3
Grant element (%)	..	44.2	77.2	52.8	63.1	46.6	19.7	55.4	60.2	63.3
Private creditors										
Interest (%)	..	7.5	0.0	7.5	7.9	8.1	6.2	6.2	6.7	6.6
Maturity (years)	..	6.6	0.0	8.1	6.0	6.5	7.6	5.6	5.4	7.4
Grace period (years)	..	1.1	0.0	1.7	1.7	1.8	2.2	0.8	1.0	1.1
Grant element (%)	..	6.9	0.0	8.6	6.3	5.1	13.7	9.5	8.3	10.2
Memorandum items										
Commitments	..	22.1	15.5	11.6	29.2	13.1	27.2	33.2	36.4	38.1
Official creditors	..	20.3	15.5	5.8	25.6	4.0	15.5	17.3	27.6	26.9
Private creditors	..	1.8	0.0	5.7	3.6	9.1	11.7	15.9	8.7	11.2

10. CONTRACTUAL OBLIGATIONS ON OUTSTANDING LONG-TERM DEBT

	2001	2002	2003	2004	2005	2006	2007	2008	2009	2010
TOTAL										
Disbursements	25.0	23.7	16.0	10.4	6.2	3.1	1.7	0.8	0.4	0.0
Principal	18.4	18.6	16.2	14.8	12.8	10.6	10.0	9.3	9.5	9.6
Interest	5.2	4.8	4.2	3.8	3.4	3.0	2.9	2.5	2.1	1.9
Official creditors										
Disbursements	18.4	20.2	14.9	10.1	6.1	3.1	1.7	0.8	0.4	0.0
Principal	7.3	8.1	8.6	9.1	9.5	9.8	9.2	8.5	8.9	8.9
Interest	2.9	3.1	3.1	3.1	3.0	2.9	2.7	2.4	2.0	1.9
Bilateral creditors										
Disbursements	5.7	6.6	4.8	3.2	1.9	1.0	0.6	0.3	0.0	0.0
Principal	3.9	4.2	4.5	4.8	4.9	4.9	4.7	3.0	3.0	3.0
Interest	1.0	1.0	1.0	0.9	0.8	0.7	0.6	0.5	0.4	0.4
Multilateral creditors										
Disbursements	12.7	13.6	10.1	7.0	4.2	2.0	1.1	0.5	0.4	0.0
Principal	3.4	3.9	4.1	4.3	4.6	4.9	4.5	5.5	5.8	5.9
Interest	1.9	2.0	2.1	2.2	2.2	2.2	2.2	1.9	1.6	1.5
Private creditors										
Disbursements	6.6	3.5	1.2	0.3	0.0	0.0	0.0	0.0	0.0	0.0
Principal	11.0	10.5	7.6	5.7	3.2	0.8	0.8	0.8	0.6	0.6
Interest	2.3	1.7	1.1	0.7	0.3	0.2	0.1	0.1	0.1	0.0
Commercial banks										
Disbursements	6.1	3.0	1.0	0.2	0.0	0.0	0.0	0.0	0.0	0.0
Principal	9.4	9.3	6.3	4.5	2.4	0.8	0.8	0.8	0.6	0.6
Interest	2.0	1.5	0.9	0.6	0.3	0.2	0.1	0.1	0.1	0.0
Other private										
Disbursements	0.5	0.4	0.2	0.1	0.0	0.0	0.0	0.0	0.0	0.0
Principal	1.6	1.3	1.3	1.3	0.8	0.0	0.0	0.0	0.0	0.0
Interest	0.3	0.2	0.2	0.1	0.0	0.0	0.0	0.0	0.0	0.0

MALI

(US$ million, unless otherwise indicated)

	1970	1980	1990	1994	1995	1996	1997	1998	1999	2000
1. SUMMARY DEBT DATA										
TOTAL DEBT STOCKS (EDT)	**249**	**727**	**2,467**	**2,694**	**2,958**	**3,006**	**3,142**	**3,202**	**3,183**	**2,956**
Long-term debt (LDOD)	**238**	**664**	**2,336**	**2,545**	**2,739**	**2,762**	**2,692**	**2,827**	**2,799**	**2,645**
Public and publicly guaranteed	238	664	2,336	2,545	2,739	2,762	2,692	2,827	2,799	2,645
Private nonguaranteed	0	0	0	0	0	0	0	0	0	0
Use of IMF credit	**9**	**39**	**69**	**108**	**147**	**165**	**176**	**187**	**193**	**176**
Short-term debt	**3**	**24**	**62**	**41**	**72**	**79**	**275**	**188**	**192**	**136**
of which interest arrears on LDOD	3	1	9	21	28	33	43	44	46	44
Official creditors	3	1	9	21	28	33	43	44	46	44
Private creditors	0	0	0	0	0	0	0	0	0	0
Memo: principal arrears on LDOD	12	75	63	273	342	415	632	664	581	580
Official creditors	7	73	63	271	340	415	632	664	581	580
Private creditors	6	2	0	2	2	0	0	0	0	0
Memo: export credits	0	0	86	44	69	65	88	42	102	97
TOTAL DEBT FLOWS										
Disbursements	**24**	**109**	**194**	**164**	**238**	**186**	**147**	**108**	**139**	**97**
Long-term debt	23	95	167	122	193	156	118	94	116	88
IMF purchases	2	14	28	42	45	30	28	14	23	9
Principal repayments	**4**	**9**	**44**	**63**	**62**	**54**	**49**	**55**	**75**	**70**
Long-term debt	0	6	25	53	55	47	42	44	64	53
IMF repurchases	4	3	18	10	7	7	7	11	12	17
Net flows on debt	**20**	**99**	**158**	**92**	**200**	**135**	**283**	**-36**	**66**	**-26**
of which short-term debt	0	-1	8	-9	24	3	186	-89	2	-53
Interest payments (INT)	**0**	**7**	**24**	**25**	**25**	**62**	**36**	**27**	**30**	**28**
Long-term debt	0	3	18	24	22	59	20	18	21	19
IMF charges	0	1	4	1	1	1	1	1	1	1
Short-term debt	0	3	3	1	2	2	15	8	8	8
Net transfers on debt	**20**	**92**	**134**	**67**	**175**	**73**	**247**	**-63**	**35**	**-54**
Total debt service paid (TDS)	**5**	**16**	**68**	**88**	**87**	**116**	**85**	**82**	**106**	**97**
Long-term debt	1	9	43	77	77	106	62	62	85	71
IMF repurchases and charges	4	4	22	10	7	9	8	12	13	18
Short-term debt (interest only)	0	3	3	1	2	2	15	8	8	8
2. AGGREGATE NET RESOURCE FLOWS AND NET TRANSFERS (LONG-TERM)										
NET RESOURCE FLOWS	**34**	**195**	**335**	**306**	**457**	**402**	**326**	**269**	**261**	**420**
Net flow of long-term debt (ex. IMF)	23	89	141	69	138	110	76	50	52	36
Foreign direct investment (net)	0	2	-7	17	111	84	39	17	19	76
Portfolio equity flows	0	0	0	0	0	0	0	0	0	0
Grants (excluding technical coop.)	12	104	201	221	208	209	211	202	190	308
Memo: technical coop. grants	8	77	93	111	132	121	125	108	108	120
official net resource flows	34	185	343	290	346	318	287	252	242	344
private net resource flows	0	10	-8	16	111	84	39	17	19	76
NET TRANSFERS	**32**	**192**	**294**	**268**	**420**	**330**	**294**	**238**	**226**	**388**
Interest on long-term debt	0	3	18	24	22	59	20	18	21	19
Profit remittances on FDI	2	0	24	14	15	13	12	13	14	13
Memo: official net transfers	34	182	326	266	324	259	267	234	221	325
private net transfers	-2	9	-33	2	96	71	27	4	5	63
3. MAJOR ECONOMIC AGGREGATES										
Gross national income (GNI)	352	1,768	2,405	1,739	2,419	2,569	2,422	2,546	2,526	2,260
Exports of goods & services (XGS)	..	322	549	516	650	639	745	747	770	804
of which workers remittances	..	59	107	103	112	107	91	84	84	80
Imports of goods & services (MGS)	..	537	889	816	1,040	1,001	959	969	1,027	1,107
International reserves (RES)	1	26	198	229	330	438	420	408	355	381
Current account balance	..	-124	-221	-163	-284	-273	-178	..	..	..
4. DEBT INDICATORS										
EDT / XGS (%)	..	225.8	449.1	521.7	455.2	470.3	421.9	428.3	413.6	367.7
EDT / GNI (%)	70.7	41.1	102.6	154.9	122.3	117.0	129.7	125.7	126.0	130.8
TDS / XGS (%)	..	5.1	12.3	17.1	13.3	18.2	11.4	11.0	13.7	12.1
INT / XGS (%)	..	2.3	4.4	4.9	3.8	9.7	4.8	3.6	3.9	3.4
INT / GNI (%)	0.1	0.4	1.0	1.5	1.0	2.4	1.5	1.1	1.2	1.2
RES / EDT (%)	0.4	3.5	8.0	8.5	11.2	14.6	13.4	12.8	11.2	12.9
RES / MGS (months)	..	0.6	2.7	3.4	3.8	5.3	5.3	5.1	4.2	4.1
Short-term / EDT (%)	1.1	3.3	2.5	1.5	2.4	2.6	8.7	5.9	6.0	4.6
Concessional / EDT (%)	93.0	84.4	91.1	91.5	89.9	89.4	83.6	86.3	86.2	87.8
Multilateral / EDT (%)	2.4	23.6	36.3	46.4	47.2	48.5	46.3	49.1	50.4	50.6

MALI

(US$ million, unless otherwise indicated)

	1970	1980	1990	1994	1995	1996	1997	1998	1999	2000
5. LONG-TERM DEBT										
DEBT OUTSTANDING (LDOD)	**238**	**664**	**2,336**	**2,545**	**2,739**	**2,762**	**2,692**	**2,827**	**2,799**	**2,645**
Public and publicly guaranteed	**238**	**664**	**2,336**	**2,545**	**2,739**	**2,762**	**2,692**	**2,827**	**2,799**	**2,645**
Official creditors	232	629	2,320	2,543	2,736	2,762	2,692	2,827	2,799	2,645
Multilateral	6	172	896	1,250	1,396	1,459	1,453	1,573	1,605	1,497
Concessional	6	163	874	1,214	1,357	1,423	1,424	1,545	1,584	1,481
Bilateral	226	457	1,424	1,293	1,340	1,303	1,239	1,254	1,194	1,148
Concessional	226	451	1,373	1,250	1,303	1,265	1,202	1,218	1,160	1,116
Private creditors	6	36	16	2	2	0	0	0	0	0
Bonds	0	0	0	0	0	0	0	0	0	0
Commercial banks	1	11	0	2	2	0	0	0	0	0
Other private	5	25	16	0	0	0	0	0	0	0
Private nonguaranteed	**0**	**0**	**0**	**0**	**0**	**0**	**0**	**0**	**0**	**0**
Bonds	0	0	0	0	0	0	0	0	0	0
Commercial banks and other	0	0	0	0	0	0	0	0	0	0
Memo:										
IBRD	0	0	0	0	0	0	0	0	0	0
IDA	6	121	498	770	863	915	939	1,009	1,035	957
DISBURSEMENTS	**23**	**95**	**167**	**122**	**193**	**156**	**118**	**94**	**116**	**88**
Public and publicly guaranteed	**23**	**95**	**167**	**122**	**193**	**156**	**118**	**94**	**116**	**88**
Official creditors	23	85	167	122	193	156	118	94	116	88
Multilateral	1	35	115	119	146	122	115	88	108	77
Concessional	1	30	111	118	141	119	115	88	108	77
Bilateral	22	50	52	2	47	35	3	6	8	11
Concessional	22	45	52	2	47	35	3	6	8	11
Private creditors	0	10	0	0	0	0	0	0	0	0
Bonds	0	0	0	0	0	0	0	0	0	0
Commercial banks	0	5	0	0	0	0	0	0	0	0
Other private	0	5	0	0	0	0	0	0	0	0
Private nonguaranteed	**0**	**0**	**0**	**0**	**0**	**0**	**0**	**0**	**0**	**0**
Bonds	0	0	0	0	0	0	0	0	0	0
Commercial banks and other	0	0	0	0	0	0	0	0	0	0
Memo:										
IBRD	0	0	0	0	0	0	0	0	0	0
IDA	1	19	44	93	86	84	75	48	57	49
PRINCIPAL REPAYMENTS	**0**	**6**	**25**	**53**	**55**	**47**	**42**	**44**	**64**	**53**
Public and publicly guaranteed	**0**	**6**	**25**	**53**	**55**	**47**	**42**	**44**	**64**	**53**
Official creditors	0	4	24	52	55	47	42	44	64	53
Multilateral	0	0	14	26	23	27	27	29	32	28
Concessional	0	0	13	21	20	23	24	25	29	26
Bilateral	0	4	11	26	32	20	15	15	31	24
Concessional	0	3	10	18	25	19	14	14	29	23
Private creditors	0	2	1	1	0	0	0	0	0	0
Bonds	0	0	0	0	0	0	0	0	0	0
Commercial banks	0	1	0	0	0	0	0	0	0	0
Other private	0	1	1	1	0	0	0	0	0	0
Private nonguaranteed	**0**	**0**	**0**	**0**	**0**	**0**	**0**	**0**	**0**	**0**
Bonds	0	0	0	0	0	0	0	0	0	0
Commercial banks and other	0	0	0	0	0	0	0	0	0	0
Memo:										
IBRD	0	0	0	0	0	0	0	0	0	0
IDA	0	0	2	6	6	7	7	9	11	9
NET FLOWS ON DEBT	**23**	**89**	**141**	**69**	**138**	**110**	**76**	**50**	**52**	**36**
Public and publicly guaranteed	**23**	**89**	**141**	**69**	**138**	**110**	**76**	**50**	**52**	**36**
Official creditors	23	81	142	69	138	110	76	50	52	36
Multilateral	1	35	101	94	123	94	88	59	75	49
Concessional	1	30	98	97	121	96	90	62	79	52
Bilateral	21	46	42	-24	15	15	-11	-9	-23	-13
Concessional	21	42	42	-16	22	16	-10	-8	-21	-12
Private creditors	0	8	-1	-1	0	0	0	0	0	0
Bonds	0	0	0	0	0	0	0	0	0	0
Commercial banks	0	4	0	0	0	0	0	0	0	0
Other private	0	4	-1	-1	0	0	0	0	0	0
Private nonguaranteed	**0**	**0**	**0**	**0**	**0**	**0**	**0**	**0**	**0**	**0**
Bonds	0	0	0	0	0	0	0	0	0	0
Commercial banks and other	0	0	0	0	0	0	0	0	0	0
Memo:										
IBRD	0	0	0	0	0	0	0	0	0	0
IDA	1	19	42	87	80	77	68	39	46	41

MALI

(US$ million, unless otherwise indicated)

	1970	1980	1990	1994	1995	1996	1997	1998	1999	2000
INTEREST PAYMENTS (LINT)	**0**	**3**	**18**	**24**	**22**	**59**	**20**	**18**	**21**	**19**
Public and publicly guaranteed	**0**	**3**	**18**	**24**	**22**	**59**	**20**	**18**	**21**	**19**
Official creditors	0	2	17	24	22	59	20	18	21	19
Multilateral	0	1	10	12	12	14	14	13	14	14
Concessional	0	1	8	11	11	12	13	12	14	13
Bilateral	0	1	7	12	10	45	7	6	7	5
Concessional	0	1	6	9	8	44	5	4	6	4
Private creditors	0	1	1	0	0	0	0	0	0	0
Bonds	0	0	0	0	0	0	0	0	0	0
Commercial banks	0	1	0	0	0	0	0	0	0	0
Other private	0	0	1	0	0	0	0	0	0	0
Private nonguaranteed	**0**	**0**	**0**	**0**	**0**	**0**	**0**	**0**	**0**	**0**
Bonds	0	0	0	0	0	0	0	0	0	0
Commercial banks and other	0	0	0	0	0	0	0	0	0	0
Memo:										
IBRD	0	0	0	0	0	0	0	0	0	0
IDA	0	1	3	6	6	7	7	7	7	7
NET TRANSFERS ON DEBT	**22**	**86**	**124**	**44**	**116**	**50**	**56**	**32**	**31**	**17**
Public and publicly guaranteed	**22**	**86**	**124**	**44**	**116**	**50**	**56**	**32**	**31**	**17**
Official creditors	22	79	126	45	116	50	56	32	31	17
Multilateral	1	34	91	81	111	81	74	47	61	35
Concessional	1	29	90	87	111	84	78	51	65	39
Bilateral	21	45	34	-36	5	-30	-18	-15	-30	-19
Concessional	21	41	37	-25	14	-28	-16	-13	-26	-17
Private creditors	0	7	-2	-1	0	0	0	0	0	0
Bonds	0	0	0	0	0	0	0	0	0	0
Commercial banks	0	3	0	0	0	0	0	0	0	0
Other private	0	4	-2	-1	0	0	0	0	0	0
Private nonguaranteed	**0**	**0**	**0**	**0**	**0**	**0**	**0**	**0**	**0**	**0**
Bonds	0	0	0	0	0	0	0	0	0	0
Commercial banks and other	0	0	0	0	0	0	0	0	0	0
Memo:										
IBRD	0	0	0	0	0	0	0	0	0	0
IDA	1	18	38	82	73	71	61	32	39	33
DEBT SERVICE (LTDS)	**1**	**9**	**43**	**77**	**77**	**106**	**62**	**62**	**85**	**71**
Public and publicly guaranteed	**1**	**9**	**43**	**77**	**77**	**106**	**62**	**62**	**85**	**71**
Official creditors	1	6	41	76	77	106	62	62	85	71
Multilateral	0	2	23	38	35	41	41	41	47	42
Concessional	0	1	21	31	30	35	37	37	43	39
Bilateral	1	5	18	38	42	65	22	21	38	29
Concessional	1	4	16	27	33	63	19	18	35	28
Private creditors	0	3	2	1	0	0	0	0	0	0
Bonds	0	0	0	0	0	0	0	0	0	0
Commercial banks	0	2	0	0	0	0	0	0	0	0
Other private	0	1	2	1	0	0	0	0	0	0
Private nonguaranteed	**0**	**0**	**0**	**0**	**0**	**0**	**0**	**0**	**0**	**0**
Bonds	0	0	0	0	0	0	0	0	0	0
Commercial banks and other	0	0	0	0	0	0	0	0	0	0
Memo:										
IBRD	0	0	0	0	0	0	0	0	0	0
IDA	0	1	5	12	12	14	14	16	18	16
UNDISBURSED DEBT	**54**	**368**	**637**	**640**	**623**	**685**	**591**	**566**	**496**	**609**
Official creditors	50	361	637	640	623	685	591	566	496	609
Private creditors	4	7	0	0	0	0	0	0	0	0
Memorandum items										
Concessional LDOD	232	614	2,247	2,464	2,660	2,687	2,626	2,763	2,744	2,596
Variable rate LDOD	0	0	6	3	3	2	2	1	1	0
Public sector LDOD	238	664	2,330	2,545	2,739	2,762	2,692	2,827	2,799	2,645
Private sector LDOD	0	0	6	0	0	0	0	0	0	0

6. CURRENCY COMPOSITION OF LONG-TERM DEBT (PERCENT)

	1970	1980	1990	1994	1995	1996	1997	1998	1999	2000
Deutsche mark	2.8	0.9	0.2	0.2	0.2	0.2	0.1	0.1	0.1	0.1
French franc	16.9	21.3	36.7	22.4	21.8	20.3	18.9	18.5	16.9	14.3
Japanese yen	0.0	0.0	0.3	1.9	2.3	2.9	2.7	2.8	3.2	2.9
Pound sterling	37.5	11.5	2.7	2.0	1.8	1.9	1.9	1.9	1.8	1.8
Swiss franc	5.9	5.6	2.3	2.0	2.1	1.8	1.7	1.7	1.5	1.5
U.S.dollars	4.9	11.6	14.9	21.2	22.5	23.9	25.9	26.9	28.3	29.9
Multiple currency	0.4	6.4	15.3	17.5	18.7	19.1	18.5	19.1	18.9	18.7
Special drawing rights	0.0	0.0	0.0	0.0	0.0	0.0	0.0	0.0	0.0	0.0
All other currencies	31.6	42.7	27.6	32.8	30.6	29.9	30.3	29.0	29.3	30.8

MALI

(US$ million, unless otherwise indicated)

	1970	1980	1990	1994	1995	1996	1997	1998	1999	2000
7. DEBT RESTRUCTURINGS										
Total amount rescheduled	..	..	11	0	0	14	0	1	0	0
Debt stock rescheduled	..	..	0	0	0	0	0	0	0	0
Principal rescheduled	..	..	7	0	0	14	0	1	0	0
Official	..	..	4	0	0	13	0	1	0	0
Private	..	..	3	0	0	1	0	0	0	0
Interest rescheduled	..	..	5	0	0	0	0	0	0	0
Official	..	..	4	0	0	0	0	0	0	0
Private	..	..	1	0	0	0	0	0	0	0
Debt forgiven	..	..	2	413	0	16	0	5	0	0
Memo: interest forgiven	..	..	2	9	0	2	0	0	0	0
Debt stock reduction	..	..	0	0	0	0	0	0	0	74
of which debt buyback	..	..	0	0	0	0	0	0	0	45
8. DEBT STOCK-FLOW RECONCILIATION										
Total change in debt stocks	..	..	340	-208	264	49	136	59	-18	-227
Net flows on debt	20	99	158	92	200	135	283	-36	66	-26
Net change in interest arrears	..	..	8	3	7	5	10	2	2	-2
Interest capitalized	..	..	5	0	0	0	0	0	0	0
Debt forgiveness or reduction	..	..	-2	-413	0	-16	0	-5	0	-29
Cross-currency valuation	..	..	119	74	-1	-115	-213	-30	-70	-177
Residual	..	..	52	36	59	39	56	128	-15	7
9. AVERAGE TERMS OF NEW COMMITMENTS										
ALL CREDITORS										
Interest (%)	1.1	2.2	1.0	0.8	1.5	1.3	0.9	1.6	0.8	0.6
Maturity (years)	25.0	23.0	29.9	37.2	30.7	35.9	45.4	28.4	38.5	35.4
Grace period (years)	9.5	5.5	8.4	9.7	8.8	9.3	10.2	7.6	9.6	8.8
Grant element (%)	68.2	50.5	67.6	77.7	68.6	73.3	80.2	64.4	77.5	76.9
Official creditors										
Interest (%)	0.3	1.8	1.0	0.8	1.5	1.3	0.9	1.6	0.8	0.6
Maturity (years)	27.4	23.9	29.9	37.2	30.7	35.9	45.4	28.4	38.5	35.4
Grace period (years)	10.6	5.6	8.4	9.7	8.8	9.3	10.2	7.6	9.6	8.8
Grant element (%)	76.4	53.2	67.6	77.7	68.6	73.3	80.2	64.4	77.5	76.9
Private creditors										
Interest (%)	6.7	9.9	0.0	0.0	0.0	0.0	0.0	0.0	0.0	0.0
Maturity (years)	8.5	6.3	0.0	0.0	0.0	0.0	0.0	0.0	0.0	0.0
Grace period (years)	1.6	2.2	0.0	0.0	0.0	0.0	0.0	0.0	0.0	0.0
Grant element (%)	11.5	-0.4	0.0	0.0	0.0	0.0	0.0	0.0	0.0	0.0
Memorandum items										
Commitments	34	146	123	135	163	238	123	51	63	235
Official creditors	30	139	123	135	163	238	123	51	63	235
Private creditors	4	7	0	0	0	0	0	0	0	0

10. CONTRACTUAL OBLIGATIONS ON OUTSTANDING LONG-TERM DEBT

	2001	2002	2003	2004	2005	2006	2007	2008	2009	2010
TOTAL										
Disbursements	137	158	120	86	57	29	17	3	1	0
Principal	82	77	76	73	78	83	87	88	86	87
Interest	21	21	21	22	21	21	20	19	17	16
Official creditors										
Disbursements	137	158	120	86	57	29	17	3	1	0
Principal	82	77	76	73	78	83	87	88	86	87
Interest	21	21	21	22	21	21	20	19	17	16
Bilateral creditors										
Disbursements	17	18	15	8	5	0	0	0	0	0
Principal	46	38	34	29	30	32	31	31	28	26
Interest	6	5	5	5	5	5	5	4	4	3
Multilateral creditors										
Disbursements	121	140	104	78	52	29	17	3	1	0
Principal	36	39	42	44	48	52	56	57	58	61
Interest	15	16	16	16	16	16	15	14	14	13
Private creditors										
Disbursements	0	0	0	0	0	0	0	0	0	0
Principal	0	0	0	0	0	0	0	0	0	0
Interest	0	0	0	0	0	0	0	0	0	0
Commercial banks										
Disbursements	0	0	0	0	0	0	0	0	0	0
Principal	0	0	0	0	0	0	0	0	0	0
Interest	0	0	0	0	0	0	0	0	0	0
Other private										
Disbursements	0	0	0	0	0	0	0	0	0	0
Principal	0	0	0	0	0	0	0	0	0	0
Interest	0	0	0	0	0	0	0	0	0	0

MAURITANIA

(US$ million, unless otherwise indicated)

	1970	1980	1990	1994	1995	1996	1997	1998	1999	2000
1. SUMMARY DEBT DATA										
TOTAL DEBT STOCKS (EDT)	**26**	**840**	**2,096**	**2,223**	**2,350**	**2,412**	**2,456**	**2,357**	**2,528**	**2,500**
Long-term debt (LDOD)	**26**	**713**	**1,789**	**1,990**	**2,081**	**2,125**	**2,040**	**2,010**	**2,138**	**2,150**
Public and publicly guaranteed	26	713	1,789	1,990	2,081	2,125	2,040	2,010	2,138	2,150
Private nonguaranteed	0	0	0	0	0	0	0	0	0	0
Use of IMF credit	**0**	**62**	**70**	**86**	**100**	**107**	**113**	**110**	**107**	**98**
Short-term debt	**0**	**65**	**238**	**148**	**169**	**180**	**304**	**237**	**283**	**252**
of which interest arrears on LDOD	0	10	64	72	79	81	86	90	135	114
Official creditors	0	9	57	70	77	81	86	90	135	114
Private creditors	0	1	7	2	3	0	0	0	0	0
Memo: principal arrears on LDOD	0	44	141	192	174	175	193	385	429	339
Official creditors	0	24	120	187	169	175	193	385	429	339
Private creditors	0	21	21	5	5	0	0	0	0	0
Memo: export credits	0	0	230	148	157	154	204	119	90	90
TOTAL DEBT FLOWS										
Disbursements	**5**	**155**	**148**	**163**	**133**	**176**	**108**	**55**	**57**	**118**
Long-term debt	5	126	137	139	111	155	89	55	49	110
IMF purchases	0	30	12	24	22	21	20	0	8	8
Principal repayments	**3**	**26**	**99**	**63**	**79**	**82**	**70**	**69**	**70**	**68**
Long-term debt	3	17	83	57	70	72	62	62	60	57
IMF repurchases	0	9	16	6	9	10	8	7	9	11
Net flows on debt	**1**	**139**	**102**	**96**	**68**	**103**	**158**	**-84**	**-12**	**40**
of which short-term debt	0	10	53	-4	14	9	119	-71	1	-10
Interest payments (INT)	**0**	**22**	**47**	**42**	**38**	**35**	**44**	**42**	**36**	**33**
Long-term debt	0	13	35	38	33	30	35	33	28	23
IMF charges	0	2	3	0	1	1	1	1	1	1
Short-term debt	0	7	9	4	5	4	8	8	7	10
Net transfers on debt	**1**	**118**	**55**	**54**	**30**	**68**	**114**	**-126**	**-48**	**7**
Total debt service paid (TDS)	**4**	**48**	**146**	**106**	**117**	**116**	**114**	**110**	**106**	**100**
Long-term debt	4	30	118	96	102	102	98	94	88	79
IMF repurchases and charges	0	11	19	6	10	11	8	8	10	12
Short-term debt (interest only)	0	7	9	4	5	4	8	8	7	10
2. AGGREGATE NET RESOURCE FLOWS AND NET TRANSFERS (LONG-TERM)										
NET RESOURCE FLOWS	**5**	**197**	**138**	**210**	**184**	**262**	**182**	**125**	**156**	**183**
Net flow of long-term debt (ex. IMF)	1	108	54	82	42	83	26	-7	-12	53
Foreign direct investment (net)	1	27	7	2	7	5	3	0	2	5
Portfolio equity flows	0	0	0	0	0	0	0	0	0	0
Grants (excluding technical coop.)	3	61	78	127	135	174	152	131	165	125
Memo: technical coop. grants	4	29	50	44	49	47	42	36	37	33
official net resource flows	6	170	133	208	177	233	180	127	156	180
private net resource flows	-1	27	6	2	7	30	2	-2	0	3
NET TRANSFERS	**-8**	**161**	**103**	**169**	**149**	**228**	**143**	**90**	**125**	**157**
Interest on long-term debt	0	13	35	38	33	30	35	33	28	23
Profit remittances on FDI	13	23	1	3	3	4	3	2	3	3
Memo: official net transfers	5	161	98	170	145	203	147	96	129	159
private net transfers	-14	1	4	-1	4	26	-3	-6	-5	-2
3. MAJOR ECONOMIC AGGREGATES										
Gross national income (GNI)	196	672	1,076	974	1,015	1,060	1,045	962	925	909
Exports of goods & services (XGS)	..	275	488	432	511	517	463	397	371	388
of which workers remittances	..	6	14	5	5	4	3	2	2	2
Imports of goods & services (MGS)	..	493	570	581	559	623	557	505	444	461
International reserves (RES)	3	146	59	44	90	145	204	206	228	..
Current account balance	..	-133	-10	-70	22	91	48	77	140	90
4. DEBT INDICATORS										
EDT / XGS (%)	..	304.9	429.4	515.1	459.8	466.7	530.9	593.4	681.3	645.1
EDT / GNI (%)	13.4	125.0	194.8	228.3	231.4	227.6	235.1	244.9	273.4	275.1
TDS / XGS (%)	..	17.3	29.9	24.4	22.9	22.5	24.5	27.7	28.4	25.9
INT / XGS (%)	..	7.9	9.7	9.8	7.5	6.7	9.5	10.5	9.7	8.5
INT / GNI (%)	0.2	3.3	4.4	4.3	3.8	3.3	4.2	4.3	3.9	3.6
RES / EDT (%)	12.2	17.4	2.8	2.0	3.8	6.0	8.3	8.8	9.0	..
RES / MGS (months)	..	3.6	1.2	0.9	1.9	2.8	4.4	4.9	6.2	..
Short-term / EDT (%)	0.0	7.7	11.3	6.7	7.2	7.5	12.4	10.1	11.2	10.1
Concessional / EDT (%)	51.7	62.6	61.1	71.9	71.8	72.1	69.2	72.8	71.6	74.3
Multilateral / EDT (%)	21.3	14.8	31.2	38.4	39.4	39.4	38.3	42.2	38.5	39.8

MAURITANIA

(US$ million, unless otherwise indicated)

	1970	1980	1990	1994	1995	1996	1997	1998	1999	2000
5. LONG-TERM DEBT										
DEBT OUTSTANDING (LDOD)	**26**	**713**	**1,789**	**1,990**	**2,081**	**2,125**	**2,040**	**2,010**	**2,138**	**2,150**
Public and publicly guaranteed	**26**	**713**	**1,789**	**1,990**	**2,081**	**2,125**	**2,040**	**2,010**	**2,138**	**2,150**
Official creditors	18	582	1,692	1,981	2,073	2,100	2,016	1,988	2,118	2,131
Multilateral	6	125	654	854	925	950	940	995	973	995
Concessional	6	106	453	634	704	755	776	835	838	877
Bilateral	13	458	1,038	1,127	1,148	1,150	1,076	993	1,146	1,136
Concessional	8	420	828	964	984	984	925	882	972	980
Private creditors	8	131	97	9	8	25	24	22	20	19
Bonds	0	0	0	0	0	0	0	0	0	0
Commercial banks	0	16	0	0	0	0	0	0	0	0
Other private	8	115	97	9	8	25	24	22	20	19
Private nonguaranteed	**0**	**0**	**0**	**0**	**0**	**0**	**0**	**0**	**0**	**0**
Bonds	0	0	0	0	0	0	0	0	0	0
Commercial banks and other	0	0	0	0	0	0	0	0	0	0
Memo:										
IBRD	0	0	54	13	11	8	6	4	2	0
IDA	5	38	210	301	336	360	373	408	415	450
DISBURSEMENTS	**5**	**126**	**137**	**139**	**111**	**155**	**89**	**55**	**49**	**110**
Public and publicly guaranteed	**5**	**126**	**137**	**139**	**111**	**155**	**89**	**55**	**49**	**110**
Official creditors	4	112	136	139	111	130	89	55	49	110
Multilateral	2	27	112	118	88	98	81	50	46	106
Concessional	2	12	65	91	78	82	74	47	43	98
Bilateral	2	85	24	21	24	33	8	5	3	4
Concessional	2	84	24	21	23	32	6	5	3	4
Private creditors	1	14	0	0	0	25	0	0	0	0
Bonds	0	0	0	0	0	0	0	0	0	0
Commercial banks	0	0	0	0	0	0	0	0	0	0
Other private	1	14	0	0	0	25	0	0	0	0
Private nonguaranteed	**0**	**0**	**0**	**0**	**0**	**0**	**0**	**0**	**0**	**0**
Bonds	0	0	0	0	0	0	0	0	0	0
Commercial banks and other	0	0	0	0	0	0	0	0	0	0
Memo:										
IBRD	0	0	0	0	0	0	0	0	0	0
IDA	2	4	39	35	31	36	34	24	19	57
PRINCIPAL REPAYMENTS	**3**	**17**	**83**	**57**	**70**	**72**	**62**	**62**	**60**	**57**
Public and publicly guaranteed	**3**	**17**	**83**	**57**	**70**	**72**	**62**	**62**	**60**	**57**
Official creditors	1	4	81	57	70	72	61	60	58	54
Multilateral	0	2	66	42	35	56	39	38	44	43
Concessional	0	1	16	18	18	20	19	22	24	26
Bilateral	1	2	15	15	34	16	22	22	14	11
Concessional	1	2	11	15	19	16	20	19	12	8
Private creditors	2	13	1	0	0	0	2	2	2	2
Bonds	0	0	0	0	0	0	0	0	0	0
Commercial banks	0	5	0	0	0	0	0	0	0	0
Other private	2	9	1	0	0	0	2	2	2	2
Private nonguaranteed	**0**	**0**	**0**	**0**	**0**	**0**	**0**	**0**	**0**	**0**
Bonds	0	0	0	0	0	0	0	0	0	0
Commercial banks and other	0	0	0	0	0	0	0	0	0	0
Memo:										
IBRD	0	0	11	8	2	2	2	2	2	2
IDA	0	0	1	1	2	2	2	3	3	4
NET FLOWS ON DEBT	**1**	**108**	**54**	**82**	**42**	**83**	**26**	**-7**	**-12**	**53**
Public and publicly guaranteed	**1**	**108**	**54**	**82**	**42**	**83**	**26**	**-7**	**-12**	**53**
Official creditors	3	108	55	82	42	58	28	-5	-10	56
Multilateral	2	25	46	77	53	42	42	12	2	63
Concessional	2	12	50	73	60	62	55	25	19	72
Bilateral	1	83	9	5	-11	17	-14	-17	-11	-7
Concessional	1	82	13	5	4	16	-14	-14	-9	-5
Private creditors	-2	0	-1	0	0	25	-2	-2	-2	-2
Bonds	0	0	0	0	0	0	0	0	0	0
Commercial banks	0	-5	0	0	0	0	0	0	0	0
Other private	-2	5	-1	0	0	25	-2	-2	-2	-2
Private nonguaranteed	**0**	**0**	**0**	**0**	**0**	**0**	**0**	**0**	**0**	**0**
Bonds	0	0	0	0	0	0	0	0	0	0
Commercial banks and other	0	0	0	0	0	0	0	0	0	0
Memo:										
IBRD	0	0	-11	-8	-2	-2	-2	-2	-2	-2
IDA	2	4	38	33	29	34	32	21	16	53

MAURITANIA

(US$ million, unless otherwise indicated)

	1970	1980	1990	1994	1995	1996	1997	1998	1999	2000
INTEREST PAYMENTS (LINT)	**0**	**13**	**35**	**38**	**33**	**30**	**35**	**33**	**28**	**23**
Public and publicly guaranteed	**0**	**13**	**35**	**38**	**33**	**30**	**35**	**33**	**28**	**23**
Official creditors	0	9	34	38	33	30	34	31	26	21
Multilateral	0	3	20	24	15	21	19	18	19	16
Concessional	0	2	7	13	8	11	11	10	11	11
Bilateral	0	6	14	15	17	9	14	13	7	5
Concessional	0	6	6	10	10	8	9	8	4	3
Private creditors	0	4	1	0	0	0	2	2	2	2
Bonds	0	0	0	0	0	0	0	0	0	0
Commercial banks	0	2	0	0	0	0	0	0	0	0
Other private	0	2	1	0	0	0	2	2	2	2
Private nonguaranteed	**0**	**0**	**0**	**0**	**0**	**0**	**0**	**0**	**0**	**0**
Bonds	0	0	0	0	0	0	0	0	0	0
Commercial banks and other	0	0	0	0	0	0	0	0	0	0
Memo:										
IBRD	0	0	5	1	1	1	1	0	0	0
IDA	0	0	1	2	2	3	3	3	3	3
NET TRANSFERS ON DEBT	**1**	**96**	**19**	**43**	**9**	**53**	**-9**	**-39**	**-40**	**30**
Public and publicly guaranteed	**1**	**96**	**19**	**43**	**9**	**53**	**-9**	**-39**	**-40**	**30**
Official creditors	3	99	21	44	10	29	-6	-35	-36	35
Multilateral	2	23	25	53	37	21	23	-6	-18	46
Concessional	2	9	43	60	52	52	45	15	9	61
Bilateral	0	77	-5	-9	-28	8	-29	-29	-18	-12
Concessional	1	76	8	-5	-6	8	-23	-21	-13	-8
Private creditors	-2	-4	-2	0	0	25	-3	-4	-4	-4
Bonds	0	0	0	0	0	0	0	0	0	0
Commercial banks	0	-7	0	0	0	0	0	0	0	0
Other private	-2	3	-2	0	0	25	-3	-4	-4	-4
Private nonguaranteed	**0**	**0**	**0**	**0**	**0**	**0**	**0**	**0**	**0**	**0**
Bonds	0	0	0	0	0	0	0	0	0	0
Commercial banks and other	0	0	0	0	0	0	0	0	0	0
Memo:										
IBRD	0	0	-16	-9	-3	-3	-2	-2	-2	-2
IDA	2	4	37	31	26	32	29	18	13	50
DEBT SERVICE (LTDS)	**4**	**30**	**118**	**96**	**102**	**102**	**98**	**94**	**88**	**79**
Public and publicly guaranteed	**4**	**30**	**118**	**96**	**102**	**102**	**98**	**94**	**88**	**79**
Official creditors	1	13	116	95	102	102	94	90	84	75
Multilateral	0	5	87	66	51	77	58	56	63	60
Concessional	0	3	22	31	26	31	29	33	35	37
Bilateral	1	8	29	30	51	25	36	34	21	16
Concessional	1	8	17	25	29	24	29	27	16	12
Private creditors	2	17	2	0	0	0	3	4	4	4
Bonds	0	0	0	0	0	0	0	0	0	0
Commercial banks	0	7	0	0	0	0	0	0	0	0
Other private	2	10	2	0	0	0	3	4	4	4
Private nonguaranteed	**0**	**0**	**0**	**0**	**0**	**0**	**0**	**0**	**0**	**0**
Bonds	0	0	0	0	0	0	0	0	0	0
Commercial banks and other	0	0	0	0	0	0	0	0	0	0
Memo:										
IBRD	0	0	16	9	3	3	2	2	2	2
IDA	0	1	2	3	4	4	5	6	6	7
UNDISBURSED DEBT	**16**	**682**	**621**	**456**	**421**	**371**	**312**	**333**	**377**	**316**
Official creditors	11	653	616	456	421	371	312	333	377	316
Private creditors	5	29	5	0	0	0	0	0	0	0
Memorandum items										
Concessional LDOD	14	526	1,281	1,598	1,688	1,739	1,701	1,717	1,809	1,857
Variable rate LDOD	0	17	131	132	136	138	131	85	156	146
Public sector LDOD	26	713	1,789	1,990	2,081	2,125	2,040	2,010	2,138	2,150
Private sector LDOD	0	0	0	0	0	0	0	0	0	0

6. CURRENCY COMPOSITION OF LONG-TERM DEBT (PERCENT)

	1970	1980	1990	1994	1995	1996	1997	1998	1999	2000
Deutsche mark	0.0	3.1	0.5	0.3	0.3	0.3	0.3	0.3	0.2	0.2
French franc	49.2	7.2	5.3	7.4	8.2	7.8	7.2	7.8	6.2	5.4
Japanese yen	0.0	0.0	1.3	3.5	3.1	3.5	3.4	3.8	3.9	3.4
Pound sterling	0.0	0.2	0.6	0.6	0.5	0.6	0.6	0.5	0.5	0.4
Swiss franc	0.0	0.3	0.0	0.0	0.0	0.0	0.0	0.0	0.0	0.0
U.S.dollars	23.7	43.1	34.6	34.7	34.8	36.4	38.1	36.4	39.6	39.5
Multiple currency	2.7	3.0	4.2	2.1	1.9	1.7	1.5	1.4	1.2	1.0
Special drawing rights	0.0	0.0	2.1	2.2	2.4	2.4	2.4	2.6	2.4	2.2
All other currencies	24.4	43.1	51.4	49.2	48.8	47.3	46.5	47.2	46.0	47.9

MAURITANIA

(US$ million, unless otherwise indicated)

	1970	1980	1990	1994	1995	1996	1997	1998	1999	2000
7. DEBT RESTRUCTURINGS										
Total amount rescheduled	..	..	11	67	60	68	12	0	157	184
Debt stock rescheduled	..	..	0	0	0	17	0	0	0	0
Principal rescheduled	..	..	7	51	39	29	5	1	0	128
Official	..	..	5	42	38	29	5	1	0	128
Private	..	..	3	9	1	0	0	0	0	0
Interest rescheduled	..	..	5	12	13	13	3	1	0	21
Official	..	..	4	11	12	13	3	1	0	21
Private	..	..	1	0	0	0	0	0	0	0
Debt forgiven	..	..	70	6	13	1	9	0	0	22
Memo: interest forgiven	..	..	1	1	2	2	2	0	0	15
Debt stock reduction	..	..	0	0	0	0	0	0	0	0
of which debt buyback	..	..	0	0	0	0	0	0	0	0
8. DEBT STOCK-FLOW RECONCILIATION										
Total change in debt stocks	..	..	140	83	126	63	44	-99	170	-28
Net flows on debt	1	139	102	96	68	103	158	-84	-12	40
Net change in interest arrears	..	..	21	-22	7	2	5	4	45	-21
Interest capitalized	..	..	5	12	13	13	3	1	0	21
Debt forgiveness or reduction	..	..	-70	-6	-13	-1	-9	0	0	-22
Cross-currency valuation	..	..	48	11	3	-100	-138	9	-56	-66
Residual	..	..	34	-8	48	47	26	-28	193	21
9. AVERAGE TERMS OF NEW COMMITMENTS										
ALL CREDITORS										
Interest (%)	6.0	3.6	3.1	2.0	1.1	3.6	2.2	1.9	1.0	1.6
Maturity (years)	10.6	22.3	31.2	28.0	34.7	27.9	30.6	24.9	40.1	33.9
Grace period (years)	3.0	9.1	8.6	7.7	9.7	6.3	6.6	6.4	9.8	8.5
Grant element (%)	18.9	47.5	56.8	61.3	75.1	49.9	60.3	56.6	77.7	68.7
Official creditors										
Interest (%)	3.2	2.7	3.1	2.0	1.1	2.2	2.2	1.9	1.0	1.6
Maturity (years)	20.9	24.5	31.2	28.0	34.7	32.4	30.6	24.9	40.1	33.9
Grace period (years)	5.4	10.4	8.6	7.7	9.7	7.9	6.6	6.4	9.8	8.5
Grant element (%)	44.4	55.2	56.8	61.3	75.1	61.7	60.3	56.6	77.7	68.7
Private creditors										
Interest (%)	6.7	7.7	0.0	0.0	0.0	8.8	0.0	0.0	0.0	0.0
Maturity (years)	8.2	11.4	0.0	0.0	0.0	10.0	0.0	0.0	0.0	0.0
Grace period (years)	2.4	2.9	0.0	0.0	0.0	0.0	0.0	0.0	0.0	0.0
Grant element (%)	13.2	10.0	0.0	0.0	0.0	3.9	0.0	0.0	0.0	0.0
Memorandum items										
Commitments	7	211	216	65	114	121	102	58	110	71
Official creditors	1	175	216	65	114	96	102	58	110	71
Private creditors	6	36	0	0	0	25	0	0	0	0

10. CONTRACTUAL OBLIGATIONS ON OUTSTANDING LONG-TERM DEBT

	2001	2002	2003	2004	2005	2006	2007	2008	2009	2010
TOTAL										
Disbursements	101	82	55	36	20	7	4	1	0	0
Principal	98	98	92	86	88	82	74	72	73	74
Interest	35	34	34	32	30	27	25	24	22	20
Official creditors										
Disbursements	100	82	55	36	20	7	4	1	0	0
Principal	96	95	89	83	85	80	73	72	73	74
Interest	33	33	33	31	29	27	25	24	22	20
Bilateral creditors										
Disbursements	19	13	7	5	2	1	1	0	0	0
Principal	44	44	44	40	40	35	31	31	34	34
Interest	15	16	17	16	15	14	14	13	13	12
Multilateral creditors										
Disbursements	81	69	48	31	18	6	3	1	0	0
Principal	52	51	45	43	45	45	42	41	40	40
Interest	18	17	16	15	14	13	11	10	9	9
Private creditors										
Disbursements	1	0	0	0	0	0	0	0	0	0
Principal	3	3	3	3	4	2	0	0	0	0
Interest	2	1	1	1	1	0	0	0	0	0
Commercial banks										
Disbursements	0	0	0	0	0	0	0	0	0	0
Principal	0	0	0	0	0	0	0	0	0	0
Interest	0	0	0	0	0	0	0	0	0	0
Other private										
Disbursements	1	0	0	0	0	0	0	0	0	0
Principal	3	3	3	3	4	2	0	0	0	0
Interest	2	1	1	1	1	0	0	0	0	0

MAURITIUS

(US$ million, unless otherwise indicated)

	1970	1980	1990	1994	1995	1996	1997	1998	1999	2000
1. SUMMARY DEBT DATA										
TOTAL DEBT STOCKS (EDT)	**32**	**467**	**984**	**1,382**	**1,757**	**1,818**	**2,472**	**2,482**	**2,464**	**2,374**
Long-term debt (LDOD)	**32**	**318**	**910**	**1,098**	**1,415**	**1,399**	**1,976**	**1,909**	**1,891**	**1,608**
Public and publicly guaranteed	32	294	762	852	1,148	1,153	1,187	1,152	1,155	889
Private nonguaranteed	0	24	148	245	267	246	789	757	736	718
Use of IMF credit	**0**	**102**	**22**	**0**	**0**	**0**	**0**	**0**	**0**	**0**
Short-term debt	**0**	**47**	**52**	**285**	**342**	**419**	**496**	**573**	**573**	**767**
of which interest arrears on LDOD	0	0	2	2	1	0	0	0	0	0
Official creditors	0	0	1	1	1	0	0	0	0	0
Private creditors	0	0	1	1	0	0	0	0	0	0
Memo: principal arrears on LDOD	0	2	5	1	0	0	0	0	0	0
Official creditors	0	2	4	1	0	0	0	0	0	0
Private creditors	0	0	1	0	0	0	0	0	0	0
Memo: export credits	0	0	201	207	226	216	286	95	77	34
TOTAL DEBT FLOWS										
Disbursements	**2**	**143**	**161**	**186**	**409**	**140**	**827**	**56**	**143**	**175**
Long-term debt	2	97	161	186	409	140	827	56	143	175
IMF purchases	0	46	0	0	0	0	0	0	0	0
Principal repayments	**5**	**19**	**104**	**103**	**154**	**108**	**136**	**158**	**113**	**404**
Long-term debt	1	19	60	103	154	108	136	158	113	404
IMF repurchases	4	0	44	0	0	0	0	0	0	0
Net flows on debt	**-3**	**104**	**76**	**260**	**312**	**110**	**768**	**-25**	**30**	**-35**
of which short-term debt	0	-20	18	177	58	78	77	77	0	194
Interest payments (INT)	**2**	**34**	**52**	**56**	**72**	**90**	**147**	**154**	**148**	**149**
Long-term debt	2	23	43	45	56	71	123	127	121	117
IMF charges	0	3	5	0	0	0	0	0	0	0
Short-term debt	0	8	5	10	16	19	23	27	27	32
Net transfers on debt	**-5**	**70**	**23**	**204**	**241**	**21**	**621**	**-179**	**-119**	**-184**
Total debt service paid (TDS)	**7**	**52**	**156**	**159**	**225**	**198**	**283**	**312**	**262**	**553**
Long-term debt	3	41	103	148	210	179	259	285	234	521
IMF repurchases and charges	4	3	49	0	0	0	0	0	0	0
Short-term debt (interest only)	0	8	5	10	16	19	23	27	27	32
2. AGGREGATE NET RESOURCE FLOWS AND NET TRANSFERS (LONG-TERM)										
NET RESOURCE FLOWS	**5**	**93**	**167**	**125**	**301**	**116**	**785**	**-69**	**97**	**46**
Net flow of long-term debt (ex. IMF)	1	79	101	83	255	32	691	-102	30	-229
Foreign direct investment (net)	2	1	41	20	19	37	55	12	49	266
Portfolio equity flows	0	0	0	10	4	34	24	8	6	0
Grants (excluding technical coop.)	3	13	25	12	24	13	15	13	12	9
Memo: technical coop. grants	2	11	20	21	24	23	23	18	18	16
official net resource flows	4	45	82	-10	2	5	12	10	-6	53
private net resource flows	1	49	86	135	298	112	773	-79	102	-8
NET TRANSFERS	**3**	**69**	**102**	**58**	**225**	**25**	**640**	**-217**	**-41**	**-92**
Interest on long-term debt	2	23	43	45	56	71	123	127	121	117
Profit remittances on FDI	1	1	22	22	20	20	22	21	17	20
Memo: official net transfers	3	37	48	-45	-33	-29	-17	-17	-31	31
private net transfers	-1	32	53	102	258	54	657	-199	-10	-123
3. MAJOR ECONOMIC AGGREGATES										
Gross national income (GNI)	222	1,109	2,635	3,485	3,946	4,271	4,084	4,056	4,199	4,349
Exports of goods & services (XGS)	..	579	1,778	2,041	2,402	2,802	2,541	2,634	2,660	2,666
of which workers remittances	..	0	0	0	0	0	0	0	0	0
Imports of goods & services (MGS)	..	718	1,994	2,377	2,525	2,884	2,757	2,726	2,895	2,763
International reserves (RES)	46	113	761	771	887	919	711	577	749	914
Current account balance	..	-117	-119	-232	-22	34	-89	3	-131	-33
4. DEBT INDICATORS										
EDT / XGS (%)	..	80.8	55.4	67.7	73.2	64.9	97.3	94.2	92.7	89.1
EDT / GNI (%)	14.3	42.1	37.3	39.7	44.5	42.6	60.5	61.2	58.7	54.6
TDS / XGS (%)	..	9.0	8.8	7.8	9.4	7.1	11.1	11.8	9.8	20.8
INT / XGS (%)	..	5.8	2.9	2.7	3.0	3.2	5.8	5.9	5.6	5.6
INT / GNI (%)	0.8	3.1	2.0	1.6	1.8	2.1	3.6	3.8	3.5	3.4
RES / EDT (%)	145.7	24.2	77.4	55.8	50.5	50.6	28.8	23.2	30.4	38.5
RES / MGS (months)	..	1.9	4.6	3.9	4.2	3.8	3.1	2.5	3.1	4.0
Short-term / EDT (%)	0.0	10.1	5.3	20.6	19.5	23.1	20.1	23.1	23.3	32.3
Concessional / EDT (%)	17.4	13.8	35.7	30.2	25.1	22.2	14.0	14.3	12.8	14.4
Multilateral / EDT (%)	17.7	16.6	31.6	19.9	15.4	13.9	9.9	10.5	10.2	9.7

MAURITIUS

(US$ million, unless otherwise indicated)

	1970	1980	1990	1994	1995	1996	1997	1998	1999	2000
5. LONG-TERM DEBT										
DEBT OUTSTANDING (LDOD)	**32**	**318**	**910**	**1,098**	**1,415**	**1,399**	**1,976**	**1,909**	**1,891**	**1,608**
Public and publicly guaranteed	**32**	**294**	**762**	**852**	**1,148**	**1,153**	**1,187**	**1,152**	**1,155**	**889**
Official creditors	21	154	647	650	664	615	554	581	529	538
Multilateral	6	78	311	275	270	253	245	261	250	230
Concessional	0	25	64	65	69	65	60	60	60	67
Bilateral	16	76	337	375	394	363	310	321	278	308
Concessional	6	39	288	352	372	338	285	294	256	276
Private creditors	10	141	115	203	484	537	632	570	626	351
Bonds	9	0	0	0	150	150	150	150	150	0
Commercial banks	2	138	102	178	315	331	426	368	416	327
Other private	0	3	13	25	19	56	56	53	61	24
Private nonguaranteed	**0**	**24**	**148**	**245**	**267**	**246**	**789**	**757**	**736**	**718**
Bonds	0	0	0	0	0	0	600	600	600	600
Commercial banks and other	0	24	148	245	267	246	189	157	136	118
Memo:										
IBRD	6	35	176	147	140	124	111	112	107	86
IDA	0	20	19	17	17	16	15	15	14	14
DISBURSEMENTS	**2**	**97**	**161**	**186**	**409**	**140**	**827**	**56**	**143**	**175**
Public and publicly guaranteed	**2**	**93**	**104**	**145**	**353**	**122**	**216**	**52**	**142**	**166**
Official creditors	2	36	96	36	39	50	75	49	35	96
Multilateral	0	18	23	14	18	33	42	32	25	26
Concessional	0	3	7	3	5	3	3	1	9	13
Bilateral	2	18	74	22	21	17	33	18	10	71
Concessional	1	13	65	22	18	10	27	12	10	59
Private creditors	0	56	8	109	313	73	141	3	106	70
Bonds	0	0	0	0	150	0	0	0	0	0
Commercial banks	0	56	0	102	159	29	121	3	92	70
Other private	0	0	7	7	5	43	20	0	14	0
Private nonguaranteed	**0**	**4**	**57**	**41**	**56**	**18**	**611**	**4**	**1**	**9**
Bonds	0	0	0	0	0	0	600	0	0	0
Commercial banks and other	0	4	57	41	56	18	11	4	1	9
Memo:										
IBRD	0	7	6	10	11	14	17	13	5	4
IDA	0	1	0	0	0	0	0	0	0	0
PRINCIPAL REPAYMENTS	**1**	**19**	**60**	**103**	**154**	**108**	**136**	**158**	**113**	**404**
Public and publicly guaranteed	**1**	**15**	**44**	**76**	**94**	**73**	**112**	**122**	**100**	**389**
Official creditors	1	5	39	58	61	58	78	52	53	52
Multilateral	0	2	22	34	33	30	31	29	30	31
Concessional	0	0	3	4	3	3	4	4	4	4
Bilateral	0	3	17	25	27	28	48	24	23	21
Concessional	0	2	12	18	22	24	44	19	19	19
Private creditors	1	10	4	18	33	15	34	69	48	337
Bonds	0	0	0	0	0	0	0	0	0	150
Commercial banks	1	8	4	14	22	11	19	62	39	153
Other private	0	1	0	3	12	4	15	8	8	34
Private nonguaranteed	**0**	**4**	**16**	**27**	**60**	**35**	**24**	**36**	**13**	**16**
Bonds	0	0	0	0	0	0	0	0	0	0
Commercial banks and other	0	4	16	27	60	35	24	36	13	16
Memo:										
IBRD	0	2	16	22	23	20	21	19	18	18
IDA	0	0	0	1	1	1	1	1	1	1
NET FLOWS ON DEBT	**1**	**79**	**101**	**83**	**255**	**32**	**691**	**-102**	**30**	**-229**
Public and publicly guaranteed	**1**	**78**	**60**	**69**	**259**	**49**	**104**	**-70**	**41**	**-223**
Official creditors	2	31	57	-22	-21	-9	-3	-3	-18	44
Multilateral	0	16	0	-20	-15	3	12	3	-5	-5
Concessional	0	3	4	-2	2	0	0	-3	5	9
Bilateral	2	15	57	-2	-6	-12	-15	-6	-12	50
Concessional	0	11	53	5	-4	-14	-17	-7	-9	40
Private creditors	-1	47	3	91	280	58	107	-67	59	-267
Bonds	0	0	0	0	150	0	0	0	0	-150
Commercial banks	-1	48	-4	88	137	18	102	-59	53	-83
Other private	0	-1	7	3	-7	39	5	-8	6	-34
Private nonguaranteed	**0**	**0**	**41**	**13**	**-4**	**-17**	**587**	**-32**	**-12**	**-6**
Bonds	0	0	0	0	0	0	600	0	0	0
Commercial banks and other	0	0	41	13	-4	-17	-13	-32	-12	-6
Memo:										
IBRD	0	5	-10	-12	-13	-7	-4	-6	-12	-14
IDA	0	1	0	-1	-1	-1	-1	-1	-1	-1

MAURITIUS

(US$ million, unless otherwise indicated)

	1970	1980	1990	1994	1995	1996	1997	1998	1999	2000
INTEREST PAYMENTS (LINT)	**2**	**23**	**43**	**45**	**56**	**71**	**123**	**127**	**121**	**117**
Public and publicly guaranteed	**2**	**20**	**37**	**41**	**50**	**66**	**61**	**66**	**60**	**56**
Official creditors	1	7	33	35	36	33	29	28	26	22
Multilateral	0	4	19	17	16	15	13	12	11	9
Concessional	0	0	1	1	1	1	1	1	1	1
Bilateral	1	3	14	18	19	18	16	16	14	13
Concessional	0	1	9	15	17	16	14	14	13	11
Private creditors	1	13	4	7	15	33	32	39	35	35
Bonds	1	0	0	0	0	10	10	10	9	5
Commercial banks	0	13	3	5	12	21	20	26	23	27
Other private	0	0	1	2	2	1	2	3	3	3
Private nonguaranteed	**0**	**3**	**6**	**4**	**6**	**5**	**62**	**61**	**61**	**61**
Bonds	0	0	0	0	0	0	60	60	60	60
Commercial banks and other	0	3	6	4	6	5	2	1	1	1
Memo:										
IBRD	0	3	14	11	11	9	8	7	6	5
IDA	0	0	0	0	0	0	0	0	0	0
NET TRANSFERS ON DEBT	**-1**	**56**	**58**	**37**	**199**	**-39**	**568**	**-229**	**-92**	**-346**
Public and publicly guaranteed	**-1**	**58**	**23**	**28**	**209**	**-17**	**43**	**-136**	**-19**	**-279**
Official creditors	1	24	24	-57	-57	-42	-32	-31	-43	23
Multilateral	-1	12	-19	-36	-32	-12	-2	-9	-17	-15
Concessional	0	3	3	-3	1	-2	-1	-4	4	8
Bilateral	1	12	43	-20	-25	-30	-31	-22	-27	37
Concessional	0	11	44	-11	-22	-31	-31	-21	-22	29
Private creditors	-2	34	-1	85	265	25	75	-105	24	-302
Bonds	-1	0	0	0	150	-10	-10	-10	-9	-155
Commercial banks	-1	35	-7	83	125	-3	82	-84	30	-110
Other private	0	-1	7	1	-9	38	3	-10	3	-37
Private nonguaranteed	**0**	**-2**	**35**	**9**	**-10**	**-22**	**525**	**-93**	**-72**	**-67**
Bonds	0	0	0	0	0	0	540	-60	-60	-60
Commercial banks and other	0	-2	35	9	-10	-22	-15	-33	-12	-7
Memo:										
IBRD	-1	2	-24	-23	-24	-16	-12	-13	-19	-19
IDA	0	1	0	-1	-1	-1	-1	-1	-1	-1
DEBT SERVICE (LTDS)	**3**	**41**	**103**	**148**	**210**	**179**	**259**	**285**	**234**	**521**
Public and publicly guaranteed	**3**	**35**	**81**	**117**	**144**	**139**	**173**	**188**	**161**	**445**
Official creditors	2	12	73	93	96	91	107	80	79	74
Multilateral	1	7	42	50	50	45	44	41	42	40
Concessional	0	0	4	5	4	4	4	4	5	5
Bilateral	1	6	31	43	47	47	64	40	37	33
Concessional	0	2	21	33	39	40	58	33	32	30
Private creditors	2	22	8	24	48	48	66	108	82	372
Bonds	1	0	0	0	0	10	10	10	9	155
Commercial banks	1	21	7	19	34	32	39	87	63	180
Other private	0	1	1	5	14	5	17	10	11	37
Private nonguaranteed	**0**	**7**	**22**	**31**	**66**	**40**	**86**	**97**	**74**	**76**
Bonds	0	0	0	0	0	0	60	60	60	60
Commercial banks and other	0	7	22	31	66	40	26	37	14	16
Memo:										
IBRD	1	4	30	33	34	30	29	26	24	23
IDA	0	0	0	1	1	1	1	1	1	1
UNDISBURSED DEBT	**15**	**175**	**246**	**296**	**485**	**383**	**299**	**280**	**230**	**149**
Official creditors	15	172	232	267	384	355	282	264	214	133
Private creditors	0	3	13	29	101	28	17	16	16	16
Memorandum items										
Concessional LDOD	6	65	351	417	441	403	345	354	316	343
Variable rate LDOD	2	150	281	488	802	780	1,333	1,275	1,241	1,000
Public sector LDOD	32	294	762	852	1,148	1,153	1,187	1,152	1,155	889
Private sector LDOD	0	24	148	245	267	246	789	757	736	718

6. CURRENCY COMPOSITION OF LONG-TERM DEBT (PERCENT)

	1970	1980	1990	1994	1995	1996	1997	1998	1999	2000
Deutsche mark	0.0	0.0	6.3	3.7	2.6	2.1	1.3	1.2	0.9	0.8
French franc	0.0	14.2	23.7	27.6	22.7	20.5	18.0	19.0	15.9	18.7
Japanese yen	0.0	0.0	1.0	2.6	1.2	4.5	4.2	4.8	5.1	6.8
Pound sterling	82.2	18.4	8.7	2.6	1.8	1.6	1.4	1.4	1.3	1.6
Swiss franc	0.0	0.0	0.5	0.3	0.2	0.1	0.1	0.2	0.3	0.3
U.S.dollars	0.0	46.0	14.4	22.5	42.3	44.2	52.5	56.3	54.2	44.5
Multiple currency	17.8	13.3	25.1	19.5	14.1	12.7	11.3	5.2	5.1	6.5
Special drawing rights	0.0	0.0	0.0	0.0	0.0	0.0	0.0	0.0	0.0	0.1
All other currencies	0.0	8.1	20.3	21.2	15.1	14.3	11.2	11.9	17.2	20.7

MAURITIUS

(US$ million, unless otherwise indicated)

	1970	1980	1990	1994	1995	1996	1997	1998	1999	2000
7. DEBT RESTRUCTURINGS										
Total amount rescheduled	..	..	0	0	0	0	0	0	0	0
Debt stock rescheduled	..	..	0	0	0	0	0	0	0	0
Principal rescheduled	..	..	0	0	0	0	0	0	0	0
Official	..	..	0	0	0	0	0	0	0	0
Private	..	..	0	0	0	0	0	0	0	0
Interest rescheduled	..	..	0	0	0	0	0	0	0	0
Official	..	..	0	0	0	0	0	0	0	0
Private	..	..	0	0	0	0	0	0	0	0
Debt forgiven	..	..	0	0	0	0	0	0	0	0
Memo: interest forgiven	..	..	0	0	0	0	0	0	0	0
Debt stock reduction	..	..	0	0	0	0	0	0	0	0
of which debt buyback	..	..	0	0	0	0	0	0	0	0
8. DEBT STOCK-FLOW RECONCILIATION										
Total change in debt stocks	..	..	138	374	374	61	654	10	-17	-90
Net flows on debt	-3	104	76	260	312	110	768	-25	30	-35
Net change in interest arrears	..	..	2	0	-1	-1	0	0	0	0
Interest capitalized	..	..	0	0	0	0	0	0	0	0
Debt forgiveness or reduction	..	..	0	0	0	0	0	0	0	0
Cross-currency valuation	..	..	40	32	21	-47	-72	24	-28	-40
Residual	..	..	20	83	41	-1	-42	11	-19	-15
9. AVERAGE TERMS OF NEW COMMITMENTS										
ALL CREDITORS										
Interest (%)	0.0	10.6	6.0	5.4	6.0	4.2	6.7	3.2	4.5	6.4
Maturity (years)	24.2	13.6	17.9	16.0	9.6	16.3	11.0	22.5	13.8	6.1
Grace period (years)	1.7	4.2	6.3	3.3	4.7	3.8	1.0	6.6	1.9	2.7
Grant element (%)	64.6	7.3	26.7	26.9	19.2	33.9	12.9	49.7	26.4	13.8
Official creditors										
Interest (%)	0.0	5.2	6.0	4.0	5.2	4.2	5.8	3.0	3.7	3.9
Maturity (years)	24.2	19.6	17.9	20.4	17.5	16.3	16.9	22.6	21.0	15.7
Grace period (years)	1.7	5.4	6.3	6.4	5.6	3.8	4.0	6.8	4.8	4.7
Grant element (%)	64.6	30.6	26.7	41.3	30.5	33.9	23.2	51.2	41.5	36.5
Private creditors										
Interest (%)	0.0	18.4	0.0	6.6	6.3	0.0	6.9	6.8	4.8	7.5
Maturity (years)	0.0	5.0	0.0	11.9	6.1	0.0	9.8	21.8	11.2	1.9
Grace period (years)	0.0	2.5	0.0	0.4	4.3	0.0	0.5	2.8	0.8	1.9
Grant element (%)	0.0	-26.5	0.0	13.3	14.3	0.0	10.8	20.8	20.9	3.7
Memorandum items										
Commitments	14	111	137	210	559	37	156	50	145	101
Official creditors	14	66	137	102	170	37	26	47	39	31
Private creditors	0	45	0	108	389	0	130	3	106	70

10. CONTRACTUAL OBLIGATIONS ON OUTSTANDING LONG-TERM DEBT

	2001	2002	2003	2004	2005	2006	2007	2008	2009	2010
TOTAL										
Disbursements	56	35	23	16	10	5	2	1	0	0
Principal	121	174	112	710	100	114	81	65	62	57
Interest	112	107	98	93	28	22	16	13	10	7
Official creditors										
Disbursements	40	35	23	16	10	5	2	1	0	0
Principal	56	58	57	56	55	54	51	48	46	41
Interest	24	23	21	19	17	15	12	10	8	6
Bilateral creditors										
Disbursements	18	15	10	6	3	2	1	0	0	0
Principal	28	31	30	30	31	30	28	27	26	24
Interest	13	13	12	10	9	8	7	5	4	3
Multilateral creditors										
Disbursements	22	20	14	10	6	4	2	1	0	0
Principal	27	27	27	26	24	24	23	21	20	18
Interest	11	11	10	9	8	7	6	5	4	3
Private creditors										
Disbursements	16	0	0	0	0	0	0	0	0	0
Principal	65	116	55	654	45	61	30	17	16	15
Interest	88	84	77	74	11	8	4	3	2	1
Commercial banks										
Disbursements	16	0	0	0	0	0	0	0	0	0
Principal	47	97	38	37	29	47	19	8	8	8
Interest	20	17	12	9	7	5	2	1	1	1
Other private										
Disbursements	0	0	0	0	0	0	0	0	0	0
Principal	18	18	17	617	16	14	11	9	8	8
Interest	68	67	66	65	4	3	2	1	1	0

MEXICO

(US$ million, unless otherwise indicated)

	1970	1980	1990	1994	1995	1996	1997	1998	1999	2000
1. SUMMARY DEBT DATA										
TOTAL DEBT STOCKS (EDT)	**6,969**	**57,378**	**104,442**	**140,193**	**166,874**	**157,496**	**148,702**	**161,404**	**167,626**	**150,288**
Long-term debt (LDOD)	**5,967**	**41,215**	**81,809**	**97,011**	**113,745**	**114,378**	**111,754**	**126,703**	**139,090**	**131,356**
Public and publicly guaranteed	3,197	33,915	75,974	79,522	95,158	94,038	84,372	88,472	89,198	81,550
Private nonguaranteed	2,770	7,300	5,835	17,489	18,587	20,340	27,382	38,231	49,893	49,806
Use of IMF credit	**0**	**0**	**6,551**	**3,860**	**15,828**	**13,279**	**9,088**	**8,380**	**4,473**	**0**
Short-term debt	**1,002**	**16,163**	**16,082**	**39,323**	**37,300**	**29,839**	**27,860**	**26,321**	**24,062**	**18,932**
of which interest arrears on LDOD	0	0	0	0	0	0	0	0	0	0
Official creditors	0	0	0	0	0	0	0	0	0	0
Private creditors	0	0	0	0	0	0	0	0	0	0
Memo: principal arrears on LDOD	0	0	0	0	0	0	0	0	0	0
Official creditors	0	0	0	0	0	0	0	0	0	0
Private creditors	0	0	0	0	0	0	0	0	0	0
Memo: export credits	0	0	15,583	26,686	19,603	17,033	14,588	4,042	3,954	3,756
TOTAL DEBT FLOWS										
Disbursements	**1,375**	**11,581**	**14,229**	**16,130**	**44,066**	**31,436**	**29,234**	**28,425**	**35,303**	**34,447**
Long-term debt	1,375	11,581	12,045	16,130	30,778	31,436	29,234	28,425	33,889	33,253
IMF purchases	0	0	2,184	0	13,288	0	0	0	1,414	1,194
Principal repayments	**1,017**	**4,894**	**4,012**	**12,704**	**15,679**	**29,071**	**32,318**	**16,568**	**27,513**	**44,537**
Long-term debt	1,017	4,760	2,821	11,500	14,535	27,019	28,878	15,504	22,417	39,044
IMF repurchases	0	134	1,191	1,204	1,144	2,052	3,439	1,063	5,096	5,493
Net flows on debt	**358**	**14,825**	**17,637**	**6,491**	**26,365**	**-5,097**	**-5,062**	**10,318**	**5,532**	**-15,221**
of which short-term debt	0	8,139	7,420	3,065	-2,022	-7,462	-1,978	-1,539	-2,259	-5,130
Interest payments (INT)	**283**	**6,068**	**7,301**	**9,216**	**11,209**	**11,960**	**11,162**	**11,423**	**12,247**	**13,722**
Long-term debt	283	4,580	5,797	6,535	8,053	8,346	8,448	9,225	10,048	11,677
IMF charges	0	4	522	233	545	651	482	423	276	153
Short-term debt	0	1,484	982	2,448	2,611	2,964	2,231	1,774	1,924	1,892
Net transfers on debt	**75**	**8,757**	**10,336**	**-2,726**	**15,157**	**-17,057**	**-16,224**	**-1,105**	**-6,716**	**-28,942**
Total debt service paid (TDS)	**1,301**	**10,962**	**11,313**	**21,920**	**26,887**	**41,031**	**43,480**	**27,990**	**39,760**	**58,259**
Long-term debt	1,301	9,340	8,619	18,035	22,587	35,365	37,327	24,729	32,464	50,721
IMF repurchases and charges	0	138	1,712	1,437	1,689	2,703	3,922	1,487	5,372	5,646
Short-term debt (interest only)	0	1,484	982	2,448	2,611	2,964	2,231	1,774	1,924	1,892

	1970	1980	1990	1994	1995	1996	1997	1998	1999	2000
2. AGGREGATE NET RESOURCE FLOWS AND NET TRANSFERS (LONG-TERM)										
NET RESOURCE FLOWS	**689**	**8,991**	**12,475**	**20,170**	**26,321**	**17,554**	**15,276**	**25,024**	**24,548**	**11,035**
Net flow of long-term debt (ex. IMF)	358	6,821	9,224	4,630	16,244	4,417	356	12,920	11,472	-5,792
Foreign direct investment (net)	323	2,156	2,634	10,972	9,526	9,185	12,831	11,312	11,915	13,286
Portfolio equity flows	0	0	563	4,521	520	3,922	2,052	730	1,129	3,517
Grants (excluding technical coop.)	8	14	54	47	31	30	37	61	31	23
Memo: technical coop. grants	6	44	81	104	122	132	101	110	105	111
official net resource flows	149	809	4,222	-536	10,383	-7,567	-4,529	-743	-1,677	-502
private net resource flows	540	8,182	8,254	20,706	15,937	25,121	19,806	25,767	26,225	11,537
NET TRANSFERS	**46**	**3,043**	**5,364**	**11,235**	**15,768**	**6,309**	**3,828**	**12,399**	**10,605**	**-4,942**
Interest on long-term debt	283	4,580	5,797	6,535	8,053	8,346	8,448	9,225	10,048	11,677
Profit remittances on FDI	359	1,368	1,314	2,400	2,500	2,900	3,000	3,400	3,895	4,300
Memo: official net transfers	89	495	2,844	-2,522	7,724	-10,093	-6,185	-2,259	-3,231	-2,051
private net transfers	-43	2,548	2,520	13,757	8,044	16,401	10,013	14,658	13,836	-2,890

	1970	1980	1990	1994	1995	1996	1997	1998	1999	2000
3. MAJOR ECONOMIC AGGREGATES										
Gross national income (GNI)	35,091	217,073	254,084	407,764	272,877	318,398	388,294	403,137	466,142	559,765
Exports of goods & services (XGS)	..	24,685	54,570	78,025	96,707	115,156	131,126	140,062	158,509	192,831
of which workers remittances	..	698	2,492	3,475	3,673	4,224	4,865	5,627	5,909	6,573
Imports of goods & services (MGS)	..	35,243	63,504	107,994	98,571	117,791	138,962	156,173	173,238	211,409
International reserves (RES)	756	4,175	10,217	6,441	17,046	19,527	28,852	31,863	31,828	35,577
Current account balance	..	-10,422	-7,451	-29,662	-1,576	-2,328	-7,454	-15,724	-14,324	-18,157

	1970	1980	1990	1994	1995	1996	1997	1998	1999	2000
4. DEBT INDICATORS										
EDT / XGS (%)	..	232.4	191.4	179.7	172.6	136.8	113.4	115.2	105.8	77.9
EDT / GNI (%)	19.9	26.4	41.1	34.4	61.2	49.5	38.3	40.0	36.0	26.9
TDS / XGS (%)	..	44.4	20.7	28.1	27.8	35.6	33.2	20.0	25.1	30.2
INT / XGS (%)	..	24.6	13.4	11.8	11.6	10.4	8.5	8.2	7.7	7.1
INT / GNI (%)	0.8	2.8	2.9	2.3	4.1	3.8	2.9	2.8	2.6	2.5
RES / EDT (%)	10.9	7.3	9.8	4.6	10.2	12.4	19.4	19.7	19.0	23.7
RES / MGS (months)	..	1.4	1.9	0.7	2.1	2.0	2.5	2.5	2.2	2.0
Short-term / EDT (%)	14.4	28.2	15.4	28.1	22.4	19.0	18.7	16.3	14.4	12.6
Concessional / EDT (%)	2.8	0.6	0.8	1.2	0.9	1.0	0.9	0.9	0.8	0.8
Multilateral / EDT (%)	10.7	5.6	13.7	12.2	11.2	11.3	11.1	10.6	10.0	11.5

MEXICO

(US$ million, unless otherwise indicated)

	1970	1980	1990	1994	1995	1996	1997	1998	1999	2000
5. LONG-TERM DEBT										
DEBT OUTSTANDING (LDOD)	**5,967**	**41,215**	**81,809**	**97,011**	**113,745**	**114,378**	**111,754**	**126,703**	**139,090**	**131,356**
Public and publicly guaranteed	**3,197**	**33,915**	**75,974**	**79,522**	**95,158**	**94,038**	**84,372**	**88,472**	**89,198**	**81,550**
Official creditors	1,150	4,481	22,621	27,368	38,995	29,340	22,977	23,054	21,783	20,801
Multilateral	749	3,189	14,303	17,075	18,642	17,733	16,443	17,093	16,690	17,251
Concessional	74	193	60	24	17	11	7	4	2	0
Bilateral	401	1,291	8,318	10,293	20,353	11,607	6,534	5,961	5,093	3,550
Concessional	123	120	822	1,603	1,514	1,516	1,358	1,397	1,376	1,180
Private creditors	2,047	29,434	53,353	52,154	56,162	64,699	61,395	65,418	67,415	60,749
Bonds	386	3,100	40,100	41,743	45,287	54,301	51,674	53,685	56,377	52,182
Commercial banks	1,267	25,637	6,630	6,446	6,529	6,384	6,217	8,822	7,795	5,387
Other private	394	698	6,624	3,965	4,347	4,014	3,504	2,912	3,243	3,180
Private nonguaranteed	**2,770**	**7,300**	**5,835**	**17,489**	**18,587**	**20,340**	**27,382**	**38,231**	**49,893**	**49,806**
Bonds	0	0	150	12,767	13,026	14,104	15,810	16,546	13,700	13,493
Commercial banks and other	2,770	7,300	5,685	4,722	5,562	6,236	11,572	21,685	36,193	36,313
Memo:										
IBRD	582	2,063	11,030	13,038	13,823	12,568	11,356	11,514	11,027	11,444
IDA	0	0	0	0	0	0	0	0	0	0
DISBURSEMENTS	**1,375**	**11,581**	**12,045**	**16,130**	**30,778**	**31,436**	**29,234**	**28,425**	**33,889**	**33,253**
Public and publicly guaranteed	**772**	**9,131**	**9,985**	**8,691**	**23,400**	**22,938**	**15,339**	**13,722**	**9,728**	**10,850**
Official creditors	229	1,081	5,454	2,117	13,424	2,465	1,752	2,189	1,455	2,849
Multilateral	161	642	3,647	1,281	2,669	2,090	1,514	1,901	1,328	2,534
Concessional	37	3	0	0	0	0	0	0	0	0
Bilateral	68	439	1,807	836	10,755	375	237	288	128	315
Concessional	9	17	636	136	10	206	39	19	9	4
Private creditors	543	8,050	4,532	6,574	9,976	20,473	13,587	11,533	8,273	8,001
Bonds	0	236	975	5,088	7,059	18,458	11,195	6,394	5,637	6,826
Commercial banks	432	7,625	2,552	500	1,699	1,072	1,826	4,769	1,820	1,006
Other private	111	189	1,005	985	1,218	943	566	371	817	169
Private nonguaranteed	**603**	**2,450**	**2,060**	**7,439**	**7,379**	**8,498**	**13,895**	**14,703**	**24,161**	**22,403**
Bonds	0	0	150	3,657	843	2,433	3,690	4,998	5,875	3,346
Commercial banks and other	603	2,450	1,910	3,782	6,535	6,065	10,205	9,705	18,285	19,057
Memo:										
IBRD	98	422	3,326	943	1,732	1,051	995	1,283	839	1,748
IDA	0	0	0	0	0	0	0	0	0	0
PRINCIPAL REPAYMENTS	**1,017**	**4,760**	**2,821**	**11,500**	**14,535**	**27,019**	**28,878**	**15,504**	**22,417**	**39,044**
Public and publicly guaranteed	**476**	**4,010**	**2,625**	**6,583**	**9,141**	**20,309**	**21,995**	**11,639**	**9,864**	**16,916**
Official creditors	88	286	1,286	2,700	3,072	10,062	6,319	2,993	3,164	3,374
Multilateral	32	141	1,037	1,423	1,714	1,713	1,625	1,603	1,695	1,817
Concessional	0	12	13	7	7	6	5	3	2	1
Bilateral	56	145	249	1,277	1,358	8,349	4,693	1,391	1,469	1,557
Concessional	9	12	0	20	99	87	80	77	91	106
Private creditors	388	3,724	1,339	3,884	6,069	10,247	15,677	8,645	6,701	13,542
Bonds	16	123	464	1,113	3,534	8,119	12,463	5,173	1,819	9,256
Commercial banks	266	3,445	185	741	1,626	1,000	2,268	2,444	4,329	3,425
Other private	106	156	690	2,029	909	1,128	946	1,028	553	862
Private nonguaranteed	**542**	**750**	**196**	**4,917**	**5,394**	**6,710**	**6,883**	**3,866**	**12,552**	**22,129**
Bonds	0	0	0	50	610	1,328	1,950	3,291	4,061	3,552
Commercial banks and other	542	750	196	4,867	4,784	5,382	4,933	575	8,492	18,577
Memo:										
IBRD	23	89	801	1,065	1,411	1,409	1,311	1,257	1,323	1,330
IDA	0	0	0	0	0	0	0	0	0	0
NET FLOWS ON DEBT	**358**	**6,821**	**9,224**	**4,630**	**16,244**	**4,417**	**356**	**12,920**	**11,472**	**-5,792**
Public and publicly guaranteed	**297**	**5,121**	**7,360**	**2,107**	**14,259**	**2,629**	**-6,657**	**2,083**	**-136**	**-6,065**
Official creditors	141	795	4,168	-583	10,352	-7,597	-4,567	-805	-1,708	-525
Multilateral	129	501	2,610	-142	955	377	-111	298	-368	718
Concessional	37	-9	-13	-7	-7	-6	-5	-3	-2	-1
Bilateral	12	294	1,558	-441	9,398	-7,974	-4,456	-1,103	-1,341	-1,242
Concessional	0	5	635	116	-90	119	-40	-58	-83	-102
Private creditors	156	4,326	3,193	2,690	3,906	10,226	-2,090	2,888	1,572	-5,541
Bonds	-16	112	511	3,975	3,525	10,339	-1,267	1,220	3,818	-2,429
Commercial banks	166	4,180	2,367	-241	73	72	-443	2,325	-2,509	-2,418
Other private	6	33	314	-1,044	309	-185	-380	-657	264	-693
Private nonguaranteed	**61**	**1,700**	**1,864**	**2,523**	**1,985**	**1,788**	**7,012**	**10,837**	**11,608**	**274**
Bonds	0	0	150	3,608	233	1,105	1,740	1,708	1,815	-206
Commercial banks and other	61	1,700	1,714	-1,085	1,752	683	5,272	9,130	9,794	480
Memo:										
IBRD	76	333	2,524	-123	321	-359	-316	26	-484	418
IDA	0	0	0	0	0	0	0	0	0	0

MEXICO

(US$ million, unless otherwise indicated)

	1970	1980	1990	1994	1995	1996	1997	1998	1999	2000
INTEREST PAYMENTS (LINT)	**283**	**4,580**	**5,797**	**6,535**	**8,053**	**8,346**	**8,448**	**9,225**	**10,048**	**11,677**
Public and publicly guaranteed	**216**	**3,880**	**5,215**	**5,177**	**6,329**	**6,431**	**6,293**	**5,971**	**6,189**	**7,250**
Official creditors	60	314	1,378	1,986	2,659	2,526	1,655	1,516	1,554	1,550
Multilateral	39	236	1,005	1,232	1,291	1,314	1,163	1,143	1,213	1,276
Concessional	2	7	2	1	1	1	0	0	0	0
Bilateral	21	78	373	755	1,368	1,212	492	373	341	274
Concessional	4	5	8	51	68	55	50	44	46	44
Private creditors	156	3,566	3,838	3,190	3,670	3,905	4,638	4,455	4,635	5,700
Bonds	27	252	1,112	2,611	2,906	3,248	3,948	3,825	3,950	4,308
Commercial banks	106	3,261	2,195	331	436	378	434	426	510	771
Other private	24	52	531	249	328	280	256	205	175	621
Private nonguaranteed	**67**	**700**	**582**	**1,358**	**1,723**	**1,914**	**2,156**	**3,255**	**3,859**	**4,427**
Bonds	0	0	0	826	1,054	1,096	1,251	1,494	1,107	1,224
Commercial banks and other	67	700	582	533	670	818	904	1,761	2,752	3,203
Memo:										
IBRD	31	166	751	924	961	962	791	767	832	890
IDA	0	0	0	0	0	0	0	0	0	0
NET TRANSFERS ON DEBT	**75**	**2,241**	**3,427**	**-1,905**	**8,191**	**-3,929**	**-8,093**	**3,695**	**1,425**	**-17,468**
Public and publicly guaranteed	**81**	**1,241**	**2,145**	**-3,069**	**7,930**	**-3,802**	**-12,949**	**-3,888**	**-6,325**	**-13,315**
Official creditors	81	481	2,790	-2,569	7,693	-10,123	-6,222	-2,321	-3,262	-2,075
Multilateral	90	264	1,605	-1,373	-336	-937	-1,274	-845	-1,581	-558
Concessional	35	-16	-15	-8	-8	-6	-5	-3	-2	-1
Bilateral	-9	216	1,185	-1,196	8,029	-9,186	-4,948	-1,476	-1,681	-1,517
Concessional	-4	0	627	65	-158	63	-90	-101	-129	-146
Private creditors	-1	760	-645	-500	237	6,321	-6,727	-1,567	-3,063	-11,241
Bonds	-42	-140	-601	1,364	618	7,091	-5,215	-2,604	-133	-6,737
Commercial banks	60	919	172	-572	-363	-306	-877	1,899	-3,019	-3,190
Other private	-18	-19	-217	-1,293	-19	-465	-636	-862	89	-1,314
Private nonguaranteed	**-6**	**1,000**	**1,282**	**1,164**	**261**	**-126**	**4,857**	**7,583**	**7,750**	**-4,153**
Bonds	0	0	150	2,782	-821	9	489	214	708	-1,430
Commercial banks and other	-6	1,000	1,132	-1,618	1,082	-136	4,368	7,369	7,042	-2,723
Memo:										
IBRD	45	167	1,773	-1,046	-641	-1,321	-1,107	-741	-1,316	-472
IDA	0	0	0	0	0	0	0	0	0	0
DEBT SERVICE (LTDS)	**1,301**	**9,340**	**8,619**	**18,035**	**22,587**	**35,365**	**37,327**	**24,729**	**32,464**	**50,721**
Public and publicly guaranteed	**692**	**7,890**	**7,841**	**11,760**	**15,470**	**26,740**	**28,288**	**17,609**	**16,053**	**24,166**
Official creditors	148	601	2,664	4,686	5,731	12,588	7,974	4,509	4,718	4,923
Multilateral	71	378	2,042	2,654	3,005	3,027	2,789	2,746	2,908	3,092
Concessional	2	18	15	8	8	6	5	3	2	1
Bilateral	77	223	622	2,032	2,726	9,561	5,185	1,764	1,809	1,832
Concessional	14	16	9	71	167	143	130	120	137	150
Private creditors	544	7,289	5,177	7,074	9,739	14,152	20,314	13,100	11,336	19,242
Bonds	42	376	1,576	3,724	6,440	11,367	16,410	8,998	5,770	13,563
Commercial banks	372	6,706	2,380	1,072	2,062	1,377	2,702	2,870	4,838	4,196
Other private	130	208	1,221	2,278	1,237	1,408	1,202	1,233	728	1,483
Private nonguaranteed	**609**	**1,450**	**778**	**6,275**	**7,117**	**8,624**	**9,039**	**7,120**	**16,411**	**26,556**
Bonds	0	0	0	876	1,664	2,424	3,201	4,784	5,168	4,776
Commercial banks and other	609	1,450	778	5,399	5,453	6,201	5,838	2,336	11,243	21,780
Memo:										
IBRD	54	255	1,553	1,989	2,372	2,372	2,102	2,024	2,155	2,220
IDA	0	0	0	0	0	0	0	0	0	0
UNDISBURSED DEBT	**557**	**4,817**	**8,114**	**13,145**	**12,774**	**11,968**	**11,479**	**11,415**	**10,943**	**7,542**
Official creditors	439	2,976	5,140	8,338	8,674	6,089	5,922	5,688	7,333	5,361
Private creditors	118	1,841	2,974	4,807	4,100	5,879	5,558	5,727	3,611	2,181
Memorandum items										
Concessional LDOD	196	313	883	1,628	1,532	1,527	1,364	1,401	1,378	1,180
Variable rate LDOD	2,951	31,271	40,382	49,267	64,415	61,902	56,637	71,080	82,064	75,772
Public sector LDOD	3,165	33,249	75,595	79,068	94,727	93,634	84,168	88,295	88,593	80,954
Private sector LDOD	2,801	7,966	6,214	17,942	19,018	20,744	27,586	38,409	50,497	50,402

6. CURRENCY COMPOSITION OF LONG-TERM DEBT (PERCENT)

	1970	1980	1990	1994	1995	1996	1997	1998	1999	2000
Deutsche mark	11.2	4.3	3.7	3.7	3.0	3.4	4.7	4.7	3.6	1.6
French franc	7.7	1.2	3.8	3.1	2.7	2.4	2.3	2.2	1.7	0.8
Japanese yen	0.5	1.4	6.3	9.1	8.2	8.3	8.6	8.1	8.4	7.6
Pound sterling	1.1	0.5	1.4	0.9	0.7	0.7	1.3	0.9	0.8	0.2
Swiss franc	3.4	2.0	0.6	0.4	0.4	0.3	0.3	0.3	0.2	0.0
U.S.dollars	51.2	78.7	64.3	60.5	65.7	67.3	64.6	75.9	77.7	85.0
Multiple currency	21.9	9.9	18.6	20.8	18.1	16.5	15.8	4.6	4.1	3.8
Special drawing rights	0.0	0.0	0.0	0.0	0.0	0.0	0.0	0.0	0.0	0.0
All other currencies	3.0	2.0	1.3	1.5	1.2	1.1	2.4	3.3	3.5	1.0

MEXICO

(US$ million, unless otherwise indicated)

	1970	1980	1990	1994	1995	1996	1997	1998	1999	2000
7. DEBT RESTRUCTURINGS										
Total amount rescheduled	..	..	36,950	0	0	0	0	0	0	0
Debt stock rescheduled	..	..	36,100	0	0	0	0	0	0	0
Principal rescheduled	..	..	570	0	0	0	0	0	0	0
Official	..	..	382	0	0	0	0	0	0	0
Private	..	..	188	0	0	0	0	0	0	0
Interest rescheduled	..	..	204	0	0	0	0	0	0	0
Official	..	..	132	0	0	0	0	0	0	0
Private	..	..	72	0	0	0	0	0	0	0
Debt forgiven	..	..	0	0	0	0	0	0	0	0
Memo: interest forgiven	..	..	0	0	0	0	0	0	0	0
Debt stock reduction	..	..	8,145	267	306	3,181	0	0	0	7,122
of which debt buyback	..	..	0	51	13	2,420	0	0	0	6,644
8. DEBT STOCK-FLOW RECONCILIATION										
Total change in debt stocks	..	..	10,601	8,467	26,680	-9,378	-8,794	12,702	6,222	-17,338
Net flows on debt	358	14,825	17,637	6,491	26,365	-5,097	-5,062	10,318	5,532	-15,221
Net change in interest arrears	..	..	0	0	0	0	0	0	0	0
Interest capitalized	..	..	204	0	0	0	0	0	0	0
Debt forgiveness or reduction	..	..	-8,145	-216	-293	-761	0	0	0	-478
Cross-currency valuation	..	..	3,254	2,511	696	-3,403	-3,805	2,031	-555	-1,803
Residual	..	..	-2,349	-319	-88	-117	73	353	1,245	164
9. AVERAGE TERMS OF NEW COMMITMENTS										
ALL CREDITORS										
Interest (%)	8.1	11.3	8.6	5.7	8.0	7.7	7.3	6.8	7.8	8.3
Maturity (years)	11.6	9.9	13.4	8.9	7.1	8.1	9.8	8.2	31.8	9.8
Grace period (years)	3.4	4.3	5.4	3.7	2.7	6.5	6.9	5.2	7.1	8.3
Grant element (%)	9.9	-5.7	7.3	16.0	6.6	6.2	12.0	11.5	9.4	6.1
Official creditors										
Interest (%)	6.7	8.0	7.8	6.9	9.1	6.5	7.1	6.4	5.7	7.0
Maturity (years)	18.5	15.3	15.6	14.6	9.2	14.1	14.5	14.3	14.9	12.7
Grace period (years)	4.0	3.3	4.5	4.3	2.9	3.9	4.4	3.6	6.7	3.5
Grant element (%)	19.4	10.1	12.3	16.4	5.5	18.1	14.8	17.9	25.7	14.5
Private creditors										
Interest (%)	8.9	12.6	9.4	5.2	6.2	7.8	7.3	6.9	8.6	8.5
Maturity (years)	7.1	7.7	11.4	6.2	3.6	7.9	9.2	7.0	38.1	9.3
Grace period (years)	3.1	4.7	6.1	3.4	2.5	6.6	7.3	5.5	7.3	9.2
Grant element (%)	3.6	-12.0	2.9	15.7	8.4	5.7	11.6	10.3	3.4	4.6
Memorandum items										
Commitments	858	7,632	12,485	10,844	24,581	23,720	15,298	14,392	11,920	8,782
Official creditors	338	2,187	5,918	3,518	15,132	865	1,903	2,350	3,239	1,382
Private creditors	520	5,445	6,567	7,326	9,450	22,855	13,394	12,043	8,682	7,400

10. CONTRACTUAL OBLIGATIONS ON OUTSTANDING LONG-TERM DEBT

	2001	2002	2003	2004	2005	2006	2007	2008	2009	2010
TOTAL										
Disbursements	4,018	1,747	831	440	262	146	82	13	1	0
Principal	24,372	17,091	13,088	12,560	15,318	6,907	6,403	5,155	6,753	4,350
Interest	11,264	8,872	7,810	6,721	5,681	4,300	3,767	3,259	2,780	2,221
Official creditors										
Disbursements	2,152	1,484	795	431	261	145	81	12	1	0
Principal	3,136	2,772	2,548	2,432	2,364	2,317	1,838	1,556	2,325	1,136
Interest	1,568	1,437	1,285	1,131	971	807	649	525	425	280
Bilateral creditors										
Disbursements	866	293	91	33	5	0	0	0	0	0
Principal	1,259	795	647	523	370	310	121	109	95	137
Interest	227	172	123	88	59	40	26	22	19	15
Multilateral creditors										
Disbursements	1,286	1,190	704	399	256	145	81	12	1	0
Principal	1,877	1,977	1,901	1,908	1,994	2,006	1,718	1,447	2,230	999
Interest	1,341	1,266	1,162	1,044	911	767	622	503	406	265
Private creditors										
Disbursements	1,867	264	36	9	2	1	1	1	1	0
Principal	21,236	14,318	10,540	10,128	12,954	4,590	4,565	3,599	4,428	3,214
Interest	9,696	7,435	6,525	5,590	4,710	3,494	3,119	2,734	2,355	1,941
Commercial banks										
Disbursements	264	75	7	2	2	1	1	1	1	0
Principal	1,876	1,356	887	465	373	299	129	28	293	17
Interest	505	213	154	115	83	59	42	34	31	3
Other private										
Disbursements	1,603	188	29	7	0	0	0	0	0	0
Principal	19,359	12,962	9,654	9,664	12,581	4,292	4,436	3,571	4,135	3,197
Interest	9,191	7,222	6,371	5,474	4,627	3,435	3,077	2,700	2,324	1,938

MOLDOVA

(US$ million, unless otherwise indicated)

	1970	1980	1990	1994	1995	1996	1997	1998	1999	2000
1. SUMMARY DEBT DATA										
TOTAL DEBT STOCKS (EDT)	..	..	..	**503**	**695**	**848**	**1,082**	**1,071**	**1,025**	**1,233**
Long-term debt (LDOD)	..	..	..	**330**	**459**	**573**	**845**	**873**	**834**	**1,051**
Public and publicly guaranteed	..	..	..	326	450	555	801	801	723	854
Private nonguaranteed	..	..	..	4	10	19	44	72	111	197
Use of IMF credit	..	..	..	**164**	**230**	**248**	**233**	**177**	**175**	**154**
Short-term debt	..	..	..	**8**	**6**	**27**	**4**	**21**	**16**	**28**
of which interest arrears on LDOD	..	..	..	7	5	1	0	14	15	22
Official creditors	..	..	..	7	5	1	0	5	7	1
Private creditors	..	..	..	0	0	0	0	9	8	22
Memo: principal arrears on LDOD	..	..	..	18	42	0	15	61	105	35
Official creditors	..	..	..	18	42	0	15	32	74	5
Private creditors	..	..	..	0	0	0	0	29	31	30
Memo: export credits	..	..	..	0	8	50	54	6	17	15
TOTAL DEBT FLOWS										
Disbursements	..	..	..	**209**	**230**	**201**	**368**	**105**	**246**	**172**
Long-term debt	..	..	..	138	166	169	347	105	177	160
IMF purchases	..	..	..	71	64	33	21	0	68	12
Principal repayments	..	..	..	**5**	**41**	**49**	**82**	**147**	**153**	**80**
Long-term debt	..	..	..	5	41	41	62	83	87	56
IMF repurchases	..	..	..	0	0	7	20	64	65	25
Net flows on debt	..	..	..	**205**	**189**	**178**	**263**	**-39**	**87**	**96**
of which short-term debt	..	..	..	1	0	25	-22	4	-6	4
Interest payments (INT)	..	..	..	**9**	**29**	**36**	**51**	**55**	**58**	**55**
Long-term debt	..	..	..	4	19	24	40	45	50	47
IMF charges	..	..	..	5	10	10	11	10	8	8
Short-term debt	..	..	..	0	0	1	0	0	0	0
Net transfers on debt	..	..	..	**196**	**159**	**142**	**212**	**-94**	**29**	**41**
Total debt service paid (TDS)	..	..	..	**14**	**71**	**84**	**133**	**202**	**211**	**135**
Long-term debt	..	..	..	9	61	65	102	128	138	102
IMF repurchases and charges	..	..	..	5	10	18	31	74	73	33
Short-term debt (interest only)	..	..	..	0	0	1	0	0	0	0
2. AGGREGATE NET RESOURCE FLOWS AND NET TRANSFERS (LONG-TERM)										
NET RESOURCE FLOWS	..	..	..	**177**	**150**	**151**	**372**	**127**	**146**	**269**
Net flow of long-term debt (ex. IMF)	..	..	..	133	124	128	285	22	90	104
Foreign direct investment (net)	..	..	..	12	26	24	76	86	34	128
Portfolio equity flows	..	..	..	0	0	0	0	0	0	0
Grants (excluding technical coop.)	..	..	..	32	0	0	12	20	23	37
Memo: technical coop. grants	..	..	..	1	0	0	16	18	45	44
official net resource flows	..	..	..	161	100	38	63	61	110	60
private net resource flows	..	..	..	16	50	114	309	67	36	209
NET TRANSFERS	..	..	..	**174**	**131**	**125**	**329**	**78**	**92**	**220**
Interest on long-term debt	..	..	..	4	19	24	40	45	50	47
Profit remittances on FDI	..	..	..	0	0	2	3	5	4	3
Memo: official net transfers	..	..	..	158	81	15	44	33	90	38
private net transfers	..	..	..	16	50	110	286	45	2	182
3. MAJOR ECONOMIC AGGREGATES										
Gross national income (GNI)	..	..	..	2,706	3,064	1,750	1,977	1,739	1,207	1,357
Exports of goods & services (XGS)	..	..	..	662	899	1,031	1,191	931	733	811
of which workers remittances	..	..	..	..	1	3	1	1	1	3
Imports of goods & services (MGS)	..	..	..	777	1,038	1,293	1,519	1,330	865	1,085
International reserves (RES)	..	..	..	180	257	312	366	144	186	230
Current account balance	..	..	..	-82	-85	-192	-275	-335	-47	-121
4. DEBT INDICATORS										
EDT / XGS (%)	..	..	..	75.9	77.4	82.2	90.9	115.0	139.8	152.0
EDT / GNI (%)	..	..	..	18.6	22.7	48.4	54.7	61.6	84.9	90.9
TDS / XGS (%)	..	..	..	2.1	7.9	8.2	11.2	21.7	28.8	16.7
INT / XGS (%)	..	..	..	1.3	3.3	3.5	4.3	5.9	7.9	6.8
INT / GNI (%)	..	..	..	0.3	1.0	2.1	2.6	3.2	4.8	4.1
RES / EDT (%)	..	..	..	35.8	37.0	36.8	33.8	13.4	18.1	18.7
RES / MGS (months)	..	..	..	2.8	3.0	2.9	2.9	1.3	2.6	2.6
Short-term / EDT (%)	..	..	..	1.6	0.9	3.2	0.4	2.0	1.6	2.3
Concessional / EDT (%)	..	..	..	9.4	14.6	12.9	13.0	14.1	18.4	16.7
Multilateral / EDT (%)	..	..	..	32.4	31.1	29.8	26.7	31.0	38.6	32.8

MOLDOVA

(US$ million, unless otherwise indicated)

	1970	1980	1990	1994	1995	1996	1997	1998	1999	2000
5. LONG-TERM DEBT										
DEBT OUTSTANDING (LDOD)	..	..	..	**330**	**459**	**573**	**845**	**873**	**834**	**1,051**
Public and publicly guaranteed	..	..	..	**326**	**450**	**555**	**801**	**801**	**723**	**854**
Official creditors	..	..	..	326	430	456	480	525	598	535
Multilateral	..	..	..	163	217	253	289	332	395	405
Concessional	..	..	..	0	0	0	35	38	77	104
Bilateral	..	..	..	164	214	203	191	193	203	131
Concessional	..	..	..	47	101	109	106	113	111	102
Private creditors	..	..	..	0	19	99	322	276	125	319
Bonds	..	..	..	0	0	0	75	75	75	75
Commercial banks	..	..	..	0	4	84	78	32	30	13
Other private	..	..	..	0	15	15	169	169	20	232
Private nonguaranteed	..	..	..	**4**	**10**	**19**	**44**	**72**	**111**	**197**
Bonds	..	..	..	0	0	0	0	0	0	0
Commercial banks and other	..	..	..	4	10	19	44	72	111	197
Memo:										
IBRD	..	..	..	99	152	142	135	169	199	191
IDA	..	..	..	0	0	0	35	38	77	103
DISBURSEMENTS	..	..	..	**138**	**166**	**169**	**347**	**105**	**177**	**160**
Public and publicly guaranteed	..	..	..	**134**	**159**	**156**	**307**	**62**	**111**	**50**
Official creditors	..	..	..	134	139	75	68	60	102	48
Multilateral	..	..	..	99	81	52	60	46	86	46
Concessional	..	..	..	0	0	0	35	2	39	31
Bilateral	..	..	..	35	58	23	8	14	16	1
Concessional	..	..	..	28	58	13	0	10	0	0
Private creditors	..	..	..	0	19	81	240	2	8	2
Bonds	..	..	..	0	0	0	75	0	0	0
Commercial banks	..	..	..	0	4	81	22	2	8	0
Other private	..	..	..	0	15	0	143	0	0	2
Private nonguaranteed	..	..	..	**4**	**7**	**13**	**40**	**43**	**67**	**110**
Bonds	..	..	..	0	0	0	0	0	0	0
Commercial banks and other	..	..	..	4	7	13	40	43	67	110
Memo:										
IBRD	..	..	..	67	50	0	5	27	35	6
IDA	..	..	..	0	0	0	35	2	39	30
PRINCIPAL REPAYMENTS	..	..	..	**5**	**41**	**41**	**62**	**83**	**87**	**56**
Public and publicly guaranteed	..	..	..	**5**	**39**	**38**	**49**	**68**	**53**	**27**
Official creditors	..	..	..	5	39	37	16	19	15	24
Multilateral	..	..	..	0	35	1	1	3	10	19
Concessional	..	..	..	0	0	0	0	0	0	0
Bilateral	..	..	..	5	4	36	15	17	5	5
Concessional	..	..	..	0	0	0	0	7	3	5
Private creditors	..	..	..	0	0	1	33	49	38	3
Bonds	..	..	..	0	0	0	0	0	0	0
Commercial banks	..	..	..	0	0	1	25	49	9	0
Other private	..	..	..	0	0	0	8	0	30	3
Private nonguaranteed	..	..	..	**0**	**2**	**3**	**13**	**15**	**34**	**29**
Bonds	..	..	..	0	0	0	0	0	0	0
Commercial banks and other	..	..	..	0	2	3	13	15	34	29
Memo:										
IBRD	..	..	..	0	0	0	0	1	4	5
IDA	..	..	..	0	0	0	0	0	0	0
NET FLOWS ON DEBT	..	..	..	**133**	**124**	**128**	**285**	**22**	**90**	**104**
Public and publicly guaranteed	..	..	..	**129**	**119**	**118**	**259**	**-6**	**57**	**23**
Official creditors	..	..	..	129	100	38	52	41	87	23
Multilateral	..	..	..	99	46	51	59	44	77	27
Concessional	..	..	..	0	0	0	35	2	39	31
Bilateral	..	..	..	30	54	-13	-7	-3	11	-4
Concessional	..	..	..	28	58	13	0	3	-3	-5
Private creditors	..	..	..	0	19	80	207	-47	-30	-1
Bonds	..	..	..	0	0	0	75	0	0	0
Commercial banks	..	..	..	0	4	80	-3	-47	-1	0
Other private	..	..	..	0	15	0	135	0	-30	-1
Private nonguaranteed	..	..	..	**4**	**5**	**10**	**26**	**27**	**32**	**82**
Bonds	..	..	..	0	0	0	0	0	0	0
Commercial banks and other	..	..	..	4	5	10	26	27	32	82
Memo:										
IBRD	..	..	..	67	50	0	5	26	31	1
IDA	..	..	..	0	0	0	35	2	39	30

MOLDOVA

(US$ million, unless otherwise indicated)

	1970	1980	1990	1994	1995	1996	1997	1998	1999	2000
INTEREST PAYMENTS (LINT)	..	..	..	**4**	**19**	**24**	**40**	**45**	**50**	**47**
Public and publicly guaranteed	..	..	..	**4**	**19**	**24**	**38**	**42**	**46**	**40**
Official creditors	..	..	..	4	19	22	20	28	20	23
Multilateral	..	..	..	4	11	15	14	25	16	18
Concessional	..	..	..	0	0	0	0	0	0	1
Bilateral	..	..	..	0	8	8	6	4	4	5
Concessional	..	..	..	0	2	2	3	3	3	3
Private creditors	..	..	..	0	0	1	19	14	26	17
Bonds	..	..	..	0	0	0	4	7	7	7
Commercial banks	..	..	..	0	0	1	6	3	3	0
Other private	..	..	..	0	0	1	9	3	15	9
Private nonguaranteed	..	..	..	**0**	**0**	**1**	**2**	**3**	**4**	**7**
Bonds	..	..	..	0	0	0	0	0	0	0
Commercial banks and other	..	..	..	0	0	1	2	3	4	7
Memo:										
IBRD	..	..	..	4	8	10	9	9	11	11
IDA	..	..	..	0	0	0	0	0	0	1
NET TRANSFERS ON DEBT	..	..	..	**129**	**105**	**103**	**245**	**-23**	**40**	**58**
Public and publicly guaranteed	..	..	..	**125**	**100**	**94**	**220**	**-48**	**11**	**-17**
Official creditors	..	..	..	125	81	15	32	13	67	1
Multilateral	..	..	..	95	35	36	45	19	61	9
Concessional	..	..	..	0	0	0	35	2	39	30
Bilateral	..	..	..	30	46	-21	-13	-6	7	-8
Concessional	..	..	..	28	56	11	-3	1	-6	-8
Private creditors	..	..	..	0	19	79	188	-60	-56	-18
Bonds	..	..	..	0	0	0	71	-7	-7	-7
Commercial banks	..	..	..	0	4	80	-10	-50	-4	0
Other private	..	..	..	0	15	-1	126	-3	-45	-10
Private nonguaranteed	..	..	..	**4**	**5**	**9**	**25**	**25**	**28**	**75**
Bonds	..	..	..	0	0	0	0	0	0	0
Commercial banks and other	..	..	..	4	5	9	25	25	28	75
Memo:										
IBRD	..	..	..	64	42	-10	-4	17	20	-10
IDA	..	..	..	0	0	0	35	2	39	30
DEBT SERVICE (LTDS)	..	..	..	**9**	**61**	**65**	**102**	**128**	**138**	**102**
Public and publicly guaranteed	..	..	..	**9**	**58**	**62**	**87**	**110**	**99**	**67**
Official creditors	..	..	..	9	58	60	36	48	35	47
Multilateral	..	..	..	4	46	16	14	27	26	37
Concessional	..	..	..	0	0	0	0	0	0	1
Bilateral	..	..	..	5	12	44	21	20	9	10
Concessional	..	..	..	0	2	2	3	9	6	8
Private creditors	..	..	..	0	0	2	51	62	64	20
Bonds	..	..	..	0	0	0	4	7	7	7
Commercial banks	..	..	..	0	0	1	31	52	12	0
Other private	..	..	..	0	0	1	16	3	45	12
Private nonguaranteed	..	..	..	**0**	**2**	**4**	**15**	**18**	**39**	**35**
Bonds	..	..	..	0	0	0	0	0	0	0
Commercial banks and other	..	..	..	0	2	4	15	18	39	35
Memo:										
IBRD	..	..	..	4	8	10	9	10	15	16
IDA	..	..	..	0	0	0	0	0	0	1
UNDISBURSED DEBT	..	..	..	**184**	**211**	**398**	**271**	**277**	**203**	**144**
Official creditors	..	..	..	175	193	208	229	236	171	117
Private creditors	..	..	..	8	18	191	42	41	32	26
Memorandum items										
Concessional LDOD	..	..	..	47	101	109	140	151	188	206
Variable rate LDOD	..	..	..	282	390	466	466	480	530	527
Public sector LDOD	..	..	..	326	450	550	778	783	700	833
Private sector LDOD	..	..	..	4	10	23	68	91	134	218

6. CURRENCY COMPOSITION OF LONG-TERM DEBT (PERCENT)

	1970	1980	1990	1994	1995	1996	1997	1998	1999	2000
Deutsche mark	..	..	..	0.0	1.9	7.5	5.7	6.2	6.9	5.3
French franc	..	..	..	0.0	0.0	0.0	0.0	0.0	0.0	0.0
Japanese yen	..	..	..	0.0	8.4	6.0	3.7	4.2	4.9	3.4
Pound sterling	..	..	..	0.0	0.0	0.0	0.0	0.0	0.0	0.0
Swiss franc	..	..	..	0.0	0.0	0.0	0.0	0.0	0.0	0.0
U.S.dollars	..	..	..	22.8	22.8	47.2	65.4	60.0	56.3	66.5
Multiple currency	..	..	..	30.3	33.9	25.5	16.9	20.8	23.5	18.7
Special drawing rights	..	..	..	0.0	0.0	0.0	0.0	0.0	0.0	0.0
All other currencies	..	..	..	46.9	33.0	13.8	8.3	8.8	8.4	6.1

MOLDOVA

(US$ million, unless otherwise indicated)

	1970	1980	1990	1994	1995	1996	1997	1998	1999	2000
7. DEBT RESTRUCTURINGS										
Total amount rescheduled	..	..	..	0	0	119	19	0	0	244
Debt stock rescheduled	..	..	..	0	0	0	0	0	0	19
Principal rescheduled	..	..	..	0	0	112	0	0	0	92
Official	..	..	..	0	0	112	0	0	0	76
Private	..	..	..	0	0	0	0	0	0	16
Interest rescheduled	..	..	..	0	0	7	0	0	0	5
Official	..	..	..	0	0	7	0	0	0	5
Private	..	..	..	0	0	0	0	0	0	0
Debt forgiven	..	..	..	0	0	0	0	0	119	0
Memo: interest forgiven	..	..	..	0	0	0	0	0	0	0
Debt stock reduction	..	..	..	0	0	0	0	0	3	0
of which debt buyback	..	..	..	0	0	0	0	0	0	0
8. DEBT STOCK-FLOW RECONCILIATION										
Total change in debt stocks	..	..	..	225	193	153	235	-12	-46	208
Net flows on debt	..	..	..	205	189	178	263	-39	87	96
Net change in interest arrears	..	..	..	6	-2	-4	0	14	1	8
Interest capitalized	..	..	..	0	0	7	0	0	0	5
Debt forgiveness or reduction	..	..	..	0	0	0	0	0	-123	0
Cross-currency valuation	..	..	..	-46	-9	-37	-46	-5	-18	-32
Residual	..	..	..	60	15	9	17	19	7	131
9. AVERAGE TERMS OF NEW COMMITMENTS										
ALL CREDITORS										
Interest (%)	..	..	..	5.6	6.9	7.1	6.1	5.7	0.5	1.1
Maturity (years)	..	..	..	16.9	9.7	9.1	17.8	17.8	34.6	35.4
Grace period (years)	..	..	..	5.4	3.0	3.0	6.3	5.5	10.1	9.4
Grant element (%)	..	..	..	27.8	13.0	11.8	29.8	31.7	80.7	74.8
Official creditors										
Interest (%)	..	..	..	5.5	6.9	6.2	3.8	5.7	0.5	0.4
Maturity (years)	..	..	..	17.2	10.5	16.8	26.6	17.8	34.6	39.7
Grace period (years)	..	..	..	5.4	3.2	5.4	7.5	5.5	10.1	10.2
Grant element (%)	..	..	..	28.4	14.0	22.9	48.9	31.7	80.7	83.4
Private creditors										
Interest (%)	..	..	..	7.5	7.0	7.5	9.3	0.0	0.0	5.9
Maturity (years)	..	..	..	10.0	5.2	5.3	5.4	0.0	0.0	3.2
Grace period (years)	..	..	..	4.5	1.5	1.9	4.6	0.0	0.0	3.2
Grant element (%)	..	..	..	11.4	7.7	6.4	2.7	0.0	0.0	10.4
Memorandum items										
Commitments	..	..	..	222	181	385	223	59	66	20
Official creditors	..	..	..	214	153	125	131	59	66	18
Private creditors	..	..	..	8	28	260	92	0	0	2

10. CONTRACTUAL OBLIGATIONS ON OUTSTANDING LONG-TERM DEBT

	2001	2002	2003	2004	2005	2006	2007	2008	2009	2010
TOTAL										
Disbursements	37	31	20	13	8	5	3	1	1	0
Principal	88	183	111	98	96	81	48	48	45	43
Interest	66	56	45	39	32	25	20	18	15	12
Official creditors										
Disbursements	37	31	20	13	8	5	3	1	1	0
Principal	42	51	52	50	42	32	30	30	31	31
Interest	26	24	22	19	17	15	13	11	9	8
Bilateral creditors										
Disbursements	0	0	0	0	0	0	0	0	0	0
Principal	12	13	13	13	13	6	6	6	5	5
Interest	5	4	4	3	2	2	2	2	1	1
Multilateral creditors										
Disbursements	36	31	20	13	8	5	3	1	1	0
Principal	31	38	40	38	29	26	24	25	26	25
Interest	21	20	18	16	14	13	11	9	8	6
Private creditors										
Disbursements	0	0	0	0	0	0	0	0	0	0
Principal	46	133	59	48	54	49	18	18	14	12
Interest	40	32	23	20	15	10	8	7	5	4
Commercial banks										
Disbursements	0	0	0	0	0	0	0	0	0	0
Principal	2	2	2	2	1	1	1	1	0	0
Interest	1	1	0	0	0	0	0	0	0	0
Other private										
Disbursements	0	0	0	0	0	0	0	0	0	0
Principal	44	131	57	46	54	48	17	17	14	12
Interest	39	32	22	20	15	10	8	7	5	4

MONGOLIA

(US$ million, unless otherwise indicated)

	1970	1980	1990	1994	1995	1996	1997	1998	1999	2000
1. SUMMARY DEBT DATA										
TOTAL DEBT STOCKS (EDT)	..	..	..	**461.3**	**525.5**	**531.3**	**607.7**	**710.6**	**890.9**	**858.8**
Long-term debt (LDOD)	..	..	..	**400.5**	**464.9**	**481.0**	**532.6**	**631.7**	**816.3**	**794.8**
Public and publicly guaranteed	..	..	..	400.5	464.9	481.0	532.6	631.7	816.3	794.8
Private nonguaranteed	..	..	..	0.0	0.0	0.0	0.0	0.0	0.0	0.0
Use of IMF credit	**0.0**	**0.0**	**0.0**	**55.3**	**47.0**	**43.6**	**47.6**	**48.3**	**51.4**	**50.3**
Short-term debt	..	..	..	**5.5**	**13.7**	**6.8**	**27.5**	**30.6**	**23.2**	**13.7**
of which interest arrears on LDOD	..	..	..	2.5	2.5	2.5	2.5	2.5	2.6	2.6
Official creditors	..	..	..	2.1	2.0	2.0	2.0	2.0	2.1	2.1
Private creditors	..	..	..	0.4	0.5	0.5	0.5	0.5	0.5	0.5
Memo: principal arrears on LDOD	..	..	..	16.0	3.9	4.1	4.8	4.9	4.6	4.5
Official creditors	..	..	..	13.5	0.0	0.0	0.0	0.0	0.0	0.0
Private creditors	..	..	..	2.6	3.9	4.1	4.8	4.9	4.6	4.5
Memo: export credits	..	..	..	63.0	50.7	39.1	51.6	43.8	13.4	5.4
TOTAL DEBT FLOWS										
Disbursements	..	..	..	**94.8**	**98.6**	**89.0**	**152.4**	**84.8**	**168.1**	**62.3**
Long-term debt	..	..	..	73.5	98.6	80.9	144.8	84.8	160.0	54.5
IMF purchases	0.0	0.0	0.0	21.3	0.0	8.1	7.7	0.0	8.1	7.8
Principal repayments	..	..	..	**33.7**	**41.6**	**44.1**	**54.1**	**25.9**	**15.7**	**18.7**
Long-term debt	..	..	..	33.7	32.1	34.1	53.2	24.6	11.9	12.3
IMF repurchases	0.0	0.0	0.0	0.0	9.5	10.0	0.9	1.3	3.8	6.4
Net flows on debt	..	..	..	**51.9**	**65.2**	**38.0**	**119.0**	**62.0**	**144.9**	**34.1**
of which short-term debt	..	..	..	-9.2	8.2	-6.9	20.7	3.1	-7.5	-9.5
Interest payments (INT)	..	..	..	**9.9**	**10.1**	**8.8**	**12.4**	**8.6**	**10.5**	**10.5**
Long-term debt	..	..	..	8.3	8.6	8.1	11.5	6.9	8.9	9.5
IMF charges	0.0	0.0	0.0	1.1	1.1	0.5	0.2	0.2	0.3	0.3
Short-term debt	..	..	..	0.5	0.4	0.2	0.6	1.5	1.3	0.8
Net transfers on debt	..	..	..	**41.9**	**55.0**	**29.2**	**106.6**	**53.4**	**134.4**	**23.6**
Total debt service paid (TDS)	..	..	..	**43.6**	**51.8**	**52.9**	**66.4**	**34.5**	**26.2**	**29.2**
Long-term debt	..	..	..	42.1	40.7	42.2	64.7	31.5	20.9	21.8
IMF repurchases and charges	0.0	0.0	0.0	1.1	10.6	10.5	1.1	1.5	4.1	6.6
Short-term debt (interest only)	..	..	..	0.5	0.4	0.2	0.6	1.5	1.3	0.8
2. AGGREGATE NET RESOURCE FLOWS AND NET TRANSFERS (LONG-TERM)										
NET RESOURCE FLOWS	..	..	..	**108.5**	**150.5**	**123.4**	**175.7**	**133.0**	**228.1**	**154.4**
Net flow of long-term debt (ex. IMF)	..	..	..	39.8	66.5	46.8	91.6	60.2	148.0	42.1
Foreign direct investment (net)	..	..	..	6.9	9.8	16.0	25.0	19.0	30.4	30.4
Portfolio equity flows	..	..	..	0.0	0.0	0.0	0.0	0.0	0.0	0.0
Grants (excluding technical coop.)	..	..	..	61.9	74.3	60.6	59.1	53.8	49.7	81.9
Memo: technical coop. grants	..	..	..	52.7	56.3	51.3	54.0	58.5	64.8	61.1
official net resource flows	..	..	..	123.3	154.4	127.6	161.9	126.4	200.5	127.4
private net resource flows	..	..	..	-14.8	-3.9	-4.2	13.8	6.6	27.6	27.0
NET TRANSFERS	..	..	..	**100.2**	**141.9**	**115.3**	**164.2**	**126.1**	**219.2**	**145.0**
Interest on long-term debt	..	..	..	8.3	8.6	8.1	11.5	6.9	8.9	9.5
Profit remittances on FDI	..	..	..	0.0	0.0	0.0	0.0	0.0	0.0	0.0
Memo: official net transfers	..	..	..	120.1	149.7	122.4	152.8	120.9	192.5	118.7
private net transfers	..	..	..	-19.9	-7.8	-7.1	11.4	5.2	26.7	26.3
3. MAJOR ECONOMIC AGGREGATES										
Gross national income (GNI)	..	..	..	648.6	928.0	1,037.0	892.4	972.5	895.4	954.5
Exports of goods & services (XGS)	..	..	..	415.6	511.3	492.5	627.3	555.8	544.0	624.8
of which workers remittances	..	..	..	..	..	..	..	5.5	7.2	7.8
Imports of goods & services (MGS)	..	..	..	447.0	549.5	599.2	576.3	680.7	663.0	784.1
International reserves (RES)	..	..	..	94.2	157.5	161.0	200.4	103.2	136.9	202.1
Current account balance	..	..	..	46.4	38.9	-36.9	102.9	-74.7	-51.9	..
4. DEBT INDICATORS										
EDT / XGS (%)	..	..	..	111.0	102.8	107.9	96.9	127.9	163.8	137.4
EDT / GNI (%)	..	..	..	71.1	56.6	51.2	68.1	73.1	99.5	90.0
TDS / XGS (%)	..	..	..	10.5	10.1	10.7	10.6	6.2	4.8	4.7
INT / XGS (%)	..	..	..	2.4	2.0	1.8	2.0	1.6	1.9	1.7
INT / GNI (%)	..	..	..	1.5	1.1	0.9	1.4	0.9	1.2	1.1
RES / EDT (%)	..	..	..	20.4	30.0	30.3	33.0	14.5	15.4	23.5
RES / MGS (months)	..	..	..	2.5	3.4	3.2	4.2	1.8	2.5	3.1
Short-term / EDT (%)	..	..	..	1.2	2.6	1.3	4.5	4.3	2.6	1.6
Concessional / EDT (%)	..	..	..	56.5	65.7	74.3	79.4	84.3	88.8	90.5
Multilateral / EDT (%)	..	..	..	24.5	32.3	38.5	47.6	50.5	49.2	51.3

MONGOLIA

(US$ million, unless otherwise indicated)

5. LONG-TERM DEBT

	1970	1980	1990	1994	1995	1996	1997	1998	1999	2000
DEBT OUTSTANDING (LDOD)	..	..	..	**400.5**	**464.9**	**481.0**	**532.6**	**631.7**	**816.3**	**794.8**
Public and publicly guaranteed	..	..	..	**400.5**	**464.9**	**481.0**	**532.6**	**631.7**	**816.3**	**794.8**
Official creditors	..	..	..	311.3	386.9	428.4	495.3	606.0	795.0	777.4
Multilateral	..	..	..	113.1	169.9	204.3	289.2	358.7	438.0	440.7
Concessional	..	..	..	113.1	169.9	204.3	289.2	358.7	438.0	440.7
Bilateral	..	..	..	198.2	217.0	224.1	206.1	247.3	357.0	336.7
Concessional	..	..	..	147.5	175.5	190.6	193.3	240.1	353.4	336.7
Private creditors	..	..	..	89.2	78.0	52.5	37.3	25.7	21.3	17.4
Bonds	..	..	..	0.0	0.0	0.0	0.0	0.0	0.0	0.0
Commercial banks	..	..	..	19.6	14.6	10.3	6.0	2.4	1.9	1.6
Other private	..	..	..	69.7	63.4	42.2	31.3	23.3	19.4	15.8
Private nonguaranteed	..	..	..	**0.0**	**0.0**	**0.0**	**0.0**	**0.0**	**0.0**	**0.0**
Bonds	..	..	..	0.0	0.0	0.0	0.0	0.0	0.0	0.0
Commercial banks and other	..	..	..	0.0	0.0	0.0	0.0	0.0	0.0	0.0
Memo:										
IBRD	0.0	0.0	0.0	0.0	0.0	0.0	0.0	0.0	0.0	0.0
IDA	0.0	0.0	0.0	49.2	58.7	67.6	97.1	118.0	129.7	137.1
DISBURSEMENTS	..	..	..	**73.5**	**98.6**	**80.9**	**144.8**	**84.8**	**160.0**	**54.5**
Public and publicly guaranteed	..	..	..	**73.5**	**98.6**	**80.9**	**144.8**	**84.8**	**160.0**	**54.5**
Official creditors	..	..	..	70.9	93.0	80.9	138.8	82.3	159.1	54.5
Multilateral	..	..	..	38.9	58.3	45.1	102.8	50.7	63.8	34.2
Concessional	..	..	..	38.9	58.3	45.1	102.8	50.7	63.8	34.2
Bilateral	..	..	..	32.0	34.8	35.8	36.0	31.6	95.3	20.3
Concessional	..	..	..	10.6	31.2	34.4	25.2	31.6	95.3	20.3
Private creditors	..	..	..	2.6	5.6	0.0	6.0	2.5	0.9	0.0
Bonds	..	..	..	0.0	0.0	0.0	0.0	0.0	0.0	0.0
Commercial banks	..	..	..	1.7	0.1	0.0	0.0	0.4	0.0	0.0
Other private	..	..	..	0.9	5.5	0.0	6.0	2.1	0.9	0.0
Private nonguaranteed	..	..	..	**0.0**	**0.0**	**0.0**	**0.0**	**0.0**	**0.0**	**0.0**
Bonds	..	..	..	0.0	0.0	0.0	0.0	0.0	0.0	0.0
Commercial banks and other	..	..	..	0.0	0.0	0.0	0.0	0.0	0.0	0.0
Memo:										
IBRD	0.0	0.0	0.0	0.0	0.0	0.0	0.0	0.0	0.0	0.0
IDA	0.0	0.0	0.0	17.4	8.4	11.0	33.8	16.7	14.2	14.1
PRINCIPAL REPAYMENTS	..	..	..	**33.7**	**32.1**	**34.1**	**53.2**	**24.6**	**11.9**	**12.3**
Public and publicly guaranteed	..	..	..	**33.7**	**32.1**	**34.1**	**53.2**	**24.6**	**11.9**	**12.3**
Official creditors	..	..	..	9.5	12.9	13.9	36.0	9.7	8.3	8.9
Multilateral	..	..	..	3.0	0.0	0.0	0.0	0.0	0.0	0.0
Concessional	..	..	..	0.0	0.0	0.0	0.0	0.0	0.0	0.0
Bilateral	..	..	..	6.5	12.9	13.9	36.0	9.7	8.3	8.9
Concessional	..	..	..	0.0	0.1	4.5	4.5	4.0	4.7	5.4
Private creditors	..	..	..	24.2	19.2	20.2	17.2	14.9	3.6	3.4
Bonds	..	..	..	0.0	0.0	0.0	0.0	0.0	0.0	0.0
Commercial banks	..	..	..	2.0	5.2	4.1	4.3	4.1	0.3	0.3
Other private	..	..	..	22.2	14.0	16.1	12.9	10.8	3.3	3.1
Private nonguaranteed	..	..	..	**0.0**	**0.0**	**0.0**	**0.0**	**0.0**	**0.0**	**0.0**
Bonds	..	..	..	0.0	0.0	0.0	0.0	0.0	0.0	0.0
Commercial banks and other	..	..	..	0.0	0.0	0.0	0.0	0.0	0.0	0.0
Memo:										
IBRD	0.0	0.0	0.0	0.0	0.0	0.0	0.0	0.0	0.0	0.0
IDA	0.0	0.0	0.0	0.0	0.0	0.0	0.0	0.0	0.0	0.0
NET FLOWS ON DEBT	..	..	..	**39.8**	**66.5**	**46.8**	**91.6**	**60.2**	**148.0**	**42.1**
Public and publicly guaranteed	..	..	..	**39.8**	**66.5**	**46.8**	**91.6**	**60.2**	**148.0**	**42.1**
Official creditors	..	..	..	61.4	80.1	67.0	102.8	72.6	150.8	45.5
Multilateral	..	..	..	35.9	58.3	45.1	102.8	50.7	63.8	34.2
Concessional	..	..	..	38.9	58.3	45.1	102.8	50.7	63.8	34.2
Bilateral	..	..	..	25.5	21.9	21.9	0.0	21.9	87.0	11.4
Concessional	..	..	..	10.6	31.1	29.9	20.7	27.6	90.5	14.9
Private creditors	..	..	..	-21.7	-13.7	-20.2	-11.2	-12.4	-2.8	-3.4
Bonds	..	..	..	0.0	0.0	0.0	0.0	0.0	0.0	0.0
Commercial banks	..	..	..	-0.3	-5.2	-4.1	-4.3	-3.7	-0.3	-0.3
Other private	..	..	..	-21.4	-8.5	-16.1	-6.9	-8.7	-2.5	-3.1
Private nonguaranteed	..	..	..	**0.0**	**0.0**	**0.0**	**0.0**	**0.0**	**0.0**	**0.0**
Bonds	..	..	..	0.0	0.0	0.0	0.0	0.0	0.0	0.0
Commercial banks and other	..	..	..	0.0	0.0	0.0	0.0	0.0	0.0	0.0
Memo:										
IBRD	0.0	0.0	0.0	0.0	0.0	0.0	0.0	0.0	0.0	0.0
IDA	0.0	0.0	0.0	17.4	8.4	11.0	33.8	16.7	14.2	14.1

MONGOLIA

(US$ million, unless otherwise indicated)

	1970	1980	1990	1994	1995	1996	1997	1998	1999	2000
INTEREST PAYMENTS (LINT)	..	..	..	**8.3**	**8.6**	**8.1**	**11.5**	**6.9**	**8.9**	**9.5**
Public and publicly guaranteed	..	..	..	**8.3**	**8.6**	**8.1**	**11.5**	**6.9**	**8.9**	**9.5**
Official creditors	..	..	..	3.2	4.7	5.2	9.1	5.5	8.0	8.7
Multilateral	..	..	..	1.0	1.1	1.6	2.0	2.7	3.5	3.9
Concessional	..	..	..	0.8	1.1	1.6	2.0	2.7	3.5	3.9
Bilateral	..	..	..	2.2	3.5	3.6	7.1	2.8	4.5	4.8
Concessional	..	..	..	0.9	2.1	2.1	5.7	2.2	4.3	4.7
Private creditors	..	..	..	5.1	3.9	2.9	2.4	1.4	0.9	0.7
Bonds	..	..	..	0.0	0.0	0.0	0.0	0.0	0.0	0.0
Commercial banks	..	..	..	1.4	1.0	0.4	0.5	0.2	0.1	0.0
Other private	..	..	..	3.7	3.0	2.4	1.9	1.2	0.9	0.7
Private nonguaranteed	..	..	..	**0.0**	**0.0**	**0.0**	**0.0**	**0.0**	**0.0**	**0.0**
Bonds	..	..	..	0.0	0.0	0.0	0.0	0.0	0.0	0.0
Commercial banks and other	..	..	..	0.0	0.0	0.0	0.0	0.0	0.0	0.0
Memo:										
IBRD	0.0	0.0	0.0	0.0	0.0	0.0	0.0	0.0	0.0	0.0
IDA	0.0	0.0	0.0	0.3	0.4	0.5	0.5	0.7	0.9	1.0
NET TRANSFERS ON DEBT	..	..	..	**31.5**	**57.9**	**38.7**	**80.1**	**53.3**	**139.1**	**32.7**
Public and publicly guaranteed	..	..	..	**31.5**	**57.9**	**38.7**	**80.1**	**53.3**	**139.1**	**32.7**
Official creditors	..	..	..	58.2	75.4	61.8	93.7	67.1	142.8	36.8
Multilateral	..	..	..	34.9	57.1	43.5	100.8	48.0	60.4	30.2
Concessional	..	..	..	38.1	57.1	43.5	100.8	48.0	60.4	30.2
Bilateral	..	..	..	23.3	18.3	18.3	-7.1	19.1	82.5	6.6
Concessional	..	..	..	9.7	29.0	27.8	15.1	25.4	86.2	10.3
Private creditors	..	..	..	-26.8	-17.6	-23.1	-13.6	-13.8	-3.7	-4.2
Bonds	..	..	..	0.0	0.0	0.0	0.0	0.0	0.0	0.0
Commercial banks	..	..	..	-1.7	-6.2	-4.6	-4.8	-3.8	-0.4	-0.3
Other private	..	..	..	-25.1	-11.4	-18.5	-8.8	-10.0	-3.3	-3.8
Private nonguaranteed	..	..	..	**0.0**	**0.0**	**0.0**	**0.0**	**0.0**	**0.0**	**0.0**
Bonds	..	..	..	0.0	0.0	0.0	0.0	0.0	0.0	0.0
Commercial banks and other	..	..	..	0.0	0.0	0.0	0.0	0.0	0.0	0.0
Memo:										
IBRD	0.0	0.0	0.0	0.0	0.0	0.0	0.0	0.0	0.0	0.0
IDA	0.0	0.0	0.0	17.1	8.0	10.5	33.3	16.0	13.3	13.1
DEBT SERVICE (LTDS)	..	..	..	**42.1**	**40.7**	**42.2**	**64.7**	**31.5**	**20.9**	**21.8**
Public and publicly guaranteed	..	..	..	**42.1**	**40.7**	**42.2**	**64.7**	**31.5**	**20.9**	**21.8**
Official creditors	..	..	..	12.7	17.6	19.1	45.1	15.2	16.3	17.6
Multilateral	..	..	..	4.0	1.1	1.6	2.0	2.7	3.5	3.9
Concessional	..	..	..	0.8	1.1	1.6	2.0	2.7	3.5	3.9
Bilateral	..	..	..	8.7	16.4	17.5	43.1	12.5	12.8	13.7
Concessional	..	..	..	0.9	2.2	6.6	10.2	6.3	9.0	10.0
Private creditors	..	..	..	29.3	23.2	23.1	19.6	16.3	4.6	4.2
Bonds	..	..	..	0.0	0.0	0.0	0.0	0.0	0.0	0.0
Commercial banks	..	..	..	3.4	6.2	4.6	4.8	4.3	0.4	0.3
Other private	..	..	..	25.9	17.0	18.5	14.8	12.0	4.2	3.8
Private nonguaranteed	..	..	..	**0.0**	**0.0**	**0.0**	**0.0**	**0.0**	**0.0**	**0.0**
Bonds	..	..	..	0.0	0.0	0.0	0.0	0.0	0.0	0.0
Commercial banks and other	..	..	..	0.0	0.0	0.0	0.0	0.0	0.0	0.0
Memo:										
IBRD	0.0	0.0	0.0	0.0	0.0	0.0	0.0	0.0	0.0	0.0
IDA	0.0	0.0	0.0	0.3	0.4	0.5	0.5	0.7	0.9	1.0
UNDISBURSED DEBT	..	..	..	**206.4**	**354.3**	**313.3**	**323.3**	**350.9**	**201.9**	**231.2**
Official creditors	..	..	..	191.9	345.4	304.4	319.9	350.0	201.9	231.2
Private creditors	..	..	..	14.5	8.9	8.9	3.4	0.9	0.0	0.0
Memorandum items										
Concessional LDOD	..	..	..	260.5	345.4	394.8	482.5	598.9	791.4	777.4
Variable rate LDOD	..	..	..	16.0	12.0	8.0	4.0	0.5	0.2	0.1
Public sector LDOD	..	..	..	384.5	443.0	463.8	513.8	612.8	800.3	781.8
Private sector LDOD	..	..	..	16.0	21.9	17.2	18.8	18.9	16.0	12.9

6. CURRENCY COMPOSITION OF LONG-TERM DEBT (PERCENT)

	1970	1980	1990	1994	1995	1996	1997	1998	1999	2000
Deutsche mark	..	..	..	4.0	5.2	5.4	5.8	5.6	4.1	4.9
French franc	..	..	..	0.0	0.0	0.0	0.0	0.0	0.0	0.0
Japanese yen	..	..	..	29.1	26.9	26.0	19.8	22.1	30.8	29.1
Pound sterling	..	..	..	0.0	0.0	0.0	0.0	0.0	0.0	0.0
Swiss franc	..	..	..	2.7	2.3	1.7	1.0	0.8	0.5	0.4
U.S.dollars	..	..	..	44.9	38.7	34.8	35.0	31.6	28.3	29.6
Multiple currency	..	..	..	16.3	24.2	29.6	34.4	35.6	32.2	31.6
Special drawing rights	..	..	..	0.0	0.0	0.3	1.8	2.3	2.1	2.0
All other currencies	..	..	..	3.0	2.7	2.2	2.2	2.0	2.0	2.4

MONGOLIA

(US$ million, unless otherwise indicated)

	1970	1980	1990	1994	1995	1996	1997	1998	1999	2000
7. DEBT RESTRUCTURINGS										
Total amount rescheduled	..	..	..	0.0	0.0	0.0	0.0	0.0	0.0	0.0
Debt stock rescheduled	..	..	..	0.0	0.0	0.0	0.0	0.0	0.0	0.0
Principal rescheduled	..	..	..	0.0	0.0	0.0	0.0	0.0	0.0	0.0
Official	..	..	..	0.0	0.0	0.0	0.0	0.0	0.0	0.0
Private	..	..	..	0.0	0.0	0.0	0.0	0.0	0.0	0.0
Interest rescheduled	..	..	..	0.0	0.0	0.0	0.0	0.0	0.0	0.0
Official	..	..	..	0.0	0.0	0.0	0.0	0.0	0.0	0.0
Private	..	..	..	0.0	0.0	0.0	0.0	0.0	0.0	0.0
Debt forgiven	..	..	..	0.0	0.0	0.0	0.8	0.0	0.0	0.0
Memo: interest forgiven	..	..	..	0.0	0.0	0.0	0.0	0.0	0.0	0.0
Debt stock reduction	..	..	..	0.0	0.0	0.0	0.0	0.0	0.0	0.0
of which debt buyback	..	..	..	0.0	0.0	0.0	0.0	0.0	0.0	0.0
8. DEBT STOCK-FLOW RECONCILIATION										
Total change in debt stocks	..	..	..	77.4	64.3	5.8	76.3	102.9	180.3	-32.2
Net flows on debt	..	..	..	51.9	65.2	38.0	119.0	62.0	144.9	34.1
Net change in interest arrears	..	..	..	0.9	0.0	0.0	0.0	0.0	0.1	0.0
Interest capitalized	..	..	..	0.0	0.0	0.0	0.0	0.0	0.0	0.0
Debt forgiveness or reduction	..	..	..	0.0	0.0	0.0	-0.8	0.0	0.0	0.0
Cross-currency valuation	..	..	..	24.7	0.1	-30.9	-39.4	36.7	18.6	-63.8
Residual	..	..	..	-0.1	-0.9	-1.3	-2.4	4.2	16.7	-2.4
9. AVERAGE TERMS OF NEW COMMITMENTS										
ALL CREDITORS										
Interest (%)	..	..	..	0.8	2.2	1.1	2.6	2.0	0.8	1.3
Maturity (years)	..	..	..	38.7	35.3	33.5	36.8	39.8	39.7	31.2
Grace period (years)	..	..	..	10.7	10.1	8.4	10.0	10.0	10.2	8.8
Grant element (%)	..	..	..	80.2	65.4	71.5	62.9	69.7	80.5	70.4
Official creditors										
Interest (%)	..	..	..	0.8	2.2	1.1	2.6	2.0	0.8	1.3
Maturity (years)	..	..	..	38.7	35.3	33.5	36.9	39.8	39.7	31.2
Grace period (years)	..	..	..	10.7	10.1	8.4	10.0	10.0	10.2	8.8
Grant element (%)	..	..	..	80.2	65.4	71.5	63.0	69.7	80.5	70.4
Private creditors										
Interest (%)	..	..	..	0.0	0.0	0.0	2.5	0.0	0.0	0.0
Maturity (years)	..	..	..	0.0	0.0	0.0	3.8	0.0	0.0	0.0
Grace period (years)	..	..	..	0.0	0.0	0.0	1.3	0.0	0.0	0.0
Grant element (%)	..	..	..	0.0	0.0	0.0	15.6	0.0	0.0	0.0
Memorandum items										
Commitments	..	..	..	77.7	250.1	58.4	177.0	91.0	12.0	96.8
Official creditors	..	..	..	77.7	250.1	58.4	176.5	91.0	12.0	96.8
Private creditors	..	..	..	0.0	0.0	0.0	0.4	0.0	0.0	0.0

10. CONTRACTUAL OBLIGATIONS ON OUTSTANDING LONG-TERM DEBT

	2001	2002	2003	2004	2005	2006	2007	2008	2009	2010
TOTAL										
Disbursements	63.2	57.1	41.4	28.5	18.6	10.7	6.4	2.9	1.9	0.6
Principal	10.3	14.4	16.0	17.3	22.1	25.3	27.9	32.7	33.9	34.3
Interest	9.9	10.1	10.2	10.1	11.0	13.2	13.8	13.5	13.1	12.5
Official creditors										
Disbursements	63.2	57.1	41.4	28.5	18.6	10.7	6.4	2.9	1.9	0.6
Principal	6.9	11.2	12.7	15.6	21.2	25.2	27.8	32.7	33.9	34.3
Interest	9.3	9.7	9.9	10.0	11.0	13.1	13.8	13.5	13.1	12.5
Bilateral creditors										
Disbursements	25.4	20.1	13.5	8.8	5.4	2.7	1.9	1.4	1.1	0.6
Principal	6.9	9.8	11.0	11.9	15.3	16.9	15.8	17.5	18.5	18.5
Interest	4.7	5.0	5.0	5.0	4.9	4.7	4.5	4.3	4.1	3.9
Multilateral creditors										
Disbursements	37.8	37.0	27.8	19.8	13.2	8.0	4.5	1.5	0.7	0.0
Principal	0.0	1.4	1.7	3.7	5.8	8.3	12.0	15.2	15.4	15.8
Interest	4.5	4.7	4.9	5.0	6.1	8.4	9.3	9.2	9.0	8.7
Private creditors										
Disbursements	0.0	0.0	0.0	0.0	0.0	0.0	0.0	0.0	0.0	0.0
Principal	3.4	3.3	3.3	1.8	0.9	0.1	0.1	0.0	0.0	0.0
Interest	0.6	0.4	0.3	0.1	0.0	0.0	0.0	0.0	0.0	0.0
Commercial banks										
Disbursements	0.0	0.0	0.0	0.0	0.0	0.0	0.0	0.0	0.0	0.0
Principal	0.2	0.1	0.1	0.1	0.1	0.1	0.1	0.0	0.0	0.0
Interest	0.0	0.0	0.0	0.0	0.0	0.0	0.0	0.0	0.0	0.0
Other private										
Disbursements	0.0	0.0	0.0	0.0	0.0	0.0	0.0	0.0	0.0	0.0
Principal	3.1	3.1	3.1	1.6	0.8	0.0	0.0	0.0	0.0	0.0
Interest	0.6	0.4	0.3	0.1	0.0	0.0	0.0	0.0	0.0	0.0

MOROCCO

(US$ million, unless otherwise indicated)

1. SUMMARY DEBT DATA

	1970	1980	1990	1994	1995	1996	1997	1998	1999	2000
TOTAL DEBT STOCKS (EDT)	**985**	**9,259**	**24,458**	**22,158**	**22,665**	**21,889**	**20,195**	**20,526**	**19,190**	**17,944**
Long-term debt (LDOD)	**886**	**8,024**	**23,301**	**21,788**	**22,416**	**21,564**	**19,964**	**20,411**	**18,906**	**17,688**
Public and publicly guaranteed	871	7,874	23,101	21,530	22,085	21,172	19,012	19,164	17,314	15,793
Private nonguaranteed	15	150	200	259	331	392	953	1,247	1,593	1,896
Use of IMF credit	**28**	**457**	**750**	**148**	**52**	**3**	**0**	**0**	**0**	**0**
Short-term debt	**71**	**778**	**407**	**222**	**198**	**322**	**231**	**116**	**284**	**256**
of which interest arrears on LDOD	0	3	182	94	92	138	113	116	110	111
Official creditors	0	3	182	91	92	137	113	115	109	111
Private creditors	0	0	0	3	0	0	0	1	1	1
Memo: principal arrears on LDOD	0	3	738	137	138	182	195	215	423	526
Official creditors	0	3	738	126	136	179	195	210	418	523
Private creditors	0	0	0	11	2	2	0	5	6	4
Memo: export credits	0	0	8,416	8,076	7,957	7,042	6,513	1,510	1,239	1,044
TOTAL DEBT FLOWS										
Disbursements	**196**	**2,262**	**1,711**	**1,802**	**2,089**	**1,757**	**1,313**	**1,587**	**1,534**	**1,571**
Long-term debt	186	1,985	1,646	1,802	2,089	1,757	1,313	1,587	1,534	1,571
IMF purchases	10	278	65	0	0	0	0	0	0	0
Principal repayments	**54**	**678**	**908**	**2,246**	**2,373**	**2,006**	**2,123**	**1,761**	**1,972**	**2,378**
Long-term debt	40	591	680	2,094	2,272	1,959	2,119	1,761	1,972	2,378
IMF repurchases	14	88	228	152	101	47	3	0	0	0
Net flows on debt	**142**	**1,624**	**889**	**-532**	**-306**	**-172**	**-876**	**-292**	**-265**	**-836**
of which short-term debt	0	40	86	-87	-22	78	-66	-118	174	-29
Interest payments (INT)	**26**	**768**	**886**	**1,393**	**1,391**	**1,346**	**1,068**	**1,021**	**1,076**	**955**
Long-term debt	26	651	794	1,363	1,360	1,335	1,061	1,018	1,068	947
IMF charges	0	12	72	13	7	2	0	0	0	0
Short-term debt	0	105	20	18	24	9	6	3	9	8
Net transfers on debt	**116**	**857**	**3**	**-1,925**	**-1,696**	**-1,517**	**-1,943**	**-1,313**	**-1,341**	**-1,791**
Total debt service paid (TDS)	**80**	**1,446**	**1,794**	**3,639**	**3,764**	**3,352**	**3,190**	**2,782**	**3,049**	**3,333**
Long-term debt	66	1,241	1,474	3,457	3,633	3,294	3,181	2,779	3,040	3,325
IMF repurchases and charges	14	100	300	165	107	49	3	0	0	0
Short-term debt (interest only)	0	105	20	18	24	9	6	3	9	8

2. AGGREGATE NET RESOURCE FLOWS AND NET TRANSFERS (LONG-TERM)

	1970	1980	1990	1994	1995	1996	1997	1998	1999	2000
NET RESOURCE FLOWS	**190**	**1,559**	**1,610**	**601**	**159**	**452**	**-278**	**365**	**-27**	**-460**
Net flow of long-term debt (ex. IMF)	146	1,394	965	-293	-183	-202	-806	-174	-439	-807
Foreign direct investment (net)	20	89	165	551	92	76	4	12	3	10
Portfolio equity flows	0	0	0	63	150	222	243	174	91	147
Grants (excluding technical coop.)	24	75	480	279	100	356	281	353	318	191
Memo: technical coop. grants	29	123	182	202	266	249	215	228	230	193
official net resource flows	144	828	1,269	-151	-187	343	-534	-101	92	-167
private net resource flows	46	731	341	752	346	109	256	467	-119	-293
NET TRANSFERS	**145**	**859**	**748**	**-872**	**-1,331**	**-1,059**	**-1,530**	**-873**	**-1,299**	**-1,640**
Interest on long-term debt	26	651	794	1,363	1,360	1,335	1,061	1,018	1,068	947
Profit remittances on FDI	20	49	69	110	130	175	190	220	205	233
Memo: official net transfers	126	692	689	-1,169	-1,110	-546	-1,363	-880	-577	-718
private net transfers	19	167	58	297	-221	-513	-166	7	-723	-921

3. MAJOR ECONOMIC AGGREGATES

	1970	1980	1990	1994	1995	1996	1997	1998	1999	2000
Gross national income (GNI)	3,945	18,402	24,835	29,181	31,668	35,330	32,239	34,636	34,138	32,457
Exports of goods & services (XGS)	..	4,324	8,328	9,606	11,265	11,984	11,575	12,175	12,749	12,890
of which workers remittances	..	1,054	2,006	1,827	1,970	2,165	1,893	2,011	1,938	2,161
Imports of goods & services (MGS)	..	5,807	8,853	10,772	12,812	12,360	11,975	12,653	13,132	13,686
International reserves (RES)	142	814	2,338	4,622	3,874	4,054	4,197	4,638	5,894	5,017
Current account balance	..	-1,407	-196	-723	-1,186	35	-87	-144	-167	-475

4. DEBT INDICATORS

	1970	1980	1990	1994	1995	1996	1997	1998	1999	2000
EDT / XGS (%)	..	214.1	293.7	230.7	201.2	182.7	174.5	168.6	150.5	139.2
EDT / GNI (%)	25.0	50.3	98.5	75.9	71.6	62.0	62.6	59.3	56.2	55.3
TDS / XGS (%)	..	33.4	21.5	37.9	33.4	28.0	27.6	22.9	23.9	25.9
INT / XGS (%)	..	17.8	10.6	14.5	12.4	11.2	9.2	8.4	8.4	7.4
INT / GNI (%)	0.7	4.2	3.6	4.8	4.4	3.8	3.3	3.0	3.2	2.9
RES / EDT (%)	14.4	8.8	9.6	20.9	17.1	18.5	20.8	22.6	30.7	28.0
RES / MGS (months)	..	1.7	3.2	5.2	3.6	3.9	4.2	4.4	5.4	4.4
Short-term / EDT (%)	7.2	8.4	1.7	1.0	0.9	1.5	1.1	0.6	1.5	1.4
Concessional / EDT (%)	63.2	29.4	32.6	27.1	28.1	30.4	31.1	31.3	31.5	31.1
Multilateral / EDT (%)	6.0	7.8	19.2	28.4	29.9	30.3	30.1	31.6	32.7	32.5

MOROCCO

(US$ million, unless otherwise indicated)

	1970	1980	1990	1994	1995	1996	1997	1998	1999	2000
5. LONG-TERM DEBT										
DEBT OUTSTANDING (LDOD)	**886**	**8,024**	**23,301**	**21,788**	**22,416**	**21,564**	**19,964**	**20,411**	**18,906**	**17,688**
Public and publicly guaranteed	**871**	**7,874**	**23,101**	**21,530**	**22,085**	**21,172**	**19,012**	**19,164**	**17,314**	**15,793**
Official creditors	742	3,519	16,991	16,127	16,515	15,964	14,220	14,255	13,157	12,031
Multilateral	59	723	4,687	6,297	6,768	6,623	6,074	6,491	6,281	5,822
Concessional	3	79	405	520	599	698	783	879	899	906
Bilateral	683	2,796	12,304	9,829	9,748	9,341	8,145	7,764	6,876	6,209
Concessional	620	2,638	7,579	5,493	5,772	5,960	5,503	5,540	5,147	4,673
Private creditors	129	4,355	6,110	5,403	5,570	5,208	4,792	4,909	4,157	3,761
Bonds	32	173	0	0	0	286	251	267	197	152
Commercial banks	0	2,343	3,394	3,424	3,523	3,301	3,295	3,380	2,892	2,713
Other private	98	1,839	2,716	1,979	2,047	1,621	1,247	1,263	1,068	895
Private nonguaranteed	**15**	**150**	**200**	**259**	**331**	**392**	**953**	**1,247**	**1,593**	**1,896**
Bonds	0	0	0	0	0	0	0	0	0	0
Commercial banks and other	15	150	200	259	331	392	953	1,247	1,593	1,896
Memo:										
IBRD	56	539	3,099	3,746	3,966	3,732	3,271	3,388	3,194	2,837
IDA	3	39	39	35	33	32	31	29	28	27
DISBURSEMENTS	**186**	**1,985**	**1,646**	**1,802**	**2,089**	**1,757**	**1,313**	**1,587**	**1,534**	**1,571**
Public and publicly guaranteed	**179**	**1,910**	**1,638**	**1,722**	**1,987**	**1,666**	**1,038**	**1,249**	**1,144**	**913**
Official creditors	145	866	1,220	1,040	1,355	1,329	851	855	912	570
Multilateral	16	109	781	655	906	797	568	641	668	405
Concessional	2	22	39	71	92	136	138	117	75	72
Bilateral	130	757	439	385	449	532	283	214	243	165
Concessional	90	709	287	368	314	335	221	176	175	124
Private creditors	34	1,044	418	681	632	337	187	394	232	342
Bonds	0	7	0	0	0	293	0	0	0	0
Commercial banks	0	482	47	266	204	0	22	289	29	179
Other private	34	555	371	416	428	44	165	104	203	163
Private nonguaranteed	**8**	**75**	**8**	**80**	**103**	**91**	**275**	**338**	**390**	**658**
Bonds	0	0	0	0	0	0	0	0	0	0
Commercial banks and other	8	75	8	80	103	91	275	338	390	658
Memo:										
IBRD	14	64	426	246	426	380	141	253	404	138
IDA	2	1	0	0	0	0	0	0	0	0
PRINCIPAL REPAYMENTS	**40**	**591**	**680**	**2,094**	**2,272**	**1,959**	**2,119**	**1,761**	**1,972**	**2,378**
Public and publicly guaranteed	**38**	**566**	**672**	**2,093**	**2,242**	**1,929**	**2,076**	**1,717**	**1,928**	**1,581**
Official creditors	25	114	430	1,471	1,642	1,342	1,666	1,310	1,137	928
Multilateral	5	39	276	476	629	571	661	515	533	554
Concessional	0	0	13	26	22	28	31	36	36	54
Bilateral	20	75	155	994	1,013	771	1,005	795	605	374
Concessional	15	61	33	317	267	199	331	234	230	237
Private creditors	13	452	242	623	600	587	409	407	791	653
Bonds	3	9	0	0	0	0	0	0	35	30
Commercial banks	0	295	40	98	111	168	148	139	500	350
Other private	10	149	202	525	489	419	261	268	256	272
Private nonguaranteed	**3**	**25**	**8**	**1**	**30**	**30**	**44**	**44**	**44**	**797**
Bonds	0	0	0	0	0	0	0	0	0	0
Commercial banks and other	3	25	8	1	30	30	44	44	44	797
Memo:										
IBRD	5	29	202	301	349	341	306	286	302	307
IDA	0	0	1	1	1	1	1	1	1	1
NET FLOWS ON DEBT	**146**	**1,394**	**965**	**-293**	**-183**	**-202**	**-806**	**-174**	**-439**	**-807**
Public and publicly guaranteed	**141**	**1,344**	**965**	**-372**	**-256**	**-263**	**-1,038**	**-468**	**-785**	**-668**
Official creditors	120	752	790	-430	-287	-13	-816	-455	-226	-358
Multilateral	11	70	506	179	277	226	-93	126	136	-149
Concessional	2	22	25	45	70	108	108	82	39	18
Bilateral	109	682	284	-609	-564	-239	-722	-581	-361	-209
Concessional	75	648	254	51	46	136	-110	-57	-54	-113
Private creditors	21	592	176	59	32	-250	-222	-14	-559	-310
Bonds	-3	-2	0	0	0	293	0	0	-35	-30
Commercial banks	0	188	7	167	93	-168	-126	150	-471	-171
Other private	24	406	169	-109	-61	-376	-96	-164	-53	-109
Private nonguaranteed	**5**	**50**	**0**	**79**	**73**	**61**	**231**	**294**	**346**	**-139**
Bonds	0	0	0	0	0	0	0	0	0	0
Commercial banks and other	5	50	0	79	73	61	231	294	346	-139
Memo:										
IBRD	9	35	224	-55	78	39	-165	-34	102	-169
IDA	2	1	-1	-1	-1	-1	-1	-1	-1	-1

MOROCCO

(US$ million, unless otherwise indicated)

	1970	1980	1990	1994	1995	1996	1997	1998	1999	2000
INTEREST PAYMENTS (LINT)	**26**	**651**	**794**	**1,363**	**1,360**	**1,335**	**1,061**	**1,018**	**1,068**	**947**
Public and publicly guaranteed	**25**	**639**	**789**	**1,362**	**1,359**	**1,324**	**1,014**	**970**	**1,010**	**876**
Official creditors	19	135	580	1,018	923	888	829	779	669	551
Multilateral	4	56	306	427	466	465	422	390	394	365
Concessional	0	1	7	17	19	24	28	32	31	32
Bilateral	15	79	274	591	458	424	407	389	275	186
Concessional	13	69	57	136	142	142	163	168	172	119
Private creditors	6	504	208	344	436	436	185	192	341	325
Bonds	2	15	0	0	0	0	17	17	16	14
Commercial banks	0	364	43	158	259	281	42	62	231	228
Other private	4	125	165	186	176	155	126	113	94	83
Private nonguaranteed	**1**	**11**	**5**	**1**	**2**	**11**	**48**	**48**	**58**	**71**
Bonds	0	0	0	0	0	0	0	0	0	0
Commercial banks and other	1	11	5	1	2	11	48	48	58	71
Memo:										
IBRD	4	49	226	271	282	258	238	206	212	190
IDA	0	0	0	0	0	0	0	0	0	0
NET TRANSFERS ON DEBT	**121**	**743**	**172**	**-1,655**	**-1,543**	**-1,537**	**-1,868**	**-1,192**	**-1,506**	**-1,754**
Public and publicly guaranteed	**116**	**705**	**177**	**-1,734**	**-1,614**	**-1,588**	**-2,052**	**-1,438**	**-1,794**	**-1,544**
Official creditors	102	617	209	-1,448	-1,210	-901	-1,645	-1,233	-895	-909
Multilateral	7	14	200	-248	-189	-238	-516	-264	-259	-514
Concessional	2	21	19	28	51	84	80	50	8	-13
Bilateral	95	603	10	-1,200	-1,022	-663	-1,129	-970	-636	-395
Concessional	62	579	197	-85	-96	-6	-272	-225	-227	-232
Private creditors	15	88	-33	-286	-404	-686	-407	-205	-900	-635
Bonds	-5	-17	0	0	0	293	-17	-17	-51	-44
Commercial banks	0	-177	-36	9	-167	-449	-168	88	-702	-399
Other private	20	281	4	-295	-237	-531	-223	-277	-147	-192
Private nonguaranteed	**4**	**39**	**-5**	**79**	**71**	**50**	**184**	**246**	**288**	**-210**
Bonds	0	0	0	0	0	0	0	0	0	0
Commercial banks and other	4	39	-5	79	71	50	184	246	288	-210
Memo:										
IBRD	5	-14	-2	-326	-204	-219	-403	-240	-109	-359
IDA	2	0	-1	-2	-2	-2	-2	-2	-2	-2
DEBT SERVICE (LTDS)	**66**	**1,241**	**1,474**	**3,457**	**3,633**	**3,294**	**3,181**	**2,779**	**3,040**	**3,325**
Public and publicly guaranteed	**62**	**1,205**	**1,461**	**3,456**	**3,601**	**3,253**	**3,089**	**2,688**	**2,938**	**2,457**
Official creditors	44	249	1,011	2,489	2,565	2,230	2,495	2,089	1,806	1,480
Multilateral	9	95	582	903	1,095	1,035	1,083	905	927	919
Concessional	0	1	20	43	41	52	58	68	68	85
Bilateral	35	154	429	1,586	1,471	1,195	1,412	1,184	879	560
Concessional	28	130	90	453	409	341	493	402	402	356
Private creditors	19	956	451	967	1,036	1,023	594	599	1,132	977
Bonds	5	23	0	0	0	0	17	17	51	44
Commercial banks	0	659	83	256	371	449	190	201	731	578
Other private	14	274	367	711	665	574	388	381	350	355
Private nonguaranteed	**3**	**36**	**13**	**2**	**32**	**41**	**92**	**92**	**102**	**868**
Bonds	0	0	0	0	0	0	0	0	0	0
Commercial banks and other	3	36	13	2	32	41	92	92	102	868
Memo:										
IBRD	9	78	428	572	630	599	545	493	514	497
IDA	0	1	1	2	2	2	2	2	2	2
UNDISBURSED DEBT	**242**	**2,291**	**4,024**	**5,210**	**5,619**	**4,277**	**4,550**	**4,274**	**4,518**	**3,411**
Official creditors	221	1,882	3,416	4,354	5,196	3,922	4,070	3,818	3,826	3,006
Private creditors	21	409	608	856	423	355	480	456	692	405
Memorandum items										
Concessional LDOD	622	2,717	7,984	6,012	6,371	6,659	6,285	6,419	6,046	5,579
Variable rate LDOD	15	2,626	7,827	8,294	8,621	8,205	8,197	8,572	8,170	7,720
Public sector LDOD	864	7,819	23,037	21,304	21,841	20,940	18,807	18,980	17,142	15,640
Private sector LDOD	23	204	264	484	575	624	1,158	1,431	1,764	2,048

6. CURRENCY COMPOSITION OF LONG-TERM DEBT (PERCENT)

	1970	1980	1990	1994	1995	1996	1997	1998	1999	2000
Deutsche mark	11.7	3.9	5.4	7.8	7.8	7.1	6.8	6.7	6.0	5.7
French franc	29.5	22.0	23.3	21.5	21.2	20.4	18.4	19.5	17.5	17.4
Japanese yen	0.0	1.9	2.3	4.3	3.9	3.5	2.5	2.7	3.4	3.7
Pound sterling	0.0	0.4	0.1	0.2	0.2	0.2	0.2	0.1	0.1	0.1
Swiss franc	0.1	0.3	0.2	0.1	0.1	0.1	0.2	0.2	0.2	0.2
U.S.dollars	40.9	54.7	41.0	29.5	28.2	29.9	32.9	40.7	40.7	39.9
Multiple currency	6.8	7.0	15.8	23.5	23.8	22.8	21.9	11.4	11.3	10.4
Special drawing rights	0.0	0.2	0.1	0.2	0.2	0.1	0.1	0.1	0.1	0.2
All other currencies	11.0	9.6	11.8	12.9	14.6	15.9	17.0	18.6	20.7	22.4

MOROCCO

(US$ million, unless otherwise indicated)

	1970	1980	1990	1994	1995	1996	1997	1998	1999	2000
7. DEBT RESTRUCTURINGS										
Total amount rescheduled	..	..	4,118	0	0	0	0	0	0	0
Debt stock rescheduled	..	..	2,732	0	0	0	0	0	0	0
Principal rescheduled	..	..	591	0	0	0	0	0	0	0
Official	..	..	389	0	0	0	0	0	0	0
Private	..	..	203	0	0	0	0	0	0	0
Interest rescheduled	..	..	219	0	0	0	0	0	0	0
Official	..	..	137	0	0	0	0	0	0	0
Private	..	..	82	0	0	0	0	0	0	0
Debt forgiven	..	..	31	0	0	0	5	0	1	118
Memo: interest forgiven	..	..	0	0	0	0	0	0	0	0
Debt stock reduction	..	..	0	0	0	0	0	0	0	0
of which debt buyback	..	..	0	0	0	0	0	0	0	0
8. DEBT STOCK-FLOW RECONCILIATION										
Total change in debt stocks	..	..	2,585	699	508	-776	-1,694	331	-1,336	-1,246
Net flows on debt	142	1,624	889	-532	-306	-172	-876	-292	-265	-836
Net change in interest arrears	..	..	43	-6	-2	46	-25	3	-6	1
Interest capitalized	..	..	219	0	0	0	0	0	0	0
Debt forgiveness or reduction	..	..	-31	0	0	0	-5	0	-1	-118
Cross-currency valuation	..	..	1,052	1,017	692	-1,037	-1,344	626	-1,029	-598
Residual	..	..	414	219	123	387	555	-6	-35	305
9. AVERAGE TERMS OF NEW COMMITMENTS										
ALL CREDITORS										
Interest (%)	4.3	7.9	6.7	4.7	4.6	6.0	4.9	3.7	3.5	2.7
Maturity (years)	27.2	17.2	20.0	16.6	19.4	14.3	16.1	17.8	16.7	19.2
Grace period (years)	7.4	4.9	6.4	4.3	5.1	3.8	5.0	5.9	4.6	5.8
Grant element (%)	38.0	15.8	24.7	31.3	34.2	21.8	30.7	40.3	38.9	48.3
Official creditors										
Interest (%)	3.9	4.1	5.4	4.1	4.4	5.7	4.5	2.9	3.0	1.8
Maturity (years)	31.7	20.7	23.7	19.2	20.3	16.9	17.8	21.2	19.2	23.1
Grace period (years)	8.8	5.3	8.3	5.7	5.4	4.5	5.3	6.3	5.8	7.3
Grant element (%)	44.0	39.5	35.9	38.7	36.0	25.9	34.8	49.1	45.9	59.2
Private creditors										
Interest (%)	6.1	12.1	9.7	6.1	6.9	6.5	6.6	5.3	4.8	5.4
Maturity (years)	8.6	13.4	11.6	11.1	8.2	9.3	9.1	11.6	10.3	6.7
Grace period (years)	1.7	4.5	2.3	1.3	0.6	2.6	3.5	5.2	1.7	1.0
Grant element (%)	13.7	-10.0	-0.1	15.7	9.5	13.8	14.1	24.4	21.2	13.5
Memorandum items										
Commitments	251	1,920	2,311	1,660	2,313	1,063	1,903	1,123	1,841	176
Official creditors	201	1,000	1,596	1,128	2,153	704	1,519	721	1,318	134
Private creditors	50	920	715	531	160	359	384	403	523	42

10. CONTRACTUAL OBLIGATIONS ON OUTSTANDING LONG-TERM DEBT

	2001	2002	2003	2004	2005	2006	2007	2008	2009	2010
TOTAL										
Disbursements	1,204	916	545	311	181	105	40	19	8	0
Principal	2,174	1,985	2,113	1,839	1,379	1,224	1,103	985	944	859
Interest	888	810	709	601	485	416	356	305	254	212
Official creditors										
Disbursements	975	798	501	298	179	105	40	19	8	0
Principal	1,194	1,105	1,088	1,085	1,083	1,048	951	875	836	764
Interest	586	546	504	456	404	351	299	253	212	174
Bilateral creditors										
Disbursements	495	338	197	103	48	22	7	0	0	0
Principal	627	517	523	505	474	411	398	364	361	349
Interest	251	226	205	182	159	137	118	101	86	72
Multilateral creditors										
Disbursements	480	461	305	195	131	83	33	19	8	0
Principal	567	588	564	580	609	638	554	511	475	414
Interest	335	321	299	274	245	214	181	152	126	102
Private creditors										
Disbursements	229	118	44	13	2	0	0	0	0	0
Principal	981	879	1,026	754	296	176	152	110	108	95
Interest	302	263	205	145	81	66	57	51	42	38
Commercial banks										
Disbursements	143	65	23	6	0	0	0	0	0	0
Principal	630	621	797	538	98	54	41	34	33	25
Interest	183	163	119	71	20	14	11	9	7	5
Other private										
Disbursements	85	53	21	7	2	0	0	0	0	0
Principal	351	259	229	216	198	122	111	76	75	70
Interest	118	100	86	74	62	52	46	42	35	32

MOZAMBIQUE

(US$ million, unless otherwise indicated)

1. SUMMARY DEBT DATA

	1970	1980	1990	1994	1995	1996	1997	1998	1999	2000
TOTAL DEBT STOCKS (EDT)	..	..	**4,650**	**7,272**	**7,458**	**7,566**	**7,632**	**8,302**	**6,982**	**7,135**
Long-term debt (LDOD)	..	..	**4,231**	**6,871**	**6,978**	**7,203**	**7,123**	**7,730**	**6,392**	**6,346**
Public and publicly guaranteed	..	..	4,211	5,219	5,209	5,358	5,211	5,973	4,645	4,599
Private nonguaranteed	..	..	19	1,652	1,769	1,845	1,912	1,757	1,747	1,747
Use of IMF credit	**0**	**0**	**74**	**212**	**202**	**181**	**189**	**207**	**200**	**220**
Short-term debt	..	..	**345**	**189**	**279**	**182**	**320**	**365**	**390**	**570**
of which interest arrears on LDOD	..	..	207	171	250	164	202	249	161	405
Official creditors	..	..	76	166	245	162	200	247	159	395
Private creditors	..	..	131	4	5	2	2	2	2	10
Memo: principal arrears on LDOD	..	..	725	884	1,087	1,117	1,177	1,184	221	587
Official creditors	..	..	373	870	1,074	1,114	1,174	1,181	219	537
Private creditors	..	..	352	14	12	3	3	3	3	50
Memo: export credits	..	..	986	1,105	1,113	999	1,492	1,096	1,261	1,010
TOTAL DEBT FLOWS										
Disbursements	..	..	**242**	**254**	**267**	**300**	**300**	**259**	**161**	**191**
Long-term debt	..	..	230	233	267	282	265	224	132	132
IMF purchases	0	0	12	21	0	18	35	34	29	60
Principal repayments	..	..	**41**	**67**	**85**	**92**	**64**	**64**	**71**	**56**
Long-term debt	..	..	41	57	71	59	49	39	40	27
IMF repurchases	0	0	0	11	14	33	15	25	31	29
Net flows on debt	..	..	**173**	**189**	**193**	**197**	**335**	**193**	**203**	**71**
of which short-term debt	..	..	-28	2	11	-11	100	-2	113	-64
Interest payments (INT)	..	..	**38**	**56**	**77**	**49**	**45**	**40**	**48**	**31**
Long-term debt	..	..	23	54	75	46	41	36	40	19
IMF charges	0	0	0	1	1	2	1	1	2	1
Short-term debt	..	..	15	1	1	1	3	4	6	11
Net transfers on debt	..	..	**136**	**133**	**116**	**148**	**290**	**153**	**155**	**40**
Total debt service paid (TDS)	..	..	**79**	**123**	**162**	**141**	**110**	**104**	**119**	**88**
Long-term debt	..	..	64	111	146	106	91	75	80	46
IMF repurchases and charges	0	0	0	12	16	34	16	25	33	30
Short-term debt (interest only)	..	..	15	1	1	1	3	4	6	11

2. AGGREGATE NET RESOURCE FLOWS AND NET TRANSFERS (LONG-TERM)

	1970	1980	1990	1994	1995	1996	1997	1998	1999	2000
NET RESOURCE FLOWS	..	..	**948**	**849**	**1,011**	**736**	**797**	**1,072**	**1,785**	**971**
Net flow of long-term debt (ex. IMF)	..	..	189	176	196	222	216	185	92	104
Foreign direct investment (net)	..	..	9	35	45	73	64	213	382	139
Portfolio equity flows	..	..	0	0	0	0	0	0	0	0
Grants (excluding technical coop.)	..	..	750	638	770	441	517	674	1,311	728
Memo: technical coop. grants	..	..	92	239	233	190	162	150	156	174
official net resource flows	..	..	913	816	942	669	732	863	1,413	833
private net resource flows	..	..	35	33	69	67	66	209	372	138
NET TRANSFERS	..	..	**925**	**793**	**936**	**687**	**754**	**1,032**	**1,730**	**912**
Interest on long-term debt	..	..	23	54	75	46	41	36	40	19
Profit remittances on FDI	..	..	0	2	0	3	2	4	15	40
Memo: official net transfers	..	..	897	763	871	624	691	835	1,381	814
private net transfers	..	..	28	30	65	63	63	197	349	98

3. MAJOR ECONOMIC AGGREGATES

	1970	1980	1990	1994	1995	1996	1997	1998	1999	2000
Gross national income (GNI)	..	..	2,320	1,984	2,133	2,673	3,218	3,662	3,789	3,603
Exports of goods & services (XGS)	..	..	300	395	470	540	572	577	639	769
of which workers remittances	..	..	0	0	0	0	0	0	..	..
Imports of goods & services (MGS)	..	..	1,164	1,427	1,254	1,186	1,181	1,320	1,783	1,767
International reserves (RES)	..	..	233	178	195	344	537	628	669	744
Current account balance	..	..	-415	-467	-445	-421	-296	-429	..	..

4. DEBT INDICATORS

	1970	1980	1990	1994	1995	1996	1997	1998	1999	2000
EDT / XGS (%)	..	..	1,550.9	1,839.1	1,585.5	1,400.3	1,333.6	1,438.5	1,092.1	927.8
EDT / GNI (%)	..	..	200.4	366.5	349.7	283.1	237.2	226.7	184.3	198.1
TDS / XGS (%)	..	..	26.2	31.2	34.5	26.0	19.2	18.0	18.5	11.4
INT / XGS (%)	..	..	12.6	14.2	16.4	9.0	7.9	6.9	7.4	4.0
INT / GNI (%)	..	..	1.6	2.8	3.6	1.8	1.4	1.1	1.3	0.9
RES / EDT (%)	..	..	5.0	2.4	2.6	4.6	7.0	7.6	9.6	10.4
RES / MGS (months)	..	..	2.4	1.5	1.9	3.5	5.5	5.7	4.5	5.1
Short-term / EDT (%)	..	..	7.4	2.6	3.7	2.4	4.2	4.4	5.6	8.0
Concessional / EDT (%)	..	..	44.8	44.6	39.4	42.4	41.7	48.8	50.4	49.3
Multilateral / EDT (%)	..	..	10.0	14.4	17.1	19.6	21.2	22.9	15.5	15.8

MOZAMBIQUE

(US$ million, unless otherwise indicated)

	1970	1980	1990	1994	1995	1996	1997	1998	1999	2000
5. LONG-TERM DEBT										
DEBT OUTSTANDING (LDOD)	..	..	**4,231**	**6,871**	**6,978**	**7,203**	**7,123**	**7,730**	**6,392**	**6,346**
Public and publicly guaranteed	..	..	**4,211**	**5,219**	**5,209**	**5,358**	**5,211**	**5,973**	**4,645**	**4,599**
Official creditors	..	..	3,560	5,128	5,163	5,331	5,193	5,960	4,633	4,588
Multilateral	..	..	464	1,050	1,277	1,483	1,618	1,900	1,079	1,130
Concessional	..	..	406	975	1,196	1,401	1,533	1,803	1,015	1,081
Bilateral	..	..	3,097	4,078	3,886	3,848	3,575	4,060	3,554	3,458
Concessional	..	..	1,677	2,265	1,741	1,803	1,651	2,251	2,502	2,436
Private creditors	..	..	651	91	46	27	18	13	12	11
Bonds	..	..	0	0	0	0	0	0	0	0
Commercial banks	..	..	147	7	7	2	2	1	1	0
Other private	..	..	504	84	39	25	17	12	11	11
Private nonguaranteed	..	..	**19**	**1,652**	**1,769**	**1,845**	**1,912**	**1,757**	**1,747**	**1,747**
Bonds	..	..	0	0	0	0	0	0	0	0
Commercial banks and other	..	..	19	1,652	1,769	1,845	1,912	1,757	1,747	1,747
Memo:										
IBRD	0	0	0	0	0	0	0	0	0	0
IDA	0	0	268	714	890	1,076	1,160	1,335	702	760
DISBURSEMENTS	..	..	**230**	**233**	**267**	**282**	**265**	**224**	**132**	**132**
Public and publicly guaranteed	..	..	**210**	**230**	**231**	**282**	**259**	**224**	**132**	**132**
Official creditors	..	..	186	229	231	282	259	224	132	132
Multilateral	..	..	96	220	219	275	244	220	121	129
Concessional	..	..	89	211	208	265	224	216	120	125
Bilateral	..	..	91	10	11	7	15	4	11	3
Concessional	..	..	91	10	11	7	15	4	10	3
Private creditors	..	..	24	1	0	0	0	0	0	0
Bonds	..	..	0	0	0	0	0	0	0	0
Commercial banks	..	..	0	0	0	0	0	0	0	0
Other private	..	..	24	1	0	0	0	0	0	0
Private nonguaranteed	..	..	**20**	**3**	**36**	**0**	**6**	**0**	**0**	**0**
Bonds	..	..	0	0	0	0	0	0	0	0
Commercial banks and other	..	..	20	3	36	0	6	0	0	0
Memo:										
IBRD	0	0	0	0	0	0	0	0	0	0
IDA	0	0	74	176	160	221	148	131	80	98
PRINCIPAL REPAYMENTS	..	..	**41**	**57**	**71**	**59**	**49**	**39**	**40**	**27**
Public and publicly guaranteed	..	..	**29**	**54**	**67**	**55**	**45**	**35**	**30**	**27**
Official creditors	..	..	23	51	58	53	44	35	29	27
Multilateral	..	..	9	13	13	17	17	19	13	14
Concessional	..	..	4	5	6	11	9	11	7	11
Bilateral	..	..	13	39	46	36	28	16	16	12
Concessional	..	..	5	11	18	18	24	13	14	11
Private creditors	..	..	7	2	9	1	1	0	0	1
Bonds	..	..	0	0	0	0	0	0	0	0
Commercial banks	..	..	3	1	0	0	0	0	0	1
Other private	..	..	3	2	9	1	1	0	0	0
Private nonguaranteed	..	..	**12**	**3**	**3**	**5**	**4**	**4**	**10**	**0**
Bonds	..	..	0	0	0	0	0	0	0	0
Commercial banks and other	..	..	12	3	3	5	4	4	10	0
Memo:										
IBRD	0	0	0	0	0	0	0	0	0	0
IDA	0	0	0	0	0	1	2	3	2	4
NET FLOWS ON DEBT	..	..	**189**	**176**	**196**	**222**	**216**	**185**	**92**	**104**
Public and publicly guaranteed	..	..	**181**	**176**	**163**	**227**	**214**	**189**	**102**	**104**
Official creditors	..	..	164	178	172	229	215	189	103	105
Multilateral	..	..	86	207	207	258	228	201	108	114
Concessional	..	..	85	206	202	255	216	206	113	114
Bilateral	..	..	77	-29	-34	-29	-13	-12	-6	-9
Concessional	..	..	85	-2	-7	-11	-9	-9	-4	-9
Private creditors	..	..	17	-2	-9	-1	-1	0	0	-1
Bonds	..	..	0	0	0	0	0	0	0	0
Commercial banks	..	..	-3	-1	0	0	0	0	0	-1
Other private	..	..	21	-1	-9	-1	-1	0	0	0
Private nonguaranteed	..	..	**8**	**0**	**33**	**-5**	**2**	**-4**	**-10**	**0**
Bonds	..	..	0	0	0	0	0	0	0	0
Commercial banks and other	..	..	8	0	33	-5	2	-4	-10	0
Memo:										
IBRD	0	0	0	0	0	0	0	0	0	0
IDA	0	0	74	176	160	220	147	128	78	94

MOZAMBIQUE

(US$ million, unless otherwise indicated)

	1970	1980	1990	1994	1995	1996	1997	1998	1999	2000
INTEREST PAYMENTS (LINT)	..	..	**23**	**54**	**75**	**46**	**41**	**36**	**40**	**19**
Public and publicly guaranteed	..	..	**23**	**54**	**74**	**45**	**41**	**28**	**32**	**19**
Official creditors	..	..	17	53	71	45	41	28	32	19
Multilateral	..	..	7	12	12	15	16	17	12	9
Concessional	..	..	3	7	7	10	11	13	12	8
Bilateral	..	..	10	40	59	30	25	11	21	10
Concessional	..	..	6	10	12	15	16	10	21	9
Private creditors	..	..	6	1	3	0	0	0	0	0
Bonds	..	..	0	0	0	0	0	0	0	0
Commercial banks	..	..	1	0	0	0	0	0	0	0
Other private	..	..	5	1	3	0	0	0	0	0
Private nonguaranteed	..	..	**0**	**0**	**1**	**1**	**1**	**8**	**8**	**0**
Bonds	..	..	0	0	0	0	0	0	0	0
Commercial banks and other	..	..	0	0	1	1	1	8	8	0
Memo:										
IBRD	0	0	0	0	0	0	0	0	0	0
IDA	0	0	1	4	6	7	8	9	11	5
NET TRANSFERS ON DEBT	..	..	**166**	**122**	**122**	**176**	**175**	**149**	**52**	**85**
Public and publicly guaranteed	..	..	**158**	**122**	**90**	**182**	**173**	**161**	**70**	**85**
Official creditors	..	..	147	125	102	183	174	161	70	86
Multilateral	..	..	80	195	195	243	212	184	96	106
Concessional	..	..	82	200	195	245	205	193	101	106
Bilateral	..	..	67	-69	-93	-60	-38	-23	-26	-20
Concessional	..	..	79	-11	-19	-26	-25	-19	-25	-17
Private creditors	..	..	11	-3	-12	-2	-1	0	-1	-1
Bonds	..	..	0	0	0	0	0	0	0	0
Commercial banks	..	..	-5	-1	0	0	0	0	-1	-1
Other private	..	..	16	-3	-12	-1	-1	0	0	0
Private nonguaranteed	..	..	**8**	**0**	**32**	**-6**	**2**	**-12**	**-18**	**0**
Bonds	..	..	0	0	0	0	0	0	0	0
Commercial banks and other	..	..	8	0	32	-6	2	-12	-18	0
Memo:										
IBRD	0	0	0	0	0	0	0	0	0	0
IDA	0	0	73	172	154	214	139	119	67	89
DEBT SERVICE (LTDS)	..	..	**64**	**111**	**146**	**106**	**91**	**75**	**80**	**46**
Public and publicly guaranteed	..	..	**52**	**108**	**141**	**100**	**86**	**63**	**62**	**46**
Official creditors	..	..	39	104	129	99	85	63	62	46
Multilateral	..	..	16	25	25	32	32	36	25	23
Concessional	..	..	7	12	13	21	20	24	19	19
Bilateral	..	..	23	79	104	66	53	28	37	22
Concessional	..	..	11	21	30	33	40	23	35	20
Private creditors	..	..	12	4	12	2	1	0	1	1
Bonds	..	..	0	0	0	0	0	0	0	0
Commercial banks	..	..	5	1	0	0	0	0	1	1
Other private	..	..	8	3	12	1	1	0	0	0
Private nonguaranteed	..	..	**12**	**3**	**5**	**6**	**5**	**12**	**18**	**0**
Bonds	..	..	0	0	0	0	0	0	0	0
Commercial banks and other	..	..	12	3	5	6	5	12	18	0
Memo:										
IBRD	0	0	0	0	0	0	0	0	0	0
IDA	0	0	1	4	6	7	9	12	12	9
UNDISBURSED DEBT	..	..	**835**	**1,336**	**1,275**	**944**	**892**	**716**	**870**	**842**
Official creditors	..	..	822	1,336	1,275	944	892	716	870	842
Private creditors	..	..	13	0	0	0	0	0	0	0
Memorandum items										
Concessional LDOD	..	..	2,083	3,240	2,936	3,204	3,185	4,055	3,517	3,518
Variable rate LDOD	..	..	290	2,221	2,313	2,324	2,352	2,156	2,122	2,119
Public sector LDOD	..	..	4,211	5,219	5,209	5,358	5,211	5,973	4,629	4,583
Private sector LDOD	..	..	20	1,652	1,769	1,845	1,912	1,757	1,763	1,763

6. CURRENCY COMPOSITION OF LONG-TERM DEBT (PERCENT)

	1970	1980	1990	1994	1995	1996	1997	1998	1999	2000
Deutsche mark	..	..	5.0	5.5	4.6	4.5	4.0	3.8	4.3	4.1
French franc	..	..	12.1	9.4	10.1	9.7	8.8	8.7	9.3	8.8
Japanese yen	..	..	1.8	1.9	1.8	1.8	1.7	1.8	2.1	1.9
Pound sterling	..	..	2.4	2.1	2.1	2.2	2.2	2.0	2.5	2.2
Swiss franc	..	..	0.0	0.0	0.0	0.0	0.0	0.0	0.0	0.0
U.S.dollars	..	..	52.8	60.8	60.4	61.8	61.8	61.9	65.9	67.7
Multiple currency	..	..	4.7	7.4	8.4	8.0	8.4	8.2	6.1	5.7
Special drawing rights	..	..	1.3	1.1	1.2	1.1	1.1	1.1	1.5	1.5
All other currencies	..	..	19.9	11.8	11.4	10.9	12.0	12.5	8.3	8.1

MOZAMBIQUE

(US$ million, unless otherwise indicated)

	1970	1980	1990	1994	1995	1996	1997	1998	1999	2000
7. DEBT RESTRUCTURINGS										
Total amount rescheduled	..	..	386	200	66	191	132	596	669	0
Debt stock rescheduled	..	..	0	0	0	0	0	1	0	0
Principal rescheduled	..	..	225	73	162	82	50	142	386	0
Official	..	..	133	66	160	73	48	141	386	0
Private	..	..	92	7	2	9	2	0	0	0
Interest rescheduled	..	..	118	62	57	105	64	84	83	0
Official	..	..	83	61	57	103	63	84	83	0
Private	..	..	35	1	0	2	1	0	0	0
Debt forgiven	..	..	210	57	311	64	215	20	41	1
Memo: interest forgiven	..	..	14	7	12	67	8	0	1	0
Debt stock reduction	..	..	950	0	0	0	0	9	819	0
of which debt buyback	..	..	0	0	0	0	0	0	325	0
8. DEBT STOCK-FLOW RECONCILIATION										
Total change in debt stocks	..	..	287	2,060	187	107	66	670	-1,320	154
Net flows on debt	..	..	173	189	193	197	335	193	203	71
Net change in interest arrears	..	..	-62	23	79	-86	38	47	-88	244
Interest capitalized	..	..	118	62	57	105	64	84	83	0
Debt forgiveness or reduction	..	..	-1,160	-57	-311	-64	-215	-29	-535	-1
Cross-currency valuation	..	..	176	137	86	-121	-322	-13	-947	-260
Residual	..	..	1,041	1,706	83	77	166	388	-37	100
9. AVERAGE TERMS OF NEW COMMITMENTS										
ALL CREDITORS										
Interest (%)	..	..	1.4	0.8	0.9	2.1	1.5	0.8	0.7	0.8
Maturity (years)	..	..	35.0	39.8	36.8	23.8	41.9	42.9	40.6	46.3
Grace period (years)	..	..	9.2	9.9	9.3	8.7	9.7	10.5	10.2	10.2
Grant element (%)	..	..	71.8	79.0	76.4	59.4	73.5	81.6	80.8	82.3
Official creditors										
Interest (%)	..	..	1.3	0.8	0.9	2.1	1.5	0.8	0.7	0.8
Maturity (years)	..	..	35.2	39.8	36.8	23.8	41.9	42.9	40.6	46.3
Grace period (years)	..	..	9.2	9.9	9.3	8.7	9.7	10.5	10.2	10.2
Grant element (%)	..	..	72.3	79.0	76.4	59.4	73.5	81.6	80.8	82.3
Private creditors										
Interest (%)	..	..	9.0	0.0	0.0	0.0	0.0	0.0	0.0	0.0
Maturity (years)	..	..	4.9	0.0	0.0	0.0	0.0	0.0	0.0	0.0
Grace period (years)	..	..	2.9	0.0	0.0	0.0	0.0	0.0	0.0	0.0
Grant element (%)	..	..	2.4	0.0	0.0	0.0	0.0	0.0	0.0	0.0
Memorandum items										
Commitments	..	..	177	570	150	11	303	51	310	163
Official creditors	..	..	176	570	150	11	303	51	310	163
Private creditors	..	..	1	0	0	0	0	0	0	0

10. CONTRACTUAL OBLIGATIONS ON OUTSTANDING LONG-TERM DEBT

	2001	2002	2003	2004	2005	2006	2007	2008	2009	2010
TOTAL										
Disbursements	200	213	154	116	80	45	30	5	0	0
Principal	374	375	352	319	282	191	188	183	177	184
Interest	128	115	100	85	75	67	62	58	54	51
Official creditors										
Disbursements	200	213	154	116	80	45	30	5	0	0
Principal	331	334	317	281	243	151	145	139	132	138
Interest	120	108	94	80	70	62	58	54	51	48
Bilateral creditors										
Disbursements	6	4	2	1	1	0	0	0	0	0
Principal	312	314	293	254	213	118	110	101	92	93
Interest	107	93	78	64	54	46	42	39	36	33
Multilateral creditors										
Disbursements	194	209	152	115	79	44	30	5	0	0
Principal	19	20	24	27	30	32	35	38	40	45
Interest	13	15	16	16	16	16	16	15	15	15
Private creditors										
Disbursements	0	0	0	0	0	0	0	0	0	0
Principal	43	41	35	37	39	41	42	44	45	47
Interest	8	7	6	6	5	4	4	4	4	3
Commercial banks										
Disbursements	0	0	0	0	0	0	0	0	0	0
Principal	0	0	0	0	0	0	0	0	0	0
Interest	0	0	0	0	0	0	0	0	0	0
Other private										
Disbursements	0	0	0	0	0	0	0	0	0	0
Principal	43	41	35	37	39	41	42	44	45	47
Interest	8	7	6	6	5	4	4	4	4	3

MYANMAR

(US$ million, unless otherwise indicated)

	1970	1980	1990	1994	1995	1996	1997	1998	1999	2000
1. SUMMARY DEBT DATA										
TOTAL DEBT STOCKS (EDT)	**123**	**1,500**	**4,695**	**6,555**	**5,771**	**5,184**	**5,503**	**5,647**	**6,004**	**6,046**
Long-term debt (LDOD)	**106**	**1,390**	**4,466**	**6,154**	**5,378**	**4,804**	**5,069**	**5,053**	**5,337**	**5,360**
Public and publicly guaranteed	106	1,390	4,466	6,154	5,378	4,804	5,069	5,053	5,337	5,360
Private nonguaranteed	0	0	0	0	0	0	0	0	0	0
Use of IMF credit	**17**	**106**	**0**	**0**	**0**	**0**	**0**	**0**	**0**	**0**
Short-term debt	**0**	**4**	**229**	**401**	**393**	**381**	**434**	**594**	**666**	**686**
of which interest arrears on LDOD	0	0	200	380	352	366	390	456	509	488
Official creditors	0	0	168	312	285	305	332	401	459	442
Private creditors	0	0	32	68	67	61	58	55	50	46
Memo: principal arrears on LDOD	0	0	377	1,431	1,359	1,289	1,349	1,532	1,803	1,738
Official creditors	0	0	291	1,178	1,100	1,042	1,113	1,290	1,562	1,516
Private creditors	0	0	85	252	259	247	236	241	241	222
Memo: export credits	0	0	282	462	573	538	747	468	422	307
TOTAL DEBT FLOWS										
Disbursements	**22**	**282**	**122**	**59**	**86**	**144**	**615**	**214**	**64**	**15**
Long-term debt	22	269	122	59	86	144	615	214	64	15
IMF purchases	0	14	0	0	0	0	0	0	0	0
Principal repayments	**20**	**89**	**46**	**42**	**180**	**140**	**101**	**79**	**64**	**71**
Long-term debt	20	66	44	42	180	140	101	79	64	71
IMF repurchases	0	23	2	0	0	0	0	0	0	0
Net flows on debt	**1**	**171**	**91**	**30**	**-74**	**-23**	**544**	**230**	**18**	**-16**
of which short-term debt	0	-22	15	13	20	-27	29	94	19	41
Interest payments (INT)	**3**	**52**	**15**	**121**	**70**	**18**	**15**	**14**	**32**	**16**
Long-term debt	3	45	13	120	68	18	13	9	24	4
IMF charges	0	4	0	0	0	0	0	0	0	0
Short-term debt	0	3	2	1	2	1	2	6	8	12
Net transfers on debt	**-2**	**119**	**76**	**-91**	**-144**	**-41**	**529**	**216**	**-14**	**-31**
Total debt service paid (TDS)	**23**	**141**	**60**	**163**	**250**	**158**	**116**	**93**	**97**	**87**
Long-term debt	23	112	57	162	248	157	114	88	88	75
IMF repurchases and charges	0	26	2	0	0	0	0	0	0	0
Short-term debt (interest only)	0	3	2	1	2	1	2	6	8	12
2. AGGREGATE NET RESOURCE FLOWS AND NET TRANSFERS (LONG-TERM)										
NET RESOURCE FLOWS	**16**	**269**	**276**	**289**	**363**	**437**	**972**	**517**	**282**	**244**
Net flow of long-term debt (ex. IMF)	1	202	78	17	-95	4	514	135	-1	-56
Foreign direct investment (net)	0	0	161	126	277	310	387	315	253	255
Portfolio equity flows	0	0	0	29	16	10	-2	0	0	0
Grants (excluding technical coop.)	15	66	37	117	164	113	73	67	29	45
Memo: technical coop. grants	6	31	34	29	45	35	32	35	39	51
official net resource flows	9	240	123	124	34	97	45	119	42	55
private net resource flows	6	29	153	165	329	340	927	398	240	188
NET TRANSFERS	**13**	**223**	**263**	**169**	**295**	**419**	**959**	**508**	**258**	**240**
Interest on long-term debt	3	45	13	120	68	18	13	9	24	4
Profit remittances on FDI	0	0	0	0	0	0	0	0	0	0
Memo: official net transfers	7	219	113	5	-31	83	35	116	22	55
private net transfers	5	5	151	164	326	337	924	392	235	185
3. MAJOR ECONOMIC AGGREGATES										
Gross national income (GNI)	..	..	..	..	..	..	..	..	..	..
Exports of goods & services (XGS)	129	556	668	1,035	1,307	1,450	1,587	1,791	1,615	1,846
of which workers remittances	..	0	0	1	10	35	21	0	0	..
Imports of goods & services (MGS)	211	869	1,270	1,670	2,173	2,331	2,726	3,003	2,745	2,863
International reserves (RES)	98	409	410	518	651	315	317	382	333	286
Current account balance	-81	-307	-526	-230	-416	-459	-696	-722	-662	-651
4. DEBT INDICATORS										
EDT / XGS (%)	94.9	270.0	703.2	633.1	441.5	357.6	346.9	315.3	371.8	327.6
EDT / GNI (%)	..	..	..	..	..	..	..	..	..	..
TDS / XGS (%)	18.0	25.4	9.1	15.7	19.1	10.9	7.3	5.2	6.0	4.7
INT / XGS (%)	2.2	9.4	2.2	11.7	5.3	1.3	1.0	0.8	2.0	0.9
INT / GNI (%)	..	..	..	..	..	..	..	..	..	..
RES / EDT (%)	80.2	27.3	8.7	7.9	11.3	6.1	5.8	6.8	5.5	4.7
RES / MGS (months)	5.6	5.6	3.9	3.7	3.6	1.6	1.4	1.5	1.5	1.2
Short-term / EDT (%)	0.0	0.3	4.9	6.1	6.8	7.3	7.9	10.5	11.1	11.4
Concessional / EDT (%)	45.8	72.7	87.6	86.6	84.7	83.5	74.1	77.5	78.4	71.0
Multilateral / EDT (%)	12.2	18.7	26.3	22.2	23.1	23.6	21.3	21.2	20.8	20.9

MYANMAR

(US$ million, unless otherwise indicated)

	1970	1980	1990	1994	1995	1996	1997	1998	1999	2000
5. LONG-TERM DEBT										
DEBT OUTSTANDING (LDOD)	**106**	**1,390**	**4,466**	**6,154**	**5,378**	**4,804**	**5,069**	**5,053**	**5,337**	**5,360**
Public and publicly guaranteed	**106**	**1,390**	**4,466**	**6,154**	**5,378**	**4,804**	**5,069**	**5,053**	**5,337**	**5,360**
Official creditors	72	1,109	4,216	5,820	5,011	4,438	4,177	4,476	4,806	4,380
Multilateral	15	280	1,234	1,458	1,331	1,223	1,171	1,199	1,251	1,266
Concessional	0	274	1,228	1,454	1,328	1,222	1,170	1,199	1,251	1,266
Bilateral	57	829	2,982	4,362	3,680	3,215	3,006	3,277	3,555	3,114
Concessional	56	817	2,884	4,225	3,558	3,109	2,909	3,175	3,453	3,024
Private creditors	34	281	250	334	367	366	892	577	531	980
Bonds	0	0	0	0	0	0	0	0	0	0
Commercial banks	0	51	0	0	0	0	440	38	4	546
Other private	34	231	250	334	367	366	452	539	527	434
Private nonguaranteed	**0**	**0**	**0**	**0**	**0**	**0**	**0**	**0**	**0**	**0**
Bonds	0	0	0	0	0	0	0	0	0	0
Commercial banks and other	0	0	0	0	0	0	0	0	0	0
Memo:										
IBRD	15	0	0	0	0	0	0	0	0	0
IDA	0	146	716	818	777	742	724	727	723	802
DISBURSEMENTS	**22**	**269**	**122**	**59**	**86**	**144**	**615**	**214**	**64**	**15**
Public and publicly guaranteed	**22**	**269**	**122**	**59**	**86**	**144**	**615**	**214**	**64**	**15**
Official creditors	3	199	119	31	17	96	33	100	35	12
Multilateral	0	38	68	12	0	-1	0	0	0	1
Concessional	0	38	68	12	0	-1	0	0	0	1
Bilateral	3	161	51	19	16	97	33	100	34	11
Concessional	2	160	51	19	16	97	33	100	34	11
Private creditors	19	70	3	28	69	47	583	114	29	3
Bonds	0	0	0	0	0	0	0	0	0	0
Commercial banks	0	15	0	0	0	0	440	0	0	0
Other private	19	55	3	28	69	47	143	114	29	3
Private nonguaranteed	**0**	**0**	**0**	**0**	**0**	**0**	**0**	**0**	**0**	**0**
Bonds	0	0	0	0	0	0	0	0	0	0
Commercial banks and other	0	0	0	0	0	0	0	0	0	0
Memo:										
IBRD	0	0	0	0	0	0	0	0	0	0
IDA	0	23	57	7	0	-1	0	0	0	0
PRINCIPAL REPAYMENTS	**20**	**66**	**44**	**42**	**180**	**140**	**101**	**79**	**64**	**71**
Public and publicly guaranteed	**20**	**66**	**44**	**42**	**180**	**140**	**101**	**79**	**64**	**71**
Official creditors	8	26	33	24	147	111	61	48	22	2
Multilateral	2	0	15	23	25	27	19	2	4	2
Concessional	0	0	14	22	24	26	18	2	4	2
Bilateral	5	25	18	1	122	85	42	46	18	0
Concessional	5	18	18	1	122	85	42	45	17	0
Private creditors	13	41	11	18	34	28	40	31	43	69
Bonds	0	0	0	0	0	0	0	0	0	0
Commercial banks	0	13	0	0	0	0	0	0	0	0
Other private	13	28	11	18	34	28	40	31	43	69
Private nonguaranteed	**0**	**0**	**0**	**0**	**0**	**0**	**0**	**0**	**0**	**0**
Bonds	0	0	0	0	0	0	0	0	0	0
Commercial banks and other	0	0	0	0	0	0	0	0	0	0
Memo:										
IBRD	2	0	0	0	0	0	0	0	0	0
IDA	0	0	4	9	10	10	7	0	0	0
NET FLOWS ON DEBT	**1**	**202**	**78**	**17**	**-95**	**4**	**514**	**135**	**-1**	**-56**
Public and publicly guaranteed	**1**	**202**	**78**	**17**	**-95**	**4**	**514**	**135**	**-1**	**-56**
Official creditors	-5	173	86	7	-130	-15	-28	52	13	10
Multilateral	-2	38	53	-10	-24	-27	-19	-2	-4	-1
Concessional	0	38	54	-10	-24	-26	-18	-2	-4	-1
Bilateral	-3	135	33	18	-106	12	-9	54	17	11
Concessional	-2	142	33	18	-106	12	-9	55	18	11
Private creditors	6	29	-8	10	36	19	542	83	-14	-66
Bonds	0	0	0	0	0	0	0	0	0	0
Commercial banks	0	2	0	0	0	0	440	0	0	0
Other private	6	27	-8	10	36	19	102	83	-14	-66
Private nonguaranteed	**0**	**0**	**0**	**0**	**0**	**0**	**0**	**0**	**0**	**0**
Bonds	0	0	0	0	0	0	0	0	0	0
Commercial banks and other	0	0	0	0	0	0	0	0	0	0
Memo:										
IBRD	-2	0	0	0	0	0	0	0	0	0
IDA	0	23	53	-2	-10	-11	-7	0	0	0

MYANMAR

(US$ million, unless otherwise indicated)

	1970	1980	1990	1994	1995	1996	1997	1998	1999	2000
INTEREST PAYMENTS (LINT)	**3**	**45**	**13**	**120**	**68**	**18**	**13**	**9**	**24**	**4**
Public and publicly guaranteed	**3**	**45**	**13**	**120**	**68**	**18**	**13**	**9**	**24**	**4**
Official creditors	2	21	11	119	66	15	10	3	20	0
Multilateral	1	3	10	12	13	12	7	1	1	0
Concessional	0	2	10	12	12	11	7	0	1	0
Bilateral	1	19	1	107	53	3	3	3	19	0
Concessional	1	17	1	107	50	1	1	2	17	0
Private creditors	1	24	2	1	2	3	3	5	4	3
Bonds	0	0	0	0	0	0	0	0	0	0
Commercial banks	0	8	0	0	0	0	0	0	0	0
Other private	1	16	2	1	2	3	3	5	4	3
Private nonguaranteed	**0**	**0**	**0**	**0**	**0**	**0**	**0**	**0**	**0**	**0**
Bonds	0	0	0	0	0	0	0	0	0	0
Commercial banks and other	0	0	0	0	0	0	0	0	0	0
Memo:										
IBRD	1	0	0	0	0	0	0	0	0	0
IDA	0	1	5	6	6	6	4	0	0	0
NET TRANSFERS ON DEBT	**-2**	**157**	**65**	**-104**	**-162**	**-14**	**501**	**127**	**-24**	**-60**
Public and publicly guaranteed	**-2**	**157**	**65**	**-104**	**-162**	**-14**	**501**	**127**	**-24**	**-60**
Official creditors	-7	152	76	-112	-196	-30	-38	49	-7	10
Multilateral	-3	36	43	-23	-37	-39	-26	-3	-5	-1
Concessional	0	36	44	-22	-36	-38	-25	-3	-5	-1
Bilateral	-4	117	33	-89	-159	9	-13	52	-2	11
Concessional	-3	125	33	-89	-156	11	-10	53	0	11
Private creditors	6	5	-10	8	33	16	539	78	-18	-70
Bonds	0	0	0	0	0	0	0	0	0	0
Commercial banks	0	-6	0	0	0	0	440	0	0	0
Other private	6	11	-10	8	33	16	99	78	-18	-70
Private nonguaranteed	**0**	**0**	**0**	**0**	**0**	**0**	**0**	**0**	**0**	**0**
Bonds	0	0	0	0	0	0	0	0	0	0
Commercial banks and other	0	0	0	0	0	0	0	0	0	0
Memo:										
IBRD	-3	0	0	0	0	0	0	0	0	0
IDA	0	22	48	-8	-16	-17	-11	0	0	0
DEBT SERVICE (LTDS)	**23**	**112**	**57**	**162**	**248**	**157**	**114**	**88**	**88**	**75**
Public and publicly guaranteed	**23**	**112**	**57**	**162**	**248**	**157**	**114**	**88**	**88**	**75**
Official creditors	10	47	44	143	212	126	71	51	41	2
Multilateral	3	3	25	35	37	38	26	3	5	2
Concessional	0	2	24	34	36	37	25	3	5	2
Bilateral	6	44	19	108	175	88	45	49	37	0
Concessional	6	35	19	108	172	85	43	47	34	0
Private creditors	14	65	13	20	36	31	43	36	47	73
Bonds	0	0	0	0	0	0	0	0	0	0
Commercial banks	0	21	0	0	0	0	0	0	0	0
Other private	14	44	13	20	36	31	43	36	47	73
Private nonguaranteed	**0**	**0**	**0**	**0**	**0**	**0**	**0**	**0**	**0**	**0**
Bonds	0	0	0	0	0	0	0	0	0	0
Commercial banks and other	0	0	0	0	0	0	0	0	0	0
Memo:										
IBRD	3	0	0	0	0	0	0	0	0	0
IDA	0	1	9	15	16	16	11	0	0	0
UNDISBURSED DEBT	**106**	**1,282**	**915**	**951**	**859**	**893**	**745**	**560**	**551**	**35**
Official creditors	74	1,072	890	874	770	674	615	507	528	32
Private creditors	32	211	24	76	89	219	130	53	23	3
Memorandum items										
Concessional LDOD	56	1,090	4,112	5,679	4,886	4,331	4,079	4,374	4,704	4,290
Variable rate LDOD	0	70	0	0	0	0	440	38	4	546
Public sector LDOD	106	1,390	4,466	6,154	5,378	4,804	5,069	5,053	5,337	5,360
Private sector LDOD	0	0	0	0	0	0	0	0	0	0

6. CURRENCY COMPOSITION OF LONG-TERM DEBT (PERCENT)

	1970	1980	1990	1994	1995	1996	1997	1998	1999	2000
Deutsche mark	15.4	11.6	12.4	11.2	12.0	12.0	10.3	10.5	8.8	8.2
French franc	0.0	2.6	3.0	1.3	1.4	1.4	1.2	1.2	1.0	0.9
Japanese yen	0.0	42.8	46.8	55.9	52.3	50.1	44.5	48.8	52.5	44.3
Pound sterling	31.2	4.3	1.7	1.2	1.3	1.5	1.5	1.4	1.3	1.2
Swiss franc	0.0	0.2	0.0	0.0	0.0	0.0	0.0	0.0	0.0	0.0
U.S.dollars	21.7	23.3	24.3	20.3	22.6	24.7	33.4	28.5	26.2	36.3
Multiple currency	14.0	7.7	7.6	7.1	7.0	6.8	6.0	6.4	6.9	6.0
Special drawing rights	0.0	0.0	0.0	0.0	0.0	0.0	0.0	0.0	0.0	0.0
All other currencies	17.7	7.5	4.2	3.0	3.4	3.5	3.1	3.2	3.3	3.1

MYANMAR

(US$ million, unless otherwise indicated)

	1970	1980	1990	1994	1995	1996	1997	1998	1999	2000
7. DEBT RESTRUCTURINGS										
Total amount rescheduled	..	..	0	0	0	0	0	0	0	0
Debt stock rescheduled	..	..	0	0	0	0	0	0	0	0
Principal rescheduled	..	..	0	0	0	0	0	0	0	0
Official	..	..	0	0	0	0	0	0	0	0
Private	..	..	0	0	0	0	0	0	0	0
Interest rescheduled	..	..	0	0	0	0	0	0	0	0
Official	..	..	0	0	0	0	0	0	0	0
Private	..	..	0	0	0	0	0	0	0	0
Debt forgiven	..	..	0	0	0	0	0	0	0	0
Memo: interest forgiven	..	..	0	0	0	0	0	0	0	0
Debt stock reduction	..	..	0	0	0	0	0	0	0	0
of which debt buyback	..	..	0	0	0	0	0	0	0	0
8. DEBT STOCK-FLOW RECONCILIATION										
Total change in debt stocks	..	..	504	803	-785	-586	319	144	357	43
Net flows on debt	1	171	91	30	-74	-23	544	230	18	-16
Net change in interest arrears	..	..	90	26	-29	15	24	66	54	-21
Interest capitalized	..	..	0	0	0	0	0	0	0	0
Debt forgiveness or reduction	..	..	0	0	0	0	0	0	0	0
Cross-currency valuation	..	..	306	706	-755	-627	-296	216	301	-459
Residual	..	..	18	42	73	49	47	-367	-16	538
9. AVERAGE TERMS OF NEW COMMITMENTS										
ALL CREDITORS										
Interest (%)	4.2	3.5	2.7	0.5	1.4	1.4	7.0	3.3	0.0	0.0
Maturity (years)	15.6	29.0	13.7	7.5	14.4	11.1	6.5	7.6	0.0	0.0
Grace period (years)	4.4	7.4	3.4	2.1	8.7	3.2	1.4	3.0	0.0	0.0
Grant element (%)	32.1	52.2	39.3	25.6	39.1	40.2	9.7	25.8	0.0	0.0
Official creditors										
Interest (%)	2.7	1.6	1.5	2.5	2.8	1.8	2.8	0.0	0.0	0.0
Maturity (years)	28.3	37.0	16.7	24.6	33.0	13.6	15.6	0.0	0.0	0.0
Grace period (years)	7.9	9.6	5.2	7.1	24.4	4.1	5.5	0.0	0.0	0.0
Grant element (%)	56.9	71.0	53.3	55.9	62.6	44.7	43.4	0.0	0.0	0.0
Private creditors										
Interest (%)	5.3	8.0	3.5	0.0	0.8	1.1	7.2	3.3	0.0	0.0
Maturity (years)	6.3	10.4	11.6	3.4	6.4	8.9	6.2	7.6	0.0	0.0
Grace period (years)	1.8	2.2	2.1	0.9	1.8	2.4	1.2	3.0	0.0	0.0
Grant element (%)	13.9	8.5	29.4	18.4	28.8	36.2	8.6	25.8	0.0	0.0
Memorandum items										
Commitments	42	605	42	37	118	342	514	27	0	0
Official creditors	18	423	17	7	36	162	16	0	0	0
Private creditors	24	182	24	30	82	181	498	27	0	0

10. CONTRACTUAL OBLIGATIONS ON OUTSTANDING LONG-TERM DEBT

	2001	2002	2003	2004	2005	2006	2007	2008	2009	2010
TOTAL										
Disbursements	9	6	3	2	1	1	0	0	0	0
Principal	445	408	404	220	206	196	180	172	154	123
Interest	80	63	47	34	30	26	23	20	17	14
Official creditors										
Disbursements	8	5	2	2	1	1	0	0	0	0
Principal	198	182	185	188	185	184	177	172	154	123
Interest	44	40	37	33	30	26	23	20	17	14
Bilateral creditors										
Disbursements	6	4	2	1	1	1	0	0	0	0
Principal	156	138	139	139	137	136	130	124	107	76
Interest	33	30	27	24	21	18	15	12	9	7
Multilateral creditors										
Disbursements	2	1	1	1	0	0	0	0	0	0
Principal	42	44	46	48	48	48	48	48	47	47
Interest	11	10	10	10	9	9	8	8	7	7
Private creditors										
Disbursements	2	1	0	0	0	0	0	0	0	0
Principal	247	227	219	33	21	12	3	0	0	0
Interest	36	23	10	1	0	0	0	0	0	0
Commercial banks										
Disbursements	0	0	0	0	0	0	0	0	0	0
Principal	182	182	182	0	0	0	0	0	0	0
Interest	33	21	9	0	0	0	0	0	0	0
Other private										
Disbursements	2	1	0	0	0	0	0	0	0	0
Principal	65	45	37	33	21	12	3	0	0	0
Interest	3	2	1	1	0	0	0	0	0	0

NEPAL

(US$ million, unless otherwise indicated)

	1970	1980	1990	1994	1995	1996	1997	1998	1999	2000
1. SUMMARY DEBT DATA										
TOTAL DEBT STOCKS (EDT)	**3**	**205**	**1,640**	**2,328**	**2,418**	**2,411**	**2,390**	**2,646**	**2,970**	**2,823**
Long-term debt (LDOD)	**3**	**156**	**1,572**	**2,210**	**2,347**	**2,346**	**2,332**	**2,591**	**2,910**	**2,784**
Public and publicly guaranteed	3	156	1,572	2,210	2,347	2,346	2,332	2,591	2,910	2,784
Private nonguaranteed	0	0	0	0	0	0	0	0	0	0
Use of IMF credit	**0**	**42**	**44**	**55**	**48**	**39**	**30**	**24**	**18**	**12**
Short-term debt	**0**	**7**	**24**	**63**	**23**	**26**	**28**	**31**	**43**	**26**
of which interest arrears on LDOD	0	0	4	2	2	2	1	2	0	0
Official creditors	0	0	4	2	2	2	1	2	0	0
Private creditors	0	0	0	0	0	0	0	0	0	0
Memo: principal arrears on LDOD	0	0	6	6	8	10	9	9	2	1
Official creditors	0	0	6	3	3	4	4	4	1	1
Private creditors	0	0	0	3	5	6	5	4	1	0
Memo: export credits	0	0	109	82	41	25	82	13	11	10
TOTAL DEBT FLOWS										
Disbursements	**1**	**69**	**168**	**198**	**164**	**158**	**214**	**177**	**145**	**155**
Long-term debt	1	50	168	191	164	158	214	177	145	155
IMF purchases	0	18	0	8	0	0	0	0	0	0
Principal repayments	**2**	**3**	**41**	**48**	**53**	**47**	**70**	**61**	**75**	**71**
Long-term debt	2	2	29	42	45	39	63	54	69	66
IMF repurchases	0	1	12	5	8	8	7	7	6	4
Net flows on debt	**-2**	**61**	**129**	**194**	**71**	**114**	**146**	**118**	**83**	**68**
of which short-term debt	0	-5	2	43	-40	3	3	2	13	-16
Interest payments (INT)	**0**	**5**	**29**	**32**	**32**	**31**	**28**	**27**	**32**	**29**
Long-term debt	0	2	25	30	29	30	26	26	30	27
IMF charges	0	1	2	0	0	0	0	0	0	0
Short-term debt	0	2	2	2	2	1	2	2	2	2
Net transfers on debt	**-2**	**56**	**100**	**162**	**39**	**83**	**119**	**91**	**51**	**39**
Total debt service paid (TDS)	**2**	**8**	**70**	**80**	**85**	**78**	**98**	**88**	**107**	**100**
Long-term debt	2	4	54	72	74	69	89	80	99	93
IMF repurchases and charges	0	1	14	6	8	8	7	7	6	4
Short-term debt (interest only)	0	2	2	2	2	1	2	2	2	2
2. AGGREGATE NET RESOURCE FLOWS AND NET TRANSFERS (LONG-TERM)										
NET RESOURCE FLOWS	**7**	**127**	**288**	**325**	**298**	**280**	**313**	**251**	**228**	**237**
Net flow of long-term debt (ex. IMF)	-2	48	139	148	119	119	151	123	76	89
Foreign direct investment (net)	0	0	6	7	8	19	23	12	4	4
Portfolio equity flows	0	0	0	0	0	0	0	0	0	0
Grants (excluding technical coop.)	9	79	143	170	171	142	140	117	148	143
Memo: technical coop. grants	8	50	106	141	142	142	133	138	107	108
official net resource flows	7	127	296	327	295	264	307	252	237	240
private net resource flows	0	0	-8	-2	3	16	6	-1	-8	-4
NET TRANSFERS	**7**	**125**	**263**	**296**	**269**	**250**	**287**	**226**	**198**	**210**
Interest on long-term debt	0	2	25	30	29	30	26	26	30	27
Profit remittances on FDI	0	0	0	0	0	0	0	0	0	0
Memo: official net transfers	7	125	282	303	271	239	285	230	209	214
private net transfers	0	0	-19	-8	-2	11	2	-4	-10	-4
3. MAJOR ECONOMIC AGGREGATES										
Gross national income (GNI)	866	1,958	3,695	4,124	4,485	4,574	5,004	4,950	5,193	5,687
Exports of goods & services (XGS)	71	269	524	1,072	1,206	1,111	1,428	1,259	1,354	1,529
of which workers remittances	..	30	61	70	101	78	98	113	152	183
Imports of goods & services (MGS)	96	368	774	1,282	1,542	1,645	1,885	1,671	1,523	1,814
International reserves (RES)	94	272	354	752	646	628	671	800	887	989
Current account balance	-1	-93	-251	-225	-356	-527	-460	-421	-168	-293
4. DEBT INDICATORS										
EDT / XGS (%)	3.9	76.0	312.9	217.2	200.5	216.9	167.4	210.1	219.4	184.7
EDT / GNI (%)	0.3	10.4	44.4	56.4	53.9	52.7	47.8	53.5	57.2	49.7
TDS / XGS (%)	3.2	2.9	13.4	7.4	7.1	7.0	6.9	7.0	7.9	6.5
INT / XGS (%)	0.1	1.9	5.5	3.0	2.7	2.8	2.0	2.2	2.4	1.9
INT / GNI (%)	0.0	0.3	0.8	0.8	0.7	0.7	0.6	0.6	0.6	0.5
RES / EDT (%)	3,364.4	133.0	21.6	32.3	26.7	26.0	28.1	30.3	29.9	35.0
RES / MGS (months)	11.8	8.9	5.5	7.0	5.0	4.6	4.3	5.8	7.0	6.5
Short-term / EDT (%)	0.0	3.4	1.5	2.7	1.0	1.1	1.2	1.2	1.4	0.9
Concessional / EDT (%)	67.9	75.7	88.5	91.9	94.2	94.7	95.8	96.7	97.5	98.5
Multilateral / EDT (%)	7.1	62.0	77.3	77.5	80.8	82.4	83.2	84.4	85.6	87.1

NEPAL

(US$ million, unless otherwise indicated)

	1970	*1980*	*1990*	*1994*	*1995*	*1996*	*1997*	*1998*	*1999*	*2000*
5. LONG-TERM DEBT										
DEBT OUTSTANDING (LDOD)	**3**	**156**	**1,572**	**2,210**	**2,347**	**2,346**	**2,332**	**2,591**	**2,910**	**2,784**
Public and publicly guaranteed	**3**	**156**	**1,572**	**2,210**	**2,347**	**2,346**	**2,332**	**2,591**	**2,910**	**2,784**
Official creditors	2	156	1,462	2,141	2,281	2,285	2,291	2,561	2,897	2,779
Multilateral	0	127	1,268	1,805	1,952	1,986	1,989	2,233	2,541	2,458
Concessional	0	126	1,259	1,802	1,950	1,984	1,987	2,231	2,541	2,458
Bilateral	2	29	193	337	329	299	302	328	356	321
Concessional	2	29	193	337	329	299	302	328	356	321
Private creditors	1	0	110	69	65	60	41	29	13	5
Bonds	0	0	0	0	0	0	0	0	0	0
Commercial banks	0	0	0	0	0	0	0	0	0	0
Other private	1	0	110	69	65	60	41	29	13	5
Private nonguaranteed	**0**	**0**	**0**	**0**	**0**	**0**	**0**	**0**	**0**	**0**
Bonds	0	0	0	0	0	0	0	0	0	0
Commercial banks and other	0	0	0	0	0	0	0	0	0	0
Memo:										
IBRD	0	0	0	0	0	0	0	0	0	0
IDA	0	76	668	932	1,023	1,049	1,047	1,131	1,147	1,134
DISBURSEMENTS	**1**	**50**	**168**	**191**	**164**	**158**	**214**	**177**	**145**	**155**
Public and publicly guaranteed	**1**	**50**	**168**	**191**	**164**	**158**	**214**	**177**	**145**	**155**
Official creditors	1	50	166	191	164	158	211	177	145	155
Multilateral	0	36	146	150	151	146	159	167	123	144
Concessional	0	36	146	150	151	146	159	167	123	144
Bilateral	0	14	20	41	13	12	52	10	22	11
Concessional	0	14	20	41	13	12	52	10	22	11
Private creditors	0	0	2	0	0	0	3	0	0	0
Bonds	0	0	0	0	0	0	0	0	0	0
Commercial banks	0	0	0	0	0	0	0	0	0	0
Other private	0	0	2	0	0	0	3	0	0	0
Private nonguaranteed	**0**	**0**	**0**	**0**	**0**	**0**	**0**	**0**	**0**	**0**
Bonds	0	0	0	0	0	0	0	0	0	0
Commercial banks and other	0	0	0	0	0	0	0	0	0	0
Memo:										
IBRD	0	0	0	0	0	0	0	0	0	0
IDA	0	25	68	75	82	62	55	63	48	50
PRINCIPAL REPAYMENTS	**2**	**2**	**29**	**42**	**45**	**39**	**63**	**54**	**69**	**66**
Public and publicly guaranteed	**2**	**2**	**29**	**42**	**45**	**39**	**63**	**54**	**69**	**66**
Official creditors	2	2	13	34	40	36	43	42	56	58
Multilateral	0	2	10	23	24	26	28	26	36	37
Concessional	0	2	10	20	24	26	28	26	33	37
Bilateral	2	0	3	11	16	9	15	15	21	21
Concessional	1	0	3	11	16	9	15	15	21	21
Private creditors	0	0	16	9	5	4	20	13	13	8
Bonds	0	0	0	0	0	0	0	0	0	0
Commercial banks	0	0	0	0	0	0	0	0	0	0
Other private	0	0	16	9	5	4	20	13	13	8
Private nonguaranteed	**0**	**0**	**0**	**0**	**0**	**0**	**0**	**0**	**0**	**0**
Bonds	0	0	0	0	0	0	0	0	0	0
Commercial banks and other	0	0	0	0	0	0	0	0	0	0
Memo:										
IBRD	0	0	0	0	0	0	0	0	0	0
IDA	0	0	2	5	7	8	9	11	14	16
NET FLOWS ON DEBT	**-2**	**48**	**139**	**148**	**119**	**119**	**151**	**123**	**76**	**89**
Public and publicly guaranteed	**-2**	**48**	**139**	**148**	**119**	**119**	**151**	**123**	**76**	**89**
Official creditors	-2	48	153	157	124	123	168	135	89	97
Multilateral	0	35	136	127	127	120	132	141	87	107
Concessional	0	35	136	130	127	120	132	141	89	107
Bilateral	-2	14	17	30	-3	3	36	-5	1	-10
Concessional	0	14	17	30	-3	3	36	-5	1	-10
Private creditors	0	0	-14	-9	-5	-4	-17	-13	-13	-8
Bonds	0	0	0	0	0	0	0	0	0	0
Commercial banks	0	0	0	0	0	0	0	0	0	0
Other private	0	0	-14	-9	-5	-4	-17	-13	-13	-8
Private nonguaranteed	**0**	**0**	**0**	**0**	**0**	**0**	**0**	**0**	**0**	**0**
Bonds	0	0	0	0	0	0	0	0	0	0
Commercial banks and other	0	0	0	0	0	0	0	0	0	0
Memo:										
IBRD	0	0	0	0	0	0	0	0	0	0
IDA	0	25	65	69	75	54	46	52	34	34

NEPAL

(US$ million, unless otherwise indicated)

	1970	1980	1990	1994	1995	1996	1997	1998	1999	2000
INTEREST PAYMENTS (LINT)	**0**	**2**	**25**	**30**	**29**	**30**	**26**	**26**	**30**	**27**
Public and publicly guaranteed	**0**	**2**	**25**	**30**	**29**	**30**	**26**	**26**	**30**	**27**
Official creditors	0	2	14	24	24	25	22	22	28	26
Multilateral	0	1	10	16	17	17	17	18	23	22
Concessional	0	1	10	15	17	17	17	18	22	22
Bilateral	0	1	4	7	8	8	5	5	5	5
Concessional	0	1	4	7	8	8	5	5	5	5
Private creditors	0	0	12	6	5	4	4	3	2	1
Bonds	0	0	0	0	0	0	0	0	0	0
Commercial banks	0	0	0	0	0	0	0	0	0	0
Other private	0	0	12	6	5	4	4	3	2	1
Private nonguaranteed	**0**	**0**	**0**	**0**	**0**	**0**	**0**	**0**	**0**	**0**
Bonds	0	0	0	0	0	0	0	0	0	0
Commercial banks and other	0	0	0	0	0	0	0	0	0	0
Memo:										
IBRD	0	0	0	0	0	0	0	0	0	0
IDA	0	0	5	7	8	8	8	8	9	9
NET TRANSFERS ON DEBT	**-2**	**46**	**114**	**119**	**90**	**89**	**124**	**97**	**46**	**62**
Public and publicly guaranteed	**-2**	**46**	**114**	**119**	**90**	**89**	**124**	**97**	**46**	**62**
Official creditors	-2	46	139	134	100	97	146	113	61	71
Multilateral	0	33	126	111	111	103	115	123	64	85
Concessional	0	34	126	115	111	103	115	123	68	85
Bilateral	-2	13	13	23	-11	-5	31	-10	-4	-14
Concessional	0	13	13	23	-11	-5	31	-10	-4	-14
Private creditors	0	0	-25	-15	-10	-8	-21	-16	-15	-9
Bonds	0	0	0	0	0	0	0	0	0	0
Commercial banks	0	0	0	0	0	0	0	0	0	0
Other private	0	0	-25	-15	-10	-8	-21	-16	-15	-9
Private nonguaranteed	**0**	**0**	**0**	**0**	**0**	**0**	**0**	**0**	**0**	**0**
Bonds	0	0	0	0	0	0	0	0	0	0
Commercial banks and other	0	0	0	0	0	0	0	0	0	0
Memo:										
IBRD	0	0	0	0	0	0	0	0	0	0
IDA	0	25	61	63	67	46	38	44	25	26
DEBT SERVICE (LTDS)	**2**	**4**	**54**	**72**	**74**	**69**	**89**	**80**	**99**	**93**
Public and publicly guaranteed	**2**	**4**	**54**	**72**	**74**	**69**	**89**	**80**	**99**	**93**
Official creditors	2	4	27	57	64	61	65	64	84	84
Multilateral	0	3	20	39	40	43	45	44	59	59
Concessional	0	3	20	35	40	43	45	44	55	59
Bilateral	2	1	7	18	24	17	21	20	26	26
Concessional	1	1	7	18	24	17	21	20	26	26
Private creditors	0	0	27	15	10	8	24	16	15	9
Bonds	0	0	0	0	0	0	0	0	0	0
Commercial banks	0	0	0	0	0	0	0	0	0	0
Other private	0	0	27	15	10	8	24	16	15	9
Private nonguaranteed	**0**	**0**	**0**	**0**	**0**	**0**	**0**	**0**	**0**	**0**
Bonds	0	0	0	0	0	0	0	0	0	0
Commercial banks and other	0	0	0	0	0	0	0	0	0	0
Memo:										
IBRD	0	0	0	0	0	0	0	0	0	0
IDA	0	1	7	12	14	16	17	19	22	24
UNDISBURSED DEBT	**26**	**366**	**1,318**	**995**	**799**	**878**	**779**	**672**	**582**	**392**
Official creditors	26	366	1,307	990	794	873	779	672	582	392
Private creditors	0	0	10	5	5	5	0	0	0	0
Memorandum items										
Concessional LDOD	2	155	1,452	2,138	2,278	2,283	2,289	2,559	2,897	2,779
Variable rate LDOD	0	0	0	0	0	0	0	0	0	0
Public sector LDOD	3	156	1,566	2,209	2,346	2,345	2,332	2,590	2,910	2,784
Private sector LDOD	0	0	5	1	1	1	1	1	1	0

6. CURRENCY COMPOSITION OF LONG-TERM DEBT (PERCENT)

	1970	1980	1990	1994	1995	1996	1997	1998	1999	2000
Deutsche mark	20.4	0.0	0.9	0.3	0.3	0.3	0.2	0.2	0.1	0.1
French franc	0.0	0.2	2.0	1.9	1.9	1.8	1.6	1.5	1.4	1.7
Japanese yen	0.0	7.9	8.4	12.3	11.2	9.8	10.2	9.9	9.5	8.5
Pound sterling	50.8	0.2	0.2	0.1	0.1	0.1	0.1	0.1	0.1	0.1
Swiss franc	0.0	0.0	0.0	0.0	0.0	0.0	0.0	0.0	0.0	0.0
U.S.dollars	8.5	49.5	49.6	44.3	43.8	43.7	42.5	41.4	37.0	39.0
Multiple currency	3.9	31.2	32.6	36.0	35.9	35.9	36.5	37.7	43.6	42.3
Special drawing rights	0.0	0.0	2.7	3.2	5.0	6.4	7.1	7.4	6.8	6.8
All other currencies	16.4	11.0	3.6	1.9	1.8	2.0	1.8	1.8	1.5	1.5

NEPAL

(US$ million, unless otherwise indicated)

	1970	1980	1990	1994	1995	1996	1997	1998	1999	2000
7. DEBT RESTRUCTURINGS										
Total amount rescheduled	..	..	0	0	0	0	0	0	0	0
Debt stock rescheduled	..	..	0	0	0	0	0	0	0	0
Principal rescheduled	..	..	0	0	0	0	0	0	0	0
Official	..	..	0	0	0	0	0	0	0	0
Private	..	..	0	0	0	0	0	0	0	0
Interest rescheduled	..	..	0	0	0	0	0	0	0	0
Official	..	..	0	0	0	0	0	0	0	0
Private	..	..	0	0	0	0	0	0	0	0
Debt forgiven	..	..	0	0	0	0	0	0	2	0
Memo: interest forgiven	..	..	0	0	0	0	0	0	0	0
Debt stock reduction	..	..	0	0	0	0	0	0	0	0
of which debt buyback	..	..	0	0	0	0	0	0	0	0
8. DEBT STOCK-FLOW RECONCILIATION										
Total change in debt stocks	..	..	272	318	90	-7	-20	255	325	-147
Net flows on debt	-2	61	129	194	71	114	146	118	83	68
Net change in interest arrears	..	..	1	-1	0	0	0	0	-2	0
Interest capitalized	..	..	0	0	0	0	0	0	0	0
Debt forgiveness or reduction	..	..	0	0	0	0	0	0	-2	0
Cross-currency valuation	..	..	127	96	9	-135	-180	119	48	-188
Residual	..	..	15	29	10	14	14	18	197	-28
9. AVERAGE TERMS OF NEW COMMITMENTS										
ALL CREDITORS										
Interest (%)	2.8	0.8	0.9	0.8	3.7	3.2	0.8	3.3	0.8	1.5
Maturity (years)	26.9	46.0	39.2	38.6	36.1	38.7	36.8	38.3	39.8	31.5
Grace period (years)	6.2	10.2	10.3	10.1	9.2	10.3	9.7	9.8	10.3	8.1
Grant element (%)	53.1	81.2	78.8	80.0	51.0	58.7	77.3	56.9	80.6	69.1
Official creditors										
Interest (%)	2.8	0.8	0.9	0.8	3.7	3.2	0.8	3.3	0.8	1.5
Maturity (years)	26.9	46.0	39.2	38.6	36.1	38.7	36.8	38.3	39.8	31.5
Grace period (years)	6.2	10.2	10.3	10.1	9.2	10.3	9.7	9.8	10.3	8.1
Grant element (%)	53.1	81.2	78.8	80.0	51.0	58.7	77.3	56.9	80.6	69.1
Private creditors										
Interest (%)	0.0	0.0	0.0	0.0	0.0	0.0	0.0	0.0	0.0	0.0
Maturity (years)	0.0	0.0	0.0	0.0	0.0	0.0	0.0	0.0	0.0	0.0
Grace period (years)	0.0	0.0	0.0	0.0	0.0	0.0	0.0	0.0	0.0	0.0
Grant element (%)	0.0	0.0	0.0	0.0	0.0	0.0	0.0	0.0	0.0	0.0
Memorandum items										
Commitments	17	92	219	107	60	290	191	84	98	65
Official creditors	17	92	219	107	60	290	191	84	98	65
Private creditors	0	0	0	0	0	0	0	0	0	0

10. CONTRACTUAL OBLIGATIONS ON OUTSTANDING LONG-TERM DEBT

	2001	2002	2003	2004	2005	2006	2007	2008	2009	2010
TOTAL										
Disbursements	144	111	66	38	18	8	4	2	2	0
Principal	61	66	70	73	80	87	91	100	103	107
Interest	30	30	30	29	29	29	33	33	32	30
Official creditors										
Disbursements	144	111	66	38	18	8	4	2	2	0
Principal	60	66	70	73	80	86	91	100	102	106
Interest	30	30	30	29	29	29	33	33	32	30
Bilateral creditors										
Disbursements	12	7	3	1	1	0	0	0	0	0
Principal	22	23	23	23	23	22	22	22	21	19
Interest	5	5	4	4	4	3	3	3	2	2
Multilateral creditors										
Disbursements	132	104	63	37	17	8	4	2	2	0
Principal	38	43	47	50	57	64	69	78	82	87
Interest	24	25	25	25	25	26	30	30	29	28
Private creditors										
Disbursements	0	0	0	0	0	0	0	0	0	0
Principal	0	0	0	0	0	0	0	0	0	0
Interest	0	0	0	0	0	0	0	0	0	0
Commercial banks										
Disbursements	0	0	0	0	0	0	0	0	0	0
Principal	0	0	0	0	0	0	0	0	0	0
Interest	0	0	0	0	0	0	0	0	0	0
Other private										
Disbursements	0	0	0	0	0	0	0	0	0	0
Principal	0	0	0	0	0	0	0	0	0	0
Interest	0	0	0	0	0	0	0	0	0	0

NICARAGUA

(US$ million, unless otherwise indicated)

	1970	1980	1990	1994	1995	1996	1997	1998	1999	2000
1. SUMMARY DEBT DATA										
TOTAL DEBT STOCKS (EDT)	**203**	**2,193**	**10,745**	**11,958**	**10,402**	**5,974**	**6,242**	**6,463**	**7,094**	**7,019**
Long-term debt (LDOD)	**147**	**1,671**	**8,313**	**9,666**	**8,578**	**5,161**	**5,377**	**5,676**	**6,010**	**5,860**
Public and publicly guaranteed	147	1,671	8,313	9,666	8,578	5,161	5,377	5,648	5,899	5,602
Private nonguaranteed	0	0	0	0	0	0	0	28	110	258
Use of IMF credit	**8**	**49**	**0**	**51**	**39**	**29**	**27**	**52**	**155**	**169**
Short-term debt	**48**	**472**	**2,432**	**2,241**	**1,785**	**784**	**838**	**736**	**930**	**990**
of which interest arrears on LDOD	0	12	1,693	1,945	1,475	481	573	688	810	868
Official creditors	0	5	1,067	1,244	1,458	475	562	673	798	855
Private creditors	0	8	626	701	18	6	12	15	13	13
Memo: principal arrears on LDOD	0	32	2,464	4,226	3,234	994	921	1,381	1,555	1,158
Official creditors	0	13	1,491	3,125	2,918	723	699	1,161	1,334	943
Private creditors	0	19	973	1,100	316	271	222	220	221	216
Memo: export credits	0	0	643	618	471	801	698	652	589	595
TOTAL DEBT FLOWS										
Disbursements	**54**	**276**	**577**	**368**	**277**	**226**	**610**	**280**	**509**	**501**
Long-term debt	44	276	577	339	277	226	610	258	402	474
IMF purchases	10	0	0	29	0	0	0	23	107	27
Principal repayments	**29**	**46**	**4**	**103**	**203**	**134**	**182**	**86**	**99**	**192**
Long-term debt	16	45	4	100	190	124	182	86	96	186
IMF repurchases	13	1	0	3	13	9	0	0	3	5
Net flows on debt	**24**	**345**	**593**	**198**	**88**	**85**	**390**	**-22**	**481**	**312**
of which short-term debt	0	115	21	-67	14	-7	-38	-217	71	3
Interest payments (INT)	**7**	**69**	**11**	**104**	**86**	**85**	**144**	**169**	**87**	**109**
Long-term debt	7	42	5	96	76	72	129	91	82	101
IMF charges	0	3	0	1	1	0	0	0	1	1
Short-term debt	0	25	6	7	8	13	15	78	5	7
Net transfers on debt	**18**	**276**	**582**	**94**	**3**	**0**	**246**	**-191**	**394**	**203**
Total debt service paid (TDS)	**36**	**115**	**16**	**207**	**288**	**219**	**326**	**255**	**186**	**300**
Long-term debt	23	86	10	196	266	196	311	176	179	288
IMF repurchases and charges	13	3	0	4	14	10	0	0	3	6
Short-term debt (interest only)	0	25	6	7	8	13	15	78	5	7
2. AGGREGATE NET RESOURCE FLOWS AND NET TRANSFERS (LONG-TERM)										
NET RESOURCE FLOWS	**43**	**279**	**813**	**460**	**573**	**817**	**819**	**712**	**931**	**797**
Net flow of long-term debt (ex. IMF)	28	231	572	239	87	101	428	172	305	288
Foreign direct investment (net)	15	0	0	40	75	97	173	184	300	254
Portfolio equity flows	0	0	0	0	0	0	0	0	0	0
Grants (excluding technical coop.)	0	48	241	181	410	619	218	356	326	255
Memo: technical coop. grants	4	19	73	130	132	119	111	95	94	116
official net resource flows	28	305	793	426	579	724	662	540	549	401
private net resource flows	14	-26	20	34	-6	93	157	171	382	395
NET TRANSFERS	**13**	**216**	**808**	**352**	**486**	**733**	**677**	**606**	**828**	**671**
Interest on long-term debt	7	42	5	96	76	72	129	91	82	101
Profit remittances on FDI	23	21	0	12	11	12	13	15	21	24
Memo: official net transfers	25	268	789	332	506	656	539	453	474	314
private net transfers	-13	-51	19	21	-21	77	138	153	354	357
3. MAJOR ECONOMIC AGGREGATES										
Gross national income (GNI)	717	2,019	988	1,233	1,479	1,598	1,718	1,815	1,958	2,110
Exports of goods & services (XGS)	..	514	404	521	694	747	960	1,054	1,167	1,304
of which workers remittances	..	0	0	50	75	95	150	200	300	320
Imports of goods & services (MGS)	..	1,049	911	1,433	1,482	1,632	1,890	1,876	2,260	2,218
International reserves (RES)	49	75	166	146	142	203	382	355	514	493
Current account balance	..	-411	-305	-667	-498	-567	-651	-496	-632	-493
4. DEBT INDICATORS										
EDT / XGS (%)	..	426.6	2,659.6	2,297.4	1,499.1	799.2	650.4	613.0	608.1	538.3
EDT / GNI (%)	28.3	108.6	1,087.8	969.5	703.5	373.8	363.2	356.0	362.3	332.7
TDS / XGS (%)	..	22.3	3.9	39.8	41.5	29.3	34.0	24.2	16.0	23.0
INT / XGS (%)	..	13.4	2.8	20.0	12.3	11.4	15.0	16.0	7.5	8.3
INT / GNI (%)	1.0	3.4	1.2	8.5	5.8	5.3	8.4	9.3	4.5	5.2
RES / EDT (%)	24.3	3.4	1.5	1.2	1.4	3.4	6.1	5.5	7.3	7.0
RES / MGS (months)	..	0.9	2.2	1.2	1.2	1.5	2.4	2.3	2.7	2.7
Short-term / EDT (%)	23.7	21.5	22.6	18.7	17.2	13.1	13.4	11.4	13.1	14.1
Concessional / EDT (%)	29.1	21.5	30.6	32.2	37.7	37.0	41.0	43.1	43.0	45.6
Multilateral / EDT (%)	23.7	19.3	8.8	11.1	14.1	26.1	33.3	35.4	34.7	30.2

NICARAGUA

(US$ million, unless otherwise indicated)

	1970	1980	1990	1994	1995	1996	1997	1998	1999	2000
5. LONG-TERM DEBT										
DEBT OUTSTANDING (LDOD)	**147**	**1,671**	**8,313**	**9,666**	**8,578**	**5,161**	**5,377**	**5,676**	**6,010**	**5,860**
Public and publicly guaranteed	**147**	**1,671**	**8,313**	**9,666**	**8,578**	**5,161**	**5,377**	**5,648**	**5,899**	**5,602**
Official creditors	102	866	6,768	7,586	7,568	4,703	4,981	5,249	5,509	5,225
Multilateral	48	424	940	1,328	1,464	1,557	2,080	2,288	2,465	2,116
Concessional	11	200	356	674	769	858	1,308	1,480	1,671	1,775
Bilateral	53	442	5,827	6,258	6,104	3,146	2,901	2,962	3,044	3,108
Concessional	49	271	2,929	3,174	3,148	1,354	1,253	1,307	1,376	1,422
Private creditors	45	805	1,545	2,080	1,010	458	396	399	391	378
Bonds	0	0	0	524	524	0	0	0	0	0
Commercial banks	38	746	1,305	1,394	383	409	362	355	344	326
Other private	8	59	240	162	103	48	34	44	47	52
Private nonguaranteed	**0**	**0**	**0**	**0**	**0**	**0**	**0**	**28**	**110**	**258**
Bonds	0	0	0	0	0	0	0	0	0	0
Commercial banks and other	0	0	0	0	0	0	0	28	110	258
Memo:										
IBRD	27	93	239	76	65	44	24	15	9	5
IDA	3	43	60	254	276	335	368	487	598	654
DISBURSEMENTS	**44**	**276**	**577**	**339**	**277**	**226**	**610**	**258**	**402**	**474**
Public and publicly guaranteed	**44**	**276**	**577**	**339**	**277**	**226**	**610**	**258**	**283**	**215**
Official creditors	32	276	554	338	258	209	605	255	277	212
Multilateral	11	90	7	248	177	139	560	219	208	170
Concessional	4	73	0	124	117	110	116	215	206	168
Bilateral	21	186	546	91	81	70	45	37	70	42
Concessional	19	108	370	70	67	55	40	27	66	33
Private creditors	12	0	23	1	20	17	5	2	6	2
Bonds	0	0	0	0	0	0	0	0	0	0
Commercial banks	12	0	0	1	20	17	5	2	0	0
Other private	0	0	23	0	0	0	0	0	6	2
Private nonguaranteed	**0**	**0**	**0**	**0**	**0**	**0**	**0**	**0**	**118**	**260**
Bonds	0	0	0	0	0	0	0	0	0	0
Commercial banks and other	0	0	0	0	0	0	0	0	118	260
Memo:										
IBRD	6	12	0	0	0	0	0	0	0	0
IDA	0	19	0	52	18	69	51	105	120	87
PRINCIPAL REPAYMENTS	**16**	**45**	**4**	**100**	**190**	**124**	**182**	**86**	**96**	**186**
Public and publicly guaranteed	**16**	**45**	**4**	**100**	**190**	**124**	**182**	**86**	**59**	**74**
Official creditors	4	19	1	93	89	104	161	71	54	66
Multilateral	3	14	1	67	47	40	85	37	28	38
Concessional	0	2	0	35	20	13	11	14	13	19
Bilateral	1	5	1	26	42	64	76	34	26	28
Concessional	0	2	0	2	2	3	15	4	6	8
Private creditors	13	26	3	7	101	21	21	15	5	8
Bonds	0	0	0	0	0	8	0	0	0	0
Commercial banks	11	20	0	0	96	8	9	10	4	5
Other private	2	6	3	7	4	4	12	5	1	3
Private nonguaranteed	**0**	**0**	**0**	**0**	**0**	**0**	**0**	**0**	**38**	**112**
Bonds	0	0	0	0	0	0	0	0	0	0
Commercial banks and other	0	0	0	0	0	0	0	0	38	112
Memo:										
IBRD	2	4	1	18	15	16	17	9	6	5
IDA	0	0	0	1	1	1	1	1	1	2
NET FLOWS ON DEBT	**28**	**231**	**572**	**239**	**87**	**101**	**428**	**172**	**305**	**288**
Public and publicly guaranteed	**28**	**231**	**572**	**239**	**87**	**101**	**428**	**172**	**225**	**141**
Official creditors	28	257	552	245	169	105	444	185	223	147
Multilateral	9	76	6	180	130	99	475	182	180	132
Concessional	4	71	0	89	98	97	105	201	193	150
Bilateral	20	181	546	65	39	6	-31	3	44	14
Concessional	18	106	370	68	65	52	25	23	61	25
Private creditors	-1	-26	20	-6	-81	-4	-16	-13	1	-6
Bonds	0	0	0	0	0	-8	0	0	0	0
Commercial banks	1	-20	0	0	-77	9	-4	-8	-4	-5
Other private	-2	-6	20	-7	-4	-4	-12	-5	5	-1
Private nonguaranteed	**0**	**0**	**0**	**0**	**0**	**0**	**0**	**0**	**81**	**148**
Bonds	0	0	0	0	0	0	0	0	0	0
Commercial banks and other	0	0	0	0	0	0	0	0	81	148
Memo:										
IBRD	4	8	-1	-18	-15	-16	-17	-9	-6	-5
IDA	0	19	0	51	17	68	49	104	119	86

NICARAGUA

(US$ million, unless otherwise indicated)

	1970	1980	1990	1994	1995	1996	1997	1998	1999	2000
INTEREST PAYMENTS (LINT)	**7**	**42**	**5**	**96**	**76**	**72**	**129**	**91**	**82**	**101**
Public and publicly guaranteed	**7**	**42**	**5**	**96**	**76**	**72**	**129**	**91**	**77**	**90**
Official creditors	3	38	4	95	73	68	123	87	76	88
Multilateral	2	29	1	55	33	45	55	50	57	64
Concessional	0	7	0	25	11	11	11	28	29	37
Bilateral	1	9	3	40	39	22	68	37	18	24
Concessional	1	3	0	18	19	11	27	9	6	10
Private creditors	4	4	1	1	3	4	6	4	1	3
Bonds	0	0	0	0	0	0	0	0	0	0
Commercial banks	3	0	0	0	3	3	6	3	1	2
Other private	0	4	1	1	1	1	1	1	0	0
Private nonguaranteed	**0**	**0**	**0**	**0**	**0**	**0**	**0**	**0**	**5**	**11**
Bonds	0	0	0	0	0	0	0	0	0	0
Commercial banks and other	0	0	0	0	0	0	0	0	5	11
Memo:										
IBRD	2	11	1	8	6	6	3	2	6	1
IDA	0	0	0	2	2	3	3	3	4	5
NET TRANSFERS ON DEBT	**21**	**190**	**567**	**143**	**12**	**30**	**299**	**81**	**223**	**187**
Public and publicly guaranteed	**21**	**190**	**567**	**143**	**12**	**30**	**299**	**81**	**148**	**51**
Official creditors	25	220	548	151	96	38	321	97	148	59
Multilateral	7	47	5	126	97	54	420	132	122	69
Concessional	4	64	0	64	87	86	94	174	164	112
Bilateral	19	173	543	25	-1	-16	-99	-35	26	-10
Concessional	18	103	370	50	46	42	-2	14	54	15
Private creditors	-5	-30	19	-8	-85	-8	-23	-16	0	-9
Bonds	0	0	0	0	0	-8	0	0	0	0
Commercial banks	-2	-20	0	0	-80	5	-9	-11	-5	-8
Other private	-2	-10	19	-8	-5	-5	-13	-5	5	-1
Private nonguaranteed	**0**	**0**	**0**	**0**	**0**	**0**	**0**	**0**	**76**	**136**
Bonds	0	0	0	0	0	0	0	0	0	0
Commercial banks and other	0	0	0	0	0	0	0	0	76	136
Memo:										
IBRD	3	-3	-2	-25	-21	-22	-20	-11	-11	-6
IDA	0	19	0	49	16	65	47	101	115	81
DEBT SERVICE (LTDS)	**23**	**86**	**10**	**196**	**266**	**196**	**311**	**176**	**179**	**288**
Public and publicly guaranteed	**23**	**86**	**10**	**196**	**266**	**196**	**311**	**176**	**136**	**164**
Official creditors	7	56	5	188	162	171	284	158	130	153
Multilateral	5	43	2	122	81	85	140	87	85	101
Concessional	0	8	0	60	30	24	22	42	42	56
Bilateral	2	13	3	66	81	86	144	71	44	52
Concessional	1	5	0	20	21	14	42	13	12	17
Private creditors	16	30	4	8	104	25	27	18	6	11
Bonds	0	0	0	0	0	8	0	0	0	0
Commercial banks	14	20	0	0	99	11	14	13	5	8
Other private	3	10	4	8	5	5	13	5	1	3
Private nonguaranteed	**0**	**0**	**0**	**0**	**0**	**0**	**0**	**0**	**43**	**124**
Bonds	0	0	0	0	0	0	0	0	0	0
Commercial banks and other	0	0	0	0	0	0	0	0	43	124
Memo:										
IBRD	3	15	1	25	21	22	20	11	11	6
IDA	0	0	0	3	3	4	4	4	5	6
UNDISBURSED DEBT	**62**	**449**	**573**	**1,086**	**1,080**	**649**	**408**	**750**	**667**	**607**
Official creditors	52	418	562	1,063	1,055	637	398	742	657	601
Private creditors	9	30	11	24	24	12	10	8	10	7
Memorandum items										
Concessional LDOD	59	471	3,285	3,848	3,918	2,211	2,561	2,787	3,047	3,197
Variable rate LDOD	0	796	1,829	2,011	1,127	1,332	1,678	1,727	1,825	1,544
Public sector LDOD	138	1,656	8,313	9,666	8,578	5,151	5,368	5,645	5,896	5,657
Private sector LDOD	9	15	0	0	0	10	9	31	113	203
6. CURRENCY COMPOSITION OF LONG-TERM DEBT (PERCENT)										
Deutsche mark	3.9	2.9	1.3	1.9	4.7	8.2	6.9	7.6	6.5	6.4
French franc	0.0	0.0	1.3	1.3	1.9	2.9	2.0	2.1	1.0	1.0
Japanese yen	0.0	0.0	0.0	1.2	1.3	2.3	1.9	2.1	2.3	2.2
Pound sterling	1.6	0.2	0.0	0.0	0.0	0.0	0.0	0.0	0.0	0.0
Swiss franc	0.0	0.0	0.0	0.0	0.0	0.1	0.1	0.1	0.0	0.0
U.S.dollars	66.4	72.5	80.0	79.0	72.8	60.2	70.3	69.6	71.0	70.4
Multiple currency	28.1	20.9	10.3	8.7	10.3	17.6	11.4	10.9	10.8	11.0
Special drawing rights	0.0	0.0	0.0	0.0	0.0	0.1	0.1	0.1	0.2	0.2
All other currencies	0.0	3.5	7.1	7.9	9.0	8.6	7.3	7.5	8.2	8.8

NICARAGUA

(US$ million, unless otherwise indicated)

	1970	1980	1990	1994	1995	1996	1997	1998	1999	2000
7. DEBT RESTRUCTURINGS										
Total amount rescheduled	..	..	30	6	263	858	466	126	138	149
Debt stock rescheduled	..	..	0	0	0	668	367	44	0	0
Principal rescheduled	..	..	0	4	210	304	37	45	41	96
Official	..	..	0	3	148	255	37	42	33	83
Private	..	..	0	1	61	49	0	3	9	13
Interest rescheduled	..	..	30	3	77	203	3	37	51	62
Official	..	..	30	3	40	193	3	36	47	58
Private	..	..	0	0	37	10	0	1	4	4
Debt forgiven	..	..	0	7	438	23	182	39	43	28
Memo: interest forgiven	..	..	0	0	723	923	2	10	8	7
Debt stock reduction	..	..	0	9	1,200	3,065	116	0	36	0
of which debt buyback	..	..	0	0	89	0	0	0	0	0
8. DEBT STOCK-FLOW RECONCILIATION										
Total change in debt stocks	..	..	1,060	651	-1,556	-4,428	268	222	631	-76
Net flows on debt	24	345	593	198	88	85	390	-22	481	312
Net change in interest arrears	..	..	346	367	-470	-994	92	115	123	58
Interest capitalized	..	..	30	3	77	203	3	37	51	62
Debt forgiveness or reduction	..	..	0	-15	-1,549	-3,088	-297	-39	-79	-28
Cross-currency valuation	..	..	82	-8	-57	-215	-314	-62	-106	-123
Residual	..	..	8	106	355	-419	395	193	161	-357
9. AVERAGE TERMS OF NEW COMMITMENTS										
ALL CREDITORS										
Interest (%)	7.1	4.0	4.6	3.1	2.7	2.0	7.1	1.8	1.3	1.6
Maturity (years)	17.9	25.3	12.1	30.4	30.6	32.8	4.5	36.0	38.3	36.9
Grace period (years)	3.9	6.7	1.7	8.1	7.9	8.1	0.6	9.2	9.8	9.7
Grant element (%)	18.9	44.1	23.6	55.5	58.9	63.7	7.6	68.8	74.5	70.8
Official creditors										
Interest (%)	5.8	3.9	4.4	3.0	2.3	2.0	7.1	1.8	1.1	1.6
Maturity (years)	27.8	26.4	12.4	31.2	32.2	32.6	4.3	36.0	39.6	36.9
Grace period (years)	6.5	7.0	1.8	8.4	8.4	8.1	0.6	9.2	10.1	9.7
Grant element (%)	32.7	45.5	24.5	57.1	62.5	63.5	7.1	68.8	77.1	70.8
Private creditors										
Interest (%)	8.6	4.3	9.4	6.0	7.4	0.0	0.8	0.0	6.8	0.0
Maturity (years)	7.0	9.2	4.9	8.3	8.2	39.7	39.6	0.0	3.3	0.0
Grace period (years)	1.0	2.1	0.4	1.9	1.0	10.2	10.1	0.0	1.3	0.0
Grant element (%)	3.7	22.7	0.9	14.0	8.1	74.9	69.0	0.0	6.1	0.0
Memorandum items										
Commitments	23	434	447	527	361	208	486	587	215	171
Official creditors	12	408	429	508	337	203	482	587	207	171
Private creditors	11	27	18	20	24	5	3	0	8	0

10. CONTRACTUAL OBLIGATIONS ON OUTSTANDING LONG-TERM DEBT

	2001	2002	2003	2004	2005	2006	2007	2008	2009	2010
TOTAL										
Disbursements	182	161	119	80	50	24	14	2	1	0
Principal	286	405	301	271	285	236	215	207	200	194
Interest	168	158	143	131	120	110	100	91	82	75
Official creditors										
Disbursements	179	160	118	79	50	24	14	2	1	0
Principal	198	331	244	220	223	229	209	200	193	187
Interest	152	145	134	123	115	107	97	88	80	72
Bilateral creditors										
Disbursements	36	21	12	6	5	4	3	1	1	0
Principal	157	291	187	163	161	161	139	143	130	120
Interest	100	93	81	72	65	57	50	43	37	30
Multilateral creditors										
Disbursements	143	138	106	73	45	20	11	2	1	0
Principal	41	40	57	57	62	68	70	57	63	67
Interest	53	53	53	51	51	50	48	45	44	42
Private creditors										
Disbursements	4	2	1	0	0	0	0	0	0	0
Principal	88	74	56	50	61	7	7	7	7	7
Interest	15	12	10	8	5	3	3	2	2	2
Commercial banks										
Disbursements	0	0	0	0	0	0	0	0	0	0
Principal	11	10	6	6	26	6	6	6	6	6
Interest	5	4	4	4	3	2	2	2	2	2
Other private										
Disbursements	4	2	1	0	0	0	0	0	0	0
Principal	77	64	51	45	36	1	1	1	1	1
Interest	11	8	6	4	2	1	1	1	1	1

NIGER

(US$ million, unless otherwise indicated)

	1970	1980	1990	1994	1995	1996	1997	1998	1999	2000
1. SUMMARY DEBT DATA										
TOTAL DEBT STOCKS (EDT)	**32**	**863**	**1,726**	**1,525**	**1,587**	**1,536**	**1,571**	**1,653**	**1,640**	**1,638**
Long-term debt (LDOD)	**32**	**687**	**1,487**	**1,425**	**1,463**	**1,439**	**1,418**	**1,515**	**1,493**	**1,481**
Public and publicly guaranteed	32	383	1,226	1,268	1,330	1,330	1,322	1,443	1,423	1,413
Private nonguaranteed	0	305	261	157	133	110	96	72	70	68
Use of IMF credit	**0**	**16**	**85**	**61**	**52**	**53**	**61**	**76**	**68**	**74**
Short-term debt	**0**	**159**	**154**	**39**	**72**	**44**	**92**	**62**	**78**	**83**
of which interest arrears on LDOD	0	0	31	24	53	24	35	33	46	58
Official creditors	0	0	16	24	53	24	35	33	46	58
Private creditors	0	0	16	0	0	0	0	0	0	0
Memo: principal arrears on LDOD	0	1	80	40	75	58	62	56	88	103
Official creditors	0	1	39	40	75	58	62	56	88	103
Private creditors	0	0	41	0	0	0	0	0	0	0
Memo: export credits	0	0	398	131	265	243	233	59	67	69
TOTAL DEBT FLOWS										
Disbursements	**12**	**290**	**148**	**89**	**28**	**55**	**111**	**111**	**48**	**79**
Long-term debt	12	281	139	73	28	41	85	85	48	68
IMF purchases	0	10	9	16	0	14	27	26	0	11
Principal repayments	**2**	**58**	**63**	**48**	**41**	**45**	**49**	**50**	**22**	**18**
Long-term debt	2	58	47	38	31	33	34	36	16	16
IMF repurchases	0	0	16	10	10	12	15	14	6	2
Net flows on debt	**11**	**286**	**123**	**27**	**-9**	**13**	**98**	**33**	**29**	**54**
of which short-term debt	0	53	38	-14	4	2	36	-28	4	-7
Interest payments (INT)	**1**	**84**	**36**	**18**	**15**	**12**	**15**	**12**	**11**	**11**
Long-term debt	1	65	23	15	13	10	13	10	10	10
IMF charges	0	0	4	1	1	1	1	1	0	0
Short-term debt	0	19	9	2	1	1	2	1	1	1
Net transfers on debt	**10**	**202**	**87**	**9**	**-24**	**1**	**83**	**21**	**17**	**44**
Total debt service paid (TDS)	**2**	**141**	**99**	**66**	**56**	**56**	**64**	**62**	**34**	**28**
Long-term debt	2	122	71	53	44	43	46	46	27	26
IMF repurchases and charges	0	0	19	11	11	13	16	15	6	2
Short-term debt (interest only)	0	19	9	2	1	1	2	1	1	1
2. AGGREGATE NET RESOURCE FLOWS AND NET TRANSFERS (LONG-TERM)										
NET RESOURCE FLOWS	**26**	**324**	**316**	**279**	**174**	**184**	**266**	**215**	**153**	**179**
Net flow of long-term debt (ex. IMF)	11	223	92	35	-3	8	51	49	31	52
Foreign direct investment (net)	1	49	-1	-11	7	20	25	9	0	15
Portfolio equity flows	0	0	0	0	0	0	0	0	0	0
Grants (excluding technical coop.)	15	51	226	255	170	155	190	158	122	112
Memo: technical coop. grants	11	62	101	102	109	88	72	72	55	48
official net resource flows	26	125	308	314	191	187	255	230	155	166
private net resource flows	0	199	9	-35	-17	-4	11	-15	-2	13
NET TRANSFERS	**23**	**248**	**293**	**264**	**162**	**173**	**253**	**205**	**143**	**170**
Interest on long-term debt	1	65	23	15	13	10	13	10	10	10
Profit remittances on FDI	2	11	0	0	0	0	0	0	0	0
Memo: official net transfers	25	118	301	305	184	182	245	221	145	157
private net transfers	-2	130	-8	-41	-22	-9	8	-16	-2	13
3. MAJOR ECONOMIC AGGREGATES										
Gross national income (GNI)	645	2,476	2,423	1,532	1,830	1,959	1,821	2,048	1,990	1,842
Exports of goods & services (XGS)	..	650	566	278	333	347	310	346	300	306
of which workers remittances	..	6	13	6	6	6	5	5	7	10
Imports of goods & services (MGS)	..	1,016	803	466	510	497	468	518	453	479
International reserves (RES)	19	132	226	115	99	83	56	56	42	80
Current account balance	..	-276	-236	-126	-152	-181	-185	-199	-174	..
4. DEBT INDICATORS										
EDT / XGS (%)	..	132.8	304.7	547.7	475.9	443.0	505.8	478.4	545.7	534.6
EDT / GNI (%)	4.9	34.9	71.2	99.5	86.7	78.4	86.3	80.7	82.4	89.0
TDS / XGS (%)	..	21.7	17.4	23.8	16.7	16.3	20.7	17.8	11.2	9.2
INT / XGS (%)	..	12.9	6.4	6.4	4.4	3.4	5.0	3.4	3.8	3.4
INT / GNI (%)	0.1	3.4	1.5	1.2	0.8	0.6	0.9	0.6	0.6	0.6
RES / EDT (%)	59.1	15.4	13.1	7.5	6.2	5.4	3.6	3.4	2.6	4.9
RES / MGS (months)	..	1.6	3.4	3.0	2.3	2.0	1.5	1.3	1.1	2.0
Short-term / EDT (%)	0.0	18.5	8.9	2.6	4.5	2.9	5.8	3.8	4.8	5.1
Concessional / EDT (%)	91.5	17.9	47.9	64.1	64.1	67.1	66.9	70.1	71.8	72.4
Multilateral / EDT (%)	13.3	16.5	40.7	54.7	55.1	56.9	56.0	57.9	58.3	59.0

NIGER

(US$ million, unless otherwise indicated)

	1970	1980	1990	1994	1995	1996	1997	1998	1999	2000
5. LONG-TERM DEBT										
DEBT OUTSTANDING (LDOD)	**32**	**687**	**1,487**	**1,425**	**1,463**	**1,439**	**1,418**	**1,515**	**1,493**	**1,481**
Public and publicly guaranteed	**32**	**383**	**1,226**	**1,268**	**1,330**	**1,330**	**1,322**	**1,443**	**1,423**	**1,413**
Official creditors	31	255	1,115	1,268	1,330	1,330	1,322	1,443	1,423	1,413
Multilateral	4	143	701	834	874	875	880	957	957	966
Concessional	4	112	651	790	828	831	842	921	927	941
Bilateral	27	112	414	435	456	455	443	486	467	447
Concessional	25	42	175	189	189	200	208	238	250	245
Private creditors	1	128	111	0	0	0	0	0	0	0
Bonds	0	0	0	0	0	0	0	0	0	0
Commercial banks	0	68	109	0	0	0	0	0	0	0
Other private	0	60	2	0	0	0	0	0	0	0
Private nonguaranteed	**0**	**305**	**261**	**157**	**133**	**110**	**96**	**72**	**70**	**68**
Bonds	0	0	0	0	0	0	0	0	0	0
Commercial banks and other	0	305	261	157	133	110	96	72	70	68
Memo:										
IBRD	0	0	0	0	0	0	0	0	0	0
IDA	4	66	461	565	598	609	625	688	694	723
DISBURSEMENTS	**12**	**281**	**139**	**73**	**28**	**41**	**85**	**85**	**48**	**68**
Public and publicly guaranteed	**12**	**167**	**96**	**73**	**28**	**41**	**85**	**85**	**48**	**68**
Official creditors	12	91	90	73	28	41	85	85	48	68
Multilateral	2	60	70	66	28	35	74	68	38	68
Concessional	2	47	68	64	28	35	74	68	38	68
Bilateral	10	31	21	7	0	6	11	17	9	0
Concessional	10	11	21	4	0	5	11	17	9	0
Private creditors	0	76	5	0	0	0	0	0	0	0
Bonds	0	0	0	0	0	0	0	0	0	0
Commercial banks	0	56	5	0	0	0	0	0	0	0
Other private	0	20	0	0	0	0	0	0	0	0
Private nonguaranteed	**0**	**113**	**43**	**0**	**0**	**0**	**0**	**0**	**0**	**0**
Bonds	0	0	0	0	0	0	0	0	0	0
Commercial banks and other	0	113	43	0	0	0	0	0	0	0
Memo:										
IBRD	0	0	0	0	0	0	0	0	0	0
IDA	2	18	55	44	24	34	50	50	26	68
PRINCIPAL REPAYMENTS	**2**	**58**	**47**	**38**	**31**	**33**	**34**	**36**	**16**	**16**
Public and publicly guaranteed	**2**	**23**	**10**	**15**	**7**	**9**	**20**	**12**	**14**	**14**
Official creditors	1	17	9	15	7	9	20	12	14	14
Multilateral	0	15	7	14	7	8	18	10	12	12
Concessional	0	14	3	6	6	7	17	10	10	10
Bilateral	1	3	2	1	0	1	2	3	2	2
Concessional	1	2	2	0	0	0	1	2	1	2
Private creditors	1	5	2	0	0	0	0	0	0	0
Bonds	0	0	0	0	0	0	0	0	0	0
Commercial banks	0	1	0	0	0	0	0	0	0	0
Other private	1	4	2	0	0	0	0	0	0	0
Private nonguaranteed	**0**	**35**	**37**	**24**	**24**	**24**	**14**	**24**	**2**	**2**
Bonds	0	0	0	0	0	0	0	0	0	0
Commercial banks and other	0	35	37	24	24	24	14	24	2	2
Memo:										
IBRD	0	0	0	0	0	0	0	0	0	0
IDA	0	0	1	3	3	5	5	7	7	8
NET FLOWS ON DEBT	**11**	**223**	**92**	**35**	**-3**	**8**	**51**	**49**	**31**	**52**
Public and publicly guaranteed	**11**	**144**	**86**	**59**	**21**	**32**	**64**	**73**	**33**	**54**
Official creditors	11	74	82	59	21	32	64	73	33	54
Multilateral	2	46	63	52	21	27	56	58	26	56
Concessional	2	33	65	58	22	28	57	58	29	58
Bilateral	9	28	19	6	0	5	8	14	7	-2
Concessional	9	10	19	4	0	5	10	15	8	-2
Private creditors	-1	71	4	0	0	0	0	0	0	0
Bonds	0	0	0	0	0	0	0	0	0	0
Commercial banks	0	55	5	0	0	0	0	0	0	0
Other private	-1	16	-2	0	0	0	0	0	0	0
Private nonguaranteed	**0**	**79**	**6**	**-24**	**-24**	**-24**	**-14**	**-24**	**-2**	**-2**
Bonds	0	0	0	0	0	0	0	0	0	0
Commercial banks and other	0	79	6	-24	-24	-24	-14	-24	-2	-2
Memo:										
IBRD	0	0	0	0	0	0	0	0	0	0
IDA	2	18	54	42	21	29	45	43	19	60

NIGER

(US$ million, unless otherwise indicated)

	1970	1980	1990	1994	1995	1996	1997	1998	1999	2000
INTEREST PAYMENTS (LINT)	**1**	**65**	**23**	**15**	**13**	**10**	**13**	**10**	**10**	**10**
Public and publicly guaranteed	**1**	**16**	**7**	**9**	**7**	**6**	**10**	**9**	**10**	**10**
Official creditors	1	7	7	9	7	6	10	9	10	10
Multilateral	0	3	6	7	7	5	8	6	6	8
Concessional	0	2	4	5	6	5	7	6	5	7
Bilateral	1	5	1	2	0	1	2	3	4	1
Concessional	1	1	1	0	0	0	1	1	2	0
Private creditors	0	9	0	0	0	0	0	0	0	0
Bonds	0	0	0	0	0	0	0	0	0	0
Commercial banks	0	6	0	0	0	0	0	0	0	0
Other private	0	3	0	0	0	0	0	0	0	0
Private nonguaranteed	**0**	**49**	**16**	**6**	**6**	**5**	**3**	**2**	**0**	**0**
Bonds	0	0	0	0	0	0	0	0	0	0
Commercial banks and other	0	49	16	6	6	5	3	2	0	0
Memo:										
IBRD	0	0	0	0	0	0	0	0	0	0
IDA	0	0	3	5	5	4	4	5	4	6
NET TRANSFERS ON DEBT	**10**	**158**	**68**	**20**	**-15**	**-2**	**38**	**38**	**21**	**43**
Public and publicly guaranteed	**10**	**128**	**78**	**50**	**14**	**27**	**55**	**64**	**23**	**45**
Official creditors	11	66	75	50	14	27	55	64	23	45
Multilateral	2	43	57	46	14	23	49	52	20	48
Concessional	2	32	62	53	16	24	50	52	23	51
Bilateral	8	23	18	4	0	4	6	11	3	-3
Concessional	8	9	18	3	0	5	9	13	7	-2
Private creditors	-1	62	4	0	0	0	0	0	0	0
Bonds	0	0	0	0	0	0	0	0	0	0
Commercial banks	0	49	5	0	0	0	0	0	0	0
Other private	-1	14	-2	0	0	0	0	0	0	0
Private nonguaranteed	**0**	**30**	**-10**	**-30**	**-29**	**-29**	**-17**	**-25**	**-2**	**-2**
Bonds	0	0	0	0	0	0	0	0	0	0
Commercial banks and other	0	30	-10	-30	-29	-29	-17	-25	-2	-2
Memo:										
IBRD	0	0	0	0	0	0	0	0	0	0
IDA	2	18	51	37	16	24	41	38	15	54
DEBT SERVICE (LTDS)	**2**	**122**	**71**	**53**	**44**	**43**	**46**	**46**	**27**	**26**
Public and publicly guaranteed	**2**	**39**	**17**	**23**	**14**	**15**	**30**	**21**	**24**	**24**
Official creditors	2	25	16	23	14	15	30	21	24	24
Multilateral	0	17	12	21	14	12	25	16	18	21
Concessional	0	16	7	11	12	11	24	15	15	17
Bilateral	2	8	3	3	1	2	5	5	6	3
Concessional	1	3	3	1	0	1	2	4	2	2
Private creditors	1	14	2	0	0	0	0	0	0	0
Bonds	0	0	0	0	0	0	0	0	0	0
Commercial banks	0	7	0	0	0	0	0	0	0	0
Other private	1	7	2	0	0	0	0	0	0	0
Private nonguaranteed	**0**	**83**	**53**	**30**	**29**	**29**	**17**	**25**	**2**	**2**
Bonds	0	0	0	0	0	0	0	0	0	0
Commercial banks and other	0	83	53	30	29	29	17	25	2	2
Memo:										
IBRD	0	0	0	0	0	0	0	0	0	0
IDA	0	1	4	7	8	9	9	12	11	14
UNDISBURSED DEBT	**41**	**415**	**368**	**354**	**310**	**333**	**299**	**399**	**243**	**208**
Official creditors	24	279	368	354	310	333	299	399	243	208
Private creditors	17	136	0	0	0	0	0	0	0	0
Memorandum items										
Concessional LDOD	29	155	826	978	1,017	1,032	1,050	1,159	1,177	1,185
Variable rate LDOD	0	387	377	169	145	124	113	91	89	85
Public sector LDOD	24	372	1,223	1,268	1,330	1,330	1,322	1,443	1,423	1,413
Private sector LDOD	7	316	264	157	133	110	96	72	70	68

6. CURRENCY COMPOSITION OF LONG-TERM DEBT (PERCENT)

	1970	1980	1990	1994	1995	1996	1997	1998	1999	2000
Deutsche mark	12.0	0.0	0.0	0.5	0.5	0.0	0.0	0.0	0.0	0.0
French franc	67.5	53.8	43.9	35.2	35.2	32.1	29.9	28.9	26.7	25.3
Japanese yen	0.0	0.0	1.3	4.8	4.4	2.0	1.8	1.8	2.0	1.8
Pound sterling	0.0	0.0	0.8	1.1	1.0	1.2	1.4	1.4	1.4	1.3
Swiss franc	0.0	0.0	0.0	0.3	0.3	0.0	0.0	0.0	0.0	0.0
U.S.dollars	7.0	30.2	27.1	36.0	36.8	38.0	40.5	41.3	43.0	46.0
Multiple currency	0.0	2.1	0.5	0.0	0.0	0.0	0.0	0.0	0.0	0.0
Special drawing rights	0.0	0.0	2.6	3.5	3.5	3.5	3.3	3.1	3.0	2.8
All other currencies	13.5	13.9	23.8	18.6	18.3	23.2	23.1	23.5	23.9	22.8

NIGER

(US$ million, unless otherwise indicated)

	1970	1980	1990	1994	1995	1996	1997	1998	1999	2000
7. DEBT RESTRUCTURINGS										
Total amount rescheduled	..	..	29	120	5	63	27	26	6	6
Debt stock rescheduled	..	..	0	0	0	0	0	0	0	0
Principal rescheduled	..	..	12	57	1	21	6	17	3	5
Official	..	..	12	56	1	21	6	17	3	5
Private	..	..	0	1	0	0	0	0	0	0
Interest rescheduled	..	..	16	32	1	29	9	8	1	1
Official	..	..	16	32	1	29	9	8	1	1
Private	..	..	0	0	0	0	0	0	0	0
Debt forgiven	..	..	0	107	4	26	4	8	1	0
Memo: interest forgiven	..	..	0	30	0	15	5	0	2	0
Debt stock reduction	..	..	0	0	0	0	0	0	0	0
of which debt buyback	..	..	0	0	0	0	0	0	0	0
8. DEBT STOCK-FLOW RECONCILIATION										
Total change in debt stocks	..	..	230	-17	62	-51	34	82	-13	-1
Net flows on debt	11	286	123	27	-9	13	98	33	29	54
Net change in interest arrears	..	..	8	-47	29	-29	11	-1	13	12
Interest capitalized	..	..	16	32	1	29	9	8	1	1
Debt forgiveness or reduction	..	..	0	-107	-4	-26	-4	-8	-1	0
Cross-currency valuation	..	..	36	-31	-37	-115	-153	-61	-87	-61
Residual	..	..	46	108	81	79	73	112	32	-7
9. AVERAGE TERMS OF NEW COMMITMENTS										
ALL CREDITORS										
Interest (%)	1.2	7.4	1.9	1.0	0.7	1.0	1.1	0.7	0.0	0.8
Maturity (years)	39.7	18.3	31.7	35.2	38.1	37.5	35.3	38.6	0.0	39.8
Grace period (years)	8.3	4.7	8.5	9.0	9.6	9.2	8.1	9.9	0.0	10.3
Grant element (%)	72.5	18.7	64.4	73.7	78.1	76.1	72.9	78.7	0.0	80.6
Official creditors										
Interest (%)	0.6	5.4	1.9	1.0	0.7	1.0	1.1	0.7	0.0	0.8
Maturity (years)	44.8	26.2	31.7	35.2	38.1	37.5	35.3	38.6	0.0	39.8
Grace period (years)	9.2	6.8	8.5	9.0	9.6	9.2	8.1	9.9	0.0	10.3
Grant element (%)	80.9	35.3	64.4	73.7	78.1	76.1	72.9	78.7	0.0	80.6
Private creditors										
Interest (%)	4.5	9.8	0.0	0.0	0.0	0.0	0.0	0.0	0.0	0.0
Maturity (years)	13.6	8.8	0.0	0.0	0.0	0.0	0.0	0.0	0.0	0.0
Grace period (years)	3.6	2.2	0.0	0.0	0.0	0.0	0.0	0.0	0.0	0.0
Grant element (%)	29.1	-1.0	0.0	0.0	0.0	0.0	0.0	0.0	0.0	0.0
Memorandum items										
Commitments	19	341	56	89	7	76	66	183	0	45
Official creditors	16	185	56	89	7	76	66	183	0	45
Private creditors	3	156	0	0	0	0	0	0	0	0

10. CONTRACTUAL OBLIGATIONS ON OUTSTANDING LONG-TERM DEBT

	2001	2002	2003	2004	2005	2006	2007	2008	2009	2010
TOTAL										
Disbursements	57	53	36	19	9	7	5	1	0	0
Principal	78	66	63	62	52	45	48	50	50	54
Interest	28	26	23	21	19	17	16	15	15	14
Official creditors										
Disbursements	57	53	36	19	9	7	5	1	0	0
Principal	71	58	55	56	45	38	41	43	46	47
Interest	27	25	22	20	18	17	16	15	14	14
Bilateral creditors										
Disbursements	0	0	0	0	0	0	0	0	0	0
Principal	49	38	35	34	23	14	14	13	12	13
Interest	19	16	14	12	11	9	9	8	8	7
Multilateral creditors										
Disbursements	57	53	36	19	9	7	5	1	0	0
Principal	23	20	19	21	22	24	27	30	34	34
Interest	8	8	8	8	8	8	7	7	7	7
Private creditors										
Disbursements	0	0	0	0	0	0	0	0	0	0
Principal	6	8	8	7	7	7	7	7	4	7
Interest	1	1	1	1	1	0	0	0	0	0
Commercial banks										
Disbursements	0	0	0	0	0	0	0	0	0	0
Principal	0	0	0	0	0	0	0	0	0	0
Interest	0	0	0	0	0	0	0	0	0	0
Other private										
Disbursements	0	0	0	0	0	0	0	0	0	0
Principal	6	8	8	7	7	7	7	7	4	7
Interest	1	1	1	1	1	0	0	0	0	0

NIGERIA

(US$ million, unless otherwise indicated)

	1970	1980	1990	1994	1995	1996	1997	1998	1999	2000
1. SUMMARY DEBT DATA										
TOTAL DEBT STOCKS (EDT)	**837**	**8,921**	**33,439**	**33,092**	**34,093**	**31,407**	**28,455**	**30,315**	**29,230**	**34,134**
Long-term debt (LDOD)	**567**	**5,368**	**31,935**	**28,266**	**28,441**	**25,731**	**22,926**	**23,740**	**22,673**	**32,950**
Public and publicly guaranteed	452	4,271	31,545	27,955	28,140	25,431	22,631	23,455	22,423	32,735
Private nonguaranteed	115	1,097	391	311	301	300	295	285	250	215
Use of IMF credit	**0**	**0**	**0**	**0**	**0**	**0**	**0**	**0**	**0**	**0**
Short-term debt	**270**	**3,553**	**1,504**	**4,827**	**5,651**	**5,676**	**5,529**	**6,575**	**6,557**	**1,184**
of which interest arrears on LDOD	1	0	1,040	3,820	4,717	4,967	4,957	5,785	5,721	107
Official creditors	0	0	465	3,361	4,211	4,468	4,483	5,235	5,124	82
Private creditors	0	0	575	459	506	499	474	550	597	25
Memo: principal arrears on LDOD	2	0	1,091	5,814	8,102	9,298	10,151	12,113	12,928	291
Official creditors	0	0	194	4,409	6,545	7,736	8,648	10,270	10,825	275
Private creditors	1	0	897	1,405	1,557	1,562	1,503	1,843	2,103	16
Memo: export credits	0	0	20,116	12,765	14,193	13,725	17,135	8,455	14,746	13,112
TOTAL DEBT FLOWS										
Disbursements	**81**	**1,753**	**927**	**599**	**433**	**308**	**314**	**276**	**175**	**153**
Long-term debt	81	1,753	927	599	433	308	314	276	175	153
IMF purchases	0	0	0	0	0	0	0	0	0	0
Principal repayments	**68**	**242**	**1,180**	**746**	**918**	**1,418**	**840**	**763**	**596**	**581**
Long-term debt	68	242	1,180	746	918	1,418	840	763	596	581
IMF repurchases	0	0	0	0	0	0	0	0	0	0
Net flows on debt	**13**	**2,780**	**-34**	**-660**	**-559**	**-1,334**	**-663**	**-269**	**-375**	**-187**
of which short-term debt	0	1,270	219	-512	-73	-224	-137	218	45	241
Interest payments (INT)	**28**	**909**	**2,155**	**1,125**	**915**	**1,091**	**576**	**557**	**457**	**429**
Long-term debt	28	529	2,123	1,075	859	1,043	544	519	416	365
IMF charges	0	0	0	0	0	0	0	0	0	0
Short-term debt	0	379	32	50	56	48	33	38	41	64
Net transfers on debt	**-15**	**1,872**	**-2,190**	**-1,785**	**-1,474**	**-2,425**	**-1,239**	**-826**	**-832**	**-615**
Total debt service paid (TDS)	**96**	**1,151**	**3,336**	**1,872**	**1,833**	**2,509**	**1,416**	**1,320**	**1,052**	**1,009**
Long-term debt	96	772	3,304	1,822	1,777	2,461	1,383	1,283	1,012	945
IMF repurchases and charges	0	0	0	0	0	0	0	0	0	0
Short-term debt (interest only)	0	379	32	50	56	48	33	38	41	64
2. AGGREGATE NET RESOURCE FLOWS AND NET TRANSFERS (LONG-TERM)										
NET RESOURCE FLOWS	**259**	**773**	**459**	**1,871**	**632**	**512**	**1,045**	**599**	**633**	**706**
Net flow of long-term debt (ex. IMF)	13	1,510	-253	-148	-486	-1,110	-525	-487	-421	-428
Foreign direct investment (net)	205	-740	588	1,959	1,079	1,593	1,539	1,051	1,005	1,083
Portfolio equity flows	0	0	0	17	6	5	4	2	2	2
Grants (excluding technical coop.)	40	3	125	43	33	24	27	33	48	49
Memo: technical coop. grants	36	48	94	78	79	84	83	51	43	80
official net resource flows	70	79	-8	211	-5	-396	-240	-429	-227	-201
private net resource flows	189	694	467	1,660	637	908	1,285	1,028	860	908
NET TRANSFERS	**-207**	**-1,354**	**-1,799**	**631**	**-372**	**-691**	**321**	**-160**	**-52**	**2**
Interest on long-term debt	28	529	2,123	1,075	859	1,043	544	519	416	365
Profit remittances on FDI	438	1,598	135	165	145	160	180	240	269	340
Memo: official net transfers	54	16	-1,308	-125	-328	-911	-606	-803	-470	-391
private net transfers	-261	-1,370	-491	756	-44	220	927	643	419	393
3. MAJOR ECONOMIC AGGREGATES										
Gross national income (GNI)	12,081	61,079	25,585	21,310	25,888	33,068	33,993	29,317	31,298	36,726
Exports of goods & services (XGS)	..	27,772	14,771	10,428	13,246	17,911	18,172	11,762	15,396	23,258
of which workers remittances	..	13	10	550	804	947	1,920	1,574	1,301	..
Imports of goods & services (MGS)	..	22,005	9,858	12,504	15,820	14,403	17,617	16,001	14,881	17,622
International reserves (RES)	223	10,640	4,129	1,649	1,709	4,329	7,580	6,485	..	..
Current account balance	..	5,178	4,988	-2,128	-2,578	3,507	552	-4,244	506	6,983
4. DEBT INDICATORS										
EDT / XGS (%)	..	32.1	226.4	317.3	257.4	175.4	156.6	257.7	189.9	146.8
EDT / GNI (%)	6.9	14.6	130.7	155.3	131.7	95.0	83.7	103.4	93.4	92.9
TDS / XGS (%)	..	4.1	22.6	18.0	13.8	14.0	7.8	11.2	6.8	4.3
INT / XGS (%)	..	3.3	14.6	10.8	6.9	6.1	3.2	4.7	3.0	1.8
INT / GNI (%)	0.2	1.5	8.4	5.3	3.5	3.3	1.7	1.9	1.5	1.2
RES / EDT (%)	26.7	119.3	12.4	5.0	5.0	13.8	26.6	21.4	..	..
RES / MGS (months)	..	5.8	5.0	1.6	1.3	3.6	5.2	4.9	..	..
Short-term / EDT (%)	32.2	39.8	4.5	14.6	16.6	18.1	19.4	21.7	22.4	3.5
Concessional / EDT (%)	15.6	4.9	1.6	3.9	4.0	4.3	4.7	5.2	5.9	4.3
Multilateral / EDT (%)	21.8	6.4	11.2	14.5	14.5	14.3	14.1	13.5	12.9	9.7

NIGERIA

(US$ million, unless otherwise indicated)

	1970	1980	1990	1994	1995	1996	1997	1998	1999	2000
5. LONG-TERM DEBT										
DEBT OUTSTANDING (LDOD)	**567**	**5,368**	**31,935**	**28,266**	**28,441**	**25,731**	**22,926**	**23,740**	**22,673**	**32,950**
Public and publicly guaranteed	**452**	**4,271**	**31,545**	**27,955**	**28,140**	**25,431**	**22,631**	**23,455**	**22,423**	**32,735**
Official creditors	358	992	17,007	19,811	20,492	18,644	17,011	17,679	16,669	29,244
Multilateral	182	571	3,732	4,807	4,944	4,493	4,013	4,083	3,768	3,302
Concessional	17	38	36	239	339	425	496	663	727	755
Bilateral	175	422	13,275	15,004	15,548	14,151	12,998	13,596	12,901	25,942
Concessional	114	401	485	1,051	1,038	929	826	919	997	702
Private creditors	94	3,279	14,537	8,144	7,648	6,786	5,620	5,776	5,753	3,491
Bonds	10	0	0	2,051	2,051	2,051	2,051	2,051	2,051	2,051
Commercial banks	18	2,634	5,714	0	0	0	0	0	0	0
Other private	66	645	8,823	6,093	5,597	4,735	3,569	3,725	3,702	1,440
Private nonguaranteed	**115**	**1,097**	**391**	**311**	**301**	**300**	**295**	**285**	**250**	**215**
Bonds	0	0	0	0	0	0	0	0	0	0
Commercial banks and other	115	1,097	391	311	301	300	295	285	250	215
Memo:										
IBRD	165	517	3,284	3,286	3,221	2,762	2,373	2,278	1,989	1,625
IDA	17	38	36	181	268	348	410	564	624	644
DISBURSEMENTS	**81**	**1,753**	**927**	**599**	**433**	**308**	**314**	**276**	**175**	**153**
Public and publicly guaranteed	**56**	**1,187**	**927**	**599**	**433**	**308**	**314**	**276**	**175**	**153**
Official creditors	45	122	642	599	433	308	314	276	175	153
Multilateral	14	73	542	599	433	308	314	276	175	153
Concessional	1	0	7	77	99	94	97	145	81	68
Bilateral	31	49	100	0	0	0	0	0	0	0
Concessional	30	49	100	0	0	0	0	0	0	0
Private creditors	11	1,065	285	0	0	0	0	0	0	0
Bonds	0	0	0	0	0	0	0	0	0	0
Commercial banks	3	492	0	0	0	0	0	0	0	0
Other private	8	573	285	0	0	0	0	0	0	0
Private nonguaranteed	**25**	**565**	**0**	**0**	**0**	**0**	**0**	**0**	**0**	**0**
Bonds	0	0	0	0	0	0	0	0	0	0
Commercial banks and other	25	565	0	0	0	0	0	0	0	0
Memo:										
IBRD	13	63	384	258	189	139	178	86	44	31
IDA	1	0	7	60	86	90	83	135	75	55
PRINCIPAL REPAYMENTS	**68**	**242**	**1,180**	**746**	**918**	**1,418**	**840**	**763**	**596**	**581**
Public and publicly guaranteed	**38**	**65**	**1,165**	**736**	**908**	**1,408**	**830**	**753**	**561**	**546**
Official creditors	16	45	774	431	470	728	582	739	450	404
Multilateral	5	25	247	431	470	447	467	419	450	404
Concessional	0	0	1	1	2	1	1	1	3	5
Bilateral	11	20	528	0	0	281	115	319	0	0
Concessional	5	14	6	0	0	0	70	319	0	0
Private creditors	22	20	391	306	438	680	248	15	111	142
Bonds	0	0	0	0	0	0	0	0	0	0
Commercial banks	0	1	388	0	0	0	0	0	0	0
Other private	22	19	3	306	438	680	248	15	111	142
Private nonguaranteed	**30**	**177**	**15**	**10**	**10**	**10**	**10**	**10**	**35**	**35**
Bonds	0	0	0	0	0	0	0	0	0	0
Commercial banks and other	30	177	15	10	10	10	10	10	35	35
Memo:										
IBRD	5	24	241	384	392	369	338	313	305	273
IDA	0	0	1	1	1	1	1	1	3	4
NET FLOWS ON DEBT	**13**	**1,510**	**-253**	**-148**	**-486**	**-1,110**	**-525**	**-487**	**-421**	**-428**
Public and publicly guaranteed	**18**	**1,122**	**-238**	**-138**	**-476**	**-1,100**	**-515**	**-477**	**-386**	**-393**
Official creditors	29	77	-132	168	-37	-420	-267	-463	-275	-251
Multilateral	10	48	295	168	-37	-139	-152	-143	-275	-251
Concessional	1	0	6	76	97	93	96	144	78	63
Bilateral	20	29	-428	0	0	-281	-115	-319	0	0
Concessional	25	35	95	0	0	0	-70	-319	0	0
Private creditors	-11	1,046	-106	-306	-438	-680	-248	-15	-111	-142
Bonds	0	0	0	0	0	0	0	0	0	0
Commercial banks	3	491	-388	0	0	0	0	0	0	0
Other private	-14	555	282	-306	-438	-680	-248	-15	-111	-142
Private nonguaranteed	**-5**	**388**	**-15**	**-10**	**-10**	**-10**	**-10**	**-10**	**-35**	**-35**
Bonds	0	0	0	0	0	0	0	0	0	0
Commercial banks and other	-5	388	-15	-10	-10	-10	-10	-10	-35	-35
Memo:										
IBRD	8	38	144	-126	-202	-231	-161	-227	-261	-242
IDA	1	0	6	59	85	89	82	134	72	51

NIGERIA

(US$ million, unless otherwise indicated)

	1970	1980	1990	1994	1995	1996	1997	1998	1999	2000
INTEREST PAYMENTS (LINT)	**28**	**529**	**2,123**	**1,075**	**859**	**1,043**	**544**	**519**	**416**	**365**
Public and publicly guaranteed	**20**	**438**	**2,120**	**1,073**	**840**	**1,025**	**532**	**510**	**402**	**347**
Official creditors	16	63	1,300	337	323	515	365	374	243	190
Multilateral	9	46	262	337	323	322	280	242	243	190
Concessional	0	0	0	2	2	3	3	4	5	6
Bilateral	7	17	1,038	0	0	193	85	132	0	0
Concessional	3	8	312	0	0	0	65	132	0	0
Private creditors	4	375	820	737	516	510	166	136	159	157
Bonds	0	0	0	127	128	128	128	128	128	128
Commercial banks	1	352	378	0	0	0	0	0	0	0
Other private	3	24	442	610	388	382	38	8	31	29
Private nonguaranteed	**8**	**91**	**3**	**2**	**19**	**18**	**12**	**9**	**14**	**18**
Bonds	0	0	0	0	0	0	0	0	0	0
Commercial banks and other	8	91	3	2	19	18	12	9	14	18
Memo:										
IBRD	9	45	243	265	266	228	181	154	138	103
IDA	0	0	0	1	2	2	3	3	4	5
NET TRANSFERS ON DEBT	**-15**	**981**	**-2,377**	**-1,223**	**-1,344**	**-2,153**	**-1,069**	**-1,007**	**-837**	**-792**
Public and publicly guaranteed	**-2**	**684**	**-2,358**	**-1,211**	**-1,315**	**-2,125**	**-1,047**	**-988**	**-788**	**-740**
Official creditors	14	14	-1,433	-169	-361	-935	-633	-836	-518	-441
Multilateral	1	2	33	-169	-361	-461	-433	-386	-518	-441
Concessional	1	-1	6	74	95	91	92	140	73	58
Bilateral	13	12	-1,466	0	0	-474	-200	-451	0	0
Concessional	22	27	-217	0	0	0	-135	-451	0	0
Private creditors	-15	670	-926	-1,043	-955	-1,190	-414	-151	-270	-299
Bonds	0	0	0	-127	-128	-128	-128	-128	-128	-128
Commercial banks	2	140	-766	0	0	0	0	0	0	0
Other private	-17	531	-160	-916	-827	-1,063	-286	-23	-142	-170
Private nonguaranteed	**-13**	**297**	**-18**	**-12**	**-29**	**-28**	**-22**	**-19**	**-49**	**-53**
Bonds	0	0	0	0	0	0	0	0	0	0
Commercial banks and other	-13	297	-18	-12	-29	-28	-22	-19	-49	-53
Memo:										
IBRD	-1	-6	-100	-390	-468	-459	-341	-381	-399	-346
IDA	1	-1	6	58	83	87	79	131	68	46
DEBT SERVICE (LTDS)	**96**	**772**	**3,304**	**1,822**	**1,777**	**2,461**	**1,383**	**1,283**	**1,012**	**945**
Public and publicly guaranteed	**58**	**503**	**3,285**	**1,810**	**1,748**	**2,433**	**1,361**	**1,264**	**963**	**893**
Official creditors	32	108	2,074	767	793	1,243	947	1,112	693	594
Multilateral	14	71	509	767	793	769	747	662	693	594
Concessional	0	1	1	3	4	4	4	5	8	10
Bilateral	18	37	1,566	0	0	474	200	451	0	0
Concessional	8	22	317	0	0	0	135	451	0	0
Private creditors	26	395	1,211	1,043	955	1,190	414	151	270	299
Bonds	0	0	0	127	128	128	128	128	128	128
Commercial banks	1	352	766	0	0	0	0	0	0	0
Other private	25	43	445	916	827	1,063	286	23	142	170
Private nonguaranteed	**38**	**269**	**18**	**12**	**29**	**28**	**22**	**19**	**49**	**53**
Bonds	0	0	0	0	0	0	0	0	0	0
Commercial banks and other	38	269	18	12	29	28	22	19	49	53
Memo:										
IBRD	14	69	484	649	657	598	519	467	443	377
IDA	0	1	1	2	3	3	4	5	7	9
UNDISBURSED DEBT	**185**	**3,714**	**5,216**	**4,864**	**4,255**	**3,073**	**1,316**	**672**	**473**	**370**
Official creditors	167	1,112	3,938	3,786	3,183	2,426	1,316	672	473	370
Private creditors	18	2,602	1,278	1,078	1,072	648	0	0	0	0
Memorandum items										
Concessional LDOD	131	439	521	1,290	1,377	1,354	1,322	1,582	1,724	1,457
Variable rate LDOD	127	4,001	11,044	5,452	5,539	5,218	4,864	4,913	4,575	1,971
Public sector LDOD	450	4,271	31,545	27,914	28,077	25,359	22,565	23,387	22,357	32,680
Private sector LDOD	117	1,097	391	352	365	372	362	353	316	271

6. CURRENCY COMPOSITION OF LONG-TERM DEBT (PERCENT)

	1970	1980	1990	1994	1995	1996	1997	1998	1999	2000
Deutsche mark	9.0	23.5	14.8	13.3	14.2	11.1	10.9	11.2	10.1	0.6
French franc	0.0	0.9	9.0	10.4	10.9	10.7	10.2	10.5	9.4	0.9
Japanese yen	0.8	2.0	8.2	13.3	12.6	12.0	11.9	12.9	15.2	2.1
Pound sterling	30.4	2.7	11.8	10.0	9.9	11.9	13.0	12.6	12.8	1.4
Swiss franc	0.3	0.4	0.7	0.5	0.6	0.5	0.5	0.6	0.5	0.0
U.S.dollars	9.9	55.0	38.8	30.5	29.6	31.5	31.9	31.3	32.5	86.3
Multiple currency	38.5	12.1	10.4	11.8	11.5	10.9	10.5	9.8	8.9	5.0
Special drawing rights	0.0	0.0	0.0	0.0	0.0	0.0	0.1	0.2	0.2	0.1
All other currencies	11.1	3.4	6.3	10.2	10.7	11.4	11.0	10.9	10.4	3.6

NIGERIA

(US$ million, unless otherwise indicated)

	1970	1980	1990	1994	1995	1996	1997	1998	1999	2000
7. DEBT RESTRUCTURINGS										
Total amount rescheduled	..	..	1,480	0	0	0	0	0	0	20,920
Debt stock rescheduled	..	..	0	0	0	0	0	0	0	0
Principal rescheduled	..	..	1,280	0	0	0	0	0	10	12,027
Official	..	..	1,090	0	0	0	0	0	0	10,024
Private	..	..	191	0	0	0	0	0	10	2,003
Interest rescheduled	..	..	169	0	0	0	0	0	4	8,471
Official	..	..	149	0	0	0	0	0	0	7,920
Private	..	..	21	0	0	0	0	0	4	551
Debt forgiven	..	..	0	0	0	0	0	0	0	0
Memo: interest forgiven	..	..	0	0	0	0	0	0	0	0
Debt stock reduction	..	..	286	13	95	1,023	700	0	0	0
of which debt buyback	..	..	0	0	0	281	0	0	0	0
8. DEBT STOCK-FLOW RECONCILIATION										
Total change in debt stocks	..	..	3,317	2,357	1,000	-2,686	-2,952	1,860	-1,085	4,905
Net flows on debt	13	2,780	-34	-660	-559	-1,334	-663	-269	-375	-187
Net change in interest arrears	..	..	820	1,345	898	249	-10	828	-63	-5,614
Interest capitalized	..	..	169	0	0	0	0	0	4	8,471
Debt forgiveness or reduction	..	..	-286	-13	-95	-742	-700	0	0	0
Cross-currency valuation	..	..	2,014	1,532	606	-1,166	-1,635	883	-647	-1,189
Residual	..	..	635	153	150	307	55	418	-5	3,423
9. AVERAGE TERMS OF NEW COMMITMENTS										
ALL CREDITORS										
Interest (%)	6.0	10.5	6.6	7.7	0.0	0.0	0.0	0.0	0.0	0.8
Maturity (years)	14.0	10.9	19.0	21.0	0.0	0.0	0.0	0.0	0.0	34.7
Grace period (years)	3.9	3.5	5.2	5.5	0.0	0.0	0.0	0.0	0.0	10.2
Grant element (%)	21.3	-2.2	23.0	15.0	0.0	0.0	0.0	0.0	0.0	78.7
Official creditors										
Interest (%)	5.9	8.2	5.8	7.7	0.0	0.0	0.0	0.0	0.0	0.8
Maturity (years)	15.4	16.1	22.4	21.0	0.0	0.0	0.0	0.0	0.0	34.7
Grace period (years)	4.3	3.9	6.1	5.5	0.0	0.0	0.0	0.0	0.0	10.2
Grant element (%)	23.2	9.2	30.3	15.0	0.0	0.0	0.0	0.0	0.0	78.7
Private creditors										
Interest (%)	6.5	11.4	7.9	0.0	0.0	0.0	0.0	0.0	0.0	0.0
Maturity (years)	6.5	8.9	13.1	0.0	0.0	0.0	0.0	0.0	0.0	0.0
Grace period (years)	1.9	3.4	3.7	0.0	0.0	0.0	0.0	0.0	0.0	0.0
Grant element (%)	11.0	-6.6	10.4	0.0	0.0	0.0	0.0	0.0	0.0	0.0
Memorandum items										
Commitments	65	1,904	2,192	472	0	0	0	0	0	80
Official creditors	55	525	1,391	472	0	0	0	0	0	80
Private creditors	10	1,380	801	0	0	0	0	0	0	0

10. CONTRACTUAL OBLIGATIONS ON OUTSTANDING LONG-TERM DEBT

	2001	2002	2003	2004	2005	2006	2007	2008	2009	2010
TOTAL										
Disbursements	170	109	60	24	7	0	0	0	0	0
Principal	1,329	1,182	1,174	1,237	1,415	1,412	1,296	1,415	1,460	1,243
Interest	574	541	483	1,049	1,607	1,529	1,453	1,366	1,289	1,213
Official creditors										
Disbursements	170	109	60	24	7	0	0	0	0	0
Principal	1,133	987	981	1,058	1,232	1,232	1,121	1,264	1,310	1,206
Interest	397	369	315	885	1,446	1,371	1,298	1,232	1,159	1,085
Bilateral creditors										
Disbursements	0	0	0	0	0	0	0	0	0	0
Principal	740	630	629	711	896	925	862	1,021	1,152	1,085
Interest	225	216	181	772	1,354	1,299	1,243	1,193	1,132	1,067
Multilateral creditors										
Disbursements	170	109	60	24	7	0	0	0	0	0
Principal	393	358	351	347	337	307	259	243	158	120
Interest	172	153	134	113	92	72	55	40	26	18
Private creditors										
Disbursements	0	0	0	0	0	0	0	0	0	0
Principal	196	194	193	178	183	180	176	151	150	37
Interest	177	173	168	164	161	158	155	134	131	128
Commercial banks										
Disbursements	0	0	0	0	0	0	0	0	0	0
Principal	0	0	0	0	0	0	0	0	0	0
Interest	0	0	0	0	0	0	0	0	0	0
Other private										
Disbursements	0	0	0	0	0	0	0	0	0	0
Principal	196	194	193	178	183	180	176	151	150	37
Interest	177	173	168	164	161	158	155	134	131	128

OMAN

(US$ million, unless otherwise indicated)

1. SUMMARY DEBT DATA

	1970	1980	1990	1994	1995	1996	1997	1998	1999	2000
TOTAL DEBT STOCKS (EDT)	..	**599**	**2,736**	**5,669**	**5,777**	**6,120**	**6,227**	**6,266**	**6,839**	**6,267**
Long-term debt (LDOD)	..	**436**	**2,400**	**5,192**	**5,235**	**5,354**	**5,195**	**4,868**	**5,004**	**4,968**
Public and publicly guaranteed	..	436	2,400	2,608	2,637	2,646	2,567	2,235	2,596	2,673
Private nonguaranteed	..	0	0	2,584	2,598	2,708	2,628	2,633	2,408	2,296
Use of IMF credit	**0**	**0**	**0**	**0**	**0**	**0**	**0**	**0**	**0**	**0**
Short-term debt	..	**163**	**335**	**477**	**541**	**766**	**1,032**	**1,398**	**1,835**	**1,299**
of which interest arrears on LDOD	..	0	1	0	2	1	1	0	0	0
Official creditors	..	0	1	0	2	1	1	0	0	0
Private creditors	..	0	0	0	0	0	0	0	0	0
Memo: principal arrears on LDOD	..	0	3	0	35	35	5	0	4	4
Official creditors	..	0	3	0	29	35	5	0	0	0
Private creditors	..	0	0	0	6	0	0	0	4	4
Memo: export credits	..	0	561	827	958	987	1,437	209	219	154
TOTAL DEBT FLOWS										
Disbursements	..	**98**	**125**	**601**	**637**	**1,298**	**492**	**442**	**821**	**480**
Long-term debt	..	98	125	601	637	1,298	492	442	821	480
IMF purchases	0	0	0	0	0	0	0	0	0	0
Principal repayments	..	**179**	**536**	**376**	**583**	**1,151**	**597**	**796**	**696**	**479**
Long-term debt	..	179	536	376	583	1,151	597	796	696	479
IMF repurchases	0	0	0	0	0	0	0	0	0	0
Net flows on debt	..	**-64**	**-425**	**360**	**116**	**373**	**161**	**13**	**561**	**-536**
of which short-term debt	..	17	-14	135	62	226	266	367	437	-537
Interest payments (INT)	..	**70**	**203**	**174**	**370**	**333**	**323**	**357**	**280**	**385**
Long-term debt	..	44	178	149	349	302	278	295	272	298
IMF charges	0	0	0	0	0	0	0	0	0	0
Short-term debt	..	26	25	25	21	31	45	62	8	87
Net transfers on debt	..	**-134**	**-627**	**186**	**-253**	**40**	**-162**	**-344**	**281**	**-921**
Total debt service paid (TDS)	..	**249**	**739**	**550**	**953**	**1,484**	**920**	**1,153**	**976**	**864**
Long-term debt	..	223	714	525	933	1,453	875	1,091	968	777
IMF repurchases and charges	0	0	0	0	0	0	0	0	0	0
Short-term debt (interest only)	..	26	25	25	21	31	45	62	8	87

2. AGGREGATE NET RESOURCE FLOWS AND NET TRANSFERS (LONG-TERM)

	1970	1980	1990	1994	1995	1996	1997	1998	1999	2000
NET RESOURCE FLOWS	..	**174**	**-213**	**398**	**120**	**252**	**32**	**-230**	**170**	**69**
Net flow of long-term debt (ex. IMF)	..	-81	-411	225	54	147	-105	-355	125	0
Foreign direct investment (net)	..	98	141	77	46	60	65	101	21	23
Portfolio equity flows	..	0	0	26	5	25	38	10	11	11
Grants (excluding technical coop.)	..	157	57	70	15	20	35	13	14	35
Memo: technical coop. grants	..	4	13	22	17	17	18	25	13	15
official net resource flows	..	140	45	57	84	80	19	-16	90	12
private net resource flows	..	34	-259	341	36	171	14	-214	80	57
NET TRANSFERS	..	**-155**	**-780**	**-216**	**-679**	**-521**	**-725**	**-1,000**	**-568**	**-739**
Interest on long-term debt	..	44	178	149	349	302	278	295	272	298
Profit remittances on FDI	..	286	390	465	450	470	480	475	466	510
Memo: official net transfers	..	127	31	32	55	52	-12	-44	60	-20
private net transfers	..	-282	-812	-249	-735	-573	-713	-956	-628	-719

3. MAJOR ECONOMIC AGGREGATES

	1970	1980	1990	1994	1995	1996	1997	1998	1999	2000
Gross national income (GNI)	..	5,338	9,445	9,360	10,531	..	..	..	..	..
Exports of goods & services (XGS)	..	3,887	5,990	5,852	6,442	7,867	8,309	6,135	7,699	11,893
of which workers remittances	..	35	39	39	39	0	0	0	0	..
Imports of goods & services (MGS)	..	2,650	3,971	5,317	5,734	6,159	6,882	7,662	6,630	7,090
International reserves (RES)	..	704	1,784	1,090	1,251	1,497	1,633	1,148	2,852	2,460
Current account balance	..	942	1,106	-805	-801	338	-73	-2,993	-369	3,347

4. DEBT INDICATORS

	1970	1980	1990	1994	1995	1996	1997	1998	1999	2000
EDT / XGS (%)	..	15.4	45.7	96.9	89.7	77.8	74.9	102.1	88.8	52.7
EDT / GNI (%)	..	11.2	29.0	60.6	54.9	..	..	..	..	..
TDS / XGS (%)	..	6.4	12.3	9.4	14.8	18.9	11.1	18.8	12.7	7.3
INT / XGS (%)	..	1.8	3.4	3.0	5.7	4.2	3.9	5.8	3.6	3.2
INT / GNI (%)	..	1.3	2.1	1.9	3.5	..	..	..	..	..
RES / EDT (%)	..	117.7	65.2	19.2	21.7	24.5	26.2	18.3	41.7	39.3
RES / MGS (months)	..	3.2	5.4	2.5	2.6	2.9	2.9	1.8	5.2	4.2
Short-term / EDT (%)	..	27.2	12.3	8.4	9.4	12.5	16.6	22.3	26.8	20.7
Concessional / EDT (%)	..	43.6	8.9	9.1	9.9	9.6	8.9	8.9	9.6	9.9
Multilateral / EDT (%)	..	5.8	4.7	2.9	3.5	3.6	3.2	3.2	4.1	4.3

OMAN

(US$ million, unless otherwise indicated)

	1970	1980	1990	1994	1995	1996	1997	1998	1999	2000
5. LONG-TERM DEBT										
DEBT OUTSTANDING (LDOD)	..	**436**	**2,400**	**5,192**	**5,235**	**5,354**	**5,195**	**4,868**	**5,004**	**4,968**
Public and publicly guaranteed	..	**436**	**2,400**	**2,608**	**2,637**	**2,646**	**2,567**	**2,235**	**2,596**	**2,673**
Official creditors	..	349	327	601	665	693	645	642	735	686
Multilateral	..	35	129	162	199	221	199	202	277	270
Concessional	..	6	49	80	108	121	111	118	203	207
Bilateral	..	314	198	439	466	473	446	439	458	416
Concessional	..	255	194	434	462	469	443	437	456	415
Private creditors	..	87	2,073	2,007	1,972	1,953	1,923	1,593	1,861	1,987
Bonds	..	0	0	0	0	0	225	225	225	225
Commercial banks	..	0	1,721	1,521	1,470	1,439	1,257	995	1,330	1,594
Other private	..	87	353	486	502	514	440	374	306	169
Private nonguaranteed	..	**0**	**0**	**2,584**	**2,598**	**2,708**	**2,628**	**2,633**	**2,408**	**2,296**
Bonds	..	0	0	0	0	0	0	0	0	0
Commercial banks and other	..	0	0	2,584	2,598	2,708	2,628	2,633	2,408	2,296
Memo:										
IBRD	0	14	52	33	25	19	13	9	6	3
IDA	0	0	0	0	0	0	0	0	0	0
DISBURSEMENTS	..	**98**	**125**	**601**	**637**	**1,298**	**492**	**442**	**821**	**480**
Public and publicly guaranteed	..	**98**	**125**	**601**	**322**	**608**	**272**	**45**	**670**	**347**
Official creditors	..	45	34	58	117	106	44	45	132	41
Multilateral	..	13	22	21	58	49	10	17	100	23
Concessional	..	6	12	15	37	28	8	14	98	21
Bilateral	..	32	13	37	58	57	34	28	33	19
Concessional	..	7	13	32	58	57	34	28	33	19
Private creditors	..	52	91	543	206	502	228	0	538	305
Bonds	..	0	0	0	0	0	225	0	0	0
Commercial banks	..	0	0	431	132	468	0	0	538	300
Other private	..	52	91	112	74	34	3	0	0	6
Private nonguaranteed	..	**0**	**0**	**0**	**315**	**691**	**220**	**397**	**151**	**133**
Bonds	..	0	0	0	0	0	0	0	0	0
Commercial banks and other	..	0	0	0	315	691	220	397	151	133
Memo:										
IBRD	0	6	10	0	0	0	0	0	0	0
IDA	0	0	0	0	0	0	0	0	0	0
PRINCIPAL REPAYMENTS	..	**179**	**536**	**376**	**583**	**1,151**	**597**	**796**	**696**	**479**
Public and publicly guaranteed	..	**179**	**536**	**376**	**282**	**570**	**297**	**404**	**321**	**234**
Official creditors	..	62	46	71	48	45	60	74	56	64
Multilateral	..	3	30	30	23	22	23	18	20	24
Concessional	..	0	10	9	10	13	13	9	11	14
Bilateral	..	60	16	41	25	23	37	56	36	40
Concessional	..	9	15	40	24	22	37	55	35	39
Private creditors	..	117	491	304	234	526	237	330	266	170
Bonds	..	0	0	0	0	0	0	0	0	0
Commercial banks	..	32	370	242	178	482	167	262	203	36
Other private	..	85	120	62	56	44	70	68	63	134
Private nonguaranteed	..	**0**	**0**	**0**	**302**	**581**	**300**	**392**	**375**	**245**
Bonds	..	0	0	0	0	0	0	0	0	0
Commercial banks and other	..	0	0	0	302	581	300	392	375	245
Memo:										
IBRD	0	1	16	17	9	5	4	4	4	3
IDA	0	0	0	0	0	0	0	0	0	0
NET FLOWS ON DEBT	..	**-81**	**-411**	**225**	**54**	**147**	**-105**	**-355**	**125**	**0**
Public and publicly guaranteed	..	**-81**	**-411**	**225**	**41**	**37**	**-25**	**-359**	**349**	**113**
Official creditors	..	-17	-12	-13	69	61	-16	-29	77	-23
Multilateral	..	11	-9	-9	35	27	-12	-1	79	-1
Concessional	..	6	2	6	27	15	-6	5	88	7
Bilateral	..	-27	-3	-4	34	34	-4	-28	-3	-21
Concessional	..	-1	-2	-8	35	35	-3	-27	-2	-20
Private creditors	..	-65	-400	238	-28	-24	-9	-330	273	135
Bonds	..	0	0	0	0	0	225	0	0	0
Commercial banks	..	-32	-370	189	-46	-14	-167	-262	335	264
Other private	..	-33	-30	50	18	-10	-67	-68	-63	-129
Private nonguaranteed	..	**0**	**0**	**0**	**13**	**110**	**-80**	**5**	**-224**	**-112**
Bonds	..	0	0	0	0	0	0	0	0	0
Commercial banks and other	..	0	0	0	13	110	-80	5	-224	-112
Memo:										
IBRD	0	5	-6	-16	-9	-5	-4	-4	-4	-3
IDA	0	0	0	0	0	0	0	0	0	0

OMAN

(US$ million, unless otherwise indicated)

	1970	1980	1990	1994	1995	1996	1997	1998	1999	2000
INTEREST PAYMENTS (LINT)	..	**44**	**178**	**149**	**349**	**302**	**278**	**295**	**272**	**298**
Public and publicly guaranteed	..	**44**	**178**	**149**	**184**	**149**	**132**	**156**	**136**	**155**
Official creditors	..	14	14	24	29	28	31	28	30	32
Multilateral	..	2	6	6	11	10	11	11	12	14
Concessional	..	0	0	0	6	6	7	7	7	10
Bilateral	..	12	8	18	18	18	20	17	18	18
Concessional	..	1	8	18	18	18	20	17	18	18
Private creditors	..	30	164	125	155	121	101	128	106	123
Bonds	..	0	0	0	0	0	0	16	16	16
Commercial banks	..	3	133	91	109	84	64	80	63	86
Other private	..	28	31	34	46	37	37	32	26	21
Private nonguaranteed	..	**0**	**0**	**0**	**166**	**153**	**146**	**139**	**136**	**143**
Bonds	..	0	0	0	0	0	0	0	0	0
Commercial banks and other	..	0	0	0	166	153	146	139	136	143
Memo:										
IBRD	0	1	5	4	2	2	1	1	1	0
IDA	0	0	0	0	0	0	0	0	0	0
NET TRANSFERS ON DEBT	..	**-125**	**-589**	**76**	**-295**	**-155**	**-383**	**-649**	**-147**	**-297**
Public and publicly guaranteed	..	**-125**	**-589**	**76**	**-143**	**-112**	**-157**	**-515**	**213**	**-43**
Official creditors	..	-30	-26	-38	40	33	-47	-57	46	-55
Multilateral	..	9	-15	-15	24	17	-24	-13	67	-15
Concessional	..	6	2	6	21	9	-12	-2	81	-2
Bilateral	..	-39	-11	-23	16	16	-23	-45	-21	-39
Concessional	..	-2	-10	-26	17	17	-22	-44	-20	-39
Private creditors	..	-95	-563	114	-183	-144	-110	-458	167	12
Bonds	..	0	0	0	0	0	225	-16	-16	-16
Commercial banks	..	-35	-503	98	-155	-98	-231	-342	272	178
Other private	..	-60	-60	15	-29	-46	-104	-100	-89	-150
Private nonguaranteed	..	**0**	**0**	**0**	**-152**	**-43**	**-226**	**-134**	**-360**	**-255**
Bonds	..	0	0	0	0	0	0	0	0	0
Commercial banks and other	..	0	0	0	-152	-43	-226	-134	-360	-255
Memo:										
IBRD	0	4	-11	-20	-11	-6	-5	-5	-4	-3
IDA	0	0	0	0	0	0	0	0	0	0
DEBT SERVICE (LTDS)	..	**223**	**714**	**525**	**933**	**1,453**	**875**	**1,091**	**968**	**777**
Public and publicly guaranteed	..	**223**	**714**	**525**	**465**	**719**	**429**	**560**	**457**	**389**
Official creditors	..	76	60	96	76	73	91	102	86	96
Multilateral	..	5	37	36	34	32	34	29	32	38
Concessional	..	0	10	9	16	19	20	16	17	23
Bilateral	..	71	23	60	43	41	57	73	54	58
Concessional	..	9	23	58	41	40	56	72	53	57
Private creditors	..	147	654	429	389	646	338	458	371	293
Bonds	..	0	0	0	0	0	0	16	16	16
Commercial banks	..	35	503	333	287	566	231	342	267	122
Other private	..	113	151	96	102	80	107	100	89	155
Private nonguaranteed	..	**0**	**0**	**0**	**468**	**734**	**446**	**531**	**511**	**388**
Bonds	..	0	0	0	0	0	0	0	0	0
Commercial banks and other	..	0	0	0	468	734	446	531	511	388
Memo:										
IBRD	0	2	20	20	11	6	5	5	4	3
IDA	0	0	0	0	0	0	0	0	0	0
UNDISBURSED DEBT	..	**499**	**897**	**490**	**407**	**230**	**196**	**323**	**696**	**580**
Official creditors	..	176	454	137	259	181	151	272	462	400
Private creditors	..	323	443	353	148	49	45	50	234	179
Memorandum items										
Concessional LDOD	..	261	243	514	570	590	554	555	659	622
Variable rate LDOD	..	0	1,386	3,945	3,925	4,028	3,783	3,636	3,744	3,892
Public sector LDOD	..	436	2,400	2,608	2,637	2,646	2,567	2,235	2,596	2,673
Private sector LDOD	..	0	0	2,584	2,598	2,708	2,628	2,633	2,408	2,296

6. CURRENCY COMPOSITION OF LONG-TERM DEBT (PERCENT)

	1970	1980	1990	1994	1995	1996	1997	1998	1999	2000
Deutsche mark	..	0.0	0.0	0.0	0.0	0.0	0.0	0.0	0.0	0.0
French franc	..	7.5	0.5	0.0	0.0	0.0	0.0	0.0	0.0	0.0
Japanese yen	..	0.0	7.3	16.2	15.2	13.1	11.3	8.1	7.3	5.8
Pound sterling	..	8.8	5.5	10.2	9.6	9.3	8.1	8.0	5.5	1.1
Swiss franc	..	0.0	0.0	0.0	0.0	0.0	0.0	0.0	0.0	0.0
U.S.dollars	..	16.8	75.5	62.1	61.1	61.4	64.1	64.8	67.3	74.1
Multiple currency	..	3.1	2.2	1.2	0.9	0.7	0.5	0.0	0.0	0.0
Special drawing rights	..	0.0	0.0	0.0	0.0	0.0	0.0	0.0	0.0	0.0
All other currencies	..	63.8	9.0	10.3	13.2	15.5	16.0	19.1	19.9	19.0

OMAN

(US$ million, unless otherwise indicated)

	1970	1980	1990	1994	1995	1996	1997	1998	1999	2000
7. DEBT RESTRUCTURINGS										
Total amount rescheduled	..	..	0	0	0	0	0	0	0	0
Debt stock rescheduled	..	..	0	0	0	0	0	0	0	0
Principal rescheduled	..	..	0	0	0	0	0	0	0	0
Official	..	..	0	0	0	0	0	0	0	0
Private	..	..	0	0	0	0	0	0	0	0
Interest rescheduled	..	..	0	0	0	0	0	0	0	0
Official	..	..	0	0	0	0	0	0	0	0
Private	..	..	0	0	0	0	0	0	0	0
Debt forgiven	..	..	0	0	0	0	0	0	0	0
Memo: interest forgiven	..	..	0	0	0	0	0	0	0	0
Debt stock reduction	..	..	0	0	0	0	0	0	0	0
of which debt buyback	..	..	0	0	0	0	0	0	0	0
8. DEBT STOCK-FLOW RECONCILIATION										
Total change in debt stocks	..	..	-233	3,012	108	344	107	39	573	-572
Net flows on debt	..	-64	-425	360	116	373	161	13	561	-536
Net change in interest arrears	..	..	1	0	2	-1	0	-1	0	0
Interest capitalized	..	..	0	0	0	0	0	0	0	0
Debt forgiveness or reduction	..	..	0	0	0	0	0	0	0	0
Cross-currency valuation	..	..	39	64	-13	-27	-55	44	14	-38
Residual	..	..	152	2,588	2	-2	1	-17	-2	2
9. AVERAGE TERMS OF NEW COMMITMENTS										
ALL CREDITORS										
Interest (%)	..	7.9	7.5	4.7	4.6	5.7	6.7	3.4	6.2	6.9
Maturity (years)	..	9.4	13.8	8.8	16.6	8.1	6.0	18.0	9.1	4.0
Grace period (years)	..	3.2	4.0	3.2	3.3	4.9	4.7	3.2	2.0	1.0
Grant element (%)	..	9.1	12.8	21.9	31.6	19.1	13.7	37.5	13.2	6.2
Official creditors										
Interest (%)	..	10.0	1.9	3.3	4.6	3.5	3.6	3.3	7.2	0.0
Maturity (years)	..	10.5	16.7	16.7	16.6	19.1	13.0	18.2	16.7	0.0
Grace period (years)	..	2.9	4.5	3.5	3.3	4.1	2.9	3.2	0.5	0.0
Grant element (%)	..	2.9	45.1	37.0	31.6	40.9	32.7	37.8	12.7	0.0
Private creditors										
Interest (%)	..	7.5	8.0	5.0	0.0	6.0	7.1	3.9	5.8	6.9
Maturity (years)	..	9.2	13.5	7.6	0.0	7.0	5.0	11.1	5.8	4.0
Grace period (years)	..	3.3	4.0	3.2	0.0	5.0	5.0	3.1	2.7	1.0
Grant element (%)	..	10.3	9.9	19.6	0.0	16.9	10.9	28.8	13.4	6.2
Memorandum items										
Commitments	..	454	412	622	245	441	258	188	1,031	263
Official creditors	..	76	34	80	245	41	33	183	308	0
Private creditors	..	379	379	542	0	400	225	6	723	263

10. CONTRACTUAL OBLIGATIONS ON OUTSTANDING LONG-TERM DEBT

	2001	2002	2003	2004	2005	2006	2007	2008	2009	2010
TOTAL										
Disbursements	261	187	82	34	11	5	0	0	0	0
Principal	1,065	1,149	993	680	430	395	372	95	65	53
Interest	273	203	155	104	72	49	29	24	19	16
Official creditors										
Disbursements	145	135	74	31	11	5	0	0	0	0
Principal	107	105	100	98	84	80	79	77	57	53
Interest	28	26	38	36	33	29	26	22	19	16
Bilateral creditors										
Disbursements	122	121	67	27	11	5	0	0	0	0
Principal	66	68	65	64	64	61	61	59	38	38
Interest	17	16	29	29	27	24	21	18	15	13
Multilateral creditors										
Disbursements	23	15	7	4	1	0	0	0	0	0
Principal	41	37	35	34	20	20	18	18	18	14
Interest	11	10	9	7	6	6	5	4	4	3
Private creditors										
Disbursements	117	52	8	3	0	0	0	0	0	0
Principal	957	1,044	893	582	347	315	293	18	9	0
Interest	244	177	118	68	39	20	3	2	0	0
Commercial banks										
Disbursements	48	20	0	0	0	0	0	0	0	0
Principal	518	373	461	213	34	18	18	18	9	0
Interest	108	71	44	16	6	4	3	2	0	0
Other private										
Disbursements	68	32	8	3	0	0	0	0	0	0
Principal	439	671	432	369	313	297	276	0	0	0
Interest	136	106	74	52	33	16	0	0	0	0

PAKISTAN

(US$ million, unless otherwise indicated)

	1970	1980	1990	1994	1995	1996	1997	1998	1999	2000
1. SUMMARY DEBT DATA										
TOTAL DEBT STOCKS (EDT)	**3,407**	**9,931**	**20,663**	**27,383**	**30,229**	**29,835**	**30,079**	**32,271**	**33,899**	**32,091**
Long-term debt (LDOD)	**3,257**	**8,520**	**16,643**	**23,887**	**25,381**	**25,623**	**26,317**	**28,752**	**30,365**	**29,043**
Public and publicly guaranteed	3,252	8,502	16,506	22,709	23,788	23,628	23,979	26,150	28,144	27,140
Private nonguaranteed	5	18	138	1,178	1,593	1,995	2,338	2,602	2,221	1,903
Use of IMF credit	**45**	**674**	**836**	**1,557**	**1,613**	**1,396**	**1,281**	**1,360**	**1,704**	**1,529**
Short-term debt	**104**	**737**	**3,185**	**1,938**	**3,235**	**2,816**	**2,481**	**2,159**	**1,830**	**1,519**
of which interest arrears on LDOD	0	0	1	0	0	0	0	213	0	0
Official creditors	0	0	1	0	0	0	0	143	0	0
Private creditors	0	0	0	0	0	0	0	70	0	0
Memo: principal arrears on LDOD	0	0	15	0	0	0	0	577	0	0
Official creditors	0	0	15	0	0	0	0	482	0	0
Private creditors	0	0	0	0	0	0	0	94	0	0
Memo: export credits	0	0	2,343	3,329	5,182	4,765	4,779	1,479	2,139	2,128
TOTAL DEBT FLOWS										
Disbursements	**572**	**1,366**	**1,746**	**3,974**	**3,288**	**3,605**	**4,801**	**2,683**	**2,659**	**1,877**
Long-term debt	572	1,058	1,746	3,553	3,086	3,450	4,520	2,505	2,048	1,682
IMF purchases	0	308	0	421	202	156	281	178	611	195
Principal repayments	**178**	**492**	**1,071**	**2,455**	**2,013**	**2,093**	**2,848**	**1,441**	**1,888**	**1,871**
Long-term debt	150	352	905	2,391	1,837	1,772	2,537	1,283	1,652	1,589
IMF repurchases	28	139	166	64	176	322	311	158	236	282
Net flows on debt	**393**	**1,170**	**1,089**	**1,511**	**2,572**	**1,093**	**1,618**	**707**	**655**	**-306**
of which short-term debt	0	296	414	-8	1,297	-419	-335	-535	-116	-312
Interest payments (INT)	**81**	**377**	**831**	**994**	**1,203**	**1,193**	**1,235**	**856**	**1,047**	**985**
Long-term debt	81	248	515	851	955	910	905	711	954	858
IMF charges	0	27	52	34	45	58	37	35	44	49
Short-term debt	0	103	264	109	203	225	294	110	49	78
Net transfers on debt	**313**	**793**	**258**	**517**	**1,369**	**-100**	**383**	**-150**	**-392**	**-1,291**
Total debt service paid (TDS)	**259**	**869**	**1,902**	**3,449**	**3,216**	**3,286**	**4,083**	**2,297**	**2,935**	**2,857**
Long-term debt	230	600	1,420	3,241	2,793	2,682	3,441	1,994	2,606	2,447
IMF repurchases and charges	28	166	218	98	221	379	348	193	280	332
Short-term debt (interest only)	0	103	264	109	203	225	294	110	49	78
2. AGGREGATE NET RESOURCE FLOWS AND NET TRANSFERS (LONG-TERM)										
NET RESOURCE FLOWS	**497**	**1,251**	**1,409**	**3,117**	**2,889**	**3,500**	**3,126**	**1,903**	**1,125**	**526**
Net flow of long-term debt (ex. IMF)	422	706	841	1,162	1,249	1,678	1,983	1,222	396	93
Foreign direct investment (net)	23	63	244	421	723	922	716	506	532	308
Portfolio equity flows	0	0	0	1,335	729	700	252	0	0	0
Grants (excluding technical coop.)	53	482	324	199	188	200	174	175	197	124
Memo: technical coop. grants	24	120	318	180	181	156	130	119	100	82
official net resource flows	433	1,021	1,228	1,352	1,119	1,316	947	1,024	1,071	578
private net resource flows	64	230	181	1,765	1,770	2,184	2,179	878	55	-53
NET TRANSFERS	**411**	**997**	**841**	**2,197**	**1,834**	**2,464**	**2,021**	**961**	**-109**	**-552**
Interest on long-term debt	81	248	515	851	955	910	905	711	954	858
Profit remittances on FDI	6	6	53	70	100	126	200	230	280	220
Memo: official net transfers	368	819	778	664	361	622	263	502	525	52
private net transfers	42	179	63	1,533	1,473	1,842	1,758	459	-635	-604
3. MAJOR ECONOMIC AGGREGATES										
Gross national income (GNI)	9,933	23,409	39,044	50,692	59,423	61,376	60,265	59,907	56,807	59,620
Exports of goods & services (XGS)	891	4,758	8,267	9,851	11,775	11,622	11,345	11,631	9,997	10,675
of which workers remittances	86	1,748	1,942	1,446	1,866	1,461	1,409	1,490	1,060	983
Imports of goods & services (MGS)	1,591	6,042	10,425	12,759	14,830	17,364	16,743	15,273	13,640	13,897
International reserves (RES)	195	1,568	1,046	3,716	2,528	1,307	1,795	1,626	2,117	2,087
Current account balance	-705	-1,137	-1,890	-1,964	-2,484	-4,820	-3,851	-1,922	-2,698	-2,208
4. DEBT INDICATORS										
EDT / XGS (%)	382.4	208.7	250.0	278.0	256.7	256.7	265.1	277.5	339.1	300.6
EDT / GNI (%)	34.3	42.4	52.9	54.0	50.9	48.6	49.9	53.9	59.7	53.8
TDS / XGS (%)	29.1	18.3	23.0	35.0	27.3	28.3	36.0	19.8	29.4	26.8
INT / XGS (%)	9.1	7.9	10.1	10.1	10.2	10.3	10.9	7.4	10.5	9.2
INT / GNI (%)	0.8	1.6	2.1	2.0	2.0	1.9	2.1	1.4	1.8	1.7
RES / EDT (%)	5.7	15.8	5.1	13.6	8.4	4.4	6.0	5.0	6.3	6.5
RES / MGS (months)	1.5	3.1	1.2	3.5	2.1	0.9	1.3	1.3	1.9	1.8
Short-term / EDT (%)	3.1	7.4	15.4	7.1	10.7	9.4	8.3	6.7	5.4	4.7
Concessional / EDT (%)	68.9	71.6	58.5	55.7	53.9	53.5	50.0	52.1	54.6	56.2
Multilateral / EDT (%)	18.0	15.4	33.4	41.9	40.3	40.9	39.4	40.7	41.7	42.1

(US$ million, unless otherwise indicated)

	1970	1980	1990	1994	1995	1996	1997	1998	1999	2000
5. LONG-TERM DEBT										
DEBT OUTSTANDING (LDOD)	**3,257**	**8,520**	**16,643**	**23,887**	**25,381**	**25,623**	**26,317**	**28,752**	**30,365**	**29,043**
Public and publicly guaranteed	**3,252**	**8,502**	**16,506**	**22,709**	**23,788**	**23,628**	**23,979**	**26,150**	**28,144**	**27,140**
Official creditors	2,942	7,953	15,791	21,539	22,691	22,396	21,544	23,715	25,977	25,076
Multilateral	614	1,532	6,894	11,462	12,179	12,190	11,860	13,125	14,132	13,521
Concessional	280	956	3,887	6,270	6,894	7,174	7,116	7,973	8,537	8,195
Bilateral	2,327	6,420	8,897	10,077	10,512	10,207	9,684	10,590	11,844	11,555
Concessional	2,067	6,154	8,207	8,982	9,392	8,786	7,926	8,852	9,965	9,844
Private creditors	311	550	714	1,170	1,097	1,231	2,436	2,436	2,168	2,064
Bonds	0	0	0	150	150	310	685	685	623	623
Commercial banks	6	115	402	421	377	303	1,360	1,390	1,158	1,103
Other private	305	435	313	599	570	619	390	360	386	338
Private nonguaranteed	**5**	**18**	**138**	**1,178**	**1,593**	**1,995**	**2,338**	**2,602**	**2,221**	**1,903**
Bonds	0	0	0	45	45	45	45	45	45	45
Commercial banks and other	5	18	138	1,133	1,548	1,950	2,293	2,557	2,176	1,858
Memo:										
IBRD	330	330	1,816	2,934	3,082	3,007	3,046	3,136	3,315	3,093
IDA	280	821	2,106	3,054	3,321	3,480	3,526	3,800	3,905	3,828
DISBURSEMENTS	**572**	**1,058**	**1,746**	**3,553**	**3,086**	**3,450**	**4,520**	**2,505**	**2,048**	**1,682**
Public and publicly guaranteed	**569**	**1,049**	**1,708**	**3,122**	**2,331**	**2,749**	**3,842**	**1,896**	**1,847**	**1,565**
Official creditors	471	793	1,629	2,644	2,199	2,347	2,616	1,738	1,749	1,561
Multilateral	94	161	978	1,465	1,167	1,276	1,195	1,006	1,218	1,081
Concessional	24	103	360	795	677	712	532	579	411	380
Bilateral	377	632	651	1,180	1,032	1,071	1,421	733	531	480
Concessional	325	539	325	826	804	456	368	638	85	256
Private creditors	98	257	78	478	132	402	1,227	158	98	4
Bonds	0	0	0	150	0	160	375	0	0	0
Commercial banks	0	101	8	134	90	84	826	125	2	0
Other private	98	156	70	194	42	158	26	32	97	4
Private nonguaranteed	**3**	**9**	**39**	**431**	**755**	**701**	**678**	**609**	**201**	**117**
Bonds	0	0	0	45	0	0	0	0	0	0
Commercial banks and other	3	9	39	386	755	701	678	609	201	117
Memo:										
IBRD	66	16	356	314	271	371	490	130	434	160
IDA	24	74	135	317	255	280	233	219	194	141
PRINCIPAL REPAYMENTS	**150**	**352**	**905**	**2,391**	**1,837**	**1,772**	**2,537**	**1,283**	**1,652**	**1,589**
Public and publicly guaranteed	**149**	**346**	**867**	**2,125**	**1,497**	**1,473**	**2,201**	**983**	**1,026**	**1,144**
Official creditors	90	253	725	1,492	1,267	1,232	1,843	889	875	1,107
Multilateral	22	41	307	634	559	486	619	479	604	830
Concessional	0	5	43	67	81	93	111	119	137	167
Bilateral	68	212	419	858	708	746	1,225	410	271	277
Concessional	46	177	359	545	462	469	569	271	12	14
Private creditors	59	92	141	634	231	241	358	94	150	37
Bonds	0	0	0	0	0	0	0	0	75	0
Commercial banks	1	10	88	585	138	157	122	48	69	35
Other private	58	83	53	49	92	85	236	46	6	2
Private nonguaranteed	**1**	**7**	**39**	**265**	**340**	**299**	**335**	**300**	**626**	**445**
Bonds	0	0	0	0	0	0	0	0	0	0
Commercial banks and other	1	7	39	265	340	299	335	300	626	445
Memo:										
IBRD	22	26	73	180	219	227	206	197	225	227
IDA	0	4	19	30	35	39	42	47	58	65
NET FLOWS ON DEBT	**422**	**706**	**841**	**1,162**	**1,249**	**1,678**	**1,983**	**1,222**	**396**	**93**
Public and publicly guaranteed	**420**	**704**	**841**	**997**	**834**	**1,276**	**1,641**	**913**	**821**	**421**
Official creditors	381	539	904	1,153	932	1,116	772	849	873	454
Multilateral	72	120	672	831	608	790	576	527	613	251
Concessional	23	99	317	728	596	619	421	460	274	213
Bilateral	309	419	232	322	324	326	196	322	260	203
Concessional	279	363	-34	281	342	-13	-200	367	74	242
Private creditors	39	164	-63	-156	-98	160	869	63	-52	-33
Bonds	0	0	0	150	0	160	375	0	-75	0
Commercial banks	-1	91	-80	-451	-48	-72	704	78	-68	-35
Other private	40	73	17	145	-50	73	-211	-14	91	2
Private nonguaranteed	**2**	**2**	**0**	**166**	**416**	**402**	**342**	**309**	**-425**	**-328**
Bonds	0	0	0	45	0	0	0	0	0	0
Commercial banks and other	2	2	0	121	416	402	342	309	-425	-328
Memo:										
IBRD	44	-10	283	134	52	144	284	-67	209	-67
IDA	23	70	116	287	219	242	191	172	136	77

PAKISTAN

(US$ million, unless otherwise indicated)

	1970	1980	1990	1994	1995	1996	1997	1998	1999	2000
INTEREST PAYMENTS (LINT)	**81**	**248**	**515**	**851**	**955**	**910**	**905**	**711**	**954**	**858**
Public and publicly guaranteed	**81**	**246**	**505**	**760**	**825**	**788**	**760**	**565**	**679**	**641**
Official creditors	65	203	450	688	759	694	684	522	545	527
Multilateral	21	61	247	422	445	411	392	342	438	383
Concessional	2	7	30	50	59	61	65	62	78	73
Bilateral	44	142	204	266	314	282	292	181	107	144
Concessional	31	128	174	199	259	210	200	76	46	57
Private creditors	16	44	54	72	66	94	77	43	133	114
Bonds	0	0	0	0	9	17	17	9	54	61
Commercial banks	0	9	38	45	32	31	18	18	69	39
Other private	16	35	16	27	26	46	41	16	10	14
Private nonguaranteed	**0**	**2**	**11**	**91**	**130**	**122**	**144**	**147**	**276**	**217**
Bonds	0	0	0	1	2	2	2	2	2	2
Commercial banks and other	0	2	11	90	128	120	142	144	274	215
Memo:										
IBRD	19	33	126	203	217	210	193	182	204	182
IDA	2	6	15	21	24	25	26	26	28	29
NET TRANSFERS ON DEBT	**341**	**458**	**326**	**312**	**294**	**768**	**1,079**	**510**	**-559**	**-765**
Public and publicly guaranteed	**339**	**457**	**337**	**237**	**9**	**488**	**881**	**348**	**143**	**-220**
Official creditors	316	337	454	465	173	422	89	327	328	-73
Multilateral	51	60	425	409	163	379	184	186	175	-133
Concessional	21	92	287	678	537	558	356	398	196	140
Bilateral	265	277	29	56	10	43	-96	142	153	60
Concessional	248	235	-207	83	83	-223	-401	291	28	185
Private creditors	24	121	-117	-228	-164	66	792	21	-185	-147
Bonds	0	0	0	150	-9	143	358	-9	-129	-61
Commercial banks	-1	82	-118	-497	-80	-103	686	60	-137	-74
Other private	25	39	1	118	-76	26	-252	-30	81	-12
Private nonguaranteed	**2**	**1**	**-11**	**75**	**285**	**280**	**198**	**162**	**-701**	**-545**
Bonds	0	0	0	44	-2	-2	-2	-2	-2	-2
Commercial banks and other	2	1	-11	31	287	282	200	164	-699	-542
Memo:										
IBRD	25	-43	157	-69	-165	-65	91	-249	5	-249
IDA	21	64	101	266	195	217	166	145	108	48
DEBT SERVICE (LTDS)	**230**	**600**	**1,420**	**3,241**	**2,793**	**2,682**	**3,441**	**1,994**	**2,606**	**2,447**
Public and publicly guaranteed	**230**	**592**	**1,371**	**2,885**	**2,322**	**2,261**	**2,962**	**1,548**	**1,704**	**1,785**
Official creditors	155	456	1,175	2,180	2,026	1,925	2,527	1,411	1,421	1,634
Multilateral	43	102	553	1,056	1,004	897	1,011	820	1,043	1,213
Concessional	2	12	73	117	140	154	176	181	215	240
Bilateral	112	355	622	1,124	1,022	1,028	1,517	591	378	420
Concessional	77	305	532	744	721	679	769	347	57	71
Private creditors	75	136	196	706	297	336	435	137	283	151
Bonds	0	0	0	0	9	17	17	9	129	61
Commercial banks	1	19	127	630	170	187	140	66	138	74
Other private	74	117	69	76	118	131	277	63	16	17
Private nonguaranteed	**1**	**8**	**49**	**356**	**470**	**421**	**479**	**447**	**902**	**662**
Bonds	0	0	0	1	2	2	2	2	2	2
Commercial banks and other	1	8	49	355	468	419	477	444	900	659
Memo:										
IBRD	41	59	199	383	436	436	399	379	429	409
IDA	2	10	34	51	59	63	68	73	86	93
UNDISBURSED DEBT	**1,609**	**2,822**	**9,153**	**10,050**	**9,506**	**8,931**	**7,118**	**6,548**	**5,175**	**3,354**
Official creditors	1,396	2,677	8,922	9,649	9,156	8,698	6,765	6,331	5,120	3,323
Private creditors	213	145	231	401	351	232	353	217	55	31
Memorandum items										
Concessional LDOD	2,347	7,110	12,094	15,252	16,287	15,960	15,041	16,826	18,501	18,039
Variable rate LDOD	5	129	2,232	5,422	6,002	6,853	8,994	9,743	8,931	8,410
Public sector LDOD	3,130	8,432	16,374	22,614	23,694	23,544	23,919	26,090	27,984	26,962
Private sector LDOD	127	88	269	1,274	1,687	2,079	2,398	2,662	2,382	2,081

6. CURRENCY COMPOSITION OF LONG-TERM DEBT (PERCENT)

	1970	1980	1990	1994	1995	1996	1997	1998	1999	2000
Deutsche mark	8.7	9.1	10.2	8.0	8.2	7.4	5.9	5.7	4.8	4.5
French franc	1.5	3.2	1.8	2.5	2.8	2.7	2.2	2.2	2.4	2.6
Japanese yen	5.6	8.4	13.6	15.6	15.2	14.3	13.0	15.6	17.6	16.9
Pound sterling	15.2	3.7	1.5	0.9	0.8	0.8	0.8	0.8	0.7	0.7
Swiss franc	0.6	0.4	0.3	0.3	0.3	0.4	0.3	0.3	0.2	0.3
U.S.dollars	45.6	53.8	35.7	31.1	31.2	33.7	40.7	38.6	39.4	41.4
Multiple currency	16.1	9.6	26.2	34.4	34.6	33.8	31.1	31.2	30.0	28.1
Special drawing rights	0.0	0.0	3.1	2.8	2.9	3.0	3.0	3.1	3.1	3.1
All other currencies	6.7	11.8	7.6	4.4	4.0	3.9	3.0	2.5	1.8	2.4

PAKISTAN

(US$ million, unless otherwise indicated)

	1970	1980	1990	1994	1995	1996	1997	1998	1999	2000
7. DEBT RESTRUCTURINGS										
Total amount rescheduled	..	..	0	0	0	0	0	0	3,421	918
Debt stock rescheduled	..	..	0	0	0	0	0	0	615	29
Principal rescheduled	..	..	0	0	0	0	0	0	2,158	741
Official	..	..	0	0	0	0	0	0	1,453	663
Private	..	..	0	0	0	0	0	0	705	78
Interest rescheduled	..	..	0	0	0	0	0	0	643	236
Official	..	..	0	0	0	0	0	0	508	200
Private	..	..	0	0	0	0	0	0	135	37
Debt forgiven	..	..	0	0	0	0	0	0	0	0
Memo: interest forgiven	..	..	0	0	0	0	0	0	0	0
Debt stock reduction	..	..	0	0	0	0	0	0	0	0
of which debt buyback	..	..	0	0	0	0	0	0	0	0
8. DEBT STOCK-FLOW RECONCILIATION										
Total change in debt stocks	..	..	2,315	2,836	2,846	-394	245	2,192	1,628	-1,808
Net flows on debt	393	1,170	1,089	1,511	2,572	1,093	1,618	707	655	-306
Net change in interest arrears	..	..	0	0	0	0	0	213	-213	0
Interest capitalized	..	..	0	0	0	0	0	0	643	236
Debt forgiveness or reduction	..	..	0	0	0	0	0	0	0	0
Cross-currency valuation	..	..	1,085	1,227	108	-1,650	-1,856	1,129	494	-1,668
Residual	..	..	141	98	166	164	482	143	50	-70
9. AVERAGE TERMS OF NEW COMMITMENTS										
ALL CREDITORS										
Interest (%)	2.6	4.4	5.3	4.3	5.2	5.0	5.2	5.1	4.8	6.2
Maturity (years)	31.7	30.1	22.5	22.5	17.4	20.9	12.0	18.1	14.8	12.8
Grace period (years)	11.5	6.6	6.1	6.4	5.0	6.0	3.4	5.0	3.9	3.1
Grant element (%)	60.7	47.9	34.7	40.7	30.5	33.2	21.5	32.0	25.5	20.6
Official creditors										
Interest (%)	2.1	2.5	5.2	3.8	5.0	5.1	5.0	4.9	4.8	6.2
Maturity (years)	35.0	35.5	22.9	24.1	18.7	22.8	18.9	19.3	14.8	12.8
Grace period (years)	13.1	8.2	6.1	6.8	5.5	6.3	5.2	5.3	3.9	3.1
Grant element (%)	67.3	62.2	35.6	44.5	32.8	35.5	32.5	34.6	25.5	20.7
Private creditors										
Interest (%)	5.7	11.3	8.8	8.5	7.0	4.6	5.5	7.1	0.0	6.8
Maturity (years)	11.2	10.8	11.3	8.0	4.4	5.2	3.3	6.5	0.0	1.1
Grace period (years)	1.9	0.9	4.8	3.0	0.9	3.3	1.2	2.1	0.0	1.1
Grant element (%)	17.9	-4.0	5.1	5.8	8.1	13.9	7.6	7.2	0.0	2.9
Memorandum items										
Commitments	1,054	1,113	2,925	3,545	2,257	2,823	3,130	1,974	940	830
Official creditors	912	873	2,843	3,197	2,044	2,515	1,738	1,790	940	828
Private creditors	143	240	82	348	213	307	1,392	184	0	2

10. CONTRACTUAL OBLIGATIONS ON OUTSTANDING LONG-TERM DEBT

	2001	2002	2003	2004	2005	2006	2007	2008	2009	2010
TOTAL										
Disbursements	1,210	908	537	287	134	70	38	8	2	0
Principal	2,768	2,114	1,877	1,955	1,820	1,636	1,604	1,589	1,280	1,298
Interest	1,034	917	817	751	658	592	530	464	406	358
Official creditors										
Disbursements	1,194	898	533	286	134	70	38	8	2	0
Principal	1,658	1,364	1,406	1,487	1,444	1,365	1,349	1,336	1,261	1,294
Interest	795	743	693	661	601	556	507	454	403	356
Bilateral creditors										
Disbursements	341	237	138	75	39	17	8	1	0	0
Principal	705	645	681	711	684	644	616	604	561	638
Interest	370	353	332	308	282	258	235	214	193	174
Multilateral creditors										
Disbursements	853	662	395	211	94	53	30	7	2	0
Principal	953	719	724	776	761	721	733	731	700	656
Interest	425	390	360	353	319	297	271	240	210	182
Private creditors										
Disbursements	16	10	4	1	0	0	0	0	0	0
Principal	1,110	751	471	468	376	272	255	253	19	5
Interest	238	174	124	90	57	37	23	10	3	2
Commercial banks										
Disbursements	6	3	1	0	0	0	0	0	0	0
Principal	684	291	21	21	21	21	19	17	16	1
Interest	64	25	9	7	6	5	3	2	1	0
Other private										
Disbursements	10	7	3	1	0	0	0	0	0	0
Principal	426	460	450	447	355	251	236	236	3	3
Interest	174	148	116	83	51	32	20	8	2	2

PANAMA

(US$ million, unless otherwise indicated)

	1970	1980	1990	1994	1995	1996	1997	1998	1999	2000
1. SUMMARY DEBT DATA										
TOTAL DEBT STOCKS (EDT)	**229**	**2,975**	**6,506**	**6,908**	**6,098**	**6,069**	**6,022**	**6,407**	**6,837**	**7,056**
Long-term debt (LDOD)	**194**	**2,271**	**3,856**	**3,799**	**3,782**	**5,211**	**5,418**	**5,768**	**6,245**	**6,503**
Public and publicly guaranteed	194	2,271	3,856	3,799	3,782	5,136	5,074	5,419	5,678	5,723
Private nonguaranteed	0	0	0	0	0	75	344	349	567	780
Use of IMF credit	**0**	**23**	**272**	**133**	**111**	**131**	**142**	**177**	**149**	**90**
Short-term debt	**35**	**681**	**2,379**	**2,976**	**2,206**	**727**	**461**	**462**	**443**	**463**
of which interest arrears on LDOD	0	1	979	1,511	1,607	48	49	21	0	0
Official creditors	0	0	266	192	225	1	0	0	0	0
Private creditors	0	1	713	1,319	1,382	47	49	21	0	0
Memo: principal arrears on LDOD	0	0	1,983	1,903	1,996	191	166	107	0	0
Official creditors	0	0	554	197	204	3	5	3	0	0
Private creditors	0	0	1,430	1,706	1,792	188	161	105	0	0
Memo: export credits	0	0	204	32	129	279	247	210	104	109
TOTAL DEBT FLOWS										
Disbursements	**67**	**404**	**6**	**54**	**113**	**403**	**1,789**	**775**	**911**	**754**
Long-term debt	67	404	6	40	99	327	1,743	735	911	754
IMF purchases	0	0	0	14	13	76	46	41	0	0
Principal repayments	**25**	**232**	**121**	**165**	**172**	**463**	**1,239**	**360**	**333**	**472**
Long-term debt	24	215	51	163	134	411	1,214	346	309	420
IMF repurchases	2	17	71	1	39	52	26	13	24	52
Net flows on debt	**42**	**361**	**-115**	**-97**	**-926**	**20**	**283**	**445**	**580**	**302**
of which short-term debt	0	189	0	14	-866	80	-267	29	2	20
Interest payments (INT)	**7**	**256**	**224**	**217**	**144**	**431**	**331**	**370**	**408**	**456**
Long-term debt	7	252	91	137	101	385	301	336	376	420
IMF charges	0	3	16	6	7	5	6	7	7	7
Short-term debt	0	2	117	74	36	41	24	27	26	30
Net transfers on debt	**35**	**105**	**-339**	**-314**	**-1,070**	**-411**	**-48**	**75**	**172**	**-154**
Total debt service paid (TDS)	**32**	**488**	**345**	**382**	**316**	**894**	**1,570**	**729**	**741**	**928**
Long-term debt	31	466	141	300	235	796	1,514	682	685	840
IMF repurchases and charges	2	20	87	8	46	57	32	20	30	58
Short-term debt (interest only)	0	2	117	74	36	41	24	27	26	30
2. AGGREGATE NET RESOURCE FLOWS AND NET TRANSFERS (LONG-TERM)										
NET RESOURCE FLOWS	**76**	**149**	**213**	**412**	**223**	**348**	**1,842**	**1,695**	**1,265**	**946**
Net flow of long-term debt (ex. IMF)	44	189	-45	-124	-34	-84	530	389	601	333
Foreign direct investment (net)	33	-47	132	402	223	416	1,299	1,296	652	603
Portfolio equity flows	0	0	0	115	20	5	2	0	0	0
Grants (excluding technical coop.)	-1	6	126	19	15	11	11	11	12	10
Memo: technical coop. grants	8	9	-16	28	43	29	25	27	23	23
official net resource flows	10	83	87	-74	-7	-130	130	146	16	-1
private net resource flows	67	65	127	486	231	478	1,712	1,549	1,249	947
NET TRANSFERS	**50**	**-174**	**80**	**236**	**79**	**-71**	**1,509**	**1,320**	**852**	**482**
Interest on long-term debt	7	252	91	137	101	385	301	336	376	420
Profit remittances on FDI	19	72	42	40	43	35	33	40	38	44
Memo: official net transfers	7	49	-1	-137	-66	-371	64	78	-63	-80
private net transfers	43	-223	81	373	146	299	1,444	1,241	914	563
3. MAJOR ECONOMIC AGGREGATES										
Gross national income (GNI)	1,034	3,393	5,051	7,505	7,542	7,834	8,246	8,820	8,816	9,368
Exports of goods & services (XGS)	..	7,855	5,595	8,669	9,271	8,819	9,756	9,819	8,577	9,154
of which workers remittances	..	2	18	17	16	16	16	16	16	16
Imports of goods & services (MGS)	..	8,222	5,588	8,784	9,776	9,240	10,494	11,138	10,101	10,230
International reserves (RES)	16	117	344	704	781	867	1,148	954	823	723
Current account balance	..	-329	209	16	-369	-302	-604	-1,176	-1,376	-927
4. DEBT INDICATORS										
EDT / XGS (%)	..	37.9	116.3	79.7	65.8	68.8	61.7	65.3	79.7	77.1
EDT / GNI (%)	22.1	87.7	128.8	92.1	80.9	77.5	73.0	72.6	77.6	75.3
TDS / XGS (%)	..	6.2	6.2	4.4	3.4	10.1	16.1	7.4	8.6	10.1
INT / XGS (%)	..	3.3	4.0	2.5	1.6	4.9	3.4	3.8	4.8	5.0
INT / GNI (%)	0.7	7.5	4.4	2.9	1.9	5.5	4.0	4.2	4.6	4.9
RES / EDT (%)	6.9	4.0	5.3	10.2	12.8	14.3	19.1	14.9	12.0	10.2
RES / MGS (months)	..	0.2	0.7	1.0	1.0	1.1	1.3	1.0	1.0	0.9
Short-term / EDT (%)	15.3	22.9	36.6	43.1	36.2	12.0	7.7	7.2	6.5	6.6
Concessional / EDT (%)	34.3	9.0	6.1	6.4	6.9	6.8	6.7	6.2	5.9	5.0
Multilateral / EDT (%)	16.5	11.0	15.7	8.6	10.2	11.2	12.8	15.4	15.0	14.6

PANAMA

(US$ million, unless otherwise indicated)

	1970	1980	1990	1994	1995	1996	1997	1998	1999	2000
5. LONG-TERM DEBT										
DEBT OUTSTANDING (LDOD)	**194**	**2,271**	**3,856**	**3,799**	**3,782**	**5,211**	**5,418**	**5,768**	**6,245**	**6,503**
Public and publicly guaranteed	**194**	**2,271**	**3,856**	**3,799**	**3,782**	**5,136**	**5,074**	**5,419**	**5,678**	**5,723**
Official creditors	93	595	1,504	1,264	1,262	1,070	1,138	1,322	1,342	1,289
Multilateral	38	327	1,020	591	619	677	773	984	1,028	1,031
Concessional	29	129	202	147	142	133	124	122	127	117
Bilateral	55	268	483	674	643	393	365	338	313	259
Concessional	49	138	194	292	277	282	280	276	273	238
Private creditors	101	1,676	2,352	2,534	2,520	4,066	3,936	4,097	4,336	4,433
Bonds	29	395	260	3	3	3,327	3,328	3,599	3,925	4,140
Commercial banks	6	1,161	1,969	2,467	2,466	690	565	488	401	282
Other private	66	120	123	65	51	49	43	10	11	11
Private nonguaranteed	**0**	**0**	**0**	**0**	**0**	**75**	**344**	**349**	**567**	**780**
Bonds	0	0	0	0	0	75	321	246	266	266
Commercial banks and other	0	0	0	0	0	0	23	103	301	514
Memo:										
IBRD	7	133	462	206	175	199	209	279	288	283
IDA	0	0	0	0	0	0	0	0	0	0
DISBURSEMENTS	**67**	**404**	**6**	**40**	**99**	**327**	**1,743**	**735**	**911**	**754**
Public and publicly guaranteed	**67**	**404**	**6**	**40**	**99**	**252**	**1,469**	**650**	**666**	**516**
Official creditors	15	95	6	15	95	192	240	247	113	99
Multilateral	6	68	0	15	93	168	201	235	94	88
Concessional	6	23	0	4	5	2	1	8	8	7
Bilateral	9	27	6	0	2	24	39	12	19	11
Concessional	8	10	0	0	0	24	39	12	19	11
Private creditors	52	309	0	25	5	61	1,230	403	553	417
Bonds	0	25	0	0	0	0	1,200	352	517	370
Commercial banks	0	272	0	25	5	55	30	51	34	46
Other private	52	13	0	0	0	5	0	0	2	2
Private nonguaranteed	**0**	**0**	**0**	**0**	**0**	**75**	**274**	**85**	**245**	**238**
Bonds	0	0	0	0	0	75	246	0	20	0
Commercial banks and other	0	0	0	0	0	0	28	85	225	238
Memo:										
IBRD	0	20	0	2	3	69	53	91	31	22
IDA	0	0	0	0	0	0	0	0	0	0
PRINCIPAL REPAYMENTS	**24**	**215**	**51**	**163**	**134**	**411**	**1,214**	**346**	**309**	**420**
Public and publicly guaranteed	**24**	**215**	**51**	**163**	**134**	**411**	**1,209**	**267**	**283**	**395**
Official creditors	5	18	45	108	117	333	121	111	109	109
Multilateral	2	9	43	92	85	72	70	60	54	58
Concessional	1	3	0	10	11	11	10	10	10	10
Bilateral	3	9	2	16	32	262	51	51	55	52
Concessional	2	2	0	9	11	10	29	29	35	33
Private creditors	19	197	6	55	17	78	1,088	155	173	286
Bonds	1	9	2	1	1	0	987	59	156	120
Commercial banks	2	165	1	47	3	70	95	94	16	164
Other private	16	23	3	8	13	8	6	3	1	1
Private nonguaranteed	**0**	**0**	**0**	**0**	**0**	**0**	**5**	**80**	**27**	**25**
Bonds	0	0	0	0	0	0	0	75	0	0
Commercial banks and other	0	0	0	0	0	0	5	5	27	25
Memo:										
IBRD	1	6	41	54	43	31	29	26	21	24
IDA	0	0	0	0	0	0	0	0	0	0
NET FLOWS ON DEBT	**44**	**189**	**-45**	**-124**	**-34**	**-84**	**530**	**389**	**601**	**333**
Public and publicly guaranteed	**44**	**189**	**-45**	**-124**	**-34**	**-159**	**260**	**384**	**383**	**121**
Official creditors	11	77	-39	-94	-22	-141	119	136	4	-11
Multilateral	5	59	-43	-78	8	96	131	175	40	30
Concessional	5	20	0	-7	-6	-10	-9	-2	-2	-2
Bilateral	6	18	4	-16	-30	-237	-12	-39	-36	-41
Concessional	6	8	0	-9	-10	15	10	-17	-16	-23
Private creditors	33	112	-5	-30	-12	-18	142	248	380	131
Bonds	-1	16	-2	-1	-1	0	213	293	361	249
Commercial banks	-2	107	-1	-22	1	-15	-65	-43	18	-118
Other private	36	-10	-3	-8	-13	-3	-6	-3	1	0
Private nonguaranteed	**0**	**0**	**0**	**0**	**0**	**75**	**269**	**5**	**218**	**213**
Bonds	0	0	0	0	0	75	246	-75	20	0
Commercial banks and other	0	0	0	0	0	0	23	80	198	213
Memo:										
IBRD	-1	15	-41	-52	-40	37	25	65	9	-2
IDA	0	0	0	0	0	0	0	0	0	0

PANAMA

(US$ million, unless otherwise indicated)

	1970	1980	1990	1994	1995	1996	1997	1998	1999	2000
INTEREST PAYMENTS (LINT)	**7**	**252**	**91**	**137**	**101**	**385**	**301**	**336**	**376**	**420**
Public and publicly guaranteed	**7**	**252**	**91**	**137**	**101**	**385**	**292**	**300**	**336**	**367**
Official creditors	3	35	88	63	59	240	66	68	79	79
Multilateral	1	20	85	44	39	39	45	53	66	69
Concessional	1	3	9	3	3	3	3	3	3	4
Bilateral	1	15	2	19	20	202	22	15	13	10
Concessional	1	4	0	10	11	10	13	9	9	8
Private creditors	4	217	3	74	42	144	226	232	258	288
Bonds	1	40	0	35	1	0	163	198	234	264
Commercial banks	0	168	0	34	36	140	59	32	23	23
Other private	3	9	3	5	5	4	3	2	1	1
Private nonguaranteed	**0**	**0**	**0**	**0**	**0**	**0**	**9**	**36**	**39**	**53**
Bonds	0	0	0	0	0	0	8	30	22	24
Commercial banks and other	0	0	0	0	0	0	2	6	17	29
Memo:										
IBRD	0	12	27	18	15	13	15	16	19	21
IDA	0	0	0	0	0	0	0	0	0	0
NET TRANSFERS ON DEBT	**37**	**-62**	**-135**	**-260**	**-135**	**-469**	**229**	**53**	**226**	**-87**
Public and publicly guaranteed	**37**	**-62**	**-135**	**-260**	**-135**	**-544**	**-31**	**83**	**47**	**-247**
Official creditors	8	42	-127	-157	-81	-382	53	68	-75	-90
Multilateral	3	39	-128	-122	-31	57	86	122	-26	-39
Concessional	4	17	-9	-10	-9	-12	-12	-5	-5	-6
Bilateral	5	4	1	-35	-50	-439	-34	-54	-49	-51
Concessional	5	4	0	-20	-21	4	-3	-27	-25	-30
Private creditors	29	-105	-9	-104	-55	-162	-84	16	122	-157
Bonds	-2	-24	-2	-36	-1	-1	50	95	127	-15
Commercial banks	-3	-61	-1	-55	-35	-155	-124	-74	-6	-141
Other private	33	-20	-6	-13	-18	-6	-9	-5	1	-1
Private nonguaranteed	**0**	**0**	**0**	**0**	**0**	**75**	**260**	**-31**	**179**	**160**
Bonds	0	0	0	0	0	75	239	-105	-2	-24
Commercial banks and other	0	0	0	0	0	0	22	74	181	184
Memo:										
IBRD	-1	3	-68	-70	-55	25	10	50	-10	-23
IDA	0	0	0	0	0	0	0	0	0	0
DEBT SERVICE (LTDS)	**31**	**466**	**141**	**300**	**235**	**796**	**1,514**	**682**	**685**	**840**
Public and publicly guaranteed	**31**	**466**	**141**	**300**	**235**	**796**	**1,501**	**567**	**619**	**763**
Official creditors	7	52	133	171	176	574	187	179	188	189
Multilateral	3	29	128	137	124	111	114	113	120	127
Concessional	2	6	9	13	14	14	12	13	13	13
Bilateral	5	23	4	35	52	463	73	66	68	62
Concessional	3	6	0	20	21	20	43	39	44	41
Private creditors	23	414	9	128	59	222	1,314	387	431	574
Bonds	2	49	2	36	1	1	1,150	257	390	385
Commercial banks	3	333	1	80	40	210	154	125	39	187
Other private	19	32	6	13	18	12	9	5	2	2
Private nonguaranteed	**0**	**0**	**0**	**0**	**0**	**0**	**14**	**116**	**66**	**78**
Bonds	0	0	0	0	0	0	8	105	22	24
Commercial banks and other	0	0	0	0	0	0	6	11	43	54
Memo:										
IBRD	1	17	68	72	58	44	44	41	40	45
IDA	0	0	0	0	0	0	0	0	0	0
UNDISBURSED DEBT	**96**	**595**	**222**	**581**	**592**	**575**	**679**	**802**	**767**	**603**
Official creditors	92	522	214	573	529	448	534	701	672	553
Private creditors	5	73	8	8	63	127	146	101	96	50
Memorandum items										
Concessional LDOD	78	267	396	439	419	414	404	398	400	355
Variable rate LDOD	0	1,197	2,186	2,540	2,527	3,955	3,055	3,008	2,984	2,938
Public sector LDOD	194	2,271	3,856	3,799	3,782	5,136	5,074	5,419	5,678	5,723
Private sector LDOD	0	0	0	0	0	75	344	349	567	780
6. CURRENCY COMPOSITION OF LONG-TERM DEBT (PERCENT)										
Deutsche mark	0.0	0.0	0.0	0.0	0.1	0.0	0.0	0.0	0.0	0.0
French franc	0.0	0.0	0.1	0.2	0.2	0.1	0.1	0.1	0.1	0.1
Japanese yen	0.0	9.6	9.8	10.6	10.4	2.2	2.5	2.2	2.2	1.8
Pound sterling	0.0	0.0	0.7	0.5	0.4	0.3	0.2	0.2	0.1	0.1
Swiss franc	0.3	0.0	0.1	0.1	0.1	0.0	0.0	0.0	0.0	0.0
U.S.dollars	94.5	71.0	62.0	70.4	70.7	85.7	86.1	89.6	90.4	91.8
Multiple currency	5.2	11.5	24.6	14.4	14.4	10.9	10.4	7.2	6.6	5.8
Special drawing rights	0.0	0.0	0.5	0.2	0.2	0.3	0.3	0.5	0.5	0.4
All other currencies	0.0	7.9	2.2	3.6	3.5	0.5	0.4	0.2	0.1	0.0

PANAMA

(US$ million, unless otherwise indicated)

	1970	1980	1990	1994	1995	1996	1997	1998	1999	2000
7. DEBT RESTRUCTURINGS										
Total amount rescheduled	..	..	0	422	5	3,328	0	0	0	0
Debt stock rescheduled	..	..	0	0	0	2	0	0	0	0
Principal rescheduled	..	..	0	241	0	1,744	0	0	0	0
Official	..	..	0	0	0	0	0	0	0	0
Private	..	..	0	241	0	1,744	0	0	0	0
Interest rescheduled	..	..	0	153	0	1,349	0	0	0	0
Official	..	..	0	0	0	0	0	0	0	0
Private	..	..	0	153	0	1,349	0	0	0	0
Debt forgiven	..	..	0	0	0	590	56	29	3	0
Memo: interest forgiven	..	..	0	0	0	0	0	0	0	0
Debt stock reduction	..	..	0	0	0	56	1,227	80	155	154
of which debt buyback	..	..	0	0	0	0	987	58	122	120
8. DEBT STOCK-FLOW RECONCILIATION										
Total change in debt stocks	..	..	274	193	-810	-29	-47	385	430	219
Net flows on debt	42	361	-115	-97	-926	20	283	445	580	302
Net change in interest arrears	..	..	330	7	96	-1,559	1	-28	-21	0
Interest capitalized	..	..	0	153	0	1,349	0	0	0	0
Debt forgiveness or reduction	..	..	0	0	0	-646	-296	-51	-35	-34
Cross-currency valuation	..	..	74	0	-52	-144	-107	11	8	-42
Residual	..	..	-16	131	72	950	72	9	-102	-7
9. AVERAGE TERMS OF NEW COMMITMENTS										
ALL CREDITORS										
Interest (%)	6.9	11.3	5.0	7.3	5.0	5.9	8.2	6.7	8.6	10.3
Maturity (years)	15.0	11.4	8.3	17.2	17.8	15.6	19.5	13.9	27.0	19.0
Grace period (years)	4.0	4.5	4.8	5.7	3.8	3.9	16.1	6.8	24.9	18.8
Grant element (%)	16.9	-4.2	22.6	16.6	28.5	22.5	11.2	18.5	9.6	-6.0
Official creditors										
Interest (%)	6.0	6.3	5.0	7.3	6.9	6.6	7.2	5.7	6.0	4.7
Maturity (years)	24.5	15.4	8.3	17.2	21.2	18.9	20.7	17.1	21.6	20.9
Grace period (years)	6.2	5.3	4.8	5.7	4.6	5.2	5.4	4.6	7.1	6.3
Grant element (%)	27.9	21.2	22.6	16.6	20.0	21.4	17.7	23.8	28.4	38.8
Private creditors										
Interest (%)	7.9	15.2	0.0	0.0	3.3	5.1	8.4	8.0	9.0	10.4
Maturity (years)	4.3	8.3	0.0	0.0	14.7	11.7	19.2	9.7	27.9	19.0
Grace period (years)	1.6	4.0	0.0	0.0	3.1	2.4	18.9	9.6	27.7	19.0
Grant element (%)	4.5	-24.0	0.0	0.0	36.4	23.7	9.5	11.4	6.7	-6.6
Memorandum items										
Commitments	111	534	4	60	116	277	1,578	832	631	377
Official creditors	59	233	4	60	57	151	329	473	84	5
Private creditors	52	300	0	0	60	127	1,249	359	548	372

10. CONTRACTUAL OBLIGATIONS ON OUTSTANDING LONG-TERM DEBT

	2001	2002	2003	2004	2005	2006	2007	2008	2009	2010
TOTAL										
Disbursements	572	409	203	117	40	8	3	1	0	0
Principal	340	917	351	277	272	279	275	566	254	255
Interest	487	481	449	360	351	339	326	326	297	281
Official creditors										
Disbursements	181	146	103	70	40	8	3	1	0	0
Principal	137	119	135	137	139	135	127	122	111	106
Interest	88	89	88	84	79	71	63	55	47	40
Bilateral creditors										
Disbursements	0	0	0	0	0	0	0	0	0	0
Principal	49	14	14	12	11	11	12	12	12	12
Interest	7	6	5	5	4	4	4	3	3	3
Multilateral creditors										
Disbursements	180	146	103	70	40	8	3	1	0	0
Principal	87	105	121	125	128	124	115	110	100	94
Interest	80	83	83	80	74	67	59	52	44	38
Private creditors										
Disbursements	391	263	100	46	0	0	0	0	0	0
Principal	204	798	216	140	133	144	148	445	143	149
Interest	399	392	361	276	273	268	263	271	249	240
Commercial banks										
Disbursements	31	16	2	1	0	0	0	0	0	0
Principal	104	73	35	30	24	21	11	8	7	7
Interest	18	12	8	6	5	3	2	2	1	1
Other private										
Disbursements	360	248	98	45	0	0	0	0	0	0
Principal	100	725	181	109	109	123	137	436	136	143
Interest	382	381	353	270	268	265	261	269	248	239

PAPUA NEW GUINEA

(US$ million, unless otherwise indicated)

1. SUMMARY DEBT DATA

	1970	1980	1990	1994	1995	1996	1997	1998	1999	2000
TOTAL DEBT STOCKS (EDT)	**209**	**719**	**2,594**	**2,792**	**2,506**	**2,509**	**2,592**	**2,718**	**2,707**	**2,604**
Long-term debt (LDOD)	**209**	**624**	**2,461**	**2,678**	**2,379**	**2,424**	**2,390**	**2,516**	**2,588**	**2,515**
Public and publicly guaranteed	36	486	1,523	1,732	1,668	1,546	1,340	1,436	1,529	1,502
Private nonguaranteed	173	139	938	946	711	878	1,050	1,080	1,059	1,014
Use of IMF credit	**0**	**31**	**61**	**16**	**50**	**51**	**48**	**46**	**22**	**39**
Short-term debt	**0**	**64**	**72**	**99**	**78**	**34**	**154**	**157**	**98**	**50**
of which interest arrears on LDOD	0	0	0	0	0	0	0	0	0	0
Official creditors	0	0	0	0	0	0	0	0	0	0
Private creditors	0	0	0	0	0	0	0	0	0	0
Memo: principal arrears on LDOD	0	0	0	0	0	0	0	0	0	0
Official creditors	0	0	0	0	0	0	0	0	0	0
Private creditors	0	0	0	0	0	0	0	0	0	0
Memo: export credits	0	0	223	554	371	354	497	96	88	85
TOTAL DEBT FLOWS										
Disbursements	**154**	**150**	**681**	**489**	**240**	**549**	**525**	**235**	**81**	**293**
Long-term debt	154	135	623	489	189	546	525	235	81	255
IMF purchases	0	15	58	0	51	3	0	0	0	38
Principal repayments	**20**	**78**	**391**	**741**	**509**	**388**	**424**	**212**	**147**	**215**
Long-term debt	20	72	388	710	493	388	424	208	125	195
IMF repurchases	0	7	3	31	16	0	0	4	23	19
Net flows on debt	**134**	**108**	**197**	**-417**	**-290**	**117**	**222**	**26**	**-126**	**30**
of which short-term debt	0	36	-93	-165	-21	-44	120	3	-59	-48
Interest payments (INT)	**10**	**72**	**162**	**157**	**117**	**100**	**107**	**98**	**64**	**90**
Long-term debt	10	52	156	144	111	97	100	88	56	85
IMF charges	0	1	0	2	1	2	2	2	1	1
Short-term debt	0	19	6	11	5	1	4	8	7	4
Net transfers on debt	**124**	**36**	**35**	**-574**	**-407**	**16**	**115**	**-72**	**-190**	**-60**
Total debt service paid (TDS)	**30**	**150**	**553**	**897**	**626**	**489**	**531**	**310**	**212**	**305**
Long-term debt	30	123	544	854	603	485	524	296	181	280
IMF repurchases and charges	0	7	3	32	17	2	2	6	24	20
Short-term debt (interest only)	0	19	6	11	5	1	4	8	7	4

2. AGGREGATE NET RESOURCE FLOWS AND NET TRANSFERS (LONG-TERM)

	1970	1980	1990	1994	1995	1996	1997	1998	1999	2000
NET RESOURCE FLOWS	**278**	**418**	**694**	**69**	**871**	**651**	**317**	**346**	**580**	**335**
Net flow of long-term debt (ex. IMF)	134	64	235	-221	-303	158	101	28	-44	59
Foreign direct investment (net)	0	76	155	57	455	111	29	110	297	130
Portfolio equity flows	0	0	0	0	450	187	0	0	232	48
Grants (excluding technical coop.)	144	279	304	233	269	195	187	208	95	98
Memo: technical coop. grants	1	13	44	71	89	121	110	111	104	144
official net resource flows	149	313	490	215	309	236	183	212	79	207
private net resource flows	128	105	204	-146	562	414	134	134	501	128
NET TRANSFERS	**268**	**163**	**538**	**-205**	**624**	**415**	**66**	**98**	**344**	**55**
Interest on long-term debt	10	52	156	144	111	97	100	88	56	85
Profit remittances on FDI	0	204	0	130	136	139	150	160	180	195
Memo: official net transfers	149	306	450	158	247	180	130	165	33	157
private net transfers	118	-143	88	-362	378	234	-64	-67	312	-103

3. MAJOR ECONOMIC AGGREGATES

	1970	1980	1990	1994	1995	1996	1997	1998	1999	2000
Gross national income (GNI)	626	2,488	3,098	5,110	4,450	4,989	4,711	3,654	3,429	3,651
Exports of goods & services (XGS)	..	1,089	1,487	2,909	3,014	2,994	2,592	2,112	2,194	2,252
of which workers remittances	..	0	0	0	0	0	0	0	0	0
Imports of goods & services (MGS)	..	1,561	1,719	2,356	2,415	2,753	2,752	2,152	2,091	2,250
International reserves (RES)	..	458	427	120	267	607	381	211	223	326
Current account balance	..	-289	-76	569	674	313	-99	47	120	-8

4. DEBT INDICATORS

	1970	1980	1990	1994	1995	1996	1997	1998	1999	2000
EDT / XGS (%)	..	66.1	174.4	96.0	83.1	83.8	100.0	128.7	123.4	115.6
EDT / GNI (%)	33.4	28.9	83.7	54.7	56.3	50.3	55.0	74.4	78.9	71.3
TDS / XGS (%)	..	13.8	37.2	30.9	20.8	16.3	20.5	14.7	9.7	13.5
INT / XGS (%)	..	6.6	10.9	5.4	3.9	3.4	4.1	4.7	2.9	4.0
INT / GNI (%)	1.6	2.9	5.2	3.1	2.6	2.0	2.3	2.7	1.9	2.5
RES / EDT (%)	..	63.7	16.5	4.3	10.6	24.2	14.7	7.8	8.3	12.5
RES / MGS (months)	..	3.5	3.0	0.6	1.3	2.7	1.7	1.2	1.3	1.7
Short-term / EDT (%)	0.0	8.9	2.8	3.6	3.1	1.4	5.9	5.8	3.6	1.9
Concessional / EDT (%)	0.5	11.9	21.5	28.5	31.9	32.8	29.8	31.6	36.6	35.0
Multilateral / EDT (%)	0.8	21.2	29.5	32.9	37.4	34.3	31.0	31.7	34.2	33.3

PAPUA NEW GUINEA

(US$ million, unless otherwise indicated)

	1970	1980	1990	1994	1995	1996	1997	1998	1999	2000
5. LONG-TERM DEBT										
DEBT OUTSTANDING (LDOD)	**209**	**624**	**2,461**	**2,678**	**2,379**	**2,424**	**2,390**	**2,516**	**2,588**	**2,515**
Public and publicly guaranteed	**36**	**486**	**1,523**	**1,732**	**1,668**	**1,546**	**1,340**	**1,436**	**1,529**	**1,502**
Official creditors	4	184	1,074	1,398	1,441	1,380	1,240	1,352	1,460	1,440
Multilateral	2	152	764	919	938	861	804	863	926	868
Concessional	1	79	359	438	449	426	395	421	490	440
Bilateral	2	32	310	479	503	519	436	490	534	572
Concessional	0	7	199	358	351	397	376	438	500	470
Private creditors	32	302	449	334	227	166	101	84	69	62
Bonds	0	85	37	30	0	0	0	0	0	0
Commercial banks	32	211	307	207	157	124	69	62	54	56
Other private	0	6	105	97	70	42	32	22	15	6
Private nonguaranteed	**173**	**139**	**938**	**946**	**711**	**878**	**1,050**	**1,080**	**1,059**	**1,014**
Bonds	0	0	0	0	0	0	0	0	0	0
Commercial banks and other	173	139	938	946	711	878	1,050	1,080	1,059	1,014
Memo:										
IBRD	1	55	235	281	299	270	270	267	241	244
IDA	1	55	115	109	108	105	101	100	97	92
DISBURSEMENTS	**154**	**135**	**623**	**489**	**189**	**546**	**525**	**235**	**81**	**255**
Public and publicly guaranteed	**43**	**120**	**280**	**232**	**135**	**161**	**140**	**101**	**79**	**220**
Official creditors	5	41	234	79	122	133	120	100	76	206
Multilateral	2	36	180	65	55	33	72	44	46	67
Concessional	1	20	74	40	19	7	11	10	7	6
Bilateral	4	4	55	13	67	100	47	56	30	139
Concessional	0	4	28	3	15	100	46	33	30	56
Private creditors	37	80	45	154	13	27	20	1	3	14
Bonds	0	0	0	0	0	0	0	0	0	0
Commercial banks	37	75	20	154	13	27	20	1	3	14
Other private	0	5	25	0	0	0	0	0	0	0
Private nonguaranteed	**111**	**15**	**343**	**256**	**54**	**385**	**386**	**134**	**2**	**35**
Bonds	0	0	0	0	0	0	0	0	0	0
Commercial banks and other	111	15	343	256	54	385	386	134	2	35
Memo:										
IBRD	1	2	64	21	34	21	48	14	8	43
IDA	1	13	0	0	0	0	0	0	0	0
PRINCIPAL REPAYMENTS	**20**	**72**	**388**	**710**	**493**	**388**	**424**	**208**	**125**	**195**
Public and publicly guaranteed	**0**	**32**	**184**	**251**	**204**	**173**	**207**	**114**	**108**	**115**
Official creditors	0	6	48	97	82	92	123	96	92	97
Multilateral	0	3	35	67	47	49	47	48	56	54
Concessional	0	1	15	31	7	7	7	6	8	10
Bilateral	0	3	13	31	35	42	76	49	36	43
Concessional	0	1	2	12	14	12	23	16	19	32
Private creditors	0	25	136	154	122	82	83	18	16	18
Bonds	0	8	0	5	32	0	0	0	0	0
Commercial banks	0	17	129	123	63	64	74	8	9	9
Other private	0	1	7	26	27	18	10	10	7	9
Private nonguaranteed	**20**	**40**	**204**	**459**	**289**	**215**	**217**	**93**	**17**	**80**
Bonds	0	0	0	0	0	0	0	0	0	0
Commercial banks and other	20	40	204	459	289	215	217	93	17	80
Memo:										
IBRD	0	2	14	24	27	30	28	29	31	29
IDA	0	0	1	2	2	2	2	2	3	3
NET FLOWS ON DEBT	**134**	**64**	**235**	**-221**	**-303**	**158**	**101**	**28**	**-44**	**59**
Public and publicly guaranteed	**43**	**89**	**96**	**-19**	**-69**	**-13**	**-67**	**-14**	**-29**	**105**
Official creditors	5	34	186	-19	40	42	-4	4	-16	110
Multilateral	2	33	145	-1	8	-16	25	-4	-9	13
Concessional	1	20	59	9	12	0	5	4	-1	-4
Bilateral	4	1	41	-17	32	58	-29	8	-7	97
Concessional	0	4	26	-9	2	88	24	17	11	24
Private creditors	37	55	-91	0	-109	-54	-64	-17	-14	-5
Bonds	0	-8	0	-5	-32	0	0	0	0	0
Commercial banks	37	58	-109	31	-50	-37	-54	-7	-7	4
Other private	0	4	18	-26	-27	-18	-10	-10	-7	-9
Private nonguaranteed	**91**	**-25**	**139**	**-203**	**-235**	**170**	**169**	**41**	**-14**	**-45**
Bonds	0	0	0	0	0	0	0	0	0	0
Commercial banks and other	91	-25	139	-203	-235	170	169	41	-14	-45
Memo:										
IBRD	1	0	50	-4	7	-9	20	-15	-23	15
IDA	1	13	-1	-2	-2	-2	-2	-2	-3	-3

PAPUA NEW GUINEA

(US$ million, unless otherwise indicated)

	1970	1980	1990	1994	1995	1996	1997	1998	1999	2000
INTEREST PAYMENTS (LINT)	**10**	**52**	**156**	**144**	**111**	**97**	**100**	**88**	**56**	**85**
Public and publicly guaranteed	**1**	**30**	**86**	**79**	**82**	**73**	**64**	**54**	**53**	**55**
Official creditors	0	7	40	57	63	56	53	47	47	50
Multilateral	0	6	27	38	44	37	34	32	33	32
Concessional	0	1	3	4	5	4	4	4	5	5
Bilateral	0	2	13	19	19	19	20	15	14	18
Concessional	0	0	5	11	12	11	12	11	12	16
Private creditors	1	23	46	22	19	17	11	7	6	5
Bonds	0	7	3	3	2	0	0	0	0	0
Commercial banks	1	15	36	8	9	11	7	5	5	3
Other private	0	0	8	11	8	7	4	2	1	1
Private nonguaranteed	**8**	**22**	**70**	**65**	**29**	**24**	**37**	**35**	**3**	**31**
Bonds	0	0	0	0	0	0	0	0	0	0
Commercial banks and other	8	22	70	65	29	24	37	35	3	31
Memo:										
IBRD	0	4	15	20	22	20	18	17	15	15
IDA	0	0	1	1	1	1	1	1	1	1
NET TRANSFERS ON DEBT	**124**	**12**	**79**	**-365**	**-414**	**61**	**1**	**-61**	**-100**	**-26**
Public and publicly guaranteed	**41**	**59**	**10**	**-98**	**-151**	**-86**	**-131**	**-67**	**-82**	**50**
Official creditors	5	27	146	-76	-23	-14	-57	-43	-63	60
Multilateral	2	28	118	-40	-36	-53	-9	-36	-42	-19
Concessional	1	19	56	5	8	-4	1	0	-5	-8
Bilateral	4	-1	28	-36	13	39	-49	-8	-21	79
Concessional	0	4	21	-20	-10	77	12	6	-1	8
Private creditors	36	32	-137	-22	-128	-72	-74	-24	-20	-9
Bonds	0	-15	-3	-8	-35	0	0	0	0	0
Commercial banks	36	43	-145	23	-59	-47	-61	-12	-12	1
Other private	0	4	11	-37	-34	-24	-14	-12	-8	-10
Private nonguaranteed	**83**	**-47**	**69**	**-268**	**-264**	**147**	**132**	**7**	**-17**	**-76**
Bonds	0	0	0	0	0	0	0	0	0	0
Commercial banks and other	83	-47	69	-268	-264	147	132	7	-17	-76
Memo:										
IBRD	1	-4	35	-24	-15	-29	1	-32	-38	-1
IDA	1	12	-2	-3	-3	-3	-3	-3	-3	-3
DEBT SERVICE (LTDS)	**30**	**123**	**544**	**854**	**603**	**485**	**524**	**296**	**181**	**280**
Public and publicly guaranteed	**1**	**61**	**270**	**330**	**286**	**247**	**271**	**168**	**161**	**169**
Official creditors	0	14	88	154	145	148	177	143	139	147
Multilateral	0	9	62	105	91	87	81	80	88	86
Concessional	0	2	18	35	11	11	10	11	12	14
Bilateral	0	5	26	50	54	61	96	64	50	61
Concessional	0	1	7	23	26	23	34	27	30	48
Private creditors	1	48	182	176	141	99	94	25	22	23
Bonds	0	15	3	8	35	0	0	0	0	0
Commercial banks	1	32	165	131	72	75	80	12	14	13
Other private	0	1	15	37	34	24	14	12	8	10
Private nonguaranteed	**29**	**62**	**274**	**524**	**318**	**239**	**254**	**128**	**20**	**111**
Bonds	0	0	0	0	0	0	0	0	0	0
Commercial banks and other	29	62	274	524	318	239	254	128	20	111
Memo:										
IBRD	0	6	28	45	49	50	47	45	46	44
IDA	0	0	2	3	3	3	3	3	3	3
UNDISBURSED DEBT	**41**	**181**	**527**	**670**	**687**	**518**	**404**	**266**	**318**	**379**
Official creditors	41	151	476	595	625	489	398	261	315	357
Private creditors	0	30	51	75	62	29	6	5	3	22
Memorandum items										
Concessional LDOD	1	86	558	796	800	823	772	859	990	910
Variable rate LDOD	173	271	1,339	1,399	1,139	1,214	1,308	1,366	1,350	1,321
Public sector LDOD	36	463	1,501	1,725	1,668	1,546	1,340	1,412	1,512	1,488
Private sector LDOD	173	162	960	952	711	878	1,050	1,104	1,077	1,028

6. CURRENCY COMPOSITION OF LONG-TERM DEBT (PERCENT)

	1970	1980	1990	1994	1995	1996	1997	1998	1999	2000
Deutsche mark	0.0	5.2	1.8	1.6	1.6	1.6	1.5	1.5	1.2	1.1
French franc	0.0	0.0	0.2	0.1	0.1	0.1	0.1	0.1	0.1	0.0
Japanese yen	0.0	4.4	20.4	24.8	21.3	25.1	26.4	28.4	30.8	29.1
Pound sterling	0.0	2.7	2.1	0.7	0.6	0.9	1.4	1.2	1.0	0.8
Swiss franc	0.0	5.8	1.5	0.0	0.0	0.0	0.0	0.0	0.0	0.0
U.S.dollars	2.7	35.0	27.3	20.7	19.4	18.6	19.2	19.6	18.4	20.6
Multiple currency	2.1	27.4	37.9	44.3	46.1	44.8	46.0	44.9	44.9	38.9
Special drawing rights	0.0	0.0	0.3	0.4	0.5	0.5	0.5	0.6	0.6	0.6
All other currencies	95.2	19.5	8.5	7.4	10.4	8.4	4.9	3.7	3.0	8.9

PAPUA NEW GUINEA

(US$ million, unless otherwise indicated)

	1970	1980	1990	1994	1995	1996	1997	1998	1999	2000
7. DEBT RESTRUCTURINGS										
Total amount rescheduled	..	..	0	0	0	0	0	0	0	0
Debt stock rescheduled	..	..	0	0	0	0	0	0	0	0
Principal rescheduled	..	..	0	0	0	0	0	0	0	0
Official	..	..	0	0	0	0	0	0	0	0
Private	..	..	0	0	0	0	0	0	0	0
Interest rescheduled	..	..	0	0	0	0	0	0	0	0
Official	..	..	0	0	0	0	0	0	0	0
Private	..	..	0	0	0	0	0	0	0	0
Debt forgiven	..	..	0	0	0	9	0	0	0	0
Memo: interest forgiven	..	..	0	0	0	0	0	0	0	0
Debt stock reduction	..	..	0	0	0	0	0	0	0	0
of which debt buyback	..	..	0	0	0	0	0	0	0	0
8. DEBT STOCK-FLOW RECONCILIATION										
Total change in debt stocks	..	..	278	-476	-286	2	83	127	-11	-103
Net flows on debt	134	108	197	-417	-290	117	222	26	-126	30
Net change in interest arrears	..	..	0	0	0	0	0	0	0	0
Interest capitalized	..	..	0	0	0	0	0	0	0	0
Debt forgiveness or reduction	..	..	0	0	0	-9	0	0	0	0
Cross-currency valuation	..	..	78	116	-26	-113	-157	91	74	-118
Residual	..	..	3	-175	30	8	19	9	41	-16
9. AVERAGE TERMS OF NEW COMMITMENTS										
ALL CREDITORS										
Interest (%)	6.4	11.2	6.0	7.4	5.2	1.8	5.6	6.3	5.7	6.5
Maturity (years)	21.7	17.7	16.0	5.6	10.6	28.8	27.5	15.6	25.5	16.0
Grace period (years)	8.1	4.8	4.6	1.5	4.4	8.6	6.2	3.6	5.7	4.8
Grant element (%)	25.4	1.1	22.7	6.8	23.2	59.6	32.9	20.6	31.4	20.4
Official creditors										
Interest (%)	5.4	5.8	5.7	6.2	5.2	1.8	5.6	6.3	5.7	6.5
Maturity (years)	20.9	29.1	17.3	18.2	10.6	28.8	27.5	15.6	25.5	17.3
Grace period (years)	5.2	6.9	4.9	4.3	4.4	8.6	6.2	3.6	5.7	5.1
Grant element (%)	30.5	34.9	24.5	22.9	23.2	59.6	32.9	20.6	31.4	21.5
Private creditors										
Interest (%)	7.7	15.5	7.2	7.5	0.0	0.0	0.0	0.0	0.0	6.2
Maturity (years)	22.9	8.8	9.5	4.1	0.0	0.0	0.0	0.0	0.0	5.3
Grace period (years)	12.2	3.1	3.2	1.2	0.0	0.0	0.0	0.0	0.0	2.5
Grant element (%)	18.0	-25.1	13.4	4.9	0.0	0.0	0.0	0.0	0.0	10.9
Memorandum items										
Commitments	91	184	247	183	175	71	64	5	132	319
Official creditors	53	80	207	19	175	71	64	5	132	285
Private creditors	37	103	41	164	0	0	0	0	0	34

10. CONTRACTUAL OBLIGATIONS ON OUTSTANDING LONG-TERM DEBT

	2001	2002	2003	2004	2005	2006	2007	2008	2009	2010
TOTAL										
Disbursements	147	79	59	40	25	17	11	2	1	0
Principal	209	228	243	244	222	201	193	199	188	121
Interest	92	76	70	63	56	51	46	41	35	30
Official creditors										
Disbursements	136	71	56	39	25	17	11	2	1	0
Principal	103	106	116	113	98	87	84	84	84	80
Interest	58	55	52	48	44	42	39	35	32	28
Bilateral creditors										
Disbursements	30	17	8	4	2	1	0	0	0	0
Principal	46	49	62	60	45	31	30	29	28	28
Interest	22	20	18	14	12	11	10	9	8	7
Multilateral creditors										
Disbursements	106	55	49	35	23	16	10	1	1	0
Principal	57	56	54	54	53	56	55	56	55	52
Interest	36	35	35	34	32	31	29	27	24	21
Private creditors										
Disbursements	11	7	3	1	0	0	0	0	0	0
Principal	106	122	128	130	124	114	109	115	105	41
Interest	34	21	18	15	12	10	8	6	3	1
Commercial banks										
Disbursements	11	7	3	1	0	0	0	0	0	0
Principal	10	9	16	18	12	4	2	2	2	2
Interest	3	3	3	2	1	1	1	0	0	0
Other private										
Disbursements	0	0	0	0	0	0	0	0	0	0
Principal	97	114	112	112	112	110	108	113	103	39
Interest	31	17	15	13	11	9	7	5	3	1

PARAGUAY

(US$ million, unless otherwise indicated)

	1970	1980	1990	1994	1995	1996	1997	1998	1999	2000
1. SUMMARY DEBT DATA										
TOTAL DEBT STOCKS (EDT)	**112**	**921**	**2,105**	**2,105**	**2,562**	**2,553**	**2,449**	**2,781**	**3,381**	**3,091**
Long-term debt (LDOD)	**112**	**747**	**1,732**	**1,496**	**1,778**	**1,811**	**1,934**	**2,112**	**2,630**	**2,511**
Public and publicly guaranteed	112	630	1,713	1,359	1,441	1,403	1,452	1,578	2,072	2,061
Private nonguaranteed	0	117	19	138	338	408	482	534	558	450
Use of IMF credit	**0**	**0**	**0**	**0**	**0**	**0**	**0**	**0**	**0**	**0**
Short-term debt	**0**	**174**	**373**	**608**	**784**	**742**	**515**	**668**	**751**	**580**
of which interest arrears on LDOD	0	0	115	28	8	10	10	9	10	11
Official creditors	0	0	29	18	4	6	6	6	4	5
Private creditors	0	0	86	11	4	4	4	4	6	6
Memo: principal arrears on LDOD	2	2	321	77	65	58	65	69	65	65
Official creditors	0	0	61	17	16	14	24	30	30	30
Private creditors	2	1	259	60	49	44	40	39	35	34
Memo: export credits	0	0	501	211	194	125	131	67	66	35
TOTAL DEBT FLOWS										
Disbursements	**14**	**206**	**77**	**213**	**224**	**246**	**408**	**283**	**616**	**190**
Long-term debt	14	206	77	213	224	246	408	283	616	190
IMF purchases	0	0	0	0	0	0	0	0	0	0
Principal repayments	**7**	**74**	**235**	**160**	**159**	**127**	**179**	**142**	**121**	**199**
Long-term debt	7	74	235	160	159	127	179	142	121	199
IMF repurchases	0	0	0	0	0	0	0	0	0	0
Net flows on debt	**7**	**161**	**-83**	**373**	**261**	**75**	**1**	**295**	**578**	**-181**
of which short-term debt	0	29	75	319	196	-44	-228	154	82	-173
Interest payments (INT)	**4**	**60**	**90**	**96**	**129**	**107**	**100**	**103**	**109**	**131**
Long-term debt	4	38	77	74	87	60	63	70	69	99
IMF charges	0	0	0	0	0	0	0	0	0	0
Short-term debt	0	22	13	22	42	47	37	34	41	33
Net transfers on debt	**4**	**102**	**-173**	**277**	**131**	**-32**	**-99**	**192**	**468**	**-313**
Total debt service paid (TDS)	**11**	**133**	**325**	**256**	**288**	**234**	**279**	**245**	**230**	**330**
Long-term debt	11	111	312	234	246	187	242	212	190	297
IMF repurchases and charges	0	0	0	0	0	0	0	0	0	0
Short-term debt (interest only)	0	22	13	22	42	47	37	34	41	33
2. AGGREGATE NET RESOURCE FLOWS AND NET TRANSFERS (LONG-TERM)										
NET RESOURCE FLOWS	**12**	**174**	**-75**	**209**	**204**	**288**	**487**	**505**	**616**	**99**
Net flow of long-term debt (ex. IMF)	7	132	-158	53	65	119	229	141	496	-9
Foreign direct investment (net)	4	32	76	137	103	149	236	342	87	82
Portfolio equity flows	0	0	0	0	0	0	0	0	0	0
Grants (excluding technical coop.)	1	10	7	19	36	21	23	22	33	26
Memo: technical coop. grants	7	21	40	54	64	54	51	43	52	56
official net resource flows	5	48	-141	50	117	86	168	93	97	115
private net resource flows	7	126	67	160	87	203	320	412	519	-16
NET TRANSFERS	**4**	**82**	**-174**	**105**	**82**	**187**	**379**	**385**	**480**	**-65**
Interest on long-term debt	4	38	77	74	87	60	63	70	69	99
Profit remittances on FDI	5	54	22	30	35	42	45	50	67	66
Memo: official net transfers	2	31	-199	-12	46	29	108	26	30	46
private net transfers	1	51	25	117	36	158	271	359	450	-111
3. MAJOR ECONOMIC AGGREGATES										
Gross national income (GNI)	585	4,621	5,381	7,967	9,126	9,738	9,645	8,604	7,772	7,554
Exports of goods & services (XGS)	90	781	2,674	4,060	5,275	4,861	4,995	4,722	3,650	3,188
of which workers remittances	..	..	43	26	200	183	182	178	173	176
Imports of goods & services (MGS)	111	1,399	2,284	4,331	5,363	5,214	5,092	4,778	3,712	3,485
International reserves (RES)	18	783	675	1,044	1,106	1,062	937	875	988	770
Current account balance	-16	-618	390	-274	-92	-353	-98	-56	-64	-299
4. DEBT INDICATORS										
EDT / XGS (%)	125.2	117.9	78.7	51.8	48.6	52.5	49.0	58.9	92.6	97.0
EDT / GNI (%)	19.2	19.9	39.1	26.4	28.1	26.2	25.4	32.3	43.5	40.9
TDS / XGS (%)	11.7	17.0	12.2	6.3	5.5	4.8	5.6	5.2	6.3	10.4
INT / XGS (%)	3.9	7.6	3.4	2.4	2.5	2.2	2.0	2.2	3.0	4.1
INT / GNI (%)	0.6	1.3	1.7	1.2	1.4	1.1	1.0	1.2	1.4	1.7
RES / EDT (%)	15.7	85.0	32.1	49.6	43.2	41.6	38.3	31.5	29.2	24.9
RES / MGS (months)	1.9	6.7	3.6	2.9	2.5	2.4	2.2	2.2	3.2	2.7
Short-term / EDT (%)	0.0	18.9	17.7	28.9	30.6	29.1	21.0	24.0	22.2	18.8
Concessional / EDT (%)	57.4	31.7	26.3	36.3	32.1	31.9	34.2	32.4	27.9	28.0
Multilateral / EDT (%)	40.2	20.9	34.8	33.8	30.4	32.0	36.2	35.3	32.1	36.9

PARAGUAY

(US$ million, unless otherwise indicated)

	1970	1980	1990	1994	1995	1996	1997	1998	1999	2000
5. LONG-TERM DEBT										
DEBT OUTSTANDING (LDOD)	**112**	**747**	**1,732**	**1,496**	**1,778**	**1,811**	**1,934**	**2,112**	**2,630**	**2,511**
Public and publicly guaranteed	**112**	**630**	**1,713**	**1,359**	**1,441**	**1,403**	**1,452**	**1,578**	**2,072**	**2,061**
Official creditors	83	409	1,182	1,223	1,320	1,311	1,372	1,510	1,618	1,613
Multilateral	45	193	733	711	778	816	885	983	1,085	1,142
Concessional	36	97	229	301	332	356	386	406	432	410
Bilateral	38	216	450	513	543	495	486	528	533	472
Concessional	29	195	325	463	491	458	452	496	511	457
Private creditors	30	221	531	136	121	92	80	68	454	448
Bonds	0	0	0	0	0	0	0	0	0	0
Commercial banks	2	105	263	46	49	42	35	32	428	426
Other private	28	116	268	90	72	50	45	36	27	23
Private nonguaranteed	**0**	**117**	**19**	**138**	**338**	**408**	**482**	**534**	**558**	**450**
Bonds	0	0	0	0	0	0	0	0	0	0
Commercial banks and other	0	117	19	138	338	408	482	534	558	450
Memo:										
IBRD	6	80	279	162	154	138	143	165	182	201
IDA	18	45	41	37	36	34	33	31	30	28
DISBURSEMENTS	**14**	**206**	**77**	**213**	**224**	**246**	**408**	**283**	**616**	**190**
Public and publicly guaranteed	**14**	**158**	**77**	**148**	**216**	**169**	**259**	**164**	**568**	**190**
Official creditors	7	55	50	142	204	169	248	164	168	190
Multilateral	4	40	31	73	129	136	167	131	153	165
Concessional	2	8	7	16	41	33	48	27	18	11
Bilateral	4	15	19	70	75	33	82	34	15	25
Concessional	3	11	18	47	72	33	73	34	15	25
Private creditors	7	103	27	6	12	0	10	0	400	0
Bonds	0	0	0	0	0	0	0	0	0	0
Commercial banks	2	33	2	3	12	0	0	0	400	0
Other private	5	69	25	2	0	0	10	0	0	0
Private nonguaranteed	**0**	**48**	**0**	**65**	**8**	**77**	**149**	**119**	**48**	**0**
Bonds	0	0	0	0	0	0	0	0	0	0
Commercial banks and other	0	48	0	65	8	77	149	119	48	0
Memo:										
IBRD	2	30	16	7	26	28	41	37	42	47
IDA	2	3	0	0	0	0	0	0	0	0
PRINCIPAL REPAYMENTS	**7**	**74**	**235**	**160**	**159**	**127**	**179**	**142**	**121**	**199**
Public and publicly guaranteed	**7**	**44**	**226**	**152**	**158**	**127**	**120**	**107**	**115**	**106**
Official creditors	3	17	199	112	123	104	104	93	104	101
Multilateral	1	4	62	76	76	67	60	59	67	59
Concessional	1	1	6	10	10	9	8	9	10	14
Bilateral	3	13	137	36	47	37	44	34	37	42
Concessional	1	9	21	32	40	26	36	30	31	37
Private creditors	4	27	27	41	34	23	16	14	11	5
Bonds	0	0	0	0	0	0	0	0	0	0
Commercial banks	0	17	10	15	10	5	6	4	3	2
Other private	3	10	18	26	24	18	10	10	8	3
Private nonguaranteed	**0**	**30**	**9**	**8**	**2**	**0**	**60**	**35**	**6**	**93**
Bonds	0	0	0	0	0	0	0	0	0	0
Commercial banks and other	0	30	9	8	2	0	60	35	6	93
Memo:										
IBRD	0	2	40	43	41	34	26	23	23	19
IDA	0	0	1	1	1	1	2	2	2	2
NET FLOWS ON DEBT	**7**	**132**	**-158**	**53**	**65**	**119**	**229**	**141**	**496**	**-9**
Public and publicly guaranteed	**7**	**114**	**-149**	**-4**	**58**	**42**	**139**	**57**	**454**	**84**
Official creditors	4	38	-149	31	81	65	145	71	64	89
Multilateral	3	36	-31	-3	53	69	107	71	86	106
Concessional	2	6	1	6	31	24	39	18	8	-2
Bilateral	1	2	-118	34	28	-4	38	-1	-22	-17
Concessional	2	2	-3	15	32	8	37	4	-16	-12
Private creditors	3	76	0	-35	-23	-23	-6	-14	389	-5
Bonds	0	0	0	0	0	0	0	0	0	0
Commercial banks	2	16	-7	-11	2	-5	-6	-4	397	-2
Other private	2	60	8	-24	-24	-18	0	-10	-8	-3
Private nonguaranteed	**0**	**18**	**-9**	**58**	**7**	**77**	**89**	**84**	**42**	**-93**
Bonds	0	0	0	0	0	0	0	0	0	0
Commercial banks and other	0	18	-9	58	7	77	89	84	42	-93
Memo:										
IBRD	1	29	-24	-36	-16	-6	15	15	19	28
IDA	2	3	-1	-1	-1	-1	-2	-2	-2	-2

PARAGUAY

(US$ million, unless otherwise indicated)

	1970	*1980*	*1990*	*1994*	*1995*	*1996*	*1997*	*1998*	*1999*	*2000*
INTEREST PAYMENTS (LINT)	**4**	**38**	**77**	**74**	**87**	**60**	**63**	**70**	**69**	**99**
Public and publicly guaranteed	**4**	**35**	**77**	**74**	**87**	**60**	**63**	**70**	**69**	**99**
Official creditors	3	17	57	62	71	57	60	66	67	69
Multilateral	1	10	47	42	41	38	40	47	50	51
Concessional	1	1	4	6	6	7	6	8	9	8
Bilateral	1	7	11	20	30	19	19	19	17	18
Concessional	1	5	10	18	22	16	17	17	14	17
Private creditors	1	18	20	12	16	3	3	4	2	29
Bonds	0	0	0	0	0	0	0	0	0	0
Commercial banks	0	12	2	3	2	1	2	2	1	29
Other private	1	7	18	10	14	2	1	2	1	1
Private nonguaranteed	**0**	**3**	**0**	**0**	**0**	**0**	**0**	**0**	**0**	**0**
Bonds	0	0	0	0	0	0	0	0	0	0
Commercial banks and other	0	3	0	0	0	0	0	0	0	0
Memo:										
IBRD	0	6	25	16	15	11	10	11	9	11
IDA	0	0	0	0	0	0	0	0	0	0
NET TRANSFERS ON DEBT	**4**	**95**	**-235**	**-21**	**-23**	**59**	**166**	**72**	**427**	**-107**
Public and publicly guaranteed	**4**	**79**	**-226**	**-78**	**-29**	**-18**	**76**	**-12**	**385**	**-14**
Official creditors	1	22	-206	-31	10	8	85	5	-3	20
Multilateral	2	26	-78	-45	12	31	67	24	36	54
Concessional	1	5	-3	0	24	18	33	10	-1	-11
Bilateral	0	-5	-128	14	-2	-23	19	-20	-39	-35
Concessional	2	-4	-13	-3	10	-8	20	-13	-30	-29
Private creditors	3	57	-20	-47	-39	-26	-9	-17	387	-34
Bonds	0	0	0	0	0	0	0	0	0	0
Commercial banks	2	4	-10	-14	0	-6	-8	-6	396	-30
Other private	1	53	-10	-33	-39	-20	-1	-12	-9	-4
Private nonguaranteed	**0**	**16**	**-9**	**58**	**7**	**77**	**89**	**84**	**42**	**-93**
Bonds	0	0	0	0	0	0	0	0	0	0
Commercial banks and other	0	16	-9	58	7	77	89	84	42	-93
Memo:										
IBRD	1	23	-49	-52	-30	-18	5	4	10	17
IDA	2	2	-1	-1	-2	-2	-2	-2	-2	-2
DEBT SERVICE (LTDS)	**11**	**111**	**312**	**234**	**246**	**187**	**242**	**212**	**190**	**297**
Public and publicly guaranteed	**11**	**79**	**303**	**226**	**245**	**187**	**182**	**177**	**184**	**204**
Official creditors	6	34	256	173	195	161	163	159	171	170
Multilateral	2	14	109	117	118	105	100	106	117	110
Concessional	1	3	9	16	16	16	15	17	19	22
Bilateral	4	20	147	56	77	56	63	53	54	60
Concessional	2	15	30	50	61	41	53	47	45	54
Private creditors	5	45	47	53	50	26	19	17	13	34
Bonds	0	0	0	0	0	0	0	0	0	0
Commercial banks	0	29	12	17	11	6	8	6	4	30
Other private	4	16	35	36	39	20	11	12	9	4
Private nonguaranteed	**0**	**33**	**9**	**8**	**2**	**0**	**60**	**35**	**6**	**93**
Bonds	0	0	0	0	0	0	0	0	0	0
Commercial banks and other	0	33	9	8	2	0	60	35	6	93
Memo:										
IBRD	1	7	65	59	56	45	36	33	33	29
IDA	0	1	1	1	2	2	2	2	2	2
UNDISBURSED DEBT	**47**	**567**	**563**	**1,030**	**1,170**	**1,041**	**1,010**	**914**	**766**	**665**
Official creditors	41	423	455	1,030	1,169	1,040	1,010	914	766	665
Private creditors	5	145	107	1	1	1	1	0	0	0
Memorandum items										
Concessional LDOD	64	292	553	764	823	813	838	902	943	867
Variable rate LDOD	0	180	287	243	471	569	703	847	1,376	1,344
Public sector LDOD	110	628	1,713	1,359	1,441	1,403	1,452	1,578	2,072	2,061
Private sector LDOD	2	118	19	138	338	408	482	534	558	450

6. CURRENCY COMPOSITION OF LONG-TERM DEBT (PERCENT)

Deutsche mark	11.4	9.4	11.4	10.1	9.1	6.8	6.2	5.5	3.2	2.6
French franc	0.0	0.3	10.5	3.6	2.8	2.5	1.8	1.6	0.9	0.8
Japanese yen	0.0	5.0	15.6	23.9	22.9	21.6	19.7	20.4	16.8	15.0
Pound sterling	0.2	0.6	2.0	0.3	0.3	0.3	0.3	0.2	0.1	0.1
Swiss franc	0.0	0.1	0.3	0.1	0.1	0.1	0.1	0.1	0.1	0.1
U.S.dollars	66.4	56.2	17.2	22.2	28.2	34.3	41.3	44.1	56.9	60.1
Multiple currency	19.6	22.9	37.8	38.8	34.9	32.1	28.5	26.4	20.9	20.2
Special drawing rights	0.0	0.0	0.8	0.7	0.7	1.4	1.3	1.1	0.7	0.7
All other currencies	2.4	5.5	4.4	0.3	1.0	0.9	0.8	0.6	0.4	0.4

PARAGUAY

(US$ million, unless otherwise indicated)

	1970	1980	1990	1994	1995	1996	1997	1998	1999	2000
7. DEBT RESTRUCTURINGS										
Total amount rescheduled	..	..	0	0	0	0	0	0	0	0
Debt stock rescheduled	..	..	0	0	0	0	0	0	0	0
Principal rescheduled	..	..	0	0	0	0	0	0	0	0
Official	..	..	0	0	0	0	0	0	0	0
Private	..	..	0	0	0	0	0	0	0	0
Interest rescheduled	..	..	0	0	0	0	0	0	0	0
Official	..	..	0	0	0	0	0	0	0	0
Private	..	..	0	0	0	0	0	0	0	0
Debt forgiven	..	..	16	0	0	0	0	0	0	0
Memo: interest forgiven	..	..	0	0	0	0	0	0	0	0
Debt stock reduction	..	..	436	0	0	0	0	0	0	0
of which debt buyback	..	..	111	0	0	0	0	0	0	0
8. DEBT STOCK-FLOW RECONCILIATION										
Total change in debt stocks	..	..	-278	508	457	-9	-105	332	600	-290
Net flows on debt	7	161	-83	373	261	75	1	295	578	-181
Net change in interest arrears	..	..	38	0	-21	2	1	-1	1	2
Interest capitalized	..	..	0	0	0	0	0	0	0	0
Debt forgiveness or reduction	..	..	-340	0	0	0	0	0	0	0
Cross-currency valuation	..	..	778	21	-28	-125	-119	2	-8	-97
Residual	..	..	-670	114	245	39	13	35	30	-13
9. AVERAGE TERMS OF NEW COMMITMENTS										
ALL CREDITORS										
Interest (%)	5.7	7.0	3.5	5.1	5.6	7.0	7.0	7.2	6.7	6.4
Maturity (years)	25.0	24.2	34.4	21.7	19.0	21.4	18.3	25.6	20.0	21.7
Grace period (years)	5.5	6.6	10.1	7.1	5.5	4.0	4.4	2.4	5.0	2.9
Grant element (%)	33.1	25.2	53.9	34.9	28.1	18.8	18.0	17.6	20.9	22.0
Official creditors										
Interest (%)	4.9	5.4	3.5	5.1	5.5	7.0	7.0	7.2	7.0	6.4
Maturity (years)	28.6	27.9	34.4	21.7	19.3	21.4	18.8	25.6	20.0	21.7
Grace period (years)	6.3	7.1	10.1	7.1	5.6	4.0	4.6	2.4	4.5	2.9
Grant element (%)	39.1	36.9	53.9	34.9	28.8	18.8	18.5	17.6	18.7	22.0
Private creditors										
Interest (%)	10.1	13.0	0.0	0.0	7.9	0.0	7.1	0.0	6.7	0.0
Maturity (years)	5.3	10.5	0.0	0.0	9.8	0.0	6.0	0.0	20.0	0.0
Grace period (years)	1.4	4.6	0.0	0.0	2.3	0.0	0.5	0.0	5.0	0.0
Grant element (%)	-0.2	-18.2	0.0	0.0	7.8	0.0	7.0	0.0	20.9	0.0
Memorandum items										
Commitments	14	99	117	338	364	74	252	61	405	125
Official creditors	12	78	117	338	352	74	242	61	5	125
Private creditors	2	21	0	0	12	0	10	0	400	0

10. CONTRACTUAL OBLIGATIONS ON OUTSTANDING LONG-TERM DEBT

	2001	2002	2003	2004	2005	2006	2007	2008	2009	2010
TOTAL										
Disbursements	214	174	117	75	41	23	14	3	2	1
Principal	261	258	252	261	269	188	162	156	152	147
Interest	143	137	129	119	106	95	85	76	67	58
Official creditors										
Disbursements	214	174	117	75	41	23	14	3	2	1
Principal	167	165	158	156	151	162	137	130	126	121
Interest	89	89	87	82	76	69	61	54	47	40
Bilateral creditors										
Disbursements	54	32	19	11	5	2	1	0	0	0
Principal	51	46	43	45	44	37	36	30	29	26
Interest	17	16	15	14	12	11	9	8	7	6
Multilateral creditors										
Disbursements	160	142	98	65	36	21	13	3	2	1
Principal	116	119	115	112	108	125	100	100	97	95
Interest	72	73	72	69	64	59	52	46	40	34
Private creditors										
Disbursements	0	0	0	0	0	0	0	0	0	0
Principal	94	93	93	105	117	26	26	26	26	26
Interest	54	48	43	37	30	26	24	22	20	18
Commercial banks										
Disbursements	0	0	0	0	0	0	0	0	0	0
Principal	2	1	1	14	26	26	26	26	26	26
Interest	29	29	29	29	27	26	24	22	20	18
Other private										
Disbursements	0	0	0	0	0	0	0	0	0	0
Principal	92	92	92	91	91	0	0	0	0	0
Interest	25	19	14	8	3	0	0	0	0	0

PERU

(US$ million, unless otherwise indicated)

	1970	1980	1990	1994	1995	1996	1997	1998	1999	2000
1. SUMMARY DEBT DATA										
TOTAL DEBT STOCKS (EDT)	**3,211**	**9,386**	**20,064**	**26,528**	**30,852**	**28,986**	**29,265**	**29,792**	**28,896**	**28,560**
Long-term debt (LDOD)	**2,655**	**6,828**	**13,959**	**18,854**	**20,215**	**21,602**	**21,701**	**22,610**	**23,563**	**24,045**
Public and publicly guaranteed	856	6,218	13,629	17,681	18,927	20,224	19,225	19,319	19,500	19,205
Private nonguaranteed	1,799	610	330	1,173	1,288	1,378	2,476	3,290	4,063	4,841
Use of IMF credit	**10**	**474**	**755**	**938**	**955**	**924**	**1,011**	**905**	**735**	**558**
Short-term debt	**546**	**2,084**	**5,350**	**6,736**	**9,681**	**6,459**	**6,553**	**6,278**	**4,598**	**3,957**
of which interest arrears on LDOD	0	0	3,733	4,450	4,606	221	81	56	46	43
Official creditors	0	0	1,386	211	211	138	45	19	20	16
Private creditors	0	0	2,347	4,239	4,395	83	36	37	27	27
Memo: principal arrears on LDOD	0	0	8,345	4,148	4,166	862	92	93	68	66
Official creditors	0	0	3,215	1,017	1,018	699	65	63	47	45
Private creditors	0	0	5,130	3,131	3,147	163	27	31	22	22
Memo: export credits	0	0	4,632	6,428	5,781	5,707	5,066	3,189	3,179	3,237
TOTAL DEBT FLOWS										
Disbursements	**405**	**1,452**	**289**	**1,223**	**880**	**528**	**3,016**	**1,433**	**3,346**	**3,729**
Long-term debt	387	1,308	289	1,223	880	528	2,795	1,433	3,346	3,729
IMF purchases	18	145	0	0	0	0	221	0	0	0
Principal repayments	**360**	**1,187**	**229**	**601**	**520**	**1,227**	**2,148**	**894**	**2,542**	**2,624**
Long-term debt	333	1,019	166	601	520	1,227	2,075	749	2,395	2,483
IMF repurchases	27	168	63	0	0	0	74	145	147	141
Net flows on debt	**45**	**775**	**126**	**1,256**	**3,149**	**464**	**1,101**	**289**	**-866**	**467**
of which short-term debt	0	510	66	634	2,789	1,164	234	-250	-1,670	-638
Interest payments (INT)	**162**	**964**	**247**	**542**	**721**	**1,705**	**1,512**	**1,512**	**1,642**	**1,681**
Long-term debt	162	670	91	393	485	1,308	1,088	1,105	1,325	1,421
IMF charges	0	35	74	47	52	42	47	45	33	33
Short-term debt	0	259	82	102	184	356	376	362	285	227
Net transfers on debt	**-117**	**-189**	**-121**	**715**	**2,429**	**-1,241**	**-411**	**-1,223**	**-2,508**	**-1,214**
Total debt service paid (TDS)	**522**	**2,151**	**476**	**1,143**	**1,240**	**2,932**	**3,660**	**2,406**	**4,184**	**4,305**
Long-term debt	495	1,689	257	993	1,004	2,535	3,163	1,854	3,720	3,904
IMF repurchases and charges	27	202	137	47	52	42	121	191	179	174
Short-term debt (interest only)	0	259	82	102	184	356	376	362	285	227
2. AGGREGATE NET RESOURCE FLOWS AND NET TRANSFERS (LONG-TERM)										
NET RESOURCE FLOWS	**2**	**347**	**344**	**4,933**	**4,306**	**5,504**	**3,418**	**3,003**	**3,778**	**2,291**
Net flow of long-term debt (ex. IMF)	54	289	124	622	360	-699	721	684	950	1,246
Foreign direct investment (net)	-70	27	41	3,108	2,056	3,225	1,781	1,905	2,390	680
Portfolio equity flows	0	0	0	977	1,611	2,740	692	174	289	205
Grants (excluding technical coop.)	18	31	180	226	279	238	225	240	149	159
Memo: technical coop. grants	13	64	127	99	127	125	142	181	210	154
official net resource flows	54	414	286	387	594	5	629	303	629	738
private net resource flows	-52	-67	59	4,546	3,712	5,499	2,789	2,700	3,150	1,553
NET TRANSFERS	**-233**	**-580**	**243**	**4,460**	**3,723**	**3,946**	**2,080**	**1,618**	**2,160**	**550**
Interest on long-term debt	162	670	91	393	485	1,308	1,088	1,105	1,325	1,421
Profit remittances on FDI	73	256	10	80	99	250	250	280	294	320
Memo: official net transfers	37	262	234	41	200	-438	48	-445	-270	-178
private net transfers	-270	-842	9	4,419	3,523	4,384	2,032	2,064	2,430	728
3. MAJOR ECONOMIC AGGREGATES										
Gross national income (GNI)	7,119	19,700	25,509	43,290	51,885	54,381	57,852	55,342	50,016	51,925
Exports of goods & services (XGS)	..	4,832	4,402	6,470	7,892	8,519	9,748	8,964	9,013	10,055
of which workers remittances	..	0	87	472	600	596	636	648	672	718
Imports of goods & services (MGS)	..	5,080	6,015	9,305	12,229	12,235	13,089	12,929	11,259	11,984
International reserves (RES)	339	2,804	1,891	7,420	8,653	10,990	11,306	9,882	9,050	8,676
Current account balance	..	-101	-1,419	-2,560	-4,125	-3,430	-3,057	-3,634	-1,923	-1,628
4. DEBT INDICATORS										
EDT / XGS (%)	..	194.2	455.8	410.0	390.9	340.3	300.2	332.4	320.6	284.0
EDT / GNI (%)	45.1	47.6	78.7	61.3	59.5	53.3	50.6	53.8	57.8	55.0
TDS / XGS (%)	..	44.5	10.8	17.7	15.7	34.4	37.5	26.8	46.4	42.8
INT / XGS (%)	..	20.0	5.6	8.4	9.1	20.0	15.5	16.9	18.2	16.7
INT / GNI (%)	2.3	4.9	1.0	1.3	1.4	3.1	2.6	2.7	3.3	3.2
RES / EDT (%)	10.6	29.9	9.4	28.0	28.1	37.9	38.6	33.2	31.3	30.4
RES / MGS (months)	..	6.6	3.8	9.6	8.5	10.8	10.4	9.2	9.7	8.7
Short-term / EDT (%)	17.0	22.2	26.7	25.4	31.4	22.3	22.4	21.1	15.9	13.9
Concessional / EDT (%)	3.5	14.4	9.1	19.6	18.2	18.8	17.8	12.3	13.3	13.8
Multilateral / EDT (%)	4.6	5.5	11.0	12.0	12.1	12.3	14.5	15.6	18.4	19.4

PERU

(US$ million, unless otherwise indicated)

	1970	1980	1990	1994	1995	1996	1997	1998	1999	2000
5. LONG-TERM DEBT										
DEBT OUTSTANDING (LDOD)	**2,655**	**6,828**	**13,959**	**18,854**	**20,215**	**21,602**	**21,701**	**22,610**	**23,563**	**24,045**
Public and publicly guaranteed	**856**	**6,218**	**13,629**	**17,681**	**18,927**	**20,224**	**19,225**	**19,319**	**19,500**	**19,205**
Official creditors	373	3,123	6,594	13,915	15,228	14,689	14,570	14,711	14,430	14,366
Multilateral	148	514	2,199	3,186	3,717	3,567	4,244	4,647	5,307	5,525
Concessional	0	36	185	158	142	139	124	112	129	94
Bilateral	225	2,610	4,395	10,729	11,511	11,121	10,326	10,064	9,123	8,841
Concessional	112	1,318	1,650	5,050	5,461	5,298	5,096	3,564	3,716	3,851
Private creditors	483	3,095	7,035	3,766	3,699	5,536	4,655	4,608	5,070	4,839
Bonds	22	2	1	0	0	4,873	4,130	4,130	3,727	3,727
Commercial banks	148	1,694	3,159	3,056	3,040	122	98	74	225	110
Other private	314	1,399	3,876	709	660	541	427	403	1,119	1,002
Private nonguaranteed	**1,799**	**610**	**330**	**1,173**	**1,288**	**1,378**	**2,476**	**3,290**	**4,063**	**4,841**
Bonds	0	0	0	60	60	60	0	150	150	150
Commercial banks and other	1,799	610	330	1,113	1,228	1,318	2,476	3,140	3,913	4,691
Memo:										
IBRD	125	359	1,188	1,554	1,729	1,633	1,920	2,128	2,417	2,590
IDA	0	0	0	0	0	0	0	0	0	0
DISBURSEMENTS	**387**	**1,308**	**289**	**1,223**	**880**	**528**	**2,795**	**1,433**	**3,346**	**3,729**
Public and publicly guaranteed	**148**	**1,248**	**289**	**613**	**725**	**378**	**1,518**	**639**	**1,089**	**1,468**
Official creditors	59	664	187	609	720	374	1,460	639	1,065	1,434
Multilateral	18	209	38	500	631	269	1,126	560	886	807
Concessional	0	10	10	5	3	5	3	3	6	8
Bilateral	41	455	149	109	89	105	334	79	178	627
Concessional	8	232	92	79	26	97	214	74	162	565
Private creditors	89	584	103	4	5	4	58	0	25	35
Bonds	0	0	0	0	0	0	0	0	0	0
Commercial banks	3	248	69	0	0	0	0	0	21	34
Other private	85	336	34	4	5	4	58	0	3	1
Private nonguaranteed	**240**	**60**	**0**	**610**	**155**	**150**	**1,278**	**794**	**2,257**	**2,261**
Bonds	0	0	0	60	0	0	0	0	0	0
Commercial banks and other	240	60	0	550	155	150	1,278	794	2,257	2,261
Memo:										
IBRD	10	140	0	171	203	108	490	271	380	266
IDA	0	0	0	0	0	0	0	0	0	0
PRINCIPAL REPAYMENTS	**333**	**1,019**	**166**	**601**	**520**	**1,227**	**2,075**	**749**	**2,395**	**2,483**
Public and publicly guaranteed	**100**	**959**	**112**	**560**	**480**	**1,167**	**1,895**	**620**	**911**	**1,000**
Official creditors	23	281	81	448	404	608	1,055	575	585	855
Multilateral	11	24	24	195	201	194	231	228	246	498
Concessional	0	0	3	13	22	16	16	16	16	13
Bilateral	12	257	57	253	203	413	825	348	339	357
Concessional	3	48	6	132	56	42	72	95	154	106
Private creditors	77	678	31	112	75	559	839	45	326	145
Bonds	7	0	0	0	0	0	742	0	255	0
Commercial banks	25	445	9	37	28	540	24	24	50	130
Other private	46	233	22	75	47	19	73	21	21	15
Private nonguaranteed	**233**	**60**	**54**	**41**	**40**	**60**	**180**	**129**	**1,484**	**1,483**
Bonds	0	0	0	0	0	0	60	0	0	0
Commercial banks and other	233	60	54	41	40	60	120	129	1,484	1,483
Memo:										
IBRD	8	15	0	80	86	79	65	64	89	93
IDA	0	0	0	0	0	0	0	0	0	0
NET FLOWS ON DEBT	**54**	**289**	**124**	**622**	**360**	**-699**	**721**	**684**	**950**	**1,246**
Public and publicly guaranteed	**48**	**289**	**178**	**53**	**245**	**-789**	**-377**	**20**	**178**	**469**
Official creditors	36	383	106	161	316	-234	405	64	480	579
Multilateral	7	185	14	305	429	75	895	332	640	309
Concessional	0	10	7	-8	-18	-11	-13	-13	-10	-5
Bilateral	29	198	92	-144	-114	-308	-491	-269	-161	270
Concessional	5	184	87	-54	-29	55	142	-22	9	459
Private creditors	11	-94	72	-108	-70	-556	-782	-44	-302	-110
Bonds	-7	0	0	0	0	0	-742	0	-255	0
Commercial banks	-22	-197	60	-37	-28	-540	-24	-24	-29	-96
Other private	40	103	12	-71	-42	-16	-15	-21	-18	-14
Private nonguaranteed	**7**	**0**	**-54**	**569**	**115**	**90**	**1,098**	**665**	**773**	**778**
Bonds	0	0	0	60	0	0	-60	0	0	0
Commercial banks and other	7	0	-54	509	115	90	1,158	665	773	778
Memo:										
IBRD	2	125	0	91	116	29	425	207	291	173
IDA	0	0	0	0	0	0	0	0	0	0

PERU

(US$ million, unless otherwise indicated)

	1970	1980	1990	1994	1995	1996	1997	1998	1999	2000
INTEREST PAYMENTS (LINT)	**162**	**670**	**91**	**393**	**485**	**1,308**	**1,088**	**1,105**	**1,325**	**1,421**
Public and publicly guaranteed	**43**	**547**	**66**	**370**	**413**	**1,218**	**927**	**923**	**1,085**	**1,104**
Official creditors	17	152	51	346	395	443	581	749	899	916
Multilateral	8	33	27	212	245	252	271	286	334	383
Concessional	0	1	3	6	7	5	4	4	3	3
Bilateral	9	118	24	135	150	191	311	463	565	533
Concessional	3	27	7	95	74	71	76	163	140	156
Private creditors	26	395	15	24	18	776	346	175	186	187
Bonds	1	0	0	0	0	0	318	159	171	179
Commercial banks	12	273	8	13	10	771	10	9	7	5
Other private	13	122	7	11	9	5	18	7	9	4
Private nonguaranteed	**119**	**124**	**25**	**22**	**71**	**89**	**161**	**182**	**240**	**318**
Bonds	0	0	0	1	6	6	4	0	11	11
Commercial banks and other	119	124	25	21	65	83	157	182	229	306
Memo:										
IBRD	7	24	0	109	118	116	117	120	155	189
IDA	0	0	0	0	0	0	0	0	0	0
NET TRANSFERS ON DEBT	**-108**	**-382**	**32**	**230**	**-124**	**-2,007**	**-368**	**-421**	**-375**	**-175**
Public and publicly guaranteed	**4**	**-258**	**111**	**-317**	**-168**	**-2,008**	**-1,304**	**-904**	**-908**	**-635**
Official creditors	20	231	54	-185	-79	-676	-177	-685	-419	-338
Multilateral	-1	152	-13	93	185	-177	625	47	306	-74
Concessional	0	9	4	-13	-25	-16	-17	-17	-13	-8
Bilateral	21	80	68	-278	-264	-499	-801	-732	-725	-263
Concessional	3	157	79	-148	-104	-16	67	-184	-132	303
Private creditors	-15	-490	57	-132	-89	-1,331	-1,128	-219	-488	-297
Bonds	-8	-1	0	0	0	0	-1,060	-159	-426	-179
Commercial banks	-34	-470	52	-50	-38	-1,311	-34	-32	-36	-101
Other private	27	-19	5	-83	-51	-21	-33	-28	-27	-17
Private nonguaranteed	**-112**	**-124**	**-79**	**547**	**44**	**1**	**937**	**483**	**533**	**460**
Bonds	0	0	0	59	-6	-6	-64	0	-11	-11
Commercial banks and other	-112	-124	-79	488	50	7	1,001	483	544	471
Memo:										
IBRD	-5	101	0	-18	-2	-87	308	87	136	-16
IDA	0	0	0	0	0	0	0	0	0	0
DEBT SERVICE (LTDS)	**495**	**1,689**	**257**	**993**	**1,004**	**2,535**	**3,163**	**1,854**	**3,720**	**3,904**
Public and publicly guaranteed	**144**	**1,506**	**178**	**930**	**893**	**2,385**	**2,822**	**1,543**	**1,997**	**2,103**
Official creditors	40	433	132	794	799	1,050	1,637	1,324	1,484	1,771
Multilateral	19	58	51	406	446	446	501	513	580	881
Concessional	0	1	6	18	28	21	20	20	19	16
Bilateral	21	375	81	387	353	604	1,135	811	904	890
Concessional	5	75	13	227	130	113	147	258	294	262
Private creditors	104	1,073	46	137	94	1,335	1,185	219	513	332
Bonds	8	1	0	0	0	0	1,060	159	426	179
Commercial banks	37	718	17	50	38	1,311	34	32	57	135
Other private	59	355	29	87	56	24	91	28	30	18
Private nonguaranteed	**352**	**184**	**79**	**63**	**111**	**149**	**341**	**311**	**1,724**	**1,801**
Bonds	0	0	0	1	6	6	64	0	11	11
Commercial banks and other	352	184	79	62	105	143	277	311	1,713	1,789
Memo:										
IBRD	15	39	0	189	205	195	182	184	244	282
IDA	0	0	0	0	0	0	0	0	0	0
UNDISBURSED DEBT	**238**	**2,397**	**1,509**	**1,611**	**1,738**	**3,052**	**2,650**	**2,105**	**3,876**	**3,219**
Official creditors	166	1,126	863	1,592	1,726	3,044	2,649	2,105	3,875	3,219
Private creditors	72	1,272	646	18	12	8	1	0	0	0
Memorandum items										
Concessional LDOD	112	1,353	1,834	5,209	5,603	5,436	5,220	3,675	3,845	3,946
Variable rate LDOD	1,799	2,130	4,626	9,220	9,970	11,887	12,954	11,875	13,600	14,654
Public sector LDOD	840	6,200	13,584	17,675	18,921	20,224	19,225	17,921	18,160	17,934
Private sector LDOD	1,816	628	376	1,179	1,294	1,378	2,476	4,689	5,403	6,112

6. CURRENCY COMPOSITION OF LONG-TERM DEBT (PERCENT)

	1970	1980	1990	1994	1995	1996	1997	1998	1999	2000
Deutsche mark	13.9	6.5	5.0	4.4	4.4	3.5	3.2	2.1	1.7	1.6
French franc	1.1	4.2	9.3	9.1	9.7	8.7	8.1	3.1	2.6	2.3
Japanese yen	0.0	10.9	6.3	14.3	14.6	11.5	11.6	10.5	12.5	13.7
Pound sterling	0.9	2.0	0.9	1.2	1.2	1.2	1.3	0.6	0.5	0.4
Swiss franc	0.1	1.4	1.5	1.2	1.2	0.9	0.6	0.6	0.5	0.5
U.S.dollars	59.0	44.1	48.0	43.6	41.9	50.3	54.3	74.0	73.8	73.7
Multiple currency	17.0	7.5	15.2	12.6	13.3	12.0	12.1	5.2	5.4	5.0
Special drawing rights	0.0	0.0	0.0	0.1	0.1	0.1	0.1	0.1	0.1	0.1
All other currencies	8.0	23.4	13.8	13.5	13.6	11.8	8.7	3.8	2.9	2.7

PERU

(US$ million, unless otherwise indicated)

	1970	1980	1990	1994	1995	1996	1997	1998	1999	2000
7. DEBT RESTRUCTURINGS										
Total amount rescheduled	..	..	0	712	919	5,732	806	4,682	0	0
Debt stock rescheduled	..	..	0	0	0	2,489	0	4,415	6	0
Principal rescheduled	..	..	0	277	304	430	329	30	0	0
Official	..	..	0	230	284	339	235	27	0	0
Private	..	..	0	48	20	91	94	3	0	0
Interest rescheduled	..	..	0	419	516	2,813	477	243	0	0
Official	..	..	0	410	511	498	393	242	0	0
Private	..	..	0	10	4	2,316	84	1	0	0
Debt forgiven	..	..	0	0	0	32	3	116	26	0
Memo: interest forgiven	..	..	0	0	0	758	1	1	1	0
Debt stock reduction	..	..	0	0	0	2,150	0	0	403	0
of which debt buyback	..	..	0	0	0	944	0	0	255	0
8. DEBT STOCK-FLOW RECONCILIATION										
Total change in debt stocks	..	..	1,482	2,954	4,324	-1,866	279	528	-896	-336
Net flows on debt	45	775	126	1,256	3,149	464	1,101	289	-866	467
Net change in interest arrears	..	..	460	360	156	-4,385	-140	-25	-10	-4
Interest capitalized	..	..	0	419	516	2,813	477	243	0	0
Debt forgiveness or reduction	..	..	0	0	0	-1,238	-3	-116	-174	0
Cross-currency valuation	..	..	642	744	267	-971	-1,198	317	-339	-488
Residual	..	..	254	176	236	1,452	42	-181	492	-312
9. AVERAGE TERMS OF NEW COMMITMENTS										
ALL CREDITORS										
Interest (%)	7.4	9.4	6.7	6.9	6.2	4.5	5.7	6.7	3.8	5.7
Maturity (years)	13.3	12.3	8.5	18.4	17.4	22.9	19.6	20.4	17.4	22.2
Grace period (years)	4.3	3.5	2.1	4.5	4.6	6.5	5.4	4.5	4.9	5.0
Grant element (%)	11.8	5.5	13.1	18.7	23.2	39.7	28.6	20.8	38.1	31.1
Official creditors										
Interest (%)	7.2	7.5	7.1	6.9	6.2	4.5	5.7	6.7	3.8	5.7
Maturity (years)	13.8	15.4	9.1	18.5	17.4	22.9	20.2	20.4	17.4	22.3
Grace period (years)	4.5	4.3	2.4	4.5	4.6	6.5	5.5	4.5	4.9	5.0
Grant element (%)	12.6	18.7	14.0	18.8	23.2	39.7	29.3	20.8	38.1	31.2
Private creditors										
Interest (%)	8.7	10.7	5.5	7.7	0.0	0.0	6.0	0.0	8.3	9.0
Maturity (years)	9.2	10.3	6.7	7.3	0.0	0.0	4.0	0.0	5.0	5.0
Grace period (years)	2.0	3.0	1.3	2.3	0.0	0.0	1.0	0.0	0.1	0.1
Grant element (%)	4.8	-3.2	10.5	7.5	0.0	0.0	8.0	0.0	3.5	1.7
Memorandum items										
Commitments	125	1,614	179	1,081	930	1,797	1,536	70	2,687	1,253
Official creditors	112	643	137	1,065	930	1,797	1,486	70	2,686	1,250
Private creditors	13	971	43	16	0	0	50	0	1	4

10. CONTRACTUAL OBLIGATIONS ON OUTSTANDING LONG-TERM DEBT

	2001	2002	2003	2004	2005	2006	2007	2008	2009	2010
TOTAL										
Disbursements	1,124	867	579	342	188	81	38	1	0	0
Principal	3,016	2,213	1,178	1,327	1,405	1,471	1,567	1,757	1,670	1,602
Interest	1,372	1,266	1,231	1,177	1,106	1,026	980	924	809	701
Official creditors										
Disbursements	1,124	867	579	342	188	81	38	1	0	0
Principal	721	746	899	1,014	1,061	1,127	1,191	1,230	1,283	1,199
Interest	931	925	898	854	798	736	668	594	517	438
Bilateral creditors										
Disbursements	695	525	340	194	98	35	19	0	0	0
Principal	326	336	455	513	553	631	704	745	803	729
Interest	510	507	495	476	451	423	390	352	311	267
Multilateral creditors										
Disbursements	430	341	239	148	90	46	18	1	0	0
Principal	395	410	444	501	508	496	486	485	481	470
Interest	421	418	402	378	347	313	278	242	206	171
Private creditors										
Disbursements	0	0	0	0	0	0	0	0	0	0
Principal	2,295	1,467	279	313	345	344	377	527	387	403
Interest	440	341	333	323	308	290	312	330	292	263
Commercial banks										
Disbursements	0	0	0	0	0	0	0	0	0	0
Principal	6	8	8	8	8	7	7	7	7	7
Interest	10	9	9	8	7	7	6	5	5	4
Other private										
Disbursements	0	0	0	0	0	0	0	0	0	0
Principal	2,288	1,459	271	304	337	337	369	519	380	396
Interest	430	331	324	315	300	284	306	325	287	259

PHILIPPINES

(US$ million, unless otherwise indicated)

1. SUMMARY DEBT DATA

	1970	1980	1990	1994	1995	1996	1997	1998	1999	2000
TOTAL DEBT STOCKS (EDT)	**2,196**	**17,417**	**30,580**	**39,412**	**37,829**	**40,146**	**45,683**	**48,266**	**53,019**	**50,063**
Long-term debt (LDOD)	**1,544**	**8,817**	**25,241**	**32,632**	**31,823**	**31,771**	**33,034**	**39,512**	**45,452**	**42,083**
Public and publicly guaranteed	625	6,363	24,040	29,687	28,292	26,868	26,200	28,637	34,566	33,429
Private nonguaranteed	919	2,454	1,201	2,945	3,531	4,902	6,834	10,875	10,886	8,654
Use of IMF credit	**69**	**1,044**	**912**	**1,064**	**728**	**405**	**855**	**1,569**	**1,822**	**2,032**
Short-term debt	**583**	**7,556**	**4,427**	**5,716**	**5,279**	**7,969**	**11,794**	**7,185**	**5,745**	**5,948**
of which interest arrears on LDOD	0	0	52	0	0	0	0	0	0	0
Official creditors	0	0	5	0	0	0	0	0	0	0
Private creditors	0	0	48	0	0	0	0	0	0	0
Memo: principal arrears on LDOD	0	1	182	0	0	0	0	0	0	0
Official creditors	0	0	13	0	0	0	0	0	0	0
Private creditors	0	1	169	0	0	0	0	0	0	0
Memo: export credits	0	0	4,366	8,412	8,309	8,186	9,751	4,095	4,062	3,883
TOTAL DEBT FLOWS										
Disbursements	**446**	**2,300**	**2,516**	**3,354**	**2,851**	**5,023**	**6,049**	**3,956**	**8,585**	**4,243**
Long-term debt	418	1,854	2,516	3,302	2,851	5,023	5,349	3,225	8,239	3,930
IMF purchases	28	446	0	52	0	0	700	730	346	313
Principal repayments	**264**	**686**	**1,818**	**2,520**	**3,099**	**3,192**	**2,340**	**2,444**	**4,001**	**4,012**
Long-term debt	261	541	1,473	2,250	2,737	2,890	2,124	2,365	3,947	4,004
IMF repurchases	3	145	345	270	363	301	216	79	54	8
Net flows on debt	**182**	**3,855**	**1,123**	**1,515**	**-685**	**4,521**	**7,533**	**-3,097**	**3,144**	**434**
of which short-term debt	0	2,241	425	681	-437	2,690	3,825	-4,609	-1,440	203
Interest payments (INT)	**44**	**1,496**	**1,772**	**2,112**	**2,249**	**2,165**	**2,201**	**2,286**	**2,424**	**2,724**
Long-term debt	44	579	1,573	1,646	1,844	1,659	1,702	1,950	2,036	2,397
IMF charges	0	42	99	62	55	27	24	49	65	94
Short-term debt	0	875	100	403	351	478	474	287	323	234
Net transfers on debt	**138**	**2,359**	**-649**	**-597**	**-2,935**	**2,357**	**5,333**	**-5,383**	**721**	**-2,291**
Total debt service paid (TDS)	**308**	**2,183**	**3,590**	**4,632**	**5,349**	**5,356**	**4,541**	**4,730**	**6,424**	**6,737**
Long-term debt	305	1,120	3,046	3,896	4,581	4,550	3,827	4,315	5,982	6,401
IMF repurchases and charges	3	187	444	333	417	329	240	128	119	102
Short-term debt (interest only)	0	875	100	403	351	478	474	287	323	234

2. AGGREGATE NET RESOURCE FLOWS AND NET TRANSFERS (LONG-TERM)

	1970	1980	1990	1994	1995	1996	1997	1998	1999	2000
NET RESOURCE FLOWS	**155**	**1,266**	**1,935**	**4,334**	**3,831**	**5,230**	**4,721**	**3,798**	**5,462**	**2,401**
Net flow of long-term debt (ex. IMF)	157	1,313	1,043	1,052	114	2,132	3,225	860	4,292	-75
Foreign direct investment (net)	-25	-106	530	1,591	1,478	1,517	1,222	2,287	573	2,029
Portfolio equity flows	0	0	0	1,407	1,961	1,333	73	454	422	290
Grants (excluding technical coop.)	23	59	362	284	277	247	201	197	175	157
Memo: technical coop. grants	16	64	243	329	381	278	246	230	256	226
official net resource flows	83	426	1,296	466	-478	241	307	204	111	-57
private net resource flows	72	840	639	3,868	4,309	4,988	4,414	3,594	5,351	2,459
NET TRANSFERS	**87**	**489**	**51**	**2,293**	**1,587**	**3,120**	**2,518**	**1,268**	**2,827**	**-646**
Interest on long-term debt	44	579	1,573	1,646	1,844	1,659	1,702	1,950	2,036	2,397
Profit remittances on FDI	24	198	311	395	400	450	500	580	599	650
Memo: official net transfers	72	286	547	-682	-1,765	-800	-616	-627	-761	-881
private net transfers	15	203	-496	2,975	3,352	3,921	3,135	1,895	3,588	236

3. MAJOR ECONOMIC AGGREGATES

	1970	1980	1990	1994	1995	1996	1997	1998	1999	2000
Gross national income (GNI)	6,576	32,436	44,092	65,730	76,165	86,258	85,606	68,845	80,729	79,317
Exports of goods & services (XGS)	..	8,202	13,290	24,476	33,294	40,118	49,120	43,617	47,195	49,395
of which workers remittances	..	205	262	443	432	569	1,057	204	102	125
Imports of goods & services (MGS)	..	10,348	16,437	27,919	35,722	44,091	53,494	42,302	39,677	40,622
International reserves (RES)	255	3,978	2,036	7,126	7,757	11,747	8,714	10,789	15,029	15,035
Current account balance	..	-1,904	-2,695	-2,950	-1,980	-3,953	-4,351	1,546	7,910	9,081

4. DEBT INDICATORS

	1970	1980	1990	1994	1995	1996	1997	1998	1999	2000
EDT / XGS (%)	..	212.4	230.1	161.0	113.6	100.1	93.0	110.7	112.3	101.4
EDT / GNI (%)	33.4	53.7	69.4	60.0	49.7	46.5	53.4	70.1	65.7	63.1
TDS / XGS (%)	..	26.6	27.0	18.9	16.1	13.4	9.2	10.8	13.6	13.6
INT / XGS (%)	..	18.2	13.3	8.6	6.8	5.4	4.5	5.2	5.1	5.5
INT / GNI (%)	0.7	4.6	4.0	3.2	3.0	2.5	2.6	3.3	3.0	3.4
RES / EDT (%)	11.6	22.8	6.7	18.1	20.5	29.3	19.1	22.4	28.4	30.0
RES / MGS (months)	..	4.6	1.5	3.1	2.6	3.2	2.0	3.1	4.6	4.4
Short-term / EDT (%)	26.6	43.4	14.5	14.5	14.0	19.9	25.8	14.9	10.8	11.9
Concessional / EDT (%)	3.1	5.5	20.0	27.4	29.5	25.9	21.9	23.7	25.3	24.8
Multilateral / EDT (%)	5.5	7.5	20.5	21.2	22.4	19.8	16.0	16.5	14.7	14.2

PHILIPPINES

(US$ million, unless otherwise indicated)

	1970	1980	1990	1994	1995	1996	1997	1998	1999	2000
5. LONG-TERM DEBT										
DEBT OUTSTANDING (LDOD)	**1,544**	**8,817**	**25,241**	**32,632**	**31,823**	**31,771**	**33,034**	**39,512**	**45,452**	**42,083**
Public and publicly guaranteed	**625**	**6,363**	**24,040**	**29,687**	**28,292**	**26,868**	**26,200**	**28,637**	**34,566**	**33,429**
Official creditors	272	2,636	15,302	23,208	22,196	20,211	18,485	20,224	21,490	19,478
Multilateral	120	1,310	6,273	8,348	8,479	7,928	7,321	7,972	7,812	7,116
Concessional	0	60	457	935	976	972	947	1,045	1,107	1,058
Bilateral	152	1,326	9,029	14,860	13,717	12,282	11,164	12,252	13,678	12,362
Concessional	68	894	5,649	9,860	10,164	9,422	9,065	10,371	12,286	11,358
Private creditors	353	3,727	8,739	6,479	6,096	6,658	7,715	8,414	13,076	13,952
Bonds	11	888	825	4,858	4,666	5,450	6,228	6,357	10,008	11,095
Commercial banks	267	2,256	6,661	575	650	581	942	1,630	2,685	2,553
Other private	75	583	1,253	1,047	780	627	546	426	382	303
Private nonguaranteed	**919**	**2,454**	**1,201**	**2,945**	**3,531**	**4,902**	**6,834**	**10,875**	**10,886**	**8,654**
Bonds	0	0	0	1,062	1,925	3,499	5,274	5,366	6,137	5,690
Commercial banks and other	919	2,454	1,201	1,883	1,606	1,404	1,560	5,509	4,749	2,964
Memo:										
IBRD	119	926	3,943	4,855	5,002	4,666	4,179	4,311	4,040	3,627
IDA	0	34	101	174	183	193	195	205	206	207
DISBURSEMENTS	**418**	**1,854**	**2,516**	**3,302**	**2,851**	**5,023**	**5,349**	**3,225**	**8,239**	**3,930**
Public and publicly guaranteed	**142**	**1,382**	**2,225**	**2,316**	**1,827**	**3,245**	**3,172**	**2,716**	**7,444**	**3,411**
Official creditors	74	461	1,373	1,770	1,425	1,596	1,803	1,419	1,618	1,323
Multilateral	17	321	854	612	621	728	620	652	315	313
Concessional	0	9	121	63	63	70	61	37	36	44
Bilateral	57	140	519	1,158	805	868	1,182	767	1,303	1,010
Concessional	15	102	462	728	745	792	1,161	755	1,287	1,007
Private creditors	68	920	852	546	402	1,649	1,370	1,297	5,826	2,089
Bonds	0	96	575	350	278	1,618	866	500	4,550	1,631
Commercial banks	51	657	167	35	102	13	453	772	1,275	457
Other private	17	167	110	162	22	18	52	24	2	0
Private nonguaranteed	**276**	**472**	**291**	**985**	**1,024**	**1,778**	**2,177**	**510**	**795**	**519**
Bonds	0	0	0	785	864	1,778	1,793	90	795	5
Commercial banks and other	276	472	291	201	161	0	384	420	0	514
Memo:										
IBRD	16	229	506	300	393	442	295	292	157	152
IDA	0	2	0	5	10	15	9	9	6	10
PRINCIPAL REPAYMENTS	**261**	**541**	**1,473**	**2,250**	**2,737**	**2,890**	**2,124**	**2,365**	**3,947**	**4,004**
Public and publicly guaranteed	**75**	**221**	**1,411**	**2,104**	**2,587**	**2,596**	**1,883**	**2,115**	**3,167**	**2,472**
Official creditors	15	95	439	1,588	2,181	1,601	1,697	1,412	1,682	1,537
Multilateral	5	45	388	520	651	608	586	566	591	561
Concessional	0	1	6	8	6	7	7	9	13	15
Bilateral	10	49	51	1,069	1,530	993	1,111	846	1,091	976
Concessional	3	24	21	420	674	495	549	473	558	665
Private creditors	61	126	972	516	406	995	186	703	1,485	934
Bonds	1	16	180	168	32	798	28	439	1,115	395
Commercial banks	41	44	743	108	101	64	67	99	296	488
Other private	19	67	49	240	273	133	91	166	74	52
Private nonguaranteed	**186**	**320**	**62**	**146**	**150**	**294**	**241**	**250**	**780**	**1,533**
Bonds	0	0	0	0	0	100	0	0	20	445
Commercial banks and other	186	320	62	146	150	194	241	250	760	1,088
Memo:										
IBRD	5	33	301	358	413	425	407	387	384	349
IDA	0	0	1	2	2	2	2	2	3	3
NET FLOWS ON DEBT	**157**	**1,313**	**1,043**	**1,052**	**114**	**2,132**	**3,225**	**860**	**4,292**	**-75**
Public and publicly guaranteed	**67**	**1,161**	**814**	**212**	**-760**	**648**	**1,289**	**600**	**4,277**	**940**
Official creditors	60	367	934	182	-756	-6	106	7	-64	-215
Multilateral	12	276	466	92	-30	120	35	86	-276	-248
Concessional	0	8	115	55	57	63	54	28	23	28
Bilateral	48	91	468	90	-726	-126	71	-79	212	34
Concessional	12	78	441	308	71	297	612	282	729	342
Private creditors	7	794	-120	30	-4	654	1,183	593	4,341	1,154
Bonds	-1	80	395	182	246	820	838	61	3,435	1,237
Commercial banks	11	614	-576	-74	1	-51	385	674	978	-31
Other private	-3	100	61	-78	-251	-115	-40	-141	-72	-52
Private nonguaranteed	**90**	**152**	**229**	**839**	**874**	**1,484**	**1,935**	**260**	**15**	**-1,014**
Bonds	0	0	0	785	864	1,678	1,793	90	775	-440
Commercial banks and other	90	152	229	55	11	-194	142	170	-760	-574
Memo:										
IBRD	11	195	206	-58	-21	18	-112	-95	-227	-198
IDA	0	2	-1	3	8	13	8	7	3	7

PHILIPPINES

(US$ million, unless otherwise indicated)

	1970	1980	1990	1994	1995	1996	1997	1998	1999	2000
INTEREST PAYMENTS (LINT)	**44**	**579**	**1,573**	**1,646**	**1,844**	**1,659**	**1,702**	**1,950**	**2,036**	**2,397**
Public and publicly guaranteed	**26**	**375**	**1,486**	**1,513**	**1,693**	**1,428**	**1,384**	**1,463**	**1,622**	**1,810**
Official creditors	11	140	749	1,148	1,287	1,042	923	830	872	824
Multilateral	7	100	444	565	604	537	485	443	447	414
Concessional	0	1	4	9	10	10	9	9	10	10
Bilateral	4	40	305	584	683	505	438	388	424	410
Concessional	2	21	125	273	404	300	289	277	329	345
Private creditors	15	235	737	365	405	387	461	632	751	987
Bonds	1	36	31	274	288	300	397	505	650	827
Commercial banks	11	165	671	33	54	45	36	103	81	145
Other private	3	34	35	58	63	41	28	24	20	15
Private nonguaranteed	**19**	**204**	**87**	**133**	**152**	**231**	**319**	**487**	**413**	**587**
Bonds	0	0	0	20	82	154	257	386	388	479
Commercial banks and other	19	204	87	113	70	77	62	101	26	108
Memo:										
IBRD	7	73	296	359	376	341	302	266	256	223
IDA	0	0	1	1	1	1	1	2	2	2
NET TRANSFERS ON DEBT	**113**	**733**	**-529**	**-595**	**-1,730**	**473**	**1,522**	**-1,090**	**2,256**	**-2,471**
Public and publicly guaranteed	**41**	**785**	**-672**	**-1,301**	**-2,452**	**-780**	**-94**	**-862**	**2,655**	**-871**
Official creditors	49	227	185	-967	-2,043	-1,047	-817	-823	-936	-1,038
Multilateral	5	176	22	-472	-634	-417	-451	-357	-723	-662
Concessional	0	8	111	46	47	53	45	19	12	18
Bilateral	43	51	163	-494	-1,409	-630	-366	-466	-212	-376
Concessional	9	57	316	35	-333	-3	324	5	400	-2
Private creditors	-8	559	-857	-334	-409	268	723	-39	3,590	168
Bonds	-2	44	364	-92	-41	519	441	-444	2,785	409
Commercial banks	0	448	-1,247	-106	-54	-96	350	570	897	-175
Other private	-6	66	25	-136	-315	-156	-68	-166	-92	-66
Private nonguaranteed	**71**	**-52**	**142**	**706**	**723**	**1,253**	**1,617**	**-228**	**-398**	**-1,601**
Bonds	0	0	0	764	782	1,524	1,536	-296	388	-919
Commercial banks and other	71	-52	142	-58	-59	-271	80	69	-786	-682
Memo:										
IBRD	4	123	-90	-417	-397	-324	-414	-361	-484	-421
IDA	0	1	-2	2	7	12	6	5	2	6
DEBT SERVICE (LTDS)	**305**	**1,120**	**3,046**	**3,896**	**4,581**	**4,550**	**3,827**	**4,315**	**5,982**	**6,401**
Public and publicly guaranteed	**101**	**596**	**2,897**	**3,617**	**4,279**	**4,025**	**3,267**	**3,578**	**4,789**	**4,282**
Official creditors	26	235	1,188	2,737	3,468	2,643	2,620	2,242	2,553	2,361
Multilateral	12	145	832	1,084	1,255	1,145	1,071	1,009	1,038	975
Concessional	0	1	10	17	16	16	16	18	23	26
Bilateral	14	90	356	1,653	2,213	1,498	1,549	1,234	1,515	1,386
Concessional	6	45	146	693	1,078	795	837	750	887	1,009
Private creditors	75	362	1,709	880	811	1,382	647	1,336	2,236	1,921
Bonds	2	52	211	441	320	1,099	425	944	1,765	1,222
Commercial banks	52	209	1,414	141	155	109	103	202	377	633
Other private	22	101	85	298	336	174	119	190	94	67
Private nonguaranteed	**204**	**524**	**149**	**279**	**302**	**525**	**560**	**737**	**1,193**	**2,119**
Bonds	0	0	0	20	82	254	257	386	408	924
Commercial banks and other	204	524	149	259	220	271	303	351	786	1,196
Memo:										
IBRD	12	106	597	717	789	766	709	654	641	573
IDA	0	0	2	3	3	3	3	4	4	5
UNDISBURSED DEBT	**193**	**4,365**	**6,590**	**8,507**	**8,726**	**8,063**	**7,100**	**9,309**	**52,500**	**13,008**
Official creditors	176	3,246	6,156	8,089	8,324	7,748	6,870	9,006	52,081	12,412
Private creditors	16	1,119	434	419	402	315	230	304	419	596
Memorandum items										
Concessional LDOD	68	954	6,105	10,795	11,140	10,395	10,011	11,416	13,393	12,416
Variable rate LDOD	924	4,399	11,066	10,644	11,638	12,852	15,151	20,524	21,683	19,052
Public sector LDOD	624	6,363	23,668	29,459	28,135	26,730	26,071	28,570	34,493	33,359
Private sector LDOD	920	2,454	1,573	3,173	3,687	5,041	6,963	10,943	10,958	8,725

6. CURRENCY COMPOSITION OF LONG-TERM DEBT (PERCENT)

	1970	1980	1990	1994	1995	1996	1997	1998	1999	2000
Deutsche mark	12.0	2.0	1.5	1.4	1.5	1.7	1.5	1.4	1.0	0.8
French franc	0.2	2.2	1.5	0.8	0.8	0.9	0.8	0.9	0.6	0.5
Japanese yen	2.7	21.9	31.0	40.4	39.5	38.1	36.8	38.0	38.9	38.6
Pound sterling	0.0	0.2	1.0	0.3	0.2	0.2	0.3	0.2	0.2	0.1
Swiss franc	3.1	0.5	0.5	0.4	0.3	0.2	0.2	0.2	0.1	0.1
U.S.dollars	62.1	51.6	36.2	28.0	27.5	29.8	33.9	34.9	39.2	42.3
Multiple currency	19.3	19.0	23.6	25.4	26.9	26.0	24.1	22.4	17.5	15.6
Special drawing rights	0.0	0.0	0.0	0.3	0.4	0.6	0.6	0.6	0.5	0.5
All other currencies	0.6	2.6	4.7	3.0	2.9	2.5	1.8	1.4	2.0	1.5

PHILIPPINES

(US$ million, unless otherwise indicated)

	1970	1980	1990	1994	1995	1996	1997	1998	1999	2000
7. DEBT RESTRUCTURINGS										
Total amount rescheduled	..	..	1,068	0	0	0	0	0	0	0
Debt stock rescheduled	..	..	0	0	0	0	0	0	0	0
Principal rescheduled	..	..	848	0	0	0	0	0	0	0
Official	..	..	172	0	0	0	0	0	0	0
Private	..	..	676	0	0	0	0	0	0	0
Interest rescheduled	..	..	186	0	0	0	0	0	0	0
Official	..	..	107	0	0	0	0	0	0	0
Private	..	..	80	0	0	0	0	0	0	0
Debt forgiven	..	..	0	0	0	0	0	0	0	0
Memo: interest forgiven	..	..	0	0	0	0	0	0	0	0
Debt stock reduction	..	..	1,803	0	0	0	0	0	1,003	0
of which debt buyback	..	..	721	0	0	0	0	0	859	0
8. DEBT STOCK-FLOW RECONCILIATION										
Total change in debt stocks	..	..	1,927	3,476	-1,582	2,316	5,537	2,583	4,753	-2,956
Net flows on debt	182	3,855	1,123	1,515	-685	4,521	7,533	-3,097	3,144	434
Net change in interest arrears	..	..	48	0	0	0	0	0	0	0
Interest capitalized	..	..	186	0	0	0	0	0	0	0
Debt forgiveness or reduction	..	..	-1,082	0	0	0	0	0	-144	0
Cross-currency valuation	..	..	1,542	1,958	-266	-2,256	-2,075	1,688	1,275	-2,193
Residual	..	..	111	3	-632	51	79	3,992	478	-1,197
9. AVERAGE TERMS OF NEW COMMITMENTS										
ALL CREDITORS										
Interest (%)	7.3	9.9	6.2	4.4	4.8	6.2	4.7	5.5	6.1	6.4
Maturity (years)	11.1	17.3	21.9	20.7	24.1	17.3	21.3	19.0	18.4	15.4
Grace period (years)	1.9	5.3	7.4	7.1	8.2	9.4	10.2	6.5	10.6	5.3
Grant element (%)	11.6	4.0	28.2	38.0	39.7	24.4	34.2	31.8	26.3	22.4
Official creditors										
Interest (%)	6.8	6.9	5.1	3.9	4.3	4.9	3.7	4.3	2.3	5.9
Maturity (years)	14.0	22.3	24.4	23.2	26.7	21.0	26.4	24.6	26.6	19.7
Grace period (years)	1.9	6.3	7.3	7.5	7.8	6.2	7.7	6.9	7.2	4.8
Grant element (%)	15.0	22.1	36.8	43.2	43.6	34.7	48.4	42.6	57.6	27.4
Private creditors										
Interest (%)	8.1	13.5	9.2	6.7	7.1	7.4	6.0	8.0	8.3	7.4
Maturity (years)	6.7	11.4	15.0	8.9	10.9	13.9	14.4	6.3	13.5	7.4
Grace period (years)	2.0	4.1	7.6	5.3	10.2	12.4	13.5	5.5	12.7	6.3
Grant element (%)	6.4	-17.4	4.1	12.7	19.0	14.6	15.2	7.2	7.5	12.8
Memorandum items										
Commitments	164	2,143	3,520	3,202	2,595	3,631	3,030	4,566	7,938	6,600
Official creditors	100	1,164	2,588	2,658	2,182	1,766	1,729	3,165	2,980	4,325
Private creditors	64	979	933	544	413	1,865	1,301	1,401	4,958	2,275

10. CONTRACTUAL OBLIGATIONS ON OUTSTANDING LONG-TERM DEBT

	2001	2002	2003	2004	2005	2006	2007	2008	2009	2010
TOTAL										
Disbursements	3,196	3,208	2,351	1,715	1,170	782	477	42	26	12
Principal	3,717	4,257	3,611	4,149	3,616	3,497	2,512	3,371	3,214	4,061
Interest	2,442	2,299	2,226	2,086	1,918	1,769	1,619	1,444	1,296	1,022
Official creditors										
Disbursements	2,887	3,024	2,277	1,688	1,168	782	477	42	26	12
Principal	1,514	1,682	1,814	1,876	1,934	2,023	1,957	1,897	1,911	1,702
Interest	832	837	901	890	866	820	752	667	584	501
Bilateral creditors										
Disbursements	2,328	1,993	1,243	734	372	192	79	3	2	1
Principal	833	947	1,008	1,039	1,057	1,107	1,048	981	947	912
Interest	426	444	441	420	391	358	321	289	260	234
Multilateral creditors										
Disbursements	559	1,031	1,035	954	796	590	398	40	24	11
Principal	681	736	806	837	877	915	910	916	963	790
Interest	406	393	460	470	475	462	431	378	324	266
Private creditors										
Disbursements	309	185	73	27	2	0	0	0	0	0
Principal	2,203	2,575	1,797	2,273	1,683	1,474	555	1,475	1,303	2,359
Interest	1,611	1,462	1,325	1,196	1,052	949	867	776	712	521
Commercial banks										
Disbursements	214	119	45	17	0	0	0	0	0	0
Principal	725	100	208	494	366	53	48	43	567	52
Interest	167	135	129	114	78	51	48	46	30	15
Other private										
Disbursements	96	65	28	10	2	0	0	0	0	0
Principal	1,478	2,475	1,589	1,779	1,317	1,421	507	1,432	736	2,306
Interest	1,443	1,328	1,196	1,082	974	898	819	730	682	506

POLAND

(US$ million, unless otherwise indicated)

	1970	1980	1990	1994	1995	1996	1997	1998	1999	2000
1. SUMMARY DEBT DATA										
TOTAL DEBT STOCKS (EDT)	..	..	**49,364**	**42,553**	**44,263**	**43,473**	**40,401**	**55,494**	**60,579**	**63,561**
Long-term debt (LDOD)	..	..	**39,261**	**40,367**	**42,086**	**40,810**	**36,589**	**49,303**	**54,635**	**56,457**
Public and publicly guaranteed	..	..	39,261	39,503	41,073	39,208	34,178	35,136	33,151	30,785
Private nonguaranteed	..	..	0	864	1,012	1,602	2,412	14,167	21,484	25,672
Use of IMF credit	**0**	**0**	**509**	**1,341**	**0**	**0**	**0**	**0**	**0**	**0**
Short-term debt	..	..	**9,595**	**845**	**2,178**	**2,663**	**3,812**	**6,191**	**5,944**	**7,105**
of which interest arrears on LDOD	..	..	8,315	139	136	0	0	0	0	139
Official creditors	..	..	6,568	139	136	0	0	0	0	0
Private creditors	..	..	1,747	0	0	0	0	0	0	139
Memo: principal arrears on LDOD	..	..	5,670	585	625	29	29	3	3	3
Official creditors	..	..	4,284	578	619	25	25	0	0	0
Private creditors	..	..	1,386	7	5	4	4	3	3	3
Memo: export credits	..	..	28,076	19,123	17,559	19,330	16,058	15,462	14,610	13,504
TOTAL DEBT FLOWS										
Disbursements	..	..	**1,025**	**2,429**	**1,279**	**1,475**	**2,394**	**4,742**	**8,262**	**10,244**
Long-term debt	..	..	540	1,512	1,279	1,475	2,394	4,742	8,262	10,244
IMF purchases	0	0	485	917	0	0	0	0	0	0
Principal repayments	..	..	**635**	**1,895**	**2,279**	**1,114**	**1,085**	**2,910**	**6,244**	**7,718**
Long-term debt	..	..	635	1,581	885	1,114	1,085	2,910	6,244	7,718
IMF repurchases	0	0	0	314	1,394	0	0	0	0	0
Net flows on debt	..	..	**423**	**97**	**335**	**982**	**2,459**	**4,210**	**1,771**	**3,549**
of which short-term debt	..	..	33	-436	1,335	621	1,149	2,379	-247	1,023
Interest payments (INT)	..	..	**332**	**1,207**	**1,868**	**1,566**	**1,477**	**1,624**	**2,130**	**2,573**
Long-term debt	..	..	203	1,123	1,719	1,433	1,286	1,374	1,802	2,237
IMF charges	0	0	23	48	47	0	0	0	0	0
Short-term debt	..	..	105	37	102	133	191	250	328	336
Net transfers on debt	..	..	**92**	**-1,110**	**-1,532**	**-584**	**982**	**2,586**	**-359**	**976**
Total debt service paid (TDS)	..	..	**966**	**3,103**	**4,147**	**2,680**	**2,562**	**4,534**	**8,374**	**10,290**
Long-term debt	..	..	838	2,704	2,604	2,547	2,371	4,284	8,047	9,955
IMF repurchases and charges	0	0	23	362	1,440	0	0	0	0	0
Short-term debt (interest only)	..	..	105	37	102	133	191	250	328	336
2. AGGREGATE NET RESOURCE FLOWS AND NET TRANSFERS (LONG-TERM)										
NET RESOURCE FLOWS	..	..	**21**	**3,499**	**8,381**	**6,537**	**7,815**	**9,717**	**10,699**	**13,413**
Net flow of long-term debt (ex. IMF)	..	..	-95	-70	394	361	1,310	1,832	2,018	2,526
Foreign direct investment (net)	..	..	89	1,875	3,659	4,498	4,908	6,365	7,270	9,342
Portfolio equity flows	..	..	0	5	921	722	945	969	721	871
Grants (excluding technical coop.)	..	..	26	1,688	3,408	956	652	551	690	674
Memo: technical coop. grants	..	..	0	101	334	147	145	215	138	110
official net resource flows	..	..	-51	2,255	3,324	1,204	512	64	247	218
private net resource flows	..	..	71	1,244	5,058	5,333	7,303	9,653	10,452	13,195
NET TRANSFERS	..	..	**-202**	**2,176**	**6,438**	**4,804**	**6,169**	**7,943**	**8,317**	**10,517**
Interest on long-term debt	..	..	203	1,123	1,719	1,433	1,286	1,374	1,802	2,237
Profit remittances on FDI	..	..	20	200	225	300	360	400	580	660
Memo: official net transfers	..	..	-164	1,519	2,108	282	-265	-695	-659	-435
private net transfers	..	..	-38	658	4,330	4,523	6,434	8,638	8,975	10,952
3. MAJOR ECONOMIC AGGREGATES										
Gross national income (GNI)	..	..	55,620	96,428	125,037	142,751	142,845	157,267	154,029	156,819
Exports of goods & services (XGS)	..	..	19,640	26,158	37,501	39,554	41,910	46,471	40,958	49,181
of which workers remittances	..	..	0	558	696	723	797	938	698	639
Imports of goods & services (MGS)	..	..	19,084	25,898	36,909	43,789	48,892	55,331	54,961	60,919
International reserves (RES)	..	..	4,674	6,023	14,957	18,019	20,670	28,276	27,314	27,469
Current account balance	..	..	3,067	954	854	-3,264	-5,744	-6,901	-12,487	-9,997
4. DEBT INDICATORS										
EDT / XGS (%)	..	..	251.4	162.7	118.0	109.9	96.4	119.4	147.9	129.2
EDT / GNI (%)	..	..	88.8	44.1	35.4	30.5	28.3	35.3	39.3	40.5
TDS / XGS (%)	..	..	4.9	11.9	11.1	6.8	6.1	9.8	20.5	20.9
INT / XGS (%)	..	..	1.7	4.6	5.0	4.0	3.5	3.5	5.2	5.2
INT / GNI (%)	..	..	0.6	1.3	1.5	1.1	1.0	1.0	1.4	1.6
RES / EDT (%)	..	..	9.5	14.2	33.8	41.5	51.2	51.0	45.1	43.2
RES / MGS (months)	..	..	2.9	2.8	4.9	4.9	5.1	6.1	6.0	5.4
Short-term / EDT (%)	..	..	19.4	2.0	4.9	6.1	9.4	11.2	9.8	11.2
Concessional / EDT (%)	..	..	7.7	25.4	25.1	23.3	19.0	14.2	12.0	10.7
Multilateral / EDT (%)	..	..	1.1	4.6	4.7	5.0	5.1	3.9	3.6	3.5

POLAND

(US$ million, unless otherwise indicated)

	1970	1980	1990	1994	1995	1996	1997	1998	1999	2000
5. LONG-TERM DEBT										
DEBT OUTSTANDING (LDOD)	..	..	**39,261**	**40,367**	**42,086**	**40,810**	**36,589**	**49,303**	**54,635**	**56,457**
Public and publicly guaranteed	..	..	**39,261**	**39,503**	**41,073**	**39,208**	**34,178**	**35,136**	**33,151**	**30,785**
Official creditors	..	..	27,919	31,040	32,232	30,502	26,578	27,075	25,059	23,655
Multilateral	..	..	524	1,957	2,067	2,175	2,079	2,156	2,185	2,229
Concessional	..	..	0	0	0	0	0	0	0	0
Bilateral	..	..	27,395	29,083	30,165	28,327	24,500	24,919	22,874	21,426
Concessional	..	..	3,822	10,797	11,097	10,111	7,692	7,904	7,292	6,786
Private creditors	..	..	11,342	8,463	8,841	8,707	7,600	8,062	8,092	7,129
Bonds	..	..	1	7,860	8,110	8,271	6,964	7,365	7,338	6,660
Commercial banks	..	..	9,760	362	556	323	573	650	725	456
Other private	..	..	1,582	241	175	113	63	47	28	13
Private nonguaranteed	..	..	**0**	**864**	**1,012**	**1,602**	**2,412**	**14,167**	**21,484**	**25,672**
Bonds	..	..	0	0	0	50	850	1,678	11,009	13,981
Commercial banks and other	..	..	0	864	1,012	1,552	1,561	12,489	10,475	11,691
Memo:										
IBRD	0	0	55	1,818	2,067	2,175	2,079	2,156	2,185	2,229
IDA	0	0	0	0	0	0	0	0	0	0
DISBURSEMENTS	..	..	**540**	**1,512**	**1,279**	**1,475**	**2,394**	**4,742**	**8,262**	**10,244**
Public and publicly guaranteed	..	..	**540**	**1,015**	**856**	**1,014**	**1,010**	**1,391**	**520**	**906**
Official creditors	..	..	70	712	248	693	280	153	247	350
Multilateral	..	..	56	672	210	464	239	153	247	349
Concessional	..	..	0	0	0	0	0	0	0	0
Bilateral	..	..	14	40	38	229	42	0	0	1
Concessional	..	..	10	16	7	199	1	0	0	1
Private creditors	..	..	470	303	608	321	730	1,239	273	557
Bonds	..	..	0	138	250	166	400	1,138	0	554
Commercial banks	..	..	300	72	353	155	326	94	270	2
Other private	..	..	171	93	5	0	3	7	3	0
Private nonguaranteed	..	..	**0**	**497**	**423**	**461**	**1,384**	**3,351**	**7,743**	**9,338**
Bonds	..	..	0	0	0	50	803	812	1,146	4,887
Commercial banks and other	..	..	0	497	423	411	581	2,539	6,596	4,451
Memo:										
IBRD	0	0	54	672	210	464	239	153	247	349
IDA	0	0	0	0	0	0	0	0	0	0
PRINCIPAL REPAYMENTS	..	..	**635**	**1,581**	**885**	**1,114**	**1,085**	**2,910**	**6,244**	**7,718**
Public and publicly guaranteed	..	..	**635**	**1,408**	**611**	**803**	**510**	**1,444**	**846**	**2,278**
Official creditors	..	..	147	146	332	445	421	640	690	805
Multilateral	..	..	46	0	158	197	155	175	188	199
Concessional	..	..	0	0	0	0	0	0	0	0
Bilateral	..	..	101	146	174	248	265	464	502	606
Concessional	..	..	43	47	44	51	80	231	195	205
Private creditors	..	..	488	1,262	279	358	90	804	156	1,473
Bonds	..	..	0	0	0	0	0	748	0	1,224
Commercial banks	..	..	400	1,179	192	312	54	35	139	235
Other private	..	..	88	83	87	46	36	21	17	14
Private nonguaranteed	..	..	**0**	**174**	**275**	**311**	**575**	**1,466**	**5,398**	**5,440**
Bonds	..	..	0	0	0	0	0	0	50	1,767
Commercial banks and other	..	..	0	174	275	311	575	1,466	5,348	3,673
Memo:										
IBRD	0	0	0	0	19	197	155	175	188	199
IDA	0	0	0	0	0	0	0	0	0	0
NET FLOWS ON DEBT	..	..	**-95**	**-70**	**394**	**361**	**1,310**	**1,832**	**2,018**	**2,526**
Public and publicly guaranteed	..	..	**-95**	**-393**	**245**	**211**	**500**	**-53**	**-327**	**-1,372**
Official creditors	..	..	-77	567	-84	248	-140	-487	-443	-456
Multilateral	..	..	10	672	52	266	84	-23	59	150
Concessional	..	..	0	0	0	0	0	0	0	0
Bilateral	..	..	-87	-106	-136	-19	-224	-464	-502	-606
Concessional	..	..	-33	-31	-37	147	-79	-231	-195	-204
Private creditors	..	..	-18	-959	329	-37	640	434	116	-917
Bonds	..	..	0	138	250	166	400	390	0	-670
Commercial banks	..	..	-100	-1,107	161	-157	272	59	131	-233
Other private	..	..	83	10	-82	-46	-32	-14	-14	-14
Private nonguaranteed	..	..	**0**	**323**	**148**	**150**	**810**	**1,884**	**2,345**	**3,899**
Bonds	..	..	0	0	0	50	803	812	1,096	3,120
Commercial banks and other	..	..	0	323	148	100	7	1,072	1,249	778
Memo:										
IBRD	0	0	54	672	191	266	84	-23	59	150
IDA	0	0	0	0	0	0	0	0	0	0

POLAND

(US$ million, unless otherwise indicated)

	1970	1980	1990	1994	1995	1996	1997	1998	1999	2000
INTEREST PAYMENTS (LINT)	..	..	**203**	**1,123**	**1,719**	**1,433**	**1,286**	**1,374**	**1,802**	**2,237**
Public and publicly guaranteed	..	..	**203**	**1,075**	**1,663**	**1,355**	**1,169**	**1,164**	**1,316**	**1,138**
Official creditors	..	..	113	736	1,216	923	777	759	906	653
Multilateral	..	..	31	152	148	147	142	131	133	122
Concessional	..	..	0	0	0	0	0	0	0	0
Bilateral	..	..	82	584	1,068	775	636	629	773	532
Concessional	..	..	56	338	478	465	405	407	343	296
Private creditors	..	..	90	339	447	433	391	405	410	484
Bonds	..	..	0	0	386	392	364	349	364	449
Commercial banks	..	..	74	318	47	32	23	53	44	34
Other private	..	..	15	21	14	8	5	3	2	1
Private nonguaranteed	..	..	**0**	**48**	**56**	**78**	**118**	**210**	**486**	**1,099**
Bonds	..	..	0	0	0	0	3	65	123	584
Commercial banks and other	..	..	0	48	56	78	114	145	363	515
Memo:										
IBRD	0	0	1	88	133	147	142	131	133	122
IDA	0	0	0	0	0	0	0	0	0	0
NET TRANSFERS ON DEBT	..	..	**-298**	**-1,192**	**-1,325**	**-1,072**	**23**	**458**	**216**	**290**
Public and publicly guaranteed	..	..	**-298**	**-1,467**	**-1,418**	**-1,144**	**-669**	**-1,217**	**-1,643**	**-2,510**
Official creditors	..	..	-190	-169	-1,300	-675	-918	-1,246	-1,349	-1,109
Multilateral	..	..	-22	520	-96	119	-58	-153	-74	28
Concessional	..	..	0	0	0	0	0	0	0	0
Bilateral	..	..	-169	-690	-1,204	-794	-859	-1,093	-1,275	-1,137
Concessional	..	..	-90	-369	-515	-318	-485	-637	-538	-500
Private creditors	..	..	-107	-1,298	-118	-469	249	30	-294	-1,401
Bonds	..	..	0	138	-136	-226	36	41	-364	-1,119
Commercial banks	..	..	-175	-1,425	114	-189	249	6	86	-267
Other private	..	..	67	-11	-96	-54	-37	-17	-16	-15
Private nonguaranteed	..	..	**0**	**275**	**93**	**72**	**692**	**1,675**	**1,859**	**2,799**
Bonds	..	..	0	0	0	50	800	748	973	2,536
Commercial banks and other	..	..	0	275	93	22	-107	927	885	263
Memo:										
IBRD	0	0	54	585	58	119	-58	-153	-74	28
IDA	0	0	0	0	0	0	0	0	0	0
DEBT SERVICE (LTDS)	..	..	**838**	**2,704**	**2,604**	**2,547**	**2,371**	**4,284**	**8,047**	**9,955**
Public and publicly guaranteed	..	..	**838**	**2,482**	**2,274**	**2,158**	**1,679**	**2,608**	**2,162**	**3,416**
Official creditors	..	..	260	882	1,548	1,368	1,198	1,399	1,596	1,459
Multilateral	..	..	77	152	306	344	297	306	321	321
Concessional	..	..	0	0	0	0	0	0	0	0
Bilateral	..	..	183	729	1,241	1,023	901	1,093	1,275	1,138
Concessional	..	..	100	385	522	516	486	637	538	500
Private creditors	..	..	578	1,601	726	790	481	1,209	566	1,957
Bonds	..	..	0	0	386	392	364	1,097	364	1,674
Commercial banks	..	..	474	1,497	239	344	77	88	184	269
Other private	..	..	103	104	102	54	40	24	19	15
Private nonguaranteed	..	..	**0**	**221**	**331**	**389**	**692**	**1,676**	**5,884**	**6,539**
Bonds	..	..	0	0	0	0	3	65	173	2,351
Commercial banks and other	..	..	0	221	331	389	689	1,612	5,711	4,188
Memo:										
IBRD	0	0	1	88	152	344	297	306	321	321
IDA	0	0	0	0	0	0	0	0	0	0
UNDISBURSED DEBT	..	..	**2,126**	**2,460**	**1,939**	**1,244**	**1,223**	**972**	**1,217**	**650**
Official creditors	..	..	1,297	2,296	1,830	1,136	1,060	912	1,165	602
Private creditors	..	..	829	164	109	108	163	61	52	48
Memorandum items										
Concessional LDOD	..	..	3,822	10,797	11,097	10,111	7,692	7,904	7,292	6,786
Variable rate LDOD	..	..	26,112	24,013	25,387	25,048	23,268	34,789	40,893	43,143
Public sector LDOD	..	..	39,259	39,488	41,071	39,208	33,970	34,934	32,949	30,783
Private sector LDOD	..	..	2	879	1,015	1,603	2,619	14,370	21,686	25,674

6. CURRENCY COMPOSITION OF LONG-TERM DEBT (PERCENT)

	1970	1980	1990	1994	1995	1996	1997	1998	1999	2000
Deutsche mark	..	..	23.3	10.1	10.2	9.9	10.1	10.6	9.4	9.1
French franc	..	..	11.0	12.7	13.1	12.7	12.6	12.9	11.5	11.2
Japanese yen	..	..	2.9	3.9	3.6	3.8	3.8	4.1	4.8	4.5
Pound sterling	..	..	3.8	2.6	2.5	2.8	3.2	3.1	3.1	3.0
Swiss franc	..	..	9.2	0.0	0.0	0.0	0.0	0.0	0.0	0.0
U.S.dollars	..	..	32.2	47.0	45.9	47.4	46.5	46.2	48.4	47.7
Multiple currency	..	..	0.1	4.6	5.0	5.5	6.0	5.3	5.2	4.8
Special drawing rights	..	..	0.0	0.0	0.0	0.0	0.0	0.0	0.0	0.0
All other currencies	..	..	17.5	19.1	19.7	17.9	17.8	17.8	17.6	19.7

POLAND

(US$ million, unless otherwise indicated)

	1970	1980	1990	1994	1995	1996	1997	1998	1999	2000
7. DEBT RESTRUCTURINGS										
Total amount rescheduled	..	..	3,559	7,723	0	0	0	0	0	0
Debt stock rescheduled	..	..	0	3,307	0	0	0	0	0	0
Principal rescheduled	..	..	1,366	325	0	70	7	3	0	0
Official	..	..	746	0	0	0	0	0	0	0
Private	..	..	620	325	0	70	7	3	0	0
Interest rescheduled	..	..	2,163	1,838	0	1	1	0	0	0
Official	..	..	1,998	0	0	0	0	0	0	0
Private	..	..	165	1,838	0	1	1	0	0	0
Debt forgiven	..	..	233	3,791	0	5	8	33	0	0
Memo: interest forgiven	..	..	61	0	0	0	0	0	0	0
Debt stock reduction	..	..	284	4,809	0	0	1,686	748	0	943
of which debt buyback	..	..	0	956	0	0	0	748	0	943
8. DEBT STOCK-FLOW RECONCILIATION										
Total change in debt stocks	..	..	6,279	-2,624	1,710	-790	-3,072	15,093	5,085	2,983
Net flows on debt	..	..	423	97	335	982	2,459	4,210	1,771	3,549
Net change in interest arrears	..	..	987	-1,375	-3	-136	0	0	0	139
Interest capitalized	..	..	2,163	1,838	0	1	1	0	0	0
Debt forgiveness or reduction	..	..	-516	-7,643	0	-5	-1,694	-33	0	0
Cross-currency valuation	..	..	2,795	2,564	1,363	-1,372	-2,309	1,056	-1,638	-1,243
Residual	..	..	427	1,896	14	-261	-1,529	9,859	4,952	539
9. AVERAGE TERMS OF NEW COMMITMENTS										
ALL CREDITORS										
Interest (%)	..	..	7.5	6.8	7.8	6.4	6.4	7.4	4.5	1.7
Maturity (years)	..	..	15.3	14.2	2.9	9.8	9.9	8.2	9.1	11.0
Grace period (years)	..	..	5.1	6.3	2.9	4.3	6.1	8.0	3.1	8.9
Grant element (%)	..	..	14.6	17.8	5.0	16.0	17.3	13.1	21.0	50.4
Official creditors										
Interest (%)	..	..	7.2	6.9	0.0	6.3	5.7	4.3	4.6	7.6
Maturity (years)	..	..	17.8	14.8	0.0	16.8	14.9	14.9	14.5	14.3
Grace period (years)	..	..	5.6	5.2	0.0	4.6	5.4	5.4	5.0	5.1
Grant element (%)	..	..	18.0	17.0	0.0	21.7	25.3	34.0	31.0	12.9
Private creditors										
Interest (%)	..	..	8.5	6.7	7.8	6.4	6.9	7.4	4.3	0.0
Maturity (years)	..	..	7.4	13.1	2.9	4.4	6.7	8.1	3.1	10.0
Grace period (years)	..	..	3.6	8.3	2.9	4.0	6.6	8.1	1.0	10.0
Grant element (%)	..	..	3.9	19.1	5.0	11.6	12.0	12.7	9.9	61.3
Memorandum items										
Commitments	..	..	1,673	462	558	568	1,347	1,231	573	717
Official creditors	..	..	1,266	289	0	249	533	20	300	161
Private creditors	..	..	407	173	558	320	813	1,211	273	556

10. CONTRACTUAL OBLIGATIONS ON OUTSTANDING LONG-TERM DEBT

	2001	2002	2003	2004	2005	2006	2007	2008	2009	2010
TOTAL										
Disbursements	188	132	114	82	59	35	20	13	6	1
Principal	7,080	5,067	5,203	4,837	4,704	5,628	5,630	6,910	5,649	2,902
Interest	2,414	2,213	2,063	1,866	1,606	1,394	1,154	861	624	765
Official creditors										
Disbursements	141	132	114	82	59	35	20	13	6	1
Principal	1,139	1,529	1,986	2,370	2,879	3,293	3,751	4,162	2,507	189
Interest	1,174	1,120	1,045	946	823	673	505	314	97	29
Bilateral creditors										
Disbursements	0	0	0	0	0	0	0	0	0	0
Principal	920	1,307	1,715	2,084	2,572	2,980	3,437	3,934	2,314	29
Interest	1,036	988	920	833	724	590	440	265	61	3
Multilateral creditors										
Disbursements	140	132	114	82	59	35	20	13	6	1
Principal	219	222	271	286	307	313	313	228	194	160
Interest	138	132	124	113	99	83	65	48	36	26
Private creditors										
Disbursements	48	0	0	0	0	0	0	0	0	0
Principal	5,941	3,538	3,216	2,468	1,825	2,335	1,879	2,748	3,142	2,712
Interest	1,240	1,093	1,018	920	784	721	649	547	526	736
Commercial banks										
Disbursements	48	0	0	0	0	0	0	0	0	0
Principal	339	153	8	1	1	1	1	0	0	0
Interest	20	3	1	0	0	0	0	0	0	0
Other private										
Disbursements	0	0	0	0	0	0	0	0	0	0
Principal	5,602	3,385	3,209	2,467	1,825	2,335	1,879	2,748	3,142	2,712
Interest	1,221	1,089	1,018	920	784	721	649	547	526	736

ROMANIA

(US$ million, unless otherwise indicated)

	1970	1980	1990	1994	1995	1996	1997	1998	1999	2000
1. SUMMARY DEBT DATA										
TOTAL DEBT STOCKS (EDT)	..	**9,762**	**1,140**	**5,609**	**6,784**	**8,345**	**9,503**	**9,899**	**9,127**	**10,224**
Long-term debt (LDOD)	..	**7,131**	**230**	**3,319**	**4,443**	**6,558**	**7,944**	**8,784**	**8,284**	**9,410**
Public and publicly guaranteed	..	7,131	223	2,925	3,909	5,523	6,213	6,428	5,753	6,430
Private nonguaranteed	..	0	7	394	534	1,035	1,731	2,356	2,531	2,980
Use of IMF credit	**0**	**328**	**0**	**1,323**	**1,038**	**651**	**641**	**539**	**458**	**453**
Short-term debt	..	**2,303**	**910**	**966**	**1,303**	**1,136**	**918**	**576**	**385**	**361**
of which interest arrears on LDOD	..	0	0	0	0	0	0	21	20	12
Official creditors	..	0	0	0	0	0	0	0	0	4
Private creditors	..	0	0	0	0	0	0	21	20	8
Memo: principal arrears on LDOD	..	0	0	0	0	0	2	44	42	17
Official creditors	..	0	0	0	0	0	2	0	0	0
Private creditors	..	0	0	0	0	0	0	44	42	17
Memo: export credits	..	0	188	1,539	1,818	1,917	1,980	666	636	514
TOTAL DEBT FLOWS										
Disbursements	..	**2,955**	**27**	**1,425**	**1,458**	**4,690**	**3,741**	**1,997**	**3,282**	**3,160**
Long-term debt	..	2,797	27	1,074	1,401	4,690	3,575	1,997	3,209	3,045
IMF purchases	0	158	0	351	57	0	166	0	73	114
Principal repayments	..	**928**	**4**	**387**	**675**	**4,063**	**2,759**	**1,888**	**3,139**	**1,753**
Long-term debt	..	824	4	259	303	3,706	2,624	1,763	3,000	1,657
IMF repurchases	0	104	0	128	373	356	135	125	140	96
Net flows on debt	..	**2,027**	**45**	**1,112**	**1,119**	**461**	**764**	**-254**	**-48**	**1,391**
of which short-term debt	..	0	22	74	337	-167	-218	-363	-190	-16
Interest payments (INT)	..	**601**	**14**	**232**	**318**	**496**	**553**	**525**	**541**	**588**
Long-term debt	..	332	0	129	202	364	471	481	498	542
IMF charges	0	20	0	63	69	39	29	29	20	24
Short-term debt	..	249	14	40	47	93	53	15	23	22
Net transfers on debt	..	**1,426**	**30**	**880**	**801**	**-35**	**211**	**-779**	**-588**	**803**
Total debt service paid (TDS)	..	**1,529**	**18**	**619**	**993**	**4,558**	**3,312**	**2,413**	**3,680**	**2,341**
Long-term debt	..	1,156	4	388	505	4,070	3,095	2,244	3,498	2,198
IMF repurchases and charges	0	124	0	191	442	395	165	154	159	120
Short-term debt (interest only)	..	249	14	40	47	93	53	15	23	22
2. AGGREGATE NET RESOURCE FLOWS AND NET TRANSFERS (LONG-TERM)										
NET RESOURCE FLOWS	..	**1,973**	**24**	**1,253**	**1,553**	**1,362**	**2,294**	**2,444**	**1,445**	**2,606**
Net flow of long-term debt (ex. IMF)	..	1,973	23	815	1,098	984	952	235	210	1,389
Foreign direct investment (net)	..	0	0	341	419	263	1,215	2,031	1,041	1,025
Portfolio equity flows	..	0	0	1	1	11	0	42	0	0
Grants (excluding technical coop.)	..	0	2	96	35	104	127	136	195	192
Memo: technical coop. grants	..	0	2	41	152	100	57	160	91	109
official net resource flows	..	613	21	566	778	843	463	5	158	706
private net resource flows	..	1,360	4	687	775	519	1,831	2,439	1,287	1,900
NET TRANSFERS	..	**1,641**	**24**	**1,118**	**1,350**	**983**	**1,803**	**1,938**	**920**	**2,029**
Interest on long-term debt	..	332	0	129	202	364	471	481	498	542
Profit remittances on FDI	..	0	0	6	0	15	20	25	28	35
Memo: official net transfers	..	495	21	466	654	607	222	-202	-72	461
private net transfers	..	1,146	3	652	696	376	1,581	2,140	992	1,569
3. MAJOR ECONOMIC AGGREGATES										
Gross national income (GNI)	..	..	38,455	29,944	35,236	35,025	34,964	41,384	34,774	36,381
Exports of goods & services (XGS)	..	12,160	6,555	7,315	9,489	9,736	10,161	9,836	10,024	12,460
of which workers remittances	..	0	0	4	4	10	2	4	4	2
Imports of goods & services (MGS)	..	14,580	9,915	8,022	11,628	12,890	12,875	13,503	11,943	14,677
International reserves (RES)	..	2,511	1,374	3,092	2,624	3,143	4,679	3,795	3,651	4,848
Current account balance	..	-2,420	-3,254	-428	-1,774	-2,571	-2,137	-2,918	-1,297	-1,359
4. DEBT INDICATORS										
EDT / XGS (%)	..	80.3	17.4	76.7	71.5	85.7	93.5	100.6	91.1	82.1
EDT / GNI (%)	..	..	3.0	18.7	19.3	23.8	27.2	23.9	26.3	28.1
TDS / XGS (%)	..	12.6	0.3	8.5	10.5	46.8	32.6	24.5	36.7	18.8
INT / XGS (%)	..	4.9	0.2	3.2	3.4	5.1	5.4	5.3	5.4	4.7
INT / GNI (%)	..	..	0.0	0.8	0.9	1.4	1.6	1.3	1.6	1.6
RES / EDT (%)	..	25.7	120.5	55.1	38.7	37.7	49.2	38.3	40.0	47.4
RES / MGS (months)	..	2.1	1.7	4.6	2.7	2.9	4.4	3.4	3.7	4.0
Short-term / EDT (%)	..	23.6	79.8	17.2	19.2	13.6	9.7	5.8	4.2	3.5
Concessional / EDT (%)	..	1.8	19.2	2.5	6.3	5.5	4.7	5.8	4.0	3.1
Multilateral / EDT (%)	..	8.3	0.0	23.4	25.0	23.3	23.5	23.9	28.6	29.2

ROMANIA

(US$ million, unless otherwise indicated)

	1970	1980	1990	1994	1995	1996	1997	1998	1999	2000
5. LONG-TERM DEBT										
DEBT OUTSTANDING (LDOD)	..	**7,131**	**230**	**3,319**	**4,443**	**6,558**	**7,944**	**8,784**	**8,284**	**9,410**
Public and publicly guaranteed	..	**7,131**	**223**	**2,925**	**3,909**	**5,523**	**6,213**	**6,428**	**5,753**	**6,430**
Official creditors	..	2,468	218	2,218	3,008	3,584	3,630	3,636	3,861	4,203
Multilateral	..	807	0	1,315	1,695	1,943	2,230	2,368	2,610	2,986
Concessional	..	0	0	0	0	0	0	0	0	3
Bilateral	..	1,661	218	903	1,313	1,642	1,401	1,268	1,251	1,217
Concessional	..	174	218	142	424	460	449	577	363	316
Private creditors	..	4,663	5	708	901	1,939	2,583	2,792	1,892	2,227
Bonds	..	0	0	0	0	757	1,016	1,118	652	597
Commercial banks	..	4,222	0	210	314	592	1,051	1,164	856	1,345
Other private	..	441	5	498	587	590	516	510	385	286
Private nonguaranteed	..	**0**	**7**	**394**	**534**	**1,035**	**1,731**	**2,356**	**2,531**	**2,980**
Bonds	..	0	0	0	0	0	75	75	75	0
Commercial banks and other	..	0	7	394	534	1,035	1,656	2,281	2,456	2,980
Memo:										
IBRD	0	807	0	695	844	1,009	1,305	1,443	1,662	1,898
IDA	0	0	0	0	0	0	0	0	0	0
DISBURSEMENTS	..	**2,797**	**27**	**1,074**	**1,401**	**4,690**	**3,575**	**1,997**	**3,209**	**3,045**
Public and publicly guaranteed	..	**2,797**	**24**	**926**	**1,130**	**2,191**	**1,796**	**1,173**	**1,881**	**1,851**
Official creditors	..	954	19	683	876	944	658	673	686	997
Multilateral	..	239	0	338	365	380	532	397	629	794
Concessional	..	0	0	0	0	0	0	0	0	3
Bilateral	..	715	19	344	511	564	126	276	57	203
Concessional	..	0	19	65	286	72	53	107	21	52
Private creditors	..	1,843	5	243	254	1,247	1,139	500	1,194	854
Bonds	..	0	0	0	0	804	347	0	0	0
Commercial banks	..	1,402	0	64	117	323	712	413	1,166	820
Other private	..	441	5	179	137	120	81	87	28	34
Private nonguaranteed	..	**0**	**3**	**148**	**271**	**2,499**	**1,779**	**825**	**1,329**	**1,194**
Bonds	..	0	0	0	0	0	75	0	0	0
Commercial banks and other	..	0	3	148	271	2,499	1,704	825	1,329	1,194
Memo:										
IBRD	0	239	0	263	129	228	399	153	315	384
IDA	0	0	0	0	0	0	0	0	0	0
PRINCIPAL REPAYMENTS	..	**824**	**4**	**259**	**303**	**3,706**	**2,624**	**1,763**	**3,000**	**1,657**
Public and publicly guaranteed	..	**824**	**0**	**259**	**217**	**1,708**	**1,541**	**1,563**	**1,513**	**935**
Official creditors	..	341	0	213	133	205	322	804	723	484
Multilateral	..	22	0	148	14	35	78	350	278	318
Concessional	..	0	0	0	0	0	0	0	0	0
Bilateral	..	319	0	65	118	171	244	454	445	166
Concessional	..	0	0	1	0	3	5	10	219	71
Private creditors	..	483	0	46	85	1,503	1,219	759	790	452
Bonds	..	0	0	0	0	0	0	0	456	0
Commercial banks	..	483	0	7	19	1,404	1,094	651	206	330
Other private	..	0	0	39	65	99	125	108	128	122
Private nonguaranteed	..	**0**	**4**	**0**	**86**	**1,998**	**1,083**	**200**	**1,487**	**721**
Bonds	..	0	0	0	0	0	0	0	0	75
Commercial banks and other	..	0	4	0	86	1,998	1,083	200	1,487	646
Memo:										
IBRD	0	22	0	0	0	0	29	69	83	91
IDA	0	0	0	0	0	0	0	0	0	0
NET FLOWS ON DEBT	..	**1,973**	**23**	**815**	**1,098**	**984**	**952**	**235**	**210**	**1,389**
Public and publicly guaranteed	..	**1,973**	**24**	**667**	**913**	**483**	**256**	**-391**	**368**	**916**
Official creditors	..	613	19	470	744	739	336	-132	-36	513
Multilateral	..	217	0	191	350	345	455	46	351	476
Concessional	..	0	0	0	0	0	0	0	0	3
Bilateral	..	396	19	280	393	393	-119	-178	-388	38
Concessional	..	0	19	65	286	69	48	97	-198	-18
Private creditors	..	1,360	5	197	170	-256	-80	-259	404	403
Bonds	..	0	0	0	0	804	347	0	-456	0
Commercial banks	..	919	0	57	98	-1,081	-382	-239	961	490
Other private	..	441	5	140	72	21	-44	-21	-100	-88
Private nonguaranteed	..	**0**	**-1**	**148**	**185**	**501**	**696**	**625**	**-158**	**473**
Bonds	..	0	0	0	0	0	75	0	0	-75
Commercial banks and other	..	0	-1	148	185	501	621	625	-158	548
Memo:										
IBRD	0	217	0	263	129	228	371	84	233	293
IDA	0	0	0	0	0	0	0	0	0	0

ROMANIA

(US$ million, unless otherwise indicated)

	1970	1980	1990	1994	1995	1996	1997	1998	1999	2000
INTEREST PAYMENTS (LINT)	..	**332**	**0**	**129**	**202**	**364**	**471**	**481**	**498**	**542**
Public and publicly guaranteed	..	**332**	**0**	**129**	**176**	**312**	**368**	**342**	**358**	**397**
Official creditors	..	118	0	100	124	236	241	207	230	245
Multilateral	..	59	0	68	70	156	159	143	173	184
Concessional	..	0	0	0	0	0	0	0	0	0
Bilateral	..	59	0	33	54	80	82	64	58	61
Concessional	..	0	0	4	7	15	15	15	14	13
Private creditors	..	214	0	29	52	76	128	135	128	152
Bonds	..	0	0	0	0	9	39	63	55	43
Commercial banks	..	173	0	8	9	22	45	43	40	81
Other private	..	42	0	21	43	46	44	29	33	28
Private nonguaranteed	..	**0**	**0**	**0**	**27**	**52**	**103**	**139**	**140**	**145**
Bonds	..	0	0	0	0	0	0	7	7	7
Commercial banks and other	..	0	0	0	27	52	103	132	133	138
Memo:										
IBRD	0	59	0	32	53	63	70	82	88	104
IDA	0	0	0	0	0	0	0	0	0	0
NET TRANSFERS ON DEBT	..	**1,641**	**22**	**686**	**896**	**620**	**481**	**-247**	**-288**	**847**
Public and publicly guaranteed	..	**1,641**	**24**	**538**	**737**	**171**	**-113**	**-732**	**10**	**519**
Official creditors	..	495	19	370	620	503	95	-338	-267	268
Multilateral	..	158	0	123	280	189	296	-97	179	292
Concessional	..	0	0	0	0	0	0	0	0	3
Bilateral	..	337	19	247	340	314	-201	-241	-445	-23
Concessional	..	0	19	61	279	54	34	82	-211	-31
Private creditors	..	1,146	5	168	118	-332	-208	-394	277	251
Bonds	..	0	0	0	0	796	308	-63	-511	-43
Commercial banks	..	747	0	50	88	-1,102	-427	-281	921	409
Other private	..	399	5	118	29	-25	-88	-50	-133	-115
Private nonguaranteed	..	**0**	**-1**	**148**	**158**	**449**	**593**	**486**	**-298**	**328**
Bonds	..	0	0	0	0	0	75	-7	-7	-82
Commercial banks and other	..	0	-1	148	158	449	518	493	-291	410
Memo:										
IBRD	0	158	0	230	76	164	301	3	145	189
IDA	0	0	0	0	0	0	0	0	0	0
DEBT SERVICE (LTDS)	..	**1,156**	**4**	**388**	**505**	**4,070**	**3,095**	**2,244**	**3,498**	**2,198**
Public and publicly guaranteed	..	**1,156**	**0**	**388**	**393**	**2,021**	**1,909**	**1,905**	**1,871**	**1,332**
Official creditors	..	459	0	313	256	441	563	1,011	953	729
Multilateral	..	81	0	216	85	191	237	494	451	502
Concessional	..	0	0	0	0	0	0	0	0	0
Bilateral	..	378	0	97	172	250	326	517	502	226
Concessional	..	0	0	4	8	18	19	25	232	84
Private creditors	..	698	0	75	137	1,579	1,346	894	918	603
Bonds	..	0	0	0	0	9	39	63	511	43
Commercial banks	..	656	0	15	29	1,426	1,139	694	246	411
Other private	..	42	0	61	108	145	169	137	161	150
Private nonguaranteed	..	**0**	**4**	**0**	**112**	**2,050**	**1,186**	**339**	**1,627**	**866**
Bonds	..	0	0	0	0	0	0	7	7	82
Commercial banks and other	..	0	4	0	112	2,050	1,186	332	1,620	785
Memo:										
IBRD	0	81	0	32	53	63	99	150	170	195
IDA	0	0	0	0	0	0	0	0	0	0
UNDISBURSED DEBT	..	**1,865**	**113**	**1,968**	**2,337**	**3,228**	**3,010**	**2,405**	**2,618**	**2,353**
Official creditors	..	1,347	0	1,506	1,879	2,555	2,570	2,095	2,106	1,735
Private creditors	..	518	113	462	458	673	441	309	513	618
Memorandum items										
Concessional LDOD	..	174	218	142	424	460	449	577	363	318
Variable rate LDOD	..	4,222	7	1,494	1,878	2,888	3,875	5,200	5,795	6,923
Public sector LDOD	..	7,131	223	2,925	3,909	5,498	6,195	6,403	5,738	6,418
Private sector LDOD	..	0	7	394	534	1,060	1,749	2,381	2,546	2,993

6. CURRENCY COMPOSITION OF LONG-TERM DEBT (PERCENT)

	1970	1980	1990	1994	1995	1996	1997	1998	1999	2000
Deutsche mark	..	2.1	0.0	4.3	10.9	8.0	12.1	12.8	11.8	9.3
French franc	..	0.0	0.8	5.0	5.0	4.5	3.9	4.1	3.6	2.7
Japanese yen	..	0.0	0.0	3.7	2.8	19.4	15.5	12.6	7.0	5.5
Pound sterling	..	0.0	0.0	0.0	0.0	0.0	0.0	0.0	0.0	0.0
Swiss franc	..	2.6	89.5	4.0	1.8	1.2	0.8	1.1	1.0	0.9
U.S.dollars	..	83.8	9.8	36.5	35.4	31.2	37.1	38.9	44.1	46.9
Multiple currency	..	11.4	0.0	23.8	21.6	18.3	16.5	17.5	20.2	16.9
Special drawing rights	..	0.0	0.0	0.0	0.0	0.0	0.0	0.0	0.0	0.0
All other currencies	..	0.1	-0.1	22.7	22.5	17.4	14.1	13.0	12.3	17.8

ROMANIA

(US$ million, unless otherwise indicated)

	1970	1980	1990	1994	1995	1996	1997	1998	1999	2000
7. DEBT RESTRUCTURINGS										
Total amount rescheduled	..	..	0	0	0	0	0	0	0	0
Debt stock rescheduled	..	..	0	0	0	0	0	0	0	0
Principal rescheduled	..	..	0	0	0	0	0	0	0	0
Official	..	..	0	0	0	0	0	0	0	0
Private	..	..	0	0	0	0	0	0	0	0
Interest rescheduled	..	..	0	0	0	0	0	0	0	0
Official	..	..	0	0	0	0	0	0	0	0
Private	..	..	0	0	0	0	0	0	0	0
Debt forgiven	..	..	0	0	0	0	0	0	0	0
Memo: interest forgiven	..	..	0	0	0	0	0	0	0	0
Debt stock reduction	..	..	0	0	0	0	0	0	0	0
of which debt buyback	..	..	0	0	0	0	0	0	0	0
8. DEBT STOCK-FLOW RECONCILIATION										
Total change in debt stocks	..	..	53	1,369	1,176	1,561	1,157	396	-772	1,097
Net flows on debt	..	2,027	45	1,112	1,119	461	764	-254	-48	1,391
Net change in interest arrears	..	..	0	0	0	0	0	21	-1	-8
Interest capitalized	..	..	0	0	0	0	0	0	0	0
Debt forgiveness or reduction	..	..	0	0	0	0	0	0	0	0
Cross-currency valuation	..	..	39	189	123	-199	-450	332	-176	-234
Residual	..	..	-30	68	-67	1,299	843	298	-547	-52
9. AVERAGE TERMS OF NEW COMMITMENTS										
ALL CREDITORS										
Interest (%)	..	14.1	7.6	6.6	6.1	5.1	8.5	5.6	6.4	8.6
Maturity (years)	..	8.5	10.7	12.1	12.2	8.3	10.4	8.6	14.4	9.1
Grace period (years)	..	3.5	4.5	3.8	3.9	3.7	3.5	2.7	3.5	2.7
Grant element (%)	..	-16.0	13.2	14.5	18.7	18.8	13.1	14.3	20.3	7.0
Official creditors										
Interest (%)	..	8.0	2.7	6.3	6.0	4.4	6.0	7.5	5.6	6.7
Maturity (years)	..	14.9	25.5	13.2	13.3	11.3	18.9	13.8	20.4	14.6
Grace period (years)	..	3.4	10.0	4.4	4.3	4.5	5.1	6.0	5.3	2.5
Grant element (%)	..	10.0	57.3	16.1	20.5	24.1	25.3	14.7	29.2	15.8
Private creditors										
Interest (%)	..	15.0	8.4	7.2	7.0	5.8	10.5	4.5	7.3	9.9
Maturity (years)	..	7.6	8.2	9.5	6.0	4.9	3.4	5.4	6.3	5.1
Grace period (years)	..	3.6	3.6	2.1	2.1	2.9	2.2	0.7	1.1	2.9
Grant element (%)	..	-19.8	5.8	10.7	8.5	12.7	3.0	14.0	8.2	0.8
Memorandum items										
Commitments	..	1,886	132	996	1,595	3,154	1,717	580	1,428	1,650
Official creditors	..	240	19	716	1,349	1,668	774	219	825	688
Private creditors	..	1,646	113	281	246	1,487	943	361	603	962

10. CONTRACTUAL OBLIGATIONS ON OUTSTANDING LONG-TERM DEBT

	2001	2002	2003	2004	2005	2006	2007	2008	2009	2010
TOTAL										
Disbursements	1,031	627	336	157	92	49	24	16	10	6
Principal	1,884	1,880	1,568	1,317	1,342	942	429	403	368	262
Interest	613	550	445	342	279	189	162	137	114	94
Official creditors										
Disbursements	663	458	268	144	92	49	24	16	10	6
Principal	568	735	648	610	431	376	351	333	318	235
Interest	309	297	258	215	191	169	148	128	109	92
Bilateral creditors										
Disbursements	101	79	29	10	2	1	0	0	0	0
Principal	280	321	325	275	88	29	23	22	22	10
Interest	93	75	52	19	11	7	5	4	3	2
Multilateral creditors										
Disbursements	563	379	239	134	90	49	24	16	10	6
Principal	288	414	324	335	342	347	328	311	296	225
Interest	216	222	206	195	180	162	143	124	106	90
Private creditors										
Disbursements	367	169	68	13	0	0	0	0	0	0
Principal	1,316	1,145	920	708	911	566	78	70	50	27
Interest	304	253	186	128	88	20	14	8	5	2
Commercial banks										
Disbursements	319	153	61	13	0	0	0	0	0	0
Principal	428	280	343	162	407	70	62	54	39	27
Interest	114	104	93	66	56	16	12	8	5	2
Other private										
Disbursements	48	16	7	1	0	0	0	0	0	0
Principal	888	865	577	546	505	497	16	16	10	0
Interest	190	149	93	62	31	4	2	1	0	0

RUSSIAN FEDERATION

(US$ million, unless otherwise indicated)

	1970	1980	1990	1994	1995	1996	1997	1998	1999	2000
1. SUMMARY DEBT DATA										
TOTAL DEBT STOCKS (EDT)	..	..	**59,340**	**122,342**	**121,735**	**126,685**	**127,706**	**177,710**	**174,360**	**160,300**
Long-term debt (LDOD)	..	..	**47,540**	**108,282**	**101,763**	**102,058**	**108,399**	**143,396**	**143,377**	**133,158**
Public and publicly guaranteed	..	..	47,540	108,282	101,763	102,058	106,494	121,233	120,794	111,419
Private nonguaranteed	..	..	0	0	0	0	1,905	22,163	22,583	21,739
Use of IMF credit	**0**	**0**	**0**	**4,198**	**9,617**	**12,508**	**13,231**	**19,335**	**15,238**	**11,613**
Short-term debt	..	..	**11,800**	**9,863**	**10,355**	**12,120**	**6,076**	**14,979**	**15,745**	**15,530**
of which interest arrears on LDOD	..	..	4,500	5,163	6,005	7,520	2,876	4,879	6,645	4,430
Official creditors	..	..	0	1,028	1,430	1,985	2,127	3,847	4,394	4,421
Private creditors	..	..	4,500	4,135	4,575	5,535	750	1,032	2,251	9
Memo: principal arrears on LDOD	..	..	0	13,756	22,435	25,595	6,516	6,427	7,171	7,553
Official creditors	..	..	0	825	4,229	4,852	4,920	4,220	6,654	7,038
Private creditors	..	..	0	12,932	18,207	20,742	1,595	2,207	517	516
Memo: export credits	..	..	15,056	41,992	42,985	44,718	37,471	30,656	30,312	27,677
TOTAL DEBT FLOWS										
Disbursements	..	..	**16,891**	**4,008**	**8,536**	**10,210**	**10,835**	**27,546**	**3,472**	**1,239**
Long-term debt	..	..	16,891	2,463	3,083	6,453	8,816	21,305	2,827	1,239
IMF purchases	0	0	0	1,544	5,453	3,757	2,019	6,241	645	0
Principal repayments	..	..	**7,893**	**2,181**	**3,273**	**3,160**	**1,813**	**5,134**	**6,845**	**6,070**
Long-term debt	..	..	7,893	2,181	3,273	2,638	1,318	4,220	2,605	3,182
IMF repurchases	0	0	0	0	0	522	495	914	4,241	2,888
Net flows on debt	..	..	**-1,403**	**1,127**	**4,913**	**7,300**	**7,623**	**21,912**	**-4,374**	**-2,831**
of which short-term debt	..	..	-10,400	-700	-350	250	-1,400	-500	-1,000	2,000
Interest payments (INT)	..	..	**3,853**	**1,289**	**2,885**	**4,155**	**5,136**	**5,817**	**5,154**	**5,601**
Long-term debt	..	..	2,611	1,114	2,591	3,685	4,554	5,100	3,927	4,281
IMF charges	0	0	0	175	294	470	582	718	723	691
Short-term debt	..	..	1,242	0	0	0	0	0	505	630
Net transfers on debt	..	..	**-5,256**	**-162**	**2,028**	**3,145**	**2,487**	**16,095**	**-9,528**	**-8,432**
Total debt service paid (TDS)	..	..	**11,747**	**3,470**	**6,159**	**7,315**	**6,948**	**10,951**	**12,000**	**11,671**
Long-term debt	..	..	10,505	3,295	5,864	6,323	5,871	9,319	6,531	7,462
IMF repurchases and charges	0	0	0	175	294	992	1,077	1,632	4,963	3,579
Short-term debt (interest only)	..	..	1,242	0	0	0	0	0	505	630
2. AGGREGATE NET RESOURCE FLOWS AND NET TRANSFERS (LONG-TERM)										
NET RESOURCE FLOWS	..	..	**8,998**	**2,757**	**2,917**	**11,761**	**15,695**	**20,322**	**4,981**	**2,508**
Net flow of long-term debt (ex. IMF)	..	..	8,998	283	-190	3,815	7,499	17,085	222	-1,943
Foreign direct investment (net)	..	..	0	638	2,016	2,478	6,638	2,764	3,309	2,714
Portfolio equity flows	..	..	0	271	141	5,008	1,206	296	644	1,075
Grants (excluding technical coop.)	..	..	0	1,566	950	460	353	177	805	661
Memo: technical coop. grants	..	..	0	263	527	820	432	828	860	587
official net resource flows	..	..	3,442	2,163	1,014	4,030	2,974	878	1,359	308
private net resource flows	..	..	5,556	594	1,902	7,731	12,721	19,444	3,622	2,200
NET TRANSFERS	..	..	**6,386**	**1,644**	**325**	**8,075**	**11,142**	**15,223**	**754**	**-2,198**
Interest on long-term debt	..	..	2,611	1,114	2,591	3,685	4,554	5,100	3,927	4,281
Profit remittances on FDI	..	..	0	0	0	0	0	0	300	425
Memo: official net transfers	..	..	3,331	1,771	-231	1,960	252	-920	731	-898
private net transfers	..	..	3,055	-127	557	6,116	10,890	16,143	23	-1,300
3. MAJOR ECONOMIC AGGREGATES										
Gross national income (GNI)	..	..	577,910	321,094	331,909	411,017	418,764	270,529	181,317	239,952
Exports of goods & services (XGS)	..	..	..	76,751	94,381	104,947	104,287	88,058	85,238	115,815
of which workers remittances	..	..	..	0	0	0	0	0	0	0
Imports of goods & services (MGS)	..	..	..	70,343	89,481	95,430	102,880	87,143	65,370	74,059
International reserves (RES)	..	..	..	7,206	18,024	16,258	17,624	12,043	12,325	27,656
Current account balance	..	..	..	6,102	4,973	9,589	1,047	506	20,410	41,846
4. DEBT INDICATORS										
EDT / XGS (%)	..	..	..	159.4	129.0	120.7	122.5	201.8	204.6	138.4
EDT / GNI (%)	..	..	10.3	38.1	36.7	30.8	30.5	65.7	96.2	66.8
TDS / XGS (%)	..	..	..	4.5	6.5	7.0	6.7	12.4	14.1	10.1
INT / XGS (%)	..	..	..	1.7	3.1	4.0	4.9	6.6	6.1	4.8
INT / GNI (%)	..	..	0.7	0.4	0.9	1.0	1.2	2.2	2.8	2.3
RES / EDT (%)	..	..	..	5.9	14.8	12.8	13.8	6.8	7.1	17.3
RES / MGS (months)	..	..	..	1.2	2.4	2.0	2.1	1.7	2.3	4.5
Short-term / EDT (%)	..	..	19.9	8.1	8.5	9.6	4.8	8.4	9.0	9.7
Concessional / EDT (%)	..	..	0.0	0.9	1.0	0.9	0.8	0.6	0.2	0.2
Multilateral / EDT (%)	..	..	0.7	1.3	1.6	2.2	4.1	3.7	4.0	4.4

RUSSIAN FEDERATION

(US$ million, unless otherwise indicated)

	1970	1980	1990	1994	1995	1996	1997	1998	1999	2000
5. LONG-TERM DEBT										
DEBT OUTSTANDING (LDOD)	..	..	**47,540**	**108,282**	**101,763**	**102,058**	**108,399**	**143,396**	**143,377**	**133,158**
Public and publicly guaranteed	..	..	**47,540**	**108,282**	**101,763**	**102,058**	**106,494**	**121,233**	**120,794**	**111,419**
Official creditors	..	..	5,857	63,261	57,678	63,314	63,724	68,653	71,162	70,933
Multilateral	..	..	416	1,532	1,985	2,762	5,289	6,577	6,916	7,040
Concessional	..	..	0	0	0	0	0	0	0	0
Bilateral	..	..	5,440	61,729	55,693	60,552	58,435	62,075	64,247	63,892
Concessional	..	..	0	1,100	1,174	1,119	1,008	1,021	346	346
Private creditors	..	..	41,683	45,021	44,085	38,743	42,770	52,580	49,632	40,486
Bonds	..	..	1,891	1,776	1,115	1,074	4,585	15,981	15,644	36,368
Commercial banks	..	..	17,840	16,380	16,674	15,628	29,288	29,305	29,033	44
Other private	..	..	21,952	26,865	26,296	22,041	8,897	7,294	4,955	4,075
Private nonguaranteed	..	..	**0**	**0**	**0**	**0**	**1,905**	**22,163**	**22,583**	**21,739**
Bonds	..	..	0	0	0	0	1,905	2,190	2,171	1,412
Commercial banks and other	..	..	0	0	0	0	0	19,974	20,413	20,327
Memo:										
IBRD	0	0	0	684	1,524	2,509	5,053	6,337	6,707	6,844
IDA	0	0	0	0	0	0	0	0	0	0
DISBURSEMENTS	..	..	**16,891**	**2,463**	**3,083**	**6,453**	**8,816**	**21,305**	**2,827**	**1,239**
Public and publicly guaranteed	..	..	**16,891**	**2,463**	**3,083**	**6,453**	**6,911**	**14,418**	**1,806**	**959**
Official creditors	..	..	3,679	876	981	4,038	3,022	1,921	1,216	738
Multilateral	..	..	178	392	856	1,187	2,748	1,293	561	574
Concessional	..	..	0	0	0	0	0	0	0	0
Bilateral	..	..	3,501	484	126	2,852	274	628	654	164
Concessional	..	..	0	158	22	0	0	0	346	0
Private creditors	..	..	13,212	1,588	2,102	2,415	3,890	12,497	591	221
Bonds	..	..	310	0	0	1,000	3,555	11,329	0	0
Commercial banks	..	..	479	3	21	6	2	6	0	0
Other private	..	..	12,422	1,585	2,081	1,409	333	1,162	591	221
Private nonguaranteed	..	..	**0**	**0**	**0**	**0**	**1,905**	**6,887**	**1,021**	**279**
Bonds	..	..	0	0	0	0	1,905	278	0	75
Commercial banks and other	..	..	0	0	0	0	0	6,609	1,021	204
Memo:										
IBRD	0	0	0	283	824	1,097	2,691	1,226	538	540
IDA	0	0	0	0	0	0	0	0	0	0
PRINCIPAL REPAYMENTS	..	..	**7,893**	**2,181**	**3,273**	**2,638**	**1,318**	**4,220**	**2,605**	**3,182**
Public and publicly guaranteed	..	..	**7,893**	**2,181**	**3,273**	**2,638**	**1,318**	**3,794**	**1,925**	**1,880**
Official creditors	..	..	238	279	917	468	400	1,220	662	1,092
Multilateral	..	..	7	193	434	291	68	129	204	312
Concessional	..	..	0	0	0	0	0	0	0	0
Bilateral	..	..	231	86	483	177	332	1,092	458	780
Concessional	..	..	0	0	0	0	26	26	26	0
Private creditors	..	..	7,656	1,902	2,356	2,170	918	2,574	1,263	788
Bonds	..	..	0	34	810	979	0	69	0	268
Commercial banks	..	..	4,086	71	51	30	29	270	35	19
Other private	..	..	3,570	1,797	1,495	1,160	889	2,235	1,228	500
Private nonguaranteed	..	..	**0**	**0**	**0**	**0**	**0**	**426**	**680**	**1,302**
Bonds	..	..	0	0	0	0	0	0	0	825
Commercial banks and other	..	..	0	0	0	0	0	426	680	477
Memo:										
IBRD	0	0	0	0	0	0	0	66	150	267
IDA	0	0	0	0	0	0	0	0	0	0
NET FLOWS ON DEBT	..	..	**8,998**	**283**	**-190**	**3,815**	**7,499**	**17,085**	**222**	**-1,943**
Public and publicly guaranteed	..	..	**8,998**	**283**	**-190**	**3,815**	**5,594**	**10,624**	**-119**	**-920**
Official creditors	..	..	3,442	597	64	3,570	2,622	701	554	-354
Multilateral	..	..	171	199	421	896	2,680	1,164	357	262
Concessional	..	..	0	0	0	0	0	0	0	0
Bilateral	..	..	3,271	398	-357	2,674	-58	-463	196	-616
Concessional	..	..	0	158	22	0	-26	-26	320	0
Private creditors	..	..	5,556	-315	-255	245	2,972	9,923	-673	-567
Bonds	..	..	310	-34	-810	21	3,555	11,260	0	-268
Commercial banks	..	..	-3,607	-68	-31	-24	-27	-264	-35	-19
Other private	..	..	8,853	-212	586	249	-557	-1,073	-638	-279
Private nonguaranteed	..	..	**0**	**0**	**0**	**0**	**1,905**	**6,461**	**341**	**-1,023**
Bonds	..	..	0	0	0	0	1,905	278	0	-750
Commercial banks and other	..	..	0	0	0	0	0	6,183	341	-273
Memo:										
IBRD	0	0	0	283	824	1,097	2,691	1,160	388	274
IDA	0	0	0	0	0	0	0	0	0	0

RUSSIAN FEDERATION

(US$ million, unless otherwise indicated)

	1970	1980	1990	1994	1995	1996	1997	1998	1999	2000
INTEREST PAYMENTS (LINT)	..	..	**2,611**	**1,114**	**2,591**	**3,685**	**4,554**	**5,100**	**3,927**	**4,281**
Public and publicly guaranteed	..	..	**2,611**	**1,114**	**2,591**	**3,685**	**4,554**	**3,507**	**2,552**	**3,204**
Official creditors	..	..	111	393	1,245	2,070	2,723	1,799	628	1,206
Multilateral	..	..	17	101	133	153	200	332	371	431
Concessional	..	..	0	0	0	0	0	0	0	0
Bilateral	..	..	94	292	1,113	1,917	2,522	1,466	257	775
Concessional	..	..	0	14	14	14	14	13	13	0
Private creditors	..	..	2,501	721	1,346	1,615	1,831	1,708	1,924	1,998
Bonds	..	..	96	121	140	58	216	670	1,639	1,845
Commercial banks	..	..	1,435	1	600	1,156	1,250	790	6	4
Other private	..	..	970	599	605	401	365	249	280	149
Private nonguaranteed	..	..	**0**	**0**	**0**	**0**	**0**	**1,593**	**1,375**	**1,077**
Bonds	..	..	0	0	0	0	0	129	170	165
Commercial banks and other	..	..	0	0	0	0	0	1,464	1,204	912
Memo:										
IBRD	0	0	0	38	57	121	178	316	359	412
IDA	0	0	0	0	0	0	0	0	0	0
NET TRANSFERS ON DEBT	..	..	**6,386**	**-831**	**-2,782**	**130**	**2,945**	**11,986**	**-3,704**	**-6,224**
Public and publicly guaranteed	..	..	**6,386**	**-831**	**-2,782**	**130**	**1,040**	**7,118**	**-2,671**	**-4,124**
Official creditors	..	..	3,331	205	-1,181	1,500	-101	-1,097	-75	-1,560
Multilateral	..	..	153	98	289	743	2,480	832	-14	-169
Concessional	..	..	0	0	0	0	0	0	0	0
Bilateral	..	..	3,177	106	-1,470	757	-2,581	-1,930	-61	-1,390
Concessional	..	..	0	144	8	-14	-41	-40	307	0
Private creditors	..	..	3,055	-1,036	-1,601	-1,370	1,141	8,215	-2,597	-2,564
Bonds	..	..	214	-155	-951	-38	3,339	10,590	-1,639	-2,113
Commercial banks	..	..	-5,042	-70	-631	-1,180	-1,277	-1,054	-41	-23
Other private	..	..	7,883	-811	-19	-153	-921	-1,322	-917	-428
Private nonguaranteed	..	..	**0**	**0**	**0**	**0**	**1,905**	**4,868**	**-1,033**	**-2,100**
Bonds	..	..	0	0	0	0	1,905	149	-170	-915
Commercial banks and other	..	..	0	0	0	0	0	4,719	-863	-1,184
Memo:										
IBRD	0	0	0	245	767	976	2,513	844	29	-139
IDA	0	0	0	0	0	0	0	0	0	0
DEBT SERVICE (LTDS)	..	..	**10,505**	**3,295**	**5,864**	**6,323**	**5,871**	**9,319**	**6,531**	**7,462**
Public and publicly guaranteed	..	..	**10,505**	**3,295**	**5,864**	**6,323**	**5,871**	**7,301**	**4,477**	**5,083**
Official creditors	..	..	348	671	2,162	2,538	3,122	3,019	1,290	2,298
Multilateral	..	..	24	293	567	444	268	461	575	744
Concessional	..	..	0	0	0	0	0	0	0	0
Bilateral	..	..	324	378	1,596	2,094	2,854	2,558	715	1,555
Concessional	..	..	0	14	14	14	41	40	39	0
Private creditors	..	..	10,156	2,624	3,702	3,785	2,749	4,282	3,188	2,785
Bonds	..	..	96	155	951	1,038	216	739	1,639	2,113
Commercial banks	..	..	5,521	73	652	1,186	1,279	1,060	41	23
Other private	..	..	4,539	2,396	2,100	1,561	1,254	2,484	1,508	649
Private nonguaranteed	..	..	**0**	**0**	**0**	**0**	**0**	**2,019**	**2,054**	**2,379**
Bonds	..	..	0	0	0	0	0	129	170	990
Commercial banks and other	..	..	0	0	0	0	0	1,889	1,884	1,389
Memo:										
IBRD	0	0	0	38	57	121	178	382	509	679
IDA	0	0	0	0	0	0	0	0	0	0
UNDISBURSED DEBT	..	..	**1,297**	**9,223**	**9,523**	**8,423**	**7,466**	**6,837**	**5,994**	**3,018**
Official creditors	..	..	62	3,517	4,814	4,849	5,096	5,440	5,202	2,519
Private creditors	..	..	1,235	5,706	4,708	3,575	2,370	1,396	792	498
Memorandum items										
Concessional LDOD	..	..	0	1,100	1,174	1,119	1,008	1,021	346	346
Variable rate LDOD	..	..	17,729	49,259	50,357	51,506	66,950	87,723	79,865	46,497
Public sector LDOD	..	..	47,540	108,282	101,763	102,058	106,494	121,233	120,794	111,419
Private sector LDOD	..	..	0	0	0	0	1,905	22,163	22,583	21,739

6. CURRENCY COMPOSITION OF LONG-TERM DEBT (PERCENT)

	1970	1980	1990	1994	1995	1996	1997	1998	1999	2000
Deutsche mark	..	..	34.4	28.1	34.6	38.2	29.3	29.2	22.2	20.6
French franc	..	..	6.1	1.2	1.4	1.8	0.5	0.5	0.4	0.4
Japanese yen	..	..	3.0	1.9	2.0	1.9	0.2	0.2	0.2	0.1
Pound sterling	..	..	2.3	0.8	0.8	0.7	0.3	0.3	0.2	0.1
Swiss franc	..	..	6.5	2.3	2.8	2.4	0.1	0.0	0.0	0.0
U.S.dollars	..	..	33.9	59.2	51.7	49.0	64.3	64.2	71.4	72.6
Multiple currency	..	..	0.0	0.6	1.5	2.5	4.7	4.9	5.1	5.7
Special drawing rights	..	..	0.0	0.0	0.0	0.0	0.0	0.0	0.0	0.0
All other currencies	..	..	13.8	5.9	5.2	3.5	0.6	0.7	0.5	0.5

RUSSIAN FEDERATION

(US$ million, unless otherwise indicated)

	1970	1980	1990	1994	1995	1996	1997	1998	1999	2000
7. DEBT RESTRUCTURINGS										
Total amount rescheduled	..	..	0	8,339	7,166	7,367	34,656	5,270	13,680	26,526
Debt stock rescheduled	..	..	0	0	0	0	121	0	0	17,369
Principal rescheduled	..	..	0	5,830	5,427	5,568	28,987	3,979	7,800	3,225
Official	..	..	0	342	2,069	2,338	3,718	2,973	6,001	2,810
Private	..	..	0	5,488	3,358	3,230	25,269	1,006	1,800	415
Interest rescheduled	..	..	0	2,186	1,122	1,006	5,263	547	5,217	4,363
Official	..	..	0	705	547	432	581	389	4,745	2,199
Private	..	..	0	1,481	575	574	4,682	158	472	2,163
Debt forgiven	..	..	0	0	0	0	0	0	0	0
Memo: interest forgiven	..	..	0	0	0	0	0	0	0	0
Debt stock reduction	..	..	0	0	0	0	5	0	0	11,600
of which debt buyback	..	..	0	0	0	0	0	0	0	0
8. DEBT STOCK-FLOW RECONCILIATION										
Total change in debt stocks	..	..	5,418	9,902	-607	4,950	1,021	50,005	-3,350	-14,059
Net flows on debt	..	..	-1,403	1,127	4,913	7,300	7,623	21,912	-4,374	-2,831
Net change in interest arrears	..	..	4,000	2,272	842	1,515	-4,644	2,003	1,766	-2,215
Interest capitalized	..	..	0	2,186	1,122	1,006	5,263	547	5,217	4,363
Debt forgiveness or reduction	..	..	0	0	0	0	-5	0	0	-11,600
Cross-currency valuation	..	..	2,872	4,419	3,428	-4,119	-7,164	3,039	-5,658	-2,995
Residual	..	..	-52	-101	-10,912	-752	-53	15,105	-302	1,218
9. AVERAGE TERMS OF NEW COMMITMENTS										
ALL CREDITORS										
Interest (%)	..	..	8.3	6.8	7.0	6.8	7.9	9.8	3.6	7.3
Maturity (years)	..	..	12.9	12.7	14.3	9.8	13.3	14.7	12.2	16.8
Grace period (years)	..	..	7.2	3.6	4.4	4.4	6.8	13.4	3.8	5.3
Grant element (%)	..	..	9.1	14.6	16.0	14.4	12.0	-2.4	30.8	16.0
Official creditors										
Interest (%)	..	..	8.4	6.8	7.0	6.3	6.4	6.4	3.6	7.3
Maturity (years)	..	..	10.8	16.2	15.9	10.9	18.1	10.6	12.2	16.8
Grace period (years)	..	..	6.0	5.1	5.0	4.1	5.3	4.1	3.8	5.3
Grant element (%)	..	..	7.6	18.8	17.3	17.0	21.5	16.6	30.8	16.0
Private creditors										
Interest (%)	..	..	8.3	6.9	7.0	8.2	9.2	10.5	0.0	0.0
Maturity (years)	..	..	13.4	9.0	8.5	7.1	8.9	15.5	0.0	0.0
Grace period (years)	..	..	7.5	1.9	2.5	5.2	8.0	15.3	0.0	0.0
Grant element (%)	..	..	9.4	10.1	11.2	8.2	3.5	-6.4	0.0	0.0
Memorandum items										
Commitments	..	..	17,842	4,333	3,154	6,897	7,921	14,175	1,207	30
Official creditors	..	..	3,721	2,224	2,474	4,891	3,759	2,465	1,207	30
Private creditors	..	..	14,121	2,109	680	2,007	4,163	11,711	0	0

10. CONTRACTUAL OBLIGATIONS ON OUTSTANDING LONG-TERM DEBT

	2001	2002	2003	2004	2005	2006	2007	2008	2009	2010
TOTAL										
Disbursements	1,186	884	426	234	113	78	43	28	20	4
Principal	11,487	10,112	11,721	8,864	11,723	5,131	7,695	5,870	6,127	5,873
Interest	7,705	7,385	6,766	6,207	5,653	5,137	4,964	4,706	4,398	4,059
Official creditors										
Disbursements	930	728	361	221	107	78	43	28	20	4
Principal	3,657	4,765	4,929	4,203	4,764	4,104	4,441	4,590	4,820	4,765
Interest	3,657	3,583	3,464	3,269	3,078	2,859	2,669	2,463	2,251	2,017
Bilateral creditors										
Disbursements	325	188	92	42	11	8	0	0	0	0
Principal	3,244	4,140	4,126	3,328	3,886	3,325	3,662	3,871	4,128	4,092
Interest	3,161	3,081	2,983	2,831	2,689	2,522	2,380	2,223	2,057	1,868
Multilateral creditors										
Disbursements	605	540	269	179	95	70	43	28	20	4
Principal	413	625	803	875	879	779	779	719	691	673
Interest	496	502	481	439	388	337	289	240	194	149
Private creditors										
Disbursements	256	156	66	13	7	0	0	0	0	0
Principal	7,830	5,347	6,792	4,661	6,959	1,027	3,254	1,280	1,307	1,108
Interest	4,048	3,802	3,303	2,938	2,575	2,279	2,295	2,244	2,147	2,042
Commercial banks										
Disbursements	0	0	0	0	0	0	0	0	0	0
Principal	19	7	6	3	2	0	0	0	0	0
Interest	2	1	1	0	0	0	0	0	0	0
Other private										
Disbursements	256	156	66	13	7	0	0	0	0	0
Principal	7,811	5,341	6,786	4,658	6,957	1,027	3,254	1,280	1,307	1,108
Interest	4,045	3,800	3,302	2,937	2,575	2,279	2,295	2,244	2,147	2,042

RWANDA

(US$ million, unless otherwise indicated)

1. SUMMARY DEBT DATA

	1970	1980	1990	1994	1995	1996	1997	1998	1999	2000
TOTAL DEBT STOCKS (EDT)	**5**	**190**	**712**	**952**	**1,029**	**1,043**	**1,111**	**1,226**	**1,292**	**1,271**
Long-term debt (LDOD)	**2**	**150**	**665**	**905**	**970**	**985**	**994**	**1,120**	**1,162**	**1,147**
Public and publicly guaranteed	2	150	665	905	970	985	994	1,120	1,162	1,147
Private nonguaranteed	0	0	0	0	0	0	0	0	0	0
Use of IMF credit	**3**	**14**	**0**	**13**	**26**	**24**	**40**	**56**	**76**	**86**
Short-term debt	**0**	**26**	**47**	**34**	**32**	**34**	**77**	**50**	**54**	**39**
of which interest arrears on LDOD	0	0	2	16	18	20	29	15	16	17
Official creditors	0	0	2	15	18	20	29	15	16	17
Private creditors	0	0	0	0	0	0	0	0	0	0
Memo: principal arrears on LDOD	0	0	8	41	46	56	68	61	67	74
Official creditors	0	0	8	39	44	54	66	60	66	73
Private creditors	0	0	0	2	2	2	1	1	1	1
Memo: export credits	0	0	41	24	32	32	26	16	20	20
TOTAL DEBT FLOWS										
Disbursements	**0**	**34**	**62**	**22**	**68**	**62**	**92**	**104**	**111**	**65**
Long-term debt	0	27	62	22	54	62	72	88	82	40
IMF purchases	0	6	0	0	14	0	21	16	29	25
Principal repayments	**1**	**3**	**10**	**2**	**11**	**10**	**13**	**11**	**20**	**24**
Long-term debt	0	3	9	2	11	9	10	9	12	13
IMF repurchases	1	0	1	0	0	1	2	2	9	11
Net flows on debt	**-1**	**36**	**55**	**-11**	**53**	**52**	**114**	**79**	**95**	**25**
of which short-term debt	0	5	2	-31	-4	0	34	-14	4	-16
Interest payments (INT)	**0**	**5**	**11**	**3**	**9**	**7**	**10**	**9**	**11**	**11**
Long-term debt	0	2	6	2	8	6	7	6	8	8
IMF charges	0	0	0	0	0	1	1	2	1	1
Short-term debt	0	3	5	1	1	1	2	2	2	2
Net transfers on debt	**-1**	**31**	**43**	**-14**	**44**	**45**	**104**	**69**	**84**	**14**
Total debt service paid (TDS)	**1**	**8**	**21**	**4**	**20**	**18**	**22**	**21**	**31**	**35**
Long-term debt	0	4	15	3	20	15	17	15	20	21
IMF repurchases and charges	1	0	1	0	0	2	3	4	10	13
Short-term debt (interest only)	0	3	5	1	1	1	2	2	2	2

2. AGGREGATE NET RESOURCE FLOWS AND NET TRANSFERS (LONG-TERM)

	1970	1980	1990	1994	1995	1996	1997	1998	1999	2000
NET RESOURCE FLOWS	**10**	**109**	**206**	**617**	**611**	**389**	**189**	**285**	**300**	**253**
Net flow of long-term debt (ex. IMF)	0	25	53	20	43	53	62	79	70	27
Foreign direct investment (net)	0	16	8	0	2	2	3	7	2	14
Portfolio equity flows	0	0	0	0	0	0	0	0	0	0
Grants (excluding technical coop.)	10	68	145	597	566	333	124	199	228	211
Memo: technical coop. grants	12	55	90	107	97	91	58	61	60	56
official net resource flows	10	95	200	617	608	387	186	278	298	238
private net resource flows	0	14	6	0	2	2	3	7	2	14
NET TRANSFERS	**10**	**98**	**194**	**614**	**602**	**383**	**182**	**279**	**292**	**245**
Interest on long-term debt	0	2	6	2	8	6	7	6	8	8
Profit remittances on FDI	0	9	6	2	0	0	0	0	0	0
Memo: official net transfers	10	93	194	616	600	380	179	272	290	230
private net transfers	0	5	0	-2	2	2	3	7	2	14

3. MAJOR ECONOMIC AGGREGATES

	1970	1980	1990	1994	1995	1996	1997	1998	1999	2000
Gross national income (GNI)	220	1,165	2,572	750	1,291	1,392	1,849	2,017	1,926	1,775
Exports of goods & services (XGS)	..	184	150	32	99	89	158	122	121	142
of which workers remittances	..	1	1	..	..	..	5	0	0	0
Imports of goods & services (MGS)	..	335	380	477	391	387	501	441	464	429
International reserves (RES)	8	187	44	51	99	107	153	169	174	191
Current account balance	..	-48	-86	-46	57	-8	-62	-83	-72	-7

4. DEBT INDICATORS

	1970	1980	1990	1994	1995	1996	1997	1998	1999	2000
EDT / XGS (%)	..	103.4	474.8	2,952.7	1,040.9	1,177.0	704.8	1,006.7	1,063.8	896.2
EDT / GNI (%)	2.2	16.3	27.7	127.0	79.6	74.9	60.1	60.8	67.1	71.6
TDS / XGS (%)	..	4.1	14.0	13.0	20.4	19.9	14.1	17.0	25.9	24.7
INT / XGS (%)	..	2.7	7.5	8.4	9.0	8.4	6.1	7.7	9.3	7.8
INT / GNI (%)	0.1	0.4	0.4	0.4	0.7	0.5	0.5	0.5	0.6	0.6
RES / EDT (%)	157.1	98.3	6.2	5.4	9.6	10.2	13.8	13.8	13.5	15.0
RES / MGS (months)	..	6.7	1.4	1.3	3.0	3.3	3.7	4.6	4.5	5.3
Short-term / EDT (%)	0.0	13.7	6.6	3.5	3.1	3.3	6.9	4.0	4.2	3.0
Concessional / EDT (%)	30.6	74.5	92.6	94.9	93.5	93.6	88.7	90.9	89.7	90.1
Multilateral / EDT (%)	2.0	47.8	76.2	79.2	78.9	79.9	76.5	78.3	78.0	78.3

RWANDA

(US$ million, unless otherwise indicated)

	1970	1980	1990	1994	1995	1996	1997	1998	1999	2000
5. LONG-TERM DEBT										
DEBT OUTSTANDING (LDOD)	**2**	**150**	**665**	**905**	**970**	**985**	**994**	**1,120**	**1,162**	**1,147**
Public and publicly guaranteed	**2**	**150**	**665**	**905**	**970**	**985**	**994**	**1,120**	**1,162**	**1,147**
Official creditors	2	143	661	904	968	983	992	1,118	1,160	1,145
Multilateral	0	91	542	754	811	834	850	959	1,008	996
Concessional	0	91	541	754	811	833	850	959	1,008	995
Bilateral	1	52	119	150	157	149	142	159	153	150
Concessional	1	51	118	149	150	143	136	155	150	150
Private creditors	0	8	4	2	2	2	1	1	1	1
Bonds	0	0	0	0	0	0	0	0	0	0
Commercial banks	0	0	0	0	0	0	0	0	0	0
Other private	0	8	4	2	2	2	1	1	1	1
Private nonguaranteed	**0**	**0**	**0**	**0**	**0**	**0**	**0**	**0**	**0**	**0**
Bonds	0	0	0	0	0	0	0	0	0	0
Commercial banks and other	0	0	0	0	0	0	0	0	0	0
Memo:										
IBRD	0	0	0	0	0	0	0	0	0	0
IDA	0	58	340	474	512	536	558	639	692	692
DISBURSEMENTS	**0**	**27**	**62**	**22**	**54**	**62**	**72**	**88**	**82**	**40**
Public and publicly guaranteed	**0**	**27**	**62**	**22**	**54**	**62**	**72**	**88**	**82**	**40**
Official creditors	0	27	62	22	54	62	72	88	82	40
Multilateral	0	21	37	20	54	62	67	88	82	40
Concessional	0	20	37	20	54	62	67	88	82	40
Bilateral	0	7	26	2	0	0	5	0	0	0
Concessional	0	7	25	2	0	0	3	0	0	0
Private creditors	0	0	0	0	0	0	0	0	0	0
Bonds	0	0	0	0	0	0	0	0	0	0
Commercial banks	0	0	0	0	0	0	0	0	0	0
Other private	0	0	0	0	0	0	0	0	0	0
Private nonguaranteed	**0**	**0**	**0**	**0**	**0**	**0**	**0**	**0**	**0**	**0**
Bonds	0	0	0	0	0	0	0	0	0	0
Commercial banks and other	0	0	0	0	0	0	0	0	0	0
Memo:										
IBRD	0	0	0	0	0	0	0	0	0	0
IDA	0	10	22	12	35	43	53	67	69	37
PRINCIPAL REPAYMENTS	**0**	**3**	**9**	**2**	**11**	**9**	**10**	**9**	**12**	**13**
Public and publicly guaranteed	**0**	**3**	**9**	**2**	**11**	**9**	**10**	**9**	**12**	**13**
Official creditors	0	0	7	2	11	9	10	9	12	13
Multilateral	0	0	5	2	11	8	9	7	10	10
Concessional	0	0	5	2	11	7	8	7	10	10
Bilateral	0	0	2	0	0	2	2	2	2	2
Concessional	0	0	2	0	0	1	1	1	1	1
Private creditors	0	2	2	0	0	0	0	0	0	0
Bonds	0	0	0	0	0	0	0	0	0	0
Commercial banks	0	0	0	0	0	0	0	0	0	0
Other private	0	2	2	0	0	0	0	0	0	0
Private nonguaranteed	**0**	**0**	**0**	**0**	**0**	**0**	**0**	**0**	**0**	**0**
Bonds	0	0	0	0	0	0	0	0	0	0
Commercial banks and other	0	0	0	0	0	0	0	0	0	0
Memo:										
IBRD	0	0	0	0	0	0	0	0	0	0
IDA	0	0	1	1	6	5	5	5	6	6
NET FLOWS ON DEBT	**0**	**25**	**53**	**20**	**43**	**53**	**62**	**79**	**70**	**27**
Public and publicly guaranteed	**0**	**25**	**53**	**20**	**43**	**53**	**62**	**79**	**70**	**27**
Official creditors	0	27	55	20	43	53	62	79	70	27
Multilateral	0	20	32	19	43	55	59	81	72	29
Concessional	0	20	32	19	43	55	59	81	72	30
Bilateral	0	7	23	2	0	-2	3	-2	-2	-2
Concessional	0	7	23	2	0	-1	2	-1	-1	-1
Private creditors	0	-2	-2	0	0	0	0	0	0	0
Bonds	0	0	0	0	0	0	0	0	0	0
Commercial banks	0	0	0	0	0	0	0	0	0	0
Other private	0	-2	-2	0	0	0	0	0	0	0
Private nonguaranteed	**0**	**0**	**0**	**0**	**0**	**0**	**0**	**0**	**0**	**0**
Bonds	0	0	0	0	0	0	0	0	0	0
Commercial banks and other	0	0	0	0	0	0	0	0	0	0
Memo:										
IBRD	0	0	0	0	0	0	0	0	0	0
IDA	0	10	21	11	29	38	48	62	64	31

RWANDA

(US$ million, unless otherwise indicated)

	1970	1980	1990	1994	1995	1996	1997	1998	1999	2000
INTEREST PAYMENTS (LINT)	**0**	**2**	**6**	**2**	**8**	**6**	**7**	**6**	**8**	**8**
Public and publicly guaranteed	**0**	**2**	**6**	**2**	**8**	**6**	**7**	**6**	**8**	**8**
Official creditors	0	1	6	2	8	6	7	6	8	8
Multilateral	0	1	4	2	8	6	7	6	7	7
Concessional	0	1	4	2	8	6	7	6	7	7
Bilateral	0	1	2	0	0	0	0	0	1	1
Concessional	0	0	1	0	0	0	0	0	1	1
Private creditors	0	0	0	0	0	0	0	0	0	0
Bonds	0	0	0	0	0	0	0	0	0	0
Commercial banks	0	0	0	0	0	0	0	0	0	0
Other private	0	0	0	0	0	0	0	0	0	0
Private nonguaranteed	**0**	**0**	**0**	**0**	**0**	**0**	**0**	**0**	**0**	**0**
Bonds	0	0	0	0	0	0	0	0	0	0
Commercial banks and other	0	0	0	0	0	0	0	0	0	0
Memo:										
IBRD	0	0	0	0	0	0	0	0	0	0
IDA	0	0	2	1	7	4	5	4	5	5
NET TRANSFERS ON DEBT	**0**	**23**	**47**	**19**	**34**	**47**	**55**	**73**	**62**	**19**
Public and publicly guaranteed	**0**	**23**	**47**	**19**	**34**	**47**	**55**	**73**	**62**	**19**
Official creditors	0	26	49	19	34	47	55	73	62	19
Multilateral	0	20	28	17	35	49	52	75	65	22
Concessional	0	19	28	17	35	49	52	75	65	22
Bilateral	0	6	22	2	0	-2	3	-2	-3	-3
Concessional	0	6	21	2	0	-1	2	-1	-2	-2
Private creditors	0	-3	-2	0	0	0	0	0	0	0
Bonds	0	0	0	0	0	0	0	0	0	0
Commercial banks	0	0	0	0	0	0	0	0	0	0
Other private	0	-3	-2	0	0	0	0	0	0	0
Private nonguaranteed	**0**	**0**	**0**	**0**	**0**	**0**	**0**	**0**	**0**	**0**
Bonds	0	0	0	0	0	0	0	0	0	0
Commercial banks and other	0	0	0	0	0	0	0	0	0	0
Memo:										
IBRD	0	0	0	0	0	0	0	0	0	0
IDA	0	10	18	11	22	35	43	58	59	26
DEBT SERVICE (LTDS)	**0**	**4**	**15**	**3**	**20**	**15**	**17**	**15**	**20**	**21**
Public and publicly guaranteed	**0**	**4**	**15**	**3**	**20**	**15**	**17**	**15**	**20**	**21**
Official creditors	0	2	13	3	20	15	17	15	20	21
Multilateral	0	1	9	3	20	14	15	13	17	18
Concessional	0	1	9	3	19	13	15	13	17	18
Bilateral	0	1	4	0	0	2	2	2	3	3
Concessional	0	0	4	0	0	1	1	1	2	2
Private creditors	0	3	2	0	0	0	0	0	0	0
Bonds	0	0	0	0	0	0	0	0	0	0
Commercial banks	0	0	0	0	0	0	0	0	0	0
Other private	0	3	2	0	0	0	0	0	0	0
Private nonguaranteed	**0**	**0**	**0**	**0**	**0**	**0**	**0**	**0**	**0**	**0**
Bonds	0	0	0	0	0	0	0	0	0	0
Commercial banks and other	0	0	0	0	0	0	0	0	0	0
Memo:										
IBRD	0	0	0	0	0	0	0	0	0	0
IDA	0	1	3	1	12	8	10	9	11	11
UNDISBURSED DEBT	**10**	**110**	**465**	**452**	**408**	**297**	**254**	**226**	**243**	**242**
Official creditors	10	110	459	452	408	297	254	226	243	242
Private creditors	0	0	6	0	0	0	0	0	0	0
Memorandum items										
Concessional LDOD	2	141	659	903	961	977	985	1,114	1,158	1,145
Variable rate LDOD	0	0	0	0	0	0	0	0	0	0
Public sector LDOD	2	150	665	905	970	985	994	1,120	1,162	1,147
Private sector LDOD	0	0	0	0	0	0	0	0	0	0

6. CURRENCY COMPOSITION OF LONG-TERM DEBT (PERCENT)

	1970	1980	1990	1994	1995	1996	1997	1998	1999	2000
Deutsche mark	46.6	0.8	0.0	0.0	0.0	0.0	0.0	0.0	0.0	0.0
French franc	0.0	7.3	3.9	5.7	7.6	8.1	7.5	5.8	5.0	4.7
Japanese yen	0.0	4.5	1.5	1.4	1.3	1.1	1.0	0.6	0.6	0.4
Pound sterling	0.0	0.0	0.0	0.0	0.0	0.0	0.0	0.0	0.0	0.0
Swiss franc	0.0	0.0	0.0	0.0	0.0	0.0	0.0	0.0	0.0	0.0
U.S.dollars	10.4	48.0	38.6	45.1	45.8	47.9	50.8	55.3	58.4	60.2
Multiple currency	0.0	5.9	14.9	12.1	11.3	11.4	10.5	9.6	8.9	8.4
Special drawing rights	0.0	0.0	6.2	4.4	4.2	4.0	3.8	3.5	3.3	3.1
All other currencies	43.0	33.5	34.9	31.3	29.8	27.5	26.4	25.2	23.8	23.2

RWANDA

(US$ million, unless otherwise indicated)

	1970	1980	1990	1994	1995	1996	1997	1998	1999	2000
7. DEBT RESTRUCTURINGS										
Total amount rescheduled	..	..	0	0	6	0	0	33	5	7
Debt stock rescheduled	..	..	0	0	0	0	0	0	0	0
Principal rescheduled	..	..	0	0	5	0	0	17	4	3
Official	..	..	0	0	5	0	0	17	4	3
Private	..	..	0	0	0	0	0	0	0	0
Interest rescheduled	..	..	0	0	2	0	0	15	1	1
Official	..	..	0	0	2	0	0	15	1	1
Private	..	..	0	0	0	0	0	0	0	0
Debt forgiven	..	..	0	0	0	0	0	1	0	0
Memo: interest forgiven	..	..	0	0	0	0	0	1	0	0
Debt stock reduction	..	..	0	0	0	0	0	0	0	0
of which debt buyback	..	..	0	0	0	0	0	0	0	0
8. DEBT STOCK-FLOW RECONCILIATION										
Total change in debt stocks	..	..	88	43	77	15	68	115	66	-21
Net flows on debt	-1	36	55	-11	53	52	114	79	95	25
Net change in interest arrears	..	..	0	6	2	2	9	-13	1	1
Interest capitalized	..	..	0	0	2	0	0	15	1	1
Debt forgiveness or reduction	..	..	0	0	0	0	0	-1	0	0
Cross-currency valuation	..	..	9	-8	-21	-70	-77	-13	-27	-37
Residual	..	..	24	56	41	30	22	48	-4	-10
9. AVERAGE TERMS OF NEW COMMITMENTS										
ALL CREDITORS										
Interest (%)	0.8	1.5	1.4	0.0	0.8	0.8	0.4	0.5	0.8	0.8
Maturity (years)	50.0	39.4	33.9	0.0	39.8	39.6	41.0	42.7	43.1	39.7
Grace period (years)	10.5	8.7	9.0	0.0	10.3	10.1	10.3	10.2	10.2	10.2
Grant element (%)	83.4	70.1	71.3	0.0	80.6	80.4	83.8	83.7	81.4	80.5
Official creditors										
Interest (%)	0.8	1.5	1.4	0.0	0.8	0.8	0.4	0.5	0.8	0.8
Maturity (years)	50.0	39.4	33.9	0.0	39.8	39.6	41.0	42.7	43.1	39.7
Grace period (years)	10.5	8.7	9.0	0.0	10.3	10.1	10.3	10.2	10.2	10.2
Grant element (%)	83.4	70.1	71.3	0.0	80.6	80.4	83.8	83.7	81.4	80.5
Private creditors										
Interest (%)	0.0	0.0	0.0	0.0	0.0	0.0	0.0	0.0	0.0	0.0
Maturity (years)	0.0	0.0	0.0	0.0	0.0	0.0	0.0	0.0	0.0	0.0
Grace period (years)	0.0	0.0	0.0	0.0	0.0	0.0	0.0	0.0	0.0	0.0
Grant element (%)	0.0	0.0	0.0	0.0	0.0	0.0	0.0	0.0	0.0	0.0
Memorandum items										
Commitments	9	48	72	0	50	5	57	76	122	55
Official creditors	9	48	72	0	50	5	57	76	122	55
Private creditors	0	0	0	0	0	0	0	0	0	0

10. CONTRACTUAL OBLIGATIONS ON OUTSTANDING LONG-TERM DEBT

	2001	2002	2003	2004	2005	2006	2007	2008	2009	2010
TOTAL										
Disbursements	34	44	30	23	18	12	8	1	0	0
Principal	27	28	29	29	30	29	29	31	33	34
Interest	10	10	10	10	9	9	9	8	8	8
Official creditors										
Disbursements	34	44	30	23	18	12	8	1	0	0
Principal	27	28	29	29	30	29	29	31	33	34
Interest	10	10	10	10	9	9	9	8	8	8
Bilateral creditors										
Disbursements	0	0	0	0	0	0	0	0	0	0
Principal	8	8	7	7	6	5	4	4	4	4
Interest	2	2	2	2	2	2	1	1	1	1
Multilateral creditors										
Disbursements	34	44	30	23	18	12	8	1	0	0
Principal	19	20	22	22	23	24	25	27	30	30
Interest	8	8	8	8	8	7	7	7	7	7
Private creditors										
Disbursements	0	0	0	0	0	0	0	0	0	0
Principal	0	0	0	0	0	0	0	0	0	0
Interest	0	0	0	0	0	0	0	0	0	0
Commercial banks										
Disbursements	0	0	0	0	0	0	0	0	0	0
Principal	0	0	0	0	0	0	0	0	0	0
Interest	0	0	0	0	0	0	0	0	0	0
Other private										
Disbursements	0	0	0	0	0	0	0	0	0	0
Principal	0	0	0	0	0	0	0	0	0	0
Interest	0	0	0	0	0	0	0	0	0	0

SAMOA

(US$ million, unless otherwise indicated)

	1970	1980	1990	1994	1995	1996	1997	1998	1999	2000
1. SUMMARY DEBT DATA										
TOTAL DEBT STOCKS (EDT)	**2.7**	**60.2**	**92.0**	**156.9**	**170.4**	**166.9**	**156.4**	**180.1**	**192.4**	**197.2**
Long-term debt (LDOD)	**2.7**	**53.4**	**91.0**	**156.7**	**168.1**	**162.8**	**148.3**	**154.3**	**156.6**	**147.0**
Public and publicly guaranteed	2.7	53.4	91.0	156.7	168.1	162.8	148.3	154.3	156.6	147.0
Private nonguaranteed	0.0	0.0	0.0	0.0	0.0	0.0	0.0	0.0	0.0	0.0
Use of IMF credit	**0.0**	**5.8**	**0.8**	**0.0**	**0.0**	**0.0**	**0.0**	**0.0**	**0.0**	**0.0**
Short-term debt	**0.0**	**1.0**	**0.2**	**0.2**	**2.3**	**4.1**	**8.0**	**25.8**	**35.8**	**50.1**
of which interest arrears on LDOD	0.0	0.0	0.0	0.0	0.0	0.0	0.0	0.0	0.0	0.0
Official creditors	0.0	0.0	0.0	0.0	0.0	0.0	0.0	0.0	0.0	0.0
Private creditors	0.0	0.0	0.0	0.0	0.0	0.0	0.0	0.0	0.0	0.0
Memo: principal arrears on LDOD	0.0	0.0	0.0	0.0	0.0	0.0	0.0	0.0	0.0	0.0
Official creditors	0.0	0.0	0.0	0.0	0.0	0.0	0.0	0.0	0.0	0.0
Private creditors	0.0	0.0	0.0	0.0	0.0	0.0	0.0	0.0	0.0	0.0
Memo: export credits	0.0	0.0	2.0	0.2	0.3	0.3	0.5	7.9	0.8	1.1
TOTAL DEBT FLOWS										
Disbursements	**2.4**	**11.2**	**15.4**	**11.8**	**12.7**	**3.7**	**2.7**	**3.2**	**0.0**	**6.4**
Long-term debt	2.4	10.5	15.4	11.8	12.7	3.7	2.7	3.2	0.0	6.4
IMF purchases	0.0	0.7	0.0	0.0	0.0	0.0	0.0	0.0	0.0	0.0
Principal repayments	**0.1**	**2.8**	**4.1**	**3.7**	**3.0**	**3.1**	**3.2**	**2.8**	**3.3**	**4.2**
Long-term debt	0.1	2.3	3.3	3.7	3.0	3.1	3.2	2.8	3.3	4.2
IMF repurchases	0.0	0.5	0.9	0.0	0.0	0.0	0.0	0.0	0.0	0.0
Net flows on debt	**2.3**	**8.4**	**11.3**	**-45.0**	**11.9**	**2.4**	**3.4**	**18.2**	**6.8**	**16.5**
of which short-term debt	0.0	0.0	0.1	-53.1	2.1	1.8	3.9	17.8	10.1	14.3
Interest payments (INT)	**0.0**	**2.7**	**1.3**	**2.8**	**1.7**	**1.9**	**1.8**	**2.3**	**3.2**	**4.3**
Long-term debt	0.0	2.3	1.2	1.4	1.6	1.6	1.5	1.4	1.4	1.4
IMF charges	0.0	0.2	0.1	0.0	0.0	0.0	0.0	0.0	0.0	0.0
Short-term debt	0.0	0.2	0.0	1.3	0.1	0.3	0.3	0.8	1.7	2.9
Net transfers on debt	**2.3**	**5.7**	**9.9**	**-47.7**	**10.2**	**0.5**	**1.6**	**15.9**	**3.6**	**12.2**
Total debt service paid (TDS)	**0.1**	**5.5**	**5.5**	**6.4**	**4.6**	**5.0**	**5.0**	**5.1**	**6.5**	**8.5**
Long-term debt	0.1	4.6	4.4	5.1	4.6	4.7	4.7	4.2	4.8	5.6
IMF repurchases and charges	0.0	0.7	1.0	0.0	0.0	0.0	0.0	0.0	0.0	0.0
Short-term debt (interest only)	0.0	0.2	0.0	1.3	0.1	0.3	0.3	0.8	1.7	2.9
2. AGGREGATE NET RESOURCE FLOWS AND NET TRANSFERS (LONG-TERM)										
NET RESOURCE FLOWS	**2.3**	**17.0**	**39.3**	**36.8**	**33.6**	**17.7**	**11.1**	**15.3**	**4.5**	**7.1**
Net flow of long-term debt (ex. IMF)	2.3	8.2	12.1	8.1	9.8	0.6	-0.5	0.4	-3.3	2.2
Foreign direct investment (net)	0.0	0.0	7.0	3.0	3.0	4.0	4.0	3.0	2.0	0.0
Portfolio equity flows	0.0	0.0	0.0	0.0	0.0	0.0	0.0	0.0	0.0	0.0
Grants (excluding technical coop.)	0.0	8.8	20.2	25.7	20.8	13.1	7.6	11.9	5.8	4.9
Memo: technical coop. grants	0.9	9.8	13.5	17.4	16.9	20.3	21.1	19.6	19.1	17.6
official net resource flows	2.4	18.8	32.3	34.4	30.6	13.7	7.1	12.3	2.5	7.1
private net resource flows	-0.1	-1.8	7.0	2.4	3.0	4.0	4.0	3.0	2.0	0.0
NET TRANSFERS	**2.3**	**14.7**	**38.1**	**35.4**	**32.0**	**16.1**	**9.6**	**13.9**	**3.1**	**5.7**
Interest on long-term debt	0.0	2.3	1.2	1.4	1.6	1.6	1.5	1.4	1.4	1.4
Profit remittances on FDI	0.0	0.0	0.0	0.0	0.0	0.0	0.0	0.0	0.0	0.0
Memo: official net transfers	2.4	17.4	31.2	33.0	29.0	12.1	5.6	10.9	1.1	5.7
private net transfers	-0.1	-2.7	6.9	2.4	3.0	4.0	4.0	3.0	2.0	0.0
3. MAJOR ECONOMIC AGGREGATES										
Gross national income (GNI)	..	..	164.3	188.6	193.8	220.2	237.8	224.6	239.0	236.3
Exports of goods & services (XGS)	..	44.4	94.1	86.9	108.4	123.3	130.5	129.1	126.9	78.6
of which workers remittances	..	18.7	42.9	36.4	39.2	42.6	45.1	40.2	44.7	..
Imports of goods & services (MGS)	..	74.3	96.5	101.4	119.9	127.5	144.3	128.4	142.6	136.4
International reserves (RES)	5.2	2.8	69.0	50.8	55.3	60.8	64.2	61.4	68.2	63.6
Current account balance	..	-12.9	8.6	5.8	9.3	12.3	9.1	20.1	-18.8	..
4. DEBT INDICATORS										
EDT / XGS (%)	..	135.5	97.8	180.5	157.2	135.4	119.9	139.5	151.6	250.8
EDT / GNI (%)	..	..	56.0	83.2	88.0	75.8	65.8	80.2	80.5	83.5
TDS / XGS (%)	..	12.4	5.8	7.4	4.2	4.1	3.8	4.0	5.1	10.8
INT / XGS (%)	..	6.1	1.4	3.2	1.6	1.5	1.4	1.8	2.5	5.5
INT / GNI (%)	..	..	0.8	1.5	0.9	0.9	0.8	1.0	1.3	1.8
RES / EDT (%)	193.3	4.6	75.1	32.4	32.5	36.4	41.1	34.1	35.5	32.2
RES / MGS (months)	..	0.5	8.6	6.0	5.5	5.7	5.3	5.7	5.7	5.6
Short-term / EDT (%)	0.0	1.7	0.2	0.1	1.4	2.5	5.1	14.3	18.6	25.4
Concessional / EDT (%)	88.9	56.3	90.4	95.5	94.7	94.0	91.8	83.3	79.7	73.3
Multilateral / EDT (%)	88.9	54.3	88.2	92.9	92.2	91.1	88.2	80.2	76.6	70.0

SAMOA

(US$ million, unless otherwise indicated)

	1970	1980	1990	1994	1995	1996	1997	1998	1999	2000
5. LONG-TERM DEBT										
DEBT OUTSTANDING (LDOD)	**2.7**	**53.4**	**91.0**	**156.7**	**168.1**	**162.8**	**148.3**	**154.3**	**156.6**	**147.0**
Public and publicly guaranteed	**2.7**	**53.4**	**91.0**	**156.7**	**168.1**	**162.8**	**148.3**	**154.3**	**156.6**	**147.0**
Official creditors	2.4	45.1	89.6	156.7	168.1	162.8	148.3	154.3	156.6	147.0
Multilateral	2.4	32.7	81.1	145.8	157.1	152.1	138.0	144.4	147.3	138.0
Concessional	2.4	32.7	76.5	138.9	150.3	146.2	133.3	140.0	144.0	135.5
Bilateral	0.0	12.5	8.5	11.0	11.0	10.7	10.3	10.0	9.3	9.1
Concessional	0.0	1.2	6.7	11.0	11.0	10.7	10.3	10.0	9.3	9.1
Private creditors	0.3	8.3	1.4	0.0	0.0	0.0	0.0	0.0	0.0	0.0
Bonds	0.0	4.5	1.4	0.0	0.0	0.0	0.0	0.0	0.0	0.0
Commercial banks	0.0	1.9	0.0	0.0	0.0	0.0	0.0	0.0	0.0	0.0
Other private	0.3	1.9	0.0	0.0	0.0	0.0	0.0	0.0	0.0	0.0
Private nonguaranteed	**0.0**	**0.0**	**0.0**	**0.0**	**0.0**	**0.0**	**0.0**	**0.0**	**0.0**	**0.0**
Bonds	0.0	0.0	0.0	0.0	0.0	0.0	0.0	0.0	0.0	0.0
Commercial banks and other	0.0	0.0	0.0	0.0	0.0	0.0	0.0	0.0	0.0	0.0
Memo:										
IBRD	0.0	0.0	0.0	0.0	0.0	0.0	0.0	0.0	0.0	0.0
IDA	0.0	6.3	18.3	43.3	44.7	43.2	41.8	45.3	44.2	47.3
DISBURSEMENTS	**2.4**	**10.5**	**15.4**	**11.8**	**12.7**	**3.7**	**2.7**	**3.2**	**0.0**	**6.4**
Public and publicly guaranteed	**2.4**	**10.5**	**15.4**	**11.8**	**12.7**	**3.7**	**2.7**	**3.2**	**0.0**	**6.4**
Official creditors	2.4	10.5	15.4	11.8	12.7	3.7	2.7	3.2	0.0	6.4
Multilateral	2.4	10.5	15.0	11.6	12.6	3.6	2.6	3.2	0.0	5.7
Concessional	2.4	10.5	14.7	11.5	12.5	3.6	2.6	3.2	0.0	5.7
Bilateral	0.0	0.0	0.4	0.2	0.2	0.0	0.0	0.0	0.0	0.7
Concessional	0.0	0.0	0.4	0.2	0.2	0.0	0.0	0.0	0.0	0.7
Private creditors	0.0	0.0	0.0	0.0	0.0	0.0	0.0	0.0	0.0	0.0
Bonds	0.0	0.0	0.0	0.0	0.0	0.0	0.0	0.0	0.0	0.0
Commercial banks	0.0	0.0	0.0	0.0	0.0	0.0	0.0	0.0	0.0	0.0
Other private	0.0	0.0	0.0	0.0	0.0	0.0	0.0	0.0	0.0	0.0
Private nonguaranteed	**0.0**	**0.0**	**0.0**	**0.0**	**0.0**	**0.0**	**0.0**	**0.0**	**0.0**	**0.0**
Bonds	0.0	0.0	0.0	0.0	0.0	0.0	0.0	0.0	0.0	0.0
Commercial banks and other	0.0	0.0	0.0	0.0	0.0	0.0	0.0	0.0	0.0	0.0
Memo:										
IBRD	0.0	0.0	0.0	0.0	0.0	0.0	0.0	0.0	0.0	0.0
IDA	0.0	2.0	3.5	1.7	0.7	0.0	0.8	2.5	0.0	5.7
PRINCIPAL REPAYMENTS	**0.1**	**2.3**	**3.3**	**3.7**	**3.0**	**3.1**	**3.2**	**2.8**	**3.3**	**4.2**
Public and publicly guaranteed	**0.1**	**2.3**	**3.3**	**3.7**	**3.0**	**3.1**	**3.2**	**2.8**	**3.3**	**4.2**
Official creditors	0.0	0.5	3.3	3.1	3.0	3.1	3.2	2.8	3.3	4.2
Multilateral	0.0	0.3	2.2	2.6	2.6	2.8	2.9	2.5	2.7	3.3
Concessional	0.0	0.3	2.0	1.8	2.1	2.2	2.3	1.9	2.1	2.8
Bilateral	0.0	0.1	1.0	0.5	0.3	0.3	0.3	0.3	0.6	0.9
Concessional	0.0	0.0	0.0	0.3	0.3	0.3	0.3	0.3	0.6	0.9
Private creditors	0.1	1.8	0.0	0.6	0.0	0.0	0.0	0.0	0.0	0.0
Bonds	0.0	0.0	0.0	0.6	0.0	0.0	0.0	0.0	0.0	0.0
Commercial banks	0.0	0.6	0.0	0.0	0.0	0.0	0.0	0.0	0.0	0.0
Other private	0.1	1.2	0.0	0.0	0.0	0.0	0.0	0.0	0.0	0.0
Private nonguaranteed	**0.0**	**0.0**	**0.0**	**0.0**	**0.0**	**0.0**	**0.0**	**0.0**	**0.0**	**0.0**
Bonds	0.0	0.0	0.0	0.0	0.0	0.0	0.0	0.0	0.0	0.0
Commercial banks and other	0.0	0.0	0.0	0.0	0.0	0.0	0.0	0.0	0.0	0.0
Memo:										
IBRD	0.0	0.0	0.0	0.0	0.0	0.0	0.0	0.0	0.0	0.0
IDA	0.0	0.0	0.1	0.1	0.2	0.3	0.3	0.3	0.4	0.7
NET FLOWS ON DEBT	**2.3**	**8.2**	**12.1**	**8.1**	**9.8**	**0.6**	**-0.5**	**0.4**	**-3.3**	**2.2**
Public and publicly guaranteed	**2.3**	**8.2**	**12.1**	**8.1**	**9.8**	**0.6**	**-0.5**	**0.4**	**-3.3**	**2.2**
Official creditors	2.4	10.0	12.1	8.7	9.8	0.6	-0.5	0.4	-3.3	2.2
Multilateral	2.4	10.2	12.8	9.0	9.9	0.9	-0.2	0.7	-2.7	2.4
Concessional	2.4	10.2	12.7	9.7	10.4	1.4	0.4	1.3	-2.1	2.9
Bilateral	0.0	-0.1	-0.7	-0.3	-0.1	-0.3	-0.3	-0.3	-0.6	-0.2
Concessional	0.0	0.0	0.3	-0.1	-0.1	-0.3	-0.3	-0.3	-0.6	-0.2
Private creditors	-0.1	-1.8	0.0	-0.6	0.0	0.0	0.0	0.0	0.0	0.0
Bonds	0.0	0.0	0.0	-0.6	0.0	0.0	0.0	0.0	0.0	0.0
Commercial banks	0.0	-0.6	0.0	0.0	0.0	0.0	0.0	0.0	0.0	0.0
Other private	-0.1	-1.2	0.0	0.0	0.0	0.0	0.0	0.0	0.0	0.0
Private nonguaranteed	**0.0**	**0.0**	**0.0**	**0.0**	**0.0**	**0.0**	**0.0**	**0.0**	**0.0**	**0.0**
Bonds	0.0	0.0	0.0	0.0	0.0	0.0	0.0	0.0	0.0	0.0
Commercial banks and other	0.0	0.0	0.0	0.0	0.0	0.0	0.0	0.0	0.0	0.0
Memo:										
IBRD	0.0	0.0	0.0	0.0	0.0	0.0	0.0	0.0	0.0	0.0
IDA	0.0	2.0	3.4	1.6	0.5	-0.3	0.5	2.2	-0.4	5.0

SAMOA

(US$ million, unless otherwise indicated)

	1970	1980	1990	1994	1995	1996	1997	1998	1999	2000
INTEREST PAYMENTS (LINT)	**0.0**	**2.3**	**1.2**	**1.4**	**1.6**	**1.6**	**1.5**	**1.4**	**1.4**	**1.4**
Public and publicly guaranteed	**0.0**	**2.3**	**1.2**	**1.4**	**1.6**	**1.6**	**1.5**	**1.4**	**1.4**	**1.4**
Official creditors	0.0	1.4	1.1	1.4	1.6	1.6	1.5	1.4	1.4	1.4
Multilateral	0.0	0.3	0.7	1.3	1.5	1.6	1.4	1.3	1.4	1.3
Concessional	0.0	0.3	0.7	1.2	1.3	1.4	1.3	1.2	1.3	1.3
Bilateral	0.0	1.1	0.4	0.1	0.1	0.1	0.1	0.1	0.1	0.0
Concessional	0.0	0.1	0.1	0.1	0.1	0.1	0.1	0.1	0.1	0.0
Private creditors	0.0	0.9	0.1	0.0	0.0	0.0	0.0	0.0	0.0	0.0
Bonds	0.0	0.3	0.1	0.0	0.0	0.0	0.0	0.0	0.0	0.0
Commercial banks	0.0	0.4	0.0	0.0	0.0	0.0	0.0	0.0	0.0	0.0
Other private	0.0	0.2	0.0	0.0	0.0	0.0	0.0	0.0	0.0	0.0
Private nonguaranteed	**0.0**	**0.0**	**0.0**	**0.0**	**0.0**	**0.0**	**0.0**	**0.0**	**0.0**	**0.0**
Bonds	0.0	0.0	0.0	0.0	0.0	0.0	0.0	0.0	0.0	0.0
Commercial banks and other	0.0	0.0	0.0	0.0	0.0	0.0	0.0	0.0	0.0	0.0
Memo:										
IBRD	0.0	0.0	0.0	0.0	0.0	0.0	0.0	0.0	0.0	0.0
IDA	0.0	0.0	0.1	0.3	0.3	0.3	0.3	0.3	0.3	0.3
NET TRANSFERS ON DEBT	**2.3**	**5.9**	**10.9**	**6.7**	**8.2**	**-1.1**	**-2.0**	**-1.0**	**-4.8**	**0.8**
Public and publicly guaranteed	**2.3**	**5.9**	**10.9**	**6.7**	**8.2**	**-1.1**	**-2.0**	**-1.0**	**-4.8**	**0.8**
Official creditors	2.4	8.6	11.0	7.3	8.2	-1.1	-2.0	-1.0	-4.8	0.8
Multilateral	2.4	9.9	12.0	7.7	8.4	-0.7	-1.6	-0.6	-4.1	1.1
Concessional	2.4	9.9	12.0	8.5	9.1	0.0	-1.0	0.1	-3.4	1.6
Bilateral	0.0	-1.3	-1.1	-0.4	-0.2	-0.4	-0.4	-0.4	-0.7	-0.3
Concessional	0.0	-0.1	0.2	-0.2	-0.2	-0.4	-0.4	-0.4	-0.7	-0.3
Private creditors	-0.1	-2.7	-0.1	-0.6	0.0	0.0	0.0	0.0	0.0	0.0
Bonds	0.0	-0.3	-0.1	-0.6	0.0	0.0	0.0	0.0	0.0	0.0
Commercial banks	0.0	-1.0	0.0	0.0	0.0	0.0	0.0	0.0	0.0	0.0
Other private	-0.1	-1.4	0.0	0.0	0.0	0.0	0.0	0.0	0.0	0.0
Private nonguaranteed	**0.0**	**0.0**	**0.0**	**0.0**	**0.0**	**0.0**	**0.0**	**0.0**	**0.0**	**0.0**
Bonds	0.0	0.0	0.0	0.0	0.0	0.0	0.0	0.0	0.0	0.0
Commercial banks and other	0.0	0.0	0.0	0.0	0.0	0.0	0.0	0.0	0.0	0.0
Memo:										
IBRD	0.0	0.0	0.0	0.0	0.0	0.0	0.0	0.0	0.0	0.0
IDA	0.0	2.0	3.3	1.3	0.2	-0.6	0.2	1.9	-0.7	4.7
DEBT SERVICE (LTDS)	**0.1**	**4.6**	**4.4**	**5.1**	**4.6**	**4.7**	**4.7**	**4.2**	**4.8**	**5.6**
Public and publicly guaranteed	**0.1**	**4.6**	**4.4**	**5.1**	**4.6**	**4.7**	**4.7**	**4.2**	**4.8**	**5.6**
Official creditors	0.0	1.9	4.4	4.5	4.6	4.7	4.7	4.2	4.8	5.6
Multilateral	0.0	0.6	3.0	3.8	4.1	4.3	4.3	3.8	4.1	4.6
Concessional	0.0	0.6	2.7	3.0	3.4	3.6	3.6	3.1	3.4	4.1
Bilateral	0.0	1.3	1.4	0.6	0.4	0.4	0.4	0.4	0.7	1.0
Concessional	0.0	0.1	0.1	0.4	0.4	0.4	0.4	0.4	0.7	1.0
Private creditors	0.1	2.7	0.1	0.6	0.0	0.0	0.0	0.0	0.0	0.0
Bonds	0.0	0.3	0.1	0.6	0.0	0.0	0.0	0.0	0.0	0.0
Commercial banks	0.0	1.0	0.0	0.0	0.0	0.0	0.0	0.0	0.0	0.0
Other private	0.1	1.4	0.0	0.0	0.0	0.0	0.0	0.0	0.0	0.0
Private nonguaranteed	**0.0**	**0.0**	**0.0**	**0.0**	**0.0**	**0.0**	**0.0**	**0.0**	**0.0**	**0.0**
Bonds	0.0	0.0	0.0	0.0	0.0	0.0	0.0	0.0	0.0	0.0
Commercial banks and other	0.0	0.0	0.0	0.0	0.0	0.0	0.0	0.0	0.0	0.0
Memo:										
IBRD	0.0	0.0	0.0	0.0	0.0	0.0	0.0	0.0	0.0	0.0
IDA	0.0	0.0	0.2	0.4	0.5	0.6	0.6	0.6	0.7	1.0
UNDISBURSED DEBT	**0.3**	**24.9**	**56.7**	**14.9**	**10.9**	**8.9**	**5.9**	**2.4**	**16.6**	**19.7**
Official creditors	0.3	24.9	56.7	14.9	10.9	8.9	5.9	2.4	16.6	19.7
Private creditors	0.0	0.0	0.0	0.0	0.0	0.0	0.0	0.0	0.0	0.0
Memorandum items										
Concessional LDOD	2.4	33.9	83.3	149.8	161.2	156.8	143.6	150.0	153.3	144.6
Variable rate LDOD	0.0	1.8	0.0	0.0	0.0	0.0	0.0	0.0	0.0	0.0
Public sector LDOD	2.7	53.4	91.0	156.7	168.1	162.8	148.3	154.3	156.6	147.0
Private sector LDOD	0.0	0.0	0.0	0.0	0.0	0.0	0.0	0.0	0.0	0.0

6. CURRENCY COMPOSITION OF LONG-TERM DEBT (PERCENT)

	1970	1980	1990	1994	1995	1996	1997	1998	1999	2000
Deutsche mark	0.0	12.0	1.7	0.0	0.0	0.0	0.0	0.0	0.0	0.0
French franc	0.0	0.0	0.1	0.3	0.3	0.3	0.2	0.2	0.2	0.2
Japanese yen	0.0	0.5	0.0	0.0	0.0	0.0	0.0	0.0	0.0	0.0
Pound sterling	0.0	0.0	0.0	0.0	0.0	0.0	0.0	0.0	0.0	0.0
Swiss franc	0.0	0.0	0.0	0.0	0.0	0.0	0.0	0.0	0.0	0.0
U.S.dollars	100.0	53.7	38.6	37.2	34.8	34.2	34.9	35.6	34.3	38.2
Multiple currency	0.0	12.8	43.9	47.6	44.3	43.2	41.3	40.9	43.8	40.5
Special drawing rights	0.0	0.0	1.3	3.3	9.6	11.6	12.8	13.3	13.0	13.0
All other currencies	0.0	21.0	14.4	11.6	11.0	10.7	10.8	10.0	8.7	8.1

SAMOA

(US$ million, unless otherwise indicated)

	1970	1980	1990	1994	1995	1996	1997	1998	1999	2000
7. DEBT RESTRUCTURINGS										
Total amount rescheduled	..	..	0.0	0.0	0.0	0.0	0.0	0.0	0.0	0.0
Debt stock rescheduled	..	..	0.0	0.0	0.0	0.0	0.0	0.0	0.0	0.0
Principal rescheduled	..	..	0.0	0.0	0.0	0.0	0.0	0.0	0.0	0.0
Official	..	..	0.0	0.0	0.0	0.0	0.0	0.0	0.0	0.0
Private	..	..	0.0	0.0	0.0	0.0	0.0	0.0	0.0	0.0
Interest rescheduled	..	..	0.0	0.0	0.0	0.0	0.0	0.0	0.0	0.0
Official	..	..	0.0	0.0	0.0	0.0	0.0	0.0	0.0	0.0
Private	..	..	0.0	0.0	0.0	0.0	0.0	0.0	0.0	0.0
Debt forgiven	..	..	0.0	0.0	0.0	0.0	0.0	0.0	0.0	0.0
Memo: interest forgiven	..	..	0.0	0.0	0.0	0.0	0.0	0.0	0.0	0.0
Debt stock reduction	..	..	0.0	0.0	0.0	0.0	0.0	0.0	0.0	0.0
of which debt buyback	..	..	0.0	0.0	0.0	0.0	0.0	0.0	0.0	0.0
8. DEBT STOCK-FLOW RECONCILIATION										
Total change in debt stocks	..	..	18.3	-36.9	13.4	-3.4	-10.6	23.7	12.3	4.8
Net flows on debt	2.3	8.4	11.3	-45.0	11.9	2.4	3.4	18.2	6.8	16.5
Net change in interest arrears	..	..	-0.1	-0.1	0.0	0.0	0.0	0.0	0.0	0.0
Interest capitalized	..	..	0.0	0.0	0.0	0.0	0.0	0.0	0.0	0.0
Debt forgiveness or reduction	..	..	0.0	0.0	0.0	0.0	0.0	0.0	0.0	0.0
Cross-currency valuation	..	..	6.0	5.4	-1.0	-8.4	-15.4	3.6	0.1	-10.2
Residual	..	..	1.1	2.8	2.6	2.6	1.5	2.0	5.4	-1.5
9. AVERAGE TERMS OF NEW COMMITMENTS										
ALL CREDITORS										
Interest (%)	4.7	0.4	0.8	0.0	0.7	0.0	0.0	0.0	0.8	1.1
Maturity (years)	20.0	40.2	39.8	0.0	40.6	20.5	0.0	0.0	39.8	35.6
Grace period (years)	6.0	20.6	10.3	0.0	9.9	10.5	0.0	0.0	10.3	9.2
Grant element (%)	36.4	86.2	80.5	0.0	80.6	76.2	0.0	0.0	80.7	75.2
Official creditors										
Interest (%)	4.7	0.4	0.8	0.0	0.7	0.0	0.0	0.0	0.8	1.1
Maturity (years)	20.0	40.2	39.8	0.0	40.6	20.5	0.0	0.0	39.8	35.6
Grace period (years)	6.0	20.6	10.3	0.0	9.9	10.5	0.0	0.0	10.3	9.2
Grant element (%)	36.4	86.2	80.5	0.0	80.6	76.2	0.0	0.0	80.7	75.2
Private creditors										
Interest (%)	0.0	0.0	0.0	0.0	0.0	0.0	0.0	0.0	0.0	0.0
Maturity (years)	0.0	0.0	0.0	0.0	0.0	0.0	0.0	0.0	0.0	0.0
Grace period (years)	0.0	0.0	0.0	0.0	0.0	0.0	0.0	0.0	0.0	0.0
Grant element (%)	0.0	0.0	0.0	0.0	0.0	0.0	0.0	0.0	0.0	0.0
Memorandum items										
Commitments	0.6	12.2	15.3	0.0	9.2	2.0	0.0	0.0	14.4	10.2
Official creditors	0.6	12.2	15.3	0.0	9.2	2.0	0.0	0.0	14.4	10.2
Private creditors	0.0	0.0	0.0	0.0	0.0	0.0	0.0	0.0	0.0	0.0

10. CONTRACTUAL OBLIGATIONS ON OUTSTANDING LONG-TERM DEBT

	2001	2002	2003	2004	2005	2006	2007	2008	2009	2010
TOTAL										
Disbursements	3.7	4.8	4.0	2.8	1.8	1.4	1.0	0.2	0.0	0.0
Principal	4.6	4.5	4.8	4.8	5.0	5.1	5.2	5.4	5.3	5.4
Interest	1.3	1.3	1.3	1.3	1.2	1.2	1.2	1.1	1.1	1.0
Official creditors										
Disbursements	3.7	4.8	4.0	2.8	1.8	1.4	1.0	0.2	0.0	0.0
Principal	4.6	4.5	4.8	4.8	5.0	5.1	5.2	5.4	5.3	5.4
Interest	1.3	1.3	1.3	1.3	1.2	1.2	1.2	1.1	1.1	1.0
Bilateral creditors										
Disbursements	0.4	0.3	0.2	0.1	0.1	0.1	0.1	0.1	0.0	0.0
Principal	0.9	0.9	0.9	0.9	0.9	0.9	0.8	0.8	0.8	0.3
Interest	0.0	0.0	0.0	0.0	0.0	0.0	0.0	0.0	0.0	0.0
Multilateral creditors										
Disbursements	3.3	4.6	3.8	2.7	1.7	1.3	0.9	0.2	0.0	0.0
Principal	3.6	3.6	3.9	4.0	4.1	4.3	4.4	4.6	4.5	5.2
Interest	1.3	1.3	1.3	1.3	1.2	1.2	1.2	1.1	1.1	1.0
Private creditors										
Disbursements	0.0	0.0	0.0	0.0	0.0	0.0	0.0	0.0	0.0	0.0
Principal	0.0	0.0	0.0	0.0	0.0	0.0	0.0	0.0	0.0	0.0
Interest	0.0	0.0	0.0	0.0	0.0	0.0	0.0	0.0	0.0	0.0
Commercial banks										
Disbursements	0.0	0.0	0.0	0.0	0.0	0.0	0.0	0.0	0.0	0.0
Principal	0.0	0.0	0.0	0.0	0.0	0.0	0.0	0.0	0.0	0.0
Interest	0.0	0.0	0.0	0.0	0.0	0.0	0.0	0.0	0.0	0.0
Other private										
Disbursements	0.0	0.0	0.0	0.0	0.0	0.0	0.0	0.0	0.0	0.0
Principal	0.0	0.0	0.0	0.0	0.0	0.0	0.0	0.0	0.0	0.0
Interest	0.0	0.0	0.0	0.0	0.0	0.0	0.0	0.0	0.0	0.0

SAO TOME AND PRINCIPE

(US$ million, unless otherwise indicated)

	1970	1980	1990	1994	1995	1996	1997	1998	1999	2000
1. SUMMARY DEBT DATA										
TOTAL DEBT STOCKS (EDT)	..	**23.5**	**150.0**	**222.3**	**245.5**	**234.8**	**237.6**	**257.6**	**320.6**	**315.9**
Long-term debt (LDOD)	..	**23.5**	**132.9**	**200.7**	**231.6**	**226.4**	**226.7**	**243.5**	**291.3**	**294.4**
Public and publicly guaranteed	..	23.5	132.9	200.7	231.6	226.4	226.7	243.5	291.3	294.4
Private nonguaranteed	..	0.0	0.0	0.0	0.0	0.0	0.0	0.0	0.0	0.0
Use of IMF credit	**0.0**	**0.0**	**1.1**	**1.1**	**0.8**	**0.6**	**0.3**	**0.1**	**0.0**	**2.5**
Short-term debt	..	**0.0**	**16.0**	**20.5**	**13.0**	**7.9**	**10.6**	**14.0**	**29.3**	**19.0**
of which interest arrears on LDOD	..	0.0	7.6	14.5	6.0	5.8	6.6	9.0	17.3	7.0
Official creditors	..	0.0	7.4	14.1	6.0	5.8	6.6	9.0	17.3	7.0
Private creditors	..	0.0	0.2	0.3	0.0	0.0	0.0	0.0	0.0	0.0
Memo: principal arrears on LDOD	..	0.0	21.4	39.1	27.2	22.5	20.4	29.1	68.6	50.2
Official creditors	..	0.0	20.4	38.0	27.2	22.5	20.4	29.1	68.6	50.2
Private creditors	..	0.0	1.0	1.1	0.0	0.0	0.0	0.0	0.0	0.0
Memo: export credits	..	0.0	18.0	0.2	17.4	18.0	42.6	45.3	51.9	42.8
TOTAL DEBT FLOWS										
Disbursements	..	**9.9**	**15.6**	**14.8**	**14.1**	**11.2**	**5.1**	**6.6**	**13.9**	**11.1**
Long-term debt	..	9.9	15.6	14.8	14.1	11.2	5.1	6.6	13.9	8.6
IMF purchases	0.0	0.0	0.0	0.0	0.0	0.0	0.0	0.0	0.0	2.5
Principal repayments	..	**0.9**	**1.1**	**1.3**	**1.0**	**1.5**	**1.9**	**2.2**	**2.6**	**2.4**
Long-term debt	..	0.9	1.1	1.2	0.8	1.3	1.6	2.0	2.5	2.4
IMF repurchases	0.0	0.0	0.0	0.1	0.2	0.2	0.2	0.2	0.1	0.0
Net flows on debt	..	**7.0**	**9.2**	**8.3**	**14.1**	**4.7**	**5.2**	**5.4**	**18.2**	**8.8**
of which short-term debt	..	-2.0	-5.3	-5.2	1.0	-5.0	2.0	1.0	7.0	0.0
Interest payments (INT)	..	**0.3**	**1.7**	**1.4**	**1.2**	**1.5**	**1.7**	**1.6**	**1.7**	**2.1**
Long-term debt	..	0.2	1.2	1.1	0.9	1.4	1.5	1.3	1.4	1.3
IMF charges	0.0	0.0	0.0	0.0	0.0	0.0	0.0	0.0	0.0	0.0
Short-term debt	..	0.1	0.5	0.3	0.3	0.1	0.2	0.3	0.3	0.8
Net transfers on debt	..	**6.7**	**7.4**	**6.9**	**12.9**	**3.2**	**3.4**	**3.8**	**16.5**	**6.7**
Total debt service paid (TDS)	..	**1.2**	**2.8**	**2.7**	**2.3**	**3.0**	**3.6**	**3.8**	**4.3**	**4.4**
Long-term debt	..	1.1	2.3	2.3	1.7	2.7	3.2	3.3	3.9	3.6
IMF repurchases and charges	0.0	0.0	0.0	0.1	0.2	0.2	0.2	0.2	0.1	0.0
Short-term debt (interest only)	..	0.1	0.5	0.3	0.3	0.1	0.2	0.3	0.3	0.8
2. AGGREGATE NET RESOURCE FLOWS AND NET TRANSFERS (LONG-TERM)										
NET RESOURCE FLOWS	..	**11.7**	**41.2**	**36.3**	**37.9**	**27.8**	**19.8**	**15.6**	**20.6**	**29.6**
Net flow of long-term debt (ex. IMF)	..	9.0	14.4	13.6	13.3	9.9	3.4	4.7	11.3	6.3
Foreign direct investment (net)	..	0.0	0.0	0.0	0.0	0.0	0.0	0.0	0.0	10.0
Portfolio equity flows	..	0.0	0.0	0.0	0.0	0.0	0.0	0.0	0.0	0.0
Grants (excluding technical coop.)	..	2.7	26.7	22.7	24.6	17.9	16.4	10.9	9.3	13.3
Memo: technical coop. grants	..	1.3	7.0	12.8	20.5	16.7	13.0	12.4	15.0	11.9
official net resource flows	..	11.7	41.3	36.3	37.9	27.8	19.8	15.6	20.6	19.6
private net resource flows	..	0.0	-0.1	0.0	0.0	0.0	0.0	0.0	0.0	10.0
NET TRANSFERS	..	**11.5**	**40.0**	**35.2**	**37.0**	**26.4**	**18.3**	**14.3**	**19.2**	**28.3**
Interest on long-term debt	..	0.2	1.2	1.1	0.9	1.4	1.5	1.3	1.4	1.3
Profit remittances on FDI	..	0.0	0.0	0.0	0.0	0.0	0.0	0.0	0.0	0.0
Memo: official net transfers	..	11.5	40.2	35.2	37.0	26.4	18.3	14.3	19.2	18.3
private net transfers	..	0.0	-0.2	0.0	0.0	0.0	0.0	0.0	0.0	10.0
3. MAJOR ECONOMIC AGGREGATES										
Gross national income (GNI)	..	49.2	52.5	44.1	40.0	40.2	39.1	35.8	42.2	43.5
Exports of goods & services (XGS)	..	23.3	8.2	10.5	9.8	9.5	11.2	10.8	14.8	13.9
of which workers remittances	..	0.8	0.1	..	..	..	..	..	..	..
Imports of goods & services (MGS)	..	22.0	22.4	22.2	24.4	22.3	22.0	16.4	21.2	19.9
International reserves (RES)	..	..	..	..	5.1	5.0	12.4	9.7	10.9	..
Current account balance	..	0.7	-12.0	..	..	..	..	..	..	..
4. DEBT INDICATORS										
EDT / XGS (%)	..	100.8	1,820.4	2,112.0	2,493.8	2,460.3	2,129.8	2,387.7	2,168.2	2,273.2
EDT / GNI (%)	..	47.7	285.9	504.0	613.6	583.8	607.9	719.4	758.8	726.1
TDS / XGS (%)	..	5.2	34.0	25.7	23.4	31.4	32.3	35.2	29.1	31.7
INT / XGS (%)	..	1.3	20.6	13.3	12.2	15.7	15.2	14.8	11.5	15.1
INT / GNI (%)	..	0.6	3.2	3.2	3.0	3.7	4.4	4.5	4.0	4.8
RES / EDT (%)	..	..	..	..	2.1	2.1	5.2	3.8	3.4	..
RES / MGS (months)	..	..	..	..	2.5	2.7	6.8	7.1	6.2	..
Short-term / EDT (%)	..	0.0	10.7	9.2	5.3	3.4	4.5	5.4	9.1	6.0
Concessional / EDT (%)	..	83.8	71.8	79.5	90.1	93.1	92.4	91.9	88.8	88.3
Multilateral / EDT (%)	..	45.1	48.4	61.5	62.2	66.4	63.7	65.2	53.4	53.9

SAO TOME AND PRINCIPE

(US$ million, unless otherwise indicated)

	1970	1980	1990	1994	1995	1996	1997	1998	1999	2000
5. LONG-TERM DEBT										
DEBT OUTSTANDING (LDOD)	..	**23.5**	**132.9**	**200.7**	**231.6**	**226.4**	**226.7**	**243.5**	**291.3**	**294.4**
Public and publicly guaranteed	..	**23.5**	**132.9**	**200.7**	**231.6**	**226.4**	**226.7**	**243.5**	**291.3**	**294.4**
Official creditors	..	23.1	131.7	199.6	231.6	226.4	226.7	243.5	291.3	290.6
Multilateral	..	10.6	72.6	136.7	152.6	155.8	151.4	167.9	171.1	170.1
Concessional	..	10.6	69.1	134.5	150.5	154.0	149.9	166.6	169.7	166.5
Bilateral	..	12.6	59.2	62.9	79.0	70.5	75.3	75.6	120.2	120.5
Concessional	..	9.1	38.6	42.2	70.7	64.5	69.6	70.2	115.1	112.5
Private creditors	..	0.4	1.1	1.1	0.0	0.0	0.0	0.0	0.0	3.8
Bonds	..	0.0	0.0	0.0	0.0	0.0	0.0	0.0	0.0	0.0
Commercial banks	..	0.0	0.0	0.0	0.0	0.0	0.0	0.0	0.0	0.0
Other private	..	0.4	1.1	1.1	0.0	0.0	0.0	0.0	0.0	3.8
Private nonguaranteed	..	**0.0**	**0.0**	**0.0**	**0.0**	**0.0**	**0.0**	**0.0**	**0.0**	**0.0**
Bonds	..	0.0	0.0	0.0	0.0	0.0	0.0	0.0	0.0	0.0
Commercial banks and other	..	0.0	0.0	0.0	0.0	0.0	0.0	0.0	0.0	0.0
Memo:										
IBRD	0.0	0.0	0.0	0.0	0.0	0.0	0.0	0.0	0.0	0.0
IDA	0.0	0.0	23.9	46.9	53.6	59.5	57.4	61.3	60.7	58.9
DISBURSEMENTS	..	**9.9**	**15.6**	**14.8**	**14.1**	**11.2**	**5.1**	**6.6**	**13.9**	**8.6**
Public and publicly guaranteed	..	**9.9**	**15.6**	**14.8**	**14.1**	**11.2**	**5.1**	**6.6**	**13.9**	**8.6**
Official creditors	..	9.9	15.6	14.8	14.1	11.2	5.1	6.6	13.9	8.6
Multilateral	..	6.5	12.8	14.1	14.1	11.2	5.1	6.4	13.3	8.4
Concessional	..	6.5	11.7	14.0	14.0	11.2	5.1	6.4	8.8	5.8
Bilateral	..	3.4	2.7	0.7	0.0	0.0	0.0	0.2	0.6	0.2
Concessional	..	1.4	2.7	0.7	0.0	0.0	0.0	0.2	0.6	0.2
Private creditors	..	0.0	0.0	0.0	0.0	0.0	0.0	0.0	0.0	0.0
Bonds	..	0.0	0.0	0.0	0.0	0.0	0.0	0.0	0.0	0.0
Commercial banks	..	0.0	0.0	0.0	0.0	0.0	0.0	0.0	0.0	0.0
Other private	..	0.0	0.0	0.0	0.0	0.0	0.0	0.0	0.0	0.0
Private nonguaranteed	..	**0.0**	**0.0**	**0.0**	**0.0**	**0.0**	**0.0**	**0.0**	**0.0**	**0.0**
Bonds	..	0.0	0.0	0.0	0.0	0.0	0.0	0.0	0.0	0.0
Commercial banks and other	..	0.0	0.0	0.0	0.0	0.0	0.0	0.0	0.0	0.0
Memo:										
IBRD	0.0	0.0	0.0	0.0	0.0	0.0	0.0	0.0	0.0	0.0
IDA	0.0	0.0	5.4	6.5	5.6	8.0	1.5	1.9	1.0	1.7
PRINCIPAL REPAYMENTS	..	**0.9**	**1.1**	**1.2**	**0.8**	**1.3**	**1.6**	**2.0**	**2.5**	**2.4**
Public and publicly guaranteed	..	**0.9**	**1.1**	**1.2**	**0.8**	**1.3**	**1.6**	**2.0**	**2.5**	**2.4**
Official creditors	..	0.9	1.0	1.2	0.8	1.3	1.6	2.0	2.5	2.4
Multilateral	..	0.0	0.4	1.2	0.8	1.0	1.3	1.4	1.7	2.0
Concessional	..	0.0	0.4	0.4	0.5	0.7	1.2	1.2	1.4	1.8
Bilateral	..	0.9	0.6	0.0	0.0	0.3	0.3	0.5	0.9	0.3
Concessional	..	0.2	0.0	0.0	0.0	0.0	0.0	0.2	0.5	0.0
Private creditors	..	0.0	0.1	0.0	0.0	0.0	0.0	0.0	0.0	0.0
Bonds	..	0.0	0.0	0.0	0.0	0.0	0.0	0.0	0.0	0.0
Commercial banks	..	0.0	0.0	0.0	0.0	0.0	0.0	0.0	0.0	0.0
Other private	..	0.0	0.1	0.0	0.0	0.0	0.0	0.0	0.0	0.0
Private nonguaranteed	..	**0.0**	**0.0**	**0.0**	**0.0**	**0.0**	**0.0**	**0.0**	**0.0**	**0.0**
Bonds	..	0.0	0.0	0.0	0.0	0.0	0.0	0.0	0.0	0.0
Commercial banks and other	..	0.0	0.0	0.0	0.0	0.0	0.0	0.0	0.0	0.0
Memo:										
IBRD	0.0	0.0	0.0	0.0	0.0	0.0	0.0	0.0	0.0	0.0
IDA	0.0	0.0	0.0	0.0	0.1	0.1	0.2	0.2	0.2	0.5
NET FLOWS ON DEBT	..	**9.0**	**14.4**	**13.6**	**13.3**	**9.9**	**3.4**	**4.7**	**11.3**	**6.3**
Public and publicly guaranteed	..	**9.0**	**14.4**	**13.6**	**13.3**	**9.9**	**3.4**	**4.7**	**11.3**	**6.3**
Official creditors	..	9.0	14.6	13.6	13.3	9.9	3.4	4.7	11.3	6.3
Multilateral	..	6.5	12.4	12.9	13.3	10.2	3.8	5.0	11.6	6.4
Concessional	..	6.5	11.3	13.6	13.6	10.5	3.9	5.2	7.3	4.0
Bilateral	..	2.5	2.2	0.7	0.0	-0.3	-0.3	-0.3	-0.3	-0.1
Concessional	..	1.2	2.7	0.7	0.0	0.0	0.0	0.0	0.1	0.2
Private creditors	..	0.0	-0.1	0.0	0.0	0.0	0.0	0.0	0.0	0.0
Bonds	..	0.0	0.0	0.0	0.0	0.0	0.0	0.0	0.0	0.0
Commercial banks	..	0.0	0.0	0.0	0.0	0.0	0.0	0.0	0.0	0.0
Other private	..	0.0	-0.1	0.0	0.0	0.0	0.0	0.0	0.0	0.0
Private nonguaranteed	..	**0.0**	**0.0**	**0.0**	**0.0**	**0.0**	**0.0**	**0.0**	**0.0**	**0.0**
Bonds	..	0.0	0.0	0.0	0.0	0.0	0.0	0.0	0.0	0.0
Commercial banks and other	..	0.0	0.0	0.0	0.0	0.0	0.0	0.0	0.0	0.0
Memo:										
IBRD	0.0	0.0	0.0	0.0	0.0	0.0	0.0	0.0	0.0	0.0
IDA	0.0	0.0	5.4	6.5	5.6	7.9	1.3	1.7	0.7	1.3

SAO TOME AND PRINCIPE

(US$ million, unless otherwise indicated)

	1970	1980	1990	1994	1995	1996	1997	1998	1999	2000
INTEREST PAYMENTS (LINT)	..	**0.2**	**1.2**	**1.1**	**0.9**	**1.4**	**1.5**	**1.3**	**1.4**	**1.3**
Public and publicly guaranteed	..	**0.2**	**1.2**	**1.1**	**0.9**	**1.4**	**1.5**	**1.3**	**1.4**	**1.3**
Official creditors	..	0.2	1.1	1.1	0.9	1.4	1.5	1.3	1.4	1.3
Multilateral	..	0.0	0.3	1.0	0.8	1.2	1.0	1.2	1.2	1.3
Concessional	..	0.0	0.3	0.9	0.7	1.2	1.0	1.2	1.2	1.2
Bilateral	..	0.2	0.9	0.1	0.1	0.1	0.6	0.1	0.2	0.0
Concessional	..	0.0	0.1	0.1	0.1	0.1	0.6	0.1	0.2	0.0
Private creditors	..	0.0	0.1	0.0	0.0	0.0	0.0	0.0	0.0	0.0
Bonds	..	0.0	0.0	0.0	0.0	0.0	0.0	0.0	0.0	0.0
Commercial banks	..	0.0	0.0	0.0	0.0	0.0	0.0	0.0	0.0	0.0
Other private	..	0.0	0.1	0.0	0.0	0.0	0.0	0.0	0.0	0.0
Private nonguaranteed	..	**0.0**	**0.0**	**0.0**	**0.0**	**0.0**	**0.0**	**0.0**	**0.0**	**0.0**
Bonds	..	0.0	0.0	0.0	0.0	0.0	0.0	0.0	0.0	0.0
Commercial banks and other	..	0.0	0.0	0.0	0.0	0.0	0.0	0.0	0.0	0.0
Memo:										
IBRD	0.0	0.0	0.0	0.0	0.0	0.0	0.0	0.0	0.0	0.0
IDA	0.0	0.0	0.1	0.3	0.3	0.5	0.4	0.4	0.4	0.5
NET TRANSFERS ON DEBT	..	**8.8**	**13.2**	**12.5**	**12.4**	**8.5**	**1.9**	**3.3**	**9.9**	**5.0**
Public and publicly guaranteed	..	**8.8**	**13.2**	**12.5**	**12.4**	**8.5**	**1.9**	**3.3**	**9.9**	**5.0**
Official creditors	..	8.8	13.4	12.5	12.4	8.5	1.9	3.3	9.9	5.0
Multilateral	..	6.5	12.1	11.9	12.6	9.0	2.8	3.8	10.4	5.1
Concessional	..	6.5	11.0	12.7	12.9	9.3	3.0	4.0	6.1	2.7
Bilateral	..	2.4	1.3	0.6	-0.1	-0.5	-0.9	-0.5	-0.4	-0.1
Concessional	..	1.2	2.7	0.6	-0.1	-0.1	-0.6	-0.1	-0.1	0.2
Private creditors	..	0.0	-0.2	0.0	0.0	0.0	0.0	0.0	0.0	0.0
Bonds	..	0.0	0.0	0.0	0.0	0.0	0.0	0.0	0.0	0.0
Commercial banks	..	0.0	0.0	0.0	0.0	0.0	0.0	0.0	0.0	0.0
Other private	..	0.0	-0.2	0.0	0.0	0.0	0.0	0.0	0.0	0.0
Private nonguaranteed	..	**0.0**	**0.0**	**0.0**	**0.0**	**0.0**	**0.0**	**0.0**	**0.0**	**0.0**
Bonds	..	0.0	0.0	0.0	0.0	0.0	0.0	0.0	0.0	0.0
Commercial banks and other	..	0.0	0.0	0.0	0.0	0.0	0.0	0.0	0.0	0.0
Memo:										
IBRD	0.0	0.0	0.0	0.0	0.0	0.0	0.0	0.0	0.0	0.0
IDA	0.0	0.0	5.3	6.2	5.2	7.4	0.9	1.3	0.3	0.8
DEBT SERVICE (LTDS)	..	**1.1**	**2.3**	**2.3**	**1.7**	**2.7**	**3.2**	**3.3**	**3.9**	**3.6**
Public and publicly guaranteed	..	**1.1**	**2.3**	**2.3**	**1.7**	**2.7**	**3.2**	**3.3**	**3.9**	**3.6**
Official creditors	..	1.1	2.2	2.3	1.7	2.7	3.2	3.3	3.9	3.6
Multilateral	..	0.0	0.7	2.2	1.5	2.2	2.3	2.6	2.9	3.3
Concessional	..	0.0	0.7	1.3	1.2	1.9	2.1	2.4	2.7	3.1
Bilateral	..	1.1	1.4	0.1	0.1	0.5	0.9	0.7	1.0	0.3
Concessional	..	0.2	0.1	0.1	0.1	0.1	0.6	0.3	0.7	0.0
Private creditors	..	0.0	0.2	0.0	0.0	0.0	0.0	0.0	0.0	0.0
Bonds	..	0.0	0.0	0.0	0.0	0.0	0.0	0.0	0.0	0.0
Commercial banks	..	0.0	0.0	0.0	0.0	0.0	0.0	0.0	0.0	0.0
Other private	..	0.0	0.2	0.0	0.0	0.0	0.0	0.0	0.0	0.0
Private nonguaranteed	..	**0.0**	**0.0**	**0.0**	**0.0**	**0.0**	**0.0**	**0.0**	**0.0**	**0.0**
Bonds	..	0.0	0.0	0.0	0.0	0.0	0.0	0.0	0.0	0.0
Commercial banks and other	..	0.0	0.0	0.0	0.0	0.0	0.0	0.0	0.0	0.0
Memo:										
IBRD	0.0	0.0	0.0	0.0	0.0	0.0	0.0	0.0	0.0	0.0
IDA	0.0	0.0	0.1	0.3	0.4	0.5	0.6	0.7	0.6	0.9
UNDISBURSED DEBT	..	**32.1**	**86.4**	**71.1**	**58.5**	**46.9**	**46.6**	**41.4**	**24.9**	**32.3**
Official creditors	..	32.1	86.4	71.1	58.5	46.9	46.6	41.4	24.9	32.3
Private creditors	..	0.0	0.0	0.0	0.0	0.0	0.0	0.0	0.0	0.0
Memorandum items										
Concessional LDOD	..	19.6	107.6	176.7	221.2	218.5	219.5	236.8	284.9	279.0
Variable rate LDOD	..	0.0	0.0	0.0	0.0	0.0	0.0	0.0	0.0	7.1
Public sector LDOD	..	23.5	132.9	200.7	231.6	226.4	226.7	243.5	291.3	294.4
Private sector LDOD	..	0.0	0.0	0.0	0.0	0.0	0.0	0.0	0.0	0.0

6. CURRENCY COMPOSITION OF LONG-TERM DEBT (PERCENT)

	1970	1980	1990	1994	1995	1996	1997	1998	1999	2000
Deutsche mark	..	0.0	0.0	0.0	0.0	0.0	0.0	0.0	0.0	0.0
French franc	..	0.0	4.0	4.5	4.2	4.0	3.5	3.4	2.3	2.2
Japanese yen	..	0.0	0.0	0.0	0.0	0.0	0.0	0.0	0.0	0.0
Pound sterling	..	0.0	0.0	0.0	0.0	0.0	0.0	0.0	0.0	0.0
Swiss franc	..	0.0	0.0	0.0	0.0	0.0	0.0	0.0	4.6	4.5
U.S.dollars	..	63.1	39.3	35.5	40.0	40.5	44.9	43.1	43.6	42.4
Multiple currency	..	0.0	43.6	51.3	48.1	47.6	45.9	45.5	38.0	36.3
Special drawing rights	..	0.0	0.0	0.0	0.0	0.0	0.0	0.0	0.0	0.0
All other currencies	..	36.9	13.1	8.7	7.7	7.9	5.7	8.0	11.5	14.6

SAO TOME AND PRINCIPE

(US$ million, unless otherwise indicated)

	1970	1980	1990	1994	1995	1996	1997	1998	1999	2000
7. DEBT RESTRUCTURINGS										
Total amount rescheduled	..	..	0.0	0.7	29.5	0.0	11.2	0.0	7.5	23.5
Debt stock rescheduled	..	..	0.0	0.0	0.0	0.0	2.1	0.0	7.5	2.4
Principal rescheduled	..	..	0.0	0.0	15.5	0.0	2.6	0.0	5.3	13.7
Official	..	..	0.0	0.0	14.4	0.0	2.6	0.0	5.3	13.7
Private	..	..	0.0	0.0	1.1	0.0	0.0	0.0	0.0	0.0
Interest rescheduled	..	..	0.0	0.7	8.5	0.0	0.0	0.0	0.2	9.8
Official	..	..	0.0	0.7	8.1	0.0	0.0	0.0	0.2	9.8
Private	..	..	0.0	0.0	0.3	0.0	0.0	0.0	0.0	0.0
Debt forgiven	..	..	0.0	0.0	0.0	0.0	0.0	0.0	0.0	4.8
Memo: interest forgiven	..	..	0.0	0.0	0.0	0.0	0.0	0.0	0.0	1.7
Debt stock reduction	..	..	0.0	0.0	0.0	0.0	0.0	0.0	0.0	4.8
of which debt buyback	..	..	0.0	0.0	0.0	0.0	0.0	0.0	0.0	0.0
8. DEBT STOCK-FLOW RECONCILIATION										
Total change in debt stocks	..	..	15.6	13.0	23.2	-10.7	2.8	20.0	63.0	-4.7
Net flows on debt	..	7.0	9.2	8.3	14.1	4.7	5.2	5.4	18.2	8.8
Net change in interest arrears	..	..	1.3	-1.1	-8.5	-0.1	0.7	2.4	8.3	-10.3
Interest capitalized	..	..	0.0	0.7	8.5	0.0	0.0	0.0	0.2	9.8
Debt forgiveness or reduction	..	..	0.0	0.0	0.0	0.0	0.0	0.0	0.0	-9.7
Cross-currency valuation	..	..	2.3	-1.0	1.3	-5.0	-7.5	-3.2	12.3	-3.2
Residual	..	..	2.9	6.0	7.9	-10.2	4.4	15.3	24.0	0.0
9. AVERAGE TERMS OF NEW COMMITMENTS										
ALL CREDITORS										
Interest (%)	..	4.0	0.8	0.8	0.0	3.0	1.2	1.5	0.0	1.0
Maturity (years)	..	11.1	35.7	49.8	0.0	16.5	45.0	12.7	0.0	39.5
Grace period (years)	..	4.4	10.1	10.3	0.0	5.0	9.7	4.2	0.0	9.6
Grant element (%)	..	31.5	76.6	82.9	0.0	43.0	76.2	44.2	0.0	77.3
Official creditors										
Interest (%)	..	4.0	0.8	0.8	0.0	3.0	1.2	1.5	0.0	1.0
Maturity (years)	..	11.1	35.7	49.8	0.0	16.5	45.0	12.7	0.0	39.5
Grace period (years)	..	4.4	10.1	10.3	0.0	5.0	9.7	4.2	0.0	9.6
Grant element (%)	..	31.5	76.6	82.9	0.0	43.0	76.2	44.2	0.0	77.3
Private creditors										
Interest (%)	..	0.0	0.0	0.0	0.0	0.0	0.0	0.0	0.0	0.0
Maturity (years)	..	0.0	0.0	0.0	0.0	0.0	0.0	0.0	0.0	0.0
Grace period (years)	..	0.0	0.0	0.0	0.0	0.0	0.0	0.0	0.0	0.0
Grant element (%)	..	0.0	0.0	0.0	0.0	0.0	0.0	0.0	0.0	0.0
Memorandum items										
Commitments	..	8.2	36.3	14.3	0.0	1.0	6.9	0.2	0.0	17.4
Official creditors	..	8.2	36.3	14.3	0.0	1.0	6.9	0.2	0.0	17.4
Private creditors	..	0.0	0.0	0.0	0.0	0.0	0.0	0.0	0.0	0.0

10. CONTRACTUAL OBLIGATIONS ON OUTSTANDING LONG-TERM DEBT

	2001	2002	2003	2004	2005	2006	2007	2008	2009	2010
TOTAL										
Disbursements	7.9	7.9	5.2	3.8	2.5	1.5	0.9	0.1	0.0	0.0
Principal	4.4	7.7	7.9	8.0	9.2	9.2	9.8	10.2	10.3	10.4
Interest	3.8	3.9	4.0	4.0	3.9	3.7	3.6	3.4	3.3	3.1
Official creditors										
Disbursements	7.9	7.9	5.2	3.8	2.5	1.5	0.9	0.1	0.0	0.0
Principal	4.4	7.5	7.7	7.8	9.0	9.0	9.6	10.0	10.0	10.1
Interest	3.6	3.6	3.6	3.5	3.4	3.3	3.1	3.0	2.9	2.7
Bilateral creditors										
Disbursements	0.2	0.1	0.1	0.1	0.0	0.0	0.0	0.0	0.0	0.0
Principal	0.8	3.2	3.5	3.5	4.6	4.6	4.5	4.4	4.4	4.3
Interest	2.2	2.2	2.2	2.1	2.0	1.9	1.8	1.7	1.6	1.5
Multilateral creditors										
Disbursements	7.7	7.8	5.1	3.7	2.5	1.4	0.8	0.1	0.0	0.0
Principal	3.6	4.3	4.1	4.2	4.3	4.4	5.0	5.5	5.6	5.8
Interest	1.4	1.4	1.4	1.4	1.4	1.4	1.3	1.3	1.2	1.2
Private creditors										
Disbursements	0.0	0.0	0.0	0.0	0.0	0.0	0.0	0.0	0.0	0.0
Principal	0.0	0.3	0.3	0.3	0.3	0.3	0.3	0.3	0.3	0.3
Interest	0.2	0.3	0.4	0.5	0.5	0.5	0.5	0.5	0.4	0.4
Commercial banks										
Disbursements	0.0	0.0	0.0	0.0	0.0	0.0	0.0	0.0	0.0	0.0
Principal	0.0	0.0	0.0	0.0	0.0	0.0	0.0	0.0	0.0	0.0
Interest	0.0	0.0	0.0	0.0	0.0	0.0	0.0	0.0	0.0	0.0
Other private										
Disbursements	0.0	0.0	0.0	0.0	0.0	0.0	0.0	0.0	0.0	0.0
Principal	0.0	0.3	0.3	0.3	0.3	0.3	0.3	0.3	0.3	0.3
Interest	0.2	0.3	0.4	0.5	0.5	0.5	0.5	0.5	0.4	0.4

SENEGAL

(US$ million, unless otherwise indicated)

	1970	1980	1990	1994	1995	1996	1997	1998	1999	2000
1. SUMMARY DEBT DATA										
TOTAL DEBT STOCKS (EDT)	**145**	**1,473**	**3,736**	**3,658**	**3,841**	**3,663**	**3,663**	**3,858**	**3,709**	**3,372**
Long-term debt (LDOD)	**145**	**1,114**	**3,000**	**3,097**	**3,234**	**3,155**	**3,158**	**3,293**	**3,129**	**2,971**
Public and publicly guaranteed	114	1,105	2,940	3,049	3,191	3,116	3,103	3,271	3,115	2,958
Private nonguaranteed	31	9	60	48	44	39	55	22	14	13
Use of IMF credit	**0**	**140**	**314**	**300**	**347**	**326**	**292**	**293**	**272**	**255**
Short-term debt	**0**	**219**	**421**	**262**	**260**	**183**	**213**	**273**	**308**	**147**
of which interest arrears on LDOD	0	0	4	39	10	2	2	2	2	2
Official creditors	0	0	3	30	4	2	2	2	2	2
Private creditors	0	0	0	10	6	1	0	0	0	0
Memo: principal arrears on LDOD	0	0	0	227	64	13	12	12	11	13
Official creditors	0	0	0	156	9	2	2	2	2	5
Private creditors	0	0	0	71	55	12	10	10	9	8
Memo: export credits	0	0	812	453	626	569	493	228	195	171
TOTAL DEBT FLOWS										
Disbursements	**20**	**395**	**252**	**201**	**241**	**216**	**270**	**255**	**92**	**145**
Long-term debt	20	327	223	132	158	181	221	206	72	127
IMF purchases	0	68	29	68	83	35	49	48	20	19
Principal repayments	**9**	**165**	**197**	**154**	**195**	**160**	**158**	**215**	**161**	**154**
Long-term debt	9	156	142	125	154	116	95	155	129	131
IMF repurchases	0	8	55	29	41	45	63	60	33	23
Net flows on debt	**11**	**246**	**222**	**-29**	**74**	**-14**	**143**	**100**	**-34**	**-170**
of which short-term debt	0	16	168	-76	28	-70	31	60	35	-161
Interest payments (INT)	**2**	**95**	**128**	**80**	**86**	**129**	**89**	**106**	**76**	**74**
Long-term debt	2	67	84	63	69	118	75	88	57	58
IMF charges	0	3	15	3	3	4	3	2	2	1
Short-term debt	0	24	29	14	14	7	11	15	17	15
Net transfers on debt	**8**	**151**	**94**	**-110**	**-13**	**-143**	**54**	**-6**	**-110**	**-244**
Total debt service paid (TDS)	**12**	**259**	**325**	**234**	**281**	**289**	**247**	**321**	**237**	**228**
Long-term debt	12	223	226	188	224	233	170	243	186	189
IMF repurchases and charges	0	12	70	31	43	48	66	63	34	24
Short-term debt (interest only)	0	24	29	14	14	7	11	15	17	15
2. AGGREGATE NET RESOURCE FLOWS AND NET TRANSFERS (LONG-TERM)										
NET RESOURCE FLOWS	**32**	**262**	**691**	**551**	**409**	**408**	**540**	**375**	**477**	**349**
Net flow of long-term debt (ex. IMF)	11	171	81	7	4	66	126	52	-56	-5
Foreign direct investment (net)	5	15	57	67	32	8	176	71	157	107
Portfolio equity flows	0	0	0	0	0	0	0	0	0	0
Grants (excluding technical coop.)	16	77	553	476	373	334	238	252	376	246
Memo: technical coop. grants	21	123	175	160	185	171	154	133	126	124
official net resource flows	22	244	649	493	402	411	349	320	325	243
private net resource flows	10	18	42	58	7	-2	191	55	151	106
NET TRANSFERS	**14**	**161**	**574**	**450**	**300**	**252**	**427**	**249**	**379**	**248**
Interest on long-term debt	2	67	84	63	69	118	75	88	57	58
Profit remittances on FDI	15	34	33	38	40	39	38	37	40	43
Memo: official net transfers	19	223	578	432	337	295	276	232	269	186
private net transfers	-5	-62	-4	17	-38	-44	151	18	111	62
3. MAJOR ECONOMIC AGGREGATES										
Gross national income (GNI)	855	2,887	5,502	3,500	4,321	4,566	4,315	4,590	4,661	4,286
Exports of goods & services (XGS)	..	905	1,628	1,368	1,680	1,530	1,437	1,560	1,656	1,580
of which workers remittances	..	75	91	73	86	82	92	91	130	167
Imports of goods & services (MGS)	..	1,337	2,053	1,679	2,033	1,814	1,708	1,888	2,006	1,921
International reserves (RES)	22	25	22	191	283	299	395	439	411	384
Current account balance	..	-386	-363	-187	-244	-200	-185	-247	-320	-310
4. DEBT INDICATORS										
EDT / XGS (%)	..	162.8	229.5	267.5	228.7	239.4	255.0	247.2	224.0	213.4
EDT / GNI (%)	17.0	51.0	67.9	104.5	88.9	80.2	84.9	84.1	79.6	78.7
TDS / XGS (%)	..	28.7	20.0	17.1	16.7	18.9	17.2	20.6	14.3	14.4
INT / XGS (%)	..	10.5	7.9	5.9	5.1	8.4	6.2	6.8	4.6	4.7
INT / GNI (%)	0.3	3.3	2.3	2.3	2.0	2.8	2.1	2.3	1.6	1.7
RES / EDT (%)	15.2	1.7	0.6	5.2	7.4	8.2	10.8	11.4	11.1	11.4
RES / MGS (months)	..	0.2	0.1	1.4	1.7	2.0	2.8	2.8	2.5	2.4
Short-term / EDT (%)	0.0	14.9	11.3	7.2	6.8	5.0	5.8	7.1	8.3	4.4
Concessional / EDT (%)	59.8	27.1	52.7	57.5	58.3	62.4	65.3	67.7	68.2	72.6
Multilateral / EDT (%)	9.2	17.9	36.6	48.2	48.1	50.6	49.5	51.0	51.3	54.8

SENEGAL

(US$ million, unless otherwise indicated)

	1970	1980	1990	1994	1995	1996	1997	1998	1999	2000
5. LONG-TERM DEBT										
DEBT OUTSTANDING (LDOD)	**145**	**1,114**	**3,000**	**3,097**	**3,234**	**3,155**	**3,158**	**3,293**	**3,129**	**2,971**
Public and publicly guaranteed	**114**	**1,105**	**2,940**	**3,049**	**3,191**	**3,116**	**3,103**	**3,271**	**3,115**	**2,958**
Official creditors	100	653	2,759	2,943	3,107	3,102	3,092	3,260	3,106	2,950
Multilateral	13	263	1,366	1,762	1,849	1,852	1,815	1,967	1,903	1,846
Concessional	9	179	1,153	1,467	1,577	1,612	1,619	1,773	1,732	1,704
Bilateral	87	390	1,393	1,181	1,258	1,249	1,277	1,292	1,203	1,104
Concessional	78	221	815	637	662	674	774	838	799	743
Private creditors	14	452	181	106	83	14	11	11	9	8
Bonds	0	4	0	0	0	0	0	0	0	0
Commercial banks	0	129	129	86	78	11	10	10	9	8
Other private	14	319	52	20	6	3	1	1	0	0
Private nonguaranteed	**31**	**9**	**60**	**48**	**44**	**39**	**55**	**22**	**14**	**13**
Bonds	0	0	0	0	0	0	0	0	0	0
Commercial banks and other	31	9	60	48	44	39	55	22	14	13
Memo:										
IBRD	2	57	88	44	35	23	14	9	4	1
IDA	9	100	747	1,005	1,126	1,194	1,187	1,301	1,310	1,330
DISBURSEMENTS	**20**	**327**	**223**	**132**	**158**	**181**	**221**	**206**	**72**	**127**
Public and publicly guaranteed	**19**	**327**	**208**	**132**	**157**	**181**	**200**	**205**	**71**	**125**
Official creditors	12	186	208	132	157	181	200	205	71	125
Multilateral	5	93	136	117	139	135	100	151	67	115
Concessional	4	63	127	84	132	135	99	136	63	109
Bilateral	7	94	72	15	17	46	100	54	4	10
Concessional	7	50	72	14	17	46	100	53	4	10
Private creditors	8	141	0	0	0	0	0	0	0	0
Bonds	0	0	0	0	0	0	0	0	0	0
Commercial banks	0	23	0	0	0	0	0	0	0	0
Other private	8	118	0	0	0	0	0	0	0	0
Private nonguaranteed	**1**	**0**	**15**	**1**	**1**	**0**	**21**	**2**	**1**	**1**
Bonds	0	0	0	0	0	0	0	0	0	0
Commercial banks and other	1	0	15	1	1	0	21	2	1	1
Memo:										
IBRD	1	18	0	0	0	0	0	0	0	0
IDA	4	12	117	54	107	110	60	85	49	92
PRINCIPAL REPAYMENTS	**9**	**156**	**142**	**125**	**154**	**116**	**95**	**155**	**129**	**131**
Public and publicly guaranteed	**7**	**152**	**130**	**119**	**149**	**111**	**91**	**138**	**122**	**129**
Official creditors	6	19	111	115	128	105	89	137	122	129
Multilateral	0	3	58	106	97	69	41	71	77	72
Concessional	0	0	29	60	59	44	20	42	53	52
Bilateral	6	16	53	9	31	36	48	67	44	56
Concessional	5	7	25	8	14	20	27	47	36	38
Private creditors	1	133	19	3	21	6	2	1	1	0
Bonds	0	1	0	0	0	0	0	0	0	0
Commercial banks	0	58	8	3	12	5	0	0	0	0
Other private	0	74	11	0	9	1	2	1	1	0
Private nonguaranteed	**3**	**4**	**12**	**7**	**5**	**5**	**5**	**17**	**7**	**3**
Bonds	0	0	0	0	0	0	0	0	0	0
Commercial banks and other	3	4	12	7	5	5	5	17	7	3
Memo:										
IBRD	0	2	13	11	12	10	7	6	5	3
IDA	0	0	3	5	6	7	8	11	12	16
NET FLOWS ON DEBT	**11**	**171**	**81**	**7**	**4**	**66**	**126**	**52**	**-56**	**-5**
Public and publicly guaranteed	**13**	**175**	**78**	**13**	**8**	**70**	**110**	**67**	**-51**	**-3**
Official creditors	6	167	96	17	29	77	111	67	-51	-3
Multilateral	5	90	77	11	43	66	59	80	-10	43
Concessional	4	63	98	24	74	91	79	95	10	57
Bilateral	1	77	19	5	-14	10	52	-13	-41	-46
Concessional	2	43	47	6	4	26	73	6	-32	-28
Private creditors	7	8	-19	-3	-21	-6	-2	-1	-1	0
Bonds	0	-1	0	0	0	0	0	0	0	0
Commercial banks	0	-35	-8	-3	-12	-5	0	0	0	0
Other private	7	43	-11	0	-9	-1	-2	-1	-1	0
Private nonguaranteed	**-2**	**-4**	**4**	**-6**	**-4**	**-5**	**16**	**-15**	**-5**	**-1**
Bonds	0	0	0	0	0	0	0	0	0	0
Commercial banks and other	-2	-4	4	-6	-4	-5	16	-15	-5	-1
Memo:										
IBRD	1	16	-13	-11	-12	-10	-7	-6	-5	-3
IDA	4	12	114	49	101	103	52	74	37	77

SENEGAL

(US$ million, unless otherwise indicated)

	1970	1980	1990	1994	1995	1996	1997	1998	1999	2000
INTEREST PAYMENTS (LINT)	**2**	**67**	**84**	**63**	**69**	**118**	**75**	**88**	**57**	**58**
Public and publicly guaranteed	**2**	**67**	**82**	**61**	**68**	**117**	**74**	**88**	**57**	**57**
Official creditors	2	22	71	61	65	116	74	88	57	57
Multilateral	0	6	26	46	38	38	27	35	29	26
Concessional	0	1	9	19	14	17	15	18	17	16
Bilateral	2	15	46	15	27	78	47	52	28	32
Concessional	2	6	20	7	8	62	15	19	17	21
Private creditors	0	45	10	0	3	1	0	0	0	0
Bonds	0	0	0	0	0	0	0	0	0	0
Commercial banks	0	23	7	0	2	1	0	0	0	0
Other private	0	22	3	0	1	0	0	0	0	0
Private nonguaranteed	**0**	**0**	**3**	**2**	**1**	**1**	**1**	**1**	**1**	**0**
Bonds	0	0	0	0	0	0	0	0	0	0
Commercial banks and other	0	0	3	2	1	1	1	1	1	0
Memo:										
IBRD	0	4	6	4	4	2	2	1	1	0
IDA	0	1	4	8	8	9	9	9	10	9
NET TRANSFERS ON DEBT	**8**	**103**	**-3**	**-56**	**-66**	**-52**	**51**	**-37**	**-114**	**-63**
Public and publicly guaranteed	**10**	**108**	**-4**	**-48**	**-61**	**-46**	**36**	**-21**	**-108**	**-61**
Official creditors	3	146	25	-44	-36	-39	38	-20	-107	-61
Multilateral	4	84	51	-35	5	29	32	45	-39	17
Concessional	4	62	89	6	60	74	65	77	-7	41
Bilateral	-1	62	-27	-9	-41	-67	5	-65	-69	-78
Concessional	1	37	27	-1	-4	-36	58	-13	-49	-48
Private creditors	7	-38	-29	-4	-25	-8	-2	-1	-1	0
Bonds	0	-1	0	0	0	0	0	0	0	0
Commercial banks	0	-58	-15	-3	-15	-6	0	0	0	0
Other private	7	21	-14	0	-10	-1	-2	-1	-1	0
Private nonguaranteed	**-2**	**-5**	**1**	**-8**	**-5**	**-6**	**15**	**-16**	**-6**	**-2**
Bonds	0	0	0	0	0	0	0	0	0	0
Commercial banks and other	-2	-5	1	-8	-5	-6	15	-16	-6	-2
Memo:										
IBRD	1	12	-19	-15	-15	-12	-9	-7	-5	-3
IDA	4	11	110	41	93	94	44	65	27	68
DEBT SERVICE (LTDS)	**12**	**223**	**226**	**188**	**224**	**233**	**170**	**243**	**186**	**189**
Public and publicly guaranteed	**9**	**219**	**212**	**180**	**217**	**228**	**164**	**226**	**179**	**186**
Official creditors	9	41	183	176	193	220	162	225	178	186
Multilateral	0	9	84	152	134	107	68	106	106	98
Concessional	0	1	38	78	73	61	35	59	70	68
Bilateral	8	32	98	24	58	113	95	119	72	88
Concessional	6	13	45	15	21	82	42	67	52	58
Private creditors	1	178	29	4	25	8	2	1	1	0
Bonds	0	1	0	0	0	0	0	0	0	0
Commercial banks	0	81	15	3	15	6	0	0	0	0
Other private	1	96	14	0	10	1	2	1	1	0
Private nonguaranteed	**3**	**5**	**14**	**9**	**6**	**6**	**6**	**17**	**7**	**3**
Bonds	0	0	0	0	0	0	0	0	0	0
Commercial banks and other	3	5	14	9	6	6	6	17	7	3
Memo:										
IBRD	0	6	19	15	15	12	9	7	5	3
IDA	0	1	7	13	14	15	17	20	22	24
UNDISBURSED DEBT	**42**	**604**	**976**	**753**	**889**	**813**	**746**	**732**	**798**	**939**
Official creditors	37	563	966	750	888	812	746	732	798	934
Private creditors	5	41	9	3	1	1	1	0	0	5
Memorandum items										
Concessional LDOD	87	400	1,968	2,104	2,239	2,286	2,393	2,611	2,531	2,447
Variable rate LDOD	31	141	140	271	305	255	236	400	349	311
Public sector LDOD	112	1,079	2,903	3,020	3,159	3,116	3,103	3,271	3,115	2,958
Private sector LDOD	33	35	97	77	76	39	55	22	14	13

6. CURRENCY COMPOSITION OF LONG-TERM DEBT (PERCENT)

	1970	1980	1990	1994	1995	1996	1997	1998	1999	2000
Deutsche mark	23.5	4.6	1.3	1.3	1.3	1.6	1.4	1.7	1.5	1.6
French franc	26.9	39.3	25.8	18.4	19.1	17.7	15.3	14.7	13.6	12.9
Japanese yen	0.0	0.0	1.5	3.9	3.7	3.3	2.9	3.1	3.7	3.4
Pound sterling	0.0	0.8	0.2	0.1	0.1	0.1	0.2	0.1	0.1	0.1
Swiss franc	0.0	0.3	0.9	0.5	0.5	0.4	0.3	0.3	0.3	0.2
U.S.dollars	1.7	23.0	32.9	35.1	36.6	38.5	41.6	42.7	44.7	47.6
Multiple currency	2.0	6.7	8.6	14.8	13.9	14.0	12.4	11.8	11.7	11.0
Special drawing rights	0.0	0.0	0.4	0.7	1.0	1.2	1.2	1.4	1.5	1.6
All other currencies	45.9	25.3	28.4	25.2	23.8	23.2	24.7	24.2	22.9	21.6

SENEGAL

(US$ million, unless otherwise indicated)

	1970	1980	1990	1994	1995	1996	1997	1998	1999	2000
7. DEBT RESTRUCTURINGS										
Total amount rescheduled	..	..	111	172	233	58	12	306	15	0
Debt stock rescheduled	..	..	0	0	0	0	0	306	0	0
Principal rescheduled	..	..	76	88	173	25	4	0	1	0
Official	..	..	58	86	166	25	4	0	1	0
Private	..	..	18	2	7	0	0	0	0	0
Interest rescheduled	..	..	27	83	49	28	1	0	0	0
Official	..	..	23	83	48	28	1	0	0	0
Private	..	..	4	0	1	0	0	0	0	0
Debt forgiven	..	..	18	219	14	3	4	0	0	4
Memo: interest forgiven	..	..	0	28	5	6	0	0	0	9
Debt stock reduction	..	..	0	0	0	65	0	16	0	0
of which debt buyback	..	..	0	0	0	5	0	0	0	0
8. DEBT STOCK-FLOW RECONCILIATION										
Total change in debt stocks	..	..	465	-106	183	-178	0	195	-149	-337
Net flows on debt	11	246	222	-29	74	-14	143	100	-34	-170
Net change in interest arrears	..	..	-7	-85	-29	-8	0	0	0	0
Interest capitalized	..	..	27	83	49	28	1	0	0	0
Debt forgiveness or reduction	..	..	-18	-219	-14	-62	-4	-16	0	-4
Cross-currency valuation	..	..	30	-125	-193	-382	-497	-182	-164	-146
Residual	..	..	211	270	297	259	357	294	49	-17
9. AVERAGE TERMS OF NEW COMMITMENTS										
ALL CREDITORS										
Interest (%)	3.9	5.9	1.9	0.7	1.1	2.4	1.4	1.0	0.9	0.9
Maturity (years)	23.2	20.0	33.4	38.4	38.7	31.1	40.0	39.2	41.9	39.4
Grace period (years)	6.8	5.6	8.7	9.2	9.4	9.7	10.2	9.5	9.9	9.7
Grant element (%)	43.8	30.2	66.1	76.8	76.0	61.5	75.0	77.0	79.7	78.2
Official creditors										
Interest (%)	2.3	5.4	1.9	0.7	1.1	2.4	1.4	1.0	0.9	0.7
Maturity (years)	30.6	21.3	33.7	38.4	38.7	31.1	40.0	39.2	41.9	40.2
Grace period (years)	8.8	6.0	8.8	9.2	9.4	9.7	10.2	9.5	9.9	9.9
Grant element (%)	59.6	33.7	66.8	76.8	76.0	61.5	75.0	77.0	79.7	80.0
Private creditors										
Interest (%)	7.5	10.8	8.3	0.0	0.0	0.0	0.0	0.0	0.0	7.6
Maturity (years)	5.9	8.3	10.1	0.0	0.0	0.0	0.0	0.0	0.0	8.3
Grace period (years)	2.2	2.5	2.6	0.0	0.0	0.0	0.0	0.0	0.0	1.3
Grant element (%)	6.8	-0.7	6.6	0.0	0.0	0.0	0.0	0.0	0.0	7.8
Memorandum items										
Commitments	7	469	366	47	309	162	182	167	178	225
Official creditors	5	421	361	47	309	162	182	167	178	220
Private creditors	2	49	4	0	0	0	0	0	0	5

10. CONTRACTUAL OBLIGATIONS ON OUTSTANDING LONG-TERM DEBT

	2001	2002	2003	2004	2005	2006	2007	2008	2009	2010
TOTAL										
Disbursements	294	254	177	106	50	22	14	3	0	0
Principal	138	142	135	228	121	116	110	112	112	114
Interest	71	71	68	57	53	50	47	44	42	39
Official creditors										
Disbursements	292	252	177	106	50	22	14	3	0	0
Principal	136	139	133	225	119	113	109	112	112	114
Interest	71	71	68	57	53	50	47	44	42	39
Bilateral creditors										
Disbursements	52	34	19	9	4	1	1	1	0	0
Principal	72	77	72	164	57	52	48	45	41	35
Interest	42	42	40	29	27	25	24	23	22	20
Multilateral creditors										
Disbursements	239	218	158	97	46	20	13	3	0	0
Principal	64	63	61	61	62	61	62	67	71	79
Interest	28	28	28	27	26	25	23	22	20	19
Private creditors										
Disbursements	3	2	1	0	0	0	0	0	0	0
Principal	2	3	3	3	3	3	1	1	0	0
Interest	0	1	0	0	0	0	0	0	0	0
Commercial banks										
Disbursements	0	0	0	0	0	0	0	0	0	0
Principal	0	0	0	0	0	0	0	0	0	0
Interest	0	0	0	0	0	0	0	0	0	0
Other private										
Disbursements	3	2	1	0	0	0	0	0	0	0
Principal	2	3	3	3	3	3	1	1	0	0
Interest	0	1	0	0	0	0	0	0	0	0

SEYCHELLES

(US$ million, unless otherwise indicated)

	1970	1980	1990	1994	1995	1996	1997	1998	1999	2000
1. SUMMARY DEBT DATA										
TOTAL DEBT STOCKS (EDT)	..	**84.1**	**163.2**	**170.9**	**158.9**	**148.0**	**149.1**	**186.6**	**172.4**	**163.2**
Long-term debt (LDOD)	..	**25.1**	**117.2**	**147.8**	**145.8**	**138.1**	**131.3**	**145.0**	**132.2**	**124.4**
Public and publicly guaranteed	..	25.1	117.2	147.8	145.8	138.1	131.3	145.0	132.2	124.4
Private nonguaranteed	..	0.0	0.0	0.0	0.0	0.0	0.0	0.0	0.0	0.0
Use of IMF credit	**0.0**	**0.0**	**0.0**	**0.0**	**0.0**	**0.0**	**0.0**	**0.0**	**0.0**	**0.0**
Short-term debt	..	**59.0**	**46.0**	**23.1**	**13.1**	**9.8**	**17.8**	**41.6**	**40.3**	**38.8**
of which interest arrears on LDOD	..	0.0	1.2	2.1	2.1	2.9	3.8	3.8	3.5	5.9
Official creditors	..	0.0	0.6	0.9	0.8	1.4	2.3	2.8	2.6	5.1
Private creditors	..	0.0	0.7	1.2	1.3	1.5	1.5	1.0	0.8	0.8
Memo: principal arrears on LDOD	..	0.0	9.3	18.6	20.8	22.4	23.7	21.7	20.0	24.8
Official creditors	..	0.0	7.1	8.3	9.3	11.6	13.2	12.3	11.9	16.9
Private creditors	..	0.0	2.1	10.3	11.5	10.8	10.4	9.4	8.1	7.9
Memo: export credits	..	0.0	45.0	41.6	51.0	37.9	46.1	13.5	20.3	12.4
TOTAL DEBT FLOWS										
Disbursements	..	**11.7**	**9.2**	**18.1**	**8.4**	**12.2**	**11.2**	**22.9**	**10.4**	**8.2**
Long-term debt	..	11.7	9.2	18.1	8.4	12.2	11.2	22.9	10.4	8.2
IMF purchases	0.0	0.0	0.0	0.0	0.0	0.0	0.0	0.0	0.0	0.0
Principal repayments	..	**0.1**	**12.7**	**10.1**	**15.6**	**10.3**	**9.5**	**13.6**	**17.8**	**11.0**
Long-term debt	..	0.1	12.7	10.1	15.6	10.3	9.5	13.6	17.8	11.0
IMF repurchases	0.0	0.0	0.0	0.0	0.0	0.0	0.0	0.0	0.0	0.0
Net flows on debt	..	**-390.3**	**6.7**	**5.5**	**-17.2**	**-2.2**	**8.8**	**33.0**	**-8.5**	**-6.7**
of which short-term debt	..	-402.0	10.2	-2.5	-10.0	-4.1	7.1	23.8	-1.0	-3.9
Interest payments (INT)	..	**37.1**	**9.0**	**6.9**	**7.9**	**5.0**	**5.3**	**7.7**	**7.6**	**6.3**
Long-term debt	..	0.2	5.5	6.2	7.1	4.5	4.8	6.4	5.5	2.5
IMF charges	0.0	0.0	0.0	0.0	0.0	0.0	0.0	0.0	0.0	0.0
Short-term debt	..	36.9	3.6	0.8	0.8	0.5	0.5	1.3	2.1	3.9
Net transfers on debt	..	**-427.5**	**-2.4**	**-1.4**	**-25.1**	**-7.3**	**3.4**	**25.3**	**-16.1**	**-13.1**
Total debt service paid (TDS)	..	**37.2**	**21.7**	**17.0**	**23.5**	**15.4**	**14.8**	**21.3**	**25.5**	**17.4**
Long-term debt	..	0.3	18.2	16.3	22.7	14.9	14.3	20.0	23.4	13.5
IMF repurchases and charges	0.0	0.0	0.0	0.0	0.0	0.0	0.0	0.0	0.0	0.0
Short-term debt (interest only)	..	36.9	3.6	0.8	0.8	0.5	0.5	1.3	2.1	3.9
2. AGGREGATE NET RESOURCE FLOWS AND NET TRANSFERS (LONG-TERM)										
NET RESOURCE FLOWS	..	**26.9**	**28.2**	**44.6**	**40.3**	**39.0**	**61.1**	**72.4**	**59.8**	**64.4**
Net flow of long-term debt (ex. IMF)	..	11.7	-3.5	8.0	-7.2	1.8	1.7	9.2	-7.4	-2.8
Foreign direct investment (net)	..	9.5	20.0	29.5	40.3	30.0	54.0	55.0	59.9	56.0
Portfolio equity flows	..	0.0	0.0	0.0	0.0	0.0	0.0	0.0	0.0	0.0
Grants (excluding technical coop.)	..	5.7	11.6	7.1	7.2	7.2	5.4	8.2	7.3	11.2
Memo: technical coop. grants	..	8.0	10.3	7.9	8.8	10.3	7.4	5.9	5.1	3.5
official net resource flows	..	17.4	14.4	10.3	8.3	13.3	10.1	12.3	4.9	12.6
private net resource flows	..	9.5	13.8	34.3	32.0	25.7	51.0	60.1	54.9	51.8
NET TRANSFERS	..	**18.7**	**8.8**	**25.4**	**20.2**	**20.5**	**41.3**	**49.1**	**33.3**	**43.0**
Interest on long-term debt	..	0.2	5.5	6.2	7.1	4.5	4.8	6.4	5.5	2.5
Profit remittances on FDI	..	8.0	14.0	13.0	13.0	14.0	15.0	17.0	21.0	19.0
Memo: official net transfers	..	17.2	10.9	6.8	3.6	10.2	6.5	7.7	0.2	10.7
private net transfers	..	1.5	-2.1	18.6	16.6	10.3	34.8	41.4	33.1	32.3
3. MAJOR ECONOMIC AGGREGATES										
Gross national income (GNI)	..	142.0	355.4	473.0	491.0	535.5	577.9	582.8	588.6	579.4
Exports of goods & services (XGS)	..	102.8	240.6	259.8	282.9	324.8	368.7	411.5	470.9	506.4
of which workers remittances	..	0.0	7.1	6.0	5.9	4.9	6.0	3.6	3.9	3.9
Imports of goods & services (MGS)	..	131.4	264.6	287.7	339.3	391.8	440.0	524.4	574.1	566.1
International reserves (RES)	..	18.4	16.6	30.2	27.1	21.8	26.3	21.6	30.3	43.8
Current account balance	..	-15.6	-13.0	-25.9	-53.9	-56.5	-63.2	-106.9	-103.5	-59.8
4. DEBT INDICATORS										
EDT / XGS (%)	..	81.8	67.8	65.8	56.2	45.6	40.4	45.4	36.6	32.2
EDT / GNI (%)	..	59.2	45.9	36.1	32.4	27.6	25.8	32.0	29.3	28.2
TDS / XGS (%)	..	36.2	9.0	6.5	8.3	4.7	4.0	5.2	5.4	3.4
INT / XGS (%)	..	36.1	3.7	2.7	2.8	1.5	1.4	1.9	1.6	1.2
INT / GNI (%)	..	26.1	2.5	1.5	1.6	0.9	0.9	1.3	1.3	1.1
RES / EDT (%)	..	21.9	10.2	17.6	17.1	14.7	17.7	11.6	17.6	26.8
RES / MGS (months)	..	1.7	0.8	1.3	1.0	0.7	0.7	0.5	0.6	0.9
Short-term / EDT (%)	..	70.2	28.2	13.5	8.2	6.6	11.9	22.3	23.4	23.8
Concessional / EDT (%)	..	22.4	43.2	39.4	42.6	45.3	45.1	37.7	39.2	41.7
Multilateral / EDT (%)	..	5.4	25.9	32.5	37.8	37.7	36.2	31.1	32.0	33.0

SEYCHELLES

(US$ million, unless otherwise indicated)

	1970	1980	1990	1994	1995	1996	1997	1998	1999	2000
5. LONG-TERM DEBT										
DEBT OUTSTANDING (LDOD)	..	**25.1**	**117.2**	**147.8**	**145.8**	**138.1**	**131.3**	**145.0**	**132.2**	**124.4**
Public and publicly guaranteed	..	**25.1**	**117.2**	**147.8**	**145.8**	**138.1**	**131.3**	**145.0**	**132.2**	**124.4**
Official creditors	..	25.1	97.9	105.3	109.5	108.4	106.1	114.0	107.8	104.5
Multilateral	..	4.5	42.3	55.6	60.0	55.8	53.9	58.1	55.1	53.8
Concessional	..	2.5	19.8	23.1	23.6	21.8	20.8	21.6	21.6	23.7
Bilateral	..	20.6	55.6	49.7	49.5	52.6	52.3	55.9	52.8	50.7
Concessional	..	16.3	50.7	44.3	44.1	45.2	46.5	48.8	45.9	44.3
Private creditors	..	0.0	19.3	42.5	36.3	29.7	25.1	31.0	24.3	19.9
Bonds	..	0.0	0.0	0.0	0.0	0.0	0.0	0.0	0.0	0.0
Commercial banks	..	0.0	16.4	24.0	21.6	16.9	14.2	17.0	13.1	11.5
Other private	..	0.0	2.8	18.5	14.8	12.8	10.9	13.9	11.2	8.3
Private nonguaranteed	..	**0.0**	**0.0**	**0.0**	**0.0**	**0.0**	**0.0**	**0.0**	**0.0**	**0.0**
Bonds	..	0.0	0.0	0.0	0.0	0.0	0.0	0.0	0.0	0.0
Commercial banks and other	..	0.0	0.0	0.0	0.0	0.0	0.0	0.0	0.0	0.0
Memo:										
IBRD	0.0	0.0	5.8	4.8	5.4	4.4	3.6	3.6	3.7	2.9
IDA	0.0	0.0	0.0	0.0	0.0	0.0	0.0	0.0	0.0	0.0
DISBURSEMENTS	..	**11.7**	**9.2**	**18.1**	**8.4**	**12.2**	**11.2**	**22.9**	**10.4**	**8.2**
Public and publicly guaranteed	..	**11.7**	**9.2**	**18.1**	**8.4**	**12.2**	**11.2**	**22.9**	**10.4**	**8.2**
Official creditors	..	11.7	7.6	8.9	8.1	11.5	11.2	13.2	9.7	8.2
Multilateral	..	3.5	3.4	8.9	7.5	6.0	5.5	7.3	4.2	3.6
Concessional	..	1.6	1.2	0.9	0.9	0.6	0.6	1.2	1.2	3.0
Bilateral	..	8.2	4.1	0.1	0.6	5.5	5.7	5.8	5.5	4.6
Concessional	..	4.5	4.1	0.1	0.6	3.5	5.6	4.5	5.1	4.5
Private creditors	..	0.0	1.6	9.1	0.3	0.7	0.0	9.7	0.6	0.0
Bonds	..	0.0	0.0	0.0	0.0	0.0	0.0	0.0	0.0	0.0
Commercial banks	..	0.0	1.3	1.0	0.0	0.7	0.0	5.1	0.4	0.0
Other private	..	0.0	0.3	8.2	0.3	0.0	0.0	4.6	0.2	0.0
Private nonguaranteed	..	**0.0**	**0.0**	**0.0**	**0.0**	**0.0**	**0.0**	**0.0**	**0.0**	**0.0**
Bonds	..	0.0	0.0	0.0	0.0	0.0	0.0	0.0	0.0	0.0
Commercial banks and other	..	0.0	0.0	0.0	0.0	0.0	0.0	0.0	0.0	0.0
Memo:										
IBRD	0.0	0.0	1.4	0.9	1.3	0.0	0.2	0.5	1.2	0.1
IDA	0.0	0.0	0.0	0.0	0.0	0.0	0.0	0.0	0.0	0.0
PRINCIPAL REPAYMENTS	..	**0.1**	**12.7**	**10.1**	**15.6**	**10.3**	**9.5**	**13.6**	**17.8**	**11.0**
Public and publicly guaranteed	..	**0.1**	**12.7**	**10.1**	**15.6**	**10.3**	**9.5**	**13.6**	**17.8**	**11.0**
Official creditors	..	0.1	4.8	5.8	6.9	5.4	6.6	9.0	12.2	6.8
Multilateral	..	0.0	2.9	3.4	4.1	3.9	3.9	5.5	6.5	2.1
Concessional	..	0.0	0.3	0.8	0.8	0.7	0.7	0.7	0.8	0.3
Bilateral	..	0.1	2.0	2.3	2.9	1.5	2.6	3.5	5.7	4.7
Concessional	..	0.1	1.8	2.3	2.8	1.5	1.0	3.5	5.2	4.3
Private creditors	..	0.0	7.9	4.3	8.6	5.0	3.0	4.6	5.6	4.2
Bonds	..	0.0	0.0	0.0	0.0	0.0	0.0	0.0	0.0	0.0
Commercial banks	..	0.0	6.8	3.3	4.6	3.0	1.0	3.0	2.7	1.3
Other private	..	0.0	1.1	1.1	4.0	1.9	1.9	1.6	2.9	2.9
Private nonguaranteed	..	**0.0**	**0.0**	**0.0**	**0.0**	**0.0**	**0.0**	**0.0**	**0.0**	**0.0**
Bonds	..	0.0	0.0	0.0	0.0	0.0	0.0	0.0	0.0	0.0
Commercial banks and other	..	0.0	0.0	0.0	0.0	0.0	0.0	0.0	0.0	0.0
Memo:										
IBRD	0.0	0.0	0.6	0.7	0.8	0.7	0.6	0.8	1.1	0.7
IDA	0.0	0.0	0.0	0.0	0.0	0.0	0.0	0.0	0.0	0.0
NET FLOWS ON DEBT	..	**11.7**	**-3.5**	**8.0**	**-7.2**	**1.8**	**1.7**	**9.2**	**-7.4**	**-2.8**
Public and publicly guaranteed	..	**11.7**	**-3.5**	**8.0**	**-7.2**	**1.8**	**1.7**	**9.2**	**-7.4**	**-2.8**
Official creditors	..	11.7	2.8	3.2	1.1	6.1	4.7	4.1	-2.4	1.4
Multilateral	..	3.5	0.6	5.5	3.4	2.1	1.6	1.8	-2.2	1.5
Concessional	..	1.6	0.9	0.2	0.1	-0.1	-0.1	0.5	0.4	2.7
Bilateral	..	8.2	2.2	-2.3	-2.3	4.0	3.1	2.3	-0.2	-0.1
Concessional	..	4.5	2.3	-2.3	-2.3	2.0	4.6	1.0	-0.1	0.2
Private creditors	..	0.0	-6.2	4.8	-8.3	-4.3	-3.0	5.1	-5.0	-4.2
Bonds	..	0.0	0.0	0.0	0.0	0.0	0.0	0.0	0.0	0.0
Commercial banks	..	0.0	-5.5	-2.3	-4.6	-2.4	-1.0	2.1	-2.3	-1.3
Other private	..	0.0	-0.8	7.1	-3.7	-1.9	-1.9	3.0	-2.7	-2.9
Private nonguaranteed	..	**0.0**	**0.0**	**0.0**	**0.0**	**0.0**	**0.0**	**0.0**	**0.0**	**0.0**
Bonds	..	0.0	0.0	0.0	0.0	0.0	0.0	0.0	0.0	0.0
Commercial banks and other	..	0.0	0.0	0.0	0.0	0.0	0.0	0.0	0.0	0.0
Memo:										
IBRD	0.0	0.0	0.8	0.2	0.5	-0.6	-0.4	-0.3	0.2	-0.6
IDA	0.0	0.0	0.0	0.0	0.0	0.0	0.0	0.0	0.0	0.0

SEYCHELLES

(US$ million, unless otherwise indicated)

	1970	1980	1990	1994	1995	1996	1997	1998	1999	2000
INTEREST PAYMENTS (LINT)	..	**0.2**	**5.5**	**6.2**	**7.1**	**4.5**	**4.8**	**6.4**	**5.5**	**2.5**
Public and publicly guaranteed	..	**0.2**	**5.5**	**6.2**	**7.1**	**4.5**	**4.8**	**6.4**	**5.5**	**2.5**
Official creditors	..	0.2	3.5	3.5	4.7	3.1	3.6	4.6	4.7	1.9
Multilateral	..	0.2	2.5	2.8	3.6	2.6	2.9	3.8	3.7	0.9
Concessional	..	0.0	0.3	0.5	0.5	0.4	0.5	0.5	0.5	0.2
Bilateral	..	0.1	1.1	0.7	1.1	0.5	0.7	0.9	1.1	1.0
Concessional	..	0.0	0.9	0.7	1.1	0.5	0.6	0.8	0.8	0.9
Private creditors	..	0.0	1.9	2.7	2.4	1.4	1.2	1.7	0.8	0.5
Bonds	..	0.0	0.0	0.0	0.0	0.0	0.0	0.0	0.0	0.0
Commercial banks	..	0.0	1.7	1.0	1.2	0.3	0.2	0.7	0.1	0.0
Other private	..	0.0	0.2	1.7	1.2	1.1	1.0	1.0	0.8	0.5
Private nonguaranteed	..	**0.0**	**0.0**	**0.0**	**0.0**	**0.0**	**0.0**	**0.0**	**0.0**	**0.0**
Bonds	..	0.0	0.0	0.0	0.0	0.0	0.0	0.0	0.0	0.0
Commercial banks and other	..	0.0	0.0	0.0	0.0	0.0	0.0	0.0	0.0	0.0
Memo:										
IBRD	0.0	0.0	0.4	0.3	0.4	0.4	0.3	0.2	0.2	0.2
IDA	0.0	0.0	0.0	0.0	0.0	0.0	0.0	0.0	0.0	0.0
NET TRANSFERS ON DEBT	..	**11.4**	**-9.0**	**1.8**	**-14.3**	**-2.7**	**-3.1**	**2.8**	**-13.0**	**-5.3**
Public and publicly guaranteed	..	**11.4**	**-9.0**	**1.8**	**-14.3**	**-2.7**	**-3.1**	**2.8**	**-13.0**	**-5.3**
Official creditors	..	11.4	-0.8	-0.3	-3.6	3.0	1.0	-0.5	-7.2	-0.6
Multilateral	..	3.3	-1.9	2.7	-0.2	-0.5	-1.4	-2.0	-5.9	0.6
Concessional	..	1.6	0.6	-0.3	-0.5	-0.5	-0.6	0.0	-0.1	2.5
Bilateral	..	8.1	1.1	-3.0	-3.4	3.5	2.4	1.5	-1.3	-1.2
Concessional	..	4.4	1.4	-2.9	-3.3	1.5	4.0	0.2	-1.0	-0.7
Private creditors	..	0.0	-8.2	2.1	-10.7	-5.7	-4.1	3.3	-5.8	-4.7
Bonds	..	0.0	0.0	0.0	0.0	0.0	0.0	0.0	0.0	0.0
Commercial banks	..	0.0	-7.2	-3.3	-5.8	-2.7	-1.2	1.4	-2.3	-1.3
Other private	..	0.0	-1.0	5.4	-4.9	-3.0	-2.9	2.0	-3.5	-3.4
Private nonguaranteed	..	**0.0**	**0.0**	**0.0**	**0.0**	**0.0**	**0.0**	**0.0**	**0.0**	**0.0**
Bonds	..	0.0	0.0	0.0	0.0	0.0	0.0	0.0	0.0	0.0
Commercial banks and other	..	0.0	0.0	0.0	0.0	0.0	0.0	0.0	0.0	0.0
Memo:										
IBRD	0.0	0.0	0.4	-0.1	0.1	-1.0	-0.7	-0.5	-0.1	-0.8
IDA	0.0	0.0	0.0	0.0	0.0	0.0	0.0	0.0	0.0	0.0
DEBT SERVICE (LTDS)	..	**0.3**	**18.2**	**16.3**	**22.7**	**14.9**	**14.3**	**20.0**	**23.4**	**13.5**
Public and publicly guaranteed	..	**0.3**	**18.2**	**16.3**	**22.7**	**14.9**	**14.3**	**20.0**	**23.4**	**13.5**
Official creditors	..	0.3	8.4	9.2	11.6	8.5	10.2	13.7	16.9	8.8
Multilateral	..	0.2	5.4	6.2	7.7	6.5	6.9	9.3	10.2	3.0
Concessional	..	0.0	0.6	1.3	1.3	1.1	1.2	1.2	1.3	0.5
Bilateral	..	0.1	3.0	3.0	4.0	2.0	3.3	4.4	6.8	5.8
Concessional	..	0.1	2.8	3.0	3.9	2.0	1.6	4.3	6.1	5.1
Private creditors	..	0.0	9.8	7.0	11.0	6.4	4.1	6.3	6.5	4.7
Bonds	..	0.0	0.0	0.0	0.0	0.0	0.0	0.0	0.0	0.0
Commercial banks	..	0.0	8.5	4.2	5.8	3.4	1.2	3.8	2.8	1.3
Other private	..	0.0	1.3	2.8	5.3	3.0	2.9	2.6	3.7	3.4
Private nonguaranteed	..	**0.0**	**0.0**	**0.0**	**0.0**	**0.0**	**0.0**	**0.0**	**0.0**	**0.0**
Bonds	..	0.0	0.0	0.0	0.0	0.0	0.0	0.0	0.0	0.0
Commercial banks and other	..	0.0	0.0	0.0	0.0	0.0	0.0	0.0	0.0	0.0
Memo:										
IBRD	0.0	0.0	1.0	1.0	1.1	1.0	0.9	1.0	1.3	0.9
IDA	0.0	0.0	0.0	0.0	0.0	0.0	0.0	0.0	0.0	0.0
UNDISBURSED DEBT	..	**23.9**	**56.6**	**40.0**	**41.6**	**46.7**	**50.7**	**49.1**	**47.0**	**36.9**
Official creditors	..	23.4	47.7	35.0	36.5	45.0	50.0	48.5	47.0	36.9
Private creditors	..	0.6	8.9	5.0	5.1	1.6	0.6	0.7	0.0	0.0
Memorandum items										
Concessional LDOD	..	18.8	70.5	67.4	67.7	67.0	67.2	70.4	67.5	67.9
Variable rate LDOD	..	0.0	5.8	6.3	7.0	5.9	5.1	14.4	12.5	9.8
Public sector LDOD	..	25.1	117.2	147.8	145.8	138.1	131.3	145.0	132.2	124.4
Private sector LDOD	..	0.0	0.0	0.0	0.0	0.0	0.0	0.0	0.0	0.0

6. CURRENCY COMPOSITION OF LONG-TERM DEBT (PERCENT)

	1970	1980	1990	1994	1995	1996	1997	1998	1999	2000
Deutsche mark	..	8.1	3.5	3.2	3.4	3.5	3.1	3.4	3.0	2.8
French franc	..	2.6	15.3	8.3	7.8	7.0	5.9	3.7	2.8	2.5
Japanese yen	..	0.0	0.0	0.0	0.0	0.0	0.0	0.0	0.0	0.0
Pound sterling	..	68.1	15.9	7.5	7.5	8.6	8.8	8.1	7.7	6.6
Swiss franc	..	0.0	8.4	6.6	7.6	6.8	6.7	6.4	6.0	6.3
U.S.dollars	..	8.4	9.9	21.9	17.9	17.1	15.1	19.1	18.4	17.4
Multiple currency	..	12.8	29.3	30.3	33.6	33.6	34.0	32.9	32.5	31.2
Special drawing rights	..	0.0	0.0	0.6	0.6	0.6	0.5	0.4	0.4	0.4
All other currencies	..	0.0	17.7	21.6	21.6	22.8	25.9	26.0	29.2	32.8

SEYCHELLES

(US$ million, unless otherwise indicated)

	1970	1980	1990	1994	1995	1996	1997	1998	1999	2000
7. DEBT RESTRUCTURINGS										
Total amount rescheduled	..	..	0.0	0.0	0.0	0.0	0.0	0.0	0.0	0.0
Debt stock rescheduled	..	..	0.0	0.0	0.0	0.0	0.0	0.0	0.0	0.0
Principal rescheduled	..	..	0.0	0.0	0.0	0.0	0.0	0.0	0.0	0.0
Official	..	..	0.0	0.0	0.0	0.0	0.0	0.0	0.0	0.0
Private	..	..	0.0	0.0	0.0	0.0	0.0	0.0	0.0	0.0
Interest rescheduled	..	..	0.0	0.0	0.0	0.0	0.0	0.0	0.0	0.0
Official	..	..	0.0	0.0	0.0	0.0	0.0	0.0	0.0	0.0
Private	..	..	0.0	0.0	0.0	0.0	0.0	0.0	0.0	0.0
Debt forgiven	..	..	0.0	0.0	0.0	0.0	0.0	0.0	0.0	0.0
Memo: interest forgiven	..	..	0.0	0.0	0.0	0.0	0.0	0.0	0.0	0.0
Debt stock reduction	..	..	0.0	0.0	0.0	0.0	0.0	0.0	0.0	0.0
of which debt buyback	..	..	0.0	0.0	0.0	0.0	0.0	0.0	0.0	0.0
8. DEBT STOCK-FLOW RECONCILIATION										
Total change in debt stocks	..	..	18.8	14.1	-12.0	-11.0	1.1	37.5	-14.1	-9.2
Net flows on debt	..	-390.3	6.7	5.5	-17.2	-2.2	8.8	33.0	-8.5	-6.7
Net change in interest arrears	..	..	0.9	0.8	0.0	0.8	0.9	-0.1	-0.3	2.5
Interest capitalized	..	..	0.0	0.0	0.0	0.0	0.0	0.0	0.0	0.0
Debt forgiveness or reduction	..	..	0.0	0.0	0.0	0.0	0.0	0.0	0.0	0.0
Cross-currency valuation	..	..	9.2	5.1	4.1	-9.4	-5.2	2.2	-4.2	-2.3
Residual	..	..	2.1	2.6	1.1	-0.2	-3.3	2.3	-1.2	-2.7
9. AVERAGE TERMS OF NEW COMMITMENTS										
ALL CREDITORS										
Interest (%)	..	6.6	4.5	6.9	4.3	3.4	6.7	5.4	0.0	0.0
Maturity (years)	..	15.6	22.1	13.2	18.2	13.8	18.6	9.6	9.6	0.0
Grace period (years)	..	5.1	7.9	5.7	4.7	4.1	5.0	2.1	3.1	0.0
Grant element (%)	..	20.2	45.0	15.7	33.1	36.3	20.4	18.9	44.3	0.0
Official creditors										
Interest (%)	..	6.6	3.3	6.9	4.3	3.3	6.7	4.0	0.0	0.0
Maturity (years)	..	15.7	25.0	20.0	18.2	14.3	18.6	11.5	9.6	0.0
Grace period (years)	..	5.1	9.0	10.0	4.7	4.3	5.0	4.0	3.1	0.0
Grant element (%)	..	20.3	52.9	23.2	33.1	37.7	20.4	30.1	44.3	0.0
Private creditors										
Interest (%)	..	7.3	11.5	6.9	0.0	6.0	0.0	7.0	0.0	0.0
Maturity (years)	..	5.0	4.8	5.0	0.0	3.0	0.0	7.4	0.0	0.0
Grace period (years)	..	0.5	0.9	0.5	0.0	0.5	0.0	0.1	0.0	0.0
Grant element (%)	..	5.7	-2.5	6.5	0.0	5.8	0.0	6.5	0.0	0.0
Memorandum items										
Commitments	..	11.4	12.4	2.1	8.7	15.5	18.4	20.3	9.2	0.0
Official creditors	..	11.4	10.6	1.2	8.7	14.8	18.4	10.6	9.2	0.0
Private creditors	..	0.1	1.8	1.0	0.0	0.7	0.0	9.7	0.0	0.0

10. CONTRACTUAL OBLIGATIONS ON OUTSTANDING LONG-TERM DEBT

	2001	2002	2003	2004	2005	2006	2007	2008	2009	2010
TOTAL										
Disbursements	14.2	9.2	5.9	4.0	2.1	0.7	0.4	0.3	0.0	0.0
Principal	15.2	14.7	16.2	13.3	12.0	11.6	10.1	9.5	7.5	5.8
Interest	4.8	4.5	4.0	3.5	3.1	2.7	2.2	1.9	1.5	1.2
Official creditors										
Disbursements	14.2	9.2	5.9	4.0	2.1	0.7	0.4	0.3	0.0	0.0
Principal	11.6	11.7	13.4	12.2	11.5	11.1	9.6	9.3	7.5	5.8
Interest	4.5	4.3	4.0	3.5	3.1	2.7	2.2	1.9	1.5	1.2
Bilateral creditors										
Disbursements	3.0	2.0	1.3	0.9	0.5	0.5	0.4	0.3	0.0	0.0
Principal	4.2	3.9	4.8	5.3	5.0	5.1	3.9	3.9	3.4	2.6
Interest	1.1	1.1	1.1	1.0	0.8	0.7	0.6	0.5	0.4	0.3
Multilateral creditors										
Disbursements	11.2	7.2	4.6	3.1	1.6	0.2	0.0	0.0	0.0	0.0
Principal	7.4	7.8	8.6	6.9	6.5	6.1	5.8	5.5	4.1	3.2
Interest	3.4	3.2	2.9	2.5	2.2	1.9	1.6	1.4	1.1	0.9
Private creditors										
Disbursements	0.0	0.0	0.0	0.0	0.0	0.0	0.0	0.0	0.0	0.0
Principal	3.6	3.0	2.7	1.1	0.5	0.5	0.5	0.1	0.0	0.0
Interest	0.3	0.2	0.1	0.0	0.0	0.0	0.0	0.0	0.0	0.0
Commercial banks										
Disbursements	0.0	0.0	0.0	0.0	0.0	0.0	0.0	0.0	0.0	0.0
Principal	1.3	1.3	1.0	0.0	0.0	0.0	0.0	0.0	0.0	0.0
Interest	0.0	0.0	0.0	0.0	0.0	0.0	0.0	0.0	0.0	0.0
Other private										
Disbursements	0.0	0.0	0.0	0.0	0.0	0.0	0.0	0.0	0.0	0.0
Principal	2.3	1.7	1.7	1.1	0.5	0.5	0.5	0.1	0.0	0.0
Interest	0.3	0.2	0.1	0.0	0.0	0.0	0.0	0.0	0.0	0.0

SIERRA LEONE

(US$ million, unless otherwise indicated)

	1970	1980	1990	1994	1995	1996	1997	1998	1999	2000
1. SUMMARY DEBT DATA										
TOTAL DEBT STOCKS (EDT)	**61**	**469**	**1,151**	**1,493**	**1,178**	**1,179**	**1,148**	**1,260**	**1,254**	**1,273**
Long-term debt (LDOD)	**61**	**357**	**604**	**849**	**906**	**903**	**890**	**959**	**941**	**969**
Public and publicly guaranteed	61	357	604	849	906	903	890	959	941	969
Private nonguaranteed	0	0	0	0	0	0	0	0	0	0
Use of IMF credit	**0**	**59**	**108**	**146**	**165**	**171**	**167**	**191**	**195**	**174**
Short-term debt	**0**	**53**	**439**	**497**	**107**	**105**	**90**	**111**	**119**	**131**
of which interest arrears on LDOD	0	7	107	14	3	3	4	17	29	39
Official creditors	0	4	82	10	3	2	4	16	28	39
Private creditors	0	4	25	4	0	0	0	1	1	1
Memo: principal arrears on LDOD	0	17	247	45	19	21	23	35	50	65
Official creditors	0	4	173	26	15	17	19	31	46	61
Private creditors	0	12	74	19	4	4	4	4	4	4
Memo: export credits	0	0	166	171	129	110	135	86	81	79
TOTAL DEBT FLOWS										
Disbursements	**8**	**104**	**24**	**200**	**115**	**90**	**47**	**62**	**36**	**91**
Long-term debt	8	84	24	64	95	75	40	46	15	77
IMF purchases	0	21	0	137	20	15	7	16	21	14
Principal repayments	**16**	**50**	**12**	**98**	**59**	**47**	**6**	**11**	**17**	**33**
Long-term debt	11	34	7	17	55	44	6	11	4	8
IMF repurchases	5	17	5	81	4	3	0	0	12	25
Net flows on debt	**-8**	**62**	**11**	**90**	**-136**	**41**	**25**	**59**	**16**	**59**
of which short-term debt	0	8	-1	-13	-192	-2	-16	8	-4	1
Interest payments (INT)	**3**	**16**	**9**	**62**	**21**	**12**	**7**	**9**	**5**	**10**
Long-term debt	3	8	4	20	19	10	6	8	3	7
IMF charges	0	2	0	38	1	1	1	1	1	3
Short-term debt	0	6	5	5	1	1	1	0	1	0
Net transfers on debt	**-11**	**47**	**2**	**28**	**-156**	**29**	**18**	**49**	**10**	**50**
Total debt service paid (TDS)	**19**	**66**	**21**	**160**	**79**	**59**	**13**	**21**	**22**	**43**
Long-term debt	13	41	11	36	74	54	12	19	8	14
IMF repurchases and charges	5	19	5	119	4	4	1	1	14	28
Short-term debt (interest only)	0	6	5	5	1	1	1	0	1	0
2. AGGREGATE NET RESOURCE FLOWS AND NET TRANSFERS (LONG-TERM)										
NET RESOURCE FLOWS	**7**	**56**	**79**	**116**	**125**	**101**	**100**	**110**	**77**	**186**
Net flow of long-term debt (ex. IMF)	-3	50	17	47	40	31	34	35	11	69
Foreign direct investment (net)	8	-19	32	-3	-2	5	4	5	1	1
Portfolio equity flows	0	0	0	0	0	0	0	0	0	0
Grants (excluding technical coop.)	1	24	30	72	87	65	61	70	65	116
Memo: technical coop. grants	5	21	28	26	24	31	17	13	12	23
official net resource flows	4	63	43	119	155	96	96	105	76	185
private net resource flows	2	-7	36	-3	-30	5	4	5	1	1
NET TRANSFERS	**0**	**43**	**24**	**93**	**104**	**88**	**92**	**99**	**69**	**176**
Interest on long-term debt	3	8	4	20	19	10	6	8	3	7
Profit remittances on FDI	5	5	51	3	2	3	2	3	5	4
Memo: official net transfers	3	60	39	99	137	86	90	97	73	179
private net transfers	-4	-17	-15	-6	-32	2	2	2	-4	-3
3. MAJOR ECONOMIC AGGREGATES										
Gross national income (GNI)	401	1,136	772	811	876	912	832	679	650	616
Exports of goods & services (XGS)	..	276	210	218	129	132	90	77	74	89
of which workers remittances	..	0	0	0	0	..	..	..	..	..
Imports of goods & services (MGS)	..	494	287	353	281	370	166	178	165	266
International reserves (RES)	39	31	5	41	35	27	38	44	39	51
Current account balance	..	-165	-69	-89	-127	..	..	..	..	..
4. DEBT INDICATORS										
EDT / XGS (%)	..	169.9	547.2	685.8	912.8	895.0	1,273.9	1,644.5	1,686.4	1,434.7
EDT / GNI (%)	15.3	41.3	149.0	184.0	134.4	129.3	137.9	185.6	193.0	206.6
TDS / XGS (%)	..	23.8	10.1	73.4	61.5	44.8	14.4	26.8	29.5	48.0
INT / XGS (%)	..	5.6	4.4	28.6	16.0	9.0	7.8	12.1	7.1	11.0
INT / GNI (%)	0.6	1.4	1.2	7.7	2.4	1.3	0.8	1.4	0.8	1.6
RES / EDT (%)	64.1	6.5	0.5	2.7	2.9	2.3	3.4	3.5	3.2	4.0
RES / MGS (months)	..	0.7	0.2	1.4	1.5	0.9	2.8	3.0	2.9	2.3
Short-term / EDT (%)	0.0	11.3	38.1	33.3	9.1	8.9	7.9	8.8	9.5	10.3
Concessional / EDT (%)	32.6	37.3	27.1	39.5	59.4	62.5	63.7	62.1	62.0	63.9
Multilateral / EDT (%)	10.3	13.2	15.8	23.3	36.8	40.7	42.6	42.6	42.4	45.2

SIERRA LEONE

(US$ million, unless otherwise indicated)

	1970	1980	1990	1994	1995	1996	1997	1998	1999	2000
5. LONG-TERM DEBT										
DEBT OUTSTANDING (LDOD)	**61**	**357**	**604**	**849**	**906**	**903**	**890**	**959**	**941**	**969**
Public and publicly guaranteed	**61**	**357**	**604**	**849**	**906**	**903**	**890**	**959**	**941**	**969**
Official creditors	34	246	505	823	898	895	884	952	934	963
Multilateral	6	62	182	348	434	480	489	536	531	575
Concessional	0	39	170	329	412	458	470	505	501	548
Bilateral	28	184	323	475	464	416	395	416	403	388
Concessional	20	136	142	261	288	278	261	277	276	266
Private creditors	27	111	99	26	8	8	6	7	6	6
Bonds	0	0	0	0	0	0	0	0	0	0
Commercial banks	3	20	17	17	0	0	0	0	0	0
Other private	24	91	83	9	8	8	6	7	6	6
Private nonguaranteed	**0**	**0**	**0**	**0**	**0**	**0**	**0**	**0**	**0**	**0**
Bonds	0	0	0	0	0	0	0	0	0	0
Commercial banks and other	0	0	0	0	0	0	0	0	0	0
Memo:										
IBRD	6	13	11	3	3	2	2	1	0	0
IDA	0	29	81	186	231	258	270	298	300	354
DISBURSEMENTS	**8**	**84**	**24**	**64**	**95**	**75**	**40**	**46**	**15**	**77**
Public and publicly guaranteed	**8**	**84**	**24**	**64**	**95**	**75**	**40**	**46**	**15**	**77**
Official creditors	4	42	20	64	95	75	40	46	15	77
Multilateral	3	9	1	61	87	73	40	41	15	74
Concessional	0	5	1	58	86	71	40	28	13	74
Bilateral	1	33	19	3	8	3	0	6	0	3
Concessional	1	28	19	3	8	3	0	6	0	3
Private creditors	4	42	4	0	0	0	0	0	0	0
Bonds	0	0	0	0	0	0	0	0	0	0
Commercial banks	0	0	0	0	0	0	0	0	0	0
Other private	4	42	4	0	0	0	0	0	0	0
Private nonguaranteed	**0**	**0**	**0**	**0**	**0**	**0**	**0**	**0**	**0**	**0**
Bonds	0	0	0	0	0	0	0	0	0	0
Commercial banks and other	0	0	0	0	0	0	0	0	0	0
Memo:										
IBRD	3	2	0	0	0	0	0	0	0	0
IDA	0	2	0	38	44	35	27	21	9	70
PRINCIPAL REPAYMENTS	**11**	**34**	**7**	**17**	**55**	**44**	**6**	**11**	**4**	**8**
Public and publicly guaranteed	**11**	**34**	**7**	**17**	**55**	**44**	**6**	**11**	**4**	**8**
Official creditors	1	4	7	17	27	44	6	11	4	8
Multilateral	0	1	2	4	4	4	3	9	4	8
Concessional	0	0	0	3	3	4	3	9	3	6
Bilateral	1	3	5	13	23	40	3	2	0	0
Concessional	1	2	2	6	4	2	3	1	0	0
Private creditors	10	29	0	0	28	0	0	0	0	0
Bonds	5	0	0	0	0	0	0	0	0	0
Commercial banks	1	3	0	0	28	0	0	0	0	0
Other private	4	27	0	0	0	0	0	0	0	0
Private nonguaranteed	**0**	**0**	**0**	**0**	**0**	**0**	**0**	**0**	**0**	**0**
Bonds	0	0	0	0	0	0	0	0	0	0
Commercial banks and other	0	0	0	0	0	0	0	0	0	0
Memo:										
IBRD	0	1	0	0	1	1	0	1	1	0
IDA	0	0	0	1	2	2	1	3	2	2
NET FLOWS ON DEBT	**-3**	**50**	**17**	**47**	**40**	**31**	**34**	**35**	**11**	**69**
Public and publicly guaranteed	**-3**	**50**	**17**	**47**	**40**	**31**	**34**	**35**	**11**	**69**
Official creditors	3	38	13	47	68	31	34	35	11	69
Multilateral	3	8	-1	57	84	69	37	32	11	67
Concessional	0	5	1	55	83	67	37	20	10	68
Bilateral	1	30	13	-10	-16	-37	-3	4	0	3
Concessional	1	26	16	-3	4	0	-3	4	0	3
Private creditors	-6	12	4	0	-28	0	0	0	0	0
Bonds	-5	0	0	0	0	0	0	0	0	0
Commercial banks	-1	-3	0	0	-28	0	0	0	0	0
Other private	-1	15	4	0	0	0	0	0	0	0
Private nonguaranteed	**0**	**0**	**0**	**0**	**0**	**0**	**0**	**0**	**0**	**0**
Bonds	0	0	0	0	0	0	0	0	0	0
Commercial banks and other	0	0	0	0	0	0	0	0	0	0
Memo:										
IBRD	3	2	0	0	-1	-1	0	-1	-1	0
IDA	0	2	0	37	42	34	26	19	7	68

SIERRA LEONE

(US$ million, unless otherwise indicated)

	1970	1980	1990	1994	1995	1996	1997	1998	1999	2000
INTEREST PAYMENTS (LINT)	**3**	**8**	**4**	**20**	**19**	**10**	**6**	**8**	**3**	**7**
Public and publicly guaranteed	**3**	**8**	**4**	**20**	**19**	**10**	**6**	**8**	**3**	**7**
Official creditors	1	2	4	20	19	10	6	8	3	7
Multilateral	0	1	2	2	3	3	2	5	3	4
Concessional	0	0	1	2	2	3	2	5	3	3
Bilateral	1	1	2	17	16	7	3	3	0	3
Concessional	1	0	1	2	3	1	3	0	0	0
Private creditors	1	5	0	0	0	0	0	0	0	0
Bonds	0	0	0	0	0	0	0	0	0	0
Commercial banks	0	1	0	0	0	0	0	0	0	0
Other private	1	4	0	0	0	0	0	0	0	0
Private nonguaranteed	**0**	**0**	**0**	**0**	**0**	**0**	**0**	**0**	**0**	**0**
Bonds	0	0	0	0	0	0	0	0	0	0
Commercial banks and other	0	0	0	0	0	0	0	0	0	0
Memo:										
IBRD	0	1	0	0	0	0	0	0	0	0
IDA	0	0	0	1	2	2	1	3	2	2
NET TRANSFERS ON DEBT	**-5**	**43**	**13**	**27**	**21**	**22**	**29**	**27**	**8**	**63**
Public and publicly guaranteed	**-5**	**43**	**13**	**27**	**21**	**22**	**29**	**27**	**8**	**63**
Official creditors	2	36	9	27	50	22	29	27	8	63
Multilateral	3	7	-3	55	81	65	35	27	8	63
Concessional	0	5	0	53	81	64	35	15	7	65
Bilateral	-1	29	12	-28	-31	-44	-6	1	0	-1
Concessional	0	26	15	-5	1	-1	-5	4	0	2
Private creditors	-7	7	4	0	-28	0	0	0	0	0
Bonds	-5	0	0	0	0	0	0	0	0	0
Commercial banks	-1	-4	0	0	-28	0	0	0	0	0
Other private	-1	11	4	0	0	0	0	0	0	0
Private nonguaranteed	**0**	**0**	**0**	**0**	**0**	**0**	**0**	**0**	**0**	**0**
Bonds	0	0	0	0	0	0	0	0	0	0
Commercial banks and other	0	0	0	0	0	0	0	0	0	0
Memo:										
IBRD	2	1	0	-1	-1	-1	0	-1	-1	0
IDA	0	2	0	36	41	32	25	16	5	66
DEBT SERVICE (LTDS)	**13**	**41**	**11**	**36**	**74**	**54**	**12**	**19**	**8**	**14**
Public and publicly guaranteed	**13**	**41**	**11**	**36**	**74**	**54**	**12**	**19**	**8**	**14**
Official creditors	2	6	11	36	45	54	12	19	8	14
Multilateral	0	2	4	6	6	7	5	14	7	11
Concessional	0	0	1	5	5	7	5	13	6	10
Bilateral	2	4	7	30	39	46	6	5	0	3
Concessional	2	2	4	8	6	4	5	1	0	1
Private creditors	11	35	0	0	28	0	0	0	0	0
Bonds	5	0	0	0	0	0	0	0	0	0
Commercial banks	1	4	0	0	28	0	0	0	0	0
Other private	5	31	0	0	0	0	0	0	0	0
Private nonguaranteed	**0**	**0**	**0**	**0**	**0**	**0**	**0**	**0**	**0**	**0**
Bonds	0	0	0	0	0	0	0	0	0	0
Commercial banks and other	0	0	0	0	0	0	0	0	0	0
Memo:										
IBRD	0	1	0	1	1	1	0	1	1	0
IDA	0	0	0	2	3	4	2	6	4	4
UNDISBURSED DEBT	**25**	**116**	**164**	**307**	**263**	**219**	**162**	**156**	**131**	**121**
Official creditors	22	95	164	307	263	219	162	156	131	121
Private creditors	2	22	0	0	0	0	0	0	0	0
Memorandum items										
Concessional LDOD	20	175	312	590	700	736	731	782	777	814
Variable rate LDOD	6	0	8	8	12	12	11	11	11	10
Public sector LDOD	61	357	604	849	906	903	890	959	941	969
Private sector LDOD	0	0	0	0	0	0	0	0	0	0

6. CURRENCY COMPOSITION OF LONG-TERM DEBT (PERCENT)

	1970	1980	1990	1994	1995	1996	1997	1998	1999	2000
Deutsche mark	11.0	15.7	4.8	2.1	1.7	1.6	1.5	1.5	1.3	1.2
French franc	19.1	2.7	6.1	3.1	2.8	2.7	2.6	2.6	2.3	2.0
Japanese yen	0.0	4.8	7.4	9.5	8.7	7.6	6.8	7.1	8.2	7.1
Pound sterling	39.0	10.0	2.2	0.5	0.6	0.7	0.7	0.7	0.6	0.6
Swiss franc	0.8	10.7	8.3	3.5	3.3	2.8	2.7	2.7	2.4	2.2
U.S.dollars	16.9	23.4	30.3	43.5	40.3	39.5	42.3	42.5	43.5	47.9
Multiple currency	10.3	4.0	5.4	8.9	11.6	12.5	12.9	12.8	12.9	12.2
Special drawing rights	0.0	0.0	11.1	9.9	10.2	10.9	10.7	10.6	10.8	9.9
All other currencies	2.9	28.7	24.4	19.0	20.8	21.7	19.8	19.5	18.0	16.9

SIERRA LEONE

(US$ million, unless otherwise indicated)

	1970	1980	1990	1994	1995	1996	1997	1998	1999	2000
7. DEBT RESTRUCTURINGS										
Total amount rescheduled	..	..	0	107	31	24	55	1	0	0
Debt stock rescheduled	..	..	0	0	0	0	0	0	0	0
Principal rescheduled	..	..	0	72	26	14	46	1	0	0
Official	..	..	0	70	25	13	45	1	0	0
Private	..	..	0	2	1	1	1	0	0	0
Interest rescheduled	..	..	0	35	4	9	9	0	0	0
Official	..	..	0	33	4	9	9	0	0	0
Private	..	..	0	2	0	0	0	0	0	0
Debt forgiven	..	..	0	28	18	5	0	0	0	0
Memo: interest forgiven	..	..	0	2	119	0	3	0	0	0
Debt stock reduction	..	..	0	0	222	0	0	0	0	0
of which debt buyback	..	..	0	0	29	0	0	0	0	0
8. DEBT STOCK-FLOW RECONCILIATION										
Total change in debt stocks	..	..	85	97	-315	1	-31	113	-6	19
Net flows on debt	-8	62	11	90	-136	41	25	59	16	59
Net change in interest arrears	..	..	32	-38	-11	-1	2	13	12	11
Interest capitalized	..	..	0	35	4	9	9	0	0	0
Debt forgiveness or reduction	..	..	0	-28	-211	-5	0	0	0	0
Cross-currency valuation	..	..	44	25	12	-50	-72	21	-31	-44
Residual	..	..	-2	14	27	6	5	21	-3	-7
9. AVERAGE TERMS OF NEW COMMITMENTS										
ALL CREDITORS										
Interest (%)	2.9	5.3	2.3	1.5	0.6	0.6	0.0	2.6	0.0	0.8
Maturity (years)	26.7	25.5	26.6	43.5	32.6	34.5	0.0	30.6	1.3	39.8
Grace period (years)	5.6	5.9	8.9	9.0	7.8	8.5	0.0	5.7	0.3	10.3
Grant element (%)	49.9	32.7	60.8	73.2	70.4	73.0	0.0	54.8	8.3	80.6
Official creditors										
Interest (%)	2.1	4.7	1.2	1.5	0.6	0.6	0.0	2.6	0.0	0.8
Maturity (years)	33.0	30.3	30.6	43.5	32.6	34.5	0.0	30.6	1.3	39.8
Grace period (years)	6.8	7.7	10.2	9.0	7.8	8.5	0.0	5.7	0.3	10.3
Grant element (%)	61.6	40.4	71.1	73.2	70.4	73.0	0.0	54.8	8.3	80.6
Private creditors										
Interest (%)	5.4	7.0	9.1	0.0	0.0	0.0	0.0	0.0	0.0	0.0
Maturity (years)	6.7	12.8	3.0	0.0	0.0	0.0	0.0	0.0	0.0	0.0
Grace period (years)	1.7	1.3	1.0	0.0	0.0	0.0	0.0	0.0	0.0	0.0
Grant element (%)	12.7	12.5	1.2	0.0	0.0	0.0	0.0	0.0	0.0	0.0
Memorandum items										
Commitments	25	68	27	35	48	69	0	34	2	65
Official creditors	19	49	23	35	48	69	0	34	2	65
Private creditors	6	19	4	0	0	0	0	0	0	0

10. CONTRACTUAL OBLIGATIONS ON OUTSTANDING LONG-TERM DEBT

	2001	2002	2003	2004	2005	2006	2007	2008	2009	2010
TOTAL										
Disbursements	57	33	17	7	3	2	1	0	0	0
Principal	25	31	34	36	36	35	35	37	37	37
Interest	17	17	16	15	14	13	12	11	10	9
Official creditors										
Disbursements	57	33	17	7	3	2	1	0	0	0
Principal	25	31	34	36	36	35	35	37	37	37
Interest	17	17	16	15	14	13	12	11	10	9
Bilateral creditors										
Disbursements	1	1	0	0	0	0	0	0	0	0
Principal	14	19	19	19	18	18	19	20	20	19
Interest	12	11	11	10	9	9	8	7	6	5
Multilateral creditors										
Disbursements	56	33	17	7	3	2	1	0	0	0
Principal	11	12	15	17	18	17	17	17	17	18
Interest	5	5	5	5	5	5	5	4	4	4
Private creditors										
Disbursements	0	0	0	0	0	0	0	0	0	0
Principal	0	0	0	0	0	0	0	0	0	0
Interest	0	0	0	0	0	0	0	0	0	0
Commercial banks										
Disbursements	0	0	0	0	0	0	0	0	0	0
Principal	0	0	0	0	0	0	0	0	0	0
Interest	0	0	0	0	0	0	0	0	0	0
Other private										
Disbursements	0	0	0	0	0	0	0	0	0	0
Principal	0	0	0	0	0	0	0	0	0	0
Interest	0	0	0	0	0	0	0	0	0	0

SLOVAK REPUBLIC

(US$ million, unless otherwise indicated)

	1970	1980	1990	1994	1995	1996	1997	1998	1999	2000
1. SUMMARY DEBT DATA										
TOTAL DEBT STOCKS (EDT)	..	..	**2,008**	**4,758**	**5,744**	**6,057**	**8,775**	**9,537**	**9,891**	**9,462**
Long-term debt (LDOD)	..	..	**1,505**	**2,879**	**3,573**	**4,509**	**6,365**	**7,366**	**8,182**	**8,304**
Public and publicly guaranteed	..	..	1,505	2,866	3,488	3,963	4,443	4,363	4,424	4,883
Private nonguaranteed	..	..	0	13	85	546	1,922	3,003	3,758	3,421
Use of IMF credit	**0**	**0**	**0**	**642**	**457**	**319**	**249**	**190**	**133**	**0**
Short-term debt	..	..	**503**	**1,236**	**1,714**	**1,229**	**2,161**	**1,981**	**1,577**	**1,158**
of which interest arrears on LDOD	..	..	0	0	0	0	0	0	0	0
Official creditors	..	..	0	0	0	0	0	0	0	0
Private creditors	..	..	0	0	0	0	0	0	0	0
Memo: principal arrears on LDOD	..	..	0	2	0	2	0	28	41	242
Official creditors	..	..	0	0	0	0	0	0	0	0
Private creditors	..	..	0	2	0	2	0	28	41	242
Memo: export credits	..	..	0	401	570	540	595	617	638	294
TOTAL DEBT FLOWS										
Disbursements	..	..	**436**	**1,146**	**1,013**	**1,766**	**1,167**	**2,536**	**1,297**	**2,023**
Long-term debt	..	..	436	1,008	1,013	1,766	1,167	2,536	1,297	2,023
IMF purchases	0	0	0	138	0	0	0	0	0	0
Principal repayments	..	..	**171**	**546**	**862**	**821**	**381**	**1,443**	**1,176**	**2,033**
Long-term debt	..	..	171	457	662	697	330	1,375	1,124	1,905
IMF repurchases	0	0	0	89	201	124	52	68	52	127
Net flows on debt	..	..	**173**	**1,121**	**629**	**460**	**1,717**	**913**	**-283**	**-428**
of which short-term debt	..	..	-91	521	478	-484	932	-181	-404	-419
Interest payments (INT)	..	..	**147**	**297**	**419**	**515**	**416**	**564**	**514**	**557**
Long-term debt	..	..	84	182	282	291	222	443	421	460
IMF charges	0	0	0	30	32	17	13	10	6	6
Short-term debt	..	..	63	85	105	206	181	110	87	92
Net transfers on debt	..	..	**26**	**824**	**210**	**-54**	**1,301**	**349**	**-797**	**-986**
Total debt service paid (TDS)	..	..	**318**	**843**	**1,281**	**1,335**	**798**	**2,007**	**1,690**	**2,590**
Long-term debt	..	..	256	639	944	988	552	1,819	1,545	2,365
IMF repurchases and charges	0	0	0	119	233	141	65	78	58	133
Short-term debt (interest only)	..	..	63	85	105	206	181	110	87	92
2. AGGREGATE NET RESOURCE FLOWS AND NET TRANSFERS (LONG-TERM)										
NET RESOURCE FLOWS	..	..	**270**	**881**	**661**	**1,477**	**1,092**	**1,776**	**585**	**2,234**
Net flow of long-term debt (ex. IMF)	..	..	264	550	352	1,069	837	1,161	173	118
Foreign direct investment (net)	..	..	0	270	236	351	174	562	354	2,053
Portfolio equity flows	..	..	0	0	60	0	48	0	0	0
Grants (excluding technical coop.)	..	..	5	60	14	57	33	53	57	63
Memo: technical coop. grants	..	..	0	18	68	33	23	30	29	16
official net resource flows	..	..	-8	304	120	138	291	221	308	49
private net resource flows	..	..	278	577	541	1,339	801	1,555	277	2,185
NET TRANSFERS	..	..	**186**	**699**	**379**	**1,180**	**860**	**1,320**	**148**	**1,754**
Interest on long-term debt	..	..	84	182	282	291	222	443	421	460
Profit remittances on FDI	..	..	0	0	0	6	10	12	16	20
Memo: official net transfers	..	..	-20	274	83	100	251	152	254	-10
private net transfers	..	..	206	426	296	1,080	609	1,168	-106	1,764
3. MAJOR ECONOMIC AGGREGATES										
Gross national income (GNI)	..	..	15,497	14,429	18,363	19,728	20,288	21,151	19,410	18,767
Exports of goods & services (XGS)	..	..	..	9,123	11,219	11,117	12,131	13,450	12,369	14,405
of which workers remittances	..	..	..	..	0	4	7	..	..	..
Imports of goods & services (MGS)	..	..	..	8,520	10,922	13,404	14,258	15,942	13,722	15,219
International reserves (RES)	..	..	..	2,186	3,863	3,895	3,605	3,240	3,745	4,376
Current account balance	..	..	..	671	390	-2,090	-1,961	-2,126	-1,155	-694
4. DEBT INDICATORS										
EDT / XGS (%)	..	..	..	52.2	51.2	54.5	72.3	70.9	80.0	65.7
EDT / GNI (%)	..	..	13.0	33.0	31.3	30.7	43.3	45.1	51.0	50.4
TDS / XGS (%)	..	..	..	9.2	11.4	12.0	6.6	14.9	13.7	18.0
INT / XGS (%)	..	..	..	3.3	3.7	4.6	3.4	4.2	4.2	3.9
INT / GNI (%)	..	..	1.0	2.1	2.3	2.6	2.1	2.7	2.7	3.0
RES / EDT (%)	..	..	..	45.9	67.3	64.3	41.1	34.0	37.9	46.3
RES / MGS (months)	..	..	..	3.1	4.2	3.5	3.0	2.4	3.3	3.5
Short-term / EDT (%)	..	..	25.1	26.0	29.8	20.3	24.6	20.8	15.9	12.2
Concessional / EDT (%)	..	..	4.1	2.6	1.6	2.0	3.0	3.3	3.8	3.4
Multilateral / EDT (%)	..	..	4.4	8.9	7.7	7.6	5.8	6.7	7.5	6.7

SLOVAK REPUBLIC

(US$ million, unless otherwise indicated)

	1970	1980	1990	1994	1995	1996	1997	1998	1999	2000
5. LONG-TERM DEBT										
DEBT OUTSTANDING (LDOD)	..	..	**1,505**	**2,879**	**3,573**	**4,509**	**6,365**	**7,366**	**8,182**	**8,304**
Public and publicly guaranteed	..	..	**1,505**	**2,866**	**3,488**	**3,963**	**4,443**	**4,363**	**4,424**	**4,883**
Official creditors	..	..	126	595	617	652	829	1,070	1,281	1,115
Multilateral	..	..	89	422	442	463	511	637	746	629
Concessional	..	..	82	40	0	0	0	0	0	0
Bilateral	..	..	36	173	175	190	319	434	535	485
Concessional	..	..	0	83	91	124	264	318	376	323
Private creditors	..	..	1,380	2,271	2,871	3,310	3,614	3,293	3,143	3,768
Bonds	..	..	0	552	581	970	1,120	686	889	1,409
Commercial banks	..	..	866	629	406	273	579	835	649	904
Other private	..	..	514	1,091	1,884	2,067	1,915	1,772	1,605	1,456
Private nonguaranteed	..	..	**0**	**13**	**85**	**546**	**1,922**	**3,003**	**3,758**	**3,421**
Bonds	..	..	0	0	0	100	100	100	251	449
Commercial banks and other	..	..	0	13	85	446	1,822	2,903	3,507	2,972
Memo:										
IBRD	0	0	0	247	263	250	228	239	219	184
IDA	0	0	0	0	0	0	0	0	0	0
DISBURSEMENTS	..	..	**436**	**1,008**	**1,013**	**1,766**	**1,167**	**2,536**	**1,297**	**2,023**
Public and publicly guaranteed	..	..	**436**	**995**	**945**	**1,273**	**881**	**712**	**609**	**1,033**
Official creditors	..	..	8	265	161	97	295	208	309	107
Multilateral	..	..	2	216	84	51	114	125	214	71
Concessional	..	..	2	0	0	0	0	0	0	0
Bilateral	..	..	6	49	78	46	181	83	95	37
Concessional	..	..	0	26	77	46	166	22	19	0
Private creditors	..	..	428	730	784	1,176	585	504	300	925
Bonds	..	..	0	267	0	390	162	126	248	748
Commercial banks	..	..	209	134	74	107	383	371	47	177
Other private	..	..	218	329	710	680	40	7	5	0
Private nonguaranteed	..	..	**0**	**12**	**68**	**493**	**286**	**1,824**	**688**	**991**
Bonds	..	..	0	0	0	100	0	0	160	208
Commercial banks and other	..	..	0	12	68	393	286	1,824	528	783
Memo:										
IBRD	0	0	0	86	8	6	13	15	3	1
IDA	0	0	0	0	0	0	0	0	0	0
PRINCIPAL REPAYMENTS	..	..	**171**	**457**	**662**	**697**	**330**	**1,375**	**1,124**	**1,905**
Public and publicly guaranteed	..	..	**171**	**457**	**658**	**664**	**275**	**899**	**414**	**578**
Official creditors	..	..	22	22	55	15	38	40	58	122
Multilateral	..	..	3	11	42	2	18	30	42	99
Concessional	..	..	0	11	0	0	0	0	0	0
Bilateral	..	..	19	11	13	13	20	10	17	23
Concessional	..	..	0	0	0	0	0	3	5	12
Private creditors	..	..	150	436	604	649	238	859	356	456
Bonds	..	..	0	63	0	0	10	570	5	199
Commercial banks	..	..	14	158	194	225	45	136	186	102
Other private	..	..	136	215	410	425	182	153	165	155
Private nonguaranteed	..	..	**0**	**0**	**3**	**32**	**55**	**476**	**710**	**1,328**
Bonds	..	..	0	0	0	0	0	0	0	0
Commercial banks and other	..	..	0	0	3	32	55	476	710	1,328
Memo:										
IBRD	0	0	0	0	0	0	15	17	20	23
IDA	0	0	0	0	0	0	0	0	0	0
NET FLOWS ON DEBT	..	..	**264**	**550**	**352**	**1,069**	**837**	**1,161**	**173**	**118**
Public and publicly guaranteed	..	..	**264**	**538**	**287**	**609**	**605**	**-187**	**195**	**455**
Official creditors	..	..	-14	244	107	82	258	168	250	-15
Multilateral	..	..	0	205	42	48	96	95	172	-28
Concessional	..	..	2	-11	0	0	0	0	0	0
Bilateral	..	..	-13	39	65	33	162	73	78	14
Concessional	..	..	0	26	77	46	166	19	14	-12
Private creditors	..	..	278	295	180	527	348	-355	-55	469
Bonds	..	..	0	204	0	390	152	-444	243	550
Commercial banks	..	..	195	-24	-120	-118	338	235	-139	75
Other private	..	..	83	115	300	256	-142	-146	-159	-155
Private nonguaranteed	..	..	**0**	**12**	**65**	**461**	**232**	**1,348**	**-22**	**-337**
Bonds	..	..	0	0	0	100	0	0	160	208
Commercial banks and other	..	..	0	12	65	361	232	1,348	-182	-545
Memo:										
IBRD	0	0	0	86	8	6	-2	-2	-18	-22
IDA	0	0	0	0	0	0	0	0	0	0

SLOVAK REPUBLIC

(US$ million, unless otherwise indicated)

	1970	1980	1990	1994	1995	1996	1997	1998	1999	2000
INTEREST PAYMENTS (LINT)	..	..	**84**	**182**	**282**	**291**	**222**	**443**	**421**	**460**
Public and publicly guaranteed	..	..	**84**	**181**	**282**	**269**	**191**	**252**	**199**	**208**
Official creditors	..	..	12	31	38	39	40	69	54	59
Multilateral	..	..	9	24	29	30	31	52	35	39
Concessional	..	..	8	11	0	0	0	0	0	0
Bilateral	..	..	3	6	8	9	10	17	19	20
Concessional	..	..	0	0	2	4	5	5	10	11
Private creditors	..	..	72	151	244	230	151	183	146	149
Bonds	..	..	0	7	53	61	72	75	47	54
Commercial banks	..	..	46	86	51	19	17	50	45	48
Other private	..	..	27	58	141	150	61	58	54	48
Private nonguaranteed	..	..	**0**	**0**	**1**	**23**	**31**	**192**	**221**	**252**
Bonds	..	..	0	0	0	0	6	7	7	21
Commercial banks and other	..	..	0	0	1	23	26	185	215	232
Memo:										
IBRD	0	0	0	12	17	17	16	14	14	11
IDA	0	0	0	0	0	0	0	0	0	0
NET TRANSFERS ON DEBT	..	..	**180**	**369**	**69**	**778**	**615**	**718**	**-248**	**-342**
Public and publicly guaranteed	..	..	**180**	**357**	**5**	**340**	**415**	**-439**	**-4**	**247**
Official creditors	..	..	-26	213	69	43	217	100	197	-73
Multilateral	..	..	-9	181	13	19	65	43	138	-67
Concessional	..	..	-6	-21	0	0	0	0	0	0
Bilateral	..	..	-17	32	56	24	152	56	59	-7
Concessional	..	..	0	26	76	42	161	13	4	-23
Private creditors	..	..	206	144	-64	297	197	-538	-201	320
Bonds	..	..	0	197	-53	329	80	-520	197	496
Commercial banks	..	..	150	-110	-170	-138	321	186	-184	27
Other private	..	..	56	57	159	106	-203	-204	-213	-203
Private nonguaranteed	..	..	**0**	**12**	**64**	**438**	**200**	**1,156**	**-244**	**-589**
Bonds	..	..	0	0	0	100	-6	-7	153	187
Commercial banks and other	..	..	0	12	64	338	206	1,163	-397	-776
Memo:										
IBRD	0	0	0	74	-9	-11	-18	-16	-32	-33
IDA	0	0	0	0	0	0	0	0	0	0
DEBT SERVICE (LTDS)	..	..	**256**	**639**	**944**	**988**	**552**	**1,819**	**1,545**	**2,365**
Public and publicly guaranteed	..	..	**256**	**638**	**940**	**933**	**466**	**1,151**	**613**	**786**
Official creditors	..	..	34	52	92	54	78	109	112	181
Multilateral	..	..	11	35	71	32	48	82	76	138
Concessional	..	..	8	21	0	0	0	0	0	0
Bilateral	..	..	22	17	21	22	29	27	36	43
Concessional	..	..	0	0	2	4	5	8	15	23
Private creditors	..	..	222	586	848	879	388	1,042	501	605
Bonds	..	..	0	70	53	61	83	646	52	253
Commercial banks	..	..	60	244	244	244	63	185	231	150
Other private	..	..	162	273	551	574	243	211	219	203
Private nonguaranteed	..	..	**0**	**1**	**4**	**55**	**86**	**668**	**931**	**1,580**
Bonds	..	..	0	0	0	0	6	7	7	21
Commercial banks and other	..	..	0	1	4	55	80	661	924	1,559
Memo:										
IBRD	0	0	0	12	17	17	30	31	34	34
IDA	0	0	0	0	0	0	0	0	0	0
UNDISBURSED DEBT	..	..	**211**	**351**	**342**	**890**	**719**	**349**	**339**	**264**
Official creditors	..	..	0	277	193	377	327	266	291	235
Private creditors	..	..	211	73	150	514	392	83	48	29
Memorandum items										
Concessional LDOD	..	..	82	123	91	124	264	318	376	323
Variable rate LDOD	..	..	182	400	734	1,214	3,100	4,604	5,302	4,864
Public sector LDOD	..	..	1,505	2,744	3,361	3,815	4,232	4,116	4,229	4,778
Private sector LDOD	..	..	0	135	212	694	2,134	3,250	3,953	3,526

6. CURRENCY COMPOSITION OF LONG-TERM DEBT (PERCENT)

	1970	1980	1990	1994	1995	1996	1997	1998	1999	2000
Deutsche mark	..	..	39.3	13.4	5.6	5.3	7.1	11.2	8.3	6.0
French franc	..	..	4.7	3.2	3.0	2.3	1.4	1.2	1.0	5.0
Japanese yen	..	..	3.7	0.8	2.6	3.1	6.0	7.3	8.5	8.6
Pound sterling	..	..	0.5	0.2	0.1	0.1	0.0	0.0	0.0	0.0
Swiss franc	..	..	5.1	0.3	0.1	0.4	0.5	0.6	0.3	0.0
U.S.dollars	..	..	35.5	12.9	1.5	12.3	17.4	25.2	23.2	16.0
Multiple currency	..	..	5.6	66.1	82.5	72.1	62.2	48.0	43.3	35.5
Special drawing rights	..	..	0.0	0.0	0.0	0.0	0.0	0.0	0.0	0.0
All other currencies	..	..	5.6	3.1	4.6	4.4	5.4	6.5	15.4	28.9

SLOVAK REPUBLIC

(US$ million, unless otherwise indicated)

	1970	1980	1990	1994	1995	1996	1997	1998	1999	2000
7. DEBT RESTRUCTURINGS										
Total amount rescheduled	..	..	0	0	0	0	0	0	0	0
Debt stock rescheduled	..	..	0	0	0	0	0	0	0	0
Principal rescheduled	..	..	0	0	0	0	0	0	0	0
Official	..	..	0	0	0	0	0	0	0	0
Private	..	..	0	0	0	0	0	0	0	0
Interest rescheduled	..	..	0	0	0	0	0	0	0	0
Official	..	..	0	0	0	0	0	0	0	0
Private	..	..	0	0	0	0	0	0	0	0
Debt forgiven	..	..	0	1	0	0	0	0	0	0
Memo: interest forgiven	..	..	0	0	0	0	0	0	0	0
Debt stock reduction	..	..	0	0	0	0	0	0	0	0
of which debt buyback	..	..	0	0	0	0	0	0	0	0
8. DEBT STOCK-FLOW RECONCILIATION										
Total change in debt stocks	..	..	181	1,365	986	314	2,718	762	354	-429
Net flows on debt	..	..	173	1,121	629	460	1,717	913	-283	-428
Net change in interest arrears	..	..	0	0	0	0	0	0	0	0
Interest capitalized	..	..	0	0	0	0	0	0	0	0
Debt forgiveness or reduction	..	..	0	-1	0	0	0	0	0	0
Cross-currency valuation	..	..	53	99	67	-74	-115	99	-84	-139
Residual	..	..	-46	145	292	-72	1,116	-250	722	138
9. AVERAGE TERMS OF NEW COMMITMENTS										
ALL CREDITORS										
Interest (%)	..	..	7.8	7.8	6.1	6.6	5.4	6.6	6.4	7.1
Maturity (years)	..	..	6.0	11.0	7.3	9.4	8.8	7.1	13.9	8.0
Grace period (years)	..	..	3.6	6.5	3.5	4.2	4.1	2.6	3.1	6.9
Grant element (%)	..	..	6.9	7.1	16.9	14.8	19.5	11.5	19.8	13.3
Official creditors										
Interest (%)	..	..	3.4	5.1	3.7	5.2	3.9	6.1	4.6	7.1
Maturity (years)	..	..	19.1	14.0	14.3	14.0	13.8	11.9	21.1	12.0
Grace period (years)	..	..	5.3	3.9	4.5	4.6	4.9	2.8	2.4	3.5
Grant element (%)	..	..	46.1	23.1	35.5	26.5	33.9	18.5	32.9	13.9
Private creditors										
Interest (%)	..	..	7.8	8.7	7.3	7.0	6.3	7.0	8.8	7.1
Maturity (years)	..	..	5.9	10.0	3.7	8.0	5.9	3.7	4.6	7.7
Grace period (years)	..	..	3.5	7.4	2.9	4.0	3.6	2.4	4.1	7.2
Grant element (%)	..	..	6.6	1.7	7.3	11.2	11.3	6.7	2.9	13.2
Memorandum items										
Commitments	..	..	265	725	273	1,236	771	322	627	1,001
Official creditors	..	..	2	184	94	292	282	131	355	81
Private creditors	..	..	263	541	179	944	489	191	273	920

10. CONTRACTUAL OBLIGATIONS ON OUTSTANDING LONG-TERM DEBT

	2001	2002	2003	2004	2005	2006	2007	2008	2009	2010
TOTAL										
Disbursements	132	69	31	17	9	4	2	0	0	0
Principal	1,243	859	856	819	474	808	748	297	1,011	655
Interest	409	372	327	274	227	196	164	98	120	53
Official creditors										
Disbursements	113	61	29	17	9	4	2	0	0	0
Principal	92	127	135	138	138	141	123	106	87	79
Interest	54	60	55	48	41	33	26	20	14	10
Bilateral creditors										
Disbursements	34	44	28	17	9	4	2	0	0	0
Principal	31	58	57	60	60	63	61	55	44	36
Interest	19	23	21	19	16	13	10	8	5	4
Multilateral creditors										
Disbursements	79	17	1	0	0	0	0	0	0	0
Principal	61	69	78	78	78	78	62	51	43	43
Interest	35	38	34	29	24	20	16	12	9	7
Private creditors										
Disbursements	19	8	2	0	0	0	0	0	0	0
Principal	1,151	731	721	681	336	667	625	191	924	576
Interest	355	312	272	226	187	163	138	79	105	43
Commercial banks										
Disbursements	19	8	2	0	0	0	0	0	0	0
Principal	106	148	112	112	77	48	47	25	3	1
Interest	51	44	32	23	14	9	5	2	0	0
Other private										
Disbursements	0	0	0	0	0	0	0	0	0	0
Principal	1,045	583	608	569	258	619	578	166	921	576
Interest	305	268	240	203	173	154	133	77	105	43

SOLOMON ISLANDS

(US$ million, unless otherwise indicated)

	1970	1980	1990	1994	1995	1996	1997	1998	1999	2000
1. SUMMARY DEBT DATA										
TOTAL DEBT STOCKS (EDT)	..	**19.4**	**120.5**	**154.9**	**158.7**	**147.5**	**139.9**	**154.6**	**165.0**	**155.4**
Long-term debt (LDOD)	..	**17.4**	**103.2**	**152.9**	**149.1**	**146.0**	**137.7**	**151.7**	**160.3**	**152.1**
Public and publicly guaranteed	..	17.4	103.2	98.4	100.3	100.5	96.5	113.7	125.3	120.7
Private nonguaranteed	..	0.0	0.0	54.5	48.8	45.6	41.2	38.1	35.0	31.5
Use of IMF credit	**0.0**	**0.0**	**0.7**	**0.0**	**0.0**	**0.0**	**0.0**	**0.0**	**0.0**	**0.0**
Short-term debt	..	**2.0**	**16.6**	**2.0**	**9.7**	**1.4**	**2.2**	**2.9**	**4.7**	**3.2**
of which interest arrears on LDOD	..	0.0	0.1	0.0	8.4	0.6	2.1	1.7	1.8	1.8
Official creditors	..	0.0	0.1	0.0	0.5	0.4	1.6	1.0	1.1	0.4
Private creditors	..	0.0	0.0	0.0	8.0	0.2	0.5	0.7	0.7	1.4
Memo: principal arrears on LDOD	..	0.0	0.2	1.2	11.4	2.4	5.0	4.1	4.3	3.3
Official creditors	..	0.0	0.2	0.0	1.5	2.2	4.0	3.1	3.2	1.0
Private creditors	..	0.0	0.0	1.2	9.9	0.2	1.0	1.1	1.1	2.3
Memo: export credits	..	0.0	29.0	62.5	70.6	54.5	54.6	44.2	50.3	44.7
TOTAL DEBT FLOWS										
Disbursements	..	**4.0**	**5.2**	**10.4**	**11.8**	**5.5**	**5.0**	**18.6**	**9.0**	**3.4**
Long-term debt	..	4.0	5.2	10.4	11.8	5.5	5.0	18.6	9.0	3.4
IMF purchases	0.0	0.0	0.0	0.0	0.0	0.0	0.0	0.0	0.0	0.0
Principal repayments	..	**0.0**	**7.9**	**12.5**	**6.5**	**6.3**	**4.4**	**7.8**	**7.3**	**6.2**
Long-term debt	..	0.0	7.0	12.5	6.5	6.3	4.4	7.8	7.3	6.2
IMF repurchases	0.0	0.0	0.8	0.0	0.0	0.0	0.0	0.0	0.0	0.0
Net flows on debt	..	**4.9**	**13.8**	**-6.3**	**4.5**	**-1.2**	**-0.1**	**11.8**	**3.5**	**-4.4**
of which short-term debt	..	1.0	16.5	-4.1	-0.8	-0.4	-0.7	1.0	1.8	-1.5
Interest payments (INT)	..	**0.3**	**3.7**	**3.3**	**1.6**	**2.1**	**1.3**	**4.1**	**3.6**	**2.9**
Long-term debt	..	0.0	3.1	3.1	1.5	2.0	1.3	4.0	3.5	2.7
IMF charges	0.0	0.0	0.1	0.0	0.0	0.0	0.0	0.0	0.0	0.0
Short-term debt	..	0.3	0.5	0.2	0.1	0.0	0.0	0.1	0.1	0.1
Net transfers on debt	..	**4.7**	**10.1**	**-9.6**	**3.0**	**-3.3**	**-1.4**	**7.7**	**-0.1**	**-7.3**
Total debt service paid (TDS)	..	**0.3**	**11.6**	**15.9**	**8.1**	**8.4**	**5.7**	**11.9**	**10.9**	**9.1**
Long-term debt	..	0.0	10.1	15.6	8.0	8.3	5.7	11.9	10.9	9.0
IMF repurchases and charges	0.0	0.0	1.0	0.0	0.0	0.0	0.0	0.0	0.0	0.0
Short-term debt (interest only)	..	0.3	0.5	0.2	0.1	0.0	0.0	0.1	0.1	0.1
2. AGGREGATE NET RESOURCE FLOWS AND NET TRANSFERS (LONG-TERM)										
NET RESOURCE FLOWS	..	**27.3**	**28.4**	**17.6**	**27.9**	**23.7**	**50.3**	**30.1**	**24.3**	**55.7**
Net flow of long-term debt (ex. IMF)	..	3.9	-1.8	-2.2	5.3	-0.8	0.6	10.8	1.7	-2.9
Foreign direct investment (net)	..	2.4	10.0	2.1	2.0	5.9	33.8	8.8	9.9	9.9
Portfolio equity flows	..	0.0	0.0	0.0	0.0	0.0	0.0	0.0	0.0	0.0
Grants (excluding technical coop.)	..	21.0	20.2	17.6	20.6	18.6	15.9	10.5	12.7	48.7
Memo: technical coop. grants	..	11.5	19.5	25.5	26.0	21.4	18.5	17.5	18.4	21.0
official net resource flows	..	24.9	21.5	17.5	24.1	21.9	20.2	24.8	17.9	49.3
private net resource flows	..	2.4	6.9	0.1	3.8	1.8	30.1	5.3	6.4	6.4
NET TRANSFERS	..	**12.4**	**23.3**	**8.5**	**21.4**	**14.6**	**41.0**	**17.1**	**11.7**	**45.0**
Interest on long-term debt	..	0.0	3.1	3.1	1.5	2.0	1.3	4.0	3.5	2.7
Profit remittances on FDI	..	14.9	2.0	6.0	5.0	7.0	8.0	9.0	9.0	8.0
Memo: official net transfers	..	24.9	19.9	16.0	23.3	20.7	19.9	23.3	16.6	48.5
private net transfers	..	-12.5	3.4	-7.5	-1.9	-6.1	21.1	-6.2	-4.9	-3.5
3. MAJOR ECONOMIC AGGREGATES										
Gross national income (GNI)	..	107.9	207.3	289.9	320.7	337.6	350.8	312.3	332.4	285.3
Exports of goods & services (XGS)	..	85.0	97.8	193.6	211.3	217.0	229.5	199.0	226.3	135.4
of which workers remittances	..	0.0	0.0	0.0	0.0	0.0	0.0	0.0	..	..
Imports of goods & services (MGS)	..	117.0	163.6	252.6	239.4	245.4	302.9	224.4	219.9	172.9
International reserves (RES)	..	29.6	17.6	17.4	15.9	32.6	36.3	49.0	51.1	31.3
Current account balance	..	-12.2	-27.8	-3.4	8.3	14.6	-37.9	8.1	21.5	..
4. DEBT INDICATORS										
EDT / XGS (%)	..	22.8	123.2	80.0	75.1	68.0	61.0	77.7	72.9	114.8
EDT / GNI (%)	..	18.0	58.1	53.4	49.5	43.7	39.9	49.5	49.7	54.5
TDS / XGS (%)	..	0.4	11.9	8.2	3.8	3.9	2.5	6.0	4.8	6.7
INT / XGS (%)	..	0.4	3.8	1.7	0.8	1.0	0.6	2.1	1.6	2.1
INT / GNI (%)	..	0.3	1.8	1.1	0.5	0.6	0.4	1.3	1.1	1.0
RES / EDT (%)	..	152.6	14.6	11.2	10.0	22.1	26.0	31.7	31.0	20.1
RES / MGS (months)	..	3.0	1.3	0.8	0.8	1.6	1.4	2.6	2.8	2.2
Short-term / EDT (%)	..	10.3	13.8	1.3	6.1	1.0	1.6	1.9	2.9	2.1
Concessional / EDT (%)	..	89.7	64.2	53.6	54.3	60.1	61.0	66.2	69.9	74.3
Multilateral / EDT (%)	..	36.6	51.0	48.3	50.1	54.8	54.5	60.7	65.4	64.6

SOLOMON ISLANDS

(US$ million, unless otherwise indicated)

	1970	1980	1990	1994	1995	1996	1997	1998	1999	2000
5. LONG-TERM DEBT										
DEBT OUTSTANDING (LDOD)	..	**17.4**	**103.2**	**152.9**	**149.1**	**146.0**	**137.7**	**151.7**	**160.3**	**152.1**
Public and publicly guaranteed	..	**17.4**	**103.2**	**98.4**	**100.3**	**100.5**	**96.5**	**113.7**	**125.3**	**120.7**
Official creditors	..	17.4	89.1	91.2	95.1	96.2	92.4	109.9	121.9	117.3
Multilateral	..	7.1	61.5	74.8	79.5	80.8	76.2	93.9	107.9	100.4
Concessional	..	7.1	61.5	74.8	78.2	79.6	75.1	92.8	106.9	99.5
Bilateral	..	10.3	27.7	16.4	15.6	15.4	16.2	16.0	14.0	16.9
Concessional	..	10.3	15.8	8.2	8.0	9.1	10.2	9.6	8.4	16.0
Private creditors	..	0.0	14.1	7.2	5.2	4.2	4.2	3.8	3.4	3.4
Bonds	..	0.0	0.0	0.0	0.0	0.0	0.0	0.0	0.0	0.0
Commercial banks	..	0.0	10.9	0.0	0.0	0.0	0.0	0.0	0.0	0.0
Other private	..	0.0	3.2	7.2	5.2	4.2	4.2	3.8	3.4	3.4
Private nonguaranteed	..	**0.0**	**0.0**	**54.5**	**48.8**	**45.6**	**41.2**	**38.1**	**35.0**	**31.5**
Bonds	..	0.0	0.0	0.0	0.0	0.0	0.0	0.0	0.0	0.0
Commercial banks and other	..	0.0	0.0	54.5	48.8	45.6	41.2	38.1	35.0	31.5
Memo:										
IBRD	0.0	0.0	0.0	0.0	0.0	0.0	0.0	0.0	0.0	0.0
IDA	0.0	0.0	16.6	22.4	25.9	29.2	29.9	32.7	39.9	38.4
DISBURSEMENTS	..	**4.0**	**5.2**	**10.4**	**11.8**	**5.5**	**5.0**	**18.6**	**9.0**	**3.4**
Public and publicly guaranteed	..	**4.0**	**5.2**	**2.8**	**9.1**	**5.5**	**5.0**	**18.6**	**9.0**	**3.4**
Official creditors	..	4.0	5.2	2.8	4.8	5.5	5.0	18.6	9.0	3.4
Multilateral	..	4.0	5.2	2.8	4.8	4.5	3.3	18.2	8.6	1.4
Concessional	..	4.0	5.2	2.8	3.5	4.5	3.3	18.2	8.6	1.4
Bilateral	..	0.0	0.0	0.0	0.0	1.0	1.7	0.4	0.4	2.0
Concessional	..	0.0	0.0	0.0	0.0	1.0	1.7	0.4	0.4	2.0
Private creditors	..	0.0	0.0	0.0	4.2	0.0	0.0	0.0	0.0	0.0
Bonds	..	0.0	0.0	0.0	0.0	0.0	0.0	0.0	0.0	0.0
Commercial banks	..	0.0	0.0	0.0	0.0	0.0	0.0	0.0	0.0	0.0
Other private	..	0.0	0.0	0.0	4.2	0.0	0.0	0.0	0.0	0.0
Private nonguaranteed	..	**0.0**	**0.0**	**7.6**	**2.8**	**0.0**	**0.0**	**0.0**	**0.0**	**0.0**
Bonds	..	0.0	0.0	0.0	0.0	0.0	0.0	0.0	0.0	0.0
Commercial banks and other	..	0.0	0.0	7.6	2.8	0.0	0.0	0.0	0.0	0.0
Memo:										
IBRD	0.0	0.0	0.0	0.0	0.0	0.0	0.0	0.0	0.0	0.0
IDA	0.0	0.0	2.5	1.8	3.2	4.3	2.6	1.9	8.0	0.6
PRINCIPAL REPAYMENTS	..	**0.0**	**7.0**	**12.5**	**6.5**	**6.3**	**4.4**	**7.8**	**7.3**	**6.2**
Public and publicly guaranteed	..	**0.0**	**7.0**	**6.0**	**1.8**	**3.1**	**0.7**	**4.7**	**4.3**	**2.7**
Official creditors	..	0.0	3.9	2.9	1.3	2.2	0.7	4.3	3.8	2.7
Multilateral	..	0.0	0.5	0.9	0.6	0.9	0.3	3.3	1.4	1.1
Concessional	..	0.0	0.5	0.9	0.6	0.9	0.3	3.3	1.4	1.1
Bilateral	..	0.0	3.4	2.0	0.7	1.3	0.4	1.0	2.4	1.6
Concessional	..	0.0	1.4	0.8	0.2	0.4	0.4	1.0	1.4	1.6
Private creditors	..	0.0	3.1	3.1	0.5	0.9	0.0	0.4	0.4	0.0
Bonds	..	0.0	0.0	0.0	0.0	0.0	0.0	0.0	0.0	0.0
Commercial banks	..	0.0	2.7	2.7	0.0	0.0	0.0	0.0	0.0	0.0
Other private	..	0.0	0.4	0.4	0.5	0.9	0.0	0.4	0.4	0.0
Private nonguaranteed	..	**0.0**	**0.0**	**6.5**	**4.7**	**3.2**	**3.7**	**3.1**	**3.1**	**3.5**
Bonds	..	0.0	0.0	0.0	0.0	0.0	0.0	0.0	0.0	0.0
Commercial banks and other	..	0.0	0.0	6.5	4.7	3.2	3.7	3.1	3.1	3.5
Memo:										
IBRD	0.0	0.0	0.0	0.0	0.0	0.0	0.0	0.0	0.0	0.0
IDA	0.0	0.0	0.0	0.1	0.1	0.2	0.2	0.2	0.2	0.2
NET FLOWS ON DEBT	..	**3.9**	**-1.8**	**-2.2**	**5.3**	**-0.8**	**0.6**	**10.8**	**1.7**	**-2.9**
Public and publicly guaranteed	..	**3.9**	**-1.8**	**-3.2**	**7.3**	**2.4**	**4.3**	**13.9**	**4.8**	**0.6**
Official creditors	..	3.9	1.3	-0.1	3.5	3.3	4.3	14.3	5.2	0.6
Multilateral	..	4.0	4.7	1.9	4.2	3.7	3.0	15.0	7.2	0.3
Concessional	..	4.0	4.7	1.9	2.9	3.7	3.0	15.0	7.2	0.3
Bilateral	..	0.0	-3.4	-2.0	-0.7	-0.4	1.4	-0.7	-2.0	0.3
Concessional	..	0.0	-1.4	-0.8	-0.2	0.6	1.4	-0.7	-1.0	0.3
Private creditors	..	0.0	-3.1	-3.1	3.8	-0.9	0.0	-0.4	-0.4	0.0
Bonds	..	0.0	0.0	0.0	0.0	0.0	0.0	0.0	0.0	0.0
Commercial banks	..	0.0	-2.7	-2.7	0.0	0.0	0.0	0.0	0.0	0.0
Other private	..	0.0	-0.4	-0.4	3.8	-0.9	0.0	-0.4	-0.4	0.0
Private nonguaranteed	..	**0.0**	**0.0**	**1.1**	**-2.0**	**-3.2**	**-3.7**	**-3.1**	**-3.1**	**-3.5**
Bonds	..	0.0	0.0	0.0	0.0	0.0	0.0	0.0	0.0	0.0
Commercial banks and other	..	0.0	0.0	1.1	-2.0	-3.2	-3.7	-3.1	-3.1	-3.5
Memo:										
IBRD	0.0	0.0	0.0	0.0	0.0	0.0	0.0	0.0	0.0	0.0
IDA	0.0	0.0	2.5	1.7	3.1	4.2	2.4	1.7	7.8	0.4

SOLOMON ISLANDS

(US$ million, unless otherwise indicated)

	1970	1980	1990	1994	1995	1996	1997	1998	1999	2000
INTEREST PAYMENTS (LINT)	..	**0.0**	**3.1**	**3.1**	**1.5**	**2.0**	**1.3**	**4.0**	**3.5**	**2.7**
Public and publicly guaranteed	..	**0.0**	**3.1**	**2.1**	**0.9**	**1.5**	**0.3**	**1.8**	**1.5**	**0.8**
Official creditors	..	0.0	1.6	1.5	0.8	1.2	0.3	1.5	1.3	0.8
Multilateral	..	0.0	0.6	0.7	0.5	0.6	0.2	1.5	1.0	0.7
Concessional	..	0.0	0.6	0.7	0.5	0.6	0.2	1.5	1.0	0.7
Bilateral	..	0.0	1.0	0.8	0.3	0.6	0.1	0.0	0.2	0.1
Concessional	..	0.0	0.0	0.1	0.0	0.1	0.1	0.0	0.0	0.1
Private creditors	..	0.0	1.5	0.6	0.1	0.4	0.0	0.3	0.2	0.0
Bonds	..	0.0	0.0	0.0	0.0	0.0	0.0	0.0	0.0	0.0
Commercial banks	..	0.0	1.2	0.1	0.0	0.0	0.0	0.0	0.0	0.0
Other private	..	0.0	0.3	0.5	0.1	0.4	0.0	0.3	0.2	0.0
Private nonguaranteed	..	**0.0**	**0.0**	**1.0**	**0.6**	**0.5**	**1.0**	**2.2**	**2.1**	**1.9**
Bonds	..	0.0	0.0	0.0	0.0	0.0	0.0	0.0	0.0	0.0
Commercial banks and other	..	0.0	0.0	1.0	0.6	0.5	1.0	2.2	2.1	1.9
Memo:										
IBRD	0.0	0.0	0.0	0.0	0.0	0.0	0.0	0.0	0.0	0.0
IDA	0.0	0.0	0.1	0.2	0.2	0.2	0.2	0.2	0.3	0.3
NET TRANSFERS ON DEBT	..	**3.9**	**-4.9**	**-5.3**	**3.8**	**-2.8**	**-0.7**	**6.7**	**-1.9**	**-5.6**
Public and publicly guaranteed	..	**3.9**	**-4.9**	**-5.3**	**6.3**	**0.9**	**4.0**	**12.1**	**3.3**	**-0.2**
Official creditors	..	3.9	-0.3	-1.6	2.7	2.1	4.0	12.8	3.9	-0.2
Multilateral	..	3.9	4.1	1.2	3.7	3.1	2.7	13.5	6.2	-0.5
Concessional	..	3.9	4.1	1.2	2.4	3.1	2.7	13.5	6.2	-0.5
Bilateral	..	0.0	-4.4	-2.8	-1.0	-0.9	1.3	-0.7	-2.3	0.2
Concessional	..	0.0	-1.4	-0.9	-0.2	0.5	1.3	-0.7	-1.0	0.2
Private creditors	..	0.0	-4.7	-3.7	3.7	-1.3	0.0	-0.6	-0.6	0.0
Bonds	..	0.0	0.0	0.0	0.0	0.0	0.0	0.0	0.0	0.0
Commercial banks	..	0.0	-3.9	-2.8	0.0	0.0	0.0	0.0	0.0	0.0
Other private	..	0.0	-0.7	-0.9	3.7	-1.3	0.0	-0.6	-0.6	0.0
Private nonguaranteed	..	**0.0**	**0.0**	**0.0**	**-2.5**	**-3.7**	**-4.6**	**-5.4**	**-5.1**	**-5.4**
Bonds	..	0.0	0.0	0.0	0.0	0.0	0.0	0.0	0.0	0.0
Commercial banks and other	..	0.0	0.0	0.0	-2.5	-3.7	-4.6	-5.4	-5.1	-5.4
Memo:										
IBRD	0.0	0.0	0.0	0.0	0.0	0.0	0.0	0.0	0.0	0.0
IDA	0.0	0.0	2.4	1.6	3.0	4.0	2.2	1.4	7.5	0.2
DEBT SERVICE (LTDS)	..	**0.0**	**10.1**	**15.6**	**8.0**	**8.3**	**5.7**	**11.9**	**10.9**	**9.0**
Public and publicly guaranteed	..	**0.0**	**10.1**	**8.1**	**2.7**	**4.6**	**1.1**	**6.5**	**5.7**	**3.6**
Official creditors	..	0.0	5.5	4.4	2.1	3.4	1.1	5.8	5.1	3.6
Multilateral	..	0.0	1.1	1.6	1.1	1.5	0.6	4.8	2.4	1.8
Concessional	..	0.0	1.1	1.6	1.1	1.5	0.6	4.8	2.4	1.8
Bilateral	..	0.0	4.4	2.8	1.0	1.9	0.5	1.1	2.7	1.7
Concessional	..	0.0	1.4	0.9	0.2	0.5	0.5	1.1	1.4	1.7
Private creditors	..	0.0	4.7	3.7	0.6	1.3	0.0	0.6	0.6	0.0
Bonds	..	0.0	0.0	0.0	0.0	0.0	0.0	0.0	0.0	0.0
Commercial banks	..	0.0	3.9	2.8	0.0	0.0	0.0	0.0	0.0	0.0
Other private	..	0.0	0.7	0.9	0.6	1.3	0.0	0.6	0.6	0.0
Private nonguaranteed	..	**0.0**	**0.0**	**7.5**	**5.3**	**3.7**	**4.6**	**5.4**	**5.1**	**5.4**
Bonds	..	0.0	0.0	0.0	0.0	0.0	0.0	0.0	0.0	0.0
Commercial banks and other	..	0.0	0.0	7.5	5.3	3.7	4.6	5.4	5.1	5.4
Memo:										
IBRD	0.0	0.0	0.0	0.0	0.0	0.0	0.0	0.0	0.0	0.0
IDA	0.0	0.0	0.1	0.3	0.3	0.4	0.4	0.4	0.5	0.4
UNDISBURSED DEBT	..	**12.9**	**25.4**	**21.0**	**25.1**	**19.0**	**13.0**	**22.0**	**26.2**	**15.8**
Official creditors	..	12.9	10.4	21.0	25.1	19.0	13.0	22.0	26.2	15.8
Private creditors	..	0.0	15.0	0.0	0.0	0.0	0.0	0.0	0.0	0.0
Memorandum items										
Concessional LDOD	..	17.4	77.2	83.0	86.2	88.6	85.3	102.4	115.3	115.5
Variable rate LDOD	..	0.0	10.9	54.5	48.8	45.6	41.2	38.1	35.0	31.5
Public sector LDOD	..	17.4	103.2	98.4	100.3	100.5	96.5	113.7	125.3	120.7
Private sector LDOD	..	0.0	0.0	54.5	48.8	45.6	41.2	38.1	35.0	31.5

6. CURRENCY COMPOSITION OF LONG-TERM DEBT (PERCENT)

	1970	1980	1990	1994	1995	1996	1997	1998	1999	2000
Deutsche mark	..	0.0	3.1	1.3	0.9	0.4	0.4	0.0	0.0	0.0
French franc	..	0.0	0.0	0.0	0.0	0.0	0.0	0.0	0.0	0.0
Japanese yen	..	0.0	4.8	10.3	3.8	2.9	2.7	2.5	2.2	3.4
Pound sterling	..	59.1	13.1	6.5	6.4	7.0	7.0	5.6	4.4	2.9
Swiss franc	..	0.0	0.0	0.0	0.0	0.0	0.0	0.0	0.0	0.0
U.S.dollars	..	40.9	52.0	48.0	53.9	55.7	57.0	63.9	66.4	67.1
Multiple currency	..	0.0	7.3	12.8	12.6	12.6	11.5	10.0	10.8	9.9
Special drawing rights	..	0.0	6.3	8.5	8.3	7.7	7.2	6.3	7.5	6.7
All other currencies	..	0.0	13.4	12.6	14.1	13.7	14.2	11.7	8.7	10.0

SOLOMON ISLANDS

(US$ million, unless otherwise indicated)

	1970	1980	1990	1994	1995	1996	1997	1998	1999	2000
7. DEBT RESTRUCTURINGS										
Total amount rescheduled	..	..	0.0	0.0	0.0	0.0	0.0	0.0	0.0	7.8
Debt stock rescheduled	..	..	0.0	0.0	0.0	0.0	0.0	0.0	0.0	0.0
Principal rescheduled	..	..	0.0	0.0	0.0	0.0	0.0	0.0	0.0	6.4
Official	..	..	0.0	0.0	0.0	0.0	0.0	0.0	0.0	6.4
Private	..	..	0.0	0.0	0.0	0.0	0.0	0.0	0.0	0.0
Interest rescheduled	..	..	0.0	0.0	0.0	0.0	0.0	0.0	0.0	1.4
Official	..	..	0.0	0.0	0.0	0.0	0.0	0.0	0.0	1.4
Private	..	..	0.0	0.0	0.0	0.0	0.0	0.0	0.0	0.0
Debt forgiven	..	..	0.0	0.0	6.3	0.0	0.0	0.0	0.0	0.0
Memo: interest forgiven	..	..	0.0	0.0	0.0	0.0	0.0	0.0	0.0	0.0
Debt stock reduction	..	..	0.0	0.0	0.0	0.0	0.0	0.0	0.0	0.0
of which debt buyback	..	..	0.0	0.0	0.0	0.0	0.0	0.0	0.0	0.0
8. DEBT STOCK-FLOW RECONCILIATION										
Total change in debt stocks	..	..	20.5	4.4	3.8	-11.2	-7.5	14.6	10.4	-9.6
Net flows on debt	..	4.9	13.8	-6.3	4.5	-1.2	-0.1	11.8	3.5	-4.4
Net change in interest arrears	..	..	0.1	0.0	8.4	-7.8	1.5	-0.4	0.0	0.0
Interest capitalized	..	..	0.0	0.0	0.0	0.0	0.0	0.0	0.0	1.4
Debt forgiveness or reduction	..	..	0.0	0.0	-6.3	0.0	0.0	0.0	0.0	0.0
Cross-currency valuation	..	..	6.6	6.8	-0.5	-2.9	-8.9	2.8	0.8	-7.0
Residual	..	..	-0.1	3.9	-2.4	0.7	-0.1	0.4	6.0	0.4
9. AVERAGE TERMS OF NEW COMMITMENTS										
ALL CREDITORS										
Interest (%)	..	1.0	2.2	2.0	4.9	0.0	0.0	3.3	1.1	0.8
Maturity (years)	..	39.8	17.7	14.7	15.9	0.0	0.0	39.7	36.1	40.0
Grace period (years)	..	10.3	11.5	14.7	2.6	0.0	0.0	10.2	9.2	10.5
Grant element (%)	..	78.4	56.9	60.2	29.4	0.0	0.0	57.7	74.0	80.9
Official creditors										
Interest (%)	..	1.0	2.2	2.0	3.4	0.0	0.0	3.3	1.1	0.8
Maturity (years)	..	39.8	17.7	14.7	18.9	0.0	0.0	39.7	36.1	40.0
Grace period (years)	..	10.3	11.5	14.7	3.6	0.0	0.0	10.2	9.2	10.5
Grant element (%)	..	78.4	56.9	60.2	40.8	0.0	0.0	57.7	74.0	80.9
Private creditors										
Interest (%)	..	0.0	0.0	0.0	7.8	0.0	0.0	0.0	0.0	0.0
Maturity (years)	..	0.0	0.0	0.0	10.2	0.0	0.0	0.0	0.0	0.0
Grace period (years)	..	0.0	0.0	0.0	0.7	0.0	0.0	0.0	0.0	0.0
Grant element (%)	..	0.0	0.0	0.0	7.6	0.0	0.0	0.0	0.0	0.0
Memorandum items										
Commitments	..	8.3	2.5	2.4	12.3	0.0	0.0	27.3	14.0	4.0
Official creditors	..	8.3	2.5	2.4	8.1	0.0	0.0	27.3	14.0	4.0
Private creditors	..	0.0	0.0	0.0	4.2	0.0	0.0	0.0	0.0	0.0

10. CONTRACTUAL OBLIGATIONS ON OUTSTANDING LONG-TERM DEBT

	2001	2002	2003	2004	2005	2006	2007	2008	2009	2010
TOTAL										
Disbursements	6.7	4.2	2.6	1.2	0.7	0.2	0.1	0.1	0.0	0.0
Principal	7.1	6.0	6.0	6.3	6.8	6.6	6.3	8.3	7.1	7.7
Interest	2.9	2.7	2.5	2.3	2.4	2.2	2.0	1.9	1.8	1.6
Official creditors										
Disbursements	6.7	4.2	2.6	1.2	0.7	0.2	0.1	0.1	0.0	0.0
Principal	3.4	3.1	3.1	3.5	4.0	4.0	3.7	5.7	4.5	5.1
Interest	1.1	1.1	1.1	1.0	1.2	1.2	1.1	1.2	1.3	1.2
Bilateral creditors										
Disbursements	0.9	0.7	0.4	0.2	0.1	0.1	0.1	0.1	0.0	0.0
Principal	1.6	1.2	1.0	1.0	1.5	1.5	1.1	1.1	1.1	1.2
Interest	0.3	0.2	0.2	0.2	0.4	0.4	0.4	0.3	0.3	0.3
Multilateral creditors										
Disbursements	5.8	3.6	2.2	1.0	0.6	0.1	0.0	0.0	0.0	0.0
Principal	1.8	2.0	2.1	2.5	2.6	2.5	2.6	4.6	3.4	3.8
Interest	0.8	0.8	0.8	0.8	0.8	0.8	0.7	0.9	1.0	0.9
Private creditors										
Disbursements	0.0	0.0	0.0	0.0	0.0	0.0	0.0	0.0	0.0	0.0
Principal	4.0	3.0	3.0	3.0	3.0	3.0	3.0	3.0	3.0	3.0
Interest	2.0	2.0	1.0	1.0	1.0	1.0	1.0	1.0	1.0	0.0
Commercial banks										
Disbursements	0.0	0.0	0.0	0.0	0.0	0.0	0.0	0.0	0.0	0.0
Principal	0.0	0.0	0.0	0.0	0.0	0.0	0.0	0.0	0.0	0.0
Interest	0.0	0.0	0.0	0.0	0.0	0.0	0.0	0.0	0.0	0.0
Other private										
Disbursements	0.0	0.0	0.0	0.0	0.0	0.0	0.0	0.0	0.0	0.0
Principal	4.0	3.0	3.0	3.0	3.0	3.0	3.0	3.0	3.0	3.0
Interest	2.0	2.0	1.0	1.0	1.0	1.0	1.0	1.0	1.0	0.0

SOMALIA

(US$ million, unless otherwise indicated)

	1970	1980	1990	1994	1995	1996	1997	1998	1999	2000
1. SUMMARY DEBT DATA										
TOTAL DEBT STOCKS (EDT)	**77**	**660**	**2,370**	**2,616**	**2,678**	**2,643**	**2,561**	**2,635**	**2,606**	**2,562**
Long-term debt (LDOD)	**77**	**595**	**1,926**	**1,935**	**1,961**	**1,918**	**1,853**	**1,886**	**1,859**	**1,825**
Public and publicly guaranteed	77	595	1,926	1,935	1,961	1,918	1,853	1,886	1,859	1,825
Private nonguaranteed	0	0	0	0	0	0	0	0	0	0
Use of IMF credit	**0**	**18**	**159**	**164**	**167**	**161**	**151**	**158**	**154**	**146**
Short-term debt	**0**	**47**	**285**	**518**	**551**	**564**	**558**	**591**	**593**	**591**
of which interest arrears on LDOD	0	8	255	487	521	533	534	562	564	569
Official creditors	0	8	249	471	504	517	518	546	549	554
Private creditors	0	0	5	16	17	17	16	16	15	15
Memo: principal arrears on LDOD	0	14	674	1,033	1,135	1,167	1,180	1,227	1,232	1,241
Official creditors	0	13	646	997	1,098	1,131	1,145	1,192	1,198	1,208
Private creditors	0	0	28	36	37	36	34	35	34	33
Memo: export credits	0	0	357	289	296	302	390	372	407	406
TOTAL DEBT FLOWS										
Disbursements	**4**	**135**	**46**	**0**	**0**	**0**	**0**	**0**	**0**	**0**
Long-term debt	4	114	46	0	0	0	0	0	0	0
IMF purchases	0	22	0	0	0	0	0	0	0	0
Principal repayments	**2**	**11**	**5**	**0**	**0**	**0**	**0**	**0**	**0**	**0**
Long-term debt	1	7	3	0	0	0	0	0	0	0
IMF repurchases	2	4	3	0	0	0	0	0	0	0
Net flows on debt	**2**	**138**	**58**	**0**	**0**	**0**	**-7**	**5**	**0**	**-7**
of which short-term debt	0	13	18	0	0	0	-7	5	0	-7
Interest payments (INT)	**0**	**2**	**5**	**0**	**1**	**3**	**0**	**0**	**1**	**0**
Long-term debt	0	2	4	0	0	3	0	0	0	0
IMF charges	0	0	1	0	1	1	0	0	1	0
Short-term debt	0	0	0	0	0	0	0	0	0	0
Net transfers on debt	**1**	**135**	**53**	**0**	**-1**	**-3**	**-7**	**5**	**-1**	**-7**
Total debt service paid (TDS)	**3**	**13**	**11**	**0**	**1**	**3**	**0**	**0**	**1**	**0**
Long-term debt	1	9	7	0	0	3	0	0	0	0
IMF repurchases and charges	2	4	4	0	1	1	0	0	1	0
Short-term debt (interest only)	0	0	0	0	0	0	0	0	0	0
2. AGGREGATE NET RESOURCE FLOWS AND NET TRANSFERS (LONG-TERM)										
NET RESOURCE FLOWS	**17**	**380**	**372**	**494**	**150**	**60**	**67**	**68**	**93**	**86**
Net flow of long-term debt (ex. IMF)	4	106	43	0	0	0	0	0	0	0
Foreign direct investment (net)	5	0	6	1	1	0	0	0	0	0
Portfolio equity flows	0	0	0	0	0	0	0	0	0	0
Grants (excluding technical coop.)	8	274	323	493	149	60	67	68	93	86
Memo: technical coop. grants	11	93	94	46	43	33	26	16	24	19
official net resource flows	13	354	366	493	149	60	67	68	93	86
private net resource flows	4	27	6	1	1	0	0	0	0	0
NET TRANSFERS	**16**	**378**	**368**	**494**	**150**	**58**	**67**	**68**	**93**	**86**
Interest on long-term debt	0	2	4	0	0	3	0	0	0	0
Profit remittances on FDI	0	0	0	0	0	0	0	0	0	0
Memo: official net transfers	12	352	362	493	149	58	67	68	93	86
private net transfers	4	27	6	1	1	0	0	0	0	0
3. MAJOR ECONOMIC AGGREGATES										
Gross national income (GNI)	323	603	835	..	..	..	..	..	..	..
Exports of goods & services (XGS)	..	262	70	..	..	..	..	..	..	..
of which workers remittances	..	57	..	..	..	..	..	..	..	..
Imports of goods & services (MGS)	..	541	..	..	..	..	..	..	..	..
International reserves (RES)	21	26	..	..	..	..	..	..	..	..
Current account balance	..	-136	..	..	..	..	..	..	..	..
4. DEBT INDICATORS										
EDT / XGS (%)	..	252.1	3,363.0	..	..	..	..	..	..	..
EDT / GNI (%)	23.9	109.5	283.9	..	..	..	..	..	..	..
TDS / XGS (%)	..	4.9	15.2	..	..	..	..	..	..	..
INT / XGS (%)	..	0.9	7.5	..	..	..	..	..	..	..
INT / GNI (%)	0.1	0.4	0.6	..	..	..	..	..	..	..
RES / EDT (%)	27.6	3.9	..	..	..	..	..	..	..	..
RES / MGS (months)	..	0.6	..	..	..	..	..	..	..	..
Short-term / EDT (%)	0.0	7.1	12.0	19.8	20.6	21.3	21.8	22.4	22.8	23.1
Concessional / EDT (%)	90.9	82.8	65.7	60.3	59.6	58.9	58.7	58.1	58.2	58.1
Multilateral / EDT (%)	9.2	24.1	31.8	29.6	29.4	28.9	28.2	28.1	28.0	27.7

SOMALIA

(US$ million, unless otherwise indicated)

	1970	1980	1990	1994	1995	1996	1997	1998	1999	2000
5. LONG-TERM DEBT										
DEBT OUTSTANDING (LDOD)	**77**	**595**	**1,926**	**1,935**	**1,961**	**1,918**	**1,853**	**1,886**	**1,859**	**1,825**
Public and publicly guaranteed	**77**	**595**	**1,926**	**1,935**	**1,961**	**1,918**	**1,853**	**1,886**	**1,859**	**1,825**
Official creditors	75	568	1,889	1,899	1,924	1,882	1,818	1,851	1,826	1,792
Multilateral	7	159	754	774	786	764	723	741	729	709
Concessional	7	147	735	756	767	745	706	723	712	693
Bilateral	68	408	1,136	1,125	1,138	1,119	1,095	1,110	1,097	1,083
Concessional	63	400	822	820	828	812	797	808	804	794
Private creditors	2	28	37	36	37	36	34	35	34	33
Bonds	0	0	0	0	0	0	0	0	0	0
Commercial banks	2	0	0	0	0	0	0	0	0	0
Other private	0	28	37	36	37	36	34	35	34	33
Private nonguaranteed	**0**	**0**	**0**	**0**	**0**	**0**	**0**	**0**	**0**	**0**
Bonds	0	0	0	0	0	0	0	0	0	0
Commercial banks and other	0	0	0	0	0	0	0	0	0	0
Memo:										
IBRD	0	0	0	0	0	0	0	0	0	0
IDA	7	72	419	425	432	422	406	416	409	396
DISBURSEMENTS	**4**	**114**	**46**	**0**	**0**	**0**	**0**	**0**	**0**	**0**
Public and publicly guaranteed	**4**	**114**	**46**	**0**	**0**	**0**	**0**	**0**	**0**	**0**
Official creditors	4	87	46	0	0	0	0	0	0	0
Multilateral	0	36	46	0	0	0	0	0	0	0
Concessional	0	25	46	0	0	0	0	0	0	0
Bilateral	4	50	0	0	0	0	0	0	0	0
Concessional	4	49	0	0	0	0	0	0	0	0
Private creditors	0	27	0	0	0	0	0	0	0	0
Bonds	0	0	0	0	0	0	0	0	0	0
Commercial banks	0	0	0	0	0	0	0	0	0	0
Other private	0	27	0	0	0	0	0	0	0	0
Private nonguaranteed	**0**	**0**	**0**	**0**	**0**	**0**	**0**	**0**	**0**	**0**
Bonds	0	0	0	0	0	0	0	0	0	0
Commercial banks and other	0	0	0	0	0	0	0	0	0	0
Memo:										
IBRD	0	0	0	0	0	0	0	0	0	0
IDA	0	10	35	0	0	0	0	0	0	0
PRINCIPAL REPAYMENTS	**1**	**7**	**3**	**0**	**0**	**0**	**0**	**0**	**0**	**0**
Public and publicly guaranteed	**1**	**7**	**3**	**0**	**0**	**0**	**0**	**0**	**0**	**0**
Official creditors	0	7	3	0	0	0	0	0	0	0
Multilateral	0	5	3	0	0	0	0	0	0	0
Concessional	0	0	2	0	0	0	0	0	0	0
Bilateral	0	2	0	0	0	0	0	0	0	0
Concessional	0	2	0	0	0	0	0	0	0	0
Private creditors	1	0	0	0	0	0	0	0	0	0
Bonds	0	0	0	0	0	0	0	0	0	0
Commercial banks	1	0	0	0	0	0	0	0	0	0
Other private	0	0	0	0	0	0	0	0	0	0
Private nonguaranteed	**0**	**0**	**0**	**0**	**0**	**0**	**0**	**0**	**0**	**0**
Bonds	0	0	0	0	0	0	0	0	0	0
Commercial banks and other	0	0	0	0	0	0	0	0	0	0
Memo:										
IBRD	0	0	0	0	0	0	0	0	0	0
IDA	0	0	2	0	0	0	0	0	0	0
NET FLOWS ON DEBT	**4**	**106**	**43**	**0**	**0**	**0**	**0**	**0**	**0**	**0**
Public and publicly guaranteed	**4**	**106**	**43**	**0**	**0**	**0**	**0**	**0**	**0**	**0**
Official creditors	4	80	43	0	0	0	0	0	0	0
Multilateral	0	31	43	0	0	0	0	0	0	0
Concessional	0	25	44	0	0	0	0	0	0	0
Bilateral	4	49	0	0	0	0	0	0	0	0
Concessional	4	47	0	0	0	0	0	0	0	0
Private creditors	-1	27	0	0	0	0	0	0	0	0
Bonds	0	0	0	0	0	0	0	0	0	0
Commercial banks	-1	0	0	0	0	0	0	0	0	0
Other private	0	27	0	0	0	0	0	0	0	0
Private nonguaranteed	**0**	**0**	**0**	**0**	**0**	**0**	**0**	**0**	**0**	**0**
Bonds	0	0	0	0	0	0	0	0	0	0
Commercial banks and other	0	0	0	0	0	0	0	0	0	0
Memo:										
IBRD	0	0	0	0	0	0	0	0	0	0
IDA	0	10	32	0	0	0	0	0	0	0

SOMALIA

(US$ million, unless otherwise indicated)

	1970	1980	1990	1994	1995	1996	1997	1998	1999	2000
INTEREST PAYMENTS (LINT)	**0**	**2**	**4**	**0**	**0**	**3**	**0**	**0**	**0**	**0**
Public and publicly guaranteed	**0**	**2**	**4**	**0**	**0**	**3**	**0**	**0**	**0**	**0**
Official creditors	0	2	4	0	0	3	0	0	0	0
Multilateral	0	1	4	0	0	3	0	0	0	0
Concessional	0	1	4	0	0	0	0	0	0	0
Bilateral	0	1	0	0	0	0	0	0	0	0
Concessional	0	1	0	0	0	0	0	0	0	0
Private creditors	0	0	0	0	0	0	0	0	0	0
Bonds	0	0	0	0	0	0	0	0	0	0
Commercial banks	0	0	0	0	0	0	0	0	0	0
Other private	0	0	0	0	0	0	0	0	0	0
Private nonguaranteed	**0**	**0**	**0**	**0**	**0**	**0**	**0**	**0**	**0**	**0**
Bonds	0	0	0	0	0	0	0	0	0	0
Commercial banks and other	0	0	0	0	0	0	0	0	0	0
Memo:										
IBRD	0	0	0	0	0	0	0	0	0	0
IDA	0	1	3	0	0	0	0	0	0	0
NET TRANSFERS ON DEBT	**3**	**104**	**39**	**0**	**0**	**-3**	**0**	**0**	**0**	**0**
Public and publicly guaranteed	**3**	**104**	**39**	**0**	**0**	**-3**	**0**	**0**	**0**	**0**
Official creditors	4	78	39	0	0	-3	0	0	0	0
Multilateral	0	31	39	0	0	-3	0	0	0	0
Concessional	0	25	40	0	0	0	0	0	0	0
Bilateral	4	47	0	0	0	0	0	0	0	0
Concessional	4	46	0	0	0	0	0	0	0	0
Private creditors	-1	27	0	0	0	0	0	0	0	0
Bonds	0	0	0	0	0	0	0	0	0	0
Commercial banks	-1	0	0	0	0	0	0	0	0	0
Other private	0	27	0	0	0	0	0	0	0	0
Private nonguaranteed	**0**	**0**	**0**	**0**	**0**	**0**	**0**	**0**	**0**	**0**
Bonds	0	0	0	0	0	0	0	0	0	0
Commercial banks and other	0	0	0	0	0	0	0	0	0	0
Memo:										
IBRD	0	0	0	0	0	0	0	0	0	0
IDA	0	9	29	0	0	0	0	0	0	0
DEBT SERVICE (LTDS)	**1**	**9**	**7**	**0**	**0**	**3**	**0**	**0**	**0**	**0**
Public and publicly guaranteed	**1**	**9**	**7**	**0**	**0**	**3**	**0**	**0**	**0**	**0**
Official creditors	0	9	7	0	0	3	0	0	0	0
Multilateral	0	6	7	0	0	3	0	0	0	0
Concessional	0	1	6	0	0	0	0	0	0	0
Bilateral	0	3	0	0	0	0	0	0	0	0
Concessional	0	3	0	0	0	0	0	0	0	0
Private creditors	1	0	0	0	0	0	0	0	0	0
Bonds	0	0	0	0	0	0	0	0	0	0
Commercial banks	1	0	0	0	0	0	0	0	0	0
Other private	0	0	0	0	0	0	0	0	0	0
Private nonguaranteed	**0**	**0**	**0**	**0**	**0**	**0**	**0**	**0**	**0**	**0**
Bonds	0	0	0	0	0	0	0	0	0	0
Commercial banks and other	0	0	0	0	0	0	0	0	0	0
Memo:										
IBRD	0	0	0	0	0	0	0	0	0	0
IDA	0	1	6	0	0	0	0	0	0	0
UNDISBURSED DEBT	**67**	**565**	**497**	**452**	**314**	**230**	**219**	**226**	**12**	**12**
Official creditors	67	494	497	452	314	230	219	226	12	12
Private creditors	0	70	0	0	0	0	0	0	0	0
Memorandum items										
Concessional LDOD	70	546	1,557	1,576	1,596	1,557	1,503	1,531	1,516	1,487
Variable rate LDOD	0	0	20	20	20	20	20	20	20	20
Public sector LDOD	77	568	1,926	1,935	1,961	1,918	1,853	1,886	1,859	1,825
Private sector LDOD	0	28	0	0	0	0	0	0	0	0

6. CURRENCY COMPOSITION OF LONG-TERM DEBT (PERCENT)

	1970	1980	1990	1994	1995	1996	1997	1998	1999	2000
Deutsche mark	18.6	0.0	0.0	0.0	0.0	0.0	0.0	0.0	0.0	0.0
French franc	0.0	0.0	4.7	4.5	4.8	4.6	4.2	4.4	3.8	3.6
Japanese yen	0.0	0.0	2.4	3.2	3.1	2.8	2.6	2.9	3.3	3.0
Pound sterling	0.0	0.4	0.2	0.1	0.1	0.1	0.1	0.1	0.1	0.1
Swiss franc	0.0	0.0	0.0	0.0	0.0	0.0	0.0	0.0	0.0	0.0
U.S.dollars	24.6	34.1	50.5	50.5	50.2	50.8	51.8	51.4	51.7	52.0
Multiple currency	47.8	16.7	7.2	7.2	7.4	7.2	7.2	7.2	7.0	7.1
Special drawing rights	0.0	0.0	1.3	1.3	1.3	1.3	1.3	1.3	1.3	1.3
All other currencies	9.0	48.8	33.7	33.2	33.1	33.2	32.8	32.7	32.8	32.9

SOMALIA

(US$ million, unless otherwise indicated)

	1970	1980	1990	1994	1995	1996	1997	1998	1999	2000
7. DEBT RESTRUCTURINGS										
Total amount rescheduled	..	..	0	0	0	0	0	0	0	0
Debt stock rescheduled	..	..	0	0	0	0	0	0	0	0
Principal rescheduled	..	..	0	0	0	0	0	0	0	0
Official	..	..	0	0	0	0	0	0	0	0
Private	..	..	0	0	0	0	0	0	0	0
Interest rescheduled	..	..	0	0	0	0	0	0	0	0
Official	..	..	0	0	0	0	0	0	0	0
Private	..	..	0	0	0	0	0	0	0	0
Debt forgiven	..	..	0	0	0	0	0	0	0	0
Memo: interest forgiven	..	..	0	0	0	0	0	0	0	0
Debt stock reduction	..	..	0	0	0	0	0	0	0	0
of which debt buyback	..	..	0	0	0	0	0	0	0	0
8. DEBT STOCK-FLOW RECONCILIATION										
Total change in debt stocks	..	..	211	116	62	-35	-82	74	-29	-44
Net flows on debt	2	138	58	0	0	0	-7	5	0	-7
Net change in interest arrears	..	..	71	68	33	13	0	28	2	5
Interest capitalized	..	..	0	0	0	0	0	0	0	0
Debt forgiveness or reduction	..	..	0	0	0	0	0	0	0	0
Cross-currency valuation	..	..	30	3	-14	-71	-89	2	-33	-36
Residual	..	..	52	45	43	23	13	39	2	-6
9. AVERAGE TERMS OF NEW COMMITMENTS										
ALL CREDITORS										
Interest (%)	0.0	3.3	0.8	0.0	0.0	0.0	0.0	0.0	0.0	0.0
Maturity (years)	20.3	24.7	46.1	0.0	0.0	0.0	0.0	0.0	0.0	0.0
Grace period (years)	15.6	5.9	10.3	0.0	0.0	0.0	0.0	0.0	0.0	0.0
Grant element (%)	79.7	44.3	81.9	0.0	0.0	0.0	0.0	0.0	0.0	0.0
Official creditors										
Interest (%)	0.0	3.0	0.8	0.0	0.0	0.0	0.0	0.0	0.0	0.0
Maturity (years)	20.3	26.1	46.1	0.0	0.0	0.0	0.0	0.0	0.0	0.0
Grace period (years)	15.6	6.2	10.3	0.0	0.0	0.0	0.0	0.0	0.0	0.0
Grant element (%)	79.7	47.0	81.9	0.0	0.0	0.0	0.0	0.0	0.0	0.0
Private creditors										
Interest (%)	0.0	7.0	0.0	0.0	0.0	0.0	0.0	0.0	0.0	0.0
Maturity (years)	0.0	6.3	0.0	0.0	0.0	0.0	0.0	0.0	0.0	0.0
Grace period (years)	0.0	2.0	0.0	0.0	0.0	0.0	0.0	0.0	0.0	0.0
Grant element (%)	0.0	9.1	0.0	0.0	0.0	0.0	0.0	0.0	0.0	0.0
Memorandum items										
Commitments	22	188	72	0	0	0	0	0	0	0
Official creditors	22	174	72	0	0	0	0	0	0	0
Private creditors	0	14	0	0	0	0	0	0	0	0

10. CONTRACTUAL OBLIGATIONS ON OUTSTANDING LONG-TERM DEBT

	2001	2002	2003	2004	2005	2006	2007	2008	2009	2010
TOTAL										
Disbursements	0	0	0	0	0	0	0	0	0	0
Principal	35	32	30	30	29	27	29	28	28	29
Interest	11	10	9	9	8	8	7	7	6	5
Official creditors										
Disbursements	0	0	0	0	0	0	0	0	0	0
Principal	35	32	30	30	29	27	29	28	28	29
Interest	11	10	9	9	8	8	7	7	6	5
Bilateral creditors										
Disbursements	0	0	0	0	0	0	0	0	0	0
Principal	18	15	14	14	13	13	13	13	12	12
Interest	7	6	6	5	5	4	4	4	3	3
Multilateral creditors										
Disbursements	0	0	0	0	0	0	0	0	0	0
Principal	17	17	16	16	16	14	16	16	16	17
Interest	4	4	4	3	3	3	3	3	3	3
Private creditors										
Disbursements	0	0	0	0	0	0	0	0	0	0
Principal	0	0	0	0	0	0	0	0	0	0
Interest	0	0	0	0	0	0	0	0	0	0
Commercial banks										
Disbursements	0	0	0	0	0	0	0	0	0	0
Principal	0	0	0	0	0	0	0	0	0	0
Interest	0	0	0	0	0	0	0	0	0	0
Other private										
Disbursements	0	0	0	0	0	0	0	0	0	0
Principal	0	0	0	0	0	0	0	0	0	0
Interest	0	0	0	0	0	0	0	0	0	0

SOUTH AFRICA

(US$ million, unless otherwise indicated)

	1970	1980	1990	1994	1995	1996	1997	1998	1999	2000
1. SUMMARY DEBT DATA										
TOTAL DEBT STOCKS (EDT)	..	..	..	**21,671**	**25,358**	**26,050**	**25,272**	**24,753**	**23,907**	**24,861**
Long-term debt (LDOD)	..	..	..	**13,035**	**14,772**	**14,335**	**13,930**	**13,309**	**13,092**	**15,308**
Public and publicly guaranteed	..	..	..	7,789	9,837	10,348	11,517	10,668	8,173	9,088
Private nonguaranteed	..	..	..	5,246	4,935	3,987	2,413	2,641	4,919	6,220
Use of IMF credit	**0**	**0**	**0**	**897**	**913**	**884**	**415**	**0**	**0**	**0**
Short-term debt	..	..	..	**7,739**	**9,673**	**10,832**	**10,928**	**11,444**	**10,815**	**9,553**
of which interest arrears on LDOD	..	..	..	0	0	0	0	0	0	0
Official creditors	..	..	..	0	0	0	0	0	0	0
Private creditors	..	..	..	0	0	0	0	0	0	0
Memo: principal arrears on LDOD	..	..	..	0	0	0	0	0	0	0
Official creditors	..	..	..	0	0	0	0	0	0	0
Private creditors	..	..	..	0	0	0	0	0	0	0
Memo: export credits	..	..	..	5,086	2,891	2,340	3,452	0	0	0
TOTAL DEBT FLOWS										
Disbursements	..	..	..	**3,518**	**3,549**	**2,291**	**4,630**	**2,046**	**2,696**	**3,523**
Long-term debt	..	..	..	3,518	3,549	2,291	4,630	2,046	2,696	3,523
IMF purchases	0	0	0	0	0	0	0	0	0	0
Principal repayments	..	..	..	**1,995**	**2,070**	**2,770**	**5,103**	**2,859**	**2,844**	**2,609**
Long-term debt	..	..	..	1,995	2,070	2,770	4,680	2,442	2,844	2,609
IMF repurchases	0	0	0	0	0	0	423	417	0	0
Net flows on debt	..	..	..	**1,524**	**3,412**	**681**	**-377**	**-297**	**-698**	**1,186**
of which short-term debt	..	..	..	0	1,934	1,159	96	516	-550	272
Interest payments (INT)	..	..	..	**907**	**1,320**	**1,467**	**1,439**	**1,530**	**1,446**	**1,251**
Long-term debt	..	..	..	617	855	923	850	892	815	741
IMF charges	0	0	0	38	50	40	34	15	1	0
Short-term debt	..	..	..	251	415	504	555	622	631	509
Net transfers on debt	..	..	..	**617**	**2,092**	**-786**	**-1,816**	**-1,827**	**-2,144**	**65**
Total debt service paid (TDS)	..	..	..	**2,902**	**3,391**	**4,236**	**6,542**	**4,388**	**4,290**	**3,860**
Long-term debt	..	..	..	2,612	2,926	3,692	5,530	3,334	3,658	3,350
IMF repurchases and charges	0	0	0	38	50	40	456	432	1	0
Short-term debt (interest only)	..	..	..	251	415	504	555	622	631	509
2. AGGREGATE NET RESOURCE FLOWS AND NET TRANSFERS (LONG-TERM)										
NET RESOURCE FLOWS	..	..	..	**2,262**	**7,454**	**2,240**	**5,354**	**1,020**	**5,456**	**2,957**
Net flow of long-term debt (ex. IMF)	..	..	..	1,524	1,478	-478	-51	-396	-148	914
Foreign direct investment (net)	..	..	..	374	1,248	816	3,811	550	1,503	961
Portfolio equity flows	..	..	..	219	4,571	1,759	1,393	619	3,855	864
Grants (excluding technical coop.)	..	..	..	146	156	144	200	248	246	219
Memo: technical coop. grants	..	..	..	149	214	207	244	210	213	225
official net resource flows	..	..	..	146	156	144	200	248	246	221
private net resource flows	..	..	..	2,117	7,297	2,097	5,154	773	5,210	2,736
NET TRANSFERS	..	..	..	**-1,355**	**3,998**	**-1,083**	**2,504**	**-2,072**	**2,312**	**-334**
Interest on long-term debt	..	..	..	617	855	923	850	892	815	741
Profit remittances on FDI	..	..	..	3,000	2,600	2,400	2,000	2,200	2,330	2,550
Memo: official net transfers	..	..	..	146	156	144	200	248	246	221
private net transfers	..	..	..	-1,501	3,842	-1,226	2,304	-2,319	2,065	-556
3. MAJOR ECONOMIC AGGREGATES										
Gross national income (GNI)	..	..	..	133,356	148,238	140,728	145,172	129,833	127,014	122,643
Exports of goods & services (XGS)	..	..	..	31,055	35,825	36,367	37,803	35,852	35,241	38,705
of which workers remittances	..	..	..	0	0	0	..	..	..	..
Imports of goods & services (MGS)	..	..	..	30,334	37,384	37,494	39,373	37,265	34,867	38,248
International reserves (RES)	..	..	..	3,295	4,464	2,341	5,957	5,508	7,497	7,702
Current account balance	..	..	..	112	-2,205	-1,880	-2,294	-2,157	-553	-469
4. DEBT INDICATORS										
EDT / XGS (%)	..	..	..	69.8	70.8	71.6	66.9	69.0	67.8	64.2
EDT / GNI (%)	..	..	..	16.3	17.1	18.5	17.4	19.1	18.8	20.3
TDS / XGS (%)	..	..	..	9.3	9.5	11.7	17.3	12.2	12.2	10.0
INT / XGS (%)	..	..	..	2.9	3.7	4.0	3.8	4.3	4.1	3.2
INT / GNI (%)	..	..	..	0.7	0.9	1.0	1.0	1.2	1.1	1.0
RES / EDT (%)	..	..	..	15.2	17.6	9.0	23.6	22.3	31.4	31.0
RES / MGS (months)	..	..	..	1.3	1.4	0.8	1.8	1.8	2.6	2.4
Short-term / EDT (%)	..	..	..	35.7	38.2	41.6	43.2	46.2	45.2	38.4
Concessional / EDT (%)	..	..	..	0.0	0.0	0.0	0.0	0.0	0.0	0.0
Multilateral / EDT (%)	..	..	..	0.0	0.0	0.0	0.0	0.0	0.0	0.0

SOUTH AFRICA

(US$ million, unless otherwise indicated)

	1970	1980	1990	1994	1995	1996	1997	1998	1999	2000
5. LONG-TERM DEBT										
DEBT OUTSTANDING (LDOD)	..	..	..	**13,035**	**14,772**	**14,335**	**13,930**	**13,309**	**13,092**	**15,308**
Public and publicly guaranteed	..	..	..	**7,789**	**9,837**	**10,348**	**11,517**	**10,668**	**8,173**	**9,088**
Official creditors	..	..	..	0	0	0	0	0	1	3
Multilateral	..	..	..	0	0	0	0	0	1	3
Concessional	..	..	..	0	0	0	0	0	0	0
Bilateral	..	..	..	0	0	0	0	0	0	0
Concessional	..	..	..	0	0	0	0	0	0	0
Private creditors	..	..	..	7,789	9,837	10,348	11,517	10,668	8,172	9,085
Bonds	..	..	..	2,062	2,454	2,749	3,631	3,649	3,969	4,749
Commercial banks	..	..	..	3,867	3,978	3,563	3,327	2,638	1,842	1,973
Other private	..	..	..	1,860	3,405	4,036	4,559	4,381	2,361	2,363
Private nonguaranteed	..	..	..	**5,246**	**4,935**	**3,987**	**2,413**	**2,641**	**4,919**	**6,220**
Bonds	..	..	..	0	350	350	395	786	395	1,110
Commercial banks and other	..	..	..	5,246	4,585	3,637	2,018	1,855	4,524	5,110
Memo:										
IBRD	0	0	0	0	0	0	0	0	1	3
IDA	0	0	0	0	0	0	0	0	0	0
DISBURSEMENTS	..	..	..	**3,518**	**3,549**	**2,291**	**4,630**	**2,046**	**2,696**	**3,523**
Public and publicly guaranteed	..	..	..	**3,068**	**3,199**	**2,152**	**3,004**	**1,290**	**1,968**	**2,763**
Official creditors	..	..	..	0	0	0	0	0	1	3
Multilateral	..	..	..	0	0	0	0	0	1	3
Concessional	..	..	..	0	0	0	0	0	0	0
Bilateral	..	..	..	0	0	0	0	0	0	0
Concessional	..	..	..	0	0	0	0	0	0	0
Private creditors	..	..	..	3,068	3,199	2,152	3,004	1,290	1,967	2,760
Bonds	..	..	..	1,510	391	632	1,278	0	1,627	765
Commercial banks	..	..	..	941	830	419	726	840	240	1,674
Other private	..	..	..	617	1,978	1,101	1,000	450	100	321
Private nonguaranteed	..	..	..	**450**	**350**	**139**	**1,626**	**756**	**728**	**760**
Bonds	..	..	..	0	350	0	45	373	0	712
Commercial banks and other	..	..	..	450	0	139	1,581	383	728	48
Memo:										
IBRD	0	0	0	0	0	0	0	0	1	3
IDA	0	0	0	0	0	0	0	0	0	0
PRINCIPAL REPAYMENTS	..	..	..	**1,995**	**2,070**	**2,770**	**4,680**	**2,442**	**2,844**	**2,609**
Public and publicly guaranteed	..	..	..	**1,145**	**1,168**	**1,568**	**1,480**	**1,896**	**363**	**1,627**
Official creditors	..	..	..	0	0	0	0	0	0	0
Multilateral	..	..	..	0	0	0	0	0	0	0
Concessional	..	..	..	0	0	0	0	0	0	0
Bilateral	..	..	..	0	0	0	0	0	0	0
Concessional	..	..	..	0	0	0	0	0	0	0
Private creditors	..	..	..	1,145	1,168	1,568	1,480	1,896	363	1,627
Bonds	..	..	..	7	10	266	253	70	16	284
Commercial banks	..	..	..	787	719	834	752	1,198	347	949
Other private	..	..	..	351	439	467	475	628	0	393
Private nonguaranteed	..	..	..	**850**	**902**	**1,202**	**3,200**	**546**	**2,481**	**982**
Bonds	..	..	..	0	0	0	0	0	358	0
Commercial banks and other	..	..	..	850	902	1,202	3,200	546	2,123	982
Memo:										
IBRD	0	0	0	0	0	0	0	0	0	0
IDA	0	0	0	0	0	0	0	0	0	0
NET FLOWS ON DEBT	..	..	..	**1,524**	**1,478**	**-478**	**-51**	**-396**	**-148**	**914**
Public and publicly guaranteed	..	..	..	**1,924**	**2,030**	**585**	**1,524**	**-606**	**1,605**	**1,136**
Official creditors	..	..	..	0	0	0	0	0	1	3
Multilateral	..	..	..	0	0	0	0	0	1	3
Concessional	..	..	..	0	0	0	0	0	0	0
Bilateral	..	..	..	0	0	0	0	0	0	0
Concessional	..	..	..	0	0	0	0	0	0	0
Private creditors	..	..	..	1,924	2,030	585	1,524	-606	1,604	1,133
Bonds	..	..	..	1,503	381	367	1,025	-70	1,611	481
Commercial banks	..	..	..	154	111	-415	-26	-358	-107	725
Other private	..	..	..	266	1,539	634	525	-178	100	-73
Private nonguaranteed	..	..	..	**-400**	**-552**	**-1,063**	**-1,574**	**210**	**-1,753**	**-222**
Bonds	..	..	..	0	350	0	45	373	-358	712
Commercial banks and other	..	..	..	-400	-902	-1,063	-1,619	-163	-1,395	-934
Memo:										
IBRD	0	0	0	0	0	0	0	0	1	3
IDA	0	0	0	0	0	0	0	0	0	0

SOUTH AFRICA

(US$ million, unless otherwise indicated)

	1970	1980	1990	1994	1995	1996	1997	1998	1999	2000
INTEREST PAYMENTS (LINT)	..	..	..	**617**	**855**	**923**	**850**	**892**	**815**	**741**
Public and publicly guaranteed	..	..	..	**339**	**597**	**667**	**669**	**759**	**681**	**545**
Official creditors	..	..	..	0	0	0	0	0	0	0
Multilateral	..	..	..	0	0	0	0	0	0	0
Concessional	..	..	..	0	0	0	0	0	0	0
Bilateral	..	..	..	0	0	0	0	0	0	0
Concessional	..	..	..	0	0	0	0	0	0	0
Private creditors	..	..	..	339	597	667	669	759	681	545
Bonds	..	..	..	56	188	194	207	266	266	275
Commercial banks	..	..	..	166	245	220	228	226	160	130
Other private	..	..	..	118	164	254	234	266	255	140
Private nonguaranteed	..	..	..	**278**	**258**	**256**	**181**	**134**	**133**	**196**
Bonds	..	..	..	0	0	25	25	27	59	27
Commercial banks and other	..	..	..	278	258	231	156	107	74	169
Memo:										
IBRD	0	0	0	0	0	0	0	0	0	0
IDA	0	0	0	0	0	0	0	0	0	0
NET TRANSFERS ON DEBT	..	..	..	**906**	**623**	**-1,401**	**-901**	**-1,288**	**-963**	**173**
Public and publicly guaranteed	..	..	..	**1,584**	**1,433**	**-83**	**854**	**-1,364**	**924**	**591**
Official creditors	..	..	..	0	0	0	0	0	1	3
Multilateral	..	..	..	0	0	0	0	0	1	3
Concessional	..	..	..	0	0	0	0	0	0	0
Bilateral	..	..	..	0	0	0	0	0	0	0
Concessional	..	..	..	0	0	0	0	0	0	0
Private creditors	..	..	..	1,584	1,433	-83	854	-1,364	923	588
Bonds	..	..	..	1,448	193	173	818	-336	1,345	206
Commercial banks	..	..	..	-12	-135	-635	-254	-584	-266	595
Other private	..	..	..	149	1,375	380	291	-445	-155	-213
Private nonguaranteed	..	..	..	**-678**	**-810**	**-1,319**	**-1,755**	**76**	**-1,886**	**-418**
Bonds	..	..	..	0	350	-25	20	346	-417	685
Commercial banks and other	..	..	..	-678	-1,160	-1,294	-1,775	-270	-1,469	-1,103
Memo:										
IBRD	0	0	0	0	0	0	0	0	1	3
IDA	0	0	0	0	0	0	0	0	0	0
DEBT SERVICE (LTDS)	..	..	..	**2,612**	**2,926**	**3,692**	**5,530**	**3,334**	**3,658**	**3,350**
Public and publicly guaranteed	..	..	..	**1,484**	**1,766**	**2,235**	**2,150**	**2,654**	**1,044**	**2,172**
Official creditors	..	..	..	0	0	0	0	0	0	0
Multilateral	..	..	..	0	0	0	0	0	0	0
Concessional	..	..	..	0	0	0	0	0	0	0
Bilateral	..	..	..	0	0	0	0	0	0	0
Concessional	..	..	..	0	0	0	0	0	0	0
Private creditors	..	..	..	1,484	1,766	2,235	2,150	2,654	1,044	2,172
Bonds	..	..	..	63	198	460	460	336	283	559
Commercial banks	..	..	..	953	965	1,054	981	1,424	506	1,079
Other private	..	..	..	469	603	721	709	895	255	534
Private nonguaranteed	..	..	..	**1,128**	**1,160**	**1,458**	**3,381**	**680**	**2,614**	**1,178**
Bonds	..	..	..	0	0	25	25	27	417	27
Commercial banks and other	..	..	..	1,128	1,160	1,433	3,356	653	2,197	1,151
Memo:										
IBRD	0	0	0	0	0	0	0	0	0	0
IDA	0	0	0	0	0	0	0	0	0	0
UNDISBURSED DEBT	..	..	..	**0**	**26**	**226**	**1,750**	**956**	**634**	**21**
Official creditors	..	..	..	0	0	0	0	46	24	21
Private creditors	..	..	..	0	26	226	1,750	910	610	0
Memorandum items										
Concessional LDOD	..	..	..	0	0	0	0	0	0	0
Variable rate LDOD	..	..	..	9,113	8,913	7,550	5,659	5,230	6,746	8,196
Public sector LDOD	..	..	..	7,789	9,837	10,348	11,517	10,528	7,733	8,054
Private sector LDOD	..	..	..	5,246	4,935	3,987	2,413	2,781	5,359	7,254

6. CURRENCY COMPOSITION OF LONG-TERM DEBT (PERCENT)

	1970	1980	1990	1994	1995	1996	1997	1998	1999	2000
Deutsche mark	..	..	..	3.3	2.8	3.1	2.4	2.8	3.1	2.6
French franc	..	..	..	0.0	0.0	0.0	0.0	0.0	0.0	0.0
Japanese yen	..	..	..	0.0	3.0	2.5	4.7	5.7	8.4	3.8
Pound sterling	..	..	..	0.0	0.0	0.0	0.0	0.0	0.0	0.0
Swiss franc	..	..	..	0.0	0.0	0.0	0.0	0.0	0.0	0.0
U.S.dollars	..	..	..	92.2	90.6	91.3	92.8	91.4	88.5	93.6
Multiple currency	..	..	..	0.0	0.0	0.0	0.0	0.0	0.0	0.0
Special drawing rights	..	..	..	0.0	0.0	0.0	0.0	0.0	0.0	0.0
All other currencies	..	..	..	4.5	3.6	3.1	0.1	0.1	0.0	0.0

SOUTH AFRICA

(US$ million, unless otherwise indicated)

	1970	1980	1990	1994	1995	1996	1997	1998	1999	2000
7. DEBT RESTRUCTURINGS										
Total amount rescheduled	..	..	..	0	0	0	0	0	60	0
Debt stock rescheduled	..	..	..	0	0	0	0	0	0	0
Principal rescheduled	..	..	..	0	0	0	0	0	0	0
Official	..	..	..	0	0	0	0	0	0	0
Private	..	..	..	0	0	0	0	0	0	0
Interest rescheduled	..	..	..	..	0	0	0	0	0	0
Official	..	..	..	0	0	0	0	0	0	0
Private	..	..	..	0	0	0	0	0	0	0
Debt forgiven	..	..	..	0	0	0	0	0	0	0
Memo: interest forgiven	..	..	..	0	0	0	0	0	0	0
Debt stock reduction	..	..	..	0	0	0	0	0	0	0
of which debt buyback	..	..	..	0	0	0	0	0	0	0
8. DEBT STOCK-FLOW RECONCILIATION										
Total change in debt stocks	..	..	..	..	3,687	692	-778	-520	-846	954
Net flows on debt	..	..	..	1,524	3,412	681	-377	-297	-698	1,186
Net change in interest arrears	..	..	..	..	0	0	0	0	0	0
Interest capitalized	..	..	..	..	0	0	0	0	0	0
Debt forgiveness or reduction	..	..	..	..	0	0	0	0	0	0
Cross-currency valuation	..	..	..	..	63	-102	-163	106	35	-95
Residual	..	..	..	..	212	113	-238	-329	-103	1,397
9. AVERAGE TERMS OF NEW COMMITMENTS										
ALL CREDITORS										
Interest (%)	..	..	..	6.2	5.4	5.9	6.3	6.0	6.0	6.1
Maturity (years)	..	..	..	9.0	14.2	12.5	11.9	12.9	9.4	8.6
Grace period (years)	..	..	..	3.1	1.8	3.3	5.3	1.5	4.2	2.3
Grant element (%)	..	..	..	15.6	21.3	18.8	15.1	17.5	18.5	15.0
Official creditors										
Interest (%)	..	..	..	0.0	0.0	0.0	0.0	6.3	0.0	0.0
Maturity (years)	..	..	..	0.0	0.0	0.0	0.0	14.3	0.0	0.0
Grace period (years)	..	..	..	0.0	0.0	0.0	0.0	2.8	0.0	0.0
Grant element (%)	..	..	..	0.0	0.0	0.0	0.0	19.2	0.0	0.0
Private creditors										
Interest (%)	..	..	..	6.2	5.4	5.9	6.3	6.0	6.0	6.1
Maturity (years)	..	..	..	9.0	14.2	12.5	11.9	12.8	9.4	8.6
Grace period (years)	..	..	..	3.1	1.8	3.3	5.3	1.4	4.2	2.3
Grant element (%)	..	..	..	15.6	21.3	18.8	15.1	17.4	18.5	15.0
Memorandum items										
Commitments	..	..	..	3,068	3,225	2,352	4,528	496	1,993	2,150
Official creditors	..	..	..	0	0	0	0	46	0	0
Private creditors	..	..	..	3,068	3,225	2,352	4,528	450	1,993	2,150

10. CONTRACTUAL OBLIGATIONS ON OUTSTANDING LONG-TERM DEBT

	2001	2002	2003	2004	2005	2006	2007	2008	2009	2010
TOTAL										
Disbursements	9	12	0	0	0	0	0	0	0	0
Principal	3,767	2,963	2,598	1,854	1,837	447	272	147	147	147
Interest	631	475	360	249	200	168	134	116	108	99
Official creditors										
Disbursements	9	12	0	0	0	0	0	0	0	0
Principal	2	2	2	2	2	2	2	2	2	2
Interest	1	1	1	1	1	1	1	1	1	0
Bilateral creditors										
Disbursements	0	0	0	0	0	0	0	0	0	0
Principal	0	0	0	0	0	0	0	0	0	0
Interest	0	0	0	0	0	0	0	0	0	0
Multilateral creditors										
Disbursements	9	12	0	0	0	0	0	0	0	0
Principal	2	2	2	2	2	2	2	2	2	2
Interest	1	1	1	1	1	1	1	1	1	0
Private creditors										
Disbursements	0	0	0	0	0	0	0	0	0	0
Principal	3,765	2,961	2,596	1,852	1,835	445	270	145	145	145
Interest	630	474	358	247	199	167	133	116	107	98
Commercial banks										
Disbursements	0	0	0	0	0	0	0	0	0	0
Principal	1,134	256	234	234	115	0	0	0	0	0
Interest	113	53	37	21	6	0	0	0	0	0
Other private										
Disbursements	0	0	0	0	0	0	0	0	0	0
Principal	2,631	2,705	2,362	1,618	1,720	445	270	145	145	145
Interest	518	421	322	226	193	167	133	116	107	98

SRI LANKA

(US$ million, unless otherwise indicated)

	1970	1980	1990	1994	1995	1996	1997	1998	1999	2000
1. SUMMARY DEBT DATA										
TOTAL DEBT STOCKS (EDT)	**433**	**1,841**	**5,863**	**7,960**	**8,370**	**8,250**	**7,983**	**8,838**	**9,797**	**9,066**
Long-term debt (LDOD)	**317**	**1,231**	**5,049**	**6,804**	**7,239**	**7,154**	**7,071**	**8,037**	**8,593**	**8,200**
Public and publicly guaranteed	317	1,227	4,947	6,722	7,150	7,066	6,987	7,951	8,506	8,035
Private nonguaranteed	0	3	102	83	90	88	84	87	86	165
Use of IMF credit	**79**	**391**	**410**	**617**	**595**	**531**	**433**	**367**	**258**	**161**
Short-term debt	**38**	**220**	**405**	**538**	**535**	**565**	**479**	**434**	**946**	**705**
of which interest arrears on LDOD	0	0	11	32	35	121	117	138	155	133
Official creditors	0	0	0	0	0	20	22	27	30	25
Private creditors	0	0	11	32	35	102	94	111	126	107
Memo: principal arrears on LDOD	0	0	0	11	42	169	190	242	284	262
Official creditors	0	0	0	2	3	37	40	58	68	61
Private creditors	0	0	0	9	39	132	149	184	216	201
Memo: export credits	0	0	566	755	906	754	672	188	205	288
TOTAL DEBT FLOWS										
Disbursements	**75**	**344**	**545**	**587**	**677**	**626**	**739**	**827**	**457**	**676**
Long-term debt	66	272	485	507	677	626	739	827	457	676
IMF purchases	10	72	61	80	0	0	0	0	0	0
Principal repayments	**57**	**94**	**214**	**261**	**312**	**316**	**366**	**388**	**480**	**520**
Long-term debt	30	51	167	248	278	271	300	306	380	434
IMF repurchases	27	43	47	13	34	45	66	82	99	86
Net flows on debt	**19**	**334**	**331**	**591**	**360**	**254**	**291**	**374**	**472**	**-62**
of which short-term debt	0	84	0	265	-6	-57	-82	-66	495	-218
Interest payments (INT)	**12**	**85**	**170**	**155**	**172**	**176**	**168**	**170**	**195**	**218**
Long-term debt	12	33	122	135	144	147	141	148	164	182
IMF charges	0	17	21	3	3	3	2	2	2	1
Short-term debt	0	36	27	17	24	26	24	19	29	34
Net transfers on debt	**7**	**248**	**161**	**437**	**188**	**78**	**124**	**204**	**277**	**-279**
Total debt service paid (TDS)	**69**	**179**	**384**	**416**	**483**	**492**	**534**	**557**	**674**	**738**
Long-term debt	42	84	289	383	422	418	441	454	544	617
IMF repurchases and charges	27	59	69	16	37	48	69	84	101	87
Short-term debt (interest only)	0	36	27	17	24	26	24	19	29	34
2. AGGREGATE NET RESOURCE FLOWS AND NET TRANSFERS (LONG-TERM)										
NET RESOURCE FLOWS	**51**	**425**	**582**	**697**	**691**	**687**	**1,080**	**835**	**371**	**530**
Net flow of long-term debt (ex. IMF)	36	221	318	259	399	355	439	521	77	242
Foreign direct investment (net)	0	43	43	166	56	120	430	193	176	173
Portfolio equity flows	0	0	0	112	61	70	98	6	6	6
Grants (excluding technical coop.)	15	161	221	160	175	142	113	115	112	109
Memo: technical coop. grants	7	57	104	98	115	97	94	81	87	78
official net resource flows	55	296	529	442	499	464	426	493	272	268
private net resource flows	-4	129	53	255	192	224	654	343	100	262
NET TRANSFERS	**31**	**377**	**435**	**522**	**513**	**500**	**895**	**637**	**156**	**302**
Interest on long-term debt	12	33	122	135	144	147	141	148	164	182
Profit remittances on FDI	8	15	25	40	34	40	44	50	51	45
Memo: official net transfers	47	270	452	336	387	349	319	386	152	142
private net transfers	-16	106	-17	186	126	152	577	251	5	160
3. MAJOR ECONOMIC AGGREGATES										
Gross national income (GNI)	2,259	3,997	7,865	11,551	12,893	13,651	14,748	15,193	15,620	16,368
Exports of goods & services (XGS)	..	1,492	2,786	4,821	5,630	5,868	6,669	6,940	6,780	7,670
of which workers remittances	..	152	401	715	790	832	922	1,002	1,052	1,142
Imports of goods & services (MGS)	..	2,269	3,224	5,658	6,342	6,477	6,974	7,070	7,198	8,553
International reserves (RES)	43	283	447	2,070	2,112	1,985	2,042	1,998	1,654	1,211
Current account balance	..	-655	-298	-757	-770	-683	-395	-228	-561	-1,042
4. DEBT INDICATORS										
EDT / XGS (%)	..	123.4	210.4	165.1	148.7	140.6	119.7	127.4	144.5	118.2
EDT / GNI (%)	19.2	46.1	74.6	68.9	64.9	60.4	54.1	58.2	62.7	55.4
TDS / XGS (%)	..	12.0	13.8	8.6	8.6	8.4	8.0	8.0	10.0	9.6
INT / XGS (%)	..	5.7	6.1	3.2	3.1	3.0	2.5	2.4	2.9	2.8
INT / GNI (%)	0.5	2.1	2.2	1.3	1.3	1.3	1.1	1.1	1.3	1.3
RES / EDT (%)	9.9	15.4	7.6	26.0	25.2	24.1	25.6	22.6	16.9	13.4
RES / MGS (months)	..	1.5	1.7	4.4	4.0	3.7	3.5	3.4	2.8	1.7
Short-term / EDT (%)	8.8	11.9	6.9	6.8	6.4	6.9	6.0	4.9	9.7	7.8
Concessional / EDT (%)	43.2	56.0	71.9	75.7	76.1	75.9	75.9	77.5	76.2	77.5
Multilateral / EDT (%)	6.7	11.7	27.7	33.4	34.2	35.7	36.1	36.5	36.8	37.5

SRI LANKA

(US$ million, unless otherwise indicated)

	1970	1980	1990	1994	1995	1996	1997	1998	1999	2000
5. LONG-TERM DEBT										
DEBT OUTSTANDING (LDOD)	**317**	**1,231**	**5,049**	**6,804**	**7,239**	**7,154**	**7,071**	**8,037**	**8,593**	**8,200**
Public and publicly guaranteed	**317**	**1,227**	**4,947**	**6,722**	**7,150**	**7,066**	**6,987**	**7,951**	**8,506**	**8,035**
Official creditors	253	1,087	4,349	6,162	6,506	6,404	6,221	7,015	7,636	7,211
Multilateral	29	216	1,623	2,656	2,858	2,942	2,878	3,222	3,607	3,403
Concessional	1	177	1,536	2,600	2,806	2,899	2,845	3,193	3,585	3,387
Bilateral	224	872	2,726	3,506	3,648	3,462	3,343	3,793	4,029	3,808
Concessional	186	854	2,681	3,428	3,564	3,360	3,216	3,660	3,883	3,634
Private creditors	64	140	598	560	644	663	766	936	870	824
Bonds	12	0	0	0	0	0	50	115	115	65
Commercial banks	3	57	253	278	338	353	433	527	448	357
Other private	49	83	345	282	306	310	283	294	308	402
Private nonguaranteed	**0**	**3**	**102**	**83**	**90**	**88**	**84**	**87**	**86**	**165**
Bonds	0	0	0	0	0	0	0	0	0	0
Commercial banks and other	0	3	102	83	90	88	84	87	86	165
Memo:										
IBRD	26	31	82	54	49	40	31	26	20	13
IDA	1	98	864	1,339	1,463	1,516	1,514	1,648	1,652	1,610
DISBURSEMENTS	**66**	**272**	**485**	**507**	**677**	**626**	**739**	**827**	**457**	**676**
Public and publicly guaranteed	**66**	**269**	**485**	**507**	**677**	**626**	**739**	**825**	**457**	**560**
Official creditors	55	174	396	415	472	467	474	559	350	371
Multilateral	4	32	234	172	197	258	176	226	149	120
Concessional	1	31	233	172	197	258	176	226	149	120
Bilateral	52	142	162	243	275	209	298	333	202	250
Concessional	40	141	162	242	262	187	265	320	180	203
Private creditors	11	96	89	92	206	160	265	266	107	189
Bonds	0	0	0	0	0	0	50	65	0	0
Commercial banks	0	57	54	62	107	71	171	157	28	15
Other private	11	39	35	30	99	89	44	45	78	174
Private nonguaranteed	**0**	**2**	**0**	**0**	**0**	**0**	**0**	**2**	**0**	**116**
Bonds	0	0	0	0	0	0	0	0	0	0
Commercial banks and other	0	2	0	0	0	0	0	2	0	116
Memo:										
IBRD	1	0	1	0	0	0	0	0	0	0
IDA	1	20	127	78	106	104	78	97	49	47
PRINCIPAL REPAYMENTS	**30**	**51**	**167**	**248**	**278**	**271**	**300**	**306**	**380**	**434**
Public and publicly guaranteed	**30**	**51**	**165**	**245**	**276**	**268**	**293**	**306**	**380**	**420**
Official creditors	16	39	89	133	148	145	161	181	191	212
Multilateral	2	5	21	26	26	29	37	43	43	50
Concessional	0	2	13	18	19	22	31	37	36	45
Bilateral	14	34	68	108	122	116	125	139	148	162
Concessional	6	28	64	101	115	113	120	129	138	148
Private creditors	14	12	76	112	129	123	132	125	189	208
Bonds	3	0	0	0	0	0	0	0	0	50
Commercial banks	1	0	29	43	54	57	78	72	109	93
Other private	10	12	47	69	75	66	54	53	81	65
Private nonguaranteed	**0**	**0**	**2**	**3**	**2**	**3**	**7**	**0**	**0**	**14**
Bonds	0	0	0	0	0	0	0	0	0	0
Commercial banks and other	0	0	2	3	2	3	7	0	0	14
Memo:										
IBRD	2	2	7	8	7	6	6	6	6	5
IDA	0	0	3	7	8	9	11	13	15	18
NET FLOWS ON DEBT	**36**	**221**	**318**	**259**	**399**	**355**	**439**	**521**	**77**	**242**
Public and publicly guaranteed	**36**	**219**	**320**	**262**	**401**	**359**	**446**	**519**	**77**	**140**
Official creditors	40	135	307	282	324	322	313	378	160	159
Multilateral	2	27	214	146	171	229	140	183	106	70
Concessional	1	30	220	154	178	236	146	189	112	76
Bilateral	38	108	94	136	153	93	173	194	53	88
Concessional	34	113	98	141	146	73	144	191	42	55
Private creditors	-4	84	13	-20	77	37	133	142	-83	-19
Bonds	-3	0	0	0	0	0	50	65	0	-50
Commercial banks	-1	57	24	19	54	14	93	85	-80	-77
Other private	1	27	-12	-39	24	23	-10	-8	-3	108
Private nonguaranteed	**0**	**2**	**-2**	**-3**	**-2**	**-3**	**-7**	**2**	**0**	**102**
Bonds	0	0	0	0	0	0	0	0	0	0
Commercial banks and other	0	2	-2	-3	-2	-3	-7	2	0	102
Memo:										
IBRD	-1	-2	-6	-8	-7	-6	-6	-6	-6	-5
IDA	1	20	124	71	98	95	68	84	34	28

SRI LANKA

(US$ million, unless otherwise indicated)

	1970	1980	1990	1994	1995	1996	1997	1998	1999	2000
INTEREST PAYMENTS (LINT)	**12**	**33**	**122**	**135**	**144**	**147**	**141**	**148**	**164**	**182**
Public and publicly guaranteed	**12**	**33**	**120**	**134**	**143**	**146**	**138**	**144**	**161**	**173**
Official creditors	8	25	77	106	112	115	107	107	120	125
Multilateral	3	5	19	26	29	28	28	27	32	32
Concessional	0	2	11	21	24	24	25	25	30	30
Bilateral	6	20	58	79	83	87	79	80	88	94
Concessional	3	19	55	77	81	83	74	73	81	86
Private creditors	4	8	43	28	31	30	30	37	41	47
Bonds	1	0	0	0	0	0	0	4	4	6
Commercial banks	0	0	16	15	20	19	19	25	31	26
Other private	3	8	27	13	11	12	11	8	6	15
Private nonguaranteed	**0**	**0**	**2**	**1**	**1**	**1**	**3**	**5**	**3**	**10**
Bonds	0	0	0	0	0	0	0	0	0	0
Commercial banks and other	0	0	2	1	1	1	3	5	3	10
Memo:										
IBRD	3	3	8	5	5	4	3	3	2	1
IDA	0	1	6	10	11	11	11	11	12	12
NET TRANSFERS ON DEBT	**24**	**188**	**196**	**124**	**255**	**208**	**298**	**373**	**-87**	**59**
Public and publicly guaranteed	**24**	**186**	**200**	**128**	**258**	**213**	**309**	**375**	**-84**	**-33**
Official creditors	32	110	230	176	212	207	206	271	40	33
Multilateral	-1	22	195	120	142	201	112	156	74	39
Concessional	1	28	209	133	154	211	121	164	82	45
Bilateral	33	87	35	56	69	6	94	115	-34	-5
Concessional	31	94	43	64	66	-9	70	118	-39	-32
Private creditors	-8	76	-30	-48	46	6	103	105	-124	-66
Bonds	-4	0	0	0	0	0	50	61	-4	-56
Commercial banks	-1	57	8	4	34	-5	74	60	-112	-104
Other private	-2	19	-38	-52	12	11	-21	-16	-9	93
Private nonguaranteed	**0**	**2**	**-4**	**-4**	**-3**	**-5**	**-10**	**-2**	**-3**	**92**
Bonds	0	0	0	0	0	0	0	0	0	0
Commercial banks and other	0	2	-4	-4	-3	-5	-10	-2	-3	92
Memo:										
IBRD	-3	-5	-13	-13	-12	-11	-9	-8	-8	-7
IDA	1	19	118	61	88	84	57	72	22	16
DEBT SERVICE (LTDS)	**42**	**84**	**289**	**383**	**422**	**418**	**441**	**454**	**544**	**617**
Public and publicly guaranteed	**42**	**84**	**285**	**379**	**419**	**414**	**431**	**450**	**541**	**593**
Official creditors	24	64	166	239	260	260	269	288	310	337
Multilateral	4	10	39	52	54	57	64	70	75	82
Concessional	0	3	24	39	43	47	55	62	67	75
Bilateral	19	54	126	187	206	203	204	218	236	256
Concessional	9	47	119	178	196	196	194	202	219	234
Private creditors	18	20	119	140	160	153	162	161	230	255
Bonds	4	0	0	0	0	0	0	4	4	56
Commercial banks	1	0	46	58	73	76	97	97	140	119
Other private	13	20	74	82	86	77	65	61	87	81
Private nonguaranteed	**0**	**0**	**4**	**4**	**3**	**5**	**10**	**5**	**3**	**24**
Bonds	0	0	0	0	0	0	0	0	0	0
Commercial banks and other	0	0	4	4	3	5	10	5	3	24
Memo:										
IBRD	4	5	14	13	12	11	9	8	8	7
IDA	0	1	8	16	19	20	22	24	27	31
UNDISBURSED DEBT	**215**	**1,147**	**2,170**	**3,036**	**2,674**	**2,966**	**2,754**	**2,719**	**3,082**	**2,577**
Official creditors	196	899	2,070	2,649	2,401	2,702	2,537	2,489	2,772	2,375
Private creditors	19	248	99	387	273	263	217	230	309	202
Memorandum items										
Concessional LDOD	187	1,031	4,217	6,028	6,370	6,259	6,060	6,852	7,468	7,021
Variable rate LDOD	0	85	256	313	355	379	495	642	562	508
Public sector LDOD	311	1,219	4,854	6,598	7,029	6,959	6,891	7,843	8,385	7,927
Private sector LDOD	5	11	194	206	210	194	180	194	207	272

6. CURRENCY COMPOSITION OF LONG-TERM DEBT (PERCENT)

	1970	1980	1990	1994	1995	1996	1997	1998	1999	2000
Deutsche mark	13.8	11.2	12.0	7.9	7.9	7.2	6.3	6.0	4.8	4.7
French franc	3.6	2.7	3.2	2.2	2.1	1.9	1.7	1.6	1.3	1.2
Japanese yen	6.4	15.0	22.7	29.5	28.7	27.0	25.4	27.5	30.2	29.5
Pound sterling	28.8	2.3	3.2	1.9	1.8	1.8	1.6	1.1	0.9	0.7
Swiss franc	0.3	2.4	0.9	0.5	0.5	0.4	0.4	0.3	0.3	0.3
U.S.dollars	19.7	37.0	36.2	34.6	35.6	37.9	41.7	40.4	36.9	38.8
Multiple currency	14.3	8.5	13.9	18.6	18.6	19.3	18.7	19.0	22.2	21.3
Special drawing rights	0.0	0.0	0.5	0.5	0.5	0.5	0.5	0.5	0.5	0.5
All other currencies	13.1	20.9	7.4	4.3	4.3	4.0	3.7	3.6	2.9	3.0

SRI LANKA

(US$ million, unless otherwise indicated)

	1970	1980	1990	1994	1995	1996	1997	1998	1999	2000
7. DEBT RESTRUCTURINGS										
Total amount rescheduled	..	..	0	0	0	0	0	0	0	0
Debt stock rescheduled	..	..	0	0	0	0	0	0	0	0
Principal rescheduled	..	..	0	0	0	0	0	0	0	0
Official	..	..	0	0	0	0	0	0	0	0
Private	..	..	0	0	0	0	0	0	0	0
Interest rescheduled	..	..	0	0	0	0	0	0	0	0
Official	..	..	0	0	0	0	0	0	0	0
Private	..	..	0	0	0	0	0	0	0	0
Debt forgiven	..	..	0	0	7	0	0	0	0	0
Memo: interest forgiven	..	..	0	0	0	0	0	0	0	0
Debt stock reduction	..	..	0	0	0	0	0	0	0	0
of which debt buyback	..	..	0	0	0	0	0	0	0	0
8. DEBT STOCK-FLOW RECONCILIATION										
Total change in debt stocks	..	..	682	1,058	410	-120	-267	856	958	-731
Net flows on debt	19	334	331	591	360	254	291	374	472	-62
Net change in interest arrears	..	..	4	7	3	86	-5	21	17	-23
Interest capitalized	..	..	0	0	0	0	0	0	0	0
Debt forgiveness or reduction	..	..	0	0	-7	0	0	0	0	0
Cross-currency valuation	..	..	296	368	-42	-555	-660	327	202	-580
Residual	..	..	51	92	96	95	107	134	267	-67
9. AVERAGE TERMS OF NEW COMMITMENTS										
ALL CREDITORS										
Interest (%)	3.0	3.9	1.8	3.9	3.5	3.6	3.6	5.1	3.8	4.5
Maturity (years)	27.1	30.6	34.8	21.7	26.0	25.7	24.6	27.5	27.0	21.9
Grace period (years)	4.9	7.7	9.5	6.3	7.0	7.6	7.4	8.1	6.9	5.2
Grant element (%)	47.9	50.4	69.3	43.1	48.8	48.5	48.2	35.5	46.7	37.8
Official creditors										
Interest (%)	2.9	1.3	1.4	2.3	3.2	3.1	2.3	4.4	2.9	2.6
Maturity (years)	27.9	40.9	36.3	30.6	30.2	28.3	30.4	37.2	32.7	32.1
Grace period (years)	5.1	9.9	10.1	9.5	8.5	8.4	9.1	9.9	9.2	8.5
Grant element (%)	49.2	75.1	73.0	62.2	56.2	54.0	61.5	46.9	58.3	59.7
Private creditors										
Interest (%)	5.9	8.7	8.5	6.6	4.8	6.3	7.2	6.4	6.6	6.6
Maturity (years)	7.4	11.9	8.8	6.5	11.2	8.5	8.8	6.5	10.1	10.4
Grace period (years)	1.4	3.8	0.8	0.8	1.9	1.8	2.9	4.4	0.1	1.3
Grant element (%)	12.6	5.8	4.3	10.3	22.9	11.8	11.6	10.8	12.2	13.2
Memorandum items										
Commitments	81	752	837	778	420	1,187	776	792	716	418
Official creditors	78	484	791	492	327	1,033	570	540	536	221
Private creditors	3	268	46	286	93	154	206	252	181	196

10. CONTRACTUAL OBLIGATIONS ON OUTSTANDING LONG-TERM DEBT

	2001	2002	2003	2004	2005	2006	2007	2008	2009	2010
TOTAL										
Disbursements	842	753	478	284	127	52	27	9	6	0
Principal	418	401	407	419	429	441	444	499	435	411
Interest	199	211	212	205	198	189	177	166	148	135
Official creditors										
Disbursements	743	688	452	272	127	52	27	9	6	0
Principal	265	298	304	317	330	345	354	382	385	392
Interest	145	162	167	166	166	162	156	150	141	132
Bilateral creditors										
Disbursements	515	476	307	180	73	25	11	1	1	0
Principal	200	227	234	243	252	259	261	268	264	267
Interest	111	128	133	132	131	125	117	109	101	93
Multilateral creditors										
Disbursements	228	212	146	93	54	27	15	8	5	0
Principal	64	71	70	74	78	86	93	114	120	124
Interest	33	34	34	34	35	38	39	41	40	39
Private creditors										
Disbursements	99	65	26	11	0	0	0	0	0	0
Principal	153	103	103	102	99	96	90	117	50	19
Interest	55	49	45	39	33	26	21	15	7	4
Commercial banks										
Disbursements	93	61	24	11	0	0	0	0	0	0
Principal	101	51	50	49	48	45	41	28	27	16
Interest	25	22	21	18	15	12	9	6	5	3
Other private										
Disbursements	7	4	2	1	0	0	0	0	0	0
Principal	53	53	54	53	51	51	49	89	23	3
Interest	30	27	24	21	18	15	12	9	2	1

ST. KITTS AND NEVIS

(US$ million, unless otherwise indicated)

	1970	1980	1990	1994	1995	1996	1997	1998	1999	2000
1. SUMMARY DEBT DATA										
TOTAL DEBT STOCKS (EDT)	..	..	**45.2**	**58.2**	**56.8**	**64.6**	**114.4**	**128.8**	**139.9**	**140.1**
Long-term debt (LDOD)	..	..	**44.2**	**55.2**	**54.1**	**62.7**	**112.3**	**125.0**	**135.7**	**135.8**
Public and publicly guaranteed	..	..	44.2	55.2	54.1	62.7	112.3	125.0	135.7	135.8
Private nonguaranteed	..	..	0.0	0.0	0.0	0.0	0.0	0.0	0.0	0.0
Use of IMF credit	**0.0**	**0.0**	**0.0**	**0.0**	**0.0**	**0.0**	**0.0**	**2.3**	**2.2**	**2.1**
Short-term debt	..	..	**1.0**	**3.0**	**2.7**	**1.9**	**2.1**	**1.5**	**2.0**	**2.2**
of which interest arrears on LDOD	..	..	0.0	1.0	1.2	0.2	0.1	0.3	0.1	0.7
Official creditors	..	..	0.0	1.0	1.2	0.2	0.1	0.3	0.1	0.1
Private creditors	..	..	0.0	0.0	0.0	0.0	0.0	0.0	0.0	0.6
Memo: principal arrears on LDOD	..	..	0.0	0.7	0.7	0.0	0.1	0.1	0.1	0.4
Official creditors	..	..	0.0	0.6	0.3	0.0	0.0	0.1	0.1	0.0
Private creditors	..	..	0.0	0.1	0.4	0.0	0.1	0.0	0.0	0.4
Memo: export credits	..	..	30.0	24.2	29.1	32.3	58.0	22.4	19.9	27.6
TOTAL DEBT FLOWS										
Disbursements	..	..	**7.3**	**9.5**	**5.6**	**13.3**	**55.2**	**24.4**	**20.9**	**13.8**
Long-term debt	..	..	7.3	9.5	5.6	13.3	55.2	22.2	20.9	13.8
IMF purchases	0.0	0.0	0.0	0.0	0.0	0.0	0.0	2.2	0.0	0.0
Principal repayments	..	..	**1.5**	**4.8**	**4.8**	**4.8**	**4.7**	**6.0**	**9.4**	**12.8**
Long-term debt	..	..	1.5	4.8	4.8	4.8	4.7	6.0	9.4	12.8
IMF repurchases	0.0	0.0	0.0	0.0	0.0	0.0	0.0	0.0	0.0	0.0
Net flows on debt	..	..	**5.8**	**3.5**	**0.3**	**8.9**	**50.7**	**17.7**	**12.1**	**0.6**
of which short-term debt	..	..	0.0	-1.1	-0.6	0.4	0.2	-0.8	0.6	-0.4
Interest payments (INT)	..	..	**1.5**	**1.9**	**2.0**	**2.1**	**2.2**	**4.9**	**7.9**	**6.8**
Long-term debt	..	..	1.4	1.7	1.9	2.0	2.1	4.8	7.8	6.6
IMF charges	0.0	0.0	0.0	0.0	0.0	0.0	0.0	0.0	0.1	0.1
Short-term debt	..	..	0.1	0.1	0.1	0.1	0.1	0.1	0.1	0.1
Net transfers on debt	..	..	**4.3**	**1.7**	**-1.7**	**6.8**	**48.6**	**12.8**	**4.2**	**-6.2**
Total debt service paid (TDS)	..	..	**3.0**	**6.7**	**6.8**	**6.9**	**6.9**	**10.9**	**17.4**	**19.6**
Long-term debt	..	..	2.9	6.6	6.6	6.8	6.8	10.8	17.2	19.4
IMF repurchases and charges	0.0	0.0	0.0	0.0	0.0	0.0	0.0	0.0	0.1	0.1
Short-term debt (interest only)	..	..	0.1	0.1	0.1	0.1	0.1	0.1	0.1	0.1
2. AGGREGATE NET RESOURCE FLOWS AND NET TRANSFERS (LONG-TERM)										
NET RESOURCE FLOWS	..	..	**56.8**	**20.1**	**21.7**	**44.8**	**70.3**	**53.8**	**70.7**	**98.8**
Net flow of long-term debt (ex. IMF)	..	..	5.8	4.6	0.9	8.6	50.5	16.2	11.5	1.0
Foreign direct investment (net)	..	..	49.0	15.0	20.0	35.0	20.0	32.0	58.0	96.0
Portfolio equity flows	..	..	0.0	0.0	0.0	0.0	0.0	0.0	0.0	0.0
Grants (excluding technical coop.)	..	..	2.0	0.4	0.8	1.2	-0.2	5.5	1.2	1.8
Memo: technical coop. grants	..	..	2.2	4.0	2.3	2.7	2.3	1.1	0.8	0.6
official net resource flows	..	..	8.2	2.8	2.6	11.0	32.9	14.3	6.9	3.8
private net resource flows	..	..	48.6	17.3	19.1	33.8	37.4	39.5	63.8	95.0
NET TRANSFERS	..	..	**50.4**	**9.4**	**10.8**	**32.8**	**57.1**	**39.0**	**50.9**	**79.2**
Interest on long-term debt	..	..	1.4	1.7	1.9	2.0	2.1	4.8	7.8	6.6
Profit remittances on FDI	..	..	5.0	9.0	9.0	10.0	11.0	10.0	12.0	13.0
Memo: official net transfers	..	..	6.8	1.3	1.1	9.3	31.0	11.1	1.8	-0.3
private net transfers	..	..	43.6	8.1	9.7	23.5	26.1	27.9	49.1	79.5
3. MAJOR ECONOMIC AGGREGATES										
Gross national income (GNI)	..	..	154.5	208.7	219.7	224.8	249.8	256.0	269.5	275.2
Exports of goods & services (XGS)	..	..	102.8	137.9	119.1	119.4	142.7	150.7	142.1	159.7
of which workers remittances	..	..	17.2	14.1	..	..	..	..	..	..
Imports of goods & services (MGS)	..	..	140.1	159.7	190.6	218.1	224.2	236.5	245.9	293.6
International reserves (RES)	..	..	16.3	31.8	33.5	32.7	36.1	46.8	49.6	45.2
Current account balance	..	..	-47.0	-26.4	-53.5	-83.3	-67.5	..	..	..
4. DEBT INDICATORS										
EDT / XGS (%)	..	..	44.0	42.2	47.7	54.1	80.2	85.5	98.5	87.7
EDT / GNI (%)	..	..	29.3	27.9	25.9	28.7	45.8	50.3	51.9	50.9
TDS / XGS (%)	..	..	2.9	4.9	5.7	5.8	4.8	7.2	12.3	12.3
INT / XGS (%)	..	..	1.5	1.4	1.7	1.8	1.5	3.3	5.6	4.3
INT / GNI (%)	..	..	1.0	0.9	0.9	0.9	0.9	1.9	2.9	2.5
RES / EDT (%)	..	..	36.0	54.7	58.9	50.7	31.5	36.3	35.4	32.3
RES / MGS (months)	..	..	1.4	2.4	2.1	1.8	1.9	2.4	2.4	1.9
Short-term / EDT (%)	..	..	2.2	5.2	4.8	2.9	1.8	1.2	1.4	1.6
Concessional / EDT (%)	..	..	76.6	67.2	72.9	80.7	73.2	68.6	65.3	66.0
Multilateral / EDT (%)	..	..	44.3	46.4	52.1	52.3	35.3	31.8	35.5	37.9

ST. KITTS AND NEVIS

(US$ million, unless otherwise indicated)

	1970	1980	1990	1994	1995	1996	1997	1998	1999	2000
5. LONG-TERM DEBT										
DEBT OUTSTANDING (LDOD)	..	..	**44.2**	**55.2**	**54.1**	**62.7**	**112.3**	**125.0**	**135.7**	**135.8**
Public and publicly guaranteed	..	..	**44.2**	**55.2**	**54.1**	**62.7**	**112.3**	**125.0**	**135.7**	**135.8**
Official creditors	..	..	41.4	48.5	48.5	58.3	90.5	95.7	100.6	101.8
Multilateral	..	..	20.0	27.0	29.6	33.8	40.4	41.0	49.6	53.1
Concessional	..	..	15.1	21.1	23.6	28.4	34.2	33.9	40.4	43.9
Bilateral	..	..	21.5	21.5	19.0	24.5	50.0	54.7	51.1	48.6
Concessional	..	..	19.5	18.0	17.8	23.7	49.5	54.5	50.9	48.5
Private creditors	..	..	2.7	6.7	5.6	4.4	21.8	29.3	35.1	34.0
Bonds	..	..	0.0	0.0	0.0	0.0	0.0	0.0	0.0	0.0
Commercial banks	..	..	0.0	0.0	0.0	0.0	18.0	18.5	24.3	26.8
Other private	..	..	2.7	6.7	5.6	4.4	3.8	10.8	10.7	7.2
Private nonguaranteed	..	..	**0.0**	**0.0**	**0.0**	**0.0**	**0.0**	**0.0**	**0.0**	**0.0**
Bonds	..	..	0.0	0.0	0.0	0.0	0.0	0.0	0.0	0.0
Commercial banks and other	..	..	0.0	0.0	0.0	0.0	0.0	0.0	0.0	0.0
Memo:										
IBRD	0.0	0.0	0.0	0.8	1.1	1.0	0.9	0.8	3.6	4.5
IDA	0.0	0.0	0.0	1.6	1.6	1.6	1.5	1.5	1.5	1.4
DISBURSEMENTS	..	..	**7.3**	**9.5**	**5.6**	**13.3**	**55.2**	**22.2**	**20.9**	**13.8**
Public and publicly guaranteed	..	..	**7.3**	**9.5**	**5.6**	**13.3**	**55.2**	**22.2**	**20.9**	**13.8**
Official creditors	..	..	7.3	6.2	5.0	12.8	36.4	12.4	12.0	7.1
Multilateral	..	..	2.4	2.7	3.8	6.2	9.6	6.5	11.6	6.7
Concessional	..	..	2.3	1.8	3.5	6.2	7.7	5.1	8.4	5.6
Bilateral	..	..	4.9	3.4	1.3	6.6	26.8	6.0	0.4	0.4
Concessional	..	..	4.9	1.3	1.3	6.6	26.8	6.0	0.4	0.4
Private creditors	..	..	0.0	3.3	0.6	0.5	18.8	9.8	8.9	6.7
Bonds	..	..	0.0	0.0	0.0	0.0	0.0	0.0	0.0	0.0
Commercial banks	..	..	0.0	0.0	0.0	0.0	18.0	1.5	7.0	6.7
Other private	..	..	0.0	3.3	0.6	0.5	0.8	8.3	1.9	0.0
Private nonguaranteed	..	..	**0.0**	**0.0**	**0.0**	**0.0**	**0.0**	**0.0**	**0.0**	**0.0**
Bonds	..	..	0.0	0.0	0.0	0.0	0.0	0.0	0.0	0.0
Commercial banks and other	..	..	0.0	0.0	0.0	0.0	0.0	0.0	0.0	0.0
Memo:										
IBRD	0.0	0.0	0.0	0.6	0.3	0.0	0.0	0.2	2.8	1.1
IDA	0.0	0.0	0.0	0.1	0.0	0.0	0.0	0.0	0.0	0.0
PRINCIPAL REPAYMENTS	..	..	**1.5**	**4.8**	**4.8**	**4.8**	**4.7**	**6.0**	**9.4**	**12.8**
Public and publicly guaranteed	..	..	**1.5**	**4.8**	**4.8**	**4.8**	**4.7**	**6.0**	**9.4**	**12.8**
Official creditors	..	..	1.1	3.8	3.3	3.1	3.3	3.7	6.3	5.1
Multilateral	..	..	0.7	1.4	1.5	1.7	2.2	2.3	2.4	2.4
Concessional	..	..	0.6	1.1	1.0	1.3	1.6	1.8	1.8	1.8
Bilateral	..	..	0.3	2.4	1.8	1.4	1.1	1.4	3.9	2.7
Concessional	..	..	0.2	1.6	1.4	1.1	0.8	1.2	3.8	2.6
Private creditors	..	..	0.4	1.0	1.5	1.7	1.4	2.3	3.1	7.7
Bonds	..	..	0.0	0.0	0.0	0.0	0.0	0.0	0.0	0.0
Commercial banks	..	..	0.0	0.0	0.0	0.0	0.0	0.9	1.2	4.2
Other private	..	..	0.4	1.0	1.5	1.7	1.4	1.4	2.0	3.5
Private nonguaranteed	..	..	**0.0**	**0.0**	**0.0**	**0.0**	**0.0**	**0.0**	**0.0**	**0.0**
Bonds	..	..	0.0	0.0	0.0	0.0	0.0	0.0	0.0	0.0
Commercial banks and other	..	..	0.0	0.0	0.0	0.0	0.0	0.0	0.0	0.0
Memo:										
IBRD	0.0	0.0	0.0	0.0	0.0	0.0	0.1	0.1	0.1	0.1
IDA	0.0	0.0	0.0	0.0	0.0	0.0	0.0	0.0	0.0	0.0
NET FLOWS ON DEBT	..	..	**5.8**	**4.6**	**0.9**	**8.6**	**50.5**	**16.2**	**11.5**	**1.0**
Public and publicly guaranteed	..	..	**5.8**	**4.6**	**0.9**	**8.6**	**50.5**	**16.2**	**11.5**	**1.0**
Official creditors	..	..	6.2	2.4	1.8	9.8	33.1	8.8	5.7	2.0
Multilateral	..	..	1.7	1.3	2.3	4.5	7.4	4.2	9.2	4.2
Concessional	..	..	1.6	0.8	2.4	4.9	6.2	3.3	6.6	3.8
Bilateral	..	..	4.6	1.1	-0.5	5.2	25.7	4.6	-3.5	-2.3
Concessional	..	..	4.7	-0.3	-0.1	5.6	26.0	4.8	-3.4	-2.2
Private creditors	..	..	-0.4	2.3	-0.9	-1.2	17.4	7.5	5.8	-1.0
Bonds	..	..	0.0	0.0	0.0	0.0	0.0	0.0	0.0	0.0
Commercial banks	..	..	0.0	0.0	0.0	0.0	18.0	0.5	5.8	2.5
Other private	..	..	-0.4	2.3	-0.9	-1.2	-0.6	6.9	0.0	-3.5
Private nonguaranteed	..	..	**0.0**	**0.0**	**0.0**	**0.0**	**0.0**	**0.0**	**0.0**	**0.0**
Bonds	..	..	0.0	0.0	0.0	0.0	0.0	0.0	0.0	0.0
Commercial banks and other	..	..	0.0	0.0	0.0	0.0	0.0	0.0	0.0	0.0
Memo:										
IBRD	0.0	0.0	0.0	0.6	0.3	0.0	-0.1	0.1	2.7	1.0
IDA	0.0	0.0	0.0	0.1	0.0	0.0	0.0	0.0	0.0	0.0

ST. KITTS AND NEVIS

(US$ million, unless otherwise indicated)

	1970	1980	1990	1994	1995	1996	1997	1998	1999	2000
INTEREST PAYMENTS (LINT)	..	..	**1.4**	**1.7**	**1.9**	**2.0**	**2.1**	**4.8**	**7.8**	**6.6**
Public and publicly guaranteed	..	..	**1.4**	**1.7**	**1.9**	**2.0**	**2.1**	**4.8**	**7.8**	**6.6**
Official creditors	..	..	1.4	1.5	1.5	1.7	1.9	3.2	5.1	4.1
Multilateral	..	..	0.7	0.9	1.0	1.1	1.0	1.3	1.5	1.9
Concessional	..	..	0.5	0.7	0.7	0.8	0.8	1.0	1.2	1.5
Bilateral	..	..	0.7	0.6	0.5	0.6	0.9	1.9	3.5	2.2
Concessional	..	..	0.6	0.4	0.4	0.5	0.8	1.9	3.5	2.1
Private creditors	..	..	0.0	0.2	0.4	0.3	0.3	1.6	2.7	2.5
Bonds	..	..	0.0	0.0	0.0	0.0	0.0	0.0	0.0	0.0
Commercial banks	..	..	0.0	0.0	0.0	0.0	0.0	1.4	2.0	1.8
Other private	..	..	0.0	0.2	0.4	0.3	0.2	0.2	0.7	0.7
Private nonguaranteed	..	..	**0.0**	**0.0**	**0.0**	**0.0**	**0.0**	**0.0**	**0.0**	**0.0**
Bonds	..	..	0.0	0.0	0.0	0.0	0.0	0.0	0.0	0.0
Commercial banks and other	..	..	0.0	0.0	0.0	0.0	0.0	0.0	0.0	0.0
Memo:										
IBRD	0.0	0.0	0.0	0.0	0.1	0.1	0.1	0.1	0.1	0.3
IDA	0.0	0.0	0.0	0.0	0.0	0.0	0.0	0.0	0.0	0.0
NET TRANSFERS ON DEBT	..	..	**4.4**	**2.9**	**-1.0**	**6.6**	**48.4**	**11.4**	**3.7**	**-5.6**
Public and publicly guaranteed	..	..	**4.4**	**2.9**	**-1.0**	**6.6**	**48.4**	**11.4**	**3.7**	**-5.6**
Official creditors	..	..	4.8	0.9	0.3	8.1	31.2	5.5	0.6	-2.1
Multilateral	..	..	1.0	0.4	1.3	3.5	6.4	2.9	7.6	2.3
Concessional	..	..	1.1	0.1	1.8	4.1	5.4	2.3	5.4	2.3
Bilateral	..	..	3.8	0.5	-1.0	4.6	24.8	2.7	-7.0	-4.4
Concessional	..	..	4.1	-0.7	-0.6	5.0	25.2	2.9	-6.9	-4.4
Private creditors	..	..	-0.5	2.0	-1.3	-1.5	17.2	5.9	3.1	-3.5
Bonds	..	..	0.0	0.0	0.0	0.0	0.0	0.0	0.0	0.0
Commercial banks	..	..	0.0	0.0	0.0	0.0	18.0	-0.9	3.8	0.7
Other private	..	..	-0.5	2.0	-1.3	-1.5	-0.8	6.8	-0.8	-4.2
Private nonguaranteed	..	..	**0.0**	**0.0**	**0.0**	**0.0**	**0.0**	**0.0**	**0.0**	**0.0**
Bonds	..	..	0.0	0.0	0.0	0.0	0.0	0.0	0.0	0.0
Commercial banks and other	..	..	0.0	0.0	0.0	0.0	0.0	0.0	0.0	0.0
Memo:										
IBRD	0.0	0.0	0.0	0.6	0.3	-0.1	-0.2	0.0	2.7	0.7
IDA	0.0	0.0	0.0	0.1	0.0	0.0	0.0	0.0	0.0	0.0
DEBT SERVICE (LTDS)	..	..	**2.9**	**6.6**	**6.6**	**6.8**	**6.8**	**10.8**	**17.2**	**19.4**
Public and publicly guaranteed	..	..	**2.9**	**6.6**	**6.6**	**6.8**	**6.8**	**10.8**	**17.2**	**19.4**
Official creditors	..	..	2.4	5.3	4.7	4.7	5.2	6.9	11.4	9.2
Multilateral	..	..	1.4	2.3	2.4	2.7	3.2	3.6	3.9	4.4
Concessional	..	..	1.2	1.7	1.7	2.1	2.3	2.8	3.0	3.3
Bilateral	..	..	1.0	3.0	2.3	2.0	1.9	3.3	7.4	4.8
Concessional	..	..	0.8	2.0	1.8	1.6	1.6	3.0	7.3	4.8
Private creditors	..	..	0.5	1.3	1.9	2.0	1.6	3.9	5.8	10.2
Bonds	..	..	0.0	0.0	0.0	0.0	0.0	0.0	0.0	0.0
Commercial banks	..	..	0.0	0.0	0.0	0.0	0.0	2.3	3.2	6.0
Other private	..	..	0.5	1.3	1.9	2.0	1.6	1.6	2.7	4.2
Private nonguaranteed	..	..	**0.0**	**0.0**	**0.0**	**0.0**	**0.0**	**0.0**	**0.0**	**0.0**
Bonds	..	..	0.0	0.0	0.0	0.0	0.0	0.0	0.0	0.0
Commercial banks and other	..	..	0.0	0.0	0.0	0.0	0.0	0.0	0.0	0.0
Memo:										
IBRD	0.0	0.0	0.0	0.0	0.1	0.1	0.2	0.1	0.2	0.3
IDA	0.0	0.0	0.0	0.0	0.0	0.0	0.0	0.0	0.0	0.0
UNDISBURSED DEBT	..	..	**15.3**	**42.1**	**46.4**	**69.1**	**49.7**	**54.8**	**78.8**	**77.2**
Official creditors	..	..	14.3	41.0	45.9	69.1	49.7	52.9	78.8	77.2
Private creditors	..	..	1.1	1.0	0.5	0.0	0.0	1.9	0.0	0.0
Memorandum items										
Concessional LDOD	..	..	34.7	39.1	41.5	52.1	83.7	88.4	91.3	92.4
Variable rate LDOD	..	..	0.0	1.4	1.7	1.7	1.6	1.4	4.7	5.6
Public sector LDOD	..	..	40.7	53.5	52.9	61.8	111.8	124.9	135.7	135.8
Private sector LDOD	..	..	3.4	1.7	1.3	0.9	0.5	0.1	0.0	0.0

6. CURRENCY COMPOSITION OF LONG-TERM DEBT (PERCENT)

	1970	1980	1990	1994	1995	1996	1997	1998	1999	2000
Deutsche mark	..	..	0.0	0.0	0.0	0.0	0.0	0.0	0.0	0.0
French franc	..	..	0.0	0.0	0.0	0.0	0.0	0.0	0.0	0.0
Japanese yen	..	..	0.0	0.0	0.0	0.0	0.0	0.0	0.0	0.0
Pound sterling	..	..	16.3	9.8	7.4	6.1	3.6	2.8	2.0	1.7
Swiss franc	..	..	0.0	0.0	0.0	0.0	0.0	0.0	0.0	0.0
U.S.dollars	..	..	37.8	51.7	51.4	55.3	72.5	74.1	74.9	76.8
Multiple currency	..	..	35.6	33.0	33.8	28.9	15.6	12.8	11.0	9.9
Special drawing rights	..	..	0.0	0.0	0.0	0.0	0.1	0.3	0.3	0.3
All other currencies	..	..	10.3	5.5	7.4	9.7	8.2	10.0	11.8	11.3

ST. KITTS AND NEVIS

(US$ million, unless otherwise indicated)

	1970	1980	1990	1994	1995	1996	1997	1998	1999	2000
7. DEBT RESTRUCTURINGS										
Total amount rescheduled	..	..	0.0	0.0	0.0	0.0	0.0	0.0	0.0	0.0
Debt stock rescheduled	..	..	0.0	0.0	0.0	0.0	0.0	0.0	0.0	0.0
Principal rescheduled	..	..	0.0	0.0	0.0	0.0	0.0	0.0	0.0	0.0
Official	..	..	0.0	0.0	0.0	0.0	0.0	0.0	0.0	0.0
Private	..	..	0.0	0.0	0.0	0.0	0.0	0.0	0.0	0.0
Interest rescheduled	..	..	0.0	0.0	0.0	0.0	0.0	0.0	0.0	0.0
Official	..	..	0.0	0.0	0.0	0.0	0.0	0.0	0.0	0.0
Private	..	..	0.0	0.0	0.0	0.0	0.0	0.0	0.0	0.0
Debt forgiven	..	..	0.0	0.0	0.0	0.0	0.0	0.0	0.0	0.0
Memo: interest forgiven	..	..	0.0	0.0	0.0	0.0	0.0	0.0	0.0	0.0
Debt stock reduction	..	..	0.0	0.0	0.0	0.0	0.0	0.0	0.0	0.0
of which debt buyback	..	..	0.0	0.0	0.0	0.0	0.0	0.0	0.0	0.0
8. DEBT STOCK-FLOW RECONCILIATION										
Total change in debt stocks	..	..	8.6	4.5	-1.4	7.8	49.8	14.4	11.1	0.2
Net flows on debt	..	..	5.8	3.5	0.3	8.9	50.7	17.7	12.1	0.6
Net change in interest arrears	..	..	-0.1	0.2	0.2	-1.1	0.0	0.2	-0.2	0.6
Interest capitalized	..	..	0.0	0.0	0.0	0.0	0.0	0.0	0.0	0.0
Debt forgiveness or reduction	..	..	0.0	0.0	0.0	0.0	0.0	0.0	0.0	0.0
Cross-currency valuation	..	..	1.3	0.7	0.1	0.0	-0.7	0.3	-0.8	-0.8
Residual	..	..	0.6	0.1	-2.0	0.0	-0.2	-3.7	-0.1	-0.2
9. AVERAGE TERMS OF NEW COMMITMENTS										
ALL CREDITORS										
Interest (%)	..	..	4.0	5.1	3.7	2.0	6.2	5.1	3.4	7.0
Maturity (years)	..	..	31.7	6.9	18.8	32.2	12.0	14.8	26.2	17.9
Grace period (years)	..	..	7.5	1.8	5.2	9.5	6.0	4.0	8.2	3.1
Grant element (%)	..	..	41.5	16.9	40.7	66.1	17.8	27.4	51.5	19.5
Official creditors										
Interest (%)	..	..	4.5	2.0	3.7	2.0	4.9	4.4	2.5	4.1
Maturity (years)	..	..	38.0	10.9	18.8	32.2	15.0	20.2	28.4	21.4
Grace period (years)	..	..	9.0	3.4	5.2	9.5	3.5	5.7	9.6	6.1
Grant element (%)	..	..	46.1	38.4	40.7	66.1	27.8	38.5	59.7	41.1
Private creditors										
Interest (%)	..	..	2.0	5.8	0.0	0.0	7.5	6.1	8.5	9.5
Maturity (years)	..	..	5.8	6.0	0.0	0.0	9.1	6.8	13.4	15.0
Grace period (years)	..	..	1.3	1.5	0.0	0.0	8.4	1.4	0.3	0.5
Grant element (%)	..	..	22.5	12.3	0.0	0.0	8.0	10.9	5.3	1.3
Memorandum items										
Commitments	..	..	5.5	5.3	11.2	36.3	37.5	29.1	46.5	12.4
Official creditors	..	..	4.4	0.9	11.2	36.3	18.6	17.4	39.5	5.7
Private creditors	..	..	1.1	4.4	0.0	0.0	18.8	11.7	7.0	6.7

10. CONTRACTUAL OBLIGATIONS ON OUTSTANDING LONG-TERM DEBT

	2001	2002	2003	2004	2005	2006	2007	2008	2009	2010
TOTAL										
Disbursements	18.3	22.3	14.7	9.3	5.6	3.4	1.9	0.9	0.8	0.0
Principal	9.1	9.6	9.7	10.0	10.6	10.8	10.3	22.6	10.5	11.1
Interest	6.6	6.8	6.8	6.6	6.3	5.8	5.5	3.9	3.5	3.0
Official creditors										
Disbursements	18.3	22.3	14.7	9.3	5.6	3.4	1.9	0.9	0.8	0.0
Principal	6.4	6.9	7.4	7.8	8.4	9.2	9.3	8.8	9.5	10.4
Interest	3.8	4.3	4.4	4.4	4.2	4.0	3.7	3.4	3.1	2.7
Bilateral creditors										
Disbursements	3.9	2.3	1.3	0.6	0.2	0.0	0.0	0.0	0.0	0.0
Principal	3.8	4.0	4.0	4.0	4.2	4.5	4.5	4.0	4.0	4.0
Interest	1.9	1.8	1.7	1.6	1.5	1.3	1.1	0.9	0.8	0.6
Multilateral creditors										
Disbursements	14.3	20.0	13.3	8.7	5.4	3.4	1.9	0.9	0.8	0.0
Principal	2.7	2.9	3.4	3.8	4.1	4.7	4.8	4.7	5.4	6.3
Interest	1.9	2.4	2.7	2.8	2.8	2.7	2.6	2.4	2.3	2.1
Private creditors										
Disbursements	0.0	0.0	0.0	0.0	0.0	0.0	0.0	0.0	0.0	0.0
Principal	2.7	2.7	2.3	2.3	2.3	1.6	1.0	13.9	1.0	0.8
Interest	2.8	2.6	2.4	2.2	2.0	1.9	1.7	0.5	0.4	0.3
Commercial banks										
Disbursements	0.0	0.0	0.0	0.0	0.0	0.0	0.0	0.0	0.0	0.0
Principal	1.3	1.3	1.0	1.0	1.0	1.0	1.0	13.9	1.0	0.8
Interest	2.3	2.2	2.1	2.0	1.9	1.8	1.7	0.5	0.4	0.3
Other private										
Disbursements	0.0	0.0	0.0	0.0	0.0	0.0	0.0	0.0	0.0	0.0
Principal	1.4	1.4	1.3	1.2	1.2	0.6	0.0	0.0	0.0	0.0
Interest	0.5	0.4	0.3	0.2	0.1	0.0	0.0	0.0	0.0	0.0

ST. LUCIA

(US$ million, unless otherwise indicated)

	1970	1980	1990	1994	1995	1996	1997	1998	1999	2000
1. SUMMARY DEBT DATA										
TOTAL DEBT STOCKS (EDT)	..	..	**79.2**	**113.6**	**128.3**	**141.6**	**152.9**	**190.0**	**198.5**	**237.0**
Long-term debt (LDOD)	..	..	**72.1**	**103.6**	**111.3**	**121.4**	**119.9**	**133.5**	**143.2**	**169.2**
Public and publicly guaranteed	..	..	72.1	103.6	111.3	121.4	119.9	133.5	143.2	169.2
Private nonguaranteed	..	..	0.0	0.0	0.0	0.0	0.0	0.0	0.0	0.0
Use of IMF credit	**0.0**	**0.0**	**0.0**	**0.0**	**0.0**	**0.0**	**0.0**	**0.0**	**0.0**	**0.0**
Short-term debt	..	..	**7.0**	**10.0**	**16.9**	**20.2**	**33.0**	**56.5**	**55.3**	**67.8**
of which interest arrears on LDOD	..	..	0.8	0.0	0.0	0.0	0.0	0.0	0.0	0.0
Official creditors	..	..	0.8	0.0	0.0	0.0	0.0	0.0	0.0	0.0
Private creditors	..	..	0.0	0.0	0.0	0.0	0.0	0.0	0.0	0.0
Memo: principal arrears on LDOD	..	..	0.1	0.2	0.0	0.0	0.0	0.0	0.0	0.0
Official creditors	..	..	0.1	0.2	0.0	0.0	0.0	0.0	0.0	0.0
Private creditors	..	..	0.0	0.0	0.0	0.0	0.0	0.0	0.0	0.0
Memo: export credits	..	..	40.0	30.8	30.3	31.8	30.7	2.3	2.7	4.9
TOTAL DEBT FLOWS										
Disbursements	..	..	**8.0**	**8.9**	**11.5**	**18.0**	**10.4**	**19.5**	**23.2**	**50.3**
Long-term debt	..	..	8.0	8.9	11.5	18.0	10.4	19.5	23.2	50.3
IMF purchases	0.0	0.0	0.0	0.0	0.0	0.0	0.0	0.0	0.0	0.0
Principal repayments	..	..	**3.2**	**5.8**	**6.2**	**6.5**	**6.9**	**8.3**	**10.4**	**21.0**
Long-term debt	..	..	3.2	5.8	6.2	6.5	6.9	8.3	10.4	21.0
IMF repurchases	0.0	0.0	0.0	0.0	0.0	0.0	0.0	0.0	0.0	0.0
Net flows on debt	..	..	**7.0**	**8.8**	**12.3**	**14.7**	**16.3**	**34.8**	**11.6**	**41.8**
of which short-term debt	..	..	2.2	5.6	6.9	3.3	12.8	23.5	-1.2	12.5
Interest payments (INT)	..	..	**3.1**	**5.0**	**5.7**	**6.2**	**6.6**	**8.1**	**8.9**	**19.3**
Long-term debt	..	..	2.8	4.5	4.8	5.3	5.2	5.8	6.4	16.5
IMF charges	0.0	0.0	0.0	0.0	0.0	0.0	0.0	0.0	0.0	0.0
Short-term debt	..	..	0.3	0.5	0.9	0.9	1.4	2.4	2.5	2.8
Net transfers on debt	..	..	**3.8**	**3.7**	**6.6**	**8.4**	**9.7**	**26.6**	**2.7**	**22.5**
Total debt service paid (TDS)	..	..	**6.3**	**10.8**	**11.9**	**12.8**	**13.5**	**16.4**	**19.3**	**40.3**
Long-term debt	..	..	6.0	10.3	10.9	11.9	12.1	14.0	16.8	37.5
IMF repurchases and charges	0.0	0.0	0.0	0.0	0.0	0.0	0.0	0.0	0.0	0.0
Short-term debt (interest only)	..	..	0.3	0.5	0.9	0.9	1.4	2.4	2.5	2.8
2. AGGREGATE NET RESOURCE FLOWS AND NET TRANSFERS (LONG-TERM)										
NET RESOURCE FLOWS	..	..	**52.9**	**53.4**	**81.2**	**57.7**	**58.5**	**108.5**	**116.3**	**88.7**
Net flow of long-term debt (ex. IMF)	..	..	4.8	3.1	5.4	11.4	3.5	11.3	12.8	29.4
Foreign direct investment (net)	..	..	45.0	32.5	33.0	18.0	50.0	83.0	83.0	49.0
Portfolio equity flows	..	..	0.0	0.0	0.0	0.0	0.0	0.0	0.0	0.0
Grants (excluding technical coop.)	..	..	3.1	17.8	42.8	28.3	5.0	14.3	20.6	10.3
Memo: technical coop. grants	..	..	3.5	7.1	4.7	5.1	4.4	4.5	3.5	4.4
official net resource flows	..	..	8.7	20.9	48.2	39.7	8.5	18.5	16.2	15.3
private net resource flows	..	..	44.2	32.5	33.0	18.0	50.0	90.0	100.1	73.4
NET TRANSFERS	..	..	**23.1**	**14.9**	**43.4**	**22.4**	**21.3**	**69.7**	**74.9**	**36.2**
Interest on long-term debt	..	..	2.8	4.5	4.8	5.3	5.2	5.8	6.4	16.5
Profit remittances on FDI	..	..	27.0	34.0	33.0	30.0	32.0	33.0	35.0	36.0
Memo: official net transfers	..	..	6.1	16.4	43.4	34.4	3.3	12.7	10.9	10.1
private net transfers	..	..	17.0	-1.5	0.0	-12.0	18.0	57.0	64.0	26.1
3. MAJOR ECONOMIC AGGREGATES										
Gross national income (GNI)	..	..	369.2	484.0	521.2	530.4	542.1	581.2	627.6	669.3
Exports of goods & services (XGS)	..	..	301.2	362.1	407.2	381.4	384.9	411.2	400.8	420.2
of which workers remittances	..	..	13.7	19.6	21.0	22.1	20.1	20.5	20.8	20.8
Imports of goods & services (MGS)	..	..	352.1	408.9	438.6	453.6	481.8	500.5	516.3	534.8
International reserves (RES)	..	..	44.6	57.8	63.1	56.1	61.0	70.6	74.5	78.8
Current account balance	..	..	-57.0	-48.5	-33.2	-80.3	-104.3	-89.7	-113.4	-112.5
4. DEBT INDICATORS										
EDT / XGS (%)	..	..	26.3	31.4	31.5	37.1	39.7	46.2	49.5	56.4
EDT / GNI (%)	..	..	21.5	23.5	24.6	26.7	28.2	32.7	31.6	35.4
TDS / XGS (%)	..	..	2.1	3.0	2.9	3.4	3.5	4.0	4.8	9.6
INT / XGS (%)	..	..	1.0	1.4	1.4	1.6	1.7	2.0	2.2	4.6
INT / GNI (%)	..	..	0.8	1.0	1.1	1.2	1.2	1.4	1.4	2.9
RES / EDT (%)	..	..	56.3	50.9	49.2	39.7	39.9	37.2	37.5	33.3
RES / MGS (months)	..	..	1.5	1.7	1.7	1.5	1.5	1.7	1.7	1.8
Short-term / EDT (%)	..	..	8.8	8.8	13.2	14.3	21.6	29.7	27.9	28.6
Concessional / EDT (%)	..	..	41.5	56.8	57.6	57.8	54.9	45.1	40.1	32.6
Multilateral / EDT (%)	..	..	53.3	62.8	61.6	60.9	56.3	48.9	46.6	41.9

ST. LUCIA

(US$ million, unless otherwise indicated)

	1970	1980	1990	1994	1995	1996	1997	1998	1999	2000
5. LONG-TERM DEBT										
DEBT OUTSTANDING (LDOD)	..	..	**72.1**	**103.6**	**111.3**	**121.4**	**119.9**	**133.5**	**143.2**	**169.2**
Public and publicly guaranteed	..	..	**72.1**	**103.6**	**111.3**	**121.4**	**119.9**	**133.5**	**143.2**	**169.2**
Official creditors	..	..	69.5	103.5	111.3	121.4	119.9	126.5	119.0	120.7
Multilateral	..	..	42.2	71.3	79.0	86.2	86.0	92.9	92.4	99.4
Concessional	..	..	32.5	48.9	56.2	60.6	61.6	61.9	59.2	58.7
Bilateral	..	..	27.3	32.3	32.3	35.1	33.9	33.6	26.6	21.3
Concessional	..	..	0.4	15.6	17.7	21.3	22.3	23.8	20.4	18.5
Private creditors	..	..	2.6	0.1	0.0	0.0	0.0	7.1	24.2	48.6
Bonds	..	..	0.0	0.0	0.0	0.0	0.0	0.0	0.0	0.0
Commercial banks	..	..	2.6	0.1	0.0	0.0	0.0	7.1	24.2	48.6
Other private	..	..	0.0	0.0	0.0	0.0	0.0	0.0	0.0	0.0
Private nonguaranteed	..	..	**0.0**	**0.0**	**0.0**	**0.0**	**0.0**	**0.0**	**0.0**	**0.0**
Bonds	..	..	0.0	0.0	0.0	0.0	0.0	0.0	0.0	0.0
Commercial banks and other	..	..	0.0	0.0	0.0	0.0	0.0	0.0	0.0	0.0
Memo:										
IBRD	0.0	0.0	0.0	1.5	2.1	3.9	3.7	5.4	6.2	6.0
IDA	0.0	0.0	0.0	5.7	7.9	8.2	9.7	11.4	11.6	11.6
DISBURSEMENTS	..	..	**8.0**	**8.9**	**11.5**	**18.0**	**10.4**	**19.5**	**23.2**	**50.3**
Public and publicly guaranteed	..	..	**8.0**	**8.9**	**11.5**	**18.0**	**10.4**	**19.5**	**23.2**	**50.3**
Official creditors	..	..	8.0	8.9	11.5	18.0	10.4	12.5	6.0	16.8
Multilateral	..	..	6.9	6.7	10.8	13.2	7.0	11.1	6.0	15.7
Concessional	..	..	4.3	4.0	9.3	7.9	5.2	2.9	1.2	3.7
Bilateral	..	..	1.1	2.2	0.8	4.8	3.3	1.4	0.0	1.1
Concessional	..	..	0.2	1.7	0.8	4.8	3.3	1.4	0.0	1.1
Private creditors	..	..	0.0	0.0	0.0	0.0	0.0	7.1	17.2	33.5
Bonds	..	..	0.0	0.0	0.0	0.0	0.0	0.0	0.0	0.0
Commercial banks	..	..	0.0	0.0	0.0	0.0	0.0	7.1	17.2	33.5
Other private	..	..	0.0	0.0	0.0	0.0	0.0	0.0	0.0	0.0
Private nonguaranteed	..	..	**0.0**	**0.0**	**0.0**	**0.0**	**0.0**	**0.0**	**0.0**	**0.0**
Bonds	..	..	0.0	0.0	0.0	0.0	0.0	0.0	0.0	0.0
Commercial banks and other	..	..	0.0	0.0	0.0	0.0	0.0	0.0	0.0	0.0
Memo:										
IBRD	0.0	0.0	0.0	1.0	0.7	2.2	0.4	1.5	0.8	0.9
IDA	0.0	0.0	0.0	0.2	2.1	0.6	2.0	1.2	0.5	0.7
PRINCIPAL REPAYMENTS	..	..	**3.2**	**5.8**	**6.2**	**6.5**	**6.9**	**8.3**	**10.4**	**21.0**
Public and publicly guaranteed	..	..	**3.2**	**5.8**	**6.2**	**6.5**	**6.9**	**8.3**	**10.4**	**21.0**
Official creditors	..	..	2.4	5.8	6.2	6.5	6.9	8.2	10.3	11.8
Multilateral	..	..	2.4	3.7	4.2	4.5	4.9	5.4	5.8	6.7
Concessional	..	..	2.0	2.3	2.6	2.7	2.8	3.3	3.4	3.1
Bilateral	..	..	0.0	2.1	2.0	2.1	2.0	2.8	4.6	5.1
Concessional	..	..	0.0	0.1	0.1	0.1	0.1	0.9	1.3	2.0
Private creditors	..	..	0.8	0.0	0.0	0.0	0.0	0.0	0.1	9.2
Bonds	..	..	0.0	0.0	0.0	0.0	0.0	0.0	0.0	0.0
Commercial banks	..	..	0.8	0.0	0.0	0.0	0.0	0.0	0.1	9.2
Other private	..	..	0.0	0.0	0.0	0.0	0.0	0.0	0.0	0.0
Private nonguaranteed	..	..	**0.0**	**0.0**	**0.0**	**0.0**	**0.0**	**0.0**	**0.0**	**0.0**
Bonds	..	..	0.0	0.0	0.0	0.0	0.0	0.0	0.0	0.0
Commercial banks and other	..	..	0.0	0.0	0.0	0.0	0.0	0.0	0.0	0.0
Memo:										
IBRD	0.0	0.0	0.0	0.0	0.1	0.2	0.2	0.2	0.2	0.5
IDA	0.0	0.0	0.0	0.0	0.0	0.0	0.0	0.0	0.0	0.1
NET FLOWS ON DEBT	..	..	**4.8**	**3.1**	**5.4**	**11.4**	**3.5**	**11.3**	**12.8**	**29.4**
Public and publicly guaranteed	..	..	**4.8**	**3.1**	**5.4**	**11.4**	**3.5**	**11.3**	**12.8**	**29.4**
Official creditors	..	..	5.6	3.1	5.4	11.4	3.5	4.2	-4.4	5.0
Multilateral	..	..	4.5	3.0	6.6	8.7	2.2	5.6	0.2	9.0
Concessional	..	..	2.2	1.7	6.7	5.1	2.4	-0.4	-2.1	0.6
Bilateral	..	..	1.1	0.1	-1.3	2.7	1.3	-1.4	-4.6	-4.0
Concessional	..	..	0.2	1.6	0.7	4.7	3.3	0.5	-1.3	-0.9
Private creditors	..	..	-0.8	0.0	0.0	0.0	0.0	7.0	17.1	24.4
Bonds	..	..	0.0	0.0	0.0	0.0	0.0	0.0	0.0	0.0
Commercial banks	..	..	-0.8	0.0	0.0	0.0	0.0	7.0	17.1	24.4
Other private	..	..	0.0	0.0	0.0	0.0	0.0	0.0	0.0	0.0
Private nonguaranteed	..	..	**0.0**	**0.0**	**0.0**	**0.0**	**0.0**	**0.0**	**0.0**	**0.0**
Bonds	..	..	0.0	0.0	0.0	0.0	0.0	0.0	0.0	0.0
Commercial banks and other	..	..	0.0	0.0	0.0	0.0	0.0	0.0	0.0	0.0
Memo:										
IBRD	0.0	0.0	0.0	1.0	0.6	2.0	0.2	1.3	0.6	0.4
IDA	0.0	0.0	0.0	0.2	2.1	0.6	2.0	1.2	0.5	0.6

ST. LUCIA

(US$ million, unless otherwise indicated)

	1970	1980	1990	1994	1995	1996	1997	1998	1999	2000
INTEREST PAYMENTS (LINT)	..	..	**2.8**	**4.5**	**4.8**	**5.3**	**5.2**	**5.8**	**6.4**	**16.5**
Public and publicly guaranteed	..	..	**2.8**	**4.5**	**4.8**	**5.3**	**5.2**	**5.8**	**6.4**	**16.5**
Official creditors	..	..	2.6	4.5	4.8	5.3	5.2	5.8	5.3	5.2
Multilateral	..	..	1.8	2.8	3.0	3.5	3.7	3.9	3.6	4.0
Concessional	..	..	1.3	1.5	1.6	1.7	1.9	2.0	1.4	1.7
Bilateral	..	..	0.8	1.7	1.8	1.9	1.5	1.8	1.7	1.2
Concessional	..	..	0.0	0.8	0.9	0.9	0.9	0.9	1.0	0.9
Private creditors	..	..	0.2	0.0	0.0	0.0	0.0	0.0	1.1	11.3
Bonds	..	..	0.0	0.0	0.0	0.0	0.0	0.0	0.0	0.0
Commercial banks	..	..	0.2	0.0	0.0	0.0	0.0	0.0	1.1	11.3
Other private	..	..	0.0	0.0	0.0	0.0	0.0	0.0	0.0	0.0
Private nonguaranteed	..	..	**0.0**	**0.0**	**0.0**	**0.0**	**0.0**	**0.0**	**0.0**	**0.0**
Bonds	..	..	0.0	0.0	0.0	0.0	0.0	0.0	0.0	0.0
Commercial banks and other	..	..	0.0	0.0	0.0	0.0	0.0	0.0	0.0	0.0
Memo:										
IBRD	0.0	0.0	0.0	0.0	0.1	0.2	0.3	0.3	0.3	0.3
IDA	0.0	0.0	0.0	0.0	0.0	0.1	0.1	0.1	0.1	0.1
NET TRANSFERS ON DEBT	..	..	**2.0**	**-1.4**	**0.6**	**6.1**	**-1.7**	**5.5**	**6.4**	**12.9**
Public and publicly guaranteed	..	..	**2.0**	**-1.4**	**0.6**	**6.1**	**-1.7**	**5.5**	**6.4**	**12.9**
Official creditors	..	..	3.0	-1.4	0.6	6.1	-1.7	-1.5	-9.7	-0.2
Multilateral	..	..	2.7	0.2	3.7	5.3	-1.5	1.7	-3.4	4.9
Concessional	..	..	1.0	0.2	5.1	3.4	0.5	-2.4	-3.5	-1.1
Bilateral	..	..	0.3	-1.6	-3.1	0.9	-0.2	-3.2	-6.3	-5.1
Concessional	..	..	0.2	0.8	-0.3	3.8	2.4	-0.4	-2.3	-1.8
Private creditors	..	..	-1.0	0.0	0.0	0.0	0.0	7.0	16.1	13.0
Bonds	..	..	0.0	0.0	0.0	0.0	0.0	0.0	0.0	0.0
Commercial banks	..	..	-1.0	0.0	0.0	0.0	0.0	7.0	16.1	13.0
Other private	..	..	0.0	0.0	0.0	0.0	0.0	0.0	0.0	0.0
Private nonguaranteed	..	..	**0.0**	**0.0**	**0.0**	**0.0**	**0.0**	**0.0**	**0.0**	**0.0**
Bonds	..	..	0.0	0.0	0.0	0.0	0.0	0.0	0.0	0.0
Commercial banks and other	..	..	0.0	0.0	0.0	0.0	0.0	0.0	0.0	0.0
Memo:										
IBRD	0.0	0.0	0.0	1.0	0.4	1.8	-0.1	1.1	0.3	0.0
IDA	0.0	0.0	0.0	0.1	2.1	0.5	1.9	1.2	0.4	0.5
DEBT SERVICE (LTDS)	..	..	**6.0**	**10.3**	**10.9**	**11.9**	**12.1**	**14.0**	**16.8**	**37.5**
Public and publicly guaranteed	..	..	**6.0**	**10.3**	**10.9**	**11.9**	**12.1**	**14.0**	**16.8**	**37.5**
Official creditors	..	..	5.0	10.3	10.9	11.9	12.1	14.0	15.6	17.0
Multilateral	..	..	4.2	6.5	7.1	7.9	8.6	9.4	9.4	10.7
Concessional	..	..	3.3	3.8	4.2	4.5	4.7	5.3	4.8	4.8
Bilateral	..	..	0.8	3.8	3.8	3.9	3.5	4.6	6.3	6.2
Concessional	..	..	0.0	0.9	1.0	1.0	0.9	1.7	2.3	2.9
Private creditors	..	..	1.0	0.0	0.0	0.0	0.0	0.0	1.1	20.5
Bonds	..	..	0.0	0.0	0.0	0.0	0.0	0.0	0.0	0.0
Commercial banks	..	..	1.0	0.0	0.0	0.0	0.0	0.0	1.1	20.5
Other private	..	..	0.0	0.0	0.0	0.0	0.0	0.0	0.0	0.0
Private nonguaranteed	..	..	**0.0**	**0.0**	**0.0**	**0.0**	**0.0**	**0.0**	**0.0**	**0.0**
Bonds	..	..	0.0	0.0	0.0	0.0	0.0	0.0	0.0	0.0
Commercial banks and other	..	..	0.0	0.0	0.0	0.0	0.0	0.0	0.0	0.0
Memo:										
IBRD	0.0	0.0	0.0	0.0	0.2	0.4	0.5	0.4	0.6	0.9
IDA	0.0	0.0	0.0	0.0	0.0	0.1	0.1	0.1	0.1	0.2
UNDISBURSED DEBT	..	..	**53.5**	**33.5**	**68.9**	**53.7**	**60.8**	**57.2**	**61.1**	**65.3**
Official creditors	..	..	53.5	33.5	68.9	53.7	46.7	45.0	42.0	56.3
Private creditors	..	..	0.0	0.0	0.0	0.0	14.1	12.1	19.0	9.0
Memorandum items										
Concessional LDOD	..	..	32.9	64.5	73.9	81.9	84.0	85.8	79.5	77.2
Variable rate LDOD	..	..	0.0	1.6	2.2	4.5	5.1	7.5	11.6	11.7
Public sector LDOD	..	..	72.1	103.6	111.3	121.4	119.9	133.5	143.2	169.2
Private sector LDOD	..	..	0.0	0.0	0.0	0.0	0.0	0.0	0.0	0.0

6. CURRENCY COMPOSITION OF LONG-TERM DEBT (PERCENT)

	1970	1980	1990	1994	1995	1996	1997	1998	1999	2000
Deutsche mark	..	..	6.0	3.0	2.7	2.0	1.6	1.3	0.9	0.6
French franc	..	..	0.3	15.1	15.9	14.0	13.2	12.0	8.7	6.1
Japanese yen	..	..	4.0	3.1	2.4	1.7	1.2	1.0	0.7	0.3
Pound sterling	..	..	40.3	16.5	13.7	12.1	10.2	7.7	4.7	1.9
Swiss franc	..	..	1.1	0.6	0.5	0.3	0.3	0.2	0.1	0.0
U.S.dollars	..	..	32.8	50.6	53.4	57.8	62.4	61.8	57.4	49.7
Multiple currency	..	..	0.0	1.9	3.3	5.2	5.1	5.8	5.9	4.9
Special drawing rights	..	..	0.8	1.8	1.8	1.6	1.7	1.9	2.3	1.8
All other currencies	..	..	14.7	7.4	6.3	5.3	4.3	8.3	19.3	34.7

ST. LUCIA

(US$ million, unless otherwise indicated)

	1970	1980	1990	1994	1995	1996	1997	1998	1999	2000
7. DEBT RESTRUCTURINGS										
Total amount rescheduled	..	..	0.0	0.0	0.0	0.0	0.0	0.0	0.0	0.0
Debt stock rescheduled	..	..	0.0	0.0	0.0	0.0	0.0	0.0	0.0	0.0
Principal rescheduled	..	..	0.0	0.0	0.0	0.0	0.0	0.0	0.0	0.0
Official	..	..	0.0	0.0	0.0	0.0	0.0	0.0	0.0	0.0
Private	..	..	0.0	0.0	0.0	0.0	0.0	0.0	0.0	0.0
Interest rescheduled	..	..	0.0	0.0	0.0	0.0	0.0	0.0	0.0	0.0
Official	..	..	0.0	0.0	0.0	0.0	0.0	0.0	0.0	0.0
Private	..	..	0.0	0.0	0.0	0.0	0.0	0.0	0.0	0.0
Debt forgiven	..	..	0.4	0.2	0.0	0.0	0.0	0.0	0.0	0.0
Memo: interest forgiven	..	..	0.0	0.0	0.0	0.0	0.0	0.0	0.0	0.0
Debt stock reduction	..	..	0.0	0.0	0.0	0.0	0.0	0.0	0.0	0.0
of which debt buyback	..	..	0.0	0.0	0.0	0.0	0.0	0.0	0.0	0.0
8. DEBT STOCK-FLOW RECONCILIATION										
Total change in debt stocks	..	..	13.5	12.7	14.7	13.3	11.4	37.1	8.5	38.5
Net flows on debt	..	..	7.0	8.8	12.3	14.7	16.3	34.8	11.6	41.8
Net change in interest arrears	..	..	0.8	0.0	0.0	0.0	0.0	0.0	0.0	0.0
Interest capitalized	..	..	0.0	0.0	0.0	0.0	0.0	0.0	0.0	0.0
Debt forgiveness or reduction	..	..	-0.4	-0.2	0.0	0.0	0.0	0.0	0.0	0.0
Cross-currency valuation	..	..	5.8	4.0	2.2	-1.1	-4.7	1.8	-3.1	-3.2
Residual	..	..	0.3	0.2	0.1	-0.3	-0.3	0.5	0.0	-0.1
9. AVERAGE TERMS OF NEW COMMITMENTS										
ALL CREDITORS										
Interest (%)	..	..	4.3	4.1	4.7	5.7	6.1	4.6	2.7	7.3
Maturity (years)	..	..	24.1	19.8	24.8	15.9	12.9	20.7	6.1	18.0
Grace period (years)	..	..	8.2	4.1	7.1	3.1	8.0	7.9	4.1	9.3
Grant element (%)	..	..	42.8	36.9	38.4	20.4	23.5	40.3	16.1	17.9
Official creditors										
Interest (%)	..	..	4.3	4.1	4.7	5.7	3.3	3.1	0.6	6.0
Maturity (years)	..	..	24.1	19.8	24.8	15.9	15.7	26.1	24.9	22.7
Grace period (years)	..	..	8.2	4.1	7.1	3.1	3.6	7.6	6.9	5.5
Grant element (%)	..	..	42.8	36.9	38.4	20.4	38.5	53.3	66.4	26.7
Private creditors										
Interest (%)	..	..	0.0	0.0	0.0	0.0	8.0	7.7	3.0	8.7
Maturity (years)	..	..	0.0	0.0	0.0	0.0	11.0	9.0	3.7	13.2
Grace period (years)	..	..	0.0	0.0	0.0	0.0	11.0	8.6	3.7	13.2
Grant element (%)	..	..	0.0	0.0	0.0	0.0	13.0	12.1	9.8	9.1
Memorandum items										
Commitments	..	..	34.9	6.9	50.4	3.5	23.9	16.2	27.1	65.3
Official creditors	..	..	34.9	6.9	50.4	3.5	9.9	11.0	3.0	32.7
Private creditors	..	..	0.0	0.0	0.0	0.0	14.1	5.1	24.1	32.5

10. CONTRACTUAL OBLIGATIONS ON OUTSTANDING LONG-TERM DEBT

	2001	2002	2003	2004	2005	2006	2007	2008	2009	2010
TOTAL										
Disbursements	19.7	20.6	11.9	7.2	2.8	1.7	0.5	0.4	0.3	0.1
Principal	10.9	10.4	10.4	10.6	10.6	11.5	10.9	38.6	10.4	9.8
Interest	9.3	10.1	10.3	10.1	9.8	9.3	8.8	7.7	5.5	5.1
Official creditors										
Disbursements	13.4	17.9	11.9	7.2	2.8	1.7	0.5	0.4	0.3	0.1
Principal	10.8	10.3	10.4	10.6	10.6	11.5	10.9	10.7	10.4	9.8
Interest	5.4	5.9	6.0	5.8	5.5	5.0	4.5	4.0	3.4	3.0
Bilateral creditors										
Disbursements	0.2	0.3	0.2	0.1	0.1	0.0	0.0	0.0	0.0	0.0
Principal	2.6	2.6	2.5	2.5	2.5	2.2	2.0	2.0	1.6	1.2
Interest	1.0	0.9	0.8	0.6	0.5	0.4	0.3	0.2	0.1	0.1
Multilateral creditors										
Disbursements	13.2	17.6	11.7	7.1	2.7	1.7	0.5	0.4	0.3	0.1
Principal	8.3	7.7	7.9	8.1	8.1	9.3	8.9	8.7	8.8	8.6
Interest	4.4	5.0	5.2	5.2	4.9	4.6	4.2	3.8	3.3	2.9
Private creditors										
Disbursements	6.3	2.7	0.0	0.0	0.0	0.0	0.0	0.0	0.0	0.0
Principal	0.0	0.0	0.0	0.0	0.0	0.0	0.0	27.9	0.0	0.0
Interest	3.9	4.2	4.3	4.3	4.3	4.3	4.3	3.8	2.1	2.1
Commercial banks										
Disbursements	6.3	2.7	0.0	0.0	0.0	0.0	0.0	0.0	0.0	0.0
Principal	0.0	0.0	0.0	0.0	0.0	0.0	0.0	27.9	0.0	0.0
Interest	3.9	4.2	4.3	4.3	4.3	4.3	4.3	3.8	2.1	2.1
Other private										
Disbursements	0.0	0.0	0.0	0.0	0.0	0.0	0.0	0.0	0.0	0.0
Principal	0.0	0.0	0.0	0.0	0.0	0.0	0.0	0.0	0.0	0.0
Interest	0.0	0.0	0.0	0.0	0.0	0.0	0.0	0.0	0.0	0.0

ST. VINCENT AND THE GRENADINES

(US$ million, unless otherwise indicated)

	1970	1980	1990	1994	1995	1996	1997	1998	1999	2000
1. SUMMARY DEBT DATA										
TOTAL DEBT STOCKS (EDT)	**1.5**	**10.6**	**61.0**	**115.1**	**119.2**	**123.3**	**118.3**	**136.5**	**194.4**	**192.4**
Long-term debt (LDOD)	**1.5**	**10.3**	**58.9**	**92.3**	**92.3**	**93.9**	**92.8**	**108.1**	**162.6**	**161.0**
Public and publicly guaranteed	1.5	10.3	58.9	92.3	92.3	93.9	92.8	108.1	162.6	161.0
Private nonguaranteed	0.0	0.0	0.0	0.0	0.0	0.0	0.0	0.0	0.0	0.0
Use of IMF credit	**0.0**	**0.3**	**0.0**	**0.0**	**0.0**	**0.0**	**0.0**	**0.0**	**0.0**	**0.0**
Short-term debt	**0.0**	**0.0**	**2.1**	**22.7**	**27.0**	**29.4**	**25.6**	**28.4**	**31.9**	**31.4**
of which interest arrears on LDOD	0.0	0.0	0.1	0.0	0.1	0.5	0.2	0.0	0.1	0.4
Official creditors	0.0	0.0	0.1	0.0	0.1	0.0	0.1	0.0	0.1	0.4
Private creditors	0.0	0.0	0.0	0.0	0.0	0.5	0.1	0.0	0.0	0.0
Memo: principal arrears on LDOD	0.0	0.0	0.1	0.1	0.6	0.9	0.1	0.2	0.3	0.9
Official creditors	0.0	0.0	0.1	0.1	0.3	0.0	0.1	0.2	0.3	0.9
Private creditors	0.0	0.0	0.0	0.0	0.2	0.9	0.0	0.0	0.0	0.0
Memo: export credits	0.0	0.0	2.0	3.4	2.6	5.4	20.4	19.5	42.9	17.1
TOTAL DEBT FLOWS										
Disbursements	**0.4**	**3.5**	**7.2**	**16.6**	**3.6**	**8.7**	**9.8**	**20.8**	**64.2**	**7.4**
Long-term debt	0.4	3.0	7.2	16.6	3.6	8.7	9.8	20.8	64.2	7.4
IMF purchases	0.0	0.5	0.0	0.0	0.0	0.0	0.0	0.0	0.0	0.0
Principal repayments	**0.0**	**0.1**	**2.4**	**4.8**	**4.7**	**5.8**	**6.9**	**6.8**	**6.2**	**8.3**
Long-term debt	0.0	0.1	2.4	4.8	4.7	5.8	6.9	6.8	6.2	8.3
IMF repurchases	0.0	0.0	0.0	0.0	0.0	0.0	0.0	0.0	0.0	0.0
Net flows on debt	**0.4**	**3.4**	**5.2**	**10.8**	**3.1**	**4.9**	**-0.7**	**17.0**	**61.5**	**-1.8**
of which short-term debt	0.0	0.0	0.4	-1.0	4.2	2.0	-3.6	3.0	3.4	-0.8
Interest payments (INT)	**0.1**	**0.3**	**1.9**	**3.9**	**4.2**	**4.5**	**4.8**	**5.0**	**8.4**	**7.0**
Long-term debt	0.1	0.3	1.7	2.5	2.7	2.9	3.2	3.4	6.6	5.2
IMF charges	0.0	0.0	0.0	0.0	0.0	0.0	0.0	0.0	0.0	0.0
Short-term debt	0.0	0.0	0.2	1.4	1.5	1.7	1.6	1.6	1.8	1.9
Net transfers on debt	**0.3**	**3.1**	**3.3**	**6.9**	**-1.2**	**0.4**	**-5.5**	**11.9**	**53.1**	**-8.8**
Total debt service paid (TDS)	**0.1**	**0.4**	**4.3**	**8.7**	**8.9**	**10.3**	**11.8**	**11.9**	**14.5**	**15.4**
Long-term debt	0.1	0.4	4.1	7.3	7.4	8.7	10.1	10.3	12.7	13.5
IMF repurchases and charges	0.0	0.0	0.0	0.0	0.0	0.0	0.0	0.0	0.0	0.0
Short-term debt (interest only)	0.0	0.0	0.2	1.4	1.5	1.7	1.6	1.6	1.8	1.9
2. AGGREGATE NET RESOURCE FLOWS AND NET TRANSFERS (LONG-TERM)										
NET RESOURCE FLOWS	**0.4**	**8.9**	**16.2**	**61.5**	**75.5**	**66.5**	**99.2**	**114.6**	**127.5**	**30.6**
Net flow of long-term debt (ex. IMF)	0.4	2.9	4.8	11.8	-1.1	2.9	2.9	14.0	58.1	-1.0
Foreign direct investment (net)	0.0	1.1	8.0	47.0	30.6	43.0	92.0	89.0	56.0	28.0
Portfolio equity flows	0.0	0.0	0.0	0.0	0.0	0.0	0.0	0.0	0.0	0.0
Grants (excluding technical coop.)	0.0	4.9	3.4	2.8	46.0	20.6	4.4	11.6	13.4	3.6
Memo: technical coop. grants	0.0	1.0	2.4	2.3	2.7	3.2	2.5	2.0	2.0	1.2
official net resource flows	0.0	7.7	8.2	9.8	44.8	23.5	8.8	26.0	14.0	3.0
private net resource flows	0.4	1.2	8.0	51.7	30.7	43.0	90.4	88.6	113.5	27.6
NET TRANSFERS	**0.3**	**8.6**	**1.5**	**47.0**	**59.7**	**45.7**	**77.0**	**90.2**	**101.0**	**4.5**
Interest on long-term debt	0.1	0.3	1.7	2.5	2.7	2.9	3.2	3.4	6.6	5.2
Profit remittances on FDI	0.0	0.0	13.0	12.0	13.0	18.0	19.0	21.0	20.0	21.0
Memo: official net transfers	0.0	7.5	6.5	7.3	42.3	20.8	6.1	22.8	10.7	-0.3
private net transfers	0.3	1.1	-5.0	39.7	17.4	24.9	70.9	67.4	90.3	4.8
3. MAJOR ECONOMIC AGGREGATES										
Gross national income (GNI)	18.5	59.4	187.3	231.3	252.3	268.0	280.9	302.3	308.6	312.3
Exports of goods & services (XGS)	..	39.6	148.7	131.1	155.3	166.9	147.4	154.8	172.6	195.9
of which workers remittances	..	0.0	13.9	14.8	15.2	16.3	..	..	..	..
Imports of goods & services (MGS)	..	65.0	167.9	186.1	190.2	197.1	..	..	..	..
International reserves (RES)	..	7.3	26.5	31.3	29.8	30.2	31.2	38.8	42.6	55.2
Current account balance	..	-9.3	-23.6	-58.0	-41.2	-35.2	..	..	..	..
4. DEBT INDICATORS										
EDT / XGS (%)	..	26.8	41.0	87.8	76.7	73.9	80.2	88.2	112.6	98.2
EDT / GNI (%)	8.1	17.8	32.6	49.8	47.3	46.0	42.1	45.2	63.0	61.6
TDS / XGS (%)	..	1.0	2.9	6.6	5.7	6.2	8.0	7.7	8.4	7.9
INT / XGS (%)	..	0.8	1.3	3.0	2.7	2.7	3.3	3.2	4.9	3.6
INT / GNI (%)	0.5	0.5	1.0	1.7	1.7	1.7	1.7	1.7	2.7	2.2
RES / EDT (%)	..	68.6	43.4	27.2	25.0	24.5	26.4	28.4	21.9	28.7
RES / MGS (months)	..	1.3	1.9	2.0	1.9	1.8	..	..	..	..
Short-term / EDT (%)	0.0	0.0	3.4	19.7	22.7	23.8	21.6	20.8	16.4	16.3
Concessional / EDT (%)	0.0	57.6	82.6	64.8	62.4	63.1	68.9	67.6	47.1	46.6
Multilateral / EDT (%)	0.0	58.5	81.0	53.5	51.5	46.6	51.1	50.9	34.1	35.0

ST. VINCENT AND THE GRENADINES

(US$ million, unless otherwise indicated)

5. LONG-TERM DEBT

	1970	1980	1990	1994	1995	1996	1997	1998	1999	2000
DEBT OUTSTANDING (LDOD)	**1.5**	**10.3**	**58.9**	**92.3**	**92.3**	**93.9**	**92.8**	**108.1**	**162.6**	**161.0**
Public and publicly guaranteed	**1.5**	**10.3**	**58.9**	**92.3**	**92.3**	**93.9**	**92.8**	**108.1**	**162.6**	**161.0**
Official creditors	0.0	9.4	58.8	87.6	87.5	89.1	91.0	106.7	103.7	102.5
Multilateral	0.0	6.2	49.4	61.6	61.4	57.4	60.5	69.5	66.3	67.4
Concessional	0.0	5.1	41.9	50.1	49.4	46.8	51.3	55.1	54.2	54.4
Bilateral	0.0	3.2	9.5	26.0	26.1	31.7	30.5	37.2	37.4	35.2
Concessional	0.0	1.0	8.5	24.5	25.0	31.0	30.2	37.2	37.4	35.2
Private creditors	1.5	0.9	0.0	4.7	4.8	4.8	1.8	1.4	58.9	58.5
Bonds	1.5	0.8	0.0	0.0	0.0	0.0	0.0	0.0	0.0	0.0
Commercial banks	0.0	0.0	0.0	4.7	4.8	4.8	1.8	1.4	58.9	58.5
Other private	0.0	0.1	0.0	0.0	0.0	0.0	0.0	0.0	0.0	0.0
Private nonguaranteed	**0.0**	**0.0**	**0.0**	**0.0**	**0.0**	**0.0**	**0.0**	**0.0**	**0.0**	**0.0**
Bonds	0.0	0.0	0.0	0.0	0.0	0.0	0.0	0.0	0.0	0.0
Commercial banks and other	0.0	0.0	0.0	0.0	0.0	0.0	0.0	0.0	0.0	0.0
Memo:										
IBRD	0.0	0.0	0.0	0.5	0.4	0.3	0.3	0.2	0.2	0.1
IDA	0.0	0.0	6.2	8.0	8.1	7.8	7.3	7.6	7.4	7.0
DISBURSEMENTS	**0.4**	**3.0**	**7.2**	**16.6**	**3.6**	**8.7**	**9.8**	**20.8**	**64.2**	**7.4**
Public and publicly guaranteed	**0.4**	**3.0**	**7.2**	**16.6**	**3.6**	**8.7**	**9.8**	**20.8**	**64.2**	**7.4**
Official creditors	0.0	2.9	7.2	11.9	3.5	8.7	9.8	20.8	6.4	7.4
Multilateral	0.0	2.8	6.6	7.5	2.6	1.8	8.6	12.4	3.6	5.5
Concessional	0.0	1.9	5.3	6.9	1.7	1.3	8.0	6.5	3.2	2.6
Bilateral	0.0	0.1	0.6	4.4	0.9	6.9	1.2	8.4	2.8	1.9
Concessional	0.0	0.0	0.6	2.9	0.9	6.9	1.2	8.4	2.8	1.9
Private creditors	0.4	0.1	0.0	4.7	0.1	0.0	0.0	0.0	57.9	0.0
Bonds	0.4	0.0	0.0	0.0	0.0	0.0	0.0	0.0	0.0	0.0
Commercial banks	0.0	0.0	0.0	4.7	0.1	0.0	0.0	0.0	57.9	0.0
Other private	0.0	0.1	0.0	0.0	0.0	0.0	0.0	0.0	0.0	0.0
Private nonguaranteed	**0.0**	**0.0**	**0.0**	**0.0**	**0.0**	**0.0**	**0.0**	**0.0**	**0.0**	**0.0**
Bonds	0.0	0.0	0.0	0.0	0.0	0.0	0.0	0.0	0.0	0.0
Commercial banks and other	0.0	0.0	0.0	0.0	0.0	0.0	0.0	0.0	0.0	0.0
Memo:										
IBRD	0.0	0.0	0.0	0.0	0.0	0.1	0.1	0.0	0.0	0.0
IDA	0.0	0.0	0.9	0.0	0.0	0.0	0.0	0.1	0.1	0.0
PRINCIPAL REPAYMENTS	**0.0**	**0.1**	**2.4**	**4.8**	**4.7**	**5.8**	**6.9**	**6.8**	**6.2**	**8.3**
Public and publicly guaranteed	**0.0**	**0.1**	**2.4**	**4.8**	**4.7**	**5.8**	**6.9**	**6.8**	**6.2**	**8.3**
Official creditors	0.0	0.1	2.4	4.8	4.7	5.8	5.4	6.4	5.8	7.9
Multilateral	0.0	0.1	2.2	3.4	3.6	4.4	3.7	4.5	3.9	4.4
Concessional	0.0	0.1	1.7	2.4	2.4	3.1	2.6	3.2	2.6	3.1
Bilateral	0.0	0.0	0.2	1.4	1.1	1.4	1.6	2.0	1.9	3.5
Concessional	0.0	0.0	0.1	1.0	0.7	1.0	1.4	1.7	1.9	3.5
Private creditors	0.0	0.0	0.0	0.0	0.0	0.0	1.6	0.4	0.4	0.4
Bonds	0.0	0.0	0.0	0.0	0.0	0.0	0.0	0.0	0.0	0.0
Commercial banks	0.0	0.0	0.0	0.0	0.0	0.0	1.6	0.4	0.4	0.4
Other private	0.0	0.0	0.0	0.0	0.0	0.0	0.0	0.0	0.0	0.0
Private nonguaranteed	**0.0**	**0.0**	**0.0**	**0.0**	**0.0**	**0.0**	**0.0**	**0.0**	**0.0**	**0.0**
Bonds	0.0	0.0	0.0	0.0	0.0	0.0	0.0	0.0	0.0	0.0
Commercial banks and other	0.0	0.0	0.0	0.0	0.0	0.0	0.0	0.0	0.0	0.0
Memo:										
IBRD	0.0	0.0	0.0	0.1	0.1	0.1	0.1	0.1	0.0	0.0
IDA	0.0	0.0	0.0	0.0	0.1	0.1	0.1	0.1	0.1	0.1
NET FLOWS ON DEBT	**0.4**	**2.9**	**4.8**	**11.8**	**-1.1**	**2.9**	**2.9**	**14.0**	**58.1**	**-1.0**
Public and publicly guaranteed	**0.4**	**2.9**	**4.8**	**11.8**	**-1.1**	**2.9**	**2.9**	**14.0**	**58.1**	**-1.0**
Official creditors	0.0	2.8	4.8	7.0	-1.2	2.9	4.4	14.4	0.6	-0.6
Multilateral	0.0	2.7	4.4	4.1	-0.9	-2.6	4.9	7.9	-0.3	1.1
Concessional	0.0	1.7	3.6	4.5	-0.7	-1.8	5.4	3.3	0.6	-0.5
Bilateral	0.0	0.1	0.4	2.9	-0.3	5.6	-0.5	6.4	0.8	-1.6
Concessional	0.0	0.0	0.6	1.9	0.2	6.0	-0.2	6.7	0.8	-1.6
Private creditors	0.4	0.1	0.0	4.7	0.1	0.0	-1.6	-0.4	57.5	-0.4
Bonds	0.4	0.0	0.0	0.0	0.0	0.0	0.0	0.0	0.0	0.0
Commercial banks	0.0	0.0	0.0	4.7	0.1	0.0	-1.6	-0.4	57.5	-0.4
Other private	0.0	0.1	0.0	0.0	0.0	0.0	0.0	0.0	0.0	0.0
Private nonguaranteed	**0.0**	**0.0**	**0.0**	**0.0**	**0.0**	**0.0**	**0.0**	**0.0**	**0.0**	**0.0**
Bonds	0.0	0.0	0.0	0.0	0.0	0.0	0.0	0.0	0.0	0.0
Commercial banks and other	0.0	0.0	0.0	0.0	0.0	0.0	0.0	0.0	0.0	0.0
Memo:										
IBRD	0.0	0.0	0.0	0.0	-0.1	0.0	0.0	-0.1	0.0	0.0
IDA	0.0	0.0	0.9	0.0	-0.1	-0.1	-0.1	0.1	0.0	-0.1

ST. VINCENT AND THE GRENADINES

(US$ million, unless otherwise indicated)

	1970	1980	1990	1994	1995	1996	1997	1998	1999	2000
INTEREST PAYMENTS (LINT)	**0.1**	**0.3**	**1.7**	**2.5**	**2.7**	**2.9**	**3.2**	**3.4**	**6.6**	**5.2**
Public and publicly guaranteed	**0.1**	**0.3**	**1.7**	**2.5**	**2.7**	**2.9**	**3.2**	**3.4**	**6.6**	**5.2**
Official creditors	0.0	0.2	1.7	2.5	2.5	2.7	2.7	3.2	3.3	3.3
Multilateral	0.0	0.2	1.5	1.9	1.8	2.0	1.9	2.2	2.2	2.2
Concessional	0.0	0.1	1.1	1.4	1.2	1.4	1.3	1.8	1.7	1.7
Bilateral	0.0	0.0	0.3	0.6	0.7	0.8	0.8	1.0	1.1	1.2
Concessional	0.0	0.0	0.2	0.5	0.6	0.7	0.8	1.0	1.1	1.2
Private creditors	0.1	0.1	0.0	0.0	0.3	0.1	0.5	0.2	3.2	1.8
Bonds	0.1	0.1	0.0	0.0	0.0	0.0	0.0	0.0	0.0	0.0
Commercial banks	0.0	0.0	0.0	0.0	0.3	0.1	0.5	0.2	3.2	1.8
Other private	0.0	0.0	0.0	0.0	0.0	0.0	0.0	0.0	0.0	0.0
Private nonguaranteed	**0.0**	**0.0**	**0.0**	**0.0**	**0.0**	**0.0**	**0.0**	**0.0**	**0.0**	**0.0**
Bonds	0.0	0.0	0.0	0.0	0.0	0.0	0.0	0.0	0.0	0.0
Commercial banks and other	0.0	0.0	0.0	0.0	0.0	0.0	0.0	0.0	0.0	0.0
Memo:										
IBRD	0.0	0.0	0.0	0.0	0.0	0.0	0.0	0.0	0.0	0.0
IDA	0.0	0.0	0.0	0.1	0.1	0.1	0.1	0.1	0.1	0.1
NET TRANSFERS ON DEBT	**0.3**	**2.6**	**3.1**	**9.3**	**-3.9**	**0.1**	**-0.3**	**10.5**	**51.5**	**-6.1**
Public and publicly guaranteed	**0.3**	**2.6**	**3.1**	**9.3**	**-3.9**	**0.1**	**-0.3**	**10.5**	**51.5**	**-6.1**
Official creditors	0.0	2.5	3.1	4.5	-3.6	0.2	1.8	11.1	-2.8	-3.9
Multilateral	0.0	2.5	3.0	2.2	-2.7	-4.6	3.0	5.7	-2.5	-1.1
Concessional	0.0	1.6	2.4	3.1	-1.9	-3.2	4.1	1.5	-1.1	-2.3
Bilateral	0.0	0.1	0.1	2.3	-0.9	4.8	-1.3	5.4	-0.3	-2.8
Concessional	0.0	0.0	0.4	1.4	-0.4	5.3	-1.0	5.7	-0.3	-2.8
Private creditors	0.3	0.1	0.0	4.7	-0.2	-0.1	-2.1	-0.6	54.3	-2.2
Bonds	0.3	-0.1	0.0	0.0	0.0	0.0	0.0	0.0	0.0	0.0
Commercial banks	0.0	0.0	0.0	4.7	-0.2	-0.1	-2.1	-0.6	54.3	-2.2
Other private	0.0	0.1	0.0	0.0	0.0	0.0	0.0	0.0	0.0	0.0
Private nonguaranteed	**0.0**	**0.0**	**0.0**	**0.0**	**0.0**	**0.0**	**0.0**	**0.0**	**0.0**	**0.0**
Bonds	0.0	0.0	0.0	0.0	0.0	0.0	0.0	0.0	0.0	0.0
Commercial banks and other	0.0	0.0	0.0	0.0	0.0	0.0	0.0	0.0	0.0	0.0
Memo:										
IBRD	0.0	0.0	0.0	-0.1	-0.1	-0.1	-0.1	-0.1	-0.1	0.0
IDA	0.0	0.0	0.8	-0.1	-0.1	-0.1	-0.1	0.0	-0.1	-0.1
DEBT SERVICE (LTDS)	**0.1**	**0.4**	**4.1**	**7.3**	**7.4**	**8.7**	**10.1**	**10.3**	**12.7**	**13.5**
Public and publicly guaranteed	**0.1**	**0.4**	**4.1**	**7.3**	**7.4**	**8.7**	**10.1**	**10.3**	**12.7**	**13.5**
Official creditors	0.0	0.4	4.1	7.3	7.1	8.5	8.1	9.7	9.1	11.3
Multilateral	0.0	0.4	3.6	5.3	5.3	6.4	5.6	6.7	6.1	6.6
Concessional	0.0	0.3	2.9	3.8	3.7	4.5	3.9	5.0	4.4	4.8
Bilateral	0.0	0.0	0.5	2.0	1.8	2.1	2.5	3.0	3.1	4.7
Concessional	0.0	0.0	0.2	1.5	1.3	1.6	2.1	2.7	3.1	4.7
Private creditors	0.1	0.1	0.0	0.0	0.3	0.1	2.1	0.6	3.6	2.2
Bonds	0.1	0.1	0.0	0.0	0.0	0.0	0.0	0.0	0.0	0.0
Commercial banks	0.0	0.0	0.0	0.0	0.3	0.1	2.1	0.6	3.6	2.2
Other private	0.0	0.0	0.0	0.0	0.0	0.0	0.0	0.0	0.0	0.0
Private nonguaranteed	**0.0**	**0.0**	**0.0**	**0.0**	**0.0**	**0.0**	**0.0**	**0.0**	**0.0**	**0.0**
Bonds	0.0	0.0	0.0	0.0	0.0	0.0	0.0	0.0	0.0	0.0
Commercial banks and other	0.0	0.0	0.0	0.0	0.0	0.0	0.0	0.0	0.0	0.0
Memo:										
IBRD	0.0	0.0	0.0	0.1	0.2	0.2	0.1	0.1	0.1	0.0
IDA	0.0	0.0	0.0	0.1	0.1	0.1	0.1	0.1	0.2	0.2
UNDISBURSED DEBT	**0.0**	**13.4**	**29.6**	**31.5**	**40.4**	**53.3**	**44.7**	**33.8**	**25.9**	**127.3**
Official creditors	0.0	12.2	29.6	31.5	40.4	53.3	44.7	33.8	25.9	127.3
Private creditors	0.0	1.2	0.0	0.1	0.0	0.0	0.0	0.0	0.0	0.0
Memorandum items										
Concessional LDOD	0.0	6.1	50.3	74.7	74.3	77.9	81.5	92.3	91.6	89.5
Variable rate LDOD	0.0	0.0	0.0	1.4	1.3	1.0	7.3	10.3	50.4	51.2
Public sector LDOD	1.5	10.3	58.9	92.3	92.3	93.9	92.8	108.1	162.6	161.0
Private sector LDOD	0.0	0.0	0.0	0.0	0.0	0.0	0.0	0.0	0.0	0.0

6. CURRENCY COMPOSITION OF LONG-TERM DEBT (PERCENT)

	1970	1980	1990	1994	1995	1996	1997	1998	1999	2000
Deutsche mark	0.0	0.0	0.7	0.5	0.6	0.5	0.4	0.4	0.2	0.0
French franc	0.0	0.0	0.2	3.6	4.1	4.1	3.6	3.0	1.9	0.6
Japanese yen	0.0	0.0	0.2	0.1	0.1	0.1	0.0	0.0	0.0	0.0
Pound sterling	0.0	36.7	4.6	5.5	5.4	5.0	4.3	5.3	3.1	2.9
Swiss franc	0.0	0.0	0.2	1.3	1.4	1.1	0.9	0.8	0.4	0.3
U.S.dollars	0.0	20.9	67.5	70.0	70.1	70.2	74.4	70.9	82.6	82.7
Multiple currency	0.0	11.3	9.8	5.2	4.5	3.7	3.0	1.9	0.9	0.5
Special drawing rights	0.0	0.0	3.6	2.8	3.1	3.0	2.9	2.7	1.3	1.8
All other currencies	0.0	31.1	13.2	11.0	10.7	12.3	10.5	15.0	9.6	11.2

ST. VINCENT AND THE GRENADINES

(US$ million, unless otherwise indicated)

	1970	1980	1990	1994	1995	1996	1997	1998	1999	2000
7. DEBT RESTRUCTURINGS										
Total amount rescheduled	..	..	0.0	0.0	0.0	0.0	0.0	0.0	0.0	0.0
Debt stock rescheduled	..	..	0.0	0.0	0.0	0.0	0.0	0.0	0.0	0.0
Principal rescheduled	..	..	0.0	0.0	0.0	0.0	0.0	0.0	0.0	0.0
Official	..	..	0.0	0.0	0.0	0.0	0.0	0.0	0.0	0.0
Private	..	..	0.0	0.0	0.0	0.0	0.0	0.0	0.0	0.0
Interest rescheduled	..	..	0.0	0.0	0.0	0.0	0.0	0.0	0.0	0.0
Official	..	..	0.0	0.0	0.0	0.0	0.0	0.0	0.0	0.0
Private	..	..	0.0	0.0	0.0	0.0	0.0	0.0	0.0	0.0
Debt forgiven	..	..	0.8	0.0	0.0	0.3	1.4	0.0	0.0	0.0
Memo: interest forgiven	..	..	0.0	0.0	0.0	0.0	0.0	0.0	0.0	0.0
Debt stock reduction	..	..	0.0	0.0	0.0	0.0	0.0	0.0	0.0	0.0
of which debt buyback	..	..	0.0	0.0	0.0	0.0	0.0	0.0	0.0	0.0
8. DEBT STOCK-FLOW RECONCILIATION										
Total change in debt stocks	..	..	8.2	12.9	4.2	4.0	-4.9	18.1	57.9	-2.0
Net flows on debt	0.4	3.4	5.2	10.8	3.1	4.9	-0.7	17.0	61.5	-1.8
Net change in interest arrears	..	..	0.0	0.0	0.0	0.4	-0.3	-0.2	0.1	0.3
Interest capitalized	..	..	0.0	0.0	0.0	0.0	0.0	0.0	0.0	0.0
Debt forgiveness or reduction	..	..	-0.8	0.0	0.0	-0.3	-1.4	0.0	0.0	0.0
Cross-currency valuation	..	..	1.3	1.5	0.9	-1.4	-2.8	0.7	-3.0	-1.8
Residual	..	..	2.6	0.6	0.1	0.4	0.3	0.7	-0.6	1.2
9. AVERAGE TERMS OF NEW COMMITMENTS										
ALL CREDITORS										
Interest (%)	7.5	4.8	4.0	1.4	3.5	4.3	4.3	3.9	4.4	5.0
Maturity (years)	13.5	17.2	20.7	16.0	19.9	22.2	15.6	21.0	18.8	29.8
Grace period (years)	13.5	4.9	4.9	3.3	4.2	5.9	3.5	5.6	4.3	5.3
Grant element (%)	18.1	32.8	39.8	45.6	41.0	38.3	32.2	42.3	34.9	37.4
Official creditors										
Interest (%)	0.0	4.0	4.0	2.0	3.5	4.3	4.3	3.9	0.0	5.0
Maturity (years)	0.0	20.1	20.7	20.0	19.9	22.2	15.6	21.0	0.0	29.8
Grace period (years)	0.0	6.1	4.9	4.0	4.2	5.9	3.5	5.6	0.0	5.3
Grant element (%)	0.0	40.2	39.8	51.6	41.0	38.3	32.2	42.3	0.0	37.4
Private creditors										
Interest (%)	7.5	7.5	0.0	0.0	0.0	0.0	0.0	0.0	4.4	0.0
Maturity (years)	13.5	7.3	0.0	6.2	0.0	0.0	0.0	0.0	18.8	0.0
Grace period (years)	13.5	0.8	0.0	1.7	0.0	0.0	0.0	0.0	4.3	0.0
Grant element (%)	18.1	7.2	0.0	30.5	0.0	0.0	0.0	0.0	34.9	0.0
Memorandum items										
Commitments	0.4	5.8	8.0	8.3	12.6	22.4	2.4	12.6	57.9	109.3
Official creditors	0.0	4.5	8.0	5.9	12.6	22.4	2.4	12.6	0.0	109.3
Private creditors	0.4	1.3	0.0	2.4	0.0	0.0	0.0	0.0	57.9	0.0

10. CONTRACTUAL OBLIGATIONS ON OUTSTANDING LONG-TERM DEBT

	2001	2002	2003	2004	2005	2006	2007	2008	2009	2010
TOTAL										
Disbursements	23.1	28.6	21.4	15.9	11.9	8.2	5.8	5.6	4.5	2.2
Principal	7.4	8.6	11.0	12.7	16.5	15.7	15.3	15.4	15.4	15.4
Interest	6.9	8.0	8.7	9.0	9.1	8.8	8.5	8.1	7.7	7.2
Official creditors										
Disbursements	23.1	28.6	21.4	15.9	11.9	8.2	5.8	5.6	4.5	2.2
Principal	7.0	8.4	9.1	8.9	12.7	11.8	11.5	11.5	11.5	11.5
Interest	4.2	5.3	6.0	6.5	6.7	6.6	6.4	6.3	6.0	5.7
Bilateral creditors										
Disbursements	17.9	25.0	19.1	14.4	11.0	7.7	5.5	5.4	4.4	2.2
Principal	3.1	3.4	3.4	3.0	7.0	7.0	7.0	7.0	7.0	7.0
Interest	1.8	2.9	3.7	4.3	4.7	4.8	4.8	4.8	4.8	4.6
Multilateral creditors										
Disbursements	5.3	3.7	2.3	1.5	0.9	0.5	0.3	0.2	0.1	0.1
Principal	3.9	5.0	5.7	5.8	5.7	4.8	4.5	4.5	4.5	4.5
Interest	2.4	2.4	2.3	2.1	1.9	1.8	1.6	1.4	1.3	1.1
Private creditors										
Disbursements	0.0	0.0	0.0	0.0	0.0	0.0	0.0	0.0	0.0	0.0
Principal	0.4	0.2	1.9	3.9	3.9	3.9	3.9	3.9	3.9	3.9
Interest	2.7	2.7	2.7	2.5	2.4	2.2	2.0	1.8	1.7	1.5
Commercial banks										
Disbursements	0.0	0.0	0.0	0.0	0.0	0.0	0.0	0.0	0.0	0.0
Principal	0.4	0.2	1.9	3.9	3.9	3.9	3.9	3.9	3.9	3.9
Interest	2.7	2.7	2.7	2.5	2.4	2.2	2.0	1.8	1.7	1.5
Other private										
Disbursements	0.0	0.0	0.0	0.0	0.0	0.0	0.0	0.0	0.0	0.0
Principal	0.0	0.0	0.0	0.0	0.0	0.0	0.0	0.0	0.0	0.0
Interest	0.0	0.0	0.0	0.0	0.0	0.0	0.0	0.0	0.0	0.0

SUDAN

(US$ million, unless otherwise indicated)

	1970	1980	1990	1994	1995	1996	1997	1998	1999	2000
1. SUMMARY DEBT DATA										
TOTAL DEBT STOCKS (EDT)	**385**	**5,177**	**14,762**	**16,918**	**17,603**	**16,972**	**16,326**	**16,843**	**16,132**	**15,741**
Long-term debt (LDOD)	**294**	**4,147**	**9,651**	**9,896**	**10,275**	**9,865**	**9,494**	**9,722**	**9,348**	**9,143**
Public and publicly guaranteed	294	3,822	9,155	9,400	9,779	9,369	8,998	9,226	8,852	8,647
Private nonguaranteed	0	325	496	496	496	496	496	496	496	496
Use of IMF credit	**31**	**431**	**956**	**980**	**960**	**893**	**797**	**772**	**715**	**625**
Short-term debt	**61**	**599**	**4,155**	**6,042**	**6,368**	**6,214**	**6,035**	**6,349**	**6,070**	**5,974**
of which interest arrears on LDOD	0	63	3,705	5,414	5,737	5,683	5,624	5,893	5,761	5,703
Official creditors	0	33	3,244	4,550	4,748	4,767	4,721	4,922	4,876	4,831
Private creditors	0	30	461	863	989	916	903	971	885	873
Memo: principal arrears on LDOD	0	551	5,704	7,155	7,637	7,467	7,321	7,608	7,414	7,307
Official creditors	0	108	3,893	5,024	5,282	5,377	5,348	5,553	5,572	5,494
Private creditors	0	444	1,811	2,131	2,355	2,090	1,973	2,055	1,843	1,813
Memo: export credits	0	0	2,972	2,748	2,921	3,148	2,912	1,816	2,316	2,045
TOTAL DEBT FLOWS										
Disbursements	**47**	**921**	**185**	**12**	**51**	**17**	**5**	**0**	**0**	**0**
Long-term debt	47	711	185	12	51	17	5	0	0	0
IMF purchases	0	210	0	0	0	0	0	0	0	0
Principal repayments	**29**	**131**	**16**	**3**	**54**	**36**	**42**	**59**	**44**	**59**
Long-term debt	21	53	15	3	15	0	0	1	6	4
IMF repurchases	8	78	1	0	39	36	42	57	38	54
Net flows on debt	**70**	**839**	**169**	**9**	**0**	**-119**	**-157**	**-14**	**-191**	**-97**
of which short-term debt	52	50	0	0	3	-100	-120	45	-147	-39
Interest payments (INT)	**13**	**133**	**34**	**1**	**15**	**12**	**15**	**3**	**13**	**3**
Long-term debt	12	49	9	0	2	0	0	2	7	2
IMF charges	0	14	0	0	13	12	15	1	7	0
Short-term debt	1	70	25	0	0	0	0	0	0	0
Net transfers on debt	**57**	**707**	**135**	**9**	**-15**	**-131**	**-173**	**-16**	**-204**	**-100**
Total debt service paid (TDS)	**42**	**264**	**50**	**3**	**69**	**48**	**58**	**61**	**57**	**61**
Long-term debt	33	102	23	3	17	0	0	3	12	7
IMF repurchases and charges	8	92	1	0	52	48	57	58	45	54
Short-term debt (interest only)	1	70	25	0	0	0	0	0	0	0
2. AGGREGATE NET RESOURCE FLOWS AND NET TRANSFERS (LONG-TERM)										
NET RESOURCE FLOWS	**29**	**1,046**	**603**	**372**	**185**	**161**	**221**	**558**	**582**	**563**
Net flow of long-term debt (ex. IMF)	26	658	171	9	36	17	5	-1	-6	-4
Foreign direct investment (net)	0	0	0	0	0	0	98	371	371	392
Portfolio equity flows	0	0	0	0	0	0	0	0	0	0
Grants (excluding technical coop.)	3	388	433	363	149	144	118	188	216	176
Memo: technical coop. grants	7	103	184	84	77	65	33	26	33	33
official net resource flows	32	908	603	372	185	161	123	187	211	171
private net resource flows	-3	138	0	0	0	0	98	371	371	392
NET TRANSFERS	**13**	**997**	**595**	**372**	**183**	**161**	**221**	**556**	**575**	**561**
Interest on long-term debt	12	49	9	0	2	0	0	2	7	2
Profit remittances on FDI	4	0	0	0	0	0	0	0	0	0
Memo: official net transfers	22	864	595	372	183	161	123	185	204	169
private net transfers	-9	133	0	0	0	0	98	371	371	392
3. MAJOR ECONOMIC AGGREGATES										
Gross national income (GNI)	2,092	7,467	12,635	7,259	6,281	7,278	9,301	9,025	8,794	9,754
Exports of goods & services (XGS)	339	1,051	665	558	690	677	641	626	850	1,897
of which workers remittances	..	257	134	..	..	..	..	..	..	..
Imports of goods & services (MGS)	380	1,856	2,237	2,140	2,272	2,586	2,732	3,128	2,774	3,190
International reserves (RES)	22	49	11	78	163	107	82	91	189	..
Current account balance	-41	-721	-1,299	-1,459	-1,479	-1,548	-1,639	-1,995	-1,467	-974
4. DEBT INDICATORS										
EDT / XGS (%)	113.6	492.6	2,219.9	3,033.5	2,551.6	2,506.9	2,546.2	2,690.6	1,897.7	829.8
EDT / GNI (%)	18.4	69.3	116.8	233.1	280.3	233.2	175.5	186.6	183.4	161.4
TDS / XGS (%)	12.3	25.1	7.5	0.6	10.0	7.1	9.0	9.8	6.7	3.2
INT / XGS (%)	3.7	12.6	5.1	0.1	2.2	1.8	2.4	0.4	1.6	0.1
INT / GNI (%)	0.6	1.8	0.3	0.0	0.2	0.2	0.2	0.0	0.2	0.0
RES / EDT (%)	5.7	0.9	0.1	0.5	0.9	0.6	0.5	0.5	1.2	..
RES / MGS (months)	0.7	0.3	0.1	0.4	0.9	0.5	0.4	0.4	0.8	..
Short-term / EDT (%)	15.7	11.6	28.2	35.7	36.2	36.6	37.0	37.7	37.6	38.0
Concessional / EDT (%)	36.0	33.4	30.2	28.2	27.5	28.0	28.4	27.9	28.9	29.0
Multilateral / EDT (%)	26.9	12.2	11.7	12.2	12.1	12.3	12.3	12.2	12.5	12.4

SUDAN

(US$ million, unless otherwise indicated)

	1970	1980	1990	1994	1995	1996	1997	1998	1999	2000
5. LONG-TERM DEBT										
DEBT OUTSTANDING (LDOD)	**294**	**4,147**	**9,651**	**9,896**	**10,275**	**9,865**	**9,494**	**9,722**	**9,348**	**9,143**
Public and publicly guaranteed	**294**	**3,822**	**9,155**	**9,400**	**9,779**	**9,369**	**8,998**	**9,226**	**8,852**	**8,647**
Official creditors	256	3,293	7,500	7,765	7,921	7,776	7,521	7,666	7,505	7,330
Multilateral	104	634	1,723	2,064	2,133	2,084	2,001	2,051	2,011	1,946
Concessional	12	368	1,549	1,880	1,928	1,871	1,798	1,839	1,806	1,750
Bilateral	153	2,659	5,777	5,701	5,787	5,692	5,521	5,615	5,494	5,384
Concessional	127	1,361	2,903	2,895	2,910	2,879	2,838	2,865	2,848	2,820
Private creditors	37	529	1,655	1,635	1,859	1,594	1,477	1,559	1,347	1,317
Bonds	1	0	0	0	0	0	0	0	0	0
Commercial banks	27	298	1,651	1,631	1,855	1,590	1,473	1,555	1,343	1,313
Other private	9	231	4	4	4	4	4	4	4	4
Private nonguaranteed	**0**	**325**	**496**	**496**	**496**	**496**	**496**	**496**	**496**	**496**
Bonds	0	0	0	0	0	0	0	0	0	0
Commercial banks and other	0	325	496	496	496	496	496	496	496	496
Memo:										
IBRD	91	46	19	6	6	6	6	6	3	1
IDA	12	190	1,028	1,251	1,272	1,244	1,198	1,226	1,208	1,167
DISBURSEMENTS	**47**	**711**	**185**	**12**	**51**	**17**	**5**	**0**	**0**	**0**
Public and publicly guaranteed	**47**	**711**	**185**	**12**	**51**	**17**	**5**	**0**	**0**	**0**
Official creditors	45	566	185	12	51	17	5	0	0	0
Multilateral	15	189	185	12	51	17	5	0	0	0
Concessional	0	80	180	10	27	2	0	0	0	0
Bilateral	30	377	0	0	0	0	0	0	0	0
Concessional	15	190	0	0	0	0	0	0	0	0
Private creditors	2	145	0	0	0	0	0	0	0	0
Bonds	0	0	0	0	0	0	0	0	0	0
Commercial banks	0	108	0	0	0	0	0	0	0	0
Other private	2	37	0	0	0	0	0	0	0	0
Private nonguaranteed	**0**	**0**	**0**	**0**	**0**	**0**	**0**	**0**	**0**	**0**
Bonds	0	0	0	0	0	0	0	0	0	0
Commercial banks and other	0	0	0	0	0	0	0	0	0	0
Memo:										
IBRD	15	1	0	0	0	0	0	0	0	0
IDA	0	37	121	8	0	0	0	0	0	0
PRINCIPAL REPAYMENTS	**21**	**53**	**15**	**3**	**15**	**0**	**0**	**1**	**6**	**4**
Public and publicly guaranteed	**21**	**53**	**15**	**3**	**15**	**0**	**0**	**1**	**6**	**4**
Official creditors	16	46	15	3	15	0	0	1	6	4
Multilateral	4	15	15	3	15	0	0	1	6	4
Concessional	0	3	4	3	9	0	0	0	0	2
Bilateral	12	32	0	0	0	0	0	0	0	0
Concessional	5	11	0	0	0	0	0	0	0	0
Private creditors	5	7	0	0	0	0	0	0	0	0
Bonds	1	0	0	0	0	0	0	0	0	0
Commercial banks	3	4	0	0	0	0	0	0	0	0
Other private	1	3	0	0	0	0	0	0	0	0
Private nonguaranteed	**0**	**0**	**0**	**0**	**0**	**0**	**0**	**0**	**0**	**0**
Bonds	0	0	0	0	0	0	0	0	0	0
Commercial banks and other	0	0	0	0	0	0	0	0	0	0
Memo:										
IBRD	4	4	10	0	0	0	0	0	3	2
IDA	0	0	4	0	0	0	0	0	0	2
NET FLOWS ON DEBT	**26**	**658**	**171**	**9**	**36**	**17**	**5**	**-1**	**-6**	**-4**
Public and publicly guaranteed	**26**	**658**	**171**	**9**	**36**	**17**	**5**	**-1**	**-6**	**-4**
Official creditors	29	520	171	9	36	17	5	-1	-6	-4
Multilateral	11	174	171	9	36	17	5	-1	-6	-4
Concessional	0	77	176	7	18	2	0	0	0	-2
Bilateral	19	346	0	0	0	0	0	0	0	0
Concessional	10	179	0	0	0	0	0	0	0	0
Private creditors	-3	138	0	0	0	0	0	0	0	0
Bonds	-1	0	0	0	0	0	0	0	0	0
Commercial banks	-3	104	0	0	0	0	0	0	0	0
Other private	1	33	0	0	0	0	0	0	0	0
Private nonguaranteed	**0**	**0**	**0**	**0**	**0**	**0**	**0**	**0**	**0**	**0**
Bonds	0	0	0	0	0	0	0	0	0	0
Commercial banks and other	0	0	0	0	0	0	0	0	0	0
Memo:										
IBRD	11	-3	-10	0	0	0	0	0	-3	-2
IDA	0	37	117	8	0	0	0	0	0	-2

SUDAN

(US$ million, unless otherwise indicated)

	1970	1980	1990	1994	1995	1996	1997	1998	1999	2000
INTEREST PAYMENTS (LINT)	**12**	**49**	**9**	**0**	**2**	**0**	**0**	**2**	**7**	**2**
Public and publicly guaranteed	**12**	**49**	**9**	**0**	**2**	**0**	**0**	**2**	**7**	**2**
Official creditors	10	44	9	0	2	0	0	2	7	2
Multilateral	5	8	9	0	2	0	0	2	7	2
Concessional	0	2	7	0	1	0	0	0	0	2
Bilateral	5	35	0	0	0	0	0	0	0	0
Concessional	3	26	0	0	0	0	0	0	0	0
Private creditors	2	5	0	0	0	0	0	0	0	0
Bonds	0	0	0	0	0	0	0	0	0	0
Commercial banks	2	2	0	0	0	0	0	0	0	0
Other private	0	3	0	0	0	0	0	0	0	0
Private nonguaranteed	**0**	**0**	**0**	**0**	**0**	**0**	**0**	**0**	**0**	**0**
Bonds	0	0	0	0	0	0	0	0	0	0
Commercial banks and other	0	0	0	0	0	0	0	0	0	0
Memo:										
IBRD	5	4	2	0	0	0	0	0	1	1
IDA	0	1	6	0	0	0	0	0	0	2
NET TRANSFERS ON DEBT	**14**	**609**	**162**	**9**	**34**	**17**	**4**	**-3**	**-12**	**-7**
Public and publicly guaranteed	**14**	**609**	**162**	**9**	**34**	**17**	**4**	**-3**	**-12**	**-7**
Official creditors	20	476	162	9	34	17	4	-3	-12	-7
Multilateral	6	166	162	9	34	17	4	-3	-12	-7
Concessional	0	75	169	7	17	2	0	0	0	-4
Bilateral	14	310	0	0	0	0	0	0	0	0
Concessional	6	153	0	0	0	0	0	0	0	0
Private creditors	-5	133	0	0	0	0	0	0	0	0
Bonds	-1	0	0	0	0	0	0	0	0	0
Commercial banks	-5	102	0	0	0	0	0	0	0	0
Other private	1	31	0	0	0	0	0	0	0	0
Private nonguaranteed	**0**	**0**	**0**	**0**	**0**	**0**	**0**	**0**	**0**	**0**
Bonds	0	0	0	0	0	0	0	0	0	0
Commercial banks and other	0	0	0	0	0	0	0	0	0	0
Memo:										
IBRD	6	-7	-11	0	0	0	0	0	-5	-3
IDA	0	35	110	8	0	0	0	0	0	-4
DEBT SERVICE (LTDS)	**33**	**102**	**23**	**3**	**17**	**0**	**0**	**3**	**12**	**7**
Public and publicly guaranteed	**33**	**102**	**23**	**3**	**17**	**0**	**0**	**3**	**12**	**7**
Official creditors	26	90	23	3	17	0	0	3	12	7
Multilateral	9	23	23	3	17	0	0	3	12	7
Concessional	0	5	10	3	10	0	0	0	0	4
Bilateral	17	67	0	0	0	0	0	0	0	0
Concessional	9	37	0	0	0	0	0	0	0	0
Private creditors	7	12	0	0	0	0	0	0	0	0
Bonds	1	0	0	0	0	0	0	0	0	0
Commercial banks	5	6	0	0	0	0	0	0	0	0
Other private	1	6	0	0	0	0	0	0	0	0
Private nonguaranteed	**0**	**0**	**0**	**0**	**0**	**0**	**0**	**0**	**0**	**0**
Bonds	0	0	0	0	0	0	0	0	0	0
Commercial banks and other	0	0	0	0	0	0	0	0	0	0
Memo:										
IBRD	9	8	11	0	0	0	0	0	5	3
IDA	0	1	10	0	0	0	0	0	0	4
UNDISBURSED DEBT	**124**	**1,310**	**1,284**	**678**	**634**	**583**	**562**	**540**	**23**	**22**
Official creditors	119	1,167	1,284	678	634	583	562	540	23	22
Private creditors	5	143	0	0	0	0	0	0	0	0
Memorandum items										
Concessional LDOD	139	1,730	4,452	4,775	4,838	4,750	4,636	4,704	4,654	4,569
Variable rate LDOD	0	408	1,927	1,909	2,103	1,874	1,772	1,844	1,660	1,634
Public sector LDOD	294	4,145	9,651	9,896	10,275	9,865	9,494	9,722	9,348	9,143
Private sector LDOD	0	2	0	0	0	0	0	0	0	0

6. CURRENCY COMPOSITION OF LONG-TERM DEBT (PERCENT)

	1970	1980	1990	1994	1995	1996	1997	1998	1999	2000
Deutsche mark	7.1	0.5	1.0	0.9	1.0	0.9	0.8	0.9	0.8	0.8
French franc	0.0	2.3	3.4	3.2	3.3	3.2	3.0	3.1	2.8	2.6
Japanese yen	0.0	2.0	2.3	3.1	2.9	2.7	2.5	2.7	3.2	2.9
Pound sterling	15.6	7.0	4.3	3.5	3.4	3.7	3.8	3.7	3.8	3.7
Swiss franc	0.0	0.6	18.6	17.9	19.6	17.5	16.9	17.4	15.6	15.6
U.S.dollars	11.1	54.4	48.1	49.3	47.6	49.3	50.8	49.9	51.7	52.5
Multiple currency	31.1	2.0	1.2	1.4	1.5	1.6	1.6	1.6	1.7	1.6
Special drawing rights	0.0	0.0	0.5	0.5	0.5	0.5	0.5	0.5	0.5	0.5
All other currencies	35.1	31.2	20.6	20.2	20.2	20.6	20.1	20.2	19.9	19.8

SUDAN

(US$ million, unless otherwise indicated)

	1970	1980	1990	1994	1995	1996	1997	1998	1999	2000
7. DEBT RESTRUCTURINGS										
Total amount rescheduled	..	..	0	0	0	0	0	0	0	0
Debt stock rescheduled	..	..	0	0	0	0	0	0	0	0
Principal rescheduled	..	..	0	0	0	0	0	0	0	0
Official	..	..	0	0	0	0	0	0	0	0
Private	..	..	0	0	0	0	0	0	0	0
Interest rescheduled	..	..	0	0	0	0	0	0	0	0
Official	..	..	0	0	0	0	0	0	0	0
Private	..	..	0	0	0	0	0	0	0	0
Debt forgiven	..	..	0	0	0	0	0	0	0	0
Memo: interest forgiven	..	..	0	0	0	0	0	0	0	0
Debt stock reduction	..	..	0	0	0	0	0	0	0	0
of which debt buyback	..	..	0	0	0	0	0	0	0	0
8. DEBT STOCK-FLOW RECONCILIATION										
Total change in debt stocks	..	..	1,403	1,082	685	-631	-646	517	-711	-391
Net flows on debt	70	839	169	9	0	-119	-157	-14	-191	-97
Net change in interest arrears	..	..	645	618	324	-54	-59	269	-133	-57
Interest capitalized	..	..	0	0	0	0	0	0	0	0
Debt forgiveness or reduction	..	..	0	0	0	0	0	0	0	0
Cross-currency valuation	..	..	518	335	274	-516	-484	167	-367	-220
Residual	..	..	71	120	88	58	54	94	-20	-17
9. AVERAGE TERMS OF NEW COMMITMENTS										
ALL CREDITORS										
Interest (%)	1.8	5.7	0.8	0.0	0.0	0.0	0.0	0.0	0.0	0.0
Maturity (years)	17.2	17.9	49.9	0.0	0.0	0.0	0.0	0.0	0.0	0.0
Grace period (years)	8.7	4.6	10.4	0.0	0.0	0.0	0.0	0.0	0.0	0.0
Grant element (%)	54.6	30.2	83.3	0.0	0.0	0.0	0.0	0.0	0.0	0.0
Official creditors										
Interest (%)	1.5	3.7	0.8	0.0	0.0	0.0	0.0	0.0	0.0	0.0
Maturity (years)	17.7	22.7	49.9	0.0	0.0	0.0	0.0	0.0	0.0	0.0
Grace period (years)	9.1	5.9	10.4	0.0	0.0	0.0	0.0	0.0	0.0	0.0
Grant element (%)	57.1	40.8	83.3	0.0	0.0	0.0	0.0	0.0	0.0	0.0
Private creditors										
Interest (%)	5.6	12.0	0.0	0.0	0.0	0.0	0.0	0.0	0.0	0.0
Maturity (years)	9.3	2.9	0.0	0.0	0.0	0.0	0.0	0.0	0.0	0.0
Grace period (years)	3.5	0.4	0.0	0.0	0.0	0.0	0.0	0.0	0.0	0.0
Grant element (%)	17.3	-3.4	0.0	0.0	0.0	0.0	0.0	0.0	0.0	0.0
Memorandum items										
Commitments	97	905	35	0	0	0	0	0	0	0
Official creditors	91	687	35	0	0	0	0	0	0	0
Private creditors	6	218	0	0	0	0	0	0	0	0

10. CONTRACTUAL OBLIGATIONS ON OUTSTANDING LONG-TERM DEBT

	2001	2002	2003	2004	2005	2006	2007	2008	2009	2010
TOTAL										
Disbursements	12	5	2	1	0	0	0	0	0	0
Principal	101	94	94	91	87	84	79	77	76	462
Interest	52	49	46	43	40	38	35	33	31	29
Official creditors										
Disbursements	12	5	2	1	0	0	0	0	0	0
Principal	101	94	94	91	87	84	79	77	76	462
Interest	52	49	46	43	40	38	35	33	31	29
Bilateral creditors										
Disbursements	0	0	0	0	0	0	0	0	0	0
Principal	42	42	41	41	38	35	31	27	26	409
Interest	35	34	32	30	28	26	25	23	22	20
Multilateral creditors										
Disbursements	12	5	2	1	0	0	0	0	0	0
Principal	58	52	53	50	49	49	48	50	50	52
Interest	16	15	14	13	12	12	11	10	9	9
Private creditors										
Disbursements	0	0	0	0	0	0	0	0	0	0
Principal	0	0	0	0	0	0	0	0	0	0
Interest	0	0	0	0	0	0	0	0	0	0
Commercial banks										
Disbursements	0	0	0	0	0	0	0	0	0	0
Principal	0	0	0	0	0	0	0	0	0	0
Interest	0	0	0	0	0	0	0	0	0	0
Other private										
Disbursements	0	0	0	0	0	0	0	0	0	0
Principal	0	0	0	0	0	0	0	0	0	0
Interest	0	0	0	0	0	0	0	0	0	0

SWAZILAND

(US$ million, unless otherwise indicated)

	1970	1980	1990	1994	1995	1996	1997	1998	1999	2000
1. SUMMARY DEBT DATA										
TOTAL DEBT STOCKS (EDT)	**37.0**	**209.5**	**253.8**	**219.6**	**234.9**	**221.7**	**368.2**	**250.8**	**257.6**	**261.6**
Long-term debt (LDOD)	**37.0**	**188.8**	**249.2**	**210.2**	**223.0**	**219.6**	**210.1**	**222.5**	**204.8**	**198.2**
Public and publicly guaranteed	37.0	188.8	249.2	210.2	223.0	219.6	210.1	222.5	204.8	198.2
Private nonguaranteed	0.0	0.0	0.0	0.0	0.0	0.0	0.0	0.0	0.0	0.0
Use of IMF credit	**0.0**	**5.7**	**0.0**	**0.0**	**0.0**	**0.0**	**0.0**	**0.0**	**0.0**	**0.0**
Short-term debt	**0.0**	**15.0**	**4.6**	**9.4**	**11.9**	**2.1**	**158.1**	**28.2**	**52.8**	**63.4**
of which interest arrears on LDOD	0.0	0.0	0.1	3.0	1.3	0.2	0.1	0.1	0.0	0.0
Official creditors	0.0	0.0	0.1	3.0	1.3	0.2	0.1	0.1	0.0	0.0
Private creditors	0.0	0.0	0.0	0.0	0.0	0.0	0.0	0.0	0.0	0.0
Memo: principal arrears on LDOD	0.0	0.0	0.2	4.1	4.5	1.2	1.1	1.2	0.3	0.3
Official creditors	0.0	0.0	0.2	3.5	4.2	1.2	1.1	1.2	0.3	0.3
Private creditors	0.0	0.0	0.0	0.5	0.3	0.0	0.0	0.0	0.0	0.0
Memo: export credits	0.0	0.0	28.0	17.8	14.1	19.0	22.0	6.5	3.4	1.6
TOTAL DEBT FLOWS										
Disbursements	**4.6**	**31.2**	**15.0**	**16.2**	**19.2**	**29.0**	**24.6**	**17.8**	**15.2**	**16.3**
Long-term debt	3.5	28.5	15.0	16.2	19.2	29.0	24.6	17.8	15.2	16.3
IMF purchases	1.2	2.7	0.0	0.0	0.0	0.0	0.0	0.0	0.0	0.0
Principal repayments	**2.5**	**7.5**	**36.2**	**19.9**	**16.1**	**21.1**	**16.3**	**14.4**	**19.4**	**13.2**
Long-term debt	1.5	7.5	35.8	19.9	16.1	21.1	16.3	14.4	19.4	13.2
IMF repurchases	1.0	0.0	0.3	0.0	0.0	0.0	0.0	0.0	0.0	0.0
Net flows on debt	**2.1**	**30.6**	**-37.9**	**-2.9**	**7.4**	**-0.8**	**164.3**	**-126.5**	**20.5**	**13.7**
of which short-term debt	0.0	7.0	-16.7	0.8	4.3	-8.8	156.1	-129.9	24.7	10.6
Interest payments (INT)	**1.9**	**10.6**	**10.7**	**6.2**	**5.5**	**12.0**	**15.1**	**9.1**	**12.0**	**10.4**
Long-term debt	1.9	9.0	10.3	6.0	5.1	11.7	7.3	7.5	10.4	6.5
IMF charges	0.0	0.0	0.0	0.0	0.0	0.0	0.0	0.0	0.0	0.0
Short-term debt	0.0	1.6	0.4	0.2	0.4	0.3	7.8	1.6	1.6	3.9
Net transfers on debt	**0.2**	**20.0**	**-48.6**	**-9.1**	**1.9**	**-12.9**	**149.2**	**-135.5**	**8.5**	**3.3**
Total debt service paid (TDS)	**4.4**	**18.1**	**46.9**	**26.1**	**21.6**	**33.1**	**31.5**	**23.4**	**31.4**	**23.6**
Long-term debt	3.4	16.5	46.1	25.9	21.2	32.8	23.7	21.9	29.8	19.8
IMF repurchases and charges	1.0	0.0	0.3	0.0	0.0	0.0	0.0	0.0	0.0	0.0
Short-term debt (interest only)	0.0	1.6	0.4	0.2	0.4	0.3	7.8	1.6	1.6	3.9
2. AGGREGATE NET RESOURCE FLOWS AND NET TRANSFERS (LONG-TERM)										
NET RESOURCE FLOWS	**5.5**	**59.3**	**29.3**	**77.7**	**73.9**	**48.5**	**10.5**	**184.4**	**96.9**	**-30.7**
Net flow of long-term debt (ex. IMF)	2.0	21.0	-20.8	-3.7	3.1	7.9	8.2	3.4	-4.2	3.1
Foreign direct investment (net)	0.0	26.5	30.0	63.3	51.8	21.7	-15.3	165.5	89.5	-43.7
Portfolio equity flows	0.0	0.0	0.0	0.0	0.0	0.0	0.0	0.0	0.0	0.0
Grants (excluding technical coop.)	3.5	11.8	20.1	18.0	18.9	18.9	17.6	15.5	11.6	9.9
Memo: technical coop. grants	2.0	22.7	27.3	23.5	28.1	25.9	14.4	19.0	11.6	9.5
official net resource flows	6.5	35.4	1.2	15.9	22.4	27.1	25.8	18.9	7.4	13.0
private net resource flows	-1.0	23.9	28.1	61.8	51.5	21.4	-15.3	165.5	89.5	-43.7
NET TRANSFERS	**3.6**	**23.0**	**-89.2**	**-28.3**	**-34.3**	**-62.2**	**-96.8**	**86.9**	**-1.5**	**-136.2**
Interest on long-term debt	1.9	9.0	10.3	6.0	5.1	11.7	7.3	7.5	10.4	6.5
Profit remittances on FDI	0.0	27.2	108.1	100.0	103.0	99.0	100.0	90.0	88.0	99.0
Memo: official net transfers	5.7	28.3	-8.4	10.1	17.4	15.4	18.5	11.4	-3.0	6.5
private net transfers	-2.1	-5.3	-80.8	-38.4	-51.6	-77.6	-115.3	75.5	1.5	-142.7
3. MAJOR ECONOMIC AGGREGATES										
Gross national income (GNI)	98.7	587.6	886.5	1,099.2	1,361.0	1,385.5	1,511.5	1,345.5	1,379.4	1,515.1
Exports of goods & services (XGS)	..	450.7	819.6	1,042.2	1,182.2	1,152.1	1,268.5	1,238.2	1,165.0	1,015.0
of which workers remittances	..	0.0	..	..	..	..	..	..	..	..
Imports of goods & services (MGS)	..	659.2	870.4	1,197.8	1,355.9	1,363.9	1,378.0	1,439.4	1,283.3	1,151.3
International reserves (RES)	..	158.7	216.5	297.0	298.2	254.0	294.8	358.6	375.9	351.8
Current account balance	..	-129.7	50.7	1.9	-29.7	-52.0	8.9	-68.4	6.4	-40.1
4. DEBT INDICATORS										
EDT / XGS (%)	..	46.5	31.0	21.1	19.9	19.2	29.0	20.3	22.1	25.8
EDT / GNI (%)	37.5	35.7	28.6	20.0	17.3	16.0	24.4	18.6	18.7	17.3
TDS / XGS (%)	..	4.0	5.7	2.5	1.8	2.9	2.5	1.9	2.7	2.3
INT / XGS (%)	..	2.4	1.3	0.6	0.5	1.0	1.2	0.7	1.0	1.0
INT / GNI (%)	1.9	1.8	1.2	0.6	0.4	0.9	1.0	0.7	0.9	0.7
RES / EDT (%)	..	75.8	85.3	135.2	127.0	114.6	80.1	143.0	145.9	134.5
RES / MGS (months)	..	2.9	3.0	3.0	2.6	2.2	2.6	3.0	3.5	3.7
Short-term / EDT (%)	0.0	7.2	1.8	4.3	5.1	1.0	42.9	11.2	20.5	24.2
Concessional / EDT (%)	33.0	41.0	62.9	69.7	71.0	69.5	38.2	57.1	50.9	45.9
Multilateral / EDT (%)	24.1	29.5	47.1	53.6	51.8	58.4	36.2	59.1	55.8	55.7

SWAZILAND

(US$ million, unless otherwise indicated)

	1970	1980	1990	1994	1995	1996	1997	1998	1999	2000
5. LONG-TERM DEBT										
DEBT OUTSTANDING (LDOD)	**37.0**	**188.8**	**249.2**	**210.2**	**223.0**	**219.6**	**210.1**	**222.5**	**204.8**	**198.2**
Public and publicly guaranteed	**37.0**	**188.8**	**249.2**	**210.2**	**223.0**	**219.6**	**210.1**	**222.5**	**204.8**	**198.2**
Official creditors	20.9	164.6	242.4	209.6	222.7	219.6	210.1	222.5	204.8	198.2
Multilateral	8.9	61.8	119.5	117.6	121.6	129.5	133.3	148.1	143.7	145.8
Concessional	2.8	16.7	46.0	63.4	66.9	64.9	64.5	69.1	69.9	67.6
Bilateral	12.0	102.8	123.0	92.0	101.1	90.1	76.7	74.5	61.1	52.4
Concessional	9.4	69.1	113.7	89.7	99.8	89.1	76.1	74.1	61.1	52.4
Private creditors	16.1	24.2	6.8	0.5	0.3	0.0	0.0	0.0	0.0	0.0
Bonds	0.0	0.0	0.0	0.0	0.0	0.0	0.0	0.0	0.0	0.0
Commercial banks	14.9	23.8	0.0	0.0	0.0	0.0	0.0	0.0	0.0	0.0
Other private	1.3	0.4	6.8	0.5	0.3	0.0	0.0	0.0	0.0	0.0
Private nonguaranteed	**0.0**	**0.0**	**0.0**	**0.0**	**0.0**	**0.0**	**0.0**	**0.0**	**0.0**	**0.0**
Bonds	0.0	0.0	0.0	0.0	0.0	0.0	0.0	0.0	0.0	0.0
Commercial banks and other	0.0	0.0	0.0	0.0	0.0	0.0	0.0	0.0	0.0	0.0
Memo:										
IBRD	6.1	17.7	36.9	20.9	19.2	14.5	9.9	9.9	9.1	9.0
IDA	2.8	7.5	6.8	6.2	5.9	5.7	5.4	5.2	4.9	4.7
DISBURSEMENTS	**3.5**	**28.5**	**15.0**	**16.2**	**19.2**	**29.0**	**24.6**	**17.8**	**15.2**	**16.3**
Public and publicly guaranteed	**3.5**	**28.5**	**15.0**	**16.2**	**19.2**	**29.0**	**24.6**	**17.8**	**15.2**	**16.3**
Official creditors	3.5	28.5	15.0	16.2	19.2	29.0	24.6	17.8	15.2	16.3
Multilateral	0.4	15.4	9.1	13.1	7.9	26.3	22.9	16.8	14.8	16.2
Concessional	0.0	0.3	3.6	12.5	3.5	3.2	4.5	4.2	5.0	2.7
Bilateral	3.1	13.1	5.9	3.1	11.3	2.7	1.7	0.9	0.5	0.2
Concessional	3.1	8.2	5.9	3.1	11.3	2.7	1.7	0.9	0.5	0.2
Private creditors	0.0	0.0	0.0	0.0	0.0	0.0	0.0	0.0	0.0	0.0
Bonds	0.0	0.0	0.0	0.0	0.0	0.0	0.0	0.0	0.0	0.0
Commercial banks	0.0	0.0	0.0	0.0	0.0	0.0	0.0	0.0	0.0	0.0
Other private	0.0	0.0	0.0	0.0	0.0	0.0	0.0	0.0	0.0	0.0
Private nonguaranteed	**0.0**	**0.0**	**0.0**	**0.0**	**0.0**	**0.0**	**0.0**	**0.0**	**0.0**	**0.0**
Bonds	0.0	0.0	0.0	0.0	0.0	0.0	0.0	0.0	0.0	0.0
Commercial banks and other	0.0	0.0	0.0	0.0	0.0	0.0	0.0	0.0	0.0	0.0
Memo:										
IBRD	0.4	2.1	1.0	0.0	0.0	2.7	1.3	2.7	1.0	0.7
IDA	0.0	0.3	0.0	0.0	0.0	0.0	0.0	0.0	0.0	0.0
PRINCIPAL REPAYMENTS	**1.5**	**7.5**	**35.8**	**19.9**	**16.1**	**21.1**	**16.3**	**14.4**	**19.4**	**13.2**
Public and publicly guaranteed	**1.5**	**7.5**	**35.8**	**19.9**	**16.1**	**21.1**	**16.3**	**14.4**	**19.4**	**13.2**
Official creditors	0.5	4.9	33.9	18.4	15.8	20.8	16.3	14.4	19.4	13.2
Multilateral	0.2	1.2	26.8	11.8	8.4	12.1	9.6	7.9	13.1	8.0
Concessional	0.0	0.1	1.1	1.3	1.7	2.3	1.7	1.8	2.6	2.3
Bilateral	0.3	3.7	7.1	6.5	7.4	8.7	6.7	6.5	6.3	5.2
Concessional	0.2	1.2	4.4	5.5	6.4	8.3	6.4	6.2	6.0	5.2
Private creditors	1.0	2.6	1.9	1.5	0.3	0.3	0.0	0.0	0.0	0.0
Bonds	0.0	0.0	0.0	0.0	0.0	0.0	0.0	0.0	0.0	0.0
Commercial banks	0.9	2.5	0.2	0.0	0.0	0.0	0.0	0.0	0.0	0.0
Other private	0.1	0.1	1.7	1.5	0.3	0.3	0.0	0.0	0.0	0.0
Private nonguaranteed	**0.0**	**0.0**	**0.0**	**0.0**	**0.0**	**0.0**	**0.0**	**0.0**	**0.0**	**0.0**
Bonds	0.0	0.0	0.0	0.0	0.0	0.0	0.0	0.0	0.0	0.0
Commercial banks and other	0.0	0.0	0.0	0.0	0.0	0.0	0.0	0.0	0.0	0.0
Memo:										
IBRD	0.2	0.7	20.4	4.4	3.5	5.9	4.8	2.7	1.7	0.9
IDA	0.0	0.0	0.2	0.2	0.3	0.3	0.3	0.3	0.3	0.3
NET FLOWS ON DEBT	**2.0**	**21.0**	**-20.8**	**-3.7**	**3.1**	**7.9**	**8.2**	**3.4**	**-4.2**	**3.1**
Public and publicly guaranteed	**2.0**	**21.0**	**-20.8**	**-3.7**	**3.1**	**7.9**	**8.2**	**3.4**	**-4.2**	**3.1**
Official creditors	3.0	23.6	-18.9	-2.1	3.5	8.2	8.2	3.4	-4.2	3.1
Multilateral	0.2	14.3	-17.7	1.3	-0.5	14.2	13.2	9.0	1.7	8.2
Concessional	0.0	0.2	2.5	11.2	1.8	0.9	2.8	2.4	2.4	0.4
Bilateral	2.8	9.4	-1.2	-3.4	3.9	-6.0	-5.0	-5.6	-5.8	-5.1
Concessional	2.9	7.0	1.5	-2.4	5.0	-5.7	-4.6	-5.2	-5.5	-5.1
Private creditors	-1.0	-2.6	-1.9	-1.5	-0.3	-0.3	0.0	0.0	0.0	0.0
Bonds	0.0	0.0	0.0	0.0	0.0	0.0	0.0	0.0	0.0	0.0
Commercial banks	-0.9	-2.5	-0.2	0.0	0.0	0.0	0.0	0.0	0.0	0.0
Other private	-0.1	-0.1	-1.7	-1.5	-0.3	-0.3	0.0	0.0	0.0	0.0
Private nonguaranteed	**0.0**	**0.0**	**0.0**	**0.0**	**0.0**	**0.0**	**0.0**	**0.0**	**0.0**	**0.0**
Bonds	0.0	0.0	0.0	0.0	0.0	0.0	0.0	0.0	0.0	0.0
Commercial banks and other	0.0	0.0	0.0	0.0	0.0	0.0	0.0	0.0	0.0	0.0
Memo:										
IBRD	0.2	1.3	-19.4	-4.4	-3.5	-3.1	-3.4	-0.1	-0.7	-0.1
IDA	0.0	0.3	-0.2	-0.2	-0.3	-0.3	-0.3	-0.3	-0.3	-0.3

SWAZILAND

(US$ million, unless otherwise indicated)

	1970	1980	1990	1994	1995	1996	1997	1998	1999	2000
INTEREST PAYMENTS (LINT)	**1.9**	**9.0**	**10.3**	**6.0**	**5.1**	**11.7**	**7.3**	**7.5**	**10.4**	**6.5**
Public and publicly guaranteed	**1.9**	**9.0**	**10.3**	**6.0**	**5.1**	**11.7**	**7.3**	**7.5**	**10.4**	**6.5**
Official creditors	0.8	7.1	9.5	5.8	5.0	11.7	7.3	7.5	10.4	6.5
Multilateral	0.4	3.1	6.6	4.0	3.2	10.0	5.7	6.0	9.1	5.5
Concessional	0.0	0.1	0.5	0.4	0.4	1.3	0.7	0.9	1.0	0.7
Bilateral	0.4	3.9	2.9	1.8	1.8	1.7	1.7	1.5	1.3	1.1
Concessional	0.2	0.7	1.7	1.5	1.6	1.6	1.6	1.4	1.3	1.1
Private creditors	1.1	2.0	0.8	0.2	0.1	0.0	0.0	0.0	0.0	0.0
Bonds	0.0	0.0	0.0	0.0	0.0	0.0	0.0	0.0	0.0	0.0
Commercial banks	1.1	1.9	0.0	0.0	0.0	0.0	0.0	0.0	0.0	0.0
Other private	0.1	0.0	0.8	0.2	0.1	0.0	0.0	0.0	0.0	0.0
Private nonguaranteed	**0.0**	**0.0**	**0.0**	**0.0**	**0.0**	**0.0**	**0.0**	**0.0**	**0.0**	**0.0**
Bonds	0.0	0.0	0.0	0.0	0.0	0.0	0.0	0.0	0.0	0.0
Commercial banks and other	0.0	0.0	0.0	0.0	0.0	0.0	0.0	0.0	0.0	0.0
Memo:										
IBRD	0.4	1.8	3.6	1.8	1.2	1.6	1.1	0.7	0.7	0.8
IDA	0.0	0.1	0.1	0.0	0.0	0.0	0.0	0.0	0.0	0.0
NET TRANSFERS ON DEBT	**0.1**	**12.0**	**-31.1**	**-9.7**	**-2.0**	**-3.8**	**0.9**	**-4.1**	**-14.6**	**-3.4**
Public and publicly guaranteed	**0.1**	**12.0**	**-31.1**	**-9.7**	**-2.0**	**-3.8**	**0.9**	**-4.1**	**-14.6**	**-3.4**
Official creditors	2.2	16.6	-28.4	-8.0	-1.6	-3.5	0.9	-4.1	-14.6	-3.4
Multilateral	-0.2	11.1	-24.2	-2.7	-3.7	4.3	7.6	3.0	-7.4	2.7
Concessional	0.0	0.1	2.0	10.7	1.4	-0.4	2.1	1.5	1.5	-0.3
Bilateral	2.4	5.4	-4.1	-5.3	2.1	-7.8	-6.6	-7.1	-7.1	-6.1
Concessional	2.7	6.3	-0.2	-4.0	3.3	-7.3	-6.2	-6.7	-6.8	-6.1
Private creditors	-2.1	-4.6	-2.7	-1.7	-0.4	-0.3	0.0	0.0	0.0	0.0
Bonds	0.0	0.0	0.0	0.0	0.0	0.0	0.0	0.0	0.0	0.0
Commercial banks	-2.0	-4.4	-0.2	0.0	0.0	0.0	0.0	0.0	0.0	0.0
Other private	-0.1	-0.2	-2.5	-1.7	-0.4	-0.3	0.0	0.0	0.0	0.0
Private nonguaranteed	**0.0**	**0.0**	**0.0**	**0.0**	**0.0**	**0.0**	**0.0**	**0.0**	**0.0**	**0.0**
Bonds	0.0	0.0	0.0	0.0	0.0	0.0	0.0	0.0	0.0	0.0
Commercial banks and other	0.0	0.0	0.0	0.0	0.0	0.0	0.0	0.0	0.0	0.0
Memo:										
IBRD	-0.2	-0.4	-23.0	-6.3	-4.8	-4.8	-4.5	-0.7	-1.3	-0.9
IDA	0.0	0.2	-0.2	-0.2	-0.3	-0.3	-0.3	-0.3	-0.3	-0.3
DEBT SERVICE (LTDS)	**3.4**	**16.5**	**46.1**	**25.9**	**21.2**	**32.8**	**23.7**	**21.9**	**29.8**	**19.8**
Public and publicly guaranteed	**3.4**	**16.5**	**46.1**	**25.9**	**21.2**	**32.8**	**23.7**	**21.9**	**29.8**	**19.8**
Official creditors	1.3	11.9	43.4	24.2	20.8	32.5	23.7	21.9	29.8	19.8
Multilateral	0.6	4.3	33.4	15.8	11.6	22.1	15.3	13.9	22.2	13.5
Concessional	0.0	0.2	1.6	1.7	2.1	3.6	2.4	2.7	3.6	3.0
Bilateral	0.7	7.6	10.0	8.4	9.2	10.4	8.4	8.0	7.6	6.3
Concessional	0.4	1.8	6.1	7.1	8.0	9.9	8.0	7.6	7.3	6.3
Private creditors	2.1	4.6	2.7	1.7	0.4	0.3	0.0	0.0	0.0	0.0
Bonds	0.0	0.0	0.0	0.0	0.0	0.0	0.0	0.0	0.0	0.0
Commercial banks	2.0	4.4	0.2	0.0	0.0	0.0	0.0	0.0	0.0	0.0
Other private	0.1	0.2	2.5	1.7	0.4	0.3	0.0	0.0	0.0	0.0
Private nonguaranteed	**0.0**	**0.0**	**0.0**	**0.0**	**0.0**	**0.0**	**0.0**	**0.0**	**0.0**	**0.0**
Bonds	0.0	0.0	0.0	0.0	0.0	0.0	0.0	0.0	0.0	0.0
Commercial banks and other	0.0	0.0	0.0	0.0	0.0	0.0	0.0	0.0	0.0	0.0
Memo:										
IBRD	0.5	2.5	24.1	6.3	4.8	7.5	5.8	3.4	2.4	1.6
IDA	0.0	0.1	0.2	0.2	0.3	0.3	0.3	0.3	0.3	0.3
UNDISBURSED DEBT	**0.0**	**64.8**	**68.6**	**120.9**	**132.7**	**134.1**	**103.1**	**80.0**	**63.2**	**44.9**
Official creditors	0.0	64.8	68.6	120.9	132.7	134.1	103.1	80.0	63.2	44.9
Private creditors	0.0	0.0	0.0	0.0	0.0	0.0	0.0	0.0	0.0	0.0
Memorandum items										
Concessional LDOD	12.2	85.8	159.7	153.1	166.7	154.0	140.6	143.3	131.0	120.0
Variable rate LDOD	0.0	23.8	8.1	5.9	5.3	6.7	6.8	8.8	9.1	9.0
Public sector LDOD	37.0	188.8	249.2	210.2	223.0	219.6	210.1	222.5	204.8	198.2
Private sector LDOD	0.0	0.0	0.0	0.0	0.0	0.0	0.0	0.0	0.0	0.0

6. CURRENCY COMPOSITION OF LONG-TERM DEBT (PERCENT)

	1970	1980	1990	1994	1995	1996	1997	1998	1999	2000
Deutsche mark	0.0	12.6	16.7	16.9	20.7	19.5	17.6	17.4	15.6	13.9
French franc	0.0	0.0	1.5	1.3	1.2	1.0	0.9	0.8	0.7	0.6
Japanese yen	0.0	0.0	0.0	0.0	0.0	0.0	0.0	0.0	0.0	0.0
Pound sterling	38.2	20.5	10.4	5.8	4.9	4.5	3.6	2.5	1.7	1.2
Swiss franc	0.0	12.6	0.0	0.0	0.0	0.0	0.0	0.0	0.0	0.0
U.S.dollars	7.6	11.4	13.1	11.7	10.5	10.0	9.7	12.5	13.0	12.7
Multiple currency	16.5	16.9	33.8	39.0	38.5	42.8	48.0	46.8	49.7	47.4
Special drawing rights	0.0	0.0	2.2	2.8	2.6	2.3	2.8	3.2	3.5	3.4
All other currencies	37.7	26.0	22.3	22.5	21.6	19.9	17.4	16.8	15.8	20.8

SWAZILAND

(US$ million, unless otherwise indicated)

	1970	1980	1990	1994	1995	1996	1997	1998	1999	2000
7. DEBT RESTRUCTURINGS										
Total amount rescheduled	..	..	0.0	0.0	0.0	0.0	0.0	0.0	0.0	0.0
Debt stock rescheduled	..	..	0.0	0.0	0.0	0.0	0.0	0.0	0.0	0.0
Principal rescheduled	..	..	0.0	0.0	0.0	0.0	0.0	0.0	0.0	0.0
Official	..	..	0.0	0.0	0.0	0.0	0.0	0.0	0.0	0.0
Private	..	..	0.0	0.0	0.0	0.0	0.0	0.0	0.0	0.0
Interest rescheduled	..	..	0.0	0.0	0.0	0.0	0.0	0.0	0.0	0.0
Official	..	..	0.0	0.0	0.0	0.0	0.0	0.0	0.0	0.0
Private	..	..	0.0	0.0	0.0	0.0	0.0	0.0	0.0	0.0
Debt forgiven	..	..	0.0	0.0	0.0	0.0	0.0	0.0	0.0	0.0
Memo: interest forgiven	..	..	0.0	0.0	0.0	0.0	0.0	0.0	0.0	0.0
Debt stock reduction	..	..	0.0	0.0	0.0	0.0	0.0	0.0	0.0	0.0
of which debt buyback	..	..	0.0	0.0	0.0	0.0	0.0	0.0	0.0	0.0
8. DEBT STOCK-FLOW RECONCILIATION										
Total change in debt stocks	..	..	-15.8	12.0	15.3	-13.2	146.5	-117.4	6.8	4.0
Net flows on debt	2.1	30.6	-37.9	-2.9	7.4	-0.8	164.3	-126.5	20.5	13.7
Net change in interest arrears	..	..	0.0	1.0	-1.8	-1.1	0.0	0.0	-0.1	0.0
Interest capitalized	..	..	0.0	0.0	0.0	0.0	0.0	0.0	0.0	0.0
Debt forgiveness or reduction	..	..	0.0	0.0	0.0	0.0	0.0	0.0	0.0	0.0
Cross-currency valuation	..	..	13.1	8.7	6.3	-14.9	-13.9	3.5	-11.3	-4.0
Residual	..	..	9.0	5.1	3.3	3.7	-3.9	5.6	-2.3	-5.8
9. AVERAGE TERMS OF NEW COMMITMENTS										
ALL CREDITORS										
Interest (%)	0.0	7.2	0.0	0.9	7.1	7.3	0.0	0.0	0.0	0.0
Maturity (years)	25.5	22.4	0.0	45.4	19.5	19.7	0.0	0.0	0.0	0.0
Grace period (years)	7.7	6.2	0.0	10.4	5.0	5.2	0.0	0.0	0.0	0.0
Grant element (%)	76.8	20.1	0.0	80.3	18.1	16.8	0.0	0.0	0.0	0.0
Official creditors										
Interest (%)	0.0	7.2	0.0	0.9	7.1	7.3	0.0	0.0	0.0	0.0
Maturity (years)	25.5	22.4	0.0	45.4	19.5	19.7	0.0	0.0	0.0	0.0
Grace period (years)	7.7	6.2	0.0	10.4	5.0	5.2	0.0	0.0	0.0	0.0
Grant element (%)	76.8	20.1	0.0	80.3	18.1	16.8	0.0	0.0	0.0	0.0
Private creditors										
Interest (%)	0.0	0.0	0.0	0.0	0.0	0.0	0.0	0.0	0.0	0.0
Maturity (years)	0.0	0.0	0.0	0.0	0.0	0.0	0.0	0.0	0.0	0.0
Grace period (years)	0.0	0.0	0.0	0.0	0.0	0.0	0.0	0.0	0.0	0.0
Grant element (%)	0.0	0.0	0.0	0.0	0.0	0.0	0.0	0.0	0.0	0.0
Memorandum items										
Commitments	3.1	16.9	0.0	18.9	29.0	35.9	0.0	0.0	0.0	0.0
Official creditors	3.1	16.9	0.0	18.9	29.0	35.9	0.0	0.0	0.0	0.0
Private creditors	0.0	0.0	0.0	0.0	0.0	0.0	0.0	0.0	0.0	0.0

10. CONTRACTUAL OBLIGATIONS ON OUTSTANDING LONG-TERM DEBT

	2001	2002	2003	2004	2005	2006	2007	2008	2009	2010
TOTAL										
Disbursements	15.2	15.1	11.9	2.8	0.0	0.0	0.0	0.0	0.0	0.0
Principal	16.0	16.0	14.7	14.4	14.7	14.7	14.5	13.5	12.8	12.3
Interest	8.0	8.0	7.9	7.6	6.9	6.1	5.4	4.7	4.0	3.4
Official creditors										
Disbursements	15.2	15.1	11.9	2.8	0.0	0.0	0.0	0.0	0.0	0.0
Principal	16.0	16.0	14.7	14.4	14.7	14.7	14.5	13.5	12.8	12.3
Interest	8.0	8.0	7.9	7.6	6.9	6.1	5.4	4.7	4.0	3.4
Bilateral creditors										
Disbursements	0.1	0.0	0.0	0.0	0.0	0.0	0.0	0.0	0.0	0.0
Principal	5.1	4.6	4.0	3.8	3.8	3.8	3.9	3.1	2.5	2.2
Interest	1.0	0.9	0.8	0.7	0.7	0.6	0.5	0.5	0.4	0.4
Multilateral creditors										
Disbursements	15.1	15.0	11.9	2.8	0.0	0.0	0.0	0.0	0.0	0.0
Principal	10.9	11.5	10.7	10.6	10.9	10.9	10.7	10.4	10.3	10.1
Interest	7.0	7.1	7.1	6.8	6.2	5.5	4.9	4.2	3.6	3.0
Private creditors										
Disbursements	0.0	0.0	0.0	0.0	0.0	0.0	0.0	0.0	0.0	0.0
Principal	0.0	0.0	0.0	0.0	0.0	0.0	0.0	0.0	0.0	0.0
Interest	0.0	0.0	0.0	0.0	0.0	0.0	0.0	0.0	0.0	0.0
Commercial banks										
Disbursements	0.0	0.0	0.0	0.0	0.0	0.0	0.0	0.0	0.0	0.0
Principal	0.0	0.0	0.0	0.0	0.0	0.0	0.0	0.0	0.0	0.0
Interest	0.0	0.0	0.0	0.0	0.0	0.0	0.0	0.0	0.0	0.0
Other private										
Disbursements	0.0	0.0	0.0	0.0	0.0	0.0	0.0	0.0	0.0	0.0
Principal	0.0	0.0	0.0	0.0	0.0	0.0	0.0	0.0	0.0	0.0
Interest	0.0	0.0	0.0	0.0	0.0	0.0	0.0	0.0	0.0	0.0

SYRIAN ARAB REPUBLIC

(US$ million, unless otherwise indicated)

	1970	1980	1990	1994	1995	1996	1997	1998	1999	2000
1. SUMMARY DEBT DATA										
TOTAL DEBT STOCKS (EDT)	**276**	**3,548**	**17,259**	**20,647**	**21,415**	**21,484**	**20,937**	**22,460**	**22,369**	**21,657**
Long-term debt (LDOD)	**231**	**2,917**	**15,108**	**16,629**	**16,853**	**16,762**	**16,326**	**16,353**	**16,142**	**15,930**
Public and publicly guaranteed	231	2,917	15,108	16,629	16,853	16,762	16,326	16,353	16,142	15,930
Private nonguaranteed	0	0	0	0	0	0	0	0	0	0
Use of IMF credit	**10**	**0**	**0**	**0**	**0**	**0**	**0**	**0**	**0**	**0**
Short-term debt	**35**	**631**	**2,151**	**4,018**	**4,562**	**4,722**	**4,611**	**6,107**	**6,227**	**5,727**
of which interest arrears on LDOD	0	0	460	1,400	1,633	1,822	1,976	2,155	2,301	2,407
Official creditors	0	0	407	1,281	1,502	1,685	1,838	2,011	2,160	2,267
Private creditors	0	0	53	119	131	137	138	144	142	140
Memo: principal arrears on LDOD	0	0	864	4,563	5,654	6,638	7,410	8,238	9,039	9,820
Official creditors	0	0	580	3,824	4,831	5,727	6,447	7,218	8,002	8,775
Private creditors	0	0	284	739	823	910	963	1,020	1,037	1,046
Memo: export credits	0	0	360	695	675	439	381	366	416	635
TOTAL DEBT FLOWS										
Disbursements	**63**	**1,147**	**186**	**265**	**242**	**168**	**104**	**64**	**35**	**19**
Long-term debt	60	1,147	186	265	242	168	104	64	35	19
IMF purchases	3	0	0	0	0	0	0	0	0	0
Principal repayments	**30**	**225**	**1,066**	**101**	**70**	**65**	**353**	**94**	**127**	**122**
Long-term debt	30	225	1,066	101	70	65	353	94	127	122
IMF repurchases	0	0	0	0	0	0	0	0	0	0
Net flows on debt	**33**	**1,239**	**-672**	**191**	**483**	**74**	**-514**	**1,287**	**-119**	**-708**
of which short-term debt	0	317	208	26	311	-29	-265	1,317	-27	-605
Interest payments (INT)	**6**	**157**	**123**	**266**	**199**	**177**	**202**	**243**	**243**	**222**
Long-term debt	6	77	41	97	60	47	63	78	79	102
IMF charges	0	0	0	0	0	0	0	0	0	0
Short-term debt	0	80	82	169	139	130	138	165	164	120
Net transfers on debt	**27**	**1,082**	**-795**	**-75**	**284**	**-103**	**-716**	**1,044**	**-362**	**-930**
Total debt service paid (TDS)	**36**	**382**	**1,189**	**367**	**269**	**243**	**554**	**337**	**370**	**344**
Long-term debt	36	302	1,108	198	130	113	416	172	206	224
IMF repurchases and charges	0	0	0	0	0	0	0	0	0	0
Short-term debt (interest only)	0	80	82	169	139	130	138	165	164	120
2. AGGREGATE NET RESOURCE FLOWS AND NET TRANSFERS (LONG-TERM)										
NET RESOURCE FLOWS	**41**	**2,573**	**-188**	**534**	**342**	**228**	**-97**	**145**	**55**	**68**
Net flow of long-term debt (ex. IMF)	30	922	-880	165	172	103	-249	-31	-93	-103
Foreign direct investment (net)	0	0	71	251	100	89	80	80	91	111
Portfolio equity flows	0	0	0	0	0	0	0	0	0	0
Grants (excluding technical coop.)	11	1,651	621	118	70	36	72	96	57	59
Memo: technical coop. grants	8	26	31	62	82	74	47	50	44	42
official net resource flows	11	2,531	-251	288	247	144	-172	69	-32	-40
private net resource flows	30	42	62	246	95	84	75	76	87	107
NET TRANSFERS	**35**	**2,496**	**-230**	**437**	**282**	**181**	**-160**	**67**	**-24**	**-34**
Interest on long-term debt	6	77	41	97	60	47	63	78	79	102
Profit remittances on FDI	0	0	0	0	0	0	0	0	0	0
Memo: official net transfers	9	2,485	-283	193	189	99	-234	-8	-110	-141
private net transfers	26	11	53	244	93	82	73	75	87	107
3. MAJOR ECONOMIC AGGREGATES										
Gross national income (GNI)	2,219	13,565	11,955	10,290	11,591	13,768	14,246	14,612	15,341	15,965
Exports of goods & services (XGS)	..	3,341	5,460	5,830	6,201	6,504	6,060	5,177	5,813	7,191
of which workers remittances	..	0	0	0	0	0	0	0	0	0
Imports of goods & services (MGS)	..	4,610	3,786	7,212	6,545	7,088	6,098	5,650	6,101	6,614
International reserves (RES)	57	828	..	..	..	..	..	..	..	..
Current account balance	..	251	1,762	-791	263	40	461	58	201	1,062
4. DEBT INDICATORS										
EDT / XGS (%)	..	106.2	316.1	354.2	345.4	330.3	345.5	433.8	384.8	301.2
EDT / GNI (%)	12.4	26.2	144.4	200.6	184.8	156.0	147.0	153.7	145.8	135.7
TDS / XGS (%)	..	11.4	21.8	6.3	4.3	3.7	9.2	6.5	6.4	4.8
INT / XGS (%)	..	4.7	2.3	4.6	3.2	2.7	3.3	4.7	4.2	3.1
INT / GNI (%)	0.3	1.2	1.0	2.6	1.7	1.3	1.4	1.7	1.6	1.4
RES / EDT (%)	20.6	23.3	..	..	..	..	..	..	..	..
RES / MGS (months)	..	2.2	..	..	..	..	..	..	..	..
Short-term / EDT (%)	12.7	17.8	12.5	19.5	21.3	22.0	22.0	27.2	27.8	26.5
Concessional / EDT (%)	14.3	51.8	76.1	72.0	70.4	70.3	71.7	67.2	67.0	68.4
Multilateral / EDT (%)	1.5	8.8	5.2	4.7	5.0	5.0	3.7	3.3	2.9	2.7

SYRIAN ARAB REPUBLIC

(US$ million, unless otherwise indicated)

	1970	1980	1990	1994	1995	1996	1997	1998	1999	2000
5. LONG-TERM DEBT										
DEBT OUTSTANDING (LDOD)	**231**	**2,917**	**15,108**	**16,629**	**16,853**	**16,762**	**16,326**	**16,353**	**16,142**	**15,930**
Public and publicly guaranteed	**231**	**2,917**	**15,108**	**16,629**	**16,853**	**16,762**	**16,326**	**16,353**	**16,142**	**15,930**
Official creditors	57	2,161	13,831	15,420	15,646	15,603	15,191	15,233	15,055	14,862
Multilateral	4	311	901	965	1,077	1,081	771	734	641	575
Concessional	4	89	205	414	517	586	599	591	563	528
Bilateral	53	1,850	12,930	14,455	14,569	14,523	14,420	14,499	14,414	14,287
Concessional	35	1,749	12,930	14,453	14,567	14,521	14,418	14,497	14,412	14,286
Private creditors	174	756	1,277	1,209	1,207	1,159	1,135	1,120	1,088	1,068
Bonds	0	0	0	0	0	0	0	0	0	0
Commercial banks	0	0	0	0	0	0	0	0	0	0
Other private	174	756	1,277	1,209	1,207	1,159	1,135	1,120	1,088	1,068
Private nonguaranteed	**0**	**0**	**0**	**0**	**0**	**0**	**0**	**0**	**0**	**0**
Bonds	0	0	0	0	0	0	0	0	0	0
Commercial banks and other	0	0	0	0	0	0	0	0	0	0
Memo:										
IBRD	0	215	479	405	428	383	85	67	42	25
IDA	4	42	44	44	44	44	34	32	31	30
DISBURSEMENTS	**60**	**1,147**	**186**	**265**	**242**	**168**	**104**	**64**	**35**	**19**
Public and publicly guaranteed	**60**	**1,147**	**186**	**265**	**242**	**168**	**104**	**64**	**35**	**19**
Official creditors	9	971	157	265	242	168	104	63	34	19
Multilateral	3	64	30	123	123	90	55	35	20	12
Concessional	3	2	8	122	122	90	54	35	20	12
Bilateral	6	907	128	142	118	78	49	28	14	7
Concessional	5	900	128	142	118	78	49	28	14	7
Private creditors	51	176	29	0	0	0	0	1	1	0
Bonds	0	0	0	0	0	0	0	0	0	0
Commercial banks	0	0	0	0	0	0	0	0	0	0
Other private	51	176	29	0	0	0	0	1	1	0
Private nonguaranteed	**0**	**0**	**0**	**0**	**0**	**0**	**0**	**0**	**0**	**0**
Bonds	0	0	0	0	0	0	0	0	0	0
Commercial banks and other	0	0	0	0	0	0	0	0	0	0
Memo:										
IBRD	0	60	0	0	0	0	0	0	0	0
IDA	3	2	0	0	0	0	0	0	0	0
PRINCIPAL REPAYMENTS	**30**	**225**	**1,066**	**101**	**70**	**65**	**353**	**94**	**127**	**122**
Public and publicly guaranteed	**30**	**225**	**1,066**	**101**	**70**	**65**	**353**	**94**	**127**	**122**
Official creditors	9	92	1,029	95	65	60	348	89	122	117
Multilateral	0	4	24	80	48	35	310	55	75	70
Concessional	0	1	8	14	17	17	31	20	36	44
Bilateral	9	88	1,005	15	16	25	37	34	48	48
Concessional	5	31	1,005	15	16	25	37	34	48	48
Private creditors	21	133	37	5	5	5	5	5	5	4
Bonds	0	0	0	0	0	0	0	0	0	0
Commercial banks	0	0	0	0	0	0	0	0	0	0
Other private	21	133	37	5	5	5	5	5	5	4
Private nonguaranteed	**0**	**0**	**0**	**0**	**0**	**0**	**0**	**0**	**0**	**0**
Bonds	0	0	0	0	0	0	0	0	0	0
Commercial banks and other	0	0	0	0	0	0	0	0	0	0
Memo:										
IBRD	0	3	1	49	13	0	262	22	21	14
IDA	0	0	2	0	0	0	10	2	2	2
NET FLOWS ON DEBT	**30**	**922**	**-880**	**165**	**172**	**103**	**-249**	**-31**	**-93**	**-103**
Public and publicly guaranteed	**30**	**922**	**-880**	**165**	**172**	**103**	**-249**	**-31**	**-93**	**-103**
Official creditors	0	880	-872	170	177	108	-244	-26	-89	-99
Multilateral	3	60	5	43	75	55	-256	-20	-54	-58
Concessional	3	2	0	108	105	73	24	15	-16	-32
Bilateral	-3	820	-877	127	102	53	12	-6	-34	-41
Concessional	0	869	-877	127	102	53	12	-6	-34	-41
Private creditors	30	42	-9	-5	-5	-5	-5	-4	-4	-4
Bonds	0	0	0	0	0	0	0	0	0	0
Commercial banks	0	0	0	0	0	0	0	0	0	0
Other private	30	42	-9	-5	-5	-5	-5	-4	-4	-4
Private nonguaranteed	**0**	**0**	**0**	**0**	**0**	**0**	**0**	**0**	**0**	**0**
Bonds	0	0	0	0	0	0	0	0	0	0
Commercial banks and other	0	0	0	0	0	0	0	0	0	0
Memo:										
IBRD	0	57	-1	-49	-13	0	-262	-22	-21	-14
IDA	3	2	-2	0	0	0	-10	-2	-2	-2

(US$ million, unless otherwise indicated)

	1970	1980	1990	1994	1995	1996	1997	1998	1999	2000
INTEREST PAYMENTS (LINT)	**6**	**77**	**41**	**97**	**60**	**47**	**63**	**78**	**79**	**102**
Public and publicly guaranteed	**6**	**77**	**41**	**97**	**60**	**47**	**63**	**78**	**79**	**102**
Official creditors	2	46	33	95	59	46	62	77	79	102
Multilateral	0	20	14	79	39	28	40	56	57	82
Concessional	0	1	5	14	20	23	27	24	25	23
Bilateral	2	26	18	16	20	17	22	21	21	20
Concessional	1	18	18	16	20	17	22	21	21	20
Private creditors	4	31	9	2	2	1	1	1	1	1
Bonds	0	0	0	0	0	0	0	0	0	0
Commercial banks	0	0	0	0	0	0	0	0	0	0
Other private	4	31	9	2	2	1	1	1	1	1
Private nonguaranteed	**0**	**0**	**0**	**0**	**0**	**0**	**0**	**0**	**0**	**0**
Bonds	0	0	0	0	0	0	0	0	0	0
Commercial banks and other	0	0	0	0	0	0	0	0	0	0
Memo:										
IBRD	0	18	1	59	12	0	9	28	30	57
IDA	0	0	1	0	0	0	3	0	0	0
NET TRANSFERS ON DEBT	**24**	**845**	**-922**	**68**	**112**	**56**	**-312**	**-109**	**-172**	**-205**
Public and publicly guaranteed	**24**	**845**	**-922**	**68**	**112**	**56**	**-312**	**-109**	**-172**	**-205**
Official creditors	-2	834	-904	75	119	63	-306	-104	-167	-201
Multilateral	3	40	-9	-36	37	27	-296	-76	-112	-140
Concessional	3	1	-5	94	85	50	-3	-9	-40	-55
Bilateral	-5	794	-895	111	82	36	-10	-27	-56	-61
Concessional	-1	851	-895	111	82	36	-10	-27	-56	-61
Private creditors	26	11	-18	-7	-7	-7	-7	-5	-5	-4
Bonds	0	0	0	0	0	0	0	0	0	0
Commercial banks	0	0	0	0	0	0	0	0	0	0
Other private	26	11	-18	-7	-7	-7	-7	-5	-5	-4
Private nonguaranteed	**0**	**0**	**0**	**0**	**0**	**0**	**0**	**0**	**0**	**0**
Bonds	0	0	0	0	0	0	0	0	0	0
Commercial banks and other	0	0	0	0	0	0	0	0	0	0
Memo:										
IBRD	0	39	-2	-107	-25	0	-271	-50	-52	-72
IDA	3	1	-2	0	0	0	-13	-2	-2	-2
DEBT SERVICE (LTDS)	**36**	**302**	**1,108**	**198**	**130**	**113**	**416**	**172**	**206**	**224**
Public and publicly guaranteed	**36**	**302**	**1,108**	**198**	**130**	**113**	**416**	**172**	**206**	**224**
Official creditors	11	138	1,062	190	123	106	410	166	201	219
Multilateral	0	24	39	160	87	64	351	111	132	152
Concessional	0	2	13	28	37	40	58	44	61	67
Bilateral	11	114	1,023	31	36	42	59	55	69	67
Concessional	6	49	1,023	31	36	42	59	55	69	67
Private creditors	25	165	46	7	7	7	7	6	5	5
Bonds	0	0	0	0	0	0	0	0	0	0
Commercial banks	0	0	0	0	0	0	0	0	0	0
Other private	25	165	46	7	7	7	7	6	5	5
Private nonguaranteed	**0**	**0**	**0**	**0**	**0**	**0**	**0**	**0**	**0**	**0**
Bonds	0	0	0	0	0	0	0	0	0	0
Commercial banks and other	0	0	0	0	0	0	0	0	0	0
Memo:										
IBRD	0	21	2	107	25	0	271	50	52	72
IDA	0	0	2	0	0	0	13	2	2	2
UNDISBURSED DEBT	**110**	**1,975**	**922**	**1,275**	**1,003**	**744**	**578**	**546**	**56**	**33**
Official creditors	11	1,393	716	1,182	919	693	531	512	49	29
Private creditors	99	583	206	93	84	51	46	33	7	4
Memorandum items										
Concessional LDOD	39	1,838	13,134	14,867	15,083	15,107	15,017	15,088	14,976	14,813
Variable rate LDOD	0	0	0	0	0	0	0	0	0	0
Public sector LDOD	231	2,917	15,107	16,629	16,853	16,762	16,326	16,352	16,142	15,930
Private sector LDOD	0	0	0	0	0	0	0	0	0	0

6. CURRENCY COMPOSITION OF LONG-TERM DEBT (PERCENT)

	1970	1980	1990	1994	1995	1996	1997	1998	1999	2000
Deutsche mark	1.7	1.5	2.1	2.3	2.4	2.2	2.0	2.1	1.8	1.7
French franc	7.0	3.6	0.8	0.7	0.8	0.7	0.6	0.7	0.6	0.6
Japanese yen	0.0	0.3	1.8	3.7	3.5	3.1	2.8	3.1	3.5	3.1
Pound sterling	4.0	0.2	0.6	1.0	1.0	0.8	0.8	0.7	0.7	0.6
Swiss franc	4.1	0.8	0.0	0.0	0.0	0.0	0.0	0.0	0.0	0.0
U.S.dollars	31.4	70.1	86.2	83.1	81.9	82.4	84.5	84.3	85.0	86.1
Multiple currency	0.0	8.0	3.3	2.5	2.7	2.4	0.6	0.5	0.4	0.3
Special drawing rights	0.0	0.0	0.0	0.0	0.0	0.0	0.0	0.0	0.0	0.0
All other currencies	51.8	15.5	5.2	6.7	7.7	8.4	8.7	8.6	8.0	7.6

SYRIAN ARAB REPUBLIC

(US$ million, unless otherwise indicated)

	1970	1980	1990	1994	1995	1996	1997	1998	1999	2000
7. DEBT RESTRUCTURINGS										
Total amount rescheduled	..	..	0	0	0	0	0	0	0	0
Debt stock rescheduled	..	..	0	0	0	0	0	0	0	0
Principal rescheduled	..	..	0	0	0	0	0	0	0	0
Official	..	..	0	0	0	0	0	0	0	0
Private	..	..	0	0	0	0	0	0	0	0
Interest rescheduled	..	..	0	0	0	0	0	0	0	0
Official	..	..	0	0	0	0	0	0	0	0
Private	..	..	0	0	0	0	0	0	0	0
Debt forgiven	..	..	0	0	0	0	0	0	0	0
Memo: interest forgiven	..	..	0	0	0	0	0	0	0	0
Debt stock reduction	..	..	0	0	0	0	0	0	0	0
of which debt buyback	..	..	0	0	0	0	0	0	0	0
8. DEBT STOCK-FLOW RECONCILIATION										
Total change in debt stocks	..	..	-342	468	768	69	-547	1,522	-91	-712
Net flows on debt	33	1,239	-672	191	483	74	-514	1,287	-119	-708
Net change in interest arrears	..	..	247	251	233	189	154	179	146	106
Interest capitalized	..	..	0	0	0	0	0	0	0	0
Debt forgiveness or reduction	..	..	0	0	0	0	0	0	0	0
Cross-currency valuation	..	..	157	151	57	-151	-264	98	-27	-112
Residual	..	..	-74	-124	-5	-43	77	-42	-91	3
9. AVERAGE TERMS OF NEW COMMITMENTS										
ALL CREDITORS										
Interest (%)	4.3	2.5	3.7	0.0	0.0	0.0	0.0	0.0	0.0	0.0
Maturity (years)	8.7	22.4	22.7	0.0	0.0	0.0	0.0	0.0	0.0	0.0
Grace period (years)	2.4	4.3	6.1	0.0	0.0	0.0	0.0	0.0	0.0	0.0
Grant element (%)	24.0	50.7	43.6	0.0	0.0	0.0	0.0	0.0	0.0	0.0
Official creditors										
Interest (%)	2.7	2.0	3.8	0.0	0.0	0.0	0.0	0.0	0.0	0.0
Maturity (years)	8.7	25.1	23.0	0.0	0.0	0.0	0.0	0.0	0.0	0.0
Grace period (years)	3.0	4.2	6.2	0.0	0.0	0.0	0.0	0.0	0.0	0.0
Grant element (%)	30.4	55.8	43.9	0.0	0.0	0.0	0.0	0.0	0.0	0.0
Private creditors										
Interest (%)	4.5	4.1	3.0	0.0	0.0	0.0	0.0	0.0	0.0	0.0
Maturity (years)	8.7	12.6	12.8	0.0	0.0	0.0	0.0	0.0	0.0	0.0
Grace period (years)	2.4	4.4	3.6	0.0	0.0	0.0	0.0	0.0	0.0	0.0
Grant element (%)	23.2	32.2	36.3	0.0	0.0	0.0	0.0	0.0	0.0	0.0
Memorandum items										
Commitments	14	1,169	344	0	0	0	0	0	0	0
Official creditors	2	918	334	0	0	0	0	0	0	0
Private creditors	13	251	10	0	0	0	0	0	0	0

10. CONTRACTUAL OBLIGATIONS ON OUTSTANDING LONG-TERM DEBT

	2001	2002	2003	2004	2005	2006	2007	2008	2009	2010
TOTAL										
Disbursements	19	11	2	1	0	0	0	0	0	0
Principal	907	901	889	884	867	858	114	107	101	100
Interest	153	132	110	89	69	49	30	25	21	17
Official creditors										
Disbursements	16	9	2	1	0	0	0	0	0	0
Principal	899	896	884	879	864	857	113	107	100	99
Interest	152	131	110	89	68	49	30	25	21	17
Bilateral creditors										
Disbursements	11	6	2	1	0	0	0	0	0	0
Principal	845	846	835	834	827	822	81	74	68	67
Interest	128	110	91	73	54	36	19	16	13	11
Multilateral creditors										
Disbursements	5	3	0	0	0	0	0	0	0	0
Principal	54	50	49	45	38	34	33	33	33	33
Interest	24	21	19	16	14	13	11	10	8	7
Private creditors										
Disbursements	3	1	0	0	0	0	0	0	0	0
Principal	8	5	4	4	3	1	0	0	0	0
Interest	1	1	0	0	0	0	0	0	0	0
Commercial banks										
Disbursements	0	0	0	0	0	0	0	0	0	0
Principal	0	0	0	0	0	0	0	0	0	0
Interest	0	0	0	0	0	0	0	0	0	0
Other private										
Disbursements	3	1	0	0	0	0	0	0	0	0
Principal	8	5	4	4	3	1	0	0	0	0
Interest	1	1	0	0	0	0	0	0	0	0

TAJIKISTAN

(US$ million, unless otherwise indicated)

	1970	1980	1990	1994	1995	1996	1997	1998	1999	2000
1. SUMMARY DEBT DATA										
TOTAL DEBT STOCKS (EDT)	..	..	..	**580.3**	**633.6**	**699.4**	**1,065.0**	**1,249.7**	**1,134.1**	**1,170.0**
Long-term debt (LDOD)	..	..	..	**562.0**	**590.4**	**656.8**	**961.0**	**1,003.4**	**942.7**	**995.3**
Public and publicly guaranteed	..	..	..	562.0	590.4	656.8	669.0	709.1	611.7	625.6
Private nonguaranteed	..	..	..	0.0	0.0	0.0	292.0	294.3	331.0	369.7
Use of IMF credit	..	..	..	**0.0**	**0.0**	**21.6**	**30.4**	**99.0**	**100.5**	**110.8**
Short-term debt	..	..	..	**18.3**	**43.2**	**21.0**	**73.7**	**147.2**	**90.9**	**64.0**
of which interest arrears on LDOD	..	..	..	18.3	43.2	13.0	36.7	35.2	29.9	31.9
Official creditors	..	..	..	16.0	37.0	4.5	14.8	15.6	10.2	10.0
Private creditors	..	..	..	2.3	6.2	8.4	22.0	19.7	19.7	21.9
Memo: principal arrears on LDOD	..	..	..	60.3	141.9	89.6	99.5	94.7	90.9	70.5
Official creditors	..	..	..	60.3	120.2	21.6	31.5	34.8	35.4	19.8
Private creditors	..	..	..	0.0	21.7	68.0	68.0	60.0	55.5	50.7
Memo: export credits	..	..	..	0.0	37.8	0.0	0.3	0.0	11.0	2.7
TOTAL DEBT FLOWS										
Disbursements	..	..	..	**177.1**	**28.4**	**58.3**	**52.3**	**136.2**	**112.1**	**132.2**
Long-term debt	..	..	..	177.1	28.4	36.5	42.0	71.4	103.0	106.7
IMF purchases	..	..	..	0.0	0.0	21.8	10.3	64.9	9.1	25.5
Principal repayments	..	..	..	**0.0**	**0.0**	**0.0**	**28.9**	**60.3**	**44.2**	**56.0**
Long-term debt	..	..	..	0.0	0.0	0.0	28.9	60.3	39.1	46.1
IMF repurchases	..	..	..	0.0	0.0	0.0	0.0	0.0	5.1	9.9
Net flows on debt	..	..	..	**177.1**	**28.4**	**58.3**	**52.4**	**150.9**	**16.9**	**47.1**
of which short-term debt	..	..	..	0.0	0.0	0.0	29.0	75.0	-51.0	-29.0
Interest payments (INT)	..	..	..	**0.4**	**0.0**	**1.1**	**18.8**	**30.8**	**25.0**	**31.4**
Long-term debt	..	..	..	0.4	0.0	0.3	16.6	28.0	19.3	27.2
IMF charges	..	..	..	0.0	0.0	0.5	0.9	1.7	1.9	2.0
Short-term debt	..	..	..	0.0	0.0	0.4	1.2	1.2	3.8	2.3
Net transfers on debt	..	..	..	**176.7**	**28.4**	**57.2**	**33.6**	**120.1**	**-8.1**	**15.7**
Total debt service paid (TDS)	..	..	..	**0.4**	**0.0**	**1.1**	**47.7**	**91.1**	**69.2**	**87.5**
Long-term debt	..	..	..	0.4	0.0	0.3	45.5	88.3	58.4	73.3
IMF repurchases and charges	..	..	..	0.0	0.0	0.5	0.9	1.7	7.0	11.9
Short-term debt (interest only)	..	..	..	0.0	0.0	0.4	1.2	1.2	3.8	2.3
2. AGGREGATE NET RESOURCE FLOWS AND NET TRANSFERS (LONG-TERM)										
NET RESOURCE FLOWS	..	..	..	**251.8**	**97.0**	**111.0**	**72.4**	**98.7**	**139.5**	**134.1**
Net flow of long-term debt (ex. IMF)	..	..	..	177.1	28.4	36.5	13.1	11.1	63.9	60.5
Foreign direct investment (net)	..	..	..	12.0	15.0	16.0	4.0	30.0	21.0	24.0
Portfolio equity flows	..	..	..	0.0	0.0	0.0	0.0	0.0	0.0	0.0
Grants (excluding technical coop.)	..	..	..	62.7	53.6	58.5	55.3	57.7	54.6	49.6
Memo: technical coop. grants	..	..	..	4.0	11.8	14.5	8.6	10.3	9.8	15.1
official net resource flows	..	..	..	239.8	82.0	95.0	68.8	75.8	85.8	70.2
private net resource flows	..	..	..	12.0	15.0	16.0	3.6	22.9	53.7	63.9
NET TRANSFERS	..	..	..	**251.4**	**97.0**	**110.7**	**55.8**	**70.8**	**120.1**	**107.0**
Interest on long-term debt	..	..	..	0.4	0.0	0.3	16.6	28.0	19.3	27.2
Profit remittances on FDI	..	..	..	0.0	0.0	0.0	0.0	0.0	0.0	0.0
Memo: official net transfers	..	..	..	239.4	82.0	94.7	63.9	61.1	83.7	66.4
private net transfers	..	..	..	12.0	15.0	16.0	-8.1	9.7	36.4	40.6
3. MAJOR ECONOMIC AGGREGATES										
Gross national income (GNI)	..	..	..	2,821.5	2,248.6	989.9	891.3	1,257.4	1,029.2	936.1
Exports of goods & services (XGS)	..	..	..	559.0	779.0	770.0	746.0	604.2	677.0	800.0
of which workers remittances	..	..	..	0.0	0.0	0.0	0.0	0.0	0.0	0.0
Imports of goods & services (MGS)	..	..	..	754.0	893.0	870.0	842.0	769.0	748.0	894.0
International reserves (RES)	..	..	..	..	..	..	38.9	55.9	..	..
Current account balance	..	..	..	-170.0	-89.0	-70.0	-56.0	-107.8	-36.0	-61.0
4. DEBT INDICATORS										
EDT / XGS (%)	..	..	..	103.8	81.3	90.8	142.8	206.8	167.5	146.3
EDT / GNI (%)	..	..	..	20.6	28.2	70.7	119.5	99.4	110.2	125.0
TDS / XGS (%)	..	..	..	0.1	0.0	0.1	6.4	15.1	10.2	10.9
INT / XGS (%)	..	..	..	0.1	0.0	0.1	2.5	5.1	3.7	3.9
INT / GNI (%)	..	..	..	0.0	0.0	0.1	2.1	2.5	2.4	3.4
RES / EDT (%)	..	..	..	..	..	..	3.7	4.5	..	..
RES / MGS (months)	..	..	..	..	..	..	0.6	0.9	..	..
Short-term / EDT (%)	..	..	..	3.2	6.8	3.0	6.9	11.8	8.0	5.5
Concessional / EDT (%)	..	..	..	3.4	3.3	79.6	52.4	50.1	47.0	46.7
Multilateral / EDT (%)	..	..	..	0.0	0.0	4.3	4.7	8.8	12.7	14.7

TAJIKISTAN

(US$ million, unless otherwise indicated)

	1970	1980	1990	1994	1995	1996	1997	1998	1999	2000
5. LONG-TERM DEBT										
DEBT OUTSTANDING (LDOD)	..	..	..	**562.0**	**590.4**	**656.8**	**961.0**	**1,003.4**	**942.7**	**995.3**
Public and publicly guaranteed	..	..	..	**562.0**	**590.4**	**656.8**	**669.0**	**709.1**	**611.7**	**625.6**
Official creditors	..	..	..	494.0	522.4	588.8	601.0	649.2	556.2	574.9
Multilateral	..	..	..	0.0	0.0	30.2	50.1	109.7	143.5	171.7
Concessional	..	..	..	0.0	0.0	30.2	50.1	109.7	143.5	171.7
Bilateral	..	..	..	494.0	522.4	558.6	550.9	539.4	412.8	403.2
Concessional	..	..	..	19.9	20.9	526.7	507.6	516.1	389.5	374.6
Private creditors	..	..	..	68.0	68.0	68.0	68.0	60.0	55.5	50.7
Bonds	..	..	..	0.0	0.0	0.0	0.0	0.0	0.0	0.0
Commercial banks	..	..	..	0.0	0.0	0.0	0.0	0.0	0.0	0.0
Other private	..	..	..	68.0	68.0	68.0	68.0	60.0	55.5	50.7
Private nonguaranteed	..	..	..	**0.0**	**0.0**	**0.0**	**292.0**	**294.3**	**331.0**	**369.7**
Bonds	..	..	..	0.0	0.0	0.0	0.0	0.0	0.0	0.0
Commercial banks and other	..	..	..	0.0	0.0	0.0	292.0	294.3	331.0	369.7
Memo:										
IBRD	..	..	..	0.0	0.0	0.0	0.0	0.0	0.0	0.0
IDA	..	..	..	0.0	0.0	30.2	50.1	91.8	126.0	142.6
DISBURSEMENTS	..	..	..	**177.1**	**28.4**	**36.5**	**42.0**	**71.4**	**103.0**	**106.7**
Public and publicly guaranteed	..	..	..	**177.1**	**28.4**	**36.5**	**42.0**	**57.6**	**35.8**	**35.5**
Official creditors	..	..	..	177.1	28.4	36.5	42.0	57.6	35.8	35.5
Multilateral	..	..	..	0.0	0.0	30.4	22.0	55.3	35.8	35.5
Concessional	..	..	..	0.0	0.0	30.4	22.0	55.3	35.8	35.5
Bilateral	..	..	..	177.1	28.4	6.1	20.0	2.3	0.0	0.0
Concessional	..	..	..	0.0	1.0	0.0	8.7	2.3	0.0	0.0
Private creditors	..	..	..	0.0	0.0	0.0	0.0	0.0	0.0	0.0
Bonds	..	..	..	0.0	0.0	0.0	0.0	0.0	0.0	0.0
Commercial banks	..	..	..	0.0	0.0	0.0	0.0	0.0	0.0	0.0
Other private	..	..	..	0.0	0.0	0.0	0.0	0.0	0.0	0.0
Private nonguaranteed	..	..	..	**0.0**	**0.0**	**0.0**	**0.0**	**13.8**	**67.2**	**71.2**
Bonds	..	..	..	0.0	0.0	0.0	0.0	0.0	0.0	0.0
Commercial banks and other	..	..	..	0.0	0.0	0.0	0.0	13.8	67.2	71.2
Memo:										
IBRD	..	..	..	0.0	0.0	0.0	0.0	0.0	0.0	0.0
IDA	..	..	..	0.0	0.0	30.4	22.0	37.9	35.8	22.8
PRINCIPAL REPAYMENTS	..	..	..	**0.0**	**0.0**	**0.0**	**28.9**	**60.3**	**39.1**	**46.1**
Public and publicly guaranteed	..	..	..	**0.0**	**0.0**	**0.0**	**28.5**	**47.5**	**9.1**	**14.8**
Official creditors	..	..	..	0.0	0.0	0.0	28.5	39.4	4.6	14.8
Multilateral	..	..	..	0.0	0.0	0.0	0.0	0.0	0.0	0.0
Concessional	..	..	..	0.0	0.0	0.0	0.0	0.0	0.0	0.0
Bilateral	..	..	..	0.0	0.0	0.0	28.5	39.4	4.6	14.8
Concessional	..	..	..	0.0	0.0	0.0	28.5	39.4	4.6	14.8
Private creditors	..	..	..	0.0	0.0	0.0	0.0	8.1	4.5	0.0
Bonds	..	..	..	0.0	0.0	0.0	0.0	0.0	0.0	0.0
Commercial banks	..	..	..	0.0	0.0	0.0	0.0	0.0	0.0	0.0
Other private	..	..	..	0.0	0.0	0.0	0.0	8.1	4.5	0.0
Private nonguaranteed	..	..	..	**0.0**	**0.0**	**0.0**	**0.4**	**12.8**	**30.0**	**31.3**
Bonds	..	..	..	0.0	0.0	0.0	0.0	0.0	0.0	0.0
Commercial banks and other	..	..	..	0.0	0.0	0.0	0.4	12.8	30.0	31.3
Memo:										
IBRD	..	..	..	0.0	0.0	0.0	0.0	0.0	0.0	0.0
IDA	..	..	..	0.0	0.0	0.0	0.0	0.0	0.0	0.0
NET FLOWS ON DEBT	..	..	..	**177.1**	**28.4**	**36.5**	**13.1**	**11.1**	**63.9**	**60.5**
Public and publicly guaranteed	..	..	..	**177.1**	**28.4**	**36.5**	**13.5**	**10.1**	**26.7**	**20.6**
Official creditors	..	..	..	177.1	28.4	36.5	13.5	18.1	31.2	20.6
Multilateral	..	..	..	0.0	0.0	30.4	22.0	55.3	35.8	35.5
Concessional	..	..	..	0.0	0.0	30.4	22.0	55.3	35.8	35.5
Bilateral	..	..	..	177.1	28.4	6.1	-8.5	-37.2	-4.6	-14.8
Concessional	..	..	..	0.0	1.0	0.0	-19.8	-37.2	-4.6	-14.8
Private creditors	..	..	..	0.0	0.0	0.0	0.0	-8.1	-4.5	0.0
Bonds	..	..	..	0.0	0.0	0.0	0.0	0.0	0.0	0.0
Commercial banks	..	..	..	0.0	0.0	0.0	0.0	0.0	0.0	0.0
Other private	..	..	..	0.0	0.0	0.0	0.0	-8.1	-4.5	0.0
Private nonguaranteed	..	..	..	**0.0**	**0.0**	**0.0**	**-0.4**	**1.0**	**37.2**	**39.9**
Bonds	..	..	..	0.0	0.0	0.0	0.0	0.0	0.0	0.0
Commercial banks and other	..	..	..	0.0	0.0	0.0	-0.4	1.0	37.2	39.9
Memo:										
IBRD	..	..	..	0.0	0.0	0.0	0.0	0.0	0.0	0.0
IDA	..	..	..	0.0	0.0	30.4	22.0	37.9	35.8	22.8

TAJIKISTAN

(US$ million, unless otherwise indicated)

	1970	1980	1990	1994	1995	1996	1997	1998	1999	2000
INTEREST PAYMENTS (LINT)	..	..	..	**0.4**	**0.0**	**0.3**	**16.6**	**28.0**	**19.3**	**27.2**
Public and publicly guaranteed	..	..	..	**0.4**	**0.0**	**0.3**	**4.9**	**14.7**	**2.6**	**7.3**
Official creditors	..	..	..	0.4	0.0	0.3	4.9	14.7	2.1	3.8
Multilateral	..	..	..	0.0	0.0	0.0	0.2	0.4	0.8	1.2
Concessional	..	..	..	0.0	0.0	0.0	0.2	0.4	0.8	1.2
Bilateral	..	..	..	0.4	0.0	0.3	4.7	14.3	1.3	2.6
Concessional	..	..	..	0.4	0.0	0.3	4.7	13.7	1.3	2.6
Private creditors	..	..	..	0.0	0.0	0.0	0.0	0.0	0.5	3.5
Bonds	..	..	..	0.0	0.0	0.0	0.0	0.0	0.0	0.0
Commercial banks	..	..	..	0.0	0.0	0.0	0.0	0.0	0.0	0.0
Other private	..	..	..	0.0	0.0	0.0	0.0	0.0	0.5	3.5
Private nonguaranteed	..	..	..	**0.0**	**0.0**	**0.0**	**11.7**	**13.2**	**16.8**	**19.8**
Bonds	..	..	..	0.0	0.0	0.0	0.0	0.0	0.0	0.0
Commercial banks and other	..	..	..	0.0	0.0	0.0	11.7	13.2	16.8	19.8
Memo:										
IBRD	..	..	..	0.0	0.0	0.0	0.0	0.0	0.0	0.0
IDA	..	..	..	0.0	0.0	0.0	0.2	0.4	0.7	0.9
NET TRANSFERS ON DEBT	..	..	..	**176.7**	**28.4**	**36.2**	**-3.5**	**-16.9**	**44.6**	**33.4**
Public and publicly guaranteed	..	..	..	**176.7**	**28.4**	**36.2**	**8.5**	**-4.7**	**24.2**	**13.3**
Official creditors	..	..	..	176.7	28.4	36.2	8.5	3.4	29.1	16.8
Multilateral	..	..	..	0.0	0.0	30.4	21.8	54.9	35.0	34.2
Concessional	..	..	..	0.0	0.0	30.4	21.8	54.9	35.0	34.2
Bilateral	..	..	..	176.7	28.4	5.8	-13.2	-51.5	-5.9	-17.4
Concessional	..	..	..	-0.4	1.0	-0.3	-24.5	-50.8	-5.9	-17.4
Private creditors	..	..	..	0.0	0.0	0.0	0.0	-8.1	-5.0	-3.5
Bonds	..	..	..	0.0	0.0	0.0	0.0	0.0	0.0	0.0
Commercial banks	..	..	..	0.0	0.0	0.0	0.0	0.0	0.0	0.0
Other private	..	..	..	0.0	0.0	0.0	0.0	-8.1	-5.0	-3.5
Private nonguaranteed	..	..	..	**0.0**	**0.0**	**0.0**	**-12.0**	**-12.2**	**20.4**	**20.1**
Bonds	..	..	..	0.0	0.0	0.0	0.0	0.0	0.0	0.0
Commercial banks and other	..	..	..	0.0	0.0	0.0	-12.0	-12.2	20.4	20.1
Memo:										
IBRD	..	..	..	0.0	0.0	0.0	0.0	0.0	0.0	0.0
IDA	..	..	..	0.0	0.0	30.4	21.8	37.5	35.1	21.9
DEBT SERVICE (LTDS)	..	..	..	**0.4**	**0.0**	**0.3**	**45.5**	**88.3**	**58.4**	**73.3**
Public and publicly guaranteed	..	..	..	**0.4**	**0.0**	**0.3**	**33.5**	**62.2**	**11.6**	**22.2**
Official creditors	..	..	..	0.4	0.0	0.3	33.5	54.2	6.7	18.6
Multilateral	..	..	..	0.0	0.0	0.0	0.2	0.4	0.8	1.2
Concessional	..	..	..	0.0	0.0	0.0	0.2	0.4	0.8	1.2
Bilateral	..	..	..	0.4	0.0	0.3	33.2	53.8	5.9	17.4
Concessional	..	..	..	0.4	0.0	0.3	33.2	53.1	5.9	17.4
Private creditors	..	..	..	0.0	0.0	0.0	0.0	8.1	5.0	3.5
Bonds	..	..	..	0.0	0.0	0.0	0.0	0.0	0.0	0.0
Commercial banks	..	..	..	0.0	0.0	0.0	0.0	0.0	0.0	0.0
Other private	..	..	..	0.0	0.0	0.0	0.0	8.1	5.0	3.5
Private nonguaranteed	..	..	..	**0.0**	**0.0**	**0.0**	**12.0**	**26.0**	**46.8**	**51.1**
Bonds	..	..	..	0.0	0.0	0.0	0.0	0.0	0.0	0.0
Commercial banks and other	..	..	..	0.0	0.0	0.0	12.0	26.0	46.8	51.1
Memo:										
IBRD	..	..	..	0.0	0.0	0.0	0.0	0.0	0.0	0.0
IDA	..	..	..	0.0	0.0	0.0	0.2	0.4	0.7	0.9
UNDISBURSED DEBT	..	..	..	**66.4**	**34.1**	**52.7**	**33.3**	**59.2**	**97.4**	**86.7**
Official creditors	..	..	..	66.4	34.1	52.7	33.3	59.2	97.4	86.7
Private creditors	..	..	..	0.0	0.0	0.0	0.0	0.0	0.0	0.0
Memorandum items										
Concessional LDOD	..	..	..	19.9	20.9	556.9	557.7	625.9	532.9	546.3
Variable rate LDOD	..	..	..	542.1	561.7	86.1	385.0	359.3	391.5	425.4
Public sector LDOD	..	..	..	562.0	590.4	656.8	669.0	709.1	611.7	625.6
Private sector LDOD	..	..	..	0.0	0.0	0.0	128.0	117.6	102.4	89.9

6. CURRENCY COMPOSITION OF LONG-TERM DEBT (PERCENT)

	1970	1980	1990	1994	1995	1996	1997	1998	1999	2000
Deutsche mark	..	..	..	0.0	0.0	0.0	0.0	0.0	0.0	0.0
French franc	..	..	..	0.0	0.0	0.0	0.0	0.0	0.0	0.0
Japanese yen	..	..	..	0.0	0.0	0.0	0.0	0.0	0.0	0.0
Pound sterling	..	..	..	0.0	0.0	0.0	0.0	0.0	0.0	0.0
Swiss franc	..	..	..	0.0	0.0	0.0	0.0	0.0	0.0	0.0
U.S.dollars	..	..	..	96.9	97.0	100.0	100.0	98.2	98.0	96.6
Multiple currency	..	..	..	0.0	0.0	0.0	0.0	0.0	0.0	0.0
Special drawing rights	..	..	..	0.0	0.0	0.0	0.0	0.0	0.0	0.0
All other currencies	..	..	..	3.1	3.0	0.0	0.0	1.8	2.0	3.4

TAJIKISTAN

(US$ million, unless otherwise indicated)

	1970	1980	1990	1994	1995	1996	1997	1998	1999	2000
7. DEBT RESTRUCTURINGS										
Total amount rescheduled	..	..	..	0.0	0.0	505.8	19.0	196.9	7.2	0.0
Debt stock rescheduled	..	..	..	0.0	0.0	259.7	18.3	151.2	0.0	0.0
Principal rescheduled	..	..	..	0.0	0.0	215.9	0.0	20.0	0.0	0.0
Official	..	..	..	0.0	0.0	215.9	0.0	20.0	0.0	0.0
Private	..	..	..	0.0	0.0	0.0	0.0	0.0	0.0	0.0
Interest rescheduled	..	..	..	0.0	0.0	22.8	0.0	5.7	0.0	0.0
Official	..	..	..	0.0	0.0	22.8	0.0	5.7	0.0	0.0
Private	..	..	..	0.0	0.0	0.0	0.0	0.0	0.0	0.0
Debt forgiven	..	..	..	0.0	0.0	0.0	0.0	0.0	125.7	1.7
Memo: interest forgiven	..	..	..	0.0	0.0	0.0	0.0	0.0	0.0	0.0
Debt stock reduction	..	..	..	0.0	0.0	0.0	0.0	0.0	0.0	0.0
of which debt buyback	..	..	..	0.0	0.0	0.0	0.0	0.0	0.0	0.0
8. DEBT STOCK-FLOW RECONCILIATION										
Total change in debt stocks	..	..	..	195.1	53.3	65.8	365.7	184.6	-115.6	35.9
Net flows on debt	..	..	..	177.1	28.4	58.3	52.4	150.9	16.9	47.1
Net change in interest arrears	..	..	..	18.0	24.9	-30.2	23.8	-1.5	-5.4	2.1
Interest capitalized	..	..	..	0.0	0.0	22.8	0.0	5.7	0.0	0.0
Debt forgiveness or reduction	..	..	..	0.0	0.0	0.0	0.0	0.0	-125.7	-1.7
Cross-currency valuation	..	..	..	-11.5	-3.9	-4.4	-3.4	-14.2	-4.5	-11.9
Residual	..	..	..	11.5	3.9	11.4	292.9	43.7	3.1	0.4
9. AVERAGE TERMS OF NEW COMMITMENTS										
ALL CREDITORS										
Interest (%)	..	..	..	7.3	0.0	0.8	0.5	0.6	0.7	0.8
Maturity (years)	..	..	..	7.2	0.0	39.8	38.0	35.8	35.1	38.0
Grace period (years)	..	..	..	2.1	0.0	10.3	9.9	9.4	9.1	9.8
Grant element (%)	..	..	..	9.6	0.0	80.7	81.5	78.4	77.5	78.7
Official creditors										
Interest (%)	..	..	..	7.3	0.0	0.8	0.5	0.6	0.7	0.8
Maturity (years)	..	..	..	7.2	0.0	39.8	38.0	35.8	35.1	38.0
Grace period (years)	..	..	..	2.1	0.0	10.3	9.9	9.4	9.1	9.8
Grant element (%)	..	..	..	9.6	0.0	80.7	81.5	78.4	77.5	78.7
Private creditors										
Interest (%)	..	..	..	0.0	0.0	0.0	0.0	0.0	0.0	0.0
Maturity (years)	..	..	..	0.0	0.0	0.0	0.0	0.0	0.0	0.0
Grace period (years)	..	..	..	0.0	0.0	0.0	0.0	0.0	0.0	0.0
Grant element (%)	..	..	..	0.0	0.0	0.0	0.0	0.0	0.0	0.0
Memorandum items										
Commitments	..	..	..	198.6	0.0	55.0	25.0	81.7	74.9	27.9
Official creditors	..	..	..	198.6	0.0	55.0	25.0	81.7	74.9	27.9
Private creditors	..	..	..	0.0	0.0	0.0	0.0	0.0	0.0	0.0

10. CONTRACTUAL OBLIGATIONS ON OUTSTANDING LONG-TERM DEBT

	2001	2002	2003	2004	2005	2006	2007	2008	2009	2010
TOTAL										
Disbursements	23.9	21.8	14.8	11.2	7.1	3.1	1.8	0.4	0.0	0.0
Principal	179.2	151.5	111.4	68.0	52.1	52.7	54.3	34.1	24.3	24.9
Interest	29.5	20.6	13.4	10.4	8.2	6.6	4.9	3.9	3.2	2.6
Official creditors										
Disbursements	23.9	21.8	14.8	11.2	7.1	3.1	1.8	0.4	0.0	0.0
Principal	45.5	46.0	41.4	40.8	41.1	41.6	43.2	34.1	24.3	24.9
Interest	11.8	10.6	9.2	8.2	7.1	6.0	4.9	3.9	3.2	2.6
Bilateral creditors										
Disbursements	5.0	2.0	0.0	0.0	0.0	0.0	0.0	0.0	0.0	0.0
Principal	45.5	46.0	40.8	40.2	40.2	40.2	40.2	29.1	18.3	18.3
Interest	10.7	9.4	7.9	6.7	5.6	4.5	3.4	2.3	1.6	1.1
Multilateral creditors										
Disbursements	18.9	19.7	14.8	11.2	7.1	3.1	1.8	0.4	0.0	0.0
Principal	0.0	0.0	0.6	0.6	0.9	1.4	3.0	5.0	6.0	6.6
Interest	1.1	1.2	1.4	1.4	1.5	1.5	1.5	1.6	1.6	1.5
Private creditors										
Disbursements	0.0	0.0	0.0	0.0	0.0	0.0	0.0	0.0	0.0	0.0
Principal	133.7	105.5	70.0	27.2	11.1	11.1	11.1	0.0	0.0	0.0
Interest	17.7	9.9	4.1	2.3	1.2	0.6	0.0	0.0	0.0	0.0
Commercial banks										
Disbursements	0.0	0.0	0.0	0.0	0.0	0.0	0.0	0.0	0.0	0.0
Principal	0.0	0.0	0.0	0.0	0.0	0.0	0.0	0.0	0.0	0.0
Interest	0.0	0.0	0.0	0.0	0.0	0.0	0.0	0.0	0.0	0.0
Other private										
Disbursements	0.0	0.0	0.0	0.0	0.0	0.0	0.0	0.0	0.0	0.0
Principal	133.7	105.5	70.0	27.2	11.1	11.1	11.1	0.0	0.0	0.0
Interest	17.7	9.9	4.1	2.3	1.2	0.6	0.0	0.0	0.0	0.0

TANZANIA

(US$ million, unless otherwise indicated)

	1970	1980	1990	1994	1995	1996	1997	1998	1999	2000
1. SUMMARY DEBT DATA										
TOTAL DEBT STOCKS (EDT)	**212**	**5,322**	**6,454**	**7,244**	**7,415**	**7,371**	**7,127**	**7,627**	**8,043**	**7,445**
Long-term debt (LDOD)	**188**	**3,381**	**5,796**	**6,147**	**6,255**	**6,134**	**6,061**	**6,468**	**6,719**	**6,353**
Public and publicly guaranteed	173	3,297	5,784	6,135	6,211	6,089	6,021	6,432	6,687	6,325
Private nonguaranteed	15	84	12	12	44	45	41	37	32	28
Use of IMF credit	**0**	**171**	**140**	**212**	**197**	**206**	**246**	**268**	**312**	**324**
Short-term debt	**24**	**1,770**	**518**	**884**	**963**	**1,031**	**820**	**891**	**1,012**	**768**
of which interest arrears on LDOD	0	1,467	402	803	903	903	681	742	854	566
Official creditors	0	1,464	280	650	740	726	536	588	698	413
Private creditors	0	3	122	153	164	177	144	155	155	153
Memo: principal arrears on LDOD	0	592	821	1,279	1,508	1,612	1,083	1,100	1,246	629
Official creditors	0	586	637	1,025	1,234	1,324	902	928	1,068	464
Private creditors	0	6	184	253	275	288	182	172	178	166
Memo: export credits	0	0	1,278	799	911	907	1,034	655	618	596
TOTAL DEBT FLOWS										
Disbursements	**57**	**433**	**328**	**259**	**258**	**244**	**336**	**264**	**336**	**280**
Long-term debt	57	367	299	259	258	207	251	216	255	227
IMF purchases	0	66	29	0	0	37	85	48	80	53
Principal repayments	**4**	**81**	**118**	**116**	**146**	**168**	**118**	**135**	**126**	**155**
Long-term debt	4	49	89	101	127	146	87	97	97	130
IMF repurchases	0	33	28	15	20	22	31	38	29	25
Net flows on debt	**52**	**405**	**226**	**162**	**90**	**145**	**230**	**139**	**219**	**169**
of which short-term debt	0	53	16	20	-22	68	12	10	10	44
Interest payments (INT)	**3**	**80**	**62**	**67**	**86**	**104**	**48**	**112**	**72**	**61**
Long-term debt	3	48	47	62	81	97	41	104	63	50
IMF charges	0	7	6	1	1	1	1	1	2	2
Short-term debt	0	26	9	5	4	6	6	7	8	10
Net transfers on debt	**49**	**325**	**164**	**95**	**4**	**41**	**182**	**26**	**147**	**107**
Total debt service paid (TDS)	**7**	**161**	**179**	**184**	**232**	**271**	**166**	**247**	**198**	**217**
Long-term debt	7	96	137	163	208	243	128	201	160	180
IMF repurchases and charges	0	39	34	16	21	23	32	39	31	27
Short-term debt (interest only)	0	26	9	5	4	6	6	7	8	10
2. AGGREGATE NET RESOURCE FLOWS AND NET TRANSFERS (LONG-TERM)										
NET RESOURCE FLOWS	**58**	**804**	**887**	**772**	**702**	**642**	**753**	**940**	**916**	**1,020**
Net flow of long-term debt (ex. IMF)	52	318	210	158	131	61	165	118	159	97
Foreign direct investment (net)	0	0	0	50	120	150	158	172	183	193
Portfolio equity flows	0	0	0	0	0	0	0	0	0	0
Grants (excluding technical coop.)	6	485	677	565	451	431	431	650	574	730
Memo: technical coop. grants	21	173	208	209	265	254	218	190	149	153
official net resource flows	48	705	882	720	567	504	614	783	744	838
private net resource flows	11	99	5	52	135	137	140	157	171	182
NET TRANSFERS	**56**	**756**	**815**	**674**	**584**	**510**	**665**	**786**	**793**	**896**
Interest on long-term debt	3	48	47	62	81	97	41	104	63	50
Profit remittances on FDI	0	0	25	36	37	35	48	50	60	74
Memo: official net transfers	46	671	838	660	490	413	575	682	683	791
private net transfers	10	86	-24	15	93	97	89	104	109	105
3. MAJOR ECONOMIC AGGREGATES										
Gross national income (GNI)	..	..	4,072	4,357	5,131	6,378	7,583	8,534	8,386	8,984
Exports of goods & services (XGS)	..	762	544	969	1,297	1,422	1,254	1,180	1,222	1,340
of which workers remittances	..	0	..	..	..	..	..	..	..	..
Imports of goods & services (MGS)	..	1,412	1,665	1,966	2,281	2,272	2,130	2,527	2,258	2,149
International reserves (RES)	65	20	193	332	270	440	622	599	775	974
Current account balance	..	-521	-559	-637	-590	-413	-473	-788	-647	-298
4. DEBT INDICATORS										
EDT / XGS (%)	..	698.6	1,185.7	747.9	571.7	518.2	568.2	646.6	658.1	555.7
EDT / GNI (%)	..	..	158.5	166.3	144.5	115.6	94.0	89.4	95.9	82.9
TDS / XGS (%)	..	21.2	32.9	19.0	17.9	19.1	13.2	21.0	16.2	16.2
INT / XGS (%)	..	10.5	11.3	6.9	6.6	7.3	3.8	9.5	5.9	4.6
INT / GNI (%)	..	..	1.5	1.5	1.7	1.6	0.6	1.3	0.9	0.7
RES / EDT (%)	30.6	0.4	3.0	4.6	3.6	6.0	8.7	7.9	9.6	13.1
RES / MGS (months)	..	0.2	1.4	2.0	1.4	2.3	3.5	2.9	4.1	5.4
Short-term / EDT (%)	11.3	33.3	8.0	12.2	13.0	14.0	11.5	11.7	12.6	10.3
Concessional / EDT (%)	76.8	50.6	53.6	60.4	60.1	60.9	71.6	72.5	72.9	76.1
Multilateral / EDT (%)	18.0	10.6	30.7	36.7	37.7	39.1	41.0	41.2	40.7	44.0

TANZANIA

(US$ million, unless otherwise indicated)

	1970	1980	1990	1994	1995	1996	1997	1998	1999	2000
5. LONG-TERM DEBT										
DEBT OUTSTANDING (LDOD)	**188**	**3,381**	**5,796**	**6,147**	**6,255**	**6,134**	**6,061**	**6,468**	**6,719**	**6,353**
Public and publicly guaranteed	**173**	**3,297**	**5,784**	**6,135**	**6,211**	**6,089**	**6,021**	**6,432**	**6,687**	**6,325**
Official creditors	168	3,041	5,315	5,743	5,806	5,709	5,778	6,199	6,465	6,129
Multilateral	38	566	1,980	2,659	2,796	2,881	2,924	3,140	3,274	3,278
Concessional	35	305	1,619	2,430	2,603	2,733	2,813	3,049	3,199	3,217
Bilateral	129	2,476	3,335	3,084	3,010	2,828	2,855	3,059	3,191	2,851
Concessional	129	2,388	1,840	1,947	1,855	1,753	2,287	2,483	2,667	2,451
Private creditors	6	256	469	392	405	380	243	233	221	197
Bonds	0	0	0	0	0	0	0	0	0	0
Commercial banks	0	28	26	4	5	4	2	1	0	10
Other private	6	228	443	388	400	376	241	232	221	186
Private nonguaranteed	**15**	**84**	**12**	**12**	**44**	**45**	**41**	**37**	**32**	**28**
Bonds	0	0	0	0	0	0	0	0	0	0
Commercial banks and other	15	84	12	12	44	45	41	37	32	28
Memo:										
IBRD	4	198	243	114	87	56	34	22	16	11
IDA	35	242	1,250	1,998	2,182	2,242	2,306	2,463	2,594	2,593
DISBURSEMENTS	**57**	**367**	**299**	**259**	**258**	**207**	**251**	**216**	**255**	**227**
Public and publicly guaranteed	**49**	**335**	**299**	**259**	**257**	**206**	**251**	**216**	**255**	**227**
Official creditors	43	245	282	241	216	201	251	216	253	217
Multilateral	11	122	203	215	187	194	244	187	251	199
Concessional	9	63	187	211	173	192	238	184	249	199
Bilateral	33	123	79	27	29	7	8	28	3	18
Concessional	32	95	50	18	28	7	6	10	3	18
Private creditors	6	90	17	17	40	4	0	0	2	10
Bonds	0	0	0	0	0	0	0	0	0	0
Commercial banks	0	8	0	1	1	1	0	0	0	10
Other private	6	82	17	16	40	3	0	0	2	0
Private nonguaranteed	**8**	**31**	**0**	**0**	**1**	**2**	**0**	**0**	**0**	**0**
Bonds	0	0	0	0	0	0	0	0	0	0
Commercial banks and other	8	31	0	0	1	2	0	0	0	0
Memo:										
IBRD	1	34	0	0	0	0	0	0	0	0
IDA	9	35	187	183	160	134	183	102	199	142
PRINCIPAL REPAYMENTS	**4**	**49**	**89**	**101**	**127**	**146**	**87**	**97**	**97**	**130**
Public and publicly guaranteed	**2**	**32**	**89**	**101**	**122**	**146**	**83**	**93**	**92**	**126**
Official creditors	2	26	77	86	100	128	68	82	83	108
Multilateral	0	8	45	68	79	76	64	65	52	55
Concessional	0	1	13	30	23	34	31	39	40	45
Bilateral	2	18	33	18	22	51	4	17	31	53
Concessional	2	18	24	11	14	20	4	9	24	21
Private creditors	0	6	12	16	22	18	14	11	10	17
Bonds	0	0	0	0	0	0	0	0	0	0
Commercial banks	0	1	0	0	0	3	2	1	1	0
Other private	0	6	12	15	22	16	13	10	9	17
Private nonguaranteed	**3**	**16**	**0**	**0**	**5**	**0**	**4**	**4**	**4**	**4**
Bonds	0	0	0	0	0	0	0	0	0	0
Commercial banks and other	3	16	0	0	5	0	4	4	4	4
Memo:										
IBRD	0	5	26	33	34	27	20	12	6	4
IDA	0	1	6	11	12	14	15	17	24	33
NET FLOWS ON DEBT	**52**	**318**	**210**	**158**	**131**	**61**	**165**	**118**	**159**	**97**
Public and publicly guaranteed	**47**	**303**	**210**	**158**	**135**	**60**	**169**	**123**	**163**	**102**
Official creditors	42	219	205	156	116	74	183	134	171	108
Multilateral	11	115	158	147	109	118	179	122	199	144
Concessional	9	63	174	181	149	158	208	145	209	154
Bilateral	31	104	47	9	8	-44	4	12	-28	-35
Concessional	30	77	26	8	14	-13	3	2	-21	-3
Private creditors	6	84	5	2	19	-14	-14	-11	-8	-7
Bonds	0	0	0	0	0	0	0	0	0	0
Commercial banks	0	8	0	0	1	-1	-2	-1	-1	10
Other private	6	77	5	1	18	-13	-13	-10	-7	-17
Private nonguaranteed	**5**	**15**	**0**	**0**	**-4**	**1**	**-4**	**-4**	**-4**	**-4**
Bonds	0	0	0	0	0	0	0	0	0	0
Commercial banks and other	5	15	0	0	-4	1	-4	-4	-4	-4
Memo:										
IBRD	1	29	-26	-33	-34	-27	-20	-12	-6	-4
IDA	9	34	181	172	148	121	168	85	175	109

TANZANIA

(US$ million, unless otherwise indicated)

	1970	1980	1990	1994	1995	1996	1997	1998	1999	2000
INTEREST PAYMENTS (LINT)	**3**	**48**	**47**	**62**	**81**	**97**	**41**	**104**	**63**	**50**
Public and publicly guaranteed	**2**	**41**	**47**	**62**	**80**	**96**	**40**	**103**	**62**	**49**
Official creditors	2	34	44	61	77	92	39	101	61	47
Multilateral	0	18	27	34	57	47	36	36	29	28
Concessional	0	2	9	17	18	33	25	22	25	24
Bilateral	2	16	17	27	20	45	3	65	32	19
Concessional	2	14	11	11	11	22	2	54	26	14
Private creditors	0	7	3	1	3	4	1	2	1	2
Bonds	0	0	0	0	0	0	0	0	0	0
Commercial banks	0	1	0	0	0	1	0	0	0	0
Other private	0	6	3	1	3	4	1	2	1	2
Private nonguaranteed	**1**	**7**	**0**	**0**	**1**	**1**	**1**	**1**	**1**	**1**
Bonds	0	0	0	0	0	0	0	0	0	0
Commercial banks and other	1	7	0	0	1	1	1	1	1	1
Memo:										
IBRD	0	15	17	10	8	6	4	2	2	1
IDA	0	2	8	14	16	17	16	17	19	19
NET TRANSFERS ON DEBT	**49**	**271**	**162**	**96**	**50**	**-35**	**124**	**15**	**96**	**47**
Public and publicly guaranteed	**45**	**262**	**162**	**96**	**55**	**-36**	**129**	**20**	**101**	**52**
Official creditors	40	185	161	95	40	-18	144	33	110	61
Multilateral	10	97	131	113	52	71	143	86	170	116
Concessional	9	61	165	165	132	125	182	123	184	130
Bilateral	29	89	30	-18	-13	-89	1	-53	-60	-54
Concessional	29	64	15	-3	3	-36	1	-53	-47	-16
Private creditors	6	77	2	1	15	-18	-15	-13	-9	-9
Bonds	0	0	0	0	0	0	0	0	0	0
Commercial banks	0	7	0	0	1	-2	-2	-1	-1	10
Other private	6	71	1	1	15	-16	-13	-12	-8	-19
Private nonguaranteed	**4**	**9**	**0**	**0**	**-5**	**1**	**-6**	**-5**	**-5**	**-5**
Bonds	0	0	0	0	0	0	0	0	0	0
Commercial banks and other	4	9	0	0	-5	1	-6	-5	-5	-5
Memo:										
IBRD	1	14	-44	-42	-42	-33	-24	-15	-8	-6
IDA	9	33	172	158	132	104	151	68	156	91
DEBT SERVICE (LTDS)	**7**	**96**	**137**	**163**	**208**	**243**	**128**	**201**	**160**	**180**
Public and publicly guaranteed	**4**	**73**	**137**	**163**	**202**	**242**	**122**	**196**	**154**	**175**
Official creditors	4	60	121	146	177	219	107	183	144	155
Multilateral	0	26	72	102	135	123	101	102	81	83
Concessional	0	2	21	47	41	67	56	61	65	68
Bilateral	4	34	49	45	42	96	7	81	63	73
Concessional	4	32	34	22	25	42	6	63	50	35
Private creditors	0	13	15	16	25	22	15	13	11	19
Bonds	0	0	0	0	0	0	0	0	0	0
Commercial banks	0	2	0	0	0	3	2	1	1	0
Other private	0	12	15	16	25	19	13	12	10	19
Private nonguaranteed	**3**	**23**	**0**	**0**	**6**	**1**	**6**	**5**	**5**	**5**
Bonds	0	0	0	0	0	0	0	0	0	0
Commercial banks and other	3	23	0	0	6	1	6	5	5	5
Memo:										
IBRD	0	20	44	42	42	33	24	15	8	6
IDA	0	2	14	25	28	31	32	33	43	51
UNDISBURSED DEBT	**315**	**1,165**	**1,170**	**1,536**	**1,303**	**1,244**	**1,157**	**1,105**	**913**	**994**
Official creditors	311	1,088	1,165	1,511	1,278	1,235	1,145	1,094	875	949
Private creditors	4	77	5	25	25	9	12	11	38	45
Memorandum items										
Concessional LDOD	163	2,693	3,458	4,376	4,458	4,486	5,099	5,532	5,866	5,668
Variable rate LDOD	15	89	467	477	515	514	336	311	305	249
Public sector LDOD	173	3,268	5,731	6,059	6,129	6,008	5,954	6,371	6,635	6,285
Private sector LDOD	15	112	65	88	126	126	108	98	84	68

6. CURRENCY COMPOSITION OF LONG-TERM DEBT (PERCENT)

	1970	1980	1990	1994	1995	1996	1997	1998	1999	2000
Deutsche mark	3.2	1.3	3.9	4.2	3.2	2.9	1.9	1.9	1.5	1.3
French franc	0.0	2.0	3.9	2.6	2.8	2.7	1.9	1.8	1.5	1.3
Japanese yen	0.0	49.7	8.5	12.1	10.9	9.8	10.2	11.7	14.2	11.6
Pound sterling	24.1	4.8	12.1	10.5	10.2	10.3	9.8	9.2	8.9	8.1
Swiss franc	0.0	0.3	0.5	0.2	0.1	0.0	0.0	0.0	0.0	0.0
U.S.dollars	15.0	12.8	35.6	38.9	39.0	40.6	45.8	45.4	45.5	47.5
Multiple currency	2.1	6.5	6.0	4.2	8.2	6.5	6.6	6.7	6.4	14.7
Special drawing rights	0.0	0.1	1.3	4.9	5.2	5.1	4.9	5.0	4.7	5.0
All other currencies	55.6	22.5	28.2	22.4	20.4	22.1	18.9	18.3	17.3	10.5

TANZANIA

(US$ million, unless otherwise indicated)

	1970	1980	1990	1994	1995	1996	1997	1998	1999	2000
7. DEBT RESTRUCTURINGS										
Total amount rescheduled	..	..	183	9	0	33	761	153	68	523
Debt stock rescheduled	..	..	0	0	0	0	0	0	0	0
Principal rescheduled	..	..	59	6	0	11	426	30	2	315
Official	..	..	35	5	0	11	328	30	2	309
Private	..	..	24	1	0	0	97	0	0	7
Interest rescheduled	..	..	96	1	0	9	229	14	2	161
Official	..	..	91	1	0	9	207	14	2	161
Private	..	..	5	0	0	0	22	0	0	0
Debt forgiven	..	..	102	85	140	30	246	70	26	361
Memo: interest forgiven	..	..	10	17	0	1	92	0	0	230
Debt stock reduction	..	..	0	0	0	0	11	0	0	0
of which debt buyback	..	..	0	0	0	0	0	0	0	0
8. DEBT STOCK-FLOW RECONCILIATION										
Total change in debt stocks	..	..	603	445	171	-44	-244	500	416	-598
Net flows on debt	52	405	226	162	90	145	230	139	219	169
Net change in interest arrears	..	..	61	107	100	0	-223	62	111	-288
Interest capitalized	..	..	96	1	0	9	229	14	2	161
Debt forgiveness or reduction	..	..	-102	-85	-140	-30	-258	-70	-26	-361
Cross-currency valuation	..	..	118	24	-136	-440	-532	-58	-73	-285
Residual	..	..	204	236	258	272	309	414	182	6
9. AVERAGE TERMS OF NEW COMMITMENTS										
ALL CREDITORS										
Interest (%)	1.4	4.1	1.1	1.2	1.7	1.3	1.0	1.5	1.6	0.9
Maturity (years)	41.0	22.9	34.9	35.7	17.5	35.4	41.5	36.2	35.2	38.2
Grace period (years)	22.5	7.5	9.3	9.4	5.7	9.2	9.8	8.2	9.7	9.8
Grant element (%)	81.0	43.0	72.5	73.8	48.3	72.7	78.2	66.9	69.8	78.2
Official creditors										
Interest (%)	1.4	3.6	1.1	1.0	1.7	1.2	0.9	1.3	1.1	0.8
Maturity (years)	41.0	24.2	35.3	37.6	22.9	35.8	42.3	37.2	39.9	39.0
Grace period (years)	22.5	8.0	9.4	10.0	7.4	9.3	10.0	8.4	10.3	10.1
Grant element (%)	81.0	46.8	72.9	77.6	61.3	73.7	79.6	68.9	77.5	79.6
Private creditors										
Interest (%)	0.0	7.6	2.5	4.2	1.9	8.9	5.0	6.5	4.5	2.5
Maturity (years)	0.0	11.6	13.3	6.1	3.7	5.9	3.0	3.9	9.1	23.8
Grace period (years)	0.0	3.2	6.8	0.7	1.6	2.4	1.0	2.2	6.1	4.3
Grant element (%)	0.0	10.3	47.7	15.7	15.4	0.4	8.6	8.2	27.6	51.7
Memorandum items										
Commitments	271	741	697	218	141	227	269	141	192	391
Official creditors	271	663	686	205	101	224	264	137	162	371
Private creditors	0	78	12	13	40	3	6	5	30	20

10. CONTRACTUAL OBLIGATIONS ON OUTSTANDING LONG-TERM DEBT

	2001	2002	2003	2004	2005	2006	2007	2008	2009	2010
TOTAL										
Disbursements	312	259	186	124	72	24	13	3	1	0
Principal	205	175	171	162	163	167	172	178	173	182
Interest	103	102	132	129	126	123	119	115	112	108
Official creditors										
Disbursements	290	244	180	123	72	24	13	3	1	0
Principal	182	166	167	158	154	154	159	165	172	181
Interest	101	99	130	127	124	121	118	115	111	108
Bilateral creditors										
Disbursements	40	24	16	10	6	4	1	0	0	0
Principal	117	98	93	77	73	71	70	70	71	69
Interest	71	69	100	97	94	92	89	87	84	82
Multilateral creditors										
Disbursements	250	220	165	113	65	20	12	3	1	0
Principal	65	68	73	80	82	83	89	95	100	112
Interest	29	30	30	30	30	30	29	28	27	26
Private creditors										
Disbursements	22	15	6	1	1	0	0	0	0	0
Principal	22	9	4	4	9	13	13	13	1	1
Interest	3	2	2	2	2	2	1	1	0	0
Commercial banks										
Disbursements	12	5	2	0	0	0	0	0	0	0
Principal	0	0	0	0	4	8	8	8	0	0
Interest	1	1	1	1	1	1	1	0	0	0
Other private										
Disbursements	10	10	4	1	1	0	0	0	0	0
Principal	22	9	4	4	5	4	4	4	1	1
Interest	2	1	1	1	1	1	1	0	0	0

THAILAND

(US$ million, unless otherwise indicated)

	1970	1980	1990	1994	1995	1996	1997	1998	1999	2000
1. SUMMARY DEBT DATA										
TOTAL DEBT STOCKS (EDT)	**1,001**	**8,297**	**28,095**	**65,533**	**100,039**	**107,736**	**109,699**	**104,916**	**96,769**	**79,675**
Long-term debt (LDOD)	**726**	**5,646**	**19,771**	**36,354**	**55,944**	**65,123**	**69,434**	**72,018**	**69,919**	**61,733**
Public and publicly guaranteed	324	3,943	12,460	16,203	16,826	16,887	22,292	28,086	31,305	29,418
Private nonguaranteed	402	1,703	7,311	20,152	39,117	48,235	47,142	43,931	38,615	32,316
Use of IMF credit	**0**	**348**	**1**	**0**	**0**	**0**	**2,429**	**3,239**	**3,431**	**3,062**
Short-term debt	**275**	**2,303**	**8,322**	**29,179**	**44,095**	**42,613**	**37,836**	**29,660**	**23,418**	**14,880**
of which interest arrears on LDOD	0	0	0	0	0	0	0	0	0	0
Official creditors	0	0	0	0	0	0	0	0	0	0
Private creditors	0	0	0	0	0	0	0	0	0	0
Memo: principal arrears on LDOD	0	0	0	0	0	0	0	0	0	0
Official creditors	0	0	0	0	0	0	0	0	0	0
Private creditors	0	0	0	0	0	0	0	0	0	0
Memo: export credits	0	0	3,106	7,613	10,489	9,278	12,211	6,367	5,754	4,458
TOTAL DEBT FLOWS										
Disbursements	**220**	**2,648**	**4,569**	**9,096**	**10,715**	**14,550**	**14,757**	**8,134**	**6,304**	**3,996**
Long-term debt	220	2,604	4,569	9,096	10,715	14,550	12,280	7,456	6,030	3,996
IMF purchases	0	45	0	0	0	0	2,477	678	274	0
Principal repayments	**131**	**804**	**3,264**	**5,141**	**4,398**	**4,306**	**6,178**	**7,812**	**9,438**	**9,166**
Long-term debt	131	782	2,983	5,141	4,398	4,306	6,178	7,812	9,438	8,968
IMF repurchases	0	22	281	0	0	0	0	0	0	198
Net flows on debt	**90**	**1,808**	**3,516**	**10,499**	**21,233**	**8,762**	**3,802**	**-7,854**	**-9,376**	**-13,708**
of which short-term debt	0	-37	2,210	6,545	14,916	-1,482	-4,777	-8,176	-6,242	-8,538
Interest payments (INT)	**33**	**814**	**2,026**	**2,710**	**4,189**	**5,218**	**5,633**	**4,942**	**6,772**	**4,850**
Long-term debt	33	473	1,355	2,019	2,646	3,111	3,468	3,755	5,629	3,778
IMF charges	0	13	21	0	0	0	15	121	129	168
Short-term debt	0	328	650	692	1,543	2,107	2,150	1,066	1,014	905
Net transfers on debt	**57**	**994**	**1,489**	**7,789**	**17,045**	**3,544**	**-1,831**	**-12,795**	**-16,148**	**-18,559**
Total debt service paid (TDS)	**164**	**1,617**	**5,290**	**7,851**	**8,587**	**9,524**	**11,810**	**12,754**	**16,210**	**14,017**
Long-term debt	164	1,254	4,338	7,160	7,044	7,417	9,645	11,566	15,067	12,746
IMF repurchases and charges	0	35	302	0	0	0	15	121	129	366
Short-term debt (interest only)	0	328	650	692	1,543	2,107	2,150	1,066	1,014	905
2. AGGREGATE NET RESOURCE FLOWS AND NET TRANSFERS (LONG-TERM)										
NET RESOURCE FLOWS	**139**	**2,087**	**4,672**	**4,888**	**10,638**	**14,228**	**9,777**	**9,381**	**5,399**	**-525**
Net flow of long-term debt (ex. IMF)	90	1,822	1,586	3,955	6,317	10,244	6,102	-356	-3,408	-4,972
Foreign direct investment (net)	43	190	2,444	1,366	2,068	2,336	3,895	7,315	6,213	3,366
Portfolio equity flows	0	0	449	-538	2,154	1,551	-308	2,341	2,527	1,044
Grants (excluding technical coop.)	6	75	193	105	99	98	88	81	67	38
Memo: technical coop. grants	49	103	230	244	267	230	218	200	192	197
official net resource flows	27	623	292	431	591	521	6,017	1,176	2,329	858
private net resource flows	111	1,464	4,380	4,457	10,047	13,707	3,760	8,206	3,070	-1,383
NET TRANSFERS	**87**	**1,576**	**3,006**	**2,404**	**7,512**	**10,608**	**5,759**	**5,047**	**-870**	**-5,012**
Interest on long-term debt	33	473	1,355	2,019	2,646	3,111	3,468	3,755	5,629	3,778
Profit remittances on FDI	19	38	312	465	480	510	550	580	640	710
Memo: official net transfers	13	506	-150	-54	71	29	5,577	377	1,239	-150
private net transfers	74	1,070	3,156	2,458	7,442	10,579	182	4,670	-2,109	-4,862
3. MAJOR ECONOMIC AGGREGATES										
Gross national income (GNI)	7,096	32,091	84,272	142,295	165,543	178,385	147,203	108,039	118,711	120,544
Exports of goods & services (XGS)	..	8,575	31,289	58,679	74,093	75,385	76,161	69,232	74,502	86,052
of which workers remittances	..	0	0	0	..	..	..	..	..	..
Imports of goods & services (MGS)	..	10,861	38,783	67,892	88,133	90,836	79,661	55,404	62,427	77,268
International reserves (RES)	911	3,026	14,258	30,280	36,939	38,645	26,897	29,537	34,781	32,665
Current account balance	..	-2,076	-7,281	-8,085	-13,554	-14,691	-3,021	14,243	12,428	9,369
4. DEBT INDICATORS										
EDT / XGS (%)	..	96.8	89.8	111.7	135.0	142.9	144.0	151.5	129.9	92.6
EDT / GNI (%)	14.1	25.9	33.3	46.1	60.4	60.4	74.5	97.1	81.5	66.1
TDS / XGS (%)	..	18.9	16.9	13.4	11.6	12.6	15.5	18.4	21.8	16.3
INT / XGS (%)	..	9.5	6.5	4.6	5.7	6.9	7.4	7.1	9.1	5.6
INT / GNI (%)	0.5	2.5	2.4	1.9	2.5	2.9	3.8	4.6	5.7	4.0
RES / EDT (%)	91.1	36.5	50.8	46.2	36.9	35.9	24.5	28.2	35.9	41.0
RES / MGS (months)	..	3.3	4.4	5.4	5.0	5.1	4.1	6.4	6.7	5.1
Short-term / EDT (%)	27.5	27.8	29.6	44.5	44.1	39.6	34.5	28.3	24.2	18.7
Concessional / EDT (%)	9.3	10.0	15.2	10.3	7.1	6.4	6.0	7.2	9.8	11.9
Multilateral / EDT (%)	16.4	12.0	13.2	4.8	3.2	2.8	3.3	4.4	5.6	6.7

THAILAND

(US$ million, unless otherwise indicated)

	1970	1980	1990	1994	1995	1996	1997	1998	1999	2000
5. LONG-TERM DEBT										
DEBT OUTSTANDING (LDOD)	**726**	**5,646**	**19,771**	**36,354**	**55,944**	**65,123**	**69,434**	**72,018**	**69,919**	**61,733**
Public and publicly guaranteed	**324**	**3,943**	**12,460**	**16,203**	**16,826**	**16,887**	**22,292**	**28,086**	**31,305**	**29,418**
Official creditors	291	2,168	8,283	10,804	11,187	10,553	15,418	18,199	21,847	21,128
Multilateral	164	992	3,716	3,118	3,206	2,978	3,590	4,602	5,427	5,330
Concessional	0	42	247	283	291	273	255	246	232	212
Bilateral	127	1,175	4,567	7,687	7,981	7,575	11,828	13,597	16,421	15,798
Concessional	93	787	4,034	6,448	6,845	6,664	6,330	7,325	9,240	9,290
Private creditors	33	1,776	4,177	5,399	5,639	6,334	6,874	9,887	9,457	8,290
Bonds	0	148	738	1,682	1,574	1,967	2,766	3,035	2,840	2,630
Commercial banks	3	1,339	2,126	2,303	2,978	3,445	3,277	6,003	5,881	5,052
Other private	30	289	1,313	1,414	1,088	921	831	850	737	607
Private nonguaranteed	**402**	**1,703**	**7,311**	**20,152**	**39,117**	**48,235**	**47,142**	**43,931**	**38,615**	**32,316**
Bonds	0	0	40	5,223	7,375	10,610	11,411	10,627	9,501	8,414
Commercial banks and other	402	1,703	7,272	14,928	31,743	37,626	35,731	33,304	29,114	23,901
Memo:										
IBRD	159	671	2,421	1,782	1,805	1,607	1,728	2,111	2,723	2,940
IDA	0	32	109	103	102	100	98	96	93	90
DISBURSEMENTS	**220**	**2,604**	**4,569**	**9,096**	**10,715**	**14,550**	**12,280**	**7,456**	**6,030**	**3,996**
Public and publicly guaranteed	**51**	**1,315**	**1,277**	**2,117**	**2,759**	**2,600**	**8,080**	**4,956**	**4,030**	**2,996**
Official creditors	38	622	887	1,190	1,417	1,354	6,576	1,824	3,128	2,486
Multilateral	21	236	263	331	358	284	1,062	1,143	1,119	751
Concessional	0	7	2	16	17	0	0	0	0	0
Bilateral	18	386	624	859	1,060	1,070	5,514	681	2,009	1,735
Concessional	11	179	504	487	1,043	995	664	674	1,304	1,729
Private creditors	13	694	391	926	1,341	1,246	1,504	3,132	902	510
Bonds	0	44	0	690	242	514	1,055	300	0	0
Commercial banks	0	606	110	230	1,094	721	407	2,812	895	455
Other private	13	44	280	7	5	11	43	20	8	55
Private nonguaranteed	**169**	**1,288**	**3,292**	**6,979**	**7,956**	**11,950**	**4,200**	**2,500**	**2,000**	**1,000**
Bonds	0	0	0	3,165	2,080	3,370	1,264	0	0	0
Commercial banks and other	169	1,288	3,292	3,814	5,876	8,580	2,936	2,500	2,000	1,000
Memo:										
IBRD	19	145	174	128	146	138	443	498	806	456
IDA	0	5	0	0	0	0	0	0	0	0
PRINCIPAL REPAYMENTS	**131**	**782**	**2,983**	**5,141**	**4,398**	**4,306**	**6,178**	**7,812**	**9,438**	**8,968**
Public and publicly guaranteed	**23**	**172**	**2,393**	**1,868**	**1,888**	**1,316**	**1,151**	**1,030**	**2,404**	**3,034**
Official creditors	17	73	788	864	925	931	646	730	866	1,666
Multilateral	9	35	438	499	360	275	263	263	313	753
Concessional	0	0	8	11	11	11	11	13	15	15
Bilateral	8	38	349	366	566	656	383	466	553	912
Concessional	5	13	102	288	447	411	282	373	361	623
Private creditors	6	99	1,605	1,004	962	384	505	300	1,538	1,368
Bonds	0	0	87	49	199	86	220	72	233	174
Commercial banks	0	52	1,324	659	425	206	231	139	1,145	1,069
Other private	6	47	194	296	338	93	54	89	160	125
Private nonguaranteed	**107**	**610**	**591**	**3,273**	**2,510**	**2,991**	**5,027**	**6,782**	**7,034**	**5,935**
Bonds	0	0	0	0	0	25	373	859	1,125	1,044
Commercial banks and other	107	610	591	3,273	2,510	2,966	4,653	5,923	5,909	4,891
Memo:										
IBRD	9	26	207	415	201	196	192	179	180	181
IDA	0	0	1	2	2	2	2	2	3	3
NET FLOWS ON DEBT	**90**	**1,822**	**1,586**	**3,955**	**6,317**	**10,244**	**6,102**	**-356**	**-3,408**	**-4,972**
Public and publicly guaranteed	**28**	**1,143**	**-1,115**	**248**	**871**	**1,284**	**6,929**	**3,926**	**1,627**	**-38**
Official creditors	21	548	99	326	492	423	5,930	1,094	2,262	820
Multilateral	12	200	-176	-168	-2	9	799	879	805	-3
Concessional	0	7	-6	6	6	-11	-11	-13	-15	-15
Bilateral	10	348	275	494	494	414	5,131	215	1,457	823
Concessional	6	166	402	199	596	584	382	301	943	1,106
Private creditors	7	595	-1,214	-78	379	861	1,000	2,832	-636	-858
Bonds	0	44	-87	641	43	429	835	228	-233	-174
Commercial banks	0	555	-1,214	-429	669	514	176	2,674	-250	-614
Other private	7	-3	86	-289	-333	-82	-11	-70	-153	-70
Private nonguaranteed	**62**	**678**	**2,702**	**3,706**	**5,446**	**8,959**	**-827**	**-4,282**	**-5,034**	**-4,935**
Bonds	0	0	0	3,165	2,080	3,345	891	-859	-1,125	-1,044
Commercial banks and other	62	678	2,702	542	3,366	5,614	-1,717	-3,423	-3,909	-3,891
Memo:										
IBRD	10	120	-34	-287	-56	-59	251	319	626	275
IDA	0	4	-1	-2	-2	-2	-2	-2	-3	-3

THAILAND

(US$ million, unless otherwise indicated)

	1970	1980	1990	1994	1995	1996	1997	1998	1999	2000
INTEREST PAYMENTS (LINT)	**33**	**473**	**1,355**	**2,019**	**2,646**	**3,111**	**3,468**	**3,755**	**5,629**	**3,778**
Public and publicly guaranteed	**16**	**269**	**874**	**764**	**874**	**875**	**853**	**1,254**	**1,681**	**1,579**
Official creditors	14	117	442	485	521	492	440	799	1,090	1,008
Multilateral	9	76	284	217	218	206	190	248	324	351
Concessional	0	1	5	6	8	7	5	7	6	6
Bilateral	5	42	158	268	302	287	250	550	766	658
Concessional	3	19	110	206	224	210	197	192	375	252
Private creditors	2	152	432	279	353	383	414	455	591	571
Bonds	0	9	46	53	97	111	160	179	204	193
Commercial banks	0	117	227	133	192	227	215	238	353	352
Other private	2	26	160	94	65	45	39	39	34	26
Private nonguaranteed	**17**	**204**	**481**	**1,254**	**1,772**	**2,236**	**2,615**	**2,501**	**3,948**	**2,199**
Bonds	0	0	2	67	222	579	560	587	521	476
Commercial banks and other	17	204	479	1,188	1,550	1,657	2,054	1,914	3,427	1,723
Memo:										
IBRD	9	53	189	144	135	122	104	122	173	178
IDA	0	0	1	1	1	1	1	1	1	1
NET TRANSFERS ON DEBT	**57**	**1,349**	**232**	**1,936**	**3,671**	**7,133**	**2,635**	**-4,110**	**-9,036**	**-8,750**
Public and publicly guaranteed	**12**	**875**	**-1,989**	**-516**	**-3**	**410**	**6,076**	**2,672**	**-54**	**-1,616**
Official creditors	7	431	-343	-159	-29	-69	5,490	296	1,173	-188
Multilateral	2	125	-460	-385	-220	-197	609	631	482	-353
Concessional	0	6	-11	-1	-2	-19	-16	-20	-21	-20
Bilateral	5	306	116	226	192	128	4,881	-335	691	165
Concessional	3	148	292	-8	372	375	185	109	568	854
Private creditors	5	444	-1,646	-357	25	479	586	2,376	-1,227	-1,429
Bonds	0	35	-133	588	-54	318	675	48	-437	-367
Commercial banks	-1	438	-1,440	-562	477	288	-39	2,436	-603	-966
Other private	5	-29	-74	-383	-398	-127	-50	-108	-187	-96
Private nonguaranteed	**45**	**475**	**2,221**	**2,452**	**3,674**	**6,723**	**-3,441**	**-6,783**	**-8,982**	**-7,134**
Bonds	0	0	-2	3,098	1,859	2,766	330	-1,446	-1,646	-1,520
Commercial banks and other	45	475	2,223	-646	1,816	3,957	-3,772	-5,337	-7,336	-5,614
Memo:										
IBRD	1	66	-222	-431	-190	-180	147	197	453	97
IDA	0	4	-2	-3	-3	-3	-3	-3	-4	-4
DEBT SERVICE (LTDS)	**164**	**1,254**	**4,338**	**7,160**	**7,044**	**7,417**	**9,645**	**11,566**	**15,067**	**12,746**
Public and publicly guaranteed	**39**	**441**	**3,267**	**2,633**	**2,762**	**2,190**	**2,004**	**2,284**	**4,084**	**4,612**
Official creditors	31	191	1,230	1,350	1,446	1,423	1,086	1,528	1,955	2,674
Multilateral	18	111	722	716	578	481	453	511	637	1,104
Concessional	0	1	13	17	19	19	16	20	21	20
Bilateral	13	80	508	634	868	942	633	1,017	1,318	1,570
Concessional	8	32	212	495	671	620	479	564	736	875
Private creditors	8	250	2,037	1,283	1,316	767	918	756	2,129	1,939
Bonds	0	9	133	102	296	197	380	252	437	367
Commercial banks	1	168	1,550	792	617	433	446	376	1,498	1,421
Other private	7	73	354	390	403	138	93	128	195	150
Private nonguaranteed	**124**	**814**	**1,071**	**4,527**	**4,282**	**5,227**	**7,641**	**9,283**	**10,982**	**8,134**
Bonds	0	0	2	67	222	604	934	1,446	1,646	1,520
Commercial banks and other	124	814	1,070	4,460	4,060	4,623	6,707	7,837	9,336	6,614
Memo:										
IBRD	18	79	396	559	336	318	296	301	353	360
IDA	0	1	2	3	3	3	3	3	4	4
UNDISBURSED DEBT	**156**	**3,015**	**3,631**	**8,314**	**7,956**	**7,464**	**7,701**	**9,458**	**9,622**	**7,206**
Official creditors	145	2,650	2,936	6,494	5,752	5,424	5,672	7,377	8,981	6,688
Private creditors	11	364	694	1,820	2,204	2,040	2,029	2,082	641	518
Memorandum items										
Concessional LDOD	93	829	4,281	6,730	7,135	6,937	6,585	7,571	9,472	9,502
Variable rate LDOD	402	2,903	10,204	22,790	41,828	51,444	51,238	52,775	48,982	42,075
Public sector LDOD	312	3,943	12,460	16,203	16,826	16,887	22,292	28,086	31,305	29,418
Private sector LDOD	414	1,703	7,311	20,152	39,117	48,235	47,142	43,931	38,615	32,316

6. CURRENCY COMPOSITION OF LONG-TERM DEBT (PERCENT)

	1970	1980	1990	1994	1995	1996	1997	1998	1999	2000
Deutsche mark	17.6	4.7	3.6	2.3	2.4	2.1	1.4	1.3	1.1	1.0
French franc	0.0	1.8	1.0	1.2	1.2	1.1	0.8	0.6	0.4	0.4
Japanese yen	6.0	25.3	42.7	50.7	47.7	44.5	38.7	40.0	45.9	46.1
Pound sterling	2.4	0.2	0.4	0.2	0.2	0.1	0.1	0.1	0.1	0.1
Swiss franc	0.0	0.1	5.7	3.0	0.9	0.6	0.1	0.1	0.0	0.0
U.S.dollars	21.6	41.0	15.8	22.9	27.2	32.4	47.0	49.1	44.5	46.4
Multiple currency	50.7	24.3	28.2	18.6	19.2	17.7	10.8	8.0	7.3	5.4
Special drawing rights	0.0	0.0	0.2	0.2	0.1	0.1	0.1	0.1	0.0	0.0
All other currencies	1.7	2.6	2.4	0.9	1.1	1.4	1.0	0.7	0.7	0.6

THAILAND

(US$ million, unless otherwise indicated)

	1970	1980	1990	1994	1995	1996	1997	1998	1999	2000
7. DEBT RESTRUCTURINGS										
Total amount rescheduled	..	..	0	0	0	0	0	0	0	0
Debt stock rescheduled	..	..	0	0	0	0	0	0	0	0
Principal rescheduled	..	..	0	0	0	0	0	0	0	0
Official	..	..	0	0	0	0	0	0	0	0
Private	..	..	0	0	0	0	0	0	0	0
Interest rescheduled	..	..	0	0	0	0	0	0	0	0
Official	..	..	0	0	0	0	0	0	0	0
Private	..	..	0	0	0	0	0	0	0	0
Debt forgiven	..	..	0	0	0	0	0	6	0	0
Memo: interest forgiven	..	..	0	0	0	0	0	0	0	0
Debt stock reduction	..	..	0	0	0	0	0	0	0	0
of which debt buyback	..	..	0	0	0	0	0	0	0	0
8. DEBT STOCK-FLOW RECONCILIATION										
Total change in debt stocks	..	..	4,606	12,895	34,505	7,697	1,963	-4,783	-8,147	-17,093
Net flows on debt	90	1,808	3,516	10,499	21,233	8,762	3,802	-7,854	-9,376	-13,708
Net change in interest arrears	..	..	0	0	0	0	0	0	0	0
Interest capitalized	..	..	0	0	0	0	0	0	0	0
Debt forgiveness or reduction	..	..	0	0	0	0	0	-6	0	0
Cross-currency valuation	..	..	1,024	1,078	-183	-1,303	-1,163	1,301	1,283	-1,966
Residual	..	..	66	1,318	13,455	239	-676	1,775	-54	-1,419
9. AVERAGE TERMS OF NEW COMMITMENTS										
ALL CREDITORS										
Interest (%)	6.8	9.6	4.8	4.8	5.7	4.7	6.0	5.0	3.8	1.5
Maturity (years)	19.2	16.8	22.1	17.0	14.8	16.9	12.4	12.7	19.1	29.0
Grace period (years)	4.4	5.3	7.2	5.2	5.2	5.9	5.9	3.8	5.4	6.9
Grant element (%)	19.6	6.4	38.2	31.4	25.7	33.6	22.1	24.8	39.6	59.9
Official creditors										
Interest (%)	6.8	7.1	4.4	4.3	4.4	4.0	5.9	3.9	3.8	1.5
Maturity (years)	19.6	21.4	25.6	20.0	23.5	23.0	12.7	17.9	20.7	38.1
Grace period (years)	4.4	6.0	7.8	5.1	6.4	6.2	5.6	5.1	5.4	8.2
Grant element (%)	19.7	20.5	43.3	37.4	40.9	43.7	22.8	36.6	40.7	71.1
Private creditors										
Interest (%)	6.0	13.8	5.8	5.7	6.6	5.9	6.6	6.3	3.4	1.6
Maturity (years)	11.5	8.7	14.7	12.5	8.9	7.9	10.9	6.8	6.7	7.3
Grace period (years)	3.0	4.1	5.9	5.2	4.3	5.3	6.9	2.2	5.5	3.6
Grant element (%)	18.6	-18.3	27.5	22.1	15.3	18.3	18.5	11.7	31.1	32.7
Memorandum items										
Commitments	106	1,869	1,755	3,471	2,930	2,729	8,941	7,085	5,009	1,327
Official creditors	100	1,191	1,196	2,096	1,190	1,639	7,445	3,751	4,446	938
Private creditors	6	678	560	1,375	1,740	1,090	1,496	3,334	563	389

10. CONTRACTUAL OBLIGATIONS ON OUTSTANDING LONG-TERM DEBT

	2001	2002	2003	2004	2005	2006	2007	2008	2009	2010
TOTAL										
Disbursements	2,462	2,046	1,100	583	320	162	77	6	0	0
Principal	8,111	6,272	8,219	6,885	6,448	5,789	4,931	5,075	3,222	2,653
Interest	3,134	2,698	2,387	1,916	1,567	1,243	948	805	554	457
Official creditors										
Disbursements	2,420	2,029	1,095	580	319	162	77	6	0	0
Principal	1,041	1,373	2,379	3,397	3,403	1,461	1,485	1,644	1,325	1,293
Interest	1,031	1,056	1,036	892	708	555	496	435	358	301
Bilateral creditors										
Disbursements	1,840	1,477	880	483	253	118	48	0	0	0
Principal	717	954	1,859	2,855	2,873	932	953	809	810	800
Interest	665	677	666	549	396	274	247	221	196	172
Multilateral creditors										
Disbursements	581	552	214	97	66	44	29	6	0	0
Principal	324	419	521	542	529	529	532	835	515	494
Interest	366	378	370	343	312	281	248	214	162	129
Private creditors										
Disbursements	42	18	5	2	1	0	0	0	0	0
Principal	7,070	4,899	5,839	3,488	3,046	4,328	3,445	3,431	1,897	1,360
Interest	2,103	1,643	1,351	1,023	859	689	453	370	196	156
Commercial banks										
Disbursements	16	5	3	1	1	0	0	0	0	0
Principal	1,043	815	706	627	398	261	411	217	468	88
Interest	283	219	168	127	89	68	54	36	20	7
Other private										
Disbursements	26	12	3	1	0	0	0	0	0	0
Principal	6,027	4,084	5,133	2,861	2,648	4,067	3,034	3,214	1,429	1,272
Interest	1,820	1,424	1,184	896	770	620	399	334	176	149

TOGO

(US$ million, unless otherwise indicated)

	1970	1980	1990	1994	1995	1996	1997	1998	1999	2000
1. SUMMARY DEBT DATA										
TOTAL DEBT STOCKS (EDT)	**40**	**1,122**	**1,281**	**1,456**	**1,476**	**1,488**	**1,347**	**1,476**	**1,526**	**1,435**
Long-term debt (LDOD)	**40**	**970**	**1,081**	**1,229**	**1,286**	**1,310**	**1,215**	**1,329**	**1,290**	**1,232**
Public and publicly guaranteed	40	970	1,081	1,229	1,286	1,310	1,215	1,329	1,290	1,232
Private nonguaranteed	0	0	0	0	0	0	0	0	0	0
Use of IMF credit	**0**	**33**	**87**	**82**	**105**	**90**	**88**	**95**	**83**	**70**
Short-term debt	**0**	**120**	**113**	**145**	**85**	**88**	**44**	**52**	**154**	**133**
of which interest arrears on LDOD	0	15	1	85	27	27	3	14	34	63
Official creditors	0	7	1	73	13	3	3	14	34	63
Private creditors	0	9	0	12	14	24	0	0	0	0
Memo: principal arrears on LDOD	0	35	3	112	64	59	2	13	35	67
Official creditors	0	14	2	79	18	9	2	13	35	67
Private creditors	0	20	1	34	46	50	0	0	0	0
Memo: export credits	0	0	351	282	299	285	277	408	392	266
TOTAL DEBT FLOWS										
Disbursements	**5**	**119**	**110**	**56**	**59**	**101**	**73**	**86**	**39**	**24**
Long-term debt	5	97	89	41	26	101	58	72	39	24
IMF purchases	0	22	21	16	33	0	15	15	0	0
Principal repayments	**2**	**19**	**43**	**13**	**18**	**32**	**40**	**28**	**32**	**19**
Long-term debt	2	19	27	6	7	20	28	17	22	10
IMF repurchases	0	0	16	7	11	12	12	12	10	9
Net flows on debt	**3**	**108**	**16**	**56**	**39**	**72**	**14**	**55**	**89**	**-45**
of which short-term debt	0	7	-51	13	-2	3	-20	-3	81	-49
Interest payments (INT)	**1**	**34**	**43**	**10**	**11**	**26**	**16**	**12**	**13**	**10**
Long-term debt	1	19	33	6	8	23	13	10	8	5
IMF charges	0	0	4	0	1	1	0	1	0	0
Short-term debt	0	14	6	4	3	2	2	2	4	5
Net transfers on debt	**2**	**74**	**-27**	**47**	**27**	**45**	**-3**	**43**	**76**	**-55**
Total debt service paid (TDS)	**2**	**52**	**86**	**23**	**29**	**58**	**56**	**41**	**45**	**30**
Long-term debt	2	38	60	12	14	44	42	27	31	15
IMF repurchases and charges	0	0	20	7	12	12	12	12	10	10
Short-term debt (interest only)	0	14	6	4	3	2	2	2	4	5
2. AGGREGATE NET RESOURCE FLOWS AND NET TRANSFERS (LONG-TERM)										
NET RESOURCE FLOWS	**11**	**136**	**182**	**123**	**168**	**168**	**109**	**148**	**102**	**93**
Net flow of long-term debt (ex. IMF)	3	78	62	34	19	81	30	55	17	14
Foreign direct investment (net)	1	42	0	15	26	17	21	30	43	30
Portfolio equity flows	0	0	0	0	0	0	0	0	0	0
Grants (excluding technical coop.)	7	15	120	73	123	70	58	63	43	49
Memo: technical coop. grants	8	29	60	23	32	29	27	27	27	23
official net resource flows	11	53	182	107	142	151	94	118	60	63
private net resource flows	0	83	0	15	26	17	15	30	43	30
NET TRANSFERS	**5**	**116**	**137**	**111**	**155**	**138**	**89**	**135**	**92**	**87**
Interest on long-term debt	1	19	33	6	8	23	13	10	8	5
Profit remittances on FDI	6	0	12	6	5	7	6	4	2	1
Memo: official net transfers	10	41	154	101	134	128	80	108	52	58
private net transfers	-6	75	-17	9	21	10	9	26	41	29
3. MAJOR ECONOMIC AGGREGATES										
Gross national income (GNI)	248	1,096	1,598	931	1,265	1,439	1,470	1,393	1,383	1,195
Exports of goods & services (XGS)	..	580	723	424	489	616	555	541	505	487
of which workers remittances	..	10	27	15	15	13	9	0	4	8
Imports of goods & services (MGS)	..	752	912	545	713	841	762	770	699	679
International reserves (RES)	35	85	358	99	135	93	122	121	126	152
Current account balance	..	-95	-84	-56	-122	-154	-117	-140	-127	..
4. DEBT INDICATORS										
EDT / XGS (%)	..	193.4	177.2	343.6	302.1	241.7	242.9	272.9	302.5	294.7
EDT / GNI (%)	16.0	102.4	80.1	156.3	116.7	103.4	91.6	105.9	110.4	120.1
TDS / XGS (%)	..	9.0	11.9	5.4	6.0	9.5	10.1	7.5	8.9	6.1
INT / XGS (%)	..	5.8	6.0	2.3	2.3	4.3	2.9	2.3	2.6	2.1
INT / GNI (%)	0.3	3.1	2.7	1.1	0.9	1.8	1.1	0.9	0.9	0.9
RES / EDT (%)	88.8	7.6	28.0	6.8	9.2	6.3	9.1	8.2	8.2	10.6
RES / MGS (months)	..	1.4	4.7	2.2	2.3	1.3	1.9	1.9	2.2	2.7
Short-term / EDT (%)	0.0	10.7	8.8	9.9	5.8	5.9	3.3	3.5	10.1	9.3
Concessional / EDT (%)	78.9	28.3	55.1	61.2	61.8	65.2	71.5	71.5	68.8	70.2
Multilateral / EDT (%)	4.8	10.3	43.7	46.5	48.3	49.7	53.3	54.3	52.0	53.4

TOGO

(US$ million, unless otherwise indicated)

	1970	1980	1990	1994	1995	1996	1997	1998	1999	2000
5. LONG-TERM DEBT										
DEBT OUTSTANDING (LDOD)	**40**	**970**	**1,081**	**1,229**	**1,286**	**1,310**	**1,215**	**1,329**	**1,290**	**1,232**
Public and publicly guaranteed	**40**	**970**	**1,081**	**1,229**	**1,286**	**1,310**	**1,215**	**1,329**	**1,290**	**1,232**
Official creditors	32	554	1,029	1,178	1,235	1,260	1,215	1,329	1,290	1,232
Multilateral	2	116	560	677	713	740	718	801	793	767
Concessional	2	90	516	646	681	718	705	777	774	750
Bilateral	30	439	469	501	522	520	497	529	497	465
Concessional	30	228	189	245	232	253	258	279	277	257
Private creditors	8	415	52	51	52	50	0	0	0	0
Bonds	0	0	0	0	0	0	0	0	0	0
Commercial banks	0	96	51	50	52	50	0	0	0	0
Other private	8	319	1	1	0	0	0	0	0	0
Private nonguaranteed	**0**	**0**	**0**	**0**	**0**	**0**	**0**	**0**	**0**	**0**
Bonds	0	0	0	0	0	0	0	0	0	0
Commercial banks and other	0	0	0	0	0	0	0	0	0	0
Memo:										
IBRD	0	4	5	0	0	0	0	0	0	0
IDA	2	43	393	513	541	576	561	620	622	604
DISBURSEMENTS	**5**	**97**	**89**	**41**	**26**	**101**	**58**	**72**	**39**	**24**
Public and publicly guaranteed	**5**	**97**	**89**	**41**	**26**	**101**	**58**	**72**	**39**	**24**
Official creditors	4	47	89	41	26	101	58	72	39	24
Multilateral	1	35	45	39	26	72	37	63	32	21
Concessional	1	30	44	39	26	70	37	52	32	21
Bilateral	3	12	44	1	0	29	21	8	7	3
Concessional	3	5	44	1	0	29	21	8	7	3
Private creditors	0	50	0	0	0	0	0	0	0	0
Bonds	0	0	0	0	0	0	0	0	0	0
Commercial banks	0	2	0	0	0	0	0	0	0	0
Other private	0	47	0	0	0	0	0	0	0	0
Private nonguaranteed	**0**	**0**	**0**	**0**	**0**	**0**	**0**	**0**	**0**	**0**
Bonds	0	0	0	0	0	0	0	0	0	0
Commercial banks and other	0	0	0	0	0	0	0	0	0	0
Memo:										
IBRD	0	0	0	0	0	0	0	0	0	0
IDA	1	13	31	28	20	56	17	44	22	15
PRINCIPAL REPAYMENTS	**2**	**19**	**27**	**6**	**7**	**20**	**28**	**17**	**22**	**10**
Public and publicly guaranteed	**2**	**19**	**27**	**6**	**7**	**20**	**28**	**17**	**22**	**10**
Official creditors	1	10	27	6	7	20	22	17	22	10
Multilateral	0	0	17	6	6	17	16	9	14	8
Concessional	0	0	5	4	6	12	9	8	11	8
Bilateral	1	9	10	0	1	4	6	8	8	2
Concessional	1	1	1	0	1	3	4	6	5	2
Private creditors	1	9	0	0	0	0	6	0	0	0
Bonds	0	0	0	0	0	0	0	0	0	0
Commercial banks	0	4	0	0	0	0	6	0	0	0
Other private	1	4	0	0	0	0	0	0	0	0
Private nonguaranteed	**0**	**0**	**0**	**0**	**0**	**0**	**0**	**0**	**0**	**0**
Bonds	0	0	0	0	0	0	0	0	0	0
Commercial banks and other	0	0	0	0	0	0	0	0	0	0
Memo:										
IBRD	0	0	8	0	0	0	0	0	0	0
IDA	0	0	1	3	3	4	4	5	8	5
NET FLOWS ON DEBT	**3**	**78**	**62**	**34**	**19**	**81**	**30**	**55**	**17**	**14**
Public and publicly guaranteed	**3**	**78**	**62**	**34**	**19**	**81**	**30**	**55**	**17**	**14**
Official creditors	3	38	62	34	19	81	36	55	17	14
Multilateral	1	35	28	33	20	55	21	54	18	12
Concessional	1	30	39	35	20	58	28	45	21	13
Bilateral	2	3	34	1	-1	25	15	1	-1	1
Concessional	2	4	44	1	-1	26	17	3	2	2
Private creditors	-1	41	0	0	0	0	-6	0	0	0
Bonds	0	0	0	0	0	0	0	0	0	0
Commercial banks	0	-2	0	0	0	0	-6	0	0	0
Other private	-1	43	0	0	0	0	0	0	0	0
Private nonguaranteed	**0**	**0**	**0**	**0**	**0**	**0**	**0**	**0**	**0**	**0**
Bonds	0	0	0	0	0	0	0	0	0	0
Commercial banks and other	0	0	0	0	0	0	0	0	0	0
Memo:										
IBRD	0	0	-8	0	0	0	0	0	0	0
IDA	1	13	30	25	17	52	13	39	15	10

TOGO

(US$ million, unless otherwise indicated)

	1970	1980	1990	1994	1995	1996	1997	1998	1999	2000
INTEREST PAYMENTS (LINT)	**1**	**19**	**33**	**6**	**8**	**23**	**13**	**10**	**8**	**5**
Public and publicly guaranteed	**1**	**19**	**33**	**6**	**8**	**23**	**13**	**10**	**8**	**5**
Official creditors	1	12	28	6	8	23	13	10	8	5
Multilateral	0	2	8	6	5	8	7	5	7	5
Concessional	0	1	4	5	4	7	6	5	6	5
Bilateral	1	9	20	0	3	15	6	5	1	0
Concessional	1	0	4	0	1	6	2	3	1	0
Private creditors	0	8	5	0	0	0	0	0	0	0
Bonds	0	0	0	0	0	0	0	0	0	0
Commercial banks	0	8	5	0	0	0	0	0	0	0
Other private	0	0	0	0	0	0	0	0	0	0
Private nonguaranteed	**0**	**0**	**0**	**0**	**0**	**0**	**0**	**0**	**0**	**0**
Bonds	0	0	0	0	0	0	0	0	0	0
Commercial banks and other	0	0	0	0	0	0	0	0	0	0
Memo:										
IBRD	0	0	1	0	0	0	0	0	0	0
IDA	0	0	3	4	4	5	4	3	5	3
NET TRANSFERS ON DEBT	**2**	**59**	**29**	**28**	**12**	**57**	**17**	**45**	**9**	**9**
Public and publicly guaranteed	**2**	**59**	**29**	**28**	**12**	**57**	**17**	**45**	**9**	**9**
Official creditors	3	26	34	28	12	57	23	45	9	9
Multilateral	1	33	20	27	15	47	14	49	11	8
Concessional	1	29	35	30	16	51	22	40	15	8
Bilateral	2	-7	14	1	-3	10	9	-4	-3	1
Concessional	2	3	40	1	-2	21	14	0	1	1
Private creditors	-1	33	-5	0	0	0	-6	0	0	0
Bonds	0	0	0	0	0	0	0	0	0	0
Commercial banks	0	-10	-5	0	0	0	-6	0	0	0
Other private	-1	43	0	0	0	0	0	0	0	0
Private nonguaranteed	**0**	**0**	**0**	**0**	**0**	**0**	**0**	**0**	**0**	**0**
Bonds	0	0	0	0	0	0	0	0	0	0
Commercial banks and other	0	0	0	0	0	0	0	0	0	0
Memo:										
IBRD	0	0	-9	0	0	0	0	0	0	0
IDA	1	12	28	21	14	47	9	36	10	7
DEBT SERVICE (LTDS)	**2**	**38**	**60**	**12**	**14**	**44**	**42**	**27**	**31**	**15**
Public and publicly guaranteed	**2**	**38**	**60**	**12**	**14**	**44**	**42**	**27**	**31**	**15**
Official creditors	2	21	55	12	14	44	36	27	31	15
Multilateral	0	3	25	12	11	25	23	14	21	13
Concessional	0	1	9	9	10	19	15	12	17	13
Bilateral	2	19	30	0	4	19	12	12	10	2
Concessional	2	2	5	0	2	8	7	9	6	2
Private creditors	1	16	5	0	0	0	6	0	0	0
Bonds	0	0	0	0	0	0	0	0	0	0
Commercial banks	0	12	5	0	0	0	6	0	0	0
Other private	1	5	0	0	0	0	0	0	0	0
Private nonguaranteed	**0**	**0**	**0**	**0**	**0**	**0**	**0**	**0**	**0**	**0**
Bonds	0	0	0	0	0	0	0	0	0	0
Commercial banks and other	0	0	0	0	0	0	0	0	0	0
Memo:										
IBRD	0	0	9	0	0	0	0	0	0	0
IDA	0	0	4	7	6	9	8	9	13	8
UNDISBURSED DEBT	**7**	**155**	**290**	**138**	**162**	**187**	**223**	**208**	**177**	**146**
Official creditors	6	152	290	138	162	187	223	208	177	146
Private creditors	1	3	0	0	0	0	0	0	0	0
Memorandum items										
Concessional LDOD	31	318	705	892	912	971	963	1,055	1,051	1,007
Variable rate LDOD	0	108	37	37	129	139	119	136	126	115
Public sector LDOD	36	969	1,081	1,229	1,286	1,310	1,215	1,329	1,290	1,232
Private sector LDOD	3	1	0	0	0	0	0	0	0	0

6. CURRENCY COMPOSITION OF LONG-TERM DEBT (PERCENT)

	1970	1980	1990	1994	1995	1996	1997	1998	1999	2000
Deutsche mark	62.3	16.3	1.9	1.9	1.8	1.7	1.4	1.4	1.2	1.3
French franc	7.8	22.3	12.9	13.0	9.0	8.6	7.3	7.4	6.7	6.6
Japanese yen	0.0	0.0	3.0	3.6	3.3	4.6	5.8	5.8	6.6	6.0
Pound sterling	0.0	5.4	1.9	1.6	1.7	1.7	1.7	1.6	1.6	1.5
Swiss franc	0.0	9.5	10.3	9.2	10.9	9.5	9.5	8.6	8.2	7.8
U.S.dollars	15.4	18.1	44.2	46.9	47.4	49.2	49.4	49.8	51.5	52.6
Multiple currency	0.0	2.1	7.5	7.3	7.4	7.1	7.1	7.0	6.9	6.7
Special drawing rights	0.0	0.0	1.0	1.0	1.0	1.1	1.2	1.2	1.3	1.3
All other currencies	14.5	26.3	17.3	15.5	17.5	16.5	16.6	17.2	16.0	16.2

TOGO

(US$ million, unless otherwise indicated)

	1970	1980	1990	1994	1995	1996	1997	1998	1999	2000
7. DEBT RESTRUCTURINGS										
Total amount rescheduled	..	..	79	0	133	31	30	19	9	0
Debt stock rescheduled	..	..	0	0	1	0	0	0	0	0
Principal rescheduled	..	..	66	0	64	11	15	7	0	0
Official	..	..	66	0	63	11	15	7	0	0
Private	..	..	0	0	1	0	0	0	0	0
Interest rescheduled	..	..	12	0	63	16	15	7	0	0
Official	..	..	12	0	63	16	15	7	0	0
Private	..	..	0	0	0	0	0	0	0	0
Debt forgiven	..	..	18	0	85	5	4	11	0	0
Memo: interest forgiven	..	..	0	0	23	3	35	1	0	0
Debt stock reduction	..	..	0	0	0	0	49	0	0	0
of which debt buyback	..	..	0	0	0	0	6	0	0	0
8. DEBT STOCK-FLOW RECONCILIATION										
Total change in debt stocks	..	..	104	162	20	12	-141	129	51	-92
Net flows on debt	3	108	16	56	39	72	14	55	89	-45
Net change in interest arrears	..	..	1	34	-58	0	-24	11	21	29
Interest capitalized	..	..	12	0	63	16	15	7	0	0
Debt forgiveness or reduction	..	..	-18	0	-85	-5	-47	-11	0	0
Cross-currency valuation	..	..	42	14	-21	-134	-194	-18	-63	-66
Residual	..	..	52	58	82	63	96	85	5	-10
9. AVERAGE TERMS OF NEW COMMITMENTS										
ALL CREDITORS										
Interest (%)	4.6	4.0	0.7	0.0	0.7	1.0	1.0	2.5	0.8	0.0
Maturity (years)	16.8	24.5	766.4	0.0	733.1	398.5	484.2	29.9	47.0	0.0
Grace period (years)	4.4	7.4	10.4	0.0	9.9	9.1	9.7	7.6	10.3	0.0
Grant element (%)	32.8	46.5	80.1	0.0	79.7	73.5	76.8	59.5	82.0	0.0
Official creditors										
Interest (%)	3.5	3.2	0.7	0.0	0.7	1.0	1.0	2.5	0.8	0.0
Maturity (years)	21.3	26.7	766.4	0.0	733.1	398.5	484.2	29.9	47.0	0.0
Grace period (years)	5.4	8.0	10.4	0.0	9.9	9.1	9.7	7.6	10.3	0.0
Grant element (%)	42.6	52.6	80.1	0.0	79.7	73.5	76.8	59.5	82.0	0.0
Private creditors										
Interest (%)	7.6	10.1	0.0	0.0	0.0	0.0	0.0	0.0	0.0	0.0
Maturity (years)	4.3	6.9	0.0	0.0	0.0	0.0	0.0	0.0	0.0	0.0
Grace period (years)	1.6	2.6	0.0	0.0	0.0	0.0	0.0	0.0	0.0	0.0
Grant element (%)	5.5	-1.3	0.0	0.0	0.0	0.0	0.0	0.0	0.0	0.0
Memorandum items										
Commitments	3	97	115	0	69	132	108	55	22	0
Official creditors	2	86	115	0	69	132	108	55	22	0
Private creditors	1	11	0	0	0	0	0	0	0	0

10. CONTRACTUAL OBLIGATIONS ON OUTSTANDING LONG-TERM DEBT

	2001	2002	2003	2004	2005	2006	2007	2008	2009	2010
TOTAL										
Disbursements	50	39	25	12	7	1	1	0	0	0
Principal	42	42	42	41	34	35	38	41	43	44
Interest	27	26	24	23	22	21	20	19	18	17
Official creditors										
Disbursements	50	39	25	12	7	1	1	0	0	0
Principal	42	42	42	41	34	35	38	41	43	44
Interest	27	26	24	23	22	21	20	19	18	17
Bilateral creditors										
Disbursements	3	4	3	2	1	1	0	0	0	0
Principal	26	27	26	22	14	13	15	16	16	17
Interest	20	19	17	16	15	14	14	13	12	12
Multilateral creditors										
Disbursements	47	35	23	10	6	1	0	0	0	0
Principal	16	15	16	19	19	22	23	25	27	27
Interest	7	7	7	7	7	7	6	6	6	6
Private creditors										
Disbursements	0	0	0	0	0	0	0	0	0	0
Principal	0	0	0	0	0	0	0	0	0	0
Interest	0	0	0	0	0	0	0	0	0	0
Commercial banks										
Disbursements	0	0	0	0	0	0	0	0	0	0
Principal	0	0	0	0	0	0	0	0	0	0
Interest	0	0	0	0	0	0	0	0	0	0
Other private										
Disbursements	0	0	0	0	0	0	0	0	0	0
Principal	0	0	0	0	0	0	0	0	0	0
Interest	0	0	0	0	0	0	0	0	0	0

TONGA

(US$ million, unless otherwise indicated)

	1970	1980	1990	1994	1995	1996	1997	1998	1999	2000
1. SUMMARY DEBT DATA										
TOTAL DEBT STOCKS (EDT)	..	..	**53.7**	**58.6**	**64.1**	**63.8**	**57.3**	**61.5**	**63.6**	**58.2**
Long-term debt (LDOD)	..	..	**44.5**	**57.6**	**62.8**	**62.5**	**56.3**	**60.8**	**63.5**	**58.0**
Public and publicly guaranteed	..	..	44.5	57.6	62.8	62.5	56.3	60.8	63.5	58.0
Private nonguaranteed	..	..	0.0	0.0	0.0	0.0	0.0	0.0	0.0	0.0
Use of IMF credit	**0.0**	**0.0**	**0.0**	**0.0**	**0.0**	**0.0**	**0.0**	**0.0**	**0.0**	**0.0**
Short-term debt	..	..	**9.2**	**1.0**	**1.3**	**1.3**	**1.0**	**0.6**	**0.2**	**0.1**
of which interest arrears on LDOD	..	..	0.0	0.0	0.0	0.0	0.0	0.0	0.0	0.0
Official creditors	..	..	0.0	0.0	0.0	0.0	0.0	0.0	0.0	0.0
Private creditors	..	..	0.0	0.0	0.0	0.0	0.0	0.0	0.0	0.0
Memo: principal arrears on LDOD	..	..	0.0	0.0	0.0	0.0	0.0	0.0	0.0	0.0
Official creditors	..	..	0.0	0.0	0.0	0.0	0.0	0.0	0.0	0.0
Private creditors	..	..	0.0	0.0	0.0	0.0	0.0	0.0	0.0	0.0
Memo: export credits	..	..	1.0	7.7	1.3	1.2	0.8	0.3	1.9	1.7
TOTAL DEBT FLOWS										
Disbursements	..	..	**3.3**	**7.7**	**6.2**	**4.5**	**2.6**	**5.2**	**2.5**	**2.9**
Long-term debt	..	..	3.3	7.7	6.2	4.5	2.6	5.2	2.5	2.9
IMF purchases	0.0	0.0	0.0	0.0	0.0	0.0	0.0	0.0	0.0	0.0
Principal repayments	..	..	**1.0**	**2.1**	**2.4**	**2.7**	**3.2**	**2.8**	**3.5**	**3.3**
Long-term debt	..	..	1.0	2.1	2.4	2.7	3.2	2.8	3.5	3.3
IMF repurchases	0.0	0.0	0.0	0.0	0.0	0.0	0.0	0.0	0.0	0.0
Net flows on debt	..	..	**10.4**	**6.0**	**4.1**	**1.9**	**-0.9**	**2.1**	**-1.4**	**-0.5**
of which short-term debt	..	..	8.2	0.4	0.3	0.0	-0.3	-0.4	-0.4	0.0
Interest payments (INT)	..	..	**0.9**	**0.6**	**0.8**	**0.8**	**0.9**	**0.8**	**0.9**	**0.7**
Long-term debt	..	..	0.5	0.6	0.7	0.7	0.9	0.8	0.8	0.7
IMF charges	0.0	0.0	0.0	0.0	0.0	0.0	0.0	0.0	0.0	0.0
Short-term debt	..	..	0.4	0.1	0.1	0.1	0.1	0.0	0.0	0.0
Net transfers on debt	..	..	**9.5**	**5.4**	**3.3**	**1.1**	**-1.9**	**1.2**	**-2.3**	**-1.2**
Total debt service paid (TDS)	..	..	**1.9**	**2.7**	**3.2**	**3.4**	**4.1**	**3.6**	**4.3**	**4.1**
Long-term debt	..	..	1.5	2.7	3.1	3.4	4.1	3.6	4.3	4.0
IMF repurchases and charges	0.0	0.0	0.0	0.0	0.0	0.0	0.0	0.0	0.0	0.0
Short-term debt (interest only)	..	..	0.4	0.1	0.1	0.1	0.1	0.0	0.0	0.0
2. AGGREGATE NET RESOURCE FLOWS AND NET TRANSFERS (LONG-TERM)										
NET RESOURCE FLOWS	..	..	**19.1**	**22.8**	**24.1**	**16.2**	**10.5**	**10.1**	**8.1**	**8.4**
Net flow of long-term debt (ex. IMF)	..	..	2.2	5.6	3.8	1.9	-0.6	2.4	-1.0	-0.4
Foreign direct investment (net)	..	..	0.0	2.0	2.0	2.0	3.0	2.0	2.0	2.0
Portfolio equity flows	..	..	0.0	0.0	0.0	0.0	0.0	0.0	0.0	0.0
Grants (excluding technical coop.)	..	..	16.9	15.2	18.3	12.3	8.1	5.6	7.1	6.9
Memo: technical coop. grants	..	..	10.9	14.0	16.4	17.5	17.0	14.1	13.6	11.2
official net resource flows	..	..	19.1	20.8	22.1	14.0	8.6	8.9	7.4	7.7
private net resource flows	..	..	0.0	2.0	2.0	2.2	1.9	1.2	0.7	0.7
NET TRANSFERS	..	..	**18.6**	**22.2**	**23.4**	**15.5**	**9.6**	**9.3**	**7.2**	**7.7**
Interest on long-term debt	..	..	0.5	0.6	0.7	0.7	0.9	0.8	0.8	0.7
Profit remittances on FDI	..	..	0.0	0.0	0.0	0.0	0.0	0.0	0.0	0.0
Memo: official net transfers	..	..	18.6	20.2	21.4	13.3	8.0	8.3	6.7	7.1
private net transfers	..	..	0.0	2.0	2.0	2.2	1.6	1.0	0.5	0.6
3. MAJOR ECONOMIC AGGREGATES										
Gross national income (GNI)	..	..	117.3	159.1	165.7	168.4	172.9	165.4	154.6	154.9
Exports of goods & services (XGS)	..	..	66.5	62.1	66.7	86.7	53.2	50.4	39.4	35.2
of which workers remittances	..	..	23.0	18.1	19.6	28.2	..	..	..	..
Imports of goods & services (MGS)	..	..	75.0	102.5	128.7	125.1	97.1	115.4	80.2	92.2
International reserves (RES)	..	..	31.3	35.5	28.7	30.6	27.5	28.7	26.8	27.0
Current account balance	..	..	5.8	-32.8	-49.3	-36.3	-10.0	-28.6	-9.5	-19.7
4. DEBT INDICATORS										
EDT / XGS (%)	..	..	80.8	94.4	96.2	73.6	107.7	122.1	161.4	165.3
EDT / GNI (%)	..	..	45.8	36.8	38.7	37.9	33.2	37.2	41.1	37.6
TDS / XGS (%)	..	..	2.9	4.4	4.8	3.9	7.7	7.1	10.9	11.6
INT / XGS (%)	..	..	1.4	1.0	1.2	0.9	1.7	1.6	2.3	2.0
INT / GNI (%)	..	..	0.8	0.4	0.5	0.5	0.5	0.5	0.6	0.5
RES / EDT (%)	..	..	58.4	60.7	44.8	48.0	48.0	46.6	42.1	46.4
RES / MGS (months)	..	..	5.0	4.2	2.7	2.9	3.4	3.0	4.0	3.5
Short-term / EDT (%)	..	..	17.1	1.7	2.0	2.0	1.8	1.0	0.3	0.2
Concessional / EDT (%)	..	..	72.3	80.4	82.4	83.4	85.5	88.8	93.6	96.6
Multilateral / EDT (%)	..	..	42.3	61.6	65.1	68.3	72.4	76.8	84.3	87.6

TONGA

(US$ million, unless otherwise indicated)

	1970	1980	1990	1994	1995	1996	1997	1998	1999	2000
5. LONG-TERM DEBT										
DEBT OUTSTANDING (LDOD)	..	..	**44.5**	**57.6**	**62.8**	**62.5**	**56.3**	**60.8**	**63.5**	**58.0**
Public and publicly guaranteed	..	..	**44.5**	**57.6**	**62.8**	**62.5**	**56.3**	**60.8**	**63.5**	**58.0**
Official creditors	..	..	44.5	53.3	58.5	58.0	52.9	58.3	62.2	58.0
Multilateral	..	..	22.7	36.1	41.7	43.6	41.5	47.2	53.6	51.0
Concessional	..	..	18.0	30.2	36.0	38.8	37.6	43.5	50.9	49.1
Bilateral	..	..	21.7	17.2	16.8	14.4	11.4	11.1	8.6	7.1
Concessional	..	..	20.8	16.9	16.8	14.4	11.4	11.1	8.6	7.1
Private creditors	..	..	0.0	4.3	4.3	4.5	3.4	2.5	1.3	0.0
Bonds	..	..	0.0	0.0	0.0	0.0	0.0	0.0	0.0	0.0
Commercial banks	..	..	0.0	0.0	0.0	0.0	0.0	0.0	0.0	0.0
Other private	..	..	0.0	4.3	4.3	4.5	3.4	2.5	1.3	0.0
Private nonguaranteed	..	..	**0.0**	**0.0**	**0.0**	**0.0**	**0.0**	**0.0**	**0.0**	**0.0**
Bonds	..	..	0.0	0.0	0.0	0.0	0.0	0.0	0.0	0.0
Commercial banks and other	..	..	0.0	0.0	0.0	0.0	0.0	0.0	0.0	0.0
Memo:										
IBRD	0.0	0.0	0.0	0.0	0.0	0.0	0.0	0.0	0.0	0.0
IDA	0.0	0.0	2.6	4.5	4.8	4.6	4.3	4.4	4.3	4.0
DISBURSEMENTS	..	..	**3.3**	**7.7**	**6.2**	**4.5**	**2.6**	**5.2**	**2.5**	**2.9**
Public and publicly guaranteed	..	..	**3.3**	**7.7**	**6.2**	**4.5**	**2.6**	**5.2**	**2.5**	**2.9**
Official creditors	..	..	3.3	7.7	6.2	3.9	2.6	5.2	2.5	2.9
Multilateral	..	..	3.3	7.7	6.2	3.9	2.6	5.2	2.5	2.9
Concessional	..	..	3.2	7.0	6.2	3.9	2.4	5.1	2.4	2.9
Bilateral	..	..	0.0	0.0	0.0	0.0	0.0	0.0	0.0	0.0
Concessional	..	..	0.0	0.0	0.0	0.0	0.0	0.0	0.0	0.0
Private creditors	..	..	0.0	0.0	0.0	0.7	0.0	0.0	0.0	0.0
Bonds	..	..	0.0	0.0	0.0	0.0	0.0	0.0	0.0	0.0
Commercial banks	..	..	0.0	0.0	0.0	0.0	0.0	0.0	0.0	0.0
Other private	..	..	0.0	0.0	0.0	0.7	0.0	0.0	0.0	0.0
Private nonguaranteed	..	..	**0.0**	**0.0**	**0.0**	**0.0**	**0.0**	**0.0**	**0.0**	**0.0**
Bonds	..	..	0.0	0.0	0.0	0.0	0.0	0.0	0.0	0.0
Commercial banks and other	..	..	0.0	0.0	0.0	0.0	0.0	0.0	0.0	0.0
Memo:										
IBRD	0.0	0.0	0.0	0.0	0.0	0.0	0.0	0.0	0.0	0.0
IDA	0.0	0.0	1.0	0.8	0.2	-0.1	0.0	0.0	0.0	0.0
PRINCIPAL REPAYMENTS	..	..	**1.0**	**2.1**	**2.4**	**2.7**	**3.2**	**2.8**	**3.5**	**3.3**
Public and publicly guaranteed	..	..	**1.0**	**2.1**	**2.4**	**2.7**	**3.2**	**2.8**	**3.5**	**3.3**
Official creditors	..	..	1.0	2.1	2.4	2.2	2.1	1.9	2.2	2.1
Multilateral	..	..	0.5	0.7	0.8	0.9	0.9	0.9	1.2	1.2
Concessional	..	..	0.3	0.2	0.2	0.3	0.3	0.4	0.5	0.6
Bilateral	..	..	0.5	1.4	1.7	1.3	1.2	1.1	1.0	0.9
Concessional	..	..	0.4	1.2	1.4	1.3	1.2	1.1	1.0	0.9
Private creditors	..	..	0.0	0.0	0.0	0.5	1.1	0.8	1.3	1.3
Bonds	..	..	0.0	0.0	0.0	0.0	0.0	0.0	0.0	0.0
Commercial banks	..	..	0.0	0.0	0.0	0.0	0.0	0.0	0.0	0.0
Other private	..	..	0.0	0.0	0.0	0.5	1.1	0.8	1.3	1.3
Private nonguaranteed	..	..	**0.0**	**0.0**	**0.0**	**0.0**	**0.0**	**0.0**	**0.0**	**0.0**
Bonds	..	..	0.0	0.0	0.0	0.0	0.0	0.0	0.0	0.0
Commercial banks and other	..	..	0.0	0.0	0.0	0.0	0.0	0.0	0.0	0.0
Memo:										
IBRD	0.0	0.0	0.0	0.0	0.0	0.0	0.0	0.0	0.0	0.0
IDA	0.0	0.0	0.0	0.0	0.0	0.0	0.0	0.0	0.0	0.1
NET FLOWS ON DEBT	..	..	**2.2**	**5.6**	**3.8**	**1.9**	**-0.6**	**2.4**	**-1.0**	**-0.4**
Public and publicly guaranteed	..	..	**2.2**	**5.6**	**3.8**	**1.9**	**-0.6**	**2.4**	**-1.0**	**-0.4**
Official creditors	..	..	2.2	5.6	3.8	1.7	0.5	3.3	0.3	0.8
Multilateral	..	..	2.8	7.0	5.4	3.0	1.7	4.3	1.3	1.7
Concessional	..	..	2.9	6.7	6.0	3.6	2.1	4.7	1.9	2.3
Bilateral	..	..	-0.5	-1.4	-1.7	-1.3	-1.2	-1.1	-1.0	-0.9
Concessional	..	..	-0.4	-1.2	-1.4	-1.3	-1.2	-1.1	-1.0	-0.9
Private creditors	..	..	0.0	0.0	0.0	0.2	-1.1	-0.8	-1.3	-1.3
Bonds	..	..	0.0	0.0	0.0	0.0	0.0	0.0	0.0	0.0
Commercial banks	..	..	0.0	0.0	0.0	0.0	0.0	0.0	0.0	0.0
Other private	..	..	0.0	0.0	0.0	0.2	-1.1	-0.8	-1.3	-1.3
Private nonguaranteed	..	..	**0.0**	**0.0**	**0.0**	**0.0**	**0.0**	**0.0**	**0.0**	**0.0**
Bonds	..	..	0.0	0.0	0.0	0.0	0.0	0.0	0.0	0.0
Commercial banks and other	..	..	0.0	0.0	0.0	0.0	0.0	0.0	0.0	0.0
Memo:										
IBRD	0.0	0.0	0.0	0.0	0.0	0.0	0.0	0.0	0.0	0.0
IDA	0.0	0.0	1.0	0.8	0.2	-0.1	0.0	0.0	0.0	-0.1

TONGA

(US$ million, unless otherwise indicated)

	1970	1980	1990	1994	1995	1996	1997	1998	1999	2000
INTEREST PAYMENTS (LINT)	..	..	**0.5**	**0.6**	**0.7**	**0.7**	**0.9**	**0.8**	**0.8**	**0.7**
Public and publicly guaranteed	..	..	**0.5**	**0.6**	**0.7**	**0.7**	**0.9**	**0.8**	**0.8**	**0.7**
Official creditors	..	..	0.5	0.6	0.7	0.7	0.6	0.6	0.7	0.6
Multilateral	..	..	0.2	0.4	0.5	0.6	0.5	0.5	0.6	0.5
Concessional	..	..	0.1	0.2	0.3	0.4	0.4	0.4	0.5	0.5
Bilateral	..	..	0.3	0.2	0.2	0.1	0.1	0.1	0.1	0.1
Concessional	..	..	0.2	0.2	0.2	0.1	0.1	0.1	0.1	0.1
Private creditors	..	..	0.0	0.0	0.0	0.0	0.3	0.2	0.2	0.1
Bonds	..	..	0.0	0.0	0.0	0.0	0.0	0.0	0.0	0.0
Commercial banks	..	..	0.0	0.0	0.0	0.0	0.0	0.0	0.0	0.0
Other private	..	..	0.0	0.0	0.0	0.0	0.3	0.2	0.2	0.1
Private nonguaranteed	..	..	**0.0**	**0.0**	**0.0**	**0.0**	**0.0**	**0.0**	**0.0**	**0.0**
Bonds	..	..	0.0	0.0	0.0	0.0	0.0	0.0	0.0	0.0
Commercial banks and other	..	..	0.0	0.0	0.0	0.0	0.0	0.0	0.0	0.0
Memo:										
IBRD	0.0	0.0	0.0	0.0	0.0	0.0	0.0	0.0	0.0	0.0
IDA	0.0	0.0	0.0	0.0	0.0	0.0	0.0	0.0	0.0	0.0
NET TRANSFERS ON DEBT	..	..	**1.7**	**5.0**	**3.1**	**1.2**	**-1.5**	**1.6**	**-1.8**	**-1.1**
Public and publicly guaranteed	..	..	**1.7**	**5.0**	**3.1**	**1.2**	**-1.5**	**1.6**	**-1.8**	**-1.1**
Official creditors	..	..	1.7	5.0	3.1	1.0	-0.1	2.7	-0.4	0.2
Multilateral	..	..	2.5	6.6	4.9	2.4	1.2	3.8	0.7	1.2
Concessional	..	..	2.8	6.5	5.7	3.2	1.7	4.3	1.4	1.8
Bilateral	..	..	-0.8	-1.6	-1.9	-1.4	-1.3	-1.2	-1.1	-1.0
Concessional	..	..	-0.5	-1.4	-1.5	-1.4	-1.3	-1.2	-1.1	-1.0
Private creditors	..	..	0.0	0.0	0.0	0.2	-1.4	-1.0	-1.4	-1.3
Bonds	..	..	0.0	0.0	0.0	0.0	0.0	0.0	0.0	0.0
Commercial banks	..	..	0.0	0.0	0.0	0.0	0.0	0.0	0.0	0.0
Other private	..	..	0.0	0.0	0.0	0.2	-1.4	-1.0	-1.4	-1.3
Private nonguaranteed	..	..	**0.0**	**0.0**	**0.0**	**0.0**	**0.0**	**0.0**	**0.0**	**0.0**
Bonds	..	..	0.0	0.0	0.0	0.0	0.0	0.0	0.0	0.0
Commercial banks and other	..	..	0.0	0.0	0.0	0.0	0.0	0.0	0.0	0.0
Memo:										
IBRD	0.0	0.0	0.0	0.0	0.0	0.0	0.0	0.0	0.0	0.0
IDA	0.0	0.0	1.0	0.8	0.2	-0.1	0.0	-0.1	-0.1	-0.1
DEBT SERVICE (LTDS)	..	..	**1.5**	**2.7**	**3.1**	**3.4**	**4.1**	**3.6**	**4.3**	**4.0**
Public and publicly guaranteed	..	..	**1.5**	**2.7**	**3.1**	**3.4**	**4.1**	**3.6**	**4.3**	**4.0**
Official creditors	..	..	1.5	2.7	3.1	2.9	2.7	2.5	2.9	2.7
Multilateral	..	..	0.7	1.1	1.3	1.5	1.4	1.4	1.7	1.7
Concessional	..	..	0.4	0.4	0.5	0.7	0.7	0.7	1.0	1.1
Bilateral	..	..	0.8	1.6	1.9	1.4	1.3	1.2	1.1	1.0
Concessional	..	..	0.5	1.4	1.5	1.4	1.3	1.2	1.1	1.0
Private creditors	..	..	0.0	0.0	0.0	0.5	1.4	1.0	1.4	1.3
Bonds	..	..	0.0	0.0	0.0	0.0	0.0	0.0	0.0	0.0
Commercial banks	..	..	0.0	0.0	0.0	0.0	0.0	0.0	0.0	0.0
Other private	..	..	0.0	0.0	0.0	0.5	1.4	1.0	1.4	1.3
Private nonguaranteed	..	..	**0.0**	**0.0**	**0.0**	**0.0**	**0.0**	**0.0**	**0.0**	**0.0**
Bonds	..	..	0.0	0.0	0.0	0.0	0.0	0.0	0.0	0.0
Commercial banks and other	..	..	0.0	0.0	0.0	0.0	0.0	0.0	0.0	0.0
Memo:										
IBRD	0.0	0.0	0.0	0.0	0.0	0.0	0.0	0.0	0.0	0.0
IDA	0.0	0.0	0.0	0.0	0.0	0.0	0.0	0.1	0.1	0.1
UNDISBURSED DEBT	..	..	**18.0**	**14.3**	**19.0**	**15.8**	**11.2**	**6.3**	**3.7**	**0.5**
Official creditors	..	..	18.0	13.7	18.3	15.8	11.2	6.3	3.7	0.5
Private creditors	..	..	0.0	0.7	0.7	0.0	0.0	0.0	0.0	0.0
Memorandum items										
Concessional LDOD	..	..	38.8	47.1	52.8	53.2	49.0	54.6	59.5	56.1
Variable rate LDOD	..	..	0.0	0.0	0.0	0.0	0.0	0.0	0.0	0.0
Public sector LDOD	..	..	44.5	57.6	62.8	62.5	56.3	60.8	63.5	58.0
Private sector LDOD	..	..	0.0	0.0	0.0	0.0	0.0	0.0	0.0	0.0

6. CURRENCY COMPOSITION OF LONG-TERM DEBT (PERCENT)

	1970	1980	1990	1994	1995	1996	1997	1998	1999	2000
Deutsche mark	..	..	40.8	27.2	25.2	21.7	19.2	17.6	13.1	12.0
French franc	..	..	0.0	0.0	0.0	0.0	0.0	0.0	0.0	0.0
Japanese yen	..	..	0.0	0.0	0.0	0.0	0.0	0.0	0.0	0.0
Pound sterling	..	..	6.0	2.1	1.6	1.4	1.1	0.7	0.4	0.2
Swiss franc	..	..	0.0	0.0	0.0	0.0	0.0	0.0	0.0	0.0
U.S.dollars	..	..	1.0	11.2	10.7	10.8	9.8	7.8	5.4	3.5
Multiple currency	..	..	45.5	54.5	57.7	60.2	63.6	67.7	75.4	78.7
Special drawing rights	..	..	0.0	1.7	2.4	3.9	4.6	4.7	4.6	4.8
All other currencies	..	..	6.7	3.3	2.4	2.0	1.7	1.5	1.1	0.8

TONGA

(US$ million, unless otherwise indicated)

	1970	1980	1990	1994	1995	1996	1997	1998	1999	2000
7. DEBT RESTRUCTURINGS										
Total amount rescheduled	..	..	0.0	0.0	0.0	0.0	0.0	0.0	0.0	0.0
Debt stock rescheduled	..	..	0.0	0.0	0.0	0.0	0.0	0.0	0.0	0.0
Principal rescheduled	..	..	0.0	0.0	0.0	0.0	0.0	0.0	0.0	0.0
Official	..	..	0.0	0.0	0.0	0.0	0.0	0.0	0.0	0.0
Private	..	..	0.0	0.0	0.0	0.0	0.0	0.0	0.0	0.0
Interest rescheduled	..	..	0.0	0.0	0.0	0.0	0.0	0.0	0.0	0.0
Official	..	..	0.0	0.0	0.0	0.0	0.0	0.0	0.0	0.0
Private	..	..	0.0	0.0	0.0	0.0	0.0	0.0	0.0	0.0
Debt forgiven	..	..	0.0	0.0	0.0	0.0	0.0	0.0	0.0	0.0
Memo: interest forgiven	..	..	0.0	0.0	0.0	0.0	0.0	0.0	0.0	0.0
Debt stock reduction	..	..	0.0	0.0	0.0	0.0	0.0	0.0	0.0	0.0
of which debt buyback	..	..	0.0	0.0	0.0	0.0	0.0	0.0	0.0	0.0
8. DEBT STOCK-FLOW RECONCILIATION										
Total change in debt stocks	..	..	14.5	14.4	5.5	-0.3	-6.5	4.2	2.2	-5.5
Net flows on debt	..	..	10.4	6.0	4.1	1.9	-0.9	2.1	-1.4	-0.5
Net change in interest arrears	..	..	0.0	0.0	0.0	0.0	0.0	0.0	0.0	0.0
Interest capitalized	..	..	0.0	0.0	0.0	0.0	0.0	0.0	0.0	0.0
Debt forgiveness or reduction	..	..	0.0	0.0	0.0	0.0	0.0	0.0	0.0	0.0
Cross-currency valuation	..	..	3.1	3.5	1.0	-2.2	-5.2	1.6	-0.3	-3.7
Residual	..	..	1.1	4.9	0.4	0.0	-0.4	0.5	4.0	-1.3
9. AVERAGE TERMS OF NEW COMMITMENTS										
ALL CREDITORS										
Interest (%)	..	..	0.9	0.0	4.4	3.5	0.0	0.0	0.0	0.0
Maturity (years)	..	..	39.7	0.0	39.0	39.7	0.0	0.0	0.0	0.0
Grace period (years)	..	..	10.2	0.0	9.5	10.2	0.0	0.0	0.0	0.0
Grant element (%)	..	..	79.5	0.0	47.6	55.8	0.0	0.0	0.0	0.0
Official creditors										
Interest (%)	..	..	0.9	0.0	4.4	3.5	0.0	0.0	0.0	0.0
Maturity (years)	..	..	39.7	0.0	39.0	39.7	0.0	0.0	0.0	0.0
Grace period (years)	..	..	10.2	0.0	9.5	10.2	0.0	0.0	0.0	0.0
Grant element (%)	..	..	79.5	0.0	47.6	55.8	0.0	0.0	0.0	0.0
Private creditors										
Interest (%)	..	..	0.0	0.0	0.0	0.0	0.0	0.0	0.0	0.0
Maturity (years)	..	..	0.0	0.0	0.0	0.0	0.0	0.0	0.0	0.0
Grace period (years)	..	..	0.0	0.0	0.0	0.0	0.0	0.0	0.0	0.0
Grant element (%)	..	..	0.0	0.0	0.0	0.0	0.0	0.0	0.0	0.0
Memorandum items										
Commitments	..	..	5.7	0.0	10.5	3.5	0.0	0.0	0.0	0.0
Official creditors	..	..	5.7	0.0	10.5	3.5	0.0	0.0	0.0	0.0
Private creditors	..	..	0.0	0.0	0.0	0.0	0.0	0.0	0.0	0.0

10. CONTRACTUAL OBLIGATIONS ON OUTSTANDING LONG-TERM DEBT

	2001	2002	2003	2004	2005	2006	2007	2008	2009	2010
TOTAL										
Disbursements	0.5	0.0	0.0	0.0	0.0	0.0	0.0	0.0	0.0	0.0
Principal	2.3	1.9	1.8	2.0	2.2	2.2	2.2	2.3	1.8	1.8
Interest	0.8	0.7	0.7	0.7	1.0	0.9	0.9	0.8	0.8	0.8
Official creditors										
Disbursements	0.5	0.0	0.0	0.0	0.0	0.0	0.0	0.0	0.0	0.0
Principal	2.3	1.9	1.8	2.0	2.2	2.2	2.2	2.3	1.8	1.8
Interest	0.8	0.7	0.7	0.7	1.0	0.9	0.9	0.8	0.8	0.8
Bilateral creditors										
Disbursements	0.0	0.0	0.0	0.0	0.0	0.0	0.0	0.0	0.0	0.0
Principal	0.9	0.8	0.8	0.8	0.8	0.8	0.8	0.8	0.2	0.2
Interest	0.1	0.1	0.1	0.0	0.0	0.0	0.0	0.0	0.0	0.0
Multilateral creditors										
Disbursements	0.5	0.0	0.0	0.0	0.0	0.0	0.0	0.0	0.0	0.0
Principal	1.4	1.2	1.0	1.2	1.4	1.4	1.4	1.5	1.5	1.6
Interest	0.7	0.7	0.7	0.7	1.0	0.9	0.9	0.8	0.8	0.8
Private creditors										
Disbursements	0.0	0.0	0.0	0.0	0.0	0.0	0.0	0.0	0.0	0.0
Principal	0.0	0.0	0.0	0.0	0.0	0.0	0.0	0.0	0.0	0.0
Interest	0.0	0.0	0.0	0.0	0.0	0.0	0.0	0.0	0.0	0.0
Commercial banks										
Disbursements	0.0	0.0	0.0	0.0	0.0	0.0	0.0	0.0	0.0	0.0
Principal	0.0	0.0	0.0	0.0	0.0	0.0	0.0	0.0	0.0	0.0
Interest	0.0	0.0	0.0	0.0	0.0	0.0	0.0	0.0	0.0	0.0
Other private										
Disbursements	0.0	0.0	0.0	0.0	0.0	0.0	0.0	0.0	0.0	0.0
Principal	0.0	0.0	0.0	0.0	0.0	0.0	0.0	0.0	0.0	0.0
Interest	0.0	0.0	0.0	0.0	0.0	0.0	0.0	0.0	0.0	0.0

TRINIDAD AND TOBAGO

(US$ million, unless otherwise indicated)

	1970	1980	1990	1994	1995	1996	1997	1998	1999	2000
1. SUMMARY DEBT DATA										
TOTAL DEBT STOCKS (EDT)	**101**	**829**	**2,512**	**2,505**	**2,746**	**2,248**	**2,166**	**2,174**	**2,462**	**2,467**
Long-term debt (LDOD)	**101**	**713**	**2,055**	**2,090**	**2,040**	**1,954**	**1,587**	**1,621**	**1,629**	**1,606**
Public and publicly guaranteed	101	713	1,782	1,972	1,950	1,876	1,533	1,478	1,485	1,496
Private nonguaranteed	0	0	273	118	90	78	54	144	144	110
Use of IMF credit	**0**	**0**	**329**	**91**	**50**	**24**	**4**	**0**	**0**	**0**
Short-term debt	**0**	**116**	**127**	**324**	**656**	**270**	**575**	**553**	**833**	**861**
of which interest arrears on LDOD	0	0	0	1	7	10	7	7	11	10
Official creditors	0	0	0	1	2	0	0	0	0	0
Private creditors	0	0	0	0	5	9	6	7	10	9
Memo: principal arrears on LDOD	0	0	37	76	111	108	92	97	53	49
Official creditors	0	0	7	14	9	2	2	2	2	2
Private creditors	0	0	31	62	102	106	91	96	51	47
Memo: export credits	0	0	591	664	653	640	875	345	304	302
TOTAL DEBT FLOWS										
Disbursements	**12**	**363**	**188**	**344**	**127**	**251**	**83**	**175**	**311**	**314**
Long-term debt	8	363	85	344	127	251	83	175	311	314
IMF purchases	5	0	103	0	0	0	0	0	0	0
Principal repayments	**14**	**176**	**233**	**392**	**243**	**282**	**399**	**188**	**297**	**332**
Long-term debt	10	176	233	320	200	257	381	184	297	332
IMF repurchases	4	0	0	72	44	25	18	4	0	0
Net flows on debt	**-2**	**137**	**-45**	**148**	**210**	**-420**	**-8**	**-35**	**291**	**10**
of which short-term debt	0	-50	0	196	326	-389	308	-23	277	28
Interest payments (INT)	**6**	**54**	**216**	**156**	**177**	**195**	**151**	**126**	**157**	**168**
Long-term debt	6	50	177	133	148	167	128	96	112	112
IMF charges	0	0	24	7	4	2	1	0	0	0
Short-term debt	0	4	15	16	25	25	22	30	45	56
Net transfers on debt	**-8**	**83**	**-262**	**-9**	**33**	**-615**	**-159**	**-161**	**134**	**-158**
Total debt service paid (TDS)	**20**	**230**	**449**	**548**	**420**	**477**	**550**	**313**	**454**	**500**
Long-term debt	16	226	410	453	347	425	509	279	409	444
IMF repurchases and charges	4	0	24	79	48	27	19	4	0	0
Short-term debt (interest only)	0	4	15	16	25	25	22	30	45	56
2. AGGREGATE NET RESOURCE FLOWS AND NET TRANSFERS (LONG-TERM)										
NET RESOURCE FLOWS	**81**	**372**	**-26**	**549**	**237**	**356**	**710**	**731**	**652**	**633**
Net flow of long-term debt (ex. IMF)	-3	187	-148	24	-72	-7	-298	-8	13	-18
Foreign direct investment (net)	83	185	109	516	299	355	999	730	633	650
Portfolio equity flows	0	0	0	0	0	0	0	0	0	0
Grants (excluding technical coop.)	0	1	13	9	10	7	8	9	6	1
Memo: technical coop. grants	1	4	5	5	5	6	5	4	5	5
official net resource flows	2	115	42	44	56	-22	-46	-30	-61	-40
private net resource flows	80	258	-69	505	181	378	755	761	713	673
NET TRANSFERS	**16**	**-157**	**-401**	**166**	**-174**	**-91**	**283**	**315**	**240**	**200**
Interest on long-term debt	6	50	177	133	148	167	128	96	112	112
Profit remittances on FDI	59	479	197	250	263	280	299	320	300	320
Memo: official net transfers	-1	99	-8	-13	-10	-92	-91	-79	-110	-89
private net transfers	17	-256	-393	179	-164	0	373	394	351	290
3. MAJOR ECONOMIC AGGREGATES										
Gross national income (GNI)	757	5,925	4,638	4,522	4,864	5,244	5,448	5,782	6,311	6,701
Exports of goods & services (XGS)	..	3,373	2,331	2,187	2,906	2,883	3,088	3,038	3,465	4,849
of which workers remittances	..	1	3	26	30	28	30	45	..	..
Imports of goods & services (MGS)	..	2,972	1,863	1,943	2,577	2,742	3,676	3,660	3,473	4,513
International reserves (RES)	43	2,813	513	373	379	564	723	800	963	1,403
Current account balance	..	357	459	218	294	105	-614	-644	..	..
4. DEBT INDICATORS										
EDT / XGS (%)	..	24.6	107.7	114.6	94.5	78.0	70.1	71.6	71.1	50.9
EDT / GNI (%)	13.3	14.0	54.2	55.4	56.5	42.9	39.8	37.6	39.0	36.8
TDS / XGS (%)	..	6.8	19.3	25.1	14.5	16.5	17.8	10.3	13.1	10.3
INT / XGS (%)	..	1.6	9.3	7.1	6.1	6.8	4.9	4.1	4.5	3.5
INT / GNI (%)	0.8	0.9	4.7	3.5	3.6	3.7	2.8	2.2	2.5	2.5
RES / EDT (%)	42.8	339.4	20.4	14.9	13.8	25.1	33.4	36.8	39.1	56.9
RES / MGS (months)	..	11.4	3.3	2.3	1.8	2.5	2.4	2.6	3.3	3.7
Short-term / EDT (%)	0.0	14.0	5.1	13.0	23.9	12.0	26.5	25.4	33.9	34.9
Concessional / EDT (%)	5.9	1.2	2.1	1.3	1.0	0.9	0.7	0.6	0.4	0.4
Multilateral / EDT (%)	23.1	8.6	4.1	16.0	19.2	25.5	27.0	28.5	26.2	26.0

TRINIDAD AND TOBAGO

(US$ million, unless otherwise indicated)

	1970	1980	1990	1994	1995	1996	1997	1998	1999	2000
5. LONG-TERM DEBT										
DEBT OUTSTANDING (LDOD)	**101**	**713**	**2,055**	**2,090**	**2,040**	**1,954**	**1,587**	**1,621**	**1,629**	**1,606**
Public and publicly guaranteed	**101**	**713**	**1,782**	**1,972**	**1,950**	**1,876**	**1,533**	**1,478**	**1,485**	**1,496**
Official creditors	45	263	634	888	957	876	778	763	688	649
Multilateral	23	71	103	400	527	573	584	620	645	641
Concessional	0	1	6	4	4	3	4	6	7	8
Bilateral	22	192	532	488	430	303	194	143	42	8
Concessional	6	8	48	27	24	17	10	6	4	2
Private creditors	56	450	1,147	1,084	993	1,000	755	715	798	847
Bonds	36	53	335	450	450	575	425	425	652	780
Commercial banks	15	348	624	495	433	347	274	241	108	47
Other private	4	50	188	139	111	79	57	49	38	20
Private nonguaranteed	**0**	**0**	**273**	**118**	**90**	**78**	**54**	**144**	**144**	**110**
Bonds	0	0	0	0	0	0	0	110	110	110
Commercial banks and other	0	0	273	118	90	78	54	34	34	0
Memo:										
IBRD	23	57	41	61	72	79	76	83	85	89
IDA	0	0	0	0	0	0	0	0	0	0
DISBURSEMENTS	**8**	**363**	**85**	**344**	**127**	**251**	**83**	**175**	**311**	**314**
Public and publicly guaranteed	**8**	**363**	**85**	**344**	**127**	**251**	**83**	**65**	**311**	**314**
Official creditors	5	125	43	95	127	101	83	65	81	64
Multilateral	3	11	39	93	125	99	83	63	79	63
Concessional	0	0	0	0	0	0	1	2	2	1
Bilateral	2	114	4	2	2	2	0	2	2	0
Concessional	2	0	0	0	0	0	0	0	0	0
Private creditors	3	238	42	249	0	150	0	0	230	250
Bonds	0	0	0	227	0	150	0	0	230	250
Commercial banks	3	197	0	0	0	0	0	0	0	0
Other private	0	41	42	22	0	0	0	0	0	0
Private nonguaranteed	**0**	**0**	**0**	**0**	**0**	**0**	**0**	**110**	**0**	**0**
Bonds	0	0	0	0	0	0	0	110	0	0
Commercial banks and other	0	0	0	0	0	0	0	0	0	0
Memo:										
IBRD	3	4	20	3	15	17	12	15	10	14
IDA	0	0	0	0	0	0	0	0	0	0
PRINCIPAL REPAYMENTS	**10**	**176**	**233**	**320**	**200**	**257**	**381**	**184**	**297**	**332**
Public and publicly guaranteed	**10**	**176**	**189**	**287**	**172**	**245**	**357**	**163**	**297**	**298**
Official creditors	3	11	14	60	82	130	137	104	147	104
Multilateral	1	6	10	11	13	15	40	47	50	71
Concessional	0	0	0	1	1	0	0	0	1	1
Bilateral	3	5	3	49	69	115	97	58	98	33
Concessional	0	0	0	5	6	5	5	4	2	2
Private creditors	7	165	176	228	91	115	220	59	150	194
Bonds	5	7	52	132	0	25	150	0	0	122
Commercial banks	1	150	99	51	51	69	55	46	135	56
Other private	0	7	25	45	40	21	15	13	15	17
Private nonguaranteed	**0**	**0**	**44**	**32**	**27**	**12**	**24**	**21**	**0**	**34**
Bonds	0	0	0	0	0	0	0	0	0	0
Commercial banks and other	0	0	44	32	27	12	24	21	0	34
Memo:										
IBRD	1	6	7	2	6	5	9	8	8	10
IDA	0	0	0	0	0	0	0	0	0	0
NET FLOWS ON DEBT	**-3**	**187**	**-148**	**24**	**-72**	**-7**	**-298**	**-8**	**13**	**-18**
Public and publicly guaranteed	**-3**	**187**	**-105**	**57**	**-45**	**6**	**-274**	**-98**	**13**	**15**
Official creditors	1	114	30	35	46	-30	-54	-39	-67	-41
Multilateral	2	5	29	82	113	84	43	17	29	-8
Concessional	0	0	0	-1	-1	0	1	2	1	0
Bilateral	-1	109	1	-47	-67	-114	-97	-56	-96	-33
Concessional	2	0	0	-5	-6	-5	-5	-4	-2	-2
Private creditors	-4	73	-134	21	-91	36	-220	-59	80	56
Bonds	-5	-7	-52	95	0	125	-150	0	230	128
Commercial banks	2	47	-99	-51	-51	-69	-55	-46	-135	-56
Other private	0	34	17	-23	-40	-21	-15	-13	-15	-17
Private nonguaranteed	**0**	**0**	**-44**	**-32**	**-27**	**-12**	**-24**	**89**	**0**	**-34**
Bonds	0	0	0	0	0	0	0	110	0	0
Commercial banks and other	0	0	-44	-32	-27	-12	-24	-21	0	-34
Memo:										
IBRD	2	-1	13	0	9	12	4	7	2	4
IDA	0	0	0	0	0	0	0	0	0	0

TRINIDAD AND TOBAGO

(US$ million, unless otherwise indicated)

	1970	1980	1990	1994	1995	1996	1997	1998	1999	2000
INTEREST PAYMENTS (LINT)	**6**	**50**	**177**	**133**	**148**	**167**	**128**	**96**	**112**	**112**
Public and publicly guaranteed	**6**	**50**	**151**	**125**	**141**	**162**	**124**	**93**	**104**	**104**
Official creditors	3	16	51	57	66	69	45	49	49	49
Multilateral	1	5	6	23	30	43	30	41	42	47
Concessional	0	0	0	0	0	0	0	0	0	0
Bilateral	1	11	45	34	36	27	15	7	7	2
Concessional	0	0	2	1	1	1	1	0	0	0
Private creditors	4	35	101	68	74	93	79	45	54	55
Bonds	2	5	25	31	32	67	59	42	42	50
Commercial banks	1	25	55	25	33	20	16	0	11	3
Other private	0	5	21	11	9	5	4	3	2	2
Private nonguaranteed	**0**	**0**	**26**	**8**	**7**	**5**	**4**	**3**	**8**	**9**
Bonds	0	0	0	0	0	0	0	0	8	8
Commercial banks and other	0	0	26	8	7	5	4	3	0	1
Memo:										
IBRD	1	5	2	4	5	5	5	5	6	7
IDA	0	0	0	0	0	0	0	0	0	0
NET TRANSFERS ON DEBT	**-9**	**137**	**-326**	**-109**	**-220**	**-174**	**-426**	**-104**	**-98**	**-130**
Public and publicly guaranteed	**-9**	**137**	**-256**	**-68**	**-186**	**-156**	**-398**	**-191**	**-90**	**-88**
Official creditors	-1	98	-21	-22	-21	-99	-99	-88	-116	-90
Multilateral	1	0	23	59	82	41	13	-25	-13	-55
Concessional	0	0	0	-1	-1	0	1	2	1	0
Bilateral	-2	98	-44	-80	-103	-140	-112	-63	-103	-35
Concessional	1	0	-2	-6	-7	-6	-5	-5	-2	-2
Private creditors	-7	39	-235	-46	-165	-57	-299	-103	26	2
Bonds	-7	-12	-77	64	-32	58	-209	-42	189	78
Commercial banks	1	22	-154	-76	-85	-89	-72	-46	-146	-58
Other private	-1	29	-4	-35	-49	-26	-18	-16	-17	-19
Private nonguaranteed	**0**	**0**	**-70**	**-41**	**-34**	**-18**	**-28**	**87**	**-8**	**-42**
Bonds	0	0	0	0	0	0	0	110	-8	-8
Commercial banks and other	0	0	-70	-41	-34	-18	-28	-23	0	-34
Memo:										
IBRD	1	-6	11	-4	5	7	-2	2	-4	-3
IDA	0	0	0	0	0	0	0	0	0	0
DEBT SERVICE (LTDS)	**16**	**226**	**410**	**453**	**347**	**425**	**509**	**279**	**409**	**444**
Public and publicly guaranteed	**16**	**226**	**340**	**412**	**313**	**407**	**481**	**256**	**401**	**402**
Official creditors	6	27	64	117	148	200	182	153	197	154
Multilateral	2	11	16	34	43	58	70	88	92	119
Concessional	0	0	1	1	1	0	0	0	1	1
Bilateral	4	16	48	83	105	142	112	65	105	35
Concessional	0	0	2	6	7	6	5	5	2	2
Private creditors	10	199	276	295	165	207	299	103	204	248
Bonds	7	12	77	163	32	92	209	42	42	172
Commercial banks	2	175	154	76	85	89	72	46	146	58
Other private	1	12	46	56	49	26	18	16	17	19
Private nonguaranteed	**0**	**0**	**70**	**41**	**34**	**18**	**28**	**23**	**8**	**42**
Bonds	0	0	0	0	0	0	0	0	8	8
Commercial banks and other	0	0	70	41	34	18	28	23	0	34
Memo:										
IBRD	2	10	9	7	10	10	14	13	14	17
IDA	0	0	0	0	0	0	0	0	0	0
UNDISBURSED DEBT	**21**	**280**	**330**	**378**	**258**	**274**	**571**	**511**	**541**	**463**
Official creditors	21	201	247	378	258	274	571	511	541	463
Private creditors	0	79	83	0	0	0	0	0	0	0
Memorandum items										
Concessional LDOD	6	10	54	31	27	20	14	13	11	9
Variable rate LDOD	0	227	1,202	1,224	1,178	1,033	858	915	751	626
Public sector LDOD	101	713	1,782	1,972	1,950	1,876	1,533	1,478	1,485	1,496
Private sector LDOD	0	0	273	118	90	78	54	144	144	110

6. CURRENCY COMPOSITION OF LONG-TERM DEBT (PERCENT)

	1970	1980	1990	1994	1995	1996	1997	1998	1999	2000
Deutsche mark	0.0	5.6	6.8	2.9	2.7	2.1	1.6	1.2	0.6	0.2
French franc	0.0	0.1	4.1	2.5	2.3	1.7	1.2	0.9	0.2	0.0
Japanese yen	0.0	18.4	34.8	21.7	19.4	14.9	13.1	12.4	4.9	1.8
Pound sterling	33.4	0.2	3.4	2.4	2.6	2.9	3.4	3.5	3.3	3.0
Swiss franc	0.0	4.3	0.0	0.2	0.2	0.1	0.1	0.1	0.1	0.1
U.S.dollars	37.7	61.3	44.9	50.8	47.8	50.3	46.6	51.5	61.0	66.3
Multiple currency	23.1	8.3	4.1	17.7	23.7	27.1	32.8	29.0	28.9	27.2
Special drawing rights	0.0	0.0	0.0	0.0	0.0	0.0	0.0	0.0	0.0	0.0
All other currencies	5.8	1.8	1.9	1.8	1.3	0.9	1.2	1.4	1.0	1.4

TRINIDAD AND TOBAGO

(US$ million, unless otherwise indicated)

	1970	1980	1990	1994	1995	1996	1997	1998	1999	2000
7. DEBT RESTRUCTURINGS										
Total amount rescheduled	..	..	262	0	0	0	0	0	0	0
Debt stock rescheduled	..	..	0	0	0	0	0	0	0	0
Principal rescheduled	..	..	262	0	0	0	0	0	0	0
Official	..	..	56	0	0	0	0	0	0	0
Private	..	..	206	0	0	0	0	0	0	0
Interest rescheduled	..	..	0	0	0	0	0	0	0	0
Official	..	..	0	0	0	0	0	0	0	0
Private	..	..	0	0	0	0	0	0	0	0
Debt forgiven	..	..	7	0	0	0	0	0	0	0
Memo: interest forgiven	..	..	0	0	0	0	0	0	0	0
Debt stock reduction	..	..	0	0	7	0	0	0	0	0
of which debt buyback	..	..	0	0	0	0	0	0	0	0
8. DEBT STOCK-FLOW RECONCILIATION										
Total change in debt stocks	..	..	374	252	241	-498	-82	8	288	5
Net flows on debt	-2	137	-45	148	210	-420	-8	-35	291	10
Net change in interest arrears	..	..	0	1	5	3	-3	1	3	-1
Interest capitalized	..	..	0	0	0	0	0	0	0	0
Debt forgiveness or reduction	..	..	-7	0	-7	0	0	0	0	0
Cross-currency valuation	..	..	111	110	11	-86	-112	-13	15	-8
Residual	..	..	315	-7	22	5	41	56	-21	3
9. AVERAGE TERMS OF NEW COMMITMENTS										
ALL CREDITORS										
Interest (%)	7.5	10.4	8.0	10.8	6.5	7.7	6.1	8.5	7.1	9.8
Maturity (years)	9.8	8.6	14.9	9.4	17.5	13.4	18.6	15.8	17.3	20.1
Grace period (years)	1.2	3.7	4.6	7.8	4.1	7.6	5.8	5.3	11.6	20.1
Grant element (%)	10.5	-2.6	10.7	-4.3	20.5	13.8	20.1	8.0	20.6	0.1
Official creditors										
Interest (%)	3.0	7.6	7.9	6.6	6.5	7.3	6.1	8.5	6.9	0.0
Maturity (years)	29.6	9.5	18.1	15.0	17.5	17.8	18.6	15.8	23.6	0.0
Grace period (years)	7.1	2.3	5.4	4.9	4.1	4.6	5.8	5.3	7.2	0.0
Grant element (%)	54.6	9.1	12.0	19.0	20.5	15.7	20.1	8.0	21.7	0.0
Private creditors										
Interest (%)	8.0	10.6	8.1	11.5	0.0	8.0	0.0	0.0	7.3	9.8
Maturity (years)	7.5	8.6	9.8	8.3	0.0	10.0	0.0	0.0	13.9	20.1
Grace period (years)	0.5	3.9	3.3	8.3	0.0	10.0	0.0	0.0	13.9	20.1
Grant element (%)	5.5	-3.6	8.6	-8.6	0.0	12.3	0.0	0.0	20.1	0.1
Memorandum items										
Commitments	3	210	187	237	18	266	385	2	353	250
Official creditors	0	16	115	37	18	116	385	2	123	0
Private creditors	3	194	73	200	0	150	0	0	230	250

10. CONTRACTUAL OBLIGATIONS ON OUTSTANDING LONG-TERM DEBT

	2001	2002	2003	2004	2005	2006	2007	2008	2009	2010
TOTAL										
Disbursements	146	122	90	64	34	7	0	0	0	0
Principal	86	87	87	238	79	228	73	72	72	67
Interest	122	132	133	123	111	106	89	84	80	75
Official creditors										
Disbursements	146	122	90	64	34	7	0	0	0	0
Principal	81	82	82	83	79	78	73	72	72	67
Interest	50	53	54	53	50	45	40	35	31	26
Bilateral creditors										
Disbursements	0	0	0	0	0	0	0	0	0	0
Principal	2	1	1	1	1	1	0	0	0	0
Interest	1	0	0	0	0	0	0	0	0	0
Multilateral creditors										
Disbursements	146	122	90	64	34	7	0	0	0	0
Principal	79	81	81	82	78	78	73	72	72	67
Interest	49	52	53	53	50	45	40	35	31	26
Private creditors										
Disbursements	0	0	0	0	0	0	0	0	0	0
Principal	5	5	5	155	0	150	0	0	0	0
Interest	72	80	79	70	61	61	49	49	49	49
Commercial banks										
Disbursements	0	0	0	0	0	0	0	0	0	0
Principal	0	0	0	0	0	0	0	0	0	0
Interest	0	0	0	0	0	0	0	0	0	0
Other private										
Disbursements	0	0	0	0	0	0	0	0	0	0
Principal	5	5	5	155	0	150	0	0	0	0
Interest	72	80	79	70	61	61	49	49	49	49

TUNISIA

(US$ million, unless otherwise indicated)

1. SUMMARY DEBT DATA

	1970	1980	1990	1994	1995	1996	1997	1998	1999	2000
TOTAL DEBT STOCKS (EDT)	**599**	**3,527**	**7,690**	**9,614**	**10,820**	**11,379**	**11,230**	**10,850**	**11,880**	**10,610**
Long-term debt (LDOD)	**541**	**3,390**	**6,880**	**8,205**	**9,217**	**9,566**	**9,517**	**9,681**	**10,267**	**9,669**
Public and publicly guaranteed	541	3,210	6,662	8,007	9,024	9,378	9,334	9,500	9,495	8,869
Private nonguaranteed	0	180	218	198	193	188	183	181	772	800
Use of IMF credit	**13**	**0**	**176**	**303**	**293**	**237**	**173**	**129**	**76**	**32**
Short-term debt	**44**	**136**	**634**	**1,106**	**1,310**	**1,576**	**1,539**	**1,040**	**1,538**	**909**
of which interest arrears on LDOD	0	0	0	0	0	0	0	0	0	0
Official creditors	0	0	0	0	0	0	0	0	0	0
Private creditors	0	0	0	0	0	0	0	0	0	0
Memo: principal arrears on LDOD	3	6	15	16	1	0	0	0	0	0
Official creditors	3	6	8	15	1	0	0	0	0	0
Private creditors	0	0	7	0	0	0	0	0	0	0
Memo: export credits	0	0	1,547	1,922	1,982	1,867	1,827	561	515	502
TOTAL DEBT FLOWS										
Disbursements	**96**	**611**	**1,017**	**1,059**	**1,389**	**1,333**	**1,480**	**648**	**1,430**	**1,520**
Long-term debt	89	611	1,017	1,059	1,389	1,333	1,480	648	1,430	1,520
IMF purchases	8	0	0	0	0	0	0	0	0	0
Principal repayments	**54**	**290**	**984**	**928**	**939**	**907**	**875**	**867**	**951**	**1,347**
Long-term debt	47	258	873	928	924	861	825	818	901	1,307
IMF repurchases	7	31	111	0	16	47	50	50	50	40
Net flows on debt	**42**	**267**	**292**	**448**	**654**	**692**	**568**	**-718**	**976**	**-456**
of which short-term debt	0	-54	259	317	204	266	-37	-499	497	-629
Interest payments (INT)	**18**	**255**	**448**	**529**	**541**	**558**	**538**	**563**	**584**	**553**
Long-term debt	18	228	394	462	486	507	479	496	502	489
IMF charges	0	1	23	15	17	12	10	7	4	3
Short-term debt	0	26	30	52	38	39	49	60	77	61
Net transfers on debt	**23**	**12**	**-156**	**-81**	**113**	**133**	**30**	**-1,281**	**393**	**-1,009**
Total debt service paid (TDS)	**73**	**545**	**1,431**	**1,457**	**1,480**	**1,466**	**1,413**	**1,430**	**1,534**	**1,900**
Long-term debt	65	486	1,267	1,390	1,409	1,368	1,303	1,314	1,403	1,796
IMF repurchases and charges	7	33	135	15	32	59	60	57	54	43
Short-term debt (interest only)	0	26	30	52	38	39	49	60	77	61

2. AGGREGATE NET RESOURCE FLOWS AND NET TRANSFERS (LONG-TERM)

	1970	1980	1990	1994	1995	1996	1997	1998	1999	2000
NET RESOURCE FLOWS	**100**	**613**	**394**	**646**	**788**	**848**	**1,131**	**585**	**987**	**1,009**
Net flow of long-term debt (ex. IMF)	42	352	144	131	465	472	655	-170	529	213
Foreign direct investment (net)	16	235	76	432	264	238	339	650	350	752
Portfolio equity flows	0	0	0	0	0	0	0	40	0	0
Grants (excluding technical coop.)	43	26	174	83	59	138	137	65	108	44
Memo: technical coop. grants	27	74	100	84	122	103	92	93	97	96
official net resource flows	83	276	516	334	31	230	209	-87	246	44
private net resource flows	17	336	-121	312	756	618	922	672	741	966
NET TRANSFERS	**62**	**232**	**-146**	**-56**	**57**	**91**	**386**	**-186**	**207**	**271**
Interest on long-term debt	18	228	394	462	486	507	479	496	502	489
Profit remittances on FDI	20	153	146	240	245	250	266	275	278	250
Memo: official net transfers	75	203	267	-28	-337	-140	-130	-415	-84	-251
private net transfers	-13	30	-413	-27	394	231	517	229	290	522

3. MAJOR ECONOMIC AGGREGATES

	1970	1980	1990	1994	1995	1996	1997	1998	1999	2000
Gross national income (GNI)	1,380	8,450	11,882	14,742	17,111	18,555	17,997	18,983	20,066	18,572
Exports of goods & services (XGS)	..	3,674	5,851	7,610	8,778	8,952	8,934	9,290	9,644	9,402
of which workers remittances	..	319	551	629	680	736	685	718	761	700
Imports of goods & services (MGS)	..	4,119	6,591	8,317	9,646	9,554	9,636	10,079	10,227	10,347
International reserves (RES)	60	700	867	1,544	1,689	1,978	2,041	1,913	2,325	1,871
Current account balance	..	-353	-463	-537	-774	-478	-595	-675	-442	-821

4. DEBT INDICATORS

	1970	1980	1990	1994	1995	1996	1997	1998	1999	2000
EDT / XGS (%)	..	96.0	131.4	126.3	123.3	127.1	125.7	116.8	123.2	112.9
EDT / GNI (%)	43.4	41.7	64.7	65.2	63.2	61.3	62.4	57.2	59.2	57.1
TDS / XGS (%)	..	14.8	24.5	19.1	16.9	16.4	15.8	15.4	15.9	20.2
INT / XGS (%)	..	6.9	7.7	7.0	6.2	6.2	6.0	6.1	6.1	5.9
INT / GNI (%)	1.3	3.0	3.8	3.6	3.2	3.0	3.0	3.0	2.9	3.0
RES / EDT (%)	10.0	19.9	11.3	16.1	15.6	17.4	18.2	17.6	19.6	17.6
RES / MGS (months)	..	2.0	1.6	2.2	2.1	2.5	2.5	2.3	2.7	2.2
Short-term / EDT (%)	7.4	3.9	8.3	11.5	12.1	13.9	13.7	9.6	12.9	8.6
Concessional / EDT (%)	55.7	39.3	36.2	32.1	28.1	24.9	22.6	23.0	21.8	24.4
Multilateral / EDT (%)	7.3	12.3	29.0	37.2	35.0	32.7	30.9	32.7	30.7	32.4

TUNISIA

(US$ million, unless otherwise indicated)

	1970	1980	1990	1994	1995	1996	1997	1998	1999	2000
5. LONG-TERM DEBT										
DEBT OUTSTANDING (LDOD)	**541**	**3,390**	**6,880**	**8,205**	**9,217**	**9,566**	**9,517**	**9,681**	**10,267**	**9,669**
Public and publicly guaranteed	**541**	**3,210**	**6,662**	**8,007**	**9,024**	**9,378**	**9,334**	**9,500**	**9,495**	**8,869**
Official creditors	364	1,961	5,242	6,886	7,400	7,480	6,987	7,059	6,414	6,030
Multilateral	44	433	2,233	3,571	3,783	3,724	3,472	3,544	3,646	3,434
Concessional	16	75	229	389	425	442	423	421	418	473
Bilateral	320	1,529	3,009	3,315	3,617	3,755	3,515	3,515	2,767	2,596
Concessional	317	1,311	2,553	2,694	2,614	2,394	2,116	2,076	2,166	2,116
Private creditors	177	1,249	1,420	1,121	1,624	1,898	2,348	2,440	3,081	2,840
Bonds	2	6	0	0	535	603	1,112	1,200	1,825	1,327
Commercial banks	0	493	339	237	237	592	573	560	484	840
Other private	175	750	1,081	884	853	703	663	680	772	673
Private nonguaranteed	**0**	**180**	**218**	**198**	**193**	**188**	**183**	**181**	**772**	**800**
Bonds	0	0	0	0	0	0	0	0	0	0
Commercial banks and other	0	180	218	198	193	188	183	181	772	800
Memo:										
IBRD	26	269	1,347	1,715	1,717	1,610	1,434	1,458	1,323	1,211
IDA	16	68	59	52	50	47	45	43	41	39
DISBURSEMENTS	**89**	**611**	**1,017**	**1,059**	**1,389**	**1,333**	**1,480**	**648**	**1,430**	**1,520**
Public and publicly guaranteed	**89**	**558**	**987**	**1,029**	**1,359**	**1,303**	**1,450**	**618**	**1,230**	**1,220**
Official creditors	54	323	699	860	611	685	656	458	791	680
Multilateral	13	82	430	481	467	504	351	289	536	400
Concessional	3	8	45	35	48	46	24	27	48	91
Bilateral	41	242	269	378	145	181	305	169	255	280
Concessional	40	197	177	242	130	118	114	117	241	278
Private creditors	34	235	288	169	747	618	794	159	439	540
Bonds	0	0	0	0	588	138	586	0	240	0
Commercial banks	0	51	88	5	56	457	74	49	19	519
Other private	34	184	200	164	103	23	134	110	180	21
Private nonguaranteed	**0**	**53**	**30**	**30**	**30**	**30**	**30**	**30**	**200**	**300**
Bonds	0	0	0	0	0	0	0	0	0	0
Commercial banks and other	0	53	30	30	30	30	30	30	200	300
Memo:										
IBRD	9	51	213	189	138	202	127	142	210	136
IDA	3	1	0	0	0	0	0	0	0	0
PRINCIPAL REPAYMENTS	**47**	**258**	**873**	**928**	**924**	**861**	**825**	**818**	**901**	**1,307**
Public and publicly guaranteed	**47**	**216**	**836**	**893**	**889**	**826**	**790**	**786**	**869**	**1,275**
Official creditors	14	72	357	608	639	592	584	610	653	680
Multilateral	1	20	168	290	363	341	344	367	391	408
Concessional	0	0	7	15	18	22	25	36	28	32
Bilateral	13	52	189	318	276	251	240	244	262	273
Concessional	11	40	142	251	189	194	186	188	181	191
Private creditors	33	144	478	285	250	233	206	176	216	595
Bonds	0	5	60	0	0	0	0	0	0	371
Commercial banks	0	24	113	88	63	98	88	63	134	133
Other private	33	114	305	197	187	135	118	113	82	90
Private nonguaranteed	**0**	**43**	**37**	**35**	**35**	**35**	**35**	**32**	**32**	**32**
Bonds	0	0	0	0	0	0	0	0	0	0
Commercial banks and other	0	43	37	35	35	35	35	32	32	32
Memo:										
IBRD	1	15	111	173	203	187	173	178	166	150
IDA	0	0	2	2	2	2	2	2	2	2
NET FLOWS ON DEBT	**42**	**352**	**144**	**131**	**465**	**472**	**655**	**-170**	**529**	**213**
Public and publicly guaranteed	**42**	**342**	**151**	**136**	**470**	**477**	**660**	**-168**	**361**	**-55**
Official creditors	40	251	342	252	-27	93	72	-152	138	-1
Multilateral	12	61	262	191	104	163	8	-77	144	-8
Concessional	3	8	38	20	30	24	-1	-10	20	60
Bilateral	29	190	80	60	-131	-70	64	-75	-7	7
Concessional	30	156	35	-9	-59	-76	-72	-71	60	87
Private creditors	1	92	-190	-115	497	385	588	-16	223	-54
Bonds	0	-5	-60	0	588	138	586	0	240	-371
Commercial banks	0	27	-26	-83	-6	359	-15	-14	-115	386
Other private	1	70	-105	-32	-85	-112	17	-2	98	-69
Private nonguaranteed	**0**	**10**	**-7**	**-5**	**-5**	**-5**	**-5**	**-2**	**168**	**268**
Bonds	0	0	0	0	0	0	0	0	0	0
Commercial banks and other	0	10	-7	-5	-5	-5	-5	-2	168	268
Memo:										
IBRD	8	36	102	15	-65	15	-46	-37	44	-15
IDA	3	1	-2	-2	-2	-2	-2	-2	-2	-2

TUNISIA

(US$ million, unless otherwise indicated)

	1970	1980	1990	1994	1995	1996	1997	1998	1999	2000
INTEREST PAYMENTS (LINT)	**18**	**228**	**394**	**462**	**486**	**507**	**479**	**496**	**502**	**489**
Public and publicly guaranteed	**18**	**212**	**384**	**454**	**478**	**499**	**469**	**488**	**492**	**479**
Official creditors	8	74	249	363	368	370	339	328	330	295
Multilateral	2	28	149	235	255	268	246	228	245	213
Concessional	0	1	6	14	13	15	15	15	16	16
Bilateral	7	46	100	128	113	102	93	100	85	82
Concessional	6	29	73	93	76	69	64	60	56	53
Private creditors	10	138	136	92	110	129	130	159	162	184
Bonds	0	1	5	0	14	33	36	66	85	99
Commercial banks	0	69	35	19	18	23	37	36	30	39
Other private	10	68	96	73	78	73	57	57	48	46
Private nonguaranteed	**0**	**16**	**10**	**7**	**8**	**8**	**9**	**8**	**10**	**10**
Bonds	0	0	0	0	0	0	0	0	0	0
Commercial banks and other	0	16	10	7	8	8	9	8	10	10
Memo:										
IBRD	1	23	103	124	129	115	103	90	103	79
IDA	0	1	1	0	0	0	0	0	0	0
NET TRANSFERS ON DEBT	**23**	**125**	**-250**	**-331**	**-21**	**-35**	**177**	**-666**	**27**	**-276**
Public and publicly guaranteed	**23**	**131**	**-233**	**-318**	**-8**	**-22**	**191**	**-656**	**-131**	**-533**
Official creditors	32	177	93	-111	-395	-277	-267	-480	-192	-295
Multilateral	10	33	113	-44	-151	-105	-238	-306	-100	-221
Concessional	3	7	32	6	18	9	-15	-25	5	44
Bilateral	22	144	-20	-68	-245	-172	-28	-174	-91	-74
Concessional	23	127	-38	-102	-135	-145	-136	-131	4	33
Private creditors	-9	-46	-326	-207	387	255	458	-175	61	-238
Bonds	0	-6	-65	0	574	105	550	-66	155	-470
Commercial banks	0	-43	-60	-102	-24	336	-52	-50	-145	347
Other private	-9	3	-201	-105	-162	-185	-40	-59	50	-115
Private nonguaranteed	**0**	**-6**	**-17**	**-12**	**-13**	**-13**	**-14**	**-10**	**158**	**258**
Bonds	0	0	0	0	0	0	0	0	0	0
Commercial banks and other	0	-6	-17	-12	-13	-13	-14	-10	158	258
Memo:										
IBRD	7	14	-1	-109	-194	-101	-148	-127	-59	-94
IDA	3	0	-2	-3	-3	-3	-3	-2	-2	-2
DEBT SERVICE (LTDS)	**65**	**486**	**1,267**	**1,390**	**1,409**	**1,368**	**1,303**	**1,314**	**1,403**	**1,796**
Public and publicly guaranteed	**65**	**428**	**1,220**	**1,347**	**1,367**	**1,325**	**1,259**	**1,273**	**1,361**	**1,753**
Official creditors	22	146	606	971	1,007	962	923	938	983	975
Multilateral	3	48	317	525	617	609	590	595	636	621
Concessional	0	1	13	29	30	37	39	51	44	47
Bilateral	20	98	289	446	389	353	333	344	347	355
Concessional	17	70	215	343	265	263	250	249	237	245
Private creditors	43	281	614	376	360	363	336	335	378	778
Bonds	0	6	65	0	14	33	36	66	85	470
Commercial banks	0	94	148	107	81	122	126	99	164	172
Other private	43	182	401	269	265	208	175	169	130	136
Private nonguaranteed	**0**	**58**	**47**	**42**	**43**	**43**	**44**	**40**	**42**	**42**
Bonds	0	0	0	0	0	0	0	0	0	0
Commercial banks and other	0	58	47	42	43	43	44	40	42	42
Memo:										
IBRD	3	37	214	297	332	303	275	268	269	229
IDA	0	1	2	3	3	3	3	2	2	2
UNDISBURSED DEBT	**319**	**2,050**	**3,861**	**3,411**	**4,006**	**3,775**	**3,544**	**4,146**	**6,168**	**4,051**
Official creditors	269	1,578	3,157	2,992	3,396	3,187	3,002	3,472	5,746	3,496
Private creditors	50	472	704	419	610	588	542	674	422	555
Memorandum items										
Concessional LDOD	333	1,386	2,782	3,082	3,039	2,836	2,539	2,497	2,584	2,589
Variable rate LDOD	0	680	1,560	2,237	2,303	2,650	2,523	2,566	3,170	3,018
Public sector LDOD	528	3,120	6,662	7,999	9,017	9,373	9,332	9,498	9,495	8,869
Private sector LDOD	13	270	218	206	200	193	186	183	772	800

6. CURRENCY COMPOSITION OF LONG-TERM DEBT (PERCENT)

	1970	1980	1990	1994	1995	1996	1997	1998	1999	2000
Deutsche mark	8.7	10.8	11.0	8.0	7.2	5.9	6.1	6.2	6.1	5.6
French franc	23.4	21.1	13.6	14.3	13.6	11.7	9.9	10.2	11.0	10.7
Japanese yen	0.0	1.7	8.6	9.4	13.5	13.3	13.9	15.1	20.6	21.6
Pound sterling	0.8	0.2	0.1	0.0	0.0	0.0	0.0	0.0	0.5	0.5
Swiss franc	0.1	0.9	0.6	0.2	0.2	0.1	0.1	0.1	0.5	0.6
U.S.dollars	37.8	33.4	21.8	16.4	17.5	24.4	28.6	41.0	31.7	30.4
Multiple currency	5.5	8.4	22.7	27.0	24.9	23.0	21.3	7.5	6.3	5.8
Special drawing rights	0.0	0.0	0.3	0.2	0.2	0.1	0.1	0.2	0.2	0.2
All other currencies	23.7	23.5	21.3	24.5	22.9	21.5	20.0	19.7	23.1	24.6

TUNISIA

(US$ million, unless otherwise indicated)

	1970	1980	1990	1994	1995	1996	1997	1998	1999	2000
7. DEBT RESTRUCTURINGS										
Total amount rescheduled	..	..	0	0	0	0	0	0	0	0
Debt stock rescheduled	..	..	0	0	0	0	0	0	0	0
Principal rescheduled	..	..	0	0	0	0	0	0	0	0
Official	..	..	0	0	0	0	0	0	0	0
Private	..	..	0	0	0	0	0	0	0	0
Interest rescheduled	..	..	0	0	0	0	0	0	0	0
Official	..	..	0	0	0	0	0	0	0	0
Private	..	..	0	0	0	0	0	0	0	0
Debt forgiven	..	..	7	1	0	0	0	0	0	0
Memo: interest forgiven	..	..	0	0	0	0	0	0	0	0
Debt stock reduction	..	..	0	0	0	0	0	0	0	0
of which debt buyback	..	..	0	0	0	0	0	0	0	0
8. DEBT STOCK-FLOW RECONCILIATION										
Total change in debt stocks	..	..	715	920	1,206	559	-150	-380	1,030	-1,270
Net flows on debt	42	267	292	448	654	692	568	-718	976	-456
Net change in interest arrears	..	..	0	0	0	0	0	0	0	0
Interest capitalized	..	..	0	0	0	0	0	0	0	0
Debt forgiveness or reduction	..	..	-7	-1	0	0	0	0	0	0
Cross-currency valuation	..	..	352	349	178	-514	-584	345	-148	-409
Residual	..	..	79	123	374	382	-134	-6	201	-405
9. AVERAGE TERMS OF NEW COMMITMENTS										
ALL CREDITORS										
Interest (%)	3.5	6.2	6.9	7.8	5.7	4.7	5.1	4.0	2.9	4.0
Maturity (years)	27.8	18.4	14.3	18.1	16.7	15.6	17.7	19.2	18.4	17.3
Grace period (years)	6.4	5.4	3.8	5.3	4.8	5.6	9.8	5.4	5.4	8.8
Grant element (%)	48.1	26.6	17.9	13.3	22.9	30.5	31.7	38.2	43.6	39.4
Official creditors										
Interest (%)	2.7	5.0	6.0	7.7	6.2	4.9	4.3	3.3	2.1	4.6
Maturity (years)	32.6	21.2	18.0	18.5	24.0	19.7	19.1	19.6	19.6	16.7
Grace period (years)	7.7	6.5	5.0	5.5	4.6	5.5	5.2	5.6	4.7	5.4
Grant element (%)	57.4	35.4	25.9	13.8	24.5	34.5	36.5	43.3	48.8	34.6
Private creditors										
Interest (%)	6.3	9.6	8.1	9.1	5.2	4.3	5.9	6.2	7.1	3.5
Maturity (years)	11.0	10.7	9.2	10.3	8.5	9.0	16.3	17.6	12.6	17.8
Grace period (years)	1.9	2.4	2.1	0.8	5.1	5.7	14.1	4.5	8.7	11.6
Grant element (%)	15.1	2.8	7.1	2.7	21.2	24.0	27.3	21.3	18.2	43.4
Memorandum items										
Commitments	144	777	799	807	1,947	1,708	1,552	1,156	1,724	1,370
Official creditors	112	567	462	770	1,022	1,054	748	888	1,429	613
Private creditors	32	210	338	37	925	655	805	268	295	756

10. CONTRACTUAL OBLIGATIONS ON OUTSTANDING LONG-TERM DEBT

	2001	2002	2003	2004	2005	2006	2007	2008	2009	2010
TOTAL										
Disbursements	1,367	1,068	662	394	226	136	72	30	15	9
Principal	1,156	1,098	1,099	1,300	1,163	1,065	1,044	697	842	914
Interest	538	512	479	432	389	346	277	225	197	156
Official creditors										
Disbursements	1,101	923	603	371	221	133	71	30	15	9
Principal	765	739	766	779	790	748	691	632	583	567
Interest	321	308	288	262	236	207	178	151	126	103
Bilateral creditors										
Disbursements	533	394	227	129	68	32	13	2	1	0
Principal	365	325	305	300	300	291	273	242	218	194
Interest	99	94	87	79	73	66	57	49	42	35
Multilateral creditors										
Disbursements	568	529	376	242	153	100	58	28	14	8
Principal	400	414	461	479	490	456	419	389	365	373
Interest	221	214	201	183	163	141	120	102	84	68
Private creditors										
Disbursements	266	145	59	23	5	3	1	0	0	0
Principal	391	359	333	521	373	318	353	65	259	347
Interest	217	204	191	170	154	139	99	74	71	53
Commercial banks										
Disbursements	155	83	33	11	0	0	0	0	0	0
Principal	137	118	98	37	34	30	31	20	18	321
Interest	45	40	34	30	27	25	24	22	21	20
Other private										
Disbursements	111	62	26	12	5	3	1	0	0	0
Principal	254	241	235	484	339	288	323	45	242	26
Interest	172	164	156	141	126	114	76	52	50	33

TURKEY

(US$ million, unless otherwise indicated)

	1970	1980	1990	1994	1995	1996	1997	1998	1999	2000
1. SUMMARY DEBT DATA										
TOTAL DEBT STOCKS (EDT)	**2,747**	**19,131**	**49,424**	**66,255**	**73,790**	**79,641**	**84,771**	**97,162**	**102,068**	**116,209**
Long-term debt (LDOD)	**1,888**	**15,575**	**39,924**	**54,601**	**57,405**	**61,634**	**66,182**	**75,557**	**77,705**	**83,121**
Public and publicly guaranteed	1,846	15,040	38,870	48,443	50,326	48,216	47,499	50,217	50,581	55,293
Private nonguaranteed	42	535	1,054	6,159	7,079	13,419	18,684	25,340	27,124	27,828
Use of IMF credit	**74**	**1,054**	**0**	**344**	**685**	**662**	**594**	**388**	**891**	**4,176**
Short-term debt	**784**	**2,502**	**9,500**	**11,310**	**15,701**	**17,345**	**17,994**	**21,217**	**23,472**	**28,912**
of which interest arrears on LDOD	0	12	0	0	0	0	0	0	0	0
Official creditors	0	12	0	0	0	0	0	0	0	0
Private creditors	0	0	0	0	0	0	0	0	0	0
Memo: principal arrears on LDOD	0	23	0	0	0	0	0	0	0	0
Official creditors	0	21	0	0	0	0	0	0	0	0
Private creditors	0	1	0	0	0	0	0	0	0	0
Memo: export credits	0	0	11,519	12,831	11,056	12,131	13,932	6,009	5,328	5,224
TOTAL DEBT FLOWS										
Disbursements	**407**	**3,115**	**5,243**	**5,982**	**6,980**	**7,774**	**10,597**	**11,643**	**21,262**	**26,097**
Long-term debt	332	2,475	5,243	5,644	6,638	7,774	10,597	11,643	20,465	22,639
IMF purchases	75	640	0	337	341	0	0	0	798	3,459
Principal repayments	**158**	**750**	**4,010**	**6,277**	**7,017**	**6,476**	**6,794**	**9,265**	**12,778**	**14,278**
Long-term debt	131	595	3,961	6,277	7,017	6,476	6,767	9,042	12,490	14,192
IMF repurchases	27	155	49	0	0	0	28	223	287	87
Net flows on debt	**249**	**1,259**	**4,988**	**-7,518**	**4,353**	**2,941**	**4,452**	**5,600**	**10,740**	**17,259**
of which short-term debt	0	-1,106	3,755	-7,223	4,391	1,644	649	3,223	2,255	5,440
Interest payments (INT)	**44**	**858**	**3,412**	**3,979**	**4,431**	**4,433**	**4,906**	**5,685**	**5,782**	**6,857**
Long-term debt	44	507	2,891	3,199	3,464	3,389	3,844	4,533	4,524	5,005
IMF charges	0	51	4	4	24	30	29	25	11	52
Short-term debt	0	299	517	776	942	1,014	1,034	1,127	1,247	1,800
Net transfers on debt	**204**	**402**	**1,576**	**-11,497**	**-77**	**-1,491**	**-455**	**-84**	**4,958**	**10,401**
Total debt service paid (TDS)	**203**	**1,607**	**7,422**	**10,255**	**11,448**	**10,909**	**11,701**	**14,950**	**18,560**	**21,136**
Long-term debt	176	1,102	6,852	9,476	10,482	9,866	10,611	13,575	17,014	19,197
IMF repurchases and charges	27	206	53	4	24	30	57	248	299	139
Short-term debt (interest only)	0	299	517	776	942	1,014	1,034	1,127	1,247	1,800
2. AGGREGATE NET RESOURCE FLOWS AND NET TRANSFERS (LONG-TERM)										
NET RESOURCE FLOWS	**300**	**2,083**	**2,805**	**1,343**	**1,575**	**3,093**	**5,270**	**4,493**	**9,677**	**12,217**
Net flow of long-term debt (ex. IMF)	201	1,880	1,282	-632	-379	1,297	3,830	2,601	7,975	8,447
Foreign direct investment (net)	58	18	684	608	885	722	805	940	783	982
Portfolio equity flows	0	0	35	1,059	630	799	577	880	800	2,701
Grants (excluding technical coop.)	41	185	804	309	439	274	58	72	119	87
Memo: technical coop. grants	14	38	148	175	198	212	177	129	130	85
official net resource flows	257	1,423	1,023	-294	-741	-566	-64	-50	-519	801
private net resource flows	43	660	1,782	1,637	2,316	3,659	5,333	4,543	10,195	11,416
NET TRANSFERS	**221**	**1,545**	**-247**	**-2,285**	**-2,329**	**-797**	**896**	**-590**	**4,613**	**6,632**
Interest on long-term debt	44	507	2,891	3,199	3,464	3,389	3,844	4,533	4,524	5,005
Profit remittances on FDI	34	31	161	430	440	500	530	550	540	580
Memo: official net transfers	219	1,212	-20	-1,272	-1,717	-1,396	-762	-856	-1,209	129
private net transfers	2	333	-227	-1,014	-612	600	1,658	266	5,822	6,503
3. MAJOR ECONOMIC AGGREGATES										
Gross national income (GNI)	18,071	69,742	152,300	130,355	172,071	184,215	194,350	206,136	187,871	201,517
Exports of goods & services (XGS)	..	5,743	25,205	32,708	41,397	50,616	58,101	62,378	52,602	58,544
of which workers remittances	..	2,071	3,246	2,627	3,327	3,542	4,197	5,356	4,529	4,560
Imports of goods & services (MGS)	..	9,251	29,077	30,542	44,904	53,958	61,449	60,765	54,608	69,028
International reserves (RES)	440	3,298	7,626	8,633	13,891	17,819	19,746	20,568	24,433	23,515
Current account balance	..	-3,408	-2,625	2,631	-2,338	-2,437	-2,679	1,984	-1,360	-9,819
4. DEBT INDICATORS										
EDT / XGS (%)	..	333.1	196.1	202.6	178.3	157.3	145.9	155.8	194.0	198.5
EDT / GNI (%)	15.2	27.4	32.5	50.8	42.9	43.2	43.6	47.1	54.3	57.7
TDS / XGS (%)	..	28.0	29.4	31.4	27.7	21.6	20.1	24.0	35.3	36.1
INT / XGS (%)	..	14.9	13.5	12.2	10.7	8.8	8.4	9.1	11.0	11.7
INT / GNI (%)	0.3	1.2	2.2	3.1	2.6	2.4	2.5	2.8	3.1	3.4
RES / EDT (%)	16.0	17.2	15.4	13.0	18.8	22.4	23.3	21.2	23.9	20.2
RES / MGS (months)	..	4.3	3.2	3.4	3.7	4.0	3.9	4.1	5.4	4.1
Short-term / EDT (%)	28.6	13.1	19.2	17.1	21.3	21.8	21.2	21.8	23.0	24.9
Concessional / EDT (%)	52.4	20.4	15.1	11.6	10.2	8.3	6.7	6.0	5.4	4.3
Multilateral / EDT (%)	14.0	11.2	19.5	14.0	12.1	9.7	7.8	6.7	5.3	4.9

TURKEY

(US$ million, unless otherwise indicated)

	1970	1980	1990	1994	1995	1996	1997	1998	1999	2000
5. LONG-TERM DEBT										
DEBT OUTSTANDING (LDOD)	**1,888**	**15,575**	**39,924**	**54,601**	**57,405**	**61,634**	**66,182**	**75,557**	**77,705**	**83,121**
Public and publicly guaranteed	**1,846**	**15,040**	**38,870**	**48,443**	**50,326**	**48,216**	**47,499**	**50,217**	**50,581**	**55,293**
Official creditors	1,766	9,636	18,150	17,848	17,333	15,202	13,728	14,542	12,913	12,845
Multilateral	383	2,149	9,627	9,298	8,962	7,708	6,606	6,469	5,439	5,698
Concessional	110	242	825	1,114	1,145	855	691	604	529	468
Bilateral	1,383	7,487	8,523	8,550	8,371	7,494	7,122	8,073	7,474	7,147
Concessional	1,328	3,661	6,625	6,566	6,413	5,718	4,991	5,266	5,021	4,563
Private creditors	81	5,405	20,720	30,595	32,993	33,014	33,771	35,675	37,668	42,448
Bonds	20	64	4,976	13,022	13,646	14,185	15,075	14,978	17,766	22,783
Commercial banks	8	4,112	13,403	13,707	15,643	15,358	15,319	17,448	17,245	18,116
Other private	53	1,229	2,341	3,865	3,705	3,470	3,377	3,248	2,658	1,549
Private nonguaranteed	**42**	**535**	**1,054**	**6,159**	**7,079**	**13,419**	**18,684**	**25,340**	**27,124**	**27,828**
Bonds	0	0	16	150	150	175	125	795	1,338	1,784
Commercial banks and other	42	535	1,038	6,009	6,929	13,244	18,559	24,546	25,786	26,044
Memo:										
IBRD	54	1,158	6,272	5,195	4,939	4,260	3,587	3,446	2,902	3,634
IDA	83	189	157	136	130	124	118	112	107	101
DISBURSEMENTS	**332**	**2,475**	**5,243**	**5,644**	**6,638**	**7,774**	**10,597**	**11,643**	**20,465**	**22,639**
Public and publicly guaranteed	**331**	**2,400**	**4,700**	**4,281**	**4,862**	**5,728**	**8,233**	**6,668**	**9,391**	**13,758**
Official creditors	310	1,618	2,139	1,250	808	1,144	1,810	1,693	980	2,509
Multilateral	126	476	1,083	474	466	634	539	426	452	1,529
Concessional	7	10	12	25	8	2	44	3	8	1
Bilateral	185	1,142	1,056	777	342	510	1,271	1,267	528	980
Concessional	177	801	900	357	117	241	380	278	236	434
Private creditors	21	782	2,562	3,030	4,053	4,584	6,423	4,975	8,412	11,249
Bonds	0	0	644	898	2,343	2,921	3,711	2,330	5,230	7,899
Commercial banks	0	600	1,435	1,294	1,256	1,100	1,958	2,235	3,014	3,245
Other private	21	182	483	838	455	563	755	410	168	106
Private nonguaranteed	**1**	**75**	**543**	**1,364**	**1,777**	**2,046**	**2,364**	**4,975**	**11,074**	**8,881**
Bonds	0	0	0	100	0	25	0	670	552	454
Commercial banks and other	1	75	543	1,264	1,777	2,021	2,364	4,305	10,522	8,427
Memo:										
IBRD	18	313	627	343	422	489	266	271	377	1,292
IDA	7	0	0	0	0	0	0	0	0	0
PRINCIPAL REPAYMENTS	**131**	**595**	**3,961**	**6,277**	**7,017**	**6,476**	**6,767**	**9,042**	**12,490**	**14,192**
Public and publicly guaranteed	**128**	**566**	**3,677**	**4,777**	**5,984**	**5,454**	**5,530**	**7,337**	**5,492**	**6,716**
Official creditors	95	379	1,920	1,853	1,988	1,985	1,931	1,815	1,617	1,795
Multilateral	70	66	825	1,180	1,229	1,259	1,090	941	953	1,046
Concessional	22	1	23	33	54	197	139	125	70	32
Bilateral	24	314	1,094	673	759	726	841	874	664	750
Concessional	18	77	364	433	465	435	531	391	407	453
Private creditors	34	186	1,758	2,924	3,996	3,470	3,599	5,522	3,875	4,921
Bonds	0	1	47	539	1,716	1,368	1,686	3,201	2,019	1,869
Commercial banks	1	154	1,204	1,827	1,579	1,454	1,259	1,677	1,200	1,925
Other private	32	31	508	558	701	648	654	643	656	1,127
Private nonguaranteed	**3**	**29**	**283**	**1,500**	**1,033**	**1,022**	**1,237**	**1,705**	**6,998**	**7,476**
Bonds	0	0	0	0	0	0	50	0	0	0
Commercial banks and other	3	29	283	1,500	1,033	1,022	1,187	1,705	6,998	7,476
Memo:										
IBRD	3	45	620	800	882	815	692	637	610	486
IDA	0	1	4	6	6	6	6	6	6	6
NET FLOWS ON DEBT	**201**	**1,880**	**1,282**	**-632**	**-379**	**1,297**	**3,830**	**2,601**	**7,975**	**8,447**
Public and publicly guaranteed	**203**	**1,834**	**1,023**	**-496**	**-1,123**	**273**	**2,703**	**-669**	**3,899**	**7,042**
Official creditors	216	1,239	219	-603	-1,180	-841	-121	-122	-638	714
Multilateral	55	410	258	-707	-763	-625	-552	-515	-501	483
Concessional	-15	9	-11	-8	-45	-195	-96	-122	-63	-31
Bilateral	160	828	-39	104	-417	-216	430	392	-137	230
Concessional	158	724	536	-77	-348	-194	-152	-113	-171	-19
Private creditors	-13	596	804	107	57	1,114	2,824	-547	4,537	6,329
Bonds	0	-1	597	360	627	1,553	2,025	-871	3,210	6,029
Commercial banks	-1	446	231	-533	-323	-354	699	557	1,814	1,320
Other private	-11	151	-25	280	-246	-85	101	-233	-487	-1,021
Private nonguaranteed	**-2**	**46**	**260**	**-136**	**744**	**1,024**	**1,127**	**3,270**	**4,075**	**1,405**
Bonds	0	0	0	100	0	25	-50	670	552	454
Commercial banks and other	-2	46	260	-236	744	999	1,177	2,600	3,523	951
Memo:										
IBRD	15	268	6	-457	-460	-326	-426	-366	-233	806
IDA	7	-1	-4	-6	-6	-6	-6	-6	-6	-6

TURKEY

(US$ million, unless otherwise indicated)

	1970	1980	1990	1994	1995	1996	1997	1998	1999	2000
INTEREST PAYMENTS (LINT)	**44**	**507**	**2,891**	**3,199**	**3,464**	**3,389**	**3,844**	**4,533**	**4,524**	**5,005**
Public and publicly guaranteed	**42**	**487**	**2,830**	**2,875**	**3,126**	**2,918**	**2,961**	**3,214**	**2,980**	**3,472**
Official creditors	37	211	1,043	978	977	830	698	805	690	672
Multilateral	11	128	688	668	656	561	466	519	407	373
Concessional	2	4	30	40	44	36	24	22	14	13
Bilateral	26	84	355	310	321	270	232	287	283	299
Concessional	25	33	172	204	204	172	154	139	142	137
Private creditors	5	276	1,787	1,897	2,149	2,088	2,262	2,409	2,290	2,800
Bonds	1	4	383	993	1,074	1,009	993	1,173	1,141	1,598
Commercial banks	1	250	1,204	662	782	780	1,045	1,005	949	1,066
Other private	3	21	200	242	293	300	224	231	200	136
Private nonguaranteed	**2**	**20**	**61**	**324**	**339**	**471**	**883**	**1,319**	**1,544**	**1,533**
Bonds	0	0	1	2	13	12	13	12	86	126
Commercial banks and other	2	20	60	322	326	459	870	1,307	1,458	1,407
Memo:										
IBRD	3	88	512	418	396	339	273	245	243	237
IDA	1	1	1	1	1	1	1	1	1	1
NET TRANSFERS ON DEBT	**156**	**1,373**	**-1,609**	**-3,831**	**-3,843**	**-2,092**	**-14**	**-1,932**	**3,451**	**3,442**
Public and publicly guaranteed	**161**	**1,347**	**-1,808**	**-3,371**	**-4,248**	**-2,645**	**-258**	**-3,883**	**919**	**3,570**
Official creditors	178	1,027	-824	-1,580	-2,157	-1,671	-820	-928	-1,328	41
Multilateral	44	283	-431	-1,374	-1,418	-1,185	-1,018	-1,033	-908	110
Concessional	-17	5	-41	-48	-89	-231	-120	-143	-77	-44
Bilateral	134	744	-394	-206	-738	-485	198	105	-420	-69
Concessional	134	691	363	-281	-552	-366	-305	-252	-313	-156
Private creditors	-18	320	-983	-1,790	-2,092	-974	562	-2,955	2,247	3,529
Bonds	-1	-5	214	-634	-447	544	1,033	-2,044	2,070	4,431
Commercial banks	-2	196	-973	-1,195	-1,106	-1,134	-347	-447	865	255
Other private	-15	130	-225	38	-539	-385	-124	-464	-687	-1,157
Private nonguaranteed	**-5**	**26**	**199**	**-461**	**405**	**553**	**244**	**1,951**	**2,532**	**-129**
Bonds	0	0	-1	98	-13	13	-63	658	466	328
Commercial banks and other	-5	26	200	-558	418	540	307	1,293	2,065	-457
Memo:										
IBRD	12	179	-505	-875	-856	-665	-699	-611	-476	569
IDA	7	-2	-5	-7	-7	-7	-7	-7	-7	-7
DEBT SERVICE (LTDS)	**176**	**1,102**	**6,852**	**9,476**	**10,482**	**9,866**	**10,611**	**13,575**	**17,014**	**19,197**
Public and publicly guaranteed	**170**	**1,053**	**6,507**	**7,651**	**9,110**	**8,372**	**8,490**	**10,551**	**8,472**	**10,188**
Official creditors	132	591	2,963	2,831	2,965	2,815	2,630	2,620	2,307	2,467
Multilateral	81	193	1,514	1,848	1,885	1,820	1,557	1,459	1,360	1,419
Concessional	24	5	53	73	98	233	163	147	85	45
Bilateral	51	398	1,449	983	1,081	995	1,073	1,161	948	1,049
Concessional	43	110	537	638	669	607	685	530	548	590
Private creditors	38	462	3,545	4,821	6,145	5,558	5,861	7,930	6,165	7,720
Bonds	1	5	430	1,532	2,790	2,377	2,678	4,375	3,160	3,467
Commercial banks	2	405	2,408	2,489	2,361	2,233	2,304	2,682	2,149	2,991
Other private	35	52	707	800	994	948	878	874	855	1,263
Private nonguaranteed	**6**	**49**	**344**	**1,824**	**1,372**	**1,493**	**2,120**	**3,024**	**8,542**	**9,009**
Bonds	0	0	1	2	13	12	63	12	86	126
Commercial banks and other	6	49	343	1,822	1,359	1,481	2,057	3,012	8,456	8,883
Memo:										
IBRD	6	133	1,132	1,218	1,278	1,154	965	882	853	723
IDA	1	3	5	7	7	7	7	7	7	7
UNDISBURSED DEBT	**857**	**3,706**	**8,563**	**8,251**	**7,624**	**7,824**	**6,938**	**8,196**	**11,286**	**11,384**
Official creditors	753	2,938	4,823	4,577	3,765	4,305	3,326	3,324	5,969	5,114
Private creditors	104	768	3,740	3,674	3,859	3,519	3,612	4,872	5,317	6,270
Memorandum items										
Concessional LDOD	1,438	3,903	7,450	7,680	7,558	6,573	5,682	5,870	5,550	5,031
Variable rate LDOD	58	4,122	13,577	18,636	19,393	24,657	30,256	36,129	36,581	38,890
Public sector LDOD	1,839	14,956	38,570	48,078	50,140	48,110	47,441	50,173	50,554	55,274
Private sector LDOD	50	620	1,354	6,524	7,265	13,524	18,742	25,384	27,151	27,847

6. CURRENCY COMPOSITION OF LONG-TERM DEBT (PERCENT)

	1970	1980	1990	1994	1995	1996	1997	1998	1999	2000
Deutsche mark	17.6	17.0	17.4	17.6	16.7	16.8	21.3	22.8	19.3	14.6
French franc	3.2	5.6	1.6	1.6	1.6	1.6	1.5	1.3	1.2	1.0
Japanese yen	0.0	4.0	12.1	23.2	23.3	22.0	18.6	15.7	14.8	12.9
Pound sterling	6.0	3.8	0.8	1.0	0.9	1.0	0.9	1.0	0.9	0.6
Swiss franc	1.6	8.6	5.2	3.0	2.9	2.0	1.6	1.1	0.7	0.3
U.S.dollars	49.3	43.5	40.0	36.2	38.3	41.4	49.2	51.5	51.4	55.2
Multiple currency	9.1	8.1	18.9	14.3	13.3	12.1	3.5	3.1	2.5	2.0
Special drawing rights	0.0	0.0	0.0	0.0	0.0	0.0	0.0	0.0	0.0	0.0
All other currencies	13.2	9.4	4.0	3.1	3.0	3.1	3.4	3.5	9.2	13.4

TURKEY

(US$ million, unless otherwise indicated)

	1970	1980	1990	1994	1995	1996	1997	1998	1999	2000
7. DEBT RESTRUCTURINGS										
Total amount rescheduled	..	..	0	0	0	0	0	0	0	0
Debt stock rescheduled	..	..	0	0	0	0	0	0	0	0
Principal rescheduled	..	..	0	0	0	0	0	0	0	0
Official	..	..	0	0	0	0	0	0	0	0
Private	..	..	0	0	0	0	0	0	0	0
Interest rescheduled	..	..	0	0	0	0	0	0	0	0
Official	..	..	0	0	0	0	0	0	0	0
Private	..	..	0	0	0	0	0	0	0	0
Debt forgiven	..	..	0	0	0	0	0	0	0	0
Memo: interest forgiven	..	..	0	0	0	0	0	0	0	0
Debt stock reduction	..	..	0	0	0	0	0	0	0	0
of which debt buyback	..	..	0	0	0	0	0	0	0	0
8. DEBT STOCK-FLOW RECONCILIATION										
Total change in debt stocks	..	..	7,847	-2,353	7,535	5,851	5,129	12,392	4,906	14,142
Net flows on debt	249	1,259	4,988	-7,518	4,353	2,941	4,452	5,600	10,740	17,259
Net change in interest arrears	..	..	0	0	0	0	0	0	0	0
Interest capitalized	..	..	0	0	0	0	0	0	0	0
Debt forgiveness or reduction	..	..	0	0	0	0	0	0	0	0
Cross-currency valuation	..	..	1,874	2,575	675	-2,825	-2,899	2,091	-1,159	-2,021
Residual	..	..	985	2,590	2,507	5,735	3,577	4,700	-4,675	-1,096
9. AVERAGE TERMS OF NEW COMMITMENTS										
ALL CREDITORS										
Interest (%)	3.6	8.3	8.4	6.2	6.2	6.5	7.5	6.2	7.8	8.3
Maturity (years)	19.0	16.4	10.2	10.4	5.4	9.0	8.0	7.6	10.0	11.2
Grace period (years)	4.8	5.1	4.6	4.7	2.9	4.3	5.0	4.0	4.4	7.7
Grant element (%)	37.5	17.4	9.2	18.6	11.5	16.6	9.8	14.2	10.7	4.8
Official creditors										
Interest (%)	3.4	7.1	6.7	6.0	5.4	4.9	6.7	7.1	5.1	7.4
Maturity (years)	19.6	18.3	17.0	13.7	17.7	16.6	11.2	12.1	15.3	14.1
Grace period (years)	4.9	5.7	7.3	4.8	5.7	4.9	4.2	4.2	4.0	4.9
Grant element (%)	39.1	22.9	23.4	22.2	27.6	31.5	16.0	15.6	28.4	13.8
Private creditors										
Interest (%)	5.5	14.4	9.4	6.2	6.3	7.2	7.6	6.0	9.0	8.4
Maturity (years)	13.7	7.5	6.5	9.5	4.5	5.5	7.4	6.3	7.8	10.6
Grace period (years)	3.1	1.9	3.2	4.7	2.7	4.0	5.1	4.0	4.6	8.2
Grant element (%)	22.7	-9.6	1.5	17.5	10.3	10.0	8.6	13.8	3.4	3.1
Memorandum items										
Commitments	489	2,925	4,628	3,800	4,435	6,395	7,899	7,307	11,909	14,887
Official creditors	440	2,426	1,624	890	318	1,981	1,228	1,660	3,489	2,436
Private creditors	49	499	3,004	2,910	4,118	4,414	6,671	5,647	8,420	12,451

10. CONTRACTUAL OBLIGATIONS ON OUTSTANDING LONG-TERM DEBT

	2001	2002	2003	2004	2005	2006	2007	2008	2009	2010
TOTAL										
Disbursements	5,871	2,983	1,253	542	266	171	97	57	35	13
Principal	11,359	9,737	11,265	9,056	9,177	6,814	7,313	4,979	3,552	3,824
Interest	5,574	5,074	4,559	3,906	3,292	2,677	2,241	1,758	1,487	1,158
Official creditors										
Disbursements	1,747	1,526	785	399	266	171	97	57	35	13
Principal	2,207	1,524	1,979	1,354	1,374	1,246	1,095	1,014	1,101	832
Interest	756	701	644	557	498	433	373	320	270	208
Bilateral creditors										
Disbursements	971	744	428	218	104	42	20	0	0	0
Principal	823	882	1,302	746	687	583	559	516	643	409
Interest	323	311	273	220	196	171	150	129	110	77
Multilateral creditors										
Disbursements	776	782	357	181	162	129	77	56	35	13
Principal	1,383	642	677	608	687	663	536	498	458	423
Interest	433	390	371	337	302	262	223	191	160	131
Private creditors										
Disbursements	4,124	1,458	468	143	0	0	0	0	0	0
Principal	9,153	8,214	9,286	7,702	7,803	5,568	6,218	3,965	2,451	2,992
Interest	4,817	4,372	3,916	3,350	2,794	2,245	1,868	1,438	1,216	951
Commercial banks										
Disbursements	3,857	1,339	446	134	0	0	0	0	0	0
Principal	2,751	2,084	2,677	1,276	1,036	847	632	532	487	406
Interest	1,134	1,077	965	817	749	685	639	604	574	545
Other private										
Disbursements	267	119	22	10	0	0	0	0	0	0
Principal	6,402	6,130	6,609	6,426	6,767	4,721	5,586	3,433	1,964	2,586
Interest	3,683	3,295	2,951	2,533	2,046	1,560	1,228	834	642	405

TURKMENISTAN

(US$ million, unless otherwise indicated)

	1970	1980	1990	1994	1995	1996	1997	1998	1999	2000
1. SUMMARY DEBT DATA										
TOTAL DEBT STOCKS (EDT)	..	..	..	**431**	**402**	**751**	**1,771**	**2,259**	..	..
Long-term debt (LDOD)	..	..	..	**346**	**385**	**464**	**1,242**	**1,748**	..	..
Public and publicly guaranteed	..	..	..	346	385	464	1,242	1,731	..	..
Private nonguaranteed	..	..	..	0	0	0	0	16	..	..
Use of IMF credit	..	..	..	**0**	**0**	**0**	**0**	**0**	**0**	**0**
Short-term debt	..	..	..	**85**	**17**	**287**	**529**	**511**	..	..
of which interest arrears on LDOD	..	..	..	5	9	14	9	9	..	..
Official creditors	..	..	..	4	5	7	3	4	..	..
Private creditors	..	..	..	1	5	8	6	5	..	..
Memo: principal arrears on LDOD	..	..	..	34	130	50	73	115	..	..
Official creditors	..	..	..	16	115	29	37	54	..	..
Private creditors	..	..	..	18	15	22	36	61	..	..
Memo: export credits	..	..	..	149	101	259	483	251	531	654
TOTAL DEBT FLOWS										
Disbursements	..	..	..	**137**	**113**	**240**	**986**	**685**	..	..
Long-term debt	..	..	..	137	113	240	986	685	..	..
IMF purchases	..	..	..	0	0	0	0	0	..	..
Principal repayments	..	..	..	**72**	**80**	**154**	**196**	**219**	..	..
Long-term debt	..	..	..	72	80	154	196	219	..	..
IMF repurchases	..	..	..	0	0	0	0	0	..	..
Net flows on debt	..	..	..	**145**	**-39**	**350**	**1,039**	**449**	..	..
of which short-term debt	..	..	..	80	-72	264	248	-18	..	..
Interest payments (INT)	..	..	..	**28**	**24**	**39**	**68**	**92**	..	..
Long-term debt	..	..	..	26	22	27	46	66	..	..
IMF charges	..	..	..	0	0	0	0	0	..	..
Short-term debt	..	..	..	2	2	12	22	26	..	..
Net transfers on debt	..	..	..	**118**	**-63**	**311**	**971**	**357**	..	..
Total debt service paid (TDS)	..	..	..	**100**	**104**	**193**	**263**	**311**	..	..
Long-term debt	..	..	..	98	102	180	242	285	..	..
IMF repurchases and charges	..	..	..	0	0	0	0	0	..	..
Short-term debt (interest only)	..	..	..	2	2	12	22	26	..	..
2. AGGREGATE NET RESOURCE FLOWS AND NET TRANSFERS (LONG-TERM)										
NET RESOURCE FLOWS	..	..	..	**77**	**34**	**196**	**903**	**603**	..	..
Net flow of long-term debt (ex. IMF)	..	..	..	65	33	86	791	466	..	..
Foreign direct investment (net)	..	..	..	0	0	108	108	130	..	..
Portfolio equity flows	..	..	..	0	0	0	0	0	..	..
Grants (excluding technical coop.)	..	..	..	11	1	1	5	7	..	..
Memo: technical coop. grants	..	..	..	3	13	11	8	17	..	..
official net resource flows	..	..	..	62	14	-78	33	130	..	..
private net resource flows	..	..	..	14	20	274	870	473	..	..
NET TRANSFERS	..	..	..	**50**	**12**	**169**	**857**	**537**	..	..
Interest on long-term debt	..	..	..	26	22	27	46	66	..	..
Profit remittances on FDI	..	..	..	0	0	0	0	0	..	..
Memo: official net transfers	..	..	..	44	2	-88	24	123	..	..
private net transfers	..	..	..	6	10	257	833	414	..	..
3. MAJOR ECONOMIC AGGREGATES										
Gross national income (GNI)	..	..	..	4,681	5,892	2,396	2,766	2,894	3,300	4,227
Exports of goods & services (XGS)	..	..	..	2,276	2,231	1,902	1,203	978	1,495	2,932
of which workers remittances	..	..	..	..	..	0	0	0	0	0
Imports of goods & services (MGS)	..	..	..	2,193	2,219	1,905	1,752	1,939	2,172	2,686
International reserves (RES)	..	..	..	929	1,168	1,169	1,256	1,376	1,513	..
Current account balance	..	..	..	84	24	2	-580	-934	-571	412
4. DEBT INDICATORS										
EDT / XGS (%)	..	..	..	18.9	18.0	39.5	147.3	231.0	..	..
EDT / GNI (%)	..	..	..	9.2	6.8	31.3	64.0	78.0	..	..
TDS / XGS (%)	..	..	..	4.4	4.7	10.1	21.9	31.8	..	..
INT / XGS (%)	..	..	..	1.2	1.1	2.1	5.6	9.4	..	..
INT / GNI (%)	..	..	..	0.6	0.4	1.6	2.5	3.2	..	..
RES / EDT (%)	..	..	..	215.6	290.4	155.7	70.9	60.9	..	..
RES / MGS (months)	..	..	..	5.1	6.3	7.4	8.6	8.5	..	..
Short-term / EDT (%)	..	..	..	19.7	4.3	38.2	29.9	22.6	..	..
Concessional / EDT (%)	..	..	..	4.6	4.9	2.6	2.2	5.2	..	..
Multilateral / EDT (%)	..	..	..	12.4	14.5	0.4	1.1	1.7	..	..

TURKMENISTAN

(US$ million, unless otherwise indicated)

	1970	1980	1990	1994	1995	1996	1997	1998	1999	2000
5. LONG-TERM DEBT										
DEBT OUTSTANDING (LDOD)	..	..	..	**346**	**385**	**464**	**1,242**	**1,748**	..	..
Public and publicly guaranteed	..	..	..	**346**	**385**	**464**	**1,242**	**1,731**	..	..
Official creditors	..	..	..	203	219	136	160	285	..	..
Multilateral	..	..	..	54	58	3	19	37	..	..
Concessional	..	..	..	0	0	0	0	0	..	..
Bilateral	..	..	..	149	161	133	141	248	..	..
Concessional	..	..	..	20	20	20	38	118	..	..
Private creditors	..	..	..	144	166	328	1,083	1,447	..	..
Bonds	..	..	..	0	0	0	0	0	..	..
Commercial banks	..	..	..	0	0	0	89	60	..	..
Other private	..	..	..	144	166	328	994	1,387	..	..
Private nonguaranteed	..	..	..	**0**	**0**	**0**	**0**	**16**	..	..
Bonds	..	..	..	0	0	0	0	0	..	..
Commercial banks and other	..	..	..	0	0	0	0	16	..	..
Memo:										
IBRD	..	..	..	0	1	3	6	9	9	28
IDA	..	..	..	0	0	0	0	0	0	0
DISBURSEMENTS	..	..	..	**137**	**113**	**240**	**986**	**685**	..	..
Public and publicly guaranteed	..	..	..	**137**	**113**	**240**	**986**	**685**	..	..
Official creditors	..	..	..	70	32	22	57	133	..	..
Multilateral	..	..	..	25	1	3	16	18	..	..
Concessional	..	..	..	0	0	0	0	0	..	..
Bilateral	..	..	..	45	31	20	41	115	..	..
Concessional	..	..	..	11	0	0	20	70	..	..
Private creditors	..	..	..	67	81	217	930	553	..	..
Bonds	..	..	..	0	0	0	0	0	..	..
Commercial banks	..	..	..	0	0	0	130	0	..	..
Other private	..	..	..	67	81	217	800	553	..	..
Private nonguaranteed	..	..	..	**0**	**0**	**0**	**0**	**0**	..	..
Bonds	..	..	..	0	0	0	0	0	..	..
Commercial banks and other	..	..	..	0	0	0	0	0	..	..
Memo:										
IBRD	..	..	..	0	1	3	3	2	0	20
IDA	..	..	..	0	0	0	0	0	0	0
PRINCIPAL REPAYMENTS	..	..	..	**72**	**80**	**154**	**196**	**219**	..	..
Public and publicly guaranteed	..	..	..	**72**	**80**	**154**	**196**	**216**	..	..
Official creditors	..	..	..	19	20	102	28	9	..	..
Multilateral	..	..	..	0	0	55	0	0	..	..
Concessional	..	..	..	0	0	0	0	0	..	..
Bilateral	..	..	..	19	20	46	28	9	..	..
Concessional	..	..	..	0	0	0	0	0	..	..
Private creditors	..	..	..	53	61	52	167	206	..	..
Bonds	..	..	..	0	0	0	0	0	..	..
Commercial banks	..	..	..	0	0	0	41	30	..	..
Other private	..	..	..	53	61	52	127	177	..	..
Private nonguaranteed	..	..	..	**0**	**0**	**0**	**0**	**3**	..	..
Bonds	..	..	..	0	0	0	0	0	..	..
Commercial banks and other	..	..	..	0	0	0	0	3	..	..
Memo:										
IBRD	..	..	..	0	0	0	0	0	0	1
IDA	..	..	..	0	0	0	0	0	0	0
NET FLOWS ON DEBT	..	..	..	**65**	**33**	**86**	**791**	**466**	..	..
Public and publicly guaranteed	..	..	..	**65**	**33**	**86**	**791**	**470**	..	..
Official creditors	..	..	..	51	13	-79	28	123	..	..
Multilateral	..	..	..	25	1	-53	16	18	..	..
Concessional	..	..	..	0	0	0	0	0	..	..
Bilateral	..	..	..	26	12	-27	12	105	..	..
Concessional	..	..	..	11	0	0	20	70	..	..
Private creditors	..	..	..	14	20	165	762	346	..	..
Bonds	..	..	..	0	0	0	0	0	..	..
Commercial banks	..	..	..	0	0	0	89	-30	..	..
Other private	..	..	..	14	20	165	673	376	..	..
Private nonguaranteed	..	..	..	**0**	**0**	**0**	**0**	**-3**	..	..
Bonds	..	..	..	0	0	0	0	0	..	..
Commercial banks and other	..	..	..	0	0	0	0	-3	..	..
Memo:										
IBRD	..	..	..	0	1	3	3	2	0	20
IDA	..	..	..	0	0	0	0	0	0	0

TURKMENISTAN

(US$ million, unless otherwise indicated)

	1970	1980	1990	1994	1995	1996	1997	1998	1999	2000
INTEREST PAYMENTS (LINT)	..	..	..	**26**	**22**	**27**	**46**	**66**	..	..
Public and publicly guaranteed	..	..	..	**26**	**22**	**27**	**46**	**66**	..	..
Official creditors	..	..	..	18	12	10	9	7	..	..
Multilateral	..	..	..	7	2	4	1	2	..	..
Concessional	..	..	..	0	0	0	0	0	..	..
Bilateral	..	..	..	12	10	6	7	5	..	..
Concessional	..	..	..	0	1	1	1	2	..	..
Private creditors	..	..	..	8	10	17	37	59	..	..
Bonds	..	..	..	0	0	0	0	0	..	..
Commercial banks	..	..	..	0	0	0	2	5	..	..
Other private	..	..	..	8	10	17	35	54	..	..
Private nonguaranteed	..	..	..	**0**	**0**	**0**	**0**	**1**	..	..
Bonds	..	..	..	0	0	0	0	0	..	..
Commercial banks and other	..	..	..	0	0	0	0	1	..	..
Memo:										
IBRD	..	..	..	0	0	0	0	0	1	1
IDA	..	..	..	0	0	0	0	0	0	0
NET TRANSFERS ON DEBT	..	..	..	**39**	**11**	**59**	**745**	**400**	..	..
Public and publicly guaranteed	..	..	..	**39**	**11**	**59**	**745**	**404**	..	..
Official creditors	..	..	..	33	1	-89	20	116	..	..
Multilateral	..	..	..	18	-1	-56	15	16	..	..
Concessional	..	..	..	0	0	0	0	0	..	..
Bilateral	..	..	..	15	2	-33	5	100	..	..
Concessional	..	..	..	11	-1	-1	19	68	..	..
Private creditors	..	..	..	6	10	149	725	288	..	..
Bonds	..	..	..	0	0	0	0	0	..	..
Commercial banks	..	..	..	0	0	0	87	-34	..	..
Other private	..	..	..	6	10	149	638	322	..	..
Private nonguaranteed	..	..	..	**0**	**0**	**0**	**0**	**-4**	..	..
Bonds	..	..	..	0	0	0	0	0	..	..
Commercial banks and other	..	..	..	0	0	0	0	-4	..	..
Memo:										
IBRD	..	..	..	0	1	2	3	2	-1	18
IDA	..	..	..	0	0	0	0	0	0	0
DEBT SERVICE (LTDS)	..	..	..	**98**	**102**	**180**	**242**	**285**	..	..
Public and publicly guaranteed	..	..	..	**98**	**102**	**180**	**242**	**281**	..	..
Official creditors	..	..	..	37	31	112	37	16	..	..
Multilateral	..	..	..	7	2	59	1	2	..	..
Concessional	..	..	..	0	0	0	0	0	..	..
Bilateral	..	..	..	30	29	53	36	15	..	..
Concessional	..	..	..	0	1	1	1	2	..	..
Private creditors	..	..	..	61	71	69	205	265	..	..
Bonds	..	..	..	0	0	0	0	0	..	..
Commercial banks	..	..	..	0	0	0	43	34	..	..
Other private	..	..	..	61	71	69	162	231	..	..
Private nonguaranteed	..	..	..	**0**	**0**	**0**	**0**	**4**	..	..
Bonds	..	..	..	0	0	0	0	0	..	..
Commercial banks and other	..	..	..	0	0	0	0	4	..	..
Memo:										
IBRD	..	..	..	0	0	0	0	0	1	2
IDA	..	..	..	0	0	0	0	0	0	0
UNDISBURSED DEBT	..	..	..	**108**	**265**	**756**	**1,038**	**597**	..	..
Official creditors	..	..	..	103	93	218	423	312	..	..
Private creditors	..	..	..	5	172	538	615	285	..	..
Memorandum items										
Concessional LDOD	..	..	..	20	20	20	38	118	..	..
Variable rate LDOD	..	..	..	281	276	284	937	1,386	..	..
Public sector LDOD	..	..	..	346	385	464	1,242	1,731	..	..
Private sector LDOD	..	..	..	0	0	0	0	16	..	..

6. CURRENCY COMPOSITION OF LONG-TERM DEBT (PERCENT)

	1970	1980	1990	1994	1995	1996	1997	1998	1999	2000
Deutsche mark	..	..	..	7.2	12.4	14.4	9.9	14.4	..	..
French franc	..	..	..	0.0	0.0	0.0	0.0	0.0	..	..
Japanese yen	..	..	..	0.0	0.0	0.0	1.1	5.9	..	..
Pound sterling	..	..	..	0.0	0.0	0.0	0.0	0.0	..	..
Swiss franc	..	..	..	0.0	0.0	0.0	0.0	0.0	..	..
U.S.dollars	..	..	..	76.9	72.1	84.7	88.3	79.2	..	..
Multiple currency	..	..	..	0.0	0.2	0.7	0.7	0.5	..	..
Special drawing rights	..	..	..	0.0	0.0	0.0	0.0	0.0	..	..
All other currencies	..	..	..	15.9	15.3	0.2	0.0	0.0	..	..

TURKMENISTAN

(US$ million, unless otherwise indicated)

	1970	1980	1990	1994	1995	1996	1997	1998	1999	2000
7. DEBT RESTRUCTURINGS										
Total amount rescheduled	..	..	..	0	0	0	0	0	..	..
Debt stock rescheduled	..	..	..	0	0	0	0	0	..	..
Principal rescheduled	..	..	..	0	0	0	0	0	..	..
Official	..	..	..	0	0	0	0	0	..	..
Private	..	..	..	0	0	0	0	0	..	..
Interest rescheduled	..	..	..	0	0	0	0	0	..	..
Official	..	..	..	0	0	0	0	0	..	..
Private	..	..	..	0	0	0	0	0	..	..
Debt forgiven	..	..	..	0	0	0	0	0	..	..
Memo: interest forgiven	..	..	..	0	0	0	0	0	..	..
Debt stock reduction	..	..	..	0	0	0	0	0	..	..
of which debt buyback	..	..	..	0	0	0	0	0	..	..
8. DEBT STOCK-FLOW RECONCILIATION										
Total change in debt stocks	..	..	..	155	-29	349	1,020	488	..	..
Net flows on debt	..	..	..	145	-39	350	1,039	449	..	..
Net change in interest arrears	..	..	..	5	5	5	-6	0	..	..
Interest capitalized	..	..	..	0	0	0	0	0	..	..
Debt forgiveness or reduction	..	..	..	0	0	0	0	0	..	..
Cross-currency valuation	..	..	..	3	6	-7	-9	11	..	..
Residual	..	..	..	2	0	0	-3	28	..	..
9. AVERAGE TERMS OF NEW COMMITMENTS										
ALL CREDITORS										
Interest (%)	..	..	..	6.3	6.6	5.9	5.8	6.7	..	..
Maturity (years)	..	..	..	10.3	8.2	9.6	7.6	5.6	..	..
Grace period (years)	..	..	..	3.2	1.9	2.8	2.2	2.1	..	..
Grant element (%)	..	..	..	14.7	11.9	16.7	13.8	9.7	..	..
Official creditors										
Interest (%)	..	..	..	6.2	3.9	3.8	4.3	0.0	..	..
Maturity (years)	..	..	..	12.1	13.9	11.8	15.7	0.0	..	..
Grace period (years)	..	..	..	4.0	2.8	3.4	4.4	0.0	..	..
Grant element (%)	..	..	..	17.2	26.3	31.3	32.1	0.0	..	..
Private creditors										
Interest (%)	..	..	..	6.7	6.8	6.5	6.3	6.7	..	..
Maturity (years)	..	..	..	5.3	7.7	9.0	5.4	5.6	..	..
Grace period (years)	..	..	..	1.0	1.8	2.6	1.5	2.1	..	..
Grant element (%)	..	..	..	7.5	10.7	12.9	8.7	9.7	..	..
Memorandum items										
Commitments	..	..	..	172	269	753	1,324	218	..	..
Official creditors	..	..	..	128	20	156	286	0	..	..
Private creditors	..	..	..	45	249	598	1,039	218	..	..

10. CONTRACTUAL OBLIGATIONS ON OUTSTANDING LONG-TERM DEBT

	2001	2002	2003	2004	2005	2006	2007	2008	2009	2010
TOTAL										
Disbursements	..	..	..	..	..	..	..	..	..	..
Principal	..	..	..	..	..	..	..	..	..	..
Interest	..	..	..	..	..	..	..	..	..	..
Official creditors										
Disbursements	..	..	..	..	..	..	..	..	..	..
Principal	..	..	..	..	..	..	..	..	..	..
Interest	..	..	..	..	..	..	..	..	..	..
Bilateral creditors										
Disbursements	..	..	..	..	..	..	..	..	..	..
Principal	..	..	..	..	..	..	..	..	..	..
Interest	..	..	..	..	..	..	..	..	..	..
Multilateral creditors										
Disbursements	..	..	..	..	..	..	..	..	..	..
Principal	..	..	..	..	..	..	..	..	..	..
Interest	..	..	..	..	..	..	..	..	..	..
Private creditors										
Disbursements	..	..	..	..	..	..	..	..	..	..
Principal	..	..	..	..	..	..	..	..	..	..
Interest	..	..	..	..	..	..	..	..	..	..
Commercial banks										
Disbursements	..	..	..	..	..	..	..	..	..	..
Principal	..	..	..	..	..	..	..	..	..	..
Interest	..	..	..	..	..	..	..	..	..	..
Other private										
Disbursements	..	..	..	..	..	..	..	..	..	..
Principal	..	..	..	..	..	..	..	..	..	..
Interest	..	..	..	..	..	..	..	..	..	..

UGANDA

(US$ million, unless otherwise indicated)

	1970	1980	1990	1994	1995	1996	1997	1998	1999	2000
1. SUMMARY DEBT DATA										
TOTAL DEBT STOCKS (EDT)	**152**	**689**	**2,583**	**3,372**	**3,573**	**3,675**	**3,914**	**4,005**	**3,454**	**3,409**
Long-term debt (LDOD)	**152**	**537**	**2,161**	**2,869**	**3,062**	**3,152**	**3,405**	**3,472**	**2,980**	**2,997**
Public and publicly guaranteed	152	537	2,161	2,869	3,062	3,152	3,405	3,472	2,980	2,997
Private nonguaranteed	0	0	0	0	0	0	0	0	0	0
Use of IMF credit	**0**	**89**	**282**	**383**	**417**	**417**	**394**	**398**	**372**	**316**
Short-term debt	**0**	**63**	**140**	**119**	**93**	**107**	**115**	**135**	**102**	**96**
of which interest arrears on LDOD	0	19	83	81	59	50	47	64	25	24
Official creditors	0	10	32	69	47	41	39	55	23	22
Private creditors	0	9	51	12	12	8	8	9	2	2
Memo: principal arrears on LDOD	0	82	215	207	208	202	214	216	43	43
Official creditors	0	30	94	145	147	140	151	165	38	38
Private creditors	0	52	122	63	61	62	63	51	5	5
Memo: export credits	0	0	270	149	138	134	129	126	97	94
TOTAL DEBT FLOWS										
Disbursements	**26**	**161**	**372**	**320**	**286**	**290**	**354**	**225**	**210**	**265**
Long-term debt	26	83	293	268	231	226	294	175	175	253
IMF purchases	0	78	79	52	56	64	60	50	35	12
Principal repayments	**5**	**45**	**109**	**111**	**98**	**106**	**116**	**125**	**125**	**113**
Long-term debt	5	32	65	87	70	56	59	63	74	64
IMF repurchases	0	13	43	24	28	50	58	62	51	49
Net flows on debt	**22**	**130**	**269**	**223**	**184**	**207**	**248**	**103**	**91**	**146**
of which short-term debt	0	14	6	14	-4	23	11	3	6	-6
Interest payments (INT)	**5**	**12**	**36**	**38**	**38**	**43**	**43**	**37**	**47**	**46**
Long-term debt	5	4	18	34	34	38	37	31	41	40
IMF charges	0	3	13	2	2	2	2	2	2	2
Short-term debt	0	5	5	3	2	3	4	4	5	4
Net transfers on debt	**17**	**118**	**233**	**185**	**146**	**164**	**205**	**66**	**44**	**100**
Total debt service paid (TDS)	**9**	**57**	**145**	**149**	**136**	**149**	**159**	**162**	**172**	**159**
Long-term debt	9	36	84	120	104	95	96	94	114	105
IMF repurchases and charges	0	16	56	26	30	52	60	64	53	51
Short-term debt (interest only)	0	5	5	3	2	3	4	4	5	4
2. AGGREGATE NET RESOURCE FLOWS AND NET TRANSFERS (LONG-TERM)										
NET RESOURCE FLOWS	**28**	**112**	**485**	**588**	**682**	**627**	**752**	**856**	**703**	**936**
Net flow of long-term debt (ex. IMF)	22	51	227	181	161	170	235	112	101	189
Foreign direct investment (net)	4	0	0	88	121	121	175	210	222	220
Portfolio equity flows	0	0	0	0	0	0	0	0	0	0
Grants (excluding technical coop.)	1	61	257	319	400	336	342	534	379	527
Memo: technical coop. grants	14	21	91	121	147	132	151	125	110	131
official net resource flows	17	68	468	515	571	513	578	647	482	705
private net resource flows	10	44	16	73	112	114	174	208	221	231
NET TRANSFERS	**10**	**109**	**466**	**542**	**636**	**574**	**694**	**803**	**629**	**866**
Interest on long-term debt	5	4	18	34	34	38	37	31	41	40
Profit remittances on FDI	13	0	0	13	12	14	20	22	33	30
Memo: official net transfers	14	66	451	483	539	475	541	619	442	665
private net transfers	-4	43	15	59	98	100	153	184	187	201
3. MAJOR ECONOMIC AGGREGATES										
Gross national income (GNI)	..	1,240	4,227	3,936	5,698	6,004	6,281	6,769	6,392	6,156
Exports of goods & services (XGS)	297	331	246	344	683	747	863	676	776	674
of which workers remittances	..	..	0	0	0	0	0	0	0	0
Imports of goods & services (MGS)	271	450	753	913	1,457	1,668	1,706	1,922	1,897	2,047
International reserves (RES)	57	3	44	321	459	528	633	725	763	808
Current account balance	20	-121	-429	-265	-444	-500	-521	-706	-746	-861
4. DEBT INDICATORS										
EDT / XGS (%)	51.1	208.3	1,051.2	980.3	523.3	491.9	453.4	592.2	445.1	506.1
EDT / GNI (%)	..	55.6	61.1	85.7	62.7	61.2	62.3	59.2	54.0	55.4
TDS / XGS (%)	3.0	17.3	58.9	43.2	20.0	20.0	18.5	24.0	22.1	23.7
INT / XGS (%)	1.5	3.7	14.6	11.1	5.6	5.8	5.0	5.5	6.0	6.8
INT / GNI (%)	..	1.0	0.9	1.0	0.7	0.7	0.7	0.6	0.7	0.8
RES / EDT (%)	37.3	0.4	1.7	9.5	12.8	14.4	16.2	18.1	22.1	23.7
RES / MGS (months)	2.5	0.1	0.7	4.2	3.8	3.8	4.5	4.5	4.8	4.7
Short-term / EDT (%)	0.0	9.1	5.4	3.5	2.6	2.9	3.0	3.4	3.0	2.8
Concessional / EDT (%)	71.3	36.9	56.2	72.9	77.5	78.3	76.0	79.7	81.4	83.4
Multilateral / EDT (%)	12.6	11.5	49.2	59.7	61.8	62.2	61.6	61.0	74.1	77.6

UGANDA

(US$ million, unless otherwise indicated)

	1970	1980	1990	1994	1995	1996	1997	1998	1999	2000
5. LONG-TERM DEBT										
DEBT OUTSTANDING (LDOD)	**152**	**537**	**2,161**	**2,869**	**3,062**	**3,152**	**3,405**	**3,472**	**2,980**	**2,997**
Public and publicly guaranteed	**152**	**537**	**2,161**	**2,869**	**3,062**	**3,152**	**3,405**	**3,472**	**2,980**	**2,997**
Official creditors	127	293	1,826	2,776	2,979	3,074	3,330	3,410	2,965	2,971
Multilateral	19	79	1,270	2,012	2,209	2,284	2,410	2,444	2,561	2,644
Concessional	13	63	1,129	1,915	2,129	2,208	2,329	2,377	2,489	2,578
Bilateral	108	214	556	764	770	790	920	965	405	328
Concessional	95	191	322	542	639	671	647	815	323	266
Private creditors	25	244	335	93	84	77	76	62	15	25
Bonds	10	0	4	4	4	4	4	4	4	4
Commercial banks	14	23	89	27	21	15	13	12	11	21
Other private	1	221	242	62	59	59	59	47	0	1
Private nonguaranteed	**0**	**0**	**0**	**0**	**0**	**0**	**0**	**0**	**0**	**0**
Bonds	0	0	0	0	0	0	0	0	0	0
Commercial banks and other	0	0	0	0	0	0	0	0	0	0
Memo:										
IBRD	6	1	34	11	0	0	0	0	0	0
IDA	13	46	935	1,604	1,792	1,849	1,954	1,947	2,043	2,115
DISBURSEMENTS	**26**	**83**	**293**	**268**	**231**	**226**	**294**	**175**	**175**	**253**
Public and publicly guaranteed	**26**	**83**	**293**	**268**	**231**	**226**	**294**	**175**	**175**	**253**
Official creditors	19	18	255	268	231	226	294	175	175	241
Multilateral	6	7	219	248	210	180	284	170	169	238
Concessional	5	2	215	245	200	167	264	168	166	236
Bilateral	14	11	36	19	21	46	10	5	6	3
Concessional	14	11	23	19	20	45	9	3	5	2
Private creditors	7	65	38	0	0	0	0	0	0	12
Bonds	0	0	0	0	0	0	0	0	0	0
Commercial banks	6	17	5	0	0	0	0	0	0	12
Other private	2	49	34	0	0	0	0	0	0	1
Private nonguaranteed	**0**	**0**	**0**	**0**	**0**	**0**	**0**	**0**	**0**	**0**
Bonds	0	0	0	0	0	0	0	0	0	0
Commercial banks and other	0	0	0	0	0	0	0	0	0	0
Memo:										
IBRD	0	0	0	0	0	0	0	0	0	0
IDA	5	1	199	221	160	124	217	113	132	190
PRINCIPAL REPAYMENTS	**5**	**32**	**65**	**87**	**70**	**56**	**59**	**63**	**74**	**64**
Public and publicly guaranteed	**5**	**32**	**65**	**87**	**70**	**56**	**59**	**63**	**74**	**64**
Official creditors	4	11	44	71	60	49	57	61	72	63
Multilateral	1	1	19	51	50	30	29	41	36	28
Concessional	0	0	4	19	19	18	19	23	20	24
Bilateral	3	10	25	21	11	19	28	21	37	35
Concessional	3	2	4	4	4	6	18	13	31	26
Private creditors	1	21	22	15	10	7	1	2	2	2
Bonds	0	0	0	0	0	0	0	0	0	0
Commercial banks	1	0	14	6	7	6	1	1	2	2
Other private	0	21	8	9	3	1	0	1	0	0
Private nonguaranteed	**0**	**0**	**0**	**0**	**0**	**0**	**0**	**0**	**0**	**0**
Bonds	0	0	0	0	0	0	0	0	0	0
Commercial banks and other	0	0	0	0	0	0	0	0	0	0
Memo:										
IBRD	0	1	5	6	12	0	0	0	0	0
IDA	0	0	2	7	8	8	9	8	10	14
NET FLOWS ON DEBT	**22**	**51**	**227**	**181**	**161**	**170**	**235**	**112**	**101**	**189**
Public and publicly guaranteed	**22**	**51**	**227**	**181**	**161**	**170**	**235**	**112**	**101**	**189**
Official creditors	16	7	211	196	171	177	237	114	103	178
Multilateral	5	5	200	197	160	151	255	129	133	210
Concessional	5	1	211	227	181	149	245	145	146	212
Bilateral	11	1	11	-1	11	27	-18	-16	-31	-32
Concessional	11	9	19	16	17	39	-10	-10	-27	-24
Private creditors	6	44	16	-15	-10	-7	-1	-2	-1	11
Bonds	0	0	0	0	0	0	0	0	0	0
Commercial banks	5	17	-10	-6	-7	-6	-1	-1	-1	10
Other private	2	28	26	-9	-3	-1	0	-1	0	1
Private nonguaranteed	**0**	**0**	**0**	**0**	**0**	**0**	**0**	**0**	**0**	**0**
Bonds	0	0	0	0	0	0	0	0	0	0
Commercial banks and other	0	0	0	0	0	0	0	0	0	0
Memo:										
IBRD	0	-1	-5	-6	-12	0	0	0	0	0
IDA	5	1	198	214	151	116	208	105	122	176

UGANDA

(US$ million, unless otherwise indicated)

	1970	1980	1990	1994	1995	1996	1997	1998	1999	2000
INTEREST PAYMENTS (LINT)	**5**	**4**	**18**	**34**	**34**	**38**	**37**	**31**	**41**	**40**
Public and publicly guaranteed	**5**	**4**	**18**	**34**	**34**	**38**	**37**	**31**	**41**	**40**
Official creditors	3	2	17	33	32	38	37	29	40	40
Multilateral	0	1	13	24	22	22	21	21	21	21
Concessional	0	1	6	13	17	18	17	18	19	19
Bilateral	3	1	5	8	10	16	16	8	19	19
Concessional	2	1	1	5	7	7	8	3	9	11
Private creditors	2	1	1	1	2	0	0	2	0	0
Bonds	1	0	0	0	0	0	0	0	0	0
Commercial banks	1	0	1	1	2	0	0	2	0	0
Other private	0	1	1	0	0	0	0	0	0	0
Private nonguaranteed	**0**	**0**	**0**	**0**	**0**	**0**	**0**	**0**	**0**	**0**
Bonds	0	0	0	0	0	0	0	0	0	0
Commercial banks and other	0	0	0	0	0	0	0	0	0	0
Memo:										
IBRD	0	0	2	1	1	0	0	0	0	0
IDA	0	0	5	11	13	13	14	14	15	15
NET TRANSFERS ON DEBT	**17**	**47**	**209**	**148**	**127**	**132**	**198**	**81**	**61**	**148**
Public and publicly guaranteed	**17**	**47**	**209**	**148**	**127**	**132**	**198**	**81**	**61**	**148**
Official creditors	13	4	194	164	138	139	200	85	62	138
Multilateral	5	4	188	173	138	128	234	109	112	189
Concessional	5	1	205	213	165	131	228	127	127	193
Bilateral	8	0	6	-9	1	11	-34	-24	-50	-51
Concessional	9	9	19	11	10	32	-18	-13	-36	-34
Private creditors	5	43	15	-16	-11	-7	-2	-4	-2	11
Bonds	-1	0	0	0	0	0	0	0	0	0
Commercial banks	4	17	-10	-7	-8	-6	-2	-3	-2	10
Other private	2	26	25	-9	-3	-1	0	-1	0	1
Private nonguaranteed	**0**	**0**	**0**	**0**	**0**	**0**	**0**	**0**	**0**	**0**
Bonds	0	0	0	0	0	0	0	0	0	0
Commercial banks and other	0	0	0	0	0	0	0	0	0	0
Memo:										
IBRD	-1	-1	-6	-7	-12	0	0	0	0	0
IDA	5	0	193	203	139	103	194	91	107	161
DEBT SERVICE (LTDS)	**9**	**36**	**84**	**120**	**104**	**95**	**96**	**94**	**114**	**105**
Public and publicly guaranteed	**9**	**36**	**84**	**120**	**104**	**95**	**96**	**94**	**114**	**105**
Official creditors	7	13	61	104	93	87	94	90	112	103
Multilateral	1	3	31	75	72	52	50	62	57	49
Concessional	0	1	10	32	35	36	36	41	39	43
Bilateral	6	11	29	29	21	35	44	28	56	54
Concessional	4	3	5	9	10	14	27	16	40	37
Private creditors	3	22	23	16	11	7	2	4	2	2
Bonds	1	0	0	0	0	0	0	0	0	0
Commercial banks	2	0	15	7	8	6	2	3	2	2
Other private	0	22	8	9	3	1	0	1	0	0
Private nonguaranteed	**0**	**0**	**0**	**0**	**0**	**0**	**0**	**0**	**0**	**0**
Bonds	0	0	0	0	0	0	0	0	0	0
Commercial banks and other	0	0	0	0	0	0	0	0	0	0
Memo:										
IBRD	1	1	6	7	12	0	0	0	0	0
IDA	0	1	7	17	21	21	22	22	25	29
UNDISBURSED DEBT	**47**	**162**	**844**	**1,262**	**1,069**	**844**	**685**	**735**	**815**	**606**
Official creditors	44	143	821	1,244	1,066	844	685	710	789	592
Private creditors	3	19	23	18	3	0	0	25	26	14
Memorandum items										
Concessional LDOD	108	254	1,451	2,456	2,767	2,878	2,977	3,192	2,812	2,844
Variable rate LDOD	4	7	49	88	78	78	77	91	81	65
Public sector LDOD	151	533	2,158	2,866	3,057	3,144	3,398	3,464	2,972	2,990
Private sector LDOD	1	4	3	4	6	8	7	8	7	7

6. CURRENCY COMPOSITION OF LONG-TERM DEBT (PERCENT)

	1970	1980	1990	1994	1995	1996	1997	1998	1999	2000
Deutsche mark	6.5	8.3	0.7	0.2	0.0	0.2	0.2	0.2	0.2	0.1
French franc	0.2	6.3	3.5	1.4	0.3	0.3	0.3	0.3	0.3	0.2
Japanese yen	0.3	0.7	0.3	1.3	1.2	1.7	1.4	1.6	2.1	1.5
Pound sterling	73.2	20.4	6.7	3.1	2.0	2.1	1.7	1.0	1.0	0.7
Swiss franc	0.0	9.9	0.0	0.0	0.0	0.0	0.0	0.0	0.0	0.0
U.S.dollars	6.9	43.8	53.4	63.6	66.8	65.9	68.3	67.1	60.5	62.3
Multiple currency	4.1	2.3	21.8	15.4	13.8	12.1	10.5	9.2	10.1	9.4
Special drawing rights	0.0	0.0	2.4	4.8	5.8	6.7	7.2	8.7	10.9	11.0
All other currencies	8.8	8.3	11.2	10.2	10.1	11.0	10.4	11.9	14.9	14.8

UGANDA

(US$ million, unless otherwise indicated)

	1970	1980	1990	1994	1995	1996	1997	1998	1999	2000
7. DEBT RESTRUCTURINGS										
Total amount rescheduled	..	..	16	0	172	0	0	149	0	0
Debt stock rescheduled	..	..	0	0	142	0	0	0	0	0
Principal rescheduled	..	..	4	0	0	0	0	133	0	0
Official	..	..	3	0	0	0	0	133	0	0
Private	..	..	0	0	0	0	0	0	0	0
Interest rescheduled	..	..	1	0	30	0	0	15	0	0
Official	..	..	1	0	30	0	0	15	0	0
Private	..	..	0	0	0	0	0	0	0	0
Debt forgiven	..	..	51	7	0	0	0	0	0	0
Memo: interest forgiven	..	..	1	0	1	0	0	522	0	0
Debt stock reduction	..	..	0	0	40	0	0	178	0	150
of which debt buyback	..	..	0	0	0	0	0	85	0	0
8. DEBT STOCK-FLOW RECONCILIATION										
Total change in debt stocks	..	..	406	343	201	103	239	91	-552	-45
Net flows on debt	22	130	269	223	184	207	248	103	91	146
Net change in interest arrears	..	..	28	10	-22	-9	-2	17	-39	-1
Interest capitalized	..	..	1	0	30	0	0	15	0	0
Debt forgiveness or reduction	..	..	-51	-7	-40	0	0	-94	0	-150
Cross-currency valuation	..	..	201	129	49	-91	-111	-182	-59	-139
Residual	..	..	-43	-11	-1	-4	103	232	-545	99
9. AVERAGE TERMS OF NEW COMMITMENTS										
ALL CREDITORS										
Interest (%)	3.9	4.9	1.0	0.9	0.9	0.8	0.8	0.8	0.8	1.6
Maturity (years)	28.4	26.2	33.0	38.4	39.2	39.7	43.0	38.4	40.3	41.0
Grace period (years)	6.7	6.0	9.0	10.1	10.0	10.2	9.7	10.7	10.1	6.8
Grant element (%)	46.3	40.0	68.4	78.5	79.4	80.6	79.8	80.4	80.3	68.3
Official creditors										
Interest (%)	3.2	2.7	1.1	0.9	0.9	0.8	0.8	0.8	0.8	1.6
Maturity (years)	33.8	38.2	36.5	38.4	39.2	39.7	43.0	39.3	40.4	41.0
Grace period (years)	8.0	8.2	9.9	10.1	10.0	10.2	9.7	10.1	10.2	6.8
Grant element (%)	55.5	62.0	74.9	78.5	79.4	80.6	79.8	79.7	80.7	68.3
Private creditors										
Interest (%)	6.9	8.2	0.5	0.0	0.0	0.0	0.0	0.2	7.0	0.0
Maturity (years)	5.3	7.8	1.3	0.0	0.0	0.0	0.0	30.5	21.5	0.0
Grace period (years)	0.8	2.4	0.7	0.0	0.0	0.0	0.0	16.0	5.0	0.0
Grant element (%)	7.2	6.4	8.8	0.0	0.0	0.0	0.0	86.3	19.4	0.0
Memorandum items										
Commitments	12	198	440	299	95	42	200	238	343	86
Official creditors	10	120	397	299	95	42	200	213	341	86
Private creditors	2	78	43	0	0	0	0	25	2	0

10. CONTRACTUAL OBLIGATIONS ON OUTSTANDING LONG-TERM DEBT

	2001	2002	2003	2004	2005	2006	2007	2008	2009	2010
TOTAL										
Disbursements	237	171	95	58	31	7	5	1	0	0
Principal	66	72	81	86	83	84	88	88	92	97
Interest	35	35	34	32	31	30	29	27	26	25
Official creditors										
Disbursements	227	167	95	58	31	7	5	1	0	0
Principal	64	71	79	85	82	83	88	87	92	97
Interest	35	35	33	32	31	30	28	27	26	25
Bilateral creditors										
Disbursements	2	1	1	0	0	0	0	0	0	0
Principal	25	24	26	23	16	16	14	13	12	13
Interest	11	10	9	8	7	6	6	5	5	4
Multilateral creditors										
Disbursements	226	166	95	58	31	7	5	1	0	0
Principal	39	46	53	62	66	68	74	74	79	85
Interest	24	25	25	24	24	23	23	22	21	21
Private creditors										
Disbursements	10	4	0	0	0	0	0	0	0	0
Principal	2	2	2	1	1	1	1	1	0	0
Interest	0	0	0	0	0	0	0	0	0	0
Commercial banks										
Disbursements	9	4	0	0	0	0	0	0	0	0
Principal	2	2	2	1	1	1	1	1	0	0
Interest	0	0	0	0	0	0	0	0	0	0
Other private										
Disbursements	1	0	0	0	0	0	0	0	0	0
Principal	0	0	0	0	0	0	0	0	0	0
Interest	0	0	0	0	0	0	0	0	0	0

UKRAINE

(US$ million, unless otherwise indicated)

	1970	1980	1990	1994	1995	1996	1997	1998	1999	2000
1. SUMMARY DEBT DATA										
TOTAL DEBT STOCKS (EDT)	..	..	..	**5,636**	**8,429**	**9,538**	**11,133**	**13,071**	**13,941**	**12,166**
Long-term debt (LDOD)	..	..	..	**4,855**	**6,664**	**6,832**	**7,642**	**9,797**	**10,820**	**9,646**
Public and publicly guaranteed	..	..	..	4,810	6,581	6,648	7,015	8,966	9,581	8,139
Private nonguaranteed	..	..	..	45	84	184	627	830	1,239	1,507
Use of IMF credit	..	..	..	**364**	**1,542**	**2,262**	**2,402**	**2,795**	**2,806**	**2,073**
Short-term debt	..	..	..	**417**	**223**	**444**	**1,089**	**479**	**315**	**447**
of which interest arrears on LDOD	..	..	..	205	35	41	43	53	78	183
Official creditors	..	..	..	191	5	1	11	0	0	25
Private creditors	..	..	..	14	30	40	33	53	78	159
Memo: principal arrears on LDOD	..	..	..	602	88	66	235	156	345	567
Official creditors	..	..	..	541	17	0	139	0	0	143
Private creditors	..	..	..	61	71	66	96	156	345	424
Memo: export credits	..	..	..	1,121	1,193	1,100	889	128	140	212
TOTAL DEBT FLOWS										
Disbursements	..	..	..	**935**	**1,997**	**1,852**	**1,775**	**3,634**	**2,074**	**1,628**
Long-term debt	..	..	..	578	801	1,074	1,490	3,251	1,436	1,377
IMF purchases	..	..	..	357	1,196	778	285	382	638	251
Principal repayments	..	..	..	**233**	**636**	**791**	**689**	**1,452**	**2,128**	**2,952**
Long-term debt	..	..	..	233	636	791	689	1,347	1,571	2,103
IMF repurchases	..	..	..	0	0	0	0	105	557	849
Net flows on debt	..	..	..	**783**	**1,338**	**1,276**	**1,729**	**1,562**	**-243**	**-1,297**
of which short-term debt	..	..	..	81	-24	215	643	-620	-189	27
Interest payments (INT)	..	..	..	**96**	**501**	**466**	**669**	**575**	**677**	**709**
Long-term debt	..	..	..	88	447	374	527	421	545	573
IMF charges	..	..	..	0	42	75	102	115	110	122
Short-term debt	..	..	..	7	12	18	40	39	22	14
Net transfers on debt	..	..	..	**687**	**836**	**809**	**1,060**	**987**	**-921**	**-2,006**
Total debt service paid (TDS)	..	..	..	**328**	**1,137**	**1,257**	**1,358**	**2,027**	**2,805**	**3,661**
Long-term debt	..	..	..	321	1,083	1,164	1,216	1,768	2,117	2,676
IMF repurchases and charges	..	..	..	0	42	75	102	220	667	971
Short-term debt (interest only)	..	..	..	7	12	18	40	39	22	14
2. AGGREGATE NET RESOURCE FLOWS AND NET TRANSFERS (LONG-TERM)										
NET RESOURCE FLOWS	..	..	..	**722**	**496**	**1,060**	**1,586**	**2,832**	**486**	**169**
Net flow of long-term debt (ex. IMF)	..	..	..	346	166	283	801	1,904	-136	-726
Foreign direct investment (net)	..	..	..	159	267	521	623	743	496	595
Portfolio equity flows	..	..	..	0	0	0	0	0	0	0
Grants (excluding technical coop.)	..	..	..	218	64	256	163	185	125	299
Memo: technical coop. grants	..	..	..	52	120	128	86	250	439	241
official net resource flows	..	..	..	355	449	493	167	434	413	-759
private net resource flows	..	..	..	367	48	566	1,419	2,398	73	927
NET TRANSFERS	..	..	..	**634**	**49**	**666**	**1,025**	**2,371**	**-106**	**-455**
Interest on long-term debt	..	..	..	88	447	374	527	421	545	573
Profit remittances on FDI	..	..	..	0	0	20	34	40	46	50
Memo: official net transfers	..	..	..	328	143	295	-117	291	258	-908
private net transfers	..	..	..	306	-94	371	1,143	2,080	-364	454
3. MAJOR ECONOMIC AGGREGATES										
Gross national income (GNI)	..	..	..	52,110	48,298	43,986	49,506	41,039	30,712	30,849
Exports of goods & services (XGS)	..	..	..	16,697	17,337	20,448	20,513	17,743	17,156	19,665
of which workers remittances	..	..	..	..	..	..	..	..	..	..
Imports of goods & services (MGS)	..	..	..	18,407	18,961	22,141	22,693	19,821	16,204	19,201
International reserves (RES)	..	..	..	665	1,069	1,972	2,359	793	1,094	1,477
Current account balance	..	..	..	-1,163	-1,152	-1,184	-1,335	-1,296	1,658	1,481
4. DEBT INDICATORS										
EDT / XGS (%)	..	..	..	33.8	48.6	46.7	54.3	73.7	81.3	61.9
EDT / GNI (%)	..	..	..	10.8	17.5	21.7	22.5	31.9	45.4	39.4
TDS / XGS (%)	..	..	..	2.0	6.6	6.2	6.6	11.4	16.4	18.6
INT / XGS (%)	..	..	..	0.6	2.9	2.3	3.3	3.2	4.0	3.6
INT / GNI (%)	..	..	..	0.2	1.0	1.1	1.4	1.4	2.2	2.3
RES / EDT (%)	..	..	..	11.8	12.7	20.7	21.2	6.1	7.8	12.1
RES / MGS (months)	..	..	..	0.4	0.7	1.1	1.3	0.5	0.8	0.9
Short-term / EDT (%)	..	..	..	7.4	2.7	4.7	9.8	3.7	2.3	3.7
Concessional / EDT (%)	..	..	..	0.7	0.8	2.3	1.9	2.0	24.1	18.6
Multilateral / EDT (%)	..	..	..	4.7	7.8	12.2	13.8	15.4	17.1	19.5

UKRAINE

(US$ million, unless otherwise indicated)

	1970	1980	1990	1994	1995	1996	1997	1998	1999	2000
5. LONG-TERM DEBT										
DEBT OUTSTANDING (LDOD)	..	..	..	**4,855**	**6,664**	**6,832**	**7,642**	**9,797**	**10,820**	**9,646**
Public and publicly guaranteed	..	..	..	**4,810**	**6,581**	**6,648**	**7,015**	**8,966**	**9,581**	**8,139**
Official creditors	..	..	..	3,797	4,346	4,525	4,422	4,743	6,162	5,007
Multilateral	..	..	..	264	659	1,165	1,531	2,018	2,382	2,368
Concessional	..	..	..	0	0	0	0	0	0	0
Bilateral	..	..	..	3,533	3,687	3,360	2,892	2,725	3,780	2,639
Concessional	..	..	..	40	64	217	212	263	3,361	2,257
Private creditors	..	..	..	1,013	2,235	2,123	2,593	4,223	3,420	3,133
Bonds	..	..	..	0	1,200	1,120	1,120	2,644	2,329	2,377
Commercial banks	..	..	..	282	301	252	742	835	571	258
Other private	..	..	..	731	734	750	731	744	520	499
Private nonguaranteed	..	..	..	**45**	**84**	**184**	**627**	**830**	**1,239**	**1,507**
Bonds	..	..	..	0	0	0	0	0	0	0
Commercial banks and other	..	..	..	45	84	184	627	830	1,239	1,507
Memo:										
IBRD	..	..	..	102	491	859	1,111	1,542	1,954	1,991
IDA	..	..	..	0	0	0	0	0	0	0
DISBURSEMENTS	..	..	..	**578**	**801**	**1,074**	**1,490**	**3,251**	**1,436**	**1,377**
Public and publicly guaranteed	..	..	..	**484**	**732**	**954**	**1,222**	**2,631**	**578**	**190**
Official creditors	..	..	..	205	550	754	508	524	469	158
Multilateral	..	..	..	166	525	552	453	430	432	129
Concessional	..	..	..	0	0	0	0	0	0	0
Bilateral	..	..	..	39	25	202	56	94	37	29
Concessional	..	..	..	20	25	163	10	34	11	16
Private creditors	..	..	..	279	182	200	714	2,108	110	32
Bonds	..	..	..	0	0	0	0	1,422	0	0
Commercial banks	..	..	..	0	0	17	523	523	69	28
Other private	..	..	..	279	182	184	190	162	40	4
Private nonguaranteed	..	..	..	**94**	**69**	**120**	**268**	**620**	**857**	**1,187**
Bonds	..	..	..	0	0	0	0	0	0	0
Commercial banks and other	..	..	..	94	69	120	268	620	857	1,187
Memo:										
IBRD	..	..	..	102	401	406	306	385	422	113
IDA	..	..	..	0	0	0	0	0	0	0
PRINCIPAL REPAYMENTS	..	..	..	**233**	**636**	**791**	**689**	**1,347**	**1,571**	**2,103**
Public and publicly guaranteed	..	..	..	**172**	**595**	**723**	**638**	**931**	**802**	**1,257**
Official creditors	..	..	..	68	165	516	504	275	181	1,215
Multilateral	..	..	..	53	127	1	3	6	15	70
Concessional	..	..	..	0	0	0	0	0	0	0
Bilateral	..	..	..	15	38	515	502	269	167	1,145
Concessional	..	..	..	0	0	0	0	0	2	1,100
Private creditors	..	..	..	104	430	207	134	656	621	42
Bonds	..	..	..	0	200	80	0	35	107	33
Commercial banks	..	..	..	6	2	0	3	445	300	2
Other private	..	..	..	98	228	127	130	177	214	7
Private nonguaranteed	..	..	..	**60**	**40**	**68**	**52**	**417**	**769**	**845**
Bonds	..	..	..	0	0	0	0	0	0	0
Commercial banks and other	..	..	..	60	40	68	52	417	769	845
Memo:										
IBRD	..	..	..	0	0	0	0	0	2	25
IDA	..	..	..	0	0	0	0	0	0	0
NET FLOWS ON DEBT	..	..	..	**346**	**166**	**283**	**801**	**1,904**	**-136**	**-726**
Public and publicly guaranteed	..	..	..	**312**	**136**	**231**	**584**	**1,701**	**-224**	**-1,068**
Official creditors	..	..	..	138	385	238	4	249	288	-1,058
Multilateral	..	..	..	113	398	551	450	424	418	59
Concessional	..	..	..	0	0	0	0	0	0	0
Bilateral	..	..	..	25	-13	-314	-446	-175	-130	-1,117
Concessional	..	..	..	20	25	163	10	34	9	-1,084
Private creditors	..	..	..	175	-249	-6	580	1,451	-511	-10
Bonds	..	..	..	0	-200	-80	0	1,387	-107	-33
Commercial banks	..	..	..	-6	-2	17	520	79	-230	26
Other private	..	..	..	181	-46	57	60	-15	-174	-3
Private nonguaranteed	..	..	..	**33**	**29**	**52**	**216**	**204**	**88**	**342**
Bonds	..	..	..	0	0	0	0	0	0	0
Commercial banks and other	..	..	..	33	29	52	216	204	88	342
Memo:										
IBRD	..	..	..	102	401	406	306	385	420	88
IDA	..	..	..	0	0	0	0	0	0	0

UKRAINE

(US$ million, unless otherwise indicated)

	1970	1980	1990	1994	1995	1996	1997	1998	1999	2000
INTEREST PAYMENTS (LINT)	..	..	..	**88**	**447**	**374**	**527**	**421**	**545**	**573**
Public and publicly guaranteed	..	..	..	**83**	**440**	**352**	**463**	**371**	**481**	**502**
Official creditors	..	..	..	27	306	198	285	144	155	150
Multilateral	..	..	..	24	13	40	71	93	116	141
Concessional	..	..	..	0	0	0	0	0	0	0
Bilateral	..	..	..	3	293	159	214	50	38	9
Concessional	..	..	..	1	1	2	7	8	9	3
Private creditors	..	..	..	56	134	153	178	227	326	352
Bonds	..	..	..	0	87	96	99	104	262	344
Commercial banks	..	..	..	12	4	1	20	78	22	8
Other private	..	..	..	45	44	56	60	45	42	0
Private nonguaranteed	..	..	..	**5**	**7**	**22**	**64**	**50**	**65**	**71**
Bonds	..	..	..	0	0	0	0	0	0	0
Commercial banks and other	..	..	..	5	7	22	64	50	65	71
Memo:										
IBRD	..	..	..	0	8	32	59	68	94	118
IDA	..	..	..	0	0	0	0	0	0	0
NET TRANSFERS ON DEBT	..	..	..	**257**	**-282**	**-91**	**274**	**1,483**	**-681**	**-1,299**
Public and publicly guaranteed	..	..	..	**229**	**-304**	**-120**	**122**	**1,330**	**-704**	**-1,569**
Official creditors	..	..	..	111	79	39	-281	106	133	-1,207
Multilateral	..	..	..	89	384	512	379	331	301	-82
Concessional	..	..	..	0	0	0	0	0	0	0
Bilateral	..	..	..	22	-306	-472	-660	-225	-169	-1,125
Concessional	..	..	..	19	24	160	3	27	1	-1,087
Private creditors	..	..	..	119	-383	-160	402	1,224	-837	-362
Bonds	..	..	..	0	-287	-176	-99	1,284	-369	-377
Commercial banks	..	..	..	-18	-6	15	500	1	-253	18
Other private	..	..	..	136	-90	1	0	-60	-216	-3
Private nonguaranteed	..	..	..	**28**	**22**	**30**	**152**	**153**	**23**	**271**
Bonds	..	..	..	0	0	0	0	0	0	0
Commercial banks and other	..	..	..	28	22	30	152	153	23	271
Memo:										
IBRD	..	..	..	102	393	374	247	317	326	-30
IDA	..	..	..	0	0	0	0	0	0	0
DEBT SERVICE (LTDS)	..	..	..	**321**	**1,083**	**1,164**	**1,216**	**1,768**	**2,117**	**2,676**
Public and publicly guaranteed	..	..	..	**255**	**1,036**	**1,075**	**1,100**	**1,302**	**1,282**	**1,759**
Official creditors	..	..	..	95	472	714	789	418	336	1,365
Multilateral	..	..	..	77	141	40	73	99	131	211
Concessional	..	..	..	0	0	0	0	0	0	0
Bilateral	..	..	..	18	331	674	716	319	205	1,154
Concessional	..	..	..	1	1	2	7	8	10	1,102
Private creditors	..	..	..	161	564	360	312	884	946	394
Bonds	..	..	..	0	287	176	99	139	369	377
Commercial banks	..	..	..	18	6	1	23	523	322	10
Other private	..	..	..	143	272	183	190	222	256	7
Private nonguaranteed	..	..	..	**66**	**47**	**90**	**116**	**467**	**834**	**917**
Bonds	..	..	..	0	0	0	0	0	0	0
Commercial banks and other	..	..	..	66	47	90	116	467	834	917
Memo:										
IBRD	..	..	..	0	8	32	59	68	96	142
IDA	..	..	..	0	0	0	0	0	0	0
UNDISBURSED DEBT	..	..	..	**898**	**816**	**1,643**	**1,211**	**1,692**	**1,213**	**1,000**
Official creditors	..	..	..	574	520	1,421	1,025	1,521	987	818
Private creditors	..	..	..	324	295	222	186	170	226	182
Memorandum items										
Concessional LDOD	..	..	..	40	64	217	212	263	3,361	2,257
Variable rate LDOD	..	..	..	4,684	5,284	5,359	5,670	6,174	4,720	4,938
Public sector LDOD	..	..	..	4,810	6,581	6,631	6,990	8,934	9,557	8,115
Private sector LDOD	..	..	..	45	84	201	652	863	1,263	1,531
6. CURRENCY COMPOSITION OF LONG-TERM DEBT (PERCENT)										
Deutsche mark	..	..	..	17.1	13.9	11.4	8.6	17.0	12.9	5.5
French franc	..	..	..	0.1	0.4	0.5	0.5	0.5	0.4	0.5
Japanese yen	..	..	..	0.0	0.0	2.6	2.3	1.9	1.9	2.0
Pound sterling	..	..	..	0.0	0.0	0.0	0.0	0.0	0.0	0.0
Swiss franc	..	..	..	0.0	0.0	0.0	0.0	0.0	0.0	0.0
U.S.dollars	..	..	..	56.5	63.3	57.1	58.7	49.6	57.3	53.1
Multiple currency	..	..	..	21.4	19.3	23.5	24.3	20.0	18.3	21.3
Special drawing rights	..	..	..	0.0	0.0	0.0	0.0	0.0	0.0	0.0
All other currencies	..	..	..	4.9	3.1	4.9	5.6	11.0	9.2	17.6

UKRAINE

(US$ million, unless otherwise indicated)

	1970	1980	1990	1994	1995	1996	1997	1998	1999	2000
7. DEBT RESTRUCTURINGS										
Total amount rescheduled	..	..	..	723	2,535	0	0	82	3,074	2,185
Debt stock rescheduled	..	..	..	0	0	0	0	0	1,895	1,870
Principal rescheduled	..	..	..	0	969	0	0	82	0	302
Official	..	..	..	0	969	0	0	0	0	0
Private	..	..	..	0	0	0	0	82	0	302
Interest rescheduled	..	..	..	0	166	0	0	0	601	12
Official	..	..	..	0	166	0	0	0	601	0
Private	..	..	..	0	0	0	0	0	0	12
Debt forgiven	..	..	..	0	0	0	0	0	0	0
Memo: interest forgiven	..	..	..	0	0	0	0	0	0	0
Debt stock reduction	..	..	..	0	0	17	0	0	0	0
of which debt buyback	..	..	..	0	0	0	0	0	0	0
8. DEBT STOCK-FLOW RECONCILIATION										
Total change in debt stocks	..	..	..	1,781	2,793	1,109	1,595	1,938	870	-1,775
Net flows on debt	..	..	..	783	1,338	1,276	1,729	1,562	-243	-1,297
Net change in interest arrears	..	..	..	176	-170	6	2	10	25	105
Interest capitalized	..	..	..	0	166	0	0	0	601	12
Debt forgiveness or reduction	..	..	..	0	0	-17	0	0	0	0
Cross-currency valuation	..	..	..	65	70	-175	-354	238	-412	-369
Residual	..	..	..	757	1,391	20	219	128	900	-226
9. AVERAGE TERMS OF NEW COMMITMENTS										
ALL CREDITORS										
Interest (%)	..	..	..	7.1	5.2	6.2	5.5	9.1	4.8	6.2
Maturity (years)	..	..	..	13.8	12.1	14.7	4.1	7.8	7.2	13.8
Grace period (years)	..	..	..	4.5	4.2	4.9	1.6	3.0	4.2	5.3
Grant element (%)	..	..	..	14.2	23.7	20.8	8.6	5.8	22.3	16.1
Official creditors										
Interest (%)	..	..	..	7.7	4.7	6.3	5.7	5.6	6.1	6.2
Maturity (years)	..	..	..	15.6	13.4	15.8	12.3	16.9	5.4	13.8
Grace period (years)	..	..	..	5.1	4.8	5.3	3.3	4.3	2.1	5.3
Grant element (%)	..	..	..	13.3	27.2	21.8	19.6	22.5	10.4	16.1
Private creditors										
Interest (%)	..	..	..	5.0	6.5	5.6	5.5	11.0	3.4	0.0
Maturity (years)	..	..	..	7.3	7.7	6.3	2.3	2.9	9.2	0.0
Grace period (years)	..	..	..	2.3	2.5	1.6	1.2	2.4	6.3	0.0
Grant element (%)	..	..	..	17.5	12.1	13.0	6.2	-3.2	34.9	0.0
Memorandum items										
Commitments	..	..	..	893	673	1,872	838	3,216	377	25
Official creditors	..	..	..	695	519	1,671	150	1,118	193	25
Private creditors	..	..	..	197	155	201	688	2,099	184	0

10. CONTRACTUAL OBLIGATIONS ON OUTSTANDING LONG-TERM DEBT

	2001	2002	2003	2004	2005	2006	2007	2008	2009	2010
TOTAL										
Disbursements	429	252	121	69	51	34	24	17	3	1
Principal	1,422	1,047	1,129	996	989	930	642	391	380	315
Interest	619	521	443	349	271	192	123	105	84	65
Official creditors										
Disbursements	306	208	105	69	51	34	24	17	3	1
Principal	491	425	371	421	418	386	366	333	328	312
Interest	196	184	175	161	143	125	108	94	79	64
Bilateral creditors										
Disbursements	17	8	4	2	1	0	0	0	0	0
Principal	326	153	137	127	124	124	126	124	119	108
Interest	29	15	13	11	9	8	6	4	3	2
Multilateral creditors										
Disbursements	290	201	102	67	51	34	24	17	3	1
Principal	165	272	235	294	294	263	240	210	210	204
Interest	167	169	162	150	134	118	102	89	76	62
Private creditors										
Disbursements	123	44	15	0	0	0	0	0	0	0
Principal	932	622	758	575	572	543	276	57	52	3
Interest	423	337	268	188	128	66	16	12	5	1
Commercial banks										
Disbursements	66	28	11	0	0	0	0	0	0	0
Principal	42	27	23	18	18	38	38	37	37	3
Interest	13	13	12	10	9	8	6	4	3	1
Other private										
Disbursements	56	16	4	0	0	0	0	0	0	0
Principal	890	595	735	558	554	505	238	20	14	0
Interest	410	324	257	178	119	58	9	7	3	0

URUGUAY

(US$ million, unless otherwise indicated)

	1970	1980	1990	1994	1995	1996	1997	1998	1999	2000
1. SUMMARY DEBT DATA										
TOTAL DEBT STOCKS (EDT)	**363**	**1,660**	**4,415**	**5,075**	**5,318**	**5,899**	**6,710**	**7,600**	**7,501**	**8,196**
Long-term debt (LDOD)	**298**	**1,338**	**3,114**	**3,812**	**3,961**	**4,231**	**4,809**	**5,431**	**5,550**	**6,131**
Public and publicly guaranteed	269	1,127	3,045	3,750	3,833	4,097	4,586	5,142	5,110	5,597
Private nonguaranteed	29	211	69	62	127	135	223	289	440	534
Use of IMF credit	**18**	**0**	**101**	**30**	**21**	**9**	**0**	**161**	**157**	**149**
Short-term debt	**47**	**322**	**1,201**	**1,233**	**1,336**	**1,659**	**1,901**	**2,009**	**1,794**	**1,917**
of which interest arrears on LDOD	0	0	0	0	0	0	0	0	0	0
Official creditors	0	0	0	0	0	0	0	0	0	0
Private creditors	0	0	0	0	0	0	0	0	0	0
Memo: principal arrears on LDOD	0	0	0	0	0	0	0	0	0	0
Official creditors	0	0	0	0	0	0	0	0	0	0
Private creditors	0	0	0	0	0	0	0	0	0	0
Memo: export credits	0	0	183	249	291	282	280	136	145	101
TOTAL DEBT FLOWS										
Disbursements	**91**	**356**	**358**	**501**	**661**	**659**	**1,005**	**1,370**	**666**	**1,089**
Long-term debt	50	356	346	501	661	659	1,005	1,215	666	1,089
IMF purchases	40	0	12	0	0	0	0	155	0	0
Principal repayments	**80**	**130**	**559**	**232**	**484**	**298**	**290**	**689**	**574**	**676**
Long-term debt	51	130	434	221	474	286	282	689	574	676
IMF repurchases	28	0	124	11	10	12	8	0	0	0
Net flows on debt	**11**	**342**	**-134**	**128**	**281**	**684**	**957**	**790**	**-123**	**535**
of which short-term debt	0	116	66	-141	104	322	242	108	-215	123
Interest payments (INT)	**17**	**169**	**428**	**304**	**379**	**367**	**453**	**448**	**491**	**637**
Long-term debt	17	121	319	237	298	272	346	334	379	506
IMF charges	0	0	16	2	2	1	0	0	6	8
Short-term debt	0	48	93	65	80	94	107	114	106	123
Net transfers on debt	**-6**	**173**	**-563**	**-176**	**-98**	**317**	**504**	**342**	**-614**	**-102**
Total debt service paid (TDS)	**97**	**299**	**987**	**536**	**862**	**665**	**744**	**1,136**	**1,065**	**1,313**
Long-term debt	69	251	753	458	771	558	629	1,023	953	1,183
IMF repurchases and charges	28	0	141	13	11	12	8	0	6	8
Short-term debt (interest only)	0	48	93	65	80	94	107	114	106	123
2. AGGREGATE NET RESOURCE FLOWS AND NET TRANSFERS (LONG-TERM)										
NET RESOURCE FLOWS	**0**	**516**	**-78**	**469**	**363**	**525**	**859**	**700**	**335**	**719**
Net flow of long-term debt (ex. IMF)	-1	226	-89	280	187	373	723	527	92	412
Foreign direct investment (net)	0	290	0	155	157	137	126	164	235	298
Portfolio equity flows	0	0	0	25	4	5	2	0	0	0
Grants (excluding technical coop.)	1	0	11	9	15	10	8	9	9	9
Memo: technical coop. grants	3	9	25	32	34	28	26	22	20	15
official net resource flows	10	37	114	125	19	59	260	202	260	145
private net resource flows	-10	479	-192	344	344	466	599	498	75	574
NET TRANSFERS	**-19**	**395**	**-396**	**232**	**65**	**253**	**513**	**365**	**-44**	**212**
Interest on long-term debt	17	121	319	237	298	272	346	334	379	506
Profit remittances on FDI	2	0	0	0	0	0	0	0	0	0
Memo: official net transfers	5	15	54	28	-105	-35	164	90	130	-2
private net transfers	-25	380	-450	203	170	287	349	275	-174	214
3. MAJOR ECONOMIC AGGREGATES										
Gross national income (GNI)	2,359	9,752	8,949	16,072	18,059	19,985	21,136	21,800	20,358	19,383
Exports of goods & services (XGS)	..	1,594	2,417	3,531	3,911	4,308	4,765	4,756	4,288	4,494
of which workers remittances	..	0	0	0	0	0	0	..	..	..
Imports of goods & services (MGS)	..	2,312	2,239	4,010	4,200	4,624	5,126	5,291	4,869	5,153
International reserves (RES)	186	2,401	1,446	1,622	1,813	1,892	2,067	2,587	2,604	2,776
Current account balance	..	-709	186	-438	-213	-233	-287	-476	-508	-593
4. DEBT INDICATORS										
EDT / XGS (%)	..	104.2	182.7	143.7	136.0	136.9	140.8	159.8	174.9	182.4
EDT / GNI (%)	15.4	17.0	49.3	31.6	29.5	29.5	31.8	34.9	36.8	42.3
TDS / XGS (%)	..	18.8	40.8	15.2	22.1	15.4	15.6	23.9	24.8	29.2
INT / XGS (%)	..	10.6	17.7	8.6	9.7	8.5	9.5	9.4	11.4	14.2
INT / GNI (%)	0.7	1.7	4.8	1.9	2.1	1.8	2.1	2.1	2.4	3.3
RES / EDT (%)	51.3	144.7	32.7	32.0	34.1	32.1	30.8	34.0	34.7	33.9
RES / MGS (months)	..	12.5	7.8	4.9	5.2	4.9	4.8	5.9	6.4	6.5
Short-term / EDT (%)	13.0	19.4	27.2	24.3	25.1	28.1	28.3	26.4	23.9	23.4
Concessional / EDT (%)	15.6	5.1	2.3	4.1	4.2	3.6	3.5	3.2	3.3	2.6
Multilateral / EDT (%)	17.2	11.0	15.8	24.0	23.7	20.4	18.9	19.5	23.7	23.4

URUGUAY

(US$ million, unless otherwise indicated)

	1970	1980	1990	1994	1995	1996	1997	1998	1999	2000
5. LONG-TERM DEBT										
DEBT OUTSTANDING (LDOD)	**298**	**1,338**	**3,114**	**3,812**	**3,961**	**4,231**	**4,809**	**5,431**	**5,550**	**6,131**
Public and publicly guaranteed	**269**	**1,127**	**3,045**	**3,750**	**3,833**	**4,097**	**4,586**	**5,142**	**5,110**	**5,597**
Official creditors	126	333	895	1,535	1,588	1,462	1,621	1,880	2,152	2,231
Multilateral	62	182	699	1,217	1,259	1,205	1,268	1,481	1,780	1,915
Concessional	2	20	22	30	28	26	24	23	30	19
Bilateral	64	151	196	318	329	257	353	399	372	315
Concessional	55	64	78	178	197	187	212	220	216	193
Private creditors	143	794	2,150	2,215	2,245	2,635	2,965	3,262	2,958	3,366
Bonds	45	263	567	1,966	1,963	2,109	2,429	2,722	2,467	2,774
Commercial banks	82	502	1,576	243	275	520	529	535	488	579
Other private	16	30	8	6	8	6	7	5	3	13
Private nonguaranteed	**29**	**211**	**69**	**62**	**127**	**135**	**223**	**289**	**440**	**534**
Bonds	0	0	0	40	110	104	196	260	351	300
Commercial banks and other	29	211	69	22	18	30	28	29	89	234
Memo:										
IBRD	49	72	359	539	513	446	393	473	476	552
IDA	0	0	0	0	0	0	0	0	0	0
DISBURSEMENTS	**50**	**356**	**346**	**501**	**661**	**659**	**1,005**	**1,215**	**666**	**1,089**
Public and publicly guaranteed	**37**	**293**	**346**	**501**	**591**	**647**	**905**	**1,105**	**496**	**927**
Official creditors	20	58	174	215	128	167	376	348	438	298
Multilateral	7	25	90	148	103	142	258	281	421	297
Concessional	1	4	3	1	0	0	0	0	0	0
Bilateral	13	34	85	68	25	25	118	67	18	1
Concessional	6	3	3	54	25	8	39	13	4	1
Private creditors	18	235	172	286	463	480	529	757	58	629
Bonds	7	0	164	271	348	180	471	694	37	616
Commercial banks	10	230	4	15	111	299	54	62	21	1
Other private	1	4	4	0	4	2	4	0	1	12
Private nonguaranteed	**13**	**63**	**0**	**0**	**70**	**13**	**100**	**110**	**170**	**162**
Bonds	0	0	0	0	70	0	100	100	100	0
Commercial banks and other	13	63	0	0	0	13	0	10	70	162
Memo:										
IBRD	2	4	51	37	32	39	50	130	66	134
IDA	0	0	0	0	0	0	0	0	0	0
PRINCIPAL REPAYMENTS	**51**	**130**	**434**	**221**	**474**	**286**	**282**	**689**	**574**	**676**
Public and publicly guaranteed	**47**	**93**	**398**	**216**	**469**	**286**	**280**	**639**	**565**	**612**
Official creditors	11	22	71	99	124	118	124	156	186	162
Multilateral	8	9	61	93	117	106	116	117	130	120
Concessional	0	0	1	2	2	2	2	2	2	2
Bilateral	3	12	10	7	7	12	8	38	56	42
Concessional	3	3	2	1	3	8	6	13	12	15
Private creditors	36	72	328	117	345	169	156	484	379	451
Bonds	9	6	180	70	273	121	122	418	322	285
Commercial banks	21	59	143	45	69	45	31	63	54	165
Other private	6	6	5	2	3	3	3	3	2	2
Private nonguaranteed	**4**	**37**	**36**	**5**	**5**	**0**	**3**	**49**	**9**	**64**
Bonds	0	0	0	0	0	0	0	40	0	47
Commercial banks and other	4	37	36	5	5	0	3	9	9	17
Memo:										
IBRD	6	6	43	56	78	70	68	64	63	58
IDA	0	0	0	0	0	0	0	0	0	0
NET FLOWS ON DEBT	**-1**	**226**	**-89**	**280**	**187**	**373**	**723**	**527**	**92**	**412**
Public and publicly guaranteed	**-10**	**200**	**-53**	**285**	**122**	**361**	**625**	**466**	**-69**	**314**
Official creditors	9	37	104	116	4	49	252	193	252	136
Multilateral	-1	15	29	55	-14	36	142	164	291	178
Concessional	1	3	2	-1	-2	-2	-2	-2	-2	-2
Bilateral	9	21	75	61	18	14	110	29	-39	-41
Concessional	2	0	1	52	23	0	33	0	-8	-14
Private creditors	-19	163	-156	169	118	311	373	273	-320	178
Bonds	-2	-6	-16	201	74	59	349	276	-286	331
Commercial banks	-11	171	-139	-30	42	254	23	-1	-33	-163
Other private	-5	-2	-1	-2	2	-1	1	-3	-2	11
Private nonguaranteed	**9**	**26**	**-36**	**-5**	**65**	**13**	**97**	**61**	**160**	**98**
Bonds	0	0	0	0	70	0	100	60	100	-47
Commercial banks and other	9	26	-36	-5	-5	13	-3	1	60	145
Memo:										
IBRD	-4	-2	8	-19	-46	-31	-18	65	3	76
IDA	0	0	0	0	0	0	0	0	0	0

URUGUAY

(US$ million, unless otherwise indicated)

	1970	1980	1990	1994	1995	1996	1997	1998	1999	2000
INTEREST PAYMENTS (LINT)	**17**	**121**	**319**	**237**	**298**	**272**	**346**	**334**	**379**	**506**
Public and publicly guaranteed	**16**	**105**	**312**	**232**	**293**	**264**	**337**	**318**	**353**	**429**
Official creditors	4	23	61	96	124	94	96	112	130	147
Multilateral	3	16	54	85	91	86	85	96	115	134
Concessional	0	0	1	1	1	1	1	1	0	0
Bilateral	1	7	7	11	33	7	11	16	16	13
Concessional	1	2	2	3	25	4	4	3	4	4
Private creditors	12	82	252	136	169	170	240	206	223	283
Bonds	3	30	61	118	151	144	192	163	183	182
Commercial banks	7	50	190	17	18	26	48	43	39	101
Other private	1	2	1	0	0	1	1	0	0	1
Private nonguaranteed	**2**	**17**	**6**	**5**	**5**	**9**	**10**	**17**	**26**	**77**
Bonds	0	0	0	3	3	9	8	15	21	30
Commercial banks and other	2	17	6	2	1	0	2	2	5	48
Memo:										
IBRD	2	7	28	39	40	33	28	29	33	42
IDA	0	0	0	0	0	0	0	0	0	0
NET TRANSFERS ON DEBT	**-19**	**105**	**-407**	**43**	**-110**	**101**	**376**	**192**	**-287**	**-94**
Public and publicly guaranteed	**-26**	**95**	**-365**	**53**	**-171**	**97**	**289**	**148**	**-421**	**-115**
Official creditors	4	14	43	20	-120	-44	156	81	122	-11
Multilateral	-4	0	-25	-30	-105	-51	57	68	176	44
Concessional	1	3	1	-2	-2	-2	-2	-2	-2	-2
Bilateral	8	14	68	50	-15	6	99	13	-55	-54
Concessional	1	-2	-1	49	-2	-4	29	-4	-11	-18
Private creditors	-30	81	-408	33	-51	141	133	67	-543	-104
Bonds	-5	-36	-77	82	-77	-85	157	113	-469	149
Commercial banks	-18	121	-329	-47	24	228	-24	-43	-72	-264
Other private	-6	-4	-2	-2	1	-2	1	-3	-2	10
Private nonguaranteed	**7**	**10**	**-42**	**-10**	**61**	**4**	**88**	**45**	**134**	**21**
Bonds	0	0	0	-3	67	-9	92	45	79	-77
Commercial banks and other	7	10	-42	-6	-6	13	-4	-1	55	97
Memo:										
IBRD	-6	-9	-19	-58	-86	-64	-45	36	-30	35
IDA	0	0	0	0	0	0	0	0	0	0
DEBT SERVICE (LTDS)	**69**	**251**	**753**	**458**	**771**	**558**	**629**	**1,023**	**953**	**1,183**
Public and publicly guaranteed	**63**	**198**	**711**	**449**	**762**	**550**	**616**	**957**	**918**	**1,042**
Official creditors	16	44	132	195	248	211	220	267	317	308
Multilateral	11	25	115	178	208	192	202	213	244	253
Concessional	0	1	1	2	2	2	2	2	2	2
Bilateral	5	19	17	17	40	19	19	54	72	55
Concessional	4	5	4	5	27	12	10	17	16	19
Private creditors	48	153	579	253	514	339	396	690	601	733
Bonds	12	36	241	189	424	265	314	581	505	466
Commercial banks	28	109	333	62	87	71	78	106	93	265
Other private	8	8	5	2	3	3	4	3	3	2
Private nonguaranteed	**6**	**54**	**42**	**10**	**9**	**9**	**12**	**66**	**36**	**141**
Bonds	0	0	0	3	3	9	8	55	21	77
Commercial banks and other	6	54	42	6	6	0	4	11	14	65
Memo:										
IBRD	9	13	70	95	117	103	96	94	96	100
IDA	0	0	0	0	0	0	0	0	0	0
UNDISBURSED DEBT	**87**	**519**	**736**	**786**	**656**	**1,002**	**1,273**	**1,167**	**791**	**564**
Official creditors	79	326	676	622	521	824	1,133	1,145	787	562
Private creditors	8	193	61	164	135	178	140	23	4	2
Memorandum items										
Concessional LDOD	57	84	100	207	224	213	236	243	246	212
Variable rate LDOD	31	474	2,286	2,051	2,016	2,196	2,448	2,540	2,846	3,149
Public sector LDOD	269	1,123	3,042	3,750	3,831	4,095	4,582	5,140	5,109	5,597
Private sector LDOD	29	215	72	62	130	137	227	290	441	534

6. CURRENCY COMPOSITION OF LONG-TERM DEBT (PERCENT)

	1970	1980	1990	1994	1995	1996	1997	1998	1999	2000
Deutsche mark	2.3	0.3	1.7	0.2	6.5	5.6	4.4	4.3	3.7	0.3
French franc	0.0	3.6	0.3	0.7	0.7	0.7	0.5	0.5	0.4	0.4
Japanese yen	0.0	1.1	5.1	4.5	6.4	4.0	5.7	4.4	4.6	3.4
Pound sterling	4.9	0.2	3.6	2.4	1.9	2.1	1.8	1.5	1.4	1.0
Swiss franc	8.0	0.0	1.5	0.0	0.0	0.0	0.0	0.0	0.0	0.0
U.S.dollars	62.9	77.9	64.9	61.2	53.8	61.3	65.4	77.2	76.8	80.9
Multiple currency	20.0	14.7	22.5	31.0	30.7	26.2	22.1	12.1	13.1	10.5
Special drawing rights	0.0	0.0	0.0	0.0	0.0	0.0	0.0	0.0	0.0	0.0
All other currencies	1.9	2.2	0.4	0.0	0.0	0.1	0.1	0.0	0.0	3.5

URUGUAY

(US$ million, unless otherwise indicated)

	1970	1980	1990	1994	1995	1996	1997	1998	1999	2000
7. DEBT RESTRUCTURINGS										
Total amount rescheduled	..	..	0	0	0	0	0	0	0	0
Debt stock rescheduled	..	..	0	0	0	0	0	0	0	0
Principal rescheduled	..	..	0	0	0	0	0	0	0	0
Official	..	..	0	0	0	0	0	0	0	0
Private	..	..	0	0	0	0	0	0	0	0
Interest rescheduled	..	..	0	0	0	0	0	0	0	0
Official	..	..	0	0	0	0	0	0	0	0
Private	..	..	0	0	0	0	0	0	0	0
Debt forgiven	..	..	0	0	0	0	0	0	0	0
Memo: interest forgiven	..	..	0	0	0	0	0	0	0	0
Debt stock reduction	..	..	0	0	0	0	0	0	96	0
of which debt buyback	..	..	0	0	0	0	0	0	85	0
8. DEBT STOCK-FLOW RECONCILIATION										
Total change in debt stocks	..	..	-34	227	243	581	812	890	-100	696
Net flows on debt	11	342	-134	128	281	684	957	790	-123	535
Net change in interest arrears	..	..	0	0	0	0	0	0	0	0
Interest capitalized	..	..	0	0	0	0	0	0	0	0
Debt forgiveness or reduction	..	..	0	0	0	0	0	0	-11	0
Cross-currency valuation	..	..	77	-10	32	-142	-144	76	-12	-80
Residual	..	..	24	109	-71	39	-1	25	47	241
9. AVERAGE TERMS OF NEW COMMITMENTS										
ALL CREDITORS										
Interest (%)	7.9	10.1	9.1	6.0	6.8	7.3	6.8	7.2	6.3	7.9
Maturity (years)	11.9	15.3	12.9	11.3	7.7	15.6	19.3	11.9	26.0	9.8
Grace period (years)	3.0	5.9	2.4	3.7	3.3	4.9	10.2	6.5	13.1	7.3
Grant element (%)	10.4	1.0	5.1	19.1	12.9	14.8	18.8	15.6	29.0	10.6
Official creditors										
Interest (%)	7.1	7.9	7.8	4.5	3.9	7.2	6.8	7.0	7.0	7.3
Maturity (years)	16.2	20.6	20.1	18.1	14.9	21.9	17.4	17.6	24.8	14.7
Grace period (years)	3.8	8.0	5.0	4.6	5.5	5.1	4.0	4.4	5.5	5.2
Grant element (%)	15.4	13.5	12.9	33.8	36.4	18.1	17.9	17.5	20.6	15.2
Private creditors										
Interest (%)	9.5	13.0	9.8	6.8	7.0	7.4	6.8	7.4	5.1	7.9
Maturity (years)	3.9	8.4	8.7	7.5	7.3	9.9	22.2	8.1	28.5	9.2
Grace period (years)	1.6	3.2	1.0	3.2	3.2	4.7	19.4	8.0	27.9	7.6
Grant element (%)	1.1	-15.4	0.6	10.9	11.4	11.9	20.1	14.2	45.3	10.0
Memorandum items										
Commitments	71	347	339	545	486	957	1,221	1,075	118	707
Official creditors	46	197	124	196	29	449	730	436	78	81
Private creditors	25	150	215	350	457	508	491	639	40	626

10. CONTRACTUAL OBLIGATIONS ON OUTSTANDING LONG-TERM DEBT

	2001	2002	2003	2004	2005	2006	2007	2008	2009	2010
TOTAL										
Disbursements	200	156	87	60	33	20	7	2	0	0
Principal	570	571	677	427	563	480	645	567	278	448
Interest	431	410	380	336	309	272	223	179	149	121
Official creditors										
Disbursements	198	155	87	60	33	20	7	2	0	0
Principal	195	220	240	222	205	195	185	180	170	160
Interest	161	157	147	135	122	110	97	85	73	62
Bilateral creditors										
Disbursements	0	0	0	0	0	0	0	0	0	0
Principal	40	41	41	25	24	19	19	19	16	13
Interest	11	9	7	6	5	4	4	3	2	2
Multilateral creditors										
Disbursements	198	155	87	60	33	20	7	2	0	0
Principal	155	180	200	197	182	177	167	162	155	147
Interest	150	148	140	129	117	106	94	82	71	60
Private creditors										
Disbursements	2	1	0	0	0	0	0	0	0	0
Principal	376	351	436	205	357	285	459	387	108	288
Interest	270	253	233	201	187	162	126	94	76	59
Commercial banks										
Disbursements	0	0	0	0	0	0	0	0	0	0
Principal	105	102	99	99	48	113	4	4	1	1
Interest	41	34	26	19	12	8	1	1	0	0
Other private										
Disbursements	2	1	0	0	0	0	0	0	0	0
Principal	271	250	337	106	309	172	455	384	107	288
Interest	229	219	207	182	175	154	125	93	75	59

UZBEKISTAN

(US$ million, unless otherwise indicated)

	1970	1980	1990	1994	1995	1996	1997	1998	1999	2000
1. SUMMARY DEBT DATA										
TOTAL DEBT STOCKS (EDT)	..	..	..	**1,244**	**1,787**	**2,384**	**2,765**	**3,208**	**4,685**	**4,340**
Long-term debt (LDOD)	..	..	..	**953**	**1,418**	**2,055**	**2,124**	**2,829**	**3,857**	**3,931**
Public and publicly guaranteed	..	..	..	953	1,418	1,996	2,033	2,591	3,445	3,578
Private nonguaranteed	..	..	..	0	0	59	91	238	412	354
Use of IMF credit	..	..	..	**0**	**158**	**238**	**223**	**233**	**202**	**127**
Short-term debt	..	..	..	**291**	**212**	**92**	**419**	**147**	**626**	**282**
of which interest arrears on LDOD	..	..	..	0	0	0	0	3	3	3
Official creditors	..	..	..	0	0	0	0	0	0	0
Private creditors	..	..	..	0	0	0	0	3	3	3
Memo: principal arrears on LDOD	..	..	..	0	0	0	0	4	20	17
Official creditors	..	..	..	0	0	0	0	0	0	0
Private creditors	..	..	..	0	0	0	0	4	20	17
Memo: export credits	..	..	..	67	366	488	960	769	691	799
TOTAL DEBT FLOWS										
Disbursements	..	..	..	**107**	**782**	**879**	**478**	**823**	**1,399**	**723**
Long-term debt	..	..	..	107	621	793	478	823	1,399	723
IMF purchases	..	..	..	0	161	86	0	0	0	0
Principal repayments	..	..	..	**97**	**149**	**188**	**321**	**224**	**347**	**619**
Long-term debt	..	..	..	97	149	188	321	224	322	554
IMF repurchases	..	..	..	0	0	0	0	0	25	65
Net flows on debt	..	..	..	**210**	**554**	**570**	**484**	**324**	**1,532**	**-240**
of which short-term debt	..	..	..	199	-79	-120	328	-275	479	-344
Interest payments (INT)	..	..	..	**41**	**95**	**104**	**187**	**145**	**201**	**280**
Long-term debt	..	..	..	35	79	92	163	129	172	248
IMF charges	..	..	..	0	3	7	10	11	9	9
Short-term debt	..	..	..	6	13	4	14	6	20	23
Net transfers on debt	..	..	..	**168**	**459**	**467**	**297**	**179**	**1,331**	**-520**
Total debt service paid (TDS)	..	..	..	**138**	**243**	**291**	**508**	**369**	**548**	**899**
Long-term debt	..	..	..	132	228	280	484	353	494	802
IMF repurchases and charges	..	..	..	0	3	7	10	11	34	74
Short-term debt (interest only)	..	..	..	6	13	4	14	6	20	23
2. AGGREGATE NET RESOURCE FLOWS AND NET TRANSFERS (LONG-TERM)										
NET RESOURCE FLOWS	..	..	..	**78**	**600**	**688**	**471**	**765**	**1,224**	**303**
Net flow of long-term debt (ex. IMF)	..	..	..	11	472	605	157	599	1,078	169
Foreign direct investment (net)	..	..	..	50	115	55	285	140	121	100
Portfolio equity flows	..	..	..	0	0	0	0	0	0	0
Grants (excluding technical coop.)	..	..	..	18	13	28	29	25	25	34
Memo: technical coop. grants	..	..	..	10	28	36	32	36	46	39
official net resource flows	..	..	..	-22	293	257	62	234	404	284
private net resource flows	..	..	..	101	308	431	409	531	820	18
NET TRANSFERS	..	..	..	**43**	**521**	**595**	**308**	**635**	**1,052**	**54**
Interest on long-term debt	..	..	..	35	79	92	163	129	172	248
Profit remittances on FDI	..	..	..	0	0	0	0	0	0	0
Memo: official net transfers	..	..	..	-49	241	202	-42	168	336	218
private net transfers	..	..	..	92	280	393	350	467	716	-163
3. MAJOR ECONOMIC AGGREGATES										
Gross national income (GNI)	..	..	..	..	..	..	..	..	..	..
Exports of goods & services (XGS)	..	..	..	..	3,801	3,897	3,999	3,414	3,131	3,413
of which workers remittances	..	..	..	..	0	0	0	0	0	0
Imports of goods & services (MGS)	..	..	..	..	3,745	4,767	4,424	3,417	3,144	2,962
International reserves (RES)	..	..	..	1,330	1,867	1,901	1,167	1,168	1,242	1,273
Current account balance	..	..	..	120	-21	-980	-583	-103	-164	184
4. DEBT INDICATORS										
EDT / XGS (%)	..	..	..	..	47.0	61.2	69.2	94.0	149.6	127.2
EDT / GNI (%)	..	..	..	..	..	..	..	..	..	..
TDS / XGS (%)	..	..	..	..	6.4	7.5	12.7	10.8	17.5	26.3
INT / XGS (%)	..	..	..	..	2.5	2.7	4.7	4.3	6.4	8.2
INT / GNI (%)	..	..	..	..	..	..	..	..	..	..
RES / EDT (%)	..	..	..	106.9	104.5	79.8	42.2	36.4	26.5	29.3
RES / MGS (months)	..	..	..	..	6.0	4.8	3.2	4.1	4.7	5.2
Short-term / EDT (%)	..	..	..	23.4	11.9	3.8	15.2	4.6	13.4	6.5
Concessional / EDT (%)	..	..	..	11.5	10.5	25.8	7.4	12.1	15.5	19.9
Multilateral / EDT (%)	..	..	..	0.4	13.8	11.5	7.6	8.5	8.2	10.5

UZBEKISTAN

(US$ million, unless otherwise indicated)

	1970	1980	1990	1994	1995	1996	1997	1998	1999	2000
5. LONG-TERM DEBT										
DEBT OUTSTANDING (LDOD)	..	..	..	**953**	**1,418**	**2,055**	**2,124**	**2,829**	**3,857**	**3,931**
Public and publicly guaranteed	..	..	..	**953**	**1,418**	**1,996**	**2,033**	**2,591**	**3,445**	**3,578**
Official creditors	..	..	..	751	1,023	1,215	1,182	1,450	1,871	2,011
Multilateral	..	..	..	5	246	275	209	272	382	455
Concessional	..	..	..	0	0	0	0	1	1	2
Bilateral	..	..	..	746	777	941	973	1,178	1,489	1,556
Concessional	..	..	..	143	188	615	206	388	725	862
Private creditors	..	..	..	202	395	780	851	1,141	1,574	1,566
Bonds	..	..	..	0	0	0	0	0	0	0
Commercial banks	..	..	..	0	0	96	267	375	610	711
Other private	..	..	..	202	395	684	584	766	964	856
Private nonguaranteed	..	..	..	**0**	**0**	**59**	**91**	**238**	**412**	**354**
Bonds	..	..	..	0	0	0	0	0	0	0
Commercial banks and other	..	..	..	0	0	59	91	238	412	354
Memo:										
IBRD	..	..	..	1	157	155	155	177	203	217
IDA	..	..	..	0	0	0	0	0	0	0
DISBURSEMENTS	..	..	..	**107**	**621**	**793**	**478**	**823**	**1,399**	**723**
Public and publicly guaranteed	..	..	..	**107**	**621**	**793**	**441**	**682**	**1,154**	**690**
Official creditors	..	..	..	43	399	369	191	289	466	393
Multilateral	..	..	..	5	246	47	21	56	115	120
Concessional	..	..	..	0	0	0	0	1	0	1
Bilateral	..	..	..	37	154	322	170	234	352	273
Concessional	..	..	..	0	46	79	116	153	291	252
Private creditors	..	..	..	65	222	424	250	392	687	298
Bonds	..	..	..	0	0	0	0	0	0	0
Commercial banks	..	..	..	0	0	96	185	131	302	182
Other private	..	..	..	65	222	327	65	261	385	116
Private nonguaranteed	..	..	..	**0**	**0**	**0**	**37**	**142**	**246**	**33**
Bonds	..	..	..	0	0	0	0	0	0	0
Commercial banks and other	..	..	..	0	0	0	37	142	246	33
Memo:										
IBRD	..	..	..	1	162	9	13	13	28	31
IDA	..	..	..	0	0	0	0	0	0	0
PRINCIPAL REPAYMENTS	..	..	..	**97**	**149**	**188**	**321**	**224**	**322**	**554**
Public and publicly guaranteed	..	..	..	**97**	**149**	**188**	**316**	**200**	**300**	**418**
Official creditors	..	..	..	83	120	140	159	81	87	142
Multilateral	..	..	..	0	0	3	67	2	3	35
Concessional	..	..	..	0	0	0	0	0	0	0
Bilateral	..	..	..	83	120	137	92	79	84	107
Concessional	..	..	..	0	0	3	5	8	12	26
Private creditors	..	..	..	14	29	48	158	119	212	276
Bonds	..	..	..	0	0	0	0	0	0	0
Commercial banks	..	..	..	0	0	0	13	28	54	73
Other private	..	..	..	14	29	48	145	91	159	203
Private nonguaranteed	..	..	..	**0**	**0**	**0**	**4**	**24**	**22**	**136**
Bonds	..	..	..	0	0	0	0	0	0	0
Commercial banks and other	..	..	..	0	0	0	4	24	22	136
Memo:										
IBRD	..	..	..	0	0	0	0	0	1	5
IDA	..	..	..	0	0	0	0	0	0	0
NET FLOWS ON DEBT	..	..	..	**11**	**472**	**605**	**157**	**599**	**1,078**	**169**
Public and publicly guaranteed	..	..	..	**11**	**472**	**605**	**125**	**482**	**854**	**273**
Official creditors	..	..	..	-40	280	229	33	208	379	251
Multilateral	..	..	..	5	246	44	-46	54	112	85
Concessional	..	..	..	0	0	0	0	1	0	1
Bilateral	..	..	..	-45	34	185	78	155	267	166
Concessional	..	..	..	0	46	76	111	145	279	226
Private creditors	..	..	..	51	193	376	92	274	475	22
Bonds	..	..	..	0	0	0	0	0	0	0
Commercial banks	..	..	..	0	0	96	172	104	249	109
Other private	..	..	..	51	193	279	-80	170	227	-87
Private nonguaranteed	..	..	..	**0**	**0**	**0**	**32**	**118**	**223**	**-104**
Bonds	..	..	..	0	0	0	0	0	0	0
Commercial banks and other	..	..	..	0	0	0	32	118	223	-104
Memo:										
IBRD	..	..	..	1	162	9	13	13	27	27
IDA	..	..	..	0	0	0	0	0	0	0

UZBEKISTAN

(US$ million, unless otherwise indicated)

	1970	1980	1990	1994	1995	1996	1997	1998	1999	2000
INTEREST PAYMENTS (LINT)	..	..	..	**35**	**79**	**92**	**163**	**129**	**172**	**248**
Public and publicly guaranteed	..	..	..	**35**	**79**	**92**	**158**	**125**	**157**	**226**
Official creditors	..	..	..	26	52	55	103	66	68	67
Multilateral	..	..	..	0	4	16	16	14	18	25
Concessional	..	..	..	0	0	0	0	0	0	0
Bilateral	..	..	..	26	47	39	87	51	51	42
Concessional	..	..	..	0	0	14	55	6	16	24
Private creditors	..	..	..	9	28	37	55	59	89	160
Bonds	..	..	..	0	0	0	0	0	0	0
Commercial banks	..	..	..	0	0	0	12	17	30	45
Other private	..	..	..	9	28	37	43	42	59	115
Private nonguaranteed	..	..	..	**0**	**0**	**0**	**5**	**5**	**15**	**22**
Bonds	..	..	..	0	0	0	0	0	0	0
Commercial banks and other	..	..	..	0	0	0	5	5	15	22
Memo:										
IBRD	..	..	..	0	2	10	10	10	11	12
IDA	..	..	..	0	0	0	0	0	0	0
NET TRANSFERS ON DEBT	..	..	..	**-25**	**393**	**513**	**-6**	**470**	**905**	**-79**
Public and publicly guaranteed	..	..	..	**-25**	**393**	**513**	**-34**	**357**	**697**	**46**
Official creditors	..	..	..	-66	228	174	-71	143	311	184
Multilateral	..	..	..	5	242	28	-62	39	94	60
Concessional	..	..	..	0	0	0	0	1	0	1
Bilateral	..	..	..	-71	-13	147	-9	104	217	124
Concessional	..	..	..	0	46	63	55	140	263	202
Private creditors	..	..	..	42	165	338	37	215	386	-138
Bonds	..	..	..	0	0	0	0	0	0	0
Commercial banks	..	..	..	0	0	96	161	87	219	64
Other private	..	..	..	42	165	242	-123	128	168	-202
Private nonguaranteed	..	..	..	**0**	**0**	**0**	**28**	**113**	**208**	**-126**
Bonds	..	..	..	0	0	0	0	0	0	0
Commercial banks and other	..	..	..	0	0	0	28	113	208	-126
Memo:										
IBRD	..	..	..	1	161	-1	3	3	16	15
IDA	..	..	..	0	0	0	0	0	0	0
DEBT SERVICE (LTDS)	..	..	..	**132**	**228**	**280**	**484**	**353**	**494**	**802**
Public and publicly guaranteed	..	..	..	**132**	**228**	**280**	**475**	**324**	**456**	**644**
Official creditors	..	..	..	109	171	195	262	147	156	209
Multilateral	..	..	..	0	4	19	83	16	21	60
Concessional	..	..	..	0	0	0	0	0	0	0
Bilateral	..	..	..	109	167	176	179	130	135	148
Concessional	..	..	..	0	0	16	60	14	29	50
Private creditors	..	..	..	23	57	85	213	178	301	436
Bonds	..	..	..	0	0	0	0	0	0	0
Commercial banks	..	..	..	0	0	0	24	44	84	118
Other private	..	..	..	23	57	85	188	133	217	318
Private nonguaranteed	..	..	..	**0**	**0**	**0**	**9**	**29**	**38**	**158**
Bonds	..	..	..	0	0	0	0	0	0	0
Commercial banks and other	..	..	..	0	0	0	9	29	38	158
Memo:										
IBRD	..	..	..	0	2	10	10	10	12	16
IDA	..	..	..	0	0	0	0	0	0	0
UNDISBURSED DEBT	..	..	..	**764**	**1,136**	**1,046**	**1,040**	**1,742**	**1,678**	**1,139**
Official creditors	..	..	..	552	845	855	766	1,103	1,148	848
Private creditors	..	..	..	212	290	191	273	640	529	291
Memorandum items										
Concessional LDOD	..	..	..	143	188	615	206	389	726	864
Variable rate LDOD	..	..	..	939	1,208	1,610	1,647	2,155	2,851	2,882
Public sector LDOD	..	..	..	889	1,290	1,772	1,806	2,378	3,260	3,421
Private sector LDOD	..	..	..	64	128	283	318	511	510	420

6. CURRENCY COMPOSITION OF LONG-TERM DEBT (PERCENT)

	1970	1980	1990	1994	1995	1996	1997	1998	1999	2000
Deutsche mark	..	..	..	1.5	10.7	14.1	14.4	14.5	10.7	8.8
French franc	..	..	..	0.0	3.0	4.3	4.4	4.5	3.1	2.5
Japanese yen	..	..	..	0.0	3.1	5.7	8.6	12.6	20.2	22.3
Pound sterling	..	..	..	0.0	0.0	0.0	0.0	0.0	0.0	0.0
Swiss franc	..	..	..	0.4	0.1	0.0	0.1	0.1	0.0	0.0
U.S.dollars	..	..	..	98.0	66.4	64.4	64.8	61.5	58.6	56.5
Multiple currency	..	..	..	0.1	11.1	7.8	7.6	6.7	5.5	5.1
Special drawing rights	..	..	..	0.0	0.0	0.0	0.0	0.0	0.0	0.0
All other currencies	..	..	..	0.0	5.6	3.7	0.1	0.1	1.9	4.8

UZBEKISTAN

(US$ million, unless otherwise indicated)

	1970	1980	1990	1994	1995	1996	1997	1998	1999	2000
7. DEBT RESTRUCTURINGS										
Total amount rescheduled	..	..	..	0	0	0	501	0	0	0
Debt stock rescheduled	..	..	..	0	0	0	501	0	0	0
Principal rescheduled	..	..	..	0	0	0	0	0	0	0
Official	..	..	..	0	0	0	0	0	0	0
Private	..	..	..	0	0	0	0	0	0	0
Interest rescheduled	..	..	..	0	0	0	0	0	0	0
Official	..	..	..	0	0	0	0	0	0	0
Private	..	..	..	0	0	0	0	0	0	0
Debt forgiven	..	..	..	0	0	0	0	0	0	0
Memo: interest forgiven	..	..	..	0	0	0	0	0	0	0
Debt stock reduction	..	..	..	0	0	0	0	0	0	0
of which debt buyback	..	..	..	0	0	0	0	0	0	0
8. DEBT STOCK-FLOW RECONCILIATION										
Total change in debt stocks	..	..	..	212	543	597	382	443	1,477	-345
Net flows on debt	..	..	..	210	554	570	484	324	1,532	-240
Net change in interest arrears	..	..	..	0	0	0	0	3	0	0
Interest capitalized	..	..	..	0	0	0	0	0	0	0
Debt forgiveness or reduction	..	..	..	0	0	0	0	0	0	0
Cross-currency valuation	..	..	..	3	-4	-40	-97	68	-34	-138
Residual	..	..	..	-1	-7	66	-6	48	-21	34
9. AVERAGE TERMS OF NEW COMMITMENTS										
ALL CREDITORS										
Interest (%)	..	..	..	7.3	5.8	4.8	6.2	5.3	4.8	6.9
Maturity (years)	..	..	..	9.5	15.3	15.9	10.7	12.2	12.0	16.3
Grace period (years)	..	..	..	2.9	4.3	4.0	2.8	2.9	3.0	3.5
Grant element (%)	..	..	..	10.5	23.6	29.7	16.4	22.0	25.0	16.3
Official creditors										
Interest (%)	..	..	..	6.7	5.2	3.9	6.0	4.3	3.4	6.7
Maturity (years)	..	..	..	7.8	18.0	20.7	15.3	16.4	18.2	23.8
Grace period (years)	..	..	..	2.0	5.1	6.5	3.9	4.0	5.3	5.2
Grant element (%)	..	..	..	12.2	28.9	41.8	22.2	31.3	40.7	23.0
Private creditors										
Interest (%)	..	..	..	7.7	7.1	5.9	6.3	6.0	5.8	7.2
Maturity (years)	..	..	..	10.5	8.9	9.6	6.2	8.8	8.0	4.8
Grace period (years)	..	..	..	3.5	2.4	0.8	1.7	2.1	1.5	1.0
Grant element (%)	..	..	..	9.4	10.9	14.2	10.7	14.7	14.6	6.3
Memorandum items										
Commitments	..	..	..	441	1,001	762	689	1,333	1,017	159
Official creditors	..	..	..	166	705	428	344	590	404	96
Private creditors	..	..	..	274	296	334	345	743	612	63

10. CONTRACTUAL OBLIGATIONS ON OUTSTANDING LONG-TERM DEBT

	2001	2002	2003	2004	2005	2006	2007	2008	2009	2010
TOTAL										
Disbursements	404	310	170	101	60	37	22	10	4	2
Principal	729	675	610	518	452	419	293	237	171	156
Interest	241	208	177	143	118	96	70	55	44	36
Official creditors										
Disbursements	251	222	137	92	60	37	22	10	4	2
Principal	272	276	275	246	247	242	163	137	114	117
Interest	103	98	89	77	70	59	49	43	38	34
Bilateral creditors										
Disbursements	131	124	74	41	21	10	5	0	0	0
Principal	217	215	206	180	177	174	109	84	71	74
Interest	68	61	52	42	34	27	20	16	14	12
Multilateral creditors										
Disbursements	121	98	63	52	39	27	17	10	4	2
Principal	55	61	69	65	70	68	53	53	43	43
Interest	35	37	37	35	35	32	30	27	24	21
Private creditors										
Disbursements	153	88	33	8	0	0	0	0	0	0
Principal	456	399	335	272	205	177	131	100	56	39
Interest	138	110	89	65	49	37	21	12	6	3
Commercial banks										
Disbursements	80	40	14	3	0	0	0	0	0	0
Principal	130	148	127	98	83	70	61	56	37	31
Interest	46	41	33	26	20	15	11	7	4	2
Other private										
Disbursements	73	49	19	5	0	0	0	0	0	0
Principal	326	251	208	174	123	106	70	44	19	8
Interest	92	69	56	40	29	22	10	5	2	1

VANUATU

(US$ million, unless otherwise indicated)

	1970	1980	1990	1994	1995	1996	1997	1998	1999	2000
1. SUMMARY DEBT DATA										
TOTAL DEBT STOCKS (EDT)	..	**4.1**	**40.2**	**46.5**	**48.2**	**47.2**	**47.9**	**63.2**	**64.6**	**68.6**
Long-term debt (LDOD)	..	**4.1**	**30.6**	**41.5**	**43.2**	**42.2**	**38.9**	**54.2**	**63.4**	**67.2**
Public and publicly guaranteed	..	4.1	30.6	41.5	43.2	42.2	38.9	54.2	63.4	67.2
Private nonguaranteed	..	0.0	0.0	0.0	0.0	0.0	0.0	0.0	0.0	0.0
Use of IMF credit	**0.0**	**0.0**	**0.0**	**0.0**	**0.0**	**0.0**	**0.0**	**0.0**	**0.0**	**0.0**
Short-term debt	..	**0.0**	**9.6**	**5.0**	**5.0**	**5.0**	**9.0**	**9.0**	**1.1**	**1.4**
of which interest arrears on LDOD	..	0.0	0.0	0.0	0.0	0.0	0.0	0.0	0.0	0.0
Official creditors	..	0.0	0.0	0.0	0.0	0.0	0.0	0.0	0.0	0.0
Private creditors	..	0.0	0.0	0.0	0.0	0.0	0.0	0.0	0.0	0.0
Memo: principal arrears on LDOD	..	0.0	0.0	0.0	0.0	0.0	0.0	0.0	0.0	0.0
Official creditors	..	0.0	0.0	0.0	0.0	0.0	0.0	0.0	0.0	0.0
Private creditors	..	0.0	0.0	0.0	0.0	0.0	0.0	0.0	0.0	0.0
Memo: export credits	..	0.0	23.0	15.3	13.8	10.7	8.9	1.9	1.1	2.6
TOTAL DEBT FLOWS										
Disbursements	..	**0.0**	**8.7**	**1.8**	**1.6**	**1.1**	**0.9**	**12.1**	**5.7**	**9.6**
Long-term debt	..	0.0	8.7	1.8	1.6	1.1	0.9	12.1	5.7	9.6
IMF purchases	0.0	0.0	0.0	0.0	0.0	0.0	0.0	0.0	0.0	0.0
Principal repayments	..	**0.4**	**1.0**	**1.0**	**0.9**	**1.0**	**0.9**	**0.6**	**0.9**	**1.0**
Long-term debt	..	0.4	1.0	1.0	0.9	1.0	0.9	0.6	0.9	1.0
IMF repurchases	0.0	0.0	0.0	0.0	0.0	0.0	0.0	0.0	0.0	0.0
Net flows on debt	..	**-0.4**	**7.8**	**2.8**	**0.7**	**0.1**	**4.0**	**11.5**	**-3.1**	**8.9**
of which short-term debt	..	0.0	0.1	2.0	0.0	0.0	4.0	0.0	-7.9	0.3
Interest payments (INT)	..	**0.2**	**1.5**	**0.9**	**1.0**	**1.0**	**1.4**	**1.1**	**1.0**	**1.1**
Long-term debt	..	0.2	0.7	0.7	0.7	0.7	0.6	0.6	0.8	0.8
IMF charges	0.0	0.0	0.0	0.0	0.0	0.0	0.0	0.0	0.0	0.0
Short-term debt	..	0.0	0.7	0.2	0.3	0.3	0.8	0.5	0.3	0.3
Net transfers on debt	..	**-0.6**	**6.4**	**1.9**	**-0.3**	**-0.8**	**2.7**	**10.4**	**-4.1**	**7.7**
Total debt service paid (TDS)	..	**0.6**	**2.4**	**1.9**	**1.9**	**1.9**	**2.2**	**1.7**	**1.9**	**2.2**
Long-term debt	..	0.6	1.7	1.6	1.6	1.6	1.4	1.2	1.6	1.8
IMF repurchases and charges	0.0	0.0	0.0	0.0	0.0	0.0	0.0	0.0	0.0	0.0
Short-term debt (interest only)	..	0.0	0.7	0.2	0.3	0.3	0.8	0.5	0.3	0.3
2. AGGREGATE NET RESOURCE FLOWS AND NET TRANSFERS (LONG-TERM)										
NET RESOURCE FLOWS	..	**19.4**	**42.8**	**44.1**	**54.2**	**45.9**	**37.2**	**38.5**	**32.4**	**40.6**
Net flow of long-term debt (ex. IMF)	..	-0.4	7.7	0.8	0.7	0.1	0.0	11.5	4.8	8.6
Foreign direct investment (net)	..	0.0	13.0	30.0	31.0	33.0	30.0	20.0	20.0	20.0
Portfolio equity flows	..	0.0	0.0	0.0	0.0	0.0	0.0	0.0	0.0	0.0
Grants (excluding technical coop.)	..	19.7	22.0	13.3	22.5	12.7	7.2	7.1	7.6	12.0
Memo: technical coop. grants	..	24.7	22.2	27.7	21.5	18.1	20.0	22.1	24.1	20.6
official net resource flows	..	19.4	30.0	14.3	23.4	13.0	7.3	18.6	12.5	20.6
private net resource flows	..	0.0	12.8	29.8	30.8	32.9	29.9	19.9	19.9	20.0
NET TRANSFERS	..	**19.2**	**26.8**	**10.5**	**19.6**	**13.3**	**1.6**	**1.9**	**-2.3**	**3.8**
Interest on long-term debt	..	0.2	0.7	0.7	0.7	0.7	0.6	0.6	0.8	0.8
Profit remittances on FDI	..	0.0	15.2	33.0	34.0	32.0	35.0	36.0	34.0	36.0
Memo: official net transfers	..	19.2	29.4	13.7	22.8	12.4	6.7	18.0	11.8	19.8
private net transfers	..	0.0	-2.6	-3.2	-3.2	0.9	-5.1	-16.1	-14.1	-16.0
3. MAJOR ECONOMIC AGGREGATES										
Gross national income (GNI)	..	95.9	162.6	190.7	216.8	231.2	233.4	229.8	228.8	223.6
Exports of goods & services (XGS)	..	..	112.7	118.9	129.1	138.8	138.5	184.3	179.4	162.2
of which workers remittances	..	..	6.9	5.8	6.1	0.0	0.0	15.6	18.7	..
Imports of goods & services (MGS)	..	..	136.5	155.5	164.5	165.2	160.6	153.0	165.0	159.6
International reserves (RES)	..	..	37.7	43.6	48.3	43.9	37.3	44.7	41.4	38.9
Current account balance	..	..	-6.2	-18.5	-18.2	-26.9	-19.3	14.7	-3.1	..
4. DEBT INDICATORS										
EDT / XGS (%)	..	..	35.7	39.1	37.3	34.0	34.6	34.3	36.0	42.3
EDT / GNI (%)	..	4.3	24.7	24.4	22.2	20.4	20.5	27.5	28.2	30.7
TDS / XGS (%)	..	..	2.1	1.6	1.5	1.4	1.6	0.9	1.1	1.4
INT / XGS (%)	..	..	1.3	0.8	0.8	0.7	1.0	0.6	0.6	0.7
INT / GNI (%)	..	0.2	0.9	0.5	0.5	0.4	0.6	0.5	0.4	0.5
RES / EDT (%)	..	..	93.8	93.7	100.2	93.1	77.9	70.7	64.0	56.7
RES / MGS (months)	..	..	3.3	3.4	3.5	3.2	2.8	3.5	3.0	2.9
Short-term / EDT (%)	..	0.0	23.9	10.8	10.4	10.6	18.8	14.2	1.7	2.0
Concessional / EDT (%)	..	78.1	62.7	84.3	85.9	86.9	79.8	85.0	97.5	97.5
Multilateral / EDT (%)	..	0.0	39.6	64.3	64.7	65.7	60.5	70.1	84.8	86.7

VANUATU

(US$ million, unless otherwise indicated)

	1970	1980	1990	1994	1995	1996	1997	1998	1999	2000
5. LONG-TERM DEBT										
DEBT OUTSTANDING (LDOD)	..	**4.1**	**30.6**	**41.5**	**43.2**	**42.2**	**38.9**	**54.2**	**63.4**	**67.2**
Public and publicly guaranteed	..	**4.1**	**30.6**	**41.5**	**43.2**	**42.2**	**38.9**	**54.2**	**63.4**	**67.2**
Official creditors	..	3.9	29.1	40.9	42.8	41.8	38.8	54.2	63.4	67.2
Multilateral	..	0.0	15.9	29.9	31.2	31.0	29.0	44.3	54.8	59.5
Concessional	..	0.0	12.9	29.0	30.5	30.7	29.0	44.3	54.8	59.5
Bilateral	..	3.9	13.3	11.0	11.6	10.9	9.7	9.9	8.7	7.7
Concessional	..	3.2	12.3	10.2	10.9	10.3	9.2	9.4	8.2	7.4
Private creditors	..	0.2	1.5	0.6	0.4	0.3	0.2	0.1	0.0	0.0
Bonds	..	0.0	0.0	0.0	0.0	0.0	0.0	0.0	0.0	0.0
Commercial banks	..	0.0	0.0	0.0	0.0	0.0	0.0	0.0	0.0	0.0
Other private	..	0.2	1.5	0.6	0.4	0.3	0.2	0.1	0.0	0.0
Private nonguaranteed	..	**0.0**	**0.0**	**0.0**	**0.0**	**0.0**	**0.0**	**0.0**	**0.0**	**0.0**
Bonds	..	0.0	0.0	0.0	0.0	0.0	0.0	0.0	0.0	0.0
Commercial banks and other	..	0.0	0.0	0.0	0.0	0.0	0.0	0.0	0.0	0.0
Memo:										
IBRD	0.0	0.0	0.0	0.0	0.0	0.0	0.0	0.0	0.0	0.0
IDA	0.0	0.0	4.0	12.5	13.2	13.2	13.0	14.1	13.8	12.9
DISBURSEMENTS	..	**0.0**	**8.7**	**1.8**	**1.6**	**1.1**	**0.9**	**12.1**	**5.7**	**9.6**
Public and publicly guaranteed	..	**0.0**	**8.7**	**1.8**	**1.6**	**1.1**	**0.9**	**12.1**	**5.7**	**9.6**
Official creditors	..	0.0	8.7	1.8	1.6	1.1	0.9	12.1	5.7	9.6
Multilateral	..	0.0	3.3	1.6	1.4	1.0	0.8	12.1	5.7	9.6
Concessional	..	0.0	3.3	1.6	1.4	1.0	0.8	12.1	5.7	9.6
Bilateral	..	0.0	5.4	0.2	0.2	0.2	0.1	0.0	0.0	0.0
Concessional	..	0.0	5.3	0.2	0.2	0.2	0.1	0.0	0.0	0.0
Private creditors	..	0.0	0.0	0.0	0.0	0.0	0.0	0.0	0.0	0.0
Bonds	..	0.0	0.0	0.0	0.0	0.0	0.0	0.0	0.0	0.0
Commercial banks	..	0.0	0.0	0.0	0.0	0.0	0.0	0.0	0.0	0.0
Other private	..	0.0	0.0	0.0	0.0	0.0	0.0	0.0	0.0	0.0
Private nonguaranteed	..	**0.0**	**0.0**	**0.0**	**0.0**	**0.0**	**0.0**	**0.0**	**0.0**	**0.0**
Bonds	..	0.0	0.0	0.0	0.0	0.0	0.0	0.0	0.0	0.0
Commercial banks and other	..	0.0	0.0	0.0	0.0	0.0	0.0	0.0	0.0	0.0
Memo:										
IBRD	0.0	0.0	0.0	0.0	0.0	0.0	0.0	0.0	0.0	0.0
IDA	0.0	0.0	0.8	0.5	0.4	0.5	0.6	0.6	0.3	0.0
PRINCIPAL REPAYMENTS	..	**0.4**	**1.0**	**1.0**	**0.9**	**1.0**	**0.9**	**0.6**	**0.9**	**1.0**
Public and publicly guaranteed	..	**0.4**	**1.0**	**1.0**	**0.9**	**1.0**	**0.9**	**0.6**	**0.9**	**1.0**
Official creditors	..	0.3	0.8	0.8	0.7	0.8	0.8	0.5	0.8	1.0
Multilateral	..	0.0	0.5	0.4	0.4	0.5	0.4	0.2	0.5	0.5
Concessional	..	0.0	0.0	0.1	0.1	0.2	0.2	0.2	0.5	0.5
Bilateral	..	0.3	0.3	0.3	0.4	0.4	0.3	0.3	0.3	0.5
Concessional	..	0.3	0.2	0.3	0.3	0.3	0.3	0.2	0.2	0.5
Private creditors	..	0.0	0.2	0.2	0.2	0.1	0.1	0.1	0.1	0.0
Bonds	..	0.0	0.0	0.0	0.0	0.0	0.0	0.0	0.0	0.0
Commercial banks	..	0.0	0.0	0.0	0.0	0.0	0.0	0.0	0.0	0.0
Other private	..	0.0	0.2	0.2	0.2	0.1	0.1	0.1	0.1	0.0
Private nonguaranteed	..	**0.0**	**0.0**	**0.0**	**0.0**	**0.0**	**0.0**	**0.0**	**0.0**	**0.0**
Bonds	..	0.0	0.0	0.0	0.0	0.0	0.0	0.0	0.0	0.0
Commercial banks and other	..	0.0	0.0	0.0	0.0	0.0	0.0	0.0	0.0	0.0
Memo:										
IBRD	0.0	0.0	0.0	0.0	0.0	0.0	0.0	0.0	0.0	0.0
IDA	0.0	0.0	0.0	0.0	0.0	0.0	0.0	0.0	0.2	0.2
NET FLOWS ON DEBT	..	**-0.4**	**7.7**	**0.8**	**0.7**	**0.1**	**0.0**	**11.5**	**4.8**	**8.6**
Public and publicly guaranteed	..	**-0.4**	**7.7**	**0.8**	**0.7**	**0.1**	**0.0**	**11.5**	**4.8**	**8.6**
Official creditors	..	-0.3	8.0	1.0	0.9	0.3	0.1	11.5	4.9	8.6
Multilateral	..	0.0	2.8	1.1	1.0	0.5	0.4	11.8	5.1	9.1
Concessional	..	0.0	3.3	1.5	1.4	0.8	0.7	11.8	5.1	9.1
Bilateral	..	-0.3	5.2	-0.1	-0.1	-0.2	-0.2	-0.3	-0.3	-0.5
Concessional	..	-0.3	5.2	0.0	-0.1	-0.1	-0.2	-0.2	-0.2	-0.5
Private creditors	..	0.0	-0.2	-0.2	-0.2	-0.1	-0.1	-0.1	-0.1	0.0
Bonds	..	0.0	0.0	0.0	0.0	0.0	0.0	0.0	0.0	0.0
Commercial banks	..	0.0	0.0	0.0	0.0	0.0	0.0	0.0	0.0	0.0
Other private	..	0.0	-0.2	-0.2	-0.2	-0.1	-0.1	-0.1	-0.1	0.0
Private nonguaranteed	..	**0.0**	**0.0**	**0.0**	**0.0**	**0.0**	**0.0**	**0.0**	**0.0**	**0.0**
Bonds	..	0.0	0.0	0.0	0.0	0.0	0.0	0.0	0.0	0.0
Commercial banks and other	..	0.0	0.0	0.0	0.0	0.0	0.0	0.0	0.0	0.0
Memo:										
IBRD	0.0	0.0	0.0	0.0	0.0	0.0	0.0	0.0	0.0	0.0
IDA	0.0	0.0	0.8	0.5	0.4	0.5	0.5	0.6	0.0	-0.2

VANUATU

(US$ million, unless otherwise indicated)

	1970	1980	1990	1994	1995	1996	1997	1998	1999	2000
INTEREST PAYMENTS (LINT)	..	**0.2**	**0.7**	**0.7**	**0.7**	**0.7**	**0.6**	**0.6**	**0.8**	**0.8**
Public and publicly guaranteed	..	**0.2**	**0.7**	**0.7**	**0.7**	**0.7**	**0.6**	**0.6**	**0.8**	**0.8**
Official creditors	..	0.2	0.6	0.6	0.6	0.6	0.6	0.6	0.7	0.8
Multilateral	..	0.0	0.2	0.3	0.3	0.3	0.3	0.3	0.5	0.5
Concessional	..	0.0	0.1	0.3	0.3	0.3	0.2	0.3	0.5	0.5
Bilateral	..	0.2	0.4	0.3	0.4	0.3	0.3	0.3	0.3	0.3
Concessional	..	0.2	0.3	0.3	0.3	0.3	0.3	0.3	0.2	0.2
Private creditors	..	0.0	0.2	0.0	0.0	0.0	0.0	0.0	0.0	0.0
Bonds	..	0.0	0.0	0.0	0.0	0.0	0.0	0.0	0.0	0.0
Commercial banks	..	0.0	0.0	0.0	0.0	0.0	0.0	0.0	0.0	0.0
Other private	..	0.0	0.2	0.0	0.0	0.0	0.0	0.0	0.0	0.0
Private nonguaranteed	..	**0.0**	**0.0**	**0.0**	**0.0**	**0.0**	**0.0**	**0.0**	**0.0**	**0.0**
Bonds	..	0.0	0.0	0.0	0.0	0.0	0.0	0.0	0.0	0.0
Commercial banks and other	..	0.0	0.0	0.0	0.0	0.0	0.0	0.0	0.0	0.0
Memo:										
IBRD	0.0	0.0	0.0	0.0	0.0	0.0	0.0	0.0	0.0	0.0
IDA	0.0	0.0	0.0	0.1	0.1	0.1	0.1	0.1	0.1	0.1
NET TRANSFERS ON DEBT	..	**-0.6**	**7.0**	**0.2**	**0.0**	**-0.5**	**-0.6**	**10.9**	**4.0**	**7.8**
Public and publicly guaranteed	..	**-0.6**	**7.0**	**0.2**	**0.0**	**-0.5**	**-0.6**	**10.9**	**4.0**	**7.8**
Official creditors	..	-0.6	7.4	0.4	0.2	-0.3	-0.4	11.0	4.1	7.8
Multilateral	..	0.0	2.6	0.9	0.7	0.2	0.1	11.5	4.7	8.6
Concessional	..	0.0	3.2	1.3	1.1	0.5	0.4	11.5	4.7	8.6
Bilateral	..	-0.6	4.8	-0.5	-0.5	-0.5	-0.6	-0.6	-0.6	-0.8
Concessional	..	-0.4	4.8	-0.3	-0.4	-0.4	-0.5	-0.5	-0.5	-0.7
Private creditors	..	0.0	-0.4	-0.3	-0.2	-0.2	-0.1	-0.1	-0.1	0.0
Bonds	..	0.0	0.0	0.0	0.0	0.0	0.0	0.0	0.0	0.0
Commercial banks	..	0.0	0.0	0.0	0.0	0.0	0.0	0.0	0.0	0.0
Other private	..	0.0	-0.4	-0.3	-0.2	-0.2	-0.1	-0.1	-0.1	0.0
Private nonguaranteed	..	**0.0**	**0.0**	**0.0**	**0.0**	**0.0**	**0.0**	**0.0**	**0.0**	**0.0**
Bonds	..	0.0	0.0	0.0	0.0	0.0	0.0	0.0	0.0	0.0
Commercial banks and other	..	0.0	0.0	0.0	0.0	0.0	0.0	0.0	0.0	0.0
Memo:										
IBRD	0.0	0.0	0.0	0.0	0.0	0.0	0.0	0.0	0.0	0.0
IDA	0.0	0.0	0.8	0.4	0.3	0.4	0.4	0.5	-0.1	-0.3
DEBT SERVICE (LTDS)	..	**0.6**	**1.7**	**1.6**	**1.6**	**1.6**	**1.4**	**1.2**	**1.6**	**1.8**
Public and publicly guaranteed	..	**0.6**	**1.7**	**1.6**	**1.6**	**1.6**	**1.4**	**1.2**	**1.6**	**1.8**
Official creditors	..	0.6	1.3	1.4	1.4	1.5	1.3	1.1	1.5	1.8
Multilateral	..	0.0	0.7	0.7	0.7	0.8	0.7	0.5	1.0	1.0
Concessional	..	0.0	0.1	0.3	0.3	0.4	0.4	0.5	1.0	1.0
Bilateral	..	0.6	0.7	0.7	0.7	0.7	0.6	0.6	0.6	0.8
Concessional	..	0.4	0.5	0.5	0.6	0.6	0.5	0.5	0.5	0.7
Private creditors	..	0.0	0.4	0.3	0.2	0.2	0.1	0.1	0.1	0.0
Bonds	..	0.0	0.0	0.0	0.0	0.0	0.0	0.0	0.0	0.0
Commercial banks	..	0.0	0.0	0.0	0.0	0.0	0.0	0.0	0.0	0.0
Other private	..	0.0	0.4	0.3	0.2	0.2	0.1	0.1	0.1	0.0
Private nonguaranteed	..	**0.0**	**0.0**	**0.0**	**0.0**	**0.0**	**0.0**	**0.0**	**0.0**	**0.0**
Bonds	..	0.0	0.0	0.0	0.0	0.0	0.0	0.0	0.0	0.0
Commercial banks and other	..	0.0	0.0	0.0	0.0	0.0	0.0	0.0	0.0	0.0
Memo:										
IBRD	0.0	0.0	0.0	0.0	0.0	0.0	0.0	0.0	0.0	0.0
IDA	0.0	0.0	0.0	0.1	0.1	0.1	0.1	0.1	0.3	0.3
UNDISBURSED DEBT	..	**0.0**	**18.1**	**9.8**	**8.4**	**15.4**	**13.1**	**22.0**	**13.8**	**3.4**
Official creditors	..	0.0	18.1	9.8	8.4	15.4	13.1	22.0	13.8	3.4
Private creditors	..	0.0	0.0	0.0	0.0	0.0	0.0	0.0	0.0	0.0
Memorandum items										
Concessional LDOD	..	3.2	25.1	39.2	41.4	40.9	38.2	53.7	63.0	66.8
Variable rate LDOD	..	0.0	0.8	0.5	0.4	0.3	0.2	0.1	0.0	0.0
Public sector LDOD	..	4.1	30.6	41.5	43.2	42.2	38.9	54.2	63.4	67.2
Private sector LDOD	..	0.0	0.0	0.0	0.0	0.0	0.0	0.0	0.0	0.0

6. CURRENCY COMPOSITION OF LONG-TERM DEBT (PERCENT)

	1970	1980	1990	1994	1995	1996	1997	1998	1999	2000
Deutsche mark	..	0.0	0.0	0.0	0.0	0.0	0.0	0.0	0.0	0.0
French franc	..	81.3	33.4	17.5	18.1	17.0	15.9	12.0	8.7	7.1
Japanese yen	..	0.0	0.0	0.0	0.0	0.0	0.0	0.0	0.0	0.0
Pound sterling	..	13.6	0.6	0.1	0.1	0.0	0.0	0.0	0.0	0.0
Swiss franc	..	0.0	0.0	0.0	0.0	0.0	0.0	0.0	0.0	0.0
U.S.dollars	..	0.0	20.9	39.9	39.4	40.3	42.1	57.2	59.1	58.8
Multiple currency	..	0.0	28.7	33.1	33.8	34.6	34.3	25.5	27.9	30.2
Special drawing rights	..	0.0	0.0	0.0	0.0	0.0	0.0	0.0	0.0	0.0
All other currencies	..	5.1	16.4	9.4	8.6	8.1	7.7	5.3	4.3	3.9

VANUATU

(US$ million, unless otherwise indicated)

	1970	1980	1990	1994	1995	1996	1997	1998	1999	2000
7. DEBT RESTRUCTURINGS										
Total amount rescheduled	..	..	0.0	0.0	0.0	0.0	0.0	0.0	0.0	0.0
Debt stock rescheduled	..	..	0.0	0.0	0.0	0.0	0.0	0.0	0.0	0.0
Principal rescheduled	..	..	0.0	0.0	0.0	0.0	0.0	0.0	0.0	0.0
Official	..	..	0.0	0.0	0.0	0.0	0.0	0.0	0.0	0.0
Private	..	..	0.0	0.0	0.0	0.0	0.0	0.0	0.0	0.0
Interest rescheduled	..	..	0.0	0.0	0.0	0.0	0.0	0.0	0.0	0.0
Official	..	..	0.0	0.0	0.0	0.0	0.0	0.0	0.0	0.0
Private	..	..	0.0	0.0	0.0	0.0	0.0	0.0	0.0	0.0
Debt forgiven	..	..	0.0	0.0	0.0	0.0	0.0	0.0	0.0	0.0
Memo: interest forgiven	..	..	0.0	0.0	0.0	0.0	0.0	0.0	0.0	0.0
Debt stock reduction	..	..	0.0	0.0	0.0	0.0	0.0	0.0	0.0	0.0
of which debt buyback	..	..	0.0	0.0	0.0	0.0	0.0	0.0	0.0	0.0
8. DEBT STOCK-FLOW RECONCILIATION										
Total change in debt stocks	..	..	9.9	4.1	1.7	-1.1	0.8	15.3	1.4	4.0
Net flows on debt	..	-0.4	7.8	2.8	0.7	0.1	4.0	11.5	-3.1	8.9
Net change in interest arrears	..	..	0.0	0.0	0.0	0.0	0.0	0.0	0.0	0.0
Interest capitalized	..	..	0.0	0.0	0.0	0.0	0.0	0.0	0.0	0.0
Debt forgiveness or reduction	..	..	0.0	0.0	0.0	0.0	0.0	0.0	0.0	0.0
Cross-currency valuation	..	..	1.1	0.6	0.0	-2.2	-3.9	3.2	0.6	-4.1
Residual	..	..	0.9	0.7	1.0	1.0	0.7	0.6	3.8	-0.7
9. AVERAGE TERMS OF NEW COMMITMENTS										
ALL CREDITORS										
Interest (%)	..	0.0	0.0	0.0	0.0	3.5	0.0	3.3	0.0	0.0
Maturity (years)	..	0.0	0.0	0.0	0.0	39.9	0.0	39.6	0.0	0.0
Grace period (years)	..	0.0	0.0	0.0	0.0	10.4	0.0	10.1	0.0	0.0
Grant element (%)	..	0.0	0.0	0.0	0.0	56.0	0.0	57.7	0.0	0.0
Official creditors										
Interest (%)	..	0.0	0.0	0.0	0.0	3.5	0.0	3.3	0.0	0.0
Maturity (years)	..	0.0	0.0	0.0	0.0	39.9	0.0	39.6	0.0	0.0
Grace period (years)	..	0.0	0.0	0.0	0.0	10.4	0.0	10.1	0.0	0.0
Grant element (%)	..	0.0	0.0	0.0	0.0	56.0	0.0	57.7	0.0	0.0
Private creditors										
Interest (%)	..	0.0	0.0	0.0	0.0	0.0	0.0	0.0	0.0	0.0
Maturity (years)	..	0.0	0.0	0.0	0.0	0.0	0.0	0.0	0.0	0.0
Grace period (years)	..	0.0	0.0	0.0	0.0	0.0	0.0	0.0	0.0	0.0
Grant element (%)	..	0.0	0.0	0.0	0.0	0.0	0.0	0.0	0.0	0.0
Memorandum items										
Commitments	..	0.0	0.0	0.0	0.0	9.9	0.0	20.5	0.0	0.0
Official creditors	..	0.0	0.0	0.0	0.0	9.9	0.0	20.5	0.0	0.0
Private creditors	..	0.0	0.0	0.0	0.0	0.0	0.0	0.0	0.0	0.0

10. CONTRACTUAL OBLIGATIONS ON OUTSTANDING LONG-TERM DEBT

	2001	2002	2003	2004	2005	2006	2007	2008	2009	2010
TOTAL										
Disbursements	1.7	1.4	0.3	0.0	0.0	0.0	0.0	0.0	0.0	0.0
Principal	0.9	1.0	1.0	1.0	1.0	1.2	1.4	1.8	2.3	2.4
Interest	0.7	0.7	0.7	0.6	0.6	0.7	0.7	1.2	1.1	1.1
Official creditors										
Disbursements	1.7	1.4	0.3	0.0	0.0	0.0	0.0	0.0	0.0	0.0
Principal	0.9	1.0	1.0	1.0	1.0	1.2	1.4	1.8	2.3	2.4
Interest	0.7	0.7	0.7	0.6	0.6	0.7	0.7	1.2	1.1	1.1
Bilateral creditors										
Disbursements	0.0	0.0	0.0	0.0	0.0	0.0	0.0	0.0	0.0	0.0
Principal	0.5	0.5	0.4	0.4	0.4	0.4	0.4	0.4	0.4	0.4
Interest	0.3	0.2	0.2	0.2	0.2	0.2	0.1	0.1	0.1	0.1
Multilateral creditors										
Disbursements	1.7	1.4	0.3	0.0	0.0	0.0	0.0	0.0	0.0	0.0
Principal	0.4	0.5	0.5	0.6	0.6	0.7	1.0	1.4	1.9	2.0
Interest	0.4	0.4	0.4	0.4	0.4	0.5	0.6	1.0	1.0	1.0
Private creditors										
Disbursements	0.0	0.0	0.0	0.0	0.0	0.0	0.0	0.0	0.0	0.0
Principal	0.0	0.0	0.0	0.0	0.0	0.0	0.0	0.0	0.0	0.0
Interest	0.0	0.0	0.0	0.0	0.0	0.0	0.0	0.0	0.0	0.0
Commercial banks										
Disbursements	0.0	0.0	0.0	0.0	0.0	0.0	0.0	0.0	0.0	0.0
Principal	0.0	0.0	0.0	0.0	0.0	0.0	0.0	0.0	0.0	0.0
Interest	0.0	0.0	0.0	0.0	0.0	0.0	0.0	0.0	0.0	0.0
Other private										
Disbursements	0.0	0.0	0.0	0.0	0.0	0.0	0.0	0.0	0.0	0.0
Principal	0.0	0.0	0.0	0.0	0.0	0.0	0.0	0.0	0.0	0.0
Interest	0.0	0.0	0.0	0.0	0.0	0.0	0.0	0.0	0.0	0.0

VENEZUELA, REPUBLICA BOLIVARIANA de

(US$ million, unless otherwise indicated)

	1970	1980	1990	1994	1995	1996	1997	1998	1999	2000
1. SUMMARY DEBT DATA										
TOTAL DEBT STOCKS (EDT)	**1,422**	**29,344**	**33,170**	**36,851**	**35,538**	**34,535**	**35,797**	**38,237**	**38,192**	**38,196**
Long-term debt (LDOD)	**954**	**13,795**	**28,159**	**30,476**	**30,236**	**29,605**	**29,934**	**34,792**	**35,388**	**36,230**
Public and publicly guaranteed	718	10,614	24,509	28,040	28,223	27,791	27,085	28,111	27,761	27,628
Private nonguaranteed	236	3,181	3,650	2,436	2,013	1,814	2,849	6,681	7,627	8,602
Use of IMF credit	**0**	**0**	**3,012**	**2,643**	**2,239**	**2,196**	**1,618**	**1,226**	**741**	**203**
Short-term debt	**468**	**15,550**	**2,000**	**3,732**	**3,063**	**2,734**	**4,245**	**2,220**	**2,063**	**1,764**
of which interest arrears on LDOD	0	15	0	293	273	148	127	101	63	59
Official creditors	0	0	0	12	12	11	10	10	8	7
Private creditors	0	15	0	280	261	137	117	91	55	52
Memo: principal arrears on LDOD	0	37	0	1,247	1,023	564	368	256	121	79
Official creditors	0	0	0	116	116	105	77	77	77	68
Private creditors	0	37	0	1,131	907	458	292	179	44	11
Memo: export credits	0	0	2,386	7,750	5,880	4,865	3,801	1,062	1,109	1,288
TOTAL DEBT FLOWS										
Disbursements	**282**	**4,761**	**4,069**	**1,045**	**1,717**	**2,887**	**7,574**	**7,692**	**3,704**	**3,925**
Long-term debt	282	4,761	2,226	1,045	1,717	2,379	7,574	7,692	3,704	3,925
IMF purchases	0	0	1,843	0	0	508	0	0	0	0
Principal repayments	**67**	**2,972**	**1,747**	**1,575**	**2,739**	**2,791**	**6,501**	**3,588**	**3,284**	**3,293**
Long-term debt	67	2,972	1,747	1,374	2,278	2,314	6,049	3,142	2,833	2,786
IMF repurchases	0	0	0	201	462	477	452	446	452	507
Net flows on debt	**215**	**5,556**	**2,037**	**-1,584**	**-1,670**	**-109**	**2,605**	**2,106**	**301**	**336**
of which short-term debt	0	3,767	-284	-1,054	-648	-205	1,532	-1,999	-119	-296
Interest payments (INT)	**53**	**3,065**	**3,242**	**2,115**	**2,431**	**2,148**	**2,315**	**2,431**	**2,467**	**2,553**
Long-term debt	53	1,475	2,993	1,768	2,095	1,870	2,021	2,172	2,300	2,423
IMF charges	0	0	37	141	142	100	93	72	44	28
Short-term debt	0	1,590	212	206	193	178	201	187	124	102
Net transfers on debt	**162**	**2,491**	**-1,205**	**-3,698**	**-4,101**	**-2,257**	**291**	**-326**	**-2,166**	**-2,217**
Total debt service paid (TDS)	**120**	**6,037**	**4,990**	**3,690**	**5,170**	**4,939**	**8,816**	**6,019**	**5,752**	**5,846**
Long-term debt	120	4,447	4,741	3,141	4,373	4,184	8,070	5,313	5,132	5,209
IMF repurchases and charges	0	0	37	342	604	577	545	518	496	535
Short-term debt (interest only)	0	1,590	212	206	193	178	201	187	124	102
2. AGGREGATE NET RESOURCE FLOWS AND NET TRANSFERS (LONG-TERM)										
NET RESOURCE FLOWS	**192**	**1,844**	**934**	**532**	**904**	**4,000**	**7,502**	**9,137**	**4,241**	**5,708**
Net flow of long-term debt (ex. IMF)	215	1,789	478	-328	-560	64	1,525	4,550	872	1,139
Foreign direct investment (net)	-23	55	451	813	985	2,183	5,536	4,495	3,290	4,464
Portfolio equity flows	0	0	0	42	461	1,740	429	64	67	71
Grants (excluding technical coop.)	0	0	5	5	18	13	12	28	12	34
Memo: technical coop. grants	6	19	24	28	35	32	30	21	24	27
official net resource flows	4	19	1,059	398	172	-167	140	1,536	321	254
private net resource flows	187	1,825	-126	134	731	4,167	7,363	7,601	3,920	5,454
NET TRANSFERS	**-429**	**47**	**-2,283**	**-1,836**	**-1,811**	**1,431**	**4,481**	**5,766**	**461**	**1,635**
Interest on long-term debt	53	1,475	2,993	1,768	2,095	1,870	2,021	2,172	2,300	2,423
Profit remittances on FDI	568	322	224	600	620	700	1,000	1,200	1,480	1,650
Memo: official net transfers	-16	-16	989	128	-124	-444	-100	1,313	-5	-75
private net transfers	-413	63	-3,272	-1,963	-1,687	1,874	4,581	4,452	466	1,710
3. MAJOR ECONOMIC AGGREGATES										
Gross national income (GNI)	12,865	69,703	47,149	56,538	75,446	68,818	86,296	93,918	101,793	119,321
Exports of goods & services (XGS)	2,833	22,232	21,464	19,307	22,620	26,859	27,331	21,323	24,242	38,318
of which workers remittances	0	0	..	..	..	0	0	0	0	195
Imports of goods & services (MGS)	2,845	17,065	12,883	16,682	20,715	18,083	23,720	24,468	20,623	24,630
International reserves (RES)	1,047	13,360	12,733	12,459	10,715	16,020	17,704	14,729	15,110	15,899
Current account balance	-104	4,728	8,279	2,541	2,014	8,914	3,467	-3,253	3,689	13,350
4. DEBT INDICATORS										
EDT / XGS (%)	50.2	132.0	154.5	190.9	157.1	128.6	131.0	179.3	157.5	99.7
EDT / GNI (%)	11.1	42.1	70.4	65.2	47.1	50.2	41.5	40.7	37.5	32.0
TDS / XGS (%)	4.2	27.2	23.3	19.1	22.9	18.4	32.3	28.2	23.7	15.3
INT / XGS (%)	1.9	13.8	15.1	11.0	10.8	8.0	8.5	11.4	10.2	6.7
INT / GNI (%)	0.4	4.4	6.9	3.7	3.2	3.1	2.7	2.6	2.4	2.1
RES / EDT (%)	73.6	45.5	38.4	33.8	30.2	46.4	49.5	38.5	39.6	41.6
RES / MGS (months)	4.4	9.4	11.9	9.0	6.2	10.6	9.0	7.2	8.8	7.8
Short-term / EDT (%)	32.9	53.0	6.0	10.1	8.6	7.9	11.9	5.8	5.4	4.6
Concessional / EDT (%)	5.8	0.2	0.3	0.3	0.3	0.3	0.2	0.2	0.1	0.2
Multilateral / EDT (%)	17.1	0.7	4.9	8.5	9.3	8.1	7.0	8.1	8.3	8.4

VENEZUELA, REPUBLICA BOLIVARIANA de

(US$ million, unless otherwise indicated)

	1970	1980	1990	1994	1995	1996	1997	1998	1999	2000
5. LONG-TERM DEBT										
DEBT OUTSTANDING (LDOD)	**954**	**13,795**	**28,159**	**30,476**	**30,236**	**29,605**	**29,934**	**34,792**	**35,388**	**36,230**
Public and publicly guaranteed	**718**	**10,614**	**24,509**	**28,040**	**28,223**	**27,791**	**27,085**	**28,111**	**27,761**	**27,628**
Official creditors	366	571	1,932	4,477	4,703	4,073	3,885	5,536	5,923	6,018
Multilateral	244	216	1,639	3,133	3,300	2,790	2,492	3,107	3,166	3,192
Concessional	1	42	12	5	4	3	1	0	0	0
Bilateral	122	355	293	1,344	1,403	1,284	1,393	2,429	2,758	2,826
Concessional	81	8	73	86	96	102	68	63	49	70
Private creditors	352	10,043	22,577	23,563	23,520	23,718	23,201	22,576	21,838	21,610
Bonds	37	1,261	19,644	21,061	20,745	20,531	19,430	18,581	17,262	16,396
Commercial banks	237	8,159	364	585	1,158	1,970	2,365	2,520	2,905	3,291
Other private	78	623	2,569	1,918	1,617	1,216	1,405	1,475	1,671	1,923
Private nonguaranteed	**236**	**3,181**	**3,650**	**2,436**	**2,013**	**1,814**	**2,849**	**6,681**	**7,627**	**8,602**
Bonds	0	0	0	114	114	134	319	2,694	3,895	3,880
Commercial banks and other	236	3,181	3,650	2,322	1,899	1,680	2,530	3,987	3,732	4,722
Memo:										
IBRD	217	133	974	1,653	1,639	1,408	1,213	1,219	1,130	972
IDA	0	0	0	0	0	0	0	0	0	0
DISBURSEMENTS	**282**	**4,761**	**2,226**	**1,045**	**1,717**	**2,379**	**7,574**	**7,692**	**3,704**	**3,925**
Public and publicly guaranteed	**216**	**2,870**	**2,226**	**1,045**	**1,637**	**1,981**	**6,314**	**3,420**	**2,291**	**2,648**
Official creditors	30	88	1,103	493	529	265	600	1,975	887	865
Multilateral	21	3	1,035	103	267	74	176	846	422	454
Concessional	1	2	0	0	0	0	0	0	0	0
Bilateral	10	85	69	391	262	191	425	1,128	466	411
Concessional	0	0	15	19	16	20	0	0	0	31
Private creditors	186	2,782	1,122	552	1,108	1,716	5,714	1,445	1,404	1,784
Bonds	0	276	599	0	349	432	4,515	500	0	462
Commercial banks	140	2,362	26	304	586	944	621	548	858	853
Other private	46	144	497	248	174	340	578	397	546	468
Private nonguaranteed	**67**	**1,891**	**0**	**0**	**80**	**398**	**1,260**	**4,272**	**1,413**	**1,277**
Bonds	0	0	0	0	0	95	200	2,450	1,213	0
Commercial banks and other	67	1,891	0	0	80	303	1,060	1,822	200	1,277
Memo:										
IBRD	15	1	840	20	47	48	91	188	119	50
IDA	0	0	0	0	0	0	0	0	0	0
PRINCIPAL REPAYMENTS	**67**	**2,972**	**1,747**	**1,374**	**2,278**	**2,314**	**6,049**	**3,142**	**2,833**	**2,786**
Public and publicly guaranteed	**42**	**1,737**	**1,574**	**488**	**1,775**	**1,717**	**5,824**	**2,702**	**2,377**	**2,499**
Official creditors	26	68	49	101	375	445	473	466	578	644
Multilateral	13	33	8	65	202	272	271	289	363	374
Concessional	0	3	3	1	1	1	1	1	0	0
Bilateral	13	35	41	36	173	173	201	177	216	270
Concessional	4	6	0	4	12	8	25	8	8	7
Private creditors	16	1,668	1,526	387	1,400	1,273	5,352	2,236	1,799	1,855
Bonds	1	13	254	145	817	503	4,891	1,467	1,079	1,213
Commercial banks	5	1,324	706	32	46	69	115	430	395	430
Other private	10	331	566	210	537	701	345	339	325	212
Private nonguaranteed	**25**	**1,235**	**173**	**886**	**503**	**597**	**225**	**440**	**455**	**287**
Bonds	0	0	0	150	0	75	15	75	0	0
Commercial banks and other	25	1,235	173	736	503	522	210	365	455	287
Memo:										
IBRD	10	23	0	0	116	169	172	179	208	208
IDA	0	0	0	0	0	0	0	0	0	0
NET FLOWS ON DEBT	**215**	**1,789**	**478**	**-328**	**-560**	**64**	**1,525**	**4,550**	**872**	**1,139**
Public and publicly guaranteed	**174**	**1,133**	**651**	**557**	**-137**	**263**	**490**	**718**	**-86**	**149**
Official creditors	4	20	1,055	393	154	-180	128	1,509	309	220
Multilateral	8	-30	1,027	38	65	-198	-96	557	59	80
Concessional	1	-1	-3	-1	-1	-1	-1	-1	0	0
Bilateral	-4	50	28	355	89	18	223	951	250	141
Concessional	-4	-6	15	15	4	12	-25	-8	-8	23
Private creditors	169	1,114	-404	165	-292	443	363	-790	-395	-71
Bonds	-1	263	345	-145	-468	-71	-376	-967	-1,079	-751
Commercial banks	134	1,038	-680	272	540	875	506	118	463	424
Other private	36	-187	-69	38	-364	-361	232	59	221	257
Private nonguaranteed	**41**	**656**	**-173**	**-886**	**-423**	**-199**	**1,035**	**3,832**	**958**	**990**
Bonds	0	0	0	-150	0	20	185	2,375	1,213	0
Commercial banks and other	41	656	-173	-736	-423	-219	850	1,457	-255	990
Memo:										
IBRD	6	-22	840	20	-69	-121	-81	9	-90	-158
IDA	0	0	0	0	0	0	0	0	0	0

VENEZUELA, REPUBLICA BOLIVARIANA de

(US$ million, unless otherwise indicated)

	1970	1980	1990	1994	1995	1996	1997	1998	1999	2000
INTEREST PAYMENTS (LINT)	**53**	**1,475**	**2,993**	**1,768**	**2,095**	**1,870**	**2,021**	**2,172**	**2,300**	**2,423**
Public and publicly guaranteed	**40**	**1,218**	**2,593**	**1,636**	**1,984**	**1,828**	**1,833**	**1,909**	**1,891**	**1,855**
Official creditors	20	36	71	270	296	277	240	223	326	328
Multilateral	15	18	59	231	231	226	191	181	247	255
Concessional	0	2	0	0	0	0	0	0	0	0
Bilateral	5	18	12	40	66	51	49	42	78	74
Concessional	3	1	0	2	3	3	4	4	3	3
Private creditors	20	1,183	2,522	1,365	1,688	1,551	1,594	1,686	1,566	1,527
Bonds	3	61	135	1,307	1,534	1,402	1,422	1,501	1,376	1,327
Commercial banks	16	1,052	2,198	19	65	87	126	132	141	145
Other private	2	70	189	40	89	62	46	54	49	54
Private nonguaranteed	**13**	**257**	**400**	**132**	**111**	**42**	**188**	**262**	**408**	**568**
Bonds	0	0	0	20	10	10	11	31	200	304
Commercial banks and other	13	257	400	112	101	32	177	231	208	264
Memo:										
IBRD	13	12	19	115	120	108	87	77	88	91
IDA	0	0	0	0	0	0	0	0	0	0
NET TRANSFERS ON DEBT	**162**	**314**	**-2,515**	**-2,096**	**-2,656**	**-1,805**	**-496**	**2,379**	**-1,428**	**-1,284**
Public and publicly guaranteed	**134**	**-85**	**-1,942**	**-1,079**	**-2,122**	**-1,564**	**-1,343**	**-1,191**	**-1,978**	**-1,706**
Official creditors	-16	-16	984	122	-142	-457	-112	1,286	-17	-108
Multilateral	-7	-48	968	-193	-166	-424	-286	376	-188	-175
Concessional	1	-3	-4	-2	-2	-1	-1	-1	0	0
Bilateral	-9	32	16	315	23	-33	174	909	171	67
Concessional	-6	-6	15	13	2	10	-29	-12	-11	21
Private creditors	150	-69	-2,926	-1,201	-1,979	-1,108	-1,231	-2,477	-1,961	-1,598
Bonds	-4	202	210	-1,452	-2,002	-1,472	-1,797	-2,468	-2,455	-2,078
Commercial banks	119	-15	-2,878	253	475	787	381	-13	322	278
Other private	35	-256	-258	-2	-453	-423	186	4	172	202
Private nonguaranteed	**28**	**399**	**-573**	**-1,018**	**-534**	**-241**	**847**	**3,570**	**550**	**422**
Bonds	0	0	0	-170	-10	10	174	2,344	1,014	-304
Commercial banks and other	28	399	-573	-848	-524	-251	673	1,226	-464	726
Memo:										
IBRD	-7	-35	821	-95	-189	-229	-168	-68	-178	-249
IDA	0	0	0	0	0	0	0	0	0	0
DEBT SERVICE (LTDS)	**120**	**4,447**	**4,741**	**3,141**	**4,373**	**4,184**	**8,070**	**5,313**	**5,132**	**5,209**
Public and publicly guaranteed	**82**	**2,955**	**4,168**	**2,124**	**3,759**	**3,545**	**7,657**	**4,611**	**4,269**	**4,354**
Official creditors	46	104	119	371	671	722	712	689	904	973
Multilateral	28	51	67	296	433	498	462	470	610	628
Concessional	0	5	4	2	2	1	1	1	0	0
Bilateral	18	53	53	76	238	223	250	219	294	344
Concessional	6	6	0	6	14	10	29	12	11	10
Private creditors	36	2,851	4,048	1,753	3,088	2,824	6,945	3,922	3,365	3,381
Bonds	4	74	389	1,452	2,351	1,904	6,312	2,968	2,455	2,540
Commercial banks	21	2,377	2,905	51	110	157	241	561	536	575
Other private	11	401	755	250	626	763	392	393	374	266
Private nonguaranteed	**38**	**1,492**	**573**	**1,018**	**614**	**639**	**413**	**702**	**864**	**855**
Bonds	0	0	0	170	10	85	26	106	200	304
Commercial banks and other	38	1,492	573	848	604	554	387	596	664	551
Memo:										
IBRD	23	35	19	115	235	277	259	256	297	299
IDA	0	0	0	0	0	0	0	0	0	0
UNDISBURSED DEBT	**196**	**364**	**2,986**	**3,199**	**2,518**	**2,198**	**5,566**	**5,966**	**3,905**	**2,547**
Official creditors	106	101	1,567	2,619	2,294	2,162	3,327	3,216	2,328	1,645
Private creditors	90	263	1,419	580	224	37	2,238	2,750	1,577	903
Memorandum items										
Concessional LDOD	82	50	84	91	100	105	69	63	49	70
Variable rate LDOD	255	11,224	17,448	17,767	17,765	18,020	18,208	21,047	20,608	20,270
Public sector LDOD	682	10,277	24,508	27,278	27,648	27,230	26,605	27,637	27,300	27,179
Private sector LDOD	272	3,518	3,650	3,198	2,588	2,375	3,329	7,155	8,088	9,051

6. CURRENCY COMPOSITION OF LONG-TERM DEBT (PERCENT)

	1970	1980	1990	1994	1995	1996	1997	1998	1999	2000
Deutsche mark	5.2	7.8	6.9	6.9	8.9	9.4	7.4	5.1	4.3	3.3
French franc	1.5	1.9	4.1	2.6	2.4	1.9	1.4	1.1	1.1	1.2
Japanese yen	0.0	4.9	0.6	4.0	4.2	3.8	3.1	2.9	2.7	1.9
Pound sterling	0.1	0.0	1.5	1.3	1.2	1.4	1.3	1.1	1.0	0.8
Swiss franc	4.6	0.0	0.9	0.7	0.7	0.6	0.5	0.5	0.4	0.4
U.S.dollars	54.3	82.8	78.2	72.1	69.1	71.0	75.3	82.6	84.0	83.8
Multiple currency	32.0	2.3	6.5	11.1	11.7	10.0	9.2	5.0	5.3	5.5
Special drawing rights	0.0	0.0	0.0	0.0	0.0	0.0	0.0	0.0	0.0	0.0
All other currencies	2.3	0.3	1.3	1.3	1.8	1.9	1.8	1.7	1.2	3.1

VENEZUELA, REPUBLICA BOLIVARIANA de

(US$ million, unless otherwise indicated)

	1970	1980	1990	1994	1995	1996	1997	1998	1999	2000
7. DEBT RESTRUCTURINGS										
Total amount rescheduled	..	..	17,659	0	0	0	0	0	0	0
Debt stock rescheduled	..	..	17,630	0	0	0	0	0	0	0
Principal rescheduled	..	..	0	0	0	0	0	0	0	0
Official	..	..	0	0	0	0	0	0	0	0
Private	..	..	0	0	0	0	0	0	0	0
Interest rescheduled	..	..	0	0	0	0	0	0	0	0
Official	..	..	0	0	0	0	0	0	0	0
Private	..	..	0	0	0	0	0	0	0	0
Debt forgiven	..	..	0	0	0	0	0	0	0	0
Memo: interest forgiven	..	..	0	0	0	0	0	0	0	0
Debt stock reduction	..	..	2,361	0	0	0	4,400	0	0	0
of which debt buyback	..	..	634	0	0	0	4,000	0	0	0
8. DEBT STOCK-FLOW RECONCILIATION										
Total change in debt stocks	..	..	793	-689	-1,313	-1,003	1,262	2,440	-45	4
Net flows on debt	215	5,556	2,037	-1,584	-1,670	-109	2,605	2,106	301	336
Net change in interest arrears	..	..	-6	103	-20	-125	-21	-27	-38	-4
Interest capitalized	..	..	0	0	0	0	0	0	0	0
Debt forgiveness or reduction	..	..	-1,727	0	0	0	-400	0	0	0
Cross-currency valuation	..	..	379	753	365	-784	-960	434	-253	-327
Residual	..	..	110	39	12	15	38	-73	-56	-1
9. AVERAGE TERMS OF NEW COMMITMENTS										
ALL CREDITORS										
Interest (%)	7.2	12.1	8.2	7.1	7.4	7.5	7.7	7.9	7.5	8.2
Maturity (years)	8.3	7.7	14.5	14.1	7.3	8.4	16.5	9.3	8.2	8.1
Grace period (years)	1.9	3.1	5.6	3.6	3.6	3.8	13.3	1.5	3.9	2.6
Grant element (%)	11.0	-8.5	9.5	15.0	9.5	9.2	9.1	6.8	15.9	6.2
Official creditors										
Interest (%)	8.0	8.3	7.8	6.9	6.8	7.3	6.7	7.0	0.3	8.0
Maturity (years)	17.7	12.4	15.6	15.8	17.2	18.0	9.7	10.2	30.0	12.7
Grace period (years)	2.9	2.7	4.9	4.3	5.2	4.5	2.2	2.5	10.5	2.6
Grant element (%)	9.4	7.1	11.8	16.9	19.1	15.9	11.9	11.4	80.6	9.9
Private creditors										
Interest (%)	7.0	12.3	8.5	7.4	7.7	7.6	8.0	8.7	9.0	8.3
Maturity (years)	6.8	7.5	13.6	9.0	3.2	7.2	18.4	8.5	3.4	6.3
Grace period (years)	1.7	3.1	6.1	1.4	3.0	3.7	16.5	0.5	2.5	2.7
Grant element (%)	11.3	-9.3	7.8	9.0	5.6	8.4	8.4	2.1	1.7	4.7
Memorandum items										
Commitments	188	2,769	3,209	777	1,033	1,731	10,140	3,956	355	1,553
Official creditors	25	133	1,362	586	298	199	2,225	2,005	64	430
Private creditors	163	2,636	1,847	191	735	1,532	7,916	1,951	291	1,123

10. CONTRACTUAL OBLIGATIONS ON OUTSTANDING LONG-TERM DEBT

	2001	2002	2003	2004	2005	2006	2007	2008	2009	2010
TOTAL										
Disbursements	1,112	731	371	181	80	40	17	7	4	3
Principal	4,760	5,212	3,993	3,520	2,719	2,310	2,448	1,106	729	957
Interest	2,612	2,341	1,974	1,718	1,524	1,299	1,156	1,010	938	880
Official creditors										
Disbursements	566	476	302	150	79	40	17	7	4	3
Principal	1,420	1,424	1,080	791	598	395	362	298	243	237
Interest	416	354	279	225	176	142	115	91	72	56
Bilateral creditors										
Disbursements	67	40	12	4	1	1	0	0	0	0
Principal	928	923	553	231	138	24	8	5	4	6
Interest	149	96	42	19	8	3	2	1	1	0
Multilateral creditors										
Disbursements	499	436	290	147	78	39	17	7	4	3
Principal	492	501	526	560	460	372	354	292	239	231
Interest	267	258	238	205	168	139	114	90	71	55
Private creditors										
Disbursements	547	254	70	31	1	0	0	0	0	0
Principal	3,340	3,787	2,913	2,729	2,121	1,914	2,086	808	486	721
Interest	2,196	1,987	1,695	1,493	1,348	1,158	1,041	919	867	824
Commercial banks										
Disbursements	464	202	63	29	0	0	0	0	0	0
Principal	1,094	1,282	728	358	200	143	82	68	51	36
Interest	240	184	97	60	37	24	15	9	5	2
Other private										
Disbursements	82	52	7	2	1	0	0	0	0	0
Principal	2,246	2,505	2,185	2,371	1,921	1,771	2,003	740	435	685
Interest	1,956	1,804	1,598	1,434	1,311	1,133	1,026	910	862	822

VIETNAM

(US$ million, unless otherwise indicated)

	1970	1980	1990	1994	1995	1996	1997	1998	1999	2000
1. SUMMARY DEBT DATA										
TOTAL DEBT STOCKS (EDT)	..	..	**23,270**	**24,800**	**25,427**	**26,257**	**21,780**	**22,502**	**23,260**	**12,787**
Long-term debt (LDOD)	..	..	**21,378**	**21,855**	**21,777**	**21,964**	**18,986**	**19,918**	**20,529**	**11,546**
Public and publicly guaranteed	..	..	21,378	21,855	21,777	21,964	18,986	19,918	20,529	11,546
Private nonguaranteed	..	..	0	0	0	0	0	0	0	0
Use of IMF credit	**0**	**0**	**112**	**282**	**377**	**539**	**452**	**391**	**355**	**316**
Short-term debt	..	..	**1,780**	**2,663**	**3,272**	**3,754**	**2,342**	**2,193**	**2,376**	**925**
of which interest arrears on LDOD	..	..	1,530	2,209	2,501	2,741	1,391	1,545	1,689	80
Official creditors	..	..	859	1,716	1,999	2,238	1,391	1,543	1,687	78
Private creditors	..	..	671	494	502	503	0	2	2	2
Memo: principal arrears on LDOD	..	..	2,011	7,205	8,915	10,574	7,360	8,046	8,601	1,386
Official creditors	..	..	1,091	6,857	8,460	10,104	7,359	8,041	8,591	1,379
Private creditors	..	..	921	347	456	470	1	5	9	7
Memo: export credits	..	..	431	515	567	866	985	1,197	929	489
TOTAL DEBT FLOWS										
Disbursements	..	..	**13**	**455**	**729**	**742**	**1,205**	**1,303**	**1,079**	**1,189**
Long-term debt	..	..	13	282	637	566	1,205	1,303	1,079	1,189
IMF purchases	0	0	0	173	92	175	0	0	0	0
Principal repayments	..	..	**104**	**210**	**225**	**200**	**589**	**665**	**1,047**	**954**
Long-term debt	..	..	99	210	225	200	535	587	1,021	932
IMF repurchases	0	0	5	0	0	0	54	78	26	21
Net flows on debt	..	..	**-95**	**95**	**821**	**784**	**554**	**335**	**71**	**393**
of which short-term debt	..	..	-4	-150	317	242	-62	-303	39	158
Interest payments (INT)	..	..	**70**	**96**	**139**	**194**	**325**	**429**	**362**	**350**
Long-term debt	..	..	46	57	82	98	268	387	326	296
IMF charges	0	0	0	7	12	10	9	6	3	3
Short-term debt	..	..	23	32	46	86	47	36	33	51
Net transfers on debt	..	..	**-165**	**-1**	**681**	**590**	**230**	**-94**	**-292**	**43**
Total debt service paid (TDS)	..	..	**174**	**306**	**364**	**393**	**913**	**1,094**	**1,410**	**1,303**
Long-term debt	..	..	146	268	306	298	803	974	1,347	1,228
IMF repurchases and charges	0	0	5	7	12	10	63	84	30	24
Short-term debt (interest only)	..	..	23	32	46	86	47	36	33	51
2. AGGREGATE NET RESOURCE FLOWS AND NET TRANSFERS (LONG-TERM)										
NET RESOURCE FLOWS	..	..	**25**	**2,740**	**3,251**	**3,381**	**3,051**	**2,623**	**1,732**	**1,790**
Net flow of long-term debt (ex. IMF)	..	..	-86	71	412	367	670	716	58	256
Foreign direct investment (net)	..	..	16	1,936	2,336	2,395	2,220	1,671	1,412	1,298
Portfolio equity flows	..	..	0	283	155	390	-94	0	0	0
Grants (excluding technical coop.)	..	..	96	449	348	230	254	236	263	236
Memo: technical coop. grants	..	..	98	189	229	237	210	204	204	246
official net resource flows	..	..	9	549	405	380	631	1,319	1,102	1,209
private net resource flows	..	..	16	2,190	2,846	3,002	2,420	1,304	631	581
NET TRANSFERS	..	..	**-21**	**2,682**	**3,169**	**3,163**	**2,632**	**2,036**	**1,067**	**1,074**
Interest on long-term debt	..	..	46	57	82	98	268	387	326	296
Profit remittances on FDI	..	..	0	0	0	120	150	200	340	420
Memo: official net transfers	..	..	-17	524	355	331	543	1,205	1,037	1,133
private net transfers	..	..	-4	2,159	2,814	2,832	2,089	831	29	-59
3. MAJOR ECONOMIC AGGREGATES										
Gross national income (GNI)	..	..	..	15,531	19,819	22,997	27,609	27,184	28,682	31,344
Exports of goods & services (XGS)	..	..	1,953	5,364	7,441	10,214	11,819	12,101	14,152	17,299
of which workers remittances	..	..	..	..	..	..	..	..	..	..
Imports of goods & services (MGS)	..	..	2,353	6,874	9,992	13,852	14,349	14,323	14,049	18,133
International reserves (RES)	..	..	..	..	1,324	1,736	1,986	2,002	3,326	3,417
Current account balance	..	..	-351	-1,340	-2,078	-2,592	-1,817	-1,271	1,154	507
4. DEBT INDICATORS										
EDT / XGS (%)	..	..	1,191.5	462.4	341.7	257.1	184.3	186.0	164.4	73.9
EDT / GNI (%)	..	..	..	159.7	128.3	114.2	78.9	82.8	81.1	40.8
TDS / XGS (%)	..	..	8.9	5.7	4.9	3.9	7.7	9.0	10.0	7.5
INT / XGS (%)	..	..	3.6	1.8	1.9	1.9	2.8	3.5	2.6	2.0
INT / GNI (%)	..	..	..	0.6	0.7	0.8	1.2	1.6	1.3	1.1
RES / EDT (%)	..	..	..	..	5.2	6.6	9.1	8.9	14.3	26.7
RES / MGS (months)	..	..	..	..	1.6	1.5	1.7	1.7	2.8	2.3
Short-term / EDT (%)	..	..	7.7	10.7	12.9	14.3	10.8	9.8	10.2	7.2
Concessional / EDT (%)	..	..	84.9	81.7	78.4	76.1	15.4	20.2	24.2	48.3
Multilateral / EDT (%)	..	..	0.6	0.9	1.3	2.0	3.8	5.6	6.9	14.4

VIETNAM

(US$ million, unless otherwise indicated)

	1970	1980	1990	1994	1995	1996	1997	1998	1999	2000
5. LONG-TERM DEBT										
DEBT OUTSTANDING (LDOD)	..	..	**21,378**	**21,855**	**21,777**	**21,964**	**18,986**	**19,918**	**20,529**	**11,546**
Public and publicly guaranteed	..	..	**21,378**	**21,855**	**21,777**	**21,964**	**18,986**	**19,918**	**20,529**	**11,546**
Official creditors	..	..	20,171	20,868	20,449	20,481	14,242	15,489	16,865	6,951
Multilateral	..	..	130	228	325	526	828	1,270	1,606	1,847
Concessional	..	..	103	228	325	526	819	1,252	1,585	1,818
Bilateral	..	..	20,042	20,640	20,124	19,955	13,414	14,220	15,260	5,104
Concessional	..	..	19,646	20,034	19,613	19,442	2,530	3,303	4,043	4,356
Private creditors	..	..	1,207	986	1,328	1,483	4,744	4,429	3,663	4,595
Bonds	..	..	0	0	0	0	560	560	560	560
Commercial banks	..	..	684	662	1,044	1,213	3,465	3,120	2,311	1,670
Other private	..	..	523	325	285	271	719	749	793	2,366
Private nonguaranteed	..	..	**0**	**0**	**0**	**0**	**0**	**0**	**0**	**0**
Bonds	..	..	0	0	0	0	0	0	0	0
Commercial banks and other	..	..	0	0	0	0	0	0	0	0
Memo:										
IBRD	0	0	0	0	0	0	0	0	0	0
IDA	0	2	59	181	231	412	569	851	989	1,113
DISBURSEMENTS	..	..	**13**	**282**	**637**	**566**	**1,205**	**1,303**	**1,079**	**1,189**
Public and publicly guaranteed	..	..	**13**	**282**	**637**	**566**	**1,205**	**1,303**	**1,079**	**1,189**
Official creditors	..	..	13	187	232	325	562	1,167	924	1,101
Multilateral	..	..	4	129	100	218	346	392	342	346
Concessional	..	..	0	129	100	218	338	384	338	338
Bilateral	..	..	9	58	132	107	216	775	583	755
Concessional	..	..	8	16	131	104	206	733	553	715
Private creditors	..	..	0	95	405	241	643	136	155	87
Bonds	..	..	0	0	0	0	0	0	0	0
Commercial banks	..	..	0	94	389	207	184	56	20	6
Other private	..	..	0	1	17	35	460	80	135	81
Private nonguaranteed	..	..	**0**	**0**	**0**	**0**	**0**	**0**	**0**	**0**
Bonds	..	..	0	0	0	0	0	0	0	0
Commercial banks and other	..	..	0	0	0	0	0	0	0	0
Memo:										
IBRD	0	0	0	0	0	0	0	0	0	0
IDA	0	1	0	126	47	189	181	254	158	174
PRINCIPAL REPAYMENTS	..	..	**99**	**210**	**225**	**200**	**535**	**587**	**1,021**	**932**
Public and publicly guaranteed	..	..	**99**	**210**	**225**	**200**	**535**	**587**	**1,021**	**932**
Official creditors	..	..	99	87	175	175	185	84	85	128
Multilateral	..	..	3	6	7	6	6	5	6	6
Concessional	..	..	3	6	7	6	6	5	6	6
Bilateral	..	..	96	81	168	169	179	79	80	123
Concessional	..	..	44	62	72	77	56	43	57	88
Private creditors	..	..	0	124	50	25	349	503	936	804
Bonds	..	..	0	0	0	0	0	0	0	0
Commercial banks	..	..	0	0	0	6	331	428	829	618
Other private	..	..	0	124	50	19	19	75	107	186
Private nonguaranteed	..	..	**0**	**0**	**0**	**0**	**0**	**0**	**0**	**0**
Bonds	..	..	0	0	0	0	0	0	0	0
Commercial banks and other	..	..	0	0	0	0	0	0	0	0
Memo:										
IBRD	0	0	0	0	0	0	0	0	0	0
IDA	0	0	1	1	1	1	1	1	2	2
NET FLOWS ON DEBT	..	..	**-86**	**71**	**412**	**367**	**670**	**716**	**58**	**256**
Public and publicly guaranteed	..	..	**-86**	**71**	**412**	**367**	**670**	**716**	**58**	**256**
Official creditors	..	..	-86	100	57	150	376	1,083	839	973
Multilateral	..	..	1	123	94	212	340	387	336	340
Concessional	..	..	-3	123	94	212	331	379	332	332
Bilateral	..	..	-87	-23	-37	-62	37	696	503	633
Concessional	..	..	-36	-46	59	27	150	689	496	627
Private creditors	..	..	0	-29	355	217	294	-367	-781	-717
Bonds	..	..	0	0	0	0	0	0	0	0
Commercial banks	..	..	0	94	389	201	-147	-373	-810	-612
Other private	..	..	0	-122	-33	16	441	5	29	-105
Private nonguaranteed	..	..	**0**	**0**	**0**	**0**	**0**	**0**	**0**	**0**
Bonds	..	..	0	0	0	0	0	0	0	0
Commercial banks and other	..	..	0	0	0	0	0	0	0	0
Memo:										
IBRD	0	0	0	0	0	0	0	0	0	0
IDA	0	1	-1	125	47	188	180	253	156	173

VIETNAM

(US$ million, unless otherwise indicated)

	1970	1980	1990	1994	1995	1996	1997	1998	1999	2000
INTEREST PAYMENTS (LINT)	..	..	**46**	**57**	**82**	**98**	**268**	**387**	**326**	**296**
Public and publicly guaranteed	..	..	**46**	**57**	**82**	**98**	**268**	**387**	**326**	**296**
Official creditors	..	..	26	26	50	48	87	114	64	75
Multilateral	..	..	2	2	3	3	5	8	12	14
Concessional	..	..	0	2	3	3	5	8	12	13
Bilateral	..	..	24	24	47	45	82	106	52	61
Concessional	..	..	3	13	21	20	53	53	38	46
Private creditors	..	..	20	32	32	50	181	273	262	220
Bonds	..	..	0	0	0	0	0	12	23	23
Commercial banks	..	..	5	11	24	43	164	232	197	155
Other private	..	..	16	20	8	7	17	29	42	43
Private nonguaranteed	..	..	**0**	**0**	**0**	**0**	**0**	**0**	**0**	**0**
Bonds	..	..	0	0	0	0	0	0	0	0
Commercial banks and other	..	..	0	0	0	0	0	0	0	0
Memo:										
IBRD	0	0	0	0	0	0	0	0	0	0
IDA	0	0	0	1	2	2	3	5	7	8
NET TRANSFERS ON DEBT	..	..	**-133**	**14**	**331**	**268**	**402**	**329**	**-268**	**-39**
Public and publicly guaranteed	..	..	**-133**	**14**	**331**	**268**	**402**	**329**	**-268**	**-39**
Official creditors	..	..	-113	74	7	101	289	969	775	898
Multilateral	..	..	-1	121	91	209	334	379	324	326
Concessional	..	..	-3	121	91	209	326	371	321	319
Bilateral	..	..	-112	-47	-84	-107	-45	590	451	571
Concessional	..	..	-39	-59	38	7	97	636	459	582
Private creditors	..	..	-20	-60	323	167	113	-640	-1,043	-937
Bonds	..	..	0	0	0	0	0	-12	-23	-23
Commercial banks	..	..	-5	82	365	158	-311	-605	-1,006	-766
Other private	..	..	-16	-143	-41	9	424	-23	-14	-148
Private nonguaranteed	..	..	**0**	**0**	**0**	**0**	**0**	**0**	**0**	**0**
Bonds	..	..	0	0	0	0	0	0	0	0
Commercial banks and other	..	..	0	0	0	0	0	0	0	0
Memo:										
IBRD	0	0	0	0	0	0	0	0	0	0
IDA	0	1	-1	125	45	186	177	248	150	165
DEBT SERVICE (LTDS)	..	..	**146**	**268**	**306**	**298**	**803**	**974**	**1,347**	**1,228**
Public and publicly guaranteed	..	..	**146**	**268**	**306**	**298**	**803**	**974**	**1,347**	**1,228**
Official creditors	..	..	125	112	224	224	273	198	149	204
Multilateral	..	..	5	8	9	9	12	13	18	20
Concessional	..	..	3	8	9	9	12	13	17	19
Bilateral	..	..	121	105	215	214	261	185	132	184
Concessional	..	..	47	75	93	97	109	97	95	134
Private creditors	..	..	20	155	82	74	530	776	1,197	1,024
Bonds	..	..	0	0	0	0	0	12	23	23
Commercial banks	..	..	5	11	24	48	495	661	1,026	772
Other private	..	..	16	144	58	26	36	104	149	229
Private nonguaranteed	..	..	**0**	**0**	**0**	**0**	**0**	**0**	**0**	**0**
Bonds	..	..	0	0	0	0	0	0	0	0
Commercial banks and other	..	..	0	0	0	0	0	0	0	0
Memo:										
IBRD	0	0	0	0	0	0	0	0	0	0
IDA	0	0	1	1	2	3	4	5	8	9
UNDISBURSED DEBT	..	..	**155**	**1,835**	**3,591**	**4,345**	**8,604**	**5,597**	**5,288**	**4,126**
Official creditors	..	..	89	1,470	3,097	3,924	8,338	5,294	5,106	4,034
Private creditors	..	..	66	365	494	421	266	303	182	92
Memorandum items										
Concessional LDOD	..	..	19,750	20,262	19,937	19,968	3,349	4,555	5,627	6,174
Variable rate LDOD	..	..	847	887	1,000	1,077	3,500	3,290	2,565	1,964
Public sector LDOD	..	..	21,378	21,855	21,777	21,964	18,986	19,918	20,529	11,546
Private sector LDOD	..	..	0	0	0	0	0	0	0	0

6. CURRENCY COMPOSITION OF LONG-TERM DEBT (PERCENT)

	1970	1980	1990	1994	1995	1996	1997	1998	1999	2000
Deutsche mark	..	..	1.7	0.6	1.0	1.0	0.9	0.9	0.7	1.0
French franc	..	..	1.0	0.9	1.0	1.0	1.6	1.9	2.3	4.0
Japanese yen	..	..	2.0	5.8	5.6	4.7	5.4	9.1	12.1	23.7
Pound sterling	..	..	0.2	0.1	0.1	0.2	0.1	0.1	0.1	0.1
Swiss franc	..	..	0.0	0.0	0.0	0.0	0.1	0.1	0.1	0.1
U.S.dollars	..	..	5.5	6.4	8.4	10.3	30.7	29.3	26.8	42.9
Multiple currency	..	..	0.2	0.1	0.3	0.4	1.1	1.8	2.5	5.1
Special drawing rights	..	..	0.0	0.0	0.0	0.0	0.1	0.1	0.2	0.3
All other currencies	..	..	89.4	86.1	83.6	82.4	60.0	56.7	55.2	22.8

VIETNAM

(US$ million, unless otherwise indicated)

	1970	1980	1990	1994	1995	1996	1997	1998	1999	2000
7. DEBT RESTRUCTURINGS										
Total amount rescheduled	..	..	410	0	90	168	887	15	1	0
Debt stock rescheduled	..	..	0	0	0	0	0	0	0	0
Principal rescheduled	..	..	0	0	61	108	407	5	0	0
Official	..	..	0	0	48	108	12	5	0	0
Private	..	..	0	0	13	0	395	0	0	0
Interest rescheduled	..	..	..	0	1	0	303	5	0	0
Official	..	..	0	0	1	0	0	5	0	0
Private	..	..	0	0	0	0	303	0	0	0
Debt forgiven	..	..	0	0	32	0	0	0	1	5
Memo: interest forgiven	..	..	0	0	0	0	0	0	0	1,631
Debt stock reduction	..	..	0	0	0	0	249	0	0	8,759
of which debt buyback	..	..	0	0	0	0	31	0	0	0
8. DEBT STOCK-FLOW RECONCILIATION										
Total change in debt stocks	..	..	..	633	627	830	-4,477	723	758	-10,473
Net flows on debt	..	..	-95	95	821	784	554	335	71	393
Net change in interest arrears	..	..	..	344	292	240	-1,351	154	144	-1,609
Interest capitalized	..	..	..	0	1	0	303	5	0	0
Debt forgiveness or reduction	..	..	..	0	-32	0	-218	0	-1	-8,763
Cross-currency valuation	..	..	..	199	1	-203	-335	183	120	-461
Residual	..	..	..	-5	-456	9	-3,431	46	424	-32
9. AVERAGE TERMS OF NEW COMMITMENTS										
ALL CREDITORS										
Interest (%)	..	..	5.7	2.7	3.3	2.5	3.2	2.4	2.4	1.4
Maturity (years)	..	..	9.6	26.3	26.3	29.6	27.1	29.1	32.4	35.2
Grace period (years)	..	..	4.2	7.8	7.9	8.6	7.6	8.2	8.4	8.8
Grant element (%)	..	..	19.9	56.9	51.9	59.3	52.6	59.5	60.3	71.9
Official creditors										
Interest (%)	..	..	5.7	0.9	2.3	1.9	2.1	2.0	2.3	1.4
Maturity (years)	..	..	9.6	33.9	31.5	33.4	32.5	30.8	34.0	35.2
Grace period (years)	..	..	4.2	9.9	9.5	9.8	9.6	8.9	9.0	8.8
Grant element (%)	..	..	19.9	76.1	63.4	67.0	65.5	63.5	62.8	71.9
Private creditors										
Interest (%)	..	..	0.0	6.3	6.7	5.8	7.0	5.6	3.6	0.0
Maturity (years)	..	..	0.0	10.9	7.1	9.1	9.8	12.2	11.6	0.0
Grace period (years)	..	..	0.0	3.5	2.0	2.0	1.1	1.6	1.7	0.0
Grant element (%)	..	..	0.0	17.7	10.3	17.7	11.1	19.8	27.6	0.0
Memorandum items										
Commitments	..	..	11	1,400	2,466	1,799	2,027	1,833	560	413
Official creditors	..	..	11	941	1,933	1,519	1,547	1,663	520	413
Private creditors	..	..	0	460	533	280	481	170	40	0

10. CONTRACTUAL OBLIGATIONS ON OUTSTANDING LONG-TERM DEBT

	2001	2002	2003	2004	2005	2006	2007	2008	2009	2010
TOTAL										
Disbursements	1,401	1,123	725	457	245	104	52	14	6	0
Principal	805	822	425	311	371	412	488	580	572	566
Interest	375	340	300	282	278	268	275	258	243	226
Official creditors										
Disbursements	1,343	1,096	719	455	245	104	52	14	6	0
Principal	110	127	151	182	237	286	330	388	389	401
Interest	113	123	131	132	136	134	148	141	136	127
Bilateral creditors										
Disbursements	745	551	325	187	99	47	21	5	1	0
Principal	104	121	141	160	203	241	267	307	293	297
Interest	89	96	99	99	96	92	101	95	87	81
Multilateral creditors										
Disbursements	598	545	394	268	145	57	31	9	5	0
Principal	6	6	10	22	33	45	63	81	96	104
Interest	24	27	31	33	40	42	46	46	49	47
Private creditors										
Disbursements	58	26	6	1	1	0	0	0	0	0
Principal	695	696	274	129	135	125	158	192	182	165
Interest	262	216	169	150	142	134	127	117	108	98
Commercial banks										
Disbursements	11	4	1	0	0	0	0	0	0	0
Principal	599	599	189	38	37	31	24	18	17	15
Interest	116	75	33	19	17	14	13	11	10	9
Other private										
Disbursements	48	22	4	1	1	0	0	0	0	0
Principal	96	97	86	78	72	68	109	148	140	125
Interest	123	118	113	107	103	98	94	87	79	72

YEMEN, REPUBLIC OF

(US$ million, unless otherwise indicated)

	1970	1980	1990	1994	1995	1996	1997	1998	1999	2000
1. SUMMARY DEBT DATA										
TOTAL DEBT STOCKS (EDT)	..	**1,684**	**6,352**	**6,593**	**6,654**	**6,425**	**3,874**	**4,907**	**5,382**	**5,616**
Long-term debt (LDOD)	..	**1,453**	**5,160**	**5,875**	**5,916**	**5,678**	**3,434**	**4,357**	**4,501**	**4,525**
Public and publicly guaranteed	..	1,453	5,160	5,875	5,916	5,678	3,434	4,357	4,501	4,525
Private nonguaranteed	..	0	0	0	0	0	0	0	0	0
Use of IMF credit	**0**	**48**	**0**	**0**	**0**	**121**	**250**	**336**	**409**	**317**
Short-term debt	..	**183**	**1,192**	**719**	**738**	**626**	**190**	**215**	**473**	**774**
of which interest arrears on LDOD	..	1	192	486	522	499	70	75	86	102
Official creditors	..	0	131	344	365	329	50	55	66	82
Private creditors	..	0	61	142	157	170	20	20	20	19
Memo: principal arrears on LDOD	..	7	845	2,592	2,796	2,641	632	684	751	803
Official creditors	..	3	383	1,613	1,718	1,474	469	522	585	644
Private creditors	..	4	463	980	1,078	1,167	163	162	166	160
Memo: export credits	..	0	338	104	120	104	143	65	137	147
TOTAL DEBT FLOWS										
Disbursements	..	**576**	**305**	**119**	**118**	**286**	**287**	**236**	**309**	**80**
Long-term debt	..	566	305	119	118	164	147	164	195	80
IMF purchases	0	10	0	0	0	122	140	72	115	0
Principal repayments	..	**36**	**81**	**58**	**65**	**58**	**60**	**73**	**79**	**125**
Long-term debt	..	25	80	58	65	58	60	73	45	54
IMF repurchases	0	11	1	0	0	0	0	0	34	71
Net flows on debt	..	**546**	**386**	**99**	**36**	**140**	**219**	**183**	**478**	**240**
of which short-term debt	..	6	161	38	-17	-89	-7	20	247	285
Interest payments (INT)	..	**37**	**88**	**48**	**37**	**29**	**38**	**52**	**77**	**96**
Long-term debt	..	10	28	23	25	21	26	45	54	51
IMF charges	0	2	0	0	0	3	7	0	9	10
Short-term debt	..	25	60	25	11	5	5	7	13	36
Net transfers on debt	..	**509**	**297**	**51**	**-1**	**111**	**181**	**131**	**401**	**144**
Total debt service paid (TDS)	..	**73**	**169**	**106**	**102**	**87**	**98**	**125**	**155**	**221**
Long-term debt	..	35	108	81	91	79	86	118	99	105
IMF repurchases and charges	0	13	1	0	0	3	7	0	43	81
Short-term debt (interest only)	..	25	60	25	11	5	5	7	13	36
2. AGGREGATE NET RESOURCE FLOWS AND NET TRANSFERS (LONG-TERM)										
NET RESOURCE FLOWS	..	**944**	**333**	**153**	**-72**	**155**	**82**	**-3**	**113**	**-12**
Net flow of long-term debt (ex. IMF)	..	542	226	61	53	106	87	91	150	26
Foreign direct investment (net)	..	34	-131	11	-218	-60	-139	-219	-194	-201
Portfolio equity flows	..	0	0	0	0	0	0	0	0	0
Grants (excluding technical coop.)	..	368	238	82	92	109	133	125	157	163
Memo: technical coop. grants	..	62	106	57	65	60	65	58	50	51
official net resource flows	..	847	303	148	147	215	221	216	307	189
private net resource flows	..	97	30	5	-220	-60	-139	-219	-194	-201
NET TRANSFERS	..	**934**	**304**	**130**	**-98**	**134**	**55**	**-48**	**59**	**-63**
Interest on long-term debt	..	10	28	23	25	21	26	45	54	51
Profit remittances on FDI	..	0	0	0	0	0	0	0	0	0
Memo: official net transfers	..	838	279	128	122	195	194	171	253	138
private net transfers	..	96	25	2	-220	-60	-139	-219	-194	-201
3. MAJOR ECONOMIC AGGREGATES										
Gross national income (GNI)	..	..	4,792	3,732	4,067	5,187	6,287	5,901	6,590	7,386
Exports of goods & services (XGS)	..	..	3,026	3,026	3,277	3,630	3,720	2,982	3,979	5,870
of which workers remittances	..	..	1,498	1,059	1,081	1,135	1,169	1,202	1,223	1,255
Imports of goods & services (MGS)	..	..	2,579	2,780	3,069	3,530	3,755	3,258	3,410	3,973
International reserves (RES)	..	..	441	274	638	1,036	1,218	1,010	1,486	2,914
Current account balance	..	..	739	250	184	106	22	-149	769	2,063
4. DEBT INDICATORS										
EDT / XGS (%)	..	..	209.9	217.9	203.0	177.0	104.1	164.6	135.3	95.7
EDT / GNI (%)	..	..	132.6	176.7	163.6	123.9	61.6	83.2	81.7	76.0
TDS / XGS (%)	..	..	5.6	3.5	3.1	2.4	2.6	4.2	3.9	3.8
INT / XGS (%)	..	..	2.9	1.6	1.1	0.8	1.0	1.7	1.9	1.6
INT / GNI (%)	..	..	1.8	1.3	0.9	0.6	0.6	0.9	1.2	1.3
RES / EDT (%)	..	..	7.0	4.2	9.6	16.1	31.4	20.6	27.6	51.9
RES / MGS (months)	..	..	2.1	1.2	2.5	3.5	3.9	3.7	5.2	8.8
Short-term / EDT (%)	..	10.8	18.8	10.9	11.1	9.8	4.9	4.4	8.8	13.8
Concessional / EDT (%)	..	72.1	50.7	59.0	58.8	55.7	79.6	82.0	77.8	75.6
Multilateral / EDT (%)	..	14.9	16.1	18.3	19.2	21.1	35.9	37.7	40.0	36.7

YEMEN, REPUBLIC OF

(US$ million, unless otherwise indicated)

	1970	1980	1990	1994	1995	1996	1997	1998	1999	2000
5. LONG-TERM DEBT										
DEBT OUTSTANDING (LDOD)	..	**1,453**	**5,160**	**5,875**	**5,916**	**5,678**	**3,434**	**4,357**	**4,501**	**4,525**
Public and publicly guaranteed	..	**1,453**	**5,160**	**5,875**	**5,916**	**5,678**	**3,434**	**4,357**	**4,501**	**4,525**
Official creditors	..	1,238	3,502	4,154	4,198	3,959	3,251	4,179	4,324	4,358
Multilateral	..	252	1,025	1,206	1,278	1,358	1,390	1,850	2,153	2,060
Concessional	..	252	989	1,183	1,239	1,303	1,331	1,806	2,127	2,056
Bilateral	..	986	2,477	2,949	2,920	2,601	1,861	2,328	2,172	2,297
Concessional	..	962	2,232	2,704	2,675	2,276	1,751	2,218	2,062	2,187
Private creditors	..	216	1,658	1,720	1,718	1,719	182	178	177	167
Bonds	..	0	0	0	0	0	0	0	0	0
Commercial banks	..	0	80	80	80	80	80	80	80	80
Other private	..	216	1,578	1,640	1,638	1,639	102	98	97	87
Private nonguaranteed	..	**0**	**0**	**0**	**0**	**0**	**0**	**0**	**0**	**0**
Bonds	..	0	0	0	0	0	0	0	0	0
Commercial banks and other	..	0	0	0	0	0	0	0	0	0
Memo:										
IBRD	0	0	0	0	0	0	0	0	0	0
IDA	0	137	602	780	828	893	934	1,075	1,216	1,217
DISBURSEMENTS	..	**566**	**305**	**119**	**118**	**164**	**147**	**164**	**195**	**80**
Public and publicly guaranteed	..	**566**	**305**	**119**	**118**	**164**	**147**	**164**	**195**	**80**
Official creditors	..	501	139	118	118	164	147	164	195	80
Multilateral	..	65	56	113	109	161	145	164	193	78
Concessional	..	65	55	95	88	134	134	160	189	78
Bilateral	..	437	84	6	9	3	2	0	1	2
Concessional	..	426	84	6	9	3	2	0	1	2
Private creditors	..	65	166	0	0	0	0	0	0	0
Bonds	..	0	0	0	0	0	0	0	0	0
Commercial banks	..	0	0	0	0	0	0	0	0	0
Other private	..	65	166	0	0	0	0	0	0	0
Private nonguaranteed	..	**0**	**0**	**0**	**0**	**0**	**0**	**0**	**0**	**0**
Bonds	..	0	0	0	0	0	0	0	0	0
Commercial banks and other	..	0	0	0	0	0	0	0	0	0
Memo:										
IBRD	0	0	0	0	0	0	0	0	0	0
IDA	0	28	27	37	42	95	89	122	173	65
PRINCIPAL REPAYMENTS	..	**25**	**80**	**58**	**65**	**58**	**60**	**73**	**45**	**54**
Public and publicly guaranteed	..	**25**	**80**	**58**	**65**	**58**	**60**	**73**	**45**	**54**
Official creditors	..	23	74	52	64	58	60	73	45	54
Multilateral	..	3	41	45	53	54	60	73	42	44
Concessional	..	3	26	44	48	45	55	52	21	23
Bilateral	..	20	34	8	10	4	0	0	2	10
Concessional	..	16	34	8	10	4	0	0	2	10
Private creditors	..	2	5	5	2	0	0	0	0	0
Bonds	..	0	0	0	0	0	0	0	0	0
Commercial banks	..	0	0	0	0	0	0	0	0	0
Other private	..	2	5	5	2	0	0	0	0	0
Private nonguaranteed	..	**0**	**0**	**0**	**0**	**0**	**0**	**0**	**0**	**0**
Bonds	..	0	0	0	0	0	0	0	0	0
Commercial banks and other	..	0	0	0	0	0	0	0	0	0
Memo:										
IBRD	0	0	0	0	0	0	0	0	0	0
IDA	0	0	2	7	8	9	10	11	12	14
NET FLOWS ON DEBT	..	**542**	**226**	**61**	**53**	**106**	**87**	**91**	**150**	**26**
Public and publicly guaranteed	..	**542**	**226**	**61**	**53**	**106**	**87**	**91**	**150**	**26**
Official creditors	..	479	65	66	55	106	87	91	150	26
Multilateral	..	62	15	68	56	107	86	91	151	35
Concessional	..	62	29	51	40	89	78	108	168	56
Bilateral	..	416	50	-2	-1	-1	2	0	-1	-9
Concessional	..	410	50	-2	-1	-1	2	0	-1	-9
Private creditors	..	63	161	-5	-2	0	0	0	0	0
Bonds	..	0	0	0	0	0	0	0	0	0
Commercial banks	..	0	0	0	0	0	0	0	0	0
Other private	..	63	161	-5	-2	0	0	0	0	0
Private nonguaranteed	..	**0**	**0**	**0**	**0**	**0**	**0**	**0**	**0**	**0**
Bonds	..	0	0	0	0	0	0	0	0	0
Commercial banks and other	..	0	0	0	0	0	0	0	0	0
Memo:										
IBRD	0	0	0	0	0	0	0	0	0	0
IDA	0	28	25	30	34	86	79	111	160	51

YEMEN, REPUBLIC OF

(US$ million, unless otherwise indicated)

	1970	1980	1990	1994	1995	1996	1997	1998	1999	2000
INTEREST PAYMENTS (LINT)	..	**10**	**28**	**23**	**25**	**21**	**26**	**45**	**54**	**51**
Public and publicly guaranteed	..	**10**	**28**	**23**	**25**	**21**	**26**	**45**	**54**	**51**
Official creditors	..	9	23	20	25	21	26	45	54	51
Multilateral	..	5	14	17	18	18	21	21	12	12
Concessional	..	5	12	16	17	16	17	17	10	11
Bilateral	..	4	9	3	7	3	6	24	42	39
Concessional	..	4	9	3	7	3	0	17	34	39
Private creditors	..	1	5	3	1	0	0	0	0	0
Bonds	..	0	0	0	0	0	0	0	0	0
Commercial banks	..	0	0	0	0	0	0	0	0	0
Other private	..	1	5	3	1	0	0	0	0	0
Private nonguaranteed	..	**0**	**0**	**0**	**0**	**0**	**0**	**0**	**0**	**0**
Bonds	..	0	0	0	0	0	0	0	0	0
Commercial banks and other	..	0	0	0	0	0	0	0	0	0
Memo:										
IBRD	0	0	0	0	0	0	0	0	0	0
IDA	0	1	4	6	6	6	7	7	8	9
NET TRANSFERS ON DEBT	..	**531**	**198**	**38**	**28**	**85**	**61**	**46**	**96**	**-24**
Public and publicly guaranteed	..	**531**	**198**	**38**	**28**	**85**	**61**	**46**	**96**	**-24**
Official creditors	..	469	42	46	30	85	61	46	96	-24
Multilateral	..	57	1	52	38	89	65	70	139	23
Concessional	..	57	17	35	23	73	61	91	159	45
Bilateral	..	412	41	-5	-8	-4	-4	-24	-43	-47
Concessional	..	405	41	-5	-8	-4	2	-17	-36	-47
Private creditors	..	62	156	-8	-2	0	0	0	0	0
Bonds	..	0	0	0	0	0	0	0	0	0
Commercial banks	..	0	0	0	0	0	0	0	0	0
Other private	..	62	156	-8	-2	0	0	0	0	0
Private nonguaranteed	..	**0**	**0**	**0**	**0**	**0**	**0**	**0**	**0**	**0**
Bonds	..	0	0	0	0	0	0	0	0	0
Commercial banks and other	..	0	0	0	0	0	0	0	0	0
Memo:										
IBRD	0	0	0	0	0	0	0	0	0	0
IDA	0	27	22	24	28	80	72	104	152	42
DEBT SERVICE (LTDS)	..	**35**	**108**	**81**	**91**	**79**	**86**	**118**	**99**	**105**
Public and publicly guaranteed	..	**35**	**108**	**81**	**91**	**79**	**86**	**118**	**99**	**105**
Official creditors	..	32	98	72	88	79	86	118	99	105
Multilateral	..	7	55	61	71	72	81	94	54	55
Concessional	..	7	38	60	65	62	73	69	31	33
Bilateral	..	24	43	11	17	7	6	24	44	49
Concessional	..	21	43	11	17	7	0	17	37	49
Private creditors	..	3	10	9	2	0	0	0	0	0
Bonds	..	0	0	0	0	0	0	0	0	0
Commercial banks	..	0	0	0	0	0	0	0	0	0
Other private	..	3	10	9	2	0	0	0	0	0
Private nonguaranteed	..	**0**	**0**	**0**	**0**	**0**	**0**	**0**	**0**	**0**
Bonds	..	0	0	0	0	0	0	0	0	0
Commercial banks and other	..	0	0	0	0	0	0	0	0	0
Memo:										
IBRD	0	0	0	0	0	0	0	0	0	0
IDA	0	1	6	13	14	15	16	18	20	23
UNDISBURSED DEBT	..	**1,589**	**1,656**	**809**	**727**	**799**	**767**	**447**	**305**	**428**
Official creditors	..	1,252	1,206	809	727	799	767	447	305	428
Private creditors	..	336	450	0	0	0	0	0	0	0
Memorandum items										
Concessional LDOD	..	1,214	3,221	3,887	3,914	3,579	3,082	4,025	4,189	4,243
Variable rate LDOD	..	0	80	80	80	80	80	80	80	80
Public sector LDOD	..	1,453	5,160	5,875	5,916	5,678	3,434	4,357	4,501	4,525
Private sector LDOD	..	0	0	0	0	0	0	0	0	0

6. CURRENCY COMPOSITION OF LONG-TERM DEBT (PERCENT)

	1970	1980	1990	1994	1995	1996	1997	1998	1999	2000
Deutsche mark	..	0.0	0.0	0.0	0.0	0.0	0.0	0.0	0.0	0.0
French franc	..	1.5	0.8	1.3	1.4	1.3	1.7	1.3	1.0	0.8
Japanese yen	..	0.6	4.4	6.1	5.7	5.0	7.3	6.1	6.2	5.1
Pound sterling	..	3.2	0.7	0.5	0.5	0.6	1.0	0.8	0.7	0.7
Swiss franc	..	2.8	0.3	0.3	0.3	0.3	0.4	0.4	0.3	0.3
U.S.dollars	..	22.4	20.2	19.3	19.8	22.9	56.3	65.2	67.2	69.6
Multiple currency	..	0.1	1.6	1.7	1.7	1.4	0.5	0.4	0.3	0.3
Special drawing rights	..	0.0	2.5	2.5	2.6	2.9	4.8	4.3	4.2	4.1
All other currencies	..	69.4	69.5	68.3	68.0	65.6	28.0	21.5	20.1	19.1

YEMEN, REPUBLIC OF

(US$ million, unless otherwise indicated)

	1970	1980	1990	1994	1995	1996	1997	1998	1999	2000
7. DEBT RESTRUCTURINGS										
Total amount rescheduled	..	..	98	0	0	80	685	360	209	24
Debt stock rescheduled	..	..	0	0	0	0	0	0	0	0
Principal rescheduled	..	..	98	0	0	24	559	24	25	17
Official	..	..	98	0	0	24	268	21	23	15
Private	..	..	0	0	0	0	292	2	2	2
Interest rescheduled	..	..	0	0	0	17	95	7	7	4
Official	..	..	0	0	0	17	61	6	6	4
Private	..	..	0	0	0	0	34	1	1	0
Debt forgiven	..	..	0	0	0	1	2,173	0	0	0
Memo: interest forgiven	..	..	0	0	0	0	338	0	0	0
Debt stock reduction	..	..	0	0	0	0	0	0	0	0
of which debt buyback	..	..	0	0	0	0	0	0	0	0
8. DEBT STOCK-FLOW RECONCILIATION										
Total change in debt stocks	..	..	759	-274	61	-228	-2,552	1,033	476	233
Net flows on debt	..	546	386	99	36	140	219	183	478	240
Net change in interest arrears	..	..	82	-8	37	-23	-429	5	11	16
Interest capitalized	..	..	0	0	0	17	95	7	7	4
Debt forgiveness or reduction	..	..	0	0	0	-1	-2,173	0	0	0
Cross-currency valuation	..	..	233	-402	-75	-445	-221	-10	-15	-125
Residual	..	..	58	36	63	83	-43	849	-5	98
9. AVERAGE TERMS OF NEW COMMITMENTS										
ALL CREDITORS										
Interest (%)	..	2.7	1.8	1.9	5.1	1.2	0.5	0.5	0.8	0.8
Maturity (years)	..	26.9	28.6	27.6	10.8	34.2	39.7	39.1	39.7	39.8
Grace period (years)	..	5.8	7.2	7.3	3.3	8.9	10.2	9.6	10.2	10.3
Grant element (%)	..	54.4	61.3	57.6	21.4	72.3	82.7	81.7	80.5	80.7
Official creditors										
Interest (%)	..	2.4	1.8	1.9	5.1	1.2	0.5	0.5	0.8	0.8
Maturity (years)	..	28.3	28.6	27.6	10.8	34.2	39.7	39.1	39.7	39.8
Grace period (years)	..	6.0	7.2	7.3	3.3	8.9	10.2	9.6	10.2	10.3
Grant element (%)	..	57.2	61.3	57.6	21.4	72.3	82.7	81.7	80.5	80.7
Private creditors										
Interest (%)	..	4.4	0.0	0.0	0.0	0.0	0.0	0.0	0.0	0.0
Maturity (years)	..	18.9	0.0	0.0	0.0	0.0	0.0	0.0	0.0	0.0
Grace period (years)	..	4.9	0.0	0.0	0.0	0.0	0.0	0.0	0.0	0.0
Grant element (%)	..	37.5	0.0	0.0	0.0	0.0	0.0	0.0	0.0	0.0
Memorandum items										
Commitments	..	553	201	49	80	276	149	60	128	222
Official creditors	..	476	201	49	80	276	149	60	128	222
Private creditors	..	78	0	0	0	0	0	0	0	0

10. CONTRACTUAL OBLIGATIONS ON OUTSTANDING LONG-TERM DEBT

	2001	2002	2003	2004	2005	2006	2007	2008	2009	2010
TOTAL										
Disbursements	101	113	87	59	35	21	11	0	0	0
Principal	115	124	130	126	124	125	121	118	118	139
Interest	86	85	84	82	80	77	75	73	71	68
Official creditors										
Disbursements	101	113	87	59	35	21	11	0	0	0
Principal	112	122	129	126	124	125	121	118	118	139
Interest	86	85	84	82	80	77	75	73	71	68
Bilateral creditors										
Disbursements	1	1	0	0	0	0	0	0	0	0
Principal	58	70	80	77	77	77	72	69	66	63
Interest	60	59	58	57	55	54	52	50	49	47
Multilateral creditors										
Disbursements	100	112	87	59	35	21	11	0	0	0
Principal	54	52	49	50	48	49	49	49	52	76
Interest	26	26	26	25	25	24	23	22	22	21
Private creditors										
Disbursements	0	0	0	0	0	0	0	0	0	0
Principal	3	2	2	0	0	0	0	0	0	0
Interest	0	0	0	0	0	0	0	0	0	0
Commercial banks										
Disbursements	0	0	0	0	0	0	0	0	0	0
Principal	0	0	0	0	0	0	0	0	0	0
Interest	0	0	0	0	0	0	0	0	0	0
Other private										
Disbursements	0	0	0	0	0	0	0	0	0	0
Principal	3	2	2	0	0	0	0	0	0	0
Interest	0	0	0	0	0	0	0	0	0	0

YUGOSLAVIA, FEDERAL REPUBLIC

(US$ million, unless otherwise indicated)

	1970	1980	1990	1994	1995	1996	1997	1998	1999	2000
1. SUMMARY DEBT DATA										
TOTAL DEBT STOCKS (EDT)	**2,258**	**18,486**	**17,792**	**11,453**	**11,137**	**9,762**	**10,968**	**11,250**	**11,253**	**11,960**
Long-term debt (LDOD)	**2,053**	**15,586**	**16,802**	**9,372**	**8,601**	**7,731**	**7,124**	**7,243**	**6,845**	**6,685**
Public and publicly guaranteed	1,199	4,581	12,942	6,613	6,827	6,566	6,148	6,500	6,234	6,074
Private nonguaranteed	854	11,005	3,860	2,759	1,773	1,165	976	743	611	611
Use of IMF credit	**0**	**760**	**467**	**83**	**85**	**81**	**76**	**79**	**76**	**152**
Short-term debt	**205**	**2,140**	**524**	**1,998**	**2,452**	**1,951**	**3,769**	**3,928**	**4,332**	**5,123**
of which interest arrears on LDOD	0	0	0	1,375	1,709	1,665	1,755	2,619	3,190	3,981
Official creditors	0	0	0	635	756	791	812	1,597	2,101	2,834
Private creditors	0	0	0	740	954	874	943	1,022	1,089	1,148
Memo: principal arrears on LDOD	1	0	298	4,032	4,182	3,983	3,961	4,955	4,889	5,436
Official creditors	0	0	298	1,826	2,595	2,925	2,964	3,851	3,664	3,801
Private creditors	1	0	0	2,206	1,588	1,059	997	1,104	1,225	1,636
Memo: export credits	0	0	5,521	58	36	448	582	0	0	0
TOTAL DEBT FLOWS										
Disbursements	**645**	**5,029**	**1,590**	**0**	**0**	**0**	**0**	**0**	**0**	**154**
Long-term debt	645	4,589	1,501	0	0	0	0	0	0	0
IMF purchases	0	441	89	0	0	0	0	0	0	154
Principal repayments	**420**	**2,450**	**3,079**	**0**	**0**	**1**	**0**	**0**	**1**	**73**
Long-term debt	375	2,381	2,726	0	0	0	0	0	0	0
IMF repurchases	45	70	353	0	0	1	0	0	1	73
Net flows on debt	**225**	**2,930**	**-1,760**	**-402**	**120**	**-458**	**1,728**	**-705**	**-168**	**81**
of which short-term debt	0	351	-271	-402	120	-457	1,728	-705	-167	0
Interest payments (INT)	**104**	**1,286**	**1,700**	**47**	**47**	**17**	**53**	**65**	**64**	**104**
Long-term debt	104	1,077	1,579	0	0	0	0	0	0	0
IMF charges	0	32	66	0	0	0	0	0	0	29
Short-term debt	0	177	55	47	47	17	53	65	63	75
Net transfers on debt	**121**	**1,644**	**-3,460**	**-449**	**73**	**-476**	**1,676**	**-770**	**-231**	**-23**
Total debt service paid (TDS)	**524**	**3,736**	**4,779**	**47**	**47**	**19**	**53**	**65**	**64**	**177**
Long-term debt	479	3,458	4,305	0	0	0	0	0	0	0
IMF repurchases and charges	45	101	419	0	0	1	0	0	1	102
Short-term debt (interest only)	0	177	55	47	47	17	53	65	63	75
2. AGGREGATE NET RESOURCE FLOWS AND NET TRANSFERS (LONG-TERM)										
NET RESOURCE FLOWS	**276**	**2,208**	**-1,151**	**999**	**487**	**451**	**132**	**183**	**1,055**	**1,298**
Net flow of long-term debt (ex. IMF)	270	2,208	-1,225	0	0	0	0	0	0	0
Foreign direct investment (net)	0	0	67	0	0	0	0	0	0	0
Portfolio equity flows	0	0	0	0	0	0	0	0	0	0
Grants (excluding technical coop.)	6	0	7	999	487	451	132	183	1,055	1,298
Memo: technical coop. grants	3	7	35	81	57	45	34	34	45	125
official net resource flows	57	372	-314	999	487	451	132	183	1,055	1,298
private net resource flows	219	1,836	-837	0	0	0	0	0	0	0
NET TRANSFERS	**172**	**1,130**	**-2,730**	**999**	**487**	**451**	**132**	**183**	**1,055**	**1,298**
Interest on long-term debt	104	1,077	1,579	0	0	0	0	0	0	0
Profit remittances on FDI	0	0	0	0	0	0	0	0	0	0
Memo: official net transfers	21	157	-1,041	999	487	451	132	183	1,055	1,298
private net transfers	152	973	-1,689	0	0	0	0	0	0	0
3. MAJOR ECONOMIC AGGREGATES										
Gross national income (GNI)	..	..	..	..	..	..	..	13,592	9,801	8,448
Exports of goods & services (XGS)	..	..	..	..	..	..	..	..	..	..
of which workers remittances	..	..	..	..	..	..	..	..	..	..
Imports of goods & services (MGS)	..	..	..	..	..	..	..	..	..	..
International reserves (RES)	..	..	..	..	..	..	..	..	..	..
Current account balance	..	..	..	..	..	..	..	..	..	..
4. DEBT INDICATORS										
EDT / XGS (%)	..	..	..	..	..	..	..	..	..	..
EDT / GNI (%)	..	..	..	..	..	..	..	82.8	114.8	141.6
TDS / XGS (%)	..	..	..	..	..	..	..	..	..	..
INT / XGS (%)	..	..	..	..	..	..	..	..	..	..
INT / GNI (%)	..	..	..	..	..	..	..	0.5	0.7	1.2
RES / EDT (%)	..	..	..	..	..	..	..	..	..	..
RES / MGS (months)	..	..	..	..	..	..	..	..	..	..
Short-term / EDT (%)	9.1	11.6	3.0	17.4	22.0	20.0	34.4	34.9	38.5	42.8
Concessional / EDT (%)	17.2	7.2	5.4	3.0	3.3	3.5	2.8	2.9	2.6	2.3
Multilateral / EDT (%)	11.1	7.6	17.1	11.0	11.8	12.6	11.4	13.5	13.2	12.0

YUGOSLAVIA, FEDERAL REPUBLIC

(US$ million, unless otherwise indicated)

	1970	1980	1990	1994	1995	1996	1997	1998	1999	2000
5. LONG-TERM DEBT										
DEBT OUTSTANDING (LDOD)	**2,053**	**15,586**	**16,802**	**9,372**	**8,601**	**7,731**	**7,124**	**7,243**	**6,845**	**6,685**
Public and publicly guaranteed	**1,199**	**4,581**	**12,942**	**6,613**	**6,827**	**6,566**	**6,148**	**6,500**	**6,234**	**6,074**
Official creditors	858	3,600	7,494	4,416	4,627	4,385	4,167	4,550	4,298	4,139
Multilateral	251	1,408	3,048	1,259	1,311	1,234	1,251	1,520	1,484	1,440
Concessional	3	0	0	0	0	0	0	0	0	0
Bilateral	606	2,192	4,446	3,157	3,316	3,151	2,916	3,029	2,815	2,699
Concessional	387	1,328	967	344	366	343	307	324	288	272
Private creditors	341	981	5,447	2,197	2,200	2,180	1,981	1,950	1,935	1,935
Bonds	21	10	0	0	0	0	0	0	0	0
Commercial banks	2	808	5,325	2,190	2,193	2,173	1,974	1,943	1,928	1,928
Other private	318	163	122	7	7	7	7	7	7	7
Private nonguaranteed	**854**	**11,005**	**3,860**	**2,759**	**1,773**	**1,165**	**976**	**743**	**611**	**611**
Bonds	0	0	0	0	0	0	0	0	0	0
Commercial banks and other	854	11,005	3,860	2,759	1,773	1,165	976	743	611	611
Memo:										
IBRD	244	1,359	2,433	1,204	1,252	1,178	1,112	1,148	1,132	1,097
IDA	0	0	0	0	0	0	0	0	0	0
DISBURSEMENTS	**645**	**4,589**	**1,501**	**0**	**0**	**0**	**0**	**0**	**0**	**0**
Public and publicly guaranteed	**179**	**1,366**	**286**	**0**	**0**	**0**	**0**	**0**	**0**	**0**
Official creditors	139	644	286	0	0	0	0	0	0	0
Multilateral	37	308	276	0	0	0	0	0	0	0
Concessional	0	0	0	0	0	0	0	0	0	0
Bilateral	102	336	10	0	0	0	0	0	0	0
Concessional	64	77	8	0	0	0	0	0	0	0
Private creditors	40	721	0	0	0	0	0	0	0	0
Bonds	0	0	0	0	0	0	0	0	0	0
Commercial banks	0	686	0	0	0	0	0	0	0	0
Other private	40	36	0	0	0	0	0	0	0	0
Private nonguaranteed	**465**	**3,223**	**1,215**	**0**	**0**	**0**	**0**	**0**	**0**	**0**
Bonds	0	0	0	0	0	0	0	0	0	0
Commercial banks and other	465	3,223	1,215	0	0	0	0	0	0	0
Memo:										
IBRD	37	281	269	0	0	0	0	0	0	0
IDA	0	0	0	0	0	0	0	0	0	0
PRINCIPAL REPAYMENTS	**375**	**2,381**	**2,726**	**0**	**0**	**0**	**0**	**0**	**0**	**0**
Public and publicly guaranteed	**170**	**368**	**1,516**	**0**	**0**	**0**	**0**	**0**	**0**	**0**
Official creditors	88	272	607	0	0	0	0	0	0	0
Multilateral	11	67	421	0	0	0	0	0	0	0
Concessional	0	0	0	0	0	0	0	0	0	0
Bilateral	78	206	186	0	0	0	0	0	0	0
Concessional	22	65	26	0	0	0	0	0	0	0
Private creditors	82	96	909	0	0	0	0	0	0	0
Bonds	2	2	0	0	0	0	0	0	0	0
Commercial banks	1	39	891	0	0	0	0	0	0	0
Other private	80	55	18	0	0	0	0	0	0	0
Private nonguaranteed	**204**	**2,012**	**1,210**	**0**	**0**	**0**	**0**	**0**	**0**	**0**
Bonds	0	0	0	0	0	0	0	0	0	0
Commercial banks and other	204	2,012	1,210	0	0	0	0	0	0	0
Memo:										
IBRD	10	66	405	0	0	0	0	0	0	0
IDA	0	0	0	0	0	0	0	0	0	0
NET FLOWS ON DEBT	**270**	**2,208**	**-1,225**	**0**	**0**	**0**	**0**	**0**	**0**	**0**
Public and publicly guaranteed	**9**	**998**	**-1,230**	**0**	**0**	**0**	**0**	**0**	**0**	**0**
Official creditors	51	372	-321	0	0	0	0	0	0	0
Multilateral	27	242	-145	0	0	0	0	0	0	0
Concessional	0	0	0	0	0	0	0	0	0	0
Bilateral	24	131	-176	0	0	0	0	0	0	0
Concessional	42	12	-18	0	0	0	0	0	0	0
Private creditors	-42	625	-909	0	0	0	0	0	0	0
Bonds	-2	-2	0	0	0	0	0	0	0	0
Commercial banks	-1	647	-891	0	0	0	0	0	0	0
Other private	-40	-19	-18	0	0	0	0	0	0	0
Private nonguaranteed	**261**	**1,211**	**5**	**0**	**0**	**0**	**0**	**0**	**0**	**0**
Bonds	0	0	0	0	0	0	0	0	0	0
Commercial banks and other	261	1,211	5	0	0	0	0	0	0	0
Memo:										
IBRD	27	216	-136	0	0	0	0	0	0	0
IDA	0	0	0	0	0	0	0	0	0	0

YUGOSLAVIA, FEDERAL REPUBLIC

(US$ million, unless otherwise indicated)

	1970	1980	1990	1994	1995	1996	1997	1998	1999	2000
INTEREST PAYMENTS (LINT)	**104**	**1,077**	**1,579**	**0**	**0**	**0**	**0**	**0**	**0**	**0**
Public and publicly guaranteed	**73**	**249**	**1,199**	**0**	**0**	**0**	**0**	**0**	**0**	**0**
Official creditors	37	215	727	0	0	0	0	0	0	0
Multilateral	14	111	247	0	0	0	0	0	0	0
Concessional	0	0	0	0	0	0	0	0	0	0
Bilateral	23	103	479	0	0	0	0	0	0	0
Concessional	10	39	17	0	0	0	0	0	0	0
Private creditors	36	34	472	0	0	0	0	0	0	0
Bonds	0	0	0	0	0	0	0	0	0	0
Commercial banks	0	17	454	0	0	0	0	0	0	0
Other private	35	17	19	0	0	0	0	0	0	0
Private nonguaranteed	**32**	**829**	**380**	**0**	**0**	**0**	**0**	**0**	**0**	**0**
Bonds	0	0	0	0	0	0	0	0	0	0
Commercial banks and other	32	829	380	0	0	0	0	0	0	0
Memo:										
IBRD	13	110	191	0	0	0	0	0	0	0
IDA	0	0	0	0	0	0	0	0	0	0
NET TRANSFERS ON DEBT	**166**	**1,131**	**-2,804**	**0**	**0**	**0**	**0**	**0**	**0**	**0**
Public and publicly guaranteed	**-64**	**749**	**-2,429**	**0**	**0**	**0**	**0**	**0**	**0**	**0**
Official creditors	14	158	-1,048	0	0	0	0	0	0	0
Multilateral	13	130	-393	0	0	0	0	0	0	0
Concessional	0	0	0	0	0	0	0	0	0	0
Bilateral	1	27	-656	0	0	0	0	0	0	0
Concessional	32	-27	-35	0	0	0	0	0	0	0
Private creditors	-78	591	-1,381	0	0	0	0	0	0	0
Bonds	-2	-2	0	0	0	0	0	0	0	0
Commercial banks	-1	630	-1,345	0	0	0	0	0	0	0
Other private	-75	-36	-36	0	0	0	0	0	0	0
Private nonguaranteed	**230**	**382**	**-375**	**0**	**0**	**0**	**0**	**0**	**0**	**0**
Bonds	0	0	0	0	0	0	0	0	0	0
Commercial banks and other	230	382	-375	0	0	0	0	0	0	0
Memo:										
IBRD	14	106	-327	0	0	0	0	0	0	0
IDA	0	0	0	0	0	0	0	0	0	0
DEBT SERVICE (LTDS)	**479**	**3,458**	**4,305**	**0**	**0**	**0**	**0**	**0**	**0**	**0**
Public and publicly guaranteed	**243**	**617**	**2,715**	**0**	**0**	**0**	**0**	**0**	**0**	**0**
Official creditors	125	487	1,334	0	0	0	0	0	0	0
Multilateral	24	178	669	0	0	0	0	0	0	0
Concessional	0	0	0	0	0	0	0	0	0	0
Bilateral	101	309	665	0	0	0	0	0	0	0
Concessional	33	103	43	0	0	0	0	0	0	0
Private creditors	118	130	1,381	0	0	0	0	0	0	0
Bonds	2	2	0	0	0	0	0	0	0	0
Commercial banks	1	56	1,345	0	0	0	0	0	0	0
Other private	115	72	36	0	0	0	0	0	0	0
Private nonguaranteed	**236**	**2,841**	**1,590**	**0**	**0**	**0**	**0**	**0**	**0**	**0**
Bonds	0	0	0	0	0	0	0	0	0	0
Commercial banks and other	236	2,841	1,590	0	0	0	0	0	0	0
Memo:										
IBRD	23	175	596	0	0	0	0	0	0	0
IDA	0	0	0	0	0	0	0	0	0	0
UNDISBURSED DEBT	**550**	**1,218**	**943**	**208**	**222**	**212**	**187**	**0**	**0**	**20**
Official creditors	462	1,205	943	208	222	212	187	0	0	20
Private creditors	87	13	0	0	0	0	0	0	0	0
Memorandum items										
Concessional LDOD	389	1,328	967	344	366	343	307	324	288	272
Variable rate LDOD	893	12,100	12,016	7,008	6,098	5,409	4,911	4,697	4,452	4,400
Public sector LDOD	980	3,826	12,485	6,482	6,693	6,433	5,930	6,050	5,802	5,651
Private sector LDOD	1,073	11,759	4,316	2,891	1,908	1,298	1,194	1,193	1,042	1,034

6. CURRENCY COMPOSITION OF LONG-TERM DEBT (PERCENT)

	1970	1980	1990	1994	1995	1996	1997	1998	1999	2000
Deutsche mark	13.9	13.3	8.5	9.6	10.1	9.7	9.0	9.1	8.1	7.7
French franc	2.0	0.0	4.4	7.5	7.9	7.7	7.2	6.8	6.1	5.8
Japanese yen	0.3	0.7	1.0	2.3	2.2	1.8	1.7	1.9	2.2	2.0
Pound sterling	3.6	0.1	0.4	0.7	0.6	0.7	0.8	0.7	0.5	0.5
Swiss franc	1.1	0.1	1.8	3.3	3.6	3.2	3.1	3.1	2.8	2.8
U.S.dollars	36.5	52.3	17.3	21.0	20.3	21.1	19.4	21.8	22.7	23.3
Multiple currency	24.8	30.7	56.5	47.5	46.7	47.4	49.6	47.4	49.2	49.9
Special drawing rights	0.0	0.0	0.0	0.0	0.0	0.0	0.0	0.0	0.0	0.0
All other currencies	17.8	2.8	10.1	8.1	8.6	8.4	9.2	9.2	8.4	8.0

YUGOSLAVIA, FEDERAL REPUBLIC

(US$ million, unless otherwise indicated)

	1970	1980	1990	1994	1995	1996	1997	1998	1999	2000
7. DEBT RESTRUCTURINGS										
Total amount rescheduled	..	..	0	0	0	0	0	0	0	0
Debt stock rescheduled	..	..	0	0	0	0	0	0	0	0
Principal rescheduled	..	..	0	0	0	0	0	0	0	0
Official	..	..	0	0	0	0	0	0	0	0
Private	..	..	0	0	0	0	0	0	0	0
Interest rescheduled	..	..	0	0	0	0	0	0	0	0
Official	..	..	0	0	0	0	0	0	0	0
Private	..	..	0	0	0	0	0	0	0	0
Debt forgiven	..	..	0	0	0	0	0	0	0	0
Memo: interest forgiven	..	..	0	0	0	0	0	0	0	0
Debt stock reduction	..	..	1,496	0	0	0	0	0	0	0
of which debt buyback	..	..	883	0	0	0	0	0	0	0
8. DEBT STOCK-FLOW RECONCILIATION										
Total change in debt stocks	..	..	-1,280	-1,256	-315	-1,376	1,207	282	3	708
Net flows on debt	225	2,930	-1,760	-402	120	-458	1,728	-705	-168	81
Net change in interest arrears	..	..	0	759	335	-44	90	864	571	791
Interest capitalized	..	..	0	0	0	0	0	0	0	0
Debt forgiveness or reduction	..	..	-613	0	0	0	0	0	0	0
Cross-currency valuation	..	..	484	285	215	-248	-318	163	-253	-164
Residual	..	..	610	-1,898	-985	-625	-294	-41	-147	-1
9. AVERAGE TERMS OF NEW COMMITMENTS										
ALL CREDITORS										
Interest (%)	7.0	15.1	8.1	0.0	0.0	0.0	0.0	0.0	0.0	0.8
Maturity (years)	17.2	8.6	16.0	0.0	0.0	0.0	0.0	0.0	0.0	34.5
Grace period (years)	6.1	3.2	5.2	0.0	0.0	0.0	0.0	0.0	0.0	10.0
Grant element (%)	17.9	-19.3	10.3	0.0	0.0	0.0	0.0	0.0	0.0	78.4
Official creditors										
Interest (%)	7.0	12.0	8.1	0.0	0.0	0.0	0.0	0.0	0.0	0.8
Maturity (years)	18.9	10.8	16.0	0.0	0.0	0.0	0.0	0.0	0.0	34.5
Grace period (years)	6.9	3.3	5.2	0.0	0.0	0.0	0.0	0.0	0.0	10.0
Grant element (%)	19.3	-7.4	10.3	0.0	0.0	0.0	0.0	0.0	0.0	78.4
Private creditors										
Interest (%)	7.0	17.0	0.0	0.0	0.0	0.0	0.0	0.0	0.0	0.0
Maturity (years)	13.1	7.1	0.0	0.0	0.0	0.0	0.0	0.0	0.0	0.0
Grace period (years)	4.1	3.0	0.0	0.0	0.0	0.0	0.0	0.0	0.0	0.0
Grant element (%)	14.2	-26.8	0.0	0.0	0.0	0.0	0.0	0.0	0.0	0.0
Memorandum items										
Commitments	199	1,187	800	0	0	0	0	0	0	20
Official creditors	143	461	800	0	0	0	0	0	0	20
Private creditors	56	726	0	0	0	0	0	0	0	0

10. CONTRACTUAL OBLIGATIONS ON OUTSTANDING LONG-TERM DEBT

	2001	2002	2003	2004	2005	2006	2007	2008	2009	2010
TOTAL										
Disbursements	0	5	4	4	3	2	1	0	0	0
Principal	413	302	177	130	114	97	7	7	7	1
Interest	80	56	38	24	15	7	2	1	1	0
Official creditors										
Disbursements	0	5	4	4	3	2	1	0	0	0
Principal	149	60	44	40	24	7	7	7	7	1
Interest	21	12	9	6	4	3	2	1	1	0
Bilateral creditors										
Disbursements	0	0	0	0	0	0	0	0	0	0
Principal	6	6	3	0	0	0	0	0	0	0
Interest	0	0	0	0	0	0	0	0	0	0
Multilateral creditors										
Disbursements	0	5	4	4	3	2	1	0	0	0
Principal	143	54	40	40	24	7	7	7	7	1
Interest	21	12	9	6	4	3	2	1	1	0
Private creditors										
Disbursements	0	0	0	0	0	0	0	0	0	0
Principal	264	242	134	90	90	90	0	0	0	0
Interest	59	44	30	17	11	5	0	0	0	0
Commercial banks										
Disbursements	0	0	0	0	0	0	0	0	0	0
Principal	90	90	90	90	90	90	0	0	0	0
Interest	36	30	24	17	11	5	0	0	0	0
Other private										
Disbursements	0	0	0	0	0	0	0	0	0	0
Principal	174	152	44	0	0	0	0	0	0	0
Interest	22	14	6	0	0	0	0	0	0	0

ZAMBIA

(US$ million, unless otherwise indicated)

	1970	1980	1990	1994	1995	1996	1997	1998	1999	2000
1. SUMMARY DEBT DATA										
TOTAL DEBT STOCKS (EDT)	**814**	**3,244**	**6,916**	**6,804**	**6,953**	**7,054**	**6,654**	**6,865**	**5,853**	**5,730**
Long-term debt (LDOD)	**654**	**2,211**	**4,554**	**5,188**	**5,299**	**5,379**	**5,257**	**5,348**	**4,571**	**4,513**
Public and publicly guaranteed	624	2,124	4,552	5,174	5,285	5,363	5,245	5,320	4,498	4,448
Private nonguaranteed	30	87	2	14	14	16	13	29	73	65
Use of IMF credit	**0**	**447**	**949**	**805**	**1,239**	**1,198**	**1,138**	**1,188**	**1,171**	**1,138**
Short-term debt	**160**	**586**	**1,414**	**812**	**415**	**477**	**259**	**329**	**111**	**79**
of which interest arrears on LDOD	0	6	739	471	178	151	138	135	37	36
Official creditors	0	3	671	443	146	119	112	120	27	26
Private creditors	0	3	68	27	32	33	26	15	10	10
Memo: principal arrears on LDOD	0	33	1,493	1,146	766	712	739	749	143	141
Official creditors	0	21	1,389	1,069	671	606	649	687	114	113
Private creditors	0	13	104	77	95	106	90	62	29	28
Memo: export credits	0	0	1,123	1,024	659	1,170	1,468	610	784	639
TOTAL DEBT FLOWS										
Disbursements	**374**	**690**	**164**	**294**	**2,606**	**236**	**286**	**84**	**264**	**287**
Long-term debt	374	599	164	294	352	236	272	84	250	261
IMF purchases	0	90	0	0	2,253	0	14	0	14	26
Principal repayments	**45**	**269**	**126**	**206**	**2,067**	**156**	**165**	**132**	**295**	**98**
Long-term debt	41	212	101	186	242	156	165	132	295	98
IMF repurchases	4	57	25	21	1,825	0	0	0	0	0
Net flows on debt	**329**	**360**	**-127**	**88**	**435**	**169**	**-84**	**25**	**-151**	**159**
of which short-term debt	0	-61	-165	0	-104	89	-205	73	-121	-31
Interest payments (INT)	**31**	**141**	**77**	**169**	**556**	**95**	**81**	**70**	**144**	**88**
Long-term debt	31	115	72	127	136	75	65	55	131	80
IMF charges	0	26	2	41	419	11	6	6	6	6
Short-term debt	0	0	3	2	1	9	10	10	8	3
Net transfers on debt	**299**	**219**	**-203**	**-82**	**-121**	**74**	**-165**	**-45**	**-295**	**71**
Total debt service paid (TDS)	**76**	**410**	**202**	**376**	**2,623**	**251**	**246**	**202**	**439**	**186**
Long-term debt	72	326	173	312	378	231	230	187	425	177
IMF repurchases and charges	4	84	27	62	2,244	11	6	6	6	6
Short-term debt (interest only)	0	0	3	2	1	9	10	10	8	3
2. AGGREGATE NET RESOURCE FLOWS AND NET TRANSFERS (LONG-TERM)										
NET RESOURCE FLOWS	**38**	**521**	**930**	**520**	**569**	**470**	**564**	**407**	**466**	**778**
Net flow of long-term debt (ex. IMF)	333	388	63	109	110	80	107	-49	-44	163
Foreign direct investment (net)	-297	62	203	56	97	117	207	198	163	200
Portfolio equity flows	0	0	0	0	0	0	0	0	0	0
Grants (excluding technical coop.)	2	72	663	355	362	273	250	257	347	415
Memo: technical coop. grants	13	87	128	135	164	142	133	97	92	108
official net resource flows	18	346	736	489	509	379	365	241	315	587
private net resource flows	20	175	194	32	60	91	200	166	151	191
NET TRANSFERS	**-53**	**322**	**743**	**346**	**383**	**350**	**446**	**302**	**277**	**629**
Interest on long-term debt	31	115	72	127	136	75	65	55	131	80
Profit remittances on FDI	60	84	115	48	50	45	53	50	58	69
Memo: official net transfers	12	293	693	377	393	312	312	193	192	511
private net transfers	-65	29	50	-32	-10	38	135	109	85	118
3. MAJOR ECONOMIC AGGREGATES										
Gross national income (GNI)	1,742	3,594	3,008	3,111	3,228	3,065	3,706	3,023	2,948	2,791
Exports of goods & services (XGS)	..	1,625	1,362	1,285	1,445	1,227	1,454	1,036	957	991
of which workers remittances	..	0	0	..	..	..	..	..	..	..
Imports of goods & services (MGS)	..	1,987	2,336	1,727	1,962	1,702	2,026	1,659	1,487	1,633
International reserves (RES)	515	206	201	268	223	223	239	69	45	245
Current account balance	..	-516	-594	..	..	..	..	..	..	..
4. DEBT INDICATORS										
EDT / XGS (%)	..	199.7	507.8	529.4	481.3	575.2	457.6	662.4	611.8	578.1
EDT / GNI (%)	46.7	90.3	229.9	218.7	215.4	230.2	179.6	227.1	198.6	205.3
TDS / XGS (%)	..	25.2	14.9	29.2	181.6	20.4	16.9	19.5	45.8	18.7
INT / XGS (%)	..	8.7	5.6	13.2	38.5	7.7	5.6	6.7	15.1	8.9
INT / GNI (%)	1.8	3.9	2.5	5.4	17.2	3.1	2.2	2.3	4.9	3.2
RES / EDT (%)	63.3	6.4	2.9	3.9	3.2	3.2	3.6	1.0	0.8	4.3
RES / MGS (months)	..	1.3	1.0	1.9	1.4	1.6	1.4	0.5	0.4	1.8
Short-term / EDT (%)	19.7	18.1	20.4	11.9	6.0	6.8	3.9	4.8	1.9	1.4
Concessional / EDT (%)	6.3	24.6	29.9	45.4	47.4	49.6	52.4	53.1	60.3	62.4
Multilateral / EDT (%)	7.6	12.1	20.2	28.5	30.6	30.7	32.6	32.7	39.8	42.0

ZAMBIA

(US$ million, unless otherwise indicated)

	1970	1980	1990	1994	1995	1996	1997	1998	1999	2000
5. LONG-TERM DEBT										
DEBT OUTSTANDING (LDOD)	**654**	**2,211**	**4,554**	**5,188**	**5,299**	**5,379**	**5,257**	**5,348**	**4,571**	**4,513**
Public and publicly guaranteed	**624**	**2,124**	**4,552**	**5,174**	**5,285**	**5,363**	**5,245**	**5,320**	**4,498**	**4,448**
Official creditors	120	1,485	4,108	4,929	5,075	5,186	5,075	5,207	4,465	4,417
Multilateral	61	393	1,400	1,940	2,127	2,169	2,167	2,242	2,331	2,409
Concessional	0	19	579	1,458	1,715	1,839	1,923	2,031	2,138	2,252
Bilateral	59	1,091	2,708	2,989	2,948	3,018	2,908	2,965	2,135	2,008
Concessional	51	778	1,487	1,629	1,579	1,663	1,565	1,617	1,393	1,325
Private creditors	503	639	444	245	210	177	170	113	33	32
Bonds	55	3	0	0	0	0	0	0	0	0
Commercial banks	0	77	70	10	16	17	21	21	1	0
Other private	449	560	374	235	194	160	149	92	32	31
Private nonguaranteed	**30**	**87**	**2**	**14**	**14**	**16**	**13**	**29**	**73**	**65**
Bonds	0	0	0	0	0	0	0	0	0	0
Commercial banks and other	30	87	2	14	14	16	13	29	73	65
Memo:										
IBRD	61	346	539	201	163	105	62	41	33	25
IDA	0	2	274	1,043	1,270	1,405	1,493	1,587	1,704	1,823
DISBURSEMENTS	**374**	**599**	**164**	**294**	**352**	**236**	**272**	**84**	**250**	**261**
Public and publicly guaranteed	**363**	**593**	**162**	**292**	**351**	**232**	**272**	**64**	**200**	**251**
Official creditors	22	311	117	259	327	224	222	64	200	251
Multilateral	6	56	106	242	251	213	211	64	198	249
Concessional	0	6	41	207	237	205	207	59	192	244
Bilateral	16	254	11	18	76	11	12	0	3	2
Concessional	16	237	9	11	72	0	3	0	2	2
Private creditors	341	282	46	33	24	8	50	0	0	0
Bonds	0	0	0	0	0	0	0	0	0	0
Commercial banks	0	9	0	10	8	5	5	0	0	0
Other private	341	273	46	22	16	4	44	0	0	0
Private nonguaranteed	**11**	**6**	**2**	**2**	**1**	**5**	**0**	**20**	**50**	**10**
Bonds	0	0	0	0	0	0	0	0	0	0
Commercial banks and other	11	6	2	2	1	5	0	20	50	10
Memo:										
IBRD	6	28	0	0	0	0	0	0	0	0
IDA	0	2	3	186	209	181	169	43	156	210
PRINCIPAL REPAYMENTS	**41**	**212**	**101**	**186**	**242**	**156**	**165**	**132**	**295**	**98**
Public and publicly guaranteed	**35**	**181**	**101**	**184**	**241**	**154**	**161**	**128**	**289**	**80**
Official creditors	6	37	44	126	180	117	108	80	233	79
Multilateral	4	18	39	101	120	88	76	57	54	51
Concessional	0	0	2	10	15	14	13	19	27	22
Bilateral	2	18	6	25	60	29	32	23	179	28
Concessional	1	3	0	11	32	19	20	8	114	18
Private creditors	29	144	57	58	61	37	53	48	56	1
Bonds	7	3	0	0	0	0	0	0	0	0
Commercial banks	0	4	0	8	2	4	1	0	20	0
Other private	22	137	57	50	59	33	53	48	36	1
Private nonguaranteed	**6**	**31**	**0**	**2**	**1**	**2**	**4**	**4**	**6**	**18**
Bonds	0	0	0	0	0	0	0	0	0	0
Commercial banks and other	6	31	0	2	1	2	4	4	6	18
Memo:										
IBRD	4	18	5	55	50	47	35	21	9	8
IDA	0	0	0	1	2	3	4	4	4	4
NET FLOWS ON DEBT	**333**	**388**	**63**	**109**	**110**	**80**	**107**	**-49**	**-44**	**163**
Public and publicly guaranteed	**328**	**413**	**61**	**108**	**110**	**78**	**111**	**-65**	**-89**	**171**
Official creditors	16	274	73	133	147	107	114	-17	-32	172
Multilateral	1	38	67	141	131	124	134	6	144	198
Concessional	0	6	39	196	222	190	194	40	165	222
Bilateral	15	236	5	-8	17	-18	-20	-23	-176	-26
Concessional	15	234	9	1	40	-19	-16	-8	-112	-17
Private creditors	312	138	-11	-25	-37	-29	-4	-48	-56	-1
Bonds	-7	-3	0	0	0	0	0	0	0	0
Commercial banks	0	5	0	3	6	1	5	0	-20	0
Other private	319	136	-11	-27	-43	-30	-8	-48	-36	-1
Private nonguaranteed	**5**	**-25**	**2**	**0**	**0**	**3**	**-4**	**16**	**44**	**-8**
Bonds	0	0	0	0	0	0	0	0	0	0
Commercial banks and other	5	-25	2	0	0	3	-4	16	44	-8
Memo:										
IBRD	1	10	-5	-55	-50	-47	-35	-21	-9	-8
IDA	0	2	3	185	207	178	166	39	152	206

ZAMBIA

(US$ million, unless otherwise indicated)

	1970	1980	1990	1994	1995	1996	1997	1998	1999	2000
INTEREST PAYMENTS (LINT)	**31**	**115**	**72**	**127**	**136**	**75**	**65**	**55**	**131**	**80**
Public and publicly guaranteed	**29**	**105**	**72**	**127**	**136**	**75**	**65**	**55**	**127**	**76**
Official creditors	6	52	43	111	116	67	53	48	123	76
Multilateral	4	33	33	61	65	46	39	29	35	33
Concessional	0	0	3	14	17	17	15	14	19	19
Bilateral	2	19	10	51	51	21	14	19	89	42
Concessional	2	13	9	22	16	12	5	9	53	22
Private creditors	23	53	29	15	20	8	12	7	4	0
Bonds	3	1	0	0	0	0	0	0	0	0
Commercial banks	0	12	0	1	1	1	1	0	1	0
Other private	20	40	29	15	19	7	12	7	3	0
Private nonguaranteed	**2**	**10**	**0**	**0**	**0**	**0**	**0**	**0**	**4**	**4**
Bonds	0	0	0	0	0	0	0	0	0	0
Commercial banks and other	2	10	0	0	0	0	0	0	4	4
Memo:										
IBRD	4	31	1	21	15	11	6	4	3	3
IDA	0	0	0	6	9	10	10	11	12	13
NET TRANSFERS ON DEBT	**302**	**273**	**-9**	**-18**	**-25**	**5**	**42**	**-103**	**-175**	**84**
Public and publicly guaranteed	**299**	**307**	**-11**	**-18**	**-25**	**3**	**45**	**-119**	**-215**	**95**
Official creditors	10	222	29	22	31	39	61	-65	-155	96
Multilateral	-2	5	34	80	66	78	95	-23	109	165
Concessional	0	6	36	182	206	174	179	26	146	203
Bilateral	12	217	-5	-58	-34	-39	-34	-42	-264	-69
Concessional	13	221	0	-21	24	-31	-22	-17	-165	-38
Private creditors	289	85	-40	-40	-57	-37	-16	-55	-60	-1
Bonds	-10	-4	0	0	0	0	0	0	0	0
Commercial banks	0	-6	0	2	5	0	4	0	-21	0
Other private	299	96	-40	-42	-62	-37	-20	-54	-39	-1
Private nonguaranteed	**3**	**-35**	**2**	**0**	**0**	**3**	**-4**	**16**	**40**	**-12**
Bonds	0	0	0	0	0	0	0	0	0	0
Commercial banks and other	3	-35	2	0	0	3	-4	16	40	-12
Memo:										
IBRD	-2	-21	-5	-76	-65	-58	-41	-25	-12	-11
IDA	0	2	3	179	198	169	155	28	140	193
DEBT SERVICE (LTDS)	**72**	**326**	**173**	**312**	**378**	**231**	**230**	**187**	**425**	**177**
Public and publicly guaranteed	**64**	**286**	**173**	**310**	**377**	**229**	**227**	**183**	**416**	**156**
Official creditors	12	89	88	237	296	184	161	128	356	155
Multilateral	8	51	72	161	185	134	116	87	89	84
Concessional	0	0	5	24	32	31	28	33	45	41
Bilateral	4	37	16	76	110	50	45	42	267	70
Concessional	3	16	9	32	48	31	25	17	167	40
Private creditors	52	197	85	73	81	45	66	55	60	1
Bonds	10	4	0	0	0	0	0	0	0	0
Commercial banks	0	16	0	8	3	5	1	0	21	0
Other private	42	177	85	64	78	40	64	54	39	1
Private nonguaranteed	**8**	**41**	**0**	**2**	**1**	**2**	**4**	**4**	**10**	**22**
Bonds	0	0	0	0	0	0	0	0	0	0
Commercial banks and other	8	41	0	2	1	2	4	4	10	22
Memo:										
IBRD	8	48	5	76	65	58	41	25	12	11
IDA	0	0	0	8	11	13	14	15	16	17
UNDISBURSED DEBT	**309**	**877**	**690**	**618**	**659**	**559**	**507**	**529**	**551**	**572**
Official creditors	291	679	587	589	641	550	503	529	551	572
Private creditors	18	198	103	29	18	9	4	0	0	0
Memorandum items										
Concessional LDOD	51	797	2,066	3,087	3,294	3,502	3,488	3,648	3,531	3,578
Variable rate LDOD	30	280	494	737	731	732	738	738	503	402
Public sector LDOD	624	2,107	4,551	5,146	5,253	5,317	5,197	5,272	4,459	4,417
Private sector LDOD	30	104	2	41	46	62	60	76	112	96

6. CURRENCY COMPOSITION OF LONG-TERM DEBT (PERCENT)

	1970	1980	1990	1994	1995	1996	1997	1998	1999	2000
Deutsche mark	0.4	9.4	10.4	10.5	10.8	10.2	9.3	9.8	6.1	4.7
French franc	0.9	3.2	3.0	2.9	3.1	2.5	2.5	2.6	2.2	1.5
Japanese yen	0.0	4.8	10.0	10.9	11.2	12.3	10.6	12.5	16.0	13.9
Pound sterling	17.7	10.6	8.5	8.0	7.7	8.4	9.2	7.7	4.7	3.9
Swiss franc	0.0	0.0	0.6	0.1	0.2	0.1	0.1	0.1	0.1	0.1
U.S.dollars	53.7	20.2	28.1	38.5	39.4	40.9	44.1	43.7	55.4	61.6
Multiple currency	9.9	16.7	17.5	10.7	9.8	8.2	7.0	6.7	7.6	6.9
Special drawing rights	0.0	0.0	1.0	0.0	0.0	0.1	0.1	0.2	0.4	0.5
All other currencies	17.4	35.1	20.9	18.4	17.8	17.3	17.1	16.7	7.5	6.9

ZAMBIA

(US$ million, unless otherwise indicated)

	1970	1980	1990	1994	1995	1996	1997	1998	1999	2000
7. DEBT RESTRUCTURINGS										
Total amount rescheduled	..	..	690	146	20	203	127	78	274	169
Debt stock rescheduled	..	..	38	0	0	0	0	0	0	0
Principal rescheduled	..	..	466	74	7	121	55	22	182	105
Official	..	..	342	74	7	121	55	22	182	105
Private	..	..	123	0	0	0	0	0	0	0
Interest rescheduled	..	..	321	72	5	81	72	55	92	64
Official	..	..	299	71	5	81	72	55	92	64
Private	..	..	22	1	0	0	0	0	0	0
Debt forgiven	..	..	114	96	1	23	1	2	53	39
Memo: interest forgiven	..	..	22	67	1	7	1	0	37	18
Debt stock reduction	..	..	26	446	2	0	0	0	0	0
of which debt buyback	..	..	0	8	0	0	0	0	0	0
8. DEBT STOCK-FLOW RECONCILIATION										
Total change in debt stocks	..	..	351	319	149	102	-400	211	-1,013	-123
Net flows on debt	329	360	-127	88	435	169	-84	25	-151	159
Net change in interest arrears	..	..	29	-115	-293	-26	-13	-3	-98	-2
Interest capitalized	..	..	321	72	5	81	72	55	92	64
Debt forgiveness or reduction	..	..	-140	-535	-3	-23	-1	-2	-53	-39
Cross-currency valuation	..	..	303	35	-102	-489	-693	-205	-100	-290
Residual	..	..	-34	774	106	390	319	341	-702	-16
9. AVERAGE TERMS OF NEW COMMITMENTS										
ALL CREDITORS										
Interest (%)	4.2	6.7	8.1	1.9	1.8	2.0	1.7	0.8	0.8	0.8
Maturity (years)	20.6	18.6	16.2	32.5	36.3	35.7	32.6	39.4	39.6	39.5
Grace period (years)	10.2	4.4	4.8	8.8	10.1	9.3	7.4	9.9	10.1	10.0
Grant element (%)	42.8	22.1	14.8	66.4	70.2	70.0	64.7	80.2	80.4	80.4
Official creditors										
Interest (%)	1.4	3.7	6.3	1.4	1.5	2.0	0.5	0.8	0.8	0.8
Maturity (years)	32.6	29.0	21.8	35.0	37.3	35.7	37.9	39.4	39.6	39.5
Grace period (years)	21.6	8.5	6.9	9.3	10.3	9.3	8.9	9.9	10.1	10.0
Grant element (%)	79.2	48.9	26.3	71.7	72.9	70.0	76.6	80.2	80.4	80.4
Private creditors										
Interest (%)	6.6	8.8	11.0	6.4	10.5	0.0	7.0	0.0	0.0	0.0
Maturity (years)	10.4	11.0	6.9	7.4	9.2	0.0	7.8	0.0	0.0	0.0
Grace period (years)	0.5	1.4	1.4	3.0	2.9	0.0	0.3	0.0	0.0	0.0
Grant element (%)	12.1	2.6	-4.1	12.3	-3.7	0.0	8.8	0.0	0.0	0.0
Memorandum items										
Commitments	557	635	192	338	382	143	253	75	213	303
Official creditors	255	267	120	307	368	143	209	75	213	303
Private creditors	302	368	72	30	14	0	44	0	0	0

10. CONTRACTUAL OBLIGATIONS ON OUTSTANDING LONG-TERM DEBT

	2001	2002	2003	2004	2005	2006	2007	2008	2009	2010
TOTAL										
Disbursements	195	158	110	71	30	4	3	1	0	0
Principal	149	168	177	170	145	137	139	136	143	146
Interest	114	127	123	116	108	103	97	93	88	83
Official creditors										
Disbursements	195	158	110	71	30	4	3	1	0	0
Principal	142	162	172	164	139	131	134	131	138	141
Interest	111	124	121	113	106	101	96	91	87	82
Bilateral creditors										
Disbursements	1	1	1	1	1	0	0	0	0	0
Principal	89	110	116	105	81	67	68	69	73	75
Interest	79	92	90	84	79	76	73	69	66	62
Multilateral creditors										
Disbursements	194	158	109	70	30	4	3	1	0	0
Principal	54	53	55	59	58	64	66	62	65	66
Interest	32	31	30	29	27	25	23	22	21	20
Private creditors										
Disbursements	0	0	0	0	0	0	0	0	0	0
Principal	6	6	6	6	6	6	5	5	5	5
Interest	4	3	3	3	2	2	2	1	1	1
Commercial banks										
Disbursements	0	0	0	0	0	0	0	0	0	0
Principal	0	0	0	0	0	0	0	0	0	0
Interest	0	0	0	0	0	0	0	0	0	0
Other private										
Disbursements	0	0	0	0	0	0	0	0	0	0
Principal	6	6	6	6	6	6	5	5	5	5
Interest	4	3	3	3	2	2	2	1	1	1

ZIMBABWE

(US$ million, unless otherwise indicated)

1. SUMMARY DEBT DATA

	1970	1980	1990	1994	1995	1996	1997	1998	1999	2000
TOTAL DEBT STOCKS (EDT)	**232**	**786**	**3,247**	**4,524**	**5,007**	**4,976**	**4,919**	**4,707**	**4,577**	**4,002**
Long-term debt (LDOD)	**229**	**696**	**2,649**	**3,651**	**3,861**	**3,737**	**3,556**	**3,532**	**3,462**	**3,158**
Public and publicly guaranteed	229	696	2,464	3,408	3,480	3,309	3,103	3,332	3,222	2,948
Private nonguaranteed	0	0	185	243	381	428	453	200	240	211
Use of IMF credit	**0**	**0**	**7**	**376**	**461**	**437**	**385**	**407**	**369**	**281**
Short-term debt	**3**	**90**	**591**	**497**	**685**	**801**	**977**	**768**	**746**	**563**
of which interest arrears on LDOD	3	0	0	1	3	0	0	0	0	50
Official creditors	3	0	0	0	1	0	0	0	0	38
Private creditors	0	0	0	1	2	0	0	0	0	12
Memo: principal arrears on LDOD	67	0	0	19	22	2	10	13	16	148
Official creditors	4	0	0	15	8	1	5	5	4	99
Private creditors	63	0	0	5	15	1	5	8	12	49
Memo: export credits	0	0	660	807	888	852	877	220	216	241
TOTAL DEBT FLOWS										
Disbursements	**0**	**132**	**424**	**504**	**651**	**447**	**496**	**603**	**522**	**150**
Long-term debt	0	132	424	428	572	447	496	550	489	150
IMF purchases	0	0	0	75	80	0	0	53	34	0
Principal repayments	**5**	**40**	**270**	**372**	**401**	**423**	**459**	**763**	**455**	**306**
Long-term debt	5	40	247	372	401	414	433	715	393	236
IMF repurchases	0	0	24	0	0	9	26	48	62	70
Net flows on debt	**-5**	**148**	**335**	**28**	**437**	**142**	**213**	**-369**	**46**	**-389**
of which short-term debt	0	55	181	-104	187	119	176	-209	-22	-233
Interest payments (INT)	**5**	**26**	**201**	**230**	**244**	**238**	**228**	**218**	**193**	**165**
Long-term debt	5	10	149	192	195	182	174	165	143	113
IMF charges	0	0	2	10	13	12	10	10	9	10
Short-term debt	0	15	49	28	35	44	44	43	41	42
Net transfers on debt	**-9**	**122**	**134**	**-202**	**193**	**-96**	**-15**	**-587**	**-147**	**-554**
Total debt service paid (TDS)	**9**	**65**	**471**	**602**	**645**	**661**	**686**	**981**	**648**	**471**
Long-term debt	9	50	396	564	596	596	607	880	536	349
IMF repurchases and charges	0	0	26	10	13	20	36	58	71	81
Short-term debt (interest only)	0	15	49	28	35	44	44	43	41	42

2. AGGREGATE NET RESOURCE FLOWS AND NET TRANSFERS (LONG-TERM)

	1970	1980	1990	1994	1995	1996	1997	1998	1999	2000
NET RESOURCE FLOWS	**-5**	**221**	**364**	**405**	**615**	**339**	**333**	**436**	**298**	**108**
Net flow of long-term debt (ex. IMF)	-5	93	177	57	171	33	63	-165	95	-85
Foreign direct investment (net)	0	2	-12	35	118	81	135	444	59	79
Portfolio equity flows	0	0	0	50	18	17	10	3	4	1
Grants (excluding technical coop.)	0	127	199	264	308	209	126	154	140	114
Memo: technical coop. grants	1	70	103	115	132	109	111	98	86	77
official net resource flows	-5	199	278	461	375	279	265	289	227	79
private net resource flows	0	22	85	-56	240	60	68	148	71	29
NET TRANSFERS	**-10**	**133**	**122**	**143**	**344**	**80**	**80**	**189**	**59**	**-80**
Interest on long-term debt	5	10	149	192	195	182	174	165	143	113
Profit remittances on FDI	0	78	92	70	75	77	80	82	96	75
Memo: official net transfers	-9	197	212	349	254	162	150	184	117	10
private net transfers	-1	-64	-90	-206	90	-82	-71	5	-57	-91

3. MAJOR ECONOMIC AGGREGATES

	1970	1980	1990	1994	1995	1996	1997	1998	1999	2000
Gross national income (GNI)	1,854	6,610	8,494	6,596	6,795	8,329	8,166	5,911	5,149	7,142
Exports of goods & services (XGS)	..	1,724	2,035	2,372	2,737	3,118	3,096	2,565	2,377	2,132
of which workers remittances	..	9	0	0	..	..	..	..	..	..
Imports of goods & services (MGS)	..	1,895	2,287	2,836	3,297	3,524	4,131	3,115	2,708	2,264
International reserves (RES)	59	419	295	585	888	834	384	310	480	321
Current account balance	..	-149	-140	-425	..	..	..	..	..	..

4. DEBT INDICATORS

	1970	1980	1990	1994	1995	1996	1997	1998	1999	2000
EDT / XGS (%)	..	45.6	159.6	190.7	182.9	159.6	158.9	183.5	192.5	187.7
EDT / GNI (%)	12.5	11.9	38.2	68.6	73.7	59.7	60.2	79.6	88.9	56.0
TDS / XGS (%)	..	3.8	23.2	25.4	23.6	21.2	22.2	38.2	27.3	22.1
INT / XGS (%)	..	1.5	9.9	9.7	8.9	7.6	7.4	8.5	8.1	7.8
INT / GNI (%)	0.3	0.4	2.4	3.5	3.6	2.9	2.8	3.7	3.7	2.3
RES / EDT (%)	25.6	53.4	9.1	12.9	17.7	16.8	7.8	6.6	10.5	8.0
RES / MGS (months)	..	2.7	1.6	2.5	3.2	2.8	1.1	1.2	2.1	1.7
Short-term / EDT (%)	1.4	11.5	18.2	11.0	13.7	16.1	19.9	16.3	16.3	14.1
Concessional / EDT (%)	18.9	1.9	27.9	31.8	29.2	28.2	27.5	31.7	34.2	36.9
Multilateral / EDT (%)	17.5	0.4	19.6	33.6	32.6	31.7	32.8	36.4	35.5	37.1

ZIMBABWE

(US$ million, unless otherwise indicated)

	1970	*1980*	*1990*	*1994*	*1995*	*1996*	*1997*	*1998*	*1999*	*2000*
5. LONG-TERM DEBT										
DEBT OUTSTANDING (LDOD)	**229**	**696**	**2,649**	**3,651**	**3,861**	**3,737**	**3,556**	**3,532**	**3,462**	**3,158**
Public and publicly guaranteed	**229**	**696**	**2,464**	**3,408**	**3,480**	**3,309**	**3,103**	**3,332**	**3,222**	**2,948**
Official creditors	85	101	1,508	2,713	2,806	2,726	2,649	2,913	2,858	2,626
Multilateral	41	3	637	1,520	1,632	1,575	1,612	1,715	1,622	1,484
Concessional	0	0	129	384	413	417	478	532	558	545
Bilateral	44	98	871	1,193	1,174	1,151	1,037	1,198	1,235	1,141
Concessional	44	15	778	1,056	1,048	988	876	961	1,007	931
Private creditors	145	595	957	695	673	583	455	419	364	322
Bonds	145	592	293	150	120	90	60	30	0	0
Commercial banks	0	3	208	139	187	192	150	176	197	184
Other private	0	0	456	406	366	301	245	213	167	138
Private nonguaranteed	**0**	**0**	**185**	**243**	**381**	**428**	**453**	**200**	**240**	**211**
Bonds	0	0	0	0	0	0	0	0	0	0
Commercial banks and other	0	0	185	243	381	428	453	200	240	211
Memo:										
IBRD	41	3	381	556	560	513	473	498	473	416
IDA	0	0	67	313	336	335	399	442	452	437
DISBURSEMENTS	**0**	**132**	**424**	**428**	**572**	**447**	**496**	**550**	**489**	**150**
Public and publicly guaranteed	**0**	**132**	**297**	**395**	**343**	**305**	**351**	**395**	**399**	**131**
Official creditors	0	77	158	313	234	238	329	325	311	110
Multilateral	0	0	72	188	149	149	275	154	122	46
Concessional	0	0	7	112	26	27	92	39	43	16
Bilateral	0	77	86	125	85	89	54	171	189	64
Concessional	0	1	76	72	71	39	28	76	155	35
Private creditors	0	55	139	82	109	67	22	70	88	21
Bonds	0	52	0	0	0	0	0	0	0	0
Commercial banks	0	3	29	47	75	54	15	53	75	16
Other private	0	0	111	35	34	13	7	17	14	5
Private nonguaranteed	**0**	**0**	**127**	**33**	**229**	**142**	**145**	**156**	**90**	**20**
Bonds	0	0	0	0	0	0	0	0	0	0
Commercial banks and other	0	0	127	33	229	142	145	156	90	20
Memo:										
IBRD	0	0	40	33	32	38	49	44	31	19
IDA	0	0	0	102	15	12	83	29	20	8
PRINCIPAL REPAYMENTS	**5**	**40**	**247**	**372**	**401**	**414**	**433**	**715**	**393**	**236**
Public and publicly guaranteed	**5**	**40**	**229**	**276**	**310**	**319**	**313**	**306**	**343**	**187**
Official creditors	5	5	78	116	167	167	190	190	223	145
Multilateral	4	3	46	73	88	111	125	125	142	94
Concessional	0	0	4	4	7	6	6	4	4	1
Bilateral	1	2	32	43	79	57	65	65	82	50
Concessional	1	2	17	30	51	41	44	44	49	20
Private creditors	0	34	151	160	143	152	124	116	120	42
Bonds	0	19	30	30	30	30	30	30	30	0
Commercial banks	0	0	46	56	33	47	43	33	38	15
Other private	0	16	75	74	80	75	50	54	52	28
Private nonguaranteed	**0**	**0**	**18**	**96**	**91**	**95**	**120**	**409**	**50**	**49**
Bonds	0	0	0	0	0	0	0	0	0	0
Commercial banks and other	0	0	18	96	91	95	120	409	50	49
Memo:										
IBRD	4	3	33	41	48	46	46	47	51	46
IDA	0	0	0	1	1	1	1	1	1	0
NET FLOWS ON DEBT	**-5**	**93**	**177**	**57**	**171**	**33**	**63**	**-165**	**95**	**-85**
Public and publicly guaranteed	**-5**	**93**	**69**	**120**	**33**	**-15**	**38**	**88**	**56**	**-56**
Official creditors	-5	72	80	198	67	71	139	135	88	-35
Multilateral	-4	-3	26	116	61	38	150	29	-20	-49
Concessional	0	0	3	108	19	21	86	35	39	16
Bilateral	-1	75	54	82	6	32	-11	106	107	14
Concessional	-1	-1	59	41	20	-2	-16	32	105	15
Private creditors	0	21	-12	-78	-34	-85	-102	-47	-32	-21
Bonds	0	34	-30	-30	-30	-30	-30	-30	-30	0
Commercial banks	0	3	-17	-9	42	7	-29	20	36	1
Other private	0	-16	36	-39	-46	-62	-43	-37	-38	-22
Private nonguaranteed	**0**	**0**	**109**	**-63**	**138**	**47**	**25**	**-253**	**40**	**-29**
Bonds	0	0	0	0	0	0	0	0	0	0
Commercial banks and other	0	0	109	-63	138	47	25	-253	40	-29
Memo:										
IBRD	-4	-3	7	-8	-16	-8	3	-3	-20	-27
IDA	0	0	0	101	15	11	83	28	20	7

ZIMBABWE

(US$ million, unless otherwise indicated)

	1970	1980	1990	1994	1995	1996	1997	1998	1999	2000
INTEREST PAYMENTS (LINT)	**5**	**10**	**149**	**192**	**195**	**182**	**174**	**165**	**143**	**113**
Public and publicly guaranteed	**5**	**10**	**141**	**159**	**169**	**160**	**151**	**135**	**136**	**83**
Official creditors	4	2	67	113	121	117	115	105	110	68
Multilateral	2	0	43	85	90	88	85	79	77	46
Concessional	0	0	1	3	4	4	4	5	4	2
Bilateral	2	1	24	28	31	29	29	26	33	23
Concessional	2	1	15	20	21	19	18	15	17	11
Private creditors	0	9	74	47	49	43	36	30	26	15
Bonds	0	7	13	7	6	5	3	2	1	0
Commercial banks	0	0	28	11	12	12	11	11	11	7
Other private	0	1	33	29	31	26	21	18	14	8
Private nonguaranteed	**0**	**0**	**9**	**33**	**26**	**22**	**23**	**30**	**6**	**30**
Bonds	0	0	0	0	0	0	0	0	0	0
Commercial banks and other	0	0	9	33	26	22	23	30	6	30
Memo:										
IBRD	2	0	33	44	46	41	36	32	32	26
IDA	0	0	1	2	3	3	2	3	3	1
NET TRANSFERS ON DEBT	**-9**	**82**	**28**	**-136**	**-25**	**-150**	**-111**	**-330**	**-48**	**-198**
Public and publicly guaranteed	**-9**	**82**	**-72**	**-40**	**-137**	**-175**	**-113**	**-47**	**-81**	**-140**
Official creditors	-9	71	13	85	-54	-47	25	30	-23	-103
Multilateral	-6	-3	-17	31	-29	-50	65	-50	-97	-95
Concessional	0	0	2	104	15	17	82	30	35	14
Bilateral	-3	74	30	54	-25	3	-40	80	74	-9
Concessional	-3	-2	43	21	-2	-20	-34	17	88	5
Private creditors	-1	12	-85	-125	-83	-128	-138	-77	-58	-36
Bonds	-1	26	-43	-37	-36	-35	-33	-32	-31	0
Commercial banks	0	3	-46	-19	30	-5	-40	10	26	-6
Other private	0	-17	3	-69	-77	-89	-65	-55	-53	-30
Private nonguaranteed	**0**	**0**	**100**	**-96**	**112**	**25**	**2**	**-283**	**33**	**-59**
Bonds	0	0	0	0	0	0	0	0	0	0
Commercial banks and other	0	0	100	-96	112	25	2	-283	33	-59
Memo:										
IBRD	-6	-3	-26	-52	-62	-49	-33	-36	-51	-53
IDA	0	0	-1	99	12	9	80	25	17	6
DEBT SERVICE (LTDS)	**9**	**50**	**396**	**564**	**596**	**596**	**607**	**880**	**536**	**349**
Public and publicly guaranteed	**9**	**50**	**370**	**435**	**479**	**479**	**464**	**441**	**480**	**270**
Official creditors	9	7	145	228	288	285	304	295	333	213
Multilateral	6	3	89	157	178	199	210	204	219	140
Concessional	0	0	5	8	11	10	10	8	8	2
Bilateral	3	4	56	71	110	86	94	91	115	73
Concessional	3	3	33	50	73	59	62	59	66	30
Private creditors	1	43	225	207	192	195	160	147	146	57
Bonds	1	26	43	37	36	35	33	32	31	0
Commercial banks	0	0	74	66	46	58	55	43	49	21
Other private	0	17	107	104	111	102	72	71	66	36
Private nonguaranteed	**0**	**0**	**27**	**129**	**117**	**117**	**143**	**439**	**56**	**79**
Bonds	0	0	0	0	0	0	0	0	0	0
Commercial banks and other	0	0	27	129	117	117	143	439	56	79
Memo:										
IBRD	6	3	67	84	94	87	82	79	83	72
IDA	0	0	1	3	3	3	3	4	3	2
UNDISBURSED DEBT	**0**	**86**	**1,042**	**1,494**	**1,348**	**1,261**	**1,065**	**1,103**	**892**	**744**
Official creditors	0	60	940	1,353	1,263	1,223	939	968	836	709
Private creditors	0	26	102	142	86	38	125	134	56	35
Memorandum items										
Concessional LDOD	44	15	906	1,440	1,462	1,405	1,354	1,492	1,565	1,476
Variable rate LDOD	0	3	699	829	967	962	945	739	750	673
Public sector LDOD	229	696	2,463	3,407	3,479	3,309	3,103	3,291	3,156	2,880
Private sector LDOD	0	0	186	244	381	428	453	241	306	278

6. CURRENCY COMPOSITION OF LONG-TERM DEBT (PERCENT)

	1970	1980	1990	1994	1995	1996	1997	1998	1999	2000
Deutsche mark	0.0	0.1	11.7	10.1	10.8	11.3	10.5	11.0	10.6	11.0
French franc	0.0	0.0	7.2	5.1	6.7	6.8	6.0	6.2	5.5	4.9
Japanese yen	0.0	0.0	2.1	3.3	3.6	3.2	2.9	4.4	9.0	9.4
Pound sterling	76.2	40.3	14.0	7.6	6.7	6.8	6.0	5.4	5.7	5.3
Swiss franc	0.0	0.0	1.2	0.8	0.9	0.8	0.6	0.5	0.3	0.4
U.S.dollars	0.3	0.4	30.3	27.9	26.0	25.8	27.5	26.6	26.0	27.3
Multiple currency	20.2	59.2	18.4	26.3	26.3	26.7	26.9	25.5	24.6	24.3
Special drawing rights	0.0	0.0	0.0	0.3	0.4	0.4	0.4	0.4	0.3	0.3
All other currencies	3.3	0.0	15.1	18.6	18.6	18.2	19.2	20.0	18.0	17.1

ZIMBABWE

(US$ million, unless otherwise indicated)

	1970	1980	1990	1994	1995	1996	1997	1998	1999	2000
7. DEBT RESTRUCTURINGS										
Total amount rescheduled	..	..	0	0	0	0	0	0	0	0
Debt stock rescheduled	..	..	0	0	0	0	0	0	0	0
Principal rescheduled	..	..	0	0	0	0	0	0	0	0
Official	..	..	0	0	0	0	0	0	0	0
Private	..	..	0	0	0	0	0	0	0	0
Interest rescheduled	..	..	0	0	0	0	0	0	0	0
Official	..	..	0	0	0	0	0	0	0	0
Private	..	..	0	0	0	0	0	0	0	0
Debt forgiven	..	..	24	0	81	0	0	0	5	0
Memo: interest forgiven	..	..	0	0	0	0	0	0	0	0
Debt stock reduction	..	..	0	0	0	0	0	0	0	0
of which debt buyback	..	..	0	0	0	0	0	0	0	0
8. DEBT STOCK-FLOW RECONCILIATION										
Total change in debt stocks	..	..	456	238	483	-31	-57	-212	-130	-575
Net flows on debt	-5	148	335	28	437	142	213	-369	46	-389
Net change in interest arrears	..	..	-1	0	2	-3	0	0	0	50
Interest capitalized	..	..	0	0	0	0	0	0	0	0
Debt forgiveness or reduction	..	..	-24	0	-81	0	0	0	-5	0
Cross-currency valuation	..	..	145	153	23	-256	-276	40	-177	-191
Residual	..	..	0	57	102	86	6	117	6	-45
9. AVERAGE TERMS OF NEW COMMITMENTS										
ALL CREDITORS										
Interest (%)	0.0	7.1	6.6	5.6	4.6	2.9	5.3	2.5	1.3	3.3
Maturity (years)	0.0	15.2	17.1	18.8	18.1	26.3	17.0	21.7	19.9	14.3
Grace period (years)	0.0	5.5	4.5	4.8	4.6	7.6	3.9	6.0	5.4	4.6
Grant element (%)	0.0	25.8	21.0	26.6	34.4	53.0	28.5	52.6	57.2	38.2
Official creditors										
Interest (%)	0.0	4.9	6.5	5.4	3.9	2.7	4.0	1.6	0.9	2.7
Maturity (years)	0.0	16.8	17.7	22.3	21.3	27.8	22.5	24.5	20.9	14.6
Grace period (years)	0.0	5.7	4.7	5.8	5.6	8.1	5.2	6.9	5.6	4.9
Grant element (%)	0.0	35.6	22.2	30.9	42.2	56.3	42.0	61.3	60.7	42.2
Private creditors										
Interest (%)	0.0	17.2	8.7	6.3	6.8	5.9	7.1	6.7	5.7	6.9
Maturity (years)	0.0	7.8	9.6	8.8	8.0	7.9	9.6	8.8	8.3	12.4
Grace period (years)	0.0	4.5	1.2	2.0	1.6	1.4	2.1	2.1	2.6	3.1
Grant element (%)	0.0	-18.7	3.5	13.9	10.3	13.5	10.0	12.4	16.2	14.6
Memorandum items										
Commitments	0	171	444	398	187	288	271	418	222	19
Official creditors	0	140	414	296	142	266	156	344	204	16
Private creditors	0	31	30	102	46	22	115	74	18	3

10. CONTRACTUAL OBLIGATIONS ON OUTSTANDING LONG-TERM DEBT

	2001	2002	2003	2004	2005	2006	2007	2008	2009	2010
TOTAL										
Disbursements	182	137	87	52	29	10	5	2	1	0
Principal	382	315	280	255	233	223	215	188	141	123
Interest	132	111	96	83	67	58	49	40	33	28
Official creditors										
Disbursements	161	128	84	51	29	10	5	2	1	0
Principal	255	234	203	191	187	184	177	163	131	120
Interest	96	86	76	68	60	53	45	38	32	27
Bilateral creditors										
Disbursements	50	33	19	11	7	3	2	1	1	0
Principal	93	92	84	83	84	80	72	63	55	54
Interest	34	31	29	26	23	21	18	16	15	14
Multilateral creditors										
Disbursements	111	95	66	41	22	7	3	1	1	0
Principal	162	142	119	108	103	104	104	101	76	66
Interest	63	55	48	42	37	32	27	22	17	14
Private creditors										
Disbursements	22	10	3	1	0	0	0	0	0	0
Principal	126	81	77	65	46	39	39	24	10	3
Interest	35	25	20	15	7	5	4	3	1	1
Commercial banks										
Disbursements	14	5	1	0	0	0	0	0	0	0
Principal	35	31	30	25	17	10	9	8	7	2
Interest	11	9	7	5	3	2	2	1	1	0
Other private										
Disbursements	8	5	2	1	0	0	0	0	0	0
Principal	91	50	47	39	29	29	29	17	3	1
Interest	24	16	13	10	3	3	2	2	1	0

Country notes

Albania

Data source. Data on long-term public and publicly guaranteed debt as of 2000 are based on reports provided by the country. Short-term debt data are from the BIS semiannual series on international bank lending and short-term export credits from the OECD.

Rescheduling. Albania concluded a rescheduling agreement with official creditors outside of formal Paris Club auspices in December 1993 and a debt buyback operation in 1996.

Algeria

Data source. Data on long-term public and publicly guaranteed debt as of 2000 are based on reports provided by the country. Short-term debt data are also as reported by the country.

Rescheduling. Projected debt service is based on contractual obligations on debt outstanding at the end of 2000. It includes the effects of the Paris Club agreement signed in June 1994 and the commercial bank agreement signed in July 1996.

Angola

Data source. Data on long-term public and publicly guaranteed debt for 2000 are based on reports provided by the country. Short-term debt data are from the BIS semiannual series on international bank lending and short-term export credits from the OECD, supplemented by World Bank staff estimates.

Rescheduling. In 1987 Angola concluded an informal agreement with Paris Club creditors that was signed in July 1989. Debt owed to Portugal and Spain was rescheduled in 1994. In late 1996 Angola reached a debt restructuring agreement with the Russian Federation, receiving an upfront discount of 70 percent on the stock and interest arrears and a rescheduling of the remainder over 20 years.

Argentina

Data source. Data on long-term public and publicly guaranteed debt for 2000 are based on reports provided by the country. Long-term private nonguaranteed debt and short-term debt data are World Bank staff estimates.

The increase in debt outstanding in 1989 is due mostly to the conversion of austral-denominated time deposits and government domestic debt into dollar-denominated bonds (BONEX 89).

Debt reduction. In March 1993 Argentina concluded a debt and debt service reduction exchanging its commercial bank debt to either par or discount bonds for a total face value of $17 billion. Interest arrears were also swapped into bonds at par with a face value of $8.2 billion, after a down payment of $910 million. These operations enabled Argentina to reduce its stock of debt by $3.3 billion in 1993, $399 million in 1994, and $863 million in 1995. Data for 2000 include debt buybacks.

Other. The residual in debt stock-flow reconciliation is due to data revisions introduced in 1993.

Armenia

Data source. Data on long-term public and publicly guaranteed debt for 2000 are actual, based on reports provided by the country. Short-term debt data are from the BIS semiannual series on international bank lending and short-term export credits from the OECD.

Rescheduling. In 1993, $30.8 million of technical credits were rescheduled with the Russian Federation, and in 1996, $34.0 million were rescheduled with bilateral creditors.

Azerbaijan

Data source. Data on long-term public and publicly guaranteed debt for 2000 are based on reports provided by the country. Short-term debt data are from the BIS semiannual series on international bank lending and short-term export credits from the OECD.

Rescheduling. In 1993, $36 million of technical credits were rescheduled with the Russian Federation.

Bangladesh

Data source. Data on long-term public and publicly guaranteed debt for 2000 are based on reports provided by the country. Short-term debt data are from the BIS semiannual series on international bank lending and short-term export credits from the OECD.

Belarus

Data source. Data on long-term public and publicly guaranteed debt for 2000 are based on reports provided by the country. Short-term debt data are from the BIS semiannual series on international bank lending and short-term export credits from the OECD.

Rescheduling. In 1993, $385 million of technical credits were rescheduled with the Russian Federation.

Belize

Data source. Data on long-term public and publicly guaranteed debt for 2000 are based on reports provided by the country. Short-term debt data are from the BIS semiannual series on international bank lending and short-term export credits from the OECD.

Benin

Data source. Data on long-term public and publicly guaranteed debt for 2000 are based on reports provided by the country. Short-term debt data are from the BIS semiannual series on international bank lending and short-term export credits from the OECD.

Rescheduling. Projected debt service is based on contractual obligations on debt outstanding at the end of 2000. It includes the effects of the Paris Club agreements signed in 1991, 1993, 1996, and 2000.

Bhutan

Data source. Data on long-term public and publicly guaranteed debt for 2000 are based on reports provided by the country. Short-term debt data are from the BIS semiannual series on international bank lending and short-term export credits from the OECD.

Bolivia

Data source. Data on long-term public and publicly guaranteed debt and on private nonguaranteed debt for 2000 are based on reports provided by the country. Short-term debt data are World Bank staff estimates.

Rescheduling. Projected debt service is based on contractual obligations on debt outstanding at the end of 2000. It includes the effects of all Paris Club agreements. The last Paris Club agreement was signed in 1998.

Bosnia and Herzegovina

Data source. Data on long-term public and publicly guaranteed debt for 2000 are based on reports provided by the country. Prior to 1999 data on long-term public and publicly guaranteed debt include only the IBRD and IMF. Short-term debt data are from the BIS semiannual series on international bank lending and short-term export credits from the OECD.

Botswana

Data source. Data on long-term public and publicly guaranteed debt for 2000 are based on reports provided by the country. Short-term debt data are from the BIS semiannual series on international bank lending and short-term export credits from the OECD.

Brazil

Data source. Data on long-term public and publicly guaranteed and private nonguaranteed debt for 2000 are preliminary, based on partial reports provided by the country. Short-term debt data are from the BIS semiannual series on international bank lending and short-term export credits from the OECD.

Rescheduling. From 1983 onward, the increase in long-term public and publicly guaranteed debt is due to the transfer of liabilities from private nonguaranteed and short-term debt as a result of Paris Club and commercial bank restructuring. In 1992 an agreement was reached with Paris Club creditors to reschedule $6.2 billion, of which $5.1 billion corresponded to rescheduling of arrears and debt service due in 1992. Brazil also rescheduled $7.1 billion of interest in arrears with commercial banks. Interest payments for 1992 include a $836 million cash payment on the interest arrears.

Debt reduction. Debt owed to commercial banks at the end of 1994 was reduced by $4.1 billion as a result of the April 1994 Brady accord. Data for 2000 include debt buybacks.

Bulgaria

Data source. Data on long-term public and publicly guaranteed and private nonguaranteed debt for 2000 are based on reports provided by the country. Short-term debt data are from the BIS semiannual series on international bank lending and short-term export credits from the OECD.

Rescheduling. Projected debt service is based on contractual obligations on debt outstanding at the end of 2000. It includes the effects of the Paris Club agreements signed in 1991, 1992, and 1994. Commercial bank creditors agreed to restructure $8.3 billion of external public debt in July 1994.

Burkina Faso

Data source. Data on long-term public and publicly guaranteed debt for 2000 are based on reports provided by the country. Short-term debt data are from the BIS semiannual series on international bank lending and short-term export credits from the OECD.

Rescheduling. Projected debt service is based on contractual obligations on debt outstanding at the end of 2000. It includes the effects of the Paris Club agreements signed in 1991, 1993, 1996, and 2000.

Burundi

Data source. Data on long-term public and publicly guaranteed debt for 2000 are World Bank staff estimates. Short-term debt data are from the BIS semiannual series on international bank lending and short-term export credits from the OECD.

Rescheduling. Projected debt service is based on contractual obligations on debt outstanding at the end of 2000. It includes the effect of the cancellation of all concessional debt owed to Belgium, France, the Republic of Korea, and the Russian Federation. In 1989 Burundi rescheduled $13.3 million of debt owed to China.

Cambodia

Data source. Data on long-term public and publicly guaranteed debt for 2000 are based on reports provided by the country and World Bank staff estimates. Short-term debt data are from the BIS semiannual series on international bank lending and short-term export credits from the OECD.

Rescheduling. Projected debt service is based on contractual obligations on debt outstanding at the end of 2000. It includes the effect of the Paris Club agreement on Naples terms signed in January 1995.

Cameroon

Data source. Data on long-term and publicly guaranteed debt for 2000 are based on reports provided by the country and World Bank staff estimates. Long-term private nonguaranteed debt data are reported by the country. Short-term debt data are from the BIS semiannual series on international bank lending and short-term export credits from the OECD.

Rescheduling. Projected debt service is based on contractual obligations on debt outstanding at the end of 2000. It includes the effects of the Paris Club agreements signed in January 1992, November 1995, and October 1997.

Cape Verde

Data source. Data on long-term public and publicly guaranteed debt for 2000 are based on the reports provided by the country. Short-term debt data are from the BIS semiannual series on international bank lending and short-term export credits from the OECD.

Central African Republic

Data source. Data on long-term public and publicly guaranteed debt for 2000 are World Bank staff estimates. Short-term debt data are from the BIS semiannual series on international bank lending and short-term export credits from the OECD.

Rescheduling. Projected debt service is based on contractual obligations on debt outstanding at the end of 2000. It includes the effects of the Paris Club agreements signed in 1988, 1990, 1994, and 1998.

Chad

Data source. Data on long-term public and publicly guaranteed debt for 2000 are World Bank staff estimates. Short-term debt data are from the BIS semiannual series on international bank lending and short-term export credits from the OECD.

Rescheduling. Projected debt service is based on contractual obligations on debt outstanding at the end of 2000. It includes the effect of the debt relief agreement signed in 1989, concluded outside the Paris Club. In addition, it includes the 1995 and 1996 Paris Club agreements. The reporting of the loans covered by this agreement remains partial, including the February 1995 and July 1996 Paris Club agreements.

Chile

Data source. Data on long-term public and publicly guaranteed, private nonguaranteed, and short-term debt for 2000 are based on reports provided by the country. Short-term debt data for 1990–99 have been revised.

Rescheduling. Projected debt service is based on contractual obligations on debt outstanding at the end of 2000. It includes the effect of a 1990 agreement with commercial banks under which there was no repayment of principal during 1991–94. The data also reflect the forgiveness of $15 million and the rescheduling of $132 million under the Enterprise for the Americas Initiative.

Debt reduction. By end-1993 reduction of debt owed to commercial banks through various debt conversion programs reached $8.7 billion, including $2.5 billion in 1988, $2.5 billion in 1989, $1.1 billion in 1990, $496 million in 1991, $279 million in 1992, and $264 million in 1993. Also, 1988 principal repayments include a $164 million cash payment in connection with a buyback.

China

Data source. Data on long-term public and publicly guaranteed debt for 2000 are World Bank staff preliminary estimates as the debt data collection and reporting method is in transition. State-owned enterprises are responsible for servicing their external debt exposures, and their obligations are not guaranteed by the Ministry of Finance. Short-term debt data for 1990–2000 are from the BIS semiannual series on international bank lending and short-term export credits from the OECD.

Colombia

Data source. Data on long-term public and publicly guaranteed debt for 2000 are based on reports provided by the country. Data on long-term private nonguaranteed debt are World Bank staff estimates. Short-term debt data are from the BIS semiannual series on international bank lending and short-term export credits from the OECD.

Comoros

Data source. Data on long-term public and publicly guaranteed debt for 2000 are based on reports provided by the country. Short-term debt data are from the BIS semiannual series on international bank lending and short-term export credits from the OECD.

Debt reduction. France wrote off all outstanding debt in 1994.

Congo, Democratic Republic of

Data source. Data on long-term public and publicly guaranteed debt for 2000 are based on reports provided by the country. Short-term debt data are from the BIS semiannual series on international bank lending and short-term export credits from the OECD.

Congo, Republic of

Data source. Data on long-term public and publicly guaranteed debt for 2000 are World Bank staff estimates. Short-term debt data are from the BIS semiannual series on international bank lending and short-term export credits from the OECD.

Rescheduling. Projected debt service is based on contractual obligations on debt outstanding at the end of 2000. It includes the effects of the Paris Club agreements signed in 1986, 1990, 1994, and 1996, but excludes the effect of the 1988 agreement with commercial banks because it has not been implemented. In 1986, in addition to Paris Club, the government rescheduled with Eastern Bloc creditors. Under the 1986 Brazzaville Club agreement, $23 million was rescheduled.

Costa Rica

Data source. Data on long-term public and publicly guaranteed debt for 2000 are based on reports provided by the country. Long-term private nonguaranteed debt data are World Bank staff estimates. Short-term debt data are from the BIS semiannual series on international bank lending and short-term export credits from the OECD.

Côte d'Ivoire

Data source. Data on long-term public and publicly guaranteed debt for 2000 are World Bank staff estimates. Long-term private nonguaranteed debt data are World Bank staff estimates. Short-term debt data are from the BIS semiannual series on international bank lending and short-term export credits from the OECD.

Rescheduling. Projected debt service is based on contractual obligations on debt outstanding at the end of 2000. It includes the effects of all Paris Club agreements beginning in 1984 and the commercial bank agreements of 1985–86. It includes the DDSR agreement of May 1997.

Croatia

Data source. Data on long-term public and publicly guaranteed and private nonguaranteed debt for 2000 are based on reports provided by the country. Short-term debt data are from BIS semiannual series on international bank lending and short-term export credits from the OECD.

Other. Croatia became a member of the World Bank in 1993. Debt data includes the effects of the Paris Club agreement signed in March 1995 and the London Club agreement signed in March 1996.

Czech Republic

Data source. Data on long-term public and publicly guaranteed, private nonguaranteed, and short-term debt for 2000 are preliminary, based on partial reports provided by the country, and include only convertible currency debt.

Other. The Czech Republic became a member of the World Bank in 1993. Data for 1985–92 are based on preliminary information on the succession of the former Czechoslovakia (effective January 1, 1993).

Djibouti

Data source. Data on long-term public and publicly guaranteed debt for 2000 are World Bank staff estimates. Short-term debt data are from the BIS semiannual series on international bank lending and short-term export credits from the OECD. The effect of the May 2000 Paris Club agreement is not implemented.

Debt reduction. France wrote off all outstanding and disbursed debt at the end of 1989.

Dominica

Data source. Data on long-term public and publicly guaranteed debt for 2000 are based on reports provided by the country. Short-term debt data are from the BIS semiannual series on international bank lending and short-term export credits from the OECD.

Debt reduction. As part of its Caribbean initiative, Canada forgave all its official development assistance loans, about $1.7 million, in 1990.

Dominican Republic

Data source. Data on long-term public and publicly guaranteed debt for 2000 are based on reports provided by the country. Short-term debt data are from the BIS semiannual series on international bank lending and short-term export credits from the OECD.

Rescheduling. Projected debt service is based on contractual obligations on debt outstanding at the end of 2000. It includes the effects of the Paris Club agreement signed in November 1991 rescheduling $843 million and of the 1994 debt and debt service reduction agreement to restructure $1.2 billion owed to commercial banks.

Ecuador

Data source. Data on long-term public and publicly guaranteed and private nonguaranteed debt for 2000 are World Bank staff estimates. Short-term debt data are from the BIS semiannual series on international bank lending and short-term export credits from the OECD.

Rescheduling. Projected debt service is based on contractual obligations on debt outstanding at the end of 2000. It includes the effects of the Paris Club agreement on Houston terms signed in September 2000 and of the 2000 bond exchange operation.

Debt reduction. The debt conversion program was continued in 1992, enabling the country to reduce its stock of debt due to private creditors by about $50 million, bringing the total for 1987–92 to $539 million. Debt reduction resulting from the 1995 DDSR operations amounts to $1.2 billion.

Egypt, Arab Republic of

Data source. Data on long-term public and publicly guaranteed debt for 2000 and revised data for 1991–95 due to the third stage of the 1991 Paris Club agreement are based on reports provided by the country. Data on private nonguaranteed debt are World Bank staff estimates. Short-term debt data are from the BIS semiannual series on international bank lending and short-term export credits from OECD.

Rescheduling. Projected debt service is based on contractual obligations on debt outstanding at the end of 2000. It includes the effects of the third stage of the Paris Club agreement signed in May 1991.

El Salvador

Data source. Data on long-term public and publicly guaranteed debt for 2000 are based on reports provided by the country. Long-term private nonguaranteed debt data are World Bank staff estimates. Short-term debt data are from the BIS semiannual series on international bank lending and short-term export credits from the OECD.

Equatorial Guinea

Data source. Data on long-term public and publicly guaranteed debt for 2000 are estimates based on the original terms of the loans. Short-term debt data are from the BIS semiannual series on international bank lending and short-term export credits from the OECD.

Rescheduling. Projected debt service is based on contractual obligations on debt outstanding at the end of 2000. It does not include the effects of the Paris Club agreements signed in April 1992 and December 1996 because of lack of information.

Eritrea

Data source. Data on long-term public and publicly guaranteed debt for 2000 are based on reports provided by the country. Short-term debt data are from the BIS semiannual series on international bank lending and short-term export credits from the OECD.

Estonia

Data source. Data on long-term public debt for 2000 are based on reports provided by the country. Private nonguaranteed and short-term debt data have been revised starting from 1996 based on International Investment Position figures, which have been compiled and published officially by the country and provided by the Country Management Unit, and World Bank staff estimates.

Ethiopia

Data source. Data on long-term public and publicly guaranteed debt for 2000 are based on reports provided by the country. The 1996 debt report included information not reported in previous years. The historical data were revised. Short-term debt data are from the BIS semiannual series on international bank lending and short-term export credits from the OECD. The data include debt contracted from commercial sources for military expenditures.

Rescheduling. Projected debt service is based on contractual obligations on debt outstanding at the end of 2000. It includes the effects of the last Paris Club agreement signed in January 24, 1997 and the debt forgiveness operation from the Russian Federation.

Fiji

Data source. Data on long-term public and publicly guaranteed debt for 2000 are based on reports provided by the country. Long-term private nonguaranteed debt data are World Bank staff estimates. Short-term debt data are from the BIS semiannual series on international bank lending and short-term export credits from the OECD.

Gabon

Data source. Data on long-term public and publicly guaranteed debt for 2000 are World Bank staff estimates. Short-term debt data are from the BIS semiannual series on international bank lending and short-term export credits from the OECD.

Rescheduling. Projected debt service is based on contractual obligations on debt outstanding at the end of 2000. It includes the effects of the Paris Club agreements signed in April 1994, December 1995, and December 2000. Projections exclude the effect of the Paris Club agreement signed in October 1991. According to Caisse Autonome d'Amortissement, the agreement was canceled because of difficulties in meeting certain conditions requested by one of the creditor countries.

Gambia, The

Data source. Data on long-term public and publicly guaranteed debt for 2000 are based on reports provided by the country. Short-term debt data are from the BIS semiannual series on international bank lending and short-term export credits from the OECD.

Georgia

Data source. Data on long-term public and publicly guaranteed debt for 2000 are based on reports provided by the country. Short-term debt data are from the BIS semiannual series on international bank lending and short-term export credits from the OECD.

Rescheduling. In 1993 a total of $366 million of technical credits were rescheduled with Armenia ($10.6 million), Azerbaijan ($2.1 million), Kazakhstan ($17.9 million), the Russian Federation ($135.0 million), and Turkmenistan ($200.8 million). In 1996, $634 million were rescheduled with bilateral creditors.

Ghana

Data source. Data on long-term public and publicly guaranteed debt for 2000 are based on reports provided by the country. Long-term private nonguaranteed debt data are World Bank staff estimates. Short-term debt data are from the BIS semiannual series on international bank lending and short-term export credits from the OECD.

Rescheduling. In 1991 the Netherlands rescheduled all payment arrears. It includes the effect of the Paris Club agreement signed in March 1996.

Grenada

Data source. Data on public and publicly guaranteed debt for 2000 are based on reports provided by the country. Short-term debt data are from the BIS semiannual series on international bank lending and short-term export credits from the OECD.

Guatemala

Data source. Data on long-term public and publicly guaranteed debt for 2000 are based on reports provided by the country. Long-term private nonguaranteed debt data are World Bank staff estimates. Short-term debt data are from the BIS semiannual series on international bank lending and short-term export credits from the OECD.

Guinea

Data source. Data on long-term public and publicly guaranteed debt for 2000 are World Bank staff estimates. Short-term debt data are from the BIS semiannual series on international bank lending and short-term export credits from the OECD.

Rescheduling. Projected debt service is based on contractual obligations on debt outstanding at the end of 2000. It includes the effects of the Paris Club agreements signed in 1986, 1989, 1992, 1995, and 1997.

Guinea-Bissau

Data source. Data on long-term public and publicly guaranteed debt for 2000 are World Bank staff estimates. Short-term debt data are from the BIS semiannual series on international bank lending and short-term export credits from the OECD.

Rescheduling. Projected debt service is based on contractual obligations on debt outstanding at the end of 2000. It includes the effects of the Paris Club agreements signed in October 1987, October 1989, and February 1995.

Guyana

Data source. Data on long-term public and publicly guaranteed and private nonguaranteed debt for 2000 are based on reports provided by the country. Short-term debt data are from the BIS semiannual series on international bank lending and short-term export credits from the OECD.

Haiti

Data source. Data on long-term public and publicly guaranteed debt as of end-September 2000 are preliminary, based on partial reports provided by the country. Short-term debt data are from the BIS semiannual series on international bank lending and short-term export credits from the OECD.

Honduras

Data source. Data on long-term public and publicly guaranteed and private nonguaranteed debt for 2000 are based on reports provided by the country. Short-term debt data are from the BIS semiannual series on international bank lending and short-term export credits from the OECD.

Rescheduling. Projected debt service is based on contractual obligations on debt outstanding at the end of 2000. It includes the effect of the Paris Club agreement signed in March 1999.

Debt reduction. Reductions of the stock of debt at the end of 1999 and 2000 as a result of the write off of the March 1999 Paris Club agreement were $32 million and $8 million, respectively.

Hungary

Data source. Data on long-term public and publicly guaranteed and private nonguaranteed debt for 2000 are based on reports provided by the country. Short-term debt data are from the BIS semiannual series on international bank lending and short-term export credits from the OECD.

India

Data source. Data relate to the year ending in March (latest data are for the year ending in March 2001). Details on long-term public and publicly guaranteed, private nonguaranteed, and short-term debt as of the end of March 2001 are based on aggregate reports provided by the country and World Bank staff estimates.

Indonesia

Data source. Data on long-term public and publicly guaranteed debt for 2000 are preliminary based on partial reports provided by the country. Short-term debt data (1993 to 2000) are from the BIS semiannual series on international bank lending and short-term export credits from the OECD. (The debt data may include indistinguishable local currency components held by nonresidents.)

Other. The residual in debt stock flow reconciliation from 1994 onward reflects the private nonguaranteed stock revisions introduced without corresponding flow data adjustments.

Rescheduling. Projected debt service is based on contractual obligations on debt outstanding at the end of 2000. It includes the effect of the Paris Club agreement signed in April 2000.

Iran, Islamic Republic of

Data source. Data relate to the year ending in March. Long-term public and publicly guaranteed debt and short-term debt as of end-March 2001 are based on aggregate reports provided by the country. Long-term private nonguaranteed debt are World Bank staff estimates.

Jamaica

Data source. Data on long-term public and publicly guaranteed debt for 2000 are based on reports provided by the country. Long-term private nonguaranteed debt data are World Bank staff estimates. Short-term debt data are from the BIS semiannual series on international bank lending and short-term export credits from the OECD.

Jordan

Data source. Data on long-term public and publicly guaranteed debt for 2000 are based on reports provided by the country. Short-term debt data are from the BIS semiannual series on international bank lending and short-term export credits from the OECD.

Rescheduling. Projected debt service is based on contractual obligations on debt outstanding at the end of 2000. It reflects the effects of all Paris Club agreements signed up to 1999.

Kazakhstan

Data source. Data on long-term public and publicly guaranteed and private nonguaranteed debt for 2000 are based on reports provided by the country. Private nonguaranteed debt includes only registered private debt of National Bank of Kazakhstan. Short-term debt data are from the BIS semiannual series on international bank lending and short-term export credits from the OECD.

Rescheduling. In 1993, $1.3 billion of technical credits were rescheduled with the Russian Federation.

Kenya

Data source. Data on long-term public and publicly guaranteed debt for 2000 are actual, based on reports provided by the country. Long-term private nonguaranteed debt are World Bank staff estimates. Short-term debt data are from the BIS semiannual series on international bank lending and short-term export credits from the OECD.

Rescheduling. Projected debt service is based on contractual obligations on debt outstanding at the end of 2000. It includes the effects of the Paris Club agreements signed in January 1994 and November 2000.

Korea, Republic of

Data source. Data on total external liabilities, including long-term public and publicly guaranteed debt for 1994–2000, are based on reports provided by the country and World Bank staff estimates. The data include 1998 debt rescheduling of short-term debt.

Kyrgyz Republic

Data source. Data on long-term public and publicly guaranteed debt for 2000 are based on reports provided by the country. Short-term debt data are from the BIS semiannual series on international bank lending and short-term export credits from the OECD.

Rescheduling. In 1993 a total of $125.8 million of technical credits were rescheduled with Kazakhstan ($31.5 million), the Russian Federation ($81.0 million), and Uzbekistan ($13.3 million). In 1996, $220.4 million were rescheduled with bilateral creditors.

Lao People's Democratic Republic

Data source. Data on long-term public and publicly guaranteed debt for 2000 are World Bank staff estimates and include both convertible and nonconvertible currency obligations. Short-term debt data are from the BIS semiannual series on international bank lending and short-term export credits from the OECD.

Rescheduling. Projected debt service is based on contractual obligations on debt outstanding at the end of 2000. It includes the effects of the bilateral debt restructuring agreements of 1988 and 1991.

Latvia

Data source. Data on long-term public debt for 2000 are based on reports provided by the country. Private nonguaranteed and short-term debt data have been revised starting from 1996, based on International Investment Position figures which have been compiled and published officially by the Central Statistical Bureau of Latvia and provided by the Country Management Unit.

Lebanon

Data source. Data on long-term public and publicly guaranteed debt for 2000 are estimates based on the original terms of the loans. Short-term debt data are from the BIS semiannual series on international bank lending and short-term export credits from the OECD.

Lesotho

Data source. Data on long-term public and publicly guaranteed debt for 2000 are based on reports provided by the country and World Bank staff estimates. Short-term debt data are World Bank staff estimates.

Liberia

Data source. Data on long-term public and publicly guaranteed debt for 2000 are estimates based on the original terms of the loans. Short-term debt data are from the BIS semiannual series on international bank lending and short-term export credits from the OECD.

Lithuania

Data source. Data on long-term public and publicly guaranteed debt for 2000 are based on reports provided by the country. Long-term private nonguaranteed debt data are World Bank staff estimates. Short-term debt data have been revised starting from 1996 based on International Investment Position figures compiled and published officially by the country, and provided by the Country Management Unit and World Bank staff estimates.

Macedonia, FYR

Data source. Data on long-term public and publicly guaranteed and private nonguaranteed debt for 2000 are based on reports provided by the country. Short-term debt data are from the BIS semiannual series on international bank lending and short-term export credits from the OECD.

Other. The former Yugoslav Republic of Macedonia became a member of the World Bank in 1993. Debt outstanding as of end-1993 reflect only loans used directly by Macedonian beneficiaries.

Madagascar

Data source. Data on long-term public and publicly guaranteed debt for 2000 are World Bank staff estimates. Short-term debt data are from the BIS semiannual series on international bank lending and short-term export credits from the OECD.

Rescheduling. Projected debt service is based on contractual obligations on debt outstanding at the end of 2000. It includes the effects of the Paris Club agreements signed during 1988–2000 and the 1990 commercial bank rescheduling arrangements.

Malawi

Data source. Data on long-term public and publicly guaranteed debt for 2000 are World Bank staff estimates. Short-term debt data are from the BIS semiannual series on international bank lending and short-term export credits from the OECD.

Rescheduling. Projected debt service is based on contractual obligations on debt outstanding at the end of 2000. It includes the effect of the Paris Club agreement signed in April 1988. The agreement to reschedule debt owed to the Commonwealth Development Corporation has not been implemented. As a result there are both principal and interest arrears due to the corporation.

Malaysia

Data source. Data on long-term public and publicly guaranteed and private nonguaranteed debt for 2000 are World Bank staff estimates. Short-term debt data are government estimates.

Maldives

Data source. Data on long-term public and publicly guaranteed debt for 2000 are based on reports provided by the country. Short-term debt data are from the BIS semiannual series on international bank lending and short-term export credits from the OECD.

Mali

Data source. Data on long-term public and publicly guaranteed debt for 2000 are based on reports provided by the country. Short-term debt data are from the BIS semiannual series on international bank lending and short-term export credits from the OECD.

Rescheduling. Projected debt service is based on contractual obligations on debt outstanding at the end of 2000. It includes the effects of all Paris Club agreements signed up to 2000.

Mauritania

Data source. Data on long-term public and publicly guaranteed debt for 2000 are based on reports provided by the country. Short-term debt data are from the BIS semiannual series on international bank lending and short-term export credits from the OECD.

Rescheduling. Projected debt service is based on contractual obligations on debt outstanding at the end of 2000. It reflects the effects of the Paris Club agreements signed in 1989, 1993, 1995, and 2000. The reporting of the loans covered by these agreements remains partial. There have also been bilateral rescheduling arrangements with Algeria, Brazil, Iraq, Kuwait, Qatar, and Saudi Arabia.

Mauritius

Data source. Data on long-term public and publicly guaranteed and private nonguaranteed debt for 2000 are based on reports provided by the country. Short-term debt data are from the BIS semiannual series on international bank lending and short-term export credits from the OECD.

Mexico

Data source. Data on long-term public and publicly guaranteed, private nonguaranteed, and short-term debt for 2000 are based on reports provided by the country. Revised data on short-term and private nonguaranteed debt were provided by the country.

Rescheduling. Projected debt service is based on contractual obligations on debt outstanding at the end of 2000. It includes the effects of all agreements concluded to date, including the effect of the zero-coupon bonds and the swap operations. In 1992, $327 million was rescheduled as a result of the 1989 Paris Club agreement. In 1993 a number of public borrowers, including the government, swapped liabilities to meet the ceiling on borrowings.

Debt reduction. The decline in private nonguaranteed debt in 1988 is due primarily to prepayment and swaps operations. The debt reduction in 1989 of $2.5 billion comprised debt-equity swaps of $800 million and buybacks of $1.7 billion. In 1990 swaps amounted to $846 million, and debt reduction from discount bonds to $7.3 billion. The debt conversion program continued in 1991 and amounted to $1.1 billion, including privatization of $431 million and debt-equity swaps of $95 million. In 1992, $7.5 billion was bought back for $5.2 billion, which is shown under principal repayments. Also, $137 million was converted from foreign debt to equity. The increase in 1995 in long-term debt includes the stock transfer of the "Tesobonos." Data for 2000 include debt buybacks.

Moldova

Data source. Data on long-term public and publicly guaranteed debt for 2000 are based on reports provided by the country. Short-term debt data have been revised starting in 1996 based on International Investment Position figures compiled and published officially by the country, and provided by the Country Management Unit and World Bank staff estimates.

Rescheduling. In 1993, $89 million of technical credits were rescheduled with the Russian Federation. In 1996, $118.8 million were rescheduled with bilateral creditors.

Mongolia

Data source. Data on long-term public and publicly guaranteed debt for 2000 are World Bank staff estimates. Short-term debt data are from the BIS semiannual series on international bank lending and short-term export credits from the OECD. Data exclude military debt of about 10.6 billion rubles owed to the Russian Federation.

Morocco

Data source. Data on long-term public and publicly guaranteed debt for 2000 are based on reports provided by the country. Data on short-term debt are World Bank staff estimates. Private nonguaranteed debt data for end-2000 are World Bank staff estimates. Major revisions to the database, especially on short-term debt and arrears, were based on information provided by the authorities. The arrears are mostly late payments to creditor countries.

Rescheduling. Projected debt service is based on contractual obligations on debt outstanding at the end of 2000. It includes the effect of the Paris Club agreement signed in February 1992.

Mozambique

Data source. Data on long-term public and publicly guaranteed debt for 2000 are based on reports provided by the country. Private nonguaranteed debt data are World Bank staff estimates and include private debt from Cahora Bassa. Short-term debt data are from the BIS semiannual series on international bank lending and short-term export credits from the OECD.

Rescheduling. Projected debt service is based on contractual obligations on debt outstanding at the end of 2000. It includes the effects of all Paris Club agreements signed up to March 2000. The 1999 rescheduling agreement with the Russian Federation has been implemented.

Debt reduction. Debt reduction in 1990 amounted to $231 million, and to $237 million in 1991. In 1991 there was a debt buyback, at a discount of 90 percent, of $124 million under the IDA Debt Reduction Facility.

Myanmar

Data source. Data relate to the year ending in March. Data on long-term public and publicly guaranteed debt for end-March 2001 are estimates based on the original terms of the loans. Short-term debt data are from the BIS semiannual series on international bank lending and short-term export credits from the OECD.

Nepal

Data source. Data on long-term public and publicly guaranteed debt for 2000 are based on reports provided by the country. Short-term debt data are from the BIS semiannual series on international bank lending and short-term export credits from the OECD.

Nicaragua

Data source. Data on long-term public and publicly guaranteed debt for 2000 are actual, based on reports provided by the country. Short-term debt data are from the BIS semiannual series on international bank lending and short-term export credits from the OECD.

Rescheduling. Projected debt service is based on contractual obligations on debt outstanding at the end of 2000. It includes the effect of agreements reached with Mexico ($950 million) and República Bolivariana de Venezuela ($159 million) in 1991, with Brazil in 1992 ($66 million), and with Argentina ($76 million) and Cuba ($7 million) in 1993; the 1995 Paris Club agreement; and agreements with the Russian Federation ($442 million), Czech Republic ($141 million), Honduras ($117 million), Mexico ($91 million), and El Salvador ($23 million) in 1996.

Debt reduction. In 1995 debt reduction was $1.2 billion using the IDA facility.

Niger

Data source. Data on long-term public and publicly guaranteed debt for 2000 are World Bank staff estimates. Short-term debt data are from the BIS semiannual series on international bank lending and short-term export credits from the OECD.

Rescheduling. Projected debt service is based on contractual obligations on debt outstanding at the end of 2000. It includes the effects of all Paris Club agreements.

Nigeria

Data source. Data on long-term public and private nonguaranteed debt for 2000 are estimates based on the original terms of the loans augmented by creditor source information and World Bank staff estimates. Nigeria has not reported external debt transactions for individual loans to the Bank since 1992. All data from 1992 forward are estimates based on aggregate data from the authorities, World Bank staff, and other sources. The promissory notes data for 1994–97 are based on partial information from the authorities. The Russian buyback is also based on partial information from the authorities. Short-term debt data are from the BIS semiannual series on international bank lending and short-term export credits from the OECD.

Rescheduling. Projected debt service is based on contractual obligations on debt outstanding at the end of 2000. It includes the effects of all Paris Club and London Club agreements signed up to 2000, as well as those signed with other bilateral creditors.

Debt reduction. Debt reduction in 1988 was $40 million and in 1989, $247 million, all of it due to debt-equity swaps. In 1990 debt reduction was $286 million, $48 million of which was due to debt forgiveness and $238 million to debt-equity swaps. In 1991 debt reduction was $243 million, of which $134 million represented a buyback, $95 million was debt-equity swaps, and $14 million was debt forgiveness. In 1992 there was a $1.3 billion buyback.

Other. The Central Bank of Nigeria reported a large cancellation of promissory notes in 1992 that led to a reduction of about $1.1 billion in the stock of notes outstanding. This reduction, classified under private suppliers' credits, is not recorded as part of the DDSR accounts and therefore is included in the residual imbalance during 1992.

Oman

Data source. Data on long-term public and publicly guaranteed debt for 2000 are based on reports provided by the country. Short-term debt data are from the BIS semiannual series on international bank lending and short-term export credits from the OECD.

Pakistan

Data source. Data on long-term public and publicly guaranteed and private nonguaranteed debt for 2000 are based on reports provided by the country. Short-term debt data are from the BIS semiannual series on international bank lending and short-term export credits from the OECD and exclude foreign currency deposits in local banks made by nonresidents.

Rescheduling. The January 1999 Paris Club rescheduling has been implemented.

Panama

Data source. Data on long-term public and publicly guaranteed debt for 2000 are based on reports provided by the country. Data on long-term private nonguaranteed debt and on short-term debt are World Bank staff estimates.

Papua New Guinea

Data source. Data on long-term public and publicly guaranteed debt for 2000 are based on reports provided by the country. Private nonguaranteed debt data are World Bank staff estimates. Short-term debt data are from the BIS semiannual series on international bank lending and short-term export credits from the OECD.

Paraguay

Data source. Data on long-term public and publicly guaranteed debt for 2000 are based on reports provided by the country. Private nonguaranteed debt data have been revised starting in 1995 based on the country's new reports. Short-term debt data are from the BIS semiannual series on international bank lending and short-term export credits from the OECD.

Peru

Data source. Data on long-term public and publicly guaranteed, private nonguaranteed, and short-term debt for 2000 are based on reports provided by the country. Historical data have been revised starting in 1997 based on aggregate data provided by the Country Management Unit.

Philippines

Data source. Data on long-term public and publicly guaranteed, private nonguaranteed, and short-term debt for 2000 are based on reports provided by the country.

Rescheduling. Projected debt service is based on contractual obligations on debt outstanding as of December 2000. It includes the effect of the Paris Club agreement signed in June 1991. The Paris Club agreement signed in July 1994 was not implemented because the Philippines decided to meet Paris Club debt service due.

Debt reduction. Cash buyback of $1.3 billion at the price of 52 cents per dollar (equivalent to $656 million) was implemented in May 1992, as was the DDSR $4.4 billion multioption package of July 1992. In October 1999 the Philippines completed a $1,006 million, 25-year (plus 7-year put option) global bond offering. The offering involved a $292 million cash sale and a $714 million exchange for $858 million in Brady bonds.

Poland

Data source. Data on long-term public and publicly guaranteed, private nonguaranteed, and short-term debt for 2000 are based on reports by the country and include both convertible and nonconvertible debt.

Rescheduling. Projected debt service is based on contractual obligations on debt outstanding at the end of 2000. It includes the effect of the Paris Club agreement signed in April 1991, which provided for cancellation of about 50 percent of the stock of debt or an equivalent reduction in scheduled debt service on a net present value basis. It also includes the effect of the DDSR operation with commercial banks that was concluded in October 1994. The 1994 DDSR agreement restructured $14.3 billion of debt.

Romania

Data source. Data on long-term public and publicly guaranteed, private nonguaranteed, and short-term debt for 2000 are based on reports provided by the country. Private nonguaranteed and short-term debt data have been revised starting in 1996 based on information from the National Bank of Romania.

Russian Federation

Data source. Data on long-term public and publicly guaranteed and short-term debt for 2000 are estimates, based on aggregate data provided by the country. Private nonguaranteed debt data are World Bank staff estimates. Data prior to 1992 are for the former Soviet Union. Beginning in 1993, the database has been revised to include obligations to members of the former Council for Mutual Economic Assistance and other countries in the form of trade-related credits amounting to $15.4 billion as of end-1996.

Rescheduling. Projected debt service is based on contractual obligations on debt outstanding at the end of 2000. It includes the effects of the Paris Club agreements signed in June 1995, April 1996, and August 1999, as well as the February 2000 rescheduling with London Club creditors.

Rwanda

Data source. Data on long-term public and publicly guaranteed debt for 2000 are World Bank staff estimates. Short-term debt data are from the BIS semiannual series on international bank lending and short-term export credits from the OECD.

Rescheduling. Projected debt service is based on contractual obligations on debt outstanding at the end of 2000. It includes the effect of rescheduling loans from Kuwait in 1996, as well as the effect of the Paris Club agreement signed in July 1998.

Samoa

Data source. Data on long-term public and publicly guaranteed debt for 2000 are based on reports provided by the country. Short-term debt data are from the BIS semiannual series on international bank lending and short-term export credits from the OECD.

São Tomé and Principe

Data source. Data on long-term public and publicly guaranteed debt for 2000 are based on reports provided by the country. Short-term debt data are from the BIS semiannual series on international bank lending and short-term export credits from the OECD.

Rescheduling. Projected debt service is based on contractual obligations on debt outstanding at the end of 2000. It includes the estimated effect of the Paris Club agreement signed in 2000.

Senegal

Data source. Data on long-term public and publicly guaranteed and private nonguaranteed debt for 2000 are based on reports provided by the country and World Bank staff estimates. Short-term debt data are from the BIS semiannual series on international bank lending and short-term export credits from the OECD.

Rescheduling. Projected debt service is based on contractual obligations on debt outstanding at the end of 2000. It includes the effects of the Paris Club agreements signed in June 1998 and October 2000.

Seychelles

Data source. Data on long-term public and publicly guaranteed debt for 2000 are estimates based on the original terms of the loans. Short-term debt data are from the BIS semiannual series on international bank lending and short-term export credits from the OECD.

Sierra Leone

Data source. Data on long-term public and publicly guaranteed debt for 2000 are based on reports provided by the country. Long-term private nonguaranteed debt data are World Bank staff estimates. Short-term debt data are from the BIS semiannual series on international bank lending and short-term export credits from the OECD. Major revisions to the database are based on information provided by the country.

Rescheduling. Projected debt service is based on contractual obligations on debt outstanding at the end of 2000. It includes the effects of Paris Club agreements signed in 1986, 1992, 1994, and 1996. It also includes the effect of a DDSR operation with commercial banks that was concluded in August 1995.

Slovak Republic

Data source. Data on long-term public and publicly guaranteed and private nonguaranteed debt for 2000 are based on reports provided by the country. Short-term debt data are from the BIS semiannual series on international bank lending and short-term export credits from the OECD.

Other. The Slovak Republic became a member of the World Bank in 1993. Data for 1985–92 are based on preliminary information on the succession of the former Czechoslovakia (effective January 1, 1993).

Solomon Islands

Data source. Data on long-term public and publicly guaranteed debt for 2000 are based on reports provided by the country. Short-term debt data are from the BIS semiannual series on international bank lending and short-term export credits from the OECD.

Somalia

Data source. Data on long-term public and publicly guaranteed debt for 2000 are estimates based on the original terms of the loans. Short-term debt data are from the BIS semiannual series on international bank lending and short-term export credits from the OECD.

South Africa

Data source. Data on long-term and publicly guaranteed debt for 2000 are aggregate information provided by the authorities and World Bank staff estimates.

Sri Lanka

Data source. Data on long-term public and publicly guaranteed debt for 2000 are based on reports provided by the country. Long-term private nonguaranteed debt data are based on reports provided by the country. Short-term debt data are from the BIS semiannual series on international bank lending and short-term export credits from the OECD.

St. Kitts and Nevis

Data source. Data on long-term public and publicly guaranteed debt for 2000 are based on reports provided by the country. Short-term debt data are from the BIS semiannual series on international bank lending and short-term export credits from the OECD.

St. Lucia

Data source. Data on long-term public and publicly guaranteed debt for 2000 are based on reports provided by the country. Short-term debt data are from the BIS semiannual series on international bank lending and short-term export credits from the OECD.

St. Vincent and the Grenadines

Data source. Data on long-term and publicly guaranteed debt for 2000 are based on reports provided by the country. Starting from 1993, short-term debt data are World Bank staff estimates.

Sudan

Data source. Data on long-term public and publicly guaranteed and private nonguaranteed debt for 2000 are estimates based on the original terms of the loans. Short-term debt data are World Bank staff estimates.

Swaziland

Data source. Data on long-term public and publicly guaranteed debt for 2000 are estimates based on the original terms of the loans. Short-term debt data are from the BIS semiannual series on international bank lending and short-term export credits from the OECD.

Syrian Arab Republic

Data source. Data on long-term public and publicly guaranteed debt for 2000 are estimates based on the original terms of the loans and include only civilian debt. Data on noncivilian debt, which is substantial and owed mainly to Eastern European countries, are estimates using creditor source information. Data on civilian debt do not reflect bilateral debt arrangements that have been agreed in recent years. Short-term debt are World Bank staff estimates.

Tajikistan

Data source. Data on long-term public and publicly guaranteed and private nonguaranteed debt for 2000 are based on reports provided by the country.

Rescheduling. In 1993, $18 million of technical credits were rescheduled with Kazakhstan. In 1996, $505.8 million were rescheduled with bilateral creditors.

Tanzania

Data source. Data on long-term public and publicly guaranteed debt for 2000 are based on reports provided by the country. Long-term private nonguaranteed debt data are World Bank staff estimates. Short-term debt data are from the BIS semiannual series on international bank lending and short-term export credits from the OECD.

Rescheduling. Projected debt service is based on contractual obligations on debt outstanding at the end of 2000. It includes the effects of all signed Paris Club agreements until the end of 1997 and the effect of the agreement signed in April 2000.

Thailand

Data source. Data on long-term public and publicly guaranteed and private nonguaranteed debt for 2000 are based on preliminary reports provided by the country. Short-term debt data are also from the country and include Bangkok International Banking Facility (BIBF) commercial bank transactions.

Togo

Data source. Data on long-term public and publicly guaranteed debt for 2000 are based on reports provided by the country. Short-term debt data are from the BIS semiannual series on international bank lending and short-term export credits from the OECD.

Rescheduling. Projected debt service is based on contractual obligations on debt outstanding at the end of 2000. It includes the effects of all signed Paris Club agreements and commercial bank arrangements until end-1996.

Tonga

Data source. Data on long-term public and publicly guaranteed debt for 2000 are estimates based on the original terms of the loans. Short-term debt data are from the BIS semiannual series on international bank lending and short-term export credits from the OECD.

Trinidad and Tobago

Data source. Data on long-term public and publicly guaranteed debt for 2000 are World Bank staff estimates. Short-term debt data are from the BIS semiannual series on international bank lending and short-term export credits from the OECD.

Tunisia

Data source. Data on long-term public and publicly guaranteed debt for 2000 are based on reports provided by the country. Private nonguaranteed debt data are World Bank staff estimates based on information from the government. Short-term debt data are World Bank staff estimates based on reports from the country.

Turkey

Data source. Data on long-term public and publicly guaranteed, private nonguaranteed, and short-term debt for 2000 are based on reports provided by the country.

Nonresident deposits. Long-term debt data include nonresident deposits made under the Dresdner Bank scheme, amounting to $9.7 billion at end-2000.

Turkmenistan

Data source. Data on long-term public and publicly guaranteed debt for 1999 and 2000 are not available due to reporting problems. Short-term debt data are from the BIS semiannual series on international bank lending and short-term export credits from the OECD.

Uganda

Data source. Data on long-term public and publicly guaranteed debt for 2000 are based on reports provided by the country. Short-term debt data are from the BIS semiannual series on international bank lending and short-term export credits from the OECD.

Rescheduling. Projected debt service is based on contractual obligations on debt outstanding at the end of 2000. It includes the effect of the Paris Club agreement signed in September 2000.

Debt reduction. As a result of the September 2000 Paris Club agreement on Lyon terms, the stock of debt was reduced by $150 million. Debt service payments to IDA and IMF repurchases and charges include payments from the HIPC Trust Fund, IDA grants, and IMF Trust Fund, under the HIPC debt initiative.

Ukraine

Data source. Data on long-term public and publicly guaranteed and private nonguaranteed debt for 2000 are based on reports provided by the country. Short-term debt data are from the BIS semiannual series on international bank lending and short-term export credits from the OECD.

Rescheduling. In 1993 a total of $2,528 million of technical credits were rescheduled with Moldova and the Russian Federation. In 1999 some $3.2 billion were rescheduled with the Russian Federation. In 2000 about $2.7 billion in bonds were rescheduled.

Uruguay

Data source. Data on long-term public and publicly guaranteed debt for 2000 are based on reports provided by the country. Private nonguaranteed and short-term debt data are World Bank staff estimates.

Rescheduling. Projected debt service is based on contractual obligations on debt outstanding at the end of 2000. It includes the effect of the September 1999 DDRS agreement.

Debt reduction. As a result of the September 1999 buyback of $85 million in Brady bonds, stock of debt was reduced by $11 million at end-1999.

Uzbekistan

Data source. Data on long-term public and publicly guaranteed and private nonguaranteed debt for 2000 are based on reports provided by the country. Short-term debt data are from the BIS semiannual series on international bank lending and short-term export credits from the OECD.

Rescheduling. In 1993 a total of $321 million of trade credits were rescheduled with Kazakhstan ($46.4 million) and the Russian Federation ($275.0 million).

Vanuatu

Data source. Data on long-term public and publicly guaranteed debt for 2000 are World Bank staff estimates. Short-term debt data are from the BIS semiannual series on international bank lending and short-term export credits from the OECD.

Venezuela, República Bolivariana de

Data source. Data on long-term public and publicly guaranteed debt for 2000 are based on reports provided by the country. Private nonguaranteed debt data are World Bank staff estimates. Short-term debt data are from the BIS semiannual series on international bank lending and short-term export credits from the OECD.

Vietnam

Data source. Data on long-term public and publicly guaranteed debt for 2000 are based on partial reports provided by the authorities and World Bank staff estimates. Short-term debt data are from the BIS semiannual series on international bank lending and short-term export credits from the OECD.

Rescheduling. Projected debt service is based on contractual obligations and existing terms on debt outstanding at the end of 2000. It includes the effect of the Paris Club agreement signed in December 1993, other bilateral arrangements outside of the Paris Club, and the 1997 DDSR agreement. The effect of the memorandum of understanding of September 1997 on the debt outstanding and disbursed owed to Russia is reflected in the table. The data are provisional and are based on World Bank staff estimates.

Yemen, Republic of

Data source. Data on long-term public and publicly guaranteed debt for 2000 are World Bank staff estimates. Short-term debt data are from the BIS semiannual series on international bank lending and short-term export credits from the OECD.

Rescheduling. Projected debt service is based on contractual obligations and existing terms on debt outstanding at the end of 2000. It includes the effects of the Paris Club agreements signed in September 1996 and November 1997.

Yugoslavia, Federal Republic of

Data source. Data on long-term public and publicly guaranteed and private nonguaranteed debt for 2000 are estimates and reflect borrowings by the former Yugoslavia that are not yet allocated to the various republics. Short-term data are from the BIS semiannual series on international bank lending and short-term export credits from the OECD.

Debt reduction. The debt reduction of 1988–91 consisted of buybacks of $128 million in 1988, $610 million in 1989, $1.5 billion in 1990, and $554 million in 1991.

Other. In 1992 the former Yugoslavia split into several republics; information on debt outstanding by the various republics are shown in the country pages for Croatia and FYR Macedonia.

Zambia

Data source. Data on long-term public and publicly guaranteed debt for 2000 are based on the reports provided by the country. Private nonguaranteed debt data are World Bank staff estimates. Short-term debt data are from the BIS semiannual series on international bank lending and sort-term export credits from the OECD.

Rescheduling. Projected debt service is based on contractual obligations on debt outstanding at the end of 2000. It includes the effect of the Paris Club agreement of April 1999. The total amounts rescheduled by end-1999 and end-2000 were $279 million and $169 million, respectively.

Debt reduction. Reduction of the stock of debt by end-2000 as a result of the write-off of the 1999 Paris Club agreement was $92 million.

Zimbabwe

Data source. Data on long-term public and private nonguaranteed debt for 2000 are based on reports provided by the country. Short-term debt data are from the BIS semiannual series on international bank lending and short-term export credits from the OECD.